Official 1996
National Football League

Record & Fact Book

A National Football League Book.
Workman Publishing Co., New York.

NATIONAL FOOTBALL LEAGUE, 1996

410 Park Avenue, New York, N.Y. 10022 (212) 758-1500

Commissioner: Paul Tagliabue
President: Neil Austrian

Executive Vice President & League Counsel: Jay Moyer
Executive Vice President-Labor Relations/Chairman NFLMC: Harold Henderson
Senior Vice President-Communications & Government Affairs: Joe Browne
Senior Vice President-League & Football Development: Roger Goodell
Senior Vice President-Broadcasting & Network Television: Val Pinchbeck, Jr.
Chief Financial Officer: Tom Spock

COMMUNICATIONS
Director of Communications: Greg Aiello
Director of International Public Relations: Pete Abitante
Director of Information, AFC: Leslie Hammond
Director of Information, NFC: Reggie Roberts
Director of Corporate Communications: Chris Widmaier

BROADCASTING
Director of Broadcasting Services: Dick Maxwell
Director of Broadcasting Research: Joe Ferreira

LEAGUE AND FOOTBALL DEVELOPMENT
Executive Director of Club Administration & Stadium Management: Joe Ellis
Director of Officiating: Jerry Seeman
League Secretary: Jan Van Duser
Director of Football Development: Gene Washington
Director of Game Operations: Peter Hadhazy
Director of Security: Milt Ahlerich

SPECIAL EVENTS
Executive Director of Special Events: Jim Steeg
Director of Special Events Operations: Don Renzulli
Director of Special Events Planning: Sue Robichek

MANAGEMENT COUNCIL
Vice President-General Counsel: Dennis Curran
Vice President-Operations & Compliance: Peter Ruocco
Director of Player Programs: Lem Burnham
Director of Player Personnel/Football Operations: Joel Bussert
Director of Labor Relations: Lal Heneghan

FINANCE AND ADMINISTRATION
Vice President-Law/Enterprises, Broadcast, & Finance: Frank Hawkins
Treasurer: Joe Siclare
Vice President-Internal Audit: Tom Sullivan
Controller: Richard Iandoli
Director of Administration: John Buzzeo
Director of Systems & Information Processing: Mary Oliveti
Director of Planning: Swan Paik
Director, Financial Planning & Analysis: Ken Saunders

NFL Internet Address: http://nfl.com

Cover Photograph by Gerald Gallegos.

NFL ENTERPRISES
President: Ron Bernard
Vice President-Programming/Media Development: Ann Kirschner
Vice President-Marketing & Sales: Tola Murphy-Baran
Vice President-International TV Distribution: Anne Murray

NFL FILMS
President: Steve Sabol
Vice President-Cinematography: Steve Andrich
Vice President-Marketing & Sales: John Collins
Vice President-In Charge of Production: Jay Gerber
Vice President-Video Operations: Jeff Howard
Vice President-Production Director: Hal Lipman
Vice President-Editor-in-Chief: Bob Ryan
Vice President-Special Projects: Phil Tuckett
Vice President-Finance & Administration: Barry Wolper

NFL PROPERTIES
President: Sara Levinson
Vice President-Retail Sales: Roger Atkin
Vice President-Advertising: Bruce Burke
Vice President-Retail Licensing: Jim Connelly
Vice President-Business Development/Special Events: Don Garber
Vice President-Legal/Business Affairs & General Counsel: Gary Gertzog
Vice President-Marketing: Howard Handler
Vice President-Club Marketing: Mark Holtzman
Vice President-Corporate Sponsorships: Jim Schwebel
Vice President-Publishing: John Wiebusch

Printed in the United States of America.

Compiled by the NFL Communications Department and Seymour Siwoff, Elias Sports Bureau.

Edited by Chris McCloskey, NFL Communications Department and Chuck Garrity, Jr., NFLP Publishing Group.
Statistics by Elias Sports Bureau.
Produced by NFL Properties, Inc., Publishing Group, Los Angeles.

Workman Publishing Co.
708 Broadway, New York, N.Y. 10003
Manufactured in the United States of America.
First printing, July 1996.
10 9 8 7 6 5 4 3 2 1

INDEX

1996 SCHEDULE AND NOTE CALENDAR

(All times local except Tokyo, which is EDT.)
Nationally televised games in parentheses.

Week	Date	Game	TV	Time
PRESEASON/FIRST WEEK	**Saturday, July 27**	Pro Football Hall of Fame Game at Canton, Ohio		
		Indianapolis ____ vs. New Orleans ____	(ABC)	2:30
		American Bowl at Tokyo, Japan		
		Pittsburgh ____ vs. San Diego ____	(ESPN)	10:00*
		Oakland ____ at Dallas ____		8:00
	Friday, August 2	New Orleans ____ at Detroit ____		7:30
		New York Giants ____ at Jacksonville ____		8:00
		New England____ at Green Bay ____		7:00
		Oakland ____ at Arizona ____		7:00
		Washington ____ at Buffalo ____		7:30
	Saturday, August 3	Atlanta ____ at Seattle ____		7:00
		Chicago ____ at Carolina ____		7:30
		Denver ____ at San Francisco ____		1:00
		Houston ____ vs. New York Jets ____ at Jackson, Miss.		7:00
		Indianapolis ____ at Cincinnati ____		7:30
		St. Louis ____ at Pittsburgh ____		6:00
		Philadelphia ____ at Baltimore ____		7:30
		San Diego ____ at Minnesota ____		7:00
		Tampa Bay____ at Miami ____		7:00
	Monday, August 5	American Bowl at Monterrey, Mexico		
		Dallas ____ vs. Kansas City ____	(ABC)	7:00

* Tokyo game actual kickoff 11:00 A.M., July 28.

Week	Date	Game	TV	Time
PRESEASON/SECOND WEEK	**Thursday, August 8**	Buffalo ____ at Minnesota ____	(TNT)	7:00
		New York Jets ____ at Philadelphia ____		7:30
		Seattle ____ at Oakland ____		5:00
	Friday, August 9	Jacksonville ____ at St. Louis ____		7:00
		Washington ____ at Detroit ____		7:30
	Saturday, August 10	Atlanta ____ at Tampa Bay ____		7:30
		Baltimore ____ at New York Giants ____	(NBC)	1:00
		Carolina ____ at Denver ____		6:00
		Cincinnati ____ at Arizona ____		7:30
		Indianapolis ____ at Houston ____		7:00
		New Orleans ____ at Kansas City ____		7:00
		San Diego ____ at San Francisco ____	(FOX)	5:00
	Sunday, August 11	Miami ____ at Chicago ____	(NBC)	12:00
		Pittsburgh____ at Green Bay ____	(TNT)	7:00
	Monday, August 12	New England ____ at Dallas ____	(ESPN)	7:00

Week	Date	Game	TV	Time
PRESEASON/THIRD WEEK	**Thursday, August 15**	Oakland ____ at Atlanta ____	(ESPN)	8:00
	Friday, August 16	Cincinnati ____ at Washington ____		8:00
		Detroit ____ at Houston ____		8:00
	Saturday, August 17	Arizona ____ at San Diego ____		7:00
		Buffalo ____ at Carolina ____		7:30
		Chicago ____ at New Orleans ____		7:00
		Denver ____ at Dallas ____	(FOX)	7:00
		Green Bay ____ at Baltimore ____		7:00
		New York Giants ____ at New York Jets ____		8:00
		St. Louis ____ at Kansas City ____		7:00
		Seattle ____ at Indianapolis ____		7:00
		Tampa Bay ____ at Pittsburgh ____		6:00
	Sunday, August 18	Philadelphia ____ at New England ____	(NBC)	1:00
		San Francisco ____ at Jacksonville ____	(TNT)	8:00
	Monday, August 19	Minnesota ____ at Miami ____	(ABC)	8:00

1996 SCHEDULE AND NOTE CALENDAR

Week	Date	Game	TV	Time
PRESEASON/FOURTH WEEK	**Thursday, August 22**	Kansas City ____ at Chicago ____	(ABC)	7:00
	Friday, August 23	Arizona ____ at Atlanta ____		7:30
		Baltimore ____ at Buffalo ____		7:30
		Carolina ____ at New York Giants ____		8:00
		Detroit ____ at Cincinnati ____		7:30
		Jacksonville ____ at Denver ____		6:00
		Miami ____ at Tampa Bay ____		7:30
		Minnesota ____ at New Orleans ____		7:00
		New York Jets ____ at Oakland ____		7:00
		Pittsburgh ____ at Philadelphia ____		7:30
		San Diego ____ at St. Louis ____		7:00
		San Francisco ____ at Seattle ____		7:00
		Washington ____ at New England ____		8:00
	Saturday, August 24	Dallas ____ vs. Houston ____ at Orlando, Fla.		6:00
		Green Bay ____ at Indianapolis ____	(FOX)	7:00
KICKOFF WEEKEND	**Sunday, September 1 (NBC-TV National Weekend)**	Arizona ____ at Indianapolis ____		12:00
		Atlanta ____ at Carolina ____		1:00
		Cincinnati ____ at St. Louis ____		12:00
		Detroit ____ at Minnesota ____		12:00
		Green Bay ____ at Tampa Bay ____		4:00
		Kansas City ____ at Houston ____		12:00
		New England ____ at Miami ____		4:00
		New Orleans ____ at San Francisco ____		1:00
		New York Jets ____ at Denver ____		2:00
		Oakland ____ at Baltimore ____		1:00
		Philadelphia ____ at Washington ____		1:00
		Pittsburgh ____ at Jacksonville ____		1:00
		Seattle ____ at San Diego ____		1:00
	Sunday Night	Buffalo ____ at New York Giants ____	(TNT)	8:00
	Monday, September 2	Dallas ____ at Chicago ____	(ABC)	8:00
SECOND WEEK	**Sunday, September 8 (FOX-TV National Weekend)**	Baltimore ____ at Pittsburgh ____		1:00
		Carolina ____ at New Orleans ____		12:00
		Chicago ____ at Washington ____		1:00
		Cincinnati ____ at San Diego ____		1:00
		Denver ____ at Seattle ____		1:00
		Houston ____ at Jacksonville ____		1:00
		Indianapolis ____ at New York Jets ____		1:00
		Minnesota ____ at Atlanta ____		1:00
		New England ____ at Buffalo ____		1:00
		New York Giants ____ at Dallas ____		3:00
		Oakland ____ at Kansas City ____		12:00
		St. Louis ____ at San Francisco ____		1:00
		Tampa Bay ____ at Detroit ____		1:00
	Sunday Night	Miami ____ at Arizona ____	(TNT)	5:00
	Monday, September 9	Philadelphia ____ at Green Bay ____	(ABC)	8:00
THIRD WEEK Open Dates: Atlanta, Carolina, St. Louis, San Francisco	**Sunday, September 15 (NBC-TV National Weekend)**	Arizona ____ at New England ____		1:00
		Baltimore ____ at Houston ____		12:00
		Detroit ____ at Philadelphia ____		1:00
		Indianapolis ____ at Dallas ____		3:00
		Jacksonville ____ at Oakland ____		1:00
		Kansas City ____ at Seattle ____		1:00
		Minnesota ____ at Chicago ____		12:00
		New Orleans ____ at Cincinnati ____		1:00
		New York Jets ____ at Miami ____		1:00
		San Diego ____ at Green Bay ____		12:00
		Washington ____ at New York Giants ____		4:00
	Sunday Night	Tampa Bay ____ at Denver ____	(TNT)	6:00
	Monday, September 16	Buffalo ____ at Pittsburgh ____	(ABC)	9:00

1996 SCHEDULE AND NOTE CALENDAR

FOURTH WEEK **Open Dates:** **Baltimore, Cincinnati, Houston, Pittsburgh**	**Sunday, September 22** **(FOX-TV National Weekend)**	Arizona ___ at New Orleans ___		12:00
		Chicago ___ at Detroit ___		4:00
		Dallas ___ at Buffalo ___		4:00
		Denver ___ at Kansas City ___		12:00
		Green Bay ___ at Minnesota ___		12:00
		Jacksonville ___ at New England ___		1:00
		New York Giants ___ at New York Jets ___		1:00
		San Diego ___ at Oakland ___		1:00
		San Francisco ___ at Carolina ___		1:00
		Seattle ___ at Tampa Bay ___		4:00
		Washington ___ at St. Louis ___		12:00
	Sunday Night	Philadelphia ___ at Atlanta ___	(TNT)	8:00
	Monday, September 23	Miami ___ at Indianapolis ___	(ABC)	8:00
FIFTH WEEK **Open Dates:** **Buffalo, Indianapolis, Miami, New England**	**Sunday, September 29** **(FOX-TV National Weekend)**	Atlanta ___ at San Francisco ___		1:00
		Carolina ___ at Jacksonville ___		1:00
		Denver ___ at Cincinnati ___		1:00
		Detroit ___ at Tampa Bay ___		1:00
		Green Bay ___ at Seattle ___		1:00
		Houston ___ at Pittsburgh ___		1:00
		Kansas City ___ at San Diego ___		1:00
		Minnesota ___ at New York Giants ___		1:00
		New Orleans ___ at Baltimore ___		1:00
		Oakland ___ at Chicago ___		12:00
		St. Louis ___ at Arizona ___		1:00
	Sunday Night	New York Jets ___ at Washington ___	(TNT)	8:00
	Monday, September 30	Dallas ___ at Philadelphia ___	(ABC)	9:00
SIXTH WEEK **Open Dates:** **Arizona, Dallas, New York Giants, Philadelphia, Tampa Bay, Washington**	**Sunday, October 6** **(NBC-TV National Weekend)**	Atlanta ___ at Detroit ___		1:00
		Carolina ___ at Minnesota ___		12:00
		Green Bay ___ at Chicago ___		12:00
		Indianapolis ___ at Buffalo ___		4:00
		Jacksonville ___ at New Orleans___		3:00
		New England ___ at Baltimore ___		1:00
		Oakland ___ at New York Jets ___		1:00
		San Diego ___ at Denver ___		2:00
		San Francisco ___ at St. Louis ___		3:00
		Seattle ___ at Miami ___		1:00
	Sunday Night	Houston ___ at Cincinnati___	(TNT)	8:00
	Monday, October 7	Pittsburgh ___ at Kansas City ___	(ABC)	8:00
SEVENTH WEEK **Open Dates:** **Denver, Kansas City, San Diego, Seattle**	**Sunday, October 13** **(FOX-TV National Weekend)**	Arizona ___ at Dallas ___		12:00
		Chicago ___ at New Orleans ___		12:00
		Cincinnati ___ at Pittsburgh ___		1:00
		Detroit ___ at Oakland ___		1:00
		Houston ___ at Atlanta ___		1:00
		Miami ___ at Buffalo ___		1:00
		Minnesota ___ at Tampa Bay ___		1:00
		New York Jets ___ at Jacksonville ___		1:00
		Philadelphia ___ at New York Giants ___		4:00
		St. Louis ___ at Carolina ___		1:00
		Washington ___ at New England ___		1:00
	Sunday Night	Baltimore ___ at Indianapolis ___	(TNT)	7:00
	Monday, October 14	San Francisco ___ at Green Bay ___	(ABC)	8:00

Week	Date	Game	TV	Time
EIGHTH WEEK	**Thursday, October 17**	Seattle ____ at Kansas City ____	(TNT)	7:00
Open Dates:	**Sunday, October 20**	Atlanta ____ at Dallas ____		12:00
Chicago, Detroit,	**(NBC-TV National Weekend)**	Baltimore ____ at Denver ____		2:00
Green Bay,		Buffalo ____ at New York Jets ____		4:00
Minnesota		Cincinnati ____ at San Francisco ____		1:00
		Jacksonville ____ at St. Louis ____		3:00
		Miami ____ at Philadelphia ____		1:00
		New England ____ at Indianapolis ____		12:00
		New Orleans ____ at Carolina ____		1:00
		New York Giants ____ at Washington ____		1:00
		Pittsburgh ____ at Houston ____		3:00
		Tampa Bay ____ at Arizona ____		1:00
	Monday, October 21	Oakland ____ at San Diego ____	(ABC)	6:00
NINTH WEEK	**Sunday, October 27**	Carolina ____ at Philadelphia ____		1:00
Open Dates:	**(FOX-TV National Weekend)**	Dallas ____ at Miami ____		4:00
New Orleans,		Indianapolis ____ at Washington ____		1:00
Oakland		Jacksonville ____ at Cincinnati ____		1:00
		Kansas City ____ at Denver ____		2:00
		New York Giants ____ at Detroit ____		1:00
		New York Jets ____ at Arizona ____		2:00
		Pittsburgh ____ at Atlanta ____		1:00
		St. Louis ____ at Baltimore ____		1:00
		San Diego ____ at Seattle ____		1:00
		San Francisco ____ at Houston ____		12:00
		Tampa Bay ____ at Green Bay ____		12:00
	Sunday Night	Buffalo ____ at New England ____	(TNT)	8:00
	Monday, October 28	Chicago ____ at Minnesota ____	(ABC)	8:00
TENTH WEEK	**Sunday, November 3**	Arizona ____ at New York Giants ____		1:00
Open Dates:	**(NBC-TV National Weekend)**	Carolina ____ at Atlanta ____		1:00
Jacksonville,		Cincinnati ____ at Baltimore ____		1:00
New York Jets		Detroit ____ at Green Bay ____		12:00
		Houston ____ at Seattle ____		1:00
		Kansas City ____ at Minnesota ____		12:00
		Miami ____ at New England ____		4:00
		Philadelphia ____ at Dallas ____		12:00
		St. Louis ____ at Pittsburgh ____		1:00
		San Diego ____ at Indianapolis ____		1:00
		Tampa Bay ____ at Chicago ____		12:00
		Washington ____ at Buffalo ____		4:00
	Sunday Night	San Francisco ____ at New Orleans ____	(ESPN)	7:00
	Monday, November 4	Denver ____ at Oakland ____	(ABC)	6:00
ELEVENTH WEEK	**Sunday, November 10**	Arizona ____ at Washington ____		1:00
	(FOX-TV National Weekend)	Atlanta ____ at St. Louis ____		12:00
		Baltimore ____ at Jacksonville ____		4:00
		Buffalo ____ at Philadelphia ____		1:00
		Chicago ____ at Denver ____		2:00
		Dallas ____ at San Francisco ____		1:00
		Green Bay ____ at Kansas City ____		12:00
		Houston ____ at New Orleans ____		12:00
		Indianapolis ____ at Miami ____		1:00
		Minnesota ____ at Seattle ____		1:00
		New England ____ at New York Jets ____		1:00
		Oakland ____ at Tampa Bay ____		1:00
		Pittsburgh ____ at Cincinnati ____		1:00
	Sunday Night	New York Giants ____ at Carolina ____	(ESPN)	8:00
	Monday, November 11	Detroit ____ at San Diego ____	(ABC)	6:00

1996 SCHEDULE AND NOTE CALENDAR

TWELFTH WEEK	**Sunday, November 17** **(NBC-TV National Weekend)**	Baltimore ___ at San Francisco ___		1:00
		Carolina ___ at St. Louis ___		12:00
		Chicago ___ at Kansas City ___		12:00
		Cincinnati ___ at Buffalo ___		1:00
		Denver ___ at New England ___		1:00
		Jacksonville ___ at Pittsburgh ___		1:00
		Miami ___ at Houston ___		3:00
		New Orleans ___ at Atlanta ___		1:00
		New York Giants ___ at Arizona ___		2:00
		New York Jets ___ at Indianapolis ___		1:00
		Seattle ___ at Detroit ___		1:00
		Tampa Bay ___ at San Diego ___		1:00
		Washington ___ at Philadelphia ___		1:00
	Sunday Night	Minnesota ___ at Oakland ___	(ESPN)	5:00
	Monday, November 18	Green Bay ___ at Dallas ___	(ABC)	8:00
THIRTEENTH WEEK	**Sunday, November 24** **(FOX-TV National Weekend)**	Atlanta ___ at Cincinnati ___		1:00
		Carolina ___ at Houston ___		12:00
		Dallas ___ at New York Giants ___		4:00
		Denver ___ at Minnesota ___		12:00
		Detroit ___ at Chicago ___		12:00
		Indianapolis ___ at New England ___		1:00
		Jacksonville ___ at Baltimore ___		1:00
		New Orleans ___ at Tampa Bay ___		1:00
		New York Jets ___ at Buffalo ___		1:00
		Oakland ___ at Seattle ___		1:00
		Philadelphia ___ at Arizona ___		2:00
		San Diego ___ at Kansas City ___		12:00
		San Francisco ___ at Washington ___		1:00
	Sunday Night	Green Bay ___ at St. Louis ___	(ESPN)	7:00
	Monday, November 25	Pittsburgh ___ at Miami ___	(ABC)	9:00
FOURTEENTH WEEK	**Thursday, November 28**	Kansas City ___ at Detroit ___	(NBC)	12:30
		Washington ___ at Dallas ___	(FOX)	3:00
	Sunday, December 1 **(NBC-TV National Weekend)**	Arizona ___ at Minnesota ___		12:00
		Buffalo ___ at Indianapolis ___		1:00
		Chicago ___ at Green Bay ___		12:00
		Cincinnati ___ at Jacksonville ___		1:00
		Houston ___ at New York Jets ___		4:00
		Miami ___ at Oakland ___		1:00
		New York Giants ___ at Philadelphia ___		1:00
		Pittsburgh ___ at Baltimore ___		1:00
		St. Louis ___ at New Orleans ___		3:00
		Seattle ___ at Denver ___		2:00
		Tampa Bay ___ at Carolina ___		1:00
	Sunday Night	New England ___ at San Diego ___	(ESPN)	5:00
	Monday, December 2	San Francisco ___ at Atlanta ___	(ABC)	9:00
FIFTEENTH WEEK	**Thursday, December 5**	Philadelphia ___ at Indianapolis ___	(ESPN)	8:00
	Sunday, December 8 **(FOX-TV National Weekend)**	Atlanta ___ at New Orleans ___		12:00
		Baltimore ___ at Cincinnati ___		1:00
		Buffalo ___ at Seattle ___		1:00
		Carolina ___ at San Francisco ___		1:00
		Dallas ___ at Arizona ___		2:00
		Denver ___ at Green Bay ___		12:00
		Jacksonville ___ at Houston ___		12:00
		New York Giants ___ at Miami ___		1:00
		New York Jets ___ at New England ___		4:00
		St. Louis ___ at Chicago ___		12:00
		San Diego ___ at Pittsburgh ___		1:00
		Washington ___ at Tampa Bay ___		1:00
	Sunday Night	Minnesota ___ at Detroit ___	(ESPN)	8:00
	Monday, December 9	Kansas City ___ at Oakland ___	(ABC)	6:00

SIXTEENTH WEEK

Saturday, December 14	Philadelphia ____ at New York Jets ____	(FOX)	12:30
	San Diego ____ at Chicago ____	(NBC)	3:00
Sunday, December 15	Baltimore ____ at Carolina ____		1:00
(NBC-TV National Weekend)	Cincinnati ____ at Houston ____		12:00
	Green Bay ____ at Detroit ____		1:00
	Indianapolis ____ at Kansas City ____		12:00
	New England ____ at Dallas ____		12:00
	New Orleans ____ at New York Giants ____		1:00
	Oakland ____ at Denver ____		2:00
	St. Louis ____ at Atlanta ____		1:00
	San Francisco ____ at Pittsburgh ____		1:00
	Tampa Bay ____ at Minnesota ____		12:00
	Washington ____ at Arizona ____		2:00
Sunday Night	Seattle ____ at Jacksonville ____	(ESPN)	8:00
Monday, December 16	Buffalo ____ at Miami ____	(ABC)	9:00

SEVENTEENTH WEEK

Saturday, December 21	New England ____ at New York Giants ____	(NBC)	12:30
	New Orleans ____ at St. Louis ____	(FOX)	3:00
Sunday, December 22	Arizona ____ at Philadelphia ____		1:00
(FOX-TV National Weekend)	Atlanta ____ at Jacksonville ____		1:00
	Chicago ____ at Tampa Bay ____		1:00
	Dallas ____ at Washington ____		4:00
	Houston ____ at Baltimore ____		1:00
	Indianapolis ____ at Cincinnati ____		1:00
	Kansas City ____ at Buffalo ____		1:00
	Miami ____ at New York Jets ____		1:00
	Minnesota ____ at Green Bay ____		12:00
	Pittsburgh ____ at Carolina ____		1:00
	Seattle ____ at Oakland ____		1:00
Sunday Night	Denver ____ at San Diego ____	(ESPN)	5:00
Monday, December 23	Detroit ____ at San Francisco ____	(ABC)	6:00

Wild Card Playoff Games
Site Priorities
Three Wild Card teams (division non-champions with best three records) from each conference and the division champion with the third-best record in each conference will enter the first round of the playoffs. The division champion with the third-best record will play host to the Wild Card team with the third-best record. The Wild Card team with the best record will play host to the Wild Card team with the second-best record. There are no restrictions on intra-division games.

Saturday, December 28, 1996

American Football Conference
__________ at __________ (ABC)

National Football Conference
__________ at __________ (ABC)

Sunday, December 29, 1996

American Football Conference
__________ at __________ (NBC)

National Football Conference
__________ at __________ (FOX)

Divisional Playoff Games
Site Priorities
In each conference, the two division champions with the highest won-lost-tied percentage during the regular season will play host to the Wild Card winners. The division champion with the best record in each conference is assured of playing the Wild Card survivor with the poorest record. There are no restrictions on intra-division games.

Saturday, January 4, 1997

American Football Conference
__________ at __________ (NBC)

National Football Conference
__________ at __________ (FOX)

Sunday, January 5, 1997

American Football Conference
__________ at __________ (NBC)

National Football Conference
__________ at __________ (FOX)

1996 SCHEDULE AND NOTE CALENDAR

Championship Games **Site Priorities for Championship Games** The home teams will be the surviving playoff winners with the best won-lost-tied percentage during the regular season. A Wild Card team cannot play host unless two Wild Card teams are in the game, in which case the Wild Card team that was seeded highest in the first round of the playoffs will be the home team.	**Sunday, January 12, 1997**	American Football Conference ____________ at ____________ (NBC) National Football Conference ____________ at ____________ (FOX)
Super Bowl XXXI	**Sunday, January 26, 1997**	Super Bowl XXXI at the Louisiana Superdome, New Orleans, Louisiana ____________ at ____________ (FOX)
AFC-NFC Pro Bowl	**Sunday, February 2, 1997**	AFC-NFC Pro Bowl at Honolulu, Hawaii AFC ____________ at NFC ____________ (ABC)

POSTSEASON AND NATIONALLY TELEVISED GAMES

POSTSEASON GAMES

Saturday, Dec. 28	AFC and NFC Wild Card Playoffs (ABC)
Sunday, Dec. 29	AFC and NFC Wild Card Playoffs (NBC and FOX)
Saturday, Jan. 4	AFC and NFC Divisional Playoffs (NBC and FOX)
Sunday, Jan. 5	AFC and NFC Divisional Playoffs (NBC and FOX)
Sunday, Jan. 12	AFC and NFC Championship Games (NBC and FOX)
Sunday, Jan. 26	Super Bowl XXXI at the Louisiana Superdome in New Orleans, Louisiana (FOX)
Sunday, Feb. 2	AFC-NFC Pro Bowl at Honolulu, Hawaii (ABC)

1996 NATIONALLY TELEVISED GAMES

Regular Season

Sunday, September 1	New England at Miami (day, NBC)
	Buffalo at New York Giants (night, TNT)
Monday, September 2	Dallas at Chicago (night, ABC)
Sunday, September 8	New York Giants at Dallas (day, FOX)
	Miami at Arizona (night, TNT)
Monday, September 9	Philadelphia at Green Bay (night, ABC)
Sunday, September 15	Indianapolis at Dallas (day, NBC)
	Tampa Bay at Denver (night, TNT)
Monday, September 16	Buffalo at Pittsburgh (night, ABC)
Sunday, September 22	Dallas at Buffalo (day, FOX)
	Philadelphia at Atlanta (night, TNT)
Monday, September 23	Miami at Indianapolis (night, ABC)
Sunday, September 29	Atlanta at San Francisco (day, FOX)
	New York Jets at Washington (night, TNT)
Monday, September 30	Dallas at Philadelphia (night, ABC)
Sunday, October 6	San Diego at Denver (day, NBC)
	Houston at Cincinnati (night, TNT)
Monday, October 7	Pittsburgh at Kansas City (night, ABC)
Sunday, October 13	Detroit at Oakland (day, FOX)
	Baltimore at Indianapolis (night, TNT)
Monday, October 14	San Francisco at Green Bay (night, ABC)
Thursday, October 17	Seattle at Kansas City (night, TNT)
Sunday, October 20	Cincinnati at San Francisco (day, NBC)
Monday, October 21	Oakland at San Diego (night, ABC)
Sunday, October 27	Dallas at Miami (day, FOX)
	Buffalo at New England (night, TNT)
Monday, October 28	Chicago at Minnesota (night, ABC)
Sunday, November 3	Miami at New England (day, NBC)
	San Francisco at New Orleans (night, ESPN)
Monday, November 4	Denver at Oakland (night, ABC)
Sunday, November 10	Dallas at San Francisco (day, FOX)
	New York Giants at Carolina (night, ESPN)
Monday, November 11	Detroit at San Diego (night, ABC)
Sunday, November 17	Baltimore at San Francisco (day, NBC)
	Minnesota at Oakland (night, ESPN)
Monday, November 18	Green Bay at Dallas (night, ABC)
Sunday, November 24	Dallas at New York Giants (day, FOX)
	Green Bay at St. Louis (night, ESPN)
Monday, November 25	Pittsburgh at Miami (night, ABC)
Thursday, November 28	Kansas City at Detroit (day, NBC)
	Washington at Dallas (day, FOX)
Sunday, December 1	Miami at Oakland (day, NBC)
	New England at San Diego (night, ESPN)
Monday, December 2	San Francisco at Atlanta (night, ABC)
Thursday, December 5	Philadelphia at Indianapolis (night, ESPN)
Sunday, December 8	Dallas at Arizona (day, FOX)
	Minnesota at Detroit (night, ESPN)
Monday, December 9	Kansas City at Oakland (night, ABC)
Saturday, December 14	Philadelphia at New York Jets (day, FOX)
	San Diego at Chicago (day, NBC)
Sunday, December 15	Oakland at Denver (day, NBC)
	Seattle at Jacksonville (night, ESPN)
Monday, December 16	Buffalo at Miami (night, ABC)
Saturday, December 21	New England at New York Giants (day, NBC)
	New Orleans at St. Louis (day, FOX)
Sunday, December 22	Dallas at Washington (day, FOX)
	Denver at San Diego (night, ESPN)
Monday, December 23	Detroit at San Francisco (night, ABC)

NATIONAL PRIMETIME TELEVISION GAMES AT A GLANCE

(All times local; Sunday and Thursday on TNT and ESPN, Monday on ABC; all on CBS radio)

Sunday, September 1	Buffalo at New York Giants (TNT)	8:00
Monday, September 2	Dallas at Chicago (ABC)	8:00
Sunday, September 8	Miami at Arizona (TNT)	5:00
Monday, September 9	Philadelphia at Green Bay (ABC)	8:00
Sunday, September 15	Tampa Bay at Denver (TNT)	6:00
Monday, September 16	Buffalo at Pittsburgh (ABC)	9:00
Sunday, September 22	Philadelphia at Atlanta (TNT)	8:00
Monday, September 23	Miami at Indianapolis (ABC)	8:00
Sunday, September 29	New York Jets at Washington (TNT)	8:00
Monday, September 30	Dallas at Philadelphia (ABC)	9:00
Sunday, October 6	Houston at Cincinnati (TNT)	8:00
Monday, October 7	Pittsburgh at Kansas City (ABC)	8:00
Sunday, October 13	Baltimore at Indianapolis (TNT)	7:00
Monday, October 14	San Francisco at Green Bay (ABC)	8:00
Thursday, October 17	Seattle at Kansas City (TNT)	7:00
Monday, October 21	Oakland at San Diego (ABC)	6:00
Sunday, October 27	Buffalo at New England (TNT)	8:00
Monday, October 28	Chicago at Minnesota (ABC)	8:00
Sunday, November 3	San Francisco at New Orleans (ESPN)	7:00
Monday, November 4	Denver at Oakland (ABC)	6:00
Sunday, November 10	New York Giants at Carolina (ESPN)	8:00
Monday, November 11	Detroit at San Diego (ABC)	6:00
Sunday, November 17	Minnesota at Oakland (ESPN)	5:00
Monday, November 18	Green Bay at Dallas (ABC)	8:00
Sunday, November 24	Green Bay at St. Louis (ESPN)	7:00
Monday, November 25	Pittsburgh at Miami (ABC)	9:00
Sunday, December 1	New England at San Diego (ESPN)	5:00
Monday, December 2	San Francisco at Atlanta (ABC)	9:00
Thursday, December 5	Philadelphia at Indianapolis (ESPN)	8:00
Sunday, December 8	Minnesota at Detroit (ESPN)	8:00
Monday, December 9	Kansas City at Oakland (ABC)	6:00
Sunday, December 15	Seattle at Jacksonville (ESPN)	8:00
Monday, December 16	Buffalo at Miami (ABC)	9:00
Sunday, December 22	Denver at San Diego (ESPN)	5:00
Monday, December 23	Detroit at San Francisco (ABC)	6:00

IMPORTANT DATES

1996

July 8	Claiming period of 24 hours begins in waiver system. All waiver requests for the rest of the year are no-recall and no-withdrawal.
Mid-July	Training camps open. Veteran players cannot be required to report earlier than 15 days prior to club's first preseason game or July 15, whichever is later.
July 15	Signing period ends at 4 P.M., Eastern Daylight Time, for Unrestricted Free Agents to whom June 1 tender was made by Old Club, and for Transition Players and Franchise Players who are subject to the rules for Transition Players. After this date and through 4 P.M., Eastern Daylight Time, on November 7, Old Club has exclusive negotiating rights with its unsigned Unrestricted Free Agents.
July 27	Hall of Fame Game, Canton, Ohio: Indianapolis vs. New Orleans.
July 27	American Bowl, Tokyo, Japan: Pittsburgh vs. San Diego.
August 2	If a drafted rookie has not signed with his club by this date, he may not be traded to any other club in 1996.
August 2	Deadline for players under contract to report in order to earn a season of free agency credit.
August 5	American Bowl, Monterrey, Mexico: Dallas vs. Kansas City.
August 20	Roster cutdown to maximum of 60 players on Active List by 4 P.M., Eastern Daylight Time.
August 25	Roster cutdown to maximum of 53 players on Active/Inactive List by 4 P.M., Eastern Daylight Time. Clubs may dress minimum of 42 and maximum of 45 players and third quarterback for each regular-season and postseason game.
August 26	After 4 P.M., Eastern Daylight Time, clubs may establish a Practice Squad of five players by signing free agents who do not have an accrued season of free-agency credit, unless that season was achieved by spending an entire regular season on Reserve/Injured or Reserve/Physically Unable to Perform.
August 30	All clubs are required to identify their 49-player Active List by 7:00 P.M., Eastern Daylight Time, on this Friday and thereafter on each Friday before a regular-season Sunday game. No later than one hour and 30 minutes prior to kickoff, clubs must identify their 45-player Active List and third quarterback, if any.
September 1-2	Regular season opens.
September 17	Priority on multiple waiver claims is now based on the current season's standing.
October 8	All trading ends at 4 P.M., Eastern Daylight Time.
October 9	Players with at least four previous pension-credited seasons are subject to the waiver system for the remainder of the regular season and postseason.
October 30-31	NFL Fall Meeting, New Orleans, Louisiana.
November 5	Deadline for clubs to sign by 4 P.M., Eastern Daylight Time, their Franchise and Transition players. If still unsigned after this date, such players are prohibited from playing in NFL in 1996.
November 5	Deadline for clubs to sign by 4 P.M., Eastern Daylight Time, their Unrestricted and Restricted Free Agents to whom June 1 tender was made. If still unsigned after this date, such players are prohibited from playing in NFL in 1996.
November 5	Deadline for clubs to sign drafted players by 4 P.M., Eastern Daylight Time. If such players remain unsigned, they are prohibited from playing in NFL in 1996.
November 23	Deadline for reinstatement of players in Reserve List categories of Retired and Did Not Report.
December 20	Deadline for waiver requests in 1996, except for "special waiver requests" which have a 10-day claiming period, with termination or assignment delayed until after the Super Bowl.
December 24	Clubs may begin signing free-agent players for the 1997 season.
December 28-29	Wild-Card Playoff Games.

1997

January 4-5	Divisional Playoff Games.
January 12	AFC and NFC Championship Games.
January 26	Super Bowl XXXI, Louisiana Superdome, New Orleans, Louisiana
February 2	AFC-NFC Pro Bowl, Honolulu, Hawaii.
February 3	Waiver system begins for 1997. Players with at least four previous pension-credited seasons that a club desires to terminate are not subject to the waiver system until after the trading deadline.
February 6-10	Combine Timing and Testing, RCA Dome, Indianapolis, Indiana.
Mid February:	Deadline for clubs to designate Franchise and Transition Players.
Mid February:	Expiration date of all player contracts due to expire in 1997.
Mid February:	Free Agency period begins.
Mid February:	Trading period begins for 1997 after expiration of all 1996 contracts.
March 9-13	NFL Annual Meeting, Palm Desert, California.
*April 14	Deadline for signing of Offer Sheets by Restricted Free Agents.
*April 19-20	Annual player selection meeting, New York, New York.
May 20-21	NFL Spring Meeting, San Diego, California.
June 1	Deadline for Old Club to send tender to its unsigned Restricted Free Agents or to extend Qualifying Offer, whichever is greater, in order to retain rights.
June 1	Deadline for Old Club to send tender to its unsigned Unrestricted Free Agents to retain rights if player is not signed by another club by July 15.
*July 26	Hall of Fame Game, Canton, Ohio.
*August 31-September 1	Regular season opens.
*December 27-28	Wild-Card Playoff Games.

1998

*January 3-4	Divisional Playoff Games.
*January 11	AFC and NFC Championship Games.
*January 25	Super Bowl XXXII, San Diego Jack Murphy Stadium, San Diego, California.
*February 1	AFC-NFC Pro Bowl, Honolulu, Hawaii.

**Tentatively scheduled.*

WAIVERS

The waiver system is a procedure by which player contracts or NFL rights to players are made available by a club to other clubs in the League. During the procedure, the 29 other clubs either file claims to obtain the players or waive the opportunity to do so—thus the term "waiver." Claiming clubs are assigned players on a priority based on the inverse of won-and-lost standing. The claiming period normally is 10 days during the offseason and 24 hours from early July through December. In some circumstances, another 24 hours is added on to allow the original club to rescind its action (known as a recall of a waiver request) and/or the claiming club to do the same (known as withdrawal of a claim). If a player passes through waivers unclaimed and is not recalled by the original club, he becomes a free agent. All waivers from July through December are no recall and no withdrawal. Under the Collective Bargaining Agreement, from the beginning of the waiver system each year through the trading deadline (October 8, 1996), any veteran who has acquired four years of pension credit is not subject to the waiver system if the club desires to release him. After the trading deadline, such players are subject to the waiver system.

ACTIVE/INACTIVE LIST

The Active/Inactive List is the principal status for players participating for a club. It consists of all players under contract who are eligible for preseason, regular-season, and postseason games. In 1996, teams will be permitted to open training camp with no more than 80 players under contract and thereafter must meet two mandatory roster reductions prior to the season opener. Teams will be permitted an Active List of 45 players and an Inactive List of eight players for each regular-season and postseason game during the 1996 season. Provided that a club has two quarterbacks on its 45-player Active List, a third quarterback from its Inactive List is permitted to dress for the game, but if he enters the game during the first three quarters, the other two quarterbacks are thereafter prohibited from playing. Teams also are permitted to establish Practice Squads of up to five players who are eligible to participate in practice, but these players remain free agents and are eligible to sign with any other team in the league.

August 20 ....Roster reduction to 60 players
August 25 ....Roster reduction to 53 players
August 26 ....Teams establish a Practice Squad of up to five players

In addition to the squad limits described above, the overall roster limit of 80 players remains in effect throughout the regular season and postseason. The overall limit is applicable to players on a team's Active, Inactive, and Exempt Lists, players on the Practice Squad, and players on the Reserve List as Injured, Physically Unable to Perform, Non-Football Illness/Injury, and Suspended by Club.

RESERVE LIST

The Reserve List is a status for players who, for reasons of injury, retirement, military service, or other circumstances, are not immediately available for participation with a club. Players on Reserve/Injured are not eligible to practice or return to the Active/Inactive List in the same season that they are placed on Reserve. Players in the category of Reserve/Retired or Reserve/Did Not Report may not be reinstated during the period from 30 days before the end of the regular season through the postseason.

TRADES

Unrestricted trading between the AFC and NFC is allowed in 1996 through October 8, after which trading will end until 1997.

ANNUAL ACTIVE PLAYER LIMITS

NFL

Year(s)	Limit
1991-96	45**
1985-90	45
1983-84	49
1982	45†-49
1978-81	45
1975-77	43
1974	47
1964-73	40
1963	37
1961-62	36
1960	38
1959	36
1957-58	35
1951-56	33
1949-50	32
1948	35
1947	35*-34
1945-46	33
1943-44	28
1940-42	33
1938-39	30
1936-37	25
1935	24
1930-34	20
1926-29	18
1925	16

**45 plus a third quarterback
† 45 for first two games
* 35 for first three games

AFL

Year(s)	Limit
1966-69	40
1965	38
1964	34
1962-63	33
1960-61	35

FIGURING THE 1997 SCHEDULE

At the conclusion of the 1996 NFL regular season, it will be possible to determine the 1997 opponents of the 30 teams.

Each 1996 team schedule is based on a "common-opponent" formula initiated for the 1978 season and most recently modified in 1995. Under the common-opponent format, all teams in a division play at least 11 of their 16 games the following season against common opponents. It is not a position scheduling format in which the strong play the strong and the weak play the weak.

In creating a schedule, the NFL seeks an easily understood and balanced formula that provides both competitive equality and a variety of opponents. Under the rotation scheduling system in effect from 1970-77, non-division opponents were determined by a pre-set formula. This often resulted in competitive imbalances.

With common opponents as the basis for scheduling, a more competitive and equitable method of determining division champions and postseason playoff representatives has developed. Teams battling for a division title are playing more than two-thirds of their games against common opponents.

In 1987, NFL owners passed a bylaw proposal designed to modify the common-opponent scheduling format and create greater equity. And in 1995, with the addition of two expansion teams, the 1987 changes were modified to include fifth-place teams in the common-opponent scheduling format for each division. The following chart shows a history of the pairings in non-division games within the conference since the change to a common-opponent format in 1978:

Prior Year's Finish in Division	Current Pairings in Non-Division Games Within Conference	Previous Pairings 1987-94	Previous Pairings 1978-86
1	1-1-2-3	1-1-2-3	1-1-4-4
2	1-2-2-4	1-2-2-4	2-2-3-3
3	1-3-3-5	1-3-3-4	2-2-3-3
4	2-4-4-5	2-3-4-4	1-1-4-4
5	3-4-5-5		

Under the common-opponent format, schedules of all NFL teams are figured according to the following formula. (The reference point for the figuring is the team's final division standing. Ties in divisions are broken according to the tie-breaking procedures outlined on page 16.)

1. Home-and-away round-robin **within the division** (8 games).
2. In the **interconference games,** each team plays four teams in a division of the other conference (4 games). In 1997, the AFC East will play the NFC Central, the AFC Central will play the NFC East, and the AFC West will play the NFC West (see chart on following page).
3. **Within the conference,** the first-place team plays the first-place teams in the other divisions plus a second- and third-place team in the conference. The second-place team plays the second-place teams in the other divisions plus a first- and fourth-place team in the conference. The third-place team plays the third-place teams in the other divisions plus a first- and fifth-place team in the conference. The fourth-place team plays the fourth-place teams in the other divisions plus a second- and fifth-place team in the conference. The fifth-place team plays the fifth-place teams in the other divisions plus a third- and fourth-place team in the conference (4 games, see chart).

This completes the 16-game schedule.

The 1997 Opponent Breakdown chart on the following page does not include the round-robin games within the division. Those are automatically scheduled on a home-and-away basis.

NOTES

1996 NFL Standings

AFC

EAST AE
1 ________
2 ________
3 ________
4 ________
5 ________

CENTRAL AC
1 ________
2 ________
3 ________
4 ________
5 ________

WEST AW
1 ________
2 ________
3 ________
4 ________
5 ________

NFC

EAST NE
1 ________
2 ________
3 ________
4 ________
5 ________

CENTRAL NC
1 ________
2 ________
3 ________
4 ________
5 ________

WEST NW
1 ________
2 ________
3 ________
4 ________
5 ________

A Team's 1997 Schedule

____
Team Name

OPPONENTS
1 ________
2 ________
3 ________
4 ________
5 ________
6 ________
7 ________
8 ________
9 ________
10 ________
11 ________
12 ________
13 ________
14 ________
15 ________
16 ________

1997 Non-Divisional Opponent Breakdown (Combined Intraconference and Interconference)

American Football Conference

AFC East

	Home	Away
AE1	AC 1	AW 1
	AW 3	AC 2
	NC 1	NC 2
	NC 3	NC 4
AE2	AC 2	AW 2
	AW 1	AC 4
	NC 2	NC 1
	NC 5	NC 3
AE3	AC 3	AW 3
	AW 5	AC 1
	NC 1	NC 2
	NC 4	NC 5
AE4	AC 4	AW 4
	AW 2	AC 5
	NC 3	NC 1
	NC 5	NC 4
AE5	AC 5	AW 5
	AW 4	AC 3
	NC 2	NC 3
	NC 4	NC 5

AFC Central

	Home	Away
AC1	AW 1	AE 1
	AE 3	AW 2
	NE 1	NE 2
	NE 3	NE 4
AC2	AW 2	AE 2
	AE 1	AW 4
	NE 2	NE 1
	NE 5	NE 3
AC3	AW 3	AE 3
	AE 5	AW 1
	NE 1	NE 2
	NE 4	NE 5
AC4	AW 4	AE 4
	AE 2	AW 5
	NE 3	NE 1
	NE 5	NE 4
AC5	AW 5	AE 5
	AE 4	AW 3
	NE 2	NE 3
	NE 4	NE 5

AFC West

	Home	Away
AW1	AE 1	AC 1
	AC 3	AE 2
	NW 1	NW 2
	NW 3	NW 4
AW2	AE 2	AC 2
	AC 1	AE 4
	NW 2	NW 1
	NW 5	NW 3
AW3	AE 3	AC 3
	AC 5	AE 1
	NW 1	NW 2
	NW 4	NW 5
AW4	AE 4	AC 4
	AC 2	AE 5
	NW 3	NW 1
	NW 5	NW 4
AW5	AE 5	AC 5
	AC 4	AE 3
	NW 2	NW 3
	NW 4	NW 5

National Football Conference

NFC East

	Home	Away
NE1	NW 1	NC 1
	NC 3	NW 2
	AC 2	AC 1
	AC 4	AC 3
NE2	NW 2	NC 2
	NC 1	NW 4
	AC 1	AC 2
	AC 3	AC 5
NE3	NW 3	NC 3
	NC 5	NW 1
	AC 2	AC 1
	AC 5	AC 4
NE4	NW 4	NC 4
	NC 2	NW 5
	AC 1	AC 3
	AC 4	AC 5
NE5	NW 5	NC 5
	NC 4	NW 3
	AC 3	AC 2
	AC 5	AC 4

NFC Central

	Home	Away
NC1	NE 1	NW 1
	NW 3	NE 2
	AE 2	AE 1
	AE 4	AE 3
NC2	NE 2	NW 2
	NW 1	NE 4
	AE 1	AE 2
	AE 3	AE 5
NC3	NE 3	NW 3
	NW 5	NE 1
	AE 2	AE 1
	AE 5	AE 4
NC4	NE 4	NW 4
	NW 2	NE 5
	AE 1	AE 3
	AE 4	AE 5
NC5	NE 5	NW 5
	NW 4	NE 3
	AE 3	AE 2
	AE 5	AE 4

NFC West

	Home	Away
NW1	NC 1	NE 1
	NE 3	NC 2
	AW 2	AW 1
	AW 4	AW 3
NW2	NC 2	NE 2
	NE 1	NC 4
	AW 1	AW 2
	AW 3	AW 5
NW3	NC 3	NE 3
	NE 5	NC 1
	AW 2	AW 1
	AW 5	AW 4
NW4	NC 4	NE 4
	NE 2	NC 5
	AW 1	AW 3
	AW 4	AW 5
NW5	NC 5	NE 5
	NE 4	NC 3
	AW 3	AW 2
	AW 5	AW 4

TIE-BREAKING PROCEDURES

The following procedures will be used to break standings ties for postseason playoffs and to determine regular-season schedules. NOTE: Tie games count as one-half win and one-half loss for both clubs.

TO BREAK A TIE WITHIN A DIVISION

If, at the end of the regular season, two or more clubs in the same division finish with identical won-lost-tied percentages, the following steps will be taken until a champion is determined.

TWO CLUBS

1. Head-to-head (best won-lost-tied percentage in games between the clubs).
2. Best won-lost-tied percentage in games played within the division.
3. Best won-lost-tied percentage in games played within the conference.
4. Best won-lost-tied percentage in common games, if applicable.
5. Best net points in division games.
6. Best net points in all games.
7. Strength of schedule.
8. Best net touchdowns in all games.
9. Coin toss.

THREE OR MORE CLUBS

(Note: If two clubs remain tied after third or other clubs are eliminated during any step, tie breaker reverts to step 1 of the two-club format).

1. Head-to-head (best won-lost-tied percentage in games among the clubs).
2. Best won-lost-tied percentage in games played within the division.
3. Best won-lost-tied percentage in games played within the conference.
4. Best won-lost-tied percentage in common games.
5. Best net points in division games.
6. Best net points in all games.
7. Strength of schedule.
8. Best net touchdowns in all games.
9. Coin toss.

TO BREAK A TIE FOR THE WILD-CARD TEAM

If it is necessary to break ties to determine the three Wild-Card clubs from each conference, the following steps will be taken.

1. If the tied clubs are from the same division, apply division tie breaker.
2. If the tied clubs are from different divisions, apply the following steps.

TWO CLUBS

1. Head-to-head, if applicable.
2. Best won-lost-tied percentage in games played within the conference.
3. Best won-lost-tied percentage in common games, minimum of four.
4. Best net points in conference games.
5. Best net points in all games.
6. Strength of schedule.
7. Best net touchdowns in all games.
8. Coin toss.

THREE OR MORE CLUBS

(Note: If two clubs remain tied after third or other clubs are eliminated, tie breaker reverts to step 1 of applicable two-club format.)

1. Apply division tie breaker to eliminate all but the highest ranked club in each division prior to proceeding to step 2. The original seeding within a division upon application of the division tie breaker remains the same for all subsequent applications of the procedure that are necessary to identify the three Wild-Card participants.
2. Head-to-head sweep. (Applicable only if one club has defeated each of the others or if one club has lost to each of the others).
3. Best won-lost-tied percentage in games played within the conference.
4. Best won-lost-tied percentage in common games, minimum of four.
5. Best net points in conference games.
6. Best net points in all games.
7. Strength of schedule.
8. Best net touchdowns in all games.
9. Coin toss.

When the first Wild-Card team has been identified, the procedure is repeated to name the second Wild-Card, i.e., eliminate all but the highest-ranked club in each division prior to proceeding to step 2, and repeated a third time, if necessary, to identify the third Wild Card. In situations where three or more teams from the same division are involved in the procedure, the original seeding of the teams remains the same for subsequent applications of the tie breaker if the top-ranked team in that division qualifies for a Wild-Card berth.

OTHER TIE-BREAKING PROCEDURES

1. Only one club advances to the playoffs in any tie-breaking step. Remaining tied clubs revert to the first step of the applicable division or Wild-Card tie breakers. As an example, if two clubs remain tied in any tie-breaker step after all other clubs have been eliminated, the procedure reverts to step one of the two-club format to determine the winner. When one club wins the tie breaker, all other clubs revert to step 1 of the applicable two-club or three-club format.
2. In comparing division and conference records or records against common opponents among tied teams, the best won-lost-tied percentage is the deciding factor since teams may have played an unequal number of games.
3. To determine home-field priority among division titlists, apply Wild-Card tie breakers.
4. To determine home-field priority for Wild-Card qualifiers, apply division tie breakers (if teams are from the same division) or Wild-Card tie breakers (if teams are from different divisions).

TIE-BREAKING PROCEDURE FOR SELECTION MEETING

If two or more clubs are tied in the selection order, the strength-of-schedule tie breaker is applied, subject to the following exceptions for playoff clubs:

1. The Super Bowl winner is last and the Super Bowl loser next-to-last.
2. Any non-Super Bowl playoff club involved in a tie shall be assigned priority within its segment below that of non-playoff clubs and in the order that the playoff clubs exited from the playoffs. Thus, within a tied segment a playoff club that loses in the Wild-Card game will have priority over a playoff club that loses in the Divisional playoff game, which in turn will have priority over a club that loses in the Conference Championship game. If two tied clubs exited the playoffs in the same round, the tie is broken by strength of schedule.

If any ties cannot be broken by strength of schedule, the divisional or conference tie breakers, whichever are applicable, are applied. Any ties that still exist are broken by a coin flip.

NFL PASSER RATING SYSTEM

The NFL rates its passers for statistical purposes against a fixed performance standard based on statistical achievements of all qualified pro passers since 1960. The current system replaced one that rated passers in relation to their position in a total group based on various criteria. The current system, which was adopted in 1973, removes inequities that existed in the former method and, at the same time, provides a means of comparing passing performances from one season to the next.

It is important to remember that the system is used to rate **passers,** not **quarterbacks.** Statistics do not reflect leadership, play-calling, and other intangible factors that go into making a successful professional quarterback. Four categories are used as a basis for compiling a rating:

—Percentage of touchdown passes per attempt
—Percentage of completions per attempt
—Percentage of interceptions per attempt
—Average yards gained per attempt

The **average** standard, is 1.000. The bottom is .000. To earn a 2.000 rating, a passer must perform at exceptional levels, i.e., 70 percent in completions, 10 percent in touchdowns, 1.5 percent in interceptions, and 11 yards average gain per pass attempt. The **maximum** a passer can receive in any category is 2.375.

For example, to gain a 2.375 in completion percentage, a passer would have to complete 77.5 percent of his passes. The NFL record is 70.55 by Ken Anderson (Cincinnati, 1982). To earn a 2.375 in percentage of touchdowns, a passer would have to achieve a percentage of 11.9. The record is 13.9 by Sid Luckman (Chicago, 1943). To gain 2.375 in percentage of interceptions, a passer would have to go the entire season without an interception. The 2.375 figure in average yards is 12.50, compared with the NFL record of 11.17 by Tommy O'Connell (Cleveland, 1957).

In order to make the rating more understandable, the point rating is then converted into a scale of 100. In rare cases, where statistical performance has been superior, it is possible for a passer to surpass a 100 rating. For example, take Steve Young's record-setting season in 1994 when he completed 324 of 461 passes for 3,969 yards, 35 touchdowns, and 10 interceptions. The four calculations would be:

—**Percentage of Completions**—324 of 461 is 70.28 percent. Subtract 30 from the completion percentage (40.28) and multiply the result by 0.05. The result is a point rating of **2.014**.
Note: If the result is less than zero (Comp. Pct. less than 30.0), award zero points. If the results are greater than 2.375 (Comp. Pct. greater than 77.5), award 2.375.

—**Percentage of Touchdown Passes**—35 touchdowns in 461 attempts is 7.59 percent. Multiply the touchdown percentage by 0.2. The result is a point rating of **1.518**.
Note: If the result is greater than 2.375 (touchdown percentage greater than 11.875), award 2.375.

—**Percentage of Interceptions**—10 interceptions in 461 attempts is 2.17 percent. Multiply the interception percentage by 0.25 (0.542) and subtract the number from 2.375. The result is **1.833**.
Note: If the result is less than zero (interception percentage greater than 9.5), award zero points.

—**Average Yards Gained Per Attempt**—3,969 yards divided by 461 attempts is 8.61. Subtract three yards from yards-per-attempt (5.61) and multiply the result by 0.25. The result is **1.403**.
Note: If the result is less than zero (yards per attempt less than 3.0), award zero points. If the result is greater than 2.375 (yards per attempt greater than 12.5), award 2.375 points.

The sum of the four steps is (2.014 + 1.518 + 1.833 + 1.403) **6.768**. The sum is then divided by six (1.128) and multiplied by 100. In this case, the result is **112.8**. This same formula can be used to determine a passer rating for any player who attempts at least one pass.

The following is a list of qualifying passers who had a single-season passer rating of 100 or higher:

Player, Team	Season	Rating	Att.	Comp.	Pct.	Yds.	Avg.	TD	TD Pct.	Int.	Int. Pct.
Steve Young, San Francisco	1994	112.8	461	324	70.2	3,969	8.61	35	7.6	10	2.2
Joe Montana, San Francisco	1989	112.4	386	271	70.2	3,521	9.12	26	6.7	8	2.1
Milt Plum, Cleveland	1960	110.4	250	151	60.4	2,297	9.19	21	8.4	5	2.0
Sammy Baugh, Washington	1945	109.9	182	128	70.3	1,669	9.17	11	6.0	4	2.2
Dan Marino, Miami	1984	108.9	564	362	64.2	5,084	9.01	48	8.5	17	3.0
Sid Luckman, Chicago Bears	1943	107.5	202	110	54.5	2,194	10.86	28	13.9	12	5.9
Steve Young, San Francisco	1992	107.0	402	268	66.7	3,465	8.62	25	6.2	7	1.7
Bart Starr, Green Bay	1966	105.0	251	156	62.2	2,257	8.99	14	5.6	3	1.2
Roger Staubach, Dallas	1971	104.8	211	126	59.7	1,882	8.92	15	7.1	4	1.9
Y.A. Tittle, N.Y. Giants	1963	104.8	367	221	60.2	3,145	8.57	36	9.8	14	3.8
Bart Starr, Green Bay	1968	104.3	171	109	63.7	1,617	9.46	15	8.8	8	4.7
Ken Stabler, Oakland	1976	103.4	291	194	66.7	2,737	9.41	27	9.3	17	5.8
Joe Montana, San Francisco	1984	102.9	432	279	64.6	3,630	8.40	28	6.5	10	2.3
Charlie Conerly, N.Y. Giants	1959	102.7	194	113	58.2	1,706	8.79	14	7.2	4	2.1
Bert Jones, Baltimore	1976	102.5	343	207	60.3	3,104	9.05	24	7.0	9	2.6
Joe Montana, San Francisco	1987	102.1	398	266	66.8	3,054	7.67	31	7.8	13	3.3
Steve Young, San Francisco	1991	101.8	279	180	64.5	2,517	9.02	17	6.1	8	2.9
Len Dawson, Kansas City	1966	101.7	284	159	56.0	2,527	8.90	26	9.2	10	3.5
Steve Young, San Francisco	1993	101.5	462	314	68.0	4,023	8.71	29	6.3	16	3.5
Jim Kelly, Buffalo	1990	101.2	346	219	63.3	2,829	8.18	24	6.9	9	2.6
Jim Harbaugh, Indianapolis	1995	100.7	314	200	63.7	2,575	8.20	17	5.4	5	1.6

AFC ACTIVE STATISTICAL LEADERS

TOP ACTIVE PASSERS, AMERICAN FOOTBALL CONFERENCE

1,000 or more attempts

	Yrs.	Att.	Comp.	Pct. Comp.	Yards	Avg. Gain	TD	Pct. TD	Had Int.	Pct. Int.	Rating Pts.
Dan Marino, Mia.	13	6531	3913	59.9	48841	7.48	352	5.4	200	3.1	88.4
Jim Kelly, Buff.	10	4400	2652	60.3	32657	7.42	223	5.1	156	3.5	85.4
Jeff Hostetler, Oak.	10	1792	1036	57.8	12983	7.24	66	3.7	47	2.6	81.8
Neil O'Donnell, N.Y.J.	5	1871	1069	57.1	12867	6.88	68	3.6	39	2.1	81.8
Bernie Kosar, Mia.	11	3333	1970	59.1	23093	6.93	123	3.7	87	2.6	81.6
Steve Bono, K.C.	10	1116	625	56.0	7031	6.30	45	4.0	25	2.2	79.1
Jim Harbaugh, Ind.	9	2275	1348	59.3	15582	6.85	76	3.3	67	2.9	78.9
John Elway, Den.	13	5926	3346	56.5	41706	7.04	225	3.8	191	3.2	77.7
Stan Humphries, S.D.	6	1875	1078	57.5	13033	6.95	66	3.5	65	3.5	76.2
Chris Chandler, Hou.	8	1598	918	57.4	10581	6.62	58	3.6	60	3.8	74.0
Rich Gannon, K.C.	7	1139	642	56.4	7218	6.34	43	3.8	43	3.8	72.3
John Friesz, Sea.	5	1047	570	54.4	6457	6.17	35	3.3	32	3.1	71.6
Bubby Brister*	10	2032	1101	54.2	13242	6.52	71	3.5	71	3.5	71.5
Vinny Testaverde, Balt.	9	3158	1704	54.0	22075	6.99	124	3.9	149	4.7	69.6
Drew Bledsoe, N.E.	3	1756	937	53.4	10556	6.01	53	3.0	58	3.3	67.9
Rick Mirer, Sea.	3	1258	678	53.9	7548	6.00	36	2.9	44	3.5	67.0
Mike Tomczak, Pitt.	11	1624	850	52.3	11298	6.96	58	3.6	77	4.7	66.8
Billy Joe Tolliver*	6	1124	578	51.4	6740	6.23	39	3.5	43	3.8	65.5
Vince Evans*	15	1390	704	50.6	9485	6.82	52	3.7	74	5.3	63.0

TOP ACTIVE RUSHERS, AFC

2,500 or more yards

	Yrs.	Att.	Yards	TD
1. Marcus Allen, K.C.	14	2692	10908	103
2. Thurman Thomas, Buff.	8	2285	9729	54
3. Earnest Byner, Balt.	12	1852	7314	52
4. Marion Butts*	7	1345	5185	43
5. Chris Warren, Sea.	6	1156	5004	35
6. Harold Green*	6	968	3727	8
7. Leonard Russell, S.D.	5	945	3260	22
8. Jerome Bettis, Pitt.	3	796	3091	13
9. Keith Byars, Mia.	10	848	3049	23
10. Harvey Williams, Oak.	5	754	2955	15
Other Leading Rushers				
Brad Baxter, N.Y.J.	7	779	2928	35
John Elway, Den.	13	637	2846	27
Erric Pegram, Pitt.	5	730	2794	10
Derrick Fenner, Oak.	7	730	2727	28
Natrone Means, Jax.	3	689	2725	25
Ronnie Harmon, Hou.	10	576	2607	9

TOP ACTIVE PASS RECEIVERS, AFC

275 or more receptions

	Yrs.	No.	Yards	TD
1. Andre Reed, Buff.	11	700	9848	69
2. Ernest Givins, Jax.	10	571	8215	49
3. Marcus Allen, K.C.	14	549	5055	21
4. Keith Byars, Mia.	10	532	4925	23
5. Webster Slaughter, K.C.	10	523	7584	42
6. Andre Rison, Balt.	7	522	7154	63
7. Ronnie Harmon, Hou.	10	522	5391	22
8. Haywood Jeffires, Hou.	9	515	6119	47
9. Anthony Miller, Den.	8	493	7768	56
Brian Blades, Sea.	8	493	6561	30
Other Leading Receivers				
Earnest Byner, Balt.	12	461	4207	14
Tim Brown, Oak.	8	405	6076	46
Thurman Thomas, Buff.	8	371	3622	20
Quinn Early, Buff.	8	325	4497	30
Tim McGee, Cin.	9	321	5203	28
Shannon Sharpe, Den.	6	313	3822	21
Fred Barnett, Mia.	6	308	4634	28
Ricky Proehl, Sea.	6	292	3869	21
David Meggett, N.E.	7	283	2528	10

TOP ACTIVE SCORERS, AFC

300 or more points

	Yrs.	TD	FG	PAT	TP
1. Nick Lowery, N.Y.J.	17	0	366	536	1634
2. Matt Bahr, N.E.	17	0	300	522	1422
3. Norm Johnson, Pitt.	14	0	277	515	1346
4. Al Del Greco, Hou.	12	0	204	368	980
5. Pete Stoyanovich, Mia.	7	0	176	246	774
6. Marcus Allen, K.C.	14	125	0	2	752
7. Jeff Jaeger, Oak.	8	0	166	244	742
8. Mike Cofer, Ind.	8	0	133	303	702
9. John Carney, S.D.	8	0	152	195	651
10. Steve Christie, Buff.	6	0	140	199	619
Other Leading Scorers					
Matt Stover, Balt.	5	0	108	156	480
Thurman Thomas, Buff.	8	74	0	0	444
Andre Reed, Buff.	11	70	0	0	420
Earnest Byner, Balt.	12	67	0	0	402
Andre Rison, Balt.	7	63	0	2	380
Jason Elam, Den.	3	0	87	109	370
Anthony Miller, Den.	8	59	0	2	356
Doug Pelfrey, Cin.	3	0	81	71	314
Ernest Givins, Jax.	10	51	0	0	306
Tim Brown, Oak.	8	50	0	0	300

TOP ACTIVE INTERCEPTORS, AFC

25 or more interceptions

	Yrs.	No.	Yards	TD
1. Eugene Robinson, Sea.	11	42	586	0
2. Albert Lewis, Oak.	13	38	329	0
3. Kevin Ross, S.D.	12	36	647	2
4. Lionel Washington, Den.	13	33	357	3
5. Rod Woodson, Pitt.	9	32	658	4
Eugene Daniel, Ind.	12	32	388	2
7. Cris Dishman, Hou.	8	30	341	1
8. Terry McDaniel, Oak.	8	28	457	4
9. James Hasty, K.C.	8	27	340	2
10. Nate Odomes, Sea.	7	26	224	1
Other Leading Interceptors				
Gene Atkins, Mia.	9	25	348	0
Don Griffin, Balt.	10	25	51	0

TOP ACTIVE PUNT RETURNERS, AFC

50 or more punt returns

	Yrs.	No.	Yards	Avg.	TD
1. Darrien Gordon, S.D.	2	67	870	13.0	2
2. Mel Gray, Hou.	10	211	2387	11.3	3
3. Jeff Burris, Buff.	2	52	561	10.8	0
4. Tamarick Vanover, K.C.	1	51	540	10.6	1
5. David Meggett, N.E.	7	247	2613	10.6	6
6. Tim Brown, Oak.	8	269	2811	10.4	2
7. Andre Hastings, Pitt.	3	50	489	9.8	1
8. Jeff Sydner, N.Y.J.	4	64	611	9.5	0
9. Dale Carter, K.C.	4	81	769	9.5	2
10. Rod Woodson, Pitt.	9	257	2362	9.2	2
Other Leading Punt Returners					
Don Griffin, Balt.	10	74	667	9.0	1
Chris Warren, Sea.	6	94	819	8.7	1
O.J. McDuffie, Mia.	3	84	708	8.4	2
Scott Miller, Mia.	4	53	436	8.2	0

TOP ACTIVE KICKOFF RETURNERS, AFC

50 or more kickoff returns

	Yrs.	No.	Yards	Avg.	TD
1. Anthony Miller, Den.	8	50	1269	25.4	2
2. Mel Gray, Hou.	10	362	8833	24.4	6
3. Andre Coleman, S.D.	2	111	2704	24.4	4
4. Ernie Mills, Pitt.	5	68	1607	23.6	0
5. Jon Vaughn, Pitt.	4	103	2390	23.2	4
6. Steve Broussard, Sea.	6	53	1224	23.1	0
7. O.J. McDuffie, Mia.	3	91	2086	22.9	0
8. Corey Harris, Sea.	4	97	2188	22.6	0
9. Rod Woodson, Pitt.	9	220	4894	22.2	2
10. Ronald Humphrey, Ind.	2	56	1236	22.1	1
Other Leading Kickoff Returners					
David Dunn, Cin.	1	50	1092	21.8	0
Tim McGee, Cin.	9	58	1249	21.5	0
Eric Ball, Oak.	7	115	2474	21.5	0
David Meggett, N.E.	7	184	3953	21.5	1
Raghib Ismail, Oak.	3	104	2234	21.5	0
Gene Atkins, Mia.	9	71	1508	21.2	0
Chris Warren, Sea.	6	86	1794	20.9	0
Harvey Williams, Oak.	5	56	1135	20.3	0
Jeff Sydner, N.Y.J.	4	50	998	20.0	0
Desmond Howard, Jax.	4	53	1045	19.7	0
Fred McAfee, Pitt.	5	60	1156	19.3	0
Todd McNair, Hou.	7	57	1079	18.9	0
Ronnie Harmon, Hou.	10	71	1330	18.7	0
Vince Workman, Ind.	7	61	980	16.1	0

TOP ACTIVE QUARTERBACK SACKERS, AFC (since 1982)

50 or more sacks

	Yrs.	No.
1. Bruce Smith, Buff.	11	126.5
2. Pat Swilling, Oak.	10	99.5
3. Simon Fletcher*	11	97.5
4. Jim Jeffcoat, Buff.	13	97.0
5. Derrick Thomas, K.C.	7	85.0
6. Neil Smith, K.C.	8	79.5
7. Ray Childress, Hou.	11	75.5
8. Freddie Joe Nunn, Ind.	11	67.5
9. Jeff Cross, Mia.	8	59.5
10. Michael Dean Perry, Den.	8	57.5
Other Leading Sackers		
Tony Bennett, Ind.	6	55.5
Bryce Paup, Buff.	6	50.0

TOP ACTIVE PUNTERS, AFC

50 or more punts

	Yrs.	No.	Avg.	LG
1. Darren Bennett, S.D.	1	72	44.7	66
2. Greg Montgomery, Balt.	7	373	43.7	77
3. Rohn Stark, Pitt.	14	1044	43.6	72
4. Reggie Roby*	13	792	43.5	77
5. Rick Tuten, Sea.	7	481	43.4	73
6. Tom Rouen, Den.	3	195	43.4	62
7. Rich Camarillo, Hou.	15	1027	42.7	76
8. Brian Hansen, N.Y.J.	11	872	42.1	73
9. Lee Johnson, Cin.	11	754	42.1	70
10. Tom Tupa, N.E.	7	151	41.9	65
Other Leading Punters				
Bryan Barker, Jax.	6	420	41.8	67
Jeff Gossett, Oak.	14	925	41.4	65
Louie Aguiar, K.C.	5	386	41.2	71
John Kidd, Mia.	12	786	40.9	67
Chris Mohr, Buff.	6	425	40.4	71
Chris Gardocki, Ind.	5	298	40.4	69
Pat O'Neill, N.Y.J.	2	113	39.3	67

** Free agent; subject to developments.*

NFC ACTIVE STATISTICAL LEADERS

TOP ACTIVE PASSERS, NATIONAL FOOTBALL CONFERENCE

1,000 or more attempts

	Yrs.	Att.	Comp.	Pct. Comp.	Yards	Avg. Gain	TD	Pct. TD	Had Int.	Pct. Int.	Rating Pts.
Steve Young, S.F.	11	2876	1845	64.2	23069	8.02	160	5.6	79	2.7	96.1
Brett Favre, G.B.	5	2150	1342	62.4	14825	6.90	108	5.0	66	3.1	86.8
Troy Aikman, Dall.	7	2713	1704	62.8	19607	7.23	98	3.6	85	3.1	83.5
Scott Mitchell, Det.	5	1070	600	56.1	7599	7.10	54	5.0	32	3.0	82.8
Erik Kramer, Chi.	6	1281	740	57.8	8934	6.97	64	5.0	42	3.3	82.3
Dave Krieg, Chi.	16	4911	2866	58.4	35668	7.26	247	5.0	187	3.8	81.9
Warren Moon, Minn.	12	5753	3380	58.8	42177	7.33	247	4.3	199	3.5	81.5
Boomer Esiason, Ariz.	12	4680	2661	56.9	34149	7.30	223	4.8	168	3.6	80.8
Jim Everett, N.O.	10	4384	2538	57.9	31583	7.20	190	4.3	155	3.5	80.1
Mark Rypien, St.L.	8	2552	1432	56.1	18070	7.08	114	4.5	86	3.4	79.2
Bobby Hebert, Atl.	10	2633	1545	58.7	18531	7.04	113	4.3	99	3.8	78.9
Randall Cunningham*	11	3362	1874	55.7	22877	6.80	150	4.5	105	3.1	78.7
Jim McMahon, G.B.	13	2569	1489	58.0	18109	7.05	100	3.9	90	3.5	78.1
Jeff George, Atl.	6	2613	1532	58.6	17428	6.67	88	3.4	75	2.9	78.0
Wade Wilson, Dall.	14	2301	1319	57.3	16521	7.18	92	4.0	97	4.2	75.5
Chris Miller, St.L.	9	2811	1534	54.6	18793	6.69	121	4.3	101	3.6	74.8
Don Majkowski, Det.	9	1803	1001	55.5	12146	6.74	63	3.5	64	3.5	73.3
Rodney Peete, Phil.	7	1556	889	57.1	10960	7.04	50	3.2	64	4.1	72.6
Steve Beuerlein, Car.	7	1425	752	52.8	10042	7.05	53	3.7	52	3.6	72.6
Steve Walsh, St.L.	6	1191	658	55.2	7368	6.19	40	3.4	39	3.3	71.5
Jack Trudeau, Car.	10	1644	873	53.1	10243	6.23	42	2.6	69	4.2	63.3

TOP ACTIVE RUSHERS, NFC

2,500 or more yards

	Yrs.	Att.	Yards	TD
1. Barry Sanders, Det.	7	2077	10172	73
2. Emmitt Smith, Dall.	6	2007	8956	96
3. Herschel Walker, N.Y.G.	10	1938	8122	60
4. Rodney Hampton, N.Y.G.	6	1547	5989	47
5. Randall Cunningham*	11	677	4482	32
6. Lorenzo White, N.O.	8	1062	4242	30
7. Ricky Watters, Phil.	4	990	4113	36
8. Terry Allen, Wash.	4	979	4104	33
9. Johnny Johnson, S.F.	5	1046	4078	21
10. Craig Heyward, Atl.	8	919	3881	26
Other Leading Rushers				
Steve Young, S.F.	11	539	3219	30
Mark Higgs, Ariz.	8	794	2959	14

TOP ACTIVE PASS RECEIVERS, NFC

275 or more receptions

	Yrs.	No.	Yards	TD
1. Jerry Rice, S.F.	11	942	15123	146
2. Art Monk*	16	940	12721	68
3. Henry Ellard, Wash.	13	723	12163	59
4. Cris Carter, Minn.	9	571	7204	66
5. Bill Brooks, Wash.	10	566	7777	46
6. Irving Fryar, Phil.	12	562	8916	58
7. Michael Irvin, Dall.	8	527	8538	50
8. Herschel Walker, N.Y.G.	10	491	4621	19
9. Ricky Sanders*	9	483	6477	37
10. Mark Carrier, Car.	9	459	7218	38
Other Leading Receivers				
Jay Novacek, Dall.	11	422	4630	30
Brett Perriman, Det.	8	406	5176	24
Keith Jackson*	8	401	4778	39
Eric Metcalf, Atl.	7	401	3921	23
Jessie Hester*	10	373	5850	29
Michael Haynes, N.O.	8	372	5648	42
Rob Moore, Ariz.	6	369	5165	27
Rodney Holman*	14	365	4771	36
Brent Jones, S.F.	9	355	4384	30
Pete Metzelaars, Det.	14	349	3396	29
John Taylor, S.F.	9	347	5598	43
Kelvin Martin*	9	342	4388	14
Herman Moore, Det.	5	318	4895	35
Larry Centers, Ariz.	6	313	2805	9
Emmitt Smith, Dall.	6	301	1951	4
Calvin Williams, Phil.	6	293	3832	34
Terance Mathis, Atl.	6	282	3623	24

TOP ACTIVE SCORERS, NFC

300 or more points

	Yrs.	TD	FG	PAT	TP
1. Eddie Murray, Wash.	16	0	325	498	1473
2. Gary Anderson, Phil.	14	0	331	448	1441
3. Morten Andersen, Atl.	14	0	333	441	1440
4. Kevin Butler, Chi.	11	0	243	387	1116
5. Jerry Rice, S.F.	11	156	0	4	940
6. Fuad Reveiz, Minn.	10	0	188	367	931
7. Tony Zendejas*	11	0	186	316	874
8. Dean Biasucci, St.L.	11	0	185	268	823
9. Chip Lohmiller, St.L.	8	0	183	273	822
10. Greg Davis, Ariz.	9	0	172	216	732
Other Leading Scorers					
Chris Jacke, G.B.	7	0	152	250	706
Emmitt Smith, Dall.	10	100	0	0	600
Herschel Walker, N.Y.G.	12	81	0	0	486
Barry Sanders, Det.	7	80	0	0	480
Jason Hanson, Det.	4	0	101	145	448
John Kasay, Car.	5	0	108	122	446
Art Monk*	16	68	0	0	408
Cris Carter, Minn.	9	67	0	4	406
Henry Ellard, Wash.	13	63	0	0	378
Irving Fryar, Phil.	12	62	0	4	376

TOP ACTIVE INTERCEPTORS, NFC

25 or more interceptions

	Yrs.	No.	Yards	TD
1. Darrell Green, Wash.	13	40	350	4
2. Eric Allen, N.O.	8	36	510	5
3. Deion Sanders, Dall.	7	32	857	6
Tim McKyer, Car.	10	32	235	2
5. Scott Case, Dall.	12	30	267	1
6. Tim McDonald, S.F.	9	29	552	4
Mike Prior, G.B.	10	29	361	1
8. Maurice Hurst, St.L.	7	27	263	1
9. Aeneas Williams, Ariz.	5	26	347	3
Donnell Woolford, Chi.	7	26	175	0
Other Leading Interceptor				
Terry Taylor*	12	25	259	2

TOP ACTIVE PUNT RETURNERS, NFC

50 or more punt returns

	Yrs.	No.	Yards	Avg.	TD
1. Henry Ellard, Wash.	13	135	1527	11.3	4
2. Darrell Green, Wash.	13	51	576	11.3	0
3. Brian Mitchell, Wash.	6	172	1938	11.3	6
4. Bobby J. Edmonds,T.B.	5	134	1471	11.0	1
5. Tyrone Hughes, N.O.	3	86	908	10.6	2
6. Eric Metcalf, Atl.	7	166	1724	10.4	6
7. Glyn Milburn, Det.	3	112	1158	10.3	0
8. Dexter Carter, S.F.	6	102	1041	10.2	2
9. Irving Fryar, Phil.	12	206	2055	10.0	3
10. Kelvin Martin*	9	220	2194	10.0	3
Other Leading Punt Returners					
Kevin Williams, Dall.	3	93	896	9.6	3
Johnny Bailey, St.L.	6	148	1420	9.6	2
David Palmer, Minn.	2	56	535	9.6	1
Jeff Query, Wash.	7	76	712	9.4	0
Eric Guliford, Car.	3	77	701	9.1	1
Deion Sanders, Dall.	7	94	843	9.0	2
Terance Mathis, Atl.	6	50	445	8.9	1
Todd Kinchen, St.L.	4	80	709	8.9	2
Robert Brooks, G.B.	4	67	589	8.8	1
Tony Smith, Car.	3	56	485	8.7	0
Vernon Turner, T.B.	6	95	817	8.6	1
Vince Buck, N.O.	6	70	569	8.1	0

TOP ACTIVE KICKOFF RETURNERS, NFC

50 or more kick returns

	Yrs.	No.	Yards	Avg.	TD
1. Tyrone Hughes, N.O.	3	159	3926	24.7	3
2. Robert Brooks, G.B.	4	51	1237	24.3	2
3. Kevin Williams, Dall.	3	123	2945	23.9	1
4. Tony Smith, Car.	3	61	1453	23.8	1
5. Glyn Milburn, Det.	3	96	2250	23.4	0
6. Brian Mitchell, Wash.	6	216	5004	23.2	0
7. Qadry Ismail, Minn.	3	119	2746	23.1	0
8. Deion Sanders, Dall.	7	148	3403	23.0	3
9. Herschel Walker, N.Y.G.	10	138	3138	22.7	2
10. Randy Baldwin*	5	97	2202	22.7	1
Other Leading Kickoff Returners					
Nate Lewis*	6	169	3825	22.6	1
Charles Wilson, T.B.	6	92	2048	22.3	1
Dexter Carter, S.F.	6	209	4503	21.5	2
Todd Kinchen, St.L.	4	66	1412	21.4	0
Alexander Wright, St.L.	6	79	1681	21.3	2
Bobby J. Edmonds, T.B.	5	173	3646	21.1	0
Johnny Bailey, St.L.	6	115	2420	21.0	0
Alton Montgomery, Atl.	6	65	1351	20.8	0
Marc Logan, Wash.	9	85	1760	20.7	1
Eric Metcalf, Atl.	7	151	3084	20.4	2
David Lang, Dall.	5	52	1048	20.2	0
Don Beebe, G.B.	7	60	1198	20.0	0
Michael Bates, Car.	3	65	1287	19.8	0
Vernon Turner, T.B.	6	134	2626	19.6	0
Dwight Stone, Car.	9	121	2355	19.5	1
Kelvin Martin*	9	76	1453	19.1	0
Terance Mathis, Atl.	6	107	1980	18.5	0

TOP ACTIVE QUARTERBACK SACKERS, NFC (since 1982)

50 or more sacks

	Yrs.	No.
1. Reggie White, G.B.	11	157.0
2. Kevin Greene, Car.	11	108.0
Sean Jones, G.B.	12	108.0
4. Leslie O'Neal, St.L.	9	105.5
5. Chris Doleman, S.F.	11	104.5
6. Charles Haley, Dall.	10	96.5
7. Clyde Simmons, Ariz.	10	93.0
8. William Fuller, Phil.	10	81.5
9. Ken Harvey, Wash.	8	68.5
10. Henry Thomas, Det.	9	66.5
Other Leading Sackers		
Clay Matthews, Atl.	18	63.0
John Randle, Minn.	6	58.5
Jumpy Geathers, Atl.	12	57.0
Wayne Martin, N.O.	7	53.5
Cornelius Bennett, Atl.	9	52.5
Duane Bickett, Car.	11	51.0

TOP ACTIVE PUNTERS, NFC

50 or more punts

	Yrs.	No.	Avg.	LG
1. Sean Landeta, St.L.	11	729	43.6	71
2. Tom Hutton, Phil.	1	85	43.3	63
3. Tommy Barnhardt, T.B.	9	549	42.6	65
4. Matt Turk, Wash.	1	74	42.4	60
5. Mike Horan, N.Y.G.	11	758	42.3	75
6. Craig Hentrich, G.B.	2	146	41.7	70
7. Mike Saxon, Minn.	11	813	41.7	67
8. John Jett, Dall.	3	179	41.6	59
9. Mark Royals, Det.	7	483	41.1	69
10. Jeff Feagles, Ariz.	8	648	40.8	77
Other Leading Punters				
Bryan Wagner, Det.	9	506	40.8	71
Tommy Thompson, S.F.	1	57	40.6	65
Klaus Wilmsmeyer, N.O.	4	218	40.5	61
Dan Stryzinski, Atl.	6	445	40.0	64
Todd Sauerbrun, Chi.	1	55	37.8	61

** Free agent; subject to developments.*

COACHES RECORDS

ACTIVE COACHES' CAREER RECORDS (Order Based on Career Victories)

Start of 1996 Season

		Regular Season					Postseason				Career			
Coach	**Team(s)**	**Yrs.**	**Won**	**Lost**	**Tied**	**Pct.**	**Won**	**Lost**	**Tied**	**Pct.**	**Won**	**Lost**	**Tied**	**Pct.**
Dan Reeves	Denver Broncos, New York Giants	15	135	96	1	.584	8	7	0	.533	143	103	1	.581
Marv Levy	Kansas City Chiefs, Buffalo Bills	15	127	96	0	.570	11	7	0	.611	138	103	0	.573
Marty Schottenheimer	Cleveland Browns, Kansas City Chiefs	12	116	66	1	.637	5	10	0	.333	121	76	1	.614
Bill Parcells	New York Giants, New England Patriots	11	98	76	1	.563	8	4	0	.667	106	80	1	.570
George Seifert	San Francisco 49ers	7	86	26	0	.768	9	4	0	.692	95	30	0	.760
Jim Mora	New Orleans Saints	10	91	68	0	.572	0	4	0	.000	91	72	0	.558
Ted Marchibroda	Baltimore-Indianapolis Colts, Baltimore Ravens	9	71	67	0	.514	2	4	0	.333	73	71	0	.507
Wayne Fontes	Detroit Lions	7	61	56	0	.521	1	4	0	.200	62	60	0	.508
Jimmy Johnson	Dallas Cowboys, Miami Dolphins	5	51	37	0	.580	7	1	0	.875	58	38	0	.604
Bill Cowher	Pittsburgh Steelers	4	43	21	0	.672	3	4	0	.429	46	25	0	.648
Mike Holmgren	Green Bay Packers	4	38	26	0	.594	4	3	0	.571	42	29	0	.592
Bobby Ross	San Diego Chargers	4	39	25	0	.609	3	3	0	.500	42	28	0	.600
Rich Kotite	Philadelphia Eagles, New York Jets	5	39	41	0	.488	1	1	0	.500	40	42	0	.488
Dennis Green	Minnesota Vikings	4	38	26	0	.594	0	3	0	.000	38	29	0	.567
Barry Switzer	Dallas Cowboys	2	24	8	0	.750	4	1	0	.800	28	9	0	.757
Dave Wannstedt	Chicago Bears	3	25	23	0	.521	1	1	0	.500	26	24	0	.520
Lindy Infante	Green Bay Packers, Indianapolis Colts	3	24	40	0	.375	0	0	0	.000	24	40	0	.375
Dave Shula	Cincinnati Bengals	4	18	46	0	.281	0	0	0	.000	18	46	0	.281
June Jones	Atlanta Falcons	2	16	16	0	.500	0	1	0	.000	16	17	0	.485
Mike Shanahan	Los Angeles Raiders, Denver Broncos	3	16	20	0	.444	0	0	0	.000	16	20	0	.444
Ray Rhodes	Philadelphia Eagles	1	10	6	0	.625	1	1	0	.500	11	7	0	.611
Norv Turner	Washington Redskins	2	9	23	0	.281	0	0	0	.000	9	23	0	.281
Dennis Erickson	Seattle Seahawks	1	8	8	0	.500	0	0	0	.000	8	8	0	.500
Jeff Fisher	Houston Oilers	2	8	14	0	.364	0	0	0	.000	8	14	0	.364
Mike White	Oakland Raiders	1	8	8	0	.500	0	0	0	.000	8	8	0	.500
Rich Brooks	St. Louis Rams	1	7	9	0	.438	0	0	0	.000	7	9	0	.438
Dom Capers	Carolina Panthers	1	7	9	0	.438	0	0	0	.000	7	9	0	.438
Tom Coughlin	Jacksonville Jaguars	1	4	12	0	.250	0	0	0	.000	4	12	0	.250
Tony Dungy	Tampa Bay Buccaneers	0	0	0	0	.000	0	0	0	.000	0	0	0	.000
Vince Tobin	Arizona Cardinals	0	0	0	0	.000	0	0	0	.000	0	0	0	.000

COACHES WITH 100 CAREER VICTORIES (Order Based on Career Victories)

Start of 1996 Season

		Regular Season					Postseason				Career			
Coach	**Team(s)**	**Yrs.**	**Won**	**Lost**	**Tied**	**Pct.**	**Won**	**Lost**	**Tied**	**Pct.**	**Won**	**Lost**	**Tied**	**Pct.**
Don Shula	Baltimore Colts, Miami Dolphins	33	328	156	6	.676	19	17	0	.528	347	173	6	.665
George Halas	Chicago Bears	40	318	148	31	.671	6	3	0	.667	324	151	31	.671
Tom Landry	Dallas Cowboys	29	250	162	6	.605	20	16	0	.556	270	178	6	.601
Earl (Curly) Lambeau	Green Bay Packers, Chicago Cardinals, Washington Redskins	33	226	132	22	.624	3	2	0	.600	229	134	22	.623
Chuck Noll	Pittsburgh Steelers	23	193	148	1	.566	16	8	0	.667	209	156	1	.572
Chuck Knox	Los Angeles Rams, Buffalo Bills, Seattle Seahawks	22	186	147	1	.558	7	11	0	.389	193	158	1	.550
Paul Brown	Cleveland Browns, Cincinnati Bengals	21	166	100	6	.621	4	8	0	.333	170	108	6	.609
Bud Grant	Minnesota Vikings	18	158	96	5	.620	10	12	0	.455	168	108	5	.607
Steve Owen	New York Giants	23	151	100	17	.595	2	8	0	.200	153	108	17	.581
Dan Reeves	Denver Broncos, New York Giants	15	135	96	1	.584	8	7	0	.533	143	103	1	.581
Joe Gibbs	Washington Redskins	12	124	60	0	.674	16	5	0	.762	140	65	0	.683
Marv Levy	Kansas City Chiefs, Buffalo Bills	15	127	96	0	.570	11	7	0	.611	138	103	0	.573
Hank Stram	Kansas City Chiefs, New Orleans Saints	17	131	97	10	.571	5	3	0	.625	136	100	10	.573
Weeb Ewbank	Baltimore Colts, New York Jets	20	130	129	7	.502	4	1	0	.800	134	130	7	.507
Sid Gillman	Los Angeles Rams, Los Angeles-San Diego Chargers, Houston Oilers	18	122	99	7	.550	1	5	0	.167	123	104	7	.541
Marty Schottenheimer	Cleveland Browns, Kansas City Chiefs	12	116	66	1	.637	5	10	0	.333	121	76	1	.614
George Allen	Los Angeles Rams, Washington Redskins	12	116	47	5	.705	2	7	0	.222	118	54	5	.681
Don Coryell	St. Louis Cardinals, San Diego Chargers	14	111	83	1	.572	3	6	0	.333	114	89	1	.561
Mike Ditka	Chicago Bears	11	106	62	0	.631	6	6	0	.500	112	68	0	.622
John Madden	Oakland Raiders	10	103	32	7	.750	9	7	0	.563	112	39	7	.731
Ray (Buddy) Parker	Chicago Cardinals, Detroit Lions, Pittsburgh Steelers	15	104	75	9	.577	3	1	0	.750	107	76	9	.581
Bill Parcells	New York Giants, New England Patriots	11	98	76	1	.563	8	4	0	.667	106	80	1	.570
Tom Flores	Oakland-Los Angeles Raiders, Seattle Seahawks	12	97	87	0	.527	8	3	0	.727	105	90	0	.538
Vince Lombardi	Green Bay Packers, Washington Redskins	10	96	34	6	.728	9	1	0	.900	105	35	6	.740
Bill Walsh	San Francisco 49ers	10	92	59	1	.609	10	4	0	.714	102	63	1	.617

Active coaches in bold.

The **Chicago Bears** need 10 victories to become the first franchise in NFL history to record 600 regular-season victories.

Jim Mora, New Orleans, can become the twenty-sixth head coach to record 100 career victories. Mora has recorded 91 wins in 10 seasons. (See Seifert note.)

George Seifert, San Francisco, can become the twenty-sixth head coach to record 100 career victories. Seifert has recorded 95 wins in seven seasons. (See Mora note.)

Marcus Allen, Kansas City, needs 2 touchdowns to surpass Walter Payton (125) and Jim Brown (126) for sole possession of second-place on the all-time touchdown list. Allen has recorded 125 touchdowns in 14 NFL seasons.

Allen need 8 rushing touchdowns to surpass John Riggins (104), Jim Brown (106), and Walter Payton (110) to become the NFL's all-time leader. Allen has 103 rushing touchdowns. (See E. Smith note).

Allen also needs 92 rushing yards to become the eighth player in NFL history to record 11,000.

Allen needs 18 catches to surpass Roger Craig (566) as the NFL's all-time receptions leader for running backs. He has recorded 549 in 14 seasons.

Emmitt Smith, Dallas, needs 15 rushing touchdowns to become the NFL's all-time leader, surpassing Walter Payton (110). Smith has recorded 96 rushing touchdowns in six seasons. (See Allen note).

Smith also can become the sixth player in NFL history to rush for six-straight 1,000-yard seasons. (See Hampton note).

Dan Marino, Miami, needs 1,159 yards passing to become the first player in NFL history to record 50,000 yards passing.

Jerry Rice, San Francisco, needs 58 receptions to become the first receiver in NFL history to record 1,000 catches. He also needs 877 receiving yards to become the first receiver in NFL history to record 16,000 yards.

Rice needs 50 receptions to become the all-time leader with 11 consecutive 50-reception seasons.

Rice can tie all-time record holder Don Hutson by leading the league in receiving yardage for the seventh season.

John Elway, Denver, needs 3,294 passing yards to reach 45,000 for his career. Elway has totaled 41,706 yards in 13 seasons.

Elway also needs 25 touchdown passes to become the seventh quarterback to reach 250.

Jim Everett, New Orleans, needs 3,417 passing yards to become the ninth player in NFL history to record 35,000 yards. Everett has 31,584 yards in 10 seasons. (See Kelly note).

Jim Kelly, Buffalo needs 2,343 passing yards to become the ninth player in NFL history to record 35,000 yards. (See Everett note).

Thurman Thomas, Buffalo, needs 455 rushing yards to surpass O.J. Simpson (10,183) and become the Bills' all-time leader. Thomas has amassed 9,729 yards in eight seasons.

Thomas also needs 271 rushing yards to become the eleventh player to reach 10,000 career.

Thomas can become the first player in NFL history to record eight-straight 1,000-yard rushing seasons. (See Sanders note).

Barry Sanders, Detroit, can become the first player in NFL history to record eight-consecutive 1,000-yard rushing seasons. (See Thomas note).

Rodney Hampton, New York Giants, can become the sixth player in NFL history to rush for 6 consecutive 1,000-yard seasons. (See E. Smith note).

Errict Rhett, Tampa Bay, can become the seventh player to record 1,000 yards rushing in each of his first three NFL seasons. (See Faulk note).

Marshall Faulk, Indianapolis, can become the seventh player to record 1,000 yards rushing in each of his first three NFL seasons. (See Rhett note).

Carl Pickens, Cincinnati, can become the first player in Bengals' history to have three consecutive 1,000-yard receiving seasons. Pickens recorded 1,127 in 1994 and 1,234 in 1995.

Cris Carter, Minnesota, needs 17 receptions to surpass Steve Jordan (498) and become the Vikings' all-time leader. Carter has 482 catches in six seasons with the Vikings.

Carter also needs 6 touchdown receptions to surpass Minnesota's all-time leader Anthony Carter (52).

Henry Ellard, Washington, needs 28 receptions to move past Charlie Joiner (750) into fifth place on the NFL's all-time list. Ellard has totaled 723 receptions in 13 NFL seasons.

Andre Reed, Buffalo, needs 152 receiving yards to become the tenth player in NFL history to reach 10,000 yards. Reed has 9,848 yards in 11 years.

Joey Galloway, Seattle, can become the fourth receiver in NFL history to record 1,000 receiving yards in each of his first two seasons. The other three are John Jefferson (1978-79), Bob Hayes (1965-66), and Bill Groman (1960-61).

Brett Perriman, Detroit, needs 3 catches to become the Lions' all-time leader, surpassing Charlie Sanders (336). Perriman has caught 334 passes in eight seasons with Detroit. (See Moore note.)

Herman Moore, Detroit, needs 325 receiving yards to become the Lions' all-time leader, surpassing Gail Cogdill (5,220). Moore has 4,896 yards in five NFL seasons. He also needs 19 receptions to surpass Charlie Sanders (336) as the Lions' record holder. See Perriman note.)

Bruce Smith, Buffalo, needs 6 1/2 sacks to surpass Richard Dent (126.5), Rickey Jackson (128), and Lawrence Taylor (132.5) and move into second place on the all-time list. Smith has totaled 126.5 sacks in 11 NFL seasons.

Bruce Matthews, Houston, needs to play in 11 games this season to become the Oilers' all-time leader, surpassing Elvin Bethea (210). Matthews has played in 200 games in 13 NFL seasons.

Paul Gruber, Tampa Bay, needs to play in 11 games to become the Buccaneers' all-time leader, surpassing Steve Wilson (126) and Richard Wood (132). Gruber has started all 122 games in his eight-year career.

Brian Mitchell, Washington, can become the third player in NFL history to lead the league in combined net yards for at least three consecutive seasons. The other two are Jim Brown (1958-1961) and Gale Sayers (1965-67).

Eric Metcalf, Atlanta, needs 2 touchdowns on punt or kickoff returns to surpass Mel Gray and Ollie Matson, and become the NFL's all-time record holder with 10. Metcalf has totaled 8 touchdowns on returns in seven NFL seasons.

Nick Lowery, New York Jets, needs 8 field goals to become the NFL's all-time leader, surpassing Jan Stenerud (373). Lowery has totaled 366 field goals in 15 seasons.

Chris Boniol, Dallas, needs 7 consecutive field goals to break Fuad Reveiz's NFL record of 31.

Eddie Murray, Washington, needs to make 7 consecutive extra points to surpass the NFL record of 228 held by San Francisco's Tommy Davis (1959-65).

Murray also needs 27 points to become the third player in NFL history to record 1,500 career points. Murray has totaled 1,473 in 16 NFL seasons. (See Bahr and Andersen notes).

Morten Andersen, Atlanta, needs to score a point in 10 consecutive games to become the first player in NFL history to score in 200 straight games.

Andersen also needs 60 points to become the third player in NFL history to record 1,500 career points. He has totaled 1,440 in 14 NFL seasons. (See Bahr and Murray notes).

Matt Bahr, New England, needs 68 points to become the third player in NFL history to record 1,500 career points. (See Andersen and Murray notes).

Chris Jacke, Green Bay, needs 118 points to move past Paul Hornung (760) and Don Hutson (823) and become the Packers' all-time leading scorer. Jacke has 706 points in seven NFL seasons.

Rohn Stark, Pittsburgh, needs 607 yards to surpass Jerrel Wilson (46,136) and move into second place on the NFL's all-time punt yardage list. Stark has 45,530 in 14 NFL seasons.

Stark also needs 40 punts to surpass Jerrel Wilson (1,072) and John James (1,083) and move into second on the all-time list.

DRAFT LIST FOR 1996

61st Annual NFL Draft, April 20-21, 1996
*Denotes Compensatory Selection

ARIZONA CARDINALS
(Drafted alternately 3-2)
1. Simeon Rice—3, DE, Illinois
2. Leeland McElroy—32, RB, Texas A&M
3. Johnny McWilliams—64, TE, Southern California
4. Choice to Minnesota
   Aaron Graham—112, C, Nebraska, from Minnesota
5. Choice to Kansas City
   James Dexter—137, T, South Carolina, from N.Y. Giants through Minnesota
   Harry Stamps—161, T, Oklahoma, from Green Bay through Kansas City
   Dell McGee—162, DB, Auburn, from Kansas City
6. Mike Foley—169, DT, New Hampshire
7. Jarius Hayes—212, TE, North Alabama

ATLANTA FALCONS
(Drafted alternately 19-18, 23-22-21-20)
1. Choice to Indianapolis
2. Choice to Houston through Oakland
3. Shannon Brown—84, DT, Alabama
4. Richard Huntley—117, RB, Winston-Salem
   Juran Bolden—127, DB, Mississippi Delta, from Dallas
5. Choice to Baltimore
   Gary Bandy—164, DE, Baylor, from Dallas
6. Craig Sauer—188, LB, Minnesota
7. Ethan Brooks—229, T, Williams

BALTIMORE RAVENS
(Drafted alternately 4-5)
1. Jonathan Ogden—4, T, UCLA
   Ray Lewis—26, LB, Miami, from San Francisco
2. Choice to Tampa Bay
   DeRon Jenkins—55, DB, Tennessee, from Detroit through Denver
3. Choice to Denver
4. Choice to Denver
5. Choice to New Orleans
   Jermaine Lewis—153, WR, Maryland, from Atlanta
6. Dexter Daniels—172, LB, Florida
   James Roe—186, WR, Norfolk State, from Jacksonville
7. Choice to Denver
   Jon Stark—238, QB, Trinity, Ill., from Philadelphia

BUFFALO BILLS
(Drafted alternately 24-23, 26-25)
1. Eric Moulds—24, WR, Mississippi State
2. Gabe Northern—53, DE, Louisiana State
3. Matt Stevens—87, DB, Appalachian State
4. Sean Moran—120, DE, Colorado State
5. Raymond Jackson—156, DB, Colorado State
6. Leon Neal—196, RB, Washington
   *Dusty Zeigler—202, C, Notre Dame
7. Dan Brandenburg—237, DE, Indiana State
   *Jay Riemersma—244, TE, Michigan
   *Eric Smedley—249, DB, Indiana

CAROLINA PANTHERS
(Drafted alternately 8-13-12-11-10-9, 27)
1. Tim Biakabutuka—8, RB, Michigan
2. Muhsin Muhammad—43, WR, Michigan State
3. Winslow Oliver—73, RB, New Mexico
   J.C. Price—88, DT, Virginia Tech
4. Norberto Garrido—106, T, Southern California
   Emmanuel McDaniel—111, DB, East Carolina, from Denver
   Choice to Denver
5. Marquette Smith—142, RB, Central Florida
   Choice to Denver
6. Choice to Kansas City
   Choice to San Diego through Pittsburgh
   Scott Greene—193, RB, Michigan State
7. Donnell Baker—217, WR, Southern
   Kerry Hicks—234, DE, Colorado
   Choice to Denver

CHICAGO BEARS
(Drafted alternately 18-22, 22-21-20-24)
1. Walt Harris—13, DB, Mississippi State, from St. Louis
   Choice to St. Louis
2. Bobby Engram—52, WR, Penn State
3. Choice to St. Louis
4. Paul Grasmanis—116, DT, Notre Dame
5. Chris Villarrial—152, G, Indiana, Pa.
6. Jon Clark—187, T, Temple
7. Marcus Keyes—233, DT, North Alabama
   *Michael Hicks—253, RB, South Carolina State

CINCINNATI BENGALS
(Drafted alternately 10-9-8-13-12-11)
1. Willie Anderson—10, T, Auburn
2. Marco Battaglia—39, TE, Rutgers
3. Ken Blackman—69, T, Illinois
4. Jevon Langford—108, DE, Oklahoma State
5. Greg Myers—144, DB, Colorado State
6. Tom Tumulty—178, LB, Pittsburgh
7. Rod Jones—219, T, Kansas

DALLAS COWBOYS
(Drafted alternately 30, 32)
1. Choice to Washington
2. Kavika Pittman—37, DE, McNeese State, from Washington
   Randall Godfrey—49, LB, Georgia, from Miami
   Choice to Jacksonville through Miami
3. Clay Shiver—67, C, Florida State, from Washington
   Choice exercised in 1995 Supplemental Draft
   *Stepfret Williams—94, WR, Northeast Louisiana
   *Mike Ulufale—95, DT, Brigham Young
4. Choice to Atlanta
   Kenneth McDaniel—157, T, Norfolk State, from Philadelphia through Baltimore
   Choice to Atlanta
   *Alan Campos—167, LB, Louisville
6. Choice to St. Louis through Chicago
   *Wendell Davis—207, DB, Oklahoma
7. Ryan Wood—243, RB, Arizona State

DENVER BRONCOS
(Drafted alternately 15-14-17-16)
1. John Mobley—15, LB, Kutztown
2. Tory James—44, DB, Louisiana State
3. Detron Smith—65, RB, Texas A&M, from Baltimore
   Mark Campbell—78, DT, Florida
4. Jeff Lewis—100, QB, Northern Arizona, from Baltimore
   Choice to Carolina
   Darrius Johnson—122, DB, Oklahoma, from Carolina
5. Choice to Philadelphia
   Patrick Jeffers—159, WR, Virginia, from Carolina
6. Tony Veland—181, DB, Nebraska
7 Leslie Ratliffe—213, T, Tennessee, from Baltimore
   Chris Banks—226, G, Kansas
   L.T. Levine—235, RB, Kansas, from Carolina
   Brian Gragert—236, P, Wyoming, from Detroit

DETROIT LIONS
(Drafted alternately 23-25-24, 26-28-27)
1. Reggie Brown—17, LB, Texas A&M, from Oakland through Houston and Seattle
   Jeff Hartings—23, G, Penn State
2. Choice to Baltimore through Denver
3. Ryan Stewart—76, DB, Georgia Tech, from Oakland through New England
   Choice to New England
4. Choice to New England
   *Brad Ford—129, DB, Alabama
5. Kerwin Waldrop—158, DT, Central State, Ohio
6. Choice to New England
7. Choice to Denver

GREEN BAY PACKERS
(Drafted alternately 27-26, 29-28)
1. John Michels—27, T, Southern California
2. Derrick Mayes—56, WR, Notre Dame
3. Mike Flanagan—90, C, UCLA
   *Tyrone Williams—93, DB, Nebraska
4. Chris Darkins—123, RB, Minnesota
5. Choice to Arizona through Kansas City
6. Choice to Philadelphia
   *Marco Rivera—208, G, Penn State
7. Kyle Wachholtz—240, QB, Southern California
   *Keith McKenzie—252, LB, Ball State

HOUSTON OILERS
(Drafted alternately 9-8-13-12-11-10)
1. Choice to Oakland
   Eddie George—14, RB, Ohio State, from Seattle
2. Bryant Mix—38, DE, Alcorn State
   Jason Layman—48, T, Tennessee, from Atlanta through Oakland
3. Terry Killens—74, LB, Penn State
4. Kendrick Burton—107, DE, Alabama
   Jon Runyan—109, T, Michigan, from Oakland
5. Rayna Stewart—143, DB, Northern Arizona
6. Anthony Dorsett—177, DB, Pittsburgh
7. Mike Archie—218, RB, Penn State

INDIANAPOLIS COLTS
(Drafted alternately 22-21, 21-20-19-24-23)
1. Marvin Harrison—19, WR, Syracuse, from Atlanta
   Choice to Tampa Bay
2. Dedric Mathis—51, DB, Houston
3. Scott Slutzker—82, TE, Iowa
4. Brian Milne—115, RB, Penn State
5. Steve Martin—151, DT, Missouri
6. Keith Conlin—191, T, Penn State
   *Mike Cawley—205, QB, James Madison
7. Adrian Robinson—232, DB, Baylor

JACKSONVILLE JAGUARS
(Drafted alternately 2-3, 18)
1. Kevin Hardy—2, LB, Illinois
2. Tony Brackens—33, DE, Texas
   Michael Cheever—60, C, Georgia Tech, from Dallas through Miami
3. Aaron Beasley—63, DB, West Virginia
   Choice to Miami
4. Choice to Kansas City through Miami
   Reggie Barlow—110, WR, Alabama State, from Seattle
   Choice to Miami through Kansas City
5. Choice to Miami
   Jimmy Herndon—146, T, Houston, from Seattle
   Choice to Miami
6. John Fisher—170, DB, Missouri Western
   Chris Doering—185, WR, Florida
   Choice to Baltimore
7. Choice to Kansas City through Pittsburgh
   Clarence Jones—227, WR, Tennessee State
   Gregory Spann—228, WR, Jackson State

KANSAS CITY CHIEFS
(Drafted alternately 28, 30)
1. Jerome Woods—28, DB, Memphis
2. Reggie Tongue—58, DB, Oregon State
3. John Browning—68, DE, West Virginia, from New England
   Choice to Seattle through Detroit
4. Donnie Edwards—98, LB, UCLA, from Jacksonville through Miami
   Choice to Miami
5. Joe Horn—135, WR, Itawamba J.C., from Arizona
   Choice to Arizona
6. Dietrich Jells—176, WR, Pittsburgh, from Carolina
   Choice to Philadelphia
7. Ben Lynch—211, C, California, from Jacksonville through Pittsburgh
   Jeff Smith—241, C, Tennessee
   *Darrell Williams—245, DB, Tennessee State

MIAMI DOLPHINS
(Drafted alternately 20-19, 19-23-22-21)
1. Daryl Gardener—20, DT, Baylor
2. Choice to Dallas
3. Dorian Brew—79, DB, Kansas, from Jacksonville
   Karim Abdul-Jabbar—80, RB, UCLA
4. Kirk Pointer—113, DB, Austin Peay, from Jacksonville through Kansas City
   Stanley Pritchett—118, RB, South Carolina
   LaCurtis Jones—125, LB, Baylor, from Kansas City
5. Jerris McPhail—134, RB, East Carolina, from Jacksonville
   Shane Burton—150, DT, Tennessee, from Jacksonville
   Zach Thomas—154, LB, Texas Tech
6. Shawn Wooden—189, DB, Notre Dame
7. Jeff Buckey—230, T, Stanford
   *Brice Hunter—251, WR, Georgia

MINNESOTA VIKINGS
(Drafted alternately 16-15-14-17)
1. Duane Clemons—16, DE, California
2. James Manley—45, DT, Vanderbilt
3. Moe Williams—75, RB, Kentucky
4. Hunter Goodwin—97, TE, Texas A&M, from Arizona
   Choice to Arizona
5. Sean Boyd—148, DB, North Carolina
6. Choice to N.Y. Giants
7. Jon Merrill—223, G, Duke

NEW ENGLAND PATRIOTS
(Drafted alternately 7-6)
1. Terry Glenn—7, WR, Ohio State
2. Lawyer Milloy—36, DB, Washington
3. Choice to Kansas City
   Tedy Bruschi—86, LB, Arizona, from Detroit
4. Heath Irwin—101, G, Colorado
   Chris Sullivan—119, DE, Boston College, from Detroit
   Kantroy Barber—124, RB, West Virginia, from San Francisco through Oakland
5. John Elmore—139, G, Texas
   Christian Peter—149, NT, Nebraska, from Oakland
6. Chris Griffin—173, TE, New Mexico
   Marrio Grier—195, RB, Tennessee-Chattanooga, from Detroit
   Devin Wyman—206, DT, Kentucky State
7. Lovett Purnell—216, TE, West Virginia
   J.R. Conrad—247, G, Oklahoma

NEW ORLEANS SAINTS
(Drafted alternately 11-10-9-8-13-12)
1. Alex Molden—11, DB, Oregon
2. Je'rod Cherry—40, DB, California
3. Brady Smith—70, DE, Colorado State
4. Ricky Whittle—103, RB, Oregon
5. Mercury Hayes—136, WR, Michigan, from Baltimore
   Tom Ackerman—145, G, Eastern Washington
   *Terry Guess—165, WR, Gardner-Webb
6. Keno Hills—179, T, Southwestern Louisiana
   *Toderick Malone—204, WR, Alabama
7. Choice to Oakland
   *Henry Lusk—246, TE, Utah

NEW YORK GIANTS
(Drafted alternately 5-4)
1. Cedric Jones—5, DE, Oklahoma
2. Amani Toomer—34, WR, Michigan
3. Roman Oben—66, T, Louisville
4. Choice to Seattle through Dallas, Miami, and Jacksonville
   *Danny Kanell—130, QB, Florida State
5. Choice to Arizona through Minnesota
6. Doug Colman—171, LB, Nebraska
   Scott Galyon—182, LB, Tennessee, from Minnesota
7. Conrad Hamilton—214, DB, Eastern New Mexico

NEW YORK JETS
(Drafted 1)
1. Keyshawn Johnson—1, WR, Southern California
2. Alex Van Dyke—31, WR, Nevada
3. Ray Mickens—62, DB, Texas A&M
4. Choice to Tampa Bay
5. Marcus Coleman—133, DB, Texas Tech
6. Hugh Hunter—168, DE, Hampton
7. Chris Hayes—210, DB, Washington State

OAKLAND RAIDERS
(Drafted alternately 17-16-15-14)
1. Rickey Dudley—9, TE, Ohio State, from Houston
   Choice to Detroit through Houston and Seattle
2. Choice to San Francisco
   Lance Johnstone—57, DE, Temple, from San Francisco through New England
3. Choice to Detroit through New England
4. Choice to Houston
5. Choice to New England
   *La'Roi Glover—166, DT, San Diego State
6. Tim Hall—183, RB, Robert Morris
7. Sedric Clark—220, LB, Tulsa, from New Orleans
   Darius Smith—224, C, Sam Houston State
   *Joey Wylie—248, G, Stephen F. Austin

PHILADELPHIA EAGLES
(Drafted alternately 25-24, 24-26-25)
1. Jermane Mayberry—25, T, Texas A&M-Kingsville
2. Jason Dunn—54, TE, Eastern Kentucky
   *Brian Dawkins—61, DB, Clemson
3. Bobby Hoying—85, QB, Ohio State
4. Ray Farmer—121, LB, Duke
5. Whit Marshall—147, LB, Georgia, from Denver
   Choice to Dallas through Baltimore
6. Steve White—194, LB, Tennessee
   Tony Johnson—197, TE, Alabama, from Green Bay
   Phillip Riley—199, WR, Florida State, from Kansas City
7. Choice to Baltimore

PITTSBURGH STEELERS
(Drafted alternately 29, 31)
1. Jamain Stephens—29, T, North Carolina A&T
2. Choice to St. Louis
3. Steven Conley—72, LB, Arkansas, from St. Louis
   Jon Witman—92, RB, Penn State
4. Earl Holmes—126, LB, Florida A&M
   *Jahine Arnold—132, WR, Fresno State
5. Israel Raybon—163, DE, North Alabama
6. Orpheus Roye—200, DE, Florida State
   *Spence Fischer—203, QB, Duke
7. Carlos Emmons—242, LB, Arkansas State

ST. LOUIS RAMS
(Drafted alternately 13-12-11-10-9-8)
1. Lawrence Phillips—6, RB, Nebraska, from Washington
   Choice to Chicago
   Eddie Kennison—18, WR, Louisiana State, from Chicago
2. Tony Banks—42, QB, Michigan State
   Ernie Conwell—59, TE, Washington, from Pittsburgh
3. Choice to Pittsburgh
   Jerald Moore—83, RB, Oklahoma, from Chicago
4. Percell Gaskins—105, LB, Kansas State
5. Fred Miller—141, T, Baylor
6. Derrick Harris—175, RB, Miami
   Hayward Clay—201, TE, Texas A&M, from Dallas through Chicago
7. Chuck Osborne—222, DT, Arizona

SAN DIEGO CHARGERS
(Drafted alternately 21-20, 20-19-23-22)
1. Choice to Seattle through Detroit
2. Bryan Still—41, WR, Virginia Tech, from Tampa Bay
   Patrick Sapp—50, LB, Clemson
3. Brian Roche—81, TE, San Jose State
4. Charlie Jones—114, WR, Fresno State
5. Junior Soli—155, DT, Arkansas
6. Jim Mills—190, T, Idaho
   Bryan Stoltenberg—192, C, Colorado, from Carolina through Pittsburgh
7. Freddie Bradley—231, RB, Sonoma State

SAN FRANCISCO 49ERS
(Drafted alternately 26-27, 28-29)
1. Choice to Baltimore
2. Israel Ifeanyi—46, DE, Southern California, from Oakland
   Choice to Oakland through New England
3. Terrell Owens—89, WR, Tennessee-Chattanooga
4. Choice to New England through Oakland
   *Daryl Price—128, DE, Colorado
5. Iheanyi Uwaezuoke—160, WR, California
6. Stephen Pitts—198, RB, Penn State
7. Sean Manuel—239, TE, New Mexico State
   *Sam Manuel—254, LB, New Mexico State

SEATTLE SEAHAWKS
(Drafted alternately 14-17-16-15)
1. Choice to Houston
   Pete Kendall—21, T, Boston College, from San Diego through Detroit
2. Fred Thomas—47, DB, Tennessee-Martin
3. Robert Barr—77, T, Rutgers
   Reggie Brown—91, RB, Fresno State, from Kansas City through Detroit
4. Phillip Daniels—99, DE, Georgia, from N.Y. Giants through Dallas, Miami, and Jacksonville
   Choice to Jacksonville
   *Eric Unverzagt—131, LB, Wisconsin
5. Choice to Jacksonville
6. Reggie Green —184, G, Florida
   *T.J. Cunningham—209, DB, Colorado
7. Johnie Church—225, DE, Florida

TAMPA BAY BUCCANEERS
(Drafted alternately 12-11-10-9-8-13)
1. Regan Upshaw—12, DE, California
   Marcus Jones—22, DT, North Carolina, from Indianapolis
2. Mike Alstott—35, RB, Purdue, from Baltimore
   Choice to San Diego
3. Donnie Abraham—71, DB, East Tennessee State
4. Jason Odom—96, T, Florida, from N.Y. Jets
   Eric Austin—104, DB, Jackson State
5. Jason Maniecki—140, DT, Wisconsin
6. Nilo Silvan—180, WR, Tennessee
7. Reggie Rusk—221, DB, Kentucky

WASHINGTON REDSKINS
(Drafted alternately 6-7)
1. Choice to St. Louis
   Andre Johnson—30, T, Penn State, from Dallas
2. Choice to Dallas
3. Choice to Dallas
4. Stephen Davis—102, RB, Auburn
5. Leomont Evans—138, DB, Clemson
6. Kelvin Kinney—174, DE, Virginia State
7. Jeremy Asher—215, LB, Oregon
   *DeAndre Maxwell—250, WR, San Diego State

DRAFT LIST FOR 1996

NUMBER OF PLAYERS DRAFTED

BY POSITION:

Defensive Backs	43
Wide Receivers	33
Running Backs	32
Linebackers	29
Tackles	27
Defensive Ends	26
Defensive Tackles	18
Tight Ends	16
Guards	11
Centers	9
Quarterbacks	8
Punters	1
Nose Tackles	1
Kick Returners	0
Kickers	0

BY COLLEGE:

Penn State	10
Tennessee	8
Florida	6
Nebraska	6
Oklahoma	6
Southern California	6
Texas A&M	6
Alabama	5
Baylor	5
California	5
Colorado	5
Michigan	5
Colorado State	4
Florida State	4
Georgia	4
Kansas	4
Notre Dame	4
Ohio State	4
UCLA	4
West Virginia	4
Auburn	3
Clemson	3
Duke	3
Fresno State	3
Illinois	3
Louisiana State	3
Michigan State	3
North Alabama	3
Oregon	3
Pittsburgh	3
Washington	3
Arizona	2
Arkansas	2
Boston College	2
East Carolina	2
Georgia Tech	2
Houston	2
Jackson State	2
Kentucky	2
Louisville	2
Miami	2
Minnesota	2
Mississippi State	2
New Mexico	2
New Mexico State	2
Norfolk State	2
North Carolina	2
Northern Arizona	2
Rutgers	2
San Diego State	2
South Carolina	2
Temple	2
Tennessee State	2
Tennessee-Chattanooga	2
Texas	2
Texas Tech	2
Virginia Tech	2
Wisconsin	2
Alabama State	1
Alcorn State	1
Appalachian State	1
Arizona State	1
Arkansas State	1
Austin Peay	1
Ball State	1
Brigham Young	1
Central Florida	1
Central State, Ohio	1
East Tennessee State	1
Eastern Kentucky	1
Eastern Michigan	1
Eastern New Mexico	1
Florida A&M	1
Gardner-Webb	1
Hampton	1
Idaho	1
Indiana	1
Indiana State	1
Indiana, Pa.	1
Iowa	1
Itawamba J.C.	1
James Madison	1
Kansas State	1
Kentucky State	1
Kutztown	1
Maryland	1
McNeese State	1
Memphis	1
Mississippi Delta C.C.	1
Missouri	1
Missouri Western	1
Nevada	1
New Hampshire	1
North Carolina A&T	1
Northeast Louisiana	1
Oklahoma State	1
Oregon State	1
Purdue	1
Robert Morris	1
Sam Houston State	1
San Jose State	1
Sonoma State	1
South Carolina State	1
Southern	1
Southwestern Louisiana	1
Stanford	1
Stephen F. Austin	1
Syracuse	1
Tennessee Martin	1
Texas A&M-Kingsville	1
Trinity, Ill.	1
Tulsa	1
Utah	1
Vanderbilt	1
Virginia	1
Virginia State	1
Washington State	1
Williams	1
Winston-Salem	1
Wyoming	1

BY CONFERENCE:

SEC	38
Big 10	32
Pac 10	27
Big 8	24
Big East	18
SWC	17
ACC	16
Independent	15
WAC	14
Big West	6
Ohio Valley	5
SWAC	5
Big Sky	4
CIAA	4
Southern	4
Gulf South	3
MEAC	3
Southland	3
J.C./C.C.	2
Lone Star	2
PSAC	2
Yankee	2
Gateway	1
MAC	1
MAIAA	1
MSFA	1
NCAC	1
NESC	1
SAC	1
SIAC	1

In April, 1995, the NFL became the first major professional sports league to launch an Internet site. Visit the following NFL web sites for quick and easy access to all the latest information.

NFL.COM—(http://nfl.com)
NFL.com is a year-round home page on the Internet, providing information on the National Football League during the regular season, postseason, and offseason. During the 1996 season, the site will feature up-to-the-minute information from around the league, live play-by-play and statistics of games in progress, in-depth weekly previews, chat areas, a kids section, a television schedule, and more.

In addition, NFL.com includes customized home pages for all 30 clubs, including rosters, team news, ticket information, and fan programs.

Fans also can chat with NFL stars weekly in one-hour live Quarterback Club "Cyberspace Showdowns." The showdowns will feature two NFL stars competing against each other on the field that weekend.

NFL offseason coverage on the Internet is highlighted by the NFL draft. The draft site includes chat sessions with top picks, live round-by-round reports, updates from team headquarters, and expert analysis.

WORLDLEAGUE.COM—(http://worldleague.com)
Worldleague.com is the official Internet site of the World League of American Football. It provides game previews and recaps, player profiles, statistics, and individual team information. In addition, fans can listen to World League games in action with live audio feeds from game broadcasts.

SUPERBOWL.COM—(http://superbowl.com)
Look for Superbowl.com in late December for complete coverage of the playoffs and Super Bowl XXXI. This multimedia site follows all postseason action and features audio and video clips of past Super Bowls.

During the week leading up to Super Bowl XXXI, the site will go "live" from New Orleans, providing coverage of events, plus live audio from players' and coaches' press conferences, and chats with Super Bowl players.

On Super Bowl Sunday, Superbowl.com will showcase a live Internet cybercast, complete with online commentators calling all of the action. The site also features digital photos from the game, live public-address audio and press-box announcements, plus postgame interviews.

The AFC

BALTIMORE RAVENS

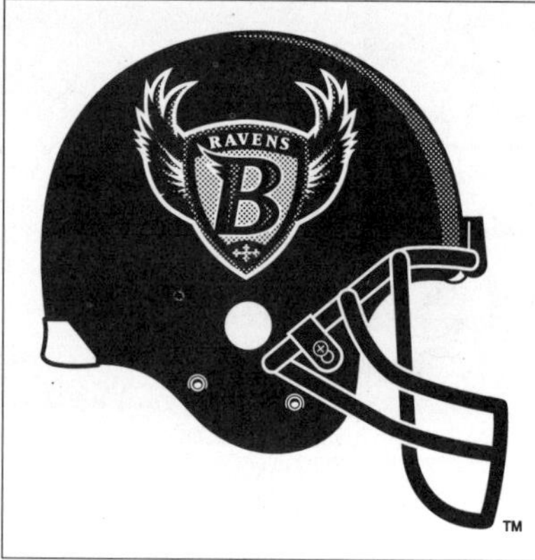

American Football Conference
Central Division
Team Colors: Black, Purple, and Gold
11001 Owings Mills Boulevard
Owings Mills, Maryland 21117
Telephone: (410) 654-6200

CLUB OFFICIALS

President and Owner: Arthur B. Modell
Executive Vice President/Legal and Administration: Jim Bailey
Assistant to the President/Executive Vice President-Marketing and Communications: David Modell
Vice President/Public Relations: Kevin Byrne
Vice President/Sales and Marketing: David Cope
Director of Business Operations-Chief Financial Officer: Pat Moriarty
Director of Football Operations: Ozzie Newsome
Director of Operations/Information: Bob Eller
Director of Publications/Assistant Director of Public Relations: Francine Lubera
Director of College Scouting: Phil Savage
Pro Personnel Coordinator: Scott Pioli
Scouts: Ron Marciniak, Terry McDonough, Vince Newsome, Ernie Plank, Ellis Rainsberger, Bill Shunkwiler, Lionel Vital
Head Trainer: Bill Tessendorf
Facilities Manager: Chuck Cusick
Equipment Manager: Ed Carroll
Stadium: Memorial Stadium • **Capacity:** 65,000
1000 East 33rd Street
Baltimore, Maryland 21218
Playing Surface: SportGrass
Training Camp: Western Maryland College
2 College Hill
Westminster, Maryland 21157

THE FOUNDING OF THE BALTIMORE RAVENS

After a 12-year absence, NFL football officially returned to the city of Baltimore on February 9, 1996, when the NFL clubs approved the transfer of Art Modell's franchise from Cleveland to Baltimore. Now owner of the Ravens, Modell's previous franchise competed in 20 postseason contests, including four NFL Championship Games, three AFC Championship Games, and a victory in the 1964 NFL title game. Former Baltimore Colts coach Ted Marchibroda, who led the Colts to three consecutive AFC East titles during his first tenure (1975-79) in Baltimore, will lead the Ravens in 1996. Baltimore will play the 1996 and 1997 seasons in Memorial Stadium, but will move into a new downtown stadium in 1998.

1996 SCHEDULE

PRESEASON

Aug. 3	**Philadelphia**	7:30
Aug. 10	at New York Giants	1:00
Aug. 17	**Green Bay**	7:00
Aug. 23	at Buffalo	7:30

REGULAR SEASON

Sept. 1	**Oakland**	1:00
Sept. 8	at Pittsburgh	1:00
Sept. 15	at Houston	12:00
Sept. 22	Open Date	
Sept. 29	**New Orleans**	1:00
Oct. 6	**New England**	1:00
Oct. 13	at Indianapolis	7:00
Oct. 20	at Denver	2:00
Oct. 27	**St. Louis**	1:00
Nov. 3	**Cincinnati**	1:00
Nov. 10	at Jacksonville	4:00
Nov. 17	at San Francisco	1:00
Nov. 24	**Jacksonville**	1:00
Dec. 1	**Pittsburgh**	1:00
Dec. 8	at Cincinnati	1:00
Dec. 15	at Carolina	1:00
Dec. 22	**Houston**	1:00

MEMORIAL STADIUM

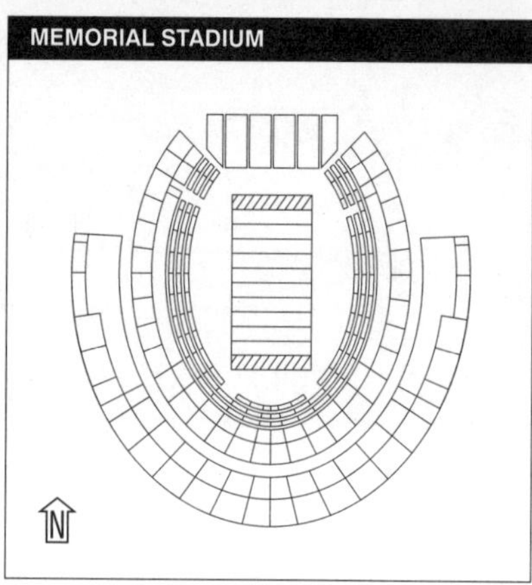

1996 DRAFT CHOICES

Round	Name	Pos.	College
1	Jonathan Ogden	T	UCLA
	Ray Lewis	LB	Miami
2	DeRon Jenkins	DB	Tennessee
5	Jermaine Lewis	WR	Maryland
6	Dexter Daniels	LB	Florida
	James Roe	WR	Norfolk State
7	Jon Stark	QB	Trinity, Ill.

BALTIMORE PROFESSIONAL FOOTBALL CHRONOLOGY

(The following chronology outlines historical highlights of the AAFC and NFL teams based in Baltimore and only reflects history while those teams were in Baltimore.)

December 28, 1946 Baltimore was awarded the bankrupt Miami Seahawks franchise of the All-American Football Conference. The team was renamed Colts via a fan contest. Bob Rodenberg heads the purchasing group.

September 7, 1947 The Colts win their first-ever AAFC game over the Brooklyn Dodgers, 16-7, in front of 27,418 fans at Baltimore Stadium. With Cecil Isbell as head coach, the Colts finish 2-11-1, drawing just under 200,000 fans.

April 28, 1948 The Colts reorganize, with more than 200 stockholders. Jake Embry is named president, and Walt Driskill is named general manager.

December 12, 1948 The Colts lose their first-ever playoff game, 28-17, against visiting Buffalo in a game marked by near riots after both teams finished tied for the Eastern Division title with 7-7 marks.

February 24, 1949 Driskill named president and general manager, with Robert C. Embry becoming vice-chairman of the board.

Fall, 1949 Isbell fired after four games and Driskill named head coach. Colts finished 1-11.

December 8, 1949 AAFC and NFL reached a merge agreement. Three AAFC teams—Cleveland, San Francisco, and Baltimore—enter the NFL for the 1950 season.

December 18, 1949 Abraham Watner named Colts' president.

December 19, 1950 Under head coach Clem Crowe, Colts finished 1-11 in first NFL season with a 15-14 loss to the New York Yanks at Yankee Stadium.

January 18, 1951 Watner withdraws franchise and receives $50,000 for his players from the NFL.

1951-1952 No Baltimore team existed.

December 3, 1952 Commissioner Bert Bell challenges Baltimore to sell 15,000 tickets in six weeks to re-enter NFL. Ticket drive reaches quota in four weeks, three days.

January, 1953 Carroll Rosenbloom heads ownership group and Baltimore awarded defunct Dallas Texans franchise. Don Kellett named president and Keith Molesworth head coach.

March 25, 1953 Baltimore and Cleveland put together one of the largest trades in sport history, with the Browns trading 10 players to the Colts for five players.

September 27, 1953 The Colts upset the Chicago Bears, 13-9, in the NFL opener at Memorial Stadium.

Spring, 1954 Weeb Ewbank named head coach.

December 28, 1958 In one of the NFL's greatest games, the Colts defeat the New York Giants, 23-17, in Yankee Stadium in sudden death for the World Championship. The game sparked the emergence of the NFL as a television sports' giant.

December 27, 1959 The Colts win their second consecutive World Championship, again over the Giants, 31-16, in Baltimore.

December 11, 1960 The Rams snap an NFL-record 47-game consecutive touchdown pass streak by Johnny Unitas.

January 8, 1963 Don Shula replaces Weeb Ewbank as head coach. Gino Marchetti and Bill Pellington were named player-coaches.

January 20, 1964 Caroll Rosenbloom purchased the remaining shares of the club to gain 100 percent ownership.

December 13, 1964 Raymond Berry catches his 506th career pass, and Lenny Moore scores his twentieth touchdown of the season against Washington, both NFL records at the time.

December 27, 1964 The Browns defeat the Colts, 27-0, in Cleveland for the NFL title. Art Modell wins his first NFL title, with Blanton Collier as head coach.

December 26, 1965 The Packers beat the Colts, 13-10, in sudden-death playoff for the Western Conference title. Running back Tom Matte quarterbacks the club with plays written on his wristband, subbing for injured quarterbacks Johnny Unitas and Gary Cuozzo.

June 8, 1966 The National Football League and the American Football League announce plan to merge in 1970. Baltimore, Cleveland, and Pittsburgh later agree join the AFC in the NFL's realignment.

March 17, 1967 Harry Hulmes, Colts' publicity director, is named general manager, succeeding Joe Campanella, who passed away on February 15 after only 23 days in GM capacity.

August 3, 1968 Art Donovan becomes the first Colts player inducted into the Pro Football Hall of Fame.

December 29, 1968 The Colts shut out the Browns, 34-0, for the NFL Championship.

January 12, 1969 The New York Jets defeat the Colts, 16-7, in Super Bowl III at the Orange Bowl after Jets quarterback Joe Namath "guarantees" a New York victory.

April 3, 1970 Don Shula resigns to become head coach of the Miami Dolphins, and is succeeded by Don McCafferty. In January, Don Klosterman is named general manager.

September 20, 1970 The Colts beat San Diego, 16-14, to win first AFC game in newly realigned NFL.

December 13, 1970 The Colts clinch their first AFC Eastern Division title with a 20-14 win at Buffalo.

December 26, 1970 The Colts beat Cincinnati, 17-0, in an AFC divisional playoff game.

January 3, 1971 The Colts beat the Oakland Raiders, 27-17, to win the AFC Championship Game.

January 17, 1971 Jim O'Brien kicks a 23-yard field goal with 5 seconds to play as the Colts win Super Bowl V over Dallas, 16-13, in the first-ever AFC-NFC Super Bowl.

January 2, 1972 Miami beats Baltimore, 21-0, in the AFC title game. The Colts had defeated Cleveland, 20-3, in the AFC playoffs to advance to the conference championship.

July 26, 1972 Robert Irsay acquires the Colts from Carroll Rosenbloom in exchange for the Los Angeles Rams. Joe Thomas named general manager.

July 29, 1972 Gino Marchetti inducted into Pro Football Hall of Fame.

October 16, 1972 John Sandusky replaces Don McCafferty as head coach after the fifth game of the season.

February 14, 1973 Howard Schnellenberger named head coach.

July 28, 1973 Raymond Berry and Jim Parker inducted into Pro Football Hall of Fame.

September 29, 1974 Joe Thomas replaces Howard Schnellenberger as head coach.

January 15, 1975 Ted Marchibroda named head coach.

August 2, 1975 Lenny Moore inducted into Pro Football Hall of Fame.

December 21, 1975 Colts win first of three consecutive AFC Eastern Division crowns by defeating New England, 34-21, at Memorial Stadium. The season capped the greatest turnaround in NFL history at the time, as Marchibroda leads the Colts to a 10-4 mark after the team was 2-12 in 1974.

December 12, 1975 Colts win second consecutive AFC East crown by defeating Buffalo, 58-20, in last home game of regular season.

January 25, 1977 Dick Szymanski named general manager and Ernie Accorsi assistant general manager.

December 18, 1977 Colts win third consecutive AFC East title.

July 28, 1979 Johnny Unitas inducted into the Pro Football Hall of Fame, a year after Weeb Ewbank was so honored.

January 16, 1980 Mike McCormack named head coach, replacing Ted Marchibroda.

December 21, 1981 Frank Kush named head coach.

May 16, 1982 Ernie Accorsi named general manager.

April 26, 1983 Colts select John Elway with the first pick in the NFL draft, but trade him on May 2 to Denver for tackle Chris Hinton, quarterback Mark Herrmann, and Denver's top pick in 1984.

March 28, 1984 The Colts' franchise relocates to Indianapolis.

November 6, 1995 The Cleveland Browns announce their intention to relocate to Baltimore for the 1996 season.

February 15, 1996 Ted Marchibroda is named Baltimore's head coach exactly 21 years and one month to the date he was hired by the Baltimore Colts.

March 29, 1996 Baltimore's NFL franchise is officially named Ravens after a *Baltimore Sun* telephone poll received a record number of calls supporting the name Ravens.

April 1, 1996 The Ravens open operations at the Owings Mills training facility.

May 16, 1996 Ravens announce season tickets and personal seat license policy in a press conference at Memorial Stadium.

June 5, 1996 Ravens unveil their new logo, colors, and uniforms in a fashion display at Harborplace.

BALTIMORE RAVENS

1996 VETERAN ROSTER

No.	Name	Pos.	Ht.	Wt.	Birthdate	NFL Exp.	College	Hometown	How Acq.	'95 Games/ Starts
43	Adams, Vashone	CB-S	5-10	196	9/12/73	2	Eastern Michigan	Aurora, Colo.	FA-'95	8/6
85	Alexander, Derrick	WR	6-2	195	11/6/71	3	Michigan	Detroit, Mich.	D1b-'94	14/2
70	Arvie, Herman	T	6-4	305	10/12/70	4	Grambling State	Opelousas, La.	D5-'93	16/2
89	Bishop, Harold	TE	6-4	250	4/8/70	3	Louisiana State	Tuscaloosa, Ala.	T(TB)-'95	13/3
69	t- Blackshear, Jeff	G	6-6	323	3/29/69	4	Northeast Louisiana	Ft. Pierce, Fla.	T(Sea)-'96	16/3
36	Booth, Isaac	CB-S	6-3	190	5/23/71	3	California	Indianapolis, Ind.	D5-'94	8/1
77	Brown, Orlando	T	6-7	340	11/12/70	4	South Carolina State	Washington, D.C.	FA-'93	16/16
90	Burnett, Rob	DE	6-4	280	8/27/67	7	Syracuse	Coram, N.Y.	D5-'90	16/16
21	Byner, Earnest	RB	5-10	215	9/15/62	13	East Carolina	Milledgeville, Ga.	UFA(Wash)-'94	16/2
56	† Caldwell, Mike	LB	6-2	235	8/31/71	4	Middle Tennessee State	Oak Ridge, Tenn.	D3-'93	16/6
26	Davis, Michael	CB	6-0	195	1/14/72	3	Cincinnati	Springfield, Ohio	W(Jax)-'95	3/0
60	Devries, Jed	G-T	6-6	300	1/6/71	2	Utah State	Ogden, Utah	FA-'94	2/0
61	† Everitt, Steve	C	6-5	290	8/21/70	4	Michigan	Miami, Fla.	D1-'93	15/14
78	† Footman, Dan	DE	6-5	290	1/13/69	4	Florida State	Tampa, Fla.	D2-'93	16/16
91	Fortune, Elliott	DE-DT	6-4	275	5/28/74	2	Georgia Tech	Roosevelt, N.Y.	FA-'95	1/0
94	Frederick, Mike	DE	6-5	280	8/6/72	2	Virginia	Neshaminy, Pa.	D3b-'95	16/0
28	Griffin, Don	CB	6-0	176	3/17/64	11	Middle Tennessee State	Camilla, Ga.	UFA(SF)-'94	16/16
48	Hartley, Frank	TE	6-2	268	12/15/67	3	Illinois	Chicago, Ill.	FA-'94	15/13
33	Hoard, Leroy	RB	5-11	225	5/15/68	7	Michigan	New Orleans, La.	D2-'90	12/12
23	Hunter, Earnest	RB	5-8	201	12/21/70	2	Oklahoma State	Longview, Tex.	FA-'95	10/0
64	Isaia, Sale	G-T	6-5	315	6/13/72	2	UCLA	Oceanside, Calif.	FA-'95	0*
81	Jackson, Michael	WR	6-4	195	4/12/69	6	Southern Mississippi	Kentwood, La.	D6-'91	13/10
52	Johnson, Pepper	LB	6-3	248	7/29/64	11	Ohio State	Detroit, Mich.	FA-'93	16/16
66	Jones, Tony	T	6-5	295	5/24/66	9	Western Carolina	Cannesville, Ga.	FA-'88	16/16
88	Kinchen, Brian	TE	6-2	240	8/6/65	9	Louisiana State	Baton Rouge, La.	FA-'91	13/12
38	Langham, Antonio	CB	6-0	180	7/31/72	3	Alabama	Town Creek, Ala.	D1a-'94	16/16
95	Lyle, Rick	DE-DT	6-5	280	2/26/71	3	Missouri	Kansas City, Mo.	FA-'94	0*
99	McKenzie, Rich	DE	6-2	258	4/15/71	2	Penn State	Ft. Lauderdale, Fla.	D6-'93	8/0
9	Montgomery, Greg	P	6-4	215	10/29/64	8	Michigan State	Little Silver, N.J.	FA-'96	0*
27	Moore, Stevon	S	5-11	210	2/9/67	8	Mississippi	Wiggins, Miss.	PB(Mia)-'92	16/16
67	Neujahr, Quentin	G-T	6-4	285	1/30/71	2	Kansas State	Seward, Neb.	FA-'94	0*
68	Palelei, Lonnie	G	6-3	320	10/15/70	4	Nevada-Las Vegas	Blue Springs, Mo.	W(Pitt)-'95	1/0
98	Pleasant, Anthony	DE	6-5	280	1/27/68	7	Tennessee State	Century, Fla.	D3-'90	16/16
59	Powell, Craig	LB	6-4	230	11/13/71	2	Ohio State	Youngstown, Ohio	D1-'95	3/0
92	Pupua, Tau	DT	6-5	290	8/25/71	2	Weber State	Salt Lake City, Utah	D5-'95	0*
80	Rison, Andre	WR	6-1	188	3/18/67	8	Michigan State	Flint, Mich.	UFA(Atl)-'95	16/14
3	Stover, Matt	K	5-11	178	1/27/68	7	Louisiana Tech	Dallas, Tex.	PB(NYG)-'91	16/0
12	Testaverde, Vinny	QB	6-5	227	11/13/63	10	Miami	Floral Park, N.Y.	UFA(TB)-'93	13/12
20	Thomas, Johnny	CB	5-9	191	8/3/64	9	Baylor	Houston, Tex.	UFA(Wash)-'95	16/0
37	Thompson, Bennie	S	6-0	214	2/10/63	7	Grambling	New Orleans, La.	FA-'94	13/0
29	Turner, Eric	S	6-1	207	9/20/68	6	UCLA	Ventura, Calif.	D1-'91	8/8
79	Webster, Larry	DT	6-5	288	1/18/69	5	Maryland	Elkton, Md.	UFA(Mia)-'95	10/0
63	Williams, Wally	C-G	6-2	300	2/19/71	4	Florida A&M	Tallahassee, Fla.	FA-'93	16/16
10	Zeier, Eric	QB	6-0	205	9/6/72	2	Georgia	Marietta, Ga.	D3a-'95	7/4

* Isaia, Lyle, and Pupua missed '95 season because of injury; Montgomery last active with Detroit in '94; Neujahr active for 1 game in '95 but did not play.

† Restricted free agent; subject to developments.

t- Ravens traded for Blackshear (Seattle).

Players lost through free agency (7): LB Gerald Dixon (Cin; 16 games in '95), WR Keenan McCardell (Jax; 16), S Louis Riddick (Atl; 16), DT Pio Sagapolutele (NE; 15), WR Rico Smith (NYJ; 4), P Tom Tupa (NE; 16), RB Tommy Vardell (SF; 5).

Also played with Browns in '95—LB Carl Banks (16 games), WR Michael Bates (13), CB-S Donny Brady (2), G Bob Dahl (16), DT Tim Goad (16), S Dana Hall (15), LB Travis Hill (4), CB Tim Jacobs (14), T Eric Moore (1), RB Ricky Powers (3), TE Walter Reeves (5), LB Frank Stams (4), LB Ed Sutter (16), RB Lorenzo White (12).

COACHING STAFF

Head Coach,
Ted Marchibroda

Pro Career: Returns to Baltimore as head coach of the city's new NFL franchise—21 years to the day of his appointment as head coach of the Baltimore Colts. Marchibroda, who coached the Baltimore Colts from 1975-79 (41-36-0) and the Indianapolis Colts from 1992-94 (32-35-0), owns a 73-71 overall record (tied with Don Shula with 73 wins), to rank as the winningest head coach in Colts' history. His 144 total games coached are a franchise record. The 1995 Colts came within one dropped "Hail Mary" touchdown pass of going to Super Bowl XXX in the thrilling 20-16 loss to the Pittsburgh Steelers at Three Rivers Stadium. The Colts finished with a 9-7 record, good for second place in the AFC East, one game behind the 10-6 Buffalo Bills. The Colts won at San Diego (35-20 in a wild-card game) and Kansas City (10-7 in Divisional Playoff game). Marchibroda easily can be described as the NFL's all-time "turnaround coach." Twice in his career he has improved his team by a margin of eight victories. Inheriting a 2-12 Colts team when he was named head coach in 1975, he led Baltimore to a 10-4 record and the AFC East title and was named NFL Coach of the Year. The Colts followed with two more division titles, earning 11-3 and 10-4 records in 1976 and 1977. Those are the most titles won by any coach in Colts' history. From October 26, 1975, through November 20, 1977, Marchibroda's Colts won 29 of 33 regular-season games. Marchibroda left the Colts following the 1979 season and was rehired as the team boss on January 28, 1992. Marchibroda achieved the eight-game swing the second time in 1992, taking Indianapolis to a 9-7 mark after the team finished 1-15 in 1991. Prior to returning to the Colts, Marchibroda served five years as an assistant with the Buffalo Bills (1987-1991), the last three as offensive coordinator. He began his career as backfield coach with the Washington Redskins in 1961. Marchibroda joined George Allen's staff with the Los Angeles Rams in 1966 and moved with Allen to the Redskins in 1971, where he served as offensive coordinator through the 1974 season. After his stint with the Colts, Marchibroda served as quarterback coach with the Chicago Bears in 1981, then moved on to Detroit as offensive coordinator with the Lions from 1982-1983. He served in that same role with the Philadelphia Eagles from 1984-85 before joining Buffalo in 1987. Marchibroda was the first draft pick of the Pittsburgh Steelers in 1953 and played one year before serving in the Army. He returned to Pittsburgh for the 1955-56 seasons. His top season was 1956, when he completed 124 of 275 passes for 1,585 yards and 12 touchdowns. His playing career ended with the Chicago Cardinals in 1957. Career record: 73-71.

Background: Quarterback at St. Bonaventure 1950-51 and University of Detroit 1952. Led nation in total offense at Detroit. He was a football, basketball (all-state selection), and baseball player at Franklin (Pa.) High School.

Personal: Born March 15, 1931, Franklin, Pa. Ted and his wife Ann reside in Owings Mills, Md. They have two daughters, Jodi and Lonni and two sons, Ted Jr. and Robert.

ASSISTANT COACHES

Maxie Baughan, linebackers; born August 3, 1938, Forkland, Ala., lives in Owings Mills, Md. Center-linebacker Georgia Tech 1957-60. Pro linebacker Philadelphia Eagles 1960-65, Los Angeles Rams 1966-70, Washington Redskins 1971, 1974. College coach: Georgia Tech 1972-73, Cornell 1983-88 (head coach). Pro coach: Baltimore Colts 1975-79, Detroit Lions 1980-82, Minnesota Vikings 1990-91, Tampa Bay Buccaneers, 1992-95, joined Baltimore in 1996.

Jacob Burney, defensive line; born January 24, 1959, Chattanooga, Tenn., lives in Owings Mills, Md. Defensive tackle Tennessee-Chattanooga 1977-80. No pro playing experience. College coach: New Mexico 1983-86, Tulsa 1987, Mississippi State 1988, Wisconsin 1989, UCLA 1990-92, Tennessee 1993. Pro coach: Joined Browns in 1994.

Kirk Ferentz, assistant head coach-offense; born August 1, 1955, Royal Oak, Mich., lives in Owings Mills, Md. Linebacker Connecticut 1973-76. No pro playing experience. College coach: Connecticut 1977, Pittsburgh 1980, Iowa 1981-89, Maine 1990-92 (head coach). Pro coach: Joined Browns in 1993.

Pat Hill, tight ends; born December 17, 1951, Los Angeles, Calif., lives in Owings Mills, Md. Center California-Riverside 1971-73. No pro playing experience. College coach: Los Angeles Valley Junior College 1974-76, Utah 1977-80, Nevada-Las Vegas 1981-82, Fresno State 1985-89, Arizona 1990-91. Pro coach: Calgary Stampeders (CFL) 1983-84, joined Browns in 1992.

Al Lavan, runing backs; born September 13, 1946, Pierce, Fla., lives in Owings Mills, Md. Defensive back Colorado State 1965-67. Pro defensive back Philadelphia Eagles 1968, Atlanta Falcons 1969-70. College coach: Colorado State 1972, Louisville 1973, Iowa State 1974, Georgia Tech 1977-78, Stanford 1979, Washington 1992-95. Pro coach: Atlanta Falcons 1975-76, Dallas Cowboys 1980-88, San Francisco 49ers 1989-90, joined Baltimore in 1996.

Marvin Lewis, defensive coordinator; born September 23, 1958, McDonald, Pa., lives in Owings Mills, Md. Linebacker Idaho State 1977-80. No pro playing experience. College coach: Idaho State 1981-84, Long Beach State 1985-86, New Mexico, 1987-89, Pittsburgh 1990-91. Pro coach: Pittsburgh Steelers, 1992-95, joined Baltimore in 1996.

Scott O'Brien, special teams; born June 25, 1957, Superior, Wis., lives in Owings Mills, Md. Defensive end Wisconsin-Superior 1975-78. Pro defensive end Green Bay Packers 1979, Toronto Argonauts (CFL) 1979. College coach: Wisconsin-Superior 1980-82, Nevada-Las Vegas 1983-85, Rice 1986, Pittsburgh 1987-90. Pro coach: Joined Browns in 1991.

Alvin Reynolds, secondary; born June 24, 1959, Pineville, La., lives in Owings Mills, Md. Safety Indiana State 1978-81. No pro playing experience. College coach: Indiana State 1982-92. Pro coach: Denver Broncos 1993-95, joined Baltimore in 1996.

Mike Sheppard, receivers; born October 29, 1951, Tulsa, Okla., lives in Owings Mills, Md. Wide receiver Cal Lutheran 1969-72. No pro playing experience. College coach: Cal Lutheran 1974-76, Brigham Young 1977-78, U.S. International 1979, Idaho State 1980-81, Long Beach State 1982, 1984-86 (head coach), Kansas 1983, New Mexico 1987-91 (head coach), California 1992. Pro coach: Joined Browns in 1993.

Jerry Simmons, strength and conditioning; born June 15, 1954, Elkhart, Kan., lives in Owings Mills, Md. Linebacker Fort Hays State 1976-77. No pro playing experience. College coach: Fort Hays State 1978, Clemson 1980, Rice 1981-82, Southern California 1983-87. Pro coach: New England Patriots 1988-90, joined Browns in 1991.

Don Strock, quarterbacks; born November 27, 1950, Pottstown, Pa., lives in Owings Mills, Md. Quarterback Virginia Tech 1970-72. Pro quarterback Miami 1973-87, Cleveland 1988, Indianapolis 1989. Pro coach: Miami (Arena Football League) 1993 (head coach), and Mass Marauders (Arena Football League) 1994 (head coach), Rhein Fire (World League) 1995, joined Baltimore in 1996.

1996 FIRST-YEAR ROSTER

Name	Pos.	Ht.	Wt.	Birthdate	College	Hometown	How Acq.
Barnard, David	DT	6-2	290	11/26/74	Florida	Miami, Fla.	FA
Bivins, Marquin	G	6-2	317	7/24/72	Alcorn State	Laurel, Miss.	FA
Bradley, Mario	CB	6-2	195	4/16/72	Southern California	Long Beach, Calif.	FA
Brady, Donny (1)	CB-S	6-2	195	11/24/73	Wisconsin	North Bellmore, N.Y.	FA
Brown, Curtis	WR	6-2	185	7/18/71	Alabama	John's Island, S.C.	FA
Cullors, Derrick	RB	5-11	185	12/26/72	Murray State	Dallas, Tex.	FA
Daniels, Dexter	LB	6-1	241	12/8/73	Florida	Valdosta, Ga.	D6a
Depaola, Dante	S	5-10	190	8/13/72	California	Monte Rio, Calif.	FA
Dowers, Donte	CB-S	5-11	183	4/18/72	Alcorn State	Belle Glade, Fla.	FA
Eaton, Chad (1)	DE-DT	6-4	292	4/4/72	Washington State	Puyallup, Wash.	FA
Ethridge, Ray (1)	WR	5-10	180	12/12/68	Pasadena C.C.	San Diego, Calif.	FA
Fields, Henry	RB	6-2	205	4/20/73	McNeese State	Wossman, La.	FA
Folau, Spencer	T	6-5	300	4/5/73	Idaho	Sequoia, Calif.	FA
Groh, Mike	QB	6-3	201	12/19/71	Virginia	Charlottesville, Va.	FA
Jenkins, Deron	CB	5-11	177	11/14/73	Tennessee	St. Louis, Mo.	D2b
Jones, Ray	CB-S	5-10	175	2/11/74	Pittsburgh	Warminster, Pa.	FA
Killian, P.J. (1)	LB	6-2	242	5/19/71	Virginia	Pittsburgh, Pa.	FA
Lewis, Jermaine	WR-KR	5-7	172	10/16/74	Maryland	Lanham, Md.	D5b
Lewis, Ray	LB	6-1	235	5/15/75	Miami	Lakeland, Fla.	D1b
MacInnis, Chris	K	5-11	190	5/10/72	Air Force	Melbourne, Fla.	FA
McSeed, Larry	LB	6-2	222	9/27/73	Delaware	Philadelphia, Pa.	FA
Ogden, Jonathan	G	6-8	318	7/31/74	UCLA	Washington, D.C.	D1a
Otis, Scott	QB	6-5	230	9/28/72	Glenville State	Southington, Conn.	FA
Poumele, Pulu (1)	T-G	6-3	300	1/31/72	Arizona	Oceanside, Calif.	FA
Powers, Ricky (1)	RB	6-0	213	11/30/70	Michigan	Akron, Ohio	FA
Randolph, Charles	TE	6-2	290	7/29/72	N.E. Louisiana	New Orleans, La.	FA
Roe, James	WR	6-1	187	9/23/73	Norfolk State	Richmond, Va.	D6b
Thomas, Richard	RB	5-9	220	3/16/72	Washington	Kent, Wash.	FA
Sears, Corey	DT	6-3	300	4/15/73	Mississippi State	Universal City, Tex.	FA
Stark, Jon	QB	6-4	222	2/22/73	Trinity International	Nashville, Tenn.	D7
Warren, Michael	TE	6-3	270	11/11/72	McNeese State	Sour Lake, Tex.	FA
Thorp, Deron	T	6-7	322	8/31/73	Nevada	Cupertino, Calif.	FA
Williams, Larry	DE	6-4	283	11/29/72	Mississippi State	Indianola, Miss.	FA

The term NFL Rookie is defined as a player who is in his first season of professional football and has not been on the roster of another professional football team for any regular-season or postseason games. A Rookie is designated by an "R" on NFL rosters. Players who have been active in another professional football league or players who have NFL experience, including either preseason training camp or being on an Active List or Inactive List, or on Reserve/Injured or Reserve/Physically Unable to Perform for fewer than six regular-season games, are termed NFL First-Year Players. An NFL First-Year Player is designated by a "1" on NFL rosters. Thereafter, a player is credited with an additional year of experience for each season in which he accumulates six games on the Active List or Inactive List, or on Reserve/Injured or Reserve/Physically Unable to Perform.

NOTES

BUFFALO BILLS

American Football Conference
Eastern Division
Team Colors: Royal Blue, Scarlet Red, and White
One Bills Drive
Orchard Park, New York 14127-2296
Telephone: (716) 648-1800

CLUB OFFICIALS

President: Ralph C. Wilson, Jr.
Exec. V.P./General Manager: John Butler
Corporate V.P.: Linda Bogdan
V.P./Head Coach: Marv Levy
Treasurer: Jeffrey C. Littmann
Director of Administration/Ticket Sales: Jerry Foran
Asst. G.M./Business Operations: Bill Munson
Director of Business Operations: Jim Overdorf
Director of Marketing and Sales: John Livsey
Director of Merchandising: Christy Wilson Hofmann
Director of Player Personnel: Dwight Adams
Director of Pro Personnel: A.J. Smith
Director of Player/Alumni Relations: Jerry Butler
Director of Public/Community Relations: Denny Lynch
Director of Media Relations: Scott Berchtold
Director of Stadium Operations: George Koch
Engineering and Operations Manager: Joseph Frandina
Director of Security: Bill Bambach
Ticket Director: June Foran
Equipment Manager: Dave Hojnowski
Strength/Conditioning Coordinator: Rusty Jones
Trainers: Ed Abramoski, Bud Carpenter, Melvin Lewis, Greg McMillen
Video Director: Henry Kunttu
Scouts: Brad Forsyth, Tom Gibbons, Doug Majeski, Buddy Nix, Bob Ryan, George (Chink) Sengel, David G. Smith, David W. Smith
Stadium: Rich Stadium • **Capacity:** 80,024
One Bills Drive
Orchard Park, New York 14127-2296
Playing Surface: AstroTurf
Training Camp: Fredonia State University
Fredonia, New York 14063

1996 SCHEDULE

PRESEASON

Aug. 2	**Washington**	7:30
Aug. 8	at Minnesota	7:00
Aug. 17	at Carolina	7:30
Aug. 23	**Baltimore**	7:30

REGULAR SEASON

Sept. 1	at New York Giants	8:00
Sept. 8	**New England**	1:00
Sept. 16	at Pittsburgh (Mon.)	9:00
Sept. 22	**Dallas**	4:00
Sept. 29	Open Date	
Oct. 6	**Indianapolis**	4:00
Oct. 13	**Miami**	1:00
Oct. 20	at New York Jets	4:00
Oct. 27	at New England	8:00
Nov. 3	**Washington**	4:00
Nov. 10	at Philadelphia	1:00
Nov. 17	**Cincinnati**	1:00
Nov. 24	**New York Jets**	1:00
Dec. 1	at Indianapolis	1:00
Dec. 8	at Seattle	1:00
Dec. 16	at Miami (Mon.)	9:00
Dec. 22	**Kansas City**	1:00

RECORD HOLDERS

INDIVIDUAL RECORDS—CAREER

Category	Name	Performance
Rushing (Yds.)	O.J. Simpson, 1969-1977	10,183
Passing (Yds.)	Jim Kelly, 1986-1995	32,657
Passing (TDs)	Jim Kelly, 1986-1995	223
Receiving (No.)	Andre Reed, 1985-1995	700
Receiving (Yds.)	Andre Reed, 1985-1995	9,848
Interceptions	George (Butch) Byrd, 1964-1970	40
Punting (Avg.)	Paul Maguire, 1964-1970	42.1
Punt Return (Avg.)	Keith Moody, 1976-79	10.5
Kickoff Return (Avg.)	Wallace Francis, 1973-74	27.2
Field Goals	Scott Norwood, 1985-1991	133
Touchdowns (Tot.)	Thurman Thomas, 1988-1995	74
Points	Scott Norwood, 1985-1991	670

INDIVIDUAL RECORDS—SINGLE SEASON

Category	Name	Performance
Rushing (Yds.)	O.J. Simpson, 1973	2,003
Passing (Yds.)	Jim Kelly, 1991	3,844
Passing (TDs)	Jim Kelly, 1991	33
Receiving (No.)	Andre Reed, 1994	90
Receiving (Yds.)	Andre Reed, 1989	1,312
Interceptions	Billy Atkins, 1961	10
	Tom Janik, 1967	10
Punting (Avg.)	Billy Atkins, 1961	44.5
Punt Return (Avg.)	Keith Moody, 1977	13.1
Kickoff Return (Avg.)	Ed Rutkowski, 1963	30.2
Field Goals	Scott Norwood, 1988	32
Touchdowns (Tot.)	O.J. Simpson, 1975	23
Points	O.J. Simpson, 1975	138

INDIVIDUAL RECORDS—SINGLE GAME

Category	Name	Performance
Rushing (Yds.)	O.J. Simpson, 11-25-76	273
Passing (Yds.)	Joe Ferguson, 10-9-83	419
Passing (TDs)	Jim Kelly, 9-8-91	6
Receiving (No.)	Andre Reed, 11-20-94	15
Receiving (Yds.)	Jerry Butler, 9-23-79	255
Interceptions	Many Times	3
	Last time by Jeff Nixon, 9-7-80	
Field Goals	Pete Gogolak, 12-5-65	5
	Scott Norwood, 9-25-88	5
	Steve Christie, 9-18-94	5
	Steve Christie, 10-8-95	5
Touchdowns (Tot.)	Cookie Gilchrist, 12-8-63	5
Points	Cookie Gilchrist, 12-8-63	30

COACHING HISTORY

(265-285-8)

1960-61	Buster Ramsey	11-16-1
1962-65	Lou Saban	38-18-3
1966-68	Joe Collier*	13-17-1
1968	Harvey Johnson	1-10-1
1969-70	John Rauch	7-20-1
1971	Harvey Johnson	1-13-0
1972-76	Lou Saban**	32-29-1
1976-77	Jim Ringo	3-20-0
1978-82	Chuck Knox	38-38-0
1983-85	Kay Stephenson***	10-26-0
1985-86	Hank Bullough****	4-17-0
1986-95	Marv Levy	107-61-0

*Released after two games in 1968
**Resigned after five games in 1976
***Released after four games in 1985
****Released after nine games in 1986

RICH STADIUM

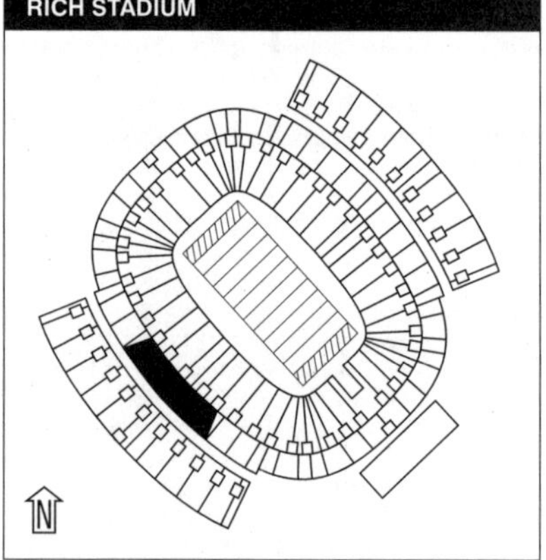

1995 TEAM RECORD

PRESEASON (2-3)

Date	Result		Opponents
7/29	L	15-21	at Dallas
8/4	L	10-31	Pittsburgh
8/12	W	9-7	vs. Dallas at Toronto
8/19	L	10-36	at Kansas City
8/25	W	20-14	Atlanta

REGULAR SEASON (10-6)

Date	Result		Opponents	Att.
9/3	L	7-22	at Denver	75,157
9/10	W	31-9	Carolina	79,190
9/17	W	20-14	Indianapolis	62,499
10/2	W	22-19	at Cleveland	76,211
10/8	W	29-10	N.Y. Jets	79,485
10/15	W	27-21	Seattle	74,362
10/23	L	14-27	at New England	60,203
10/29	L	6-23	at Miami	71,060
11/5	W	16-10	at Indianapolis	59,612
11/12	W	23-17	Atlanta	62,690
11/19	W	28-26	at N.Y. Jets	54,436
11/26	L	25-35	New England	69,384
12/3	L	17-27	at San Francisco	65,568
12/10	W	45-27	at St. Louis	64,623
12/17	W	23-20	Miami	79,531
12/24	L	17-28	Houston	45,253

POSTSEASON (1-1)

Date	Result		Opponents	Att.
12/30	W	37-22	Miami	73,103
1/6	L	21-40	at Pittsburgh	59,072

(OT) Overtime

SCORE BY PERIODS

Bills	73	115	97	65	0	—	350
Opponents	64	79	89	103	0	—	335

ATTENDANCE

Home 552,394 Away 526,870 Total 1,079,264
Single-game home record, 80,366 (9/29/91)
Single-season home record, 635,899 (1991)*
*NFL record

1995 TEAM STATISTICS

	Bills	Opp.
Total First Downs	300	287
Rushing	130	93
Passing	142	180
Penalty	28	14
Third Down: Made/Att.	71/225	84/244
Third Down Pct.	31.6	34.4
Fourth Down: Made/Att.	7/13	13/23
Fourth Down Pct.	53.8	56.5
Total Net Yards	5117	5128
Avg. Per Game	319.8	320.5
Total Plays	1059	1084
Avg. Per Play	4.8	4.7
Net Yards Rushing	1993	1626
Avg. Per Game	124.6	101.6
Total Rushes	521	453
Net Yards Passing	3124	3502
Avg. Per Game	195.3	218.9
Sacked/Yards Lost	32/224	49/362
Gross Yards	3348	3864
Att./Completions	506/279	582/310
Completion Pct.	55.1	53.3
Had Intercepted	14	17
Punts/Avg.	86/40.4	90/42.8
Net Punting Avg.	86/36.2	90/35.1
Penalties/Yards Lost	89/672	115/890
Fumbles/Ball Lost	25/12	23/11
Touchdowns	37	33
Rushing	10	16
Passing	24	14
Returns	3	3
Avg. Time of Possession	28:10	31.50

1995 INDIVIDUAL STATISTICS

PASSING	Att.	Comp.	Yds.	Pct.	TD	Int.	Tkld.	Rate
Kelly	458	255	3130	55.7	22	13	26/181	81.1
Collins	29	14	112	48.3	0	1	6/43	44.0
Van Pelt	18	10	106	55.6	2	0	0/0	110.0
Armour	1	0	0	0.0	0	0	0/0	39.6
Bills	506	279	3348	55.1	24	14	32/224	79.9
Opponents	582	310	3864	53.3	14	17	49/362	70.0

SCORING	TD R	TD P	TD Rt	PAT	FG	Saf	PTS
Christie	0	0	0	33/35	31/40	0	126
Brooks	0	11	0	0/0	0/0	0	66
T. Thomas	6	2	0	0/0	0/0	0	48
Holmes	4	0	0	0/0	0/0	0	24
Armour	0	3	0	0/0	0/0	0	18
Reed	0	3	0	0/0	0/0	0	18
Tasker	0	3	0	0/0	0/0	0	18
Gardner	0	0	1	0/0	0/0	0	8
Bennett	0	0	1	0/0	0/0	0	6
Copeland	0	1	0	0/0	0/0	0	6
L. Johnson	0	1	0	0/0	0/0	0	6
Schulz	0	0	1	0/0	0/0	0	6
Bills	10	24	3	33/35	31/40	0	350
Opponents	16	14	3	29/29	34/43	1	335

2-Point conversions: Gardner. Team: 1-2.

RUSHING	Att.	Yds.	Avg.	LG	TD
T. Thomas	267	1005	3.8	49	6
Holmes	172	698	4.1	38t	4
Gardner	20	77	3.9	17	0
Tasker	8	74	9.3	17	0
Reed	7	48	6.9	14	0
Jourdain	8	31	3.9	19	0
Collins	9	23	2.6	10	0
Kelly	17	20	1.2	17	0
Tindale	5	16	3.2	6	0
Brooks	3	7	2.3	9	0
Copeland	1	-1	-1.0	-1	0
Armour	4	-5	-1.2	6	0
Bills	521	1993	3.8	49	10
Opponents	453	1626	3.6	39	16

RECEIVING	No.	Yds.	Avg.	LG	TD
Brooks	53	763	14.4	51t	11
L. Johnson	49	504	10.3	52	1
Copeland	42	646	15.4	77t	1
Armour	26	300	11.5	28t	3
T. Thomas	26	220	8.5	60	2
Reed	24	312	13.0	41t	3
Holmes	24	214	8.9	47	0
Tasker	20	255	12.8	43	3
Cline	8	64	8.0	17	0
Coons	3	28	9.3	13	0
Gardner	2	17	8.5	13	0
D. Thomas	1	18	18.0	18	0
Jourdain	1	7	7.0	7	0
Bills	279	3348	12.0	77t	24
Opponents	310	3864	12.5	54t	14

INTERCEPTIONS	No.	Yds.	Avg.	LG	TD
Schulz	6	48	8.0	32t	1
Darby	2	37	18.5	37	0
T. Smith	2	23	11.5	13	0
Paup	2	0	0.0	0	0
Bennett	1	69	69.0	69t	1
Burris	1	19	19.0	19	0
Evans	1	18	18.0	18	0
Jones	1	10	10.0	10	0
White	1	9	9.0	9	0
Bills	17	233	13.7	69t	2
Opponents	14	187	13.4	49	0

PUNTING	No.	Yds.	Avg.	In 20	LG
Mohr	86	3473	40.4	23	60
Bills	86	3473	40.4	23	60
Opponents	90	3854	42.8	19	73

PUNT RETURNS	No.	FC	Yds.	Avg.	LG	TD
Burris	20	1	229	11.5	40	0
Tasker	17	7	204	12.0	44	0
Brooks	6	2	35	5.8	15	0
Copeland	2	1	8	4.0	7	0
Jourdain	1	0	0	0.0	0	0
D. Thomas	1	0	0	0.0	0	0
Bills	47	11	476	10.1	44	0
Opponents	23	30	224	9.7	69t	1

KICKOFF RETURNS	No.	Yds.	Avg.	LG	TD
Holmes	39	799	20.5	42	0
Jourdain	19	348	18.3	41	0
Tindale	6	62	10.3	20	0
Green	2	37	18.5	22	0
Cline	1	11	11.0	11	0
Irvin	1	12	12.0	12	0
Louchiey	1	13	13.0	13	0
Pike	1	20	20.0	20	0
Bills	70	1302	18,6	42	0
Opponents	73	1615	22.1	46	0

SACKS	No.
Paup	17.5
B. Smith	10.5
Hansen	10.0
Jeffcoat	2.5
Washington	2.5
Bennett	2.0
Rogers	2.0
White	1.0
Wilson	1.0
Bills	49.0
Opponents	32.0

1996 DRAFT CHOICES

Round	Name	Pos.	College
1	Eric Moulds	WR	Mississippi State
2	Gabe Northern	DE	Louisiana State
3	Matt Stevens	DB	Appalachian State
4	Sean Moran	DE	Colorado State
5	Raymond Jackson	DB	Colorado State
6	Leon Neal	RB	Washington
	Dusty Zeigler	C	Notre Dame
7	Dan Brandenburg	DE	Indiana State
	Jay Riemersma	TE	Michigan
	Eric Smedley	DB	Indiana

BUFFALO BILLS

1996 VETERAN ROSTER

No.	Name	Pos.	Ht.	Wt.	Birthdate	NFL Exp.	College	Hometown	How Acq.	'95 Games/ Starts
81	Armour, Justin	WR	6-4	209	1/1/73	2	Stanford	Colorado Springs, Colo.	D4b-'95	15/9
18	Brantley, Chris	WR	5-10	180	12/12/70	2	Rutgers	Teaneck, N.J.	FA-'96	0*
79	Brown, Ruben	G	6-3	304	2/13/70	2	Pittsburgh	Lynchburg, Va.	D1-'95	16/16
22	Burris, Jeff	CB-S	6-0	204	6/7/72	3	Notre Dame	Rock Hill, S.C.	D1-'94	9/9
2	Christie, Steve	K	6-0	185	11/13/67	7	William & Mary	Oakville, Canada	PB(TB)-'92	16/0
88	Cline, Tony	TE	6-4	247	11/24/71	2	Stanford	Davis, Calif.	D4c-'95	16/1
15	Collins, Todd	QB	6-4	224	11/5/71	2	Michigan	Walpole, Mass.	D2-'95	7/1
87	Coons, Robert	TE	6-5	249	9/18/69	2	Pittsburgh	Anaheim, Calif.	FA-'95	4/0
85	† Copeland, Russell	WR	6-0	200	11/4/71	4	Memphis	Tupelo, Miss.	D4-'93	16/15
57	Covington, Damien	LB	5-11	236	12/4/72	2	North Carolina State	Berlin, N.J.	D3b-'95	13/1
	Early, Quinn	WR	6-0	190	4/13/65	10	Iowa	West Hempstead, N.Y	UFA(NO)-'96	16/15*
41	Evans, Greg	S	6-1	208	6/28/71	2	Texas Christian	Dangerfield, Tex.	FA-'94	16/4
70	Fina, John	T	6-4	285	3/11/69	5	Arizona	Tucson, Ariz.	D1-'92	16/16
90	Hansen, Phil	DE	6-5	278	5/20/68	6	North Dakota State	Ellendale, N.D.	D2-'91	16/16
44	Holmes, Darick	RB	6-0	226	7/1/71	2	Portland State	Pasadena, Calif.	D7b-'95	16/2
67	Hull, Kent	C	6-5	284	1/13/61	11	Mississippi State	Greenwood, Miss.	FA-'86	16/16
27	Irvin, Ken	CB	5-10	182	7/11/72	2	Memphis	Rome, Ga.	D4a-'95	16/3
77	Jeffcoat, Jim	DE	6-5	280	4/1/61	14	Arizona State	Cliffwood, N.J.	UFA(Dall)-'95	16/2
84	Johnson, Lonnie	TE	6-3	240	2/14/71	3	Florida State	Miami, Fla.	D2b-'94	16/16
20	Jones, Henry	S	5-11	197	12/29/67	6	Illinois	St. Louis, Mo.	D1-'91	13/13
30	Jourdain, Yonel	RB	5-11	204	4/20/71	3	Southern Illinois	Evanston, Ill.	FA-'93	8/0
12	Kelly, Jim	QB	6-3	226	2/14/60	11	Miami	East Brady, Pa.	D1b-'83	15/15
46	Kerner, Marlon	CB	5-10	187	3/18/73	2	Ohio State	Columbus, Ohio	D3a-'95	14/5
68	Lacina, Corbin	G	6-4	297	11/2/70	4	Augustana	Woodbury, Minn.	D6-'93	16/3
72	Louchiey, Corey	T	6-8	305	10/10/71	2	South Carolina	Greenville, S.C.	D3b-'94	13/3
55	Maddox, Mark	LB	6-1	233	3/23/68	6	Northern Michigan	Milwaukee, Wis.	D9-'91	4/4
9	Mohr, Chris	P	6-5	215	5/11/66	7	Alabama	Thomson, Ga.	FA-'91	16/0
60	Ostroski, Jerry	G	6-4	310	7/12/70	3	Tulsa	Collegeville, Pa.	FA-'93	16/13
74	Parker, Glenn	G-T	6-5	305	4/22/66	7	Arizona	Huntington Beach, Calif.	D3-'90	13/13
95	Paup, Bryce	LB	6-5	247	2/29/68	7	Northern Iowa	Jefferson, Iowa	UFA(GB)-'95	15/15
58	Perry, Marlo	LB	6-4	250	8/25/72	3	Jackson State	Forest, Miss.	D3a-'94	16/11
75	Philion, Ed	DT	6-2	277	3/27/70	3	Ferris State	Essex, Canada	FA-'94	2/0
94	Pike, Mark	DE	6-4	272	12/27/63	10	Georgia Tech	Villa Hills, Ky.	D7b-'86	16/0
83	Reed, Andre	WR	6-2	190	1/29/64	12	Kutztown	Allentown, Pa.	D4a-'85	6/6
59	Rogers, Sam	LB	6-3	245	5/30/70	3	Colorado	Pontiac, Mich.	D2c-'94	16/8
24	Schulz, Kurt	S	6-1	208	12/28/68	5	Eastern Washington	Yakima, Wash.	D7-'92	13/13
78	Smith, Bruce	DE	6-4	273	6/18/63	12	Virginia Tech	Norfolk, Va.	D1a-'85	15/15
28	Smith, Thomas	CB	5-11	188	12/5/70	4	North Carolina	Gates, N.C.	D1-'93	16/16
54	Spielman, Chris	LB	6-0	247	10/11/65	9	Ohio State	Canton, Ohio	UFA(Det)-'96	16/16*
89	Tasker, Steve	WR	5-9	181	4/10/62	12	Northwestern	Leoti, Kan.	W(Hou)-'86	13/3
82	Thomas, Damon	WR	6-2	208	12/15/70	3	Wayne State	Clovis, Calif.	FA-'94	14/0
34	Thomas, Thurman	RB	5-10	198	5/16/66	9	Oklahoma State	Missouri City, Tex.	D2-'88	14/14
33	Tindale, Tim	RB	5-10	220	4/15/71	2	Western Ontario	London, Canada	FA-'94	16/0
10	Van Pelt, Alex	QB	6-0	220	5/1/70	2	Pittsburgh	Pittsburgh, Pa.	FA-'94	1/0
92	Washington, Ted	NT	6-4	325	4/13/68	6	Louisville	Tampa, Fla.	UFA(Den)-'95	16/15
50	White, David	LB	6-2	235	2/27/70	3	Nebraska	New Orleans, La.	FA-'95	15/1

* Brantley last active with L.A. Rams in '94; Early played 16 games with New Orleans; Spielman played 16 games with Detroit.

† Restricted free agent; subject to developments.

Players lost through free agency (3): LB Cornelius Bennett (Atl; 14 games in '95), WR Bill Brooks (Wash; 15), LB Monty Brown (NE; 16).

Also played with Bills in '95—S Matt Darby (7 games), G-C Mike Devlin (16), RB Carwell Gardner (15), S Chris Green (16), DB Filmel Johnson (2), C Adam Lingner (16).

COACHING STAFF

Head Coach,
Marv Levy

Pro Career: Begins his eleventh season as Bills head coach. Guided Bills to their sixth AFC crown in past eight years in 1995. Led Bills to four consecutive AFC Championships in 1990-93. Under Levy, the Bills recorded 13-3 records in 1990 and 1991, the best regular-season marks in club history. He guided the Bills to their second consecutive AFC East title with a 9-7 record in 1989. Finished 1988 season with a 12-4 record and a berth in the AFC Championship Game. In his first full year with Bills in 1987, he led team to a 7-8 record. Replaced Hank Bullough on November 3, 1986, and compiled a 2-5 record over the final seven weeks of the season. Previously served as head coach of the Kansas City Chiefs from 1978-1982 and produced a 31-42 mark. Levy began his pro coaching career in 1969 as an assistant with the Philadelphia Eagles. He joined George Allen and the Los Angeles Rams as an assistant one-year later and followed Allen to Washington, where he remained with the Redskins through the 1972 season when Washington played in Super Bowl VII. He was named head coach of the Montreal Alouettes (CFL) in 1973 and posted a 50-34-4 record and two Grey Cup victories (1974, 1977) in five seasons in Canada. After two seasons away from football, he became head coach of the Chicago Blitz of the USFL in 1984. No pro playing experience. Career record: 138-103.

Background: Running back at Coe College 1948-50. Coached at high school level for two years before returning to alma mater from 1953-55. Joined New Mexico staff in 1956 and served as head coach there in 1958-59. Head coach at California from 1960-63 before becoming head coach at William & Mary from 1964-68.

Personal: Born August 3, 1928, Chicago, Ill. Levy was Phi Beta Kappa at Coe College and earned master's degree in English history from Harvard. He lives with his wife Mary Frances in Hamburg, N.Y.

ASSISTANT COACHES

Tom Bresnahan, offensive coordinator-offensive line; born January 21, 1935, Springfield, Mass., lives in Orchard Park, N.Y. Tackle Holy Cross 1953-55. No pro playing experience. College coach: Williams 1963-67, Columbia 1968-72, Navy 1973-80. Pro coach: Kansas City Chiefs 1981-82, New York Giants 1983-84, St. Louis/Phoenix Cardinals 1986-88, joined Bills in 1989.

Ted Cottrell, linebackers; born June 13, 1947, Chester, Pa., lives in Orchard Park, N.Y. Linebacker Delaware Valley College 1966-68. Pro linebacker Atlanta Falcons 1969-70, Winnepeg Blue Bombers (CFL) 1971. College coach: Rutgers 1973-80, 1983. Pro coach: Kansas City Chiefs 1981-82, New Jersey Generals (USFL) 1983-84, Buffalo Bills 1986-89, Arizona Cardinals 1990-94, rejoined Bills in 1995.

Bruce DeHaven, special teams; born September 6, 1952, Trousdale, Kan., lives in East Aurora, N.Y. No college or pro playing experience. College coach: Kansas 1979-81, New Mexico State 1982. Pro coach: New Jersey Generals (USFL) 1983, Pittsburgh Maulers (USFL) 1984, Orlando Renegades (USFL) 1985, joined Bills in 1987.

Charlie Joiner, receivers; born October 14, 1947, Many, La., lives in Orchard Park, N.Y. Wide receiver Grambling 1965-68. Defensive back-wide receiver Houston Oilers 1969-72, Cincinnati Bengals 1972-75, San Diego Chargers 1976-86. Inducted into Pro Football Hall of Fame in 1996. Pro coach: San Diego Chargers 1987-91, joined Bills in 1992.

Rusty Jones, strength and conditioning; born August 14, 1953, Berwick, Maine, lives in Hamburg, N.Y. No college or pro playing experience. College coach: Springfield 1978-79. Pro coach: Pittsburgh Maulers (USFL) 1983-84, joined Bills in 1985.

Don Lawrence, offensive quality control-tight ends; born June 4, 1937, Cleveland, Ohio, lives in Orchard Park, N.Y. Offensive-defensive lineman Notre Dame 1957-58. Pro offensive-defensive lineman Washington Redskins 1959-61. College coach: Notre Dame 1961-63, Kansas State 1964-65, Cincinnati 1966, Virginia 1970-73 (head coach 1971-73), Texas Christian 1974-75, Missouri 1976-77. Pro coach: British Columbia Lions (CFL) 1978-79, Kansas City Chiefs 1980-82, 1987-88, Buffalo Bills 1983-84, Tampa Bay Buccaneers 1985-86, Winnipeg Blue Bombers (CFL) 1989, rejoined Bills in 1990.

Chuck Lester, administrative assistant to head coach, assistant linebackers coach; born May 18, 1955, Chicago, Ill., lives in Orchard Park, N.Y. Linebacker Oklahoma 1974. No pro playing experience. College coach: Iowa State 1980-81, Oklahoma 1982-84. Pro coach: Kansas City Chiefs 1984-86 (scout), joined Bills in 1987.

Wade Phillips, defensive coordinator; born June 21, 1947, Orange, Tex., lives in Orchard Park, N.Y. Linebacker Houston 1966-68. No pro playing experience. College coach: Houston, 1969, Oklahoma State 1973-74, Kansas 1975. Pro coach: Houston Oilers 1976-80, New Orleans Saints 1981-85 (head coach last four games of 1985), Philadelphia Eagles 1986-88, Denver Broncos 1989-94 (head coach 1993-94), joined Bills in 1995.

Elijah Pitts, assistant head coach-running backs; born February 3, 1938, Mayflower, Ark., lives in Orchard Park, N.Y. Running back Philander Smith 1957-60. Pro running back Green Bay Packers 1961-69, 1971, Los Angeles Rams 1970, Chicago Bears 1970, New Orleans Saints 1970. Pro coach: Los Angeles Rams 1974-77, Buffalo Bills 1978-80, Houston Oilers 1981-83, Hamilton Tiger-Cats (CFL) 1984, rejoined Bills in 1985.

Dick Roach, defensive backs; born August 23, 1937, Rapid City, S.D., lives in Orchard Park, N.Y. Defensive back Black Hills State 1952-55. No pro playing experience. College coach: Montana State 1966-69, Oregon State 1970, Wyoming 1971-72, Fresno State 1973, Washington State 1974-75. Pro coach: Montreal Alouettes (CFL) 1976-77, Kansas City Chiefs 1978-80, New England Patriots 1981, Michigan Panthers (USFL) 1983-84, Tampa Bay Buccaneers 1985-86, joined Bills in 1987.

Dan Sekanovich, defensive line; born July 27, 1933, West Hazelton, Pa., lives in Depew, N.Y. End Tennessee 1951-53. Pro defensive end Montreal Alouettes (CFL) 1954. College coach: Susquehanna 1961-63, Connecticut 1964-67, Pittsburgh 1968, Navy 1969-70, Kentucky 1971-72. Pro coach: Montreal Alouettes (CFL) 1973-76, New York Jets 1977-82, Atlanta Falcons 1983-85, Miami Dolphins 1986-91, joined Bills in 1992.

Jim Shofner, quarterbacks; born December 18, 1935, Grapevine, Tex., lives in Depew, N.Y. Running back Texas Christian 1955-57. Pro defensive back Cleveland Browns 1958-63. College coach: Texas Christian 1964-66, 1974-76 (head coach). Pro coach: San Francisco 49ers 1967-73, 1977, Cleveland Browns 1978-80, 1990-91 (head coach last 7 games in 1990, director of player personnel in 1991), Houston Oilers 1981-82, Dallas Cowboys 1983-85, St. Louis/Phoenix Cardinals 1986-89, joined Bills in 1992.

1996 FIRST-YEAR ROSTER

Name	Pos.	Ht.	Wt.	Birthdate	College	Hometown	How Acq.
Allen, Dennis	CB-S	6-1	193	9/22/72	Texas A&M	Hurst, Tex.	FA
Avina, Armando	K-P	6-2	205	4/21/73	Nevada	Reno, Nev.	FA
Bailey, Henry	WR	5-9	183	2/28/73	Nevada-Las Vegas	Chicago, Ill.	FA
Bender, Carey (1)	RB	5-8	185	1/28/72	Coe College	Marion, Iowa	FA-'95
Brandenburg, Dan	LB	6-2	255	2/2/73	Indiana State	Rensselaer, Ind.	D7a
Bratton, Jason	RB	6-1	252	10/19/72	Grambling State	Longview, Tex.	FA
Colston, Tim	DE	6-0	275	12/18/73	Kansas State	Tampa, Fla.	FA
Deshotel, Robert	LB	6-3	246	1/17/73	Louisiana State	Lake Charles, La.	FA
Hack, Dave	T-G	6-6	277	4/22/72	Maryland	Holland, N.Y.	FA
Hammonds, Juan	LB	6-3	260	3/5/72	Michigan State	Louisville, Ky.	FA
Harris, Ken	WR	5-10	190	4/15/68	Arkansas-Pine Bluff	Pine Bluff, Ark.	FA
Holecek, John (1)	LB	6-2	238	5/7/72	Illinois	Steger, Ill.	D5-'95
Houston, Artis	CB	5-7	179	11/29/72	California	Los Angeles, Calif.	FA
Jackson, Raymond	CB-S	5-10	189	2/17/73	Colorado State	Denver, Colo.	D5
Johnson, Demeris	WR	6-1	185	8/26/69	Western Illinois	Detroit, Mich.	FA
Lillibridge, Marc	LB	6-1	240	2/18/72	Iowa State	Vermillon, S.D.	FA
Martin, Emanuel	CB	5-11	184	7/31/69	Alabama State	Miami, Fla.	FA
Maxwell, Mike	QB	6-4	203	3/17/72	Nevada	Temecula, Calif.	FA
Meservey, Matt	G	6-4	305	1/10/71	Brigham Young	Idaho Faces, Idaho	FA
Moran, Sean	DE	6-3	255	6/5/73	Colorado State	Aurora, Colo.	D4
Moulds, Eric	WR	6-0	204	7/17/73	Mississippi State	Lucedale, Miss.	D1
Neal, Leon	RB	5-9	185	9/11/72	Washington	Long Beach, Calif.	D6a
Northern, Gabe	DE	6-2	240	6/8/74	Louisiana State	Baton Rouge, La.	D2
Nutten, Tom (1)	C	6-4	295	6/8/71	Western Michigan	Magog, Canada	D7a-'95
Riemersma, Jay	TE	6-5	254	5/17/73	Michigan	Leeland, Mich.	D7b
Rockwood, Mike	T	6-10	345	6/5/73	Nevada	Mira Loma, Calif.	FA
Schulte, Ross	P-K	6-5	190	8/14/72	Western Illinois	Fowler, Ill.	FA
Shamsid-Deen, Muhamed	RB	5-10	196	11/6/69	Tenn.-Chattanooga	Ellenwood, Calif.	FA
Sheldon, Michael	T	6-4	295	6/8/73	Grand Valley State	Villa Park, Ill.	FA
Smedley, Eric	CB-S	5-11	199	7/23/73	Indiana	Charleston, W.Va.	D7c
Stevens, Matt	CB	6-0	206	6/15/73	Appalachian State	Chapel Hill, N.C.	D3
Van Hofwegen, Harry	DE	6-4	250	6/9/70	Carleton, Canada	Nepean, Canada	FA
Zeigler, Dusty	C-G	6-5	298	9/27/73	Notre Dame	Rincon, Ga.	D6b

The term NFL Rookie is defined as a player who is in his first season of professional football and has not been on the roster of another professional football team for any regular-season or postseason games. A Rookie is designated by an "R" on NFL rosters. Players who have been active in another professional football league or players who have NFL experience, including either preseason training camp or being on an Active List or Inactive List, or on Reserve/Injured or Reserve/Physically Unable to Perform for fewer than six regular-season games, are termed NFL First-Year Players. An NFL First-Year Player is designated by a "1" on NFL rosters. Thereafter, a player is credited with an additional year of experience for each season in which he accumulates six games on the Active List or Inactive List, or on Reserve/Injured or Reserve/Physically Unable to Perform.

NOTES

CINCINNATI BENGALS

American Football Conference
Central Division
Team Colors: Black, Orange, and White
Spinney Field
One Bengals Drive
Cincinnati, Ohio 45204
Telephone: (513) 621-3550

CLUB OFFICIALS

Chairman of the Board: Austin E. Knowlton
President/General Manager: Michael Brown
Vice President: John Sawyer
Assistant General Manager/Director of Player Personnel: Pete Brown
General Counsel/Corporate Secretary: Katherine Blackburn
Assistant Secretary/Treasurer; Scouting/Player Personnel: Paul H. Brown
Business Manager: Bill Connelly
Director of Stadium Development: Troy Blackburn
Director of Community Affairs: Jeff Berding
Director of Pro Personnel/Scouting: Jim Lippincott
Comptroller: Jay Reis
Director of Finance: Bill Scanlon
Public Relations Director: Jack Brennan
Assistant Public Relations Director: Patrick J. Combs
Director of Marketing: Mike Hoffbauer
Entertainment Director/Assistant Director of Marketing: Dave Slyby
Ticket Manager: Paul Kelly
Trainer: Paul Sparling
Assistant Trainers: Billy Brooks, Rob Recker
Equipment Manager: Tom Gray
Video Director: Al Davis
Assistant Video Director: Travis Brammer
Stadium: Riverfront Stadium • **Capacity:** 60,389
200 Riverfront Stadium
Cincinnati, Ohio 45202
Playing Surface: AstroTurf-8
Training Camp: Wilmington College
Wilmington, Ohio 45177

1996 SCHEDULE

PRESEASON

Aug. 3	**Indianapolis**	7:30
Aug. 10	at Arizona	7:30
Aug. 16	at Washington	8:00
Aug. 23	**Detroit**	7:30

REGULAR SEASON

Sept. 1	at St. Louis	12:00
Sept. 8	at San Diego	1:00
Sept. 15	**New Orleans**	1:00
Sept. 22	Open Date	
Sept. 29	**Denver**	1:00
Oct. 6	**Houston**	8:00
Oct. 13	at Pittsburgh	1:00
Oct. 20	at San Francisco	1:00
Oct. 27	**Jacksonville**	1:00
Nov. 3	at Baltimore	1:00
Nov. 10	**Pittsburgh**	1:00
Nov. 17	at Buffalo	1:00
Nov. 24	**Atlanta**	1:00
Dec. 1	at Jacksonville	1:00
Dec. 8	**Baltimore**	1:00
Dec. 15	at Houston	12:00
Dec. 22	**Indianapolis**	1:00

RECORD HOLDERS

INDIVIDUAL RECORDS—CAREER

Category	Name	Performance
Rushing (Yds.)	James Brooks, 1984-1991	6,447
Passing (Yds.)	Ken Anderson, 1971-1986	32,838
Passing (TDs)	Ken Anderson, 1971-1986	197
Receiving (No.)	Cris Collinsworth, 1981-88	417
Receiving (Yds.)	Isaac Curtis, 1973-1984	7,101
Interceptions	Ken Riley, 1969-1983	65
Punting (Avg.)	Dave Lewis, 1970-73	43.9
Punt Return (Avg.)	Mitchell Price, 1990-92	10.4
Kickoff Return (Avg.)	Lemar Parrish, 1970-77	24.7
Field Goals	Jim Breech, 1980-1992	225
Touchdowns (Tot.)	Pete Johnson, 1977-1983	70
Points	Jim Breech, 1980-1992	1,151

INDIVIDUAL RECORDS—SINGLE SEASON

Category	Name	Performance
Rushing (Yds.)	James Brooks, 1989	1,239
Passing (Yds.)	Boomer Esiason, 1986	3,959
Passing (TDs)	Ken Anderson, 1981	29
Receiving (No.)	Carl Pickens, 1995	99
Receiving (Yds.)	Eddie Brown, 1988	1,273
Interceptions	Ken Riley, 1976	9
Punting (Avg.)	Dave Lewis, 1970	46.2
Punt Return (Avg.)	Mike Martin, 1984	15.7
Kickoff Return (Avg.)	Lemar Parrish, 1970	30.2
Field Goals	Doug Pelfrey, 1995	29
Touchdowns (Tot.)	Carl Pickens, 1995	17
Points	Doug Pelfrey, 1995	121

INDIVIDUAL RECORDS—SINGLE GAME

Category	Name	Performance
Rushing (Yds.)	James Brooks, 12-23-90	201
Passing (Yds.)	Boomer Esiason, 10-7-90	490
Passing (TDs)	Boomer Esiason, 12-21-86	5
	Boomer Esiason, 10-29-89	5
Receiving (No.)	James Brooks, 12-25-89	12
Receiving (Yds.)	Eddie Brown, 11-6-88	216
Interceptions	Many times	3
	Last time by David Fulcher, 12-17-89	
Field Goals	Doug Pelfrey, 11-6-94	6
Touchdowns (Tot.)	Larry Kinnebrew, 10-28-84	4
Points	Larry Kinnebrew, 10-28-84	24

COACHING HISTORY

(197-234-1)

1968-75	Paul Brown	55-59-1
1976-78	Bill Johnson*	18-15-0
1978-79	Homer Rice	8-19-0
1980-83	Forrest Gregg	34-27-0
1984-91	Sam Wyche	64-68-0
1992-95	Dave Shula	18-46-0

*Resigned after five games in 1978

RIVERFRONT STADIUM

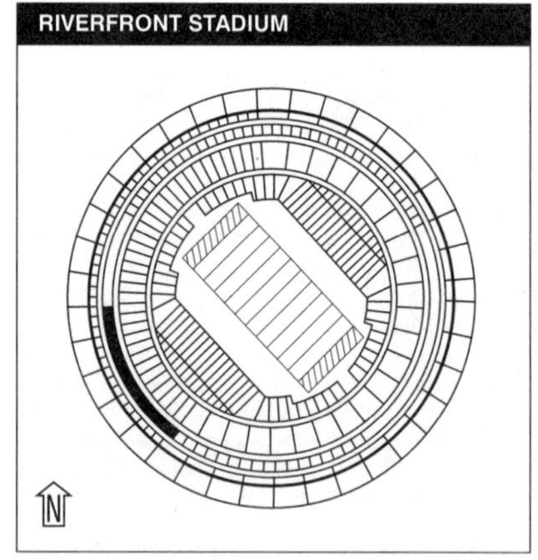

1995 TEAM RECORD

PRESEASON (1-3)

Date	Result		Opponents
8/4	W	34-21	at Indianapolis
8/11	L	7-31	Tampa Bay
8/19	L	13-20	at Detroit
8/25	L	24-30	N.Y. Jets

REGULAR SEASON (7-9)

Date	Result		Opponents	Att.
9/3	W	24-21	at Indianapolis (OT)	42,445
9/10	W	24-17	Jacksonville	48,318
9/17	L	21-24	at Seattle	39,492
9/24	L	28-38	Houston	46,332
10/1	L	23-26	Miami	52,671
10/8	L	16-19	at Tampa Bay	41,732
10/19	W	27-9	at Pittsburgh	56,684
10/29	L	26-29	Cleveland (OT)	58,639
11/5	L	17-20	Oakland	51,265
11/12	W	32-35	at Houston	32,998
11/19	L	31-49	Pittsburgh	54,636
11/26	W	17-13	at Jacksonville	68,249
12/3	L	10-24	at Green Bay	60,318
12/10	W	16-10	Chicago	38,642
12/17	L	10-26	at Cleveland	55,875
12/24	W	27-24	Minnesota	34,568

(OT) Overtime

SCORE BY PERIODS

Bengals	52	99	93	102	3	—	349
Opponents	70	131	56	114	3	—	374

ATTENDANCE

Home 385,071 Away 397,793 Total 782,864
Single-game home record, 60,284 (10/17/71)
Single-season home record, 473,288 (1990)

1995 TEAM STATISTICS

	Bengals	Opp.
Total First Downs	288	354
Rushing	76	117
Passing	184	215
Penalty	28	22
Third Down: Made/Att	72/205	107/243
Third Down Pct.	35.1	44.0
Fourth Down: Made/Att	10/19	8/15
Fourth Down Pct.	52.6	53.3
Total Net Yards	5192	6349
Avg. Per Game	324.5	396.8
Total Plays	975	1127
Avg. Per Play	5.3	5.6
Net Yards Rushing	1439	2104
Avg. Per Game	89.9	131.5
Total Rushes	364	483
Net Yards Passing	3753	4245
Avg. Per Game	234.6	265.3
Sacked/Yards Lost	25/162	42/267
Gross Yards	3915	4512
Att./Completions	586/334	602/364
Completion Pct.	57.0	60.5
Had Intercepted	18	12
Punts/Avg.	70/41.6	64/38.4
Net Punting Avg.	70/38.3	64/33.3
Penalties/Yards Lost	103/835	116/1143
Fumbles/Ball Lost	23/14	27/12
Touchdowns	37	37
Rushing	7	10
Passing	29	25
Returns	1	2
Avg. Time of Possession	26:57	33:03

1995 INDIVIDUAL STATISTICS

PASSING	Att.	Comp.	Yds.	Pct.	TD	Int.	Tkld.	Rate
Blake	567	326	3822	57.5	28	17	24/152	82.1
Klingler	15	7	88	46.7	1	1	1/10	59.9
Bieniemy	2	0	0	0.0	0	0	0/0	39.6
Dunn	1	0	0	0.0	0	0	0/0	39.6
Johnson	1	1	5	100.0	0	0	0/0	87.5
Bengals	586	334	3915	57.0	29	18	25/162	81.1
Opponents	602	364	4512	60.5	25	12	42/267	89.2

SCORING	TD R	TD P	TD Rt	PAT	FG	Saf	PTS
Pelfrey	0	0	0	34/34	29/36	0	121
Pickens	0	17	0	0/0	0/0	0	102
Scott	0	5	0	0/0	0/0	0	30
To. McGee	0	4	0	0/0	0/0	0	24
Bieniemy	3	0	0	0/0	0/0	0	18
Green	2	1	0	0/0	0/0	0	18
Blake	2	0	0	0/0	0/0	0	14
Dunn	0	1	0	0/0	0/0	0	6
Rog. Jones	0	0	1	0/0	0/0	0	6
Tuten	0	1	0	0/0	0/0	0	6
A. Williams	0	0	0	0/0	0/0	1	2
Bengals	7	29	1	34/34	29/36	2	349
Opponents	10	25	2	34/34	38/49	0	374

2-Point conversions: Blake. Team: 1-3.

RUSHING	Att.	Yds.	Avg.	LG	TD
Green	171	661	3.9	23t	2
Bieniemy	98	381	3.9	27	3
Blake	53	309	5.8	30	2
Cothran	16	62	3.9	15	0
Joseph	16	40	2.5	8	0
Scott	5	11	2.2	9	0
Pickens	1	6	6.0	6	0
Burns	1	1	1.0	1	0
Hill	1	-3	-3.0	-3	0
Dunn	1	-13	-13.0	-13	0
Johnson	1	-16	-16.0	-16	0
Bengals	364	1439	4.0	30	7
Opponents	483	2104	4.4	38	10

RECEIVING	No.	Yds.	Avg.	LG	TD
Pickens	99	1234	12.5	68t	17
To. McGee	55	754	13.7	41	4
Scott	52	821	15.8	88t	5
Bieniemy	43	424	9.9	33	0
Green	27	182	6.7	24	1
Joseph	20	118	5.9	13	0
Dunn	17	209	12.3	37	1
Cothran	8	44	5.5	15	0
Sadowski	5	37	7.4	12	0
Hill	4	44	11.0	18	0
Ware	2	36	18.0	21	0
Tuten	2	12	6.0	9	1
Bengals	334	3915	11.7	88t	29
Opponents	364	4512	12.4	71t	25

INTERCEPTIONS	No.	Yds.	Avg.	LG	TD
Walker	4	56	14.0	23	0
Sawyer	2	61	30.5	61	0
A. Collins	2	3	1.5	3	0
Rod Jones	1	24	24.0	24	0
Roger Jones	1	17	17.0	17t	1
Tovar	1	13	13.0	13	0
Williams	1	1	1.0	1	0
Bengals	12	175	14.6	61	1
Opponents	18	307	17.1	74	2

PUNTING	No.	Yds.	Avg.	In 20	LG
Johnson	68	2861	42.1	26	61
Pelfrey	2	52	26.0	0	27
Bengals	70	2913	41.6	26	61
Opponents	64	2455	38.4	22	64

PUNT RETURNS	No.	FC	Yds.	Avg.	LG	TD
Sawyer	9	8	58	6.4	21	0
Bieniemy	7	1	47	6.7	10	0
Pickens	5	2	-2	-0.4	4	0
Bailey	0	1	0	—	—	0
Query	0	1	0	—	—	0
Bengals	21	13	103	4.9	21	0
Opponents	27	20	154	5.7	19	0

KICKOFF RETURNS	No.	Yds.	Avg.	LG	TD
Dunn	50	1092	21.8	45	0
Hill	17	454	26.7	55	0
Bieniemy	8	168	21.0	34	0
Sawyer	2	50	25.0	28	0
A. Collins	1	-3	-3.0	-3	0
Joseph	1	17	17.0	17	0
Von Oelhoffen	1	10	10.0	10	0
Bengals	80	1788	22.4	62	0
Opponents	65	1475	22.7	64	0

SACKS	No.
Copeland	9.0
Wilkinson	8.0
McDonald	5.0
A. Collins	4.0
Francis	3.0
Rog. Jones	2.0
Rucker	2.0
Sawyer	2.0
Smith	2.0
Kelly	1.0
Oglesby	1.0
Stallings	1.0
Tovar	1.0
Williams	1.0
Bengals	42.0
Opponents	25.0

1996 DRAFT CHOICES

Round	Name	Pos.	College
1	Willie Anderson	T	Auburn
2	Marco Battaglia	TE	Rutgers
3	Ken Blackman	T	Illinois
4	Jevon Langford	DE	Oklahoma State
5	Greg Myers	DB	Colorado State
6	Tom Tumulty	LB	Pittsburgh
7	Rod Jones	T	Kansas

CINCINNATI BENGALS

1996 VETERAN ROSTER

No.	Name	Pos.	Ht.	Wt.	Birthdate	NFL Exp.	College	Hometown	How Acq.	'95 Games/ Starts
33	Ambrose, Ashley	CB	5-10	192	9/17/70	5	Mississippi Valley State	New Orleans, La.	UFA(Ind)-'96	16/0*
18	Bailey, Thomas	WR	6-0	196	12/6/71	2	Auburn	Dallas, Tex.	FA-'95	1/0
21	Bieniemy, Eric	RB	5-7	198	8/15/69	6	Colorado	New Orleans, La.	UFA(SD)-'95	16/1
8	Blake, Jeff	QB	6-0	202	12/4/70	5	East Carolina	Sanford, Fla.	W(NYJ)-'94	16/16
74	Braham, Rich	T	6-4	290	11/6/70	3	West Virginia	Morgantown, W. Va.	W(Ariz)-'94	0*
65	Brilz, Darrick	G	6-3	287	2/14/64	10	Oregon State	Pinole Valley, Calif.	UFA(Sea)-'94	16/16
75	Brown, Anthony	T	6-5	310	11/6/72	2	Utah	Salt Lake City, Utah	FA-'95	7/1
72	Brumfield, Scott	G	6-8	320	8/19/70	4	Brigham Young	Spanish Fork, Utah	FA-'94	14/11
38	Burns, Jason	RB	5-7	195	11/27/72	2	Wisconsin	Chicago, Ill.	FA-'95	1/0
32	Carter, Ki-Jana	RB	5-10	227	9/12/73	2	Penn State	Westerville, Ohio	D1-'95	0*
55	# Collins, Andre	LB	6-1	231	5/4/68	7	Penn State	Cinaminson, N.J.	FA-'95	16/5
90	Collins, Gerald	LB	6-2	250	2/13/71	2	Vanderbilt	St. Louis, Mo.	FA-'95	3/0
92	Copeland, John	DE	6-3	286	9/20/70	4	Alabama	Lanett, Ala.	D1-'93	16/16
46	Cothran, Jeff	RB	6-1	249	6/28/71	3	Ohio State	Middletown, Ohio	D3-'94	14/13
19	Davis, Tyree	WR	5-9	175	9/23/70	2	Central Arkansas	Altheimer, Ark.	FA-'96	1/0*
51	Dixon, Gerald	LB	6-3	250	6/20/69	5	South Carolina	Rock Hill, S.C.	UFA(Balt)-'96	16/9*
80	Dunn, David	WR	6-3	210	6/10/72	2	Fresno State	San Diego, Calif.	D5-'95	16/0
50	Francis, James	LB	6-5	252	8/4/68	7	Baylor	Houston, Tex.	D1-'90	11/11
28	# Green, Harold	RB	6-2	222	1/29/68	7	South Carolina	Ladson, S.C.	D2-'90	15/15
19	Hill, Jeff	WR	5-11	178	9/24/72	2	Purdue	Cincinnati, Ohio	FA-'94	16/0
57	Jefferson, Kevin	LB	6-1	232	1/14/74	3	Lehigh	Greensburg, Pa.	FA-'94	16/0
11	Johnson, Lee	P-K	6-2	200	11/27/61	12	Brigham Young	Conroe, Tex.	W(Clev)-'88	16/0
25	Jones, Rod	CB	6-0	185	3/31/64	11	Southern Methodist	Dallas, Tex.	T(TB)-'90	13/7
24	Jones, Roger	CB	5-9	175	4/22/69	6	Tennessee State	Nashville, Tenn.	W(TB)-'94	16/16
32	Joseph, James	RB	6-2	222	10/28/67	6	Auburn	Phenix City, Ala.	UFA(Phil)-'95	16/3
98	Kelly, Todd	DE	6-2	259	11/27/70	4	Tennessee	Hampton, Va.	W(SF)-'95	16/0
7	# Klingler, David	QB	6-2	205	2/17/69	5	Houston	Stratford, Tex.	D1-'92	3/0
64	Kozerski, Bruce	G	6-4	287	4/2/62	13	Holy Cross	Plains, Pa.	D9-'84	8/8
56	McDonald, Ricardo	LB	6-2	235	11/8/69	5	Pittsburgh	Kingston, Jamaica	D4-'92	16/16
85	# McGee, Tim	WR	5-10	183	8/7/64	11	Tennessee	Cleveland, Ohio	FA-'94	0*
82	† McGee, Tony	TE	6-3	246	4/21/71	4	Michigan	Terre Haute, Ind.	D2-'93	16/16
26	Orlando, Bo	S	5-10	180	4/3/66	7	West Virginia	Berwick, Pa.	UFA(SD)-'96	16/16*
9	† Pelfrey, Doug	K	5-11	185	9/25/70	4	Kentucky	Ft. Thomas, Ky.	D8-'93	16/0
81	Pickens, Carl	WR	6-2	206	3/23/70	5	Tennessee	Murphy, N.C.	D2-'92	16/16
76	Pollard, Trent	G	6-4	330	11/20/72	3	Eastern Washington	Seattle, Wash.	D5-'94	9/0
39	Prior, Anthony	CB	5-11	185	3/27/70	4	Washington State	Riverside, Calif.	W(NYJ)-'96	11/0*
95	Rucker, Keith	DT	6-4	332	11/20/68	5	Ohio Wesleyan	University Park, Ill.	FA-'94	15/14
87	Sadowski, Troy	TE	6-5	250	12/8/65	7	Georgia	Atlanta, Ga.	UFA(NYJ)-'94	12/0
77	Sargent, Kevin	T	6-6	284	3/31/69	5	Eastern Washington	Bremerton, Wash.	FA-'92	15/15
23	Sawyer, Corey	CB	5-11	171	10/4/71	3	Florida State	Key West, Fla.	D4-'94	12/8
86	Scott, Darnay	WR	6-1	180	7/7/72	3	San Diego State	St. Louis, Mo.	D2-'94	16/16
35	Shade, Sam	S	6-1	191	6/14/73	2	Alabama	Birmingham, Ala.	D4-'95	16/2
30	Shelling, Chris	CB	5-10	180	11/3/72	2	Auburn	Columbus, Ga.	FA-'95	13/0
70	Smith, Artie	DE	6-4	285	5/15/70	4	Louisiana Tech	Stillwater, Okla.	W(SF)-'94	16/16
22	Spencer, Jimmy	CB	5-9	180	3/29/69	5	Florida	South Bay, Fla.	UFA(NO)-'96	16/15*
79	Stallings, Ramondo	DE	6-7	285	11/21/71	3	San Diego State	Winston-Salem, N.C.	D7-'94	13/2
51	Tovar, Steve	LB	6-3	244	4/25/70	4	Ohio State	Elyria, Ohio	D3-'93	14/14
59	Truitt, Greg	LS	6-0	235	12/8/65	3	Penn State	Sarasota, Fla.	FA-'94	16/0
61	Tuten, Melvin	T	6-6	305	11/11/71	2	Syracuse	Washington, D.C.	D3-'95	16/2
67	von Oelhoffen, Kimo	DT	6-4	300	1/30/71	3	Boise State	Molokai, Hawaii	D6-'94	16/1
27	Walker, Bracey	S	5-11	200	10/28/70	3	North Carolina	Pine Forest, N.C.	W(KC)-'94	14/14
91	Wallerstedt, Brett	LB	6-1	240	11/24/70	4	Arizona State	Manhattan, Kan.	W(Den)-'94	11/2
63	Walter, Joe	T	6-7	292	6/18/63	12	Texas Tech	Dallas, Tex.	D7a-'85	16/16
88	# Ware, Derek	TE	6-2	255	9/17/67	5	Central State, Okla.	Sacramento, Calif.	W(Ariz)-'94	7/0
37	Wheeler, Leonard	S-CB	5-11	189	1/15/69	5	Troy State	Toccoa, Ga.	D3-'92	16/1
4	Wilhelm, Erik	QB	6-3	217	11/9/65	7	Oregon State	Lake Oswego, Ore.	UFA-'96	0*
99	Wilkinson, Dan	DT	6-5	313	3/13/73	3	Ohio State	Dayton, Ohio	D1-'94	14/14

* Ambrose played 16 games with Indianapolis in '95; Braham, Carter, and Tim McGee missed '95 season because of injury; Davis played 1 game with Tampa Bay; Dixon played 16 games with Cleveland; Orlando played 16 games with San Diego; Prior played 11 games with N.Y. Jets; Spencer played 16 games with New Orleans; Wilhelm active for 7 games but did not play and inactive with N.Y. Jets for 6 games.

Unrestricted free agent; subject to developments.

† Restricted free agent; subject to developments.

Players lost through free agency (1): S Darryl Williams (Sea; 16 games in '95).

Also played with Bengals in '95—CB Mike Brim (1 game), CB Adrian Hardy (10), G Dan Jones (5), G Todd Kalis (15), LB James Logan (1), DT Alfred Oglesby (6), DE Ty Parten (1), WR Jeff Query (1).

COACHING STAFF

Head Coach, Dave Shula

Pro Career: Shula is in his fifth year as head coach of the Cincinnati Bengals. He became the sixth head coach in Bengals history on December 27, 1991. Shula was offensive coordinator and quarterbacks coach for Dallas in 1989-90 before joining Cincinnati in 1991 as receivers coach. Shula began his coaching career with the Miami Dolphins in 1982. In 1988, Shula was named assistant head coach with the Dolphins. He was a wide receiver and kick return specialist with the Baltimore Colts in 1981. Career record: 18-46.

Background: Outstanding wide receiver at Dartmouth where he was a two-time All-Ivy League selection.

Personal: Born May 28, 1959, Lexington, Ky. Dave and his wife, Leslie, live in Cincinnati, and have three sons—Daniel, Christopher, and Matthew.

ASSISTANT COACHES

Paul Alexander, offensive line; born February 12, 1960, Rochester, N.Y., lives in Cincinnati. Tackle Cortland State 1979-81. No pro playing experience. College coach: Penn State 1982-84, Michigan 1985-86, Central Michigan 1987-91. Pro coach: New York Jets 1992-93, joined Bengals in 1994.

Jim Anderson, running backs; born March 27, 1948, Harrisburg, Pa., lives in Cincinnati. Linebacker-defensive end Cal Western (U.S. International) 1967-70. No pro playing experience. College coach: Cal Western 1970-71, Scottsdale, Ariz., Community College 1973, Nevada-Las Vegas 1974-75, Southern Methodist 1976-80, Stanford 1981-83. Pro coach: Joined Bengals in 1984.

Ken Anderson, quarterbacks; born February 15, 1949, Batavia, Ill., lives in Lakeside Park, Ky. Quarterback Augustana (Ill.) 1967-70. Pro quarterback Cincinnati Bengals 1971-86. Pro coach: Joined Bengals in 1992.

Bruce Coslet, offensive coordinator; born August 5, 1946, Oakdale, Calif., lives in Cincinnati. Tight end University of Pacific 1965-67. Pro tight end Cincinnati Bengals 1969-76. Pro coach: San Francisco 49ers 1980, Cincinnati Bengals 1981-89, New York Jets (head coach) 1990-93, rejoined Bengals in 1994.

Bobby DePaul, staff assistant; born January 24, 1963, Bowie, Md., lives in Cincinnati. Linebacker Maryland 1981-84. No pro playing experience. College coach: Catholic University 1986-88. Pro coach: Washington Redskins 1989-93, joined Bengals in 1994.

John Garrett, wide receivers; born March 2, 1965, Danville, Pa., lives in Cincinnati. Wide receiver Columbia 1983-84, Princeton 1987. Pro wide receiver Cincinnati Bengals 1989, San Antonio Riders (World League) 1991. Pro coach: Tampa Bay Buccaneers 1992-94 (Pro Personnel Assistant), joined Bengals in 1995.

Tim Krumrie, defensive line, born May 20, 1960, Menomonie, Wis., lives in Cincinnati. Defensive tackle Wisconsin 1979-82. Pro defensive tackle Cincinnati Bengals 1983-94. Pro coach: Joined Bengals in 1995.

Ron Meeks, defensive backfield; born August 27, 1954, Jacksonville, Fla., lives in Cincinnati. Defensive back Arkansas State 1975-76. Pro defensive back Hamilton Tiger-Cats (CFL) 1977-79, Ottawa Roughriders (CFL) 1979, Toronto Argonauts (CFL) 1980-81. College coach: Arkansas State 1984-85, Miami 1986-87, New Mexico State 1988, Fresno State 1989-90. Pro coach: Dallas Cowboys 1991, joined Bengals in 1992.

Gary Moeller, tight ends; born January 26, 1941, Lima, Ohio, lives in Cincinnati. Center-linebacker Ohio State 1960-62. No pro playing experience. College coach: Miami (Ohio) 1967-68, Michigan 1969-76, 1980-94 (head coach 1990-94), Illinois 1977-79. Pro coach: Joined Bengals in 1995.

Joe Pascale, linebackers; born April 4, 1946, New York, N.Y., lives in Cincinnati. Linebacker Connecticut 1963-66. No pro playing experience. College coach: Connecticut 1967-68, Rhode Island 1969-73, Idaho State 1974-76 (head coach 1976), Princeton 1977-79. Pro coach: Montreal Alouettes (CFL) 1980-81. Ottawa Rough Riders (CFL) 1982-83, New Jersey Generals (USFL) 1984-85, St. Louis/Phoenix Cardinals 1986-93, joined Bengals in 1994.

Larry Peccatiello, defensive coordinator; born December 21, 1937, Newark, N.J., lives in Cincinnati. Receiver William & Mary 1955-58. No pro playing experience. College coach: William & Mary 1961-68, Navy 1969-70, Rice 1971. Pro coach: Houston Oilers 1972-75, Seattle Seahawks 1976-80, Washington Redskins 1981-93, joined Bengals in 1994.

Joe Wessel, special teams; born January 5, 1962, Miami, Fla., lives in Cincinnati. Quarterback-safety Florida State 1981-84. No pro playing experience. College coach: Louisiana State 1985-90, Notre Dame 1991-93. Pro coach: Joined Bengals in 1994.

Kim Wood, strength; born July 12, 1945, Barrington, Ill., lives in Cincinnati. Running back Wisconsin 1965-68. No pro playing experience. Pro coach: Joined Bengals in 1975.

1996 FIRST-YEAR ROSTER

Name	Pos.	Ht.	Wt.	Birthdate	College	Hometown	How Acq.
Anderson, Willie	T	6-5	325	7/11/75	Auburn	Mobile, Ala.	D1
Banks, Shawn	LB	6-1	228	10/14/72	Texas Tech	Dallas, Tex.	FA
Battaglia, Marco	TE	6-2	250	1/25/73	Rutgers	Howard Beach, N.Y.	D2
Blackman, Ken	G-T	6-5	315	11/8/72	Illinois	Abiline, Tex.	D3
Daigle, Anthony (1)	RB	5-11	214	4/5/71	Fresno State	Benicia, Calif.	W(Pitt)-'96
Davis, Joel	G	6-5	310	4/6/73	Army	Binghamton, N.Y.	FA
Del Ricco, George	LB	6-1	220	1/21/73	Virginia Tech	Seabrook, Md.	FA
Estes, Marlon	WR	5-9	188	6/28/73	Wake Forest	Raleigh, N.C.	FA
Ferguson, Nicholas	CB	5-10	187	11/27/73	Georgia Tech	Miami, Fla.	FA
Gilman, Mark	TE	6-3	233	7/5/72	Nebraska	Kalispell, Mont.	FA
Gorrie, Steve	RB	5-10	220	1/26/74	Presbyterian	Snellville, Ga.	FA
Gutierrez, Brock	C	6-3	300	9/25/73	Central Michigan	Charlotte, Mich.	FA
Hetherington, Chris	RB	6-2	233	11/27/72	Yale	North Branford, Conn.	FA
Huard, Damon	QB	6-3	220	7/9/73	Washington	Yakima, Wash.	FA
Hundon, James	WR	6-1	195	4/9/71	Portland State	Daly City, Calif.	FA
Jones, Rod	G-T	6-4	315	1/11/74	Kansas	Detroit, Mich.	D7
Joseph, Kerry	QB	6-1	205	10/4/73	McNeese State	New Iberia, La.	FA
Langford, Jevon	DE	6-3	275	2/16/74	Oklahoma State	Washington, D.C.	D4
Libiano, Mark	LB	6-3	235	8/8/74	East Carolina	Easton, Pa.	FA
McCullough, Deland	RB	5-11	195	12/1/72	Miami, Ohio	Youngstown, Ohio	FA
McGaughey, Thomas	S	6-0	207	5/8/73	Houston	Houston, Tex.	FA
Morabito, Tim	DT	6-3	288	10/12/73	Boston College	Garnerville, N.Y.	FA
Myers, Greg	S	6-1	197	9/30/72	Colorado State	Tampa, Fla.	D5
Neal, Randy (1)	LB	6-3	236	12/29/72	Virginia	Hackensack, N.J.	FA
Rhodes, David (1)	WR	6-1	200	3/15/72	Central Florida	Mulberry, Fla.	FA
Tagoai, Junior	DT	5-11	300	4/29/70	Hawaii	Honolulu, Hawaii	FA
Tumulty, Tom	LB	6-2	242	2/11/73	Pittsburgh	Penn Hills, Pa.	D6
Twyner, Gunnard	WR	5-10	167	7/14/73	Western Illinois	Bettendorf, Ill.	FA
Washel, Jayme	DT	6-2	290	12/20/73	Purdue	Greenwood, Ind.	FA

The term NFL Rookie is defined as a player who is in his first season of professional football and has not been on the roster of another professional football team for any regular-season or postseason games. A Rookie is designated by an "R" on NFL rosters. Players who have been active in another professional football league or players who have NFL experience, including either preseason training camp or being on an Active List or Inactive List, or on Reserve/Injured or Reserve/Physically Unable to Perform for fewer than six regular-season games, are termed NFL First-Year Players. An NFL First-Year Player is designated by a "1" on NFL rosters. Thereafter, a player is credited with an additional year of experience for each season in which he accumulates six games on the Active List or Inactive List, or on Reserve/Injured or Reserve/Physically Unable to Perform.

NOTES

CLEVELAND BROWNS

AGREEMENT BETWEEN THE NFL AND THE CITY OF CLEVELAND

On February 8, 1996, the NFL and the city of Cleveland announced the terms of a historic public-private partnership that continues the Browns franchise in Cleveland and guarantees a new state-of-the-art stadium for the Browns in Cleveland by 1999.

The agreement includes the following key points:

• **Cleveland Browns Franchise:** With the relocation of Art Modell's NFL franchise to Baltimore in 1996, the Browns franchise will remain in Cleveland and will resume playing no later than the 1999 season. This team will be either an expansion franchise or an existing club from another city.

• **New Cleveland Stadium:** A new 72,000-seat stadium will be built in Cleveland, and the NFL will provide substantial funds for stadium construction costs. The new stadium will be owned by the city of Cleveland and will have a 30-year lease with the NFL franchise beginning in 1999.

• **Cleveland Browns Logo, Colors, and Heritage:** The heritage and records, including the Browns' name, logo, colors, history, playing records, trophies, and memorabilia, will remain in Cleveland as property of the Cleveland Browns franchise.

COACHING HISTORY

(385-285-10)

1950-62	Paul Brown	115-49-5
1963-70	Blanton Collier	79-38-2
1971-74	Nick Skorich	30-26-2
1975-77	Forrest Gregg*	18-23-0
1977	Dick Modzelewski	0-1-0
1978-84	Sam Rutigliano**	47-52-0
1984-88	Marty Schottenheimer	46-31-0
1989-90	Bud Carson***	12-14-1
1990	Jim Shofner	1-6-0
1991-95	Bill Belichick	37-45-0

*Resigned after 13 games in 1977
**Released after eight games in 1984
***Released after nine games in 1990

RECORD HOLDERS

INDIVIDUAL RECORDS—CAREER

Category	Name	Performance
Rushing (Yds.)	Jim Brown, 1957-1965	12,312
Passing (Yds.)	Brian Sipe, 1974-1983	23,713
Passing (TDs)	Brian Sipe, 1974-1983	154
Receiving (No.)	Ozzie Newsome, 1978-1990	662
Receiving (Yds.)	Ozzie Newsome, 1978-1990	7,980
Interceptions	Thom Darden, 1972-74, 1976-1981	45
Punting (Avg.)	Horace Gillom, 1950-56	43.8
Punt Return (Avg.)	Greg Pruitt, 1973-1981	11.8
Kickoff Return (Avg.)	Greg Pruitt, 1973-1981	26.3
Field Goals	Lou Groza, 1950-59, 1961-67	234
Touchdowns (Tot.)	Jim Brown, 1957-1965	126
Points	Lou Groza, 1950-59, 1961-67	1,349

INDIVIDUAL RECORDS—SINGLE SEASON

Category	Name	Performance
Rushing (Yds.)	Jim Brown, 1963	1,863
Passing (Yds.)	Brian Sipe, 1980	4,132
Passing (TDs)	Brian Sipe, 1980	30
Receiving (No.)	Ozzie Newsome, 1983	89
	Ozzie Newsome, 1984	89
Receiving (Yds.)	Webster Slaughter, 1989	1,236
Interceptions	Thom Darden, 1978	10
Punting (Avg.)	Gary Collins, 1965	46.7
Punt Return (Avg.)	Leroy Kelly, 1965	15.6
Kickoff Return (Avg.)	Billy Reynolds, 1954	29.5
Field Goals	Matt Stover, 1995	29
Touchdowns (Tot.)	Jim Brown, 1965	21
Points	Jim Brown, 1965	126

INDIVIDUAL RECORDS—SINGLE GAME

Category	Name	Performance
Rushing (Yds.)	Jim Brown, 11-24-57	237
	Jim Brown, 11-19-61	237
Passing (Yds.)	Bernie Kosar, 1-3-87	489
Passing (TDs)	Frank Ryan, 12-12-64	5
	Bill Nelsen, 11-2-69	5
	Brian Sipe, 10-7-79	5
Receiving (No.)	Ozzie Newsome, 10-14-84	14
Receiving (Yds.)	Ozzie Newsome, 10-14-84	191
Interceptions	Many times	3
	Last time by Frank Minnifield, 11-22-87	
Field Goals	Don Cockroft, 10-19-75	5
Touchdowns (Tot.)	Dub Jones, 11-25-51	*6
Points	Dub Jones, 11-25-51	36

*NFL Record

1995 TEAM RECORD

PRESEASON (2-2)

Date	Result		Opponents
8/6	L	13-19	N.Y. Giants
8/14	W	55-13	Chicago
8/19	L	10-19	at Atlanta
8/25	W	31-17	at Arizona

REGULAR SEASON (5-11)

Date	Result		Opponents	Att.
9/3	L	14-17	at New England	60,126
9/10	W	22-6	Tampa Bay	61,083
9/17	W	14-7	at Houston	36,077
9/24	W	35-17	Kansas City	74,280
10/2	L	19-22	Buffalo	76,211
10/8	L	20-38	at Detroit	74,171
10/22	L	15-23	Jacksonville	64,405
10/29	W	29-26	at Cincinnati (OT)	58,639
11/5	L	10-37	Houston	57,881
11/13	L	3-20	at Pittsburgh	58,675
11/19	L	20-31	Green Bay	55,388
11/26	L	17-20	Pittsburgh	67,269
12/3	L	13-31	at San Diego	56,358
12/9	L	11-27	at Minnesota	47,984
12/17	W	26-10	Cincinnati	55,875
12/24	L	21-24	at Jacksonville	66,007

(OT) Overtime

SCORE BY PERIODS

Browns	37	97	59	93	3	—	289
Opponents	89	91	43	133	0	—	356

ATTENDANCE

Home 512,392 Away 458,037 Total 970,429
Single-game home record, 85,073 (9/21/70)
Single-season home record, 620,496 (1980)

1995 TEAM STATISTICS

	Browns	Opp.
Total First Downs	293	342
Rushing	83	112
Passing	189	200
Penalty	21	30
Third Down: Made/Att	85/211	112/226
Third Down Pct.	40.3	49.6
Fourth Down: Made/Att	10/21	7/14
Fourth Down Pct.	47.6	50.0
Total Net Yards	5076	5648
Avg. Per Game	317.3	353.0
Total Plays	985	1082
Avg. Per Play	5.2	5.2
Net Yards Rushing	1482	1826
Avg. Per Game	92.6	114.1
Total Rushes	398	480
Net Yards Passing	3594	3822
Avg. Per Game	224.6	238.9
Sacked/Yards Lost	32/178	29/191
Gross Yards	3772	4013
Att./Completions	555/324	573/360
Completion Pct.	58.4	62.8
Had Intercepted	20	17
Punts/Avg.	65/43.6	59/41.7
Net Punting Avg.	65/36.2	59/34.4
Penalties/Yards Lost	107/966	108/736
Fumbles/Ball Lost	25/11	20/7
Touchdowns	29	40
Rushing	5	15
Passing	21	23
Returns	3	2
Avg. Time of Possession	28:25	31:35

1995 INDIVIDUAL STATISTICS

PASSING	Att.	Comp.	Yds.	Pct.	TD	Int.	Tkld.	Rate
Testaverde	392	241	2883	61.5	17	10	17/87	87.8
Zeier	161	82	864	50.9	4	9	15/91	51.9
Jackson	1	0	0	0.0	0	1	0/0	0.0
Tupa	1	1	25	100.0	0	0	0/0	118.8
Browns	555	324	3772	58.4	21	20	32/178	76.6
Opponents	573	360	4013	62.8	23	17	29/191	84.6

SCORING	TD R	TD P	TD Rt	PAT	FG	Saf	PTS
Stover	0	0	0	26/26	29/33	0	113
Jackson	0	9	0	0/0	0/0	0	54
Byner	2	2	0	0/0	0/0	0	24
McCardell	0	4	0	0/0	0/0	0	24
Rison	0	3	0	0/0	0/0	0	18
Testaverde	2	0	0	0/0	0/0	0	12
Alexander	0	0	1	0/0	0/0	0	6
Caldwell	0	0	1	0/0	0/0	0	6
Dixon	0	0	1	0/0	0/0	0	6
Hartley	0	1	0	0/0	0/0	0	6
Reeves	0	1	0	0/0	0/0	0	6
Smith	0	1	0	0/0	0/0	0	6
White	1	0	0	0/0	0/0	0	6
Zeier	0	0	0	0/0	0/0	0	2
Browns	5	21	3	26/26	29/33	0	289
Opponents	15	23	2	34/36	26/34	0	256

2-Point conversions: Zeier. Team: 1-3.

RUSHING	Att.	Yds.	Avg.	LG	TD
Hoard	136	547	4.0	25	0
Byner	115	432	3.8	23	2
White	62	163	2.6	11	1
Hunter	30	100	3.3	15	0
Zeier	15	80	5.3	17	0
Testaverde	18	62	3.4	14	2
Powers	14	51	3.6	15	0
Alexander	1	29	29.0	29	0
Tupa	1	9	9.0	9	0
Vardell	4	9	2.3	6	0
Rison	2	0	0/0	5	0
Browns	398	1482	3.7	29	5
Opponents	480	1826	3.8	75t	15

RECEIVING	No.	Yds.	Avg.	LG	TD
Byner	61	494	8.1	29t	2
McCardell	56	709	12.7	36	4
Rison	47	701	14.9	59	3
Jackson	44	714	16.2	70t	9
Kinchen	20	216	10.8	41	0
Bishop	16	135	8.4	21	0
Alexander	15	216	14.4	40	0
Smith	13	173	13.3	29t	1
Hoard	13	103	7.9	24	0
Hartley	11	137	12.5	23	1
White	8	64	8.0	28	0
Vardell	6	18	3.0	7	0
Reeves	6	12	2.0	3	1
Hunter	5	42	8.4	17	0
Riddick	1	25	25.0	25	0
Testaverde	1	7	7.0	7	0
Powers	1	6	6.0	6	0
Browns	324	3772	11.6	70t	21
Opponents	360	4013	11.1	52	23

INTERCEPTIONS	No.	Yds.	Avg.	LG	TD
S. Moore	5	55	11.0	28	0
Dixon	2	48	24.0	30	1
Hall	2	41	20.5	36	0
Langham	2	29	14.5	29	0
Caldwell	2	24	12.0	24t	1
Johnson	2	22	11.0	22	0
Booth	1	11	11.0	11	0
Griffin	1	0	0.0	0	0
Browns	17	230	13.5	36	2
Opponents	20	276	13.8	76	2

PUNTING	No.	Yds.	Avg.	In 20	LG
Tupa	65	2831	43.6	18	64
Browns	65	2831	43.6	18	64
Opponents	59	2462	41.7	18	61

PUNT RETURNS	No.	FC	Yds.	Avg.	LG	TD
McCardell	13	14	93	7.2	17	0
Alexander	9	0	122	13.6	69t	1
Hunter	3	0	40	13.3	17	0
Griffin	0	2	0	—	—	0
Browns	25	16	255	10.2	69t	1
Opponents	34	9	296	8.7	56	0

KICKOFF RETURNS	No.	Yds.	Avg.	LG	TD
Hunter	23	508	22.1	37	0
Alexander	21	419	20.0	42	0
Bates	9	176	19.6	38	0
McCardell	9	161	17.9	28	0
Byner	5	98	19.6	27	0
Powers	3	54	18.0	20	0
Frederick	2	16	8.0	11	0
Dixon	1	10	10.0	10	0
Hoard	1	13	13.0	13	0
Browns	74	1455	19.7	42	0
Opponents	63	1172	18.6	45	0

SACKS	No.
Pleasant	8.0
Burnett	7.5
Footman	5.0
Johnson	2.0
Frederick	1.5
McKenzie	1.5
Banks	1.0
Hall	1.0
S. Moore	1.0
Sagapolutele	0.5
Browns	29.0
Opponents	32.0

DENVER BRONCOS

American Football Conference
Western Division
Team Colors: Orange, Royal Blue, and White
13655 Broncos Parkway
Englewood, Colorado 80112
Telephone: (303) 649-9000

CLUB OFFICIALS

President-Chief Executive Officer: Pat Bowlen
General Manager: John Beake
Head Coach: Mike Shanahan
Director of Player Personnel: Neal Dahlen
Controller: Alex Rohr
Director of Ticket Operations/Business Development: Rick Nichols
Executive Assistant to the President: Yolanda Saltus
Director of Media Relations: Jim Saccomano
Stadium Operations Manager: Gail Stuckey
Director of Operations: Bill Harpole
Director of Marketing: Rosemary Hanratty
Assistant to the General Manager/Community Relations: Fred Fleming
Director of Player Relations: Bill Thompson
Community Relations Coordinator: Steve Sewell
Trainer: Steve Antonopulos
Equipment Manager: Doug West
Video Director: Kent Erickson
Stadium: Denver Mile High Stadium
•**Capacity:** 76,273
1900 West Eliot
Denver, Colorado 80204
Playing Surface: Grass (PAT)
Training Camp: University of Northern Colorado
Greeley, Colorado 80639

1996 SCHEDULE

PRESEASON

Aug. 3	at San Francisco	1:00
Aug. 10	**Carolina**	6:00
Aug. 17	at Dallas	7:00
Aug. 23	**Jacksonville**	6:00

REGULAR SEASON

Sept. 1	**New York Jets**	2:00
Sept. 8	at Seattle	1:00
Sept. 15	**Tampa Bay**	6:00
Sept. 22	at Kansas City	12:00
Sept. 29	at Cincinnati	1:00
Oct. 6	**San Diego**	2:00
Oct. 13	Open Date	
Oct. 20	**Baltimore**	2:00
Oct. 27	**Kansas City**	2:00
Nov. 4	at Oakland (Mon.)	6:00
Nov. 10	**Chicago**	2:00
Nov. 17	at New England	1:00
Nov. 24	at Minnesota	12:00
Dec. 1	**Seattle**	2:00
Dec. 8	at Green Bay	12:00
Dec. 15	**Oakland**	2:00
Dec. 22	at San Diego	5:00

RECORD HOLDERS

INDIVIDUAL RECORDS—CAREER

Category	Name	Performance
Rushing (Yds.)	Floyd Little, 1967-1975	6,323
Passing (Yds.)	John Elway, 1983-1995	41,706
Passing (TDs)	John Elway, 1983-1995	225
Receiving (No.)	Lionel Taylor, 1960-66	543
Receiving (Yds.)	Lionel Taylor, 1960-66	6,872
Interceptions	Steve Foley, 1976-1986	44
Punting (Avg.)	Jim Fraser, 1962-64	45.2
Punt Return (Avg.)	Rick Upchurch, 1975-1983	12.1
Kickoff Return (Avg.)	Abner Haynes, 1965-66	26.3
Field Goals	Jim Turner, 1971-79	151
Touchdowns (Tot.)	Floyd Little, 1967-1975	54
Points	Jim Turner, 1971-79	742

INDIVIDUAL RECORDS—SINGLE SEASON

Category	Name	Performance
Rushing (Yds.)	Otis Armstrong, 1974	1,407
Passing (Yds.)	John Elway, 1993	4,030
Passing (TDs)	John Elway, 1995	26
Receiving (No.)	Lionel Taylor, 1961	100
Receiving (Yds.)	Steve Watson, 1981	1,244
Interceptions	Goose Gonsoulin, 1960	11
Punting (Avg.)	Jim Fraser, 1963	46.1
Punt Return (Avg.)	Floyd Little, 1967	16.9
Kickoff Return (Avg.)	Bill Thompson, 1969	28.5
Field Goals	Jason Elam, 1995	31
Touchdowns (Tot.)	Sammy Winder, 1986	14
	Anthony Miller, 1995	14
Points	Gene Mingo, 1962	137

INDIVIDUAL RECORDS—SINGLE GAME

Category	Name	Performance
Rushing (Yds.)	Otis Armstrong, 12-8-74	183
Passing (Yds.)	Frank Tripucka, 9-15-62	447
Passing (TDs)	Frank Tripucka, 10-28-62	5
	John Elway, 11-18-84	5
Receiving (No.)	Lionel Taylor, 11-29-64	13
	Bobby Anderson, 9-30-73	13
Receiving (Yds.)	Lionel Taylor, 11-27-60	199
Interceptions	Goose Gonsoulin, 9-18-60	*4
	Willie Brown, 11-15-64	*4
Field Goals	Gene Mingo, 10-6-63	5
	Rich Karlis, 11-20-83	5
	Jason Elam, 9-3-95	5
Touchdowns (Tot.)	Many times	3
	Last time by Terrell Davis, 9-17-95	
Points	Gene Mingo, 12-10-60	21

*NFL Record

COACHING HISTORY

(265-276-10)

1960-61	Frank Filchock	7-20-1
1962-64	Jack Faulkner*	9-22-1
1964-66	Mac Speedie**	6-19-1
1966	Ray Malavasi	4-8-0
1967-71	Lou Saban***	20-42-3
1971	Jerry Smith	2-3-0
1972-76	John Ralston	34-33-3
1977-80	Robert (Red) Miller	42-25-0
1981-92	Dan Reeves	117-79-1
1993-94	Wade Phillips	16-17-0
1995	Mike Shanahan	8-8-0

*Released after four games in 1964
**Resigned after two games in 1966
***Resigned after nine games in 1971

DENVER MILE HIGH STADIUM

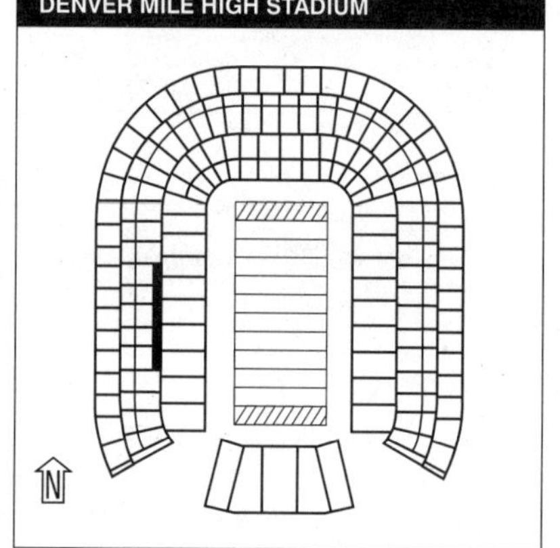

1995 TEAM RECORD

PRESEASON (3-2)

Date	Result		Opponents
7/29	W	9-7	San Francisco
8-5	W	24-10	vs. San Francisco at Tokyo
8/12	L	10-19	at Carolina
8/21	W	20-17	Dallas
8/25	L	17-23	at Jacksonville

REGULAR SEASON (8-8)

Date	Result		Opponents	Att.
9/3	W	22-7	Buffalo	75,157
9/10	L	21-31	at Dallas	64,578
9/17	W	38-31	Washington	71,930
9/24	L	6-17	at San Diego	58,987
10/1	L	10-27	at Seattle	49,914
10/8	W	37-3	at New England	60,074
10/16	W	27-0	Oakland	75,491
10/22	L	7-21	Kansas City	71,044
11/5	W	38-6	Arizona	71,488
11/12	L	13-31	at Philadelphia	60,842
11/19	W	30-27	San Diego	74,681
11/26	L	33-42	at Houston	36,113
12/3	W	31-23	Jacksonville	72,231
12/10	L	27-31	Seattle	71,488
12/17	L	17-20	at Kansas City	75,061
12/24	W	31-28	at Oakland	50,074

SCORE BY PERIODS

Broncos	96	137	64	91	—	388
Opponents	72	103	68	102	—	345

ATTENDANCE

Home 583,510 Away 455,643 Total 1,039,153
Single-game home record, 76,105 (1/4/87)
Single-season home record, 598,224 (1981)

1995 TEAM STATISTICS

	Broncos	Opp.
Total First Downs	344	322
Rushing	114	114
Passing	205	186
Penalty	25	22
Third Down: Made/Att	89/207	92/212
Third Down Pct.	43.0	43.4
Fourth Down: Made/Att	8/18	10/21
Fourth Down Pct.	44.4	47.6
Total Net Yards	6040	5193
Avg. Per Game	377.5	324.6
Total Plays	1060	1010
Avg. Per Play	5.7	5.1
Net Yards Rushing	1995	1895
Avg. Per Game	124.7	118.4
Total Rushes	440	451
Net Yards Passing	4045	3298
Avg. Per Game	252.8	206.1
Sacked/Yards Lost	26/215	30/220
Gross Yards	4260	3518
Att./Completions	594/350	529/297
Completion Pct.	58.9	56.1
Had Intercepted	14	8
Punts/Avg.	54/40.9	76/42.8
Net Punting Avg.	54/37.3	76/34.9
Penalties/Yards Lost	109/851	103/848
Fumbles/Ball Lost	25/16	20/13
Touchdowns	42	44
Rushing	14	19
Passing	27	20
Returns	1	5
Avg. Time of Possession	30:09	29:51

1995 INDIVIDUAL STATISTICS

PASSING	Att.	Comp.	Yds.	Pct.	TD	Int.	Tkld.	Rate
Elway	542	316	3970	58.3	26	14	22/180	86.4
Millen	40	26	197	65.0	1	0	4/35	85.1
Musgrave	12	8	93	66.7	0	0	0/0	89.9
Broncos	594	350	4260	58.9	27	14	26/215	86.4
Opponents	529	297	3518	56.1	20	8	30/220	82.9

SCORING	TD R	TD P	TD Rt	PAT	FG	Saf	PTS
Elam	0	0	0	39/39	31/38	0	132
Miller	0	14	0	0/0	0/0	0	84
Davis	7	1	0	0/0	0/0	0	48
Craver	5	1	0	0/0	0/0	0	36
Sharpe	0	4	0	0/0	0/0	0	24
Pritchard	0	3	0	0/0	0/0	0	18
McCaffrey	0	2	0	0/0	0/0	0	14
Elway	1	0	0	0/0	0/0	0	8
Bernstine	1	0	0	0/0	0/0	0	6
Crockett	0	0	1	0/0	0/0	0	6
Evans	0	1	0	0/0	0/0	0	6
Smith	0	1	0	0/0	0/0	0	6
Broncos	14	27	1	39/39	31/38	0	388
Opponents	19	20	5	42/42	13/19	0	345

2-Point conversions: Elway, McCaffrey. Team: 2-3.

RUSHING	Att.	Yds.	Avg.	LG	TD
Davis	237	1117	4.7	60t	7
Craver	73	333	4.6	23	5
Milburn	49	266	5.4	29	0
Elway	41	176	4.3	25	1
Bernstine	23	76	3.3	18	1
Pritchard	6	17	2.8	9	0
Millen	3	8	2.7	7	0
Miller	1	5	5.0	5	0
Rivers	2	2	1.0	1	0
McCaffrey	1	-1	-1.0	-1	0
Musgrave	4	-4	-1.0	0	0
Broncos	440	1995	4.5	60t	14
Opponents	451	1895	4.2	74t	19

RECEIVING	No.	Yds.	Avg.	LG	TD
Sharpe	63	756	12.0	49	4
Miller	59	1079	18.3	62t	14
Davis	49	367	7.5	31	1
Craver	43	369	8.6	32	1
McCaffrey	39	477	12.2	35	2
Pritchard	33	441	13.4	45t	3
Milburn	22	191	8.7	23	0
Johnson	12	170	14.2	23	0
Evans	12	124	10.3	22	1
Smith	6	152	25.3	43t	1
Bernstine	5	54	10.8	38	0
Carswell	3	37	12.3	23	0
Rivers	3	32	10.7	23	0
Chamberlain	1	11	11.0	11	0
Broncos	350	4260	12.2	62t	27
Opponents	297	3518	11.8	57	20

INTERCEPTIONS	No.	Yds.	Avg.	LG	TD
Atwater	3	54	18.0	25	0
Braxton	2	36	18.0	36	0
Alexander	2	5	2.5	4	0
Hager	1	19	19.0	19	0
Broncos	8	114	14.3	36	0
Opponents	14	103	7.4	29	0

PUNTING	No.	Yds.	Avg.	In 20	LG
Rouen	52	2192	42.2	22	61
Elam	1	17	17.0	1	17
Broncos	54	2209	40.9	23	61
Opponents	76	3253	42.8	18	62

PUNT RETURNS	No.	FC	Yds.	Avg.	LG	TD
Milburn	31	17	354	11.4	44	0
Crockett	0	0	4	—	4	0
Smith	0	1	0	—	—	0
Broncos	31	18	358	11.5	44	0
Opponents	25	12	137	5.5	52	0

KICKOFF RETURNS	No.	Yds.	Avg.	LG	TD
Milburn	47	1269	27.0	86	0
Craver	7	50	7.1	13	0
Smith	4	54	13.5	17	0
Burns	1	5	5.0	5	0
Robinson	1	14	14.0	14	0
Davis	0	0	—	—	0
Broncos	60	1392	23.2	86	0
Opponents	77	1671	21.7	94t	2

SACKS	No.
Perry	6.0
Fletcher	5.0
Hasselbach	4.0
Crockett	3.0
Cadrez	2.0
Dronett	2.0
Williams	2.0
Aldridge	1.5
Burns	1.5
J. Jones	1.0
Robinson	1.0
Alexander	0.5
Wilson	0.5
Broncos	30.0
Opponents	26.0

1996 DRAFT CHOICES

Round	Name	Pos.	College
1	John Mobley	LB	Kutztown
2	Tory James	DB	Louisiana State
3	Detron Smith	RB	Texas A&M
	Mark Campbell	DT	Florida
4	Jeff Lewis	QB	Northern Arizona
	Darrius Johnson	DB	Oklahoma
5	Patrick Jeffers	WR	Virginia
6	Tony Veland	DB	Nebraska
7	Leslie Ratliffe	T	Tennessee
	Chris Banks	G	Kansas
	L.T. Levine	RB	Kansas
	Brian Gragert	P	Wyoming

DENVER BRONCOS

1996 VETERAN ROSTER

No.	Name	Pos.	Ht.	Wt.	Birthdate	NFL Exp.	College	Hometown	How Acq.	'95 Games/ Starts
57	Aldridge, Allen	LB	6-1	245	5/30/72	3	Houston	Houston, Tex.	D2-'94	16/12
27	Atwater, Steve	S	6-3	217	10/28/66	8	Arkansas	Chicago, Ill.	D1-'89	16/16
81	Beach, Sanjay	WR	6-1	190	2/21/66	4	Colorado State	Chandler, Ariz.	FA-'96	0*
23	Bradford, Ronnie	CB	5-10	188	10/1/70	4	Colorado	Commerce City, Colo.	FA-'93	4/0
34	Braxton, Tyrone	S	5-11	185	12/17/64	10	North Dakota State	Madison, Wis.	FA-'95	16/0
70	Brown, Jamie	T	6-8	320	4/24/72	2	Florida A&M	Miami, Fla.	D4a-'95	6/0
55	Brown, Ken	LB	6-1	235	5/5/71	2	Virginia Tech	Richmond, Va.	D4b-'95	2/0
56	Burns, Keith	LB	6-2	245	5/16/72	3	Oklahoma State	Greeleyville, S.C.	D7a-'94	16/0
59	Cadrez, Glenn	LB	6-3	245	1/2/70	5	Houston	El Centro, Calif.	FA-'95	10/7
89	Carswell, Dwayne	TE	6-3	261	1/18/72	2	Liberty	Jacksonville, Fla.	FA-'94	9/2
77	Childs, Jason	T	6-4	292	1/6/69	2	North Dakota State	White Bear Lake, Minn.	FA-'96	0*
43	Clark, Derrick	RB	6-3	230	5/4/71	2	Evangel	Orlando, Fla.	FA-'96	0*
41	Cook, Toi	CB	5-11	188	12/3/64	10	Stanford	Van Nuys, Calif.	UFA(SF)-'96	2/0*
29	Craver, Aaron	RB	6-0	220	12/18/68	6	Fresno State	Compton, Calif.	UFA(Mia)-'95	16/10
39	Crockett, Ray	CB	5-10	185	1/5/67	8	Baylor	Dallas, Tex.	UFA(Det)-'94	16/16
30	Davis, Terrell	RB	5-11	200	10/28/72	2	Georgia	San Diego, Calif.	D6b-'95	14/14
63	Diaz-Infante, David	C-G	6-3	292	3/31/64	3	San Jose State	San Jose, Calif.	FA-'95	0
45	Downs, Gary	RB	6-0	212	6/28/71	3	North Carolina State	Columbus, Ga.	FA-'95	2/0
1	Elam, Jason	K	5-11	192	3/8/70	4	Hawaii	Ft. Walton Beach, Fla.	D3b-'93	16/0
7	Elway, John	QB	6-3	215	6/28/60	14	Stanford	Port Angeles, Wash.	T(Balt)-'83	16/16
88	Evans, Jerry	TE	6-4	250	9/28/68	4	Toledo	Lorain, Ohio	FA-'93	13/4
61	Floyd, Eric	G-T	6-5	310	10/28/65	6	Auburn	Rome, Ga.	FA-'95	1/0*
75	Habib, Brian	G	6-7	299	12/2/64	9	Washington	Ellensburg, Wash.	UFA(Minn)-'93	16/16
54	Hager, Britt	LB	6-1	225	2/20/66	8	Texas	Odessa, Tex.	UFA(Phil)-'95	16/5
17	Hargain, Tony	WR	6-0	194	12/26/67	2	Oregon	Palo Alto, Calif.	FA-'96	0*
96	Hasselbach, Harald	DE	6-6	280	9/22/67	3	Washington	Amsterdam, Holland	FA-'94	16/10
37	Hauck, Tim	S	5-10	185	12/20/66	7	Montana	Big Timber, Mont.	UFA(GB)-'95	16/0
21	Hilliard, Randy	CB	5-11	165	2/6/67	7	Northwestern State, La.	Metairie, La.	FA-'94	12/0
50	Jacobs, Ray	LB	6-2	244	8/18/72	3	North Carolina	Hamstead, N.C.	FA-'94	15/0
72	Jones, Ernest	DE	6-2	255	4/1/71	2	Oregon	Utica, N.Y.	FA-'96	0*
93	Jones, James	DT	6-2	290	2/6/69	6	Northern Iowa	Davenport, Iowa	UFA(Clev)-'95	16/16
31	Jones, Rondell	S	6-2	210	5/7/71	4	North Carolina	Sunderland, Mass.	D3a-'93	14/0
62	Kalaniuvala, Alai	G-T	6-3	298	10/23/71	3	Oregon State	Honolulu, Hawaii	FA-'96	0*
97	Lodish, Mike	T	6-3	280	8/11/67	7	UCLA	Birmingham, Mich.	UFA(Buff)-'95	16/0
87	McCaffrey, Ed	WR	6-5	215	8/17/68	6	Stanford	Allentown, Pa.	UFA(SF)-'95	16/5
68	McElroy, Reggie	T	6-6	290	3/4/60	14	West Texas State	Beaumont, Tex.	FA-'95	16/0
33	McMillan, Erik	S	6-2	200	5/3/65	7	Missouri	Silver Spring, Md.	FA-'96	0*
83	Miller, Anthony	WR	5-11	190	4/15/65	9	Tennessee	Pasadena, Calif.	UFA(SD)-'94	14/14
14	Musgrave, Bill	QB	6-3	215	11/11/67	6	Oregon	Grand Junction, Colo.	UFA(SF)-'95	4/0
66	Nalen, Tom	C	6-2	280	5/13/71	3	Boston College	Foxboro, Mass.	D7c-'94	15/15
91	Oshodin, Willie	DE	6-4	260	9/16/69	5	Villanova	Benn City, Nigeria	FA-'95	2/0
95	Perry, Michael Dean	DT	6-1	285	8/27/65	9	Clemson	Aiken, S.C.	FA-'95	14/14
81	Pritchard, Mike	WR	5-10	190	10/26/69	6	Colorado	Shaw AFB, S.C.	T(Atl)-'94	15/13
38	Rivers, Reggie	RB	6-1	215	2/22/68	6	Southwest Texas State	Dayton, Ohio	FA-'91	16/0
94	Robinson, Jeff	DE	6-4	265	2/20/70	4	Idaho	Kennewick, Wash.	D4-'93	16/0
53	Romanowski, Bill	LB	6-4	241	4/2/66	9	Boston College	Vernon, Conn.	UFA(Phil)-'96	16/16*
16	Rouen, Tom	P	6-3	215	6/9/68	4	Colorado	Hindsdale, Ill.	FA-'93	16/0
12	Rubley, T.J.	QB	6-3	212	11/29/68	5	Tulsa	Davenport, Iowa	FA-'96	1/0*
69	Schlereth, Mark	G	6-3	278	1/25/66	8	Idaho	Anchorage, Alaska	UFA(Wash)-'95	16/16
74	Schultz, Bill	G-T	6-5	305	5/1/67	7	Southern California	Granada Hills, Calif.	FA-'95	2/0
36	Scott, Kevin	CB-S	5-9	175	10/24/64	5	Stanford	Scottsdale, Ariz.	FA-'96	0*
84	Sharpe, Shannon	TE	6-2	230	6/26/68	7	Savannah State	Glennville, Ga.	D7-'90	13/12
82	Sherrard, Mike	WR	6-2	187	6/21/63	11	UCLA	Los Angeles, Calif.	UFA(NYG)-'96	13/13*
58	Shufelt, Pete	LB	6-3	242	10/28/69	2	Texas-El Paso	Tucson, Ariz.	FA-'96	0*
80	Smith, Rod	WR	6-0	183	5/15/70	2	Missouri Southern	Texarkana, Ark.	FA-'95	16/1
64	Tamm, Ralph	G	6-4	280	3/11/66	9	West Chester	Bensalem, Pa.	FA-'95	13/1
98	Tanuvasa, Maa	DT	6-2	277	11/6/70	3	Hawaii	Mililani, Hawaii	FA-'95	1/0
76	Thompson, Broderick	T	6-5	295	8/14/60	11	Kansas	Cerritos, Calif.	UFA(Phil)-'95	16/16
99	Wallace, Aaron	DE	6-3	240	4/17/67	7	Texas A&M	Dallas, Tex.	UFA(Oak)-'96	13/0*
48	Washington, Lionel	CB	6-0	185	10/21/60	14	Tulane	Lutcher, La.	UFA(Oak)-'95	16/16
91	Williams, Alfred	DE	6-6	265	11/6/68	6	Colorado	Houston, Tex.	UFA(SF)-'96	16/1*
90	Williams, Dan	DE	6-4	290	12/15/69	4	Toledo	Ypsilanti, Mich.	D1-'93	6/6
85	Wilner, Jeff	TE	6-4	245	12/31/71	2	Wesleyan	East Meadowbrook, N.Y.	FA-'95	3/0*
92	# Wyman, Dave	LB	6-2	248	3/31/64	10	Stanford	San Diego, Calif.	UFA(Sea)-'93	11/11
65	Zimmerman, Gary	T	6-6	294	12/13/61	11	Oregon	Walnut, Calif.	T(Minn)-'94	16/16

* Beach last active with San Francisco in '93; Childs inactive for one game with Carolina; Clark last active with Denver in '94; Cook played 2 games with San Francisco; Floyd active for 1 game with Arizona; Hargain last active with L.A. Rams in '93; E. Jones last active with Rams in '94; Kalaniuvala last active with Green Bay in '94; McMillan last active with Kansas City in '93: Romanowski played 16 games with Philadelphia; Rubley played 1 game with Green Bay; Scott last active with Detroit in '94; Sherrard played 13 games with N.Y. Giants; Shufelt last active with N.Y. Giants in '94; Wallace played 13 games wiith Oakland; A. Williams played 16 games with San Francisco; Wilner played 3 games with Green Bay and was inactive for 1 game with Denver.

Unrestricted free agent; subject to developments.

Also played with Broncos in '95—LB Elijah Alexander (9 games), RB Rod Bernstine (3), DT Shane Dronett (13), DE Simon Fletcher (16), LB Dave Garnett (3), CB Clifford Hicks (6), WR Vance Johnson (10), LB Dante Jones (5), QB Hugh Millen (3), CB Eric Thomas (14), DB Troy Wilson (3).

COACHING STAFF

Head Coach,
Mike Shanahan

Pro Career: Became the eleventh head coach in Broncos history on January 31, 1995, coming to Denver from the 1994 world champion San Francisco 49ers, where he served as offensive coordinator from 1992-94. In his first year as the Broncos' head coach Shanahan returned the team to a .500 record (8-8) while stamping the Denver offense with his signature as the most productive unit in the AFC, finishing third in the entire NFL. Under Shanahan, the Broncos had the most prolific offense in franchise history, breaking team records in points scored (388), total yards (6,040), total passing yardage (4,260), first downs passing (205), highest average gain per play (5.7), while tying the team records for touchdown passes (27) and average gain per rush (4.5). San Francisco's three-year average under Shanahan's direction was the most-productive offense in the history of pro football. San Francisco's quarterback Steve Young rewrote many NFL passing records and was named the NFL most valuable player twice in his three years under Shanahan's guidance. During his NFL career, Shanahan has been a part of teams that have played in seven AFC or NFC Championship Games, in addition to his four Super Bowl appearances, three with Denver and Super Bowl XXIX with San Francisco. In his 21 seasons coaching in the NFL and at the college level, Shanahan's teams have participated in postseason playoffs or bowl games 15 times. A driving force behind the Broncos' offense for all three of the team's most recent Super Bowl appearances (following the 1986, 1987, and 1989 seasons), he first came to Denver in 1984 as wide receivers coach. Shanahan was Broncos' offensive coordinator from 1985-87, and then returned to Denver as quarterbacks coach on October 16, 1989, after serving as head coach of the Los Angeles Raiders in 1988 and through the first four games of the 1989 campaign. His record with the Raiders was 8-12. Career record: 16-20.

Background: Shanahan began his coaching career at Oklahoma in 1975-76, also coaching at Northern Arizona (1977), Eastern Illinois (1978), and Minnesota (1979), before moving on to Florida (1980-83), where he led the Gators to an NCAA-record 4,540 yards as assistant head coach in 1983. During his tenure on the college level, Shanahan's teams had a combined record of 77-29-3 (.720), including national championship seasons at Oklahoma in 1975 and at Eastern Illinois in 1978.

Personal: Shanahan was born in Oak Park, Illinois, on August 24, 1952. He attended East Leyden High School in Franklin Park and was a wishbone quarterback/defensive back at Eastern Illinois, graduating in 1974 with a degree in physical education. He earned a master's degree there in 1975. Mike and his wife, Peggy, have two children, son Kyle and daughter Krystal.

ASSISTANT COACHES

Frank Bush, linebackers; born January 10, 1963, Athens, Ga., lives in Englewood, Colo. Linebacker North Carolina State 1981-84. Pro linebacker Houston Oilers 1985-86. Pro coach: Houston Oilers 1992-94, joined Broncos in 1995.

Barney Chavous, assistant offensive line-assistant strength and conditioning; born March 22, 1951, Aiken, S.C., lives in Englewood, Colo. Defensive end South Carolina State 1969-72. Pro defensive end Denver Broncos 1973-85. Pro coach: Joined Broncos in 1989.

Rick Dennison, offensive assistant; born June 22, 1958, in Kalispel, Mont., lives in Englewood, Colo. Tight end Colorado State 1976-79. Pro linebacker Denver Broncos 1982-90. Pro coach: Joined Broncos in 1995.

Ed Donatell, defensive backs; born February 4, 1957, Akron, Ohio, lives in Littleton, Colo. Safety Glenville State 1975-78. No pro playing experience. College coach: Kent State 1979-80, Washington 1981-82, Pacific 1983-85, Idaho 1986-88, Cal State-Fullerton 1989. Pro coach: New York Jets 1990-94, joined Broncos in 1995.

George Dyer, defensive line; born May 4, 1940, Alhambra, Calif., lives in Aurora, Colo. Center-linebacker U.C. Santa Barbara 1961-63. No pro playing experience. College coach: Humboldt State 1964-66, Coalinga (Calif.) J.C. 1967 (head coach), Portland State 1968-71, Idaho 1972, San Jose State 1973, Michigan State 1977-79, Arizona State 1980-81. Pro coach: Winnipeg Blue Bombers (CFL) 1974-76, Buffalo Bills 1982, Seattle Seahawks 1983-91, Los Angeles Rams 1992-94, joined Broncos in 1995.

Alex Gibbs, assistant head coach-offensive line; born February 11, 1941, Morganton, N.C., lives in Greenwood Village, Colo. Running back-defensive back Davidson College 1959-63. No pro playing experience. College coach: Duke 1969-70, Kentucky 1971-72, West Virginia 1973-74, Ohio State 1975-78, Auburn 1979-81, Georgia 1982-83. Pro coach: Denver Broncos 1984-87, Los Angeles Raiders 1988-89, San Diego Chargers 1990-91, Indianapolis Colts 1992, Kansas City Chiefs 1993-94, rejoined Broncos in 1995.

Mike Heimerdinger, wide receivers; born October 13, 1952, DeKalb, Ill., lives in Englewood, Colo. Wide receiver Eastern Illinois 1970-74. No pro playing experience. College coach: Florida 1980, Air Force 1981, North Texas State 1982, Florida 1983-87, Cal State-Fullerton 1988, Rice 1989-93, Duke 1994. Pro coach: Joined Broncos in 1995.

Gary Kubiak, offensive coordinator-quarterbacks; born August 15, 1961, Houston, Tex., lives in Englewood, Colo. Quarterback Texas A&M 1979-82. Pro quarterback Denver Broncos 1983-91. College coach: Texas A&M 1992-93. Pro coach: San Francisco 49ers 1994, joined Broncos in 1995.

Brian Pariani, tight ends; born July 2, 1965, San Francisco, Calif., lives in Castle Pines, Colo. No college or pro playing experience. College coach: UCLA 1989. Pro coach: San Francisco 49ers 1991-94, joined Broncos in 1995.

Greg Robinson, defensive coordinator; born October 9, 1951, Los Angeles, Calif., lives in Aurora, Colo. Linebacker-tight end Pacific 1972-74. No pro playing experience. College coach: Pacific 1975-76, Cal State-Fullerton 1977-79, North Carolina State 1980-81, UCLA 1982-89. Pro coach: New York Jets 1990-94, joined Broncos in 1995.

Greg Saporta, assistant strength and conditioning; born February 2, 1957, New York, N.Y., lives in Englewood, Colo. Wide receiver Buffalo State 1977-79. No pro playing experience. College coach: Florida 1981-88, 1993-94, North Carolina 1989-92. Pro coach: Joined Broncos in 1995.

Richard Smith, special teams; born October 17, 1955, Los Angeles, Calif., lives in Larkspur, Colo. Offensive lineman Rio Hondo (Calif.) J.C. 1975-76, Fresno State 1977-78. No pro playing experience. College coach: Rio Hondo (Calif.) J.C. 1979-80, Cal State-Fullerton 1981-83, California 1984-86, Arizona 1987. Pro coach: Houston Oilers 1988-92, joined Broncos in 1993.

Rick Smith, defensive assistant; born September 3, 1969, Petersburg, Va., lives in Aurora, Colo. Safety Purdue 1987-91. No pro playing experience. College coach: Purdue 1992-95. Pro coach: Joined Broncos in 1996.

Bobby Turner, running backs; born May 6, 1949, East Chicago, Ind., lives in Englewood, Colo. Defensive back Indiana State 1968-71. No pro playing experience. College coach: Indiana State 1975-82, Fresno State 1983-88, Ohio State 1989-90, Purdue 1991-94. Pro coach: Joined Broncos in 1995.

Rich Tuten, strength and conditioning; born December 30, 1953, Columbia, S.C., lives in Englewood, Colo. Nose guard Clemson 1976-78. No pro playing experience. College coach: Florida 1979-88, 1993-94, North Carolina 1989-92. Pro coach: Joined Broncos in 1995.

1996 FIRST-YEAR ROSTER

Name	Pos.	Ht.	Wt.	Birthdate	College	Hometown	How Acq.
Banks, Chris	G	6-1	286	4/4/73	Kansas	Lexington, Mo.	D7b
Bryant, Blaise (1)	RB	5-11	201	11/23/69	Iowa State	Huntington Bch., Calif.	FA
Burnett, Bryce (1)	TE	6-2	238	3/9/69	San Jose State	Chicago Heights, Ill.	FA
Campbell, Mark	DT	6-1	290	9/12/72	Florida	Miami, Fla.	D3b
Chamberlain, Byron (1)	WR	6-1	240	10/17/71	Wayne State	Ft. Worth, Tex.	D7b-'95
Ellis, Jamal (1)	CB	5-11	190	6/21/72	Duke	Dallas, Tex.	FA
Gamble, David (1)	WR	6-1	190	6/14/71	New Hampshire	Albany, N.Y.	FA
Gragen, Brian	P	6-0	228	8/14/72	Wyoming	Lincoln, Neb.	D7d
Jackson, Larry (1)	DE-DT	6-3	262	10/7/71	Texas A&M	Rockdale, Tex.	FA-'95
James, Tory	CB	6-1	188	5/18/73	Louisiana State	New Orleans, La.	D2
Jasper, Shane (1)	LB	6-2	256	12/23/71	UCLA	Troup, Tex.	FA
Jeffers, Patrick	WR	6-3	217	2/2/73	Virginia	Ft. Campbell, Ky.	D5
Johnson, Darrius	CB	5-9	177	9/17/72	Oklahoma	Terrell, Tex.	D4b
Levine, L.T.	RB	5-10	210	12/27/73	Kansas	Colonia, N.J.	D7c
Lewis, Jeff	QB	6-1	215	4/17/73	Northern Arizona	Columbus, Ohio	D4a
Mobley, John	LB	6-1	230	10/10/73	Kutztown	Chester, Pa.	D1
Ratliffe, Leslie	T	6-7	296	5/22/73	Tennessee	Newport, Ark.	D7a
Russ, Steve (1)	LB	6-4	237	9/16/72	Air Force	Stetsonville, Wis.	D7a-'95
Smith, Detron	RB	5-9	231	2/25/74	Texas A&M	Dallas, Tex.	D3a
Veland, Tony	S	6-0	205	3/11/73	Nebraska	Omaha, Neb.	D6

The term NFL Rookie is defined as a player who is in his first season of professional football and has not been on the roster of another professional football team for any regular-season or postseason games. A Rookie is designated by an "R" on NFL rosters. Players who have been active in another professional football league or players who have NFL experience, including either preseason training camp or being on an Active List or Inactive List, or on Reserve/Injured or Reserve/Physically Unable to Perform for fewer than six regular-season games, are termed NFL First-Year Players. An NFL First-Year Player is designated by a "1" on NFL rosters. Thereafter, a player is credited with an additional year of experience for each season in which he accumulates six games on the Active List or Inactive List, or on Reserve/Injured or Reserve/Physically Unable to Perform.

NOTES

HOUSTON OILERS

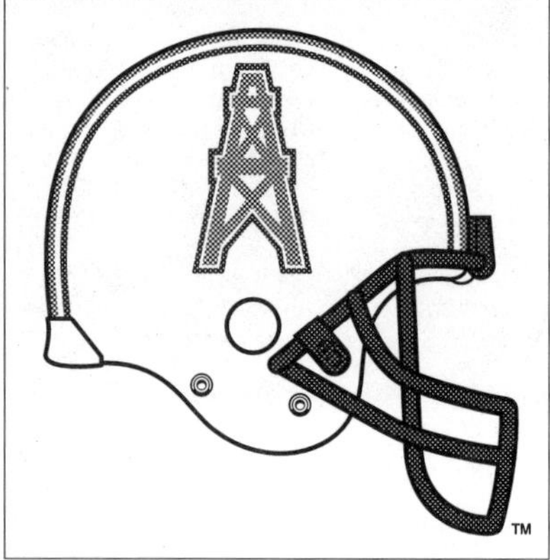

American Football Conference
Central Division
Team Colors: Columbia Blue, Scarlet, and White
8030 El Rio
Houston, Texas 77054
Telephone: (713) 881-3500

CLUB OFFICIALS

President: K.S. (Bud) Adams, Jr.
Exec. V.P./General Manager: Floyd Reese
Exec. V.P./Administration: Mike McClure
Exec. Assistant to President: Thomas S. Smith
Vice President/General Counsel: Steve Underwood
Vice President/Player Personnel and Scouting: Mike Holovak
Senior Vice President/Marketing and Broadcasting: Don MacLachlan
Director of Pro Personnel: Rich Snead
Director of Business Operations: Lewis Mangum
Director of Media Services: Dave Pearson
Director of Public and Community Relations: Rod St. Clair
Director of Ticket Administration Services: Mike Mullis
Assistant Ticket Manager: Ralph Stolarski
Director of Security: Grady Sessums
Director of Player Relations: Willie Alexander
Head Trainer: Brad Brown
Assistant Trainers: Don Moseley, Geoff Kaplan
Equipment Manager: Dan Murray
Video Coordinator: Ken Sparacino
Stadium: Astrodome • **Capacity:** 59,969
8400 Kirby Drive
Houston, Texas 77054
Playing Surface: AstroTurf-8
Training Camp: Prassel Residence Hall
Trinity University
San Antonio, Texas 78212

1996 SCHEDULE

PRESEASON

Aug. 3	vs. New York Jets at Jackson, Miss.	7:00
Aug. 10	**Indianapolis**	7:00
Aug. 16	**Detroit**	8:00
Aug. 24	vs. Dallas at Orlando, Florida	6:00

REGULAR SEASON

Sept. 1	**Kansas City**	12:00
Sept. 8	at Jacksonville	1:00
Sept. 15	**Baltimore**	12:00
Sept. 22	Open Date	
Sept. 29	at Pittsburgh	1:00
Oct. 6	at Cincinnati	8:00
Oct. 13	at Atlanta	1:00
Oct. 20	**Pittsburgh**	3:00
Oct. 27	**San Francisco**	12:00
Nov. 3	at Seattle	1:00
Nov. 10	at New Orleans	12:00
Nov. 17	**Miami**	3:00
Nov. 24	**Carolina**	12:00
Dec. 1	at New York Jets	4:00
Dec. 8	**Jacksonville**	12:00
Dec. 15	**Cincinnati**	12:00
Dec. 22	at Baltimore	1:00

RECORD HOLDERS

INDIVIDUAL RECORDS—CAREER

Category	Name	Performance
Rushing (Yds.)	Earl Campbell, 1978-1984	8,574
Passing (Yds.)	Warren Moon, 1984-1993	33,685
Passing (TDs)	Warren Moon, 1984-1993	196
Receiving (No.)	Ernest Givins, 1986-1994	542
Receiving (Yds.)	Ernest Givins, 1986-1994	7,935
Interceptions	Jim Norton, 1960-68	45
Punting (Avg.)	Greg Montgomery, 1988-1993	43.6
Punt Return (Avg.)	Billy Johnson, 1974-1980	13.2
Kickoff Return (Avg.)	Bobby Jancik, 1962-67	26.5
Field Goals	Tony Zendejas, 1985-1990	117
Touchdowns (Tot.)	Earl Campbell, 1978-1984	73
Points	George Blanda, 1960-66	596

INDIVIDUAL RECORDS—SINGLE SEASON

Category	Name	Performance
Rushing (Yds.)	Earl Campbell, 1980	1,934
Passing (Yds.)	Warren Moon, 1991	4,690
Passing (TDs)	George Blanda, 1961	36
Receiving (No.)	Charlie Hennigan, 1964	101
Receiving (Yds.)	Charlie Hennigan, 1961	1,746
Interceptions	Fred Glick, 1963	12
	Mike Reinfeldt, 1979	12
Punting (Avg.)	Greg Montgomery, 1992	46.9
Punt Return (Avg.)	Billy Johnson, 1977	15.4
Kickoff Return (Avg.)	Ken Hall, 1960	31.3
Field Goals	Al Del Greco, 1993	29
Touchdowns (Tot.)	Earl Campbell, 1979	19
Points	Al Del Greco, 1993	126

INDIVIDUAL RECORDS—SINGLE GAME

Category	Name	Performance
Rushing (Yds.)	Billy Cannon, 12-10-61	216
Passing (Yds.)	Warren Moon, 12-16-90	527
Passing (TDs)	George Blanda, 11-19-61	*7
Receiving (No.)	Charlie Hennigan, 10-13-61	13
	Haywood Jeffires, 10-13-91	13
Receiving (Yds.)	Charlie Hennigan, 10-13-61	272
Interceptions	Many times	3
	Last time by Marcus Robertson, 11-21-93	
Field Goals	Skip Butler, 10-12-75	6
Touchdowns (Tot.)	Billy Cannon, 12-10-61	5
Points	Billy Cannon, 12-10-61	30

*NFL Record

COACHING HISTORY

(252-296-6)

1960-61	Lou Rymkus*	12-7-1
1961	Wally Lemm	10-0-0
1962-63	Frank (Pop) Ivy	17-12-0
1964	Sammy Baugh	4-10-0
1965	Hugh Taylor	4-10-0
1966-70	Wally Lemm	28-40-4
1971	Ed Hughes	4-9-1
1972-73	Bill Peterson**	1-18-0
1973-74	Sid Gillman	8-15-0
1975-80	O.A. (Bum) Phillips	59-38-0
1981-83	Ed Biles***	8-23-0
1983	Chuck Studley	2-8-0
1984-85	Hugh Campbell****	8-22-0
1985-89	Jerry Glanville	35-35-0
1990-94	Jack Pardee#	44-35-0
1994-95	Jeff Fisher	8-14-0

*Released after five games in 1961
**Released after five games in 1973
***Resigned after six games in 1983
****Released after 14 games in 1985
#Released after 10 games in 1994

ASTRODOME

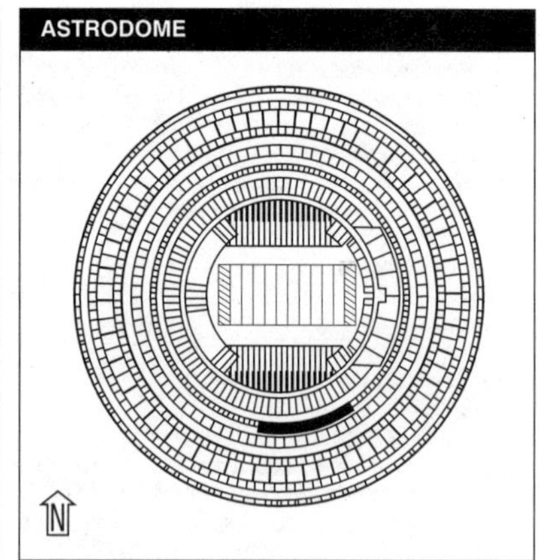

1995 TEAM RECORD

PRESEASON (0-3)

Date	Result		Opponents
8/5	L	13-16	Arizona
8/12	L	13-16	vs. Washington (OT) at Knoxville, Tenn.
8/19	Cancelled		San Diego
8/26	L	0-10	vs. Dallas at San Antonio, Tex.

REGULAR SEASON (7-9)

Date	Result		Opponents	Att.
9/3	W	10-3	at Jacksonville	72,363
9/10	L	17-34	Pittsburgh	44,122
9/17	L	7-14	Cleveland	36,077
9/24	W	38-28	at Cincinnati	46,332
10/1	L	16-17	Jacksonville	36,346
10/8	L	17-23	at Minnesota (OT)	56,430
10/22	L	32-35	at Chicago	63,545
10/29	W	19-7	Tampa Bay	31,489
11/5	W	37-10	at Cleveland	57,881
11/12	L	25-32	Cincinnati	32,998
11/19	L	13-20	at Kansas City	77,576
11/26	W	42-33	Denver	36,113
12/3	L	7-21	at Pittsburgh	56,013
12/10	L	17-24	Detroit	35,842
12/17	W	23-6	N.Y. Jets	35,873
12/24	W	28-17	at Buffalo	45,253

(OT) Overtime

SCORE BY PERIODS

Oilers	70	103	85	90	0	—	348
Opponents	83	98	36	101	6	—	324

ATTENDANCE

Home 288,860 Away 475,393 Total 764,253

Single-game home record, 63,705 (9/6/92)

Single-season home record, 494,447 (1992)

1995 TEAM STATISTICS

	Oilers	Opp.
Total First Downs	295	267
Rushing	109	85
Passing	157	157
Penalty	29	25
Third Down: Made/Att	99/228	71/212
Third Down Pct.	43.4	33.5
Fourth Down: Made/Att	7/12	5/15
Fourth Down Pct.	58.3	33.3
Total Net Yards	4905	4651
Avg. Per Game	306.6	290.7
Total Plays	1046	983
Avg. Per Play	4.7	4.7
Net Yards Rushing	1664	1526
Avg. Per Game	104.0	95.4
Total Rushes	478	400
Net Yards Passing	3241	3125
Avg. Per Game	202.6	195.3
Sacked/Yards Lost	32/271	30/200
Gross Yards	3512	3325
Att./Completions	536/314	553/289
Completion Pct.	58.6	52.3
Had Intercepted	18	21
Punts/Avg.	79/40.3	86/42.4
Net Punting Avg.	79/34.6	86/36.1
Penalties/Yards Lost	98/791	118/962
Fumbles/Ball Lost	36/20	28/17
Touchdowns	38	38
Rushing	12	11
Passing	22	24
Returns	4	3
Avg. Time of Possession	32:12	27:48

1995 INDIVIDUAL STATISTICS

PASSING	Att.	Comp.	Yds.	Pct.	TD	Int.	Tkld.	Rate
Chandler	356	225	2460	63.2	17	10	21/173	87.8
Furrer	99	48	483	48.5	2	7	5/35	40.1
S. McNair	80	41	569	51.3	3	1	6/63	81.7
Camarillo	1	0	0	0.0	0	0	0/0	39.6
Oilers	536	314	3512	58.6	22	18	32/271	77.9
Opponents	553	289	3325	52.3	24	21	30/200	69.3

SCORING	TD R	TD P	TD Rt	PAT	FG	Saf	PTS
Del Greco	0	0	0	33/33	27/31	0	114
Sanders	0	9	0	0/0	0/0	0	54
Jeffires	0	8	0	0/0	0/0	0	48
R. Thomas	5	2	0	0/0	0/0	0	44
Butts	4	0	0	0/0	0/0	0	24
Chandler	2	0	0	0/0	0/0	0	14
Wycheck	1	1	0	0/0	0/0	0	12
Bishop	0	0	1	0/0	0/0	0	6
Cecil	0	0	1	0/0	0/0	0	6
D. Lewis	0	0	1	0/0	0/0	0	6
T. McNair	0	1	0	0/0	0/0	0	6
Robinson	0	0	1	0/0	0/0	0	6
Seabron	0	1	0	0/0	0/0	0	6
Cook	0	0	0	0/0	0/0	1	2
Oilers	12	22	4	33/33	27/31	1	348
Opponents	11	24	3	35/35	19/24	2	324

2-Point conversions: Chandler, R. Thomas. Team: 2-5.

RUSHING	Att.	Yds.	Avg.	LG	TD
R. Thomas	251	947	3.8	74t	5
Brown	86	293	3.4	21	0
Butts	71	185	2.6	9	4
T. McNair	19	136	7.2	22	0
Chandler	28	58	2.1	9	2
S. McNair	11	38	3.5	13	0
Furrer	8	20	2.5	11	0
Hannah	1	5	5.0	5	0
Wycheck	1	1	1.0	1t	1
Sanders	2	-19	-9.5	-6	0
Oilers	478	1664	3.5	74t	12
Opponents	400	1526	3.8	60t	11

RECEIVING	No.	Yds.	Avg.	LG	TD
Jeffires	61	684	11.2	35t	8
T. McNair	60	501	8.4	25	1
Wycheck	40	471	11.8	36t	1
R. Thomas	39	204	5.2	19	2
Sanders	35	823	23.5	76t	9
Russell	24	321	13.4	57	0
R. Lewis	16	116	7.3	16	0
Seabron	12	167	13.9	34	1
Hannah	10	142	14.2	42	0
Roan	8	46	5.8	11	0
Brown	6	16	2.7	7	0
Butts	2	10	5.0	10	0
Lundy	1	11	11.0	11	0
Oilers	314	3512	11.2	76t	22
Opponents	289	3325	11.5	76t	24

INTERCEPTIONS	No.	Yds.	Avg.	LG	TD
D. Lewis	6	145	24.2	98t	1
Cecil	3	35	11.7	20t	1
Dishman	3	17	5.7	17	0
Barnes	2	6	3.0	6	0
Harris	2	0	0.0	0	0
Jackson	2	0	0.0	0	0
Bishop	1	62	62.0	62t	1
Robinson	1	49	49.0	49t	1
Davidson	1	3	3.0	3	0
Oilers	21	317	15.1	98t	4
Opponents	18	265	14.7	32t	1

PUNTING	No.	Yds.	Avg.	In 20	LG
Camarillo	77	3165	41.1	26	60
Del Greco	1	15	15.0	0	15
Oilers	79	3180	40.3	26	60
Opponents	86	3645	42.4	29	58

PUNT RETURNS	No.	FC	Yds.	Avg.	LG	TD
Gray	30	20	303	10.1	20	0
Hannah	5	1	36	7.2	11	0
Oilers	35	21	339	9.7	20	0
Opponents	35	17	288	8.2	72t	1

KICKOFF RETURNS	No.	Yds.	Avg.	LG	TD
Gray	53	1183	22.3	54	0
R. Thomas	3	48	16.0	23	0
Butts	2	14	7.0	14	0
Lundy	2	28	14.0	17	0
Barnes	1	-4	-4.0	-4	0
Bowden	1	6	6.0	6	0
R. Lewis	1	5	5.0	5	0
Wortham	1	-3	-3.0	-3	0
Oilers	64	1277	20.0	54	0
Opponents	78	1467	18.8	47	0

SACKS	No.
Cook	4.5
Ford	4.5
Robinson	3.5
Barrow	3.0
Walker	2.5
Davidson	2.0
Montgomery	2.0
Bishop	1.5
McGhee	1.5
Bowden	1.0
Childress	1.0
Jackson	1.0
D. Lewis	1.0
Wortham	1.0
Oilers	30.0
Opponents	32.0

1996 DRAFT CHOICES

Round	Name	Pos.	College
1	Eddie George	RB	Ohio State
2	Bryant Mix	DE	Alcorn State
	Jason Layman	T	Tennessee
3	Terry Killens	LB	Penn State
4	Kendrick Burton	DE	Alabama
	Jon Runyan	T	Michigan
5	Rayna Stewart	DB	Northern Arizona
6	Anthony Dorsett	DB	Pittsburgh
7	Mike Archie	RB	Penn State

HOUSTON OILERS

1996 VETERAN ROSTER

No.	Name	Pos.	Ht.	Wt.	Birthdate	NFL Exp.	College	Hometown	How Acq.	'95 Games/ Starts
22	Barnes, Tomur	CB	5-10	188	9/8/70	2	North Texas	McNair, Tex.	FA-'94	15/0
56	† Barrow, Micheal	LB	6-1	236	4/19/70	4	Miami	Homestead, Fla.	D2-'93	13/12
23	Bishop, Blaine	S	5-9	197	7/24/70	4	Ball State	Indianapolis, Ind.	D8-'93	16/16
58	Bowden, Joe	LB	5-11	230	2/25/70	5	Oklahoma	Mesquite, Tex.	D5a-'92	16/14
35	# Butts, Marion	RB	6-1	248	8/1/66	8	Florida State	Sylvester, Ga.	FA-'95	12/2
16	# Camarillo, Rich	P	5-11	202	11/29/59	16	Washington	Pico Rivera, Calif.	UFA(Ariz)-'94	16/0
12	Chandler, Chris	QB	6-4	225	10/12/65	9	Washington	Everett, Wash.	UFA(StL)-'95	13/13
78	Cook, Anthony	DE-DT	6-3	293	5/30/72	2	South Carolina State	Bennettsville, S.C.	D2-'95	10/4
86	Davis, Willie	WR	6-0	181	10/10/67	5	Central Arkansas	Little Rock, Ark.	UFA(KC)-'96	16/16*
3	Del Greco, Al	K	5-10	200	3/2/62	13	Auburn	Coral Gables, Fla.	FA-'91	16/0
28	Dishman, Cris	CB	6-0	188	8/13/65	9	Purdue	Louisville, Ky.	D5a-'88	15/15
77	Donnalley, Kevin	G-T	6-5	305	6/10/68	6	North Carolina	Raleigh, N.C.	D3b-'91	16/16
75	Eatman, Irv	T	6-7	305	1/1/61	11	UCLA	Dayton, Ohio	UFA(Atl)-'95	16/7
60	El-Mashtoub, Hicham	C-G	6-2	288	5/11/72	2	Arizona	Laval, Canada	D6-'95	2/0
91	Evans, Josh	DT-DE	6-0	280	9/6/72	2	Alabama-Birmingham	West Shawmut, Ala.	FA-'95	7/0
92	Ford, Henry	DE	6-3	284	10/30/71	3	Arkansas	Ft. Worth, Tex.	D1-'94	16/16
21	Gray, Mel	KR-WR	5-9	171	3/16/61	11	Purdue	Williamsburg, Va.	UFA(Det)-'95	15/0
51	Hall, Lemanski	LB	6-0	229	11/24/70	2	Alabama	Valley, Ala.	D7-'94	12/0
33	Harmon, Ronnie	RB	5-11	200	5/7/64	11	Iowa	Queens, N.Y.	UFA(SD)-'96	16/1*
48	# Harris, Odie	S-CB	6-0	190	4/1/66	9	Sam Houston State	Bryan, Tex.	FA-'95	16/1
11	Hollas, Donald	QB	6-3	215	11/22/67	4	Rice	Rosenberg, Tex.	FA-'96	0*
72	Hopkins, Brad	T	6-3	306	9/5/70	4	Illinois	Moline, Ill.	D1-'93	16/16
61	Hunt, Purvis	G	6-4	378	11/25/70	2	Mississippi State	Ruston, La.	FA-'95	0*
25	Hunter, Torey	CB	5-9	176	2/10/72	2	Washington State	Tacoma, Wash.	D3c-'95	12/0
24	Jackson, Steve	CB	5-8	182	4/8/69	6	Purdue	Houston, Tex.	D3a-'91	10/1
29	Lewis, Darryll	CB	5-9	183	12/16/68	6	Arizona	La Puente, Calif.	D2b-'91	16/15
88	Lewis, Roderick	TE	6-5	254	6/9/71	3	Arizona	Dallas, Tex.	D5a-'94	16/9
74	# Matthews, Bruce	G-C	6-5	298	8/8/61	14	Southern California	Arcadia, Calif.	D1-'83	16/16
95	# McGhee, Kanavis	DE	6-4	257	10/4/68	5	Colorado	Houston, Tex.	FA-'95	9/0
9	McNair, Steve	QB	6-2	224	2/14/73	2	Alcorn State	Mount Olive, Miss.	D1-'95	4/2
55	† Mills, John Henry	LB	6-0	222	10/31/69	4	Wake Forest	Tallahassee, Fla.	D5-'93	16/0
64	Norgard, Erik	G-C	6-1	282	11/4/65	7	Colorado	Arlington, Wash.	FA-'90	15/0
67	Reid, Jim	T-G	6-6	306	2/13/71	2	Virginia	Newport News, Va.	D5b-'94	6/0
80	Roan, Michael	TE	6-3	251	8/29/72	2	Wisconsin	Iowa City, Iowa	D4-'95	5/2
31	Robertson, Marcus	S	5-11	197	10/2/69	6	Iowa State	Pasadena, Calif.	D4b-'91	2/2
37	Robinson, Rafael	S	5-11	200	6/19/69	5	Wisconsin	Jefferson, Tex.	UFA(Sea)-'96	13/3*
85	Russell, Derek	WR	6-0	195	7/22/69	6	Arkansas	Little Rock, Ark.	UFA(Den)-'95	11/5
81	Sanders, Chris	WR	6-0	184	5/8/72	2	Ohio State	Denver, Colo.	D3a-'95	16/11
83	Seabron, Malcolm	WR	6-0	194	12/29/72	3	Fresno State	Sacramento, Calif.	D3-'94	15/1
54	Smith, Al	LB	6-1	244	11/26/64	10	Utah State	Los Angeles, Calif.	D6a-'87	2/2
53	Stepnoski, Mark	C	6-2	269	1/20/67	8	Pittsburgh	Erie, Pa.	UFA(Dall)-'95	16/16
20	Thomas, Rodney	RB	5-10	213	3/30/73	2	Texas A&M	Groveton, Tex.	D3b-'95	16/10
96	Walker, Gary	DT-DE	6-2	285	2/28/73	2	Auburn	Lavonia, Ga.	D5-'95	15/9
52	Wortham, Barron	LB	5-11	244	11/1/69	3	Texas-El Paso	Everman, Tex.	D6b-'94	16/5
89	† Wycheck, Frank	TE	6-3	247	10/14/71	4	Maryland	Philadelphia, Pa.	W(Wash)-'95	16/10

* Davis played 16 games with Kansas City in '95; Harmon played 16 games with San Diego; Hollas last active with Cincinnati in '94; Hunt missed '95 season because of injury; Robinson played 13 games with Seattle.

\# Unrestricted free agent; subject to developments.

† Restricted free agent; subject to developments.

Traded—DT Glenn Montgomery to Seattle.

Players lost through free agency (1): LB Eddie Robinson (Jax; 16 games in '95).

Also played with Oilers in '95—RB Gary Brown (10 games), S Chuck Cecil (14), DT Ray Childress (6), DE Kenny Davidson (15), QB Will Furrer (7), WR Travis Hannah (16), RB-TE Steve Hendrickson (5), WR Haywood Jeffires (16), LB James Logan (3), RB Dennis Lundy (7), RB Todd McNair (15), TE James Thornton (4), DE-DT Natu Tuatagaloa (1), DT-DE Craig Veasey (15), T David Williams (10).

COACHING STAFF

Head Coach,
Jeff Fisher

Pro Career: Officially named as Oilers' fifteenth head coach on January 5, 1995. Led Oilers to 7-9 record (tied for second in AFC Central) in his first full season as head coach. Was elevated to head coach-defensive coordinator on November 14, 1994, after head coach Jack Pardee and assistant head coach-offense Kevin Gilbride were relieved of their duties. Took over a 1-9 team and guided them through the final six games of the season, picking up his first victory against the New York Jets in the season finale. Originally joined the Oilers on February 9, 1994, as defensive coordinator after spending two seasons as defensive backs coach for the San Francisco 49ers (1992-93). Prior to stint with the 49ers, worked as defensive coordinator for the Los Angeles Rams (1991). From 1986-1990, was an assistant for Buddy Ryan's Philadelphia Eagles, serving as defensive backs coach from 1986-88 before becoming the NFL's youngest defensive coordinator in 1989. Drafted by Chicago in seventh round in 1981, spent five seasons as a cornerback and kick returner for the Bears (1981-85). Did not play in Bears' 1985 Super Bowl championship season after being placed on injured reserve with an ankle injury. That season he assisted defensive coordinator Buddy Ryan. Career record: 8-14.

Background: Played at Southern California (1977-1980) for John Robinson in a star-studded defensive backfield that included Ronnie Lott, Dennis Smith, and Joey Browner. Member of the USC team that won the national championship in 1978. Also served as the Trojans' backup placekicker and was a Pac-10 All-Academic selection in 1980.

Personal: Born February 25, 1958, in Culver City, Calif. Jeff and his wife Juli have three children, sons Brandon and Trenton, and daughter Tara. The family resides in Sugar Land, Tex.

ASSISTANT COACHES

Dick Coury, offensive assistant; born September 29, 1929, Athens, Ohio, lives in Pearland, Tex. No pro playing experience. College coach: Southern California 1967-69, Cal State-Fullerton 1970-71 (head coach). Pro coach: Denver Broncos 1972-73, Portland Storm (WFL) 1974 (head coach), San Diego Chargers 1975, Philadelphia Eagles 1976-81, Boston/New Orleans/Portland Breakers (USFL) 1983-85 (head coach), Los Angeles Rams 1986-90, New England Patriots 1991-92, Minnesota Vikings 1993, joined Oilers in 1994.

Alan Lowry, defensive assistant/quality control; born November 21, 1950, Miami, Okla., lives in Houston, Tex. Defensive back/quarterback Texas 1970-72. No pro playing experience. College coach: Virginia Tech 1974, Wyoming 1975, Texas 1977-81. Pro coach: Dallas Cowboys 1982-90 (scout, 1976), Tampa Bay Buccaneers 1991, San Francisco 49ers 1992-95, joined Oilers in 1996.

Mike Munchak, offensive assistant-quality control; born March 5, 1960, Scranton, Pa., lives in Sugar Land, Tex. Guard-tackle Penn State 1979-81. Pro guard Houston Oilers 1982-93. Pro coach: Joined Oilers in 1994.

Rex Norris, defensive line; born December 10, 1939, Tipton, Ind., lives in Sugar Land, Tex. Linebacker San Angelo (Tex.) J.C. 1959-60, East Texas State 1961-62. No pro playing experience. College coach: Navarro (Tex.) J.C. 1970-71, Texas A&M 1972, Oklahoma 1973-83, Arizona State 1984, Florida 1988-89, Tennessee 1990-91, Texas 1992-93. Pro coach: Detroit Lions 1985-87, Denver Broncos 1994, joined Oilers in 1995.

Rod Perry, defensive backs; born September 11, 1953, Fresno, Calif., lives in Sugar Land, Tex. Defensive back Colorado 1972-74. Pro cornerback Los Angeles Rams 1975-82, Cleveland Browns 1983-84. College coach: Columbia 1985, Fresno City College 1986, Fresno State 1987-88. Pro coach: Seattle Seahawks 1989-91, Los Angeles Rams 1992-94, joined Oilers in 1995.

1996 FIRST-YEAR ROSTER

Name	Pos.	Ht.	Wt.	Birthdate	College	Hometown	How Acq.
Archie, Mike	RB	5-8	205	10/14/72	Penn State	Sharon, Pa.	D7
Bell, Shonn	TE	6-5	238	10/25/74	Clinch Valley	Waynesboro, Va.	FA
Burton, Kendrick	DE	6-5	288	9/7/73	Alabama	Hartselle, Ala.	D4a
Cole, Lee	CB	5-11	188	6/25/74	Arizona State	Riverside, Calif.	FA
Davis, Andre	RB	5-8	187	4/8/73	Texas Christian	Longview, Tex.	FA
Dorsett, Anthony	CB	5-11	190	9/14/73	Pittsburgh	Dallas, Tex.	D6
Earle, Guy (1)	T-G	6-5	300	4/1/68	Western Kentucky	Keyport, N.J.	FA
George, Eddie	RB	6-3	232	9/24/73	Ohio State	Philadelphia, Pa.	D1
Halapin, Mike	DT	6-4	294	7/1/73	Pittsburgh	Apollo, Pa.	FA
Hatfield, Mark (1)	T	6-6	305	8/21/70	Bishop's, Canada	Ottawa, Canada	FA
Jackson, Chris	S	6-0	202	9/21/73	Iowa	Missouri City, Tex.	FA
Jones, Lenoy	LB	6-1	232	9/25/74	Texas Christian	Groesbeck, Tex.	FA
Killens, Terry	LB	6-1	232	3/24/74	Penn State	Cincinnati, Ohio	D3
Layman, Jason	T-G	6-5	306	7/29/73	Tennessee	Sevierville, Tenn.	D2b
Makovicka, Jeff	RB	5-10	227	9/24/72	Nebraska	Brainard, Neb.	FA
McKeehan, James (1)	TE	6-3	251	8/9/73	Texas A&M	Willis, Tex.	FA
Mix, Bryant	DE-DT	6-3	301	7/28/72	Alcorn State	Water Valley, Miss.	D2a
Montana, Denis	WR	6-0	193	1/6/72	Concordia, Canada	St. Jean, Canada	FA
Nelson, Picasso	S	6-0	208	5/1/73	Jackson State	Hattiesburg, Miss.	FA
Nyquist, Matt	TE	6-2	244	6/8/72	Wisconsin	Cokato, Minn.	FA
Reeves, Chad	LB	6-2	245	4/29/73	McNeese State	Moss Bluff, La.	FA
Rhodes, Kevin	CB	5-11	188	11/9/72	Northwestern St., La.	New Orleans, La.	FA
Running, Mitch	WR	5-11	184	9/7/72	Kansas State	Decorah, Iowa	FA
Runyan, Jon	T	6-7	308	11/27/73	Michigan	Flint, Mich.	D4b
Sanders, Chris	WR	6-2	221	4/22/73	Texas A&M	Austin, Tex.	FA
Stewart, Rayna	CB	5-10	192	6/18/73	Northern Arizona	Chatsworth, Calif.	D5
Stocz, Eric	TE	6-3	278	5/25/74	Westminster	Cortland, Ohio	FA
Strong, Jasper (1)	WR	6-1	177	8/28/72	Illinois	Chicago, Ill.	FA
White, Dan	QB	6-4	211	9/14/72	Arizona	San Diego, Calif.	FA
Wilson, Sheddrick	WR	6-2	210	11/23/73	Louisiana State	Thomasville, Ga.	FA

The term NFL Rookie is defined as a player who is in his first season of professional football and has not been on the roster of another professional football team for any regular-season or postseason games. A Rookie is designated by an "R" on NFL rosters. Players who have been active in another professional football league or players who have NFL experience, including either preseason training camp or being on an Active List or Inactive List, or on Reserve/Injured or Reserve/Physically Unable to Perform for fewer than six regular-season games, are termed NFL First-Year Players. An NFL First-Year Player is designated by a "1" on NFL rosters. Thereafter, a player is credited with an additional year of experience for each season in which he accumulates six games on the Active List or Inactive List, or on Reserve/Injured or Reserve/Physically Unable to Perform.

NOTES

Russ Purnell, special teams; born June 12, 1948, Chicago, Ill., lives in Sugar Land, Tex. Center Orange Coast (Calif.) J.C. 1966-67, Whittier College 1968-69. No pro playing experience. College coach: Whittier College 1970-71, Southern California 1982-84. Pro coach: Seattle Seahawks 1986-94, joined Oilers in 1995.

Jerry Rhome, offensive coordinator; born March 6, 1942, Dallas, Tex., lives in Missouri City, Tex. Quarterback Southern Methodist 1960-61, Tulsa 1963-64. Pro quarterback Dallas Cowboys 1965-68, Cleveland Browns 1969, Houston Oilers 1970, Los Angeles Rams 1971-72. College coach: Tulsa 1973-75. Pro coach: Seattle Seahawks 1976-82, Washington Redskins 1983-87, San Diego Chargers 1988, Dallas Cowboys 1989, Phoenix Cardinals 1990-93, Minnesota Vikings 1994, joined Oilers in 1995.

Steve Sidwell, defensive coordinator; born August 30, 1944, Winfield, Kan., lives in Sugar Land, Tex. Linebacker Colorado 1962-65. No pro playing experience. College coach: Colorado 1966-73, Nevada-Las Vegas 1974-75, Southern Methodist 1976-81. Pro coach: New England Patriots 1982-84, Indianapolis Colts 1985, New Orleans Saints 1986-94, joined Oilers in 1995.

Warren "Rennie" Simmons, offensive line; born February 25, 1942, Poughkeepsie, N.Y., lives in Houston, Tex. Center San Diego State 1961-65. No pro playing experience. College coach: Cal State-Fullerton 1974-78, Cerritos (Calif.) J.C. 1978-80, Vanderbilt 1995. Pro coach: Washington Redskins 1981-93, Los Angeles Rams 1994, joined Oilers in 1996.

Sherman Smith, running backs; born November 1, 1954, Youngstown, Ohio, lives in Missouri City, Tex. Quarterback Miami, Ohio 1972-75. Pro running back Seattle Seahawks 1976-82, San Diego Chargers 1983-84. College coach: Miami, Ohio 1990-91, Illinois 1992-94. Pro coach: Joined Oilers in 1995.

Les Steckel, wide receiver-tight ends; born July 1, 1946, North Hampton, Pa., lives in Sugar Land, Tex. Running back Kansas 1964-68. No pro playing experience. College coach: Colorado 1972-76, 1991-92, Navy 1977, Brown 1989. Pro coach: San Francisco 49ers 1978, Minnesota Vikings 1979-84 (head coach, 1984), New England Patriots 1985-88, Denver Broncos 1993-94, joined Oilers in 1995.

Steve Watterson, strength and rehabilitation; born November 27, 1956, Newport, R.I., lives in Sugar Land, Tex. Attended Rhode Island. No college or pro playing experience. Pro coach: Philadelphia Eagles 1984-85 (assistant trainer), joined Oilers in 1986 (strength and rehabilitation coordinator), named assistant coach in 1988.

Gregg Williams, linebackers; born July 15, 1958 in Excelsior Springs, Mo., lives in Katy, Tex. Quarterback Northeast Missouri State 1976-79. No pro playing experience. College coach: Houston 1988-89. Pro coach: Joined Oilers in 1990 (quality control coordinator), named assistant coach in 1993.

INDIANAPOLIS COLTS

American Football Conference
Eastern Division
Team Colors: Royal Blue and White
P.O. Box 535000
Indianapolis, Indiana 46253
Telephone: (317) 297-2658

CLUB OFFICIALS

President-Treasurer: Robert Irsay
Senior Executive Vice President, General Manager, & Chief Operating Officer: James Irsay
Executive Vice President and Chief Financial Officer: Michael G. Chernoff
Vice President-Director of Football Operations: Bill Tobin
Assistant General Manager: Bob Terpening
Director of Pro Player Personnel: Clyde Powers
Director of College Player Personnel: George Boone
Controller: Kurt Humphrey
Director of Operations: Pete Ward
Director of Public Relations: Craig Kelley
Ticket Manager: Larry Hall
Director of Sales: Rene Longoria
Asst. Director of Public Relations: Todd Stewart
Purchasing Administrator: David Filar
Administrative Assistant: Nicole Kucharski
Equipment Manager: Jon Scott
Assistant Equipment Manager: Mike Mays
Video Director: Marty Heckscher
Assistant Video Director: John Starliper
Head Trainer: Hunter Smith
Assistant Trainer: Dave Hammer
Team Physician and Orthopedic Surgeon: K. Donald Shelbourne
Orthopedic Surgeon: Arthur C. Rettig
Physician: Douglas Robertson
Stadium: RCA Dome • **Capacity:** 60,272
100 South Capitol Avenue
Indianapolis, Indiana 46225
Playing Surface: AstroTurf
Training Camp: Anderson University
Anderson, Indiana 46011

1996 SCHEDULE

PRESEASON

July 27	vs. New Orleans at Canton, Ohio	2:30
Aug. 3	at Cincinnati	7:30
Aug. 10	at Houston	7:00
Aug. 17	**Seattle**	7:00
Aug. 24	**Green Bay**	7:00

REGULAR SEASON

Sept. 1	**Arizona**	12:00
Sept. 8	at New York Jets	1:00
Sept. 15	at Dallas	3:00
Sept. 23	**Miami** (Mon.)	8:00
Sept. 29	Open Date	
Oct. 6	at Buffalo	4:00
Oct. 13	**Baltimore**	7:00
Oct. 20	**New England**	12:00
Oct. 27	at Washington	1:00
Nov. 3	**San Diego**	1:00
Nov. 10	at Miami	1:00
Nov. 17	**New York Jets**	1:00
Nov. 24	at New England	1:00
Dec. 1	**Buffalo**	1:00
Dec. 5	**Philadelphia** (Thurs.)	8:00
Dec. 15	at Kansas City	12:00
Dec. 22	at Cincinnati	1:00

RECORD HOLDERS

INDIVIDUAL RECORDS—CAREER

Category	Name	Performance
Rushing (Yds.)	Lydell Mitchell, 1972-77	5,487
Passing (Yds.)	Johnny Unitas, 1956-1972	39,768
Passing (TDs)	Johnny Unitas, 1956-1972	287
Receiving (No.)	Raymond Berry, 1955-1967	631
Receiving (Yds.)	Raymond Berry, 1955-1967	9,275
Interceptions	Bob Boyd, 1960-68	57
Punting (Avg.)	Rohn Stark, 1982-1994	43.8
Punt Return (Avg.)	Wendell Harris, 1964	12.6
Kickoff Return (Avg.)	Jim Duncan, 1969-1971	32.5
Field Goals	Dean Biasucci 1984, 1986-1994	176
Touchdowns (Tot.)	Lenny Moore, 1956-1967	113
Points	Dean Biasucci, 1984, 1986-1994	783

INDIVIDUAL RECORDS—SINGLE SEASON

Category	Name	Performance
Rushing (Yds.)	Eric Dickerson, 1988	1,659
Passing (Yds.)	Johnny Unitas, 1963	3,481
Passing (TDs)	Johnny Unitas, 1959	32
Receiving (No.)	Reggie Langhorne, 1993	85
Receiving (Yds.)	Raymond Berry, 1960	1,298
Interceptions	Tom Keane, 1953	11
Punting (Avg.)	Rohn Stark, 1985	45.9
Punt Return (Avg.)	Clarence Verdin, 1989	12.9
Kickoff Return (Avg.)	Jim Duncan, 1970	35.4
Field Goals	Raul Allegre, 1983	30
Touchdowns (Tot.)	Lenny Moore, 1964	20
Points	Lenny Moore, 1964	120

INDIVIDUAL RECORDS—SINGLE GAME

Category	Name	Performance
Rushing (Yds.)	Norm Bulaich, 9-19-71	198
Passing (Yds.)	Johnny Unitas, 9-17-67	401
Passing (TDs)	Gary Cuozzo, 11-14-65	5
	Gary Hogeboom, 10-4-87	5
Receiving (No.)	Lydell Mitchell, 12-15-74	13
	Joe Washington, 9-2-79	13
Receiving (Yds.)	Raymond Berry, 11-10-57	224
Interceptions	Many times.	3
	Last time by Mike Prior, 12-20-92	
Field Goals	Many times	5
	Last time by Dean Biasucci, 9-25-88	
Touchdowns (Tot.)	Many times	4
	Last time by Eric Dickerson, 10-31-88	
Points	Many times	24
	Last time by Eric Dickerson, 10-31-88	

COACHING HISTORY

BALTIMORE 1953-1983
(308-318-7)

1953	Keith Molesworth	3-9-0
1954-62	Weeb Ewbank	61-52-1
1963-69	Don Shula	73-26-4
1970-72	Don McCafferty*	26-11-1
1972	John Sandusky	4-5-0
1973-74	Howard Schnellenberger**	4-13-0
1974	Joe Thomas	2-9-0
1975-79	Ted Marchibroda	41-36-0
1980-81	Mike McCormack	9-23-0
1982-84	Frank Kush***	11-28-1
1984	Hal Hunter	0-1-0
1985-86	Rod Dowhower****	5-24-0
1986-91	Ron Meyer#	36-36-0
1991	Rick Venturi	1-10-0
1992-95	Ted Marchibroda	32-35-0

*Released after five games in 1972
**Released after three games in 1974
***Resigned after 15 games in 1984
****Released after 13 games in 1986
#Released after five games in 1991

RCA DOME

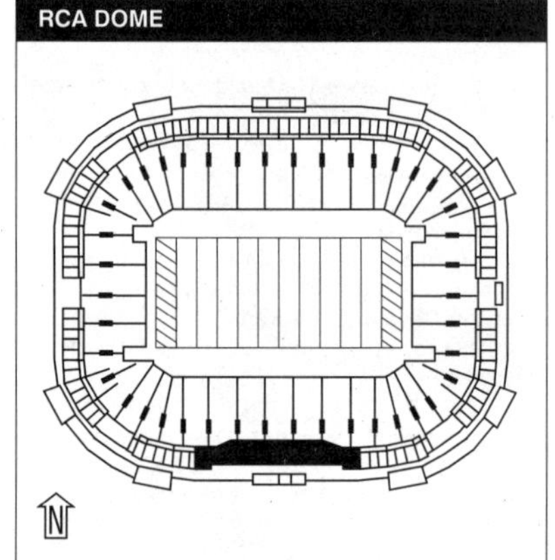

1995 TEAM RECORD

PRESEASON (3-1)

Date	Result		Opponents
8/4	L	21-34	Cincinnati
8/12	W	20-17	at Seattle
8/19	W	20-17	at Green Bay (OT)
8/24	W	29-7	Chicago

REGULAR SEASON (9-7)

Date	Result		Opponents	Att.
9/3	L	21-24	Cincinnati (OT)	42,445
9/10	W	27-24	at N.Y. Jets (OT)	65,134
9/17	L	14-20	at Buffalo	62,499
10/1	W	21-18	St. Louis	58,616
10/8	W	27-24	at Miami (OT)	68,471
10/15	W	18-17	San Francisco	60,273
10/22	L	17-30	at Oakland	53,543
10/29	W	17-10	N.Y. Jets	49,250
11/5	L	10-16	Buffalo	59,612
11/12	L	14-17	at New Orleans	44,122
11/19	W	24-10	at New England	59,544
11/26	W	36-28	Miami	60,414
12/3	L	10-13	at Carolina	49,841
12/10	W	41-31	at Jacksonville	66,099
12/17	L	24-27	San Diego	55,318
12/23	W	10-7	New England	54,685

POSTSEASON (2-1)

12/31	W	35-20	at San Diego	61,182
1/7	W	10-7	at Kansas City	77,594
1/14	L	16-20	at Pittsburgh	61,062

(OT) Overtime

SCORE BY PERIODS

Colts	78	98	52	97	6	—	331
Opponents	75	86	74	78	3	—	316

ATTENDANCE

Home 440,613 Away 469,253 Total 909,866
Single-game home record, 61,479 (11/13/83)
Single-season home record, 481,305 (1984)

1995 TEAM STATISTICS

	Colts	Opp.
Total First Downs	281	304
Rushing	110	92
Passing	147	182
Penalty	24	30
Third Down: Made/Att	80/205	85/212
Third Down Pct.	39.0	40.1
Fourth Down: Made/Att	12/19	7/14
Fourth Down Pct.	63.2	50.0
Total Net Yards	4919	5027
Avg. Per Game	307.4	314.2
Total Plays	961	1016
Avg. Per Play	5.1	4.9
Net Yards Rushing	1855	1457
Avg. Per Game	115.9	91.1
Total Rushes	478	418
Net Yards Passing	3064	3570
Avg. Per Game	191.5	223.1
Sacked/Yards Lost	49/309	29/169
Gross Yards	3373	3739
Att./Completions	434/270	569/336
Completion Pct.	62.2	59.1
Had Intercepted	11	13
Punts/Avg.	63/42.6	63/41.0
Net Punting Avg.	63/33.4	63/36.6
Penalties/Yards Lost	97/943	111/935
Fumbles/Ball Lost	21/11	24/13
Touchdowns	37	34
Rushing	14	8
Passing	20	23
Returns	3	3
Avg. Time of Possession	31:40	28:20

1995 INDIVIDUAL STATISTICS

PASSING	Att.	Comp.	Yds.	Pct.	TD	Int.	Tkld.	Rate
Harbaugh	314	200	2575	63.7	17	5	36/219	100.7
Erickson	83	50	586	60.2	3	4	10/68	73.7
Justin	36	20	212	55.6	0	2	3/22	49.8
Gardocki	1	0	0	0.0	0	0	0/0	39.6
Colts	434	270	3373	62.2	20	11	49/309	91.1
Opponents	569	336	3739	59.1	23	13	29/169	82.6

SCORING	TD R	TD P	TD Rt	PAT	FG	Saf	PTS
Faulk	11	3	0	0/0	0/0	0	84
Blanchard	0	0	0	25/25	19/24	0	82
Turner	0	4	0	0/0	0/0	0	28
Bailey	0	3	1	0/0	0/0	0	24
Dilger	0	4	0	0/0	0/0	0	24
Cofer	0	0	0	9/9	4/9	0	21
Dawkins	0	3	0	0/0	0/0	0	18
Anderson	0	2	0	0/0	0/0	0	12
Harbaugh	2	0	0	0/0	0/0	0	12
Bennett	0	0	1	0/0	0/0	1	8
Daniel	0	0	1	0/0	0/0	0	6
Potts	0	1	0	0/0	0/0	0	6
Warren	1	0	0	0/0	0/0	0	6
Colts	14	20	3	34/34	23/33	1	331
Opponents	8	23	3	29/29	25/38	1	316

2-Point conversions: Turner 2. Team: 2-3.

RUSHING	Att.	Yds.	Avg.	LG	TD
Faulk	289	1078	3.7	40	11
Potts	65	309	4.8	37	0
Harbaugh	52	235	4.5	21	2
Warren	47	152	3.2	42	1
Bailey	1	34	34.0	34	0
Workman	9	26	2.9	13	0
Erickson	9	14	1.6	15	0
Humphrey	2	6	3.0	5	0
Justin	3	1	0.3	2	0
Crockett	1	0	0.0	0	0
Colts	478	1855	3.9	42	14
Opponents	418	1457	3.5	30	8

RECEIVING	No.	Yds.	Avg.	LG	TD
Faulk	56	475	8.5	34	3
Dawkins	52	784	15.1	52	3
Dilger	42	635	15.1	42	4
Turner	35	431	12.3	47t	4
Bailey	21	379	18.0	45	3
Potts	21	228	10.9	52	1
Warren	17	159	9.4	18	0
Anderson	8	111	13.9	28	2
Stablein	8	95	11.9	16	0
Arbuckle	4	33	8.3	12	0
Crockett	2	35	17.5	19	0
Humphrey	2	11	5.5	6	0
Banta	1	6	6.0	6	0
Harbaugh	1	-9	-9.0	-9	0
Colts	270	3373	12.5	52	20
Opponents	336	3739	11.1	73t	23

INTERCEPTIONS	No.	Yds.	Avg.	LG	TD
Daniel	3	142	47.3	97t	1
Ambrose	3	12	4.0	7	0
Buchanan	2	60	30.0	60	0
Gray	1	10	10.0	10	0
Grant	1	9	9.0	9	0
Watts	1	9	9.0	9	0
Coryatt	1	6	6.0	6	0
Belser	1	0	0.0	0	0
Colts	13	248	19.1	97t	1
Opponents	11	156	14.2	49t	1

PUNTING	No.	Yds.	Avg.	In 20	LG
Gardocki	63	2681	42.6	16	69
Colts	63	2681	42.6	16	69
Opponents	63	2580	41.0	19	57

PUNT RETURNS	No.	FC	Yds.	Avg.	LG	TD
Buchanan	16	4	113	7.1	17	0
Bronson	13	6	79	6.1	32	0
Stablein	0	2	0	—	—	0
Colts	29	12	192	6.6	32	0
Opponents	37	5	436	11.8	62	0

KICKOFF RETURNS	No.	Yds.	Avg.	LG	TD
Bailey	21	495	23.6	95t	1
Humphrey	21	453	21.6	64	0
Warren	15	315	21.0	34	0
Morrison	2	6	3.0	6	0
Belser	1	15	15.0	15	0
Bronson	1	31	31.0	31	0
Buchanan	1	22	22.0	22	0
Radecic	1	-5	-5.0	-5	0
Colts	63	1332	21.1	95t	1
Opponents	68	1546	22.7	84t	1

SACKS	No.
Bennett	10.5
Johnson	4.5
Coryatt	2.5
McCoy	2.5
Alberts	2.0
Grant	2.0
Siragusa	2.0
Whittington	2.0
Buchanan	1.0
Colts	29.0
Opponents	49.0

1996 DRAFT CHOICES

Round	Name	Pos.	College
1	Marvin Harrison	WR	Syracuse
2	Dedric Mathis	DB	Houston
3	Scott Slutzker	TE	Iowa
4	Brian Milne	RB	Penn State
5	Steve Martin	DT	Missouri
6	Keith Conlin	T	Penn State
	Mike Cawley	QB	James Madison
7	Adrian Robinson	DB	Baylor

INDIANAPOLIS COLTS

1996 VETERAN ROSTER

No.		Name	Pos.	Ht.	Wt.	Birthdate	NFL Exp.	College	Hometown	How Acq.	'95 Games/ Starts
51		Alberts, Trev	LB	6-4	245	8/8/70	3	Nebraska	Cedar Falls, Iowa	D1b-'94	15/3
84		Anderson, Willie	WR	6-0	173	3/7/65	9	UCLA	Paulsboro, N.J.	UFA(StL)-'95	2/2
68		Auzenne, Troy	T	6-7	300	6/26/69	5	California	El Monte, Calif.	UFA(Chi)-'96	11/0*
80		Bailey, Aaron	WR	5-10	184	10/24/71	3	Louisville	Ann Arbor, Mich.	FA-'94	15/3
83		Banta, Bradford	TE	6-6	260	12/14/70	3	Southern California	Baton Rouge, La.	D4-'94	16/2
29		Belser, Jason	CB-S	5-9	180	5/28/70	5	Oklahoma	Kansas City, Mo.	D8a-'92	16/16
56		Bennett, Tony	LB	6-2	250	7/1/67	7	Mississippi	Clarksdale, Miss.	FA-'94	16/16
14		Blanchard, Cary	K	6-1	227	11/5/68	4	Oklahoma State	Hurst, Tex.	FA-'95	12/0
34		Buchanan, Ray	CB	5-9	195	9/29/71	4	Louisville	Chicago, Ill.	D3-'93	16/16
35		Clarks, Conrad	S-CB	5-10	218	4/21/69	2	Northeast Louisiana	Franklin, La.	FA-'95	6/0
55		Coryatt, Quentin	LB	6-3	250	8/1/70	5	Texas A&M	St. Croix, Virgin Islands	D1b-'92	16/16
32		Crockett, Zack	RB	6-2	246	12/2/72	2	Florida State	Pompano Beach, Fla.	D3-'95	16/0
38		Daniel, Eugene	CB	5-11	178	5/4/61	13	Louisiana State	Baton Rouge, La.	D8-'84	16/16
87		Dawkins, Sean	WR	6-4	211	2/3/71	4	California	Red Bank, N.J.	D1-'93	16/13
85		Dilger, Ken	TE	6-5	259	2/2/71	2	Illinois	Mariah Hill, Ind.	D2-'95	16/13
69	#	Dixon, Randy	G	6-3	290	3/12/65	10	Pittsburgh	Clewiston, Fla.	D4-'87	12/9
7		Erickson, Craig	QB	6-2	209	5/17/69	5	Miami	Boynton Beach, Fla.	T(TB)-'95	6/3
28		Faulk, Marshall	RB	5-10	211	2/26/73	3	San Diego State	New Orleans, La.	D1a-'94	16/16
17		Gardocki, Chris	P	6-1	260	2/7/70	6	Clemson	Stone Mountain, Ga.	UFA(Chi)-'95	16/0
59		Grant, Stephen	LB	6-0	240	12/23/69	5	West Virginia	Miami, Fla.	D10-'92	15/15
30	†	Gray, Derwin	CB-S	5-11	210	4/9/71	4	Brigham Young	San Antonio, Tex.	D4a-'93	16/0
4		Harbaugh, Jim	QB	6-3	215	12/23/63	10	Michigan	Ann Arbor, Mich.	FA-'94	15/12
75		Harper, Shawn	T	6-3	290	7/9/68	4	Indiana	Columbus, Ohio	FA-'95	8/0
54		Herrod, Jeff	LB	6-0	249	7/29/66	9	Mississippi	Birmingham, Ala.	D9-'88	16/16
25	†	Humphrey, Ronald	RB	5-10	211	3/3/69	3	Mississippi Valley State	Marland, Tex.	D8b-'92	11/0
62		Johnson, Ellis	DE-DT	6-2	292	10/10/73	2	Florida	Wildwood, Fla.	D1-'95	16/2
11		Justin, Paul	QB	6-4	211	5/19/68	2	Arizona State	Schaumburg, Ill.	FA-'95	3/1
58		Leeuwenberg, Jay	C-G	6-3	297	6/18/69	5	Colorado	St. Louis, Mo.	UFA(Chi)-'96	16/16*
63	#	Lowdermilk, Kirk	C	6-4	284	4/10/63	12	Ohio State	Canton, Ohio	UFA(Minn)-'93	16/16
65		Mahlum, Eric	G	6-4	290	12/6/70	3	California	San Diego, Calif.	D2-'94	7/7
78		Mandarich, Tony	G-T	6-5	317	9/23/66	5	Michigan State	Ontario, Canada	FA-'96	0*
74		Mathews, Jason	T	6-5	288	2/9/71	3	Texas A&M	Orange, Tex.	D3-'94	16/16
61		McCoy, Tony	DT	6-0	282	6/10/69	5	Florida	Orlando, Fla.	D4b-'92	16/16
57		McDonald, Devon	LB	6-4	240	11/8/69	4	Notre Dame	Kingston, Jamaica	D4b-'93	15/0
40		McElroy, Ray	S	5-11	207	7/31/72	2	Eastern Illinois	Bellwood, Ill.	D4-'95	16/0
81		McLemore, Thomas	TE	6-5	261	3/14/70	4	Southern	Shreveport, La.	FA-'95	1/0
92		Morrison, Steve	LB	6-3	243	12/28/71	2	Michigan	Birmingham, Mich.	FA-'95	10/0
93		Nunn, Freddie Joe	DE	6-5	262	4/9/62	12	Mississippi	Noxubee, Miss.	FA-'94	10/1
1		Olive, Bobby	WR	5-11	170	4/22/69	2	Ohio State	Paris, Tenn.	FA-'95	1/0
99		Pelton, Mike	DT	6-2	305	12/13/71	2	Auburn	Goshen, Ala.	FA-'95	0*
48		Pollard, Marcus	TE	6-4	257	2/8/72	2	Bradley	Valley, Ala.	FA-'95	8/0
42	†	Potts, Roosevelt	RB	6-0	250	1/8/71	4	Northeast Louisiana	Rayville, La.	D2-'93	15/15
98		Siragusa, Tony	DT	6-3	320	5/14/67	7	Pittsburgh	Kenilworth, N.J.	FA-'90	14/14
15		Smith, Terry	WR	6-0	206	4/20/71	2	Clemson	Clemson, S.C.	FA-'95	0*
86		Stablein, Brian	WR	6-1	190	4/14/70	3	Ohio State	Erie, Pa.	FA-'94	15/0
79	#	Staysniak, Joe	G	6-4	292	12/8/66	6	Ohio State	Elyria, Ohio	FA-'92	16/16
49		Tate, David	S-CB	6-1	209	11/22/64	9	Colorado	Buffalo Grove, Ill.	FA-'94	16/16
88	#	Turner, Floyd	WR	5-11	199	5/29/66	8	Northwestern State, La.	Shreveport, La.	UFA(NO)-'94	14/12
71		Vickers, Kipp	G-T	6-2	296	8/27/69	2	Miami	Holiday, Fla.	FA-'93	9/0
21		Warren, Lamont	RB	5-11	211	1/4/73	3	Colorado	Indianapolis, Ind.	D6-'94	12/1
36		Watts, Damon	CB-S	5-10	173	4/8/72	3	Indiana	Indianapolis, Ind.	FA-'94	13/0
72		West, Derek	T	6-8	312	3/28/72	2	Colorado	Indianapolis, Ind.	D5-'95	3/0
95		Whittington, Bernard	DE	6-6	283	8/20/71	3	Indiana	St. Louis, Mo.	FA-'94	16/13
67		Widell, Doug	G	6-4	290	9/23/66	8	Boston College	Hartford, Conn.	UFA(Det)-'96	11/11*
96		Wilmot, Trevor	LB	6-2	228	10/30/72	2	Indiana	Evanston, Ill.	FA-'95	7/0
46		Workman, Vince	RB	5-10	215	5/9/68	8	Ohio State	Buffalo, N.Y.	FA-'95	1/0

* Auzenne played 11 games with Chicago in '95; Leeuwenberg played 16 games with Chicago; Mandarich last active with Green Bay in '91; Pelton inactive for 13 games; Smith missed '95 season because of injury; Widell played 11 games with Detroit.

Unrestricted free agent; subject to developments.

† Restricted free agent; subject to developments.

Players lost through free agency (2): CB Ashley Ambrose (Cin; 16 games in '95), T Will Wolford (Pitt; 16).

Also played with Colts in '95—TE Charles Arbuckle (3 games), WR Ben Bronson (9), K Mike Cofer (4), G-T Garin Patrick (5), LB Scott Radecic (13), LB Glen Sanders (9).

COACHING STAFF

Head Coach,
Lindy Infante

Pro Career: Infante enters his first season as the Colts' head coach and his second overall with the club. With Infante as offensive coordinator in 1995, the Colts improved from twenty-seventh to twenty-second in total offense, from twenty-eighth to twenty-third in passing offense and from eighteenth to sixteenth in scoring. The Colts placed three offensive players (Marshall Faulk, Jim Harbaugh, and Will Wolford) in the Pro Bowl for the first time since 1989. Under Infante's tutelage, Harbaugh led the NFL in passing rating (100.7) and became the first Colts quarterback named to the Pro Bowl since 1976 (Bert Jones). Infante helped seven players total more than 15 receptions, tying for the most with 15+ receptions since 1986 (8). In addition, five players had at least three touchdown receptions for the first time since 1980, and tight end Ken Dilger set a Colts rookie tight end reception record (42 receptions for 635 yards and 4 touchdowns). Infante previously served as head coach of the Green Bay Packers from 1988-1991. He was named NFL Coach of the Year in 1989 by the *Associated Press* and *The Sporting News* and NFC Coach of the Year by *United Press International,* the Pro Football Writers Association of America, *Football News,* and *College and Pro Football Newsweekly* after guiding Green Bay to a 10-6 record. He entered the coaching ranks as an assistant on the staff of Miami Senior High School in 1965. He served as freshman coach at Florida from 1966-68 and coached the Gators' defensive backs from 1969-71. Infante served as offensive coordinator and assistant head coach at Memphis State from 1972-74 before joining the staff of the Charlotte Hornets of the World Football League in 1975. He was offensive coordinator at Tulane in 1976 and 1979, a tenure sandwiched around a two-year stint as receivers coach with the New York Giants (1977-78). Infante left Tulane for the Cincinnati Bengals (1980-82). He served as quarterbacks/receivers coach in 1980-81 and was named the team's first-ever offensive coordinator prior to the 1982 season. Infante served as head coach of the Jacksonville Bulls of the United States Football League in 1984-85. He served as offensive coordinator/quarterbacks coach with the Cleveland Browns in 1986-87.

Background: Was three-year letterman (1960-62) as running back at Florida. In 1963, he was a twelfth-round selection of the Cleveland Browns and an eleventh-round choice of the Buffalo Bills of the American Football League. He signed with Buffalo, was released before the season began, and then played briefly with the Hamilton Tiger Cats of the Canadian Football League.

Personal: Born May 27, 1940, Miami, Fla. Lindy and his wife, Stephanie, live in Indianapolis, and have two sons, Brett (25) and Brad (24).

ASSISTANT COACHES

Tom Batta, tight ends-quality control; born October 6, 1942, Youngstown, Ohio, lives in Indianapolis. Offensive-defensive line Kent State 1961-63. No pro playing experience. College coach: Akron 1973, Colorado 1974-78, Kansas 1979-82, North Carolina State 1983. Pro coach: Minnesota Vikings 1984-93, joined Colts in 1994.

Greg Blache, defensive line; born March 9, 1949, New Orleans, La., lives in Indianapolis. No college or pro playing experience. College coach: Notre Dame 1973-75, 1981-83, Tulane 1976-80, Southern University 1986, Kansas 1987. Pro coach: Jacksonville Bulls (USFL) 1984-85, Green Bay Packers 1988-93, joined Colts in 1994.

Ron Blackledge, offensive line; born April 15, 1938, Canton, Ohio, lives in Indianapolis. Tight end-defensive end Bowling Green 1957-59. No pro playing experience. College coach: Ashland 1968-69, Cincinnati 1970-72, Kentucky 1973-75, Princeton 1976, Kent State 1977-81 (head coach 1979-81). Pro coach: Pittsburgh Steelers 1982-91, joined Colts in 1992.

Chuck Bresnahan, linebackers; born September 8, 1960, Springfield, Mass., lives in Indianapolis. Linebacker Navy 1979-83. No pro playing experience. College coach: Navy 1983-84, 1986-87, Georgia Tech 1987-91, Maine 1992-93. Pro coach: Cleveland Browns 1994-95, joined Colts in 1996.

Fred Bruney, defensive assistant; born December 30, 1931, Martins Ferry, Ohio, lives in Indianapolis. Running back-defensive back Ohio State 1950-52. Pro defensive back San Francisco 49ers 1953-56, Pittsburgh Steelers 1957, Los Angeles Rams 1958, Boston Patriots 1960-62. College coach: Ohio State 1959. Pro coach: Boston Patriots 1962-63, Philadelphia Eagles 1964-68, 1977-85, Atlanta Falcons 1969-76, 1986-89, Tampa Bay Buccaneers 1990, New York Giants 1991-92, joined Colts in 1993.

Charlie Davis, assistant to the offensive line; born August 7, 1944, San Diego, Calif., lives in Indianapolis. Linebacker UCLA 1962-64. No pro playing experience. College coach: UCLA 1966, San Francisco State 1967-68, San Diego City College 1969-70, Xavier 1971-73, Ball State 1974-75, Tulane 1976-80. Pro coach: Jacksonville Bulls (USFL) 1984-85, Cleveland Browns 1986-87, Green Bay Packers 1988-91, joined Colts in 1996.

Wayne "Buddy" Geis, offensive assistant/assistant quarterbacks coach; born September 16, 1946, Altoona, Pa., lives in Indianapolis. Wide receiver Northern Arizona 1965. No pro playing experience. College coach: Arizona 1974-76, Tulane 1977-82, Memphis State 1986-87, Duke 1993, Tulane 1994. Pro coach: Jacksonville Bulls (USFL) 1984-85, Green Bay Packers 1988-91, Memphis Mad Dogs (CFL) 1995, joined Colts in 1996.

Gene Huey, running backs; born July 20, 1947, Uniontown, Pa., lives in Indianapolis. Defensive back-wide receiver Wyoming 1966-69. No pro playing experience. College coach: Wyoming 1970-74, New Mexico 1975-77, Nebraska 1978-87, Ohio State 1988-91. Pro coach: Joined Colts in 1992.

Jim Johnson, defensive coordinator; born May 26, 1941, Maywood, Ill., lives in Indianapolis. Quarterback Missouri 1959-62. Pro tight end Buffalo Bills 1963-64. College coach: Missouri Southern 1967-68 (head coach), Drake 1969-72, Indiana 1973-76, Notre Dame 1977-80. Pro coach: Oklahoma Outlaws (USFL) 1984, Jacksonville Bulls (USFL) 1985, Phoenix Cardinals 1986-93, joined Colts in 1994.

Hank Kuhlmann, special teams; born October 6, 1937, Webster Groves, Mo., lives in Indianapolis. Running back Missouri 1956-59. No pro playing experience. College coach: Missouri 1962-71, Notre Dame 1975-77. Pro coach: Green Bay Packers 1972-74, Chicago Bears 1978-82, Birmingham Stallions (USFL) 1983-85, Phoenix Cardinals 1986-90 (scout, 1990), Tampa Bay Buccaneers 1991, joined Colts in 1994.

Jimmy Robinson, wide receivers; born January 3, 1953, Atlanta, Ga., lives in Indianapolis. Wide receiver Georgia Tech 1972-74. Pro wide receiver Atlanta Falcons 1975, New York Giants 1976-79, San Francisco 49ers 1980, Denver Broncos 1981. College coach: Georgia Tech 1986-89. Pro coach: Memphis Showboats (USFL) 1984-85, Atlanta Falcons 1990-93, joined Colts in 1994.

Pat Thomas, secondary; born September 1, 1954, Plano, Tex., lives in Indianapolis. Cornerback Texas A&M 1972-75. Pro cornerback Los Angeles Rams 1976-82. College coach: Houston 1987-89. Pro coach: Houston Gamblers (USFL) 1984-85, Houston Oilers 1990-92, joined Colts in 1994.

Tom Zupancic, strength and conditioning; born September 14, 1955, Indianapolis, lives in Indianapolis. Defensive tackle-offensive tackle Indiana Central 1975-78. No pro playing experience. Pro coach: Joined Colts in 1984.

1996 FIRST-YEAR ROSTER

Name	Pos.	Ht.	Wt.	Birthdate	College	Hometown	How Acq.
Anderson, Avery	WR	6-2	200	3/16/73	UCLA	Bellflower, Calif.	FA
Abdullah, Joe	RB	5-11	215	2/21/73	Pacific	Stockton, Calif.	FA
Atterberry, Derrick	CB-S	5-11	184	11/1/72	Vanderbilt	Dayton, Ohio	FA
Burroughs, Sammie	CB-S	6-0	215	6/21/73	Portland State	Pomona, Calif.	FA
Cawley, Mike	QB	6-1	200	8/28/72	James Madison	Edna, Tex.	D6b
Conlin, Keith	T	6-7	305	11/9/72	Penn State	Glenside, Pa.	D6a
Dittman, Seth	T	6-7	290	7/23/72	Stanford	Tigard, Ore.	FA
Groce, Clif	RB	5-11	242	7/30/72	Texas A&M	College Station, Tex.	FA
Hall, Steven	CB-S	6-0	205	4/15/73	Kentucky	Fort Wayne, Ind.	FA
Hardin, Steve (1)	G	6-7	334	12/30/71	Oregon	Shohomish, Wash.	FA
Harrison, Marvin	WR	6-0	181	8/25/72	Syracuse	Philadelphia, Pa.	D1
Horn, Jason	DE-DT	6-5	280	10/31/72	Michigan	Lafayette, Ind.	FA
Jones, Richard	CB-S	5-9	180	8/4/73	Texas A&M-Kingsville	Waco, Tex.	FA
Jones, Tyronne (1)	WR	5-8	161	9/12/71	Grambling State	New Orleans, La.	FA
Martin, Steve	DT	6-4	292	5/31/74	Missouri	St. Paul, Minn.	D5
Mathis, Dedric	CB-S	5-10	196	9/26/73	Houston	Cuero, Tex.	D2
McLemore, Cristin	WR	5-11	190	10/8/73	Oregon	San Diego, Calif.	FA
Mickens, Arnold	RB	5-11	220	10/12/72	Butler	Indianapolis, Ind.	FA
Milne, Brian	RB	6-3	254	1/7/73	Penn State	Waterford, Pa.	D4
Milwee, David	C-G-T	6-3	277	4/23/73	Tulsa	Houston, Tex.	FA
Powell, Dion	DE-DT	6-1	280	8/17/73	Western Michigan	East Chicago, Ill.	FA
Presley, Bruce	RB	5-10	215	2/26/73	Rutgers	Highland Park, N.J.	FA
Proctor, Michael	K	5-10	190	11/4/73	Alabama	Pleham, Ala.	FA
Robinson, Adrian	CB-S	6-2	216	7/25/74	Baylor	Mt. Lebanon, Pa.	D7
Shello, Kendel	DE-DT	6-3	295	11/24/73	Southern	New Iberia, La.	FA
Slutzker, Scott	TE	6-4	250	12/20/72	Iowa	Hasbrouck Heights, N.J.	D3
Summerday, John	C-G-T	6-2	290	6/28/73	Temple	California, Md.	FA
Wallace, Leon	TE	6-3	272	7/29/74	Notre Dame	Bedford, Tex.	FA
Wiegmann, Casey	C-G-T	6-3	290	7/20/73	Iowa	Parkersburg, Iowa	FA
Williams, Clay	C-G-T	6-6	295	5/6/73	Indiana	Toboso, Ohio	FA

The term NFL Rookie is defined as a player who is in his first season of professional football and has not been on the roster of another professional football team for any regular-season or postseason games. A Rookie is designated by an "R" on NFL rosters. Players who have been active in another professional football league or players who have NFL experience, including either preseason training camp or being on an Active List or Inactive List, or on Reserve/Injured or Reserve/Physically Unable to Perform for fewer than six regular-season games, are termed NFL First-Year Players. An NFL First-Year Player is designated by a "1" on NFL rosters. Thereafter, a player is credited with an additional year of experience for each season in which he accumulates six games on the Active List or Inactive List, or on Reserve/Injured or Reserve/Physically Unable to Perform.

NOTES

JACKSONVILLE JAGUARS

American Football Conference
Central Division
Team Colors: Teal, Black, and Gold
One Stadium Place
Jacksonville, Florida 32202
Telephone: (904) 633-6000

CLUB OFFICIALS

Chairman and Chief Executive Officer: Wayne Weaver
President and Chief Operating Officer: David Seldin
Chief Financial Officer: Bill Prescott
Head Coach: Tom Coughlin
Senior Vice President/Football Operations: Michael Huyghue
General Counsel: Paul Vance
Senior Vice President/Marketing: Dan Connell
Vice President/Ticket Operations: Judy Seldin
Executive Director of Communications: Dan Edwards
Director of Pro Personnel: Ron Hill
Director of College Scouting: Rick Reiprish
Director of Finance: Kim Dodson
Director of Special Events & Promotions: Ann Carroll
Director of Corporate Sponsorship: David Rowan
Director of Facilities: Jeff Cannon
Director of Computer Services: Bruce Swindell
Director of Player Programs: Paul Lankford
Director of Security: Skip Richardson
Head Athletic Trainer: Michael Ryan
Video Director: Mike Perkins
Equipment Manager: Bob Monica

Chair & Chief Executive Officer, Jaguars Foundation: Delores Barr Weaver
President, Jaguars Foundation: Dr. Gregory Gross
Stadium: Jacksonville Municipal Stadium
•**Capacity:** 73,000
One Stadium Place
Jacksonville, Florida 32202
Playing Surface: Grass
Training Camp: Jacksonville Municipal Stadium
One Stadium Place
Jacksonville, Florida 32202

RECORD HOLDERS

INDIVIDUAL RECORDS—CAREER

Category	Name	Performance
Rushing (Yds.)	James Stewart, 1995	525
Passing (Yds.)	Mark Brunell, 1995	2,168
Passing (TDs)	Mark Brunell, 1995	15
Receiving (No.)	Willie Jackson, 1995	53
Receiving (Yds.)	Willie Jackson, 1995	589
Interceptions	Harry Colon, 1995	3
Punting (Avg.)	Bryan Barker, 1995	43.8
Punt Return (Avg.)	Desmond Howard, 1995	10.3
Kickoff Return (Avg.)	Jimmy Smith, 1995	22.5
Field Goals	Mike Hollis, 1995	20
Touchdowns (Tot.)	Willie Jackson, 1995	5
	Jimmy Smith, 1995	5
Points	Mike Hollis, 1995	87

INDIVIDUAL RECORDS—SINGLE SEASON

Category	Name	Performance
Rushing (Yds.)	James Stewart, 1995	525
Passing (Yds.)	Mark Brunell, 1995	2,168
Passing (TDs)	Mark Brunell, 1995	15
Receiving (No.)	Willie Jackson, 1995	53
Receiving (Yds.)	Willie Jackson, 1995	589
Interceptions	Harry Colon, 1995	3
Punting (Avg.)	Bryan Barker, 1995	43.8
Punt Return (Avg.)	Desmond Howard, 1995	10.3
Kickoff Return (Avg.)	Jimmy Smith, 1995	22.5
Field Goals	Mike Hollis, 1995	20
Touchdowns (Tot.)	Willie Jackson, 1995	5
	Jimmy Smith, 1995	5
Points	Mike Hollis, 1995	87

INDIVIDUAL RECORDS—SINGLE GAME

Category	Name	Performance
Rushing (Yds.)	James Stewart, 10-15-95	97
Passing (Yds.)	Mark Brunell, 12-10-95	312
Passing (TDs)	Mark Brunell, 10-15-95, 12-10-95	3
Receiving (No.)	Pete Mitchell, 11-19-95	10
Receiving (Yds.)	Pete Mitchell, 11-19-95	161
Interceptions	Many times.	1
	Last time by Harry Colon, 12-24-95	
Field Goals	Mike Hollis, 11-12-95, 12-24-95	3
Touchdowns (Tot.)	Jimmy Smith, 12-3-95	3
Points	Jimmy Smith, 12-3-95	18

1996 SCHEDULE

PRESEASON

Aug. 2	**New York Giants**	8:00
Aug. 9	at St. Louis	7:00
Aug. 18	**San Francisco**	8:00
Aug. 23	at Denver	6:00

REGULAR SEASON

Sept. 1	**Pittsburgh**	1:00
Sept. 8	**Houston**	1:00
Sept. 15	at Oakland	1:00
Sept. 22	at New England	1:00
Sept. 29	**Carolina**	1:00
Oct. 6	at New Orleans	3:00
Oct. 13	**New York Jets**	1:00
Oct. 20	at St. Louis	3:00
Oct. 27	at Cincinnati	1:00
Nov. 3	Open Date	
Nov. 10	**Baltimore**	4:00
Nov. 17	at Pittsburgh	1:00
Nov. 24	at Baltimore	1:00
Dec. 1	**Cincinnati**	1:00
Dec. 8	at Houston	12:00
Dec. 15	**Seattle**	8:00
Dec. 22	**Atlanta**	1:00

JACKSONVILLE MUNICIPAL STADIUM

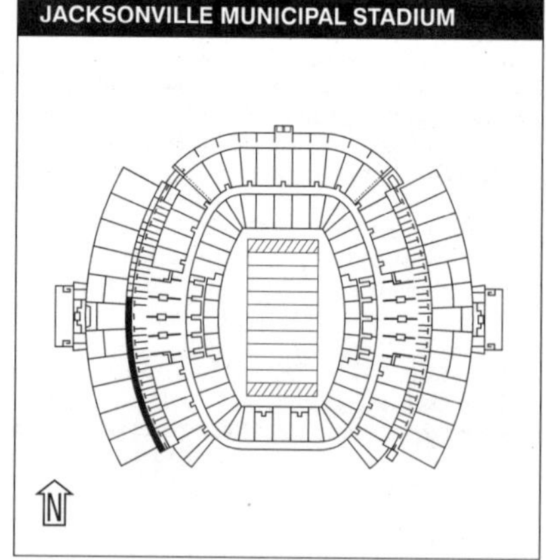

COACHING HISTORY

(4-12)

1995 Tom Coughlin 4-12

1995 TEAM RECORD

PRESEASON (2-3)

Date	Result		Opponents
7/29	L	14-20	vs. Carolina at Canton
8/4	W	24-21	at Miami
8/10	L	3-19	at Detroit
8/18	L	10-27	St. Louis
8/25	W	23-17	Denver

REGULAR SEASON (4-12)

Date	Result		Opponents	Att.
9/3	L	3-10	Houston	72,363
9/10	L	17-24	at Cincinnati	48,318
9/17	L	10-27	at N.Y. Jets	49,970
9/24	L	14-24	Green Bay	66,744
10/1	W	17-16	at Houston	36,346
10/8	W	20-16	Pittsburgh	72,042
10/15	L	27-30	Chicago	72,020
10/22	W	23-15	at Cleveland	64,405
10/29	L	7-24	at Pittsburgh	54,516
11/12	L	30-47	Seattle	71,290
11/19	L	16-17	at Tampa Bay	71,629
11/26	L	13-17	Cincinnati	68,249
12/3	L	23-31	at Denver	72,231
12/10	L	31-41	Indianapolis	66,099
12/17	L	0-44	at Detroit	70,204
12/24	W	24-21	Cleveland	66,007

SCORE BY PERIODS

Jaguars	64	67	28	116	—	275
Opponents	75	138	91	100	—	404

ATTENDANCE

Home 554,814 Away 467,619 Total 1,022,433
Single-game home record, 72,363 (9/3/95)
Single-season home record, 554,814 (1995)

1995 TEAM STATISTICS

	Jaguars	Opp.
Total First Downs	283	320
Rushing	100	121
Passing	154	177
Penalty	29	22
Third Down: Made/Att	74/205	107/222
Third Down Pct.	36.1	48.2
Fourth Down: Made/Att	6/15	10/16
Fourth Down Pct.	40.0	62.5
Total Net Yards	4495	5515
Avg. Per Game	280.9	344.7
Total Plays	962	1030
Avg. Per Play	4.7	5.4
Net Yards Rushing	1705	2003
Avg. Per Game	106.6	125.2
Total Rushes	410	504
Net Yards Passing	2790	3512
Avg. Per Game	174.4	219.5
Sacked/Yards Lost	57/354	17/72
Gross Yards	3144	3584
Att./Completions	495/275	509/304
Completion Pct.	55.6	59.7
Had Intercepted	15	13
Punts/Avg.	82/43.8	61/42.0
Net Punting Avg.	82/38.6	61/36.1
Penalties/Yards Lost	121/970	102/958
Fumbles/Ball Lost	23/13	22/11
Touchdowns	31	46
Rushing	9	17
Passing	19	28
Returns	3	1
Avg. Time of Possession	28:37	31:23

1995 INDIVIDUAL STATISTICS

PASSING	Att.	Comp.	Yds.	Pct.	TD	Int.	Tkld.	Rate
Brunell	346	201	2168	58.1	15	7	39/238	82.6
Beuerlein	142	71	952	50.0	4	7	17/103	60.5
R. Johnson	7	3	24	42.9	0	1	1/13	12.5
Jaguars	495	275	3144	55.6	19	15	57/354	75.0
Opponents	509	304	3584	59.7	28	13	17/72	88.9

SCORING	TD R	TD P	TD Rt	PAT	FG	Saf	PTS
Hollis	0	0	0	27/28	20/27	0	87
W. Jackson	0	5	0	0/0	0/0	0	32
Smith	0	3	2	0/0	0/0	0	30
Brunell	4	0	0	0/0	0/0	0	24
Givins	0	3	0	0/0	0/0	0	18
Stewart	2	1	0	0/0	0/0	0	18
Tillman	0	3	0	0/0	0/0	0	18
Dunbar	2	0	0	0/0	0/0	0	12
Mitchell	0	2	0	0/0	0/0	0	12
Christopherson	1	0	0	0/0	0/0	0	6
Howard	0	1	0	0/0	0/0	0	6
Jordan	0	1	0	0/0	0/0	0	6
Washington	0	0	1	0/0	0/0	0	6
Jaguars	9	19	3	27/28	20/27	0	275
Opponents	17	28	1	45/45	27/31	1	404

2-Point conversions: W. Jackson. Team: 1-3.

RUSHING	Att.	Yds.	Avg.	LG	TD
Stewart	137	525	3.8	22	2
Brunell	67	480	7.2	27t	4
Dunbar	110	361	3.3	26	2
Maston	41	186	4.5	21	0
Jordan	21	62	3.0	10	0
Beuerlein	5	32	6.4	13	0
Cobb	9	18	2.0	5	0
R. Johnson	3	17	5.7	7	0
Christopherson	16	16	1.0	10	1
Howard	1	8	8.0	8	0
Jaguars	410	1705	4.2	27t	9
Opponents	504	2003	4.0	86t	17

RECEIVING	No.	Yds.	Avg.	LG	TD
W. Jackson	53	589	11.1	45	5
Mitchell	41	527	12.9	35	2
Tillman	30	368	12.3	28	3
Givins	29	280	9.7	18	3
Howard	26	276	10.6	24	1
Smith	22	288	13.1	33	3
Stewart	21	190	9.0	38	1
Maston	18	131	7.3	19	0
Griffith	16	243	15.2	39	0
Marsh	7	127	18.1	34	0
Jordan	5	89	17.8	71t	1
Keith	3	20	6.7	9	0
Dunbar	2	11	5.5	8	0
Laro	1	6	6.0	6	0
Christopherson	1	-1	-1.0	-1	0
Jaguars	275	3144	11.4	71t	19
Opponents	304	3584	11.8	68t	28

INTERCEPTIONS	No.	Yds.	Avg.	LG	TD
Colon	3	46	15.3	41	0
J. Williams	2	19	9.5	16	0
Goganious	2	11	5.5	6	0
Washington	1	48	48.0	48t	1
Carrington	1	17	17.0	17	0
Smeenge	1	12	12.0	12	0
Grow	1	2	2.0	2	0
V. Clark	1	0	0.0	0	0
Dumas	1	0	0.0	0	0
Jaguars	13	155	11.9	48t	1
Opponents	15	178	11.9	45	0

PUNTING	No.	Yds.	Avg.	In 20	LG
Barker	82	3591	43.8	19	63
Jaguars	82	3591	43.8	19	63
Opponents	61	2564	42.0	30	58

PUNT RETURNS	No.	FC	Yds.	Avg.	LG	TD
Howard	24	8	246	10.3	40	0
Givins	2	0	-7	-3.5	-1	0
Tillman	2	0	6	3.0	9	0
W. Jackson	1	0	-2	-2.0	-2	0
Jaguars	29	8	243	8.4	40	0
Opponents	45	11	323	7.2	25	0

KICKOFF RETURNS	No.	Yds.	Avg.	LG	TD
Smith	24	540	22.5	89t	1
W. Jackson	19	404	21.3	47	0
Marsh	15	323	21.5	39	0
Howard	10	178	17.8	24	0
Dunbar	2	32	16.0	21	0
Jordan	2	41	20.5	21	0
Griffith	1	9	9.0	9	0
Maston	1	5	5.0	5	0
Jaguars	74	1532	20.7	89t	1
Opponents	54	1278	23.7	95t	1

SACKS	No.
Smeenge	4.0
Davey	3.0
Lageman	3.0
Logan	3.0
Mayfield	1.5
Pritchett	1.5
Frase	1.0
Jaguars	17.0
Opponents	57.0

1996 DRAFT CHOICES

Round	Name	Pos.	College
1	Kevin Hardy	LB	Illinois
2	Tony Brackens	DE	Texas
	Michael Cheever	C	Georgia Tech
3	Aaron Beasley	DB	West Virginia
4	Reggie Barlow	WR	Alabama State
5	Jimmy Herndon	T	Houston
6	John Fisher	DB	Missouri Western
	Chris Doering	WR	Florida
7	Clarence Jones	WR	Tennessee State
	Gregory Spann	WR	Jackson State

JACKSONVILLE JAGUARS

1996 VETERAN ROSTER

No.	Name	Pos.	Ht.	Wt.	Birthdate	NFL Exp.	College	Hometown	How Acq.	'95 Games/ Starts
4	Barker, Bryan	P	6-2	189	6/28/64	7	Santa Clara	Miramonte, Calif.	UFA(Phil)-'95	16/0
71	Boselli, Tony	T	6-7	323	4/17/72	2	Southern California	Boulder, Colo.	D1a-'95	13/12
66	Bouwens, Shawn	G	6-5	293	5/25/68	6	Nebraska Wesleyan	Lincoln, Neb.	UFA(Det)-'95	10/9
52	Boyer, Brant	LB	6-1	235	6/27/71	3	Arizona	Ogden, Utah	FA-'95	2/0
86	Brown, Derek	TE	6-6	262	3/31/70	5	Notre Dame	Fairfax, Va.	ED24(NYG)-'95	0*
8	Brunell, Mark	QB	6-0	217	9/17/70	4	Washington	Santa Maria, Calif.	T(GB)-'95	13/10
96	Carter, Bernard	LB	6-3	238	8/22/71	2	East Carolina	Tallahassee, Fla.	FA-'95	5/0
36	Christopherson, Ryan	RB	5-11	237	7/26/72	2	Wyoming	Glendale, Ariz.	D5-'95	11/0
59	Clark, Reggie	LB	6-3	245	10/17/67	3	North Carolina	Charlotte, N.C.	FA-'95	5/0
27	Clark, Vinnie	CB	6-0	204	1/22/69	6	Ohio State	Cincinnati, Ohio	UFA(NO)-'95	16/16
62	† Coleman, Ben	G-T	6-6	315	5/18/71	4	Wake Forest	South Hill, Va.	W(Ariz)-'95	10/5
92	Davey, Don	DT	6-4	275	4/8/68	6	Wisconsin	Manitowoc, Wis.	UFA(GB)-'95	16/16
45	Davis, Travis	S	6-0	200	1/10/73	2	Notre Dame	Wilmington, Calif.	FA-'95	9/5
73	DeMarco, Brian	G-T	6-7	321	4/9/72	2	Michigan State	Lorain, Ohio	D2a-'95	16/16
38	Dumas, Mike	S	5-11	198	3/18/69	6	Indiana	Lowell, Mich.	UFA(Buff)-'95	14/8
91	Frase, Paul	DE	6-5	276	5/5/65	8	Syracuse	Barrington, N.H.	ED9(NYJ)-'95	9/5
85	Griffith, Rich	TE	6-5	256	7/31/69	3	Arizona	Tucson, Ariz.	FA-'95	16/15
22	Grow, Monty	S	6-4	214	9/4/71	3	Florida	Inverness, Fla.	ED20(KC)-'95	4/1
28	Hall, Dana	S	6-2	206	7/8/69	5	Washington	Diamond Bar, Calif.	UFA(Balt)-'96	15/2*
97	Hall, Ray	DT	6-4	294	3/2/71	2	Washington State	Seattle, Wash.	FA-'95	12/0
49	Hallock, Ty	TE	6-3	249	4/30/71	3	Michigan State	Greenville, Mich.	T(Det)-'95	0*
1	Hollis, Mike	K	5-7	180	5/5/72	2	Idaho	Spokane, Wash.	FA-'95	16/0
37	Hudson, Chris	S	5-10	203	10/6/71	2	Colorado	Houston, Tex.	D3-'95	1/0
78	Huntington, Greg	G	6-4	293	9/22/70	3	Penn State	Cincinnati, Ohio	FA-'95	4/0
47	Jackson, Al	CB	5-10	191	9/7/71	3	Georgia	Pensacola, Fla.	ED7(Phil)-'95	0*
80	Jackson, Willie	WR	6-1	203	8/16/71	3	Florida	Gainesville, Fla.	ED11(Dall)-'95	14/10
11	Johnson, Rob	QB	6-3	222	3/18/73	2	Southern California	El Toro, Calif.	D4a-'95	1/0
21	Johnson, Tommy	CB	5-10	183	12/5/71	2	Alabama	Rome, Ga.	FA-'95	1/0
23	Jordan, Randy	RB	5-10	216	6/6/70	3	North Carolina	Manson, N.C.	FA-'94	12/3
64	Jurkovic, John	DT	6-2	295	8/18/67	5	Eastern Illinois	Calumet City, Ill.	UFA(GB)-'96	16/14*
19	Kimbrough, Tony	WR	6-2	192	9/17/70	3	Jackson State	Weir, Miss.	FA-'96	0*
56	Lageman, Jeff	DE	6-6	268	7/18/67	8	Virginia	Sterling, Va.	UFA(NYJ)-'95	11/11
93	Logan, Ernie	DE	6-3	283	5/18/68	5	East Carolina	Fayetteville, N.C.	FA-'94	15/1
89	Marsh, Curtis	WR	6-2	201	11/24/70	2	Utah	Simi Valley, Calif.	D7-'95	9/0
40	Massey, Robert	CB	5-11	195	2/27/67	8	North Carolina Central	Charlotte, N.C.	FA-'96	16/3*
35	Maston, Le'Shai	RB	6-0	229	10/7/70	4	Baylor	Dallas, Tex.	ED18(Hou)-'95	16/10
98	Mayfield, Corey	DT	6-3	302	2/25/70	3	Oklahoma	Tyler, Tex.	FA-'95	16/4
87	McCardell, Keenan	WR	6-1	175	1-6-70	5	Nevada-Las Vegas	Houston, Tex.	UFA(Balt)-'96	16/5*
55	McManus, Tom	LB	6-2	252	7/30/70	2	Boston College	Edgewater, Fla.	FA-'95	14/2
20	Means, Natrone	RB	5-10	245	4/26/72	4	North Carolina	Harrisburg, N.C.	W(SD)-'96	10/9*
83	Mitchell, Pete	TE	6-2	243	10/9/71	2	Boston College	Birmingham, Mich.	T(Mia)-'95	16/5
67	Novak, Jeff	G-T	6-5	296	7/27/67	3	Southwest Texas State	Arlington Heights, Ill.	ED3(Mia)-'95	16/13
5	Philcox, Todd	QB	6-4	225	9/25/66	6	Syracuse	Norwalk, Conn.	UFA(TB)-'96	0*
94	Pritchett, Kelvin	DT	6-3	290	10/24/69	6	Mississippi	Atlanta, Ga.	UFA(Det)-'95	16/16
50	Robinson, Eddie	LB	6-1	245	4/13/70	5	Alabama State	New Orleans, La.	UFA(Hou)-'96	16/16*
58	Schwartz, Bryan	LB	6-4	250	12/5/71	2	Augustana (South Dakota)	St. Lawrence, S.D.	D2b-'95	14/9
72	Searcy, Leon	T	6-3	304	12/21/69	5	Miami	Washington, D.C.	UFA(Pitt)-'96	16/16*
99	Smeenge, Joel	LB	6-6	260	4/1/68	7	Western Michigan	Grand Rapids, Mich.	UFA(NO)-'95	15/15
82	Smith, Jimmy	WR	6-1	207	2/9/69	4	Jackson State	Jackson, Miss.	FA-'95	16/4
53	Stephens, Santo	LB	6-4	244	6/16/69	4	Temple	Capital Heights, Md.	ED13(Cin)-'95	13/0
33	Stewart, James	RB	6-1	221	12/27/71	2	Tennessee	Morristown, Tenn.	D1b-'95	14/8
30	Studstill, Darren	S	6-1	186	8/9/70	2	West Virginia	Palm Beach Gardens, Fla.	FA-'95	8/0
77	Thomas, Cornell	DE	6-3	270	11/11/72	2	West Georgia	Livingston, N.J.	FA-'96	0*
41	† Thomas, Dave	CB	6-3	213	8/25/68	4	Tennessee	Miami, Fla.	ED1(Dall)-'95	16/2
95	Thompson, Mike	DT	6-3	279	12/22/72	2	Wisconsin	Portage, Wis.	D4b-'95	2/0
84	Warren, Terrence	WR	6-1	205	8/2/69	3	Hampton	Suffolk, Va.	FA-'95	0*
25	Washington, Mickey	CB	5-10	191	7/8/68	6	Texas A&M	Beaumont, Tex.	UFA(Buff)-'95	16/16
79	Widell, Dave	C	6-7	308	5/14/65	9	Boston College	Hartford, Conn.	UFA(Den)-'95	16/16
51	Williams, Mark	LB	6-3	243	5/17/71	3	Ohio State	Upper Marlboro, Md.	D6(GB)-'95	11/10

* Brown and A. Jackson missed '95 season because of injury; D. Hall played 15 games with Cleveland in '95; Hallock last active with Detroit in '94; Jurkovic played 16 games with Green Bay; Kimbrough last active with Denver in '94; Massey played 16 games with Detroit; McCardell played 16 games with Cleveland; Means played 10 games with San Diego; Philcox inactive for 16 games with Tampa Bay; Robinson played 16 games with Houston; Searcy played 16 games with Pittsburgh; C. Thomas last active with San Diego in '94; Warren active for 1 game with San Francisco but did not play.

† Restricted free agent; subject to developments.

Players lost through free agency (3): QB Steve Beuerlein (Car; 7 games in '95), S Darren Carrington (Oak; 6), G Eugene Chung (SF; 11).

Also played with Jaguars in '95—S Deral Boykin (5 games), RB Reggie Cobb (1), S Harry Colon (16), G Frank Cornish (3), RB Vaughn Dunbar (14), WR Ernest Givins (9), LB Keith Goganious (16), CB Rogerick Green (14), WR Desmond Howard (13), TE Craig Keith (11), TE Gordon Laro (2), G Tom Myslinski (9), LB Ashley Sheppard (2), WR Cedric Tillman (13), T Bruce Wilkerson (10), LB James Williams (12).

COACHING STAFF

Head Coach,
Tom Coughlin

Pro Career: Became the first head coach of the NFL's newest franchise on February 21, 1994, following a successful three seasons as head coach at Boston College. A veteran of 25 years in coaching, including 17 at the collegiate level and seven as an NFL assistant, Coughlin previously coached wide receivers for the Philadelphia Eagles (1984-85), Green Bay Packers (1986-87), and New York Giants (1988-1990). He was a member of the Giants' Super Bowl XXV champion coaching staff prior to being named head coach at Boston College in 1991. In three seasons at Boston College, he turned a struggling program into a top-20 team, posting a 21-13-1 record. His final season at Boston College was highlighted by eight consecutive wins, including a 41-39 victory over top-ranked Notre Dame, and a 9-3 finish. Despite an 0-2 start to the season, Boston College ranked thirteenth in the *Associated Press* poll and twelfth in the *USA Today/CNN* coaches poll at the end of the 1993 season. Coughlin's previous 14 seasons as a college coach were at Rochester Institute of Technology 1970-73 (head coach), Syracuse 1974-80, and Boston College 1981-83. No pro playing experience. Career record: 4-12.

Background: Played wingback for Syracuse from 1965-67 under legendary coach Ben Schwartzwalder, along with teammates Larry Czonka and Floyd Little. Received Syracuse 1967 Orange Key Award as outstanding scholar athlete, and graduated in 1968 with bachelor's degree in education. Received master's degree in education from Syracuse in 1969.

Personal: Born August 31, 1947, Waterloo, N.Y. Was standout scholastic star for Waterloo Central High School. Tom and his wife, Judy, reside in Jacksonville. They have two daughters, Keli and Katie, and two sons, Tim and Brian.

ASSISTANT COACHES

Joe Baker, assistant special teams; born June 29, 1969, Glen Ridge, N.J., lives in Jacksonville. Wide receiver Princeton 1987-90. No pro playing experience. College coach: Samford 1993. Pro coach: Joined Jaguars in 1995.

Pete Carmichael, wide receivers; born March 4, 1941, North Plainfield, N.J., lives in Jacksonville. Quarterback Dayton 1961, Montclair State College 1962-63. No pro playing experience. College coach: Virginia Military 1965-66, New Hampshire 1967, Boston College 1968-72, 1981-93, Trenton State College 1973 (head coach), Columbia 1974-77, Merchant Marine Academy 1977-80 (head coach). Pro coach: Joined Jaguars in 1995.

Randy Edsall, secondary; Born August 27, 1958, Glen Rock, Pa., lives in Jacksonville. Quarterback Syracuse 1976-79. No pro playing experience. College coach: Syracuse 1983-90, Boston College 1991-93. Pro coach: Joined Jaguars in 1995.

Kevin Gilbride, offensive coordinator; born August 27, 1951, New Haven, Conn., lives in Jacksonville. Quarterback-tight end Southern Connecticut State 1970-73. No pro playing experience. College coach: Idaho State 1974-75, Tufts 1976-77, American International 1978-79, Southern Connecticut State 1980-84 (head coach), East Carolina 1987-88. Pro coach: Ottawa Rough Riders (CFL) 1985-86, Houston Oilers 1989-94, joined Jaguars in 1995.

Jerald Ingram, running backs; born December 24, 1960, Beaver, Pa., lives in Jacksonville. Fullback Michigan 1979-84. No pro playing experience. College coach: Ball State 1985-90, Boston College 1991-93. Pro coach: Joined Jaguars in 1995.

Dick Jauron, defensive coordinator; born October 7, 1950, Peoria, Ill., lives in Jacksonville. Defensive back Yale 1970-72. Pro defensive back Detroit Lions 1973-77, Cincinnati Bengals 1978-80. Pro coach: Buffalo Bills 1985, Green Bay Packers 1986-94, joined Jaguars in 1995.

Mike Maser, offensive line; born March 2, 1947, Clayton, N.Y., lives in Jacksonville. Guard Buffalo 1967-70. No pro playing experience. College coach: Marshall 1973, Bluefield State College 1974-78, Maine 1979-80, Boston College 1981-93. Pro coach: Joined Jaguars in 1995.

Nick Nicolau, tight ends; born May 5, 1933, New York, N.Y., lives in Jacksonville. Running back Southern Connecticut State 1957-59. No pro playing experience. College coach: Southern Connecticut State 1960, Springfield 1961, Bridgeport 1962-69 (head coach 1965-69), Massachusetts 1970, Connecticut 1971-72, Kentucky 1973-75, Kent State 1976. Pro coach: Hamilton Tiger-Cats (CFL) 1977, Montreal Alouettes (CFL) 1978-79, New Orleans Saints 1980, Denver Broncos 1981-87, Los Angeles Raiders 1988, Buffalo Bills 1989-91, Indianapolis Colts 1992-94, joined Jaguars in 1995.

Jerry Palmieri, strength and conditioning; born October 30, 1958, Englewood, N.J., lives in Jacksonville. No college or pro playing experience. College coach: Oklahoma State 1984-87, Kansas State 1988-92, Boston College 1993-94. Pro coach: Joined Jaguars in 1995.

Larry Pasquale, special teams coordinator; born April 21, 1941, Brooklyn, N.Y., lives in Jacksonville. Quarterback Bridgeport 1961-63. No pro playing experience. College coach: Slippery Rock State 1967, Boston University 1968, Navy 1969-70, Massachusetts 1971-75, Idaho State 1976. Pro coach: Montreal Alouettes (CFL) 1977-78, Detroit Lions 1979, New York Jets 1980-89, San Diego Chargers 1990-91, Philadelphia Eagles 1992-94, joined Jaguars in 1995.

John Pease, defensive line; born October 14, 1943, Pittsburgh, Pa., lives in Jacksonville. Wingback Utah 1963-64. No pro playing experience. College coach: Fullerton, Calif., J.C. 1970-73, Long Beach State 1974-76, Utah 1977, Washington 1978-83. Pro coach: Philadelphia/Baltimore Stars (USFL) 1983-85, New Orleans Saints 1986-94, joined Jaguars in 1995.

Lucious Selmon, outside linebackers; born March 15, 1951, Muskogee, Okla., lives in Jacksonville. Defensive tackle Oklahoma 1970-73. Pro defensive tackle Memphis Southmen (WFL) 1974-75. College coach: Oklahoma 1976-94. Pro Coach: Joined Jaguars in 1995.

Steve Szabo, inside linebackers; born September 11, 1943, Chicago, Ill., lives in Jacksonville. Halfback/defensive back Navy 1961-64. No pro playing experience. College coach: Johns Hopkins 1969, Toledo 1970, Iowa 1971-73, Syracuse 1974-76, Iowa State 1977-78, Ohio State 1979-81, Western Michigan 1982-84, Edinboro 1985-87 (head coach), Northern Iowa 1988, Colorado State 1989-90, Boston College 1991-93. Pro coach: Joined Jaguars in 1995.

1996 FIRST-YEAR ROSTER

Name	Pos.	Ht.	Wt.	Birthdate	College	Hometown	How Acq.
Barlow, Reggie	WR	5-11	187	1/22/73	Alabama State	Montgomery, Ala.	D4
Beasley, Aaron	CB-S	5-11	194	7/7/73	West Virginia	Pottstown, Pa.	D3
Brackens, Tony	DE	6-4	260	12/26/74	Texas	Fairfield, Tex.	D2a
Cheever, Michael	C	6-3	296	6/24/73	Georgia Tech	Newnan, Ga.	D2b
Dickerson, Bryan (1)	RB	6-1	245	3/22/71	Eastern Kentucky	Louisville, Ky.	FA
Doering, Chris	WR	6-3	191	5/19/73	Florida	Gainesville, Fla.	D6b
Dukes, Jason	T	6-6	310	12/22/72	Georgia Tech	Augusta, Ga.	FA
Fayak, Craig (1)	K	6-1	188	7/22/72	Penn State	Belle Vernon, Pa.	FA
Fisher, John	S	5-10	197	7/28/73	Missouri Western	Oakland, Calif.	D6a
Gayle, Rashid	CB	5-8	175	4/16/74	Boise State	Roseville, Calif.	FA
Geter, Thomas	S	6-2	200	12/2/74	Northern Arizona	Compton, Calif.	FA
Graham, Roger (1)	RB	5-10	212	11/8/72	New Haven	Spring Valley, N.Y.	FA
Hardy, Kevin	LB	6-4	245	7/24/73	Illinois	Evansville, Ind.	D1
Herndon, Jimmy	T	6-8	304	8/30/73	Houston	Baytown, Tex.	D5
Jones, Clarence	WR	6-0	184	3/12/73	Tennessee State	Vero Beach, Fla.	D7a
Mangram, Omari	T	6-6	322	7/31/73	Indiana State	Robbins, Ill.	FA
McCoy, Ryan (1)	LB	6-2	247	3/13/72	Houston	Waterloo, Iowa	FA
Miller, Bronzell (1)	DE	6-4	245	10/12/71	Utah	Federal Way, Wash.	FA
Parker, Chris	RB	5-11	202	12/31/72	Marshall	Lynchburg, Va.	FA
Price, Marcus (1)	T	6-5	316	3/3/72	Louisiana State	Port Arthur, Tex.	D6-'95
Smith, Gene	LB	6-3	230	11/29/73	Fresno State	Hanford, Calif.	FA
Spann, Gregory	WR	6-0	215	4/16/73	Jackson State	Macon, Miss.	D7b
Taneyhill, Steve	QB	6-3	215	7/21/73	South Carolina	Altoona, Pa.	FA
Thornton, Cedric	LB	6-1	246	11/11/72	Alabama State	Jackson, Miss.	FA
Tylski, Rich (1)	G-C	6-4	290	2/27/71	Utah State	San Diego, Calif.	FA
Walsh, Pat	T	6-9	350	1/29/74	Connecticut	East Islip, N.Y.	FA
Wiltshire, Kelly	CB	5-11	193	6/28/72	James Madison	St. Laurent, Canada	FA

The term NFL Rookie is defined as a player who is in his first season of professional football and has not been on the roster of another professional football team for any regular-season or postseason games. A Rookie is designated by an "R" on NFL rosters. Players who have been active in another professional football league or players who have NFL experience, including either preseason training camp or being on an Active List or Inactive List, or on Reserve/Injured or Reserve/Physically Unable to Perform for fewer than six regular-season games, are termed NFL First-Year Players. An NFL First-Year Player is designated by a "1" on NFL rosters. Thereafter, a player is credited with an additional year of experience for each season in which he accumulates six games on the Active List or Inactive List, or on Reserve/Injured or Reserve/Physically Unable to Perform.

NOTES

KANSAS CITY CHIEFS

American Football Conference
Western Division
Team Colors: Red, Gold, and White
One Arrowhead Drive
Kansas City, Missouri 64129
Telephone: (816) 924-9300

CLUB OFFICIALS

Founder: Lamar Hunt
Chairman of the Board: Jack Steadman
President/General Manager and Chief Executive Officer: Carl Peterson
Executive Vice President, Assistant General Manager: Dennis Thum
Vice President of Player Personnel: Lynn Stiles
Vice President of Administration: Dennis Watley
Secretary: Jim Seigfreid
Director of Finance/Treasurer: Dale Young
Director of Public Relations: Bob Moore
Director of Sales and Marketing: Wallace Bennett
Director of Operations: Jeff Klein
Director of Development: Ken Blume
Assistant Director of Public Relations: Jim Carr
Director of Corporate Sponsorships: Anita McDonald
Community Relations Manager: Brenda Sniezek
Director of Ticket Operations: Doug Hopkins
Equipment Manager: Mike Davidson
Asst. Equipment Managers: Allen Wright, Darin Kerns
Trainer: Dave Kendall
Assistant Trainer: Bud Epps
Director of Video Operations: John Wuehrmann
Assistant Video Directors: Mike Kirk, Mike Portz
Stadium: Arrowhead Stadium • **Capacity:** 79,101
One Arrowhead Drive
Kansas City, Missouri 64129
Playing Surface: Grass
Training Camp: University of Wisconsin-River Falls
River Falls, Wisconsin 54022

1996 SCHEDULE

PRESEASON

Aug. 5	vs. Dallas at Monterrey, Mexico	7:00
Aug. 10	**New Orleans**	7:00
Aug. 17	**St. Louis**	7:00
Aug. 22	at Chicago	7:00

REGULAR SEASON

Sept. 1	at Houston	12:00
Sept. 8	**Oakland**	12:00
Sept. 15	at Seattle	1:00
Sept. 22	**Denver**	12:00
Sept. 29	at San Diego	1:00
Oct. 7	**Pittsburgh** (Mon.)	8:00
Oct. 13	Open Date	
Oct. 17	**Seattle** (Thurs.)	7:00
Oct. 27	at Denver	2:00
Nov. 3	at Minnesota	12:00
Nov. 10	**Green Bay**	12:00
Nov. 17	**Chicago**	12:00
Nov. 24	**San Diego**	12:00
Nov. 28	at Detroit (Thurs.)	12:30
Dec. 9	at Oakland (Mon.)	6:00
Dec. 15	**Indianapolis**	12:00
Dec. 22	at Buffalo	1:00

RECORD HOLDERS

INDIVIDUAL RECORDS—CAREER

Category	Name	Performance
Rushing (Yds.)	Christian Okoye, 1987-1992	4,897
Passing (Yds.)	Len Dawson, 1962-1975	28,507
Passing (TDs)	Len Dawson, 1962-1975	237
Receiving (No.)	Henry Marshall, 1976-1987	416
Receiving (Yds.)	Otis Taylor, 1965-1975	7,306
Interceptions	Emmitt Thomas, 1966-1978	58
Punting (Avg.)	Jerrel Wilson, 1963-1977	43.5
Punt Return (Avg.)	J.T. Smith, 1979-1984	10.6
Kickoff Return (Avg.)	Noland Smith, 1967-69	26.8
Field Goals	Nick Lowery, 1980-1993	329
Touchdowns (Tot.)	Otis Taylor, 1965-1975	60
Points	Nick Lowery, 1980-1993	1,466

INDIVIDUAL RECORDS—SINGLE SEASON

Category	Name	Performance
Rushing (Yds.)	Christian Okoye, 1989	1,480
Passing (Yds.)	Bill Kenney, 1983	4,348
Passing (TDs)	Len Dawson, 1964	30
Receiving (No.)	Carlos Carson, 1983	80
Receiving (Yds.)	Carlos Carson, 1983	1,351
Interceptions	Emmitt Thomas, 1974	12
Punting (Avg.)	Jerrel Wilson, 1965	46.0
Punt Return (Avg.)	Abner Haynes, 1960	15.4
Kickoff Return (Avg.)	Dave Grayson, 1962	29.7
Field Goals	Nick Lowery, 1990	34
Touchdowns (Tot.)	Abner Haynes, 1962	19
Points	Nick Lowery, 1990	139

INDIVIDUAL RECORDS—SINGLE GAME

Category	Name	Performance
Rushing (Yds.)	Barry Word, 10-14-90	200
Passing (Yds.)	Len Dawson, 11-1-64	435
Passing (TDs)	Len Dawson, 11-1-64	6
Receiving (No.)	Ed Podolak, 10-7-73	12
Receiving (Yds.)	Stephone Paige, 12-22-85	309
Interceptions	Bobby Ply, 12-16-62	*4
	Bobby Hunt, 12-4-64	*4
	Deron Cherry, 9-29-85	*4
Field Goals	Many times	5
	Last time by Nick Lowery, 9-20-93	
Touchdowns (Tot.)	Abner Haynes, 11-26-61	5
Points	Abner Haynes, 11-26-61	30

*NFL Record

COACHING HISTORY

DALLAS TEXANS 1960-62
(285-253-12)

1960-74	Hank Stram	129-79-10
1975-77	Paul Wiggin*	11-24-0
1977	Tom Bettis	1-6-0
1978-82	Marv Levy	31-42-0
1983-86	John Mackovic	30-35-0
1987-88	Frank Gansz	8-22-1
1989-95	Marty Schottenheimer	75-45-1

*Released after seven games in 1977

ARROWHEAD STADIUM

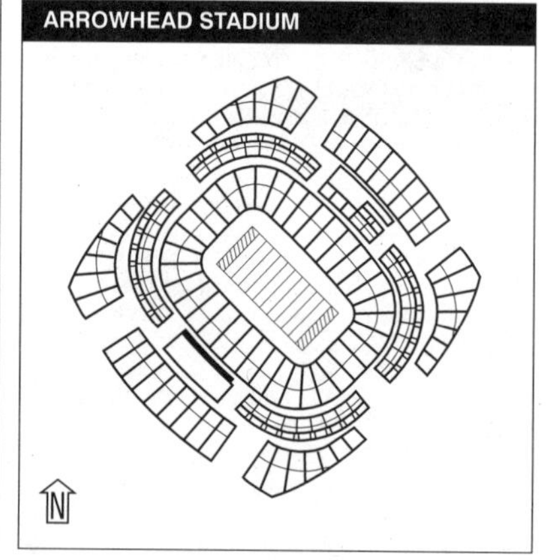

1995 TEAM RECORD

PRESEASON (3-1)

Date	Result		Opponents
8/5	W	37-21	Washington
8/11	L	17-22	at Arizona
8/19	W	36-10	Buffalo
8/26	W	17-13	at Minnesota

REGULAR SEASON (13-3)

Date	Result		Opponents	Att.
9/3	W	34-10	at Seattle	47,564
9/10	W	20-17	N.Y. Giants (OT)	77,962
9/17	W	23-17	Oakland (OT)	78,696
9/24	L	17-35	at Cleveland	74,280
10/1	W	24-3	at Arizona	50,211
10/9	W	29-23	San Diego (OT)	79,288
10/15	W	31-26	New England	77,992
10/22	W	21-7	at Denver	71,044
11/5	W	24-3	Washington	77,821
11/12	W	22-7	at San Diego	59,285
11/19	W	20-13	Houston	77,576
11/23	L	12-24	at Dallas	64,901
12/3	W	29-23	at Oakland	53,930
12/11	L	6-13	at Miami	70,321
12/17	W	20-17	Denver	75,061
12/24	W	26-3	Seattle	75,784

POSTSEASON (0-1)

1/7	L	7-10	Indianapolis	77,594

(OT) Overtime

SCORE BY PERIODS

Chiefs	70	120	56	97	15	—	358
Opponents	68	59	29	85	0	—	241

ATTENDANCE

Home 620,180 Away 491,536 Total 1,111,716
Single-game home record, 82,094 (11/5/72)
Single-season home record, 620,180 (1995)

1995 TEAM STATISTICS

	Chiefs	Opp.
Total First Downs	295	289
Rushing	113	83
Passing	164	178
Penalty	18	28
Third Down: Made/Att	82/231	78/229
Third Down Pct.	35.5	34.1
Fourth Down: Made/Att	15/22	7/18
Fourth Down Pct.	68.2	38.9
Total Net Yards	5242	4549
Avg. Per Game	327.6	284.3
Total Plays	1059	1047
Avg. Per Play	4.9	4.3
Net Yards Rushing	2222	1327
Avg. Per Game	138.9	82.9
Total Rushes	507	404
Net Yards Passing	3020	3222
Avg. Per Game	188.8	201.4
Sacked/Yards Lost	21/158	47/347
Gross Yards	3178	3569
Att./Completions	531/300	596/329
Completion Pct.	56.5	55.2
Had Intercepted	10	16
Punts/Avg.	91/43.8	102/41.8
Net Punting Avg.	91/36.5	102/35.1
Penalties/Yards Lost	116/851	108/828
Fumbles/Ball Lost	17/11	35/17
Touchdowns	42	28
Rushing	14	7
Passing	21	16
Returns	7	5
Avg. Time of Possession	31:08	28:52

1995 INDIVIDUAL STATISTICS

PASSING	Att.	Comp.	Yds.	Pct.	TD	Int.	Tkld.	Rate
Bono	520	293	3121	56.3	21	10	21/158	79.5
Gannon	11	7	57	63.6	0	0	0/0	76.7
Chiefs	531	300	3178	56.5	21	10	21/158	79.4
Opponents	596	329	3569	55.2	16	16	47/347	70.8

SCORING	TD R	TD P	TD Rt	PAT	FG	Saf	PTS
Elliott	0	0	0	34/37	24/30	0	106
Allen	5	0	0	0/0	0/0	0	30
Bono	5	0	0	0/0	0/0	0	30
W. Davis	0	5	0	0/0	0/0	0	30
Dawson	0	5	0	0/0	0/0	0	30
Vanover	0	2	3	0/0	0/0	0	30
Slaughter	0	4	0	0/0	0/0	0	24
Anders	2	1	0	0/0	0/0	0	18
Booker	0	0	1	0/0	0/0	0	6
Cash	0	1	0	0/0	0/0	0	6
Collins	0	0	1	0/0	0/0	0	6
Gannon	1	0	0	0/0	0/0	0	6
Hasty	0	0	1	0/0	0/0	0	6
Hill	1	0	0	0/0	0/0	0	6
Hughes	0	1	0	0/0	0/0	0	6
Valerio	0	1	0	0/0	0/0	0	6
Walker	0	1	0	0/0	0/0	0	6
Washington	0	0	1	0/0	0/0	0	6
Chiefs	14	21	7	34/37	24/30	0	358
Opponents	7	16	5	25/25	16/19	0	241

2-Point conversions: 0. Team: 0-3.

RUSHING	Att.	Yds.	Avg.	LG	TD
Allen	207	890	4.3	38	5
Hill	155	667	4.3	27	1
Anders	58	398	6.9	44	2
Bono	28	113	4.0	76t	5
Thompson	28	73	2.6	10	0
Vanover	6	31	5.2	13	0
Gannon	8	25	3.1	12t	1
Richardson	8	18	2.3	5	0
Bennett	7	11	1.6	11	0
Hughes	1	5	5.0	5	0
Dawson	1	-9	-9.0	-9	0
Chiefs	507	2222	4.4	76t	14
Opponents	404	1327	3.3	27	7

RECEIVING	No.	Yds.	Avg.	LG	TD
Anders	55	349	6.3	28	1
Cash	42	419	10.0	38t	1
Dawson	40	513	12.8	45t	5
Slaughter	34	514	15.1	38	4
W. Davis	33	527	16.0	60t	5
Allen	27	210	7.8	20	0
Walker	25	205	8.2	18t	1
Hughes	14	103	7.4	16	1
Vanover	11	231	21.0	57	2
Thompson	9	37	4.1	7	0
Hill	7	45	6.4	13	0
Bennett	1	12	12.0	12	0
Penn	1	12	12.0	12	0
Valerio	1	1	1.0	1t	1
Chiefs	300	3178	10.6	60t	21
Opponents	329	3569	10.8	49	16

INTERCEPTIONS	No.	Yds.	Avg.	LG	TD
D. Carter	4	45	11.3	29	0
Washington	3	100	33.3	74t	1
Hasty	3	89	29.7	64t	1
White	2	48	24.0	30	0
A. Davis	1	11	11.0	11	0
Collins	1	8	8.0	8	0
Phillips	1	2	2.0	2	0
Saleaumua	1	0	0.0	0	0
Chiefs	16	303	18.9	74t	2
Opponents	10	123	12.3	42t	3

PUNTING	No.	Yds.	Avg.	In 20	LG
Aguiar	91	3990	43.8	29	65
Chiefs	91	3990	43.8	29	65
Opponents	102	4266	41.8	27	66

PUNT RETURNS	No.	FC	Yds.	Avg.	LG	TD
Vanover	51	4	540	10.6	86t	1
Penn	4	2	12	3.0	5	0
Hughes	3	1	9	3.0	8	0
Chiefs	58	7	561	9.7	86t	1
Opponents	42	18	433	10.3	38	0

KICKOFF RETURNS	No.	Yds.	Avg.	LG	TD
Vanover	43	1095	25.5	99t	2
Thompson	6	152	25.3	40	0
Penn	2	26	13.0	25	0
Valerio	2	15	7.5	13	0
Hughes	1	18	18.0	18	0
McDaniels	1	0	0.0	0	0
Chiefs	55	1306	23.7	99t	2
Opponents	71	1448	20.4	70	0

SACKS	No.
N. Smith	12.0
Thomas	8.0
Saleaumua	7.0
Mickell	5.5
Phillips	4.5
A. Davis	2.0
McDaniels	2.0
Booker	1.5
Traylor	1.5
Bayless	1.0
Simien	1.0
White	1.0
Chiefs	47.0
Opponents	21.0

1996 DRAFT CHOICES

Round	Name	Pos.	College
1	Jerome Woods	DB	Memphis
2	Reggie Tongue	DB	Oregon State
3	John Browning	DE	West Virginia
4	Donnie Edwards	LB	UCLA
5	Joe Horn	WR	Itawamba J.C.
6	Dietrich Jells	WR	Pittsburgh
7	Ben Lynch	C	California
	Jeff Smith	C	Tennessee
	Darrell Williams	DB	Tennessee State

KANSAS CITY CHIEFS

1996 VETERAN ROSTER

No.	Name	Pos.	Ht.	Wt.	Birthdate	NFL Exp.	College	Hometown	How Acq.	'95 Games/ Starts
5	Aguiar, Louie	P	6-2	219	6/30/66	6	Utah State	Livermore, Calif.	FA-'94	16/0
32	Allen, Marcus	RB	6-2	210	3/26/60	15	Southern California	San Diego, Calif.	UFA(Raid)-'93	16/15
76	Alt, John	T	6-8	307	5/30/62	13	Iowa	Columbia Heights, Minn.	D1b-'84	16/16
38	Anders, Kimble	RB	5-11	230	9/10/66	6	Houston	Galveston, Tex.	FA-'91	16/13
44	Anderson, Darren	CB	5-10	187	1/11/69	4	Toledo	Cincinnati, Ohio	T(TB)-'94	16/1
88	† Bailey, Victor	WR	6-2	203	7/3/70	4	Missouri	Ft. Worth, Tex.	T(Phil)-'95	0*
21	# Bayless, Martin	S	6-2	219	10/11/62	13	Bowling Green	Dayton, Ohio	FA-'95	11/1
30	Bennett, Donnell	RB	6-0	241	9/14/72	3	Miami	Ft. Lauderdale, Fla.	D2-'94	3/1
13	Bono, Steve	QB	6-4	215	5/11/62	12	UCLA	Norristown, Pa.	T(SF)-'94	16/16
99	Booker, Vaughn	DE	6-5	293	2/24/68	3	Cincinnati	Cincinnati, Ohio	FA-'94	16/10
34	Carter, Dale	CB	6-1	188	11/28/69	5	Tennessee	Covington, Ga.	D1-'92	16/14
89	Cash, Keith	TE	6-4	242	8/7/69	5	Texas	San Antonio, Tex.	PB(Pitt)-'92	14/14
45	Cobb, Trevor	RB	5-9	220	11/20/70	3	Rice	Pasadena, Tex.	FA-'96	0*
25	Collins, Mark	S-CB	5-10	196	1/16/64	11	Cal State-Fullerton	San Bernardino, Calif.	UFA(NYG)-'94	16/15
69	Criswell, Jeff	T	6-7	294	3/7/64	9	Graceland, Iowa	Searsboro, Iowa	UFA(NYJ)-'95	15/4
50	Davis, Anthony	LB	6-0	231	3/7/69	3	Utah	Pasco, Wash.	FA-'94	16/3
80	Dawson, Lake	WR	6-1	207	1/2/72	3	Notre Dame	Federal Way, Wash.	D3a-'94	16/9
55	Dumas, Troy	LB	6-3	233	9/30/72	2	Nebraska	Cheyenne, Wyo.	D3b-'95	0*
12	Gannon, Rich	QB	6-3	205	1/20/66	9	Delaware	Philadelphia, Pa.	FA-'95	2/0
61	Grunhard, Tim	C	6-2	299	5/17/68	7	Notre Dame	Chicago, Ill.	D2-'90	16/16
40	Hasty, James	CB	6-0	207	5/23/65	9	Washington State	Seattle, Wash.	UFA(NYJ)-'95	16/16
27	Hill, Greg	RB	5-11	207	2/23/72	3	Texas A&M	Dallas, Tex.	D1-'94	16/1
83	† Hughes, Danan	WR	6-2	211	12/11/70	4	Iowa	Bayonne, N.J.	D7-'93	16/0
57	Jamison, George	LB	6-1	235	9/30/62	11	Cincinnati	Bridgeton, N.J.	UFA(Det)-'94	14/13
74	Jenkins, Trezelle	T	6-7	322	3/13/73	2	Michigan	Chicago, Ill.	D1-'95	1/0
47	Johnson, Reggie	TE	6-2	256	1/27/68	5	Florida State	Pensacola, Fla.	UFA(Phil)-'96	9/2*
10	LaChapelle, Sean	WR	6-3	205	7/29/70	2	UCLA	Sacramento, Calif.	FA-'95	0*
51	Manusky, Greg	LB	6-1	243	8/12/66	9	Colgate	Dallas, Pa.	FA-'94	16/1
77	McDaniels, Pellom	DE	6-3	292	2/21/68	4	Oregon State	San Jose, Calif.	FA-'93	16/2
9	Nittmo, Bjorn	K	5-11	188	7/26/66	2	Appalachian State	Lomma, Sweden	FA-'96	0*
81	Penn, Chris	WR	6-0	198	4/20/71	3	Tulsa	Lenapah, Okla.	D3b-'94	2/0
75	Phillips, Joe	DT	6-5	310	7/15/63	10	Southern Methodist	Vancouver, Wash.	FA-'92	16/16
67	Proby, Bryan	DE	6-5	285	11/30/71	2	Arizona State	Los Angeles, Calif.	D6a-'95	4/0
7	Richardson, Bucky	QB	6-1	228	2/7/69	4	Texas A&M	Baton Rouge, La.	FA-'96	15/1
49	Richardson, Tony	RB	6-1	232	12/17/71	2	Auburn	Daleville, Ala.	FA-'95	14/1
52	Rogers, Tracy	LB	6-2	244	8/13/67	7	Fresno State	Taft, Calif.	FA-'90	16/0
97	Saleaumua, Dan	DT	6-0	315	11/25/64	10	Arizona State	San Diego, Calif.	PB(Det)-'89	16/16
68	Shields, Will	G	6-3	308	9/15/71	4	Nebraska	Lawton, Okla.	D3-'93	16/16
66	Siglar, Ricky	T	6-7	316	6/14/66	5	San Jose State	Albuquerque, N.M.	FA-'93	16/12
54	Simien, Tracy	LB	6-1	255	5/21/67	6	Texas Christian	Bay City, Tex.	FA-'91	16/15
92	Sims, Tom	DT	6-2	208	4/18/67	6	Pittsburgh	Detroit, Mich.	FA-'96	0*
22	Smith, J.J.	RB	6-0	203	10/14/72	2	Kansas State	Kansas City, Mo.	FA-'95	0*
90	Smith, Neil	DE	6-4	273	4/10/66	9	Nebraska	New Orleans, La.	D1-'88	16/14
41	Swann, Charles	S	6-1	188	10/29/70	2	Indiana State	South Bend, Ind.	FA-'96	0*
79	Szott, Dave	G	6-4	290	12/12/67	7	Penn State	Clifton, N.J.	D7-'90	16/16
24	Terry, Doug	S	5-11	204	12/12/69	5	Kansas	Liberal, Kan.	FA-'92	16/0
58	Thomas, Derrick	LB	6-3	247	1/1/67	8	Alabama	Miami, Fla.	D1-'89	15/15
94	Traylor, Keith	DT	6-2	295	9/3/69	5	Central Oklahoma	Malvern, Ark.	FA-'95	16/0
73	Valerio, Joe	T-C	6-5	295	2/11/69	6	Pennsylvania	Ridley, Pa.	D2-'91	16/0
87	Vanover, Tamarick	WR-KR	5-11	213	2/25/74	2	Florida State	Tallahassee, Fla.	D3a-'95	15/0
72	Villa, Danny	G	6-5	308	9/21/64	10	Arizona State	Nogales, Ariz.	UFA(Phx)-'93	16/0
82	Walker, Derrick	TE	6-0	249	6/23/67	7	Michigan	Chicago Heights, Ill.	FA-'94	16/3
48	Washington, Brian	S	6-1	210	9/10/65	8	Nebraska	Richmond, Va.	FA-'95	15/15
35	White, William	S	5-10	205	2/19/66	9	Ohio State	Lima, Ohio	T(Det)-'94	16/5
62	Wilson, Troy	DE	6-4	250	11/22/70	3	Pittsburg State	Topeka, Kan.	FA-'96	3/0*

* Bailey inactive for 16 games in '95; Cobb last active with Chicago in '94; Dumas missed '95 season because of injury; Johnson played 9 games with Philadelphia; LaChapelle last active with L.A. Rams in '93; Nittmo last active with Houston in '92; Sims last active with Indianapolis in '93; J. Smith inactive for 16 games; Swann last active with Denver in '94; Wilson played 3 games with Denver.

Unrestricted free agent; subject to developments.

† Restricted free agent; subject to developments.

Players lost through free agency (2): Willie Davis (Hou; 16 games in '95), Darren Mickell (NO; 12).

Also played with Chiefs in '95—CB Perry Carter (2 games), K Lin Elliot (16), WR Webster Slaughter (16), LB Frank Stams (1), RB Leroy Thompson (16), S Tim Watson (4).

COACHING STAFF

Head Coach,
Marty Schottenheimer

Pro Career: In seven seasons as head coach of the Kansas City Chiefs, Schottenheimer has established the highest winning percentage in franchise history (.647). In directing the Chiefs to seven of their nine winning seasons since 1974, Schottenheimer has led the club to six consecutive postseason berths, the longest current streak of any NFL club. He also has claimed division titles two of the past three seasons. Schottenheimer, who has been in the playoffs 10 of his 11 full seasons as an NFL head coach, is the only coach in league history to direct two clubs (Chiefs and Cleveland Browns) to five-year playoff streaks. He also is the only NFL coach who has taken his club to the playoffs 10 times since 1985, accumulating more regular-season victories (116) than any other NFL coach during that span. In 1995, he became just the eighth coach in NFL history to direct his club into the playoffs six straight seasons. Schottenheimer's career winning percentage (.637) is second among active NFL coaches with at least five full seasons of experience. As head coach of the Cleveland Browns from midseason in 1984 through 1988, he led the club to four playoff berths, three AFC Central Division titles, two AFC Championship Game appearances, and captured AFC coach of the years honors (1986). He first joined the Browns in 1980 as defensive coordinator after serving as linebackers coach of the Detroit Lions in 1978-79. His first NFL coaching job came with the New York Giants, where he was linebackers coach and later defensive coordinator from 1975-77. He also served as an assistant coach with the Portland Storm (WFL) in 1974. A seventh-round draft choice of the Buffalo Bills in 1965, he played linebacker with the Bills until 1968 and finished his pro playing career with the Boston Patriots in 1969-70. Career record: 121-76-1.

Background: Schottenheimer was an All-America linebacker at the University of Pittsburgh 1962-64. Following his retirement from pro football, he worked as a real estate developer in both Miami and Denver from 1971-74.

Personal: Born September 23, 1943, Canonsburg, Pa. Marty and his wife, Patricia, live in Overland Park, Kan., and have one daughter, Kristen, and one son, Brian.

ASSISTANT COACHES

Russ Ball, assistant strength and conditioning; born August 28, 1959, Moberly, Mo., lives in Kansas City. Center Central Missouri State 1977-80. No pro playing experience. College coach: Missouri 1981-88. Pro coach: Joined Chiefs in 1989.

John Bunting, linebackers; born July 15, 1950, Portland, Me., lives in Stanley, Kan. Linebacker North Carolina 1968-71. Pro linebacker Philadelphia Eagles 1972-82, Philadelphia Stars (USFL) 1983-84. College coach: Brown 1986, Rowan College 1987-92 (head coach 1988-92). Pro coach: Baltimore Stars (USFL) 1985, joined Chiefs in 1993.

Gunther Cunningham, defensive coordinator; born December 6, 1944, Munich, Germany, lives in Leawood, Kan. Linebacker-placekicker Oregon 1966-68. No pro playing experience. College coach: Oregon 1969-71, Arkansas 1972, Stanford 1973-76, California 1977-80. Pro coach: Hamilton Tiger-Cats (CFL) 1981, Baltimore/Indianapolis Colts 1982-84, San Diego Chargers 1985-90, Los Angeles Raiders 1991-94, joined Chiefs in 1995.

Jim Erkenbeck, tight ends-offensive assistant; born September 10, 1933, Los Angeles, Calif., lives in Kansas City. Linebacker-end San Diego State 1949-51. No pro playing experience. College coach: San Diego State 1961-63, Grossmont (Calif.) J.C. 1964-67 (head coach), Utah State 1968, Washington State 1969-71, California 1972-76. Pro coach: Winnepeg Blue Bombers (CFL) 1977, Montreal Alouettes (CFL) 1978-81, Calgary Stampeders (CFL) 1982, Philadelphia/Baltimore Stars (USFL) 1983-85, New Orleans Saints 1986, Dallas Cowboys 1987-88, Kansas City Chiefs 1989-91, Los Angeles Rams 1992-94, rejoined Chiefs in 1995.

Paul Hackett, offensive coordinator; born July 5, 1947, Burlington, Vt., lives in Overland Park, Kan. Quarterback Cal-Davis 1965-68. No pro playing experience. College coach: Cal-Davis 1970-71, California 1972-75, Southern California 1976-80, Pittsburgh 1989-92 (head coach 1990-92). Pro coach: Cleveland Browns 1981-82, San Francisco 49ers 1983-85, Dallas Cowboys 1986-88, joined Chiefs in 1993.

Carl Hairston, defensive line; born December 15, 1952, Martinsville, Va., lives in Independence, Mo. Defensive end-linebacker Maryland-Eastern Shore 1972-75. Pro defensive end Philadelphia Eagles 1976-83, Cleveland Browns 1984-89, Phoenix Cardinals 1990. Pro scout: Phoenix Cardinals 1991-93, Kansas City Chiefs 1994. Pro coach: Joined Chiefs in 1995.

Woodrow Lowe, defensive assistant-assistant special teams; born June 9, 1954, Columbus, Ga., lives in Lenexa, Kan. Linebacker Alabama 1973-75. Pro linebacker San Diego Chargers 1976-86. Pro coach: Joined Chiefs in 1995.

Mike McCarthy, quarterbacks; born November 10, 1963, Pittsburgh, Pa., lives in Lenexa, Kan. Tight end Baker University 1985-86. No pro playing experience. College coach: Fort Hays State 1987-88, Pittsburgh 1989-92. Pro coach: Joined Chiefs in 1993.

Jimmy Raye, running backs; born March 26, 1946, Fayetteville, N.C., lives in Kansas City. Quarterback Michigan State 1965-67. Pro defensive back Philadelphia Eagles 1969. College coach: Michigan State 1971-75, Wyoming 1976. Pro coach: San Francisco 49ers 1977, Detroit Lions 1978-79, Atlanta Falcons 1980-82, 1987-89, Los Angeles Rams 1983-84, 1991, Tampa Bay Buccaneers 1985-86, New England Patriots 1990, joined Chiefs in 1992.

Dave Redding, strength and conditioning; born June 14, 1952, North Platte, Neb., lives in Lee's Summit, Mo. Defensive end Nebraska 1972-75. No pro playing experience. College coach: Nebraska 1976, Washington State 1977, Missouri 1978-81. Pro coach: Cleveland Browns 1982-88, joined Chiefs in 1989.

Al Saunders, assistant head coach-receivers; born February 1, 1947, London, England, lives in Overland Park, Kan. Defensive back San Jose State 1966-68. No pro playing experience. College coach: Southern California 1970-71, Missouri 1972, Utah State 1973-75, California 1976-81, Tennessee 1982. Pro coach: San Diego Chargers 1983-88 (head coach 1986-88), joined Chiefs in 1989.

Kurt Schottenheimer, defensive backs; born October 1, 1949, McDonald, Pa., lives in Leawood, Kan. Defensive back Miami 1969-70. No pro playing experience. College coach: William Patterson 1974, Michigan State 1978-82, Tulane 1983, Louisiana State 1984-85, Notre Dame 1986. Pro coach: Cleveland Browns 1987-88, joined Chiefs in 1989.

Art Shell, offensive line; born November 26, 1946, Charleston, S.C., lives in Overland Park, Kan. Offensive-defensive tackle Maryland State 1965-67. Pro offensive tackle Oakland/Los Angeles Raiders 1968-82. Pro coach: Los Angeles Raiders 1983-94 (head coach 1989-94), joined Chiefs in 1995.

Mike Stock, special teams; born September 29, 1939, Barberton, Ohio, lives in Overland Park, Kan. Fullback Northwestern 1957-60. Pro running back Saskatchewan Roughriders (CFL) 1961. College coach: Northwestern 1961, Buffalo 1966-67, Navy 1968, Notre Dame 1969-74, Wisconsin 1975-78, Eastern Michigan 1979-83 (head coach), Notre Dame 1984-86, Ohio State 1992-94. Pro coach: Cincinnati Bengals 1987-91, joined Chiefs in 1995.

Darvin Wallis, special assistant-quality control; born February 14, 1949, Ft. Branch, Ind., lives in Overland Park, Kan. Defensive end Arizona 1970-71. No pro playing experience. College coach: Adams State 1976-77, Tulane 1978-79, Mississippi 1980-81. Pro coach: Cleveland Browns 1982-88, joined Chiefs in 1989.

1996 FIRST-YEAR ROSTER

Name	Pos.	Ht.	Wt.	Birthdate	College	Hometown	How Acq.
Anderson, John (1)	S	5-10	190	11/30/71	Oklahoma	Sugar Land, Tex.	FA
Anderson, Roman (1)	K	5-10	190	4/19/69	Houston	Houston, Tex.	FA
Barndt, Tom (1)	C-G	6-3	285	3/14/72	Pittsburgh	Mentor, Ohio	D8b-'95
Browning, John	DE	6-4	264	9/30/73	West Virginia	Miami, Fla.	D3
Carter, Perry (1)	CB	5-11	206	8/15/71	Southern Mississippi	McComb, Miss.	FA
Davis, Don (1)	LB	6-1	239	12/17/72	Kansas	Olathe, Kan.	FA
Davis, Robert (1)	DT	6-2	270	12/10/68	Shippensburg	Greenbelt, Md.	FA
Dingle, Nate (1)	LB	6-2	242	9/22/72	Cincinnati	Berwick, Maine	FA
Dritlein, Michael	WR	6-1	185	1/14/74	Washburn	Olathe, Kan.	FA
Edwards, Donnie	LB	6-2	225	4/6/73	UCLA	Chula Vista, Calif.	D4
Florine, Ron (1)	T	6-6	305	9/27/71	Central Missouri State	Marceline, Mo.	FA
Horn, Joe	WR	6-1	195	1/16/72	Itawamba J.C.	Fayetteville, N.C.	D5
Jells, Dietrich	WR	5-10	186	4/11/72	Pittsburgh	Erie, Pa.	D6
Lynch, Ben	C	6-3	291	11/18/72	California	Sebastopol, Calif.	D7a
Matthews, Steve (1)	QB	6-3	209	10/13/70	Memphis	Tullahoma, Tenn.	D7a-'94
McEntyre, Kenny (1)	CB	5-10	180	12/2/70	Kansas State	Plano, Tex.	FA
Rutherford, Reynard	RB	6-0	202	5/15/73	California	Benica, Calif.	FA
Simmons, Jason (1)	DE	6-5	266	12/20/70	Ohio State	Akron, Ohio	FA
Smith, Eric	WR	5-11	183	1/5/71	Louisiana State	Vero Beach, Fla.	FA
Smith, Jeff	C	6-3	334	5/25/73	Tennessee	Decatur, Tenn.	D7b
Szeredy, Scott (1)	K	6-1	210	5/27/71	Texas	La Habra, Calif.	FA
Tagoai, Mu (1)	G-DT	6-3	350	4/10/72	Arizona	Honolulu, Hawaii	FA
Tate, Willy (1)	TE	6-3	243	9/7/72	Oregon	Elk Grove, Calif.	FA
Tongue, Reggie	CB-S	6-0	201	4/11/73	Oregon State	Fairbanks, Alaska	D2
Willard, Jerrott (1)	LB	6-1	233	7/11/72	California	Newport Beach, Calif.	D5b-'95
Williams, Darrell	CB-S	5-11	196	6/29/73	Tennessee State	Augusta, Ga.	D7c
Williams, Robert (1)	TE	6-3	240	2/1/72	Valdosta State	Washington, Ga.	FA
Woods, Jerome	CB-S	6-2	198	3/17/73	Memphis	Memphis, Tenn.	D1
Young, Alan (1)	LB	6-4	255	1/20/71	Vanderbilt	Woodstock, N.Y.	FA

The term NFL Rookie is defined as a player who is in his first season of professional football and has not been on the roster of another professional football team for any regular-season or postseason games. A Rookie is designated by an "R" on NFL rosters. Players who have been active in another professional football league or players who have NFL experience, including either preseason training camp or being on an Active List or Inactive List, or on Reserve/Injured or Reserve/Physically Unable to Perform for fewer than six regular-season games, are termed NFL First-Year Players. An NFL First-Year Player is designated by a "1" on NFL rosters. Thereafter, a player is credited with an additional year of experience for each season in which he accumulates six games on the Active List or Inactive List, or on Reserve/Injured or Reserve/Physically Unable to Perform.

MIAMI DOLPHINS

American Football Conference
Eastern Division
Team Colors: Aqua, Coral, and White
7500 S.W. 30th Street
Davie, Florida 33314
(954) 452-7000

CLUB OFFICIALS

Owner/Chairman of the Board: H. Wayne Huizenga
Vice-Chairman of the Board: Don Shula
President/Chief Operating Officer: Eddie J. Jones
General Manager/Head Coach: Jimmy Johnson
Vice President-Administration: Bryan Wiedmeier
Vice President-Finance: Jill R. Strafaci
Director of Football Operations: Bob Ackles
Director of Pro Personnel: Tom Heckert
Director of College Scouting: Tom Braatz
Senior Director-Media Relations: Harvey Greene
Media Relations Coordinator: Mike Hanson
Director of Publications: Scott Stone
Senior Director-Marketing: David Evans
Senior Director-Information Systems: Burt Gilner
Community Relations Director: Fudge Browne
Ticket Director: Bill Galante
Head Athletic Trainer: Kevin O'Neill
Equipment Manager: Tony Egues
Stadium: Joe Robbie Stadium • **Capacity:** 74,916
2269 N.W. 199th Street
Miami, Florida 33056
Playing Surface: Grass (PAT)
Training Camp: Nova University
7500 S.W. 30th Street
Davie, Florida 33314

1996 SCHEDULE

PRESEASON

Aug. 3	**Tampa Bay**	7:00
Aug. 11	at Chicago	12:00
Aug. 19	**Minnesota**	8:00
Aug. 23	at Tampa Bay	7:30

REGULAR SEASON

Sept. 1	**New England**	4:00
Sept. 8	at Arizona	5:00
Sept. 15	**New York Jets**	1:00
Sept. 23	at Indianapolis (Mon.)	8:00
Sept. 29	Open Date	
Oct. 6	**Seattle**	1:00
Oct. 13	at Buffalo	1:00
Oct. 20	at Philadelphia	1:00
Oct. 27	**Dallas**	4:00
Nov. 3	at New England	4:00
Nov. 10	**Indianapolis**	1:00
Nov. 17	at Houston	3:00
Nov. 25	**Pittsburgh** (Mon.)	9:00
Dec. 1	at Oakland	1:00
Dec. 8	**New York Giants**	1:00
Dec. 16	**Buffalo** (Mon.)	9:00
Dec. 22	at New York Jets	1:00

RECORD HOLDERS

INDIVIDUAL RECORDS—CAREER

Category	Name	Performance
Rushing (Yds.)	Larry Csonka, 1968-1974, 1979	6,737
Passing (Yds.)	Dan Marino, 1983-1995	*48,841
Passing (TDs)	Dan Marino, 1983-1995	*352
Receiving (No.)	Mark Clayton, 1983-1992	550
Receiving (Yds.)	Mark Duper, 1982-1992	8,869
Interceptions	Jake Scott, 1970-75	35
Punting (Avg.)	Reggie Roby, 1983-1992	43.3
Punt Return (Avg.)	Freddie Solomon, 1975-77	11.4
Kickoff Return (Avg.)	Mercury Morris, 1969-1975	26.5
Field Goals	Pete Stoyanovich, 1989-1995	176
Touchdowns (Tot.)	Mark Clayton, 1983-1992	82
Points	Garo Yepremian, 1970-78	830

INDIVIDUAL RECORDS—SINGLE SEASON

Category	Name	Performance
Rushing (Yds.)	Delvin Williams, 1978	1,258
Passing (Yds.)	Dan Marino, 1984	*5,084
Passing (TDs)	Dan Marino, 1984	*48
Receiving (No.)	Mark Clayton, 1988	86
Receiving (Yds.)	Mark Clayton, 1984	1,389
Interceptions	Dick Westmoreland, 1967	10
Punting (Avg.)	Reggie Roby, 1991	45.7
Punt Return (Avg.)	Freddie Solomon, 1975	12.3
Kickoff Return (Avg.)	Duriel Harris, 1976	32.9
Field Goals	Pete Stoyanovich, 1991	31
Touchdowns (Tot.)	Mark Clayton, 1984	18
Points	Pete Stoyanovich, 1992	124

INDIVIDUAL RECORDS—SINGLE GAME

Category	Name	Performance
Rushing (Yds.)	Mercury Morris, 9-30-73	197
Passing (Yds.)	Dan Marino, 10-23-88	521
Passing (TDs)	Bob Griese, 11-24-77	6
	Dan Marino, 9-21-86	6
Receiving (No.)	Jim Jensen, 11-6-88	12
Receiving (Yds.)	Mark Duper, 11-10-85	217
Interceptions	Dick Anderson, 12-3-73	*4
Field Goals	Garo Yepremian, 9-26-71	5
Touchdowns (Tot.)	Paul Warfield, 12-15-73	4
Points	Paul Warfield, 12-15-73	24

*NFL Record

COACHING HISTORY

(289-186-4)

1966-69	George Wilson	15-39-2
1970-95	Don Shula	274-147-2

JOE ROBBIE STADIUM

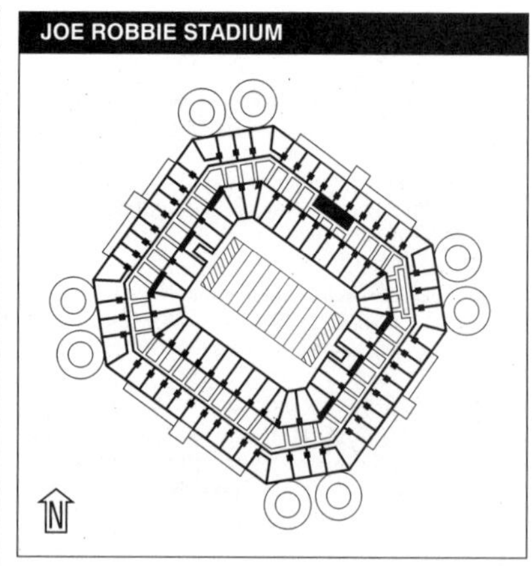

1995 TEAM RECORD

PRESEASON (1-3)

Date	Result		Opponents
8/4	L	21-24	Jacksonville
8/11	L	0-37	at Atlanta
8/19	W	27-13	Washington
8/25	L	17-24	vs.Tampa Bay at Orlando, Fla.

REGULAR SEASON (9-7)

Date	Result		Opponents	Att.
9/3	W	52-14	N.Y. Jets	71,317
9/10	W	20-3	at New England	60,239
9/18	W	23-10	Pittsburgh	72,874
10/1	W	26-23	at Cincinnati	52,671
10/8	L	24-27	Indianapolis (OT)	68,471
10/15	L	30-33	at New Orleans	55,628
10/22	L	16-17	at N.Y. Jets	67,228
10/29	W	23-6	Buffalo	71,060
11/5	W	24-14	at San Diego	61,996
11/12	L	17-34	New England	70,399
11/20	L	20-44	San Francisco	73,080
11/26	L	28-36	at Indianapolis	60,414
12/3	W	21-20	Atlanta	63,395
12/11	W	13-6	Kansas City	70,321
12/17	L	20-23	at Buffalo	79,531
12/24	W	41-22	at St. Louis	63,876

POSTSEASON (0-1)

12/30	L	22-37	at Buffalo	73,103

(OT) Overtime

SCORE BY PERIODS

Dolphins	62	137	93	106	0	—	398
Opponents	44	105	95	85	3	—	332

ATTENDANCE

Home 560,917 Away 501,583 Total 1,062,500

Single-game home record, 73,080 (11/20/95)

Single-season home record, 560,917 (1995)

1995 TEAM STATISTICS

	Dolphins	Opp.
Total First Downs	345	309
Rushing	98	93
Passing	225	192
Penalty	22	24
Third Down: Made/Att	96/209	68/199
Third Down Pct.	45.9	34.2
Fourth Down: Made/Att	10/13	15/32
Fourth Down Pct.	76.9	46.9
Total Net Yards	5716	5244
Avg. Per Game	357.3	327.8
Total Plays	1034	1000
Avg. Per Play	5.5	5.2
Net Yards Rushing	1506	1675
Avg. Per Game	94.1	104.7
Total Rushes	413	415
Net Yards Passing	4210	3569
Avg. Per Game	263.1	223.1
Sacked/Yards Lost	29/188	29/187
Gross Yards	4398	3756
Att./Completions	592/384	556/327
Completion Pct.	64.9	58.8
Had Intercepted	20	14
Punts/Avg.	57/42.7	59/41.0
Net Punting Avg.	57/36.3	59/34.5
Penalties/Yards Lost	110/907	82/739
Fumbles/Ball Lost	24/12	30/16
Touchdowns	46	38
Rushing	16	7
Passing	28	30
Returns	2	1
Avg. Time of Possession	31:22	28:38

1995 INDIVIDUAL STATISTICS

PASSING	Att.	Comp.	Yds.	Pct.	TD	Int.	Tkld.	Rate
Marino	482	309	3668	64.1	24	15	22/153	90.8
Kosar	108	74	699	68.5	3	5	6/28	76.1
Kirby	1	1	31	100.0	1	0	0/0	158.3
McGwire	1	0	0	0.0	0	0	1/7	39.6
Dolphins	592	384	4398	64.9	28	20	29/188	88.8
Opponents	556	327	3756	58.8	30	14	29/187	86.7

SCORING	TD R	TD P	TD Rt	PAT	FG	Saf	PTS
Stoyanovich	0	0	0	37/37	27/34	0	118
Parmalee	9	1	0	0/0	0/0	0	60
McDuffie	0	8	0	0/0	0/0	0	50
Fryar	0	8	0	0/0	0/0	0	48
Kirby	4	3	0	0/0	0/0	0	42
Green	0	3	0	0/0	0/0	0	20
Byars	1	2	0	0/0	0/0	0	18
Clark	0	2	0	0/0	0/0	0	12
Spikes	1	1	0	0/0	0/0	0	12
Johnson	0	0	1	0/0	0/0	0	6
Kosar	1	0	0	0/0	0/0	0	6
Vincent	0	0	1	0/0	0/0	0	6
Dolphins	16	28	2	37/37	27/34	0	398
Opponents	7	30	1	31/33	23/31	1	332

2-Point conversions: Green, McDuffie. Team: 2-9.

RUSHING	Att.	Yds.	Avg.	LG	TD
Parmalee	236	878	3.7	40	9
Kirby	108	414	3.8	38	4
Spikes	32	126	3.9	17t	1
Byars	15	44	2.9	15	1
Kosar	7	19	2.7	14	1
Marino	11	14	1.3	12	0
McDuffie	3	6	2.0	11	0
Wilson	1	5	5.0	5	0
Dolphins	413	1506	3.6	40	16
Opponents	415	1675	4.0	44	7

RECEIVING	No.	Yds.	Avg.	LG	TD
Kirby	66	618	9.4	46	3
Fryar	62	910	14.7	67t	8
McDuffie	62	819	13.2	48	8
Byars	51	362	7.1	26	2
Green	43	499	11.6	31t	3
Parmalee	39	345	8.8	35	1
Clark	37	525	14.2	42t	2
R. Hill	12	260	21.7	58	0
Spikes	5	18	3.6	13	1
R. Williams	3	28	9.3	13	0
M. Williams	2	17	8.5	15	0
Wilson	1	3	3.0	3	0
Marino	1	-6	-6.0	-6	0
Dolphins	384	4398	11.5	67t	28
Opponents	327	3756	11.5	50t	30

INTERCEPTIONS	No.	Yds.	Avg.	LG	TD
Vincent	5	95	19.0	69t	1
Brown	2	20	10.0	20	0
Jackson	1	23	23.0	23	0
Cox	1	12	12.0	12	0
Beavers	1	8	8.0	8	0
Singleton	1	3	3.0	3	0
Atkins	1	0	0.0	0	0
Buckley	1	0	0.0	0	0
Stewart	1	0	0.0	0	0
Dolphins	14	161	11.5	69t	1
Opponents	20	210	10.5	45	0

PUNTING	No.	Yds.	Avg.	In 20	LG
Kidd	57	2433	42.7	15	56
Dolphins	57	2433	42.7	15	56
Opponents	59	2420	41.0	11	61

PUNT RETURNS	No.	FC	Yds.	Avg.	LG	TD
McDuffie	24	12	163	6.8	24	0
Dolphins	24	12	163	6.8	24	0
Opponents	35	10	265	7.6	27	0

KICKOFF RETURNS	No.	Yds.	Avg.	LG	TD
McDuffie	23	564	24.5	47	0
Spikes	18	378	21.0	55	0
R. Hill	12	287	23.9	33	0
R. Williams	2	20	10.0	12	0
Buckley	1	16	16.0	16	0
Dar Dar	1	22	22.0	22	0
S. Hill	1	38	38.0	38	0
Milner	1	13	13.0	13	0
Wainright	0	0	—	—	0
Dolphins	59	1338	22.7	55	0
Opponents	85	1782	21.0	62	0

SACKS	No.
Cox	7.5
Coleman	6.5
Cross	6.0
T. Armstrong	4.5
Bowens	2.0
Emtman	1.0
Singleton	1.0
Foxx	0.5
Dolphins	29.0
Opponents	29.0

1996 DRAFT CHOICES

Round	Name	Pos.	College
1	Daryl Gardener	DT	Baylor
3	Dorian Brew	DB	Kansas
	Karim Abdul-Jabbar	RB	UCLA
4	Kirk Pointer	DB	Austin Peay
	Stanley Pritchett	RB	South Carolina
	La Curtis Jones	LB	Baylor
5	Jerris McPhail	RB	East Carolina
	Shane Burton	DT	Tennessee
	Zach Thomas	LB	Texas Tech
6	Shawn Wooden	DB	Notre Dame
7	Jeff Buckey	T	Stanford
	Brice Hunter	WR	Georgia

MIAMI DOLPHINS

1996 VETERAN ROSTER

No.	Name	Pos.	Ht.	Wt.	Birthdate	NFL Exp.	College	Hometown	How Acq.	'95 Games/ Starts
71	Albright, Ethan	T	6-5	283	5/1/71	2	North Carolina	Greensboro, N.C.	FA-'95	10/0
58	Armstrong, Antonio	LB	6-1	234	10/15/73	2	Texas A&M	Houston, Tex.	FA-'95	4/0
93	Armstrong, Trace	DE	6-4	265	10/5/65	8	Florida	Birmingham, Ala.	T(Chi)-'95	15/0
28	Atkins, Gene	S	5-11	201	11/22/64	10	Florida A&M	Tallahassee, Fla.	UFA(NO)-'94	16/11
23	Bailey, Robert	CB	5-9	174	9/3/68	6	Miami	Miami, Fla.	UFA(Dall)-'96	13/0*
80	Barnett, Fred	WR	6-0	199	6/17/66	7	Arkansas State	Rosedale, Miss.	UFA(Phil)-'96	14/14*
53	Beavers, Aubrey	LB	6-3	231	8/30/71	3	Oklahoma	Houston, Tex.	D2a-'94	16/1
95	Bowens, Tim	DT	6-4	310	2/7/73	3	Mississippi	Okolona, Miss.	D1-'94	16/16
37	Brown, J.B.	CB	6-0	191	1/5/67	8	Maryland	Washington, D.C.	D12-'89	13/12
76	t- Brown, James	T	6-6	329	11/30/70	4	Virginia State	Philadelphia, Pa.	T(NYJ)-'96	15/12*
7	Buck, Mike	QB	6-3	227	4/22/67	5	Maine	Sayville, N.Y.	UFA(Ariz)-'96	3/0*
27	Buckley, Terrell	CB	5-9	178	7/7/71	5	Florida State	Pascagoula, Miss.	T(GB)-'95	16/4
41	Byars, Keith	RB	6-1	255	10/14/63	11	Ohio State	Dayton, Ohio	UFA(Phil)-'93	16/16
91	Cross, Jeff	DE	6-4	280	3/25/66	9	Missouri	Blythe, Calif.	D9-'88	16/16
44	Dotson, Dewayne	RB	6-1	256	6/10/71	2	Mississippi	Hendersonville, Tenn.	FA-'95	15/0
94	Emtman, Steve	DE	6-4	284	4/16/70	5	Washington	Spokane, Wash.	FA-'95	16/1
62	Gray, Chris	G-T	6-4	292	6/19/70	4	Auburn	Birmingham, Ala.	D5-'93	10/10
86	Green, Eric	TE	6-5	280	6/22/67	7	Liberty	Savannah, Ga.	UFA(Pitt)-'95	14/14
98	Hand, Norman	DT	6-3	329	9/4/72	2	Mississippi	Waterboro, S.C.	D5-'95	0*
74	Hawthorne, Ed	DT	6-1	305	7/30/70	2	Minnesota	St. Louis, Mo.	FA-'95	1/0
73	Heller, Ron	T	6-6	290	8/25/62	13	Penn State	Farmingdale, N.Y.	UFA(Phil)-'93	7/7
89	Hill, Randal	WR	5-11	180	9/21/69	6	Miami	Miami, Fla.	UFA(Ariz)-'95	12/0
31	Hill, Sean	CB	5-10	179	8/14/71	3	Montana State	Ft. Carson, Colo.	D7-'94	16/0
50	Hollier, Dwight	LB	6-2	250	4/21/69	5	North Carolina	Hampton, Va.	D4-'92	16/14
38	Jackson, Calvin	CB	5-9	185	10/28/72	2	Auburn	Ft. Lauderdale, Fla.	FA-'95	9/1
24	Johnson, Pat	S	6-1	204	6/10/72	2	Purdue	Mineral Point, Mo.	FA-'95	14/0
97	Jones, Aaron	DE	6-5	267	12/18/66	9	Eastern Kentucky	Apopka, Fla.	UFA(NE)-'96	9/0*
88	Jordan, Charles	WR	5-11	183	10/9/69	4	Long Beach C.C.	Inglewood, Calif.	RFA(GB)-'96	6/1*
47	Keith, Craig	TE	6-3	262	4/27/71	4	Lenoir-Rhyne	Raleigh, N.C.	FA-'96	13/2*
17	Kidd, John	P	6-3	214	8/22/61	13	Northwestern	Findlay, Ohio	FA-'94	16/0
42	Kirby, Terry	RB	6-1	218	1/20/70	4	Virginia	Tabb, Va.	D3-'93	16/15
99	Klingbeil, Chuck	NT	6-1	288	11/2/65	6	Northern Michigan	Houghton, Mich.	FA-'91	16/15
52	Kopp, Jeff	LB	6-3	243	7/8/71	2	Southern California	Danville, Calif.	D6-'95	16/0
13	Marino, Dan	QB	6-4	224	9/15/61	14	Pittsburgh	Pittsburgh, Pa.	D1-'83	14/14
81	McDuffie, O.J.	WR	5-10	188	12/2/69	4	Penn State	Gates Mills, Ohio	D1-'93	16/16
67	McGuire, Gene	C	6-4	300	7/17/70	4	Notre Dame	Lynn Haven, Fla.	FA-'95	1/0
11	McGwire, Dan	QB	6-8	239	12/18/67	6	San Diego State	Claremont, Calif.	UFA(Sea)-'95	1/0
83	Miller, Scott	WR	5-11	185	10/20/68	6	UCLA	El Toro, Calif.	D9-'91	0*
79	Milner, Billy	T	6-5	293	6/21/72	2	Houston	Atlanta, Ga.	D1-'95	16/9
18	Myers, Shannon	WR	6-0	170	6/16/73	2	Lenoir-Rhyne	Salisbury, N.C.	D7a-'95	0*
25	Oliver, Louis	S	6-2	224	3/9/66	8	Florida	Belle Glade, Fla.	FA-'95	15/5
30	Parmalee, Bernie	RB	5-11	196	9/16/67	5	Ball State	Jersey City, N.J.	FA-'92	16/12
61	Ruddy, Tim	C	6-3	290	4/27/72	3	Notre Dame	Dunmore, Pa.	D2b-'94	16/16
69	Sims, Keith	G	6-3	309	6/17/67	7	Iowa State	Watchung, N.J.	D2-'90	16/16
55	Singleton, Chris	LB	6-2	246	2/20/67	7	Arizona	Parsippany, N.J.	FA-'93	15/15
40	Spikes, Irving	RB	5-8	206	12/21/70	3	Northeast Louisiana	Ocean Springs, Miss.	FA-'94	9/0
35	Stewart, Michael	S	5-11	202	7/12/65	10	Fresno State	Bakersfield, Calif.	UFA(Rams)-'94	16/16
10	Stoyanovich, Pete	K	5-11	195	4/28/67	8	Indiana	Dearborn Heights, Mich.	D8-'89	16/0
92	Stubbs, Daniel	DE	6-4	272	1/3/65	8	Miami	Red Bank, N.J.	UFA(Phil)-'96	16/6*
82	Wainright, Frank	TE	6-3	245	10/10/67	6	Northern Colorado	Arvada, Colo.	FA-'95	6/0
78	Webb, Richmond	T	6-6	303	1/11/67	7	Texas A&M	Dallas, Tex.	D1-'90	16/16
85	Williams, Ronnie	TE	6-3	258	1/19/66	5	Oklahoma State	North Natchez, Miss.	FA-'93	16/2
49	Wilson, Robert	RB	6-0	255	1/13/69	4	Texas A&M	Houston, Tex.	FA-'94	16/0

* Bailey played 4 games with Washington, 9 games with Dallas in '95; Barnett played 14 games with Philadelphia; James Brown played 15 games with N.Y. Jets; Buck played 3 games with Arizona; Hand was inactive for 16 games; Jones played 9 games with New England; Jordan played 6 games with Green Bay; Keith played 11 games with Jacksonville; Miller and Myers missed '95 season because of injury; Stubbs played 16 games with Philadelphia.

t- Dolphins traded for James Brown (N.Y. Jets).

Players lost through free agency (4): DE Marco Coleman (SD; 16 games in '95), LB Bryan Cox (Chi; 16), WR Irving Fryar (Phil; 16), CB Troy Vincent (Phil; 16).

Also played with Dolphins in '95—WR Gary Clark (16 games), WR Kirby Dar Dar (1), LB Dion Foxx (1), G Andrew Greene (6), QB Bernie Kosar (9), G Tom McHale (7), T Eric Moore (2), TE Joe Planansky (2), CB Frankie Smith (11), WR Mike Williams (12).

COACHING STAFF

Head Coach,
Jimmy Johnson

Pro Career: Begins his sixth season as an NFL head coach and his first with the Miami Dolphins. Named general manager/head coach of the Dolphins on January 11, 1996, becoming the third head coach in club history, joining George Wilson (1966-69) and Don Shula (1970-1995). Became the first, and one of only two head coaches ever in football history, to win both a Super Bowl title (Dallas Cowboys - 1992 and 1993) and a national collegiate championship (University of Miami - 1987). Served as head coach of the Cowboys from 1989 through 1993. Became only the third man in NFL history to coach consecutive Super Bowl winners, winning Super Bowl XXVII in 1992 and following that with a victory in Super Bowl XXVIII in 1993. In his five years in Dallas, Johnson led the Cowboys to two NFL championships, with their first title in 1992 coming just three years after the franchise produced a 1-15 mark in 1989. In three of the four years that followed, Johnson's initial season with the Cowboys, he was named the NFL Coach of the Year by at least one national news media outlet. During that time, Johnson's clubs compiled a four-year record of 50-22 (.694) and the Cowboys won 39 of their last 50 games (.780) under Johnson. In addition, Johnson's postseason winning percentage of .875 (7-1 record) is the second best in NFL history, behind only Vince Lombardi's mark of .900 (9-1). Career record: 51-37.

Background: At the University of Miami (1984-88), Johnson led the Hurricanes to a 52-9 (.853) record, including a 44-4 mark over the final four seasons. His Hurricane teams also captured two Orange Bowl titles, a national championship in 1987 and two number two finishes (1986, 1988). In his first head coaching job, Johnson took over a losing program at Oklahoma State in 1979 and brought it to national prominence, compiling a 29-25 record in five seasons, including two bowl appearances. Johnson was named Big Eight Coach of the Year following his first season. Served as assistant head coach/defensive coordinator at the University of Pittsburgh (1977-78), defensive coordinator at the University of Arkansas (1973-76), defensive line coach at the University of Oklahoma (1970-72), defensive coordinator at Iowa State University (1968-69), assistant coach at Wichita State (1967), and defensive line coach at Louisiana Tech University (1965). Before beginning his coaching career, Johnson was an All-Southwest Conference defensive lineman at Arkansas and helped lead the Razorbacks to the 1964 national championship. A three-year letterman, Johnson was named to Arkansas' All-Decade Team of the 1960s.

Personal: Born July 16, 1943, in Port Arthur, Texas. Lives in Miami. Johnson has two sons, Brent and Chad.

ASSISTANT COACHES

Larry Beightol, assistant head coach/offensive line; born November 21, 1942, Morrisville, Pa., lives in Pembroke Pines, Fla. Guard-linebacker Catawba College 1961-63. No pro playing experience. College coach: William & Mary 1968-71, North Carolina State 1972-75, Auburn 1976, Arkansas 1977-78, 1980-82, Louisiana Tech 1979 (head coach), Missouri 1983-84. Pro coach: Atlanta Falcons 1985-86, Tampa Bay Buccaneers 1987-88, San Diego Chargers 1989, New York Jets 1990-94, Houston Oilers 1995, joined Dolphins in 1996.

Kippy Brown, running backs; born March 6, 1955, Sweetwater, Tenn., lives in Plantation, Fla. Quarterback Memphis State 1974-77. No pro playing experience. College coach: Memphis State 1978-80, Louisville 1982, Tennessee 1983-89, 1993-94. Pro coach: New York Jets 1990-92, Tampa Bay Buccaneers 1995, joined Dolphins in 1996.

Joel Collier, defensive staff assistant; born December 25, 1963, Buffalo, N.Y., lives in Plantation, Fla. Linebacker Northern Colorado 1984-87. No pro playing experience. College coach: Syracuse 1988-89. Pro coach: Tampa Bay Buccaneers 1990, New England Patriots 1991-93, joined Dolphins in 1994.

John Gamble, strength and conditioning; born June 26, 1957, Richmond, Va., lives in Ft. Lauderdale, Fla. Linebacker Hampton Institute 1975-78. No pro playing experience. College coach: Virginia 1982-93. Pro coach: Joined Dolphins in 1994.

Cary Godette, defensive line; born March 20, 1954, New Bern, N.C., lives in Plantation, Fla. Defensive end East Carolina 1973-76. No pro playing experience. College coach: East Carolina 1977-79, 1990-91, Wyoming 1980-82, Cincinnati 1983-88, Georgia Tech 1992-93, North Carolina State 1994. Pro coach: Carolina Panthers 1995, joined Dolphins in 1996.

George Hill, defensive coordinator/linebackers; born April 28, 1933, Bay Village, Ohio, lives in Plantation, Fla. Tackle-fullback Denison 1954-57. No pro playing experience. College coach: Findlay 1959, Denison 1960-64, Cornell 1965, Duke 1966-70, Ohio State 1971-78. Pro coach: Philadelphia Eagles 1979-84, Indianapolis Colts 1985-88, joined Dolphins in 1989.

Pat Jones, tight ends; born November 4, 1947, Memphis, Tenn., lives in Ft. Lauderdale, Fla. Nose guard Arkansas Tech 1965, linebacker/nose guard Arkansas 1966-67. No pro playing experience. College coach: Arkansas 1974-75, Southern Methodist 1976-77, Pittsburgh 1978, Oklahoma State 1979-94 (1984-94 head coach). Pro coach: Joined Dolphins in 1996.

Bill Lewis, defensive nickel package; born August 5, 1941, Bristol, Pa., lives in Ft. Lauderdale, Fla. Quarterback East Stroudsburg State 1959-62. No pro playing experience. College coach: East Stroudsburg State 1963-65, Pittsburgh 1966-68, Wake Forest 1969-70, Georgia Tech 1971-72, 1992-94 (head coach), Arkansas 1973-76, Wyoming 1977-79, Georgia 1980-88, East Carolina 1989-91 (head coach). Pro coach: Joined Dolphins in 1996.

Rich McGeorge, assistant offensive line; born September 14, 1948, Roanoke, Va., lives in Plantation, Fla. Tight end Elon College 1966-69. Pro tight end Green Bay Packers 1970-78. College coach: Duke 1981-82, 1987-89, Florida 1990-92. Pro coach: Birmingham Stallions (USFL) 1983-84, Tampa Bay Bandits (USFL) 1985, joined Dolphins in 1993.

Mel Phillips, secondary; born January 6, 1942, Shelby, N.C., lives in Miami Lakes, Fla. Defensive back-running back North Carolina A&T 1964-65. Pro defensive back San Francisco 49ers 1966-77. Pro coach: Detroit Lions 1980-84, joined Dolphins in 1985.

Brad Roll, assistant strength and conditioning; born July 4, 1958, Houston, Tex., lives in Davie, Fla. Center Blinn (Tex.) J.C. 1976-77, Stephen F. Austin 1978-79. No pro playing experience. College coach: Stephen F. Austin 1980, Southwestern Louisiana 1981-86, Kansas 1987-88, Miami 1989-92. Pro coach: Tampa Bay Buccaneers 1993-95, joined Dolphins in 1996.

Larry Seiple, wide receivers; born February 14, 1945, Allentown, Pa., lives in Pembroke Pines, Fla. Running back-receiver-punter Kentucky 1964-66. Pro punter-tight end-receiver-running back Miami Dolphins 1966-77. College coach: Miami 1978-79. Pro coach: Detroit Lions 1980-84, Tampa Bay Buccaneers 1985-86, joined Dolphins in 1988.

Gary Stevens, offensive coordinator; born March 19, 1943, Cleveland, Ohio, lives in Ft. Lauderdale, Fla. Running back John Carroll 1963-65. No pro playing experience. College coach: Louisville 1971-74, Kent State 1975, West Virginia 1976-79, Miami 1980-88. Pro coach: Joined Dolphins in 1989.

Mike Westhoff, special teams; born January 10, 1948, Pittsburgh, Pa., lives in Plantation, Fla. Center-linebacker Wichita State 1967-69. No pro playing experience. College coach: Indiana 1974-75, Dayton 1976, Indiana State 1977, Northwestern 1978-80, Texas Christian 1981. Pro coach: Baltimore/Indianapolis Colts 1982-84, Arizona Outlaws (USFL) 1985, joined Dolphins in 1986.

1996 FIRST-YEAR ROSTER

Name	Pos.	Ht.	Wt.	Birthdate	College	Hometown	How Acq.
Abdul Jabbar, Karim	RB	5-10	194	6/28/74	UCLA	Los Angeles, Calif.	D3b
Brew, Dorian	CB	5-10	182	7/19/74	Kansas	Florissant, Mo.	D3a
Buckey, Jeff	G	6-5	300	8/7/74	Stanford	Bakersfield, Calif.	D7a
Burton, Shane	DT	6-6	300	1/18/74	Tennessee	Catawba, N.C.	D5b
Dar Dar, Kirby (1)	WR	5-9	183	3/27/72	Syracuse	Tampa, Fla.	FA
Fuller, Andy	TE	6-1	258	9/8/74	Auburn	Huntsville, Ala.	FA
Gardener, Daryl	DT	6-6	320	2/25/73	Baylor	Lawton, Okla.	D1
Harris, Anthony	LB	6-1	224	1/25/73	Auburn	Fort Pierce, Fla.	FA
Hunter, Brice	WR	6-0	214	4/21/74	Georgia	Valdosta, Ga.	D7b
Izzo, Larry	LB	5-10	220	9/26/74	Rice	Houston, Tex.	FA
Jones, LaCurtis	LB	6-0	200	6/23/72	Baylor	Waco, Tex.	D4c
Kushner, Bill (1)	P	6-0	203	1/13/70	Boston College	San Diego, Calif.	FA
McClinton, Lee (1)	RB	5-11	252	8/2/72	New Hampshire	Highland, N.Y.	FA
McPhail, Jerris	RB	5-11	201	6/26/72	East Carolina	Clinton, N.C.	D5a
Neal, Henry (1)	WR	5-10	181	10/28/70	Texas Southern	West Palm Beach, Fla.	FA
Nedney, Joe (1)	K	6-4	205	3/22/73	San Jose State	San Jose, Calif.	FA
Planansky, Joe (1)	TE	6-4	250	10/21/71	Chadron State	Hemingford, Neb.	FA
Pointer, Kirk	CB	5-11	178	2/13/74	Austin Peay	White House, Tenn.	D4a
Pritchett, Stanley	RB	6-1	232	12/12/73	South Carolina	College Park, Ga.	D4b
Ray, Rodney	CB	5-10	185	2/2/73	Northwestern	Ferguson, Mo.	FA
Smith, Walter (1)	S	5-9	191	10/19/70	Michigan	Detroit, Mich.	FA
Tellison, A.C. (1)	WR	6-2	208	9/5/71	Miami	Bay City, Tex.	FA
Thomas, Zach	LB	5-11	231	9/1/73	Texas Tech	Pampa, Tex.	D5c
Wilson, Sir Mahn	WR	6-2	210	6/4/73	Syracuse	Tampa, Fla.	FA
Wooden, Shawn	CB	5-11	186	10/23/73	Notre Dame	Abington, Pa.	D6
Yarborough, William	CB	6-0	166	4/8/73	Virginia Tech	Newport News, Va.	FA

The term NFL Rookie is defined as a player who is in his first season of professional football and has not been on the roster of another professional football team for any regular-season or postseason games. A Rookie is designated by an "R" on NFL rosters. Players who have been active in another professional football league or players who have NFL experience, including either preseason training camp or being on an Active List or Inactive List, or on Reserve/Injured or Reserve/Physically Unable to Perform for fewer than six regular-season games, are termed NFL First-Year Players. An NFL First-Year Player is designated by a "1" on NFL rosters. Thereafter, a player is credited with an additional year of experience for each season in which he accumulates six games on the Active List or Inactive List, or on Reserve/Injured or Reserve/Physically Unable to Perform.

NOTES

NEW ENGLAND PATRIOTS

American Football Conference
Eastern Division
Team Colors: Blue, Red, Silver, and White
Foxboro Stadium
60 Washington Street
Foxboro, Massachusetts 02035
Telephone: (508) 543-8200

CLUB OFFICIALS

President/Chief Executive Officer: Robert K. Kraft
Vice President-Owner's Repesentative: Jonathan A. Kraft
Vice President-Business Operations: Andrew Wasynczuk
Vice President-Finance: James Hausmann
Corporate Marketing and Sales: Daniel A. Kraft
Director of Public and Community Relations: Donald Lowery
Director of Media Relations: Stacey James
Director of Player Resources: Andre Tippett
Controller: Jim Nolan
Director of Pro Personnel: Bobby Grier
Director of College Scouting: Charles Armey
Director of Ticketing: Mike Nichols
Operations Manager: Dan Murphy
Building Services Manager: Bernie Reinhart
Head Trainer: Ron O'Neil
Equipment Manager: Don Brocher
Video Director: Ken Deininger
Stadium: Foxboro Stadium • **Capacity:** 60,292
60 Washington Street
Foxboro, Massachusetts 02035
Playing Surface: Grass
Training Camp: Bryant College
Route 7
Smithfield, Rhode Island 02917

1996 SCHEDULE

PRESEASON

Aug. 2	at Green Bay	7:00
Aug. 12	at Dallas	7:00
Aug. 18	**Philadelphia**	1:00
Aug. 23	**Washington**	8:00

REGULAR SEASON

Sept. 1	at Miami	4:00
Sept. 8	at Buffalo	1:00
Sept. 15	**Arizona**	1:00
Sept. 22	**Jacksonville**	1:00
Sept. 29	Open Date	
Oct. 6	at Baltimore	1:00
Oct. 13	**Washington**	1:00
Oct. 20	at Indianapolis	12:00
Oct. 27	**Buffalo**	8:00
Nov. 3	**Miami**	4:00
Nov. 10	at New York Jets	1:00
Nov. 17	**Denver**	1:00
Nov. 24	**Indianapolis**	1:00
Dec. 1	at San Diego	5:00
Dec. 8	**New York Jets**	4:00
Dec. 15	at Dallas	12:00
Dec. 21	at New York Giants (Sat.)	12:30

RECORD HOLDERS

INDIVIDUAL RECORDS—CAREER

Category	Name	Performance
Rushing (Yds.)	Sam Cunningham, 1973-79, 1981-82	5,453
Passing (Yds.)	Steve Grogan, 1975-1990	26,886
Passing (TDs)	Steve Grogan, 1975-1990	182
Receiving (No.)	Stanley Morgan, 1977-1989	534
Receiving (Yds.)	Stanley Morgan, 1977-1989	10,352
Interceptions	Raymond Clayborn, 1977-1989	36
Punting (Avg.)	Rich Camarillo, 1981-87	42.6
Punt Return (Avg.)	Mack Herron, 1973-75	12.0
Kickoff Return (Avg.)	Allen Carter, 1975-76	27.2
Field Goals	Gino Cappelletti, 1960-1970	176
Touchdowns (Tot.)	Stanley Morgan, 1977-1989	68
Points	Gino Cappelletti, 1960-1970	1,130

INDIVIDUAL RECORDS—SINGLE SEASON

Category	Name	Performance
Rushing (Yds.)	Curtis Martin, 1995	1,487
Passing (Yds.)	Drew Bledsoe, 1994	4,555
Passing (TDs)	Vito (Babe) Parilli, 1964	31
Receiving (No.)	Ben Coates, 1994	96
Receiving (Yds.)	Stanley Morgan, 1986	1,491
Interceptions	Ron Hall, 1964	11
Punting (Avg.)	Rich Camarillo, 1983	44.6
Punt Return (Avg.)	Mack Herron, 1974	14.8
Kickoff Return (Avg.)	Raymond Clayborn, 1977	31.0
Field Goals	Tony Franklin, 1986	32
Touchdowns (Tot.)	Curtis Martin, 1995	15
Points	Gino Cappelletti, 1964	155

INDIVIDUAL RECORDS—SINGLE GAME

Category	Name	Performance
Rushing (Yds.)	Tony Collins, 9-18-83	212
Passing (Yds.)	Drew Bledsoe, 11-13-94	426
Passing (TDs)	Vito (Babe) Parilli, 11-15-64	5
	Vito (Babe) Parilli, 10-15-67	5
	Steve Grogan, 9-9-79	5
Receiving (No.)	Ben Coates, 11-27-94	12
Receiving (Yds.)	Stanley Morgan, 11-8-81	182
Interceptions	Many times	3
	Last time by Roland James, 10-23-83	
Field Goals	Gino Cappelletti, 10-4-64	6
Touchdowns (Tot.)	Many times	3
	Last time by Stanley Morgan, 9-21-86	
Points	Gino Cappelletti, 12-18-65	28

COACHING HISTORY

BOSTON 1960-1970
(241-293-9)

1960-61	Lou Saban*	7-12-0
1961-68	Mike Holovak	53-47-9
1969-70	Clive Rush**	5-16-0
1970-72	John Mazur***	9-21-0
1972	Phil Bengtson	1-4-0
1973-78	Chuck Fairbanks****	46-41-0
1978	Hank Bullough-Ron Erhardt#	0-1-0
1979-81	Ron Erhardt	21-27-0
1982-84	Ron Meyer##	18-16-0
1984-89	Raymond Berry	51-41-0
1990	Rod Rust	1-15-0
1991-92	Dick MacPherson	8-24-0
1993-95	Bill Parcells	21-28-0

*Released after five games in 1961
**Released after seven games in 1970
***Resigned after nine games in 1972
****Suspended for final regular-season game in 1978
#Co-coaches
##Released after eight games in 1984

FOXBORO STADIUM

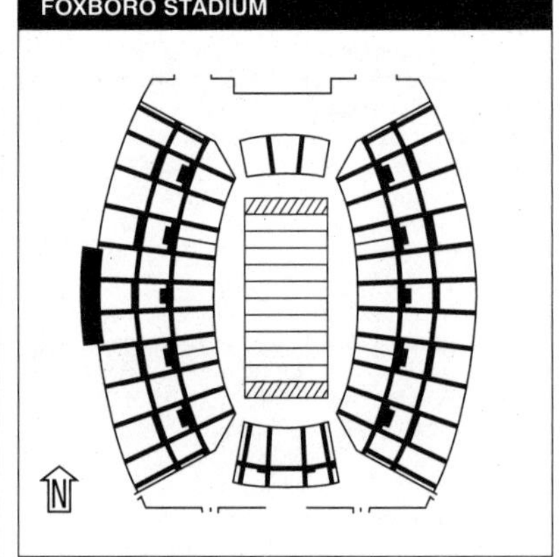

1995 TEAM RECORD

PRESEASON (1-3)

Date	Result		Opponents
8/4	L	17-30	Detroit
8/12	W	21-14	Minnesota
8/17	L	7-31	at Philadelphia
8/25	L	24-32	vs. Oakland at Stanford, Calif.

REGULAR SEASON (6-10)

Date	Result		Opponents	Att.
9/3	W	17-14	Cleveland	60,126
9/10	L	3-20	Miami	60,239
9/17	L	3-28	at San Francisco	66,179
10/1	L	17-30	at Atlanta	47,114
10/8	L	3-37	Denver	60,074
10/15	L	26-31	at Kansas City	77,992
10/23	W	27-14	Buffalo	60,203
10/29	L	17-20	Carolina (OT)	60,064
11/5	W	20-7	at N.Y. Jets	61,462
11/12	W	34-17	at Miami	70,399
11/19	L	10-24	Indianapolis	59,544
11/26	W	35-25	at Buffalo	69,384
12/3	L	17-31	New Orleans	59,876
12/10	W	31-28	N.Y. Jets	46,617
12/16	L	27-41	at Pittsburgh	57,158
12/23	L	7-10	at Indianapolis	54,685

(OT) Overtime

SCORE BY PERIODS

Patriots	49	84	59	102	0	—	294
Opponents	60	143	72	99	3	—	377

ATTENDANCE

Home 466,743 Away 504,313 Total 971,056
Single-game home record, 61,457 (12/5/71)
Single-season home record, 482,572 (1986)

1995 TEAM STATISTICS

	Patriots	Opp.
Total First Downs	335	308
Rushing	106	106
Passing	207	181
Penalty	22	21
Third Down: Made/Att	99/260	80/215
Third Down Pct.	38.1	37.2
Fourth Down: Made/Att	17/39	7/13
Fourth Down Pct.	43.6	53.8
Total Net Yards	5457	5764
Avg. Per Game	341.1	360.3
Total Plays	1187	1034
Avg. Per Play	4.6	5.6
Net Yards Rushing	1866	1878
Avg. Per Game	116.6	117.4
Total Rushes	474	448
Net Yards Passing	3591	3886
Avg. Per Game	224.4	242.9
Sacked/Yards Lost	27/198	37/221
Gross Yards	3789	4107
Att./Completions	686/351	549/342
Completion Pct.	51.2	62.3
Had Intercepted	16	15
Punts/Avg.	79/39.2	86/38.8
Net Punting Avg.	79/32.9	86/32.0
Penalties/Yards Lost	84/676	104/816
Fumbles/Ball Lost	32/20	24/14
Touchdowns	32	44
Rushing	16	12
Passing	14	29
Returns	2	3
Avg. Time of Possession	29:32	30:28

1995 INDIVIDUAL STATISTICS

PASSING	Att.	Comp.	Yds.	Pct.	TD	Int.	Tkld.	Rate
Bledsoe	636	323	3507	50.8	13	16	23/170	63.7
Zolak	49	28	282	57.1	1	0	4/28	80.5
Meggett	1	0	0	0.0	0	0	0/0	39.6
Patriots	686	351	3789	51.2	14	16	27/198	64.8
Opponents	549	342	4107	62.3	29	15	37/221	91.4

SCORING	TD R	TD P	TD Rt	PAT	FG	Saf	PTS
Bahr	0	0	0	27/27	23/33	0	96
Martin	14	1	0	0/0	0/0	0	92
Coates	0	6	0	0/0	0/0	0	36
Brisby	0	3	0	0/0	0/0	0	18
Meggett	2	0	0	0/0	0/0	0	16
Graham	0	2	0	0/0	0/0	0	12
T. Brown	0	0	1	0/0	0/0	0	6
Gash	0	1	0	0/0	0/0	0	6
W. Moore	0	1	0	0/0	0/0	0	6
Slade	0	0	1	0/0	0/0	0	6
Patriots	16	14	2	27/27	23/33	0	294
Opponents	12	29	3	40/41	23/32	0	377

2-Point conversions: Meggett 2, Martin. Team: 3-5.

RUSHING	Att.	Yds.	Avg.	LG	TD
Martin	368	1487	4.0	49	14
Meggett	60	250	4.2	25	2
Croom	13	54	4.2	12	0
Bledsoe	20	28	1.4	15	0
Gash	8	24	3.0	9	0
Zolak	4	19	4.8	12	0
Lee	1	4	4.0	4	0
Patriots	474	1866	3.9	49	16
Opponents	448	1878	4.2	66t	12

RECEIVING	No.	Yds.	Avg.	LG	TD
Coates	84	915	10.9	35	6
Brisby	66	974	14.8	72	3
Meggett	52	334	6.4	19	0
W. Moore	43	502	11.7	33	1
Martin	30	261	8.7	27	1
Gash	26	242	9.3	30	1
Burke	15	136	9.1	21	0
T. Brown	14	159	11.4	31	0
Graham	10	156	15.6	37t	2
Lee	8	107	13.4	33	0
Croom	1	8	8.0	8	0
Grant	1	4	4.0	4	0
Bledsoe	1	-9	-9.0	-9	0
Patriots	351	3789	10.8	72	14
Opponents	342	4107	12.0	70t	29

INTERCEPTIONS	No.	Yds.	Avg.	LG	TD
V. Brown	4	1	0.3	1	0
Guyton	3	68	22.7	45	0
Law	3	47	15.7	38	0
Reynolds	3	6	2.0	4	0
Ray	1	21	21.0	21	0
Hurst	1	0	0.0	0	0
Patriots	15	143	9.5	45	0
Opponents	16	161	10.1	69t	2

PUNTING	No.	Yds.	Avg.	In 20	LG
O'Neill	41	1514	36.9	14	57
Wagner	37	1557	42.1	13	57
Bahr	1	29	29.0	0	29
Patriots	79	3100	39.2	27	57
Opponents	86	3339	38.8	21	64

PUNT RETURNS	No.	FC	Yds.	Avg.	LG	TD
Meggett	45	17	383	8.5	23	0
Patriots	45	17	383	8.5	23	0
Opponents	40	11	342	8.6	42	0

KICKOFF RETURNS	No.	Yds.	Avg.	LG	TD
Meggett	38	964	25.4	62	0
T. Brown	31	672	21.7	38	0
Gisler	2	19	9.5	11	0
Burke	1	7	7.0	7	0
Frisch	1	8	8.0	8	0
Grant	1	7	7.0	7	0
Lee	1	14	14.0	14	0
Patriots	75	1691	22.5	62	0
Opponents	67	1405	21.0	58	0

SACKS	No.
McGinest	11.0
V. Brown	4.0
Collons	4.0
Slade	4.0
M. Jones	3.0
Reynolds	2.5
Barnett	2.0
Lewis	1.5
White	1.5
A. Jones	1.0
Law	1.0
T. Roberts	1.0
Johnson	0.5
Patriots	37.0
Opponents	27.0

1996 DRAFT CHOICES

Round	Name	Pos.	College
1	Terry Glenn	WR	Ohio State
2	Lawyer Milloy	DB	Washington
3	Tedy Bruschi	LB	Arizona
4	Heath Irwin	G	Colorado
	Chris Sullivan	DE	Boston College
	Kantroy Barber	RB	West Virginia
5	John Elmore	G	Texas
	Christian Peter	NT	Nebraska
6	Chris Griffin	TE	New Mexico
	Marrio Grier	RB	Tenn.-Chattanooga
	Devin Wyman	DT	Kentucky State
7	Lovett Purnell	TE	West Virginia
	J.R. Conrad	G	Oklahoma

NEW ENGLAND PATRIOTS

1996 VETERAN ROSTER

No.	Name	Pos.	Ht.	Wt.	Birthdate	NFL Exp.	College	Hometown	How Acq.	'95 Games/ Starts
50	Abrams, Bobby	LB	6-3	240	4/12/67	7	Michigan	Detroit, Mich.	UFA(Minn)-'95	9/1
78	Armstrong, Bruce	T	6-4	295	9/7/65	10	Louisville	Miami, Fla.	D1-'87	16/16
3	Bahr, Matt	K	5-10	175	7/6/56	18	Penn State	Langhorne, Pa.	W(Phil)-'93	16/0
7	Barker, Jay	QB	6-3	215	7/20/72	2	Alabama	Trussville, Ala.	FA-'95	0*
98	Barnett, Troy	DE	6-5	293	5/24/71	3	North Carolina	Jacksonville, N.C.	FA-'94	16/15
11	Bledsoe, Drew	QB	6-5	233	2/14/72	4	Washington State	Walla Walla, Wash.	D1-'93	15/15
51	Bowden, Andre	LB	6-3	240	5/4/68	2	Fayetteville State	Raleigh, N.C.	FA-'94	0*
82	Brisby, Vincent	WR	6-2	188	1/25/71	4	Northeast Louisiana	Lake Charles, La.	D2c-'93	16/16
30	Brown, Corwin	S	6-1	200	4/25/70	4	Michigan	Chicago, Ill.	D4b-'93	16/2
93	Brown, Monty	LB	6-0	228	4/13/70	4	Ferris State	Bridgeport, Mich.	RFA(Buff)-'96	16/6*
80	Brown, Troy	WR	5-9	190	7/2/71	4	Marshall	Blackville, S.C.	FA-'94	16/0
59	Brown, Vincent	LB	6-2	245	1/9/65	9	Mississippi Valley State	Decatur, Ga.	D2-'88	16/16
85	Burke, John	TE	6-3	255	9/7/71	3	Virginia Tech	Holmdel, N.J.	D4-'94	16/4
41	Cade, Eddie	S	6-1	206	8/4/73	2	Arizona State	Eloy, Ariz.	FA-'95	10/0
54	Catanho, Alcides	LB	6-3	216	1/20/72	2	Rutgers	Elizabeth, N.J.	FA-'95	12/0
32	Clay, Willie	S	5-9	184	9/5/70	5	Georgia Tech	Pittsburgh, Pa.	UFA(Det)-'96	16/16*
87	Coates, Ben	TE	6-5	245	8/16/69	6	Livingstone College	Greenwood, S.C.	D5b-'91	16/15
92	Collons, Ferric	DE	6-6	285	12/4/69	3	California	Sacramento, Calif.	T(GB)-'95	16/4
26	Croom, Corey	RB	5-11	208	5/22/71	4	Ball State	Sandusky, Ohio	FA-'93	13/1
66	Dellenbach, Jeff	C	6-6	300	2/14/63	12	Wisconsin	Wausau, Wis.	UFA(Mia)-'95	15/5
99	DeOssie, Steve	LB	6-2	248	11/22/62	13	Boston College	Boston, Mass.	UFA(NYJ)-'94	16/0
33	Gash, Sam	RB	5-11	224	3/7/69	5	Penn State	Hendersonville, N.C.	D8b-'92	15/12
67	Gisler, Mike	G-C	6-4	300	8/26/69	4	Houston	Range, Tex.	FA-'93	16/0
81	Graham, Hason	WR	5-10	176	3/21/71	2	Georgia	Decatur, Ga.	FA-'95	10/1
34	Grant, Rupert	RB	6-1	233	11/5/73	2	Howard	Washington, D.C.	FA-'95	7/1
38	Green, David	RB	5-11	193	4/18/72	2	Boston College	Mt. Kisco, N.Y.	FA-'95	2/0
77	Harlow, Pat	T	6-6	290	3/16/69	6	Southern California	Norco, Calif.	D1a-'91	10/0
84	Jefferson, Shawn	WR	5-11	180	2/22/69	6	Central Florida	Jacksonville, Fla.	FA-'96	16/15*
52	Johnson, Ted	LB	6-3	240	12/4/72	2	Colorado	Carlsbad, Calif.	D2-'95	12/12
96	Jones, Mike	DE	6-4	295	8/25/69	6	North Carolina State	Columbus, S.C.	FA-'94	13/3
61	Kratch, Bob	G	6-3	288	1/6/66	8	Iowa	Mahwah, N.J.	UFA(NYG)-'94	16/16
68	Lane, Max	T	6-6	295	2/22/71	3	Navy	Norborne, Mo.	D6b-'94	16/16
24	Law, Ty	CB	5-11	196	2/10/74	2	Michigan	Aliquippa, Pa.	D1-'95	14/7
86	Lee, Kevin	WR	6-1	194	1/1/71	3	Alabama	Mobile, Ala.	D2-'94	7/2
43	Lewis, Vernon	CB	5-10	192	10/27/70	4	Pittsburgh	Houston, Tex.	FA-'93	16/2
28	Martin, Curtis	RB	5-11	203	5/1/73	2	Pittsburgh	Pittsburgh, Pa.	D3a-'95	16/15
55	McGinest, Willie	LB	6-5	255	12/11/71	3	Southern California	Long Beach, Calif.	D1-'94	16/16
27	McGruder, Michael	CB	5-10	182	5/6/64	7	Kent State	Cleveland Heights, Ohio	UFA(TB)-'96	16/2*
22	Meggett, David	RB	5-7	195	4/30/66	8	Towson State	Charleston, S.C.	UFA(NYG)-'95	16/0
58	Moore, Marty	LB	6-1	244	3/19/71	3	Kentucky	Ft. Thomas, Ky.	D7b-'94	16/2
83	Moore, Will	WR	6-2	180	2/21/70	2	Texas Southern	Dallas, Tex.	FA-'95	14/13
23	Ray, Terry	S	6-1	205	10/12/69	5	Oklahoma	Killeen, Tex.	W(Atl)-'93	16/16
21	Reynolds, Ricky	CB	5-11	190	1/19/65	10	Washington State	Sacramento, Calif.	UFA(TB)-'95	16/16
94	Roberts, Tim	DE	6-6	318	4/14/69	4	Southern Mississippi	Atlanta, Ga.	RFA(Hou)-'95	13/12
76	Roberts, William	G	6-5	292	8/5/62	13	Ohio State	Miami, Fla.	FA-'95	16/11
71	Rucci, Todd	G	6-5	291	7/14/70	4	Penn State	Upper Darby, Pa.	D2b-'93	6/5
95	Sabb, Dwayne	LB	6-4	248	10/9/69	5	New Hampshire	Union, N.J.	D5-'92	12/0
75	Sagapolutele, Pio	DT	6-6	297	11/28/69	6	San Diego State	Honolulu, Hawaii	UFA(Balt)-'96	15/3*
18	Schroeder, Bill	WR	6-2	198	1/9/71	2	Wisconsin-La Crosse	Sheboygan, Wis.	T(GB)-'95	0*
53	Slade, Chris	LB	6-5	242	1/30/71	4	Virginia	Newport News, Va.	D2a-'93	16/16
77	Tharpe, Larry	T	6-4	299	11/19/70	5	Tennessee State	Macon, Ga.	UFA(Ariz)-'96	16/16*
19	Tupa, Tom	P	6-4	230	2/6/66	8	Ohio State	Cleveland, Ohio	UFA(Balt)-'96	16/0*
91	Walker, Bruce	NT	6-4	310	7/18/72	2	UCLA	Compton, Calif.	FA-'94	11/5
97	Wheeler, Mark	DT	6-2	285	4/1/70	5	Texas A&M	San Marcos, Tex.	UFA(TB)-'96	14/12*
25	Whigham, Larry	S	6-2	202	6/23/72	3	Northeast Louisiana	Hattiesburg, Miss.	FA-'94	16/0
90	White, Reggie	NT	6-4	315	3/22/70	5	North Carolina A&T	Baltimore, Md.	FA-'95	16/7
64	Wohlabaugh, Dave	C-G	6-3	304	4/13/72	2	Syracuse	Hamburg, N.Y.	D4-'95	11/11
16	Zolak, Scott	QB	6-5	222	12/13/67	6	Maryland	Monongahela, Pa.	D4-'91	16/1

* Barker inactive for 12 games; Bowden missed '95 season because of injury; M. Brown played 16 games with Buffalo; Clay played 16 games with Detroit in '95; Jefferson played 16 games with San Diego; McGruder played 16 games with Tampa Bay; Sagapolutele played 15 games with Cleveland; Schroeder missed '95 season because of injury; Tharpe played 16 games with Arizona; Tupa played 16 games with Cleveland; Wheeler played 14 games with Tampa Bay.

\# Unrestricted free agent; subject to developments.

† Restricted free agent; subject to developments.

Traded— T Pat Harlow to Oakland.

Players lost through free agency (1): P Bryan Wagner (Det; 8 games in '95).

Also played for Patriots in '95—LB Vincent Brown (16 games), TE David Frisch (2), S Myron Guyton (14), CB Maurice Hurst (10), DE Aaron Jones (10), T Brandon Moore (6), P Pat O'Neill (8), TE Andre President (1).

COACHING STAFF

Head Coach,
Bill Parcells

Pro Career: On January 21, 1993, Parcells became the franchise's thirteenth head coach since the Patriots' inception in 1960. It took Parcells just two seasons to resurrect the 2-14 team he inherited in 1992 into a playoff team in 1994. The Patriots finished 1994 with seven consecutive victories to tie a franchise record and qualified for the playoffs with a 10-6 regular-season record. Parcells made his NFL coaching debut with the New England Patriots as the linebackers coach on Ron Erhardt's staff in 1980. He accepted the same position on the New York Giants staff in 1981 and was named the Giants head coach in 1983. In eight seasons at the helm of the Giants, Parcells led his teams to two Super Bowl championships. His first title came in 1986, with a 39-20 victory over the Denver Broncos. Four years later, the Giants claimed another championship with a 20-19 victory over the Buffalo Bills. On May 15, 1991, health concerns caused Parcells to resign from the Giants. During his two seasons away from coaching, Parcells entertained football audiences from the broadcast booth, in 1991 as a studio analyst and in 1992 as a color commentator for NBC Sports. Career record: 106-80-1.

Background: Linebacker at Wichita State 1961-63. College assistant Hastings (Neb.) 1964, Wichita State 1965, Army 1966-69, Florida State 1970-72, Vanderbilt 1973-74, Texas Tech 1975-77, Air Force 1978 (head coach).

Personal: Born August 22, 1941, Englewood, N.J. Bill and his wife, Judy, live in Foxboro, Mass., and have three daughters—Suzy, Jill, and Dallas.

ASSISTANT COACHES

Bill Belichick, assistant head coach/defensive backs; born April 16, 1952, Nashville, Tenn., lives in Weston, Mass. Center/tight end Wesleyan 1971-75. No pro playing experience. Pro coach: Baltimore Colts 1975, Detroit Lions 1976-77, Denver Broncos 1978, New York Giants 1979-90, Cleveland Browns 1991-95 (head coach), joined Patriots in 1996.

Maurice Carthon, running backs; born April 24, 1961, Chicago, Ill., lives in Foxboro, Mass. Running back Arkansas State 1979-82. Pro running back New Jersey Generals (USFL) 1983-85, New York Giants 1985-91, Indianapolis Colts 1992. Pro coach: Joined Patriots in 1994.

Romeo Crennel, defensive line; born June 18, 1947, Lynchburg, Va., lives in Walpole, Mass. Defensive tackle, linebacker Western Kentucky 1966-69. No pro playing experience. College coach: Western Kentucky 1970-74, Texas Tech 1975-77, Mississippi 1978-79, Georgia Tech 1980. Pro coach: New York Giants 1981-92, joined Patriots in 1993.

Al Groh, defensive coordinator-linebackers; born July 13, 1944, New York, N.Y. Defensive end Virginia 1964-67. No pro playing experience. College coach: Army 1968-69, Virginia 1970-72, North Carolina 1973-77, Air Force 1978-79, Texas Tech 1980, Wake Forest 1981-86 (head coach), South Carolina 1988. Pro coach: Atlanta Falcons 1987, New York Giants 1989-91, Cleveland Browns 1992, joined Patriots in 1993.

Fred Hoaglin, offensive line; born January 28, 1944, Alliance, Ohio, lives in Cumberland, R.I. Center Pittsburgh 1962-65. Pro center Cleveland Browns 1966-72, Baltimore Colts 1973, Houston Oilers 1974-75, Seattle Seahawks 1976. Pro coach: Detroit Lions 1978-84, New York Giants 1985-92, joined Patriots in 1993.

Chris Palmer, quarterbacks; born September 23, 1949, Mt. Kisco, N.Y., lives in Foxboro, Mass. Quarterback Southern Connecticut State 1968-71. No pro playing experience. College coach: Connecticut 1972-74, Lehigh 1975, Colgate 1976-82, New Haven 1986-87 (head coach), Boston University 1988-89 (head coach). Pro coach: Montreal Concordes (CFL) 1983, New Jersey Generals (USFL) 1984-85, Houston Oilers 1990-92, joined Patriots in 1993.

Johnny Parker, strength and conditioning; born February 1, 1947, Greenville, S.C., lives in Foxboro, Mass. Graduate of Mississippi, master's degree from Delta State University. No college or pro playing experience. College coach: South Carolina 1974-76, Indiana 1977-79, Louisiana State 1980, Mississippi 1981-83. Pro coach: New York Giants 1984-92, joined Patriots in 1993.

Ray Perkins, offensive coordinator; born November 6, 1941, Mount Olive, Miss., lives in Foxboro, Mass. Wide receiver Alabama 1964-66. Pro receiver Baltimore Colts 1967-71. College coach: Mississippi State 1973, Alabama 1983-86 (head coach), Arkansas State 1992 (head coach). Pro coach: New England Patriots 1974-77, San Diego Chargers 1978, New York Giants 1979-82 (head coach), Tampa Bay Buccaneers 1987-90 (head coach), rejoined Patriots in 1993.

Michael Pope, tight ends; born March 15, 1942, Monroe, N.C., lives in Foxboro, Mass. Quarterback Lenoir Rhyne 1962-64. No pro playing experience. College coach: Florida State 1970-74, Texas Tech 1975-77, Mississippi 1978-82. Pro coach: New York Giants 1983-91, Cincinnati Bengals 1992-93, joined Patriots in 1994.

Dante Scarnecchia, defensive assistant-linebackers; born February 15, 1948, Los Angeles, Calif., lives in Wrentham, Mass. Center-guard California Western 1968-70. No pro playing experience. College coach: California Western (now U.S. International) 1970-72, Iowa State 1973, Southern Methodist 1975-76, 1980-81, Pacific 1977-78, Northern Arizona 1979. Pro coach: New England Patriots 1982-89, Indianapolis Colts 1990, rejoined Patriots in 1991.

Mike Sweatman, special teams, born October 23, 1947, Kansas City, Mo., lives in Foxboro, Mass. Linebacker Kansas 1964-67. No pro playing experience. College coach: Kansas 1973-74, 1979-82, Tulsa 1977-78, Tennessee 1983. Pro coach: Minnesota Vikings 1984, New York Giants 1985-92, joined Patriots in 1993.

Charlie Weis, wide receivers; born March 30, 1956, Trenton, N.J., lives in Foxboro, Mass. Graduate of Notre Dame. No college or pro playing experience. College coach: South Carolina 1985-88. Pro coach: New York Giants 1990-92, joined Patriots in 1993.

1996 FIRST-YEAR ROSTER

Name	Pos.	Ht.	Wt.	Birthdate	College	Hometown	How Acq.
Barber, Kantroy	RB	6-1	243	10/4/73	West Virginia	Miami, Fla.	D4c
Bruschi, Tedy	LB	6-1	245	6/9/73	Arizona	Roseville, Calif.	D3
Conrad, J.R.	T	6-3	300	2/2/74	Oklahoma	Fairland, Okla.	D7b
Culley, Blair (1)	K	6-1	190	11/29/68	Oklahoma	Sand Springs, Okla.	FA
Elmore, John	G	6-3	302	3/2/73	Texas	Sherman, Tex.	D5a
Glenn, Terry	WR	5-10	184	7/23/74	Ohio State	Columbus, Ohio	D1
Grier, Marrio	RB	5-10	225	12/5/71	Tenn.-Chattanooga	Charlotte, N.C.	D6b
Griffin, Chris	TE	6-4	257	7/26/74	New Mexico	Oklahoma City, Okla.	D6a
Hitchcock, Jimmy (1)	CB	5-10	188	11/9/71	North Carolina	Concord, N.C.	D3b-'95
Holcomb, Sean (1)	LB	6-3	250	3/9/71	Texas A&M-Kingsville	Midland, Tex.	FA
Irwin, Heath	G	6-4	300	6/27/73	Colorado	Boulder, Colo.	D4a
Milloy, Lawyer	S	6-1	208	11/14/73	Washington	Tacoma, Wash.	D2
Nelson, Chico (1)	S	6-1	198	12/25/69	Ohio State	Sarasota, Fla.	FA
Oman, Ryan	G	6-5	294	5/12/73	Wyoming	Bemedji, Minn.	FA
Purnell, Lovett	TE	6-2	250	4/7/72	West Virginia	Seaford, Del.	D7a
Sullivan, Chris	DE	6-4	279	3/14/73	Boston College	North Attleboro, Mass.	D4b
Thompson, Byron	DE	6-5	260	4/20/73	Baylor	Killeen, Tex.	FA
Wall, Marcus	WR-KR	5-9	165	12/10/73	North Carolina	Fayetteville, N.C.	FA
Wyman, Devin	DE	6-7	307	8/29/73	Kentucky State	Palo Alto, Calif.	D6c
Yancy, Carlos (1)	CB	6-0	185	6/24/70	Georgia	Sarasota, Fla.	D7-'95

The term NFL Rookie is defined as a player who is in his first season of professional football and has not been on the roster of another professional football team for any regular-season or postseason games. A Rookie is designated by an "R" on NFL rosters. Players who have been active in another professional football league or players who have NFL experience, including either preseason training camp or being on an Active List or Inactive List, or on Reserve/Injured or Reserve/Physically Unable to Perform for fewer than six regular-season games, are termed NFL First-Year Players. An NFL First-Year Player is designated by a "1" on NFL rosters. Thereafter, a player is credited with an additional year of experience for each season in which he accumulates six games on the Active List or Inactive List, or on Reserve/Injured or Reserve/Physically Unable to Perform.

NOTES

NEW YORK JETS

American Football Conference
Eastern Division
Team Colors: Kelly Green and White
1000 Fulton Avenue
Hempstead, New York 11550
Telephone: (516) 538-6600

CLUB OFFICIALS

Chairman of the Board: Leon Hess
President: Steve Gutman
Director of Player Personnel: Dick Haley
Assistant General Manager: James Harris
Director of Player Administration: Pat Kirwan
Director of Public Relations: Frank Ramos
Treasurer & C.F.O.: Mike Gerstle
Director of Operations: Mike Kensil
Executive Director of Business Operations: Bob Parente
Talent Scouts: Joey Clinkscales, Sid Hall, Jesse Kaye, Bob Schmitz, Marv Sunderland
College Scouting Coordinator: John Griffin
Asst. Director of Public Relations: Doug Miller
Public Relations Assistants: Sharon Czark, Berj Najarian
Coordinator of Special Projects: Ken Ilchuk
Travel Coordinator: Kevin Coyle
Controller: Mike Minarczyk
Marketing Manager: Beth Conroy
Director of Ticket Operations: John Buschhorn
Computer Ticket Operations Manager: Carol Anne Coppola
Director of Computer Technology: Hal Masure
Video Director: Jim Pons
Assistant Video Director: John Seiter
Head Trainer: David Price
Assistant Head Trainer: John Mellody
Equipment Manager: Bill Hampton
Equipment Director: Clay Hampton
Stadium: Giants Stadium • **Capacity:** 77,803
East Rutherford, New Jersey 07073
Playing Surface: AstroTurf
Training Center: 1000 Fulton Avenue
Hempstead, New York 11550

1996 SCHEDULE

PRESEASON

Aug. 3	vs. Houston at Jackson, Miss.	7:00
Aug. 8	at Philadelphia	7:30
Aug. 17	**New York Giants**	8:00
Aug. 23	at Oakland	7:00

REGULAR SEASON

Sept. 1	at Denver	2:00
Sept. 8	**Indianapolis**	1:00
Sept. 15	at Miami	1:00
Sept. 22	**New York Giants**	1:00
Sept. 29	at Washington	8:00
Oct. 6	**Oakland**	1:00
Oct. 13	at Jacksonville	1:00
Oct. 20	**Buffalo**	4:00
Oct. 27	at Arizona	2:00
Nov. 3	Open Date	
Nov. 10	**New England**	1:00
Nov. 17	at Indianapolis	1:00
Nov. 24	at Buffalo	1:00
Dec. 1	**Houston**	4:00
Dec. 8	at New England	4:00
Dec. 14	**Philadelphia** (Sat.)	12:30
Dec. 22	**Miami**	1:00

RECORD HOLDERS

INDIVIDUAL RECORDS—CAREER

Category	Name	Performance
Rushing (Yds.)	Freeman McNeil, 1981-1992	8,074
Passing (Yds.)	Joe Namath, 1965-1976	27,057
Passing (TDs)	Joe Namath, 1965-1976	170
Receiving (No.)	Don Maynard, 1960-1972	627
Receiving (Yds.)	Don Maynard, 1960-1972	11,732
Interceptions	Bill Baird, 1963-69	34
Punting (Avg.)	Curley Johnson, 1961-68	42.8
Punt Return (Avg.)	Dick Christy, 1961-63	16.2
Kickoff Return (Avg.)	Bobby Humphery, 1984-89	22.8
Field Goals	Pat Leahy, 1974-1991	304
Touchdowns (Tot.)	Don Maynard, 1960-1972	88
Points	Pat Leahy, 1974-1991	1,470

INDIVIDUAL RECORDS—SINGLE SEASON

Category	Name	Performance
Rushing (Yds.)	Freeman McNeil, 1985	1,331
Passing (Yds.)	Joe Namath, 1967	4,007
Passing (TDs)	Al Dorow, 1960	26
	Joe Namath, 1967	26
Receiving (No.)	Al Toon, 1988	93
Receiving (Yds.)	Don Maynard, 1967	1,434
Interceptions	Dainard Paulson, 1964	12
Punting (Avg.)	Curley Johnson, 1965	45.3
Punt Return (Avg.)	Dick Christy, 1961	21.3
Kickoff Return (Avg.)	Bobby Humphery, 1984	30.7
Field Goals	Jim Turner, 1968	34
Touchdowns (Tot.)	Art Powell, 1960	14
	Don Maynard, 1965	14
	Emerson Boozer, 1972	14
Points	Jim Turner, 1968	145

INDIVIDUAL RECORDS—SINGLE GAME

Category	Name	Performance
Rushing (Yds.)	Freeman McNeil, 9-15-85	192
Passing (Yds.)	Joe Namath, 9-24-72	496
Passing (TDs)	Joe Namath, 9-24-72	6
Receiving (No.)	Clark Gaines, 9-21-80	17
Receiving (Yds.)	Don Maynard, 11-17-68	228
Interceptions	Many times	3
	Last time by Marcus Turner, 11-20-94	
Field Goals	Jim Turner, 11-3-68	6
	Bobby Howfield, 12-3-72	6
Touchdowns (Tot.)	Wesley Walker, 9-21-86	4
Points	Wesley Walker, 9-21-86	24

COACHING HISTORY

New York Titans 1960-62
(235-300-8)

1960-61	Sammy Baugh	14-14-0
1962	Clyde (Bulldog) Turner	5-9-0
1963-73	Weeb Ewbank	73-78-6
1974-75	Charley Winner*	9-14-0
1975	Ken Shipp	1-4-0
1976	Lou Holtz**	3-10-0
1976	Mike Holovak	0-1-0
1977-82	Walt Michaels	41-49-1
1983-89	Joe Walton	54-59-1
1990-93	Bruce Coslet	26-39-0
1994	Pete Carroll	6-10-0
1995	Rich Kotite	3-13-0

*Released after nine games in 1975
**Resigned after 13 games in 1976

GIANTS STADIUM

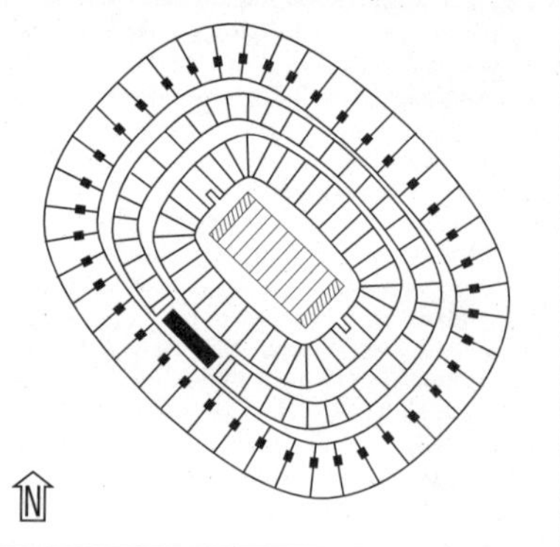

1995 TEAM RECORD

PRESEASON (2-2)

Date	Result		Opponents
8/5	W	9-3	at Tampa Bay
8/12	L	10-13	vs. Philadelphia at Jackson, Miss.
8/19	L	31-32	at N.Y. Giants
8/25	W	30-24	at Cincinnati

REGULAR SEASON (3-13)

Date	Result		Opponents	Att.
9/3	L	14-52	at Miami	71,317
9/10	L	24-27	Indianapolis (OT)	65,134
9/17	W	27-10	Jacksonville	49,970
9/24	L	3-13	at Atlanta	40,778
10/1	L	10-47	Oakland	68,941
10/8	L	10-29	at Buffalo	79,485
10/15	L	15-26	at Carolina	52,613
10/22	W	17-16	Miami	67,228
10/29	L	10-17	at Indianapolis	49,250
11/5	L	7-20	New England	61,462
11/19	L	26-28	Buffalo	54,436
11/26	W	16-10	at Seattle	41,160
12/3	L	20-23	St. Louis	52,023
12/10	L	28-31	at New England	46,617
12/17	L	6-23	at Houston	35,873
12/24	L	0-12	New Orleans	28,885

(OT) Overtime

SCORE BY PERIODS

Jets	37	61	65	70	0	—	233
Opponents	59	128	98	96	3	—	384

ATTENDANCE

Home 448,079 Away 417,093 Total 865,172
Single-game home record, 75,945 (9/20/92)
Single-season home record, 603,619 (1992)

1995 TEAM STATISTICS

	Jets	Opp.
Total First Downs	254	301
Rushing	78	123
Passing	159	149
Penalty	17	29
Third Down: Made/Att	65/223	75/225
Third Down Pct.	29.1	33.3
Fourth Down: Made/Att	10/22	9/14
Fourth Down Pct.	45.5	64.3
Total Net Yards	4067	4756
Avg. Per Game	254.2	297.3
Total Plays	1001	1066
Avg. Per Play	4.1	4.5
Net Yards Rushing	1279	2016
Avg. Per Game	79.9	126.0
Total Rushes	365	526
Net Yards Passing	2788	2740
Avg. Per Game	174.3	171.3
Sacked/Yards Lost	47/341	43/315
Gross Yards	3129	3055
Att./Completions	589/330	497/263
Completion Pct.	56.0	52.9
Had Intercepted	24	17
Punts/Avg.	105/41.2	85/41.1
Net Punting Avg.	105/32.0	85/34.3
Penalties/Yards Lost	121/1078	97/759
Fumbles/Ball Lost	38/18	27/17
Touchdowns	26	42
Rushing	2	15
Passing	20	21
Returns	4	6
Avg. Time of Possession	29:15	30:45

1995 INDIVIDUAL STATISTICS

PASSING	Att.	Comp.	Yds.	Pct.	TD	Int.	Tkld.	Rate
Esiason	389	221	2275	56.8	16	15	27/198	71.4
Brister	170	93	726	54.7	4	8	16/122	53.7
Foley	29	16	128	55.2	0	1	4/21	52.1
Anderson	1	0	0	0.0	0	0	0/0	39.6
Jets	589	330	3129	56.0	20	24	47/341	65.2
Opponents	497	263	3055	52.9	21	17	43/315	71.6

SCORING	TD R	TD P	TD Rt	PAT	FG	Saf	PTS
Lowery	0	0	0	24/24	17/21	0	75
Mitchell	0	5	0	0/0	0/0	0	30
Chrebet	0	4	0	0/0	0/0	0	24
Wilson	0	4	0	0/0	0/0	0	24
Murrell	1	2	0	0/0	0/0	0	18
Brady	0	2	0	0/0	0/0	0	12
Yarborough	0	2	0	0/0	0/0	0	12
F. Baxter	0	1	0	0/0	0/0	0	6
B. Baxter	1	0	0	0/0	0/0	0	6
Brock	0	0	1	0/0	0/0	0	6
G. Jones	0	0	1	0/0	0/0	0	6
Lewis	0	0	1	0/0	0/0	0	6
Smith	0	0	1	0/0	0/0	0	6
Howard	0	0	0	0/0	0/0	1	2
Jets	2	20	4	24/24	17/21	1	233
Opponents	15	21	6	40/41	30/41	1	384

2-Point conversions: 0. Team: 0-2.

RUSHING	Att.	Yds.	Avg.	LG	TD
Murrell	192	795	4.1	30	1
B. Baxter	85	296	3.5	26	1
Moore	43	121	2.8	14	0
Brister	16	18	1.1	7	0
Anderson	5	17	3.4	10	0
Esiason	19	14	0.7	19	0
Foley	1	9	9.0	9	0
May	2	5	2.5	3	0
Rasheed	1	3	3.0	3	0
Chrebet	1	1	1.0	1	0
Jets	365	1279	3.5	30	2
Opponents	526	2016	3.8	49	15

RECEIVING	No.	Yds.	Avg.	LG	TD
Murrell	71	465	6.5	43	2
Chrebet	66	726	11.0	32	4
Mitchell	45	497	11.0	43t	5
Wilson	41	484	11.8	24	4
Brady	26	252	9.7	29	2
B. Baxter	26	160	6.2	20	0
Yarborough	18	230	12.8	38	2
F. Baxter	18	222	12.3	32	1
Moore	8	50	6.3	13	0
Anderson	5	26	5.2	9	0
Rasheed	2	15	7.5	9	0
Davis	1	9	9.0	9	0
Brister	1	2	2.0	2	0
Carter	1	0	0.0	0	0
Foley	1	-9	-9.0	-9	0
Jets	330	3129	9.5	43t	20
Opponents	263	3055	11.6	66t	21

INTERCEPTIONS	No.	Yds.	Avg.	LG	TD
Smith	6	101	16.8	49t	1
G. Jones	2	51	25.5	49t	1
Joseph	2	39	19.5	39	0
Lewis	2	22	11.0	15t	1
Marshall	2	20	10.0	20	0
Glenn	1	17	17.0	17	0
Brock	1	9	9.0	9	0
Green	1	2	2.0	2	0
Jets	17	261	15.4	49t	3
Opponents	24	404	16.8	97t	3

PUNTING	No.	Yds.	Avg.	In 20	LG
Hansen	99	4090	41.3	23	67
Silvestri	5	238	47.6	0	61
Jets	105	4328	41.2	23	67
Opponents	85	3497	41.1	24	63

PUNT RETURNS	No.	FC	Yds.	Avg.	LG	TD
Carter	21	8	145	6.9	20	0
Sydner	17	9	178	10.5	22	0
Jets	38	17	323	8.5	22	0
Opponents	62	13	753	12.1	32	0

KICKOFF RETURNS	No.	Yds.	Avg.	LG	TD
Carter	33	705	21.4	57	0
Carpenter	20	553	27.7	58	0
Moore	8	166	20.8	46	0
F. Baxter	6	36	6.0	12	0
Sydner	4	80	20.0	35	0
Brady	2	25	12.5	14	0
Benfatti	1	25	25.0	25	0
Glenn	1	12	12.0	12	0
Murrell	1	5	5.0	5	0
Smith	1	6	6.0	6	0
Jets	77	1613	20.9	58	0
Opponents	42	987	23.5	42	0

SACKS	No.
Douglas	10.0
Washington	6.0
Brock	5.0
Lewis	5.0
Casillas	3.0
Houston	3.0
Howard	2.5
Barber	2.0
Evans	2.0
Green	2.0
M. Jones	1.5
Marshall	1.0
Jets	43.0
Opponents	47.0

1996 DRAFT CHOICES

Round	Name	Pos.	College
1	Keyshawn Johnson	WR	Southern California
2	Alex Van Dyke	WR	Nevada
3	Ray Mickens	DB	Texas A&M
5	Marcus Coleman	DB	Texas Tech
6	Hugh Hunter	DE	Hampton
7	Chris Hayes	DB	Washington State

NEW YORK JETS

1996 VETERAN ROSTER

No.	Name	Pos.	Ht.	Wt.	Birthdate	NFL Exp.	College	Hometown	How Acq.	'95 Games/ Starts
72	Alexander, Dave	C	6-3	275	7/28/64	10	Tulsa	Broken Arrow, Okla.	FA-'95	0*
20	Anderson, Richie	RB	6-2	225	9/13/71	4	Penn State	Sandy Spring, Md.	D6-'93	10/0
30	Baxter, Brad	RB	6-1	235	5/5/67	7	Alabama State	Slocomb, Ala.	FA-'89	15/13
84	Baxter, Fred	TE	6-3	260	6/14/71	4	Auburn	Brundidge, Ala.	D5a-'93	15/3
78	Benfatti, Lou	DT	6-4	278	3/9/71	3	Penn State	Green Pond, N.J.	D3-'94	12/0
69	Boatswain, Harry	T	6-4	295	6/26/69	6	New Haven	Brooklyn, N.Y.	UFA(Phil)-'96	13/7*
68	Bock, John	C	6-3	285	2/11/71	2	Indiana State	Crystal Lake, Ill.	FA-'95	10/7
81	Brady, Kyle	TE	6-6	260	1/14/72	2	Penn State	New Cumberland, Pa.	D1a-'95	15/11
94	Brock, Matt	DE-DT	6-5	290	1/14/66	8	Oregon	San Diego, Calif.	UFA(GB)-'95	16/15
26	Carpenter, Ron	S	6-1	189	1/20/70	3	Miami, Ohio	Cincinnati, Ohio	FA-'95	13/4
53	Cascadden, Chad	LB	6-1	225	5/14/72	2	Wisconsin	Chippewa Falls, Wis.	FA-'95	12/0
80	Chrebet, Wayne	WR	5-10	180	8/14/73	2	Hofstra	Garfield, N.J.	FA-'95	16/16
59	Clifton, Kyle	LB	6-4	236	8/23/62	13	Texas Christian	Bridgeport, Tex.	D3-'84	16/0
99	Douglas, Hugh	DE	6-2	265	8/23/71	2	Central State, Ohio	Mansfield, Ohio	D1b-'95	15/3
62	Duffy, Roger	G-C	6-3	311	7/16/67	7	Penn State	Canton, Ohio	D8-'90	16/16
76	Elliott, John	T	6-7	308	4/1/65	9	Michigan	Lake Ronkonkoma, N.Y.	UFA(NYG)-'96	16/16*
96	Faulkner, Jeff	DT	6-4	305	4/4/64	7	Southern	St. Thomas, Virgin Islands	FA-'96	0*
4	Foley, Glenn	QB	6-2	210	10/10/70	3	Boston College	Cherry Hill, N.J.	D7-'94	1/0
31	Glenn, Aaron	CB	5-9	185	7/16/72	3	Texas A&M	Aldine, Tex.	D1-'94	16/16
1	Graham, Jeff	WR	6-2	200	2/14/69	6	Ohio State	Kettering, Ohio	UFA(Chi)-'96	16/16*
21	Green, Victor	CB-S	5-9	195	12/8/69	4	Akron	Americus, Ga.	FA-'93	16/12
22	Greenwood, Carl	CB	5-11	186	3/11/72	2	UCLA	Corpus Christi, Tex.	D5-'95	10/0
11	Hansen, Brian	P	6-4	215	10/26/60	12	Sioux Falls	Hawarden, Iowa	UFA(Clev)-'94	16/0
79	Hayes, Melvin	T	6-6	329	4/28/73	2	Mississippi State	New Orleans, La.	D4a-'95	3/0
55	Houston, Bobby	LB	6-2	245	10/26/67	6	North Carolina State	Hyattsville, Md.	PB(Atl)-'91	16/15
74	Howard, Erik	DT-DE	6-4	275	11/12/64	11	Washington State	San Jose, Calif.	UFA(NYG)-'95	16/16
65	Hudson, John	T	6-2	276	1/29/68	7	Auburn	Paris, Tenn.	UFA(Phil)-'96	16/16*
25	Jones, Gary	S	6-1	217	11/30/67	7	Texas A&M	Dallas, Tex.	UFA(Pitt)-'95	11/8
54	Jones, Marvin	LB	6-2	249	6/28/72	4	Florida State	Miami, Fla.	D1-'93	10/10
43	Joseph, Vance	CB	6-0	202	9/20/72	2	Colorado	Marrero, La.	FA-'95	13/6
57	Lewis, Mo	LB	6-3	250	10/21/69	6	Georgia	Peachtree, Ga.	D3-'91	16/16
8	Lowery, Nick	K	6-4	215	5/27/56	17	Dartmouth	Washington, D.C.	FA-'94	14/0
75	Malamala, Siupeli	G-T	6-5	315	1/15/69	5	Washington	Kalaheo, Hawaii	D3-'92	6/4
51	Mason, Eddie	LB	6-0	230	1/9/72	2	North Carolina	Siler City, N.C.	D6-'95	15/0
67	McIver, Everett	G-T	6-6	315	8/5/70	3	Elizabeth City State	Fayetteville, N.C.	FA-'93	14/4
33	Moore, Ronald	RB-KR	5-10	225	1/26/70	4	Pittsburg State	Spencer, Okla.	T(Ariz)-'95	15/3
29	Murrell, Adrian	RB	5-11	214	10/16/70	4	West Virginia	Wahiawa, Hawaii	D5b-'93	15/9
14	O'Donnell, Neil	QB	6-3	226	7/3/66	7	Maryland	Madison, N.J.	UFA(Pitt)-'96	12/12*
70	O'Dwyer, Matt	G	6-5	308	9/1/72	2	Northwestern	Lincolnshire, Ill.	D2-'95	12/2
3	O'Neill, Pat	P-K	6-1	200	2/9/71	3	Syracuse	Harrisburg, Pa.	FA-'95	9/0*
34	Rasheed, Kenyon	RB	5-10	235	8/23/70	3	Oklahoma	Kansas City, Mo.	FA-'95	3/0
7	Reich, Frank	QB	6-4	210	12/4/61	12	Maryland	Lebanon, Pa.	UFA(Car)-'96	3/3*
5	Silvestri, Don	K	6-4	210	12/25/68	2	Pittsburgh	Perkasie, Pa.	FA-'95	16/0
45	Smith, Otis	CB	5-11	190	10/22/65	7	Missouri	New Orleans, La.	UFA(Phil)-'95	11/10
82	Smith, Rico	WR	6-0	185	1/14/69	5	Colorado	Los Angeles, Calif.	UFA(Balt)-'96	4/2*
93	Spindler, Marc	DT-DE	6-5	290	11/28/69	7	Pittsburgh	West Scranton, Pa.	T(TB)-'95	10/4
85	Sydner, Jeff	WR-KR	5-6	177	11/11/69	5	Hawaii	Columbus, Ohio	FA-'95	6/0
97	Washington, Marvin	DE	6-6	280	10/22/65	8	Idaho	Dallas, Tex.	D6a-'89	16/16
73	Williams, David	T	6-5	292	6/21/66	8	Florida	Lakeland, Fla.	FA-'96	10/9*
77	Willig, Matt	T-G	6-8	317	1/21/69	4	Southern California	La Mirada, Calif.	FA-'92	15/12
89	Wilson, Charles	WR	5-10	185	7/1/68	6	Memphis State	Tallahassee, Fla.	T(TB)-'95	15/11
87	Yarborough, Ryan	WR	6-2	195	4/26/71	3	Wyoming	Park Forest, Ill.	D2-'94	16/2
44	Young, Lonnie	CB-S	6-1	196	7/18/63	12	Michigan State	Flint, Mich.	FA-'95	7/0

* Alexander missed '95 season because of injury; Boatswain played 13 games with Philadelphia in '95; Elliott played 16 games with N.Y. Giants; Faulkner last active with New Orleans in '93; Graham played 16 games with Chicago; Hudson played 16 games with Philadelphia; O'Donnell played 12 games with Pittsburgh; O'Neill played 8 games with New England and 1 game with Chicago; Reich played 3 games with Carolina; R. Smith played 4 games with Cleveland; Williams played 10 games with Houston.

Traded—T James Brown to Miami, CB Marcus Turner to Green Bay.

Players lost through free agency (3): C Cal Dixon (Mia; 13 games in '95), QB Boomer Esiason (Ariz; 12), QB Erik Wilhelm (Cin; 0).

Also played with Jets in '95—DE Kurt Barber (6 games), QB Bubby Brister (9), T James Brown (14), LB Glenn Cadrez (1), RB Dexter Carter (10), DT Tony Casillas (11), WR Curtis Ceaser (4), C Cal Dixon (13), QB Boomer Esiason (12), DE Donald Evans (4), G Carlton Haselrig (11), LB Wilber Marshall (15), TE Johnny Mitchell (12), CB Anthony Prior (11), S Todd Scott (10), CB Marcus Turner (6),

COACHING STAFF

Head Coach,
Rich Kotite

Pro Career: Entering his second season as head coach of the New York Jets and sixth as a head coach in the NFL. Kotite rejoined the Jets on January 10, 1995, after spending five years with the Philadelphia Eagles (1990-94), the last four as head coach. Kotite led the Eagles to a 36-28 regular-season record and guided them to their first playoff victory since 1980 when they defeated New Orleans 36-20 in the 1992 NFL Wild Card game. In his first year as a head coach, Kotite led Philadelphia to 10 wins despite losing Randall Cunningham, the starting quarterback, in the first game and playing the rest of the season with four other quarterbacks. The second year, the Eagles won 12 games including a playoff win, despite losing one of their best players, Jerome Brown, in a car crash. In 1993, the Eagles lost 15 starters and still won eight games and went down to the final game of the season before missing the playoffs. As the Eagles' offensive coordinator in 1990, Kotite's squad led the NFL in rushing and topped the NFC in scoring and touchdown passes. Kotite had served previously as the Jets' offensive coordinator and receivers coach from 1985-89 after originally joining the club as receivers coach in 1983. In each of Kotite's years at the helm of the New York offense, the Jets finished near the top in the AFC in total offense, including a third-place ranking in 1985. Kotite began his pro coaching career with the New Orleans Saints in 1977 before joining the Cleveland Browns as a receivers coach from 1978-1982. During his playing days, Kotite was known as a tenacious tight end and outstanding special teams performer with the New York Giants (1967 and 1969-72) and Pittsburgh Steelers (1968). Career record: 40-42.

Background: Attended Poly Prep in Brooklyn, N.Y. After a brief boxing career at the University of Miami where he was the school's heavyweight champion, he served as a sparring partner for Cassius Clay, later known as Muhammad Ali. Kotite became a Little All-America tight end at Wagner College on Staten Island, N.Y.

Personal: Born in Brooklyn on October 13, 1942. He and his wife, Elizabeth, live on Staten Island and have one daughter, Alexandra.

ASSISTANT COACHES

Zeke Bratkowski, assistant to the head coach; born October 20, 1931, Danville, Ill., lives on Long Island, N.Y. Quarterback Georgia 1951-1953. Pro quarterback Chicago Bears 1954, 1957-60, Los Angeles Rams 1961-63, Green Bay Packers 1963-68, 1971. Pro coach: Green Bay Packers 1969-70, 1975-81, Chicago Bears 1972-74, Baltimore-Indianapolis Colts 1982-84, New York Jets 1985-89, Cleveland Browns 1990, Philadelphia Eagles 1991-1994, rejoined Jets in 1995.

Ron Erhardt, offensive coordinator-quarterbacks; born February 27, 1931, Mandan, N.D., lives on Long Island. Quarterback Jamestown (N.D.) College 1951-54. No pro playing experience. College coach: North Dakota State 1963-72 (head coach in 1966-72). Pro coach: New England Patriots 1973-81 (head coach 1979-81), New York Giants 1982-91, Pittsburgh Steelers 1992-1995, joined Jets in 1996.

Chip Falivene, assistant to the head coach; born March 10, 1953, Schenectady, N.Y., lives on Long Island, N.Y. Center Baldwin-Wallace College 1972-74. No pro playing experience. No college coaching experience. Pro coach: Joined Jets in 1995.

Tom Gamble, defensive assistant-quality control; born February 14, 1963, Woodbury, N.J. No college or pro playing experience. Pro coach: Joined Jets in 1995.

Peter Giunta, defensive secondary; born August 11, 1956, Salem, Mass., lives on Long Island, N.Y. Running back-defensive back Northeastern 1974-77. No pro playing experience. College coach: Penn State 1981-83, Brown 1984-87, Lehigh 1988-90. Pro coach: Philadelphia Eagles 1991-1994, joined Jets in 1995.

1996 FIRST-YEAR ROSTER

Name	Pos.	Ht.	Wt.	Birthdate	College	Hometown	How Acq.
Allen, Alan (1)	WR	6-1	186	8/9/71	Idaho	Tacoma, Wash.	FA
Bianchin, Mike	T	6-4	290	12/18/73	Virginia Tech	Pittsburgh, Pa.	FA
Clark, Brian	S	6-3	205	5/5/74	Hofstra	Toms River, N.J.	FA
Coleman, Marcus	S	6-2	208	5/24/74	Texas Tech	Dallas, Tex.	D5
Crawford, Melvin (1)	CB-S	5-11	187	2/18/73	Hampton	Potomac, Md.	FA
Davis, Tyrone (1)	WR	6-4	229	6/30/72	Virginia	Halifax, Va.	D4b-'95
Ellis, Kwame	CB	5-10	185	2/27/74	Stanford	Oakland, Calif.	FA
Frost, Johnny	LB	6-1	252	11/27/73	Louisville	Miami, Fla.	FA
Hayes, Chris	S	5-11	191	5/7/72	Washington State	San Bernadino, Calif.	D7
Howard, Rawle	LB	6-4	260	2/26/72	Lafayette	Bayshore, N.Y.	FA
Hunter, Hugh	DE	6-3	260	6/19/72	Hampton	Portsmouth, Va.	D6
Johnson, Eric	DE	6-4	261	3/31/73	Texas Southern	Dakalb, Miss.	FA
Johnson, Keyshawn	WR	6-3	215	7/22/72	Southern California	Los Angeles, Calif.	D1
Marshall, Malcolm (1)	RB	6-1	240	6/29/72	North Carolina	Winston-Salem, N.C.	FA
May, Sherriden (1)	RB	6-0	215	8/10/73	Idaho	Tacoma, Wash.	FA
Mickens, Ray	CB	5-8	178	1/4/73	Texas A&M	El Paso, Tex.	D3
Owens, Darrick (1)	WR	6-2	200	11/5/70	Mississippi	Tallahassee, Fla.	FA
Paci, John	QB	6-3	218	7/19/72	Indiana	Huntington, N.Y.	FA
Sanders, Dwayne	DE	6-5	244	9/23/74	Washington State	Los Angeles, Calif.	FA
Simpson, Tim (1)	G-C	6-3	296	3/5/69	Illinois	East Peoria, Ill.	FA
Stark, Steve	G	6-3	296	5/16/73	Wisconsin	Rockton, Ill.	FA
Van Dyke, Alex	WR	6-0	200	7/24/74	Nevada	Sacramento, Calif.	D2
Willis, Terrell	RB	5-11	200	7/12/73	Rutgers	Orange, N.J.	FA

The term NFL Rookie is defined as a player who is in his first season of professional football and has not been on the roster of another professional football team for any regular-season or postseason games. A Rookie is designated by an "R" on NFL rosters. Players who have been active in another professional football league or players who have NFL experience, including either preseason training camp or being on an Active List or Inactive List, or on Reserve/Injured or Reserve/Physically Unable to Perform for fewer than six regular-season games, are termed NFL First-Year Players. An NFL First-Year Player is designated by a "1" on NFL rosters. Thereafter, a player is credited with an additional year of experience for each season in which he accumulates six games on the Active List or Inactive List, or on Reserve/Injured or Reserve/Physically Unable to Perform.

NOTES

Ray Hamilton, defensive line; born January 20, 1951, Omaha, Neb., lives on Long Island, N.Y. Nose tackle Oklahoma 1969-72. Pro nose tackle-defensive end New England Patriots 1973-81. College coach: Tennessee 1992. Pro coach: New England Patriots 1985-89, Tampa Bay Buccaneers 1991, Los Angeles Raiders 1993-94, joined Jets in 1995.

Pat Hodgson, tight ends; born January 30, 1944, Columbus, Ga., lives on Long Island. Tight end Georgia 1963-65. Pro tight end Washington Redskins 1966, Minnesota Vikings 1967. College coach: Georgia 1968-70, 1972-77, Florida State 1971, Texas Tech 1978. Pro coach: San Diego Chargers 1978, New York Giants 1979-87, Pittsburgh Steelers 1992-95, joined Jets in 1996.

Richard Mann, receivers; born April 20, 1947, Aliquippa, Pa., lives on Long Island, N.Y. Wide receiver Arizona State 1966-68. No pro playing experience. College coach: Arizona State 1974-79, Louisville 1980-81. Pro coach: Baltimore-Indianapolis Colts 1982-84, Cleveland Browns 1985-93, joined Jets in 1994.

Bill Muir, offensive line; born Ocrtober 26, 1942, Pittsburgh, Pa., lives on Long Island, N.Y. Tackle Susquehanna 1962-64. No pro playing experience. College coach: Susquehanna 1965, Delaware Valley 1966-67. Rhode Island 1970-71, Idaho State 1972-73, Southern Methodist 1976-77. Pro coach: Orlando (Continental Football League) 1968-69, Houston-Shreveport Steamer (WFL) 1975, New England Patriots 1982-84, Detroit Lions 1985-88, Indianapolis Colts 1989-91, Philadelphia Eagles 1992-94, joined Jets in 1995.

Ken Rose, special teams; born June 9, 1962, Sacramento, Calif. lives on Long Island, N.Y. Linebacker Nevada-Las Vegas 1979-82. Pro linebacker Saskatchewan Rough Riders (CFL) 1983-84, Tampa Bay Bandits (USFL) 1986, New York Jets 1987-89, Cleveland Browns 1990, Philadelphia Eagles 1990-94. Pro coach: Joined Jets in 1995.

Jim Vechiarella, defensive coordinator-linebackers; born February 20, 1937, Youngstown, Ohio, lives on Long Island, N.Y. Linebacker Youngstown State 1955-57. No pro playing experience. College coach: Youngstown State 1964-74, Southern Illinois 1976-77, Tulane 1978-80. Pro coach: Charlotte (WFL) 1975, Los Angeles Rams 1981-82, Kansas City Chiefs 1983-85, New York Jets 1986-89, Cleveland Browns 1990, Philadelphia Eagles 1991-94, rejoined Jets in 1995.

Jim Williams, strength and conditioning; born March 29, 1948, Kingston, Pa., lives on Long Island, N.Y. No college or pro playing experience. College coach: Nebraska 1972-74, Arkansas 1974-77, Wyoming 1977-79. Pro coach: New York Giants 1979-81, New York Jets 1982-89, Philadelphia Eagles 1991-1994, rejoined Jets in 1995.

Dick Wood, running backs; born February 2, 1936, Lanett, Ala., lives on Long Island, N.Y. Quarterback Auburn 1956-59. Pro quarterback Baltimore Colts 1960-61, San Diego Chargers 1962, Denver Broncos 1962, New York Jets 1963-64, Oakland Raiders 1965, Miami Dolphins 1966. College coach: Georgia 1967-68, Mississippi 1971-73, Auburn 1986. Pro coach: Oakland Raiders 1969-70, Cleveland Browns 1974, New Orleans Saints 1976-77, Atlanta Falcons 1978-82, Philadelphia Eagles 1983, 1991-94, Kansas City Chiefs 1987-88, New England Patriots 1989-90, joined Jets in 1995.

OAKLAND RAIDERS

American Football Conference
Western Division
Team Colors: Silver and Black
Oakland Office: 1220 Harbor Bay Parkway
Alameda, California 94502
Telephone: (510) 864-5000

CLUB OFFICIALS

President of the Managing General Partner: Al Davis
Executive Assistant: Al LoCasale
Pro Football Scout: George Karras
Legal Affairs: Jeff Birren, Amy Trask
Senior Assistant: Bruce Allen
Finance: Mark Fletcher, Tom Blanda, Marc Badain
Senior Administrator: Morris Bradshaw
Business Manager: John Novak
Senior Executive: John Herrera
Publications: Mike Taylor
Community Relations: Gil Lafferty-Hernandez
Administrative Assistants: Mario Perez, Marc McKinney
Ticket Operations: Peter Eiges
Trainers: H. Rod Martin, Jonathan Jones, Scott Touchet
Equipment Manager: Bob Romanski
Video Director: Dave Nash
Stadium: Oakland-Alameda County Coliseum
•**Capacity:** 62,500
Playing Surface: Grass
Training Camp: Napa Valley Marriott
Napa, California 94558

1996 SCHEDULE

PRESEASON

July 27	at Dallas	8:00
Aug. 2	at Arizona	7:00
Aug. 8	**Seattle**	5:00
Aug. 15	at Atlanta	8:00
Aug. 23	**New York Jets**	7:00

REGULAR SEASON

Sept. 1	at Baltimore	1:00
Sept. 8	at Kansas City	12:00
Sept. 15	**Jacksonville**	1:00
Sept. 22	**San Diego**	1:00
Sept. 29	at Chicago	12:00
Oct. 6	at New York Jets	1:00
Oct. 13	**Detroit**	1:00
Oct. 21	at San Diego (Mon.)	6:00
Oct. 27	Open Date	
Nov. 4	**Denver** (Mon.)	6:00
Nov. 10	at Tampa Bay	1:00
Nov. 17	**Minnesota**	5:00
Nov. 24	at Seattle	1:00
Dec. 1	**Miami**	1:00
Dec. 9	**Kansas City** (Mon.)	6:00
Dec. 15	at Denver	2:00
Dec. 22	**Seattle**	1:00

RECORD HOLDERS

INDIVIDUAL RECORDS—CAREER

Category	Name	Performance
Rushing (Yds.)	Marcus Allen, 1982-1992	8,545
Passing (Yds.)	Ken Stabler, 1970-79	19,078
Passing (TDs)	Ken Stabler, 1970-79	150
Receiving (No.)	Fred Biletnikoff, 1965-1978	589
Receiving (Yds.)	Fred Biletnikoff, 1965-1978	8,974
Interceptions	Willie Brown, 1967-1978	39
	Lester Hayes, 1977-1986	39
Punting (Avg.)	Ray Guy, 1973-1986	42.5
Punt Return (Avg.)	Claude Gibson, 1963-65	12.6
Kickoff Return (Avg.)	Jack Larscheid, 1960-61	28.4
Field Goals	Chris Bahr, 1980-88	162
Touchdowns (Tot.)	Marcus Allen, 1982-1992	98
Points	George Blanda, 1967-1975	863

INDIVIDUAL RECORDS—SINGLE SEASON

Category	Name	Performance
Rushing (Yds.)	Marcus Allen, 1985	1,759
Passing (Yds.)	Ken Stabler, 1979	3,615
Passing (TDs)	Daryle Lamonica, 1969	34
Receiving (No.)	Todd Christensen, 1986	95
Receiving (Yds.)	Art Powell, 1964	1,361
Interceptions	Lester Hayes, 1980	13
Punting (Avg.)	Ray Guy, 1973	45.3
Punt Return (Avg.)	Claude Gibson, 1964	14.4
Kickoff Return (Avg.)	Harold Hart, 1975	30.5
Field Goals	Jeff Jaeger, 1993	*35
Touchdowns (Tot.)	Marcus Allen, 1984	18
Points	Jeff Jaeger, 1993	132

INDIVIDUAL RECORDS—SINGLE GAME

Category	Name	Performance
Rushing (Yds.)	Bo Jackson, 11-30-87	221
Passing (Yds.)	Jeff Hostetler, 10-31-93	424
Passing (TDs)	Tom Flores, 12-22-63	6
	Daryle Lamonica, 10-19-69	6
Receiving (No.)	Dave Casper, 10-3-76	12
	Tim Brown, 12-19-95	12
Receiving (Yds.)	Art Powell, 12-22-63	247
Interceptions	Many times	3
	Last time by Terry McDaniel, 10-9-94	
Field Goals	Jeff Jaeger, 12-11-94	5
Touchdowns (Tot.)	Art Powell, 12-22-63	4
	Marcus Allen, 9-24-84	4
Points	Art Powell, 12-22-63	24
	Marcus Allen, 9-24-84	24

*NFL Record

COACHING HISTORY

OAKLAND 1960-1981
LOS ANGELES 1982-1994
(342-215-11)

1960-61	Eddie Erdelatz*	6-10-0
1961-62	Marty Feldman**	2-15-0
1962	Red Conkright	1-8-0
1963-65	Al Davis	23-16-3
1966-68	John Rauch	35-10-1
1969-78	John Madden	112-39-7
1979-87	Tom Flores	91-56-0
1988-89	Mike Shanahan***	8-12-0
1989-94	Art Shell	56-41-0
1995	Mike White	8-8-0

*Released after two games in 1961
**Released after five games in 1962
***Released after four games in 1989

OAKLAND-ALAMEDA COUNTY COLISEUM

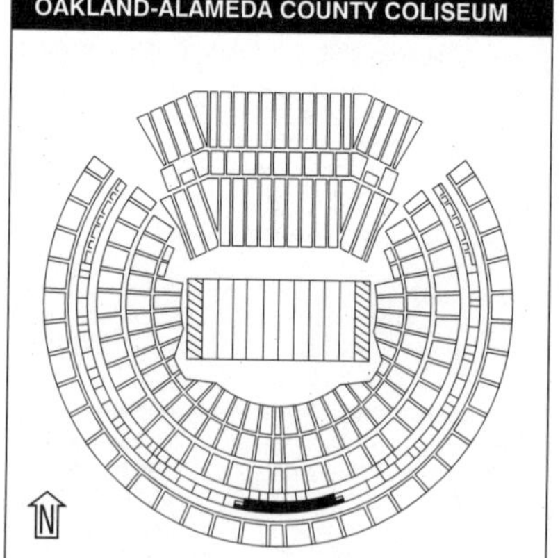

1995 TEAM RECORD

PRESEASON (3-1)

Date	Result		Opponents
8/5	W	27-14	at Dallas
8/12	W	27-22	St. Louis
8/18	L	17-20	at Minnesota
8/25	W	32-24	vs. New England at Stanford,Calif.

REGULAR SEASON (8-8)

Date	Result		Opponents	Att.
9/3	W	17-7	San Diego	50,323
9/10	W	20-8	at Washington	54,548
9/17	L	17-23	at Kansas City (OT)	78,696
9/24	W	48-17	Philadelphia	48,875
10/1	W	47-10	at N.Y. Jets	68,941
10/8	W	34-14	Seattle	50,213
10/16	L	0-27	at Denver	75,491
10/22	W	30-17	Indianapolis	53,543
11/5	W	20-17	at Cincinnati	51,265
11/12	W	17-13	at N.Y. Giants	71,160
11/19	L	21-34	Dallas	54,092
11/27	L	6-12	at San Diego	60,607
12/3	L	23-29	Kansas City	53,930
12/10	L	10-29	Pittsburgh	53,516
12/17	L	10-44	at Seattle	58,428
12/24	L	28-31	Denver	50,074

(OT) Overtime

SCORE BY PERIODS

Raiders	54	112	97	85	0	—	348
Opponents	67	99	88	72	6	—	332

ATTENDANCE

Home 414,556 Away 519,136 Total 933,692

Single-game home record, 91,494 (9/29/91; Los Angeles Memorial Coliseum)

Single-season home record, 516,205 (1986; Los Angeles Memorial Coliseum)

1995 TEAM STATISTICS

	Raiders	Opp.
Total First Downs	317	293
Rushing	104	90
Passing	189	177
Penalty	24	26
Third Down: Made/Att	85/213	69/210
Third Down Pct.	39.9	32.9
Fourth Down: Made/Att	7/14	6/17
Fourth Down Pct.	50.0	35.3
Total Net Yards	5505	5104
Avg. Per Game	344.1	319.0
Total Plays	1042	1016
Avg. Per Play	5.3	5.0
Net Yards Rushing	1932	1794
Avg. Per Game	120.8	112.1
Total Rushes	463	446
Net Yards Passing	3573	3310
Avg. Per Game	223.3	206.9
Sacked/Yards Lost	36/214	43/332
Gross Yards	3787	3642
Att./Completions	543/317	527/301
Completion Pct.	58.4	57.1
Had Intercepted	21	11
Punts/Avg.	76/40.6	70/43.5
Net Punting Avg.	76/34.7	70/36.1
Penalties/Yards Lost	134/1059	94/730
Fumbles/Ball Lost	25/13	37/22
Touchdowns	41	33
Rushing	10	15
Passing	25	14
Returns	6	4
Avg. Time of Possession	30:42	29:18

1995 INDIVIDUAL STATISTICS

PASSING	Att.	Comp.	Yds.	Pct.	TD	Int.	Tkld.	Rate
Hostetler	286	172	1998	60.1	12	9	22/133	82.2
Evans	175	100	1236	57.1	6	8	11/70	71.5
Hobert	80	44	540	55.0	6	4	3/11	80.2
Hobbs	1	0	0	0.0	0	0	0/0	39.6
Williams	1	1	13	100.0	1	0	0/0	158.3
Raiders	543	317	3787	58.4	25	21	36/214	79.0
Opponents	527	301	3642	57.1	14	11	43/332	78.6

SCORING	TD R	TD P	TD Rt	PAT	FG	Saf	PTS
Jaeger	0	0	0	22/22	13/18	0	61
Brown	0	10	0	0/0	0/0	0	60
Williams	9	0	0	0/0	0/0	0	54
Ford	0	0	0	17/18	8/9	0	41
Fenner	0	3	0	0/0	0/0	0	18
Glover	0	3	0	0/0	0/0	0	18
Hobbs	0	3	0	0/0	0/0	0	18
Ismail	0	3	0	0/0	0/0	0	18
Cash	0	2	0	0/0	0/0	0	12
Kaufman	1	0	1	0/0	0/0	0	12
Bruce	0	0	1	0/0	0/0	0	6
Fredrickson	0	0	1	0/0	0/0	0	6
Jett	0	1	0	0/0	0/0	0	6
M. Jones	0	0	1	0/0	0/0	0	6
McDaniel	0	0	1	0/0	0/0	0	6
A. Robbins	0	0	1	0/0	0/0	0	6
Raiders	10	25	6	39/40	21/27	0	348
Opponents	15	14	4	27/29	33/41	1	332

2-Point conversions: 0. Team: 0-1.

RUSHING	Att.	Yds.	Avg.	LG	TD
Williams	255	1114	4.4	60	9
Kaufman	108	490	4.5	28	1
Hostetler	31	119	3.8	18	0
Fenner	39	110	2.8	10	0
Evans	14	36	2.6	11	0
Ismail	6	29	4.8	13	0
C. Jones	5	19	3.8	15	0
E. Ball	2	10	5.0	10	0
Hobert	3	5	1.7	6	0
Raiders	463	1932	4.2	60	10
Opponents	446	1794	4.0	38	15

RECEIVING	No.	Yds.	Avg.	LG	TD
Brown	89	1342	15.1	80t	10
Williams	54	375	6.9	28	0
Hobbs	38	612	16.1	54t	3
Fenner	35	252	7.2	23	3
Ismail	28	491	17.5	73t	3
Glover	26	220	8.5	25	3
Cash	25	254	10.2	23	2
Jett	13	179	13.8	26t	1
Kaufman	9	62	6.9	18	0
Raiders	317	3787	11.9	80t	25
Opponents	301	3642	12.1	52	14

INTERCEPTIONS	No.	Yds.	Avg.	LG	TD
McDaniel	6	46	7.7	42t	1
Hoskins	1	26	26.0	26	0
M. Jones	1	23	23.0	23	0
Fredrickson	1	14	14.0	14	0
Bruce	1	1	1.0	1t	1
Anderson	1	0	0.0	0	0
Raiders	11	110	10.0	42t	2
Opponents	21	344	16.4	74t	2

PUNTING	No.	Yds.	Avg.	In 20	LG
Gossett	75	3089	41.2	22	60
Raiders	76	3089	40.6	22	60
Opponents	70	3044	43.5	25	67

PUNT RETURNS	No.	FC	Yds.	Avg.	LG	TD
Brown	36	9	364	10.1	38	0
Hobbs	1	0	10	10.0	10	0
Raiders	37	9	374	10.1	38	0
Opponents	38	8	294	7.7	32	0

KICKOFF RETURNS	No.	Yds.	Avg.	LG	TD
Ismail	36	706	19.6	43	0
Kaufman	22	572	26.0	84t	1
C. Jones	5	92	18.4	22	0
Hobbs	1	20	20.0	20	0
Raiders	64	1390	21.7	84t	1
Opponents	68	1469	21.6	57	0

SACKS	No.
Swilling	13.0
McGlockton	7.5
A. Smith	7.0
Bruce	5.5
Ball	3.0
A. Robbins	2.0
Wallace	2.0
Biekert	1.0
Holmberg	1.0
Lewis	1.0
Raiders	43.0
Opponents	36.0

1996 DRAFT CHOICES

Round	Name	Pos.	College
1	Rickey Dudley	TE	Ohio State
2	Lance Johnstone	DE	Temple
5	La'Roi Glover	DT	San Diego State
6	Tim Hall	RB	Robert Morris
7	Sedric Clark	LB	Tulsa
	Darius Smith	C	Sam Houston State
	Joey Wylie	G	Stephen F. Austin

OAKLAND RAIDERS

1996 VETERAN ROSTER

No.	Name	Pos.	Ht.	Wt.	Birthdate	NFL Exp.	College	Hometown	How Acq.	'95 Games/ Starts
33	Anderson, Eddie	S	6-1	210	7/22/63	11	Ft. Valley State	Warner Robins, Ga.	FA-'87	14/14
35	Aska, Joe	RB	5-11	235	7/14/72	2	Central Oklahoma	Putnam City, Okla.	D3-'95	1/0
42	# Ball, Eric	RB	6-2	230	7/1/66	8	UCLA	Ypsilanti, Mich.	FA-'95	16/0
93	Ball, Jerry	DT	6-1	320	12/15/64	10	Southern Methodist	Beaumont, Tex.	UFA(Clev)-'94	15/14
54	Biekert, Greg	LB	6-2	240	3/14/69	4	Colorado	Longmont, Colo.	D7-'93	16/14
24	Brown, Larry	CB	5-11	185	11/30/69	6	Texas Christian	Los Angeles, Calif.	UFA(Dall)-'96	16/15*
81	Brown, Tim	WR	6-0	195	7/22/66	9	Notre Dame	Dallas, Tex.	D1-'88	16/16
99	Bruce, Aundray	DE	6-5	265	4/30/66	9	Auburn	Montgomery, Ala.	PB(Atl)-'92	14/0
49	Carrington, Darren	S	6-2	200	10/10/66	8	Northern Arizona	Bronx, N.Y.	FA-'96	6/2*
88	Cash, Kerry	TE	6-4	245	8/7/69	6	Texas	San Antonio, Tex.	UFA(Ind)-'95	16/10
59	Dyson, Matt	DE	6-3	275	8/1/72	2	Michigan	La Plata, Md.	D5-'95	4/0
34	Fenner, Derrick	RB	6-3	240	4/6/67	8	North Carolina	Oxon Hill, Md.	UFA(Cin)-'95	16/10
55	Folston, James	LB	6-3	235	8/14/71	3	Northeast Louisiana	Cocoa, Fla.	D2-'94	14/0
5	Ford, Cole	K	6-2	205	12/31/72	2	Southern California	Tucson, Ariz.	FA-'95	5/0
53	Fredrickson, Rob	LB	6-4	240	5/13/71	3	Michigan State	St. Joseph, Mich.	D1-'94	16/15
70	Freeman, Russell	T	6-7	295	9/2/69	5	Georgia Tech	Homestead, Pa.	FA-'95	15/1
87	Glover, Andrew	TE	6-6	250	8/12/67	6	Grambling State	Geismar, La.	D10-'91	16/9
66	Gogan, Kevin	G	6-7	325	11/2/64	10	Washington	San Francisco, Calif.	UFA(Dall)-'94	16/16
7	Gossett, Jeff	P	6-2	195	1/25/57	15	Eastern Illinois	Charleston, Ill.	T(Hou)-'88	16/0
75	Harlow, Pat	T	6-6	290	3/16/69	6	Southern California	Norco, Calif.	T(NE)-'96	10/0*
74	Harrison, Nolan	DT	6-5	280	1/25/69	6	Indiana	Flossmoor, Ill.	D6-'91	7/6
80	Hobbs, Daryl	WR	6-2	175	5/23/68	4	Pacific	Los Angeles, Calif.	FA-'93	16/3
9	Hobert, Billy Joe	QB	6-3	230	1/8/71	4	Washington	Puyallup, Wash.	D3-'93	4/2
57	Holmberg, Rob	LB	6-3	230	5/6/71	3	Penn State	Mt. Pleasant, Pa.	D7-'94	16/0
15	Hostetler, Jeff	QB	6-3	215	4/22/61	13	West Virginia	Davidsville, Pa.	UFA(NYG)-'93	11/11
86	† Ismail, Raghib	WR	5-11	180	11/18/69	4	Notre Dame	Wilkes-Barre, Pa.	D4-'91	16/15
18	Jaeger, Jeff	K	5-11	195	11/26/64	10	Washington	Kent, Wash.	PB(Clev)-'89	11/0
64	Jenkins, Robert	T	6-5	295	12/30/63	10	UCLA	Dublin, Calif.	FA-'94	15/13
82	Jett, James	WR	5-10	165	12/28/70	4	West Virginia	Kearneysville, W.Va.	FA-'93	16/0
44	Jones, Calvin	RB	5-11	205	11/27/70	3	Nebraska	Omaha, Neb.	D3-'94	8/0
52	Jones, Mike	LB	6-1	230	4/15/69	6	Missouri	Kansas City, Mo.	FA-'91	16/16
26	Kaufman, Napoleon	RB	5-9	180	6/7/73	2	Washington	Lompoc, Calif.	D1-'95	16/1
72	Kennedy, Lincoln	T	6-6	350	2/12/71	4	Washington	San Diego, Calif.	T(Atl)-'96	16/4*
46	Kidd, Carl	CB	6-1	205	6/14/73	2	Arkansas	Pine Bluff, Ark.	FA-'95	13/0
31	King, Joe	S	6-2	200	5/7/68	5	Oklahoma State	Dallas, Tex.	FA-'95	16/2
79	Kysar, Jeff	T	6-7	330	6/14/72	2	Arizona State	San Diego, Calif.	D5-'95	1/0
25	Land, Dan	S	6-0	195	7/3/65	8	Albany State	Donalsonville, Ga.	FA-'89	16/3
29	Lewis, Albert	CB	6-2	200	10/6/60	14	Grambling State	Mansfield, La.	UFA(KC)-'94	16/15
43	Lynch, Lorenzo	S	5-11	200	4/6/63	10	Cal State-Sacramento	Oakland, Calif.	FA-'96	13/12*
97	Maryland, Russell	DT	6-1	285	3/22/69	6	Miami	Chicago, Ill.	UFA(Dall)-'96	13/13*
36	McDaniel, Terry	CB	5-10	180	2/8/65	9	Tennessee	Saginaw, Mich.	D1-'88	16/16
91	McGlockton, Chester	DT	6-4	320	9/16/69	5	Clemson	Whiteville, N.C.	D1-'92	16/16
73	McRae, Charles	T	6-7	305	9/16/68	6	Tennessee	Clinton, Tenn.	UFA(TB)-'96	11/4*
50	Morton, Mike	LB	6-4	235	3/28/72	2	North Carolina	Kannapolis, N.C.	D4-'95	12/0
39	Pickens, Bruce	CB	5-11	190	5/9/68	5	Nebraska	Kansas City, Mo.	FA-'95	16/1
95	Robbins, Austin	DT	6-6	290	3/1/71	3	North Carolina	Washington, D.C.	D4-'94	16/0
63	Robbins, Barret	C	6-3	305	8/26/73	2	Texas Christian	Houston, Tex.	D2-'95	16/0
94	Smith, Anthony	DE	6-3	265	6/28/67	7	Arizona	Elizabeth City, N.C.	D1-'90	16/12
77	† Stephens, Rich	T	6-7	315	1/1/65	4	Tulsa	House Springs, Mo.	FA-'92	13/1
56	Swilling, Pat	DE	6-3	245	10/25/64	11	Georgia Tech	Toccoa, Ga.	UFA(Det)-'95	16/16
27	Trapp, James	CB	6-0	185	12/28/69	4	Clemson	Lawton, Okla.	D3-'93	14/2
17	Truitt, Orlanda	WR	6-0	195	1/4/71	4	Mississippi State	Birmingham, Ala.	FA-'96	5/2*
67	Turk, Dan	C	6-4	290	8/25/62	12	Wisconsin	Milwaukee, Wis.	FA-'89	16/16
22	Williams, Harvey	RB	6-2	215	4/22/67	6	Louisiana State	Hempstead, Tex.	UFA(KC)-'94	16/16
76	Wisniewski, Steve	G	6-4	295	4/7/67	8	Penn State	Houston, Tex.	D2-'89	16/16

* L. Brown played 16 games with Dallas in '95; Carrington played 6 games with Jacksonville; Harlow played 10 games with New England; Kennedy played 16 games with Atlanta; Lynch played 13 games with Arizona; Maryland played 13 games with Dallas; McRae played 11 games with Tampa Bay; Truitt played 5 games with Washington.

\# Unrestricted free agent; subject to developments.

† Restricted free agent; subject to developments.

Traded—CB-S Patrick Bates to Atlanta.

t- Raiders traded for Harlow (New England) and Kennedy (Atlanta).

Retired—Don Mosebar, 13-year center, last active with Raiders in '94.

Players lost through free agency (2): T Greg Skrepenak (Car; 14 games in '95), DE Aaron Wallace (Den; 16).

Also played with Raiders in '95—QB Vince Evans (9 games), LB Keith Franklin (2), S Derrick Hoskins (13), CB Najee Mustafaa (12), T Gerald Perry (3).

COACHING STAFF

Head Coach,
Mike White

Pro Career: Named tenth head coach in Raiders history on February 2, 1995, after five years as an assistant coach with the organization. First joined Raiders in 1990 as quarterback coach. In 1992, he became offensive line coach. During these five seasons Raiders were 47-33 in league play and made AFC playoffs three times (1990, 1991, 1993). First came into pro coaching as an assistant with San Francisco 49ers in 1978-79 on Bill Walsh's staff.
Background: Offensive end at California 1955-57. Also lettered in basketball and track while earning degree in business. Began a 37-year coaching career at California as an assistant coach in 1958. He then joined staff at Stanford University as an assistant coach in 1964, remaining there through 1972, including Rose Bowl seasons of 1970 and 1971. In 1973, was named head coach at California where he remained through 1977, building 31-23-0 record. Was named college football coach-of-the-year in 1975. In 1980, was selected as head coach at Illinois, serving in that capacity through 1987 with a record of 47-38-3, earning berths in the Rose Bowl, Liberty Bowl, and Peach Bowl. He also coached in 11 college all-star games—two East-West Shrine Games, two Hula Bowls, two Blue-Grey games, and five Japan Bowls. Leaving college coaching after the 1987 season, he spent the next two years with the National Football League helping to plan and organize the World League of American Football before coming to the Raiders in April, 1990.
Personal: Born January 4, 1936, Berkeley, Calif. Mike and wife, Marilyn, live in Alameda, Calif. Their family includes daughter Carrie and sons Chris and Matt.

ASSISTANT COACHES

Fred Biletnikoff, quality control-offense; born February 23, 1943, Erie, Pa., lives in Danville, Calif. Wide receiver Florida State 1962-64. Pro wide receiver Oakland Raiders 1965-78, Montreal Alouettes (CFL) 1980. College coach: Palomar, (Calif.), J.C. 1983, Diablo Valley, (Calif.), J.C. 1984, 1986. Pro coach: Oakland Invaders (USFL) 1985, Calgary Stampeders (CFL) 1987-88, joined Raiders in 1989.
Willie Brown, squad development; born December 2, 1940, Yazoo City, Miss., lives in San Ramon, Calif. Defensive back Grambling 1959-62. Pro defensive back Denver Broncos 1963-66, Oakland Raiders 1967-78. College coach: Long Beach State 1990-91 (head coach 1991). Pro coach: Oakland/Los Angeles Raiders 1979-88, re-joined Raiders in 1995.
Joe Bugel, assistant head coach-offense; born March 10, 1940, Pittsburgh, Pa., lives in Danville, Calif. Offensive guard at Western Kentucky 1960-62. No pro playing experience. College coach: Western Kentucky 1964-68, Navy 1969-72, Iowa State 1973, Ohio State 1974. Pro coach: Detroit Lions 1975-76, Houston Oilers 1977-80, Washington Redskins 1981-89, Phoenix Cardinals 1990-93 (head coach), joined Raiders in 1995.
John Fox, defensive coordinator; born February 8, 1955, Virginia Beach, Va., lives in Alameda, Calif. Defensive back San Diego State 1975-77. No pro playing experience. College coach: U.S. International 1979, Boise State 1980, Long Beach State 1981, Utah 1982, Kansas 1983, 1985, Iowa State 1984, Pittsburgh 1986-88. Pro coach: Los Angeles Express (USFL) 1985, Pittsburgh Steelers 1989-91, San Diego Chargers 1992-93, joined Raiders in 1994.
Garrett Giemont, strength and conditioning; born August 31, 1957, Fullerton, Calif., lives in Alameda, Calif. No college or pro playing experience. Pro coach: Los Angeles Rams 1990-91, joined Raiders in 1995.
John Guy, defensive assistant; born May 26, 1951, Greensboro, N.C., lives in Alameda, Calif. Defensive back-kicker North Carolina A&T 1969-72. No pro playing experience. College coach: North Carolina 1973-77, Virginia Tech 1978, Duke 1978-80, Georgia Tech 1981-86, Alabama 1987-89, Kentucky 1990-91. Pro coach: Pittsburgh Steelers 1992-93, joined Raiders in 1995.
Bishop Harris, running backs; born November 23, 1941, Phenix City, Ala., lives in Alameda, Calif. Running back and defensive back North Carolina College 1960-63. No pro playing experience. College coach: Duke 1972-75, North Carolina State 1977-79, Louisiana State 1980-83, Notre Dame 1984-85, Minnesota 1986-90, North Carolina Central 1991-92 (head coach). Pro coach: Denver Broncos 1993-94, joined Raiders in 1995.
Larry Kennan, quarterbacks; born June 13, 1944, Pomona, Calif., lives in Alameda, Calif. Quarterback LaVerne College 1962-65. No pro playing experience. College coach: Colorado 1969-71, Nevada-Las Vegas 1973-75, Southern Methodist 1976-77, Lamar 1978-81 (head coach). Pro coach: Los Angeles Raiders 1982-87, Denver Broncos 1988, Indianapolis Colts 1989-90, London Monarchs (World League) 1991 (head coach), Seattle Seahawks 1992-94, New Orleans Saints 1995, re-joined Raiders in 1996.
Bill Meyers, tight ends; born October 8, 1946, Chippewa Falls, Wis., lives in Alameda, Calif. Tackle Stanford 1970-71. No pro playing experience. College coach: California 1972-73, 1977-78, Santa Clara 1974-76, Notre Dame 1979-81, Missouri 1985-86, Pittsburgh 1987-92. Pro coach: Green Bay Packers 1982-83, Pittsburgh Steelers 1984, joined Raiders in 1993.
Floyd Peters, defensive line; born May 21, 1936, Council Bluffs, Iowa, lives in Alameda, Calif. Defensive lineman San Francisco State 1954-57. Defensive tackle Baltimore Colts 1958, Cleveland Browns 1959-62, Detroit Lions 1963, Philadelphia Eagles 1964-69, Washington Redskins 1970. Pro coach Miami Dolphins 1971-73, New York Giants 1974-75, San Francisco 49ers 1976-77, Detroit Lions 1978-81, St. Louis Cardinals 1982-85, Minnesota Vikings 1986-90, Tampa Bay Buccaneers 1991-94, joined Raiders in 1995.
Steve Shafer, defensive backs; born December 8, 1940, Glendale, Calif., lives in Alameda, Calif. Quarterback-defensive back Utah State 1961-62. Pro defensive back British Columbia Lions (CFL) 1963-67. College coach: San Mateo (Calif.) J.C. 1968-74 (head coach 1973-74), San Diego State 1975-82, 1994. Pro coach: Los Angeles Rams 1983-90, Tampa Bay Buccaneers 1991-93, joined Raiders in 1995.
Kevin Spencer, quality control-defense; born November 2, 1953, Queens, N.Y., lives in Alameda, Calif. No college or pro playing experience. College coach: State University of New York 1975-76, Cornell 1979-80. Ithaca 1981-86, Wesleyan 1987-91 (head coach). Pro coach: Cleveland Browns 1991-94, joined Raiders in 1995.
Rusty Tillman, special teams; born February 27, 1946, Beloit, Wis., lives in Alameda, Calif. Linebacker Arizona 1966-67, Northern Arizona 1968-69. Pro linebacker Washington Redskins 1970-77. Pro coach: Seattle Seahawks 1979-94, Tampa Bay Buccaneers 1995, joined Raiders in 1996.
Fred Whittingham, linebackers; born February 4, 1939, Boston, Mass., lives in Alameda, Calif. Tight end-linebacker Brigham Young 1957-58, Cal Poly-SLO 1961-62. Pro linebacker Los Angeles Rams 1963-64, Philadelphia Eagles 1965-66, 1971, New Orleans Saints 1967-70. College coach: Brigham Young 1973-81, Utah 1992-94. Pro coach: Los Angeles Rams 1982-91, joined Raiders in 1995.
Mike Wilson, wide receivers; born December 19, 1958, Los Angeles, Calif., lives in Alameda, Calif. Wide receiver Washington State 1977-80. Pro wide receiver San Francisco 49ers 1981-90. College coach: Stanford 1992-94. Pro coach: Joined Raiders in 1995.

1996 FIRST-YEAR ROSTER

Name	Pos.	Ht.	Wt.	Birthdate	College	Hometown	How Acq.
Bobo, Phillip (1)	WR	5-11	205	12/6/71	Washington State	Moreno Valley, Calif.	FA
Bussey, Kendall	RB	6-1	230	2/14/73	Northeast Louisiana	Marrero, La.	FA
Caswell, A.C. (1)	WR	5-9	165	9/17/68	Glendale C.C.	Phoenix, Ariz.	FA
Clark, Sedric	LB	6-2	245	1/28/73	Tulsa	Missouri City, Tex.	D7
Cotton, Curtis (1)	S	5-11	210	10/15/69	Nebraska	Omaha, Neb.	FA
Dudley, Rickey	TE	6-6	245	7/15/72	Ohio State	Hendersonville, Tex.	D1
Foster, Sean (1)	WR	6-0	190	12/22/67	Long Beach State	Los Angeles, Calif.	FA
Franklin, Keith (1)	LB	6-2	230	3/4/70	South Carolina	Los Angeles, Calif.	FA
Glover, La'Roi	DT	6-1	280	7/4/74	San Diego State	San Diego, Calif.	D5
Hall, Tim	RB	5-11	220	2/15/74	Robert Morris	Kansas City, Mo.	D6
Hinton, Marcus (1)	TE	6-4	260	12/27/71	Alcorn State	Wiggins, Miss.	FA
Johnstone, Lance	DE	6-4	245	6/11/73	Temple	Philadelphia, Pa.	D2
Montez, Alfred	QB	6-2	225	10/18/72	Western New Mexico	Grenada, Colo.	FA
Morton, John (1)	WR	6-0	185	9/24/69	Western Michigan	Auburn Hills, Mich.	FA
Robsock, Tom (1)	G	6-4	280	12/1/71	West Virginia	Berwick, Pa.	FA
Smith, Darius	C	6-2	285	10/9/72	Sam Houston State	Dallas, Tex.	D7
Wylie, Joey	C	6-3	290	4/25/74	Stephen F. Austin	Sante Fe, Tex.	D7

The term NFL Rookie is defined as a player who is in his first season of professional football and has not been on the roster of another professional football team for any regular-season or postseason games. A Rookie is designated by an "R" on NFL rosters. Players who have been active in another professional football league or players who have NFL experience, including either preseason training camp or being on an Active List or Inactive List, or on Reserve/Injured or Reserve/Physically Unable to Perform for fewer than six regular-season games, are termed NFL First-Year Players. An NFL First-Year Player is designated by a "1" on NFL rosters. Thereafter, a player is credited with an additional year of experience for each season in which he accumulates six games on the Active List or Inactive List, or on Reserve/Injured or Reserve/Physically Unable to Perform.

NOTES

PITTSBURGH STEELERS

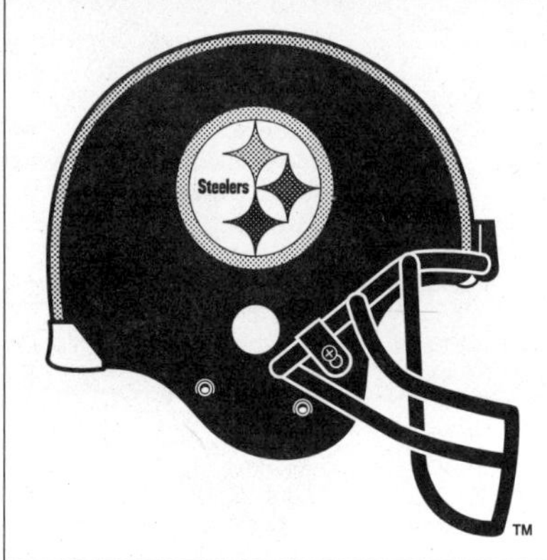

American Football Conference
Central Division
Team Colors: Black and Gold
Three Rivers Stadium
300 Stadium Circle
Pittsburgh, Pennsylvania 15212
Telephone: (412) 323-1200

CLUB OFFICIALS

President: Daniel M. Rooney
Vice President: John R. McGinley
Vice President: Arthur J. Rooney, Jr.
Vice President/General Counsel: Arthur J. Rooney II
Administration Advisor: Charles H. Noll
Director of Marketing: Joe Gordon
Public Relations Coordinator: Rob Boulware
Controller: Michael J. Hagan
Assistant Controller: Dan Ferens
Assistant Controller: Jim Ellenberger
Director of Football Operations: Tom Donahoe
College Personnel Coordinator: Tom Modrak
Pro Personnel Coordinator: Charles Bailey
College Scouts: Phil Kreidler, Bob Lane, Max McCartney, Bob Schmitz
Office/Ticket Manager: Geraldine R. Glenn
Player Development Coordinator: Anthony Griggs
Trainers: John Norwig, Rick Burkholder
Equipment Manager: Anthony Parisi
Equipment/Field Manager: Rodgers Freyvogel
Stadium: Three Rivers Stadium
•**Capacity:** 59,600
300 Stadium Circle
Pittsburgh, Pennsylvania 15212
Playing Surface: AstroTurf
Training Camp: St. Vincent College
Latrobe, Pennsylvania 15650

1996 SCHEDULE

PRESEASON

July 27	vs. San Diego at Tokyo, Japan	10:00
Aug. 3	**St. Louis**	6:00
Aug. 11	at Green Bay	7:00
Aug. 17	**Tampa Bay**	6:00
Aug. 23	at Philadelphia	7:30

REGULAR SEASON

Sept. 1	at Jacksonville	1:00
Sept. 8	**Baltimore**	1:00
Sept. 16	**Buffalo** (Mon.)	9:00
Sept. 22	Open Date	
Sept. 29	**Houston**	1:00
Oct. 7	at Kansas City (Mon.)	8:00
Oct. 13	**Cincinnati**	1:00
Oct. 20	at Houston	3:00
Oct. 27	at Atlanta	1:00
Nov. 3	**St. Louis**	1:00
Nov. 10	at Cincinnati	1:00
Nov. 17	**Jacksonville**	1:00
Nov. 25	at Miami (Mon.)	9:00
Dec. 1	at Baltimore	1:00
Dec. 8	**San Diego**	1:00
Dec. 15	**San Francisco**	1:00
Dec. 22	at Carolina	1:00

RECORD HOLDERS

INDIVIDUAL RECORDS—CAREER

Category	Name	Performance
Rushing (Yds.)	Franco Harris, 1972-1983	11,950
Passing (Yds.)	Terry Bradshaw, 1970-1983	27,989
Passing (TDs)	Terry Bradshaw, 1970-1983	212
Receiving (No.)	John Stallworth, 1974-1987	537
Receiving (Yds.)	John Stallworth, 1974-1987	8,723
Interceptions	Mel Blount, 1970-1983	57
Punting (Avg.)	Bobby Joe Green, 1960-61	45.7
Punt Return (Avg.)	Bobby Gage, 1949-1950	14.9
Kickoff Return (Avg.)	Lynn Chandnois, 1950-56	29.6
Field Goals	Gary Anderson, 1982-1994	309
Touchdowns (Tot.)	Franco Harris, 1972-1983	100
Points	Gary Anderson, 1982-1994	1,343

INDIVIDUAL RECORDS—SINGLE SEASON

Category	Name	Performance
Rushing (Yds.)	Barry Foster, 1992	1,690
Passing (Yds.)	Terry Bradshaw, 1979	3,724
Passing (TDs)	Terry Bradshaw, 1978	28
Receiving (No.)	Yancey Thigpen, 1995	85
Receiving (Yds.)	John Stallworth, 1984	1,395
Interceptions	Mel Blount, 1975	11
Punting (Avg.)	Bobby Joe Green, 1961	47.0
Punt Return (Avg.)	Bobby Gage, 1949	16.0
Kickoff Return (Avg.)	Lynn Chandnois, 1952	35.2
Field Goals	Norm Johnson, 1995	34
Touchdowns (Tot.)	Louis Lipps, 1985	15
Points	Norm Johnson, 1995	141

INDIVIDUAL RECORDS—SINGLE GAME

Category	Name	Performance
Rushing (Yds.)	John Fuqua, 12-20-70	218
Passing (Yds.)	Bobby Layne, 12-3-58	409
Passing (TDs)	Terry Bradshaw, 11-15-81	5
	Mark Malone, 9-8-85	5
Receiving (No.)	J.R. Wilburn, 10-22-67	12
Receiving (Yds.)	Buddy Dial, 10-22-61	235
Interceptions	Jack Butler, 12-13-53	*4
Field Goals	Gary Anderson, 10-23-88	6
Touchdowns (Tot.)	Ray Mathews, 10-17-54	4
	Roy Jefferson, 11-3-68	4
Points	Ray Mathews, 10-17-54	24
	Roy Jefferson, 11-3-68	24

*NFL Record

COACHING HISTORY

Pittsburgh Pirates 1933-1940
(416-437-20)

1933	Forrest (Jap) Douds	3-6-2
1934	Luby DiMelio	2-10-0
1935-36	Joe Bach	10-14-0
1937-39	Johnny (Blood) McNally*	6-19-0
1939-40	Walt Kiesling	3-13-3
1941	Bert Bell**	0-2-0
	Aldo (Buff) Donelli***	0-5-0
1941-44	Walt Kiesling****	13-20-2
1945	Jim Leonard	2-8-0
1946-47	Jock Sutherland	13-10-1
1948-51	Johnny Michelosen	20-26-2
1952-53	Joe Bach	11-13-0
1954-56	Walt Kiesling	14-22-0
1957-64	Raymond (Buddy) Parker	51-48-6
1965	Mike Nixon	2-12-0
1966-68	Bill Austin	11-28-3
1969-91	Chuck Noll	209-156-1
1992-95	Bill Cowher	46-25-0

*Released after three games in 1939
**Resigned after two games in 1941
***Released after five games in 1941
****Co-coach with Earle (Greasy) Neale in Philadelphia-Pittsburgh merger in 1943 and with Phil Handler in Chicago Cardinals-Pittsburgh merger in 1944

THREE RIVERS STADIUM

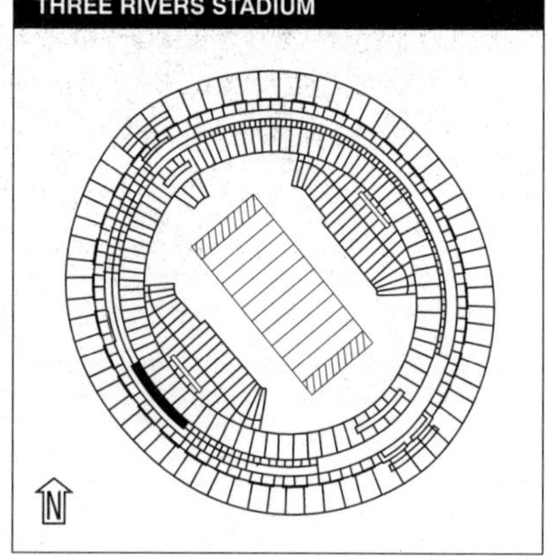

1995 TEAM RECORD

PRESEASON (1-3)

Date	Result		Opponents
8/4	W	31-10	at Buffalo
8/13	L	13-36	Green Bay
8/19	L	7-20	at Tampa Bay
8/24	L	6-16	Philadelphia

REGULAR SEASON (11-5)

Date	Result		Opponents	Att.
9/3	W	23-20	Detroit	58,002
9/10	W	34-17	at Houston	44,122
9/18	L	10-23	at Miami	72,874
9/24	L	24-44	Minnesota	57,853
10/1	W	31-16	San Diego	57,012
10/8	L	16-20	at Jacksonville	72,042
10/19	L	9-27	Cincinnati	56,684
10/29	W	24-7	Jacksonville	54,516
11/5	W	37-34	at Chicago (OT)	61,838
11/13	W	20-3	Cleveland	58,675
11/19	W	49-31	at Cincinnati	54,636
11/26	W	20-17	at Cleveland	67,269
12/3	W	21-7	Houston	56,013
12/10	W	29-10	at Oakland	53,516
12/16	W	41-27	New England	57,158
12/24	L	19-24	at Green Bay	60,649

POSTSEASON (2-1)

Date	Result		Opponents	Att.
1/6	W	40-21	Buffalo	59,072
1/14	W	20-16	Indianapolis	61,062
1/28	L	17-27	Dallas	76,347

(OT) Overtime

SCORE BY PERIODS

Steelers	72	137	60	135	3	—	407
Opponents	33	124	109	61	0	—	327

ATTENDANCE

Home 455,913 Away 486,946 Total 942,859
Single-game home record, 60,808 (12/18/94)
Single-season home record, 471,306 (1992)

1995 TEAM STATISTICS

	Steelers	Opp.
Total First Downs	344	272
Rushing	117	67
Passing	193	181
Penalty	34	24
Third Down: Made/Att	97/230	68/202
Third Down Pct.	42.2	33.7
Fourth Down: Made/Att	11/20	8/13
Fourth Down Pct.	55.0	61.5
Total Net Yards	5769	4561
Avg. Per Game	360.6	285.1
Total Plays	1110	943
Avg. Per Play	5.2	4.8
Net Yards Rushing	1852	1321
Avg. Per Game	115.8	82.6
Total Rushes	494	370
Net Yards Passing	3917	3240
Avg. Per Game	244.8	202.5
Sacked/Yards Lost	24/176	42/272
Gross Yards	4093	3512
Att./Completions	592/348	531/314
Completion Pct.	58.8	59.1
Had Intercepted	21	22
Punts/Avg.	59/40.1	85/43.3
Net Punting Avg.	59/33.3	85/36.3
Penalties/Yards Lost	109/839	101/931
Fumbles/Ball Lost	24/13	30/12
Touchdowns	44	37
Rushing	17	9
Passing	21	24
Returns	6	4
Avg. Time of Possession	32:36	27:24

1995 INDIVIDUAL STATISTICS

PASSING	Att.	Comp.	Yds.	Pct.	TD	Int.	Tkld.	Rate
O'Donnell	416	246	2970	59.1	17	7	15/126	87.7
Tomczak	113	65	666	57.5	1	9	6/42	44.3
Miller	56	32	397	57.1	2	5	2/8	53.9
Stewart	7	5	60	71.4	1	0	1/0	136.9
Steelers	592	348	4093	58.8	21	21	24/176	76.9
Opponents	531	314	3512	59.1	24	22	42/272	76.7

SCORING	TD R	TD P	TD Rt	PAT	FG	Saf	PTS
N. Johnson	0	0	0	39/39	34/41	0	141
Morris	9	0	0	0/0	0/0	0	54
Mills	0	8	0	0/0	0/0	0	48
Pegram	5	1	0	0/0	0/0	0	38
Thigpen	0	5	0	0/0	0/0	0	30
Bruener	0	3	0	0/0	0/0	0	18
Hastings	0	1	1	0/0	0/0	0	12
Stewart	1	1	0	0/0	0/0	0	12
Avery	0	1	0	0/0	0/0	0	6
Buckner	0	0	1	0/0	0/0	0	6
Lake	0	0	1	0/0	0/0	0	6
Lester	1	0	0	0/0	0/0	0	6
A. Mays	0	0	1	0/0	0/0	0	6
McAfee	1	0	0	0/0	0/0	0	6
Oldham	0	0	1	0/0	0/0	0	6
J. Williams	0	1	0	0/0	0/0	0	6
W. Williams	0	0	1	0/0	0/0	0	6
Steelers	17	21	6	39/39	34/41	0	407
Opponents	9	24	4	34/34	23/25	0	327

2-Point conversions: Pegram. Team: 1-5.

RUSHING	Att.	Yds.	Avg.	LG	TD
Pegram	213	813	3.8	38	5
Morris	148	559	3.8	30t	9
McAfee	39	156	4.0	22t	1
J. Williams	29	110	3.8	31	0
Stewart	15	86	5.7	22t	1
O'Donnell	24	45	1.9	14	0
Mills	5	39	7.8	20	0
Tomczak	11	25	2.3	11	0
Hastings	1	14	14.0	14	0
Lester	5	9	1.8	3	1
Avery	1	3	3.0	3	0
Miller	1	2	2.0	2	0
Thigpen	1	1	1.0	1	0
C. Johnson	1	-10	-10.0	-10	0
Steelers	494	1852	3.7	38	17
Opponents	370	1321	3.6	58t	9

RECEIVING	No.	Yds.	Avg.	LG	TD
Thigpen	85	1307	15.4	43	5
Hastings	48	502	10.5	36	1
Mills	39	679	17.4	62t	8
C. Johnson	38	432	11.4	33	0
Bruener	26	238	9.2	29	3
Pegram	26	206	7.9	22	1
J. Williams	24	127	5.3	20	1
McAfee	15	88	5.9	18	0
Stewart	14	235	16.8	71t	1
Hayes	11	113	10.3	32	0
Avery	11	82	7.5	18t	1
Morris	8	36	4.5	13	0
Barnes	3	48	16.0	25	0
Steelers	348	4093	11.8	71t	21
Opponents	314	3512	11.2	76t	24

INTERCEPTIONS	No.	Yds.	Avg.	LG	TD
W. Williams	7	122	17.4	63t	1
Perry	4	71	17.8	26	0
Lloyd	3	85	28.3	52	0
A. Mays	2	35	17.5	32t	1
Bell	2	4	2.0	4	0
Lake	1	32	32.0	32t	1
Oldham	1	12	12.0	12	0
K. Greene	1	0	0.0	0	0
Seals	1	0	0.0	0	0
Steelers	22	361	16.4	63t	3
Opponents	21	185	8.8	60t	3

PUNTING	No.	Yds.	Avg.	In 20	LG
Stark	59	2368	40.1	20	64
Steelers	59	2368	40.1	20	64
Opponents	85	3682	43.3	19	66

PUNT RETURNS	No.	FC	Yds.	Avg.	LG	TD
Hastings	48	8	474	9.9	72t	1
Steelers	48	8	474	9.9	72t	1
Opponents	22	9	186	8.5	16	0

KICKOFF RETURNS	No.	Yds.	Avg.	LG	TD
Mills	54	1306	24.2	57	0
McAfee	5	56	11.2	25	0
Pegram	4	85	21.3	28	0
Bruener	2	19	9.5	10	0
C. Johnson	2	47	23.5	40	0
Gibson	1	10	10.0	10	0
T. Greene	1	7	7.0	7	0
Steelers	69	1530	22.2	57	0
Opponents	88	1544	17.5	62	0

SACKS	No.
K. Greene	9.0
Seals	8.5
Lloyd	6.5
C. Brown	5.5
Buckner	3.0
Gildon	3.0
Henry	2.0
Lake	1.5
Kirkland	1.0
Olsavsky	1.0
Steed	1.0
Steelers	42.0
Opponents	24.0

1996 DRAFT CHOICES

Round	Name	Pos.	College
1	Jamain Stephens	T	North Carolina A&T
3	Steven Conley	LB	Arkansas
	Jon Witman	RB	Penn State
4	Earl Holmes	LB	Florida A&M
	Jahine Arnold	WR	Fresno State
5	Israel Raybon	DE	North Alabama
6	Orpheus Roye	DE	Florida State
	Spence Fischer	QB	Duke
7	Carlos Emmons	LB	Arkansas State

PITTSBURGH STEELERS

1996 VETERAN ROSTER

No.	Name	Pos.	Ht.	Wt.	Birthdate	NFL Exp.	College	Hometown	How Acq.	'95 Games/ Starts
43	Avery, Steve	RB	6-2	229	8/18/66	3	Northern Michigan	Oconomowoc, Wis.	FA-'93	11/3
80	Barnes, Johnnie	WR	6-1	185	7/21/68	5	Hampton	Suffolk, Va.	FA-'95	3/0
40	Bell, Myron	S	5-11	203	9/15/71	3	Michigan State	Toledo, Ohio	D5a-'94	16/9
36	t- Bettis, Jerome	RB	5-11	243	2/16/72	4	Notre Dame	Detroit, Mich.	T(StL)-'96	15/13*
94	Brown, Chad	LB	6-2	240	7/12/70	4	Colorado	Altadena, Calif.	D2-'93	10/10
87	Bruener, Mark	TE	6-4	254	9/16/72	2	Washington	Aberdeen, Wash.	D1-'95	16/13
96	Buckner, Brentson	DE	6-2	305	9/30/71	3	Clemson	Columbus, Ga.	D2-'94	16/16
72	Dafney, Bernard	T-G	6-5	329	11/1/68	5	Tennessee	Los Angeles, Calif.	FA-'96	11/8*
63	Dawson, Dermontti	C	6-2	288	6/17/65	9	Kentucky	Lexington, Ky.	D2-'88	16/16
78	Faumui, Taase	DE-DT	6-3	278	3/19/71	3	Hawaii	Honolulu, Hawaii	D4-'94	3/0
21	Figures, Deon	CB-KR	6-0	192	1/10/70	4	Colorado	Compton, Calif.	D1-'93	14/1
41	Flowers, Lethon	CB-S	6-0	207	1/14/73	2	Georgia Tech	Spring Valley, N.C.	D5a-'95	10/0
29	Fuller, Randy	CB-S	5-10	175	6/2/70	3	Tennessee State	Columbus, Ga.	FA-'95	13/0
60	Gammon, Kendall	C	6-4	288	10/23/68	5	Pittsburg State	Wichita, Kan.	D11-'92	16/0
98	Gibson, Oliver	DE-DT	6-2	283	3/15/72	2	Notre Dame	Romeoville, Ill.	D4a-'95	12/0
92	Gildon, Jason	LB	6-3	245	7/31/72	3	Oklahoma State	Altus, Okla.	D3a-'94	16/0
84	Greene, Tracy	TE	6-5	270	11/5/72	3	Grambling State	Grambling, La.	T(KC)-'95	16/0
88	† Hastings, Andre	WR	6-1	190	11/7/70	4	Georgia	Atlanta, Ga.	D3-'93	16/0
85	Hayes, Jonathan	TE	6-5	248	8/11/62	12	Iowa	Oxford, Ala.	FA-'94	16/7
76	† Henry, Kevin	DE	6-4	282	10/23/68	4	Mississippi State	Mound Bayou, Miss.	D4-'93	14/5
65	Jackson, John	T	6-6	297	1/4/65	9	Eastern Kentucky	Cincinnati, Ohio	D10-'88	11/9
90	Johnson, Bill	DE-DT	6-4	300	12/9/68	5	Michigan State	Chicago, Ill.	FA-'95	9/0
81	Johnson, Charles	WR	6-0	193	1/3/72	3	Colorado	San Bernardino, Calif.	D1-'94	15/10
9	Johnson, Norm	K	6-2	202	5/31/60	15	UCLA	Garden Grove, Calif.	UFA(Atl)-'95	16/0
54	Jones, Donta	LB	6-2	226	8/27/72	2	Nebraska	Pomfret, Md.	D4b-'95	16/0
99	Kirkland, Levon	LB	6-1	264	2/17/69	5	Clemson	Lamar, S.C.	D2-'92	16/16
37	Lake, Carnell	S	6-1	210	7/15/67	8	UCLA	Inglewood, Calif.	D2-'89	16/16
34	Lester, Tim	RB	5-9	227	6/15/68	5	Eastern Kentucky	Miami, Fla.	FA-'95	6/1
95	Lloyd, Greg	LB	6-2	228	5/26/65	10	Ft. Valley State	Ft. Valley, Ga.	D6b-'87	16/16
28	Mays, Alvoid	CB	5-9	180	7/10/66	7	West Virginia	Bradenton, Fla.	UFA(Wash)-'95	13/6
86	Mays, Damon	WR	5-9	170	5/20/68	4	Missouri	Phoenix, Ariz.	FA-'95	0*
25	McAfee, Fred	RB	5-10	193	6/20/68	6	Mississippi	Philadelphia, Miss.	FA-'94	16/1
49	Miles, Barron	CB-S	5-8	165	1/1/72	2	Nebraska	Roselle, N.J.	D6-'95	0*
16	Miller, Jim	QB	6-2	210	2/9/71	3	Michigan State	Waterford, Mich.	D6a-'94	3/0
89	Mills, Ernie	WR	5-11	192	10/28/68	6	Florida	Dunnellon, Fla.	D3-'91	16/6
33	Morris, Byron "Bam"	RB	6-0	246	1/13/72	3	Texas Tech	Cooper, Tex.	D3b-'94	13/4
62	Myslinski, Tom	T-G	6-3	287	12/7/68	4	Tennessee	Rome, N.Y.	FA-'96	9/9*
66	Newberry, Tom	G	6-2	285	12/20/62	11	Wisconsin-La Crosse	Onalaska, Wis.	UFA(StL)-'95	16/15
24	Oldham, Chris	CB	5-9	193	10/26/68	6	Oregon	Sacramento, Calif.	UFA(Ariz)-'94	15/0
55	Olsavsky, Jerry	LB	6-1	224	3/29/67	8	Pittsburgh	Youngstown, Ohio	FA-'94	15/5
79	Parrish, James	T-G	6-6	310	5/19/68	4	Temple	Jessup, Md.	FA-'95	16/1
20	Pegram, Erric	RB	5-10	195	1/7/69	6	North Texas State	Dallas, Tex.	UFA(Atl)-'95	15/11
39	Perry, Darren	S	5-11	196	12/29/68	5	Penn State	Deep Creek, Va.	D8a-'92	16/16
57	Ravotti, Eric	LB	6-3	246	3/16/71	3	Penn State	Freeport, Pa.	D6b-'94	6/1
97	Seals, Ray	DE	6-3	306	6/17/65	9	No College	Syracuse, N.Y.	UFA(TB)-'94	16/16
68	Stai, Brenden	G	6-4	297	3/30/72	2	Nebraska	Anaheim, Calif.	D3-'95	16/9
3	Stark, Rohn	P	6-3	203	5/4/59	15	Florida State	Minneapolis, Minn.	UFA(Ind)-'95	16/0
93	Steed, Joel	NT	6-2	300	2/17/69	5	Colorado	Denver, Colo.	D3-'92	12/11
10	Stewart, Kordell	QB-WR	6-1	212	10/16/72	2	Colorado	Marreo, La.	D2-'95	10/2
73	Strzelczyk, Justin	G-T	6-6	302	8/18/68	7	Maine	Seneca, N.Y.	D11-'90	16/14
82	Thigpen, Yancey	WR	6-1	202	8/15/69	5	Winston-Salem State	Tarboro, N.C.	FA-'92	16/16
18	Tomczak, Mike	QB	6-1	201	10/23/62	12	Ohio State	Calumet City, Ill.	UFA(Clev)-'93	7/4
22	Vaughn, Jon	RB	5-9	203	3/12/70	5	Michigan	Florissant, Mo.	FA-'96	0*
27	† Williams, Willie	CB	5-9	180	12/26/70	4	Western Carolina	Columbia, S.C.	D6-'93	16/15
77	Wolford, Will	G-T	6-5	300	5/18/64	11	Vanderbilt	Louisville, Ky.	UFA(Ind)-'96	16/16*
26	Woodson, Rod	CB-KR	6-0	200	3/10/65	10	Purdue	Ft. Wayne, Ind.	D1-'87	1/1

* Bettis played 15 games with St. Louis in '95; Dafney played 11 games with Arizona; D. Mays and Miles missed '95 season because of injury; Myslinski played 9 games with Jacksonville; Vaughn last active with Kansas City in '94; Wolford played 16 games with Indianapolis.

\# Unrestricted free agent; subject to developments.

† Restricted free agent, subject to developments.

t- Steelers traded for Bettis (St. Louis).

Players lost through free agency (4): QB Neil O'Donnell (NYJ; 12 games in '95), LB Kevin Greene (Car; 16), T Leon Searcy (Jax; 16), C-G Ariel Solomon (Minn; 4).

Also played with Steelers in '95—T-G Lonnie Paleli (1 game), RB John L. Williams (11).

COACHING STAFF

Head Coach,
Bill Cowher

Pro Career: Begins his fifth season as the fifteenth head coach in Steelers' history, replacing Chuck Noll on January 21, 1992. Cowher led the Steelers to an 11-5 regular-season record in 1995 and at age 38, became the youngest coach to lead his team to a Super Bowl. With four straight playoff berths. Cowher is the fourth head coach in NFL history to lead his team to the playoffs during his first four seasons as a head coach. During Cowher's 11-year coaching career, teams he has been associated with have made the postseason 10 times. Began his NFL career as a free-agent linebacker with the Philadelphia Eagles in 1979, and then signed with the Cleveland Browns the following year. Cowher played three seasons (1980-82) in Cleveland before being traded back to the Eagles, where he played two more years (1983-84). Cowher began his coaching career in 1985 at age 28 under Marty Schottenheimer with the Cleveland Browns. He was the Browns' special teams coach in 1985-86 and secondary coach in 1987-88 before following Schottenheimer to the Kansas City Chiefs in 1989 as defensive coordinator. Career record: 46-25.

Background: Excelled in football, basketball, and track for Carlynton High in Crafton, Pa. Was a three-year starter at linebacker for North Carolina State, serving as captain and earning team MVP honors as senior. Graduated in 1979 with education degree.

Personal: Born in Pittsburgh, Pa., on May 8, 1957. His wife Kaye, also a North Carolina State graduate, played professional basketball for the New York Stars of the Women's Professional Basketball League with twin sister Faye. Bill and Kaye live in Pittsburgh and have three daughters—Meagan Lyn, Lauren Marie, and Lindsay Morgan.

ASSISTANT COACHES

Mike Archer, linebackers; born July 26, 1953, State College, Pa., lives in Pittsburgh. Safety/punter Miami 1972-75. No pro playing experience. College coach: Miami 1978-83, Louisiana State 1984-90, Virginia 1991-92, Kentucky 1993-95. Pro coach: Joined the Steelers in 1996.

Dave Culley, receivers; born September 17, 1955, Sparta, Tenn., lives in Pittsburgh. Quarterback Vanderbilt 1973-77. No pro playing experience. College coach: Austin Peay 1978, Vanderbilt 1979-81, Middle Tennessee State 1982, Tennessee-Chattanooga 1983, Western Kentucky 1984, Southwestern Louisiana 1985-88, Texas-El Paso 1989-90, Texas A&M 1991-93. Pro coach: Tampa Bay Buccaneers 1994-95, joined Steelers in 1996.

Chan Gailey, wide receivers; born January 5, 1952, Gainesville, Ga., lives in Pittsburgh. Quarterback Florida 1970-73. No pro playing experience. College coach: Troy State 1976-78, 1983-84, Air Force 1979-82, Samford (head coach) 1992. Pro coach: Denver Broncos 1985-90, Birmingham Fire (WL) 1991-92, joined Steelers in 1994.

Dick Hoak, running backs; born December 8, 1939, Jeannette, Pa., lives in Greensburg, Pa. Halfback-quarterback Penn State 1958-60. Pro running back Pittsburgh Steelers 1961-70. Pro coach: Joined Steelers in 1972.

Dick LeBeau, defensive coordinator; born September 9, 1937, London, Ohio, lives in Pittsburgh. Defensive back-offensive back Ohio State 1954-57. Pro cornerback Detroit Lions 1959-72. Pro coach: Philadelphia Eagles 1972-75, Green Bay Packers 1976-79, Cincinnati Bengals 1980-91, joined Steelers in 1992.

Tim Lewis, defensive backs; born December 18, 1961, Quakertown, Pa., lives in Pittsburgh. Defensive back Pittsburgh 1979-82. Pro cornerback Green Bay Packers 1983-86. College coach: Texas A&M 1987-88, Southern Methodist 1989-92, Pittsburgh 1993-94. Pro coach: Joined Steelers in 1995.

Mike Mularkey, tight ends; born November 19, 1961, Ft. Lauderdale, Fla., lives in Pittsburgh. Tight end Florida 1979-82. Pro tight end Minnesota Vikings 1983-88, Pittsburgh Steelers 1989-91. College coach: Concordia 1993. Pro coach: Tampa Bay Buccaneers 1994-95, joined Steelers in 1996.

John Mitchell, defensive line; born October 14, 1951, Mobile, Ala., lives in Pittsburgh. Defensive end Eastern Arizona J.C. 1969-70, Alabama 1971-72. No pro playing experience. College coach: Alabama 1973-76, Arkansas 1977-82, Temple 1986, Louisiana State 1987-90. Pro coach: Birmingham Stallions (USFL) 1983-85, Cleveland Browns 1991-93, joined Steelers in 1994.

Kent Stephenson, offensive line; born February 4, 1942, Anita, Iowa, lives in Pittsburgh. Guard-nose tackle Northern Iowa 1962-64. No pro playing experience. College coach: Wayne State 1965-68, North Dakota 1969-71, Southern Methodist 1972-73, Iowa 1974-76, Oklahoma State 1977-78, Kansas 1979-82. Pro coach: Michigan Panthers (USFL) 1983-84, Seattle Seahawks 1985-91, joined Steelers in 1992.

Ron Zook, special teams; born April 28, 1954, Ashland, Ohio, lives in Pittsburgh. Defensive back Miami (Ohio) 1972-75. No pro playing experience. College coach: Murray State 1978-80, Cincinnati 1981-82, Kansas 1983, Tennessee 1984-86, Virginia Tech 1987, Ohio State 1988-90, Florida 1991-95. Pro coach: Joined the Steelers in 1996.

1996 FIRST-YEAR ROSTER

Name	Pos.	Ht.	Wt.	Birthdate	College	Hometown	How Acq.
Arnold, Jahine	WR	6-0	187	6/19/73	Fresno State	Cupertino, Calif.	D4b
Bell, Ricky	CB-S	5-10	186	10/2/74	North Carolina State	Columbia, S.C.	FA
Black, Greg (1)	T-G	6-4	306	9/14/73	North Carolina	Gastonia, N.C.	FA
Coleman, LaMonte (1)	RB	5-10	227	6/24/71	Slippery Rock	Pittsburgh, Pa.	FA
Conley, Steven	LB	6-5	231	1/18/72	Arkansas	Chicago, Ill.	D3a
Edge, Shayne (1)	P	5-11	180	8/21/71	Florida	Lake City, Fla.	FA
Emmons, Carlos	LB	6-4	240	9/3/73	Arkansas State	Greenwood, Miss.	D7
Farquhar, John (1)	TE	6-6	240	3/22/72	Duke	Stanford, Calif.	FA
Fischer, Spence	QB	6-4	220	11/30/72	Duke	Atlanta, Ga.	D6b
George, Chris (1)	WR	5-11	190	11/27/71	Glenville State	Clarksburg, W.Va.	FA
Green, Lorenzo	DE-DT	6-2	270	1/8/73	Oklahoma State	Miami Springs, Fla.	FA
Holliday, Corey (1)	WR	6-2	208	1/31/71	North Carolina	Richmond, Va.	FA
Holmes, Earl	LB	6-1	238	4/28/73	Florida A&M	Tallahassee, Fla.	D4a
Jones, Chris	WR	6-3	202	6/3/72	Mississippi State	Tupelo, Miss.	FA
Martin, Emerson (1)	G	6-3	302	5/6/70	Hampton	Elizabeth, N.C.	FA
Ofodile, A.J. (1)	TE	6-7	260	10/9/73	Missouri	Detroit, Mich.	FA
Parker, Cornell	CB-S	5-11	195	2/17/73	Southern Methodist	Washington, D.C.	FA
Raybon, Israel	DE	6-6	293	2/5/73	North Alabama	Lee, Ala.	D5
Roye, Orpheus	DE	6-3	295	1/21/74	Florida State	Miami Springs, Fla.	D6a
Scott, Patrick (1)	LB	6-4	229	6/4/71	South Carolina State	Durham, N.C.	FA
Stephens, Jamain	T	6-5	315	1/9/74	North Carolina A&T	Lumberton, N.C.	D1
Tyre, Lewis	C-G-T	6-4	274	12/8/72	Florida State	Surrency, Ga.	FA
Witman, Jon	RB	6-1	242	6/1/72	Penn State	Wrightsville, Pa.	D3b
Wood, Joseph (1)	K	6-2	220	12/29/68	Air Force	Capistrano, Calif.	FA

The term NFL Rookie is defined as a player who is in his first season of professional football and has not been on the roster of another professional football team for any regular-season or postseason games. A Rookie is designated by an "R" on NFL rosters. Players who have been active in another professional football league or players who have NFL experience, including either preseason training camp or being on an Active List or Inactive List, or on Reserve/Injured or Reserve/Physically Unable to Perform for fewer than six regular-season games, are termed NFL First-Year Players. An NFL First-Year Player is designated by a "1" on NFL rosters. Thereafter, a player is credited with an additional year of experience for each season in which he accumulates six games on the Active List or Inactive List, or on Reserve/Injured or Reserve/Physically Unable to Perform.

NOTES

SAN DIEGO CHARGERS

American Football Conference
Western Division
Team Colors: Navy Blue, White, and Gold
San Diego Jack Murphy Stadium
P.O. Box 609609
San Diego, California 92160-9609
Telephone: (619) 280-2111

CLUB OFFICIALS

Chairman of the Board: Alex G. Spanos
President-Vice Chairman: Dean A. Spanos
Executive Vice President: Michael A. Spanos
General Manager: Bobby Beathard
Vice President-Finance: Jeremiah T. Murphy
Chief Financial and Administrative Officer: Jeanne Bonk
Director of Player Personnel: Billy Devaney
Director of Pro Personnel: Rudy Feldman
Coordinator of Football Operations: Marty Hurney
Business Manager: John Hinek
Director of Public Relations: Bill Johnston
Director of Marketing: Rich Israel
Director of Premium Seating: Eric Ashlock
Director of Ticket Operations: Ron Tuck
Director of Video Operations: Dusty Alves
Head Trainer: Keoki Kamau
Equipment Manager: Sid Brooks
Stadium: San Diego Jack Murphy Stadium
• **Capacity:** 60,794
9449 Friars Road
San Diego, California 92108
Playing Surface: Grass
Training Camp: University of California-San Diego
Third College
La Jolla, California 92037

1996 SCHEDULE

PRESEASON

July 27	vs. Pittsburgh at Tokyo, Japan	10:00
Aug. 3	at Minnesota	7:00
Aug. 10	at San Francisco	5:00
Aug. 17	**Arizona**	7:00
Aug. 23	at St. Louis	7:00

REGULAR SEASON

Sept. 1	**Seattle**	1:00
Sept. 8	**Cincinnati**	1:00
Sept. 15	at Green Bay	12:00
Sept. 22	at Oakland	1:00
Sept. 29	**Kansas City**	1:00
Oct. 6	at Denver	2:00
Oct. 13	Open Date	
Oct. 21	**Oakland** (Mon.)	6:00
Oct. 27	at Seattle	1:00
Nov. 3	at Indianapolis	1:00
Nov. 11	**Detroit** (Mon.)	6:00
Nov. 17	**Tampa Bay**	1:00
Nov. 24	at Kansas City	12:00
Dec. 1	**New England**	5:00
Dec. 8	at Pittsburgh	1:00
Dec. 14	at Chicago (Sat.)	3:00
Dec. 22	**Denver**	5:00

RECORD HOLDERS

INDIVIDUAL RECORDS—CAREER

Category	Name	Performance
Rushing (Yds.)	Paul Lowe, 1960-67	4,963
Passing (Yds.)	Dan Fouts, 1973-1987	43,040
Passing (TDs)	Dan Fouts, 1973-1987	254
Receiving (No.)	Charlie Joiner, 1976-1986	586
Receiving (Yds.)	Lance Alworth, 1962-1970	9,585
Interceptions	Gill Byrd, 1983-1992	42
Punting (Avg.)	Ralf Mojsiejenko, 1985-88	42.9
Punt Return (Avg.)	Leslie (Speedy) Duncan, 1964-1970	12.3
Kickoff Return (Avg.)	Leslie (Speedy) Duncan, 1964-1970	25.2
Field Goals	John Carney, 1990-95	150
Touchdowns (Tot.)	Lance Alworth, 1962-1970	83
Points	Rolf Benirschke, 1977-1986	766

INDIVIDUAL RECORDS—SINGLE SEASON

Category	Name	Performance
Rushing (Yds.)	Natrone Means, 1994	1,350
Passing (Yds.)	Dan Fouts, 1981	4,802
Passing (TDs)	Dan Fouts, 1981	33
Receiving (No.)	Tony Martin, 1995	90
Receiving (Yds.)	Lance Alworth, 1965	1,602
Interceptions	Charlie McNeil, 1961	9
Punting (Avg.)	Darren Bennett, 1995	44.7
Punt Return (Avg.)	Leslie (Speedy) Duncan, 1965	15.5
Kickoff Return (Avg.)	Keith Lincoln, 1962	28.4
Field Goals	John Carney, 1994	34
Touchdowns (Tot.)	Chuck Muncie, 1981	19
Points	John Carney, 1994	135

INDIVIDUAL RECORDS—SINGLE GAME

Category	Name	Performance
Rushing (Yds.)	Gary Anderson, 12-18-88	217
Passing (Yds.)	Dan Fouts, 10-19-80	444
	Dan Fouts, 12-11-82	444
Passing (TDs)	Dan Fouts, 11-22-81	6
Receiving (No.)	Kellen Winslow, 10-7-84	15
Receiving (Yds.)	Wes Chandler, 12-20-82	260
Interceptions	Many times	3
	Last time by Dwayne Harper, 11-27-95	
Field Goals	John Carney, 9-5-93	6
	John Carney, 9-18-93	6
Touchdowns (Tot.)	Kellen Winslow, 11-22-81	5
Points	Kellen Winslow, 11-22-81	30

COACHING HISTORY

(272-267-11)

1960-69	Sid Gillman*	83-51-6
1969-70	Charlie Waller	9-7-3
1971	Sid Gillman**	4-6-0
1971-73	Harland Svare***	7-17-2
1973	Ron Waller	1-5-0
1974-78	Tommy Prothro****	21-39-0
1978-86	Don Coryell#	72-60-0
1986-88	Al Saunders	17-22-0
1989-91	Dan Henning	16-32-0
1992-95	Bobby Ross	42-28-0

*Retired after nine games in 1969
**Resigned after 10 games in 1971
***Resigned after eight games in 1973
****Resigned after four games in 1978
#Resigned after eight games in 1986

SAN DIEGO JACK MURPHY STADIUM

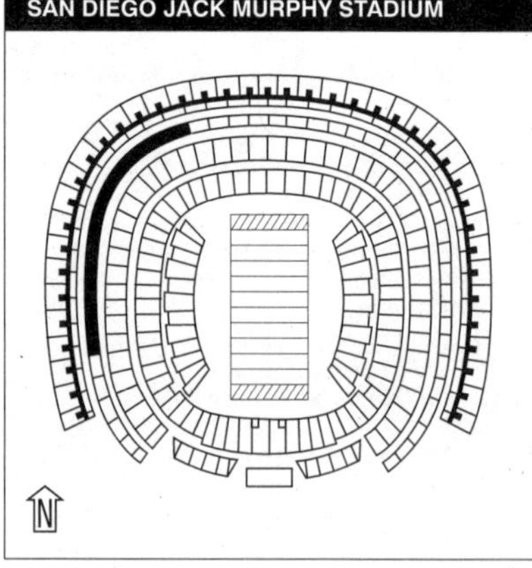

1995 TEAM RECORD

PRESEASON (1-2)

Date	Result		Opponents
8/7	L	19-23	Minnesota
8/13	L	6-17	San Francisco
8/19	Cancelled		at Houston
8/25	W	17-9	St. Louis

REGULAR SEASON (9-7)

Date	Result		Opponents	Att.
9/3	L	7-17	at Oakland	50,323
9/10	W	14-10	Seattle	54,420
9/17	W	27-21	at Philadelphia	63,081
9/24	W	17-6	Denver	58,987
10/1	L	16-31	at Pittsburgh	57,012
10/9	L	23-29	at Kansas City (OT)	79,288
10/15	L	9-23	Dallas	62,664
10/22	W	35-25	at Seattle	45,821
11/5	L	14-24	Miami	61,996
11/12	L	7-22	Kansas City	59,285
11/19	L	27-30	at Denver	74,681
11/27	W	12-6	Oakland	60,607
12/3	W	31-13	Cleveland	56,358
12/9	W	28-25	Arizona	55,258
12/17	W	27-24	at Indianapolis	55,318
12/23	W	27-17	at N.Y. Giants	50,243

POSTSEASON (0-1)

12/31	L	20-35	Indianapolis	61,182

(OT) Overtime

SCORE BY PERIODS

Chargers	49	102	69	101	0	—	321
Opponents	86	107	58	66	6	—	323

ATTENDANCE

Home 469,575 Away 475,767 Total 945,342
Single-game home record, 64,411 (12/15/84)
Single-season home record, 494,103 (1988)

1995 TEAM STATISTICS

	Chargers	Opp.
Total First Downs	314	313
Rushing	108	112
Passing	185	178
Penalty	21	23
Third Down: Made/Att	95/222	90/214
Third Down Pct.	42.8	42.1
Fourth Down: Made/Att	12/21	6/11
Fourth Down Pct.	57.1	54.5
Total Net Yards	5213	5074
Avg. Per Game	325.8	317.1
Total Plays	1051	1020
Avg. Per Play	5.0	5.0
Net Yards Rushing	1747	1691
Avg. Per Game	109.2	105.7
Total Rushes	479	441
Net Yards Passing	3466	3383
Avg. Per Game	216.6	211.4
Sacked/Yards Lost	32/240	36/222
Gross Yards	3706	3605
Att./Completions	540/318	543/321
Completion Pct.	58.9	59.1
Had Intercepted	18	17
Punts/Avg.	72/44.7	73/43.4
Net Punting Avg.	72/36.6	73/36.0
Penalties/Yards Lost	107/953	117/951
Fumbles/Ball Lost	30/12	24/10
Touchdowns	37	35
Rushing	14	15
Passing	17	16
Returns	6	4
Avg. Time of Possession	29:34	30:26

1995 INDIVIDUAL STATISTICS

PASSING	Att.	Comp.	Yds.	Pct.	TD	Int.	Tkld.	Rate
Humphries	478	282	3381	59.0	17	14	23/197	80.4
Gilbert	61	36	325	59.0	0	4	9/43	46.1
Martin	1	0	0	0.0	0	0	0/0	39.6
Chargers	540	318	3706	58.9	17	18	32/240	76.4
Opponents	543	321	3605	59.1	16	17	36/222	75.8

SCORING	TD R	TD P	TD Rt	PAT	FG	Saf	PTS
Carney	0	0	0	32/33	21/26	0	95
Harmon	1	5	0	0/0	0/0	0	36
Martin	0	6	0	0/0	0/0	0	36
Means	5	0	0	0/0	0/0	0	30
Seay	0	3	0	0/0	0/0	0	20
Coleman	0	0	3	0/0	0/0	0	18
Culver	3	0	0	0/0	0/0	0	18
Hayden	3	0	0	0/0	0/0	0	18
Gayle	0	0	2	0/0	0/0	0	12
Jefferson	0	2	0	0/0	0/0	0	12
Fletcher	1	0	0	0/0	0/0	0	6
Humphries	1	0	0	0/0	0/0	0	6
Mitchell	0	1	0	0/0	0/0	0	6
Seau	0	0	1	0/0	0/0	0	6
R. Davis	0	0	0	0/0	0/0	1	2
Chargers	14	17	6	32/33	21/26	1	321
Opponents	15	16	4	28/29	27/32	0	323

2-Point conversions: Seay. Team: 1-4.

RUSHING	Att.	Yds.	Avg.	LG	TD
Means	186	730	3.9	36	5
Hayden	128	470	3.7	20	3
Harmon	51	187	3.7	48t	1
Culver	47	155	3.3	17	3
Fletcher	26	140	5.4	46	1
Humphries	33	53	1.6	18	1
Gilbert	6	11	1.8	8	0
Jefferson	2	1	0.5	11	0
Chargers	479	1747	3.6	48t	14
Opponents	441	1691	3.8	60	15

RECEIVING	No.	Yds.	Avg.	LG	TD
Martin	90	1224	13.6	51t	6
Harmon	63	673	10.7	44	5
Jefferson	48	621	12.9	45	2
Seay	45	537	11.9	38t	3
Pupunu	35	315	9.0	26	0
D. Young	9	90	10.0	22	0
Means	7	46	6.6	14	0
Hayden	5	53	10.6	16	0
Culver	5	21	4.2	12	0
Coleman	3	67	22.3	41	0
Mitchell	3	31	10.3	24	1
Fletcher	3	26	8.7	15	0
Ellison	1	6	6.0	6	0
Humphries	1	-4	-4.0	-4	0
Chargers	318	3706	11.7	51t	17
Opponents	321	3605	11.2	50	16

INTERCEPTIONS	No.	Yds.	Avg.	LG	TD
Harrison	5	22	4.4	17	0
Harper	4	12	3.0	15	0
Gayle	2	99	49.5	99t	1
Clark	2	14	7.0	13	0
Seau	2	5	2.5	3	0
Shaw	1	31	31.0	31	0
Bush	1	0	0.0	0	0
Orlando	0	37	—	37	0
Chargers	17	220	12.9	99t	1
Opponents	18	164	9.1	63t	3

PUNTING	No.	Yds.	Avg.	In 20	LG
Bennett	72	3221	44.7	28	66
Chargers	72	3221	44.7	28	66
Opponents	73	3168	43.4	24	63

PUNT RETURNS	No.	FC	Yds.	Avg.	LG	TD
Coleman	28	14	326	11.6	88t	1
Fletcher	3	1	12	4.0	11	0
Chargers	31	15	338	10.9	88t	1
Opponents	35	13	429	12.3	86t	1

KICKOFF RETURNS	No.	Yds.	Avg.	LG	TD
Coleman	62	1411	22.8	92t	2
Fletcher	4	65	16.3	30	0
Harmon	4	25	6.3	9	0
Engel	0	1	---	1	0
Chargers	70	1502	21.5	92t	2
Opponents	63	1496	23.7	86	0

SACKS	No.
O'Neal	12.5
Lee	8.0
R. Davis	3.5
R. Johnson	3.0
Mims	2.0
Parrella	2.0
Seau	2.0
Brandon	1.0
Dw. Gordon	1.0
G. Young	1.0
Chargers	36.0
Opponents	32.0

1996 DRAFT CHOICES

Round	Name	Pos.	College
2	Bryan Still	WR	Virginia Tech
	Patrick Sapp	LB	Clemson
3	Brian Roche	TE	San Jose State
4	Charlie Jones	WR	Fresno State
5	Junior Soli	DT	Arkansas
6	Jim Mills	T	Idaho
	Bryan Stoltenberg	C	Colorado
7	Freddie Bradley	RB	Sonoma State

SAN DIEGO CHARGERS

1996 VETERAN ROSTER

No.	Name	Pos.	Ht.	Wt.	Birthdate	NFL Exp.	College	Hometown	How Acq.	'95 Games/ Starts
2	Bennett, Darren	P	6-5	235	1/9/65	2	No College	Western, Australia	FA-'95	16/0
75	Berti, Tony	G-T	6-6	300	6/21/72	2	Colorado	Thornton, Colo.	D6d-'95	1/0
50	Binn, David	LS	6-3	240	2/6/72	3	California	San Mateo, Calif.	FA-'94	16/0
58	† Bush, Lewis	LB	6-2	245	12/2/69	4	Washington State	Tacoma, Wash.	D4b-'93	16/15
3	Carney, John	K	5-11	170	4/20/64	7	Notre Dame	West Palm Beach, Fla.	FA-'90	16/0
44	Castle, Eric	S	6-3	212	3/15/70	4	Oregon	Lebanon, Ore.	D6-'93	16/0
31	Clark, Willie	CB	5-10	186	1/6/72	3	Notre Dame	Wheatland, Calif.	D3b-'94	16/2
68	† Cocozzo, Joe	G	6-4	300	8/7/70	4	Michigan	Mechanicville, N.Y.	D3-'93	16/7
83	Coleman, Andre	WR-KR	5-9	165	1/18/71	3	Kansas State	Hermitage, Pa.	D3a-'94	15/0
90	Coleman, Marco	DE	6-3	267	12/18/69	5	Georgia Tech	Dayton, Ohio	UFA(Mia)-'96	16/16*
73	Davis, Isaac	G	6-3	320	4/8/72	3	Arkansas	Malvern, Ark.	D2a-'94	16/10
93	Davis, Reuben	DT	6-5	320	5/7/65	9	North Carolina	Greensboro, N.C.	UFA(Phx)-'94	16/16
84	Ellison, 'OMar	WR	6-1	200	10/8/71	2	Florida State	Griffin, Ga.	D5-'95	2/0
60	Engel, Greg	C	6-3	285	1/18/71	3	Illinois	Bloomington, Ill.	FA-'94	10/0
41	Fletcher, Terrell	RB	5-8	196	9/14/73	2	Wisconsin	St. Louis, Mo.	D2b-'95	16/0
23	Gayle, Shaun	S	5-11	202	3/8/62	13	Ohio State	Bethel, Va.	UFA(Chi)-'95	16/16
21	Gordon, Darrien	CB	5-11	182	11/14/70	4	Stanford	Shawnee, Okla.	D1-'93	0*
52	† Gordon, Dwayne	LB	6-1	245	11/2/69	4	New Hampshire	LaGrangeville, N.Y.	FA-'95	16/3
54	Gouveia, Kurt	LB	6-1	240	9/14/64	11	Brigham Young	Honolulu, Hawaii	UFA(Phil)-'96	16/16*
53	Hall, Courtney	C	6-1	281	8/26/68	8	Rice	Wilmington, Calif.	D2a-'89	16/16
28	Harper, Dwayne	CB	5-11	175	3/29/66	9	South Carolina State	Orangeburg, S.C.	UFA(Sea)-'94	16/16
37	Harrison, Rodney	S	6-0	201	12/15/72	3	Western Illinois	Marion, Ill.	D5b-'94	11/0
24	Hayden, Aaron	RB	6-0	218	4/13/73	2	Tennessee	Detroit, Mich.	D4b-'95	6/4
38	Hendrix, David	S	6-1	213	5/29/72	2	Georgia Tech	Norcross, Ga.	FA-'95	5/0
12	Humphries, Stan	QB	6-2	223	4/14/65	8	Northeast Louisiana	Shreveport, La.	T(Wash)-'92	15/15
99	Johnson, Raylee	DE	6-3	265	6/1/70	4	Arkansas	Fordyce, Ark.	D4a-'93	16/1
98	Lee, Shawn	DT	6-2	300	10/24/66	9	North Alabama	Brooklyn, N.Y.	FA-'92	16/15
81	Martin, Tony	WR	6-0	181	9/5/65	7	Mesa, Colo.	Miami, Fla.	T(Mia)-'94	16/16
88	May, Deems	TE	6-4	263	3/6/69	5	North Carolina	Lexington, N.C.	D7-'92	5/0
94	Mims, Chris	DE	6-5	290	9/29/70	5	Tennessee	Los Angeles, Calif.	D1-'92	15/15
89	Mitchell, Shannon	TE	6-2	245	3/28/72	3	Georgia	Alcoa, Tenn.	FA-'94	16/2
40	Montreuil, Mark	CB	6-1	200	12/29/71	2	Concordia, Canada	Montreal, Canada	D7-'95	16/0
77	Moten, Eric	G-T	6-2	306	4/11/68	6	Michigan State	Cleveland Heights, Ohio	D2c-'91	16/15
85	Oliver, Jimmy	WR	5-10	173	1/30/73	2	Texas Christian	Dallas, Tex.	D2c-'95	0*
70	Parker, Vaughn	T	6-3	296	6/5/71	3	UCLA	Buffalo, N.Y.	D2b-'94	15/7
97	† Parrella, John	DT	6-3	290	11/22/69	4	Nebraska	Topeka, Kan.	FA-'94	16/1
86	Pupunu, Alfred	TE	6-2	265	10/17/69	5	Weber State	Salt Lake City, Utah	W(KC)-'92	13/10
82	Reeves, Walter	TE	6-4	270	12/16/65	8	Auburn	Eufaula, Ala.	FA-'96	5/3*
36	Ross, Kevin	S	5-9	185	1/16/62	13	Temple	Mickleton, N.J.	FA-'96	16/15*
42	Russell, Leonard	RB	6-2	240	11/17/69	6	Arizona State	Long Beach, Calif.	FA-'96	13/3*
8	Salisbury, Sean	QB	6-5	225	3/9/63	8	Southern California	Escondido, Calif.	FA-'96	0*
96	Sasa, Don	DT	6-2	286	9/16/72	2	Washington State	Long Beach, Calif.	D3a-'95	5/0
55	Seau, Junior	LB	6-3	250	1/19/69	7	Southern California	Oceanside, Calif.	D1-'90	16/16
29	Shaw, Terrence	CB	5-11	190	11/11/73	2	Stephen F. Austin	Marshall, Tex.	D2a-'95	16/14
65	Sienkiewicz, Troy	G-T	6-5	310	5/27/72	2	New Mexico State	Alamogordo, N.M.	D6a-'95	0*
72	# Swayne, Harry	T	6-5	295	2/2/65	10	Rutgers	Philadelphia, Pa.	PB(TB)-'91	16/16
5	Whelihan, Craig	QB	6-5	204	4/15/71	2	Pacific	San Jose, Calif.	D6c-'95	0*
59	Young, Glen	LB	6-3	240	5/2/69	2	Syracuse	Scarborough, Canada	FA-'95	16/0

* M. Coleman played 16 games with Miami in '95; Da. Gordon missed '95 season because of injury; Gouveia played 16 games with Philadelphia; Oliver was inactive for 9 games; Reeves played 5 games with Cleveland; Ross played 16 games with Atlanta; Russell played 13 games with St. Louis; Salisbury last active with Minnesota in '94; Sienkiewicz inactive for 16 games; Whelihan inactive for 16 games.

\# Unrestricted free agent; subject to developments.

† Restricted free agent; subject to developments.

Players lost through free agency (4): LB David Brandon (Atl; 16 games in '95), RB Ronnie Harmon (Hou; 16), S Bo Orlando (Cin; 16), DE Leslie O'Neal (StL; 16).

Also played with Chargers in '95—DT Sebastian Barrie (7 games), LB David Brandon (16), T Stan Brock (16), RB Rodney Culver (8), LB Dennis Gibson (13), QB Gale Gilbert (16), WR Shawn Jefferson (16), CB AJ Johnson (1), RB Natrone Means (10), TE Ron Middleton (3), WR Mark Seay (16), TE Duane Young (16).

COACHING STAFF

Head Coach,
Bobby Ross

Pro Career: Begins fifth season as San Diego's head coach. In 1995, led Chargers to third playoff appearance in four seasons as head coach. In 1994, led the Chargers to second AFC Western Division title in the last four years, and first-ever AFC Championship. Named ninth head coach in Chargers' history on January 2, 1992. Ross began his pro coaching career in 1978 as an assistant with the Kansas City Chiefs, where he coached special teams and defense in 1978-79 and offensive backs in 1980-81. No pro playing experience. Career record: 42-28.

Background: Played quarterback and defensive back for Virginia Military Institute. Began coaching career in 1965 at VMI. Moved on as an assistant at William & Mary 1967-70, Rice 1971, and Maryland 1972. Head coach at The Citadel 1973-77. Compiled 39-19-1 (.672) record as he led Maryland (1982-86) to three Atlantic Coast Conference titles and made four bowl game appearances in five seasons. Guided Georgia Tech (1987-91) to first ACC title in school history. Under Ross, the Yellow Jackets won first national championship as country's only undefeated team (11-0-1) in 1990. Named consensus national coach of the year in 1990. Career collegiate head coaching record: 94-76-2.

Personal: Born December 23, 1936, Richmond, Va. Bobby and wife, Alice, live in San Diego and have five children—Chris, Kevin, Robbie, Mary, and Teresa.

ASSISTANT COACHES

Dave Adolph, defensive coordinator; born June 6, 1937, Akron, Ohio, lives in San Diego. Guard-linebacker Akron 1955-58. No pro playing experience. College coach: Akron 1963-64, Connecticut 1965-68, Kentucky 1969-72, Illinois 1973-76, Ohio State 1977-78. Pro coach: Cleveland Browns 1979-84, 1986-88, San Diego Chargers 1985, Los Angeles Raiders 1989-91, Kansas City Chiefs 1992-94, rejoined Chargers in 1995.

Brian Baker, defensive line; born June 20, 1962, Baltimore, Maryland, lives in San Diego. Linebacker Maryland 1980-83. No pro playing experience. College coach: Maryland 1984-85, Army 1986, Georgia Tech 1987-95. Pro coach: Joined Chargers in 1996.

Greg Brown, secondary; born October 10, 1957, Denver, Colo., lives in San Diego. Defensive back Texas-El Paso 1978-79. No pro playing experience. College coach: Wyoming 1987-88, Purdue 1989-90, Colorado 1991-93. Pro coach: Denver Gold (USFL) 1983-84, Tampa Bay Buccaneers 1984-86, Atlanta Falcons 1994, joined Chargers in 1995.

Sylvester Croom, offensive backs; born September 25, 1954, Tuscaloosa, Ala., lives in San Diego. Center Alabama 1971-74. Pro center New Orleans Saints 1975. College coach: Alabama 1976-86. Pro coach: Tampa Bay Buccaneers 1987-90, Indianapolis Colts 1991, joined Chargers in 1992.

John Dunn, strength and conditioning; born July 22, 1956, Hillsdale, N.Y., lives in San Diego. Guard Penn State 1974-77. No pro playing experience. College coach: Penn State 1978. Pro coach: Washington Redskins 1984-86, Los Angeles Raiders 1987-89, joined Chargers in 1990.

Frank Falks, tight ends/H-Backs; born March 9, 1943, Tampa, Fla., lives in San Diego. Linebacker Joplin (Missouri) J.C. 1963-64, Parsons College 1965-66. No pro playing experience. College coach: Parsons College 1967-69, Kansas State 1970-72, Arkansas 1973-77, Wyoming 1978-79, San Diego State 1980, Oklahoma State 1981-82, Southern California 1983-86, Arizona State 1987-91, Ohio State 1992-93. Pro coach: Joined Chargers in 1994.

Ralph Friedgen, offensive coordinator; born April 4, 1947, Harrison, N.Y., lives in San Diego. Guard Maryland 1967-68. No pro playing experience. College coach: The Citadel 1973-79, William & Mary 1980, Murray State 1981, Maryland 1982-86, Georgia Tech 1987-91. Pro coach: Joined Chargers in 1992.

Jack Henry, offensive line; born March 14, 1946, Wilmerding, Pa., lives in San Diego. Linebacker Penn State 1964-65, guard Indiana (Pa.) University 1967-68. No pro playing experience. College coach: West Virginia 1970, 1978-79, Edinboro 1973, Louisville 1974, Millersville 1975-76, Southern Illinois 1977, Appalachian State 1980, Wake Forest 1981-85, Indiana (Pa.) University 1986-89, Pittsburgh 1993-95. Pro coach: Pittsburgh Steelers 1990-91, joined Chargers in 1996.

Dale Lindsey, linebackers; born January 18, 1943, Bedford, Ind., lives in San Diego. Linebacker Western Kentucky 1961-64. Pro linebacker Cleveland Browns 1965-73. College coach: Southern Methodist 1988-89. Pro coach: Cleveland Browns 1974, Portland Storm (WFL) 1975, Toronto Argonauts (CFL) 1979-82, Boston Breakers (USFL) 1983, New Jersey Generals (USFL) 1984-85, Green Bay Packers 1986-87, New England Patriots 1990, Tampa Bay Buccaneers 1991, joined Chargers in 1992.

John Misciagna, quality control; born December 11, 1954, Brooklyn, N.Y., lives in San Diego. Guard Dickinson College 1973-76. No pro playing experience. College coach: Indiana (Pa.) University 1977, Columbia 1978-79, Maryland 1980-88, Georgia Tech 1989-91. Pro coach: Joined Chargers in 1992.

Dennis Murphy, defensive assistant/special teams; born October 22, 1940, Endicott, N.Y., lives in San Diego. Tight end-defensive lineman Notre Dame 1959-61. No pro playing experience. College coach: Notre Dame 1968-74, Colgate 1975, Holy Cross 1976-77, Eastern Michigan 1978-81, Maryland 1982-91, Navy 1992-93. Pro coach: Joined Chargers in 1994.

Dwain Painter, quarterbacks; born February 13, 1942, Monroeville, Pa., lives in San Diego. Quarterback-defensive back Rutgers 1961-64. No pro playing experience. College coach: San Jose State 1971-72, UCLA 1976-78, Northern Arizona 1979-81 (head coach), Georgia Tech 1982-85, Texas 1986, Illinois 1987. Pro coach: Pittsburgh Steelers 1988-91, Indianapolis Colts 1992-93, joined Chargers in 1994.

Chuck Priefer, special teams; born July 26, 1944, Cleveland, Ohio, lives in San Diego. No college or pro playing experience. College coach: Miami (Ohio) 1977, North Carolina 1978-83, Kent State 1986, Georgia Tech 1987-91. Pro coach: Green Bay Packers 1984-85, joined Chargers in 1992.

Jerry Sullivan, wide receivers; born July 13, 1944, Miami, Fla., lives in San Diego. Quarterback Florida State 1963-64. No pro playing experience. College coach: Kansas State 1971-72, Texas Tech 1973-75, South Carolina 1976-82, Indiana 1983, Louisiana State 1984-90, Ohio State 1991. Pro coach: Joined Chargers in 1992.

1996 FIRST-YEAR ROSTER

Name	Pos.	Ht.	Wt.	Birthdate	College	Hometown	How Acq.
Bartlett, Jason	T	6-6	304	6/23/73	Wyoming	Chadron, Neb.	FA
Benton, Phillip	LB	6-1	244	7/8/71	Georgia	Covington, Ga.	FA
Bockert, Jeff	LB	6-3	247	10/29/72	Portland State	Vancouver, Wash.	FA
Bradley, Freddie	RB	5-10	208	6/12/70	Sonoma State	Oxnard, Calif.	D7
Brook, Mark	LB	6-5	255	1/26/73	Wyoming	Ft. Collins, Colo.	FA
Brown, Matt	G	6-2	309	10/27/71	Rutgers	Trenton, N.J.	FA
Camp, Tim	T	6-7	315	4/9/73	Oregon State	Gresham, Ore.	FA
Cavil, Ben (1)	G	6-2	310	1/31/72	Oklahoma	La Marque, Tex.	FA
Edwards, Vernon (1)	DE	6-4	255	6/23/72	Southern Methodist	Houston, Tex.	FA
Evans, Brandon	G	6-4	285	1/26/73	Colorado State	Ventura, Calif.	FA
Gillyard, James	DE	6-2	253	3/30/74	Louisiana State	Shreveport, La.	FA
Greenfield, Brian (1)	P	5-11	220	6/6/69	Pittsburgh	Sepulveda, Calif.	FA
Harrell, Maurice (1)	TE	6-4	245	4/10/72	Georgia	Eastman, Ga.	FA
Harrison, Brandon (1)	WR	5-10	181	9/10/71	Howard Payne	Dallas, Tex.	D6b-'95
Higgins, Robert	QB	6-3	225	5/23/71	Rutgers	Brooklyn, N.Y.	FA
Hippler, Werner	TE	6-5	262	7/30/70	Sacramento State	Cologne, Germany	FA
Ivey, Pat	DE	6-4	255	12/27/72	Missouri	Detroit, Mich.	FA
Jones, Charlie	WR	5-8	175	12/1/72	Fresno State	Hanford, Calif.	D4
Jones, Jo Jo	RB	5-6	184	3/16/71	Lambuth	Savannah, Ga.	FA
Kight, Danny	K	6-1	200	8/18/71	Augusta	Atlanta, Ga.	FA
Malone, Tyrone	DE	6-4	260	1/15/70	Lambuth	Houston, Tex.	FA
McKinzie, Dwight	WR	5-11	175	5/4/74	Idaho	Ft. Lauderdale, Fla.	FA
McWilliams, Robert	CB	6-0	175	12/2/72	Temple	Miami, Fla.	FA
Mills, Jim	T	6-4	290	3/30/73	Idaho	Marysville, Wash.	D6a
Miller, Tony (1)	WR	5-11	180	3/15/69	UCLA	San Francisco, Calif.	FA
Parker, Matt	DE	6-3	290	6/8/72	Alabama	Lawton, Okla.	FA
Peterson, Ray	WR	5-8	165	12/12/73	San Diego State	New Orleans, La.	FA
Roche, Brian	TE	6-4	255	5/5/73	San Jose State	La Verne, Calif.	D3
Sapp, Patrick	LB	6-4	258	5/11/73	Clemson	Jacksonville, Fla.	D2b
Shorter, Tyrone	CB	5-11	178	10/6/73	Austin Peay	Port Gibson, Miss.	FA
Soli, Junior	DT	6-2	290	11/15/74	Arkansas	Ft. Benning, Ga.	D5
Stallworth, Larry	WR	5-11	187	8/9/73	Sacramento C.C.	Sacramento, Calif.	FA
Still, Bryan	WR	5-11	174	6/3/74	Virginia Tech	Richmond, Va.	D2a
Stoltenberg, Bryan	C	6-1	293	8/25/72	Colorado	Sugarland, Tex.	D6b
Swift, Michael	CB	5-10	165	2/28/74	Austin Peay	Tiptonville, Tenn.	FA
Wright, Tyron	S	6-0	185	3/8/72	San Diego State	Gardena, Calif.	FA

The term NFL Rookie is defined as a player who is in his first season of professional football and has not been on the roster of another professional football team for any regular-season or postseason games. A Rookie is designated by an "R" on NFL rosters. Players who have been active in another professional football league or players who have NFL experience, including either preseason training camp or being on an Active List or Inactive List, or on Reserve/Injured or Reserve/Physically Unable to Perform for fewer than six regular-season games, are termed NFL First-Year Players. An NFL First-Year Player is designated by a "1" on NFL rosters. Thereafter, a player is credited with an additional year of experience for each season in which he accumulates six games on the Active List or Inactive List, or on Reserve/Injured or Reserve/Physically Unable to Perform.

NOTES

SEATTLE SEAHAWKS

American Football Conference
Western Division
Team Colors: Blue, Green, and Silver
11220 N.E. 53rd Street
Kirkland, Washington 98033
Telephone: (206) 827-9777

CLUB OFFICIALS

Ownership
Owner: Ken Behring
President: David Behring
Football Northwest, Inc.
Chairman: Paul Allen
Vice Chairman: Bert Kolde
President: Bob Whitsitt
Administration
Executive Vice President: Mickey Loomis
Vice President/Football Operations: Randy Mueller
Vice President/Administration and Communications: Gary Wright
Player Personnel Director: Mike Allman
Public Relations Director: Dave Neubert
Community Relations Director: Sandy Gregory
Player Programs Director: Reggie McKenzie
Assistant Public Relations Director: Steve Wright
Information Systems Director: Sterling Monroe
Ticket Manager: James Nagaoka
Trainer: Jim Whitesel
Equipment Manager: Terry Sinclair
Team Physicians: Dr. Kevin Auld, Dr. Stan Herring, Dr. Pierce Scranton, Dr. James Trombold
Stadium: Kingdome • **Capacity:** 66,400
201 South King Street
Seattle, Washington 98104
Playing Surface: AstroTurf
Training Camp: 11220 N.E. 53rd Street
Kirkland, Washington 98033

1996 SCHEDULE

PRESEASON

Aug. 3	**Atlanta**	7:00
Aug. 8	at Oakland	5:00
Aug. 17	at Indianapolis	7:00
Aug. 23	**San Francisco**	7:00

REGULAR SEASON

Sept. 1	at San Diego	1:00
Sept. 8	**Denver**	1:00
Sept. 15	**Kansas City**	1:00
Sept. 22	at Tampa Bay	4:00
Sept. 29	**Green Bay**	1:00
Oct. 6	at Miami	1:00
Oct. 13	Open Date	
Oct. 17	at Kansas City (Thurs.)	7:00
Oct. 27	**San Diego**	1:00
Nov. 3	**Houston**	1:00
Nov. 10	**Minnesota**	1:00
Nov. 17	at Detroit	1:00
Nov. 24	**Oakland**	1:00
Dec. 1	at Denver	2:00
Dec. 8	**Buffalo**	1:00
Dec. 15	at Jacksonville	8:00
Dec. 22	at Oakland	1:00

RECORD HOLDERS

INDIVIDUAL RECORDS—CAREER

Category	Name	Performance
Rushing (Yds.)	Curt Warner, 1983-89	6,705
Passing (Yds.)	Dave Krieg, 1980-1991	26,132
Passing (TDs)	Dave Krieg, 1980-1991	195
Receiving (No.)	Steve Largent, 1976-1989	819
Receiving (Yds.)	Steve Largent, 1976-1989	13,089
Interceptions	Dave Brown, 1976-1986	50
Punting (Avg.)	Rick Tuten, 1991-95	43.9
Punt Return (Avg.)	Paul Johns, 1981-84	11.4
Kickoff Return (Avg.)	Bobby Joe Edmonds, 1986-88	22.1
Field Goals	Norm Johnson, 1982-1990	159
Touchdowns (Tot.)	Steve Largent, 1976-1989	101
Points	Norm Johnson, 1982-1990	810

INDIVIDUAL RECORDS—SINGLE SEASON

Category	Name	Performance
Rushing (Yds.)	Chris Warren, 1994	1,545
Passing (Yds.)	Dave Krieg, 1984	3,671
Passing (TDs)	Dave Krieg, 1984	32
Receiving (No.)	Brian Blades, 1994	81
Receiving (Yds.)	Steve Largent, 1985	1,287
Interceptions	John Harris, 1981	10
	Kenny Easley, 1984	10
Punting (Avg.)	Rick Tuten, 1995	45.0
Punt Return (Avg.)	Bobby Joe Edmonds, 1987	12.6
Kickoff Return (Avg.)	Al Hunter, 1978	24.1
Field Goals	John Kasay, 1991	25
Touchdowns (Tot.)	Chris Warren, 1995	16
Points	Norm Johnson, 1984	110

INDIVIDUAL RECORDS—SINGLE GAME

Category	Name	Performance
Rushing (Yds.)	Curt Warner, 11-27-83	207
Passing (Yds.)	Dave Krieg, 11-20-83	418
Passing (TDs)	Dave Krieg, 12-2-84	5
	Dave Krieg, 9-15-85	5
	Dave Krieg, 11-28-88	5
Receiving (No.)	Steve Largent, 10-18-87	15
Receiving (Yds.)	Steve Largent, 10-18-87	261
Interceptions	Kenny Easley, 9-3-84	3
	Eugene Robinson, 12-6-92	3
Field Goals	Norm Johnson, 9-20-87	5
	Norm Johnson, 12-18-88	5
Touchdowns (Tot.)	Daryl Turner, 9-15-85	4
	Curt Warner, 12-11-88	4
Points	Daryl Turner, 9-15-85	24
	Curt Warner, 12-11-88	24

COACHING HISTORY

(144-171-0)

1976-82	Jack Patera*	35-59-0
1982	Mike McCormack	4-3-0
1983-91	Chuck Knox	83-67-0
1992-94	Tom Flores	14-34-0
1995	Dennis Erickson	8-8-0

*Released after two games in 1982

KINGDOME

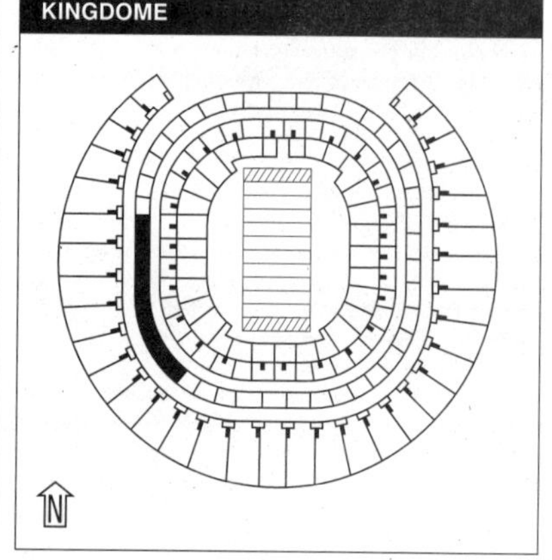

1995 TEAM RECORD

PRESEASON (2-2)

Date	Result		Opponents
8/5	W	34-20	St. Louis
8/12	L	17-20	Indianapolis
8/20	W	24-19	at New Orleans
8/26	L	7-17	at San Francisco

REGULAR SEASON (8-8)

Date	Result		Opponents	Att.
9/3	L	10-34	Kansas City	47,564
9/10	L	10-14	at San Diego	54,420
9/17	W	24-21	Cincinnati	39,492
10/1	W	27-10	Denver	49,914
10/8	L	14-34	at Oakland	50,213
10/15	L	21-27	at Buffalo	74,362
10/22	L	25-35	San Diego	45,821
10/29	L	14-20	at Arizona (OT)	39,600
11/5	W	30-28	N.Y. Giants	42,100
11/12	W	47-30	at Jacksonville	71,290
11/19	W	27-20	at Washington	51,298
11/26	L	10-16	N.Y. Jets	41,160
12/3	W	26-14	Philadelphia	39,893
12/10	W	31-27	at Denver	71,488
12/17	W	44-10	Oakland	58,428
12/24	L	3-26	at Kansas City	75,784

(OT) Overtime

SCORE BY PERIODS

Seahawks	79	77	88	119	0	—	363
Opponents	90	128	48	94	6	—	366

ATTENDANCE

Home 364,372 Away 488,455 Total 852,827
Single-game home record, 65,536 (9/18/94, Husky Stadium)
Single-season home record, 514,984 (1992)

1995 TEAM STATISTICS

	Seahawks	Opp.
Total First Downs	311	321
Rushing	121	116
Passing	171	181
Penalty	19	24
Third Down: Made/Att	82/217	81/218
Third Down Pct.	37.8	37.2
Fourth Down: Made/Att	9/13	10/18
Fourth Down Pct.	69.2	55.6
Total Net Yards	5270	5669
Avg. Per Game	329.4	354.3
Total Plays	1033	1078
Avg. Per Play	5.1	5.3
Net Yards Rushing	2178	2130
Avg. Per Game	136.1	133.1
Total Rushes	477	496
Net Yards Passing	3092	3539
Avg. Per Game	193.3	221.2
Sacked/Yards Lost	45/267	28/167
Gross Yards	3359	3706
Att./Completions	511/273	554/310
Completion Pct.	53.4	56.0
Had Intercepted	23	16
Punts/Avg.	83/45.0	81/42.6
Net Punting Avg.	83/36.5	81/36.4
Penalties/Yards Lost	100/852	114/901
Fumbles/Ball Lost	24/9	17/9
Touchdowns	42	43
Rushing	20	11
Passing	19	26
Returns	3	6
Avg. Time of Possession	28:30	31:30

1995 INDIVIDUAL STATISTICS

PASSING	Att.	Comp.	Yds.	Pct.	TD	Int.	Tkld.	Rate
Mirer	391	209	2564	53.5	13	20	42/255	63.7
Friesz	120	64	795	53.3	6	3	3/12	80.4
Seahawks	511	273	3359	53.4	19	23	45/267	67.6
Opponents	554	310	3706	56.0	26	16	28/167	80.2

SCORING	TD R	TD P	TD Rt	PAT	FG	Saf	PTS
Peterson	0	0	0	40/40	23/28	0	109
Warren	15	1	0	0/0	0/0	0	96
Galloway	1	7	1	0/0	0/0	0	54
Blades	0	4	0	0/0	0/0	0	24
Strong	1	3	0	0/0	0/0	0	24
Broussard	1	0	0	0/0	0/0	0	6
Crumpler	0	1	0	0/0	0/0	0	6
Edwards	0	0	1	0/0	0/0	0	6
Fauria	0	1	0	0/0	0/0	0	6
C. Harris	0	0	1	0/0	0/0	0	6
Johnson	1	0	0	0/0	0/0	0	6
Mirer	1	0	0	0/0	0/0	0	6
S. Smith	0	1	0	0/0	0/0	0	6
Thomas	0	1	0	0/0	0/0	0	6
Adams	0	0	0	0/0	0/0	1	2
Seahawks	20	19	3	40/40	23/28	1	363
Opponents	11	26	6	36/37	24/35	0	366

2-Point conversions: 0. Team: 0-2.

RUSHING	Att.	Yds.	Avg.	LG	TD
Warren	310	1346	4.3	52	15
Broussard	46	222	4.8	21t	1
L. Smith	36	215	6.0	68	0
Mirer	43	193	4.5	24	1
Galloway	11	154	14.0	86t	1
Strong	8	23	2.9	9	1
S. Smith	9	19	2.1	4	0
Blades	2	4	2.0	4	0
Johnson	1	2	2.0	2t	1
Friesz	11	0	0.0	2	0
Seahawks	477	2178	4.6	86t	20
Opponents	496	2130	4.3	46	11

RECEIVING	No.	Yds.	Avg.	LG	TD
Blades	77	1001	13.0	49	4
Galloway	67	1039	15.5	59t	7
Warren	35	247	7.1	20t	1
Crumpler	23	254	11.0	24	1
Fauria	17	181	10.6	20t	1
Thomas	12	239	19.9	50t	1
Strong	12	117	9.8	25	3
Broussard	10	94	9.4	25	0
S. Smith	7	59	8.4	17	1
McKnight	6	91	15.2	24	0
Proehl	5	29	5.8	9	0
L. Smith	1	10	10.0	10	0
Johnson	1	-2	-2.0	-2	0
Seahawks	273	3359	12.3	59t	19
Opponents	310	3706	12.0	88t	26

INTERCEPTIONS	No.	Yds.	Avg.	LG	TD
Blackmon	5	46	9.2	21	0
Gray	4	45	11.3	26	0
C. Harris	3	-5	-1.7	0	0
E. Robinson	1	32	32.0	21	0
Wooden	1	9	9.0	9	0
Jones	1	0	0.0	0	0
Moss	1	0	0.0	0	0
Seahawks	16	127	7.9	32	0
Opponents	23	384	16.7	72t	2

PUNTING	No.	Yds.	Avg.	In 20	LG
Tuten	83	3735	45.0	21	73
Seahawks	83	3735	45.0	21	73
Opponents	81	3449	42.6	24	62

PUNT RETURNS	No.	FC	Yds.	Avg.	LG	TD
Galloway	36	12	360	10.0	89t	1
R. Harris	3	0	23	7.7	10	0
E. Robinson	1	1	1	1.0	1	0
Seahawks	40	13	384	9.6	89t	1
Opponents	48	7	549	11.4	44	0

KICKOFF RETURNS	No.	Yds.	Avg.	LG	TD
Broussard	43	1064	24.7	70	0
C. Harris	19	397	20.9	35	0
Strong	4	65	16.3	30	0
Galloway	2	30	15.0	18	0
R. Harris	1	29	29.0	29	0
McKnight	1	4	4.0	4	0
L. Smith	1	20	20.0	20	0
S. Smith	1	11	11.0	11	0
Seahawks	72	1620	22.5	70	0
Opponents	70	1669	23.8	99t	2

SACKS	No.
Kennedy	6.5
Edwards	5.5
Sinclair	5.5
Adams	3.5
Moss	2.0
Bickett	1.0
Blackmon	1.0
McCrary	1.0
Nash	1.0
Williams	1.0
Seahawks	28.0
Opponents	45.0

1996 DRAFT CHOICES

Round	Name	Pos.	College
1	Pete Kendall	T	Boston College
2	Fred Thomas	DB	Tennessee-Martin
3	Robert Barr	T	Rutgers
	Reggie Brown	RB	Fresno State
4	Phillip Daniels	DE	Georgia
	Eric Unverzagt	LB	Wisconsin
6	Reggie Green	G	Florida
	T.J. Cunningham	DB	Colorado
7	Johnie Church	DE	Florida

SEATTLE SEAHAWKS

1996 VETERAN ROSTER

No.	Name	Pos.	Ht.	Wt.	Birthdate	NFL Exp.	College	Hometown	How Acq.	'95 Games/ Starts
98	Adams, Sam	DT	6-3	297	6/13/73	3	Texas A&M	Houston, Tex.	D1-'94	16/5
74	Atkins, James	T	6-6	303	1/28/70	3	Southwestern Louisiana	Amite, La.	FA-'93	16/16
75	Ballard, Howard	T	6-6	325	11/3/63	9	Alabama A&M	Ashland, Ala.	UFA(Buff)-'94	16/16
54	Barber, Michael	LB	6-1	252	11/9/71	2	Clemson	Edgemore, S.C.	FA-'95	2/0
20	Bellamy, Jay	S	5-11	198	7/8/72	3	Rutgers	Aberdeen, N.J.	FA-'94	15/0
25	Blackmon, Robert	S	6-0	208	5/12/67	7	Baylor	Van Vleck, Tex.	D2b-'90	13/13
89	Blades, Brian	WR	5-11	188	7/24/65	9	Miami	Ft. Lauderdale, Fla.	D2-'88	16/16
31	Broussard, Steve	RB	5-7	201	2/22/67	7	Washington State	Los Angeles, Calif.	FA-'95	15/1
27	Covington, Tony	S	5-11	197	12/26/67	6	Virginia	Winston-Salem, N.C.	UFA(TB)-'95	11/0
87	Crumpler, Carlester	TE	6-6	260	9/5/71	3	East Carolina	Greenville, N.C.	D7-'94	16/7
94	Edwards, Antonio	DE	6-3	271	3/10/70	4	Valdosta State	Moultrie, Ga.	D8b-'93	13/7
85	Fauria, Christian	TE	6-4	245	9/22/71	2	Colorado	Encino, Calif.	D2-'95	14/9
17	Friesz, John	QB	6-4	211	5/19/67	7	Idaho	Coeur d'Alene, Idaho	UFA(Wash)-'95	6/3
84	Galloway, Joey	WR	5-11	188	11/20/71	2	Ohio State	Bellaire, Ohio	D1-'95	16/16
8	# Gelbaugh, Stan	QB	6-3	215	12/4/62	8	Maryland	Mechanicsburg, Pa.	PB(Ariz)-'92	0*
73	Graham, Derrick	G	6-4	315	3/18/67	7	Appalachian State	Groveland, Fla.	UFA(Car)-'96	11/7*
26	† Gray, Carlton	CB	6-0	200	6/26/71	4	UCLA	Cincinnati, Ohio	D2-'93	16/16
30	Harris, Corey	CB	5-11	199	10/25/69	5	Vanderbilt	Indianapolis, Ind.	RFA(GB)-'95	16/16
81	Harris, Ronnie	WR	5-11	175	6/4/70	2	Oregon	San Jose, Calif.	FA-'94	13/0
24	Jones, Selwyn	CB	6-0	185	5/13/70	5	Colorado State	Missouri City, Tex.	FA-'95	15/0
77	Joyce, Matt	G	6-7	316	3/30/72	2	Richmond	St. Petersburg, Fla.	FA-'95	16/13
78	† Keim, Mike	T	6-7	302	11/12/65	4	Brigham Young	Springerville, Ariz.	FA-'92	7/0
96	Kennedy, Cortez	DT	6-3	293	8/23/68	7	Miami	Wilson, Ark.	D1-'90	16/16
57	Kyle, Jason	LB	6-3	242	5/12/72	2	Arizona State	Tempe, Ariz.	D4b-'95	16/0
56	Logan, James	LB	6-2	214	12/6/72	2	Memphis	Opp, Ala.	W(Cin)-'95	6/0
52	Mawae, Kevin	C	6-4	288	1/23/71	3	Louisiana State	Leesville, La.	D2-'94	16/16
99	† McCrary, Michael	DE	6-4	267	7/7/70	4	Wake Forest	Vienna, Va.	D7-'93	11/0
82	McKnight, James	WR	6-0	186	6/17/72	3	Liberty	Apoka, Fla.	FA-'94	16/0
92	McMillian, Henry	DT	6-3	275	10/17/71	2	Florida	Folkston, Ga.	D6a-'95	1/0
3	Mirer, Rick	QB	6-2	214	3/19/70	4	Notre Dame	Goshen, Ind.	D1-'93	15/13
97	t- Montgomery, Glenn	DT	6-0	282	3/31/67	8	Houston	Harvey, La.	T(Hou)-'96	15/14*
55	Moss, Winston	LB	6-3	245	12/24/65	10	Miami	Miami, Fla.	UFA(Oak)-'95	16/16
37	Odomes, Nate	CB	5-10	188	8/25/65	9	Wisconsin	Columbus, Ga.	UFA(Buff)-'94	0*
2	Peterson, Todd	K	5-10	173	2/4/70	2	Georgia	Valdosta, Ga.	FA-'95	16/0
88	Proehl, Ricky	WR	6-0	189	3/7/68	7	Wake Forest	Hillsborough, N.J.	T(Ariz)-'95	8/0
41	Robinson, Eugene	S	6-0	195	5/28/63	12	Colgate	Hartford, Conn.	FA-'85	16/16
70	Sinclair, Michael	DE	6-4	267	1/31/68	5	Eastern New Mexico	Beaumont, Tex.	D6-'91	16/15
36	Smith, Lamar	RB	5-11	223	11/29/70	3	Houston	Ft. Wayne, Ind.	D3-'94	12/0
35	Smith, Steve	RB	6-1	242	8/30/64	10	Penn State	Hyattsville, Md.	FA-'94	9/7
59	Stowe, Tyronne	LB	6-2	239	5/30/65	10	Rutgers	Passaic, N.J.	UFA(Wash)-'93	6/6
38	Strong, Mack	RB	6-0	224	9/11/71	3	Georgia	Columbus, Ga.	FA-'93	16/2
53	Sweeney, Jim	C	6-4	295	8/8/62	13	Pittsburgh	Pittsburgh, Pa.	FA-'95	16/16
86	# Thomas, Robb	WR	5-11	175	3/29/66	8	Oregon State	Corvallis, Ore.	FA-'92	15/2
14	# Tuten, Rick	P	6-2	221	1/5/65	7	Florida State	Ocala, Fla.	FA-'91	16/0
42	Warren, Chris	RB	6-2	225	1/24/68	7	Ferrum	Burke, Va.	D4-'90	16/16
95	Wells, Dean	LB	6-3	244	7/20/70	4	Kentucky	Louisville, Ky.	D4-'93	14/10
33	Williams, Darryl	S	6-0	191	1/7/70	5	Miami	Hialeah, Fla.	UFA(Cin)-'96	16/16*
90	Wooden, Terry	LB	6-3	239	1/14/67	7	Syracuse	Farmington, Conn.	D2a-'90	16/16

* Gelbaugh active for one game but did not play in '95; Graham played 11 games with Carolina in '95; Montgomery played 15 games with Houston; Odomes missed '95 season because of injury; Williams played 16 games with Cincinnati.

Unrestricted free agent; subject to developments.

† Restricted free agent; subject to developments.

Traded—G Jeff Blackshear to Baltimore.

t- Seahawks traded for Montgomery (Houston).

Players lost through free agency (3): LB Duane Bickett (Car; 15 games in '95), T Ray Roberts (Det; 11), S Rafael Robinson (Hou; 13).

Also played with Seahawks in '95—G Jeff Blackshear (16 games in '95), CB Tony Brown (16), RB Tracy Johnson (15), TE Trey Junkin (16), DT Joe Nash (16), DE Brent Williams (11).

COACHING STAFF

Head Coach,
Dennis Erickson

Pro Career: Named the fifth head coach in franchise history on January 12, 1995. Quarterback at Montana State from 1966-68. Career record: 8-8-0.

Background: Started his coaching career at Montana State as a graduate assistant in 1969. Also served as a graduate assistant at Washington State in 1970. Was an assistant at Montana State, Idaho, and Fresno State before becoming the head coach at Idaho in 1982. Twice advanced to NCAA I-AA playoffs and was a two-time All-Big Sky Conference coach of the year. Head coach one season (1986) at Wyoming before moving to Washington State in 1987. Took Cougars to their first bowl game since 1981 and posted their first bowl game win in 72 years in 1988. Finished the season with a national ranking of sixteenth, the school's best ever. Spent the last six seasons at the University of Miami, where he won national championships in 1989 (his first season) and in 1991, compiling an undefeated (12-0) record. Played in six New Year's Day bowl games, including five with national championship implications. Twice finished third in the country and once sixth in addition to the two national titles. Posted an NCAA-best 63-9 record during tenure at Miami and reached 100 career wins in just 137 games, the fourth fastest among Division I coaches active in 1994. Was 35-2 at the Orange Bowl, including being part of an NCAA-record 58-game winning streak. Career record: 137-40-1.

Personal: Born March 24, 1947, in Everett, Washington. Graduated from Montana State with a bachelor of arts degree in Physical Education. Dennis and his wife, Marilyn, have two sons, Bryce and Ryan, and live in Redmond, Washington.

ASSISTANT COACHES

Dave Arnold, special teams; born September 18, 1944, Jackson, Mich., lives in Bellevue, Wash. Tight end Drake 1963-66. No pro playing experience. College coach: Michigan State 1980-81, Montana State 1982-86 (head coach 1983-86), Washington State 1987-88, Miami 1989-94. Pro coach: Joined Seahawks in 1995.

Tommy Brasher, defensive line; born December 30, 1940, El Dorado, Ark., lives in Redmond, Wash. Linebacker Arkansas 1962-63. No pro playing experience. College coach: Arkansas 1970, Virginia Tech 1971, Northeast Louisiana 1974, 1976, Southern Methodist 1977-81. Pro coach: Shreveport Steamer (WFL) 1975, New England Patriots 1982-84, Philadelphia Eagles 1985, Atlanta Falcons 1986-89, Tampa Bay Buccaneers 1990, joined Seahawks in 1992.

Bob Bratkowski, offensive coordinator-wide receivers; born December 2, 1955, San Angelo, Tex., lives in Redmond, Wash. Wide receiver Washington State 1974, 1976-77. No pro playing experience. College coach: Missouri 1978-80, Weber State 1981-85, Wyoming 1986, Washington State 1987-88, Miami 1989-91. Pro coach: Joined Seahawks in 1992.

Dave Brown, defensive assistant; born January 16, 1953, Akron, Ohio, lives in Woodinville, Wash. Defensive back Michigan 1972-74. Pro defensive back Pittsburgh Steelers 1975, Seattle Seahawks 1976-86, Green Bay Packers 1987-90. Pro coach: Joined Seahawks in 1992.

Keith Gilbertson, defensive assistant; born May 15, 1948, Snohomish, Wash; lives in Kirkland, Wash. Lineman Hawaii 1969-70. No pro playing experience. College coach: 1971-73 Idaho State, 1974 Western Washington, 1976, 1989-91 Washington, 1977-81 Utah State, 1982, 1985-88 Idaho (head coach 1986-88), 1992-95 California (head coach).

Ned James, offensive staff assistant; born January 18, 1964, Syracuse, N.Y., lives in Kirkland, Wash. Quarterback New Mexico 1965-66. Pro quarterback Montreal Alouettes (CFL) 1987, Dallas Texans (Arena Football) 1990. College coach: Arizona State 1987-88, Long Beach State 1988-89, Texas Christian 1989-90, Winona State 1992-94. Pro coach: London Monarchs (World League) 1991-92, joined Seahawks in 1995.

Dana LeDuc, strength and conditioning; born March 22, 1953, Tacoma, Wash., lives in Bellevue, Wash. No college or pro playing experience. College coach: Texas 1977-92, Miami 1993-94. Pro Coach: Joined Seahawks in 1995.

Greg McMakin, defensive coordinator; born April 24, 1947, Springfield, Ore., lives in Redmond, Wash. Defensive back Southern Oregon 1964-68. No pro playing experience. College coach: Arizona 1968-69, Western Oregon State 1973-76, Idaho 1976-78, San Jose State 1978-85, Stanford 1984-85, Oregon Tech 1986-90, Utah 1990-92, Miami 1993-94. Pro coach: Denver Gold (USFL) 1985-86, joined Seahawks in 1995.

Howard Mudd, offensive line; born February 10, 1942, Midland, Mich., lives in Kirkland, Wash. Guard Hillsdale College 1961-63. Pro guard San Francisco 49ers 1964-69, Chicago Bears 1969-71. College coach: California 1972-73. Pro coach: San Diego Chargers 1974-76, San Francisco 49ers 1977, Seattle Seahawks 1978-82, Cleveland Browns 1983-88, Kansas City Chiefs 1989-92, rejoined Seahawks in 1993.

Mike Murphy, linebackers; born September 25, 1944, New York City, N.Y., lives in Bellevue, Wash. Guard-linebacker Huron College 1963-1965. No pro playing experience. College coach: Vermont 1970-73, Idaho State 1974-76, Western Illinois 1977-78. Pro coach: Saskatchewan Roughriders (CFL) 1979, Chicago Blitz (USFL) 1984, Detroit Lions 1985-89, Arizona Cardinals 1990-93, joined Seahawks in 1995.

Rich Olson, quarterbacks; born July 7, 1948, Wilmington, Calif., lives in Bellevue, Wash. Quarterback/free safety Washington State 1968-69. No pro playing experience. College coach: Washington State 1970, Fresno State 1976, Southern California 1977, Southern Methodist 1978-80, Arkansas 1981-83, Fresno State 1984-91, Miami 1992-94. Pro coach: Joined Seahawks in 1995.

Willy Robinson, defensive backs; born February 10, 1956, Fort Carson, Colo., lives in Bellevue, Wash. No college or pro playing experience. College coach: Fresno State 1978, 1980-83, San Jose State 1979, Miami 1994. Pro coach: Joined Seahawks in 1995.

Clarence Shelmon, running backs; born September 17, 1952, Bossier City, La., lives in Kirkland, Wash. Running back Houston 1971-75. No pro playing experience. College coach: Army 1978-80, Indiana 1981-83, Arizona 1984-86, Southern California 1987-90. Pro coach: Los Angeles Rams 1991, joined Seahawks in 1992.

Gregg Smith, assistant head coach-tight ends; born October 28, 1946, Oklahoma City, Okla., lives in Bellevue, Wash. Tight end Idaho 1965-66. No pro playing experience. College coach: Idaho 1967-68, 1982-85, Wyoming 1986, Washington State 1987-88, Miami 1989-94. Pro coach: Joined Seahawks in 1995.

1996 FIRST-YEAR ROSTER

Name	Pos.	Ht.	Wt.	Birthdate	College	Hometown	How Acq.
Barr, Robert	T	6-4	307	6/7/73	Rutgers	Hanover, Pa.	D3a
Beede, Frank	C	6-4	292	5/1/73	Panhandle State	Antioch, Calif.	FA
Benford, Clarence	TE	6-3	249	8/18/73	Albany State	Windsor Forest, Ga.	FA
Bloedorn, Greg	C	6-6	278	11/15/72	Cornell	Glen Ellyn, Ill.	FA
Brown, Reggie	RB	6-0	233	6/26/73	Fresno State	Detroit, Mich.	D3b
Brown, Willie	LB	6-0	212	5/19/72	Temple	Syracuse, N.Y.	FA
Bryant, Keif (1)	DT	6-4	282	3/12/73	Rutgers	Largo, Fla.	D7-'95
Church, Johnie	DE	6-3	259	1/1/74	Florida	Ft. Myers, Fla.	D7
Collins, Marc	P	6-4	209	4/24/74	Eastern Kentucky	Crestview Hills, Ky.	FA
Cunningham, T.J.	S	6-0	191	10/24/72	Colorado	Aurora, Colo.	D6b
Daniels, Phillip	DE	6-5	263	3/4/73	Georgia	Donalsonville, Ga.	D4a
Fletcher, Tom (1)	LS	6-3	245	10/24/72	San Diego State	San Marcos, Calif.	FA
Goines, Eddie (1)	WR	6-0	186	8/16/72	North Carolina State	Lakeland, Fla.	D6b-'95
Gary, Jimmy	RB	5-11	209	11/7/72	West Virginia	Okechobee, Fla.	FA
Gray, Oscar (1)	RB	6-1	255	8/7/72	Arkansas	Houston, Tex.	FA
Green, Reggie	G	6-5	310	11/23/73	Florida	Bradenton, Fla.	D6a
Ingram, Kelvin (1)	T	6-5	276	10/25/70	Oklahoma State	Ft. Pierce, Fla.	FA
Kendall, Pete	G	6-5	292	7/9/72	Boston College	Weymouth, Mass.	D1
Kitna, Jon	QB	6-2	217	9/21/72	Central Washington	Tacoma, Wash.	FA
Miller, Josh (1)	P	6-3	215	7/14/70	Arizona	East Brunswick, N.J.	FA
Newby, Henry (1)	LB	6-2	231	6/21/68	Fairmont State	Farrell, Pa.	FA
Norman, Todd (1)	G	6-5	300	9/11/71	Notre Dame	Huntington Bch., Calif.	FA
Seigler, Dexter (1)	CB	5-9	178	1/11/72	Miami	Miami, Fla.	FA
Shillingford, Grayson	WR	6-0	192	12/25/74	British Columbia	Toronto, Canada	FA
Solomon, John (1)	DE	6-3	233	11/10/73	Sam Houston State	Houston, Tex.	FA
Thomas, Fred	CB	5-9	172	9/11/73	Tennessee-Martin	Bruce, Miss.	D2
Thompson, Larry (1)	WR	5-11	170	5/25/71	Solano C.C.	Fairfield, Calif.	FA
Unverzagt, Eric	LB	6-1	236	12/18/72	Wisconsin	Central Islip, N.Y.	D4c
Williams, Grant	T	6-7	323	5/10/74	Louisiana Tech	Clinton, Miss.	FA
Woods, Manley (1)	WR	6-2	169	7/28/72	New Mexico	Gardena, Calif.	FA

The term NFL Rookie is defined as a player who is in his first season of professional football and has not been on the roster of another professional football team for any regular-season or postseason games. A Rookie is designated by an "R" on NFL rosters. Players who have been active in another professional football league or players who have NFL experience, including either preseason training camp or being on an Active List or Inactive List, or on Reserve/Injured or Reserve/Physically Unable to Perform for fewer than six regular-season games, are termed NFL First-Year Players. An NFL First-Year Player is designated by a "1" on NFL rosters. Thereafter, a player is credited with an additional year of experience for each season in which he accumulates six games on the Active List or Inactive List, or on Reserve/Injured or Reserve/Physically Unable to Perform.

NOTES

The NFC

ARIZONA CARDINALS

National Football Conference
Eastern Division
Team Colors: Cardinal Red, Black, and White
P.O. Box 888
Phoenix, Arizona 85001-0888
Telephone: (602) 379-0101

CLUB OFFICIALS

President: William V. Bidwill
Vice President: Larry Wilson
Vice President of Sales and Marketing: John Shean
Secretary and General Counsel: Thomas J. Guilfoil
Treasurer and Chief Financial Officer: Charley Schlegel
Assistant to the General Manager: Joe Woolley
Assistant to the President: Bob Ferguson
Public Relations Director: Paul Jensen
Media Coordinator: Greg Gladysiewski
Director of Community Relations: Adele Harris
Director of Marketing: Joe Castor
Business Manager: Steve Walsh
Ticket Manager: Steve Bomar
Trainer: John Omohundro
Assistant Trainers: Jim Shearer, Jeff Herndon
Equipment Manager: Mark Ahlemeier
Assistant Equipment Manager: Steve Christensen
Stadium: Sun Devil Stadium • **Capacity:** 73,273
Fifth Street
Tempe, Arizona 85287
Playing Surface: Grass
Training Camp: Northern Arizona University
Flagstaff, Arizona 86011

1996 SCHEDULE

PRESEASON

Aug. 2	**Oakland**	7:00
Aug. 10	**Cincinnati**	7:30
Aug. 17	at San Diego	7:00
Aug. 23	at Atlanta	7:30

REGULAR SEASON

Sept. 1	at Indianapolis	12:00
Sept. 8	**Miami**	5:00
Sept. 15	at New England	1:00
Sept. 22	at New Orleans	12:00
Sept. 29	**St. Louis**	1:00
Oct. 6	Open Date	
Oct. 13	at Dallas	12:00
Oct. 20	**Tampa Bay**	1:00
Oct. 27	**New York Jets**	2:00
Nov. 3	at New York Giants	1:00
Nov. 10	at Washington	1:00
Nov. 17	**New York Giants**	2:00
Nov. 24	**Philadelphia**	2:00
Dec. 1	at Minnesota	12:00
Dec. 8	**Dallas**	2:00
Dec. 15	**Washington**	2:00
Dec. 22	at Philadelphia	1:00

RECORD HOLDERS

INDIVIDUAL RECORDS—CAREER

Category	Name	Performance
Rushing (Yds.)	Ottis Anderson, 1979-1986	7,999
Passing (Yds.)	Jim Hart, 1966-1983	34,639
Passing (TDs)	Jim Hart, 1966-1983	209
Receiving (No.)	Roy Green, 1979-1990	522
Receiving (Yds.)	Roy Green, 1979-1990	8,497
Interceptions	Larry Wilson, 1960-1972	52
Punting (Avg.)	Jerry Norton, 1959-1961	44.9
Punt Return (Avg.)	Charley Trippi, 1947-1955	13.7
Kickoff Return (Avg.)	Ollie Matson, 1952, 1954-58	28.5
Field Goals	Jim Bakken, 1962-1978	282
Touchdowns (Tot.)	Roy Green, 1979-1990	70
Points	Jim Bakken, 1962-1978	1,380

INDIVIDUAL RECORDS—SINGLE SEASON

Category	Name	Performance
Rushing (Yds.)	Ottis Anderson, 1979	1,605
Passing (Yds.)	Neil Lomax, 1984	4,614
Passing (TDs)	Charley Johnson, 1963	28
	Neil Lomax, 1984	28
Receiving (No.)	Larry Centers, 1995	101
Receiving (Yds.)	Roy Green, 1984	1,555
Interceptions	Bob Nussbaumer, 1949	12
Punting (Avg.)	Jerry Norton, 1960	45.6
Punt Return (Avg.)	John (Red) Cochran, 1949	20.9
Kickoff Return (Avg.)	Ollie Matson, 1958	35.5
Field Goals	Greg Davis, 1995	30
Touchdowns (Tot.)	John David Crow, 1962	17
Points	Jim Bakken, 1967	117
	Neil O'Donoghue, 1984	117

INDIVIDUAL RECORDS—SINGLE GAME

Category	Name	Performance
Rushing (Yds.)	John David Crow, 12-18-60	203
Passing (Yds.)	Neil Lomax, 12-16-84	468
Passing (TDs)	Jim Hardy, 10-2-50	6
	Charley Johnson, 9-26-65	6
	Charley Johnson, 11-2-69	6
Receiving (No.)	Sonny Randle, 11-4-62	16
Receiving (Yds.)	Sonny Randle, 11-4-62	256
Interceptions	Bob Nussbaumer, 11-13-49	*4
	Jerry Norton, 11-20-60	*4
Field Goals	Jim Bakken, 9-24-67	*7
Touchdowns (Tot.)	Ernie Nevers, 11-28-29	*6
Points	Ernie Nevers, 11-28-29	*40

*NFL Record

COACHING HISTORY

Chicago 1920-1959, St. Louis 1960-1987
(398-546-39)

1920-22	John (Paddy) Driscoll	17-8-4
1923-24	Arnold Horween	13-8-1
1925-26	Norman Barry	16-8-2
1927	Guy Chamberlin	3-7-1
1928	Fred Gillies	1-5-0
1929	Dewey Scanlon	6-6-1
1930	Ernie Nevers	5-6-2
1931	LeRoy Andrews*	0-1-0
1931	Ernie Nevers	5-3-0
1932	Jack Chevigny	2-6-2
1933-34	Paul Schissler	6-15-1
1935-38	Milan Creighton	16-26-4
1939	Ernie Nevers	1-10-0
1940-42	Jimmy Conzelman	8-22-3
1943-45	Phil Handler**	1-29-0
1946-48	Jimmy Conzelman	27-10-0
1949	Phil Handler-Buddy Parker***	2-4-0
1949	Raymond (Buddy) Parker	4-1-1
1950-51	Earl (Curly) Lambeau****	7-15-0
1951	Phil Handler-Cecil Isbell#	1-1-0
1952	Joe Kuharich	4-8-0
1953-54	Joe Stydahar	3-20-1
1955-57	Ray Richards	14-21-1
1958-61	Frank (Pop) Ivy##	17-29-2
1961	Chuck Drulis-Ray Prochaska-Ray Willsey###	2-0-0
1962-65	Wally Lemm	27-26-3
1966-70	Charley Winner	35-30-5
1971-72	Bob Hollway	8-18-2
1973-77	Don Coryell	42-29-1
1978-79	Bud Wilkinson####	9-20-0
1979	Larry Wilson	2-1-0
1980-85	Jim Hanifan	39-50-1
1986-89	Gene Stallings@	23-34-1
1989	Hank Kuhlmann	0-5-0
1990-93	Joe Bugel	20-44-0
1994-95	Buddy Ryan	12-20-0

* Resigned after one game in 1931
** Co-coach with Walt Kiesling in Chicago Cardinals-Pittsburgh merger in 1944
*** Co-coaches for first six games in 1949
**** Resigned after 10 games in 1951
# Co-coaches
Resigned after 12 games in 1961
Co-coaches
Released after 13 games in 1979
@ Released after 11 games in 1989

SUN DEVIL STADIUM

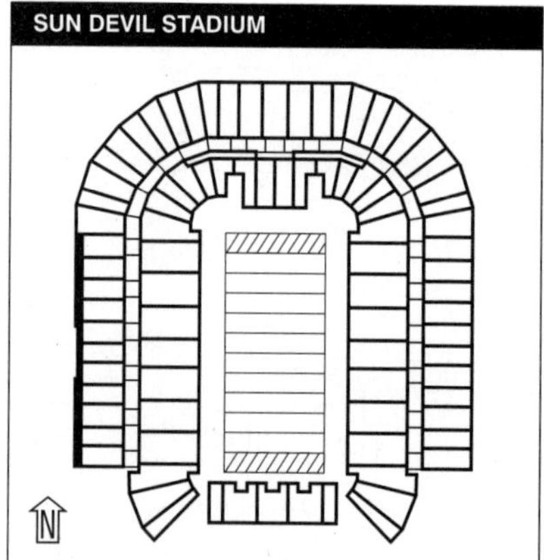

1995 TEAM RECORD

PRESEASON (3-1)

Date	Result		Opponents
8/5	W	16-13	at Houston
8/11	W	22-17	Kansas City
8/20	W	17-16	at Chicago
8/25	L	17-31	Cleveland

REGULAR SEASON (4-12)

Date	Result		Opponents	Att.
9/3	L	7-27	at Washington	52,731
9/10	L	19-31	Philadelphia	45,004
9/17	W	20-17	at Detroit	58,727
9/24	L	20-34	at Dallas	64,560
10/1	L	3-24	Kansas City	50,211
10/8	L	21-27	at N.Y. Giants (OT)	68,463
10/15	W	24-20	Washington	42,370
10/29	W	20-14	Seattle (OT)	39,600
11/5	L	6-38	at Denver	71,488
11/12	L	24-30	Minnesota (OT)	51,342
11/19	L	7-27	at Carolina	49,582
11/26	W	40-37	Atlanta (OT)	35,147
11/30	L	6-10	N.Y. Giants	44,246
12/9	L	25-28	at San Diego	55,258
12/17	L	20-21	at Philadelphia	62,076
12/25	L	13-37	Dallas	72,394

(OT) Overtime

SCORE BY PERIODS

Cardinals	35	108	53	70	9	—	275
Opponents	75	136	109	90	12	—	422

ATTENDANCE

Home 380,314 Away 482,885 Total 863,199
Single-game home record, 72,394 (12/25/95)
Single-season home record, 497,330 (1994)

1995 TEAM STATISTICS

	Cardinals	Opp.
Total First Downs	285	310
Rushing	65	105
Passing	184	180
Penalty	36	25
Third Down: Made/Att	71/205	90/203
Third Down Pct.	34.6	44.3
Fourth Down: Made/Att	2/13	3/8
Fourth Down Pct.	15.4	37.5
Total Net Yards	4866	5704
Avg. Per Game	304.1	356.5
Total Plays	1002	995
Avg. Per Play	4.9	5.7
Net Yards Rushing	1363	2249
Avg. Per Game	85.2	140.6
Total Rushes	387	503
Net Yards Passing	3503	3455
Avg. Per Game	218.9	215.9
Sacked/Yards Lost	55/390	31/200
Gross Yards	3893	3655
Att./Completions	560/327	461/264
Completion Pct.	58.4	57.3
Had Intercepted	24	19
Punts/Avg.	72/43.8	62/43.5
Net Punting Avg.	72/38.2	62/38.1
Penalties/Yards Lost	119/835	117/860
Fumbles/Ball Lost	41/19	39/23
Touchdowns	26	53
Rushing	3	14
Passing	17	33
Returns	6	6
Avg. Time of Possession	30:54	29:06

1995 INDIVIDUAL STATISTICS

PASSING	Att.	Comp.	Yds.	Pct.	TD	Int.	Tkld.	Rate
Krieg	521	304	3554	58.3	16	21	53/380	72.6
Buck	32	20	271	62.5	1	0	2/10	99.9
Case	2	1	19	50.0	0	1	0/0	43.8
Hearst	2	1	16	50.0	0	0	0/0	77.1
R. Moore	2	1	33	50.0	0	1	0/0	56.3
Centers	1	0	0	0.0	0	1	0/0	0.0
Cardinals	560	327	3893	58.4	17	24	55/390	72.0
Opponents	461	264	3655	57.3	33	19	31/200	89.5

SCORING	TD R	TD P	TD Rt	PAT	FG	Saf	PTS
G. Davis	0	0	0	19/19	30/39	0	109
R. Moore	0	5	0	0/0	0/0	0	32
Centers	2	2	0	0/0	0/0	0	24
Williams	0	0	3	0/0	0/0	0	18
Sanders	0	2	0	0/0	0/0	0	16
Edwards	0	2	0	0/0	0/0	0	12
Gaines	0	2	0	0/0	0/0	0	12
Hearst	1	1	0	0/0	0/0	0	12
McBride	0	2	0	0/0	0/0	0	12
Anderson	0	1	0	0/0	0/0	0	10
Lynch	0	0	1	0/0	0/0	0	6
McCants	0	0	1	0/0	0/0	0	6
Simmons	0	0	1	0/0	0/0	0	6
Cardinals	3	17	6	19/19	30/39	0	275
Opponents	14	33	6	50/51	18/25	0	422

2-Point conversions: Anderson 2, Sanders 2, R. Moore. Team: 5-6.

RUSHING	Att.	Yds.	Avg.	LG	TD
Hearst	284	1070	3.8	38	1
Centers	78	254	3.3	20	2
Krieg	19	29	1.5	17	0
Case	1	4	4.0	4	0
Feagles	2	4	2.0	4	0
Lassiter	1	1	1.0	1	0
Sanders	1	1	1.0	1	0
Buck	1	0	0.0	0	0
Cardinals	387	1363	3.5	38	3
Opponents	503	2249	4.5	76t	14

RECEIVING	No.	Yds.	Avg.	LG	TD
Centers	101	962	9.5	32	2
R. Moore	63	907	14.4	45	5
Sanders	52	883	17.0	48	2
Edwards	29	417	14.4	28t	2
Hearst	29	243	8.4	39	1
Gaines	14	117	8.4	22t	2
McBride	13	112	8.6	24	2
Dowdell	10	96	9.6	23	0
Reeves	6	62	10.3	22	0
Fann	5	41	8.2	13	0
Anderson	3	34	11.3	18	1
Samuels	2	19	9.5	12	0
Cardinals	327	3893	11.9	48	17
Opponents	264	3655	13.8	73t	33

INTERCEPTIONS	No.	Yds.	Avg.	LG	TD
Williams	6	86	14.3	48t	2
Joyner	3	9	3.0	11	0
Hunter	2	21	10.5	21	0
Alexander	2	14	7.0	14	0
Hoage	2	0	0.0	0	0
Lynch	1	72	72.0	72t	1
Bankston	1	28	28.0	28	0
Simmons	1	25	25.0	25t	1
Paul	1	4	4.0	4	0
Cardinals	19	259	13.6	72t	4
Opponents	24	307	12.8	58t	4

PUNTING	No.	Yds.	Avg.	In 20	LG
Feagles	72	3150	43.8	20	60
Cardinals	72	3150	43.8	20	60
Opponents	62	2694	43.5	21	65

PUNT RETURNS	No.	FC	Yds.	Avg.	LG	TD
Edwards	18	11	131	7.3	16	0
Reeves	4	0	41	10.3	14	0
Dowdell	1	0	0	0.0	0	0
Cardinals	23	11	172	7.5	16	0
Opponents	32	14	242	7.6	25	0

KICKOFF RETURNS	No.	Yds.	Avg.	LG	TD
Terry	37	808	21.8	53	0
Dowdell	18	344	19.1	28	0
Johnson	11	259	23.5	70	0
Edwards	3	50	16.7	24	0
Higgs	2	26	13.0	17	0
Anderson	1	17	17.0	17	0
Centers	1	15	15.0	15	0
Cardinals	73	1519	20.8	70	0
Opponents	65	1593	24.5	92t	2

SACKS	No.
Simmons	11.0
Swann	8.5
Bankston	2.0
Hill	2.0
Hoage	1.0
Irving	1.0
Joyner	1.0
Lynch	1.0
Miller	1.0
Wilson	1.0
Alexander	0.5
C. Brown	0.5
McCants	0.5
Cardinals	31.0
Opponents	55.0

1996 DRAFT CHOICES

Round	Name	Pos.	College
1	Simeon Rice	DE	Illinois
2	Leeland McElroy	RB	Texas A&M
3	Johnny McWilliams	TE	Southern California
4	Aaron Graham	C	Nebraska
5	James Dexter	T	South Carolina
	Harry Stamps	T	Oklahoma
	Dell McGee	DB	Auburn
6	Mike Foley	DT	New Hampshire
7	Jarius Hayes	TE	North Alabama

ARIZONA CARDINALS

1996 VETERAN ROSTER

No.	Name	Pos.	Ht.	Wt.	Birthdate	NFL Exp.	College	Hometown	How Acq.	'95 Games/ Starts
46	Alexander, Brent	CB-S	5-10	184	7/10/71	3	Tennessee State	Gallatin, Tenn.	FA-'94	16/13
82	Anderson, Stevie	WR	6-5	215	5/12/70	3	Grambling State	Monroe, La.	W(NYJ)-'95	5/0
63	Bankston, Michael	DE	6-3	280	3/12/70	5	Sam Houston State	East Bernard, Tex.	D4b-'92	16/16
25	Brooks, Carlos	CB	6-0	200	5/8/71	2	Bowling Green	Middletown, Ohio	FA-'95	7/0
78	Brown, Chadrick	DE	6-7	265	7/9/71	4	Mississippi	Thomasville, Ga.	D8a-'93	5/4
21	Brown, Lance	CB-S	6-0	200	2/2/72	2	Indiana	Jacksonville, Fla.	FA-'95	11/5
75	Brown, Lomas	T	6-4	275	3/30/63	12	Florida	Miami, Fla.	UFA(Det)-'96	15/14*
80	Carter, Pat	TE	6-4	258	8/1/66	9	Florida State	Sarasota, Fla.	UFA(StL)-'96	16/6*
15	Case, Stoney	QB	6-2	206	7/7/72	2	New Mexico	Odessa, Tex.	D3-'95	2/0
37	Centers, Larry	RB	5-11	215	6/1/68	7	Stephen F. Austin	Tatum, Tex.	D5-'90	16/10
21	Davis, Cedric	CB	5-9	170	9/7/72	2	Tennessee State	Brandon, Fla.	D5a-'95	0*
5	Davis, Greg	K	6-0	205	10/29/65	9	Citadel	Atlanta, Ga.	PB(Atl)-'91	16/0
62	Devlin, Mike	G-T	6-2	300	11/16/69	4	Iowa	Blacksburg, Va.	UFA(Buff)-'96	16/0*
84	Dowdell, Marcus	WR-KR	5-10	179	5/22/70	3	Tennessee State	Birmingham, Ala.	FA-'95	13/0
93	Dunbar, Karl	DT	6-4	275	5/18/67	5	Louisiana State	Opelousas, La.	FA-'95	4/0
65	Dye, Ernest	T	6-6	325	7/15/71	4	South Carolina	Greenwood, S.C.	D1-'93	6/6
83	Edwards, Anthony	WR	5-10	190	5/26/66	8	New Mexico Highlands	Casa Grande, Ariz.	FA-'91	15/0
92	England, Eric	DE	6-2	283	4/25/71	3	Texas A&M	Sugar Land, Tex.	D3b-'94	15/0
7	Esiason, Boomer	QB	6-5	224	4/17/61	13	Maryland	Islip, N.Y.	UFA(NYJ)-'96	12/12*
86	† Fann, Chad	TE	6-3	250	6/7/70	4	Florida A&M	Jacksonville, Fla.	FA-'93	16/3
10	Feagles, Jeff	P	6-1	205	3/7/66	9	Miami	Scottsdale, Ariz.	UFA(Phil)-'94	16/0
89	Gaines, Wendall	TE	6-4	293	1/17/72	3	Oklahoma State	Frederick, Okla.	FA-'94	16/11
11	Graham, Kent	QB	6-5	242	11/1/68	5	Ohio State	Wheaton, Ill.	UFA(Det)-'96	0*
23	† Hearst, Garrison	RB	5-11	215	1/4/71	4	Georgia	Lincolnton, Ga.	D1a-'93	16/15
58	Hill, Eric	LB	6-2	255	11/14/66	8	Louisiana State	Galveston, Tex.	D1a-'89	14/14
34	Hoage, Terry	S	6-2	201	4/11/62	13	Georgia	Huntsville, Tex.	FA-'94	12/7
56	Irving, Terry	LB	6-0	224	7/3/71	3	McNeese State	Galveston, Tex.	D4c-'94	16/8
53	Jax, Garth	LB	6-2	250	9/16/93	11	Florida State	Houston, Tex.	PB(Dall)-'89	16/4
32	Johnson, LeShon	RB	5-11	195	1/15/71	3	Northern Illinois	Haskell, Okla.	W(GB)-'95	5/0*
59	Joyner, Seth	LB	6-2	235	11/18/64	11	Texas-El Paso	Spring Valley, N.Y.	UFA(Phil)-'94	16/16
17	Krieg, Dave	QB	6-1	202	10/20/58	17	Milton	Schofield, Wis.	UFA(Det)-'95	16/16
42	Lassiter, Kwamie	CB-S	5-11	180	12/3/69	2	Kansas	Newport News, Va.	FA-'95	5/0
52	Leasy, Wesley	LB	6-2	234	9/7/71	2	Mississippi State	Greenville, Miss.	D7b-'95	12/0
67	Love, Duval	G	6-3	288	6/24/63	12	UCLA	Fountain Valley, Calif.	UFA(Pitt)-'95	16/16
97	Maumalanga, Chris	DT	6-2	292	12/15/71	3	Kansas	Hawthorne, Calif.	FA-'95	6/0
87	McBride, Oscar	TE	6-5	266	7/23/72	2	Notre Dame	Chiefland, Fla.	FA-'95	16/10
50	Merritt, David	LB	6-1	237	9/8/71	4	North Carolina State	Raleigh, N.C.	FA-'93	15/0
95	Miller, Jamir	LB	6-4	242	11/19/73	3	UCLA	Oakland, Calif.	D1-'94	10/9
72	Moore, Brandon	T	6-7	295	6/21/70	4	Duke	Ardmore, Pa.	W(NE)-'95	6/0*
85	Moore, Rob	WR	6-3	205	9/27/68	7	Syracuse	Hempstead, N.Y.	T(NYJ)-'95	15/15
27	Paul, Tito	CB-S	6-0	195	5/24/72	2	Ohio State	Kissimmee, Fla.	D5c-'95	14/4
60	Redmon, Anthony	G	6-4	308	4/9/71	3	Auburn	Brewton, Ala.	D5b-'94	12/9
39	Richardson, C.J.	S	5-10	209	6/10/72	2	Miami	Dallas, Tex.	FA-'95	1/0
44	Samuels, Terry	RB-TE	6-2	254	9/26/70	3	Kentucky	Louisville, Ky.	FA-'95	4/1
81	Sanders, Frank	WR	6-1	202	2/17/73	2	Auburn	Fort Lauderdale, Fla.	D2-'95	16/15
70	Scott, Lance	G-T	6-3	285	2/15/72	2	Utah	Salt Lake City, Utah	D5b-'95	0*
74	Selby, Rob	G	6-3	286	10/11/67	6	Auburn	Birmingham, Ala.	FA-'95	7/4
51	Shanks, Simon	LB	6-1	215	10/16/71	2	Coahoma, Miss., J.C.	Laurel, Miss.	FA-'95	15/0
96	Simmons, Clyde	DE	6-6	280	8/4/64	11	Western Carolina	Wilmington, N.C.	UFA(Phil)-'94	16/16
98	Swann, Eric	DT	6-5	295	8/16/70	6	No College	Swann Station, N.C.	D1-'91	12/12
31	Terry, Ryan	RB-KR	5-11	203	9/20/71	2	Iowa	Steubenville, Ohio	FA-'95	15/0
35	Williams, Aeneas	CB	5-10	190	1/29/69	6	Southern	New Orleans, La.	D3-'90	16/16
94	Wilson, Bernard	DT	6-2	295	8/17/70	4	Tennessee State	Nashville, Tenn.	W(TB)-'94	16/14
68	Wolf, Joe	G	6-6	296	12/28/66	8	Boston College	Allentown, Pa.	D1b-'89	6/1

* Lo. Brown played 15 games with Detroit in '95; Carter played 11 games with St. Louis; C. Davis missed '95 season because of injury; Devlin played 16 games with Buffalo; Esiason played 12 games with N.Y. Jets; Graham inactive for 15 games with Detroit; Johnson played 2 games with Green Bay, 3 with Arizona; Moore played 6 games with New England; Scott active for 3 games but did not play.

† Restricted free agent; subject to developments.

Players lost through free agency (5): QB Mike Buck (Mia; 4 games in '95), C Ed Cunningham (Chi; 9), T Bernard Daffney (Pitt; 11), LB Randy Kirk (SF; 16), T Larry Tharpe (NE; 16).

Also played for Cardinals in '95—LB Melvin Aldridge (2 games), C Jamie Dukes (8), T Eric Floyd (1), T Cecil Gray (7), LB Darryl Hardy (4), RB Mark Higgs (1), CB Patrick Hunter (5), CB-S Lorenzo Lynch (12), DE Keith McCants (16), WR Bryan Reeves (5), CB Ben Smith (2), S Andre Waters (7).

COACHING STAFF

Head Coach,
Vince Tobin

Pro Career: Named Cardinals' head coach on February 7, 1996. Became thirty-third coach in the history of the franchise dating back to 1920. As a defensive coordinator of the Indianapolis Colts from 1994-95, oversaw a defense that was a principal reason Indianapolis finished 9-7 during the 1995 regular season before defeating San Diego (35-10) and Kansas City (10-7) in the first two rounds of postseason play. Tobin earned credit for rebuilding a Colts defense he inherited that ranked last in overall defense in 1993. Tobin's first unit improved to twentieth in 1994 and tied for seventh with Carolina in 1995 at 314.2 yards per game. In four seasons prior to Tobin's arrival, the Colts' defense finished twenty-fourth or lower against the run. In 1994, Tobin's first Indianapolis defense ranked twelfth against the rush, then improved to sixth in 1995 at 91.1 yards per game, the second lowest figure in team history. It also was just the third time in Colts history the opposition averaged less than 100 yards per game on the ground. Over the past two seasons, Tobin's defensive unit did not allow an individual to rush for 100 yards in 24 consecutive games (final 13 games in 1994, first 11 games in 1995). His 1994 Colts' defense also boasted the lowest red-zone touchdown percentage (40) in the NFL and did not allow a touchdown at home in the final 12 quarters of the season. Tobin previously served as defensive coordinator of the Chicago Bears (1986-1992), tutoring a Bears' defense that set an NFL record for fewest points allowed in a 16-game season (187 in 1986). His 1986 Chicago unit topped the league by allowing just 258 yards per contest. The 1987 Bears surrendered the league's fewest points (215) and sported the best rushing defense (82.9). Tobin also earned victories over Tampa Bay and Washington as Chicago's interim head coach for Mike Ditka. Tobin's other coaching stops have been with the USFL Philadelphia/Baltimore Stars (1983-85), the CFL British Columbia Lions (1977-1982), and his alma mater, the University of Missouri (1967-1976). Tobin's defensive units in the CFL ranked second overall during his six seasons, while his defensive schemes in the USFL helped the Stars rank first defensively in 1983 and 1984 and second in 1985 while allowing the fewest points all three seasons. The Stars reached the league championship game each season, winning the final two times.
Background: Tobin played defensive back at Missouri from 1961-64. He joined the Missouri coaching staff as a defensive assistant from 1967-1976, serving the final six years as defensive coordinator. Tobin owns a bachelor's degree in education and a master's degree in guidance and counseling.
Personal: Born September 29, 1943, in Burlington Junction, Missouri. He and his wife, Kathy, have two children—son Ryan (16) and daughter Shannon (14).

ASSISTANT COACHES

George (Geep) Chryst, tight ends/quality control; born June 25, 1962, Madison, Wis., lives in Phoenix. No college or pro playing experience. College coach: Wisconsin-Platteville 1987, Wisconsin 1988-90. Pro coach: Orlando Thunder (World League) 1991, Chicago Bears 1991-95, joined Cardinals in 1996.
Alan Everest, special teams; born August 22, 1950, Santa Barbara, Calif., lives in Phoenix. Safety Southern Methodist 1970-71. No pro playing experience. College coach: Southern Methodist 1972, North Texas State 1973-74, Cameron (Okla.) 1974-75, U.S. International 1981-87. Pro coach: Arkansas Miners (PSFL) 1991-92, Birmingham Barracudas (CFL) 1995, joined Cardinals in 1996.
Jim Fassel, offensive coordinator; born August 31, 1949, Anaheim, Calif., lives in Phoenix. Quarterback Southern California 1969-70, Long Beach State 1971. Pro quarterback Chicago Bears 1972, Houston Oilers 1972, San Diego Chargers 1972. College coach: Fullerton (Calif.) J.C. 1973, Utah 1976, 1985-89 (head coach), Weber State 1977-78, Stanford 1979-83. Pro Coach: Hawaii (WFL) 1974, Portland Breakers (USFL) 1984, New York Giants 1991-92, Denver Broncos 1993-94, Oakland Raiders 1995, joined Cardinals in 1996.
Joe Greene, defensive line; born September 24, 1946, Temple, Tex., lives in Phoenix. Defensive tackle North Texas State 1966-68. Pro defensive tackle Pittsburgh Steelers 1969-81. Inducted into Pro Football Hall of Fame in 1987. Pro coach: Pittsburgh Steelers 1987-91, Miami Dolphins 1992-95, joined Cardinals in 1996.
Larry Marmie, defensive backs; born October 17, 1942, Barnesville, Ohio, lives in Phoenix. Quarterback Eastern Kentucky 1962-65. No pro playing experience. College coach: Eastern Kentucky 1967-68, 1972-76, Morehead State 1968-71, Tulsa 1977-78, North Carolina 1979-82, Tennessee 1983-84, 1992-94, Arizona State 1988-91 (head coach), UCLA 1995. Pro coach: Joined Cardinals in 1996.
Carl Mauck, offensive line; born July 7, 1947, McLeansboro, Ill., lives in Phoenix. Linebacker-center Southern Illinois 1966-68. Pro center Baltimore Colts 1969, Miami Dolphins 1970, San Diego Chargers 1971-74, Houston Oilers 1975-81. Pro coach: New Orleans Saints 1982-85, Kansas City Chiefs 1986-88, Tampa Bay Buccaneers 1991, San Diego Chargers 1992-95, joined Cardinals in 1996.
Dave McGinnis, defensive coordinator; born August 7, 1951, Independence, Kan., lives in Phoenix. Defensive back Texas Christian 1970-72. No pro playing experience. College coach: Texas Christian 1973-74, 1982, Missouri 1975-77, Indiana State 1978-81, Kansas State 1983-85. Pro coach: Chicago Bears 1986-95, joined Cardinals in 1996.
Glenn Pires, linebackers; born September 13, 1958, New Bedford, Mass., lives in Phoenix. Linebacker Springfield College 1978-80. No pro playing experience. College coach: Syracuse 1983-84, Dartmouth 1985-88, Michigan State 1989-95. Pro coach: Joined Cardinals in 1996.
Vic Rapp, wide receivers; born December 23, 1935, Marionville, Mo., lives in Phoenix. Running back Southwest Missouri State 1954-57. No pro playing experience. Pro coach: Edmonton Eskimos (CFL) 1972-76, British Columbia Lions (CFL) 1977-82 (head coach), Houston Oilers 1983, Los Angeles Rams 1984, Tampa Bay Buccaneers 1985-86, Detroit Lions 1987, Chicago Bears 1989-92, joined Cardinals in 1996.
Bob Rogucki, strength and conditioning; born September 27, 1953, Clarksburg, W.Va., lives in Phoenix. No college or pro playing experience. College coach: Penn State 1981, Weber State 1982, Army 1983-89. Pro coach: Joined Cardinals in 1990.
Jim Skipper, running backs; born January 23, 1949, Breaux Bridge, La., lives in Phoenix. Defensive back Whittier College 1971-72. No pro playing experience. College coach: Cal Poly-Pomona 1974-76, San Jose State 1977-78, Pacific 1979, Oregon 1980-82. Pro coach: Philadelphia/Baltimore Stars (USFL) 1983-85, New Orleans Saints 1986-95, joined Cardinals in 1996.

1996 FIRST-YEAR ROSTER

Name	Pos.	Ht.	Wt.	Birthdate	College	Hometown	How Acq.
Bennett, Tommy	S	6-1	204	2/19/73	UCLA	San Diego, Calif.	FA
Bonhaus, Matt	DT	6-5	285	10/13/72	Ohio State	Cincinnati, Ohio	FA
Brock, Fred	WR	5-10	175	11/15/74	Southern Mississippi	Montgomery, Ala.	FA
Butterfield, Mark	QB	6-4	215	7/14/73	Stanford	Antioch, Calif.	FA
Carollo, Joe	C-G-T	6-1	280	8/29/73	Oklahoma	Sacramento, Calif.	FA
Celestine, Art	CB	5-8	192	7/12/73	New Mexico	Riverside, Calif.	FA
Claro, Tom	C-G-T	6-5	300	12/14/74	Holy Cross	Floral Park, N.Y.	FA
Davis, Cedric (1)	CB	5-9	170	9/7/72	Tennessee State	Brandon, Fla.	D5a-'95
Dexter, James	T	6-5	300	3/3/73	South Carolina	Springfield, Va.	D5
Drake, Jerry	DE-DT	6-4	292	7/6/69	Hastings College	Kingston, N.Y.	FA
Foley, Mike	DT	6-3	290	11/12/71	New Hampshire	Worcester, Mass.	D6
Graham, Aaron	C	6-3	295	5/22/73	Nebraska	Denton, Tex.	D4
Hayes, Jarius	TE	6-3	255	3/23/73	North Alabama	Muscle Shoals, Ala.	D7
Jones, Alton	DT	6-5	275	4/16/73	Louisville	Moultire, Ga.	FA
Jones, Tony	S	6-4	200	3/2/72	Syracuse	Tampa, Fla.	FA
Jordan, Kevin	WR	6-1	188	12/14/72	UCLA	Washington, D.C.	FA
Larsen, Atle	K	5-11	201	3/24/73	Virginia Tech	Sola, Norway	FA
Leahy, Ryan	C-G-T	6-3	290	8/30/72	Notre Dame	Yakima, Wash.	FA
Matthews, Clarence	RB	5-8	160	5/8/74	Northwestern St., La.	New Orleans, La.	FA
McElroy, Leeland	RB	5-9	198	6/25/74	Texas A&M	Beaumont, Tex.	D2
McGee, Dell	CB	5-8	180	9/7/73	Auburn	Columbus, Ga.	D5
McKinnon, Ronald	LB	5-11	230	9/20/73	North Alabama	Elba, Ala.	FA
McWilliams, Johnny	TE	6-4	261	12/14/72	Southern California	Ontario, Calif.	D3
Player, Scott (1)	P	6-0	220	12/17/69	Florida State	St. Augustine, Fla.	FA
Rice, Simeon	DE	6-5	265	2/24/74	Illinois	Chicago, Ill.	D1
Stamps, Harry	T	6-4	305	6/6/74	Oklahoma	Houston, Tex.	D5
Whitehead, Ervin	WR	6-2	170	5/8/70	Westmar College	St. Petersburg, Fla.	FA

The term NFL Rookie is defined as a player who is in his first season of professional football and has not been on the roster of another professional football team for any regular-season or postseason games. A Rookie is designated by an "R" on NFL rosters. Players who have been active in another professional football league or players who have NFL experience, including either preseason training camp or being on an Active List or Inactive List, or on Reserve/Injured or Reserve/Physically Unable to Perform for fewer than six regular-season games, are termed NFL First-Year Players. An NFL First-Year Player is designated by a "1" on NFL rosters. Thereafter, a player is credited with an additional year of experience for each season in which he accumulates six games on the Active List or Inactive List, or on Reserve/Injured or Reserve/Physically Unable to Perform.

NOTES

ATLANTA FALCONS

National Football Conference
Western Division
Team Colors: Black, Red, Silver, and White
One Falcon Place
Suwanee, Georgia 30174
Telephone: (770) 945-1111

CLUB OFFICIALS

Chairman of the Board: Rankin M. Smith, Sr.
President: Taylor Smith
Vice President & Chief Financial Officer: Jim Hay
Vice President of Player Personnel: Ken Herock
Vice President of Administration: Rob Jackson
Director of Public Relations: Charlie Taylor
Asst. Director of Public Relations: Frank Kleha
Public Relations Assistant: Gary Glenn
Sales & Marketing: Todd Marble, Chris Demos, Trisha Williamson
Director of Community Relations: Carol Breeding
Director of Player Programs: Billy Johnson
Director of Ticket Operations: Jack Ragsdale
Asst. Director of Ticket Operations: Mike Jennings
Administrative Assts./Finance: Kevin Anthony, John Knox
Administrative Asst./Player Personnel: Danny Mock
Scouts: Bill Baker, Scott Campbell, Dick Corrick, Elbert Dubenion, Bill Groman
Director of Pro Personnel: Chuck Connor
Director of Player Development: Tommy Nobis
Controller: Wallace Norman
Director of Information Systems: Randy Kopp
Trainer: Ron Medlin
Assistant Trainers: Arnold Gamber, Matt Smith
Equipment Manager: Craig Campanozzi
Senior Equipment Manager: Horace Daniel
Video Director: Tom Atcheson
Stadium: Georgia Dome • **Capacity:** 71,228
One Georgia Dome Drive
Atlanta, Georgia 30313
Playing Surface: Artificial turf
Training Camp: One Falcon Place
Suwanee, Georgia 30174

1996 SCHEDULE

PRESEASON

Aug. 3	at Seattle	7:00
Aug. 10	at Tampa Bay	7:30
Aug. 15	**Oakland**	8:00
Aug. 23	**Arizona**	7:30

REGULAR SEASON

Sept. 1	at Carolina	1:00
Sept. 8	**Minnesota**	1:00
Sept. 15	Open Date	
Sept. 22	**Philadelphia**	8:00
Sept. 29	at San Francisco	1:00
Oct. 6	at Detroit	1:00
Oct. 13	**Houston**	1:00
Oct. 20	at Dallas	12:00
Oct. 27	**Pittsburgh**	1:00
Nov. 3	**Carolina**	1:00
Nov. 10	at St. Louis	12:00
Nov. 17	**New Orleans**	1:00
Nov. 24	at Cincinnati	1:00
Dec. 2	**San Francisco** (Mon.)	9:00
Dec. 8	at New Orleans	12:00
Dec. 15	**St. Louis**	1:00
Dec. 22	at Jacksonville	1:00

RECORD HOLDERS

INDIVIDUAL RECORDS—CAREER

Category	Name	Performance
Rushing (Yds.)	Gerald Riggs, 1982-88	6,631
Passing (Yds.)	Steve Bartkowski, 1975-1985	23,468
Passing (TDs)	Steve Bartkowski, 1975-1985	154
Receiving (No.)	Andre Rison, 1990-94	423
Receiving (Yds.)	Andre Rison, 1990-94	5,635
Interceptions	Rolland Lawrence, 1973-1980	39
Punting (Avg.)	Rick Donnelly, 1985-89	42.6
Punt Return (Avg.)	Al Dodd, 1973-74	11.8
Kickoff Return (Avg.)	Tony Smith, 1992-94	24.9
Field Goals	Mick Luckhurst, 1981-87	115
Touchdowns (Tot.)	Andre Rison, 1990-94	56
Points	Mick Luckhurst, 1981-87	558

INDIVIDUAL RECORDS—SINGLE SEASON

Category	Name	Performance
Rushing (Yds.)	Gerald Riggs, 1985	1,719
Passing (Yds.)	Jeff George, 1995	4,143
Passing (TDs)	Steve Bartkowski, 1980	31
Receiving (No.)	Terance Mathis, 1994	111
Receiving (Yds.)	Alfred Jenkins, 1981	1,358
Interceptions	Scott Case, 1988	10
Punting (Avg.)	Billy Lothridge, 1968	44.3
Punt Return (Avg.)	Gerald Tinker, 1974	13.9
Kickoff Return (Avg.)	Sylvester Stamps, 1987	27.5
Field Goals	Morten Andersen, 1995	31
Touchdowns (Tot.)	Andre Rison, 1993	15
Points	Morten Andersen, 1995	122

INDIVIDUAL RECORDS—SINGLE GAME

Category	Name	Performance
Rushing (Yds.)	Gerald Riggs, 9-2-84	202
Passing (Yds.)	Steve Bartkowski, 11-15-81	416
Passing (TDs)	Wade Wilson, 12-13-92	5
Receiving (No.)	William Andrews, 11-15-81	15
Receiving (Yds.)	Alfred Jackson, 12-2-84	193
	Andre Rison, 9-4-94	193
Interceptions	Many times	2
	Last time by Vinnie Clark, 10-9-94	
Field Goals	Norm Johnson, 11-13-94	6
Touchdowns (Tot.)	Many times	3
	Last time by Terance Mathis, 11-19-95	
Points	Norm Johnson, 11-13-94	20

COACHING HISTORY

(174-275-5)

1966-68	Norb Hecker*	4-26-1
1968-74	Norm Van Brocklin**	37-49-3
1974-76	Marion Campbell***	6-19-0
1976	Pat Peppler	3-6-0
1977-82	Leeman Bennett	47-44-0
1983-86	Dan Henning	22-41-1
1987-89	Marion Campbell****	11-32-0
1989	Jim Hanifan	0-4-0
1990-93	Jerry Glanville	28-38-0
1994-95	June Jones	16-16

*Released after three games in 1968
**Released after eight games in 1974
***Released after five games in 1976
****Retired after 12 games in 1989

GEORGIA DOME

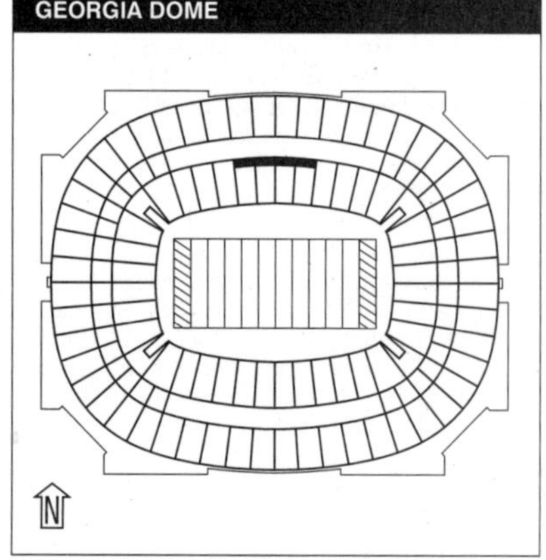

1995 TEAM RECORD

PRESEASON (2-2)

Date	Result		Opponents
8/5	L	17-25	at Philadelphia
8/11	W	37-0	Miami
8/19	W	19-10	Cleveland
8/25	L	14-20	at Buffalo

REGULAR SEASON (9-7)

Date	Result		Opponents	Att.
9/3	W	23-20	Carolina (OT)	58,808
9/10	L	10-41	at San Francisco	63,627
9/17	W	27-24	at New Orleans (OT)	57,442
9/24	W	13-3	N.Y. Jets	40,778
10/1	W	30-17	New England	47,114
10/12	L	19-21	at St. Louis	59,700
10/22	W	24-21	at Tampa Bay	66,135
10/29	L	13-28	Dallas	70,089
11/5	W	34-22	Detroit	49,619
11/12	L	17-23	at Buffalo	62,690
11/19	W	31-6	St. Louis	46,309
11/26	L	37-40	at Arizona (OT)	35,147
12/3	L	20-21	at Miami	63,395
12/10	W	19-14	New Orleans	54,603
12/17	L	17-21	at Carolina	53,833
12/24	W	28-27	San Francisco	51,785

POSTSEASON (0-1)

12/31	L	20-37	at Green Bay	60,453

(OT) Overtime

SCORE BY PERIODS

Falcons	73	144	80	59	6	—	362
Opponents	94	103	57	92	3	—	349

ATTENDANCE

Home 419,105 Away 461,969 Total 881,074
Single-game home record, 70,089 (10/29/95)
Single-season home record, 553,979 (1992)

1995 TEAM STATISTICS

	Falcons	Opp.
Total First Downs	317	340
Rushing	85	96
Passing	216	230
Penalty	16	14
Third Down: Made/Att	80/198	95/231
Third Down Pct.	40.4	41.1
Fourth Down: Made/Att	7/13	18/28
Fourth Down Pct.	53.8	64.3
Total Net Yards	5579	6088
Avg. Per Game	348.7	380.5
Total Plays	983	1084
Avg. Per Play	5.7	5.6
Net Yards Rushing	1393	1547
Avg. Per Game	87.1	96.7
Total Rushes	337	404
Net Yards Passing	4186	4541
Avg. Per Game	261.6	283.8
Sacked/Yards Lost	43/270	30/210
Gross Yards	4456	4751
Att./Completions	603/364	650/405
Completion Pct.	60.4	62.3
Had Intercepted	12	18
Punts/Avg.	67/41.2	70/43.3
Net Punting Avg.	67/36.2	70/36.1
Penalties/Yards Lost	96/737	94/688
Fumbles/Ball Lost	21/9	21/12
Touchdowns	38	43
Rushing	8	12
Passing	26	28
Returns	4	3
Avg. Time of Possession	29:27	30:33

1995 INDIVIDUAL STATISTICS

Passing	Att.	Comp.	Yds.	Pct.	TD	Int.	Tkld.	Rate
J. George	557	336	4143	60.3	24	11	43/270	89.5
Hebert	45	28	313	62.2	2	1	0/0	88.5
Metcalf	1	0	0	0.0	0	0	0/0	39.6
Falcons	603	364	4456	60.4	26	12	43/270	89.3
Opponents	650	405	4751	62.3	28	18	30/210	87.3

SCORING	TD R	TD P	TD Rt	PAT	FG	Saf	PTS
Andersen	0	0	0	29/30	31/37	0	122
Mathis	0	9	0	0/0	0/0	0	60
Metcalf	1	8	1	0/0	0/0	0	60
Heyward	6	2	0	0/0	0/0	0	48
Emanuel	0	5	0	0/0	0/0	0	30
Anderson	1	0	0	0/0	0/0	0	6
Birden	0	1	0	0/0	0/0	0	6
Montgomery	0	0	1	0/0	0/0	0	6
Preston	0	1	0	0/0	0/0	0	6
Ross	0	0	1	0/0	0/0	0	6
Tuggle	0	0	1	0/0	0/0	0	6
Zendejas	0	0	0	0/0	2/3	0	6
Falcons	8	26	4	29/30	33/40	0	362
Opponents	12	28	3	38/38	17/22	1	349

2-Point conversions: Mathis 3. Team: 3-8.

RUSHING	Att.	Yds.	Avg.	LG	TD
Heyward	236	1083	4.6	31	6
Anderson	39	161	4.1	13	1
Metcalf	28	133	4.8	23t	1
J. George	27	17	0.6	6	0
Emanuel	1	0	0.0	0	0
Stryzinski	1	0	0.0	0	0
Hebert	5	-1	-.2	2	0
Falcons	337	1393	4.1	31	8
Opponents	404	1547	3.8	41	12

RECEIVING	No.	Yds.	Avg.	LG	TD
Metcalf	104	1189	11.4	62t	8
Mathis	78	1039	13.3	54t	9
Emanuel	74	1039	14.0	52	5
Heyward	37	350	9.5	25	2
Birden	31	303	9.8	24	1
Brown	17	198	11.6	26	0
Preston	7	129	18.4	61t	1
Lyons	5	83	16.6	34	0
Spencer	5	60	12.0	22	0
Anderson	4	42	10.5	17	0
Sanders	2	24	12.0	21	0
Falcons	364	4456	12.2	62t	26
Opponents	405	4751	11.7	89t	28

INTERCEPTIONS	No.	Yds.	Avg.	LG	TD
Tuggle	3	84	28.0	49	1
Ross	3	70	23.3	33	0
Taylor	3	31	10.3	31	0
Johnson	2	4	2.0	2	0
Matthews	2	1	0.5	1	0
Montgomery	1	71	71.0	71t	1
Phillips	1	43	43.0	43	0
Bush	1	0	0.0	0	0
Harper	1	0	0.0	0	0
Tippins	1	0	0.0	0	0
Falcons	18	304	16.9	71t	2
Opponents	12	49	4.1	21	2

PUNTING	No.	Yds.	Avg.	In 20	LG
Stryzinski	67	2759	41.2	21	64
Falcons	67	2759	41.2	21	64
Opponents	70	3031	43.3	23	60

PUNT RETURNS	No.	FC	Yds.	Avg.	LG	TD
Metcalf	39	14	383	9.8	66t	1
Falcons	39	14	383	9.8	66t	1
Opponents	28	21	236	8.4	52	0

KICKOFF RETURNS	No.	Yds.	Avg.	LG	TD
Preston	30	627	20.9	44	0
Anderson	24	541	22.5	35	0
Metcalf	12	278	23.2	47	0
George	3	45	15.0	21	0
Tippins	1	15	15.0	15	0
Falcons	70	1506	21.5	47	0
Opponents	59	1323	22.4	46	0

SACKS	No.
Doleman	9.0
Geathers	7.0
Smith	5.5
Archambeau	3.0
Montgomery	3.0
Holt	1.0
Tuggle	1.0
Gardner	0.5
Falcons	30.0
Opponents	43.0

1996 DRAFT CHOICES

Round	Name	Pos.	College
3	Shannon Brown	DT	Alabama
4	Richard Huntley	RB	Winston-Salem
	Juran Bolden	DB	Mississippi Delta C.C.
5	Gary Bandy	DE	Baylor
6	Craig Sauer	LB	Minnesota
7	Ethan Brooks	T	Williams

ATLANTA FALCONS

1996 VETERAN ROSTER

No.		Name	Pos.	Ht.	Wt.	Birthdate	NFL Exp.	College	Hometown	How Acq.	'95 Games/ Starts
5		Andersen, Morten	K	6-2	225	8/19/60	15	Michigan State	Struer, Denmark	FA-'95	16/0
32		Anderson, Jamal	RB	5-10	234	9/30/72	3	Utah	El Camino, Calif.	D7-'94	16/0
92		Archambeau, Lester	DE	6-5	275	6/27/67	7	Stanford	Montville, N.J.	T(GB)-'93	16/6
24	t-	Bates, Patrick	S	6-3	215	11/27/70	4	Texas A&M	Galveston, Tex.	T(Oak)-'96	0*
97		Bennett, Cornelius	LB	6-2	238	8/25/65	10	Alabama	Birmingham, Ala.	UFA(Buff)-'96	14/14*
89		Birden, J.J.	WR	5-9	170	6/16/65	8	Oregon	Portland, Ore.	UFA(KC)-'95	10/10
51		Brandon, David	LB	6-4	234	2/9/65	10	Memphis State	Memphis, Tenn.	UFA(SD)-'96	16/1*
80		Brown, Tyrone	WR	5-11	168	1/3/73	2	Toledo	Cincinnati, Ohio	FA-'95	6/5
91		Burrough, John	DT	6-5	275	5/17/72	2	Wyoming	Pinedale, Wyo.	D7-'95	16/0
42		Bush, Devin	S	5-11	210	7/3/73	2	Florida State	Miami, Fla.	D1-'95	11/5
41		Coleman, Lincoln	RB	6-1	235	8/12/69	3	Baylor	Dallas, Tex.	FA-'96	0*
76		Davis, Antone	T	6-4	330	2/28/67	6	Tennessee	Ft. Valley, Ga.	UFA(Phil)-'96	15/14*
28		Davis, Ron	CB	5-10	190	2/24/72	2	Tennessee	Bartlett, Tenn.	D2-'95	12/5
99		Dronett, Shane	DE	6-6	288	1/12/71	5	Texas	Orange, Tex.	UFA(Den)-'96	13/2*
27		Edwards, Brad	S	6-2	208	3/22/66	8	South Carolina	Fayetteville, N.C.	FA-'94	13/0
87		Emanuel, Bert	WR	5-10	180	10/26/70	3	Rice	Houston, Tex.	D2-'94	16/16
65		Fortin, Roman	C	6-5	297	2/26/67	7	San Diego State	Ventura, Calif.	PB(Det)-'92	16/15
67		Gardner, Moe	NT	6-2	265	8/10/68	6	Illinois	Indianapolis, Ind.	D4-'91	16/16
1		George, Jeff	QB	6-4	215	12/8/67	7	Illinois	Indianapolis, Ind.	T(Ind)-'94	16/16
50	†	George, Ron	LB	6-2	242	3/20/70	4	Stanford	Heidelberg, Germany	D5-'93	16/0
98		Hall, Travis	DE	6-5	287	8/3/72	2	Brigham Young	Kenal, Alaska	D6-'95	1/0
54		Hamilton, Ruffin	LB	6-1	238	3/2/71	2	Tulane	Zachary, La.	FA-'96	0*
95		Hayworth, Tracy	LB	6-3	250	12/18/67	7	Tennessee	Franklin, Tenn.	FA-'96	16/14*
3		Hebert, Bobby	QB	6-4	215	8/19/60	11	Northwestern State, La.	Mandeville, La.	UFA(NO)-'93	4/0
34		Heyward, Craig	RB	5-11	250	9/26/66	9	Pittsburgh	Passaic, N.J.	UFA(Chi)-'94	16/16
39		Jack, Eric	CB	5-10	175	4/19/72	3	New Mexico	El Paso, Tex.	FA-'94	0*
44		Johnson, D.J.	CB	6-0	190	7/14/66	8	Kentucky	Lexington, Ky.	UFA(Pitt)-'94	13/13
15		Johnson, Tyrone	WR	5-11	178	9/4/71	2	Western State	Denver, Colo.	FA-'96	0*
7		Klein, Perry	QB	6-2	215	3/25/71	3	C.W. Post	Santa Monica, Calif.	D4-'94	0*
88		Le Bel, Harper	TE	6-4	255	7/14/63	8	Colorado State	Sherman Oaks, Calif.	PB(Phil)-'91	16/0
86	†	Lyons, Mitch	TE	6-4	265	5/13/70	4	Michigan State	Grand Rapids, Mich.	D6-'93	14/4
81		Mathis, Terance	WR	5-10	180	6/7/67	7	New Mexico	Stone Mountain, Ga.	UFA(NYJ)-'94	14/12
57		Matthews, Clay	LB	6-2	245	3/15/56	19	Southern California	Los Angeles, Calif.	UFA(Clev)-'94	16/16
2		McLaughlin, Steve	K	6-1	167	10/2/71	2	Arizona	Tuscon, Ariz.	FA-'96	8/0*
21		Metcalf, Eric	WR-RB	5-10	188	1/23/68	8	Texas	Seattle, Wash.	T(Clev)-'95	16/15
19		Mitchell, Derrell	WR	5-9	187	9/16/71	2	Texas Tech	Miami, Fla.	FA-'96	0*
22	#	Montgomery, Alton	S	6-0	211	6/16/68	7	Houston	Griffin, Ga.	T(Den)-'93	15/0
13		Nagle, Browning	QB	6-3	220	4/29/68	6	Louisville	Philadelphia, Pa.	UFA(Ind)-'95	0*
93		Owens, Dan	DE-DT	6-3	280	3/16/67	7	Southern California	Whittier, Calif.	UFA(Det)-'96	16/0*
64		Pahukoa, Jeff	G-T	6-2	298	2/9/69	5	Washington	Vancouver, Wash.	FA-'95	6/2
26		Phillips, Anthony	CB	6-2	209	10/5/70	3	Texas A&M-Kingsville	Galveston, Tex.	D3-'94	6/4
85		Preston, Roell	WR	5-10	185	6/23/72	2	Mississippi	Miami, Fla.	D5-'95	14/0
62		Richards, Dave	G	6-5	315	4/11/66	9	UCLA	Dallas, Tex.	UFA(Det)-'94	14/12
29		Riddick, Louis	S	6-2	215	3/15/69	5	Pittsburgh	Quakertown, Pa.	UFA(Balt)-'96	16/0*
37		Shelley, Elbert	CB	5-11	190	12/24/64	10	Arkansas State	Tyronza, Ark.	D11-'87	13/0
90		Smith, Chuck	DE	6-2	262	12/21/69	5	Tennessee	Athens, Ga.	D2-'92	14/14
4		Stryzinski, Dan	P	6-2	200	5/15/65	7	Indiana	Vincennes, Ind.	UFA(TB)-'95	16/0
59		Styles, Lorenzo	LB	6-1	245	1/31/74	2	Ohio State	Columbus, Ohio	D3-'95	12/0
61		Tobeck, Robbie	G-C	6-4	295	3/6/70	3	Washington State	Tarpon Springs, Fla.	FA-'93	16/16
58		Tuggle, Jessie	LB	5-11	230	2/14/65	10	Valdosta State	Spalding, Ga.	FA-'87	16/16
45	†	Walker, Darnell	CB	5-8	168	1/17/70	4	Oklahoma	St. Louis, Mo.	D7-'93	16/7
70		Whitfield, Bob	T	6-5	312	10/18/71	5	Stanford	Carson, Calif.	D1a-'92	16/16
69		Williams, Gene	G-T	6-2	306	10/14/68	6	Iowa State	Omaha, Neb.	T(Clev)-'95	12/3
40		Williams, James	LB	6-0	243	10/10/68	7	Mississippi	North Natchez, Miss.	FA-'96	12/6*
77	t-	Willig, Matt	T	6-8	317	1/21/69	4	Southern California	La Mirada, Calif.	FA-'96	15/12*
72		Zandofsky, Mike	G	6-2	308	11/30/65	8	Washington	Corvallis, Ore.	UFA(SD)-'94	12/12

* Bates last active with L.A. Raiders in '94; Bennett played 14 games with Buffalo in '95; Brandon played 16 games with San Diego; Coleman last active with Dallas in '94; A. Davis played 15 games with Philadelphia; Dronett played 13 games with Denver; Hamilton last active with Green Bay in '94; Hayworth played 16 games with Detroit; Jack missed the '95 season because of injury; T. Johnson last active with New Orleans in '94; Klein active for one game but did not play; McLaughlin played 8 games with St. Louis; Mitchell last active with New Orleans in '94; Nagle inactive for 15 games; Owens played 16 games with Detroit; Riddick played 16 games with Cleveland; J. Williams played 12 games with Jacksonville; Willig played 15 games with N.Y. Jets.

Unrestricted free agent; subject to developments.

† Restricted free agent; subject to developments.

Traded—S Roger Harper to Dallas, G-T Lincoln Kennedy to Oakland.

t- Falcons traded for Bates (Oakland), Willig (N.Y. Jets).

Players lost through free agency (1): DE Chris Doleman (SF; 16 games in '95).

Also played with Falcons in '95—DT Mel Agee (16 games), DT Jumpy Geathers (16), S Roger Harper (16), DT Pierce Holt (11), G-T Lincoln Kennedy (16), S Rich Miano (11), G Jim Richter (13), S Kevin Ross (16), WR Ricky Sanders (3), WR Darryl Spencer (5), LB Darryl Talley (16), CB Terry Taylor (16), LB Ken Tippins (16), K Tony Zendejas (1).

COACHING STAFF

Head Coach,
June Jones

Pro Career: Led Falcons to a playoff berth in only his second season as head coach. Became the eighth head coach in Falcons history on January 24, 1994, succeeding Jerry Glanville. Most recently was Falcons' assistant head coach-offense since 1991. He played five seasons (1977-1981) in NFL mainly as a backup quarterback to Falcons' all-time leading passer Steve Bartkowski. He was a member of the Falcons' first-ever playoff team in 1978. Jones began his coaching career as wide receivers coach of Houston Gamblers of the USFL in 1984. He became the offensive coordinator of the Denver Gold (USFL) in 1985 and then moved on to Ottawa Roughriders of the CFL in 1986. He was quarterbacks coach of the Houston Oilers in 1987-89. Was the quarterbacks and receivers coach for Detroit Lions in 1989-90. Career record: 16-16.

Background: Guided Portland State to back-to-back 8-3 seasons, serving as team captain during his senior year, after also playing at Hawaii and Oregon. Jones and new Redskins head coach, Norv Turner, were backups to Hall of Famer quarterback Dan Fouts at Oregon. Jones has been to a Grey Cup final in the CFL, a division title with Jim Kelly in the USFL, and has advanced to the postseason in both NFL conferences.

Personal: Born on February 19, 1953, in Portland, Oregon. June and his wife, Diane, live in Lake Lanier, Ga., and have three daughters—Jennifer, Kelli, Nicole, and son June, IV.

ASSISTANT COACHES

Keith Armstrong, secondary; born December 15, 1963, Philadelphia, Pa., lives in Duluth, Ga. Running back Temple 1983-86. No pro playing experience. College coach: Akron 1989, Oklahoma State 1990-92, Notre Dame 1993. Pro coach: Joined Falcons in 1994.

Darrell (Mouse) Davis, quarterbacks; born September 6, 1932, Palouse, Wash., lives in Alpharetta, Ga. Quarterback Western Oregon State 1952-55. No pro playing experience. College coach: Portland State 1974-80 (head coach 1975-80). Pro coach: Toronto Argonauts (CFL) 1982-83, Houston Gamblers (USFL) 1984, Denver Gold (USFL) 1985, Detroit Lions 1989-90, NY/NJ Knights (WL) 1991-92, joined Falcons in 1994.

Frank Gansz, assistant head coach-special teams; born November 22, 1938, Altoona, Pa., lives in Braselton, Ga. Center-linebacker Navy 1957-59. No pro playing experience. College coach: Air Force 1964-66, Colgate 1968, Navy 1969-72, Oklahoma State 1973, 1975, Army 1974, UCLA 1976-77. Pro coach: San Francisco 49ers 1978, Cincinnati Bengals 1979-80, Kansas City Chiefs 1981-82, 1986-88 (head coach 1987-88), Philadelphia Eagles 1983-85, Detroit Lions 1989-93, joined Falcons in 1994.

Joe Haering, linebackers; born February 1, 1946, Pittsburgh, Pa., lives in Lawrenceville, Ga. Linebacker Bucknell 1961-65. No pro playing experience. College coach: Bucknell 1969, Kentucky 1970-72, Boston University 1973-74, Kent State 1975-77. Pro coach: New York Jets 1978-79, Hamilton Tiger-Cats (CFL) 1980, Chicago Blitz (USFL) 1982-83, Pittsburgh Maulers (USFL) 1984, Denver Gold (USFL) 1985, NY/NJ Knights (WL) 1992, joined Falcons in 1994.

Milt Jackson, assistant head coach-offense; born October 16, 1943, Groesbeck, Tex., lives in Suwanee, Ga. Defensive back Tulsa 1965-66. Pro defensive back San Francisco 49ers 1967. College coach: Oregon State 1973, Rice 1974, California 1975-76, Oregon 1977-78, UCLA 1979. Pro coach: San Francisco 49ers 1980-82, Buffalo Bills 1983-84, Philadelphia Eagles 1985, Houston Oilers 1986-88, Indianapolis Colts 1989-91, Los Angeles Rams 1992-93, joined Falcons in 1994.

Tim Jorgensen, strength and conditioning; born April 21, 1955, St. Louis, Mo., lives in Snellville, Ga. Guard Southwest Missouri State 1974-76. No pro playing experience. College coach: Southwest Missouri State 1977-78, Alabama 1979, Louisiana State 1980-83. Pro coach: Philadelphia Eagles 1984-86, joined Falcons in 1987.

Bill Kollar, defensive line; born November 27, 1952, Warren, Ohio, lives in Duluth, Ga. Defensive end Montana State 1971-74. Pro defensive end Cincinnati Bengals 1974-76, Tampa Bay Buccaneers 1977-81. College coach: Illinois 1985-87, Purdue 1988-89. Pro coach: Tampa Bay Buccaneers 1984, joined Falcons in 1990.

Will Lewis, defensive assistant; born January 16, 1958, Quarkerstown, Pa., lives in Suwanee, Ga. Defensive back Millersville State 1976-79. Pro defensive back Seattle Seahawks 1980-81, Kansas City Chiefs 1981, Houston Gamblers (USFL) 1984-86, Ottawa Roughriders (CFL) 1986-88, Hamilton Tiger-Cats (CFL) 1989. College coach: Houston 1989, Lock Haven 1990-91, Millersville State 1992-93, Maine 1994. Pro coach: New York/New Jersey Knights (World League) 1991-92, joined Falcons in 1995.

Bob Palcic, offensive line; born July 2, 1948, Gowanda, N.Y., lives in Lawrenceville, Ga. Linebacker Dayton 1968-70. No pro playing experience. College coach: Dayton 1974-75, Ball State 1976-77, Wisconsin 1978-81, Arizona 1984-85, Ohio State 1986-91, Southern California 1992, UCLA 1993. Pro coach: Joined Falcons in 1994.

Rod Rust, assistant head coach-defense; born August 2, 1928, Cedar Rapids, Iowa, lives in Lawrenceville, Ga. Center-linebacker Iowa State 1947-49. No pro playing experience. College coach: New Mexico 1960-62, Stanford 1963-66, North Texas State 1967-72 (head coach). Pro coach: Montreal Alouettes 1973-75, Philadelphia Eagles 1976-77, Kansas City Chiefs 1978-82, 1988, New England Patriots 1983-87, 1990 (head coach), Pittsburgh Steelers 1989, New York Giants 1992, Winnepeg Blue Bombers (CFL) 1994, joined Falcons in 1995.

Ollie Wilson, running backs; born March 31, 1951, Worcester, Mass., lives in Roswell, Ga. Wide receiver Springfield 1971-73. No pro playing experience. College coach: Springfield 1975, Northeastern 1976-82, California 1983-90. Pro coach: Joined Falcons in 1991.

1996 FIRST-YEAR ROSTER

Name	Pos.	Ht.	Wt.	Birthdate	College	Hometown	How Acq.
Allen, Demetrius	WR	5-10	160	7/8/74	Virginia	Cincinnati, Ohio	FA
Baldwin, Robert (1)	RB	5-11	230	9/1/72	Duke	Deland, Fla.	FA
Bandy, Gary	DE	6-3	237	12/6/72	Baylor	Kansas City, Mo.	D5
Bolden, Juran	CB	6-2	201	6/27/74	Delta State	Tampa, Fla.	D4
Brooks, Ethan	T	6-6	270	4/27/72	Williams	Simsbury, Conn.	D7
Brown, Shannon	DT	6-5	290	5/23/72	Alabama	Millbrook, Ala.	D3
Cherry, Ronald (1)	G	6-4	330	4/15/72	McNeese State	New Orleans, La.	FA
Christensen, James	G	6-3	305	2/22/73	UCLA	Anaheim, Calif.	FA
Couch, Robert	T	6-5	301	9/4/73	Vanderbilt	Irving, Tex.	FA
Denton, Tim	CB	5-11	180	2/2/73	Sam Houston State	Galveston, Tex.	FA
Fagan, Tommy (1)	DE-DT	6-0	270	3/26/71	N.E. Louisiana	Lamont, Fla.	FA
Fields, Scott	LB	6-2	220	4/22/73	Southern California	Ontario, Calif.	FA
Henry, Mario (1)	WR	6-1	188	9/14/71	Rutgers	Chicago, Ill.	FA
Howard, Ed (1)	WR	6-4	195	1/14/73	Rice	Houston, Tex.	FA
Huntley, Richard	RB	5-11	224	9/18/72	Winston-Salem State	Monroe, N.C.	D4
Ivy, Greg	P	6-1	191	9/28/72	Oklahoma State	Atlanta, Tex.	FA
Johnson, Akili (1)	CB-S	5-10	192	5/10/72	Grambling State	Little Rock, Ark.	FA
Lee, Robert	CB	5-11	195	8/6/73	North Carolina	Clinton, N.C.	FA
Miller, Nate (1)	T-G	6-3	310	10/8/71	Louisiana State	Tuscaloosa, Ala.	FA
Mitchell, Verl	G	6-4	292	11/3/72	Arkansas	Paragould, Ark.	FA
Roques, Burnell	WR	5-11	170	12/26/72	Claremont College	Moreno Valley, Calif.	FA
Sauer, Craig	LB	6-1	226	12/13/72	Minnesota	Sartell, Minn.	D6
Schlegel, Mike	DT	6-4	265	9/9/73	Kentucky	New Orleans, La.	FA
Scott, Freddie	WR	5-10	189	8/26/74	Penn State	Southfield, Mich.	FA
Vinson, Tony (1)	RB	6-1	230	3/13/71	Towson State	Newport News, Va.	FA
Yurkiewicz, Rich (1)	LB	6-3	235	5/2/73	Kent	Valley Forge, Ohio	FA
Zenkewicz, Trent	DT	6-5	280	9/29/72	Michigan	Cleveland, Ohio	FA

The term NFL Rookie is defined as a player who is in his first season of professional football and has not been on the roster of another professional football team for any regular-season or postseason games. A Rookie is designated by an "R" on NFL rosters. Players who have been active in another professional football league or players who have NFL experience, including either preseason training camp or being on an Active List or Inactive List, or on Reserve/Injured or Reserve/Physically Unable to Perform for fewer than six regular-season games, are termed NFL First-Year Players. An NFL First-Year Player is designated by a "1" on NFL rosters. Thereafter, a player is credited with an additional year of experience for each season in which he accumulates six games on the Active List or Inactive List, or on Reserve/Injured or Reserve/Physically Unable to Perform.

NOTES

CAROLINA PANTHERS

National Football Conference
Western Division
Team Colors: Black, Panther Blue, and Silver
800 South Mint Street
Charlotte, North Carolina 28202-1502
Telephone: (704) 358-7000

CLUB OFFICIALS

Founder/Owner: Jerry Richardson
President: Mike McCormack
General Manager: Bill Polian
Director of Business Operations: Mark Richardson
Director of Stadium Operations: Jon Richardson
Assistant Director of Business Operations: Charles Waddell
Counsel: Richard Thigpen, Jr.
Chief Financial Officer: Dave Olsen
Controller: Lisa Garber
Assistant General Manager: Joe Mack
Director Player Personnel: Dom Anile
Pro Scouts: Chris Polian, Hal Hunter
Regional Scouts: Jack Bushofsky, Ralph Hawkins
Area Scouts: Hal Athon, Joe Bushofsky, Boyd Dowler, Bob Guarini, Steve Hinshaw, Tony Softli, Todd Vasvari
Scouting Assistant: Tom Telesco
Director of Communications: Charlie Dayton
Media Relations Assistant: Lex Sant
Media Relations and Marketing Assistant: Bruce Speight
Director of Ticket Sales: Phil Youtsey
Assistant Ticket Manager: Kati Hynes
Director of Player Relations: Donnie Shell
Director of Community Relations/Family Programs: B.J. Harrison Waymer
Director of Special Events: Leslie Matz
Director of Information Systems: Roger Goss
Systems Analyst: Antoine Speller
Football Systems: Rob Rogers
Video Director: Dave Sutherby
Assistant Video Director: Mark Hobbs
Head Trainer: John Kasik
Assistant Trainers: Al Shuford, Dan Ruiz
Equipment Manager: Jackie Miles
Assistant Equipment Manager: Don Toner
Director of Football Security: Ed Stillwell
Manager of Football Administration: Mark Koncz
Director of Facilities: Tom Fellows
Director of Stadium Security: Gene Brown
Stadium Operations Coordinator: Mitch Silverman
Office Manager: Jackie Jeffries
Stadium: Carolinas Stadium • **Capacity:** 72,520
Charlotte, North Carolina 28202-1502
Playing Surface: Grass
Training Camp: Wofford College
Spartanburg, South Carolina
29303

RECORD HOLDERS

INDIVIDUAL RECORDS—CAREER

Category	Name	Performance
Rushing (Yds.)	Derrick Moore, 1995	740
Passing (Yds.)	Kerry Collins, 1995	2,717
Passing (TDs)	Kerry Collins, 1995	14
Receiving (No.)	Mark Carrier, 1995	66
Receiving (Yds.)	Mark Carrier, 1995	1,002
Interceptions	Brett Maxie, 1995	6
Punting (Avg.)	Tommy Barnhardt, 1995	41.1
Punt Return (Avg.)	Eric Guliford, 1995	11.0
Kickoff Return (Avg.)	Randy Baldwin, 1995	22.6
Field Goals	John Kasay, 1995	26
Touchdowns (Tot.)	Willie Green, 1995	6
Points	John Kasay, 1995	105

INDIVIDUAL RECORDS—SINGLE SEASON

Category	Name	Performance
Rushing (Yds.)	Derrick Moore, 1995	740
Passing (Yds.)	Kerry Collins, 1995	2,717
Passing (TDs)	Kerry Collins 1995	14
Receiving (No.)	Mark Carrier, 1995	66
Receiving (Yds.)	Mark Carrier, 1995	1,002
Interceptions	Brett Maxie, 1995	6
Punting (Avg.)	Tommy Barnhardt, 1995	41.1
Punt Return (Avg.)	Eric Guliford, 1995	11.0
Kickoff Return (Avg.)	Randy Baldwin, 1995	22.6
Field Goals	John Kasay, 1995	26
Touchdowns (Tot.)	Willie Green, 1995	6
Points	John Kasay, 1995	105

INDIVIDUAL RECORDS—SINGLE GAME

Category	Name	Performance
Rushing (Yds.)	Derrick Moore, 10-1-95	123
Passing (Yds.)	Kerry Collins, 11-26-95	335
Passing (TDs)	Kerry Collins, 11-26-95	3
Receiving (No.)	Vince Workman, 9-17-95	8
Receiving (Yds.)	Willie Green, 11-12-95	157
Interceptions	Brett Maxie, 10-22-95	2
Field Goals	John Kasay, 10-15-95	4
Touchdowns (Tot.)	Howard Griffith, 10-22-95	2
	Mark Carrier, 11-26-95	2
Points	John Kasay, 10-15-95	14

1996 SCHEDULE

PRESEASON

Aug. 3	**Chicago**	7:30
Aug. 10	at Denver	6:00
Aug. 17	**Buffalo**	7:30
Aug. 23	at New York Giants	8:00

REGULAR SEASON

Sept. 1	**Atlanta**	1:00
Sept. 8	at New Orleans	12:00
Sept. 15	Open Date	
Sept. 22	**San Francisco**	1:00
Sept. 29	at Jacksonville	1:00
Oct. 6	at Minnesota	12:00
Oct. 13	**St. Louis**	1:00
Oct. 20	**New Orleans**	1:00
Oct. 27	at Philadelphia	1:00
Nov. 3	at Atlanta	1:00
Nov. 10	**New York Giants**	8:00
Nov. 17	at St. Louis	12:00
Nov. 24	at Houston	12:00
Dec. 1	**Tampa Bay**	1:00
Dec. 8	at San Francisco	1:00
Dec. 15	**Baltimore**	1:00
Dec. 22	**Pittsburgh**	1:00

CAROLINAS STADIUM

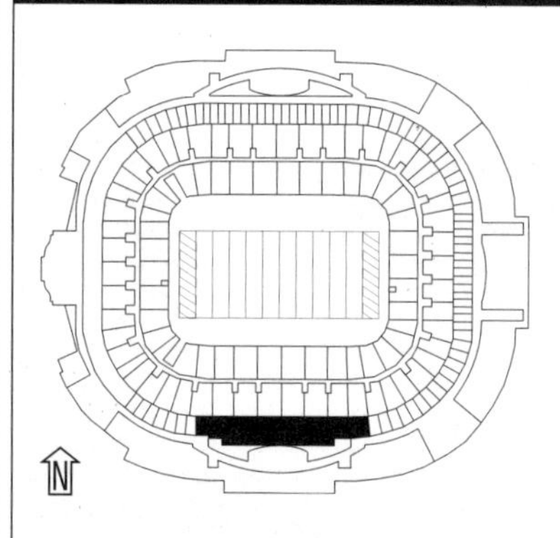

COACHING HISTORY

(7-9-0)

1995	Dom Capers	7-9-0

1995 TEAM RECORD

PRESEASON (3-2)

Date	Result		Opponents
7/29	W	20-14	vs. Jacksonville at Canton
8/4	L	15-18	at Chicago
8/12	W	19-10	Denver
8/19	L	10-17	at San Francisco
8/26	W	6-3	N.Y. Giants

REGULAR SEASON (7-9)

Date	Result		Opponents	Att.
9/3	L	20-23	at Atlanta (OT)	58,808
9/20	L	9-31	at Buffalo	79,190
9/17	L	10-31	St. Louis	54,060
10/1	L	13-20	Tampa Bay	50,076
10/8	L	27-31	at Chicago	59,668
10/15	W	26-15	N.Y. Jets	52,613
10/22	W	20-3	New Orleans	55,484
10/29	W	20-17	at New England (OT)	60,064
11/5	W	13-7	at San Francisco	61,722
11/12	L	17-28	at St. Louis	65,598
11/19	W	27-7	Arizona	49,582
11/26	L	26-34	at New Orleans	39,580
12/3	W	13-10	Indianapolis	49,841
12/10	L	10-31	San Francisco	76,136
12/17	W	21-17	Atlanta	53,833
12/24	L	17-20	at Washington	42,903

(OT) Overtime

SCORE BY PERIODS

Panthers	35	98	78	75	3	—	289
Opponents	62	106	72	82	3	—	325

ATTENDANCE

Home 441,625 Away 467,533 Total 909,158
Single-game home record, 76,136 (12/10/95; Clemson Memorial Stadium)
Single-season home record, 441,625 (1995)

1995 TEAM STATISTICS

	Panthers	Opp.
Total First Downs	250	288
Rushing	74	99
Passing	157	175
Penalty	19	14
Third Down: Made/Att	93/244	98/240
Third Down Pct.	38.1	40.8
Fourth Down: Made/Att	4/9	7/12
Fourth Down Pct.	44.4	58.3
Total Net Yards	4619	5027
Avg. Per Game	288.7	314.2
Total Plays	1029	1072
Avg. Per Play	4.5	4.7
Net Yards Rushing	1573	1576
Avg. Per Game	98.3	98.5
Total Rushes	454	450
Net Yards Passing	3046	3451
Avg. Per Game	190.4	215.7
Sacked/Yards Lost	38/258	36/265
Gross Yards	3304	3716
Att./Completions	537/263	586/310
Completion Pct.	49.0	52.9
Had Intercepted	25	21
Punts/Avg.	96/41.0	94/40.4
Net Punting Avg.	96/35.2	94/34.0
Penalties/Yards Lost	94/683	112/808
Fumbles/Ball Lost	28/16	28/16
Touchdowns	30	38
Rushing	10	17
Passing	16	15
Returns	4	6
Avg. Time of Possession	29:27	30:33

1995 INDIVIDUAL STATISTICS

PASSING	Att.	Comp.	Yds.	Pct.	TD	Int.	Tkld.	Rate
Collins	433	214	2717	49.4	14	19	24/150	61.9
Reich	84	37	441	44.0	2	2	12/100	58.7
Trudeau	17	11	100	64.7	0	3	2/8	40.9
Guliford	2	1	46	50.0	0	1	0/0	56.3
Workman	1	0	0	0.0	0	0	0/0	39.6
Panthers	537	263	3304	49.0	16	25	38/258	59.1
Opponents	586	310	3716	52.9	15	21	36/265	66.2

SCORING	TD R	TD P	TD Rt	PAT	FG	Saf	PTS
Kasay	0	0	0	27/28	26/33	0	105
Green	0	6	0	0/0	0/0	0	36
Moore	4	0	0	0/0	0/0	0	24
Carrier	0	3	0	0/0	0/0	0	18
Collins	3	0	0	0/0	0/0	0	18
Metzelaars	0	3	0	0/0	0/0	0	18
Griffith	1	1	0	0/0	0/0	0	12
Guliford	0	1	1	0/0	0/0	0	12
Christian	0	1	0	0/0	0/0	0	8
Beebe	0	1	0	0/0	0/0	0	6
Johnson	1	0	0	0/0	0/0	0	6
Kragen	0	0	1	0/0	0/0	0	6
McKyer	0	0	1	0/0	0/0	0	6
Mills	0	0	1	0/0	0/0	0	6
Workman	1	0	0	0/0	0/0	0	6
Rasby	0	0	0	0/0	0/0	0	2
Panthers	10	16	4	27/28	26/33	0	289
Opponents	17	15	6	38/38	19/26	1	325

2-Point conversions: Christian, Rasby. Team: 2-2.

RUSHING	Att.	Yds.	Avg.	LG	TD
Moore	195	740	3.8	53t	4
Griffith	65	197	3.0	15	1
Christian	41	158	3.9	17	0
Johnson	24	110	4.6	23t	1
Workman	35	139	4.0	14	1
B. Thomas	22	90	4.1	13	0
Collins	42	74	1.8	10	3
Baldwin	23	61	2.7	9	0
Reich	1	3	3.0	3	0
Stone	1	3	3.0	3	0
Guliford	2	2	1.0	1	0
Carrier	3	-4	-1.3	4	0
Panthers	454	1573	3.5	53t	10
Opponents	450	1576	3.5	35t	17

RECEIVING	No.	Yds.	Avg.	LG	TD
Carrier	66	1002	15.2	66t	3
Green	47	882	18.8	89t	6
Guliford	29	444	15.3	49	1
Christian	29	255	8.8	23	1
Johnson	16	121	7.6	37	0
Metzelaars	20	171	8.6	27	3
Beebe	14	152	10.9	24	1
Workman	13	74	5.7	14	0
Griffith	11	63	5.7	15	1
Rasby	5	47	9.4	15	0
Moore	4	12	3.0	5	0
Campbell	3	32	10.7	12	0
B. Thomas	3	24	8.0	14	0
Tillman	2	22	11.0	12	0
Dennis	1	3	3.0	3	0
Panthers	263	3304	12.6	89t	16
Opponents	310	3716	12.0	77t	15

INTERCEPTIONS	No.	Yds.	Avg.	LG	TD
Maxie	6	59	9.8	49	0
Mills	5	58	11.6	36t	1
McKyer	3	99	33.0	96t	1
Terrell	3	33	11.0	21	0
Poole	2	8	4.0	4	0
McDowell	1	33	33.0	33	0
Kragen	1	29	29.0	29	0
Panthers	21	319	15.2	96t	2
Opponents	25	221	8.8	35	3

PUNTING	No.	Yds.	Avg.	In 20	LG
Barnhardt	95	3906	41.1	27	54
Kasay	1	32	32.0	1	32
Panthers	96	3938	41.0	28	54
Opponents	94	3796	40.4	23	58

PUNT RETURNS	No.	FC	Yds.	Avg.	LG	TD
Guliford	43	22	475	11.0	62t	1
Carrier	6	1	25	4.2	9	0
Panthers	49	23	500	10.2	62t	1
Opponents	39	23	342	8.8	45	0

KICKOFF RETURNS	No.	Yds.	Avg.	LG	TD
By'Not'e	18	335	18.6	35	0
Baldwin	14	316	22.6	36	0
Stone	12	269	22.4	40	0
Beebe	9	215	23.9	38	0
Butcher	1	5	5.0	5	0
Philyaw	1	23	23.0	23	0
Panthers	55	1163	21.1	40	0
Opponents	62	1159	18.7	83	0

SACKS	No.
Lathon	8.0
Conner	7.0
Fox	4.5
Mills	4.5
Bailey	3.0
King	2.0
Poole	2.0
M. Thomas	2.0
Kragen	1.0
Price	1.0
Panthers	35.0
Opponents	38.0

1996 DRAFT CHOICES

Round	Name	Pos.	College
1	Tim Biakabutuka	RB	Michigan
2	M. Muhammad	WR	Michigan State
3	Winslow Oliver	RB	New Mexico
	J.C. Price	DT	Virginia Tech
4	Norberto Garrido	T	Southern California
	E. McDaniel	DB	East Carolina
5	Marquette Smith	RB	Central Florida
6	Scott Green	RB	Michigan State
7	Donnell Baker	WR	Southern
	Kerry Hicks	DE	Colorado

CAROLINA PANTHERS

1996 VETERAN ROSTER

No.	Name	Pos.	Ht.	Wt.	Birthdate	NFL Exp.	College	Hometown	How Acq.	'95 Games/ Starts
54	Bailey, Carlton	LB	6-3	242	12/15/64	9	North Carolina	Baltimore, Md.	FA-'95	16/14
6	Barnhardt, Tommy	P	6-2	218	6/11/63	10	North Carolina	China Grove, N.C.	UFA(NO)-'95	16/0
17	Bates, Michael	WR	5-10	189	12/19/69	4	Arizona	Tucson, Ariz.	FA-'96	13/0*
55	Bickett, Duane	LB	6-5	245	12/1/62	12	Southern California	Glendale, Calif.	UFA(Sea)-'96	15/0*
26	Brewer, Dewell	RB	5-8	201	5/22/70	3	Oklahoma	Lawton, Okla.	ED(Ind)-'95	0*
68	Brockermeyer, Blake	T	6-4	300	4/11/73	2	Texas	Ft. Worth, Tex.	D1c-'95	16/16
53	# Butcher, Paul	LB	6-0	233	11/8/63	9	Wayne State	Dearborn, Mich.	ED(Ind)-'95	16/0
33	By'not'e, Butler	CB	5-9	190	9/29/72	3	Ohio State	St. Louis, Mo.	W(Den)-'95	7/0
87	Campbell, Mathew	G	6-4	270	7/14/72	2	South Carolina	North Augusta, S.C.	FA-'95	10/2
83	Carrier, Mark	WR	6-0	186	10/28/65	10	Nicholls State	Church Point, La.	ED(Clev)-'95	16/14
44	† Christian, Bob	RB	5-10	230	11/14/68	4	Northwestern	Florissant, Mo.	ED(Chi)-'95	14/12
12	Collins, Kerry	QB	6-5	240	12/30/72	2	Penn State	Lancaster, Pa.	D1a-'95	15/13
56	† Conner, Darion	LB	6-2	250	9/28/67	7	Jackson State	Noxubee, Miss.	UFA(NO)-'95	16/16
37	Cota, Chad	S	6-1	195	8/13/71	2	Oregon	Ashland, Ore.	D7a-'95	16/0
11	Crittenden, Ray	WR	6-1	188	3/1/70	3	Virginia Tech	Alexandria, Va.	FA-'96	0*
24	Davis, Eric	CB	5-11	185	1/26/68	7	Jacksonville State	Anniston, Ala.	UFA(SF)-'96	15/15*
62	Dennis, Mark	T	6-6	288	4/15/65	10	Illinois	Washington, Ill.	FA-'95	12/9
52	† Elliott, Matt	G	6-3	295	10/1/68	4	Michigan	Carmel, Ind.	FA-'95	15/14
55	Faryniarz, Brett	LB	6-3	230	7/23/65	7	San Diego State	Sacramento, Calif.	FA-'95	15/1
50	Fountaine, Jamal	LB	6-3	240	1/29/71	2	Washington	San Francisco, Calif.	FA-'95	0*
93	Fox, Mike	DE	6-8	295	8/5/67	7	West Virginia	Akron, Ohio	UFA(NYG)-'95	16/16
65	Garcia, Frank	G	6-1	295	1/28/72	2	Washington	Phoenix, Ariz.	D4-'95	15/14
86	Green, Willie	WR	6-4	185	4/2/66	7	Mississippi	Clarke, Ga.	FA-'95	16/7
91	Greene, Kevin	LB	6-3	247	7/31/62	12	Auburn	Oxford, Ala.	UFA(Pitt)-'96	16/16*
30	† Griffith, Howard	RB	6-0	240	11/17/67	4	Illinois	Chicago, Ill.	ED(Rams)-'95	15/7
67	Hayes, Brandon	T	6-4	305	3/11/73	2	Central State, Ohio	Muncie, Ind.	FA-'95	0*
23	Johnson, Anthony	RB	6-0	225	10/15/67	7	Notre Dame	South Bend, Ind.	W(Chi)-'95	7/0
81	Jones, Reggie	WR	6-0	175	5/5/71	2	Louisiana State	Kansas City, Mo.	FA-'95	1/0
4	Kasay, John	K	5-10	198	10/27/69	6	Georgia	Athens, Ga.	UFA(Sea)-'95	16/0
96	King, Shawn	DE	6-3	278	6/24/72	2	Northeast Louisiana	Monroe, La.	D2-'95	14/0
71	Kragen, Greg	NT	6-3	267	3/4/62	12	Utah State	Pleasanton, Calif.	ED(KC)-'95	16/14
57	Lathon, Lamar	LB	6-3	260	12/23/67	7	Houston	Wharton, Tex.	UFA(Hou)-'95	15/15
27	Lofton, Steve	CB	5-9	177	11/26/68	5	Texas A&M	Alto, Tex.	FA-'95	10/2
79	Love, Sean	G	6-3	304	9/6/68	4	Penn State	Tamaqua, Pa.	FA-'95	11/1
39	Maxie, Brett	S	6-2	210	1/13/62	12	Texas Southern	Dallas, Tex.	UFA(Atl)-'95	16/16
25	McDowell, Bubba	S	6-1	206	11/4/66	8	Miami	Merritt Island, Fla.	FA-'95	16/3
22	# McKyer, Tim	CB	6-0	184	9/5/63	11	Texas-Arlington	Port Arthur, Tex.	ED(Pitt)-'95	16/16
69	Miller, Les	DE-DT	6-7	285	3/1/65	9	Ft. Hayes State	Arkansas City, Kan.	FA-'96	0*
51	Mills, Sam	LB	5-9	232	6/3/59	11	Montclair State	Long Branch, N.J.	UFA(NO)-'95	16/16
99	Nunley, Jeremy	DE	6-5	278	9/19/71	3	Alabama	Winchester, Tenn.	FA-'95	0*
60	Peterson, Andrew	G-T	6-5	308	6/11/72	2	Washington	Port Orchard, Wash.	D5b-'95	4/2
34	Philyaw, Dino	RB	5-10	199	10/6/70	2	Oregon	Kenansville, N.C.	FA-'95	1/0
27	Pieri, Damon	S	6-0	186	9/25/70	2	San Diego State	Phoenix, Ariz.	FA-'96	0*
38	Poole, Tyrone	CB	5-8	188	2/3/72	2	Ft. Valley State	La Grange, Ga.	D1b-'95	16/13
89	Rasby, Walter	TE	6-3	247	9/7/72	3	Wake Forest	Washington, N.C.	FA-'95	9/2
45	Reed, Michael	CB	5-9	180	8/16/72	2	Boston College	Wilmington, Del.	D7b-'95	1/0
63	Rodenhauser, Mark	C	6-5	280	6/1/61	9	Illinois State	Addison, Ill.	ED(Det)-'95	16/0
58	Royal, Andre	LB	6-2	220	12/1/72	2	Alabama	Tuscaloosa, Ala.	FA-'95	12/0
47	Senters, Mike	CB	5-11	183	12/14/71	2	Northwestern	Dallas, Tex.	D5a-'95	0*
75	Skrepenak, Greg	T	6-7	325	1/31/70	5	Michigan	Wilkes Barre, Pa.	UFA(Oak)-'96	14/14*
28	Smith, Tony	RB	6-1	212	6/29/70	4	Southern Mississippi	Vicksburg, Miss.	FA-'95	0*
80	Stone, Dwight	WR	6-0	195	1/28/64	10	Middle Tennessee State	Florala, Ala.	UFA(Pitt)-'95	16/0
7	Stouffer, Kelly	QB	6-4	218	7/6/64	6	Colorado State	Rushville, Neb.	FA-'96	0*
40	Terrell, Pat	S	6-2	210	3/18/68	7	Notre Dame	St. Petersburg, Fla.	FA-'95	16/13
31	# Thomas, Blair	RB	5-10	202	10/7/67	7	Penn State	Philadelphia, Pa.	FA-'95	7/0
95	Thomas, Mark	DE	6-5	275	5/6/69	5	North Carolina State	Lilburn, Ga.	ED(SF)-'95	10/0
10	Trudeau, Jack	RB	6-3	220	9/9/62	11	Illinois	Livermore, Calif.	ED(NYJ)-'95	1/0
32	# Turner, Nate	RB	6-1	255	5/28/69	5	Nebraska	Chicago, Ill.	FA-'95	2/0
85	Walls, Wesley	TE	6-5	250	3/26/66	8	Mississippi	Pontoloc, Miss.	UFA(NO)-'96	16/11*
64	Whitley, Curtis	C	6-1	295	5/10/69	5	Clemson	Smithfield, N.C.	ED(SD)-'95	16/16
98	Williams, Gerald	DE	6-3	290	9/8/63	11	Auburn	Valley, Ala.	UFA(Pitt)-'95	16/16
90	Zgonina, Jeff	DE-DT	6-1	284	5/24/70	4	Purdue	Lake Grove, Ill.	W(Pitt)-'95	2/0

* Bates played 13 games with Cleveland in '95; Bickett played 15 games with Seattle; Brewer, Hayes, Senters, and T. Smith missed '95 season because of injuries; Crittenden last active with New England in '94; Davis played 15 games with San Francisco; Fountaine active for 2 games but did not play; Greene played 16 games with Pittsburgh; Miller last active with San Diego in '94; Nunley inactive for 3 games in '95; Pieri inactive for 10 games; Skrepenak played 14 games with Oakland; Stouffer last active with Seattle in '92; Walls played 16 games with New Orleans.

\# Unrestricted free agent; subject to developments.

† Restricted free agent; subject to developments.

Players lost through free agency (3): RB Derrick Moore (Det; 13 games in '95), QB Frank Reich (NYJ; 3), CB Rod Smith (Minn; 16).

Also played with Panthers in '95—RB Randy Baldwin (7 games), WR Don Beebe (14), DE-DT Jeff Fields (2), T Derrick Graham (11), CB Alan Haller (2), LB Travis Hill (3), G Emerson Martin (2), TE Pete Metzelaars (14), TE Lawyer Tillman (5), RB Vince Workman (9).

COACHING STAFF

Head Coach,
Dom Capers

Pro Career: Enters his second season as head coach of the Carolina Panthers after guiding the team from an 0-5 start to a 7-9 finish, the best expansion record in NFL history. Capers also directed the Panthers to other expansion records including the first to win four consecutive games; the first to defeat the reigning world champions; the first to win four games in a row at home; the first to win two straight on the road; and the first team to post a winning record at home (5-3). Also, the Panthers were just the third team in NFL history to begin the season 0-5 and win the next four games. He was named first head coach in Carolina Panthers history on January 23, 1995 after spending three seasons as defensive coordinator for the Pittsburgh Steelers where he oversaw a unit that allowed the fewest points in the league from 1992-94. His 1994 defense was the best overall in the AFC for the second consecutive year and second best in the NFL. The Steelers led the league in sacks and finished second in points allowed, opponents' average gain per play, first downs allowed, and opponents' third-down efficiency. In addition to leading the league in overall defense in 1993, Capers' unit led all teams in forced fumbles, finished second with an opponent passer rating of 64.9, and tied for second in interceptions. In 1992, the Steelers' defense led the NFL in takeaways, fumble recoveries, tied for the league lead in touchdowns allowed, while ranking second in points allowed. Capers entered the professional coaching ranks in 1984 as an assistant under Jim Mora with the USFL Baltimore/Philadelphia Stars where he helped them earn championships in 1984 and 1985. He then moved with Mora to the New Orleans Saints where he coached the secondary from 1986-1991. Career Record: 7-9.

Background: Capers played defensive back for Mount Union College under Ron Lynn, who now is the Washington Redskins' defensive coordinator. He entered the coaching ranks as a graduate assistant at Kent State before taking a graduate assistant position at the University of Washington with Mora. Capers also served full-time coaching stints at Hawaii (1975-76), San Jose State (1977), California (1978-79), Tennessee (1980-81), and Ohio State (1982-83).

Personal: Born August 5, 1950, in Cambridge, Ohio. Capers and his wife, Karen, were married in June, 1994.

ASSISTANT COACHES

Don Breaux, tight ends; born August 3, 1940, Jennings, La., lives in Charlotte, N.C. Quarterback McNeese State 1959-61. Pro quarterback Denver Broncos 1963, San Diego Chargers 1964-65. College coach: Florida State 1966-67, Arkansas 1968-71, 1977-80, Florida 1973-74, Texas 1975-76. Pro coach: Houston Oilers 1972, Washington Redskins 1981-1993, New York Jets 1994, joined Panthers in 1995.

George Catavolos, defensive backs; born May 8,1945, Chicago, Ill., lives in Charlotte, N.C. Defensive back Purdue 1963-67. No pro playing experience. College coach: Purdue 1967-68, 1971-76, Middle Tennessee State 1969, Louisville 1970, Kentucky 1977-81, Tennessee 1982-83. Pro coach: Indianapolis Colts 1984-93, joined Panthers in 1995.

Billy Davis, outside linebackers; born November 5, 1965, Youngstown, Ohio, lives in Charlotte, N.C. Quarterback Cincinnati 1984-88. No pro playing experience. College coach: Michigan State 1990-91. Pro coach: Pittsburgh Steelers 1992-94, joined Panthers in 1995.

Vic Fangio, defensive coordinator; born August 22, 1958, Dunmore, Pa., lives in Charlotte, N.C. Defensive back East Stroudsburg State 1976-78. No pro playing experience. College coach: North Carolina 1983. Pro coach: Philadelphia/Baltimore Stars (USFL) 1984-85, New Orleans Saints 1986-94, joined Panthers in 1995.

Ted Gill, defensive line; born October 3, 1948, Washington, D.C., lives in Charlotte, N.C. Defensive tackle Idaho State. No pro playing experience. College coach: Utah 1974-76, New Mexico State 1977, Ball State 1978-81, Cornell 1982, Army 1983, North Carolina 1984-87, Rice 1988-89, Iowa 1990-94, Oklahoma State 1995. Pro coach: Joined Panthers in 1996.

Chick Harris, running backs; born September 21, 1945, Durham, N.C., lives in Charlotte, N.C. Running back Northern Arizona 1966-69. No pro playing experience. College coach: Colorado State 1970-72, Long Beach State 1973-74, Washington 1975-80. Pro coach: Buffalo Bills 1981-82, Seattle Seahawks 1983-91, Los Angeles Rams 1992-94, joined Panthers in 1995

Jim McNally, offensive line; born December 13, 1943, Buffalo, N.Y., lives in Charlotte, N.C. Guard Buffalo 1961-65. No pro playing experience. College coach: Buffalo 1966-69, Marshall 1973-75, Boston College 1976-78, Wake Forest 1979. Pro coach: Cincinnati Bengals 1980-94, joined Panthers in 1995.

Chip Morton, strength and conditioning; born November 27, 1962, Hamden, Conn., lives in Charlotte, N.C. No college or pro playing experience. College coach: Ohio State 1985-86, Penn State 1987-91. Pro coach: San Diego Chargers 1992-94, joined Panthers in 1995.

Joe Pendry, offensive coordinator; born August 5, 1947, Matheny, W. Va., lives in Charlotte, N.C. Tight end West Virginia 1966-67. No pro playing experience. College coach: West Virginia 1967-74, 1976-77, Kansas State 1975, Pittsburgh 1978-79, Michigan State 1980-81. Pro coach: Philadelphia Stars (USFL) 1983, Pittsburgh Maulers (USFL) 1984 (head coach), Cleveland Browns 1985-88, Kansas City Chiefs 1989-92, Chicago Bears 1993-94, joined Panthers in 1995.

Brad Seely, special teams; born September 6, 1956, Vinton, Iowa, lives in Charlotte, N.C. Tackle-guard South Dakota State 1974-77. No pro playing experience. College coach: Colorado State 1980, Southern Methodist 1981, North Carolina State 1982, Pacific 1983, Oklahoma State 1984-88. Pro coach: Indianapolis Colts 1989-93, New York Jets 1994, joined Panthers in 1995.

John Shoop, quality control-offense; born August 1, 1969, Pittsburgh, Pa., lives in Charlotte, N.C. Quarterback University of the South 1987-91. No pro playing experience. College coach: Dartmouth 1991, Vanderbilt 1992-94. Pro coach: Joined Panthers in 1995.

Kevin Steele, linebackers; born March 17, 1958, La Jolla, Calif., lives in Matthews, N.C. Linebacker Tennessee 1976-79. No pro playing experience. College coach: Tennessee 1981-82, 1987-88, New Mexico State 1983, Oklahoma State 1984-86, Nebraska, 1989-94. Pro coach: Joined Panthers in 1995.

Richard Williamson, wide receivers; born April 13, 1941, Ft. Deposit, Ala., lives in Charlotte, N.C. Receiver Alabama 1961-62. No pro playing experience. College coach: Alabama 1963-67, 1970-71, Arkansas 1968-69, 1972-74, Memphis State 1975-80 (head coach). Pro coach: Kansas City Chiefs 1983-86, Tampa Bay Buccaneers 1987-91 (interim head coach final three games of 1990 season, head coach 1991), Cincinnati Bengals 1992-94, joined Panthers in 1995.

1996 FIRST-YEAR ROSTER

Name	Pos.	Ht.	Wt.	Birthdate	College	Hometown	How Acq.
Baker, Donnell	WR	6-0	180	12/21/73	Southern	Baton Rouge, La.	D7a
Biakabutuka, Tim	RB	6-0	210	1/24/74	Michigan	Lonqueuil, Canada	D1
Burke, Paul (1)	TE	6-3	250	2/16/69	Idaho	Detroit, Mich.	FA
Denton, Robert	G	6-3	315	6/3/73	Michigan State	Martinsville, Ind.	FA
Dragoo, Justin	LB	6-3	240	1/30/72	Arizona State	Napa, Calif.	FA
Feighery, Kevin (1)	P	6-4	215	12/2/73	Merchant Marine	Carmel, N.Y.	FA
Garrido, Norberto	T	6-6	313	10/4/72	Southern California	La Puente, Calif.	D4a
Greeley, Bucky	C	6-2	276	7/30/72	Penn State	Wilkes-Barre, Pa.	FA
Greene, Scott	RB	5-11	230	6/1/72	Michigan State	Canandiagua, N.Y.	D6
Hicks, Kerry	DE-DT	6-6	282	12/29/72	Colorado	Salt Lake City, Utah	D7b
Kanner, Aaron (1)	P	6-1	220	9/25/70	Catawba	Manalapan, N.J.	FA
Knight, William	G	6-8	340	4/27/73	Brigham Young	Lancaster, Calif.	FA
Kubiak, Jim	QB	6-2	211	5/12/72	Navy	Buffalo, N.Y.	FA
Lauder, David (1)	K	6-2	210	2/18/69	Brigham Young	Bountiful, Utah	FA
McDaniel, Emmanuel	CB	5-9	178	7/27/72	East Carolina	Jonesboro, Ga.	D4b
Muhammad, Muhsin	WR	6-2	217	5/5/73	Michigan State	Lansing, Mich.	D2
Oliver, Winslow	RB	5-7	180	3/3/73	New Mexico	Houston, Tex.	D3a
Price, J.C.	DE-DT	6-2	280	1/13/73	Virginia Tech	Dunkirk, Md.	D3b
Smith, Marquette	RB	5-7	190	7/14/72	Central Florida	Lake Howell, Fla.	D5
Terry, Sean	P	6-1	214	4/11/72	Texas A&M	Evadale, Tex.	FA
Tucker, Syii	TE	6-4	236	7/31/73	Miami	Oklahoma City, Okla.	FA
Walters, John	LB	6-2	225	2/23/74	Alabama	Dallas, Tex.	FA
Wiggins, Brian (1)	WR	5-11	183	6/14/68	Texas Southern	New Rochelle, N.Y.	FA
Williams, Johnnie	S	5-11	217	4/22/73	Miami, Ohio	Cleveland, Ohio	FA
Yeboah-Kodie, Phil (1)	LB	6-2	225	1/22/71	Penn State	Montreal, Canada	FA

The term NFL Rookie is defined as a player who is in his first season of professional football and has not been on the roster of another professional football team for any regular-season or postseason games. A Rookie is designated by an "R" on NFL rosters. Players who have been active in another professional football league or players who have NFL experience, including either preseason training camp or being on an Active List or Inactive List, or on Reserve/Injured or Reserve/Physically Unable to Perform for fewer than six regular-season games, are termed NFL First-Year Players. An NFL First-Year Player is designated by a "1" on NFL rosters. Thereafter, a player is credited with an additional year of experience for each season in which he accumulates six games on the Active List or Inactive List, or on Reserve/Injured or Reserve/Physically Unable to Perform.

NOTES

CHICAGO BEARS

National Football Conference
Central Division
Team Colors: Navy Blue, Orange, and White
Halas Hall, 250 North Washington
Lake Forest, Illinois 60045
Telephone: (847) 295-6600

CLUB OFFICIALS

Chairman of the Board: Edward W. McCaskey
President and CEO: Michael B. McCaskey
Secretary: Virginia H. McCaskey
Vice President: Tim McCaskey
Vice President of Operations: Ted Phillips
Director of Player Personnel: Rod Graves
Director of Administration: Tim LeFevour
Ticket Manager: George McCaskey
Director of Community Relations: Pat McCaskey
Player Liaison: Brian McCaskey
Director of Marketing/Communications: Ken Valdiserri
Manager of Promotions: John Bostrom
Manager of Sales: Jack Trompeter
Director of Public Relations: Bryan Harlan
Asst. Director of Public Relations: Doug Green
Computer Systems: Greg Gershuny
Controller: Scott Worthem
Video Director: Dean Pope
Trainer: Fred Caito
Assistant Trainers: Tim Bream, Jeff Hay
Strength Coordinator: Clyde Emrich
Physical Development Coordinator: Russ Riederer
Assistant Physical Development Coordinator: Steve Little
Equipment Manager: Gary Haeger
Quality Control: Craig VerSteeg
Assistant Equipment Manager: Tony Medlin
Scouts: Gary Smith, Jeff Shiver, Charlie Mackey, Bobby Riggle, Mike McCartney, Charles Garcia
Stadium: Soldier Field • **Capacity:** 66,944
425 McFetridge Place
Chicago, Illinois 60605
Playing Surface: Grass
Training Camp: University of Wisconsin-Platteville
Platteville, Wisconsin 53818

1996 SCHEDULE

PRESEASON

Aug. 3	at Carolina	7:30
Aug. 11	**Miami**	12:00
Aug. 17	at New Orleans	7:00
Aug. 22	**Kansas City**	7:00

REGULAR SEASON

Sept. 2	**Dallas** (Mon.)	8:00
Sept. 8	at Washington	1:00
Sept. 15	**Minnesota**	12:00
Sept. 22	at Detroit	4:00
Sept. 29	**Oakland**	12:00
Oct. 6	**Green Bay**	12:00
Oct. 13	at New Orleans	12:00
Oct. 20	Open Date	
Oct. 28	at Minnesota (Mon.)	8:00
Nov. 3	**Tampa Bay**	12:00
Nov. 10	at Denver	2:00
Nov. 17	at Kansas City	12:00
Nov. 24	**Detroit**	12:00
Dec. 1	at Green Bay	12:00
Dec. 8	**St. Louis**	12:00
Dec. 14	**San Diego** (Sat.)	3:00
Dec. 22	at Tampa Bay	1:00

RECORD HOLDERS

INDIVIDUAL RECORDS—CAREER

Category	Name	Performance
Rushing (Yds.)	Walter Payton, 1975-1987	*16,726
Passing (Yds.)	Sid Luckman, 1939-1950	14,686
Passing (TDs)	Sid Luckman, 1939-1950	137
Receiving (No.)	Walter Payton, 1975-1987	492
Receiving (Yds.)	Johnny Morris, 1958-1967	5,059
Interceptions	Gary Fencik, 1976-1987	38
Punting (Avg.)	George Gulyanics, 1947-1952	44.5
Punt Return (Avg.)	Ray (Scooter) McLean, 1940-47	14.8
Kickoff Return (Avg.)	Gale Sayers, 1965-1971	30.6
Field Goals	Kevin Butler, 1985-1995	243
Touchdowns (Tot.)	Walter Payton, 1975-1987	125
Points	Kevin Butler, 1985-1995	1,116

INDIVIDUAL RECORDS—SINGLE SEASON

Category	Name	Performance
Rushing (Yds.)	Walter Payton, 1977	1,852
Passing (Yds.)	Erik Kramer, 1995	3,838
Passing (TDs)	Erik Kramer, 1995	29
Receiving (No.)	Johnny Morris, 1964	93
Receiving (Yds.)	Jeff Graham, 1995	1,301
Interceptions	Mark Carrier, 1990	10
Punting (Avg.)	Bobby Joe Green, 1963	46.5
Punt Return (Avg.)	Harry Clark, 1943	15.8
Kickoff Return (Avg.)	Gale Sayers, 1967	37.7
Field Goals	Kevin Butler, 1985	31
Touchdowns (Tot.)	Gale Sayers, 1965	22
Points	Kevin Butler, 1985	144

INDIVIDUAL RECORDS—SINGLE GAME

Category	Name	Performance
Rushing (Yds.)	Walter Payton, 11-20-77	*275
Passing (Yds.)	Johnny Lujack, 12-11-49	468
Passing (TDs)	Sid Luckman, 11-14-43	*7
Receiving (No.)	Jim Keane, 10-23-49	14
Receiving (Yds.)	Harlon Hill, 10-31-54	214
Interceptions	Many times	3
	Last time by Mark Carrier, 12-9-90	
Field Goals	Roger LeClerc, 12-3-61	5
	Mac Percival, 10-20-68	5
Touchdowns (Tot.)	Gale Sayers, 12-12-65	*6
Points	Gale Sayers, 12-12-65	36

*NFL Record

COACHING HISTORY

Decatur Staleys 1920,
Chicago Staleys 1921
(605-399-42)

1920-29	George Halas	84-31-19
1930-32	Ralph Jones	24-10-7
1933-42	George Halas*	88-24-4
1942-45	Hunk Anderson-Luke Johnsos**	24-12-2
1946-55	George Halas	76-43-2
1956-57	John (Paddy) Driscoll	14-10-1
1958-67	George Halas	76-53-6
1968-71	Jim Dooley	20-36-0
1972-74	Abe Gibron	11-30-1
1975-77	Jack Pardee	20-23-0
1978-81	Neill Armstrong	30-35-0
1982-92	Mike Ditka	112-68-0
1993-95	Dave Wannstedt	26-24-0

*Retired after five games to enter U.S. Navy
**Co-coaches

SOLDIER FIELD

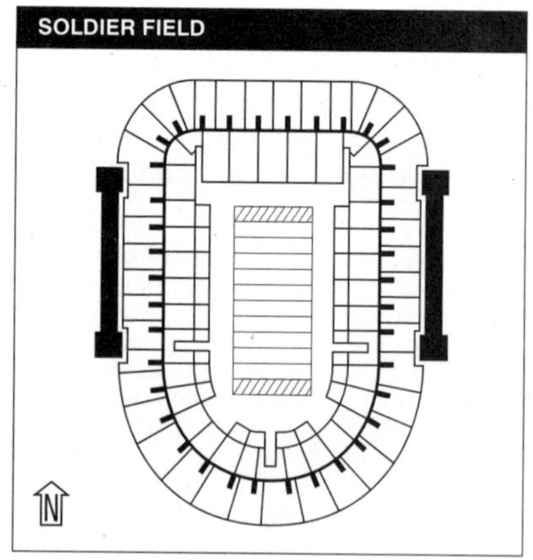

1995 TEAM RECORD

PRESEASON (1-3)

Date	Result		Opponents
8/4	W	18-15	Carolina
8/14	L	13-55	at Cleveland
8/20	L	16-17	Arizona
8/24	L	7-29	at Indianapolis

REGULAR SEASON (9-7)

Date	Result		Opponents	Att.
9/3	W	31-14	Minnesota	63,036
9/11	L	24-27	Green Bay	64,855
9/17	W	25-6	at Tampa Bay	71,507
9/24	L	28-34	at St. Louis	59,679
10/8	W	31-27	Carolina	59,668
10/15	W	30-27	at Jacksonville	72,020
10/22	W	35-32	Houston	63,545
10/30	W	14-6	at Minnesota	61,238
11/5	L	34-37	Pittsburgh (OT)	61,838
11/12	L	28-35	at Green Bay	59,996
11/19	L	17-24	Detroit	61,779
11/26	W	27-24	at N.Y. Giants	70,015
12/4	L	7-27	at Detroit	77,230
12/10	L	10-16	at Cincinnati	38,642
12/17	W	31-10	Tampa Bay	49,475
12/24	W	20-14	Philadelphia	52,391

(OT) Overtime

SCORE BY PERIODS

Bears	73	130	91	98	0	— 392
Opponents	93	112	66	86	3	— 360

ATTENDANCE

Home 476,587 Away 510,337 Total 986,924
Single-game home record, 66,900 (9/5/93)
Single-season home record, 528,465 (1992)

1995 TEAM STATISTICS

	Bears	Opp.
Total First Downs	340	316
Rushing	116	81
Passing	201	212
Penalty	23	23
Third Down: Made/Att	88/207	101/217
Third Down Pct.	42.5	46.5
Fourth Down: Made/Att	13/19	10/17
Fourth Down Pct.	68.4	58.8
Total Net Yards	5673	5442
Avg. Per Game	354.6	340.1
Total Plays	1030	1035
Avg. Per Play	5.5	5.3
Net Yards Rushing	1930	1441
Avg. Per Game	120.6	90.1
Total Rushes	492	405
Net Yards Passing	3743	4001
Avg. Per Game	233.9	250.1
Sacked/Yards Lost	15/95	35/239
Gross Yards	3838	4240
Att./Completions	523/315	595/374
Completion Pct.	60.2	62.9
Had Intercepted	10	16
Punts/Avg.	58/37.4	62/37.3
Net Punting Avg.	58/30.9	62/31.8
Penalties/Yards Lost	71/601	104/821
Fumbles/Ball Lost	26/16	25/13
Touchdowns	46	41
Rushing	15	9
Passing	29	27
Returns	2	5
Avg. Time of Possession	29:55	30:05

1995 INDIVIDUAL STATISTICS

PASSING	Att.	Comp.	Yds.	Pct.	TD	Int.	Tkld.	Rate
Kramer	522	315	3838	60.3	29	10	15/95	93.5
Conway	1	0	0	0.0	0	0	0/0	39.6
Bears	523	315	3838	60.2	29	10	15/95	93.4
Opponents	595	374	4240	62.9	27	16	35/239	88.1

SCORING	TD R	TD P	TD Rt	PAT	FG	Saf	PTS
Butler	0	0	0	45/45	23/31	0	114
Conway	0	12	0	0/0	0/0	0	72
Salaam	10	0	0	0/0	0/0	0	60
Jennings	0	6	0	0/0	0/0	0	36
Graham	0	4	0	0/0	0/0	0	24
Green	3	0	0	0/0	0/0	0	18
Timpson	1	2	0	0/0	0/0	0	18
Flanigan	0	2	0	0/0	0/0	0	12
Wetnight	0	2	0	0/0	0/0	0	12
T. Carter	0	1	0	0/0	0/0	0	6
Kramer	1	0	0	0/0	0/0	0	6
Marshall	0	0	1	0/0	0/0	0	6
MInter	0	0	1	0/0	0/0	0	6
A. Fontenot	0	0	0	0/0	0/0	1	2
Bears	15	29	2	45/45	21/31	1	392
Opponents	9	27	5	40/40	24/29	0	360

2-Point conversions: 0. Team: 0-1.

RUSHING	Att.	Yds.	Avg.	LG	TD
Salaam	296	1074	3.6	42	10
Green	107	570	5.3	38	3
Tillman	29	78	2.7	9	0
Conway	5	77	15.4	20	0
Kramer	35	39	1.1	11	1
T. Carter	10	34	3.4	7	0
A. Johnson	6	30	5.0	11	0
Timpson	3	28	9.3	16	1
Flanigan	1	0	0.0	0	0
Bears	492	1930	3.9	42	15
Opponents	405	1441	3.6	29t	9

RECEIVING	No.	Yds.	Avg.	LG	TD
Graham	82	1301	15.9	51	4
Conway	62	1037	16.7	76t	12
T. Carter	40	329	8.2	27	1
Green	28	246	8.8	28	0
Jennings	25	217	8.7	20	6
Timpson	24	289	12.0	36	2
Wetnight	24	193	8.0	22	2
A. Johnson	13	86	6.6	18	0
Salaam	7	56	8.0	18	0
Gedney	5	52	10.4	15	0
Faulkerson	2	22	11.0	12	0
Flanigan	2	6	3.0	4t	2
R. Harris	1	4	4.0	4	0
Bears	315	3838	12.2	76t	29
Opponents	374	4240	11.3	99t	27

INTERCEPTIONS	No.	Yds.	Avg.	Long	TD
Woolford	4	21	5.3	16	0
Miniefield	3	37	12.3	37	0
Joseph	2	31	15.5	31	0
M. Carter	2	20	10.0	15	0
Lincoln	1	32	32.0	32	0
Mangum	1	2	2.0	2	0
Minter	1	2	2.0	2t	1
Cox	1	1	1.0	1	0
Marshall	1	0	0.0	0	0
Bears	16	146	9.1	37	1
Opponents	10	203	20.3	98t	1

PUNTING	No.	Yds.	Avg.	In 20	LG
Sauerbrun	55	2080	37.8	16	61
O'Neill	3	89	29.7	0	39
Bears	58	2169	37.4	16	61
Opponents	62	2311	37.3	21	57

PUNT RETURNS	No.	FC	Yds.	Avg.	LG	TD
Graham	23	14	183	8.0	39	0
Lundy	1	0	-4	-4.0	-4	0
Bears	24	14	179	7.5	39	0
Opponents	28	13	257	9.2	62t	1

KICKOFF RETURNS	No.	Yds.	Avg.	LG	TD
N. Lewis	42	904	21.5	52	0
Timpson	18	420	23.3	51	0
T. Carter	3	24	8.0	9	0
Green	3	29	9.7	19	0
Lundy	1	11	11.0	11	0
Primus	2	39	19.5	22	0
Graham	1	12	12.0	12	0
Tillman	1	20	20.0	20	0
Bears	71	1459	20.5	61	0
Opponents	72	1570	21.8	54	0

SACKS	No.
Flanigan	11.0
Spellman	8.5
Smith	4.0
Thierry	4.0
A. Fontenot	2.5
Lincoln	1.0
Mangum	1.0
Simpson	1.0
Zorich	1.0
Bears	35.0
Opponents	15.0

1996 DRAFT CHOICES

Round	Name	Pos.	College
1	Walt Harris	DB	Mississippi State
2	Bobby Engram	WR	Penn State
4	Paul Grasmanis	DT	Notre Dame
5	Chris Villarrial	G	Indiana, Pa.
6	Jon Clark	T	Temple
7	Marcus Keyes	DT	North Alabama
	Michael Hicks	RB	South Carolina State

CHICAGO BEARS

1996 VETERAN ROSTER

No.		Name	Pos.	Ht.	Wt.	Birthdate	NFL Exp.	College	Hometown	How Acq.	'95 Games/ Starts
91	†	Baker, Myron	LB	6-1	232	1/6/71	4	Louisiana Tech	Haughton, La.	D4b-'93	16/0
63		Burger, Todd	G	6-3	301	3/20/70	3	Penn State	Clark, N.J.	FA-'93	16/1
35		Burton, James	CB	5-9	181	4/22/71	3	Fresno State	Long Beach, Calif.	FA-'94	11/2
6		Butler, Kevin	K	6-1	205	7/24/62	12	Georgia	Redan, Ga.	D4-'85	16/0
59		Cain, Joe	LB	6-1	239	6/11/65	8	Oregon Tech	Compton, Calif.	RFA(Sea)-'93	16/16
20		Carrier, Mark	S	6-1	190	4/28/68	7	Southern California	Long Beach, Calif.	D1-'90	16/15
23		Carter, Marty	S	6-1	209	12/27/69	6	Middle Tennessee State	La Grange, Ga.	UFA(TB)-'95	16/16
30		Carter, Tony	RB	5-11	232	8/23/72	3	Minnesota	Columbus, Ohio	FA-'94	16/11
80		Conway, Curtis	WR-KR	6-0	193	3/13/71	4	Southern California	Hawthorne, Calif.	D1-'93	16/16
52		Cox, Bryan	LB	6-4	248	2/17/68	6	Western Illinois	East St. Louis, Ill.	UFA(Mia)-'96	16/16*
54		Cunningham, Ed	G-C	6-3	285	8/14/69	5	Washington	Alexandria, Va.	UFA(Ariz)-'96	9/8*
25	#	Eilers, Pat	S	5-11	195	9/3/66	6	Notre Dame	St. Paul, Minn.	UFA(Wash)-'95	9/0
99		Flanigan, Jim	DT	6-2	280	8/27/71	3	Notre Dame	Green Bay, Wis.	D3-'94	16/12
96		Fontenot, Albert	DE	6-4	275	9/17/70	4	Baylor	Houston, Tex.	D4c-'93	13/5
67	†	Fontenot, Jerry	C	6-3	290	11/21/66	8	Texas A&M	Lafayette, La.	D3-'89	16/16
48		Gales, Kenny	CB	5-11	173	4/1/72	2	Wisconsin	Bayside, N.Y.	D6a-'95	0*
84		Gedney, Chris	TE	6-5	265	8/9/70	4	Syracuse	Liverpool, N.Y.	D3-'93	14/1
22		Green, Robert	RB	5-8	212	9/10/70	5	William & Mary	Ft. Washington, Md.	W(Wash)-'93	12/3
29		Harris, Raymont	RB	6-0	225	12/23/70	3	Ohio State	Lorain, Ohio	D4-'94	1/1
57		Harris, Sean	LB	6-3	244	2/25/72	2	Arizona	Magnet, Ariz.	D3a-'95	11/0
64		Heck, Andy	T	6-6	296	1/1/67	8	Notre Dame	Fairfax, Va.	RFA(Sea)-'94	16/16
8		Huerta, Carlos	K	5-7	185	6/29/69	2	Miami	Coral Gables, Fla.	FA-'96	0*
88		Jackson, Jack	WR	5-8	171	11/11/72	2	Florida	Moss Point, Miss.	D4-'95	0*
85		Jennings, Keith	TE	6-4	270	5/19/66	7	Clemson	Summerville, S.C.	FA-'91	16/16
37		Johnson, Keshon	CB	5-10	177	7/17/70	4	Arizona	Fresno, Calif.	UFA(Det)-'95	12/0
32		Joseph, Dwayne	CB	5-9	180	6/2/72	2	Syracuse	Carol City, Fla.	FA-'94	16/1
12		Kramer, Erik	QB	6-1	200	11/6/64	8	North Carolina State	Burbank, Calif.	UFA(Det)-'94	16/16
82	#	Lewis, Nate	WR-KR	5-11	189	10/19/66	7	Oregon Tech	Klamath Falls, Ore.	UFA(Atl)-'95	11/0
79		Lewis, Scotty	DE	6-3	273	12/30/71	2	Baylor	Sulphur Springs, Tex.	FA-'95	0*
39		Lincoln, Jeremy	CB	5-10	180	4/7/69	5	Tennessee	Toledo, Ohio	D3-'92	16/14
43		Lundy, Dennis	RB	5-8	187	7/6/72	2	Northwestern	Tampa, Fla.	FA-'95	2/0
26		Mangum, John	S	5-10	186	3/16/67	7	Alabama	Magee, Miss.	D7-'90	11/1
36		Marshall, Anthony	S	6-1	205	9/16/70	2	Louisiana State	Mobile, Ala.	FA-'94	16/2
9		Matthews, Shane	QB	6-3	196	6/1/70	3	Florida	Pascagoula, Miss.	FA-'93	0*
24		Miniefield, Kevin	CB-S	5-9	180	3/2/70	4	Arizona State	Phoenix, Ariz.	FA-'93	15/7
92		Minter, Barry	LB	6-2	240	1/28/70	4	Tulsa	Mt. Pleasant, Tex.	T(Dall)-'93	16/3
75		Perry, Todd	G	6-5	310	11/28/70	4	Kentucky	Elizabethtown, Ky.	D4a-'93	15/15
65		Pilgrim, Evan	G	6-4	300	8/14/72	2	Brigham Young	Anioch, Calif.	D3b-'95	0*
87		President, Andre	TE	6-3	255	6/16/71	2	Angelo State	Ft. Worth, Tex.	FA-'95	2/0
68		Reeves, Carl	DE	6-4	247	12/17/71	2	North Carolina State	Durham, N.C.	D6b-'95	0*
78		Riley, Pat	DE	6-5	286	3/8/72	2	Miami	Marrero, La.	D2a-'95	1/0
31		Salaam, Rashaan	RB	6-1	226	10/8/74	2	Colorado	La Jolla, Calif.	D1-'95	16/11
16		Sauerbrun, Todd	P-K	5-10	206	1/4/73	2	West Virginia	Setauket, N.Y.	D2b-'95	15/0
98		Simpson, Carl	DT	6-2	295	4/18/70	4	Florida State	Appling County, Ga.	D2-'93	16/8
55		Smith, Vinson	LB	6-2	247	7/3/65	9	East Carolina	Statesville, N.C.	T(Dall)-'93	16/13
76		Spears, Marcus	T	6-4	300	9/28/71	3	Northwestern State, La.	Baton Rouge, La.	D2-'94	0*
90		Spellman, Alonzo	DE	6-4	290	9/27/71	5	Ohio State	Rancocas, N.J.	D1-'92	16/16
18		Stenstrom, Steve	QB	6-1	200	12/23/71	2	Stanford	El Toro, Calif.	W(KC)-'95	0*
11		Sullivan, Kent	P	6-1	206	5/15/67	3	Cal Lutheran	Middlebury, Ind.	FA-'96	0*
53		Sullivan, Mike	G-C	6-3	292	12/22/67	5	Miami	Chicago, Ill.	UFA(TB)-'96	12/0*
94		Thierry, John	DE	6-4	260	9/4/71	3	Alcorn State	Opelousas, La.	D1-'94	16/7
27		Tillman, Lewis	RB	6-0	204	4/16/66	8	Jackson State	Hazelhurst, Miss.	UFA(NYG)-'94	13/1
86		Timpson, Michael	WR	5-10	180	6/6/67	8	Penn State	Miami Lakes, Fla.	UFA(NE)-'95	16/1
89		Wetnight, Ryan	TE	6-2	240	11/5/70	4	Stanford	Fresno, Calif.	FA-'93	12/2
71		Williams, James	T	6-7	335	3/29/68	6	Cheyney State	Allerdice, Pa.	FA-'91	16/16
21		Woolford, Donnell	CB	5-9	188	1/6/66	8	Clemson	Byrd, N.C.	D1a-'89	9/9
97		Zorich, Chris	DT	6-1	280	3/13/69	6	Notre Dame	Chicago, Ill.	D2-'91	16/15

* B. Cox played 16 games with Miami in '95; Cunningham played 9 games with Arizona; Gales, Jackson, and Reeves missed '95 season because of injury; Huerta was last active with Houston in '93; S. Lewis inactive for 9 games; Matthews inactive for 2 games; Pilgrim inactive for 16 games; Spears active for 5 games but did not play; Stenstrom inactive for 12 games; K. Sullivan last active with San Diego in '93; M. Sullivan played 12 games with Tampa Bay.

Unrestricted free agent; subject to developments.

† Restricted free agent; subject to developments.

Players lost through free agency (6): T Scott Adams (TB; 4 games in '95), T Troy Auzenne (Ind; 11), LB Ron Cox (GB; 16), WR Jeff Graham (NYJ; 16), G Jay Leeuwenburg (Ind; 16), QB Steve Walsh (StL; 1).

Also played with Bears in '95—LB Robert Bass (2 games), DE Richard Dent (3), LB Garland Hawkins (1), LB Darwin Ireland (1), RB Anthony Johnson (8), P Pat O'Neill (1), WR Greg Primus (4).

COACHING STAFF

Head Coach,
Dave Wannstedt

Pro Career: Has guided Bears to back-to-back 9-7 marks after a 7-9 record in his rookie season. Named Chicago's head coach on January 19, 1993. He was an integral part of one of the most successful turnarounds in NFL history, helping to turn the 1989 Dallas Cowboys, which finished the season 1-15, into Super Bowl champions four years later. In January, 1992, he was named Dallas's assistant head coach and defensive coordinator. He was the defensive coordinator for the Cowboys in 1989. Selected by the Green Bay Packers in the fifteenth round of the 1974 draft, but spent the entire season on injured reserve. Career record: 26-24.
Background: Played offensive tackle at the University of Pittsburgh from 1970-73. Began coaching career at Pittsburgh in 1975 and was part of the staff that led the Panthers to a 12-0 record and the NCAA championship in 1976. In 1979, he took a job with Jimmy Johnson at Oklahoma State as defensive line coach. After two seasons, he was promoted to defensive coordinator. In 1983, Wannstedt was the defensive line coach for Southern California before rejoining Johnson at the University of Miami as the Hurricanes' defensive coordinator. In his first year (1986), Miami went 11-0 before losing to Penn State in the Fiesta Bowl. The following season Miami was crowned NCAA champion with a perfect 12-0 record.
Personal: Born May 21, 1952, Pittsburgh, Pa. Dave and his wife, Jan, live in Lake Forest, Ill. and have two children—Keri and Jami.

ASSISTANT COACHES

Danny Abramowicz, special teams; born July 13, 1945, Steubenville, Ohio, lives in Lake Forest, Ill. Wide receiver Xavier 1964-66. Pro wide receiver New Orleans Saints 1967-73, San Francisco 49ers 1973-74. Pro coach: Joined Bears in 1992.
Clarence Brooks, defensive line; born May 20, 1951, New York, N.Y., lives in Lake Forest, Ill. Guard Massachusetts 1970-73. No pro playing experience. College coach: Massachusetts 1976-80, Syracuse 1981-89, Arizona 1990-92. Pro coach: Joined Bears in 1993.
Ivan Fears, wide receivers; born November 15, 1954, Portsmouth, Va., lives in Lake Forest, Ill. Running back William and Mary 1973-75. No pro playing experience. College coach: William and Mary 1977-80, Syracuse 1981-90. Pro coach: New England Patriots 1991-92, joined Bears in 1993.
Carlos Mainord, defensive backs; born August 26, 1944, Greenville, Tex., lives in Lake Forest, Ill. Linebacker Navarro (Tex.) Junior College 1962-63, McMurry College 1964-65. No pro playing experience. College coach: McMurry College 1966-68, Texas Tech 1969, 1983-85, 1987-92, Ranger (Tex.) Junior College 1970-71, 1972-77 (head coach), Rice 1978-82, Miami 1986. Pro coach: Joined Bears in 1993.
Willie Peete, running backs; born July 14, 1937, Mesa, Ariz., lives in Chicago. Fullback Arizona 1956-59. No pro playing experience. College coach: Arizona 1960-62, 1971-82. Pro coach: Kansas City Chiefs 1983-86, Green Bay Packers 1987-91, Tampa Bay Buccaneers 1992-94, joined Bears in 1995.
Ted Plumb, receivers-tight ends; born August 20, 1939, Reno, Nev., lives in Lake Forest, Ill. Wide receiver Baylor 1960-61. Pro wide receiver Buffalo Bills 1962. College coach: Cerritos, Calif., J.C. 1966-67, Texas Christian 1968-70, Tulsa 1971, Kansas 1972-73. Pro coach: New York Giants 1974-76, Atlanta Falcons 1977-79, Chicago Bears 1980-85, Philadelphia Eagles 1986-89, Arizona Cardinals 1990-95, rejoined Bears in 1996.
Greg Schiano, defensive assistant; born June 1, 1966, Paterson, N.J., lives in Lake Forest, Ill. Linebacker Bucknell 1984-88. No pro playing experience. College coach: Rutgers 1989, Penn State 1990-95. Pro coach: Joined Bears in 1996.
Bob Slowik, defensive coordinator-linebackers; born May 16, 1954, Pittsburgh, Pa., lives in Lake Forest, Ill. Cornerback Delaware 1973-76. No pro playing experience. College coach: Delaware 1977, Florida 1978-81, Drake 1982, Rutgers 1983, East Carolina 1984-91. Pro coach: Dallas Cowboys 1992, joined Bears in 1993.
Ron Turner, offensive coordinator-quarterbacks; born December 5, 1953, Martinez, Calif., lives in Lake Forest, Ill. Running back-defensive back Pacific 1973-76. No pro playing experience. College coach: Pacific 1977, Arizona 1978-80, Northwestern 1981-82, Pittsburgh 1983-84, Southern California 1985-87, Texas A&M 1988, Stanford 1989-91, San Jose State 1992 (head coach). Pro coach: Joined Bears in 1993.
Tony Wise, assistant head coach-offensive line; born December 28, 1951, Albany, N.Y., lives in Lake Forest, Ill. Offensive lineman Ithaca College 1971-72. No pro playing experience. College coach: Albany State 1973, Bridgeport 1974, Central Connecticut State 1975, Washington State 1976, Pittsburgh 1977-78, Oklahoma State 1979-83, Syracuse 1984, Miami 1985-88. Pro coach: Dallas Cowboys 1989-92, joined Bears in 1993.

1996 FIRST-YEAR ROSTER

Name	Pos.	Ht.	Wt.	Birthdate	College	Hometown	How Acq.
Augustino, Jason	T	6-6	272	3/31/73	Virginia	Wexford, Pa.	FA
Bennett, Brandon (1)	RB	5-11	202	2/3/73	South Carolina	Taylors, S.C.	FA
Blair, Don	WR	5-11	202	4/6/72	Calgary	Calgary, Canada	FA
Bownes, Fabien (1)	WR	5-11	180	2/29/72	Western Illinois	Aurora, Ill.	FA
Clark, Jon	T	6-6	339	4/11/73	Temple	Philadelphia, Pa.	D6a
Coleman, Mill(1)	WR	5-9	175	6/19/72	Michigan State	Farmington, Mich.	FA
Coleman, Shaston	WR	5-11	201	1/18/72	Mississippi State	Ackerman, Miss.	FA
Crowe, Andy	C	6-3	270	6/19/74	Florida State	Tallahassee, Fla.	FA
Engram, Bobby	WR	5-10	187	1/7/73	Penn State	Camden, S.C.	D2
Faulkerson, Mike (1)	RB	6-1	237	9/9/70	North Carolina	Kingsport, Tenn.	FA
Forbes, Marlon (1)	CB	6-1	202	12/25/71	Penn State	Long Island, N.Y.	FA
Grasmanis, Paul	DT	6-2	295	8/2/74	Notre Dame	Jenison, Mich.	D4
Harris, Walt	CB	5-11	188	8/10/74	Mississippi State	La Grange, Ga.	D1
Hicks, Michael	RB	6-1	190	2/1/73	South Carolina	Barnsville, Ga.	D7b
Hobbs, Ed	RB	6-1	243	4/5/71	Albany State	Atlanta, Ga.	FA
Horton, Jeff	S	5-11	190	3/30/72	East Tennessee State	Rome, Ga.	FA
Johnson, Ahmani	LB	6-3	247	1/23/73	Oregon State	Lynnwood, Wash.	FA
Keyes, Marcus	DT	6-3	310	10/20/73	North Alabama	Taylorsville, Miss.	D7a
Littleton, Seth	G	6-4	290	6/20/74	Mesa College	Los Alamos, N.M.	FA
Lowery, Michael	LB	6-1	218	2/14/74	Mississippi	McComb, Miss.	FA
Lumelski, Zev (1)	T	6-8	304	4/14/72	Miami	Miami Beach, Fla.	FA
Martin, Chris	CB	5-9	184	9/1/74	Northwestern	Tampa Bay, Fla.	FA
Neely, Bobby	TE	6-3	251	3/22/74	Virginia	Atlanta, Ga.	FA
Polk, Octus (1)	G	6-3	340	9/17/71	Stephen F. Austin	Sulphur Springs, Tex.	FA
Sutton, Clarence	S	6-1	196	12/25/72	Appalachian State	Chicago, Ill.	FA
Turner, Derrick	T	6-4	315	8/27/73	Florida A&M	Orlando, Fla.	FA
Villarrial, Chris	C-G	6-4	300	6/9/73	Indiana, Pa.	Hummelstown, Pa.	D5

The term NFL Rookie is defined as a player who is in his first season of professional football and has not been on the roster of another professional football team for any regular-season or postseason games. A Rookie is designated by an "R" on NFL rosters. Players who have been active in another professional football league or players who have NFL experience, including either preseason training camp or being on an Active List or Inactive List, or on Reserve/Injured or Reserve/Physically Unable to Perform for fewer than six regular-season games, are termed NFL First-Year Players. An NFL First-Year Player is designated by a "1" on NFL rosters. Thereafter, a player is credited with an additional year of experience for each season in which he accumulates six games on the Active List or Inactive List, or on Reserve/Injured or Reserve/Physically Unable to Perform.

NOTES

DALLAS COWBOYS

National Football Conference
Eastern Division
Team Colors: Royal Blue, Metallic Silver Blue, and White
Cowboys Center
One Cowboys Parkway
Irving, Texas 75063
Telephone: (214) 556-9900

CLUB OFFICIALS

Owner/President/General Manager: Jerry Jones
Executive Vice President-Player Personnel: Stephen Jones
Vice President/Marketing: George Hays
Vice President/Director of Marketing and Special Events: Charlotte Anderson
Vice President/Legal Operations: Jerry Jones, Jr.
Public Relations Director: Rich Dalrymple
Assistant Director of Public Relations: Brett Daniels
Director of College and Pro Scouting: Larry Lacewell
Director of Operations: Bruce Mays
Director of Human Resources: Debbie Ross
Ticket Manager: Carol Padgett
Trainer: Jim Maurer
Equipment Manager: Mike McCord
Video Director: Robert Blackwell
Cheerleader Director: Kelli McGonagill
Stadium: Texas Stadium • **Capacity:** 65,921 Irving, Texas 75062
Playing Surface: Texas Turf
Training Camp: St. Edward's University Austin, Texas 78704

1996 SCHEDULE

PRESEASON

July 27	**Oakland**	8:00
Aug. 5	vs. Kansas City at Monterrey, Mexico	7:00
Aug. 12	**New England**	7:00
Aug. 17	**Denver**	7:00
Aug. 24	vs. Houston at Orlando, Florida	6:00

REGULAR SEASON

Sept. 2	at Chicago (Mon.)	8:00
Sept. 8	**New York Giants**	3:00
Sept. 15	**Indianapolis**	3:00
Sept. 22	at Buffalo	4:00
Sept. 30	at Philadelphia (Mon.)	9:00
Oct. 6	Open Date	
Oct. 13	**Arizona**	12:00
Oct. 20	**Atlanta**	12:00
Oct. 27	at Miami	4:00
Nov. 3	**Philadelphia**	12:00
Nov. 10	at San Francisco	1:00
Nov. 18	**Green Bay** (Mon.)	8:00
Nov. 24	at New York Giants	4:00
Nov. 28	**Washington** (Thurs.)	3:00
Dec. 8	at Arizona	2:00
Dec. 15	**New England**	12:00
Dec. 22	at Washington	4:00

RECORD HOLDERS

INDIVIDUAL RECORDS—CAREER

Category	Name	Performance
Rushing (Yds.)	Tony Dorsett, 1977-1987	12,036
Passing (Yds.)	Roger Staubach, 1969-1979	22,700
Passing (TDs)	Danny White, 1976-1988	155
Receiving (No.)	Michael Irvin, 1988-1995	527
Receiving (Yds.)	Michael Irvin, 1988-1995	8,538
Interceptions	Mel Renfro, 1964-1977	52
Punting (Avg.)	Mike Saxon, 1985-1992	41.5
Punt Return (Avg.)	Bob Hayes, 1965-1974	11.1
Kickoff Return (Avg.)	Mel Renfro, 1964-1977	26.4
Field Goals	Rafael Septien, 1978-1986	162
Touchdowns (Tot.)	Emmitt Smith, 1990-95	100
Points	Rafael Septien, 1978-1986	874

INDIVIDUAL RECORDS—SINGLE SEASON

Category	Name	Performance
Rushing (Yds.)	Emmitt Smith, 1995	1,773
Passing (Yds.)	Danny White, 1983	3,980
Passing (TDs)	Danny White, 1983	29
Receiving (No.)	Michael Irvin, 1995	111
Receiving (Yds.)	Michael Irvin, 1995	1,603
Interceptions	Everson Walls, 1981	11
Punting (Avg.)	Sam Baker, 1962	45.4
Punt Return (Avg.)	Bob Hayes, 1968	20.8
Kickoff Return (Avg.)	Mel Renfro, 1965	30.0
Field Goals	Eddie Murray, 1993	28
Touchdowns (Tot.)	Emmitt Smith, 1995	*25
Points	Emmitt Smith, 1995	150

INDIVIDUAL RECORDS—SINGLE GAME

Category	Name	Performance
Rushing (Yds.)	Emmitt Smith, 10-31-93	237
Passing (Yds.)	Don Meredith, 11-10-63	460
Passing (TDs)	Many times.	5
	Last time by Danny White, 10-30-83	
Receiving (No.)	Lance Rentzel, 11-19-67	13
Receiving (Yds.)	Bob Hayes, 11-13-66	246
Interceptions	Herb Adderley, 9-26-71	3
	Lee Roy Jordan, 11-4-73	3
	Dennis Thurman, 12-13-81	3
Field Goals	Roger Ruzek, 12-21-87	5
	Eddie Murray, 10-3-93	5
	Chris Boniol, 12-17-95	5
Touchdowns (Tot.)	Many times	4
	Last time by Emmitt Smith, 9-4-95	
Points	Many times	24
	Last time by Emmitt Smith, 9-4-95	

*NFL Record

COACHING HISTORY

(349-224-6)

1960-88	Tom Landry	270-178-6
1989-93	Jimmy Johnson	51-37-0
1994-95	Barry Switzer	28-9-0

TEXAS STADIUM

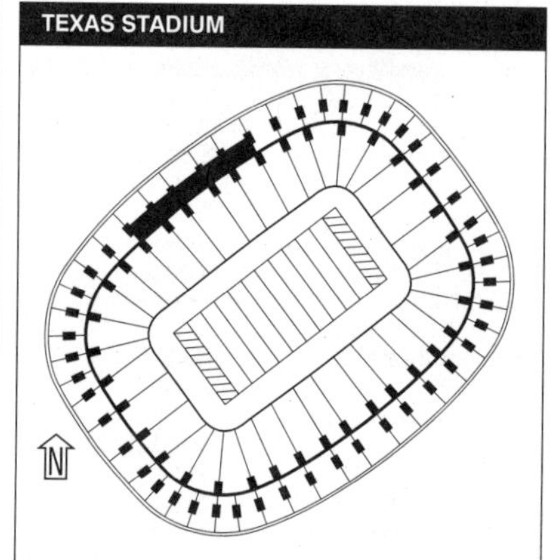

1995 TEAM RECORD

PRESEASON (2-3)

Date	Result		Opponents
7/29	W	21-15	Buffalo
8/5	L	14-27	Oakland
8/12	L	7-9	vs. Buffalo at Toronto
8/21	L	17-20	Denver
8/26	W	10-0	vs. Houston at San Antonio, Tex.

REGULAR SEASON (12-4)

Date	Result		Opponents	Att.
9/4	W	35-0	at N.Y. Giants	77,454
9/10	W	31-21	Denver	64,578
9/17	W	23-17	at Minnesota (OT)	60,088
9/24	W	34-20	Arizona	64,560
10/1	L	23-27	at Washington	55,489
10/8	W	34-24	Green Bay	64,806
10/15	W	23-9	at San Diego	62,664
10/29	W	28-13	at Atlanta	70,089
11/6	W	34-12	Philadelphia	64,876
11/12	L	20-38	San Francisco	65,180
11/19	W	34-21	at Oakland	54,092
11/23	W	24-12	Kansas City	64,901
12/3	L	17-24	Washington	64,866
12/10	L	17-20	at Philadelphia	66,198
12/17	W	21-20	N.Y. Giants	64,400
12/25	W	37-13	at Arizona	72,394

POSTSEASON (3-0)

Date	Result		Opponents	Att.
1/7	W	30-11	Philadelphia	64,371
1/14	W	38-27	Green Bay	65,135
1/28	W	27-17	Pittsburgh	76,347

(OT) Overtime

SCORE BY PERIODS

Cowboys	102	133	83	111	6	—	435
Opponents	38	104	78	71	0	—	291

ATTENDANCE

Home 518,167 Away 518,468 Total 1,036,635
Single-game home record, 80,259 (11/24/66)
Single-season home record, 518,167 (1995)

1995 TEAM STATISTICS

	Cowboys	Opp.
Total First Downs	364	303
Rushing	141	113
Passing	195	165
Penalty	28	25
Third Down: Made/Att	83/186	97/216
Third Down Pct.	44.6	44.9
Fourth Down: Made/Att	8/13	8/19
Fourth Down Pct.	61.5	42.1
Total Net Yards	5824	5044
Avg. Per Game	364.0	315.3
Total Plays	1007	1001
Avg. Per Play	5.8	5.0
Net Yards Rushing	2201	1772
Avg. Per Game	137.6	110.8
Total Rushes	495	442
Net Yards Passing	3623	3272
Avg. Per Game	226.4	204.5
Sacked/Yards Lost	18/118	36/219
Gross Yards	3741	3491
Att./Completions	494/322	523/293
Completion Pct.	65.2	56.0
Had Intercepted	10	19
Punts/Avg.	55/40.8	65/42.7
Net Punting Avg.	55/34.7	65/37.8
Penalties/Yards Lost	90/695	112/913
Fumbles/Ball Lost	24/13	16/6
Touchdowns	51	32
Rushing	29	13
Passing	18	17
Returns	4	2
Avg. Time of Possession	31:15	28:45

1995 INDIVIDUAL STATISTICS

PASSING	Att.	Comp.	Yds.	Pct.	TD	Int.	Tkld.	Rate
Aikman	432	280	3304	64.8	16	7	14/89	93.6
Wilson	57	38	391	66.7	1	3	4/29	70.1
Garrett	5	4	46	80.0	1	0	0/0	144.6
Cowboys	494	322	3741	65.2	18	10	18/118	91.7
Opponents	523	293	3491	56.0	17	19	36/219	72.3

SCORING	TD R	TD P	TD Rt	PAT	FG	Saf	PTS
E. Smith	25	0	0	0/0	0/0	0	150
Boniol	0	0	0	46/48	27/28	0	127
Irvin	0	10	0	0/0	0/0	0	60
Novacek	0	5	0	0/0	0/0	0	32
Johnston	2	1	0	0/0	0/0	0	18
Brown	0	0	2	0/0	0/0	0	12
K. Williams	0	2	0	0/0	0/0	0	12
Aikman	1	0	0	0/0	0/0	0	6
Marion	0	0	1	0/0	0/0	0	6
S. Williams	1	0	0	0/0	0/0	0	6
Woodson	0	0	1	0/0	0/0	0	6
Cowboys	29	18	4	46/48	27/28	0	435
Opponents	13	17	2	29/29	22/27	1	291

2-Point conversions: Novacek. Team:1-2.

RUSHING	Att.	Yds.	Avg.	LG	TD
E. Smith	377	1773	4.7	60t	25
S. Williams	48	205	4.3	44t	1
Johnston	25	111	4.4	18	2
K. Williams	10	53	5.3	14	0
Aikman	21	32	1.5	12	1
Wilson	10	12	1.2	11	0
Sanders	2	9	4.5	8	0
Lang	1	7	7.0	7	0
Garrett	1	-1	-1.0	-1	0
Cowboys	495	2201	4.4	60t	29
Opponents	442	1772	4.0	48t	13

RECEIVING	No.	Yds.	Avg.	LG	TD
Irvin	111	1603	14.4	50	10
Novacek	62	705	11.4	33t	5
E. Smith	62	375	6.0	40	0
K. Williams	38	613	16.1	48t	2
Johnston	30	248	8.3	24	1
Bjornson	7	53	7.6	16	0
Fleming	6	83	13.8	16	0
S. Williams	3	28	9.3	24	0
Sanders	2	25	12.5	19	0
Watkins	1	8	8.0	8	0
Cowboys	322	3741	11.6	50	18
Opponents	293	3491	11.9	81t	17

INTERCEPTIONS	No.	Yds.	Avg.	LG	TD
Brown	6	124	20.7	65t	2
Marion	6	40	6.7	32t	1
Woodson	2	46	23.0	37t	1
Sanders	2	34	17.0	34	0
Myles	1	15	15.0	15	0
Brice	1	2	2.0	2	0
Holmes	1	0	0.0	0	0
Cowboys	19	261	13.7	65t	4
Opponents	10	155	15.5	48t	1

PUNTING	No.	Yds.	Avg.	In 20	LG
Jett	53	2166	40.9	17	58
Boniol	2	77	38.5	2	56
Cowboys	55	2243	40.8	19	58
Opponents	65	2775	42.7	22	60

PUNT RETURNS	No.	FC	Yds.	Avg.	LG	TD
K. Williams	18	15	166	9.2	30	0
Holmes	4	1	35	8.8	13	0
Sanders	1	1	54	54.0	43	0
Cowboys	23	17	255	11.1	45	1
Opponents	22	10	216	9.8	21	0

KICKOFF RETURNS	No.	Yds.	Avg.	LG	TD
K. Williams	49	1108	22.6	43	0
Holmes	5	134	26.8	46	0
Marion	1	16	16.0	16	0
Sanders	1	15	15.0	15	0
Schwantz	1	9	9.0	9	0
Watkins	1	-6	-6.0	-6	0
Cowboys	58	1276	22.0	46	0
Opponents	85	1661	19.5	59	0

SACKS	No.
Haley	10.5
Hennings	5.5
Tolbert	5.5
Lett	3.0
D. Smith	3.0
Carver	2.5
Maryland	2.0
McCormack	2.0
Jones	1.0
Cowboys	36.0
Opponents	18.0

1996 DRAFT CHOICES

Round	Name	Pos.	College
2	Kavika Pittman	DE	McNeese State
	Randall Godfrey	LB	Georgia
3	Clay Shiver	C	Florida State
	Stepfret Williams	WR	N.E. Louisiana
	Mike Ulufale	DT	Brigham Young
5	Kenneth McDaniel	T	Norfolk State
	Alan Campos	LB	Louisville
6	Wendell Davis	DB	Oklahoma
7	Ryan Wood	RB	Arizona State

DALLAS COWBOYS

1996 VETERAN ROSTER

No.		Name	Pos.	Ht.	Wt.	Birthdate	NFL Exp.	College	Hometown	How Acq.	'95 Games/ Starts
8		Aikman, Troy	QB	6-4	223	11/21/66	8	UCLA	Henryetta, Okla.	D1-'89	16/16
73		Allen, Larry	G	6-3	326	11/27/71	3	Sonoma State	Napa, Calif.	D2-'94	16/16
40		Bates, Bill	S	6-1	211	6/6/61	14	Tennessee	Knoxville, Tenn.	FA-'83	16/0
68		Batiste, Michael	G-C	6-3	305	12/24/70	2	Tulane	Beaumont, Tex.	FA-'95	2/0
91		Benson, Darren	DT	6-7	308	8/25/74	2	Trinity Valley	Memphis, Tenn.	SD3-'95	6/0
86		Bjornson, Eric	TE	6-4	236	12/15/71	2	Washington	Oakland, Calif.	D4a-'95	14/1
18		Boniol, Chris	K	5-11	167	12/9/71	3	Louisiana Tech	Alexandria, La.	FA-'94	16/0
29		Brice, Alundis	CB	5-10	178	5/1/70	2	Mississippi	Brookhaven, Miss.	D4b-'95	10/1
96		Carver, Shante	DE	6-5	253	2/12/71	3	Arizona State	Stockton, Calif.	D1-'94	16/3
25	#	Case, Scott	S	6-1	188	5/17/62	13	Oklahoma	Edmond, Okla.	FA-'95	16/1
87		Davis, Billy	WR	6-1	197	7/6/72	2	Pittsburgh	El Paso, Tex.	FA-'95	16/0
53		Donaldson, Ray	C	6-3	311	5/18/58	17	Georgia	Rome, Ga.	UFA(Sea)-'95	12/12
17		Garrett, Jason	QB	6-2	195	3/28/66	4	Princeton	Chagrin, Ohio	FA-'93	1/0
94		Haley, Charles	DE	6-5	255	1/6/64	11	James Madison	Campbell County, Va.	T(SF)-'92	13/11
63		Hannah, Shane	G	6-5	329	10/21/71	2	Michigan State	Germantown, Ohio	D2c-'95	0*
54		Hardy, Darryl	LB	6-2	230	11/22/68	2	Tennessee	Cincinnati, Ohio	W(Ariz)-'95	5/0
24	t-	Harper, Roger	S	6-2	223	10/26/70	4	Ohio State	Columbus, Ohio	T(Atl)-'96	16/12*
69		Hegamin, George	T	6-7	331	2/14/73	3	North Carolina State	Camden, N.J.	D3-'94	0*
70		Hellestrae, Dale	G-C	6-5	286	7/11/62	12	Southern Methodist	Scottsdale, Ariz.	T(Raid)-'90	16/0
95		Hennings, Chad	DT	6-6	295	10/20/65	5	Air Force	Elberon, Iowa	D11-'88	16/7
81		Hervey, Edward	WR	6-3	189	5/4/73	2	Southern California	Compton, Calif.	D5a-'95	0*
88		Irvin, Michael	WR	6-2	207	3/5/66	9	Miami	Ft. Lauderdale, Fla.	D1-'88	16/16
19		Jett, John	P	6-0	199	11/11/68	4	East Carolina	Reedville, Va.	FA-'93	16/0
48		Johnston, Daryl	RB	6-2	242	2/10/66	8	Syracuse	Youngstown, N.Y.	D2-'89	16/16
38	#	Lang, David	RB	5-11	210	3/28/68	6	Northern Arizona	Rialto, Calif.	UFA(StL)-'95	16/0
78		Lett, Leon	DT-DE	6-6	291	10/12/68	6	Emporia State	Fair Hope, Ala.	D7-'91	12/12
31		Marion, Brock	S	5-11	193	6/11/70	4	Nevada	Bakersfield, Calif.	D7-'93	16/16
99		McCormack, Hurvin	DT-DE	6-5	278	4/6/72	3	Indiana	Brooklyn, N.Y.	FA-'94	15/2
98		Myles, Godfrey	LB	6-1	240	9/22/68	6	Florida	Miami, Fla.	D3a-'91	16/11
61		Newton, Nate	G	6-3	320	12/20/61	11	Florida A&M	Orlando, Fla.	FA-'86	16/16
84		Novacek, Jay	TE	6-4	234	10/24/62	12	Wyoming	Gothenburg, Neb.	PB(Phx)-'90	15/15
21		Sanders, Deion	CB-WR	6-1	190	8/9/67	8	Florida State	Ft. Myers, Fla.	UFA(SF)-'95	9/9
52		Schwantz, Jim	LB	6-2	240	1/23/70	3	Purdue	Palatine, Ill.	T(Chi)-'94	16/0
59	†	Smith, Darrin	LB	6-1	230	4/15/70	4	Miami	Miami, Fla.	D2b-'93	9/9
22		Smith, Emmitt	RB	5-9	209	5/15/69	7	Florida	Escambia, Fla.	D1-'90	16/16
26		Smith, Kevin	CB	5-11	188	4/7/70	5	Texas A&M	Orange, Tex.	D1a-'92	1/1
55		Strickland, Fred	LB	6-2	250	8/15/66	9	Purdue	Wanaque, N.J.	UFA(GB)-'96	14/10*
90		Sturgis, Oscar	DE	6-5	278	1/12/71	2	North Carolina	Hamlet, N.C.	D7-'95	1/0
51		Thomas, Broderick	LB	6-4	242	2/20/67	8	Nebraska	Houston, Tex.	FA-'96	16/16*
92		Tolbert, Tony	DE	6-6	263	12/29/67	8	Texas-El Paso	Englewood, N.J.	D4-'89	16/16
71		Tuinei, Mark	T	6-5	314	3/31/60	14	Hawaii	Honolulu, Hawaii	FA-'83	16/16
83		Watkins, Kendell	TE	6-1	282	3/8/73	2	Mississippi State	Jackson, Miss.	D2b-'95	16/0
42		Williams, Charlie	S	6-0	189	2/2/72	2	Bowling Green	Detroit, Mich.	D3-'95	16/0
79		Williams, Erik	T	6-6	324	9/7/68	6	Central State, Ohio	Philadelphia, Pa.	D3c-'91	15/15
85		Williams, Kevin	WR	5-9	194	1/25/71	4	Miami	Dallas, Tex.	D2a-'93	16/16
20		Williams, Sherman	RB	5-8	191	8/13/73	2	Alabama	Mobile, Ala.	D2a-'95	11/0
11		Wilson, Wade	QB	6-3	206	2/1/59	16	East Texas State	Commerce, Tex.	FA-'95	7/0
28		Woodson, Darren	S	6-1	216	4/25/69	5	Arizona State	Phoenix, Ariz.	D2b-'92	16/16

* Hannah missed '95 season because of injury; Harper played 16 games with Atlanta in '95; Hegamin active for four games but did not play; Hervey inactive for 16 games; Strickland played 14 games with Green Bay; Thomas played 16 games with Minnesota.

\# Unrestricted free agent; subject to developments.

† Restricted free agent; subject to developments.

t- Cowboys traded for Harper (Atlanta).

Players lost through free agency (6): CB Robert Bailey (Mia; 9 games in '95), CB Larry Brown (Oak; 16), LB Dixon Edwards (Minn; 15), LB Robert Jones (StL; 12), DT Russell Maryland (Oak; 13), G-T Ron Stone (NYG; 16).

Also played with Cowboys in '95— K Jon Baker (3 games), LB Reggie Barnes (7), S Greg Briggs (11), S Anthony Fieldings (4), WR Cory Fleming (16), CB Clayton Holmes (8), G-C Derek Kennard (9), RB Dominique Ross (1), S Greg Tremble (7).

COACHING STAFF

Head Coach, Barry Switzer

Pro Career: Led Cowboys to Super Bowl XXX victory over the Pittsburgh Steelers in January, 1996. In two seasons with the Cowboys, Switzer has claimed two NFC East titles, reached two NFC title games, and captured a Super Bowl win. Dallas finished the 1995 regular season with a 12-4 record (second best in the NFL). Named the third head coach in Cowboys history on March 30, 1994. No pro playing experience. Career record: 28-9.

Background: Played at Arkansas from 1955-59 before beginning his assistant coaching career at his alma mater in 1962. Moved on to Oklahoma in 1966, and was named the Sooners' offensive coordinator in 1967. As head coach at Oklahoma from 1973-88, Switzer registered a career record of 157-29-4. His .837 winning percentage at Oklahoma is the fourth highest mark in college history, behind only Notre Dame's Knute Rockne (.881) and Frank Leahy (.864) and Carlisle's George Woodruff (.846). He guided the Sooners to 28 consecutive wins from 1973-75 and went 37 straight games without a defeat. Switzer's Oklahoma teams won three national championships (1974, 1975, and 1985) and 12 Big Eight Conference championships.

Personal: Born October 5, 1937, Crossett, Arkansas. Switzer lives in Coppell, Texas. He has two sons—Greg and Doug and one daughter Kathy.

ASSISTANT COACHES

Hubbard Alexander, wide receivers; born February 14, 1939, Winston-Salem, N.C., lives in Coppell, Tex. Center Tennessee State 1958-61. No pro playing experience. College coach: Tennessee State 1962-63, Vanderbilt 1974-78, Miami 1979-88. Pro coach: Joined Cowboys in 1989.

Joe Avezzano, special teams; born November 17, 1943, Yonkers, N.Y., lives in Coppell, Tex. Guard Florida State 1961-65. Pro center Boston Patriots 1966. College coach: Florida State 1968, Iowa State 1969-72, Pittsburgh 1973-76, Tennessee 1977-79, Oregon State 1980-84 (head coach), Texas 1985-88. Pro coach: Joined Cowboys in 1990.

Jim Bates, linebackers; born May 31, 1946, Pontiac, Mich., lives in Irving, Tex. Linebacker Tennessee 1964-67. No pro playing experience. College coach: Tennessee 1968, Southern Mississippi 1972, Villanova 1973-74, Kansas State 1975-76, West Virginia 1977, Texas Tech 1978-83, Tennessee 1989, Florida 1990. Pro coach: San Antonio Gunslingers (USFL) 1984-85 (head coach 1985), Arizona Outlaws (USFL) 1986, Detroit Drive (AFL) 1988, Cleveland Browns 1991-93, 1995, Atlanta Falcons 1994, joined Dallas in 1996.

Craig Boller, defensive tackles; born January 29, 1948, Belmond, Iowa, lives in Irving, Tex. Defensive tackle Iowa State 1966-70. No pro playing experience. College coach: William Penn College 1974-76 (head coach 1976), Tennessee 1977, Memphis State 1978-79, Oregon State 1980-86, Iowa State 1987-94. Pro coach: Joined Dallas in 1995.

Joe Brodsky, running backs; born June 9, 1934, Miami, Fla., lives in Coppell, Tex. Fullback-linebacker Florida 1953-56. No pro playing experience. College coach: Miami 1978-88. Pro coach: Joined Cowboys in 1989.

Dave Campo, defensive coordinator; born July 18, 1947, New London, Conn., lives in Coppell, Tex. Defensive back Central Connecticut State 1967-70. No pro playing experience. College coach: Central Connecticut State 1971-72, Albany State 1973, Bridgeport 1974, Pittsburgh 1975, Washington State 1976, Boise State 1977-79, Oregon State 1980, Weber State 1981-82, Iowa State 1983, Syracuse 1984-86, Miami 1987-88. Pro coach: Joined Cowboys in 1989.

Robert Ford, tight ends; born June 21, 1951, Belton, Tex., lives in Coppell, Tex. Wide receiver Houston 1970-72. No pro playing experience. College coach: Western Illinois 1974-76, New Mexico 1977-79, Oregon State 1980-81, Mississippi State 1982-83, Kansas 1986, Texas Tech 1987-88, Texas A&M 1989-90. Pro coach: Houston Gamblers (USFL) 1985, joined Cowboys in 1991.

Tommy Hart, defensive ends; born November 11, 1944, Macon, Ga., lives in Irving, Tex. Offensive guard/defensive end Morris Brown 1964-68. Pro defensive end San Francisco 49ers 1968-77, Chicago Bears 1978-79, New Orleans Saints 1980. Pro coach: San Francisco 49ers 1983-91, 1992-93 (scout), joined Dallas in 1996.

Steve Hoffman, kickers-research and development; born September 8, 1958, Camden, N.J., lives in Coppell, Tex. Quarterback-running back-wide receiver Dickinson College 1979-82. Pro punter Washington Federals (USFL) 1983. College coach: Miami 1985-87. Pro coach: Joined Cowboys in 1989.

Hudson Houck, assistant head coach/offensive line; born January 7, 1943, Los Angeles, Calif., lives in Irving, Tex. Center Southern California 1962-64. No pro playing experience. College coach: Southern California 1970-72, 1976-82, Stanford 1973-75. Pro coach: Los Angeles Rams 1983-91, Seattle Seahawks 1992, joined Cowboys in 1993.

Clancy Pendergast, defensive assistant; born November 29, 1967, Phoenix, Ariz., lives in Irving, Tex. No college or pro playing experience. College coach: Mississippi State 1991, Southern California 1992, Oklahoma 1993-94. Pro coach: Houston Oilers 1995, joined Cowboys in 1996.

Mike Woicik, strength and conditioning; born September 26, 1956, Westwood, Mass., lives in Coppell, Tex. Boston College 1974-78. No college or pro playing experience. College coach: Springfield 1978-80, Syracuse 1980-89. Pro coach: Joined Cowboys in 1990.

Ernie Zampese, offensive coordinator/quarterbacks; born March 12, 1936, Santa Barbara, Calif., lives in Mission Viejo, Calif. Halfback Southern California 1956-58. No pro playing experience. College coach: Hancock, Calif., J.C. 1962-65, Cal Poly-SLO 1966, San Diego State 1967-75. Pro coach: San Diego Chargers 1976, 1979-86, New York Jets 1977-78 (scout), Los Angeles Rams 1987-93, joined Cowboys in 1994.

Mike Zimmer, defensive backs; born June 5, 1956, Peoria, Ill., lives in Irving, Tex. Quarterback-linebacker Illinois State 1974-76. No pro playing experience. College coach: Missouri 1979-80, Weber State 1981-88, Washington State 1989-93. Pro coach: Joined Cowboys in 1994.

1996 FIRST-YEAR ROSTER

Name	Pos.	Ht.	Wt.	Birthdate	College	Hometown	How Acq.
Alsbury, Paul (1)	P	6-1	203	9/15/68	Southwest Texas State	Edinburg, Tex.	FA
Brown, Teka	T	6-5	350	9/18/71	Central State, Ohio	Wildwood, Fla.	FA
Bullard, Kendricke (1)	WR	6-2	190	4/30/72	Arkansas State	Pine Bluff, Ark.	FA
Campos, Alan	LB	6-3	236	3/3/73	Louisville	Miami, Fla.	D5b
Davis, Wendell	CB	5-10	183	6/27/73	Oklahoma	Wichita, Kan.	D6
Dillard, Barry (1)	CB	5-10	185	2/14/73	Memphis	Memphis, Tenn.	FA
Dogins, Kevin	C	6-1	290	12/7/72	Texas A&M-Kingsville	Eagle Lake, Tex.	FA
Gadsden, Oronde (1)	WR	6-3	218	8/20/71	Winston-Salem	Charleston, S.C.	FA
Godfrey, Randall	LB	6-2	237	4/6/73	Georgia	Valdosta, Ga.	D2b
Goodwin, Matt	S	6-1	205	7/15/70	Iowa State	Ames, Iowa	FA
Harris, Mark	WR	6-3	195	4/28/70	Stanford	Brigham City, Utah	FA
Harrison, Mike	DT	6-3	303	6/28/74	North Carolina State	Camden, N.J.	FA
Hatch, Lawrence (1)	CB	6-0	196	5/22/71	Florida	Long Beach, Calif.	FA
Herrin, Errick	LB	6-1	235	4/3/69	Southern California	Akron, Ohio	FA
Higbee, Rob	TE	6-6	260	6/1/72	Delaware	Linwood, N.J.	FA
Hutson, Tony	G	6-3	313	3/13/74	N.E. Oklahoma St.	Houston, Tex.	FA
Jones, John (1)	G	6-1	309	12/8/72	Kansas	Los Angeles, Calif.	FA
McDaniel, Kenneth	G-T	6-3	322	12/20/73	Norfolk State	Mechanicsville, Va.	D5a
Mock, Kerry (1)	LB	6-1	232	8/17/73	North Carolina	Thomasville, N.C.	FA
Morrow, Harold	RB	5-11	210	2/24/73	Auburn	Maplesville, Ala.	FA
Owens, Buster	CB	5-11	202	1/30/73	Georgia	La Grange, Ga.	FA
Perry, Jarvis	RB	6-0	205	2/3/70	Rowan	Camden, N.J.	FA
Pittman, Kavika	DE	6-6	263	10/9/74	McNeese State	Leesville, La.	D2a
Reser, Reggie	CB	5-9	176	1/17/73	Washington	Pasadena, Calif.	FA
Ross, Dominique (1)	RB	6-0	203	1/12/72	Valdosta State	Jacksonville, Fla.	FA
Semptimphelter, Scott (1)	QB	6-2	215	5/15/72	Lehigh	Florence, N.J.	FA
Shelley, Jason	WR	6-1	192	8/5/74	Central State, Ohio	Vallejo, Calif.	FA
Shiver, Clay	C	6-2	294	12/7/72	Florida State	Tifton, Ga.	D3a
Simmons, Haywood	DE	6-3	260	1/13/73	Wisconsin	Macon, Ga.	FA
Smith, Rudy	DE	6-5	250	4/11/73	Rutgers	Stony Point, N.Y.	FA
Ulufale, Mike	DT	6-4	277	2/1/72	Brigham Young	Honolulu, Hawaii	D3c
Whitlock, Stan	K	5-11	215	1/19/74	Wingate	Laurens, S.C.	FA
Williams, Germaine (1)	RB	5-10	228	2/4/71	Louisiana State	Donaldsonville, La.	FA
Williams, Stepfret	WR	6-0	170	6/14/73	Northeast Louisiana	Minden, La.	D3b
Wood, Ryan	RB	5-11	236	6/13/72	Arizona State	Boulder, Colo.	D7

The term NFL Rookie is defined as a player who is in his first season of professional football and has not been on the roster of another professional football team for any regular-season or postseason games. A Rookie is designated by an "R" on NFL rosters. Players who have been active in another professional football league or players who have NFL experience, including either preseason training camp or being on an Active List or Inactive List, or on Reserve/Injured or Reserve/Physically Unable to Perform for fewer than six regular-season games, are termed NFL First-Year Players. An NFL First-Year Player is designated by a "1" on NFL rosters. Thereafter, a player is credited with an additional year of experience for each season in which he accumulates six games on the Active List or Inactive List, or on Reserve/Injured or Reserve/Physically Unable to Perform.

NOTES

DETROIT LIONS

National Football Conference
Central Division
Team Colors: Honolulu Blue and Silver
Pontiac Silverdome
1200 Featherstone Road
Pontiac, Michigan 48342
Telephone: (810) 335-4131

CLUB OFFICIALS

Chairman and President: William Clay Ford
Vice Chairman: William Clay Ford, Jr.
Executive Vice President and Chief Operating Officer: Chuck Schmidt
Vice President of Player Personnel: Ron Hughes
Vice President of Communications, Sales and Marketing: Bill Keenist
Vice President of Football Administration: Larry Lee
Vice President of Finance and Chief Financial Officer: Tom Lesnau
Vice President-General Counsel: David Potts
Secretary: David Hempstead
Administrator/Salary Cap Matters: Tom Lewand
Scouts: Rass Bolinger, Dirk Dierking, Thomas Dimitroff, Allen Hughes, Scott McEwen, Jim Owens, Rick Spielman
Director of Marketing: Steve Harms
Director of Media Relations: Mike Murray
Media Relations Assistant: James Petrylka
Director of Sales and Ticket Operations: Fred Otto
Director of Community Relations and Detroit Lions Charities: Tim Pendell
Community Relations Assistant: Kim French
Promotions Manager: Paula Buckhaulter
Head Athletic Trainer: Kent Falb
Equipment Manager: Dan Jaroshewich
Video Director: Steve Hermans
Stadium: Pontiac Silverdome • **Capacity:** 80,368
1200 Featherstone Road
Pontiac, Michigan 48342
Playing Surface: AstroTurf
Training Camp: Pontiac Silverdome
1200 Featherstone Road
Pontiac, Michigan 48342

1996 SCHEDULE

PRESEASON

Aug. 2	**New Orleans**	7:30
Aug. 9	**Washington**	7:30
Aug. 16	at Houston	8:00
Aug. 23	at Cincinnati	7:30

REGULAR SEASON

Sept. 1	at Minnesota	12:00
Sept. 8	**Tampa Bay**	1:00
Sept. 15	at Philadelphia	1:00
Sept. 22	**Chicago**	4:00
Sept. 29	at Tampa Bay	1:00
Oct. 6	**Atlanta**	1:00
Oct. 13	at Oakland	1:00
Oct. 20	Open Date	
Oct. 27	**New York Giants**	1:00
Nov. 3	at Green Bay	12:00
Nov. 11	at San Diego (Mon.)	6:00
Nov. 17	**Seattle**	1:00
Nov. 24	at Chicago	12:00
Nov. 28	**Kansas City** (Thurs.)	12:30
Dec. 8	**Minnesota**	8:00
Dec. 15	**Green Bay**	1:00
Dec. 23	at San Francisco (Mon.)	6:00

RECORD HOLDERS

INDIVIDUAL RECORDS—CAREER

Category	Name	Performance
Rushing (Yds.)	Barry Sanders, 1989-1995	10,172
Passing (Yds.)	Bobby Layne, 1950-58	15,710
Passing (TDs)	Bobby Layne, 1950-58	118
Receiving (No.)	Charlie Sanders, 1968-1977	336
Receiving (Yds.)	Gail Cogdill, 1960-68	5,220
Interceptions	Dick LeBeau, 1959-1972	62
Punting (Avg.)	Yale Lary, 1952-53, 1956-1964	44.3
Punt Return (Avg.)	Jack Christiansen, 1951-58	12.8
Kickoff Return (Avg.)	Pat Studstill, 1961-67	25.7
Field Goals	Eddie Murray, 1980-1991	243
Touchdowns (Tot.)	Barry Sanders, 1989-1995	80
Points	Eddie Murray, 1980-1991	1,113

INDIVIDUAL RECORDS—SINGLE SEASON

Category	Name	Performance
Rushing (Yds.)	Barry Sanders, 1994	1,883
Passing (Yds.)	Scott Mitchell, 1995	4,338
Passing (TDs)	Scott Mitchell, 1995	32
Receiving (No.)	Herman Moore, 1995	*123
Receiving (Yds.)	Herman Moore, 1995	1,686
Interceptions	Don Doll, 1950	12
	Jack Christiansen, 1953	12
Punting (Avg.)	Yale Lary, 1963	48.9
Punt Return (Avg.)	Jack Christiansen, 1952	21.5
Kickoff Return (Avg.)	Tom Watkins, 1965	34.4
Field Goals	Jason Hanson, 1993	34
Touchdowns (Tot.)	Barry Sanders, 1991	17
Points	Jason Hanson, 1995	132

INDIVIDUAL RECORDS—SINGLE GAME

Category	Name	Performance
Rushing (Yds.)	Barry Sanders, 11-13-94	237
Passing (Yds.)	Scott Mitchell, 11-23-95	410
Passing (TDs)	Gary Danielson, 12-9-78	5
Receiving (No.)	Herman Moore, 12-4-95	14
Receiving (Yds.)	Cloyce Box, 12-3-50	302
Interceptions	Don Doll, 10-23-49	*4
Field Goals	Garo Yepremian, 11-13-66	6
Touchdowns (Tot.)	Dutch Clark, 10-22-34	4
	Cloyce Box, 12-3-50	4
	Barry Sanders, 11-24-91	4
Points	Dutch Clark, 10-22-34	24
	Cloyce Box, 12-3-50	24
	Barry Sanders, 11-24-91	24

*NFL Record

COACHING HISTORY

Portsmouth Spartans 1930-33
(428-436-32)

1930	Hal (Tubby) Griffen	5-6-3
1931-36	George (Potsy) Clark	49-20-6
1937-38	Earl (Dutch) Clark	14-8-0
1939	Elmer (Gus) Henderson	6-5-0
1940	George (Potsy) Clark	5-5-1
1941-42	Bill Edwards*	4-9-1
1942	John Karcis	0-8-0
1943-47	Charles (Gus) Dorais	20-31-2
1948-50	Alvin (Bo) McMillin	12-24-0
1951-56	Raymond (Buddy) Parker	50-24-2
1957-64	George Wilson	55-45-6
1965-66	Harry Gilmer	10-16-2
1967-72	Joe Schmidt	43-35-7
1973	Don McCafferty	6-7-1
1974-76	Rick Forzano**	15-17-0
1976-77	Tommy Hudspeth	11-13-0
1978-84	Monte Clark	43-63-1
1985-88	Darryl Rogers***	18-40-0
1988-95	Wayne Fontes	62-60-0

*Released after three games in 1942
**Resigned after four games in 1976
***Released after 11 games in 1988

PONTIAC SILVERDOME

1995 TEAM RECORD

PRESEASON (3-1)

Date	Result		Opponents
8/4	W	30-17	at New England
8/10	W	19-3	Jacksonville
8/17	W	20-13	Cincinnati
8/25	L	10-24	at New Orleans

REGULAR SEASON (10-6)

Date	Result		Opponents	Att.
9/3	L	20-23	at Pittsburgh	58,002
9/10	L	10-20	at Minnesota	52,234
9/17	L	17-20	Arizona	58,727
9/25	W	27-24	San Francisco	76,236
10/8	W	38-20	Cleveland	74,171
10/15	L	21-30	at Green Bay	60,302
10/22	L	30-36	at Washington (OT)	52,332
10/29	W	24-16	Green Bay	73,462
11/5	L	22-34	at Atlanta	49,619
11/12	W	27-24	Tampa Bay	60,644
11/19	W	24-17	at Chicago	61,779
11/23	W	44-38	Minnesota	74,559
12/4	W	27-7	Chicago	77,230
12/10	W	24-17	at Houston	35,842
12/17	W	44-0	Jacksonville	70,204
12/23	W	37-10	at Tampa Bay	50,049

POSTSEASON (0-1)

12/30	L	37-58	at Philadelphia	66,099

(OT) Overtime

SCORE BY PERIODS

Lions	113	125	87	111	0	—	436
Opponents	53	114	67	96	6	—	336

ATTENDANCE

Home 565,233 Away 420,159 Total 985,392
Single-game home record, 80,444 (12/20/81)
Single-season home record, 622,593 (1980)

1995 TEAM STATISTICS

	Lions	Opp.
Total First Downs	349	350
Rushing	91	110
Passing	230	201
Penalty	28	39
Third Down: Made/Att	95/208	76/200
Third Down Pct.	45.7	38.0
Fourth Down: Made/Att	8/13	10/16
Fourth Down Pct.	61.5	62.5
Total Net Yards	6113	5599
Avg. Per Game	382.1	349.9
Total Plays	1024	1031
Avg. Per Play	6.0	5.4
Net Yards Rushing	1753	1795
Avg. Per Game	109.6	112.2
Total Rushes	387	409
Net Yards Passing	4360	3804
Avg. Per Game	272.5	237.8
Sacked/Yards Lost	32/150	42/317
Gross Yards	4510	4121
Att./Completions	605/362	580/354
Completion Pct.	59.8	61.0
Had Intercepted	12	22
Punts/Avg.	60/40.5	61/42.7
Net Punting Avg.	60/30.8	61/38.6
Penalties/Yards Lost	134/1032	120/1001
Fumbles/Ball Lost	21/13	24/13
Touchdowns	50	36
Rushing	16	15
Passing	33	17
Returns	1	4
Avg. Time of Possession	28:43	31:17

1995 INDIVIDUAL STATISTICS

PASSING	Att.	Comp.	Yds.	Pct.	TD	Int.	Tkld.	Rate
Mitchell	583	346	4338	59.3	32	12	31/145	92.3
Majkowski	20	15	161	75.0	1	0	1/5	114.8
Sanders	2	1	11	50.0	0	0	0/0	66.7
Lions	605	362	4510	59.8	33	12	32/150	92.9
Opponents	580	354	4121	61.0	17	22	42/317	76.5

SCORING	TD R	TD P	TD Rt	PAT	FG	Saf	PTS
Hanson	0	0	0	48/48	28/34	0	132
Moore	0	14	0	0/0	0/0	0	84
Sanders	11	1	0	0/0	0/0	0	72
Perriman	0	9	0	0/0	0/0	0	56
Morton	0	8	0	0/0	0/0	0	48
Mitchell	4	0	0	0/0	0/0	0	24
Rivers	1	0	0	0/0	0/0	0	6
Scroggins	0	0	1	0/0	0/0	0	6
Sloan	0	1	0	0/0	0/0	0	6
Blades	0	0	0	0/0	0/0	1	2
Lions	16	33	1	48/48	28/34	1	436
Opponents	15	17	4	32/32	28/42	0	336

2-Point conversions: Perriman. Team: 1-2.

RUSHING	Att.	Yds.	Avg.	LG	TD
Sanders	314	1500	4.8	75t	11
Mitchell	36	104	2.9	18	4
Rivers	18	73	4.1	19	1
Perriman	5	48	9.6	16	0
Morton	3	33	11.0	18	0
Majkowski	9	1	0.1	4	0
Schlesinger	1	1	1.0	1	0
Royals	1	-7	-7.0	-7	0
Lions	387	1753	4.5	75t	16
Opponents	409	1795	4.4	75	15

RECEIVING	No.	Yds.	Avg.	LG	TD
Moore	123	1686	13.7	69t	14
Perriman	108	1488	13.8	91t	9
Sanders	48	398	8.3	40	1
Morton	44	590	13.4	32t	8
Sloan	17	184	10.8	24	1
Hall	11	81	7.4	15	0
Holman	5	35	7.0	9	0
Matthews	4	41	10.3	12	0
Rivers	1	5	5.0	5	0
Schlesinger	1	2	2.0	2	0
Lions	362	4510	12.5	91t	33
Opponents	354	4121	11.6	85t	17

INTERCEPTIONS	No.	Yds.	Avg.	LG	TD
Clay	8	173	21.6	39	0
Raymond	6	44	7.3	18	0
McNeil	2	26	13.0	21	0
M. Johnson	2	23	11.5	14	0
Spielman	1	4	4.0	4	0
Blades	1	0	0.0	0	0
Malone	1	0	0.0	0	0
Vanhorse	1	0	0.0	0	0
Lions	22	270	12.3	39	0
Opponents	12	219	18.3	71t	2

PUNTING	No.	Yds.	Avg.	In 20	LG
Royals	57	2393	42.0	15	69
Hanson	1	34	34.0	0	34
Lions	60	2427	40.5	15	69
Opponents	61	2604	42.7	19	60

PUNT RETURNS	No.	FC	Yds.	Avg.	LG	TD
Morton	7	4	48	6.9	16	0
Turner	6	1	39	6.5	16	0
Clay	5	5	49	9.8	28	0
Perriman	5	6	50	10.0	13	0
Carter	1	1	3	3.0	3	0
Lions	24	17	189	7.9	28	0
Opponents	29	6	442	15.2	74t	1

KICKOFF RETURNS	No.	Yds.	Avg.	LG	TD
Rivers	19	420	22.1	51	0
Morton	18	390	21.7	32	0
Turner	17	323	19.0	43	0
Perriman	5	65	13.0	23	0
Williams	4	100	25.0	32	0
Carter	2	46	23.0	23	0
Owens	1	9	9.0	9	0
Sloan	1	14	14.0	14	0
Lions	67	1367	20.4	51	0
Opponents	80	1828	22.9	61	0

SACKS	No.
Thomas	10.5
Scroggins	9.5
London	7.0
Porcher	5.0
M. Johnson	2.0
Raymond	2.0
Blades	1.0
Bonham	1.0
Boyd	1.0
Hayworth	1.0
Spielman	1.0
Jeffries	0.5
Wells	0.5
Lions	42.0
Opponents	32.0

1996 DRAFT CHOICES

Round	Name	Pos.	College
1	Reggie Brown	LB	Texas A&M
	Jeff Hartings	G	Penn State
3	Ryan Stewart	DB	Georgia Tech
4	Brad Ford	DB	Alabama
5	Kerwin Waldrop	DT	Central State, Ohio

DETROIT LIONS

1996 VETERAN ROSTER

No.		Name	Pos.	Ht.	Wt.	Birthdate	NFL Exp.	College	Hometown	How Acq.	'95 Games/ Starts
51		Beer, Tom	LB-RB	6-1	237	3/27/69	3	Wayne State	Bay Port, Mich.	D7-'94	16/0
36		Blades, Bennie	S	6-1	221	9/3/66	9	Miami	Ft. Lauderdale, Fla.	D1-'88	16/16
96		Bonham, Shane	DE-DT	6-2	275	10/18/70	3	Tennessee	Fairbanks, Alaska	D3-'94	16/0
27		Borgella, Jocelyn	CB	5-10	180	8/26/71	3	Cincinnati	Miami, Fla.	D6-'94	0*
57		Boyd, Stephen	LB	6-0	247	8/22/72	2	Boston College	Valley Stream, N.Y.	D5a-'95	16/0
50		Brooks, Michael	LB	6-1	236	10/2/64	10	Louisiana State	Ruston, La.	UFA(NYG)-'96	16/16*
77		Compton, Mike	C-G	6-6	297	9/18/70	4	West Virginia	Richland, Va.	D3b-'93	16/7
76		Conover, Scott	T	6-4	285	9/27/68	6	Purdue	Freehold, N.J.	D5-'91	14/2
94		Elliss, Luther	DE	6-5	291	3/22/73	2	Utah	Mancos, Colo.	D1-'95	16/16
53		Glover, Kevin	C	6-2	282	6/17/63	12	Maryland	Upper Marlboro, Md.	D2-'85	16/16
79		Grigson, Ryan	G-T	6-6	300	2/23/72	2	Purdue	Highland, Ind.	W(Cin)-'95	0*
4		Hanson, Jason	K	5-11	183	6/17/70	5	Washington State	Spokane, Wash.	D2b-'92	16/0
66		Hempstead, Hessley	G	6-1	295	1/29/72	2	Kansas	Upland, Calif.	D7-'95	2/0
81		Hickman, Kevin	TE	6-4	258	8/20/71	2	Navy	Delran, N.J.	D6a-'95	6/0
25		Jeffries, Greg	CB	5-9	184	10/16/71	4	Virginia	High Point, N.C.	D6-'93	14/0
70		Jones, Jeff	T	6-6	310	5/30/72	2	Texas A&M	Killeen, Tex.	FA-'95	1/0
52		Kowalkowski, Scott	LB	6-2	228	8/23/68	6	Notre Dame	Orchard Lake, Mich.	FA-'94	16/0
55		London, Antonio	LB	6-2	234	4/14/71	4	Alabama	Tullahoma, Tenn.	D3a-'93	15/0
26		Lynch, Eric	RB	5-10	224	5/16/70	3	Grand Valley State	Woodhaven, Mich.	FA-'92	4/0
1		Majkowski, Don	QB	6-3	208	2/25/64	10	Virginia	Depew, N.Y.	UFA(Ind)-'95	5/0
39		Malone, Van	S	5-11	186	7/1/70	3	Texas	Houston, Tex.	D2-'94	16/0
83		Matthews, Aubrey	WR	5-7	165	9/15/62	11	Delta State	Moss Point, Miss.	FA-'90	11/0
10		McCorvey, Kez	WR	6-0	180	1/23/72	2	Florida State	Pascagoula, Miss.	D5b-'95	1/0
47	†	McNeil, Ryan	CB	6-2	192	10/4/70	4	Miami	Fort Pierce, Fla.	D2-'93	16/0
89		Metzelaars, Pete	TE	6-7	254	5/24/60	15	Wabash	Portage, Mich.	FA-'96	14/14*
33	t-	Milburn, Glyn	RB-KR	5-8	177	2/19/71	4	Stanford	Santa Monica, Calif.	T(Den)-'96	16/1*
19		Mitchell, Scott	QB	6-6	230	1/2/68	7	Utah	Springville, Utah	UFA(Mia)-'94	16/16
40		Moore, Derrick	RB	6-1	227	10/13/67	5	Northeast Oklahoma State	Albany, Ga.	UFA(Car)-'96	13/10*
84		Moore, Herman	WR	6-3	210	10/20/69	6	Virginia	Danville, Va.	D1-'91	16/16
87		Morton, Johnnie	WR	6-0	190	10/7/71	3	Southern California	Torrance, Calif.	D1-'94	16/13
71		Moss, Zefross	T	6-6	324	8/17/66	8	Alabama State	Holt, Ala.	UFA(Ind)-'95	14/14
80		Perriman, Brett	WR	5-9	180	10/10/65	9	Miami	Miami, Fla.	T(NO)-'91	16/16
91		Porcher, Robert	DE	6-3	270	7/30/69	5	South Carolina State	Wando, S.C.	D1-'92	16/16
31		Raymond, Corey	CB	5-11	185	7/28/69	5	Louisiana State	New Iberia, La.	T(Jax)-'95	16/15
28		Rice, Ron	S	6-1	206	11/9/72	2	Eastern Michigan	Detroit, Mich.	FA-'95	0*
34		Rivers, Ron	RB	5-8	205	11/13/71	2	Fresno State	Highland, Calif.	FA-'94	16/0
72		Roberts, Ray	T	6-6	308	6/3/69	5	Virginia	Asheville, N.C.	UFA(Sea)-'96	11/0*
3	#	Royals, Mark	P	6-5	215	6/22/65	7	Appalachian State	Matthews, Va.	UFA(Pitt)-'95	16/0
20		Sanders, Barry	RB	5-8	203	7/16/68	8	Oklahoma State	Wichita, Kan.	D1-'89	16/16
30		Schlesinger, Cory	RB	6-0	230	6/23/72	2	Nebraska	Duncan, Neb.	D6b-'95	16/2
97		Scroggins, Tracy	LB	6-2	255	9/11/69	5	Tulsa	Checotah, Okla.	D2a-'92	16/16
62		Semple, Tony	G	6-4	286	12/20/70	3	Memphis State	Lincoln, Ill.	D5-'94	16/0
86		Sloan, David	TE	6-6	254	6/8/72	2	New Mexico	Tollhouse, Calif.	D3-'95	16/7
12		Strom, Rick	QB	6-2	197	3/11/65	7	Georgia Tech	Pittsburgh, Pa.	FA-'96	0*
98		Thomas, Henry	DT	6-2	277	1/12/65	10	Louisiana State	Houston, Tex.	UFA(Minn)-'95	16/16
29	#	Vanhorse, Sean	CB	5-10	180	7/22/68	7	Howard	Baltimore, Md.	UFA(SD)-'95	14/2
9		Wagner, Bryan	P	6-1	196	3/18/62	10	Cal State-Northridge	Chula Vista, Calif.	FA-'96	8/0*
95		Wells, Mike	DE	6-3	287	1/6/71	3	Iowa	Arnold, Mo.	FA-'94	15/0
21		Williams, Allen	RB-KR	5-10	205	9/17/72	1	Maryland	Thomasville, Ga.	FA-'95	5/0

* Borgella was active for 2 games but did not play; Brooks played 16 games with N.Y. Giants; Grigson inactive for 16 games; Metzelaars played 14 games with Carolina; Milburn played 16 games with Denver; Moore played 13 games with Carolina; Rice inactive for 8 games; Roberts played 11 games with Seattle; Strom last active with Buffalo in '94; Wagner played 8 games with New England.

\# Unrestricted free agent; subject to developments.

† Restricted free agent; subject to developments.

t- Lions traded for Milburn (Denver).

Players lost to free agency (6): T Lomas Brown (Ariz; 15 games in '95), S Willie Clay (NE; 16), QB Kent Graham (Ariz, 0), DE Dan Owens (Atl, 16), LB Chris Spielman (Buff; 16), G Doug Widell (Ind; 11).

Also played with Lions in '95—WR Anthony Carter (3 games), TE Rodney Hollman (16), G Dave Lutz (16), CB Robert Massey (16), RB Vernon Turner (6), RB Allen Williams (5).

COACHING STAFF

Head Coach,
Wayne Fontes

Pro Career: Became the Lions' seventeenth head coach on December, 22, 1988, after serving five weeks as interim head coach (2-3 record). Fontes hold the Lions' record for most victories with 62 (61 regular season, one postseason). He also has coached the most games in team history (122) and is tied with Monte Clark for second most seasons as head coach. Has led the Lions to two Central Division championships and four playoff appearances in last five seasons. The Lions won their last seven games in 1995 to earn a wild-card berth with a 10-6 record, but were defeated by Philadelphia 58-37 in the first round of the playoffs. In 1994, the Lions earned a wild-card spot, but failed to advance beyond the first round of the playoffs. The Lions captured the NFC Central title with a 10-6 record in 1993, but were eliminated in the first round of the playoffs. Detroit finished 5-11 in 1992. In 1991, Fontes led the Lions to a 12-4 record and the team's first NFC Central Division title since 1983. The Lions notched their first playoff victory since 1957 and reached the NFC Championship Game in 1991. The Lions were 6-10 in 1990. In 1989, Fontes's first full season, the Lions finished 7-9, including five consecutive season-ending wins. He began the 1988 season as Detroit's defensive coordinator and secondary coach, following a nine-year stint with the Tampa Bay Buccaneers. A former defensive back with the New York Jets, Fontes advanced from secondary coach to defensive coordinator to assistant head coach of the Buccaneers during his years with Tampa Bay. As a player with the Jets, his brief pro career was cut short by a broken leg after two seasons (1963-64). However, his 83-yard interception return against Houston (12-15-63) did stand as the Jets' team record until it was broken in 1989 by Erik McMillan's 93-yard return. Career record: 62-60.

Background: A former two-sport star (football and baseball) at Michigan State, Fontes earned all-Big Ten honors at defensive back for the Spartans. He earned his bachelor's degree in education and biological science and later earned his master's degree in administration, all from Michigan State. Fontes became defensive backfield coach at Dayton in 1968. He also served in the same capacity at Iowa (1969-71) and Southern California (1972-75).

Personal: Born February 17, 1939, New Bedford, Mass. Fontes and his wife, Evelyn, live in Rochester Hills, Mich., and have three children—Mike, Scott, and Kim.

ASSISTANT COACHES

Paul Boudreau, offensive line; born December 30, 1949, Somerville, Mass., lives in Rochester Hills, Mich. Guard Boston College 1971-73. No pro playing experience. College coach: Boston College 1974-76, Maine 1977-78, Dartmouth 1979-81, Navy 1983. Pro coach: Edmonton Eskimos (CFL) 1983-86, New Orleans Saints 1987-93, joined Lions in 1994.

Don Clemons, defensive assistant-linebackers, defensive backs; born February 15, 1954, Newark, N.J., lives in Rochester, Mich. Defensive end Muehlenberg College 1973-76. No pro playing experience. College coach: Kutztown State 1977-78, New Mexico 1979, Arizona State 1980-84. Pro coach: Joined Lions in 1985.

Jim Eddy, defensive coordinator; born May 2, 1939, Checotah, Okla., lives in Carrollton, Tex. Defensive back-running back New Mexico State 1956-59. No pro playing experience. College coach: New Mexico State 1965-70, Texas El-Paso 1971-72, Houston 1987-89. Pro coach: Saskatchewan Rough Riders (CFL) 1974-78 (head coach 1977-78), Hamilton Tiger Cats (CFL) 1979-80, Montreal Alouettes (CFL) 1981 (head coach), Toronto Argonauts (CFL) 1982-83, Houston Gamblers (USFL) 1984-85, Houston Oilers 1990-92, Dallas Cowboys 1993-95, joined Lions in 1996.

John Fontes, defensive backs; born June 24, 1949, New Bedford, Mass., lives in Rochester Hills, Mich. Defensive back Iowa 1969-70. No pro playing experience. College coach: Iowa 1971-72, Oregon State 1976-80, Northwestern 1985, Miami 1986, Louisiana State 1987-89. Pro coach: Tampa Bay Storm (Arena League) 1991, Sacramento Surge (World League) 1992, joined Lions in 1992.

Mo Forte, running backs; born March 1, 1947, Hannibal, Mo., lives in Rochester Hills, Mich. Running back Minnesota 1965-68. No pro playing experience. College coach: Minnesota 1970-75, Duke 1976-77, Michigan State 1978-79, Arizona State 1980-81, North Carolina A&T 1982-87 (head coach). Pro coach: Denver Broncos 1988-94, joined Lions in 1995.

Bert Hill, strength and conditioning-defensive assistant; born January 25, 1958, Montgomery, Ala., lives in Rochester Hills, Mich. Linebacker Marion (Ala.) Military Institute 1976-77, Wichita State 1978. No pro playing experience. College coach: Nicholls State 1981-82, Auburn 1983, Texas A&M 1984-88, Ohio State 1989. Pro coach: Joined Lions in 1990.

Steve Kazor, tight ends-offensive assistant; born February 24, 1948, New Kensington, Pa., lives in Oxford, Mich. Nose tackle Westminster College 1967-70. No pro playing experience. College coach: Emporia State 1973 (head coach), Texas Arlington 1974, Colorado State 1975, Wyoming 1976, Texas 1977-78, Texas-El Paso 1979-80, Iowa Wesleyan 1993 (head coach). Pro coach: Chicago Bears 1982-92, joined Lions in 1994.

Greg Landry, quarterbacks; born December 18, 1946, Nashua, N.H., lives in Rochester Hills, Mich. Quarterback Massachusetts 1965-67. Pro quarterback Detroit Lions 1968-78, Baltimore Colts 1979-81, Chicago Blitz/Arizona Wranglers (USFL) 1983-84, Chicago Bears 1984. College coach: Illinois 1993-94. Pro coach: Cleveland Browns 1985, Chicago Bears 1986-92, joined Lions in 1995.

Dave Levy, assistant head coach; born October 25, 1932, Carrollton, Mo., lives in Southfield, Mich. Guard UCLA 1952-53. No pro playing experience. College coach: UCLA 1954, Long Beach City College 1955, Southern California 1960-75. Pro coach: San Diego Chargers 1980-88, joined Lions in 1989.

Tom Moore, offensive coordinator; born November 7, 1938, Owatanna, Minn., lives in Rochester Hills, Mich. Quarterback Iowa 1957-60. No pro playing experience. College coach: Iowa 1961-62, Dayton 1965-68, Wake Forest 1969, Georgia Tech 1970-71, Minnesota 1972-73, 1975-76. Pro coach: New York Stars (WFL) 1974, Pittsburgh Steelers 1977-89, Minnesota Vikings 1990-93, joined Lions in 1994.

Frank Novak, special teams; born May 18, 1938, Worcester, Mass., lives in Rochester Hills, Mich. Quarterback Northern Michigan 1959-61. No pro playing experience. College coach: Northern Michigan 1966-72, East Carolina 1973, Virginia 1974-75, Western Illinois 1976-77, Holy Cross 1978-83, Massachusetts 1986, Missouri 1988. Pro coach: Oklahoma Outlaws (USFL) 1984, Birmingham Stallions (USFL) 1985, Houston Oilers 1989-94, joined Lions in 1995.

Charlie Sanders, receivers; born August 25, 1946, Greensboro, N.C., lives in Rochester, Mich. Tight end Minnesota 1966-67. Pro tight end Detroit Lions 1968-77. Pro coach: Joined Lions in 1989.

John Teerlinck, assistant head coach-defense; born April 9, 1951, Rochester, N.Y., lives in Rochester Hills, Mich. Defensive lineman Western Illinois 1970-73. Pro defensive tackle San Diego Chargers 1974-76. College coach: Iowa Lakes J.C. 1977, Eastern Illinois 1978-79, Illinois 1980-82. Pro coach: Chicago Blitz (USFL) 1983, Arizona Wranglers/Outlaws (USFL) 1984-85, Cleveland Browns 1989-90, Los Angeles Rams 1991, Minnesota Vikings 1992-94, joined Lions in 1995.

Howard Tippett, linebackers; born September 23, 1938, Tallassee, Ala., lives in Rochester Hills, Mich. Quarterback-safety East Tennessee State 1956-58. No pro playing experience. College coach: Tulane 1963-65, West Virginia 1966, 1970-71, Houston 1967-69, Wake Forest 1972, Mississippi State 1973, 1979, Washington State 1976, Oregon 1977-78, UCLA 1980, Illinois 1987. Pro coach: Jacksonville Express (WFL) 1974-75, Tampa Bay Buccaneers 1981-86, Green Bay Packers 1988-91, Los Angeles Rams 1992-93, joined Lions in 1994.

1996 FIRST-YEAR ROSTER

Name	Pos.	Ht.	Wt.	Birthdate	College	Hometown	How Acq.
Adair, Gene	K	6-2	190	8/16/70	New Haven	Mercer Island, Wash.	FA
Bailey, Troy	DE	6-3	271	3/9/73	Oregon	Honolulu, Hawaii	FA
Baron, James	DE	6-4	263	6/8/73	Virginia Tech	Maywood, Ill.	FA
Bellot, Desmond	WR	6-0	195	5/12/73	Northeastern	North Quincy, Mass.	FA
Boyd, Tommy	WR	6-0	195	12/21/71	Toledo	Lansing, Mich.	FA
Brown, Reggie	LB	6-2	241	9/28/74	Texas A&M	Austin, Tex.	D1a
Ford, Brad	CB	5-10	170	1/11/74	Alabama	Alexander City, Ala.	D4
Davis, Ed	RB-WR	5-9	197	4/16/73	Michigan	Detroit, Mich.	FA
Green, Damacio	CB-S	5-10	185	2/18/72	Virginia State	Pahokee, Fla.	FA
Harrison, Chris	G	6-3	290	2/25/72	Virginia	Washington, D.C.	FA
Hartings, Jeff	G	6-3	283	9/7/72	Penn State	St. Henry, Ohio	D1b
Heinrich-Taves, Josh (1)	DE	6-7	260	5/13/72	Northeastern	Yarmouth, Mass.	FA
Horacek, Mike	WR	6-0	201	7/7/73	Iowa State	Omaha, Neb.	FA
Johnson, Johnny	QB	6-1	202	1/21/73	Illinois	North Chicago, Ill.	FA
Knott, David	S	6-1	195	3/18/72	Mississippi	Brandon, Miss.	FA
London, Michael	WR	5-9	160	11/22/73	Wisconsin	Sicklerville, N.J.	FA
Macik, Miles	WR	6-4	210	9/15/73	Pennsylvania	Mayfield Heights, Ohio	FA
Mose, Diriki	WR	5-9	170	7/19/73	Grand Valley State	South Bend, Ind.	FA
O'Shea, Mike (1)	LB	6-3	230	9/21/70	Guelph, Canada	North Bay, Canada	FA
Price, Derek	TE	6-3	240	8/17/72	Iowa	Tempe, Ariz.	FA
Robique, Shannon	C	6-1	275	4/28/73	Auburn	Denham Springs, La.	FA
Steinhauer, Orlondo	CB	5-10	179	6/9/73	Western Washington	Seattle, Wash.	FA
Steward, Ryan	S	6-1	207	9/30/73	Georgia Tech	Moncks Corner, S.C.	D3
Stokes, Barry	G	6-4	288	12/20/73	Eastern Michigan	Flint, Mich.	FA
Waldroup, Kerwin	DE-DT	6-3	260	8/1/74	Central State, Ohio	Country Club Hills, Ill.	D5

The term NFL Rookie is defined as a player who is in his first season of professional football and has not been on the roster of another professional football team for any regular-season or postseason games. A Rookie is designated by an "R" on NFL rosters. Players who have been active in another professional football league or players who have NFL experience, including either preseason training camp or being on an Active List or Inactive List, or on Reserve/Injured or Reserve/Physically Unable to Perform for fewer than six regular-season games, are termed NFL First-Year Players. An NFL First-Year Player is designated by a "1" on NFL rosters. Thereafter, a player is credited with an additional year of experience for each season in which he accumulates six games on the Active List or Inactive List, or on Reserve/Injured or Reserve/Physically Unable to Perform.

GREEN BAY PACKERS

National Football Conference
Central Division
Team Colors: Dark Green, Gold, and White
1265 Lombardi Avenue
Green Bay, Wisconsin 54304
Telephone: (414) 496-5700

CLUB OFFICIALS

President, CEO: Robert E. Harlan
Vice President: John Fabry
Secretary: Peter M. Platten III
Treasurer: John R. Underwood
Vice President-Administration/ Chief Financial Officer: Michael R. Reinfeldt
Exec. V.P. and General Manager: Ron Wolf
Exec. Assistant to the President: Phil Pionek
General Counsel: Lance Lopes
Exec. Director of Public Relations: Lee Remmel
Director of Marketing: Jeff Cieply
Assistant Director of Public Relations: Jeff Blumb
Assistant Director of Public Relations/Travel Coordinator: Mark Schiefelbein
Director of Family Programs/Player Speakers Bureau: Sherry Schuldes
Director of Pro Personnel: Ted Thompson
Director of College Scouting: John Math
Ticket Director: Mark Wagner
Accountants: Duke Copp, Vicki Vannieuwenhoven
Director of Computer Services: Wayne Wichlacz
Video Director: Al Treml
Trainer: Pepper Burruss
Equipment Manager: Gordon Batty
Corporate Security Officer: Jerry Parins
Stadium Supervisor: Ted Eisenreich
Stadium: Lambeau Field •**Capacity:** 60,790
1265 Lombardi Avenue
Green Bay, Wisconsin 54304
Playing Surface: Grass
Training Camp: St. Norbert College
De Pere, Wisconsin 54115

1996 SCHEDULE

PRESEASON

Aug. 2	**New England**	7:00
Aug. 11	**Pittsburgh**	7:00
Aug. 17	at Baltimore	7:00
Aug. 24	at Indianapolis	7:00

REGULAR SEASON

Sept. 1	at Tampa Bay	4:00
Sept. 9	**Philadelphia** (Mon.)	8:00
Sept. 15	**San Diego**	12:00
Sept. 22	at Minnesota	12:00
Sept. 29	at Seattle	1:00
Oct. 6	at Chicago	12:00
Oct. 14	**San Francisco** (Mon.)	8:00
Oct. 20	Open Date	
Oct. 27	**Tampa Bay**	12:00
Nov. 3	**Detroit**	12:00
Nov. 10	at Kansas City	12:00
Nov. 18	at Dallas (Mon.)	8:00
Nov. 24	at St. Louis	7:00
Dec. 1	**Chicago**	12:00
Dec. 8	**Denver**	12:00
Dec. 15	at Detroit	1:00
Dec. 22	**Minnesota**	12:00

RECORD HOLDERS

INDIVIDUAL RECORDS—CAREER

Category	Name	Performance
Rushing (Yds.)	Jim Taylor, 1958-1966	8,207
Passing (Yds.)	Bart Starr, 1956-1971	24,718
Passing (TDs)	Bart Starr, 1956-1971	152
Receiving (No.)	Sterling Sharpe, 1988-1994	595
Receiving (Yds.)	James Lofton, 1978-1986	9,656
Interceptions	Bobby Dillon, 1952-59	52
Punting (Avg.)	Dick Deschaine, 1955-57	42.6
Punt Return (Avg.)	Billy Grimes, 1950-52	13.2
Kickoff Return (Avg.)	Travis Williams, 1967-1970	26.7
Field Goals	Chris Jacke, 1989-1995	152
Touchdowns (Tot.)	Don Hutson, 1935-1945	105
Points	Don Hutson, 1935-1945	823

INDIVIDUAL RECORDS—SINGLE SEASON

Category	Name	Performance
Rushing (Yds.)	Jim Taylor, 1962	1,474
Passing (Yds.)	Lynn Dickey, 1983	4,458
Passing (TDs)	Brett Favre, 1995	38
Receiving (No.)	Sterling Sharpe, 1993	112
Receiving (Yds.)	Robert Brooks, 1995	1,497
Interceptions	Irv Comp, 1943	10
Punting (Avg.)	Jerry Norton, 1963	44.7
Punt Return (Avg.)	Billy Grimes, 1950	19.1
Kickoff Return (Avg.)	Travis Williams, 1967	*41.1
Field Goals	Chester Marcol, 1972	33
Touchdowns (Tot.)	Jim Taylor, 1962	19
Points	Paul Hornung, 1960	*176

INDIVIDUAL RECORDS—SINGLE GAME

Category	Name	Performance
Rushing (Yds.)	Jim Taylor, 12-3-61	186
Passing (Yds.)	Lynn Dickey, 10-12-80	418
Passing (TDs)	Many times	5
	Last time by Brett Favre, 11-12-95	
Receiving (No.)	Don Hutson, 11-22-42	14
Receiving (Yds.)	Bill Howton, 10-21-56	257
Interceptions	Bobby Dillon, 11-26-53	*4
	Willie Buchanon, 9-24-78	*4
Field Goals	Chris Jacke, 11-11-90	5
Touchdowns (Tot.)	Paul Hornung, 12-12-65	5
Points	Paul Hornung, 10-8-61	33

*NFL Record

COACHING HISTORY

(531-442-36)

1921-49	Earl (Curly) Lambeau	212-106-21
1950-53	Gene Ronzani*	14-31-1
1953	Hugh Devore- Ray (Scooter) McLean**	0-2-0
1954-57	Lisle Blackbourn	17-31-0
1958	Ray (Scooter) McLean	1-10-1
1959-67	Vince Lombardi	98-30-4
1968-70	Phil Bengtson	20-21-1
1971-74	Dan Devine	25-28-4
1975-83	Bart Starr	53-77-3
1984-87	Forrest Gregg	25-37-1
1988-91	Lindy Infante	24-40-0
1992-95	Mike Holmgren	42-29-0

*Resigned after 10 games in 1953
**Co-coaches

LAMBEAU FIELD

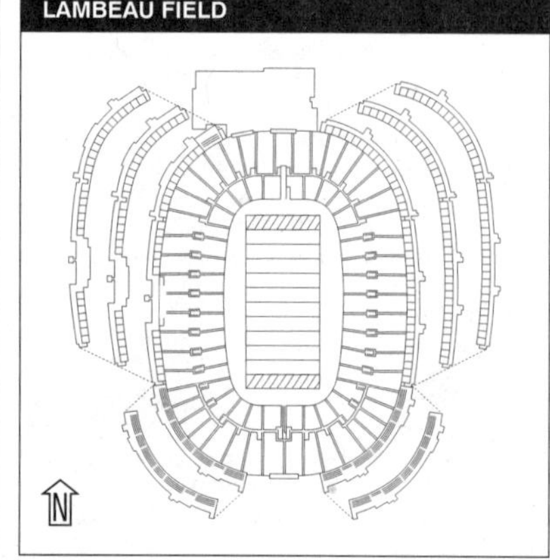

1995 TEAM RECORD

PRESEASON (3-1)

Date	Result		Opponents
8/5	W	27-17	New Orleans
8/13	W	36-13	at Pittsburgh
8/19	L	17-20	Indianapolis (OT)
8/25	W	35-23	Washington

REGULAR SEASON (11-5)

Date	Result		Opponents	Att.
9/3	L	14-17	St. Louis	60,104
9/11	W	27-24	at Chicago	64,855
9/17	W	14-6	N.Y. Giants	60,117
9/24	W	24-14	at Jacksonville	66,744
10/8	L	24-34	at Dallas	64,806
10/15	W	30-21	Detroit	60,302
10/22	W	38-21	Minnesota	60,332
10/29	L	16-24	at Detroit	73,462
11/5	L	24-27	at Minnesota	62,839
11/12	W	35-28	Chicago	59,996
11/19	W	31-20	at Cleveland	55,388
11/26	W	35-13	Tampa Bay	59,218
12/3	W	24-10	Cincinnati	60,318
12/10	L	10-13	at Tampa Bay (OT)	67,557
12/16	W	34-23	at New Orleans	50,132
12/24	W	24-19	Pittsburgh	60,649

POSTSEASON (2-1)

12/31	W	37-20	Atlanta	60,453
1/6	W	27-17	at San Francisco	69,311
1/14	L	27-38	at Dallas	65,135

(OT) Overtime

SCORE BY PERIODS

Packers	83	146	81	94	0	— 404
Opponents	41	106	72	92	3	— 314

ATTENDANCE

Home 481,036 Away 545,773 Total 1,026,809
Single-game home record, 60,649 (12/24/95)
Single-season home record, 481,036 (1995)

1995 TEAM STATISTICS

	Packers	Opp.
Total First Downs	339	303
Rushing	84	99
Passing	235	188
Penalty	20	16
Third Down: Made/Att	108/220	75/214
Third Down Pct.	49.1	35.0
Fourth Down: Made/Att	5/8	12/26
Fourth Down Pct.	62.5	46.2
Total Net Yards	5750	5155
Avg. Per Game	359.4	322.2
Total Plays	1036	1029
Avg. Per Play	5.6	5.0
Net Yards Rushing	1428	1515
Avg. Per Game	89.3	94.7
Total Rushes	410	374
Net Yards Passing	4322	3640
Avg. Per Game	270.1	227.5
Sacked/Yards Lost	33/217	39/275
Gross Yards	4539	3915
Att./Completions	593/372	616/351
Completion Pct.	62.7	57.0
Had Intercepted	15	13
Punts/Avg.	67/40.9	88/42.6
Net Punting Avg.	67/34.6	88/35.6
Penalties/Yards Lost	85/604	98/738
Fumbles/Ball Lost	22/6	12/3
Touchdowns	49	37
Rushing	9	12
Passing	39	25
Returns	1	0
Avg. Time of Possession	31:12	28:48

1995 INDIVIDUAL STATISTICS

PASSING	Att.	Comp.	Yds.	Pct.	TD	Int.	Tkld.	Rate
Favre	570	359	4413	63.0	38	13	33/217	99.5
Detmer	16	8	81	50.0	1	1	0/0	59.6
Rubley	6	4	39	66.7	0	1	0/0	45.1
McMahon	1	1	6	100.0	0	0	0/0	91.7
Packers	593	372	4539	62.7	39	15	33/217	97.6
Opponents	616	351	3915	57.0	25	13	39/275	80.8

SCORING	TD R	TD P	TD Rt	PAT	FG	Saf	PTS
Jacke	0	0	0	43/43	17/23	0	94
R. Brooks	0	13	0	0/0	0/0	0	78
Chmura	0	7	0	0/0	0/0	0	44
Bennett	3	4	0	0/0	0/0	0	42
Levens	3	4	0	0/0	0/0	0	42
Morgan	0	4	0	0/0	0/0	0	24
Favre	3	0	0	0/0	0/0	0	18
Ingram	0	3	0	0/0	0/0	0	18
Hentrich	0	0	0	5/5	3/5	0	14
Jordan	0	2	0	0/0	0/0	0	12
Freeman	0	1	0	0/0	0/0	0	6
Jackson	0	1	0	0/0	0/0	0	6
Jones	0	0	1	0/0	0/0	0	6
Packers	9	39	1	48/48	20/28	0	404
Opponents	12	25	0	35/35	19/21	0	314

2-Point conversion: Chmura. Team: 1-1.

RUSHING	Att.	Yds.	Avg.	LG	TD
Bennett	316	1067	3.4	23	3
Favre	39	181	4.6	40	3
Levens	36	120	3.3	22	3
Henderson	7	35	5.0	17	0
R. Brooks	4	21	5.3	21	0
Rubley	2	6	3.0	6	0
Detmer	3	3	1.0	5	0
L. Johnson	2	-2	-1.0	0	0
Ingram	1	-3	-3.0	-3	0
Packers	410	1428	3.5	40	9
Opponents	374	1515	4.1	37	12

RECEIVING	No.	Yds.	Avg.	LG	TD
R. Brooks	102	1497	14.7	99t	13
Bennett	61	648	10.6	35	4
Chmura	54	679	12.6	33	7
Levens	48	434	9.0	27	4
Ingram	39	469	12.0	29	3
Morgan	31	344	11.1	29t	4
Jackson	13	142	10.9	22	1
Freeman	8	106	13.3	28	1
Jordan	7	117	16.7	35	2
Mickens	3	50	16.7	24	0
Thomason	3	32	10.7	15	0
Henderson	3	21	7.0	9	0
Packers	372	4539	12.2	99t	39
Opponents	351	3915	11.2	69t	25

INTERCEPTIONS	No.	Yds.	Avg.	LG	TD
Butler	5	105	21.0	76	0
Teague	2	100	50.0	74	0
Evans	2	24	12.0	24	0
Koonce	1	12	12.0	12	0
Prior	1	9	9.0	9	0
Newsome	1	3	3.0	3	0
Kelly	1	0	0.0	0	0
Packers	13	253	19.5	76	0
Opponents	15	243	16.2	61	0

PUNTING	No.	Yds.	Avg.	In 20	LG
Hentrich	65	2740	42.2	26	61
Packers	67	2740	40.9	26	61
Opponents	88	3746	42.6	17	58

PUNT RETURNS	No.	FC	Yds.	Avg.	LG	TD
Freeman	37	3	292	7.9	26	0
Jordan	21	2	213	10.1	18	0
Evans	1	0	0	0.0	0	0
Ingram	1	0	0	0.0	0	0
Prior	1	2	10	10.0	10	0
Packers	61	7	515	8.4	26	0
Opponents	36	11	279	7.8	40	0

KICKOFF RETURNS	No.	Yds.	Avg.	LG	TD
Freeman	24	556	23.2	45	0
Jordan	21	444	21.1	33	0
Jervey	8	165	20.6	28	0
Morgan	3	46	15.3	20	0
Arthur	1	10	10.0	10	0
R. Brooks	1	28	28.0	28	0
Jurkovic	1	17	17.0	17	0
Mickens	1	0	0.0	0	0
Thomason	1	16	16.0	16	0
Packers	61	1282	21.0	45	0
Opponents	74	1581	21.4	46	0

SACKS	No.
R. White	12.0
Jones	9.0
Simmons	4.0
LaBounty	3.0
Wilkins	3.0
Kuberski	2.0
Holland	1.5
Prior	1.5
Butler	1.0
Evans	1.0
Koonce	1.0
Packers	39.0
Opponents	33.0

1996 DRAFT CHOICES

Round	Name	Pos.	College
1	John Michels	T	Southern Califonia
2	Derrick Mayes	WR	Notre Dame
3	Mike Flanagan	C	UCLA
	Tyrone Williams	DB	Nebraska
4	Chris Darkins	RB	Minnesota
6	Marco Rivera	G	Penn State
7	Kyle Wachholtz	QB	Southern Califonia
	Keith McKenzie	LB	Ball State

GREEN BAY PACKERS

1996 VETERAN ROSTER

No.	Name	Pos.	Ht.	Wt.	Birthdate	NFL Exp.	College	Hometown	How Acq.	'95 Games/ Starts
50	Arthur, Mike	C	6-3	280	5/7/68	6	Texas A&M	Houston, Tex.	T(NE)-'95	11/0
48	Baldwin, Randy	RB	5-11	216	8/19/67	6	Mississippi	Griffin, Ga.	W(SF)-'96	7/2*
44	Barnes, Reggie	LB	6-1	237	10/23/69	3	Oklahoma	Grand Prairie, Tex.	FA-'96	7/0*
84	Bartrum, Mike	TE	6-5	243	6/23/70	3	Marshall	Pomeroy, Ohio	FA-'95	4/0
58	Bass, Robert	LB	6-1	239	11/10/70	2	Miami	Brooklyn, N.Y.	FA-'95	0*
82	Beebe, Don	WR	5-11	183	12/18/64	8	Chadron State	Maple Park, Ill.	FA-'96	14/1*
34	Bennett, Edgar	RB	6-0	217	2/15/69	5	Florida State	Jacksonville, Fla.	D4-'92	16/16
43	Bostic, James	RB	6-0	225	3/13/72	2	Auburn	Ft. Lauderdale, Fla.	FA-'96	0*
40	Brabham, Cary	S	6-0	195	8/11/70	2	Southern Methodist	Hughes Springs, Tex.	FA-'96	0*
47	Brooks, Bucky	CB	6-0	185	1/22/71	2	North Carolina	Raleigh, N.C.	FA-'95	0*
87	Brooks, Robert	WR	6-0	180	6/23/70	5	South Carolina	Greenwood, S.C.	D3-'92	16/16
68	Brown, Gary	T	6-4	315	6/25/71	3	Georgia Tech	Brentwood, N.Y.	W(Pitt)-'94	16/0
93	Brown, Gilbert	NT	6-2	325	2/22/71	4	Kansas	Detroit, Mich.	W(Minn)-'93	13/7
36	Butler, LeRoy	S	6-0	200	7/19/68	7	Florida State	Jacksonville, Fla.	D2-'90	16/16
89	Chmura, Mark	TE	6-5	250	2/22/69	5	Boston College	South Deerfield, Mass.	D6-'92	16/15
91	Clavelle, Shannon	DE	6-2	287	10/12/72	2	Colorado	New Orleans, La.	FA-'95	1/0
54	Cox, Ron	LB	6-2	235	2/27/68	7	Fresno State	Fresno, Calif.	UFA(Chi)-'96	16/13*
45	Crawford, Keith	CB	6-2	198	11/21/70	3	Howard Payne	Palestine, Tex.	FA-'94	13/0
23	Dorsett, Matthew	CB	5-11	187	8/23/73	2	Southern	New Orleans, La.	FA-'95	10/0
72	Dotson, Earl	T	6-4	310	12/17/70	4	Texas A&I	Beaumont, Tex.	D3-'93	16/16
71	Dotson, Santana	DT	6-5	275	12/19/69	5	Baylor	Houston, Tex.	UFA(TB)-'96	16/8*
33	Evans, Doug	CB	6-1	190	5/13/70	4	Louisiana Tech	Haynesville, La.	D6a-'93	16/16
4	Favre, Brett	QB	6-2	220	10/10/69	6	Southern Mississippi	Kiln, Miss.	T(Atl)-'92	16/16
86	Freeman, Antonio	WR	6-1	187	5/27/72	2	Virginia Tech	Baltimore, Md.	D3d-'95	11/0
95	Freeman, Reggie	LB	6-2	232	5/8/70	2	Florida State	Clewiston, Fla.	FA-'96	0*
76	# Galbreath, Harry	G	6-1	295	1/1/65	9	Tennessee	Clarksville, Tenn.	UFA(Mia)-'93	16/16
42	Goodwin, Marvin	S	6-1	204	9/21/72	2	UCLA	Camden, N.J.	FA-'96	0*
56	Harris, Bernardo	LB	6-2	243	10/15/71	2	North Carolina	Chapel Hill, N.C.	FA-'95	11/0
30	Henderson, William	RB	6-2	248	2/19/71	2	North Carolina	Chester, Va.	D3b-'95	15/1
17	Hentrich, Craig	P	6-3	200	5/18/71	3	Notre Dame	Alton, Ill.	FA-'93	16/0
90	Holland, Darius	DT	6-5	305	11/10/73	2	Colorado	Las Cruces, N.M.	D3a-'93	14/4
99	Holinquest, Lamont	LB	6-3	243	10/24/70	3	Southern California	Downey, Calif.	FA-'96	0*
13	Jacke, Chris	K	6-0	205	3/12/66	8	Texas-El Paso	Richardson, Tex.	D6-'89	14/0
88	# Jackson, Keith	TE	6-2	258	4/9/65	9	Oklahoma	Little Rock, Ark.	T(Mia)-'95	9/1
32	Jervey, Travis	RB	5-11	225	5/5/72	2	Citadel	Mount Pleasant, S.C.	D5b-'95	16/0
96	Jones, Sean	DE	6-7	283	12/19/62	13	Northeastern	Montclair, N.J.	UFA(Hou)-'94	16/16
65	† Knapp, Lindsay	G-T	6-6	290	2/25/70	4	Notre Dame	Deerfield, Ill.	T(KC)-'95	0*
53	Koonce, George	LB	6-1	243	10/15/68	5	East Carolina	Vanceboro, N.C.	FA-'92	16/16
94	Kuberski, Bob	NT	6-5	300	4/5/71	2	Navy	Folsom, Pa.	D7-'93	9/0
97	LaBounty, Matt	DE	6-4	278	1/3/69	4	Oregon	San Marin, Calif.	W(SF)-'93	14/2
25	Levens, Dorsey	RB	6-1	240	5/21/70	3	Georgia Tech	Syracuse, N.Y.	D5b-'94	15/12
22	McGill, Lenny	CB	6-2	198	5/31/71	3	Arizona State	Escondido, Calif.	FA-'94	15/1
78	t- McIntosh, Toddrick	DT	6-3	277	1/22/72	3	Florida State	Richardson, Tex.	T(NO)-'96	11/1*
9	McMahon, Jim	QB	6-1	195	8/21/59	15	Brigham Young	Roy, Utah	W(Clev)-'95	1/0
85	Mickens, Terry	WR	6-1	198	2/21/71	3	Florida A&M	Tallahassee, Fla.	D5a-'94	16/0
70	Miller, Jeff	T	6-4	295	11/23/72	2	Mississippi	Vero Beach, Fla.	D4-'95	0*
81	Morgan, Anthony	WR	6-1	200	11/15/67	6	Tennessee	Cleveland, Ohio	W(Chi)-'93	16/8
28	Mullen, Roderick	CB	6-1	204	12/5/72	2	Grambling State	St. Francisville, La.	FA-'95	8/0
21	Newsome, Craig	CB	6-0	188	8/10/71	2	Arizona State	Rialto, Calif.	D1-'95	16/16
18	Pederson, Doug	QB	6-3	215	1/31/68	4	Northeast Lousiana	Ferndale, Wash.	FA-'95	0*
39	Prior, Mike	S	6-0	208	11/14/63	11	Illinois State	Chicago Heights, Ill.	UFA(Ind)-'93	16/2
75	Ruettgers, Ken	T	6-6	292	8/20/62	12	Southern California	Bakersfield, Calif.	D1-'85	15/15
38	Satterfield, Brian	RB	6-0	225	12/22/69	2	North Alabama	Blue Ridge, Ga.	FA-'95	0*
59	Simmons, Wayne	LB	6-3	248	12/15/69	4	Clemson	Hilton Head, S.C.	D1a-'93	16/16
49	Smith, Kevin	TE	6-4	265	7/25/69	3	UCLA	Oakland, Calif.	FA-'96	2/0*
73	Taylor, Aaron	G	6-4	305	11/14/72	3	Notre Dame	Concord, Calif.	D1-'94	16/16
31	Teague, George	S	6-1	195	2/18/71	4	Alabama	Montgomery, Ala.	D1b-'93	15/15
83	Thomason, Jeff	TE	6-5	250	12/30/69	4	Oregon	Newport Beach, Calif.	FA-'95	16/1
63	Timmerman, Adam	G	6-4	288	8/14/71	2	South Dakota State	Cherokee, Iowa	D7-'95	13/0
92	White, Reggie	DE	6-5	300	12/19/61	12	Tennessee	Chattanooga, Tenn.	UFA(Phil)-'93	15/13
98	Wilkins, Gabe	DE	6-5	310	9/1/71	3	Gardner-Webb	Spartanburg, S.C.	D4-'94	13/8
51	Williams, Brian	LB	6-2	240	12/17/72	2	Southern California	Dallas, Tex.	D3c-'95	13/0
29	# Wilson, Marcus	RB	6-1	215	4/16/68	5	Virginia	Rochester, N.Y	FA-'95	14/0
52	Winters, Frank	C	6-3	295	1/23/64	10	Western Illinois	Union City, N.J.	PB(KC)-'92	16/16

* Baldwin played 7 games with Carolina in '95; Barnes played in 7 games with Dallas; Bass inactive for 16 games; Beebe played 14 games with Carolina; Bostic last active with L.A. Rams in '94; Brabham last active with L.A. Raiders in '94; B. Brooks inactive for 2 games; Cox played 16 games with Chicago; Dotson played 16 games with Tampa Bay; R. Freeman last active with New Orleans in '93; Goodwin last active with Philadelphia in '94; Holinquest last active with Cincinnati in '94; Knapp active for 1 game but did not play; McIntosh played 11 games with Tampa Bay; Miller and Satterfield missed '95 season because of injury; Pederson inactive for 5 games; Smith played 2 games with Oakland.

Unrestricted free agent; subject to developments.

† Restricted free agent; subject to developments.

t- Packers traded for McIntosh (New Orleans).

Players lost through free agency (4): QB Ty Detmer (Phil; 1 game in '95), WR Charles Jordan (Mia; 6), NT John Jurkovik (Jax; 16), LB Fred Strickland (Dall; 14).

Also played with Packers in '95—K Dirk Borgognone (2 games), WR Mark Ingram (16), RB LeShon Johnson (2), LB Joe Kelly (13), QB T.J. Rubley (1), G Joe Sims (4), TE Jeff Wilner (2).

COACHING STAFF

Head Coach,
Mike Holmgren

Pro Career: Became Packers' eleventh head coach on January 11, 1992. In 1995, he directed Packers to their first division title since 1972 and first NFC Championship Game appearance since 1967. Has led team to four consecutive winning seasons (9-7 each year from 1992-94 and 11-5 in 1995) for the first time since 1964-67 and three straight playoff berths (1993-95) for the first time since 1965-67. Holmgren was offensive coordinator for the San Francisco 49ers under George Seifert (1989-91) after spending three previous seasons (1986-88) as quarterbacks coach under Bill Walsh. During his six-year tenure with San Francisco, the 49ers won five consecutive NFC Western Division championships (1986-1990) and back-to-back Super Bowls (XXIII and XXIV). In that span, San Francisco compiled the NFL's best overall record (71-23-1, a .753 percentage). The 49ers never ranked lower than third overall in his three years as offensive coordinator. Career record: 42-29.

Background: Quarterback at Southern California (1966-69) and was drafted by the St. Louis Cardinals in the eighth round of the 1970 NFL draft. He served as an assistant coach at San Francisco State (1981) and Brigham Young (1982-85) before his tenure with the 49ers. Earned his bachelor of science degree in business finance at Southern California (1970).

Personal: Born June 15, 1948, in San Francisco. He and his wife, Kathy, live in Green Bay and have four daughters—Calla, Jenny, Emily, and Gretchen.

ASSISTANT COACHES

Larry Brooks, defensive line; born June 10, 1950, Prince George, Va., lives in Green Bay. Defensive lineman Virginia State 1968-71. Pro defensive tackle Los Angeles Rams 1972-82. College coach: Virginia State 1992-93. Pro coach: Los Angeles Rams 1983-90, joined Packers in 1994.

Nolan Cromwell, special teams; born January 30, 1955, Smith Center, Kan., lives in Green Bay. Quarterback-safety Kansas 1973-76. Pro defensive back Los Angeles Rams 1977-87. Pro coach: Los Angeles Rams 1991, joined Packers in 1992.

Gil Haskell, wide receivers; born September 24, 1943, San Francisco, Calif., lives in Green Bay. Defensive back San Francisco State 1961, 1963-65. No pro playing experience. College coach: Southern California 1978-82. Pro coach: Los Angeles Rams 1983-91, joined Packers in 1992.

Johnny Holland, defensive assistant-quality control; born March 11, 1965, Hempstead, Tex., lives in Green Bay. Linebacker Texas A&M 1983-86. Pro linebacker Green Bay Packers 1987-1993. Pro coach: Joined Packers in 1995.

Kent Johnston, strength and conditioning; born February 21, 1956, Mexia, Tex., lives in Green Bay. Defensive back Stephen F. Austin 1974-77. No pro playing experience. College coach: Northwestern State (Louisiana) 1979, Northeast Louisiana 1980-81, Alabama 1983-86. Pro coach: Tampa Bay Buccaneers 1987-91, joined Packers in 1992.

Sherman Lewis, offensive coordinator; born June 29, 1942, Louisville, Ky., lives in Green Bay. Running back Michigan State 1961-63. Pro running back Toronto Argonauts (CFL) 1964-65, New York Jets 1966. College coach: Michigan State 1969-82. Pro coach: San Francisco 49ers 1983-91, joined Packers in 1992.

Jim Lind, linebackers; born November 11, 1947, Isle, Minn., lives in Green Bay. Linebacker Bethel College 1965-66; defensive back Bemidji State 1971-72. No pro playing experience. College coach: St. Cloud State 1977-78, St. John's (Minn.) 1979-80, Brigham Young 1981-82, Minnesota-Morris 1983-86 (head coach), Wisconsin-Eau Claire 1987-91 (head coach). Pro coach: Joined Packers in 1992.

Tom Lovat, offensive line; born December 28, 1938, Bingham, Utah, lives in Green Bay. Guard-linebacker Utah 1958-60. No pro playing experience. College coach: Utah 1967, 1972-76 (head coach 1974-76), Idaho State 1968-70, Stanford 1977-79, Wyoming 1989. Pro coach: Saskatchewan Roughriders (CFL) 1971, Green Bay Packers 1980, St. Louis-Phoenix Cardinals 1981-84, 1990-91, Indianapolis Colts 1985-88, rejoined Packers in 1992.

Marty Mornhinweg, quarterbacks; born March 29, 1962, Edmond, Okla., lives in Green Bay. Quarterback Montana 1981-84. Pro quarterback Denver Dynamite (Arena Football) 1986. College coach: Montana 1985, Texas-El Paso 1986-87, Northern Arizona 1988, Southeast Missouri State 1989-90, Missouri 1991-93, Northern Arizona 1994. Pro coach: Joined Packers in 1995.

Andy Reid, tight ends-assistant offensive line; born March 19, 1958, Los Angeles, Calif., lives in Green Bay. Offensive tackle-guard Brigham Young 1978-80. No pro playing experience. College coach: Brigham Young 1982, San Francisco State 1983-85, Northern Arizona 1986, Texas-El Paso 1987, Missouri 1988-91. Pro coach: Joined Packers in 1992.

Fritz Shurmur, defensive coordinator; born July 15, 1932, Riverview, Mich., lives in Green Bay. No pro playing experience. College coach: Albion 1956-61, Wyoming 1962-74 (head coach 1971-74). Pro coach: Detroit Lions 1975-77, New England Patriots 1978-81, Los Angeles Rams 1982-90, Phoenix Cardinals 1991-93, joined Packers in 1994.

Harry Sydney, running backs; born June 26, 1959, Petersburg, Va., lives in Green Bay. Quarterback/running back Kansas 1978-81. Pro running back Denver Gold (USFL) 1983-84, Memphis Showboats (USFL) 1985, Montreal Alouettes (CFL) 1986, San Francisco 49ers 1987-91, Green Bay Packers 1992. Pro coach: Joined Packers in 1994.

Bob Valesente, defensive backs; born July 19, 1940, Seneca Falls, N.Y., lives in Green Bay. Halfback Ithaca College 1958-61. No pro playing experience. College coach: Cornell 1964-74, Cincinnati 1975-76, Arizona 1977-79, Mississippi State 1980-81, Kansas 1984-87 (head coach 1986-87), Maryland 1988, Pittsburgh 1989. Pro coach: Baltimore Colts 1982-83, Pittsburgh Steelers 1990-91, joined Packers in 1992.

1996 FIRST-YEAR ROSTER

Name	Pos.	Ht.	Wt.	Birthdate	College	Hometown	How Acq.
Caflisch, Andy (1)	P	6-3	200	8/7/70	Wisconsin-Stout	River Falls, Wis.	FA
Cunningham, Richie (1)	K	5-10	165	8/18/70	S.W. Louisiana	Houma, La.	FA
Darkins, Chris	RB	6-0	211	4/30/74	Minnesota	Houston, Tex.	D4
DeGraffenreid, Allen (1)	WR	6-2	210	5/1/70	Ohio State	Cincinnati, Ohio	FA
Flanagan, Mike	C	6-5	290	11/10/73	UCLA	Sacramento, Calif.	D3a
Holt, Reggie (1)	S	5-11	198	2/18/71	Wisconsin	North Miami, Fla.	FA
Keeney, Brad	DT	6-3	294	11/20/73	Citadel	Wilmington, N.C.	FA
Matthews, Eric	WR	5-11	169	3/22/72	Indiana	Boynton Beach, Fla.	FA
Mayes, Derrick	WR	6-0	201	1/28/74	Notre Dame	Indianapolis, Ind.	D2
McCoy, Mike (1)	QB	6-3	204	4/1/72	Utah	Novato, Calif.	FA
McKenzie, Keith	LB	6-2	242	10/17/73	Ball State	Detroit, Mich.	D7b
Michels, John	T	6-7	290	3/19/73	Southern California	La Jolla, Calif.	D1
Ochs, Dirk	DE	6-3	245	7/8/73	Kansas State	Overland Park, Kan.	FA
Rivera, Marco	G	6-4	295	4/26/72	Penn State	Elmont, N.Y.	D6
Scott, Walter	DT	6-3	282	5/18/73	East Carolina	Trenton, S.C.	FA
Simmons, Charlie (1)	WR	6-2	210	8/25/72	Georgia Tech	Macon, Ga.	D6-'95
Stark, Troy	T	6-5	302	1/2/73	Georgia	Canandaigua, N.Y.	FA
Wachholtz, Kyle	QB	6-4	238	5/17/72	Southern California	Corona, Calif.	D7a
Williams, Tyrone	CB	5-11	190	5/31/73	Nebraska	Bradenton, Fla.	D3b

The term NFL Rookie is defined as a player who is in his first season of professional football and has not been on the roster of another professional football team for any regular-season or postseason games. A Rookie is designated by an "R" on NFL rosters. Players who have been active in another professional football league or players who have NFL experience, including either preseason training camp or being on an Active List or Inactive List, or on Reserve/Injured or Reserve/Physically Unable to Perform for fewer than six regular-season games, are termed NFL First-Year Players. An NFL First-Year Player is designated by a "1" on NFL rosters. Thereafter, a player is credited with an additional year of experience for each season in which he accumulates six games on the Active List or Inactive List, or on Reserve/Injured or Reserve/Physically Unable to Perform.

NOTES

MINNESOTA VIKINGS

National Football Conference
Central Division
Team Colors: Purple, Gold, and White
9520 Viking Drive
Eden Prairie, Minnesota 55344
Telephone: (612) 828-6500

CLUB OFFICERS

Chairman of the Board: John C. Skoglund
Vice Chairmen: Jaye F. Dyer, Philip S. Maas
Directors: James Binger, N. Bud Grossman, Roger L. Headrick, James R. Jundt, Elizabeth MacMillan, Carol S. Sperry, Wheelock Whitney

CLUB OFFICIALS

President/CEO: Roger L. Headrick
Vice President Administration/Team Operations: Jeff Diamond
Vice President Player Personnel: Frank Gilliam
Vice President of Marketing and Business Development: Stew Widdess
Assistant General Manager/National Scouting: Jerry Reichow
Assistant General Manager/Pro Personnel: Paul Wiggin
Director of Finance: Nick Valentine
Director of Research and Dev.: Mike Eayrs
Director of Marketing: Kernal Buhler
Director of Public Relations: David Pelletier
Director of Team Operations: Breck Spinner
Ticket Manager: Gina Dillon
Director of Security: Steve Rollins
Player Personnel Coordinator: Scott Studwell
Equipment Manager: Dennis Ryan
Trainer: Fred Zamberletti
Video Director: Larry Kohout
Stadium: Hubert H. Humphrey Metrodome
•**Capacity:** 64,035
500 11th Avenue South
Minneapolis, Minnesota 55415
Playing Surface: AstroTurf
Training Camp: Mankato State University
Mankato, Minnesota 56001

1996 SCHEDULE

PRESEASON

Aug. 3	**San Diego**	7:00
Aug. 8	**Buffalo**	7:00
Aug. 19	at Miami	8:00
Aug. 23	at New Orleans	7:00

REGULAR SEASON

Sept. 1	**Detroit**	12:00
Sept. 8	at Atlanta	1:00
Sept. 15	at Chicago	12:00
Sept. 22	**Green Bay**	12:00
Sept. 29	at New York Giants	1:00
Oct. 6	**Carolina**	12:00
Oct. 13	at Tampa Bay	1:00
Oct. 20	Open Date	
Oct. 28	**Chicago** (Mon.)	8:00
Nov. 3	**Kansas City**	12:00
Nov. 10	at Seattle	1:00
Nov. 17	at Oakland	5:00
Nov. 24	**Denver**	12:00
Dec. 1	**Arizona**	12:00
Dec. 8	at Detroit	8:00
Dec. 15	**Tampa Bay**	12:00
Dec. 22	at Green Bay	12:00

RECORD HOLDERS

INDIVIDUAL RECORDS—CAREER

Category	Name	Performance
Rushing (Yds.)	Chuck Foreman, 1973-79	5,879
Passing (Yds.)	Fran Tarkenton, 1961-66, 1972-78	33,098
Passing (TDs)	Fran Tarkenton, 1961-66, 1972-78	239
Receiving (No.)	Steve Jordan, 1982-1994	498
Receiving (Yds.)	Anthony Carter, 1985-1993	7,636
Interceptions	Paul Krause, 1968-1979	53
Punting (Avg.)	Harry Newsome, 1990-93	43.8
Punt Return (Avg.)	Tommy Mason, 1961-66	10.4
Kickoff Return (Avg.)	Charlie West, 1968-1973	25.5
Field Goals	Fred Cox, 1963-1977	282
Touchdowns (Tot.)	Bill Brown, 1962-1974	76
Points	Fred Cox, 1963-1977	1,365

INDIVIDUAL RECORDS—SINGLE SEASON

Category	Name	Performance
Rushing (Yds.)	Terry Allen, 1992	1,201
Passing (Yds.)	Warren Moon, 1994	4,264
Passing (TDs)	Warren Moon, 1995	33
Receiving (No.)	Cris Carter, 1994, 1995	122
Receiving (Yds.)	Cris Carter, 1995	1,371
Interceptions	Paul Krause, 1975	10
Punting (Avg.)	Bobby Walden, 1964	46.4
Punt Return (Avg.)	David Palmer, 1995	13.2
Kickoff Return (Avg.)	John Gilliam, 1972	26.3
Field Goals	Fuad Reveiz, 1994	34
Touchdowns (Tot.)	Chuck Foreman, 1975	22
Points	Chuck Foreman, 1975	132
	Fuad Reveiz, 1994	132

INDIVIDUAL RECORDS—SINGLE GAME

Category	Name	Performance
Rushing (Yds.)	Chuck Foreman, 10-24-76	200
Passing (Yds.)	Tommy Kramer, 11-2-86	490
Passing (TDs)	Joe Kapp, 9-28-69	*7
Receiving (No.)	Rickey Young, 12-16-79	15
Receiving (Yds.)	Sammy White, 11-7-76	210
Interceptions	Many times	3
	Last time by Jack Del Rio, 12-5-93	
Field Goals	Rich Karlis, 11-5-89	*7
Touchdowns (Tot.)	Chuck Foreman, 12-20-75	4
	Ahmad Rashad, 9-2-79	4
Points	Chuck Foreman, 12-20-75	24
	Ahmad Rashad, 9-2-79	24

*NFL Record

VIKINGS COACHING HISTORY

(293-247-9)

1961-66	Norm Van Brocklin	29-51-4
1967-83	Bud Grant	161-99-5
1984	Les Steckel	3-13-0
1985	Bud Grant	7-9-0
1986-91	Jerry Burns	55-46-0
1992-95	Dennis Green	38-29-0

METRODOME

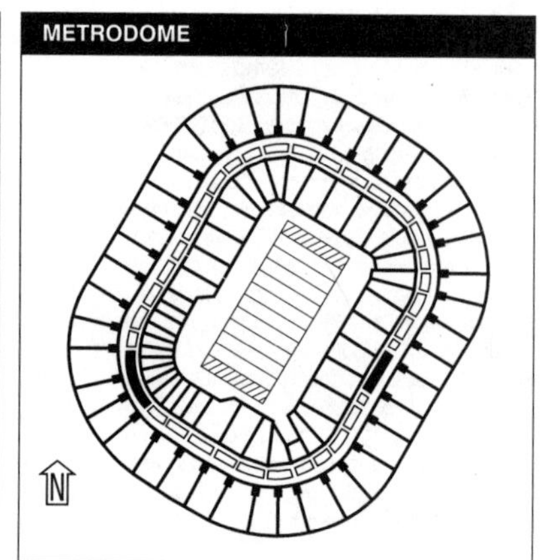

1995 TEAM RECORD

PRESEASON (2-2)

Date	Result		Opponents
8/7	W	23-19	at San Diego
8/12	L	14-21	at New England
8/18	W	20-7	Oakland
8/26	L	13-17	Kansas City

REGULAR SEASON (8-8)

Date	Result		Opponents	Att.
9/3	L	14-31	at Chicago	63,036
9/10	W	20-10	Detroit	52,234
9/17	L	17-23	Dallas (OT)	60,088
9/24	W	44-24	at Pittsburgh	57,853
10/8	W	23-17	Houston (OT)	56,430
10/15	L	17-20	at Tampa Bay (OT)	55,703
10/22	L	21-38	at Green Bay	60,332
10/30	L	6-14	Chicago	61,238
11/5	W	27-24	Green Bay	62,839
11/12	W	30-24	at Arizona (OT)	51,342
11/19	W	43-24	New Orleans	58,108
11/23	L	38-44	at Detroit	74,559
12/3	W	31-17	Tampa Bay	52,879
12/9	W	27-11	Cleveland	47,984
12/18	L	30-37	at San Francisco	64,975
12/24	L	24-27	at Cincinnati	34,568

(OT) Overtime

SCORE BY PERIODS

Vikings	81	176	67	76	12	— 412
Opponents	85	99	71	121	9	— 385

ATTENDANCE

Home 451,800 Away 462,368 Total 914,168
Single-game home record, 64,035 (9/25/94)
Single-season home record, 485,616 (1992)

1995 TEAM STATISTICS

	Vikings	Opp.
Total First Downs	342	312
Rushing	91	75
Passing	223	212
Penalty	28	25
Third Down: Made/Att	114/239	93/224
Third Down Pct.	47.7	41.5
Fourth Down: Made/Att	4/11	7/11
Fourth Down Pct.	36.4	63.6
Total Net Yards	5938	5451
Avg. Per Game	371.1	340.7
Total Plays	1115	1016
Avg. Per Play	5.3	5.4
Net Yards Rushing	1733	1329
Avg. Per Game	108.3	83.1
Total Rushes	433	352
Net Yards Passing	4205	4122
Avg. Per Game	262.8	257.6
Sacked/Yards Lost	40/295	44/294
Gross Yards	4500	4416
Att./Completions	642/402	620/369
Completion Pct.	62.6	59.5
Had Intercepted	16	25
Punts/Avg.	72/40.9	68/42.2
Net Punting Avg.	72/33.1	68/34.9
Penalties/Yards Lost	105/797	100/707
Fumbles/Ball Lost	29/13	30/15
Touchdowns	48	44
Rushing	10	11
Passing	33	29
Returns	5	4
Avg. Time of Possession	31:50	28:10

1995 INDIVIDUAL STATISTICS

PASSING	Att.	Comp.	Yds.	Pct.	TD	Int.	Tkld.	Rate
Moon	606	377	4228	62.2	33	14	38/277	91.5
Johnson	36	25	272	69.4	0	2	2/18	68.3
Vikings	642	402	4500	62.6	33	16	40/295	90.2
Opponents	620	369	4416	59.5	29	25	44/294	80.1

SCORING	TD R	TD P	TD Rt	PAT	FG	Saf	PTS
Reveiz	0	0	0	44/44	26/36	0	122
Carter	0	17	0	0/0	0/0	0	102
Reed	0	9	0	0/0	0/0	0	54
R. Smith	5	0	0	0/0	0/0	0	32
Ismail	0	3	0	0/0	0/0	0	18
Lee	2	1	0	0/0	0/0	0	18
Evans	1	1	0	0/0	0/0	0	12
Graham	2	0	0	0/0	0/0	0	12
Jordan	0	2	0	0/0	0/0	0	12
O. Thomas	0	0	2	0/0	0/0	0	12
Fuller	0	0	1	0/0	0/0	0	6
Jackson	0	0	1	0/0	0/0	0	6
Palmer	0	0	1	0/0	0/0	0	6
Vikings	10	33	5	44/44	26/36	0	412
Opponents	11	29	4	29/32	26/35	0	385

2-Point conversions: R. Smith. Team: 1-2.

RUSHING	Att.	Yds.	Avg.	LG	TD
R. Smith	139	632	4.5	58t	5
Graham	110	406	3.7	26	2
Lee	69	371	5.4	66t	2
Stewart	31	144	4.6	51	0
Moon	33	82	2.5	16	0
Evans	19	59	3.1	12	1
Phillips	14	26	1.9	7	0
Palmer	7	15	2.1	9	0
Ismail	1	7	7.0	7	0
Carter	1	0	0.0	0	0
Johnson	9	-9	-1.0	3	0
Vikings	433	1733	4.0	66t	10
Opponents	352	1329	3.8	53	11

RECEIVING	No.	Yds.	Avg.	LG	TD
Carter	122	1371	11.2	60t	17
Reed	72	1167	16.2	55t	9
Lee	71	558	7.9	33	1
Ismail	32	597	18.7	85t	3
Jordan	27	185	6.9	17	2
Cooper	18	207	11.5	41	0
Evans	18	119	6.6	24	1
Palmer	12	100	8.3	19	0
Walsh	7	66	9.4	16	0
R. Smith	7	35	5.0	11	0
DeLong	6	38	6.3	9	0
Graham	4	30	7.5	11	0
Tice	3	22	7.3	9	0
Gerak	1	3	3.0	3	0
Stewart	1	3	3.0	3	0
Stringer	1	-1	-1.0	-1	0
Vikings	402	4500	11.2	85t	33
Opponents	369	4416	12.0	73t	29

INTERCEPTIONS	No.	Yds.	Avg.	LG	TD
O.Thomas	9	108	12.0	45t	1
Frank	3	72	24.0	42	0
Mincy	3	37	12.3	20	0
Jackson	2	46	23.0	37t	1
Brady	2	7	3.5	9	0
D. Washington	1	25	25.0	25	0
Del Rio	1	15	15.0	15	0
Harrison	1	15	15.0	15	0
E. McDaniel	1	3	3.0	3	0
Fuller	1	0	0.0	0	0
Barker	1	-2	-2.0	-2	0
Vikings	25	326	13.0	60t	2
Opponents	16	172	10.8	36	1

PUNTING	No.	Yds.	Avg.	In 20	LG
Saxon	72	2948	40.9	21	60
Vikings	72	2948	40.9	21	60
Opponents	68	2867	42.2	26	69

PUNT RETURNS	No.	FC	Yds.	Avg.	LG	TD
Palmer	26	13	342	13.2	74t	1
Lee	5	1	50	10.0	17	0
Mincy	4	0	22	5.5	8	0
Vikings	35	14	414	11.8	74t	1
Opponents	41	10	446	10.9	78t	1

KICKOFF RETURNS	No.	Yds.	Avg.	LG	TD
Ismail	42	1037	24.7	71	0
Palmer	17	354	20.8	42	0
Lee	5	100	20.0	24	0
Phillips	4	60	15.0	23	0
Walsh	3	42	14.0	18	0
Gerak	1	19	19.0	19	0
Vikings	72	1612	22.4	71	0
Opponents	74	1581	21.4	52	0

SACKS	No.
Randle	10.5
B. Thomas	6.0
Harrison	4.5
E. McDaniel	4.5
Barker	3.0
Brady	3.0
Del Rio	3.0
Tuaolo	3.0
F. Smith	2.5
Alexander	2.0
Harris	1.0
Fuller	0.5
Griffith	0.5
Vikings	44.0
Opponents	40.0

1996 DRAFT CHOICES

Round	Name	Pos.	College
1	Duane Clemons	DE	California
2	James Manley	DT	Vanderbilt
3	Moe Williams	RB	Kentucky
4	Hunter Goodwin	TE	Texas A&M
5	Sean Boyd	DB	North Carolina
7	Jon Merrill	G	Duke

MINNESOTA VIKINGS

1996 VETERAN ROSTER

No.	Name	Pos.	Ht.	Wt.	Birthdate	NFL Exp.	College	Hometown	How Acq.	'95 Games/ Starts
63	Alex, Keith	G	6-4	307	6/9/69	3	Texas A&M	Beaumont, Tex.	FA-'95	0*
90	Alexander, Derrick	DE	6-4	265	11/13/73	2	Florida State	Jacksonville, Fla.	D1a-'95	15/12
53	Alipate, Tuineau	LB	6-2	239	8/21/67	3	Washington State	Union City, Calif.	FA-'95	16/0
42	Barnett, Harlon	S	5-11	203	1/2/67	7	Michigan State	Cincinnati, Ohio	UFA(NE)-'95	15/11
56	Bercich, Pete	LB	6-1	237	12/23/71	2	Notre Dame	Joliet, Ill.	D7-'94	9/0
50	Brady, Jeff	LB	6-1	238	11/9/68	6	Kentucky	Melbourne, Ky.	UFA(TB)-'95	16/7
52	Brown, Richard	LB	6-3	240	9/21/65	8	San Diego State	Westminister, Calif.	FA-'94	16/0
80	Carter, Cris	WR	6-3	206	11/25/65	10	Ohio State	Middletown, Ohio	W(Phil)-'90	16/16
62	Christy, Jeff	C	6-3	284	2/3/69	4	Pittsburgh	Freeport, Pa.	FA-'93	16/16
85	DeLong, Greg	TE	6-4	245	4/3/73	2	North Carolina	Orefield, Pa.	FA-'95	2/2
71	Dixon, David	G	6-5	359	1/5/69	3	Arizona State	Auckland, New Zealand	FA-'94	15/6
59	Edwards, Dixon	LB	6-1	225	3/25/68	6	Michigan State	Cincinnati, Ohio	UFA(Dall)-'96	15/15*
29	Evans, Charles	RB	6-1	240	4/16/67	4	Clark	Augusta, Ga.	D11-'92	16/8
72	Fisk, Jason	DT	6-3	284	9/4/72	2	Stanford	Davis, Calif.	D7b-'95	8/0
37	Frank, Donald	CB	6-0	192	10/24/65	7	Winston-Salem State	Tarboro, N.C.	UFA(Oak)-'95	12/6
83	Frisch, David	TE	6-7	260	6/22/70	4	Colorado State	House Springs, Mo.	FA-'96	2/0*
27	Fuller, Corey	CB	5-10	198	5/11/71	2	Florida State	Rickards, Fla.	D2b-'95	16/10
54	Garnett, Dave	LB	6-2	219	12/6/70	3	Stanford	Naperville, Ill.	FA-'96	3/0*
46	Gerak, John	G	6-3	269	1/6/70	4	Penn State	Struthers, Ohio	D3a-'93	16/6
31	† Graham, Scottie	RB	5-9	222	3/28/69	4	Ohio State	Long Island, N.Y.	FA-'93	16/6
24	Griffith, Robert	S	5-11	193	11/30/70	3	San Diego State	San Diego, Calif.	FA-'94	16/1
91	Harrison, Martin	DE	6-5	251	9/20/67	6	Washington	Bellevue, Wash.	FA-'94	11/0
82	Ismail, Qadry	WR	6-0	196	11/8/70	4	Syracuse	Wilkes-Barre, Pa.	D2-'93	16/1
25	Jackson, Alfred	CB	6-0	183	7/10/67	6	San Diego State	Tulare, Calif.	FA-'95	8/2
14	Johnson, Brad	QB	6-5	223	9/13/68	5	Florida State	Black Mountain, N.C.	D9a-'92	5/0
89	Jordan, Andrew	TE	6-4	258	6/21/72	3	Western Carolina	Charlotte, N.C.	D6-'94	13/7
32	Lee, Amp	RB	5-11	197	10/1/71	5	Florida State	Chipley, Fla.	FA-'94	16/3
61	Lindsay, Everett	G-C	6-4	305	9/18/70	4	Mississippi	Raleigh, N.C.	D5-'93	16/0
5	May, Chad	QB	6-1	219	9/28/71	2	Kansas State	La Verne, Calif.	D4-'95	0*
58	McDaniel, Ed	LB	5-11	230	2/23/69	5	Clemson	Batesburg, S.C.	D5-'92	16/16
64	McDaniel, Randall	G	6-3	277	12/19/64	9	Arizona State	Avondale, Ariz.	D1-'88	16/16
1	Moon, Warren	QB	6-3	213	11/18/56	13	Washington	Los Angeles, Calif.	T(Hou)-'94	16/16
68	Morris, Mike	C	6-5	275	2/22/61	10	Northeast Missouri State	Centerville, Iowa	FA-'91	16/0
22	Palmer, David	RB	5-8	169	11/19/72	3	Alabama	Birmingham, Ala.	D2a-'94	14/0
30	Phillips, Bobby	RB	5-9	187	12/8/69	2	Virginia Union	Richmond, Va.	FA-'95	8/0
93	Randle, John	DT	6-1	277	12/12/67	7	Texas A&I	Hearne, Tex.	FA-'90	16/16
86	Reed, Jake	WR	6-3	216	9/28/67	6	Grambling	Covington, Ga.	D3b-'91	16/16
7	Reveiz, Fuad	K	5-11	225	2/24/63	12	Tennessee	Miami, Fla.	FA-'90	16/0
4	Saxon, Mike	P	6-3	205	7/10/62	12	San Diego State	Whittier, Calif.	FA-'94	16/0
95	Smith, Fernando	DE	6-6	283	8/2/71	3	Jackson State	Flint, Mich.	D2b-'94	12/1
26	† Smith, Robert	RB	6-0	205	3/4/72	4	Ohio State	Euclid, Ohio	D1-'93	9/7
47	Smith, Rod	CB	5-11	187	3/12/70	5	Notre Dame	St. Paul, Minn.	UFA(Car)-'96	16/5*
69	Solomon, Ariel	T	6-5	290	7/16/68	6	Colorado	Boulder, Colo.	UFA(Pitt)-'96	4/0*
73	Steussie, Todd	T	6-6	313	12/1/70	3	California	Canoga Park, Calif.	D1b-'94	16/16
28	Stewart, James	RB	6-2	238	12/8/71	2	Miami	Vero Beach, Fla.	D5-'95	4/0
77	Stringer, Korey	T	6-4	339	5/8/74	2	Ohio State	Warren, Ohio	D1b-'95	16/15
43	Thomas, Orlando	S	6-1	210	10/21/72	2	Southwestern Louisiana	Crowley, La.	D2a-'95	16/11
98	Tuaolo, Esera	DT	6-2	276	7/11/68	6	Oregon State	Chino, Calif.	FA-'92	16/16
6	Walker, Jay	QB	6-3	230	1/24/72	2	Howard	Los Angeles, Calif.	FA-'96	0*
81	Walsh, Chris	WR	6-1	194	12/12/68	4	Stanford	Concord, Calif.	FA-'94	16/0
20	Washington, Dewayne	CB	5-11	191	12/27/72	3	North Carolina State	Durham, N.C.	D1a-'94	15/14
96	Washington, Keith	DE	6-4	257	12/18/73	2	Nevada-Las Vegas	Dallas, Tex.	FA-'95	0*

* Alex active for 2 games but did not play; Edwards played 15 games with Dallas in '95; Frisch played 2 games with New England; Garnett played 3 games with Denver; May inactive for 16 games; Rod Smith played 16 games with Carolina; Solomon played 4 games with Pittsburgh; Walker last active with New England in '94; K. Washington inactive for 5 games.

† Restricted free agent; subject to developments.

Players lost through free agency (2): TE Adrian Cooper (SF; 13 games in '95), DE Roy Barker (SF; 16).

Also played with Vikings in '95—T Rick Cunningham (11 games), LB Jack Del Rio (9), CB Shelly Hammonds (1), DE James Harris (12), G Chris Hinton (4), S Charles Mincy (16), LB Broderick Thomas (16), TE Mike Tice (3).

COACHING STAFF

Head Coach
Dennis Green

Pro Career: Named the fifth head coach in Vikings history on January 10, 1992, Green is one of only seven people in the history of the league to lead his team to the playoffs in each of his first three seasons as an NFL head coach. He also won two NFC Central titles in his first three seasons in Minnesota. In 1994, NFL Commissioner Paul Tagliabue appointed Green to the league's Competition Committee. His best coaching job may have come in 1993, when the Vikings qualified as a wild-card entrant with a 9-7 mark and won their final three regular-season games for the first time since 1974. In '92, Green led the Vikings to their best record (11-5) and first division title under a first-year head coach. He earned NFL coach of the year honors from the Washington Touchdown Club and NFC coach of the year honors from *United Press International* and *College & Pro Football Newsweekly*. As receivers coach at San Francisco from 1986-89, Green developed Pro Bowl players Jerry Rice and John Taylor. Green's first pro coaching opportunity came as special teams coach for the 49ers in 1979. Green briefly played defensive back with British Columbia (CFL) in 1971. Career record: 38-29.

Background: A running back at Iowa from 1968-70, Green began his coaching career as a graduate assistant for Iowa in 1972. He coached running backs and receivers at Dayton in 1973 then running backs and receivers at Iowa from 1974-76. Green worked with running backs at Stanford in 1977-78. He returned to Stanford as offensive coordinator in 1980 then was head coach at Northwestern from 1981-85. Green was named Big Ten coach of the year in 1982. As head coach at Stanford from 1989-91, he led the school to the 1991 Aloha Bowl, its first bowl game since 1986.

Personal: Born February 17, 1949 in Harrisburg, Pa., Green earned his degree in recreation from Iowa. He and his wife, Marie, live in Wayzata, Minn. Green has two children, Patti and Jeremy.

ASSISTANT COACHES

Brian Billick, offensive coordinator; born February 28, 1954, Redlands, Calif., lives in Eden Prairie, Minn. Tight end Brigham Young 1974-76. Pro tight end Dallas Cowboys 1977. College coach: Brigham Young 1978, Redlands 1979, San Diego State 1981-85, Utah State 1986-88, Stanford 1989-91. Pro coach: Joined Vikings in 1992.

Foge Fazio, defensive coordinator; born February 28, 1939, Dawmont, W.Va., lives in Eden Prairie, Minn. Linebacker-center Pittsburgh 1957-60. No pro playing experience. College coach: Boston University 1967, Harvard 1968, Pittsburgh 1969-72, 1977-81, 1982-85 (head coach), Cincinnati 1973-76, Notre Dame 1986-87. Pro coach: Atlanta Falcons 1988-89, New York Jets 1990-94, joined Vikings in 1995.

Jeff Friday, assistant strength and conditioning; born October 11, 1966, Milwaukee, Wis., lives in Eden Prairie, Minn. No college or pro playing experience. College coach: Illinois State 1991-92, Northwestern 1992-95. Pro coach: Joined Vikings in 1996.

Carl Hargrave, running backs; born November 8, 1954, Frankfurt, Germany, lives in Eden Prairie, Minn. Defensive back Upper Iowa 1972-75. No pro playing experience. College coach: Upper Iowa 1977-80, Northwestern 1981-85, Pittsburgh 1986, Houston 1987-91, Iowa 1992-93. Pro coach: Joined Vikings in 1994.

John Levra, defensive line; born October 2, 1937, Arma, Kan., lives in Eden Prairie, Minn. Guard-linebacker Pittsburg (Kan.) State 1963-65. No pro playing experience. College coach: New Mexico Highlands 1966-70, Stephen F. Austin 1971-74, Kansas 1975-78, North Texas State 1979. Pro coach: British Columbia Lions (CFL) 1980, New Orleans Saints 1981-85, Chicago Bears 1986-92, Denver Broncos 1993-94, joined Vikings in 1995.

Chip Myers, wide receivers; born July 9, 1945, Panama City, Fla., lives in Eden Prairie, Minn. Receiver Northwestern Oklahoma 1964-66. Pro receiver San Francisco 49ers 1967, Cincinnati Bengals 1969-76. College coach: Illinois 1980-82. Pro coach: Tampa Bay Buccaneers 1983-84, Indianapolis Colts 1985-88, New York Jets 1990-93, New Orleans Saints 1994, joined Vikings in 1995.

Tom Olivadotti, inside linebackers; born September 22, 1945, Long Branch, N.J., lives in Eden Prairie, Minn. Defensive back-wide receiver Upsala 1963-66. No pro playing experience. College coach: Princeton 1975-77, Boston College 1978-79, Miami 1980-83. Pro coach: Cleveland Browns 1985-86, Miami Dolphins 1987-95, joined Vikings in 1996.

Keith Rowen, offensive line; born September 2, 1952, New York, N.Y., lives in Eden Prairie, Minn. Offensive tackle Stanford 1972-74. No pro playing experience. College coach: Stanford 1975-76, Long Beach State 1977-78, Arizona 1979-82. Pro coach: Boston/New Orleans Breakers (USFL) 1983-84, Cleveland Browns 1984, Indianapolis Colts 1985-88, New England Patriots 1989, Atlanta Falcons 1990-93, joined Vikings in 1994.

Ray Sherman, quarterbacks; born November 27, 1951, Berkeley, Calif., lives in Eden Prairie, Minn. Wide receiver Laney (Calif.) J.C. 1969-70, Fresno State 1971-72. Pro defensive back Green Bay Packers 1973. College coach: San Jose State 1974, California 1975, 1981, Michigan State 1976-77, Wake Forest 1978-80, Purdue 1982-85, Georgia 1986-87. Pro coach: Houston Oilers 1988-89, San Francisco 49ers 1991-93, New York Jets 1994, joined Vikings in 1995.

Richard Solomon, defensive backs; born December 8, 1949, New Orleans, La., lives in Eden Prairie, Minn. Running back-defensive back Iowa 1970-73. No pro playing experience. College coach: Dubuque 1973-75, Southern Illinois 1976, Iowa 1977-78, Syracuse 1979, Illinois 1980-86. Pro coach: New York Giants 1987-91 (scout), joined Vikings in 1992.

Mike Tice, tight ends; born February 2, 1959, Bayshore, N.Y., lives in Eden Prairie, Minn. Quarterback Maryland 1977-80. Pro tight end Seattle Seahawks 1981-88, 1990-91, Washington Redskins 1989, Minnesota Vikings 1992-93, 1995. Pro coach: Joined Vikings in 1996.

Trent Walters, outside linebackers; born November 20, 1943, Knoxville, Tenn., lives in Eden Prairie, Minn. Defensive back Indiana 1963-65. Pro defensive back Edmonton Eskimos (CFL) 1966-67. College coach: Indiana 1968-71, Louisville 1972, Indiana 1973-80, Washington 1981-83, Pittsburgh 1985, Louisville 1986-90, Texas A&M 1991-93. Pro coach: Cincinnati Bengals 1984, joined Vikings in 1994.

Steve Wetzel, strength and conditioning; born May 11, 1963, Washington D.C., lives in Eden Prairie, Minn. No college or pro playing experience. College coach: Maryland 1985-89, George Mason 1990. Pro coach: Washington Redskins 1990-91, joined Vikings in 1992.

Gary Zauner, special teams; born November 2, 1950, Milwaukee, Wis., lives in Eden Prairie, Minn. Kicker Wisconsin-LaCrosse 1968-72. No pro playing experience. College coach: Brigham Young 1979-80, San Diego State 1981-86, New Mexico 1987-88, Long Beach State 1990-91. Pro coach: Joined Vikings in 1994.

1996 FIRST-YEAR ROSTER

Name	Pos.	Ht.	Wt.	Birthdate	College	Hometown	How Acq.
Bland, Tony	WR	6-3	210	12/12/72	Florida A&M	St. Petersburg, Fla.	FA
Bobo, Orlando	G	6-3	308	2/9/74	N.E. Louisiana	West Point, Miss.	FA
Boyd, Sean	S	6-2	206	12/19/72	North Carolina	Gastonia, N.C.	D5
Clemons, Duane	LB	6-5	261	5/23/74	California	Riverside, Calif.	D1
Coleman, Jamie	CB	5-9	184	6/16/75	Appalachian State	Laurinburg, N.C.	FA
Gissendaner, Lee (1)	WR	5-9	175	10/25/71	Northwestern	Stow, Ohio	FA
Goodwin, Hunter	T	6-5	277	10/10/72	Texas A&M	Bellville, Tex.	D4
Goynes, Brynton	DT	6-3	288	11/5/73	Rice	Katy, Tex.	FA
Grantlin, Gilbert	WR	5-11	187	11/25/72	Edinboro State	Belle Glade, Fla.	FA
Hammonds, Shelly(1)	S	5-10	189	2/13/71	Penn State	Barnwell, S.C.	D5-'94
Hanks, Ben	LB	6-2	223	7/31/72	Florida	Miami, Fla.	FA
Johnson, Chris (1)	S	6-0	205	8/7/71	San Diego State	San Diego, Calif.	FA
Lee, Mark	DE	6-4	259	6/4/72	Western State	Colorado Spgs., Colo.	FA
Mackey, Earl (1)	LB	6-0	233	5/25/73	Southern	Jonesville, La.	FA-'95
Maddox, Markco	S	6-2	210	9/2/71	Albany State	Albany, Ga.	FA
Manley, James	DT	6-2	302	7/11/74	Vanderbilt	Birmingham, Ala.	D2
Merrill, Jon	T-G	6-3	292	6/22/73	Duke	Brevard, N.C.	D7
Nesbitt, Mike (1)	P	6-2	180	2/3/71	New Mexico	Delen, N.M.	FA
Reem, Matt	TE	6-6	270	12/23/72	Minnesota	Roseville, Minn.	FA
Robinson, Michael	CB	6-1	192	6/24/73	Hampton	Newtown, Va.	FA
Ryan, Chris	RB	6-0	250	3/9/73	Clark	Sulphur, La.	FA
Ware, Moses (1)	WR	6-4	191	8/12/73	N. Carolina Central	Washington, D.C.	FA-'95
Washington, Keith (1)	DE	6-4	257	12/27/72	Nevada-Las Vegas	Dallas, Tex.	FA-'95
White, Jose (1)	DT	6-3	274	3/2/73	Howard	Washington, D.C.	D7a-'95
Williams, Moe	RB	6-1	203	7/26/74	Kentucky	Columbus, Ga.	D3

The term NFL Rookie is defined as a player who is in his first season of professional football and has not been on the roster of another professional football team for any regular-season or postseason games. A Rookie is designated by an "R" on NFL rosters. Players who have been active in another professional football league or players who have NFL experience, including either preseason training camp or being on an Active List or Inactive List, or on Reserve/Injured or Reserve/Physically Unable to Perform for fewer than six regular-season games, are termed NFL First-Year Players. An NFL First-Year Player is designated by a "1" on NFL rosters. Thereafter, a player is credited with an additional year of experience for each season in which he accumulates six games on the Active List or Inactive List, or on Reserve/Injured or Reserve/Physically Unable to Perform.

NOTES

NEW ORLEANS SAINTS

National Football Conference
Western Division
Team Colors: Old Gold, Black, and White
5800 Airline Highway
Metairie, Louisiana 70003
Telephone: (504) 733-0255

CLUB OFFICIALS

Owner: Tom Benson
Vice President/General Manager: Bill Kuharich
Vice President/Head Coach: Jim Mora
Vice President/Marketing: Greg Suit
Director of Pro Personnel: Chet Franklin
Director of College Scouting: Bruce Lemmerman
Treasurer: Bruce Broussard
Administrative Coordinator: Austin Dejan
Comptroller: Charleen Sharpe
Director of Corporate Sales: Bill Ferrante
Director of Media Relations: Rusty Kasmiersky
Assistant Director of Media Relations: Neal Gulkis
Data Processing Manager: Jay Romig
Director of Travel/Entertainment/Special Projects: Barra Birrcher
Player Personnel Scouts: Bill Baker, Hamp Cook, Hokie Gajan, Tom Marino
Director of Ticket Sales: Greg Seeling
Trainer: Dean Kleinschmidt
Equipment Manager: Dan Simmons
Video Director: Albert Aucoin
Stadium: Louisiana Superdome
•**Capacity:** 64,992
1500 Poydras Street
New Orleans, Louisiana 70112
Playing Surface: AstroTurf
Training Camp: University of Wisconsin-La Crosse
La Crosse, Wisconsin 54601

1996 SCHEDULE

PRESEASON

Date	Opponent	Time
July 27	vs. Indianapolis at Canton, Ohio	2:30
Aug. 2	at Detroit	7:30
Aug. 10	at Kansas City	7:00
Aug. 17	**Chicago**	7:00
Aug. 23	**Minnesota**	7:00

REGULAR SEASON

Date	Opponent	Time
Sept. 1	at San Francisco	1:00
Sept. 8	**Carolina**	12:00
Sept. 15	at Cincinnati	1:00
Sept. 22	**Arizona**	12:00
Sept. 29	at Baltimore	1:00
Oct. 6	**Jacksonville**	3:00
Oct. 13	**Chicago**	12:00
Oct. 20	at Carolina	1:00
Oct. 27	Open Date	
Nov. 3	**San Francisco**	7:00
Nov. 10	**Houston**	12:00
Nov. 17	at Atlanta	1:00
Nov. 24	at Tampa Bay	1:00
Dec. 1	**St. Louis**	3:00
Dec. 8	**Atlanta**	12:00
Dec. 15	at New York Giants	1:00
Dec. 21	at St. Louis (Sat.)	3:00

RECORD HOLDERS

INDIVIDUAL RECORDS—CAREER

Category	Name	Performance
Rushing (Yds.)	George Rogers, 1981-84	4,267
Passing (Yds.)	Archie Manning, 1971-1982	21,734
Passing (TDs)	Archie Manning, 1971-1982	115
Receiving (No.)	Eric Martin, 1985-1993	532
Receiving (Yds.)	Eric Martin, 1985-1993	7,854
Interceptions	Dave Waymer, 1980-89	37
Punting (Avg.)	Tommy Barnhardt, 1987, 1989-1994	43.0
Punt Return (Avg.)	Mel Gray, 1986-88	13.4
Kickoff Return (Avg.)	Walter Roberts, 1967	26.3
Field Goals	Morten Andersen, 1982-1994	302
Touchdowns (Tot.)	Dalton Hilliard, 1986-1993	53
Points	Morten Andersen, 1982-1994	1,318

INDIVIDUAL RECORDS—SINGLE SEASON

Category	Name	Performance
Rushing (Yds.)	George Rogers, 1981	1,674
Passing (Yds.)	Jim Everett, 1995	3,970
Passing (TDs)	Jim Everett, 1995	26
Receiving (No.)	Eric Martin, 1988	85
Receiving (Yds.)	Eric Martin, 1989	1,090
Interceptions	Dave Whitsell, 1967	10
Punting (Avg.)	Tommy Barnhardt, 1992	44.0
Punt Return (Avg.)	Mel Gray, 1987	14.7
Kickoff Return (Avg.)	Don Shy, 1969	27.9
Field Goals	Morten Andersen, 1985	31
Touchdowns (Tot.)	Dalton Hilliard, 1989	18
Points	Morten Andersen, 1987	121

INDIVIDUAL RECORDS—SINGLE GAME

Category	Name	Performance
Rushing (Yds.)	George Rogers, 9-4-83	206
Passing (Yds.)	Archie Manning, 12-7-80	377
Passing (TDs)	Billy Kilmer, 11-2-69	6
Receiving (No.)	Tony Galbreath, 9-10-78	14
Receiving (Yds.)	Wes Chandler, 9-2-79	205
Interceptions	Tommy Myers, 9-3-78	3
	Dave Waymer, 10-6-85	3
	Reggie Sutton, 10-18-87	3
	Gene Atkins, 12-22-91	3
Field Goals	Morten Andersen, 12-1-85	5
	Morten Andersen, 11-15-87	5
	Morten Andersen, 12-3-92	5
	Morten Andersen, 12-11-94	5
Touchdowns (Tot.)	Many times	3
	Last time by Mario Bates, 12-4-94	
Points	Many times	18

COACHING HISTORY

(174-259-5)

Years	Coach	Record
1967-70	Tom Fears*	13-34-2
1970-72	J.D. Roberts	7-25-3
1973-75	John North**	11-23-0
1975	Ernie Hefferle	1-7-0
1976-77	Hank Stram	7-21-0
1978-80	Dick Nolan***	15-29-0
1980	Dick Stanfel	1-3-0
1981-85	O.A. (Bum) Phillips****	27-42-0
1985	Wade Phillips	1-3-0
1986-95	Jim Mora	91-72-0

*Released after seven games in 1970
**Released after six games in 1975
***Released after 12 games in 1980
****Resigned after 12 games in 1985

LOUISIANA SUPERDOME

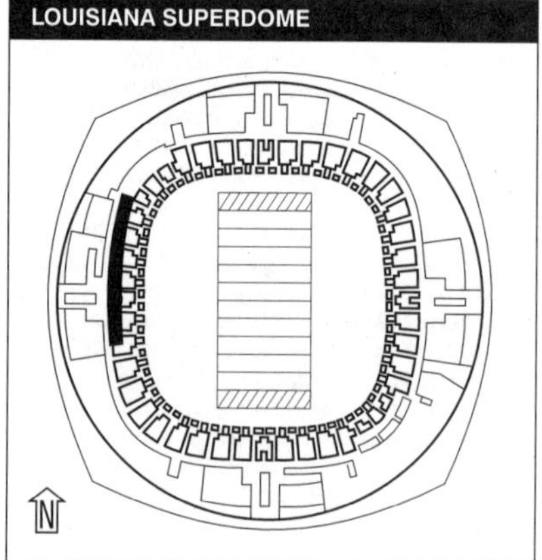

1995 TEAM RECORD

PRESEASON (1-3)

Date	Result		Opponents
8/5	L	17-27	at Green Bay
8/11	L	13-14	at N.Y. Giants
8/20	L	19-24	Seattle
8/25	W	24-10	Detroit

REGULAR SEASON (7-9)

Date	Result		Opponents	Att.
9/3	L	22-24	San Francisco	66,627
9/10	L	13-17	at St. Louis	59,335
9/17	L	24-27	Atlanta (OT)	57,442
9/24	L	29-45	at N.Y. Giants	72,619
10/1	L	10-15	Philadelphia	43,938
10/15	W	33-30	Miami	55,628
10/22	L	3-20	at Carolina	55,484
10/29	W	11-7	at San Francisco	65,272
11/5	W	19-10	St. Louis	43,120
11/12	W	17-14	Indianapolis	44,122
11/19	L	24-43	at Minnesota	58,108
11/26	W	34-26	Carolina	39,580
12/3	W	31-17	at New England	59,876
12/10	L	14-19	at Atlanta	54,603
12/16	L	23-34	Green Bay	50,132
12/24	W	12-0	at N.Y. Jets	28,885

(OT) Overtime

SCORE BY PERIODS

Saints	61	75	74	109	0	—	319
Opponents	71	132	81	61	3	—	348

ATTENDANCE

Home 400,589 Away 454,182 Total 854,771
Single-game home record, 70,940 (11/4/79)
Single-season home record, 548,655 (1991)

1995 TEAM STATISTICS

	Saints	Opp.
Total First Downs	294	320
Rushing	75	107
Passing	202	195
Penalty	17	18
Third Down: Made/Att	91/215	97/222
Third Down Pct.	42.3	43.7
Fourth Down: Made/Att	5/11	8/13
Fourth Down Pct.	45.5	61.5
Total Net Yards	5178	5561
Avg. Per Game	323.6	347.6
Total Plays	984	1056
Avg. Per Play	5.3	5.3
Net Yards Rushing	1390	1838
Avg. Per Game	86.9	114.9
Total Rushes	383	469
Net Yards Passing	3788	3723
Avg. Per Game	236.8	232.7
Sacked/Yards Lost	28/214	44/275
Gross Yards	4002	3998
Att./Completions	573/349	543/329
Completion Pct.	60.9	60.6
Had Intercepted	14	17
Punts/Avg.	74/40.1	66/41.8
Net Punting Avg.	74/35.6	66/35.6
Penalties/Yards Lost	86/688	109/830
Fumbles/Ball Lost	19/11	29/12
Touchdowns	38	38
Rushing	11	13
Passing	26	23
Returns	1	2
Avg. Time of Possession	28:15	31:45

1995 INDIVIDUAL STATISTICS

PASSING	Att.	Comp.	Yds.	Pct.	TD	Int.	Tkld.	Rate
Everett	567	345	3970	60.8	26	14	27/210	87.0
Hodson	5	3	14	60.0	0	0	0/0	64.6
Wilmsmeyer	1	1	18	100.0	0	0	0/0	118.8
Small	0	0	0	—	0	0	1/4	—
Saints	573	349	4002	60.9	26	14	28/214	86.9
Opponents	543	329	3998	60.6	23	17	44/275	84.3

SCORING	TD R	TD P	TD Rt	PAT	FG	Saf	PTS
Brien	0	0	0	16/16	12/17	0	52
Early	0	8	0	0/0	0/0	0	48
Bates	7	0	0	0/0	0/0	0	42
Small	1	5	0	0/0	0/0	0	36
Lohmiller	0	0	0	11/13	8/14	0	35
Walls	0	4	0	0/0	0/0	0	26
Haynes	0	4	0	0/0	0/0	0	24
Smith	0	3	0	0/0	0/0	0	20
Brown	1	1	0	0/0	0/0	0	12
Zellars	2	0	0	0/0	0/0	0	12
Lumpkin	0	0	1	0/0	0/0	0	6
Neal	0	1	0	0/0	0/0	0	6
Saints	11	26	1	27/29	20/31	0	319
Opponents	13	23	2	33/33	27/33	0	348

2-Point conversions: Smith, Walls. Team: 2-9.

RUSHING	Att.	Yds.	Avg.	LG	TD
Bates	244	951	3.9	66t	7
Zellars	50	162	3.2	11	2
Brown	49	159	3.2	35t	1
Small	6	75	12.5	44t	1
Everett	24	42	1.8	9	0
Neal	5	3	0.6	3	0
Ned	3	1	0.3	5	0
Early	2	-3	-1.5	9	0
Saints	383	1390	3.6	66t	11
Opponents	469	1838	3.9	51	13

RECEIVING	No.	Yds.	Avg.	LG	TD
Early	81	1087	13.4	70t	8
Walls	57	694	12.2	29	4
Smith	45	466	10.4	43	3
Haynes	41	597	14.6	48	4
Small	38	461	12.1	32t	5
Brown	35	266	7.6	19	1
Bates	18	114	6.3	26	0
Neal	12	123	10.3	69t	1
Zellars	7	33	4.7	9	0
DeRamus	6	76	12.7	27	0
Rhem	4	50	12.5	20	0
Ned	3	9	3.0	9	0
Newman	1	18	18.0	18	0
Botkin	1	8	8.0	8	0
Saints	349	4002	11.5	70t	26
Opponents	329	3998	12.2	77	23

INTERCEPTIONS	No.	Yds.	Avg.	LG	TD
Spencer	4	11	2.8	9	0
Allen	2	28	14.0	28	0
Hughes	2	19	9.5	19	0
Dixon	2	17	8.5	11	0
Pahukoa	2	12	6.0	12	0
Lumpkin	1	47	47.0	47t	1
Legette	1	43	43.0	43	0
Martin	1	12	12.0	12	0
Tubbs	1	6	6.0	6	0
McCleskey	1	0	0.0	0	0
Saints	17	195	11.5	47t	1
Opponents	14	273	19.5	60	2

PUNTING	No.	Yds.	Avg.	In 20	LG
Wilmsmeyer	73	2965	40.6	21	53
Saints	74	2965	40.1	21	53
Opponents	66	2756	41.8	24	61

PUNT RETURNS	No.	FC	Yds.	Avg.	LG	TD
Hughes	28	22	262	9.4	74	0
Legette	1	0	6	6.0	6	0
Buck	0	1	0	—	—	0
Saints	29	23	268	9.2	74	0
Opponents	36	22	233	6.5	33	0

KICKOFF RETURNS	No.	Yds.	Avg.	LG	TD
Hughes	66	1617	24.5	83	0
Neal	2	28	14.0	16	0
Ned	2	33	16.5	19	0
McCleskey	1	0	0.0	0	0
Smith	1	6	6.0	6	0
Walls	1	6	6.0	6	0
Saints	73	1690	23.2	83	0
Opponents	68	1348	19.8	62	0

SACKS	No.
Martin	13.0
Turnbull	7.0
Joe Johnson	5.5
Dixon	4.0
Porter	3.0
Broughton	2.0
Harvey	2.0
McIntosh	2.0
Stanley	2.0
Goff	1.5
Fields	1.0
B. Jones	1.0
Legette	1.0
Tubbs	1.0
Saints	44.0
Opponents	28.0

1996 DRAFT CHOICES

Round	Name	Pos.	College
1	Alex Molden	DB	Oregon
2	Je'Rod Cherry	DB	California
3	Brady Smith	DE	Colorado State
4	Ricky Whittle	RB	Oregon
5	Mercury Hayes	WR	Michigan
	Tom Ackerman	G	Eastern Washington
	Terry Guess	WR	Gardner-Webb
6	Keno Hills	T	Southwestern La.
	Toderick Malone	WR	Alabama
7	Henry Lusk	TE	Utah

NEW ORLEANS SAINTS

1996 VETERAN ROSTER

No.	Name	Pos.	Ht.	Wt.	Birthdate	NFL Exp.	College	Hometown	How Acq.	'95 Games/ Starts
21	Allen, Eric	CB	5-10	180	11/22/65	9	Arizona State	San Diego, Calif.	UFA(Phil)-'95	16/16
24	Bates, Mario	RB	6-1	217	1/16/73	3	Arizona State	Tucson, Ariz.	D2-'94	16/16
86	Botkin, Kirk	TE	6-3	245	3/19/71	2	Arkansas	Baytown, Tex.	FA-'94	16/0
27	Boyd, Malik	CB	5-10	185	11/5/70	2	Southern	Houston, Tex.	FA-'96	0*
10	Brien, Doug	K	6-0	180	11/24/70	3	California	Concord, Calif.	FA-'95	14/0*
99	Broughton, Willie	DT	6-5	285	9/9/64	10	Miami	Ft. Pierce, Fla.	T(Oak)-'95	16/10
20	Brown, Derek	RB	5-9	205	4/15/71	4	Nebraska	Anaheim, Calif.	D4b-'93	16/0
26	Buck, Vince	S	6-0	198	1/12/68	7	Central State, Ohio	Owensboro, Ky.	D2-'90	13/13
45	Byrd, Israel	CB	5-11	184	2/1/71	2	Utah State	St. Louis, Mo.	FA-'94	4/0
51	Childs, Ron	LB	5-11	212	9/18/71	2	Washington State	Kennewick, Wash.	W(KC)-'95	9/0
39	Covington, John	S	6-0	206	4/22/72	2	Notre Dame	Winter Haven, Fla.	FA-'95	0*
28	Dawkins, Ralph	RB	5-8	195	3/20/70	2	Louisville	Jacksonville, Fla.	FA-'94	0*
87	DeRamus, Lee	WR	6-0	205	8/24/72	2	Wisconsin	Atco, N.J.	D6-'95	8/0
56	Dixon, Ernest	LB	6-1	240	10/17/71	3	South Carolina	Ft. Mill, S.C.	FA-'94	16/5
72	Dombrowski, Jim	G	6-5	300	10/19/63	11	Virginia	Williamsville, N.Y.	D1-'86	16/16
47	Duckett, Forey	CB	6-3	195	2/5/70	3	Nevada	Pinole, Calif.	FA-'96	0*
79	Epps, Tory	DT	6-1	280	5/28/67	7	Memphis	Uniontown, Pa.	UFA(Chi)-'95	12/0
17	Everett, Jim	QB	6-5	212	1/3/63	11	Purdue	Albuquerque, N.M.	T(Rams)-'94	16/16
55	Fields, Mark	LB	6-2	244	11/9/72	2	Washington State	Cerritos, Calif.	D1-'95	16/3
40	Fuller, James	S	5-11	208	8/5/69	3	Portland State	Tacoma, Wash.	FA-'96	0*
85	Green, Paul	TE	6-3	253	10/8/66	4	Southern California	Clovis, Calif.	FA-'96	0*
52	Harvey, Richard	LB	6-1	242	9/11/66	7	Tulane	Pascagoula, Miss.	UFA(Den)-'95	16/14
81	Haynes, Michael	WR	6-0	184	12/24/65	9	Northern Arizona	New Orleans, La.	UFA(Atl)-'95	16/15
14	Hodson, Tom	QB	6-3	195	1/28/67	5	Louisiana State	Mathews, La.	FA-'95	4/0
33	Hughes, Tyrone	CB	5-9	175	1/14/70	4	Nebraska	New Orleans, La.	D5-'93	16/2
96	Jeffries, Dameian	DE	6-4	277	5/7/73	2	Alabama	Sylacauga, Ala.	D4-'95	2/0
94	Johnson, Joe	DT	6-4	270	7/11/72	3	Louisville	St. Louis, Mo.	D1-'94	14/14
58	Jones, Brian	LB	6-1	250	1/22/68	3	Texas	Lubbock, Tex.	FA-'95	16/7
74	Jones, Clarence	T	6-6	280	5/6/68	6	Maryland	Central Islip, N.Y.	UFA(StL)-'96	13/0*
61	King, Ed	G	6-4	300	12/3/69	5	Auburn	Phenix City, Ala.	FA-'95	1/0
68	Kline, Alan	T	6-5	290	2/25/71	2	Ohio State	Tiffin, Ohio	FA-'94	3/0
25	Mack, Milton	CB	5-11	195	9/20/63	9	Alcorn State	Jackson, Miss.	FA-'96	0*
93	Martin, Wayne	DT	6-5	275	10/26/65	8	Arkansas	Cherry Valley, Ark.	D1-'89	16/16
44	McCleskey, J.J.	S	5-7	177	4/10/70	3	Tennessee	Knoxville, Tenn.	FA-'94	14/1
67	McCollum, Andy	C-G	6-4	295	6/2/70	3	Toledo	Akron, Ohio	FA-'94	11/9
29	McMillian, Mark	CB	5-7	148	4/29/70	5	Alabama	Los Angeles, Calif.	UFA(Phil)-'96	16/16*
38	McNabb, Dexter	RB	6-2	250	7/8/69	3	Florida	De Funiak Springs, Fla.	FA-'96	1/0*
92	Mickell, Darren	DE	6-4	291	8/3/70	5	Florida	Miami, Fla.	UFA(KC)-'96	12/5*
12	Millen, Hugh	QB	6-5	216	11/22/63	11	Washington	Seattle, Wash.	FA-'96	3/0*
22	† Neal, Lorenzo	RB	5-11	240	12/27/70	4	Fresno State	Lemoore, Calif.	D4a-'93	16/5
30	Newman, Anthony	S	6-0	200	11/25/65	9	Oregon	Beaverton, Ore.	FA-'95	12/1
60	Novitsky, Craig	C-T	6-5	295	5/21/71	3	UCLA	Dumfries, Va.	D5b-'94	16/3
13	Nussmeier, Doug	QB	6-3	211	12/11/70	3	Idaho	Lake Oswego, Ore.	D4-'94	0*
35	Pahukoa, Shane	S	6-2	202	11/25/70	3	Washington	Marysville, Wash.	FA-'94	15/2
59	Porter, Rufus	LB	6-1	230	5/18/65	9	Southern	Baton Rouge, La.	UFA(Sea)-'95	13/12
65	Reese, Darren	G	6-4	295	10/25/70	2	Ohio University	Elida, Ohio	FA-'96	0*
84	Rhem, Steve	WR	6-2	212	11/9/71	3	Minnesota	Ocala, Fla.	FA-'94	8/0
77	Roaf, William	T	6-5	300	4/18/70	4	Louisiana Tech	Pine Bluff, Ark.	D1a-'93	16/16
78	Roth, Tom	G	6-5	285	9/19/68	2	Southern Illinois	Godfrey, Ill.	FA-'96	0*
83	Small, Torrance	WR	6-3	201	9/6/70	5	Alcorn State	Tampa, Fla.	D5-'92	16/1
82	Smith, Irv	TE	6-3	246	10/13/71	4	Notre Dame	Pemberton, N.J.	D1b-'93	16/16
95	Stanley, Buster	DT	6-2	290	5/14/70	2	Michigan	Youngstown, Ohio	FA-'96	0*
90	Stanley, Israel	DE	6-3	260	4/21/70	2	Arizona State	San Diego, Calif.	FA-'95	14/0
71	Stokes, Fred	DE	6-3	274	3/14/64	10	Georgia Southern	Vidalia, Ga.	UFA(StL)-'96	14/2*
54	Tubbs, Winfred	LB	6-4	250	9/24/70	3	Texas	Fairfield, Tex.	D3-'94	7/6
70	Tucker, Mark	C-G	6-3	300	4/29/68	3	Southern California	Los Angeles, Calif.	FA-'96	0*
97	Turnbull, Renaldo	DE	6-4	250	1/5/66	7	West Virginia	St. Thomas, Virgin Islands	D1-'90	15/15
66	Verstegen, Mike	G	6-6	311	10/24/71	2	Wisconsin	Kimberly, Wis.	D3-'95	0*
63	Willis, Donald	G	6-3	330	7/15/73	2	North Carolina A&T	Lompoc, Calif.	W(Sea)-'95	0*
4	Wilmsmeyer, Klaus	P	6-1	210	12/4/67	5	Louisville	Mississauga, Canada	FA-'95	16/0
34	Zellars, Ray	RB	5-11	233	3/25/73	2	Notre Dame	Pittsburgh, Pa.	D2-'95	12/0

* Boyd last active with Minnesota in '94; Brien played 6 games with San Francisco and 8 with New Orleans in '95; Covington inactive for 1 game; Dawkins missed '95 season because of injury; Duckett last active with Seattle in '94; Fuller last active with San Diego in '94; Green last active with Seattle in '94; C. Jones played 13 games with St. Louis; Mack last active with Detroit in '94; McMillian played 16 games with Philadelphia; McNabb played 1 game with Philadelphia; Mickell played 12 games with Kansas City; Millen played 3 games with Denver; Nussmeier inactive for 16 games; Reese last active with N.Y. Giants in '94; Roth last active with New Orleans in '94; B. Stanley last active with New England in '94; Stokes played 14 games with St. Louis; Tucker last active with Arizona in '94; Verstegen active for 3 games but did not play; Willis inactive for 16 games.

† Restricted free agent; subject to developments.

Traded—DT Toddrick McIntosh to Green Bay.

Players lost through free agency (4): T Richard Cooper (Phil; 14 games in '95), WR Quinn Early (Buff; 16), CB Jimmy Spencer (Cin; 16), TE Wesley Walls (Car; 16).

Also played with Saints in '95—RB Vaughn Dunbar (1 game), DE Robert Goff (11), LB John Johnson (1), DE Earnest Jones (1), K Chip Lohmiller (8), RB Derrick Ned (12), G Chris Port (8).

COACHING STAFF

Vice President-Head Coach, Jim Mora

Pro Career: Begins eleventh year as an NFL head coach, the most-tenured head coach with the same team. His 91 career victories are sixth most among active NFL coaches. Led Saints to a 12-4 record and their third straight playoff appearance in 1992. Guided Saints to an 11-5 mark and the club's first-ever NFC West title in 1991. Was named 1987 NFL coach of the year after leading Saints to a 12-3 record and the team's first playoff appearance. Came to New Orleans following a three-year career as the winningest coach in USFL history as head coach of the Philadelphia/Baltimore Stars. Directed Stars to championship game in each of his three seasons and won league championship in 1984 and 1985. He won USFL coach of the year honors following the 1984 season. Mora began his pro coaching career in 1978 as defensive line coach of the Seattle Seahawks. In 1982, he became defensive coordinator of the New England Patriots and played a vital role in the Patriots' march to the playoffs that year. No pro playing experience. Career record: 91-72.

Background: Played tight end and defensive end at Occidental College. Assistant coach at Occidental from 1960-63 and head coach from 1964-66. Linebacker coach at Stanford (1967) on a staff that included former Eagles head coach Dick Vermeil. Defensive assistant at Colorado 1968-73. Linebacker coach under Vermeil at UCLA 1974. Defensive coordinator at Washington 1975-77. Received bachelor's degree in physical education from Occidental in 1957. Also holds master's degree in education from Southern California.

Personal: Born May 24, 1935, in Glendale, Calif. Jim and his wife, Connie, live in Metairie, La., and have three sons—Michael, Stephen, and Jim (defensive backs coach for the Saints).

ASSISTANT COACHES

Bobby April, special teams; born April 15, 1953, New Orleans, La., lives in Metairie, La. Defensive end/linebacker Nicholls State 1972-75. No pro playing experience. College coach: Tulane 1979, Arizona 1980-86, Southern California 1987-90. Pro coach: Atlanta Falcons 1991-93, Pittsburgh Steelers 1994-95, joined Saints in 1996.

Bruce Arians, tight ends; born October 3, 1952, Paterson, N.J., lives in Metairie, La. Quarterback Virginia Tech 1972-74. No pro playing experience. College coach: Virginia Tech 1975-77, Mississippi State 1978-80, 1993-95, Alabama 1981-82, Temple 1983-88 (head coach). Pro coach: Kansas City Chiefs 1989-92, joined Saints in 1996.

Dave Atkins, running backs; born May 18, 1949, Victoria, Tex., lives in Metairie, La. Running back Texas-El Paso 1970-72. Pro running back San Francisco 49ers 1973, Honolulu Hawaiians (WFL) 1974, San Diego Chargers 1975. College coach: Texas-El Paso 1979-80, San Diego State 1981-85. Pro coach: Philadelphia Eagles 1986-92, New England Patriots 1993, Arizona Cardinals 1994-95, joined Saints in 1996.

Jeff Davidson, offensive assistant; born October 3, 1967, Akron, Ohio, lives in Metairie, La. Offensive lineman Ohio State 1986-89. Pro offensive lineman Denver Broncos 1990-92, New Orleans Saints 1994. Pro coach: Joined Saints in 1996.

Jim Haslett, linebackers; born December 9, 1955, Pittsburgh, Pa., lives in Destrehan, La. Defensive end Indiana University (Pa.) 1975-78. Linebacker Buffalo Bills 1979-86, New York Jets 1987. College coach: Buffalo 1988-90. Pro coach: Sacramento Surge (World League) 1991-92, Los Angeles Raiders 1993-94, joined Saints in 1995.

John Matsko, offensive line; born February 2, 1951, Cleveland, Ohio, lives in Mandeville, La. Fullback Kent State 1970-73. No pro playing experience. College coach: Kent State 1973, Miami, Ohio 1974-75, 1977, North Carolina 1978-84, Navy 1985, Arizona 1986, Southern California 1987-91. Pro coach: Phoenix Cardinals 1992-93, joined Saints in 1994.

1996 FIRST-YEAR ROSTER

Name	Pos.	Ht.	Wt.	Birthdate	College	Hometown	How Acq.
Ackerman, Tom	C-G	6-3	290	9/6/72	Eastern Washington	Nooksack, Wash.	D5b
Becksvoort, John	K	6-1	177	2/26/73	Tennessee	Chattanooga, Tenn.	FA
Brooks, Steve (1)	TE	6-5	245	6/2/71	Occidental	Ventura, Calif.	FA
Cherry, Je'Rod	S	6-0	196	5/30/73	California	Berkeley, Calif.	D2
Dowden, Corey (1)	CB	5-11	190	10/18/68	Tulane	New Orleans, La.	FA
Esposito, Dan (1)	RB	5-11	205	5/11/72	Millersville State	Philadelphia, Pa.	FA
Farkas, Kevin (1)	T	6-9	345	2/4/71	Appalachian State	Richmond, Va.	FA
Fields, Jeff (1)	DT	6-3	320	7/3/67	Arkansas State	Jackson, Miss.	FA
Gardere, Peter (1)	P	6-0	190	9/28/69	Texas	Houston, Tex.	FA
Goosby, Michael (1)	WR	6-3	207	10/15/70	North Texas	Arlington, Tex.	FA
Guess, Terry	WR	6-0	200	9/22/74	Gardner-Webb	Orangeburg, S.C.	D5c
Hayes, Mercury	WR	5-11	195	1/1/73	Michigan	Houston, Tex.	D5a
Hills, Keno	T	6-6	305	6/13/73	Southwestern La.	Tampa, Fla.	D6a
Lusk, Hendrick	TE	6-1	240	5/8/72	Utah	Monterey, Calif.	D7
Malone, Toderick	WR	5-11	177	1/11/74	Alabama	Attalla, Ala.	D6b
Molden, Alex	CB	5-10	190	8/4/73	Oregon	Colorado Spgs., Colo.	D1
Palmer, Emile	DT	6-3	320	4/5/73	Syracuse	Cheverly, Md.	FA
Payton, Elfrid (1)	LB	6-1	230	9/22/67	Grambling State	Harvey, La.	FA
Smith, Brady	DE	6-5	260	6/5/73	Colorado State	Barrington, Ill.	D3
Strong, William (1)	CB	5-10	191	11/3/71	North Carolina St.	Lewisville, S.C.	D5
Whittle, Ricky	RB	5-9	200	12/21/71	Oregon	Fresno, Calif.	D4

The term NFL Rookie is defined as a player who is in his first season of professional football and has not been on the roster of another professional football team for any regular-season or postseason games. A Rookie is designated by an "R" on NFL rosters. Players who have been active in another professional football league or players who have NFL experience, including either preseason training camp or being on an Active List or Inactive List, or on Reserve/Injured or Reserve/Physically Unable to Perform for fewer than six regular-season games, are termed NFL First-Year Players. An NFL First-Year Player is designated by a "1" on NFL rosters. Thereafter, a player is credited with an additional year of experience for each season in which he accumulates six games on the Active List or Inactive List, or on Reserve/Injured or Reserve/Physically Unable to Perform.

NOTES

Glenn Mayeaux, strength and conditioning assistant; born July 19, 1949, New Orleans, lives in Metairie, La. No college or pro playing experience. Pro coach: Joined Saints in 1996.

Jim Mora, defensive backs; born November 19, 1961, Los Angeles, Calif., lives in New Orleans. Defensive back Washington 1980-83. No pro playing experience. College coach: Washington 1984. Pro coach: San Diego Chargers 1985-91, joined Saints in 1992.

Wayne Nunnely, defensive line; born March 29, 1952, Los Angeles, Calif., lives in Kenner, La. Fullback Nevada-Las Vegas 1972-75. No pro playing experience. College coach: Nevada-Las Vegas 1976, 1982-89 (head coach 1986-89), Cal Poly-Pomona 1977-78, Cal State-Fullerton 1979, Pacific 1980-81, Southern California 1991-92, UCLA 1993-94. Pro coach: Joined Saints in 1995.

John Pagano, defensive assistant; born March 30, 1967, Boulder, Colo., lives in Harahan, La. Linebacker Mesa College 1985-88. No pro playing experience. College coach: Mesa College 1989, Nevada-Las Vegas1990-91, Louisiana Tech 1994, Mississippi 1995. Pro coach: Bergamo Lions (Italian League) 1992, joined Saints in 1996.

Russell Paternostro, strength and conditioning; born July 21, 1940, New Orleans, La., lives in Covington, La. San Diego State. No college or pro playing experience. Pro coach: Joined Saints in 1981.

Carl Smith, offensive coordinator-quarterbacks; born April 26, 1948, Wasco, Calif., lives in Kenner, La. Defensive back Cal Poly-SLO 1968-70. No pro playing experience. College coach: Cal Poly-SLO 1971, Colorado 1972-73, Southwestern Louisiana 1974-78, Lamar 1979-81, North Carolina State 1982. Pro coach: Philadelphia/Baltimore Stars (USFL) 1983-85, joined Saints in 1986.

Rick Venturi, linebackers; born February 23, 1946, Taylorville, Ill., lives in Metairie, La. Quarterback-defensive back Northwestern 1965-67. No pro playing experience. College coach: Northwestern 1968-72, 1978-80 (head coach), Purdue 1973-76, Illinois 1977. Pro coach: Hamilton Tiger-Cats (CFL) 1981, Indianapolis Colts 1982-93 (interim head coach for final 11 games of 1991), Cleveland Browns 1994-95, joined Saints in 1996.

Steve Walters, wide receivers; born June 16, 1948, Jonesboro, Ark., lives in Destrehan, La. Quarterback-defensive back Arkansas 1967-70. No pro playing experience. College coach: Tampa 1973, Northeast Louisiana 1974-75, Morehead State 1976, Tulsa 1977-78, Memphis State 1979, Southern Methodist 1980-81, Alabama 1985. Pro coach: New England Patriots 1982-84, joined Saints in 1986.

NEW YORK GIANTS

National Football Conference
Eastern Division
Team Colors: Blue, Red, and White
Giants Stadium
East Rutherford, New Jersey 07073
Telephone: (201) 935-8111

CLUB OFFICIALS

President/Co-CEO: Wellington T. Mara
Chairman/Co-CEO: Preston Robert Tisch
Executive Vice President/General Counsel: John K. Mara, Esq.
Treasurer: Jonathan Tisch
Senior Vice President-General Manager: George Young
Vice President-Chief Financial Officer: John Pasquali
Vice President-Marketing: Rusty Hawley
Vice President-Public Relations: Pat Hanlon
Assistant General Manager: Ernie Accorsi
Special Assistant to the General Manager: Harry Hulmes
Director of Player Personnel: Tom Boisture
Director of Pro Personnel: Tim Rooney
Assistant Director of Player Personnel: Rick Donohue
Director of Administration: Tom Power
Director of Promotion: Frank Mara
Ticket Manager: John Gorman
Controller: Christine Procops
Assistant Director of Public Relations: Aaron Salkin
Assistant Director of Marketing: Bill Smith
Manager of Creative Services: Doug Murphy
Community Relations Coordinator: Allison Stangeby
Head Trainer: Ronnie Barnes
Assistant Trainers: John Johnson, Michael Colello, Steve Kennelly
Equipment Manager: Ed Wagner, Jr.
Stadium: Giants Stadium • **Capacity:** 78,148
East Rutherford, New Jersey 07073
Playing Surface: AstroTurf
Training Camp: University at Albany
1400 Washington Avenue
Albany, N.Y. 12222

1996 SCHEDULE

PRESEASON

Aug. 2	at Jacksonville	8:00
Aug. 10	**Baltimore**	1:00
Aug. 17	at New York Jets	8:00
Aug. 23	**Carolina**	8:00

REGULAR SEASON

Sept. 1	**Buffalo**	8:00
Sept. 8	at Dallas	3:00
Sept. 15	**Washington**	4:00
Sept. 22	at New York Jets	1:00
Sept. 29	**Minnesota**	1:00
Oct. 6	Open Date	
Oct. 13	**Philadelphia**	4:00
Oct. 20	at Washington	1:00
Oct. 27	at Detroit	1:00
Nov. 3	**Arizona**	1:00
Nov. 10	at Carolina	8:00
Nov. 17	at Arizona	2:00
Nov. 24	**Dallas**	4:00
Dec. 1	at Philadelphia	1:00
Dec. 8	at Miami	1:00
Dec. 15	**New Orleans**	1:00
Dec. 21	**New England** (Sat.)	12:30

RECORD HOLDERS

INDIVIDUAL RECORDS—CAREER

Category	Name	Performance
Rushing (Yds.)	Rodney Hampton, 1990-95	5,989
Passing (Yds.)	Phil Simms, 1979-1993	33,462
Passing (TDs)	Phil Simms, 1979-1993	199
Receiving (No.)	Joe Morrison, 1959-1972	395
Receiving (Yds.)	Frank Gifford, 1952-1960, 1962-64	5,434
Interceptions	Emlen Tunnell, 1948-1958	74
Punting (Avg.)	Don Chandler, 1956-1964	43.8
Punt Return (Avg.)	David Meggett, 1989-1994	11.0
Kickoff Return (Avg.)	Rocky Thompson, 1971-72	27.2
Field Goals	Pete Gogolak, 1966-1974	126
Touchdowns (Tot.)	Frank Gifford, 1952-1960, 1962-64	78
Points	Pete Gogolak, 1966-1974	646

INDIVIDUAL RECORDS—SINGLE SEASON

Category	Name	Performance
Rushing (Yds.)	Joe Morris, 1986	1,516
Passing (Yds.)	Phil Simms, 1984	4,044
Passing (TDs)	Y.A. Tittle, 1963	36
Receiving (No.)	Earnest Gray, 1983	78
Receiving (Yds.)	Homer Jones, 1967	1,209
Interceptions	Otto Schnellbacher, 1951	11
	Jim Patton, 1958	11
Punting (Avg.)	Don Chandler, 1959	46.6
Punt Return (Avg.)	Merle Hapes, 1942	15.5
Kickoff Return (Avg.)	John Salscheider, 1949	31.6
Field Goals	Ali Haji-Sheikh, 1983	35
Touchdowns (Tot.)	Joe Morris, 1985	21
Points	Ali Haji-Sheikh, 1983	127

INDIVIDUAL RECORDS—SINGLE GAME

Category	Name	Performance
Rushing (Yds.)	Gene Roberts, 11-12-50	218
Passing (Yds.)	Phil Simms, 10-13-85	513
Passing (TDs)	Y.A. Tittle, 10-28-62	*7
Receiving (No.)	Mark Bavaro, 10-13-85	12
Receiving (Yds.)	Del Shofner, 10-28-62	269
Interceptions	Many times	3
	Last time by Terry Kinard, 9-27-87	
Field Goals	Joe Danelo, 10-18-81	6
Touchdowns (Tot.)	Ron Johnson, 10-2-72	4
	Earnest Gray, 9-7-80	4
	Rodney Hampton, 9-24-95	4
Points	Ron Johnson, 10-2-72	24
	Earnest Gray, 9-7-80	24
	Rodney Hampton, 9-24-95	24

*NFL Record

COACHING HISTORY

(521-432-32)

1925	Bob Folwell	8-4-0
1926	Joe Alexander	8-4-1
1927-28	Earl Potteiger	15-8-3
1929-30	LeRoy Andrews*	24-5-1
1930	Benny Friedman	2-0-0
1930-53	Steve Owen	155-108-17
1954-60	Jim Lee Howell	55-29-4
1961-68	Allie Sherman	57-54-4
1969-73	Alex Webster	29-40-1
1974-76	Bill Arnsparger**	7-28-0
1976-78	John McVay	14-23-0
1979-82	Ray Perkins	24-35-0
1983-90	Bill Parcells	85-52-1
1991-92	Ray Handley	14-18-0
1993-95	Dan Reeves	26-24-0

*Released after 15 games in 1930
**Released after seven games in 1976

GIANTS STADIUM

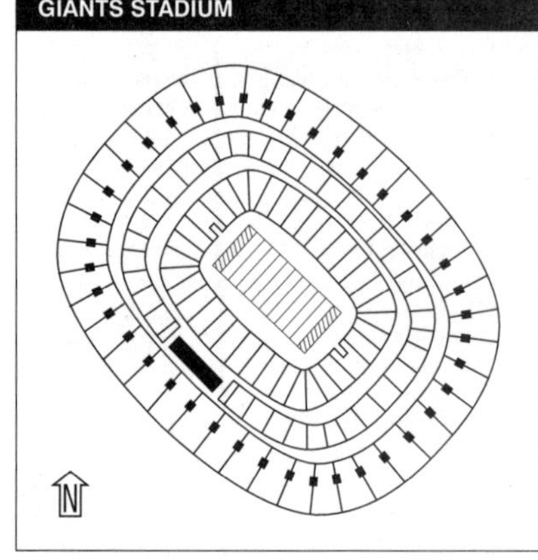

1995 TEAM RECORD

PRESEASON (3-1)

Date	Result		Opponents
8/6	W	19-13	at Cleveland
8/11	W	14-13	New Orleans
8/19	W	32-31	N.Y. Jets
8/26	L	3-6	at Carolina

REGULAR SEASON (5-11)

Date	Result		Opponents	Att.
9/4	L	0-35	Dallas	77,454
9/10	L	17-20	at Kansas City (OT)	77,962
9/17	L	6-14	at Green Bay	60,117
9/24	W	45-29	New Orleans	72,619
10/1	L	6-20	at San Francisco	65,536
10/8	W	27-21	Arizona (OT)	68,463
10/15	L	14-17	Philadelphia	74,252
10/29	W	24-15	at Washington	53,310
11/5	L	28-30	at Seattle	42,100
11/12	L	13-17	Oakland	71,160
11/19	L	19-28	at Philadelphia	63,562
11/26	L	24-27	Chicago	70,015
11/30	W	10-6	at Arizona	44,246
12/10	W	20-13	Washington	48,247
12/17	L	20-21	at Dallas	64,400
12/23	L	17-27	San Diego	50,243

(OT) Overtime

SCORE BY PERIODS

Giants	54	116	47	67	6	—	290
Opponents	81	105	53	98	3	—	340

ATTENDANCE

Home 532,453 Away 471,233 Total 1,003,686

Single-game home record, 77,454 (9/4/95)

Single-season home record, 608,706 (1992)

1995 TEAM STATISTICS

	Giants	Opp.
Total First Downs	288	335
Rushing	113	120
Passing	150	187
Penalty	25	28
Third Down: Made/Att	85/209	89/213
Third Down Pct.	40.7	41.8
Fourth Down: Made/Att	7/14	14/21
Fourth Down Pct.	50.0	66.7
Total Net Yards	4483	5293
Avg. Per Game	280.2	330.8
Total Plays	1003	1037
Avg. Per Play	4.5	5.1
Net Yards Rushing	1833	2109
Avg. Per Game	114.6	131.8
Total Rushes	478	500
Net Yards Passing	2650	3184
Avg. Per Game	165.6	199.0
Sacked/Yards Lost	46/213	29/177
Gross Yards	2863	3361
Att./Completions	479/260	508/299
Completion Pct.	54.3	58.9
Had Intercepted	13	16
Punts/Avg.	73/42.2	63/42.2
Net Punting Avg.	73/35.9	63/36.5
Penalties/Yards Lost	92/772	94/662
Fumbles/Ball Lost	27/15	29/15
Touchdowns	33	37
Rushing	17	17
Passing	11	17
Returns	5	3
Avg. Time of Possession	29:23	30:37

1995 INDIVIDUAL STATISTICS

PASSING	Att.	Comp.	Yds.	Pct.	TD	Int.	Tkld.	Rate
Brown	456	254	2814	55.7	11	10	44/206	73.1
Maddox	23	6	49	26.1	0	3	2/7	0.0
Giants	479	260	2863	54.3	11	13	46/213	68.6
Opponents	508	299	3361	58.9	17	16	29/177	76.7

SCORING	TD R	TD P	TD Rt	PAT	FG	Saf	PTS
Daluiso	0	0	0	28/28	20/28	0	88
Hampton	10	0	0	0/0	0/0	0	62
Brown	4	0	0	0/0	0/0	0	24
Sherrard	0	4	0	0/0	0/0	0	24
Calloway	0	3	0	0/0	0/0	0	18
Wheatley	3	0	0	0/0	0/0	0	18
Lewis	0	1	1	0/0	0/0	0	12
Armstead	0	0	1	0/0	0/0	0	6
Douglas	0	0	1	0/0	0/0	0	6
Glenn	0	0	1	0/0	0/0	0	6
Marshall	0	1	0	0/0	0/0	0	6
Walker	0	1	0	0/0	0/0	0	6
Way	0	1	0	0/0	0/0	0	6
Wooten	0	0	1	0/0	0/0	0	6
Strahan	0	0	0	0/0	0/0	1	2
Giants	17	11	5	28/28	20/28	1	290
Opponents	17	17	3	32/33	28/35	0	340

2-Point conversions: Hampton. Team: 1-4.

RUSHING	Att.	Yds.	Avg.	LG	TD
Hampton	306	1182	3.9	32	10
Wheatley	78	245	3.1	19t	3
Brown	45	228	5.1	23	4
Walker	31	126	4.1	36	0
Elias	10	44	4.4	8	0
Pierce	1	6	6.0	6	0
Way	2	6	3.0	6	0
Maddox	1	4	4.0	4	0
Marshall	1	1	1.0	1	0
Horan	1	0	0.0	0	0
Calloway	2	-9	-4.5	-3	0
Giants	478	1833	3.8	36	17
Opponents	500	2109	4.2	60t	17

RECEIVING	No.	Yds.	Avg.	LG	TD
Calloway	56	796	14.2	49	3
Sherrard	44	577	13.1	57t	4
Pierce	33	310	9.4	26	0
Walker	31	234	7.5	34	1
Hampton	24	142	5.9	18	0
Cross	18	197	10.9	26	0
Marshall	17	195	11.5	27	1
Lewis	12	208	17.3	46t	1
Elias	9	69	7.7	18	0
Way	7	76	10.9	34	1
Wheatley	5	27	5.4	16	0
Kozlowski	2	17	8.5	12	0
Douglas	2	15	7.5	11	0
Giants	260	2863	11.0	57t	11
Opponents	299	3361	11.2	47	17

INTERCEPTIONS	No.	Yds.	Avg.	LG	TD
Glenn	5	91	18.2	75t	1
Sparks	5	11	2.2	6	0
Strahan	2	56	28.0	56	0
Randolph	2	15	7.5	15	0
Armstead	1	58	58.0	58t	1
Wooten	1	38	38.0	38	0
Giants	16	269	16.8	75t	2
Opponents	13	241	18.5	99t	1

PUNTING	No.	Yds.	Avg.	In 20	LG
Horan	72	3063	42.5	15	60
Brown	1	15	15.0	0	15
Giants	73	3078	42.2	15	60
Opponents	63	2660	42.2	18	61

PUNT RETURNS	No.	FC	Yds.	Avg.	LG	TD
Harrell	12	3	76	6.3	17	0
Marshall	12	7	96	8.0	21	0
Lewis	6	0	46	7.7	14	0
Young	1	0	0	0.0	0	0
Giants	31	10	218	7.0	21	0
Opponents	34	12	297	8.7	89t	1

KICKOFF RETURNS	No.	Yds.	Avg.	LG	TD
Walker	41	881	21.5	67	0
Wheatley	10	186	18.6	32	0
Lewis	9	257	28.6	91t	1
Kozlowski	5	75	15.0	17	0
Douglas	1	13	13.0	13	0
Harrell	1	23	23.0	23	0
Way	1	8	8.0	8	0
Widmer	1	0	0.0	0	0
Zatechka	1	5	5.0	5	0
Giants	70	1448	20.7	91t	1
Opponents	54	1129	20.9	54	0

SACKS	No.
Strahan	7.5
Harris	5.0
Duff	4.0
Rudolph	4.0
Hamilton	2.0
Agnew	1.0
Brooks	1.0
Croel	1.0
Dillard	1.0
Douglass	1.0
Armstead	0.5
Giants	29.0
Opponents	46.0

1996 DRAFT CHOICES

Round	Name	Pos.	College
1	Cedric Jones	DE	Oklahoma
2	Amani Toomer	WR	Michigan
3	Roman Oben	T	Louisville
4	Danny Kanell	QB	Florida State
6	Doug Colman	LB	Nebraska
	Scott Galyon	LB	Tennessee
7	Conrad Hamilton	DB	Eastern New Mexico

NEW YORK GIANTS

1996 VETERAN ROSTER

No.		Name	Pos.	Ht.	Wt.	Birthdate	NFL Exp.	College	Hometown	How Acq.	'95 Games/ Starts
93		Agnew, Ray	DT	6-3	285	12/9/67	7	North Carolina State	Winston-Salem, N.C.	FA-'95	16/15
69		Allen, Derek	C	6-4	305	1/30/71	2	Illinois	Geneseo, Ill.	FA-'95	1/0
98		Armstead, Jessie	LB	6-1	232	10/26/70	4	Miami	Dallas, Tex.	D8-'93	16/2
21	†	Beamon, Willie	CB	5-11	184	6/14/70	4	Northern Iowa	Riviera Beach, Fla.	FA-'93	16/0
78		Bishop, Greg	T	6-5	300	5/2/71	4	Pacific	Lodi, Calif.	D4-'93	16/16
77		Bratzke, Chad	DE	6-4	273	9/15/71	3	Eastern Kentucky	Brandon, Fla.	D5-'94	6/0
17		Brown, Dave	QB	6-5	223	2/25/70	5	Duke	Westfield, N.J.	SD1-'92	16/16
55		Buckley, Marcus	LB	6-3	240	2/3/71	4	Texas A&M	Ft. Worth, Tex.	D3-'93	16/5
80		Calloway, Chris	WR	5-10	191	3/29/68	7	Michigan	Chicago, Ill.	FA-'92	16/15
37		Campbell, Jesse	S	6-1	215	4/11/69	6	North Carolina State	Vanceboro, N.C.	FA-'92	16/16
51	#	Croel, Mike	LB	6-3	235	6/6/69	6	Nebraska	Detroit, Mich.	FA-'95	16/14
87		Cross, Howard	TE	6-5	265	8/8/67	8	Alabama	Huntsville, Ala.	D6-'89	15/15
3		Daluiso, Brad	K	6-2	210	12/31/67	6	UCLA	San Diego, Calif.	FA-'93	16/0
62		Davis, Scott	G	6-3	292	1/29/70	4	Iowa	Glenwood, Iowa	D6-'93	0*
71		Dillard, Stacey	DT	6-5	290	9/17/68	5	Oklahoma	Clarksville, Tex.	D6-'92	15/3
82		Douglas, Omar	WR	5-10	182	6/3/72	3	Minnesota	New Orleans, La.	FA-'94	8/1
24		Douglass, Maurice	S	5-11	210	2/12/64	10	Kentucky	Dayton, Ohio	UFA(Chi)-'95	8/0
96		Duff, Jamal	DE	6-7	271	3/11/72	2	San Diego State	Tustin, Calif.	D6a-'95	15/2
20		Elias, Keith	RB	5-9	203	2/3/72	3	Princeton	Lacey Township, N.J.	FA-'94	15/0
25		Glenn, Vencie	S	6-0	205	10/26/64	11	Indiana State	Silver Spring, Md.	T(Minn)-'95	15/15
74		Gragg, Scott	T	6-8	325	2/28/72	2	Montana	Silverton, Ore.	D2-'95	13/0
75		Hamilton, Keith	DE	6-6	285	5/25/71	5	Pittsburgh	Lynchburg, Va.	D4-'92	14/14
27		Hampton, Rodney	RB	5-11	230	4/3/69	7	Georgia	Houston, Tex.	D1-'90	16/15
89		Harrell, Gary	WR	5-7	170	1/23/72	2	Howard	Miami, Fla.	FA-'95	4/0
97		Harris, Robert	DE	6-4	295	6/13/69	5	Southern	Riviera Beach, Fla.	RFA(Minn)-'95	15/15
2		Horan, Mike	P	5-11	192	2/1/59	12	Long Beach State	Orange, Calif.	FA-'93	16/0
85		Kozlowski, Brian	TE	6-3	255	10/4/70	3	Connecticut	Rochester, N.Y.	FA-'94	16/0
81		Lewis, Thomas	WR	6-1	195	1/10/72	3	Indiana	Akron, Ohio	D1-'94	8/2
12		Maddox, Tommy	QB	6-4	218	9/2/71	5	UCLA	Hurst, Tex.	FA-'95	16/0
86	#	Marshall, Arthur	WR	5-11	186	4/29/69	5	Georgia	Hephzibah, Ga.	T(Den)-'94	15/0
57		Miller, Corey	LB	6-2	245	10/25/68	6	South Carolina	Pageland, S.C.	D6-'91	14/9
84		Pierce, Aaron	TE	6-5	250	9/6/69	5	Washington	Seattle, Wash.	D3-'92	16/11
23		Randolph, Thomas	CB	5-9	178	10/5/70	3	Kansas State	Norfolk, Va.	D2a-'94	16/16
66		Reynolds, Jerry	G-T	6-6	315	4/2/70	3	Nevada-Las Vegas	Ft. Thomas, Ky.	FA-'95	0*
72		Riesenberg, Doug	T	6-5	288	7/22/65	10	California	Moscow, Idaho	D6a-'87	16/16
91		Rudolph, Coleman	DE	6-4	262	10/22/70	4	Georgia Tech	Valdosta, Ga.	FA-'94	16/0
67		Schreiber, Adam	C	6-4	298	2/20/62	12	Texas	Galveston, Tex.	FA-'94	16/0
31		Sehorn, Jason	S	6-2	210	4/15/71	3	Southern California	Mt. Shasta, Calif.	D2b-'94	14/0
61		Smith, Lance	G	6-3	282	1/1/63	12	Louisiana State	Kannapolis, N.C.	UFA(Ariz)-'94	13/13
22		Sparks, Phillippi	CB	5-11	190	4/15/69	5	Arizona State	Glendale, Calif.	D2-'92	16/16
65		Stone, Ron	G-T	6-5	325	7/20/71	4	Boston College	Roxbury, Mass.	RFA(Dall)-'96	16/1*
92	†	Strahan, Michael	DE	6-4	268	11/21/71	4	Texas Southern	Westbury, Tex.	D2-'93	15/15
54		Talley, Ben	LB	6-3	245	7/14/72	2	Tennessee	Griffin, Ga.	D4b-'95	4/0
34		Walker, Herschel	RB	6-1	225	3/3/62	11	Georgia	Wrightsville, Ga.	FA-'95	16/3
30		Way, Charles	RB	6-0	245	12/27/72	2	Virginia	Philadelphia, Pa.	D6b-'95	16/4
28		Wheatley, Tyrone	RB	6-0	228	1/19/72	2	Michigan	Inkster, Mich.	D1-'95	13/1
8		White, Stan	QB	6-2	218	8/14/71	3	Auburn	Birmingham, Ala.	FA-'94	0*
90		Widmer, Corey	LB	6-3	250	12/25/68	5	Montana State	Bozeman, Mont.	D7-'92	16/0
59		Williams, Brian	C	6-5	300	6/8/66	8	Minnesota	Mt. Lebanon, Pa.	D1-'89	16/16
29		Wooten, Tito	S	6-0	195	12/12/71	3	Northeast Louisiana	Goldsboro, N.C.	SD4-'94	16/3
47		Young, Rodney	S	6-1	212	1/25/73	2	Louisiana State	Grambling, La.	D3-'95	10/0
73		Zatechka, Rob	G	6-4	315	12/1/71	2	Nebraska	Lincoln, Neb.	D4a-'95	16/3

* Davis missed '95 season because of injury; Reynolds active for 4 games but did not play; Stone played 16 games with Dallas; White active for 1 game but did not play.

\# Unrestricted free agent; subject to developments.

† Restricted free agent; subject to developments.

Players lost through free agency (3): LB Michael Brooks (Det; 16 games in '95), T John Elliot (NYJ; 16), WR Mike Sherrard (Den; 13).

Also played with Giants in '95—S Tim Watson (1 game).

COACHING STAFF

Head Coach,
Dan Reeves

Pro Career: Head coach Dan Reeves suffered through a losing season in 1995 for only the third time in his 30 years in professional football. It was a frustrating season for Reeves and the Giants. The 1995 Giants lost seven games that were decided on the final drive of the game. In six of those games, the Giants were either tied or leading at some point in the fourth quarter. Reeves followed each of his previous two losing seasons with playoff berths. The last time that a Reeves-coached team finished with a losing record was 1990 when the Denver Broncos went 5-11. Reeves helped the Broncos rebound the following year by leading them to a 12-4 record and a berth in the AFC Championship Game. With the retirement of Miami's Don Shula, Reeves with 143 career victoriers now is the winningest active coach in the NFL. Shula retired with 347 career victories. Buffalo's Marv Levy is the second-winningest active coach with 138 victories. The Giants' win over Arizona on October 8, 1995, was Reeves' 132nd regular-season victory, which gave him sole possesion of tenth place in NFL history. Former Giants head coach Steve Owen is in ninth place with 151 victories. General Manager George Young named Reeves the fourteenth head coach of the New York Giants on January 27, 1993. Reeves quickly proved just what kind of winner he is when he was named the *Associated Press* Coach of the Year after helping turn the Giants' 1992 record of 6-10 into a playoff-qualifying 11-5 mark in 1993, the best-ever record for a first-year Giants coach. He became just the second head coach in Giants' history to lead his team to the playoffs in his first season. Following a 3-0 start in 1994, the Giants suffered through a seven-game losing streak, the longest of Reeves' NFL career. In what many say may have been his best coaching job ever, Reeves and his coaching staff managed to keep the team together as the Giants won their final six games to get back into playoff contention and finish the year with a 9-7 record. Reeves came to the Giants after spending 12 years as head coach of the Denver Broncos, where he produced five first-place finishes in the AFC Western Division, three Super Bowl appearances, and four AFC Championship Game appearances. He also led Denver to seven 10-victory seasons in his 12 years. Until he was named head coach in Denver, Reeves had been a member of the Dallas coaching staff since 1970 when he spent two seasons as a player coach. In 1977, he was named offensive coordinator on Tom Landry's staff. Reeves began his football career as a free-agent running back for Dallas in 1965. Reeves has played or coached in a record eight Super Bowls. He has participated in 45 NFL postseason games, 15 games as head coach, 16 as an assistant, 6 as a player-coach, and 8 as a player. Career record: 143-103-1.

Background: Quarterback at South Carolina from 1962-64. He was inducted into the school's Hall of Fame in 1978.

Personal: Born January 19, 1944, Americus, Ga. Dan and his wife, Pam, live in Hohokus, N.J., and have three children—Dana, Laura, and Lee.

ASSISTANT COACHES

Don Blackmon, linebackers; born March 14, 1958, Pompano Beach, Fla., lives in Morristown, N.J. Linebacker Tulsa 1977-80. Pro linebacker New England Patriots 1981-87. Pro coach: New England Patriots 1988-90, Cleveland Browns 1991-92, joined Giants in 1993.

Dave Brazil, defensive quality control; born March 25, 1936, Detroit, Mich., lives in East Rutherford, N.J. No college or pro playing experience. College coach: Holy Cross 1968, Tulsa 1969-70, Eastern Michigan 1971-73, Boston College 1980, Kent State 1981-82. Pro coach: Detroit Wheels (WFL) 1974, Chicago Wind (WFL) 1975, Kansas City Chiefs 1984-88, Pittsburgh Steelers 1989-91, joined Giants in 1992.

James Daniel, tight ends; born January 17, 1953, Wetumpka, Ala., lives in Clifton, N.J. Offensive guard Alabama State 1970-73. No pro playing experience. College coach: Auburn 1981-92. Pro coach: Joined Giants in 1993.

Steve DeBerg, quarterbacks; born January 19, 1954, Oakland, Calif., lives in East Rutherford, N.J. Quarterback San Jose State 1974-1977. Pro quarterback San Francisco 49ers 1978-80, Denver Broncos 1981-83, Tampa Bay Buccaneers 1984-87, Kansas City Chiefs 1988-1991, Tampa Bay Buccaneers 1992, Miami Dolphins 1993. Pro coach: Joined Giants in 1995.

Joe DeCamillis, special teams; born June 29, 1965, Arvada, Colo., lives in Morris Township, N.J. Wrestler Wyoming 1983-87. No pro playing experience. College coach: Wyoming 1988. Pro coach: Denver Broncos 1989-92, joined Giants 1993.

Kerry Goode, assistant strength and conditioning; born July 28, 1965, Town Creek, Ala., lives in Mahwah, N.J. Tailback Alabama 1983-87. Pro running back Tampa Bay Buccaneers 1988, Denver Broncos 1989, Miami Dolphins 1990. Pro coach: Joined Giants in 1993.

George Henshaw, offensive coordinator; born January 22, 1948, Midlothian, Va., lives in Smoke Rise, N.J. Defensive tackle West Virginia 1967-69. No pro playing experience. College coach: West Virginia 1970-75, Florida State 1976-82, Alabama 1983-86, Tulsa 1987 (head coach). Pro coach: Denver Broncos 1988-92, joined Giants in 1993.

Earl Leggett, defensive line, born March 5, 1935, Jacksonville, Fla., lives in Randolph, N.J. Tackle Hinds J.C. 1953-54, Louisiana State 1955-56. Pro defensive tackle Chicago Bears 1957-65, Los Angeles Rams 1966, New Orleans Saints 1967-68. College coach: Nicholls State 1971, Texas Christian 1972-73. Pro coach: Southern California Sun (WFL) 1974-75, Seattle Seahawks 1976-77, San Francisco 49ers 1978, Oakland/Los Angeles Raiders 1980-88, Denver Broncos 1989-92, joined Giants in 1993.

Pete Mangurian, offensive line; born June 17, 1955, Los Angeles, Calif., lives in Denville, N.J. Defensive lineman Louisiana State 1975-78. No pro playing experience. College coach: Southern Methodist 1979-80, New Mexico State 1981, Stanford 1982-83, Louisiana State 1984-87. Pro coach: Denver Broncos 1988-92, joined Giants in 1993.

Al Miller, strength and conditioning; born August 29, 1947, El Dorado, Ark., lives in Randolph, N.J. Wide receiver Northeast Louisiana 1965-69. No pro playing experience. College coach: Northwestern Louisiana 1974-78, Mississippi State 1980. Northeast Louisiana 1981, Alabama 1982-84. Pro coach: Denver Broncos 1987-92, joined Giants in 1993.

Mike Nolan, defensive coordinator, born March 7, 1959, Baltimore, Md., lives in Chatham, N.J. Safety Oregon 1977-80. No pro playing experience. College coach: Stanford 1982-83, Rice 1984-85, Louisiana State 1986. Pro coach: Denver Broncos 1987-92, joined Giants in 1993.

Dick Rehbein, wide receivers; born November 22, 1955, Green Bay, Wis., lives in Wayne, N.J. Center Ripon 1973-77. No pro playing experience. Pro coach: Green Bay Packers 1979-83, Los Angeles Express (USFL) 1984, Minnesota Vikings 1984-91, joined Giants in 1992.

George Sefcik, running backs, born December 27, 1939, Cleveland, Ohio, lives in Cranford, N.J. Halfback Notre Dame 1959-61. No pro playing experience. College coach: Notre Dame 1963-68, Kentucky 1969-72. Pro coach: Baltimore Colts 1973-74, Cleveland Browns 1975-77, 1989-90, Cincinnati Bengals 1978-83, Green Bay Packers 1984-87, Kansas City Chiefs 1988, joined Giants in 1991.

Zaven Yaralian, defensive backs, born February 5, 1952, lives in Mountain Lakes, N.J. Defensive back Nebraska 1972-73. Pro defensive back Green Bay Packers 1974, Philadelphia Bell (WFL) 1975. College coach: Nebraska 1975, Washington State 1976-77, Missouri 1978-83, Florida 1984-87, Colorado 1988-89. Pro coach: Chicago Bears 1990-92, joined Giants in 1993.

1996 FIRST-YEAR ROSTER

Name	Pos.	Ht.	Wt.	Birthdate	College	Hometown	How Acq.
Alcorn, Daron (1)	K	6-3	234	5/12/71	Akron	Vancouver, Wash.	FA
Alexander, Kevin	WR	5-9	184	1/23/75	Utah State	Phoenix, Ariz.	FA
Burkett, Jeremy (1)	RB	6-1	215	4/15/73	Colorado State	Denver, Colo.	FA
Colman, Doug	LB	6-2	252	6/4/73	Nebraska	Somers Point, N.J.	D6a
Dammann, Ken (1)	G	6-4	300	1/17/72	Rutgers	Little Silver, N.J.	FA
Ellsworth, Percy	S	6-2	199	10/19/74	Virginia	Drewryville, Va.	FA
Galyon, Scott	LB	6-2	237	3/23/74	Tennessee	Seymour, Tenn.	D6b
Gilliard, Darnell	DT	6-5	304	3/24/73	Troy State	Anderson, S.C.	FA
Grenier, Geoff	RB	6-2	240	1/25/73	Oklahoma State	Fullerton, Calif.	FA
Hamilton, Conrad	CB	5-10	184	11/5/74	Eastern New Mexico	Alamogordo, N.M.	D7
Holsey, Bernard	DT	6-2	284	12/10/73	Duke	Cave Spring, Ga.	FA
Jones, Cedric	DE	6-4	275	4/30/74	Oklahoma	Houston, Tex.	D1
Kanell, Danny	QB	6-3	222	11/21/73	Florida State	Ft. Lauderdale, Fla.	D4
Kennedy, Chris	G	6-4	285	4/26/73	Rutgers	Downingtown, Pa.	FA
Oben, Roman	T	6-4	297	10/9/72	Louisville	Washington, D.C.	D3
Phillips, Micah	S	5-10	189	4/14/73	Southern California	Dallas, Tex.	FA
Regular, Moses	LB	6-3	255	10/30/71	Missouri Valley	Kissimmee, Fla.	FA
Rodgers, Jeff (1)	LB	6-3	247	6/10/71	Texas A&M-Kingsville	Lufkin, Tex.	FA
Saxton, Brian (1)	TE	6-6	256	3/13/72	Boston College	Whippany, N.J.	FA
Sensley, Tim	CB	5-9	165	1/15/73	S.W. Louisiana	Baton Rouge, La.	FA
Sparks, Kenyatta	WR	5-8	185	8/24/73	Southern	New Orleans, La.	FA
Stinson, Jason	C	6-4	289	9/16/72	Louisville	Louisville, Ky.	FA
Stonehouse, John	P	5-11	234	1/16/74	Southern California	Los Angeles, Calif.	FA
Stretz, Grady	DT	6-5	278	11/8/72	UCLA	Tempe, Ariz.	FA
Toomer, Amani	WR	6-3	202	9/8/74	Michigan	Berkeley, Calif.	D2
Walker, Robert	RB	5-10	197	6/26/72	West Virginia	Huntington, W.Va.	FA
Washington, Mark	S	5-9	180	4/16/73	Rutgers	Temple Hills, Md.	FA
Yeaman, Todd (1)	DT	6-5	298	1/7/71	Northeast Oklahoma	Ft. Worth, Tex.	FA

The term NFL Rookie is defined as a player who is in his first season of professional football and has not been on the roster of another professional football team for any regular-season or postseason games. A Rookie is designated by an "R" on NFL rosters. Players who have been active in another professional football league or players who have NFL experience, including either preseason training camp or being on an Active List or Inactive List, or on Reserve/Injured or Reserve/Physically Unable to Perform for fewer than six regular-season games, are termed NFL First-Year Players. An NFL First-Year Player is designated by a "1" on NFL rosters. Thereafter, a player is credited with an additional year of experience for each season in which he accumulates six games on the Active List or Inactive List, or on Reserve/Injured or Reserve/Physically Unable to Perform.

PHILADELPHIA EAGLES

National Football Conference
Eastern Division
Team Colors: Midnight Green, Silver, Black, and White
Veterans Stadium
3501 South Broad Street
Philadelphia, Pennsylvania 19148
Telephone: (215) 463-2500

CLUB OFFICIALS

Owner/Chief Executive Officer: Jeffrey Lurie
Senior Vice President-Administration: Joe Banner
Senior Vice President-Chief Financial Officer: Mimi Box
Vice President-Sales and Marketing: Len Komoroski
Vice President of Sales: Vic Gregovits
Director of Football Operations: Dick Daniels
Executive Direcotor of Eagles Youth Partnership: Sarah Helfman
Director of Pro Scouting: Chuck Banker
Director of College Scouting: John Wooten
Director of Administration: Vicki Chatley
Director of Corporate Sales: Scott O'Neil
Director of Public Relations: Ron Howard
Assistant Director of Public Relations: Derek Boyko
Ticket Manager: Leo Carlin
Office Manager/Traveling Secretary: Andrea Minassian
Director of Advertising and Promotions: Christine Callabrese
Assistant Director of Penthouse Sales: Ken Iman
Director of Penthouse Operations: Christiana Noyalas
Trainer: James Collins
Assistant Trainer: Scottie Patton
Peak Performance Specialist: Baron Baptiste
Video Director: Mike Dougherty
Equipment Manager: Rusty Sweeney
Stadium: Veterans Stadium • **Capacity:** 64,899
3501 South Broad Street
Philadelphia, Pennsylvania 19148
Playing Surface: AstroTurf-8
Training Camp: Lehigh University
Bethlehem, Pennsylvania 18015

1996 SCHEDULE

PRESEASON

Aug. 3	at Baltimore	7:30
Aug. 8	**New York Jets**	7:30
Aug. 18	at New England	1:00
Aug. 23	**Pittsburgh**	7:30

REGULAR SEASON

Sept. 1	at Washington	1:00
Sept. 9	at Green Bay (Mon.)	8:00
Sept. 15	**Detroit**	1:00
Sept. 22	at Atlanta	8:00
Sept. 30	**Dallas** (Mon.)	9:00
Oct. 6	Open Date	
Oct. 13	at New York Giants	4:00
Oct. 20	**Miami**	1:00
Oct. 27	**Carolina**	1:00
Nov. 3	at Dallas	12:00
Nov. 10	**Buffalo**	1:00
Nov. 17	**Washington**	1:00
Nov. 24	at Arizona	2:00
Dec. 1	**New York Giants**	1:00
Dec. 5	at Indianapolis (Thurs.)	8:00
Dec. 14	at New York Jets (Sat.)	12:30
Dec. 22	**Arizona**	1:00

RECORD HOLDERS

INDIVIDUAL RECORDS—CAREER

Category	Name	Performance
Rushing (Yds.)	Wilbert Montgomery, 1977-1984	6,538
Passing (Yds.)	Ron Jaworski, 1977-1986	26,963
Passing (TDs)	Ron Jaworski, 1977-1986	175
Receiving (No.)	Harold Carmichael, 1971-1983	589
Receiving (Yds.)	Harold Carmichael, 1971-1983	8,978
Interceptions	Bill Bradley, 1969-1976	34
Punting (Avg.)	Joe Muha, 1946-1950	42.9
Punt Return (Avg.)	Steve Van Buren, 1944-1951	13.9
Kickoff Return (Avg.)	Steve Van Buren, 1944-1951	26.7
Field Goals	Paul McFadden, 1984-87	91
Touchdowns (Tot.)	Harold Carmichael, 1971-1983	79
Points	Bobby Walston, 1951-1962	881

INDIVIDUAL RECORDS—SINGLE SEASON

Category	Name	Performance
Rushing (Yds.)	Wilbert Montgomery, 1979	1,512
Passing (Yds.)	Randall Cunningham, 1988	3,808
Passing (TDs)	Sonny Jurgensen, 1961	32
Receiving (No.)	Keith Jackson, 1988	81
	Keith Byars, 1990	81
Receiving (Yds.)	Mike Quick, 1983	1,409
Interceptions	Bill Bradley, 1971	11
Punting (Avg.)	Joe Muha, 1948	47.2
Punt Return (Avg.)	Steve Van Buren, 1944	15.3
Kickoff Return (Avg.)	Al Nelson, 1972	29.1
Field Goals	Paul McFadden, 1984	30
Touchdowns (Tot.)	Steve Van Buren, 1945	18
Points	Paul McFadden, 1984	116

INDIVIDUAL RECORDS—SINGLE GAME

Category	Name	Performance
Rushing (Yds.)	Steve Van Buren, 11-27-49	205
Passing (Yds.)	Randall Cunningham, 9-17-89	447
Passing (TDs)	Adrian Burk, 10-17-54	*7
Receiving (No.)	Don Looney, 12-1-40	14
Receiving (Yds.)	Tommy McDonald, 12-10-60	237
Interceptions	Russ Craft, 9-24-50	*4
Field Goals	Tom Dempsey, 11-12-72	6
Touchdowns (Tot.)	Many times	4
	Last time by Wilbert Montgomery, 10-7-79	
Points	Bobby Walston, 10-17-54	25

*NFL Record

COACHING HISTORY

(381-450-24)

1933-35	Lud Wray	9-21-1
1936-40	Bert Bell	10-44-2
1941-50	Earle (Greasy) Neale*	66-44-5
1951	Alvin (Bo) McMillin**	2-0-0
1951	Wayne Millner	2-8-0
1952-55	Jim Trimble	25-20-3
1956-57	Hugh Devore	7-16-1
1958-60	Lawrence (Buck) Shaw	20-16-1
1961-63	Nick Skorich	15-24-3
1964-68	Joe Kuharich	28-41-1
1969-71	Jerry Williams***	7-22-2
1971-72	Ed Khayat	8-15-2
1973-75	Mike McCormack	16-25-1
1976-82	Dick Vermeil	57-51-0
1983-85	Marion Campbell****	17-29-1
1985	Fred Bruney	1-0-0
1986-90	Buddy Ryan	43-38-1
1991-94	Rich Kotite	37-29-0
1995	Ray Rhodes	11-7

*Co-coach with Walt Kiesling in Philadelphia-Pittsburgh merger in 1943
**Retired after two games in 1951
***Released after three games in 1971
****Released after 15 games in 1985

VETERANS STADIUM

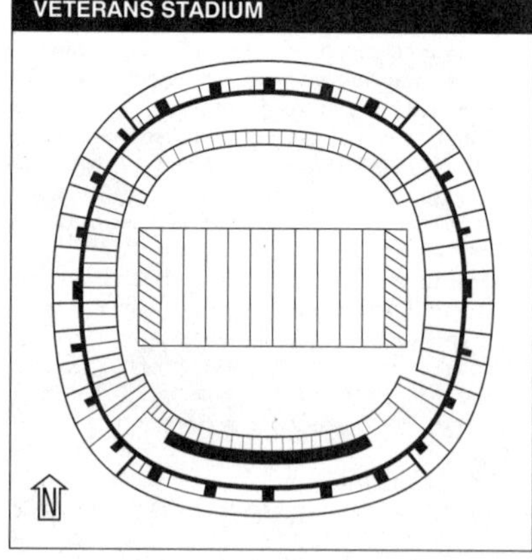

1995 TEAM RECORD

PRESEASON (4-0)

Date	Result		Opponents
8/5	W	25-17	Atlanta
8/12	W	13-10	vs. N.Y. Jets in Jackson, Miss.
8/17	W	31-7	New England
8/24	W	16-6	at Pittsburgh

REGULAR SEASON (10-6)

Date	Result		Opponents	Att.
9/3	L	6-21	Tampa Bay	66,266
9/10	W	31-19	at Arizona	45,004
9/17	L	21-27	San Diego	63,081
9/24	L	17-48	at Oakland	48,875
10/1	W	15-10	at New Orleans	43,938
10/8	W	37-34	Washington (OT)	65,498
10/15	W	17-14	at N.Y. Giants	74,252
10/29	W	20-9	St. Louis	62,172
11/6	L	12-34	at Dallas	64,876
11/12	W	31-13	Denver	60,842
11/19	W	28-19	N.Y. Giants	63,562
11/26	W	14-7	at Washington	50,539
12/3	L	14-26	at Seattle	39,893
12/10	W	20-17	Dallas	66,198
12/17	W	21-20	Arizona	62,076
12/24	L	14-20	at Chicago	52,391

POSTSEASON (1-1)

Date	Result		Opponents	Att.
12/30	W	58-37	Detroit	66,099
1/7	L	11-30	at Dallas	64,371

(OT) Overtime

SCORE BY PERIODS

Eagles	83	99	55	78	3	—	318
Opponents	71	101	59	107	0	—	338

ATTENDANCE

Home 509,695 Away 419,768 Total 929,463
Single-game home record, 72,111 (11/1/81)
Single-season home record, 557,325 (1980)

1995 TEAM STATISTICS

	Eagles	Opp.
Total First Downs	290	281
Rushing	126	102
Passing	145	154
Penalty	19	25
Third Down: Made/Att	89/233	84/220
Third Down Pct.	38.2	38.2
Fourth Down: Made/Att	10/17	12/17
Fourth Down Pct.	58.8	70.6
Total Net Yards	4807	4638
Avg. Per Game	300.4	289.9
Total Plays	1050	1013
Avg. Per Play	4.6	4.6
Net Yards Rushing	2121	1822
Avg. Per Game	132.6	113.9
Total Rushes	508	466
Net Yards Passing	2686	2816
Avg. Per Game	167.9	176.0
Sacked/Yards Lost	46/245	48/305
Gross Yards	2931	3121
Att./Completions	496/284	499/268
Completion Pct.	57.3	53.7
Had Intercepted	19	19
Punts/Avg.	86/42.8	74/41.3
Net Punting Avg.	86/33.7	74/35.2
Penalties/Yards Lost	112/838	87/727
Fumbles/Ball Lost	31/17	30/19
Touchdowns	36	36
Rushing	19	14
Passing	11	14
Returns	6	8
Avg. Time of Possession	30:26	29:34

1995 INDIVIDUAL STATISTICS

PASSING	Att.	Comp.	Yds.	Pct.	TD	Int.	Tkld.	Rate
Peete	375	215	2326	57.3	8	14	33/166	67.3
Cunningham	121	69	605	57.0	3	5	13/79	61.5
Eagles	496	284	2931	57.3	11	19	46/245	65.9
Opponents	499	268	3121	53.7	14	19	48/305	66.4

SCORING	TD R	TD P	TD Rt	PAT	FG	Saf	PTS
Anderson	0	0	0	32/33	22/30	0	98
Watters	11	1	0	0/0	0/0	0	72
Garner	6	0	0	0/0	0/0	0	36
Barnett	0	5	0	0/0	0/0	0	32
C. Williams	0	2	0	0/0	0/0	0	14
R. Johnson	0	2	0	0/0	0/0	0	12
Henderson	0	0	1	0/0	0/0	0	6
Jackson	0	0	1	0/0	0/0	0	6
K. Johnson	0	0	1	0/0	0/0	0	6
McCrary	1	0	0	0/0	0/0	0	6
Peete	1	0	0	0/0	0/0	0	6
Thomas	0	0	1	0/0	0/0	0	6
West	0	1	0	0/0	0/0	0	6
Witherspoon	0	0	1	0/0	0/0	0	6
Zordich	0	0	1	0/0	0/0	0	6
Eagles	19	11	6	32/33	22/30	0	318
Opponents	14	14	8	32/32	28/37	1	338

2-Point conversions: Barnett, C. Williams. Team: 0-2.

RUSHING	Att.	Yds.	Avg.	LG	TD
Watters	337	1273	3.8	57	11
Garner	108	588	5.4	55t	6
Peete	32	147	4.6	18	1
Cunningham	21	98	4.7	20	0
Turner	2	9	4.5	12	0
Witherspoon	2	7	3.5	5	0
McCrary	3	1	0.3	1t	1
Hutton	1	0	0.0	0	0
Saxon	1	0	0.0	0	0
C. Williams	1	-2	-2.0	-2	0
Eagles	508	2121	4.2	57	19
Opponents	466	1822	3.9	44t	14

RECEIVING	No.	Yds.	Avg.	LG	TD
C. Williams	63	768	12.2	37t	2
Watters	62	434	7.0	24	1
Barnett	48	585	12.2	33	5
Carpenter	29	318	11.0	29	0
West	20	190	9.5	26	1
Martin	17	206	12.1	22	0
Garner	10	61	6.1	29	0
McCrary	9	60	6.7	11	0
Monk	6	114	19.0	36	0
J. Johnson	6	37	6.2	9	0
R. Johnson	5	68	13.6	33	2
Jones	5	61	12.2	17	0
Turner	4	29	7.3	11	0
Eagles	284	2931	10.3	37t	11
Opponents	268	3121	11.6	64t	14

INTERCEPTIONS	No.	Yds.	Avg.	LG	TD
Thomas	7	104	14.9	37t	1
McMillian	3	27	9.0	19	0
Taylor	2	52	26.0	35	0
Romanowski	2	5	2.5	7	0
Gouveia	1	20	20.0	20	0
Jackson	1	18	18.0	18	0
Zordich	1	10	10.0	10	0
Frazier	1	3	3.0	3	0
Wilburn	1	0	0.0	0	0
Eagles	19	239	12.6	37t	1
Opponents	19	240	12.6	65t	2

PUNTING	No.	Yds.	Avg.	In 20	LG
Hutton	85	3682	43.3	20	63
Eagles	86	3682	42.8	20	63
Opponents	74	3055	41.3	25	63

PUNT RETURNS	No.	FC	Yds.	Avg.	LG	TD
Martin	17	10	214	12.6	38	0
Carpenter	12	6	79	6.6	22	0
Eagles	29	16	293	10.1	38	0
Opponents	38	17	527	13.9	88t	2

KICKOFF RETURNS	No.	Yds.	Avg.	LG	TD
Garner	29	590	20.3	41	0
Martin	20	388	19.4	38	0
Witherspoon	18	459	25.5	86t	1
Jones	2	46	23.0	26	0
McCrary	1	1	1.0	1	0
Saxon	1	3	3.0	3	0
Eagles	71	1487	20.9	86t	1
Opponents	61	1576	25.8	70	0

SACKS	No.
Fuller	13.0
Harmon	11.0
K. Johnson	6.0
Mamula	5.5
Stubbs	5.5
Thomas	2.0
Woodard	1.5
Hall	1.0
Romanowski	1.0
Zordich	1.0
Gunn	0.5
Eagles	48.0
Opponents	46.0

1996 DRAFT CHOICES

Round	Name	Pos.	College
1	Jermane Mayberry	T	Texas A&M-Kingsville
2	Jason Dunn	TE	Eastern Kentucky
	Brian Dawkins	DB	Clemson
3	Bobby Hoying	QB	Ohio State
4	Ray Farmer	LB	Duke
5	Whit Marshall	LB	Georgia
6	Steve White	LB	Tennessee
	Tony Johnson	TE	Alabama
	Phillip Riley	WR	Florida State

PHILADELPHIA EAGLES

1996 VETERAN ROSTER

No.	Name	Pos.	Ht.	Wt.	Birthdate	NFL Exp.	College	Hometown	How Acq.	'95 Games/ Starts
1	Anderson, Gary	K	5-11	178	7/16/59	15	Syracuse	Durban, South Africa	FA-'95	16/0
93	Barrie, Sebastian	DT	6-2	280	5/26/70	4	Liberty	Dallas, Tex.	FA-'96	7/0*
33	Bouie, Kevin	RB	6-1	230	8/18/71	2	Mississippi State	Pahokee, Fla.	D7a-'95	0*
25	Boykin, Deral	S	5-11	198	9/2/70	4	Louisville	Kent, Ohio	FA-'96	5/0*
76	Brooks, Barrett	T	6-4	309	5/5/72	2	Kansas State	Florissant, Mo.	D2b-'95	16/16
77	Cooper, Richard	T	6-5	290	11/1/64	7	Tennessee	Memphis, Tenn.	UFA(NO)-'96	14/14*
14	Detmer, Ty	QB	6-0	194	10/30/67	5	Brigham Young	San Antonio, Tex.	UFA(GB)-'96	4/0*
90	Dixon, Ronnie	DT	6-3	292	5/10/71	3	Cincinnati	Clinton, N.C.	T(Clev)-'95	16/10
75	Drake, Troy	T	6-6	289	5/15/72	2	Indiana	Byron, Ill.	FA-'95	1/0
11	Fiedler, Jay	QB	6-1	214	12/29/71	3	Dartmouth	Oceanside, N.Y.	FA-'94	0*
80	Fryar, Irving	WR	6-0	200	9/28/62	13	Nebraska	Mount Holly, N.J.	UFA(Mia)-'96	16/16*
95	Fuller, William	DE	6-3	280	3/8/62	11	North Carolina	Chesapeake, Va.	UFA(Hou)-'94	14/13
30	Garner, Charlie	RB	5-9	187	2/13/72	3	Tennessee	Falls Church, Va.	D2b-'94	15/3
96	Gunn, Mark	DE	6-5	297	7/24/68	6	Pittsburgh	Cleveland, Ohio	UFA(NO)-'95	12/5
97	Hall, Rhett	DT	6-2	276	12/5/68	6	California	Morgan Hill, Calif.	UFA(SF)-'95	2/1
91	Harmon, Andy	DT	6-4	278	4/6/69	6	Kent State	Centerville, Ohio	D6-'91	15/15
20	Hebron, Vaughn	RB	5-8	195	10/7/70	4	Virginia Tech	Baltimore, Md.	FA-'93	0*
26	Henderson, Jerome	CB	5-10	188	8/8/69	6	Clemson	Statesville, N.C.	UFA(Buff)-'95	15/0
73	† Holmes, Lester	G	6-3	305	9/27/69	4	Jackson State	Tylertown, Miss.	D1a-'93	2/2
4	Hutton, Tom	P-K	6-1	193	7/8/72	2	Tennessee	Memphis, Tenn.	FA-'95	16/0
79	Jefferson, Greg	DE	6-3	257	8/31/71	2	Central Florida	Bartow, Fla.	D3a-'95	3/0
88	Johnson, Jimmie	TE	6-2	257	10/6/66	8	Howard	Augusta, Ga.	FA-'95	9/2
94	Johnson, Kevin	DT	6-1	306	10/30/70	2	Texas Southern	Los Angeles, Calif.	W(Oak)-'95	11/1
61	Jonassen, Eric	T	6-5	310	8/16/68	3	Bloomsburg	Glen Burnie, Md.	FA-'96	0*
82	Jones, Chris T.	WR	6-3	209	8/7/71	2	Miami	West Palm Beach, Fla.	D3b-'95	12/0
59	Mamula, Mike	LB-DE	6-4	252	8/14/73	2	Boston College	Lackawanna, N.Y.	D1-'95	14/13
41	McCrary, Fred	RB	6-0	219	9/19/72	2	Mississippi State	Naples, Fla.	D6-'95	13/4
63	McKenzie, Raleigh	C	6-2	283	2/8/63	12	Tennessee	Knoxville, Tenn.	UFA(Wash)-'95	16/16
72	Panos, Joe	G-C	6-2	293	1/24/71	3	Wisconsin	Brookfield, Wis.	D3a-'94	9/9
9	Peete, Rodney	QB	6-0	225	3/16/66	8	Southern California	Tucson, Ariz.	UFA(Dall)-'95	15/12
64	Rudolph, Joe	G	6-1	285	7/21/72	2	Wisconsin	Belle Vernon, Pa.	FA-'95	4/0
81	Seay, Mark	WR	6-0	175	4/11/67	5	Long Beach State	San Bernardino, Calif.	FA-'96	16/0*
21	Taylor, Bobby	CB	6-3	216	12/28/73	2	Notre Dame	Longview, Tex.	D2a-'95	16/12
51	Thomas, William	LB	6-2	223	8/13/68	6	Texas A&M	Amarillo, Tex.	D4-'91	16/16
34	Turner, Kevin	RB	6-1	231	6/12/69	5	Alabama	Prattville, Ala.	RFA(NE)-'95	2/2
23	Vincent, Troy	CB	6-0	184	6/8/70	5	Wisconsin	Trenton, N.J.	RFA(Mia)-'96	16/16*
74	Wallace, Steve	T	6-5	302	12/27/64	11	Auburn	Atlanta, Ga.	FA-'96	13/12*
32	Watters, Ricky	RB	6-1	217	4/7/69	6	Notre Dame	Harrisburg, Pa.	RFA(SF)-'95	16/16
83	West, Ed	TE	6-1	250	8/2/61	13	Auburn	Leighton, Ala.	FA-'95	16/14
89	Williams, Calvin	WR	5-11	187	3/3/67	7	Purdue	Baltimore, Md.	D5-'90	16/15
50	Willis, James	LB	6-2	237	9/2/72	4	Auburn	Huntsville, Ala.	FA-'95	5/0
31	Witherspoon, Derrick	RB	5-10	196	2/14/71	2	Clemson	Sumter, S.C.	FA-'95	15/0
57	Woodard, Marc	LB	6-0	238	2/21/70	3	Mississippi State	Kosciusko, Mich.	FA-'93	16/0
52	Wright, Sylvester	LB	6-2	258	12/30/71	2	Kansas	Detroit, Mich.	FA-'95	6/0
27	Zomalt, Eric	S	5-11	201	8/9/72	3	California	Los Angeles, Calif.	D3b-'94	15/1
36	Zordich, Michael	S	6-1	212	10/12/63	10	Penn State	Youngstown, Ohio	FA-'94	15/15

* Barrie played 7 games with San Diego in '95; Bouie and Hebron, missed '95 season because of injury; Boykin played 5 games with Jacksonville; Cooper played 14 games with New Orleans; Detmer played 4 games with Green Bay; Fiedler inactive for 16 games; Fryar played 16 games with Miami; Jones last active with San Diego in '94; Seay played 16 games with San Diego; Vincent played 16 games with Miami; Wallace played 13 games with San Francisco.

† Restricted free agent; subject to developments.

Players lost to free agency (9): WR Fred Barnett (Mia; 14 games), T Harry Boatswain (NYJ; 13), T Antone Davis (Atl; 15), LB Kurt Gouveia (SD; 16), C John Hudson (NYJ; 16), TE Reggie Johnson (KC; 16), CB Mark McMillian (NO; 16), LB Bill Romanowski (Den; 16), DE Daniel Stubbs (Mia; 16).

Also played with Eagles in '95—WR Rob Carpenter (16 games), DT Mike Chalenski (9), C Frank Cornish (2), QB Randall Cunningham (7), LB Nate Dingle (6), T Moe Elewonibi (6), CB Derrick Frazier (7), LB Steve Hendrickson (3), S Greg Jackson (16), TE Reggie Johnson (16), WR Kelvin Martin (9), G Guy McIntyre (16), WR Art Monk (3), LB Derrick Oden (12), RB James Saxon (9), S Greg Tremble (4), TE Frank Wainright (7), S David Whitmore (3), S Barry Wilburn (16).

COACHING STAFF

Head Coach

Ray Rhodes

Pro Career: Named the nineteenth head coach in Eagles history on February 2, 1995, after serving as the defensive coordinator for the San Francisco 49ers. In just his first year at the Eagles' helm, Rhodes revamped the club's roster with 33 new players and guided Philadelphia to a 10-6 record and back into the playoffs after a three-year absence. Under Rhodes, the Eagles captured the top Wild Card playoff spot in the NFC and subsequently defeated Detroit, 58-37, in a record-setting playoff game that advanced Philadelphia into the divisional round of postseason play. Rhodes's effort was rewarded when numerous organizations named him the 1995 NFL coach of the year, including the *Associated Press, The Sporting News, Sports Illustrated, Football Digest,* and *USA Today.* Rhodes came to Philadelphia after assisting George Seifert and the 49ers to that franchise's unprecedented fifth Super Bowl championship. In fact, Rhodes was an assistant on each of the 49ers' championship teams, making him one of only four men in NFL history to have served on the staffs of five Super Bowl winners. Before his most recent stint with San Francisco, Rhodes served two seasons in Green Bay as defensive coordinator under ex-49ers assistant Mike Holmgren, where he elevated the Packers' defense to the second-ranked unit overall in just two seasons. Rhodes ended his seven-year NFL playing career with San Francisco in 1980 and then joined Bill Walsh's coaching staff as an assistant defensive backs coach the following season. In 1982, he was promoted to defensive backs coach and held that position through 1991. Over that period, he developed four Pro Bowl defenders, cornerbacks Ronnie Lott and Eric Wright, and safeties Dwight Hicks and Carlton Williamson. Career record: 11-7.

Background: After spending two years at Texas Christian University, Rhodes finished his collegiate career at the University of Tulsa and was selected by the New York Giants in the tenth round of the 1974 NFL draft. He played wide receiver for his first three seasons with the Giants but was switched to defensive back in 1977. In 1979, he was traded to San Francisco in a deal that also saw 49ers defensive back Tony Dungy, presently the head coach of the Tampa Bay Buccaneers, sent to the Giants.

Personal: Born October 20, 1950, in Mexia, Tex. Rhodes and his wife, Carmen, have four daughters: Detra, Candra, Tynesha, and Raven, and reside in Marlton, New Jersey.

Assistant Coaches

Bill Callahan, offensive line; born July 31, 1956, Chicago, Ill., lives in Mt. Laurel, N.J. Quarterback Illinois Benedictine 1975-77. No pro playing experience. College coach: Illinois 1980-87, Northern Arizona 1987-88, Southern Illinois 1989, Wisconsin 1990-94. Pro coach: Joined Eagles in 1995.

Gerald Carr, wide receivers; born June 28, 1959, Davidson, N.C., lives in Siclerville, N.J. Quarterback Southern Illinois 1977-80. No pro playing experience. College coach: Southern Illinois 1982, Davidson 1983-85, Akron 1986-88, Washington State 1989-90, Arizona 1991, North Carolina 1992-94. Pro coach: Joined Eagles in 1995.

Juan Castillo, offensive assistant; born October 8, 1959, Port Isabel, Tex., lives in Moorestown, N.J. Linebacker Texas A&M-Kingsville (formerly Texas A&I) 1978-80. Pro linebacker San Antonio Gunslingers (USFL) 1984-85. College coach: Texas A&M-Kingsville 1982-85, 1990-94. Pro coach: Joined Eagles in 1995.

Jon Gruden, offensive coordinator; born August 17, 1963, Sandusky, Ohio, lives in Mt. Laurel, N.J. Quarterback Dayton 1983-85. No pro playing experience. College coach: Tennessee 1986-87, Southeast Missouri 1988, Pacific 1989, Pittsburgh 1991. Pro coach: San Francisco 49ers 1990, Green Bay Packers 1992-94, joined Eagles in 1995.

Dick Jamieson, running backs; born November 13, 1937, Streator, Ill., lives in Cherry Hill, N.J. Quarterback Bradley 1955-58. Pro quarterback Baltimore Colts 1959, New York Titans (AFL) 1960. College coach: Bradley 1962-64, Missouri 1972-77, Indiana State 1978-79, Northwestern 1990-91, Rutgers 1992-94. Pro coach: St. Louis Cardinals 1980-85, Houston Oilers 1986-87, joined Eagles in 1995.

Chuck Knox, Jr., defensive assistant; born June 19, 1965, Englewood, N.J., lives in Mt. Laurel, N.J. Running back Arizona 1984-85. No pro playing experience. Pro coach: Los Angeles Rams 1993-94, joined Eagles in 1995.

Danny Smith, special teams; born November 7, 1953, Pittsburgh, Pa., lives in Mt. Laurel, N.J. Defensive back Edinboro State 1972-75. No pro playing experience. College coach: Edinboro State 1976, Clemson 1979, William & Mary 1980-83, Citadel 1984-86, Georgia Tech 1987-94. Pro coach: Joined Eagles in 1995.

Emmitt Thomas, defensive coordinator; born June 3, 1943, Angleton, Tex., lives in Voorhees, N.J. Quarterback-wide receiver Bishop (Tex.) College 1963-65. Pro defensive back Kansas City Chiefs 1966-78. College coach: Central Missouri State 1979-80. Pro coach: St. Louis Cardinals 1981-85, Washington Redskins 1986-94, joined Eagles in 1995.

Mike Trgovac, defensive line; born February 27, 1959, Youngstown, Ohio, lives in Marlton, N.J. Defensive lineman Michigan 1977-80. No pro playing experience. College coach: Michigan 1984-85, Ball State 1986-88, Navy 1989, Colorado State 1990-91, Notre Dame 1992-94. Pro coach: Joined Eagles in 1995.

Joe Vitt, linebackers; born August 23, 1954, Camden, N.J., lives in Mt. Laurel, N.J. Linebacker Towson State 1973-75. No pro playing experience. Pro coach: Baltimore Colts 1979-81, Seattle Seahawks 1982-91, Los Angeles Rams 1992-94, joined Eagles in 1995.

Ted Williams, tight ends; born November 17, 1943, Lyons, Tex., lives in Siclerville, N.J. No college or pro playing experience. College coach: UCLA 1980-89, Washington State 1991-93, Arizona 1994. Pro coach: Joined Eagles in 1995.

Mike Wolf, strength and conditioning; born May 15, 1965, Allentown, Pa., lives in Marlton, N.J. Center Penn State 1983-87. No pro playing experience. College coach: Vanderbilt 1988-89, Lehigh 1990, Penn State 1991. Pro coach: Minnesota Vikings 1992-94, joined Eagles in 1995.

1996 FIRST-YEAR ROSTER

Name	Pos.	Ht.	Wt.	Birthdate	College	Hometown	How Acq.
Buckhalter, Chris	RB	5-9	203	5/23/73	Southern Mississippi	Collins, Miss.	FA
Campbell, Alex	P-K	6-0	200	2/21/72	Morris Brown	De Funiak Springs, Fla.	FA
Cummings, Joe	LB	6-2	242	6/8/72	Wyoming	Stevensville, Mont.	FA
Dawkins, Brian	S	5-11	188	10/13/73	Clemson	Jacksonville, Fla.	D2b
Dunn, Jason	TE	6-4	257	11/15/73	Eastern Kentucky	Harrodsburg, Ky.	D2a
Farmer, Ray	S	6-3	225	7/1/72	Duke	Kernersville, N.C.	D4
Feanny, Maxwell	LB	6-0	250	7/22/72	Albany State	Port Charlotte, Fla.	FA
Ford, Frederick	CB	6-3	196	1/2/73	Mississippi Valley St.	Greenwood, Miss.	FA
Gillock, Mike (1)	CB	5-10	175	5/20/72	Indianapolis	Greenwood, Ind.	FA
Graham, Renaldo	TE	6-4	260	3/9/72	Grambling State	St. Petersburg, Fla.	FA
Hoying, Bobby	QB	6-3	221	9/20/72	Ohio State	St. Henry, Ohio	D3
Johnson, Tony	TE	6-5	256	2/5/72	Alabama	Como, Miss.	D6b
Kinsler, Latish (1)	S	6-2	193	8/16/71	Cincinnati	Montclair, N.J.	FA
Marshall, Whit	LB	6-2	247	1/6/73	Georgia	Atlanta, Ga.	D5
Mayberry, Jermane	G-T	6-4	325	8/29/73	Texas A&M-Kingsville	Floresville, Tex.	D1
McKinley, Verone	S	6-0	191	9/20/73	Texas Tech	Dallas, Tex.	FA
Miller, Bubba	C	6-1	300	1/24/73	Tennessee	Franklin, Tenn.	D6a
Montgomery, Bill (1)	S	6-0	186	12/23/70	Georgia	Carrollton, Ga.	FA
Moss, Tristan	CB	5-10	175	11/22/72	Western Michigan	Cincinnati, Ohio	FA
Nord, Kendrick	WR	6-2	211	4/28/72	Grambling State	Mobile, Ala.	FA
Oltmanns, Chris	G	6-5	315	11/21/72	Kansas State	Delmar, Iowa	FA
Pratt, Khevin	WR	5-10	180	5/16/70	Cal State-Chico	Los Angeles, Calif.	FA
Purdy, Matt	G	6-1	299	12/13/72	Iowa	Cedar Falls, Iowa	FA
Reed, Robert	LB	6-1	241	2/4/73	Texas	Converse, Tex.	FA
Riley, Phillip	WR	5-11	189	9/24/72	Florida State	Orlando, Fla.	D6c
Samson, Michael	DT	6-3	294	2/17/73	Grambling State	Heidelberg, Miss.	FA
Simonson, Eric	T	6-3	291	10/2/72	Montana	Plentywood, Mont.	FA
Smith, Greg	WR	5-9	174	1/16/72	Western State	Alexandria, La.	FA
Solomon, Freddie (1)	WR	5-10	180	8/15/72	South Carolina State	Alachus, Fla.	FA
Thomas, Hollis	DT	6-0	306	1/10/74	Northern Illinois	St. Louis, Mo.	FA
Unutoa, Morris	C	6-1	284	3/10/71	Brigham Young	Carson, Calif.	FA
White, Steve	LB	6-2	246	10/25/73	Tennessee	Memphis, Tenn.	FA
Zachery, Cedric	WR	5-11	178	11/10/72	Georgia Tech	Decatur, Ga.	FA

The term NFL Rookie is defined as a player who is in his first season of professional football and has not been on the roster of another professional football team for any regular-season or postseason games. A Rookie is designated by an "R" on NFL rosters. Players who have been active in another professional football league or players who have NFL experience, including either preseason training camp or being on an Active List or Inactive List, or on Reserve/Injured or Reserve/Physically Unable to Perform for fewer than six regular-season games, are termed NFL First-Year Players. An NFL First-Year Player is designated by a "1" on NFL rosters. Thereafter, a player is credited with an additional year of experience for each season in which he accumulates six games on the Active List or Inactive List, or on Reserve/Injured or Reserve/Physically Unable to Perform.

NOTES

ST. LOUIS RAMS

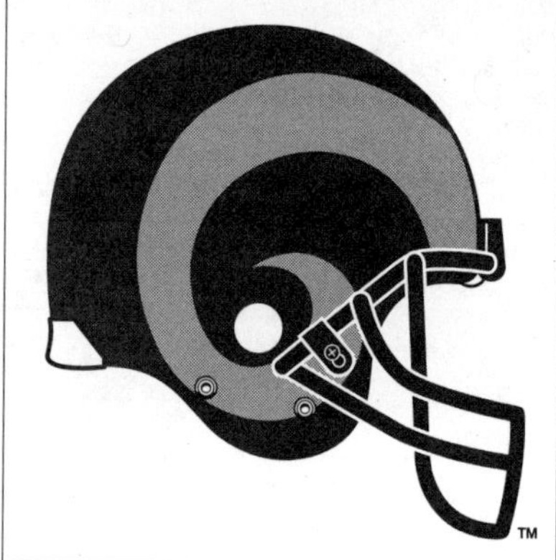

National Football Conference
Western Division
Team Colors: Royal Blue, Gold, and White
Business Address:
One Rams Way
St. Louis County, Missouri 63045
Telephone: (314) 982-7267

CLUB OFFICIALS

Chairman: Georgia Frontiere
Vice Chairman: Stan Kroenke
President: John Shaw
Executive Vice President: Jay Zygmunt
Senior Vice President-Administration, General Counsel: Bob Wallace
Vice President-Football Operations: Steve Ortmayer
Vice President-Marketing: Phil Thomas
Vice President-Media and Community Relations: Marshall Klein
Vice President-Sales: Brian Ulione
Vice President-Finance: Adrian Barr
Director of Pro Personnel: John Becker
Treasurer: Jeff Brewer
Director of Operations: John Oswald
Director of Public Relations: Rick Smith
Assistant Director-Public Relations: Tony Wyllie
Player Relations Coordinator: Doug Wilkerson
Head Trainer: Jim Anderson
Assistant Trainers: Dake Walden, Ron DuBuque
Equipment Manager: Todd Hewitt
Scouts: Lawrence McCutcheon, David Razzano, Pete Russell, Harley Sewell
Stadium: Trans World Dome at America's Center
• **Capacity:** 66,000
701 Convention Plaza
St. Louis County, Missouri 63101
Playing Surface: AstroTurf
Training Camp: Western Illinois University
Macomb, Illinois 61455

1996 SCHEDULE

PRESEASON

Aug. 3	at Pittsburgh	6:00
Aug. 9	**Jacksonville**	7:00
Aug. 17	at Kansas City	7:00
Aug. 23	**San Diego**	7:00

REGULAR SEASON

Sept. 1	**Cincinnati**	12:00
Sept. 8	at San Francisco	1:00
Sept. 15	Open Date	
Sept. 22	**Washington**	12:00
Sept. 29	at Arizona	1:00
Oct. 6	**San Francisco**	3:00
Oct. 13	at Carolina	1:00
Oct. 20	**Jacksonville**	3:00
Oct. 27	at Baltimore	1:00
Nov. 3	at Pittsburgh	1:00
Nov. 10	**Atlanta**	12:00
Nov. 17	**Carolina**	12:00
Nov. 24	**Green Bay**	7:00
Dec. 1	at New Orleans	3:00
Dec. 8	at Chicago	12:00
Dec. 15	at Atlanta	1:00
Dec. 21	**New Orleans** (Sat.)	3:00

RECORD HOLDERS

INDIVIDUAL RECORDS—CAREER

Category	Name	Performance
Rushing (Yds.)	Eric Dickerson, 1983-87	7,245
Passing (Yds.)	Jim Everett, 1986-1993	23,758
Passing (TDs)	Roman Gabriel, 1962-1972	154
Receiving (No.)	Henry Ellard, 1983-1993	593
Receiving (Yds.)	Henry Ellard, 1983-1993	9,761
Interceptions	Ed Meador, 1959-1970	46
Punting (Avg.)	Danny Villanueva, 1960-64	44.2
Punt Return (Avg.)	Henry Ellard, 1983-1992	11.3
Kickoff Return (Avg.)	Tom Wilson, 1956-1961	27.1
Field Goals	Mike Lansford, 1982-1990	158
Touchdowns (Tot.)	Eric Dickerson, 1983-87	58
Points	Mike Lansford, 1982-1990	789

INDIVIDUAL RECORDS—SINGLE SEASON

Category	Name	Performance
Rushing (Yds.)	Eric Dickerson, 1984	*2,105
Passing (Yds.)	Jim Everett, 1989	4,310
Passing (TDs)	Jim Everett, 1988	31
Receiving (No.)	Isaac Bruce, 1995	119
Receiving (Yds.)	Isaac Bruce, 1995	1,781
Interceptions	Dick (Night Train) Lane, 1952	*14
Punting (Avg.)	Danny Villanueva, 1962	45.5
Punt Return (Avg.)	Woodley Lewis, 1952	18.5
Kickoff Return (Avg.)	Verda (Vitamin T) Smith, 1950	33.7
Field Goals	David Ray, 1973	30
Touchdowns (Tot.)	Eric Dickerson, 1983	20
Points	David Ray, 1973	130

INDIVIDUAL RECORDS—SINGLE GAME

Category	Name	Performance
Rushing (Yds.)	Eric Dickerson, 1-4-86	248
Passing (Yds.)	Norm Van Brocklin, 9-28-51	*554
Passing (TDs)	Many times	5
	Last time by Jim Everett, 9-25-88	
Receiving (No.)	Tom Fears, 12-3-50	*18
Receiving (Yds.)	Willie Anderson, 11-26-89	*336
Interceptions	Many times	3
	Last time by Pat Thomas, 10-7-79	
Field Goals	Bob Waterfield, 12-9-51	5
Touchdowns (Tot.)	Bob Shaw, 12-11-49	4
	Elroy (Crazylegs) Hirsch, 9-28-51	4
	Harold Jackson, 10-14-73	4
Points	Bob Shaw, 12-11-49	24
	Elroy (Crazylegs) Hirsch, 9-28-51	24
	Harold Jackson, 10-14-73	24

*NFL Record

COACHING HISTORY

Cleveland 1937-1945, Los Angeles 1946-1994
(418-378-20)

1937-38	Hugo Bezdek*	1-13-0
1938	Art Lewis	4-4-0
1939-42	Earl (Dutch) Clark	16-26-2
1944	Aldo (Buff) Donelli	4-6-0
1945-46	Adam Walsh	16-5-1
1947	Bob Snyder	6-6-0
1948-49	Clark Shaughnessy	14-8-3
1950-52	Joe Stydahar**	19-9-0
1952-54	Hamp Pool	23-11-2
1955-59	Sid Gillman	28-32-1
1960-62	Bob Waterfield***	9-24-1
1962-65	Harland Svare	14-31-3
1966-70	George Allen	49-19-4
1971-72	Tommy Prothro	14-12-2
1973-77	Chuck Knox	57-20-1
1978-82	Ray Malavasi	43-36-0
1983-91	John Robinson	79-74-0
1992-94	Chuck Knox	15-33-0
1995	Rich Brooks	7-9-0

*Released after three games in 1938
**Resigned after one game in 1952
***Resigned after eight games in 1962

TRANS WORLD DOME

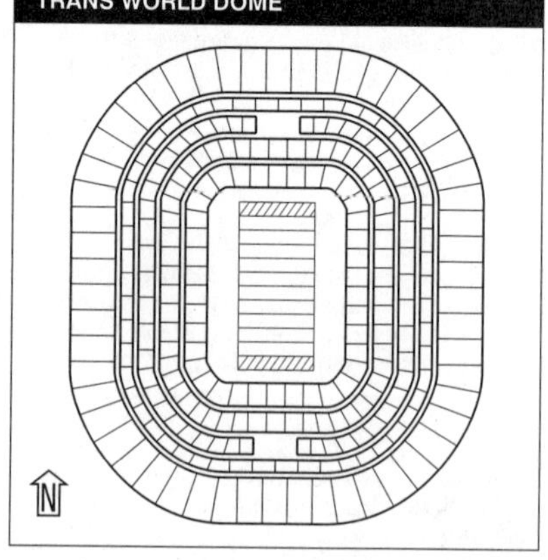

1995 TEAM RECORD

PRESEASON (1-3)

Date	Result		Opponents
8/5	L	20-34	at Seattle
8/12	L	22-27	at Oakland
8/18	W	27-10	at Jacksonville
8/25	L	9-17	at San Diego

REGULAR SEASON (7-9)

Date	Result		Opponents	Att.
9/3	W	17-14	at Green Bay	60,104
9/10	W	17-13	New Orleans	59,335
9/17	W	31-10	at Carolina	54,060
9/24	W	34-28	Chicago	59,679
10/1	L	18-21	at Indianapolis	58,616
10/12	W	21-19	Atlanta	59,700
10/22	L	10-44	San Francisco	59,915
10/29	L	9-20	at Philadelphia	62,172
11/5	L	10-19	at New Orleans	43,120
11/12	W	28-17	Carolina	65,598
11/19	L	6-31	at Atlanta	46,309
11/26	L	13-41	at San Francisco	66,049
12/3	W	23-20	at N.Y. Jets	52,023
12/10	L	27-45	Buffalo	64,623
12/17	L	23-35	Washington	63,760
12/24	L	22-41	Miami	63,876

SCORE BY PERIODS

Rams	78	87	60	84	—	309
Opponents	62	151	101	104	—	418

ATTENDANCE

Home 496,486 Away 442,453 Total 938,939

Single-game home record, 69,898 (11/9/92; Anaheim Stadium)

Single-season home record, 553,979 (1992; Anaheim Stadium)

1995 TEAM STATISTICS

	Rams	Opp.
Total First Downs	292	301
Rushing	77	101
Passing	199	178
Penalty	16	22
Third Down: Made/Att	87/239	85/204
Third Down Pct.	36.4	41.7
Fourth Down: Made/Att	15/26	5/8
Fourth Down Pct.	57.7	62.5
Total Net Yards	5236	5118
Avg. Per Game	327.3	319.9
Total Plays	1067	980
Avg. Per Play	4.9	5.2
Net Yards Rushing	1431	1677
Avg. Per Game	89.4	104.8
Total Rushes	392	410
Net Yards Passing	3805	3441
Avg. Per Game	237.8	215.1
Sacked/Yards Lost	43/308	36/258
Gross Yards	4113	3699
Att./Completions	632/366	534/320
Completion Pct.	57.9	59.9
Had Intercepted	23	22
Punts/Avg.	83/44.3	79/43.5
Net Punting Avg.	83/36.7	79/34.3
Penalties/Yards Lost	117/916	87/681
Fumbles/Ball Lost	27/16	27/14
Touchdowns	37	51
Rushing	5	14
Passing	27	27
Returns	5	10
Avg. Time of Possession	31:10	28:50

1995 INDIVIDUAL STATISTICS

PASSING	Att.	Comp.	Yds.	Pct.	TD	Int.	Tkld.	Rate
Miller	405	232	2623	57.3	18	15	31/244	76.2
Rypien	217	129	1448	59.4	9	8	11/60	77.9
Barr	9	5	42	55.6	0	0	1/4	67.8
Kinchen	1	0	0	0.0	0	0	0/0	39.6
Rams	632	366	4113	57.9	27	23	43/308	76.5
Opponents	534	320	3699	59.9	27	22	36/258	80.6

SCORING	TD R	TD P	TD Rt	PAT	FG	Saf	PTS
Bruce	0	13	0	0/0	0/0	0	80
McLaughlin	0	0	0	17/17	8/16	0	41
Biasucci	0	0	0	13/14	9/12	0	40
Drayton	0	4	0	0/0	0/0	0	24
Kinchen	0	4	0	0/0	0/0	0	24
Bettis	3	0	0	0/0	0/0	0	18
Hester	0	3	0	0/0	0/0	0	18
Bailey	2	0	0	0/0	0/0	0	14
Dorn	0	0	2	0/0	0/0	0	12
A. Wright	0	2	0	0/0	0/0	0	12
Cook	0	1	0	0/0	0/0	0	6
Lyght	0	0	1	0/0	0/0	0	6
Parker	0	0	1	0/0	0/0	0	6
T. Wright	0	0	1	0/0	0/0	0	6
K. Carter	0	0	0	0/0	0/0	1	2
Rams	5	27	5	30/31	17/28	1	309
Opponents	14	27	10	47/48	21/27	0	418

2-Point conversions: Bailey, Bruce. Team: 2-6.

RUSHING	Att.	Yds.	Avg.	LG	TD
Bettis	183	637	3.5	41	3
Russell	66	203	3.1	18	0
Bailey	36	182	5.1	17	2
Robinson	40	165	4.1	37	0
Moss	22	90	4.1	18	0
Miller	22	67	3.0	13	0
Bruce	3	17	5.7	12	0
A. Wright	1	17	17.0	17	0
Kinchen	4	16	4.0	15	0
Rypien	9	10	1.1	5	0
Wolfley	3	9	3.0	4	0
T. Wright	1	9	9.0	9	0
Barr	1	5	5.0	5	0
Lyle	1	4	4.0	4	0
Rams	392	1431	3.7	41	5
Opponents	410	1677	4.1	49	14

RECEIVING	No.	Yds.	Avg.	LG	TD
Bruce	119	1781	15.0	72	13
Drayton	47	458	9.7	31	4
Bailey	38	265	7.0	25	0
Kinchen	36	419	11.6	35	4
Hester	30	399	13.3	38t	3
Cook	26	135	5.2	16	1
A. Wright	23	368	16.0	50	2
Bettis	18	106	5.9	19	0
Russell	16	89	5.6	17	0
Thomas	5	42	8.4	12	0
Price	4	29	7.3	24	0
Robinson	2	12	6.0	6	0
Pinkney	1	13	13.0	13	0
Moss	1	-3	-3.0	-3	0
Rams	366	4113	11.2	72	27
Opponents	320	3699	11.6	52	27

INTERCEPTIONS	No.	Yds.	Avg.	LG	TD
T. Wright	6	79	13.2	27	0
Lyght	4	34	8.5	29t	1
Phifer	3	52	17.3	25	0
Lyle	3	42	14.0	31	0
Parker	2	-5	-2.5	3	0
Dorn	1	24	24.0	24t	1
Scurlock	1	13	13.0	13	0
Farr	1	5	5.0	5	0
Conlan	1	1	1.0	1	0
Rams	22	245	11.1	31	2
Opponents	23	497	21.6	86t	5

PUNTING	No.	Yds.	Avg.	In 20	LG
Landeta	83	3679	44.3	23	63
Rams	83	3679	44.3	23	63
Opponents	79	3435	43.5	21	65

PUNT RETURNS	No.	FC	Yds.	Avg.	LG	TD
Kinchen	53	7	416	7.8	27	0
Bailey	2	0	42	21.0	22	0
Bruce	0	0	52	—	52	0
Lyght	0	0	16	—	16	0
Thomas	0	0	61	—	61	0
Rams	55	7	587	10.7	62	0
Opponents	38	16	393	10.3	66t	1

KICKOFF RETURNS	No.	Yds.	Avg.	LG	TD
Kinchen	35	743	21.2	50	0
Thomas	32	752	23.5	46	0
Bailey	5	97	19.4	28	0
Pinkney	1	26	26.0	26	0
Rams	73	1618	22.2	50	0
Opponents	59	1247	21.1	55	0

SACKS	No.
Farr	11.5
Gilbert	6.5
K. Carter	6.0
Phifer	3.0
Stokes	2.5
Jenkins	1.5
D. Davis	1.0
Figaro	1.0
McBurrows	1.0
A. White	1.0
T. Wright	1.0
Rams	36.0
Opponents	43.0

1996 DRAFT CHOICES

Round	Name	Pos.	College
1	Lawrence Phillips	RB	Nebraska
	Eddie Kennison	WR	Louisiana State
2	Tony Banks	QB	Michigan State
	Ernie Conwell	TE	Washington
3	Jerald Moore	RB	Oklahoma
4	Percell Gaskins	LB	Kansas State
5	Fred Miller	T	Baylor
6	Derrick Harris	RB	Miami
	Hayward Clay	TE	Texas A&M
7	Chuck Osborne	DT	Arizona

ST. LOUIS RAMS

1996 VETERAN ROSTER

No.	Name	Pos.	Ht.	Wt.	Birthdate	NFL Exp.	College	Hometown	How Acq.	'95 Games/ Starts
77	Ashmore, Darryl	T	6-7	310	11/1/69	5	Northwestern	Peoria, Ill.	D7-'92	16/15
20	# Bailey, Johnny	RB	5-8	180	3/17/67	7	Texas A&I	Houston, Tex.	FA-'94	12/1
16	Barr, Dave	QB	6-3	210	5/9/72	2	California	Oakland, Calif.	W(Phil)-'95	2/0
71	† Belin, Chuck	G	6-2	305	10/27/70	4	Wisconsin	Milwaukee, Wis.	D5b-'93	6/0
4	# Biasucci, Dean	K	6-0	190	7/25/62	12	Western Carolina	Miramar, Fla.	FA-'95	8/0
26	Blake, Ricky	RB	6-2	225	7/15/67	2	Alabama A&M	Fayetville, Tenn.	FA-'96	0*
61	Brostek, Bern	C	6-3	300	9/11/66	7	Washington	Honolulu, Hawaii	D1-'90	16/16
80	Bruce, Isaac	WR	6-0	178	11/10/72	3	Memphis	Ft. Lauderdale, Fla.	D2a-'94	16/16
93	Carter, Kevin	DE	6-5	274	9/21/73	2	Florida	Tallahassee, Fla.	D1-'95	16/16
56	# Conlan, Shane	LB	6-3	235	3/4/64	10	Penn State	Frewsburg, N.Y.	UFA(Buff)-'93	13/11
47	† Cook, Marv	TE	6-4	234	2/24/66	8	Iowa	West Branch, La.	UFA(Chi)-'95	16/9
29	Davis, Dexter	CB	5-10	184	3/20/70	6	Clemson	Sumter, S.C.	FA-'93	16/0
46	Dorn, Torin	CB	6-0	190	2/29/68	6	North Carolina	Southfield, Mich.	FA-'95	12/3
84	Drayton, Troy	TE	6-3	255	6/29/70	4	Penn State	Steelton, Pa.	D2-'93	16/16
75	Farr, D'Marco	DT	6-1	270	6/9/71	3	Washington	Richmond, Calif.	FA-'94	16/16
53	# Figaro, Cedric	LB	6-3	242	8/17/66	7	Notre Dame	Lafayette, La.	FA-'95	16/1
70	Gandy, Wayne	T	6-4	292	2/10/71	3	Auburn	Haines City, Fla.	D1-'94	16/16
79	# Goeas, Leo	G	6-4	300	8/15/66	7	Hawaii	Honolulu, Hawaii	T(SD)-'93	15/14
98	Harris, James	DE	6-6	225	5/13/68	4	Temple	East St. Louis, Ill.	FA-'96	12/3*
86	Hester, Jessie	WR	5-11	175	1/21/63	11	Florida State	Belle Glade, Fla.	UFA(Ind)-'94	12/7
57	Homco, Thomas	LB	6-0	245	1/8/70	4	Northwestern	Highland, Ind.	FA-'92	11/0
50	Howard, Dana	LB	6-0	238	2/25/72	2	Illinois	East St. Louis, Ill.	W(Dall)-'95	16/0*
37	Hurst, Maurice	CB	5-10	185	9/17/67	8	Southern	New Orleans, La.	FA-'96	10/0*
69	James, Jesse	C	6-4	311	9/16/71	2	Mississippi State	Mobile, Ala.	D2b-'95	1/0
51	Jenkins, Carlos	LB	6-3	217	7/12/68	6	Michigan State	Lantana, Fla.	UFA(Minn)-'95	16/13
98	Jones, Jimmie	DT	6-4	285	1/9/66	7	Miami	Lake Okeechobee, Fla.	UFA(Dall)-'94	16/16
55	Jones, Robert	LB	6-3	244	9/27/69	5	East Carolina	Reedville, Va.	UFA(Dall)-'96	12/12*
81	Kinchen, Todd	WR	5-11	187	1/7/69	5	Louisiana State	Baton Rouge, La.	D3b-'92	16/1
48	Laing, Aaron	TE	6-3	264	7/19/71	2	New Mexico State	Houston, Tex.	FA-'96	0*
5	Landeta, Sean	P	6-0	210	1/6/62	12	Towson State	Baltimore, Md.	FA-'93	16/0
8	Lohmiller, Chip	K	6-3	215	7/16/66	9	Minnesota	Woodbury, Minn.	FA-'96	8/0*
64	Loneker, Keith	G	6-3	325	6/21/71	4	Kansas	Roselle Park, N.J.	FA-'93	13/1
35	Lyle, Keith	S	6-2	204	4/17/72	3	Virginia	Vienna, Va.	D3a-'94	16/16
10	Martin, Jamie	QB	6-2	215	2/8/70	3	Weber State	Arroyo Grande, Calif.	FA-'94	0*
23	McBurrows, Gerald	S	5-11	195	10/7/73	2	Kansas	Detroit, Mich.	D7a-'95	14/3
25	Montgomery, Tyrone	RB	6-0	190	8/3/70	3	Mississippi	Greenville, Miss.	FA-'95	0*
31	Moss, Brent	RB	5-8	211	1/30/72	2	Wisconsin	Milwaukee, Wis.	FA-'95	4/0
91	O'Neal, Leslie	DE	6-4	265	5/7/64	11	Oklahoma State	Little Rock, Ark.	UFA(SD)-'96	16/16*
95	Ottis, Brad	DE	6-4	272	8/2/72	3	Wayne State	Wahoo, Neb.	D2c-'94	12/0
27	Parker, Anthony	CB	5-10	181	2/1/66	6	Arizona State	Tempe, Ariz.	UFA(Minn)-'95	16/16
58	Phifer, Roman	LB	6-2	235	3/5/68	6	UCLA	Pineville, N.C.	D2-'91	16/16
17	# Price, Jim	TE	6-4	247	10/2/66	5	Stanford	Pine Brook, N.J.	FA-'95	13/0
21	Reece, John	CB	6-0	203	1/24/71	2	Nebraska	Houston, Tex.	FA-'95	5/0
28	† Robinson, Greg	RB	5-10	205	8/8/69	4	Northeast Louisiana	Grenada, Miss.	FA-'95	5/1
82	Ross, Jermaine	WR	6-0	192	4/27/71	2	Purdue	Jeffersonville, Ind.	FA-'94	0*
11	† Rypien, Mark	QB	6-4	231	10/2/62	11	Washington State	Spokane, Wash.	UFA(Clev)-'95	11/3
22	Scurlock, Mike	CB	5-10	197	2/26/72	2	Arizona	Tucson, Ariz.	D5-'95	14/1
59	Sheppard, Ashley	LB	6-3	240	1/21/69	4	Clemson	Bethel, N.C.	FA-'95	4/0*
18	Thomas, J.T.	WR	5-10	173	7/11/71	2	Arizona State	San Bernardino, Calif.	D7d-'95	15/1
4	Walsh, Steve	QB	6-3	200	12/1/66	8	Miami	St. Paul, Minn.	UFA(Chi)-'96	1/0*
68	White, Dwayne	G	6-2	315	2/10/67	7	Alcorn State	Philadelphia, Pa.	UFA(NYJ)-'95	15/15
73	Wiegert, Zach	T	6-4	305	8/16/72	2	Nebraska	Fremont, Neb.	D2a-'95	5/2
96	Williams, Jay	DT	6-3	270	10/13/71	2	Wake Forest	Washington, D.C.	FA-'94	7/0
89	Wright, Alexander	WR	6-0	195	7/19/67	7	Auburn	Albany, Ga.	UFA(Oak)-'95	8/6
32	Wright, Toby	S	5-11	203	11/19/70	3	Nebraska	Phoenix, Ariz.	D2b-'94	16/16
76	Young, Robert	DE	6-6	273	1/29/69	6	Mississippi State	Jackson, Miss.	D5-'91	14/0
63	Zeno, Lance	G	6-4	279	4/15/67	3	UCLA	Fountain Valley, Calif.	FA-'95	0*

* Blake last active with Dallas in '91; Harris played 12 games with Minnesota in '95; Hurst played 10 games with New England; R. Jones played 12 games with Dallas; Laing last active with San Diego in '94; Lohmiller played 8 games with New Orleans; Martin missed '95 season because of injury; Montgomery inactive for 2 games; O'Neal played 16 games with San Diego; Ross missed '95 season because of injury; Sheppard played 2 games with Jacksonville, 2 with St. Louis; Walsh played 1 game with Chicago; Zeno last active with Green Bay in '93.

\# Unrestricted free agent; subject to developments.

† Restricted free agent; subject to developments.

Traded—RB Jerome Bettis to Pittsburgh, DT Sean Gilbert to Washington.

Retired—Chris Miller, 9-year quarterback, 13 games in '95. Jackie Slater, 20-year tackle, 1 game in '95.

Players lost through free agency (3): TE Pat Carter (Ariz; 16 games in '95), T Clarence Jones (NO; 13), DE Fred Stokes (NO; 14).

Also played with Rams in '95—RB Jerome Bettis (15 games), LB Paschall Davis (3), DT Sean Gilbert (14), CB Todd Lyght (16), K Steve McLaughlin (8), TE Lovell Pinkney (8), RB Leonard Russell (13), DE Alberto White (2), RB Ron Wolfley (9).

COACHING STAFF

Head Coach,
Rich Brooks

Pro Career: Named nineteenth head coach of the Rams on February 10, 1995. Coached special teams and fundamentals in 1971-72 for the Los Angeles Rams under head coach Tommy Prothro. During that time, Rams kick returner Travis Williams led the NFL in 1971 with 29.72-yard average and set an NFL record with a 105-yard kickoff return versus New Orleans. Returned to the NFL in 1974 as defensive back and special teams coach with the San Francisco 49ers. Career record: 7-9.

Background: Played single-wing tailback, defensive back, and quarterback for Tommy Prothro at Oregon State from 1959-1962. Was an assistant coach at Oregon State in 1963, then spent 1964 season at Norte Del Rio High School in Sacramento, Calif. In 1965, Brooks returned to his alma mater as a defensive end and line coach. Rejoined Prothro at UCLA in 1970 as linebackers coach. Returned to Oregon State in 1973 as defensive coordinator. Returned to UCLA as linebacker coach in 1976. Head coach at Oregon from 1977-1994.

Personal: Born August 10, 1941, in Forest, Calif. Graduated from Oregon State in 1963 with bachelor of science degree in physical education and earned a master's degree in education from Oregon State in 1964. Brooks and wife, Karen, live in St. Louis, and have four children: Denny, Kasey, Kerri, and Brady.

Assistant Coaches

Nick Aliotti, special teams; born May 29, 1954, Pittsburg, Calif., lives in St. Louis. Running back U.C.-Davis 1972-75. No pro playing experience. College coach: U.C.-Davis 1976-77, Oregon 1978-79, 1988-94, Oregon State 1980-83, Chico State 1984-87. Pro coach: Joined Rams in 1995.

Steve Brown, cornerbacks; born March 20, 1960, Sacramento, Calif., lives in St. Louis. Defensive back Oregon 1978-82. Pro cornerback Houston Oilers 1983-90. Pro coach: Joined Rams in 1995.

Chris Clausen, strength and conditioning coordinator; born February 21, 1958, Evergreen Park, Ill., lives in St. Louis. Cornerback Indiana 1976-79. No pro playing experience. College coach: San Diego State 1987-88. Pro coach: San Diego Chargers 1989-91, joined Rams in 1992.

Michael Gray, defensive assistant-quality control; born February 11, 1960, Baltimore, Md., lives in St. Louis. Defensive end West Hills (Calif.)C.C. 1979-80, Oregon 1981-82. Pro defensive end British Columbia Lions (CFL) 1983-86, Winnipeg Blue Bombers (CFL) 1987-92. College coach: Weber State 1995. Pro coach: British Columbia Lions (CFL) 1993-94, joined Rams in 1996.

Steve Greatwood, offensive line; born August 15, 1958, Portland, Ore., lives in St. Louis. Guard Oregon 1976-79. No pro playing experience. College coach: Oregon 1982-94. Pro coach: Joined Rams in 1995.

Mike Martz, receivers; born May 13, 1951, Sioux Falls, S.D., lives in St. Louis. Tight end San Diego Mesa (Calif.) J.C. 1969-1970, U.C. Santa Barbara 1971, Fresno State 1972. No pro playing experience. College coach: San Diego Mesa (Calif.) J.C. 1974, 1976-77, San Jose State 1975, Santa Ana (Calif.) J.C. 1978-79, Fresno State 1979, Pacific 1980-81, Minnesota 1982-83, Arizona State 1984-91. Pro coach: Joined Rams in 1992.

Don (Deek) Pollard, defensive line; born September 16, 1939, Roodhouse, Ill., lives in St. Louis. Defensive back Western Illinois 1957-61. No pro playing experience. College coach: Western Illinois 1971-73, Florida State 1974-75, Oklahoma State 1976-78, Central Florida 1990-93, Boston College 1994. Pro coach: New York Giants 1979-1981, Denver Gold (USFL) 1983, Arizona Wranglers (USFL) 1984-85, Cleveland Browns 1989, joined Rams in 1995.

John Ramsdell, tight ends; born August 16, 1954, Lafayette, Ind., lives in St. Louis. Running back Springfield (Mass.) College 1972-75. No pro playing experience. College coach: San Francisco State 1976-77, Long Beach State 1978, Pacific 1979-82, Oregon 1983-94. Pro coach: Joined Rams in 1995.

Johnny Roland, assistant head coach-running backs; born May 21, 1943, Corpus Christi, Tex., lives in St. Louis. Running back Missouri 1961-65. Pro running back St. Louis Cardinals 1966-72, New York Giants 1973. College coach: Notre Dame 1975. Pro coach: Green Bay Packers 1974, Philadelphia Eagles 1976-78, Chicago Bears 1983-92, New York Jets 1993-94, joined Rams in 1995.

Jack Reilly, offensive coordinator-quarterbacks; born May 22, 1945, Boston, Mass., lives in St. Louis. Quarterback Washington State 1963, Santa Monica (Calif.) J.C. 1964, Long Beach State 1965-66. No pro playing experience. College coach: El Camino (Calif.) J.C. 1980-84 (head coach 1981-84), Utah 1985-89. Pro coach: San Diego Chargers 1990-93, Los Angeles Raiders 1994, joined Rams in 1995.

Richard Selcer, linebackers; born August 22, 1937, Cincinnati, Ohio., lives in St. Louis. Running back Notre Dame 1955-58. No pro playing experience. College coach: Xavier, Ohio 1962-64, 1970-71 (head coach), Cincinnati 1965-66, Brown 1967-69, Wisconsin 1972-74, Kansas State 1975-77, Southwestern Louisiana 1978-1980. Pro coach: Houston Oilers 1981-83, Cincinnati Bengals 1984-91, joined Rams in 1992.

Willie Shaw, defensive coordinator; born January 11, 1944, San Diego, Calif., lives in St. Louis. Cornerback New Mexico 1966-68. No pro playing experience. College coach: San Diego City College 1970-73, Stanford 1974-76, 1989-91, Long Beach State 1977-78, Oregon 1979, Arizona State 1980-84. Pro coach: Detroit Lions 1985-88, Minnesota Vikings 1992-93, San Diego Chargers 1994, joined Rams in 1995.

George Warhop, offensive line; born September 19, 1961, Riverside, Calif., lives in St. Louis. Guard Mt. San Jacinto (Calif.) J.C. 1979-80, Center Cincinnati 1981-82. No pro playing experience. College coach: Cincinnati 1983, Kansas 1984-86, Vanderbilt 1987-89, New Mexico 1990, Southern Methodist 1993, Boston College 1994-95. Pro coach: London Monarchs (World League) 1991-92, joined Rams in 1996.

1996 FIRST-YEAR ROSTER

Name	Pos.	Ht.	Wt.	Birthdate	College	Hometown	How Acq.
Banks, Tony	QB	6-4	220	4/5/73	Michigan State	San Diego, Calif.	D2a
Clay, Hayward	TE	6-3	256	7/25/73	Texas A&M	Snyder, Tex.	D6b
Conwell, Ernie	TE	6-1	253	8/17/72	Washington	Kent, Wash.	D2b
Davis, Paschall (1)	LB	6-2	225	7/5/69	Texas A&I	Bryan, Tex.	FA
Earle, John	G	6-5	315	4/1/68	Western Illinois	Red Bank, N.J.	FA
Gaskins, Percell	LB	6-0	225	4/25/72	Kansas State	Daytona Beach, Fla.	D4
Gruttadauria, Mike (1)	C	6-3	273	12/6/72	Central Florida	Tarpon Springs, Fla.	FA
Harris, Derrick	RB	6-0	253	9/18/72	Miami	Angleton, Tex.	D6a
Hooks, Bryan	DT	6-3	286	9/15/70	Arizona State	Tempe, Ariz.	FA
Kennison, Eddie	WR	6-0	191	1/20/73	Louisiana State	Lake Charles, La.	D1b
Kirksey, Jon (1)	G-T	6-4	350	2/21/70	Sacramento State	Greenville, S.C.	FA
Miller, Fred	T	6-7	305	2/6/73	Baylor	Houston, Tex.	D5
Moore, Jerald	RB	5-9	233	11/20/74	Oklahoma	Houston, Tex.	D3
O'Berry, Herman (1)	CB-S	5-9	195	7/11/71	Oregon	Highlands, Calif.	FA
Osborne, Chuck	DT	6-2	281	11/2/73	Arizona	Canyon Country, Calif.	D7
Phillips, Lawrence	RB	6-0	229	5/12/75	Nebraska	West Covina, Calif.	D1a
Swinson, Corey (1)	G-T	6-5	234	12/15/69	Hampton	Bay Shore, N.Y.	FA
Thomas, LeMay	WR	5-10	175	9/12/71	Mississippi	Delhi, La.	FA
Walker, Marquis	CB	5-10	165	7/6/72	S.E. Missouri State	St. Louis, Mo.	FA
Williams, Billy (1)	WR	5-11	175	6/7/71	Tennessee	Alcoa, Tenn.	FA
Wright, Claudius (1)	CB	5-10	180	7/10/72	Arizona	West Covina, Calif.	FA
Wright, Sean	K	5-11	160	5/27/71	Boston College	Kansas City, Mo.	FA

The term NFL Rookie is defined as a player who is in his first season of professional football and has not been on the roster of another professional football team for any regular-season or postseason games. A Rookie is designated by an "R" on NFL rosters. Players who have been active in another professional football league or players who have NFL experience, including either preseason training camp or being on an Active List or Inactive List, or on Reserve/Injured or Reserve/Physically Unable to Perform for fewer than six regular-season games, are termed NFL First-Year Players. An NFL First-Year Player is designated by a "1" on NFL rosters. Thereafter, a player is credited with an additional year of experience for each season in which he accumulates six games on the Active List or Inactive List, or on Reserve/Injured or Reserve/Physically Unable to Perform.

NOTES

SAN FRANCISCO 49ERS

National Football Conference
Western Division
Team Colors: Forty Niners Gold and Cardinal
4949 Centennial Boulevard
Santa Clara, California 95054
Telephone: (408) 562-4949

CLUB OFFICIALS

Owner: Edward J. DeBartolo, Jr.
President: Carmen Policy
Vice President and Director of Football Operations: Dwight Clark
Vice President-Business Operations & C.F.O.: Bill Duffy
Director of Player Personnel: Vinny Cerrato
Pro Personnel-NFC: Joe Collins
Pro Personnel-AFC: George Streeter
Director of Public/Community Relations: Rodney Knox
Director of Marketing/Promotions: Laurie Albrecht
Ticket Manager: Lynn Carrozzi
Director of Stadium Operations: Murlan (Mo) Fowell
Video Director: Robert Yanagi
Trainer: Lindsy McLean
Equipment Manager: Bronco Hinek
Stadium: 3Com Park •**Capacity:** 70,207
San Francisco, California 94124
Playing Surface: Grass
Training Camp: Sierra Community College
Rocklin, California 95677

1996 SCHEDULE

PRESEASON

Aug. 3	**Denver**	1:00
Aug. 10	**San Diego**	5:00
Aug. 18	at Jacksonville	8:00
Aug. 23	at Seattle	7:00

REGULAR SEASON

Sept. 1	**New Orleans**	1:00
Sept. 8	**St. Louis**	1:00
Sept. 15	Open Date	
Sept. 22	at Carolina	1:00
Sept. 29	**Atlanta**	1:00
Oct. 6	at St. Louis	3:00
Oct. 14	at Green Bay (Mon.)	8:00
Oct. 20	**Cincinnati**	1:00
Oct. 27	at Houston	12:00
Nov. 3	at New Orleans	7:00
Nov. 10	**Dallas**	1:00
Nov. 17	**Baltimore**	1:00
Nov. 24	at Washington	1:00
Dec. 2	at Atlanta (Mon.)	9:00
Dec. 8	**Carolina**	1:00
Dec. 15	at Pittsburgh	1:00
Dec. 23	**Detroit** (Mon.)	6:00

RECORD HOLDERS

INDIVIDUAL RECORDS—CAREER

Category	Name	Performance
Rushing (Yds.)	Joe Perry, 1950-1960, 1963	7,344
Passing (Yds.)	Joe Montana, 1979-1992	35,124
Passing (TDs)	Joe Montana, 1979-1992	244
Receiving (No.)	Jerry Rice, 1985-1995	*942
Receiving (Yds.)	Jerry Rice, 1985-1995	*15,123
Interceptions	Ronnie Lott, 1981-1990	51
Punting (Avg.)	Tommy Davis, 1959-1969	44.7
Punt Return (Avg.)	Manfred Moore, 1974-75	14.7
Kickoff Return (Avg.)	Abe Woodson, 1958-1964	29.4
Field Goals	Ray Wersching, 1977-1987	190
Touchdowns (Tot.)	Jerry Rice, 1985-1995	*156
Points	Ray Wersching, 1977-1987	979

INDIVIDUAL RECORDS—SINGLE SEASON

Category	Name	Performance
Rushing (Yds.)	Roger Craig, 1988	1,502
Passing (Yds.)	Steve Young, 1993	4,023
Passing (TDs)	Steve Young, 1994	35
Receiving (No.)	Jerry Rice, 1995	122
Receiving (Yds.)	Jerry Rice, 1995	*1,848
Interceptions	Dave Baker, 1960	10
	Ronnie Lott, 1986	10
Punting (Avg.)	Tommy Davis, 1965	45.8
Punt Return (Avg.)	Dana McLemore, 1982	22.3
Kickoff Return (Avg.)	Joe Arenas, 1953	34.4
Field Goals	Mike Cofer, 1989	29
Touchdowns (Tot.)	Jerry Rice, 1987	23
Points	Jerry Rice, 1987	138

INDIVIDUAL RECORDS—SINGLE GAME

Category	Name	Performance
Rushing (Yds.)	Delvin Williams, 10-31-76	194
Passing (Yds.)	Joe Montana, 10-14-90	476
Passing (TDs)	Joe Montana, 10-14-90	6
Receiving (No.)	Jerry Rice, 11-20-94	16
Receiving (Yds.)	Jerry Rice, 12-18-95	289
Interceptions	Dave Baker, 12-4-60	*4
Field Goals	Ray Wersching, 10-16-83	6
Touchdowns (Tot.)	Jerry Rice, 10-14-90	5
Points	Jerry Rice, 10-14-90	30

*NFL Record

COACHING HISTORY

(377-293-13)

1950-54	Lawrence (Buck) Shaw	33-25-2
1955	Norman (Red) Strader	4-8-0
1956-58	Frankie Albert	19-17-1
1959-63	Howard (Red) Hickey*	27-27-1
1963-67	Jack Christiansen	26-38-3
1968-75	Dick Nolan	56-56-5
1976	Monte Clark	8-6-0
1977	Ken Meyer	5-9-0
1978	Pete McCulley**	1-8-0
1978	Fred O'Connor	1-6-0
1979-88	Bill Walsh	102-63-1
1989-95	George Seifert	95-30-0

*Resigned after three games in 1963
**Released after nine games in 1978

3COM PARK

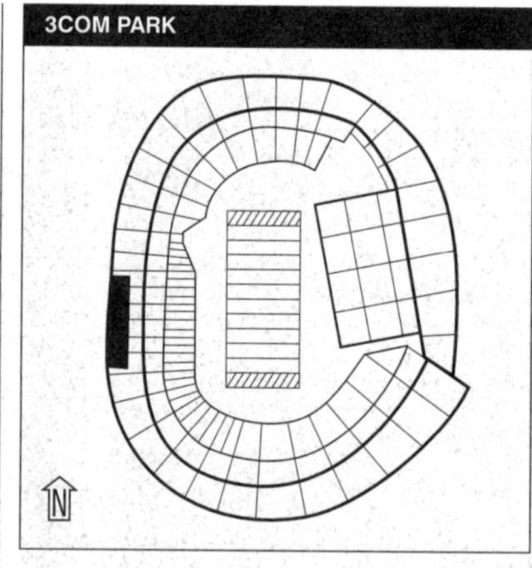

1995 TEAM RECORD

PRESEASON (3-2)

Date	Result		Opponents
7/29	L	7-9	at Denver
8/5	L	10-24	vs. Denver at Tokyo
8/13	W	17-6	at San Diego
8/19	W	17-10	Carolina
8/26	W	17-7	Seattle

REGULAR SEASON (11-5)

Date	Result		Opponents	Att.
9/3	W	24-22	at New Orleans	66,627
9/10	W	41-10	Atlanta	63,627
9/17	W	28-3	New England	66,179
9/25	L	24-27	at Detroit	76,236
10/1	W	20-6	N.Y. Giants	65,536
10/15	L	17-18	at Indianapolis	60,273
10/22	W	44-10	at St. Louis	59,915
10/29	L	7-11	New Orleans	65,272
11/5	L	7-13	Carolina	61,722
11/12	W	38-20	at Dallas	65,180
11/20	W	44-20	at Miami	73,080
11/26	W	41-13	St. Louis	66,049
12/3	W	27-17	Buffalo	65,568
12/10	W	31-10	at Carolina	76,136
12/18	W	37-30	Minnesota	64,975
12/24	L	27-28	at Atlanta	51,785

POSTSEASON (0-1)

1/6	L	17-27	Green Bay	69,311

SCORE BY PERIODS

49ers	114	161	96	86	—	457
Opponents	35	91	81	51	—	258

ATTENDANCE

Home 518,928 Away 529,232 Total 1,048,160
Single-game home record, 69,014 (11/13/94)
Single-season home record, 523,355 (1992)

1995 TEAM STATISTICS

	49ers	Opp.
Total First Downs	355	264
Rushing	109	57
Passing	231	192
Penalty	15	15
Third Down: Made/Att	109/223	85/224
Third Down Pct.	48.9	37.9
Fourth Down: Made/Att	11/18	9/23
Fourth Down Pct.	61.1	39.1
Total Net Yards	6087	4398
Avg. Per Game	380.4	274.9
Total Plays	1092	999
Avg. Per Play	5.6	4.4
Net Yards Rushing	1479	1061
Avg. Per Game	92.4	66.3
Total Rushes	415	348
Net Yards Passing	4608	3337
Avg. Per Game	288.0	208.6
Sacked/Yards Lost	33/171	40/240
Gross Yards	4779	3577
Att./Completions	644/432	611/330
Completion Pct.	67.1	54.0
Had Intercepted	16	26
Punts/Avg.	57/40.6	70/41.7
Net Punting Avg.	57/33.7	70/34.7
Penalties/Yards Lost	88/711	74/556
Fumbles/Ball Lost	21/12	23/8
Touchdowns	57	26
Rushing	19	5
Passing	29	19
Returns	9	2
Avg. Time of Possession	31:56	28:04

1995 INDIVIDUAL STATISTICS

PASSING	Att.	Comp.	Yds.	Pct.	TD	Int.	Tkld.	Rate
S. Young	447	299	3200	66.9	20	11	25/115	92.3
Grbac	183	127	1469	69.4	8	5	6/36	96.6
Conklin	12	4	48	33.3	0	0	2/20	46.5
Rice	1	1	41	100.0	1	0	0/0	158.3
Taylor	1	1	21	100.0	0	0	0/0	118.8
49ers	644	432	4779	67.1	29	16	33/171	93.6
Opponents	611	330	3577	54.0	19	26	40/240	64.1

SCORING	TD R	TD P	TD Rt	PAT	FG	Saf	PTS
Rice	1	15	1	0/0	0/0	0	104
Loville	10	3	0	0/0	0/0	0	80
Wilkins	0	0	0	27/29	12/13	0	63
Brien	0	0	0	19/19	7/12	0	40
Stokes	0	4	0	0/0	0/0	0	24
Floyd	2	1	0	0/0	0/0	0	18
Jones	0	3	0	0/0	0/0	0	18
S. Young	3	0	0	0/0	0/0	0	18
Grbac	2	0	0	0/0	0/0	0	12
McDonald	0	0	2	0/0	0/0	0	12
Norton	0	0	2	0/0	0/0	0	12
Taylor	0	2	0	0/0	0/0	0	12
Zendejas	0	0	0	5/6	1/3	0	8
Carter	0	0	1	0/0	0/0	0	6
Davis	0	0	1	0/0	0/0	0	6
Hanks	0	0	1	0/0	0/0	0	6
Singleton	0	1	0	0/0	0/0	0	6
Walker	1	0	0	0/0	0/0	0	6
Woodall	0	0	1	0/0	0/0	0	6
49ers	19	29	9	51/54	20/28	0	457
Opponents	5	19	2	17/18	27/32	0	258

2-Point conversions: Loville, Rice. Team: 2-3.

RUSHING	Att.	Yds.	Avg.	LG	TD
Loville	218	723	3.3	27	10
S. Young	50	250	5.0	29	3
Floyd	64	237	3.7	23	2
Ervins	23	88	3.8	13	0
Walker	14	44	3.1	16	1
Rice	5	36	7.2	20t	1
Willis	12	35	2.9	15	0
Grbac	20	33	1.7	11	2
Carter	7	22	3.1	15	0
Lynn	2	11	5.5	6	0
49ers	415	1479	3.6	29	19
Opponents	348	1061	3.0	33	5

RECEIVING	No.	Yds.	Avg.	LG	TD
Rice	122	1848	15.1	81t	15
Loville	87	662	7.6	31	3
Jones	60	595	9.9	39	3
Floyd	47	348	7.4	23	1
Stokes	38	517	13.6	41t	4
Taylor	29	387	13.3	40	2
Popson	16	128	8.0	16	0
Walker	11	78	7.1	15	0
Singleton	8	108	13.5	23	1
Thomas	6	73	12.2	23	0
Willis	3	8	2.7	5	0
Ervins	2	21	10.5	11	0
Carter	1	4	4.0	4	0
Carolan	1	3	3.0	3	0
Dalman	1	-1	-1.0	-1	0
49ers	432	4779	11.1	81t	29
Opponents	330	3577	10.8	53	19

INTERCEPTIONS	No.	Yds.	Avg.	LG	TD
Drakeford	5	54	10.8	37	0
Hanks	5	31	6.2	23	0
McDonald	4	135	33.8	52t	2
Norton	3	102	34.0	46	2
Davis	3	84	28.0	86t	1
Woodall	2	0	0.0	0	0
Dodge	1	13	13.0	13	0
Stubblefield	1	12	12.0	12	0
Jackson	1	1	1.0	1	0
Pope	1	-7	-7.0	-7	0
49ers	26	425	16.3	86t	5
Opponents	16	247	15.4	96t	2

PUNTING	No.	Yds.	Avg.	In 20	LG
Thompson	57	2312	40.6	13	65
49ers	57	2312	40.6	13	65
Opponents	70	2918	41.7	19	55

PUNT RETURNS	No.	FC	Yds.	Avg.	LG	TD
Carter	9	7	164	18.2	78t	1
Taylor	11	9	56	5.1	11	0
Singleton	5	1	27	5.4	19	0
Hanks	1	0	0	0.0	0	0
Thomas	1	0	25	25.0	25	0
49ers	27	17	272	10.1	78t	1
Opponents	26	20	292	11.2	74	0

KICKOFF RETURNS	No.	Yds.	Avg.	LG	TD
Carter	23	522	22.7	46	0
Willis	17	427	25.1	39	0
Ervins	5	32	6.4	14	0
Warren	4	67	16.8	21	0
Dalman	3	29	9.7	12	0
Thomas	3	49	16.3	20	0
Caldwell	2	40	20.0	20	0
Walker	1	17	17.0	17	0
49ers	58	1183	20.4	46	0
Opponents	82	1857	22.6	71	0

SACKS	No.
Jackson	9.5
B. Young	6.0
Stubblefield	4.5
A. Williams	4.5
Harris	4.0
Woodall	3.0
Brown	1.5
Barnett	1.0
Bryant	1.0
Davis	1.0
Drakeford	1.0
Fountaine	1.0
Norton	1.0
Plummer	1.0
49ers	40.0
Opponents	33.0

1996 DRAFT CHOICES

Round	Name	Pos.	College
2	Israel Ifeanyi	DE	Southern California
3	Terrell Owens	WR	Tenn.-Chattanooga
4	Daryl Price	DE	Colorado
5	Iheanyi Uwaezuoke	WR	California
6	Stephen Pitts	RB	Penn State
7	Sean Manuel	TE	New Mexico State
	Sam Manuel	LB	New Mexico State

SAN FRANCISCO 49ERS

1996 VETERAN ROSTER

No.	Name	Pos.	Ht.	Wt.	Birthdate	NFL Exp.	College	Hometown	How Acq.	'95 Games/ Starts
92	Barker, Roy	DE	6-5	290	2/14/69	5	North Carolina	New York, N.Y.	UFA(Minn)-'96	16/16*
72	Barnett, Oliver	DE	6-3	285	4/9/66	7	Kentucky	Jefferson, Ky.	UFA(Buff)-'95	7/0
79	Barton, Harris	T	6-4	286	4/19/64	10	North Carolina	Atlanta, Ga.	D1a-'87	12/12
78	Brandon, Michael	DE	6-4	290	7/30/68	3	Florida	Perry, Fla.	FA-'95	11/0
11	Brohm, Jeff	QB	6-1	205	4/24/71	2	Louisville	Louisville, Ky.	FA-'95	0*
65	Brown, Ray	G	6-5	315	12/12/62	11	Arkansas State	Marion, Ark.	UFA(Wash)-'96	16/16*
90	Bryant, Junior	DE	6-4	275	1/16/71	2	Notre Dame	Omaha, Neb.	FA-'95	16/4
28	Buckley, Curtis	S	5-10	190	9/25/70	4	East Texas State	Silsbee, Tex.	RFA(TB)-'96	15/0*
81	Caldwell, Mike	WR	6-2	200	3/28/71	2	California	Danville, Calif.	FA-'96	2/0
86	Carolan, Brett	TE	6-3	241	3/16/71	3	Washington State	Novato, Calif.	FA-'94	14/0
35	Carter, Dexter	RB-KR	5-9	170	9/15/67	7	Florida State	Baxley, Ga.	FA-'95	17/0*
68	Chung, Eugene	G-T	6-5	311	6/14/69	5	Virginia Tech	Oakton, Va.	UFA(Jax)-'96	11/0*
49	Cooper, Adrian	TE	6-5	268	4/27/68	6	Oklahoma	Denver, Colo.	UFA(Minn)-'96	13/13*
67	Dalman, Chris	C-G	6-3	285	3/15/70	4	Stanford	Salinas, Calif.	D6-'93	15/1
17	Davenport, Charles	WR	6-3	210	11/22/68	4	North Carolina State	Fayetteville, N.C.	FA-'96	0*
33	Dodge, Dedrick	S	6-2	184	6/14/67	5	Florida State	Mulberry, Fla.	FA-'94	16/1
56	Doleman, Chris	DE	6-5	275	10/16/61	12	Pittsburgh	York, Pa.	UFA(Atl)-'96	16/16*
22	Drakeford, Tyronne	CB	5-9	185	6/21/71	3	Virginia Tech	Camden, S.C.	D2b-'94	16/4
40	Floyd, William	RB	6-1	242	2/17/72	3	Florida State	St. Petersburg, Fla.	D1b-'94	8/8
59	Gordon, Steve	C	6-4	290	4/15/69	2	California	Nevada City, Calif.	FA-'96	0*
98	Goss, Antonio	LB	6-4	228	8/11/66	7	North Carolina	Randleman, N.C.	FA-'94	16/0
18	Grbac, Elvis	QB	6-5	232	8/13/70	4	Michigan	Willoughby Hills, Ohio	D8-'93	16/5
36	Hanks, Merton	S	6-2	185	3/12/68	6	Iowa	Dallas, Tex.	D5a-'91	16/16
77	Hanshaw, Tim	G	6-5	300	4/27/70	2	Brigham Young	Spokane, Wash.	D4-'95	0*
31	Israel, Steve	CB	5-11	186	3/16/69	5	Pittsburgh	Haddon Heights, N.J.	FA-'95	8/0
32	Johnson, Johnny	RB	6-3	220	6/11/68	5	San Jose State	Santa Cruz, Calif.	FA-'96	0*
84	Jones, Brent	TE	6-4	230	2/12/63	10	Santa Clara	San Jose, Calif.	FA-'87	16/16
57	Kirk, Randy	LB	6-2	235	12/27/64	9	San Diego State	San Diego, Calif.	UFA(Ariz)-'96	16/0*
25	Lassic, Derrick	RB	5-10	188	1/26/70	4	Alabama	Haverstraw, N.Y.	FA-'96	0*
20	Loville, Derek	RB	5-10	205	7/4/68	6	Oregon	San Francisco, Calif.	FA-'94	16/16
29	Lynn, Anthony	RB	6-3	230	12/21/68	3	Texas Tech	McKinney, Tex.	FA-'95	6/0
46	McDonald, Tim	S	6-2	215	1/6/65	10	Southern California	Fresno, Calif.	FA-'93	16/16
69	Milstead, Rod	G	6-2	278	11/10/69	5	Delaware State	Bryans Road, Md.	FA-'94	16/12
55	Mitchell, Kevin	LB	6-1	260	1/1/71	3	Syracuse	Harrisburg, Pa.	D2a-'94	15/0
51	Norton, Ken	LB	6-2	241	9/29/66	9	UCLA	Los Angeles, Calif.	UFA(Dall)-'94	16/16
26	O'Neill, Brian	RB	6-0	233	2/25/70	3	Penn State	Cincinnati, Ohio	FA-'95	3/0
53	Peterson, Anthony	LB	6-0	223	1/23/72	3	Notre Dame	Monongahela, Pa.	D5-'94	15/0
50	Plummer, Gary	LB	6-2	247	1/26/60	11	California	Fremont, Calif.	UFA(SD)-'94	16/14
23	Pope, Marquez	CB	5-11	193	10/29/70	5	Fresno State	Long Beach, Calif.	RFA(StL)-'95	16/15
85	Popson, Ted	TE	6-4	250	9/10/66	3	Portland State	Lake Tahoe, Calif.	FA-'94	12/0
80	Rice, Jerry	WR	6-2	200	10/13/62	12	Mississippi Valley State	Crawford, Miss.	D1-'85	16/16
61	Sapolu, Jesse	G	6-4	278	3/10/61	14	Hawaii	Honolulu, Hawaii	D11-'83	16/16
76	Scrafford, Kirk	T	6-6	275	3/15/67	7	Montana	Billings, Mont.	UFA(Den)-'95	16/11
88	Singleton, Nate	WR	5-11	190	7/5/68	4	Grambling State	Marrero, La.	FA-'93	6/2
83	Stokes, J.J.	WR	6-4	217	10/6/72	2	UCLA	San Diego, Calif.	D1-'95	12/2
94	Stubblefield, Dana	DT	6-2	290	11/14/70	4	Kansas	Cleves, Ohio	D1a-'93	16/16
3	Thompson, Tommy	P	5-10	192	4/27/72	2	Oregon	Lompoc, Calif.	FA-'95	16/0
44	Vardell, Tommy	RB	6-2	230	2/20/69	5	Stanford	El Cajon, Calif.	UFA(Balt)-'96	5/0*
14	Wilkins, Jeff	K	6-2	192	4/19/72	3	Youngstown State	Austintown, Ohio	FA-'95	7/0
24	Willis, Jamal	RB	6-2	218	12/12/72	2	Brigham Young	Las Vegas, Nev.	FA-'95	11/1
54	Woodall, Lee	LB	6-0	220	10/31/69	3	West Chester	Carlisle, Pa.	D6-'94	16/15
97	Young, Bryant	DT	6-2	276	1/27/72	3	Notre Dame	Chicago Heights, Ill.	D1a-'94	12/12
8	Young, Steve	QB	6-2	205	10/11/61	12	Brigham Young	Greenwich, Conn.	T(TB)-'87	11/11

* Barker played 16 games with Minnesota in '95; Brohm inactive for 3 games with San Francisco and 1 game with Washington; Brown played 16 games with Washington; Buckley played 15 games with Tampa Bay; Carter played 10 games with N.Y. Jets and 7 games with San Francisco; Chung played 11 games with Jacksonville; Cooper played 13 games with Minnesota; Davenport last active with Pittsburgh in '94; Doleman played 16 games with Atlanta; Gordon last active with New England in '92; Hanshaw inactive for 16 games; Johnson last active with N.Y. Jets in '94; Kirk played 16 games with Arizona; Lassic missed '95 season because of injury; Vardell played 5 games with Cleveland.

Retired—John Taylor, 10-year wide receiver, 12 games in '95.

Players lost through free agency (3): CB Toi Cook (Den; 2 games in '95), CB Eric Davis (Car; 15), DE Alfred Williams (Den; 16).

Also played with 49ers in '95—K Doug Brien (6 games), DE Dennis Brown (16), QB Cary Conklin (2), G Derrick Deese (2), RB Ricky Ervins (14), CB Darryl Hall (12), DE Tim Harris (10), LB Rickey Jackson (16), C Bart Oates (16), T Frank Pollack (15), LB Chris Thomas (15), RB Adam Walker (13), T Steve Wallace (13), WR Terrence Warren (1), CB Michael Williams (4), K Tony Zendejas (3).

COACHING STAFF

Head Coach,
George Seifert

Pro Career: After leading the 49ers to an 11-5 mark and their fourth consecutive NFC West title in 1995, Seifert is closing in on becoming the team's all-time winnest coach, needing only eight victories to claim the top spot (Bill Walsh has 102 career wins). Named 49ers' head coach on January 26, 1989, after serving as the team's defensive coordinator since 1983. Immediately earned a place in league history, winning a record 17 games his first year and becoming only the second rookie head coach to lead his team to a Super Bowl title (Don McCafferty of Baltimore in 1970 was the first). Recorded the NFL's best won-loss mark in 1990, posting a 14-2 record and guided San Francisco to its fifth consecutive NFC West title. In 1991, the 49ers recorded a 10-6 mark, missing the playoffs for the first time since 1982. Earned consecutive trips to the NFC Championship Game in 1992-93 winning the NFC West each season. In 1994, guided San Francisco to a record fifth Super Bowl championship, posting an NFL-best 16-3 record. Joined 49ers as secondary coach in 1980. In only his second season in the pro ranks, San Francisco had the second best defense in the league and won a Super Bowl (XVI) title, despite starting three rookies in the defensive backfield. Appointed the team's defensive coordinator in 1983. No pro playing experience. Career record: 95-30.

Background: Linebacker at University of Utah (1960-62). Served a six-month tour of duty with the U.S. Army following graduation. Returned to Utah as a graduate assistant in 1964. Named head coach at Westminster College in Salt Lake City in 1965. Assistant at Iowa (1966), Oregon (1967-71), and Stanford (1972-74). Left Stanford to become head coach at Cornell (1975-76). Joined Bill Walsh's staff at Stanford in 1977 and helped the Cardinal to a two-year mark of 17-7, including victories in the Sun and Bluebonnet Bowls. Received bachelor's degree in zoology (1963) and master's degree in physical education (1966) from Utah.

Personal: Born January 22, 1940, in San Francisco. He and his wife, Linda, have two children—Eve and Jason—and live in Los Altos, Calif.

ASSISTANT COACHES

Jerry Attaway, conditioning; born January 3, 1946, Susanville, Calif., lives in San Jose, Calif. Defensive back Yuba, Calif., J.C. 1964-65, Cal-Davis 1967. No pro playing experience. College coach: Cal-Davis 1970-71, Idaho 1972-74, Utah State 1975-77, Southern California 1978-82. Pro coach: Joined 49ers in 1983.

Mike Barnes, conditioning assistant; born March 13, 1966, Rochester N.Y., lives in Dublin, Calif. No college or pro playing experience. College coach: Texas A&M 1990, California 1991-93. Pro coach: Joined 49ers in 1994.

Dwaine Board, defensive line; born November 29, 1956, Rocky Mount, Va., lives in Redwood City, Calif. Defensive lineman North Carolina A&T 1974-77. Pro defensive lineman San Francisco 49ers 1979-87, New Orleans Saints 1988. Pro coach: Joined 49ers in 1991.

Pete Carroll, defensive coordinator; born September 15, 1951, San Francisco, Calif., lives in Santa Clara, Calif. Defensive back Pacific 1969-72. No pro playing experience. College coach: Arkansas 1977, Iowa State 1978, Ohio State 1979, North Carolina State 1980-82, Pacific 1983. Pro coach: Buffalo Bills 1984, Minnesota Vikings 1985-89, New York Jets 1990-94 (head coach 1994), joined 49ers in 1995.

Matt Cavanaugh, quarterbacks; born October 27, 1956, Youngstown, Ohio, lives in Santa Clara, Calif. Quarterback Pittsburgh 1974-77. Pro quarterback New England Patriots 1978-82, San Francisco 49ers 1983-85, Philadelphia Eagles 1986-89, New York Giants 1990-91. College coach: Pittsburgh 1993. Pro coach: Arizona Cardinals 1994-95, joined 49ers in 1996.

Carl Jackson, running backs; born August 16, 1940, Bay City, Tex., lives in San Jose, Calif. Quarterback Prairie View A&M 1959-62. No pro playing experience. College coach: North Texas State 1976-78, Iowa 1979-91. Pro coach: Joined 49ers in 1992.

Larry Kirksey, wide receivers; born January 6, 1951, Harlan, Ky., lives in Pleasanton, Calif. Wide receiver Eastern Kentucky 1970-72. No pro playing experience. College coach: Miami, Ohio 1974-76, Kentucky 1977-81, Kansas 1982, Kentucky State 1983 (head coach), Florida 1984-88, Pittsburgh 1989, Alabama 1990-93. Pro coach: Joined 49ers in 1994.

Greg Knapp, offensive assistant; born March 5, 1963, Long Beach, Calif., lives in Santa Clara, Calif. Quarterback Sacramento State 1982-85. No pro playing experience. College coach: Sacramento State 1986-94. Pro coach: Joined 49ers in 1995.

Johnnie Lynn, defensive backs; born December 19, 1956, Los Angeles, Calif., lives in Santa Clara, Calif. Defensive back UCLA 1975-78. Pro defensive back New York Jets 1979-86. College coach: Arizona 1988-93. Pro coach: Tampa Bay Buccaneers 1994-95, joined 49ers in 1996.

John Marshall, linebackers; born October 2, 1945, Arroyo Grande, Calif., lives in Pleasanton, Calif. Linebacker Washington State 1964. No pro playing experience. College coach: Oregon 1970-76, Southern California 1977-79. Pro coach: Green Bay Packers 1980-82, Atlanta Falcons 1983-85, Indianapolis Colts 1986-88, joined 49ers in 1989.

Bobb McKittrick, offensive line; born December 29, 1935, Baker, Ore., lives in San Mateo, Calif. Guard Oregon State 1955-57. No pro playing experience. College coach: Oregon State 1961-64, UCLA 1965-70. Pro coach: Los Angeles Rams 1971-72, San Diego Chargers 1974-78, joined 49ers in 1979.

Bill McPherson, assistant head coach; born October 24, 1931, Santa Clara, Calif., lives in San Jose, Calif. Tackle Santa Clara 1950-52. No pro playing experience. College coach: Santa Clara 1963-74, UCLA 1975-77. Pro coach: Philadelphia Eagles 1978, joined 49ers in 1979.

Bo Pellini, defensive assistant; born December 13, 1967, Youngstown, Ohio, lives in Sunnyvale, Calif. Defensive back Ohio State 1986-90. No pro playing experience. College coach: Iowa 1991-92. Pro coach: Joined 49ers in 1994.

Mike Solari, tight ends-offensive line assistant; born January 16, 1955, Daly City, Calif., lives in Pleasanton, Calif. Offensive lineman San Diego State 1975-76. No pro playing experience. College coach: Mira Vista (Calif.) Junior College 1977-78, U.S. International 1979, Boise State 1980, Cincinnati 1981-82, Kansas 1983-85, Pittsburgh 1986, Alabama 1990-91. Pro coach: Dallas Cowboys 1987-88, Phoenix Cardinals 1989, joined 49ers in 1992.

George Stewart, special teams; born December 29, 1958, Little Rock, Ark., lives in Santa Clara, Calif. Guard Arkansas 1977-80. No pro playing experience. College coach: Minnesota 1984-85, Notre Dame 1986-88. Pro coach: Pittsburgh Steelers 1989-91, Tampa Bay Buccaneers 1992-95, joined 49ers in 1996.

Marc Trestman, offensive coordinator; born January 15, 1956, Minneapolis, Minn., lives in Santa Clara, Calif. Quarterback Minnesota 1975-77, Moorhead (Minn.) State 1978. Pro quarterback Minnesota Vikings 1979. College coach: Miami 1981-84. Pro coach: Minnesota Vikings 1985-86, 1990-91, Tampa Bay Buccaneers 1987, Cleveland Browns 1988-89, joined 49ers in 1995.

Bill Walsh, administrative assistant to the coaching staff; born November 30, 1931, Los Angeles, Calif., lives in Atherton, Calif. End San Jose State 1953-54. No pro playing experience. College coach: California 1960-62, Stanford 1963-66, 1977-78 (head coach), 1992-94 (head coach). Pro coach: Oakland Raiders 1966-67, Cincinnati Bengals 1968-75, San Diego Chargers 1976, San Francisco 49ers 1979-88 (head coach), re-joined 49ers in 1996.

1996 FIRST-YEAR ROSTER

Name	Pos.	Ht.	Wt.	Birthdate	College	Hometown	How Acq.
Anthony, Charles (1)	CB	6-2	195	10/12/69	Nevada-Las Vegas	Las Vegas, Nev.	FA
Benefield, Daved (1)	LB	6-4	231	2/16/68	Cal State-Northridge	Arcadia, Calif.	FA
Branch, Darrick (1)	WR	6-0	196	2/10/70	Hawaii	Dallas, Tex.	FA
Carter, Eric (1)	S	6-0	195	1/23/69	Knoxville	Jesup, Ga.	FA
Fiore, Dave	T	6-4	275	8/10/74	Hofstra	Waldwick, N.J.	FA
Guarnera, James	DE	6-5	270	4/7/74	Rutgers	S. Huntington, N.Y.	FA
Ifeanyi, Israel	DE	6-3	246	11/21/70	Southern California	Lagos, Nigeria	D2
Manuel, Sam	LB	6-2	235	12/1/73	New Mexico State	Los Gatos, Calif.	D7b
Manuel, Sean	TE	6-2	245	12/1/73	New Mexico State	Los Gatos, Calif.	D7a
Moore, LaRon	CB	5-9	190	4/22/73	Notre Dame	Indianapolis, Ind.	FA
Owens, Terrell	WR	6-2	213	12/7/73	Tenn.-Chattanooga	Alexander City, Ala.	D3
Pitts, Stephen	RB	5-10	192	2/16/73	Penn State	Middletown, N.J.	D6
Pope, Marvin (1)	LB	6-1	240	1/18/69	Central State, Ohio	Gainesville, Fla.	FA
Price, Daryl	DE	6-3	274	10/23/72	Colorado	Beaumont, Tex.	D4
Reese, Albert	DT	6-6	275	4/29/73	Grambling State	Mobile, Ala.	FA
Richter, Jim	K	6-4	212	6/1/74	Furman	Columbia, S.C.	FA
Soenksen, Matt	G	6-4	316	10/8/73	UCLA	Arroyo Grande, Calif.	FA
Thompson, Chris (1)	LB	6-4	265	6/17/69	Bowie State	Clinton, Md.	FA
Uwaezuoke, Iheanyi	WR	6-2	195	7/24/73	California	Inglewood, Calif.	D5
Walker, James	LB	6-3	203	10/10/73	North Carolina State	Walterboro, S.C.	FA
Williams, Michael (1)	CB	5-10	185	5/28/70	UCLA	Los Angeles, Calif.	FA

The term NFL Rookie is defined as a player who is in his first season of professional football and has not been on the roster of another professional football team for any regular-season or postseason games. A Rookie is designated by an "R" on NFL rosters. Players who have been active in another professional football league or players who have NFL experience, including either preseason training camp or being on an Active List or Inactive List, or on Reserve/Injured or Reserve/Physically Unable to Perform for fewer than six regular-season games, are termed NFL First-Year Players. An NFL First-Year Player is designated by a "1" on NFL rosters. Thereafter, a player is credited with an additional year of experience for each season in which he accumulates six games on the Active List or Inactive List, or on Reserve/Injured or Reserve/Physically Unable to Perform.

NOTES

TAMPA BAY BUCCANEERS

National Football Conference
Central Division
Team Colors: Florida Orange, White, and Red
One Buccaneer Place
Tampa, Florida 33607
Telephone: (813) 870-2700

CLUB OFFICIALS

Owner/President: Malcolm Glazer
Executive Vice President: Bryan Glazer
Executive Vice President: Joel Glazer
General Manager: Rich McKay
Director of Player Personnel: Jerry Angelo
Director of College Scouting: Tim Ruskell
Director of Ticket Sales and Operations: Rick Odioso
Director of Public Relations: Chip Namias
Director of Corporate Sales/Broadcasting: Jim Overton
Director of Sales & Advertising: Paul Sickmon
Controller: Patrick Smith
College Scouts: Mike Ackerley, Dave Boller, Ruston Webster, Mike Yowarsky
Pro Personnel Assistants: John Idzik, Mark Dominik
Asst. Director/Ticket Operations: Lori Grimm
Asst. Director/Public Relations: Scott Smith
Public Relations Assistant: Nelson Luis
Computer Services Coordinator: Terri Kimbell
Assistant Director/Sales & Advertising: Jayne Portnoy
Assistant Director/Sales & Fundraising: Sherry Gruden
Corporate Sales Assistant: Heidi Soderholm
Trainer: Chris Smith
Assistant Trainer: Joe Joe Petrone
Equipment Manager: Frank Pupello
Video Director: Davy Levy
Assistant Video Director: Pat Brazil
Stadium: Tampa Stadium • **Capacity:** 74,301
Tampa, Florida 33607
Playing Surface: Grass
Training Camp: University of Tampa
Tampa, Florida 33606

1996 SCHEDULE

PRESEASON

Aug. 3	at Miami	7:00
Aug. 10	**Atlanta**	7:30
Aug. 17	at Pittsburgh	6:00
Aug. 23	**Miami**	7:30

REGULAR SEASON

Sept. 1	**Green Bay**	4:00
Sept. 8	at Detroit	1:00
Sept. 15	at Denver	6:00
Sept. 22	**Seattle**	4:00
Sept. 29	**Detroit**	1:00
Oct. 6	Open Date	
Oct. 13	**Minnesota**	1:00
Oct. 20	at Arizona	1:00
Oct. 27	at Green Bay	12:00
Nov. 3	at Chicago	12:00
Nov. 10	**Oakland**	1:00
Nov. 17	at San Diego	1:00
Nov. 24	**New Orleans**	1:00
Dec. 1	at Carolina	1:00
Dec. 8	**Washington**	1:00
Dec. 15	at Minnesota	12:00
Dec. 22	**Chicago**	1:00

RECORD HOLDERS

INDIVIDUAL RECORDS—CAREER

Category	Name	Performance
Rushing (Yds.)	James Wilder, 1981-89	5,957
Passing (Yds.)	Vinny Testaverde, 1987-1992	14,820
Passing (TDs)	Vinny Testaverde, 1987-1992	77
Receiving (No.)	James Wilder, 1981-89	430
Receiving (Yds.)	Mark Carrier, 1987-1992	5,018
Interceptions	Cedric Brown, 1977-1984	29
Punting (Avg.)	Frank Garcia, 1983-87	41.1
Punt Return (Avg.)	Willie Drewrey, 1989-1992	9.4
Kickoff Return (Avg.)	Isaac Hagins, 1976-1980	21.9
Field Goals	Donald Igwebuike, 1985-89	94
Touchdowns (Tot.)	James Wilder, 1981-89	46
Points	Donald Igwebuike, 1985-89	416

INDIVIDUAL RECORDS—SINGLE SEASON

Category	Name	Performance
Rushing (Yds.)	James Wilder, 1984	1,544
Passing (Yds.)	Doug Williams, 1981	3,563
Passing (TDs)	Doug Williams, 1980	20
	Vinny Testaverde, 1989	20
Receiving (No.)	Mark Carrier, 1989	86
Receiving (Yds.)	Mark Carrier, 1989	1,422
Interceptions	Cedric Brown, 1981	9
Punting (Avg.)	Reggie Roby, 1995	42.8
Punt Return (Avg.)	Courtney Hawkins, 1993	11.1
Kickoff Return (Avg.)	Isaac Hagins, 1977	23.5
Field Goals	Steve Christie, 1990	23
	Michael Husted, 1994	23
Touchdowns (Tot.)	James Wilder, 1984	13
Points	Donald Igwebuike, 1989	99

INDIVIDUAL RECORDS—SINGLE GAME

Category	Name	Performance
Rushing (Yds.)	James Wilder, 11-6-83	219
Passing (Yds.)	Doug Williams, 11-16-80	486
Passing (TDs)	Steve DeBerg, 9-13-87	5
Receiving (No.)	James Wilder, 9-15-85	13
Receiving (Yds.)	Mark Carrier, 12-6-87	212
Interceptions	Many times.	2
	Last time by Martin Mayhew, 12-3-95	
Field Goals	Many times.	4
	Last time by Michael Husted, 10-8-95	
Touchdowns (Tot.)	Jimmie Giles, 10-20-85	4

COACHING HISTORY

(95-216-1)

1976-84	John McKay	45-91-1
1985-86	Leeman Bennett	4-28-0
1987-90	Ray Perkins*	19-41-0
1990-91	Richard Williamson	4-15-0
1992-95	Sam Wyche	23-41-0

*Released after 13 games in 1990

TAMPA STADIUM

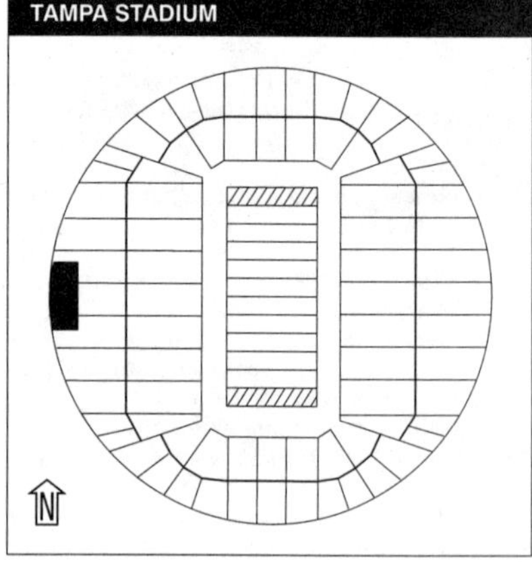

1995 TEAM RECORD

PRESEASON (3-1)

Date	Result		Opponents
8/5	L	3-9	N.Y. Jets
8/11	W	31-7	at Cincinnati
8/19	W	20-7	Pittsburgh
8/25	W	24-17	vs. Miami at Orlando, Fla.

REGULAR SEASON (7-9)

Date	Result		Opponents	Att.
9/3	W	21-6	at Philadelphia	66,266
9/10	L	6-22	at Cleveland	61,083
9/17	L	6-25	Chicago	71,507
9/24	W	14-6	Washington	49,234
10/1	W	20-13	at Carolina	50,076
10/8	W	19-16	Cincinnati	41,732
10/15	W	20-17	Minnesota (OT)	55,703
10/22	L	21-24	Atlanta	66,135
10/29	L	7-19	at Houston	31,489
11/12	L	24-27	at Detroit	60,644
11/19	W	17-16	Jacksonville	71,629
11/26	L	13-35	at Green Bay	59,218
12/3	L	17-31	at Minnesota	52,879
12/10	W	13-10	Green Bay (OT)	67,557
12/17	L	10-31	at Chicago	49,475
12/23	L	10-37	Detroit	50,049

(OT) Overtime

SCORE BY PERIODS

Buccaneers	48	77	36	71	6	—	238
Opponents	73	106	69	87	0	—	335

ATTENDANCE

Home 473,546 Away 431,130 Total 904,676
Single-game home record, 72,077 (10/8/89)
Single-season home record, 545,980 (1979)

1995 TEAM STATISTICS

	Buccaneers	Opp.
Total First Downs	283	336
Rushing	101	104
Passing	159	202
Penalty	23	30
Third Down: Made/Att	68/195	93/211
Third Down Pct.	34.9	44.1
Fourth Down: Made/Att	7/13	4/7
Fourth Down Pct.	53.8	57.1
Total Net Yards	4542	5712
Avg. Per Game	283.9	357.0
Total Plays	961	1031
Avg. Per Play	4.7	5.5
Net Yards Rushing	1587	1754
Avg. Per Game	99.2	109.6
Total Rushes	398	449
Net Yards Passing	2955	3958
Avg. Per Game	184.7	247.4
Sacked/Yards Lost	56/386	25/140
Gross Yards	3341	4098
Att./Completions	507/267	557/346
Completion Pct.	52.7	62.1
Had Intercepted	20	14
Punts/Avg.	78/42.3	59/40.0
Net Punting Avg.	78/36.2	59/32.3
Penalties/Yards Lost	113/882	87/698
Fumbles/Ball Lost	25/14	26/16
Touchdowns	26	35
Rushing	19	14
Passing	5	19
Returns	2	2
Avg. Time of Possession	28:35	31:25

1995 INDIVIDUAL STATISTICS

PASSING	Att.	Comp.	Yds.	Pct.	TD	Int.	Tkld.	Rate
Dilfer	415	224	2774	54.0	4	18	47/331	60.1
Weldon	91	42	519	46.2	1	2	9/55	58.8
Roby	1	1	48	100.0	0	0	0/0	118.8
Buccaneers	507	267	3341	52.7	5	20	56/386	60.3
Opponents	557	346	4098	62.1	19	14	25/140	85.4

SCORING	TD R	TD P	TD Rt	PAT	FG	Saf	PTS
Husted	0	0	0	25/25	19/26	0	82
Rhett	11	0	0	0/0	0/0	0	66
Ellison	5	0	0	0/0	0/0	0	30
Copeland	0	2	0	0/0	0/0	0	12
Dilfer	2	0	0	0/0	0/0	0	12
Harper	0	2	0	0/0	0/0	0	12
Harris	0	1	0	0/0	0/0	0	6
Mayhew	0	0	1	0/0	0/0	0	6
Sapp	0	0	1	0/0	0/0	0	6
Weldon	1	0	0	0/0	0/0	0	6
Buccaneers	19	5	2	25/25	19/26	0	238
Opponents	14	19	2	30/31	31/40	0	335

2-Point conversions: 0. Team: 0-1.

RUSHING	Att.	Yds.	Avg.	LG	TD
Rhett	332	1207	3.6	21	11
Ellison	26	218	8.4	75	5
Dilfer	23	115	5.0	21t	2
Edmonds	5	28	5.6	9	0
Hawkins	4	5	1.3	11	0
Thomas	1	5	5.0	5	0
Weldon	5	5	1.0	6	1
Moore	1	4	4.0	4	0
Roby	1	0	0.0	0	0
Buccaneers	398	1587	4.0	75	19
Opponents	449	1754	3.9	66t	14

RECEIVING	No.	Yds.	Avg.	LG	TD
Harris	62	751	12.1	33	1
Harper	46	633	13.8	49	2
Hawkins	41	493	12.0	47	0
Copeland	35	605	17.3	64t	2
Dawsey	30	372	12.4	26	0
Rhett	14	110	7.9	18	0
Moore	13	102	7.8	21	0
Thomas	10	107	10.7	24	0
Armstrong	7	68	9.7	29	0
Ellison	7	44	6.3	14	0
Booty	1	48	48.0	48	0
Edmonds	1	8	8.0	8	0
Buccaneers	267	3341	12.5	64t	5
Opponents	346	4098	11.8	91t	19

INTERCEPTIONS	No.	Yds.	Avg.	LG	TD
Mayhew	5	81	16.2	40	0
Lynch	3	3	1.0	3	0
Booty	1	21	21.0	21	0
Bouie	1	19	19.0	19	0
Marts	1	8	8.0	8	0
Sapp	1	5	5.0	5t	1
Dimry	1	0	0.0	0	0
Johnson	1	0	0.0	0	0
Buccaneers	14	137	9.8	40	1
Opponents	20	204	10.2	32	0

PUNTING	No.	Yds.	Avg.	In 20	LG
Roby	77	3296	42.8	23	61
Buccaneers	78	3296	42.3	23	61
Opponents	59	2358	40.0	12	61

PUNT RETURNS	No.	FC	Yds.	Avg.	LG	TD
Edmonds	29	10	293	10.1	45	0
Buccaneers	29	10	293	10.1	45	0
Opponents	41	11	335	8.2	38	0

KICKOFF RETURNS	No.	Yds.	Avg.	LG	TD
Edmonds	58	1147	19.8	44	0
Ellison	15	261	17.4	33	0
Buckley	2	29	14.5	18	0
Armstrong	1	6	6.0	6	0
Buccaneers	76	1443	19.0	44	0
Opponents	46	856	18.6	37	0

SACKS	No.
Dotson	5.0
Culpepper	4.0
Ahanotu	3.0
Sapp	3.0
Curry	2.0
McIntosh	2.0
Nickerson	1.5
Brooks	1.0
Everett	1.0
Powe	1.0
Wheeler	1.0
Rouse	0.5
Buccaneers	25.0
Opponents	56.0

1996 DRAFT CHOICES

Round	Name	Pos.	College
1	Regan Upshaw	DE	California
	Marcus Jones	DT	North Carolina
2	Mike Alstott	RB	Purdue
3	Donnie Abraham	DB	E. Tennessee State
4	Jason Odom	T	Florida
	Eric Austin	DB	Jackson State
5	Jason Maniecki	DT	Wisconsin
6	Nilo Silvan	WR	Tennessee
7	Reggie Rusk	DB	Kentucky

TAMPA BAY BUCCANEERS

1996 VETERAN ROSTER

No.		Name	Pos.	Ht.	Wt.	Birthdate	NFL Exp.	College	Hometown	How Acq.	'95 Games/ Starts
26		Abraham, Clifton	CB	5-9	184	12/9/71	2	Florida State	Dallas, Tex.	D5-'95	6/0
71		Adams, Scott	T	6-5	305	9/28/66	5	Georgia	Lake City, Fla.	UFA(Chi)-'96	4/0*
72		Ahanotu, Chidi	DE-DT	6-2	288	10/11/70	4	California	Berkeley, Calif.	D6-'93	16/15
86		Armstrong, Tyji	TE	6-4	277	10/3/70	5	Mississippi	Inkster, Mich.	D3b-'92	16/5
62		Beckles, Ian	G	6-1	304	7/20/67	7	Indiana	Montreal, Canada	D5-'90	15/15
44		Booty, John	S	6-0	185	10/9/65	9	Texas Christian	Carthage, Tex.	UFA(NYG)-'95	7/2
23		Bouie, Tony	S	5-10	187	8/7/72	2	Arizona	New Orleans, La.	FA-'95	9/3
53	#	Brady, Ed	LB	6-2	238	6/17/62	13	Illinois	Morris, Ill.	FA(Cin)-'92	16/0
55		Brooks, Derrick	LB	6-0	225	4/18/73	2	Florida State	Pensacola, Fla.	D1b-'95	16/13
27		Bussey, Barney	S	6-0	210	5/20/62	11	South Carolina State	Lincolnton, Ga.	UFA(Cin)-'93	8/5
88		Copeland, Horace	WR	6-3	202	1/2/71	4	Miami	Orlando, Fla.	D4b-'93	15/7
77		Culpepper, Brad	DT	6-1	270	5/8/69	5	Florida	Tallahassee, Fla.	W(Minn)-'94	16/4
75		Curry, Eric	DE	6-5	270	2/3/70	4	Alabama	Thomasville, Ga.	D1-'93	16/16
80		Dawsey, Lawrence	WR	6-0	192	11/16/67	6	Florida State	Dothan, Ala.	D3-'91	12/10
12		Dilfer, Trent	QB	6-4	235	3/13/72	3	Fresno State	Aptos, Calif.	D1-'94	16/16
76		Dill, Scott	T-G	6-5	295	4/5/66	9	Memphis State	Birmingham, Ala.	FA-'90	12/12
39		Dimry, Charles	CB	6-0	176	1/31/66	9	Nevada-Las Vegas	Oceanside, Calif.	UFA(Den)-'94	16/16
93	†	DuBose, Demetrius	LB	6-1	235	3/23/71	4	Notre Dame	Seattle, Wash.	D2-'93	15/0
41		Edmonds, Bobby Joe	RB	5-11	190	9/26/64	6	Arkansas	St. Louis, Mo.	FA-'95	16/0
37		Ellison, Jerry	RB	5-10	198	12/20/71	2	Tennessee-Chattanooga	Augusta, Ga.	FA-'94	16/3
29		Gant, Kenneth	S	5-11	195	4/18/67	7	Albany State	Lakeland, Fla.	UFA(Dall)-'95	16/3
74		Gruber, Paul	T	6-5	296	2/24/65	9	Wisconsin	Prairie du Sac, Wis.	D1-'88	16/16
82		Harper, Alvin	WR	6-4	218	7/6/68	6	Tennessee	Frostproof, Fla.	UFA(Dall)-'95	13/12
81		Harris, Jackie	TE	6-4	239	1/4/68	7	Northeast Louisiana	Pine Bluff, Ark.	RFA(GB)-'94	16/16
85		Hawkins, Courtney	WR	5-9	183	12/12/69	5	Michigan State	Flint, Mich.	D2-'92	16/3
5		Husted, Michael	K	6-0	195	6/16/70	4	Virginia	Hampton, Va.	FA-'93	16/0
65		Ingram, Stephen	T-G	6-4	311	5/8/71	2	Maryland	Seat Pleasant, Md.	D7a-'95	2/0
40		Johnson, Tracy	RB	6-0	242	11/29/66	8	Clemson	Kannapolis, N.C.	FA-'96	15/4*
25		Johnson, Melvin	S	6-0	191	4/15/72	2	Kentucky	Cincinnati, Ohio	D2-'95	11/3
47	†	Lynch, John	S	6-2	210	9/25/71	4	Stanford	Solana Beach, Calif.	D3b-'93	9/6
51		Marts, Lonnie	LB	6-2	236	11/10/68	7	Tulane	New Orleans, La.	UFA(KC)-'94	15/13
61		Mayberry, Tony	C	6-4	292	12/8/67	7	Wake Forest	Springfield, Va.	D4b-'90	16/16
35		Mayhew, Martin	CB	5-8	178	10/8/65	9	Florida State	Tallahassee, Fla.	UFA(Wash)-'93	13/13
96		Mills, Lamar	DT	6-4	307	1/26/71	2	Indiana	Detroit, Mich.	FA-'96	0*
66		Moore, Darryl	G	6-3	293	1/27/69	3	Texas-El Paso	Minden, La.	FA-'96	0*
83	†	Moore, Dave	TE-RB	6-2	243	11/11/69	4	Pittsburgh	Succasunna, N.J.	FA-'92	16/8
56		Nickerson, Hardy	LB	6-2	229	9/1/65	10	California	Compton, Calif.	UFA(Pitt)-'93	16/16
69		Pierson, Pete	T	6-5	295	2/4/71	2	Washington	Portland, Ore.	D5-'94	12/4
95		Powe, Keith	DE	6-3	265	6/5/69	3	Texas-El Paso	Houston, Tex.	FA-'94	3/0
60		Pyne, Jim	G-C	6-2	282	11/23/71	3	Virginia Tech	Milford, Mass.	D7-'94	15/13
32		Rhett, Errict	RB	5-11	211	12/11/70	3	Florida	Pembroke Pines, Fla.	D2-'94	16/16
1		Roby, Reggie	P	6-3	253	7/30/61	14	Iowa	East Waterloo, Iowa	UFA(Wash)-'95	16/0
52		Rouse, Wardell	LB	6-2	235	6/9/72	2	Clemson	Clewiston, Fla.	D6-'95	16/1
14		Ryans, Larry	WR	5-11	182	7/28/71	2	Clemson	Greenwood, S.C.	FA-'96	0*
99		Sapp, Warren	DT	6-2	281	12/19/72	2	Miami	Apopka, Fla.	D1a-'95	16/8
84		Saunders, Cedric	TE	6-3	240	9/30/72	2	Ohio State	Sarasota, Fla.	FA-'94	3/0
38		Scott, Todd	S	5-11	205	1/23/68	6	Southwestern Louisiana	Galveston, Tex.	W(NYJ)-'95	11/9*
91		Smith, Herman	DE	6-5	261	1/25/71	2	Portland State	Ft. Lauderdale, Fla.	FA-'95	3/0
45	#	Stargell, Tony	CB	5-11	186	8/7/66	7	Tennessee State	La Grange, Ga.	UFA(Ind)-'94	14/6
54		Stephens, Darnell	LB	5-11	243	1/29/73	2	Clemson	San Antonio, Tex.	FA-'95	13/0
87		Thomas, Lamar	WR	6-2	173	2/12/70	4	Miami	Gainesville, Fla.	D3a-'93	11/0
11		Weldon, Casey	QB	6-1	206	2/3/69	5	Florida State	Tallahassee, Fla.	FA-'93	16/0
24		Wilson, Jerry	CB	5-10	184	7/17/73	2	Southern	Lake Charles, La.	D4-'95	0*

* Adams played 4 games with Chicago in '95; Johnson played 15 games with Seattle; Mills last active with Washington in '94; Moore last active with Washington in '93; Ryans last active with Detroit in '94; Scott played 10 games with N.Y. Jets, 1 game with Tampa Bay; Wilson missed '95 season because of injury.

\# Unrestricted free agent; subject to developments.

† Restricted free agent; subject to developments.

Retired—Barney Bussey, 10-year safety, 8 games in '95.

Players lost through free agency (7): S Curtis Buckley (SF; 15 games in '95), DT Santana Dotson (GB; 16), CB Mike McGruder (NE; 16), G-T Charles McRae (Oak; 11), QB Todd Philcox (Jax; 0), C-G Mike Sullivan (Chi; 12), DT Mark Wheeler (NE; 14).

Also played with Buccaneers in '95—WR Tyree Davis (1 game), S Thomas Everett (13), DT Toddrick McIntosh (11).

COACHING STAFF

Head Coach,
Tony Dungy

Pro Career: After 15 years as an NFL assistant coach, was named as the Buccaneers' sixth head coach on January 22, 1996, when he signed a six-year contract. Joined Tampa Bay after serving as Minnesota Vikings' defensive coordinator from 1992-95. Helped Vikings' defense lead NFL with 95 interceptions during his four years in Minnesota. Prior to going to Vikings, spent 1989-1991 as defensive backs coach for Kansas City Chiefs. Also worked eight years as an assistant coach for the Pittsburgh Steelers under Chuck Noll as a defensive assistant (1981), defensive backs coach (1982-83), and as defensive coordinator (1984-88). At 25, was NFL's youngest assistant coach when hired by Steelers in 1981, then became league's youngest coordinator at age of 28. Began coaching career coaching defensive backs at University of Minnesota in 1980. As an NFL player, signed with Pittsburgh as a free agent in 1977 and played safety for Steelers for two seasons (1977-78). Had nine interceptions (second in AFC with 6 in 1978) in 30 games for Pittsburgh and played in Super Bowl XIII victory over Dallas Cowboys. Had unusual distinction of making and throwing an interception in same 1977 game versus Houston Oilers. Traded to San Francisco 49ers during 1979 training camp and played 15 games for 49ers. Was traded again prior to 1980 season to New York Giants in multi-player deal that sent current Philadelphia Eagle head coach Ray Rhodes to 49ers.
Background: Starred as quarterback at University of Minnesota from 1973-76. Finished career as school's all-time leader in attempts, completions, passing yards, and touchdown passes. Left Minnesota in fourth place in Big Ten history in total offense. Two-time team most valuable player, played in Hula Bowl, East-West Shrine Game, and Japan Bowl. Attended Parkside High School in Jackson, Michigan.
Personal: Born October 6, 1955, in Jackson, Michigan. Tony and his wife, Lauren, have three children including daughter Tiara (11), and sons James (9) and Eric (4). The family resides in Tampa.

ASSISTANT COACHES

Mark Asanovich, strength and conditioning; born May 20, 1959, Duluth, Minn., lives in Clearwater, Fla. No college or pro playing experience. College coach: Ohio State 1985, Citadel 1986. Pro coach: Minnesota Vikings 1995, joined Buccaneers in 1996.
Clyde Christensen, tight ends; born January 28, 1958, Corvine, Calif., lives in Tampa. Quarterback Fresno (Calif.) J.C. 1975, North Carolina 1976-78. No pro playing experience. College coach: East Tennessee State 1980-82, Temple 1983-85, East Carolina 1986-88, Holy Cross 1989-90, South Carolina 1991, Maryland 1992-93, Clemson 1994-95. Pro coach: Joined Buccaneers in 1996.
Herman Edwards, assistant head coach/defensive backs; born April 27, 1954, Monmouth, N.J., lives in Tampa. Defensive back California 1972, 1974, Monterrey Peninsula (Calif.) J.C. 1973, San Diego State 1975-76. Pro defensive back: Philadelphia Eagles 1977-85, Los Angeles Rams 1986, Atlanta Falcons 1986. College coach: San Jose State 1987-89. Pro coach: Kansas City Chiefs 1992-94 (scout 1990-91, 1995), joined Buccaneers in 1996.
Chris Foerster, offensive line; born October 12, 1961, Milwaukee, Wis., lives in Tampa. Center Colorado State 1979-82. No pro playing experience. College coach: Colorado State 1983-87, Stanford 1988-91, Minnesota 1992. Pro coach: Minnesota Vikings 1993-95, joined Buccaneers in 1996.
Monte Kiffin, defensive coordinator; born February 29, 1940, Lexington, Neb., lives in Tampa. Offensive/defensive tackle Nebraska 1959-63. Pro defensive end Winnipeg Blue Bombers (CFL) 1965. College coach: Nebraska 1966-76, Arkansas 1977-79, North Carolina State 1980-82 (head coach). Pro coach: Green Bay Packers 1983, Buffalo Bills 1984-85, Minnesota Vikings 1986-89, 1991-94, New York Jets 1990, New Orleans Saints 1995, joined Buccaneers in 1996.
Joe Marciano, special teams; born February 10, 1954, Scranton, Pa., lives in Tampa. Quarterback Temple 1972-75. No pro playing experience. College coach: East Stroudsburg 1977, Rhode Island 1978-79, Villanova 1980, Penn State 1981, Temple 1982. Pro coach: Philadelphia/Baltimore Stars (USFL) 1983-85, New Orleans Saints 1986-95, joined Buccaneers in 1996.
Rod Marinelli, defensive line; born July 13, 1949, Rosemead, Calif., lives in Tampa. Offensive/defensive tackle Utah 1968, offensive tackle California Lutheran 1970-72 (military service 1969-70). No pro playing experience. College coach: Utah State 1976-82, California 1983-91, Arizona State 1992-94, Southern California 1995. Pro coach: Joined Buccaneers in 1996.
Tony Nathan, running backs; born December 14, 1956, Birmingham, Ala., lives in Tampa. Running back Alabama 1975-78. Pro running back Miami Dolphins 1979-87. Pro coach: Miami Dolphins 1988-95, joined Buccaneers in 1996.
Kevin O'Dea, defensive assistant; born June 9, 1960, Williamsport, Va., lives in Tampa. Defensive back/wide receiver Lock Haven 1982-85. No pro playing experience. College coach: Lock Haven 1986, Cornell 1987, Virginia 1988-90, Penn State 1991-93. Pro coach: San Diego Chargers 1994-95, joined Buccaneers in 1996.
Ricky Porter, offensive assistant; born January 14, 1960, Sylacaga, Ala., lives in Tampa. Running back Slippery Rock 1978-81. Pro running back Detroit Lions 1982, Baltimore Colts 1983, Memphis Showboats (USFL) 1985, Montreal Alouettes (CFL) 1986-87, Buffalo Bills 1987. College coach: Slippery Rock 1990-91, Kent 1992-93. Pro coach: Joined Buccaneers in 1996.
Mike Shula, offensive coordinator; born June 3, 1965, Baltimore, Md., lives in Tampa. Quarterback Alabama 1983-86. Pro quarterback Tampa Bay Buccaneers 1987. Pro coach: Tampa Bay Buccaneers 1988-90, Miami Dolphins 1991-92, Chicago Bears 1993-95, rejoined Buccaneers in 1996.
Lovie Smith, linebackers; born May 8, 1958, Gladewater, Tex., lives in Tampa. Linebacker Tulsa 1976-79. No pro playing experience. College coach: Tulsa 1983-86, Wisconsin 1987, Arizona State 1988-91, Kentucky 1992, Tennessee 1993-94, Ohio State 1995. Pro coach: Joined Buccaneers in 1996.
Charlie Williams, wide receivers; born January 31, 1958, Long Beach, Calif., lives in Tampa. Defensive back Long Beach City College 1977-78, Colorado State 1979-80. No pro playing experience. College coach: Colorado State 1981, Long Beach City College 1984-85, New Mexico State 1986-87, Texas Christian 1988-91, Minnesota 1992, Miami 1993-95. Pro coach: Joined Buccaneers in 1996.

1996 FIRST-YEAR ROSTER

Name	Pos.	Ht.	Wt.	Birthdate	College	Hometown	How Acq.
Abraham, Donnie	CB	5-10	181	10/8/73	East Tennessee St.	Orangeburg, S.C.	D3
Alstott, Mike	RB	6-0	240	12/21/73	Purdue	Joliet, Ill.	D2
Austin, Eric	S	5-10	217	6/7/73	Jackson State	Moss Point, Miss.	D4
Clark, Stonie	DT	6-0	324	7/6/74	Texas	Gladewater, Tex.	FA
Crisman, Joel (1)	G	6-5	300	2/3/71	Southern California	Grundy Center, Iowa	FA
Davis, Terrence	WR	5-10	191	2/27/73	McNeese State	Jasper, Tex.	FA
Diaz, Jorge	G	6-4	295	11/15/73	Texas A&M-Kingsville	Katy, Tex.	FA
Ekiyor, Emil	DE	6-2	253	12/25/73	Central Florida	Port Orange, Fla.	FA
Gooch, Jeff	LB	5-11	218	10/31/74	Austin Peay	Nashville, Tenn.	FA
Harris, George	CB	5-10	185	11/13/73	Kentucky	Oakland, Calif.	FA
Holcomb, Kelly (1)	QB	6-2	202	7/9/73	Middle Tennessee St.	Fayetteville, Tenn.	FA
Holmes, Jermaine	WR	6-1	177	3/1/72	Virginia Tech	St. Petersburg, Fla.	FA
Jackson, Tyoka (1)	DE	6-2	266	11/22/71	Penn State	Washington, D.C.	FA
Johnson, Curtis (1)	RB	5-9	204	11/11/71	North Carolina	Greensboro, N.C.	FA
Jones, Marcus	DT	6-6	280	8/15/73	North Carolina	Jacksonville, N.C.	D1b
Lester, Fred (1)	FB	6-1	244	8/1/71	Alabama A&M	Miami, Fla.	FA
Long, Juan (1)	LB	6-2	244	11/21/71	Mississippi State	Tupelo, Miss.	FA
Maniecki, Jason	DT	6-4	295	8/15/72	Wisconsin	Wisconsin Dells, Wis.	D5
Marshall, Marvin (1)	WR-KR	5-10	162	6/21/72	South Carolina State	Augusta, Ga.	FA
Milanovich, Scott	QB	6-3	227	1/29/73	Maryland	Butler, Pa.	FA
Odom, Jason	T	6-4	290	3/31/74	Florida	Bartow, Fla.	D4a
Rusk, Reggie	CB	5-10	182	10/19/72	Kentucky	Texas City, Tex.	D7
Sanders, Jesse	LB	5-11	222	11/12/72	Tennessee	Sebring, Fla.	FA
Silvan, Nilo	WR	5-9	176	10/2/73	Tennessee	Covington, La.	D6
Singleton, Toraino	RB	6-2	235	4/28/73	Texas-El Paso	El Paso, Tex.	FA
Thomas, Dwayne	RB	5-10	205	2/12/73	Virginia Tech	Ft. Myers, Fla.	FA
Upshaw, Regan	DE	6-4	260	8/12/75	California	Pittsburg, Calif.	D1a
Williams, Karl	WR	5-10	163	4/10/71	Texas A&M-Kingsville	Rowlett, Tex.	FA

The term NFL Rookie is defined as a player who is in his first season of professional football and has not been on the roster of another professional football team for any regular-season or postseason games. A Rookie is designated by an "R" on NFL rosters. Players who have been active in another professional football league or players who have NFL experience, including either preseason training camp or being on an Active List or Inactive List, or on Reserve/Injured or Reserve/Physically Unable to Perform for fewer than six regular-season games, are termed NFL First-Year Players. An NFL First-Year Player is designated by a "1" on NFL rosters. Thereafter, a player is credited with an additional year of experience for each season in which he accumulates six games on the Active List or Inactive List, or on Reserve/Injured or Reserve/Physically Unable to Perform.

NOTES

WASHINGTON REDSKINS

National Football Conference
Eastern Division
Team Colors: Burgundy and Gold
Redskin Park
P.O. Box 17247
Washington, D.C. 20041
Telephone: (703) 478-8900

CLUB OFFICIALS

Chairman of the Board-CEO: Jack Kent Cooke
Executive Vice President: John Kent Cooke
House Counsel: Stuart Haney
Controller: Mark Francis
Board of Directors: Jack Kent Cooke, John Kent Cooke
General Manager: Charley Casserly
Assistant General Manager: Bobby Mitchell
Director of Player Development: Joe Mendes
Director of College Scouting: George Saimes
Scouts: Gene Bates, Larry Bryan, Scott Cohen, Mike Hagen, Reed Johnson, Mel Kaufman, Mike Maccagnan, Miller McCalmon
Scouting Administrator: Barry Asimos
Director of Public Relations: Mike McCall
Director of Media Relations: Chris Helein
Public Relations Assistant: Reggie Saunders
Community Relations Coordinator: Wendy Brinker
Director of Stadium Operations/Club Promotions: John Kent Cooke, Jr.
Assistant Promotions/Advertising Director: John Wagner
Video Director: Donnie Schoenmann
Asst. Video Director: Hugh McPhillips
Video Analyst: Mike Bean
Ticket Manager: Jeff Ritter
Head Trainer: Bubba Tyer
Assistant Trainers: Al Bellamy, Kevin Bastin
Equipment Manager: Jay Brunetti
Asst. Equipment Manager: Jeff Parsons
Stadium: RFK Stadium • **Capacity:** 56,454
Washington, D.C. 20003
Playing Surface: Grass
Training Camp: Frostburg State University
Frostburg, Maryland 21532-1099

1996 SCHEDULE

PRESEASON

Aug. 2	at Buffalo	7:30
Aug. 9	at Detroit	7:30
Aug. 16	**Cincinnati**	8:00
Aug. 23	at New England	8:00

REGULAR SEASON

Sept. 1	**Philadelphia**	1:00
Sept. 8	**Chicago**	1:00
Sept. 15	at New York Giants	4:00
Sept. 22	at St. Louis	12:00
Sept. 29	**New York Jets**	8:00
Oct. 6	Open Date	
Oct. 13	at New England	1:00
Oct. 20	**New York Giants**	1:00
Oct. 27	**Indianapolis**	1:00
Nov. 3	at Buffalo	4:00
Nov. 10	**Arizona**	1:00
Nov. 17	at Philadelphia	1:00
Nov. 24	**San Francisco**	1:00
Nov. 28	at Dallas (Thurs.)	3:00
Dec. 8	at Tampa Bay	1:00
Dec. 15	at Arizona	2:00
Dec. 22	**Dallas**	4:00

RECORD HOLDERS

INDIVIDUAL RECORDS—CAREER

Category	Name	Performance
Rushing (Yds.)	John Riggins, 1976-79, 1981-85	7,472
Passing (Yds.)	Joe Theismann, 1974-1985	25,206
Passing (TDs)	Sammy Baugh, 1937-1952	187
Receiving (No.)	Art Monk, 1980-1993	888
Receiving (Yds.)	Art Monk, 1980-1993	12,028
Interceptions	Darrell Green, 1983-1995	40
Punting (Avg.)	Sammy Baugh, 1937-1952	*45.1
Punt Return (Avg.)	Johnny Williams, 1952-53	12.8
Kickoff Return (Avg.)	Bobby Mitchell, 1962-68	28.5
Field Goals	Mark Moseley, 1974-1986	263
Touchdowns (Tot.)	Charley Taylor, 1964-1977	90
Points	Mark Moseley, 1974-1986	1,206

INDIVIDUAL RECORDS—SINGLE SEASON

Category	Name	Performance
Rushing (Yds.)	John Riggins, 1983	1,347
Passing (Yds.)	Jay Schroeder, 1986	4,109
Passing (TDs)	Sonny Jurgensen, 1967	31
Receiving (No.)	Art Monk, 1984	106
Receiving (Yds.)	Bobby Mitchell, 1963	1,436
Interceptions	Dan Sandifer, 1948	13
Punting (Avg.)	Sammy Baugh, 1940	*51.4
Punt Return (Avg.)	Johnny Williams, 1952	15.3
Kickoff Return (Avg.)	Mike Nelms, 1981	29.7
Field Goals	Mark Moseley, 1983	33
Touchdowns (Tot.)	John Riggins, 1983	24
Points	Mark Moseley, 1983	161

INDIVIDUAL RECORDS—SINGLE GAME

Category	Name	Performance
Rushing (Yds.)	Gerald Riggs, 9-17-89	221
Passing (Yds.)	Sammy Baugh, 10-31-43	446
Passing (TDs)	Sammy Baugh, 10-31-43, 11-23-47	6
	Mark Rypien, 11-10-91	6
Receiving (No.)	Art Monk, 12-15-85	13
	Kelvin Bryant, 12-7-86	13
	Art Monk, 11-4-90	13
Receiving (Yds.)	Anthony Allen, 10-4-87	255
Interceptions	Sammy Baugh, 11-14-43	*4
	Dan Sandifer, 10-31-48	*4
Field Goals	Many times	5
	Last time by Chip Lohmiller, 10-25-92	
Touchdowns (Tot.)	Dick James, 12-17-61	4
	Larry Brown, 12-4-73	4
Points	Dick James, 12-17-61	24
	Larry Brown, 12-4-73	24

*NFL Record

COACHING HISTORY

Boston 1932-36
(459-400-26)

1932	Lud Wray	4-4-2
1933-34	William (Lone Star) Dietz	11-11-2
1935	Eddie Casey	2-8-1
1936-42	Ray Flaherty	56-23-3
1943	Arthur (Dutch) Bergman	7-4-1
1944-45	Dudley DeGroot	14-6-1
1946-48	Glen (Turk) Edwards	16-18-1
1949	John Whelchel*	3-3-1
1949-51	Herman Ball**	4-16-0
1951	Dick Todd	5-4-0
1952-53	Earl (Curly) Lambeau	10-13-1
1954-58	Joe Kuharich	26-32-2
1959-60	Mike Nixon	4-18-2
1961-65	Bill McPeak	21-46-3
1966-68	Otto Graham	17-22-3
1969	Vince Lombardi	7-5-2
1970	Bill Austin	6-8-0
1971-77	George Allen	69-35-1
1978-80	Jack Pardee	24-24-0
1981-92	Joe Gibbs	140-65-0
1993	Richie Petitbon	4-12-0
1994-95	Norv Turner	9-23-0

*Released after seven games in 1949
**Released after three games in 1951

ROBERT F. KENNEDY STADIUM

1995 TEAM RECORD

PRESEASON (1-3)

Date	Result		Opponents
8/5	L	21-37	at Kansas City
8/12	W	16-13	vs. Houston (OT) at Knoxville, Tenn.
8/19	L	13-27	at Miami
8/25	L	23-35	at Green Bay

REGULAR SEASON (6-10)

Date	Result		Opponents	Att.
9/3	W	27-7	Arizona	52,731
9/10	L	8-20	Oakland	54,548
9/17	L	31-38	at Denver	71,930
9/24	L	6-14	at Tampa Bay	49,234
10/1	W	27-23	Dallas	55,489
10/8	L	34-37	at Philadelphia (OT)	65,498
10/15	L	20-24	at Arizona	42,370
10/22	W	36-30	Detroit (OT)	52,332
10/29	L	15-24	N.Y. Giants	53,310
11/5	L	3-24	at Kansas City	77,821
11/19	L	20-27	Seattle	51,298
11/26	L	7-14	Philadelphia	50,539
12/3	W	24-17	at Dallas	64,866
12/10	L	13-20	at N.Y. Giants	48,247
12/17	W	35-23	at St. Louis	63,760
12/24	W	20-17	Carolina	42,903

(OT) Overtime

SCORE BY PERIODS

Redskins	59	90	85	86	6	—	326
Opponents	65	126	48	117	3	—	359

ATTENDANCE

Home 413,150 Away 483,726 Total 896,876
Single-game home record, 56,345 (9/6/93)
Single-season home record, 443,678 (1992)

1995 TEAM STATISTICS

	Redskins	Opp.
Total First Downs	297	323
Rushing	105	127
Passing	169	182
Penalty	23	14
Third Down: Made/Att	93/230	100/220
Third Down Pct.	40.4	45.5
Fourth Down: Made/Att	10/17	12/16
Fourth Down Pct.	58.8	75.0
Total Net Yards	5184	5400
Avg. Per Game	324.0	337.5
Total Plays	1026	1059
Avg. Per Play	5.1	5.1
Net Yards Rushing	1956	2132
Avg. Per Game	122.3	133.3
Total Rushes	469	483
Net Yards Passing	3228	3268
Avg. Per Game	201.8	204.3
Sacked/Yards Lost	36/268	30/135
Gross Yards	3496	3403
Att./Completions	521/265	546/338
Completion Pct.	50.9	61.9
Had Intercepted	20	16
Punts/Avg.	74/42.4	72/41.4
Net Punting Avg.	74/37.7	72/35.1
Penalties/Yards Lost	78/563	100/780
Fumbles/Ball Lost	24/10	31/19
Touchdowns	35	42
Rushing	15	18
Passing	16	20
Returns	4	4
Avg. Time of Possession	28:42	31:18

1995 INDIVIDUAL STATISTICS

PASSING	Att.	Comp.	Yds.	Pct.	TD	Int.	Tkld.	Rate
Frerotte	396	199	2751	50.3	13	13	23/192	70.2
Shuler	125	66	745	52.8	3	7	13/76	55.6
Redskins	521	265	3496	50.9	16	20	36/268	66.7
Opponents	546	338	3403	61.9	20	16	30/135	79.6

SCORING	TD R	TD P	TD Rt	PAT	FG	Saf	PTS
Murray	0	0	0	33/33	27/36	0	114
Allen	10	1	0	0/0	0/0	0	66
Ellard	0	5	0	0/0	0/0	0	30
Logan	1	2	0	0/0	0/0	0	18
Mitchell	1	1	1	0/0	0/0	0	18
Shepherd	1	2	0	0/0	0/0	0	18
Galbraith	0	2	0	0/0	0/0	0	12
Westbrook	1	1	0	0/0	0/0	0	12
C. Bell	0	1	0	0/0	0/0	0	6
Carter	0	0	1	0/0	0/0	0	6
Frerotte	1	0	0	0/0	0/0	0	6
D. Green	0	0	1	0/0	0/0	0	6
Truitt	0	1	0	0/0	0/0	0	6
Woods	0	0	1	0/0	0/0	0	6
Brownlow	0	0	0	0/0	0/0	1	2
Redskins	15	16	4	33/33	27/36	1	326
Opponents	18	20	4	39/40	22/27	0	359

2-Point conversions: 0. Team: 0-1.

RUSHING	Att.	Yds.	Avg.	LG	TD
Allen	338	1309	3.9	28	10
Mitchell	46	301	6.5	36t	1
Westbrook	6	114	19.0	58t	1
Logan	23	72	3.1	13	1
Shepherd	7	63	9.0	26	1
Shuler	18	57	3.2	13	0
Frerotte	22	16	0.7	10	1
W. Bell	4	13	3.3	5	0
C. Smith	3	13	4.3	5	0
Brooks	2	-2	-1.0	-1	0
Redskins	469	1956	4.2	58t	15
Opponents	483	2132	4.4	55t	18

RECEIVING	No.	Yds.	Avg.	LG	TD
Ellard	56	1005	17.9	59	5
Mitchell	38	324	8.5	22t	1
Westbrook	34	522	15.4	45	1
Allen	31	232	7.5	24	1
Shepherd	29	486	16.8	73t	2
Logan	25	276	11.0	32	2
Asher	14	172	12.3	20	0
C. Bell	14	166	11.9	29t	1
Galbraith	10	80	8.0	25	2
Truitt	9	154	17.1	47	1
Winans	4	77	19.3	32	0
Jenkins	1	2	2.0	2	0
Redskins	265	3496	13.2	73t	16
Opponents	338	3403	10.1	59t	20

INTERCEPTIONS	No.	Yds.	Avg.	LG	TD
Carter	4	116	29.0	51t	1
D. Green	3	42	14.0	22	1
Richard	3	24	8.0	24	0
Washington	2	35	17.5	21	0
M. Patton	2	7	3.5	6	0
Pounds	1	26	26.0	26	0
Turner	1	0	0.0	0	0
Redskins	16	250	15.6	51t	2
Opponents	20	338	16.9	75t	3

PUNTING	No.	Yds.	Avg.	In 20	LG
Turk	74	3140	42.4	29	60
Redskins	74	3140	42.4	29	60
Opponents	72	2984	41.4	25	60

PUNT RETURNS	No.	FC	Yds.	Avg.	LG	TD
Mitchell	25	15	315	12.6	59t	1
Turner	1	0	0	0.0	0	0
Redskins	26	15	315	12.1	59t	1
Opponents	26	13	173	6.7	35	0

KICKOFF RETURNS	No.	Yds.	Avg.	LG	TD
Mitchell	55	1408	25.6	59	0
W. Bell	8	121	15.1	34	0
Shepherd	3	85	28.3	36	0
Asher	1	13	13.0	13	0
Jenkins	1	12	12.0	12	0
Vanderbeek	1	7	7.0	7	0
Redskins	69	1646	23.9	59	0
Opponents	70	1434	20.5	91t	1

SACKS	No.
Harvey	7.5
Palmer	4.5
Ti. Johnson	3.0
Owens	3.0
Boutte	2.0
Gaines	2.0
M. Patton	2.0
Woods	2.0
Flores	1.0
Taylor	1.0
Turner	1.0
Redskins	29.0
Opponents	36.0

1996 DRAFT CHOICES

Round	Name	Pos.	College
1	Andre Johnson	T	Penn State
4	Stephen Davis	RB	Auburn
5	Leomont Evans	DB	Clemson
6	Kelvin Kinney	DE	Virginia State
7	Jeremy Asher	LB	Oregon
	DeAndre Maxwell	WR	San Diego State

WASHINGTON REDSKINS

1996 VETERAN ROSTER

No.	Name	Pos.	Ht.	Wt.	Birthdate	NFL Exp.	College	Hometown	How Acq.	'95 Games/ Starts
21	Allen, Terry	RB	5-10	208	2/21/68	7	Clemson	Commerce, Ga.	FA-'95	16/16
84	Asher, Jamie	TE	6-3	243	10/31/72	2	Louisville	Galveston, Tex.	D5a-'95	7/2
72	Bandison, Romeo	DT	6-5	290	2/12/71	3	Oregon	Mill Valley, Calif.	FA-'95	4/0
87	Bell, Coleman	TE	6-2	243	4/22/70	2	Miami	Tampa, Fla.	FA-'94	11/1
36	Bell, William	RB	5-11	212	7/22/71	3	Georgia Tech	Miami, Fla.	FA-'94	16/0
4	Blanton, Scott	K	6-2	223	7/1/73	2	Oklahoma	Norman, Okla.	FA-'95	0*
93	Boutte, Marc	DT	6-4	311	7/26/69	5	Louisiana State	Lake Charles, La.	FA-'94	16/16
19	Brooks, Bill	WR	6-0	189	4/6/64	11	Boston University	Framingham, Mass.	UFA(Buff)-'96	15/10*
40	† Brooks, Reggie	RB	5-8	202	1/19/71	4	Notre Dame	Tulsa, Okla.	D2-'93	1/0
50	Brownlow, Darrick	LB	6-0	243	12/28/68	6	Illinois	Indianapolis, Ind.	FA-'95	16/0
25	Carter, Tom	CB	5-11	181	9/5/72	4	Notre Dame	St. Petersburg, Fla.	D1-'93	16/16
90	Crews, Terry	DE	6-2	245	7/30/68	4	Western Michigan	Flint, Mich.	FA-'95	16/0
75	Dahl, Bob	G	6-5	330	1/15/68	5	Notre Dame	Chagrin Falls, Ohio	UFA(Balt)-'96	16/16*
85	Ellard, Henry	WR	5-11	182	7/21/61	14	Fresno State	Fresno, Calif.	UFA(Rams)-'94	15/15
73	# Flores, Mike	DE	6-3	256	12/1/66	6	Louisville	Marlton, N.J.	FA-'95	11/0
56	Foxx, Dion	LB	6-3	250	6/11/71	3	James Madison	Richmond, Va.	FA-'95	2/0*
12	Frerotte, Gus	QB	6-2	221	7/3/71	3	Tulsa	Ford Cliff, Pa.	D7-'94	16/11
95	Gaines, William	DT	6-5	303	6/20/71	3	Florida	Jackson, Miss.	FA-'95	15/11
89	Galbraith, Scott	TE	6-2	255	1/7/67	7	Southern California	Sacramento, Calif.	UFA(Dall)-'95	16/16
75	Gesek, John	C	6-5	282	2/18/63	10	Cal State-Sacramento	Danville, Calif.	UFA(Dall)-'94	16/16
94	t- Gilbert, Sean	DT	6-5	310	4/10/70	5	Pittsburgh	Aliquippa, Pa.	T(StL)-'96	14/14*
28	Green, Darrell	CB	5-8	170	2/15/60	14	Texas A&I	Houston, Tex.	D1-'83	16/16
10	Green, Trent	QB	6-3	212	7/9/70	3	Indiana	St. Louis, Mo.	FA-'95	0*
32	Harris, Rudy	RB	6-2	240	9/18/71	3	Clemson	Brockton, Mass.	FA-'96	0*
57	Harvey, Ken	LB	6-2	245	5/6/65	9	California	Austin, Tex.	UFA(Ariz)-'94	16/16
19	Houston, Harris	WR	5-9	179	1/26/72	2	Florida	Pensacola, Fla.	FA-'96	0*
88	Jenkins, James	TE	6-2	241	8/17/67	5	Rutgers	Staten Island, N.Y.	FA-'91	16/5
78	# Johnson, Tim	DT	6-3	275	1/29/65	10	Penn State	Sarasota, Fla.	T(Pitt)-'90	14/5
77	Johnson, Tré	T	6-2	338	8/30/71	3	Temple	Peekskill, N.Y.	D2-'94	10/9
23	Jones, Larry	RB	6-0	244	2/16/71	2	Miami	Gainesville, Fla.	D4-'95	0*
79	Lachey, Jim	T	6-6	294	6/4/63	12	Ohio State	St. Henry, Ohio	T(Raid)-'88	3/3
71	Lewis, Ron	G	6-3	299	11/17/72	2	Washington State	Los Angeles, Calif.	UFA(SF)-'95	4/0
20	Logan, Marc	RB	6-0	212	5/9/65	9	Kentucky	Lexington, Ky.	UFA(SF)-'95	16/8
59	Matich, Trevor	C	6-4	297	10/9/61	12	Brigham Young	Sacramento, Calif.	UFA(Ind)-'94	16/0
34	McDowell, Anthony	RB	5-11	240	11/12/68	4	Texas Tech	Killeen, Tex.	FA-'96	0*
80	McMurtry, Greg	WR	6-2	210	10/25/67	6	Michigan	Brockton, Mass.	FA-'96	0*
30	Mitchell, Brian	RB-KR	5-10	203	8/18/68	7	Southwestern Louisiana	Plaquemine, La.	D5-'90	16/1
38	Morrison, Darryl	S	5-11	200	5/19/71	3	Arizona	Phoenix, Ariz.	D6a-'93	16/0
2	Murray, Eddie	K	5-11	195	8/29/56	17	Tulane	Victoria, Canada	FA-'95	16/0
92	Nottage, Dexter	DE	6-4	290	11/14/70	3	Florida A&M	Miami, Fla.	D6-'94	16/0
26	Oliver, Muhammad	DE	5-11	185	3/12/69	5	Oregon	Brooklyn, N.Y.	FA-'96	1/0
96	Owens, Rich	DE	6-6	270	5/22/72	2	Lehigh	Philadelphia, Pa.	D5b-'95	10/3
97	Palmer, Sterling	DE	6-5	256	2/4/71	4	Florida State	Ft. Lauderdale, Fla.	D4-'93	13/13
68	Patton, Joe	G	6-5	290	1/5/72	3	Alabama A&M	Birmingham, Ala.	D3b-'94	16/13
53	Patton, Marvcus	LB	6-2	240	5/1/67	7	UCLA	Lawndale, Calif.	UFA(Buff)-'95	16/16
31	Pounds, Darryl	CB	5-10	177	7/21/72	2	Nicholls State	Ft. Worth, Tex.	D3-'95	9/0
52	Raymer, Cory	C	6-2	302	3/3/73	2	Wisconsin	Fond du Lac, Wis.	D2-'95	3/2
15	Reeves, Bryan	WR	5-11	195	7/10/70	3	Nevada	Los Angeles, Calif.	FA-'96	5/0*
62	Renfro, Leonard	DT	6-3	308	6/29/70	3	Colorado	Detroit, Mich.	FA-'96	0*
24	Richard, Stanley	S	6-2	197	10/21/67	6	Texas	Miniola, Tex.	UFA(SD)-'95	16/16
86	Shepherd, Leslie	WR	5-11	189	11/3/69	2	Temple	Forestville, Md.	FA-'94	14/4
5	Shuler, Heath	QB	6-2	221	12/31/71	3	Tennessee	Bryson City, N.C.	D1-'94	7/5
76	Simmons, Ed	T	6-5	300	12/31/63	10	Eastern Washington	Seattle, Wash.	D6-'87	16/16
61	# Smith, Vernice	G	6-3	300	10/24/65	7	Florida A&M	Orlando, Fla.	FA-'93	9/5
99	Stephens, Rod	LB	6-1	237	6/14/66	7	Georgia Tech	Atlanta, Ga.	UFA(Sea)-'95	16/16
27	# Taylor, Keith	S	5-11	212	12/21/64	8	Illinois	Pennsauken, N.J.	UFA(NO)-'94	16/4
74	Thure, Brian	T	6-5	300	9/3/73	2	California	Downey, Calif.	D6-'95	4/0
1	Turk, Matt	P	6-5	230	6/16/68	2	Wisconsin-Whitewater	Greenfield, Wis.	FA-'95	16/0
29	Turner, Scott	CB	5-10	178	2/26/72	2	Illinois	Richardson, Tex.	D7-'95	16/0
91	Vanderbeek, Matt	LB	6-3	243	8/16/67	7	Michigan State	Holland, Mich.	FA-'95	16/0
37	Washington, James	S	6-1	209	1/10/65	9	Abilene Christian	Los Angeles, Calif.	FA-'96	12/12
82	Westbrook, Michael	WR	6-3	215	7/7/72	2	Colorado	Detroit, Mich.	D1-'95	11/9
83	Winans, Tydus	WR	5-11	180	7/26/72	3	Fresno State	Los Angeles, Calif.	D3a-'95	8/1
98	# Woods, Tony	DE	6-4	269	9/11/65	10	Pittsburgh	South Orange, N.J.	UFA(Rams)-'94	16/16

* Blanton missed '95 season because of injury; Brooks played 15 games with Buffalo in '95; Dahl played 16 games with Cleveland; Foxx played 2 games with Miami; Gilbert played 14 games with St. Louis; T. Green active for 5 games but did not play; Harris last active with Tampa Bay in '94; Houston last active with Atlanta '94; Jones inactive for 16 games; McDowell last active with Tampa Bay in '94; McMurtry last active with Chicago in '94; Reeves played 5 games with Arizona; Renfro last active with Philadelphia in '94.

Unrestricted free agent; subject to developments.

† Restricted free agent; subject to developments.

t- Redskins traded for Gilbert (St. Louis).

Players lost through free agency (1): G Ray Brown (SF; 16 games).

Also played with Redskins in '95—CB Robert Bailey (4 games), WR Jeff Query (1), S Sebastian Savage (2), RB Cedric Smith (6), WR Olanda Truitt (5).

COACHING STAFF

Head Coach,
Norv Turner

Pro Career: Enters his third season as head coach of the Washington Redskins after serving three years as the Dallas Cowboys' offensive coordinator. Turner guided the Cowboys' prolific offense during back-to-back Super Bowl championship seasons. He inherited a Cowboys offense that finished twenty-eighth in total offense in 1990, and a year later improved to ninth. The Cowboys finished fourth in the league offensively in 1992-93. In three seasons under Turner, quarterback Troy Aikman compiled a 91.7 rating, and running back Emmitt Smith won three consecutive NFL rushing titles. Prior to joining the Cowboys, Turner coached six seasons (1985-1990) with the Los Angeles Rams where he oversaw the passing game. Quarterback Jim Everett enjoyed his best seasons under Turner, while Willie Anderson led the NFL in yards per catch in 1989 and 1990, and Henry Ellard was the league's leading receiver in 1988. Career record: 9-23.

Background: Turner played quarterback for three seasons at the University of Oregon (1972-74). He began his coaching career as a graduate assistant at Oregon in 1975. A year later, he moved to the University of Southern California, where he coached from 1976-1984.

Personal: Born May 17, 1952, in LeJeune, N.C. Turner and his wife, Nancy, live in Oakton, Va., and have three children—Scott, Stephanie, and Drew.

ASSISTANT COACHES

Jason Arapoff, assistant conditioning; born July 8, 1965, Weymouth, Mass., lives in Centreville,Va. Defensive back Springfield College 1985-88. No pro playing experience. Pro coach: Joined Redskins in 1992.

Cam Cameron, quarterbacks; born February 6, 1961, Chapel Hill, N.C., lives in Ashburn, Va. Quarterback Indiana 1980-83. No pro playing experience. College coach: Michigan 1984-93. Pro coach: Joined Redskins in 1994.

Russ Grimm, tight ends; born May 2, 1959, Scottdale, Pa., lives in Fairfax, Va. Guard-center Pittsburgh 1977-80. Pro guard Washington Redskins 1981-91. Pro coach: Joined Redskins in 1992.

Mike Haluchak, linebackers; born November 28, 1949, Concord, Calif., lives in Ashburn, Va. Linebacker Southern California 1967-70. No pro playing experience. College coach: Southern California 1976-77, Cal State-Fullerton 1978, Pacific 1979-80, California 1981, North Carolina State 1982. Pro coach: Oakland Invaders (USFL) 1983-85, San Diego Chargers 1986-91, Cincinnati Bengals 1992-93, joined Redskins in 1994.

Jim Hanifan, offensive line; born September 21, 1933, Compton, Calif., lives in Ashburn, Va. Tight end California 1952-54. Pro tight end Toronto Argonauts (CFL) 1955. College coach: Glendale, Calif., J.C. 1964-66, Utah 1967-70, California 1971-72, San Diego State 1972-73. Pro coach: St. Louis Cardinals 1974-85 (head coach 1980-85), Atlanta Falcons 1987-89 (interim head coach last four games of 1989), joined Redskins in 1990.

Tom Hayes, defensive backs; born March 26, 1949, Keokuk, Iowa, lives in Ashburn, Va. Defensive back Iowa 1968-71. No pro playing experience. College coach: Coe College 1973, Iowa 1977-78, Cal State-Fullerton 1979, UCLA 1980-88, Texas A&M 1989, Oklahoma 1990-94. Pro coach: Joined Redskins in 1995.

Ray Horton, secondary assistant; born April 12, 1960, Tacoma, Wash., lives in Ashburn, Va. Defensive back Washington 1979-82. Pro defensive back Cincinnati Bengals 1983-88, Dallas Cowboys 1989-92. Pro coach: Joined Redskins in 1994.

Bobby Jackson, running backs; born February 16, 1940, Forsyth, Ga., lives in Sterling, Va. Linebacker-running back Samford (Ga.) 1959-62. No pro playing experience. College coach: Florida State 1965-69, Kansas State 1970-74, Louisville 1975-76, Tennessee 1977-82. Pro coach: Atlanta Falcons 1983-86, San Diego Chargers 1987-91, Phoenix Cardinals 1992-93, joined Redskins in 1994.

Bob Karmelowicz, defensive line; born July 22, 1949, New Britain, Conn., lives in Ashburn, Va. Nose tackle Bridgeport 1972. No pro playing experience. College coach: Arizona State 1974-79, Massachusetts 1979-80, Texas-El Paso 1980-81, Illinois 1982-87, Washington State 1987-89, Miami 1990-91. Pro coach: Cincinnati Bengals 1992-93, joined Redskins in 1994.

Ron Lynn, defensive coordinator, born December 6, 1944, Youngstown, Ohio, lives in Sterling, Va. Quarterback-defensive back Mt. Union (Ohio) 1963-65. No pro playing experience. College coach: Toledo 1966, Mt. Union (Ohio) 1967-73, Kent State 1974-76, San Jose State 1977-78, Pacific 1979, California 1980-82. Pro coach: Oakland Invaders (USFL) 1983-85, San Diego Chargers 1986-91, Cincinnati Bengals 1992-93, joined Redskins in 1994.

Dan Riley, conditioning; born October 19, 1949, Syracuse, N.Y., lives in Ashburn, Va. No college or pro playing experience. College coach: Army 1973-76, Penn State 1977-81. Pro coach: Joined Redskins in 1982.

Terry Robiskie, receivers; born November 12, 1954, New Orleans, La., lives in Clifton, Va. Running back Louisiana State 1973-76. Pro running back Oakland Raiders 1977-79, Miami Dolphins 1980-81. Pro coach: Oakland/Los Angeles Raiders 1982-1993, joined Redskins in 1994.

Pete Rodriguez, special teams; born July 25, 1940, Chicago, Ill., lives in Sterling, Va. Guard-linebacker Denver University 1959-60, Western State, Colo. 1961-63. No pro playing experience. College coach: Western State, Colo. 1964, Arizona 1968-69, Western Illinois 1970-73, 1979-82 (head coach), Florida State 1974-75, Iowa State 1976-78, Northern Iowa 1986. Pro coach: Michigan Panthers (USFL) 1983-84, Denver Gold (USFL) 1985, Jacksonville Bulls (USFL) 1986, Ottawa Rough Riders (CFL) 1987, Los Angeles Raiders 1988-89, Phoenix Cardinals 1990-93, joined Redskins in 1994.

1996 FIRST-YEAR ROSTER

Name	Pos.	Ht.	Wt.	Birthdate	College	Hometown	How Acq.
Alexandria, Patrise (1)	LB	6-1	255	10/23/72	S.W. Louisiana	Galveston, Tex.	FA
Asher, Jeremy	LB	6-0	235	10/5/72	Oregon	Medford, Ore.	D7a
Bowie, Larry	RB	6-0	224	3/21/73	Georgia	Anniston, Ala.	FA
Browning, Alphonso (1)	WR	6-2	203	7/27/72	Kentucky	Kansas City, Mo.	FA
Collier, Ervin (1)	DT	6-3	307	5/12/71	Florida A&M	Jacksonville, Fla.	FA
Davis, Stephen	RB	6-0	227	3/10/74	Auburn	Spartanburg, S.C.	D4
Evans, Leomont	S	6-1	200	7/12/74	Clemson	Abbeville, S.C.	D5
Fleming, Sean	P	6-3	205	3/19/70	Wyoming	Edmonton, Canada	FA
Johnson, Allen	CB	6-0	190	9/10/71	North Carolina State	Washington, D.C.	FA
Johnson, Andre	T	6-5	300	8/25/73	Penn State	Long Island, N.Y.	D1
Kinney, Kelvin	DE	6-6	250	12/31/72	Virginia State	Montgomery, W. Va.	D6
Kinney, Phil (1)	G	6-2	319	2/18/72	Southwest Baptist	Lawton, Okla.	FA
Kuehl, Ryan (1)	DT	6-4	276	1/18/72	Virginia	Washington, D.C.	FA
Mahone, Elic (1)	DE	6-4	260	3/7/72	Southern California	Pasadena, Calif.	FA
Maxwell, Deandre	WR	6-1	200	4/6/73	San Diego State	Fresno, Calif.	D7b
Perez, Louis	K	5-9	195	4/11/71	UCLA	Carson, Calif.	FA
Pourdanesh, Shar (1)	T	6-6	300	7/19/70	Nevada	Teheran, Iran	FA
Reynolds, Don (1)	DE	6-2	285	11/25/69	Virginia	Martinsville, Va.	FA
Seagraves, Ca'Dell	TE	6-3	252	2/12/72	Pittsburgh	Greensboro, N.C.	FA
Sedoris, Christopher	C	6-3	295	4/25/73	Purdue	Columbus, Ind.	FA
Storm, Matt (1)	T	6-3	297	9/23/72	Georgia	Edmonds, Wash.	FA
Sutton, Eric (1)	CB	5-10	170	10/24/72	San Diego State	Inglewood, Calif.	FA
Wagner, Keith (1)	T	6-4	300	1/22/70	Abilene Christian	Corpus Christi, Tex.	FA
Walker, Bryan	S	6-2	190	5/31/72	Washington State	Colorado Springs, Colo.	FA
Watkins, Michael (1)	WR	5-10	173	12/28/71	Northeast Louisiana	Hickory, N.C.	FA

The term NFL Rookie is defined as a player who is in his first season of professional football and has not been on the roster of another professional football team for any regular-season or postseason games. A Rookie is designated by an "R" on NFL rosters. Players who have been active in another professional football league or players who have NFL experience, including either preseason training camp or being on an Active List or Inactive List, or on Reserve/Injured or Reserve/Physically Unable to Perform for fewer than six regular-season games, are termed NFL First-Year Players. An NFL First-Year Player is designated by a "1" on NFL rosters. Thereafter, a player is credited with an additional year of experience for each season in which he accumulates six games on the Active List or Inactive List, or on Reserve/Injured or Reserve/Physically Unable to Perform.

NOTES

1995 Season in Review

TRADES

1995 INTERCONFERENCE TRADES

Tight end **Harold Bishop** from Tampa Bay to Cleveland for the Browns' second-round selection in 1996. (5/19)

Running back **Barry Foster** from Pittsburgh to Carolina for the Panthers' first supplemental selection in the sixth round in 1996. (5/30)

Tight end **Ty Hallock** from Detroit to Jacksonville for defensive back **Corey Raymond.** (5/31)

Wide receiver **Bill Schroeder** and tight end **Jeff Wilner** from Green Bay to New England for center **Mike Arthur.** (8/11)

Defensive tackle **Ronnie Dixon** from Cleveland to Philadelphia for the Eagles' seventh-round selection in 1996. (8/21)

Running back **Greg Robinson** from Oakland to Green Bay for the Packers' fifth-round selection in 1996. (8/21)

Wide receiver **Ray Ethridge** from Cleveland to Carolina for past considerations. (8/21)

Defensive tackle **Ferric Collons** from Green Bay to New England for past considerations. (8/26)

Defensive end **Willie Broughton** from Oakland to New Orleans for the Saints' seventh-round selection in 1996. (8/27)

Tackle **Lindsay Knapp** from Kansas City to Green Bay for the Packers' fifth-round selection in 1996. (8/27)

Wide receiver **Charles Wilson** and defensive tackle **Marc Spindler** from Tampa Bay to the New York Jets for the Jets' fourth-round selection in 1996. (8/27)

Guard **Gene Williams** from Cleveland to Atlanta for the Falcons' fifth-round selection in 1996. (8/29)

Linebacker **Travis Hill** from Cleveland to Carolina for past considerations. (8/29)

1996 INTERCONFERENCE TRADES

Defensive back **Marcus Turner** from the New York Jets to Green Bay for the Packers' sixth-round selection in 1997. (3/13)

Running back **Glyn Milburn** from Denver to Detroit for the Lions' second- and seventh-round selections in 1996. (4/12)

Oakland's second-round selection in 1996 to San Francisco for the 49ers' second- and fourth-round selections in 1996. (4/17)

Safety **Patrick Bates** from Oakland to Atlanta for the Falcons' second-round selection in 1996. (4/18)

Detroit's first- and third-round selectons in 1996 to Seattle for the Seahawks' first-round selection in 1996. Seattle selected tackle **Pete Kendall** (Boston College) and running back **Reggie Brown** (Fresno State). Detroit selected linebacker **Reggie Brown** (Texas A&M). (4/20)

Running back **Jerome Bettis** and Rams' third-round selection in 1996 to Pittsburgh for the Steelers' second-round selection in 1996 and fourth-round selection in 1997. Pittsburgh selected linebacker **Steven Conley** (Arkansas). St. Louis selected tight end **Ernie Conwell** (Washington). (4/20)

Tampa Bay's second-round selection in 1996 to San Diego for the Chargers' first-round selection in 1997. San Diego selected wide receiver **Bryan Still** (Virginia Tech). (4/20)

Miami's second-round selection in 1996 to Dallas for the Cowboys' second- and fourth-round selections in 1996. Dallas selected linebacker **Randall Godfrey** (Georgia). Miami traded the second- and fourth-round selections to Jacksonville. (4/20)

New England's third-round selection in 1996 to Detroit for the Lions' third-, fourth-, and sixth-round selections in 1996. Detroit selected defensive back **Ryan Stewart** (Georgia Tech). New England selected linebacker **Tedy Bruschi** (Arizona), defensive end **Chris Sullivan** (Boston College), and running back **Marrio Grier** (Tennessee-Chattanooga). (4/20)

Denver's fourth-round selection in 1996 to Carolina for the Panthers' fourth-, fifth-, and seventh-round selections in 1996. Carolina selected defensive back **Emmanuel McDaniel** (East Carolina). Denver selected defensive back **Darrius Johnson** (Oklahoma), wide receiver **Patrick Jeffers** (Virginia), and running back **L.T. Levine** (Kansas). (4/21)

Kansas City's two fifth-round selections in 1996 to Arizona for the Cardinals' fifth-round selection in 1996. Arizona selected tackle **Harry Stamps** (Oklahoma) and defensive back **Dell McGee** (Auburn). Kansas City selected wide receiver **Joe Horn** (Itawamba J.C.). (4/21)

Baltimore's fifth-round selection in 1996 to Dallas for the Cowboys' fourth-round selection in 1997. Dallas selected tackle **Kenneth McDaniel** (Norfolk State). (4/21)

Defensive tackle **Matt Willig** from New York Jets to Atlanta for the Falcons' unannounced selection. (4/22)

Tackle **Lincoln Kennedy** from Atlanta to Oakland for the Raiders' unannounced selection. (4/22)

1995 AFC TRADES

Tight end **Craig Keith** from Pittsburgh to Jacksonville for the Jaguars' regular seventh-round selection in 1996. (8/26)

Wide receiver **Mike Williams** from Jacksonville to Miami for tight end **Pete Mitchell.** (8/27)

Tight end **Tracy Green** from Kansas City to Pittsburgh for Jacksonville's regular seventh-round selection in 1996. (8/27)

1996 AFC TRADES

Tackle **James Brown** from New York Jets to Miami for the Dolphins' fifth-round selection in 1997. (3/5)

Guard **Jeff Blackshear** from Seattle to Baltimore for the Ravens' fourth-round selection in 1997. (3/11)

Tackle **Pat Harlow** from New England to Oakland for the Raiders' second-round selection in 1996. (4/17)

Oakland's first-, second-, and fourth-round selection in 1996 to Houston for the Oilers' first-round selection in 1996. Houston traded the first-round selection acquired from Oakland to Seattle and selected tackle **Jason Layman** (Tennessee) and tackle **Jon Runyan** (Michigan). Oakland selected tight end **Rickey Dudley** (Ohio State). (4/20)

Defensive tackle **Glenn Montgomery** and Houston's first-round selection in 1996 to Seattle for the Seahawks' first-round selection in 1996. Seattle traded the first-round selection to Detroit. Houston selected running back **Eddie George** (Ohio State). (4/20)

Baltimore's third-, fourth-, and seventh-round selections in 1996 to Denver for the Broncos' second-round selection in 1996. Denver selected running back **Detron Smith** (Texas A&M), quarterback **Jeff Lewis** (Northern Arizona), and tackle **Leslie Ratliffe** (Tennessee). Baltimore selected defensive back **DeRon Jenkins** (Tennessee). (4/20)

Miami's second- and fourth-round selections in 1996 to Jacksonville for the Jaguars' third-, fourth-, and two fifth-round selections in 1996. Jacksonville selected center **Michael Cheever** (Georgia Tech) and traded the fourth-round selection acquired from Miami to Seattle. Miami selected defensive back **Dorian Brew** (Kansas), traded fourth-round selection acquired from Jacksonville to Kansas City, and selected running back **Jerris McPhail** (East Carolina) and defensive tackle **Shane Burton** (Tennessee). (4/20)

New England's second-round selection in 1996 to Oakland for the Raiders' third-, fourth-, and fifth-round selections in 1996. The Raiders selected defensive end **Lance Johnstone** (Temple). New England traded the third-round selection acquired from Oakland to Detroit, and selected running back **Kantroy Barber** (West Virginia) and nose tackle **Christian Peter** (Nebraska). (4/20)

Miami's fourth-round selection in 1996 and seventh-round selection in 1997 to Kansas City for the Chiefs' two fourth-round selections in 1996. Kansas City selected linebacker **Donnie Edwards** (UCLA). Miami selected defensive back **Kirk Pointer** (Austin Peay) and linebacker **LaCurtis Jones** (Baylor). (4/21)

Jacksonville's fourth-round selection in 1996 to Seattle for the Seahawks' fourth- and fifth-round selections in 1996. Seattle selected defensive end **Phillip Daniels** (Georgia). Jacksonville selected wide receiver **Reggie Barlow** (Alabama State) and tackle **Jimmy Herndon** (Houston). (4/21)

Pittsburgh's sixth-round selection in 1996 to San Diego for the Chargers' fifth-round selection in 1997. San Diego selected center **Bryan Stoltenberg** (Colorado). (4/21)

1995 NFC TRADES

Defensive tackle **Ferric Collons** from Atlanta to Green Bay for past considerations. (5/19)

Tackle **Joe Sims** from Philadelphia to Green Bay for the Packers' sixth-round selection in 1996. (8/27)

1996 NFC TRADES

Defensive end **Sean Gilbert** from St. Louis to Washington for the Redskins' first-round selection in 1996. (3/13)

Defensive back **Roger Harper** from Atlanta to Dallas for Cowboys' fourth- and fifth-round selections in 1996. Atlanta selected defensive back **Juran Bolden** (Mississippi Delta C.C.) and defensive end **Gary Bandy** (Baylor). (4/20)

Chicago's first-, third-, and sixth-round selections in 1996 to St. Louis for the Rams' first-round selection in 1996. St. Louis selected wide receiver **Eddie Kennison** (Louisiana State), running back **Jerald Moore** (Oklahoma), and tight end **Hayward Clay** (Texas A&M). Chicago selected defensive back **Walt Harris** (Mississippi State). (4/20)

Washington's second- and third-round selections in 1996 to Dallas for the Cowboys' first-round selection in 1996. Dallas selected defensive end **Kavika Pittman** (McNeese State) and center **Clay Shiver** (Florida State). Washington selected tackle **Andre Johnson** (Penn State). (4/20)

Arizona's fourth-round selection in 1996 to Minnesota for the Vikings' fourth-, and fifth-round selections in 1996. Minnesota selected tight end **Hunter Goodwin** (Texas A&M). Arizona selected center **Aaron Graham** (Nebraska) and tackle **James Dexter** (South Carolina). (4/21)

Defensive tackle **Toddrick McIntosh** from New Orleans to Green Bay for past considerations. (5/13)

FINAL STANDINGS

AMERICAN FOOTBALL CONFERENCE

Eastern Division

	W	L	T	Pct.	Pts.	OP
Indianapolis	3	1	0	.750	90	75
N.Y. Jets	2	2	0	.500	80	72
Buffalo	2	3	0	.400	64	109
Miami	1	3	0	.250	65	98
New England	1	3	0	.250	69	107

Central Division

	W	L	T	Pct.	Pts.	OP
Cleveland	2	2	0	.500	109	68
Jacksonville	2	3	0	.400	74	104
Cincinnati	1	3	0	.250	78	102
Pittsburgh	1	3	0	.250	57	82
Houston	0	3	0	.000	26	42

Western Division

	W	L	T	Pct.	Pts.	OP
Kansas City	3	1	0	.750	107	66
Oakland	3	1	0	.750	103	80
Denver	3	2	0	.600	80	76
Seattle	2	2	0	.500	82	76
San Diego	1	2	0	.333	42	49

NATIONAL FOOTBALL CONFERENCE

Eastern Division

	W	L	T	Pct.	Pts.	OP
Philadelphia	4	0	0	1.000	85	40
Arizona	3	1	0	.750	72	77
N.Y. Giants	3	1	0	.750	68	63
Dallas	2	3	0	.400	69	71
Washington	1	3	0	.250	73	112

Central Division

	W	L	T	Pct.	Pts.	OP
Detroit	3	1	0	.750	79	57
Green Bay	3	1	0	.750	115	73
Tampa Bay	3	1	0	.750	78	40
Minnesota	2	2	0	.500	70	74
Chicago	1	3	0	.250	54	116

Western Division

	W	L	T	Pct.	Pts.	OP
Carolina	3	2	0	.600	70	62
San Francisco	3	2	0	.600	68	56
Atlanta	2	2	0	.500	87	55
New Orleans	1	3	0	.250	73	75
St. Louis	1	3	0	.250	78	88

AFC PRESEASON RECORDS—TEAM BY TEAM

Eastern Division

BUFFALO (2-3)

15	at Dallas	21
10	PITTSBURGH	31
9	vs. Dallas**	7
10	at Kansas City	36
20	ATLANTA	14
64		109

INDIANAPOLIS (3-1)

21	CINCINNATI	34
20	at Seattle	17
20	at Green Bay (OT)	17
29	CHICAGO	7
90		75

MIAMI (1-3)

21	JACKSONVILLE	24
0	at Atlanta	37
27	WASHINGTON	13
17	vs. T.B. (ORL)	24
65		98

NEW ENGLAND (1-3)

17	DETROIT	30
21	MINNESOTA	14
7	at Philadelphia	31
24	vs. Oak. (STA)	32
69		107

N.Y. JETS (2-2)

9	at Tampa Bay	3
10	vs. Phil.(JAC)	13
31	at N.Y. Giants	32
30	at Cincinnati	24
80		72

Central Division

CINCINNATI (1-3)

34	at Indianapolis	21
7	TAMPA BAY	31
13	at Detroit	20
24	N.Y. JETS	30
78		102

CLEVELAND (2-2)

13	N.Y. GIANTS	19
55	CHICAGO	13
10	at Atlanta	19
31	at Arizona	17
109		68

HOUSTON (0-3)

13	ARIZONA	16
13	vs. Wash.(KNX) (OT)	16
-	SAN DIEGO†	-
0	vs. Dallas (SA)	10
26		42

JACKSONVILLE (2-3)

14	Carolina***	20
24	at Miami	21
3	at Detroit	19
10	ST. LOUIS	27
23	DENVER	17
74		104

PITTSBURGH (1-3)

31	at Buffalo	10
13	GREEN BAY	36
7	at Tampa Bay	20
6	PHILADELPHIA	16
57		82

Western Division

DENVER (3-2)

9	SAN FRANCISCO	7
24	San Francisco*	10
10	at Carolina	19
20	DALLAS	17
17	at Jacksonville	23
80		76

KANSAS CITY (3-1)

37	WASHINGTON	21
17	at Arizona	22
36	BUFFALO	10
17	at Minnesota	13
107		66

OAKLAND (3-1)

27	at Dallas	14
27	ST. LOUIS	22
17	at Minnesota	20
32	vs. N.E. (STA)	24
103		80

SAN DIEGO (1-2)

19	MINNESOTA	23
6	SAN FRANCISCO	17
-	at Houston†	-
17	ST. LOUIS	9
42		49

SEATTLE (2-2)

34	ST. LOUIS	20
17	INDIANAPOLIS	20
24	at New Orleans	19
7	at San Francisco	17
82		76

NFC PRESEASON RECORDS—TEAM BY TEAM

Eastern Division

ARIZONA (3-1)

16	at Houston	13
22	KANSAS CITY	17
17	at Chicago	16
17	CLEVELAND	31
72		77

DALLAS (2-3)

21	BUFFALO	15
14	OAKLAND	27
7	Buffalo**	9
17	at Denver	20
10	vs. Hous.(SA)	0
69		71

N.Y. GIANTS (3-1)

19	at Cleveland	13
14	NEW ORLEANS	13
32	N.Y. JETS	31
3	at Carolina	6
68		63

PHILADELPHIA (4-0)

25	ATLANTA	17
13	vs. N.Y.J.(JAC)	10
31	NEW ENGLAND	7
16	at Pittsburgh	6
85		40

WASHINGTON (1-3)

21	at Kansas City	37
16	vs. Hou.(KNX)(OT)	13
13	at Miami	27
23	at Green Bay	35
73		112

Central Division

CHICAGO (1-3)

18	CAROLINA	15
13	at Cleveland	55
16	ARIZONA	17
7	at Indianapolis	29
54		116

DETROIT (3-1)

30	at New England	17
19	JACKSONVILLE	3
20	CINCINNATI	13
10	at New Orleans	24
79		57

GREEN BAY (3-1)

27	NEW ORLEANS	17
36	at Pittsburgh	13
17	INDIANAPOLIS (OT)	20
35	WASHINGTON	23
115		73

MINNESOTA (2-2)

23	at San Diego	19
14	at New England	21
20	OAKLAND	17
13	KANSAS CITY	17
70		74

TAMPA BAY (3-1)

3	N.Y. JETS	9
31	at Cincinnati	7
20	PITTSBURGH	7
24	vs. Miami (ORL)	17
78		40

Western Division

ATLANTA (2-2)

17	at Philadelphia	25
37	MIAMI	0
19	CLEVELAND	10
14	at Buffalo	20
87		55

CAROLINA (3-2)

20	Jacksonville***	14
15	at Chicago	18
19	DENVER	10
10	at San Francisco	17
6	N.Y. GIANTS	3
70		62

NEW ORLEANS (1-3)

17	at Green Bay	27
13	at N.Y. Giants	14
19	SEATTLE	24
24	DETROIT	10
73		75

ST. LOUIS (1-3)

20	at Seattle	34
22	at Oakland	27
27	at Jacksonville	10
9	at San Diego	17
78		88

SAN FRANCISCO (3-2)

7	at Denver	9
10	vs. Denver*	24
17	at San Diego	6
17	CAROLINA	10
17	SEATTLE	7
68		56

(OT) denotes overtime game
* denotes American Bowl '95 in Tokyo
** denotes American Bowl '95 in Toronto
*** denotes Pro Football Hall of Fame Game
† game cancelled
(JAC) denotes game played in Jackson, Miss.
(KNX) denotes game played in Knoxville, Tenn.
(ORL) denotes game played in Orlando, Fla.
(SA) denotes game played in San Antonio, Tex.
(STA) denotes game played in Stanford, Calif.

1995 NFL STANDINGS/RESULTS

FINAL STANDINGS

AMERICAN FOOTBALL CONFERENCE

Eastern Division	W	L	T	Pct.	Pts.	OP
Buffalo	10	6	0	.625	350	335
*Indianapolis	9	7	0	.563	331	316
*Miami	9	7	0	.563	398	332
New England	6	10	0	.375	294	377
New York Jets	3	13	0	.188	233	384
Central Division						
Pittsburgh	11	5	0	.688	407	327
Cincinnati	7	9	0	.438	349	374
Houston	7	9	0	.438	348	324
Cleveland	5	11	0	.313	289	356
Jacksonville	4	12	0	.250	275	404
Western Division						
Kansas City	13	3	0	.813	358	241
*San Diego	9	7	0	.563	321	323
Seattle	8	8	0	.500	363	366
Denver	8	8	0	.500	388	345
Oakland	8	8	0	.500	348	332

NATIONAL FOOTBALL CONFERENCE

Eastern Division	W	L	T	Pct.	Pts.	OP
Dallas	12	4	0	.750	435	291
*Philadelphia	10	6	0	.625	318	338
Washington	6	10	0	.375	326	359
New York Giants	5	11	0	.313	290	340
Arizona	4	12	0	.250	275	422
Central Division						
Green Bay	11	5	0	.688	404	314
*Detroit	10	6	0	.625	436	336
Chicago	9	7	0	.563	392	360
Minnesota	8	8	0	.500	412	385
Tampa Bay	7	9	0	.438	238	335
Western Division						
San Francisco	11	5	0	.688	457	258
*Atlanta	9	7	0	.563	362	349
St. Louis	7	9	0	.438	309	418
Carolina	7	9	0	.438	289	325
New Orleans	7	9	0	.438	319	348

**Wild-Card qualifier for playoffs*

Indianapolis finished ahead of Miami based on head-to-head sweep (2-0). San Diego was first Wild Card based on head-to-head victory over Indianapolis (1-0). Cincinnati finished ahead of Houston based on better division record (4-4 to Oilers' 3-5). Seattle finished ahead of Denver and Oakland based on best head-to-head record (3-1 to Broncos' 2-2 and Raiders' 1-3). Denver finished ahead of Oakland based on head-to-head sweep (2-0). Philadelphia was first Wild Card based on better conference record (9-3) than Detroit (7-5). Atlanta was third Wild Card ahead of Chicago based on better record against common opponents (4-2) than Chicago (3-3). St. Louis finished ahead of Carolina and New Orleans based on best head-to-head record (3-1 to Panthers' 1-3 and Saints' 2-2). Carolina finished ahead of New Orleans based on better conference record (4-8 to 3-9).

WILD CARD PLAYOFFS

AFC

Buffalo 37, Miami 22, December 30, at Buffalo
Indianapolis 35, San Diego 20, December 31, at San Diego

NFC

Philadelphia 58, Detroit 37, December 30, at Philadelphia
Green Bay 37, Atlanta 20, December 31, at Green Bay

DIVISIONAL PLAYOFFS

AFC

Pittsburgh 40, Buffalo 21, January 6, at Pittsburgh
Indianapolis 10, Kansas City 7, January 7, at Kansas City

NFC

Green Bay 27, San Francisco 17, January 6, at San Francisco
Dallas 30, Philadelphia 11, January 7, at Dallas

CHAMPIONSHIP GAMES

AFC

Pittsburgh 20, Indianapolis 16, January 14, at Pittsburgh

NFC

Dallas 38, Green Bay 27, January 14, at Dallas

SUPER BOWL XXX

Dallas 27, Pittsburgh 17, January 28, at Sun Devil Stadium, Arizona

AFC-NFC PRO BOWL

NFC 20, AFC 13, February 4, at Aloha Stadium, Honolulu, Hawaii

AFC SEASON RECORDS—TEAM BY TEAM

BUFFALO (10-6)

7	at Denver	22
31	CAROLINA	9
20	INDIANAPOLIS	14
	OPEN DATE	
22	at Cleveland	19
29	N.Y. JETS	10
27	SEATTLE	21
14	at New England	27
6	at Miami	23
16	at Indianapolis	10
23	ATLANTA	17
28	at N.Y. Jets	26
25	NEW ENGLAND	35
17	at San Francisco	27
45	at St. Louis	27
23	MIAMI	20
17	HOUSTON	28
350		335

HOUSTON (7-9)

10	at Jacksonville	3
17	PITTSBURGH	34
7	CLEVELAND	14
38	at Cincinnati	28
16	JACKSONVILLE	17
17	at Minnesota (OT)	23
	OPEN DATE	
32	at Chicago	35
19	TAMPA BAY	7
37	at Cleveland	10
25	CINCINNATI	32
13	at Kansas City	20
42	DENVER	33
7	at Pittsburgh	21
17	DETROIT	24
23	N.Y. JETS	6
28	at Buffalo	17
348		324

MIAMI (9-7)

52	N.Y. JETS	14
20	at New England	3
23	PITTSBURGH	10
	OPEN DATE	
26	at Cincinnati	23
24	INDIANAPOLIS (OT)	27
30	at New Orleans	33
16	at N.Y. Jets	17
23	BUFFALO	6
24	at San Diego	14
17	NEW ENGLAND	34
20	SAN FRANCISCO	44
28	at Indianapolis	36
21	ATLANTA	20
13	KANSAS CITY	6
20	at Buffalo	23
41	at St. Louis	22
398		332

PITTSBURGH (11-5)

23	DETROIT	20
34	at Houston	17
10	at Miami	23
24	MINNESOTA	44
31	SAN DIEGO	16
16	at Jacksonville	20
	OPEN DATE	
9	CINCINNATI	27
24	JACKSONVILLE	7
37	at Chicago (OT)	34
20	CLEVELAND	3
49	at Cincinnati	31
20	at Cleveland	17
21	HOUSTON	7
29	at Oakland	10
41	NEW ENGLAND	27
19	at Green Bay	24
407		327

CINCINNATI (7-9)

24	at Indianapolis (OT)	21
24	JACKSONVILLE	17
21	at Seattle	24
28	HOUSTON	38
23	MIAMI	26
16	at Tampa Bay	19
	OPEN DATE	
27	at Pittsburgh	9
26	CLEVELAND (OT)	29
17	OAKLAND	20
32	at Houston	25
31	PITTSBURGH	49
17	at Jacksonville	13
10	at Green Bay	24
16	CHICAGO	10
10	at Cleveland	26
27	MINNESOTA	24
349		374

INDIANAPOLIS (9-7)

21	CINCINNATI (OT)	24
27	at N.Y. Jets (OT)	24
14	at Buffalo	20
	OPEN DATE	
21	ST. LOUIS	18
27	at Miami (OT)	24
18	SAN FRANCISCO	17
17	at Oakland	30
17	N.Y. JETS	10
10	BUFFALO	16
14	at New Orleans	17
24	at New England	10
36	MIAMI	28
10	at Carolina	13
41	at Jacksonville	31
24	SAN DIEGO	27
10	NEW ENGLAND	7
331		316

NEW ENGLAND (6-10)

17	CLEVELAND	14
3	MIAMI	20
3	at San Francisco	28
	OPEN DATE	
17	at Atlanta	30
3	DENVER	37
26	at Kansas City	31
27	BUFFALO	14
17	CAROLINA (OT)	20
20	at N.Y. Jets	7
34	at Miami	17
10	INDIANAPOLIS	24
35	at Buffalo	25
17	NEW ORLEANS	31
31	N.Y. JETS	28
27	at Pittsburgh	41
7	at Indianapolis	10
294		377

SAN DIEGO (9-7)

7	at Oakland	17
14	SEATTLE	10
27	at Philadelphia	21
17	DENVER	6
16	at Pittsburgh	31
23	at Kansas City (OT)	29
9	DALLAS	23
35	at Seattle	25
	OPEN DATE	
14	MIAMI	24
7	KANSAS CITY	22
27	at Denver	30
12	OAKLAND	6
31	CLEVELAND	13
28	ARIZONA	25
27	at Indianapolis	24
27	at N.Y. Giants	17
321		323

CLEVELAND (5-11)

14	at New England	17
22	TAMPA BAY	6
14	at Houston	7
35	KANSAS CITY	17
19	BUFFALO	22
20	at Detroit	38
	OPEN DATE	
15	JACKSONVILLE	23
29	at Cincinnati (OT)	26
10	HOUSTON	37
3	at Pittsburgh	20
20	GREEN BAY	31
17	PITTSBURGH	20
13	at San Diego	31
11	at Minnesota	27
26	CINCINNATI	10
21	at Jacksonville	24
289		356

JACKSONVILLE (4-12)

3	HOUSTON	10
17	at Cincinnati	24
10	at N.Y. Jets	27
14	GREEN BAY	24
17	at Houston	16
20	PITTSBURGH	16
27	CHICAGO	30
23	at Cleveland	15
7	at Pittsburgh	24
	OPEN DATE	
30	SEATTLE	47
16	at Tampa Bay	17
13	CINCINNATI	17
23	at Denver	31
31	INDIANAPOLIS	41
0	at Detroit	44
24	CLEVELAND	21
275		404

N.Y. JETS (3-13)

14	at Miami	52
24	INDIANAPOLIS (OT)	27
27	JACKSONVILLE	10
3	at Atlanta	13
10	OAKLAND	47
10	at Buffalo	29
15	at Carolina	26
17	MIAMI	16
10	at Indianapolis	17
7	NEW ENGLAND	20
	OPEN DATE	
26	BUFFALO	28
16	at Seattle	10
20	ST. LOUIS	23
28	at New England	31
6	at Houston	23
0	NEW ORLEANS	12
233		384

SEATTLE (8-8)

10	KANSAS CITY	34
10	at San Diego	14
24	CINCINNATI	21
	OPEN DATE	
27	DENVER	10
14	at Oakland	34
21	at Buffalo	27
25	SAN DIEGO	35
14	at Arizona (OT)	20
30	N.Y. GIANTS	28
47	at Jacksonville	30
27	at Washington	20
10	N.Y. JETS	16
26	PHILADELPHIA	14
31	at Denver	27
44	OAKLAND	10
3	at Kansas City	26
363		366

DENVER (8-8)

22	BUFFALO	7
21	at Dallas	31
38	WASHINGTON	31
6	at San Diego	17
10	at Seattle	27
37	at New England	3
27	OAKLAND	0
7	KANSAS CITY	21
	OPEN DATE	
38	ARIZONA	6
13	at Philadelphia	31
30	SAN DIEGO	27
33	at Houston	42
31	JACKSONVILLE	23
27	SEATTLE	31
17	at Kansas City	20
31	at Oakland	28
388		345

KANSAS CITY (13-3)

34	at Seattle	10
20	N.Y. GIANTS (OT)	17
23	OAKLAND (OT)	17
17	at Cleveland	35
24	at Arizona	3
29	SAN DIEGO (OT)	23
31	NEW ENGLAND	26
21	at Denver	7
	OPEN DATE	
24	WASHINGTON	3
22	at San Diego	7
20	HOUSTON	13
12	at Dallas	24
29	at Oakland	23
6	at Miami	13
20	DENVER	17
26	SEATTLE	3
358		241

OAKLAND (8-8)

17	SAN DIEGO	7
20	at Washington	8
17	at Kansas City (OT)	23
48	PHILADELPHIA	17
47	at N.Y. Jets	10
34	SEATTLE	14
0	at Denver	27
30	INDIANAPOLIS	17
	OPEN DATE	
20	at Cincinnati	17
17	at N.Y. Giants	13
21	DALLAS	34
6	at San Diego	12
23	KANSAS CITY	29
10	PITTSBURGH	29
10	at Seattle	44
28	DENVER	31
348		332

(OT) denotes overtime

NFC SEASON RECORDS—TEAM BY TEAM

ARIZONA (4-12)

7	at Washington	27
19	PHILADELPHIA	31
20	at Detroit	17
20	at Dallas	34
3	KANSAS CITY	24
21	at N.Y. Giants (OT)	27
24	WASHINGTON	20
	OPEN DATE	
20	SEATTLE (OT)	14
6	at Denver	38
24	MINNESOTA (OT)	30
7	at Carolina	27
40	ATLANTA (OT)	37
6	N.Y. GIANTS	10
25	at San Diego	28
20	at Philadelphia	21
13	DALLAS	37
275		422

ATLANTA (9-7)

23	CAROLINA (OT)	20
10	at San Francisco	41
27	at New Orleans (OT)	24
13	N.Y. JETS	3
30	NEW ENGLAND	17
	OPEN DATE	
19	at St. Louis	21
24	at Tampa Bay	21
13	DALLAS	28
34	DETROIT	22
17	at Buffalo	23
31	ST. LOUIS	6
37	at Arizona (OT)	40
20	at Miami	21
19	NEW ORLEANS	14
17	at Carolina	21
28	SAN FRANCISCO	27
362		349

CAROLINA (7-9)

20	at Atlanta (OT)	23
9	at Buffalo	31
10	ST. LOUIS	31
	OPEN DATE	
13	TAMPA BAY	20
27	at Chicago	31
26	N.Y. JETS	15
20	NEW ORLEANS	3
20	at New England (OT)	17
13	at San Francisco	7
17	at St. Louis	28
27	ARIZONA	7
26	at New Orleans	34
13	INDIANAPOLIS	10
10	SAN FRANCISCO	31
21	ATLANTA	17
17	at Washington	20
289		325

CHICAGO (9-7)

31	MINNESOTA	14
24	GREEN BAY	27
25	at Tampa Bay	6
28	at St. Louis	34
	OPEN DATE	
31	CAROLINA	27
30	at Jacksonville	27
35	HOUSTON	32
14	at Minnesota	6
34	PITTSBURGH (OT)	37
28	at Green Bay	35
17	DETROIT	24
27	at N.Y. Giants	24
7	at Detroit	27
10	at Cincinnati	16
31	TAMPA BAY	10
20	PHILADELPHIA	14
392		360

(OT) denotes overtime

DALLAS (12-4)

35	at N.Y. Giants	0
31	DENVER	21
23	at Minnesota (OT)	17
34	ARIZONA	20
23	at Washington	27
34	GREEN BAY	24
23	at San Diego	9
	OPEN DATE	
28	at Atlanta	13
34	PHILADELPHIA	12
20	SAN FRANCISCO	38
34	at Oakland	21
24	KANSAS CITY	12
17	WASHINGTON	24
17	at Philadelphia	20
21	N.Y. GIANTS	20
37	at Arizona	13
435		291

DETROIT (10-6)

20	at Pittsburgh	23
10	at Minnesota	20
17	ARIZONA	20
27	SAN FRANCISCO	24
	OPEN DATE	
38	CLEVELAND	20
21	at Green Bay	30
30	at Washington (OT)	36
24	GREEN BAY	16
22	at Atlanta	34
27	TAMPA BAY	24
24	at Chicago	17
44	MINNESOTA	38
27	CHICAGO	7
24	at Houston	17
44	JACKSONVILLE	0
37	at Tampa Bay	10
436		336

GREEN BAY (11-5)

14	ST. LOUIS	17
27	at Chicago	24
14	N.Y. GIANTS	6
24	at Jacksonville	14
	OPEN DATE	
24	at Dallas	34
30	DETROIT	21
38	MINNESOTA	21
16	at Detroit	24
24	at Minnesota	27
35	CHICAGO	28
31	at Cleveland	20
35	TAMPA BAY	13
24	CINCINNATI	10
10	at Tampa Bay (OT)	13
34	at New Orleans	23
24	PITTSBURGH	19
404		314

MINNESOTA (8-8)

14	at Chicago	31
20	DETROIT	10
17	DALLAS (OT)	23
44	at Pittsburgh	24
	OPEN DATE	
23	HOUSTON (OT)	17
17	at Tampa Bay (OT)	20
21	at Green Bay	38
6	CHICAGO	14
27	GREEN BAY	24
30	at Arizona (OT)	24
43	NEW ORLEANS	24
38	at Detroit	44
31	TAMPA BAY	17
27	CLEVELAND	11
30	at San Francisco	37
24	at Cincinnati	27
412		385

NEW ORLEANS (7-9)

22	SAN FRANCISCO	24
13	at St. Louis	17
24	ATLANTA (OT)	27
29	at N.Y. Giants	45
10	PHILADELPHIA	15
	OPEN DATE	
33	MIAMI	30
3	at Carolina	20
11	at San Francisco	7
19	ST. LOUIS	10
17	INDIANAPOLIS	14
24	at Minnesota	43
34	CAROLINA	26
31	at New England	17
14	at Atlanta	19
23	GREEN BAY	34
12	at N.Y. Jets	0
319		348

N.Y. GIANTS (5-11)

0	DALLAS	35
17	at Kansas City (OT)	20
6	at Green Bay	14
45	NEW ORLEANS	29
6	at San Francisco	20
27	ARIZONA (OT)	21
14	PHILADELPHIA	17
	OPEN DATE	
24	at Washington	15
28	at Seattle	30
13	OAKLAND	17
19	at Philadelphia	28
24	CHICAGO	27
10	at Arizona	6
20	WASHINGTON	13
20	at Dallas	21
17	SAN DIEGO	27
290		340

PHILADELPHIA (10-6)

6	TAMPA BAY	21
31	at Arizona	19
21	SAN DIEGO	27
17	at Oakland	48
15	at New Orleans	10
37	WASHINGTON (OT)	34
17	at N.Y. Giants	14
	OPEN DATE	
20	ST. LOUIS	9
12	at Dallas	34
31	DENVER	13
28	N.Y. GIANTS	19
14	at Washington	7
14	at Seattle	26
20	DALLAS	17
21	ARIZONA	20
14	at Chicago	20
318		338

ST. LOUIS (7-9)

17	at Green Bay	14
17	NEW ORLEANS	13
31	at Carolina	10
34	CHICAGO	28
18	at Indianapolis	21
	OPEN DATE	
21	ATLANTA	19
10	SAN FRANCISCO	44
9	at Philadelphia	20
10	at New Orleans	19
28	CAROLINA	17
6	at Atlanta	31
13	at San Francisco	41
23	at N.Y. Jets	20
27	BUFFALO	45
23	WASHINGTON	35
22	MIAMI	41
309		418

SAN FRANCISCO (11-5)

24	at New Orleans	22
41	ATLANTA	10
28	NEW ENGLAND	3
24	at Detroit	27
20	N.Y. GIANTS	6
	OPEN DATE	
17	at Indianapolis	18
44	at St. Louis	10
7	NEW ORLEANS	11
7	CAROLINA	13
38	at Dallas	20
44	at Miami	20
41	ST. LOUIS	13
27	BUFFALO	17
31	at Carolina	10
37	MINNESOTA	10
27	at Atlanta	28
457		258

TAMPA BAY (7-9)

21	at Philadelphia	6
6	at Cleveland	22
6	CHICAGO	25
14	WASHINGTON	6
20	at Carolina	13
19	CINCINNATI	16
20	MINNESOTA (OT)	17
21	ATLANTA	24
7	at Houston	19
	OPEN DATE	
24	at Detroit	27
17	JACKSONVILLE	16
13	at Green Bay	35
17	at Minnesota	31
13	GREEN BAY (OT)	10
10	at Chicago	31
10	DETROIT	37
238		335

WASHINGTON (6-10)

27	ARIZONA	7
8	OAKLAND	20
31	at Denver	38
6	at Tampa Bay	14
27	DALLAS	23
34	at Philadelphia (OT)	37
20	at Arizona	24
36	DETROIT (OT)	30
15	N.Y. GIANTS	24
3	at Kansas City	24
	OPEN DATE	
20	SEATTLE	27
7	PHILADELPHIA	14
24	at Dallas	17
13	at N.Y. Giants	20
35	at St. Louis	23
20	CAROLINA	17
326		359

1995 WEEK BY WEEK

Attendance figures as they appear in the following, and in the club-by-club sections starting on page 28, are turnstile counts and not paid attendance. Paid attendance totals are on page 235.

FIRST WEEK SUMMARIES

AMERICAN FOOTBALL CONFERENCE

Eastern Division	W	L	T	Pct.	Pts.	OP
Miami	1	0	0	1.000	52	14
New England	1	0	0	1.000	17	14
Buffalo	0	1	0	.000	7	22
Indianapolis	0	1	0	.000	21	24
N.Y. Jets	0	1	0	.000	14	52
Central Division						
Cincinnati	1	0	0	1.000	24	21
Houston	1	0	0	1.000	10	3
Pittsburgh	1	0	0	1.000	23	20
Cleveland	0	1	0	.000	14	17
Jacksonville	0	1	0	.000	3	10
Western Division						
Denver	1	0	0	1.000	22	7
Kansas City	1	0	0	1.000	34	10
Oakland	1	0	0	1.000	17	7
San Diego	0	1	0	.000	7	17
Seattle	0	1	0	.000	10	34

NATIONAL FOOTBALL CONFERENCE

Eastern Division	W	L	T	Pct.	Pts.	OP
Dallas	1	0	0	1.000	35	0
Washington	1	0	0	1.000	27	7
Arizona	0	1	0	.000	7	27
N.Y. Giants	0	1	0	.000	0	35
Philadelphia	0	1	0	.000	6	21
Central Division						
Chicago	1	0	0	1.000	31	14
Tampa Bay	1	0	0	1.000	21	6
Detroit	0	1	0	.000	20	23
Green Bay	0	1	0	.000	14	17
Minnesota	0	1	0	.000	14	31
Western Division						
Atlanta	1	0	0	1.000	23	20
St. Louis	1	0	0	1.000	17	14
San Francisco	1	0	0	1.000	24	22
Carolina	0	1	0	.000	20	23
New Orleans	0	1	0	.000	22	24

SUNDAY, SEPTEMBER 3

WASHINGTON 27, ARIZONA 7—at RFK Stadium, attendance 52,731. Gus Frerotte came off the bench to throw 2 touchdown passes as the Redskins easily beat the Cardinals. Frerotte replaced injured starting quarterback Heath Shuler late in the first half with Washington leading 10-7. He teamed with Leslie Shepherd on a 73-yard touchdown pass late in the third quarter to put the Redskins ahead 20-7, then put the game out of reach with a 2-yard touchdown pass to tight end Scott Galbraith with 5:23 to go in the game. He finished with 9 completions in 15 attempts for 157 yards. Free-agent Terry Allen ran 131 yards on 26 carries for Washington, and became the first running back to gain 100 yards against a Buddy Ryan-coached defense since 1989. Rookie wide receiver Michael Westbrook added a 58-yard touchdown run on a reverse in the first quarter, as the Redskins amassed 259 yards on the ground. They had 456 yards in all, while Arizona managed just 197.

Arizona	0	7	0	0	—	7
Washington	10	0	10	7	—	27

Wash — FG Murray 36
Wash — Westbrook 58 run (Murray kick)
Ariz — McBride 3 pass from Krieg (Davis kick)
Wash — FG Murray 22
Wash — Shepherd 73 pass from Frerotte (Murray kick)
Wash — Galbraith 2 pass from Frerotte (Murray kick)

ATLANTA 23, CAROLINA 20—at Georgia Dome, attendance 58,808. Morten Andersen kicked a 35-yard field goal 6:17 into overtime as the Falcons narrowly escaped defeat in the expansion Panthers' inaugural game. The Panthers, who scored on their first three possessions to build a 13-3 lead in the opening period, had a chance to win the game at the end of regulation after Frank Reich's 44-yard touchdown pass to Willie Green pulled them within 20-19 with 26 seconds remaining. Carolina elected to go for 2 points, but after tackle Derrick Graham was penalized for a false start, the Panthers settled for the tying conversion kick by John Kasay. Carolina had the first chance in overtime, but Reich was stripped of the ball by defensive end Lester Archambeau, who recovered on the Panthers' 31-yard line. Six plays later, Andersen made the winning kick. Archambeau's sack was the club-record-tying ninth for Atlanta. Defensive end Chris Doleman had 3½. Falcons quarterback Jeff George completed 27 of 45 passes for 290 yards, and helped rally his team with 2 touchdown passes. Reich completed 23 of 44 passes for 329 yards for the Panthers. Green caught 7 passes for 121 yards.

Carolina	13	0	0	7	0	—	20
Atlanta	3	10	7	0	3	—	23

Car — Metzelaars 8 pass from Reich (Kasay kick)
Car — FG Kasay 39
Atl — FG Andersen 27
Car — FG Kasay 41
Atl — Birden 12 pass from George (Andersen kick)
Atl — FG Andersen 51
Atl — Emanuel 5 pass from George (Andersen kick)
Car — Green 44 pass from Reich (Kasay kick)
Atl — FG Andersen 35

CINCINNATI 24, INDIANAPOLIS 21—at RCA Dome, attendance 42,445. Doug Pelfrey kicked 5 field goals, including the game winner from 47 yards 2:36 into overtime, to give the Bengals the victory. The winning kick came four plays after Colts defensive back Ray Buchanan was whistled for a 34-yard pass interference penalty that positioned Cincinnati at Indianapolis's 33-yard line. The Colts sent the game into overtime on Jim Harbaugh's 5-yard touchdown pass to Willie Anderson and a subsequent 2-point conversion pass to Floyd Turner with three seconds remaining in regulation. Harbaugh completed 9 of 12 passes for 86 yards after taking over for starting quarterback Craig Erickson, who passed for 196 yards but was intercepted 3 times. Bengals quarterback Jeff Blake completed 19 of 33 passes for 249 yards and 1 touchdown. Tight end Tony McGee caught 6 passes for 118 yards.

Cincinnati	3	10	8	0	3	—	24
Indianapolis	7	3	0	11	0	—	21

Ind — Anderson 16 pass from Erickson (Cofer kick)
Cin — FG Pelfrey 25
Cin — Pickens 3 pass from Blake (Pelfrey kick)
Ind — FG Cofer 27
Cin — FG Pelfrey 44
Cin — FG Pelfrey 32
Cin — Safety, ball snapped out of end zone
Cin — FG Pelfrey 38
Ind — FG Cofer 40
Ind — Anderson 5 pass from Harbaugh (Turner pass from Harbaugh)
Cin — FG Pelfrey 47

NEW ENGLAND 17, CLEVELAND 14—at Foxboro Stadium, attendance 60,126. Rookie Curtis Martin's 1-yard touchdown run with 19 seconds remaining gave the Patriots a dramatic victory and avenged last season's playoff loss to the Browns. New England trailed 14-9 when they took possession at their own 15-yard line with 4:29 remaining in the game. Minutes later, the Patriots reached Cleveland's 12-yard line, only to find themselves facing third-and-10. Quarterback Drew Bledsoe completed a 9-yard pass to tight end Ben Coates, and on fourth-and-1 from the 3-yard line, dove 1 yard for a first down. Martin's winning touchdown gave him 102 yards on 19 carries for the afternoon. Bledsoe completed 30 of 47 passes for 302 yards. Tight end Ben Coates caught 9 passes for 106 yards. The Browns built a 14-6 lead in the first half on 2 touchdown passes from Vinny Testaverde to Michael Jackson. Testaverde passed for 254 yards, while Jackson caught 7 passes for 157 yards.

Cleveland	7	7	0	0	—	14
New England	6	0	0	11	—	17

NE — FG Bahr 21
Cleve — Jackson 70 pass from Testaverde (Stover kick)
NE — FG Bahr 21
Cleve — Jackson 30 pass from Testaverde (Stover kick)
NE — FG Bahr 28
NE — Martin 1 run (Meggett run)

PITTSBURGH 23, DETROIT 20—at Three Rivers Stadium, attendance 58,002. Norm Johnson's 31-yard field goal as time expired lifted the Steelers to a hard-fought but costly victory over the Lions. Pittsburgh's triumph was tempered by the loss of cornerback Rod Woodson and quarterback Neil O'Donnell to injury. Woodson likely was lost for the season with a knee injury, while O'Donnell broke a finger on his throwing hand and was expected to miss at least two weeks. Still, Byron (Bam) Morris rushed for 2 touchdowns as the Steelers rallied from a 10-6 halftime deficit to take a 20-10 lead in the fourth quarter. After Detroit tied it at 20-20 on Scott Mitchell's 27-yard touchdown pass to Herman Moore and Jason Hanson's 36-yard field goal with 3:01 to go, the Steelers drove 67 yards in 12 plays to the winning score. Backup quarterback Mike Tomczak, who had to leave the game himself early in the fourth quarter with a bruised sternum, completed all 6 of his passes on the final drive. Barry Sanders rushed for 108 yards on 21 carries for the Lions. Moore caught 10 passes for 131 yards.

Detroit	0	10	0	10	—	20
Pittsburgh	3	3	7	10	—	23

Pitt — FG N. Johnson 39
Pitt — FG N. Johnson 47
Det — Perriman 5 pass from Mitchell (Hanson kick)
Det — FG Hanson 43
Pitt — Morris 5 run (N. Johnson kick)
Pitt — Morris 1 run (N. Johnson kick)
Det — Moore 27 pass from Mitchell (Hanson kick)
Det — FG Hanson 36
Pitt — FG N. Johnson 31

HOUSTON 10, JACKSONVILLE 3—at Jacksonville Municipal Stadium, attendance 72,363. Chris Chandler's 4-yard touchdown pass to Haywood Jeffires 8:17 into the first quarter accounted for the game's only touchdown and spoiled the debut of the expansion Jaguars. The Oilers drove 78 yards in 13 plays to their touchdown the first time they had the ball. Gary Brown carried 8 times for 45 yards on the drive and eventually finished with 101 yards on 29 attempts. But for the most part the defenses dominated. Houston managed only 240 total yards, Jacksonville only 152. Jaguars quarterbacks Steve Beuerlein and Mark Brunell combined to complete only 10 of 26 passes for 75 yards, and suffered 4 sacks. Brunell accounted for a large chunk of Jacksonville's offense with 2 rushes for a team-high 36 yards.

Houston	7	0	3	0	—	10
Jacksonville	0	0	0	3	—	3

Hou — Jeffires 4 pass from Chandler (Del Greco kick)
Hou — FG Del Greco 19
Jack — FG Hollis 26

KANSAS CITY 34, SEATTLE 10—at Kingdome, attendance 54,062. Steve Bono, taking over for retired Joe Montana, was nearly perfect in his debut as the Chiefs' regular starter. Bono, making only the twelfth start of his 11-year career, completed 18 of 23 passes for 278 yards and 3 touchdowns, with no interceptions. He helped Kansas City build a 20-3 lead at halftime with touchdown bombs of 60 and 40 yards to Willie Davis. The Chiefs put the game away when Tamarick Vanover returned the second-half kickoff 99 yards for a touchdown, and, midway through the third quarter, Bono threw a 16-yard touchdown pass to Lake Dawson. Davis caught 6 passes for 155 yards and Greg Hill rushed for 109 yards for Kansas City, which amassed 419 total yards. The Seahawks drove to a field goal on the opening possession, but did not score again until late in the fourth quarter, long after the issue was decided.

Kansas City	7	13	14	0	—	34
Seattle	3	0	0	7	—	10

Sea — FG Peterson 49
KC — Davis 60 pass from Bono (Elliott kick)
KC — FG Elliott 46
KC — Davis 40 pass from Bono (Elliott kick)
KC — FG Elliott 49
KC — Vanover 99 kickoff return (Elliott kick)
KC — Dawson 16 pass from Bono (Elliott kick)
Sea — Blades 21 pass from Friesz (Peterson kick)

CHICAGO 31, MINNESOTA 14—at Soldier Field, attendance 63,036. Erik Kramer threw 3 touchdown passes to lead the Bears past the Vikings. Despite Kramer's 2 touchdown passes to Curtis Conway in the first half, Chicago found itself tied at 14-14 at the intermission. But the Bears marched 66 yards in seven plays following the second-half kickoff, taking the lead for good on Kramer's 2-yard touchdown pass to tight end Keith Jennings 3:22 into the second half. Rookie Rashaan Salaam capped an 81-yard march later in the quarter with a 3-yard touchdown run for a 28-14 lead. Chicago, which ranked twenty-third in the NFL in offense in 1994, moved the ball effectively all day, totaling 397 yards. Kramer finished with 19 completions in 28 attempts for 262 yards. Jeff Graham caught 8 passes for 107 yards, and Conway added 5 receptions for 110 yards. Warren Moon completed 26 of 36 passes for 247 yards for Minnesota.

Minnesota	7	7	0	0	—	14
Chicago	7	7	14	3	—	31

Minn — Jordan 11 pass from Moon (Reveiz kick)
Chi — Conway 73 pass from Kramer (Butler kick)
Minn — R. Smith 1 run (Reveiz kick)
Chi — Conway 5 pass from Kramer (Butler kick)
Chi — Jennings 2 pass from Kramer (Butler kick)
Chi — Salaam 3 run (Butler kick)
Chi — FG Butler 21

MIAMI 52, N.Y. JETS 14—at Joe Robbie Stadium, attendance 71,317. Dan Marino threw 3 touchdown passes in the Dolphins' rout of the Jets. Marino, who completed 16 of 26 passes for 250 yards, broke a 14-14 tie with a 1-yard touchdown pass to running back Keith Byars four seconds before halftime. Miami then broke open the game with 3 touchdowns in a span of 5:20 of the third quarter. The Dolphins took advantage of 6 takeaways, including 4 interceptions. Cornerback Troy Vincent had 2 interceptions, and returned one of them 69 yards for a touchdown. Bernie Parmalee rushed for 2 touchdowns, while Irving Fryar caught 2 touchdown passes. Fryar had 5 receptions for 110 yards. Miami raised its record to a league-best 22-4 in home openers since the 1970 AFL-NFL merger.

N.Y. Jets	0	14	0	0	—	14
Miami	0	21	21	10	—	52

Mia — Parmalee 24 run (Stoyanovich kick)
Mia — Fryar 4 pass from Marino (Stoyanovich kick)
Jets — Brock 3 fumble return (Lowery kick)
Jets — Wilson 6 pass from Esiason (Lowery kick)
Mia — Byars 1 pass from Marino (Stoyanovich kick)
Mia — Parmalee 4 run (Stoyanovich kick)
Mia — Vincent 69 interception return (Stoyanovich kick)
Mia — Fryar 50 pass from Marino (Stoyanovich kick)
Mia — FG Stoyanovich 29
Mia — Spikes 17 run (Stoyanovich kick)

ST. LOUIS 17, GREEN BAY 14—at Lambeau Field, attendance 60,104. Isaac Bruce blocked a punt and caught a touchdown pass to spark the Rams to victory. The game was scoreless late in the second quarter when Bruce blocked Craig Hentrich's punt and fell on it at the Packers' 23-yard line. The second-year wide receiver, making his first NFL start, then caught a 23-yard touchdown pass from Chris Miller on the next play. Miller also had a 30-yard touchdown pass to Alexander Wright to break a 7-7 tie late in the third quarter. Steve McLaughlin's 19-yard field goal with 5:22 remaining in the game provided the eventual margin of victory. The field goal came six plays after linebacker Roman Phifer's interception and 25-yard return to Green Bay's 20-yard line. It was St. Louis's third interception of Brett Favre. Green Bay's quarterback completed 29 of 51 passes for 299 yards and 2 touchdowns, but was picked off twice deep in Rams' territory and also was sacked 4 times. The Rams snapped a seven-game losing streak dating to last season and ended the Packers' 10-game winning streak at Lambeau Field.

St. Louis	0	7	7	3	—	17
Green Bay	0	0	7	7	—	14

StL — Bruce 23 pass from Miller (McLaughlin kick)
GB — Chmura 7 pass from Favre (Jacke kick)
StL — Wright 30 pass from Miller (McLaughlin kick)
StL — FG McLaughlin 19
GB — Jordan 11 pass from Favre (Jacke kick)

OAKLAND 17, SAN DIEGO 7—at Oakland-Alameda County Coliseum, attendance 50,323. The Raiders beat the defending AFC-champion Chargers in their return to Oakland after 14 years in Los Angeles. Rookie kicker Cole Ford, playing in place of injured Jeff Jaeger, kicked a 46-yard field goal 1:14 into the second half to break a 7-7 tie and give the Raiders the lead for good. Ford's field goal came three plays after defensive tackle Jerry Ball recovered Chargers running back Natrone Means's fumble on the first play of the second half. Another turnover, on a fumbled punt by San Diego's Andre Coleman, led to the 16-yard touchdown run by rookie Napoleon Kaufman late in the third quarter that provided the final margin of victory. Oakland managed only 247 total yards, but did march 99 yards in 14 plays to a touchdown early in the second quarter. Jeff Hostetler capped the march with a 5-yard touchdown pass to Tim Brown. San Diego's lone score came on Stan Humphries's 39-yard touchdown pass to Shawn Jefferson 1:17 before halftime. Humphries passed for 305 yards, but completed only 23 of 47 passes and was intercepted once. Jefferson caught 6 passes for 120 yards.

San Diego	0	7	0	0	—	7
Oakland	0	7	10	0	—	17

Oak — Brown 5 pass from Hostetler (Ford kick)
SD — Jefferson 39 pass from Humphries (Carney kick)
Oak — FG Ford 46
Oak — Kaufman 16 run (Ford kick)

SAN FRANCISCO 24, NEW ORLEANS 22—at Louisiana Superdome, attendance 66,627. Steve Young threw 2 touchdown passes and the 49ers held off the Saints to win. Young completed 21 of 27 passes for 260 yards despite suffering a sprained neck on a sack in the second quarter. He had to leave the game with San Francisco leading 14-0, and, in his absence, New Orleans safety Sean Lumpkin intercepted Elvis Grbac's first pass and returned it 47 yards for a touchdown. But Young returned at the start of the second half and directed an 86-yard, 14-play drive that took eight minutes, capping the march with a 4-yard touchdown pass to running back William Floyd to put the 49ers ahead 24-9. The Saints rallied behind 2 touchdown passes from Jim Everett, but their last chance ended when cornerback Tyronne Drakeford stripped Everett of the ball on fourth-and-10 from New Orleans's 40-yard line in the final minute. Everett finished with 23 completions in 38 attempts for 266 yards. Young was the game's leading rusher with 50 yards on 9 carries. San Francisco scored first on a 50-yard touchdown pass from Young to Jerry Rice 52 seconds into the second quarter. That marked the 275th consecutive game in which San Francisco scored, an NFL record.

San Francisco	0	17	7	0	—	24
New Orleans	0	9	6	7	—	22

SF — Rice 50 pass from Young (Brien kick)
SF — McDonald 52 interception return (Brien kick)
NO — Lumpkin 47 interception return (kick failed)
SF — FG Brien 28
NO — FG Lohmiller 51
SF — Floyd 4 pass from Young (Brien kick)
NO — Early 28 pass from Everett (pass failed)
NO — Haynes 29 pass from Everett (Lohmiller kick)

TAMPA BAY 21, PHILADELPHIA 6—at Veterans Stadium, attendance 66,266. Trent Dilfer threw 2 touchdown passes as the Buccaneers stunned the Eagles. Philadelphia struck first on Gary Anderson's 21-yard field goal 7:32 into the game. But on the next play from scrimmage, Dilfer teamed with Horace Copeland on a 64-yard touchdown bomb to put Tampa Bay ahead for good. Dilfer also threw a 10-yard touchdown pass to tight end Jackie Harris early in the fourth quarter. That came 8 plays after Eagles running back Ricky Watters lost a fumble at the Buccaneers' 46-yard line. Watters, a key free-agent acquisition from the 49ers, managed only 37 yards on 17 carries. Tampa Bay put the game out of reach with an 80-yard drive capped by Errict Rhett's 19-yard run with 4:01 left in the game. The march was highlighted by Dilfer's 44-yard pass to Copeland. Rhett finished with 85 yards on 26 rushes. Copeland caught 5 passes for 155 yards. Philadelphia quarterback Randall Cunningham completed 25 of 36 passes, but for only 191 yards.

Tampa Bay	7	0	0	14	—	21
Philadelphia	6	0	0	0	—	6

Phil — FG Anderson 21
TB — Copeland 64 pass from Dilfer (Husted kick)
Phil — FG Anderson 28
TB — Harris 10 pass from Dilfer (Husted kick)
TB — Rhett 19 run (Husted kick)

SUNDAY NIGHT, SEPTEMBER 3

DENVER 22, BUFFALO 7—at Denver Mile High Stadium, attendance 75,743. Jason Elam kicked 5 field goals to pace the Broncos to the victory. Elam's field goals, including a 52-yarder to start the second quarter, staked Denver to a 15-7 lead before rookie Terrell Davis put the game out of reach by running 3 yards for a touchdown with 3:22 left in the game. John Elway completed 22 of 41 passes for 317 yards as the Broncos had little trouble moving the football. Denver had 24 first downs and 439 total yards, and maintained possession for more than 37 of the game's 60 minutes. Buffalo, meanwhile, fared poorly on offense. The Bills drove 77 yards to a touchdown in the first quarter, but finished with only 234 total yards. Jim Kelly had a 34-yard touchdown pass to Andre Reed, but finished with just 12 completions in 28 attempts for 154 yards.

Buffalo	7	0	0	0	—	7
Denver	3	9	0	10	—	22

Den — FG Elam 22
Buff — Reed 34 pass from Kelly (Christie kick)
Den — FG Elam 52
Den — FG Elam 20
Den — FG Elam 38
Den — FG Elam 37
Den — Davis 3 run (Elam kick)

MONDAY, SEPTEMBER 4

DALLAS 35, N.Y. GIANTS 0—at Giants Stadium, attendance 77,454. Emmitt Smith rushed for 4 touchdowns, including a 60-yard score the first time he touched the ball, as the Cowboys blasted the Giants. Smith, who passed Pro Football Hall of Fame running back Tony Dorsett to become Dallas's career leader in rushing touchdowns (with 75 by game's end), got the Cowboys rolling with his long touchdown run 3:04 into the game. Each of his 3 other touchdowns covered 1 yard, and he finished the game with 163 yards on 21 carries. Quarterback Troy Aikman completed 15 of 20 passes for 228 yards, including a 7-yard touchdown to Michael Irvin in the second quarter. Irvin caught 7 passes for 109 yards. The Cowboys amassed 459 total yards while limiting the Giants to only 211.

Dallas	7	14	7	7	—	35
N.Y. Giants	0	0	0	0	—	0

Dall — E. Smith 60 run (Boniol kick)
Dall — Irvin 7 pass from Aikman (Boniol kick)
Dall — E. Smith 1 run (Boniol kick)
Dall — E. Smith 1 run (Boniol kick)
Dall — E. Smith 1 run (Boniol kick)

SECOND WEEK SUMMARIES

AMERICAN FOOTBALL CONFERENCE

Eastern Division	W	L	T	Pct.	Pts.	OP
Miami	2	0	0	1.000	72	17
Buffalo	1	1	0	.500	38	31
Indianapolis	1	1	0	.500	48	48
New England	1	1	0	.500	20	34
N.Y. Jets	0	2	0	.000	38	79
Central Division						
Cincinnati	2	0	0	1.000	48	38
Pittsburgh	2	0	0	1.000	57	37
Cleveland	1	1	0	.500	36	23
Houston	1	1	0	.500	27	37
Jacksonville	0	2	0	.000	20	34
Western Division						
Kansas City	2	0	0	1.000	54	27
Oakland	2	0	0	1.000	37	15
Denver	1	1	0	.500	43	38
San Diego	1	1	0	.500	21	27
Seattle	0	2	0	.000	20	48

NATIONAL FOOTBALL CONFERENCE

Eastern Division	W	L	T	Pct.	Pts.	OP
Dallas	2	0	0	1.000	66	21
Philadelphia	1	1	0	.500	37	40
Washington	1	1	0	.500	35	27
Arizona	0	2	0	.000	26	58
N.Y. Giants	0	2	0	.000	17	55
Central Division						
Chicago	1	1	0	.500	55	41
Green Bay	1	1	0	.500	41	41
Minnesota	1	1	0	.500	34	41
Tampa Bay	1	1	0	.500	27	28
Detroit	0	2	0	.000	30	43
Western Division						
St. Louis	2	0	0	1.000	34	27
San Francisco	2	0	0	1.000	65	32
Atlanta	1	1	0	.500	33	61
Carolina	0	2	0	.000	29	54
New Orleans	0	2	0	.000	35	41

SUNDAY, SEPTEMBER 10

SAN FRANCISCO 41, ATLANTA 10—at 3Com Park, attendance 63,627. Steve Young threw 3 touchdown passes in the 49ers' rout. San Francisco took the opening kickoff, drove 67 yards to a touchdown, and never looked back. Young completed all 6 of his attempts for 66 yards on the first drive, capping the march with an 18-yard touchdown pass to Jerry Rice 4:19 into the game. Cornerback Tyronne Drakeford intercepted Jeff George's pass on the next play from scrimmage, leading to Doug Brien's field goal and a 10-0 lead, and the 49ers went on to lead 24-0 before the Falcons managed a first down. Young finished with 27 completions in 40 attempts for 331 yards. Two of his scoring passes went to Rice, who caught 11 balls for 167 yards. The 49ers rolled up 489 yards against Atlanta's defense, which they shredded for 92 points in a pair of victories a year ago. San Francisco safety Tim McDonald returned an interception for a touchdown for the second consecutive week.

Atlanta	0	3	7	0	—	10
San Francisco	17	7	7	10	—	41

SF — Rice 18 pass from Young (Brien kick)
SF — FG Brien 27
SF — Loville 1 run (Brien kick)
SF — Jones 2 pass from Young (Brien kick)
Atl — FG Andersen 26
Atl — Mathis 23 pass from George (Andersen kick)
SF — McDonald 13 interception return (Brien kick)
SF — FG Brien 45
SF — Rice 29 pass from Young (Brien kick)

BUFFALO 31, CAROLINA 9—at Rich Stadium, attendance 79,190. The Bills scored 4 touchdowns in a span of 9:46 of the third quarter to turn the game around. Buffalo trailed 9-0 in the third quarter and had yet to cross midfield until quarterback Jim Kelly, just 1 of 14 passing with 3 interceptions to that point, teamed with wide receiver Russell Copeland on a 77-yard scoring play to cut the deficit to 9-7 3:11 into the second half. The Bills then scored on each of their next two possessions—Thurman Thomas ran 4 yards for a touchdown, then took a screen pass 60 yards to set up Darick Holmes's 3-yard run—to take a 21-9 lead, and capped the barrage with safety Kurt Schulz's 32-yard interception return for a touchdown with 2:03 to go in the third period. Kelly finished the day with only 4 completions in 21 attempts, but was bailed out by Thomas, who rushed for 91 yards and caught 2 passes for 64 yards, and a stingy defense that permitted the expansion Panthers only 113 total yards. Former Buffalo quarterback Frank Reich completed just 6 of 21 passes for 44 yards for Carolina, which managed only 6 first downs (2 by penalty) and averaged 1.9 yards on its 58 offensive plays.

Carolina	0	6	3	0	—	9
Buffalo	0	0	28	3	—	31

Car — FG Kasay 34
Car — FG Kasay 52
Car — FG Kasay 32
Buff — Copeland 77 pass from Kelly (Christie kick)
Buff — Thomas 4 run (Christie kick)
Buff — Holmes 3 run (Christie kick)
Buff — Schulz 32 interception return (Christie kick)
Buff — FG Christie 39

DALLAS 31, DENVER 21—at Texas Stadium, attendance 64,576. Troy Aikman threw 2 touchdown passes and ran for another in the Cowboys' victory. Aikman's 5-yard touchdown pass to fullback Daryl Johnston and the quarterback's 2-yard touchdown run staked Dallas to a 14-0 lead midway through the second quarter, and the Cowboys never allowed the Broncos to get closer than 7 points after that. While nursing a 14-7 halftime advantage that grew to 28-14 in the first minute of the fourth quarter, Dallas maintained possession for 14:08 to Denver's 1:34. Aikman completed 18 of 31 passes for 196 yards, and was complemented by running back Emmitt Smith, who gained 114 yards on 26 carries. The Broncos never seriously threatened the Cowboys' lead, but stayed close on the strength of 3 touchdown catches by Anthony Miller. John Elway passed for 2 touchdowns, but completed only 11 of 24 passes for 152 yards. Miller had 6 receptions for 108 yards.

Denver	0	7	7	7	—	21
Dallas	0	14	7	10	—	31

Dall — Johnston 5 pass from Aikman (Boniol kick)
Dall — Aikman 2 run (Boniol kick)
Den — Miller 11 pass from Elway (Elam kick)
Dall — Novacek 7 pass from Aikman (Boniol kick)
Den — Miller 59 pass from Elway (Elam kick)
Dall — E. Smith 1 run (Boniol kick)
Dall — FG Boniol 45
Den — Miller 3 pass from Millen (Elam kick)

MINNESOTA 20, DETROIT 10—at Metrodome, attendance 52,234. Robert Smith rushed for 111 yards and 1 touchdown in the Vikings' victory. Smith carried 20 times and outperformed Lions Pro Bowl running back Barry Sanders, who managed only 35 yards on 13 carries. The game was tied 10-10 at halftime before Fuad Reveiz broke the deadlock with a 27-yard field goal in the final minute of the third quarter. It was Reveiz's NFL-record thirtieth consecutive field goal, breaking John Carney's previous mark of 29. Minnesota's clinching touchdown came with 4:50 to play, when Warren Moon's pass bounced off a pair of Detroit defenders and into the arms of Qadry Ismail, who went on to complete an 85-yard touchdown. Moon completed 19 of 29 passes for 233 yards. The Lions' Scott Mitchell was 27 of 47 for 279 yards and 1 touchdown.

Detroit	10	0	0	0	—	10
Minnesota	7	3	3	7	—	20

Minn — R. Smith 1 run (Reveiz kick)
Det — Moore 47 pass from Mitchell (Hanson kick)
Det — FG Hanson 33
Minn — FG Reveiz 32
Minn — FG Reveiz 27
Minn — Ismail 85 pass from Moon (Reveiz kick)

INDIANAPOLIS 27, N.Y. JETS 24—at Giants Stadium, attendance 65,134. The Colts rallied from a 21-point deficit late in the third quarter to win in overtime on Mike Cofer's 52-yard field goal. Indianapolis trailed 24-3 before beginning its comeback when linebacker Tony Bennett recovered Jets running back Ron Moore's fumble and returned it 32 yards for a touchdown with 2:11 remaining in the third quarter. The next time they had the ball, the Colts drove 80 yards in 12 plays, capping the march with Jim Harbaugh's 15-yard touchdown pass to Sean Dawkins to pull within 24-17 with 8:46 left. New York threatened to put the game out of reach by driving to Indianapolis's 23-yard line, but on second down Boomer Esiason fumbled the center snap and Colts linebacker Stephen Grant recovered at the 25. Seven plays later, Harbaugh's 14-yard touchdown pass to running back Marshall Faulk tied the score, and Indianapolis won the game on its first possession of overtime. Harbaugh's 24-yard pass to Dawkins positioned Cofer for the winning field goal 4:27 into the extra session. Harbaugh, who relieved starter Craig Erickson for the second consecutive week, completed 11 of 16 passes for 123 yards. Faulk rushed for 81 yards and caught 8 passes for 58 yards. The Jets drove 80 yards for a touchdown following the game's opening kickoff, then converted a pair of turnovers into 14 points to build their big advantage.

Indianapolis	0	3	7	14	3	—	27
N.Y. Jets	14	3	7	0	0	—	24

Jets — Wilson 5 pass from Esiason (Lowery kick)
Jets — Smith 49 interception return (Lowery kick)
Jets — FG Lowery 28
Ind — FG Cofer 20
Jets — Chrebet 5 pass from Esiason (Lowery kick)
Ind — Bennett 32 fumble return (Cofer kick)
Ind — Dawkins 15 pass from Harbaugh (Cofer kick)
Ind — Faulk 14 pass from Harbaugh (Cofer kick)
Ind — FG Cofer 52

CINCINNATI 24, JACKSONVILLE 17—at Riverfront Stadium, attendance 48,318. Jeff Blake threw 2 touchdown passes, and the Bengals' defense recorded 7 sacks as Cincinnati improved to 2-0. Blake's 68-yard touchdown pass to Carl Pickens gave the Bengals a 24-10 lead over the expansion Jaguars early in the fourth quarter, but Jacksonville made it close by scoring on quarterback Mark Brunell's 8-yard run midway through the fourth period and then driving inside Cincinnati territory in the final minute. The Jaguars' last threat, however, ended when Bengals defensive tackle Dan Wilkinson sacked Brunell on fourth down from the 41. Brunell was in the game because starting quarterback Steve Beuerlein injured his knee when sacked in the second quarter. Blake completed 20 of 30 passes for 247 yards for Cincinnati. His 3-yard touchdown pass to tackle-eligible Melvin Tuten 16 seconds before halftime gave the Bengals a 10-7 lead at the intermission.

Jacksonville	7	0	3	7	—	17
Cincinnati	3	7	7	7	—	24

Cin — FG Pelfrey 27
Jack — Jordan 71 pass from Beuerlein (Hollis kick)
Cin — Tuten 3 pass from Blake (Pelfrey kick)
Jack — FG Hollis 29
Cin — Green 10 run (Pelfrey kick)
Cin — Pickens 68 pass from Blake (Pelfrey kick)
Jack — Brunell 8 run (Hollis kick)

MIAMI 20, NEW ENGLAND 3—at Foxboro Stadium, attendance 60,239. Irving Fryar caught a pair of touchdown passes and the Dolphins' defense kept the Patriots out of the end zone as Miami improved to 2-0. Fryar, whose 3 catches in the game went for 113 yards, grabbed a 67-yard touchdown bomb from Dan Marino in the first quarter, then gave the Dolphins a 17-3 lead when he caught a 31-yard halfback-option pass from Terry Kirby 2:22 before halftime. Miami then preserved its lead by limiting New England to 292 total yards for the game and stopping the Patriots inside the Dolphins' 20-yard line on each of their last four possessions. New England quarterback Drew Bledsoe passed for 267 yards, but completed only 25 of 51 passes and was intercepted twice. Kirby rushed for 82 yards for Miami, which accumulated 182 yards on the ground and 224 through the air.

Miami	10	7	0	3	—	20
New England	0	3	0	0	—	3

Mia — FG Stoyanovich 22
Mia — Fryar 67 pass from Marino (Stoyanovich kick)
NE — FG Bahr 29
Mia — Fryar 31 pass from Kirby (Stoyanovich kick)
Mia — FG Stoyanovich 19

ST. LOUIS 17, NEW ORLEANS 13—at Busch Memorial Stadium, attendance 58,186. The Rams won their inaugural game in St. Louis before a record crowd at Busch Stadium. Chris Miller threw a touchdown pass, and Todd Lyght returned an interception 29 yards for a touchdown as the Rams improved to 2-0 and won back-to-back games for the first time since 1991. Quarterback Jim Everett, who completed 24 of 40 passes for 246 yards, rallied the Saints from a 17-3 halftime deficit to close within 4 points in the fourth quarter, but after Chip Lohmiller's 34-yard field goal with 6:13 to play, New Orleans never got the ball back. St. Louis ran out the clock with the help of safety Keith Lyle's 4-yard run on fourth-and-1 from the Saints' 48-yard line with less than three minutes to play. The Rams had lined up in punt formation with Lyle as the blocking back. The victory was the 400th in Rams' franchise history.

New Orleans	3	0	7	3	—	13
St. Louis	7	10	0	0	—	17

NO — FG Lohmiller 33
StL — Bruce 33 pass from Miller (McLaughlin kick)
StL — FG McLaughlin 31
StL — Lyght 29 interception return (McLaughlin kick)
NO — Small 1 pass from Everett (Lohmiller kick)
NO — FG Lohmiller 34

KANSAS CITY 20, N.Y. GIANTS 17—at Arrowhead Stadium, attendance 77,962. The Chiefs rallied from a 14-point, fourth-quarter deficit and won the game on Lin Elliott's 23-yard field goal 7:49 into overtime. The Giants led 17-3 after safety Tito Wooten recovered teammate Keith Hamilton's fumble and returned it 1 yard for a touchdown with 10:56 remaining in regulation play. Hamilton, a defensive end, had picked up a fumble by Kansas City quarterback Steve Bono and rumbled 87 yards before fumbling himself. But Bono rebounded to march his team 73 yards in nine plays to Marcus Allen's 1-yard touchdown run with 5:03 to go, and then 67 yards in 14 plays to the game-tying 3-yard touchdown pass to Danan Hughes with 1:22 left. In overtime, Louie Aguiar's punt pinned New York at its own 3-yard line, and after the Chiefs' defense forced a punt, Kansas City took over possession at the Giants' 41. Six consecutive running plays advanced the ball to the 6, and Elliott converted his game-winning kick.

N.Y. Giants	7	3	0	7	0	—	17
Kansas City	3	0	0	14	3	—	20

Giants— Calloway 26 pass from Brown (Daluiso kick)
KC — FG Elliott 42
Giants— FG Daluiso 23
Giants— Wooten 1 fumble return (Daluiso kick)
KC — Allen 1 run (Elliott kick)
KC — Hughes 3 pass from Bono (Elliott kick)
KC — FG Elliott 23

OAKLAND 20, WASHINGTON 8—at RFK Stadium, attendance 54,548. Jeff Hostetler threw 2 touchdown passes to lead the Raiders to victory. Hostetler teamed with nine different pass catchers, and finished with 22 completions in 29 attempts for 205 yards. His 1-yard touchdown pass to tight end Andrew Glover broke a 6-6 tie late in the third quarter, and his 8-yard touchdown pass to running back Derrick Fenner broke open the game with 10:55 left. The Redskins matched Oakland with 358 total yards, but turned over the ball 3 times and failed to crack the end zone despite six trips inside the Raiders' 25-yard line. Gus Frerotte, starting in place of injured Heath Shuler, completed 20 of 34 passes for 272 yards. Harvey Williams had 84 of Oakland's 153 rushing yards.

Oakland	0	3	10	7	—	20
Washington	0	3	3	2	—	8

Oak — FG Ford 19
Wash — FG Murray 21
Wash — FG Murray 43
Oak — FG Ford 34
Oak — Glover 1 pass from Hostetler (Ford kick)
Oak — Fenner 8 pass from Hostetler (Ford kick)
Wash — Safety, Brownlow blocked punt out of end zone

PITTSBURGH 34, HOUSTON 17—at Astrodome, attendance 44,122. Andre Hastings returned a punt 72 yards for a touchdown just 71 seconds into the game, sparking the Steelers to the victory. Pittsburgh went on to build a 24-3 lead in the third quarter, and put the game away when safety Carnell Lake returned an interception 32 yards for a touchdown and a 31-10 advantage with 5:02 to play. Steelers quarterback Mike Tomczak, playing in place of injured starter Neil O'Donnell, was efficient, completing 13 of 22 passes for 123 yards and 1 touchdown with no interceptions or sacks. The Oilers' Chris Chandler, meanwhile, was harassed into completing only 15 of 30 attempts for 176 yards. He was intercepted twice and sacked 4 times, 3 by linebacker Chad Brown.

Pittsburgh	14	3	7	10	—	34
Houston	3	0	7	7	—	17

Pitt — Hastings 72 punt return (Johnson kick)
Hou — FG Del Greco 43
Pitt — Bruener 15 pass from Tomczak (Johnson kick)
Pitt — FG Johnson 43
Pitt — McAfee 22 run (Johnson kick)
Hou — Chandler 1 run (Del Greco kick)
Pitt — Lake 32 interception return (Johnson kick)
Hou — Thomas 6 run (Del Greco kick)
Pitt — FG Johnson 40

SAN DIEGO 14, SEATTLE 10—at San Diego Jack Murphy Stadium, attendance 54,420. Stan Humphries threw 2 touchdown passes as the defending AFC-champion Chargers rebounded from their opening-day loss to the Raiders to beat the Seahawks. San Diego took the opening kickoff and drove 75 yards in 12 plays, the last a 5-yard touchdown pass from Humphries to Tony Martin, to take an early lead. The Chargers trailed 10-7 before Humphries's 15-yard touchdown pass to running back Ronnie Harmon 1:19 into the fourth quarter proved decisive. Humphries completed all 5 of his passes for 52 yards on the 80-yard drive, and finished with 23 completions in 35 attempts for 260 yards. Natrone Means added 115 yards on 26 carries, and Martin caught a career-high 13 passes for 163 yards for San Diego, which amassed 397 total yards while limiting Seattle to only 209. Seahawks quarterback Rick Mirer was held to only 13 completions in 29 attempts for 127 yards, and was intercepted twice.

Seattle	0	7	3	0	—	10
San Diego	7	0	0	7	—	14

SD — Martin 5 pass from Humphries (Carney kick)
Sea — Fauria 20 pass from Mirer (Peterson kick)
Sea — FG Peterson 23
SD — Harmon 15 pass from Humphries (Carney kick)

CLEVELAND 22, TAMPA BAY 6—at Cleveland Stadium, attendance 61,083. Vinny Testaverde threw 2 touchdown passes to Keenan McCardell in a 58-second span of the second quarter to lead the Browns to the victory. Testaverde, playing against his former teammates for the first time, completed 14 of 18 passes as Cleveland built a 19-0 lead at halftime. He threw a 6-yard touchdown pass to McCardell with 1:14 left in the second period, and after the Browns' defense forced a punt, he teamed with McCardell on a 32-yard scoring strike 16 seconds before the intermission. He finished with 17 completions in 27 attempts for 256 yards, with no interceptions. Trent Dilfer completed 20 of 36 passes for 255 yards for the Buccaneers, but was intercepted twice and sacked 7 times.

Tampa Bay	0	0	0	6	—	6
Cleveland	0	19	0	3	—	22

Cleve — FG Stover 43
Cleve — FG Stover 23
Cleve — McCardell 6 pass from Testaverde (pass failed)
Cleve — McCardell 32 pass from Testaverde (Stover kick)
TB — Rhett 2 run (run failed)
Cleve — FG Stover 20

SUNDAY NIGHT, SEPTEMBER 10

PHILADELPHIA 31, ARIZONA 19—at Sun Devil Stadium, attendance 45,004. Rodney Peete came off the bench to pass for 145 yards and 1 touchdown in the Eagles' victory. Peete relieved starting quarterback Randall Cunningham in the second quarter and sparked Philadelphia's offense by completing 8 of 13 passes. His 19-yard touchdown pass to Fred Barnett 3:41 into the fourth quarter gave the Eagles a 24-6 lead and effectively put the game out of reach. Barnett caught 5 passes for 97 yards, while Ricky Watters rushed for 94 yards for the Eagles. Rookie wide receiver Frank Sanders caught 5 passes for 102 yards for the Cardinals, but Arizona's ground game was limited to only 30 yards on 23 carries.

Philadelphia	0	10	7	14	—	31
Arizona	0	3	3	13	—	19

Phil — Thomas 37 interception return (Anderson kick)
Ariz — FG Davis 21
Phil — FG Anderson 43
Phil — Garner 1 run (Anderson kick)
Ariz — FG Davis 29
Phil — Barnett 19 pass from Peete (Anderson kick)
Ariz — Hearst 1 run (Davis kick)
Phil — McCrary 1 run (Anderson kick)
Ariz — Moore 5 pass from Buck (run failed)

MONDAY, SEPTEMBER 11

GREEN BAY 27, CHICAGO 24—at Soldier Field, attendance 64,855. Brett Favre threw 3 touchdown passes as the Packers built a big lead at Chicago and held on for the victory. Favre's third scoring pass was a 99-yarder to Robert Brooks to tie the NFL record for longest pass completion shared by seven others. That came 4:52 into the second quarter and gave Green Bay a 21-0 lead en route to a 24-7 advantage at the intermission. It was 27-7 late in the third quarter before the Bears mounted their rally, scoring 17 points in a span of 6:26 to pull within a field goal. But Chicago's last chance was snuffed when Packers defensive end Reggie White sacked Erik Kramer, forcing a fumble that linebacker Wayne Simmons recovered at the Bears' 22-yard line with 1:59 left. Favre completed 21 of 37 passes for 312 yards, though he also threw a fourth-quarter interception that led to Rashaan Salaam's 8-yard touchdown run. Brooks caught 8 passes for 161 yards, and Edgar Bennett rushed for 96 yards for Green Bay, which enjoyed a sizable 431-243 edge in total yards, and maintained possession for 37:17 of the game's 60 minutes.

Green Bay	14	10	3	0	—	27
Chicago	0	7	7	10	—	24

GB — Brooks 5 pass from Favre (Jacke kick)
GB — Morgan 15 pass from Favre (Jacke kick)
GB — Brooks 99 pass from Favre (Jacke kick)
Chi — Salaam 1 run (Butler kick)
GB — FG Hentrich 32
GB — FG Hentrich 39
Chi — Flanigan 2 pass from Kramer (Butler kick)
Chi — Salaam 8 run (Butler kick)
Chi — FG Butler 20

THIRD WEEK SUMMARIES

AMERICAN FOOTBALL CONFERENCE						
Eastern Division	**W**	**L**	**T**	**Pct.**	**Pts.**	**OP**
Miami	3	0	0	1.000	95	27
Buffalo	2	1	0	.667	58	45
Indianapolis	1	2	0	.333	62	68
New England	1	2	0	.333	23	62
N.Y. Jets	1	2	0	.333	65	89
Central Division						
Cincinnati	2	1	0	.667	69	62
Cleveland	2	1	0	.667	50	30
Pittsburgh	2	1	0	.667	67	60
Houston	1	2	0	.333	34	51
Jacksonville	0	3	0	.000	30	61
Western Division						
Kansas City	3	0	0	1.000	77	44
Denver	2	1	0	.667	81	69
Oakland	2	1	0	.667	54	38
San Diego	2	1	0	.667	48	48
Seattle	1	2	0	.333	44	69
NATIONAL FOOTBALL CONFERENCE						
Eastern Division	**W**	**L**	**T**	**Pct.**	**Pts.**	**OP**
Dallas	3	0	0	1.000	89	38
Arizona	1	2	0	.333	46	75
Philadelphia	1	2	0	.333	58	67
Washington	1	2	0	.333	66	65
N.Y. Giants	0	3	0	.000	23	69
Central Division						
Chicago	2	1	0	.667	80	47
Green Bay	2	1	0	.667	55	47
Minnesota	1	2	0	.333	51	64
Tampa Bay	1	2	0	.333	33	53
Detroit	0	3	0	.000	47	63
Western Division						
St. Louis	3	0	0	1.000	65	37
San Francisco	3	0	0	1.000	93	35
Atlanta	2	1	0	.667	60	85
Carolina	0	3	0	.000	39	85
New Orleans	0	3	0	.000	59	68

SUNDAY, SEPTEMBER 17

ARIZONA 20, DETROIT 17—at Pontiac Silverdome, attendance 58,727. Dave Krieg's fourth-down, 24-yard touchdown pass to Anthony Edwards with 2:31 remaining gave the Cardinals the come-from-behind victory. The winning score came nine plays after Arizona linebacker Terry Irving recovered Barry Sanders's fumble at the Cardinals' 31-yard line with 5:06 to play and the Lions ahead 17-12. It was Sanders's first fumble in 803 carries dating to December, 1992. Krieg, who led the Lions to the playoffs in 1995 but signed with Arizona this season as a free agent, threw a desperation heave on fourth-and-10 for the go-ahead touchdown. On the ensuing series, Sanders fumbled again, turning over the ball at the Cardinals' 37 with 1:35 to play and ending Detroit's last hope. It marred an otherwise brilliant day for the all-pro running back, who ran for 147 yards, including a 47-yard touchdown, and caught 4 passes for 36 yards. Scott Mitchell passed for 217 yards and Brett Perriman caught 7 passes for 114 yards for the Lions, who amassed 358 total yards but were stymied by 3 turnovers and 15 penalties. Garrison Hearst had the first 100-yard rushing day of his career for Arizona, gaining 121 yards on 22 carries.

Arizona	0	6	0	14	—	20
Detroit	3	7	7	0	—	17

Det — FG Hanson 21
Det — Perriman 39 pass from Mitchell (Hanson kick)
Ariz — FG Davis 55
Ariz — FG Davis 41
Det — Sanders 47 run (Hanson kick)
Ariz — FG Davis 25
Ariz — FG Davis 25
Ariz — Edwards 24 pass from Krieg (F. Sanders pass from Krieg)

ATLANTA 27, NEW ORLEANS 24—at Louisiana Superdome, attendance 57,442. Morten Andersen kicked 4 field goals, including the game-winner from 21 yards with 4:02 remaining in overtime, to beat his former teammates. The winning kick capped a 91-yard drive and was set up by Jeff George's 38-yard pass to Eric Metcalf to the Saints' 3-yard line. The Falcons trailed 24-16 until forcing the extra session when Craig Heyward ran 7 yards for a touchdown and George completed a 2-point conversion pass to Terance Mathis with 6:11 left in the fourth quarter. George completed 27 of 39 passes for 386 yards as Atlanta amassed 461 total yards. Heyward ran for 102 yards on 25 carries, while Metcalf had 11 catches for 155 yards, and Bert Emanuel added 6 receptions for 104 yards. Jim Everett was 29 of 43 for 370 yards and 3 touchdowns for the Saints, who fell to 0-3. Andersen played 13 seasons with New Orleans before signing with the Falcons this year. The Saints had beaten Atlanta 13 of the last 17 times they'd played, with Andersen making the winning kick eight times.

Atlanta	3	10	3	8	3	—	27
New Orleans	10	0	7	7	0	—	24

Atl — FG Andersen 19
NO — Early 70 pass from Everett (Lohmiller kick)
NO — FG Lohmiller 21
Atl — Mathis 31 pass from George (Andersen kick)
Atl — FG Andersen 33
Atl — FG Andersen 46
NO — Haynes 9 pass from Everett (Lohmiller kick)
NO — Walls 28 pass from Everett (Lohmiller kick)
Atl — Heyward 7 run (Mathis pass from George)
Atl — FG Andersen 21

CHICAGO 25, TAMPA BAY 6—at Tampa Stadium, attendance 71,507. Defense and special teams made the difference as the Bears forced 7 turnovers, kicked 4 field goals, and blocked a punt for a touchdown. Kevin Butler kicked 3 of his field goals in the first half as Chicago built a 9-3 advantage before breaking open the game early in the third quarter. Cornerback Jeremy Lincoln's interception and 32-yard return set up Robert Green's 7-yard touchdown run 1:25 into the second half, and four plays later Anthony Marshall blocked Reggie Roby's punt and returned it 11 yards for a touchdown and a 22-3 lead. The Buccaneers never threatened after that, and turned over the ball repeatedly on 4 interceptions and 3 fumbles. Starting quarterback Trent Dilfer completed only 11 of 27 passes for 149 yards and the 4 interceptions before giving way to Casey Weldon early in the fourth quarter. Weldon did not throw an interception, but twice lost fumbles when sacked. Erik Kramer passed for 207 yards and Green (72 yards) and rookie Rashaan Salaam (55 yards) combined to rush for 127 yards for the Bears.

Chicago	3	6	13	3	—	25
Tampa Bay	0	3	3	0	—	6

Chi — FG Butler 24
TB — FG Husted 43
Chi — FG Butler 37
Chi — FG Butler 22
Chi — Green 7 run (Butler kick)
Chi — Marshall 11 blocked punt return (run failed)
TB — FG Husted 40
Chi — FG Butler 27

SEATTLE 24, CINCINNATI 21—at Kingdome, attendance 39,492. Rick Mirer passed for 279 yards and 2 touchdowns to help give Dennis Erickson his first victory as the Seahawks' coach. Mirer's 50-yard touchdown pass to Robb Thomas 1:10 before halftime broke a 7-7 tie and gave Seattle the lead for good. It was 17-7 at the intermission and 24-14 midway through the fourth quarter, but the Seahawks' victory was not secured until Doug Pelfrey's 49-yard field-goal attempt was wide right with 1:18 left. Bengals quarterback Jeff Blake kept his team close by passing for 286 yards and 2 touchdowns, including a 22-yard strike to Carl Pickens with 3:18 remaining.

Cincinnati	7	0	0	14	—	21
Seattle	7	10	0	7	—	24

Sea — Smith 5 pass from Mirer (Peterson kick)
Cin — Scott 88 pass from Blake (Pelfrey kick)
Sea — Thomas 50 pass from Mirer (Peterson kick)
Sea — FG Peterson 38
Cin — Rog. Jones 17 interception return (Pelfrey kick)
Sea — Warren 11 run (Peterson kick)
Cin — Pickens 22 pass from Blake (Pelfrey kick)

CLEVELAND 14, HOUSTON 7—at Astrodome, attendance 36,077. Vinny Testaverde threw 2 touchdown passes, including the game-winner to Michael Jackson with 9:17 remaining, in the Browns' victory. The touchdowns overcame a sluggish performance by Cleveland's offense, which netted only 270 yards. Testaverde completed just 10 of 23 passes for 147 yards. But the Browns' defense intercepted Oilers quarterback Will Furrer 4 times and kept Houston out of the end zone until Haywood Jeffires caught a 4-yard touchdown pass from Furrer 2:43 into the fourth quarter. That tied the game at 7-7, but Testaverde's 29-yard pass to Keenan McCardell set up the winning, 35-yard touchdown pass to Jackson on the next possession. Furrer, in the starting lineup because Chris Chandler was out with a bruised shoulder, completed 22 of 41 passes for 268 yards. He was intercepted 3 times in the first half by Browns safety Stevon Moore.

Cleveland	0	7	0	7	—	14
Houston	0	0	0	7	—	7

Cleve — McCardell 15 pass from Testaverde (Stover kick)
Hou — Jeffires 4 pass from Furrer (Del Greco kick)
Cleve — Jackson 35 pass from Testaverde (Stover kick)

BUFFALO 20, INDIANAPOLIS 14—at Rich Stadium, attendance 62,499. Steve Christie kicked a pair of field goals in the second half to lift the Bills past the Colts. Christie's 35-yard field goal 7:10 into the third quarter broke a 14-14 halftime tie, and his 38-yard kick with 4:27 left in the game provided the final margin of victory, though Buffalo's win wasn't secured until Indianapolis quarterback Jim Harbaugh's fourth-down pass from the Bills' 34-yard line fell incomplete with 20 seconds left. The teams traded touchdowns in the first half, with the Colts taking the opening kickoff and maintaining possession for 7:45 on a 12-play, 65-yard march before Buffalo countered with a 14-play, 80-yard touchdown drive that lasted nearly seven minutes to tie the score. Marshall Faulk, who ran 13 yards for Indianapolis's first touchdown, caught an 18-yard pass from Harbaugh for another touchdown 6:18 before halftime, but it took the Bills only five plays to answer on Thurman Thomas's 2-yard touchdown run. Buffalo quarterback Jim Kelly completed 19 of 35 passes for 201 yards and surpassed 30,000 passing yards for his career (30,058). He reached that plateau in 135 NFL games, faster than all but three quarterbacks in league history. Harbaugh, who earned a starting assignment by rallying the Colts from big deficits the first two weeks, was 19 of 33 for 241 yards, but was sacked 5 times. Bills linebacker Bryce Paup had 3 of the sacks and forced 2 fumbles.

Indianapolis	7	7	0	0	—	14
Buffalo	7	7	3	3	—	20

Ind — Faulk 13 run (Cofer kick)
Buff — Gardner recovered fumble in end zone (Christie kick)
Ind — Faulk 18 pass from Harbaugh (Cofer kick)
Buff — Thomas 2 run (Christie kick)
Buff — FG Christie 35
Buff — FG Christie 38

N.Y. JETS 27, JACKSONVILLE 10—at Giants Stadium, attendance 49,970. Boomer Esiason passed for 296 yards and 3 touchdowns in the Jets' easy victory. New York took the opening kickoff and drove 60 yards in 9 plays, the last Esiason's 11-yard touchdown pass to rookie Wayne Chrebet, to take the lead for good 4:57 into the game. Esiason also threw a 20-yard touchdown pass to rookie tight end Kyle Brady the first time the Jets had the ball in the second half, and his 15-yard touchdown pass to Charles Wilson late in the third quarter put New York ahead 27-3. The veteran quarterback finished the game with 27 completions in 43 attempts. The Jaguars, on the other hand, mustered little offense, gaining only 251 total yards, with 73 coming on their lone touchdown drive late in the fourth quarter. Jacksonville quarterback Mark Brunell made his first NFL start and completed only 15 of 33 passes for 138 yards. He was sacked 6 times, including 3 by rookie defensive end Hugh Douglas. Jets linebacker Bobby Houston had a sack and 2 fumble recoveries.

Jacksonville	0	3	0	7	—	10
N.Y. Jets	7	6	14	0	—	27

Jets — Chrebet 11 pass from Esiason (Lowery kick)
Jets — FG Lowery 21
Jack — FG Hollis 34
Jets — FG Lowery 48
Jets — Brady 20 pass from Esiason (Lowery kick)
Jets — Wilson 15 pass from Esiason (Lowery kick)
Jack — Givins 7 pass from Brunell (Hollis kick)

SAN FRANCISCO 28, NEW ENGLAND 3—at 3Com Park, attendance 66,179. Steve Young passed for 3 touchdowns and ran for another to pace the 49ers to their third consecutive victory. Young, who completed 29 of 42 passes for 284 yards, put San Francisco ahead for good with a 21-yard touchdown pass to Jerry Rice 35 seconds before halftime, then opened the third quarter by driving his team 70 yards to a 16-yard touchdown pass to Rice to give the 49ers a 14-3 advantage 4:36 into the second half. Young's 1-yard sneak for a touchdown on the first play of the fourth quarter broke open the game. Patriots quarterback Drew Bledsoe had a much rougher time, completing only 21 of 51 passes for 241 yards, with no touchdowns, 3 interceptions, and a lost fumble. He was sacked four times, and suffered a mildly separated left shoulder when hit by linebacker Ken Norton in the first quarter.

New England	0	3	0	0	—	3
San Francisco	0	7	7	14	—	28

NE — FG Bahr 43
SF — Rice 21 pass from Young (Brien kick)
SF — Rice 16 pass from Young (Brien kick)
SF — Young 1 run (Brien kick)
SF — Loville 3 pass from Young (Brien kick)

GREEN BAY 14, N.Y. GIANTS 6—at Lambeau Field, attendance 60,117. Brett Favre threw 2 touchdown passes as the Packers handed the Giants their third consecutive defeat. Green Bay jumped to a 14-0 lead behind Favre's scoring strikes to Mark Ingram (11 yards on the game's first possession) and Robert Brooks (19 yards 5:54 into the second quarter). And though the Packers managed only 36 total yards in the second half and 198 for the game, the lead held up because the Giants could not crack the end zone. Brad Daluiso's second field goal, from 32 yards with 3:21 to play, pulled New York within eight points, but the Giants' last chance ended when Dave Brown's pass was intercepted by safety Mike Prior at Green Bay's 22-yard line with 15 seconds left.

N.Y. Giants	0	3	0	3	—	6
Green Bay	7	7	0	0	—	14

GB — Ingram 11 pass from Favre (Hentrich kick)
GB — Brooks 19 pass from Favre (Hentrich kick)
Giants— FG Daluiso 37
Giants— FG Daluiso 32

KANSAS CITY 23, OAKLAND 17—at Arrowhead Stadium, attendance 78,696. James Hasty's 64-yard interception return 4:27 into overtime gave the Chiefs another dramatic victory. A week earlier, Kansas City rallied from a 14-point, fourth-quarter deficit to beat the Giants in overtime. This time, they had to come back from 10 points down in the fourth period. They pulled within a field goal at 17-14 on Steve Bono's 19-yard touchdown pass to Willie Davis with 13:32 remaining, then tied it on Lin Elliott's 35-yard field goal with 7:57 to play. Elliott had a chance to win the game in regulation, but missed a 24-yard field goal with 1:42 left. Then in the extra session, Kansas City running back Marcus Allen lost a fumble at the Raiders' 38-yard line, but Hasty made his game-winning play after Oakland had reached the Chiefs' 38 seven plays later. Bono completed 9 of 10 passes for 125 yards in the fourth quarter and overtime to finish 19 of 28 for 164 yards. Jeff Hostetler passed for 203 yards, and Harvey Williams had a pair of 1-yard touchdown runs for Oakland. Kansas City's victory was its eleventh in the last 12 meetings against the AFC West-rival Raiders.

Oakland	0	14	3	0	0	—	17
Kansas City	7	0	0	10	6	—	23

KC — Dawson 4 pass from Bono (Elliott kick)
Oak — Williams 1 run (Ford kick)
Oak — Williams 1 run (Ford kick)
Oak — FG Ford 33
KC — Davis 19 pass from Bono (Elliott kick)
KC — FG Elliott 35
KC — Hasty 64 interception return

ST. LOUIS 31, CAROLINA 10—at Clemson Memorial Stadium, attendance 54,060. The Rams improved to 3-0 for the first time since 1989 by forcing 7 turnovers and spoiling the expansion Panthers' home debut. Cornerback Anthony Parker returned a fumble 28 yards for 1 touchdown and cornerback Torin Dorn brought back an interception 24 yards for another score as St. Louis recovered 2 fumbles and harried three Carolina quarterbacks into 5 interceptions. Rams quarterback Chris Miller, meanwhile, completed 15 of 26 passes for 225 yards and 1 touchdown, with no interceptions. Isaac Bruce caught 5 passes for 100 yards, and Jerome Bettis ran for 67 yards for St. Louis.

St. Louis	0	14	10	7	—	31
Carolina	0	3	0	7	—	10

StL — Bettis 2 run (McLaughlin kick)
StL — Hester 23 pass from Miller (McLaughlin kick)
Car — FG Kasay 45
StL — Parker 28 fumble return (McLaughlin kick)
StL — FG McLaughlin 34
StL — Dorn 24 interception return (McLaughlin kick)
Car — Collins 1 run (Kasay kick)

SAN DIEGO 27, PHILADELPHIA 21—at Veterans Stadium, attendance 63,081. Natrone Means rushed for 122 yards, and the Chargers rallied from a 14-point deficit to beat the Eagles. San Diego trailed 14-0 in the second quarter before Stan Humphries's 38-yard touchdown pass to Shawn Jefferson 1:50 into the period trimmed the deficit to 7 points, then sandwiched 17 points in a span of 3:11 around halftime to take command. John Carney's 35-yard field goal 1:29 before the intermission began the spurt, and on the next play from scrimmage, Chargers linebacker Junior Seau recovered Philadelphia wide receiver Calvin Williams's fumble and returned it 29 yards for a touchdown and a 17-14 lead. After the Eagles failed to make a first down on the initial possession of the second half, Andre Coleman returned a punt 88 yards for a touchdown 1:42 into the third quarter. San Diego then protected its lead by handing the ball to Means, who ran for 87 yards in the second half. The Chargers overcame 3 touchdown passes from Philadelphia's Randall Cunningham.

San Diego	0	17	10	0	—	27
Philadelphia	7	7	7	0	—	21

Phil — Watters 4 pass from Cunningham (Anderson kick)
Phil — Barnett 1 pass from Cunningham (Anderson kick)
SD — Jefferson 38 pass from Humphries (Carney kick)
SD — FG Carney 35
SD — Seau 29 fumble return (Carney kick)
SD — Coleman 88 punt return (Carney kick)
SD — FG Carney 21
Phil — West 3 pass from Cunningham (Anderson kick)

DENVER 38, WASHINGTON 31—at Denver Mile High Stadium, attendance 71,930. John Elway and Rod Smith teamed on a 43-yard touchdown bomb as time expired to give the Broncos the victory. The Redskins had tied the wild game at 31-31 on Gus Frerotte's 1-yard touchdown pass to tight end Scott Galbraith with 1:07 remaining. But Elway, who has rallied his team to victory in the fourth quarter or overtime 35 times in his career, drove Denver 80 yards in eight plays for the winning score. Smith outjumped Washington cornerback Darrell Green on the decisive play. It was the first catch of his career. The Redskins trailed by as many as 17 points in the game, but rallied behind 3 touchdown passes from Frerotte and a spectacular all-around game from multi-purpose running back Brian Mitchell. Frerotte completed 16 of 26 passes for 233 yards, while Mitchell returned 5 kickoffs for 188 yards, brought back a punt 52 yards, scored on a 36-yard touchdown run, and caught 1 pass for 14 yards. Elway finished with 30 completions in 47 attempts for 327 yards and 2 touchdowns, with no interceptions. The Broncos amassed 476 total yards, while Washington had 354.

Washington	0	14	10	7	—	31
Denver	0	24	0	14	—	38

Den — FG Elam 20
Wash — Mitchell 36 run (Murray kick)
Den — Bernstine 1 run (Elam kick)
Den — Davis 8 pass from Elway (Elam kick)
Den — Davis 6 run (Elam kick)
Wash — Logan 5 pass from Frerotte (Murray kick)
Wash — Shepherd 7 pass from Frerotte (Murray kick)
Wash — FG Murray 21
Den — Davis 1 run (Elam kick)
Wash — Galbraith 1 pass from Frerotte (Murray kick)
Den — Smith 43 pass from Elway (Elam kick)

SUNDAY NIGHT, SEPTEMBER 17

DALLAS 23, MINNESOTA 17—at Metrodome, attendance 60,088. Emmitt Smith's 31-yard touchdown run 2:26 into overtime kept the Cowboys unbeaten. Smith, who carried 20 times for 150 yards, also had a 2-yard touchdown run in the fourth quarter, giving Dallas a 17-10 lead with 9:57 to go in the game. The Vikings rallied to tie the game on Warren Moon's 8-yard touchdown pass to Cris Carter with 30 seconds left, but the Cowboys needed only five plays in the extra session to win it. Troy Aikman's 22-yard pass to Michael Irvin started the winning drive, and Aikman's 16-yard completion to Cory Fleming set up Smith's winning run. Aikman completed 24 of 38 passes for 246 yards, while Irvin caught 8 passes for 107 yards. Moon was 22 of 38 for 185 yards and 2 touchdowns for Minnesota. Jake Reed caught 7 passes for 107 yards.

Dallas	6	3	0	8	6	—	23
Minnesota	3	7	0	7	0	—	17

Dall — Irvin 19 pass from Aikman (kick failed)
Minn — FG Reveiz 42
Minn — Reed 3 pass from Moon (Reveiz kick)
Dall — FG Boniol 39
Dall — Smith 2 run (Novacek pass from Aikman)
Minn — Carter 8 pass from Moon (Reveiz kick)
Dall — Smith 31 run

MONDAY, SEPTEMBER 18

MIAMI 23, PITTSBURGH 10—at Joe Robbie Stadium, attendance 72,874. The Dolphins remained unbeaten with a decisive victory over the Steelers. Miami scored all of its points off turnovers while building a 17-3 halftime lead and holding on to win. J.B. Brown and Troy Vincent set up 10 points with interceptions, and Jeff Cross's fumble recovery late in the second quarter led to Dan Marino's 28-yard touchdown pass to running back Terry Kirby 47 seconds before halftime. Marino completed 16 of 27 passes for 183 yards before leaving the game with a bruised sternum after a hit by Pittsburgh linebacker Greg Lloyd late in the third quarter. Steelers quarterbacks Mike Tomczak and Jim Miller combined to pass for 314 yards but suffered 3 interceptions and 4 sacks. Pittsburgh's Andre Hastings caught 10 passes for 86 yards.

Pittsburgh	0	3	0	7	—	10
Miami	3	14	3	3	—	23

Mia — FG Stoyanovich 37
Mia — Parmalee 2 run (Stoyanovich kick)
Pitt — FG N. Johnson 40
Mia — Kirby 28 pass from Marino (Stoyanovich kick)
Mia — FG Stoyanovich 39
Mia — FG Stoyanovich 21
Pitt — Mills 27 pass from Miller (N. Johnson kick)

FOURTH WEEK SUMMARIES

AMERICAN FOOTBALL CONFERENCE

Eastern Division	W	L	T	Pct.	Pts.	OP
Miami	3	0	0	1.000	95	27
Buffalo	2	1	0	.667	58	45
Indianapolis	1	2	0	.333	62	68
New England	1	2	0	.333	23	62
N.Y. Jets	1	3	0	.250	68	102
Central Division						
Cleveland	3	1	0	.750	85	47
Cincinnati	2	2	0	.500	97	100
Houston	2	2	0	.500	72	79
Pittsburgh	2	2	0	.500	91	104
Jacksonville	0	4	0	.000	44	85
Western Division						
Kansas City	3	1	0	.750	94	79
Oakland	3	1	0	.750	102	55
San Diego	3	1	0	.750	65	54
Denver	2	2	0	.500	87	86
Seattle	1	2	0	.333	44	69

NATIONAL FOOTBALL CONFERENCE

Eastern Division	W	L	T	Pct.	Pts.	OP
Dallas	4	0	0	1.000	123	58
Arizona	1	3	0	.250	66	109
N.Y. Giants	1	3	0	.250	68	98
Philadelphia	1	3	0	.250	75	115
Washington	1	3	0	.250	72	79
Central Division						
Green Bay	3	1	0	.750	79	61
Chicago	2	2	0	.500	108	81
Minnesota	2	2	0	.500	95	88
Tampa Bay	2	2	0	.500	47	59
Detroit	1	3	0	.250	74	87
Western Division						
St. Louis	4	0	0	1.000	99	65
Atlanta	3	1	0	.750	73	88
San Francisco	3	1	0	.750	117	62
Carolina	0	3	0	.000	39	85
New Orleans	0	4	0	.000	88	113

SUNDAY, SEPTEMBER 24

DALLAS 34, ARIZONA 20—at Texas Stadium, attendance 64,560. Emmitt Smith rushed for 116 yards as the Cowboys improved to 4-0 for the first time since 1983. Smith, who surpassed the 100-yard mark for the fourth consecutive week, carried 21 times and also caught 3 passes for 53 yards. His 6-yard touchdown run in the final minute of the first quarter gave Dallas a 14-0 lead, and his 1-yard touchdown run 5:37 into the second period broke open the game at 21-3. The Cowboys amassed 440 total yards, including 251 yards passing from Troy Aikman. Wide receiver Michael Irvin caught 5 passes for 105 yards. Dave Krieg tried to keep the Cardinals close by taking to the air after they fell behind early. He completed 24 of 33 passes for 324 yards and 2 touchdowns, but also was intercepted 3 times. Arizona's Rob Moore caught 9 passes for 154 yards and 1 touchdown. Dallas beat the Cardinals for the tenth consecutive time.

Arizona	0	10	3	7	—	20
Dallas	14	10	3	7	—	34

Dall — Novacek 2 pass from Aikman (Boniol kick)
Dall — E. Smith 6 run (Boniol kick)
Ariz — FG Davis 31
Dall — E. Smith 1 run (Boniol kick)
Ariz — Centers 13 pass from Krieg (Davis kick)
Dall — FG Boniol 25
Dall — FG Boniol 30
Ariz — FG Davis 19
Dall — S. Williams 44 run (Boniol kick)
Ariz — Moore 25 pass from Krieg (Davis kick)

ST. LOUIS 34, CHICAGO 28—at Busch Memorial Stadium, attendance 59,679. Chris Miller threw 3 touchdown passes, and the Rams matched their victory total for all of 1995 by improving to 4-0. Erik Kramer threw 3 touchdown passes in the second quarter to rally the Bears from an early 10-0 deficit to a 21-17 lead by halftime. But Miller countered with a pair of touchdown passes in a span of 4:29 of the third quarter as St. Louis took control. His 1-yard touchdown pass to tight end Marv Cook midway through the third quarter capped a 67-yard drive and gave the Rams the lead for good, and his 12-yard touchdown pass to tight end Troy Drayton the next time St. Louis had the ball capped a 69-yard march that upped the advantage to 31-21. Miller completed 21 of 31 passes for 231 yards before suffering a concussion in the fourth quarter and giving way to backup Mark Rypien. Kramer was 27 of 38 for 317 yards and 4 touchdowns for Chicago. Drayton caught 8 passes for 106 yards for the Rams, while Jeff Graham had 6 receptions for 145 yards for the Bears. St. Louis did not commit a turnover and thus became the first team in NFL history to go four games into the regular season without a miscue.

Chicago	0	21	0	7	—	28
St. Louis	10	7	14	3	—	34

StL — Wright 73 fumble return (McLaughlin kick)
StL — FG McLaughlin 45
Chi — Jennings 15 pass from Kramer (Butler kick)
StL — Kinchen 6 pass from Miller (McLaughlin kick)
Chi — Conway 20 pass from Kramer (Butler kick)
Chi — Timpson 12 pass from Kramer (Butler kick)
StL — Cook 1 pass from Miller (McLaughlin kick)
StL — Drayton 12 pass from Miller (McLaughlin kick)
Chi — Graham 47 pass from Kramer (Butler kick)
StL — FG McLaughlin 25

SAN DIEGO 17, DENVER 6—at San Diego Jack Murphy Stadium, attendance 58,978. Natrone Means rushed for 115 yards and 2 touchdowns to pace the Chargers to the victory. Means carried 27 times and helped San Diego amass 158 yards on the ground while maintaining possession for 36:10 of the game's 60 minutes. The Chargers' defense, meanwhile, limited John Elway to only 186 passing yards, and kept the Broncos' quarterback from leading his team to a touchdown for the first time in nearly three years. Denver managed only 246 total yards and suffered 13 penalties. Means put San Diego ahead for good with a 3-yard touchdown run 2:42 before halftime, capping a 73-yard drive on which he carried 6 times for 30 yards. He ran for 38 yards on an 86-yard march that resulted in his 2-yard touchdown run 1:14 into the fourth quarter. The Chargers put the game out of reach the next time they had the ball when John Carney kicked a 45-yard field goal.

Denver	0	3	3	0	—	6
San Diego	0	7	0	10	—	17

Den — FG Elam 23
SD — Means 3 run (Carney kick)
Den — FG Elam 52
SD — Means 2 run (Elam kick)
SD — FG Carney 45

HOUSTON 38, CINCINNATI 28—at Riverfront Stadium, attendance 46,332. Chris Chandler completed 23 of 26 passes for 352 yards and 4 touchdowns to lead the Oilers. Chandler threw all 4 of his touchdown passes in the first half as Houston built a 28-14 lead at the intermission. Two of his scoring tosses were touchdown bombs of 58 and 46 yards to rookie Chris Sanders. Among Chandler's 3 incompletions was a spike to stop the clock late in the first half. His final pass was incomplete, costing him the NFL record for completion percentage in a game. Bengals quarterback Jeff Blake completed 24 of 46 passes for 356 yards and 3 touchdowns, but could not pull his team any closer than 7 points after Chandler's 2 touchdown passes in the first 10:43 staked the Oilers to a 14-0 lead. Tony McGee caught 8 passes for 109 yards, and Darnay Scott had 4 receptions for 125 yards for Cincinnati.

Houston	14	14	10	0	—	38
Cincinnati	0	14	7	7	—	28

Hou — Sanders 58 pass from Chandler (Del Greco kick)
Hou — Jeffires 23 pass from Chandler (Del Greco kick)
Cin — Green 23 run (Pelfrey kick)
Hou — Thomas 8 pass from Chandler (Del Greco kick)
Cin — Pickens 8 pass from Blake (Pelfrey kick)
Hou — Sanders 46 pass from Chandler (Del Greco kick)
Cin — Scott 51 pass from Blake (Pelfrey kick)
Hou — Thomas 1 run (Del Greco kick)
Hou — FG Del Greco 41
Cin — To. McGee 1 pass from Blake (Pelfrey kick)

CLEVELAND 35, KANSAS CITY 17—at Cleveland Stadium, attendance 74,280. Vinny Testaverde threw 2 touchdown passes, and the Browns broke open the game with a pair of defensive touchdowns 19 seconds apart in the fourth quarter. Testaverde, who completed 21 of 36 passes for 204 yards, threw short touchdown passes to Andre Rison (4 yards) and running back Earnest Byner (3 yards) as Cleveland built a 21-3 lead early in the fourth quarter. The Chiefs tried to rally, pulling within 11 points on Steve Bono's 38-yard touchdown pass to tight end Keith Cash and then forcing a punt. But linebacker Gerald Dixon intercepted Bono's pass and returned it 18 yards for a touchdown with 5:45 left in the game. Two plays later, linebacker Mike Caldwell intercepted another Bono pass and brought it back 24 yards for a touchdown and an insurmountable 35-10 lead at the 5:26 mark.

Kansas City	0	3	0	14	—	17
Cleveland	7	0	7	21	—	35

Cleve — Byner 7 run (Stover kick)
KC — FG Elliott 25
Cleve — Rison 4 pass from Testaverde (Stover kick)
Cleve — Byner 3 pass from Testaverde (Stover kick)
KC — Cash 38 pass from Bono (Elliott kick)
Cleve — Dixon 18 interception return (Stover kick)
Cleve — Caldwell 24 interception return (Stover kick)
KC — Slaughter 2 pass from Bono (Elliott kick)

MINNESOTA 44, PITTSBURGH 24—at Three Rivers Stadium, attendance 57,853. Rookie defensive backs Corey Fuller and Orlando Thomas scored touchdowns in a 24-point third-quarter onslaught that propelled the Vikings to the victory. Minnesota led 13-6 until Fuller returned Byron (Bam) Morris's fumble 12 yards for a touchdown 24 seconds into the second half. Alfred Jackson's interception led to Warren Moon's 18-yard touchdown pass to Cris Carter two minutes later, and after linebacker Jack Del Rio intercepted a pass and lateraled to Thomas, who raced 45 yards for a touchdown, the Vikings had broken open the game at 34-6. Minnesota went on to force 5 turnovers in the third quarter and 7 in the game. In addition to his touchdown, Thomas intercepted 2 passes. On offense, Robert Smith ran for 115 yards, including a 58-yard touchdown, and Moon passed for 213 yards as the Vikings amassed 378 total yards. The Steelers had 405 yards themselves but could not overcome the turnovers and 11 penalties. Mike Tomczak passed for 143 yards and reserve Jim Miller threw for 195, but each was intercepted 3 times. Pittsburgh's Yancey Thigpen caught 10 passes for 141 yards.

Minnesota	0	13	24	7	—	44
Pittsburgh	0	6	0	18	—	24

Pitt — FG Johnson 32
Minn — R. Smith 58 run (Reveiz kick)
Minn — FG Reveiz 33
Pitt — FG Johnson 35
Minn — FG Reveiz 43
Minn — Fuller 12 fumble return (Reveiz kick)
Minn — Carter 18 pass from Moon (Reveiz kick)
Minn — Thomas 45 lateral from Del Rio (Reveiz kick)
Minn — FG Reveiz 40
Pitt — Pegram 5 run (run failed)
Pitt — Thigpen 42 pass from Miller (pass failed)
Minn — Carter 22 pass from Moon (Reveiz kick)
Pitt — Pegram 1 run (run failed)

N.Y. GIANTS 45, NEW ORLEANS 29—at Giants Stadium, attendance 72,619. Rodney Hampton rushed for 149 yards and a club-record 4 touchdowns in the Giants' victory. Hampton carried 33 times and scored on touchdown runs of 1, 5, 2, and 3 yards. He helped New York amass 31 first downs, 218 rushing yards, and 474 total yards. The Giants maintained possession for nearly 40 minutes. The Saints twice held leads in the first half, the last time at 17-14 on Chip Lohmiller's 20-yard field goal midway through the second quarter. But New York countered with a 74-yard touchdown drive capped by Dave Brown's 38-yard pass to Chris Calloway, and the Giants were not headed after that. They put the game away with 2 touchdown runs by Hampton in the third quarter, each of which was set up by interceptions by safety Vencie Glenn. Brown completed 19 of 27 passes for 258 yards for New York, which had scored only 23 points while losing its first 3 games. Jim Everett passed for 256 yards and 3 touchdowns for 0-4 New Orleans, off to its worst start since 1980.

New Orleans	7	10	0	12	—	29
N.Y. Giants	7	17	14	7	—	45

Giants— Hampton 1 run (Daluiso kick)
NO — Bates 3 run (Lohmiller kick)
NO — Walls 9 pass from Everett (Lohmiller kick)
Giants— Hampton 5 run (Daluiso kick)
NO — FG Lohmiller 20
Giants— Calloway 38 pass from Brown (Daluiso kick)
Giants— FG Daluiso 50
Giants— Hampton 2 run (Daluiso kick)
Giants— Hampton 3 run (Daluiso kick)
NO — Small 1 pass from Everett (kick failed)
Giants— Wheatley 19 run (Daluiso kick)
NO — Brown 4 pass from Everett (pass failed)

ATLANTA 13, N.Y. JETS 3—at Georgia Dome, attendance 40,778. Craig Heyward rushed for 120 yards on only 19 carries, and Jeff George passed for 1 touchdown in the Falcons' victory. George's touchdown pass, from 4 yards to Bert Emanuel 3:26 before halftime, broke a 3-3 tie and gave Atlanta all the points it would need. The Jets managed only a 37-yard field goal by Nick Lowery late in the first quarter and would go on to turn over the ball 4 times, twice in the end zone and twice on balls intercepted inside the Falcons' 10-yard line. Safety Kevin Ross had an interception and a fumble recovery for Atlanta, which won for the third time in four games and was off to its best start since 1986.

N.Y. Jets	3	0	0	0	—	3
Atlanta	3	7	3	0	—	13

Atl — FG Andersen 37
Jets — FG Lowery 37
Atl — Emanuel 4 pass from George (Andersen kick)
Atl — FG Andersen 37

OAKLAND 48, PHILADELPHIA 17—at Oakland Alameda County Coliseum, attendance 48,875. The Raiders fell behind by 17 points in the first quarter, but roared back to win. Oakland began its comeback when Cole Ford kicked a 35-yard field goal nine seconds into the second quarter, then pulled within 17-10 when Harvey Williams capped an 81-yard drive with a 1-yard run 1:53 before halftime. Just 16 seconds later, the game was tied after Raiders safety Eddie Anderson forced Eagles running back Ricky Watters to fumble and defensive tackle Austin Robbins ran 6 yards with the loose ball for a touchdown. Oakland's defense made the difference in the second half, too, with turnovers leading to 21 points late in the third quarter and early in the fourth. The decisive blow came when defensive end Aundray Bruce sacked Eagles quarterback Rodney Peete, forcing a fumble that linebacker Rob Fredrickson returned 35 yards for a touchdown and a 41-17 lead with 9:15 to play. The Raiders' defense finished the day with 2 touchdowns and 7 sacks, and forced 5 turnovers that resulted in 28 points. Linebacker Pat Swilling had 3 of the sacks, while Bruce added 2. Fredrickson had an interception to go along with his fumble recovery. Jeff Hostetler passed for 272 yards for Oakland. Daryl Hobbs caught 7 passes for 135 yards, including a 54-yard touchdown to cap the scoring in the fourth quarter.

Philadelphia	17	0	0	0	—	17
Oakland	0	17	10	21	—	48

Phil — Garner 7 run (Anderson kick)
Phil — FG Anderson 30
Phil — Jackson 45 fumble return (Anderson kick)
Oak — FG Ford 35
Oak — Williams 1 run (Ford kick)
Oak — Robbins 6 fumble return (Ford kick)
Oak — FG Ford 28
Oak — Fenner 7 pass from Hostetler (Ford kick)
Oak — H. Williams 4 run (Ford kick)
Oak — Fredrickson 35 fumble return (Ford kick)
Oak — Hobbs 54 pass from Evans (Ford kick)

TAMPA BAY 14, WASHINGTON 6—at Tampa Stadium, attendance 49,234. Errict Rhett rushed for 104 yards and 1 touchdown to lead the Buccaneers to the victory. Tampa Bay trailed 6-0 until taking the second-half kickoff and marching 68 yards in eight plays to the go-ahead score, Rhett's 10-yard touchdown run. The next time they had the ball, the Buccaneers drove 78 yards to Trent Dilfer's 7-yard touchdown pass to Alvin Harper on the first play of the fourth quarter. The Redskins had a chance to tie late in the game, driving to Tampa Bay's 1-yard line in the final minute. But Gus Frerotte's pass was intercepted in the end zone by cornerback Martin Mayhew with two seconds left. Frerotte passed for 230 yards as Washington outgained the Buccaneers 311-236. Tampa Bay quarterback Trent Dilfer was conservative but efficient, and completed 13 of 18 passes for 136 yards, with no interceptions.

Washington	3	3	0	0	—	6
Tampa Bay	0	0	7	7	—	14

Wash — FG Murray 37
Wash — FG Murray 28
TB — Rhett 10 run (Husted kick)
TB — Harper 7 pass from Dilfer (Husted kick)

SUNDAY NIGHT, SEPTEMBER 24

GREEN BAY 24, JACKSONVILLE 14—at Jacksonville Municipal Stadium, attendance 66,744. Brett Favre tied an NFL record when he threw 2 touchdown passes in the Packers' victory. It was the twelfth consecutive game that Favre passed for at least 2 touchdowns, tying the record shared by Dan Marino, Johnny Unitas, and Don Meredith. His first touchdown came in the final minute of the first half on a 6-yard pass to Robert Brooks that gave Green Bay a 10-0 lead. He tied the record on a 29-yard strike to Anthony Morgan that put the game out of reach at 24-7 with 4:52 left in the fourth quarter. Favre finished with 20 completions in 30 attempts for 202 yards. The expansion Jaguars struggled on offense while losing their fourth consecutive game. They managed only 201 total yards, much of it on their 78-yard drive which concluded with Willie Jackson's second touchdown with 1:02 left in the game.

Green Bay	0	10	7	7	—	24
Jacksonville	0	0	0	14	—	14

GB — FG Hentrich 49
GB — Brooks 6 pass from Favre (Hentrich kick)
GB — Levens 2 run (Hentrich kick)
Jack — W. Jackson 8 pass from Brunell (Hollis kick)

GB — Morgan 29 pass from Favre (Hentrich kick)
Jack — W. Jackson 3 pass from Brunell (Hollis kick)

MONDAY, SEPTEMBER 25

DETROIT 27, SAN FRANCISCO 24—at Pontiac Silverdome, attendance 76,236. Jason Hanson's 32-yard field goal with 1:12 remaining gave the winless Lions an upset victory over the unbeaten 49ers. After Hanson's kick, San Francisco drove from its own 20-yard line to Detroit's 23, only to see Doug Brien's potential game-tying field goal bounce off the upright as time expired. While all-pro running back Barry Sanders managed only 24 yards on 17 carries, the Lions beat the 49ers through the air. Scott Mitchell completed 28 of 42 passes for 291 yards and 1 touchdown, a 20-yard strike to Herman Moore to give the Lions a 24-17 advantage 4:19 into the fourth quarter. After San Francisco tied the game on Steve Young's 26-yard touchdown pass to John Taylor less than five minutes later, Detroit began its winning drive from its own 26. Mitchell's 22-yard completion to Brett Perriman moved the ball into 49ers' territory, and his quarterback sneak on fourth-and-1 from the 16 consumed valuable time and positioned Hanson for the winning kick. Perriman finished with 9 catches for 115 yards. For San Francisco, Young completed 27 of 44 passes for 348 yards and 2 touchdowns. Jerry Rice caught 11 passes for 181 yards.

San Francisco	0	10	7	7	—	24
Detroit	3	10	3	11	—	27

Det — FG Hanson 30
Det — Mitchell 1 run (Hanson kick)
SF — FG Brien 23
Det — FG Hanson 38
SF — Singleton 8 pass from Young (Brien kick)
Det — FG Hanson 18
SF — Loville 1 run (Brien kick)
Det — Moore 20 pass from Mitchell (Perriman pass from Mitchell)
SF — Taylor 26 pass from Young (Brien kick)
Det — FG Hanson 32

FIFTH WEEK SUMMARIES

AMERICAN FOOTBALL CONFERENCE

Eastern Division	W	L	T	Pct.	Pts.	OP
Miami	4	0	0	1.000	121	50
Buffalo	3	1	0	.750	80	64
Indianapolis	2	2	0	.500	83	86
New England	1	3	0	.250	40	92
N.Y. Jets	1	4	0	.200	78	149
Central Division						
Cleveland	3	2	0	.600	104	69
Pittsburgh	3	2	0	.600	122	120
Cincinnati	2	3	0	.400	120	126
Houston	2	3	0	.400	88	96
Jacksonville	1	4	0	.200	61	101
Western Division						
Kansas City	4	1	0	.800	118	82
Oakland	4	1	0	.800	149	65
San Diego	3	2	0	.600	81	85
Seattle	2	2	0	.500	71	79
Denver	2	3	0	.400	97	113

NATIONAL FOOTBALL CONFERENCE

Eastern Division	W	L	T	Pct.	Pts.	OP
Dallas	4	1	0	.800	146	85
Philadelphia	2	3	0	.400	90	125
Washington	2	3	0	.400	99	102
Arizona	1	4	0	.200	69	133
N.Y. Giants	1	4	0	.200	74	118
Central Division						
Green Bay	3	1	0	.750	79	61
Tampa Bay	3	2	0	.600	67	72
Chicago	2	2	0	.500	108	81
Minnesota	2	2	0	.500	95	88
Detroit	1	3	0	.250	74	87
Western Division						
Atlanta	4	1	0	.800	103	105
St. Louis	4	1	0	.800	117	86
San Francisco	4	1	0	.800	137	68
Carolina	0	4	0	.000	52	105
New Orleans	0	5	0	.000	98	128

SUNDAY, OCTOBER 1

WASHINGTON 27, DALLAS 23—at RFK Stadium, attendance 55,489. Terry Allen rushed for 121 yards and scored 2 touchdowns as the Redskins stunned the Cowboys. Allen carried 30 times and also led Washington with 4 receptions for 34 yards. His touchdowns came late in the second quarter and early in the third to break open a close game. The Redskins led 13-10 before marching 86 yards to a touchdown shortly before halftime. Gus Frerotte's 41-yard completion to Leslie Shepherd was the big play on the drive, and his 5-yard pass to Allen increased Washington's advantage to 20-10 with 17 seconds left in the half. Three minutes into the second half, Redskins safety Keith Taylor recovered Emmitt Smith's fumble at Dallas's 47-yard line. It took Washington seven plays to cover the distance, with Allen carrying on six of them, and open a 27-10 lead on the veteran running back's 1-yard run. The Redskins hung on to win, in part by forcing the Cowboys to kick a field goal after reaching the 5-yard line with the score 27-20 and 4:20 remaining. Dallas's last chance ended when Wade Wilson's desperation heave was intercepted by cornerback Tom Carter in the closing seconds. Wilson was in the game because starting quarterback Troy Aikman pulled a calf muscle on the Cowboys' first series and did not return. The reserve quarterback completed 21 of 29 passes for 224 yards and 1 touchdown. Frerotte passed for 192 yards and a pair of touchdowns for Washington. The victory was the first in four games for the Redskins over Dallas, which had won the previous three games by a combined score of 103-17.

Dallas	10	0	3	10	—	23
Washington	3	17	7	0	—	27

Dall — FG Boniol 32
Wash — FG Murray 38
Dall — Woodson 37 interception return (Boniol kick)
Wash — Logan 9 pass from Frerotte (Murray kick)
Wash — FG Murray 46
Wash — Allen 5 pass from Frerotte (Murray kick)
Wash — Allen 1 run (Murray kick)
Dall — FG Boniol 34
Dall — Irvin 28 pass from Wilson (Boniol kick)
Dall — FG Boniol 23

SEATTLE 27, DENVER 10—at Kingdome, attendance 56,483. Chris Warren rushed for 115 yards and 3 touchdowns in the Seahawks' victory. Rick Mirer complemented Warren's rushing by passing for 222 yards as Seattle amassed 422 total yards. The Seahawks' defense, meanwhile, entered the game ranked twenty-ninth in the NFL but limited the Broncos' prolific attack to 318 total yards and a lone touchdown midway through the fourth quarter. By that time, Seattle had a 24-3 advantage. The Seahawks built that lead while consuming large chunks of time on their scoring drives, much of it behind Warren, who carried 24 times. His 1-yard touchdown run 1:42 before halftime capped a 5-minute, 1-second, 88-yard drive that broke a scoreless tie. Then, after Todd Peterson's 45-yard field goal with two seconds left in the first half, Seattle broke open the game by taking the second-half kickoff and marching 92 yards on a 7-minute, 22-second drive capped by Warren's 4-yard touchdown run. Warren's third touchdown, also from 4 yards, came early in the fourth quarter and capped a 73-yard drive that consumed 6:45. The Seahawks finished the game with a whopping 37:03-22:57 edge in time of possession. Denver quarterback John Elway completed just 19 of 37 passes for 209 yards.

Denver	0	0	3	7	—	10
Seattle	0	10	7	10	—	27

Sea — Warren 1 run (Peterson kick)
Sea — FG Peterson 45
Sea — Warren 4 run (Peterson kick)
Den — FG Elam 30
Sea — Warren 4 run (Peterson kick)
Den — Pritchard 26 pass from Elway (Elam kick)
Sea — FG Peterson 19

JACKSONVILLE 17, HOUSTON 16—at Astrodome, attendance 36,346. Mark Brunell's 15-yard touchdown pass to Desmond Howard with 1:03 remaining gave the expansion Jaguars the first victory in franchise history. Jacksonville trailed 16-10 late in the game until safety Darren Carrington recovered Rodney Thomas's fumble at the Oilers' 45-yard line. After a 4-yard run by Le'Shai Maston took the clock to the two-minute warning, quarterback Mark Brunell completed a pair of passes and scrambled 12 yards to move the ball to the 15, and the winning touchdown came on the next play. Houston still had a chance to rally and marched from its own 25-yard line to the Jaguars' 34 with four seconds remaining, but Al Del Greco's 52-yard field goal as time ran out was wide left. Del Greco had made a 53-yard field goal in the closing seconds of the first half. Chris Chandler completed 27 of 47 passes for 225 yards for the Oilers. Carrington also set up Jacksonville's first touchdown with an interception and 17-yard return on the second play of the game.

Jacksonville	10	0	0	7	—	17
Houston	0	6	7	3	—	16

Jack — Christopherson 1 run (Hollis kick)
Jack — FG Hollas 22
Hou — FG Del Greco 29
Hou — FG Del Greco 53
Hou — Thomas 17 pass from Chandler (Del Greco kick)
Hou — FG Del Greco 32
Jack — Howard 15 pass from Brunell (Hollis kick)

KANSAS CITY 24, ARIZONA 3—at Sun Devil Stadium, attendance 50,211. Steve Bono's 76-yard touchdown run, the longest scoring run by a quarterback in NFL history, sparked the Chiefs to an easy victory. Bono rumbled untouched on his bootleg on the first play of the second quarter to give Kansas City a 7-0 advantage, and the Chiefs were not headed after that. Bono completed only 7 of 17 passes for 78 yards on the day, but had touchdown passes of 1 yard to offensive lineman Joe Valerio on a tackle-eligible play midway through the second quarter and 14 yards to Lake Dawson to give Kansas City a 21-0 lead 4:18 into the second half. It was 24-0 before the Cardinals averted a shutout on Greg Davis's 48-yard field goal in the first minute of the fourth quarter. Arizona quarterback Dave Krieg completed 25 of 41 passes for 308 yards, but was sacked 7 times and intercepted once.

Kansas City	0	14	10	0	—	24
Arizona	0	0	0	3	—	3

KC — Bono 76 run (Elliott kick)
KC — Valerio 1 pass from Bono (Elliott kick)
KC — Dawson 14 pass from Bono (Elliott kick)
KC — FG Elliott 28
Ariz — FG Davis 48

MIAMI 26, CINCINNATI 23—at Riverfront Stadium, attendance 52,671. Dan Marino threw a 16-yard touchdown pass to O.J. McDuffie with 1:03 remaining, and the Dolphins hung on to win when Doug Pelfrey's 45-yard field goal attempt on the last play of the game sailed wide left. Miami thus remained the NFL's lone unbeaten team, and head coach Don Shula remained unbeaten in two games against his son, Bengals head coach Dave Shula. The Dolphins led 13-10 at halftime, but the lead changed hands four times in the second half, swinging in Cincinnati's favor for the last time when Jeff Blake threw a 10-yard touchdown pass to Carl Pickens for a 23-19 advantage with 3:39 left. Miami's winning touchdown drive then started on its own 9-yard line and came strictly through the air, with Marino completing 8 of 10 passes. He finished with 33 completions in 48 attempts for 450 yards. Blake passed for 201 yards and 3 touchdowns, all to Pickens, for the Bengals. Pickens caught 9 passes for 117 yards.

Miami	3	10	3	10	—	26
Cincinnati	0	10	7	6	—	23

Mia — FG Stoyanovich 21
Cin — Pickens 3 pass from Blake (Pelfrey kick)
Mia — E. Green 8 pass from Marino (Stoyanovich kick)
Cin — FG Pelfrey 28
Mia — FG Stoyanovich 46
Mia — FG Stoyanovich 36
Cin — Pickens 44 pass from Blake (Pelfrey kick)
Mia — FG Stoyanovich 35
Cin — Pickens 10 pass from Blake (pass failed)
Mia — McDuffie 16 pass from Marino (Stoyanovich kick)

ATLANTA 30, NEW ENGLAND 17—at Georgia Dome, attendance 47,114. Morten Andersen kicked 5 field goals to help the Falcons win their third consecutive game. Jeff George passed for 295 yards and Craig Heyward rushed for 84 for Atlanta, whose 4-1 start was its best since 1986. Andersen kicked 3 field goals in the first half, then broke a 17-17 tie with his 32-yard kick with 9:42 left in the game. His 33-yard field goal with 4:05 left to play increased the advantage to 23-17, and the Falcons put the game away by stopping the Patriots on downs at their 41-yard line with 2:09 to go, then converting that into George's 33-yard touchdown pass to Eric Metcalf with 1:45 remaining. George finished the game with 26 completions in 38 attempts. New England quarterback Scott Zolak, subbing for injured Drew Bledsoe, was 24 of 45 for 252 yards. His 2-yard touchdown pass to Sam Gash seven seconds before halftime was the first touchdown pass of the season for the Patriots. New England wide receiver Vincent Brisby caught 9 passes for 161 yards.

New England	7	7	3	0	—	17
Atlanta	3	14	0	13	—	30

Atl — FG Andersen 34
NE — Martin 1 run (Bahr kick)
Atl — FG Andersen 54
Atl — Heyward 9 run (Mathis pass from George)
Atl — FG Andersen 31
NE — Gash 2 pass from Zolak (Bahr kick)
NE — FG Bahr 27
Atl — FG Andersen 32
Atl — FG Andersen 33
Atl — Metcalf 33 pass from George (Andersen kick)

SAN FRANCISCO 20, N.Y. GIANTS 6—at 3Com Park, attendance 65,536. The 49ers scored a pair of touchdowns 1:09 apart just before halftime, then relied on its stingy defense to defeat the Giants. The game was tied 3-3 before San Francisco fullback William Floyd capped a 64-yard drive with a 1-yard touchdown run with 1:57 remaining in the second quarter. Three plays later, the 49ers forced a punt and took possession at their own 37-yard line at the 1:24 mark. It took only 58 seconds for them to cover 63 yards and take a 17-3 advantage on Steve Young's 16-yard touchdown pass to Jerry Rice 26 seconds before the intermission. New York got no closer after that. The Giants managed only 47 rushing yards and 251 total yards and failed to crack the end zone. Running back Rodney Hampton gained only 27 yards on 11 carries before leaving the game in the third quarter with a broken hand. Young completed 26 of 40 passes for 202 yards for San Francisco.

N.Y. Giants	3	0	3	0	—	6
San Francisco	3	14	3	0	—	20

Giants— FG Daluiso 37
SF — FG Brien 22
SF — Floyd 1 run (Brien kick)
SF — Rice 16 pass from Young (Brien kick)
SF — FG Brien 46
Giants— FG Daluiso 32

PHILADELPHIA 15, NEW ORLEANS 10—at Louisiana Superdome, attendance 43,938. Gary Anderson kicked 5 field goals to lift the Eagles over the winless Saints. Philadelphia's ball-control attack kept possession away from New Orleans and resulted in one-sided advantages in plays (76-47), first downs (20-9), total yards (307-200), and time of possession (39:36-20:24). Ricky Watters gained 79 of the Eagles' 155 rushing yards, and quarterback Rodney Peete, making his first start of the season, was efficient while completing 18 of 29 passes for 173 yards. But Philadelphia could not reach the end zone and found itself trailing 10-9 after the Saints got a large chunk of their total offense on wide receiver Torrance Small's 44-yard touchdown run on a reverse midway through the third quarter. The Eagles countered on their next possession with Anderson's fourth field goal, from 37 yards with 1:18 remaining in the period, to take the lead for good. Anderson's 42-yard field goal with 7:24 to go in the game provided the final margin of victory. Philadelphia limited New Orleans quarterback Jim Everett to only 10 completions in 24 attempts for 102 yards.

Philadelphia	3	3	6	3	—	15
New Orleans	3	0	7	0	—	10

NO — FG Lohmiller 34
Phil — FG Anderson 20
Phil — FG Anderson 43
Phil — FG Anderson 36
NO — Small 44 run (Lohmiller kick)
Phil — FG Anderson 37
Phil — FG Anderson 42

INDIANAPOLIS 21, ST. LOUIS 18—at RCA Dome, attendance 58,616. Marshall Faulk rushed for 177 yards and 3 touchdowns as the Colts handed the Rams their first defeat of the season. Faulk, who carried 19 times and also caught 5 passes for 45 yards, tied the game at 7-7 with a 32-yard touchdown run 6:07 into the first quarter. That came three plays after Damon Watts's interception and 9-yard return, the first time St. Louis had turned over the ball all season. Steve McLaughlin gave the Rams a 10-7 lead with a 29-yard field goal on the first play of the second quarter, but it took Indianapolis only two plays to cover 85 yards and take the lead for good, with Jim Harbaugh's 52-yard pass to Roosevelt Potts preceding Faulk's 33-yard touchdown run. Faulk's 1-yard run late in the third quarter rendered meaningless St. Louis's touchdown in the final minute of the game. Chris Miller completed 26 of 45 passes for 326 yards and 2 touchdowns, both to Isaac Bruce, for the Rams, but was intercepted twice. Bruce caught 8 passes for 181 yards.

St. Louis	7	3	0	8	—	18
Indianapolis	7	7	7	0	—	21

StL — Bruce 4 pass from Miller (McLaughlin kick)
Ind — Faulk 32 run (Cofer kick)
StL — FG McLaughlin 29
Ind — Faulk 33 run (Cofer kick)
Ind — Faulk 1 run (Cofer kick)
StL — Bruce 34 pass from Miller (Bruce pass from Miller)

PITTSBURGH 31, SAN DIEGO 16—at Three Rivers Stadium, attendance 57,012. Cornerbacks Willie Williams and Alvoid Mays returned first-quarter interceptions for touchdowns to spark the Steelers to an easy victory. The game was a rematch of the 1994 AFC title game, which the Chargers rallied to win 17-13. There would be no rally in this one, however, after Pittsburgh jumped to a 21-0 lead after the first period and led 31-6 by the intermission. The key blows were the touchdowns by the two cornerbacks who were starting in place of injured Rod Woodson and Deon Figures. Williams returned his theft 63 yards for a touchdown 8:50 into the game, and Mays followed with a 32-yard touchdown return less than five minutes later. Both players also intercepted passes later in the game, as San Diego quarterback Stan Humphries suffered a career-high 4 interceptions. The Steelers were content to nurse their lead on the ground and got 95 rushing yards from Erric Pegram in his first start of the season. Byron (Bam) Morris, the regular starter, had 2 short touchdown runs, a 1-yard run to cap the game's opening drive, and a 2-yard run 48 seconds before halftime.

San Diego	0	6	7	3	—	16
Pittsburgh	21	10	0	0	—	31

Pitt — Morris 1 run (N. Johnson kick)
Pitt — W. Williams 63 interception return (N. Johnson kick)
Pitt — Mays 32 interception return (N. Johnson kick)
Pitt — FG N. Johnson 25
SD — Means 13 run (pass failed)
Pitt — Morris 2 run (N. Johnson kick)
SD — Martin 19 pass from Humphries (Carney kick)
SD — FG Carney 28

TAMPA BAY 20, CAROLINA 13—at Clemson Memorial Stadium, attendance 50,076. Casey Weldon's 1-yard quarterback sneak on the first play of the fourth quarter broke a 13-13 tie and lifted the Buccaneers to the victory. Weldon, in the game only because starting quarterback Trent Dilfer suffered a mild concussion late in the first half, completed 5 of 7 passes for 72 yards on the winning drive. After the touchdown, the Panthers drove inside Tampa Bay's 40-yard line on each of its remaining three possessions, only to turn over the ball twice and then see their last threat end when Kerry Collins's fourth-down pass from the Buccaneers' 22-yard line with 1 minute left fell incomplete. Collins, the Panthers' top pick in the 1995 NFL Draft who was making his first NFL start, completed 18 of 32 passes for 234 yards and 1 touchdown, with 1 interception. Derrick Moore added 123 rushing yards for Carolina, which outgained Tampa Bay 393-308, but turned over the ball 4 times.

Tampa Bay	7	6	0	7	—	20
Carolina	0	7	6	0	—	13

TB — Rhett 1 run (Husted kick)
Car — Moore 53 run (Kasay kick)
TB — FG Husted 25
TB — FG Husted 27
Car — Metzelaars 4 pass from Collins (kick failed)
TB — Weldon 1 run (Husted kick)

SUNDAY NIGHT, OCTOBER 1

OAKLAND 47, N.Y. JETS 10—at Giants Stadium, attendance 68,941. Jeff Hostetler threw 4 touchdown passes, including 3 in the first half, to key the Raiders' rout. Hostetler passed for 261 yards, Harvey Williams rushed for 97, and Napoleon Kaufman added 95 on the ground as Oakland's balanced attack amassed 25 first downs and 457 total yards. Each of Hostetler's 14 completions (in 23 attempts) went for a first down or a touchdown. Oakland jumped to a 14-0 lead in the first quarter and never looked back. The Raiders put the game away with a pair of touchdowns 2:14 apart shortly before halftime. First, Hostetler's 48-yard pass to Raghib Ismail set up an 17-yard touchdown pass to Tim Brown to give Oakland a 24-3 lead with 2:22 left in the second quarter. Moments later, defensive end Aaron Wallace recovered New York punt returner Dexter Carter's fumble at the Jets' 16-yard line, and Hostetler's 6-yard touchdown pass to Daryl Hobbs four plays later increased the advantage to 31-3 eight seconds before intermission. Brown, who also caught a 66-yard touchdown pass in the third quarter, finished with 8 receptions for 156 yards.

Oakland	14	17	9	7	—	47
N.Y. Jets	0	3	7	0	—	10

Oak — Glover 2 pass from Hostetler (Ford kick)
Oak — Williams 8 run (Ford kick)
Oak — FG Ford 29
Jets — FG Lowery 33
Oak — Brown 17 pass from Hostetler (Ford kick)
Oak — Hobbs 6 pass from Hostetler (Ford kick)
Jets — Brady 3 pass from Esiason (Lowery kick)
Oak — Brown 66 pass from Hostetler (kick blocked)
Oak — FG Ford 26
Oak — Jones 47 fumble return (Ford kick)

MONDAY, OCTOBER 2

BUFFALO 22, CLEVELAND 19—at Cleveland Stadium, attendance 76,211. Steve Christie's second-chance, 33-yard field goal with five seconds remaining gave the Bills the victory. Christie apparently had missed his opportunity to win the game a few seconds earlier when he pulled his kick wide, but was given a reprieve because the Browns had called time out just before the ball was snapped on his kick attempt. The winning kick capped a drive that began on Buffalo's 26-yard line with 3:38 remaining. The key play on the march was Jim Kelly's 20-yard completion to Russell Copeland. Kelly was 27 of 34 passing for 256 yards and 2 touchdowns, including a 41-yard strike to Andre Reed in the fourth quarter. Matt Stover kept Cleveland in the game by kicking 4 field goals, the last from 33 yards to tie the score at 19-19 with 3:49 to go.

Buffalo	10	0	3	9	—	22
Cleveland	7	3	6	3	—	19

Buff — Armour 14 pass from Kelly (Christie kick)
Cleve — Alexander 69 punt return (Stover kick)
Buff — FG Christie 38
Cleve — FG Stover 32
Buff — FG Christie 31
Cleve — FG Stover 47
Cleve — FG Stover 23
Buff — Reed 41 pass from Kelly (kick failed)
Cleve — FG Stover 38
Buff — FG Christie 33

SIXTH WEEK SUMMARIES

AMERICAN FOOTBALL CONFERENCE

Eastern Division	**W**	**L**	**T**	**Pct.**	**Pts.**	**OP**
Buffalo	4	1	0	.800	109	74
Miami	4	1	0	.800	145	77
Indianapolis	3	2	0	.600	110	110
New England	1	4	0	.200	43	129
N.Y. Jets	1	5	0	.167	88	178
Central Division						
Cleveland	3	3	0	.500	124	107
Pittsburgh	3	3	0	.500	138	140
Cincinnati	2	4	0	.333	136	145
Houston	2	4	0	.333	105	119
Jacksonville	2	4	0	.333	81	117
Western Division						
Kansas City	5	1	0	.833	147	105
Oakland	5	1	0	.833	183	79
Denver	3	3	0	.500	134	116
San Diego	3	3	0	.500	104	114
Seattle	2	3	0	.400	85	113

NATIONAL FOOTBALL CONFERENCE

Eastern Division	**W**	**L**	**T**	**Pct.**	**Pts.**	**OP**
Dallas	5	1	0	.833	180	109
Philadelphia	3	3	0	.500	127	159
N.Y. Giants	2	4	0	.333	101	139
Washington	2	4	0	.333	133	139
Arizona	1	5	0	.167	90	160

Central Division

Tampa Bay	4	2	0	.667	86	88
Chicago	3	2	0	.600	139	108
Green Bay	3	2	0	.600	103	95
Minnesota	3	2	0	.600	118	105
Detroit	2	3	0	.400	112	107
Western Division						
Atlanta	4	1	0	.800	103	105
St. Louis	4	1	0	.800	117	86
San Francisco	4	1	0	.800	137	68
Carolina	0	5	0	.000	79	136
New Orleans	0	5	0	.000	98	128

SUNDAY, OCTOBER 8

N.Y. GIANTS 27, ARIZONA 21—at Giants Stadium, attendance 68,463. Giants linebacker Jessie Armstead returned an interception 58 yards for the game-winning touchdown 4:05 into overtime. Armstead's interception capped a flurry of activity in the extra session, beginning when New York linebacker Mike Croel sacked Cardinals quarterback Dave Krieg on the fourth play, forcing a fumble that teammate Keith Hamilton recovered at Arizona's 35-yard line. Two plays later, Cardinals safety Lorenzo Lynch sacked Dave Brown and recovered his fumble at the 38. But after two running plays netted 7 yards, Krieg's pass intended for Anthony Edwards was picked off by Armstead. Krieg did help Arizona amass 431 total yards by completing 23 of 38 passes for 305 yards and a pair of touchdowns. The Cardinals' Garrison Hearst ran for 122 yards on 23 carries, and Frank Sanders caught 6 passes for 108 yards. Brown threw 2 touchdown passes for the Giants and tied the game at 21-21 early in the fourth quarter with a 2-yard touchdown run.

Arizona	3	7	11	0	0	—	21
N.Y. Giants	7	0	7	7	6	—	27

Ariz — FG Davis 23
Giants— Sherrard 6 pass from Brown (Daluiso kick)
Ariz — Sanders 11 pass from Krieg (Davis kick)
Ariz — FG Davis 36
Giants— Way 2 pass from Brown (Daluiso kick)
Ariz — Sanders 6 pass from Krieg (Sanders pass from Krieg)
Giants— Brown 2 run (Daluiso kick)
Giants— Armstead 58 interception return

CHICAGO 31, CAROLINA 27—at Soldier Field, attendance 59,668. Robert Green's 1-yard run with 38 seconds remaining capped a wild fourth quarter and lifted the Bears past the Panthers. Chicago's winning drive began at its 40-yard line with Carolina leading 27-24. Erik Kramer's 19-yard pass to Green moved the ball into Panthers' territory, and his 14-yard toss to Jeff Graham on third-and-3 from the 20 set up the go-ahead touchdown. Cornerback Donnell Woolford secured the victory when he intercepted Kerry Collins's pass two plays after Green's score. The lead changed hands four times in the final period, which began with the Bears leading 17-13. Carolina, bidding for the first victory in franchise history, went ahead when Greg Kragen sacked Kramer, forcing a fumble that the veteran nose tackle recovered and returned 1 yard for a touchdown 1:08 into the quarter. Chicago rallied to take a 24-20 lead 4:30 later when Kramer threw a 1-yard touchdown pass to tight end Ryan Wetnight, only to see the Panthers forge ahead again when Eric Guliford returned a punt 62 yards for a touchdown with 2:37 to play. Kramer finished with 23 completions in 41 attempts for 259 yards and 3 touchdowns. Rookie Rashaan Salaam added 105 yards on 28 carries for the Bears, who outgained Carolina 390-297. Collins passed for 228 yards and 1 touchdown for the Panthers.

Carolina	3	10	0	14	—	27
Chicago	7	7	3	14	—	31

Chi — Conway 41 pass from Kramer (Butler kick)
Car — FG Kasay 21
Car — Carrier 66 pass from Collins (Kasay kick)
Chi — Jennings 1 pass from Kramer (Butler kick)
Car — FG Kasay 49
Chi — FG Butler 23
Car — Kragen 1 fumble return (Kasay kick)
Chi — Wetnight 1 pass from Kramer (Butler kick)
Car — Guliford 62 punt return (Kasay kick)
Chi — Green 1 run (Butler kick)

TAMPA BAY 19, CINCINNATI 16—at Tampa Stadium, attendance 41,732. Michael Husted's 53-yard field goal with 29 seconds remaining propelled the Buccaneers to their third consecutive victory and into first place in the NFC Central Division. Husted kicked 4 field goals, including a 33-yarder to tie the game at 16-16 with 3:38 remaining. That kick was set up by safety John Lynch's interception of Bengals quarterback Jeff Blake. Twenty-seven seconds after the tying field goal, Tampa Bay cornerback Tony Stargell forced Blake to fumble, and cornerback Charles Dimry recovered at the Buccaneers' 44. Husted's winning kick came six plays later. Blake turned over the ball 5 times in all, 3 times on interceptions and twice on fumbles. Errict Rhett rushed for 91 yards and 1 touchdown for Tampa Bay. Alvin Harper caught 6 passes for 117 yards. Dimry intercepted a pass and recovered 2 fumbles.

Cincinnati	3	3	3	7	—	16
Tampa Bay	3	7	3	6	—	19

Cin — FG Pelfrey 34
TB — FG Husted 25
TB — Rhett 2 run (Husted kick)
Cin — FG Pelfrey 45
TB — FG Husted 27
Cin — FG Pelfrey 44
Cin — Dunn 10 pass from Blake (Pelfrey kick)
TB — FG Husted 33
TB — FG Husted 53

DETROIT 38, CLEVELAND 20—at Pontiac Silverdome, attendance 74,171. Scott Mitchell's passing and Barry Sanders's running lifted the Lions to their second consecutive victory after an 0-3 start. Mitchell completed 24 of 38 passes for 273 yards and 2 touchdowns, both to Brett Perriman. Sanders ran for 157 yards on only 18 carries and scored 3 touchdowns. Herman Moore caught 9 passes for 125 yards and Perriman had 6 receptions for 78 yards as Detroit exploded for 429 total yards. Sanders rushed for 129 yards in the first half to help the Lions build a 24-3 lead. His 11-yard touchdown run capped Detroit's first possession 4:17 into the game, and his 75-yard scamper late in the first quarter gave the Lions a 14-3 advantage. His third touchdown, from 2 yards 5:44 into the second half, made it 31-3 and effectively ended any doubt about the game's outcome.

Cleveland	3	0	7	10	—	20
Detroit	14	10	7	7	—	38

Det — Sanders 11 run (Hanson kick)
Cleve — FG Stover 22
Det — Sanders 75 run (Hanson kick)
Det — Perriman 14 pass from Mitchell (Hanson kick)
Det — FG Hanson 56
Det — Sanders 2 run (Hanson kick)
Cleve — Jackson 17 pass from Testaverde (Stover kick)
Det — Perriman 28 pass from Mitchell (Hanson kick)
Cleve — FG Stover 38
Cleve — Reeves 1 pass from Zeier (Stover kick)

DALLAS 34, GREEN BAY 24—at Texas Stadium, attendance 64,806. Troy Aikman passed for 316 yards and 2 touchdowns to pace the Cowboys. Aikman, who missed most of the previous game at Washington with an injured calf, returned to complete 11 of his first 12 passes and finish 24 of 31. His 10-yard touchdown pass to Jay Novacek in the first minute of the second quarter gave Dallas a lead it would not relinquish, and his 48-yard touchdown pass to Michael Irvin midway through the third quarter broke open the game at 24-3. It was 31-10 before Brett Favre rallied the Packers to a pair of touchdowns in a span of 4:07, drawing Green Bay within 7 points with 8:13 left in the game. But the Cowboys responded with a 13-play drive that consumed more than six minutes and ended with Chris Boniol's game-clinching, 35-yard field goal at the two-minute warning. Emmitt Smith rushed for 106 yards and 2 touchdowns on 31 carries for Dallas, which accumulated 448 total yards against the league's top-ranked defense. Irvin caught 8 passes for 150 yards. Favre had his NFL record-tying streak of 12 consecutive games with at least 2 touchdown passes snapped, but did pass for 295 yards and 1 score and scrambled for 2 touchdowns. Green Bay's Robert Brooks caught 10 passes for 124 yards.

Green Bay	0	3	7	14	—	24
Dallas	0	17	7	10	—	34

Dall — Novacek 10 pass from Aikman (Boniol kick)
GB — FG Jacke 42
Dall — FG Boniol 24
Dall — Smith 1 run (Boniol kick)
Dall — Irvin 48 pass from Aikman (Boniol kick)
GB — Favre 4 run (Jacke kick)
Dall — Smith 16 run (Boniol kick)
GB — Chmura 11 pass from Favre (Jacke kick)
GB — Favre 21 run (Jacke kick)
Dall — FG Boniol 35

MINNESOTA 23, HOUSTON 17—at Metrodome, attendance 56,430. Robert Smith's 20-yard touchdown run 7:10 into overtime gave the Vikings the victory. Smith's score was set up by cornerback Dewayne Washington, who intercepted Oilers quarterback Will Furrer's pass near midfield and returned it 25 yards to Houston's 28-yard line. Smith carried for 3 yards and then 5 yards before breaking his winning run on third-and-2. Furrer was in the game only because starting quarterback Chris Chandler injured his throwing shoulder when he was sacked by Minnesota linebacker Ed McDaniel with 18 seconds left in regulation. The outcome spoiled a second-half comeback by the Oilers, who rallied from a 17-6 halftime deficit. Chuck Cecil's 20-yard interception return for a touchdown and Rodney Thomas's two-point conversion run pulled Houston within 3 points in the third quarter, and Al Del Greco's 44-yard field goal with 6:40 remaining in the fourth period tied the game. Former Oilers quarterback Warren Moon passed for 289 yards and 2 touchdowns in his first game against his old team since being traded in 1994. Cris Carter had 12 receptions for 115 yards and 2 touchdowns for the Vikings, who amassed 388 total yards to only 203 for Houston, but were stymied by 3 turnovers and 12 penalties.

Houston	3	3	8	3	0	—	17
Minnesota	0	17	0	0	6	—	23

Hou — FG Del Greco 19
Minn — FG Reveiz 38
Hou — FG Del Greco 50
Minn — Carter 4 pass from Moon (Reveiz kick)
Minn — Carter 17 pass from Moon (Reveiz kick)
Hou — Cecil 20 interception return (Thomas run)
Hou — FG Del Greco 44
Minn — R. Smith 20 run

INDIANAPOLIS 27, MIAMI 24—at Joe Robbie Stadium, attendance 68,471. Jim Harbaugh's 3 touchdown passes rallied the Colts from a 24-3 halftime deficit, and Cary Blanchard's 27-yard field goal 4:58 into overtime handed the Dolphins their first defeat. It was the second time this season that Indianapolis rallied from a 24-3 deficit to win, having already victimized the Jets in week 2. Miami dominated the first half, building its big advantage behind 2 touchdown runs from Terry Kirby, Dan Marino's touchdown pass to Irving Spikes, and Pete Stoyanovich's 51-yard field goal. But the Colts pulled within 24-10 on Harbaugh's 3-yard touchdown pass to Floyd Turner late in the third quarter, and got a break when Stoyanovich missed a 27-yard field goal try with 9:56 left in the game. Six plays later, Harbaugh teamed with Turner on a 47-yard touchdown pass, and Indianapolis was within a touchdown with 6:37 left. They tied it on their next possession when Harbaugh capped a 12-play, 76-yard touchdown drive with a 21-yard pass to Aaron Bailey at the 1:09 mark. After Stoyanovich missed a 49-yard field-goal try in the closing seconds of regulation, the Colts received the kickoff in the extra session and drove 57 yards in nine plays to the winning field goal. Harbaugh completed all 5 of his attempts for 48 yards on the march. He finished 25 of 33 for 319 yards. Marino completed 19 of 30 passes for 194 yards for the Dolphins. His 6-yard pass to Keith Byars in the second quarter broke Fran Tarkenton's NFL record for career pass completions. Marino finished the day with 3,702. Tarkenton had 3,686 in his 18-year career with the Giants and Vikings.

Indianapolis	0	3	7	14	3	—	27
Miami	14	10	0	0	0	—	24

Mia — Kirby 3 run (Stoyanovich kick)
Mia — Spikes 5 pass from Marino (Stoyanovich kick)
Ind — FG Blanchard 21
Mia — Kirby 2 run (Stoyanovich kick)
Mia — FG Stoyanovich 51
Ind — Turner 3 pass from Harbaugh (Blanchard kick)
Ind — Turner 47 pass from Harbaugh (Blanchard kick)
Ind — Bailey 21 pass from Harbaugh (Blanchard kick)
Ind — FG Blanchard 27

BUFFALO 29, N.Y. JETS 10—at Rich Stadium, attendance 79,485. Thurman Thomas's 133 rushing yards and a stifling defense lifted the Bills to their fourth consecutive victory. Thomas carried 27 times and helped Buffalo accumulate 220 of its 311 total yards on the ground. He had a 1-yard touchdown run in the fourth quarter. The Bills took control of the game during a 10-second span late in the first half that produced 10 points. After Steve Christie's third field goal of the game, from 32 yards 26 seconds before intermission, gave Buffalo a 9-3 advantage, Tim Tindale recovered Dexter Carter's fumble on the ensuing kickoff and returned it to the Jets' 15. Jim Kelly threw a 15-yard touchdown pass to Bill Brooks on the next play. The Bills limited New York to only 63 total yards in the first half and 173 for the game. Jets starting quarterback Boomer Esiason had to leave the game with a concussion early in the second quarter. Backup Bubby Brister passed for 112 yards and his team's lone touchdown, a 16-yard strike to Wayne Chrebet to pull New York within 16-10 5:57 into the second half. But Thomas's touchdown run and 2 more field goals by Christie secured Buffalo's victory.

N.Y. Jets	0	3	7	0	—	10
Buffalo	3	13	3	10	—	29

Buff — FG Christie 38
Jets — FG Lowery 26
Buff — FG Christie 24
Buff — FG Christie 32
Buff — Brooks 15 pass from Kelly (Christie kick)
Jets — Chrebet 16 pass from Brister (Lowery kick)
Buff — FG Christie 51
Buff — Thomas 1 run (Christie kick)
Buff — FG Christie 27

JACKSONVILLE 20, PITTSBURGH 16—at Jacksonville Municipal Stadium, attendance 72,042. The expansion Jaguars jumped out to a 14-0 lead and held on to stun the Steelers for their second consecutive victory. Jacksonville took the opening kickoff and marched 79 yards in seven plays, the bulk of it on completions from Mark Brunell to Rich Griffith (39 yards) and Willie Jackson (20 yards). Brunell's 10-yard toss to Cedric Tillman gave the Jaguars a 7-0 lead 4:42 into the game. Late in the quarter, Le'Shai Maston recovered a fumbled punt to set up James Stewart's 6-yard touchdown, and the Jaguars led 14-0. It was 17-7 at halftime and 20-10 midway through the fourth quarter, and Jacksonville hung on to win by limiting Pittsburgh to only a pair of field goals on three trips inside the 20-yard line after that. Brunell finished with 17 completions in 30 attempts for 189 yards. Neil O'Donnell was 19 of 35 for 282 yards and 1 touchdown for the Steelers. Yancey Thigpen caught 6 passes for 160 yards.

Pittsburgh	0	7	6	3	—	16
Jacksonville	7	10	3	0	—	20

Jack — Tillman 10 pass from Brunell (Hollis kick)
Jack — Stewart 6 run (Hollis kick)
Pitt — Avery 18 pass from O'Donnell (Johnson kick)
Jack — FG Hollis 53
Pitt — FG Johnson 41
Jack — FG Hollis 32
Pitt — FG Johnson 19
Pitt — FG Johnson 22

OAKLAND 34, SEATTLE 14—at Oakland-Alameda County Coliseum, attendance 60,213. Harvey Williams rushed for a career-high 160 yards, scored 1 touchdown, and passed for another as the Raiders defeated the Seahawks for their third consecutive victory. Jeff Hostetler passed for 333 yards, and Tim Brown caught 5 passes for 143 yards for Oakland, which extensively used a No-Huddle offense to pile up 531 total yards. Still, the Raiders led just 6-0 until Hostetler teamed with Brown on an 80-yard touchdown pass 44 seconds before halftime. After Seattle closed to within 13-7, Williams put the game out of reach by running 25 yards for a touchdown with 8:54 left in the third quarter and passing 13 yards to tight end Andrew Glover for another touchdown and a 27-7 lead 1:52 before the end of the period. Hostetler, who completed 20 of 33 attempts, threw his second touchdown pass of the game early in the fourth quarter to tight end Kerry Cash to make it 34-7. The offensive explosion gave the Raiders 129 points in their winning streak, the most in franchise history over a three-week stretch. Rick Mirer passed for 236 yards and 1 touchdown for the Seahawks.

Seattle	0	0	7	7	—	14
Oakland	3	10	14	7	—	34

Oak — FG Jaeger 37
Oak — FG Jaeger 24
Oak — Brown 80 pass from Hostetler (Jaeger kick)
Sea — Broussard 21 run (Peterson kick)
Oak — H. Williams 25 run (Jaeger kick)
Oak — Glover 13 pass from H. Williams (Jaeger kick)
Oak — Cash 16 pass from Hostetler (Jaeger kick)
Sea — Galloway 35 pass from Mirer (Peterson kick)

PHILADELPHIA 37, WASHINGTON 34—at Veterans Stadium, attendance 65,498. Gary Anderson's 35-yard field goal 10:06 into overtime gave the Eagles the victory. Philadelphia amassed 524 total yards in the game, including a whopping 272 yards on the ground. Ricky Watters ran for 139 yards on 25 carries, while Charlie Garner added 120 yards on only 9 rushes. Garner also scored 3 times, once on a 55-yard run to open the scoring 2:29 into the game. The Eagles were nearly as effective through the air, with quarterback Rodney Peete completing 30 of 45 passes for 256 yards. But they stymied themselves by turning over the ball 4 times and committing 11 penalties. And they could not hold on to a 10-point lead in the fourth quarter. Quarterback Gus Frerotte rallied the Redskins by passing for 252 yards and 2 touchdowns, including a 12-yard strike to Henry Ellard to pull Washington within 34-31 with 7:13 remaining in regulation. Eddie Murray then kicked a 46-yard field with 52 seconds left to force the extra session. In overtime, the Redskins threatened to win it when they drove to Philadelphia's 45-yard line. But the Eagles forced a punt and then drove 73 yards to the winning field goal. Watters finished with 229 total yards from scrimmage, including 90 yards on 11 receptions. Ellard caught 5 passes for 110 yards for Washington. Defensive tackle Andy Harmon had 3 sacks for the Eagles.

Washington	10	7	7	10	0	—	34
Philadelphia	10	14	7	3	3	—	37

Phil — Garner 55 run (Anderson kick)
Wash — FG Murray 36
Wash — Mitchell 59 punt return (Murray kick)
Phil — FG Anderson 40
Wash — Ellard 40 pass from Frerotte (Murray kick)
Phil — Garner 1 run (Anderson kick)
Phil — Barnett 2 pass from Peete (Anderson kick)
Wash — Frerotte 1 run (Murray kick)
Phil — Garner 17 run (Anderson kick)
Phil — FG Anderson 43
Wash — Ellard 12 pass from Frerotte (Murray kick)
Wash — FG Murray 46
Phil — FG Anderson 35

SUNDAY NIGHT, OCTOBER 8

DENVER 37, NEW ENGLAND 3—at Foxboro Stadium, attendance 60,074. John Elway passed for 287 yards and 2 touchdowns as the Broncos blasted the Patriots, handing New England its fourth consecutive defeat. Denver dominated from the start, building a 14-0 first-quarter lead on 1-yard touchdown runs by Aaron Craver and Terrell Davis. Jason Elam kicked 3 field goals in the second quarter, and Elway quashed any comeback hopes by the Patriots when he teamed with Anthony Miller on a 60-yard touchdown bomb and Shannon Sharpe on a 1-yard touchdown pass in the third quarter. Elway finished with 21 completions in 34 attempts. Davis rushed for 97 yards on 24 carries. Drew Bledsoe passed for 248 yards for New England but completed only 24 of 56 passes.

Denver	14	9	14	0	—	37
New England	3	0	0	0	—	3

Den — Craver 1 run (Elam kick)
Den — Davis 1 run (Elam kick)
NE — FG Bahr 51
Den — FG Elam 37
Den — FG Elam 31
Den — FG Elam 51
Den — Miller 60 pass from Elway (Elam kick)
Den — Sharpe 1 pass from Elway (Elam kick)

MONDAY, OCTOBER 9

KANSAS CITY 29, SAN DIEGO 23—at Arrowhead Stadium, attendance 79,288. Tamarick Vanover's 86-yard punt return for a touchdown gave the Chiefs a dramatic victory, their NFL-record-tying third in overtime this season. Vanover's touchdown marked the first time in NFL history that a punt return ended an overtime game. Kansas City had forced the extra period by driving 79 yards to a touchdown late in the fourth quarter. After the Chargers' John Carney kicked a 29-yard field goal with 1:12 remaining in regulation to give San Diego a 23-16 lead, the Chiefs began the tying drive at their own 21-yard line with 1:06 left and no time outs available. Steve Bono completed 5 of 8 passes, including a 27-yarder to Lake Dawson to move the ball out to midfield and an 18-yard touchdown to tight end Derrick Walker to tie the game with 15 seconds left. In overtime, the Chargers failed to score on their two possessions. San Diego was forced to play the extra session without starting quarterback Stan Humphries, who was injured when hit late in the fourth quarter. Humphries had completed 24 of 34 passes for 315 yards. Backup Gale Gilbert was 4 of 8 for 22 yards, with an interception. Bono completed 27 of 41 passes for 329 yards for Kansas City. The Chiefs limited Chargers running back Natrone Means to only 33 yards on 24 carries.

San Diego	3	10	0	10	0	—	23
Kansas City	0	13	0	10	6	—	29

SD — FG Carney 20
KC — FG Elliott 20
SD — Means 2 run (Carney kick)
KC — FG Elliott 28
KC — Anders 1 pass from Bono (Elliott kick)
SD — FG Carney 36
KC — FG Elliott 49
SD — Mitchell 4 pass from Humphries (Carney kick)
SD — FG Carney 29
KC — Walker 18 pass from Bono (Elliott kick)
KC — Vanover 86 punt return

SEVENTH WEEK SUMMARIES

AMERICAN FOOTBALL CONFERENCE

Eastern Division	**W**	**L**	**T**	**Pct.**	**Pts.**	**OP**
Buffalo	5	1	0	.833	136	95
Indianapolis	4	2	0	.667	128	127
Miami	4	2	0	.667	175	110
New England	1	5	0	.167	69	160
N.Y. Jets	1	6	0	.143	103	204
Central Division						
Cleveland	3	3	0	.500	124	107
Pittsburgh	3	3	0	.500	138	140
Cincinnati	2	4	0	.333	136	145
Houston	2	4	0	.333	105	119
Jacksonville	2	5	0	.286	108	147
Western Division						
Kansas City	6	1	0	.857	178	131
Oakland	5	2	0	.714	183	106
Denver	4	3	0	.571	161	116
San Diego	3	4	0	.429	113	137
Seattle	2	4	0	.333	106	140

NATIONAL FOOTBALL CONFERENCE

Eastern Division	**W**	**L**	**T**	**Pct.**	**Pts.**	**OP**
Dallas	6	1	0	.857	203	118
Philadelphia	4	3	0	.571	144	173
Arizona	2	5	0	.286	114	180
N.Y. Giants	2	5	0	.286	115	156
Washington	2	5	0	.286	153	163
Central Division						
Tampa Bay	5	2	0	.714	106	105
Chicago	4	2	0	.667	169	135
Green Bay	4	2	0	.667	133	116
Minnesota	3	3	0	.500	135	125
Detroit	2	4	0	.333	133	137
Western Division						
St. Louis	5	1	0	.833	138	105
Atlanta	4	2	0	.667	122	126
San Francisco	4	2	0	.667	154	86
Carolina	1	5	0	.167	105	151
New Orleans	1	5	0	.167	131	158

THURSDAY, OCTOBER 12

ST. LOUIS 21, ATLANTA 19—at Busch Memorial Stadium, attendance 59,700. Isaac Bruce caught 10 passes for 191 yards and 2 touchdowns to help the Rams move into first place in the NFC Western Division. Bruce caught a 59-yard touchdown pass from Chris Miller late in the first quarter, then had a 9-yard touchdown reception 41 seconds before the end of the first half. That gave St. Louis a 21-7 lead and proved to be the game winner. Two field goals by Tony Zendejas and Eric Metcalf's 66-yard punt return for a touchdown made it close, but the Falcons' last drive stalled near midfield, and the Rams maintained possession for the game's last 6:36. Atlanta entered the week averaging nearly 370 total yards per game, but managed only 192 yards against St. Louis. The Falcons' other touchdown besides Metcalf's punt return came when safety Kevin Ross returned a blocked field goal 83 yards for a touchdown in the second quarter. Rams quarterback Chris Miller completed 27 of 38 passes for 328 yards. St. Louis also got 88 rushing yards from Jerome Bettis and finished with 451 total yards.

Atlanta	0	10	6	3	—	19
St. Louis	7	14	0	0	—	21

StL — Bruce 59 pass from Miller (McLaughlin kick)
StL — Bailey 12 run (McLaughlin kick)
Atl — Ross 83 blocked field goal return (Andersen kick)
StL — Bruce 9 pass from Miller (McLaughlin kick)
Atl — FG Zendejas 40
Atl — Metcalf 66 punt return (pass failed)
Atl — FG Zendejas 45

SUNDAY, OCTOBER 15

CHICAGO 30, JACKSONVILLE 27—at Jacksonville Municipal Stadium, attendance 72,020. Quarterback Erik Kramer and wide receiver Curtis Conway teamed on 3 touchdown passes as the Bears snapped the expansion Jaguars' two-game winning streak. Kramer completed 17 of 29 passes for 245 yards; Conway caught 4 passes for 74 yards; and Kevin Butler kicked 3 field goals for Chicago, including a 20-yarder to give the Bears a seemingly secure 30-20 lead with just 2:18 to play. But Jacksonville, which entered the game averaging a league-low 224 total yards per game before amassing 409 against Chicago, drove 60 yards in 10 plays, the last a 23-yard touchdown pass from Mark Brunell to Cedric Tillman, to pull within 30-27 with 27 seconds remaining. Safety Mike Dumas recovered the ensuing onside kickoff, and Brunell drove the Jaguars to Chicago's 36-yard line before Mike Hollis's 54-yard field goal try as time expired sailed wide left. Brunell finished with 30 completions in 48 attempts for 302 yards for Jacksonville, while James Stewart added 97 rushing yards on 17 carries. With the victory, the Bears became the first NFL franchise to win 600 games.

Chicago	3	7	10	10	—	30
Jacksonville	7	3	0	17	—	27

Chi — FG Butler 25
Jack — Stewart 7 pass from Brunell (Hollis kick)
Jack — FG Hollis 49
Chi — Conway 10 pass from Kramer (Butler kick)
Chi — Conway 6 pass from Kramer (Butler kick)
Chi — FG Butler 21
Jack — Givins 12 pass from Brunell (Hollis kick)
Chi — Conway 46 pass from Kramer (Butler kick)
Jack — FG Hollis 40
Chi — FG Butler 20
Jack — Tillman 23 pass from Brunell (Hollis kick)

DALLAS 23, SAN DIEGO 9—at San Diego Jack Murphy Stadium, attendance 62,664. Emmitt Smith ran for 2 touchdowns as the Cowboys handed the defending AFC-champion Chargers their third consecutive defeat. Smith helped Dallas build a 14-2 halftime lead with touchdown runs of 4 yards in the first quarter and 1 yard in the second period. San Diego pulled within 14-9 on Ronnie Harmon's 48-yard touchdown run 3:20 into the second half, but the Cowboys countered with a 14-play, 80-yard drive that consumed 7:51 and ended with fullback Daryl Johnston's 1-yard run with 3:40 left in the third quarter. The Chargers outgained Dallas 329-323 but stymied themselves with 4 turnovers and 9 penalties. Gale Gilbert, playing in place of injured Stan Humphries, made only the fourth start of his 10-year career and completed 20 of 32 passes for 206 yards, but was intercepted 3 times and fumbled once, all before the second quarter was five minutes old. Troy Aikman passed for 222 yards, and Michael Irvin caught 7 passes for 103 yards for Dallas.

Dallas	7	7	6	3	—	23
San Diego	2	0	7	0	—	9

SD — Safety, R. Davis sacked Aikman in end zone
Dall — E. Smith 4 run (Boniol kick)
Dall — E. Smith 1 run (Boniol kick)
SD — Harmon 48 run (Carney kick)
Dall — Johnston 1 run (kick failed)
Dall — FG Boniol 30

GREEN BAY 30, DETROIT 21—at Lambeau Field, attendance 60,302. The Packers built a 20-point lead in the first half, then held off the Lions in the second half. Brett Favre passed for 215 yards in the first two periods, and Green Bay forced Detroit to punt on each of its first six possessions en route to a 20-0 lead by the intermission. But the Lions, who managed only 69 total yards in the first half, began their rally by driving 55 yards following the second-half kickoff to Scott Mitchell's 17-yard touchdown pass to Herman Moore. Mitchell threw a 16-yard touchdown pass to Johnnie Morton later in the third quarter, then teamed with Moore again on an 8-yard touchdown pass to pull Detroit within 27-21 1:10 into the fourth quarter. The Packers countered, however, with a drive that lasted nearly six minutes and culminated with Chris Jacke's 20-yard field goal with 7:58 left, and the Lions did not threaten after that. Favre, who completed 15 of 19 passes in the first half, finished 23 of 34 for 342 yards and 2 touchdowns. Mitchell passed for 205 yards, and Barry Sanders rushed for 124 yards for Detroit.

Detroit	0	0	14	7	—	21
Green Bay	3	17	7	3	—	30

GB — FG Jacke 42
GB — Levens 7 pass from Favre (Jacke kick)
GB — FG Jacke 43
GB — Bennett 1 run (Jacke kick)
Det — Moore 17 pass from Mitchell (Hanson kick)
GB — Brooks 12 pass from Favre (Jacke kick)
Det — Morton 16 pass from Mitchell (Hanson kick)
Det — Moore 8 pass from Mitchell (Hanson kick)
GB — FG Jacke 20

NEW ORLEANS 33, MIAMI 30—at Louisiana Superdome, attendance 55,628. Jim Everett threw 4 touchdown passes, and the Saints held off the Dolphins to win for the first time after five defeats to start the season. The mistake-filled game included 7 turnovers (5 by Miami), 4 missed field goals, and 3 missed conversion attempts. But New Orleans prevailed behind Everett, who completed 20 of 32 passes for 242 yards and directed the Saints to 4 touchdowns following Dolphins turnovers. The last came on his 12-yard scoring toss to tight end Irv Smith for a 33-17 lead with 12 minutes to go in the game. That came five plays after linebacker Ernest Dixon's interception and 9-yard return. Miami pulled within a field goal by driving 84 and 77 yards to touchdowns, but never had a chance to tie or win after New Orleans ran out the game's final 1:54. Bernie Kosar started at quarterback for the Dolphins in place of injured Dan Marino and completed 29 of 42 passes for 368 yards and 3 touchdowns. But he was intercepted twice, and hampered by a running attack that netted only 28 yards. Michael Haynes caught 2 touchdown passes for the Saints.

Miami	0	10	7	13	—	30
New Orleans	7	6	13	7	—	33

NO — Bates 1 run (Lohmiller kick)
NO — Haynes 23 pass from Everett (run failed)
Mia — Green 31 pass from Kosar (Stoyanovich kick)
Mia — FG Stoyanovich 20
NO — Early 25 pass from Everett (kick failed)
Mia — McDuffie 12 pass from Kosar (Stoyanovich kick)
NO — Haynes 22 pass from Everett (Lohmiller kick)
NO — I. Smith 2 pass from Everett (Lohmiller kick)
Mia — Kosar 1 run (run failed)
Mia — Kirby 16 pass from Kosar (Stoyanovich kick)

TAMPA BAY 20, MINNESOTA 17—at Tampa Stadium, attendance 55,703. Michael Husted's 51-yard field goal 6:23 into overtime gave the Buccaneers their fourth consecutive victory and maintained their hold on first place in the NFC Central Division. Husted's winning kick came five plays after Vikings safety Orlando Thomas recovered a fumble at Minnesota's 41-yard line, only to fumble it back to Tampa Bay after a 2-yard return. Trent Dilfer then passed 15 yards to Alvin Harper to move the ball into Husted's range. Dilfer completed 24 of 37 passes for 249 yards and was not intercepted. Warren Moon was 33 of 48 for 332 yards and 1 touchdown for the Vikings, but was intercepted twice by Buccaneers safety John Lynch deep in Tampa Bay territory in the first half. Fuad Reveiz kicked 3 field goals for Minnesota, including a 23-yarder to tie the game with 56 seconds remaining in regulation, but missed a 53-yard attempt in overtime that would have won the game.

Minnesota	3	3	0	11	0	—	17
Tampa Bay	7	7	3	0	3	—	20

Minn — FG Reveiz 51
TB — Rhett 6 run (Husted kick)
TB — Mayhew 78 fumble return (Husted kick)
Minn — FG Reveiz 43
TB — FG Husted 36
Minn — Reed 26 pass from Moon (Smith run)
Minn — FG Reveiz 23
TB — FG Husted 51

KANSAS CITY 31, NEW ENGLAND 26—at Arrowhead Stadium, attendance 77,992. Steve Bono threw 2 touchdown passes as the Chiefs won for the sixth time in seven games. Bono's scoring tosses came within a span of 2:14 late in the second quarter and broke a 10-10 tie. The Patriots pulled within 5 points twice in the second half, the final time on Drew Bledsoe's 6-yard touchdown pass to Will Moore with 2:07 remaining. They got the ball back at their own 6-yard line at the 1:41 mark, but their last chance ended when Bledsoe was intercepted by Kansas City cornerback Dale Carter. Bono, who completed only 16 of 40 passes for 209 yards, also ran 2 yards for 1 touchdown in the second quarter. Bledsoe was 25 of 47 for 237 yards and 2 touchdowns. The Chiefs' 6-1 start was their best since their Super Bowl-winning season of 1969.

New England	7	3	9	7	—	26
Kansas City	3	21	0	7	—	31

KC — FG Elliott 27
NE — Meggett 16 run (Bahr kick)
KC — Bono 2 run (Elliott kick)
NE — FG Bahr 29
KC — Davis 18 pass from Bono (Elliott kick)
KC — Vanover 26 pass from Bono (Elliott kick)
NE — FG Bahr 20
NE — Brisby 22 pass from Bledsoe (run failed)
KC — Hill 9 run (Elliott kick)
NE — Moore 6 pass from Bledsoe (Bahr kick)

CAROLINA 26, N.Y. JETS 15—at Clemson Memorial Stadium, attendance 52,613. Linebacker Sam Mills's 36-yard interception return sparked the expansion Panthers to their first win in franchise history. Mills's big play came just 13 seconds before halftime and gave Carolina a 13-12 edge, a lead it would not relinquish. He stepped in front of Bubby Brister's shovel pass intended for running back Adrian Murrell and was not touched en route to the end zone. Vince Workman's 5-yard touchdown run 8:57 into the second half and a pair of field goals by John Kasay in the fourth quarter gave the Panthers some breathing room. Carolina's defense did the rest, limiting the Jets to only 7 first downs, 25 yards rushing, and 138 total yards. Brister started in place of injured Boomer Esiason and completed only 17 of 41 passes for 143 yards. He was sacked 3 times and intercepted 3 times. The Panthers did not fare much better on offense, accumulating 15 first downs and 265 total yards, but they maintained possession for 36:46 of the game's 60 minutes. New York lost its fourth consecutive game.

N.Y. Jets	0	12	0	3	—	15
Carolina	3	10	7	6	—	26

Car — FG Kasay 23
Jets — Safety, Howard sacked Collins in end zone
Jets — FG Lowery 50
Jets — Lewis 13 interception return (Lowery kick)
Car — FG Kasay 39
Car — Mills 36 interception return (Kasay kick)
Car — Workman 5 run (Kasay kick)
Car — FG Kasay 40
Jets — FG Lowery 39
Car — FG Kasay 30

PHILADELPHIA 17, N.Y. GIANTS 14—at Giants Stadium, attendance 74,252. Safety Michael Zordich intercepted a pass and returned a fumble 58 yards for a touchdown to lead the Eagles to their third consecutive victory. Zordich's fumble return gave Philadelphia a 14-0 lead 4:56 into the second quarter, and his interception secured the win in the game's final minute. The Giants had pulled within three points after Keith Elias forced Eagles punter Tom Hutton to fumble and Omar Douglas returned the loose ball 41 yards for a touchdown with 4:45 left in the game. New York's last chance began at its 20-yard line with 3:02 remaining. Backup quarterback Tommy Maddox converted a fourth-down opportunity, but was intercepted by Zordich on second down from Philadelphia's 43 with 43 seconds left. Maddox replaced ineffective starting quarterback Dave Brown early in the second half after Brown completed only 9 of 18 passes for 82 yards. But Maddox could complete only 6 of 23 passes for 49 yards, and was intercepted 3 times. Eagles quarterbacks Rodney Peete and Randall Cunningham fared little better, combining for 7 completions in 16 attempts for 73 yards. Peete did not play in the second half after suffering a concussion. Philadelphia running back Ricky Watters supplied much of the game's offense by rushing for 122 yards and 1 touchdown on 30 carries.

Philadelphia	0	14	0	3	—	17
N.Y. Giants	0	6	0	8	—	14

Phil — Watters 8 run (Anderson kick)
Phil — Zordich 58 fumble return (Anderson kick)
Giants— FG Daluiso 20
Giants— FG Daluiso 21
Phil — FG Anderson 40
Giants— Douglas 41 fumble return (Hampton run)

INDIANAPOLIS 18, SAN FRANCISCO 17—at RCA Dome, attendance 60,273. Cary Blanchard kicked 4 field goals, including the game-winner from 41 yards with 2:36 remaining, to give the Colts another dramatic victory. Indianapolis, which rallied from a 21-point deficit to beat the Dolphins in overtime a week earlier, hung on to beat the defending Super Bowl champions when Doug Brien's 46-yard field-goal try in the final minute sailed wide. Brien had given San Francisco a 17-15 edge when he kicked a career-best 51-yard field goal with 7:39 left in the game. But the Colts countered with a 62-yard drive to the winning field goal. The key plays on the march were Jim Harbaugh's 33-yard completion to tight end Ken Dilger and his 16-yard strike to Floyd Turner on third-and-15 from Indianapolis's 47-yard line. Harbaugh finished with 12 completions in 18 attempts for 175 yards. Dilger caught 7 passes for 125 yards. The Colts limited San Francisco's powerful offense to only 269 total yards. Quarterback Steve Young was harassed most of the afternoon and sacked 6 times. He bruised his shoulder and back while completing 28 of 40 attempts for 229 yards. The 49ers squandered a critical scoring opportunity while leading 7-6 in the closing seconds of the first half. After driving to Indianapolis's 1-yard line, they were unable to get off a field goal before time apparently ran out. When the officials put two seconds back on the clock, San Francisco elected to try for a touchdown, but running back Derek Loville was stopped for a loss by safety Jason Belser.

San Francisco	0	7	7	3	—	17
Indianapolis	3	3	9	3	—	18

Ind — FG Blanchard 32
SF — Rice 5 pass from Young (Brien kick)
Ind — FG Blanchard 46
Ind — Dilger 15 pass from Harbaugh (pass failed)
SF — Loville 4 run (Brien kick)
Ind — FG Blanchard 45
SF — FG Brien 51
Ind — FG Blanchard 41

BUFFALO 27, SEATTLE 21—at Rich Stadium, attendance 74,362. Jim Kelly threw 3 touchdown passes to lead the Bills to their fifth consecutive victory. Despite swirling winds that reached 35 miles per hour, Kelly completed 21 of 36 passes for 275 yards, and was not intercepted. His 2-yard touchdown pass to tight end Lonnie Johnson gave Buffalo a 17-7 lead 7:07 into the third quarter, and his 30-yard strike to Bill Brooks 2:02 later increased the advantage to 24-7. Seattle rallied behind the passing of Rick Mirer and pulled within 27-21, then drove to the Bills' 40-yard line in the closing seconds. But Mirer's pass on the final play of the game was intercepted by Buffalo cornerback Thomas Smith. Mirer passed for 218 yards and 1 touchdown, but completed only 15 of 34 attempts and was intercepted 3 times. Rookie Joey Galloway caught 5 passes for 102 yards for the Seahawks, including a 54-yard touchdown. Bill Brooks had 6 receptions for 109 yards and 2 touchdowns for the Bills.

Seattle	0	7	7	7	—	21
Buffalo	0	10	14	3	—	27

Sea — Warren 3 run (Peterson kick)
Buff — Brooks 28 pass from Kelly (Christie kick)
Buff — FG Christie 43
Buff — Johnson 2 pass from Kelly (Christie kick)
Buff — Brooks 30 pass from Kelly (Christie kick)
Sea — Galloway 54 pass from Mirer (Peterson kick)
Buff — FG Christie 26
Sea — Warren 4 run (Peterson kick)

ARIZONA 24, WASHINGTON 20—at Sun Devil Stadium, attendance 42,370. Dave Krieg's 1-yard touchdown pass to running back Garrison Hearst with 1:16 remaining snapped the Cardinals' three-game losing streak. Arizona began its winning drive at its own 42-yard line, trailing 20-17 with 6:44 to play. Hearst ran 6 times and caught 2 passes on the 9-play drive, but the play that set up the winning pass was Krieg's 20-yard completion to Frank Sanders to move the ball to the 1. Krieg finished with 22 completions in 33 attempts for 207 yards. Hearst ran for 79 yards and caught 3 passes for 13 yards. Arizona's defense got a boost from the return of defensive tackle Eric Swann, who missed four games with a knee injury. Swann dropped Redskins running back Terry Allen for a 7-yard loss on the game's first play and later added 1½ sacks, forced a fumble, and pressured Washington quarterback Gus Frerotte into an intentional grounding call to end the Redskins' last chance. Frerotte passed for 242 yards and 2 touchdowns for Washington.

Washington	7	6	7	0	—	20
Arizona	3	7	7	7	—	24

Wash — Ellard 46 pass from Frerotte (Murray kick)
Ariz — FG Davis 24
Ariz — Williams 28 interception return (Davis kick)
Wash — FG Murray 38
Wash — FG Murray 25
Ariz — Centers 9 run (Davis kick)
Wash — Bell 29 pass from Frerotte (Murray kick)
Ariz — Hearst 1 pass from Krieg (Davis kick)

MONDAY, OCTOBER 16

DENVER 27, OAKLAND 0—at Denver Mile High Stadium, attendance 75,491. John Elway threw 2 touchdown passes to Anthony Miller, and Jason Elam kicked 4 field goals as the Broncos crushed the Raiders. Denver's statistical edge was as big as its edge on the scoreboard. The Broncos outgained Oakland 475-169, and had more first downs (24-10), plays (84-61), and time of possession (36:08-23:52). Denver also forced 4 turnovers. Elway completed 23 of 46 passes for 324 yards. Miller caught 7 passes for 149 yards. Raiders quarterbacks Jeff Hostetler and Vince Evans combined to complete only 19 of 45 passes for 175 yards. Broncos coach Mike Shanahan won in his first game against the team for whom he coached in 1988 and the first four games of 1989.

Oakland	0	0	0	0	—	0
Denver	3	11	10	3	—	27

Den — FG Elam 30
Den — FG Elam 32
Den — Miller 33 pass from Elway (McCaffrey pass from Elway)
Den — FG Elam 33
Den — Miller 36 pass from Elway (Elam kick)
Den — FG Elam 37

EIGHTH WEEK SUMMARIES

AMERICAN FOOTBALL CONFERENCE

Eastern Division	**W**	**L**	**T**	**Pct.**	**Pts.**	**OP**
Buffalo	5	2	0	.714	150	122
Indianapolis	4	3	0	.571	145	157
Miami	4	3	0	.571	191	127
New England	2	5	0	.286	96	174
N.Y. Jets	2	6	0	.250	120	220
Central Division						
Cincinnati	3	4	0	.429	139	130
Cleveland	3	4	0	.429	120	108
Pittsburgh	3	4	0	.429	147	167
Jacksonville	3	5	0	.375	131	162
Houston	2	5	0	.286	137	154
Western Division						
Kansas City	7	1	0	.875	199	138
Oakland	6	2	0	.750	213	123
Denver	4	4	0	.500	168	137
San Diego	4	4	0	.500	148	162
Seattle	2	5	0	.286	131	175

NATIONAL FOOTBALL CONFERENCE

Eastern Division	**W**	**L**	**T**	**Pct.**	**Pts.**	**OP**
Dallas	6	1	0	.857	203	118
Philadelphia	4	3	0	.571	144	173
Washington	3	5	0	.375	189	193
Arizona	2	5	0	.286	114	180
N.Y. Giants	2	5	0	.286	115	156
Central Division						
Chicago	5	2	0	.714	204	167
Green Bay	5	2	0	.714	171	137
Tampa Bay	5	3	0	.625	127	129
Minnesota	3	4	0	.429	156	163
Detroit	2	5	0	.286	163	173
Western Division						
Atlanta	5	2	0	.714	146	147
St. Louis	5	2	0	.714	148	149
San Francisco	5	2	0	.714	198	96
Carolina	2	5	0	.286	125	154
New Orleans	1	6	0	.143	134	178

THURSDAY, OCTOBER 19

CINCINNATI 27, PITTSBURGH 9—at Three Rivers Stadium, attendance 56,684. Quarterback Jeff Blake nearly was perfect as the Bengals stunned the Steelers. Blake completed 18 of 22 passes for 275 yards, 3 touchdowns, and no interceptions against the defending Central Division champions. He helped Cincinnati snap its four-game losing streak and hand Pittsburgh its fourth loss in five games. The two teams were joined by Cleveland later in the weekend in a three-way tie for the division lead. Blake spread his touchdown passes around, completing bombs of 47 yards to Darnay Scott and 41 yards to Carl Pickens, and a 12-yard strike to Tony McGee. The Steelers, meanwhile, had little trouble moving the ball, amassing 24 first downs and 468 total yards, but could not crack the end zone. They drove into Bengals' territory on all eight of their possessions (excluding a kneeldown on the final play of the first half), but managed only 3 field goals by Norm Johnson. They also turned over the ball once on downs and once by interception, and missed a pair of field-goal tries. Pittsburgh quarterback Neil O'Donnell completed 30 of 52 passes for 359 yards. Pickens caught 8 passes for 108 yards for Cincinnati.

Cincinnati	0	10	14	3	—	27
Pittsburgh	0	3	3	3	—	9

Cin — Scott 47 pass from Blake (Pelfrey kick)
Pitt — FG N. Johnson 25
Cin — FG Pelfrey 31
Cin — To. McGee 12 pass from Blake (Pelfrey kick)
Pitt — FG N. Johnson 28
Cin — Pickens 41 pass from Blake (Pelfrey kick)
Pitt — FG N. Johnson 38
Cin — FG Pelfrey 23

SUNDAY, OCTOBER 22

ATLANTA 24, TAMPA BAY 21—at Tampa Stadium, attendance 66,135. Jeff George threw 3 touchdown passes, and Morten Andersen kicked a 30-yard field goal with 7:18 remaining as the Falcons beat the Buccaneers and moved into a three-way tie for first place in the NFC Western Division. The two teams traded touchdowns through the third quarter, which ended tied at 21-21. Andersen's decisive field goal capped a 13-play, 59-yard drive that took nearly six minutes. Tampa Bay never got past its own 42-yard line after that. George completed 24 of 37 passes for 295 yards. Two of his scoring tosses went to Bert Emanuel, who caught 9 passes for 121 yards. Eric Metcalf had 4 receptions for 106 yards, including a 62-yard touchdown. Trent Dilfer passed for 177 yards and Errict Rhett rushed for 88 yards for the Buccaneers.

Atlanta	0	14	7	3	—	24
Tampa Bay	7	7	7	0	—	21

TB — Sapp 5 interception return (Husted kick)
Atl — Metcalf 62 pass from George (Andersen kick)
Atl — Emanuel 32 pass from George (Andersen kick)
TB — Rhett 1 run (Husted kick)
Atl — Emanuel 30 pass from George (Andersen kick)
TB — Rhett 2 run (Husted kick)
Atl — FG Andersen 30

WASHINGTON 36, DETROIT 30—at RFK Stadium, attendance 52,332. Cornerback Darrell Green's interception and 7-yard return 3:41 into overtime enabled the Redskins to maintain their mastery over the Lions. Washington's victory was its seventeenth in a row against Detroit, dating to 1968. It also was its eighteenth without a defeat in Washington, a streak that began in 1939. Lions quarterback Scott Mitchell, who passed for 327 yards and 3 touchdowns, gave his team a 30-27 lead by throwing 51 yards for a touchdown to Brett Perriman with 3:21 left in the game. But the Redskins forced overtime when Eddie Murray kicked a 39-yard field goal with four seconds left. Washington had the ball first in the extra session, and drove from its own 27-yard line to Detroit's 36 before Matt Turk's punt was downed at the 4-yard line. Green made his winning play on the Lions' first snap from there. Mitchell completed 30 of his 50 pass attempts for Detroit. Herman Moore caught 10 passes for 102 yards, and Perriman had 115 yards on his 6 receptions for the Lions, who rolled up 421 total yards. The Redskins amassed 405 total yards, including 166 on the ground. Terry Allen rushed for 110 yards and 2 touchdowns on 24 carries. Quarterback Gus Frerotte completed 21 of 39 attempts for 245 yards and 1 touchdown. Henry Ellard caught 6 passes for 112 yards and became only the sixth player in NFL history to surpass 700 career receptions. Washington forced 4 turnovers and committed none.

Detroit	3	10	7	10	0	—	30
Washington	6	7	7	10	6	—	36

Wash — FG Murray 26
Det — FG Hanson 42
Wash — FG Murray 36
Wash — Allen 1 run (Murray kick)
Det — FG Hanson 20
Det — Moore 17 pass from Mitchell (Hanson kick)
Det — Morton 7 pass from Mitchell (Hanson kick)
Wash — Allen 2 run (Murray kick)
Det — FG Hanson 39
Wash — Ellard 13 pass from Frerotte (Murray kick)
Det — Perriman 51 pass from Mitchell (Hanson kick)
Wash — FG Murray 39
Wash — D. Green 7 interception return

CHICAGO 35, HOUSTON 32—at Soldier Field, attendance 63,545. The Bears built a 25-0 first half lead, then got a scare from the Oilers. Erik Kramer's 76-yard touchdown bomb highlighted Chicago's early spurt. But the Bears' quarterback, who completed 24 of 41 passes for 349 yards and 2 touchdowns in all, also threw a costly interception late in the first half that helped Houston stay in the game. Chicago led 28-8 and had reached the Oilers' 3-yard line when cornerback Darryll Lewis stepped in front of Kramer's pass and returned it 98 yards for a touchdown just eight seconds before halftime. Frank Wycheck's 1-yard run and Al Del Greco's 39-yard field goal pulled Houston within 28-25 late in the third quarter before the Bears regained control with a 12-play, 73-yard drive that consumed nearly seven minutes and culminated with Kramer's 18-yard touchdown pass to Jeff Graham with 10:18 left in the game. Chris Chandler's 6-yard touchdown pass to Haywood Jeffires drew the Oilers within a field goal again with 2:23 to go, but Chicago wide receiver Michael Timpson recovered the ensuing onside kick and the Bears ran out the clock. Graham finished with 9 catches for 137 yards, and Conway had 3 receptions for 111 yards for Chicago, which also got 109 rushing yards from rookie Rashaan Salaam and finished with 480 total yards. Chandler completed 24 of 38 passes for 296 yards and 2 touchdowns for Houston.

Houston	0	15	10	7	—	32
Chicago	15	13	0	7	—	35

Chi — FG Butler 28
Chi — FG Butler 22
Chi — Conway 76 pass from Kramer (Butler kick)
Chi — Safety, Fontenot tackled Chandler in end zone
Chi — Salaam 1 run (Butler kick)
Chi — FG Butler 47
Hou — T. McNair 24 pass from Chandler (Chandler run)
Chi — FG Butler 35
Hou — Lewis 98 interception return (Del Greco kick)
Hou — Wycheck 1 run (Del Greco kick)
Hou — FG Del Greco 39
Chi — Graham 18 pass from Kramer (Butler kick)
Hou — Jeffires 6 pass from Chandler (Del Greco kick)

OAKLAND 30, INDIANAPOLIS 17—at Oakland-Alameda County Coliseum, attendance 53,543. Vince Evans passed for a career-high 335 yards as the Raiders snapped the Colts' three-game winning streak. The 40-year-old Evans, starting in place of injured Jeff Hostetler, completed 23 of 35 passes, including touchdown bombs of 46 and 73 yards to Raghib Ismail. The first came 2:32 into the second half and broke a 10-10 tie, and the latter came on the first play from scrimmage after Indianapolis had pulled within 20-17 late in the third quarter. Ismail finished with 125 yards on his 3 receptions. Oakland also got a big play from rookie running back Napoleon Kaufman, who returned a kickoff 84 yards for a touchdown in the first quarter. Evans, a veteran of 15 NFL seasons, established his previous career high of 316 yards passing while with the Bears in 1980.

Indianapolis	3	7	7	0	—	17
Oakland	7	3	17	3	—	30

Ind — FG Blanchard 25
Oak — Kaufman 84 kickoff return (Jaeger kick)
Ind — Faulk 7 run (Blanchard kick)
Oak — FG Jaeger 28
Oak — Ismail 46 pass from Evans (Jaeger kick)
Oak — FG Jaeger 24
Ind — Faulk 9 run (Blanchard kick)
Oak — Ismail 73 pass from Evans (Jaeger kick)
Oak — FG Jaeger 35

JACKSONVILLE 23, CLEVELAND 15—at Cleveland Stadium, attendance 64,405. Mark Brunell's passing and scrambling led the Jaguars to their third victory in four games. Jacksonville thus equaled the NFL record for first-year wins by an expansion team, and pulled within a half game of three teams in the race for the AFC Central Division lead. Brunell ran for 34 yards on the Jaguars' first drive, an 80-yard march that took more than eight minutes, and threw a 6-yard touchdown pass to Cedric Tillman to give his team a 7-0 lead 11:18 into the game. Two minutes, 49 seconds later, cornerback Mickey Washington intercepted Vinny Testaverde's pass and returned it 48 yards for a touchdown to make it 13-0. It was the first time Testaverde had been intercepted in 174 pass attempts. Testaverde came back to throw a 29-yard touchdown pass to Rico Smith in the closing seconds of the first half, then directed a field- goal drive that pulled the Browns within 20-15 with 4:24 to play in the third quarter. But he lost a fumble in Jacksonville territory in the fourth quarter and had his long pass intercepted by safety Mike Dumas at the Jaguars' 3-yard line in the closing seconds of the game. He finished with 20 completions in 34 attempts for 299 yards. Smith caught 6 passes for 106 yards. Brunell was 16 of 28 for 164 yards for Jacksonville.

Jacksonville	13	7	0	3	—	23
Cleveland	0	12	3	0	—	15

Jack — Tillman 6 pass from Brunell (Hollis kick)
Jack — Washington 48 interception return (kick failed)
Cleve — FG Stover 36
Cleve — FG Stover 29
Jack — Dunbar 1 run (Hollis kick)
Cleve — Smith 29 pass from Testaverde (pass failed)
Cleve — FG Stover 21
Jack — FG Hollis 31

KANSAS CITY 21, DENVER 7—at Denver Mile High Stadium, attendance 71,044. Marcus Allen's 100th career rushing touchdown highlighted the Chiefs' victory. Allen, who gained 121 yards on 21 rushes, carried 7 times for 34 yards on Kansas City's 12-play, 52-yard touchdown drive to open the second half. He capped the march with a 1-yard touchdown run, and joined Walter Payton, Jim Brown, and John Riggins as the only players in NFL history to rush for 100 touchdowns. After leading 14-7 at halftime, the Chiefs combatted a snowstorm by keeping the ball mostly on the ground the rest of the way, rushing on 28 of their 33 plays in the second half. Forced to play catchup, the Broncos took to the air, but quarterback John Elway completed only 21 of his 40 attempts for 214 yards, and was intercepted twice. His 10-yard touchdown pass to tight end Shannon Sharpe 9:16 into the game provided Denver's only points.

Kansas City	7	7	7	0	—	21
Denver	7	0	0	0	—	7

Den — Sharpe 10 pass from Elway (Elam kick)
KC — Bono 1 run (Elliott kick)
KC — Dawson 14 pass from Bono (Elliott kick)
KC — Allen 1 run (Elliott kick)

N.Y. JETS 17, MIAMI 16—at Giants Stadium, attendance 67,228. Bubby Brister threw 2 touchdown passes, and the Jets stunned the Dolphins. New York, which entered the game with a four-game losing streak and one week earlier became the expansion Panthers' first victims, handed Miami its third consecutive defeat after a 4-0 start. The Jets did it while managing only 200 total yards for the game and despite falling behind 9-0 at halftime. But Dexter Carter returned the second-half kickoff 57 yards, and five plays later Brister teamed with rookie Wayne Chrebet on a 12-yard touchdown pass to trim the deficit to 9-7. Three plays later, linebacker Mo Lewis intercepted Bernie Kosar's pass, and Nick Lowery's 50-yard field goal gave New York its first lead. The Dolphins' Terry Kirby ran 2 yards for a touchdown late in the third quarter, but Carter gave his team good field position again with a 31-yard kickoff return, setting up a 61-yard drive that was capped by Brister's 3-yard touchdown pass to tight end Johnny Mitchell with 13:05 left in the game. Miami drove into Jets' territory twice after that, only to come away empty, once when Kosar fumbled when sacked by Marvin Washington and again when he was intercepted by Vance Joseph. The Dolphins' last threat ended with cornerback Victor Green's interception with 1:11 left. Kosar, playing in place of injured Dan Marino for the second consecutive week, completed 27 of 42 passes for 191 yards. Miami's Bernie Parmalee rushed for 120 yards on 24 carries. Brister completed 15 of 26 passes for 152 yards for New York.

Miami	3	6	7	0	—	16
N.Y. Jets	0	0	10	7	—	17

Mia — FG Stoyanovich 49
Mia — FG Stoyanovich 44
Mia — FG Stoyanovich 48
Jets — Chrebet 12 pass from Brister (Lowery kick)
Jets — FG Lowery 50
Mia — Kirby 2 run (Stoyanovich kick)
Jets — Mitchell 3 pass from Brister (Lowery kick)

GREEN BAY 38, MINNESOTA 21—at Lambeau Field, attendance 60,332. Brett Favre threw 4 touchdown passes to lead the Packers to the victory. Green Bay, which moved into a tie for first place in the NFC Central Division, broke open the game with a pair of touchdowns within 48 seconds of the fourth quarter. Favre's fourth touchdown pass, from 6 yards to running back Edgar Bennett 3:09 into the fourth quarter, capped an 82-yard drive that gave the Packers a 28-14 lead. Two plays later, defensive end Reggie White sacked Vikings quarterback Warren Moon, forcing a fumble that teammate Sean Jones recovered in the end zone for a touchdown and a 35-14 advantage with 11:03 to go. Minnesota got no closer than 14 points after that. Favre, who threw his touchdown passes to four different receivers, completed 22 of 43 attempts for 295 yards. Tight end Mark Chmura had 5 catches for 101 yards. Bennett had 105 yards rushing and receiving. Moon completed only 16 of 35 passes for 119 yards, 1 touchdown, and 2 interceptions before giving way to Brad Johnson midway throught the fourth quarter.

Minnesota	7	7	0	7	—	21
Green Bay	7	7	7	17	—	38

GB — Chmura 12 pass from Favre (Jacke kick)
Minn — Smith 4 run (Reveiz kick)
GB — C. Jordan 5 pass from Favre (Jacke kick)
Minn — Reed 2 pass from Moon (Reveiz kick)
GB — Levens 5 pass from Favre (Jacke kick)
GB — Bennett 6 pass from Favre (Jacke kick)
GB — Jones recovered fumble in end zone (Jacke kick)
Minn — Lee 3 run (Reveiz kick)
GB — FG Jacke 26

CAROLINA 20, NEW ORLEANS 3—at Clemson Memorial Stadium, attendance 55,484. An opportunistic offense and a stifling defense lifted the Panthers to their second consecutive victory. Carolina managed only 10 first downs and 155 total yards, and quarterback Kerry Collins completed just 8 of 21 passes for 48 yards, but the defense set up 2 short touchdown drives with interceptions and forced 5 turnovers in all. The game was tied 3-3 in the third quarter when safety Brett Maxie intercepted Jim Everett's pass and returned it 8 yards to the Saints' 23. Three plays later, Howard Griffth ran 2 yards for a touchdown to put the Panthers ahead for good. Later in the quarter, safety Bubba McDowell's interception and 33-yard return set up a 20-yard touchdown drive capped by Griffith's 1-yard run for a 17-3 lead. Maxie, who played for the Saints from 1985-1993, finished with 2 interceptions. Another ex-New Orleans star, linebacker Sam Mills, deflected a pass into Maxie's hands and intercepted a pass in the end zone in the fourth quarter. Everett completed 27 of 48 passes for 241 yards, but suffered 4 interceptions.

New Orleans	0	3	0	0	—	3
Carolina	0	3	14	3	—	20

NO — FG Lohmiller 29
Car — FG Kasay 45
Car — Griffith 2 run (Kasay kick)
Car — Griffith 1 run (Kasay kick)
Car — FG Kasay 37

SAN DIEGO 35, SEATTLE 25—at Kingdome, attendance 45,821. Stan Humphries threw 3 touchdown passes as the Chargers handed the Seahawks their third consecutive defeat. San Diego built a 25-10 halftime lead on 2 touchdown passes from Humphries, Natrone Means's 7-yard touchdown run, and safety Shaun Gayle's fumble recovery in the end zone for a touchdown. Seattle closed within 25-16 on Chris Warren's 1-yard touchdown run 5:35 into the second half, but cornerback Dwayne Harper's interception set up Humphries's third touchdown pass, of 23 yards to running back Ronnie Harmon in the first minute of the fourth quarter, to put the game out of reach. Humphries completed 14 of 26 passes for 166 yards, and Means rushed for 91 yards for the Chargers. The Seahawks outgained San Diego 383-299, but had 4 turnovers. Warren rushed for 112 yards and 2 touchdowns. Rick Mirer passed for 216 yards and 1 touchdown, but also was intercepted 3 times.

San Diego	6	19	0	10	—	35
Seattle	7	3	6	9	—	25

Sea — Blades 41 pass from Mirer (Peterson kick)
SD — Harmon 12 pass from Humphries (kick blocked)
SD — Seay 2 pass from Humphries (pass failed)
SD — Gayle recovered Mirer's fumble in end zone (pass failed)
Sea — FG Peterson 48
SD — Means 7 run (Carney kick)
Sea — Warren 1 run (pass failed)
SD — Harmon 23 pass from Humphries (Carney kick)
Sea — FG Peterson 27
SD — FG Carney 25
Sea — Warren 6 run (run failed)

SAN FRANCISCO 44, ST. LOUIS 10—at Busch Memorial Stadium, attendance 59,915. Linebacker Ken Norton, Jr., returned 2 interceptions for touchdowns as the defense keyed the 49ers' rout of the Rams. Less than three minutes into the game, San Francisco safety Dedrick Dodge intercepted Chris Miller's pass, and the 49ers scored on their first play when backup quarterback Elvis Grbac, playing in place of injured Steve Young, teamed with John Taylor on a 35-yard touchdown pass. Three plays later, Norton intercepted another of Miller's passes, returned it 21 yards for his first career touchdown, and gave San Francisco a 14-0 lead just 4:14 into the game. Jerry Rice caught a 4-yard touchdown pass from Grbac and ran 20 yards on a reverse for another touchdown to help increase the 49ers' advantage to 30-3 early in the second half, and then Norton delivered the knockout blow by returning an interception 35 yards for a touchdown and a 37-3 bulge with 11:19 still to play in the third quarter. Miller, who threw only 3 interceptions in the first six games, was picked off 4 times by San Francisco. Grbac, meanwhile, was efficient, and completed 11 of 14 passes for 119 yards and 2 touchdowns. Isaac Bruce caught 9 passes for 173 yards for St. Louis.

San Francisco	14	10	20	0	—	44
St. Louis	3	0	0	7	—	10

SF — Taylor 35 pass from Grbac (kick failed)
SF — Norton 21 interception return (Rice pass from Grbac)
StL — FG McLaughlin 25
SF — FG Zendejas 38
SF — Rice 4 pass from Grbac (Zendejas kick)
SF — Rice 20 run (kick blocked)
SF — Norton 35 interception return (Zendejas kick)
SF — Floyd 3 run (Zendejas kick)
StL — Hester 38 pass from Rypien (McLaughlin kick)

MONDAY, OCTOBER 23

NEW ENGLAND 27, BUFFALO 14—at Foxboro Stadium, attendance 60,203. Rookie Curtis Martin ran for 127 yards and 1 touchdown on 36 carries to power the Patriots past the Bills. The victory snapped New England's five-game losing streak and halted Buffalo's five-game winning streak. Martin's touchdown came on a 20-yard run 4:26 into the game and gave the Patriots a lead they would not relinquish. The score was set up when New England safety Terry Ray recovered Thurman Thomas's fumble at the Bills' 43-yard line. Thomas gained 42 yards on only 4 carries but had to leave the game midway through the first quarter after pulling a hamstring. Patriots quarterback Drew Bledsoe completed 23 of 40 passes for 262 yards and 1 touchdown. Jim Kelly passed for 211 yards and 1 touchdown for Buffalo. The Bills played without head coach Marv Levy, who was recovering from surgery for prostate cancer. Assistant head coach Elijah Pitts filled in for Levy.

Buffalo	6	8	0	0	—	14
New England	7	14	3	3	—	27

NE — Martin 20 run (Bahr kick)
Buff — FG Christie 23
Buff — FG Christie 23
NE — Brisby 5 pass from Bledsoe (Bahr kick)
NE — Meggett 3 run (Bahr kick)
Buff — Brooks 45 pass from Kelly (Gardner pass from Kelly)
NE — FG Bahr 39
NE — FG Bahr 24

NINTH WEEK SUMMARIES

AMERICAN FOOTBALL CONFERENCE

Eastern Division	W	L	T	Pct.	Pts.	OP
Buffalo	5	3	0	.625	156	145
Indianapolis	5	3	0	.625	162	167
Miami	5	3	0	.625	214	133
New England	2	6	0	.250	113	194
N.Y. Jets	2	7	0	.222	130	237
Central Division						
Cleveland	4	4	0	.500	168	156
Pittsburgh	4	4	0	.500	171	174
Cincinnati	3	5	0	.375	189	183
Houston	3	5	0	.375	156	161
Jacksonville	3	6	0	.333	138	186
Western Division						
Kansas City	7	1	0	.875	199	138
Oakland	6	2	0	.750	213	123
Denver	4	4	0	.500	168	137
San Diego	4	4	0	.500	148	162
Seattle	2	6	0	.250	145	195

NATIONAL FOOTBALL CONFERENCE

Eastern Division	W	L	T	Pct.	Pts.	OP
Dallas	7	1	0	.875	231	131
Philadelphia	5	3	0	.625	164	182
Arizona	3	5	0	.375	134	194
N.Y. Giants	3	5	0	.375	139	171
Washington	3	6	0	.333	204	217
Central Division						
Chicago	6	2	0	.750	218	173
Green Bay	5	3	0	.625	187	161
Tampa Bay	5	4	0	.556	134	148
Detroit	3	5	0	.375	187	189
Minnesota	3	5	0	.375	162	177
Western Division						
Atlanta	5	3	0	.625	159	175
St. Louis	5	3	0	.625	157	169
San Francisco	5	3	0	.625	205	107
Carolina	3	5	0	.375	145	171
New Orleans	2	6	0	.250	145	185

SUNDAY, OCTOBER 29

MIAMI 23, BUFFALO 6—at Joe Robbie Stadium, attendance 71,060. The Dolphins snapped a three-game losing streak and moved into a tie for first place in the AFC East by beating the Bills. Dan Marino returned to the lineup after missing two games with hip and knee injuries, and completed 20 of 35 passes for 232 yards. But it was touchdown runs by Bernie Parmalee and Terry Kirby that broke a 6-6 tie and lifted Miami to its first victory over Buffalo at Joe Robbie Stadium since 1990. Parmalee ran for 83 yards on 20 carries, including a 20-yard touchdown run in the third quarter. Kirby had 60 yards on 12 carries, one an 11-yard touchdown run 3:25 into the fourth period. The Bills, playing without injured running back Thurman Thomas and injured wide receiver Andre Reed, managed only 11 first downs and 186 total yards. Jim Kelly completed 17 of 32 passes for just 147 yards.

Buffalo	0	3	3	0	—	6
Miami	3	3	7	10	—	23

Mia — FG Stoyanovich 24
Buff — FG Christie 33
Mia — FG Stoyanovich 33
Buff — FG Christie 32
Mia — Parmalee 20 run (Stoyanovich kick)
Mia — Kirby 11 run (Stoyanovich kick)
Mia — FG Stoyanovich 22

CAROLINA 20, NEW ENGLAND 17—at Foxboro Stadium, attendance 60,064. John Kasay's 29-yard field goal 7:08 into overtime lifted the Panthers to their third consecutive victory, an expansion-team record. Carolina led 17-3 until Curtis Martin's 2 fourth-quarter touchdown runs, the last from 2 yards with 52 seconds to play, tied the game at 17-17. Kasay had a chance to win the game in the final seconds of regulation, but hit the upright from 39 yards. In the extra session, the Panthers had to drive only 20 yards to the winning kick after forcing the Patriots to punt from their own 1-yard line. Carolina, which entered the game averaging only 261 total yards per game, exploded for a club-record 434 total yards against New England. Derrick Moore ran for 119 yards on 28 carries, and Kerry Collins passed for 309 yards and 2 touchdowns. Drew Bledsoe passed for 228 yards for the Patriots.

Carolina	0	0	17	0	3	—	20
New England	0	3	0	14	0	—	17

NE — FG Bahr 19
Car — FG Kasay 27
Car — Guliford 24 pass from Collins (Kasay kick)
Car — Green 33 pass from Collins (Kasay kick)
NE — Martin 3 run (Bahr kick)
NE — Martin 2 run (Bahr kick)
Car — FG Kasay 29

CLEVELAND 29, CINCINNATI 26—at Riverfront Stadium, attendance 58,632. Rookie Eric Zeier passed for 310 yards and a touchdown to lead the Browns to victory in his first NFL start. Matt Stover's 28-yard field goal 6:30 into overtime won it, and spoiled a dramatic comeback engineered by Bengals backup quarterback David Klingler. Cleveland's Earnest Byner gave his team a 26-16 lead with a 3-yard touchdown run with 2:51 left in the game, and Klingler came on two plays later when Cincinnati starting quarterback Jeff Blake suffered a concussion when sacked by Browns defensive end Rob Burnett. Klingler completed passes of 33 yards to Eric Bieniemy and 21 yards to Tony McGee to set up Doug Pelfrey's 41-yard field goal that trimmed the Bengals' deficit to 26-19 with 1:04 to play. Lee Johnson's onside kick was recovered by Leonard Wheeler at Cincinnati's 46, and two pass-interference penalties on Cleveland cornerback Antonio Langham led to Klingler's game-tying 1-yard touchdown pass to Carl Pickens with 15 seconds left. Blake returned in the extra session, but had his pass intercepted at midfield by safety Dana Hall on the first play of the Bengals' second possession. Byner's 23-yard run to the 9 positioned Stover for the winning kick. Zeier finished with 26 completions in 46 attempts, and threw a 17-yard touchdown pass to Andre Rison to put the Browns ahead 19-16 in the fourth quarter. Rison caught 7 passes for 173 yards, while Byner added 74 yards rushing and 43 yards on 4 receptions. Blake was 20 of 35 for 249 yards for Cincinnati.

Cleveland	3	6	3	14	3	—	29
Cincinnati	6	3	7	10	0	—	26

Cin — Green 1 pass from Blake (pass failed)
Cleve — FG Stover 44
Cleve — FG Stover 25
Cin — FG Pelfrey 37
Cleve — FG Stover 36
Cleve — FG Stover 38
Cin — Pickens 8 pass from Blake (Pelfrey kick)
Cleve — Rison 17 pass from Zeier (Stover kick)
Cleve — Byner 3 run (Stover kick)
Cin — FG Pelfrey 41
Cin — Pickens 1 pass from Klingler (Pelfrey kick)
Cleve — FG Stover 28

DALLAS 28, ATLANTA 13—at Georgia Dome, attendance 70,089. The Cowboys overcame an early 10-point deficit to beat the Falcons. Atlanta received the opening kickoff and took only six plays to drive 71 yards, taking a 7-0 lead on Jeff George's 42-yard touchdown pass to Eric Metcalf 3:25 into the game. The next time they had the ball, the Falcons marched 80 yards in 11 plays, consuming 6:11 of the clock, to take a 10-0 advantage on Morten Andersen's 21-yard field goal early in the second quarter. But Dallas responded with a six-minute drive of its own, pulling within three points on Emmitt Smith's 1-yard run, and then took the lead for good on Troy Aikman's 1-yard touchdown pass to tight end Jay Novacek 15 seconds before halftime. Aikman's 43-yard touchdown pass to Michael Irvin 3:29 into the second half put the Cowboys ahead 21-10. Smith rushed for 167 yards on 26 carries, while Aikman completed 19 of 25 passes for 198 yards. Most of his completions went to Irvin, who had 10 receptions for 135 yards. After Atlanta's first two possessions, Dallas limited the Falcons to only 113 total yards.

Dallas	0	14	7	7	—	28
Atlanta	7	3	3	0	—	13

Atl — Metcalf 42 pass from George (Andersen kick)
Atl — FG Andersen 21
Dall — Smith 1 run (Boniol kick)
Dall — Novacek 1 pass from Aikman (Boniol kick)
Dall — Irvin 43 pass from Aikman (Boniol kick)
Atl — FG Andersen 40
Dall — Johnston 8 run (Boniol kick)

DETROIT 24, GREEN BAY 16—at Pontiac Silverdome, attendance 73,462. Scott Mitchell and Herman Moore teamed on 3 touchdown passes in the Lions' victory. Safety Willie Clay's interception and 24-yard return on the game's third play set up Mitchell's 10-yard touchdown pass to Moore to give Detroit a 7-0 lead 3:39 into the first quarter, and the Lions never trailed. When the Packers pulled within 7-3 on Chris Jacke's 20-yard field goal on the first play of the second quarter, Mitchell and Moore responded on the next play from scrimmage with a 69-yard touchdown bomb. And when Green Bay pulled within 14-10 late in the first half, the pair countered again, this time on a 29-yard touchdown pass in the final minute of the first half. By halftime, Moore already had 5 catches for 126 yards en route to a 6-reception, 147-yard day. Mitchell finished with 15 completions in 23 attempts for 249 yards, and Barry Sanders added 167 yards on 22 rushes. After trailing by 11 points at intermission, the Packers had only three possessions in the second half, and converted the first two into field goals before a time-consuming drive in the fourth quarter carried them to the Lions' 3-yard line. But Brett Favre, who passed for 304 yards and a touchdown but also was intercepted 3 times, fumbled when sacked Detroit's Tracy Scroggins, and Chris Spielman recovered at the 9 with 2:41 to play. It was the first fumble Green Bay had lost all season. Sanders carried 6 times for 64 yards on the ensuing possession to help run out the clock. The two teams amassed 850 total yards, including 443 by the Packers. Edgar Bennett rushed for a career-high 121 yards and caught 6 passes for 50 yards for Green Bay, while Robert Brooks caught 6 passes for 127 yards. Clay finished with 2 interceptions for the Lions.

Green Bay	0	10	6	0	—	16
Detroit	7	14	0	3	—	24

Det — Moore 10 pass from Mitchell (Hanson kick)
GB — FG Jacke 20
Det — Moore 69 pass from Mitchell (Hanson kick)
GB — Brooks 77 pass from Favre (Jacke kick)
Det — Moore 29 pass from Mitchell (Hanson kick)
GB — FG Jacke 50
GB — FG Jacke 28
Det — FG Hanson 38

PITTSBURGH 24, JACKSONVILLE 7—at Three Rivers Stadium, attendance 54,516. Neil O'Donnell threw 2 touchdown passes, and the Steelers avenged an earlier loss to the expansion Jaguars. Eric Pegram ran for 28 yards and caught 2 passes for 29 yards on an 83-yard drive that he capped with a 6-yard touchdown run to give Pittsburgh a 7-0 advantage 10:43 into the game. O'Donnell then teamed with Yancey Thigpen (15 yards) and John L. Williams (6 yards) on touchdown passes in the second quarter to increase the lead to 21-0. That advantage never was threatened, as the Steelers limited Jacksonville to only 229 total yards and sacked quarterback Mark Brunell 7 times. O'Donnell finished with 17 completions in 25 attempts for 178 yards. Brunell passed for 189 yards and led the Jaguars with 53 yards rushing.

Jacksonville	0	0	7	0	—	7
Pittsburgh	7	14	0	3	—	24

Pitt — Pegram 6 run (N.Johnson kick)
Pitt — Thigpen 15 pass from O'Donnell (N.Johnson kick)
Pitt — J.L.Williams 6 pass from O'Donnell (N.Johnson kick)
Jack — Mitchell 16 pass from Brunell (Hollis kick)
Pitt — FG N.Johnson 36

NEW ORLEANS 11, SAN FRANCISCO 7—at 3Com Park, attendance 65,272. Mario Bates's running and Tyrone Hughes's kick returns lifted the Saints past the 49ers. Bates ran for 106 yards on 26 carries, and scored on an 11-yard run for what proved to be the winning touchdown 2:48 into the third quarter. Hughes set up all of New Orleans's points with a 74-yard punt return in the second quarter and a 38-yard return of the second-half kickoff. San Francisco quarterback Elvis Grbac, playing in place on injured Steve Young, completed 29 of 42 passes for 243 yards and scored the 49ers' lone touchdown on a 1-yard quarterback sneak in the second quarter, but could not move his team inside the Saints' 40-yard line in the second half. In addition to losing for the third time in five games after a 3-0 start, the defending Super Bowl champions also lost fullback William Floyd for the season with a knee injury suffered in the fourth quarter. San Francisco's Jerry Rice caught 8 passes for 108 yards and became the NFL's career leader in receiving yards. He finished the day with 14,040 yards, surpassing the previous mark of 14,004 by James Lofton.

New Orleans	0	3	8	0	—	11
San Francisco	0	7	0	0	—	7

SF — Grbac 1 run (Zendejas kick)
NO — FG Lohmiller 20
NO — Bates 11 run (Walls pass from Hodson)

INDIANAPOLIS 17, N.Y. JETS 10—at RCA Dome, attendance 49,250. Cornerback Eugene Daniel's 97-yard interception return for a touchdown helped the Colts overcome a poor offensive performance and win for the fourth time in their last five games. Indianapolis managed only 10 first downs and 114 total yards for the game. After halftime, the Colts had only 1 first down and 3 total yards. But the big play of the game came on the final snap of the first half. The Jets, trailing 10-3, drove to Indianapolis's 2-yard line, where quarterback Bubby Brister spiked the ball to stop the clock with eight seconds left. But on the next play, Daniel stepped in front of intended receiver Wayne Chrebet to intercept Brister's pass. His 97-yard return was a club record and gave the Colts all the points they would need. Brister pulled New York within seven points with a 13-yard touchdown pass to tight end Johnny Mitchell 3:15 into the fourth quarter, but the Jets' last chance ended with an incomplete pass from Indianapolis's 9-yard line with 1:03 to play.

N.Y. Jets	3	0	0	7	—	10
Indianapolis	3	14	0	0	—	17

Jets — FG Lowery 42
Ind — FG Blanchard 46
Ind — Harbaugh 4 run (Blanchard kick)
Ind — Daniel 97 interception return (Blanchard kick)
Jets — Mitchell 13 pass from Brister (Lowery kick)

PHILADELPHIA 20, ST. LOUIS 9—at Veterans Stadium, attendance 62,172. The NFL's top-ranked defense forced 4 second-half turnovers and scored the clinching touchdown in the Eagles' victory. Philadelphia led 13-9 until defensive end William Fuller sacked Rams quarterback Chris Miller, forcing a fumble that linebacker Kevin Johnson picked up and ran 37 yards for a score with 6:16 left in the game. Fuller had 2 of the Eagles' 6 sacks of Miller, as did defensive tackle Andy Harmon. Linebacker William Thomas intercepted a pass, recovered a fumble, and made a critical stop on St. Louis's two-point conversion attempt with the score 10-9 3:14 into the fourth quarter. Miller finished with 26 completions in 43 attempts for 262 yards and a touchdown, but was intercepted twice. Wide receiver Isaac Bruce caught 9 passes for 105 yards. Rodney Peete was just 15 of 34 for 166 yards for Philadelphia, but gave his team the lead for good with a 33-yard touchdown pass to Calvin Williams two minutes into the second quarter.

St. Louis	0	0	3	6	—	9
Philadelphia	0	10	0	10	—	20

Phil — Williams 33 pass from Peete (Anderson kick)
Phil — FG Anderson 20
StL — FG McLaughlin 29
StL — Bruce 12 pass from Miller (run failed)
Phil — FG Anderson 36
Phil — K.Johnson 37 fumble return (Anderson kick)

ARIZONA 20, SEATTLE 14—at Sun Devil Stadium, attendance 39,600. Safety Lorenzo Lynch returned an interception 72 yards for a touchdown with 3:44 left in overtime to give the Cardinals the victory. Arizona took possession first in the extra session and drove from its 25-yard line to the Seahawks' 10, only to see Greg Davis's 27-yard field-goal attempt blocked by Sam Adams. Seattle then marched from its 10 to the Cardinals' 33, when John Friesz's pass bounced off running back Mack Strong's hands and into Lynch's. It was that way throughout the game, which featured 733 total yards (428 by the Seahawks) but also 6 interceptions, 11 fumbles, 22 penalties, and a pair of blocked field goals. Seattle suffered 4 of the interceptions, 8 of the fumbles (losing 3), and 13 of the penalties. Still, the Seahawks had a chance to win when Todd Peterson lined up for a 43-yard field-goal attempt with 2:27 left in regulation, but the try was blocked by Eric Swann. Chris Warren ran for 127 yards for Seattle, which amassed 230 yards on the ground. Defensive end Keith McCants recovered 2 fumbles for Arizona, one of which he returned 5 yards for a touchdown after teammate Michael Bankston fumbled at the end of a 28-yard interception return.

Seattle	0	0	7	7	0	—	14
Arizona	14	0	0	0	6	—	20

Ariz — Moore 8 pass from Krieg (Davis kick)
Ariz — McCants 5 fumble return (Davis kick)
Sea — Strong 17 pass from Friesz (Peterson kick)
Sea — Strong 2 pass from Friesz (Peterson kick)
Ariz — Lynch 72 interception return

HOUSTON 19, TAMPA BAY 7—at Astrodome, attendance 31,489. Marion Butts ran 4 yards for a touchdown and Al Del Greco kicked 3 field goals as the Oilers snapped a three-game losing streak. Houston's defense limited the Buccaneers to only 155 total yards, much of it on a 92-yard touchdown drive to take a 7-6 lead on quarterback Trent Dilfer's 21-yard run 4:18 into the second quarter. But Houston countered with a 16-play march that consumed 9:17 and culminated in Del Greco's 41-yard field goal for a 9-7 halftime lead. In the third quarter, cornerback Cris Dishman snapped Dilfer's club-record streak of 142 passes without an interception, setting up Butts's touchdown run 26 seconds before the end of the period. Del Greco's third field goal clinched the outcome with 21 seconds left in the game. Dilfer managed only 10 completions in 23 attempts for 82 yards for Tampa Bay. He was intercepted 3 times, including twice by Dishman. Rodney Thomas rushed for 89 yards for the Oilers.

Tampa Bay	0	7	0	0	—	7
Houston	6	3	7	3	—	19

Hou — FG Del Greco 19
Hou — FG Del Greco 45
TB — Dilfer 21 run (Husted kick)
Hou — FG Del Greco 41
Hou — Butts 4 run (Del Greco kick)
Hou — FG Del Greco 39

SUNDAY NIGHT, OCTOBER 29

N.Y. GIANTS 24, WASHINGTON 15—at RFK Stadium, attendance 53,310. Safety Vencie Glenn's 75-yard interception return for a touchdown sparked the Giants to the victory. The Redskins took the opening kickoff and marched from their own 18-yard line to New York's 34 in only four plays. But on the next play, Gus Frerotte's pass was bobbled by running back Marc Logan, and Glenn picked it off and gave the Giants a 7-0 lead 2:47 into the game. It was 7-3 early in the second quarter when defensive end Michael Strahan returned another interception 62 yards to Washington's 2. Two plays later, Tyrone Wheatley ran 1 yard for a touchdown. New York broke open the game at 21-3 the next time it had the ball on Dave Brown's 57-yard touchdown bomb to Mike Sherrard, took a 24-6 lead into the intermission, and held on in the second half to win. The Redskins outgained the Giants 409-243, but turned over the ball 5 times. Frerotte passed for 345 yards, but was intercepted 4 times. Leslie Shepherd caught 7 passes for 135 yards, and Henry Ellard had 6 receptions for 111 yards for Washington. In addition to his interception, Glenn forced and recovered a fumble in the second quarter that led to a field goal.

N.Y. Giants	7	17	0	0	—	24
Washington	3	3	6	3	—	15

Giants— Glenn 75 interception return (Daluiso kick)
Wash — FG Murray 47
Giants— Wheatley 1 run (Daluiso kick)
Giants— Sherrard 57 pass from Brown (Daluiso kick)
Giants— FG Daluiso 31
Wash — FG Murray 52
Wash — Logan 3 run (run failed)
Wash — FG Murray 27

MONDAY, OCTOBER 30

CHICAGO 14, MINNESOTA 6—at Metrodome, attendance 58,217. Erik Kramer threw 2 second-quarter touchdown passes as the Bears took over sole possession of first place in the NFC Central Division. Chicago trailed 3-0 until Kramer completed all 5 of his passes for 73 yards on a 78-yard drive capped by his 4-yard touchdown pass to Jim Flanigan, a defensive tackle who also lines up in the backfield in goal-line situations, with 2:23 left in the first half. The Bears' defense then forced a punt, and Kramer's 48-yard touchdown bomb to Curtis Conway made it 14-3 25 seconds before halftime. The Vikings had a chance to tie late in the game, but wide receiver Qadry Ismail's fumble was recovered by defensive end Albert Fontentot at Chicago's 19-yard line with 1:32 remaining. Kramer finished with 18 completions in 25 attempts for 231 yards. Warren Moon was 28 of 42 for 252 yards for Minnesota. The Bears snapped an eight-game losing streak in Monday-night games.

Chicago	0	14	0	0	—	14
Minnesota	0	3	3	0	—	6

Minn — FG Reveiz 22
Chi — Flanigan 4 pass from Kramer (Butler kick)
Chi — Conway 48 pass from Kramer (Butler kick)
Minn — FG Reveiz 43

TENTH WEEK SUMMARIES

AMERICAN FOOTBALL CONFERENCE

Eastern Division	W	L	T	Pct.	Pts.	OP
Buffalo	6	3	0	.667	172	155
Miami	6	3	0	.667	238	147
Indianapolis	5	4	0	.556	172	183
New England	3	6	0	.333	133	201
N.Y. Jets	2	8	0	.200	137	257
Central Division						
Pittsburgh	5	4	0	.556	208	208
Cleveland	4	5	0	.444	178	193
Houston	4	5	0	.444	193	171
Cincinnati	3	6	0	.333	206	203
Jacksonville	3	6	0	.333	138	186
Western Division						
Kansas City	8	1	0	.889	223	141
Oakland	7	2	0	.778	233	140
Denver	5	4	0	.556	206	143
San Diego	4	5	0	.444	162	186
Seattle	3	6	0	.333	175	223

NATIONAL FOOTBALL CONFERENCE

Eastern Division	W	L	T	Pct.	Pts.	OP
Dallas	8	1	0	.889	265	143
Philadelphia	5	4	0	.556	176	216
Arizona	3	6	0	.333	140	232
N.Y. Giants	3	6	0	.333	167	201
Washington	3	7	0	.300	207	241
Central Division						
Chicago	6	3	0	.667	252	210
Green Bay	5	4	0	.556	211	188
Tampa Bay	5	4	0	.556	134	148
Minnesota	4	5	0	.444	189	201
Detroit	3	6	0	.333	209	223
Western Division						
Atlanta	6	3	0	.667	193	197
St. Louis	5	4	0	.556	167	188
San Francisco	5	4	0	.556	212	120
Carolina	4	5	0	.444	158	178
New Orleans	3	6	0	.333	164	195

SUNDAY, NOVEMBER 5

DENVER 38, ARIZONA 6—at Denver Mile High Stadium, attendance 71,488. John Elway's personal milestone highlighted the Broncos' rout of the Cardinals. Denver took the opening kickoff and marched 69 yards, with Terrell Davis running for 61 yards on the drive, including a 5-yard touchdown. A fumble recovery at Arizona's 28 set up Aaron Craver's 1-yard touchdown run, which gave the Broncos a 14-0 lead less than seven minutes into the game. Elway fired scoring passes in each of the final three quarters as Denver coasted to victory. Elway completed 16 of 21 passes for 256 yards to increase his career total to 40,008 yards, making him only the seventh player in NFL history to surpass 40,000 passing yards. Davis gained 135 yards on 22 carries.

Arizona	3	3	0	0	—	6
Denver	14	10	7	7	—	38

Den — Davis 5 run (Elam kick)
Den — Craver 1 run (Elam kick)
Ariz — FG Davis 31
Den — Craver 1 pass from Elway (Elam kick)
Den — FG Elam 53
Ariz — FG Davis 20
Den — Miller 47 pass from Elway (Elam kick)
Den — McCaffrey 23 pass from Elway (Elam kick)

BUFFALO 16, INDIANAPOLIS 10—at RCA Dome, attendance 59,612. Several big stands by Buffalo's defense saved the Bills' victory over the Colts. Jim Kelly's 51-yard scoring strike to Bill Brooks gave Buffalo a 7-0 first-quarter lead, but Indianapolis answered with a 76-yard drive that was capped by Marshall Faulk's 4-yard touchdown run. The Bills took a 16-7 halftime lead on 3 field goals by Steve Christie, then turned to their defense. Protecting a 16-10 lead, Buffalo stopped Faulk three times inside the 3-yard line in the third quarter. Early in the fourth quarter, the Bills forced a fumble to snuff out an Indianapolis drive at the Buffalo 20. The Colts' last chance ended when nose tackle Ted Washington stopped Faulk on fourth down at the Buffalo 4-yard line with less than two minutes to play. Linebacker Bryce Paup led the Bills' defense with 9 tackles, including 3 sacks. Kelly completed 15 of 24 passes for 250 yards. Faulk ran for 87 yards on 25 carries and caught 5 passes for 36 yards. Injuries forced the Colts to use three quarterbacks during the game.

Buffalo	10	6	0	0	—	16
Indianapolis	7	0	3	0	—	10

Buff — Brooks 51 pass from Kelly (Christie kick)
Ind — Faulk 4 run (Blanchard kick)
Buff — FG Christie 39
Buff — FG Christie 23
Buff — FG Christie 33
Ind — FG Blanchard 37

CAROLINA 13, SAN FRANCISCO 7—at 3Com Park, attendance 61,722. The Panthers forced 5 turnovers to shock the 49ers and become the first expansion team to defeat a reigning NFL champion. San Francisco's opening possession set the tone, as Carolina linebacker Sam Mills forced a fumble to set up John Kasay's 39-yard field goal. The 49ers responded by driving inside the Panthers' 10, but Elvis Grbac's pass to Derek Loville was intercepted by former 49ers cornerback Tim McKyer, who raced 96 yards for a touchdown and a 10-0 Carolina lead. Another Kasay field goal gave the Panthers a 13-0 second-quarter lead. They protected that lead thanks to cornerback Tyrone Poole, who forced 2 fumbles inside the Panthers' 5-yard line. The 49ers finally scored early in the fourth quarter on Loville's 1-yard run. But Grbac's second interception and a missed field goal thwarted San Francisco after that. Grbac, playing in place of an injured Steve Young, passed for 327 yards before leaving late in the fourth quarter with a sprained ankle. Poole led the Panthers with 11 tackles as Carolina became the first expansion team to win four games in its inaugural season.

Carolina	10	3	0	0	—	13
San Francisco	0	0	0	7	—	7

Car — FG Kasay 39
Car — McKyer 96 interception return (Kasay kick)
Car — FG Kasay 47
SF — Loville 1 run (Zendejas kick)

ATLANTA 34, DETROIT 22—at Georgia Dome, attendance 49,619. Jeff George completed 31 of 40 passes for 362 yards to lead the Falcons over the Lions. Alton Montgomery's 71-yard interception return for a touchdown gave Atlanta a 10-0 first-quarter lead, and then George's passing helped produce 17 second-quarter points as the Falcons built a 27-7 halftime advantage. Craig Heyward's second touchdown—on a 2-yard run—made it 34-7 with 4:59 to play in the third quarter. Detroit then mounted a comeback, closing the gap to 34-20 until Jessie Tuggle's goal-line interception snuffed out the Lions' last hope with 1:37 left in the game. Eric Metcalf (9 catches for 65 yards) and Bert Emanuel (7 for 104) were George's favorite targets. The Lions' Scott Mitchell passed for 321 yards, including 176 yards on 9 receptions by Herman Moore.

Detroit	0	7	6	9	—	22
Atlanta	10	17	7	0	—	34

Atl — FG Andersen 32
Atl — Montgomery 71 interception return (Andersen kick)
Atl — FG Andersen 47
Atl — Metcalf 7 pass from George (run failed)
Atl — Heyward 3 run (Mathis pass from George)
Det — Morton 32 pass from Mitchell (Hanson kick)
Atl — Heyward 2 run (Andersen kick)
Det — Perriman 16 pass from Mitchell (pass failed)
Det — Mitchell 10 run (Hanson kick)
Det — Safety, George pushed out of end zone

MINNESOTA 27, GREEN BAY 24—at Metrodome, attendance 62,839. Fuad Reveiz's 39-yard field goal as time expired lifted the Vikings over the Packers. Warren Moon fired 3 scoring passes for Minnesota, including third-quarter touchdown strikes to Cris Carter (5 yards) and Jake Reed (9 yards) that turned a 16-10 deficit into a 24-16 lead. Ty Detmer replaced an injured Brett Favre (sprained ankle) and led Green Bay to the tying points early in the fourth quarter, tossing a 2-yard touchdown pass to Mark Chmura, then connecting with Chmura again on the two-point conversion. A wild fourth quarter saw a go-ahead field goal by Reveiz nullified by a penalty and Detmer injured after throwing an interception with 4:56 to play. Detmer's replacement, T.J. Rubley, fumbled the snap on his first play and Minnesota recovered. The Packers got the ball back in the final two minutes, but Rubley's pass bounced off his intended receiver and was intercepted by Minnesota linebacker Jeff Brady at the Vikings' 28 with 50 seconds left. Moon found Reed for 22- and 23-yard passes to set up Reveiz's winning kick. Moon finished with 237 passing yards to become the sixth player in NFL history (and second-fastest) to surpass 40,000 yards. Brady, subbing for an injured Jack Del Rio, had a sack, a forced fumble, and an interception. The Packers had 6 turnovers.

Green Bay	7	9	0	8	—	24
Minnesota	10	0	14	3	—	27

GB — Bennett 13 run (Jacke kick)
Minn — Jordan 3 pass from Moon (Reveiz kick)
Minn — FG Reveiz 36
GB — FG Jacke 42
GB — FG Jacke 50
GB — FG Jacke 46
Minn — Carter 5 pass from Moon (Reveiz kick)
Minn — Reed 9 pass from Moon (Reveiz kick)
GB — Chmura 2 pass from Detmer (Chmura pass from Detmer)
Minn — FG Reveiz 39

HOUSTON 37, CLEVELAND 10—at Cleveland Stadium, attendance 57,881. Chris Chandler passed for 2 scores and ran for another to lead the Oilers' rout of the Browns. Cleveland led 7-0 after Eric Zeier's 4-yard touchdown pass to Andre Rison (it was Rison's 500th career reception), but Houston proceeded to score on seven consecutive possessions. Chandler's 2-yard touchdown run and 23-yard scoring pass to Haywood Jeffires gave Houston a 17-7 halftime lead. Chandler added another scoring toss in the third quarter, and Houston capped the win with Blaine Bishop's 62-yard interception return for a score. Chandler was 16 of 20 for 149 yards. Oilers rookie Rodney Thomas ran for 108 yards on 17 carries.

Houston	3	14	10	10	—	37
Cleveland	7	0	3	0	—	10

Cleve — Rison 4 pass from Zeier (Stover kick)
Hou — FG Del Greco 44
Hou — Chandler 2 run (Del Greco kick)
Hou — Jeffires 23 pass from Chandler (Del Greco kick)
Cleve — FG Stover 20
Hou — Seabron 15 pass from Chandler (Del Greco kick)
Hou — FG Del Greco 45
Hou — FG Del Greco 37
Hou — Bishop 62 interception return (Del Greco kick)

NEW ENGLAND 20, N.Y. JETS 7—at Giants Stadium, attendance 61,462. Rookie Curtis Martin ran for 170 yards and 2 touchdowns on 34 carries to power the Patriots past the Jets. Martin ran for 112 yards in the first half, including a 29-yard run to set up his 2-yard touchdown and a 49-yard run to set up a field goal. His 9-yard scoring run in the third quarter increased the Patriots' lead to 20-0. The Jets drove 99 yards for their only score in the fourth period. Drew Bledsoe completed 13 of 27 passes for 173 yards. New York quarterback Glenn Foley, who played the final 2½ quarters, suffered a season-ending shoulder injury on the game's last play.

New England	3	10	7	0	—	20
N.Y. Jets	0	0	0	7	—	7

NE — FG Bahr 41
NE — Martin 2 run (Bahr kick)
NE — FG Bahr 29

NE — Martin 9 run (Bahr kick)
Jets — B. Baxter 1 run (Lowery kick)

SEATTLE 30, N.Y. GIANTS 28—at Kingdome, attendance 42,100. Todd Peterson's third field goal of the game—from 32 yards with 1:27 left—gave the Seahawks a victory over the Giants. Seattle raced to a 21-3 first-quarter lead on 2 touchdown passes from Rick Mirer to Brian Blades and Joey Galloway's 89-yard punt return for a score. But New York rallied to take a 22-21 halftime advantage on Dave Brown's 2 scoring tosses and Rodney Hampton's 1-yard touchdown run. Seattle reclaimed the lead on Peterson's 23-yard field goal in the third quarter, then upped its advantage to 27-22 on Peterson's 41-yard field goal with 13:33 left in the game. New York countered immediately, as Herschel Walker's 50-yard kickoff return set up Hampton's second touchdown run, allowing the Giants to reclaim the lead at 28-27 with 8:15 remaining. The teams traded punts, and then Seattle embarked on a 13 play, 77-yard drive to Peterson's winning kick. Mirer passed for 253 yards. Blades caught 6 passes for 153 yards. Brown passed for a career-high 299 yards, finding Mike Sherrard 6 times for 128 yards and 1 score.

N.Y. Giants	3	19	0	6	—	28
Seattle	21	0	3	6	—	30

Sea — Blades 33 pass from Mirer (Peterson kick)
Giants— FG Daluiso 23
Sea — Blades 44 pass from Mirer (Peterson kick)
Sea — Galloway 89 punt return (Peterson kick)
Giants— Walker 8 pass from Brown (Daluiso kick)
Giants— Sherrard 28 pass from Brown (run failed)
Giants— Hampton 1 run (pass failed)
Sea — FG Peterson 23
Sea — FG Peterson 41
Giants— Hampton 1 run (pass failed)
Sea — FG Peterson 32

OAKLAND 20, CINCINNATI 17—at Riverfront Stadium, attendance 51,265. Harvey Williams ran for 134 yards and 1 score on 24 carries to lead a punishing Raiders ground attack. Oakland amassed 184 yards on the ground, building a 17-3 halftime advantage on Williams's 2-yard touchdown run, Jeff Hostetler's 34-yard touchdown pass to Tim Brown, and Jeff Jaeger's 37-yard field goal. Cincinnati closed to 17-9 with 4:10 to play in the game, but Jaeger's second field goal with 2:46 remaining clinched the victory. Oakland's defense limited Cincinnati to 241 total yards, sacking Bengals quarterback Jeff Blake 4 times.

Oakland	7	10	0	3	—	20
Cincinnati	0	3	0	14	—	17

Oak — H. Williams 2 run (Jaeger kick)
Oak — Brown 34 pass from Hostetler (Jaeger kick)
Cin — FG Pelfrey 45
Oak — FG Jaeger 37
Cin — FG Pelfrey 28
Cin — FG Pelfrey 48
Oak — FG Jaeger 46
Cin — Pickens 4 pass from Blake (Blake run)

PITTSBURGH 37, CHICAGO 34—at Soldier Field, attendance 61,838. Neil O'Donnell made big play after big play to help the Steelers prevail in an overtime shootout. Pittsburgh converted 12 of 21 third downs, thanks largely to O'Donnell's pinpoint passing. The Bears' Erik Kramer passed for 3 touchdowns, including 2 in the third quarter that turned the Bears' 17-10 deficit into a 24-17 lead. Chicago led 27-20 in the fourth quarter when O'Donnell drove the Steelers 44 yards to the tying score. The Bears reclaimed the lead at 34-27 with 8:46 left when defensive end Alonzo Spellman deflected a pass that linebacker Barry Minter intercepted and returned 2 yards for a score. Pittsburgh forced overtime when O'Donnell capped a 65-yard march by firing an 11-yard touchdown pass to Ernie Mills with 1:06 to play. The drive featured two third-down conversions on passes from O'Donnell to Charles Johnson. Two more third-down conversions in overtime keyed the Steelers' drive to Norm Johnson's winning 24-yard field goal. O'Donnell was 34 of 52 for 341 yards, including 10 to Yancey Thigpen for 108 yards.

Pittsburgh	0	17	3	14	3	—	37
Chicago	3	7	14	10	0	—	34

Chi — FG Butler 40
Pitt — Pegram 1 run (N. Johnson kick)
Chi — Conway 6 pass from Kramer (Butler kick)
Pitt — FG N. Johnson 40
Pitt — Pegram 7 pass from O'Donnell (N. Johnson kick)
Chi — Carter 12 pass from Kramer (Butler kick)
Chi — Wetnight 14 pass from Kramer (Butler kick)
Pitt — FG N.Johnson 46
Chi — FG Butler 27
Pitt — Pegram 6 run (N. Johnson kick)
Chi — Minter 2 interception return (Butler kick)
Pitt — Mills 11 pass from O'Donnell (N. Johnson kick)
Pitt — FG N. Johnson 24

NEW ORLEANS 19, ST. LOUIS 10—at Louisiana Superdome, attendance 43,120. Doug Brien, playing in his first game for New Orleans, kicked 4 field goals to propel the Saints' victory. New Orleans controlled the ball for 38 minutes 6 seconds, gaining 153 yards on the ground, led by Mario Bates (22 carries for 106 yards). St. Louis continued to be plagued by turnovers, fumbling once to set up one of Brien's field goals and having a promising drive killed by an end-zone interception. Isaac Bruce led St. Louis with 8 receptions for 135 yards and 1 touchdown. The Saints' Jim Everett completed 17 of 25 passes for 189 yards.

St. Louis	7	0	3	0	—	10
New Orleans	0	10	3	6	—	19

StL — Bruce 55 pass from Miller (Biasucci kick)
NO — Zellars 1 run (Brien kick)
NO — FG Brien 35
NO — FG Brien 26
StL — FG Biasucci 32
NO — FG Brien 47
NO — FG Brien 42

KANSAS CITY 24, WASHINGTON 3—at Arrowhead Stadium, attendance 77,821. The Chiefs overcame a sluggish offensive performance with an outstanding defensive effort in their victory over the Redskins. Kansas City limited Washington to 201 total yards and 12 completions in 39 attempts. The Chiefs' offense, which held the ball for 36 minutes 13 seconds, was unable to put Washington away because of 3 turnovers and several penalties. Kimble Anders led Kansas City with 75 rushing yards, including a 40-yard scoring run with 2:26 left in the game. Steve Bono passed for 201 yards.

Washington	0	3	0	0	—	3
Kansas City	7	10	0	7	—	24

KC — Allen 1 run (Elliott kick)
KC — Davis 19 pass from Bono (Elliott kick)
Wash — FG Murray 29
KC — FG Elliott 38
KC — Anders 40 run (Elliott kick)

SUNDAY NIGHT, NOVEMBER 5

MIAMI 24, SAN DIEGO 14—at San Diego Jack Murphy Stadium, attendance 61,966. Dan Marino passed for 291 yards and 2 touchdowns to lead the Dolphins to their first victory at San Diego since 1978. Marino found Irving Fryar for a 23-yard score in the first quarter and combined with Terry Kirby on a 5-yard touchdown pass in the third quarter to give Miami a 14-6 lead. San Diego tied the game on Stan Humphries's 50-yard scoring strike to Tony Martin and Humphries's two-point conversion pass to Mark Seay. But Marino led the Dolphins on a 62-yard drive to Pete Stoyanovich's 36-yard field goal for a 17-14 lead with 10:04 remaining in the game. On the Chargers' next possession, Chris Singleton intercepted Humphries's pass and returned it 4 yards to San Diego's 18-yard line. Three plays later Keith Byars scored on a 1-yard run to seal Miami's triumph. Marino completed 25 of 39 passes. The Dolphins' Bernie Parmalee gained 103 yards on 19 carries. San Diego played most of the game without leading rusher Natrone Means, who suffered an injury on the game's fifth play. Humphries completed 19 of 28 passes for 258 yards. Martin had 7 catches for 121 yards.

Miami	7	0	7	10	—	24
San Diego	3	0	11	0	—	14

SD — FG Carney 33
Mia — Fryar 23 pass from Marino (Stoyanovich kick)
SD — FG Carney 39
Mia — Kirby 5 pass from Marino (Stoyanovich kick)
SD — Martin 50 pass from Humphries (Seay pass from Humphries)
Mia — FG Stoyanovich 36
Mia — Byars 1 run (Stoyanovich kick)

MONDAY, NOVEMBER 6

DALLAS 34, PHILADELPHIA 12—at Texas Stadium, attendance 64,876. Troy Aikman and Emmitt Smith led a balanced Dallas attack as the Cowboys defeated the Eagles. Smith ran for 158 yards on 27 carries, highlighted by scoring runs of 39 and 3 yards. Smith's first touchdown gave Dallas a 7-3 first-quarter lead, and his second touchdown made it 24-12 with 4:23 to play in the third quarter. Aikman completed 17 of 24 passes for 202 yards, including an 11-yard touchdown pass to Michael Irvin early in the second period. The Cowboys' defense limited Philadelphia to 232 total yards and intercepted 2 passes, one of which Larry Brown returned 20 yards for the game's final score. Irvin finished with 8 receptions for 115 yards.

Philadelphia	3	3	6	0	—	12
Dallas	10	7	7	10	—	34

Phil — FG Anderson 36
Dall — E. Smith 39 run (Boniol kick)
Dall — FG Boniol 42
Dall — Irvin 11 pass from Aikman (Boniol kick)
Phil — FG Anderson 37
Phil — Watters 2 run (pass failed)
Dall — E. Smith 3 run (Boniol kick)
Dall — FG Boniol 37
Dall — L. Brown 20 interception return (Boniol kick)

ELEVENTH WEEK SUMMARIES

AMERICAN FOOTBALL CONFERENCE

Eastern Division	W	L	T	Pct.	Pts.	OP
Buffalo	7	3	0	.700	195	172
Miami	6	4	0	.600	255	181
Indianapolis	5	5	0	.500	186	200
New England	4	6	0	.400	167	218
N.Y. Jets	2	8	0	.200	137	257
Central Division						
Pittsburgh	6	4	0	.600	228	211
Cincinnati	4	6	0	.400	238	228
Cleveland	4	6	0	.400	181	213
Houston	4	6	0	.400	218	203
Jacksonville	3	7	0	.300	168	233
Western Division						
Kansas City	9	1	0	.900	245	148
Oakland	8	2	0	.800	250	153
Denver	5	5	0	.500	219	174
San Diego	4	6	0	.400	169	208
Seattle	4	6	0	.400	222	253

NATIONAL FOOTBALL CONFERENCE

Eastern Division	W	L	T	Pct.	Pts.	OP
Dallas	8	2	0	.800	285	181
Philadelphia	6	4	0	.600	207	229
Arizona	3	7	0	.300	164	262
N.Y. Giants	3	7	0	.300	180	218
Washington	3	7	0	.300	207	241
Central Division						
Chicago	6	4	0	.600	280	245
Green Bay	6	4	0	.600	246	216
Minnesota	5	5	0	.500	219	225
Tampa Bay	5	5	0	.500	158	175
Detroit	4	6	0	.400	236	247
Western Division						
Atlanta	6	4	0	.600	210	220
St. Louis	6	4	0	.600	195	205
San Francisco	6	4	0	.600	250	140
Carolina	4	6	0	.400	175	206
New Orleans	4	6	0	.400	181	209

SUNDAY, NOVEMBER 12

BUFFALO 23, ATLANTA 17—at Rich Stadium, attendance 62,690. Jim Kelly passed for 272 yards and 2 touchdowns to lead the Bills to victory. Kelly teamed with Bill Brooks on 30- and 15-yard scoring passes to give Buffalo a 14-10 halftime lead. Atlanta tied the game at 17-17 midway through the third quarter when Craig Heyward ran for his second touchdown of the day. But Kelly answered by leading the Bills on 13- and 14-play drives, both of which ended with field goals by Steve Christie, the latter kick coming with 1:56 left in the game. Atlanta quickly marched to the Bills' 20, but Jeff George's pass was intercepted in the end zone by Buffalo safety Kurt Schulz with 52 seconds remaining to preserve the win. Kelly completed 22 of 36 passes, including 7 receptions by Brooks for 101 yards. Bills rookie running back Darick Holmes ran for 100 yards on 23 carries. George was 17 of 34 for 279 yards.

Atlanta	7	3	7	0	—	17
Buffalo	7	7	6	3	—	23

Atl — Heyward 1 run (Andersen kick)
Buff — Brooks 30 pass from Kelly (Christie kick)
Buff — Brooks 15 pass from Kelly (Christie kick)

Atl — FG Andersen 50
Buff — FG Christie 23
Atl — Heyward 1 run (Andersen kick)
Buff — FG Christie 38
Buff — FG Christie 21

ST. LOUIS 28, CAROLINA 17—at Trans World Dome, attendance 65,598. The Rams, playing their first game in the new Trans World Dome, christened their new stadium by forcing 6 turnovers to defeat the Panthers. Jerome Bettis's 1-yard touchdown run and Isaac Bruce's 12-yard scoring catch gave St. Louis a 14-0 second-quarter advantage. The Panthers responded with a 77-yard drive, capped by Kerry Collins's 21-yard scoring pass to Don Beebe 1:12 before halftime. The Rams' defense took over after that, stopping the Panthers inside the 5-yard line in the third quarter and forcing them to settle for a field goal. Later in the period, the Rams recovered a Panthers' fumble at the St. Louis 46. Quarterback Chris Miller then led a 54-yard drive, capped by his 2-yard touchdown pass to Troy Drayton on the first play of the fourth quarter. On the Panthers' next possession, Rams defensive tackle D'Marco Farr hit Collins, forcing a fumble that cornerback Torin Dorn scooped up and returned 26 yards for the clinching score. Bruce caught 9 passes for 110 yards, his sixth consecutive 100-yard game. Miller was 19 of 32 for 216 yards. Bettis gained 91 yards on 26 carries. Collins passed for 228 yards, but was intercepted 4 times. Carolina's Willie Green had 6 receptions for 157 yards.

Carolina	0	7	3	7	—	17
St. Louis	0	14	0	14	—	28

StL — Bettis 1 run (Biasucci kick)
StL — Bruce 12 pass from Miller (Biasucci kick)
Car — Beebe 21 pass from Collins (Kasay kick)
Car — FG Kasay 23
StL — Drayton 2 pass from Miller (Biasucci kick)
StL — Dorn 26 fumble return (Biasucci kick)
Car — Green 17 pass from Collins (Kasay kick)

GREEN BAY 35, CHICAGO 28—at Lambeau Field, attendance 59,996. Brett Favre tied a Packers' record with 5 scoring passes to rally Green Bay over the Bears. The seesaw battle began when Erik Kramer connected with Curtis Conway on a 21-yard touchdown pass 5:19 into the game. The Packers answered, as Favre teamed with Edgar Bennett on a screen pass for a 17-yard touchdown, then hit Robert Brooks for a 29-yard score that was set up by Antonio Freeman's 26-yard punt return. Rashaan Salaam tied the game at 14-14 on the first play of the second quarter on a 2-yard touchdown run. Green Bay reclaimed the lead at 21-14 on Favre's 1-yard touchdown pass to Dorsey Levens. Chicago tied the game again seven seconds before halftime on Kramer's 46-yard scoring strike to Conway. Salaam's second touchdown run gave the Bears a 28-21 lead with 2:47 left in the third quarter, but Freeman's 45-yard kickoff return placed Green Bay at the Bears' 44. On the next play, Favre beat the blitz and found Brooks down the left sideline for the tying touchdown. The Bears answered by driving to the Packers' 31, but Kramer's fourth-down pass was knocked down by cornerback Lenny McGill. Back came the Packers, with Favre leading a 69-yard march, the last 16 coming on another screen pass to Bennett to give Green Bay a 35-28 lead with 9:17 remaining in the game. The Bears drove to the Packers' 14 in the final minute, but Kramer's last-ditch pass fell incomplete as time expired. Favre completed 25 of 33 passes for 336 yards, including 6 to Brooks for 138 yards. Kramer was 23 of 38 for 318 yards. Conway had 6 catches for 126 yards and teammate Jeff Graham had 7 for 108.

Chicago	7	14	7	0	—	28
Green Bay	14	7	7	7	—	35

Chi — Conway 21 pass from Kramer (Butler kick)
GB — Bennett 17 pass from Favre (Jacke kick)
GB — Brooks 29 pass from Favre (Jacke kick)
Chi — Salaam 2 run (Butler kick)
GB — Levens 1 pass from Favre (Jacke kick)
Chi — Conway 46 pass from Kramer (Butler kick)
Chi — Salaam 1 run (Butler kick)
GB — Brooks 44 pass from Favre (Jacke kick)
GB — Bennett 16 pass from Favre (Jacke kick)

CINCINNATI 32, HOUSTON 25—at Astrodome, attendance 32,998. The Bengals used 2 touchdown passes from Jeff Blake and several big plays by their defense and special teams to defeat the Oilers. Cincinnati forced 4 turnovers, recorded 4 sacks, and blocked a punt for a safety. Eric Bieniemy's 41-yard kickoff return set up the Bengals' first touchdown, and 2 fumble recoveries led to 10 more points for Cincinnati. Blake teamed with Carl Pickens on 30- and 12-yard touchdown passes in the second half, the latter score giving Cincinnati a 32-16 lead with 9:45 left in the game. Blake completed 21 of 34 passes for 220 yards. Pickens had 7 receptions for 108 yards. The Oilers' Chris Chandler passed for 155 yards before leaving in the third quarter with an injury.

Cincinnati	10	6	9	7	—	32
Houston	10	3	0	12	—	25

Cin — Bieniemy 1 run (Pelfrey kick)
Hou — FG Del Greco 40
Hou — Robinson 49 interception return (Del Greco kick)
Cin — FG Pelfrey 33
Cin — FG Pelfrey 49
Cin — FG Pelfrey 27
Hou — FG Del Greco 34
Cin — Pickens 30 pass from Blake (Pelfrey kick)
Cin — Safety, Williams blocked punt out of end zone
Hou — FG Del Greco 34
Cin — Pickens 12 pass from Blake (Pelfrey kick)
Hou — Sanders 3 pass from Furrer (pass failed)
Hou — FG Del Greco 23

NEW ORLEANS 17, INDIANAPOLIS 14—at Louisiana Superdome, attendance 44,122. Jim Everett passed for 2 scores, but it was a huge penalty on the Colts that saved the day for the Saints. Everett capped a 73-yard drive with a 32-yard touchdown pass to Torrance Small that tied the game at 7-7 just 1:09 before halftime. Everett's second scoring toss, a 2-yard pass to Quinn Early late in the third quarter, gave New Orleans a 14-7 lead. The Colts' Jim Harbaugh, who sat out most of the first three quarters with an injury, came off the bench to drive the Colts 73 yards to the tying touchdown on a 40-yard pass to Rossevelt Potts. The Saints then embarked on a 12-play drive that consumed 6:41 and ended with Doug Brien's 25-yard field goal to break the tie with 6:33 left. Back came Harbaugh, leading the Colts to the Saints' 19 with 1:11 left. On third down, Harbaugh escaped the pressure and fired an 18-yard pass to Brian Stablein to apparently give Indianapolis a first-and-goal. But Harbaugh had crossed the line of scrimmage, so the play was nullified by the 5-yard penalty and the Colts turned to Cary Blanchard for an attempt at a game-tying 41-yard field goal. Blanchard's kick was wide left. Everett completed 27 of 37 passes for 228 yards, including 9 to tight end Irv Smith for 83 yards.

Indianapolis	0	7	0	7	—	14
New Orleans	0	7	7	3	—	17

Ind — Faulk 6 run (Blanchard kick)
NO — Small 32 pass from Everett (Brien kick)
NO — Early 2 pass from Everett (Brien kick)
Ind — Potts 40 pass from Harbaugh (Blanchard kick)
NO — FG Brien 25

KANSAS CITY 22, SAN DIEGO 7—at San Diego Jack Murphy Stadium, attendance 59,285. The Chiefs used a ball-control offense and outstanding defense to defeat the Chargers. Kansas City held the ball for 35 minutes 40 seconds, including 4:23 in the first quarter on a 59-yard touchdown drive. San Diego answered with an 80-yard touchdown drive to tie the game, but mustered few offensive threats after that. Meanwhile, the Chiefs took a 13-7 halftime advantage on 2 field goals by Lin Elliott. In the third quarter, Kansas City drove 82 yards in 12 plays, capped by Marcus Allen's 1-yard touchdown run, for a 19-7 lead. The Chiefs added another field goal by Elliott in the fourth quarter after a 12-play, 54-yard drive. Kansas City rushed for 166 yards, led by Greg Hill (78) and Allen (63). Kansas City recorded 4 sacks while limiting San Diego to 283 total yards. The Chargers, playing without injured running back Natrone Means, relied mostly on Stan Humphries (21 of 42 for 244 yards).

Kansas City	7	6	6	3	—	22
San Diego	7	0	0	0	—	7

KC — Bono 2 run (Elliott kick)
SD — Culver 1 run (Carney kick)
KC — FG Elliott 47
KC — FG Elliott 48
KC — Allen 1 run (pass failed)
KC — FG Elliott 34

MINNESOTA 30, ARIZONA 24—at Sun Devil Stadium, attendance 51,342. Warren Moon's fourth touchdown pass of the day—a 50-yard strike to Qadry Ismail—gave the Vikings an overtime victory over the Cardinals. Moon teamed with Jake Reed (32 yards) and Cris Carter (5 yards) in the first half as the Vikings built a 17-10 halftime advantage. Another touchdown toss to Carter gave Minnesota a 24-16 lead with 12:17 remaining. The Cardinals tied the game at 24-24, though, as Dave Krieg capped an 80-yard march with a 2-yard touchdown pass to Wendall Gaines with 8:36 left, followed by a two-point conversion pass to Rob Moore. The Vikings took the kickoff in the extra period and marched to the 50, where Moon beat a nine-man blitz and found Ismail streaking over the middle. Ismail broke a tackle, then broke free and sprinted the last 35 yards for the winning score. Moon, who was sacked 4 times, still completed 24 of 43 passes for 342 yards with no interceptions. Carter had 12 catches for 157 yards and Reed had 7 for 96. Krieg was 19 of 36 for 231 yards. Arizona's Garrison Hearst ran 18 times for 103 yards.

Minnesota	3	14	0	7	6	—	30
Arizona	0	10	6	8	0	—	24

Minn — FG Reveiz 43
Minn — Reed 32 pass from Moon (Reveiz kick)
Ariz — Moore 9 pass from Krieg (Davis kick)
Minn — Carter 5 pass from Moon (Reveiz kick)
Ariz — FG Davis 39
Ariz — FG Davis 44
Ariz — FG Davis 44
Minn — Carter 2 pass from Moon (Reveiz kick)
Ariz — Gaines 2 pass from Krieg (Moore pass from Krieg)
Minn — Ismail 50 pass from Moon

NEW ENGLAND 34, MIAMI 17—at Joe Robbie Stadium, attendance 70,399. Drew Bledsoe passed for 2 scores and Curtis Martin ran for 2 scores as the Patriots defeated the Dolphins to mar Dan Marino's record day. Marino passed for 333 yards to give him 47,299 career yards and surpass Fran Tarkenton (47,003) as the NFL's all-time leader. Marino's 31-yard touchdown pass to Bernie Parmalee tied the game at 7-7 in the first quarter, and his 20-yard scoring pass to O.J. McDuffie tied it at 17-17 in the third period. But the Patriots recovered a fumble at the Miami 7, and broke the tie three plays later when Bledsoe's pass slipped through the hands of running back David Meggett and into the hands of teammate Ben Coates for an 8-yard touchdown pass. Martin's second touchdown made it 31-17 with 8:36 left, and Matt Bahr added a late field goal. The 39-year-old Bahr also had a 55-yard field goal in the first half, the longest of his 17-year career. The Patriots did not commit a turnover while forcing 3 miscues by the Dolphins. Bledsoe was 14 of 25 for 209 yards, including 6 for 118 to Vincent Brisby. Martin ran for 142 yards on 30 carries.

New England	0	10	14	10	—	34
Miami	0	10	7	0	—	17

NE — Martin 3 run (Bahr kick)
Mia — Parmalee 31 pass from Marino (Stoyanovich kick)
Mia — FG Stoyanovich 36
NE — FG Bahr 55
NE — Brisby 47 pass from Bledsoe (Bahr kick)
Mia — McDuffie 20 pass from Marino (Stoyanovich kick)
NE — Coates 8 pass from Bledsoe (Bahr kick)
NE — Martin 1 run (Bahr kick)
NE — FG Bahr 47

OAKLAND 17, N.Y. GIANTS 13—at Giants Stadium, attendance 71,160. Harvey Williams's 6-yard touchdown run rallied the Raiders over the Giants on a blustery day in the Meadowlands. The Raiders led 3-0 when defensive end Anthony Smith recovered a Giants' fumble at the Oakland 40. Three plays later, Jeff Hostetler teamed with Raghib Ismail on a 40-yard touchdown bomb for a 10-0 lead. The Giants, trailing 10-3, had the wind at their back for the third quarter and used it to their advantage. Brad Daluiso's second field goal made it 10-6, and after a short punt, New York marched 47 yards to the go-ahead score on Dave Brown's 11-yard quarterback draw. Trailing 13-10 in the fourth quarter, the Raiders drove 71 yards in 10 plays to the decisive score on Williams's run. The Giants advanced into Raiders territory in the final minutes, but they were thwarted by defensive tackle Chester McGlockton's fourth-down deflection. Williams ran for 85 yards on 21 carries as the Raiders amassed 153 rushing yards while limiting New York to 76. Brown completed 18 of 31 passes for 215 yards.

Oakland	3	7	0	7	—	17
N.Y. Giants	0	3	10	0	—	13

Oak — FG Jaeger 30
Oak — Ismail 40 pass from Hostetler (Jaeger kick)
Giants— FG Daluiso 32
Giants— FG Daluiso 32
Giants— Brown 11 run (Daluiso kick)
Oak — H. Williams 6 run (Jaeger kick)

SAN FRANCISCO 38, DALLAS 20—at Texas Stadium, attendance 65,180. The 49ers scored 2 touchdowns in the first 1:24 of the game and the Cowboys never recovered. Jerry Rice turned a short pass from Elvis Grbac into an 81-yard touchdown with 1:01 gone in the first quarter. Twenty-three seconds later, 49ers cornerback Marquez Pope stripped Cowboys wide receiver Michael Irvin and safety Merton Hanks picked up the loose ball and returned it 38 yards for a touchdown and a 14-0 lead. An interception by linebacker Rickey Jackson on the next possession set up a field goal and a 17-0 49ers advantage less than five minutes into the game. An 82-yard drive upped the lead to 24-0 in the second quarter and the rout was on, as the Cowboys never got closer than 18 points. Grbac finished 20 of 30 for 305 yards and 2 touchdowns, with no interceptions. Rice had 5 catches for 161 yards. Dallas's efforts to rally were hampered by the loss of Troy Aikman, who was sidelined the final 3½ quarters by an injury. Emmitt Smith ran for 100 yards on 18 carries.

San Francisco	17	14	0	7	—	38
Dallas	0	7	6	7	—	20

SF — Rice 81 pass from Grbac (Wilkins kick)
SF — Hanks 38 fumble return (Wilkins kick)
SF — FG Wilkins 26
SF — Loville 1 run (Wilkins kick)
Dall — E. Smith 1 run (Boniol kick)
SF — Loville 19 pass from Grbac (Wilkins kick)
Dall — FG Boniol 26
Dall — FG Boniol 37
SF — Grbac 1 run (Wilkins kick)
Dall — Irvin 8 pass from Garrett (Boniol kick)

SEATTLE 47, JACKSONVILLE 30—at Jacksonville Municipal Stadium, attendance 71,290. Joey Galloway's 3 touchdowns highlighted the Seahawks' highest scoring output in 10 years. Galloway already had a 38-yard touchdown reception to his credit when, in the second quarter, he took a handoff on a reverse. He evaded one tackler in the backfield, then escaped from six Jaguars along the right sideline, cut back to the left, and raced to the end zone to complete a dazzling 86-yard touchdown play, the longest run in Seattle history. Galloway's run gave Seattle a 21-14 lead, but Jacksonville rallied to score 13 points in the final 7:30 of the quarter to take a 27-21 lead at intermission. The Seahawks reclaimed the lead on Galloway's 23-yard touchdown catch, and went on to score 19 fourth-quarter points to seal the victory. Galloway caught 5 passes for 114 yards. Chris Warren rushed 27 times for 121 yards, including a 29-yard touchdown run. Rick Mirer completed 18 of 31 passes for 244 yards while directing a Seahawks' offense that produced 481 yards. Jacksonville's Mark Brunell passed for 121 yards and 1 touchdown and ran for 60 yards and another score.

Seattle	14	7	7	19	—	47
Jacksonville	7	20	0	3	—	30

Sea — Warren 29 run (Peterson kick)
Jack — Brunell 3 run (Hollis kick)
Sea — Galloway 38 pass from Mirer (Peterson kick)
Jack — Dunbar 2 run (Hollis kick)
Sea — Galloway 86 run (Peterson kick)
Jack — Givens 15 pass from Brunell (Hollis kick)
Jack — FG Hollis 26
Jack — FG Hollis 50
Sea — Galloway 23 pass from Mirer (Peterson kick)
Sea — Strong 4 run (Peterson kick)
Jack — FG Hollis 29
Sea — FG Peterson 25
Sea — Johnson 2 run (Peterson kick)
Sea — Safety, Brunell sacked in end zone

DETROIT 27, TAMPA BAY 24—at Pontiac Silverdome, attendance 60,644. The Lions' defense forced 4 turnovers and recorded 4 sacks to stymie a potent Buccaneers offense. An interception set up the Lions' first score, a 17-yard touchdown pass from Scott Mitchell to tight end David Sloan, and Barry Sanders raced 55 yards for another Detroit touchdown. Tampa Bay, however, led 17-14 at halftime thanks to scoring runs by Trent Dilfer (7 yards) and Jerry Ellison (36 yards) and Michael Husted's 34-yard field goal. Detroit tied the game on a field goal by Jason Hanson, then converted a fumble recovery into Hanson's tiebreaking 18-yard field goal early in the fourth quarter. The Lions clinched the victory with a 95-yard drive that featured 24- and 37-yard passes by Mitchell and was capped by his 1-yard quarterback sneak with 5:21 remaining. Mitchell completed 21 of 34 passes for 260 yards, mostly to Brett Perriman (10 receptions for 125 yards) and Herman Moore (9 for 104). Errict Rhett led Tampa Bay with 144 yards on 25 carries. The Buccaneers' offense totaled 411 yards.

Tampa Bay	7	10	0	7	—	24
Detroit	7	7	3	10	—	27

Det — Sloan 17 pass from Mitchell (Hanson kick)
TB — Dilfer 7 run (Husted kick)
TB — FG Husted 34
Det — Sanders 55 run (Hanson kick)
TB — Ellison 36 run (Husted kick)
Det — FG Hanson 29
Det — FG Hanson 18
Det — Mitchell 1 run (Hanson kick)
TB — Ellison 1 run (Husted kick)

SUNDAY NIGHT, NOVEMBER 12

PHILADELPHIA 31, DENVER 13—at Veterans Stadium, attendance 60,842. Rodney Peete passed for 1 score and ran for another while the Eagles' defense bottled up the Broncos. Peete led the Eagles on scoring drives of 77, 73, and 70 yards as Philadelphia built a 21-10 halftime lead. Mike Mamula's 25-yard fumble return set up the Eagles' last touchdown, which gave them a 28-13 lead in the fourth quarter. Denver's John Elway teamed with Anthony Miller on a 46-yard touchdown pass before leaving the game in the second quarter with a concussion. Elway's replacement, Hugh Millen, completed 20 of 29 passes, but for only 127 yards as Philadelphia's defense limited Denver to short passes. Peete enjoyed his best day as an Eagle, completing 25 of 37 attempts for 264 yards with no interceptions. The Eagles' Fred Barnett caught 7 passes for 105 yards.

Denver	7	3	3	0	—	13
Philadelphia	14	7	0	10	—	31

Phil — R. Johnson 1 pass from Peete (Anderson kick)
Den — Miller 46 pass from Elway (Elam kick)
Phil — Watters 5 run (Anderson kick)
Den — FG Elam 44
Phil — Peete 2 run (Anderson kick)
Den — FG Elam 48
Phil — Watters 1 run (Anderson kick)
Phil — FG Anderson 39

MONDAY, NOVEMBER 13

PITTSBURGH 20, CLEVELAND 3—at Three Rivers Stadium, attendance 58,675. The Steelers limited the Browns to 120 total yards while Kordell Stewart shined on offense. Stewart, Pittsburgh's rookie quarterback/running back/receiver, scrambled all over the field before completing a 2-yard touchdown pass to Ernie Mills for the Steelers' first score. Stewart also ran twice for 13 yards and caught 2 passes for 21 yards. Pittsburgh held the ball for 40 minutes 36 seconds, thanks to quarterback Neil O'Donnell (17 of 31 for 167 yards) and running back Erric Pegram (26 carries for 112 yards). Cleveland managed just 43 passing yards and 7 first downs.

Cleveland	0	3	0	0	—	3
Pittsburgh	0	7	6	7	—	20

Pitt — Mills 2 pass from Stewart (N. Johnson kick)
Cleve — FG Stover 29
Pitt — FG N. Johnson 38
Pitt — FG N. Johnson 34
Pitt — Thigpen 9 pass from O'Donnell (N. Johnson kick)

TWELFTH WEEK SUMMARIES

AMERICAN FOOTBALL CONFERENCE

Eastern Division	**W**	**L**	**T**	**Pct.**	**Pts.**	**OP**
Buffalo	8	3	0	.727	223	198
Indianapolis	6	5	0	.545	210	210
Miami	6	5	0	.545	275	225
New England	4	7	0	.364	177	242
N.Y. Jets	2	9	0	.182	163	285
Central Division						
Pittsburgh	7	4	0	.636	277	242
Cincinnati	4	7	0	.364	269	277
Cleveland	4	7	0	.364	201	244
Houston	4	7	0	.364	231	223
Jacksonville	3	8	0	.273	184	250
Western Division						
Kansas City	10	1	0	.909	265	161
Oakland	8	3	0	.727	271	187
Denver	6	5	0	.545	249	201
Seattle	5	6	0	.455	249	273
San Diego	4	7	0	.364	196	238

NATIONAL FOOTBALL CONFERENCE

Eastern Division	**W**	**L**	**T**	**Pct.**	**Pts.**	**OP**
Dallas	9	2	0	.818	319	202
Philadelphia	7	4	0	.636	235	248
Arizona	3	8	0	.273	171	289
N.Y. Giants	3	8	0	.273	199	246
Washington	3	8	0	.273	227	268
Central Division						
Green Bay	7	4	0	.636	277	236
Chicago	6	5	0	.545	297	269
Minnesota	6	5	0	.545	262	249
Tampa Bay	6	5	0	.545	175	191
Detroit	5	6	0	.455	260	264
Western Division						
Atlanta	7	4	0	.636	241	226
San Francisco	7	4	0	.636	294	160
St. Louis	6	5	0	.545	201	236
Carolina	5	6	0	.455	202	213
New Orleans	4	7	0	.364	205	252

SUNDAY, NOVEMBER 19

CAROLINA 27, ARIZONA 7—at Clemson Memorial Stadium, attendance 49,582. The Panthers allowed only 96 total yards while winning for the fifth time in six weeks and handing the Cardinals their third consecutive defeat. Arizona managed only 7 first downs, 34 rushing yards, and 62 passing yards, and had its defense on the field for 37:45 of the game's 60 minutes. The Cardinals' offense did not penetrate Carolina's 30-yard line. Kerry Collins threw 2 touchdown passes as the Panthers built a 14-7 halftime lead. It could have been worse for Arizona, but cornerback Aeneas Williams picked up the ball on a blocked field-goal attempt and raced 72 yards for a touchdown on the final play of the first half. John Kasay kicked 2 field goals in the third quarter, and Anthony Johnson ran 23 yards for a touchdown to put the game out of reach with 11:18 remaining. Collins completed 15 of 23 passes for 201 yards for Carolina. Howard Griffith rushed for 88 yards.

Arizona	0	7	0	0	—	7
Carolina	0	14	6	7	—	27

Car — Metzelaars 7 pass from Collins (Kasay kick)
Car — Christian 2 pass from Collins (Kasay kick)
Ariz — A. Williams 72 blocked field goal return (Davis kick)
Car — FG Kasay 42
Car — FG Kasay 30
Car — Johnson 23 run (Kasay kick)

BUFFALO 28, N.Y. JETS 26—at Giants Stadium, attendance 54,436. Jim Kelly threw 2 touchdown passes as the Bills built a 28-10 lead before holding off the Jets. Kelly, who completed 22 of 37 passes for 316 yards, gave Buffalo the lead for good with a 45-yard touchdown bomb to Bill Brooks late in the first quarter. His 18-yard touchdown pass to Brooks with 2:26 to go in the first half gave the Bills a 21-3 advantage, and they maintained an 18-point lead until midway through the third quarter. But Nick Lowery's 35-yard field goal and Boomer Esiason's 6-yard touchdown pass to Fred Baxter pulled New York within 28-20 with 6:51 left in the game. On their final possession, the Jets took over on their 1-yard line with 1:47 to play. Esiason passed 22 yards to Wayne Chrebet and 20 yards to Charles Wilson to move the ball into Buffalo territory, then teamed with running back Adrian Murrell on a 41-yard desperation pass for a touchdown as time ran out. The ensuing 2-point conversion try, however, was broken up by cornerback Thomas Smith. Esiason finished with 24 completions in 43 attempts for 312 yards and 3 touchdowns. Brooks caught 7 passes for 107 yards for the Bills.

Buffalo	7	14	7	0	—	28
N.Y. Jets	3	0	10	13	—	26

Jets — FG Lowery 30
Buff — Brooks 45 pass from Kelly (Christie kick)
Buff — Thomas 12 run (Christie kick)
Buff — Brooks 18 pass from Kelly (Christie kick)

Jets — Mitchell 43 pass from Esiason (Lowery kick)
Buff — Holmes 6 run (Christie kick)
Jets — FG Lowery 35
Jets — F. Baxter 6 pass from Esiason (Lowery kick)
Jets — Murrell 41 pass from Esiason (pass failed)

DALLAS 34, OAKLAND 21—at Oakland-Alameda County Coliseum, attendance 54,444. Emmitt Smith rushed for 3 touchdowns as the Cowboys easily beat the Raiders. Smith carried 29 times for 110 yards and broke open the game with 2 touchdowns in a span of 7:20 of the third quarter. The Cowboys led 17-7 at halftime, then took the second-half kickoff and marched 69 yards in 7 plays to Smith's 13-yard touchdown run 4:05 into the third quarter. The next time Dallas had the ball, it drove 51 yards to a touchdown, with Smith's 4-yard touchdown run increasing the Cowboys' advantage to 31-7. Quarterback Troy Aikman complemented Smith's running by completing 19 of 24 passes for 227 yards, including a 17-yard touchdown pass to Michael Irvin in the first quarter. Irvin caught 7 passes for 109 yards. Oakland piled up 448 total yards, but also turned over the ball 3 times and committed 13 penalties. Vince Evans threw 2 touchdown passes in the second half after replacing starting quarterback Jeff Hostetler, who aggravated a shoulder injury. Raiders wide receiver Tim Brown caught 12 passes for 161 yards.

Dallas	7	10	14	3	—	34
Oakland	0	7	7	7	—	21

Dall — Irvin 17 pass from Aikman (Boniol kick)
Dall — E. Smith 4 run (Boniol kick)
Oak — Williams 7 run (Jaeger kick)
Dall — FG Boniol 26
Dall — E. Smith 13 run (Boniol kick)
Dall — E. Smith 4 run (Boniol kick)
Oak — Brown 24 pass from Evans (Jaeger kick)
Oak — Cash 16 pass from Evans (Jaeger kick)
Dall — FG Boniol 38

DETROIT 24, CHICAGO 17—at Soldier Field, attendance 61,779. Don Majkowski came off the bench to pass for 161 yards and the winning touchdown late in the game as the Lions handed the Bears their third consecutive defeat. Majkowski entered the game late in the first half after starting quarterback Scott Mitchell sprained an ankle. He went on to complete 15 of 19 passes, the last an 11-yard touchdown to Herman Moore to break a 17-17 tie with 2:32 remaining in the game. Chicago still had a chance to rally, and drove to a first down at Detroit's 11-yard line. But an offensive pass interference penalty and an incomplete pass on fourth down with 49 seconds left ended the threat. Brett Perriman caught a career-high 12 passes for 142 yards, and Barry Sanders rushed for 120 yards on 24 carries for the Lions, who amassed 422 total yards. Erik Kramer passed for 231 for the Bears. Jeff Graham caught 5 passes for 109 yards.

Detroit	7	3	7	7	—	24
Chicago	7	0	3	7	—	17

Chi — Jennings 5 pass from Kramer (Butler kick)
Det — Sanders 2 run (Hanson kick)
Det — FG Hanson 25
Chi — FG Butler 39
Det — Sanders 29 run (Hanson kick)
Chi — Kramer 1 run (Butler kick)
Det — Moore 11 pass from Majkowski (Hanson kick)

GREEN BAY 31, CLEVELAND 20—at Cleveland Stadium, attendance 55,388. Brett Favre threw 3 touchdown passes and ran for another in the Packers' victory. Favre teamed with three different receivers for scores in the first half as Green Bay built a 21-3 lead at the intermission. His 4-yard touchdown run with 8:23 remaining in the game gave the Packers an insurmountable 31-13 advantage. Vinny Testaverde came off the bench to lead the slumping Browns to a pair of fourth-quarter touchdowns, but also threw a costly interception that Green Bay safety LeRoy Butler returned 76 yards to set up Favre's touchdown run. Testaverde replaced rookie Eric Zeier in the third quarter and completed 16 of 22 passes for 244 yards and 2 touchdowns. Favre was 23 of 29 for 210 yards for the Packers.

Green Bay	7	14	3	7	—	31
Cleveland	3	0	3	14	—	20

Cleve — FG Stover 46
GB — Levens 6 pass from Favre (Jacke kick)
GB — Chmura 3 pass from Favre (Jacke kick)
GB — Morgan 13 pass from Favre (Jacke kick)
Cleve — FG Stover 38
GB — FG Jacke 28
Cleve — Jackson 8 pass from Testaverde (Stover kick)
GB — Favre 4 run (Jacke kick)
Cleve — Jackson 37 pass from Testaverde (Stover kick)

INDIANAPOLIS 24, NEW ENGLAND 10—at Foxboro Stadium, attendance 59,544. The Colts scored on three consecutive possessions in the second quarter, then relied on a stingy defense to stop the Patriots. Jim Harbaugh's 3-yard touchdown pass to tight end Ken Dilger capped an 80-yard drive that gave Indianapolis a 7-3 lead 5:13 into the second quarter. Twenty-one seconds later, linebacker Quentin Coryatt recovered New England tight end Ben Coates's fumble at the Patriots' 46-yard line, and the Colts converted that into a 36-yard field goal by Cary Blanchard. Marshall Faulk then capped the scoring spree, 1:20 before halftime, with a 10-yard touchdown run that increased Indianapolis's advantage to 17-3. The Colts' defense limited New England to only 14 first downs and 202 total yards. Patriots quarterback Drew Bledsoe completed 20 of 39 passes for 180 yards, but was sacked 5 times and constantly harassed. Harbaugh was 20 of 26 for 232 yards and 2 touchdowns for Indianapolis. Faulk rushed 24 times for 96 yards and caught 8 passes for 71 yards.

Indianapolis	0	17	0	7	—	24
New England	3	0	7	0	—	10

NE — FG Bahr 41
Ind — Dilger 3 pass from Harbaugh (Blanchard kick)
Ind — FG Blanchard 36
Ind — Faulk 10 run (Blanchard kick)
NE — Martin 2 run (Bahr kick)
Ind — Turner 14 pass from Harbaugh (Blanchard kick)

TAMPA BAY 17, JACKSONVILLE 16—at Tampa Stadium, attendance 71,629. Errict Rhett ran for 2 touchdowns, and the Buccaneers held on to win when the Jaguars' 2-point conversion attempt failed with 37 seconds left. Rhett rushed for 100 yards on 24 carries and broke a 10-10 tie with a 6-yard touchdown run 6:49 into the fourth quarter. But in the closing minutes, Jacksonville drove from its own 4-yard line to the end zone on Steve Beuerlein's 12-yard touchdown pass to tight end Pete Mitchell. The Jaguars went for the win, but Beuerlein's pass to Jimmy Smith was caught out of bounds. Jacksonville still had another chance after recovering the ensuing onside kick, but cornerback Martin Mayhew intercepted a pass from Beuerlein to secure the victory. Beuerlein replaced injured starting quarterback Mark Brunell in the fourth quarter and completed 9 of 12 passes for 104 yards. Brunell was 15 of 21 for 169 yards. Mitchell caught 10 passes for 161 yards.

Jacksonville	0	0	3	13	—	16
Tampa Bay	3	7	0	7	—	17

TB — FG Husted 33
TB — Rhett 1 run (Husted kick)
Jack — FG Hollis 22
Jack — Brunell 9 run (Hollis kick)
TB — Rhett 6 run (Husted kick)
Jack — Mitchell 12 pass from Beuerlein (pass failed)

MINNESOTA 43, NEW ORLEANS 24—at Metrodome, attendance 58,108. Warren Moon threw 4 touchdown passes, and the Vikings scored on their first eight possessions to rout the Saints. Moon, who turned 39 the day before the game, completed 25 of 32 passes for 338 yards. He threw touchdown passes to three different receivers as Minnesota built a 30-7 halftime lead, then teamed with Cris Carter for the second time late in the third quarter to make it 36-10. Scottie Graham added a 2-yard touchdown run in the fourth quarter and Fuad Reveiz kicked 3 field goals for the Vikings, who amassed 544 total yards. Carter caught 12 passes for 137 yards, and Qadry Ismail had 5 receptions for 142 yards, including a 77-yard touchdown. Jim Everett passed for 335 yards and 3 touchdowns for New Orleans, though most of New Orleans's offense came long after the issue had been decided. Quinn Early caught 9 passes for 150 yards and 2 touchdowns.

New Orleans	0	7	3	14	—	24
Minnesota	14	16	6	7	—	43

Minn — Carter 15 pass from Moon (Reveiz kick)
Minn — Lee 2 pass from Moon (Reveiz kick)
Minn — FG Reveiz 37
Minn — FG Reveiz 20
NO — Early 13 pass from Everett (Brien kick)
Minn — Ismail 77 pass from Moon (Reveiz kick)
Minn — FG Reveiz 19
NO — FG Brien 30
Minn — Carter 20 pass from Moon (pass failed)
Minn — Graham 2 run (Reveiz kick)
NO — Walls 2 pass from Everett (I. Smith pass from Everett)
NO — Early 47 pass from Everett (pass failed)

PHILADELPHIA 28, N.Y. GIANTS 19—at Veterans Stadium, attendance 63,562. Ricky Watters had 2 short touchdown runs, and Rodney Peete threw 2 touchdown passes to Fred Barnett to pace the Eagles to their sixth victory in seven games. Peete's 13-yard touchdown pass to Barnett 5:35 into the first quarter tied the game at 7-7, and Philadelphia then took control by converting a pair of Giants turnovers into touchdowns. First, cornerback Mark McMillian's interception and 7-yard return set up Watters's 3-yard touchdown run with 5:49 left in the opening period. Then in the second quarter, linebacker Kurt Gouveia recovered Tyrone Wheatley's fumble on New York's 4-yard line, and three plays later Peete threw 4 yards to Barnett to make it 21-7 8:29 before halftime. Watters's second touchdown, on a 1-yard run, gave the Eagles a 28-10 lead in the third quarter. Philadelphia's defense forced 4 turnovers in all and recorded 8 sacks. Defensive end William Fuller had 2 sacks, forced a fumble, and recovered another. Wide receiver Thomas Lewis supplied most of the Giants' 225 total yards by catching 7 passes for 126 yards.

N.Y. Giants	7	0	3	9	—	19
Philadelphia	14	7	7	0	—	28

Giants— Lewis 46 pass from Brown (Daluiso kick)
Phil — Barnett 13 pass from Peete (Anderson kick)
Phil — Watters 3 run (Anderson kick)
Phil — Barnett 4 pass from Peete (Anderson kick)
Giants— FG Daluiso 44
Phil — Watters 1 run (Anderson kick)
Giants— Hampton 1 run (Daluiso kick)
Giants— Safety, Strahan blocked punt out of end zone

PITTSBURGH 49, CINCINNATI 31—at Riverfront Stadium, attendance 54,636. Neil O'Donnell passed for 377 yards and 3 touchdowns, and the Steelers wiped out an 18-point third-quarter deficit by exploding for 36 second-half points to beat the Bengals. Cincinnati, which upset Pittsburgh 27-9 earlier in the season, moved the ball at will while building a 31-13 advantage. Quarterback Jeff Blake threw touchdown passes to three different receivers, and Carl Pickens was en route to an 8-catch, 129-yard day. But after Blake's final touchdown pass, a 20-yarder to Tony McGee with 10:31 left in the third quarter, the Steelers turned things around. They took the ensuing kickoff and drove 62 yards, capping the march on Byron (Bam) Morris's 1-yard touchdown run at the 6:46 mark. The next time Pittsburgh had the ball, it drove 83 yards to a touchdown and pulled within 31-28 on O'Donnell's 15-yard touchdown pass to Andre Hastings and Erric Pegram's 2-point conversion run. Thirty-five seconds into the fourth quarter, O'Donnell teamed with backup quarterback Kordell Stewart, who lined up as a wide receiver, on a 71-yard touchdown bomb to give the Steelers their first lead of the game. Morris secured the victory with 2 subsequent touchdown runs. O'Donnell completed 11 of 15 passes for 212 yards in the second half and finished 24 of 31. Morris gained 101 yards on 16 carries as Pittsburgh amassed a whopping 556 total yards against the league's worst-ranked defense.

Pittsburgh	3	10	15	21	—	49
Cincinnati	14	10	7	0	—	31

Cin — Scott 4 pass from Blake (Pelfrey kick)
Pitt — FG N. Johnson 50
Cin — Blake 1 run (Pelfrey kick)
Cin — Pickens 1 pass from Blake (Pelfrey kick)
Pitt — Mills 42 pass from O'Donnell (N. Johnson kick)
Cin — FG Pelfrey 27
Pitt — FG N. Johnson 26
Cin — McGee 20 pass from Blake (Pelfrey kick)
Pitt — Morris 1 run (N. Johnson kick)
Pitt — Hastings 15 pass from O'Donnell (Pegram run)
Pitt — Stewart 71 pass from O'Donnell (N. Johnson kick)
Pitt — Morris 3 run (N. Johnson kick)
Pitt — Morris 8 run (N. Johnson kick)

ATLANTA 31, ST. LOUIS 6—at Georgia Dome, attendance 46,309. Jeff George threw 4 touchdown passes, and the Falcons remained tied for first place in the NFC West by sending the Rams to their fifth loss in seven games. George completed 20 of 34 passes for 352 yards and teamed with wide receiver Terance Mathis on 3 of his touchdown passes. Mathis caught 10 passes for 184 yards in all, while running back Craig Heyward added 117 yards on the ground. Atlanta's defense forced 3 St. Louis turnovers. Chris Miller passed for 236 yards and 1 touchdown for St. Louis.

St. Louis	0	6	0	0	—	6
Atlanta	7	7	10	7	—	31

Atl — Mathis 18 pass from George (Andersen kick)
Atl — Mathis 17 pass from George (Andersen kick)
StL — Drayton 2 pass from Miller (pass failed)
Atl — Metcalf 41 pass from George (Andersen kick)
Atl — FG Andersen 23
Atl — Mathis 39 pass from George (Andersen kick)

DENVER 30, SAN DIEGO 27—at Denver Mile High Stadium, attendance 74,681. Jason Elam's 32-yard field goal with two seconds remaining won it for the Broncos. With the score tied 27-27 and 3:43 left in the game, Denver took over possession at its own 33-yard line. Rookie running back Terrell Davis positioned Elam for the winning kick by carrying on six consecutive plays for 53 yards. Davis finished the game with 176 yards on 30 attempts. That bailed out the Broncos, who failed to protect a 21-0 first-quarter lead. Andre Coleman's 91-yard kickoff return helped spark the Chargers' comeback. Stan Humphries threw a 12-yard touchdown pass to running back Ronnie Harmon on the first play of the fourth quarter, and Rodney Culver's 4-yard touchdown run tied it with 9:57 to play. Humphries completed 17 of 28 passes for 206 yards. John Elway was 19 of 34 for 190 yards and 2 touchdowns for the Broncos, who amassed 463 total yards. Tight end Shannon Sharpe caught 8 passes for 137 yards, including 1 touchdown.

San Diego	7	3	3	14	—	27
Denver	21	6	0	3	—	30

Den — Davis 2 run (Elam kick)
Den — Miller 34 pass from Elway (Elam kick)
Den — Sharpe 4 pass from Elway (Elam kick)
SD — Coleman 91 kickoff return (Carney kick)
Den — FG Elam 20
SD — FG Carney 29
Den — FG Elam 35
SD — FG Carney 32
SD — Harmon 12 pass from Humphries (Carney kick)
SD — Culver 4 run (Carney kick)
Den — FG Elam 32

SEATTLE 27, WASHINGTON 20—at RFK Stadium, attendance 51,298. Chris Warren rushed for 136 yards and 1 touchdown as the Seahawks won their third consecutive game. Warren rushed for 61 yards in the fourth quarter, and his 5-yard touchdown run with 7:46 to play gave Seattle its biggest lead of the game at 24-13. Safety Robert Blackmon set up that 2-play touchdown drive by intercepting Redskins quarterback Heath Shuler and returning the ball 14 yards to the 15. Earlier in the game, Blackmon intercepted Washington's Gus Frerotte. The Seahawks, who entered the week with a league-worst turnover differential of minus-14, intercepted 4 passes and recovered 1 fumble. Starting quarterback Frerotte passed for 200 yards and 1 touchdown for the Redskins, but completed only 14 of 32 attempts and was intercepted twice. Shuler replaced him in the fourth quarter and was 10 of 12 for 98 yards and 1 touchdown, but he also was intercepted twice. Rick Mirer threw for 185 yards and 2 touchdowns for Seattle.

Seattle	3	7	7	10	—	27
Washington	3	7	0	10	—	20

Sea — FG Peterson 39
Wash — FG Murray 18
Sea — Galloway 59 pass from Mirer (Peterson kick)
Wash — Truitt 18 pass from Frerotte (Murray kick)
Sea — Crumpler 10 pass from Mirer (Peterson kick)
Wash — FG Murray 48
Sea — Warren 5 run (Peterson kick)
Sea — FG Peterson 47
Wash — Westbrook 5 pass from Shuler (Murray kick)

SUNDAY NIGHT, NOVEMBER 19

KANSAS CITY 20, HOUSTON 13—at Arrowhead Stadium, attendance 77,576. Safety Mark Collins scooped up a fumble and raced 34 yards for a touchdown with 15 seconds left to give the Chiefs a stunning victory. The Oilers apparently had forced the overtime period after Chris Chandler threw a fourth-and-25, 40-yard touchdown pass to Chris Sanders with 1:46 remaining, and then their defense forced a punt. But former Kansas City running back Todd McNair fumbled, and the Chiefs improved to 10-1 for the first time in franchise history. Kansas City won despite managing only 11 first downs and 181 yards total offense. The Chiefs' defense set up all 20 points with 3 interceptions and the decisive fumble recovery.

Houston	0	6	0	7	—	13
Kansas City	3	7	0	10	—	20

KC — FG Elliott 27
KC — Slaughter 3 pass from Bono (Elliott kick)
Hou — Sanders 1 pass from Chandler (pass failed)
KC — FG Elliott 21
Hou — Sanders 40 pass from Chandler (Del Greco kick)
KC — Collins 34 fumble return (Elliott kick)

MONDAY, NOVEMBER 20

SAN FRANCISCO 44, MIAMI 20—at Joe Robbie Stadium, attendance 73,080. Elvis Grbac threw 4 touchdown passes to lead the 49ers' rout of the Dolphins. Grbac, in the final week of a five-game stint as San Francisco's starting quarterback in place of injured Steve Young, completed 31 of 41 passes for 382 yards. His 47-yard touchdown pass to Jerry Rice broke a 7-7 tie in the second quarter and gave the 49ers the lead for good, and his 23-yard strike to tight end Brent Jones nine seconds before halftime broke open the game at 24-7. Rice and Jones also caught touchdown passes in the second half to keep Miami from narrowing its deficit. Rice finished with 8 catches for 149 yards. Running back Derek Loville rushed for 51 yards and caught 8 passes for 78 yards. Dolphins quarterback Dan Marino completed 23 of 38 passes for 255 yards and 2 touchdowns, but was let down by a running game that produced only 52 yards and a defense that allowed 497 total yards.

San Francisco	7	17	14	6	—	44
Miami	0	7	13	0	—	20

SF — Loville 3 run (Wilkins kick)
Mia — Clark 42 pass from Marino (Stoyanovich kick)
SF — Rice 47 pass from Grbac (Wilkins kick)
SF — FG Wilkins 33
SF — Jones 23 pass from Grbac (Wilkins kick)
SF — Jones 2 pass from Grbac (Wilkins kick)
Mia — Parmalee 3 run (pass failed)
SF — Rice 46 pass from Grbac (Wilkins kick)
Mia — McDuffie 4 pass from Marino (Stoyanovich kick)
SF — FG Wilkins 31
SF — FG Wilkins 20

THIRTEENTH WEEK SUMMARIES

AMERICAN FOOTBALL CONFERENCE

Eastern Division	**W**	**L**	**T**	**Pct.**	**Pts.**	**OP**
Buffalo	8	4	0	.667	248	233
Indianapolis	7	5	0	.583	246	238
Miami	6	6	0	.500	303	261
New England	5	7	0	.417	212	267
N.Y. Jets	3	9	0	.250	179	295
Central Division						
Pittsburgh	8	4	0	.667	297	259
Cincinnati	5	7	0	.417	286	290
Houston	5	7	0	.417	273	256
Cleveland	4	8	0	.333	218	264
Jacksonville	3	9	0	.250	197	267
Western Division						
Kansas City	10	2	0	.833	277	185
Oakland	8	4	0	.667	277	199
Denver	6	6	0	.500	282	243
San Diego	5	7	0	.417	208	244
Seattle	5	7	0	.417	259	289

NATIONAL FOOTBALL CONFERENCE

Eastern Division	**W**	**L**	**T**	**Pct.**	**Pts.**	**OP**
Dallas	10	2	0	.833	343	214
Philadelphia	8	4	0	.667	249	255
Arizona	4	8	0	.333	211	326
N.Y. Giants	3	9	0	.250	223	273
Washington	3	9	0	.250	234	282
Central Division						
Green Bay	8	4	0	.667	312	249
Chicago	7	5	0	.583	324	293
Detroit	6	6	0	.500	304	302
Minnesota	6	6	0	.500	300	293
Tampa Bay	6	6	0	.500	188	226
Western Division						
San Francisco	8	4	0	.667	335	173
Atlanta	7	5	0	.583	278	266
St. Louis	6	6	0	.500	214	277
Carolina	5	7	0	.417	228	247
New Orleans	5	7	0	.417	239	278

THURSDAY, NOVEMBER 23

DALLAS 24, KANSAS CITY 12—at Texas Stadium, attendance 64,901. Troy Aikman threw 2 touchdown passes to lead the Cowboys over the Chiefs in a Thanksgiving Day showdown between the teams with the league's best records. Dallas struck quickly, building a 14-0 lead in the first quarter before Kansas City could record a first down. Aikman, who threw a 33-yard touchdown pass to Michael Irvin in the final minute of the first period, also teamed with tight end Jay Novacek on a 33-yard score 8:57 into the second half to put the Cowboys ahead 21-6. The Chiefs pulled within 21-12 late in the third quarter and drove deep into Dallas's territory early in the fourth, but defensive end Tony Tolbert sacked quarterback Steve Bono, forcing a fumble that linebacker Darrin Smith recovered and returned 63 yards. That set up a short field goal by Chris Boniol to give the Cowboys their final margin of victory. Aikman finished with 21 completions in 29 attempts for 192 yards. Irvin caught 11 passes for 121 yards. Bono passed for 276 yards for Kansas City.

Kansas City	0	6	6	0	—	12
Dallas	14	0	7	3	—	24

Dall — E. Smith 15 run (Boniol kick)
Dall — Irvin 33 pass from Aikman (Boniol kick)
KC — FG Elliott 34
KC — FG Elliott 37
Dall — Novacek 33 pass from Aikman (Boniol kick)
KC — Dawson 45 pass from Bono (pass failed)
Dall — FG Boniol 20

DETROIT 44, MINNESOTA 38—at Pontiac Silverdome, attendance 74,559. Scott Mitchell passed for a club-record 410 yards and 4 touchdowns as the Lions outlasted the Vikings in a wild game on Thanksgiving Day. Mitchell completed 30 of 45 passes and broke Pro Football Hall of Fame member Bobby Layne's 45-year-old Detroit record for yards in a game. He threw 3 touchdown passes as the Lions built a 21-7 lead in the first half, then, after Minnesota rallied to lead 31-27 in the second half, put the Lions ahead for good with a 27-yard touchdown pass to Herman Moore with 3:47 to go in the third quarter. Barry Sanders's 50-yard touchdown run with 5:18 left in the game turned out to be the game winner, although the outcome was in doubt until Warren Moon's desperation pass in the end zone was intercepted on the final play of the game. The teams combined to account for 919 total yards, 534 of them from the Lions. Sanders, limited to 1 yard in the first half, finished with 138 yards on 24 carries. Detroit's Brett Perriman caught a club-record-tying 12 passes for 153 yards and 2 touchdowns, while Moore had 8 receptions for 127 yards, and Johnnie Morton added 7 catches for 102 yards. Moon completed 30 of 47 passes for 384 yards for Minnesota but was given little help by a running game that managed only 34 yards on 15 attempts. Vikings wide receiver Jake Reed had 149 yards on 6 catches.

Minnesota	7	21	3	7	—	38
Detroit	14	10	10	10	—	44

Det — Perriman 2 pass from Mitchell (Hanson kick)
Det — Perriman 20 pass from Mitchell (Hanson kick)
Minn — Reed 55 pass from Moon (Reveiz kick)
Det — Morton 16 pass from Mitchell (Hanson kick)
Minn — Palmer 74 punt return (Reveiz kick)
Minn — O. Thomas 17 fumble return (Reveiz kick)
Det — FG Hanson 32
Minn — Carter 10 pass from Moon (Reveiz kick)
Minn — FG Reveiz 49
Det — FG Hanson 40
Det — Moore 27 pass from Mitchell (Hanson kick)
Det — Sanders 50 run (Hanson kick)

Minn — Carter 7 pass from Moon (Reveiz kick)
Det — FG Hanson 39

SUNDAY, NOVEMBER 26

ARIZONA 40, ATLANTA 37—at Sun Devil Stadium, attendance 35,147. Greg Davis's 28-yard field goal 1:43 into overtime capped a wild finish and snapped the Cardinals' three-game losing streak. The winning kick came on the first play after Arizona cornerback Aeneas Williams stripped Falcons punter Dan Stryzinski of the ball, and defensive end Eric England recovered at the 10. Stryzinski had to run after fielding a poor snap on the punt. Turnovers (there were 8 in all, 4 by each team) also were prominent at the end of regulation. Atlanta extended its 4-point lead late in the game after cornerback D.J. Johnson intercepted a pass to set up Morten Andersen's 21-yard field goal with 5:07 to play. The Cardinals were forced to punt following their next possession, but Eric Metcalf muffed the kick and Arizona's Marcus Dowdell recovered at the Falcons' 19-yard line. Five plays later, Dave Krieg's 2-yard touchdown pass to tight end Oscar McBride tied the game at 37-37 with 1:57 to go in the fourth quarter. Linebacker Seth Joyner then intercepted a pass from Jeff George, and the Cardinals had a chance to win the game on the last play of regulation, but Davis missed a 45-yard field-goal try. Arizona amassed 513 total yards in the game, a dramatic turnaround from the paltry 96 they managed in a loss to the expansion Panthers the previous week. Krieg completed 27 of 43 passes for 413 yards and 4 touchdowns, while running back Larry Centers caught 7 passes for 101 yards and rushed for 62 yards. Rob Moore caught 8 passes for 121 yards. George passed for 280 yards and 3 touchdowns for Atlanta.

Atlanta	0	20	7	10	0	—	37
Arizona	6	14	7	10	3	—	40

Ariz — FG Davis 44
Ariz — FG Davis 29
Atl — Metcalf 5 pass from George (kick blocked)
Atl — Tuggle 27 interception return (Andersen kick)
Atl — Preston 61 pass from George (Andersen kick)
Ariz — Moore 18 pass from Krieg (Davis kick)
Ariz — Edwards 28 pass from Krieg (Davis kick)
Atl — Mathis 54 pass from George (Andersen kick)
Ariz — Gaines 22 pass from Krieg (Davis kick)
Ariz — FG Davis 23
Atl — J. Anderson 3 run (Andersen kick)
Atl — FG Andersen 21
Ariz — McBride 2 pass from Krieg (Davis kick)
Ariz — FG Davis 28

CHICAGO 27, N.Y. GIANTS 24—at Giants Stadium, attendance 70,015. Kevin Butler's 37-yard field goal with seven seconds to go gave the Bears the victory. With the score tied at 24-24, the Giants drove from their 21-yard line to Chicago's 32 late in the game. But on fourth down, New York eschewed a 49-yard field-goal attempt into the wind, and Dave Brown's pass to tight end Howard Cross was knocked away by Bears cornerback Keshon Johnson. Chicago then marched 48 yards in eight plays to the winning score. Quarterback Erik Kramer completed 4 of 5 passes on the winning drive. He finished 25 of 38 for 268 yards and 2 touchdowns. Rashaan Salaam (76 yards) and Robert Green (59 yards) combined to rush for 135 yards for the Bears, who outgained the Giants 409-338. Rodney Hampton had 2 short touchdown runs for New York.

Chicago	7	7	3	10	—	27
N.Y. Giants	7	7	3	7	—	24

Chi — Timpson 6 run (Butler kick)
Giants— Marshall 5 pass from Brown (Daluiso kick)
Giants— Hampton 1 run (Daluiso kick)
Chi — Graham 6 pass from Kramer (Butler kick)
Giants— FG Daluiso 22
Chi — FG Butler 34
Chi — Timpson 9 pass from Kramer (Butler kick)
Giants— Hampton 2 run (Daluiso kick)
Chi — FG Butler 37

CINCINNATI 17, JACKSONVILLE 13—at Jacksonville Municipal Stadium, attendance 68,249. Jeff Blake's 5-yard touchdown pass to Carl Pickens with 17 seconds remaining lifted the Bengals to the victory. The Jaguars had taken a 13-10 lead on Mike Hollis's 39-yard field goal with 3:19 left. But Cincinnati began the winning drive on its own 12-yard line. On third-and-15 from the 47, Jacksonville safety Travis Davis was whistled for a 34-yard pass interference penalty that moved the ball to the Jaguars' 19. Pickens, who entered the game as the AFC's leading receiver but had not caught a pass to that point, caught a 14-yard pass down to the 5, and two plays later teamed with Blake on the winning score.

Cincinnati	0	7	0	10	—	17
Jacksonville	0	7	3	3	—	13

Cin — Blake 8 run (Pelfrey kick)
Jack — J. Smith 31 pass from Beuerlein (Hollis kick)
Jack — FG Hollis 36
Cin — FG Pelfrey 31
Jack — FG Hollis 39
Cin — Pickens 5 pass from Blake (Pelfrey kick)

HOUSTON 42, DENVER 33—at Astrodome, attendance 36,113. Chris Chandler threw 3 touchdown passes and Rodney Thomas rushed for 104 yards as the Oilers upset the Broncos. Houston, which entered the game with the NFL's twenty-fourth-ranked offense, erupted for 6 touchdowns and 448 total yards. Chandler completed 18 of 26 passes for 280 yards. His 36-yard touchdown pass to Chris Sanders late in the first quarter gave the Oilers the lead for good at 14-10, and his 2 touchdown passes sandwiched around halftime helped put the game out of reach. First, he teamed with Sanders again on a 35-yard strike 80 seconds before intermission to give Houston a 28-17 lead, and then marched the Oilers 72 yards in 12 plays following the second-half kickoff, capping the drive with a 12-yard touchdown pass to Haywood Jeffires to make it 35-17. Denver tried to rally behind the passing of John Elway, who completed 27 of 41 passes for 332 yards and 2 touchdowns, but could pull no closer than 8 points. Terrell Davis ran for 110 yards on 19 carries as the Broncos piled up 472 total yards. For Houston, Rodney Thomas rushed for 104 yards on only 13 carries, one a 74-yard touchdown run in the first quarter. Sanders caught 5 passes for 147 yards.

Denver	10	7	7	9	—	33
Houston	14	14	7	7	—	42

Den — FG Elam 56
Hou — Thomas 74 run (Del Greco kick)
Den — Miller 50 pass from Elway (Elam kick)
Hou — Sanders 36 pass from Chandler (Del Greco kick)
Hou — Butts 1 run (Del Greco kick)
Den — T. Davis 60 run (Elam kick)
Hou — Sanders 35 pass from Chandler (Del Greco kick)
Hou — Jeffires 12 pass from Chandler (Del Greco kick)
Den — Craver 1 run (Elam kick)
Den — FG Elam 35
Hou — Butts 5 run (Del Greco kick)
Den — Miller 35 pass from Elway (pass failed)

INDIANAPOLIS 36, MIAMI 28—at RCA Dome, attendance 60,414. Jim Harbaugh threw 3 touchdown passes as the Colts handed the Dolphins their third consecutive defeat and their sixth loss in eight games. Indianapolis, which swept the season series from Miami for the first time since 1988, scored on its first four possessions to build a 24-point lead midway through the second quarter. Harbaugh completed all 5 of his attempts on the game's opening drive, capping the 77-yard march with a 5-yard touchdown pass to Sean Dawkins 6:11 into the game. Four minutes and 34 seconds later, after linebacker Quentin Coryatt recovered Dan Marino's fumble at the Dolphins' 37-yard line, Harbaugh teamed with Aaron Bailey on a 34-yard touchdown pass to increase the advantage to 14-0. Harbaugh's third touchdown pass, of 7 yards to running back Marshall Faulk 7:40 before halftime, made it 24-0. Miami rallied behind 4 touchdown passes from Dan Marino, but could get no closer than the final score. Marino, who completed 23 of 36 passes for 254 yards, broke Fran Tarkenton's NFL record of 342 career touchdown passes with a 6-yard toss to running back Keith Byars with 1:06 to go in the second quarter. It was the third time this season that Marino broke a major passing record (he'd already set new standards for career yards and attempts), but each time the Dolphins lost. Miami's Bernie Parmalee rushed for 102 yards on 20 carries. Harbaugh completed 12 of 18 passes for 180 yards for Indianapolis, and also ran for 47 yards.

Miami	0	6	8	14	—	28
Indianapolis	14	10	2	10	—	36

Ind — Dawkins 5 pass from Harbaugh (Blanchard kick)
Ind — Bailey 34 pass from Harbaugh (Blanchard kick)
Ind — FG Blanchard 29
Ind — Faulk 7 pass from Harbaugh (Blanchard kick)
Mia — Byars 6 pass from Marino (pass failed)
Mia — McDuffie 5 pass from Marino (Green pass from Marino)
Ind — Safety, Bennett sacked Marino in end zone
Ind — FG Blanchard 31
Mia — Fryar 5 pass from Marino (pass failed)
Ind — Harbaugh 1 run (Blanchard kick)
Mia — McDuffie 19 pass from Marino (McDuffie pass from Marino)

NEW ENGLAND 35, BUFFALO 25—at Rich Stadium, attendance 69,384. The Patriots rallied from a 12-point deficit in the fourth quarter to snap the Bills' three-game winning streak. Jim Kelly threw 1 touchdown pass, Thurman Thomas ran for 1 touchdown, and linebacker Cornelius Bennett returned an interception 69 yards for another score as Buffalo built a 25-13 advantage through three quarters. But New England quarterback Drew Bledsoe pulled his team within 25-20 with a 4-yard touchdown pass to tight end Ben Coates on the first play of the fourth quarter, then capped an 80-yard drive with a 15-yard touchdown pass to Coates to give the Patriots a 28-25 lead with 1:23 left in the game. Three plays later, linebacker Willie McGinest hit Kelly as he threw, and linebacker Chris Slade intercepted the ball and returned it 27 yards for the clinching touchdown with 57 seconds to go. Bledsoe completed 21 of 45 passes for 263 yards, with 3 touchdowns and 3 interceptions, for the Patriots, who amassed 430 total yards. Rookie Curtis Martin rushed for 148 yards on 27 carries.

New England	3	7	3	22	—	35
Buffalo	3	16	6	0	—	25

Buff — FG Christie 51
NE — FG Bahr 29
NE — Coates 6 pass from Bledsoe (Bahr kick)
Buff — Brooks 32 pass from Kelly (kick blocked)
Buff — FG Christie 48
Buff — Bennett 69 interception return (Christie kick)
NE — FG Bahr 43
Buff — Thomas 1 run (run failed)
NE — Coates 4 pass from Bledsoe (Bahr kick)
NE — Coates 15 pass from Bledsoe (Martin pass from Bledsoe)
NE — Slade 27 interception return (Bahr kick)

N.Y. JETS 16, SEATTLE 10—at Kingdome, attendance 41,160. Adrian Murrell rushed for a career-high 116 yards, and the Jets snapped a three-game losing streak while halting the Seahawks' three-game winning streak. Murrell carried 24 times and scored New York's lone touchdown on a 2-yard run 3:02 into the game. That capped a 26-yard touchdown drive set up when Lonnie Young recovered Seattle quarterback Rick Mirer's fumbled snap. The Seahawks turned over the ball on each of their first three possessions (Jets cornerback Aaron Glenn had an interception and a fumble recovery) and managed only 192 total yards all afternoon. Still, they trimmed a 13-0 halftime deficit to 13-10 in the third quarter when Mirer threw a 6-yard touchdown pass to Mack Strong and Todd Peterson kicked a 42-yard field goal. But the Jets consumed 7:21 of the fourth quarter on a 13-play drive to Nick Lowery's third field goal, from 41 yards with 6:15 to play, and held on for their first victory on the road this season.

N.Y. Jets	7	6	0	3	—	16
Seattle	0	0	10	0	—	10

Jets — Murrell 2 run (Lowery kick)
Jets — FG Lowery 38
Jets — FG Lowery 33
Sea — Strong 6 pass from Mirer (Peterson kick)
Sea — FG Peterson 42
Jets — FG Lowery 41

PHILADELPHIA 14, WASHINGTON 7—at RFK Stadium, attendance 50,539. Ricky Watters rushed for 124 yards and 2 touchdowns to lead the Eagles to their seventh victory in the last eight games. Watters ran 9 yards for a touchdown late in the first quarter, then capped the winning 75-yard drive in the fourth quarter by rushing 1 yard for a touchdown with 11:28 left in the game. Eagles quarterback Rodney Peete, who was benched for two series in the third quarter, returned to spark the winning drive by completing all 3 of his attempts on the march for 55 yards, including a 31-yard strike to Fred Barnett. In all, Peete completed 16 of 23 passes for 150 yards. Terry Allen ran 7 yards for 1 touchdown 38 seconds into the fourth quarter to account for the Redskins' lone score.

Philadelphia	6	0	0	8	—	14
Washington	0	0	0	7	—	7

Phil — Watters 9 run (kick failed)
Wash — Allen 7 run (Murray kick)
Phil — Watters 1 run (Williams pass from Peete)

PITTSBURGH 20, CLEVELAND 17—at Cleveland Stadium, attendance 67,269. Neil O'Donnell passed for 251 yards and 1 touchdown to lead the Steelers to their fifth consecutive victory. Cornerback Willie Williams intercepted a pass and recovered a fumble on the Browns' first two offensive plays, helping Pittsburgh build a 10-point advantage 8:17 into the game. Cleveland rallied behind quarterback Vinny Testaverde, who passed for 1 touchdown and ran for another, the latter a 1-yard run to tie the game at 17 midway through the third quarter. But the Steelers countered with a 14-play, 70-yard drive to Norm Johnson's 27-yard field goal seven seconds into the fourth quarter, then dashed the Browns' comeback hopes with a 16-play drive that consumed the last 8:52 of the game. O'Donnell completed 21 of 30 passes, including 5 to wide receiver Yancey Thigpen for 106 yards.

Pittsburgh	10	7	0	3	—	20
Cleveland	0	10	7	0	—	17

Pitt — FG N. Johnson 33
Pitt — Bruener 12 pass from O'Donnell (N. Johnson kick)
Cleve — FG Stover 44
Pitt — Morris 1 run (N. Johnson kick)
Cleve — Jackson 11 pass from Testaverde (Stover kick)
Cleve — Testaverde 1 run (Stover kick)
Pitt — FG N. Johnson 27

SAN FRANCISCO 41, ST. LOUIS 13—at 3Com Park, attendance 66,049. Quarterback Steve Young, out for five weeks with an injured shoulder, returned to the lineup and threw 3 touchdown passes as the 49ers overwhelmed the Rams for the second time this season. San Francisco, which beat St. Louis 44-10 last month, extended its winning streak over the Rams to 11 games. Young, two weeks removed from arthroscopic surgery, overcame a shaky start to complete 21 of 32 passes for 226 yards before coming out of the game one play into the fourth quarter. Young's first pass was intercepted, and the 49ers failed to make a first down on their first four possessions. But after spotting St. Louis a 7-0 lead, San Francisco roared back to lead 28-7 at halftime after Young threw 2 touchdown passes to rookie J.J. Stokes, Derek Loville ran for a touchdown, and cornerback Eric Davis returned an interception 86 yards for a score just 49 seconds before the intermission. Young's third touchdown pass, a 2-yard strike to Jerry Rice, came 8:18 into the second half and increased the advantage to 35-7. The 49ers intercepted St. Louis quarterbacks Chris Miller and Mark Rypien 4 times (cornerback Tyronne Drakeford had 2 thefts), which led to 24 points.

St. Louis	7	0	6	0	—	13
San Francisco	7	21	7	6	—	41

StL — Kinchen 2 pass from Miller (Biasucci kick)
SF — Stokes 16 pass from Young (Wilkins kick)
SF — Stokes 18 pass from Young (Wilkins kick)
SF — Loville 2 run (Wilkins kick)
SF — Davis 86 interception return (Wilkins kick)
SF — Rice 2 pass from Young (Wilkins kick)
StL — Bruce 21 pass from Rypien (kick blocked)
SF — FG Wilkins 35
SF — FG Wilkins 19

GREEN BAY 35, TAMPA BAY 13—at Lambeau Field, attendance 59,218. Brett Favre passed for 267 yards and 3 touchdowns, and the Packers stayed atop the NFC Central Division by beating the Buccaneers. After Tampa Bay took its only lead of the game at 10-7 on Michael Husted's 19-yard field goal with 3:29 to go in the first half, it took Green Bay only three plays to counter, the last a 54-yard touchdown pass from Favre to Robert Brooks with 2:12 remaining. Moments later, an 18-yard punt positioned the Packers for a 36-yard touchdown drive, with Dorsey Levens's 1-yard run making it 21-10 38 seconds before halftime. Levens ran for another touchdown in the final minute of the third quarter to increase Green Bay's lead to 28-13, and Favre added a touchdown pass to Brooks midway through the fourth quarter. Brooks finished with 6 catches for 114 yards. Trent Dilfer completed 28 of 49 passes for 324 yards for the Buccaneers, but Errict Rhett, the NFC's third-leading rusher entering the game, was limited to minus-1 yard on 13 carries. Tampa Bay tight end Jackie Harris caught 10 passes for 122 yards.

Tampa Bay	0	10	3	0	—	13
Green Bay	7	14	7	7	—	35

GB — Ingram 9 pass from Favre (Jacke kick)
TB — Rhett 1 run (Husted kick)
TB — FG Husted 19
GB — Brooks 54 pass from Favre (Jacke kick)
GB — Levens 1 run (Jacke kick)
TB — FG Husted 48
GB — Levens 1 run (Jacke kick)
GB — Brooks 3 pass from Favre (Jacke kick)

SUNDAY NIGHT, NOVEMBER 26

NEW ORLEANS 34, CAROLINA 26—at Louisiana Superdome, attendance 39,580. Mario Bates ran for 2 touchdowns to help the Saints win for the fourth time in five games. Bates rushed for 71 yards on 19 carries as New Orleans amassed 180 yards on the ground against the Panthers' defense, which entered the game having allowed only 92 rushing yards per game. Carolina turned over the ball 6 times, but still managed to keep the game in reach, and pulled within 27-19 on Kerry Collins's 3-yard touchdown pass to Mark Carrier and a subsequent 2-point conversion pass to running back Bob Christian with one second left in the third quarter. But the Saints' Derek Brown ran 35 yards with 4:54 left in the game for the clinching touchdown. Collins's third touchdown pass of the game, a 60-yarder to Carrier, came with only 23 seconds left. Collins passed for 335 yards, but completed only 17 of 46 attempts and was intercepted 4 times. New Orleans cornerback Jimmy Spencer had 2 of the interceptions.

Carolina	3	8	8	7	—	26
New Orleans	7	10	10	7	—	34

Car — FG Kasay 22
NO — Bates 4 run (Brien kick)
NO — Early 27 pass from Everett (Brien kick)
Car — Green 60 pass from Collins (Rasby pass from Collins)
NO — FG Brien 45
NO — FG Brien 39
NO — Bates 6 run (Brien kick)
Car — Carrier 3 pass from Collins (Christian pass from Collins)
NO — Brown 35 run (Brien kick)
Car — Carrier 60 pass from Collins (Kasay kick)

MONDAY, NOVEMBER 27

SAN DIEGO 12, OAKLAND 6—at San Diego Jack Murphy Stadium, attendance 60,607. John Carney kicked 4 field goals as the defending AFC-champion Chargers kept their playoff hopes alive by beating the Raiders. San Diego's defense did the rest, limiting Oakland to only a pair of field goals and 285 total yards. Cornerback Dwayne Harper intercepted Oakland quarterback Vince Evans 3 times, the last coming with 56 seconds to play to seal the victory. Evans, playing in place of injured starter Jeff Hostetler, completed 17 of 32 passes for 192 yards, but turned over the ball 4 times. In addition to the interceptions, he lost a fumble in the fourth quarter when he was sacked by defensive end Chris Mims. That led to Carney's fourth field goal, from 38 yards with 4:02 to play. The Raiders could not advance the ball out of their own territory after that. Stan Humphries completed 24 of 34 passes for 236 yards for the Chargers. Harvey Williams ran for 101 yards on 20 carries for Oakland.

Oakland	3	0	0	3	—	6
San Diego	0	6	3	3	—	12

Oak — FG Jaeger 30
SD — FG Carney 39
SD — FG Carney 24
SD — FG Carney 28
Oak — FG Jaeger 26
SD — FG Carney 38

FOURTEENTH WEEK SUMMARIES

AMERICAN FOOTBALL CONFERENCE						
Eastern Division	**W**	**L**	**T**	**Pct.**	**Pts.**	**OP**
Buffalo	8	5	0	.615	265	260
Indianapolis	7	6	0	.538	256	251
Miami	7	6	0	.538	324	281
New England	5	8	0	.385	229	298
N.Y. Jets	3	10	0	.231	199	318
Central Division						
Pittsburgh	9	4	0	.692	318	266
Cincinnati	5	8	0	.385	296	314
Houston	5	8	0	.385	280	277
Cleveland	4	9	0	.308	231	295
Jacksonville	3	10	0	.231	220	298
Western Division						
Kansas City	11	2	0	.846	306	208
Oakland	8	5	0	.615	300	228
Denver	7	6	0	.538	313	266
San Diego	6	7	0	.462	239	257
Seattle	6	7	0	.462	285	303

NATIONAL FOOTBALL CONFERENCE						
Eastern Division	**W**	**L**	**T**	**Pct.**	**Pts.**	**OP**
Dallas	10	3	0	.769	360	238
Philadelphia	8	5	0	.615	263	281
Arizona	4	9	0	.308	217	336
N.Y. Giants	4	9	0	.308	233	279
Washington	4	9	0	.308	258	299
Central Division						
Green Bay	9	4	0	.692	336	259
Chicago	7	6	0	.538	331	320
Detroit	7	6	0	.538	331	309
Minnesota	7	6	0	.538	331	310
Tampa Bay	6	7	0	.462	205	257
Western Division						
San Francisco	9	4	0	.692	362	190
Atlanta	7	6	0	.538	298	287
St. Louis	7	6	0	.538	237	297
Carolina	6	7	0	.462	241	257
New Orleans	6	7	0	.462	270	295

THURSDAY, NOVEMBER 30

N.Y. GIANTS 10, ARIZONA 6—at Sun Devil Stadium, attendance 44,246. Dave Brown threw 1 touchdown pass, and the Giants turned back a last-gasp drive by the Cardinals to snap a four-game losing streak. New York trailed 6-3 until taking the second-half kickoff and marching 83 yards in 12 plays to Brown's 12-yard touchdown pass to Mike Sherrard 6:48 into the third quarter. Arizona had a chance to win the game after driving from its own 10-yard line beginning with 1:50 to play to the Giants' 8, where they had a first down in the closing seconds. But from there, Dave Krieg threw four consecutive incompletions, the last with 14 seconds remaining. The Cardinals finished with a sizable advantage in total yards (342-199), but were stymied by 8 penalties, 2 interceptions, and 1 lost fumble. Safety Vencie Glenn made the key play for New York, intercepting Stoney Case's pass at the Giants' 2 with 6:39 to play. Case was in the game because Krieg was hurt while being sacked on the drive. Krieg returned and finished with 22 completions in 37 attempts for 235 yards.

N.Y. Giants	0	3	7	0	—	10
Arizona	0	6	0	0	—	6

Ariz — FG Davis 44
Ariz — FG Davis 28
Giants— FG Daluiso 51
Giants— Sherrard 12 pass from Brown (Daluiso kick)

SUNDAY, DECEMBER 3

MIAMI 21, ATLANTA 20—at Joe Robbie Stadium, attendance 63,395. Dan Marino's 21-yard touchdown pass to Irving Fryar with 11 seconds remaining gave the Dolphins a dramatic victory over the Falcons. Miami trailed 20-9 early in the fourth quarter, but drove 80 yards to Bernie Parmalee's 3-yard touchdown run with 7:54 to play. After a 2-point conversion pass failed, the Dolphins still trailed 20-15. Late in the game, Atlanta marched to Miami's 28-yard line. But on third-and-1, Jeff George was stopped short of a first down on a quarterback sneak, and on fourth down, the Falcons passed up a field-goal try, only to see fullback Craig Heyward also fail to convert the first down. The Dolphins gained possession, and it took Marino 8 plays to cover the 72 yards to the winning touchdown. The key gain was Marino's 12-yard scramble to Atlanta's 21. The winning pass came on the next play. Marino finished with 35 completions in 50 attempts for 343 yards and 2 touchdowns. He passed for more than 300 yards for the fifty-second time in his career, breaking the NFL record he shared with Pro Football Hall of Fame quarterback Dan Fouts. Jeff George threw 2 touchdown passes for the Falcons.

Atlanta	7	7	0	6	—	20
Miami	3	6	0	12	—	21

Mia — FG Stoyanovich 42
Atl — Emanuel 1 pass from George (Andersen kick)
Atl — Metcalf 23 run (Andersen kick)
Mia — Clark 6 pass from Marino (pass failed)
Atl — Mathis 16 pass from George (pass failed)
Mia — Parmalee 3 run (pass failed)
Mia — Fryar 21 pass from Marino (pass failed)

GREEN BAY 24, CINCINNATI 10—at Lambeau Field, attendance 60,318. Brett Favre threw 3 touchdown passes, and the Packers moved closer to their first NFC Central Division title in 23 years by winning their fourth consecutive game. Favre, who completed 31 of 43 passes for 339 yards, has thrown 14 touchdown passes and only 1 interception in the winning streak. His 14-yard touchdown pass to running back Edgar Bennett with 5:48 to go in the third quarter broke a 10-10 tie, and his 8-yard touchdown pass to Mark Chmura in the first minute of the fourth quarter provided Green Bay's margin of victory. The Packers' defense took over from there and limited Cincinnati to only 12 first downs and 223 total yards.

Cincinnati	0	10	0	0	—	10
Green Bay	3	7	7	7	—	24

GB — FG Jacke 41
Cin — FG Pelfrey 28
Cin — Pickens 5 pass from Blake (Pelfrey kick)
GB — Ingram 13 pass from Favre (Jacke kick)
GB — Bennett 14 pass from Favre (Jacke kick)
GB — Chmura 8 pass from Favre (Jacke kick)

SAN DIEGO 31, CLEVELAND 13—at San Diego Jack Murphy Stadium, attendance 56,358. Rookie Aaron Hayden carried 32 times for 127 yards and 2 touchdowns as the Chargers sent the Browns reeling to their fifth consecutive defeat. Hayden, playing in place of injured Natrone Means, put San Diego ahead to stay with a 3-yard touchdown run 2:44 into the game. That came five plays after linebacker Lewis Bush recovered a fumble on the opening kickoff at Cleveland's 23-yard line. Hayden's second touchdown run came from 1 yard and capped an 80-yard drive that gave the Chargers a 17-3 lead just 41 seconds before halftime. Ahead 17-10 in the fourth quarter, San Diego put the game away with a 10-play, 96-yard drive on which quarterback Stan Humphries completed all 6 of his attempts for 78 yards. The touchdown came on his 25-yard pass to Tony Martin with seven minutes remaining. Humphries completed 18 of 25 passes in all for 230 yards. Martin had 9 receptions for 132 yards. Vinny Testaverde supplied most of the Browns' offense by completing 28 of 41 passes for 303 yards. Cleveland, considered a Super Bowl contender before the start of the season, had not won since owner Art Modell announced in November that he planned to move the team to Baltimore next season.

Cleveland	0	3	7	3	—	13
San Diego	7	10	0	14	—	31

SD — Hayden 3 run (Carney kick)
SD — FG Carney 31
Cleve — FG Stover 34
SD — Hayden 1 run (Carney kick)
Cleve — Jackson 28 pass from Testaverde (Stover kick)
SD — Martin 25 pass from Humphries (Carney kick)
SD — Fletcher 16 run (Carney kick)
Cleve — FG Stover 40

PITTSBURGH 21, HOUSTON 7—at Three Rivers Stadium, attendance 56,013. The Steelers won their sixth consecutive game to clinch their third AFC Central Division title in four seasons under coach Bill Cowher. Pittsburgh quarterback Neil O'Donnell struggled, completing only 15 of 39 passes for 209 yards with 2 interceptions. But he did throw 2 touchdown passes in the first half, the last a 7-yard strike to tight end Mark Bruener that gave the Steelers the lead for good with 19 seconds left in the first half. Byron (Bam) Morris's 30-yard touchdown run with 3:27 to play in the game secured the victory. Morris finished with 102 yards on 18 carries. Oilers quarterback Chris Chandler completed 8 of 11 passes for 111 yards and 1 touchdown in the first half, but had to sit out the second half because of effects of mononucleosis. Backup Will Furrer completed only 9 of 22 attempts for 96 yards and 1 interception.

Houston	0	7	0	0	—	7
Pittsburgh	7	7	0	7	—	21

Pitt — Thigpen 33 pass from O'Donnell (N. Johnson kick)
Hou — Sanders 76 pass from Chandler (Del Greco kick)
Pitt — Bruener 7 pass from O'Donnell (N. Johnson kick)
Pitt — Morris 30 run (N. Johnson kick)

CAROLINA 13, INDIANAPOLIS 10—at Clemson Memorial Stadium, attendance 49,841. John Kasay's 38-yard field goal with eight seconds remaining gave the expansion Panthers their sixth victory in the last eight games. With the score tied 10-10, Eric Guliford's 17-yard punt return gave Carolina the ball at the Colts' 43-yard line with two minutes remaining. On third-and-5 from the 38, Kerry Collins's pass to Guliford was incomplete, but Indianapolis defensive back Derwin Gray was whistled for a 15-yard facemask penalty that gave the Panthers a first down. Three plays later, Kasay made his winning kick. The Colts, who managed only 200 total yards, played most of the second half without starting quarterback Jim Harbaugh, the league's top-rated passer. Harbaugh, who completed 7 of 12 passes for 102 yards, was sacked 6 times and left the game with a sprained knee. Backup Paul Justin completed just 7 of 17 passes for 71 yards.

Indianapolis	10	0	0	0	—	10
Carolina	0	10	0	3	—	13

Ind — Dawkins 31 pass from Harbaugh (Blanchard kick)
Ind — FG Blanchard 47
Car — Collins 2 run (Kasay kick)
Car — FG Kasay 34
Car — FG Kasay 38

DENVER 31, JACKSONVILLE 23—at Denver Mile High Stadium, attendance 72,231. John Elway threw touchdown passes to four different receivers in the Broncos' victory. Denver spotted the Jaguars a 3-point lead on Mike Hollis's 47-yard field goal 8:25 into the game, then took the lead for good only two plays later on Elway's 62-yard touchdown pass to Anthony Miller. It was 21-10 at halftime, and Elway's 45-yard touchdown pass to Mike Pritchard gave the Broncos a seemingly comfortable 28-10 lead with 14 seconds remaining in the third quarter. But Jacksonville's Desmond Howard took the ensuing kickoff at the 6-yard line, returned it 9 yards, and threw a cross-field lateral to Jimmy Smith, who raced 89 yards for a touchdown. Smith, who also recovered a blocked punt in the end zone eight seconds before halftime, caught a 14-yard touchdown pass from Steve Beuerlein with 6:31 left in the game to trim the Jaguars' deficit to eight points. Moments later, cornerback Mickey Washington stripped the ball from Denver tight end Jerry Evans at the Broncos' 31, but the Jaguars' last chance ended when Beuerlein was sacked on consecutive plays by linebacker Glenn Cadrez. Elway finished with 22 completions in 34 attempts for 286 yards. Denver rookie Terrell Davis added 84 rushing yards.

Jacksonville	3	7	6	7	—	23
Denver	7	14	7	3	—	31

Jack — FG Hollis 47
Den — Miller 62 pass from Elway (Elam kick)
Den — Sharpe 6 pass from Elway (Elam kick)
Den — Evans 5 pass from Elway (Elam kick)
Jack — Smith recovered blocked punt in end zone (Hollis kick)
Den — Pritchard 45 pass from Elway (Elam kick)
Jack — Smith 89 lateral from Howard (pass failed)
Den — FG Elam 38
Jack — Smith 14 pass from Beuerlein (Hollis kick)

KANSAS CITY 29, OAKLAND 23—at Oakland-Alameda County Coliseum, attendance 53,930. Marcus Allen rushed for 124 yards as the Chiefs clinched the AFC Western Division title by beating the Raiders for the sixth consecutive time and the twelfth time in 13 meetings. Allen, who rushed 21 times and also caught 3 passes for 33 yards, became the first player in NFL history to accumulate 10,000 rushing yards and 5,000 receiving yards in a career. He also scored 1 touchdown on a 1-yard run six minutes into the second half to give Kansas City a 19-10 advantage. After a field goal by Lin Elliott increased the advantage to 12 points, the Chiefs put the game away when Brian Washington intercepted Vince Evans's pass and returned it 74 yards for 1 touchdown and a 29-10 lead with 7:37 to go in the game. It was the fourth consecutive possession that Evans, playing in place of injured Jeff Hostetler, turned over the ball. He completed 24 of 38 passes for 227 yards, but was replaced by Billy Joe Hobert after the interception return. Hobert threw 2 touchdown passes in the final 6:37 to make the final score close. Tim Brown caught 10 passes for 150 yards for Oakland.

Kansas City	6	6	10	7	—	29
Oakland	7	3	0	13	—	23

Oak — McDaniel 42 interception return (Jaeger kick)
KC — Gannon 12 run (kick failed)
Oak — FG Jaeger 46
KC — Anders 23 run (kick failed)
KC — Allen 1 run (Elliott kick)
KC — FG Elliott 35
KC — B. Washington 74 interception return (Elliott kick)
Oak — Jett 26 pass from Hobert (run failed)
Oak — Brown 1 pass from Hobert (Jaeger kick)

NEW ORLEANS 31, NEW ENGLAND 17—at Foxboro Stadium, attendance 59,876. The Saints used three big plays to win for the fifth time in six games and keep their playoff hopes alive, while all but eliminating the Patriots from postseason competition. New Orleans's first big play came 4:11 into the game, when quarterback Jim Everett teamed with wide receiver Quinn Early on a 50-yard touchdown bomb. The Saints led 17-14 at halftime, but New England's Matt Bahr tied the game with a 39-yard field goal four seconds into the fourth quarter. But two plays later, running back Lorenzo Neal took a short swing pass from Everett and raced 69 yards for the touchdown that gave New Orleans the lead for good. Mario Bates added some insurance on the Saints' next play from scrimmage with a 66-yard touchdown run with 8:30 remaining. Bates finished the game with 123 yards on 15 carries. Everett completed 17 of 26 passes for 293 yards. Curtis Martin rushed for 112 yards for the Patriots. Drew Bledsoe was intercepted twice by Saints safety Shane Pahukoa, once in the end zone.

New Orleans	14	3	0	14	—	31
New England	7	7	0	3	—	17

NO — Early 50 pass from Everett (Brien kick)
NE — Martin 9 run (Bahr kick)
NO — Bates 2 run (Brien kick)
NE — Martin 3 run (Bahr kick)
NO — FG Brien 24
NE — FG Bahr 39
NO — Neal 69 pass from Everett (Brien kick)
NO — Bates 66 run (Brien kick)

SEATTLE 26, PHILADELPHIA 14—at Kingdome, attendance 39,893. Running back Chris Warren and quarterback Rick Mirer rushed for touchdowns to lead the Seahawks over the Eagles. Warren's 5-yard touchdown run capped a 40-yard drive for the game's first points 11:26 into the opening quarter. Seattle marched 61 yards the next time it had the ball, with Mirer's 12-yard run increasing the Seahawks' lead to 14-0. Todd Peterson took over from there, kicking a career-high 4 field goals to keep the game out of reach. The biggest came 1:17 into the fourth quarter after Ricky Watters's 3-yard touchdown run trimmed Philadelphia's deficit to 20-14. Warren's 18-yard run highlighted a 41-yard drive that culminated in a 37-yard field goal with 9:09 to play. Peterson's fourth field goal, from 45 yards, came with 3:55 remaining. Safety Robert Blackmon squashed any Eagles' comeback hopes with an interception at Seattle's 34-yard line with 2:13 left. Warren finished with 93 yards on 27 carries. Watters had 2 touchdown runs for Philadelphia.

Philadelphia	0	7	0	7	—	14
Seattle	7	10	3	6	—	26

Sea — Warren 5 run (Peterson kick)
Sea — Mirer 12 run (Peterson kick)
Phil — Watters 1 run (Anderson kick)
Sea — FG Peterson 47
Sea — FG Peterson 35
Phil — Watters 3 run (Anderson kick)
Sea — FG Peterson 37
Sea — FG Peterson 45

ST. LOUIS 23, N.Y. JETS 20—at Giants Stadium, attendance 52,023. Backup quarterback Mark Rypien threw 2 touchdown passes to help keep the Rams' playoff hopes alive. After starting quarterback Chris Miller suffered a concussion, Rypien entered the game with 2:30 remaining in the first half and St. Louis ahead 7-0. But the veteran quarterback's first pass was intercepted by Jets safety Gary Jones, who returned it 49 yards for a touchdown and a 7-7 tie at halftime. New York took a 10-7 lead on Nick Lowery's 34-yard field goal 3:59 into the third quarter, but Rypien gave his team the lead for good with a 1-yard touchdown pass to Isaac Bruce with 1:41 remaining in the third quarter. The pair teamed again on an 11-yard touchdown pass to give the Rams a 21-13 edge with 10:45 to play. Rypien finished with 12 completions in 23 attempts for 101 yards, with 3 interceptions. Defensive tackle D'Marco Farr had 3½ sacks and an interception for St. Louis.

St. Louis	7	0	7	9	—	23
N.Y. Jets	0	7	3	10	—	20

StL — Drayton 28 pass from Miller (Biasucci kick)
Jets — G. Jones 49 interception return (Lowery kick)
Jets — FG Lowery 34
StL — Bruce 1 pass from Rypien (Biasucci kick)
Jets — FG Lowery 23
StL — Bruce 11 pass from Rypien (Biasucci kick)
StL — Safety, Carter sacked Esiason in end zone
Jets — Wilson 23 pass from Esiason (Lowery kick)

MINNESOTA 31, TAMPA BAY 17—at Metrodome, attendance 52,879. Warren Moon threw 2 touchdown passes, and the Vikings built a 28-7 first-half lead en route to an easy victory over the slumping Buccaneers. Amp Lee's 66-yard touchdown run 9:14 into the game capped a 99-yard drive and got Minnesota going. Three minutes later, Moon passed 27 yards for a touchdown to Cris Carter. Then, ahead 14-7, the Vikings broke open the game with a pair of touchdowns in a 59-second span in the second quarter. Moon threw a 60-yard touchdown pass to Carter with 9:26 left in the first half, and Scottie Graham ran 23 yards for a touchdown at the 8:27 mark. That came two plays after defensive end Derrick Alexander recovered Trent Dilfer's fumble at Tampa Bay's 30-yard line. By intermission, Minnesota had outgained the Buccaneers 351 yards to 83, and the Vikings finished the game with an advantage of 452-256. Moon completed 20 of 32 passes for 272 yards, while Graham added 98 yards and Lee had 90 on the ground. Carter caught 6 passes for 136 yards. Minnesota's defense sacked Buccaneers quarterbacks Dilfer and Casey Weldon 8 times. Linebacker Broderick Thomas had 2½ sacks, and defensive end Martin Harrison had 2.

Tampa Bay	0	7	3	7	—	17
Minnesota	14	14	0	3	—	31

Minn — Lee 66 run (Reveiz kick)
Minn — Carter 27 pass from Moon (Reveiz kick)
TB — Ellison 1 run (Husted kick)
Minn — Carter 60 pass from Moon (Reveiz kick)
Minn — Graham 23 run (Reveiz kick)
TB — FG Husted 47
Minn — FG Reveiz 42
TB — Harper 38 pass from Weldon (Husted kick)

WASHINGTON 24, DALLAS 17—at Texas Stadium, attendance 64,866. Terry Allen ran for 2 touchdowns as the Redskins snapped a four-game losing streak by stunning the Cowboys for the second time this season. Dallas led 10-7 until Washington quarterback Heath Shuler capped a 12-play, 83-yard drive with a 10-yard touchdown pass to Henry Ellard with 5:01 to play in the third quarter. In the fourth quarter, safety Stanley Richard intercepted Troy Aikman's pass near midfield and returned it 24 yards to the Cowboys' 27-yard line. Seven plays later, Allen's 1-yard touchdown run gave the Redskins an 11-point lead, and they were en route to their first season sweep of Dallas since 1987. Aikman completed 29 of 48 passes for 285 yards for the Cowboys, with 10 passes for 101 yards going to wide receiver Michael Irvin. Emmitt Smith rushed for 91 yards and 1 touchdown but also lost a fumble out of the end zone for a touchback as Dallas was driving in the fourth quarter.

Washington	0	7	7	10	—	24
Dallas	0	10	0	7	—	17

Dall — E. Smith 7 run (Boniol kick)
Wash — Allen 2 run (Murray kick)
Dall — FG Boniol 37
Wash — Ellard 10 pass from Shuler (Murray kick)
Wash — Allen 1 run (Murray kick)
Wash — FG Murray 47
Dall — Irvin 3 pass from Aikman (Boniol kick)

SUNDAY NIGHT, DECEMBER 3

SAN FRANCISCO 27, BUFFALO 17—at 3Com Park, attendance 65,568. Linebacker Lee Woodall returned a fumble 96 yards for a touchdown to spark the 49ers to the victory and a two-game lead in the NFC Western Division. Buffalo was threatening to break a 10-10 tie five minutes into the third quarter, and had the ball first-and-goal at San Francisco's 1-yard line. But on the ensuing play, linebacker Gary Plummer launched himself into Bills running back Darick Holmes, forcing a fumble that Woodall scooped up and took the length of the field. Jeff Wilkins's 40-yard field goal and Derek Loville's 8-yard touchdown run with 7:57 left in the game provided the 49ers' eventual margin of victory. Loville finished the game with career highs of 88 rushing yards and 86 yards on 10 catches. Quarterback Steve Young completed 28 of 44 passes for 243 yards. Jim Kelly passed for 214 yards and 2 touchdowns for Buffalo, but completed only 18 of 41 passes and was intercepted 3 times.

Buffalo	3	7	0	7	—	17
San Francisco	7	3	7	10	—	27

SF — Walker 1 run (Wilkins kick)
Buff — FG Christie 23
Buff — Armour 28 pass from Kelly (Christie kick)
SF — FG Wilkins 20
SF — Woodall 96 fumble return (Wilkins kick)
SF — FG Wilkins 40
Buff — Tasker 13 pass from Kelly (Christie kick)
SF — Loville 8 run (Wilkins kick)

MONDAY, DECEMBER 4

DETROIT 27, CHICAGO 7—at Pontiac Silverdome, attendance 77,230. Herman Moore caught a club-record 14 passes for a career-high 183 yards and 1 touchdown as the Lions won their fourth consecutive game. Detroit took control early, and got 3 touchdown passes from Scott Mitchell for a 21-0 lead at halftime. Mitchell finished with 26 completions in 38 attempts for 320 yards. He completed 5 consecutive attempts on a 90-yard drive exclusively through the air in the first quarter, capping the march with a short pass that Moore turned into a 46-yard touchdown, and the Lions never trailed. Barry Sanders added 90 rushing yards as Detroit enjoyed a whopping 419-185 advantage in total yards. Chicago lost for the fourth time in five weeks.

Chicago	0	0	7	0	—	7
Detroit	14	7	3	3	—	27

Det — Moore 46 pass from Mitchell (Hanson kick)
Det — Morton 4 pass from Mitchell (Hanson kick)
Det — Sanders 9 pass from Mitchell (Hanson kick)
Det — FG Hanson 42
Chi — Green 11 run (Butler kick)
Det — FG Hanson 36

FIFTEENTH WEEK SUMMARIES

AMERICAN FOOTBALL CONFERENCE

Eastern Division	W	L	T	Pct.	Pts.	OP
Buffalo	9	5	0	.643	310	287
Indianapolis	8	6	0	.571	297	282
Miami	8	6	0	.571	337	287
New England	6	8	0	.429	260	326
N.Y. Jets	3	11	0	.214	227	349
Central Division						
Pittsburgh	10	4	0	.714	347	276
Cincinnati	6	8	0	.429	312	324
Houston	5	9	0	.357	297	301
Cleveland	4	10	0	.286	242	322
Jacksonville	3	11	0	.214	251	339
Western Division						
Kansas City	11	3	0	.786	312	221
Oakland	8	6	0	.571	310	257
Denver	7	7	0	.500	340	297
San Diego	7	7	0	.500	267	282
Seattle	7	7	0	.500	316	330

NATIONAL FOOTBALL CONFERENCE

Eastern Division	W	L	T	Pct.	Pts.	OP
Dallas	10	4	0	.714	377	258
Philadelphia	9	5	0	.643	283	298
N.Y. Giants	5	9	0	.357	253	292
Arizona	4	10	0	.286	242	364
Washington	4	10	0	.286	271	319
Central Division						
Green Bay	9	5	0	.643	346	272
Detroit	8	6	0	.571	355	326
Minnesota	8	6	0	.571	358	321
Chicago	7	7	0	.500	341	336
Tampa Bay	7	7	0	.500	218	267
Western Division						
San Francisco	10	4	0	.714	393	200
Atlanta	8	6	0	.571	317	301
St. Louis	7	7	0	.500	264	342
Carolina	6	8	0	.429	251	288
New Orleans	6	8	0	.429	284	314

SATURDAY, DECEMBER 9

SAN DIEGO 28, ARIZONA 25—at San Diego Jack Murphy Stadium, attendance 55,258. The Chargers overcame 6 turnovers to defeat the Cardinals and keep their playoff hopes alive. San Diego's Stan Humphries passed for 288 yards, but he was intercepted 4 times, including 1 that Arizona defensive end Clyde Simmons returned 25 yards for a touchdown to give the Cardinals a 14-7 lead with 2:21 remaining in the first half. Humphries quickly led the Chargers down the field, tying the game just before halftime on a 3-yard scoring toss to Ronnie Harmon. San Diego took the lead for good when Andre Coleman returned the second-half kickoff 92 yards for a touchdown. Mark Seay's 38-yard scoring catch from Humphries—the Chargers' third touchdown in a span of 6:18—gave San Diego a 28-14 third-quarter lead. Seay caught 7 passes for 114 yards and 2 touchdowns. Arizona's Dave Krieg passed for 283 yards and 2 scores, but he was sacked 5 times.

Arizona	0	14	3	8	—	25
San Diego	0	14	14	0	—	28

SD — Seay 15 pass from Humphries (Carney kick)
Ariz — Centers 22 pass from Krieg (Davis kick)
Ariz — Simmons 25 interception return (Davis kick)
SD — Harmon 3 pass from Humphries (Carney kick)
SD — Coleman 92 kickoff return (Carney kick)
SD — Seay 38 pass from Humphries (Carney kick)
Ariz — FG Davis 36
Ariz — Anderson 12 pass from Krieg (Anderson pass from Krieg)

MINNESOTA 27, CLEVELAND 11—at Metrodome, attendance 47,984. The Vikings' defense collected 4 interceptions and 5 sacks to send the Browns to their sixth consecutive loss. Cleveland starter Vinny Testaverde left in the first quarter with an injury, and his replacement, rookie Eric Zeier, was smothered by Minnesota's pressure. Rookie safety Orlando Thomas had 2 of the Vikings' 4 interceptions off Zeier. The Vikings limited the Browns to 201 total yards, including just 29 on the ground. Meanwhile, Minnesota's offense produced 436 total yards and held the ball for nearly 40 minutes. Warren Moon passed for 267 yards and 2 scores, including 8 receptions by Cris Carter for 124 yards.

Cleveland	0	3	0	8	—	11
Minnesota	3	10	7	7	—	27

Minn — FG Reveiz 23
Minn — Evans 1 pass from Moon (Reveiz kick)
Cleve — FG Stover 26
Minn — FG Reveiz 28
Minn — Reed 9 pass from Moon (Reveiz kick)
Minn — Evans 2 run (Reveiz kick)
Cleve — Byner 29 pass from Zeier (Zeier run)

SUNDAY, DECEMBER 10

BUFFALO 45, ST. LOUIS 27—at Trans World Dome, attendance 64,623. Jim Kelly fired 4 touchdown passes and Thurman Thomas ran for 129 yards to lead the Bills over the Rams. Kelly's second score—a 1-yard toss to Thomas—capped a 98-yard drive and gave Buffalo a 14-10 lead midway through the second period. In the third quarter, Kelly teamed with Steve Tasker on scoring passes of 6 and 28 yards to give the Bills a 35-16 lead. Thomas set a club record with his forty-second 100-yard game, and Darick Holmes added 90 rushing yards, scoring on runs of 1 and 38 yards. Kelly completed 19 of 25 passes for 237 yards while directing a Bills' offense that amassed 454 total yards (222 rushing). The Rams' Mark Rypien, playing in place of an injured Chris Miller, completed 31 of 55 passes for 372 yards (with no interceptions) despite being sacked 4 times. Isaac Bruce had 9 catches for 136 yards.

Buffalo	7	14	14	10	—	45
St. Louis	10	3	3	11	—	27

Buff — Brooks 23 pass from Kelly (Christie kick)
StL — Kinchen 6 pass from Rypien (Biasucci kick)
StL — FG Biasucci 28
Buff — Thomas 1 pass from Kelly (Christie kick)
Buff — Holmes 1 run (Christie kick)

StL — FG Biasucci 37
Buff — Tasker 6 pass from Kelly (Christie kick)
StL — FG Biasucci 51
Buff — Tasker 28 pass from Kelly (Christie kick)
StL — FG Biasucci 25
Buff — Holmes 38 run (Christie kick)
StL — Hester 5 pass from Rypien (Bailey pass from Rypien)
Buff — FG Christie 45

CINCINNATI 16, CHICAGO 10—at Riverfront Stadium, attendance 38,642. The Bengals controlled the ball with their short passing game and held off a late rally to defeat the Bears. Cincinnati's Jeff Blake completed 30 of 41 passes for 253 yards, leading the Bengals to 3 field goals and a 38-yard touchdown pass to Darnay Scott with 3:34 left in the third quarter. Scott's touchdown, which came one play after a 14-yard punt that was tipped by the Bengals, gave Cincinnati a 16-3 lead. The Bears' offense, which struggled most of the day, mounted an 82-yard drive early in the fourth quarter, culminating with Rashaan Salaam's 5-yard scoring run to pull close at 16-10. Chicago had two possessions in the final five minutes, but one drive ended in a fumble and another ended a yard short on fourth down at the Bengals' 44. Carl Pickens led Cincinnati with 11 catches for 99 yards. Salaam gained 105 yards on 22 carries. Chicago's Erik Kramer passed for 196 yards.

Chicago	0	3	0	7	—	10
Cincinnati	3	3	10	0	—	16

Cin — FG Pelfrey 28
Cin — FG Pelfrey 37
Chi — FG Butler 27
Cin — FG Pelfrey 39
Cin — Scott 38 pass from Blake (Pelfrey kick)
Chi — Salaam 5 run (Butler kick)

PHILADELPHIA 20, DALLAS 17—at Veterans Stadium, attendance 66,198. A magnificent game by the Eagles' defense propelled Philadelphia to victory over Dallas. The Cowboys scored all their points in the first half, on Emmitt Smith's 10-yard touchdown run, Chris Boniol's 21-yard field goal, and Larry Brown's 65-yard interception return. Brown's score came with 58 seconds left in the half, but the Eagles countered with a 64-yard field-goal drive that made it 17-6 at halftime. In the second half, Philadelphia's defense shut down the Cowboys (their only scoring chance ended with a fumble at the Eagles' 2) while its offense closed the deficit to 17-14 on Ricky Watters's 1-yard touchdown run and Rodney Peete's two-point conversion pass to Fred Barnett. The Eagles tied the game with three minutes to play on Gary Anderson's 38-yard field goal. On the Cowboys' next possession, Dallas faced a fourth-and-1 from its 29. Eschewing a punt into the wind, the Cowboys went for the first down and Smith was stopped short. However, the clock had reached 2:00 just prior to the snap, nullifying the play. Alas, the Cowboys ran the same play, with Smith once again being stopped for no gain. Anderson's third field goal, with 1:26 left, gave the Eagles their first lead, and a key deflection by rookie cornerback Bobby Taylor helped preserve the victory in the final minute. Philadelphia limited Dallas to 196 total yards, posting 4 sacks of Troy Aikman (11 of 28 for 110 yards). Smith ran for 108 yards, but only 10 in the second half. Watters ran for 112 yards on 33 carries. Peete passed for 187 yards and ran for 35 more

Dallas	7	10	0	0	—	17
Philadelphia	3	3	8	6	—	20

Phil — FG Anderson 42
Dall — Smith 10 run (Boniol kick)
Dall — FG Boniol 21
Dall — Brown 65 interception return (Boniol kick)
Phil — FG Anderson 27
Phil — Watters 1 run (Barnett pass from Peete)
Phil — FG Anderson 38
Phil — FG Anderson 42

DETROIT 24, HOUSTON 17—at Astrodome, attendance 35,842. Scott Mitchell and Herman Moore teamed on 2 scoring passes and the Lions held off a late Oilers rally to win their fifth consecutive game. Mitchell's 13-yard touchdown pass to Moore opened the scoring, and his 14-yard touchdown pass to Moore gave Detroit a 24-10 lead with 13:54 to play in the game. Houston mounted a comeback behind rookie quarterback Steve McNair, who played the second half. McNair's 39-yard scoring pass to Chris Sanders made it 24-17 with 8:47 left. McNair led the Oilers inside the Lions' 20 in the final minute, but his last-ditch pass fell incomplete in the end zone as time expired. Mitchell passed for 283 yards, mostly to Moore (7 catches for 105 yards) and Brett Perriman (6 for 128). McNair completed 16 of 27 passes for 203 yards. Houston controlled the ball for 37 minutes 7 seconds but committed 6 turnovers.

Detroit	7	10	0	7	—	24
Houston	0	7	3	7	—	17

Det — Moore 13 pass from Mitchell (Hanson kick)
Hou — Jeffires 9 pass from Chandler (Del Greco kick)
Det — FG Hanson 36
Det — Sanders 9 run (Hanson kick)
Hou — FG Del Greco 47
Det — Moore 14 pass from Mitchell (Hanson kick)
Hou — Sanders 39 pass from S. McNair (Del Greco kick)

INDIANAPOLIS 41, JACKSONVILLE 31—at Jacksonville Municipal Stadium, attendance 66,099. Special teams played a big role as the Colts gained only 219 total yards but still managed to defeat the Jaguars. Aaron Bailey returned the opening kickoff 95 yards for a touchdown, and later in the first quarter scored on a 14-yard catch that was set up by a blocked field goal. In the second period, Indianapolis recovered a fumbled punt return at the Jacksonville 2 to set up a 1-yard touchdown run by Marshall Faulk that made it 21-7. Leading 27-17 in the fourth quarter, the Colts covered a Jaguars' onside kick and drove 44 yards to a touchdown and a 34-17 advantage. Faulk surpassed the 1,000-yard mark before leaving with a bruised knee. The Colts' Craig Erickson, starting in place of an injured Jim Harbaugh, was 9 of 16 for 129 yards and 2 touchdowns. Jacksonville lost despite gaining 424 total yards, led by Mark Brunell (26 of 39 for 312 yards and 3 scores). The Jaguars' Willie Jackson caught 6 passes for 113 yards and 2 touchdowns.

Indianapolis	14	10	3	14	—	41
Jacksonville	0	7	3	21	—	31

Ind — Bailey 95 kickoff return (Blanchard kick)
Ind — Bailey 14 pass from Erickson (Blanchard kick)
Jack — Stewart 6 run (Hollis kick)
Ind — Faulk 1 run (Blanchard kick)
Ind — FG Blanchard 22
Jack — FG Hollis 37
Ind — FG Blanchard 44
Jack — Jackson 15 pass from Brunell (Hollis kick)
Ind — Dilger 16 pass from Erickson (Blanchard kick)
Jack — Smith 4 pass from Brunell (Hollis kick)
Ind — Warren 2 run (Blanchard kick)
Jack — Jackson 7 pass from Brunell (Hollis kick)

ATLANTA 19, NEW ORLEANS 14—at Georgia Dome, attendance 54,603. The Falcons' Morten Andersen kicked 4 field goals to help defeat his former team. Andersen, who played 13 seasons in New Orleans, set an NFL record with 3 field goals of 50 or more yards in one game. His 51-yard field goal made it 6-0 in the first quarter, his 55-yard kick just before halftime upped the lead to 9-0 at the break, and his 55-yard field goal with 4:17 left to play not only established the mark but gave Atlanta a 19-14 lead. Linebacker Jessie Tuggle preserved the victory with an end zone interception in the final minute. The Saints' offense struggled most of the day until driving 71 and 86 yards to fourth-quarter touchdowns. Jim Everett completed 31 of 47 passes for 287 yards. The Falcons' Jeff George passed for 251 yards while leading a mistake-free offense.

New Orleans	0	0	0	14	—	14
Atlanta	6	3	7	3	—	19

Atl — FG Andersen 25
Atl — FG Andersen 51
Atl — FG Andersen 55
Atl — Heyward 5 pass from George (Andersen kick)
NO — Smith 1 pass from Everett (Brien kick)
NO — Smith 5 pass from Everett (Brien kick)
Atl — FG Andersen 55

NEW ENGLAND 31, N.Y. JETS 28—at Foxboro Stadium, attendance 46,617. The Patriots edged the Jets in a mistake-filled game. The teams combined for 7 turnovers and numerous other miscues, but New England capitalized on one of its mistakes. After the Jets scored with 5:58 remaining to take a 21-17 lead, the Patriots' David Meggett fumbled the ensuing kickoff. Meggett's teammate, Troy Brown, scooped up the loose ball and raced 75 yards for a touchdown and a 24-21 lead. The stunned Jets gave the ball right back on an interception, and Curtis Martin's 1-yard touchdown run gave New England a 31-21 advantage with 2:23 left. Martin ran for 148 yards on 31 carries. New York's Boomer Esiason completed 27 of 42 passes for 296 yards and 4 touchdowns. Johnny Mitchell had 9 catches for 108 yards and 1 touchdown, and rookie Ryan Yarborough caught 6 for 105 yards and 2 scores.

N.Y. Jets	0	7	7	14	—	28
New England	0	7	7	17	—	31

Jets — Yarborough 31 pass from Esiason (Lowery kick)
NE — Graham 37 pass from Bledsoe (Bahr kick)
Jets — Mitchell 3 pass from Esiason (Lowery kick)
NE — Martin 9 run (Bahr kick)
NE — FG Bahr 31
Jets — Murrell 3 pass from Esiason (Lowery kick)
NE — T. Brown 75 fumble return (Bahr kick)
NE — Martin 1 run (Bahr kick)
Jets — Yarborough 3 pass from Esiason (Lowery kick)

PITTSBURGH 29, OAKLAND 10—at Oakland-Alameda County Coliseum, attendance 53,516. The Steelers manhandled the Raiders on both sides of the line to hand Oakland its fourth consecutive defeat. Pittsburgh controlled the ball for 37 minutes 28 seconds, outgaining Oakland 355 to 190. Neil O'Donnell passed for 230 yards, including touchdown strikes of 37 and 14 yards to Ernie Mills that gave the Steelers a 20-7 halftime advantage. Eric Pegram ran for 122 yards on 26 carries. The Raiders' only touchdown came on Aundray Bruce's 1-yard interception return. Billy Joe Hobert, making his first NFL start, was pressured all day (although he avoided being sacked) and intercepted 4 times.

Pittsburgh	7	13	3	6	—	29
Oakland	0	7	3	0	—	10

Pitt — Mills 37 pass from O'Donnell (N. Johnson kick)
Pitt — FG N. Johnson 41
Oak — Bruce 1 interception return (Jaeger kick)
Pitt — FG N. Johnson 35
Pitt — Mills 14 pass from O'Donnell (N. Johnson kick)
Oak — FG Jaeger 39
Pitt — FG N. Johnson 32
Pitt — FG N. Johnson 20
Pitt — FG N. Johnson 22

SAN FRANCISCO 31, CAROLINA 10—at Clemson Memorial Stadium, attendance 76,136. Steve Young passed for 2 scores and ran for another as the 49ers routed the Panthers for their fifth consecutive victory. San Francisco opened the scoring with Young's 4-yard touchdown pass to Derek Loville, and Loville made it 14-0 in the second quarter with a 1-yard touchdown run. Young's 20-yard scoring pass to J.J. Stokes 30 seconds before halftime made it 21-3 at intermission. Young's 1-yard touchdown run in the third quarter gave San Francisco a commanding 28-10 lead. Young completed 31 of 45 passes for 336 yards. Jerry Rice had 6 catches for 121 yards. San Francisco limited Carolina to 195 total yards.

San Francisco	7	14	7	3	—	31
Carolina	0	3	7	0	—	10

SF — Loville 4 pass from Young (Wilkins kick)
SF — Loville 1 run (Wilkins kick)
Car — FG Kasay 43
SF — Stokes 20 pass from Young (Wilkins kick)
Car — Moore 2 run (Kasay kick)
SF — Young 1 run (Wilkins kick)
SF — FG Wilkins 20

SEATTLE 31, DENVER 27—at Denver Mile High Stadium, attendance 71,488. The Seahawks rallied from a 20-3 deficit to defeat the Broncos and overcome a record-setting day by Glyn Milburn. Denver held that lead in the third quarter, and was threatening to increase it as John Elway led a drive inside the Seahawks' 20. But safety Robert Blackmon blindsided Elway, forcing a fumble that defensive end Antonio Edwards picked up and carried 83 yards for a touchdown to make it 20-10. Another Denver advance was halted by an interception, and Seattle drove 87 yards (the last 24 on Chris Warren's run) to make it 20-17 with 11:06 left to play. The Broncos answered via Milburn, who returned the ensuing kickoff 45 yards to set up Elway's 1-yard touchdown run. Back came Seattle, as reserve quarterback John Friesz crafted an Elway-like comeback by leading the Seahawks on 76- and 56-yard touchdown drives in the final 7:16. Friesz's 5-yard touchdown pass to Joey Galloway made it 27-24 with 4:10 remaining, and his 20-yard touchdown pass to Warren with 49 seconds was the game winner. Brian Blades had 7 catches for 127 yards for Seattle, and Warren ran for 101 yards on 18 carries. Milburn set an NFL single-game record with 404 all-purpose yards (131 on 18 rushes, 45 on 5 receptions, 95 on 5 punt returns, and 133 on 5 kickoff returns). Denver committed 5 turnovers.

Seattle	0	3	7	21	—	31
Denver	10	10	0	7	—	27

Den — Craver 2 run (Elam kick)
Den — FG Elam 29
Den — Miller 15 pass from Elway (Elam kick)
Den — FG Elam 46
Sea — FG Peterson 36
Sea — Edwards 83 fumble return (Peterson kick)
Sea — Warren 24 run (Peterson kick)
Den — Elway 1 run (Elam kick)
Sea — Galloway 5 pass from Friesz (Peterson kick)
Sea — Warren 20 pass from Friesz (Peterson kick)

N.Y. GIANTS 20, WASHINGTON 13—at Giants Stadium, attendance 48,247. Dave Brown's 40-yard touchdown pass to Chris Calloway with 1:12 remaining lifted the Giants over the Redskins. New York built a 13-3 halftime advantage thanks to 2 field goals by Brad Daluiso and Thomas Lewis's 90-yard kickoff return for a touchdown. Washington rallied to tie in the second half, mounting a 13-play, 78-yard drive to a field goal and a 16-play, 80-yard march to a touchdown on Terry Allen's fourth-down run with 3:35 left in the game. New York took the ensuing kickoff and drove 68 yards to the winning score, the key play a 2-yard run by Rodney Hampton on fourth-and-1 at the Giants' 41. Hampton's run gave New York a first down (its first of the second half), and three plays later Brown found Calloway for the winning score. Washington had another chance, though, as Brian Mitchell's 53-yard kickoff return and a facemask penalty put the Redskins at the Giants' 23. But they failed on 4 pass attempts, the last batted away by cornerback Thomas Randolph at the Giants' 2. New York won despite gaining just 160 total yards and holding the ball for only 21 minutes 20 seconds. Allen ran for 120 yards on 30 carries.

Washington	0	3	0	10	—	13
N.Y. Giants	3	10	0	7	—	20

Giants— FG Daluiso 36
Wash — FG Murray 34
Giants— Lewis 90 kickoff return (Daluiso kick)
Giants— FG Daluiso 42
Wash — FG Murray 30
Wash — Allen 1 run (Murray kick)
Giants— Calloway 40 pass from Brown (Daluiso kick)

SUNDAY NIGHT, DECEMBER 10

TAMPA BAY 13, GREEN BAY 10—at Tampa Stadium, attendance 67,557. Michael Husted's 47-yard field goal 3:46 into overtime lifted the Buccaneers over the Packers. It was the Buccaneers' seventh victory, their most since 1981. Tampa Bay, which had a first-and-goal at the Packers' 1 in the first half only to be thwarted by an end-zone interception, scored its only touchdown on Jerry Ellison's 1-yard run in the third quarter. Green Bay moved the ball throughout the game but did not get into the end zone until Brett Favre teamed with tight end Keith Jackson on an 8-yard touchdown pass. Jackson's score gave the Packers a 10-7 lead with 8:59 to play. Errict Rhett's 18-yard run keyed the Buccaneers' drive to the tying field goal, a 38-yard kick by Husted less than five minutes remaining. Green Bay had a chance to win in regulation, but Chris Jacke missed a 45-yard field-goal attempt in the final minute. Tampa Bay drove 48 yards in overtime to set up Husted, who delivered his third winning field goal of the season just inside the right upright. Favre completed 27 of 46 passes for 285 yards, hitting Robert Brooks 9 times for 122 yards. Rhett ran for 118 yars on 22 carries. Packers defensive end Reggie White sat out the game with a hamstring injury, the first game he had missed in his career because of injury.

Green Bay	0	3	0	7	0	—	10
Tampa Bay	0	0	7	3	3	—	13

GB — FG Jacke 51
TB — Ellison 1 run (Husted kick)
GB — Jackson 8 pass from Favre (Jacke kick)
TB — FG Husted 38
TB — FG Husted 47

MONDAY, DECEMBER 11

MIAMI 13, KANSAS CITY 6—at Joe Robbie Stadium, attendance 70,321. The Dolphins' defense stopped the Chiefs on downs three times and forced 3 turnovers in Miami's victory. An interception and a fumble recovery set up each of the Dolphins' first two scores, 33-yard field goals by Pete Stoyanovich. A 63-yard drive in the second quarter led to Miami's only touchdown, a 3-yard pass from Dan Marino to O.J. McDuffie. The Chiefs had several scoring chances in the fourth quarter, but Marcus Allen was stopped on fourth down at the Dolphins' 4, and on their next possession, Donnell Bennett was stuffed on fourth down at the Dolphins' 27. Kansas City finally got on the board with 5:04 left on a 5-yard touchdown pass from Steve Bono to Tamarick Vanover, and had a chance to win after recovering a fumble at the Miami 36 with 3:38 left. The Chiefs drove to the 9-yard line, but were denied on fourth-and-6 when cornerback Terrell Buckley deflected a pass away from Webster Slaughter in the end zone with 1:31 left. Defensive tackle Tim Bowens led the Miami defense with 2 forced fumbles, 1 fumble recovery, and assisted tackles on both fourth-down runs.

Kansas City	0	0	0	6	—	6
Miami	6	7	0	0	—	13

Mia — FG Stoyanovich 33
Mia — FG Stoyanovich 33
Mia — McDuffie 3 pass from Marino (Stoyanovich kick)
KC — Slaughter 5 pass from Bono (kick failed)

SIXTEENTH WEEK SUMMARIES

AMERICAN FOOTBALL CONFERENCE

Eastern Division	**W**	**L**	**T**	**Pct.**	**Pts.**	**OP**
Buffalo	10	5	0	.667	333	307
Indianapolis	8	7	0	.533	321	309
Miami	8	7	0	.533	357	310
New England	6	9	0	.400	287	367
N.Y. Jets	3	12	0	.200	233	372
Central Division						
Pittsburgh	11	4	0	.733	388	303
Cincinnati	6	9	0	.400	322	350
Houston	6	9	0	.400	320	307
Cleveland	5	10	0	.333	268	332
Jacksonville	3	12	0	.200	251	383
Western Division						
Kansas City	12	3	0	.800	332	238
Oakland	8	7	0	.533	320	301
San Diego	8	7	0	.533	294	306
Seattle	8	7	0	.533	360	340
Denver	7	8	0	.467	357	317

NATIONAL FOOTBALL CONFERENCE

Eastern Division	**W**	**L**	**T**	**Pct.**	**Pts.**	**OP**
Dallas	11	4	0	.733	398	278
Philadelphia	10	5	0	.667	304	318
N.Y. Giants	5	10	0	.333	273	313
Washington	5	10	0	.333	306	342
Arizona	4	11	0	.267	262	385
Central Division						
Green Bay	10	5	0	.667	380	295
Detroit	9	6	0	.600	399	326
Chicago	8	7	0	.533	372	346
Minnesota	8	7	0	.533	388	358
Tampa Bay	7	8	0	.467	228	298
Western Division						
San Francisco	11	4	0	.733	430	230
Atlanta	8	7	0	.533	334	322
Carolina	7	8	0	.467	272	305
St. Louis	7	8	0	.467	287	377
New Orleans	6	9	0	.400	307	348

SATURDAY, DECEMBER 16

GREEN BAY 34, NEW ORLEANS 23—at Louisiana Superdome, attendance 50,132. Brett Favre completed 21 of 30 passes for 308 yards and 4 touchdowns (with no interceptions) to lead the Packers over the Saints. The victory clinched a playoff berth for Green Bay. Favre teamed with Anthony Morgan (19 yards) and Robert Brooks (17 yards) on first-quarter touchdowns, then gave Green Bay a 28-14 halftime advantage with second-quarter scoring passes to Brooks (40 yards) and Antonio Freeman (11 yards). Two field goals by Chris Jacke upped the Packers' lead to 34-14 entering the fourth quarter. Brooks finished with 5 catches for 118 yards. The Saints' Jim Everett completed 29 of 45 passes for 364 yards, including 8 receptions for 117 yards by Quinn Early.

Green Bay	14	14	6	0	—	34
New Orleans	7	7	0	9	—	23

GB — Morgan 19 pass from Favre (Jacke kick)
NO — Zellars 2 run (Brien kick)
GB — Brooks 17 pass from Favre (Jacke kick)
GB — Brooks 40 pass from Favre (Jacke kick)
GB — Freeman 11 pass from Favre (Jacke kick)
NO — Small 4 pass from Everett (Brien kick)
GB — FG Jacke 47
GB — FG Jacke 20
NO — FG Brien 43
NO — Small 6 pass from Everett (pass failed)

PITTSBURGH 41, NEW ENGLAND 27—at Three Rivers Stadium, attendance 57,158. The Steelers scored 14 points in the final 1:30 of each half to defeat the Patriots. Pittsburgh used Neil O'Donnell's 14-yard touchdown pass to Yancey Thigpen and defensive end Brentson Buckner's 46-yard fumble for a score—both in the final 1:30 of the first half—to build a 17-6 lead at intermission. New England rallied behind Drew Bledsoe, who teamed with tight end Ben Coates on a pair of 6-yard touchdown passes, the latter score pulling the Patriots close at 24-19 with 12:05 left. After a Steelers' field goal, New England tied the game on Bledsoe's 22-yard touchdown pass to Curtis Martin with 4:38 left, followed by Bledsoe's two-point conversion pass to David Meggett. The Steelers answered with 1:28 remaining when O'Donnell found Ernie Mills for a 62-yard touchdown pass. New England's last hope was dashed 19 seconds later when cornerback Chris Oldham picked up a fumble and returned it 23 yards for the clinching score. O'Donnell completed 14 of 25 passes for 195 yards, while Kordell Stewart passed for 41 yards and ran 22 yards for a touchdown. Bledsoe completed 39 of 60 passes for 336 yards. Coates had 11 receptions for 83 yards and Martin had 20 carries for 120 yards.

New England	3	3	6	15	—	27
Pittsburgh	0	17	7	17	—	41

NE — FG Bahr 23
Pitt — FG N. Johnson 32
NE — FG Bahr 22
Pitt — Thigpen 14 pass from O'Donnell (N. Johnson kick)
Pitt — Buckner 46 fumble return (N. Johnson kick)
NE — Coates 6 pass from Bledsoe (run failed)
Pitt — Stewart 22 run (N. Johnson kick)
NE — Coates 6 pass from Bledsoe (Bahr kick)
Pitt — FG N. Johnson 32
NE — Martin 22 pass from Bledsoe (Meggett pass from Bledsoe)
Pitt — Mills 62 pass from O'Donnell (N. Johnson kick)
Pitt — Oldham 23 fumble return (N. Johnson kick)

SUNDAY, DECEMBER 17

PHILADELPHIA 21, ARIZONA 20—at Veterans Stadium, attendance 62,076. The Eagles' defense forced 5 second-half turnovers to rally the team from a 17-0 deficit and defeat the Cardinals. Arizona built its lead on 3 field goals by Greg Davis and Larry Centers's 1-yard touchdown (followed by a two-point conversion pass). The Eagles came to life after Davis's third field goal, when Derrick Witherspoon returned the ensuing kickoff 86 yards for a touchdown to make it 17-7 at halftime. A fumble recovery on the Cardinals' first possession of the second half led to Rodney Peete's 21-yard touchdown pass to Reggie Johnson, closing the gap to 17-14. Davis's fourth field goal made it 20-14, but otherwise the Cardinals kept turning the ball over and the Eagles were unable to capitalize until early in the fourth quarter. Peete teamed with Calvin Williams for passes of 11 and 37 yards, the latter catch going for a touchdown that gave Philadelphia a 21-20 lead with 12:10 remaining. Arizona drove to the Eagles' 22 with 1:55 to play, but the Eagles' defense saved the day with a 7-yard sack on third down. In came Davis, but his 47-yard field goal into a stiff wind came up short. Peete passed for 213 yards and 2 scores but was intercepted 3 times. Williams had 7 catches for 105 yards. Arizona was led by Dave Krieg (253 passing yards) and Garrison Hearst (95 yards on 26 carries).

Arizona	6	11	3	0	—	20
Philadelphia	0	7	7	7	—	21

Ariz — FG Davis 37
Ariz — FG Davis 35
Ariz — Centers 1 run (Anderson pass from Krieg)
Ariz — FG Davis 37

Phil — Witherspoon 86 kickoff return (Anderson kick)
Phil — Johnson 21 pass from Peete (Anderson kick)
Ariz — FG Davis 35
Phil — Williams 37 pass from Peete (Anderson kick)

CAROLINA 21, ATLANTA 17—at Clemson Memorial Stadium, attendance 53,833. Rookie quarterback Kerry Collins rallied the Panthers from a 17-7 deficit to defeat the Falcons. Atlanta's Jeff George started fast, hitting Eric Metcalf (15 yards) and Craig Heyward (5 yards) for first-quarter touchdown passes. But the Panthers kept the Falcons out of the end zone the rest of the game, and halved the lead by driving 98 yards to a second-quarter touchdown. Morten Andersen's 34-yard field goal just before halftime made it 17-7 at intermission. In the third quarter, Collins's passing keyed a 70-yard drive that ended with Derrick Moore's 1-yard touchdown run to make it 17-14. Atlanta had a chance to increase its lead in the fourth quarter, but George's pass was tipped and intercepted by Sam Mills, who returned it to the Panthers' 11. Two plays later, Collins audibilized, telling Willie Green to fake a slant and go deep.The Falcons' secondary fell for the fake, and Collins hit Green for an 89-yard touchdown pass with 7:06 remaining. The victory was secured with 1:07 left when Carolina defensive back Pat Terrell knocked a fourth-and-goal pass away from Bert Emanuel in the end zone. Collins finished 18 of 28 for 283 yards, including 4 to Green for 147 yards. George was 29 of 53 for 310 yards, with 8 completions to Terance Mathis for 102 yards and 9 to Metcalf for 84 yards.

Atlanta 14 3 0 0 — 17
Carolina 0 7 7 7 — 21

Atl — Metcalf 15 pass from George (Andersen kick)
Atl — Heyward 5 pass from George (Andersen kick)
Car — Collins 1 run (Kasay kick)
Atl — FG Andersen 34
Car — Moore 1 run (Kasay kick)
Car — Green 89 pass from Collins (Kasay kick)

CLEVELAND 26, CINCINNATI 10—at Cleveland Stadium, attendance 55,875. Vinny Testaverde passed for 2 touchdowns and the Browns' defense collared the Bengals in the club's last home game ever at Cleveland Stadium. Testaverde led a 17-point second quarter with a 1-yard touchdown pass to Frank Hartley and a 16-yard scoring pass to Keenan McCardell. Matt Stover kicked 3 of his 4 field goals in the second half to increase the Browns' lead to 26-3. Cleveland's defense kept the Bengals out of the end zone until 6:51 remained, limiting Cincinnati to 65 rushing yards and Jeff Blake to 22 completions in 46 attempts. Testaverde completed 22 of 32 passes for 241 yards, with no interceptions. Earnest Byner ran for 121 yards on 31 carries for his first 100-yard game since 1992.

Cincinnati 0 3 0 7 — 10
Cleveland 0 17 6 3 — 26

Cleve — Hartley 1 pass from Testaverde (Stover kick)
Cin — FG Pelfrey 30
Cleve — FG Stover 37
Cleve — McCardell 16 pass from Testaverde (Stover kick)
Cleve — FG Stover 42
Cleve — FG Stover 19
Cleve — FG Stover 35
Cin — Bieniemy 1 run (Pelfrey kick)

KANSAS CITY 20, DENVER 17—at Arrowhead Stadium, attendance 75,061. Two fumble recoveries led to 14 points as the Chiefs defeated the Broncos. Defensive end Neil Smith recovered a fumble at the Broncos' 35 early in the first quarter, and six plays later, Steve Bono connected with Webster Slaughter on a 5-yard touchdown pass. Bono capped an 80-yard drive with a 5-yard touchdown run in the second quarter for a 14-0 Kansas City lead. The Chiefs' only mistake came just before halftime, when their offensive line stopped because they thought the play had been blown dead by the officials. It had not been blown dead, and Denver cornerback Ray Crockett swooped in untouched and hit Bono, forcing a fumble that Crockett returned 50 yards for a touchdown with three seconds left in the half. Denver closed to 14-10 with a third-quarter field goal, and John Elway was poised for another comeback as he led the Broncos to the Denver 39 in the final minutes of the game. But defensive end Darren Mickell sacked Elway, and defensive end Vaughn Booker finally corralled the ball at the 14 and returned it for the clinching touchdown with 1:52 left. Elway completed 24 of 36 passes for 242 yards. Bono was 23 of 37 for 232 yards.

Denver 0 7 3 7 — 17
Kansas City 7 7 0 6 — 20

KC — Slaughter 5 pass from Bono (Elliott kick)
KC — Bono 5 run (Elliott kick)
Den — Crockett 50 fumble return (Elam kick)
Den — FG Elam 49
KC — Booker 14 fumble return (pass failed)
Den — Pritchard 3 pass from Elway (Elam kick)

DETROIT 44, JACKSONVILLE 0—at Pontiac Silverdome, attendance 70,204. The Lions' top-ranked offense was running on all cylinders as they crushed the Jaguars for their sixth straight victory. The 44-point margin was the largest in franchise history. Scott Mitchell passed for 2 touchdowns, both to Johnnie Morton (23 and 17 yards). Barry Sanders ran for 76 yards and 2 scores, and Jason Hanson kicked 3 field goals. Detroit held the ball for 36 minutes 1 second and limited Jacksonville to 235 total yards while forcing 5 turnovers. Mitchell completed 19 of 28 passes for 233 yards, and Morton had 4 catches for 80 yards.

Jacksonville 0 0 0 0 — 0
Detroit 10 17 10 7 — 44

Det — FG Hanson 38
Det — Morton 23 pass from Mitchell (Hanson kick)
Det — Sanders 4 run (Hanson kick)
Det — FG Hanson 39
Det — Sanders 2 run (Hanson kick)
Det — FG Hanson 33
Det — Morton 17 pass from Mitchell (Hanson kick)
Det — Rivers 2 run (Hanson kick)

BUFFALO 23, MIAMI 20—at Rich Stadium, attendance 79,531. The Bills won their sixth AFC East title in eight seasons with a hard-fought victory over the Dolphins. The game was a battle of field goals until 38 seconds before halftime, when Thurman Thomas ran 2 yards for a touchdown to give Buffalo a 13-3 advantage at intermission. Miami parlayed a fumble recovery and an interception into 10 third-quarter points and a 13-13 tie, only to have the Bills reclaim the lead with five seconds left in the quarter on Thomas's 11-yard touchdown reception from Jim Kelly. Miami tied the game again on Bernie Parmalee's 5-yard touchdown run with 9:11 to play, then quickly got the ball back after a Buffalo punt. But reserve linebacker David White made a leaping interception of Dan Marino's pass to Irving Fryar and returned the ball to the Dolphins' 11. White's interception set up Steve Christie's 25-yard field goal with 6:11 remaining. The Dolphins punted on their next possession, and then Buffalo ran off the final 4:32 of the game behind Thomas (35 carries for 148 yards). The Bills ran for 208 yards, including 6 carries for 50 yards by special-teams whiz Steve Tasker. Miami managed just 42 rushing yards while Marino was 17 of 27 for 244 yards.

Miami 0 3 10 7 — 20
Buffalo 3 10 7 3 — 23

Buff — FG Christie 20
Buff — FG Christie 24
Mia — FG Stoyanovich 50
Buff — Thomas 2 run (Christie kick)
Mia — FG Stoyanovich 30
Mia — E. Green 25 pass from Marino (Stoyanovich kick)
Buff — Thomas 11 pass from Kelly (Christie kick)
Mia — Parmalee 5 run (Stoyanovich kick)
Buff — FG Christie 25

DALLAS 21, N.Y. GIANTS 20—at Texas Stadium, attendance 64,400. The Cowboys overcame a career day by the Giants' Rodney Hampton to outlast New York. The Giants' offensive line led the way as the Giants drove 52 and 73 yards to first-half touchdowns and a 14-6 lead at intermission. Meanwhile, the Cowboys could not get into the end zone, relying on Chris Boniol's 4 field goals to cut the gap to 14-12 entering the fourth quarter. Hampton's running keyed a Giants' drive to Brad Daluiso's 20-yard field goal that gave New York a 17-12 lead seven seconds into the fourth quarter. Dallas answered with an 82-yard drive, capped by Emmitt Smith's 5-yard touchdown run, to take an 18-17 lead (the two-point conversion failed). Back came the Giants, as Hampton carried 8 times for 57 yards to set up Daluiso's 27-yard field goal for a 20-18 lead with 5:17 left. Dallas got its last chance at its 25 with 2:59 left, and took advantage, as Troy Aikman converted three third-down passes to position Boniol for his fifth field goal, a 35-yard kick that won the game as time expired. Hampton ran for 187 yards on 34 carries as the Giants amassed 244 rushing yards. Smith had 24 carries for 103 yards. Aikman was 16 of 34 for 222 yards.

N.Y. Giants 0 14 0 6 — 20
Dallas 3 3 6 9 — 21

Dall — FG Boniol 27
Giants— Wheatley 1 run (Daluiso kick)
Dall — FG Boniol 32
Giants— D. Brown 5 run (Daluiso kick)
Dall — FG Boniol 23
Dall — FG Boniol 45
Giants— FG Daluiso 20
Dall — E. Smith 5 run (pass failed)
Giants— FG Daluiso 27
Dall — FG Boniol 35

HOUSTON 23, N.Y. JETS 6—at Astrodome, attendance 35,873. Rookie quarterback Steve McNair guided the Oilers to victory in his first NFL start. McNair, the third player chosen in the 1995 draft, completed 13 of 27 passes for 198 yards and 1 touchdown while leading a turnover-free offense. McNair's 35-yard touchdown pass to Haywood Jeffires near the end of the first quarter gave Houston a 10-0 lead. McNair's 53-yard bomb to Chris Sanders set up the Oilers' last score, a 1-yard touchdown run by Marion Butts with 4:35 to play in the game. Houston limited New York to 30 rushing yards and 164 total yards. Tight end Johnny Mitchell had 7 catches for 72 yards, scoring the Jets' only points on a 17-yard reception.

N.Y. Jets 0 0 0 6 — 6
Houston 10 3 0 10 — 23

Hou — FG Del Greco 49
Hou — Jeffires 35 pass from S. McNair (Del Greco kick)
Hou — FG Del Greco 53
Hou — FG Del Greco 24
Hou — Butts 1 run (Del Greco kick)
Jets — Mitchell 17 pass from Esiason (pass failed)

SAN DIEGO 27, INDIANAPOLIS 24—at RCA Dome, attendance 55,318. John Carney kicked 2 field goals in the final two minutes to lift the Chargers over the Colts. Stan Humphries passed for 2 scores and ran for another to lead San Diego. His 51-yard touchdown pass to Tony Martin gave the Chargers a 7-3 first-quarter lead, and his 1-yard touchdown run gave San Diego a 14-10 third-quarter lead. After the Colts closed to 14-13, Humphries found Martin again, this time for a 38-yard touchdown pass that made it 21-13 with 11:21 left. The Colts countered with an 85-yard drive, scoring on Marshall Faulk's 1-yard run and tying the game on Jim Harbaugh's 2-point conversion pass to Floyd Turner. An interception set up Carney's first kick, a 33-yard field goal with 1:59 left that gave San Diego a 24-21 lead. Harbaugh's passing brought the Colts to the Chargers' 33, where Cary Blanchard kicked a tying 50-yard field goal with 48 seconds left. That was just enough time for Humphries, who completed 2 passes to position Carney for the winning 43-yard field goal with three seconds left. Humphries completed 21 of 40 passes for 272 yards, while Aaron Hayden ran for 96 yards on 26 carries. Martin had 10 catches for 168 yards. Harbaugh completed 20 of 43 passes for 285 yards, including 6 to Sean Dawkins for 123 yards.

San Diego 7 0 7 13 — 27
Indianapolis 3 7 0 14 — 24

Ind — FG Blanchard 36
SD — Martin 51 pass from Humphries (Carney kick)
Ind — Dilger 13 pass from Harbaugh (Blanchard kick)
SD — Humphries 1 run (Carney kick)
Ind — FG Blanchard 42
SD — Martin 38 pass from Humphries (Carney kick)
Ind — Faulk 1 run (Turner pass from Harbaugh)
SD — FG Carney 33
Ind — FG Blanchard 50
SD — FG Carney 43

CHICAGO 31, TAMPA BAY 10—at Soldier Field, attendance 49,475. The Bears' offense awoke from its slumber to defeat the Buccaneers and keep Chicago's playoff hopes alive. Rashaan Salaam's 15-yard touchdown run gave Chicago a 7-0 lead 22 seconds into the game. Salaam's score was set up by an interception. Trent

Dilfer's 20-yard touchdown pass to Horace Copeland made it 7-7 less than five minutes into the game. Salaam's second touchdown early in the second period made it 14-7, but Tampa Bay hung tough, closing to 14-10 on Michael Husted's 50-yard field goal. The Bears took over in the second half, as Erik Kramer found Jeff Graham for a 47-yard touchdown pass, Kevin Butler kicked a 23-yard field goal, and Salaam clinched the victory with his third touchdown run. Salaam rushed for 134 yards on 27 carries. Kramer was 20 of 28 for 256, with no interceptions. The Bears amassed 429 yards of total offense. Graham had 5 catches for 102 yards, and Curtis Conway had 8 for 88. Dilfer was 22 of 37 for 226 yards. Tampa Bay had 4 turnovers, 3 of which led to 17 points for the Bears.

Tampa Bay	7	3	0	0	—	10
Chicago	7	7	10	7	—	31

Chi — Salaam 15 run (Butler kick)
TB — Copeland 20 pass from Dilfer (Husted kick)
Chi — Salaam 1 run (Butler kick)
TB — FG Husted 50
Chi — Graham 47 pass from Kramer (Butler kick)
Chi — FG Butler 23
Chi — Salaam 3 run (Butler kick)

WASHINGTON 35, ST. LOUIS 23—at Trans World Dome, attendance 63,760. The Redskins' defense forced 4 turnovers and scored twice in Washington's victory. The Redskins trailed 10-0 before reeling off 28 consecutive points. Heath Shuler's 22-yard touchdown pass to Brian Mitchell started the scoring, followed by cornerback Tom Carter's 51-yard interception return for a touchdown to make it 14-10 at halftime. Two touchdown runs in the third quarter—the second one was set up by a fumble recovery—upped Washington's lead to 28-10. The Rams then went without a huddle, producing 2 touchdowns in the first four minutes of the fourth quarter to pull close at 28-23. But St. Louis's hopes ended when linebacker Marvcus Patton forced a fumble that defensive end Tony Woods returned 3 yards for a touchdown. Patton had 15 tackles and 2 forced fumbles. St. Louis quarterback Mark Rypien completed 34 of 50 passes for 347 yards against his former team. The Rams' Alexander Wright had 8 catches for 132 yards.

Washington	7	7	14	7	—	35
St. Louis	10	0	0	13	—	23

StL — FG Biasucci 25
StL — Bettis 1 run (Biasucci kick)
Wash — Mitchell 22 pass from Shuler (Murray kick)
Wash — Carter 51 interception return (Murray kick)
Wash — Allen 1 run (Murray kick)
Wash — Shepherd 8 run (Murray kick)
StL — Bailey 5 run (Biasucci kick)
StL — Wright 21 pass from Rypien (pass failed)
Wash — Woods 3 fumble return (Murray kick)

SUNDAY NIGHT, DECEMBER 17

SEATTLE 44, OAKLAND 10—at Kingdome, attendance 58,428. Chris Warren ran for 3 touchdowns as the Seahawks overwhelmed the Raiders. Warren's scoring runs of 15 and 14 yards gave Seattle a 14-0 lead 8:09 into the game. That lead was 27-3 at halftime thanks to 2 field goals by Todd Peterson and John Friesz's 43-yard touchdown pass to Joey Galloway. Any Raider comeback hopes were dashed when Corey Harris picked up a fumble and rambled 53 yards for a touchdown on Oakland's first possession of the second half. Warren added a 35-yard touchdown run and finished with 105 yards on 17 carries. Galloway had 5 catches for 108 yards. Friesz was 16 of 25 for 220 yards. Raiders quarterback Jeff Hostetler, who returned after missing three games, re-injured his left shoulder and was sidelined for the season.

Oakland	3	0	0	7	—	10
Seattle	17	10	14	3	—	44

Sea — Warren 15 run (Peterson kick)
Sea — Warren 14 run (Peterson kick)
Oak — FG Jaeger 42
Sea — FG Peterson 39
Sea — Galloway 43 pass from Friesz (Peterson kick)
Sea — FG Peterson 19
Sea — C.Harris 57 fumble return (Peterson kick)
Sea — Warren 35 run (Peterson kick)
Sea — FG Peterson 38
Oak — Brown 80 pass from Hobert (Jaeger kick)

MONDAY, DECEMBER 18

SAN FRANCISCO 37, MINNESOTA 30—at 3Com Park, attendance 64,975. Steve Young passed for 425 yards and 3 scores and ran for the decisive touchdown to lead the 49ers to their sixth consecutive victory. Jerry Rice caught 14 passes for a career-high 289 yards (the fifth-highest single-game total in NFL history) and 3 scores. Young teamed with Rice on scoring passes of 8 and 46 yards during a 21-point first-quarter blitz. Minnesota cut the lead to 21-10, only to have Young and Rice strike again on a 31-yard pass play that made it 27-10 with 6:10 remaining in the first half. Back came the Vikings, as a 42-yard interception return set up Warren Moon's second touchdown pass and Fuad Reveiz kicked a field goal as the first half expired to close the gap to 27-20. A fumble recovery at the 49ers' 19 set up the tying touchdown, on a 6-yard pass from Moon to Jake Reed. San Francisco answered with an 67-yard drive to a tiebreaking field goal, with 41 of the yards coming on a pass from Young to Rice. Those two were at it again on an 80-yard drive, connecting twice for 62 yards en route to Young's 5-yard touchdown run for a 37-27 lead. Young completed 30 of 49 passes. Moon was 22 of 39 for 224 yards and 3 scores. Cris Carter led Minnesota with 12 receptions for 88 yards.

Minnesota	0	20	7	3	—	30
San Francisco	21	6	3	7	—	37

SF — Rice 8 pass from Young (kick failed)
SF — Carter 78 punt return (Loville run)
SF — Rice 46 pass from Young (Wilkins kick)
Minn — FG Reveiz 29
Minn — Carter 6 pass from Moon (Reveiz kick)
SF — Rice 31 pass from Young (kick failed)
Minn — Carter 2 pass from Moon (Reveiz kick)
Minn — FG Reveiz 43
Minn — Reed 6 pass from Moon (Reveiz kick)
SF — FG Wilkins 20
SF — Young 6 run (Wilkins kick)
Minn — FG Reveiz 38

SEVENTEENTH WEEK SUMMARIES

AMERICAN FOOTBALL CONFERENCE

Eastern Division	**W**	**L**	**T**	**Pct.**	**Pts.**	**OP**
Buffalo	10	6	0	.625	350	335
Indianapolis	9	7	0	.563	331	316
Miami	9	7	0	.563	398	332
New England	6	10	0	.375	294	377
N.Y. Jets	3	13	0	.188	233	384
Central Division						
Pittsburgh	11	5	0	.689	407	327
Cincinnati	7	9	0	.438	349	374
Houston	7	9	0	.438	348	324
Cleveland	5	11	0	.313	289	356
Jacksonville	4	12	0	.250	275	404
Western Division						
Kansas City	13	3	0	.813	358	241
San Diego	9	7	0	.563	321	323
Seattle	8	8	0	.500	363	366
Denver	8	8	0	.500	388	345
Oakland	8	8	0	.500	348	332

NATIONAL FOOTBALL CONFERENCE

Eastern Division	**W**	**L**	**T**	**Pct.**	**Pts.**	**OP**
Dallas	12	4	0	.750	435	291
Philadelphia	10	6	0	.625	318	338
Washington	6	10	0	.375	326	359
N.Y. Giants	5	11	0	.313	290	340
Arizona	4	12	0	.250	275	422
Central Division						
Green Bay	11	5	0	.689	404	314
Detroit	10	6	0	.625	436	336
Chicago	9	7	0	.563	392	360
Minnesota	8	8	0	.500	412	385
Tampa Bay	7	9	0	.438	238	335
Western Division						
San Francisco	11	5	0	.688	457	258
Atlanta	9	7	0	.563	362	349
St. Louis	7	9	0	.438	309	418
Carolina	7	9	0	.438	289	325
New Orleans	7	9	0	.438	319	348

SATURDAY, DECEMBER 23

SAN DIEGO 27, NEW YORK GIANTS 17—at Giants Stadium, attendance 50,243. The Chargers rallied from a 17-3 deficit to win their fifth consecutive game and secure a wild-card berth. The Giants built their lead in the first half, with a fumble recovery setting up Dave Brown's 3-yard touchdown run and New York driving 71 yards to its other touchdown on a 1-yard run by Rodney Hampton. With quarterback Stan Humphries sidelined by an injury, San Diego's defense led the charge. Linebacker Junior Seau's fumble recovery set up Aaron Hayden's 8-yard scoring run, which made it 17-10 in the third quarter. Gale Gilbert, Humphries's replacement, led a 55-yard drive to the tying touchdown in the fourth quarter. Gilbert's 13-yard pass on fourth-and-6 kept the drive alive, and Rodney Culver finished it with an 8-yard run. New York answered by advancing to the Chargers' 12, but Brown, hit by Seau as he threw, was intercepted by safety Shaun Gayle at the 1-yard line. Gayle returned the interception 99 yards for the tiebreaking touchdown with 5:44 left. Brown's fumble on the Giants' next possession led to a Chargers' field goal that clinched the victory. San Diego forced 4 turnovers, which led to 20 points. Hayden had 80 yards on 22 carries, and Seau tallied 13 tackles. Brown was 21 of 36 for 209 yards.

San Diego	0	3	7	17	—	27
N.Y. Giants	3	14	0	0	—	17

Giants— FG Daluiso 30
Giants— Brown 3 run (Daluiso kick)
SD — FG Carney 30
Giants— Hampton 1 run (Daluiso kick)
SD — Hayden 8 run (Carney kick)
SD — Culver 8 run (Carney kick)
SD — Gayle 99 interception return (Carney kick)
SD — FG Carney 45

DETROIT 37, TAMPA BAY 10—at Tampa Stadium, attendance 50,049. Scott Mitchell passed for 352 yards and 2 scores as the Lions rolled to their seventh consecutive victory. Mitchell capped the Lions' first possession with a 5-yard touchdown pass to Johnnie Morton. Later in the first quarter, Detroit made it 14-0 as linebacker Tracy Scroggins returned a fumble 81 yards for a score. In the third quarter, Mitchell combined with Brett Perriman on a 91-yard scoring strike that upped Detroit's advantage to 24-3. Mitchell completed 26 of 41 passes and also ran for a score. Herman Moore caught 10 passes (for 105 yards) to finish with an NFL single-season record of 123 receptions. Perriman had 5 catches for 135 yards.

Detroit	14	3	10	10	—	37
Tampa Bay	0	3	0	7	—	10

Det — Morton 5 pass from Mitchell (Hanson kick)
Det — Scroggins 81 fumble return (Hanson kick)
Det — FG Hanson 33
TB — FG Husted 27
Det — Perriman 91 pass from Mitchell (Hanson kick)
Det — FG Hanson 39
Det — FG Hanson 45
TB — Ellison 1 run (Husted kick)
Det — Mitchell 1 run (Hanson kick)

SATURDAY NIGHT, DECEMBER 23

INDIANAPOLIS 10, NEW ENGLAND 7—at RCA Dome, attendance 54,685. Lamont Warren replaced an injured Marshall Faulk and produced 157 yards from scrimmage to lead the Colts over the Patriots and into the playoffs. New England scored its only touchdown with 1:54 left in the first half, as Drew Bledsoe finished a 79-yard march with a 31-yard touchdown pass to Hanson Graham. In the third quarter, the Colts' Jim Harbaugh completed all 7 of his passes on a 65-yard drive that ended with Harbaugh's 13-yard scoring pass to Floyd Turner. Warren had a key reception on that drive, then added a key run on the Colts' march to the winning field goal, Cary Blanchard's 30-yard kick with 4:51 left in the game. Warren finished with 90 yards on 22 carries and 67 yards on 6 receptions. Harbaugh completed 20 of 30 passes for 225 yards, including 14 of 19 for 171 in the second half. Patriots rookie Curtis Martin ran for 103 yards to finish with an AFC-high 1,487 yards.

New England	0	7	0	0	—	7
Indianapolis	0	0	7	3	—	10

NE — Graham 31 pass from Bledsoe (Bahr kick)
Ind — Turner 13 pass from Harbaugh (Blanchard kick)
Ind — FG Blanchard 30

SUNDAY, DECEMBER 24

WASHINGTON 20, CAROLINA 17—at RFK Stadium, attendance 42,903. Two big plays broke a 10-10 tie and propelled the Redskins past the Panthers. Washington quarterback Gus Frerotte hit Henry Ellard on a 53-yard bomb to get the Redskins out of a hole at their 7-yard line, and on the next play, wide receiver Michael Westbrook took a reverse 33 yards to put Washington at Carolina's 1. One play later, Terry Allen's second touchdown of the day gave the Redskins a 17-10 lead. Eddie Murray's fourth-quarter field goal upped their advantage to 20-10 before Carolina closed the gap with a touchdown in the final minute. Allen finished with 92 yards on 28 carries. Frerrotte passed for 185 yards. Despite the loss, Carolina finished the season with seven victories, the most ever by an expansion team. Mark Carrier led the Panthers with 7 receptions for 101 yards.

Carolina	3	7	0	7	—	17
Washington	7	3	7	3	—	20

Car — FG Kasay 42
Wash — Allen 1 run (Murray kick)
Wash — FG Murray 29
Car — Moore 1 run (Kasay kick)
Wash — Allen 1 run (Murray kick)
Wash — FG Murray 32
Car — Green 2 pass from Collins (Kasay kick)

JACKSONVILLE 24, CLEVELAND 21—at Jacksonville Municipal Stadium, attendance 66,007. Mike Hollis's 34-yard field goal as time expired lifted the Jaguars over the Browns. Cleveland outgained Jacksonville 450 to 373, but 3 interceptions committed by the Browns made the difference. Mark Brunell's 33-yard touchdown pass to Willie Jackson gave Jacksonville a 10-0 first-quarter lead. Cleveland pulled close on Vinny Testaverde's 39-yard scoring strike to Michael Jackson, but Hollis's second field goal gave the Jaguars a 13-7 halftime lead. The Browns took the second-half kickoff and embarked on a 15-play, 91-yard drive, taking a 14-13 lead on Lorenzo White's 3-yard touchdown run. That lead would not stand, however, as Harry Colon's interception set up Brunell's 27-yard touchdown run. Brunell's two-point conversion pass to Willie Jackson made it 21-14 with 7:28 to play in the game. With three minutes to play, Testaverde mounted one last drive, leading the Browns 79 yards in 1:48 and scoring the tying touchdown on a 1-yard run with 1:13 remaining. That proved to be enough time for Jacksonville, which used a 35-yard pass interference penalty to position Hollis for the winning kick. His 39-yard attempt hit the right upright, but an offsides penalty gave him another shot and Hollis drilled it for the game winner. Brunell completed 17 of 29 passes for 275 yards, and he also ran for a team-high 51 yards. Testaverde was 28 of 45 for 325 yards, including 7 for 130 yards to Michael Jackson.

Cleveland	0	7	7	7	—	21
Jacksonville	10	3	0	11	—	24

Jack — FG Hollis 42
Jack — Jackson 33 pass from Brunell (Hollis kick)
Cleve — Jackson 39 pass from Testaverde (Stover kick)
Jack — FG Hollis 20
Cleve — White 3 run (Stover kick)
Jack — Brunell 27 run (Jackson pass from Brunell)
Cleve — Testaverde 1 run (Stover kick)
Jack — FG Hollis 34

DENVER 31, OAKLAND 28—at Oakland-Alameda County Coliseum, attendance 50,074. The Broncos' Jason Elam kicked a 37-yard field goal—his third of the day—with 48 seconds left to hand the Raiders their sixth consecutive defeat. Oakland, which would have made the playoffs with a victory, finished the season 8-8 after starting 8-2. Denver also finished 8-8. Denver entered the second half with a 17-14 cushion, but Billy Joe Hobert, who alternated as the Raiders' quarterback, quickly changed that. Cornerback Albert Lewis's 38-yard fumble return set up Hobert's 4-yard touchdown pass to Tim Brown 1:05 into the third quarter. Three minutes later, cornerback Terry McDaniel's interception set up Hobert's 48-yard scoring pass to Brown for a 28-17 Oakland lead. Elam's second field goal cut the deficit to 28-20, and then Denver tied the game with 5:45 remaining on John Elway's touchdown pass and two-point conversion run. The Raiders answered by advancing to the Broncos' 28, but fumbled the ball back to Denver. Elway then led a 53-yard drive to the winning kick. Elway completed 24 of 41 passes for 320 yards, including 225 in the second half. Aaron Craver led Denver with 108 yards and 1 touchdown on 20 carries. Hobert completed 11 of 19 passes for 133 yards and 3 scores while Vince Evans completed 9 of 11 passes for 107 yards and 1 score. Neither threw an interception. Brown had 8 catches for 127 yards.

Denver	0	17	0	14	—	31
Oakland	7	7	14	0	—	28

Oak — Hobbs 11 pass from Hobert (Jaeger kick)
Den — Miller 2 pass from Elway (Elam kick)
Den — Craver 1 run (Elam kick)
Oak — Fenner 9 pass from Evans (Jaeger kick)
Den — FG Elam 45
Oak — Brown 4 pass from Hobert (Jaeger kick)
Oak — Brown 48 pass from Hobert (Jaeger kick)
Den — FG Elam 27
Den — McCaffrey 4 pass from Elway (Elway run)
Den — FG Elam 37

HOUSTON 28, BUFFALO 17—at Rich Stadium, attendance 45,253. Rodney Thomas ran for 2 touchdowns and the Oilers' defense shut down the Bills. Buffalo, which had already clinched the AFC East, rested many of its regulars. Todd Collins made his first NFL start in place of Jim Kelly and was sacked 5 times before giving way to Alex Van Pelt. Meanwhile, Houston's Steve McNair, in his second career start, posted his second victory by passing for 168 yards and 1 score. McNair's 44-yard pass to Chris Sanders set up Thomas's 4-yard touchdown run, which gave Houston a 14-3 lead less than five minutes into the third quarter. Six minutes later, McNair's passing set up Thomas's second touchdown, a 7-yard run that gave Houston a 21-3 advantage. McNair closed the Oilers' scoring with a 36-yard touchdown pass to Frank Wycheck. Thomas finished with 80 yards on 24 carries. Houston limited Buffalo to 172 total yards, most of which came in the fourth quarter as Van Pelt led the Bills on 2 scoring drives.

Houston	0	8	13	7	—	28
Buffalo	0	0	3	14	—	17

Hou — Safety, Cook tackled Collins in end zone
Hou — FG Del Greco 39
Hou — FG Del Greco 33
Buff — FG Christie 44
Hou — Thomas 4 run (run failed)
Hou — Thomas 7 run (Del Greco kick)
Hou — Wycheck 36 pass from S. McNair (Del Greco kick)
Buff — Reed 15 pass from Van Pelt (Christie kick)
Buff — Armour 19 pass from Van Pelt (Christie kick)

MIAMI 41, ST. LOUIS 22—at Trans World Dome, attendance 63,876. The Dolphins converted 3 turnovers into 21 points to defeat the Rams. The Dolphins' victory gave them a 9-7 record and, coupled with the Raiders' loss to Denver, a wild-card berth in the playoffs. St. Louis, which started the season 4-0, finished 7-9. Miami's special teams produced the first turnover, a fumbled punt return at the Rams' 22 that led to Bernie Parmalee's 3-yard touchdown run and a 10-3 Miami lead. The Rams closed the gap to 10-6, but lost a golden opportunity in the second quarter when linebacker Roman Phifer intercepted a pass from Dan Marino only to fumble it right back to Miami. Marino took advantage of his good fortune, finding Irving Fryar for a 6-yard touchdown pass. Four minutes later, Marino teamed with O.J. McDuffie for a 7-yard touchdown pass and a 24-6 lead. Mark Rypien rallied the Rams, firing 2 scoring passes to pull St. Louis close at 27-22 with 7:01 remaining in the game. The Rams got no closer, however, as Irving Spikes returned a kickoff 55 yards to St. Louis' 35, and five plays later Parmalee scored his second touchdown to increase Miami's lead to 34-22 with 3:57 left. Miami completed the scoring with 1:19 left when safety Pat Johnson returned a fumble 37 yards for a touchdown. Marino completed 23 of 35 passes for 290 yards. Rypien was 27 of 42 for 320 yards. The Rams' Isaac Bruce caught 15 passes—an NFL single-game high for 1995—for 210 yards and 1 touchdown.

Miami	10	17	0	14	—	41
St. Louis	3	9	7	3	—	22

StL — FG Biasucci 42
Mia — FG Stoyanovich 33
Mia — Parmalee 3 run (Stoyanovich kick)
StL — FG Biasucci 27
Mia — Fryar 6 pass from Marino (Stoyanovich kick)
Mia — McDuffie 7 pass from Marino (Stoyanovich kick)
StL — Kinchen 7 pass from Rypien (pass failed)
Mia — FG Stoyanovich 48
StL — Bruce 5 pass from Rypien (Biasucci kick)
StL — FG Biasucci 38
Mia — Parmalee 7 run (Stoyanovich kick)
Mia — Johnson 37 fumble return (Stoyanovich kick)

CINCINNATI 27, MINNESOTA 24—at Riverfront Stadium, attendance 34,568. The Bengals rallied from a 24-3 deficit to defeat the Vikings, tying the biggest comeback in franchise history. Minnesota built its lead with a 21-point second-quarter blitz—2 touchdown passes by Warren Moon sandwiched around Alfred Jackson's 37-yard interception return for a score. Cincinnati, trailing 24-3, got back in the game in the third quarter with 65- and 96-yard touchdown marches. After that, the Bengals got some help from the Vikings. First, Fuad Reveiz slipped while attempting a field goal, and his 38-yard kick went wide right. Second, a 15-yard punt by the Vikings set up the Bengals' tying score, as Cincinnati took over at the Minnesota 40 and Jeff Blake completed passes for 35 and 5 yards to make it 24-24 with 8:01 left. Third, Minnesota advanced to the Bengals' 7, but Reveiz's tie-breaking 25-yard field-goal attempt went wide left with 2:06 left. Blake completed 5 passes for 46 yards to lead a drive to the Vikings' 34, where Doug Pelfrey kicked a 51-yard field goal as time expired. Blake passed for 231 yards. Minnesota, which was eliminated from playoff contention when Chicago and Atlanta won, finished 8-8 and out of the postseason for the first time in Dennis Green's four years as coach. The Vikings gained 448 yards in total offense, led by Moon (26 of 43 for 294 yards, with no interceptions) and Scottie Graham (25 carries for 115 yards).

Minnesota	3	21	0	0	—	24
Cincinnati	3	0	14	10	—	27

Minn — FG Reveiz 20
Cin — FG Pelfrey 44
Minn — Reed 51 pass from Moon (Reveiz kick)
Minn — Jackson 37 interception return (Reveiz kick)
Minn — Carter 14 pass from Moon (Reveiz kick)
Cin — Bieniemy 5 run (Pelfrey kick)
Cin — Pickens 11 pass from Blake (Pelfrey kick)
Cin — McGee 5 pass from Blake (Pelfrey kick)
Cin — FG Pelfrey 51

NEW ORLEANS 12, NEW YORK JETS 0—at Giants Stadium, attendance 28,885. The Saints played mistake-free football while forcing 3 turnovers in their victory over the Jets. The Saints took a 3-0 first-quarter lead on Doug Brien's 32-yard field goal after an 11-play, 51-yard drive. It stayed that way until the third period, when Brien culminated a 14-play, 48-yard march with a 23-yard field goal. In the fourth quarter, after stopping the Jets on downs, the Saints drove 38 yards to the clinching touchdown on Jim Everett's 12-yard pass to tight end Wesley Walls. Everett completed 20 of 38 passes for 199 yards. New Orleans limited New York to 206 total yards.

New Orleans	3	0	3	6	—	12
N.Y. Jets	0	0	0	0	—	0

NO — FG Brien 32
NO — FG Brien 23
NO — Walls 12 pass from Everett (pass failed)

CHICAGO 20, PHILADELPHIA 14—at Soldier Field, attendance 52,391. The Bears' defense delivered one of its best performances of the season in their victory over the Eagles. Despite the win, Chicago (9-7) missed the playoffs when Atlanta defeated San Francisco. Philadelphia (10-6) had already clinched a playoff berth. The Bears held the Eagles to 211 total yards (just 44 on the ground) and 12 first downs while controlling the ball for nearly 40 minutes. Safety Mark Carrier's fumble recovery set up Chicago's first score, a 13-yard pass from Erik Kramer to tight end Keith Jennings. Philadelphia answered with a 70-yard drive to the tying touchdown on Charlie Garner's 8-yard run on the first play of the second quarter. But the Bears came right back with a 13-play drive to a field goal and an 11-play march that culminated in Kramer's second touchdown pass to Jennings (1 yard) for a 17-7 halftime lead. Philadelphia mounted little offensive output in the second half, scoring only when a punt inadvertently bounced off the feet of a Bears' blocker and into the end zone, where the Eagles' Jerome Henderson recovered it for a touchdown. Henderson's score closed the deficit to 17-14 early in the fourth quarter, but the Bears countered with a 45-yard drive to a field goal and a 20-14 lead. Kramer finished 15 of 30 for 169 yards. Chicago's Rashaan Salaam ran for 122 yards on 30 carries.

Philadelphia	0	7	0	7	—	14
Chicago	7	10	0	3	—	20

Chi — Jennings 13 pass from Kramer (Butler kick)
Phil — Garner 8 run (Anderson kick)
Chi — FG Butler 27
Chi — Jennings 1 pass from Kramer (Butler kick)
Phil — Henderson fumble recovery in end zone (Anderson kick)
Chi — FG Butler 28

GREEN BAY 24, PITTSBURGH 19—at Lambeau Field, attendance 60,649. Brett Favre completed 23 of 32 passes for 301 yards and 2 touchdowns to lead the Packers to victory and their first NFC Central title since 1972. Green Bay finished 11-5, as did Pittsburgh, which already had clinched the AFC Central title. Edgar Bennett's 9-yard touchdown run, which he set up with a 23-yard run on a third-and-1 play, gave Green Bay a 7-0 second-quarter lead. After a Steelers' field goal, Favre led an 82-yard drive, the last 19 coming on a touchdown pass to Robert Brooks with 1:56 left in the half. That was enough time for the Steelers, who drove 70 yards (the last 8 on a pass from Neil O'Donnell to Ernie Mills) to make it 14-10 at halftime. Favre answered with a 1-yard touchdown pass to tight end Mark Chmura for a 21-10 Packers lead in the third quarter. The teams traded field goals, and then Pittsburgh pulled within striking distance at 24-19 on Tim Lester's 2-yard scoring run with 9:49 left in the game. In the final minutes, O'Donnell led the Steelers to the Packers' 6, but Green Bay escaped with the victory when O'Donnell's fourth-down pass was dropped by a wide-open Yancey Thigpen in the end zone with 11 seconds left. Despite the miscue, Thigpen had 6 catches to finish the season with a club-record 85 receptions. O'Donnell completed 33 of 55 passes for 318 yards, with no interceptions. Brooks had 11 receptions for 137 yards.

Pittsburgh	0	10	3	6	—	19
Green Bay	0	14	7	3	—	24

GB — Bennett 9 run (Jacke kick)
Pitt — FG N. Johnson 33
GB — Brooks 19 pass from Favre (Jacke kick)
Pitt — Mills 8 pass from O'Donnell (N. Johnson kick)
GB — Chmura 1 pass from Favre (Jacke kick)
Pitt — FG N. Johnson 25
GB — FG Jacke 47
Pitt — Lester 2 run (pass failed)

ATLANTA 28, SAN FRANCISCO 27—at Georgia Dome, attendance 51,785. Bobby Hebert came off the bench to rally the Falcons over the 49ers and secure a playoff berth for Atlanta. The Falcons finished 9-7 to claim the last wild-card spot in the NFC. The NFC-West champion 49ers finished 11-5, but the loss cost them home-field advantage throughout the NFC playoffs. San Francisco scored on its first three possessions in unconventional fashion. First, Jerry Rice, the NFL's all-time touchdown leader, found a new way to score when he recovered a teammate's fumble in the end zone. Second, Rice took a handoff from Steve Young on a reverse and lofted a 41-yard touchdown pass to J.J. Stokes to give the 49ers a 14-3 first-quarter lead. Third, Rice caught a 57-yard pass from Young that he took to the Falcons' 8, and two plays later Derek Loville made it 21-10 with a 1-yard touchdown run. Morten Andersen's 59-yard field goal—his second 50-yard kick of the game and league-record eighth of the season—pulled Atlanta to within 21-16 at halftime. Hebert, who had replaced an injured Jeff George just before intermission, engineered a 68-yard drive to start the second half. He converted a third-and-8 and a fourth-and-1 en route to hitting Terance Mathis for a 7-yard touchdown pass that gave Atlanta a 22-21 lead. Two fourth-quarter field goals put the 49ers in front 27-22 with 3:36 remaining, but it only took Hebert 6 plays and 1:51 to move Atlanta 80 yards to the winning score on a 37-yard pass to Mathis. Hebert was 17 of 27 for 197 yards. Mathis had 8 catches for 84 yards. Young completed 31 of 44 passes for 316 yards. Rice had 12 catches for 153 yards. He set NFL records for receiving yards in a season (1,848) and career receptions (942).

San Francisco	14	7	0	6	—	27
Atlanta	3	13	6	6	—	28

SF — Rice fumble recovery in end zone (Wilkins kick)
Atl — FG Andersen 52
SF — Stokes 41 pass from Rice (Wilkins kick)
Atl — Metcalf 12 pass from George (Andersen kick)
SF — Loville 1 run (Wilkins kick)
Atl — FG Andersen 28
Atl — FG Andersen 59
Atl — Mathis 7 pass from Hebert (pass failed)
SF — FG Wilkins 39
SF — FG Wilkins 32
Atl — Mathis 37 pass from Hebert (pass failed)

KANSAS CITY 26, SEATTLE 3—at Arrowhead Stadium, attendance 75,784. The Chiefs' defense dominated the Seahawks as Kansas City completed a franchise-best 13-victory season. The Chiefs finished 13-3, the NFL's best record, and were assured of home-field advantage throughout the AFC playoffs. Seattle, which entered the game with playoff hopes, finished 8-8. The Chiefs limited Seattle to 89 total yards, the fewest allowed by any team in 1995. Tamarick Vanover set the tone by taking the opening kickoff 89 yards for a touchdown. Lin Elliott kicked 2 field goals and Kansas City led 13-0 at the end of the first quarter. Seattle's only points—Todd Peterson's 34-yard field goal—were set up by Steve Broussard's 70-yard kickoff return. Steve Bono's 9-yard touchdown pass to Vanover made it 20-3 at halftime, and the Chiefs added 2 more field goals by Elliott in the second half. Bono passed for 209 yards and Greg Hill ran for 113 yards on 21 carries as Kansas City controlled the ball for nearly 40 minutes. Seattle managed just 8 first downs.

Seattle	0	3	0	0	—	3
Kansas City	13	7	3	3	—	26

KC — Vanover 89 kickoff return (Elliott kick)
KC — FG Elliott 37
KC — FG Elliott 20
Sea — FG Peterson 34
KC — Vanover 9 pass from Bono (Elliott kick)
KC — FG Elliott 20
KC — FG Elliott 27

MONDAY, DECEMBER 25

DALLAS 37, ARIZONA 13—at Sun Devil Stadium, attendance 72,394. Troy Aikman passed for 350 yards and 2 touchdowns as the Cowboys romped over the Cardinals. Dallas, which had already clinched the NFC East, finished 12-4 to secure home-field advantage throughout the NFC playoffs. Arizona finished 4-12. Kevin Williams had a career-high 9 catches for 203 yards, including first-half touchdowns of 25 and 48 yards. Dallas also scored in the first half on Brock Marion's 32-yard interception return and Chris Boniol's 39-yard field goal to build a 24-3 lead at intermission. Arizona scored its only touchdown on cornerback Aeneas Williams's 48-yard interception return in the third quarter. A Cardinals' field goal cut the Cowboys' lead to 24-13, but Boniol kicked 2 more field goals and Emmitt Smith scored on a 3-yard run. Smith's touchdown was his twenty-fifth of the season, establishing an NFL single-season record. Smith also won his fourth league rushing crown. Aikman completed 21 of 32 passes as Dallas amassed 474 total yards. The Cardinals' Larry Centers caught 12 passes for 172 yards to finish with 101 receptions, the most ever in a season by a running back.

Dallas	17	7	3	10	—	37
Arizona	0	3	10	0	—	13

Dall — K. Williams 25 pass from Aikman (Boniol kick)
Dall — Marion 32 interception return (Boniol kick)
Dall — FG Boniol 39
Dall — K. Williams 48 pass from Aikman (Boniol kick)
Ariz — FG Davis 21
Ariz — Williams 48 interception return (Davis kick)
Ariz — FG Davis 23
Dall — FG Boniol 23
Dall — E. Smith 3 run (Boniol kick)
Dall — FG Boniol 24

EIGHTEENTH WEEK SUMMARIES
SATURDAY, DECEMBER 30
NFC WILD CARD PLAYOFF GAME

PHILADELPHIA 58, DETROIT 37—at Veterans Stadium, attendance 66,099. Rodney Peete passed for 270 yards and 3 touchdowns as the Eagles blasted the Lions. The game was tied 7-7 before Philadelphia put the game away by exploding for 31 points in the second quarter. Gary Anderson began the onslaught with a 21-yard field goal 2:04 into the second quarter, and just 2:13 later Peete teamed with Fred Barnett on a 22-yard touchdown pass for a 17-7 lead. Two plays after that, cornerback Barry Wilburn returned an interception 24 yards for a touchdown, and when Ricky Watters ran 1 yard for a touchdown 4:59 before halftime, the Eagles led 31-7. They ended any remaining suspense when Peete threw a 43-yard desperation pass for a touchdown to Rob Carpenter on the final play of the second quarter. By midway through the third quarter it was 51-7 and Detroit's seven-game winning streak was in tatters. Peete completed 17 of 25 passes in all and was not intercepted. Lions quarterbacks Scott Mitchell and Don Majkowski, meanwhile, combined for 361 yards and 4 touchdowns, but suffered 6 interceptions. The 95 points scored by the two clubs set an NFL postseason record. Philadelphia's second-quarter barrage has been bettered only once in NFL postseason play. Washington scored 35 points in the second quarter of Super Bowl XXII against Denver.

Detroit	7	0	14	16	—	37
Philadelphia	7	31	13	7	—	58

Phil — Garner 15 run (Anderson kick)
Det — Sloan 32 pass from Mitchell (Hanson kick)
Phil — FG Anderson 21
Phil — Barnett 22 pass from Peete (Anderson kick)
Phil — Wilburn 24 interception return (Anderson kick)
Phil — Watters 1 run (Anderson kick)
Phil — Carpenter 43 pass from Peete (Anderson kick)
Phil — Watters 45 pass from Peete (Anderson kick)
Phil — FG Anderson 31
Phil — FG Anderson 39
Det — Moore 68 pass from Majkowski (Hanson kick)
Det — Morton 7 pass from Majkowski (Hanson kick)
Phil — Thomas 30 interception return (Anderson kick)
Det — Sloan 2 pass from Majkowski (Rivers run)
Det — Rivers 1 run (Moore pass from Majkowski)

AFC WILD CARD PLAYOFF GAME

BUFFALO 37, MIAMI 22—at Rich Stadium, attendance 73,103. Thurman Thomas ran for 158 yards and 1 touchdown as the Bills routed the Dolphins. Buffalo amassed an NFL postseason-record 341 yards on the ground, averaging 6.6 yards per carry. Reserve running back Darick Holmes gained 87 yards, and seldom-used third-stringer Tim Tindale added 68 yards on only 4 carries, one a 44-yard touchdown. The Bills marched 58 yards to Thomas's 1-yard touchdown run the first time they had the ball, and they never looked back, building a 24-0 advantage by the intermission and leading 27-0 before Miami could score. Buffalo finished with 536 total yards, and combined with the Dolphins' 502 to set another postseason record of 1,038 yards total offense in the game. Most of Miami's yardage came long after the issue was decided, however. Quarterback Dan Marino completed 33 of 64 passes for 422 yards and 2 touchdowns, but was intercepted 3 times. Wide receiver O.J. McDuffie caught 11 passes for 154 yards. For the Bills, Steve Tasker caught 5 passes for a career-high 108 yards. Tasker, a special-teams player most of his 11-year career, was thrust into the lineup at wide receiver because of injuries to others this season. He had 3 catches for 45 yards on Buffalo's opening drive.

Miami	0	0	0	22	—	22
Buffalo	10	14	3	10	—	37

Buff — Thomas 1 run (Christie kick)
Buff — FG Christie 48
Buff — Holmes 21 run (Christie kick)
Buff — Tasker 37 pass from Kelly (Christie kick)
Buff — FG Christie 23
Mia — McDuffie 5 pass from Marino (Stoyanovich kick)
Buff — Tindale 44 run (Christie kick)
Mia — Hill 45 pass from Marino (Stoyanovich kick)
Buff — FG Christie 42
Mia — Kirby 1 run (McDuffie pass from Marino)

SUNDAY, DECEMBER 31
NFC WILD CARD PLAYOFF GAME

GREEN BAY 37, ATLANTA 20—at Lambeau Field, attendance 60,453. Edgar Bennett rushed for a club playoff-record 108 yards, and Antonio Freeman returned a punt 76 yards for a touchdown in the Packers' victory. Green Bay led just 14-10 in the second quarter before Freeman's punt return and an 85-yard drive just before halftime broke open the game at 27-10. The latter, a 14-play march capped by Brett Favre's 2-yard touchdown pass to tight end Mark

Chmura with 49 seconds left in the second quarter, featured 34 rushing yards by Bennett and completions to seven different receivers. The Falcons pulled within 27-17 on Jeff George's 27-yard touchdown pass to J.J. Birden in the first minute of the fourth quarter, but the Packers countered with another lengthy drive to put the game out of reach. The 12-play, 70-yard march took 6:22 and concluded with Favre's 18-yard touchdown pass to running back Dorsey Levens. Favre, who also threw a 14-yard touchdown pass to Robert Brooks in the first quarter, completed 24 of 35 attempts for 199 yards. Bennett, who carried 24 times, broke the Packers' postseason rushing record of 105 yards shared by Pro Football Hall of Fame members Jim Taylor and Paul Hornung. George completed 30 of 54 passes for 366 yards and 2 touchdowns for the Falcons. Eric Metcalf caught 8 passes for 114 yards.

Atlanta	7	3	0	10	—	20
Green Bay	14	13	0	10	—	37

Atl — Metcalf 65 pass from George (Andersen kick)
GB — Bennett 8 run (Jacke kick)
GB — Brooks 14 pass from Favre (Jacke kick)
Atl — FG Andersen 31
GB — Freeman 76 punt return (bad snap)
GB — Chmura 2 pass from Favre (Jacke kick)
Atl — Birden 27 pass from George (Andersen kick)
GB — Levens 18 pass from Favre (Jacke kick)
Atl — FG Andersen 22
GB — FG Jacke 25

AFC WILD CARD PLAYOFF GAME

INDIANAPOLIS 35, SAN DIEGO 20—at San Diego Jack Murphy Stadium, attendance 61,182. Unheralded rookie Zack Crockett rushed for a Colts' playoff-record 147 yards as Indianapolis stunned the defending AFC champions. Crockett, who carried only one time for no yards during the regular season, was in the game because starting running back Marshall Faulk reinjured his knee on the first play from scrimmage, and fullback Roosevelt Potts was out for the season with an injured knee. But the third-round draft choice from Florida State averaged 11.3 yards on his 13 carries against a defense that had allowed only 105.7 rushing yards per game during the regular season. The Chargers, who entered the playoffs with a five-game winning streak, took a 3-0 lead on John Carney's 54-yard field goal 5:32 into the first quarter. The lead changed hands five times after that—once on Crockett's 33-yard touchdown run 1:47 before halftime—until Jim Harbaugh's 42-yard touchdown pass to Sean Dawkins in the final minute of the third quarter put the Colts ahead for good at 21-17. San Diego pulled within 21-20 on Carney's 30-yard field goal with 11:53 to play, but Crockett raced 66 yards for a touchdown on the next play from scrimmage to give Indianapolis a 28-20 lead. Harbaugh's 3-yard touchdown run with 6:55 to play provided the final margin of victory. The Chargers had 429 total yards to Indianapolis's 333, but were victimized by 4 interceptions of quarterback Stan Humphries. Jason Belser had 2 of the thefts, including 1 he returned 33 yards to set up Indianapolis's final touchdown. The Colts' victory was their first in a postseason game since 1971.

Indianapolis	0	14	7	14	—	35
San Diego	3	7	7	3	—	20

SD — FG Carney 54
Ind — Dilger 2 pass from Harbaugh (Blanchard kick)
SD — Pupunu 6 pass from Humphries (Carney kick)
Ind — Crockett 33 run (Blanchard kick)
SD — Jefferson 11 pass from Humphries (Carney kick)
Ind — Dawkins 42 pass from Harbaugh (Blanchard kick)
SD — FG Carney 30
Ind — Crockett 66 run (Blanchard kick)
Ind — Harbaugh 3 run (Blanchard kick)

NINETEENTH WEEK SUMMARIES
SATURDAY, JANUARY 6
AFC DIVISIONAL PLAYOFF GAME

PITTSBURGH 40, BUFFALO 21—at Three Rivers Stadium, attendance 59,072. Neil O'Donnell passed for 262 yards and Byron (Bam) Morris ran for 2 game-clinching touchdowns in the fourth quarter as the Steelers advanced to the AFC Championship Game for the second consecutive year. O'Donnell completed 19 of 35 passes, including a 10-yard touchdown to Ernie Mills to give Pittsburgh a 14-0 lead 42 seconds into the second quarter. Norm Johnson added 3 field goals before halftime and another 6:36 into the second half to increase the Steelers' advantage to 26-7. After the Bills pulled within 26-21 on Jim Kelly's 9-yard touchdown pass to running back Thurman Thomas with 11:23 left in the game, Pittsburgh answered with a 9-play, 76-yard drive capped by Morris's 13-yard touchdown run with 6:16 to go. Moments later, linebacker Levon Kirkland's interception and 4-yard return set up Morris's 2-yard touchdown run at the 1:58 mark. Morris finished with 106 yards on 25 carries, helping the Steelers' balanced offense produce 409 total yards. Buffalo, which had amassed a record 341 rushing yards and more than 500 total yards in its victory over the Dolphins a week earlier, managed only 94 rushing yards and 250 total yards in this one. Quarterback Jim Kelly completed only 14 of 29 passes for 135 yards and was intercepted 3 times. Buffalo played without defensive end Bruce Smith, who missed the game because of the flu.

Buffalo	0	7	7	7	—	21
Pittsburgh	7	16	3	14	—	40

Pitt — J.L. Williams 1 run (N. Johnson kick)
Pitt — Mills 10 pass from O'Donnell (N. Johnson kick)
Pitt — FG N. Johnson 45
Pitt — FG N. Johnson 38
Buff — Thomas 1 run (Christie kick)
Pitt — FG N. Johnson 34
Pitt — FG N. Johnson 39
Buff — Cline 2 pass from Van Pelt (Christie kick)
Buff — Thomas 9 pass from Kelly (Christie kick)
Pitt — Morris 13 run (N. Johnson kick)
Pitt — Morris 2 run (N. Johnson kick)

NFC DIVISIONAL PLAYOFF GAME

GREEN BAY 27, SAN FRANCISCO 17—at 3Com Park, attendance 69,311. The Packers jumped to a 21-0 lead and never were seriously threatened as they dethroned the defending Super Bowl champions. Green Bay dominated the game early, taking the opening kickoff and maintaining possession for 11 plays and 7:11 before Chris Jacke's 44-yard field-goal attempt was blocked by Tim McDonald. But on the 49ers' first play from scrimmage, fullback Adam Walker fumbled because of a hard hit by linebacker Wayne Simmons, after catching a pass from Steve Young. Packers cornerback Craig Newsome picked up the loose ball and returned it 31 yards for a touchdown. After San Francisco failed to make a first down on its ensuing possession, the Packers took only 4 plays to drive 62 yards to Brett Favre's 3-yard touchdown pass to tight end Keith Jackson. Green Bay scored again the next time it had the ball, with Favre's 13-yard touchdown pass to tight end Mark Chmura coming early in the second quarter. By halftime, Favre had completed 15 of 17 passes for 222 yards. He finished the game 21 of 28 for 299 yards, and was not intercepted. Trailing 21-3, the 49ers opened the second half with an 80-yard, 14-play touchdown drive that consumed 7:14, but Jacke kicked a pair of field goals to keep the game out of reach. San Francisco quarterback Steve Young passed for 328 yards and led all rushers with 77 yards, but was forced to attempt a postseason-record 65 passes and completed only 32. He also was intercepted twice, lost a fumble, was sacked 3 times, and consistently harassed by the Packers' pass rush.

Green Bay	14	7	3	3	—	27
San Francisco	0	3	7	7	—	17

GB — Newsome 31 fumble return (Jacke kick)
GB — Jackson 3 pass from Favre (Jacke kick)
GB — Chmura 13 pass from Favre (Jacke kick)
SF — FG Wilkins 21
SF — Young 1 run (Wilkins kick)
GB — FG Jacke 27
GB — FG Jacke 26
SF — Loville 2 run (Wilkins kick)

SUNDAY, JANUARY 7
AFC DIVISIONAL PLAYOFF GAME

INDIANAPOLIS 10, KANSAS CITY 7—at Arrowhead Stadium, attendance 77,594. Cary Blanchard broke a 7-7 tie with a 30-yard field goal late in the third quarter, and the Colts held on to stun the Chiefs. Kansas City, which had compiled the NFL's best record during the regular season by winning 13 of 16 games, had a chance to tie the game in the final minute, but Lin Elliott's 42-yard field-goal try with 37 seconds left was wide left. Elliott also missed a 35-yard attempt in the first half and a 39-yard try early in the fourth quarter. Indianapolis, which won on the road for the second consecutive week, relied on a ground game that produced 147 yards and a stingy defense that forced 4 turnovers and shut out the Chiefs after the first quarter. Kansas City quarterback Steve Bono completed only 11 of 25 passes for 122 yards and was intercepted 3 times before being lifted in favor of backup Rich Gannon late in the fourth quarter. Colts quarterback Jim Harbaugh did not fare any better, completing only 12 of 27 passes for 112 yards, but tied the game with a 5-yard touchdown pass to Floyd Turner midway through the second quarter and scrambled for 48 yards. The Chiefs' Marcus Allen led all rushers with 94 yards on 21 carries.

Indianapolis	0	7	3	0	—	10
Kansas City	7	0	0	0	—	7

KC — Dawson 20 pass from Bono (Elliott kick)
Ind — Turner 5 pass from Harbaugh (Blanchard kick)
Ind — FG Blanchard 30

NFC DIVISIONAL PLAYOFF GAME

DALLAS 30, PHILADELPHIA 11—at Texas Stadium, attendance 64,371. Emmitt Smith rushed for 99 yards and 1 touchdown to lead the Cowboys to the NFC Championship Game for the fourth consecutive year. Smith's 1-yard touchdown run 3:42 before halftime capped a 79-yard drive and helped break open the game at 17-3. Quarterback Troy Aikman accounted for most of the yards on the march with a 37-yard completion to wide receiver Kevin Williams and a 26-yard toss to fullback Daryl Johnston. A pair of field goals by Chris Boniol extended Dallas's lead to 23-3 in the third quarter, and Aikman made it 30-3 with a 9-yard touchdown pass to Michael Irvin with 5:43 left in the game. Aikman finished with 17 completions in 24 attempts for 253 yards. Williams caught 6 passes for 124 yards. The Eagles mounted little opposition after tying the game at 3-3 on Gary Anderson's 26-yard field goal on the first play of the second quarter. Starting quarterback Rodney Peete had suffered a concussion on the previous play, and backup Randall Cunningham came on to complete only 11 of 26 passes for 161 yards.

Philadelphia	0	3	0	8	—	11
Dallas	3	14	6	7	—	30

Dall — FG Boniol 24
Phil — FG Anderson 26
Dall — Sanders 21 run (Boniol kick)
Dall — E. Smith 1 run (Boniol kick)
Dall — FG Boniol 18
Dall — FG Boniol 51
Dall — Irvin 9 pass from Aikman (Boniol kick)
Phil — Cunningham 4 run (R. Johnson pass from Cunningham)

TWENTIETH WEEK SUMMARIES
SUNDAY, JANUARY 14
NFC CHAMPIONSHIP GAME

DALLAS 38, GREEN BAY 27—at Texas Stadium, attendance 65,135. Emmitt Smith rushed for 150 yards and 3 touchdowns to help the Cowboys reach the Super Bowl for the third time in four years and a record eighth time overall. Dallas, playing in the NFC Championship Game for the fourth consecutive year, jumped to a 14-3 lead in the first quarter on a pair of touchdown passes from Troy Aikman to Michael Irvin. But the Packers rallied behind 2 touchdown passes from Brett Favre, and the score was tied 17-17 late in the first half when Smith took control. With 4:05 left in the second quarter and the Cowboys pinned at their own 1-yard line by a punt that rolled out of bounds, Smith got his team out of the shadow of its goal line with a 25-yard run. Six plays later, Aikman's 28-yard completion to Irvin moved Dallas into scoring position, and Smith capped the 11-play, 99-yard drive with a 1-yard touchdown run 24 seconds before halftime. Green Bay rallied again, taking a 27-24 lead on Chris Jacke's 37-yard field goal and Brett Favre's 1-yard touchdown pass to Robert Brooks, only to see Smith rush for 2 more touchdowns to win the game in the fourth quarter. The first was a 5-yard run that capped a 14-play, 90-yard drive, and the latter was a 16-yard run with 9:28 remaining. It was set up by cornerback Larry Brown's interception and 28-yard return. The Cowboys wore down the Packers by controlling the ball for nearly 39 of the game's 60 minutes. Dallas ran more plays (77-55) for more first downs (27-17) and more total yards (419-328), and did not commit a turnover. Aikman completed 21 of 33 passes for 255 yards. Irvin caught 7 passes for 100 yards. Favre, who misfired on his first six attempts and then had his first two completions go for touchdowns, finished with 21 completions in 39 attempts for 307 yards and 3 touchdowns, but was intercepted twice. Brooks caught 6 passes for 105 yards and 2 touchdowns.

Green Bay	10	7	10	0	—	27
Dallas	14	10	0	14	—	38

GB — FG Jacke 46
Dall — Irvin 6 pass from Aikman (Boniol kick)

Dall	—	Irvin 4 pass from Aikman (Boniol kick)
GB	—	Brooks 73 pass from Favre (Jacke kick)
GB	—	Jackson 24 pass from Favre (Jacke kick)
Dall	—	FG Boniol 34
Dall	—	E. Smith 1 run (Boniol kick)
GB	—	FG Jacke 37
GB	—	Brooks 1 pass from Favre (Jacke kick)
Dall	—	E. Smith 5 run (Boniol kick)
Dall	—	E. Smith 16 run (Boniol kick)

AFC CHAMPIONSHIP GAME

PITTSBURGH 20, INDIANAPOLIS 16—at Three Rivers Stadium, attendance 61,062. Byron (Bam) Morris ran 1 yard for a touchdown with 1:34 remaining to lift the Steelers to their first AFC championship in 16 years. Despite the late touchdown, however, Pittsburgh didn't secure its Super Bowl berth until Colts quarterback Jim Harbaugh's desperation pass on the game's final play fell incomplete in the end zone. The Steelers, who lost the 1994 AFC title game to San Diego when their final possession ended three yards short of the end zone in the final minute, began their last possession in this game at their own 33-yard line and trailing 16-13 with 3:03 left. Five plays later, quarterback Neil O'Donnell kept the winning drive alive by completing a 9-yard pass to Andre Hastings on fourth-and-3 from the 47. A 37-yard pass to Ernie Mills moved the ball to the Colts' 1, and two plays later Morris bulled his way into the end zone. Indianapolis's final chance began at its 16-yard line with 1:30 to go. Harbaugh passed for 38 yards and scrambled for 17 as the Colts reached Pittsburgh's 29 with five seconds remaining. His final heave into the end zone nearly was caught by Aaron Bailey, but Bailey was not able to cradle the ball as he hit the ground. Harbaugh finished with 21 completions in 33 attempts for 267 yards and 1 touchdown. O'Donnell was 25 of 41 for 205 yards and 1 touchdown for the Steelers. Upstart Indianapolis was bidding to become only the second team (the 1985 Patriots were the first) to win three consecutive road games en route to the Super Bowl.

Indianapolis	3	3	3	7	—	16
Pittsburgh	3	7	3	7	—	20

Ind	—	FG Blanchard 34
Pitt	—	FG N. Johnson 31
Ind	—	FG Blanchard 36
Pitt	—	Stewart 5 pass from O'Donnell (N. Johnson kick)
Ind	—	FG Blanchard 37
Pitt	—	FG N. Johnson 36
Ind	—	Turner 47 pass from Harbaugh (Blanchard kick)
Pitt	—	Morris 1 run (N. Johnson kick)

TWENTY-FIRST WEEK SUMMARY
SUNDAY, JANUARY 28
SUPER BOWL XXX
TEMPE, ARIZONA

DALLAS 27, PITTSBURGH 17—at Sun Devil Stadium, attendance 76,347. Cornerback Larry Brown's 2 interceptions led to 14 second-half points and helped lift the Cowboys to their third Super Bowl victory in the last four seasons and their record-tying fifth title overall. Brown's interceptions foiled the comeback efforts of the Steelers, and earned him the Pete Rozelle Trophy as the game's most valuable player. Dallas scored on each of its first three possessions, taking a 13-0 lead on Troy Aikman's 3-yard touchdown pass to Jay Novacek and a pair of field goals by Chris Boniol. Neil O'Donnell's 6-yard touchdown pass to Yancey Thigpen 13 seconds before halftime pulled Pittsburgh within 6 points, and the Steelers had the ball near midfield midway through the third quarter. But O'Donnell's third-down pass was intercepted by Brown at the Cowboys' 38-yard line, and his 44-yard return carried to Pittsburgh's 18. After Aikman's 17-yard completion to Michael Irvin, Emmitt Smith ran 1 yard for the touchdown that put Dallas ahead again by 13 points. The Steelers rallied, though, behind Norm Johnson's 46-yard field goal, a successful surprise onside kick, and Byron (Bam) Morris's 1-yard touchdown run with 6:36 to play in the game. And when they forced a punt and took possession at their own 32-yard line trailing only 20-17 with 4:15 remaining, it appeared they might have a chance to break the NFC's recent domination in the Super Bowl. But on second down, Brown struck again, intercepting O'Donnell's pass at the 39 and returning it 33 yards to the 6. Two plays later, Smith barreled over from 4 yards out for the clinching touchdown with 3:43 to go. Pittsburgh limited the Cowboys' powerful running game to only 56 yards and enjoyed a whopping 201-61 advantage in total yards in the second half, but could not overcome the 3 interceptions (another came on the game's final play) thrown by O'Donnell, the NFL's career leader for fewest interceptions per pass attempt. In all, O'Donnell completed 28 of 49 passes for 239 yards. Morris rushed for a game-high 73 yards on 19 carries. For Dallas, Aikman completed 15 of 23 pass attempts for 209 yards. The Cowboys' victory was the twelfth in a row for NFC teams over AFC teams in the Super Bowl.

Dallas	10	3	7	7	—	27
Pittsburgh	0	7	0	10	—	17

Dall	—	FG Boniol 42
Dall	—	Novacek 3 pass from Aikman (Boniol kick)
Dall	—	FG Boniol 35
Pitt	—	Thigpen 6 pass from O'Donnell (N. Johnson kick)
Dall	—	E. Smith 1 run (Boniol kick)
Pitt	—	FG N. Johnson 46
Pitt	—	Morris 1 run (N. Johnson kick)
Dall	—	E. Smith 4 run (Boniol kick)

TWENTY-SECOND WEEK SUMMARY
SUNDAY, FEBRUARY 4
AFC-NFC PRO BOWL
HONOLULU, HAWAII

NFC 20, AFC 13—at Aloha Stadium, attendance 50,034. Jerry Rice had 6 receptions for 82 yards and 1 touchdown to earn player of the game honors in the NFC's victory. The 49ers' wide receiver, who was named to the Pro Bowl for the tenth consecutive year, caught a 1-yard touchdown pass from Packers quarterback Brett Favre 1:41 into the second quarter to cap an 80-yard drive and give the NFC the lead for good at 10-7. The AFC had taken a 7-0 lead 2:26 into the game when Bengals quarterback Jeff Blake connected with Steelers wide receiver Yancey Thigpen on a Pro Bowl-record 93-yard touchdown pass. The NFC increased its advantage to 20-7 at halftime on Redskins linebacker Ken Harvey's 36-yard interception return for a touchdown and Falcons kicker Morten Andersen's 24-yard field goal. The AFC trimmed its deficit to 20-13 when Colts quarterback Jim Harbaugh teamed with Patriots running back Curtis Martin on a 17-yard touchdown pass in the final minute of the third quarter, but its bid to win or tie was rebuffed twice in the final minutes of the fourth quarter. First, 49ers safety Tim McDonald intercepted Harbaugh's pass in the end zone with 1:50 remaining. Then, after the AFC forced a punt and got the ball back near midfield, Harbaugh drove his team to the NFC's 9-yard line in the closing seconds. But he spiked the ball once to stop the clock and threw 3 consecutive incompletions as time ran out. The AFC outgained the NFC 390 total yards to 287, but its quarterbacks suffered 4 interceptions, including 3 off Harbaugh, the NFL's leading passer during the regular season. The NFC raised its edge to 15-11 in Pro Bowl games since the AFL-NFL merger in 1970.

NFC	3	17	0	0	—	20
AFC	7	0	6	0	—	13

AFC	—	Thigpen 93 pass from Blake (Elam kick)
NFC	—	FG Andersen 36
NFC	—	Rice 1 pass from Favre (Andersen kick)
NFC	—	Harvey 36 interception return (Andersen kick)
NFC	—	FG Andersen 24
AFC	—	Martin 17 pass from Harbaugh (kick failed)

1995 PRO FOOTBALL AWARDS

	NFL	AFC	NFC
PRO FOOTBALL WRITERS OF AMERICA			
Most Valuable Player	Brett Favre		
Rookie of the Year	Curtis Martin		
Coach of the Year	Dom Capers		
ASSOCIATED PRESS			
Most Valuable Player	Brett Favre		
Offensive Player of the Year	Brett Favre		
Defensive Player of the Year	Bryce Paup		
Offensive Rookie of the Year	Curtis Martin		
Defensive Rookie of the Year	Hugh Douglas		
Coach of the Year	Ray Rhodes		
UNITED PRESS INTERNATIONAL			
Offensive Player of the Year		Jim Harbaugh	Brett Favre
Defensive Player of the Year		Bryce Paup	Reggie White
Rookie of the Year		Curtis Martin	Rashaan Salaam
Coach of the Year		Marv Levy	Ray Rhodes
THE SPORTING NEWS			
Player of the Year	Brett Favre		
Rookie of the Year	Curtis Martin		
Coach of the Year	Ray Rhodes		
FOOTBALL NEWS			
Player of the Year		Bryce Paup	Brett Favre
Coach of the Year		Marty Schottenheimer	Ray Rhodes
PRO FOOTBALL WEEKLY			
Most Valuable Player	Brett Favre		
Offensive Player of the Year	Brett Favre		
Defensive Player of the Year	Bryce Paup		
Offensive Rookie of the Year	Curtis Martin		
Defensive Rookie of the Year	Hugh Douglas		
Coach of the Year	Dom Capers		
FOOTBALL DIGEST			
Player of the Year	Brett Favre		
Defensive Player of the Year	Merton Hanks		
Offensive Rookie of the Year	Terrell Davis		
Defensive Rookie of the Year	Hugh Douglas		
Coach of the Year	Ray Rhodes		
SPORTS ILLUSTRATED			
Most Valuable Player	Brett Favre		
Rookie of the Year	Curtis Martin		
Coach of the Year	Ray Rhodes		
MAXWELL CLUB PLAYER OF THE YEAR (Bert Bell Trophy)	Brett Favre		
MAXWELL CLUB COACH OF THE YEAR (Earle "Greasy" Neale Trophy)	Ray Rhodes		
SUPER BOWL MOST VALUABLE PLAYER (Pete Rozelle Trophy)	Larry Brown		
AFC-NFC PRO BOWL PLAYER OF THE GAME (Dan McGuire Award)	Jerry Rice		

1995 AFC PLAYERS OF THE WEEK

		Offense		Defense		Special Teams
Week 1	QB	Steve Bono, Kansas City	LB	Chris Slade, New England	K	Doug Pelfrey, Cincinnati
Week 2	QB	Jeff Hostetler, Oakland	S	Rodney Harrison, San Diego	PR	Andre Hastings, Pittsburgh
Week 3	QB	John Elway, Denver	LB	Bryce Paup, Buffalo	KR-PR	Andre Coleman, San Diego
Week 4	QB	Chris Chandler, Houston	DE	Pat Swilling, Oakland	LB	John Henry Mills, Houston
Week 5	RB	Marshall Faulk, Indianapolis	S	Darren Carrington, Jacksonville	P	Louie Aguiar, Kansas City
Week 6	QB	Jim Harbaugh, Indianapolis	LB	Mike Jones, Oakland	KR-PR	Tamarick Vanover, Kansas City
Week 7	WR	Anthony Miller, Denver	LB	Bryce Paup, Buffalo	K	Cary Blanchard, Indianapolis
Week 8	QB	Vince Evans, Oakland	DE	Leslie O'Neal, San Diego	KR-PR	Tamarick Vanover, Kansas City
Week 9	WR	Andre Rison, Cleveland	CB	Cris Dishman, Houston	K	Matt Stover, Cleveland
Week 10	RB	Curtis Martin, New England	DE	Pat Swilling, Oakland	KR	Ernie Mills, Pittsburgh
Week 11	WR	Joey Galloway, Seattle	LB	Greg Lloyd, Pittsburgh	K	Matt Bahr, New England
Week 12	QB	Neil O'Donnell, Pittsburgh	CB	Robert Blackmon, Seattle	KR-PR	Glyn Milburn, Denver
Week 13	RB	Curtis Martin, New England	LB	Tony Bennett, Indianapolis	LB	Chad Cascadden, New York Jets
Week 14	QB	Dan Marino, Miami	S	Brian Washington, Kansas City	K	Todd Peterson, Seattle
Week 15	QB	Jim Kelly, Buffalo	CB	Robert Blackmon, Seattle	KR-PR	Glyn Milburn, Denver
Week 16	WR	Tony Martin, San Diego	LB	Greg Lloyd, Pittsburgh	P	Rick Tuten, Seattle
Week 17	QB	John Elway, Denver	CB	Terrell Buckley, Miami	KR-PR	Tamarick Vanover, Kansas City

1995 AFC PLAYERS OF THE MONTH

		Offense		Defense		Special Teams
September	QB	Vinny Testaverde, Cleveland	CB	James Hasty, Kansas City	KR-PR	Andre Coleman, San Diego
October	QB	Jim Harbaugh, Indianapolis	DE	Neil Smith, Kansas City	KR-PR	Tamarick Vanover, Kansas City
November	QB	Neil O'Donnell, Pittsburgh	LB	Bryce Paup, Buffalo	PR	Joey Galloway, Seattle
December	WR	Tony Martin, San Diego	CB	Willie Williams, Pittsburgh	KR-PR	Tamarick Vanover, Kansas City

1995 NFC PLAYERS OF THE WEEK

		Offense		Defense		Special Teams
Week 1	RB	Emmitt Smith, Dallas	DE	Chris Doleman, Atlanta	WR	Isaac Bruce, St. Louis
Week 2	WR	Robert Brooks, Green Bay	DE	Charles Haley, Dallas	K	Fuad Reveiz, Minnesota
Week 3	RB	Emmitt Smith, Dallas	S	Merton Hanks, San Francisco	K	Morten Andersen, Atlanta
Week 4	QB	Chris Miller, St. Louis	S	Orlando Thomas, Minnesota	K	Jason Hanson, Detroit
Week 5	RB	Terry Allen, Washington	DE	Chris Doleman, Atlanta	K	Gary Anderson, Philadelphia
Week 6	RB	Barry Sanders, Detroit	DT	Andy Harmon, Philadelphia	P	John Jett, Dallas
Week 7	WR	Isaac Bruce, St. Louis	LB	Sam Mills, Carolina	K	Michael Husted, Tampa Bay
Week 8	QB	Brett Favre, Green Bay	LB	Ken Norton, San Francisco	K	Kevin Butler, Chicago
Week 9	QB	Scott Mitchell, Detroit	S	Vencie Glenn, New York Giants	KR-PR	Tyrone Hughes, New Orleans
Week 10	QB	Jeff George, Atlanta	LB	Jeff Brady, Minnesota	K	Doug Brien, New Orleans
Week 11	QB	Brett Favre, Green Bay	S	Merton Hanks, San Francisco	P	Sean Landeta, St. Louis
Week 12	QB	Elvis Grbac, San Francisco	DE	Mike Mamula, Philadelphia	K	Jeff Wilkins, San Francisco
Week 13	WR	Brett Perriman, Detroit	S	Tim McDonald, San Francisco	P	Jeff Feagles, Arizona
Week 14	WR	Herman Moore, Detroit	S	Stanley Richard, Washington	P	Sean Landeta, St. Louis
Week 15	RB	Errict Rhett, Tampa Bay	CB	Bobby Taylor, Philadelphia	K	Morten Andersen, Atlanta
Week 16	WR	Jerry Rice, San Francisco	LB	William Thomas, Philadelphia	K	Chris Boniol, Dallas
Week 17	QB	Bobby Hebert, Atlanta	S	Willie Clay, Detroit	K	Morten Andersen, Atlanta

1995 NFC PLAYERS OF THE MONTH

		Offense		Defense		Special Teams
September	RB	Emmitt Smith, Dallas	LB	Roman Phifer, St. Louis	K	Morten Andersen, Atlanta
October	WR	Isaac Bruce, St. Louis	LB	Ken Norton, San Francisco	K	Kevin Butler, Chicago
November	QB	Warren Moon, Minnesota	LB	Sam Mills, Carolina	P	Sean Landeta, St. Louis
December	QB	Brett Favre, Green Bay	DE	William Fuller, Philadelphia	K	Morten Andersen, Atlanta

1995 ALL-PRO TEAMS

1995 PFWA ALL-PRO TEAM

Selected by the Professional Football Writers of America

Offense

Jerry Rice, San Francisco	Wide Receiver
Herman Moore, Detroit	Wide Receiver
Ben Coates, New England	Tight End
William Roaf, New Orleans	Tackle
Lomas Brown, Detroit	Tackle
Randall McDaniel, Minnesota	Guard
Nate Newton, Dallas	Guard
Dermontti Dawson, Pittsburgh	Center
Brett Favre, Green Bay	Quarterback
Barry Sanders, Detroit	Running Back
Emmitt Smith, Dallas	Running Back

Defense

Bruce Smith, Buffalo	End
Reggie White, Green Bay	End
John Randle, Minnesota	Tackle
Chester McGlockton, Oakland	Tackle
Greg Lloyd, Pittsburgh	Linebacker
Bryce Paup, Buffalo	Linebacker
Junior Seau, San Diego	Linebacker
Eric Davis, San Francisco	Cornerback
Aeneas Williams, Arizona	Cornerback
Darren Woodson, Dallas	Safety
Merton Hanks, San Francisco	Safety

Specialists

Morten Andersen, Atlanta	Kicker
Darren Bennett, San Diego	Punter
Brian Mitchell, Washington	Kick Returner
Brian Mitchell, Washington	Punt Returner
Steve Tasker, Buffalo	Special Teams Player

1995 ASSOCIATED PRESS ALL-PRO TEAM

Selected by the Associated Press

Offense

Jerry Rice, San Francisco	Wide Receiver
Herman Moore, Detroit	Wide Receiver
Ben Coates, New England	Tight End
William Roaf, New Orleans	Tackle
Lomas Brown, Detroit	Tackle
Nate Newton, Dallas	Guard
Randall McDaniel, Minnesota	Guard
Dermontti Dawson, Pittsburgh	Center
Brett Favre, Green Bay	Quarterback
Barry Sanders, Detroit	Running Back
Emmitt Smith, Dallas	Running Back

Defense

Reggie White, Green Bay	End
Bruce Smith, Buffalo	End
John Randle, Minnesota	Tackle
Chester McGlockton, Oakland	Tackle
Greg Lloyd, Pittsburgh	Linebacker
Bryce Paup, Buffalo	Linebacker
Ken Norton, San Francisco	Linebacker
Eric Davis, San Francisco	Cornerback
Aeneas Williams, Arizona	Cornerback
Merton Hanks, San Francisco	Safety
Darren Woodson, Dallas	Safety

Specialists

Morten Andersen, Atlanta	Kicker
Darren Bennett, San Diego	Punter
Brian Mitchell, Washington	Kick Returner

1995 ALL-NFL TEAM

Selected by the Associated Press *and the Professional Football Writers of America*

Offense

Jerry Rice, San Francisco (AP, PFWA)	Wide Receiver
Herman Moore, Detroit (AP, PFWA)	Wide Receiver
Ben Coates, New England (AP, PFWA)	Tight End
William Roaf, New Orleans (AP, PFWA)	Tackle
Lomas Brown, Detroit (AP, PFWA)	Tackle
Nate Newton, Dallas (AP, PFWA)	Guard
Randall McDaniel, Minnesota (AP, PFWA)	Guard
Dermontti Dawson, Pittsburgh (AP, PFWA)	Center
Brett Favre, Green Bay (AP, PFWA)	Quarterback
Barry Sanders, Detroit (AP, PFWA)	Running Back
Emmitt Smith, Dallas (AP, PFWA)	Running Back

Defense

Reggie White, Green Bay (AP, PFWA)	End
Bruce Smith, Buffalo (AP, PFWA)	End
John Randle, Minnesota (AP, PFWA)	Tackle
Chester McGlockton, Oakland (AP, PFWA)	Tackle
Greg Lloyd, Pittsburgh (AP, PFWA)	Linebacker
Bryce Paup, Buffalo (AP, PFWA)	Linebacker
Ken Norton, San Francisco (AP)	Linebacker
Junior Seau, San Diego (PFWA)	Linebacker
Eric Davis, San Francisco (AP, PFWA)	Cornerback
Aeneas Williams, Arizona (AP, PFWA)	Cornerback
Merton Hanks, San Francisco (AP, PFWA)	Safety
Darren Woodson, Dallas (AP, PFWA)	Safety

Specialists

Morten Andersen, Atlanta (AP, PFWA)	Kicker
Darren Bennett, San Diego (AP, PFWA)	Punter
Brian Mitchell, Washington (AP, PFWA)	Kick Returner
Brian Mitchell, Washington (PFWA)	Punt Returner
Steve Tasker, Buffalo (PFWA)	Special Teams Player

1995 UPI ALL-AFC TEAM

Selected by United Press International

Offense

Carl Pickens, Cincinnati	Wide Receiver
Tim Brown, Oakland	Wide Receiver
Ben Coates, New England	Tight End
Gary Zimmerman, Denver	Tackle
Richmond Webb, Miami	Tackle
Steve Wisniewski, Oakland	Guard
Bruce Matthews, Houston	Guard
Dermontti Dawson, Pittsburgh	Center
Jim Harbaugh, Indianapolis	Quaterback
Curtis Martin, New England	Running Back
Chris Warren, Seattle	Running Back

Defense

Bruce Smith, Buffalo	End
Neil Smith, Kansas City	End
Chester McGlockton, Oakland	Tackle
Dan Saleaumua, Kansas City	Tackle
Greg Lloyd, Pittsburgh	Linebacker
Bryce Paup, Green Bay	Linebacker
Junior Seau, San Diego	Linebacker
Dale Carter, Kansas City	Cornerback
Carnell Lake, Pittsburgh	Cornerback
Steve Atwater, Denver	Safety
Blaine Bishop, Houston	Safety

Specialists

Jason Elam, Denver	Kicker
Darren Bennett, San Diego	Punter

1995 UPI ALL-NFC TEAM

Selected by United Press International

Offense

Jerry Rice, San Francisco	Wide Receiver
Herman Moore, Detroit	Wide Receiver
Jay Novacek, Dallas	Tight End
William Roaf, New Orleans	Tackle
Lomas Brown, Detroit	Tackle
Nate Newton, Dallas	Guard
Randall McDaniel, Minnesota	Guard
Kevin Glover, Detroit	Center
Brett Favre, Green Bay	Quarterback
Barry Sanders, Detroit	Running Back
Emmitt Smith, Dallas	Running Back

Defense

William Fuller, Philadelphia	End
Reggie White, Green Bay	End
John Randle, Minnesota	Tackle
Dana Stubblefield, San Francisco	Tackle
Lee Woodall, San Francisco	Linebacker
Ken Harvey, Washington	Linebacker
Ken Norton, San Francisco	Linebacker
Eric Davis, San Francisco	Cornerback
Aeneas Williams, Arizona	Cornerback
Darren Woodson, Dallas	Safety
Merton Hanks, San Francisco	Safety

Specialists

Morten Andersen, Atlanta	Kicker
Jeff Feagles, Arizona	Punter

1995 PFWA ALL-ROOKIE TEAM

Selected by the Professional Football Writers of America

Offense

Joey Galloway, Seattle	Wide Receiver
Chris Sanders, Houston	Wide Receiver
Ken Dilger, Indianapolis	Tight End
Tony Boselli, Jacksonville	Tackle
Blake Brockermeyer, Carolina	Tackle
Ruben Brown, Buffalo	Guard
Brenden Stai, Pittsbugh	Guard
Dave Wohlabaugh, New England	Center
Kerry Collins, Carolina	Quarterback
Curtis Martin, New England	Running Back
Terrell Davis, Denver	Running Back

Defense

Hugh Douglas, New York Jets	End
Mike Mamula, Philadelphia	End
Warren Sapp, Tampa Bay	Tackle
Gary Walker, Houston	Tackle
Derrick Brooks, Tampa Bay	Linebacker
Mark Fields, New Orleans	Linebacker
Ted Johnson, New England	Linebacker
Tyrone Poole, Carolina	Cornerback
Bobby Taylor, Philadelphia	Cornerback
Devin Bush, Atlanta	Safety
Orlando Thomas, Minnesota	Safety

Specialists

Cole Ford, Oakland	Kicker
Tom Hutton, Philadelphia	Punter
Tamarick Vanover, Kansas City	Kick Returner
Tamarick Vanover, Kansas City	Punt Returner
Chad Cascadden, New York Jets	Special Teams Player

1995 BEST PERFORMANCES

TEN BEST RUSHING PERFORMANCES, 1995

	Att.	Yards	TD
1. Rodney Hampton N.Y. Giants vs. Dallas, December 17	34	187	0
2. Marshall Faulk Indianapolis vs. St. Louis, October 1	19	177	3
3. Terrell Davis Denver vs. San Diego, November 19	30	176	1
4. Curtis Martin New England vs. N.Y. Jets, November 5	34	170	2
5. Barry Sanders Detroit vs. Green Bay, October 29	22	167	0
Emmitt Smith Dallas vs. Atlanta, October 29	26	167	1
7. Emmitt Smith Dallas vs. N.Y. Giants, September 4	21	163	4
8. Harvey Williams Oakland vs. Seattle, October 8	19	160	1
9. Emmitt Smith Dallas vs. Philadelphia, November 6	27	158	2
10. Barry Sanders Detroit vs. Cleveland, October 8	18	157	3

100-YARD RUSHING PERFORMANCES, 1995

First Week
Emmitt Smith, Dallas — 163 yards vs. N.Y. Giants
Terry Allen, Washington — 131 yards vs. Arizona
Greg Hill, Kansas City — 109 yards vs. Seattle
Barry Sanders, Detroit — 108 yards vs. Pittsburgh
Curtis Martin, New England — 102 yards vs. Cleveland
Gary Brown, Houston — 101 yards vs. Jacksonville

Second Week
Natrone Means, San Diego — 115 yards vs. Seattle
Emmitt Smith, Dallas — 114 yards vs. Denver
Robert Smith, Minnesota — 111 yards vs. Detroit

Third Week
Emmitt Smith, Dallas — 150 yards vs. Minnesota
Barry Sanders, Detroit — 147 yards vs. Arizona
Natrone Means, San Diego — 122 yards vs. Philadelphia
Garrison Hearst, Arizona — 121 yards vs. Detroit
Chris Warren, Seattle — 109 yards vs. Cincinnati
Craig Heyward, Atlanta — 102 yards vs. New Orleans

Fourth Week
Rodney Hampton, N.Y. Giants — 149 yards vs. New Orleans
Craig Heyward, Atlanta — 120 yards vs. N.Y. Jets
Emmitt Smith, Dallas — 116 yards vs. Arizona
Natrone Means, San Diego — 115 yards vs. Denver
Robert Smith, Minnesota — 115 yards vs. Pittsburgh
Errict Rhett, Tampa Bay — 104 yards vs. Washington

Fifth Week
Marshall Faulk, Indianapolis — 177 yards vs. St. Louis
Derrick Moore, Carolina — 123 yards vs. Tampa Bay
Terry Allen, Washington — 121 yards vs. Dallas
Chris Warren, Seattle — 115 yards vs. Denver

Sixth Week
Harvey Williams, Oakland — 160 yards vs. Seattle
Barry Sanders, Detroit — 157 yards vs. Cleveland
Ricky Watters, Philadelphia — 139 yards vs. Washington
Thurman Thomas, Buffalo — 133 yards vs. N.Y. Jets
Garrison Hearst, Arizona — 122 yards vs. N.Y. Giants
Charlie Garner, Philadelphia — 120 yards vs. Washington
Emmitt Smith, Dallas — 106 yards vs. Green Bay
Rashaan Salaam, Chicago — 105 yards vs. Carolina

Seventh Week
Barry Sanders, Detroit — 124 yards vs. Green Bay
Ricky Watters, Philadelphia — 122 yards vs. N.Y. Giants

Eighth Week
Curtis Martin, New England — 127 yards vs. Buffalo
Marcus Allen, Kansas City — 121 yards vs. Denver
Bernie Parmalee, Miami — 120 yards vs. N.Y. Jets
Chris Warren, Seattle — 112 yards vs. San Diego
Terry Allen, Washington — 110 yards vs. Detroit
Rashaan Salaam, Chicago — 109 yards vs. Houston

Ninth Week
Barry Sanders, Detroit — 167 yards vs. Green Bay
Emmitt Smith, Dallas — 167 yards vs. Atlanta
Chris Warren, Seattle — 127 yards vs. Arizona
Edgar Bennett, Green Bay — 121 yards vs. Detroit
Derrick Moore, Carolina — 119 yards vs. New England
Mario Bates, New Orleans — 106 yards vs. San Francisco

Tenth Week
Curtis Martin, New England — 170 yards vs. N.Y. Jets
Emmitt Smith, Dallas — 158 yards vs. Philadelphia
Terrell Davis, Denver — 135 yards vs. Arizona
Harvey Williams, Oakland — 134 yards vs. Cincinnati
Rodney Thomas, Houston — 108 yards vs. Cleveland
Mario Bates, New Orleans — 106 yards vs. St. Louis
Bernie Parmalee, Miami — 103 yards vs. San Diego

Eleventh Week
Errict Rhett, Tampa Bay — 144 yards vs. Detroit
Curtis Martin, New England — 142 yards vs. Miami
Chris Warren, Seattle — 121 yards vs. Jacksonville
Erric Pegram, Pittsburgh — 112 yards vs. Cleveland
Garrison Hearst, Arizona — 103 yards vs. Minnesota
Darick Holmes, Buffalo — 100 yards vs. Atlanta
Emmitt Smith, Dallas — 100 yards vs. San Francisco

Twelfth Week
Terrell Davis, Denver — 176 yards vs. San Diego
Chris Warren, Seattle — 136 yards vs. Washington
Barry Sanders, Detroit — 120 yards vs. Chicago
Craig Heyward, Atlanta — 117 yards vs. St. Louis
Emmitt Smith, Dallas — 110 yards vs. Oakland
Byron (Bam) Morris, Pittsburgh — 101 yards vs. Cincinnati
Errict Rhett, Tampa Bay — 100 yards vs. Jacksonville

Thirteenth Week
Curtis Martin, New England — 148 yards vs. Buffalo
Barry Sanders, Detroit — 138 yards vs. Minnesota
Ricky Watters, Philadelphia — 124 yards vs. Washington
Adrian Murrell, N.Y. Jets — 116 yards vs. Seattle
Terrell Davis, Denver — 110 yards vs. Houston
Rodney Thomas, Houston — 104 yards vs. Denver
Bernie Parmalee, Miami — 102 yards vs. Indianapolis
Harvey Williams, Oakland — 101 yards vs. San Diego

Fourteenth Week
Aaron Hayden, San Diego — 127 yards vs. Cleveland
Marcus Allen, Kansas City — 124 yards vs. Oakland
Mario Bates, New Orleans — 123 yards vs. New England
Curtis Martin, New England — 112 yards vs. New Orleans
Byron (Bam) Morris, Pittsburgh — 102 yards vs. Houston

Fifteenth Week
Curtis Martin, New England — 148 yards vs. N.Y. Jets
Glyn Milburn, Denver — 131 yards vs. Seattle
Thurman Thomas, Buffalo — 129 yards vs. St. Louis
Erric Pegram, Pittsburgh — 122 yards vs. Oakland
Terry Allen, Washington — 120 yards vs. N.Y Giants
Errict Rhett, Tampa Bay — 118 yards vs. Green Bay
Ricky Watters, Philadelphia — 112 yards vs. Dallas
Emmitt Smith, Dallas — 108 yards vs. Philadelphia
Rashaan Salaam, Chicago — 105 yards vs. Cincinnati
Chris Warren, Seattle — 101 yards vs. Denver

Sixteenth Week

Rodney Hampton, N.Y. Giants	187 yards vs. Dallas
Thurman Thomas, Buffalo	148 yards vs. Miami
Rashaan Salaam, Chicago	134 yards vs. Tampa Bay
Earnest Byner, Cleveland	121 yards vs. Cincinnati
Curtis Martin, New England	120 yards vs. Pittsburgh
Chris Warren, Seattle	105 yards vs. Oakland
Emmitt Smith, Dallas	103 yards vs. N.Y. Giants

Seventeenth Week

Rashaan Salaam, Chicago	122 yards vs. Philadelphia
Scottie Graham, Minnesota	115 yards vs. Cincinnati
Greg Hill, Kansas City	113 yards vs. Seattle
Aaron Craver, Denver	108 yards vs. Oakland
Curtis Martin, New England	103 yards vs. Indianapolis

Times 100 or More (103)
E. Smith, 11; Martin, 9; Warren, 8; Sanders, 7; Salaam, 5; T. Allen, Rhett, Watters, 4; Bates, Davis, Heyward, Means, Parmalee, T. Thomas, Williams, 3; M. Allen, Hampton, Hearst, Hill, Moore, Morris, Pegram, R. Smith, R. Thomas, 2.

TEN BEST PASSING PERFORMANCES, 1995

	Att.	Comp.	Yards	TD
1. Dan Marino Miami vs. Cincinnati, October 1	48	33	450	2
2. Steve Young S.F. vs. Minnesota, December 18	49	30	425	3
3. Dave Krieg Arizona vs. Atlanta, November 26	43	27	413	4
4. Scott Mitchell Detroit vs. Minnesota, November 23	45	30	410	4
5. Jeff George Atlanta vs. New Orleans, September 17	39	27	386	1
6. Warren Moon Minnesota vs. Detroit, November 23	47	30	384	3
7. Elvis Grbac San Francisco vs. Miami, November 20	41	31	382	4
8. Neil O'Donnell Pittsburgh vs. Cincinnati, November 19	31	24	377	3
9. Mark Rypien St. Louis vs. Buffalo, December 10	55	31	372	2
10. Jim Everett New Orleans vs. Atlanta, September 17	43	29	370	3

300-YARD PASSING PERFORMANCES, 1995

First Week

Frank Reich, Carolina	329 yards vs. Atlanta
John Elway, Denver	317 yards vs. Buffalo
Stan Humphries, San Diego	305 yards vs. Oakland
Drew Bledsoe, New England	302 yards vs. Cleveland

Second Week

Steve Young, San Francisco	331 yards vs. Atlanta
Brett Favre, Green Bay	312 yards vs. Chicago

Third Week

Jeff George, Atlanta	386 yards vs. New Orleans
Jim Everett, New Orleans	370 yards vs. Atlanta
John Elway, Denver	327 yards vs. Washington

Fourth Week

Jeff Blake, Cincinnati	356 yards vs. Houston
Chris Chandler, Houston	352 yards vs. Cincinnati
Steve Young, San Francisco	349 yards vs. Detroit
Dave Krieg, Arizona	324 yards vs. Dallas
Erik Kramer, Chicago	317 yards vs. St. Louis

Fifth Week

Dan Marino, Miami	450 yards vs. Cincinnati
Chris Miller, St. Louis	326 yards vs. Indianapolis
Dave Krieg, Arizona	308 yards vs. Kansas City

Sixth Week

Jeff Hostetler, Oakland	333 yards vs. Seattle
Steve Bono, Kansas City	329 yards vs. San Diego
Jim Harbaugh, Indianapolis	319 yards vs. Miami
Troy Aikman, Dallas	316 yards vs. Green Bay
Stan Humphries, San Diego	315 yards vs. Kansas City
Dave Krieg, Arizona	305 yards vs. N.Y. Giants

Seventh Week

Bernie Kosar, Miami	368 yards vs. New Orleans
Brett Favre, Green Bay	342 yards vs. Detroit
Warren Moon, Minnesota	332 yards vs. Tampa Bay
Chris Miller, St. Louis	328 yards vs. Atlanta
John Elway, Denver	324 yards vs. Oakland
Mark Brunell, Jacksonville	302 yards vs. Chicago

Eighth Week

Neil O'Donnell, Pittsburgh	359 yards vs. Cincinnati
Erik Kramer, Chicago	349 yards vs. Houston
Vince Evans, Oakland	335 yards vs. Indianapolis
Scott Mitchell, Detroit	327 yards vs. Washington

1995 BEST PERFORMANCES

Ninth Week

Gus Frerotte, Washington 345 yards vs. N.Y. Giants
Eric Zeier, Cleveland 310 yards vs. Cincinnati
Kerry Collins, Carolina 309 yards vs. New England
Brett Favre, Green Bay 304 yards vs. Detroit

Tenth Week

Jeff George, Atlanta 362 yards vs. Detroit
Neil O'Donnell, Pittsburgh 341 yards vs. Chicago
Elvis Grbac, San Francisco 327 yards vs. Carolina
Scott Mitchell, Detroit 321 yards vs. Atlanta

Eleventh Week

Warren Moon, Minnesota 342 yards vs. Arizona
Brett Favre, Green Bay 336 yards vs. Chicago
Dan Marino, Miami 333 yards vs. New England
Erik Kramer, Chicago 318 yards vs. Green Bay
Elvis Grbac, San Francisco 305 yards vs. Dallas

Twelfth Week

Elvis Grbac, San Francisco 382 yards vs. Miami
Neil O'Donnell, Pittsburgh 377 yards vs. Cincinnati
Jeff George, Atlanta 352 yards vs. St. Louis
Warren Moon, Minnesota 338 yards vs. New Orleans
Jim Everett, New Orleans 335 yards vs. Minnesota
Jim Kelly, Buffalo 316 yards vs. N.Y. Jets
Boomer Esiason, N.Y. Jets 312 yards vs. Buffalo

Thirteenth Week

Dave Krieg, Arizona 413 yards vs. Atlanta
Scott Mitchell, Detroit 410 yards vs. Minnesota
Warren Moon, Minnesota 384 yards vs. Detroit
Kerry Collins, Carolina 335 yards vs. New Orleans
John Elway, Denver 332 yards vs. Houston
Trent Dilfer, Tampa Bay 324 yards vs. Green Bay

Fourteenth Week

Dan Marino, Miami 343 yards vs. Atlanta
Brett Favre, Green Bay 339 yards vs. Cincinnati
Scott Mitchell, Detroit 320 yards vs. Chicago
Vinny Testaverde, Cleveland 303 yards vs. San Diego

Fifteenth Week

Mark Rypien, St. Louis 372 yards vs. Buffalo
Steve Young, San Francisco 336 yards vs. Carolina
Mark Brunell, Jacksonville 312 yards vs. Indianapolis

Sixteenth Week

Steve Young, San Francisco 425 yards vs. Minnesota
Jim Everett, New Orleans 364 yards vs. Green Bay
Mark Rypien, St. Louis 347 yards vs. Washington
Drew Bledsoe, New England 336 yards vs. Pittsburgh
Jeff George, Atlanta 310 yards vs. Carolina
Brett Favre, Green Bay 308 yards vs. New Orleans

Seventeenth Week

Scott Mitchell, Detroit 352 yards vs. Tampa Bay
Troy Aikman, Dallas 350 yards vs. Arizona
Vinny Testaverde, Cleveland 325 yards vs. Jacksonville
John Elway, Denver 320 yards vs. Oakland
Mark Rypien, St. Louis 320 yards vs. Miami
Neil O'Donnell, Pittsburgh 318 yards vs. Green Bay
Steve Young, San Francisco 316 yards vs. Atlanta
Brett Favre, Green Bay 301 yards vs. Pittsburgh

Times 300 or More (80)
Favre, 7; Elway, Mitchell, Young, 5; George, Krieg, Moon, O'Donnell, 4; Everett, Grbac, Kramer, Marino, Rypien, 3; Bledsoe, Brunell, Collins, Humphries, Miller, Testaverde, 2.

TEN BEST RECEIVING PERFORMANCES, 1995

	Yards	No.	TD
1. Jerry Rice S.F. vs. Minnesota, December 18	14	289	3
2. Isaac Bruce St. Louis vs. Miami, December 24	15	210	1
3. Kevin Williams Dallas vs. Arizona, December 25	9	203	2
4. Isaac Bruce St. Louis vs. Atlanta, October 12	10	191	2
5. Terance Mathis Atlanta vs. St. Louis, November 19	10	184	3
6. Herman Moore Detroit vs. Chicago, December 4	14	183	1
7. Isaac Bruce St. Louis vs. Indianapolis, October 1	8	181	2
Jerry Rice S.F. vs. Detroit, September 25	11	181	0
9. Shannon Sharpe Denver vs. Buffalo, September 3	10	180	0
10. Herman Moore Detroit vs. Atlanta, November 5	9	176	0

100-YARD RECEIVING PERFORMANCES, 1995

First Week

Shannon Sharpe, Denver 180 yards vs. Buffalo
Michael Jackson, Cleveland 157 yards vs. New England
Horace Copeland, Tampa Bay 155 yards vs. Philadelphia
Willie Davis, Kansas City 155 yards vs. Seattle
Herman Moore, Detroit 131 yards vs. Pittsburgh
Willie Green, Carolina 121 yards vs. Atlanta
Sean Jefferson, San Diego 120 yards vs. Oakland
Tony McGee, Cincinnati 118 yards vs. Indianapolis
Curtis Conway, Chicago 110 yards vs. Minnesota
Irving Fryar, Miami 110 yards vs. N.Y. Jets
Michael Irvin, Dallas 109 yards vs. N.Y. Giants
Brian Blades, Seattle 107 yards vs. Kansas City
Jeff Graham, Chicago 107 yards vs. Minnesota
Ben Coates, New England 106 yards vs. Cleveland

Second Week

Jerry Rice, San Francisco 167 yards vs. Atlanta
Tony Martin, San Diego 163 yards vs. Seattle
Robert Brooks, Green Bay 161 yards vs. Chicago
Irving Fryar, Miami 113 yards vs. New England
Horace Copeland, Buffalo 112 yards vs. Carolina
Will Moore, New England 112 yards vs. Miami
Anthony Miller, Denver 108 yards vs. Dallas
Carl Pickens, Cincinnati 102 yards vs. Jacksonville
Frank Sanders, Arizona 102 yards vs. Philadelphia
Chris Calloway, N.Y. Giants 100 yards vs. Kansas City

Third Week

Eric Metcalf, Atlanta 155 yards vs. New Orleans
Brett Perriman, Detroit 114 yards vs. Arizona
Michael Irvin, Dallas 107 yards vs. Minnesota
Jake Reed, Minnesota 107 yards vs. Dallas
Bert Emanuel, Atlanta 104 yards vs. New Orleans
Isaac Bruce, St. Louis 100 yards vs. Carolina

Fourth Week

Jerry Rice, San Francisco 181 yards vs. Detroit
Rob Moore, Arizona 154 yards vs. Dallas
Jeff Graham, Chicago 145 yards vs. St. Louis
Yancey Thigpen, Pittsburgh 141 yards vs. Minnesota
Daryl Hobbs, Oakland 135 yards vs. Philadelphia
Darnay Scott, Cincinnati 125 yards vs. Houston
Brett Perriman, Detroit 115 yards vs. San Francisco
Keith Cash, Kansas City 111 yards vs. Cleveland
Tony McGee, Cincinnati 109 yards vs. Houston

Troy Drayton, St. Louis — 106 yards vs. Chicago
Michael Irvin, Dallas — 105 yards vs. Arizona
Chris Sanders, Houston — 104 yards vs. Cincinnati

Fifth Week

Isaac Bruce, St. Louis — 181 yards vs. Indianapolis
Vincent Brisby, New England — 161 yards vs. Atlanta
Tim Brown, Oakland — 156 yards vs. N.Y. Jets
Andre Rison, Cleveland — 126 yards vs. Buffalo
Carl Pickens, Cincinnati — 117 yards vs. Miami
Jackie Harris, Tampa Bay — 108 yards vs. Carolina
Michael Irvin, Dallas — 105 yards vs. Washington

Sixth Week

Yancey Thigpen, Pittsburgh — 160 yards vs. Jacksonville
Michael Irvin, Dallas — 150 yards vs. Green Bay
Tim Brown, Oakland — 143 yards vs. Seattle
Herman Moore, Detroit — 125 yards vs. Cleveland
Robert Brooks, Green Bay — 124 yards vs. Dallas
Alvin Harper, Tampa Bay — 117 yards vs. Cincinnati
Cris Carter, Minnesota — 115 yards vs. Houston
Mark Carrier, Carolina — 114 yards vs. Chicago
Henry Ellard, Washington — 110 yards vs. Philadelphia
Frank Sanders, Arizona — 108 yards vs. N.Y. Giants

Seventh Week

Isaac Bruce, St. Louis — 191 yards vs. Atlanta
Anthony Miller, Denver — 149 yards vs. Oakland
Ken Dilger, Indianapolis — 125 yards vs. San Francisco
Billy Brooks, Buffalo — 109 yards vs. Seattle
Michael Irvin, Dallas — 103 yards vs. San Diego
Joey Galloway, Seattle — 102 yards vs. Buffalo

Eighth Week

Isaac Bruce, St. Louis — 173 yards vs. San Francisco
Jeff Graham, Chicago — 137 yards vs. Houston
Raghib Ismail, Oakland — 125 yards vs. Indianapolis
Bert Emanuel, Atlanta — 121 yards vs. Tampa Bay
Brett Perriman, Detroit — 115 yards vs. Washington
Henry Ellard, Washington — 112 yards vs. Detroit
Curtis Conway, Chicago — 111 yards vs. Houston
Carl Pickens, Cincinnati — 108 yards vs. Pittsburgh
Eric Metcalf, Atlanta — 106 yards vs. Tampa Bay
Rico Smith, Cleveland — 106 yards vs. Jacksonville
Herman Moore, Detroit — 102 yards vs. Washington
Mark Chmura, Green Bay — 101 yards vs. Minnesota

Ninth Week

Andre Rison, Cleveland — 173 yards vs. Cincinnati
Herman Moore, Detroit — 147 yards vs. Green Bay
Michael Irvin, Dallas — 135 yards vs. Atlanta
Leslie Shepherd, Washington — 135 yards vs. N.Y. Giants
Robert Brooks, Green Bay — 127 yards vs. Detroit
Henry Ellard, Washington — 111 yards vs. N.Y. Giants
Jerry Rice, San Francisco — 108 yards vs. New Orleans
Isaac Bruce, St. Louis — 105 yards vs. Philadelphia

Tenth Week

Herman Moore, Detroit — 176 yards vs. Atlanta
Brian Blades, Seattle — 153 yards vs. N.Y. Giants
Isaac Bruce, St. Louis — 135 yards vs. New Orleans
Mike Sherrard, N.Y. Giants — 128 yards vs. Seattle
Tony Martin, San Diego — 121 yards vs. Miami
Robert Brooks, Green Bay — 120 yards vs. Minnesota
Michael Irvin, Dallas — 115 yards vs. Philadelphia
Jeff Graham, Chicago — 111 yards vs. Pittsburgh
Jerry Rice, San Francisco — 111 yards vs. Carolina
Yancey Thigpen, Pittsburgh — 108 yards vs. Chicago
Bert Emanuel, Atlanta — 104 yards vs. Detroit

Eleventh Week

Jerry Rice, San Francisco — 161 yards vs. Dallas
Cris Carter, Minnesota — 157 yards vs. Arizona
Willie Green, Carolina — 157 yards vs. St. Louis
Robert Brooks, Green Bay — 138 yards vs. Chicago
Curtis Conway, Chicago — 126 yards vs. Green Bay
Brett Perriman, Detroit — 125 yards vs. Tampa Bay
Vincent Brisby, New England — 118 yards vs. Miami
Joey Galloway, Seattle — 114 yards vs. Jacksonville
Isaac Bruce, St. Louis — 110 yards vs. Carolina
Jeff Graham, Chicago — 108 yards vs. Green Bay
Carl Pickens, Cincinnati — 108 yards vs. Houston
Fred Barnett, Philadelphia — 105 yards vs. Denver
Herman Moore, Detroit — 104 yards vs. Tampa Bay
Robert Brooks, Buffalo — 101 yards vs. Atlanta
Bert Emanuel, Atlanta — 100 yards vs. Buffalo

Twelfth Week

Terance Mathis, Atlanta — 184 yards vs. St. Louis
Tim Brown, Oakland — 161 yards vs. Dallas
Pete Mitchell, Jacksonville — 161 yards vs. Tampa Bay
Quinn Early, New Orleans — 150 yards vs. Minnesota
Jerry Rice, San Francisco — 149 yards vs. Miami
Qadry Ismail, Minnesota — 142 yards vs. New Orleans
Brett Perriman, Detroit — 142 yards vs. Chicago
Cris Carter, Minnesota — 137 yards vs. New Orleans
Shannon Sharpe, Denver — 137 yards vs. San Diego
Carl Pickens, Cincinnati — 129 yards vs. Pittsburgh
Thomas Lewis, N.Y. Giants — 126 yards vs. Philadelphia
Jeff Graham, Chicago — 109 yards vs. Detroit
Michael Irvin, Dallas — 109 yards vs. Oakland
Robert Brooks, Buffalo — 107 yards vs. N.Y. Jets
Keenan McCardell, Cleveland — 102 yards vs. Green Bay
Sean Dawkins, Indianapolis — 101 yards vs. New England

Thirteenth Week

Brett Perriman, Detroit — 153 yards vs. Minnesota
Anthony Miller, Denver — 152 yards vs. Houston
Jake Reed, Minnesota — 149 yards vs. Detroit
Chris Sanders, Houston — 147 yards vs. Denver
Mark Carrier, Carolina — 132 yards vs. New Orleans
Herman Moore, Detroit — 127 yards vs. Minnesota
Jackie Harris, Tampa Bay — 122 yards vs. Green Bay
Michael Irvin, Dallas — 121 yards vs. Kansas City
Rob Moore, Arizona — 121 yards vs. Atlanta
Robert Brooks, Green Bay — 114 yards vs. Tampa Bay
Yancey Thigpen, Pittsburgh — 106 yards vs. Cleveland
Willie Green, Carolina — 105 yards vs. New Orleans
Johnnie Morton, Detroit — 102 yards vs. Minnesota
Vincent Brisby, New England — 101 yards vs. Buffalo
Larry Centers, Arizona — 101 yards vs. Atlanta

Fourteenth Week

Herman Moore, Detroit — 183 yards vs. Chicago
Tim Brown, Oakland — 150 yards vs. Kansas City
Cris Carter, Minnesota — 136 yards vs. Tampa Bay
Tony Martin, San Diego — 132 yards vs. Cleveland
Mark Chmura, Green Bay — 109 yards vs. Cincinnati
Michael Irvin, Dallas — 101 yards vs. Washington

Fifteenth Week

Isaac Bruce, St. Louis — 136 yards vs. Buffalo
Brett Perriman, Detroit — 128 yards vs. Houston
Brian Blades, Seattle — 127 yards vs. Denver
Cris Carter, Minnesota — 124 yards vs. Cleveland
Robert Brooks, Green Bay — 122 yards vs. Tampa Bay
Horace Copeland, Tampa Bay — 122 yards vs. Green Bay
Jerry Rice, San Francisco — 121 yards vs. Carolina
Mark Seay, San Diego — 114 yards vs. Arizona
Willie Jackson, Jacksonville — 113 yards vs. Indianapolis
Johnny Mitchell, N.Y. Jets — 108 yards vs. New England
Herman Moore, Detroit — 105 yards vs. Houston
Ryan Yarborough, N.Y. Jets — 105 yards vs. New England
Rob Moore, Arizona — 104 yards vs. San Diego

1995 BEST PERFORMANCES

Sixteenth Week

Jerry Rice, San Francisco	289 yards vs. Minnesota
Tony Martin, San Diego	168 yards vs. Indianapolis
Willie Green, Carolina	147 yards vs. Atlanta
Alexander Wright, St. Louis	132 yards vs. Washington
Sean Dawkins, Indianapolis	123 yards vs. San Diego
Robert Brooks, Green Bay	118 yards vs. New Orleans
Quinn Early, New Orleans	117 yards vs. Green Bay
Joey Galloway, Seattle	108 yards vs. Oakland
Calvin Williams, Philadelphia	105 yards vs. Arizona
Tim Brown, Oakland	102 yards vs. Seattle
Jeff Graham, Chicago	102 yards vs. Tampa Bay
Terance Mathis, Atlanta	102 yards vs. Carolina

Seventeenth Week

Isaac Bruce, St. Louis	210 yards vs. Miami
Kevin Williams, Dallas	203 yards vs. Arizona
Larry Centers, Arizona	172 yards vs. Dallas
Jerry Rice, San Francisco	153 yards vs. Atlanta
Robert Brooks, Green Bay	137 yards vs. Pittsburgh
Brett Perriman, Detroit	135 yards vs. Tampa Bay
Michael Jackson, Cleveland	130 yards vs. Jacksonville
Tim Brown, Oakland	127 yards vs. Denver
Jake Reed, Minnesota	111 yards vs. Cincinnati
J.J. Stokes, San Francisco	106 yards vs. Atlanta
Herman Moore, Detroit	105 yards vs. Tampa Bay
Mark Carrier, Carolina	101 yards vs. Washington

Times 100 or More (185)
Irvin, 11; H. Moore, 10; R. Brooks, Bruce, Rice, 9; Perriman, 8; Graham, 7; Brown, 6; Carter, Pickens, 5; Emanuel, Green, Martin, Thigpen, 4; Blades, Brisby, B. Brooks, Carrier, Conway, Ellard, Galloway, Miller, R. Moore, Reed, 3; Centers, Chmura, Copeland, Dawkins, Early, Fryar, Harris, Jackson, Mathis, McGee, Metcalf, Rison, C. Sanders, F. Sanders, Sharpe, 2.

TOP QUARTERBACK SACK PERFORMANCES, 1995

(2.5 or More Sacks Per Game Needed to Qualify)

First Week

Chris Doleman, Atlanta	4.0 vs. Carolina
Reggie White, Green Bay	2.5 vs. St. Louis

Second Week

Chad Brown, Pittsburgh	3.0 vs. Houston

Third Week

Hugh Douglas, N.Y. Jets	3.0 vs. Jacksonville
Bryce Paup, Buffalo	3.0 vs. Indianapolis
Tracy Scroggins, Detroit	3.0 vs. Arizona
Michael Strahan, N.Y. Giants	3.0 vs. Green Bay

Fourth Week

Pat Swilling, Oakland	3.0 vs. Philadelphia

Fifth Week

None

Sixth Week

Andy Harmon, Philadelphia	3.0 vs. Washington
Ricardo McDonald, Cincinnati	3.0 vs. Tampa Bay

Seventh Week

None

Eighth Week

Leslie O'Neal, San Diego	3.5 vs. Seattle
Neil Smith, Kansas City	2.5 vs. Denver

Ninth Week

Rob Burnett, Cleveland	3.5 vs. Cincinnati

Tenth Week

Bryce Paup, Buffalo	3.0 vs. Indianapolis
Pat Swilling, Oakland	3.0 vs. Cincinnati
Rickey Jackson, San Francisco	2.5 vs. Carolina

Eleventh Week

None

Twelfth Week

Mike Mamula, Philadelphia	3.0 vs. N.Y. Giants

Thirteenth Week

Ken Harvey, Washington	3.0 vs. Philadelphia
Antonio London, Detroit	3.0 vs. Minnesota

Fourteenth Week

D'Marco Farr, St. Louis	3.5 vs. N.Y. Jets
Darion Conner, Carolina	3.0 vs. Indianapolis
Bruce Smith, Buffalo	3.0 vs. San Francisco
Broderick Thomas, Minnesota	2.5 vs. Tampa Bay

Fifteenth Week

Leslie O'Neal, San Diego	3.0 vs. Arizona

Sixteenth Week

None

Seventeenth Week

Alonzo Spellman, Chicago	3.0 vs. Philadelphia

AMERICAN FOOTBALL CONFERENCE OFFENSE

	Buff	Cin	Clev	Den	Hou	Ind	Jax	KC	Mia	NE	NYJ	Oak	Pitt	SD	Sea
First Downs	300	288	293	344	295	281	283	295	345	335	254	317	344	314	311
Rushing	130	76	83	114	109	110	100	113	98	106	78	104	117	108	121
Passing	142	184	189	205	157	147	154	164	225	207	159	189	193	185	171
Penalty	28	28	21	25	29	24	29	18	22	22	17	24	34	21	19
Rushes	521	364	398	440	478	478	410	507	413	474	365	463	494	479	477
Net Yds. Gained	1993	1439	1482	1995	1664	1855	1705	2222	1506	1866	1279	1932	1852	1747	2178
Avg. Gain	3.8	4.0	3.7	4.5	3.5	3.9	4.2	4.4	3.6	3.9	3.5	4.2	3.7	3.6	4.6
Avg. Yds. per Game	124.6	89.9	92.6	124.7	104.0	115.9	106.6	138.9	94.1	116.6	79.9	120.8	115.8	109.2	136.1
Passes Attempted	506	586	555	594	536	434	495	531	592	686	589	543	592	540	511
Completed	279	334	324	350	314	270	275	300	384	351	330	317	348	318	273
% Completed	55.1	57.0	58.4	58.9	58.6	62.2	55.6	56.5	64.9	51.2	56.0	58.4	58.8	58.9	53.4
Total Yds. Gained	3348	3915	3772	4260	3512	3373	3144	3178	4398	3789	3129	3787	4093	3706	3359
Times Sacked	32	25	32	26	32	49	57	21	29	27	47	36	24	32	45
Yds. Lost	224	162	178	215	271	309	354	158	188	198	341	214	176	240	267
Net Yds. Gained	3124	3753	3594	4045	3241	3064	2790	3020	4210	3591	2788	3573	3917	3466	3092
Avg. Yds. per Game	195.3	234.6	224.6	252.8	202.6	191.5	174.4	188.8	263.1	224.4	174.3	223.3	244.8	216.6	193.3
Net Yds. per Pass Play	5.81	6.14	6.12	6.52	5.71	6.34	5.05	5.47	6.78	5.04	4.38	6.17	6.36	6.06	5.56
Yds. Gained per Comp.	12.00	11.72	11.64	12.17	11.18	12.49	11.43	10.59	11.45	10.79	9.48	11.95	11.76	11.65	12.30
Combined Net Yds. Gained	5117	5192	5076	6040	4905	4919	4495	5242	5716	5457	4067	5505	5769	5213	5270
% Total Yds. Rushing	38.9	27.7	29.2	33.0	33.9	37.7	37.9	42.4	26.3	34.2	31.4	35.1	32.1	33.5	41.3
% Total Yds. Passing	61.1	72.3	70.8	67.0	66.1	62.3	62.1	57.6	73.7	65.8	68.6	64.9	67.9	66.5	58.7
Avg. Yds. per Game	319.8	324.5	317.3	377.5	306.6	307.4	280.9	327.6	357.3	341.1	254.2	344.1	360.6	325.8	329.4
Ball Control Plays	1059	975	985	1060	1046	961	962	1059	1034	1187	1001	1042	1110	1051	1033
Avg. Yds. per Play	4.8	5.3	5.2	5.7	4.7	5.1	4.7	4.9	5.5	4.6	4.1	5.3	5.2	5.0	5.1
Avg. Time of Poss.	28:10	26:57	28:25	30:09	32:12	31:40	28:37	31:08	31:22	29:32	29:15	30:42	32:36	29:34	28:30
Third Down Efficiency	31.6	35.1	40.3	43.0	43.4	39.0	36.1	35.5	45.9	38.1	29.1	39.9	42.2	42.8	37.8
Had Intercepted	14	18	20	14	18	11	15	10	20	16	24	21	21	18	23
Yds. Opp. Returned	187	307	276	103	265	156	178	123	210	161	404	344	185	164	384
Ret. by Opp. for TD	0	2	2	0	1	1	0	3	0	1	3	2	3	3	2
Punts	86	70	65	54	79	63	82	91	57	79	105	76	59	72	83
Yds. Punted	3473	2913	2831	2209	3180	2681	3591	3990	2433	3100	4328	3089	2368	3221	3735
Avg. Yds. per Punt	40.4	41.6	43.6	40.9	40.3	42.6	43.8	43.8	42.7	39.2	41.2	40.6	40.1	44.7	45.0
Punt Returns	47	21	25	31	35	29	29	58	24	45	38	37	48	31	40
Yds. Returned	476	103	255	358	339	192	243	561	163	383	323	374	474	338	384
Avg. Yds. per Return	10.1	4.9	10.2	11.5	9.7	6.6	8.4	9.7	6.8	8.5	8.5	10.1	9.9	10.9	9.6
Returned for TD	0	0	1	0	0	0	0	1	0	0	0	0	1	1	1
Kickoff Returns	70	80	74	60	64	63	74	55	59	75	77	64	69	70	72
Yds. Returned	1302	1788	1455	1392	1277	1332	1532	1306	1338	1691	1613	1390	1530	1502	1620
Avg. Yds. per Return	18.6	22.4	19.7	23.2	20.0	21.1	20.7	23.7	22.7	22.5	20.9	21.7	22.2	21.5	22.5
Returned for TD	0	0	0	0	0	1	1	2	0	0	0	1	0	2	0
Fumbles	25	23	25	25	36	21	23	17	24	32	38	25	24	30	24
Lost	12	14	11	16	20	11	13	11	12	20	18	13	13	12	9
Out of Bounds	0	4	3	1	0	2	2	0	0	1	3	2	2	2	5
Own Rec. for TD	1	0	0	0	0	0	0	0	0	1	0	0	0	0	0
Opp. Rec. by	11	12	7	13	17	13	11	17	16	14	17	22	12	10	9
Opp. Rec. for TD	0	0	0	1	0	1	0	2	1	1	1	3	2	2	2
Penalties	89	103	107	109	98	97	121	116	110	84	121	134	109	107	100
Yds. Penalized	672	835	966	851	791	943	970	851	907	676	1078	1059	839	953	852
Total Points Scored	350	349	289	388	348	331	275	358	398	294	233	348	407	321	363
Total TDs	37	37	29	42	38	37	31	42	46	32	26	41	44	37	42
TDs Rushing	10	7	5	14	12	14	9	14	16	16	2	10	17	14	20
TDs Passing	24	29	21	27	22	20	19	21	28	14	20	25	21	17	19
TDs on Ret. and Rec.	3	1	3	1	4	3	3	7	2	2	4	6	6	6	3
Extra Points	34	35	27	41	35	36	28	34	39	30	24	39	40	33	40
Kicks Made	33	34	26	39	33	34	27	34	37	27	24	39	39	32	40
2-Pt. Conversions	1	1	1	2	2	2	1	0	2	3	0	0	1	1	0
Safeties	0	2	0	0	1	1	0	0	0	0	1	0	0	1	1
Field Goals Made	31	29	29	31	27	23	20	24	27	23	17	21	34	21	23
Field Goals Attempted	40	36	33	38	31	33	27	30	34	33	21	27	41	26	28
% Successful	77.5	80.6	87.9	81.6	87.1	69.7	74.1	80.0	79.4	69.7	81.0	77.8	82.9	80.8	82.1

1995 TEAM STATISTICS

AMERICAN FOOTBALL CONFERENCE DEFENSE

	Buff	Cin	Clev	Den	Hou	Ind	Jax	KC	Mia	NE	NYJ	Oak	Pitt	SD	Sea
First Downs	287	354	342	322	267	304	320	289	309	308	301	293	272	313	321
Rushing	93	117	112	114	85	92	121	83	93	106	123	90	67	112	116
Passing	180	215	200	186	157	182	177	178	192	181	149	177	181	178	181
Penalty	14	22	30	22	25	30	22	28	24	21	29	26	24	23	24
Rushes	453	483	480	451	400	418	504	404	415	448	526	446	370	441	496
Net Yds. Gained	1626	2104	1826	1895	1526	1457	2003	1327	1675	1878	2016	1794	1321	1691	2130
Avg. Gain	3.6	4.4	3.8	4.2	3.8	3.5	4.0	3.3	4.0	4.2	3.8	4.0	3.6	3.8	4.3
Avg. Yds. per Game	101.6	131.5	114.1	118.4	95.4	91.1	125.2	82.9	104.7	117.4	126.0	112.1	82.6	105.7	133.1
Passes Attempted	582	602	573	529	553	569	509	596	556	549	497	527	531	543	554
Completed	310	364	360	297	289	336	304	329	327	342	263	301	314	321	310
% Completed	53.3	60.5	62.8	56.1	52,3	59.1	59.7	55.2	58.8	62.3	52.9	57.1	59.1	59.1	56.0
Total Yds. Gained	3864	4512	4013	3518	3325	3739	3584	3569	3756	4107	3055	3642	3512	3605	3706
Times Sacked	49	42	29	30	30	29	17	47	29	37	43	43	42	36	28
Yds. Lost	362	267	191	220	200	169	72	347	187	221	315	332	272	222	167
Net Yds. Gained	3502	4245	3822	3298	3125	3570	3512	3222	3569	3886	2740	3310	3240	3383	3539
Avg. Yds. per Game	218.9	265.3	238.9	206.1	195.3	223.1	219.5	201.4	223.1	242.9	171.3	206.9	202.5	211.4	221.2
Net Yds. per Pass Play	5.55	6.59	6.35	5.90	5.36	5.97	6.68	5.01	6.10	6.63	5.07	5.81	5.65	5.84	6.08
Yds. Gained per Comp.	12.46	12.40	11.15	11.85	11.51	11.13	11.79	10.85	11.49	12.01	11.62	12.10	11.18	11.23	11.95
Combined Net Yds. Gained	5128	6349	5648	5193	4651	5027	5515	4549	5244	5764	4756	5104	4561	5074	5669
% Total Yds. Rushing	31.7	33.1	32.3	36.5	32.8	29.0	36.3	29.2	31.9	32.6	42.4	35.1	29.0	33.3	37.6
% Total Yds. Passing	68.3	66.9	67.7	63.5	67.2	71.0	63.7	70.8	68.1	67.4	57.6	64.9	71.0	66.7	62.4
Avg. Yds. per Game	320.5	396.8	353.0	324.6	290.7	314.2	344.7	284.3	327.8	360.3	297.3	319.0	285.1	317.1	354.3
Ball Control Plays	1084	1127	1082	1010	983	1016	1030	1047	1000	1034	1066	1016	943	1020	1078
Avg. Yds. per Play	4.7	5.6	5.2	5.1	4.7	4.9	5.4	4.3	5.2	5.6	4.5	5.0	4.8	5.0	5.3
Avg. Time of Poss.	31:50	33:03	31:35	29:51	27:48	28:20	31:23	28:52	28:38	30:28	30:45	29:18	27:24	30:26	31:30
Third Down Efficiency	34.4	44.0	49.6	43.4	33.5	40.1	48.2	34.1	34.2	37.2	33.3	32.9	33.7	42.1	37.2
Intercepted By	17	12	17	8	21	13	13	16	14	15	17	11	22	17	16
Yds. Returned By	233	175	230	114	317	248	155	303	161	143	261	110	361	220	127
Returned for TD	2	1	2	0	4	1	1	2	1	0	3	2	3	1	0
Punts	90	64	59	76	86	63	61	102	59	86	85	70	85	73	81
Yds. Punted	3854	2455	2462	3253	3645	2580	2564	4266	2420	3339	3497	3044	3682	3168	3449
Avg. Yds. per Punt	42.8	38.4	41.7	42.8	42.4	41.0	42.0	41.8	41.0	38.8	41.1	43.5	43.3	43.4	42.6
Punt Returns	23	27	34	25	35	37	45	42	35	40	62	38	22	35	48
Yds. Returned	224	154	296	137	288	436	323	433	265	342	753	294	186	429	549
Avg. Yds. per Return	9.7	5.7	8.7	5.5	8.2	11.8	7.2	10.3	7.6	8.6	12.1	7.7	8.5	12.3	11.4
Returned for TD	1	0	0	0	1	0	0	0	0	0	0	0	0	1	0
Kickoff Returns	73	65	63	77	78	68	54	71	85	67	42	68	88	63	70
Yds. Returned	1615	1475	1172	1671	1467	1546	1278	1448	1782	1405	987	1469	1544	1496	1669
Avg. Yds. per Return	22.1	22.7	18.6	21.7	18.8	22.7	23.7	20.4	21.0	21.0	23.5	21.6	17.5	23.7	23.8
Returned for TD	0	0	0	2	0	1	1	0	0	0	0	0	0	0	2
Fumbles	23	27	20	20	28	24	22	35	30	24	27	37	30	24	17
Lost	11	12	7	13	17	13	11	17	16	14	17	22	12	10	9
Out of Bounds	4	6	4	1	2	1	0	1	1	2	0	2	2	4	0
Own Rec. for TD	0	0	0	0	0	1	0	1	0	0	1	0	0	0	1
Opp. Rec. by	12	14	11	16	20	11	13	11	12	20	18	13	13	12	9
Opp. Rec. for TD	2	0	0	2	1	0	0	1	1	2	2	2	1	0	1
Penalties	115	116	108	103	118	111	102	108	82	104	97	94	101	117	114
Yds. Penalized	890	1143	736	848	962	935	958	828	739	816	759	730	931	951	901
Total Points Scored	335	374	356	345	324	316	404	241	332	377	384	332	327	323	366
Total TDs	33	37	40	44	38	34	46	28	38	44	42	33	37	35	43
TDs Rushing	16	10	15	19	11	8	17	7	7	12	15	15	9	15	11
TDs Passing	14	25	23	20	24	23	28	16	30	29	21	14	24	16	26
TDs on Ret. and Rec.	3	2	2	5	3	3	1	5	1	3	6	4	4	4	6
Total Extra Points	31	36	36	42	35	32	45	25	32	42	40	30	35	30	36
Kicks Made	29	34	34	42	35	29	45	25	31	40	40	27	34	28	36
2-Pt. Conversions	2	2	2	0	0	3	0	0	1	2	0	3	1	2	0
Safeties	1	0	0	0	2	1	1	0	1	0	1	1	0	0	0
Field Goals Made	34	38	26	13	19	25	27	16	23	23	30	33	23	27	24
Field Goals Attempted	43	49	34	19	24	38	31	19	31	32	41	41	25	32	35
% Successful	79.1	77.6	76.5	68.4	79.2	65.8	87.1	84.2	74.2	71.9	73.2	80.5	92.0	84.4	68.6

NATIONAL FOOTBALL CONFERENCE OFFENSE

	Ariz	Atl	Car	Chi	Dall	Det	GB	Minn	NO	NYG	Phi	StL	SF	TB	Wash
First Downs	285	317	250	340	364	349	339	342	294	288	290	292	355	283	297
Rushing	65	85	74	116	141	91	84	91	75	113	126	77	109	101	105
Passing	184	216	157	201	195	230	235	223	202	150	145	199	231	159	169
Penalty	36	16	19	23	28	28	20	28	17	25	19	16	15	23	23
Rushes	387	337	454	492	495	387	410	433	383	478	508	392	415	398	469
Net Yds. Gained	1363	1393	1573	1930	2201	1753	1428	1733	1390	1833	2121	1431	1479	1587	1956
Avg. Gain	3.5	4.1	3.5	3.9	4.4	4.5	3.5	4.0	3.6	3.8	4.2	3.7	3.6	4.0	4.2
Avg. Yds. per Game	85.2	87.1	98.3	120.6	137.6	109.6	89.3	108.3	86.9	114.6	132.6	89.4	92.4	99.2	122.3
Passes Attempted	560	603	537	523	494	605	593	642	573	479	496	632	644	507	521
Completed	327	364	263	315	322	362	372	402	349	260	284	366	432	267	265
% Completed	58.4	60.4	49.0	60.2	65.2	59.8	62.7	62.6	60.9	54.3	57.3	57.9	67.1	52.7	50.9
Total Yds. Gained	3893	4456	3304	3838	3741	4510	4539	4500	4002	2863	2931	4113	4779	3341	3496
Times Sacked	55	43	38	15	18	32	33	40	28	46	46	43	33	56	36
Yds. Lost	390	270	258	95	118	150	217	295	214	213	245	308	171	386	268
Net Yds. Gained	3503	4186	3046	3743	3623	4360	4322	4205	3788	2650	2686	3805	4608	2955	3228
Avg. Yds. per Game	218.9	261.6	190.4	233.9	226.4	272.5	270.1	262.8	236.8	165.6	167.9	237.8	288.0	184.7	201.8
Net Yds. per Pass Play	5.70	6.48	5.30	6.96	7.08	6.84	6.90	6.17	6.30	5.05	4.96	5.64	6.81	5.25	5.80
Yds. Gained per Comp.	11.91	12.24	12.56	12.18	11.62	12.46	12.20	11.19	11.47	11.01	10.32	11.24	11.06	12.51	13.19
Combined Net Yds. Gained	4866	5579	4619	5673	5824	6113	5750	5938	5178	4483	4807	5236	6087	4542	5184
% Total Yds. Rushing	28.0	25.0	34.1	34.0	37.8	28.7	24.8	29.2	26.8	40.9	44.1	27.3	24.3	34.9	37.7
% Total Yds. Passing	72.0	75.0	65.9	66.0	62.2	71.3	75.2	70.8	73.2	59.1	55.9	72.7	75.7	65.1	62.3
Avg. Yds. per Game	304.1	348.7	288.7	354.6	364.0	382.1	359.4	371.1	323.6	280.2	300.4	327.3	380.4	283.9	324.0
Ball Control Plays	1002	983	1029	1030	1007	1024	1036	1115	984	1003	1050	1067	1092	961	1026
Avg. Yds. per Play	4.9	5.7	4.5	5.5	5.8	6.0	5.6	5.3	5.3	4.5	4.6	4.9	5.6	4.7	5.1
Avg. Time of Poss.	30:54	29:27	29:27	29:55	31:15	28:43	31:12	31:50	28:15	29:23	30:26	31:10	31:56	28:35	28:42
Third Down Efficiency	34.6	40.4	38.1	42.5	44.6	45.7	49.1	47.7	42.3	40.7	38.2	36.4	48.9	34.9	40.4
Had Intercepted	24	12	25	10	10	12	15	16	14	13	19	23	16	20	20
Yds. Opp. Returned	307	49	221	203	155	219	243	172	273	241	240	497	247	204	338
Ret. by Opp. for TD	4	2	3	1	1	2	0	1	2	1	2	5	2	0	3
Punts	72	67	96	58	55	60	67	72	74	73	86	83	57	78	74
Yds. Punted	3150	2759	3938	2169	2243	2427	2740	2948	2965	3078	3682	3679	2312	3296	3140
Avg. Yds. per Punt	43.8	41.2	41.0	37.4	40.8	40.5	40.9	40.9	40.1	42.2	42.8	44.3	40.6	42.3	42.4
Punt Returns	23	39	49	24	23	24	61	35	29	31	29	55	27	29	26
Yds. Returned	172	383	500	179	255	189	515	414	268	218	293	587	272	293	315
Avg. Yds. per Return	7.5	9.8	10.2	7.5	11.1	7.9	8.4	11.8	9.2	7.0	10.1	10.7	10.1	10.1	12.1
Returned for TD	0	1	1	0	0	0	0	1	0	0	0	0	1	0	1
Kickoff Returns	73	70	55	71	58	67	61	72	73	70	71	73	58	76	69
Yds. Returned	1519	1506	1163	1459	1276	1367	1282	1612	1690	1448	1487	1618	1183	1443	1646
Avg. Yds. per Return	20.8	21.5	21.1	20.5	22.0	20.4	21.0	22.4	23.2	20.7	20.9	22.2	20.4	19.0	23.9
Returned for TD	0	0	0	0	0	0	0	0	0	1	1	0	0	0	0
Fumbles	41	21	28	26	24	21	22	29	19	27	31	27	21	25	24
Lost	19	9	16	16	13	13	6	13	11	15	17	16	12	14	10
Out of Bounds	3	0	2	1	3	1	1	2	3	3	3	2	2	1	2
Own Rec. for TD	1	0	0	0	0	0	0	0	0	1	0	0	1	0	0
Opp. Rec. by	23	12	15	13	6	13	3	15	12	15	19	14	8	16	18
Opp. Rec. for TD	0	0	1	0	0	1	1	2	0	1	4	3	2	1	1
Penalties	119	96	94	71	90	134	85	105	86	92	112	117	88	113	78
Yds. Penalized	835	737	683	601	695	1032	604	797	688	772	838	916	711	882	563
Total Points Scored	275	362	289	392	435	436	404	412	319	290	318	309	457	238	326
Total TDs	26	38	30	46	51	50	49	48	38	33	36	37	57	26	35
TDs Rushing	3	8	10	15	29	16	9	10	11	17	19	5	19	19	15
TDs Passing	17	26	16	29	18	33	39	33	26	11	11	27	29	5	16
TDs on Ret. and Rec.	6	4	4	2	4	1	1	5	1	5	6	5	9	2	4
Extra Points	24	32	29	45	47	49	49	45	29	29	34	32	53	25	33
Kicks Made	19	29	27	45	46	48	48	44	27	28	32	30	51	25	33
2-Pt. Conversions	5	3	2	0	1	1	1	1	2	1	2	2	2	0	0
Safeties	0	0	0	1	0	1	0	0	0	1	0	1	0	0	1
Field Goals Made	30	33	26	23	27	28	20	26	20	20	22	17	20	19	27
Field Goals Attempted	39	40	33	31	28	34	28	36	31	28	30	28	28	26	36
% Successful	76.9	82.5	78.8	74.2	96.4	82.4	71.4	72.2	64.5	71.4	73.3	60.7	71.4	73.1	75.0

1995 TEAM STATISTICS

NATIONAL FOOTBALL CONFERENCE DEFENSE

	Ariz	Atl	Car	Chi	Dall	Det	GB	Minn	NO	NYG	Phil	StL	SF	TB	Wash
First Downs	310	340	288	316	303	350	303	312	320	335	281	301	264	336	323
Rushing	105	96	99	81	113	110	99	75	107	120	102	101	57	104	127
Passing	180	230	175	212	165	201	188	212	195	187	154	178	192	202	182
Penalty	25	14	14	23	25	39	16	25	18	28	25	22	15	30	14
Rushes	503	404	450	405	442	409	374	352	469	500	466	410	348	449	483
Net Yds. Gained	2249	1547	1576	1441	1772	1795	1515	1329	1838	2109	1822	1677	1061	1754	2132
Avg. Gain	4.5	3.8	3.5	3.6	4.0	4.4	4.1	3.8	3.9	4.2	3.9	4.1	3.0	3.9	4.4
Avg. Yds. per Game	140.6	96.7	98.5	90.1	110.8	112.2	94.7	83.1	114.9	131.8	113.9	104.8	66.3	109.6	133.3
Passes Attempted	461	650	586	595	523	580	616	620	543	508	499	534	611	557	546
Completed	264	405	310	374	293	354	351	369	329	299	268	320	330	346	338
% Completed	57.3	62.3	52.9	62.9	56.0	61.0	57.0	59.5	60.6	58.9	53.7	59.9	54.0	62.1	61.9
Total Yds. Gained	3655	4751	3716	4240	3491	4121	3915	4416	3998	3361	3121	3699	3577	4098	3403
Times Sacked	31	30	36	35	36	42	39	44	44	29	48	36	40	25	30
Yds. Lost	200	210	265	239	219	317	275	294	275	177	305	258	240	140	135
Net Yds. Gained	3455	4541	3451	4001	3272	3804	3640	4122	3723	3184	2816	3441	3337	3958	3268
Avg. Yds. per Game	215.9	283.8	215.7	250.1	204.5	237.8	227.5	257.6	232.7	199.0	176.0	215.1	208.6	247.4	204.3
Net Yds. per Pass Play	7.02	6.68	5.55	6.35	5.85	6.12	5.56	6.21	6.34	5.93	5.15	6.04	5.13	6.80	5.67
Yds. Gained per Comp.	13.84	11.73	11.99	11.34	11.91	11.64	11.15	11.97	12.15	11.24	11.65	11.56	10.84	11.84	10.07
Combined Net Yds. Gained	5704	6088	5027	5442	5044	5599	5155	5451	5561	5293	4638	5118	4398	5712	5400
% Total Yds. Rushing	39.4	25.4	31.4	26.5	35.1	32.1	29.4	24.4	33.1	39.8	39.3	32.8	24.1	30.7	39.5
% Total Yds. Passing	60.6	74.6	68.6	73.5	64.9	67.9	70.6	75.6	66.9	60.2	60.7	67.2	75.9	69.3	60.5
Avg. Yds. per Game	356.5	380.5	314.2	340.1	315.3	349.9	322.2	340.7	347.6	330.8	289.9	319.9	274.9	357.0	337.5
Ball Control Plays	995	1084	1072	1035	1001	1031	1029	1016	1056	1037	1013	980	999	1031	1059
Avg. Yds. per Play	5.7	5.6	4.7	5.3	5.0	5.4	5.0	5.4	5.3	5.1	4.6	5.2	4.4	5.5	5.1
Avg. Time of Poss.	29:06	30:33	30:33	30:05	28:45	31:17	28:48	28:10	31:45	30:37	29:34	28:50	28:04	31:25	31:18
Third Down Efficiency	44.3	41.1	40.8	46.5	44.9	38.0	35.0	41.5	43.7	41.8	38.2	41.7	37.9	44.1	45.5
Intercepted By	19	18	21	16	19	22	13	25	17	16	19	22	26	14	16
Yds. Returned By	259	304	319	146	261	270	253	326	195	269	239	245	425	137	250
Returned for TD	4	2	2	1	4	0	0	2	1	2	1	2	5	1	2
Punts	62	70	94	62	65	61	88	68	66	63	74	79	70	59	72
Yds. Punted	2694	3031	3796	2311	2775	2604	3746	2867	2756	2660	3055	3435	2918	2358	2984
Avg. Yds. per Punt	43.5	43.3	40.4	37.3	42.7	42.7	42.6	42.2	41.8	42.2	41.3	43.5	41.7	40.0	41.4
Punt Returns	32	28	39	28	22	29	36	41	36	34	38	38	26	41	26
Yds. Returned	242	236	342	257	216	442	279	446	233	297	527	393	292	335	173
Avg. Yds. per Return	7.6	8.4	8.8	9.2	9.8	15.2	7.8	10.9	6.5	8.7	13.9	10.3	11.2	8.2	6.7
Returned for TD	0	0	0	1	0	1	0	1	0	1	2	1	0	0	0
Kickoff Returns	65	59	62	72	85	80	74	74	68	54	61	59	82	46	70
Yds. Returned	1593	1323	1159	1570	1661	1828	1581	1581	1348	1129	1576	1247	1857	856	1434
Avg. Yds. per Return	24.5	22.4	18.7	21.8	19.5	22.9	21.4	21.4	19.8	20.9	25.8	21.1	22.6	18.6	20.5
Returned for TD	2	0	0	0	0	0	0	0	0	0	0	0	0	0	1
Fumbles	39	21	28	25	16	24	12	30	29	29	30	27	23	26	31
Lost	23	12	16	13	6	13	3	15	12	15	19	14	8	16	19
Out of Bounds	5	0	1	1	4	0	0	2	2	4	1	0	3	1	2
Own Rec. for TD	0	1	0	0	0	0	0	0	0	0	0	0	0	0	0
Opp. Rec. by	19	9	16	16	12	13	6	13	11	15	17	16	11	14	10
Opp. Rec. for TD	0	0	2	3	1	1	0	2	0	1	4	3	0	1	0
Penalties	117	94	112	104	112	120	98	100	109	94	87	87	74	87	100
Yds. Penalized	860	688	808	821	913	1001	738	707	830	662	727	681	556	698	780
Total Points Scored	422	349	325	360	291	336	314	385	348	340	338	418	258	335	359
Total TDs	53	43	38	41	32	36	37	44	38	37	36	51	26	35	42
TDs Rushing	14	12	17	9	13	15	12	11	13	17	14	14	5	14	18
TDs Passing	33	28	15	27	17	17	25	29	23	17	14	27	19	19	20
TDs on Ret. and Rec.	6	3	6	5	2	4	0	4	2	3	8	10	2	2	4
Total Extra Points	50	38	38	41	30	34	35	36	36	33	34	48	19	31	40
Kicks Made	50	38	38	40	29	32	35	29	33	32	32	47	17	30	39
2-Pt. Conversions	0	0	0	1	1	2	0	7	3	1	2	1	2	1	1
Safeties	0	1	1	0	1	0	0	0	0	0	1	0	0	0	0
Field Goals Made	18	17	19	24	22	28	19	26	27	28	28	21	27	31	22
Field Goals Attempted	25	22	26	29	27	42	21	35	35	35	37	27	32	40	27
% Successful	72.0	77.3	73.1	82.8	81.5	66.7	90.5	74.3	77.1	80.0	75.7	77.8	84.4	77.5	81.5

AFC, NFC, AND NFL SUMMARY

	AFC Offense Total	AFC Offense Average	AFC Defense Total	AFC Defense Average	NFC Offense Total	NFC Offense Average	NFC Defense Total	NFC Defense Average	NFL Total	NFL Average
First Downs	4599	306.6	4602	306.8	4685	312.3	4682	312.1	9284	309.5
Rushing	1567	104.5	1524	101.6	1453	96.9	1496	99.7	3020	100.7
Passing	2671	178.1	2714	180.9	2896	193.1	2853	190.2	5567	185.6
Penalty	361	24.1	364	24.3	336	22.4	333	22.2	697	23.2
Rushes	6761	450.7	6735	449.0	6438	429.2	6464	430.9	13199	440.0
Net Yds. Gained	26715	1781.0	26269	1751.3	25171	1678.1	25617	1707.8	51886	1729.5
Avg. Gain	—	4.0	—	3.9	—	3.9	—	4.0	—	3.9
Avg. Yds. per Game	—	111.3	—	109.5	—	104.9	—	106.7	—	108.1
Passes Attempted	8290	552.7	8270	551.3	8409	560.6	8429	561.9	16699	556.6
Completed	4767	317.8	4767	317.8	4950	330.0	4950	330.0	9717	323.9
% Completed	—	57.5	—	57.6	—	58.9	—	58.7	—	58.2
Total Yds. Gained	54763	3650.9	55507	3700.5	58306	3887.1	57562	3837.5	113069	3769.0
Times Sacked	514	34.3	531	35.4	562	37.5	545	36.3	1076	35.9
Yds. Lost	3495	233.0	3544	236.3	3598	239.9	3549	236.6	7093	236.4
Net Yds. Gained	51268	3417.9	51963	3464.2	54708	3647.2	54013	3600.9	105976	3532.5
Avg. Yds. per Game	—	213.6	—	216.5	—	228.0	—	225.1	—	220.8
Net Yds. per Pass Play	—	5.82	—	5.90	—	6.10	—	6.02	—	5.96
Yds. Gained per Comp.	—	11.49	—	11.64	—	11.78	—	11.63	—	11.64
Combined Net Yds. Gained	77983	5198.9	78232	5215.5	79879	5325.3	79630	5308.7	157862	5262.1
% Total Yds. Rushing	—	34.3	—	33.6	—	31.5	—	32.2	—	32.9
% Total Yds. Passing	—	65.7	—	66.4	—	68.5	—	67.8	—	67.1
Avg. Yds. per Game	—	324.9	—	326.0	—	332.8	—	331.8	—	328.9
Ball Control Plays	15565	1037.7	15536	1035.7	15409	1027.3	15438	1029.2	30974	1032.5
Avg. Yds. per Play	—	5.0	—	5.0	—	5.2	—	5.2	—	5.1
Third Down Efficiency	—	38.6	—	38.6	—	41.6	—	41.7	—	40.1
Interceptions	263	17.5	229	15.3	249	16.6	283	18.9	512	17.1
Yds. Returned	3447	229.8	3158	210.5	3609	240.6	3898	259.9	7056	235.2
Returned for TD	23	1.5	23	1.5	29	1.9	29	1.9	52	1.7
Punts	1121	74.7	1140	76.0	1072	71.5	1053	70.2	2193	73.1
Yds. Punted	47142	3142.8	47678	3178.5	44526	2968.4	43990	2932.7	91668	3055.6
Avg. Yds. per Punt	—	42.1	—	41.8	—	41.5	—	41.8	—	41.8
Punt Returns	538	35.9	548	36.5	504	33.6	494	32.9	1042	34.7
Yds. Returned	4966	331.1	5109	340.6	4853	323.5	4710	314.0	9819	327.3
Avg. Yds. per Return	—	9.2	—	9.3	—	9.6	—	9.5	—	9.4
Returned for TD	5	0.3	3	0.2	5	0.3	7	0.5	10	0.3
Kickoff Returns	1026	68.4	1032	68.8	1017	67.8	1011	67.4	2043	68.1
Yds. Returned	22068	1471.2	22024	1468.3	21699	1446.6	21743	1449.5	43767	1458.9
Avg. Yds. per Return	—	21.5	—	21.3	—	21.3	—	21.5	—	21.4
Returned for TD	7	0.5	6	0.4	2	0.1	3	0.2	9	0.3
Fumbles	392	26.1	388	25.9	386	25.7	390	26.0	778	25.9
Lost	205	13.7	201	13.4	200	13.3	204	13.6	405	13.5
Out of Bounds	27	1.8	30	2.0	29	1.9	26	1.7	56	1.9
Own Rec. for TD	2	0.1	4	0.3	3	0.2	1	0.1	5	0.2
Opp. Rec.	201	13.4	205	13.7	202	13.5	198	13.2	403	13.4
Opp. Rec. for TD	16	1.1	15	1.0	17	1.1	18	1.2	33	1.1
Penalties	1605	107.0	1590	106.0	1480	98.7	1495	99.7	3085	102.8
Yds. Penalized	13243	882.9	13127	875.1	11354	756.9	11470	764.7	24597	819.9
Total Points Scored	5052	336.8	5136	342.4	5262	350.8	5178	345.2	10314	343.8
Total TDs	561	37.4	572	38.1	600	40.0	589	39.3	1161	38.7
TDs Rushing	180	12.0	187	12.5	205	13.7	198	13.2	385	12.8
TDs Passing	327	21.8	333	22.2	336	22.4	330	22.0	663	22.1
TDs on Ret. and Rec.	54	3.6	52	3.5	59	3.9	61	4.1	113	3.8
Total Extra Points	515	34.3	527	35.1	555	37.0	543	36.2	1070	35.7
Kicks Made	498	33.2	509	33.9	532	35.5	521	34.7	1030	34.3
2-Pt. Conversions	17	1.1	18	1.2	23	1.5	22	1.5	40	1.3
Safeties	7	0.5	8	0.5	5	0.3	4	0.3	12	0.4
Field Goals Made	380	25.3	381	25.4	358	23.9	357	23.8	738	24.6
Field Goals Attempted	478	31.9	494	32.9	476	31.7	460	30.7	954	31.8
% Successful	—	79.5	—	77.1	—	75.2	—	77.6	—	77.4

1995 TEAM STATISTICS

CLUB LEADERS

	Offense	Defense
First Downs	Dall. 364	S.F. 264
Rushing	Dall. 141	S.F. 57
Passing	G.B. 235	NYJ 149
Penalty	Ariz. 36	Four tied 14
Rushes	Buff. 521	S.F. 348
Net Yds. Gained	K.C. 2222	S.F. 1061
Avg. Gain	Sea. 4.6	S.F. 3.0
Passes Attempted	N.E. 686	Ariz. 461
Completed	S.F. 432	NYJ 263
% Completed	S.F. 67.1	Hou. 52.3
Total Yds. Gained	S.F. 4779	NYJ 3055
Times Sacked	Chi. 15	Buff. 49
Yds. Lost	Chi. 95	Buff. 362
Net Yds. Gained	S.F. 4608	NYJ 2740
Net Yds. per Pass Play	Dall. 7.08	K.C. 5.01
Yds. Gained per Comp.	Wash. 13.19	Wash. 10.07
Combined Net Yds. Gained	Det. 6113	S.F. 4398
% Total Yds. Rushing	Phil. 44.1	S.F. 24.1
% Total Yds. Passing	S.F. 75.7	NYJ 57.6
Ball Control Plays	N.E. 1187	Pitt. 943
Avg. Yds. per Play	Det. 6.0	K.C. 4.3
Avg. Time of Poss.	Pitt. 32:36	—
Third Down Efficiency	G.B. 49.1	Oak. 32.9
Interceptions	—	S.F. 26
Yds. Returned	—	S.F. 425
Returned for TD	—	S.F. 5
Punts	NYJ 105	—
Yds. Punted	NYJ 4328	—
Avg. Yds. per Punt	Sea. 45.0	—
Punt Returns	G.B. 61	Pitt. & Dall. 22
Yds. Returned	St.L. 587	Den. 137
Avg. Yds. per Return	Wash. 12.1	Den. 5.5
Returned for TD	10 tied 1	—
Kickoff Returns	Cin. 80	NYJ 42
Yds. Returned	Cin. 1788	T.B. 856
Avg. Yds. per Return	Wash. 23.9	Pitt. 17.5
Returned for TD	K.C. & S.D. 2	—
Total Points Scored	S.F. 457	K.C. 241
Total TDs	S.F. 57	S.F. 26
TDs Rushing	Dall. 29	S.F. 5
TDs Passing	G.B. 39	Three tied 14
TDs on Ret. and Rec.	S.F. 9	G.B. 0
Extra Points	S.F. 53	S.F. 19
2-Point Conversions	Ariz. 5	—
Safeties	Cin. 2	—
Field Goals Made	Pitt. 34	Den. 13
Field Goals Attempted	Pitt. 41	Den. & K.C. 19
% Successful	Dall. 96.4	Ind. 65.8

NFL CLUB RANKINGS BY YARDS

	Offense			Defense		
	Total	Rush	Pass	Total	Rush	Pass
Arizona	24	29	17	26	30	15
Atlanta	10	27	6	29	9	30
Buffalo	20	6	21	13	11	16
Carolina	26	20	24	7T	10	14
Chicago	9	9	12	19	5	27
Cincinnati	17	24	11	30	26	29
Cleveland	21	22	14	24	20	24
Dallas	5	2	13	9	16	8
Denver	3	5	7	15	23	9
Detroit	*1	14	2	23	18	23
Green Bay	7	26	3	14	7	21
Houston	23	18	19	5	8	3
Indianapolis	22	11	23	7T	6	20
Jacksonville	28	17	27	21	24	17
Kansas City	14	*1	25	2	3	5
Miami	8	21	4	16	12	19
Minnesota	4	16	5	20	4	28
New England	12	10	15	28	22	25
New Orleans	19	28	10	22	21	22
N.Y. Giants	29	13	30	17	27	4
N.Y. Jets	30	30	28	6	25	*1
Oakland	11	8	16	11	17	10
Philadelphia	25	4	29	4	19	2
Pittsburgh	6	12	8	3	2	6
St. Louis	15	25	9	12	13	13
San Diego	16	15	18	10	14	12
San Francisco	2	23	*1	*1	*1	11
Seattle	13	3	22	25	28	18
Tampa Bay	27	19	26	27	15	26
Washington	18	7	20	18	29	7

T = Tied for position
** = League Leader*

AFC TAKEAWAYS/GIVEAWAYS

	Takeaways			Giveaways			Net
	Int	Fum	Total	Int	Fum	Total	Diff.
Kansas City	16	17	33	10	11	21	+12
Indianapolis	13	13	26	11	11	22	+4
Buffalo	17	11	28	14	12	26	+2
Pittsburgh	22	12	34	21	13	34	0
Houston	21	17	38	18	20	38	0
Oakland	11	22	33	21	13	34	-1
Miami	14	16	30	20	12	32	-2
San Diego	17	10	27	18	12	30	-3
Jacksonville	13	11	24	15	13	28	-4
New England	15	14	29	16	20	36	-7
Seattle	16	9	25	23	9	32	-7
Cleveland	17	7	24	20	11	31	-7
Cincinnati	12	12	24	18	14	32	-8
N.Y. Jets	17	17	34	24	18	42	-8
Denver	8	13	21	14	16	30	-9

NFC TAKEAWAYS/GIVEAWAYS

	Takeaways			Giveaways			Net
	Int	Fum	Total	Int	Fum	Total	Diff.
Minnesota	25	15	40	16	13	29	+11
Detroit	22	13	35	12	13	25	+10
Atlanta	18	12	30	12	9	21	+9
San Francisco	26	8	34	16	12	28	+6
Washington	16	19	35	20	10	30	+5
New Orleans	17	12	29	14	11	25	+4
N.Y. Giants	16	15	31	13	15	28	+3
Chicago	16	13	29	10	16	26	+3
Dallas	19	6	25	10	13	23	+2
Philadelphia	19	19	38	19	17	36	+2
Arizona	19	23	42	24	19	43	-1
St. Louis	22	14	36	23	16	39	-3
Tampa Bay	14	16	30	20	14	34	-4
Carolina	21	16	37	25	16	41	-4
Green Bay	13	3	16	15	6	21	-5

SCORING

Points
NFC: 150—Emmitt Smith, Dallas
AFC: 141—Norm Johnson, Pittsburgh

Touchdowns
NFC: 25—Emmitt Smith, Dallas
AFC: 17—Carl Pickens, Cincinnati

Extra Points
NFC: 48—Jason Hanson, Detroit
AFC: 40—Todd Peterson, Seattle

Field Goals
AFC: 34—Norm Johnson, Pittsburgh
NFC: 31—Morten Andersen, Atlanta

Field Goal Attempts
AFC: 41—Norm Johnson, Pittsburgh
NFC: 39—Greg Davis, Arizona

Longest Field Goal
NFC: 59—Morten Andersen, Atlanta vs. San Francisco, December 24
AFC: 56—Jason Elam, Denver at Houston, November 26

Most Points, Game
NFC: 24—Emmitt Smith, Dallas at N.Y. Giants, September 4 (4 TD)
Rodney Hampton, N.Y. Giants vs. New Orleans, September 24 (4 TD)
AFC: 18—Anthony Miller, Denver at Dallas, September 10 (3 TD)
Terrell Davis, Denver vs. Washington, September 17 (3 TD)
Marshall Faulk, Indianapolis vs. St. Louis, October 1 (3 TD)
Carl Pickens, Cincinnati vs. Miami, October 1 (3 TD)
Chris Warren, Seattle vs. Denver, October 1 (3 TD)
Eric Pegram, Pittsburgh at Chicago, November 5 (OT) (3 TD)
Joey Galloway, Seattle at Jacksonville, November 12 (3 TD)
Byron (Bam) Morris, Pittsburgh at Cincinnati, November 19 (3 TD)
Ben Coates, New England at Buffalo, November 26 (3 TD)
Jimmy Smith, Jacksonville at Denver, December 3 (3 TD)

Team Leaders, Points
AFC: BUFFALO: 126, Steve Christie; CINCINNATI: 121, Doug Pelfrey; CLEVELAND: 113, Matt Stover; DENVER: 132, Jason Elam; HOUSTON: 114, Al Del Greco; INDIANAPOLIS: 84, Marshall Faulk; JACKSONVILLE: 87, Mike Hollis; KANSAS CITY: 106, Lin Elliott; MIAMI: 118, Pete Stoyanovich; NEW ENGLAND: 96, Matt Bahr; N.Y. JETS: 75, Nick Lowery; OAKLAND: 61, Jeff Jaeger; PITTSBURGH: 141, Norm Johnson; SAN DIEGO: 95, John Carney; SEATTLE: 109, Todd Peterson
NFC: ARIZONA: 109, Greg Davis; ATLANTA: 122, Morten Andersen; CAROLINA: 105, John Kasay; CHICAGO: 114, Kevin Butler; DALLAS: 150, Emmitt Smith; DETROIT: 132, Jason Hanson; GREEN BAY: 94, Chris Jacke; MINNESOTA: 122, Fuad Reveiz; NEW ORLEANS: 52, Doug Brien; N.Y. GIANTS: 88, Brad Daluiso; PHILADELPHIA: 98, Gary Anderson; ST. LOUIS: 80, Isaac Bruce; SAN FRANCISCO: 104, Jerry Rice; TAMPA BAY: 82, Michael Husted; WASHINGTON: 114, Eddie Murray

Team Champion
NFC: 457—San Francisco
AFC: 407—Pittsburgh

AFC SCORING—TEAM

	TD	TDR	TDP	TDM	EXTRA PT. KICKS MADE	EXTRA PT. KICKS ATT.	2-POINT TRIES MADE	2-POINT TRIES ATT.	FG	FGA	SAF	PTS
Pittsburgh	44	17	21	6	39	39	1	5	34	41	0	407
Miami	46	16	28	2	37	37	2	9	27	34	0	398
Denver	42	14	27	1	39	39	2	3	31	38	0	388
Seattle	42	20	19	3	40	40	0	2	23	28	1	363
Kansas City	42	14	21	7	34	37	0	3	24	30	0	358
Buffalo	37	10	24	3	33	35	1	2	31	40	0	350
Cincinnati	37	7	29	1	34	34	1	3	29	36	2	349
Houston	38	12	22	4	33	33	2	5	27	31	1	348
Oakland	41	10	25	6	39	40	0	1	21	27	0	348
Indianapolis	37	14	20	3	34	34	2	3	23	33	1	331
San Diego	37	14	17	6	32	33	1	4	21	26	1	321
New England	32	16	14	2	27	27	3	5	23	33	0	294
Cleveland	29	5	21	3	26	26	1	3	29	33	0	289
Jacksonville	31	9	19	3	27	28	1	3	20	27	0	275
N.Y. Jets	26	2	20	4	24	24	0	2	17	21	1	233
AFC Total	561	180	327	54	498	506	17	53	380	478	7	5052
AFC Average	37.4	12.0	21.8	3.6	33.2	33.7	1.1	3.5	25.3	31.9	0.5	336.8

NFC SCORING—TEAM

	TD	TDR	TDP	TDM	EXTRA PT. KICKS MADE	EXTRA PT. KICKS ATT.	2-POINT TRIES MADE	2-POINT TRIES ATT.	FG	FGA	SAF	PTS
San Francisco	57	19	29	9	51	54	2	3	20	28	0	457
Detroit	50	16	33	1	48	48	1	2	28	34	1	436
Dallas	51	29	18	4	46	48	1	2	27	28	0	435
Minnesota	48	10	33	5	44	44	1	2	26	36	0	412
Green Bay	49	9	39	1	48	48	1	1	20	28	0	404
Chicago	46	15	29	2	45	45	0	1	23	31	1	392
Atlanta	38	8	26	4	29	30	3	8	33	40	0	362
Washington	35	15	16	4	33	33	0	1	27	36	1	326
New Orleans	38	11	26	1	27	29	2	9	20	31	0	319
Philadelphia	36	19	11	6	32	33	2	3	22	30	0	318
St. Louis	37	5	27	5	30	31	2	6	17	28	1	309
N.Y. Giants	33	17	11	5	28	28	1	4	20	28	1	290
Carolina	30	10	16	4	27	28	2	2	26	33	0	289
Arizona	26	3	17	6	19	19	5	6	30	39	0	275
Tampa Bay	26	19	5	2	25	25	0	1	19	26	0	238
NFC Total	600	205	336	59	532	543	23	51	358	476	5	5262
NFC Average	40.0	13.7	22.4	3.9	35.5	36.2	1.5	3.4	23.9	31.7	0.3	350.8
NFL Total	1161	385	663	113	1030	1049	40	104	738	954	12	10314
NFL Average	38.7	12.8	22.1	3.8	34.3	35.0	1.3	3.5	24.6	31.8	0.4	343.8

1995 INDIVIDUAL STATISTICS

NFL TOP TEN SCORERS—NONKICKERS

	TD	TDR	TDP	TDM	2-PT	PTS
Smith, Emmitt, Dall	25	25	0	0	0	150
Rice, Jerry, SF	17	1	15	1	1	104
Carter, Cris, Minn	17	0	17	0	0	102
Pickens, Carl, Cin	17	0	17	0	0	102
Warren, Chris, Sea	16	15	1	0	0	96
Martin, Curtis, NE	15	14	1	0	1	92
Faulk, Marshall, Ind	14	11	3	0	0	84
Miller, Anthony, Den	14	0	14	0	0	84
Moore, Herman, Det	14	0	14	0	0	84
Loville, Derek, SF	13	10	3	0	1	80
Bruce, Isaac, StL	13	0	13	0	1	80

NFL TOP TEN SCORERS—KICKERS

	XP	XPA	FG	FGA	PTS
Johnson, Norm, Pitt	39	39	34	41	141
Hanson, Jason, Det	48	48	28	34	132
Elam, Jason, Den	39	39	31	38	132
Boniol, Chris, Dall	46	48	27	28	127
Christie, Steve, Buff	33	35	31	40	126
Andersen, Morten, Atl	29	30	31	37	122
Reveiz, Fuad, Minn	44	44	26	36	122
Pelfrey, Doug, Cin	34	34	29	36	121
Stoyanovich, Pete, Mia	37	37	27	34	118
Butler, Kevin, Chi	45	45	23	31	114
Murray, Eddie, Wash	33	33	27	36	114
Del Greco, Al, Hou	33	33	27	31	114

AFC SCORERS—INDIVIDUAL

Kickers

	XP	XPA	FG	FGA	PTS
Johnson, Norm, Pitt	39	39	34	41	141
Elam, Jason, Den	39	39	31	38	132
Christie, Steve, Buff	33	35	31	40	126
Pelfrey, Doug, Cin	34	34	29	36	121
Stoyanovich, Pete, Mia	37	37	27	34	118
Del Greco, Al, Hou	33	33	27	31	114
Stover, Matt, Cle	26	26	29	33	113
Peterson, Todd, Sea	40	40	23	28	109
Elliott, Lin, KC	34	37	24	30	106
Bahr, Matt, NE	27	27	23	33	96
Carney, John, SD	32	33	21	26	95
Hollis, Mike, Jax	27	28	20	27	87
Blanchard, Cary, Ind	25	25	19	24	82
Lowery, Nick, NYJ	24	24	17	21	75
Jaeger, Jeff, Oak	22	22	13	18	61
Ford, Cole, Oak	17	18	8	9	41
Cofer, Mike, Ind	9	9	4	9	21

Nonkickers

	TD	TDR	TDP	TDM	2-PT	PTS
Pickens, Carl, Cin	17	0	17	0	0	102
Warren, Chris, Sea	16	15	1	0	0	96
Martin, Curtis, NE	15	14	1	0	1	92
Faulk, Marshall, Ind	14	11	3	0	0	84
Miller, Anthony, Den	14	0	14	0	0	84
Brooks, Bill, Buff	11	0	11	0	0	66
Brown, Tim, Oak	10	0	10	0	0	60
Parmalee, Bernie, Mia	10	9	1	0	0	60
Galloway, Joey, Sea	9	1	7	1	0	54
Jackson, Michael, Cle	9	0	9	0	0	54
Morris, Byron (Bam), Pitt	9	9	0	0	0	54
Sanders, Chris, Hou	9	0	9	0	0	54
Williams, Harvey, Oak	9	9	0	0	0	54
McDuffie, O. J., Mia	8	0	8	0	1	50
Davis, Terrell, Den	8	7	1	0	0	48
Fryar, Irving, Mia	8	0	8	0	0	48
Jeffires, Haywood, Hou	8	0	8	0	0	48
Mills, Ernie, Pitt	8	0	8	0	0	48
Thomas, Thurman, Buff	8	6	2	0	0	48
Thomas, Rodney, Hou	7	5	2	0	1	44
Kirby, Terry, Mia	7	4	3	0	0	42
Pegram, Erric, Pitt	6	5	1	0	1	38
Coates, Ben, NE	6	0	6	0	0	36
Craver, Aaron, Den	6	5	1	0	0	36
Harmon, Ronnie, SD	6	1	5	0	0	36
Martin, Tony, SD	6	0	6	0	0	36
Jackson, Willie, Jax	5	0	5	0	1	32
Allen, Marcus, KC	5	5	0	0	0	30
Bono, Steve, KC	5	5	0	0	0	30
Davis, Willie, KC	5	0	5	0	0	30
Dawson, Lake, KC	5	0	5	0	0	30
Means, Natrone, SD	5	5	0	0	0	30
Mitchell, Johnny, NYJ	5	0	5	0	0	30
Scott, Darnay, Cin	5	0	5	0	0	30
Smith, Jimmy L., Jax	5	0	3	2	0	30
Thigpen, Yancey, Pitt	5	0	5	0	0	30
Vanover, Tamarick, KC	5	0	2	3	0	30
Turner, Floyd, Ind	4	0	4	0	2	28
Bailey, Aaron, Ind	4	0	3	1	0	24
Blades, Brian, Sea	4	0	4	0	0	24
Brunell, Mark, Jax	4	4	0	0	0	24
Butts, Marion, Hou	4	4	0	0	0	24
Byner, Earnest, Cle	4	2	2	0	0	24
Chrebet, Wayne, NYJ	4	0	4	0	0	24
Dilger, Ken, Ind	4	0	4	0	0	24
Holmes, Darick, Buff	4	4	0	0	0	24
McCardell, Keenan, Cle	4	0	4	0	0	24
McGee, Tony, Cin	4	0	4	0	0	24
Sharpe, Shannon, Den	4	0	4	0	0	24
Slaughter, Webster, KC	4	0	4	0	0	24
Strong, Mack, Sea	4	1	3	0	0	24
Wilson, Charles, NYJ	4	0	4	0	0	24
Green, Eric, Mia	3	0	3	0	1	20
Seay, Mark, SD	3	0	3	0	1	20
Anders, Kimble, KC	3	2	1	0	0	18
Armour, Justin, Buff	3	0	3	0	0	18
Bieniemy, Eric, Cin	3	3	0	0	0	18
Brisby, Vincent, NE	3	0	3	0	0	18
Bruener, Mark, Pitt	3	0	3	0	0	18
Byars, Keith, Mia	3	1	2	0	0	18
Coleman, Andre, SD	3	0	0	3	0	18
Culver, Rodney, SD	3	3	0	0	0	18
Dawkins, Sean, Ind	3	0	3	0	0	18
Fenner, Derrick, Oak	3	0	3	0	0	18
Givins, Ernest, Jax	3	0	3	0	0	18
Glover, Andrew, Oak	3	0	3	0	0	18
Green, Harold, Cin	3	2	1	0	0	18
Hayden, Aaron, SD	3	3	0	0	0	18
Hobbs, Daryl, Oak	3	0	3	0	0	18
Ismail, Raghib, Oak	3	0	3	0	0	18
Murrell, Adrian, NYJ	3	1	2	0	0	18
Pritchard, Mike, Den	3	0	3	0	0	18
Reed, Andre, Buff	3	0	3	0	0	18
Rison, Andre, Cle	3	0	3	0	0	18
Stewart, James, Jax	3	2	1	0	0	18
Tasker, Steve, Buff	3	0	3	0	0	18
Tillman, Cedric, Jax	3	0	3	0	0	18
Meggett, David, NE	2	2	0	0	2	16
Blake, Jeff, Cin	2	2	0	0	1	14
Chandler, Chris, Hou	2	2	0	0	1	14
McCaffrey, Ed, Den	2	0	2	0	1	14
Anderson, Flipper, Ind	2	0	2	0	0	12
Brady, Kyle, NYJ	2	0	2	0	0	12
Cash, Kerry, Oak	2	0	2	0	0	12
Clark, Gary, Mia	2	0	2	0	0	12
Dunbar, Vaughn, Jax	2	2	0	0	0	12
Gayle, Shaun, SD	2	0	0	2	0	12
Graham, Hason, NE	2	0	2	0	0	12
Harbaugh, Jim, Ind	2	2	0	0	0	12
Hastings, Andre, Pitt	2	0	1	1	0	12
Jefferson, Shawn, SD	2	0	2	0	0	12
Kaufman, Napoleon, Oak	2	1	0	1	0	12
Mitchell, Pete, Jax	2	0	2	0	0	12
Spikes, Irving, Mia	2	1	1	0	0	12
Stewart, Kordell, Pitt	2	1	1	0	0	12
Testaverde, Vinny, Cle	2	2	0	0	0	12
Wycheck, Frank, Hou	2	1	1	0	0	12
Yarborough, Ryan, NYJ	2	0	2	0	0	12
Bennett, Tony, Ind	1	0	0	1	0	*8
Elway, John, Den	1	1	0	0	1	8
Gardner, Carwell, Buff	1	0	0	1	1	8
Alexander, Derrick, Cle	1	0	0	1	0	6
Avery, Steve, Pitt	1	0	1	0	0	6
Baxter, Fred, NYJ	1	0	1	0	0	6
Baxter, Brad, NYJ	1	1	0	0	0	6
Bennett, Cornelius, Buff	1	0	0	1	0	6
Bernstine, Rod, Den	1	1	0	0	0	6
Bishop, Blaine, Hou	1	0	0	1	0	6
Booker, Vaughn, KC	1	0	0	1	0	6
Brock, Matt, NYJ	1	0	0	1	0	6
Broussard, Steve, Sea	1	1	0	0	0	6
Brown, Troy, NE	1	0	0	1	0	6
Bruce, Aundray, Oak	1	0	0	1	0	6
Buckner, Brentson, Pitt	1	0	0	1	0	6

	TD	TDR	TDP	TDM	2-PT	PTS
Caldwell, Mike, Cle	1	0	0	1	0	6
Cash, Keith, KC	1	0	1	0	0	6
Cecil, Chuck, Hou	1	0	0	1	0	6
Christopherson, Ryan, Jax	1	1	0	0	0	6
Collins, Mark, KC	1	0	0	1	0	6
Copeland, Russell, Buff	1	0	1	0	0	6
Crockett, Ray, Den	1	0	0	1	0	6
Crumpler, Carlester, Sea	1	0	1	0	0	6
Daniel, Eugene, Ind	1	0	0	1	0	6
Dixon, Gerald, Cle	1	0	0	1	0	6
Dunn, David, Cin	1	0	1	0	0	6
Edwards, Antonio, Sea	1	0	0	1	0	6
Evans, Jerry, Den	1	0	1	0	0	6
Fauria, Christian, Sea	1	0	1	0	0	6
Fletcher, Terrell, SD	1	1	0	0	0	6
Fredrickson, Rob, Oak	1	0	0	1	0	6
Gannon, Rich, KC	1	1	0	0	0	6
Gash, Sam, NE	1	0	1	0	0	6
Harris, Corey, Sea	1	0	0	1	0	6
Hartley, Frank, Cle	1	0	1	0	0	6
Hasty, James, KC	1	0	0	1	0	6
Hill, Greg, KC	1	1	0	0	0	6
Howard, Desmond, Jax	1	0	1	0	0	6
Hughes, Danan, KC	1	0	1	0	0	6
Humphries, Stan, SD	1	1	0	0	0	6
Jett, James, Oak	1	0	1	0	0	6
Johnson, Lonnie, Buff	1	0	1	0	0	6
Johnson, Pat, Mia	1	0	0	1	0	6
Johnson, Tracy, Sea	1	1	0	0	0	6
Jones, Gary, NYJ	1	0	0	1	0	6
Jones, Mike, Oak	1	0	0	1	0	6
Jones, Roger, Cin	1	0	0	1	0	6
Jordan, Randy, Jax	1	0	1	0	0	6
Kosar, Bernie, Mia	1	1	0	0	0	6
Lake, Carnell, Pitt	1	0	0	1	0	6
Lester, Tim, Pitt	1	1	0	0	0	6
Lewis, Darryll, Hou	1	0	0	1	0	6
Lewis, Mo, NYJ	1	0	0	1	0	6
Mays, Alvoid, Pitt	1	0	0	1	0	6
McAfee, Fred, Pitt	1	1	0	0	0	6
McDaniel, Terry, Oak	1	0	0	1	0	6
McNair, Todd, Hou	1	0	1	0	0	6
Mirer, Rick, Sea	1	1	0	0	0	6
Mitchell, Shannon, SD	1	0	1	0	0	6
Moore, Will, NE	1	0	1	0	0	6
Oldham, Chris, Pitt	1	0	0	1	0	6
Potts, Roosevelt, Ind	1	0	1	0	0	6
Reeves, Walter, Cle	1	0	1	0	0	6
Robbins, Austin, Oak	1	0	0	1	0	6
Robinson, Eddie, Hou	1	0	0	1	0	6
Schulz, Kurt, Buff	1	0	0	1	0	6
Seabron, Malcolm, Hou	1	0	1	0	0	6
Seau, Junior, SD	1	0	0	1	0	6
Slade, Chris, NE	1	0	0	1	0	6
Smith, Otis, NYJ	1	0	0	1	0	6
Smith, Rico, Cle	1	0	1	0	0	6
Smith, Rod, Den	1	0	1	0	0	6
Smith, Steve, Sea	1	0	1	0	0	6
Thomas, Robb, Sea	1	0	1	0	0	6
Tuten, Melvin, Cin	1	0	1	0	0	6
Valerio, Joe, KC	1	0	1	0	0	6
Vincent, Troy, Mia	1	0	0	1	0	6
Walker, Derrick, KC	1	0	1	0	0	6
Warren, Lamont, Ind	1	1	0	0	0	6
Washington, Brian, KC	1	0	0	1	0	6
Washington, Mickey, Jax	1	0	0	1	0	6
White, Lorenzo, Cle	1	1	0	0	0	6
Williams, John L., Pitt	1	0	1	0	0	6
Williams, Willie, Pitt	1	0	0	1	0	6
Adams, Sam, Sea	0	0	0	0	0	*2
Cook, Anthony, Hou	0	0	0	0	0	*2
Davis, Reuben, SD	0	0	0	0	0	*2
Howard, Erik, NYJ	0	0	0	0	0	*2
Williams, Darryl, Cin	0	0	0	0	0	*2
Zeier, Eric, Cle	0	0	0	0	1	2

** Safety*
Team safety credited to Cincinnati.

NFC SCORERS—INDIVIDUAL

Kickers

	XP	XPA	FG	FGA	PTS
Hanson, Jason, Det	48	48	28	34	132
Boniol, Chris, Dall	46	48	27	28	127
Andersen, Morten, Atl	29	30	31	37	122
Reveiz, Fuad, Minn	44	44	26	36	122
Butler, Kevin, Chi	45	45	23	31	114
Murray, Eddie, Wash	33	33	27	36	114
Davis, Greg, Ariz	19	19	30	39	109
Kasay, John, Car	27	28	26	33	105
Anderson, Gary, Phil	32	33	22	30	98
Jacke, Chris, GB	43	43	17	23	94
Brien, Doug, SF-NO	35	35	19	29	92
Daluiso, Brad, NYG	28	28	20	28	88
Husted, Michael, TB	25	25	19	26	82
Wilkins, Jeff, SF	27	29	12	13	63
McLaughlin, Steve, StL	17	17	8	16	41
Biasucci, Dean, StL	13	14	9	12	40
Lohmiller, Chip, NO	11	13	8	14	35
Hentrich, Craig, GB	5	5	3	5	14
Zendejas, Tony, Atl-SF	5	6	3	6	14

Nonkickers

	TD	TDR	TDP	TDM	2-PT	PTS
Smith, Emmitt, Dall	25	25	0	0	0	150
Rice, Jerry, SF	17	1	15	1	1	104
Carter, Cris, Minn	17	0	17	0	0	102
Moore, Herman, Det	14	0	14	0	0	84
Bruce, Isaac, StL	13	0	13	0	1	80
Loville, Derek, SF	13	10	3	0	1	80
Brooks, Robert, GB	13	0	13	0	0	78
Conway, Curtis, Chi	12	0	12	0	0	72
Sanders, Barry, Det	12	11	1	0	0	72
Watters, Ricky, Phil	12	11	1	0	0	72
Allen, Terry, Wash	11	10	1	0	0	66
Rhett, Errict, TB	11	11	0	0	0	66
Hampton, Rodney, NYG	10	10	0	0	1	62
Irvin, Michael, Dall	10	0	10	0	0	60
Mathis, Terance, Atl	9	0	9	0	3	60
Metcalf, Eric, Atl	10	1	8	1	0	60
Salaam, Rashaan, Chi	10	10	0	0	0	60
Perriman, Brett, Det	9	0	9	0	1	56
Reed, Jake, Minn	9	0	9	0	0	54
Early, Quinn, NO	8	0	8	0	0	48
Heyward, Craig, Atl	8	6	2	0	0	48
Morton, Johnnie, Det	8	0	8	0	0	48
Chmura, Mark, GB	7	0	7	0	1	44
Bates, Mario, NO	7	7	0	0	0	42
Bennett, Edgar, GB	7	3	4	0	0	42
Levens, Dorsey, GB	7	3	4	0	0	42
Garner, Charlie, Phil	6	6	0	0	0	36
Green, Willie, Car	6	0	6	0	0	36
Jennings, Keith, Chi	6	0	6	0	0	36
Small, Torrance, NO	6	1	5	0	0	36
Barnett, Fred, Phil	5	0	5	0	1	32
Moore, Rob, Ariz	5	0	5	0	1	32
Novacek, Jay, Dall	5	0	5	0	1	32
Smith, Robert, Minn	5	5	0	0	1	32
Ellard, Henry, Wash	5	0	5	0	0	30
Ellison, Jerry, TB	5	5	0	0	0	30
Emanuel, Bert, Atl	5	0	5	0	0	30
Walls, Wesley, NO	4	0	4	0	1	26
Brown, Dave, NYG	4	4	0	0	0	24
Centers, Larry, Ariz	4	2	2	0	0	24
Drayton, Troy, StL	4	0	4	0	0	24
Graham, Jeff, Chi	4	0	4	0	0	24
Haynes, Michael, NO	4	0	4	0	0	24
Kinchen, Todd, StL	4	0	4	0	0	24
Mitchell, Scott, Det	4	4	0	0	0	24
Moore, Derrick, Car	4	4	0	0	0	24
Morgan, Anthony, GB	4	0	4	0	0	24
Sherrard, Mike, NYG	4	0	4	0	0	24
Stokes, J.J., SF	4	0	4	0	0	24
Smith, Irv, NO	3	0	3	0	1	20
Bettis, Jerome, StL	3	3	0	0	0	18
Calloway, Chris, NYG	3	0	3	0	0	18
Carrier, Mark, Car	3	0	3	0	0	18
Collins, Kerry, Car	3	3	0	0	0	18
Favre, Brett, GB	3	3	0	0	0	18
Floyd, William, SF	3	2	1	0	0	18
Green, Robert, Chi	3	3	0	0	0	18
Hester, Jessie, StL	3	0	3	0	0	18
Ingram, Mark, GB	3	0	3	0	0	18

1995 INDIVIDUAL STATISTICS

	TD	TDR	TDP	TDM	2-PT	PTS
Ismail, Qadry, Minn	3	0	3	0	0	18
Johnston, Daryl, Dall	3	2	1	0	0	18
Jones, Brent, SF	3	0	3	0	0	18
Lee, Amp, Minn	3	2	1	0	0	18
Logan, Marc, Wash	3	1	2	0	0	18
Metzelaars, Pete, Car	3	0	3	0	0	18
Mitchell, Brian, Wash	3	1	1	1	0	18
Shepherd, Leslie, Wash	3	1	2	0	0	18
Timpson, Michael, Chi	3	1	2	0	0	18
Wheatley, Tyrone, NYG	3	3	0	0	0	18
Williams, Aeneas, Ariz	3	0	0	3	0	18
Young, Steve, SF	3	3	0	0	0	18
Sanders, Frank, Ariz	2	0	2	0	2	16
Bailey, Johnny, StL	2	2	0	0	1	14
Williams, Calvin, Phil	2	0	2	0	1	14
Brown, Derek, NO	2	1	1	0	0	12
Brown, Larry, Dall	2	0	0	2	0	12
Copeland, Horace, TB	2	0	2	0	0	12
Dilfer, Trent, TB	2	2	0	0	0	12
Dorn, Torin, StL	2	0	0	2	0	12
Edwards, Anthony, Ariz	2	0	2	0	0	12
Evans, Chuck, Minn	2	1	1	0	0	12
Flanigan, Jim, Chi	2	0	2	0	0	12
Gaines, Wendall, Ariz	2	0	2	0	0	12
Galbraith, Scott, Wash	2	0	2	0	0	12
Graham, Scottie, Minn	2	2	0	0	0	12
Grbac, Elvis, SF	2	2	0	0	0	12
Griffith, Howard, Car	2	1	1	0	0	12
Guliford, Eric, Car	2	0	1	1	0	12
Harper, Alvin, TB	2	0	2	0	0	12
Hearst, Garrison, Ariz	2	1	1	0	0	12
Johnson, Reggie, Phil	2	0	2	0	0	12
Jordan, Andrew, Minn	2	0	2	0	0	12
Jordan, Charles, GB	2	0	2	0	0	12
Lewis, Thomas, NYG	2	0	1	1	0	12
McBride, Oscar, Ariz	2	0	2	0	0	12
McDonald, Tim, SF	2	0	0	2	0	12
Norton, Ken, SF	2	0	0	2	0	12
Taylor, John, SF	2	0	2	0	0	12
Thomas, Orlando, Minn	2	0	0	2	0	12
Westbrook, Michael, Wash	2	1	1	0	0	12
Wetnight, Ryan, Chi	2	0	2	0	0	12
Williams, Kevin, Dall	2	0	2	0	0	12
Wright, Alexander, StL	2	0	2	0	0	12
Zellars, Ray, NO	2	2	0	0	0	12
Anderson, Steve, Ariz	1	0	1	0	2	10
Christian, Bob, Car	1	0	1	0	1	8
Aikman, Troy, Dall	1	1	0	0	0	6
Anderson, Jamal, Atl	1	1	0	0	0	6
Armstead, Jessie, NYG	1	0	0	1	0	6
Beebe, Don, Car	1	0	1	0	0	6
Bell, Coleman, Wash	1	0	1	0	0	6
Birden, J. J., Atl	1	0	1	0	0	6
Carter, Dexter, SF	1	0	0	1	0	6
Carter, Tom, Wash	1	0	0	1	0	6
Carter, Tony, Chi	1	0	1	0	0	6
Cook, Marv, StL	1	0	1	0	0	6
Davis, Eric, SF	1	0	0	1	0	6
Douglas, Omar, NYG	1	0	0	1	0	6
Freeman, Antonio, GB	1	0	1	0	0	6
Frerotte, Gus, Wash	1	1	0	0	0	6
Fuller, Corey, Minn	1	0	0	1	0	6
Glenn, Vencie, NYG	1	0	0	1	0	6
Green, Darrell, Wash	1	0	0	1	0	6
Hanks, Merton, SF	1	0	0	1	0	6
Harris, Jackie, TB	1	0	1	0	0	6
Henderson, Jerome, Phil	1	0	0	1	0	6
Jackson, Alfred M., Minn	1	0	0	1	0	6
Jackson, Greg, Phil	1	0	0	1	0	6
Jackson, Keith, GB	1	0	1	0	0	6
Johnson, Anthony, Car	1	1	0	0	0	6
Johnson, Kevin, Phil	1	0	0	1	0	6
Jones, Sean, GB	1	0	0	1	0	6
Kragen, Greg, Car	1	0	0	1	0	6
Kramer, Erik, Chi	1	1	0	0	0	6
Lumpkin, Sean, NO	1	0	0	1	0	6
Lyght, Todd, StL	1	0	0	1	0	6
Lynch, Lorenzo, Ariz	1	0	0	1	0	6
Marion, Brock, Dall	1	0	0	1	0	6
Marshall, Anthony, Chi	1	0	0	1	0	6
Marshall, Arthur, NYG	1	0	1	0	0	6
Mayhew, Martin, TB	1	0	0	1	0	6
McCants, Keith, Ariz	1	0	0	1	0	6
McCrary, Fred, Phil	1	1	0	0	0	6
McKyer, Tim, Car	1	0	0	1	0	6
Mills, Sam, Car	1	0	0	1	0	6
Minter, Barry, Chi	1	0	0	1	0	6
Montgomery, Alton, Atl	1	0	0	1	0	6
Neal, Lorenzo, NO	1	0	1	0	0	6
Palmer, David, Minn	1	0	0	1	0	6
Parker, Anthony, StL	1	0	0	1	0	6
Peete, Rodney, Phil	1	1	0	0	0	6
Preston, Roell, Atl	1	0	1	0	0	6
Rivers, Ron, Det	1	1	0	0	0	6
Ross, Kevin, Atl	1	0	0	1	0	6
Sapp, Warren, TB	1	0	0	1	0	6
Scroggins, Tracy, Det	1	0	0	1	0	6
Simmons, Clyde, Ariz	1	0	0	1	0	6
Singleton, Nate, SF	1	0	1	0	0	6
Sloan, David, Det	1	0	1	0	0	6
Thomas, William, Phil	1	0	0	1	0	6
Truitt, Olanda, Wash	1	0	1	0	0	6
Tuggle, Jessie, Atl	1	0	0	1	0	6
Walker, Adam, SF	1	1	0	0	0	6
Walker, Herschel, NYG	1	0	1	0	0	6
Way, Charles, NYG	1	0	1	0	0	6
Weldon, Casey, TB	1	1	0	0	0	6
West, Ed, Phil	1	0	1	0	0	6
Williams, Sherman, Dall	1	1	0	0	0	6
Witherspoon, Derrick, Phil	1	0	0	1	0	6
Woodall, Lee, SF	1	0	0	1	0	6
Woods, Tony, Wash	1	0	0	1	0	6
Woodson, Darren, Dall	1	0	0	1	0	6
Wooten, Tito, NYG	1	0	0	1	0	6
Workman, Vince, Car	1	1	0	0	0	6
Wright, Toby, StL	1	0	0	1	0	6
Zordich, Mike, Phil	1	0	0	1	0	6
Blades, Bennie, Det	0	0	0	0	0	*2
Brownlow, Darrick, Wash	0	0	0	0	0	*2
Carter, Kevin, StL	0	0	0	0	0	*2
Fontenot, Albert, Chi	0	0	0	0	0	*2
Rasby, Walter, Car	0	0	0	0	1	2
Strahan, Michael, NYG	0	0	0	0	0	*2

** Safety*

FIELD GOALS

Field Goal Percentage

NFC: .964—Chris Boniol, Dallas
AFC: .879—Matt Stover, Cleveland

Field Goals

AFC: 34—Norm Johnson, Pittsburgh
NFC: 31—Morten Andersen, Atlanta

Field Goal Attempts

AFC: 41—Norm Johnson, Pittsburgh
NFC: 39—Greg Davis, Arizona

Longest Field Goal

NFC: 59—Morten Andersen, Atlanta vs. San Francisco, December 24
AFC: 56—Jason Elam, Denver at Houston, November 26

Average Yards Made

NFC: 37.8—Chris Jacke, Green Bay
AFC: 37.6—Al Del Greco, Houston

AFC FIELD GOALS—TEAM

	FG	FGA	Pct.	Long
Cleveland	29	33	.879	47
Houston	27	31	.871	53
Pittsburgh	34	41	.829	50
Seattle	23	28	.821	49
Denver	31	38	.816	56
N.Y. Jets	17	21	.810	50
San Diego	21	26	.808	45
Cincinnati	29	36	.806	51
Kansas City	24	30	.800	49
Miami	27	34	.794	51
Oakland	21	27	.778	46
Buffalo	31	40	.775	51
Jacksonville	20	27	.741	53
Indianapolis	23	33	.697	52
New England	23	33	.697	55
AFC Total	380	478	—	56
AFC Average	25.3	31.9	.795	—

NFC FIELD GOALS—TEAM

	FG	FGA	Pct.	Long
Dallas	27	28	.964	45
Atlanta	33	40	.825	59
Detroit	28	34	.824	56
Carolina	26	33	.788	52
Arizona	30	39	.769	55
Washington	27	36	.750	52
Chicago	23	31	.742	47
Philadelphia	22	30	.733	43
Tampa Bay	19	26	.731	53
Minnesota	26	36	.722	51
Green Bay	20	28	.714	51
N.Y. Giants	20	28	.714	51
San Francisco	20	28	.714	51
New Orleans	20	31	.645	51
St. Louis	17	28	.607	51
NFC Total	358	476	—	59
NFC Average	23.9	31.7	.752	—
League Total	738	954	—	59
League Average	24.6	31.8	.774	—

AFC FIELD GOALS—INDIVIDUAL

	1-19 Yards	20-29 Yards	30-39 Yards	40-49 Yards	50 or Longer	Totals	Avg. Yds. Att.	Avg. Yds. Made	Avg. Yds. Miss	Long
Stover, Matt, Cle	1-1	12-12	9-10	7-9	0-1	29-33	33.7	32.5	42.5	47
	1.000	1.000	.900	.778	.000	.879				
Del Greco, Al, Hou	3-3	3-3	8-8	10-12	3-5	27-31	38.8	37.6	47.3	53
	1.000	1.000	1.000	.833	.600	.871				
Johnson, Norm, Pitt	1-1	10-10	14-16	8-13	1-1	34-41	35.0	33.2	43.3	50
	1.000	1.000	.875	.615	1.000	.829				
Peterson, Todd, Sea	1-1	5-5	9-10	8-10	0-2	23-28	37.9	36.0	46.6	49
	1.000	1.000	.900	.800	.000	.821				
Elam, Jason, Den	0-0	7-9	14-15	5-7	5-7	31-38	37.9	36.7	43.0	56
	—	.778	.933	.714	.714	.816				
Lowery, Nick, NYJ	0-0	4-4	8-10	3-3	2-4	17-21	36.9	35.8	41.8	50
	—	1.000	.800	1.000	.500	.810				
Carney, John, SD	0-0	8-8	10-11	3-5	0-2	21-26	35.3	32.9	45.6	45
	—	1.000	.909	.600	.000	.808				
Pelfrey, Doug, Cin	0-0	8-9	10-11	10-14	1-2	29-36	37.9	36.4	43.9	51
	—	.889	.909	.714	.500	.806				
Elliott, Lin, KC	0-0	10-11	7-9	7-10	0-0	24-30	34.9	34.1	38.0	49
	—	.909	.778	.700	—	.800				
Stoyanovich, Pete, Mia	1-1	7-10	11-11	6-7	2-5	27-34	35.9	34.6	40.9	51
	1.000	.700	1.000	.857	.400	.794				
Blanchard, Cary, Ind	0-0	5-5	6-8	7-10	1-1	19-24	37.1	36.2	40.8	50
	—	1.000	.750	.700	1.000	.792				
Christie, Steve, Buff	0-0	13-14	13-15	3-6	2-5	31-40	34.5	32.4	41.7	51
	—	.929	.867	.500	.400	.775				
Hollis, Mike, Jax	0-0	7-9	7-8	4-7	2-3	20-27	36.2	35.0	39.9	53
	—	.778	.875	.571	.667	.741				
Jaeger, Jeff, Oak	0-0	4-5	6-7	3-5	0-1	13-18	36.1	34.2	41.2	46
	—	.800	.857	.600	.000	.722				
Bahr, Matt, NE	1-2	12-12	3-7	5-7	2-5	23-33	34.7	32.7	39.3	55
	.500	1.000	.429	.714	.400	.697				
Nonqualifiers										
Cofer, Mike, Ind	0-0	2-2	0-4	1-2	1-1	4-9	37.0	34.8	38.8	52
	—	1.000	.000	.500	1.000	.444				
Ford, Cole, Oak	1-1	3-3	3-3	1-1	0-1	8-9	33.7	31.3	53.0	46
	1.000	1.000	1.000	1.000	.000	.889				
AFC Totals	9-10	120-131	138-163	91-128	22-46	380-478	36.1	34.6	42.0	56
	.900	.916	.847	.711	.478	.795				
League Totals	18-19	243-265	262-318	169-261	46-91	738-954	36.0	34.3	42.0	59
	.947	.917	.824	.648	.505	.774				

Leader based on percentage, minimum 16 field goal attempts

1995 INDIVIDUAL STATISTICS

NFC FIELD GOALS—INDIVIDUAL

	1-19 Yards	20-29 Yards	30-39 Yards	40-49 Yards	50 or Longer	Totals	Avg. Yds. Att.	Avg. Yds. Made	Avg. Yds. Miss	Long
Boniol, Chris, Dall	0-0	11-12	13-13	3-3	0-0	27-28	31.0	31.4	20.0	45
	—	.917	1.000	1.000	—	.964				
Andersen, Morten, Atl	1-1	8-8	11-11	3-8	8-9	31-37	38.2	36.7	46.2	59
	1.000	1.000	1.000	.375	.889	.838				
Hanson, Jason, Det	2-2	4-4	16-17	5-10	1-1	28-34	35.8	34.6	41.3	56
	1.000	1.000	.941	.500	1.000	.824				
Kasay, John, Car	0-0	6-6	10-14	9-12	1-1	26-33	37.1	36.3	40.0	52
	—	1.000	.714	.750	1.000	.788				
Davis, Greg, Ariz	1-1	13-14	9-10	6-8	1-6	30-39	35.8	32.5	46.9	55
	1.000	.929	.900	.750	.167	.769				
Murray, Eddie, Wash	1-1	9-9	10-13	6-11	1-2	27-36	36.4	34.5	42.0	52
	1.000	1.000	.769	.545	.500	.750				
Butler, Kevin, Chi	0-0	16-19	5-6	2-4	0-2	23-31	30.9	28.4	38.0	47
	—	.842	.833	.500	.000	.742				
Jacke, Chris, GB	0-0	6-7	0-2	8-10	3-4	17-23	38.3	37.8	39.8	51
	—	.857	.000	.800	.750	.739				
Anderson, Gary, Phil	0-0	5-5	9-10	8-12	0-3	22-30	38.1	35.2	46.0	43
	—	1.000	.900	.667	.000	.733				
Husted, Michael, TB	1-1	5-6	5-7	5-9	3-3	19-26	37.9	37.0	40.4	53
	1.000	.833	.714	.556	1.000	.731				
Reveiz, Fuad, Minn	1-1	8-9	7-10	9-12	1-4	26-36	36.9	34.7	42.5	51
	1.000	.889	.700	.750	.250	.722				
Daluiso, Brad, NYG	0-0	7-7	9-10	2-9	2-2	20-28	35.4	32.2	43.4	51
	—	1.000	.900	.222	1.000	.714				
Brien, Doug, SF-NO	0-0	8-8	4-7	6-12	1-2	19-29	36.9	34.4	41.7	51
	—	1.000	.571	.500	.500	.655				
McLaughlin, Steve, StL	1-1	4-5	2-6	1-3	0-1	8-16	34.7	29.6	39.8	45
	1.000	.800	.333	.333	.000	.500				
Nonqualifiers										
Lohmiller, Chip, NO	0-0	4-6	3-4	0-2	1-2	8-14	34.0	30.3	39.0	51
	—	.667	.750	.000	.500	.571				
Wilkins, Jeff, SF	1-1	5-5	5-5	1-2	0-0	12-13	29.3	27.9	46.0	40
	1.000	1.000	1.000	.500	—	.923				
Biasucci, Dean, StL	0-0	4-4	3-4	1-1	1-3	9-12	36.9	33.9	46.0	51
	—	1.000	.750	1.000	.333	.750				
Zendejas, Tony, Atl-SF	0-0	0-0	1-3	2-3	0-0	3-6	40.0	41.0	39.0	45
	—	—	.333	.667	—	.500				
Hentrich, Craig, GB	0-0	0-0	2-3	1-2	0-0	3-5	40.8	39.7	42.5	49
	—	—	.667	.500	—	.600				
NFC Totals	9-9	123-134	124-155	78-133	24-45	358-476	35.9	33.9	41.9	59
	1.000	.918	.800	.586	.533	.752				
League Totals	18-19	243-265	262-318	169-261	46-91	738-954	36.0	34.3	42.0	59
	.947	.917	.824	.648	.505	.774				

Leader based on percentage, minimum 16 field goal attempts

RUSHING

Yards
- **NFC:** 1773—Emmitt Smith, Dallas
- **AFC:** 1487—Curtis Martin, New England

Yards, Game
- **NFC:** 187—Rodney Hampton, N.Y. Giants at Dallas, December 17, (34 attempts, 0 TD)
- **AFC:** 177—Marshall Faulk, Indianapolis vs. St. Louis, October 1, (19 attempts, 3 TD)

Longest
- **AFC:** 86—Joey Galloway, Seattle at Jacksonville, November 12 - TD
- **NFC:** 75—Barry Sanders, Detroit vs. Cleveland, October 8 - TD
  Jerry Ellison, Tampa Bay vs. Detroit, December 23

Attempts
- **NFC:** 377—Emmitt Smith, Dallas
- **AFC:** 368—Curtis Martin, New England

Attempts, Game
- **AFC:** 36—Curtis Martin, New England vs. Buffalo, October 23 (127 yards - TD)
- **NFC:** 34—Rodney Hampton, N.Y. Giants at Dallas, December 17 (187 yards)

Yards Per Attempt
- **NFC:** 5.4—Charlie Garner, Philadelphia
- **AFC:** 4.7—Terrell Davis, Denver

Touchdowns
- **NFC:** 25—Emmitt Smith, Dallas
- **AFC:** 15—Chris Warren, Seattle

Team Leaders, Yards
- **AFC:** BUFFALO: 1005, Thurman Thomas; CINCINNATI: 661, Harold Green; CLEVELAND: 547, Leroy Hoard; DENVER: 1117, Terrell Davis; HOUSTON: 947, Rodney Thomas; INDIANAPOLIS: 1078, Marshall Faulk; JACKSONVILLE: 525, James Stewart; KANSAS CITY: 890, Marcus Allen; MIAMI: 878, Bernie Parmalee; NEW ENGLAND: 1487, Curtis Martin; N.Y. JETS: 795, Adrian Murrell; OAKLAND: 1114, Harvey Williams; PITTSBURGH: 813, Erric Pegram; SAN DIEGO: 730, Natrone Means; SEATTLE: 1346, Chris Warren
- **NFC:** ARIZONA: 1070, Garrison Hearst; ATLANTA: 1083, Craig Heyward; CAROLINA: 740, Derrick Moore; CHICAGO: 1074, Rashaan Salaam; DALLAS: 1773, Emmitt Smith; DETROIT: 1500, Barry Sanders; GREEN BAY: 1067, Edgar Bennett; MINNESOTA: 632, Robert Smith; NEW ORLEANS: 951, Mario Bates; N.Y. GIANTS: 1182, Rodney Hampton; PHILADELPHIA: 1273, Ricky Watters; ST. LOUIS: 637, Jerome Bettis; SAN FRANCISCO: 723, Derek Loville; TAMPA BAY: 1207, Errict Rhett; WASHINGTON: 1309, Terry Allen

Team Champion
- **AFC:** 2222—Kansas City
- **NFC:** 2201—Dallas

AFC RUSHING—TEAM

	Att.	Yards	Avg.	Long	TD
Kansas City	507	2222	4.4	76t	14
Seattle	477	2178	4.6	86t	20
Denver	440	1995	4.5	60t	14
Buffalo	521	1993	3.8	49	10
Oakland	463	1932	4.2	60	10
New England	474	1866	3.9	49	16
Indianapolis	478	1855	3.9	42	14
Pittsburgh	494	1852	3.7	38	17
San Diego	479	1747	3.6	48t	14

	Att.	Yards	Avg.	Long	TD
Jacksonville	410	1705	4.2	27t	9
Houston	478	1664	3.5	74t	12
Miami	413	1506	3.6	40	16
Cleveland	398	1482	3.7	29	5
Cincinnati	364	1439	4.0	30	7
N.Y. Jets	365	1279	3.5	30	2
AFC Total	6761	26715	4.0	86t	180
AFC Average	450.7	1781.0	4.0	—	12.0

NFC RUSHING—TEAM

	Att.	Yards	Avg.	Long	TD
Dallas	495	2201	4.4	60t	29
Philadelphia	508	2121	4.2	57	19
Washington	469	1956	4.2	58t	15
Chicago	492	1930	3.9	42	15
N.Y. Giants	478	1833	3.8	36	17
Detroit	387	1753	4.5	75t	16
Minnesota	433	1733	4.0	66t	10
Tampa Bay	398	1587	4.0	75	19
Carolina	454	1573	3.5	53t	10
San Francisco	415	1479	3.6	29	19
St. Louis	392	1431	3.7	41	5
Green Bay	410	1428	3.5	40	9
Atlanta	337	1393	4.1	31	8
New Orleans	383	1390	3.6	66t	11
Arizona	387	1363	3.5	38	3
NFC Total	6438	25171	3.9	75t	205
NFC Average	429.2	1678.1	3.9	—	13.7
League Total	13199	51886	—	86t	385
League Average	440.0	1729.5	3.9	—	12.8

NFL TOP TEN RUSHERS

	Att.	Yards	Avg.	Long	TD
Smith, Emmitt, Dall	377	1773	4.7	60t	25
Sanders, Barry, Det	314	1500	4.8	75t	11
Martin, Curtis, NE	368	1487	4.0	49	14
Warren, Chris, Sea	310	1346	4.3	52	15
Allen, Terry, Wash	338	1309	3.9	28	10
Watters, Ricky, Phil	337	1273	3.8	57	11
Rhett, Errict, TB	332	1207	3.6	21	11
Hampton, Rodney, NYG	306	1182	3.9	32	10
Davis, Terrell, Den	237	1117	4.7	60t	7
Williams, Harvey, Oak	255	1114	4.4	60	9

AFC RUSHERS—INDIVIDUAL

	Att.	Yards	Avg.	Long	TD
Martin, Curtis, NE	368	1487	4.0	49	14
Warren, Chris, Sea	310	1346	4.3	52	15
Davis, Terrell, Den	237	1117	4.7	60t	7
Williams, Harvey, Oak	255	1114	4.4	60	9
Faulk, Marshall, Ind	289	1078	3.7	40	11
Thomas, Thurman, Buff	267	1005	3.8	49	6
Thomas, Rodney, Hou	251	947	3.8	74t	5
Allen, Marcus, KC	207	890	4.3	38	5
Parmalee, Bernie, Mia	236	878	3.7	40	9
Pegram, Erric, Pitt	213	813	3.8	38	5
Murrell, Adrian, NYJ	192	795	4.1	30	1
Means, Natrone, SD	186	730	3.9	36	5
Holmes, Darick, Buff	172	698	4.1	38t	4
Hill, Greg, KC	155	667	4.3	27	1
Green, Harold, Cin	171	661	3.9	23t	2
Morris, Byron (Bam), Pitt	148	559	3.8	30t	9
Hoard, Leroy, Cle	136	547	4.0	25	0
Stewart, James, Jax	137	525	3.8	22	2
Kaufman, Napoleon, Oak	108	490	4.5	28	1
Brunell, Mark, Jax	67	480	7.2	27t	4
Hayden, Aaron, SD	128	470	3.7	20	3
Byner, Earnest, Cle	115	432	3.8	23	2
Kirby, Terry, Mia	108	414	3.8	38	4
Anders, Kimble, KC	58	398	6.9	44	2
Bieniemy, Eric, Cin	98	381	3.9	27	3
Dunbar, Vaughn, Jax	110	361	3.3	26	2
Craver, Aaron, Den	73	333	4.6	23	5
Blake, Jeff, Cin	53	309	5.8	30	2
Potts, Roosevelt, Ind	65	309	4.8	37	0
Baxter, Brad, NYJ	85	296	3.5	26	1
Brown, Gary, Hou	86	293	3.4	21	0
Milburn, Glyn, Den	49	266	5.4	29	0
Meggett, David, NE	60	250	4.2	25	2
Harbaugh, Jim, Ind	52	235	4.5	21	2
Broussard, Steve, Sea	46	222	4.8	21t	1
Smith, Lamar, Sea	36	215	6.0	68	0
Mirer, Rick, Sea	43	193	4.5	24	1
Harmon, Ronnie, SD	51	187	3.7	48t	1
Maston, Le'Shai, Jax	41	186	4.5	21	0
Butts, Marion, Hou	71	185	2.6	9	4
Elway, John, Den	41	176	4.3	25	1
Workman, Vince, Car-Ind	44	165	3.8	14	1
White, Lorenzo, Cle	62	163	2.6	11	1
McAfee, Fred, Pitt	39	156	4.0	22t	1
Culver, Rodney, SD	47	155	3.3	17	3
Galloway, Joey, Sea	11	154	14.0	86t	1
Warren, Lamont, Ind	47	152	3.2	42	1
Fletcher, Terrell, SD	26	140	5.4	46	1
McNair, Todd, Hou	19	136	7.2	22	0
Spikes, Irving, Mia	32	126	3.9	17t	1
Moore, Ronald, NYJ	43	121	2.8	14	0
Hostetler, Jeff, Oak	31	119	3.8	18	0
Bono, Steve, KC	28	113	4.0	76t	5
Fenner, Derrick, Oak	39	110	2.8	10	0
Williams, John L., Pitt	29	110	3.8	31	0
Hunter, Ernest, Cle	30	100	3.3	15	0
Stewart, Kordell, Pitt	15	86	5.7	22t	1
Zeier, Eric, Cle	15	80	5.3	17	0
Gardner, Carwell, Buff	20	77	3.9	17	0
Bernstine, Rod, Den	23	76	3.3	18	1
Tasker, Steve, Buff	8	74	9.3	17	0
Thompson, Leroy, KC	28	73	2.6	10	0
Cothran, Jeff, Cin	16	62	3.9	15	0
Jordan, Randy, Jax	21	62	3.0	10	0
Testaverde, Vinny, Cle	18	62	3.4	14	2
Chandler, Chris, Hou	28	58	2.1	9	2
Croom, Corey, NE	13	54	4.2	12	0
Humphries, Stan, SD	33	53	1.6	18	1
Powers, Ricky, Cle	14	51	3.6	15	0
Reed, Andre, Buff	7	48	6.9	14	0
O'Donnell, Neil, Pitt	24	45	1.9	14	0
Byars, Keith, Mia	15	44	2.9	15	1
Joseph, James, Cin	16	40	2.5	8	0
Mills, Ernie, Pitt	5	39	7.8	20	0
McNair, Steve, Hou	11	38	3.5	13	0
Evans, Vince, Oak	14	36	2.6	11	0
Bailey, Aaron, Ind	1	34	34.0	34	0
Beuerlein, Steve, Jax	5	32	6.4	13	0
Jourdain, Yonel, Buff	8	31	3.9	19	0
Vanover, Tamarick, KC	6	31	5.2	13	0
Alexander, Derrick, Cle	1	29	29.0	29	0
Ismail, Raghib, Oak	6	29	4.8	13	0
Bledsoe, Drew, NE	20	28	1.4	15	0
Gannon, Rich, KC	8	25	3.1	12t	1
Tomczak, Mike, Pitt	11	25	2.3	11	0
Gash, Sam, NE	8	24	3.0	9	0
Collins, Todd, Buff	9	23	2.6	10	0
Strong, Mack, Sea	8	23	2.9	9	1
Furrer, Will, Hou	8	20	2.5	11	0
Kelly, Jim, Buff	17	20	1.2	17	0
Jones, Calvin, Oak	5	19	3.8	15	0
Kosar, Bernie, Mia	7	19	2.7	14	1
Smith, Steve, Sea	9	19	2.1	4	0
Zolak, Scott, NE	4	19	4.8	12	0
Brister, Bubby, NYJ	16	18	1.1	7	0
Cobb, Reggie, Jax	9	18	2.0	5	0
Richardson, Tony, KC	8	18	2.3	5	0
Anderson, Richie, NYJ	5	17	3.4	10	0
Johnson, Rob, Jax	3	17	5.7	7	0
Pritchard, Mike, Den	6	17	2.8	9	0
Christopherson, Ryan, Jax	16	16	1.0	10	1
Tindale, Tim, Buff	5	16	3.2	6	0
Erickson, Craig, Ind	9	14	1.6	15	0
Esiason, Boomer, NYJ	19	14	0.7	19	0
Hastings, Andre, Pitt	1	14	14.0	14	0
Marino, Dan, Mia	11	14	1.3	12	0
Bennett, Donnell, KC	7	11	1.6	11	0
Gilbert, Gale, SD	6	11	1.8	8	0
Scott, Darnay, Cin	5	11	2.2	9	0
Ball, Eric, Oak	2	10	5.0	10	0
Foley, Glenn, NYJ	1	9	9.0	9	0
Lester, Tim, Pitt	5	9	1.8	3	1
Tupa, Tom, Cle	1	9	9.0	9	0

1995 INDIVIDUAL STATISTICS

	Att.	Yards	Avg.	Long	TD
Vardell, Tommy, Cle	4	9	2.3	6	0
Howard, Desmond, Jax	1	8	8.0	8	0
Millen, Hugh, Den	3	8	2.7	7	0
Brooks, Bill, Buff	3	7	2.3	9	0
Humphrey, Ronald, Ind	2	6	3.0	5	0
McDuffie, O. J., Mia	3	6	2.0	11	0
Pickens, Carl, Cin	1	6	6.0	6	0
Hannah, Travis, Hou	1	5	5.0	5	0
Hobert, Billy Joe, Oak	3	5	1.7	6	0
Hughes, Danan, KC	1	5	5.0	5	0
May, Sheriden, NYJ	2	5	2.5	3	0
Miller, Anthony, Den	1	5	5.0	5	0
Wilson, Robert, Mia	1	5	5.0	5	0
Blades, Brian, Sea	2	4	2.0	4	0
Lee, Kevin, NE	1	4	4.0	4	0
Avery, Steve, Pitt	1	3	3.0	3	0
Rasheed, Kenyon, NYJ	1	3	3.0	3	0
Johnson, Tracy, Sea	1	2	2.0	2t	1
Miller, Jim, Pitt	1	2	2.0	2	0
Rivers, Reggie, Den	2	2	1.0	1	0
Burns, Jason, Cin	1	1	1.0	1	0
Chrebet, Wayne, NYJ	1	1	1.0	1	0
Jefferson, Shawn, SD	2	1	0.5	11	0
Justin, Paul, Ind	3	1	0.3	2	0
Thigpen, Yancey, Pitt	1	1	1.0	1	0
Wycheck, Frank, Hou	1	1	1.0	1t	1
Crockett, Zack, Ind	1	0	0.0	0	0
Friesz, John, Sea	11	0	0.0	2	0
Rison, Andre, Cle	2	0	0.0	5	0
Copeland, Russell, Buff	1	-1	-1.0	-1	0
McCaffrey, Ed, Den	1	-1	-1.0	-1	0
Hill, Jeff, Cin	1	-3	-3.0	-3	0
Musgrave, Bill, Den	4	-4	-1.0	0	0
Armour, Justin, Buff	4	-5	-1.2	6	0
Dawson, Lake, KC	1	-9	-9.0	-9	0
Johnson, Charles, Pitt	1	-10	-10.0	-10	0
Dunn, David, Cin	1	-13	-13.0	-13	0
Johnson, Lee, Cin	1	-16	-16.0	-16	0
Sanders, Chris, Hou	2	-19	-9.5	-6	0

t = Touchdown
Leader based on most yards gained

NFC RUSHERS—INDIVIDUAL

	Att.	Yards	Avg.	Long	TD
Smith, Emmitt, Dall	377	1773	4.7	60t	25
Sanders, Barry, Det	314	1500	4.8	75t	11
Allen, Terry, Wash	338	1309	3.9	28	10
Watters, Ricky, Phil	337	1273	3.8	57	11
Rhett, Errict, TB	332	1207	3.6	21	11
Hampton, Rodney, NYG	306	1182	3.9	32	10
Heyward, Craig, Atl	236	1083	4.6	31	6
Salaam, Rashaan, Chi	296	1074	3.6	42	10
Hearst, Garrison, Ariz	284	1070	3.8	38	1
Bennett, Edgar, GB	316	1067	3.4	23	3
Bates, Mario, NO	244	951	3.9	66t	7
Moore, Derrick, Car	195	740	3.8	53t	4
Loville, Derek, SF	218	723	3.3	27	10
Bettis, Jerome, StL	183	637	3.5	41	3
Smith, Robert, Minn	139	632	4.5	58t	5
Garner, Charlie, Phil	108	588	5.4	55t	6
Green, Robert, Chi	107	570	5.3	38	3
Graham, Scottie, Minn	110	406	3.7	26	2
Lee, Amp, Minn	69	371	5.4	66t	2
Mitchell, Brian, Wash	46	301	6.5	36t	1
Centers, Larry, Ariz	78	254	3.3	20	2
Young, Steve, SF	50	250	5.0	29	3
Wheatley, Tyrone, NYG	78	245	3.1	19t	3
Floyd, William, SF	64	237	3.7	23	2
Brown, Dave, NYG	45	228	5.1	23	4
Ellison, Jerry, TB	26	218	8.4	75	5
Williams, Sherman, Dall	48	205	4.3	44t	1
Russell, Leonard, StL	66	203	3.1	18	0
Griffith, Howard, Car	65	197	3.0	15	1
Bailey, Johnny, StL	36	182	5.1	17	2
Favre, Brett, GB	39	181	4.6	40	3
Robinson, Greg, StL	40	165	4.1	37	0
Zellars, Ray, NO	50	162	3.2	11	2
Anderson, Jamal, Atl	39	161	4.1	13	1
Brown, Derek, NO	49	159	3.2	35t	1
Christian, Bob, Car	41	158	3.9	17	0
Peete, Rodney, Phil	32	147	4.6	18	1
Stewart, James, Minn	31	144	4.6	51	0
Johnson, Anthony, Chi-Car	30	140	4.7	23t	1
Metcalf, Eric, Atl	28	133	4.8	23t	1
Walker, Herschel, NYG	31	126	4.1	36	0
Levens, Dorsey, GB	36	120	3.3	22	3
Dilfer, Trent, TB	23	115	5.0	21t	2
Westbrook, Michael, Wash	6	114	19.0	58t	1
Johnston, Daryl, Dall	25	111	4.4	18	2
Mitchell, Scott, Det	36	104	2.9	18	4
Cunningham, Randall, Phil	21	98	4.7	20	0
Moss, Brent, StL	22	90	4.1	18	0
Thomas, Blair, Car	22	90	4.1	13	0
Ervins, Ricky, SF	23	88	3.8	13	0
Moon, Warren, Minn	33	82	2.5	16	0
Tillman, Lewis, Chi	29	78	2.7	9	0
Conway, Curtis, Chi	5	77	15.4	20	0
Small, Torrance, NO	6	75	12.5	44t	1
Collins, Kerry, Car	42	74	1.8	10	3
Rivers, Ron, Det	18	73	4.1	19	1
Logan, Marc, Wash	23	72	3.1	13	1
Miller, Chris, StL	22	67	3.0	13	0
Shepherd, Leslie, Wash	7	63	9.0	26	1
Baldwin, Randy, Car	23	61	2.7	9	0
Evans, Chuck, Minn	19	59	3.1	12	1
Shuler, Heath, Wash	18	57	3.2	13	0
Williams, Kevin, Dall	10	53	5.3	14	0
Perriman, Brett, Det	5	48	9.6	16	0
Elias, Keith, NYG	10	44	4.4	8	0
Walker, Adam, SF	14	44	3.1	16	1
Everett, Jim, NO	24	42	1.8	9	0
Kramer, Erik, Chi	35	39	1.1	11	1
Rice, Jerry, SF	5	36	7.2	20t	1
Henderson, William, GB	7	35	5.0	17	0
Willis, Jamal, SF	12	35	2.9	15	0
Carter, Tony, Chi	10	34	3.4	7	0
Grbac, Elvis, SF	20	33	1.7	11	2
Morton, Johnnie, Det	3	33	11.0	18	0
Aikman, Troy, Dall	21	32	1.5	12	1
Krieg, Dave, Ariz	19	29	1.5	17	0
Edmonds, Bobby Joe, TB	5	28	5.6	9	0
Timpson, Michael, Chi	3	28	9.3	16	1
Phillips, Bobby, Minn	14	26	1.9	7	0
Carter, Dexter, SF	7	22	3.1	15	0
Brooks, Robert, GB	4	21	5.3	21	0
Bruce, Isaac, StL	3	17	5.7	12	0
George, Jeff, Atl	27	17	0.6	6	0
Wright, Alexander, StL	1	17	17.0	17	0
Frerotte, Gus, Wash	22	16	0.7	10	1
Kinchen, Todd, StL	4	16	4.0	15	0
Palmer, David, Minn	7	15	2.1	9	0
Bell, William, Wash	4	13	3.3	5	0
Smith, Cedric, Wash	3	13	4.3	5	0
Wilson, Wade, Dall	10	12	1.2	11	0
Lynn, Anthony, SF	2	11	5.5	6	0
Rypien, Mark, StL	9	10	1.1	5	0
Sanders, Deion, Dall	2	9	4.5	8	0
Turner, Kevin, Phil	2	9	4.5	12	0
Wolfley, Ron, StL	3	9	3.0	4	0
Wright, Toby, StL	1	9	9.0	9	0
Ismail, Qadry, Minn	1	7	7.0	7	0
Lang, David, Dall	1	7	7.0	7	0
Witherspoon, Derrick, Phil	2	7	3.5	5	0
Pierce, Aaron, NYG	1	6	6.0	6	0
Rubley, T. J., GB	2	6	3.0	6	0
Way, Charles, NYG	2	6	3.0	6	0
Barr, Dave, StL	1	5	5.0	5	0
Hawkins, Courtney, TB	4	5	1.3	11	0
Thomas, Lamar, TB	1	5	5.0	5	0
Weldon, Casey, TB	5	5	1.0	6	1
Case, Stoney, Ariz	1	4	4.0	4	0
Feagles, Jeff, Ariz	2	4	2.0	4	0
Lyle, Keith, StL	1	4	4.0	4	0
Maddox, Tommy, NYG	1	4	4.0	4	0
Moore, Dave, TB	1	4	4.0	4	0
Detmer, Ty, GB	3	3	1.0	5	0
Neal, Lorenzo, NO	5	3	0.6	3	0
Reich, Frank, Car	1	3	3.0	3	0
Stone, Dwight, Car	1	3	3.0	3	0
Guliford, Eric, Car	2	2	1.0	1	0
Lassiter, Kwamie, Ariz	1	1	1.0	1	0
Majkowski, Don, Det	9	1	0.1	4	0
Marshall, Arthur, NYG	1	1	1.0	1	0

	Att.	Yards	Avg.	Long	TD
McCrary, Fred, Phil	3	1	0.3	1t	1
Ned, Derrick, NO	3	1	0.3	5	0
Sanders, Frank, Ariz	1	1	1.0	1	0
Schlesinger, Cory, Det	1	1	1.0	1	0
Buck, Mike, Ariz	1	0	0.0	0	0
Carter, Cris, Minn	1	0	0.0	0	0
Emanuel, Bert, Atl	1	0	0.0	0	0
Flanigan, Jim, Chi	1	0	0.0	0	0
Horan, Mike, NYG	1	0	0.0	0	0
Hutton, Tom, Phil	1	0	0.0	0	0
Roby, Reggie, TB	1	0	0.0	0	0
Saxon, James, Phil	1	0	0.0	0	0
Stryzinski, Dan, Atl	1	0	0.0	0	0
Garrett, Jason, Dall	1	-1	-1.0	-1	0
Hebert, Bobby, Atl	5	-1	-0.2	2	0
Brooks, Reggie, Wash	2	-2	-1.0	-1	0
Johnson, LeShon, GB	2	-2	-1.0	0	0
Williams, Calvin, Phil	1	-2	-2.0	-2	0
Early, Quinn, NO	2	-3	-1.5	9	0
Ingram, Mark, GB	1	-3	-3.0	-3	0
Carrier, Mark, Car	3	-4	-1.3	4	0
Royals, Mark, Det	1	-7	-7.0	-7	0
Calloway, Chris, NYG	2	-9	-4.5	-3	0
Johnson, Brad, Minn	9	-9	-1.0	3	0

t = Touchdown
Leader based on most yards gained

PASSING

Highest Rating
AFC: 100.7—Jim Harbaugh, Indianapolis
NFC: 99.5—Brett Favre, Green Bay

Completion Percentage
NFC: 66.9—Steve Young, San Francisco
AFC: 64.1—Dan Marino, Miami

Attempts
AFC: 636—Drew Bledsoe, New England
NFC: 606—Warren Moon, Minnesota

Completions
NFC: 377—Warren Moon, Minnesota
AFC: 326—Jeff Blake, Cincinnati

Yards
NFC: 4413—Brett Favre, Green Bay
AFC: 3970—John Elway, Denver

Yards, Game
AFC: 450—Dan Marino, Miami at Cincinnati, October 1 (33-48, 2 TD)
NFC: 425—Steve Young, San Francisco vs. Minnesota, December 18 (30-49, 3 TD)

Longest
NFC: 99—Brett Favre (to Robert Brooks), Green Bay at Chicago, September 11 - TD
AFC: 88—Jeff Blake (to Darnay Scott), Cincinnati at Seattle, September 17 - TD

Yards Per Attempt
AFC: 8.20—Jim Harbaugh, Indianapolis
NFC: 7.74—Brett Favre, Green Bay

Touchdown Passes
NFC: 38—Brett Favre, Green Bay
AFC: 28—Jeff Blake, Cincinnati

Touchdown Passes, Game
NFC: 5—Brett Favre, Green Bay vs. Chicago, November 12 (25-33, 313 yards)
AFC: 4—Chris Chandler, Houston at Cincinnati, September 24 (23-26, 350 yards)
Jeff Hostetler, Oakland at N.Y. Jets, October 1 (14-23, 237 yards)
Dan Marino, Miami at Indianapolis, November 26 (23-36, 231 yards)
John Elway, Denver vs. Jacksonville, December 3 (22-34, 286 yards)
Boomer Esiason, N.Y. Jets at New England, December 10 (27-42, 254 yards)
Jim Kelly, Buffalo at St. Louis, December 10 (19-25, 232 yards)

Lowest Interception Percentage
AFC: 1.6—Jim Harbaugh, Indianapolis
NFC: 1.6—Troy Aikman, Dallas

Team Champion (Most Net Yards)
NFC: 4608—San Francisco
AFC: 4210—Miami

AFC PASSING—TEAM

	Att.	Comp.	Pct. Comp.	Gross Yards	Sacked	Yds. Lost	Net Yards	Yds./ Att.	Yds./ Comp.	TD	Pct. TD	Long	Int.	Pct. Int.
Miami	592	384	64.9	4398	29	188	4210	7.43	11.45	28	4.73	67t	20	3.4
Denver	594	350	58.9	4260	26	215	4045	7.17	12.17	27	4.55	62t	14	2.4
Pittsburgh	592	348	58.8	4093	24	176	3917	6.91	11.76	21	3.55	71t	21	3.5
Cincinnati	586	334	57.0	3915	25	162	3753	6.68	11.72	29	4.95	88t	18	3.1
New England	686	351	51.2	3789	27	198	3591	5.52	10.79	14	2.04	72	16	2.3
Oakland	543	317	58.4	3787	36	214	3573	6.97	11.95	25	4.60	80t	21	3.9
Cleveland	555	324	58.4	3772	32	178	3594	6.80	11.64	21	3.78	70t	20	3.6
San Diego	540	318	58.9	3706	32	240	3466	6.86	11.65	17	3.15	51t	18	3.3
Houston	536	314	58.6	3512	32	271	3241	6.55	11.18	22	4.10	76t	18	3.4
Indianapolis	434	270	62.2	3373	49	309	3064	7.77	12.49	20	4.61	52	11	2.5
Seattle	511	273	53.4	3359	45	267	3092	6.57	12.30	19	3.72	59t	23	4.5
Buffalo	506	279	55.1	3348	32	224	3124	6.62	12.00	24	4.74	77t	14	2.8
Kansas City	531	300	56.5	3178	21	158	3020	5.98	10.59	21	3.95	60t	10	1.9
Jacksonville	495	275	55.6	3144	57	354	2790	6.35	11.43	19	3.84	71t	15	3.0
N.Y. Jets	589	330	56.0	3129	47	341	2788	5.31	9.48	20	3.40	43t	24	4.1
AFC Total	8290	4767	—	54763	514	3495	51268	—	—	327	—	88t	263	—
AFC Average	552.7	317.8	57.5	3650.9	34.3	233	3417.9	6.61	11.49	21.8	3.9	—	17.5	3.2

1995 INDIVIDUAL STATISTICS

NFC PASSING—TEAM

	Att.	Comp.	Pct. Comp.	Gross Yards	Sacked	Yds. Lost	Net Yards	Yds./ Att.	Yds./ Comp.	TD	Pct. TD	Long	Int.	Pct. Int.
San Francisco	644	432	67.1	4779	33	171	4608	7.42	11.1	29	4.50	81t	16	2.5
Green Bay	593	372	62.7	4539	33	217	4322	7.65	12.2	39	6.58	99t	15	2.5
Detroit	605	362	59.8	4510	32	150	4360	7.45	12.5	33	5.45	91t	12	2.0
Minnesota	642	402	62.6	4500	40	295	4205	7.01	11.2	33	5.14	85t	16	2.5
Atlanta	603	364	60.4	4456	43	270	4186	7.39	12.2	26	4.31	62t	12	2.0
St. Louis	632	366	57.9	4113	43	308	3805	6.51	11.2	27	4.27	72	23	3.6
New Orleans	573	349	60.9	4002	28	214	3788	6.98	11.5	26	4.54	70t	14	2.4
Arizona	560	327	58.4	3893	55	390	3503	6.95	11.9	17	3.04	48	24	4.3
Chicago	523	315	60.2	3838	15	95	3743	7.34	12.2	29	5.54	76t	10	1.9
Dallas	494	322	65.2	3741	18	118	3623	7.57	11.6	18	3.64	50	10	2.0
Washington	521	265	50.9	3496	36	268	3228	6.71	13.2	16	3.07	73t	20	3.8
Tampa Bay	507	267	52.7	3341	56	386	2955	6.59	12.5	5	0.99	64t	20	3.9
Carolina	537	263	49.0	3304	38	258	3046	6.15	12.6	16	2.98	89t	25	4.7
Philadelphia	496	284	57.3	2931	46	245	2686	5.91	10.3	11	2.22	37t	19	3.8
N.Y. Giants	479	260	54.3	2863	46	213	2650	5.98	11.0	11	2.30	57t	13	2.7
NFC Total	8409	4950	—	58306	562	3598	54708	—	—	336	—	99t	249	—
NFC Average	560.6	330.0	58.9	3887.1	37.5	239.9	3647.2	6.93	11.8	22.4	4.0	—	16.6	3.0
League Total	16699	9717	—	113069	1076	7093	105976	—	—	663	—	99t	512	—
League Average	556.6	323.9	58.2	3769.0	35.9	236.4	3532.5	6.77	11.6	22.1	4.0	—	17.1	3.1

Leader based on net yards

NFL TOP TEN PASSERS

	Att.	Comp.	Pct. Comp.	Yds.	Avg. Gain	TD	Pct. TD	Long	Int.	Pct. Int.	Sack	Yds. Lost	Rating Points
Harbaugh, Jim, Ind	314	200	63.7	2575	8.20	17	5.4	52	5	1.6	36	219	100.7
Favre, Brett, GB	570	359	63.0	4413	7.74	38	6.7	99t	13	2.3	33	217	99.5
Aikman, Troy, Dall	432	280	64.8	3304	7.65	16	3.7	50	7	1.6	14	89	93.6
Kramer, Erik, Chi	522	315	60.3	3838	7.35	29	5.6	76t	10	1.9	15	95	93.5
Young, Steve, SF	447	299	66.9	3200	7.16	20	4.5	57	11	2.5	25	115	92.3
Mitchell, Scott, Det	583	346	59.3	4338	7.44	32	5.5	91t	12	2.1	31	145	92.3
Moon, Warren, Minn	606	377	62.2	4228	6.98	33	5.4	85t	14	2.3	38	277	91.5
Marino, Dan, Mia	482	309	64.1	3668	7.61	24	5.0	67t	15	3.1	22	153	90.8
George, Jeff, Atl	557	336	60.3	4143	7.44	24	4.3	62t	11	2.0	43	270	89.5
Testaverde, Vinny, Cle	392	241	61.5	2883	7.35	17	4.3	70t	10	2.6	17	87	87.8

AFC PASSING—INDIVIDUAL

	Att.	Comp.	Pct. Comp.	Yds.	Avg. Gain	TD	Pct. TD	Long	Int.	Pct. Int.	Sack	Yds. Lost	Rating Points
Harbaugh, Jim, Ind	314	200	63.7	2575	8.20	17	5.4	52	5	1.6	36	219	100.7
Marino, Dan, Mia	482	309	64.1	3668	7.61	24	5.0	67t	15	3.1	22	153	90.8
Testaverde, Vinny, Cle	392	241	61.5	2883	7.35	17	4.3	70t	10	2.6	17	87	87.8
Chandler, Chris, Hou	356	225	63.2	2460	6.91	17	4.8	76t	10	2.8	21	173	87.8
O'Donnell, Neil, Pitt	416	246	59.1	2970	7.14	17	4.1	71t	7	1.7	15	126	87.7
Elway, John, Den	542	316	58.3	3970	7.32	26	4.8	62t	14	2.6	22	180	86.4
Brunell, Mark, Jax	346	201	58.1	2168	6.27	15	4.3	45	7	2.0	39	238	82.6
Hostetler, Jeff, Oak	286	172	60.1	1998	6.99	12	4.2	80t	9	3.1	22	133	82.2
Blake, Jeff, Cin	567	326	57.5	3822	6.74	28	4.9	88t	17	3.0	24	152	82.1
Kelly, Jim, Buff	458	255	55.7	3130	6.83	22	4.8	77t	13	2.8	26	181	81.1
Humphries, Stan, SD	478	282	59.0	3381	7.07	17	3.6	51t	14	2.9	23	197	80.4
Bono, Steve, KC	520	293	56.3	3121	6.00	21	4.0	60t	10	1.9	21	158	79.5
Esiason, Boomer, NYJ	389	221	56.8	2275	5.85	16	4.1	43t	15	3.9	27	198	71.4
Mirer, Rick, Sea	391	209	53.5	2564	6.56	13	3.3	59t	20	5.1	42	255	63.7
Bledsoe, Drew, NE	636	323	50.8	3507	5.51	13	2.0	47t	16	2.5	23	170	63.7
Nonqualifiers													
Van Pelt, Alex, Buff	18	10	55.6	106	5.89	2	11.1	19t	0	0.0	0	0	110.0
Musgrave, Bill, Den	12	8	66.7	93	7.75	0	0.0	23	0	0.0	0	0	89.9
Millen, Hugh, Den	40	26	65.0	197	4.93	1	2.5	18	0	0.0	4	35	85.1
McNair, Steve, Hou	80	41	51.3	569	7.11	3	3.8	53	1	1.3	6	63	81.7
Zolak, Scott, NE	49	28	57.1	282	5.76	1	2.0	72	0	0.0	4	28	80.5
Friesz, John, Sea	120	64	53.3	795	6.63	6	5.0	43t	3	2.5	3	12	80.4
Hobert, Billy Joe, Oak	80	44	55.0	540	6.75	6	7.5	80t	4	5.0	3	11	80.2
Gannon, Rich, KC	11	7	63.6	57	5.18	0	0.0	18	0	0.0	0	0	76.7
Kosar, Bernie, Mia	108	74	68.5	699	6.47	3	2.8	31t	5	4.6	6	28	76.1
Erickson, Craig, Ind	83	50	60.2	586	7.06	3	3.6	39	4	4.8	10	68	73.7
Evans, Vince, Oak	175	100	57.1	1236	7.06	6	3.4	73t	8	4.6	11	70	71.5
Beuerlein, Steve, Jax	142	71	50.0	952	6.70	4	2.8	71t	7	4.9	17	103	60.5
Klingler, David, Cin	15	7	46.7	88	5.87	1	6.7	33	1	6.7	1	10	59.9
Miller, Jim, Pitt	56	32	57.1	397	7.09	2	3.6	42t	5	8.9	2	8	53.9
Brister, Bubby, NYJ	170	93	54.7	726	4.27	4	2.4	32	8	4.7	16	122	53.7
Foley, Glenn, NYJ	29	16	55.2	128	4.41	0	0.0	32	1	3.4	4	21	52.1
Zeier, Eric, Cle	161	82	50.9	864	5.37	4	2.5	59	9	5.6	15	91	51.9
Justin, Paul, Ind	36	20	55.6	212	5.89	0	0.0	20	2	5.6	3	22	49.8
Gilbert, Gale, SD	61	36	59.0	325	5.33	0	0.0	41	4	6.6	9	43	46.1
Tomczak, Mike, Pitt	113	65	57.5	666	5.89	1	0.9	29	9	8.0	6	42	44.3

	Att.	Comp.	Pct. Comp.	Yds.	Avg. Gain	TD	Pct. TD	Long	Int.	Pct. Int.	Sack	Yds. Lost	Rating Points
Collins, Todd, Buff	29	14	48.3	112	3.86	0	0.0	18	1	3.4	6	43	44.0
Furrer, Will, Hou	99	48	48.5	483	4.88	2	2.0	48	7	7.1	5	35	40.1
Fewer than 10 attempts													
Anderson, Richie, NYJ	1	0	0.0	0	0.00	0	0.0	0	0	0.0	0	0	39.6
Armour, Justin, Buff	1	0	0.0	0	0.00	0	0.0	0	0	0.0	0	0	39.6
Bieniemy, Eric, Cin	2	0	0.0	0	0.00	0	0.0	0	0	0.0	0	0	39.6
Camarillo, Rich, Hou	1	0	0.0	0	0.00	0	0.0	0	0	0.0	0	0	39.6
Dunn, David, Cin	1	0	0.0	0	0.00	0	0.0	0	0	0.0	0	0	39.6
Gardocki, Chris, Ind	1	0	0.0	0	0.00	0	0.0	0	0	0.0	0	0	39.6
Hobbs, Daryl, Oak	1	0	0.0	0	0.00	0	0.0	0	0	0.0	0	0	39.6
Jackson, Michael, Cle	1	0	0.0	0	0.00	0	0.0	0	1	100.0	0	0	0.0
Johnson, Lee, Cin	1	1	100.0	5	5.00	0	0.0	5	0	0.0	0	0	87.5
Johnson, Rob, Jax	7	3	42.9	24	3.43	0	0.0	19	1	14.3	1	13	12.5
Kirby, Terry, Mia	1	1	100.0	31	31.00	1	100.0	31t	0	0.0	0	0	158.3
Martin, Tony, SD	1	0	0.0	0	0.00	0	0.0	0	0	0.0	0	0	39.6
McGwire, Dan, Mia	1	0	0.0	0	0.00	0	0.0	0	0	0.0	1	7	39.6
Meggett, David, NE	1	0	0.0	0	0.00	0	0.0	0	0	0.0	0	0	39.6
Stewart, Kordell, Pitt	7	5	71.4	60	8.57	1	14.3	32	0	0.0	1	0	136.9
Tupa, Tom, Cle	1	1	100.0	25	25.00	0	0.0	25	0	0.0	0	0	118.8
Williams, Harvey, Oak	1	1	100.0	13	13.00	1	100.0	13t	0	0.0	0	0	158.3

t = Touchdown
Leader based on rating points, minimum 224 attempts

NFC PASSING—INDIVIDUAL

	Att.	Comp.	Pct. Comp.	Yds.	Avg. Gain	TD	Pct. TD	Long	Int.	Pct. Int.	Sack	Yds. Lost	Rating Points
Favre, Brett, GB	570	359	63.0	4413	7.74	38	6.7	99t	13	2.3	33	217	99.5
Aikman, Troy, Dall	432	280	64.8	3304	7.65	16	3.7	50	7	1.6	14	89	93.6
Kramer, Erik, Chi	522	315	60.3	3838	7.35	29	5.6	76t	10	1.9	15	95	93.5
Young, Steve, SF	447	299	66.9	3200	7.16	20	4.5	57	11	2.5	25	115	92.3
Mitchell, Scott, Det	583	346	59.3	4338	7.44	32	5.5	91t	12	2.1	31	145	92.3
Moon, Warren, Minn	606	377	62.2	4228	6.98	33	5.4	85t	14	2.3	38	277	91.5
George, Jeff, Atl	557	336	60.3	4143	7.44	24	4.3	62t	11	2.0	43	270	89.5
Everett, Jim, NO	567	345	60.8	3970	7.00	26	4.6	70t	14	2.5	27	210	87.0
Miller, Chris, StL	405	232	57.3	2623	6.48	18	4.4	72	15	3.7	31	244	76.2
Brown, Dave, NYG	456	254	55.7	2814	6.17	11	2.4	57t	10	2.2	44	206	73.1
Krieg, Dave, Ariz	521	304	58.3	3554	6.82	16	3.1	48	21	4.0	53	380	72.6
Frerotte, Gus, Wash	396	199	50.3	2751	6.95	13	3.3	73t	13	3.3	23	192	70.2
Peete, Rodney, Phil	375	215	57.3	2326	6.20	8	2.1	37t	14	3.7	33	166	67.3
Collins, Kerry, Car	433	214	49.4	2717	6.27	14	3.2	89t	19	4.4	24	150	61.9
Dilfer, Trent, TB	415	224	54.0	2774	6.68	4	1.0	64t	18	4.3	47	331	60.1
Nonqualifiers													
Majkowski, Don, Det	20	15	75.0	161	8.05	1	5.0	22	0	0.0	1	5	114.8
Buck, Mike, Ariz	32	20	62.5	271	8.47	1	3.1	28	0	0.0	2	10	99.9
Grbac, Elvis, SF	183	127	69.4	1469	8.03	8	4.4	81t	5	2.7	6	36	96.6
Hebert, Bobby, Atl	45	28	62.2	313	6.96	2	4.4	37t	1	2.2	0	0	88.5
Rypien, Mark, StL	217	129	59.4	1448	6.67	9	4.1	50	8	3.7	11	60	77.9
Wilson, Wade, Dall	57	38	66.7	391	6.86	1	1.8	38	3	5.3	4	29	70.1
Johnson, Brad, Minn	36	25	69.4	272	7.56	0	0.0	39	2	5.6	2	18	68.3
Cunningham, Randall, Phil	121	69	57.0	605	5.00	3	2.5	33	5	4.1	13	79	61.5
Detmer, Ty, GB	16	8	50.0	81	5.06	1	6.3	25	1	6.3	0	0	59.6
Weldon, Casey, TB	91	42	46.2	519	5.70	1	1.1	40	2	2.2	9	55	58.8
Reich, Frank, Car	84	37	44.0	441	5.25	2	2.4	46	2	2.4	12	100	58.7
Shuler, Heath, Wash	125	66	52.8	745	5.96	3	2.4	44	7	5.6	13	76	55.6
Conklin, Cary, SF	12	4	33.3	48	4.00	0	0.0	28	0	0.0	2	20	46.5
Trudeau, Jack, Car	17	11	64.7	100	5.88	0	0.0	19	3	17.6	2	8	40.9
Maddox, Tommy, NYG	23	6	26.1	49	2.13	0	0.0	13	3	13.0	2	7	0.0
Fewer than 10 attempts													
Barr, Dave, StL	9	5	55.6	42	4.67	0	0.0	18	0	0.0	1	4	67.8
Case, Stoney, Ariz	2	1	50.0	19	9.50	0	0.0	19	1	50.0	0	0	43.8
Centers, Larry, Ariz	1	0	0.0	0	0.00	0	0.0	0	1	100.0	0	0	0.0
Conway, Curtis, Chi	1	0	0.0	0	0.00	0	0.0	0	0	0.0	0	0	39.6
Garrett, Jason, Dall	5	4	80.0	46	9.20	1	20.0	24	0	0.0	0	0	144.6
Guliford, Eric, Car	2	1	50.0	46	23.00	0	0.0	46	1	50.0	0	0	56.3
Hearst, Garrison, Ariz	2	1	50.0	16	8.00	0	0.0	16	0	0.0	0	0	77.1
Hodson, Tommy, NO	5	3	60.0	14	2.80	0	0.0	9	0	0.0	0	0	64.6
Kinchen, Todd, StL	1	0	0.0	0	0.00	0	0.0	0	0	0.0	0	0	39.6
McMahon, Jim, GB	1	1	100.0	6	6.00	0	0.0	6	0	0.0	0	0	91.7
Metcalf, Eric, Atl	1	0	0.0	0	0.00	0	0.0	0	0	0.0	0	0	39.6
Moore, Rob, Ariz	2	1	50.0	33	16.50	0	0.0	33	1	50.0	0	0	56.3
Rice, Jerry, SF	1	1	100.0	41	41.00	1	100.0	41t	0	0.0	0	0	158.3
Roby, Reggie, TB	1	1	100.0	48	48.00	0	0.0	48	0	0.0	0	0	118.8
Rubley, T. J., GB	6	4	66.7	39	6.50	0	0.0	17	1	16.7	0	0	45.1
Sanders, Barry, Det	2	1	50.0	11	5.50	0	0.0	11	0	0.0	0	0	66.7
Taylor, John, SF	1	1	100.0	21	21.00	0	0.0	21	0	0.0	0	0	118.8
Wilmsmeyer, Klaus, NO	1	1	100.0	18	18.00	0	0.0	18	0	0.0	0	0	118.8
Workman, Vince, Car	1	0	0.0	0	0.00	0	0.0	0	0	0.0	0	0	39.6

t = Touchdown
Leader based on rating points, minimum 224 attempts

1995 INDIVIDUAL STATISTICS

PASS RECEIVING

Receptions

NFC: 123—Herman Moore, Detroit
AFC: 99—Carl Pickens, Cincinnati

Receptions, Game

NFC: 15—Isaac Bruce, St. Louis vs. Miami, December 24 (210 yards - TD)
AFC: 13—Tony Martin, San Diego vs. Seattle, September 10 (163 yards - TD)

Yards

NFC: 1848—Jerry Rice, San Francisco
AFC: 1342—Tim Brown, Oakland

Yards, Game

NFC: 289—Jerry Rice, San Francisco vs. Minnesota, December 18 (14 receptions - 3 TD)
AFC: 180—Shannon Sharpe, Denver vs. Buffalo, September 3 (10 receptions)

Longest

NFC: 99—Robert Brooks (from Brett Favre), Green Bay at Chicago, September 11 - TD
AFC: 88—Darnay Scott (from Jeff Blake), Cincinnati at Seattle, September 17 - TD

Yards Per Reception

AFC: 23.5—Chris Sanders, Houston
NFC: 18.8—Willie Green, Carolina

Touchdowns

AFC: 17—Carl Pickens, Cincinnati
NFC: 17—Cris Carter, Minnesota

Team Leaders, Receptions

AFC: BUFFALO: 53, Bill Brooks; CINCINNATI: 99, Carl Pickens; CLEVELAND: 61, Earnest Byner; DENVER: 63, Shannon Sharpe; HOUSTON: 61, Haywood Jeffires; INDIANAPOLIS: 56, Marshall Faulk; JACKSONVILLE: 53, Willie Jackson; KANSAS CITY: 55, Kimble Anders; MIAMI: 66, Terry Kirby; NEW ENGLAND: 84, Ben Coates; N.Y. JETS: 71, Adrian Murrell; OAKLAND: 89, Tim Brown; PITTSBURGH: 85, Yancey Thigpen; SAN DIEGO: 90, Tony Martin; SEATTLE: 77, Brian Blades

NFC: ARIZONA: 101, Larry Centers; ATLANTA: 104, Eric Metcalf; CAROLINA: 66, Mark Carrier; CHICAGO: 82, Jeff Graham; DALLAS: 111, Michael Irvin; DETROIT: 123, Herman Moore; GREEN BAY: 102, Robert Brooks; MINNESOTA: 122, Cris Carter; NEW ORLEANS: 81, Quinn Early; N.Y. GIANTS: 56, Chris Calloway; PHILADELPHIA: 63, Calvin Williams; ST. LOUIS: 119, Isaac Bruce; SAN FRANCISCO: 122, Jerry Rice; TAMPA BAY: 62, Jackie Harris; WASHINGTON: 56, Henry Ellard

NFL TOP TEN PASS RECEIVERS

	No.	Yards	Avg.	Long	TD
Moore, Herman, Det	123	1686	13.7	69t	14
Carter, Cris, Minn	122	1371	11.2	60t	17
Rice, Jerry, SF	122	1848	15.1	81t	15
Bruce, Isaac, StL	119	1781	15.0	72	13
Irvin, Michael, Dall	111	1603	14.4	50	10
Perriman, Brett, Det	108	1488	13.8	91t	9
Metcalf, Eric, Atl	104	1189	11.4	62t	8
Brooks, Robert, GB	102	1497	14.7	99t	13
Centers, Larry, Ariz	101	962	9.5	32	2
Pickens, Carl, Cin	99	1234	12.5	68t	17

NFL TOP TEN RECEIVERS BY YARDS

	Yards	No.	Avg.	Long	TD
Rice, Jerry, SF	1848	122	15.1	81t	15
Bruce, Isaac, StL	1781	119	15.0	72	13
Moore, Herman, Det	1686	123	13.7	69t	14
Irvin, Michael, Dall	1603	111	14.4	50	10
Brooks, Robert, GB	1497	102	14.7	99t	13
Perriman, Brett, Det	1488	108	13.8	91t	9
Carter, Cris, Minn	1371	122	11.2	60t	17
Brown, Tim, Oak	1342	89	15.1	80t	10
Thigpen, Yancey, Pitt	1307	85	15.4	43	5
Graham, Jeff, Chi	1301	82	15.9	51	4

AFC RECEIVERS—INDIVIDUAL

	No.	Yards	Avg.	Long	TD
Pickens, Carl, Cin	99	1234	12.5	68t	17
Martin, Tony, SD	90	1224	13.6	51t	6
Brown, Tim, Oak	89	1342	15.1	80t	10
Thigpen, Yancey, Pitt	85	1307	15.4	43	5
Coates, Ben, NE	84	915	10.9	35	6
Blades, Brian, Sea	77	1001	13.0	49	4
Murrell, Adrian, NYJ	71	465	6.5	43	2
Galloway, Joey, Sea	67	1039	15.5	59t	7
Brisby, Vincent, NE	66	974	14.8	72	3
Chrebet, Wayne, NYJ	66	726	11.0	32	4
Kirby, Terry, Mia	66	618	9.4	46	3
Sharpe, Shannon, Den	63	756	12.0	49	4
Harmon, Ronnie, SD	63	673	10.7	44	5
Fryar, Irving, Mia	62	910	14.7	67t	8
McDuffie, O. J., Mia	62	819	13.2	48	8
Jeffires, Haywood, Hou	61	684	11.2	35t	8
Byner, Earnest, Cle	61	494	8.1	29t	2
McNair, Todd, Hou	60	501	8.4	25	1
Miller, Anthony, Den	59	1079	18.3	62t	14
McCardell, Keenan, Cle	56	709	12.7	36	4
Faulk, Marshall, Ind	56	475	8.5	34	3
McGee, Tony, Cin	55	754	13.7	41	4
Anders, Kimble, KC	55	349	6.3	28	1
Williams, Harvey, Oak	54	375	6.9	28	0
Brooks, Bill, Buff	53	763	14.4	51t	11
Jackson, Willie, Jax	53	589	11.1	45	5
Scott, Darnay, Cin	52	821	15.8	88t	5
Dawkins, Sean, Ind	52	784	15.1	52	3
Meggett, David, NE	52	334	6.4	19	0
Byars, Keith, Mia	51	362	7.1	26	2
Johnson, Lonnie, Buff	49	504	10.3	52	1
Davis, Terrell, Den	49	367	7.5	31	1
Jefferson, Shawn, SD	48	621	12.9	45	2
Hastings, Andre, Pitt	48	502	10.5	36	1
Rison, Andre, Cle	47	701	14.9	59	3
Seay, Mark, SD	45	537	11.9	38t	3
Mitchell, Johnny, NYJ	45	497	11.0	43t	5
Jackson, Michael, Cle	44	714	16.2	70t	9
Moore, Will, NE	43	502	11.7	33	1
Green, Eric, Mia	43	499	11.6	31t	3
Bieniemy, Eric, Cin	43	424	9.9	33	0
Craver, Aaron, Den	43	369	8.6	32	1
Copeland, Russell, Buff	42	646	15.4	77t	1
Dilger, Ken, Ind	42	635	15.1	42	4
Cash, Keith, KC	42	419	10.0	38t	1
Mitchell, Pete, Jax	41	527	12.9	35	2
Wilson, Charles, NYJ	41	484	11.8	24	4
Dawson, Lake, KC	40	513	12.8	45t	5
Wycheck, Frank, Hou	40	471	11.8	36t	1
Mills, Ernie, Pitt	39	679	17.4	62t	8
McCaffrey, Ed, Den	39	477	12.2	35	2
Parmalee, Bernie, Mia	39	345	8.8	35	1
Thomas, Rodney, Hou	39	204	5.2	19	2
Hobbs, Daryl, Oak	38	612	16.1	54t	3
Johnson, Charles, Pitt	38	432	11.4	33	0
Clark, Gary, Mia	37	525	14.2	42t	2
Sanders, Chris, Hou	35	823	23.5	76t	9
Turner, Floyd, Ind	35	431	12.3	47t	4
Pupunu, Alfred, SD	35	315	9.0	26	0
Fenner, Derrick, Oak	35	252	7.2	23	3
Warren, Chris, Sea	35	247	7.1	20t	1
Slaughter, Webster, KC	34	514	15.1	38	4
Davis, Willie, KC	33	527	16.0	60t	5
Pritchard, Mike, Den	33	441	13.4	45t	3
Tillman, Cedric, Jax	30	368	12.3	28	3
Martin, Curtis, NE	30	261	8.7	27	1
Givins, Ernest, Jax	29	280	9.7	18	3
Ismail, Raghib, Oak	28	491	17.5	73t	3
Allen, Marcus, KC	27	210	7.8	20	0
Green, Harold, Cin	27	182	6.7	24	1
Armour, Justin, Buff	26	300	11.5	28t	3
Howard, Desmond, Jax	26	276	10.6	24	1
Brady, Kyle, NYJ	26	252	9.7	29	2
Gash, Sam, NE	26	242	9.3	30	1
Bruener, Mark, Pitt	26	238	9.2	29	3
Glover, Andrew, Oak	26	220	8.5	25	3
Thomas, Thurman, Buff	26	220	8.5	60	2
Pegram, Erric, Pitt	26	206	7.9	22	1
Baxter, Brad, NYJ	26	160	6.2	20	0
Cash, Kerry, Oak	25	254	10.2	23	2
Walker, Derrick, KC	25	205	8.2	18t	1
Russell, Derek, Hou	24	321	13.4	57	0
Reed, Andre, Buff	24	312	13.0	41t	3
Holmes, Darick, Buff	24	214	8.9	47	0
Williams, John L., Pitt	24	127	5.3	20	1
Crumpler, Carlester, Sea	23	254	11.0	24	1
Smith, Jimmy L., Jax	22	288	13.1	33	3
Milburn, Glyn, Den	22	191	8.7	23	0
Bailey, Aaron, Ind	21	379	18.0	45	3
Potts, Roosevelt, Ind	21	228	10.9	52	1
Stewart, James, Jax	21	190	9.0	38	1
Tasker, Steve, Buff	20	255	12.8	43	3
Kinchen, Brian, Cle	20	216	10.8	41	0

	No.	Yards	Avg.	Long	TD
Joseph, James, Cin	20	118	5.9	13	0
Yarborough, Ryan, NYJ	18	230	12.8	38	2
Baxter, Fred, NYJ	18	222	12.3	32	1
Maston, Le'Shai, Jax	18	131	7.3	19	0
Dunn, David, Cin	17	209	12.3	37	1
Fauria, Christian, Sea	17	181	10.6	20t	1
Warren, Lamont, Ind	17	159	9.4	18	0
Griffith, Richard, Jax	16	243	15.2	39	0
Bishop, Harold, Cle	16	135	8.4	21	0
Lewis, Roderick, Hou	16	116	7.3	16	0
Alexander, Derrick, Cle	15	216	14.4	40	0
Burke, John, NE	15	136	9.1	21	0
McAfee, Fred, Pitt	15	88	5.9	18	0
Stewart, Kordell, Pitt	14	235	16.8	71t	1
Brown, Troy, NE	14	159	11.4	31	0
Hughes, Danan, KC	14	103	7.4	16	1
Jett, James, Oak	13	179	13.8	26t	1
Smith, Rico, Cle	13	173	13.3	29t	1
Hoard, Leroy, Cle	13	103	7.9	24	0
Hill, Randal, Mia	12	260	21.7	58	0
Thomas, Robb, Sea	12	239	19.9	50t	1
Johnson, Vance, Den	12	170	14.2	23	0
Seabron, Malcolm, Hou	12	167	13.9	34	1
Evans, Jerry, Den	12	124	10.3	22	1
Strong, Mack, Sea	12	117	9.8	25	3
Vanover, Tamarick, KC	11	231	21.0	57	2
Hartley, Frank, Cle	11	137	12.5	23	1
Hayes, Jonathan, Pitt	11	113	10.3	32	0
Avery, Steve, Pitt	11	82	7.5	18t	1
Graham, Hason, NE	10	156	15.6	37t	2
Hannah, Travis, Hou	10	142	14.2	42	0
Broussard, Steve, Sea	10	94	9.4	25	0
Young, Duane, SD	9	90	10.0	22	0
Kaufman, Napoleon, Oak	9	62	6.9	18	0
Thompson, Leroy, KC	9	37	4.1	7	0
Anderson, Flipper, Ind	8	111	13.9	28	2
Lee, Kevin, NE	8	107	13.4	33	0
Stablein, Brian, Ind	8	95	11.9	16	0
Cline, Tony, Buff	8	64	8.0	17	0
White, Lorenzo, Cle	8	64	8.0	28	0
Moore, Ronald, NYJ	8	50	6.3	13	0
Roan, Michael, Hou	8	46	5.8	11	0
Cothran, Jeff, Cin	8	44	5.5	15	0
Morris, Byron (Bam), Pitt	8	36	4.5	13	0
Marsh, Curtis, Jax	7	127	18.1	34	0
Smith, Steve, Sea	7	59	8.4	17	1
Means, Natrone, SD	7	46	6.6	14	0
Hill, Greg, KC	7	45	6.4	13	0
Smith, Rod, Den	6	152	25.3	43t	1
McKnight, James, Sea	6	91	15.2	24	0
Vardell, Tommy, Cle	6	18	3.0	7	0
Brown, Gary, Hou	6	16	2.7	7	0
Reeves, Walter, Cle	6	12	2.0	3	1
Jordan, Randy, Jax	5	89	17.8	71t	1
Bernstine, Rod, Den	5	54	10.8	38	0
Hayden, Aaron, SD	5	53	10.6	16	0
Hunter, Ernest, Cle	5	42	8.4	17	0
Sadowski, Troy, Cin	5	37	7.4	12	0
Proehl, Ricky, Sea	5	29	5.8	9	0
Anderson, Richie, NYJ	5	26	5.2	9	0
Culver, Rodney, SD	5	21	4.2	12	0
Spikes, Irving, Mia	5	18	3.6	13	1
Hill, Jeff, Cin	4	44	11.0	18	0
Arbuckle, Charles, Ind	4	33	8.3	12	0
Coleman, Andre, SD	3	67	22.3	41	0
Barnes, Johnnie, Pitt	3	48	16.0	25	0
Carswell, Dwayne, Den	3	37	12.3	23	0
Rivers, Reggie, Den	3	32	10.7	23	0
Mitchell, Shannon, SD	3	31	10.3	24	1
Coons, Robert, Buff	3	28	9.3	13	0
Williams, Ronnie, Mia	3	28	9.3	13	0
Fletcher, Terrell, SD	3	26	8.7	15	0
Keith, Craig, Jax	3	20	6.7	9	0
Ware, Derek, Cin	2	36	18.0	21	0
Crockett, Zack, Ind	2	35	17.5	19	0
Gardner, Carwell, Buff	2	17	8.5	13	0
Williams, Mike, Mia	2	17	8.5	15	0
Rasheed, Kenyon, NYJ	2	15	7.5	9	0
Tuten, Melvin, Cin	2	12	6.0	9	1
Dunbar, Vaughn, Jax	2	11	5.5	8	0
Humphrey, Ronald, Ind	2	11	5.5	6	0
Butts, Marion, Hou	2	10	5.0	10	0
Riddick, Louis, Cle	1	25	25.0	25	0
Thomas, Damon, Buff	1	18	18.0	18	0
Bennett, Donnell, KC	1	12	12.0	12	0
Penn, Chris, KC	1	12	12.0	12	0
Chamberlain, Byron, Den	1	11	11.0	11	0
Lundy, Dennis, Hou	1	11	11.0	11	0
Smith, Lamar, Sea	1	10	10.0	10	0
Davis, Tyrone, NYJ	1	9	9.0	9	0
Croom, Corey, NE	1	8	8.0	8	0
Jourdain, Yonel, Buff	1	7	7.0	7	0
Testaverde, Vinny, Cle	1	7	7.0	7	0
Banta, Brad, Ind	1	6	6.0	6	0
Ellison, 'OMar, SD	1	6	6.0	6	0
Laro, Gordon, Jax	1	6	6.0	6	0
Powers, Ricky, Cle	1	6	6.0	6	0
Grant, Rupert, NE	1	4	4.0	4	0
Wilson, Robert, Mia	1	3	3.0	3	0
Brister, Bubby, NYJ	1	2	2.0	2	0
Valerio, Joe, KC	1	1	1.0	1t	1
Christopherson, Ryan, Jax	1	-1	-1.0	-1	0
Johnson, Tracy, Sea	1	-2	-2.0	-2	0
Humphries, Stan, SD	1	-4	-4.0	-4	0
Marino, Dan, Mia	1	-6	-6.0	-6	0
Bledsoe, Drew, NE	1	-9	-9.0	-9	0
Foley, Glenn, NYJ	1	-9	-9.0	-9	0
Harbaugh, Jim, Ind	1	-9	-9.0	-9	0

t = Touchdown
Leader based on receptions

NFC RECEIVERS—INDIVIDUAL

	No.	Yards	Avg.	Long	TD
Moore, Herman, Det	123	1686	13.7	69t	14
Rice, Jerry, SF	122	1848	15.1	81t	15
Carter, Cris, Minn	122	1371	11.2	60t	17
Bruce, Isaac, StL	119	1781	15.0	72	13
Irvin, Michael, Dall	111	1603	14.4	50	10
Perriman, Brett, Det	108	1488	13.8	91t	9
Metcalf, Eric, Atl	104	1189	11.4	62t	8
Brooks, Robert, GB	102	1497	14.7	99t	13
Centers, Larry, Ariz	101	962	9.5	32	2
Loville, Derek, SF	87	662	7.6	31	3
Graham, Jeff, Chi	82	1301	15.9	51	4
Early, Quinn, NO	81	1087	13.4	70t	8
Mathis, Terance, Atl	78	1039	13.3	54t	9
Emanuel, Bert, Atl	74	1039	14.0	52	5
Reed, Jake, Minn	72	1167	16.2	55t	9
Lee, Amp, Minn	71	558	7.9	33	1
Carrier, Mark, Car	66	1002	15.2	66t	3
Moore, Rob, Ariz	63	907	14.4	45	5
Williams, Calvin, Phil	63	768	12.2	37t	2
Conway, Curtis, Chi	62	1037	16.7	76t	12
Harris, Jackie, TB	62	751	12.1	33	1
Novacek, Jay, Dall	62	705	11.4	33t	5
Watters, Ricky, Phil	62	434	7.0	24	1
Smith, Emmitt, Dall	62	375	6.0	40	0
Bennett, Edgar, GB	61	648	10.6	35	4
Jones, Brent, SF	60	595	9.9	39	3
Walls, Wesley, NO	57	694	12.2	29	4
Ellard, Henry, Wash	56	1005	17.9	59	5
Calloway, Chris, NYG	56	796	14.2	49	3
Chmura, Mark, GB	54	679	12.6	33	7
Sanders, Frank, Ariz	52	883	17.0	48	2
Barnett, Fred, Phil	48	585	12.2	33	5
Levens, Dorsey, GB	48	434	9.0	27	4
Sanders, Barry, Det	48	398	8.3	40	1
Green, Willie, Car	47	882	18.8	89t	6
Drayton, Troy, StL	47	458	9.7	31	4
Floyd, William, SF	47	348	7.4	23	1
Harper, Alvin, TB	46	633	13.8	49	2
Smith, Irv, NO	45	466	10.4	43	3
Morton, Johnnie, Det	44	590	13.4	32t	8
Sherrard, Mike, NYG	44	577	13.1	57t	4
Haynes, Michael, NO	41	597	14.6	48	4
Hawkins, Courtney, TB	41	493	12.0	47	0
Carter, Tony, Chi	40	329	8.2	27	1
Ingram, Mark, GB	39	469	12.0	29	3
Williams, Kevin, Dall	38	613	16.1	48t	2
Stokes, J.J., SF	38	517	13.6	41t	4
Small, Torrance, NO	38	461	12.1	32t	5
Mitchell, Brian, Wash	38	324	8.5	22t	1
Bailey, Johnny, StL	38	265	7.0	25	0

1995 INDIVIDUAL STATISTICS

	No.	Yards	Avg.	Long	TD
Heyward, Craig, Atl	37	350	9.5	25	2
Kinchen, Todd, StL	36	419	11.6	35	4
Copeland, Horace, TB	35	605	17.3	64t	2
Brown, Derek, NO	35	266	7.6	19	1
Westbrook, Michael, Wash	34	522	15.4	45	1
Pierce, Aaron, NYG	33	310	9.4	26	0
Ismail, Qadry, Minn	32	597	18.7	85t	3
Morgan, Anthony, GB	31	344	11.1	29t	4
Birden, J. J., Atl	31	303	9.8	24	1
Walker, Herschel, NYG	31	234	7.5	34	1
Allen, Terry, Wash	31	232	7.5	24	1
Hester, Jessie, StL	30	399	13.3	38t	3
Dawsey, Lawrence, TB	30	372	12.4	26	0
Johnston, Daryl, Dall	30	248	8.3	24	1
Shepherd, Leslie, Wash	29	486	16.8	73t	2
Guliford, Eric, Car	29	444	15.3	49	1
Edwards, Anthony, Ariz	29	417	14.4	28t	2
Taylor, John, SF	29	387	13.3	40	2
Carpenter, Rob, Phil	29	318	11.0	29	0
Christian, Bob, Car	29	255	8.8	23	1
Hearst, Garrison, Ariz	29	243	8.4	39	1
Johnson, Anthony, Chi-Car	29	207	7.1	37	0
Green, Robert, Chi	28	246	8.8	28	0
Jordan, Andrew, Minn	27	185	6.9	17	2
Cook, Marv, StL	26	135	5.2	16	1
Logan, Marc, Wash	25	276	11.0	32	2
Jennings, Keith, Chi	25	217	8.7	20	6
Timpson, Michael, Chi	24	289	12.0	36	2
Wetnight, Ryan, Chi	24	193	8.0	22	2
Hampton, Rodney, NYG	24	142	5.9	18	0
Wright, Alexander, StL	23	368	16.0	50	2
West, Ed, Phil	20	190	9.5	26	1
Metzelaars, Pete, Car	20	171	8.6	27	3
Cooper, Adrian, Minn	18	207	11.5	41	0
Cross, Howard, NYG	18	197	10.9	26	0
Evans, Chuck, Minn	18	119	6.6	24	1
Bates, Mario, NO	18	114	6.3	26	0
Bettis, Jerome, StL	18	106	5.9	19	0
Martin, Kelvin, Phil	17	206	12.1	22	0
Brown, Tyrone, Atl	17	198	11.6	26	0
Marshall, Arthur, NYG	17	195	11.5	27	1
Sloan, David, Det	17	184	10.8	24	1
Popson, Ted, SF	16	128	8.0	16	0
Russell, Leonard, StL	16	89	5.6	17	0
Asher, Jamie, Wash	14	172	12.3	20	0
Bell, Coleman, Wash	14	166	11.9	29t	1
Beebe, Don, Car	14	152	10.9	24	1
Gaines, Wendall, Ariz	14	117	8.4	22t	2
Rhett, Errict, TB	14	110	7.9	18	0
Jackson, Keith, GB	13	142	10.9	22	1
McBride, Oscar, Ariz	13	112	8.6	24	2
Moore, Dave, TB	13	102	7.8	21	0
Workman, Vince, Car	13	74	5.7	14	0
Lewis, Thomas, NYG	12	208	17.3	46t	1
Neal, Lorenzo, NO	12	123	10.3	69t	1
Palmer, David, Minn	12	100	8.3	19	0
Hall, Ron, Det	11	81	7.4	15	0
Walker, Adam, SF	11	78	7.1	15	0
Griffith, Howard, Car	11	63	5.7	15	1
Thomas, Lamar, TB	10	107	10.7	24	0
Dowdell, Marcus, Ariz	10	96	9.6	23	0
Galbraith, Scott, Wash	10	80	8.0	25	2
Garner, Charlie, Phil	10	61	6.1	29	0
Truitt, Olanda, Wash	9	154	17.1	47	1
Elias, Keith, NYG	9	69	7.7	18	0
McCrary, Fred, Phil	9	60	6.7	11	0
Singleton, Nate, SF	8	108	13.5	23	1
Freeman, Antonio, GB	8	106	13.3	28	1
Preston, Roell, Atl	7	129	18.4	61t	1
Jordan, Charles, GB	7	117	16.7	35	2
Way, Charles, NYG	7	76	10.9	34	1
Armstrong, Tyji, TB	7	68	9.7	29	0
Walsh, Chris, Minn	7	66	9.4	16	0
Salaam, Rashaan, Chi	7	56	8.0	18	0
Bjornson, Eric, Dall	7	53	7.6	16	0
Ellison, Jerry, TB	7	44	6.3	14	0
Smith, Robert, Minn	7	35	5.0	11	0
Zellars, Ray, NO	7	33	4.7	9	0
Monk, Art, Phil	6	114	19.0	36	0
Fleming, Cory, Dall	6	83	13.8	16	0
DeRamus, Lee, NO	6	76	12.7	27	0
Thomas, Chris, SF	6	73	12.2	23	0
Reeves, Bryan, Ariz	6	62	10.3	22	0
DeLong, Greg, Minn	6	38	6.3	9	0
Johnson, Jimmie, Phil	6	37	6.2	9	0
Lyons, Mitch, Atl	5	83	16.6	34	0
Johnson, Reggie, Phil	5	68	13.6	33	2
Jones, Chris T., Phil	5	61	12.2	17	0
Spencer, Darryl, Atl	5	60	12.0	22	0
Gedney, Chris, Chi	5	52	10.4	15	0
Rasby, Walter, Car	5	47	9.4	15	0
Thomas, Johnny, StL	5	42	8.4	12	0
Fann, Chad, Ariz	5	41	8.2	13	0
Holman, Rodney, Det	5	35	7.0	9	0
Wheatley, Tyrone, NYG	5	27	5.4	16	0
Winans, Tydus, Wash	4	77	19.3	32	0
Rhem, Steve, NO	4	50	12.5	20	0
Anderson, Jamal, Atl	4	42	10.5	17	0
Matthews, Aubrey, Det	4	41	10.3	12	0
Graham, Scottie, Minn	4	30	7.5	11	0
Price, Jim, StL	4	29	7.3	24	0
Turner, Kevin, Phil	4	29	7.3	11	0
Moore, Derrick, Car	4	12	3.0	5	0
Mickens, Terry, GB	3	50	16.7	24	0
Anderson, Steve, Ariz	3	34	11.3	18	1
Campbell, Matthew, Car	3	32	10.7	12	0
Thomason, Jeff, GB	3	32	10.7	15	0
Williams, Sherman, Dall	3	28	9.3	24	0
Thomas, Blair, Car	3	24	8.0	14	0
Tice, Mike, Minn	3	22	7.3	9	0
Henderson, William, GB	3	21	7.0	9	0
Ned, Derrick, NO	3	9	3.0	9	0
Willis, Jamal, SF	3	8	2.7	5	0
Sanders, Deion, Dall	2	25	12.5	19	0
Sanders, Ricky, Atl	2	24	12.0	21	0
Faulkerson, Mike, Chi	2	22	11.0	12	0
Tillman, Lawyer, Car	2	22	11.0	12	0
Ervins, Ricky, SF	2	21	10.5	11	0
Samuels, Terry, Ariz	2	19	9.5	12	0
Kozlowski, Brian, NYG	2	17	8.5	12	0
Douglas, Omar, NYG	2	15	7.5	11	0
Robinson, Greg, StL	2	12	6.0	6	0
Flanigan, Jim, Chi	2	6	3.0	4t	2
Carter, Dexter, NYJ-SF	2	4	2.0	4	0
Booty, John, TB	1	48	48.0	48	0
Newman, Anthony, NO	1	18	18.0	18	0
Pinkney, Lovell, StL	1	13	13.0	13	0
Botkin, Kirk, NO	1	8	8.0	8	0
Edmonds, Bobby Joe, TB	1	8	8.0	8	0
Watkins, Kendell, Dall	1	8	8.0	8	0
Rivers, Ron, Det	1	5	5.0	5	0
Harris, Raymont, Chi	1	4	4.0	4	0
Carolan, Brett, SF	1	3	3.0	3	0
Dennis, Mark, Car	1	3	3.0	3	0
Gerak, John, Minn	1	3	3.0	3	0
Stewart, James, Minn	1	3	3.0	3	0
Jenkins, James, Wash	1	2	2.0	2	0
Schlesinger, Cory, Det	1	2	2.0	2	0
Dalman, Chris, SF	1	-1	-1.0	-1	0
Stringer, Korey, Minn	1	-1	-1.0	-1	0
Moss, Brent, StL	1	-3	-3.0	-3	0

t = Touchdown
Leader based on receptions

INTERCEPTIONS

Interceptions
- NFC: 9—Orlando Thomas, Minnesota
- AFC: 7—Willie Williams, Pittsburgh

Interceptions, Game
- AFC: 3—Stevon Moore, Cleveland at Houston, September 17
  Dwayne Harper, San Diego vs. Oakland, November 27
- NFC: 2—Tyronne Drakeford, San Francisco vs. Atlanta, September 10
  Merton Hanks, San Francisco vs. New England, September 17
  Vencie Glenn, N.Y. Giants vs. New Orleans, September 24
  Orlando Thomas, Minnesota at Pittsburgh, September 24 - TD
  William Thomas, Philadelphia at N.Y. Giants, October 15

Yards
- NFC: 173—Willie Clay, Detroit
- AFC: 145—Darryll Lewis, Houston

Longest
- AFC: 99—Shaun Gayle, San Diego at N.Y. Giants, December 23 - TD
- NFC: 96—Tim McKyer, Carolina at San Francisco, November 5 - TD

Touchdowns
- NFC: 2—Larry Brown, Dallas
  Tim McDonald, San Francisco
  Ken Norton, San Francisco
  Aeneas Williams, Arizona
- AFC: 1—by many

Team Leaders, Interceptions
- AFC: BUFFALO: 6, Kurt Schulz; CINCINNATI: 4, Bracey Walker; CLEVELAND: 5, Stevon Moore; DENVER: 3, Steve Atwater; HOUSTON: 6, Darryll Lewis; INDIANAPOLIS: 3, Ashley Ambrose, Eugene Daniel; JACKSONVILLE: 3, Harry Colon; KANSAS CITY: 4, Dale Carter; MIAMI: 5, Troy Vincent; NEW ENGLAND: 4, Vincent Brown; N.Y. JETS: 6, Otis Smith; OAKLAND: 6, Terry McDaniel; PITTSBURGH: 7, Willie Williams; SAN DIEGO: 5, Rodney Harrison; SEATTLE: 5, Robert Blackmon
- NFC: ARIZONA: 6, Aeneas Williams; ATLANTA: 3, Kevin Ross, Terry Taylor, Jessie Tuggle; CAROLINA: 6, Brett Maxie; CHICAGO: 4, Donnell Woolford; DALLAS: 6, Larry Brown, Brock Marion; DETROIT: 8, Willie Clay; GREEN BAY: 5, LeRoy Butler; MINNESOTA: 9, Orlando Thomas; NEW ORLEANS: 4, Jimmy Spencer; N.Y. GIANTS: 5, Vencie Glenn, Phillippi Sparks; PHILADELPHIA: 7, William Thomas; ST. LOUIS: 6, Toby Wright; SAN FRANCISCO: 5, Tyronne Drakeford, Merton Hanks; TAMPA BAY: 5, Martin Mayhew; WASHINGTON: 4, Tom Carter

Team Champion
- NFC: 26—San Francisco
- AFC: 22—Pittsburgh

AFC INTERCEPTIONS—TEAM

	No.	Yards	Avg.	Long	TD
Pittsburgh	22	361	16.4	63t	3
Houston	21	317	15.1	98t	4
Buffalo	17	233	13.7	69t	2
Cleveland	17	230	13.5	36	2
N.Y. Jets	17	261	15.4	49t	3
San Diego	17	220	12.9	99t	1
Kansas City	16	303	18.9	74t	2
Seattle	16	127	7.9	32	0
New England	15	143	9.5	45	0
Miami	14	161	11.5	69t	1
Indianapolis	13	248	19.1	97t	1
Jacksonville	13	155	11.9	48t	1
Cincinnati	12	175	14.6	61	1
Oakland	11	110	10.0	42t	2
Denver	8	114	14.3	36	0
AFC Total	229	3158	13.8	99t	23
AFC Average	15.3	210.5	13.8	—	1.5

NFC INTERCEPTIONS—TEAM

	No.	Yards	Avg.	Long	TD
San Francisco	26	425	16.3	86t	5
Minnesota	25	326	13.0	60t	2
Detroit	22	270	12.3	39	0
St. Louis	22	245	11.1	31	2
Carolina	21	319	15.2	96t	2
Arizona	19	259	13.6	72t	4
Dallas	19	261	13.7	65t	4
Philadelphia	19	239	12.6	37t	1
Atlanta	18	304	16.9	71t	2
New Orleans	17	195	11.5	47t	1
Chicago	16	146	9.1	37	1
N.Y. Giants	16	269	16.8	75t	2
Washington	16	250	15.6	51t	2
Tampa Bay	14	137	9.8	40	1
Green Bay	13	253	19.5	76	0
NFC Total	283	3898	13.8	96t	29
NFC Average	18.9	259.9	13.8	—	1.9
League Total	512	7056	—	99t	52
League Average	17.1	235.2	13.8	—	1.7

NFL TOP TEN INTERCEPTORS

	No.	Yards	Avg.	Long	TD
Thomas, Orlando, Minn	9	108	12.0	45t	1
Clay, Willie, Det	8	173	21.6	39	0
Thomas, William, Phil	7	104	14.9	37t	1
Williams, Willie, Pitt	7	122	17.4	63t	1
Brown, Larry, Dall	6	124	20.7	65t	2
Lewis, Darryll, Hou	6	145	24.2	98t	1
Marion, Brock, Dall	6	40	6.7	32t	1
Maxie, Brett, Car	6	59	9.8	49	0
McDaniel, Terry, Oak	6	46	7.7	42t	1
Raymond, Corey, Det	6	44	7.3	18	0
Schulz, Kurt, Buff	6	48	8.0	32t	1
Smith, Otis, NYJ	6	101	16.8	49t	1
Williams, Aeneas, Ariz	6	86	14.3	48t	2
Wright, Toby, StL	6	79	13.2	27	0

AFC INTERCEPTIONS—INDIVIDUAL

	No.	Yards	Avg.	Long	TD
Williams, Willie, Pitt	7	122	17.4	63t	1
Lewis, Darryll, Hou	6	145	24.2	98t	1
Smith, Otis, NYJ	6	101	16.8	49t	1
Schulz, Kurt, Buff	6	48	8.0	32t	1
McDaniel, Terry, Oak	6	46	7.7	42t	1
Vincent, Troy, Mia	5	95	19.0	69t	1
Moore, Stevon, Cle	5	55	11.0	28	0
Blackmon, Robert, Sea	5	46	9.2	21	0
Harrison, Rodney, SD	5	22	4.4	17	0
Perry, Darren, Pitt	4	71	17.8	26	0
Walker, Bracey, Cin	4	56	14.0	23	0
Carter, Dale, KC	4	45	11.3	29	0
Gray, Carlton, Sea	4	45	11.3	26	0
Harper, Dwayne, SD	4	12	3.0	15	0
Brown, Vincent, NE	4	1	0.3	1	0
Daniel, Eugene, Ind	3	142	47.3	97t	1
Washington, Brian, KC	3	100	33.3	74t	1
Hasty, James, KC	3	89	29.7	64t	1
Lloyd, Greg, Pitt	3	85	28.3	52	0
Guyton, Myron, NE	3	68	22.7	45	0
Atwater, Steve, Den	3	54	18.0	25	0
Law, Ty, NE	3	47	15.7	38	0
Colon, Harry, Jax	3	46	15.3	41	0
Cecil, Chuck, Hou	3	35	11.7	20t	1
Dishman, Cris, Hou	3	17	5.7	17	0
Ambrose, Ashley, Ind	3	12	4.0	7	0
Reynolds, Ricky, NE	3	6	2.0	4	0
Harris, Corey, Sea	3	-5	-1.7	0	0
Gayle, Shaun, SD	2	99	49.5	99t	1
Sawyer, Corey, Cin	2	61	30.5	61	0
Buchanan, Ray, Ind	2	60	30.0	60	0
Jones, Gary, NYJ	2	51	25.5	49t	1
Dixon, Gerald, Cle	2	48	24.0	30	1
White, William, KC	2	48	24.0	30	0
Hall, Dana, Cle	2	41	20.5	36	0
Joseph, Vance, NYJ	2	39	19.5	39	0
Darby, Matt, Buff	2	37	18.5	37	0
Braxton, Tyrone, Den	2	36	18.0	36	0

	No.	Yards	Avg.	Long	TD
Mays, Alvoid, Pitt	2	35	17.5	32t	1
Langham, Antonio, Cle	2	29	14.5	29	0
Caldwell, Mike, Cle	2	24	12.0	24t	1
Smith, Thomas, Buff	2	23	11.5	13	0
Johnson, Pepper, Cle	2	22	11.0	22	0
Lewis, Mo, NYJ	2	22	11.0	15t	1
Brown, J. B., Mia	2	20	10.0	20	0
Marshall, Wilber, NYJ	2	20	10.0	20	0
Williams, James, Jax	2	19	9.5	16	0
Clark, Willie, SD	2	14	7.0	13	0
Goganious, Keith, Jax	2	11	5.5	6	0
Barnes, Tomur, Hou	2	6	3.0	6	0
Alexander, Elijah, Den	2	5	2.5	4	0
Seau, Junior, SD	2	5	2.5	3	0
Bell, Myron, Pitt	2	4	2.0	4	0
Collins, Andre, Cin	2	3	1.5	3	0
Harris, Odie, Hou	2	0	0.0	0	0
Jackson, Steve, Hou	2	0	0.0	0	0
Paup, Bryce, Buff	2	0	0.0	0	0
Bennett, Cornelius, Buff	1	69	69.0	69t	1
Bishop, Blaine, Hou	1	62	62.0	62t	1
Robinson, Eddie, Hou	1	49	49.0	49t	1
Washington, Mickey, Jax	1	48	48.0	48t	1
Lake, Carnell, Pitt	1	32	32.0	32t	1
Robinson, Eugene, Sea	1	32	32.0	21	0
Shaw, Terrance, SD	1	31	31.0	31	0
Hoskins, Derrick, Oak	1	26	26.0	26	0
Jones, Rod, Cin	1	24	24.0	24	0
Jackson, Calvin, Mia	1	23	23.0	23	0
Jones, Mike, Oak	1	23	23.0	23	0
Ray, Terry, NE	1	21	21.0	21	0
Burris, Jeff, Buff	1	19	19.0	19	0
Hager, Britt, Den	1	19	19.0	19	0
Evans, Greg, Buff	1	18	18.0	18	0
Carrington, Darren, Jax	1	17	17.0	17	0
Glenn, Aaron, NYJ	1	17	17.0	17	0
Jones, Roger, Cin	1	17	17.0	17t	1
Fredrickson, Rob, Oak	1	14	14.0	14	0
Tovar, Steve, Cin	1	13	13.0	13	0
Cox, Bryan, Mia	1	12	12.0	12	0
Oldham, Chris, Pitt	1	12	12.0	12	0
Smeenge, Joel, Jax	1	12	12.0	12	0
Booth, Issac, Cle	1	11	11.0	11	0
Davis, Anthony, KC	1	11	11.0	11	0
Gray, Derwin, Ind	1	10	10.0	10	0
Jones, Henry, Buff	1	10	10.0	10	0
Brock, Matt, NYJ	1	9	9.0	9	0
Grant, Steve, Ind	1	9	9.0	9	0
Watts, Damon, Ind	1	9	9.0	9	0
White, David, Buff	1	9	9.0	9	0
Wooden, Terry, Sea	1	9	9.0	9	0
Beavers, Aubrey, Mia	1	8	8.0	8	0
Collins, Mark, KC	1	8	8.0	8	0
Coryatt, Quentin, Ind	1	6	6.0	6	0
Davidson, Kenny, Hou	1	3	3.0	3	0
Singleton, Chris, Mia	1	3	3.0	3	0
Green, Victor, NYJ	1	2	2.0	2	0
Grow, Monty, Jax	1	2	2.0	2	0
Phillips, Joe, KC	1	2	2.0	2	0
Bruce, Aundray, Oak	1	1	1.0	1t	1
Williams, Darryl, Cin	1	1	1.0	1	0
Anderson, Eddie, Oak	1	0	0.0	0	0
Atkins, Gene, Mia	1	0	0.0	0	0
Belser, Jason, Ind	1	0	0.0	0	0
Buckley, Terrell, Mia	1	0	0.0	0	0
Bush, Lewis, SD	1	0	0.0	0	0
Clark, Vinnie, Jax	1	0	0.0	0	0
Dumas, Mike, Jax	1	0	0.0	0	0
Greene, Kevin, Pitt	1	0	0.0	0	0
Griffin, Don, Cle	1	0	0.0	0	0
Hurst, Maurice, NE	1	0	0.0	0	0
Jones, Selwyn, Sea	1	0	0.0	0	0
Moss, Winston, Sea	1	0	0.0	0	0
Saleaumua, Dan, KC	1	0	0.0	0	0
Seals, Ray, Pitt	1	0	0.0	0	0
Stewart, Michael, Mia	1	0	0.0	0	0
Orlando, Bo, SD	0	37	—	37	0

t = Touchdown
Leader based on interceptions

NFC INTERCEPTIONS—INDIVIDUAL

	No.	Yards	Avg.	Long	TD
Thomas, Orlando, Minn	9	108	12.0	45t	1
Clay, Willie, Det	8	173	21.6	39	0
Thomas, William, Phil	7	104	14.9	37t	1
Brown, Larry, Dall	6	124	20.7	65t	2
Williams, Aeneas, Ariz	6	86	14.3	48t	2
Wright, Toby, StL	6	79	13.2	27	0
Maxie, Brett, Car	6	59	9.8	49	0
Raymond, Corey, Det	6	44	7.3	18	0
Marion, Brock, Dall	6	40	6.7	32t	1
Butler, LeRoy, GB	5	105	21.0	76	0
Glenn, Vencie, NYG	5	91	18.2	75t	1
Mayhew, Martin, TB	5	81	16.2	40	0
Mills, Sam, Car	5	58	11.6	36t	1
Drakeford, Tyronne, SF	5	54	10.8	37	0
Hanks, Merton, SF	5	31	6.2	23	0
Sparks, Phillippi, NYG	5	11	2.2	6	0
McDonald, Tim, SF	4	135	33.8	52t	2
Carter, Tom, Wash	4	116	29.0	51t	1
Lyght, Todd, StL	4	34	8.5	29t	1
Woolford, Donnell, Chi	4	21	5.3	16	0
Spencer, Jimmy, NO	4	11	2.8	9	0
Norton, Ken, SF	3	102	34.0	46	2
McKyer, Tim, Car	3	99	33.0	96t	1
Davis, Eric, SF	3	84	28.0	86t	1
Tuggle, Jessie, Atl	3	84	28.0	49	1
Frank, Donald, Minn	3	72	24.0	42	0
Ross, Kevin, Atl	3	70	23.3	33	0
Phifer, Roman, StL	3	52	17.3	25	0
Green, Darrell, Wash	3	42	14.0	22	1
Lyle, Keith, StL	3	42	14.0	31	0
Mincy, Charles, Minn	3	37	12.3	20	0
Miniefield, Kevin, Chi	3	37	12.3	37	0
Terrell, Pat, Car	3	33	11.0	21	0
Taylor, Terry, Atl	3	31	10.3	31	0
McMillian, Mark, Phil	3	27	9.0	19	0
Richard, Stanley, Wash	3	24	8.0	24	0
Joyner, Seth, Ariz	3	9	3.0	11	0
Lynch, John, TB	3	3	1.0	3	0
Teague, George, GB	2	100	50.0	74	0
Strahan, Michael, NYG	2	56	28.0	56	0
Taylor, Bobby, Phil	2	52	26.0	35	0
Jackson, Alfred M., Minn	2	46	23.0	37t	1
Woodson, Darren, Dall	2	46	23.0	37t	1
Washington, James, Wash	2	35	17.5	21	0
Sanders, Deion, Dall	2	34	17.0	34	0
Joseph, Dwayne, Chi	2	31	15.5	31	0
Allen, Eric, NO	2	28	14.0	28	0
McNeil, Ryan, Det	2	26	13.0	21	0
Evans, Doug, GB	2	24	12.0	24	0
Johnson, Mike, Det	2	23	11.5	14	0
Hunter, Patrick, Ariz	2	21	10.5	21	0
Carter, Marty, Chi	2	20	10.0	15	0
Hughes, Tyrone, NO	2	19	9.5	19	0
Dixon, Ernest, NO	2	17	8.5	11	0
Randolph, Thomas, NYG	2	15	7.5	15	0
Alexander, Brent, Ariz	2	14	7.0	14	0
Pahukoa, Shane, NO	2	12	6.0	12	0
Poole, Tyrone, Car	2	8	4.0	4	0
Brady, Jeff, Minn	2	7	3.5	9	0
Patton, Marvcus, Wash	2	7	3.5	6	0
Romanowski, Bill, Phil	2	5	2.5	7	0
Johnson, D. J., Atl	2	4	2.0	2	0
Matthews, Clay, Atl	2	1	0.5	1	0
Hoage, Terry, Ariz	2	0	0.0	0	0
Woodall, Lee, SF	2	0	0.0	0	0
Parker, Anthony, StL	2	-5	-2.5	3	0
Lynch, Lorenzo, Ariz	1	72	72.0	72t	1
Montgomery, Alton, Atl	1	71	71.0	71t	1
Armstead, Jessie, NYG	1	58	58.0	58t	1
Lumpkin, Sean, NO	1	47	47.0	47t	1
Legette, Tyrone, NO	1	43	43.0	43	0
Phillips, Anthony, Atl	1	43	43.0	43	0
Wooten, Tito, NYG	1	38	38.0	38	0
McDowell, Bubba, Car	1	33	33.0	33	0
Lincoln, Jeremy, Chi	1	32	32.0	32	0
Kragen, Greg, Car	1	29	29.0	29	0
Bankston, Michael, Ariz	1	28	28.0	28	0
Pounds, Darryl, Wash	1	26	26.0	26	0
Simmons, Clyde, Ariz	1	25	25.0	25t	1
Washington, DeWayne, Minn	1	25	25.0	25	0
Dorn, Torin, StL	1	24	24.0	24t	1

	No.	Yards	Avg.	Long	TD
Booty, John, TB	1	21	21.0	21	0
Gouveia, Kurt, Phil	1	20	20.0	20	0
Bouie, Tony, TB	1	19	19.0	19	0
Jackson, Greg, Phil	1	18	18.0	18	0
Del Rio, Jack, Minn	1	15	15.0	15	0
Harrison, Martin, Minn	1	15	15.0	15	0
Myles, Godfrey, Dall	1	15	15.0	15	0
Dodge, Dedrick, SF	1	13	13.0	13	0
Scurlock, Mike, StL	1	13	13.0	13	0
Koonce, George, GB	1	12	12.0	12	0
Martin, Wayne, NO	1	12	12.0	12	0
Stubblefield, Dana, SF	1	12	12.0	12	0
Zordich, Mike, Phil	1	10	10.0	10	0
Prior, Mike, GB	1	9	9.0	9	0
Marts, Lonnie, TB	1	8	8.0	8	0
Tubbs, Winfred, NO	1	6	6.0	6	0
Farr, D'Marco, StL	1	5	5.0	5	0
Sapp, Warren, TB	1	5	5.0	5t	1
Paul, Tito, Ariz	1	4	4.0	4	0
Spielman, Chris, Det	1	4	4.0	4	0
Frazier, Derrick, Phil	1	3	3.0	3	0
McDaniel, Ed, Minn	1	3	3.0	3	0
Newsome, Craig, GB	1	3	3.0	3	0
Brice, Alundis, Dall	1	2	2.0	2	0
Mangum, John, Chi	1	2	2.0	2	0
Minter, Barry, Chi	1	2	2.0	2t	1
Conlan, Shane, StL	1	1	1.0	1	0
Cox, Ron, Chi	1	1	1.0	1	0
Jackson, Rickey, SF	1	1	1.0	1	0
Blades, Bennie, Det	1	0	0.0	0	0
Bush, Devin, Atl	1	0	0.0	0	0
Dimry, Charles, TB	1	0	0.0	0	0
Fuller, Corey, Minn	1	0	0.0	0	0
Harper, Roger, Atl	1	0	0.0	0	0
Holmes, Clayton, Dall	1	0	0.0	0	0
Johnson, Melvin, TB	1	0	0.0	0	0
Kelly, Joe, GB	1	0	0.0	0	0
Malone, Van, Det	1	0	0.0	0	0
Marshall, Anthony, Chi	1	0	0.0	0	0
McCleskey, J. J., NO	1	0	0.0	0	0
Tippins, Ken, Atl	1	0	0.0	0	0
Turner, Scott, Wash	1	0	0.0	0	0
Vanhorse, Sean, Det	1	0	0.0	0	0
Wilburn, Barry, Phil	1	0	0.0	0	0
Barker, Roy, Minn	1	-2	-2.0	-2	0
Pope, Marquez, SF	1	-7	-7.0	-7	0

t = Touchdown
Leader based on interceptions

PUNTING

Average Yards Per Punt
AFC: 45.0—Rick Tuten, Seattle
NFC: 44.3—Sean Landeta, St. Louis

Net Average Yards Per Punt
AFC: 38.6—Bryan Barker, Jacksonville
NFC: 38.2—Jeff Feagles, Arizona

Longest
AFC: 73—Rick Tuten, Seattle at Buffalo, October 15
NFC: 69—Mark Royals, Detroit at Minnesota, September 10

Punts
AFC: 99—Brian Hansen, N.Y. Jets
NFC: 95—Tommy Barnhardt, Carolina

Punts, Game
AFC: 11—Rich Camarillo, Houston at Pittsburgh, December 3 (409 yards)
NFC: 10—Tommy Barnhardt, Carolina at Atlanta, September 3 (OT) (406 yards)
Tommy Barnhardt, Carolina vs. New Orleans, October 22 (446 yards)
Matt Turk, Washington at Kansas City, November 5 (397 yards)
Sean Landeta, St. Louis at N.Y. Jets, December 3 (484 yards)

Team Champion
AFC: 45.0—Seattle
NFC: 44.3—St. Louis

AFC PUNTING—TEAM

	Total Punts	Yards	Long	Avg.	TB	Blk.	Opp. Ret.	Return Yards	Inside the 20	Net. Avg.
Seattle	83	3735	73	45.0	8	0	48	549	21	36.5
San Diego	72	3221	66	44.7	8	0	35	429	28	36.6
Kansas City	91	3990	65	43.8	12	0	42	433	29	36.5
Jacksonville	82	3591	63	43.8	5	0	45	323	19	38.6
Cleveland	65	2831	64	43.6	9	0	34	296	18	36.2
Miami	57	2433	56	42.7	5	0	35	265	15	36.3
Indianapolis	63	2681	69	42.6	7	0	37	436	16	33.4
Cincinnati	70	2913	61	41.6	4	0	27	154	26	38.3
N.Y. Jets	105	4328	67	41.2	11	1	62	753	23	32.0
Denver	54	2209	61	40.9	3	1	25	137	23	37.3
Oakland	76	3089	60	40.6	8	1	38	294	22	34.7
Buffalo	86	3473	60	40.4	7	0	23	224	23	36.2
Houston	79	3180	60	40.3	8	1	35	288	26	34.6
Pittsburgh	59	2368	64	40.1	11	0	22	186	20	33.3
New England	79	3100	57	39.2	8	0	40	342	27	32.9
AFC Total	1121	47142	73	—	114	4	548	5109	336	—
AFC Average	74.7	3142.8	—	42.1	7.6	0.3	36.5	340.6	22.4	35.5

NFC PUNTING—TEAM

	Total Punts	Yards	Long	Avg.	TB	Blk.	Opp. Ret.	Return Yards	Inside the 20	Net. Avg.
St. Louis	83	3679	63	44.3	12	0	38	393	23	36.7
Arizona	72	3150	60	43.8	8	0	32	242	20	38.2
Philadelphia	86	3682	63	42.8	13	1	38	527	20	33.7
Washington	74	3140	60	42.4	9	0	26	173	29	37.7
Tampa Bay	78	3296	61	42.3	7	1	41	335	23	36.2
N.Y. Giants	73	3078	60	42.2	8	0	34	297	15	35.9
Atlanta	67	2759	64	41.2	5	0	28	236	21	36.2
Carolina	96	3938	54	41.0	11	0	39	342	28	35.2
Minnesota	72	2948	60	40.9	6	0	41	446	21	33.1
Green Bay	67	2740	61	40.9	7	2	36	279	26	34.6
Dallas	55	2243	58	40.8	6	0	22	216	19	34.7
San Francisco	57	2312	65	40.6	5	0	26	292	13	33.7
Detroit	60	2427	69	40.5	7	2	29	442	15	30.8
New Orleans	74	2965	53	40.1	5	1	36	233	21	35.6
Chicago	58	2169	61	37.4	6	0	28	257	16	30.9
NFC Total	1072	44526	69	—	115	7	494	4710	310	—
NFC Average	71.5	2968.4	—	41.5	7.7	0.5	32.9	314.0	20.7	35.0
NFL Total	2193	91668	73	—	229	11	1042	9819	646	—
NFL Average	73.1	3055.6	—	41.8	7.6	0.4	34.7	327.3	21.5	35.2

1995 INDIVIDUAL STATISTICS

NFL TOP TEN PUNTERS

	No.	Yards	Long	Avg.	Total Punts	TB	Blk.	Opp. Ret.	Ret. Yds.	In 20	Net. Avg.
Tuten, Rick, Sea	83	3735	73	45.0	83	8	0	48	549	21	36.5
Bennett, Darren, SD	72	3221	66	44.7	72	8	0	35	429	28	36.6
Landeta, Sean, StL	83	3679	63	44.3	83	12	0	38	393	23	36.7
Aguiar, Louie, KC	91	3990	65	43.8	91	12	0	42	433	29	36.5
Barker, Bryan, Jax	82	3591	63	43.8	82	5	0	45	323	19	38.6
Feagles, Jeff, Ariz	72	3150	60	43.8	72	8	0	32	242	20	38.2
Tupa, Tom, Cle	65	2831	64	43.6	65	9	0	34	296	18	36.2
Hutton, Tom, Phil	85	3682	63	43.3	86	13	1	38	527	20	33.7
Roby, Reggie, TB	77	3296	61	42.8	78	7	1	41	335	23	36.2
Kidd, John, Mia	57	2433	56	42.7	57	5	0	35	265	15	36.3

AFC PUNTERS—INDIVIDUAL

	No.	Yards	Long	Avg.	Total Punts	TB	Blk.	Opp. Ret.	Ret. Yds.	In 20	Net. Avg.
Tuten, Rick, Sea	83	3735	73	45.0	83	8	0	48	549	21	36.5
Bennett, Darren, SD	72	3221	66	44.7	72	8	0	35	429	28	36.6
Aguiar, Louie, KC	91	3990	65	43.8	91	12	0	42	433	29	36.5
Barker, Bryan, Jax	82	3591	63	43.8	82	5	0	45	323	19	38.6
Tupa, Tom, Cle	65	2831	64	43.6	65	9	0	34	296	18	36.2
Kidd, John, Mia	57	2433	56	42.7	57	5	0	35	265	15	36.3
Gardocki, Chris, Ind	63	2681	69	42.6	63	7	0	37	436	16	33.4
Rouen, Tom, Den	52	2192	61	42.2	53	3	1	25	137	22	37.6
Johnson, Lee, Cin	68	2861	61	42.1	68	4	0	27	154	26	38.6
Hansen, Brian, NYJ	99	4090	67	41.3	100	10	1	59	703	23	31.9
Gossett, Jeff, Oak	75	3089	60	41.2	76	8	1	38	294	22	34.7
Camarillo, Rich, Hou	77	3165	60	41.1	78	8	1	35	288	26	34.8
Mohr, Chris, Buff	86	3473	60	40.4	86	7	0	23	224	23	36.2
Stark, Rohn, Pitt	59	2368	64	40.1	59	11	0	22	186	20	33.3
Nonqualifiers											
Wagner, Bryan, NE	37	1557	57	42.1	37	4	0	20	168	13	35.4
Silvestri, Don, NYJ	5	238	61	47.6	5	1	0	3	50	0	33.6
Pelfrey, Doug, Cin	2	52	27	26.0	2	0	0	0	0	0	26.0
Bahr, Matt, NE	1	29	29	29.0	1	1	0	0	0	0	9.0
Elam, Jason, Den	1	17	17	17.0	1	0	0	0	0	1	17.0
Del Greco, Al, Hou	1	15	15	15.0	1	0	0	0	0	0	15.0

Leader based on average, minimum 40 punts

NFC PUNTERS—INDIVIDUAL

	No.	Yards	Long	Avg.	Total Punts	TB	Blk.	Opp. Ret.	Ret. Yds.	In 20	Net. Avg.
Landeta, Sean, StL	83	3679	63	44.3	83	12	0	38	393	23	36.7
Feagles, Jeff, Ariz	72	3150	60	43.8	72	8	0	32	242	20	38.2
Hutton, Tom, Phil	85	3682	63	43.3	86	13	1	38	527	20	33.7
Roby, Reggie, TB	77	3296	61	42.8	78	7	1	41	335	23	36.2
Horan, Mike, NYG	72	3063	60	42.5	72	8	0	34	297	15	36.2
Turk, Matt, Wash	74	3140	60	42.4	74	9	0	26	173	29	37.7
Hentrich, Craig, GB	65	2740	61	42.2	67	7	2	36	279	26	34.6
Royals, Mark, Det	57	2393	69	42.0	59	6	2	29	442	15	31.0
Stryzinski, Dan, Atl	67	2759	64	41.2	67	5	0	28	236	21	36.2
Barnhardt, Tommy, Car	95	3906	54	41.1	95	11	0	39	342	27	35.2
Saxon, Mike, Minn	72	2948	60	40.9	72	6	0	41	446	21	33.1
Jett, John, Dall	53	2166	58	40.9	53	6	0	22	216	17	34.5
Wilmsmeyer, Klaus, NO	73	2965	53	40.6	74	5	1	36	233	21	35.6
Thompson, Tommy, SF	57	2312	65	40.6	57	5	0	26	292	13	33.7
Sauerbrun, Todd, Chi	55	2080	61	37.8	55	6	0	27	248	16	31.1
O'Neill, Pat, NE-Chi	44	1603	57	36.4	44	3	0	21	183	14	30.9
Nonqualifiers											
Boniol, Chris, Dall	2	77	56	38.5	2	0	0	0	0	2	38.5
Hanson, Jason, Det	1	34	34	34.0	1	1	0	0	0	0	14.0
Kasay, John, Car	1	32	32	32.0	1	0	0	0	0	1	32.0
Brown, Dave, NYG	1	15	15	15.0	1	0	0	0	0	0	15.0

Leader based on average, minimum 40 punts

PUNT RETURNS

Yards Per Return
- **NFC:** 13.2—David Palmer, Minnesota
- **AFC:** 11.6—Andre Coleman, San Diego

Yards
- **AFC:** 540—Tamarick Vanover, Kansas City
- **NFC:** 475—Eric Guliford, Carolina

Yards, Game
- **AFC:** 133—Andre Coleman, San Diego at Philadelphia, September 17 (4 returns - TD)
- **NFC:** 126—Dexter Carter, San Francisco vs. Minnesota, December 18 (4 returns - TD)

Longest
- **AFC:** 89—Joey Galloway, Seattle vs. N.Y. Giants, November 5 - TD
- **NFC:** 78—Dexter Carter, San Francisco vs. Minnesota, December 18 - TD

Returns
- **NFC:** 53—Todd Kinchen, St. Louis
- **AFC:** 51—Tamarick Vanover, Kansas City

Returns, Game
- **AFC:** 9—Andre Hastings, Pittsburgh vs. Cleveland, November 13 (131 yards)
- **NFC:** 7—Eric Guliford, Carolina vs. Indianapolis, December 3 (107 yards)
  Todd Kinchen, St. Louis at N.Y. Jets, December 3 (65 yards)

Fair Catches
- **NFC:** 22—Eric Guliford, Carolina
  Tyrone Hughes, New Orleans
- **AFC:** 20—Mel Gray, Houston

Touchdowns
- **AFC:** 1—Derrick Alexander, Cleveland
  Andre Coleman, San Diego
  Joey Galloway, Seattle
  Andre Hastings, Pittsburgh
  Tamarick Vanover, Kansas City
- **NFC:** 1—Dexter Carter, San Francisco
  Eric Guliford, Carolina
  Eric Metcalf, Atlanta
  Brian Mitchell, Washington
  David Palmer, Minnesota

Team Champion
- **NFC:** 12.1—Washington
- **AFC:** 11.5—Denver

AFC PUNT RETURNS—TEAM

	No.	FC	Yards	Avg.	Long	TD
Denver	31	18	358	11.5	44	0
San Diego	31	15	338	10.9	88t	1
Cleveland	25	16	255	10.2	69t	1
Buffalo	47	11	476	10.1	44	0
Oakland	37	9	374	10.1	38	0
Pittsburgh	48	8	474	9.9	72t	1
Houston	35	21	339	9.7	20	0
Kansas City	58	7	561	9.7	86t	1
Seattle	40	13	384	9.6	89t	1
New England	45	17	383	8.5	23	0
N.Y. Jets	38	17	323	8.5	22	0
Jacksonville	29	8	243	8.4	40	0
Miami	24	12	163	6.8	24	0
Indianapolis	29	12	192	6.6	32	0
Cincinnati	21	13	103	4.9	21	0
AFC Total	538	197	4966	9.2	89t	5
AFC Average	35.9	13.1	331.1	9.2	—	0.3

NFC PUNT RETURNS—TEAM

	No.	FC	Yards	Avg.	Long	TD
Washington	26	15	315	12.1	59t	1
Minnesota	35	14	414	11.8	74t	1
Dallas	23	17	255	11.1	45	0
St. Louis	55	7	587	10.7	62	0
Carolina	49	23	500	10.2	62t	1
Philadelphia	29	16	293	10.1	38	0
San Francisco	27	17	272	10.1	78t	1
Tampa Bay	29	10	293	10.1	45	0
Atlanta	39	14	383	9.8	66t	1
New Orleans	29	23	268	9.2	74	0
Green Bay	61	7	515	8.4	26	0
Detroit	24	17	189	7.9	28	0
Arizona	23	11	172	7.5	16	0
Chicago	24	14	179	7.5	39	0
N.Y. Giants	31	10	218	7.0	21	0
NFC Total	504	215	4853	9.6	78t	5
NFC Average	33.6	14.3	323.5	9.6	—	0.3
League Total	1042	412	9819	—	89t	10
League Average	34.7	13.7	327.3	9.4	—	0.3

NFL TOP TEN PUNT RETURNERS

	No.	FC	Yards	Avg.	Long	TD
Palmer, David, Minn	26	13	342	13.2	74t	1
Mitchell, Brian, Wash	25	15	315	12.6	59t	1
Coleman, Andre, SD	28	14	326	11.6	88t	1
Burris, Jeff, Buff	20	1	229	11.5	40	0
Milburn, Glyn, Den	31	17	354	11.4	44	0
Guliford, Eric, Car	43	22	475	11.0	62t	1
Vanover, Tamarick, KC	51	4	540	10.6	86t	1
Carter, Dexter, NYJ-SF	30	15	309	10.3	78t	1
Howard, Desmond, Jax	24	8	246	10.3	40	0
Jordan, Charles, GB	21	2	213	10.1	18	0

AFC—INDIVIDUAL PUNT RETURNERS

	No.	FC	Yards	Avg.	Long	TD
Coleman, Andre, SD	28	14	326	11.6	88t	1
Burris, Jeff, Buff	20	1	229	11.5	40	0
Milburn, Glyn, Den	31	17	354	11.4	44	0
Vanover, Tamarick, KC	51	4	540	10.6	86t	1
Howard, Desmond, Jax	24	8	246	10.3	40	0
Brown, Tim, Oak	36	9	364	10.1	38	0
Gray, Mel, Hou	30	20	303	10.1	20	0
Galloway, Joey, Sea	36	12	360	10.0	89t	1
Hastings, Andre, Pitt	48	8	474	9.9	72t	1
Meggett, David, NE	45	17	383	8.5	23	0
McDuffie, O. J., Mia	24	12	163	6.8	24	0
Nonqualifiers						
Tasker, Steve, Buff	17	7	204	12.0	44	0
Sydner, Jeff, NYJ	17	9	178	10.5	22	0
Buchanan, Ray, Ind	16	4	113	7.1	17	0
McCardell, Keenan, Cle	13	14	93	7.2	17	0
Bronson, Ben, Ind	13	6	79	6.1	32	0
Alexander, Derrick, Cle	9	0	122	13.6	69t	1
Sawyer, Corey, Cin	9	8	58	6.4	21	0
Bieniemy, Eric, Cin	7	1	47	6.7	10	0
Brooks, Bill, Buff	6	2	35	5.8	15	0
Hannah, Travis, Hou	5	1	36	7.2	11	0
Pickens, Carl, Cin	5	2	-2	-0.4	4	0
Penn, Chris, KC	4	2	12	3.0	5	0
Hunter, Ernest, Cle	3	0	40	13.3	17	0
Harris, Ronnie, Sea	3	0	23	7.7	10	0
Fletcher, Terrell, SD	3	1	12	4.0	11	0
Hughes, Danan, KC	3	1	9	3.0	8	0
Copeland, Russell, Buff	2	1	8	4.0	7	0
Tillman, Cedric, Jax	2	0	6	3.0	9	0
Givins, Ernest, Jax	2	0	-7	-3.5	-1	0
Hobbs, Daryl, Oak	1	0	10	10.0	10	0
Robinson, Eugene, Sea	1	1	1	1.0	1	0
Jourdain, Yonel, Buff	1	0	0	0.0	0	0
Thomas, Damon, Buff	1	0	0	0.0	0	0
Jackson, Willie, Jax	1	0	-2	-2.0	-2	0
Crockett, Ray, Den	0	0	4	—	4	0
Bailey, Thomas, Cin	0	1	0	—	—	0
Griffin, Don, Cle	0	2	0	—	—	0
Query, Jeff, Cin	0	1	0	—	—	0

1995 INDIVIDUAL STATISTICS

	No.	FC	Yards	Avg.	Long	TD
Smith, Rod, Den	0	1	0	—	—	0
Stablein, Brian, Ind	0	2	0	—	—	0

t = Touchdown
Leader based on average return, minimum 20 returns

NFC—INDIVIDUAL PUNT RETURNERS

	No.	FC	Yards	Avg.	Long	TD
Palmer, David, Minn	26	13	342	13.2	74t	1
Mitchell, Brian, Wash	25	15	315	12.6	59t	1
Guliford, Eric, Car	43	22	475	11.0	62t	1
Carter, Dexter, NYJ-SF	30	15	309	10.3	78t	1
Jordan, Charles, GB	21	2	213	10.1	18	0
Edmonds, Bobby Joe, TB	29	10	293	10.1	45	0
Metcalf, Eric, Atl	39	14	383	9.8	66t	1
Hughes, Tyrone, NO	28	22	262	9.4	74	0
Graham, Jeff, Chi	23	14	183	8.0	39	0
Freeman, Antonio, GB	37	3	292	7.9	26	0
Kinchen, Todd, StL	53	7	416	7.8	27	0

Nonqualifiers	No.	FC	Yards	Avg.	Long	TD
Williams, Kevin, Dall	18	15	166	9.2	30	0
Edwards, Anthony, Ariz	18	11	131	7.3	16	0
Martin, Kelvin, Phil	17	10	214	12.6	38	0
Marshall, Arthur, NYG	12	7	96	8.0	21	0
Carpenter, Rob, Phil	12	6	79	6.6	22	0
Harrell, Gary, NYG	12	3	76	6.3	17	0
Taylor, John, SF	11	9	56	5.1	11	0
Morton, Johnnie, Det	7	4	48	6.9	16	0
Lewis, Thomas, NYG	6	0	46	7.7	14	0
Turner, Vernon, Det	6	1	39	6.5	16	0
Carrier, Mark, Car	6	1	25	4.2	9	0
Lee, Amp, Minn	5	1	50	10.0	17	0
Perriman, Brett, Det	5	6	50	10.0	13	0
Clay, Willie, Det	5	5	49	9.8	28	0
Singleton, Nate, SF	5	1	27	5.4	19	0
Reeves, Bryan, Ariz	4	0	41	10.3	14	0
Holmes, Clayton, Dall	4	1	35	8.8	13	0
Mincy, Charles, Minn	4	0	22	5.5	8	0
Bailey, Johnny, StL	2	0	42	21.0	22	0
Sanders, Deion, Dall	1	1	54	54.0	43	0
Thomas, Chris, SF	1	0	25	25.0	25	0
Prior, Mike, GB	1	2	10	10.0	10	0
Legette, Tyrone, NO	1	0	6	6.0	6	0
Carter, Anthony, Det	1	1	3	3.0	3	0
Dowdell, Marcus, Ariz	1	0	0	0.0	0	0
Evans, Doug, GB	1	0	0	0.0	0	0
Hanks, Merton, SF	1	0	0	0.0	0	0
Ingram, Mark, GB	1	0	0	0.0	0	0
Turner, Scott, Wash	1	0	0	0.0	0	0
Young, Rodney, NYG	1	0	0	0.0	0	0
Lundy, Dennis, Chi	1	0	-4	-4.0	-4	0
Thomas, Johnny, StL	0	0	61	—	61	0
Bruce, Isaac, StL	0	0	52	—	52	0
Lyght, Todd, StL	0	0	16	—	16	0
Buck, Vince, NO	0	1	0	—	—	0

t = Touchdown
Leader based on average return, minimum 20 returns

KICKOFF RETURNS

Yards Per Return
AFC: 27.7—Ron Carpenter, N.Y. Jets
NFC: 25.6—Brian Mitchell, Washington

Yards
NFC: 1617—Tyrone Hughes, New Orleans
AFC: 1411—Andre Coleman, San Diego

Yards, Game
NFC: 207—Qadry Ismail, Minnesota at Detroit, November 23 (8 returns)
AFC: 191—Dexter Carter, N.Y. Jets vs. Oakland, October 1 (7 returns)

Longest
AFC: 99—Tamarick Vanover, Kansas City at Seattle, September 3 - TD
NFC: 91—Thomas Lewis, N.Y. Giants vs. Washington, December 10 - TD

Returns
NFC: 66—Tyrone Hughes, New Orleans
AFC: 62—Andre Coleman, San Diego

Returns, Game
AFC: 8—Raghib Ismail, Oakland at Seattle, December 17 (137 yards)
NFC: 8—Tyrone Hughes, New Orleans at Minnesota, November 19 (156 yards)
Qadry Ismail, Minnesota at Detroit, November 23 (207 yards)
Jamal Anderson, Atlanta at Arizona, November 26 (OT) (180 yards)

Touchdowns
AFC: 2—Andre Coleman, San Diego
Tamarick Vanover, Kansas City
NFC: 1—Thomas Lewis, N.Y. Giants
Derrick Witherspoon, Philadelphia

Team Champion
NFC: 23.9—Washington
AFC: 23.7—Kansas City

AFC KICKOFF RETURNS—TEAM

	No.	Yards	Avg.	Long	TD
Kansas City	55	1306	23.7	99t	2
Denver	60	1392	23.2	86	0
Miami	59	1338	22.7	55	0
New England	75	1691	22.5	62	0
Seattle	72	1620	22.5	70	0
Cincinnati	80	1788	22.4	62	0
Pittsburgh	69	1530	22.2	57	0
Oakland	64	1390	21.7	84t	1
San Diego	70	1502	21.5	92t	2
Indianapolis	63	1332	21.1	95t	1
N.Y. Jets	77	1613	20.9	58	0
Jacksonville	74	1532	20.7	94t	1
Houston	64	1277	20.0	54	0
Cleveland	74	1455	19.7	42	0
Buffalo	70	1302	18.6	42	0
AFC Total	1026	22068	21.5	99t	7
AFC Average	68.4	1471.2	21.5	—	0.5

NFC KICKOFF RETURNS—TEAM

	No.	Yards	Avg.	Long	TD
Washington	69	1646	23.9	59	0
New Orleans	73	1690	23.2	83	0
Minnesota	72	1612	22.4	71	0
St. Louis	73	1618	22.2	50	0
Dallas	58	1276	22.0	46	0
Atlanta	70	1506	21.5	47	0
Carolina	55	1163	21.1	40	0
Green Bay	61	1282	21.0	45	0
Philadelphia	71	1487	20.9	86t	1
Arizona	73	1519	20.8	70	0
N.Y. Giants	70	1448	20.7	91t	1
Chicago	71	1459	20.5	61	0
Detroit	67	1367	20.4	51	0
San Francisco	58	1183	20.4	46	0
Tampa Bay	76	1443	19.0	44	0
NFC Total	1017	21699	21.3	91t	2
NFC Average	67.8	1446.6	21.3	—	0.1
League Total	2043	43767	—	99t	9
League Average	68.1	1458.9	21.4	—	0.3

NFL TOP TEN KICKOFF RETURNERS

	No.	Yards	Avg.	Long	TD
Carpenter, Ron, NYJ	20	553	27.7	58	0
Milburn, Glyn, Den	47	1269	27.0	86	0
Kaufman, Napoleon, Oak	22	572	26.0	84t	1
Mitchell, Brian, Wash	55	1408	25.6	59	0
Vanover, Tamarick, KC	43	1095	25.5	99t	2
Meggett, David, NE	38	964	25.4	62	0
Broussard, Steve, Sea	43	1064	24.7	70	0
Ismail, Qadry, Minn	42	1037	24.7	71	0
Hughes, Tyrone, NO	66	1617	24.5	83	0
McDuffie, O. J., Mia	23	564	24.5	47	0

AFC KICKOFF RETURNERS—INDIVIDUAL

	No.	Yards	Avg.	Long	TD
Carpenter, Ron, NYJ	20	553	27.7	58	0
Milburn, Glyn, Den	47	1269	27.0	86	0
Kaufman, Napoleon, Oak	22	572	26.0	84t	1

	No.	Yards	Avg.	Long	TD
Vanover, Tamarick, KC	43	1095	25.5	99t	2
Meggett, David, NE	38	964	25.4	62	0
Broussard, Steve, Sea	43	1064	24.7	70	0
McDuffie, O. J., Mia	23	564	24.5	47	0
Mills, Ernie, Pitt	54	1306	24.2	57	0
Bailey, Aaron, Ind	21	495	23.6	95t	1
Coleman, Andre, SD	62	1411	22.8	92t	2
Smith, Jimmy L., Jax	24	540	22.5	89t	1
Gray, Mel, Hou	f53	1183	22.3	54	0
Hunter, Ernest, Cle	23	508	22.1	37	0
Dunn, David, Cin	50	1092	21.8	45	0
Brown, Troy, NE	31	672	21.7	38	0
Humphrey, Ronald, Ind	21	453	21.6	64	0
Holmes, Darick, Buff	39	799	20.5	42	0
Alexander, Derrick, Cle	21	419	20.0	42	0
Ismail, Raghib, Oak	36	706	19.6	43	0
Nonqualifiers					
Jackson, Willie, Jax	19	404	21.3	47	0
Harris, Corey, Sea	19	397	20.9	35	0
Jourdain, Yonel, Buff	19	348	18.3	41	0
Spikes, Irving, Mia	18	378	21.0	55	0
Hill, Jeff, Cin	17	454	26.7	55	0
Marsh, Curtis, Jax	15	323	21.5	39	0
Warren, Lamont, Ind	15	315	21.0	34	0
Hill, Randal, Mia	12	287	23.9	33	0
Howard, Desmond, Jax	10	178	17.8	24	0
Bates, Michael, Cle	9	176	19.6	38	0
McCardell, Keenan, Cle	9	161	17.9	28	0
Bieniemy, Eric, Cin	8	168	21.0	34	0
Moore, Ronald, NYJ	8	166	20.8	46	0
Craver, Aaron, Den	7	50	7.1	13	0
Thompson, Leroy, KC	6	152	25.3	40	0
Tindale, Tim, Buff	6	62	10.3	20	0
Baxter, Fred, NYJ	6	36	6.0	12	0
Byner, Earnest, Cle	5	98	19.6	27	0
Jones, Calvin, Oak	5	92	18.4	22	0
McAfee, Fred, Pitt	5	56	11.2	25	0
Pegram, Erric, Pitt	4	85	21.3	28	0
Sydner, Jeff, NYJ	4	80	20.0	35	0
Fletcher, Terrell, SD	4	65	16.3	30	0
Strong, Mack, Sea	4	65	16.3	30	0
Smith, Rod, Den	4	54	13.5	17	0
Harmon, Ronnie, SD	4	25	6.3	9	0
Powers, Ricky, Cle	3	54	18.0	20	0
Thomas, Rodney, Hou	3	48	16.0	23	0
Sawyer, Corey, Cin	2	50	25.0	28	0
Johnson, Charles, Pitt	2	47	23.5	40	0
Jordan, Randy, Jax	2	41	20.5	21	0
Green, Chris, Buff	2	37	18.5	22	0
Dunbar, Vaughn, Jax	2	32	16.0	21	0
Galloway, Joey, Sea	2	30	15.0	18	0
Penn, Chris, KC	2	26	13.0	25	0
Brady, Kyle, NYJ	2	25	12.5	14	0
Williams, Ronnie, Mia	2	20	10.0	12	0
Bruener, Mark, Pitt	2	19	9.5	10	0
Gisler, Mike, NE	2	19	9.5	11	0
Frederick, Mike, Cle	2	16	8.0	11	0
Valerio, Joe, KC	2	15	7.5	13	0
Butts, Marion, Hou	2	14	7.0	14	0
Morrison, Steve, Ind	2	6	3.0	6	0
Hill, Sean, Mia	1	38	38.0	38	0
Bronson, Ben, Ind	1	31	31.0	31	0
Harris, Ronnie, Sea	1	29	29.0	29	0
Benfatti, Lou, NYJ	1	25	25.0	25	0
Buchanan, Ray, Ind	1	22	22.0	22	0
Dar Dar, Kirby, Mia	1	22	22.0	22	0
Hobbs, Daryl, Oak	1	20	20.0	20	0
Pike, Mark, Buff	1	20	20.0	20	0
Smith, Lamar, Sea	1	20	20.0	20	0
Hughes, Danan, KC	1	18	18.0	18	0
Joseph, James, Cin	1	17	17.0	17	0
Buckley, Terrell, Mia	1	16	16.0	16	0
Belser, Jason, Ind	1	15	15.0	15	0
Lee, Kevin, NE	1	14	14.0	14	0
Robinson, Jeff, Den	1	14	14.0	14	0
Hoard, Leroy, Cle	1	13	13.0	13	0
Louchiey, Corey, Buff	1	13	13.0	13	0
Milner, Billy, Mia	1	13	13.0	13	0
Glenn, Aaron, NYJ	1	12	12.0	12	0
Irvin, Ken, Buff	1	12	12.0	12	0
Cline, Tony, Buff	1	11	11.0	11	0
Smith, Steve, Sea	1	11	11.0	11	0
Dixon, Gerald, Cle	1	10	10.0	10	0
Gibson, Oliver, Pitt	1	10	10.0	10	0
Von Oelhoffen, Kimo, Cin	1	10	10.0	10	0
Griffith, Richard, Jax	1	9	9.0	9	0
Frisch, David, NE	1	8	8.0	8	0
Burke, John, NE	1	7	7.0	7	0
Grant, Rupert, NE	1	7	7.0	7	0
Greene, Tracy, Pitt	1	7	7.0	7	0
Bowden, Joe, Hou	1	6	6.0	6	0
Smith, Otis, NYJ	1	6	6.0	6	0
Burns, Keith, Den	1	5	5.0	5	0
Lewis, Roderick, Hou	1	5	5.0	5	0
Maston, Le'Shai, Jax	1	5	5.0	5	0
Murrell, Adrian, NYJ	1	5	5.0	5	0
McKnight, James, Sea	1	4	4.0	4	0
McDaniels, Pellom, KC	1	0	0.0	0	0
Collins, Andre, Cin	1	-3	-3.0	-3	0
Wortham, Barron, Hou	1	-3	-3.0	-3	0
Barnes, Tomur, Hou	1	-4	-4.0	-4	0
Radecic, Scott, Ind	1	-5	-5.0	-5	0
Engel, Greg, SD	0	1	—	1	0
Wainright, Frank, Phil-Mia	f0	0	—	—	0

t = Touchdown
f = Fair Catch
Leader based on average return, minimum 20 returns

NFC KICKOFF RETURNERS—INDIVIDUAL

	No.	Yards	Avg.	Long	TD
Mitchell, Brian, Wash	55	1408	25.6	59	0
Ismail, Qadry, Minn	42	1037	24.7	71	0
Hughes, Tyrone, NO	66	1617	24.5	83	0
Thomas, Johnny, StL	32	752	23.5	46	0
Freeman, Antonio, GB	24	556	23.2	45	0
Williams, Kevin, Dall	49	1108	22.6	43	0
Anderson, Jamal, Atl	24	541	22.5	35	0
Carter, Dexter, NYJ-SF	56	1227	21.9	57	0
Terry, Ryan, Ariz	37	808	21.8	53	0
Lewis, Nate, Chi	42	904	21.5	52	0
Walker, Herschel, NYG	41	881	21.5	67	0
Kinchen, Todd, StL	35	743	21.2	50	0
Jordan, Charles, GB	21	444	21.1	33	0
Preston, Roell, Atl	30	627	20.9	44	0
Garner, Charlie, Phil	29	590	20.3	41	0
Edmonds, Bobby Joe, TB	58	1147	19.8	44	0
Martin, Kelvin, Phil	20	388	19.4	38	0
Nonqualifiers					
Rivers, Ron, Det	19	420	22.1	51	0
Witherspoon, Derrick, Phil	18	459	25.5	86t	1
Timpson, Michael, Chi	18	420	23.3	51	0
Morton, Johnnie, Det	18	390	21.7	32	0
Dowdell, Marcus, Ariz	18	344	19.1	28	0
By'Not'e, Butler, Car	18	335	18.6	35	0
Willis, Jamal, SF	17	427	25.1	39	0
Palmer, David, Minn	17	354	20.8	42	0
Turner, Vernon, Det	17	323	19.0	43	0
Ellison, Jerry, TB	15	261	17.4	33	0
Baldwin, Randy, Car	14	316	22.6	36	0
Metcalf, Eric, Atl	12	278	23.2	47	0
Stone, Dwight, Car	12	269	22.4	40	0
Johnson, LeShon, Ariz	11	259	23.5	70	0
Wheatley, Tyrone, NYG	10	186	18.6	32	0
Lewis, Thomas, NYG	9	257	28.6	91t	1
Beebe, Don, Car	9	215	23.9	38	0
Jervey, Travis, GB	8	165	20.6	28	0
Bell, William, Wash	8	121	15.1	34	0
Holmes, Clayton, Dall	5	134	26.8	46	0
Lee, Amp, Minn	5	100	20.0	24	0
Bailey, Johnny, StL	5	97	19.4	28	0
Kozlowski, Brian, NYG	5	75	15.0	17	0
Perriman, Brett, Det	5	65	13.0	23	0
Ervins, Ricky, SF	5	32	6.4	14	0
Williams, Allen, Det	4	100	25.0	32	0
Warren, Terrence, SF	4	67	16.8	21	0
Phillips, Bobby, Minn	4	60	15.0	23	0
Shepherd, Leslie, Wash	3	85	28.3	36	0
Edwards, Anthony, Ariz	3	50	16.7	24	0
Thomas, Chris, SF	3	49	16.3	20	0
Morgan, Anthony, GB	3	46	15.3	20	0
George, Ron, Atl	3	45	15.0	21	0
Walsh, Chris, Minn	3	42	14.0	18	0
Lundy, Dennis, Hou-Chi	3	39	13.0	17	0

	No.	Yards	Avg.	Long	TD
Dalman, Chris, SF	3	29	9.7	12	0
Green, Robert, Chi	3	29	9.7	19	0
Carter, Tony, Chi	3	24	8.0	9	0
Carter, Anthony, Det	2	46	23.0	23	0
Jones, Chris T., Phil	2	46	23.0	26	0
Caldwell, Mike, SF	2	40	20.0	20	0
Primus, Greg, Chi	2	39	19.5	22	0
Ned, Derrick, NO	2	33	16.5	19	0
Buckley, Curtis, TB	2	29	14.5	18	0
Neal, Lorenzo, NO	2	28	14.0	16	0
Higgs, Mark, Ariz	2	26	13.0	17	0
Brooks, Robert, GB	1	28	28.0	28	0
Pinkney, Lovell, StL	1	26	26.0	26	0
Harrell, Gary, NYG	1	23	23.0	23	0
Philyaw, Dino, Car	1	23	23.0	23	0
Tillman, Lewis, Chi	1	20	20.0	20	0
Gerak, John, Minn	1	19	19.0	19	0
Anderson, Steve, Ariz	1	17	17.0	17	0
Jurkovic, John, GB	1	17	17.0	17	0
Walker, Adam, SF	1	17	17.0	17	0
Marion, Brock, Dall	1	16	16.0	16	0
Thomason, Jeff, GB	1	16	16.0	16	0
Centers, Larry, Ariz	1	15	15.0	15	0
Sanders, Deion, Dall	1	15	15.0	15	0
Tippins, Ken, Atl	1	15	15.0	15	0
Sloan, David, Det	1	14	14.0	14	0
Asher, Jamie, Wash	1	13	13.0	13	0
Douglas, Omar, NYG	1	13	13.0	13	0
Graham, Jeff, Chi	1	12	12.0	12	0
Jenkins, James, Wash	1	12	12.0	12	0
Arthur, Mike, GB	1	10	10.0	10	0
Owens, Dan, Det	1	9	9.0	9	0
Schwantz, Jim, Dall	1	9	9.0	9	0
Way, Charles, NYG	1	8	8.0	8	0
Vanderbeek, Matt, Wash	1	7	7.0	7	0
Armstrong, Tyji, TB	1	6	6.0	6	0
Smith, Irv, NO	1	6	6.0	6	0
Walls, Wesley, NO	1	6	6.0	6	0
Butcher, Paul, Car	1	5	5.0	5	0
Zatechka, Rob, NYG	1	5	5.0	5	0
Saxon, James, Phil	1	3	3.0	3	0
McCrary, Fred, Phil	1	1	1.0	1	0
McCleskey, J. J., NO	1	0	0.0	0	0
Mickens, Terry, GB	1	0	0.0	0	0
Widmer, Corey, NYG	1	0	0.0	0	0
Watkins, Kendell, Dall	1	-6	-6.0	-6	0

t = Touchdown
f = Fair Catch
Leader based on average return, minimum 20 returns

FUMBLES

Most Fumbles
NFC: 16—Dave Krieg, Arizona
AFC: 12—Chris Chandler, Houston
Boomer Esiason, N.Y. Jets

Most Fumbles, Game
AFC: 4—Scott Zolak, New England at Atlanta, October 1
NFC: 3—Dave Krieg, Arizona vs. Minnesota, November 12 (OT)
Kerry Collins, Carolina at New Orleans, November 26
Trent Dilfer, Tampa Bay at Minnesota, December 3
Garrison Hearst, Arizona at Philadelphia, December 17
Warren Moon, Minnesota at San Francisco, December 18
Rashaan Salaam, Chicago vs. Philadelphia, December 24

Own Fumbles Recovered
AFC: 7—Stan Humphries, San Diego
NFC: 7—Dave Krieg, Arizona

Most Own Fumbles Recovered, Game
AFC: 2—Chris Chandler, Houston at Jacksonville, September 3
Bubby Brister, N.Y. Jets vs. Miami, October 22
Stan Humphries, San Diego vs. Kansas City, November 12
Justin Armour, Buffalo at N.Y. Jets, November 19
NFC: 2—Gus Frerotte, Washington vs. Oakland, September 10
Dave Krieg, Arizona at Detroit, September 17
Kerry Collins, Carolina vs. New Orleans, October 22
Rodney Peete, Philadelphia vs. St. Louis, October 29
Dave Krieg, Arizona vs. Minnesota, November 12 (OT)

Opponents' Fumbles Recovered
AFC: 4—Blaine Bishop, Houston
Rob Fredrickson, Oakland
Harald Hasselbach, Denver
NFC: 4—Vince Buck, New Orleans
Mike Johnson, Detroit
Sam Mills, Carolina
Anthony Parker, St. Louis
John Thierry, Chicago
Orlando Thomas, Minnesota

Most Opponents' Fumbles Recovered, Game
NFC: 3—John Thierry, Chicago vs. Houston, October 22
AFC: 2—Bobby Houston, N.Y. Jets vs. Jacksonville, September 17
Levon Kirkland, Pittsburgh vs. Minnesota, September 24
Darren Perry, Pittsburgh at Chicago, November 5 (OT)
Ted Johnson, New England vs. N.Y. Jets, December 10

Yards
NFC: 98—Lee Woodall, San Francisco
AFC: 83—Antonio Edwards, Seattle

Longest
NFC: 96—Lee Woodall, San Francisco vs. Buffalo, December 3 - TD
AFC: 83—Antonio Edwards, Seattle at Denver, December 10 - TD

AFC FUMBLES—TEAM

	Fum.	Own. Rec.	Fum. OB	TD	Opp. Rec.	TD	Fum. Yards	Tot. Rec.
Kansas City	17	6	0	0	17	2	74	23
Indianapolis	21	8	2	0	13	1	22	21
Cincinnati	23	5	4	0	12	0	10	17
Jacksonville	23	8	2	0	11	0	4	19
Miami	24	12	0	0	16	1	28	28
Pittsburgh	24	9	2	0	12	2	74	21
Seattle	24	10	5	0	9	2	158	19
Buffalo	25	13	0	1	11	0	4	24
Cleveland	25	11	3	0	7	0	17	18
Denver	25	8	1	0	13	1	90	21
Oakland	25	10	2	0	22	3	123	32
San Diego	30	16	2	0	10	2	20	26
New England	32	11	1	1	14	1	133	25
Houston	36	16	0	0	17	0	22	33
N.Y. Jets	38	17	3	0	17	1	9	34
AFC Total	392	160	27	2	201	16	788	361
AFC Average	26.1	10.7	1.8	0.1	13.4	1.1	52.5	24.1

NFC FUMBLES—TEAM

	Fum.	Own. Rec.	Fum. OB	TD	Opp. Rec.	TD	Fum. Yards	Tot. Rec.
New Orleans	19	5	3	0	12	0	18	17
Atlanta	21	12	0	0	12	0	-9	24
Detroit	21	7	1	0	13	1	101	20
San Francisco	21	8	2	1	8	2	178	16
Green Bay	22	15	1	0	3	1	4	18
Dallas	24	9	3	0	6	0	47	15
Washington	24	12	2	0	18	1	-15	30
Tampa Bay	25	10	1	0	16	1	73	26
Chicago	26	9	1	0	13	0	-1	22
N.Y. Giants	27	9	3	1	15	1	112	24
St. Louis	27	9	2	0	14	3	140	23
Carolina	28	10	2	0	15	1	8	25
Minnesota	29	14	2	0	15	2	33	29
Philadelphia	31	11	3	0	19	4	140	30
Arizona	41	19	3	1	23	0	-8	42
NFC Total	386	159	29	3	202	17	821	361
NFC Average	25.7	10.6	1.9	0.2	13.5	1.1	54.7	24.1
NFL Total	778	319	56	5	403	33	1609	722
NFL Average	25.9	10.6	1.9	0.2	13.4	1.1	53.6	24.1

Fum OB = Fumbled out of bounds, includes fumbled through the end zone. Fumbled through the end zone, ball awarded to opponents: Dallas (ball awarded to Washington), San Francisco (ball awarded to Carolina).

AFC FUMBLES—INDIVIDUAL

	Fum.	Own Rec.	Opp. Rec.	Yards	Tot. Rec.
Aldridge, Allen, Den	0	0	1	0	1
Alexander, Derrick, Cle	3	1	0	0	1
Allen, Marcus, KC	2	1	0	0	1
Anders, Kimble, KC	1	0	0	0	0
Anderson, Eddie, Oak	0	0	2	0	2
Anderson, Richie, NYJ	2	0	0	0	0
Armour, Justin, Buf	1	2	0	0	2

	Fum.	Own Rec.	Opp. Rec.	Yards	Tot. Rec.
Armstrong, Bruce, NE	0	1	0	0	1
Armstrong, Trace, Mia	0	0	1	0	1
Atkins, Gene, Mia	0	0	1	1	1
Atkins, James, Sea	0	1	0	0	1
Bailey, Aaron, Ind	0	1	0	0	1
Ball, Eric, Oak	0	0	1	0	1
Ball, Jerry, Oak	0	0	1	0	1
Barnes, Tomur, Hou	0	0	1	0	1
Barnett, Troy, NE	0	0	1	0	1
Barrow, Micheal, Hou	0	0	1	0	1
Baxter, Fred, NYJ	1	1	1	8	2
Bayless, Martin, KC	0	0	1	0	1
Bell, Myron, Pitt	0	1	0	0	1
Belser, Jason, Ind	0	0	2	0	2
Bennett, Cornelius, Buf	0	0	2	0	2
Bennett, Tony, Ind	0	0	1	32	1
Bernstine, Rod, Den	0	1	0	0	1
Beuerlein, Steve, Jax	3	0	0	0	0
Bieniemy, Eric, Cin	1	0	1	0	1
Bishop, Blaine, Hou	0	0	4	6	4
Blake, Jeff, Cin	10	0	0	-7	0
Bledsoe, Drew, NE	11	1	0	-8	1
Bock, John, NYJ	1	0	0	-1	0
Bono, Steve, KC	10	1	0	-5	1
Booker, Vaughn, KC	0	0	1	14	1
Bowden, Joe, Hou	0	0	1	0	1
Bowens, Tim, Mia	0	0	2	0	2
Brister, Bubby, NYJ	4	3	0	-9	3
Brock, Matt, NYJ	0	0	2	3	2
Bronson, Ben, Ind	2	0	0	0	0
Broussard, Steve, Sea	4	1	0	0	1
Brown, Corwin, NE	0	0	1	0	1
Brown, Gary, Hou	2	1	0	0	1
Brown, J. B., Mia	1	1	1	0	2
Brown, Orlando, Cle	0	1	0	0	1
Brown, Tim, Oak	0	1	0	3	1
Brown, Troy, NE	1	1	0	75	1
Brown, Vincent, NE	0	0	1	0	1
Brunell, Mark, Jax	5	3	0	0	3
Buchanan, Ray, Ind	1	1	1	0	2
Buckner, Brentson, Pitt	0	0	1	46	1
Burke, John, NE	0	0	1	0	1
Burnett, Rob, Cle	0	0	1	0	1
Burns, Keith, Den	0	0	2	0	2
Bush, Lewis, SD	0	0	2	0	2
Byner, Earnest, Cle	1	1	0	0	1
Cadrez, Glenn, NYJ-Den	0	0	1	0	1
Camarillo, Rich, Hou	1	1	0	0	1
Carpenter, Ron, NYJ	2	0	0	0	0
Carrington, Darren, Jax	0	0	1	0	1
Carter, Dale, KC	0	1	1	0	2
Carter, Dexter, NYJ	8	4	0	0	4
Cash, Keith, KC	0	1	0	0	1
Cash, Kerry, Oak	2	2	0	3	2
Catanho, Alcides, NE	0	0	1	0	1
Chandler, Chris, Hou	12	5	0	-9	5
Childress, Ray, Hou	0	0	1	0	1
Chrebet, Wayne, NYJ	1	0	0	0	0
Christopherson, Ryan, Jax	1	0	0	0	0
Clark, Reggie, Jax	0	0	1	0	1
Clark, Willie, SD	0	1	0	0	1
Coates, Ben, NE	4	0	0	0	0
Cobb, Reggie, Jax	1	0	0	0	0
Coleman, Andre, SD	10	3	0	0	3
Coleman, Ben, Jax	0	1	0	0	1
Collins, Mark, KC	1	0	1	34	1
Copeland, Russell, Buff	1	1	0	0	1
Coryatt, Quentin, Ind	0	0	3	13	3
Cothran, Jeff, Cin	1	0	0	0	0
Cox, Bryan, Mia	0	0	1	0	1
Craver, Aaron, Den	1	1	0	0	1
Crockett, Ray, Den	0	0	1	50	1
Cross, Jeff, Mia	1	0	2	11	2
Crumpler, Carlester, Sea	1	0	0	0	0
Davidson, Kenny, Hou	0	0	1	0	1
Davis, Terrell, Den	5	1	0	0	1
Davis, Travis, Jax	0	0	1	0	1
Dawkins, Sean, Ind	1	0	0	0	0
Dishman, Cris, Hou	0	0	2	15	2
Dixon, Cal, NYJ	0	1	0	0	1
Dixon, Gerald, Cle	0	0	1	0	1
Donnalley, Kevin, Hou	0	1	0	0	1
Dotson, DeWayne, Mia	0	0	1	0	1
Douglas, Hugh, NYJ	0	0	2	0	2
Duffy, Roger, NYJ	0	2	0	0	2
Dumas, Mike, Jax	0	0	2	0	2
Dunn, David, Cin	2	0	0	0	0
Eatman, Irv, Hou	0	0	1	0	1
Edwards, Antonio, Sea	0	0	1	83	1
Elway, John, Den	9	1	0	-7	1
Emtman, Steve, Mia	0	0	1	0	1
Erickson, Craig, Ind	2	0	0	-4	0
Esiason, Boomer, NYJ	12	4	0	-27	4
Evans, Donald, NYJ	0	0	1	0	1
Evans, Greg, Buf	0	0	1	3	1
Evans, Jerry, Den	1	0	0	0	0
Evans, Vince, Oak	5	0	0	-4	0
Everitt, Steve, Cle	0	1	0	0	1
Faulk, Marshall, Ind	8	1	0	0	1
Fenner, Derrick, Oak	2	2	0	0	2
Fletcher, Terrell, SD	2	1	1	0	2
Footman, Dan, Cle	0	0	1	0	1
Fredrickson, Rob, Oak	0	0	4	35	4
Friesz, John, Sea	2	1	0	-3	1
Furrer, Will, Hou	3	0	0	0	0
Galloway, Joey, Sea	1	0	0	0	0
Gardner, Carwell, Buf	0	1	1	0	2
Gayle, Shaun, SD	0	0	1	0	1
Gilbert, Gale, SD	2	0	0	0	0
Gildon, Jason, Pitt	0	0	1	1	1
Gisler, Mike, NE	1	0	0	0	0
Givins, Ernest, Jax	1	0	0	0	0
Glenn, Aaron, NYJ	0	0	1	20	1
Goad, Tim, Cle	0	0	2	24	2
Gordon, Dwayne, SD	0	1	0	0	1
Grant, Rupert, NE	0	1	0	0	1
Grant, Steve, Ind	0	0	3	2	3
Gray, Carlton, Sea	1	0	0	0	0
Gray, Derwin, Ind	0	0	1	0	1
Gray, Mel, Hou	5	1	0	0	1
Green, Harold, Cin	2	1	0	0	1
Green, Victor, NYJ	0	0	1	0	1
Grunhard, Tim, KC	0	1	0	0	1
Guyton, Myron, NE	1	0	1	0	1
Hall, Courtney, SD	0	1	0	0	1
Hannah, Travis, Hou	0	0	1	0	1
Hansen, Phil, Buf	0	0	1	0	1
Harbaugh, Jim, Ind	4	1	0	-20	1
Harmon, Ronnie, SD	1	0	0	0	0
Harper, Dwayne, SD	0	0	1	1	1
Harris, Corey, Sea	0	0	1	57	1
Hartley, Frank, Cle	1	1	0	0	1
Hasselbach, Harald, Den	0	0	4	0	4
Hastings, Andre, Pitt	1	0	0	0	0
Hasty, James, KC	0	0	1	20	1
Hill, Greg, KC	2	0	0	0	0
Hoard, Leroy, Cle	5	0	0	0	0
Hollier, Dwight, Mia	0	0	1	0	1
Holmberg, Rob, Oak	0	0	1	0	1
Holmes, Darick, Buf	4	2	0	0	2
Hopkins, Brad, Hou	0	3	0	0	3
Hostetler, Jeff, Oak	5	1	0	-15	1
Houston, Bobby, NYJ	0	0	3	0	3
Howard, Erik, NYJ	0	0	1	0	1
Hull, Kent, Buf	1	1	0	-1	1
Humphrey, Ronald, Ind	1	0	0	0	0
Humphries, Stan, SD	9	7	0	-11	7
Hunter, Ernest, Cle	4	0	0	0	0
Ismail, Raghib, Oak	4	1	0	0	1
Jackson, Michael, Cle	1	1	0	0	1
Jackson, Willie, Jax	2	1	0	0	1
Jacobs, Ray, Den	0	0	1	0	1
Jamison, George, KC	0	0	2	0	2
Jefferson, Kevin, Cin	0	0	1	6	1
Jett, James, Oak	1	0	0	0	0
Johnson, Bill, Pitt	0	0	1	0	1
Johnson, Charles, Pitt	0	1	0	0	1
Johnson, Lee, Cin	1	0	0	0	0
Johnson, Lonnie, Buff	0	1	0	0	1
Johnson, Pat, Mia	0	0	1	37	1
Johnson, Ted, NE	0	0	2	0	2
Jones, Calvin, Oak	1	0	0	0	0

1995 INDIVIDUAL STATISTICS

	Fum.	Own Rec.	Opp. Rec.	Yards	Tot. Rec.
Jones, Henry, Buf	0	0	1	0	1
Jones, James, Den	0	1	1	0	2
Jones, Mike, Oak	0	0	2	52	2
Jones, Rod, Cin	0	0	1	0	1
Jones, Tony, Cle	0	1	0	0	1
Joseph, James, Cin	1	2	1	2	3
Jourdain, Yonel, Buff	2	2	0	0	2
Joyce, Matt, Sea	0	1	0	0	1
Justin, Paul, Ind	1	1	0	-1	1
Kelly, Jim, Buf	7	2	0	0	2
Kelly, Todd, Cin	0	0	1	0	1
Kinchen, Brian, Cle	1	1	0	0	1
Kirby, Terry, Mia	2	0	0	0	0
Kirkland, Levon, Pitt	0	0	2	0	2
Kosar, Bernie, Mia	3	1	0	-7	1
Lageman, Jeff, Jax	0	0	1	0	1
Lake, Carnell, Pitt	0	0	1	0	1
Lane, Max, NE	0	1	0	30	1
Lee, Shawn, SD	0	0	1	0	1
Lewis, Albert, Oak	0	0	1	29	1
Lewis, Vernon, NE	0	0	1	0	1
Mahlum, Eric, Ind	0	2	0	0	2
Marino, Dan, Mia	7	3	0	-14	3
Marsh, Curtis, Jax	2	1	0	0	1
Marshall, Wilber, NYJ	0	0	2	11	2
Martin, Curtis, NE	5	3	0	0	3
Martin, Tony, SD	3	0	0	0	0
Maston, Le'Shai, Jax	3	0	1	4	1
Mayfield, Corey, Jax	0	0	1	0	1
McAfee, Fred, Pitt	0	0	1	0	1
McCaffrey, Ed, Den	1	0	0	0	0
McDonald, Ricardo, Cin	0	0	1	0	1
McDuffie, O. J., Mia	4	1	1	0	2
McGee, Tony, Cin	2	0	0	0	0
McGlockton, Chester, Oak	0	0	2	0	2
McKenzie, Rich, Cle	0	0	1	3	1
McKnight, James, Sea	1	1	0	0	1
McNair, Steve, Hou	3	2	0	-2	2
McNair, Todd, Hou	1	0	0	0	0
Means, Natrone, SD	2	0	0	0	0
Meggett, David, NE	5	0	0	0	0
Mickell, Darren, KC	0	0	1	0	1
Milburn, Glyn, Den	2	0	0	0	0
Millen, Hugh, Den	1	0	0	0	0
Miller, Anthony, Den	1	1	0	9	1
Miller, Jim, Pitt	1	0	0	0	0
Mills, Ernie, Pitt	2	1	0	0	1
Milner, Billy, Mia	0	2	0	0	2
Mims, Chris, SD	0	0	1	0	1
Mirer, Rick, Sea	5	1	0	-1	1
Mitchell, Johnny, NYJ	2	0	0	0	0
Montgomery, Glenn, Hou	0	0	2	0	2
Montreuil, Mark, SD	0	1	0	0	1
Moore, Ronald, NYJ	3	0	1	0	1
Morris, Byron (Bam), Pitt	3	0	0	0	0
Morton, Mike, Oak	0	1	0	0	1
Moss, Winston, Sea	0	0	2	0	2
Moten, Eric, SD	0	1	0	0	1
Murrell, Adrian, NYJ	2	2	0	0	2
Musgrave, Bill, Den	1	0	0	0	0
Newberry, Tom, Pitt	0	1	0	0	1
O'Donnell, Neil, Pitt	2	1	0	0	1
Oldham, Chris, Pitt	0	0	1	23	1
Parker, Glenn, Buff	0	1	0	0	1
Parmalee, Bernie, Mia	5	0	0	0	0
Paup, Bryce, Buf	0	0	1	0	1
Pegram, Erric, Pitt	9	1	0	0	1
Perry, Darren, Pitt	1	0	2	0	2
Phillips, Joe, KC	0	0	1	0	1
Pickens, Bruce, Oak	0	0	1	10	1
Pickens, Carl, Cin	1	0	0	0	0
Pritchard, Mike, Den	1	0	0	0	0
Pupunu, Alfred, SD	1	0	0	0	0
Ray, Terry, NE	0	0	2	0	2
Reed, Andre, Buf	2	0	0	0	0
Reynolds, Ricky, NE	0	0	1	0	1
Rison, Andre, Cle	1	1	0	0	1
Roan, Michael, Hou	1	1	0	0	1
Robbins, Austin, Oak	0	0	2	6	2
Robinson, Eddie, Hou	0	0	1	0	1
Robinson, Eugene, Sea	0	0	1	0	1
Robinson, Jeff, Den	0	0	1	0	1
Rogers, Sam, Buf	0	0	1	0	1
Ruddy, Tim, Mia	1	0	0	0	0
Sadowski, Troy, Cin	0	1	0	0	1
Saleaumua, Dan, K.C	0	0	1	0	1
Sanders, Glenell, Ind	0	1	0	0	1
Sargent, Kevin, Cin	0	1	0	0	1
Sawyer, Corey, Cin	1	0	0	0	0
Schwartz, Bryan, Jax	0	0	1	0	1
Seals, Ray, Pitt	0	0	1	4	1
Searcy, Leon, Pitt	0	1	0	0	1
Seau, Junior, SD	0	0	3	30	3
Sharpe, Shannon, Den	1	1	0	0	1
Shields, Will, KC	0	1	0	0	1
Simien, Tracy, KC	0	0	3	0	3
Sims, Keith, Mia	0	1	0	0	1
Sinclair, Mike, Sea	0	0	2	0	2
Singleton, Chris, Mia	0	0	2	0	2
Slade, Chris, NE	0	0	2	38	2
Smeenge, Joel, Jax	1	0	0	0	0
Smith, Anthony, Oak	0	0	3	4	3
Smith, Bruce, Buf	0	0	1	0	1
Smith, Jimmy L., Jax	2	1	0	0	1
Smith, Lamar, Sea	1	0	0	0	0
Smith, Neil, KC	0	0	1	0	1
Smith, Rico, Cle	1	0	0	0	0
Stallings, Ramondo, Cin	1	0	1	0	1
Stewart, James, Jax	1	0	0	0	0
Stewart, Michael, Mia	0	1	0	0	1
Strong, Mack, Sea	2	1	0	0	1
Tamm, Ralph, Den	0	1	0	0	1
Tate, David, Ind	0	0	1	0	1
Testaverde, Vinny, Cle	4	0	0	-5	0
Thigpen, Yancey, Pitt	1	0	0	0	0
Thomas, Damon, Buff	1	0	0	0	0
Thomas, Dave, Jax	0	1	0	0	1
Thomas, Derrick, KC	0	0	1	0	1
Thomas, Johnny, Cle	0	0	1	0	1
Thomas, Rodney, Hou	8	0	0	0	0
Thomas, Thurman, Buff	6	0	0	0	0
Tillman, Cedric, Jax	1	0	0	0	0
Tindale, Tim, Buf	0	0	1	2	1
Tomczak, Mike, Pitt	2	1	0	0	1
Trapp, James, Oak	0	0	1	0	1
Traylor, Keith, KC	0	0	1	9	1
Vanover, Tamarick, KC	1	0	0	0	0
Wainright, Frank, Mia	0	1	0	0	1
Walker, Bracey, Cin	0	0	2	9	2
Wallace, Aaron, Oak	0	0	1	0	1
Warren, Chris, Sea	5	2	0	0	2
Warren, Lamont, Ind	1	0	0	0	0
Washington, Brian, KC	0	0	1	2	1
Washington, Lionel, Den	1	0	1	38	1
Washington, Mickey, Jax	0	0	2	0	2
Webb, Richmond, Mia	0	1	0	0	1
Wells, Dean, Sea	0	0	1	3	1
Whigham, Larry, NE	0	1	0	0	1
White, David, Buf	0	0	1	0	1
White, Lorenzo, Cle	0	2	0	0	2
Whittington, Bernard, Ind	0	0	1	0	1
Williams, Brent, Sea	1	0	1	-1	1
Williams, Darryl, Cin	0	0	3	0	3
Williams, Harvey, Oak	5	1	0	0	1
Williams, John L., Pitt	2	1	0	0	1
Williams, Willie, Pitt	0	0	1	0	1
Wilson, Charles, NYJ	1	0	0	0	0
Wilson, Robert, Mia	0	0	1	0	1
Wisniewski, Steve, Oak	0	1	0	0	1
Wohlabaugh, Dave, NE	0	1	0	0	1
Wooden, Terry, Sea	0	1	0	20	1
Wycheck, Frank, Hou	0	1	0	-6	1
Young, Lonnie, NYJ	0	0	2	4	2
Zeier, Eric, Cle	3	0	0	-5	0
Zolak, Scott, NE	4	1	0	-2	1

Yards includes aborted plays, own recoveries and opponents' recoveries.

NFC FUMBLES—INDIVIDUAL

	Fum.	Own Rec.	Opp. Rec.	Yards	Tot. Rec.
Agnew, Ray, NYG	0	0	1	0	1
Aikman, Troy, Dall	5	2	0	-15	2
Alexander, Brent, Ariz	0	1	0	0	1
Alexander, Derrick, Minn	0	0	1	0	1
Allen, Larry, Dall	0	1	0	0	1
Allen, Terry, Wash	6	1	0	0	1
Archambeau, Lester, Atl	0	0	1	0	1
Armstead, Jessie, NYG	0	0	1	0	1
Armstrong, Tyji, TB	1	1	0	0	1
Bailey, Johnny, StL	1	1	0	0	1
Baldwin, Randy, Car	1	0	0	0	0
Bankston, Michael, Ariz	1	0	0	0	0
Barnes, Reggie, Dall	0	1	0	0	1
Barnett, Fred, Phil	0	0	1	0	1
Bates, Mario, NO	2	1	0	0	1
Beckles, Ian, TB	0	1	1	0	2
Bell, Coleman, Wash	1	0	0	0	0
Bennett, Edgar, GB	2	1	0	0	1
Bettis, Jerome, StL	4	2	0	0	2
Birden, J. J., Atl	0	1	0	0	1
Bishop, Greg, NYG	0	1	0	0	1
Boatswain, Harry, Phil	0	1	0	0	1
Boutte, Marc, Wash	0	0	1	0	1
Brady, Ed, TB	1	0	0	-18	0
Brady, Jeff, Minn	0	0	2	0	2
Brown, Dave, NYG	10	2	0	-8	2
Brown, Dennis, SF	0	0	2	0	2
Brown, Lance, Ariz	0	0	1	0	1
Brown, Tyrone, Atl	1	0	0	0	0
Bruce, Isaac, StL	2	1	0	0	1
Buck, Mike, Ariz	1	1	0	0	1
Buck, Vince, NO	1	0	4	10	4
Buckley, Marcus, NYG	0	0	1	0	1
Bush, Devin, Atl	0	1	0	0	1
Bussey, Barney, TB	0	0	1	0	1
Campbell, Matthew, Car	1	0	0	0	0
Carpenter, Rob, Phil	2	1	0	0	1
Carrier, Mark, Car	0	1	0	0	1
Carrier, Mark, Chi	0	0	1	0	1
Carter, Kevin, StL	0	0	1	0	1
Carter, Marty, Chi	0	0	1	0	1
Carter, Tony, Chi	1	0	0	0	0
Carver, Shante, Dall	0	0	1	0	1
Centers, Larry, Ariz	2	1	0	0	1
Christian, Bob, Car	1	1	0	0	1
Collins, Kerry, Car	13	4	0	-15	4
Conlan, Shane, StL	0	0	2	0	2
Cook, Marv, StL	1	0	0	0	0
Cooper, Adrian, Minn	0	1	0	1	1
Cooper, Richard, NO	0	1	0	0	1
Cota, Chad, Car	0	0	1	0	1
Culpepper, Brad, TB	0	0	1	12	1
Cunningham, Ed, Ariz	1	0	0	-25	0
Cunningham, Randall, Phil	3	1	0	-5	1
Cunningham, Rick, Minn	0	1	0	0	1
Curry, Eric, TB	0	0	1	0	1
Dalman, Chris, SF	0	1	0	0	1
Davis, Dexter, StL	0	0	1	7	1
Davis, Ronald, Atl	0	0	1	0	1
Del Rio, Jack, Minn	0	0	1	0	1
Detmer, Ty, GB	1	1	0	0	1
Dilfer, Trent, TB	13	1	0	-9	1
Dimry, Charles, TB	0	0	2	0	2
Dixon, Ernest, NO	1	0	0	0	0
Doleman, Chris, Atl	0	0	2	0	2
Dorn, Torin, StL	0	0	1	26	1
Dotson, Santana, TB	0	0	2	0	2
Douglas, Omar, NYG	1	1	1	41	2
Douglass, Maurice, NYG	0	0	2	5	2
Dowdell, Marcus, Ariz	1	0	1	0	1
Drakeford, Tyronne, SF	1	0	1	12	1
Drayton, Troy, StL	2	0	0	0	0
Early, Quinn, NO	1	0	0	0	0
Edmonds, Bobby Joe, TB	1	1	0	0	1
Edwards, Anthony, Ariz	0	0	1	0	1
Eilers, Pat, Chi	0	1	0	0	1
Elewonibi, Mohammed, Phil	0	1	0	0	1
Ellard, Henry, Wash	1	0	0	0	0
Ellison, Jerry, TB	0	1	0	0	1
Emanuel, Bert, Atl	2	0	0	0	0
England, Eric, Ariz	0	0	2	0	2
Evans, Doug, GB	1	0	0	0	0
Everett, Jim, NO	6	0	0	-5	0
Everett, Thomas, TB	0	0	1	0	1
Fann, Chad, Ariz	1	0	0	0	0
Favre, Brett, GB	8	0	0	0	0
Feagles, Jeff, Ariz	1	0	0	-22	0
Figaro, Cedric, StL	0	1	0	0	1
Flanigan, Jim, Chi	0	1	0	0	1
Floyd, William, SF	1	0	0	0	0
Fontenot, Albert, Chi	0	0	1	0	1
Fortin, Roman, Atl	2	0	0	-6	0
Freeman, Antonio, GB	7	4	0	0	4
Frerotte, Gus, Wash	7	4	0	-16	4
Fuller, Corey, Minn	0	0	1	12	1
Fuller, William, Phil	0	0	1	0	1
Gaines, Wendall, Ariz	0	1	0	0	1
Gant, Kenneth, TB	0	0	1	13	1
Garcia, Frank, Car	1	1	0	10	1
Garner, Charlie, Phil	2	0	0	0	0
George, Jeff, Atl	6	2	0	-15	2
Gilbert, Sean, StL	0	0	1	0	1
Glenn, Vencie, NYG	0	0	2	0	2
Glover, Kevin, Det	2	1	0	-14	1
Gouveia, Kurt, Phil	0	0	1	0	1
Graham, Jeff, Chi	3	0	0	0	0
Grbac, Elvis, SF	2	2	0	-1	2
Green, Robert, Chi	2	1	0	0	1
Green, Willie, Car	1	0	0	0	0
Griffith, Howard, Car	1	1	0	0	1
Gruber, Paul, TB	0	2	0	0	2
Guliford, Eric, Car	1	0	1	0	1
Gunn, Mark, Phil	0	0	1	0	1
Hamilton, Keith, NYG	1	0	3	87	3
Hampton, Rodney, NYG	5	1	0	0	1
Hanks, Merton, SF	0	0	2	69	2
Harmon, Andy, Phil	0	0	1	0	1
Harris, Jackie, TB	2	0	0	0	0
Harris, James, Minn	0	0	1	0	1
Harris, Robert, NYG	0	0	2	5	2
Harvey, Ken, Wash	0	0	2	0	2
Hawkins, Courtney, TB	1	0	0	0	0
Hayworth, Tracy, Det	0	0	1	0	1
Hearst, Garrison, Ariz	12	2	0	0	2
Henderson, Jerome, Phil	0	0	1	0	1
Hennings, Chad, Dall	0	0	1	0	1
Heyward, Craig, Atl	3	3	0	0	3
Hoage, Terry, Ariz	0	0	2	0	2
Holmes, Clayton, Dall	1	1	0	0	1
Horan, Mike, NYG	1	1	0	-18	1
Howard, Dana, StL	0	0	1	0	1
Hughes, Tyrone, NO	2	0	0	0	0
Hutton, Tom, Phil	1	0	0	-19	0
Ingram, Mark, GB	1	0	0	0	0
Irvin, Michael, Dall	1	0	0	0	0
Irving, Terry, Ariz	0	1	2	-2	3
Ismail, Qadry, Minn	3	0	0	0	0
Jackson, Greg, Phil	0	0	3	45	3
Jenkins, Carlos, StL	0	0	1	0	1
Jenkins, James, Wash	0	0	1	0	1
Jervey, Travis, GB	0	1	0	0	1
Johnson, Anthony, Chi	2	0	0	0	0
Johnson, Brad, Minn	2	0	0	0	0
Johnson, Kevin, Phil	0	0	1	37	1
Johnson, LeShon, Ariz	1	1	0	0	1
Johnson, Mike, Det	0	0	4	6	4
Johnson, Tim, Wash	0	0	1	0	1
Johnston, Daryl, Dall	1	1	0	0	1
Jones, Brent, SF	3	1	0	0	1
Jones, Brian, NO	0	0	1	0	1
Jones, Sean, GB	0	0	1	0	1
Jordan, Andrew, Minn	1	0	0	0	0
Jordan, Charles, GB	1	1	0	0	1
Joyner, Seth, Ariz	1	0	3	0	3
Kennard, Derek, Dall	1	1	0	-1	1
Kinchen, Todd, StL	8	1	0	0	1
Kozlowski, Brian, NYG	1	0	1	0	1
Kragen, Greg, Car	0	0	2	3	2
Kramer, Erik, Chi	6	2	0	-13	2
Krieg, Dave, Ariz	16	7	0	-13	7
Lathon, Lamar, Car	0	0	1	0	1

1995 INDIVIDUAL STATISTICS

	Fum.	Own Rec.	Opp. Rec.	Yards	Tot. Rec.
LeBel, Harper, Atl	1	0	0	-8	0
Lee, Amp, Minn	3	2	0	3	2
Leeuwenburg, Jay, Chi	0	1	0	0	1
Lett, Leon, Dall	0	0	2	0	2
Lewis, Thomas, NYG	1	0	0	0	0
Logan, Marc, Wash	1	0	0	0	0
Love, Duval, Ariz	0	1	0	0	1
Loville, Derek, SF	1	0	0	0	0
Lundy, Dennis, Chi	1	0	1	18	1
Lynch, Lorenzo, Ariz	0	0	1	0	1
Maddox, Tommy, NYG	1	0	0	0	0
Mamula, Mike, Phil	0	0	1	25	1
Marshall, Arthur, NYG	1	0	0	0	0
Martin, Kelvin, Phil	2	0	0	0	0
Martin, Wayne, NO	0	0	1	0	1
Marts, Lonnie, TB	0	0	1	0	1
Mathis, Terance, Atl	1	0	0	0	0
Matich, Trevor, Wash	1	0	0	-2	0
Matthews, Clay, Atl	0	0	1	0	1
Maxie, Brett, Car	0	0	1	0	1
Mayhew, Martin, TB	0	0	1	78	1
McCants, Keith, Ariz	0	1	1	16	2
McCleskey, J. J., NO	0	0	1	0	1
McDaniel, Ed, Minn	0	0	1	0	1
McDowell, Bubba, Car	0	0	1	0	1
McGill, Lenny, GB	0	1	0	0	1
McGruder, Mike, TB	0	0	1	0	1
McKenzie, Raleigh, Phil	0	1	0	0	1
McKyer, Tim, Car	0	0	2	0	2
McMillian, Mark, Phil	0	0	2	-1	2
McNeil, Ryan, Det	0	1	1	0	2
Metcalf, Eric, Atl	4	2	0	0	2
Miller, Chris, StL	4	2	0	-6	2
Miller, Jamir, Ariz	1	0	2	26	2
Mills, Sam, Car	0	0	4	7	4
Mincy, Charles, Minn	0	1	1	10	2
Mitchell, Brian, Wash	2	1	0	0	1
Mitchell, Scott, Det	8	1	0	0	1
Moon, Warren, Minn	13	5	0	-12	5
Moore, Derrick, Car	4	0	0	0	0
Moore, Herman, Det	2	0	0	0	0
Morrison, Darryl, Wash	0	0	1	0	1
Morton, Johnnie, Det	1	0	0	0	0
Myles, Godfrey, Dall	0	1	1	0	2
Neal, Lorenzo, NO	2	0	0	0	0
Ned, Derrick, NO	1	0	0	0	0
Nickerson, Hardy, TB	0	0	3	0	3
Nottage, Dexter, Wash	0	0	3	0	3
Novacek, Jay, Dall	1	0	0	0	0
Palmer, David, Minn	1	0	0	0	0
Palmer, Sterling, Wash	0	0	1	0	1
Parker, Anthony, StL	0	0	4	35	4
Patton, Joe, Wash	0	0	1	0	1
Patton, Marvcus, Wash	0	0	1	0	1
Peete, Rodney, Phil	13	5	0	0	5
Perriman, Brett, Det	1	1	0	0	1
Phifer, Roman, StL	1	0	0	0	0
Phillips, Bobby, Minn	1	0	0	0	0
Pierce, Aaron, NYG	0	1	0	0	1
Pierson, Pete, TB	0	1	0	0	1
Popson, Ted, SF	1	0	0	0	0
Port, Chris, NO	0	1	0	0	1
Porter, Rufus, NO	0	0	1	13	1
Pounds, Darryl, Wash	1	0	0	0	0
Preston, Roell, Atl	1	0	0	0	0
Prior, Mike, GB	0	1	0	0	1
Pyne, Jim, TB	0	1	0	0	1
Randolph, Thomas, NYG	0	0	1	0	1
Raymond, Corey, Det	0	0	1	9	1
Reed, Jake, Minn	1	1	0	0	1
Reich, Frank, Car	3	1	0	0	1
Rhett, Errict, TB	2	1	0	0	1
Rice, Jerry, SF	3	1	0	0	1
Richard, Stanley, Wash	0	0	1	0	1
Richards, David, Atl	0	1	0	0	1
Riesenberg, Doug, NYG	0	1	0	0	1
Rivers, Ron, Det	2	1	0	0	1
Romanowski, Bill, Phil	0	0	1	0	1
Ross, Kevin, Atl	0	0	2	0	2
Rubley, T. J., GB	1	0	0	0	0
Ruettgers, Ken, GB	0	2	0	0	2
Russell, Leonard, StL	2	0	0	0	0
Rypien, Mark, StL	1	0	0	0	0
Salaam, Rashaan, Chi	9	1	0	0	1
Sanders, Barry, Det	3	1	0	0	1
Schlesinger, Cory, Det	0	1	0	11	1
Scroggins, Tracy, Det	0	0	1	81	1
Scurlock, Mike, StL	0	0	1	0	1
Shanks, Simon, Ariz	0	0	1	0	1
Shepherd, Leslie, Wash	0	1	0	0	1
Sherrard, Mike, NYG	2	0	0	0	0
Shuler, Heath, Wash	1	1	0	0	1
Simmons, Clyde, Ariz	0	0	1	12	1
Simmons, Ed, Wash	0	2	0	0	2
Simmons, Wayne, GB	0	0	1	0	1
Simpson, Carl, Chi	0	0	2	6	2
Singleton, Nate, SF	1	1	0	0	1
Small, Torrance, NO	0	1	0	0	1
Smith, Chuck, Atl	0	0	2	0	2
Smith, Darrin, Dall	0	0	1	63	1
Smith, Emmitt, Dall	7	0	0	0	0
Smith, Irv, NO	1	0	0	0	0
Smith, Robert, Minn	1	0	0	0	0
Smith, Vernice, Wash	0	1	0	0	1
Smith, Vinson, Chi	1	0	1	2	1
Spellman, Alonzo, Chi	0	0	1	4	1
Spielman, Chris, Det	0	0	3	8	3
Stanley, Israel, NO	0	0	1	0	1
Stephens, Rod, Wash	0	0	1	0	1
Stewart, James, Minn	2	1	0	0	1
Stringer, Korey, Minn	0	2	0	0	2
Stubbs, Danny, Phil	0	0	1	0	1
Swann, Eric, Ariz	0	0	2	0	2
Talley, Darryl, Atl	0	0	2	12	2
Taylor, Aaron, GB	0	2	0	0	2
Taylor, John, SF	2	0	0	0	0
Taylor, Keith, Wash	0	0	1	0	1
Taylor, Terry, Atl	0	1	1	8	2
Teague, George, GB	0	0	1	4	1
Terrell, Pat, Car	0	0	1	0	1
Terry, Ryan, Ariz	1	1	0	0	1
Tharpe, Larry, Ariz	0	1	0	0	1
Thierry, John, Chi	0	0	4	0	4
Thomas, Broderick, Minn	0	0	1	0	1
Thomas, Henry, Det	0	0	2	0	2
Thomas, Johnny, StL	1	1	0	5	1
Thomas, Orlando, Minn	1	0	4	19	4
Thomas, William, Phil	0	0	1	0	1
Thomason, Jeff, GB	0	1	0	0	1
Tillman, Lewis, Chi	0	0	1	0	1
Timpson, Michael, Chi	1	1	0	0	1
Trudeau, Jack, Car	1	0	0	0	0
Truitt, Olanda, Wash	1	0	0	0	0
Tuaolo, Esera, Minn	0	0	2	0	2
Tubbs, Winfred, NO	0	0	1	0	1
Turnbull, Renaldo, NO	0	0	2	0	2
Turner, Scott, Wash	1	1	0	0	1
Turner, Vernon, Det	1	0	0	0	0
Vanderbeek, Matt, Wash	0	0	1	0	1
Walker, Adam, SF	2	0	0	0	0
Walls, Wesley, NO	1	1	0	0	1
Watkins, Kendell, Dall	1	0	0	0	0
Watters, Ricky, Phil	6	0	0	0	0
Weldon, Casey, TB	4	0	0	-3	0
West, Ed, Phil	0	1	0	0	1
Wheatley, Tyrone, NYG	2	0	0	0	0
Whitley, Curtis, Car	0	1	0	0	1
Wilburn, Barry, Phil	0	0	1	0	1
Williams, Aeneas, Ariz	1	0	3	0	3
Williams, Alfred, SF	0	1	0	0	1
Williams, Allen, Det	1	0	0	0	0
Williams, Calvin, Phil	2	0	0	0	0
Williams, Kevin, Dall	3	0	0	0	0
Williams, Sherman, Dall	2	0	0	0	0
Wilson, Wade, Dall	1	1	0	0	1
Winans, Tydus, Wash	1	0	0	0	0
Woodall, Lee, SF	0	0	2	98	2
Woods, Tony, Wash	0	0	2	3	2
Wooten, Tito, NYG	0	1	0	0	1
Workman, Vince, Car	0	0	1	0	1
Wright, Toby, StL	0	0	1	73	1
Young, Bryant, SF	0	1	1	0	2

Young, Rodney, NYG	1	0	0	0	0
Young, Steve, SF	3	0	0	0	0
Zandofsky, Mike, Atl	0	1	0	0	1
Zellars, Ray, NO	1	0	0	0	0
Zordich, Mike, Phil	0	0	2	58	2
Zorich, Chris, Chi	0	1	1	0	2

Yards includes aborted plays, own recoveries, and opponents' recoveries.

SACKS

Most Sacks

AFC: 17.5—Bryce Paup, Buffalo

NFC: 13.0—William Fuller, Philadelphia
Wayne Martin, New Orleans

Most Sacks, Game

AFC: 4.0—Leslie O'Neal, San Diego at Seattle, October 22

NFC: 3.5—Chris Doleman, Atlanta vs. Carolina, September 3 (OT)
D'Marco Farr, St. Louis at N.Y. Jets, December 3

Team Champion

AFC: 49—Buffalo

NFC: 48—Philadelphia

AFC SACKS—TEAM

	Sacks	Yards
Buffalo	49	362
Kansas City	47	347
N.Y. Jets	43	315
Oakland	43	332
Cincinnati	42	267
Pittsburgh	42	272
New England	37	221
San Diego	36	222
Denver	30	220
Houston	30	200
Cleveland	29	191
Indianapolis	29	169
Miami	29	187
Seattle	28	167
Jacksonville	17	72
AFC Total	531	3544
AFC Average	35.4	236.3

NFC SACKS—TEAM

	Sacks	Yards
Philadelphia	48	305
Minnesota	44	294
New Orleans	44	275
Detroit	42	317
San Francisco	40	240
Green Bay	39	275
Carolina	36	265
Dallas	36	219
St. Louis	36	258
Chicago	35	239
Arizona	31	200
Atlanta	30	210
Washington	30	135
N.Y. Giants	29	177
Tampa Bay	25	140
NFC Total	545	3549
NFC Average	36.3	236.6
League Total	1076	7093
League Average	35.9	236.4

NFL TOP TEN LEADERS

	Total		
Paup, Bryce, Buff	17.5	White, Reggie, GB	12.0
Fuller, William, Phil	13.0	Farr, D'Marco, StL	11.5
Martin, Wayne, NO	13.0	Flanigan, Jim, Chi	11.0
Swilling, Pat, Oak	13.0	Harmon, Andy, Phil	11.0
O'Neal, Leslie, SD	12.5	McGinest, Willie, NE	11.0
Smith, Neil, KC	12.0	Simmons, Clyde, Ariz	11.0

AFC SACKS—INDIVIDUAL

Paup, Bryce, Buff	17.5
Swilling, Pat, Oak	13.0
O'Neal, Leslie, SD	12.5
Smith, Neil, KC	12.0
McGinest, Willie, NE	11.0
Bennett, Tony, Ind	10.5
Smith, Bruce, Buff	10.5
Douglas, Hugh, NYJ	10.0
Hansen, Phil, Buff	10.0
Copeland, John, Cin	9.0
Greene, Kevin, Pitt	9.0
Seals, Ray, Pitt	8.5
Lee, Shawn, SD	8.0
Pleasant, Anthony, Cle	8.0
Thomas, Derrick, KC	8.0
Wilkinson, Dan, Cin	8.0
Burnett, Rob, Cle	7.5
Cox, Bryan, Mia	7.5
McGlockton, Chester, Oak	7.5
Saleaumua, Dan, KC	7.0
Smith, Anthony, Oak	7.0
Coleman, Marco, Mia	6.5
Kennedy, Cortez, Sea	6.5
Lloyd, Greg, Pitt	6.5
Cross, Jeff, Mia	6.0
Perry, Michael Dean, Den	6.0
Washington, Marvin, NYJ	6.0
Brown, Chad, Pitt	5.5
Bruce, Aundray, Oak	5.5
Edwards, Antonio, Sea	5.5
Mickell, Darren, KC	5.5
Sinclair, Mike, Sea	5.5
Brock, Matt, NYJ	5.0
Fletcher, Simon, Den	5.0
Footman, Dan, Cle	5.0
Lewis, Mo, NYJ	5.0
McDonald, Ricardo, Cin	5.0
Armstrong, Trace, Mia	4.5
Cook, Anthony, Hou	4.5
Ford, Henry, Hou	4.5
Johnson, Ellis, Ind	4.5
Phillips, Joe, KC	4.5
Brown, Vincent, NE	4.0
Collins, Andre, Cin	4.0
Collons, Ferric, NE	4.0
Hasselbach, Harald, Den	4.0
Slade, Chris, NE	4.0
Smeenge, Joel, Jax	4.0
Adams, Sam, Sea	3.5
Davis, Reuben, SD	3.5
Robinson, Eddie, Hou	3.5
Ball, Jerry, Oak	3.0
Barrow, Micheal, Hou	3.0
Buckner, Brentson, Pitt	3.0
Casillas, Tony, NYJ	3.0
Crockett, Ray, Den	3.0
Davey, Don, Jax	3.0
Francis, James, Cin	3.0
Gildon, Jason, Pitt	3.0
Houston, Bobby, NYJ	3.0
Johnson, Raylee, SD	3.0
Jones, Mike, NE	3.0
Lageman, Jeff, Jax	3.0
Logan, Ernie, Jax	3.0
Coryatt, Quentin, Ind	2.5
Howard, Erik, NYJ	2.5
Jeffcoat, Jim, Buff	2.5
McCoy, Tony, Ind	2.5
Reynolds, Ricky, NE	2.5
Walker, Gary, Hou	2.5
Washington, Ted, Buff	2.5
Alberts, Trev, Ind	2.0
Barber, Kurt, NYJ	2.0
Barnett, Troy, NE	2.0
Bennett, Cornelius, Buff	2.0
Bowens, Tim, Mia	2.0
Cadrez, Glenn, Den	2.0
Davidson, Kenny, Hou	2.0
Davis, Anthony, KC	2.0
Dronett, Shane, Den	2.0
Evans, Donald, NYJ	2.0
Grant, Steve, Ind	2.0
Green, Victor, NYJ	2.0
Henry, Kevin, Pitt	2.0
Johnson, Pepper, Cle	2.0
Jones, Roger, Cin	2.0
McDaniels, Pellom, KC	2.0
Mims, Chris, SD	2.0
Montgomery, Glenn, Hou	2.0
Moss, Winston, Sea	2.0
Parrella, John, SD	2.0
Robbins, Austin, Oak	2.0
Rogers, Sam, Buff	2.0
Rucker, Keith, Cin	2.0
Sawyer, Corey, Cin	2.0
Seau, Junior, SD	2.0
Siragusa, Tony, Ind	2.0
Smith, Artie, Cin	2.0
Wallace, Aaron, Oak	2.0
Whittington, Bernard, Ind	2.0
Williams, Dan, Den	2.0
Aldridge, Allen, Den	1.5
Bishop, Blaine, Hou	1.5
Booker, Vaughn, KC	1.5
Burns, Keith, Den	1.5
Frederick, Mike, Cle	1.5
Jones, Marvin, NYJ	1.5
Lake, Carnell, Pitt	1.5
Lewis, Vernon, NE	1.5
Mayfield, Corey, Jax	1.5
McGhee, Kanavis, Hou	1.5
McKenzie, Rich, Cle	1.5
Pritchett, Kelvin, Jax	1.5
Traylor, Keith, KC	1.5
White, Reggie, NE	1.5
Banks, Carl, Cle	1.0
Bayless, Martin, KC	1.0
Bickett, Duane, Sea	1.0
Biekert, Greg, Oak	1.0
Blackmon, Robert, Sea	1.0
Bowden, Joe, Hou	1.0
Brandon, David, SD	1.0
Buchanan, Ray, Ind	1.0
Childress, Ray, Hou	1.0
Emtman, Steve, Mia	1.0
Frase, Paul, Jax	1.0
Gordon, Dwayne, SD	1.0
Hall, Dana, Cle	1.0
Holmberg, Rob, Oak	1.0
Jackson, Steve, Hou	1.0
Jones, Aaron, NE	1.0
Jones, James, Den	1.0
Kelly, Todd, Cin	1.0
Kirkland, Levon, Pitt	1.0
Law, Ty, NE	1.0
Lewis, Albert, Oak	1.0
Lewis, Darryll, Hou	1.0
Marshall, Wilber, NYJ	1.0
McCrary, Michael, Sea	1.0
Moore, Stevon, Cle	1.0
Nash, Joe, Sea	1.0
Oglesby, Alfred, Cin	1.0
Olsavsky, Jerry, Pitt	1.0
Roberts, Tim, NE	1.0
Robinson, Jeff, Den	1.0
Simien, Tracy, KC	1.0
Singleton, Chris, Mia	1.0
Stallings, Ramondo, Cin	1.0
Steed, Joel, Pitt	1.0
Tovar, Steve, Cin	1.0
White, David, Buff	1.0
White, William, KC	1.0
Williams, Brent, Sea	1.0
Williams, Darryl, Cin	1.0
Wilson, Karl, Buff	1.0
Wortham, Barron, Hou	1.0
Young, Glen, SD	1.0
Alexander, Elijah, Den	0.5
Foxx, Dion, Mia	0.5
Johnson, Ted, NE	0.5
Sagapolutele, Pio, Cle	0.5
Wilson, Troy, Den	0.5

NFC SACKS—INDIVIDUAL

Fuller, William, Phil	13.0
Martin, Wayne, NO	13.0
White, Reggie, GB	12.0
Farr, D'Marco, StL	11.5
Flanigan, Jim, Chi	11.0
Harmon, Andy, Phil	11.0
Simmons, Clyde, Ariz	11.0
Haley, Charles, Dall	10.5
Randle, John, Minn	10.5
Thomas, Henry, Det	10.5
Jackson, Rickey, SF	9.5
Scroggins, Tracy, Det	9.5
Doleman, Chris, Atl	9.0
Jones, Sean, GB	9.0
Spellman, Alonzo, Chi	8.5
Swann, Eric, Ariz	8.5
Lathon, Lamar, Car	8.0
Harvey, Ken, Wash	7.5
Strahan, Michael, NYG	7.5
Conner, Darion, Car	7.0
Geathers, Jumpy, Atl	7.0
London, Antonio, Det	7.0
Turnbull, Renaldo, NO	7.0
Carter, Kevin, StL	6.0
Johnson, Kevin, Phil	6.0
Thomas, Broderick, Minn	6.0
Young, Bryant, SF	6.0
Gilbert, Sean, StL	5.5
Hennings, Chad, Dall	5.5
Johnson, Joe, NO	5.5
Mamula, Mike, Phil	5.5
Smith, Chuck, Atl	5.5
Stubbs, Danny, Phil	5.5
Tolbert, Tony, Dall	5.5
Dotson, Santana, TB	5.0
Harris, Robert, NYG	5.0
Porcher, Robert, Det	5.0
Fox, Mike, Car	4.5
Harrison, Martin, Minn	4.5
McDaniel, Ed, Minn	4.5
Mills, Sam, Car	4.5
Palmer, Sterling, Wash	4.5
Stubblefield, Dana, SF	4.5
Williams, Alfred, SF	4.5
Culpepper, Brad, TB	4.0
Dixon, Ernest, NO	4.0
Duff, Jamal, NYG	4.0
Harris, Tim, SF	4.0
Rudolph, Coleman, NYG	4.0
Simmons, Wayne, GB	4.0
Smith, Vinson, Chi	4.0
Thierry, John, Chi	4.0
Stokes, Fred, StL	3.5
Ahanotu, Chidi, TB	3.0
Archambeau, Lester, Atl	3.0
Bailey, Carlton, Car	3.0
Barker, Roy, Minn	3.0
Brady, Jeff, Minn	3.0
Del Rio, Jack, Minn	3.0
Johnson, Tim, Wash	3.0
LaBounty, Matt, GB	3.0
Lett, Leon, Dall	3.0
Montgomery, Alton, Atl	3.0
Owens, Rich, Wash	3.0
Phifer, Roman, StL	3.0
Porter, Rufus, NO	3.0
Sapp, Warren, TB	3.0
Smith, Darrin, Dall	3.0
Tuaolo, Esera, Minn	3.0
Wilkins, Gabe, GB	3.0
Woodall, Lee, SF	3.0
Carver, Shante, Dall	2.5
Fontenot, Albert, Chi	2.5
Smith, Fernando, Minn	2.5
Alexander, Derrick, Minn	2.0
Bankston, Michael, Ariz	2.0
Boutte, Marc, Wash	2.0
Broughton, Willie, NO	2.0
Curry, Eric, TB	2.0
Gaines, William, Wash	2.0
Hamilton, Keith, NYG	2.0
Harvey, Richard, NO	2.0
Hill, Eric, Ariz	2.0
Johnson, Mike, Det	2.0
King, Shawn, Car	2.0
Kuberski, Bob, GB	2.0
Maryland, Russell, Dall	2.0
McCormack, Hurvin, Dall	2.0
McIntosh, Toddrick, TB	2.0
Patton, Marvcus, Wash	2.0
Poole, Tyrone, Car	2.0
Raymond, Corey, Det	2.0
Stanley, Israel, NO	2.0
Thomas, Mark, Car	2.0
Thomas, William, Phil	2.0
Woods, Tony, Wash	2.0
Brown, Dennis, SF	1.5
Goff, Robert, NO	1.5
Holland, Darius, GB	1.5
Jenkins, Carlos, StL	1.5
Nickerson, Hardy, TB	1.5
Prior, Mike, GB	1.5
Woodard, Marc, Phil	1.5
Agnew, Ray, NYG	1.0
Barnett, Oliver, SF	1.0
Blades, Bennie, Det	1.0
Bonham, Shane, Det	1.0
Boyd, Stephen, Det	1.0
Brooks, Derrick, TB	1.0
Brooks, Michael, NYG	1.0
Bryant, Junior, SF	1.0
Butler, LeRoy, GB	1.0
Croel, Mike, NYG	1.0
Davis, Dexter, StL	1.0
Davis, Eric, SF	1.0
Dillard, Stacey, NYG	1.0
Douglass, Maurice, NYG	1.0
Drakeford, Tyronne, SF	1.0
Evans, Doug, GB	1.0
Everett, Thomas, TB	1.0
Fields, Mark, NO	1.0
Figaro, Cedric, StL	1.0
Flores, Mike, Wash	1.0
Fountaine, Jamal, SF	1.0
Hall, Rhett, Phil	1.0
Harris, James, Minn	1.0
Hayworth, Tracy, Det	1.0
Hoage, Terry, Ariz	1.0
Holt, Pierce, Atl	1.0
Irving, Terry, Ariz	1.0
Jones, Brian, NO	1.0
Jones, Robert, Dall	1.0
Joyner, Seth, Ariz	1.0
Koonce, George, GB	1.0
Kragen, Greg, Car	1.0
Legette, Tyrone, NO	1.0
Lincoln, Jeremy, Chi	1.0
Lynch, Lorenzo, Ariz	1.0
Mangum, John, Chi	1.0
McBurrows, Gerald, StL	1.0
Miller, Jamir, Ariz	1.0
Norton, Ken, SF	1.0
Plummer, Gary, SF	1.0
Powe, Keith, TB	1.0
Price, Shawn, Car	1.0
Romanowski, Bill, Phil	1.0
Simpson, Carl, Chi	1.0
Spielman, Chris, Det	1.0
Taylor, Keith, Wash	1.0
Tubbs, Winfred, NO	1.0
Tuggle, Jessie, Atl	1.0
Turner, Scott, Wash	1.0
Wheeler, Mark, TB	1.0
White, Alberto, StL	1.0
Wilson, Bernard, Ariz	1.0
Wright, Toby, StL	1.0
Zordich, Mike, Phil	1.0
Zorich, Chris, Chi	1.0
Alexander, Brent, Ariz	0.5
Armstead, Jessie, NYG	0.5
Brown, Chad, Ariz	0.5
Fuller, Corey, Minn	0.5
Gardner, Moe, Atl	0.5
Griffith, Robert, Minn	0.5
Gunn, Mark, Phil	0.5
Jeffries, Greg, Det	0.5
McCants, Keith, Ariz	0.5
Rouse, Wardell, TB	0.5
Wells, Mike, Det	0.5

1995 NFL PAID ATTENDANCE BREAKDOWN

	Games	Attendance	Average
AFC Preseason	9	467,980	51,998
NFC Preseason	8	481,114	60,139
AFC-NFC Preseason, Interconference	46	2,419,195	52,591
NFL Preseason Total	**63**	**3,368,289**	**53,465**
AFC Regular Season	90	5,694,189	63,269
NFC Regular Season	90	5,647,847	62,754
AFC-NFC Regular Season, Interconference	60	3,701,526	61,692
NFL Regular Season Total	**240**	***15,043,562**	***62,682**
AFC Wild Card Playoffs	2		
Miami at Buffalo		79,663	
Indianapolis at San Diego		60,731	
AFC Divisional Playoffs	2		
Indianapolis at Kansas City		78,896	
Buffalo at Pittsburgh		60,432	
AFC Championship Game	1		
Indianapolis at Pittsburgh		61,001	
NFC Wild Card Playoffs	2		
Atlanta at Green Bay		60,311	
Detroit at Philadelphia		65,913	
NFC Divisional Playoffs	2		
Philadelphia at Dallas		63,617	
Green Bay at San Francisco		69,097	
NFC Championship Game	1		
Green Bay at Dallas		64,864	
Super Bowl XXX at Tempe, Arizona	1		
Dallas vs. Pittsburgh		76,347	
AFC-NFC Pro Bowl at Honolulu, Hawaii	1	50,034	
NFL Postseason Total	**12**	**790,906**	**65,909**
NFL All Games	**315**	***19,202,757**	**60,961**

**All-time record*

ONE MILLION PLUS CLUB

During the 1995 season, 14 clubs drew a combined home and away paid attendance of more than 1 million. The Kansas City Chiefs drew an NFL-leading 1,137,262 fans in 1995.

Team	Total Paid Home Attendance	Total Paid Visiting Attendance	Total Paid Attendance
Kansas City	625,936	511,326	1,137,262
Miami	593,242	519,355	1,112,597
New York Giants	613,232	492,580	1,105,812
Buffalo	546,537	554,506	1,101,043
Jacksonville	573,941	511,451	1,085,392
San Francisco	550,423	531,580	1,082,003
Chicago	527,921	542,042	1,069,963
Denver	591,152	476,656	1,067,808
Cleveland	566,894	492,805	1,059,699
New York Jets	611,655	442,699	1,054,354
Detroit	586,372	453,361	1,039,733
Dallas	508,167	518,212	1,026,379
Green Bay	479,209	545,773	1,024,982
New England	478,351	530,553	1,008,904

Note: *For complete year-by-year paid attendance and attendance records,* *see page 361.*

Inside the Numbers

INSIDE THE NUMBERS

RECORDS FOR NFL TEAMS FOR MOST POINTS IN A GAME (REGULAR SEASON ONLY)

Note: *When the record has been achieved more than once, only the most recent game is shown; summaries are listed in alphabetical order by conference. Bold face indicates team holding record.*

BUFFALO BILLS

September 18, 1966, at Buffalo

Miami .... 3 7 0 14 — 24
Buffalo .... 21 27 3 7 — 58

TDs: Buff—Bobby Burnett 2, Butch Byrd 2, Jack Spikes 2, Bobby Crockett, Jack Kemp; Mia—Dave Kocourek, Bo Roberson, John Roderick. TD Passes: Buff—Jack Kemp, Daryle Lamonica; Mia—George Wilson 3. FGs: Buff—Booth Lusteg; Mia—Gene Mingo.

CINCINNATI BENGALS

December 17, 1989, at Cincinnati

Houston .... 0 0 0 7 — 7
Cincinnati .... 21 10 21 9 — 61

TDs: Cin—Eddie Brown 2, Eric Ball, James Brooks, Ira Hillary, Rodney Holman, Tim McGee, Craig Taylor; Hou—Lorenzo White. TD Passes: Cin—Boomer Esiason 4, Erik Wilhelm. FGs: Cin—Jim Breech 2.

CLEVELAND BROWNS

November 7, 1954, at Cleveland

Washington .... 0 3 0 0 — 3
Cleveland .... 13 14 21 14 — 62

TDs: Clev—Darrell Brewster 2, Mo Bassett, Ken Gorgal, Otto Graham, Dub Jones, Dante Lavelli, Curley Morrison. TD Passes: Clev—George Ratterman 3, Otto Graham. FGs: Clev—Lou Groza 2; Wash—Vic Janowicz.

DENVER BRONCOS

October 6, 1963, at Denver

San Diego .... 13 7 0 14 — 34
Denver .... 3 14 9 24 — 50

TDs: Den—Lionel Taylor 2, Goose Gonsoulin, Gene Prebola, Donnie Stone; SD—Keith Lincoln 2, Lance Alworth, Paul Lowe, Jacque MacKinnon. TD Passes: Den—John McCormick 3; SD—Tobin Rote 3, John Hadl 2. FGs: Den—Gene Mingo 5.

HOUSTON OILERS

December 9, 1990, at Houston

Cleveland .... 0 7 7 0 — 14
Houston .... 14 31 7 6 — 58

TDs: Hou—Lorenzo White 4, Ernest Givins, Leonard Harris, Tony Jones, Terry Kinard; Clev—Eric Metcalf 2. TD Passes: Hou—Warren Moon 2, Cody Carlson; Clev—Bernie Kosar. FG: Hou—Teddy Garcia.

INDIANAPOLIS COLTS

December 12, 1976, at Baltimore

Buffalo .... 3 3 7 7 — 20
Baltimore Colts .... 7 13 28 10 — 58

TDs: Balt—Roger Carr, Raymond Chester, Glenn Doughty, Roosevelt Leaks, Derrel Luce, Lydell Mitchell, Howard Stevens; Buff—Bob Chandler, O.J. Simpson. TD Passes: Balt—Bert Jones 3; Buff—Gary Marangi. FGs: Balt—Toni Linhart 3; Buff—George Jakowenko 2.

JACKSONVILLE JAGUARS

December 10, 1995, at Jacksonville

Indianapolis .... 14 10 3 14 — 41
Jacksonville .... 0 7 3 21 — 31

TDs: Jax—Willie Jackson 2, Jimmy Smith, James Stewart; Ind—Aaron Bailey 2, Ken Dilger, Marshall Faulk, Lamont Warren. TD Passes: Jax—Mark Brunell 3; Ind—Craig Erickson 2. FGs: Jax—Mike Hollis; Ind—Cary Blanchard 2.

KANSAS CITY CHIEFS

September 7, 1963, at Denver

Kansas City .... 14 14 21 10 — 59
Denver .... 0 7 0 0 — 7

TDs: KC—Chris Burford 2, Frank Jackson 2, Dave Grayson, Abner Haynes, Sherrill Headrick, Curtis McClinton; Den—Lionel Taylor. TD Passes: KC—Len Dawson 4, Curtis McClinton; Den—Mickey Slaughter. FG: KC—Tommy Brooker.

MIAMI DOLPHINS

November 24, 1977, at St. Louis

Miami .... 14 14 20 7 — 55
St. Louis Cardinals .... 7 0 0 7 — 14

TDs: Mia—Nat Moore 3, Gary Davis, Duriel Harris, Leroy Harris, Benny Malone, Andre Tillman; StL—Ike Harris, Terry Metcalf. TD Passes: Mia—Bob Griese 6; StL—Jim Hart.

NEW ENGLAND PATRIOTS

September 9, 1979, at New England

New York Jets .... 3 0 0 0 — 3
New England .... 14 21 7 14 — 56

TDs: NE—Harold Jackson 3, Stanley Morgan 2, Allan Clark, Andy Johnson, Don Westbrook. TD Passes: NE—Steve Grogan 5, Tom Owen. FG: NYJ—Pat Leahy.

NEW YORK JETS

November 17, 1985, at New York

Tampa Bay .... 14 7 7 0 — 28
New York Jets .... 17 24 14 7 — 62

TDs: NYJ—Mickey Shuler 3, Johnny Hector 2, Tony Paige, Al Toon, Wesley Walker; TB—James Wilder 2, Kevin House, Calvin Magee. TD Passes: NYJ—Ken O'Brien 5; TB—Steve DeBerg 2. FGs: NYJ—Pat Leahy 2.

OAKLAND RAIDERS

December 22, 1963, at Oakland

Houston .... 14 21 14 0 — 49
Oakland Raiders .... 7 28 7 10 — 52

TDs: Oak—Art Powell 4, Clem Daniels, Claude Gibson, Ken Herock; Hou—Willard Dewveall 2, Dave Smith 2, Charley Hennigan, Bob McLeod, Charley Tolar. TD Passes: Oak—Tom Flores 6; Hou—George Blanda 5. FG: Oak—Mike Mercer.

PITTSBURGH STEELERS

November 30, 1952, at Pittsburgh

New York Giants .... 0 0 7 0 — 7
Pittsburgh .... 14 14 7 28 — 63

TDs: Pitt—Lynn Chandnois 2, Dick Hensley 2, Jack Butler, George Hays, Ray Mathews, Ed Modzelewski, Elbie Nickel; NYG—Bill Stribling. TD Passes: Pitt—Jim Finks 4, Gary Kerkorian; NYG—Tom Landry.

SAN DIEGO CHARGERS

December 22, 1963, at San Diego

Denver .... 7 10 3 0 — 20
San Diego .... 10 16 10 22 — 58

TDs: SD—Paul Lowe 2, Chuck Allen, Bobby Jackson, Dave Kocourek, Keith Lincoln, Jacque MacKinnon; Den—Billy Joe, Donnie Stone. TD Passes: SD—John Hadl, Tobin Rote; Den—Don Breaux. FGs: SD—George Blair 3; Den—Gene Mingo 2.

SEATTLE SEAHAWKS

October 30, 1977, at Seattle

Buffalo .... 3 0 7 7 — 17
Seattle .... 14 28 7 7 — 56

TDs: Sea—Steve Largent 2, Duke Fergerson, Al Hunter, David Sims, Sherman Smith, Don Testerman, Jim Zorn; Buff—Joe Ferguson, John Kimbrough. TD Passes: Sea—Jim Zorn 4; Buff—Joe Ferguson. FG: Buff—Carson Long.

ARIZONA CARDINALS

November 13, 1949, at New York

Chicago Cardinals .... 7 31 14 13 — 65
New York Bulldogs .... 7 0 6 7 — 20

TDs: Chi—Red Cochran 2, Pat Harder 2, Bill Dewell, Mel Kutner, Bob Ravensburg, Vic Schwall, Charlie Trippi; NY—Joe Golding, Frank Muehlheuser, Johnny Rauch. TD Passes: Chi—Paul Christman 3, Jim Hardy 3; NY—Bobby Layne. FG: Chi—Pat Harder.

ATLANTA FALCONS

September 16, 1973, at New Orleans

Atlanta .... 0 24 21 17 — 62
New Orleans .... 0 0 7 0 — 7

TDs: Atl—Ken Burrow 2, Eddie Ray 2, Wes Chesson, Tom Hayes, Art Malone, Joe Profit; NO—Bill Butler. TD Passes: Atl—Dick Shiner 3, Bob Lee; NO—Archie Manning. FGs: Atl—Nick Mike-Mayer 2.

CAROLINA PANTHERS

November 19, 1995, at Carolina

Arizona .... 0 7 0 0 — 7
Carolina .... 0 14 6 7 — 27

TDs: Car—Bob Christian, Anthony Johnson, Pete Metzelaars; Ariz—Aeneas Williams. TD Passes: Car—Kerry Collins 2. FGs: Car—John Kasay 2.

CHICAGO BEARS

December 7, 1980, at Chicago

Green Bay .... 0 7 0 0 — 7
Chicago .... 0 28 13 20 — 61

TDs: Chi—Walter Payton 3, Brian Baschnagel, Robin Earl, Roland Harper, Willie McClendon, Len Walterscheid, Rickey Watts; GB—James Lofton. TD Passes: Chi—Vince Evans 3; GB—Lynn Dickey.

DALLAS COWBOYS

October 12, 1980, at Dallas

San Francisco .... 0 7 0 7 — 14
Dallas .... 14 24 14 7 — 59

TDs: Dall—Drew Pearson 3, Ron Springs 2, Tony Dorsett, Billy Joe DuPree, Robert Newhouse; SF—Dwight Clark 2. TD Passes: Dall—Danny White 4; SF—Steve DeBerg 2. FG: Dall—Rafael Septien.

DETROIT LIONS

October 26, 1952, at Green Bay

Detroit .... 14 14 14 10 — 52
Green Bay .... 7 3 7 0 — 17

TDs: Det—Jug Girard 2, Bob Hoernschemeyer 2, Jack Christiansen, Jim Smith, Bill Swiacki; GB—Billy Howton, Jim Keane. TD Passes: Det—Bobby Layne 3; GB—Babe Parilli, Tobin Rote. FGs: Det—Pat Harder; GB—Bill Reichardt.

GREEN BAY PACKERS

October 7, 1945, at Milwaukee

Detroit .... 0 7 7 7 — 21
Green Bay .... 0 41 9 7 — 57

TDs: GB—Don Hutson 4, Charley Brock, Irv Comp, Ted Fritsch, Clyde Goodnight; Det—Chuck Fenenbock, John Greene, Bob Westfall. TD Passes: GB—Tex McKay 4, Lou Brock, Irv Comp; Det—Dave Ryan.

MINNESOTA VIKINGS

October 18, 1970, at Minnesota

Dallas .... 3 3 0 7 — 13
Minnesota .... 14 20 17 3 — 54

TDs: Minn—Clint Jones 2, Ed Sharockman 2, John Beasley, Dave Osborn; Dall—Calvin Hill. TD Pass: Minn—Gary Cuozzo. FGs: Minn—Fred Cox 4; Dall—Mike Clark 2.

NEW ORLEANS SAINTS

November 21, 1976, at Seattle

New Orleans .... 3 17 28 3 — 51
Seattle .... 6 0 7 14 — 27

TDs: NO—Bobby Douglass 2, Tony Galbreath, Chuck Muncie, Tom Myers, Elex Price; Sea—Sherman Smith 2, Steve Largent, Jim Zorn. TD Pass: Sea—Bill Munson. FGs: NO—Rich Szaro 3.

NEW YORK GIANTS

November 26, 1972, at New York

Philadelphia .... 3 7 0 0 — 10
New York Giants .... 14 24 10 14 — 62

TDs: NYG—Don Herrmann 2, Ron Johnson 2, Bob Tucker 2, Randy Johnson; Phil—Harold Jackson. TD Passes: NYG—Norm Snead 3, Randy Johnson 2; Phil—John Reaves. FGs: NYG—Pete Gogolak 2; Phil—Tom Dempsey.

PHILADELPHIA EAGLES

November 6, 1934, at Philadelphia

Cincinnati Reds .... 0 0 0 0 — 0
Philadelphia .... 26 6 12 20 — 64

TDs: Phil—Joe Carter 3, Swede Hanson 3, Marvin Ellstrom, Roger Kirkman, Ed Matesic, Ed Storm. TD Passes: Phil—Ed Matesic 2, Albert Weiner 2, Marvin Elstrom.

ST. LOUIS RAMS

October 22, 1950, at Los Angeles

Baltimore .... 13 0 7 7 — 27
Los Angeles .... 21 14 14 21 — 70

TDs: LA—Bob Boyd 2, Vitamin T. Smith 2, Tom Fears, Elroy (Crazylegs) Hirsch, Dick Hoerner, Ralph Pasquariello, Dan Towler, Bob Waterfield; Balt—Chet Mutryn 2, Adrian Burk, Billy Stone. TD Passes: LA—Norm Van Brocklin 2, Bob Waterfield 2, Glenn Davis; Balt—Adrian Burk 3.

SAN FRANCISCO 49ERS
October 18, 1992, at San Francisco

Atlanta	7	3	0	7	— 17
San Francisco	21	21	14	0	— 56

TDs: SF—Jerry Rice 3, Ricky Watters 3, Brent Jones, Tom Rathman; Atl—Michael Haynes, Jason Phillips. TD Passes: SF—Steve Young 3; Atl—Chris Miller, Wade Wilson. FG: Atl—Norm Johnson.

TAMPA BAY BUCCANEERS
September 13, 1987, at Tampa Bay

Atlanta	0	3	0	7	— 10
Tampa Bay	14	13	7	14	— 48

TDs: TB—Gerald Carter 2, Cliff Austin, Steve Bartalo, Mark Carrier, Phil Freeman, Calvin Magee; Atl—Stacey Bailey. TD Passes: TB—Steve DeBerg 5; Atl—Scott Campbell. FG: Atl—Mick Luckhurst.

WASHINGTON REDSKINS
November 27, 1966, at Washington

New York Giants	0	14	14	13	— 41
Washington	13	21	14	24	— 72

TDs: Wash—A.D. Whitfield 3, Brig Owens 2, Charley Taylor 2, Rickie Harris, Joe Don Looney, Bobby Mitchell; NYG—Allen Jacobs, Homer Jones, Dan Lewis, Joe Morrison, Aaron Thomas, Gary Wood. TD Passes: Wash—Sonny Jurgensen 3; NYG—Gary Wood 2, Tom Kennedy. FG: Wash—Charlie Gogolak.

TEAMS THAT FINISHED IN FIRST PLACE IN THEIR DIVISION THE SEASON AFTER FINISHING IN LAST PLACE

Season	Team	Record	Previous Season
1967	Houston	9-4-1	*3-11
1968	Minnesota	8-6	3-8-3
1970	Cincinnati	8-6	4-9-1
1970	San Francisco	10-3-1	4-8-2
1972	Green Bay	10-4	4-8-2
1975	Baltimore	10-4	2-12
1979	Tampa Bay	10-6	5-11
1981	Cincinnati	12-4	6-10
1987	Indianapolis	9-6	3-13
1988	Cincinnati	12-4	4-11
1990	Cincinnati	9-7	8-8
1991	Denver	12-4	5-11
1992	San Diego	11-5	4-12
1993	Detroit	10-6	5-11

**tied for last place*

RECORDS OF NFL TEAMS, 1986-1995

AFC	W	L	T	Pct.	Division Titles	Playoff Berths	Postseason Record	Super Bowl Record
Buffalo	98	61	0	.616	6	7	11-7	0-4
Kansas City	90	67	2	.566	2	7	3-7	0-0
Denver	89	69	1	.563	4	5	7-5	0-3
Miami	89	70	0	.560	2	4	3-4	0-0
Pittsburgh	87	72	0	.547	3	5	4-5	0-1
Houston	84	75	0	.528	2	7	3-7	0-0
Oakland	83	76	0	.522	1	3	2-3	0-0
Cleveland	80	78	1	.506	3	5	4-5	0-0
San Diego	73	86	0	.459	2	3	3-3	0-1
Seattle	73	86	0	.459	1	2	0-2	0-0
Indianapolis	67	92	0	.421	1	2	2-2	0-0
Cincinnati	64	95	0	.403	2	2	3-2	0-1
N.Y. Jets	63	95	1	.399	0	2	1-2	0-0
New England	63	96	0	.396	1	2	0-2	0-0
Jacksonville	4	12	0	.250	0	0	0-0	0-0

Oakland totals include L.A. Raiders, 1986-94

NFC	W	L	T	Pct.	Division Titles	Playoff Berths	Postseason Record	Super Bowl Record
San Francisco	119	39	1	.752	9	9	12-6	3-0
Chicago	95	64	0	.597	4	6	3-6	0-0
N.Y. Giants	94	65	0	.591	3	4	7-2	2-0
New Orleans	91	68	0	.572	1	4	0-4	0-0
Minnesota	90	69	0	.566	3	6	3-6	0-0
Philadelphia	89	69	1	.563	1	5	2-5	0-0
Washington	86	73	0	.541	2	5	10-3	2-0
Dallas	85	74	0	.535	4	5	11-2	3-0
Detroit	72	87	0	.453	2	4	1-4	0-0
Green Bay	71	87	1	.450	1	3	4-3	0-0
Carolina	7	9	0	.438	0	0	0-0	0-0
St. Louis	67	92	0	.421	0	3	2-3	0-0
Atlanta	61	97	1	.387	0	2	1-2	0-0
Arizona	55	103	1	.349	0	0	0-0	0-0
Tampa Bay	48	111	0	.302	0	0	0-0	0-0

Arizona totals include St. Louis, 1986-87, and Phoenix, 1988-93
St. Louis totals include L.A. Rams, 1986-94

HOME RECORDS, 1986-1995

AFC	W-L-T	Pct.	NFC	W-L-T	Pct.
Denver	59-21-0	.738	San Francisco	61-18-0	.772
Buffalo	58-22-0	.725	Chicago	54-26-0	.675
Kansas City	57-22-0	.722	Minnesota	54-26-0	.675
Pittsburgh	53-26-0	.671	N.Y. Giants	54-26-0	.675
Houston	52-27-0	.658	Carolina	5- 3-0	.625
Miami	49-30-0	.620	Philadelphia	49-30-1	.619
Cleveland	44-34-1	.563	New Orleans	48-31-0	.608
Oakland	45-35-0	.563	Washington	48-31-0	.608
Seattle	44-36-0	.550	Dallas	43-36-0	.544
San Diego	39-40-0	.494	Green Bay	42-37-1	.531
Cincinnati	39-41-0	.488	Atlanta	41-38-1	.519
Indianapolis	36-44-0	.450	Detroit	40-39-0	.506
New England	35-45-0	.438	St. Louis	37-42-0	.468
N.Y. Jets	34-45-1	.431	Arizona	33-46-0	.418
Jacksonville	2-6-0	.250	Tampa Bay	30-49-0	.380

Arizona totals include St. Louis, 1986-87, and Phoenix, 1988-93
Oakland totals include L.A. Raiders, 1986-94
St. Louis totals include L.A. Rams, 1986-94

ROAD RECORDS, 1986-1995

AFC	W-L-T	Pct.	NFC	W-L-T	Pct.
Buffalo	40-39-0	.506	San Francisco	58-21-1	.731
Miami	40-40-0	.500	New Orleans	43-37-0	.538
Oakland	38-41-0	.481	Dallas	42-38-0	.525
Cleveland	36-44-0	.450	Chicago	41-38-0	.519
Kansas City	33-45-2	.425	N.Y. Giants	40-39-0	.506
Pittsburgh	34-46-0	.425	Philadelphia	40-39-0	.506
San Diego	34-46-0	.425	Washington	38-42-0	.475
Houston	32-48-0	.400	Minnesota	36-43-0	.456
Indianapolis	31-48-0	.392	Detroit	32-48-0	.400
Denver	30-48-1	.386	St. Louis	30-50-0	.375
N.Y. Jets	29-50-0	.367	Green Bay	29-50-0	.367
Seattle	29-50-0	.367	Arizona	22-57-1	.281
New England	28-51-0	.354	Atlanta	20-59-0	.253
Cincinnati	25-54-0	.316	Carolina	2- 6-0	.250
Jacksonville	2- 6-0	.250	Tampa Bay	18-62-0	.225

Arizona totals include St. Louis, 1986-87, and Phoenix, 1988-93
Oakland totals include L.A. Raiders, 1986-94
St. Louis totals include L.A. Rams, 1986-94

RECORDS BY MONTHS, 1986-1995

AFC	Sept. W-L-T	Oct. W-L-T	Nov. W-L-T	Dec. W-L-T	Total W-L-T	Pct.
Buffalo	27- 9	25-14	27-17	19-21	98-61-0	.616
Kansas City	23-14	18-22-1	23-17-1	26-14	90-67-2	.566
Denver	22-14-1	23-17	26-16	18-22	89-69-1	.563
Miami	20-15	26-15	23-20	20-20	89-70-0	.560
Pittsburgh	16-21	21-19	25-18	25-14	87-72-0	.547
Houston	18-19	20-20	22-20	24-16	84-75-0	.528
Oakland	19-18	25-16	20-21	19-21	83-76-0	.522
Cleveland	20-17	25-15	17-24-1	18-22	80-78-1	.506
San Diego	15-22	16-25	22-20	20-19	73-86-0	.459
Seattle	16-20	20-23	17-23	20-20	73-86-0	.459
Indianapolis	8-27	21-21	16-26	22-18	67-92-0	.421
Cincinnati	16-20	13-28	17-25	18-22	64-95-0	.403
N.Y. Jets	18-19	15-25-1	22-20	8-31	63-95-1	.399
New England	11-25	14-27	20-22	18-22	63-96-0	.396
Jacksonville	0- 4	3- 2	0- 3	1- 3	4-12-0	.250

Oakland totals include L.A. Raiders, 1986-94
December totals include January

NFC	Sept. W-L-T	Oct. W-L-T	Nov. W-L-T	Dec. W-L-T	Total W-L-T	Pct.
San Francisco	26-11	30- 9-1	30-11	33- 8	119- 39-1	.752
Chicago	26-11	27-12	27-17	15-24	95- 64-0	.597
N.Y. Giants	22-13	23-18	24-19	25-15	94- 65-0	.591
New Orleans	19-18	23-17	26-16	23-17	91- 68-0	.572
Minnesota	22-15	19-21	27-16	22-17	90- 69-0	.566
Philadelphia	18-17	23-18	25-18	23-16-1	89- 69-1	.563
Washington	21-15	22-19	19-23	24-16	86- 73-0	.541
Dallas	20-15	24-18	21-23	20-18	85- 74-0	.535
Detroit	14-24	17-22	17-26	24-15	72- 87-0	.453
Green Bay	12-24-1	18-21	22-21	19-21	71- 87-1	.450
Carolina	0- 3	3- 2	2- 2	2- 2	7- 9-0	.438
St. Louis	23-14	14-26	15-27	15-25	67- 92-0	.421
Atlanta	16-21	15-24-1	18-24	12-28	61- 97-1	.387
Arizona	11-25	16-26	15-28	13-24-1	55-103-1	.349
Tampa Bay	14-23	12-29	10-32	12-27	48-111-0	.302

Arizona totals include St. Louis, 1986-87, and Phoenix, 1988-93
St. Louis totals include L.A. Rams, 1986-94
December totals include January

INSIDE THE NUMBERS

TAKEAWAYS/GIVEAWAYS IN 1986-1995

AFC	Takeaways Int.	Fum.	Total	Giveaways Int.	Fum.	Total	Net.Diff.
Kansas City	183	184	367	144	143	287	80
Pittsburgh	216	154	370	165	146	311	59
N.Y. Jets	187	158	345	172	153	325	20
Denver	169	152	321	173	148	321	0
Cleveland	177	130	307	164	146	310	- 3
Jacksonville	13	11	24	15	13	28	- 4
Indianapolis	157	156	313	182	140	322	- 9
San Diego	188	128	316	197	128	325	- 9
Seattle	177	152	329	197	148	345	- 16
Buffalo	185	142	327	179	166	345	- 18
Houston	204	153	357	207	177	384	- 27
Cincinnati	156	134	290	177	147	324	- 34
New England	168	160	328	214	149	363	- 35
Oakland	154	135	289	187	142	329	- 40
Miami	159	123	282	190	147	337	- 55

Oakland totals include L.A. Raiders, 1986-94

NFC	Takeaways Int.	Fum.	Total	Giveaways Int.	Fum.	Total	Net.Diff.
Philadelphia	235	172	407	165	150	315	92
San Francisco	221	128	349	140	131	271	78
Minnesota	238	141	379	180	127	307	72
N.Y. Giants	180	139	319	137	124	261	58
New Orleans	193	172	365	179	144	323	42
Detroit	182	155	337	191	147	338	- 1
Carolina	21	16	37	25	16	41	- 4
Washington	204	119	323	200	128	328	- 5
Chicago	204	126	330	184	158	342	- 12
Green Bay	181	149	330	196	159	355	- 25
Dallas	152	130	282	179	134	313	- 31
Atlanta	181	132	313	197	148	345	- 32
St. Louis	175	127	302	186	155	341	- 39
Arizona	156	152	308	213	138	351	- 43
Tampa Bay	159	156	315	240	134	374	- 59

Arizona totals include St. Louis, 1986-87, and Phoenix, 1988-93
St. Louis totals include L.A. Rams, 1986-94

HIGH AND LOW SINGLE-GAME YARDAGE TOTALS, 1986-1995

Most Total Yards, Game
676 Washington vs. Detroit, Nov. 4, 1990 (OT)
621 Cincinnati vs. N.Y. Jets, Dec. 21, 1986
598 San Francisco vs. Buffalo, Sept. 13, 1992
597 N.Y. Jets vs. Miami, Nov. 27, 1988
590 San Francisco vs. Atlanta, Oct. 18, 1992

Fewest Total Yards, Game
53 Pittsburgh vs. Cleveland, Sept. 10, 1989
60 Detroit vs. Minnesota, Nov. 24, 1988
62 Seattle vs. Dallas, Oct. 11, 1992
65 Seattle vs. New England, Dec. 4, 1988
82 Denver vs. Philadelphia, Sept. 20, 1992

Most Yards Rushing, Game
356 L.A. Raiders vs. Seattle, Nov. 30, 1987
315 Buffalo vs. Atlanta, Nov. 22, 1992
310 Kansas City vs. Detroit, Oct. 14, 1990
305 Pittsburgh vs. Miami, Dec. 18, 1988
304 Philadelphia vs. New England, Nov. 4, 1990

Fewest Yards Rushing, Game
0 Buffalo vs. Chicago, Oct. 2, 1988
1 Tampa Bay vs. Washington, Oct. 22, 1989
2 New England vs. New Orleans, Nov. 30, 1986
4 Indianapolis vs. Detroit, Sept. 22, 1991
6 N.Y. Giants vs. L.A. Rams, Nov. 12, 1989

Most Yards Passing, Game
521 Miami vs. N.Y. Jets, Oct. 23, 1988
505 Houston vs. Kansas City, Dec. 16, 1990
483 Cincinnati vs. L.A. Rams, Oct. 7, 1990
482 Washington vs. Detroit, Nov. 4, 1990 (OT)
475 San Francisco vs. L.A. Rams, Nov. 28, 1993

Fewest Yards Passing, Game
–13 Cincinnati vs. San Diego, Oct. 4, 1987
4 St. Louis vs. New Orleans, Oct. 11, 1987
12 Carolina vs. Buffalo, Sept. 10, 1995
15 New England vs. Atlanta, Nov. 29, 1992
17 Pittsburgh vs. Cleveland, Sept. 10, 1989

NFL INDIVIDUAL LEADERS, 1986-1995

Points		Touchdowns		Field Goals	
1,123	Morten Andersen	152	Jerry Rice	262	Morten Andersen
1,014	Gary Anderson	100	Emmitt Smith	237	Gary Anderson
1,014	Nick Lowery	81	Herschel Walker	230	Nick Lowery
1,008	Norm Johnson	80	Barry Sanders	215	Norm Johnson
972	Kevin Butler	74	Thurman Thomas	212	Kevin Butler

Rushes		Rushing Yards		Rushing TDs	
2,285	Thurman Thomas	10,172	Barry Sanders	96	Emmitt Smith
2,077	Barry Sanders	9,729	Thurman Thomas	73	Barry Sanders
2,007	Emmitt Smith	8,956	Emmitt Smith	60	Herschel Walker
1,938	Herschel Walker	8,122	Herschel Walker	59	Marcus Allen
1,935	Eric Dickerson	8,112	Eric Dickerson	54	Thurman Thomas

Passes		Completions		Passing Yards	
5,104	Dan Marino	3,042	Dan Marino	37,410	Dan Marino
4,926	Warren Moon	2,921	Warren Moon	36,130	Warren Moon
4,682	John Elway	2,682	John Elway	33,554	John Elway
4,400	Jim Kelly	2,652	Jim Kelly	32,657	Jim Kelly
4,384	Jim Everett	2,538	Jim Everett	31,583	Jim Everett

TD Passes		Receptions		Reception Yards	
254	Dan Marino	893	Jerry Rice	14,196	Jerry Rice
223	Jim Kelly	652	Andre Reed	10,462	Henry Ellard
220	Warren Moon	627	Gary Clark	9,930	Gary Clark
193	Boomer Esiason	619	Henry Ellard	9,211	Andre Reed
190	Jim Everett	595	Sterling Sharpe	8,215	Ernest Givins

Receiving TDs		Interceptions		Sacks	
143	Jerry Rice	40	Ronnie Lott	144.0	Reggie White
66	Cris Carter	40	Eugene Robinson	120.0	Bruce Smith
65	Andre Reed	36	Eric Allen	108.0	Kevin Greene
65	Sterling Sharpe	36	Gill Byrd	105.5	Leslie O'Neal
63	Andre Rison	35	Vencie Glenn	104.0	Chris Doleman

NFL GAMES IN WHICH A TEAM HAS SCORED 60 OR MORE POINTS

(Home team in capitals)

Regular Season
WASHINGTON 72, New York Giants 41 .... November 27, 1966
LOS ANGELES RAMS 70, Baltimore 27 .... October 22, 1950
Chicago Cardinals 65, NEW YORK BULLDOGS 20 .... November 13, 1949
LOS ANGELES RAMS 65, Detroit 24 .... October 29, 1950
PHILADELPHIA 64, Cincinnati 0 .... November 6, 1934
CHICAGO CARDINALS 63, New York Giants 35 .... October 17, 1948
AKRON 62, Oorang 0 .... October 29,1922
PITTSBURGH 62, New York Giants 7 .... November 30, 1952
CLEVELAND 62, New York Giants 14 .... December 6, 1953
CLEVELAND 62, Washington 3 .... November 7, 1954
NEW YORK GIANTS 62, Philadelphia 10 .... November 26, 1972
Atlanta 62, NEW ORLEANS 7 .... September 16, 1973
NEW YORK JETS 62, Tampa Bay 28 .... November 17, 1985
CHICAGO 61, San Francisco 20 .... December 12, 1965
Cincinnati 61, HOUSTON 17 .... December 17, 1972
CHICAGO 61, Green Bay 7 .... December 7, 1980
CINCINNATI 61, Houston 7 .... December 17, 1989
ROCK ISLAND 60, Evansville 0 .... October 15, 1922
CHICAGO CARDINALS 60, Rochester 0 .... October 7, 1923

Postseason
Chicago Bears 73, WASHINGTON 0 .... December 8, 1940

YOUNGEST AND OLDEST PLAYERS IN NFL IN 1995

10 Youngest Players	Birthdate	Games	Starts	Position
Rashaan Salaam, Chicago	10/8/74	16	11	RB
Darren Benson, Dallas	8/25/74	6	0	DT
Korey Stringer, Minnesota	5/8/74	16	15	T
Tamarick Vanover, Kansas City	2/25/74	15	0	WR
Ty Law, New England	2/10/74	14	7	CB
Lorenzo Styles, Atlanta	1/31/74	12	0	LB
Kevin Jefferson, Cincinnati	1/14/74	16	0	LB
Bobby Taylor, Philadelphia	12/28/73	16	12	CB
Donny Brady, Cleveland	11/24/73	2	0	DB
Jamir Miller, Arizona	11/19/73	10	9	LB

10 Oldest Players	Birthdate	Games	Starts	Position
Jackie Slater, St. Louis	5/27/54	1	1	T
Vince Evans, Oakland	6/14/55	9	3	QB
Clay Matthews, Atlanta	3/15/56	16	16	LB
Nick Lowery, N.Y. Jets	5/27/56	14	0	K
Matt Bahr, New England	7/6/56	16	0	K
Eddie Murray, Washington	8/29/56	16	0	K
Warren Moon, Minnesota	11/18/56	16	16	QB
Jeff Gossett, Oakland	1/25/57	16	0	P
Art Monk, Philadelphia	12/5/57	3	1	WR
Rickey Jackson, San Francisco	3/20/58	16	15	DE

YOUNGEST AND OLDEST REGULAR STARTERS BY POSITION IN 1995

Minimum: 8 Games Started

	Youngest		Oldest	
QB	12/30/72	Kerry Collins, Car.	11/18/56	Warren Moon, Minn.
RB	10/8/74	Rashaan Salaam, Chi.	3/26/60	Marcus Allen, K.C.
WR	8/14/73	Wayne Chrebet, N.Y. Jets	7/21/61	Henry Ellard, Wash.
TE	9/16/72	Mark Bruener, Pitt.	5/24/60	Pete Metzelaars, Car.
C	4/27/72	Tim Ruddy, Mia.	5/18/58	Ray Donaldson, Dall.
G	11/14/72	Aaron Taylor, G.B.	12/20/59	Dave Lutz, Det.
T	5/8/74	Korey Stringer, Minn.	6/8/58	Stan Brock, S.D.
DE	11/3/73	Derrick Alexander, Minn.	3/20/58	Rickey Jackson, S.F.
DT	3/13/73	Dan Wilkinson, Cin.	10/11/60	Joe Nash, Sea.
LB	11/19/73	Jamir Miller, Ariz.	3/15/56	Clay Matthews, Atl.
CB	12/28/73	Bobby Taylor, Phil.	2/15/60	Darrell Green, Wash.
S	10/21/72	Orlando Thomas, Minn.	1/13/62	Brett Maxie, Car.

MARCUS ALLEN'S CAREER RUSHING VS. EACH OPPONENT

Opponent	Games	Rushes	Yards	Yards Per Rush	Yards Per Game	TD
Arizona	3	33	158	4.8	52.7	1
Atlanta	4	55	241	4.4	60.3	1
Buffalo	8	128	439	3.4	54.9	5
Chicago	4	61	252	4.1	63.0	4
Cincinnati	8	101	363	3.6	45.4	5
Cleveland	5	56	227	4.1	45.4	0
Dallas	4	28	97	3.5	24.3	1
Denver	24	350	1,476	4.2	61.5	10
Detroit	3	46	153	3.3	51.0	2
Green Bay	4	75	269	3.6	67.3	5
Houston	7	100	372	3.7	53.1	3
Indianapolis	2	28	141	5.0	70.5	0
Kansas City	17	264	961	3.6	56.5	8
Miami	8	110	558	5.1	69.8	7
Minnesota	4	44	150	3.4	37.5	1
New England	3	50	200	4.0	66.7	1
New Orleans	4	70	316	4.5	79.0	3
N.Y. Giants	5	49	203	4.1	40.6	2
N.Y. Jets	2	30	119	4.0	59.5	2
Oakland	6	120	480	4.0	80.0	3
Philadelphia	2	30	82	2.7	41.0	0
Pittsburgh	2	24	82	3.4	41.0	1
St. Louis	4	78	328	4.2	82.0	3
San Diego	23	355	1,403	4.0	61.0	21
San Francisco	4	69	302	4.4	75.5	2
Seattle	25	288	1,279	4.4	51.2	11
Tampa Bay	1	13	79	6.1	79.0	0
Washington	4	37	178	4.8	44.5	1
Totals	190	2,692	10,908	4.1	57.4	103

Arizona totals include one game vs. St. Louis, one game vs. Phoenix
Oakland totals include four games vs. L.A. Raiders
St. Louis totals include four games vs. L.A. Rams

EMMITT SMITH'S CAREER RUSHING VS. EACH OPPONENT

Opponent	Games	Rushes	Yards	Yards Per Rush	Yards Per Game	TD
Arizona	12	237	998	4.2	83.2	17
Atlanta	5	99	536	5.4	107.2	5
Chicago	1	20	131	6.6	131.0	1
Cincinnati	2	44	154	3.5	77.0	1
Cleveland	2	58	224	3.9	112.0	1
Denver	2	52	176	3.4	88.0	2
Detroit	3	64	276	4.3	92.0	4
Green Bay	4	108	432	4.0	108.0	5
Houston	2	39	139	3.6	69.5	1
Indianapolis	1	25	104	4.2	104.0	1
Kansas City	2	42	151	3.6	75.5	2
Miami	1	16	51	3.2	51.0	0
Minnesota	2	39	254	6.5	127.0	3
New Orleans	3	66	271	4.1	90.3	2
N.Y. Giants	11	229	1,126	4.9	102.4	13
N.Y. Jets	2	35	146	4.2	73.0	0
Oakland	2	58	262	4.5	131.0	6
Philadelphia	12	273	1,334	4.9	111.2	8
Pittsburgh	2	63	280	4.4	140.0	2
St. Louis	2	40	134	3.4	67.0	1
San Diego	2	24	70	2.9	35.0	2
San Francisco	4	77	310	4.0	77.5	4
Seattle	1	22	78	3.5	78.0	2
Tampa Bay	2	39	169	4.3	84.5	1
Washington	11	238	1,150	4.8	104.5	12
Totals	93	2,007	8,956	4.5	96.3	96

Arizona totals include eight games vs. Phoenix
Oakland totals include one game vs. L.A. Raiders
St. Louis totals include two games vs. L.A. Rams

BARRY SANDERS'S CAREER RUSHING VS. EACH OPPONENT

Opponent	Games	Rushes	Yards	Yards Per Rush	Yards Per Game	TD
Arizona	3	56	308	5.5	102.7	2
Atlanta	5	103	467	4.5	93.4	5
Buffalo	2	45	153	3.4	76.5	2
Chicago	13	252	1,203	4.8	92.5	8
Cincinnati	2	47	265	5.6	132.5	2
Cleveland	3	76	389	5.1	129.7	4
Dallas	3	79	357	4.5	119.0	0
Denver	1	23	147	6.4	147.0	1
Green Bay	13	250	1,360	5.4	104.6	5
Houston	3	60	199	3.3	66.3	4
Indianapolis	1	30	179	6.0	179.0	2
Jacksonville	1	22	76	3.5	76.0	2
Kansas City	1	16	90	5.6	90.0	1
Miami	2	44	195	4.4	97.5	0
Minnesota	13	235	1,119	4.8	86.1	10
New England	2	50	279	5.6	139.5	2
New Orleans	4	57	194	3.4	48.5	2
N.Y. Giants	3	49	272	5.6	90.7	1
N.Y. Jets	2	43	241	5.6	120.5	2
Oakland	1	25	176	7.0	176.0	2
Pittsburgh	3	47	203	4.3	67.7	1
St. Louis	2	52	148	2.8	74.0	1
San Francisco	4	65	249	3.8	62.3	1
Seattle	2	31	124	4.0	62.0	1
Tampa Bay	13	275	1,565	5.7	120.4	11
Washington	3	45	214	4.8	71.3	1
Totals	105	2,077	10,172	4.9	96.9	73

Arizona totals include two games vs. Phoenix
Oakland totals include one game vs. L.A. Raiders
St. Louis totals include two games vs. L.A. Rams

THURMAN THOMAS'S CAREER RUSHING VS. EACH OPPONENT

Opponent	Games	Rushes	Yards	Yards Per Rush	Yards Per Game	TD
Arizona	1	26	112	4.3	112.0	0
Atlanta	3	51	264	5.2	88.0	1
Carolina	1	22	91	4.1	91.0	1
Chicago	2	30	129	4.3	64.5	1
Cincinnati	3	50	234	4.7	78.0	0
Cleveland	2	40	144	3.6	72.0	2
Dallas	1	25	75	3.0	75.0	0
Denver	5	84	343	4.1	68.6	3
Detroit	1	17	58	3.4	58.0	0
Green Bay	3	78	302	3.9	100.7	2
Houston	6	100	433	4.3	72.2	2
Indianapolis	15	258	1,048	4.1	69.9	7
Kansas City	3	49	153	3.1	51.0	1
Miami	14	300	1,333	4.4	95.2	7
Minnesota	2	34	136	4.0	68.0	1
New England	16	331	1,517	4.6	94.8	8
New Orleans	2	40	155	3.9	77.5	2
N.Y. Giants	2	47	182	3.9	91.0	1
N.Y. Jets	16	278	1,334	4.8	83.4	6
Oakland	5	79	356	4.5	71.2	3
Philadelphia	2	31	84	2.7	42.0	0
Pittsburgh	5	102	442	4.3	88.4	1

Opponent	Games	Rushes	Yards	Yards Per Rush	Yards Per Game	TD
St. Louis	3	70	337	4.8	112.3	3
San Francisco	3	35	132	3.8	44.0	1
Seattle	3	51	151	3.0	50.3	0
Tampa Bay	2	24	55	2.3	27.5	0
Washington	2	33	129	3.9	64.5	1
Totals	123	2,285	9,729	4.3	79.1	54

Arizona totals include one game vs. Phoenix
Oakland totals include five games vs. L.A. Raiders
St. Louis totals include two games vs. L.A. Rams

DAN MARINO'S CAREER PASSING VS. EACH OPPONENT

Opponent	Games	Att.	Cmp.	Pct.	Yards	Avg. Gain	TD	Int.	Sacked
Arizona	2	61	42	68.9	634	10.39	5	0	1/9
Atlanta	3	130	75	57.7	896	6.89	4	6	1/2
Buffalo	24	828	514	62.1	6,374	7.70	44	31	31/259
Chicago	4	117	63	53.8	855	7.31	6	4	8/50
Cincinnati	6	219	143	65.3	1,680	7.67	11	2	6/47
Cleveland	6	205	126	61.5	1,661	8.10	11	5	4/33
Dallas	3	115	66	57.4	860	7.48	6	3	4/36
Denver	1	43	25	58.1	390	9.07	3	0	3/25
Detroit	3	113	65	57.5	706	6.25	2	2	4/28
Green Bay	5	171	112	65.5	1,328	7.77	11	6	6/37
Houston	7	220	116	52.7	1,464	6.65	10	11	7/36
Indianapolis	25	831	505	60.8	6,042	7.27	43	14	23/156
Kansas City	6	212	123	58.0	1,428	6.74	11	4	3/30
Minnesota	2	91	49	53.8	695	7.64	5	6	1/5
New England	23	784	461	58.8	5,741	7.32	39	35	17/134
New Orleans	3	105	65	61.9	650	6.19	5	2	6/42
N.Y. Giants	1	30	14	46.7	115	3.83	0	2	1/7
N.Y. Jets	22	813	487	59.9	6,622	8.15	58	27	29/160
Oakland	7	241	133	55.2	1,655	6.87	14	7	10/81
Philadelphia	3	127	72	56.7	987	7.77	6	2	5/45
Pittsburgh	8	247	157	63.6	1,828	7.40	11	10	7/47
St. Louis	4	156	98	62.8	1,195	7.66	11	5	3/14
San Diego	5	202	128	63.4	1,534	7.59	11	3	6/42
San Francisco	4	144	84	58.3	942	6.54	5	5	8/56
Seattle	2	68	40	58.8	504	7.41	3	4	3/25
Tampa Bay	3	117	74	63.2	875	7.48	7	1	1/10
Washington	4	141	76	53.9	1,180	8.37	10	3	2/7
Totals	186	6,531	3,913	59.9	48,841	7.48	352	200	200/1,423

Arizona totals include one game vs. St. Louis, one game vs. Phoenix
Indianapolis totals include two games vs. Baltimore Colts
Oakland totals include seven games vs. L.A. Raiders
St. Louis totals include three games vs. L.A. Rams

JOHN ELWAY'S CAREER PASSING VS. EACH OPPONENT

Opponent	Games	Att.	Cmp.	Pct.	Yards	Avg. Gain	TD	Int.	Sacked
Arizona	3	83	55	66.3	748	9.01	6	5	4/26
Atlanta	3	106	62	58.5	908	8.57	6	3	9/72
Buffalo	6	196	103	52.6	1,336	6.82	6	6	14/108
Chicago	5	118	65	55.1	763	6.47	3	4	12/73
Cincinnati	4	113	69	61.1	856	7.58	7	1	6/46
Cleveland	9	251	147	58.6	2,005	7.99	14	7	16/126
Dallas	2	48	23	47.9	352	7.33	5	1	3/24
Detroit	3	88	56	63.6	699	7.94	2	2	7/72
Green Bay	4	153	88	57.5	913	5.97	2	5	5/38
Houston	4	139	81	58.3	1,081	7.78	8	6	11/109
Indianapolis	7	213	118	55.4	1,545	7.25	8	2	17/129
Jacksonville	1	34	22	64.7	286	8.41	4	1	0/0
Kansas City	24	753	422	56.0	5,286	7.02	22	31	68/490
Miami	1	37	18	48.6	250	6.76	0	1	3/24
Minnesota	5	130	84	64.6	923	7.10	10	2	13/100
New England	7	226	129	57.1	1,573	6.96	9	5	9/59
New Orleans	2	79	46	58.2	519	6.57	4	2	4/35
N.Y. Giants	3	103	58	56.3	724	7.03	2	3	3/19
N.Y. Jets	4	132	80	60.6	994	7.53	4	4	8/45
Oakland	22	680	367	54.0	4,606	6.77	26	25	58/471
Philadelphia	5	105	54	51.4	680	6.48	5	6	16/119
Pittsburgh	7	192	105	54.7	1,366	7.11	6	5	14/109
St. Louis	3	119	63	52.9	742	6.24	7	2	4/29
San Diego	25	791	453	57.3	5,415	6.85	23	31	58/391
San Francisco	3	99	51	51.5	531	5.36	3	4	11/80
Seattle	24	783	436	55.7	5,643	7.21	30	25	55/391
Tampa Bay	1	41	26	63.4	225	5.49	0	0	1/0
Washington	3	114	65	57.0	737	6.46	3	2	9/68
Totals	190	5,926	3,346	56.5	41,706	7.04	225	191	438/3,253

Arizona totals include two games vs. Phoenix
Oakland totals include 20 games vs. L.A. Raiders
St. Louis totals include three games vs. L.A. Rams

BRETT FAVRE'S CAREER PASSING VS. EACH OPPONENT

Opponent	Games	Att.	Cmp.	Pct.	Yards	Avg. Gain	TD	Int.	Sacked
Atlanta	2	87	62	71.3	597	6.86	3	2	4/26
Buffalo	1	40	22	55.0	214	5.35	3	1	1/9
Chicago	8	255	158	62.0	1,941	7.61	17	7	15/92
Cincinnati	2	82	53	64.6	628	7.66	5	1	6/36
Cleveland	2	61	43	70.5	433	7.10	3	0	4/22
Dallas	3	118	69	58.5	726	6.15	5	1	3/31
Denver	1	32	20	62.5	235	7.34	1	3	0/0
Detroit	8	282	186	66.0	2,124	7.53	15	12	11/77
Houston	1	30	19	63.3	155	5.17	1	1	3/1
Jacksonville	1	30	20	66.7	202	6.73	2	1	2/9
Kansas City	1	34	20	58.8	213	6.26	1	3	4/25
Miami	1	51	31	60.8	362	7.10	2	1	4/17
Minnesota	7	218	130	59.6	1,282	5.88	7	9	13/85
New England	1	47	25	53.2	294	6.26	1	2	4/30
New Orleans	2	62	39	62.9	458	7.39	5	0	8/39
N.Y. Giants	2	69	41	59.4	420	6.09	2	3	5/34
N.Y. Jets	1	28	20	71.4	183	6.54	2	0	1/11
Oakland	1	28	14	50.0	190	6.79	1	0	2/9
Philadelphia	3	102	59	57.8	666	6.53	5	6	9/55
Pittsburgh	2	51	37	72.5	511	10.02	4	0	4/27
St. Louis	5	144	87	60.4	973	6.76	7	6	12/102
San Diego	1	23	13	56.5	146	6.35	0	1	2/22
Tampa Bay	8	271	174	64.2	1,872	6.91	16	4	11/53
Washington	1	5	0	0.0	0	0.0	0	2	1/11
Totals	65	2,150	1,342	62.4	14,825	6.90	108	66	129/823

Oakland totals include one game vs. L.A. Raiders
St. Louis totals include four games vs. L.A. Rams

WARREN MOON'S CAREER PASSING VS. EACH OPPONENT

Opponent	Games	Att.	Cmp.	Pct.	Yards	Avg. Gain	TD	Int.	Sacked
Arizona	4	151	84	55.6	1,150	7.62	9	4	9/76
Atlanta	4	156	87	55.8	1,189	7.62	9	5	9/43
Buffalo	8	206	117	56.8	1,528	7.42	7	9	12/94
Chicago	6	211	131	62.1	1,562	7.40	7	6	15/112
Cincinnati	20	649	383	59.0	4,902	7.55	37	22	37/310
Cleveland	19	590	336	56.9	4,315	7.31	25	22	42/314
Dallas	4	149	89	59.7	1,058	7.10	4	4	19/130
Denver	3	87	50	57.5	777	8.93	5	2	9/66
Detroit	6	209	137	65.6	1,767	8.45	9	8	9/71
Green Bay	5	182	102	56.0	1,011	5.55	6	8	12/116
Houston	1	43	28	65.1	289	6.72	2	2	1/8
Indianapolis	7	255	160	62.7	2,156	8.45	13	7	14/97
Kansas City	8	267	166	62.2	2,006	7.51	10	7	26/180
Miami	6	148	102	68.9	1,236	8.35	8	6	11/112
Minnesota	3	95	58	61.1	592	6.23	2	2	14/106
New England	4	136	76	55.9	946	6.96	6	4	5/41
New Orleans	6	202	121	59.9	1,495	7.40	10	4	13/85
N.Y. Giants	3	117	71	60.7	865	7.39	4	3	6/53
N.Y. Jets	4	171	118	69.0	1,411	8.25	8	6	10/86
Oakland	4	138	68	49.3	1,004	7.28	6	5	13/115
Philadelphia	1	46	24	52.2	262	5.70	0	0	4/36
Pittsburgh	20	621	350	56.4	4,421	7.12	24	29	42/320
St. Louis	4	157	85	54.1	1,163	7.41	4	7	10/71
San Diego	6	201	108	53.7	1,362	6.78	7	6	10/71
San Francisco	5	167	93	55.7	1,127	6.75	10	8	13/81
Seattle	3	115	73	63.5	783	6.81	4	4	5/34
Tampa Bay	5	182	110	60.4	1,221	6.71	7	6	6/41
Washington	3	102	53	52.0	579	5.68	4	3	6/46
Totals	172	5,753	3,380	58.8	42,177	7.33	247	199	382/2,915

Arizona totals include one game vs. St. Louis, one game vs. Phoenix
Oakland totals include four games vs. L.A. Raiders
St. Louis totals include four games vs. L.A. Rams

JIM KELLY'S CAREER PASSING VS. EACH OPPONENT

Opponent	Games	Att.	Cmp.	Pct.	Yards	Avg. Gain	TD	Int.	Sacked
Arizona	2	26	17	65.4	270	10.38	4	1	5/34
Atlanta	3	73	46	63.0	596	8.16	6	3	5/29
Carolina	1	21	4	19.0	176	8.38	1	3	0/0
Chicago	3	99	58	58.6	692	6.99	4	3	11/96
Cincinnati	4	99	65	65.7	1,008	10.18	10	7	5/49
Cleveland	4	127	83	65.4	993	7.82	7	1	7/41
Dallas	1	27	16	59.3	155	5.74	1	1	4/26
Denver	6	178	99	55.6	1,145	6.43	4	8	12/86
Detroit	1	35	29	82.9	273	7.80	2	2	2/18
Green Bay	3	93	59	63.4	677	7.28	5	3	7/41
Houston	7	207	128	61.8	1,625	7.85	14	7	20/148
Indianapolis	18	500	300	60.0	3,752	7.50	28	10	20/154
Kansas City	5	153	95	62.1	1,068	6.98	7	7	13/105

Opponent	Games	Att.	Cmp.	Pct.	Yards	Avg. Gain	TD	Int.	Sacked
Miami	18	560	350	62.5	4,073	7.27	22	15	27/198
Minnesota	2	57	32	56.1	377	6.61	2	2	4/28
New England	18	526	311	59.1	3,955	7.52	26	24	49/375
New Orleans	2	63	30	47.6	346	5.49	2	4	3/16
N.Y. Giants	2	36	21	58.3	257	7.14	2	1	5/30
N.Y. Jets	19	597	351	58.8	4,363	7.31	30	21	35/247
Oakland	6	208	125	60.1	1,550	7.45	8	5	12/89
Philadelphia	3	98	56	57.1	698	7.12	4	5	3/26
Pittsburgh	6	192	117	60.9	1,341	6.98	12	5	15/116
St. Louis	2	44	32	72.7	343	7.80	6	2	2/5
San Francisco	3	116	66	56.9	882	7.60	5	7	8/59
Seattle	3	84	47	56.0	599	7.13	4	2	4/37
Tampa Bay	3	114	72	63.2	913	8.01	4	3	5/54
Washington	2	67	43	64.2	530	7.91	3	4	3/33
Totals	147	4,400	2,652	60.3	32,657	7.42	223	156	286/2,140

Arizona totals include one game vs. St. Louis, one game vs. Phoenix
Oakland totals include six games vs. L.A. Raiders
St. Louis totals include one game vs. L.A. Rams

TROY AIKMAN'S CAREER PASSING VS. EACH OPPONENT

Opponent	Games	Att.	Cmp.	Pct.	Yards	Avg. Gain	TD	Int.	Sacked
Arizona	12	299	190	63.5	2,609	8.73	14	9	14/94
Atlanta	3	69	50	72.5	678	9.83	6	3	1/4
Buffalo	1	45	28	62.2	297	6.60	0	2	1/7
Chicago	1	20	10	50.0	78	3.90	0	0	1/2
Cincinnati	2	55	34	61.8	548	9.96	3	3	1/12
Cleveland	2	73	45	61.6	462	6.33	3	2	4/20
Denver	2	66	43	65.2	427	6.47	5	1	2/9
Detroit	3	106	70	66.0	765	7.22	3	3	4/30
Green Bay	4	123	91	74.0	1,045	8.50	4	4	5/33
Houston	2	64	38	59.4	488	7.63	2	1	6/22
Indianapolis	1	28	21	75.0	245	8.75	1	0	2/14
Kansas City	2	58	42	72.4	384	6.62	3	2	3/26
Miami	2	76	53	69.7	442	5.82	2	2	0/0
Minnesota	2	67	43	64.2	454	6.78	2	0	2/13
New Orleans	3	84	53	63.1	532	6.33	1	4	4/46
N.Y. Giants	14	320	214	66.9	2,340	7.31	11	6	17/101
N.Y. Jets	2	67	46	68.7	501	7.48	2	5	6/40
Oakland	2	49	35	71.4	461	9.41	1	0	6/31
Philadelphia	12	307	161	52.4	1,763	5.74	9	13	36/217
Pittsburgh	1	32	21	65.6	245	7.66	1	1	0/0
St. Louis	3	103	58	56.3	754	7.32	7	2	4/25
San Diego	2	59	34	57.6	415	7.03	1	1	6/39
San Francisco	4	104	57	54.8	707	6.80	1	5	8/55
Seattle	1	23	15	65.2	173	7.52	0	2	1/3
Tampa Bay	2	53	30	56.6	332	6.26	2	2	5/38
Washington	13	363	222	61.2	2,462	6.78	14	12	28/199
Totals	98	2,713	1,704	62.8	19,607	7.23	98	85	167/1,080

Arizona totals include eight games vs. Phoenix
Oakland totals include one game vs. L.A. Raiders
St. Louis totals include three games vs. L.A. Rams

STEVE YOUNG'S CAREER PASSING VS. EACH OPPONENT

Opponent	Games	Att.	Cmp.	Pct.	Yards	Avg. Gain	TD	Int.	Sacked
Arizona	5	131	69	52.7	885	6.76	5	2	10/71
Atlanta	14	361	237	65.7	3,206	8.88	27	12	17/107
Buffalo	4	124	77	62.1	1,051	8.48	4	4	12/88
Carolina	1	45	31	68.9	336	7.47	2	1	3/14
Chicago	6	136	75	55.1	993	7.30	8	3	9/52
Cincinnati	1	25	13	52.0	179	7.16	0	2	1/6
Cleveland	3	34	19	55.9	274	8.06	0	3	1/8
Dallas	4	72	49	68.1	624	8.67	5	1	8/42
Denver	2	32	20	62.5	350	10.94	3	3	1/8
Detroit	8	204	138	67.6	1,668	8.18	11	3	15/115
Green Bay	5	109	59	54.1	668	6.13	2	6	24/177
Houston	2	29	15	51.7	178	6.14	0	2	2/10
Indianapolis	2	65	42	64.6	480	7.38	2	3	8/43
Kansas City	3	58	37	63.8	433	7.47	2	3	9/55
Miami	1	27	19	70.4	220	8.15	2	1	0/0
Minnesota	9	243	154	63.4	1,938	7.98	12	9	28/129
New England	3	81	59	72.8	706	8.72	8	2	7/30
New Orleans	13	271	186	68.6	2,014	7.43	14	4	33/193
N.Y. Giants	5	87	53	60.9	506	5.82	3	1	5/26
N.Y. Jets	2	43	28	65.1	345	8.02	3	0	1/4
Oakland	2	67	37	55.2	525	7.84	4	3	4/20
Philadelphia	4	92	60	65.2	702	7.63	5	2	8/52
Pittsburgh	2	36	24	66.7	240	6.67	3	3	1/0
St. Louis	13	313	210	67.1	2,692	8.60	20	4	17/82
San Diego	3	71	53	74.6	666	9.38	5	0	2/10
Seattle	1	6	4	66.7	49	8.17	1	0	0/0
Tampa Bay	4	87	62	71.3	850	9.77	8	0	5/28
Washington	2	27	15	55.6	291	10.78	1	2	2/8
Totals	124	2,876	1,845	64.2	23,069	8.02	160	79	233/1,378

Arizona totals include two games vs. St. Louis, three games vs. Phoenix
Oakland totals include two games vs. L.A. Raiders
St. Louis totals include 12 games vs. L.A. Rams

JERRY RICE'S CAREER RECEIVING VS. EACH OPPONENT

Opponent	Games	Rec.	Yards	Yards Per Rec.	Yards Per Game	TD
Arizona	5	25	465	18.6	93.0	5
Atlanta	21	125	2,000	16.0	95.2	21
Buffalo	3	11	104	9.5	34.7	1
Carolina	2	14	232	16.6	116.0	0
Chicago	5	24	424	17.7	84.8	7
Cincinnati	3	16	269	16.8	89.7	2
Cleveland	3	19	275	14.5	91.7	4
Dallas	6	38	622	16.4	103.7	4
Denver	3	16	266	16.6	88.7	1
Detroit	7	33	484	14.7	69.1	2
Green Bay	4	23	432	18.8	108.0	4
Houston	3	23	238	10.3	79.3	2
Indianapolis	3	18	378	21.0	126.0	5
Kansas City	3	13	178	13.7	59.3	2
Miami	3	18	304	16.9	101.3	5
Minnesota	9	50	874	17.5	97.1	10
New England	4	19	294	15.5	73.5	5
New Orleans	22	112	1,618	14.4	73.5	12
N.Y. Giants	7	34	525	15.4	75.0	5
N.Y. Jets	3	15	265	17.7	88.3	2
Oakland	4	18	362	20.1	90.5	2
Philadelphia	6	31	490	15.8	81.7	5
Pittsburgh	3	19	215	11.3	71.7	3
St. Louis	22	120	1,927	16.1	87.6	17
San Diego	3	27	465	17.2	155.0	4
Seattle	3	14	272	19.4	90.7	4
Tampa Bay	7	43	672	15.6	96.0	10
Washington	5	24	473	19.7	94.6	2
Totals	172	942	15,123	16.1	88.0	146

Arizona totals include one game vs. St. Louis, four games vs. Phoenix
Oakland totals include four games vs. L.A. Raiders
St. Louis totals include 20 games vs. L.A. Rams

ANDRE REED'S CAREER RECEIVING VS. EACH OPPONENT

Opponent	Games	Rec.	Yards	Yards Per Rec.	Yards Per Game	TD
Arizona	2	0	0	—	0.0	0
Atlanta	2	9	170	18.9	85.0	1
Carolina	1	0	0	—	0.0	0
Chicago	3	14	156	11.1	52.0	0
Cincinnati	5	11	171	15.5	34.2	2
Cleveland	5	25	347	13.9	69.4	2
Dallas	1	1	10	10.0	10.0	0
Denver	6	30	408	13.6	68.0	2
Detroit	2	10	89	8.9	44.5	1
Green Bay	3	21	249	11.9	83.0	3
Houston	9	44	663	15.1	73.7	6
Indianapolis	20	93	1,288	13.8	64.4	13
Kansas City	5	26	368	14.2	73.6	4
Miami	20	90	1,291	14.3	64.6	9
Minnesota	3	11	105	9.5	35.0	0
New England	18	80	1,295	16.2	71.9	6
New Orleans	2	6	54	9.0	27.0	0
N.Y. Giants	2	7	95	13.6	47.5	1
N.Y. Jets	21	84	1,130	13.5	53.8	8
Oakland	5	28	406	14.5	81.2	1
Philadelphia	3	15	161	10.7	53.7	3
Pittsburgh	7	28	358	12.8	51.1	3
St. Louis	2	10	135	13.5	67.5	1
San Diego	2	9	138	15.3	69.0	0
San Francisco	2	20	259	13.0	129.5	0
Seattle	2	5	116	23.2	58.0	1
Tampa Bay	3	8	119	14.9	39.7	0
Washington	3	15	267	17.8	89.0	2
Totals	159	700	9,848	14.1	61.9	69

Arizona totals include one game vs. St. Louis, one game vs. Phoenix
Oakland totals include five games vs. L.A. Raiders
St. Louis totals include two games vs. L.A. Rams

MICHAEL IRVIN'S CAREER RECEIVING VS. EACH OPPONENT

Opponent	Games	Rec.	Yards	Yards Per Rec.	Yards Per Game	TD
Arizona	14	53	1,061	20.0	75.8	7
Atlanta	7	34	541	15.9	77.3	3
Buffalo	1	8	115	14.4	115.0	0
Chicago	1	5	46	9.2	46.0	0
Cincinnati	3	15	314	20.9	104.7	1
Cleveland	3	18	248	13.8	82.7	1
Denver	2	12	156	13.0	78.0	2
Detroit	3	16	304	19.0	101.3	1
Green Bay	5	29	510	17.6	102.0	4
Houston	3	11	141	12.8	47.0	1
Indianapolis	1	7	112	16.0	112.0	0
Kansas City	2	17	205	12.1	102.5	1
Miami	1	3	31	10.3	31.0	0
Minnesota	3	18	274	15.2	91.3	2
New Orleans	5	17	268	15.8	53.6	0
N.Y. Giants	13	53	841	15.9	64.7	4
N.Y. Jets	2	10	184	18.4	92.0	2
Oakland	2	10	163	16.3	81.5	1
Philadelphia	14	42	732	17.4	52.3	4
Pittsburgh	3	19	369	19.4	123.0	2
St. Louis	2	10	239	23.9	119.5	2
San Diego	1	7	103	14.7	103.0	0
San Francisco	5	31	369	11.9	73.8	2
Seattle	1	6	113	18.8	113.0	0
Tampa Bay	2	2	42	21.0	21.0	1
Washington	13	74	1,057	14.3	81.3	9
Totals	112	527	8,538	16.2	76.2	50

Arizona totals include 10 games vs. Phoenix
Oakland totals include one game vs. L.A. Raiders
St. Louis totals include two games vs. L.A. Rams

HERMAN MOORE'S CAREER RECEIVING VS. EACH OPPONENT

Opponent	Games	Rec.	Yards	Yards Per Rec.	Yards Per Game	TD
Arizona	3	14	212	15.1	70.7	1
Atlanta	3	19	373	19.6	124.3	2
Buffalo	2	9	194	21.6	97.0	1
Chicago	10	47	647	13.8	64.7	3
Cincinnati	1	5	86	17.2	86.0	0
Cleveland	2	11	177	16.1	88.5	0
Dallas	3	12	156	13.0	52.0	1
Green Bay	10	36	590	16.4	59.0	9
Houston	2	9	193	21.4	96.5	3
Indianapolis	1	0	0	—	0.0	0
Jacksonville	1	5	59	11.8	59.0	0
Miami	2	6	69	11.5	34.5	0
Minnesota	9	27	560	20.7	62.2	4
New England	2	10	141	14.1	70.5	0
New Orleans	1	4	42	10.5	42.0	0
N.Y. Giants	1	9	106	11.8	106.0	2
N.Y. Jets	1	6	70	11.7	70.0	0
Pittsburgh	2	15	202	13.5	101.0	1
St. Louis	1	6	120	20.0	120.0	0
San Francisco	5	21	301	14.3	60.2	3
Seattle	1	8	98	12.3	98.0	2
Tampa Bay	7	29	397	13.7	56.7	2
Washington	2	10	102	10.2	51.0	1
Totals	72	318	4,895	15.4	68.0	35

Arizona totals includes two games vs. Phoenix
St. Louis totals include one game vs. L.A. Rams

CRIS CARTER'S CAREER RECEIVING VS. EACH OPPONENT

Opponent	Games	Rec.	Yards	Yards Per Rec.	Yards Per Game	TD
Arizona	10	42	670	16.0	67.0	9
Atlanta	2	9	179	19.9	89.5	4
Buffalo	2	10	121	12.1	60.5	0
Chicago	13	76	812	10.7	62.5	4
Cincinnati	3	20	223	11.2	74.3	3
Cleveland	3	12	166	13.8	55.3	0
Dallas	6	22	252	11.5	42.0	5
Denver	4	12	185	15.4	46.3	2
Detroit	12	54	581	10.8	48.4	4
Green Bay	11	55	635	11.5	57.7	5
Houston	3	17	211	12.4	70.3	3
Kansas City	2	5	88	17.6	44.0	2
Miami	2	7	81	11.6	40.5	3
Minnesota	2	5	30	6.0	15.0	1
New England	3	16	160	10.0	53.3	0
New Orleans	6	31	362	11.7	60.3	3
N.Y. Giants	8	13	274	21.1	34.3	2
N.Y. Jets	2	12	114	9.5	57.0	2
Oakland	3	15	201	13.4	67.0	1
Philadelphia	1	6	151	25.2	151.0	2
Pittsburgh	2	9	140	15.6	70.0	2
St. Louis	3	8	105	13.1	35.0	0
San Diego	2	9	122	13.6	61.0	0
San Francisco	6	28	240	8.6	40.0	3
Seattle	2	5	75	15.0	37.5	1
Tampa Bay	13	52	713	13.7	54.8	4
Washington	7	21	313	14.9	44.7	1
Totals	133	571	7,204	12.6	54.2	66

Arizona totals include two games vs. St. Louis, six games vs. Phoenix
Oakland totals include three games vs. L.A. Raiders
St. Louis totals include three games vs. L.A. Rams

STARTING RECORDS OF ACTIVE NFL QUARTERBACKS

Minimum: 10 starts

Quarterback	W-L-T	Pct.
Steve Bono	20- 7	.741
Jim McMahon	67-30	.691
Stan Humphries	40-20	.667
Neil O'Donnell	39-22	.639
Jim Kelly	93-54	.633
Dan Marino	116-68	.630
Jeff Hostetler	42-25	.627
Troy Aikman	60-38	.612
Steve Young	60-38	.612
Bobby Hebert	53-34	.609
Brett Favre	37-24	.607
John Elway	113-74-1	.604
Mark Rypien	47-31	.603
Randall Cunningham	63-43-1	.593
Mike Tomczak	31-22	.585
Dave Krieg	92-71	.564
Erik Kramer	21-17	.553
Steve Walsh	19-16	.543
Kerry Collins	7- 6	.538
Wade Wilson	35-30	.538
Jim Harbaugh	46-40	.535
Scott Mitchell	17-15	.531
Rodney Peete	31-29	.517
Rich Gannon	20-19	.513
Warren Moon	87-83	.512
Bernie Kosar	53-54-1	.495
Drew Bledsoe	21-22	.488
Steve Beuerlein	22-24	.478
Bubby Brister	33-38	.465
Don Majkowski	25-29-1	.464
Boomer Esiason	73-87	.456
Dave Brown	14-17	.452
Jim Everett	60-77	.438
Rick Mirer	18-24	.429
Craig Erickson	13-19	.406
Jeff Blake	10-15	.400
Trent Dilfer	7-11	.389
Vinny Testaverde	40-63	.388
Jack Trudeau	19-30	.388
Chris Chandler	22-36	.379
Jeff George	30-51	.370
Frank Reich	4- 7	.364
Chris Miller	32-57	.360
Vince Evans	14-25	.359
Heath Shuler	4- 9	.308
Mark Brunell	3- 7	.300
Browning Nagle	4-10	.286
Hugh Millen	7-18	.280
Gus Frerotte	4-11	.267
John Friesz	8-22	.267
David Klingler	4-20	.167
Stan Gelbaugh	0-11	.000

ALL-TIME RANKINGS OF PLAYERS IN FOUR CATEGORIES THAT DETERMINE NFL PASSER RATING

Minimum: 1500 Attempts

COMPLETION PERCENTAGE	Pct.	Att.	Comp.
Steve Young	64.15	2876	1845
Joe Montana	63.24	5391	3409
Troy Aikman	62.81	2713	1704
Brett Favre	62.42	2150	1342
Jim Kelly	60.27	4400	2652
Dan Marino	59.91	6531	3913
Ken Stabler	59.85	3793	2270
Danny White	59.69	2950	1761
Ken Anderson	59.31	4475	2654
Jim Harbaugh	59.25	2275	1348

TOUCHDOWN PERCENTAGE	Pct.	Att.	TD
Sid Luckman	7.86	1744	137
Frank Ryan	6.99	2133	149
Len Dawson	6.39	3741	239
Daryle Lamonica	6.31	2601	164
Sammy Baugh	6.24	2995	187
Charley Conerly	6.11	2833	173
Bob Waterfield	6.00	1617	97
Earl Morrall	5.99	2689	161
Sonny Jurgensen	5.98	4262	255
Norm Van Brocklin	5.98	2895	173

AVERAGE YARDS PER PASS	Avg.	Att.	Yards
Otto Graham	8.63	1565	13,499
Sid Luckman	8.42	1744	14,686
Norm Van Brocklin	8.16	2895	23,611
Steve Young	8.02	2876	23,069
Ed Brown	7.85	1987	15,600
Bart Starr	7.85	3149	24,718
Johnny Unitas	7.76	5186	40,239
Earl Morrall	7.74	2689	20,809
Dan Fouts	7.68	5604	43,040
Len Dawson	7.67	3741	28,711

INTERCEPTION PERCENTAGE	Pct.	Att.	Int.
Neil O'Donnell	2.08	1871	39
Joe Montana	2.58	5391	139
Bernie Kosar	2.61	3333	87
Jeff Hostetler	2.62	1792	47
Ken O'Brien	2.72	3602	98
Steve Young	2.75	2876	79
Neil Lomax	2.85	3153	90
Jeff George	2.87	2613	75
Jim Harbaugh	2.95	2275	67
Dan Marino	3.06	6531	200

NFL INDIVIDUAL LEADERS OVER RECENT SEASONS

	Last 2 Seasons	Last 3 Seasons	Last 4 Seasons
Points			
	282 Emmitt Smith	370 Jason Elam	475 Morten Andersen
	254 Fuad Reveiz	359 Fuad Reveiz	467 John Carney
	251 Jason Elam	355 Morten Andersen	461 Fuad Reveiz
	241 Chris Boniol	355 Jason Hanson	458 Pete Stoyanovich
	238 Morten Andersen	354 John Carney	456 Steve Christie
			456 Emmitt Smith
Touchdowns			
	47 Emmitt Smith	57 Emmitt Smith	76 Emmitt Smith
	32 Jerry Rice	48 Jerry Rice	59 Jerry Rice
	28 Carl Pickens	34 Carl Pickens	45 Ricky Watters
	27 Chris Warren	34 Chris Warren	42 Sterling Sharpe
	26 Marshall Faulk	33 Ricky Watters	39 Cris Carter
Field Goals			
	61 Jason Elam	87 Morten Andersen	116 Morten Andersen
	60 Fuad Reveiz	87 Jason Elam	112 John Carney
	59 Morten Andersen	86 John Carney	105 Fuad Reveiz
	57 Doug Pelfrey	86 Fuad Reveiz	105 Pete Stoyanovich
	55 Four players	81 Norm Johnson	102 Gary Anderson
		81 Doug Pelfrey	102 Steve Christie
Rushes			
	745 Emmitt Smith	1,028 Emmitt Smith	1,401 Emmitt Smith
	645 Barry Sanders	925 Rodney Hampton	1,221 Thurman Thomas
	643 Chris Warren	916 Chris Warren	1,200 Barry Sanders
	633 Rodney Hampton	909 Thurman Thomas	1,182 Rodney Hampton
	616 Errict Rhett	888 Barry Sanders	1,139 Chris Warren
Rushing Yards			
	3,383 Barry Sanders	4,743 Emmitt Smith	6,456 Emmitt Smith
	3,257 Emmitt Smith	4,498 Barry Sanders	5,850 Barry Sanders
	2,891 Chris Warren	3,963 Chris Warren	4,980 Chris Warren
	2,360 Marshall Faulk	3,413 Thurman Thomas	4,900 Thurman Thomas
	2,340 Terry Allen	3,334 Rodney Hampton	4,475 Rodney Hampton
Rushing TDs			
	46 Emmitt Smith	55 Emmitt Smith	73 Emmitt Smith
	24 Chris Warren	31 Chris Warren	36 Ricky Watters
	22 Marshall Faulk	27 Ricky Watters	35 Rodney Hampton
	18 Terry Allen	25 Natrone Means	34 Chris Warren
	18 Errict Rhett	24 Marcus Allen	31 Terry Allen
	18 Barry Sanders		
Passes			
	1,327 Drew Bledsoe	1,756 Drew Bledsoe	2,145 Brett Favre
	1,207 Warren Moon	1,727 Warren Moon	2,073 Warren Moon
	1,152 Brett Favre	1,674 Brett Favre	1,903 John Elway
	1,107 Jim Everett	1,587 John Elway	1,856 Jim Everett
	1,097 Dan Marino	1,488 Jeff George	1,838 Jim Kelly

HIGHEST NFL POSTSEASON PASSER RATINGS (MINIMUM: 150 ATTEMPTS)

	Games	Att.	Comp.	Pct.	Yds.	Avg. Gain	TD	Int.	Rating
Bart Starr	10	213	130	61.0	1753	8.23	15	3	104.8
Troy Aikman	12	350	239	68.3	3029	8.65	21	9	104.3
Joe Montana	23	734	460	62.7	5772	7.86	45	21	95.6
Ken Anderson	6	166	110	66.3	1321	7.96	9	6	93.5
Joe Theismann	10	211	128	60.7	1782	8.45	11	7	91.4
Brett Favre	7	246	150	61.0	1813	7.37	13	6	91.1
Steve Young	16	308	191	62.0	2212	7.18	14	7	89.4
Warren Moon	10	403	259	64.3	2870	7.12	17	14	84.9
Ken Stabler	13	351	203	57.8	2641	7.52	19	13	84.2
Bernie Kosar	10	270	152	56.3	1953	7.23	16	10	83.5

HIGHEST NFL POSTSEASON PASSER RATINGS, ACTIVE PLAYERS (MINIMUM: 150 ATTEMPTS)

	Games	Att.	Comp.	Pct.	Yds.	Avg. Gain	TD	Int.	Rating
Troy Aikman	12	350	239	68.3	3029	8.65	21	9	104.3
Brett Favre	7	246	150	61.0	1813	7.37	13	6	91.1
Steve Young	16	308	191	62.0	2212	7.18	14	7	89.4
Warren Moon	10	403	259	64.3	2870	7.12	17	14	84.9
Bernie Kosar	10	270	152	56.3	1953	7.23	16	10	83.5
Dan Marino	13	518	291	56.2	3600	6.95	29	17	82.8
Jim McMahon	8	155	82	52.9	1112	7.17	5	4	76.1
John Elway	14	431	229	53.1	3321	7.71	19	18	75.8
Wade Wilson	6	185	99	53.5	1322	7.15	7	6	75.6
Neil O'Donnell	7	273	158	57.9	1690	6.19	9	8	74.9

INSIDE THE NUMBERS

Last 2 Seasons	Last 3 Seasons	Last 4 Seasons
Completions		
748 Warren Moon	1,051 Warren Moon	1,342 Brett Favre
723 Drew Bledsoe	1,040 Brett Favre	1,275 Warren Moon
722 Brett Favre	971 John Elway	1,205 Steve Young
694 Dan Marino	937 Drew Bledsoe	1,145 John Elway
691 Jim Everett	937 Steve Young	1,115 Dan Marino
Passing Yards		
8,492 Warren Moon	11,977 Warren Moon	14,825 Brett Favre
8,295 Brett Favre	11,598 Brett Favre	14,657 Steve Young
8,121 Dan Marino	11,490 John Elway	14,498 Warren Moon
8,062 Drew Bledsoe	11,192 Steve Young	13,732 John Elway
7,877 Jeff George	10,556 Drew Bledsoe	13,455 Dan Marino
Touchdown Passes		
71 Brett Favre	90 Brett Favre	109 Steve Young
55 Steve Young	84 Steve Young	108 Brett Favre
54 Dan Marino	72 Warren Moon	90 Warren Moon
51 Warren Moon	67 John Elway	86 Dan Marino
48 Jim Everett	62 Jim Kelly	85 Jim Kelly
	62 Dan Marino	
Receptions		
244 Cris Carter	332 Jerry Rice	416 Jerry Rice
234 Jerry Rice	330 Cris Carter	383 Cris Carter
195 Herman Moore	278 Michael Irvin	356 Michael Irvin
190 Michael Irvin	258 Tim Brown	314 Sterling Sharpe
189 Terance Mathis	256 Herman Moore	307 Three players
Reception Yards		
3,347 Jerry Rice	4,850 Jerry Rice	6,051 Jerry Rice
2,859 Herman Moore	4,174 Michael Irvin	5,570 Michael Irvin
2,844 Michael Irvin	3,831 Tim Brown	4,760 Herman Moore
2,651 Tim Brown	3,794 Herman Moore	4,524 Tim Brown
2,627 Cris Carter	3,698 Cris Carter	4,408 Anthony Miller
Receiving Touchdowns		
28 Carl Pickens	43 Jerry Rice	53 Jerry Rice
28 Jerry Rice	34 Carl Pickens	42 Sterling Sharpe
25 Herman Moore	33 Cris Carter	39 Cris Carter
24 Cris Carter	31 Herman Moore	37 Andre Rison
20 Terance Mathis	29 Sterling Sharpe	35 Herman Moore
		35 Carl Pickens
Interceptions		
15 Aeneas Williams	18 Terry McDaniel	22 Terry McDaniel
13 Terry McDaniel	17 Aeneas Williams	21 Darren Perry
12 Merton Hanks	15 Merton Hanks	20 Eugene Robinson
11 Willie Clay	15 Darren Perry	20 Aeneas Williams
11 Darryll Lewis	15 Deion Sanders	19 Vencie Glenn
11 Darren Perry		
Sacks		
25.0 Leslie O'Neal	38.5 Neil Smith	54.0 Leslie O'Neal
25.0 Bryce Paup	37.0 Leslie O'Neal	53.0 Neil Smith
24.0 John Randle	36.5 John Randle	48.5 Bruce Smith
23.5 Neil Smith	36.0 Bryce Paup	48.0 John Randle
23.0 Three players	35.5 Kevin Greene	47.0 Reggie White

NFL TEAM LEADERS OVER RECENT SEASONS

Last 2 Seasons	Last 3 Seasons	Last 4 Seasons
Highest Won-Lost Percentage		
.750 Dallas	.750 Dallas	.766 Dallas
.750 San Francisco	.708 San Francisco	.750 San Francisco
.719 Pittsburgh	.688 Kansas City	.672 Kansas City
.688 Kansas City	.667 Pittsburgh	.672 Pittsburgh
.625 Green Bay	.604 Three teams	.625 Buffalo
.625 San Diego		
Most Points		
962 San Francisco	1,435 San Francisco	1,866 San Francisco
849 Dallas	1,225 Dallas	1,634 Dallas
793 Denver	1,136 Miami	1,476 Miami
787 Miami	1,126 Green Bay	1,419 Minnesota
786 Green Bay	1,108 Denver	1,402 Green Bay

Last 2 Seasons	Last 3 Seasons	Last 4 Seasons
Most Total Yards		
12,147 San Francisco	18,582 San Francisco	24,777 San Francisco
11,794 Miami	17,606 Miami	23,106 Miami
11,786 Minnesota	16,988 Denver	22,366 Dallas
11,527 Denver	16,760 Dallas	21,514 Buffalo
11,233 New England	16,610 Minnesota	21,509 Minnesota
Most Rushing Yards		
4,262 Seattle	6,315 Dallas	8,436 Dallas
4,154 Dallas	6,277 Seattle	8,203 Buffalo
4,032 Pittsburgh	6,035 Pittsburgh	8,191 Pittsburgh
3,954 Kansas City	5,797 N.Y. Giants	8,031 Philadelphia
3,915 Indianapolis	5,777 Detroit	7,874 N.Y. Giants
Most Passing Yards		
8,771 San Francisco	13,073 San Francisco	16,958 Miami
8,630 Miami	12,983 Miami	16,953 San Francisco
8,529 Minnesota	11,830 Denver	15,451 Atlanta
8,298 Atlanta	11,818 Atlanta	14,760 Denver
8,095 Green Bay	11,729 Minnesota	14,598 Minnesota
***Fewest Turnovers**		
43 Green Bay	69 Dallas	93 Dallas
47 Dallas	70 N.Y. Giants	93 N.Y. Giants
47 Kansas City	72 San Diego	96 Kansas City
49 Detroit	75 Kansas City	104 San Francisco
51 Pittsburgh	77 Green Bay	105 San Diego
***Fewest Points Allowed**		
539 Dallas	768 Dallas	1,011 Dallas
539 Kansas City	830 Kansas City	1,067 Pittsburgh
554 San Francisco	842 Pittsburgh	1,085 San Francisco
560 Cleveland	849 San Francisco	1,112 Kansas City
561 Pittsburgh	850 N.Y. Giants	1,142 Cleveland
***Fewest Total Yards Allowed**		
8,887 Pittsburgh	13,418 Pittsburgh	18,055 Dallas
9,237 San Francisco	14,124 Dallas	18,076 Pittsburgh
9,348 Philadelphia	14,234 San Francisco	18,644 Kansas City
9,357 Dallas	14,320 Kansas City	18,651 Houston
9,549 Kansas City	14,367 Philadelphia	18,778 Philadelphia
***Fewest Rushing Yards Allowed**		
2,399 San Francisco	3,955 Minnesota	5,617 San Francisco
2,419 Minnesota	4,141 Pittsburgh	5,688 Minnesota
2,773 Pittsburgh	4,199 San Francisco	5,804 San Diego
2,878 Green Bay	4,409 San Diego	5,982 Pittsburgh
3,061 Kansas City	4,460 Green Bay	6,228 Dallas
***Fewest Passing Yards Allowed**		
5,910 Philadelphia	8,849 Philadelphia	11,779 Philadelphia
5,920 Houston	9,140 Dallas	11,827 Dallas
6,024 Dallas	9,277 Pittsburgh	12,094 Pittsburgh
6,114 Pittsburgh	9,508 N.Y. Jets	12,098 Houston
6,296 N.Y. Jets	9,521 Houston	12,176 Kansas City
Most Opponents' Turnovers		
78 Arizona	109 Kansas City	150 Minnesota
74 Minnesota	109 N.Y. Jets	148 Kansas City
73 Philadelphia	108 Minnesota	148 N.Y. Jets
72 N.Y. Jets	108 Philadelphia	146 Pittsburgh
71 Kansas City	107 Houston	145 Philadelphia

**Carolina and Jacksonville excluded*

RECORDS OF TEAMS ON OPENING DAY, 1933-1995

AFC	W	L	T	Pct.	Longest W Strk.	Longest L Strk.	Current Streak
Denver	22	13	1	.629	3	4	W-1
Kansas City	21	15	0	.583	6	4	W-6
Oakland	21	15	0	.583	5	5	W-1
Cleveland	26	20	0	.565	5	5	L-1
San Diego	20	16	0	.556	6	6	L-1
Pittsburgh	30	27	4	.526	4	3	W-1
Miami	15	14	1	.517	4	5	W-4
Indianapolis	22	21	0	.512	8	8	L-1
Houston	18	18	0	.500	4	3	W-1
Cincinnati	14	14	0	.500	4	4	W-1
New England	17	19	0	.472	6	3	W-1
Buffalo	15	21	0	.417	6	5	L-2
N.Y. Jets	15	21	0	.417	3	5	L-1
Seattle	5	15	0	.250	3	8	L-1
Jacksonville	0	1	0	.000	0	1	L-1

NFC	W	L	T	Pct.	Longest W Strk.	Longest L Strk.	Current Streak
Dallas	27	8	1	.771	17	3	W-2
Chicago	37	25	1	.597	9	6	W-2
N.Y. Giants	35	24	4	.593	4	3	L-1
St. Louis	31	27	0	.534	5	6	W-2
Atlanta	16	14	0	.533	5	3	W-1
Minnesota	18	16	1	.529	4	3	L-3
Washington	31	28	4	.525	6	5	W-1
Detroit	32	29	2	.525	7	4	L-1
Green Bay	31	29	3	.517	5	6	L-1
San Francisco	23	22	1	.511	4	3	W-4
Arizona	26	35	1	.426	6	6	L-4
Philadelphia	25	36	1	.410	5	9	L-2
Tampa Bay	8	12	0	.400	3	5	W-1
New Orleans	7	22	0	.241	1	6	L-2
Carolina	0	1	0	.000	0	1	L-1

Kansas City totals include Dallas Texans, 1960-62.
Oakland totals include L.A. Raiders, 1982-94.
San Diego totals include L.A. Chargers, 1960.
Indianapolis totals include Baltimore, 1953-83.
New England totals include Boston, 1960-70.
St. Louis totals include Cleveland, 1937-42 and 1944-45, and L.A. Rams, 1946-94.
Detroit totals include Portsmouth, 1933.
Arizona totals include Chi. Cardinals, 1933-59, St. Louis, 1960-87, and Phoenix, 1988-93.
NOTE: All tied games occurred prior to 1972, when calculation of ties in percentages as half-win, half-loss was begun.

OLDEST INDIVIDUAL SINGLE-SEASON OR SINGLE-GAME RECORDS IN NFL RECORD & FACT BOOK

Regular-Season Records That Have Not Been Surpassed or Tied

Most Points, Game—40, Ernie Nevers, Chi. Cardinals vs. Chi. Bears, Nov. 28, 1929 (6-td, 4-pat)
Most Touchdowns Rushing, Game—6, Ernie Nevers, Chi. Cardinals vs. Chi. Bears, Nov. 28, 1929
Highest Punting Average, Season (Qualifiers)—51.40, Sammy Baugh, Washington, 1940 (35-1,799)
Highest Punting Average, Game (minimum: 4 punts)—61.75, Bob Cifers, Detroit vs. Chi. Bears, Nov. 24, 1946 (4-247)
Highest Average Gain, Pass Receptions, Season (minimum: 24 receptions)—32.58, Don Currivan, Boston, 1947 (24-782)
Highest Average Gain, Passing, Game (minimum: 20 passes)—18.58, Sammy Baugh, Washington vs. Boston, Oct. 31, 1948 (24-446)
Most Touchdowns, Fumble Recoveries, Game—2, Fred (Dippy) Evans, Chi. Bears vs. Washington, Nov. 28, 1948
Most Yards Gained, Intercepted Passes, Rookie, Season—301, Don Doll, Detroit, 1949
Most Passes Had Intercepted, Game—8, Jim Hardy, Chi. Cardinals vs. Philadelphia, Sept. 24, 1950
Highest Average Gain, Rushing, Game (minimum: 10 attempts)—17.09, Marion Motley, Cleveland vs. Pittsburgh, Oct. 29, 1950 (11-188)
Highest Kickoff Return Average, Game (minimum: 3 returns)—73.50, Wally Triplett, Detroit vs. Los Angeles, Oct. 29, 1950 (4-294)
Most Pass Receptions, Game—18, Tom Fears, Los Angeles vs. Green Bay, Dec. 3, 1950
Highest Punt Return Average, Season (Qualifiers)—23.00, Herb Rich, Baltimore, 1950 (12-276)
Highest Punt Return Average, Rookie, Season (Qualifiers)—23.00, Herb Rich, Baltimore, 1950 (12-276)
Most Yards Passing, Game—554, Norm Van Brocklin, Los Angeles vs. N.Y. Yanks, Sept. 28, 1951
Most Touchdowns, Punt Returns, Rookie, Season—4, Jack Christiansen, Detroit, 1951
Most Interceptions By, Season—14, Dick (Night Train) Lane, Los Angeles, 1952
Most Interceptions By, Rookie, Season—14, Dick (Night Train) Lane, Los Angeles, 1952
Highest Average Gain, Passing, Season (Qualifiers)—11.17, Tommy O'Connell, Cleveland, 1957 (110-1,229)
Most Points, Season—176, Paul Hornung, Green Bay, 1960 (15-td, 41-pat,15-fg)
Most Yards Gained, Pass Receptions, Rookie, Season—1,473, Bill Groman, Houston, 1960

LARGEST TRADES IN NFL HISTORY

(Based on number of players or draft choices involved)

18—October 13, 1989—RB Herschel Walker from the Dallas Cowboys to Minnesota. Dallas also traded its third-round choice in 1990, its tenth-round choice in 1990, and its third-round choice in 1991 to Minnesota. Minnesota traded LB Jesse Solomon, LB David Howard, CB Issiac Holt, and DE Alex Stewart along with its first-round choice in 1990, its second-round choice in 1990, its sixth-round choice in 1990, its first-round choice in 1991, its second-round choice in 1991, its first-round choice in 1992, its second-round choice in 1992, and its third-round choice in 1992 to Dallas. Minnesota traded RB Darrin Nelson to Dallas, which traded Nelson to San Diego for the Chargers' fifth-round choice in 1990, which Dallas then sent to Minnesota.
15—March 26, 1953—T Mike McCormack, DT Don Colo, LB Tom Catlin, DB John Petitbon, and G Herschell Forester from Baltimore to Cleveland for DB Don Shula, DB Bert Rechichar, DB Carl Taseff, LB Ed Sharkey, E Gern Nagler, QB Harry Agganis, T Dick Batten, T Stu Sheets, G Art Spinney, and G Elmer Willhoite.
15—January 28, 1971—LB Marlin McKeever, first- and third-round choices in 1971, and third-, fourth-, fifth-, sixth-, and seventh-round choices in 1972 from Washington to the Los Angeles Rams for LB Maxie Baughan, LB Jack Pardee, LB Myron Pottios, RB Jeff Jordan, G John Wilbur, DT Diron Talbert, and a fifth-round choice in 1971.
12—June 13, 1952—Selection rights to Les Richter from the Dallas Texans to the Los Angeles Rams for RB Dick Hoerner, DB Tom Keane, DB George Sims, C Joe Reid, HB Billy Baggett, T Jack Halliday, FB Dick McKissack, LB Vic Vasicek, E Richard Wilkins, C Aubrey Phillips, and RB Dave Anderson.
10—March 23, 1959—HB Ollie Matson from the Chicago Cardinals to the Los Angeles Rams for T Frank Fuller, DE Glenn Holtzman, T Ken Panfil, DT Art Hauser, E John Tracey, FB Larry Hickman, HB Don Brown, the Rams second-round choice in 1960, and a player to be delivered during the 1959 training camp.
10—October 31, 1987—RB Eric Dickerson from the Los Angeles Rams to Indianapolis. The rights to LB Cornelius Bennett from Indianapolis to Buffalo. Indianapolis running back Owen Gill and the Colts' first- and second-round choices in 1988 and second-round choice in 1989, plus Bills running back Greg Bell and Buffalo's first-round choice in 1988 and first- and second-round choices in 1989 to the Rams.

RETIRED UNIFORM NUMBERS IN NFL

AFC

Buffalo:	None	
Cincinnati:	Bob Johnson	54
Cleveland:	Otto Graham	14
	Jim Brown	32
	Ernie Davis	45
	Don Fleming	46
	Lou Groza	76
Denver:	Frank Tripucka	18
	Floyd Little	44
Houston:	Earl Campbell	34
	Jim Norton	43
	Mike Munchak	63
	Elvin Bethea	65
Indianapolis:	Johnny Unitas	19
	Buddy Young	22
	Lenny Moore	24
	Art Donovan	70
	Jim Parker	77
	Raymond Berry	82
	Gino Marchetti	89
Kansas City:	Jan Stenerud	3
	Len Dawson	16
	Abner Haynes	28
	Stone Johnson	33
	Mack Lee Hill	36
	Willie Lanier	63
	Bobby Bell	78
	Buck Buchanan	86
Miami:	Bob Griese	12
New England:	Steve Grogan	14
	Gino Cappelletti	20
	Mike Haynes	40
	Steve Nelson	57
	John Hannah	73
	Jim Hunt	79
	Bob Dee	89
New York Jets:	Joe Namath	12
	Don Maynard	13
Oakland:	None	
Pittsburgh:	None	
San Diego:	Dan Fouts	14
Seattle:	"Fans/the twelfth man"	12
	Steve Largent	80

INSIDE THE NUMBERS

NFC

Arizona:	Larry Wilson	8
	Stan Mauldin	77
	J.V. Cain	88
	Marshall Goldberg	99
Atlanta:	Steve Bartowski	10
	William Andrews	31
	Jeff Van Note	57
	Tommy Nobis	60
Chicago:	Bronko Nagurski	3
	George McAfee	5
	George Halas	7
	Willie Galimore	28
	Walter Payton	34
	Gale Sayers	40
	Brian Piccolo	41
	Sid Luckman	42
	Dick Butkus	51
	Bill Hewitt	56
	Bill George	61
	Bulldog Turner	66
	Red Grange	77
Dallas:	None	
Detroit:	Dutch Clark	7
	Bobby Layne	22
	Doak Walker	37
	Joe Schmidt	56
	Chuck Hughes	85
	Charlie Sanders	88
Green Bay:	Tony Canadeo	3
	Don Hutson	14
	Bart Starr	15
	Ray Nitschke	66
Minnesota:	Fran Tarkenton	10
	Alan Page	88
New Orleans:	Jim Taylor	31
	Doug Atkins	81
New York Giants:	Ray Flaherty	1
	Mel Hein	7
	Phil Simms	11
	Y.A. Tittle	14
	Al Blozis	32
	Joe Morrison	40
	Charlie Conerly	42
	Ken Strong	50
	Lawrence Taylor	56
Philadelphia:	Steve Van Buren	15
	Tom Brookshier	40
	Pete Retzlaff	44
	Chuck Bednarik	60
	Al Wistert	70
	Jerome Brown	99
St. Louis:	Bob Waterfield	7
	Merlin Olsen	74
San Francisco:	John Brodie	12
	Joe Perry	34
	Jimmy Johnson	37
	Hugh McElhenny	39
	Charlie Krueger	70
	Leo Nomellini	73
	Dwight Clark	87
Tampa Bay:	Lee Roy Selmon	63
Washington:	Sammy Baugh	33

1995 NFL SCORE BY QUARTERS

AFC Offense	1	2	3	4	OT	PTS
Pittsburgh	72	137	60	135	3	407
Miami	62	137	93	106	0	398
Denver	96	137	64	91	0	388
Seattle	79	77	88	119	0	363
Kansas City	70	120	56	97	15	358
Buffalo	73	115	97	65	0	350
Cincinnati	52	99	93	102	3	349
Oakland	54	112	97	85	0	348
Houston	70	103	85	90	0	348
Indianapolis	78	98	52	97	6	331
San Diego	49	102	69	101	0	321
New England	49	84	59	102	0	294
Cleveland	37	97	59	93	3	289
Jacksonville	64	67	28	116	0	275
N.Y. Jets	37	61	65	70	0	233

NFC Offense	1	2	3	4	OT	PTS
San Francisco	114	161	96	86	0	457
Detroit	113	125	87	111	0	436
Dallas	102	133	83	111	6	435
Minnesota	81	176	67	76	12	412
Green Bay	83	146	81	94	0	404
Chicago	73	130	91	98	0	392
Atlanta	73	144	80	59	6	362
Washington	59	90	85	86	6	326
New Orleans	61	75	74	109	0	319
Philadelphia	83	99	55	78	3	318
St. Louis	78	87	60	84	0	309
N.Y. Giants	54	116	47	67	6	290
Carolina	35	98	78	75	3	289
Arizona	35	108	53	70	9	275
Tampa Bay	48	77	36	71	6	238

AFC Defense	1	2	3	4	OT	PTS
Kansas City	68	59	29	85	0	241
Indianapolis	75	86	74	78	3	316
San Diego	86	107	58	66	6	323
Houston	83	98	36	101	6	324
Pittsburgh	33	124	109	61	0	327
Miami	44	105	95	85	3	332
Oakland	67	99	88	72	6	332
Buffalo	64	79	89	103	0	335
Denver	72	103	68	102	0	345
Cleveland	89	91	43	133	0	356
Seattle	90	128	48	94	6	366
Cincinnati	70	131	56	114	3	374
New England	60	143	72	99	3	377
N.Y. Jets	59	128	98	96	3	384
Jacksonville	75	138	91	100	0	404

NFC Defense	1	2	3	4	OT	PTS
San Francisco	35	91	81	51	0	258
Dallas	38	104	78	71	0	291
Green Bay	41	106	72	92	3	314
Carolina	62	106	72	82	3	325
Tampa Bay	73	106	69	87	0	335
Detroit	53	114	67	96	6	336
Philadelphia	71	101	59	107	0	338
N.Y. Giants	81	105	53	98	3	340
New Orleans	71	132	81	61	3	348
Atlanta	94	103	57	92	3	349
Washington	65	126	48	117	3	359
Chicago	93	112	66	86	3	360
Minnesota	85	99	71	121	9	385
St. Louis	62	151	101	104	0	418
Arizona	75	136	109	90	12	422

NFL Totals	1	2	3	4	OT	PTS
	2034	3311	2138	2744	87	10,314

TEAM LEADERS

Offense	Most Scored	Fewest Scored
1st Quarter	114 San Francisco	35 Ariz. & Car.
2nd Quarter	176 Minnesota	61 N.Y. Jets
3rd Quarter	97 Buff. & Oak.	28 Jacksonville
4th Quarter	135 Pittsburgh	59 Atlanta

Defense	Most Allowed	Fewest Allowed
1st Quarter	94 Atlanta	33 Pittsburgh
2nd Quarter	151 St. Louis	59 Kansas City
3rd Quarter	109 Ariz. & Pitt.	29 Kansas City
4th Quarter	133 Cleveland	51 San Francisco

GREATEST COMEBACKS IN NFL HISTORY
(Most Points Overcome To Win Game)

REGULAR SEASON GAMES

FROM 28 POINTS BEHIND TO WIN:
December 7, 1980, at San Francisco

New Orleans	14	21	0	0	0	— 35
San Francisco	0	7	14	14	3	— 38

NO — Harris 33 pass from Manning (Ricardo kick)
NO — Childs 21 pass from Manning (Ricardo kick)
NO — Holmes 1 run (Ricardo kick)
SF — Solomon 57 punt return (Wersching kick)
NO — Holmes 1 run (Ricardo kick)
NO — Harris 41 pass from Manning (Ricardo kick)
SF — Montana 1 run (Wersching kick)
SF — Clark 71 pass from Montana (Wersching kick)
SF — Solomon 14 pass from Montana (Wersching kick)
SF — Elliott 7 run (Wersching kick)
SF — FG Wersching 36

	N.O.	S.F.
First Downs	27	24
Total Yards	519	430
Yards Rushing	143	176
Yards Passing	376	254
Turnovers	3	0

FROM 25 POINTS BEHIND TO WIN:
November 8, 1987, at St. Louis

Tampa Bay	7	7	14	0	— 28
St. Louis	0	3	0	28	— 31

TB — Carrier 5 pass from DeBerg (Igwebuike kick)
TB — Carter 3 pass from DeBerg (Igwebuike kick)
StL — FG Gallery 31
TB — Smith 34 pass from DeBerg (Igwebuike kick)
TB — Smith 3 run (Igwebuike kick)
StL — Awalt 4 pass from Lomax (Gallery kick)
StL — Noga 23 fumble recovery (Gallery kick)
StL — J. Smith 11 pass from Lomax (Gallery kick)
StL — J. Smith 17 pass from Lomax (Gallery kick)

	T.B.	St.L.
First Downs	26	26
Total Yards	377	415
Yards Rushing	83	137
Yards Passing	294	278
Turnovers	1	2

FROM 24 POINTS BEHIND TO WIN:
October 27, 1946, at Washington

Philadelphia	0	0	14	14	— 28
Washington	10	14	0	0	— 24

Wash — Rosato 2 run (Poillon kick)
Wash — FG Poillon 28
Wash — Rosato 4 run (Poillon kick)
Wash — Lapka recovered fumble in end zone (Poillon kick)
Phil — Steele 1 run (Lio kick)
Phil — Pritchard 45 pass from Thompson (Lio kick)
Phil — Steinke 7 pass from Thompson (Lio kick)
Phil — Ferrante 30 pass from Thompson (Lio kick)

	Phil.	Wash.
First Downs	14	8
Total Yards	262	127
Yards Rushing	34	66
Yards Passing	228	61
Turnovers	6	3

FROM 24 POINTS BEHIND TO WIN:
October 20, 1957, at Detroit

Baltimore	7	14	6	0	— 27
Detroit	0	3	7	21	— 31

Balt — Mutscheller 15 pass from Unitas (Rechichar kick)
Det — FG Martin 47
Balt — Moore 72 pass from Unitas (Rechichar kick)
Balt — Mutscheller 52 pass from Unitas (Rechichar kick)
Balt — Moore 4 pass from Unitas (kick failed)
Det — Junker 14 pass from Rote (Layne kick)
Det — Cassady 26 pass from Layne (Layne kick)
Det — Johnson 1 run (Layne kick)
Det — Cassady 29 pass from Layne (Layne kick)

	Balt.	Det.
First Downs	15	20
Total Yards	322	369
Yards Rushing	117	178
Yards Passing	205	191
Turnovers	6	4

FROM 24 POINTS BEHIND TO WIN:
October 25, 1959, at Minneapolis

Philadelphia	0	0	21	7	— 28
Chicago Cardinals	7	10	7	0	— 24

Cardinals — Crow 10 pass from Roach (Conrad kick)
Cardinals — J. Hill 77 blocked field goal return (Conrad kick)
Cardinals — FG Conrad 15
Cardinals — Lane 37 interception return (Conrad kick)
Phil — Barnes 1 run (Walston kick)
Phil — McDonald 29 pass from Van Brocklin (Walston kick)
Phil — Barnes 2 run (Walston kick)
Phil — McDonald 22 pass from Van Brocklin (Walston kick)

	Phil.	Cardinals
First Downs	22	14
Total Yards	399	313
Yards Rushing	168	163
Yards Passing	231	150
Turnovers	2	6

FROM 24 POINTS BEHIND TO WIN:
October 23, 1960, at Denver

Boston	10	7	7	0	— 24
Denver	0	0	14	17	— 31

Bos — FG Cappelletti 12
Bos — Colclough 10 pass from Songin (Cappelletti kick)
Bos — Wells 6 pass from Songin (Cappelletti kick)
Bos — Miller 47 pass from Songin (Cappelletti kick)
Den — Carmichael 21 pass from Tripucka (Mingo kick)
Den — Jessup 19 pass from Tripucka (Mingo kick)
Den — Carmichael 35 lateral from Taylor, pass from Tripucka (Mingo kick)
Den — Taylor 8 pass from Tripucka (Mingo kick)
Den — FG Mingo 9

	Bos.	Den.
First Downs	19	16
Total Yards	434	326
Yards Rushing	211	65
Yards Passing	223	261
Turnovers	7	4

FROM 24 POINTS BEHIND TO WIN:
December 15, 1974, at Miami

New England	21	3	0	3	— 27
Miami	0	17	7	10	— 34

NE — Hannah recovered fumble in end zone (J. Smith kick)
NE — Sanders 23 interception return (J. Smith kick)
NE — Herron 4 pass from Plunkett (J. Smith kick)
NE — FG J. Smith 46
Mia — Nottingham 1 run (Yepremian kick)
Mia — Baker 37 pass from Morrall (Yepremian kick)
Mia — FG Yepremian 28
Mia — Baker 46 pass from Morrall (Yepremian kick)
NE — FG J. Smith 34
Mia — Nottingham 2 run (Yepremian kick)
Mia — FG Yepremian 40

	N.E.	Mia.
First Downs	18	18
Total Yards	333	333
Yards Rushing	114	61
Yards Passing	219	272
Turnovers	3	4

FROM 24 POINTS BEHIND TO WIN:
December 4, 1977, at Minnesota

San Francisco	0	10	14	3	— 27
Minnesota	0	0	7	21	— 28

SF — Delvin Williams 2 run (Wersching kick)
SF — FG Wersching 31
SF — Dave Williams 80 kickoff return (Wersching kick)
SF — Delvin Williams 5 run (Wersching kick)
Minn — McClanahan 15 pass from Lee (Cox kick)
Minn — Rashad 8 pass from Kramer (Cox kick)
Minn — Tucker 9 pass from Kramer (Cox kick)
SF — FG Wersching 31
Minn — S. White 69 pass from Kramer (Cox kick)

	S.F.	Minn.
First Downs	19	18
Total Yards	243	309
Yards Rushing	196	52
Yards Passing	47	257
Turnovers	2	5

FROM 24 POINTS BEHIND TO WIN:
September 23, 1979, at Denver

Seattle	10	10	14	0	— 34
Denver	0	10	21	6	— 37

Sea — FG Herrera 28
Sea — Doornink 5 run (Herrera kick)
Den — FG Turner 27
Sea — Doornink 5 run (Herrera kick)
Den — Armstrong 2 run (Turner kick)
Sea — FG Herrera 22
Sea — McCullum 13 pass from Zorn (Herrera kick)
Sea — Smith 1 run (Herrera kick)
Den — Studdard 2 pass from Morton (Turner kick)
Den — Moses 11 pass from Morton (Turner kick)
Den — Upchurch 35 pass from Morton (Turner kick)
Den — Lytle 1 run (kick failed)

	Sea.	Den.
First Downs	22	23
Total Yards	350	344
Yards Rushing	153	90
Yards Passing	197	254
Turnovers	4	3

FROM 24 POINTS BEHIND TO WIN:
September 23, 1979, at Cincinnati

Houston	0	10	17	0	3	—30
Cincinnati	14	10	0	3	0	—27

Cin — Johnson 1 run (Bahr kick)
Cin — Alexander 2 run (Bahr kick)
Cin — Johnson 1 run (Bahr kick)
Cin — FG Bahr 52
Hou — Burrough 35 pass from Pastorini (Fritsch kick)
Hou — FG Fritsch 33
Hou — Campbell 8 run (Fritsch kick)
Hou — Caster 22 pass from Pastorini (Fritsch kick)
Hou — FG Fritsch 47
Cin — FG Bahr 55
Hou — FG Fritsch 29

	Hou.	Cin.
First Downs	19	21
Total Yards	361	265
Yards Rushing	177	165
Yards Passing	184	100
Turnovers	3	2

FROM 24 POINTS BEHIND TO WIN:
November 22, 1982, at Los Angeles

San Diego	10	14	0	0	— 24
L.A. Raiders	0	7	14	7	— 28

SD — FG Benirschke 19
SD — Scales 29 pass from Fouts (Benirschke kick)
SD — Muncie 2 run (Benirschke kick)
SD — Muncie 1 run (Benirschke kick)
Raiders — Christensen 1 pass from Plunkett (Bahr kick)

INSIDE THE NUMBERS

Raiders — Allen 3 run (Bahr kick)
Raiders — Allen 6 run (Bahr kick)
Raiders — Hawkins 1 run (Bahr kick)

	S.D.	Raiders
First Downs	26	23
Total Yards	411	326
Yards Rushing	72	181
Yards Passing	339	145
Turnovers	4	2

FROM 24 POINTS BEHIND TO WIN:
September 26, 1988, at Denver

L.A. Raiders	0	0	14	13	3	— 30
Denver	7	17	0	3	0	— 27

Den — Dorsett 1 run (Karlis kick)
Den — Dorsett 1 run (Karlis kick)
Den — Sewell 7 pass from Elway (Karlis kick)
Den — FG Karlis 39
Raiders — Smith 40 pass from Schroeder (Bahr kick)
Raiders — Smith 42 pass from Schroeder (Bahr kick)
Raiders — FG Bahr 28
Raiders — Allen 4 run (Bahr kick)
Den — FG Karlis 25
Raiders — FG Bahr 44
Raiders — FG Bahr 35

	Raiders	Den.
First Downs	20	23
Total Yards	363	398
Yards Rushing	128	189
Yards Passing	235	209
Turnovers	1	5

FROM 24 POINTS BEHIND TO WIN:
December 6, 1992, at Tampa

L.A. Rams	0	3	21	7	— 31
Tampa Bay	6	21	0	0	— 27

TB — FG Murray 34
TB — FG Murray 47
TB — Armstrong 81 pass from Testaverde (Murray kick)
TB — Jones 26 fumble recovery (Murray kick)
Rams — FG Zendejas 18
TB — Carrier 10 pass from Testaverde (Murray kick)
Rams — Anderson 40 pass from Everett (Zendejas kick)
Rams — Chadwick 27 pass from Everett (Zendejas kick)
Rams — Lang 1 run (Zendejas kick)
Rams — Carter 8 pass from Everett (Zendejas kick)

	Rams	T.B.
First Downs	21	16
Total Yards	405	313
Yards Rushing	63	150
Yards Passing	342	163
Turnovers	3	3

POSTSEASON GAMES

FROM 32 POINTS BEHIND TO WIN:
AFC First-Round Playoff Game
January 3, 1993, at Buffalo

Houston	7	21	7	3	0 — 38
Buffalo	3	0	28	7	3 — 41

Hou — Jeffires 3 pass from Moon (Del Greco kick)
Buff — FG Christie 36
Hou — Slaughter 7 pass from Moon (Del Greco kick)
Hou — Duncan 26 pass from Moon (Del Greco kick)
Hou — Jeffires 27 pass from Moon (Del Greco kick)
Hou — McDowell 58 interception return (Del Greco kick)
Buff — Davis 1 run (Christie kick)
Buff — Beebe 38 pass from Reich (Christie kick)
Buff — Reed 26 pass from Reich (Christie kick)
Buff — Reed 18 pass from Reich (Christie kick)
Buff — Reed 17 pass from Reich (Christie kick)
Hou — FG Del Greco 26
Buff — FG Christie 32

	Hou.	Buff.
First Downs	27	19
Total Yards	429	366
Yards Rushing	82	98
Yards Passing	347	268
Turnovers	2	1

FROM 20 POINTS BEHIND TO WIN:
Western Conference Playoff Game
December 22, 1957, at San Francisco

Detroit	0	7	14	10	— 31
San Francisco	14	10	3	0	— 27

SF — Owens 34 pass from Tittle (Soltau kick)
SF — McElhenny 47 pass from Tittle (Soltau kick)
Det — Junker 4 pass from Rote (Martin kick)
SF — Wilson 12 pass from Tittle (Soltau kick)
SF — FG Soltau 25
SF — FG Soltau 10
Det — Tracy 2 run (Martin kick)
Det — Tracy 58 run (Martin kick)
Det — Gedman 3 run (Martin kick)
Det — FG Martin 14

	Det.	S.F.
First Downs	22	20
Total Yards	324	351
Yards Rushing	129	127
Yards Passing	195	224
Turnovers	5	4

FROM 18 POINTS BEHIND TO WIN:
NFC Divisional Playoff Game
December 23, 1972, at San Francisco

Dallas	3	10	0	17	— 30
San Francisco	7	14	7	0	— 28

SF — Washington 97 kickoff return (Gossett kick)
Dall — FG Fritsch 37
SF — Schreiber 1 run (Gossett kick)
SF — Schreiber 1 run (Gossett kick)
Dall — FG Fritsch 45
Dall — Alworth 28 pass from Morton (Fritsch kick)
SF — Schreiber 1 run (Gossett kick)
Dall — FG Fritsch 27
Dall — Parks 20 pass from Staubach (Fritsch kick)
Dall — Sellers 10 pass from Staubach (Fritsch kick)

	Dall.	S.F.
First Downs	22	13
Total Yards	402	255
Yards Rushing	165	105
Yards Passing	237	150
Turnovers	5	3

FROM 18 POINTS BEHIND TO WIN:
AFC Divisional Playoff Game
January 4, 1986, at Miami

Cleveland	7	7	7	0	— 21
Miami	3	0	14	7	— 24

Mia — FG Reveiz 51
Clev — Newsome 16 pass from Kosar (Bahr kick)
Clev — Byner 21 run (Bahr kick)
Clev — Byner 66 run (Bahr kick)
Mia — Moore 6 pass from Marino (Reveiz kick)
Mia — Davenport 31 run (Reveiz kick)
Mia — Davenport 1 run (Reveiz kick)

	Clev.	Mia.
First Downs	17	20
Total Yards	313	330
Yards Rushing	251	92
Yards Passing	62	238
Turnovers	1	1

RECORDS OF NFL TEAMS SINCE 1970 AFL-NFL MERGER

AFC	W - L - T	Pct.	Division Titles	Playoff Berths	Post-season Record	Super Bowl Record
Miami	257-133-2	.659	11	16	17-14	2-3
Oakland	244-142-6	.631	9	15	18-12	3-0
Pittsburgh	235-156-1	.601	12	16	19-12	4-1
Denver	217-169-6	.562	7	10	9-10	0-4
Cleveland	194-195-3	.499	6	10	4-10	0-0
Kansas City	190-195-7	.494	3	8	3-8	0-0
Buffalo	186-204-2	.477	7	10	12-10	0-4
Cincinnati	185-207-0	.472	5	7	5-7	0-2
San Diego	179-208-5	.463	5	7	6-7	0-1
Seattle*	141-167-0	.458	1	4	3-4	0-0
New England	174-218-0	.444	2	6	3-6	0-1
Houston	173-217-2	.444	2	10	7-10	0-0
Indianapolis	165-225-2	.423	5	7	6-6	1-0
N.Y. Jets	161-229-2	.413	0	5	3-5	0-0
Jacksonville**	4- 12-0	.250	0	0	0-0	0-0

NFC	W - L - T	Pct.	Division Titles	Playoff Berths	Post-season Record	Super Bowl Record
Dallas	251-141-0	.640	13	19	30-14	5-3
San Francisco	236-153-3	.606	15	16	21-11	5-0
Washington	234-157-1	.598	5	13	18-10	3-2
Minnesota	228-162-2	.584	12	16	11-16	0-3
St. Louis	214-174-4	.551	8	14	10-14	0-1
Chicago	204-187-1	.522	6	10	7-9	1-0
Philadelphia	188-198-6	.487	2	9	5-9	0-1
N.Y. Giants	183-207-2	.469	3	7	10-5	2-0
Detroit	179-209-4	.462	3	7	1-7	0-0
Green Bay	170-214-8	.444	2	5	5-5	0-0
Carolina**	7- 9-0	.438	0	0	0-0	0-0
Arizona	163-223-6	.423	2	3	0-3	0-0
New Orleans	162-226-4	.418	1	4	0-4	0-0
Atlanta	160-228-4	.413	1	5	2-5	0-0
Tampa Bay*	94-213-1	.307	2	3	1-3	0-0

*entered NFL in 1976.
**entered NFL in 1995.
Oakland totals include L.A. Raiders, 1982-94.
Indianapolis totals include Baltimore, 1970-83.
St. Louis totals include L.A. Rams, 1970-94.
Arizona totals include St. Louis, 1970-87, and Phoenix, 1988-93.
Tie games before 1972 are not calculated in won-lost percentage.
In 1982, because of players' strike, the divisional format was abandoned; L.A. Raiders and Washington won regular-season conference titles, not included in "Division Titles" totals listed above. Sixteen teams were awarded playoff berths, included in totals listed above.

LONGEST WINNING STREAKS SINCE 1970

Regular-Season Games

16	Miami, 1971-73	(1 in 1971, 14 in 1972, 1 in 1973)
16	Miami, 1983-84	(5 in 1983, 11 in 1984)
15	San Francisco, 1989-90	(5 in 1989, 10 in 1990)
14	Oakland, 1976-77	(10 in 1976, 4 in 1977)
13	Minnesota, 1974-75	(3 in 1974, 10 in 1975)
13	Chicago, 1984-85	(1 in 1984, 12 in 1985)
13	N.Y. Giants, 1989-90	(3 in 1989, 10 in 1990)
12	Washington, 1990-91	(1 in 1990, 11 in 1991)
11	Pittsburgh, 1975	
11	Baltimore, 1975-76	(9 in 1975, 2 in 1976)
11	Chicago, 1986-87	(7 in 1986, 4 in 1987)
11	Houston, 1993	
10	Miami, 1973	
10	Pittsburgh, 1976-77	(9 in 1976, 1 in 1977)
10	Denver, 1984	
10	San Francisco, 1994	

NFL PLAYOFF APPEARANCES BY SEASONS

Team	Number of Seasons in Playoffs
Cleveland	23
Dallas	23
N.Y. Giants	23
St. Louis	22
Chicago	21
Washington	19
Minnesota	18
Oakland	18
Pittsburgh	17
San Francisco	17
Green Bay	16
Miami	16
Houston	15
Buffalo	14
Philadelphia	13
Detroit	12
Indianapolis	12
Kansas City	12
San Diego	12
Denver	10
Cincinnati	7
New England	7
N.Y. Jets	7
Arizona	5
Atlanta	5
New Orleans	4
Seattle	4
Tampa Bay	3

TEAMS IN SUPER BOWL CONTENTION, 1978-1995

	With 3 Weeks to Play	With 2 Weeks to Play	With 1 Week to Play
1995	27	21	*18
1994	*25	*22	15
1993	20	18	16
1992	20	16	14
1991	20	18	13
1990	23	20	15
1989	21	18	17
1988	21	18	15
1987	19	19	15
1986	19	17	14
1985	21	18	13
1984	18	14	13
1983	24	19	15
1982	20	17	16
1981	21	20	16
1980	20	14	12
1979	19	15	13
1978	20	17	12

*NFL Record

GAMES DECIDED BY 7 POINTS OR LESS AND 3 POINTS OR LESS (1970-1995)

	Games Decided by 7 Points or Less	Games Decided by 3 Points or Less
1970	59 of 182 (32.4%)	34 of 182 (18.7%)
1971	76 of 182 (41.8%)	35 of 182 (19.2%)
1972	71 of 182 (39.0%)	38 of 182 (20.9%)
1973	60 of 182 (32.9%)	28 of 182 (15.4%)
1974	91 of 182 (50.0%)	37 of 182 (20.3%)
1975	62 of 182 (34.1%)	35 of 182 (19.2%)
1976	73 of 196 (37.2%)	38 of 196 (19.4%)
1977	85 of 196 (43.4%)	36 of 196 (18.4%)
1978	108 of 224 (48.2%)	49 of 224 (21.9%)
1979	104 of 224 (46.4%)	51 of 224 (22.8%)
1980	108 of 224 (48.2%)	58 of 224 (25.9%)
1981	91 of 224 (40.6%)	**60 of 224 (26.8%)
1982	61 of 126 (48.4%)	33 of 126 (26.2%)
1983	106 of 224 (47.3%)	54 of 224 (24.1%)
1984	95 of 224 (42.4%)	58 of 224 (25.9%)
1985	87 of 224 (38.8%)	38 of 224 (17.0%)
1986	106 of 224 (47.3%)	48 of 224 (21.4%)
1987	99 of 210 (47.1%)	40 of 210 (19.0%)
1988	113 of 224 (50.4%)	*62 of 224 (27.7%)
1989	107 of 224 (47.8%)	55 of 224 (24.6%)
1990	97 of 224 (43.3%)	54 of 224 (24.1%)
1991	112 of 224 (50.0%)	57 of 224 (25.4%)
1992	88 of 224 (39.3%)	**48 of 224 (21.4%)
1993	*105 of 224 (46.9%)	53 of 224 (23.7%)
1994	115 of 224 (51.3%)	60 of 224 (26.8%)
1995	115 of 240 (47.9%)	61 of 240 (25.4%)

*Week record: Dec. 11-13, 1993 (Week 15), 12 of 14 games (86%) decided by 7 points or less.
**Week Record: Nov. 8-9, 1981 (Week 10), 8 of 14 games (57%), and Nov. 15-16, 1992 (Week 11), 8 of 14 games (57%) decided by 3 points or less.

1995 RECORDS OF TEAMS IN CLOSE GAMES

AFC	Overall Record	Decided by 8 Pts. or Less	Decided By 3 Pts. or Less
Buffalo	10-6	7-0	3-0
Cincinnati	7-9	6-5	2-5
Cleveland	5-11	2-5	1-4
Denver	8-8	4-2	2-1
Houston	7-9	1-7	0-2
Indianapolis	9-7	7-6	5-4
Jacksonville	4-12	4-6	2-2
Kansas City	13-3	7-1	2-0
Miami	9-7	3-5	2-4
New England	6-10	2-3	2-2
N.Y. Jets	3-13	2-5	1-4
Oakland	8-8	2-4	1-1
Pittsburgh	11-5	3-2	3-0
San Diego	9-7	5-2	2-1
Seattle	8-8	4-4	2-0

NFC	Overall Record	Decided by 8 Pts. or Less	Decided By 3 Pts. or Less
Arizona	4-12	4-5	2-2
Atlanta	9-7	5-5	4-3
Carolina	7-9	4-5	2-2
Chicago	9-7	6-6	3-2
Dallas	12-4	2-3	1-1
Detroit	10-6	6-3	2-2
Green Bay	11-5	4-4	1-3
Minnesota	8-8	3-6	1-2
New Orleans	7-9	4-5	2-2
N.Y. Giants	5-11	3-7	0-5
Philadelphia	10-6	6-2	4-0
St. Louis	7-9	5-1	3-1
San Francisco	11-5	2-5	1-3
Tampa Bay	7-9	6-2	4-2
Washington	6-10	4-7	1-1

SUPER BOWL CHAMPIONS WHO DID NOT MAKE PLAYOFFS THE FOLLOWING YEAR

N.Y. Giants—Super Bowl XXV champions did not make playoffs in the 1991 season.
Washington—Super Bowl XXII champions did not make playoffs in the 1988 season.
N.Y. Giants—Super Bowl XXI champions did not make playoffs in the 1987 season.
San Francisco—Super Bowl XVI champions did not make playoffs in the 1982 season.
Oakland—Super Bowl XV champions did not make playoffs in the 1981 season.
Pittsburgh—Super Bowl XIV champions did not make playoffs in the 1980 season.
Kansas City—Super Bowl IV champions did not make playoffs in the 1970 season.
Green Bay—Super Bowl II champions did not make playoffs in the 1968 season.

NON-DIVISION WINNERS THAT PLAYED IN SUPER BOWL

1992	Buffalo Bills (Lost to Dallas, 52-17)	Super Bowl XXVII
1985	New England Patriots (Lost to Chicago, 46-10)	Super Bowl XX
1980	Oakland Raiders (Defeated Philadelphia, 27-10)	Super Bowl XV
1975	Dallas Cowboys (Lost to Pittsburgh, 21-17)	Super Bowl X
1969	Kansas City Chiefs (Defeated Minnesota, 23-7)	Super Bowl IV

TEAMS AT OR UNDER .500 IN POSTSEASON PLAY

1991	New York Jets	8-8
1990	New Orleans Saints	8-8
1985	Cleveland Browns	8-8
1982	Cleveland Browns	4-5
1982	Detroit Lions	4-5
1969	Houston Oilers	6-6-2

COLDEST NFL GAMES ON RECORD

-13 degrees (-48 degree wind chill)—December 31, 1967, Lambeau Field, Green Bay, Wisconsin, NFL Championship (Green Bay 21, Dallas 17)
-9 degrees (-59 degree wind chill)—January 10, 1982, Riverfront Stadium, Cincinnati, Ohio, AFC Championship (Cincinnati 27, San Diego 7)
0 degrees (-32 degree wind chill)—January 15, 1994, Rich Stadium, Orchard Park, New York, AFC Divisional Playoff (Buffalo 29, Los Angeles Raiders 23)
1 degree (wind chill not recorded)—January 4, 1981, Cleveland Stadium, Cleveland, Ohio, AFC Divisional Playoff (Oakland 14, Cleveland 12)

ALL-TIME RECORDS OF CURRENT NFL TEAMS

AFC

BUFFALO BILLS

	All Games			Home Games			Road Games		
Season	W	L	T	W	L	T	W	L	T
1960	5	8	1	3	4		2	4	1
1961	6	8		2	5		4	3	
1962	7	6	1	3	3	1	4	3	
1963	7	6	1	4	2	1	3	4	
1964	12	2		6	1		6	1	
1965	10	3	1	5	2		5	1	1
1966	9	4	1	4	2	1	5	2	
1967	4	10		2	5		2	5	
1968	1	12	1	1	6		0	6	1
1969	4	10		4	3		0	7	
1970	3	10	1	1	6		2	4	1
1971	1	13		1	6		0	7	
1972	4	9	1	2	4	1	2	5	
1973	9	5		5	2		4	3	
1974	9	5		5	2		4	3	
1975	8	6		3	4		5	2	
1976	2	12		1	6		1	6	
1977	3	11		1	6		2	5	
1978	5	11		4	4		1	7	
1979	7	9		3	5		4	4	
1980	11	5		6	2		5	3	
1981	10	6		7	1		3	5	
1982	4	5		4	1		0	4	
1983	8	8		3	5		5	3	
1984	2	14		2	6		0	8	
1985	2	14		2	6		0	8	
1986	4	12		3	5		1	7	
1987	7	8		4	4		3	4	
1988	12	4		8	0		4	4	

	All Games			Home Games			Road Games		
Season	W	L	T	W	L	T	W	L	T
1989	9	7		6	2		3	5	
1990	13	3		8	0		5	3	
1991	13	3		7	1		6	2	
1992	11	5		6	2		5	3	
1993	12	4		6	2		6	2	
1994	7	9		4	4		3	5	
1995	10	6		6	2		4	4	
Total	251	273	8	142	121	4	109	152	4

CINCINNATI BENGALS

	All Games			Home Games			Road Games		
Season	W	L	T	W	L	T	W	L	T
1968	3	11		2	5		1	6	
1969	4	9	1	4	3		0	6	1
1970	8	6		5	2		3	4	
1971	4	10		3	4		1	6	
1972	8	6		4	3		4	3	
1973	10	4		7	0		3	4	
1974	7	7		4	3		3	4	
1975	11	3		6	1		5	2	
1976	10	4		6	1		4	3	
1977	8	6		5	2		3	4	
1978	4	12		3	5		1	7	
1979	4	12		4	4		0	8	
1980	6	10		3	5		3	5	
1981	12	4		6	2		6	2	
1982	7	2		4	0		3	2	
1983	7	9		4	4		3	5	
1984	8	8		5	3		3	5	
1985	7	9		5	3		2	6	
1986	10	6		6	2		4	4	
1987	4	11		1	7		3	4	
1988	12	4		8	0		4	4	
1989	8	8		5	3		3	5	
1990	9	7		5	3		4	4	
1991	3	13		3	5		0	8	
1992	5	11		3	5		2	6	
1993	3	13		3	5		0	8	
1994	3	13		2	6		1	7	
1995	7	9		3	5		4	4	
Total	192	227	1	119	91		73	136	1

CLEVELAND BROWNS

	All Games			Home Games			Road Games		
Season	W	L	T	W	L	T	W	L	T
1950	10	2		5	1		5	1	
1951	11	1		6	0		5	1	
1952	8	4		4	2		4	2	
1953	11	1		6	0		5	1	
1954	9	3		5	1		4	2	
1955	9	2	1	5	1		4	1	1
1956	5	7		1	5		4	2	
1957	9	2	1	6	0		3	2	1
1958	9	3		4	2		5	1	
1959	7	5		3	3		4	2	
1960	8	3	1	4	2		4	1	1
1961	8	5	1	4	3		4	2	1
1962	7	6	1	4	2	1	3	4	
1963	10	4		5	2		5	2	
1964	10	3	1	5	1	1	5	2	
1965	11	3		5	2		6	1	
1966	9	5		5	2		4	3	
1967	9	5		6	1		3	4	
1968	10	4		5	2		5	2	
1969	10	3	1	5	1	1	5	2	
1970	7	7		4	3		3	4	
1971	9	5		4	3		5	2	
1972	10	4		4	3		6	1	
1973	7	5	2	5	1	1	2	4	1
1974	4	10		3	4		1	6	
1975	3	11		3	4		0	7	
1976	9	5		6	1		3	4	
1977	6	8		2	5		4	3	
1978	8	8		5	3		3	5	
1979	9	7		5	3		4	4	
1980	11	5		6	2		5	3	
1981	5	11		3	5		2	6	
1982	4	5		2	2		2	3	
1983	9	7		6	2		3	5	
1984	5	11		2	6		3	5	
1985	8	8		5	3		3	5	
1986	12	4		6	2		6	2	
1987	10	5		5	2		5	3	
1988	10	6		6	2		4	4	
1989	9	6	1	5	2	1	4	4	
1990	3	13		2	6		1	7	
1991	6	10		3	5		3	5	
1992	7	9		4	4		3	5	
1993	7	9		4	4		3	5	
1994	11	5		6	2		5	3	
1995	5	11		3	5		2	6	
Total	374	266	10	202	117	5	172	149	5

DENVER BRONCOS

	All Games			Home Games			Road Games		
Season	W	L	T	W	L	T	W	L	T
1960	4	9	1	2	4	1	2	5	
1961	3	11		2	5		1	6	
1962	7	7		3	4		4	3	
1963	2	11	1	2	5		0	6	1
1964	2	11	1	2	4	1	0	7	
1965	4	10		2	5		2	5	
1966	4	10		3	4		1	6	
1967	3	11		1	6		2	5	
1968	5	9		3	4		2	5	
1969	5	8	1	4	2	1	1	6	
1970	5	8	1	3	3	1	2	5	
1971	4	9	1	2	4	1	2	5	
1972	5	9		3	4		2	5	
1973	7	5	2	3	3	1	4	2	1
1974	7	6	1	3	3	1	4	3	
1975	6	8		5	2		1	6	
1976	9	5		6	1		3	4	
1977	12	2		6	1		6	1	
1978	10	6		6	2		4	4	
1979	10	6		6	2		4	4	
1980	8	8		4	4		4	4	
1981	10	6		8	0		2	6	
1982	2	7		1	4		1	3	
1983	9	7		6	2		3	5	
1984	13	3		7	1		6	2	
1985	11	5		6	2		5	3	
1986	11	5		7	1		4	4	
1987	10	4	1	7	1		3	3	1
1988	8	8		6	2		2	6	
1989	11	5		6	2		5	3	
1990	5	11		4	4		1	7	
1991	12	4		7	1		5	3	
1992	8	8		7	1		1	7	
1993	9	7		5	3		4	4	
1994	7	9		4	4		3	5	
1995	8	8		6	2		2	6	
Total	256	266	10	158	102	7	98	164	3

HOUSTON OILERS

	All Games			Home Games			Road Games		
Season	W	L	T	W	L	T	W	L	T
1960	10	4		6	1		4	3	
1961	10	3	1	6	1		4	2	1
1962	11	3		6	1		5	2	
1963	6	8		4	3		2	5	
1964	4	10		3	4		1	6	
1965	4	10		3	4		1	6	
1966	3	11		3	4		0	7	
1967	9	4	1	5	2		4	2	1
1968	7	7		3	4		4	3	
1969	6	6	2	4	2	1	2	4	1
1970	3	10	1	1	6		2	4	1
1971	4	9	1	3	3	1	1	6	
1972	1	13		1	6		0	7	
1973	1	13		0	7		1	6	
1974	7	7		3	4		4	3	
1975	10	4		5	2		5	2	
1976	5	9		3	4		2	5	
1977	8	6		5	2		3	4	
1978	10	6		5	3		5	3	
1979	11	5		6	2		5	3	
1980	11	5		6	2		5	3	
1981	7	9		5	3		2	6	
1982	1	8		1	4		0	4	
1983	2	14		2	6		0	8	
1984	3	13		2	6		1	7	
1985	5	11		4	4		1	7	
1986	5	11		4	4		1	7	
1987	9	6		5	2		4	4	
1988	10	6		7	1		3	5	
1989	9	7		6	2		3	5	
1990	9	7		6	2		3	5	
1991	11	5		7	1		4	4	
1992	10	6		5	3		5	3	
1993	12	4		7	1		5	3	
1994	2	14		2	6		0	8	
1995	7	9		3	5		4	4	
Total	243	283	6	147	117	2	96	166	4

INDIANAPOLIS COLTS*

	All Games			Home Games			Road Games		
Season	W	L	T	W	L	T	W	L	T
1953	3	9		2	4		1	5	
1954	3	9		2	4		1	5	
1955	5	6	1	4	1	1	1	5	
1956	5	7		4	2		1	5	
1957	7	5		4	2		3	3	
1958	9	3		6	0		3	3	
1959	9	3		4	2		5	1	
1960	6	6		4	2		2	4	
1961	8	6		5	2		3	4	
1962	7	7		3	4		4	3	
1963	8	6		4	3		4	3	
1964	12	2		7	1		5	1	
1965	10	3	1	5	2		5	1	1
1966	9	5		5	2		4	3	
1967	11	1	2	6	0	1	5	1	1
1968	13	1		6	1		7	0	
1969	8	5	1	4	2	1	4	3	
1970	11	2	1	5	1	1	6	1	
1971	10	4		5	2		5	2	
1972	5	9		2	5		3	4	
1973	4	10		3	4		1	6	
1974	2	12		0	7		2	5	
1975	10	4		5	2		5	2	
1976	11	3		6	1		5	2	
1977	10	4		6	1		4	3	
1978	5	11		2	6		3	5	
1979	5	11		3	5		2	6	
1980	7	9		2	6		5	3	
1981	2	14		1	7		1	7	
1982	0	8	1	0	3	1	0	5	
1983	7	9		3	5		4	4	
1984	4	12		2	6		2	6	
1985	5	11		4	4		1	7	
1986	3	13		1	7		2	6	
1987	9	6		4	4		5	2	
1988	9	7		6	2		3	5	
1989	8	8		6	2		2	6	
1990	7	9		3	5		4	4	
1991	1	15		0	8		1	7	
1992	9	7		4	4		5	3	
1993	4	12		2	6		2	6	
1994	8	8		5	3		3	5	
1995	9	7		5	3		4	4	
Total	298	309	7	160	143	5	138	166	2

**includes Baltimore Colts (1953-83).*

JACKSONVILLE JAGUARS

	All Games			Home Games			Road Games		
Season	W	L	T	W	L	T	W	L	T
1995	4	12		2	6		2	6	

KANSAS CITY CHIEFS*

	All Games			Home Games			Road Games		
Season	W	L	T	W	L	T	W	L	T
1960	8	6		5	2		3	4	
1961	6	8		4	3		2	5	
1962	11	3		6	1		5	2	
1963	5	7	2	4	3		1	4	2
1964	7	7		4	3		3	4	
1965	7	5	2	5	2		2	3	2
1966	11	2	1	4	2	1	7	0	
1967	9	5		4	3		5	2	
1968	12	2		6	1		6	1	
1969	11	3		6	1		5	2	
1970	7	5	2	4	1	2	3	4	

Season	All Games W	L	T	Home Games W	L	T	Road Games W	L	T
1971	10	3	1	7	0		3	3	1
1972	8	6		3	4		5	2	
1973	7	5	2	5	1	1	2	4	1
1974	5	9		1	6		4	3	
1975	5	9		3	4		2	5	
1976	5	9		1	6		4	3	
1977	2	12		1	6		1	6	
1978	4	12		3	5		1	7	
1979	7	9		3	5		4	4	
1980	8	8		3	5		5	3	
1981	9	7		5	3		4	4	
1982	3	6		2	2		1	4	
1983	6	10		5	3		1	7	
1984	8	8		5	3		3	5	
1985	6	10		5	3		1	7	
1986	10	6		6	2		4	4	
1987	4	11		3	4		1	7	
1988	4	11	1	4	4		0	7	1
1989	8	7	1	5	3		3	4	1
1990	11	5		6	2		5	3	
1991	10	6		6	2		4	4	
1992	10	6		7	1		3	5	
1993	11	5		7	1		4	4	
1994	9	7		5	3		4	4	
1995	13	3		8	0		5	3	
Total	277	243	12	161	100	4	116	143	8

**includes Dallas Texans (1960-62).*

MIAMI DOLPHINS

Season	All Games W	L	T	Home Games W	L	T	Road Games W	L	T
1966	3	11		2	5		1	6	
1967	4	10		4	3		0	7	
1968	5	8	1	1	5	1	4	3	
1969	3	10	1	2	4	1	1	6	
1970	10	4		6	1		4	3	
1971	10	3	1	6	1		4	2	1
1972	14	0		7	0		7	0	
1973	12	2		7	0		5	2	
1974	11	3		7	0		4	3	
1975	10	4		5	2		5	2	
1976	6	8		3	4		3	4	
1977	10	4		6	1		4	3	
1978	11	5		7	1		4	4	
1979	10	6		6	2		4	4	
1980	8	8		5	3		3	5	
1981	11	4	1	6	1	1	5	3	
1982	7	2		4	0		3	2	
1983	12	4		7	1		5	3	
1984	14	2		7	1		7	1	
1985	12	4		8	0		4	4	
1986	8	8		4	4		4	4	
1987	8	7		4	3		4	4	
1988	6	10		4	4		2	6	
1989	8	8		4	4		4	4	
1990	12	4		7	1		5	3	
1991	8	8		5	3		3	5	
1992	11	5		6	2		5	3	
1993	9	7		4	4		5	3	
1994	10	6		6	2		4	4	
1995	9	7		5	3		4	4	
Total	272	172	4	155	65	3	117	107	1

NEW ENGLAND PATRIOTS*

Season	All Games W	L	T	Home Games W	L	T	Road Games W	L	T
1960	5	9		3	4		2	5	
1961	9	4	1	4	2	1	5	2	
1962	9	4	1	6	1		3	3	1
1963	7	6	1	5	1	1	2	5	
1964	10	3	1	4	2	1	6	1	
1965	4	8	2	1	4	2	3	4	
1966	8	4	2	4	2	1	4	2	1
1967	3	10	1	2	4		1	6	1
1968	4	10		2	5		2	5	
1969	4	10		2	5		2	5	
1970	2	12		1	6		1	6	
1971	6	8		5	2		1	6	
1972	3	11		2	5		1	6	
1973	5	9		3	4		2	5	
1974	7	7		3	4		4	3	
1975	3	11		2	5		1	6	
1976	11	3		6	1		5	2	
1977	9	5		6	1		3	4	
1978	11	5		5	3		6	2	
1979	9	7		6	2		3	5	
1980	10	6		6	2		4	4	
1981	2	14		2	6		0	8	
1982	5	4		3	1		2	3	
1983	8	8		5	3		3	5	
1984	9	7		5	3		4	4	
1985	11	5		7	1		4	4	
1986	11	5		4	4		7	1	
1987	8	7		5	3		3	4	
1988	9	7		7	1		2	6	
1989	5	11		3	5		2	6	
1990	1	15		0	8		1	7	
1991	6	10		4	4		2	6	
1992	2	14		1	7		1	7	
1993	5	11		3	5		2	6	
1994	10	6		5	3		5	3	
1995	6	10		3	5		3	5	
Total	237	286	9	135	124	6	102	162	3

**includes Boston Patriots (1960-70).*

NEW YORK JETS*

Season	All Games W	L	T	Home Games W	L	T	Road Games W	L	T
1960	7	7		3	4		4	3	
1961	7	7		5	2		2	5	
1962	5	9		2	5		3	4	
1963	5	8	1	4	2	1	1	6	
1964	5	8	1	5	1	1	0	7	
1965	5	8	1	3	3	1	2	5	
1966	6	6	2	4	3		2	3	2
1967	8	5	1	4	2	1	4	3	
1968	11	3		6	1		5	2	
1969	10	4		5	2		5	2	
1970	4	10		2	5		2	5	
1971	6	8		4	3		2	5	
1972	7	7		4	3		3	4	
1973	4	10		2	4		2	6	
1974	7	7		3	4		4	3	
1975	3	11		1	6		2	5	
1976	3	11		2	5		1	6	
1977	3	11		1	6		2	5	
1978	8	8		4	4		4	4	
1979	8	8		6	2		2	6	
1980	4	12		2	6		2	6	
1981	10	5	1	6	2		4	3	1
1982	6	3		3	1		3	2	
1983	7	9		2	6		5	3	
1984	7	9		3	5		4	4	
1985	11	5		7	1		4	4	
1986	10	6		5	3		5	3	
1987	6	9		4	4		2	5	
1988	8	7	1	5	2	1	3	5	
1989	4	12		1	7		3	5	
1990	6	10		3	5		3	5	
1991	8	8		4	4		4	4	
1992	4	12		3	5		1	7	
1993	8	8		3	5		5	3	
1994	6	10		4	4		2	6	
1995	3	13		2	6		1	7	
Total	230	294	8	127	133	5	103	161	3

**includes New York Titans (1960-62).*

OAKLAND RAIDERS*

Season	All Games W	L	T	Home Games W	L	T	Road Games W	L	T
1960	6	8		3	4		3	4	
1961	2	12		1	6		1	6	
1962	1	13		1	6		0	7	
1963	10	4		6	1		4	3	
1964	5	7	2	5	2		0	5	2
1965	8	5	1	5	2		3	3	1
1966	8	5	1	3	3	1	5	2	
1967	13	1		7	0		6	1	
1968	12	2		6	1		6	1	
1969	12	1	1	7	0		5	1	1
1970	8	4	2	6	1		2	3	2
1971	8	4	2	5	1	1	3	3	1
1972	10	3	1	5	1	1	5	2	
1973	9	4	1	5	2		4	2	1
1974	12	2		6	1		6	1	
1975	11	3		6	1		5	2	
1976	13	1		7	0		6	1	
1977	11	3		6	1		5	2	
1978	9	7		4	4		5	3	
1979	9	7		6	2		3	5	
1980	11	5		6	2		5	3	
1981	7	9		4	4		3	5	
1982	8	1		4	0		4	1	
1983	12	4		6	2		6	2	
1984	11	5		6	2		5	3	
1985	12	4		7	1		5	3	
1986	8	8		3	5		5	3	
1987	5	10		3	5		2	5	
1988	7	9		3	5		4	4	
1989	8	8		7	1		1	7	
1990	12	4		6	2		6	2	
1991	9	7		5	3		4	4	
1992	7	9		5	3		2	6	
1993	10	6		5	3		5	3	
1994	9	7		4	4		5	3	
1995	8	8		4	4		4	4	
Total	321	200	11	178	85	3	143	115	8

**includes Los Angeles Raiders (1982-94).*

PITTSBURGH STEELERS*

Season	All Games W	L	T	Home Games W	L	T	Road Games W	L	T
1933	3	6	2	2	3		1	3	2
1934	2	10		1	5		1	5	
1935	4	8		2	5		2	3	
1936	6	6		4	1		2	5	
1937	4	7		2	4		2	3	
1938	2	9		0	5		2	4	
1939	1	9	1	1	4		0	5	1
1940	2	7	2	1	2	2	1	5	
1941	1	9	1	1	4		0	5	1
1942	7	4		3	2		4	2	
1945	2	8		1	4		1	4	
1946	5	5	1	4	1		1	4	1
1947	8	4		5	1		3	3	
1948	4	8		4	2		0	6	
1949	6	5	1	3	2	1	3	3	
1950	6	6		2	4		4	2	
1951	4	7	1	1	4	1	3	3	
1952	5	7		2	4		3	3	
1953	6	6		3	3		3	3	
1954	5	7		4	2		1	5	
1955	4	8		3	2		1	6	
1956	5	7		3	3		2	4	
1957	6	6		4	2		2	4	
1958	7	4	1	5	1		2	3	1
1959	6	5	1	3	2	1	3	3	
1960	5	6	1	4	2		1	4	1
1961	6	8		4	3		2	5	
1962	9	5		4	3		5	2	
1963	7	4	3	5	0	2	2	4	1
1964	5	9		2	5		3	4	
1965	2	12		1	6		1	6	
1966	5	8	1	3	3	1	2	5	
1967	4	9	1	1	6		3	3	1
1968	2	11	1	1	6		1	5	1
1969	1	13		1	6		0	7	
1970	5	9		4	3		1	6	
1971	6	8		5	2		1	6	
1972	11	3		7	0		4	3	
1973	10	4		7	1		3	3	
1974	10	3	1	5	2		5	1	1
1975	12	2		6	1		6	1	
1976	10	4		6	1		4	3	
1977	9	5		6	1		3	4	
1978	14	2		7	1		7	1	
1979	12	4		8	0		4	4	
1980	9	7		6	2		3	5	
1981	8	8		5	3		3	5	
1982	6	3		4	0		2	3	
1983	10	6		4	4		6	2	
1984	9	7		6	2		3	5	
1985	7	9		5	3		2	6	

	All Games			Home Games			Road Games		
Season	W	L	T	W	L	T	W	L	T
1986	6	10		4	4		2	6	
1987	8	7		4	3		4	4	
1988	5	11		4	4		1	7	
1989	9	7		4	4		5	3	
1990	9	7		6	2		3	5	
1991	7	9		5	3		2	6	
1992	11	5		7	1		4	4	
1993	9	7		6	2		3	5	
1994	12	4		7	1		5	3	
1995	11	5		6	2		5	3	
Total	392	409	19	234	164	8	158	245	11

**includes Pittsburgh Pirates (1933-40).*

SAN DIEGO CHARGERS*

	All Games			Home Games			Road Games		
Season	W	L	T	W	L	T	W	L	T
1960	10	4		5	2		5	2	
1961	12	2		6	1		6	1	
1962	4	10		3	4		1	6	
1963	11	3		6	1		5	2	
1964	8	5	1	4	3		4	2	1
1965	9	2	3	4	1	2	5	1	1
1966	7	6	1	5	2		2	4	1
1967	8	5	1	5	2	1	3	3	
1968	9	5		4	3		5	2	
1969	8	6		5	2		3	4	
1970	5	6	3	2	3	2	3	3	1
1971	6	8		6	1		0	7	
1972	4	9	1	2	5		2	4	1
1973	2	11	1	2	5		0	6	1
1974	5	9		3	4		2	5	
1975	2	12		1	6		1	6	
1976	6	8		3	4		3	4	
1977	7	7		3	4		4	3	
1978	9	7		5	3		4	4	
1979	12	4		7	1		5	3	
1980	11	5		6	2		5	3	
1981	10	6		5	3		5	3	
1982	6	3		3	1		3	2	
1983	6	10		4	4		2	6	
1984	7	9		4	4		3	5	
1985	8	8		6	2		2	6	
1986	4	12		2	6		2	6	
1987	8	7		4	3		4	4	
1988	6	10		3	5		3	5	
1989	6	10		4	4		2	6	
1990	6	10		3	5		3	5	
1991	4	12		3	5		1	7	
1992	11	5		6	2		5	3	
1993	8	8		4	4		4	4	
1994	11	5		5	3		6	2	
1995	9	7		5	3		4	4	
Total	265	256	11	148	113	5	117	143	6

**includes Los Angeles Chargers (1960).*

SEATTLE SEAHAWKS

	All Games			Home Games			Road Games		
Season	W	L	T	W	L	T	W	L	T
1976	2	12		1	6		1	6	
1977	5	9		3	4		2	5	
1978	9	7		5	3		4	4	
1979	9	7		5	3		4	4	
1980	4	12		0	8		4	4	
1981	6	10		5	3		1	7	
1982	4	5		3	2		1	3	
1983	9	7		5	3		4	4	
1984	12	4		7	1		5	3	
1985	8	8		5	.3		3	5	
1986	10	6		7	1		3	5	
1987	9	6		6	2		3	4	
1988	9	7		5	3		4	4	
1989	7	9		3	5		4	4	
1990	9	7		5	3		4	4	
1991	7	9		5	3		2	6	
1992	2	14		1	7		1	7	
1993	6	10		4	4		2	6	
1994	6	10		3	5		3	5	
1995	8	8		5	3		3	5	
Total	141	167		83	72		58	95	

NFC

ARIZONA CARDINALS*

	All Games			Home Games			Road Games		
Season	W	L	T	W	L	T	W	L	T
1920	6	2	2	5	1	1	1	1	1
1921	3	3	2	3	3	1	0	0	1
1922	8	3		8	3		0	0	
1923	8	4		8	3		0	1	
1924	5	4	1	5	3	1	0	1	
1925	11	2	1	11	2		0	0	1
1926	5	6	1	3	3		2	3	1
1927	3	7	1	2	3	1	1	4	
1928	1	5		1	1		0	4	
1929	6	6	1	3	2		3	4	1
1930	5	6	2	3	2		2	4	2
1931	5	4		3	0		2	4	
1932	2	6	2	1	2	1	1	4	1
1933	1	9	1	0	4	1	1	5	
1934	5	6		2	2		3	4	
1935	6	4	2	2	2		4	2	2
1936	3	8	1	3	1	1	0	7	
1937	5	5	1	1	3		4	2	1
1938	2	9		1	4		1	5	
1939	1	10		0	4		1	6	
1940	2	7	2	2	1	1	0	6	1
1941	3	7	1	0	3	1	3	4	
1942	3	8		2	2		1	6	
1943	0	10		0	3		0	7	
1945	1	9		0	3		1	6	
1946	6	5		2	2		4	3	
1947	9	3		5	0		4	3	
1948	11	1		5	1		6	0	
1949	6	5	1	2	3	1	4	2	
1950	5	7		3	3		2	4	
1951	3	9		1	5		2	4	
1952	4	8		2	4		2	4	
1953	1	10	1	0	5	1	1	5	
1954	2	10		2	4		0	6	
1955	4	7	1	3	2	1	1	5	
1956	7	5		4	2		3	3	
1957	3	9		0	6		3	3	
1958	2	9	1	1	4	1	1	5	
1959	2	10		2	4		0	6	
1960	6	5	1	3	2	1	3	3	
1961	7	7		3	4		4	3	
1962	4	9	1	2	4	1	2	5	
1963	9	5		3	4		6	1	
1964	9	3	2	4	1	1	5	2	1
1965	5	9		2	5		3	4	
1966	8	5	1	5	1	1	3	4	
1967	6	7	1	3	3	1	3	4	
1968	9	4	1	4	2	1	5	2	
1969	4	9	1	3	4		1	5	1
1970	8	5	1	6	1		2	4	1
1971	4	9	1	1	5	1	3	4	
1972	4	9	1	2	5		2	4	1
1973	4	9	1	2	4	1	2	5	
1974	10	4		5	2		5	2	
1975	11	3		6	1		5	2	
1976	10	4		6	1		4	3	
1977	7	7		4	3		3	4	
1978	6	10		3	5		3	5	
1979	5	11		3	5		2	6	
1980	5	11		2	6		3	5	
1981	7	9		5	3		2	6	
1982	5	4		1	3		4	1	
1983	8	7	1	4	3	1	4	4	
1984	9	7		5	3		4	4	
1985	5	11		4	4		1	7	
1986	4	11	1	3	5		1	6	1
1987	7	8		4	3		3	5	
1988	7	9		4	4		3	5	
1989	5	11		2	6		3	5	
1990	5	11		3	5		2	6	
1991	4	12		2	6		2	6	
1992	4	12		3	5		1	7	
1993	7	9		4	4		3	5	
1994	8	8		5	3		3	5	
1995	4	12		3	5		1	7	
Total	395	534	39	225	235	22	170	299	17

**includes Chicago Cardinals (1920-59), St. Louis Cardinals (1960-87), and Phoenix Cardinals (1988-93).*

ATLANTA FALCONS

	All Games			Home Games			Road Games		
Season	W	L	T	W	L	T	W	L	T
1966	3	11		1	6		2	5	
1967	1	12	1	1	5	1	0	7	
1968	2	12		1	6		1	6	
1969	6	8		4	3		2	5	
1970	4	8	2	3	4		1	4	2
1971	7	6	1	4	3		3	3	1
1972	7	7		4	3		3	4	
1973	9	5		4	3		5	2	
1974	3	11		2	5		1	6	
1975	4	10		3	4		1	6	
1976	4	10		3	4		1	6	
1977	7	7		4	3		3	4	
1978	9	7		7	1		2	6	
1979	6	10		3	5		3	5	
1980	12	4		6	2		6	2	
1981	7	9		4	4		3	5	
1982	5	4		2	3		3	1	
1983	7	9		4	4		3	5	
1984	4	12		2	6		2	6	
1985	4	12		3	5		1	7	
1986	7	8	1	2	5	1	5	3	
1987	3	12		2	6		1	6	
1988	5	11		2	6		3	5	
1989	3	13		3	5		0	8	
1990	5	11		5	3		0	8	
1991	10	6		6	2		4	4	
1992	6	10		5	3		1	7	
1993	6	10		4	4		2	6	
1994	7	9		5	3		2	6	
1995	9	7		7	1		2	6	
Total	172	271	5	106	117	2	66	154	3

CAROLINA PANTHERS

	All Games			Home Games			Road Games		
Season	W	L	T	W	L	T	W	L	T
1995	7	9		5	3		2	6	

CHICAGO BEARS*

	All Games			Home Games			Road Games		
Season	W	L	T	W	L	T	W	L	T
1920	10	1	2	6	0	1	4	1	1
1921	9	1	1	9	1	1	0	0	
1922	9	3		7	1		2	2	
1923	9	2	1	7	1	1	2	1	
1924	6	1	4	5	0	3	1	1	1
1925	9	5	3	7	1	1	2	4	2
1926	12	1	3	10	0	2	2	1	1
1927	9	3	2	7	1	1	2	2	1
1928	7	5	1	6	3		1	2	1
1929	4	9	2	1	5	2	3	4	
1930	9	4	1	5	2	1	4	2	
1931	8	5		6	3		2	2	
1932	7	1	6	6	1	1	1	0	5
1933	10	2	1	6	0		4	2	1
1934	13	0		5	0		8	0	
1935	6	4	2	1	2	2	5	2	
1936	9	3		3	1		6	2	
1937	9	1	1	4	1		5	0	1
1938	6	5		2	3		4	2	
1939	8	3		4	1		4	2	
1940	8	3		5	0		3	3	
1941	10	1		5	1		5	0	
1942	11	0		6	0		5	0	
1943	8	1	1	5	0		3	1	1
1944	6	3	1	4	0	1	2	3	
1945	3	7		2	3		1	4	
1946	8	2	1	4	1	1	4	1	
1947	8	4		4	2		4	2	
1948	10	2		5	1		5	1	
1949	9	3		5	1		4	2	
1950	9	3		6	0		3	3	
1951	7	5		3	3		4	2	
1952	5	7		3	3		2	4	
1953	3	8	1	1	4	1	2	4	
1954	8	4		4	2		4	2	
1955	8	4		5	1		3	3	
1956	9	2	1	6	0		3	2	1
1957	5	7		2	4		3	3	
1958	8	4		5	1		3	3	
1959	8	4		4	2		4	2	

Season	All Games W	L	T	Home Games W	L	T	Road Games W	L	T
1960	5	6	1	4	2		1	4	1
1961	8	6		5	2		3	4	
1962	9	5		4	3		5	2	
1963	11	1	2	6	0	1	5	1	1
1964	5	9		2	5		3	4	
1965	9	5		5	2		4	3	
1966	5	7	2	4	1	2	1	6	
1967	7	6	1	3	3	1	4	3	
1968	7	7		2	5		5	2	
1969	1	13		1	6		0	7	
1970	6	8		3	4		3	4	
1971	6	8		4	3		2	5	
1972	4	9	1	1	5	1	3	4	
1973	3	11		1	6		2	5	
1974	4	10		4	3		0	7	
1975	4	10		3	4		1	6	
1976	7	7		4	3		3	4	
1977	9	5		5	2		4	3	
1978	7	9		4	4		3	5	
1979	10	6		6	2		4	4	
1980	7	9		5	3		2	6	
1981	6	10		4	4		2	6	
1982	3	6		2	2		1	4	
1983	8	8		5	3		3	5	
1984	10	6		6	2		4	4	
1985	15	1		8	0		7	1	
1986	14	2		7	1		7	1	
1987	11	4		6	2		5	2	
1988	12	4		7	1		5	3	
1989	6	10		4	4		2	6	
1990	11	5		7	1		4	4	
1991	11	5		6	2		5	3	
1992	5	11		4	4		1	7	
1993	7	9		3	5		4	4	
1994	9	7		5	3		4	4	
1995	9	7		5	3		4	4	
Total	591	385	42	346	161	24	245	224	18

**includes Decatur Staleys (1920) and Chicago Staleys (1921).*

DALLAS COWBOYS

Season	All Games W	L	T	Home Games W	L	T	Road Games W	L	T
1960	0	11	1	0	6		0	5	1
1961	4	9	1	2	4	1	2	5	
1962	5	8	1	2	4	1	3	4	
1963	4	10		3	4		1	6	
1964	5	8	1	2	4	1	3	4	
1965	7	7		5	2		2	5	
1966	10	3	1	6	1		4	2	1
1967	9	5		5	2		4	3	
1968	12	2		5	2		7	0	
1969	11	2	1	6	0	1	5	2	
1970	10	4		6	1		4	3	
1971	11	3		6	1		5	2	
1972	10	4		5	2		5	2	
1973	10	4		6	1		4	3	
1974	8	6		5	2		3	4	
1975	10	4		5	2		5	2	
1976	11	3		6	1		5	2	
1977	12	2		6	1		6	1	
1978	12	4		7	1		5	3	
1979	11	5		6	2		5	3	
1980	12	4		8	0		4	4	
1981	12	4		8	0		4	4	
1982	6	3		3	2		3	1	
1983	12	4		6	2		6	2	
1984	9	7		5	3		4	4	
1985	10	6		7	1		3	5	
1986	7	9		3	5		4	4	
1987	7	8		3	4		4	4	
1988	3	13		1	7		2	6	
1989	1	15		0	8		1	7	
1990	7	9		5	3		2	6	
1991	11	5		6	2		5	3	
1992	13	3		7	1		6	2	
1993	12	4		6	2		6	2	
1994	12	4		6	2		6	2	
1995	12	4		6	2		6	2	
Total	318	206	6	174	87	4	144	119	2

DETROIT LIONS*

Season	All Games W	L	T	Home Games W	L	T	Road Games W	L	T
1930	5	6	3	5	1	2	0	5	1
1931	11	3		8	0		3	3	
1932	6	2	4	3	0	2	3	2	2
1933	6	5		4	1		2	4	
1934	10	3		6	2		4	1	
1935	7	3	2	5	0	1	2	3	1
1936	8	4		5	1		3	3	
1937	7	4		4	2		3	2	
1938	7	4		4	3		3	1	
1939	6	5		4	2		2	3	
1940	5	5	1	3	3		2	2	1
1941	4	6	1	3	2		1	4	1
1942	0	11		0	7		0	4	
1943	3	6	1	2	2	1	1	4	
1944	6	3	1	4	2		2	1	1
1945	7	3		4	1		3	2	
1946	1	10		1	5		0	5	
1947	3	9		2	4		1	5	
1948	2	10		2	4		0	6	
1949	4	8		2	4		2	4	
1950	6	6		4	2		2	4	
1951	7	4	1	3	3	1	4	1	
1952	9	3		6	1		3	2	
1953	10	2		5	1		5	1	
1954	9	2	1	5	0	1	4	2	
1955	3	9		3	4		0	5	
1956	9	3		5	1		4	2	
1957	8	4		5	1		3	3	
1958	4	7	1	2	4		2	3	1
1959	3	8	1	2	4		1	4	1
1960	7	5		5	1		2	4	
1961	8	5	1	2	5		6	0	1
1962	11	3		7	0		4	3	
1963	5	8	1	3	3	1	2	5	
1964	7	5	2	3	3	1	4	2	1
1965	6	7	1	2	4	1	4	3	
1966	4	9	1	3	4		1	5	1
1967	5	7	2	3	4		2	3	2
1968	4	8	2	1	4	2	3	4	
1969	9	4	1	5	2		4	2	1
1970	10	4		6	1		4	3	
1971	7	6	1	3	4		4	2	1
1972	8	5	1	5	2		3	3	1
1973	6	7	1	4	3		2	4	1
1974	7	7		5	2		2	5	
1975	7	7		4	3		3	4	
1976	6	8		5	2		1	6	
1977	6	8		5	2		1	6	
1978	7	9		5	3		2	6	
1979	2	14		2	6		0	8	
1980	9	7		6	2		3	5	
1981	8	8		7	1		1	7	
1982	4	5		2	3		2	2	
1983	9	7		6	2		3	5	
1984	4	11	1	2	5	1	2	6	
1985	7	9		6	2		1	7	
1986	5	11		1	7		4	4	
1987	4	11		1	6		3	5	
1988	4	12		2	6		2	6	
1989	7	9		4	4		3	5	
1990	6	10		3	5		3	5	
1991	12	4		8	0		4	4	
1992	5	11		3	5		2	6	
1993	10	6		5	3		5	3	
1994	9	7		6	2		3	5	
1995	10	6		7	1		3	5	
Total	421	428	32	258	179	14	163	249	18

**includes Portsmouth Spartans (1930-33).*

GREEN BAY PACKERS

Season	All Games W	L	T	Home Games W	L	T	Road Games W	L	T
1921	3	2	1	2	1		1	1	1
1922	4	3	3	4	1	1	0	2	2
1923	7	2	1	4	2	1	3	0	
1924	7	4		5	0		2	4	
1925	8	5		6	0		2	5	
1926	7	3	3	4	1	2	3	2	1
1927	7	2	1	6	1		1	1	1
1928	6	4	3	2	2	2	4	2	1
1929	12	0	1	5	0		7	0	1
1930	10	3	1	6	0		4	3	1
1931	12	2		8	0		4	2	
1932	10	3	1	5	0	1	5	3	
1933	5	7	1	3	2	1	2	5	
1934	7	6		4	2		3	4	
1935	8	4		5	2		3	2	
1936	10	1	1	5	1		5	0	1
1937	7	4		3	2		4	2	
1938	8	3		4	2		4	1	
1939	9	2		4	1		5	1	
1940	6	4	1	4	2		2	2	1
1941	10	1		4	1		6	0	
1942	8	2	1	4	1		4	1	1
1943	7	2	1	2	1	1	5	1	
1944	8	2		5	0		3	2	
1945	6	4		4	1		2	3	
1946	6	5		2	3		4	2	
1947	6	5	1	4	2		2	3	1
1948	3	9		2	4		1	5	
1949	2	10		1	5		1	5	
1950	3	9		3	3		0	6	
1951	3	9		2	4		1	5	
1952	6	6		3	3		3	3	
1953	2	9	1	1	5		1	4	1
1954	4	8		2	4		2	4	
1955	6	6		5	1		1	5	
1956	4	8		2	4		2	4	
1957	3	9		1	5		2	4	
1958	1	10	1	1	4	1	0	6	
1959	7	5		4	2		3	3	
1960	8	4		4	2		4	2	
1961	11	3		6	1		5	2	
1962	13	1		7	0		6	1	
1963	11	2	1	6	1		5	1	1
1964	8	5	1	4	3		4	2	1
1965	10	3	1	6	1		4	2	1
1966	12	2		6	1		6	1	
1967	9	4	1	4	2	1	5	2	
1968	6	7	1	2	5		4	2	1
1969	8	6		5	2		3	4	
1970	6	8		4	3		2	5	
1971	4	8	2	3	3	1	1	5	1
1972	10	4		4	3		6	1	
1973	5	7	2	3	2	2	2	5	
1974	6	8		4	3		2	5	
1975	4	10		3	4		1	6	
1976	5	9		4	3		1	6	
1977	4	10		2	5		2	5	
1978	8	7	1	5	2	1	3	5	
1979	5	11		4	4		1	7	
1980	5	10	1	4	4		1	6	1
1981	8	8		4	4		4	4	
1982	5	3	1	3	1		2	2	1
1983	8	8		5	3		3	5	
1984	8	8		5	3		3	5	
1985	8	8		5	3		3	5	
1986	4	12		1	7		3	5	
1987	5	9	1	2	5	1	3	4	
1988	4	12		2	6		2	6	
1989	10	6		6	2		4	4	
1990	6	10		3	5		3	5	
1991	4	12		2	6		2	6	
1992	9	7		6	2		3	5	
1993	9	7		6	2		3	5	
1994	9	7		7	1		2	6	
1995	11	5		7	1		4	4	
Total	514	434	36	295	180	16	219	254	20

MINNESOTA VIKINGS

Season	All Games W	L	T	Home Games W	L	T	Road Games W	L	T
1961	3	11		3	4		0	7	
1962	2	11	1	1	5	1	1	6	
1963	5	8	1	3	4		2	4	1
1964	8	5	1	4	3		4	2	1
1965	7	7		2	5		5	2	
1966	4	9	1	2	5		2	4	1
1967	3	8	3	1	4	2	2	4	1
1968	8	6		4	3		4	3	
1969	12	2		7	0		5	2	

Season	All Games W	L	T	Home Games W	L	T	Road Games W	L	T
1970	12	2		7	0		5	2	
1971	11	3		5	2		6	1	
1972	7	7		3	4		4	3	
1973	12	2		7	0		5	2	
1974	10	4		4	3		6	1	
1975	12	2		7	0		5	2	
1976	11	2	1	6	0	1	5	2	
1977	9	5		5	2		4	3	
1978	8	7	1	5	3		3	4	1
1979	7	9		5	3		2	6	
1980	9	7		5	3		4	4	
1981	7	9		5	3		2	6	
1982	5	4		4	1		1	3	
1983	8	8		3	5		5	3	
1984	3	13		2	6		1	7	
1985	7	9		4	4		3	5	
1986	9	7		5	3		4	4	
1987	8	7		5	3		3	4	
1988	11	5		7	1		4	4	
1989	10	6		8	0		2	6	
1990	6	10		4	4		2	6	
1991	8	8		4	4		4	4	
1992	11	5		5	3		6	2	
1993	9	7		4	4		5	3	
1994	10	6		6	2		4	4	
1995	8	8		6	2		2	6	
Total	280	229	9	158	98	4	122	131	5

NEW ORLEANS SAINTS

Season	All Games W	L	T	Home Games W	L	T	Road Games W	L	T
1967	3	11		2	5		1	6	
1968	4	9	1	3	4		1	5	1
1969	5	9		3	4		2	5	
1970	2	11	1	2	5		0	6	1
1971	4	8	2	2	4	1	2	4	1
1972	2	11	1	2	5		0	6	1
1973	5	9		5	2		0	7	
1974	5	9		4	3		1	6	
1975	2	12		2	5		0	7	
1976	4	10		2	5		2	5	
1977	3	11		2	5		1	6	
1978	7	9		3	5		4	4	
1979	8	8		3	5		5	3	
1980	1	15		0	8		1	7	
1981	4	12		2	6		2	6	
1982	4	5		2	3		2	2	
1983	8	8		5	3		3	5	
1984	7	9		3	5		4	4	
1985	5	11		3	5		2	6	
1986	7	9		4	4		3	5	
1987	12	3		6	1		6	2	
1988	10	6		5	3		5	3	
1989	9	7		5	3		4	4	
1990	8	8		5	3		3	5	
1991	11	5		6	2		5	3	
1992	12	4		6	2		6	2	
1993	8	8		4	4		4	4	
1994	7	9		3	5		4	4	
1995	7	9		4	4		3	5	
Total	174	255	5	98	118	1	76	137	4

NEW YORK GIANTS

Season	All Games W	L	T	Home Games W	L	T	Road Games W	L	T
1925	8	4		7	2		1	2	
1926	8	4	1	5	2	1	3	2	
1927	11	1	1	7	1		4	0	1
1928	4	7	2	1	2	2	3	5	
1929	13	1	1	7	1		6	0	1
1930	13	4		6	2		7	2	
1931	7	6	1	4	2	1	3	4	
1932	4	6	2	3	2	1	1	4	1
1933	11	3		7	0		4	3	
1934	8	5		5	1		3	4	
1935	9	3		4	2		5	1	
1936	5	6	1	3	3	1	2	3	
1937	6	3	2	4	2	1	2	1	1
1938	8	2	1	6	1		2	1	1
1939	9	1	1	6	0		3	1	1
1940	6	4	1	4	3		2	1	1
1941	8	3		5	2		3	1	
1942	5	5	1	3	2	1	2	3	
1943	6	3	1	4	2		2	1	1
1944	8	1	1	5	1		3	0	1
1945	3	6	1	2	4		1	2	1
1946	7	3	1	5	1	1	2	2	
1947	2	8	2	2	3	1	0	5	1
1948	4	8		2	4		2	4	
1949	6	6		2	4		4	2	
1950	10	2		5	1		5	1	
1951	9	2	1	5	1		4	1	1
1952	7	5		2	4		5	1	
1953	3	9		2	4		1	5	
1954	7	5		4	2		3	3	
1955	6	5	1	4	1	1	2	4	
1956	8	3	1	4	1	1	4	2	
1957	7	5		3	3		4	2	
1958	9	3		5	1		4	2	
1959	10	2		5	1		5	1	
1960	6	4	2	1	3	2	5	1	
1961	10	3	1	4	2	1	6	1	
1962	12	2		6	1		6	1	
1963	11	3		5	2		6	1	
1964	2	10	2	2	5		0	5	2
1965	7	7		3	4		4	3	
1966	1	12	1	1	6		0	6	1
1967	7	7		5	2		2	5	
1968	7	7		3	4		4	3	
1969	6	8		5	2		1	6	
1970	9	5		5	2		4	3	
1971	4	10		1	6		3	4	
1972	8	6		4	3		4	3	
1973	2	11	1	2	4	1	0	7	
1974	2	12		0	7		2	5	
1975	5	9		2	5		3	4	
1976	3	11		3	4		0	7	
1977	5	9		3	4		2	5	
1978	6	10		5	3		1	7	
1979	6	10		4	4		2	6	
1980	4	12		2	6		2	6	
1981	9	7		4	4		5	3	
1982	4	5		2	3		2	2	
1983	3	12	1	1	7		2	5	1
1984	9	7		6	2		3	5	
1985	10	6		6	2		4	4	
1986	14	2		8	0		6	2	
1987	6	9		5	3		1	6	
1988	10	6		5	3		5	3	
1989	12	4		7	1		5	3	
1990	13	3		7	1		6	2	
1991	8	8		5	3		3	5	
1992	6	10		4	4		2	6	
1993	11	5		6	2		5	3	
1994	9	7		4	4		5	3	
1995	5	11		3	5		2	6	
Total	507	414	32	287	191	16	220	223	16

PHILADELPHIA EAGLES

Season	All Games W	L	T	Home Games W	L	T	Road Games W	L	T
1933	3	5	1	2	3	1	1	2	
1934	4	7		2	4		2	3	
1935	2	9		0	5		2	4	
1936	1	11		1	6		0	5	
1937	2	8	1	0	5	1	2	3	
1938	5	6		2	3		3	3	
1939	1	9	1	1	3	1	0	6	
1940	1	10		1	4		0	6	
1941	2	8	1	1	4	1	1	4	
1942	2	9		0	5		2	4	
1944	7	1	2	3	1	2	4	0	
1945	7	3		6	0		1	3	
1946	6	5		3	2		3	3	
1947	8	4		6	1		2	3	
1948	9	2	1	6	0		3	2	1
1949	11	1		6	0		5	1	
1950	6	6		2	4		4	2	
1951	4	8		1	5		3	3	
1952	7	5		4	2		3	3	
1953	7	4	1	5	0	1	2	4	
1954	7	4	1	5	1		2	3	1
1955	4	7	1	4	2		0	5	1
1956	3	8	1	2	3	1	1	5	
1957	4	8		3	3		1	5	
1958	2	9	1	2	4		0	5	1
1959	6	5		4	1		2	4	
1960	10	2		5	1		5	1	
1961	10	4		5	2		5	2	
1962	3	10	1	2	5		1	5	1
1963	2	10	2	1	5	1	1	5	1
1964	6	8		3	4		3	4	
1965	5	9		2	5		3	4	
1966	9	5		5	2		4	3	
1967	6	7	1	5	2		1	5	1
1968	2	12		1	6		1	6	
1969	4	9	1	2	5		2	4	1
1970	3	10	1	3	3	1	0	7	
1971	6	7	1	3	4		3	3	1
1972	2	11	1	0	6	1	2	5	
1973	5	8	1	4	3		1	5	1
1974	7	7		5	2		2	5	
1975	4	10		2	5		2	5	
1976	4	10		2	5		2	5	
1977	5	9		4	3		1	6	
1978	9	7		5	3		4	4	
1979	11	5		5	3		6	2	
1980	12	4		7	1		5	3	
1981	10	6		6	2		4	4	
1982	3	6		1	4		2	2	
1983	5	11		1	7		4	4	
1984	6	9	1	5	3		1	6	1
1985	7	9		4	4		3	5	
1986	5	10	1	2	5	1	3	5	
1987	7	8		4	4		3	4	
1988	10	6		5	3		5	3	
1989	11	5		6	2		5	3	
1990	10	6		6	2		4	4	
1991	10	6		4	4		6	2	
1992	11	5		8	0		3	5	
1993	8	8		3	5		5	3	
1994	7	9		5	3		2	6	
1995	10	6		6	2		4	4	
Total	366	436	23	209	196	12	157	240	11

ST. LOUIS RAMS*

Season	All Games W	L	T	Home Games W	L	T	Road Games W	L	T
1937	1	10		0	5		1	5	
1938	4	7		2	2		2	5	
1939	5	5	1	3	2	1	2	3	
1940	4	6	1	3	1	1	1	5	
1941	2	9		1	4		1	5	
1942	5	6		3	2		2	4	
1944	4	6		1	2		3	4	
1945	9	1		4	0		5	1	
1946	6	4	1	3	2		3	2	1
1947	6	6		3	3		3	3	
1948	6	5	1	3	2	1	3	3	
1949	8	2	2	5	1		3	1	2
1950	9	3		5	1		4	2	
1951	8	4		5	2		3	2	
1952	9	3		5	1		4	2	
1953	8	3	1	5	1		3	2	1
1954	6	5	1	3	2	1	3	3	
1955	8	3	1	5	1		3	2	1
1956	4	8		4	2		0	6	
1957	6	6		5	1		1	5	
1958	8	4		4	2		4	2	
1959	2	10		0	6		2	4	
1960	4	7	1	2	3	1	2	4	
1961	4	10		4	3		0	7	
1962	1	12	1	0	7		1	5	1
1963	5	9		3	4		2	5	
1964	5	7	2	3	2	2	2	5	
1965	4	10		3	4		1	6	
1966	8	6		5	2		3	4	
1967	11	1	2	5	1	1	6	0	1
1968	10	3	1	5	2		5	1	1
1969	11	3		5	2		6	1	
1970	9	4	1	3	3	1	6	1	
1971	8	5	1	4	2	1	4	3	
1972	6	7	1	4	3		2	4	1

Season	All Games W	L	T	Home Games W	L	T	Road Games W	L	T
1973	12	2		7	0		5	2	
1974	10	4		6	1		4	3	
1975	12	2		6	1		6	1	
1976	10	3	1	5	2		5	1	1
1977	10	4		7	0		3	4	
1978	12	4		6	2		6	2	
1979	9	7		4	4		5	3	
1980	11	5		6	2		5	3	
1981	6	10		4	4		2	6	
1982	2	7		1	4		1	3	
1983	9	7		5	3		4	4	
1984	10	6		5	3		5	3	
1985	11	5		6	2		5	3	
1986	10	6		6	2		4	4	
1987	6	9		3	4		3	5	
1988	10	6		4	4		6	2	
1989	11	5		6	2		5	3	
1990	5	11		2	6		3	5	
1991	3	13		2	6		1	7	
1992	6	10		4	4		2	6	
1993	5	11		3	5		2	6	
1994	4	12		3	5		1	7	
1995	7	9		4	4		3	5	
Total	405	358	20	223	153	10	182	205	10

includes Cleveland Rams (1937-42, 1944-45) and Los Angeles Rams (1946-94).

SAN FRANCISCO 49ERS

Season	All Games W	L	T	Home Games W	L	T	Road Games W	L	T
1950	3	9		3	3		0	6	
1951	7	4	1	5	1		2	3	1
1952	7	5		3	3		4	2	
1953	9	3		5	1		4	2	
1954	7	4	1	4	2		3	2	1
1955	4	8		2	4		2	4	
1956	5	6	1	3	3		2	3	1
1957	8	4		5	1		3	3	
1958	6	6		4	2		2	4	
1959	7	5		4	2		3	3	
1960	7	5		3	3		4	2	
1961	7	6	1	5	1	1	2	5	
1962	6	8		1	6		5	2	
1963	2	12		2	5		0	7	
1964	4	10		3	4		1	6	
1965	7	6	1	4	2	1	3	4	
1966	6	6	2	4	2	1	2	4	1
1967	7	7		3	4		4	3	
1968	7	6	1	3	3	1	4	3	
1969	4	8	2	3	3	1	1	5	1
1970	10	3	1	5	1	1	5	2	
1971	9	5		4	3		5	2	
1972	8	5	1	4	2	1	4	3	
1973	5	9		3	4		2	5	
1974	6	8		3	4		3	4	
1975	5	9		2	5		3	4	
1976	8	6		4	3		4	3	
1977	5	9		3	4		2	5	
1978	2	14		2	6		0	8	
1979	2	14		2	6		0	8	
1980	6	10		4	4		2	6	
1981	13	3		7	1		6	2	
1982	3	6		0	5		3	1	
1983	10	6		4	4		6	2	
1984	15	1		7	1		8	0	
1985	10	6		5	3		5	3	
1986	10	5	1	6	2		4	3	1
1987	13	2		6	1		7	1	
1988	10	6		4	4		6	2	
1989	14	2		6	2		8	0	
1990	14	2		6	2		8	0	
1991	10	6		7	1		3	5	
1992	14	2		7	1		7	1	
1993	10	6		6	2		4	4	
1994	13	3		7	1		6	2	
1995	11	5		6	2		5	3	
Total	356	281	13	189	129	7	167	152	6

TAMPA BAY BUCCANEERS

Season	All Games W	L	T	Home Games W	L	T	Road Games W	L	T
1976	0	14		0	7		0	7	
1977	2	12		1	6		1	6	
1978	5	11		3	5		2	6	
1979	10	6		5	3		5	3	
1980	5	10	1	2	5	1	3	5	
1981	9	7		6	2		3	5	
1982	5	4		4	1		1	3	
1983	2	14		1	7		1	7	
1984	6	10		6	2		0	8	
1985	2	14		2	6		0	8	
1986	2	14		1	7		1	7	
1987	4	11		2	5		2	6	
1988	5	11		3	5		2	6	
1989	5	11		2	6		3	5	
1990	6	10		4	4		2	6	
1991	3	13		3	5		0	8	
1992	5	11		3	5		2	6	
1993	5	11		3	5		2	6	
1994	6	10		4	4		2	6	
1995	7	9		5	3		2	6	
Total	94	213	1	60	93	1	34	120	

WASHINGTON REDSKINS*

Season	All Games W	L	T	Home Games W	L	T	Road Games W	L	T
1932	4	4	2	2	3	1	2	1	1
1933	5	5	2	4	2		1	3	2
1934	6	6		4	3		2	3	
1935	2	8	1	2	5		0	3	1
1936	7	5		4	3		3	2	
1937	8	3		4	2		4	1	
1938	6	3	2	3	1	1	3	2	1
1939	8	2	1	5	0	1	3	2	
1940	9	2		6	0		3	2	
1941	6	5		4	2		2	3	
1942	10	1		5	1		5	0	
1943	6	3	1	4	2		2	1	1
1944	6	3	1	4	2		2	1	1
1945	8	2		6	0		2	2	
1946	5	5	1	3	2	1	2	3	
1947	4	8		4	2		0	6	
1948	7	5		4	2		3	3	
1949	4	7	1	3	3		1	4	1
1950	3	9		1	5		2	4	
1951	5	7		2	4		3	3	
1952	4	8		1	5		3	3	
1953	6	5	1	3	3		3	2	1
1954	3	9		3	3		0	6	
1955	8	4		3	3		5	1	
1956	6	6		4	2		2	4	
1957	5	6	1	2	3	1	3	3	
1958	4	7	1	3	2	1	1	5	
1959	4	8		2	4		2	4	
1960	1	9	2	1	4	1	0	5	1
1961	1	12	1	1	6		0	6	1
1962	5	7	2	3	4		2	3	2
1963	3	11		1	6		2	5	
1964	6	8		4	3		2	5	
1965	6	8		3	4		3	4	
1966	7	7		4	3		3	4	
1967	5	6	3	2	4	1	3	2	2
1968	5	9		3	4		2	5	
1969	7	5	2	4	2	1	3	3	1
1970	6	8		4	3		2	5	
1971	9	4	1	4	2	1	5	2	
1972	11	3		6	1		5	2	
1973	10	4		7	0		3	4	
1974	10	4		6	1		4	3	
1975	8	6		5	2		3	4	
1976	10	4		5	2		5	2	
1977	9	5		5	2		4	3	
1978	8	8		5	3		3	5	
1979	10	6		6	2		4	4	
1980	6	10		4	4		2	6	
1981	8	8		5	3		3	5	
1982	8	1		3	1		5	0	
1983	14	2		7	1		7	1	
1984	11	5		7	1		4	4	
1985	10	6		5	3		5	3	
1986	12	4		7	1		5	3	
1987	11	4		6	1		5	3	
1988	7	9		4	4		3	5	
1989	10	6		4	4		6	2	
1990	10	6		7	1		3	5	
1991	14	2		7	1		7	1	
1992	9	7		6	2		3	5	
1993	4	12		3	5		1	7	
1994	3	13		0	8		3	5	
1995	6	10		4	4		2	6	
Total	439	385	26	253	171	10	186	214	16

includes Boston Braves (1932) and Boston Redskins (1933-36).

History

PRO FOOTBALL HALL OF FAME

The Professional Football Hall of Fame is located in Canton, Ohio, site of the organizational meeting on September 17, 1920, from which the National Football League evolved. The NFL recognized Canton as the Hall of Fame site on April 27, 1961. Canton area individuals, foundations, and companies donated almost $400,000 in cash and services to provide funds for the construction of the original two-building complex, which was dedicated on September 7, 1963. Since that time, the Hall added three buildings with major expansion projects in 1971, 1978, and 1995. The Hall's largest-ever expansion, a $9.2 million project, was completed in early fall 1995. With the new fifth building, the Hall's size is now 82,307-square feet, more than four times its original size.

The expanded Hall represents the sport of pro football in many ways—through (1) GameDay Stadium, a dynamic two-part turntable theater featuring NFL action in Cinemascope for the first time, (2) a standard theater showing NFL films hourly, (3) six large exhibition areas where the history of pro football is detailed in memento, picture, and story form, (4) an extensive library and research center, and (5) a new and enlarged museum store.

In recent years, the Pro Football Hall of Fame has become an extremely popular tourist attraction. At the end of 1995, a total of 5,897,618 fans had visited the Hall of Fame.

New members of the Pro Football Hall of Fame are elected annually by a 36-member National Board of Selectors, made up of media representatives from every league city, 5 at-large representatives, and a representative of the Pro Football Writers of America. Between four and seven new members are elected each year. An affirmative vote of approximately 80 percent is needed for election.

Any fan may nominate any eligible player or contributor simply by writing to the Pro Football Hall of Fame. Players must be retired five years to be eligible, while a coach need only to be retired with no time limit specified. Contributors (administrators, owners, *et al.*) may be elected while they are still active.

The charter class of 17 enshrinees was elected in 1963 and the honor roll now stands at 185 with the election of a five-man class in 1996. That class consists of Lou Creekmur, Dan Dierdorf, Joe Gibbs, Charlie Joiner, and Mel Renfro.

ROSTER OF MEMBERS

HERB ADDERLEY
Defensive back. 6-1, 200. Born in Philadelphia, Pennsylvania, June 8, 1939. Michigan State. Inducted in 1980. 1961-69 Green Bay Packers, 1970-72 Dallas Cowboys. **Highlights:** 48 interceptions, 7 touchdowns. Played in four Super Bowls, five Pro Bowls.

LANCE ALWORTH
Wide receiver. 6-0, 184. Born in Houston, Texas, August 3, 1940. Arkansas. Inducted in 1978. 1962-70 San Diego Chargers, 1971-72 Dallas Cowboys. **Highlights:** 542 receptions for 10,266 yards, 85 touchdowns. All-AFL seven times, seven All-Star games.

DOUG ATKINS
Defensive end. 6-8, 275. Born in Humboldt, Tennessee, May 8, 1930. Tennessee. Inducted in 1982. 1953-54 Cleveland Browns, 1955-66 Chicago Bears, 1967-69 New Orleans Saints. **Highlights:** Eight Pro Bowls, All-NFL three times. Played for 17 years, 205 games.

MORRIS (RED) BADGRO
End. 6-0, 190. Born in Orilla, Washington, December 1, 1902. Southern California. Inducted in 1981. 1927 New York Yankees, 1930-35 New York Giants, 1936 Brooklyn Dodgers. **Highlights:** All-NFL four times. Scored first touchdown in NFL championship game series.

LEM BARNEY
Cornerback. 6-0, 190. Born in Gulfport, Mississippi, September 8, 1945. Jackson State. Inducted in 1992. 1967-77 Detroit Lions. **Highlights:** 56 interceptions for 1,077 yards, 11 defensive touchdowns. Seven Pro Bowls, All-NFL/NFC three times.

CLIFF BATTLES
Halfback. 6-1, 201. Born in Akron, Ohio, May 1, 1910. Died April 28, 1981. West Virginia Wesleyan. Inducted in 1968. 1932 Boston Braves, 1933-36 Boston Redskins, 1937 Washington Redskins. **Highlights:** NFL rushing champion 1932, 1937. First to gain more than 200 yards in a game, 1933.

SAMMY BAUGH
Quarterback. 6-2, 180. Born in Temple, Texas, March 17, 1914. Texas Christian. Inducted in 1963. 1937-52 Washington Redskins. **Highlights:** Charter enshrinee. Six-time NFL passing leader. NFL passing, punting, interception champ, 1943.

CHUCK BEDNARIK
Center-linebacker. 6-3, 230. Born in Bethlehem, Pennsylvania, May 1, 1925. Pennsylvania. Inducted in 1967. 1949-62 Philadelphia Eagles. **Highlights:** Eight Pro Bowls. Missed three games in 14 years. Named NFL all-time center, 1969.

BERT BELL
Team owner. Commissioner. Born in Philadelphia, Pennsylvania, February 25, 1895. Died October 11, 1959. Pennsylvania. Inducted in 1963. 1933-40 Philadelphia Eagles, 1941-42 Pittsburgh Steelers, 1943 Phil-Pitt, 1944 Card-Pitt, 1945-46 Pittsburgh Steelers. Commissioner, 1946-59. **Highlights:** Charter enshrinee. Built NFL image as commissioner, 1946-1959. Set up long-term television policies.

BOBBY BELL
Linebacker. 6-4, 225. Born in Shelby, North Carolina, June 17, 1940. Minnesota. Inducted in 1983. 1963-74 Kansas City Chiefs. **Highlights:** 25 interceptions. All-AFL/AFC nine times. Eight career touchdowns, 1 on onside kick return.

RAYMOND BERRY
End. 6-2, 187. Born in Corpus Christi, Texas, February 27, 1933. Southern Methodist. Inducted in 1973. 1955-67 Baltimore Colts. **Highlights:** 631 receptions for 9,275 yards, 68 touchdowns. Set NFL title game mark with 12 catches for 178 yards, 1958.

CHARLES W. BIDWILL, SR.
Team owner. Born in Chicago, Illinois, September 16, 1895. Died April 19, 1947. Loyola of Chicago. Inducted in 1967. 1933-43 Chicago Cardinals, 1944 Card-Pitt, 1945-47 Chicago Cardinals. **Highlights:** Guiding light for NFL during depression years. Built famous "Dream Backfield."

FRED BILETNIKOFF
Wide receiver. 6-1, 190. Born in Erie, Pennsylvania, February 23, 1943. Florida State. Inducted in 1988. 1965-78 Oakland Raiders. **Highlights:** 589 receptions for 8,974 yards, 76 touchdowns. 40 catches 10 straight years. MVP, Super Bowl XI.

GEORGE BLANDA
Quarterback-kicker. 6-2, 215. Born in Youngwood, Pennsylvania, September 17, 1927. Kentucky. Inducted in 1981. 1949-58 Chicago Bears, 1950 Baltimore Colts, 1960-66 Houston Oilers, 1967-75 Oakland Raiders. **Highlights:** Record 2,002 career points. 26-season, 340-game career longest in NFL history.

MEL BLOUNT
Cornerback. 6-3, 205. Born in Vidalia, Georgia, April 10, 1948. Southern University. Inducted in 1989. 1970-83 Pittsburgh Steelers. **Highlights:** 57 interceptions for 736 yards. NFL defensive MVP, 1975. Played in five Pro Bowls.

TERRY BRADSHAW
Quarterback. 6-3, 210. Born in Shreveport, Louisiana, September 2, 1948. Louisiana Tech. Inducted in 1989. 1970-83 Pittsburgh Steelers. **Highlights:** 27,989 yards passing, 212 touchdowns. MVP in Super Bowls XIII, XIV.

JIM BROWN
Fullback. 6-2, 232. Born in St. Simons, Georgia, February 17, 1936. Syracuse. Inducted in 1971. 1957-65 Cleveland Browns. **Highlights:** 12,312 yards rushing, 756 points. Led NFL rushers eight years. Nine consecutive Pro Bowls.

PAUL BROWN
Coach. Born in Norwalk, Ohio, September 7, 1908. Died August 5, 1991. Miami, Ohio. Inducted in 1967. 1946-49 Cleveland Browns (AAFC), 1950-62 Cleveland Browns, 1968-75 Cincinnati Bengals. **Highlights:** Built Cleveland dynasty with 167-53-8 record, four AAFC titles, three NFL crowns.

ROOSEVELT BROWN
Tackle. 6-3, 255. Born in Charlottesville, Virginia, October 20, 1932. Morgan State. Inducted in 1975. 1953-65 New York Giants. **Highlights:** All-NFL eight consecutive years, nine Pro Bowls. NFL's Lineman of Year, 1956.

WILLIE BROWN
Cornerback. 6-1, 210. Born in Yazoo City, Mississippi, December 2, 1940. Grambling. Inducted in 1984. 1963-66 Denver Broncos, 1967-78 Oakland Raiders. **Highlights:** 54 interceptions for 472 yards. Scored on 75-yard interception in Super Bowl XI.

BUCK BUCHANAN
Defensive tackle. 6-7, 274. Born in Gainesville, Alabama, September 10, 1940. Died July 16, 1992. Grambling. Inducted in 1990. 1963-75 Kansas City Chiefs. **Highlights:** Led Chiefs defensive efforts in Super Bowl I, IV. Missed one game in 13 years.

DICK BUTKUS
Linebacker. 6-3, 245. Born in Chicago, Illinois, December 9, 1942. Illinois. Inducted in 1979. 1965-73 Chicago Bears. **Highlights:** All-NFL seven years, eight consecutive Pro Bowls. 25 fumble recoveries.

EARL CAMPBELL
Running back. 5-11, 233. Born in Tyler, Texas, March 29, 1955. Texas. Inducted in 1991. 1978-84 Houston Oilers, 1984-85 New Orleans Saints. **Highlights:** 9,407 yards rushing, 74 touchdowns. 1,934 yards rushing in 1980, including four games with at least 200 yards.

TONY CANADEO
Halfback. 5-11, 195. Born in Chicago, Illinois, May 5, 1919. Gonzaga. Inducted in 1974. 1941-44, 1946-52 Green Bay Packers. **Highlights:** Two-way player. Third player to rush for 1,000 yards in single season, 1949.

JOE CARR
NFL president. Born in Columbus, Ohio, October 22, 1880. Died May 20, 1939. Did not attend college. Inducted in 1963. President, 1921-39 National Football League. **Highlights:** Charter enshrinee. NFL co-organizer, 1920. Introduced standard player's contract.

GUY CHAMBERLIN
End. Coach. 6-2, 210. Born in Blue Springs, Nebraska, January 16, 1894. Died April 4, 1967. Nebraska. Inducted in 1965. 1920 Decatur Staleys, 1921 Chicago Staleys, player-coach 1922-23 Canton Bulldogs, 1924 Cleveland Bulldogs, 1925-26 Frankford Yellow Jackets, 1927-28 Chicago Cardinals. **Highlights:** Player-coach of four NFL championship teams. Six-year coaching record 56-14-5.

JACK CHRISTIANSEN
Safety. 6-1, 185. Born in Sublette, Kansas, December 20, 1928. Died June 29, 1986. Colorado State. Inducted in 1970. 1951-58 Detroit Lions. **Highlights:** 46 interceptions. NFL interception leader, 1953, 1957. NFL record 8 punt returns for touchdowns.

EARL (DUTCH) CLARK
Quarterback. 6-0, 185. Born in Fowler, Colorado, October 11, 1906. Died August 5, 1978. Colorado College. Inducted in 1963. 1931-32 Portsmouth

Spartans, 1934-38 Detroit Lions. **Highlights:** Charter enshrinee. NFL scoring champion three years. Led Lions to 1935 NFL title.

GEORGE CONNOR
Tackle-linebacker. 6-3, 240. Born in Chicago, Illinois, January 21, 1925. Holy Cross, Notre Dame. Inducted in 1975. 1948-55 Chicago Bears. **Highlights:** All-NFL at three positions—T, DT, LB. All-NFL five years. Played in first four Pro Bowls.

JIMMY CONZELMAN
Quarterback. Coach. Team owner. 6-0, 180. Born in St. Louis, Missouri, March 6, 1898. Died July 31, 1970. Washington, Missouri. Inducted in 1964. 1920 Decatur Staleys, 1921-22 Rock Island, Ill., Independents, 1923-24 Milwaukee Badgers; owner-coach 1925-26 Detroit Panthers; player-coach 1927-29, coach 1930 Providence Steam Roller; coach 1940-42, 1946-48 Chicago Cardinals. **Highlights:** Player-coach of four NFL teams in 1920's. Coached Cardinals to 1947 NFL crown.

LOU CREEKMUR
Tackle-guard. 6-4, 255. Born in Hopelawn, New Jersey. January 22, 1927. William & Mary. Inducted in 1996. 1950-59 Detroit Lions. **Highlights:** All-NFL six times, twice at guard and four times at tackle. Selected to eight Pro Bowls and played on three NFL Championship teams.

LARRY CSONKA
Running back. 6-3, 235. Born in Stow, Ohio, December 25, 1946. Syracuse. Inducted in 1987. 1968-74, 1979 Miami Dolphins, 1976-78 New York Giants. **Highlights:** 8,081 yards rushing, 68 touchdowns. MVP Super Bowl VIII. Only 21 fumbles in 1,997 carries.

AL DAVIS
Team, League Administrator. Born in Brockton, Massachusetts, July 4, 1929. Wittenberg, Syracuse. Inducted in 1992. 1963-81, 1995-present Oakland Raiders, 1982-94 Los Angeles Raiders, 1966 American Football League. **Highlights:** Only person to serve in pros as personnel assistant, scout, assistant coach, head coach, general manager, commissioner, team owner/CEO.

WILLIE DAVIS
Defensive end. 6-3, 245. Born in Lisbon, Louisiana, July 24, 1934. Grambling. Inducted in 1981. 1958-59 Cleveland Browns, 1960-69 Green Bay Packers. **Highlights:** All-NFL five seasons, five Pro Bowls. Did not miss game in 12-year career.

LEN DAWSON
Quarterback. 6-0, 190. Born in Alliance, Ohio, June 20, 1935. Purdue. Inducted in 1987. 1957-59 Pittsburgh Steelers, 1960-61 Cleveland Browns, 1962 Dallas Texans, 1963-75 Kansas City Chiefs. **Highlights:** 28,711 yards passing, 239 touchdowns. Four AFL passing crowns. MVP, Super Bowl IV.

DAN DIERDORF
Tackle. 6-3, 290. Born in Canton, Ohio, June 29, 1949. Michigan. Inducted in 1996. 1971-83 St. Louis Cardinals. **Highlights:** All-Pro five times, played in six Pro Bowls, named NFL's best blocker three times.

MIKE DITKA
Tight end. 6-3, 225. Born in Carnegie, Pennsylvania, October 18, 1939. Pittsburgh. Inducted in 1988. 1961-66 Chicago Bears, 1967-68 Philadelphia Eagles, 1969-72 Dallas Cowboys. **Highlights:** 427 receptions for 5,812 yards, 43 touchdowns. First tight end selected to Hall of Fame. Five consecutive Pro Bowls.

ART DONOVAN
Defensive tackle. 6-3, 265. Born in Bronx, New York, June 5, 1925. Boston College. Inducted in 1968. 1950 Baltimore Colts, 1951 New York Yanks, 1952 Dallas Texans, 1953-61 Baltimore Colts. **Highlights:** Five Pro Bowls. Vital part of Baltimore's climb to powerhouse status in 1950s.

TONY DORSETT
Running back. 5-11, 184. Born in Rochester, Pennsylvania, April 7, 1954. Pittsburgh. Inducted in 1994. 1977-87 Dallas Cowboys, 1988 Denver Broncos. **Highlights:** 12,739 yards rushing, 398 receptions, 90 touchdowns. Ran record 99 yards for touchdown vs. Minnesota, January, 1983.

JOHN (PADDY) DRISCOLL
Quarterback. 5-11, 160. Born in Evanston, Illinois, January 11, 1896. Died June 29, 1968. Northwestern. Inducted in 1965. 1920 Decatur Staleys, 1920-25 Chicago Cardinals, 1926-29 Chicago Bears. Coach, 1956-57 Chicago Bears. **Highlights:** All-NFL six times. Dropkicked record 4 field goals in one game, 1925.

BILL DUDLEY
Halfback. 5-10, 176. Born in Bluefield, Virginia, December 24, 1921. Virginia. Inducted in 1966. 1942, 1945-46 Pittsburgh Steelers, 1947-49 Detroit Lions, 1950-51, 1953 Washington Redskins. **Highlights:** Won NFL rushing, interception, punt return titles, 1946. All-NFL 1942, 1946.

ALBERT GLEN (TURK) EDWARDS
Tackle. 6-2, 260. Born in Mold, Washington, September 28, 1907. Died January 12, 1973. Washington State. Inducted in 1969. 1932 Boston Braves, 1933-36 Boston Redskins, 1937-40 Washington Redskins. **Highlights:** All-NFL 1932-33, 1936, 1937. Steamrolling blocker, smothering tackler.

WEEB EWBANK
Coach. Born in Richmond, Indiana, May 6, 1907. Miami, Ohio. Inducted in 1978. 1954-62 Baltimore Colts, 1963-73 New York Jets. **Highlights:** Only coach to win championships in both NFL, AFL. Led both Colts (1958) and Jets (1968) to championships.

TOM FEARS
End. 6-2, 215. Born in Los Angeles, California, December 3, 1923. Santa Clara, UCLA. Inducted in 1970. 1948-56 Los Angeles Rams. **Highlights:** 400 receptions for 5,397 yards, 38 touchdowns. Led NFL receivers first three seasons. Record 18 receptions in single game.

JIM FINKS
Administrator. Born in St. Louis, Missouri, August 31, 1927. Died May 8, 1994. Tulsa. Inducted 1995. 1964-73 Minnesota Vikings, 1974-82 Chicago Bears, 1986-93 New Orleans Saints. **Highlights:** Developed Vikings, Bears, Saints—all teams with losing records—into winners.

RAY FLAHERTY
Coach. Born in Spokane, Washington, September 1, 1903. Died July 19, 1994. Gonzaga. Inducted in 1976. 1936 Boston Redskins, 1937-42 Washington Redskins, 1946-48 New York Yankees (AAFC), 1949 Chicago Hornets (AAFC). **Highlights:** 80-37-5 coaching record. Introduced screen pass in 1937 title game and platoon system.

LEN FORD
Defensive end. 6-5, 260. Born in Washington, D.C., February 18, 1926. Died March 14, 1972. Morgan State, Michigan. Inducted in 1976. 1948-49 Los Angeles Dons (AAFC), 1950-57 Cleveland Browns, 1958 Green Bay Packers. **Highlights:** All-NFL five times, four Pro Bowls. Recovered 20 opponent's fumbles.

DAN FORTMANN
Guard. 6-0, 210. Born in Pearl River, New York, April 11, 1916. Died May 24, 1995. Colgate. Inducted in 1965. 1936-43 Chicago Bears. **Highlights:** At 19, became youngest starter in NFL. All-NFL six consecutive years.

DAN FOUTS
Quarterback. 6-3, 210. Born in San Francisco, California, June 10, 1951. Oregon. Inducted in 1993. 1973-1987 San Diego Chargers. **Highlights:** 43,040 passing yards, 254 touchdowns. Six Pro Bowls, NFL MVP, 1982.

FRANK GATSKI
Center. 6-3, 240. Born in Farmington, West Virginia, March 18, 1922. Marshall, Auburn. Inducted in 1985. 1946-49 Cleveland Browns (AAFC), 1950-56 Cleveland Browns, 1957 Detroit Lions. **Highlights:** Never missed game in high school, college, or pro football. Played 11 championship games, winning eight.

BILL GEORGE
Linebacker. 6-2, 230. Born in Waynesburg, Pennsylvania, October 27, 1930. Died September 30, 1982. Wake Forest. Inducted in 1974. 1952-65 Chicago Bears, 1966 Los Angeles Rams. **Highlights:** All-NFL eight years, eight consecutive Pro Bowls. 14 years of service, longest of any Bears player.

JOE GIBBS
Coach. Born in Mocksville, North Carolina, November 25, 1940. Cerritos (Calif.) J.C., San Diego State. Inducted in 1996. 1981-92 Washington Redskins. **Highlights:** 124-60-0 record in regular season, 16-5 in postseason, including four Super Bowl appearances—winning three. Won 10 or more games eight times.

FRANK GIFFORD
Halfback. 6-1, 195. Born in Santa Monica, California, August 16, 1930. Southern California. Inducted in 1977. 1952-60, 1962-64 New York Giants. **Highlights:** Starred on both offense and defense. Seven Pro Bowls, 1956 NFL Player of the Year.

SID GILLMAN
Coach. Born in Minneapolis, Minnesota, October 26, 1911. Ohio State. Inducted in 1983. 1955-59 Los Angeles Rams, 1960 Los Angeles Chargers, 1961-69, 1971 San Diego Chargers, 1973-74 Houston Oilers. **Highlights:** 123-104-7 coaching record. First to win division titles in both NFL, AFL.

OTTO GRAHAM
Quarterback. 6-1, 195. Born in Waukegan, Illinois, December 6, 1921. Northwestern. Inducted in 1965. 1946-49 Cleveland Browns (AAFC), 1950-55 Cleveland Browns. **Highlights:** 23,584 passing yards, 174 touchdowns. Guided Browns to 10 division or league crowns in 10 years.

HAROLD (RED) GRANGE
Halfback. 6-0, 185. Born in Forksville, Pennsylvania, June 13, 1903. Died January 28, 1991. Illinois. Inducted in 1963. 1925 Chicago Bears, 1926 New York Yankees (AFL), 1927 New York Yankees, 1929-34 Chicago Bears. **Highlights:** Nicknamed "Galloping Ghost." Name produced first huge pro football crowds.

BUD GRANT
Coach. Born in Superior, Wisconsin, May 20, 1927. Minnesota. Inducted in 1994. 1967-83, 1985 Minnesota Vikings. **Highlights:** 168-108-5 coaching record. Led Vikings to 11 division championships, four Super Bowls.

JOE GREENE
Defensive tackle. 6-4, 260. Born in Temple, Texas, September 24, 1946. North Texas State. Inducted in 1987. 1969-81 Pittsburgh Steelers. **Highlights:** NFL Defensive Player of the Year, 1972, 1974. Four-time Super Bowl champion, 10 Pro Bowls.

FORREST GREGG
Tackle. 6-4, 250. Born in Birthright, Texas, October 18, 1933. Southern Methodist. Inducted in 1977. 1956, 1958-70 Green Bay Packers, 1971 Dallas Cowboys. **Highlights:** Played 188 consecutive games. Nine Pro Bowls. Played on seven NFL championship teams, three Super Bowl winners.

BOB GRIESE
Quarterback. 6-1, 190. Born in Evansville, Indiana, February 3, 1945. Purdue. Inducted in 1990. 1967-80 Miami Dolphins. **Highlights:** 25,092 passing yards, 192 touchdowns. Led Miami to three AFC titles, Super Bowl VII, VIII wins.

LOU GROZA
Tackle-kicker. 6-3, 250. Born in Martins Ferry, Ohio, January 25, 1924. Ohio State. Inducted in 1974. 1946-49

Cleveland Browns (AAFC), 1950-59, 1961-67 Cleveland Browns. **Highlights:** 1,608 points in 21 years. Nine Pro Bowls, All-NFL six years. NFL Player of the Year, 1954.

JOE GUYON
Halfback. 6-1, 180. Born on White Earth Indian Reservation, Minnesota, November 26, 1892. Died November 27, 1971. Carlisle, Georgia Tech. Inducted in 1966. 1920 Canton Bulldogs, 1921 Cleveland Indians, 1922-23 Oorang Indians, 1924 Rock Island, Ill., Independents, 1924-25 Kansas City Cowboys, 1927 New York Giants. **Highlights:** Touchdown pass gave Giants win over Bears in 1927 NFL Championship Game.

GEORGE HALAS
End. Coach. Team owner. Born in Chicago, Illinois, February 2, 1895. Died October 31, 1983. Illinois. Inducted in 1963. Player-coach 1920 Decatur Staleys, 1921 Chicago Staleys, 1922-29 Chicago Bears; coach 1933-42, 1946-55, 1958-67 Chicago Bears. **Highlights:** Charter enshrinee. 324 coaching wins. Only person associated with NFL throughout first 50 years. Coached Bears 40 seasons, won seven NFL titles.

JACK HAM
Linebacker. 6-1, 225. Born in Johnstown, Pennsylvania, December 23, 1948. Penn State. Inducted in 1988. 1971-82 Pittsburgh Steelers. **Highlights:** won four Super Bowls, 21 opponent's fumbles recovered, 32 interceptions. Eight consecutive Pro Bowls.

JOHN HANNAH
Guard. 6-3, 265. Born in Canton, Georgia, April 4, 1951. Alabama. Inducted in 1991. 1973-85 New England Patriots. **Highlights:** Renowned as premier guard of era. All-Pro 10 years, eight Pro Bowls.

FRANCO HARRIS
Running back. 6-2, 225. Born in Fort Dix, New Jersey, March 7, 1950. Penn State. Inducted in 1990. 1972-83 Pittsburgh Steelers, 1984 Seattle Seahawks. **Highlights:** 12,120 rushing yards, 100 total touchdowns. 1,556 rushing yards in 19 postseason games. MVP in Super Bowl IX.

ED HEALEY
Tackle. 6-3, 220. Born in Indian Orchard, Massachusetts, December 28, 1894. Died December 9, 1978. Dartmouth. Inducted in 1964. 1920-22 Rock Island, Ill., Independents, 1922-27 Chicago Bears. **Highlights:** Two-way star. Perennial all-pro with Bears.

MEL HEIN
Center. 6-2, 225. Born in Redding, California, August 22, 1909. Died January 31, 1992. Washington State. Inducted in 1963. 1931-45 New York Giants. **Highlights:** Charter enshrinee. 60-minute regular for 15 years. All-NFL eight consecutive years.

TED HENDRICKS
Linebacker. 6-7, 235. Born in Guatemala City, Guatemala, November 1, 1947. Miami. Inducted in 1990. 1969-73 Baltimore Colts, 1974 Green Bay Packers, 1975-81 Oakland Raiders, 1982-83 Los Angeles Raiders. **Highlights:** 25 blocked field goals or extra points, 26 interceptions. Played in 215 consecutive games.

WILBUR (PETE) HENRY
Tackle. 6-0, 250. Born in Mansfield, Ohio, October 31, 1897. Died February 7, 1952. Washington & Jefferson. Inducted in 1963. 1920-23, 1925-26 Canton Bulldogs, 1927 New York Giants, 1927-28 Pottsville Maroons. **Highlights:** Largest player of his time at 250 pounds. Bulwark of Canton's championship lines.

ARNIE HERBER
Quarterback. 6-0, 200. Born in Green Bay, Wisconsin, April 2, 1910. Died October 14, 1969. Wisconsin, Regis College. Inducted in 1966. 1930-40 Green Bay Packers, 1944-45 New York Giants. **Highlights:** NFL passing leader 1932, 1934, 1936. Came out of retirement to lead 1944 Giants to NFL Eastern crown.

BILL HEWITT
End. 5-11, 191. Born in Bay City, Michigan, October 8, 1909. Died January 14, 1947. Michigan. Inducted in 1971. 1932-36 Chicago Bears, 1937-39 Philadelphia Eagles, 1943 Phil-Pitt. **Highlights:** First to be named all-NFL with two teams—1933, 1934, 1936 Bears; 1937 Eagles.

CLARKE HINKLE
Fullback. 5-11, 201. Born in Toronto, Ohio, April 10, 1909. Died November 9, 1988. Bucknell. Inducted in 1964. 1932-41 Green Bay Packers. **Highlights:** 3,860 yards rushing, 373 points, 43.4 punting average. Fullback on offense, linebacker on defense.

ELROY (CRAZYLEGS) HIRSCH
Halfback-end. 6-2, 190. Born in Wausau, Wisconsin, June 17, 1923. Wisconsin, Michigan. Inducted in 1968. 1946-48 Chicago Rockets (AAFC), 1949-57 Los Angeles Rams. **Highlights:** 387 receptions for 7,029 yards, 60 touchdowns. Key part of Rams' revolutionary "three end" offense, 1949.

PAUL HORNUNG
Halfback. 6-2, 220. Born in Louisville, Kentucky, December 23, 1935. Notre Dame. Inducted in 1986. 1957-62, 1964-66 Green Bay Packers. **Highlights:** 760 points. Led NFL scorers three years, including record 176 points, 1960. Record 19 points scored in 1961 NFL title game.

KEN HOUSTON
Safety. 6-3, 198. Born in Lufkin, Texas, November 12, 1944. Prairie View A&M. Inducted in 1986. 1967-72 Houston Oilers, 1973-80 Washington Redskins. **Highlights:** 49 interceptions, 898 yards, 9 touchdowns. NFL's premier strong safety of 1970s. 10 Pro Bowls.

CAL HUBBARD
Tackle. 6-5, 250. Born in Keytesville, Missouri, October 31, 1900. Died October 17, 1977. Centenary, Geneva. Inducted in 1963. 1927-28 New York Giants, 1929-33, 1935 Green Bay Packers, 1936 New York Giants, 1936 Pittsburgh Pirates. **Highlights:** Charter enshrinee. Most feared lineman of his time. All-NFL six years, 1928-33.

SAM HUFF
Linebacker. 6-1, 230. Born in Morgantown, West Virginia, October 4, 1934. West Virginia. Inducted in 1982. 1956-63 New York Giants, 1964-67, 1969 Washington Redskins. **Highlights:** 30 interceptions. Played in six NFL title games, five Pro Bowls. Redskins player-coach, 1969.

LAMAR HUNT
Team owner. Born in El Dorado, Arkansas, August 2, 1932. Southern Methodist. Inducted in 1972. 1960-62 Dallas Texans, 1963-present Kansas City Chiefs. **Highlights:** Driving force behind organization of AFL. Spearheaded merger negotiations with NFL, 1966.

DON HUTSON
End. 6-1, 180. Born in Pine Bluff, Arkansas, January 31, 1913. Alabama. Inducted in 1963. 1935-45 Green Bay Packers. **Highlights:** 488 receptions for 7,991 yards, 99 touchdowns. NFL receiving champion eight years. NFL MVP, 1941, 1942.

JIMMY JOHNSON
Cornerback. 6-2, 187. Born in Dallas, Texas, March 31, 1938. UCLA. Inducted in 1994. 1961-76 San Francisco 49ers. **Highlights:** 47 interceptions for 615 yards. Five Pro Bowls. Opposing passers avoided throwing in his area.

JOHN HENRY JOHNSON
Fullback. 6-2, 225. Born in Waterproof, Louisiana, November 24, 1929. St. Mary's, Arizona State. Inducted in 1987. 1954-56 San Francisco 49ers, 1957-59 Detroit Lions, 1960-65 Pittsburgh Steelers, 1966 Houston Oilers. **Highlights:** 6,803 yards rushing, 48 touchdowns. Member of San Francisco's "Fabulous Foursome" backfield.

CHARLIE JOINER
Wide receiver. 5-11, 180. Born in Many, Louisiana, October 14, 1947. Grambling. Inducted in 1996. 1969-72 Houston Oilers, 1972-75 Cincinnati Bengals, 1976-86 San Diego Chargers. **Highlights:** 750 receptions for 12,146 yards and 65 touchdowns. Played 18 seasons, 239 games, most ever for wide receiver.

DAVID (DEACON) JONES
Defensive end. 6-5, 260. Born in Eatonville, Florida, December 9, 1938. Mississippi Vocational, South Carolina State. Inducted in 1980. 1961-71 Los Angeles Rams, 1972-73 San Diego Chargers, 1974 Washington Redskins. **Highlights:** Specialized in quarterback 'sacks,' a name he invented. Unanimous all-league six consecutive years.

STAN JONES
Guard-defensive tackle. 6-1, 250. Born in Altoona, Pennsylvania, November 24, 1931. Maryland. Inducted in 1991. 1954-65 Chicago Bears, 1966 Washington Redskins. **Highlights:** Seven consecutive Pro Bowls. First to rely on weightlifting for football preparation.

HENRY JORDAN
Defensive tackle, 6-3, 240. Born in Emporia, Virginia, January 26, 1935. Died February 21, 1977. Virginia. Inducted in 1995. 1957-58 Cleveland Browns, 1959-69 Green Bay Packers. **Highlights:** 11-year fixture at DT. Played in four Pro Bowls, seven NFL title games, Super Bowls I, II.

SONNY JURGENSEN
Quarterback. 6-0, 203. Born in Wilmington, North Carolina, August 23, 1934. Duke. Inducted in 1983. 1957-63 Philadelphia Eagles, 1964-74 Washington Redskins. **Highlights:** 32,224 yards passing, 255 touchdowns, 82.63 passer rating. Surpassed 3,000 yards passing in five seasons.

LEROY KELLY
Running back. 6-0, 205. Born in Philadelphia, Pennsylvania, May 20, 1942. Morgan State. Inducted in 1994. 1964-73 Cleveland Browns. **Highlights:** 7,274 yards rushing, 90 total touchdowns, 1,000-yard rusher first three years. Two-time punt return champion.

WALT KIESLING
Guard. Coach. 6-2, 245. Born in St. Paul, Minnesota, March 27, 1903. Died March 2, 1962. St. Thomas (Minnesota). Inducted in 1966. 1926-27 Duluth Eskimos, 1928 Pottsville Maroons, 1929-33 Chicago Cardinals, 1934 Chicago Bears, 1935-36 Green Bay Packers, 1937-38 Pittsburgh Pirates; coach, 1939 Pittsburgh Pirates, 1940-42 Pittsburgh Steelers; co-coach, 1943 Phil-Pitt, 1944 Card-Pitt; coach, 1954-56 Pittsburgh Steelers. **Highlights:** 34-year career as pro player, assistant coach, head coach. Led Steelers to first winning season, 1942.

FRANK (BRUISER) KINARD
Tackle. 6-1, 210. Born in Pelahatchie, Mississippi, October 23, 1914. Died September 7, 1985. Mississippi. Inducted in 1971. 1938-44 Brooklyn Dodgers-Tigers, 1946-47 New York Yankees (AAFC). **Highlights:** First man to earn both All-NFL, All-AAFC honors. Out because of injury only once.

EARL (CURLY) LAMBEAU
Coach. Born in Green Bay, Wisconsin, April 9, 1898. Died June 1, 1965. Notre Dame. Inducted in 1963. 1919-49 Green Bay Packers, 1950-51 Chicago Cardinals, 1952-53 Washington Redskins. **Highlights:** 229-134-22 coaching record with six NFL championships. Founded pre-NFL Packers, 1919.

JACK LAMBERT
Linebacker. 6-4, 220. Born in Mantua, Ohio, July 8, 1952. Kent State. Inducted in 1990. 1974-84 Pittsburgh Steelers. **Highlights:** Prototype middle linebacker. Two-time NFL Defensive Player of Year, nine Pro Bowls.

TOM LANDRY
Coach. Born in Mission, Texas, September 11, 1924. Texas. Inducted in 1990. 1960-88 Dallas Cowboys. **Highlights:** 270-178-6 coaching record. 20 consecutive winning seasons. Perfected flex defense, shotgun offense.

DICK (NIGHT TRAIN) LANE
Cornerback. 6-2, 210. Born in Austin, Texas, April 16, 1928. Scottsbluff Junior College. Inducted in 1974. 1952-53 Los Angeles Rams, 1954-59 Chicago Cardinals, 1960-65 Detroit Lions. **Highlights:** 68 interceptions for 1,207 yards, 5 touchdowns. Record 14 interceptions as rookie. Six Pro Bowls.

JIM LANGER
Center. 6-2, 255. Born in Little Falls, Minnesota, May 16, 1948. South Dakota State. Inducted in 1987. 1970-79 Miami Dolphins, 1980-81 Minnesota Vikings. **Highlights:** Played every offensive down in Dolphins' perfect 1972 season. Six Pro Bowls.

WILLIE LANIER
Linebacker. 6-1, 245. Born in Clover, Virginia, August 21, 1945. Morgan State. Inducted in 1986. 1967-77 Kansas City Chiefs. **Highlights:** 27 interceptions. Defensive star in Super Bowl IV upset. Nicknamed 'Contact' for ferocious tackling.

STEVE LARGENT
Wide receiver. 5-11, 191. Born in Tulsa, Oklahoma, September 28, 1954, Tulsa. Inducted in 1995. 1976-89 Seattle Seahawks. **Highlights:** 819 receptions for 13,089 yards, 100 touchdowns. Receptions in 177 consecutive games.

YALE LARY
Defensive back-punter. 5-11, 189. Born in Fort Worth, Texas, November 24, 1930. Texas A&M. Inducted in 1979. 1952-53, 1956-64 Detroit Lions. **Highlights:** 50 interceptions. Three NFL punting crowns, three touchdowns on punt returns. Nine Pro Bowls.

DANTE LAVELLI
End. 6-0, 199. Born in Hudson, Ohio, February 23, 1923. Ohio State. Inducted in 1975. 1946-49 Cleveland Browns (AAFC), 1950-56 Cleveland Browns. **Highlights:** 386 receptions for 6,488 yards, 62 touchdowns. 24 catches in six NFL title games.

BOBBY LAYNE
Quarterback. 6-2, 190. Born in Santa Anna, Texas, December 19, 1926. Died December 1, 1986. Texas. Inducted in 1967. 1948 Chicago Bears, 1949 New York Bulldogs, 1950-58 Detroit Lions, 1958-62 Pittsburgh Steelers. **Highlights:** 26,768 yards passing, 196 touchdowns, 2,451 yards rushing. Last-second touchdown pass won 1953 NFL title game.

ALPHONSE (TUFFY) LEEMANS
Fullback. 6-0, 200. Born in Superior, Wisconsin, November 12, 1912. Died January 19, 1979. Oregon, George Washington. Inducted in 1978. 1936-43 New York Giants. **Highlights:** 3,142 yards rushing, 2,324 yards passing, 442 yards receiving. Led NFL rushers as rookie, 1936.

BOB LILLY
Defensive tackle. 6-5, 260. Born in Olney, Texas, July 26, 1939. Texas Christian. Inducted in 1980. 1961-74 Dallas Cowboys. **Highlights:** 11 Pro Bowls. Missed one game in 14 years. Foundation of great Dallas defensive units.

LARRY LITTLE
Guard. 6-1, 255. Born in Groveland, Georgia, November 2, 1945. Bethune-Cookman. Inducted in 1993. 1967-68 San Diego Chargers, 1969-80 Miami Dolphins. **Highlights:** Five Pro Bowls, started in three Super Bowls. Epitome of powerful Dolphins rushing game of 1970s.

VINCE LOMBARDI
Coach. Born in Brooklyn, New York, June 11, 1913. Died September 3, 1970. Fordham. Inducted in 1971. 1959-67 Green Bay Packers, 1969 Washington Redskins. **Highlights:** 105-35-6 coaching record in 10 years, including five NFL titles and victories in Super Bowl I and II.

SID LUCKMAN
Quarterback. 6-0, 195. Born in Brooklyn, New York, November 21, 1916. Columbia. Inducted in 1965. 1939-50 Chicago Bears. **Highlights:** 139 touchdown passes. All-NFL team five times. League MVP in 1943.

WILLIAM ROY (LINK) LYMAN
Tackle. 6-2, 252. Born in Table Rock, Nebraska, November 30, 1898. Died December 16, 1972. Nebraska. Inducted in 1964. 1922-23, 1925 Canton Bulldogs, 1924 Cleveland Bulldogs, 1925 Frankford Yellow Jackets, 1926-28, 1930-31, 1933-34 Chicago Bears. **Highlights:** Played for four NFL champions. In 16 seasons of college and pro football, played on one losing team.

JOHN MACKEY
Tight end. 6-2, 224. Born in New York, New York, September 24, 1941. Syracuse. Inducted in 1992. 1963-71 Baltimore Colts, 1972 San Diego Chargers. **Highlights:** 331 receptions for 5,236 yards, 38 touchdowns. Second tight end to enter Hall of Fame.

TIM MARA
Team owner. Born in New York, New York, July 29, 1887. Died February 17, 1959. Did not attend college. Inducted in 1963. 1925-59 New York Giants. **Highlights:** Charter enshrinee. Founder of New York Giants. Built team into powerhouse winning three NFL titles, eight division titles.

GINO MARCHETTI
Defensive end. 6-4, 245. Born in Smithers, West Virginia, January 2, 1927. San Francisco. Inducted in 1972. 1952 Dallas Texans, 1953-64, 1966 Baltimore Colts. **Highlights:** Named top defensive end of NFL's first 50 years. 11 consecutive Pro Bowls. All-NFL seven times.

GEORGE PRESTON MARSHALL
Team owner. Born in Grafton, West Virginia, October 11, 1897. Died August 9, 1969. Randolph-Macon. Inducted in 1963. 1932 Boston Braves, 1933-36 Boston Redskins, 1937-69 Washington Redskins. **Highlights:** Charter enshrinee. Sponsored progressive rules changes. Organized first team band, pioneered halftime shows.

OLLIE MATSON
Halfback. 6-2, 220. Born in Trinity, Texas, May 1, 1930. San Francisco. Inducted in 1972. 1952, 1954-58 Chicago Cardinals, 1959-62 Los Angeles Rams, 1963 Detroit Lions, 1964-66 Philadelphia Eagles. **Highlights:** NFL-record 9 touchdowns on kickoff, punt returns. Traded for nine players in 1959.

DON MAYNARD
Wide receiver. 6-1, 185. Born in Crosbyton, Texas, January 25, 1935. Texas Western. Inducted in 1987. 1958 New York Giants, 1960-62 New York Titans, 1963-72 New York Jets, 1973 St. Louis Cardinals. **Highlights:** 633 receptions for 11,834 yards, 88 touchdowns. At least 50 catches and 1,000 yards in five different seasons.

GEORGE McAFEE
Halfback. 6-0, 177. Born in Corbin, Kentucky, March 13, 1918. Duke. Inducted in 1966. 1940-41, 1945-50 Chicago Bears. **Highlights:** Two-way star. 21 interceptions, 234 points. Career punt return record of 12.78 yards per return.

MIKE McCORMACK
Tackle. 6-4, 250. Born in Chicago, Illinois, June 21, 1930. Kansas. Inducted in 1984. 1951 New York Yanks, 1954-62 Cleveland Browns. **Highlights:** Excelled as offensive right tackle for eight years. Six Pro Bowls.

HUGH McELHENNY
Halfback. 6-1, 198. Born in Los Angeles, California, December 31, 1928. Washington. Inducted in 1970. 1952-60 San Francisco 49ers, 1961-62 Minnesota Vikings, 1963 New York Giants, 1964 Detroit Lions. **Highlights:** 5,281 rushing yards, 360 points. Scored 40-yard touchdown run on first pro play.

JOHNNY (BLOOD) McNALLY
Halfback. 6-0, 185. Born in New Richmond, Wisconsin, November 27, 1903. Died November 28, 1985. St. John's (Minnesota). Inducted in 1963. 1925-26 Milwaukee Badgers, 1926-27 Duluth Eskimos, 1928 Pottsville Maroons, 1929-33, 1935-36 Green Bay Packers, 1934 Pittsburgh Pirates; player-coach, 1937-39 Pittsburgh Pirates. **Highlights:** 37 touchdowns, 224 points in 15 seasons with five teams. Pittsburgh player-coach 1937-39.

MIKE MICHALSKE
Guard. 6-0, 209. Born in Cleveland, Ohio, April 24, 1903. Died October 26, 1983. Penn State. Inducted in 1964. 1926 New York Yankees (AFL), 1927-28 New York Yankees, 1929-35, 1937 Green Bay Packers. **Highlights:** Anchored Packers' championship lines, 1929-1931, 1935. First-ever guard enshrined in Canton.

WAYNE MILLNER
End. 6-0, 191. Born in Roxbury, Massachusetts, January 31, 1913. Died November 19, 1976. Notre Dame. Inducted in 1968. 1936 Boston Redskins, 1937-41, 1945 Washington Redskins. **Highlights:** Redskins' all-time leader with 124 catches when retired. 55- and 78-yard touchdown receptions in 1937 NFL championship.

BOBBY MITCHELL
Running back-wide receiver. 6-0, 195. Born in Hot Springs, Arkansas, June 6, 1935. Illinois. Inducted in 1983. 1958-61 Cleveland Browns, 1962-68 Washington Redskins. **Highlights:** 91 touchdowns, including 8 on kickoff and punt returns. 14,078 combined yards.

RON MIX
Tackle. 6-4, 255. Born in Los Angeles, California, March 10, 1938. Southern California. Inducted in 1979. 1960 Los Angeles Chargers, 1961-69 San Diego Chargers, 1971 Oakland Raiders. **Highlights:** All-AFL tackle eight times. Only two holding penalties in 10-year career.

LENNY MOORE
Flanker-running back. 6-1, 198. Born in Reading, Pennsylvania, November 25, 1933. Penn State. Inducted in 1975. 1956-67 Baltimore Colts. **Highlights:** From 1963-65, scored touchdowns in record 18 consecutive games. 113 career touchdowns, 11,213 combined net yards.

MARION MOTLEY
Fullback. 6-1, 238. Born in Leesburg, Georgia, June 5, 1920. South Carolina State, Nevada. Inducted in 1968. 1946-49 Cleveland Browns (AAFC), 1950-53 Cleveland Browns, 1955 Pittsburgh Steelers. **Highlights:** AAFC's all-time rushing champion. Led league in rushing in first NFL season.

GEORGE MUSSO
Guard-tackle. 6-2, 270. Born in Collinsville, Illinois. April 8, 1910. Millikin. Inducted in 1982. 1933-44 Chicago Bears. **Highlights:** First player to achieve All-NFL status at two positions—tackle in 1935 and guard in 1937.

BRONKO NAGURSKI
Fullback. 6-2, 225. Born in Rainy River, Ontario, Canada, November 3, 1908. Died January 7, 1990. Minnesota. Inducted in 1963. 1930-37, 1943 Chicago Bears. **Highlights:** Charter enshrinee. 4,031 rushing yards in nine seasons. All-NFL three times.

JOE NAMATH
Quarterback. 6-2, 200. Born in Beaver Falls, Pennsylvania, May 31, 1943. Alabama. Inducted in 1985. 1965-76 New York Jets, 1977 Los Angeles Rams. **Highlights:** First quarterback to pass for more than 4,000 yards in

season, 1967. Guaranteed, delivered victory over Colts in Super Bowl III.

EARLE (GREASY) NEALE
Coach. Born in Parkersburg, West Virginia, November 5, 1891. Died November 2, 1973. West Virginia Wesleyan. Inducted in 1969. 1941-42, 1944-50 Philadelphia Eagles; co-coach, 1943 Phil-Pitt. **Highlights:** Turned Eagles into winners with three consecutive division crowns, NFL championships in 1948 and 1949.

ERNIE NEVERS
Fullback. 6-1, 205. Born in Willow River, Minnesota, June 11, 1903. Died May 3, 1976. Stanford. Inducted in 1963. 1926-27 Duluth Eskimos, 1929-31 Chicago Cardinals. **Highlights:** Charter enshrinee. Holds NFL's longest-standing record, 40 points in one game in 1929.

RAY NITSCHKE
Linebacker. 6-3, 235. Born in Elmwood Park, Illinois, December 29, 1936. Illinois. Inducted in 1978. 1958-72 Green Bay Packers. **Highlights:** MVP of 1962 title game. Named NFL's all-time linebacker in 1969.

CHUCK NOLL
Coach. Born in Cleveland, Ohio, January 5, 1932. Dayton. Inducted in 1993. 1969-91 Pittsburgh Steelers. **Highlights:** Coached for 23 years. Only coach to win four Super Bowl titles (IX, X, XIII, XIV).

LEO NOMELLINI
Defensive tackle. 6-3, 264. Born in Lucca, Italy, June 19, 1924. Minnesota. Inducted in 1969. 1950-63 San Francisco 49ers. **Highlights:** Played every 49ers game for 14 seasons. 10 Pro Bowls.

MERLIN OLSEN
Defensive tackle. 6-5, 270. Born in Logan, Utah, September 15, 1940. Utah State. Inducted in 1982. 1962-76 Los Angeles Rams. **Highlights:** Member of the Fearsome Foursome. Named to 14 consecutive Pro Bowls, Rams' all-time team.

JIM OTTO
Center. 6-2, 255. Born in Wausau, Wisconsin, January 5, 1938. Miami. Inducted in 1980. 1960-74 Oakland Raiders. **Highlights:** Named AFL's all-time center. Played in 308 games, 12 all-star games, six AFL/AFC title games.

STEVE OWEN
Tackle. Coach. 6-2, 235. Born in Cleo Springs, Oklahoma, April 21, 1898. Died May 17, 1964. Phillips. Inducted in 1966. 1924-25 Kansas City Cowboys, 1925 Cleveland Bulldogs, 1926-31, 1933 New York Giants; coach, 1931-53 New York Giants. **Highlights:** Both player and coach. Coached Giants to record of 153-108-17, eight divisional titles, two NFL championships.

ALAN PAGE
Defensive tackle. 6-4, 225. Born in Canton, Ohio, August 7, 1945. Notre Dame. Inducted in 1988. 1967-78 Minnesota Vikings, 1978-81 Chicago Bears. **Highlights:** NFL iron man. Played in 236 consecutive games, four Super Bowls. League MVP in 1971.

CLARENCE (ACE) PARKER
Quarterback. 5-11, 168. Born in Portsmouth, Virginia, May 17, 1912. Duke. Inducted in 1972. 1937-41 Brooklyn Dodgers, 1945 Boston Yanks, 1946 New York Yankees (AAFC). **Highlights:** Two-way threat. Two-time All-NFL performer, league MVP in 1940.

JIM PARKER
Guard-tackle. 6-3, 273. Born in Macon, Georgia, April 3, 1934. Ohio State. Inducted in 1973. 1957-67 Baltimore Colts. **Highlights:** First full-time offensive lineman elected to Hall of Fame. All-NFL eight consecutive years, eight Pro Bowls.

WALTER PAYTON
Running back. 5-10, 202. Born in Columbia, Mississippi, July 25, 1954. Jackson State. Inducted in 1993. 1975-87 Chicago Bears. **Highlights:** NFL's all-time leading rusher with 16,726 yards. Holds single-game rushing record of 275 yards.

JOE PERRY
Fullback. 6-0, 200. Born in Stevens, Arkansas, January 22, 1927. Compton Junior College. Inducted in 1969. 1948-49 San Francisco 49ers (AAFC), 1950-60, 1963 San Francisco 49ers, 1961-62 Baltimore Colts. **Highlights:** First player in NFL history to gain 1,000 yards two consecutive seasons. 12,505 combined yards.

PETE PIHOS
End. 6-1, 210. Born in Orlando, Florida, October 22, 1923. Indiana. Inducted in 1970. 1947-55 Philadelphia Eagles. **Highlights:** Three-time NFL receiving champion. Caught winning touchdown in 1949 NFL Championship Game.

HUGH (SHORTY) RAY
Supervisor of officials 1938-52. Born in Highland Park, Illinois, September 21, 1884. Died September 16, 1956. Illinois. Inducted in 1966. **Highlights:** Supervisor of Officials, 1938-1952. Streamlined rules to improve game tempo, player safety.

DAN REEVES
Team owner. Born in New York, New York, June 30, 1912. Died April 15, 1971. Georgetown. Inducted in 1967. 1941-45 Cleveland Rams, 1946-71 Los Angeles Rams. **Highlights:** Moved Rams to Los Angeles in 1946 and opened up west coast to pro football. First post-war owner to sign African-American player.

MEL RENFRO
Cornerback-safety. 6-0, 192. Born in Houston, Texas, December 30, 1941. Oregon. Inducted in 1996. 1964-77 Dallas Cowboys. **Highlights:** 52 interceptions for 626 yards and 3 touchdowns. Also added 849 yards on punt returns, 2,246 yards on kickoff returns. Elected to Pro Bowl first 10 seasons.

JOHN RIGGINS
Running back. 6-2, 240. Born in Seneca, Kansas, August 4, 1949. Kansas. Inducted in 1992. 1971-75 New York Jets, 1976-79, 1981-85 Washington Redskins. **Highlights:** 11,352 rushing yards, 104 touchdowns. MVP of Super Bowl XVII with 166 rushing yards including game-winning 43-yard touchdown.

JIM RINGO
Center. 6-2, 230. Born in Orange, New Jersey, November 21, 1931. Syracuse. Inducted in 1981. 1953-63 Green Bay Packers, 1964-67 Philadelphia Eagles. **Highlights:** Ten-time Pro Bowl selection, six-time All-NFL selection. Started in then-record 182 consecutive games.

ANDY ROBUSTELLI
Defensive end. 6-0, 230. Born in Stamford, Connecticut, December 6, 1925. Arnold College. Inducted in 1971. 1951-55 Los Angeles Rams, 1956-64 New York Giants. **Highlights:** Anchored defense in eight championship games. Named NFL's top player in 1962.

ART ROONEY
Team owner. Born in Coulterville, Pennsylvania, January 27, 1901. Died August 25, 1988. Georgetown, Duquesne. Inducted in 1964. 1933-39 Pittsburgh Pirates, 1940-42, 1945-88 Pittsburgh Steelers, 1943 Phil-Pitt, 1944 Card-Pitt. **Highlights:** Bought Pittsburgh Pirates in 1933 and renamed them Steelers in 1940. Team won four Super Bowls in 1970s.

PETE ROZELLE
Commissioner. Born in South Gate, California, March 1, 1926. San Francisco. Inducted in 1985. Commissioner, 1960-89. **Highlights:** Negotiated first league-wide television contract in 1962. Generally recognized as premiere commissioner in all of sports. Credited with making NFL the nation's most popular sport.

BOB ST. CLAIR
Tackle. 6-9, 265. Born in San Francisco, California, February 18, 1931. San Francisco, Tulsa. Inducted in 1990. 1953-63 San Francisco 49ers. **Highlights:** Exceptional offensive lineman. Also played goal-line defense and had 10 blocked field goals, 1956.

GALE SAYERS
Running back. 6-0, 200. Born in Wichita, Kansas, May 30, 1943. Kansas. Inducted in 1977. 1965-71 Chicago Bears. **Highlights:** Broke into league by scoring rookie-record 22 touchdowns. Led league in rushing in 1966, 1969. MVP of three Pro Bowls.

JOE SCHMIDT
Linebacker. 6-0, 222. Born in Pittsburgh, Pennsylvania, January 18, 1932. Pittsburgh. Inducted in 1973. 1953-65 Detroit Lions. **Highlights:** 24 interceptions. Lions team captain for nine years. Mastered middle linebacker position which evolved in 1950s.

TEX SCHRAMM
Team president-general manager. Born in San Gabriel, California, June 2, 1920. Texas. Inducted in 1991. 1947-56 Los Angeles Rams. 1960-89 Dallas Cowboys. **Highlights:** Played prominent role in AFL-NFL merger. Chairman of Competition Committee from 1966-1988.

LEE ROY SELMON
Defensive end. 6-3, 250. Born in Eufaula, Oklahoma, October 20, 1954. Oklahoma. Inducted in 1995. 1976-84 Tampa Bay Buccaneers. **Highlights:** 78½ sacks, 380 quarterback pressures, forced 28 fumbles. Five consecutive Pro Bowls.

ART SHELL
Tackle. 6-5, 285. Born in Charleston, South Carolina, November 26, 1946. Maryland State-Eastern Shore. Inducted in 1989. 1968-81 Oakland Raiders, 1982 Los Angeles Raiders. **Highlights:** Cornerstone of Raiders' offensive line in 1970s. 207 regular-season games, 24 postseason games, eight Pro Bowls.

O.J. SIMPSON
Running back. 6-1, 212. Born in San Francisco, California, July 9, 1947. Southern California. Inducted in 1985. 1969-77 Buffalo Bills, 1978-79 San Francisco 49ers. **Highlights:** In 1973, became first player to rush for 2,000 yards in season. Finished career with four rushing titles, 11,236 yards.

JACKIE SMITH
Tight end. 6-4, 232. Born in Columbia, Mississippi, February 23, 1940. Northwestern State (Louisiana). Inducted in 1994. 1963-77 St. Louis Cardinals,1978 Dallas Cowboys. **Highlights:** 480 receptions for 7,918 yards, 40 touchdowns. Third tight end to be elected to Hall of Fame.

BART STARR
Quarterback. 6-1, 200. Born in Montgomery, Alabama, January 9, 1934. Alabama. Inducted in 1977. 1956-71 Green Bay Packers. **Highlights:** Quarterbacked Packers to six division titles, five NFL titles including first two Super Bowls in which he was MVP.

ROGER STAUBACH
Quarterback. 6-3, 202. Born in Cincinnati, Ohio, February 5, 1942. Navy. Inducted in 1985. 1969-79 Dallas Cowboys. **Highlights:** Led Cowboys to four NFC titles and victories in Super Bowls VI, XII. When retired, 83.4 career passer rating was best of all time.

ERNIE STAUTNER
Defensive tackle. 6-2, 235. Born in Prinzing-by-Cham, Bavaria, Germany, April 20, 1925. Boston College. Inducted in 1969. 1950-63 Pittsburgh Steelers. **Highlights:** Played in nine Pro Bowls and won the best lineman award in 1957. Scored three safeties.

JAN STENERUD
Kicker. 6-2, 190. Born in Fetsund, Norway, November 26, 1942. Montana State. Inducted in 1991. 1967-79 Kansas City Chiefs, 1980-83 Green

Bay Packers, 1984-85 Minnesota Vikings. **Highlights:** 1,699 points on 580 extra points, 373 field goals. First pure placekicker to enter Hall of Fame.

KEN STRONG
Halfback. 5-11, 210. Born in West Haven, Connecticut, August 6, 1906. Died October 5, 1979. New York University. Inducted in 1967. 1929-32 Staten Island Stapletons, 1933-35, 1939, 1944-47 New York Giants, 1936-37 New York Yanks (AFL). **Highlights:** Scored 17 points to lead Giants to victory in 1934 'Sneakers' game, led NFL with 64 points, 1933.

JOE STYDAHAR
Tackle. 6-4, 230. Born in Kaylor, Pennsylvania, March 3, 1912. Died March 23, 1977. West Virginia. Inducted in 1967. 1936-42, 1945-46 Chicago Bears. **Highlights:** One of stalwarts of Bears' 'Monsters of the Midway.' Played on five divisional, three NFL championship teams.

FRAN TARKENTON
Quarterback. 6-0, 185. Born in Richmond, Virginia, February 3, 1940. Georgia. Inducted in 1986. 1961-66, 1972-78 Minnesota Vikings, 1967-71 New York Giants. **Highlights:** At retirement, held NFL records for attempts (6,467), completions (3,686), yards (47,003), and touchdowns (342). Four touchdowns passes in first NFL game.

CHARLEY TAYLOR
Running back-wide receiver. 6-3, 210. Born in Grand Prairie, Texas, September 28, 1941. Arizona State. Inducted in 1984. 1964-75, 1977 Washington Redskins. **Highlights:** Won Rookie of Year honors as running back. Switched to wide receiver and won receiving titles in 1966, 1967.

JIM TAYLOR
Fullback. 6-0, 216. Born in Baton Rouge, Louisiana, September 20, 1935. Louisiana State. Inducted in 1976. 1958-66 Green Bay Packers, 1967 New Orleans Saints. **Highlights:** 8,597 rushing yards, 558 points. In 1962, led league in rushing and scoring with 19 touchdowns.

JIM THORPE
Halfback. 6-1, 190. Born in Prague, Oklahoma, May 28, 1888. Died March 28, 1953. Carlisle. Inducted in 1963. 1915-17, 1919-20, 1926 Canton Bulldogs, 1921 Cleveland Indians, 1922-23 Oorang Indians, 1924 Rock Island, Ill., Independents, 1925 New York Giants, 1928 Chicago Cardinals. **Highlights:** Charter enshrinee. First president of American Professional Football Association, 1920. Played for 12 seasons.

Y.A. TITTLE
Quarterback. 6-0, 200. Born in Marshall, Texas, October 24, 1926. Louisiana State. Inducted in 1971. 1948-49 Baltimore Colts (AAFC), 1950 Baltimore Colts, 1951-60 San Francisco 49ers, 1961-64 New York Giants. **Highlights:** 33,070 yards, 242 touchdowns. 33 touchdown passes in 1962 and 36 in 1963. Two-time league MVP.

GEORGE TRAFTON
Center. 6-2, 235. Born in Chicago, Illinois, December 6, 1896. Died September 5, 1971. Notre Dame. Inducted in 1964. 1920 Decatur Staleys, 1921 Chicago Staleys, 1922-32 Chicago Bears. **Highlights:** First center to snap with one hand. Named top NFL center of 1920s.

CHARLEY TRIPPI
Halfback. 6-0, 185. Born in Pittston, Pennsylvania, December 14, 1922. Georgia. Inducted in 1968. 1947-55 Chicago Cardinals. **Highlights:** One of football's most versatile performers. Played halfback five years, quarterback for two, defense for two.

EMLEN TUNNELL
Safety. 6-1, 200. Born in Bryn Mawr, Pennsylvania, March 29, 1925. Died July 22, 1975. Toledo, Iowa. Inducted in 1967. 1948-58 New York Giants, 1959-61 Green Bay Packers. **Highlights:** 79 interceptions. Gained more yards on kickoffs and interceptions (923) in 1952 than that season's NFL rushing leader.

CLYDE (BULLDOG) TURNER
Center. 6-2, 235. Born in Sweetwater, Texas, November 10, 1919. Hardin-Simmons. Inducted in 1966. 1940-52 Chicago Bears. **Highlights:** Anchored defense for four NFL championship teams, including 4 interceptions in five title games.

JOHNNY UNITAS
Quarterback. 6-1, 195. Born in Pittsburgh, Pennsylvania, May 7, 1933. Louisville. Inducted in 1979. 1956-72 Baltimore Colts, 1973 San Diego Chargers. **Highlights:** 40,239 passing yards, 290 touchdowns. Led Colts to two NFL championships. Passed for at least one touchdown in 47 consecutive games.

GENE UPSHAW
Guard. 6-5, 255. Born in Robstown, Texas, August 15, 1945. Texas A & I. Inducted in 1987. 1967-81 Oakland Raiders. **Highlights:** Played in 10 AFL/AFC Championship Games, three Super Bowls, seven Pro Bowls—307 total games.

NORM VAN BROCKLIN
Quarterback. 6-1, 190. Born in Eagle Butte, South Dakota, March 15, 1926. Died May 2, 1983. Oregon. Inducted in 1971. 1949-57 Los Angeles Rams, 1958-60 Philadelphia Eagles. **Highlights:** NFL-record 554 yards passing in 1951 season opener. Guided Eagles to NFL crown as league MVP in 1960.

STEVE VAN BUREN
Halfback. 6-1, 200. Born in La Ceiba, Honduras, December 28, 1920. Louisiana State. Inducted in 1965. 1944-51 Philadelphia Eagles. **Highlights:** Four-time rushing champion. Won 1944 punt return title and was 1945 kick return champion.

DOAK WALKER
Halfback. 5-11, 172. Born in Dallas, Texas, January 1, 1927. Southern Methodist. Inducted in 1986. 1950-55 Detroit Lions. **Highlights:** 534 points. Won two NFL scoring titles. Had winning 62-yard scoring run in 1952 title game.

BILL WALSH
Coach. Born in Los Angeles, California, November 30, 1931. San Jose State. Inducted in 1993. 1979-88 San Francisco 49ers. **Highlights:** 102-63-1 coaching record. Guided 49ers to three Super Bowl titles (XVI, XIX, XXIII) in 10 years.

PAUL WARFIELD
Wide receiver. 6-0, 188. Born in Warren, Ohio, November 28, 1942. Ohio State. Inducted in 1983. 1964-69, 1976-77 Cleveland Browns, 1970-74 Miami Dolphins. **Highlights:** 8,565 yards receiving, 85 touchdowns. Eight-time Pro Bowl player. Key to both Cleveland and Miami offenses.

BOB WATERFIELD
Quarterback. 6-2, 200. Born in Elmira, New York, July 26, 1920. Died March 25, 1983. UCLA. Inducted in 1965. 1945 Cleveland Rams, 1946-52 Los Angeles Rams. **Highlights:** NFL MVP as rookie in 1945 and led Rams to NFL title. Grabbed 20 interceptions in limited defensive duties.

ARNIE WEINMEISTER
Defensive tackle. 6-4, 235. Born in Rhein, Saskatchewan, Canada, March 23, 1923. Washington. Inducted in 1984. 1948-49 New York Yankees (AAFC), 1950-53 New York Giants. **Highlights:** Dominant defensive tackle of his time. Four-time All-NFL selection, four Pro Bowls.

RANDY WHITE
Defensive tackle. 6-4, 265. Born in Pittsburgh, Pennsylvania, January 15, 1953. Maryland. Inducted in 1994. 1975-88 Dallas Cowboys. **Highlights:** Missed only one game in 14 seasons. Co-MVP of Super Bowl XII. Nine-time Pro Bowl selection.

BILL WILLIS
Guard. 6-2, 215. Born in Columbus, Ohio, October 5, 1921. Ohio State. Inducted in 1977. 1946-49 Cleveland Browns (AAFC), 1950-53 Cleveland Browns. **Highlights:** Two-way player who excelled on defense. Four-time All-NFL player, played in three Pro Bowls.

LARRY WILSON
Safety. 6-0, 190. Born in Rigby, Idaho, March 24, 1938. Utah. Inducted in 1978. 1960-72 St. Louis Cardinals. **Highlights:** 52 interceptions. Had interception in seven consecutive games in 1966. Made "safety blitz" famous.

KELLEN WINSLOW
Tight end. 6-5, 250. Born in St. Louis, Missouri, November 5, 1957. Missouri. Inducted in 1995. 1979-87 San Diego Chargers **Highlights:** 541 receptions for 6,741 yards, 45 touchdowns. 13 catches, blocked field goal in 1981 playoff win over Miami.

ALEX WOJCIECHOWICZ
Center. 6-0, 235. Born in South River, New Jersey, August 12, 1915. Died July 13, 1992. Fordham. Inducted in 1968. 1938-46 Detroit Lions, 1946-50 Philadelphia Eagles. **Highlights:** One of league's first iron men. Played both ways for eight years with Lions.

WILLIE WOOD
Safety. 5-10, 190. Born in Washington, D.C., December 23, 1936. Southern California. Inducted in 1989. 1960-71 Green Bay Packers. **Highlights:** 48 interceptions. Competed in six NFL championship games including Super Bowls I and II.

CHRONOLOGY OF PROFESSIONAL FOOTBALL

1869
Rutgers and Princeton played a college soccer football game, the first ever, November 6. The game used modified London Football Association rules. During the next seven years, rugby gained favor with the major eastern schools over soccer, and modern football began to develop from rugby.

1876
At the Massasoit convention, the first rules for American football were written. Walter Camp, who would become known as the father of American football, first became involved with the game.

1892
In an era in which football was a major attraction of local athletic clubs, an intense competition between two Pittsburgh-area clubs, the Allegheny Athletic Association (AAA) and the Pittsburgh Athletic Club (PAC), led to the making of the first professional football player. Former Yale All-America guard William (Pudge) Heffelfinger was paid $500 by the AAA to play in a game against the PAC, becoming the first person to be paid to play football, November 12. The AAA won the game 4-0 when Heffelfinger picked up a PAC fumble and ran 25 yards for a touchdown.

1893
The Pittsburgh Athletic Club signed one of its players, probably halfback Grant Dibert, to the first known pro football contract, which covered all of the PAC's games for the year.

1895
John Brallier became the first football player to openly turn pro, accepting $10 and expenses to play for the Latrobe YMCA against the Jeannette Athletic Club.

1896
The Allegheny Athletic Association team fielded the first completely professional team for its abbreviated two-game season.

1897
The Latrobe Athletic Association football team went entirely professional, becoming the first team to play a full season with only professionals.

1898
A touchdown was changed from four points to five.

1899
Chris O'Brien formed a neighborhood team, which played under the name the Morgan Athletic Club, on the south side of Chicago. The team later became known as the Normals, then the Racine (for a street in Chicago) Cardinals, the Chicago Cardinals, the St. Louis Cardinals, the Phoenix Cardinals, and, in 1994, the Arizona Cardinals. The team remains the oldest continuing operation in pro football.

1900
William C. Temple took over the team payments for the Duquesne Country and Athletic Club, becoming the first known individual club owner.

1902
Baseball's Philadelphia Athletics, managed by Connie Mack, and the Philadelphia Phillies formed professional football teams, joining the Pittsburgh Stars in the first attempt at a pro football league, named the National Football League. The Athletics won the first night football game ever played, 39-0 over Kanaweola AC at Elmira, New York, November 21.

All three teams claimed the pro championship for the year, but the league president, Dave Berry, named the Stars the champions. Pitcher Rube Waddell was with the Athletics, and pitcher Christy Mathewson a fullback for Pittsburgh.

The first World Series of pro football, actually a five-team tournament, was played among a team made up of players from both the Athletics and the Phillies, but simply named New York; the New York Knickerbockers; the Syracuse AC; the Warlow AC; and the Orange (New Jersey) AC at New York's original Madison Square Garden. New York and Syracuse played the first indoor football game before 3,000, December 28. Syracuse, with Glen (Pop) Warner at guard, won 6-0 and went on to win the tournament.

1903
The Franklin (Pa.) Athletic Club won the second and last World Series of pro football over the Oreos AC of Asbury Park, New Jersey; the Watertown Red and Blacks; and the Orange AC.

Pro football was popularized in Ohio when the Massillon Tigers, a strong amateur team, hired four Pittsburgh pros to play in the season-ending game against Akron. At the same time, pro football declined in the Pittsburgh area, and the emphasis on the pro game moved west from Pennsylvania to Ohio.

1904
A field goal was changed from five points to four.

Ohio had at least seven pro teams, with Massillon winning the Ohio Independent Championship, that is, the pro title. Talk surfaced about forming a state-wide league to end spiraling salaries brought about by constant bidding for players and to write universal rules for the game. The feeble attempt to start the league failed.

Halfback Charles Follis signed a contract with the Shelby AC, making him the first known black pro football player.

1905
The Canton AC, later to become known as the Bulldogs, became a professional team. Massillon again won the Ohio League championship.

1906
The forward pass was legalized. The first authenticated pass completion in a pro game came on October 27, when George (Peggy) Parratt of Massillon threw a completion to Dan (Bullet) Riley in a victory over a combined Benwood-Moundsville team.

Arch-rivals Canton and Massillon, the two best pro teams in America, played twice, with Canton winning the first game but Massillon winning the second and the Ohio League championship. A betting scandal and the financial disaster wrought upon the two clubs by paying huge salaries caused a temporary decline in interest in pro football in the two cities and, somewhat, throughout Ohio.

1909
A field goal dropped from four points to three.

1912
A touchdown was increased from five points to six.

Jack Cusack revived a strong pro team in Canton.

1913
Jim Thorpe, a former football and track star at the Carlisle Indian School (Pa.) and a double gold medal winner at the 1912 Olympics in Stockholm, played for the Pine Village Pros in Indiana.

1915
Massillon again fielded a major team, reviving the old rivalry with Canton. Cusack signed Thorpe to play for Canton for $250 a game.

1916
With Thorpe and former Carlisle teammate Pete Calac starring, Canton went 9-0-1, won the Ohio League championship, and was acclaimed the pro football champion.

1917
Despite an upset by Massillon, Canton again won the Ohio League championship.

1919
Canton again won the Ohio League championship, despite the team having been turned over from Cusack to Ralph Hay. Thorpe and Calac were joined in the backfield by Joe Guyon.

Earl (Curly) Lambeau and George Calhoun organized the Green Bay Packers. Lambeau's employer at the Indian Packing Company provided $500 for equipment and allowed the team to use the company field for practices. The Packers went 10-1.

1920
Pro football was in a state of confusion due to three major problems: dramatically rising salaries; players continually jumping from one team to another following the highest offer; and the use of college players still enrolled in school. A league in which all the members would follow the same rules seemed the answer. An organizational meeting, at which the Akron Pros, Canton Bulldogs, Cleveland Indians, and Dayton Triangles were represented, was held at the Jordan and Hupmobile auto showroom in Canton, Ohio, August 20. This meeting resulted in the formation of the American Professional Football Conference.

A second organizational meeting was held in Canton, September 17. The teams were from four states—Akron, Canton, Cleveland, and Dayton from Ohio; the Hammond Pros and Muncie Flyers from Indiana; the Rochester Jeffersons from New York; and the Rock Island Independents, Decatur Staleys, and Racine Cardinals from Illinois. The name of the league was changed to the American Professional Football Association. Hoping to capitalize on his fame, the members elected Thorpe president; Stanley Cofall of Cleveland was elected vice president. A membership fee of $100 per team was charged to give an appearance of respectability, but no team ever paid it. Scheduling was left up to the teams, and there were wide variations, both in the overall number of games played and in the number played against APFA member teams.

Four other teams—the Buffalo All-Americans, Chicago Tigers, Columbus Panhandles, and Detroit Heralds—joined the league sometime during the year. On September 26, the first game featuring an APFA team was played at Rock Island's Douglas Park. A crowd of 800 watched the Independents defeat the St. Paul Ideals 48-0. A week later, October 3, the first game matching two APFA teams was held. At Triangle Park, Dayton defeated Columbus 14-0, with Lou Partlow of Dayton scoring the first touchdown in a game between Association teams. The same day, Rock Island defeated Muncie 45-0.

By the beginning of December, most of the teams in the APFA had abandoned their hopes for a championship, and some of them, including the Chicago Tigers and the Detroit Heralds, had finished their seasons, disbanded, and had their franchises canceled by the Association. Four teams—Akron, Buffalo, Canton, and Decatur—still had championship aspirations, but a series of late-season games among them left Akron as the only undefeated team in the Association. At one of these games, Akron sold tackle Bob Nash to Buffalo for $300 and five percent of the gate receipts—the first APFA player deal.

1921
At the league meeting in Akron, April 30, the championship of the 1920 season was awarded to the Akron Pros. The APFA was reorganized, with Joe Carr of the Columbus Panhandles named president and Carl Storck of Dayton secretary-treasurer. Carr moved the Association's headquarters to Columbus, drafted a league constitution and by-laws, gave teams territorial rights, restricted player movements, developed membership criteria for the franchises, and issued standings for the first time, so that the APFA would have a clear champion.

The Association's membership increased to 22 teams, including the Green Bay Packers, who were awarded to John Clair of the Acme Packing Company.

Thorpe moved from Canton to the Cleveland Indians, but he was hurt early in the season and played very little.

A.E. Staley turned the Decatur Staleys over to player-coach George Halas, who moved the team to Cubs

Park in Chicago. Staley paid Halas $5,000 to keep the name Staleys for one more year. Halas made halfback Ed (Dutch) Sternaman his partner.

The Staleys claimed the APFA championship with a 9-1-1 record, as did Buffalo at 9-1-2. Carr ruled in favor of the Staleys, giving Halas his first championship.

1922
After admitting the use of players who had college eligibility remaining during the 1921 season, Clair and the Green Bay management withdrew from the APFA, January 28. Curly Lambeau promised to obey league rules and then used $50 of his own money to buy back the franchise. Bad weather and low attendance plagued the Packers, and Lambeau went broke, but local merchants arranged a $2,500 loan for the club. A public nonprofit corporation was set up to operate the team, with Lambeau as head coach and manager.

The American Professional Football Association changed its name to the National Football League, June 24. The Chicago Staleys became the Chicago Bears.

The NFL fielded 18 teams, including the new Oorang Indians of Marion, Ohio, an all-Indian team featuring Thorpe, Joe Guyon, and Pete Calac, and sponsored by the Oorang dog kennels.

Canton, led by player-coach Guy Chamberlin and tackles Link Lyman and Wilbur (Pete) Henry, emerged as the league's first true powerhouse, going 10-0-2.

1923
For the first time, all of the franchises considered to be part of the NFL fielded teams. Thorpe played first for Oorang, then for the Toledo Maroons. Against the Bears, Thorpe fumbled, and Halas picked up the ball and returned it 98 yards for a touchdown, a record that would last until 1972.

Canton had its second consecutive undefeated season, going 11-0-1 for the NFL title.

1924
The league had 18 franchises, including new ones in Kansas City, Kenosha, and Frankford, a section of Philadelphia. League champion Canton, successful on the field but not at the box office, was purchased by the owner of the Cleveland franchise, who kept the Canton franchise inactive, while using the best players for his Cleveland team, which he renamed the Bulldogs. Cleveland won the title with a 7-1-1 record.

1925
Five new franchises were admitted to the NFL—the New York Giants, who were awarded to Tim Mara and Billy Gibson for $500; the Detroit Panthers, featuring Jimmy Conzelman as owner, coach, and tailback; the Providence Steam Roller; a new Canton Bulldogs team; and the Pottsville Maroons, who had been perhaps the most successful independent pro team. The NFL established its first player limit, at 16 players.

Late in the season, the NFL made its greatest coup in gaining national recognition. Shortly after the University of Illinois season ended in November, All-America halfback Harold (Red) Grange signed a contract to play with the Chicago Bears. On Thanksgiving Day, a crowd of 36,000—the largest in pro football history—watched Grange and the Bears play the Chicago Cardinals to a scoreless tie at Wrigley Field. At the beginning of December, the Bears left on a barnstorming tour that saw them play eight games in 12 days, in St. Louis, Philadelphia, New York City, Washington, Boston, Pittsburgh, Detroit, and Chicago. A crowd of 73,000 watched the game against the Giants at the Polo Grounds, helping assure the future of the troubled NFL franchise in New York. The Bears then played nine more games in the South and West, including a game in Los Angeles, in which 75,000 fans watched them defeat the Los Angeles Tigers in the Los Angeles Memorial Coliseum.

Pottsville and the Chicago Cardinals were the top contenders for the league title, with Pottsville winning a late-season meeting 21-7. Pottsville scheduled a game against a team of former Notre Dame players for Shibe Park in Philadelphia. Frankford lodged a protest not only because the game was in Frankford's protected territory, but because it was being played the same day as a Yellow Jackets home game. Carr gave three different notices forbidding Pottsville to play the game, but Pottsville played anyway, December 12. That day, Carr fined the club, suspended it from all rights and privileges (including the right to play for the NFL championship), and returned its franchise to the league. The Cardinals, who ended the season with the best record in the league, were named the 1925 champions.

1926
Grange's manager, C.C. Pyle, told the Bears that Grange wouldn't play for them unless he was paid a five-figure salary and given one-third ownership of the team. The Bears refused. Pyle leased Yankee Stadium in New York City, then petitioned for an NFL franchise. After he was refused, he started the first American Football League. It lasted one season and included Grange's New York Yankees and eight other teams. The AFL champion Philadelphia Quakers played a December game against the New York Giants, seventh in the NFL, and the Giants won 31-0. At the end of the season, the AFL folded.

Halas pushed through a rule that prohibited any team from signing a player whose college class had not graduated.

The NFL grew to 22 teams, including the Duluth Eskimos, who signed All-America fullback Ernie Nevers of Stanford, giving the league a gate attraction to rival Grange. The 15-member Eskimos, dubbed the Iron Men of the North, played 29 exhibition and league games, 28 on the road, and Nevers played in all but 29 minutes of them.

Frankford edged the Bears for the championship, despite Halas having obtained John (Paddy) Driscoll from the Cardinals. On December 4, the Yellow Jackets scored in the final two minutes to defeat the Bears 7-6 and move ahead of them in the standings.

1927
At a special meeting in Cleveland, April 23, Carr decided to secure the NFL's future by eliminating the financially weaker teams and consolidating the quality players onto a limited number of more successful teams. The new-look NFL dropped to 12 teams, and the center of gravity of the league left the Midwest, where the NFL had started, and began to emerge in the large cities of the East. One of the new teams was Grange's New York Yankees, but Grange suffered a knee injury and the Yankees finished in the middle of the pack. The NFL championship was won by the cross-town rival New York Giants, who posted 10 shutouts in 13 games.

1928
Grange and Nevers both retired from pro football, and Duluth disbanded, as the NFL was reduced to only 10 teams. The Providence Steam Roller of Jimmy Conzelman and Pearce Johnson won the championship, playing in the Cycledrome, a 10,000-seat oval that had been built for bicycle races.

1929
Chris O'Brien sold the Chicago Cardinals to David Jones, July 27.

The NFL added a fourth official, the field judge, July 28.

Grange and Nevers returned to the NFL. Nevers scored six rushing touchdowns and four extra points as the Cardinals beat Grange's Bears 40-6, November 28. The 40 points set a record that remains the NFL's oldest.

Providence became the first NFL team to host a game at night under floodlights, against the Cardinals, November 3.

The Packers added back Johnny Blood (McNally), tackle Cal Hubbard, and guard Mike Michalske, and won their first NFL championship, edging the Giants, who featured quarterback Benny Friedman.

1930
Dayton, the last of the NFL's original franchises, was purchased by William B. Dwyer and John C. Depler, moved to Brooklyn, and renamed the Dodgers. The Portsmouth, Ohio, Spartans entered the league.

The Packers edged the Giants for the title, but the most improved team was the Bears. Halas retired as a player and replaced himself as coach of the Bears with Ralph Jones, who refined the T-formation by introducing wide ends and a halfback in motion. Jones also introduced rookie All-America fullback-tackle Bronko Nagurski.

The Giants defeated a team of former Notre Dame players coached by Knute Rockne 22-0 before 55,000 at the Polo Grounds, December 14. The proceeds went to the New York Unemployment Fund to help those suffering because of the Great Depression, and the easy victory helped give the NFL credibility with the press and the public.

1931
The NFL decreased to 10 teams, and halfway through the season the Frankford franchise folded. Carr fined the Bears, Packers, and Portsmouth $1,000 each for using players whose college classes had not graduated.

The Packers won an unprecedented third consecutive title, beating out the Spartans, who were led by rookie backs Earl (Dutch) Clark and Glenn Presnell.

1932
George Preston Marshall, Vincent Bendix, Jay O'Brien, and M. Dorland Doyle were awarded a franchise for Boston, July 9. Despite the presence of two rookies—halfback Cliff Battles and tackle Glen (Turk) Edwards—the new team, named the Braves, lost money and Marshall was left as the sole owner at the end of the year.

NFL membership dropped to eight teams, the lowest in history. Official statistics were kept for the first time. The Bears and the Spartans finished the season in the first-ever tie for first place. After the season finale, the league office arranged for the first playoff game in NFL history. The game was moved indoors to Chicago Stadium because of bitter cold and heavy snow. The arena allowed only an 80-yard field that came right to the walls. The goal posts were moved from the end lines to the goal lines and, for safety, inbounds lines or hashmarks where the ball would be put in play were drawn 10 yards from the walls that butted against the sidelines. The Bears won 9-0, December 18, scoring the winning touchdown on a two-yard pass from Nagurski to Grange. The Spartans claimed Nagurski's pass was thrown from less than five yards behind the line of scrimmage, violating the existing passing rule, but the play stood.

1933
The NFL, which long had followed the rules of college football, made a number of significant changes from the college game for the first time and began to develop rules serving its needs and the style of play it preferred. The innovations from the 1932 championship game—inbounds line or hashmarks and goal posts on the goal lines—were adopted. Also the forward pass was legalized from anywhere behind the line of scrimmage, February 25.

Marshall and Halas pushed through a proposal that divided the NFL into two divisions, with the winners to meet in an annual championship game, July 8.

Three new franchises joined the league—the Pittsburgh Pirates of Art Rooney, the Philadelphia Eagles of Bert Bell and Lud Wray, and the Cincinnati Reds. The Staten Island Stapletons suspended operations for a year, but never returned to the league.

Halas bought out Sternaman, became sole owner of the Bears, and reinstated himself as head coach. Marshall changed the name of the Boston

Braves to the Redskins. David Jones sold the Chicago Cardinals to Charles W. Bidwill.

In the first NFL Championship Game scheduled before the season, the Western Division champion Bears defeated the Eastern Division champion Giants 23-21 at Wrigley Field, December 17.

1934

G.A. (Dick) Richards purchased the Portsmouth Spartans, moved them to Detroit, and renamed them the Lions.

Professional football gained new prestige when the Bears were matched against the best college football players in the first Chicago College All-Star Game, August 31. The game ended in a scoreless tie before 79,432 at Soldier Field.

The Cincinnati Reds lost their first eight games, then were suspended from the league for defaulting on payments. The St. Louis Gunners, an independent team, joined the NFL by buying the Cincinnati franchise and went 1-2 the last three weeks.

Rookie Beattie Feathers of the Bears became the NFL's first 1,000-yard rusher, gaining 1,004 on 101 carries. The Thanksgiving Day game between the Bears and the Lions became the first NFL game broadcast nationally, with Graham McNamee the announcer for NBC radio.

In the championship game, on an extremely cold and icy day at the Polo Grounds, the Giants trailed the Bears 13-3 in the third quarter before changing to basketball shoes for better footing. The Giants won 30-13 in what has come to be known as the Sneakers Game, December 9.

The player waiver rule was adopted, December 10.

1935

The NFL adopted Bert Bell's proposal to hold an annual draft of college players, to begin in 1936, with teams selecting in an inverse order of finish, May 19. The inbounds line or hashmarks were moved nearer the center of the field, 15 yards from the sidelines.

All-America end Don Hutson of Alabama joined Green Bay. The Lions defeated the Giants 26-7 in the NFL Championship Game, December 15.

1936

There were no franchise transactions for the first year since the formation of the NFL. It also was the first year in which all member teams played the same number of games.

The Eagles made University of Chicago halfback and Heisman Trophy winner Jay Berwanger the first player ever selected in the NFL draft, February 8. The Eagles traded his rights to the Bears, but Berwanger never played pro football. The first player selected to actually sign was the number-two pick, Riley Smith of Alabama, who was selected by Boston.

A rival league was formed, and it became the second to call itself the American Football League. The Boston Shamrocks were its champions.

Because of poor attendance, Marshall, the owner of the host team, moved the Championship Game from Boston to the Polo Grounds in New York. Green Bay defeated the Redskins 21-6, December 13.

1937

Homer Marshman was granted a Cleveland franchise, named the Rams, February 12. Marshall moved the Redskins to Washington, D.C., February 13. The Redskins signed TCU All-America tailback Sammy Baugh, who led them to a 28-21 victory over the Bears in the NFL Championship Game, December 12.

The Los Angeles Bulldogs had an 8-0 record to win the AFL title, but then the 2-year-old league folded.

1938

At the suggestion of Halas, Hugh (Shorty) Ray became a technical advisor on rules and officiating to the NFL. A new rule called for a 15-yard penalty for roughing the passer.

Rookie Byron (Whizzer) White of the Pittsburgh Pirates led the NFL in rushing. The Giants defeated the Packers 23-17 for the NFL title, December 11.

Marshall, *Los Angeles Times* sports editor Bill Henry, and promoter Tom Gallery established the Pro Bowl game between the NFL champion and a team of pro all-stars.

1939

The New York Giants defeated the Pro All-Stars 13-10 in the first Pro Bowl, at Wrigley Field, Los Angeles, January 15.

Carr, NFL president since 1921, died in Columbus, May 20. Carl Storck was named acting president, May 25.

An NFL game was televised for the first time when NBC broadcast the Brooklyn Dodgers-Philadelphia Eagles game from Ebbets Field to the approximately 1,000 sets then in New York.

Green Bay defeated New York 27-0 in the NFL Championship Game, December 10 at Milwaukee. NFL attendance exceeded 1 million in a season for the first time, reaching 1,071,200.

1940

A six-team rival league, the third to call itself the American Football League, was formed, and the Columbus Bullies won its championship.

Halas's Bears, with additional coaching by Clark Shaughnessy of Stanford, defeated the Redskins 73-0 in the NFL Championship Game, December 8. The game, which was the most decisive victory in NFL history, popularized the Bears' T-formation with a man-in-motion. It was the first championship carried on network radio, broadcast by Red Barber to 120 stations of the Mutual Broadcasting System, which paid $2,500 for the rights.

Art Rooney sold the Pittsburgh franchise to Alexis Thompson, December 9, then bought part interest in the Philadelphia Eagles.

1941

Elmer Layden was named the first Commissioner of the NFL, March 1; Storck, the acting president, resigned, April 5. NFL headquarters were moved to Chicago.

Bell and Rooney traded the Eagles to Thompson for the Pirates, then re-named their new team the Steelers. Homer Marshman sold the Rams to Daniel F. Reeves and Fred Levy, Jr.

The league by-laws were revised to provide for playoffs in case there were ties in division races, and sudden-death overtimes in case a playoff game was tied after four quarters. An official *NFL Record Manual* was published for the first time.

Columbus again won the championship of the AFL, but the two-year-old league then folded.

The Bears and the Packers finished in a tie for the Western Division championship, setting up the first divisional playoff game in league history. The Bears won 33-14, then defeated the Giants 37-9 for the NFL championship, December 21.

1942

Players departing for service in World War II depleted the rosters of NFL teams. Halas left the Bears in midseason to join the Navy, and Luke Johnsos and Heartley (Hunk) Anderson served as co-coaches as the Bears went 11-0 in the regular season. The Redskins defeated the Bears 14-6 in the NFL Championship Game, December 13.

1943

The Cleveland Rams, with co-owners Reeves and Levy in the service, were granted permission to suspend operations for one season, April 6. Levy transferred his stock in the team to Reeves, April 16.

The NFL adopted free substitution, April 7. The league also made the wearing of helmets mandatory and approved a 10-game schedule for all teams.

Philadelphia and Pittsburgh were granted permission to merge for one season, June 19. The team, known as Phil-Pitt (and called the Steagles by fans), divided home games between the two cities, and Earle (Greasy) Neale of Philadelphia and Walt Kiesling of Pittsburgh served as co-coaches. The merger automatically dissolved the last day of the season, December 5.

Ted Collins was granted a franchise for Boston, to become active in 1944.

Sammy Baugh led the league in passing, punting, and interceptions. He led the Redskins to a tie with the Giants for the Eastern Division title, and then to a 28-0 victory in a divisional playoff game. The Bears beat the Redskins 41-21 in the NFL Championship Game, December 26.

1944

Collins, who had wanted a franchise in Yankee Stadium in New York, named his new team in Boston the Yanks. Cleveland resumed operations. The Brooklyn Dodgers changed their name to the Tigers.

Coaching from the bench was legalized, April 20.

The Cardinals and the Steelers were granted permission to merge for one year under the name Card-Pitt, April 21. Phil Handler of the Cardinals and Walt Kiesling of the Steelers served as co-coaches. The merger automatically dissolved the last day of the season, December 3.

In the NFL Championship Game, Green Bay defeated the New York Giants 14-7, December 17.

1945

The inbounds lines or hashmarks were moved from 15 yards away from the sidelines to nearer the center of the field—20 yards from the sidelines.

Brooklyn and Boston merged into a team that played home games in both cities and was known simply as The Yanks. The team was coached by former Boston head coach Herb Kopf. In December, the Brooklyn franchise withdrew from the NFL to join the new All-America Football Conference; all the players on its active and reserve lists were assigned to The Yanks, who once again became the Boston Yanks.

Halas rejoined the Bears late in the season after service with the U.S. Navy. Although Halas took over much of the coaching duties, Anderson and Johnsos remained the coaches of record throughout the season.

Steve Van Buren of Philadelphia led the NFL in rushing, kickoff returns, and scoring.

After the Japanese surrendered ending World War II, a count showed that the NFL service roster, limited to men who had played in league games, totaled 638, 21 of whom had died in action.

Rookie quarterback Bob Waterfield led Cleveland to a 15-14 victory over Washington in the NFL Championship Game, December 16.

1946

The contract of Commissioner Layden was not renewed, and Bert Bell, the co-owner of the Steelers, replaced him, January 11. Bell moved the league headquarters from Chicago to the Philadelphia suburb of Bala-Cynwyd.

Free substitution was withdrawn and substitutions were limited to no more than three men at a time. Forward passes were made automatically incomplete upon striking the goal posts, January 11.

The NFL took on a truly national appearance for the first time when Reeves was granted permission by the league to move his NFL champion Rams to Los Angeles.

The rival All-America Football Conference began play with eight teams. The Cleveland Browns, coached by Paul Brown, won the AAFC's first championship, defeating the New York Yankees 14-9.

Bill Dudley of the Steelers led the NFL in rushing, interceptions, and punt returns, and won the league's most valuable player award.

Backs Frank Filchock and Merle Hapes of the Giants were questioned about an attempt by a New York man to fix the championship game with the Bears. Bell suspended Hapes but allowed Filchock to play; he played well, but Chicago won 24-14, December 15.

1947
The NFL added a fifth official, the back judge.

A bonus choice was made for the first time in the NFL draft. One team each year would select the special choice before the first round began. The Chicago Bears won a lottery and the rights to the first choice and drafted back Bob Fenimore of Oklahoma A&M.

The Cleveland Browns again won the AAFC title, defeating the New York Yankees 14-3.

Charles Bidwill, Sr., owner of the Cardinals, died April 19, but his wife and sons retained ownership of the team. On December 28, the Cardinals won the NFL Championship Game 28-21 over the Philadelphia Eagles, who had beaten Pittsburgh 21-0 in a playoff.

1948
Plastic helmets were prohibited. A flexible artificial tee was permitted at the kickoff. Officials other than the referee were equipped with whistles, not horns, January 14.

Fred Mandel sold the Detroit Lions to a syndicate headed by D. Lyle Fife, January 15.

Halfback Fred Gehrke of the Los Angeles Rams painted horns on the Rams' helmets, the first modern helmet emblems in pro football.

The Cleveland Browns won their third straight championship in the AAFC, going 14-0 and then defeating the Buffalo Bills 49-7.

In a blizzard, the Eagles defeated the Cardinals 7-0 in the NFL Championship Game, December 19.

1949
Alexis Thompson sold the champion Eagles to a syndicate headed by James P. Clark, January 15. The Boston Yanks became the New York Bulldogs, sharing the Polo Grounds with the Giants.

Free substitution was adopted for one year, January 20.

The NFL had two 1,000-yard rushers in the same season for the first time—Steve Van Buren of Philadelphia and Tony Canadeo of Green Bay.

The AAFC played its season with a one-division, seven-team format. On December 9, Bell announced a merger agreement in which three AAFC franchises—Cleveland, San Francisco, and Baltimore—would join the NFL in 1950. The Browns won their fourth consecutive AAFC title, defeating the 49ers 21-7, December 11.

In a heavy rain, the Eagles defeated the Rams 14-0 in the NFL Championship Game, December 18.

1950
Unlimited free substitution was restored, opening the way for the era of two platoons and specialization in pro football, January 20.

Curly Lambeau, founder of the franchise and Green Bay's head coach since 1921, resigned under fire, February 1.

The name National Football League was restored after about three months as the National-American Football League. The American and National conferences were created to replace the Eastern and Western divisions, March 3.

The New York Bulldogs became the Yanks and divided the players of the former AAFC Yankees with the Giants. A special allocation draft was held in which the 13 teams drafted the remaining AAFC players, with special consideration for Baltimore, which received 15 choices compared to 10 for other teams.

The Los Angeles Rams became the first NFL team to have all of its games—both home and away—televised. The Washington Redskins followed the Rams in arranging to televise their games; other teams made deals to put selected games on television.

In the first game of the season, former AAFC champion Cleveland defeated NFL champion Philadelphia 35-10. For the first time, deadlocks occurred in both conferences and playoffs were necessary. The Browns defeated the Giants in the American and the Rams defeated the Bears in the National. Cleveland defeated Los Angeles 30-28 in the NFL Championship Game, December 24.

1951
The Pro Bowl game, dormant since 1942, was revived under a new format matching the all-stars of each conference at the Los Angeles Memorial Coliseum. The American Conference defeated the National Conference 28-27, January 14.

Abraham Watner returned the Baltimore franchise and its player contracts back to the NFL for $50,000. Baltimore's former players were made available for drafting at the same time as college players, January 18.

A rule was passed that no tackle, guard, or center would be eligible to catch a forward pass, January 18.

The Rams reversed their television policy and televised only road games.

The NFL Championship Game was televised coast-to-coast for the first time, December 23. The DuMont Network paid $75,000 for the rights to the game, in which the Rams defeated the Browns 24-17.

1952
Ted Collins sold the New York Yanks' franchise back to the NFL, January 19. A new franchise was awarded to a group in Dallas after it purchased the assets of the Yanks, January 24. The new Texans went 1-11, with the owners turning the franchise back to the league in midseason. For the last five games of the season, the commissioner's office operated the Texans as a road team, using Hershey, Pennsylvania, as a home base. At the end of the season the franchise was canceled, the last time an NFL team failed.

The Pittsburgh Steelers abandoned the Single-Wing for the T-formation, the last pro team to do so.

The Detroit Lions won their first NFL championship in 17 years, defeating the Browns 17-7 in the title game, December 28.

1953
A Baltimore group headed by Carroll Rosenbloom was granted a franchise and was awarded the holdings of the defunct Dallas organization, January 23. The team, named the Colts, put together the largest trade in league history, acquiring 10 players from Cleveland in exchange for five.

The names of the American and National conferences were changed to the Eastern and Western conferences, January 24.

Jim Thorpe died, March 28.

Mickey McBride, founder of the Cleveland Browns, sold the franchise to a syndicate headed by Dave R. Jones, June 10.

The NFL policy of blacking out home games was upheld by Judge Allan K. Grim of the U.S. District Court in Philadelphia, November 12.

The Lions again defeated the Browns in the NFL Championship Game, winning 17-16, December 27.

1954
The Canadian Football League began a series of raids on NFL teams, signing quarterback Eddie LeBaron and defensive end Gene Brito of Washington and defensive tackle Arnie Weinmeister of the Giants, among others.

Fullback Joe Perry of the 49ers became the first player in league history to gain 1,000 yards rushing in consecutive seasons.

Cleveland defeated Detroit 56-10 in the NFL Championship Game, December 26.

1955
The sudden-death overtime rule was used for the first time in a preseason game between the Rams and Giants at Portland, Oregon, August 28. The Rams won 23-17 three minutes into overtime.

A rule change declared the ball dead immediately if the ball carrier touched the ground with any part of his body except his hands or feet while in the grasp of an opponent.

The Baltimore Colts made an 80-cent phone call to Johnny Unitas and signed him as a free agent. Another quarterback, Otto Graham, played his last game as the Browns defeated the Rams 38-14 in the NFL Championship Game, December 26. Graham had quarterbacked the Browns to 10 championship-game appearances in 10 years.

NBC replaced DuMont as the network for the title game, paying a rights fee of $100,000.

1956
The NFL Players Association was founded.

Grabbing an opponent's facemask (other than the ball carrier) was made illegal. Using radio receivers to communicate with players on the field was prohibited. A natural leather ball with white end stripes replaced the white ball with black stripes for night games.

The Giants moved from the Polo Grounds to Yankee Stadium.

Halas retired as coach of the Bears, and was replaced by Paddy Driscoll.

CBS became the first network to broadcast some NFL regular-season games to selected television markets across the nation.

The Giants routed the Bears 47-7 in the NFL Championship Game, December 30.

1957
Pete Rozelle was named general manager of the Rams. Anthony J. Morabito, founder and co-owner of the 49ers, died of a heart attack during a game against the Bears at Kezar Stadium, October 28. An NFL-record crowd of 102,368 saw the 49ers-Rams game at the Los Angeles Memorial Coliseum, November 10.

The Lions came from 20 points down to post a 31-27 playoff victory over the 49ers, December 22. Detroit defeated Cleveland 59-14 in the NFL Championship Game, December 29.

1958
The bonus selection in the draft was eliminated, January 29. The last selection was quarterback King Hill of Rice by the Chicago Cardinals.

Halas reinstated himself as coach of the Bears.

Jim Brown of Cleveland gained an NFL-record 1,527 yards rushing. In a divisional playoff game, the Giants held Brown to eight yards and defeated Cleveland 10-0.

Baltimore, coached by Weeb Ewbank, defeated the Giants 23-17 in the first sudden-death overtime in an NFL Championship Game, December 28. The game ended when Colts fullback Alan Ameche scored on a one-yard touchdown run after 8:15 of overtime.

1959
Vince Lombardi was named head coach of the Green Bay Packers, January 28. Tim Mara, the co-founder of the Giants, died, February 17.

Lamar Hunt of Dallas announced his intentions to form a second pro football league. The first meeting was held in Chicago, August 14, and consisted of Hunt representing Dallas; Bob Howsam, Denver; K.S. (Bud) Adams, Houston; Barron Hilton, Los Angeles; Max Winter and Bill Boyer, Minneapolis; and Harry Wismer, New York City. They made plans to begin play in 1960.

The new league was named the American Football League, August 22. Buffalo, owned by Ralph Wilson, became the seventh franchise, October 28. Boston, owned by William H. Sullivan, became the eighth team, November 22. The first AFL draft, lasting 33 rounds, was held, November 22. Joe Foss was named AFL Commissioner, November 30. An additional draft of 20 rounds was held by the AFL, December 2.

NFL Commissioner Bert Bell died of a heart attack suffered at Franklin Field, Philadelphia, during the last two minutes of a game between the Eagles and the Steelers, October 11. Treasurer Austin Gunsel was named president in the office of the commissioner, October 14.

The Colts again defeated the Giants in the NFL Championship Game, 31-16, December 27.

1960
Pete Rozelle was elected NFL Commissioner as a compromise choice on

the twenty-third ballot, January 26. Rozelle moved the league offices to New York City.

Hunt was elected AFL president for 1960, January 26. Minneapolis withdrew from the AFL, January 27, and the same ownership was given an NFL franchise for Minnesota (to start in 1961), January 28. Dallas received an NFL franchise for 1960, January 28. Oakland received an AFL franchise, January 30.

The AFL adopted the two-point option on points after touchdown, January 28. A no-tampering verbal pact, relative to players' contracts, was agreed to between the NFL and AFL, February 9.

The NFL owners voted to allow the transfer of the Chicago Cardinals to St. Louis, March 13.

The AFL signed a five-year television contract with ABC, June 9.

The Boston Patriots defeated the Buffalo Bills 28-7 before 16,000 at Buffalo in the first AFL preseason game, July 30. The Denver Broncos defeated the Patriots 13-10 before 21,597 at Boston in the first AFL regular-season game, September 9.

Philadelphia defeated Green Bay 17-13 in the NFL Championship Game, December 26.

1961
The Houston Oilers defeated the Los Angeles Chargers 24-16 before 32,183 in the first AFL Championship Game, January 1.

Detroit defeated Cleveland 17-16 in the first Playoff Bowl, or Bert Bell Benefit Bowl, between second-place teams in each conference in Miami, January 7.

End Willard Dewveall of the Bears played out his option and joined the Oilers, becoming the first player to move deliberately from one league to the other, January 14.

Ed McGah, Wayne Valley, and Robert Osborne bought out their partners in the ownership of the Raiders, January 17. The Chargers were transferred to San Diego, February 10. Dave R. Jones sold the Browns to a group headed by Arthur B. Modell, March 22. The Howsam brothers sold the Broncos to a group headed by Calvin Kunz and Gerry Phipps, May 26.

NBC was awarded a two-year contract for radio and television rights to the NFL Championship Game for $615,000 annually, $300,000 of which was to go directly into the NFL Player Benefit Plan, April 5.

Canton, Ohio, where the league that became the NFL was formed in 1920, was chosen as the site of the Pro Football Hall of Fame, April 27. Dick McCann, a former Redskins executive, was named executive director.

A bill legalizing single-network television contracts by professional sports leagues was introduced in Congress by Representative Emanuel Celler. It passed the House and Senate and was signed into law by President John F. Kennedy, September 30.

Houston defeated San Diego 10-3 for the AFL championship, December 24. Green Bay won its first NFL championship since 1944, defeating the New York Giants 37-0, December 31.

1962
The Western Division defeated the Eastern Division 47-27 in the first AFL All-Star Game, played before 20,973 in San Diego, January 7.

Both leagues prohibited grabbing any player's facemask. The AFL voted to make the scoreboard clock the official timer of the game.

The NFL entered into a single-network agreement with CBS for telecasting all regular-season games for $4.65 million annually, January 10.

Judge Roszel Thompson of the U.S. District Court in Baltimore ruled against the AFL in its antitrust suit against the NFL, May 21. The AFL had charged the NFL with monopoly and conspiracy in areas of expansion, television, and player signings. The case lasted two and a half years, the trial two months.

McGah and Valley acquired controlling interest in the Raiders, May 24. The AFL assumed financial responsibility for the New York Titans, November 8. With Commissioner Rozelle as referee, Daniel F. Reeves regained the ownership of the Rams, outbidding his partners in sealed-envelope bidding for the team, November 27.

The Dallas Texans defeated the Oilers 20-17 for the AFL championship at Houston after 17 minutes, 54 seconds of overtime on a 25-yard field goal by Tommy Brooker, December 23. The game lasted a record 77 minutes, 54 seconds.

Judge Edward Weinfeld of the U.S. District Court in New York City upheld the legality of the NFL's television blackout within a 75-mile radius of home games and denied an injunction that would have forced the championship game between the Giants and the Packers to be televised in the New York City area, December 28. The Packers beat the Giants 16-7 for the NFL title, December 30.

1963
The Dallas Texans transferred to Kansas City, becoming the Chiefs, February 8. The New York Titans were sold to a five-man syndicate headed by David (Sonny) Werblin, March 28. Weeb Ewbank became the Titans' new head coach and the team's name was changed to the Jets, April 15. They began play in Shea Stadium.

NFL Properties, Inc., was founded to serve as the licensing arm of the NFL.

Rozelle indefinitely suspended Green Bay halfback Paul Hornung and Detroit defensive tackle Alex Karras for placing bets on their own teams and on other NFL games; he also fined five other Detroit players $2,000 each for betting on one game in which they did not participate, and the Detroit Lions Football Company $2,000 on each of two counts for failure to report information promptly and for lack of sideline supervision.

Paul Brown, head coach of the Browns since their inception, was fired and replaced by Blanton Collier. Don Shula replaced Weeb Ewbank as head coach of the Colts.

The AFL allowed the Jets and Raiders to select players from other franchises in hopes of giving the league more competitive balance, May 11.

NBC was awarded exclusive network broadcasting rights for the 1963 AFL Championship Game for $926,000, May 23.

The Pro Football Hall of Fame was dedicated at Canton, Ohio, September 7.

The U.S. Fourth Circuit Court of Appeals reaffirmed the lower court's finding for the NFL in the $10-million suit brought by the AFL, ending three and a half years of litigation, November 21.

Jim Brown of Cleveland rushed for an NFL single-season record 1,863 yards.

Boston defeated Buffalo 26-8 in the first divisional playoff game in AFL history, December 28.

The Bears defeated the Giants 14-10 in the NFL Championship Game, a record sixth and last title for Halas in his thirty-sixth season as the Bears' coach, December 29.

1964
The Chargers defeated the Patriots 51-10 in the AFL Championship Game, January 5.

William Clay Ford, the Lions' president since 1961, purchased the team, January 10. A group representing the late James P. Clark sold the Eagles to a group headed by Jerry Wolman, January 21. Carroll Rosenbloom, the majority owner of the Colts since 1953, acquired complete ownership of the team, January 23.

The AFL signed a five-year, $36-million television contract with NBC to begin with the 1965 season, January 29.

Commissioner Rozelle negotiated an agreement on behalf of the NFL clubs to purchase Ed Sabol's Blair Motion Pictures, which was renamed NFL Films, March 5.

Hornung and Karras were reinstated by Rozelle, March 16.

CBS submitted the winning bid of $14.1 million per year for the NFL regular-season television rights for 1964 and 1965, January 24. CBS acquired the rights to the championship games for 1964 and 1965 for $1.8 million per game, April 17.

Pete Gogolak of Cornell signed a contract with Buffalo, becoming the first soccer-style kicker in pro football.

Buffalo defeated San Diego 20-7 in the AFL Championship Game, December 26. Cleveland defeated Baltimore 27-0 in the NFL Championship Game, December 27.

1965
The NFL teams pledged not to sign college seniors until completion of all their games, including bowl games, and empowered the Commissioner to discipline the clubs up to as much as the loss of an entire draft list for a violation of the pledge, February 15.

The NFL added a sixth official, the line judge, February 19. The color of the officials' penalty flags was changed from white to bright gold, April 5.

Atlanta was awarded an NFL franchise for 1966, with Rankin Smith, Sr., as owner, June 30. Miami was awarded an AFL franchise for 1966, with Joe Robbie and Danny Thomas as owners, August 16.

Green Bay defeated Baltimore 13-10 in sudden-death overtime in a Western Conference playoff game. Don Chandler kicked a 25-yard field goal for the Packers after 13 minutes, 39 seconds of overtime, December 26. The Packers then defeated the Browns 23-12 in the NFL Championship Game, January 2.

In the AFL Championship Game, the Bills again defeated the Chargers, 23-0, December 26.

CBS acquired the rights to the NFL regular-season games in 1966 and 1967, with an option for 1968, for $18.8 million per year, December 29.

1966
The AFL-NFL war reached its peak, as the leagues spent a combined $7 million to sign their 1966 draft choices. The NFL signed 75 percent of its 232 draftees, the AFL 46 percent of its 181. Of the 111 common draft choices, 79 signed with the NFL, 28 with the AFL, and 4 went unsigned.

The rights to the 1966 and 1967 NFL Championship Games were sold to CBS for $2 million per game, February 14.

Foss resigned as AFL Commissioner, April 7. Al Davis, the head coach and general manager of the Raiders, was named to replace him, April 8.

Goal posts offset from the goal line, painted bright yellow, and with uprights 20 feet above the cross-bar were made standard in the NFL, May 16.

A series of secret meetings regarding a possible AFL-NFL merger were held in the spring between Hunt of Kansas City and Tex Schramm of Dallas. Rozelle announced the merger, June 8. Under the agreement, the two leagues would combine to form an expanded league with 24 teams, to be increased to 26 in 1968 and to 28 by 1970 or soon thereafter. All existing franchises would be retained, and no franchises would be transferred outside their metropolitan areas. While maintaining separate schedules through 1969, the leagues agreed to play an annual AFL-NFL World Championship Game beginning in January, 1967, and to hold a combined draft, also beginning in 1967. Preseason games would be held between teams of each league starting in 1967. Official regular-season play would start in 1970 when the two leagues would officially merge to form one league with two conferences. Rozelle was named Commissioner of the expanded league setup.

Davis rejoined the Raiders, and Milt Woodard was named president of the AFL, July 25.

The St. Louis Cardinals moved into newly constructed Busch Memorial Stadium.

Barron Hilton sold the Chargers to a group headed by Eugene Klein and Sam Schulman, August 25.

Congress approved the AFL-NFL merger, passing legislation exempting the agreement itself from antitrust action, October 21.

New Orleans was awarded an NFL franchise to begin play in 1967, November 1. John Mecom, Jr., of Houston was designated majority stockholder and president of the franchise, December 15.

The NFL was realigned for the 1967-69 seasons into the Capitol and Century Divisions in the Eastern Conference and the Central and Coastal Divisions in the Western Conference, December 2. New Orleans and the New York Giants agreed to switch divisions in 1968 and return to the 1967 alignment in 1969.

The rights to the Super Bowl for four years were sold to CBS and NBC for $9.5 million, December 13.

1967

Green Bay earned the right to represent the NFL in the first AFL-NFL World Championship Game by defeating Dallas 34-27, January 1. The same day, Kansas City defeated Buffalo 31-7 to represent the AFL. The Packers defeated the Chiefs 35-10 before 61,946 fans at the Los Angeles Memorial Coliseum in the first game between AFL and NFL teams, January 15. The winning players' share for the Packers was $15,000 each, and the losing players' share for the Chiefs was $7,500 each. The game was televised by both CBS and NBC.

The "sling-shot" goal post and a six-foot-wide border around the field were made standard in the NFL, February 22.

Baltimore made Bubba Smith, a Michigan State defensive lineman, the first choice in the first combined AFL-NFL draft, March 14.

The AFL awarded a franchise to begin play in 1968 to Cincinnati, May 24. A group with Paul Brown as part owner, general manager, and head coach, was awarded the Cincinnati franchise, September 27.

Arthur B. Modell, the president of the Cleveland Browns, was elected president of the NFL, May 28.

An AFL team defeated an NFL team for the first time, when Denver beat Detroit 13-7 in a preseason game, August 5.

Green Bay defeated Dallas 21-17 for the NFL championship on a last-minute 1-yard quarterback sneak by Bart Starr in 13-below-zero temperature at Green Bay, December 31. The same day, Oakland defeated Houston 40-7 for the AFL championship.

1968

Green Bay defeated Oakland 33-14 in Super Bowl II at Miami, January 14. The game had the first $3-million gate in pro football history.

Vince Lombardi resigned as head coach of the Packers, but remained as general manager, January 28.

Werblin sold his shares in the Jets to his partners Don Lillis, Leon Hess, Townsend Martin, and Phil Iselin, May 21. Lillis assumed the presidency of the club, but then died July 23. Iselin was appointed president, August 6.

Halas retired for the fourth and last time as head coach of the Bears, May 27.

The Oilers left Rice Stadium for the Astrodome and became the first NFL team to play its home games in a domed stadium.

The movie *Heidi* became a footnote in sports history when NBC didn't show the last 1:05 of the Jets-Raiders game in order to permit the children's special to begin on time. The Raiders scored two touchdowns in the last 42 seconds to win 43-32, November 17.

Ewbank became the first coach to win titles in both the NFL and AFL when his Jets defeated the Raiders 27-23 for the AFL championship, December 29. The same day, Baltimore defeated Cleveland 34-0.

1969

The AFL established a playoff format for the 1969 season, with the winner in one division playing the runner-up in the other, January 11.

An AFL team won the Super Bowl for the first time, as the Jets defeated the Colts 16-7 at Miami, January 12 in Super Bowl III. The title Super Bowl was recognized by the NFL for the first time.

Vince Lombardi became part owner, executive vice-president, and head coach of the Washington Redskins, February 7.

Wolman sold the Eagles to Leonard Tose, May 1.

Baltimore, Cleveland, and Pittsburgh agreed to join the AFL teams to form the 13-team American Football Conference of the NFL in 1970, May 17. The NFL also agreed on a playoff format that would include one "wild-card" team per conference—the second-place team with the best record.

Monday Night Football was signed for 1970. ABC acquired the rights to televise 13 NFL regular-season Monday night games in 1970, 1971, and 1972.

George Preston Marshall, president emeritus of the Redskins, died at 72, August 9.

The NFL marked its fiftieth year by the wearing of a special patch by each of the 16 teams.

1970

Kansas City defeated Minnesota 23-7 in Super Bowl IV at New Orleans, January 11. The gross receipts of approximately $3.8 million were the largest ever for a one-day sports event.

Four-year television contracts, under which CBS would televise all NFC games and NBC all AFC games (except Monday night games) and the two would divide televising the Super Bowl and AFC-NFC Pro Bowl games, were announced, January 26.

Art Modell resigned as president of the NFL, March 12. Milt Woodard resigned as president of the AFL, March 13. Lamar Hunt was elected president of the AFC and George Halas was elected president of the NFC, March 19.

The merged 26-team league adopted rules changes putting names on the backs of players' jerseys, making a point after touchdown worth only one point, and making the scoreboard clock the official timing device of the game, March 18.

The Players Negotiating Committee and the NFL Players Association announced a four-year agreement guaranteeing approximately $4,535,000 annually to player pension and insurance benefits, August 3. The owners also agreed to contribute $250,000 annually to improve or implement items such as disability payments, widows' benefits, maternity benefits, and dental benefits. The agreement also provided for increased preseason game and per diem payments, averaging approximately $2.6 million annually.

The Pittsburgh Steelers moved into Three Rivers Stadium. The Cincinnati Bengals moved to Riverfront Stadium.

Lombardi died of cancer at 57, September 3.

Tom Dempsey of New Orleans kicked a game-winning NFL-record 63-yard field goal against Detroit, November 8.

1971

Baltimore defeated Dallas 16-13 on Jim O'Brien's 32-yard field goal with five seconds to go in Super Bowl V at Miami, January 17. The NBC telecast was viewed in an estimated 23,980,000 homes, the largest audience ever for a one-day sports event.

The NFC defeated the AFC 27-6 in the first AFC-NFC Pro Bowl at Los Angeles, January 24.

The Boston Patriots changed their name to the New England Patriots, March 25. Their new stadium, Schaefer Stadium, was dedicated in a 20-14 preseason victory over the Giants.

The Philadelphia Eagles left Franklin Field and played their games at the new Veterans Stadium.

The San Francisco 49ers left Kezar Stadium and moved their games to Candlestick Park.

Daniel F. Reeves, the president and general manager of the Rams, died at 58, April 15.

The Dallas Cowboys moved from the Cotton Bowl into their new home, Texas Stadium, October 24.

Miami defeated Kansas City 27-24 in sudden-death overtime in an AFC Divisional Playoff Game, December 25. Garo Yepremian kicked a 37-yard field goal for the Dolphins after 22 minutes, 40 seconds of overtime, as the game lasted 82 minutes, 40 seconds overall, making it the longest game in history.

1972

Dallas defeated Miami 24-3 in Super Bowl VI at New Orleans, January 16. The CBS telecast was viewed in an estimated 27,450,000 homes, the top-rated one-day telecast ever.

The inbounds lines or hashmarks were moved nearer the center of the field, 23 yards, 1 foot, 9 inches from the sidelines, March 23. The method of determining won-lost percentage in standings changed. Tie games, previously not counted in the standings, were made equal to a half-game won and a half-game lost, May 24.

Robert Irsay purchased the Los Angeles Rams and transferred ownership of the club to Carroll Rosenbloom in exchange for the Baltimore Colts, July 13.

William V. Bidwill purchased the stock of his brother Charles (Stormy) Bidwill to become the sole owner of the St. Louis Cardinals, September 2.

The National District Attorneys Association endorsed the position of professional leagues in opposing proposed legalization of gambling on professional team sports, September 28.

Franco Harris's "Immaculate Reception" gave the Steelers their first postseason win ever, 13-7 over the Raiders, December 23.

1973

Rozelle announced that all Super Bowl VII tickets were sold and that the game would be telecast in Los Angeles, the site of the game, on an experimental basis, January 3.

Miami defeated Washington 14-7 in Super Bowl VII at Los Angeles, completing a 17-0 season, the first perfect-record regular-season and postseason mark in NFL history, January 14. The NBC telecast was viewed by approximately 75 million people.

The AFC defeated the NFC 33-28 in the Pro Bowl in Dallas, the first time since 1942 that the game was played outside Los Angeles, January 21.

A jersey numbering system was adopted, April 5: 1-19 for quarterbacks and specialists, 20-49 for running backs and defensive backs, 50-59 for centers and linebackers, 60-79 for defensive linemen and interior offensive linemen other than centers, and 80-89 for wide receivers and tight ends. Players who had been in the NFL In 1972 could continue to use old numbers.

NFL Charities, a nonprofit organization, was created to derive an income from monies generated from NFL Properties' licensing of NFL trademarks and team names, June 26. NFL Charities was set up to support education and charitable activities and to supply economic support to persons formerly associated with professional football who were no longer able to support themselves.

Congress adopted experimental legislation (for three years) requiring any NFL game that had been declared a sellout 72 hours prior to kickoff to be made available for local televising, September 14. The legislation provided for an annual review to be made by the Federal Communications Commission.

The Buffalo Bills moved their home games from War Memorial Stadium to Rich Stadium in nearby Orchard Park. The Giants tied the Eagles 23-23 in the final game in Yankee Stadium, September 23. The Giants played the rest of their home games at the Yale Bowl in New Haven, Connecticut.

A rival league, the World Football League, was formed and was reported in operation, October 2. It had plans to start play in 1974.

O.J. Simpson of Buffalo became the first player to rush for more than 2,000 yards in a season, gaining 2,003.

1974

Miami defeated Minnesota 24-7 in Super Bowl VIII at Houston, the second consecutive Super Bowl championship for the Dolphins, January 13. The CBS telecast was viewed by approximately 75 million people.

Rozelle was given a 10-year contract effective January 1, 1973, February 27.

Tampa Bay was awarded a franchise to begin operation in 1976, April 24.

Sweeping rules changes were adopted to add action and tempo to games: one sudden-death overtime period was added for preseason and regular-season games; the goal posts were moved from the goal line to the end lines; kickoffs were moved from the 40- to the 35-yard line; after missed field goals from beyond the 20, the ball was to be returned to the line of scrimmage; restrictions were placed on members of the punting team to open up return possibilities; roll-blocking and cutting of wide receivers was eliminated; the extent of downfield contact a defender could have with an eligible receiver was restricted; the penalties for offensive holding, illegal use of the hands, and tripping were reduced from 15 to 10 yards; wide receivers blocking back toward the ball within three yards of the line of scrimmage were prevented from blocking below the waist, April 25.

The Toronto Northmen of the WFL signed Larry Csonka, Jim Kiick, and Paul Warfield of Miami, March 31.

Seattle was awarded an NFL franchise to begin play in 1976, June 4. Lloyd W. Nordstrom, president of the Seattle Seahawks, and Hugh Culverhouse, president of the Tampa Bay Buccaneers, signed franchise agreements, December 5.

The Birmingham Americans defeated the Florida Blazers 22-21 in the WFL World Bowl, winning the league championship, December 5.

1975

Pittsburgh defeated Minnesota 16-6 in Super Bowl IX at New Orleans, the Steelers' first championship since entering the NFL in 1933. The NBC telecast was viewed by approximately 78 million people.

The divisional winners with the highest won-loss percentage were made the home team for the divisional playoffs, and the surviving winners with the highest percentage made home teams for the championship games, June 26.

Referees were equipped with wireless microphones for all preseason, regular-season, and playoff games.

The Lions moved to the new Pontiac Silverdome. The Giants played their home games in Shea Stadium. The Saints moved into the Louisiana Superdome.

The World Football League folded, October 22.

1976

Pittsburgh defeated Dallas 21-17 in Super Bowl X in Miami. The Steelers joined Green Bay and Miami as the only teams to win two Super Bowls; the Cowboys became the first wild-card team to play in the Super Bowl. The CBS telecast was viewed by an estimated 80 million people, the largest television audience in history.

Lloyd Nordstrom, the president of the Seahawks, died at 66, January 20. His brother Elmer succeeded him as majority representative of the team.

The owners awarded Super Bowl XII, to be played on January 15, 1978, to New Orleans. They also adopted the use of two 30-second clocks for all games, visible to both players and fans to note the official time between the ready-for-play signal and snap of the ball, March 16.

A veteran player allocation was held to stock the Seattle and Tampa Bay franchises with 39 players each, March 30-31. In the college draft, Seattle and Tampa Bay each received eight extra choices, April 8-9.

The Giants moved into new Giants Stadium in East Rutherford, New Jersey.

The Steelers defeated the College All-Stars in a storm-shortened Chicago College All-Star Game, the last of the series, July 23. St. Louis defeated San Diego 20-10 in a preseason game before 38,000 in Korakuen Stadium, Tokyo, in the first NFL game outside of North America, August 16.

1977

Oakland defeated Minnesota 32-14 before a record crowd of 100,421 in Super Bowl XI at Pasadena, January 9. The paid attendance was a pro record 103,438. The NBC telecast was viewed by 81.9 million people, the largest ever to view a sports event. The victory was the fifth consecutive for the AFC in the Super Bowl.

The NFL Players Association and the NFL Management Council ratified a collective bargaining agreement extending until 1982, covering five football seasons while continuing the pension plan—including years 1974, 1975, and 1976—with contributions totaling more than $55 million. The total cost of the agreement was estimated at $107 million. The agreement called for a college draft at least through 1986; contained a no-strike, no-suit clause; established a 43-man active player limit; reduced pension vesting to four years; provided for increases in minimum salaries and preseason and postseason pay; improved insurance, medical, and dental benefits; modified previous practices in player movement and control; and reaffirmed the NFL Commissioner's disciplinary authority. Additionally, the agreement called for the NFL member clubs to make payments totaling $16 million the next 10 years to settle various legal disputes, February 25.

The San Francisco 49ers were sold to Edward J. DeBartolo, Jr., March 28.

A 16-game regular season, 4-game preseason was adopted to begin in 1978, March 29. A second wild-card team was adopted for the playoffs beginning in 1978, with the wild-card teams to play each other and the winners advancing to a round of eight postseason series.

The Seahawks were permanently aligned in the AFC Western Division and the Buccaneers in the NFC Central Division, March 31.

The owners awarded Super Bowl XIII, to be played on January 21, 1979, to Miami, to be played in the Orange Bowl; Super Bowl XIV, to be played January 20, 1980, was awarded to Pasadena, to be played in the Rose Bowl, June 14.

Rules changes were adopted to open up the passing game and to cut down on injuries. Defenders were permitted to make contact with eligible receivers only once; the head slap was outlawed; offensive linemen were prohibited from thrusting their hands to an opponent's neck, face, or head; and wide receivers were prohibited from clipping, even in the legal clipping zone.

Rozelle negotiated contracts with the three television networks to televise all NFL regular-season and postseason games, plus selected preseason games, for four years beginning with the 1978 season. ABC was awarded yearly rights to 16 Monday night games, four prime-time games, the AFC-NFC Pro Bowl, and the Hall of Fame games. CBS received the rights to all NFC regular-season and postseason games (except those in the ABC package) and to Super Bowls XIV and XVI. NBC received the rights to all AFC regular-season and postseason games (except those in the ABC package) and to Super Bowls XIII and XV. Industry sources considered it the largest single television package ever negotiated, October 12.

Chicago's Walter Payton set a single-game rushing record with 275 yards (40 carries) against Minnesota, November 20.

1978

Dallas defeated Denver 27-10 in Super Bowl XII, held indoors for the first time, at the Louisiana Superdome in New Orleans, January 15. The CBS telecast was viewed by more than 102 million people, meaning the game was watched by more viewers than any other show of any kind in the history of television. Dallas's victory was the first for the NFC in six years.

According to a Louis Harris Sports Survey, 70 percent of the nation's sports fans said they followed football, compared to 54 percent who followed baseball. Football increased its lead as the country's favorite, 26 percent to 16 percent for baseball, January 19.

A seventh official, the side judge, was added to the officiating crew, March 14.

The NFL continued a trend toward opening up the game. Rules changes permitted a defender to maintain contact with a receiver within five yards of the line of scrimmage, but restricted contact beyond that point. The pass-blocking rule was interpreted to permit the extending of arms and open hands, March 17.

A study on the use of instant replay as an officiating aid was made during seven nationally televised preseason games.

The NFL played for the first time in Mexico City, with the Saints defeating the Eagles 14-7 in a preseason game, August 5.

Bolstered by the expansion of the regular-season schedule from 14 to 16 weeks, NFL paid attendance exceeded 12 million (12,771,800) for the first time. The per-game average of 57,017 was the third-highest in league history and the most since 1973.

1979

Pittsburgh defeated Dallas 35-31 in Super Bowl XIII at Miami to become the first team ever to win three Super Bowls, January 21. The NBC telecast was viewed in 35,090,000 homes, by an estimated 96.6 million fans.

The owners awarded three future Super Bowl sites: Super Bowl XV to the Louisiana Superdome in New Orleans, to be played on January 25, 1981; Super Bowl XVI to the Pontiac Silverdome in Pontiac, Michigan, to be played on January 24, 1982; and Super Bowl XVII to Pasadena's Rose Bowl, to be played on January 30, 1983, March 13.

NFL rules changes emphasized additional player safety. The changes prohibited players on the receiving team from blocking below the waist during kickoffs, punts, and field-goal attempts; prohibited the wearing of torn or altered equipment and exposed pads that could be hazardous; extended the zone in which there could be no crackback blocks; and instructed officials to quickly whistle a play dead when a quarterback was clearly in the grasp of a tackler, March 16.

Rosenbloom, the president of the Rams, drowned at 72, April 2. His widow, Georgia, assumed control of the club.

1980

Pittsburgh defeated the Los Angeles Rams 31-19 in Super Bowl XIV at Pasadena to become the first team to win four Super Bowls, January 20. The game was viewed in a record 35,330,000 homes.

The AFC-NFC Pro Bowl, won 37-27 by the NFC, was played before 48,060 fans at Aloha Stadium in Honolulu, Hawaii. It was the first time in the 30-year history of the Pro Bowl that the game was played in a non-NFL city.

Rules changes placed greater restrictions on contact in the area of the head, neck, and face. Under the heading of "personal foul," players were prohibited from directly striking, swinging, or clubbing on the head, neck, or face. Starting in 1980, a penalty could be called for such contact whether or not the initial contact was made below the neck area.

CBS, with a record bid of $12 million, won the national radio rights to 26 NFL regular-season games and all 10 postseason games for the 1980-83 seasons.

The Los Angeles Rams moved their home games to Anaheim Stadium in nearby Orange County, California.

The Oakland Raiders joined the Los Angeles Coliseum Commission's antitrust suit against the NFL. The suit contended the league violated antitrust laws in declining to approve a proposed move by the Raiders from Oakland to Los Angeles.

NFL regular-season attendance of nearly 13.4 million set a record for the third year in a row. The average paid attendance for the 224-game 1980 regular season was 59,787, the highest in the league's 61-year history. NFL games in 1980 were played before 92.4 percent of total stadium capacity.

Television ratings in 1980 were the second-best in NFL history, trailing only the combined ratings of the 1976 season. All three networks posted gains, and NBC's 15.0 rating was its best ever. CBS and ABC had their best ratings since 1977, with 15.3 and 20.8 ratings, respectively. CBS Radio reported a record audience of 7 million for Monday night and special games.

1981
Oakland defeated Philadelphia 27-10 in Super Bowl XV at the Louisiana Superdome in New Orleans, to become the first wild-card team to win a Super Bowl, January 25.

Edgar F. Kaiser, Jr., purchased the Denver Broncos from Gerald and Allan Phipps, February 26.

The owners adopted a disaster plan for re-stocking a team should the club be involved in a fatal accident, March 20.

The owners awarded Super Bowl XVIII to Tampa, to be played in Tampa Stadium on January 22, 1984, June 3.

A CBS-New York Times poll showed that 48 percent of sports fans preferred football to 31 percent for baseball.

The NFL teams hosted 167 representatives from 44 predominantly black colleges during training camps for a total of 289 days. The program was adopted for renewal during each training camp period.

NFL regular-season attendance—13.6 million for an average of 60,745—set a record for the fourth year in a row. It also was the first time the per-game average exceeded 60,000. NFL games in 1981 were played before 93.8 percent of total stadium capacity.

ABC and CBS set all-time rating highs. ABC finished with a 21.7 rating and CBS with a 17.5 rating. NBC was down slightly to 13.9.

1982
San Francisco defeated Cincinnati 26-21 in Super Bowl XVI at the Pontiac Silverdome, in the first Super Bowl held in the North, January 24. The CBS telecast achieved the highest rating of any televised sports event ever, 49.1 with a 73.0 share. The game was viewed by a record 110.2 million fans. CBS Radio reported a record 14 million listeners for the game.

The NFL signed a five-year contract with the three television networks (ABC, CBS, and NBC) to televise all NFL regular-season and postseason games starting with the 1982 season.

The owners awarded the 1983, 1984, and 1985 AFC-NFC Pro Bowls to Honolulu's Aloha Stadium.

A jury ruled against the NFL in the antitrust trial brought by the Los Angeles Coliseum Commission and the Oakland Raiders, May 7. The verdict cleared the way for the Raiders to move to Los Angeles, where they defeated Green Bay 24-3 in their first preseason game, August 29.

The 1982 season was reduced from a 16-game schedule to nine as the result of a 57-day players' strike. The strike was called by the NFLPA at midnight on Monday, September 20, following the Green Bay at New York Giants game. Play resumed November 21-22 following ratification of the Collective Bargaining Agreement by NFL owners, November 17 in New York.

Under the Collective Bargaining Agreement, which was to run through the 1986 season, the NFL draft was extended through 1992 and the veteran free-agent system was left basically unchanged. A minimum salary schedule for years of experience was established; training camp and postseason pay were increased; players' medical, insurance, and retirement benefits were increased; and a severance-pay system was introduced to aid in career transition, a first in professional sports.

Despite the players' strike, the average paid attendance in 1982 was 58,472, the fifth-highest in league history.

The owners awarded the sites of two Super Bowls, December 14: Super Bowl XIX, to be played on January 20, 1985, to Stanford University Stadium in Stanford, California, with San Francisco as host team; and Super Bowl XX, to be played on January 26, 1986, to the Louisiana Superdome in New Orleans.

1983
Because of the shortened season, the NFL adopted a format of 16 teams competing in a Super Bowl Tournament for the 1982 playoffs. The NFC's number-one seed, Washington, defeated the AFC's number-two seed, Miami, 27-17 in Super Bowl XVII at the Rose Bowl in Pasadena, January 30.

Super Bowl XVII was the second-highest rated live television program of all time, giving the NFL a sweep of the top 10 live programs in television history. The game was viewed in more than 40 million homes, the largest ever for a live telecast.

Halas, the owner of the Bears and the last surviving member of the NFL's second organizational meeting, died at 88, October 31.

1984
The Los Angeles Raiders defeated Washington 38-9 in Super Bowl XVIII at Tampa Stadium, January 22. The game achieved a 46.4 rating and 71.0 share.

An 11-man group headed by H.R. (Bum) Bright purchased the Dallas Cowboys from Clint Murchison, Jr., March 20. Club president Tex Schramm was designated as managing general partner.

Patrick Bowlen purchased a majority interest in the Denver Broncos from Edgar Kaiser, Jr., March 21.

The Colts relocated to Indianapolis, March 28. Their new home became the Hoosier Dome.

The owners awarded two Super Bowl sites at their May 23-25 meetings: Super Bowl XXI, to be played on January 25, 1987, to the Rose Bowl in Pasadena; and Super Bowl XXII, to be played on January 31, 1988, to San Diego Jack Murphy Stadium.

The New York Jets moved their home games to Giants Stadium in East Rutherford, New Jersey.

Alex G. Spanos purchased a majority interest in the San Diego Chargers from Eugene V. Klein, August 28.

Houston defeated Pittsburgh 23-20 to mark the one-hundredth overtime game in regular-season play since overtime was adopted in 1974, December 2.

On the field, many all-time records were set: Dan Marino of Miami passed for 5,084 yards and 48 touchdowns; Eric Dickerson of the Los Angeles Rams rushed for 2,105 yards; Art Monk of Washington caught 106 passes; and Walter Payton of Chicago broke Jim Brown's career rushing mark, finishing the season with 13,309 yards.

According to a CBS Sports/*New York Times* survey, 53 percent of the nation's sports fans said they most enjoyed watching football, compared to 18 percent for baseball, December 2-4.

NFL paid attendance exceeded 13 million for the fifth consecutive complete regular season when 13,398,112, an average of 59,813, attended games. The figure was the second-highest in league history. Teams averaged 42.4 points per game, the second-highest total since the 1970 merger.

1985
San Francisco defeated Miami 38-16 in Super Bowl XIX at Stanford Stadium in Stanford, California, January 20. The game was viewed on television by more people than any other live event in history. President Ronald Reagan, who took his second oath of office before tossing the coin for the game, was one of 115,936,000 viewers. The game drew a 46.4 rating and a 63.0 share. In addition, 6 million people watched the Super Bowl in the United Kingdom and a similar number in Italy. Super Bowl XIX had a direct economic impact of $113.5 million on the San Francisco Bay area.

NBC Radio and the NFL entered into a two-year agreement granting NBC the radio rights to a 37-game package in each of the 1985-86 seasons, March 6. The package included 27 regular-season games and 10 postseason games.

The owners awarded two Super Bowl sites at their annual meeting, March 10-15: Super Bowl XXIII, to be played on January 22, 1989, to the proposed Dolphins Stadium in Miami; and Super Bowl XXIV, to be played on January 28, 1990, to the Louisiana Superdome in New Orleans.

Norman Braman, in partnership with Edward Leibowitz, bought the Philadelphia Eagles from Leonard Tose, April 29.

Bruce Smith, a Virginia Tech defensive lineman selected by Buffalo, was the first player chosen in the fiftieth NFL draft, April 30.

A group headed by Tom Benson, Jr., was approved to purchase the New Orleans Saints from John W. Mecom, Jr., June 3.

The NFL owners adopted a resolution calling for a series of overseas preseason games, beginning in 1986, with one game to be played in England/Europe and/or one game in Japan each year. The game would be a fifth preseason game for the clubs involved and all arrangements and selection of the clubs would be under the control of the Commissioner, May 23.

The league-wide conversion to videotape from movie film for coaching study was approved.

Commissioner Rozelle was authorized to extend the commitment to Honolulu's Aloha Stadium for the AFC-NFC Pro Bowl for 1988, 1989, and 1990, October 15.

The NFL set a single-weekend paid attendance record when 902,657 tickets were sold for the weekend of October 27-28.

A Louis Harris poll in December revealed that pro football remained the sport most followed by Americans. Fifty-nine percent of those surveyed followed pro football, compared with 54 percent who followed baseball.

The Chicago-Miami Monday game had the highest rating, 29.6, and share, 46.0, of any prime-time game in NFL history, December 2. The game was viewed in more than 25 million homes.

The NFL showed a ratings increase on all three networks for the season, gaining 4 percent on NBC, 10 on CBS, and 16 on ABC.

1986
Chicago defeated New England 46-10 in Super Bowl XX at the Louisiana Superdome, January 26. The Patriots had earned the right to play the Bears by becoming the first wild-card team to win three consecutive games on the road. The NBC telecast replaced the final episode of *M*A*S*H* as the most-viewed television program in history, with an audience of 127 million viewers, according to A.C. Nielsen figures. In addition to drawing a 48.3 rating and a 70 percent share in the United States, Super Bowl XX was televised to 59 foreign countries and beamed via satellite to the QE II. An estimated 300 million Chinese viewed a tape delay of the game in March. NBC Radio figures indicated an audience of 10 million for the game.

Super Bowl XX injected more than $100 million into the New Orleans-area economy, and fans spent $250 per day and a record $17.69 per person on game day.

The owners adopted limited use of instant replay as an officiating aid, prohibited players from wearing or otherwise displaying equipment, apparel, or other items that carry commercial names, names of organizations, or personal messages of any type, March 11.

After an 11-week trial, a jury in U.S. District Court in New York awarded the United States Football League one dollar in its $1.7 billion antitrust suit against the NFL. The jury rejected all of the USFL's television-related claims, which were the self-proclaimed heart of the USFL's case, July 29.

Chicago defeated Dallas 17-6 at Wembley Stadium in London in the first American Bowl. The game drew a sellout crowd of 82,699 and the NBC national telecast in this country produced a 12.4 rating and 36 percent share, making it the second-highest-rated daytime preseason game and highest daytime preseason television audience ever with 10.65-million viewers, August 3.

Monday Night Football became the longest-running prime-time series in the history of the ABC network.

Instant replay was used to reverse two plays in 31 preseason games. During the regular season, 374 plays were closely reviewed by replay officials, leading to 38 reversals in 224 games. Eighteen plays were closely reviewed by instant replay in 10 postseason games with three reversals.

1987

The New York Giants defeated Denver 39-20 in Super Bowl XXI and captured their first NFL title since 1956. The game, played in Pasadena's Rose Bowl, drew a sellout crowd of 101,063. According to A.C. Nielsen figures, the CBS broadcast of the game was viewed in the U.S. on television by 122.64-million people, making the telecast the second most-watched television show of all-time behind Super Bowl XX. The game was watched live or on tape in 55 foreign countries and NBC Radio's broadcast of the game was heard by a record 10.1 million people.

The NFL set an all-time paid attendance mark of 17,304,463 for all games, including preseason, regular-season, and postseason. Average regular-season game attendance (60,663) exceeded the 60,000 figure for only the second time in league history.

New three-year TV contracts with ABC, CBS, and NBC were announced for 1987-89 at the NFL annual meeting in Maui, Hawaii, March 15. Commissioner Rozelle and Broadcast Committee Chairman Art Modell also announced a three-year contract with ESPN to televise 13 prime-time games each season. The ESPN contract was the first with a cable network. However, NFL games on ESPN also were scheduled for regular television in the city of the visiting team and in the home city if the game was sold out 72 hours in advance.

Owners also voted to continue in effect for one year the instant replay system used during the 1986 season.

A special payment program was adopted to benefit nearly 1,000 former NFL players who participated in the League before the current Bert Bell NFL Pension Plan was created and made retroactive to the 1959 season. Players covered by the new program spent at least five years in the League and played all or part of their career prior to 1959. Each vested player would receive $60 per month for each year of service in the League for life.

Possible sites for Super Bowl XXV were reduced to five locations by the NFL Super Bowl XXV Site Selection Committee: Anaheim Stadium, Los Angeles Memorial Coliseum, Joe Robbie Stadium, San Diego Jack Murphy Stadium, and Tampa Stadium.

NFL and CBS Radio jointly announced agreement granting CBS the radio rights to a 40-game package in each of the next three NFL seasons, 1987-89, April 7.

NFL owners awarded Super Bowl XXV, to be played on January 27, 1991, to Tampa Stadium, May 20.

Over 400 former NFL players from the pre-1959 era received first payments from NFL owners, July 1.

The NFL's debut on ESPN produced the two highest-rated and most-watched sports programs in basic cable history. The Chicago at Miami game on August 16 drew an 8.9 rating in 3.81 million homes. Those records fell two weeks later when the Los Angeles Raiders at Dallas game achieved a 10.2 cable rating in 4.36 million homes.

Fifty-eight preseason games drew a record paid attendance of 3,116,870.

The 1987 season was reduced from a 16-game season to 15 as the result of a 24-day players' strike. The strike was called by the NFLPA on Tuesday, September 22, following the New England at New York Jets game. Games scheduled for the third weekend were canceled but the games of weeks four, five, and six were played with replacement teams. Striking players returned for the seventh week of the season, October 25.

In a three-team deal involving 10 players and/or draft choices, the Los Angeles Rams traded running back Eric Dickerson to the Indianapolis Colts for six draft choices and two players. Buffalo obtained the rights to linebacker Cornelius Bennett from Indianapolis, sending Greg Bell and three draft choices to the Rams. The Colts added Owen Gill and three draft choices of their own to complete the deal with the Rams, October 31.

The Chicago at Minnesota game became the highest-rated and most-watched sports program in basic cable history when it drew a 14.4 cable rating in 6.5 million homes, December 6.

Instant replay was used to reverse eight plays in 52 preseason games. During the strike-shortened 210-game regular season, 490 plays were closely reviewed by replay officials, leading to 57 reversals. Eighteen plays were closely reviewed by instant replay in 10 postseason games, with three reversals.

1988

Washington defeated Denver 42-10 in Super Bowl XXII to earn its second victory this decade in the NFL Championship Game. The game, played for the first time in San Diego Jack Murphy Stadium, drew a sellout crowd of 73,302. According to A.C. Nielsen figures, the ABC broadcast of the game was viewed in the U.S. on television by 115,000,000 people. The game was seen live or on tape in 60 foreign countries, including the People's Republic of China, and CBS's radio broadcast of the game was heard by 13.7 million people.

A total of 811 players shared in the postseason pool of $16.9 million, the most ever distributed in a single season.

In a unanimous 3-0 decision, the 2nd Circuit Court of Appeals in New York upheld the verdict of the jury that in July, 1986, had awarded the United States Football League one dollar in its $1.7 billion antitrust suit against the NFL. In a 91-page opinion, Judge Ralph K. Winter said the USFL sought through court decree the success it failed to gain among football fans, March 10.

By a 23-5 margin, owners voted to continue the instant replay system for the third consecutive season with the Instant Replay Official to be assigned to a regular seven-man, on-the-field crew. At the NFL annual meeting in Phoenix, Arizona, a 45-second clock was also approved to replace the 30-second clock. For a normal sequence of plays, the interval between plays was changed to 45 seconds from the time the ball is signaled dead until it is snapped on the succeeding play.

NFL owners approved the transfer of the Cardinals' franchise from St. Louis to Phoenix; approved two supplemental drafts each year—one prior to training camp and one prior to the regular season; and voted to initiate an annual series of games in Japan/Asia as early as the 1989 preseason, March 14-18.

The NFL Annual Selection Meeting returned to a separate two-day format and for the first time originated on a Sunday. ESPN drew a 3.6 rating during their seven-hour coverage of the draft, which was viewed in 1.6 million homes, April 24-25.

Art Rooney, founder and owner of the Steelers, died at 87, August 25.

Paid and average attendance of 934,271 and 66,734 at 14 games on October 16-17 set single weekend records.

Commissioner Rozelle announced that two teams would play a preseason game as part of the American Bowl series on August 6, 1989, in the Korakuen Tokyo Dome in Japan, December 16.

NFL regular-season paid attendance of 13,535,335 and the average of 60,427 was the third highest all-time. Buffalo set an NFL team single-season, in-house attendance mark of 622,793.

1989

San Francisco defeated Cincinnati 20-16 in Super Bowl XXIII. The game, played for the first time at Joe Robbie Stadium in Miami, was attended by a sellout crowd of 75,129. NBC's telecast of the game was watched by an estimated 110,780,000 viewers, according to A.C. Nielsen, making it the sixth most-watched program in television history. The game was seen live or on tape in 60 foreign countries, including an estimated 300 million in China. The CBS Radio broadcast of the game was heard by 11.2 million people.

Commissioner Rozelle announced his retirement, pending the naming of a successor, March 22 at the NFL annual meeting in Palm Desert, California.

Following the announcement, AFC president Lamar Hunt and NFC president Wellington Mara announced the formation of a six-man search committee composed of Art Modell, Robert Parins, Dan Rooney, and Ralph Wilson. Hunt and Mara served as co-chairmen.

By a 24-4 margin, owners voted to continue the instant replay system for the fourth straight season. A strengthened policy regarding anabolic steroids and masking agents was announced by Commissioner Rozelle. NFL clubs called for strong disciplinary measures in cases of feigned injuries and adopted a joint proposal by the Long-Range Planning and Finance committees regarding player personnel rules, March 19-23.

Two hundred twenty-nine unconditional free agents signed with new teams under management's Plan B system, April 1.

Jerry Jones purchased a majority interest in the Dallas Cowboys from H.R. (Bum) Bright, April 18.

Tex Schramm was named president of the new World League of American Football to work with a six-man committee of Dan Rooney, chairman; Norman Braman, Lamar Hunt, Victor Kiam, Mike Lynn, and Bill Walsh, April 18.

NFL and CBS Radio jointly announced agreement extending CBS's radio rights to an annual 40-game package through the 1994 season, April 18.

NFL owners awarded Super Bowl XXVI, to be played on January 26, 1992, to Minneapolis, May 24.

As of opening day, September 10, of the 229 Plan B free agents, 111 were active and 23 others were on teams' reserve lists. Ninety-two others were waived and three retired.

Art Shell was named head coach of the Los Angeles Raiders making him the NFL's first black head coach since Fritz Pollard coached the Akron Pros in 1921, October 3.

The site of the New England Patriots at San Francisco 49ers game scheduled for Candlestick Park on October 22 was switched to Stanford Stadium in the aftermath of the Bay Area Earthquake of October 17. The change was announced on October 19.

Paul Tagliabue became the seventh chief executive of the NFL on October 26 when he was chosen to succeed Commissioner Pete Rozelle on the sixth ballot of a three-day meeting in Cleveland, Ohio.

In all, 12 ballots were required to select Tagliabue. Two were conducted at a meeting in Chicago on July 6, and four at a meeting in Dallas on October 10-11. On the twelfth ballot, with Seattle absent, Tagliabue received more than the 19 affirmative votes required for election from among the 27 clubs present.

The transfer from Commissioner Rozelle to Commissioner Tagliabue took place at 12:01 A.M. on Sunday, November 5.

NFL Charities donated $1 million through United Way to benefit Bay Area earthquake victims, November 6.

NFL paid attendance of 17,399,538 was the highest total in league history. This included a total of 13,625,662 for an average of 60,829—both NFL records—for the 224-game regular season.

1990

San Francisco defeated Denver 55-10 in Super Bowl XXIV at the Louisiana

Superdome, January 28. San Francisco joined Pittsburgh as the NFL's only teams to win four Super Bowls.

The NFL announced revisions in its 1990 draft eligibility rules. College juniors became eligible but must renounce their collegiate football eligibility before applying for the NFL Draft, February 16.

Commissioner Tagliabue announced NFL teams will play their 16-game schedule over 17 weeks in 1990 and 1991 and 16 games over 18 weeks in 1992 and 1993, February 27.

The NFL revised its playoff format to include two additional wild-card teams (one per conference).

Commissioner Tagliabue and Broadcast Committee Chairman Art Modell announced a four-year contract with Turner Broadcasting to televise nine Sunday-night games.

New four-year TV agreements were ratified for 1990-93 for ABC, CBS, NBC, ESPN, and TNT at the NFL annual meeting in Orlando, Florida, March 12. The contracts totaled $3.6 billion, the largest in TV history.

The NFL announced plans to expand its American Bowl series of preseason games. In addition to games in London and Tokyo, American Bowl games were scheduled for Berlin, Germany, and Montreal, Canada, in 1990.

For the fifth straight year, NFL owners voted to continue a limited system of Instant Replay. Beginning in 1990, the replay official will have a two-minute time limit to make a decision. The vote was 21-7, March 12.

Commissioner Tagliabue announced the formation of a Committee on Expansion and Realignment, March 13. He also named a Player Advisory Council, comprised of 12 former NFL players, March 14.

One-hundred eighty-four Plan B unconditional free agents signed with new teams, April 2.

Commissioner Tagliabue appointed Dr. John Lombardo as the League's Drug Advisor for Anabolic Steroids, April 25 and named Dr. Lawrence Brown as the League's Advisor for Drugs of Abuse, May 17.

NFL owners awarded Super Bowl XXVIII, to be played in 1994, to the proposed Georgia Dome, May 23.

Commissioner Tagliabue named NFL referee Jerry Seeman as NFL Director of Officiating, replacing Art McNally, who announced his retirement, July 12.

NFL International Week was celebrated with four preseason games in seven days in Tokyo, London, Berlin, and Montreal. More than 200,000 fans on three continents attended the four games, August 4-11.

Commissioner Tagliabue announced the NFL Teacher of the Month program in which the League furnishes grants and scholarships in recognition of teachers who provided a positive influence upon NFL players in elementary and secondary schools, September 20.

For the first time since 1957, every NFL club won at least one of its first four games, October 1.

NFL total paid attendance of 17,665,671 was the highest total in League history. The regular-season total paid attendance of 13,959,896 and average of 62,321 for 224 games were the highest ever, surpassing the previous records set in the 1989 season.

1991

The New York Giants defeated Buffalo 20-19 in Super Bowl XXV to capture their second title in five years. The game was played before a sellout crowd of 73,813 at Tampa Stadium and became the first Super Bowl decided by one point, January 26. The ABC broadcast of the game was seen by more than 112-million people in the United States and was seen live or taped in 60 other countries.

NFL playoff games earned the top television rating spot of the week for each week of the month-long playoffs, January 29.

A total of 693 players shared in the postseason pool of $14.9 million.

New York businessman Robert Tisch purchased a 50 percent interest in the New York Giants from Mrs. Helen Mara Nugent and her children, Tim Mara and Maura Mara Concannon, February 2.

Commissioner Tagliabue named Neil Austrian to the newly created position of President of the NFL to be chief operating officer for League-wide business and financial operations, February 27.

NFL clubs voted to continue a limited system of Instant Replay for the sixth consecutive year. The vote was 21-7, March 19.

The NFL launched the World League of American Football, the first sports league to operate on a weekly basis on two separate continents, March 23.

NFL Charities presented a $250,000 donation to the United Service Organization. The donation was the second largest single grant ever by NFL Charities, April 5.

Commissioner Tagliabue named Harold Henderson as Executive Vice President for Labor Relations and Chairman of the NFL Management Council Executive Committee, April 8.

Russell Maryland, a University of Miami defensive lineman, was selected by Dallas, becoming the first player chosen in the 1991 NFL draft, April 21.

NFL clubs approved a recommendation by the Expansion and Realignment Committee to add two teams for the 1994 season, resulting in six divisions of five teams each, May 22.

NFL clubs awarded Super Bowl XXIX, to be played on January 29, 1995, to Miami, May 23.

"NFL International Week" featured six 1990 playoff teams playing nationally televised games in London, Berlin, and Tokyo on July 28 and August 3-4. The games drew more than 150,000 fans.

Paul Brown, founder of the Cleveland Browns and Cincinnati Bengals, died at age 82, August 5.

NFL clubs approved a resolution establishing an international division, reporting to the President of the NFL. A three-year financial plan for the World League was approved by NFL clubs at a meeting in Dallas, October 23.

1992

The NFL agreed to provide a minimum of $2.5 million in financial support to the NFL Alumni Association and assistance to NFL Alumni-related programs. The agreement included contributions from NFL Charities to the Pre-59ers and Dire Need Programs for former players, January 25.

The Washington Redskins defeated the Buffalo Bills 37-24 in Super Bowl XXVI to capture their third world championship in 10 years, January 26. The game was played before a sellout crowd of 63,130 at the Hubert H. Humphrey Metrodome in Minneapolis and attracted the second largest television audience in Super Bowl history. The CBS broadcast was seen by more than 123 million people nationally, second only to the 127 million who viewed Super Bowl XX.

For the third consecutive season, NFL total paid attendance reached a record level. Total paid attendance was 17,752,139 for the 296 preseason, regular-season, and postseason games, February 3.

The use in officiating of a limited system of Instant Replay for a seventh consecutive year was not approved. The vote was 17-11 in favor of approval (21 votes were required), March 18.

Steve Emtman, a University of Washington defensive lineman, was selected by Indianapolis, becoming the first player chosen in the 1992 NFL draft, April 26.

St. Louis businessman James Orthwein purchased controlling interest in the New England Patriots from Victor Kiam, May 11.

In a Harris Poll taken during the NFL offseason, professional football again was declared the nation's most popular sport. Professional football finished atop similar surveys conducted by Harris in 1985 and 1989, May 23.

NFL clubs accepted the report of the Expansion Committee at a league meeting in Pasadena. The report names five cities as finalists for the two expansion teams—Baltimore, Charlotte, Jacksonville, Memphis, and St. Louis, May 19.

At a league meeting in Dallas, NFL clubs approved a proposal by the World League Board of Directors to restructure the World League and place future emphasis on its international success, September 17.

1993

The NFL and lawyers for the players announced a settlement of various lawsuits and an agreement on the terms of a seven-year deal that included a new player system to be in place through the 1999 season, January 6.

Commissioner Tagliabue announced the establishment of the "NFL World Partnership Program" to develop amateur football internationally through a series of clinics conducted by former NFL players and coaches, January 14.

As part of Super Bowl XXVII, the NFL announced the creation of the first NFL Youth Education Town, a facility located in south central Los Angeles for inner city youth. January 25.

The Dallas Cowboys defeated the Buffalo Bills 52-17 in Super Bowl XXVII to capture their first NFL title since 1978. The game was played before a crowd of 98,374 at the Rose Bowl in Pasadena, California. The NBC broadcast of the game was the most watched program in television history and was seen by 133,400,000 people in the United States. The game also was seen live or taped in 101 other countries. The rating for the game was 45.1, the tenth highest for any televised sports event, January 31.

A total of 695 players shared in the postseason pool of $14.9 million, February 15.

For the fourth consecutive season, the NFL total paid attendance reached a record level. Total paid attendance was 17,784,354 for the 296 preseason, regular-season, and postseason games, March 4.

NFL clubs awarded Super Bowl XXX to the city of Phoenix, to be played on January 28, 1996, at Sun Devil Stadium, March 23.

Drew Bledsoe, a quarterback from Washington State, was selected by New England, becoming the first player chosen in the 1993 NFL draft, April 25.

The NFL and the NFL Players Association officially signed a 7-year Collective Bargaining Agreement in Washington, D.C., which guarantees more than $1 billion in pension, health, and post-career benefits for current and retired players—the most extensive benefits plan in pro sports. It was the NFL's first CBA since the 1982 agreement expired in 1987, June 29.

Ron Bernard was named president of NFL Enterprises, a newly formed division of the NFL responsible for NFL Films, home video, and special domestic and international television programming, August 19.

NFL announced plans to allow fans, for the first time ever, to join players and coaches in selecting the annual AFC and NFC Pro Bowl teams, October 12.

NFL clubs unanimously awarded the league's twenty-ninth franchise to the Carolina Panthers at a meeting in Chicago. NFL clubs also awarded Super Bowl XXXI to New Orleans and Super Bowl XXXII to San Diego, October 26.

At the same meeting in Chicago, NFL clubs approved a plan to form a European league with joint venture partners, October 27.

Don Shula became the winningest coach in NFL history when Miami beat Philadelphia to give Shula his 325th victory, one more than George Halas, November 14.

NFL clubs awarded the league's thirtieth franchise to the Jacksonville Jaguars at a meeting in Chicago, November 30.

The NFL announced new 4-year television agreements with ABC, ESPN, TNT, and NFL newcomer FOX, which took over the NFC package from CBS, December 18.

The NFL completed its new TV agreements by announcing that NBC would retain the rights to the AFC package, December 20.

1994

The NFL announced that a regular-season paid attendance record was set in 1993. Attendance averaged 62,354, topping the previous record of 62,321 set in 1990, January 6.

The Dallas Cowboys defeated the Buffalo Bills 30-13 in Super Bowl XXVIII to become the fifth team to win back-to-back Super Bowl titles. The game was viewed by the largest U.S. audience in television history—134.8 million people. The game's 45.5 rating was the highest for a Super Bowl since 1987 and the tenth highest-rated Super Bowl ever, January 30.

NFL clubs unanimously approved the transfer of the New England Patriots from James Orthwein to Robert Kraft at a meeting in Orlando, February 22.

In an effort to increase offensive production, NFL clubs at the league's annual meeting in Orlando adopted a package of changes, including modifications in line play, chucking rules, and the roughing-the-passer rule, plus the adoption of the two-point conversion and moving the spot of the kickoff back to the 30-yard line, March 22.

NFL clubs approved the transfer of the majority interest in the Miami Dolphins from the Robbie family to H. Wayne Huizenga, March 23.

The NFL and FOX announced the formation of a joint venture to create a six-team World League to begin play in Europe in April, 1995, March 23.

The NFL announced a total paid attendance record for the fifth consecutive year, with 17,951,831 in paid attendance for all 1993 games, March 23.

Dan Wilkinson, a defensive tackle from Ohio State, was selected by Cincinnati as the first overall selection in the draft, April 24.

The Carolina Panthers earned the right to select first in the 1995 NFL draft by winning a coin toss with the Jacksonville Jaguars. The Jaguars received the second selection in the 1995 draft, April 24.

NFL clubs approved the transfer of the Philadelphia Eagles from Norman Braman to Jeffrey Lurie, May 6.

The NFL launched "NFL Sunday Ticket," a new season subscription service for satellite television dish owners, June 1.

Sara Levinson, president/business director of MTV, was named president of NFL Properties, July 12.

An all-time NFL record crowd of 112,376 attended the American Bowl game between Dallas and Houston in Mexico City. It concluded the biggest American Bowl series in NFL history with four games attracting a record 256,666 fans, August 15.

The NFL 75th Anniversary All-Time Team was announced at a press conference at Radio City Music Hall, August 30.

The NFL reached agreement on a new seven-year contract with its game officials, September 22.

The NFL Management Council and the NFL Players Association announced an agreement on the formulation and implementation of the most comprehensive drug and alcohol policy in sports, October 28.

At an NFL meeting in Chicago, Commissioner Tagliabue slotted the two new expansion teams into the AFC Central (Jacksonville Jaguars) and NFC West (Carolina Panthers) for the 1995 season only. He also appointed a special committee on realignment to make recommendations on the 1996 season and beyond, November 2.

The NFL set a regular-season paid attendance record for the second consecutive year, topping 14 million for the first time (14,034,977), December 27.

1995

The San Francisco 49ers became the first team to win five Super Bowls when they defeated the San Diego Chargers 49-26 in Super Bowl XXIX at Joe Robbie Stadium in Miami, January 29.

Carolina and Jacksonville stocked their expansion rosters with a total of 66 players from other NFL teams in a veteran player allocation draft in New York, February 16.

CBS Radio and the NFL agreed to a new four-year contract for an annual 53-game package of games, continuing a relationship that spanned 15 of the past 17 years, February 22.

NFL total paid attendance for all 1994 season games reached a record level for the sixth consecutive year, exceeding 18 million for the first time (18,010,264), March 9.

NFL clubs approved the transfer of the Tampa Bay Buccaneers from the estate of the late Hugh Culverhouse to South Florida businessman Malcolm Glazer, March 13.

A total of $20.3 million, the largest NFL postseason pool ever, was divided among 729 players who participated in the 1994 playoffs, March 13.

A series of safety-related rules changes were adopted at a league meeting in Phoenix, primarily related to the use of the helmet against defenseless players, March 14.

After a two-year hiatus, the World League of American Football returned to action with six teams in Europe, April 8.

The NFL became the first major sports league to establish a site on the Internet system of on-line computer communication, April 10.

The transfer of the Rams from Los Angeles to St. Louis was approved by a vote of the NFL clubs at a meeting in Dallas, April 12.

ABC's *NFL Monday Night Football* finished the 1994-95 television season as the fifth highest-rated show out of 146 with a 17.8 average rating, the highest finish in the 25-year history of the series, April 18.

Ki-Jana Carter, a running back from Penn State, was selected by the Cincinnati Bengals as the first overall selection in the draft, April 22.

In an ABC News Poll taken during the NFL offseason, America's sports fans chose football as their favorite spectator sport by more than a 2-to-1 margin over basketball and baseball (35%-16%-12%), April 26.

The Frankfurt Galaxy defeated the Amsterdam Admirals 26-22 to win the 1995 World Bowl before a crowd of 23,847 in Amsterdam's Olympic Stadium, June 23.

Former NFL quarterback and Rhein Fire general manager Oliver Luck was named President of the World League, July 13.

The transfer of the Raiders from Los Angeles to Oakland was approved by a vote of the NFL clubs at a meeting in Chicago, July 22.

Jacksonville Municipal Stadium opened before a sold-out crowd of more than 70,000 for the first preseason game in Jaguars history, August 18.

NFL Charities and 50 NFL players donated $1 million to the United Negro College Fund in honor of the fiftieth anniversary of the UNCF and the integration of the modern NFL, September 15.

The Pro Football Hall Of Fame in Canton, Ohio, completed an $8.9 million expansion including a $4 million contribution by the NFL clubs, October 14.

The Trans World Dome opened in St. Louis before a sold-out crowd of 65,598 as the Rams defeated the Carolina Panthers 28-17, November 12.

NFL paid attendance totaled 963,521 for 15 games in Week 15, the highest weekend total in the league's 76-year history, November 19-20.

On the field, many significant records and milestones were achieved: Miami's Dan Marino surpassed Pro Football Hall of Famer Fran Tarkenton in four major passing categories—attempts, completions, yards, and touchdowns—to become the NFL's all-time career leader. San Francisco's Jerry Rice became the all-time reception and receiving-yardage leader with career totals of 942 catches and 15,123 yards. Dallas' Emmitt Smith scored 25 touchdowns, breaking the season record of 24 set by Washington's John Riggins in 1983.

1996

The Dallas Cowboys won their third Super Bowl title in four years when they defeated the Pittsburgh Steelers 27-17 in Super Bowl XXX at Sun Devil Stadium in Tempe, Arizona. The game was viewed by the largest audience in U.S. television history—138.5 million people, January 28.

An agreement between the NFL and the city of Cleveland regarding the Cleveland Browns' relocation was approved by a vote of the NFL clubs, February 9. According to the agreement, the city of Cleveland retained the Browns' heritage and records, including the name, logo, colors, history, playing records, trophies, and memorabilia, and committed to building a new 72,000-seat stadium for a reactivated Browns' franchise to begin play there no later than 1999. Art Modell received approval to move his franchise to Baltimore and rename it.

NFL total paid attendance for all 1995 games reached a record level for the seventh consecutive year, exceeding 19 million for the first time (19,202,757), March 7.

A total of $21.5 million, the largest NFL postseason pool ever, was divided among 717 players who participated in the 1995 playoffs, March 11.

Keyshawn Johnson, a wide receiver from Southern California, was selected by the New York Jets as the first overall selection in the draft, April 20.

The transfer of the Oilers from Houston to Nashville for the 1998 season was approved by a vote of the NFL clubs at a meeting in Atlanta, April 30.

NFL COMMISSIONERS AND PRESIDENTS*

1920 ....Jim Thorpe, President
1921-39................Joe Carr, President
1939-41 ....Carl Storck, President
1941-46 ....Elmer Layden, Commissioner
1946-59 ....Bert Bell, Commissioner
1960-89 ....Pete Rozelle, Commissioner
1989-present..............Paul Tagliabue, Commissioner

**NFL treasurer Austin Gunsel served as president in the office of the commissioner following the death of Bert Bell (Oct. 11, 1959) until the election of Pete Rozelle (Jan. 26, 1960).*

1995

AMERICAN CONFERENCE

Eastern Division

	W	L	T	Pct.	Pts.	OP
Buffalo	10	6	0	.625	350	335
Indianapolis*	9	7	0	.563	331	316
Miami*	9	7	0	.563	398	332
New England	6	10	0	.375	294	377
N.Y. Jets	3	13	0	.188	233	384

Central Division

	W	L	T	Pct.	Pts.	OP
Pittsburgh	11	5	0	.688	407	327
Cincinnati	7	9	0	.438	349	374
Houston	7	9	0	.438	348	324
Cleveland	5	11	0	.313	289	356
Jacksonville	4	12	0	.250	275	404

Western Division

	W	L	T	Pct.	Pts.	OP
Kansas City	13	3	0	.813	358	241
San Diego*	9	7	0	.563	321	323
Seattle	8	8	0	.500	363	366
Denver	8	8	0	.500	388	345
Oakland	8	8	0	.500	348	332

NATIONAL CONFERENCE

Eastern Division

	W	L	T	Pct.	Pts.	OP
Dallas	12	4	0	.750	435	291
Philadelphia*	10	6	0	.625	318	338
Washington	6	10	0	.375	326	359
N.Y. Giants	5	11	0	.313	290	340
Arizona	4	12	0	.250	275	422

Central Division

	W	L	T	Pct.	Pts.	OP
Green Bay	11	5	0	.688	404	314
Detroit*	10	6	0	.625	436	336
Chicago	9	7	0	.563	392	360
Minnesota	8	8	0	.500	412	385
Tampa Bay	7	9	0	.438	238	335

Western Division

	W	L	T	Pct.	Pts.	OP
San Francisco	11	5	0	.688	457	258
Atlanta*	9	7	0	.563	362	349
St. Louis	7	9	0	.438	309	418
Carolina	7	9	0	.438	289	325
New Orleans	7	9	0	.438	319	348

**Wild-Card qualifier for playoffs*

Indianapolis finished ahead of Miami based on head-to-head sweep (2-0). San Diego was first Wild Card based on head-to-head victory over Indianapolis (1-0). Cincinnati finished ahead of Houston based on better division record (4-4 to Oilers' 3-5). Seattle finished ahead of Denver and Oakland based on best head-to-head record (3-1 to Broncos' 2-2 and Raiders' 1-3). Denver finished ahead of Oakland based on head-to-head sweep (2-0). Philadelphia was first Wild Card ahead of Detroit based on better conference record (9-3 to Lions' 7-5). Atlanta was third Wild Card ahead of Chicago based on better record against common opponents (4-2 to Bears' 3-3). St. Louis finished ahead of Carolina and New Orleans based on best head-to-head record (3-1 to Panthers' 1-3 and Saints' 2-2). Carolina finished ahead of New Orleans based on better conference record (4-8 to 3-9).

Wild-Card playoffs: BUFFALO 37, Miami 22; Indianapolis 35, SAN DIEGO 20
Divisional playoffs: PITTSBURGH 40, Buffalo 21; Indianapolis 10, KANSAS CITY 7
AFC championship: PITTSBURGH 20, Indianapolis 16
Wild-Card playoffs: PHILADELPHIA 58, Detroit 37; GREEN BAY 37, Atlanta 20
Divisional playoffs: Green Bay 27, SAN FRANCISCO 17; DALLAS 30, Philadelphia 11
NFC championship: DALLAS 38, Green Bay 27
Super Bowl XXX: Dallas (NFC) 27, Pittsburgh (AFC)17, at Sun Devil Stadium, Tempe, Arizona.

In Past Standings section, home teams in playoff games are indicated by capital letters.

1994

AMERICAN CONFERENCE

Eastern Division

	W	L	T	Pct.	Pts.	OP
Miami	10	6	0	.625	389	327
New England*	10	6	0	.625	351	312
Indianapolis	8	8	0	.500	307	320
Buffalo	7	9	0	.438	340	356
N.Y. Jets	6	10	0	.375	264	320

Central Division

	W	L	T	Pct.	Pts.	OP
Pittsburgh	12	4	0	.750	316	234
Cleveland*	11	5	0	.688	340	204
Cincinnati	3	13	0	.188	276	406
Houston	2	14	0	.125	226	352

Western Division

	W	L	T	Pct.	Pts.	OP
San Diego	11	5	0	.688	381	306
Kansas City*	9	7	0	.563	319	298
L.A. Raiders	9	7	0	.563	303	327
Denver	7	9	0	.438	347	396
Seattle	6	10	0	.375	287	323

NATIONAL CONFERENCE

Eastern Division

	W	L	T	Pct.	Pts.	OP
Dallas	12	4	0	.750	414	248
N.Y. Giants	9	7	0	.563	279	305
Arizona	8	8	0	.500	235	267
Philadelphia	7	9	0	.438	308	308
Washington	3	13	0	.188	320	412

Central Division

	W	L	T	Pct.	Pts.	OP
Minnesota	10	6	0	.625	356	314
Green Bay*	9	7	0	.563	382	287
Detroit*	9	7	0	.563	357	342
Chicago*	9	7	0	.563	271	307
Tampa Bay	6	10	0	.375	251	351

Western Division

	W	L	T	Pct.	Pts.	OP
San Francisco	13	3	0	.813	505	296
New Orleans	7	9	0	.438	348	407
Atlanta	7	9	0	.438	317	385
L.A. Rams	4	12	0	.250	286	365

**Wild-Card qualifier for playoffs*

Miami finished ahead of New England based on a head-to-head sweep (2-0). Kansas City finished ahead of L.A. Raiders based on a head-to-head sweep (2-0). Green Bay was first Wild Card based on best head-to-head record (3-1) vs. Detroit (2-2) and Chicago (1-3) and better conference record (8-4) than N.Y. Giants (6-6). Detroit was second Wild Card based on better division record (4-4) than Chicago (3-5) and head-to-head sweep of N.Y. Giants (1-0). Chicago was third Wild Card based on better record vs. common opponents (4-4) than N.Y. Giants (3-5). New Orleans finished ahead of Atlanta based on a head-to-head sweep (2-0).

Wild-Card playoffs: MIAMI 27, Kansas City 17; CLEVELAND 20, New England 13
Divisional playoffs: PITTSBURGH 29, Cleveland 9; SAN DIEGO 22, Miami 21
AFC championship: San Diego 17, PITTSBURGH 13
Wild-Card playoffs: GREEN BAY 16, Detroit 12; Chicago 35, MINNESOTA 18
Divisional playoffs: SAN FRANCISCO 44, Chicago 15; DALLAS 35, Green Bay 9
NFC championship: SAN FRANCISCO 38, Dallas 28
Super Bowl XXIX: San Francisco (NFC) 49, San Diego (AFC) 26, at Joe Robbie Stadium, Miami, Florida

1993

AMERICAN CONFERENCE

Eastern Division

	W	L	T	Pct.	Pts.	OP
Buffalo	12	4	0	.750	329	242
Miami	9	7	0	.563	349	351
N.Y. Jets	8	8	0	.500	270	247
New England	5	11	0	.313	238	286
Indianapolis	4	12	0	.250	189	378

Central Division

	W	L	T	Pct.	Pts.	OP
Houston	12	4	0	.750	368	238
Pittsburgh*	9	7	0	.563	308	281
Cleveland	7	9	0	.438	304	307
Cincinnati	3	13	0	.188	187	319

Western Division

	W	L	T	Pct.	Pts.	OP
Kansas City	11	5	0	.688	328	291
L.A. Raiders*	10	6	0	.625	306	326
Denver*	9	7	0	.563	373	284
San Diego	8	8	0	.500	322	290
Seattle	6	10	0	.375	280	314

NATIONAL CONFERENCE

Eastern Division

	W	L	T	Pct.	Pts.	OP
Dallas	12	4	0	.750	376	229
N.Y. Giants*	11	5	0	.688	288	205
Philadelphia	8	8	0	.500	293	315
Phoenix	7	9	0	.438	326	269
Washington	4	12	0	.250	230	345

Central Division

	W	L	T	Pct.	Pts.	OP
Detroit	10	6	0	.625	298	292
Minnesota*	9	7	0	.563	277	290
Green Bay*	9	7	0	.563	340	282
Chicago	7	9	0	.438	234	230
Tampa Bay	5	11	0	.313	237	376

Western Division

	W	L	T	Pct.	Pts.	OP
San Francisco	10	6	0	.625	473	295
New Orleans	8	8	0	.500	317	343
Atlanta	6	10	0	.375	316	385
L.A. Rams	5	11	0	.313	221	367

**Wild-Card qualifier for playoffs*

Minnesota finished ahead of Green Bay based on a head-to-head sweep (2-0).

Wild-Card playoffs: KANSAS CITY 27, Pittsburgh 24 (OT); L.A. RAIDERS 42, Denver 24
Divisional playoffs: BUFFALO 29, L.A. Raiders 23; Kansas City 28, HOUSTON 20
AFC championship: BUFFALO 30, Kansas City 13
Wild-Card playoffs: Green Bay 28, DETROIT 24; N.Y. GIANTS 17, Minnesota 10
Divisional playoffs: SAN FRANCISCO 44, N.Y. Giants 3; DALLAS 27, Green Bay 17
NFC championship: DALLAS 38, San Francisco 21
Super Bowl XXVIII: Dallas (NFC) 30, Buffalo (AFC) 13, at Georgia Dome, Atlanta, Georgia

1992

AMERICAN CONFERENCE

Eastern Division

	W	L	T	Pct.	Pts.	OP
Miami	11	5	0	.688	340	281
Buffalo*	11	5	0	.688	381	283
Indianapolis	9	7	0	.563	216	302
N.Y. Jets	4	12	0	.250	220	315
New England	2	14	0	.125	205	363

Central Division

	W	L	T	Pct.	Pts.	OP
Pittsburgh	11	5	0	.688	299	225
Houston*	10	6	0	.625	352	258
Cleveland	7	9	0	.438	272	275
Cincinnati	5	11	0	.313	274	364

Western Division

	W	L	T	Pct.	Pts.	OP
San Diego	11	5	0	.688	335	241
Kansas City*	10	6	0	.625	348	282
Denver	8	8	0	.500	262	329
L.A. Raiders	7	9	0	.438	249	281
Seattle	2	14	0	.125	140	312

NATIONAL CONFERENCE

Eastern Division

	W	L	T	Pct.	Pts.	OP
Dallas	13	3	0	.813	409	243
Philadelphia*	11	5	0	.688	354	245
Washington*	9	7	0	.563	300	255
N.Y. Giants	6	10	0	.375	306	367
Phoenix	4	12	0	.250	243	332

Central Division

	W	L	T	Pct.	Pts.	OP
Minnesota	11	5	0	.688	374	249
Green Bay	9	7	0	.563	276	296
Tampa Bay	5	11	0	.313	267	365
Chicago	5	11	0	.313	295	361
Detroit	5	11	0	.313	273	332

Western Division

	W	L	T	Pct.	Pts.	OP
San Francisco	14	2	0	.875	431	236
New Orleans*	12	4	0	.750	330	202
Atlanta	6	10	0	.375	327	414
L.A. Rams	6	10	0	.375	313	383

**Wild-Card qualifier for playoffs*

Miami finished ahead of Buffalo based on better conference record (9-3 to 7-5). Tampa Bay finished ahead of Chicago and Detroit based on better conference record (5-9 to Bears' 4-8 and Lions' 3-9). Atlanta finished ahead of L.A. Rams based on better record versus common opponents (5-7 to 4-8).

Wild-Card playoffs: SAN DIEGO 17, Kansas City 0; BUFFALO 41, Houston 38 (OT)
Divisional playoffs: Buffalo 24, PITTSBURGH 3; MIAMI 31, San Diego 0
AFC championship: Buffalo 29, MIAMI 10
Wild-Card playoffs: Washington 24, MINNESOTA 7; Philadelphia 36, NEW ORLEANS 20
Divisional playoffs: SAN FRANCISCO 20, Washington 13; DALLAS 34, Philadelphia 10
NFC championship: Dallas 30, SAN FRANCISCO 20
Super Bowl XXVII: Dallas (NFC) 52, Buffalo (AFC) 17, at Rose Bowl, Pasadena, California.

PAST STANDINGS

1991

AMERICAN CONFERENCE

Eastern Division

	W	L	T	Pct.	Pts.	OP
Buffalo	13	3	0	.813	458	318
N.Y. Jets*	8	8	0	.500	314	293
Miami	8	8	0	.500	343	349
New England	6	10	0	.375	211	305
Indianapolis	1	15	0	.063	143	381

Central Division

	W	L	T	Pct.	Pts.	OP
Houston	11	5	0	.688	386	251
Pittsburgh	7	9	0	.438	292	344
Cleveland	6	10	0	.375	293	298
Cincinnati	3	13	0	.188	263	435

Western Division

	W	L	T	Pct.	Pts.	OP
Denver	12	4	0	.750	304	235
Kansas City*	10	6	0	.625	322	252
L.A. Raiders*	9	7	0	.563	298	297
Seattle	7	9	0	.438	276	261
San Diego	4	12	0	.250	274	342

NATIONAL CONFERENCE

Eastern Division

	W	L	T	Pct.	Pts.	OP
Washington	14	2	0	.875	485	224
Dallas*	11	5	0	.688	342	310
Philadelphia	10	6	0	.625	285	244
N.Y. Giants	8	8	0	.500	281	297
Phoenix	4	12	0	.250	196	344

Central Division

	W	L	T	Pct.	Pts.	OP
Detroit	12	4	0	.750	339	295
Chicago*	11	5	0	.688	299	269
Minnesota	8	8	0	.500	301	306
Green Bay	4	12	0	.250	273	313
Tampa Bay	3	13	0	.188	199	365

Western Division

	W	L	T	Pct.	Pts.	OP
New Orleans	11	5	0	.688	341	211
Atlanta*	10	6	0	.625	361	338
San Francisco	10	6	0	.625	393	239
L.A. Rams	3	13	0	.188	234	390

**Wild-Card qualifiers for playoffs*

New York Jets finished ahead of Miami based on head-to-head sweep (2-0). Atlanta finished ahead of San Francisco based on head-to-head sweep (2-0).

Wild-Card playoffs: KANSAS CITY 10, L.A. Raiders 6;
HOUSTON 17, N.Y. Jets 10

Divisional playoffs: DENVER 26, Houston 24; BUFFALO 37, Kansas City 14

AFC championship: BUFFALO 10, Denver 7

Wild-Card playoffs: Atlanta 27, NEW ORLEANS 20; Dallas 17, CHICAGO 13

Divisional playoffs: WASHINGTON 24, Atlanta 7; DETROIT 38, Dallas 6

NFC championship: WASHINGTON 41, Detroit 10

Super Bowl XXVI: Washington (NFC) 37, Buffalo (AFC) 24, at Hubert H. Humphrey Metrodome, Minneapolis, Minnesota.

1990

AMERICAN CONFERENCE

Eastern Division

	W	L	T	Pct.	Pts.	OP
Buffalo	13	3	0	.813	428	263
Miami*	12	4	0	.750	336	242
Indianapolis	7	9	0	.438	281	353
N.Y. Jets	6	10	0	.375	295	345
New England	1	15	0	.063	181	446

Central Division

	W	L	T	Pct.	Pts.	OP
Cincinnati	9	7	0	.563	360	352
Houston*	9	7	0	.563	405	307
Pittsburgh	9	7	0	.563	292	240
Cleveland	3	13	0	.188	228	462

Western Division

	W	L	T	Pct.	Pts.	OP
L.A. Raiders	12	4	0	.750	337	268
Kansas City*	11	5	0	.688	369	257
Seattle	9	7	0	.563	306	286
San Diego	6	10	0	.375	315	281
Denver	5	11	0	.313	331	374

NATIONAL CONFERENCE

Eastern Division

	W	L	T	Pct.	Pts.	OP
N.Y. Giants	13	3	0	.813	335	211
Philadelphia*	10	6	0	.625	396	299
Washington*	10	6	0	.625	381	301
Dallas	7	9	0	.438	244	308
Phoenix	5	11	0	.313	268	396

Central Division

	W	L	T	Pct.	Pts.	OP
Chicago	11	5	0	.688	348	280
Tampa Bay	6	10	0	.375	264	367
Detroit	6	10	0	.375	373	413
Green Bay	6	10	0	.375	271	347
Minnesota	6	10	0	.375	351	326

Western Division

	W	L	T	Pct.	Pts.	OP
San Francisco	14	2	0	.875	353	239
New Orleans*	8	8	0	.500	274	275
L.A. Rams	5	11	0	.313	345	412
Atlanta	5	11	0	.313	348	365

**Wild-Card qualifiers for playoffs*

Cincinnati won AFC Central title based on best head-to-head record (3-1) vs. Houston (2-2) and Pittsburgh (1-3). Houston was Wild Card based on better conference record (8-4) than Seattle (7-5) and Pittsburgh (6-6). Philadelphia finished second in the NFC East based on better division record (5-3) than Washington (4-4). Tampa Bay was second in NFC Central based on 5-1 record vs. Detroit, Green Bay, and Minnesota. Detroit finished third based on best net division points (minus 8) vs. Green Bay (minus 40) in fourth. Minnesota was fifth based on 4-8 conference record. The Los Angeles Rams finished third in NFC West based on net points in division (plus 1) vs. Atlanta (minus 31).

Wild-Card playoffs: MIAMI 17, Kansas City 16; CINCINNATI 41, Houston 14

Divisional playoffs: BUFFALO 44, Miami 34; L.A. RAIDERS 20, Cincinnati 10

AFC championship: BUFFALO 51, L.A. Raiders 3

Wild-Card playoffs: Washington 20, PHILADELPHIA 6; CHICAGO 16, New Orleans 6

Divisional playoffs: SAN FRANCISCO 28, Washington 10; N.Y. GIANTS 31, Chicago 3

NFC championship: N.Y. Giants 15, SAN FRANCISCO 13

Super Bowl XXV: N.Y. Giants (NFC) 20, Buffalo (AFC) 19, at Tampa Stadium, Tampa, Florida.

1989

AMERICAN CONFERENCE

Eastern Division

	W	L	T	Pct.	Pts.	OP
Buffalo	9	7	0	.563	409	317
Indianapolis	8	8	0	.500	298	301
Miami	8	8	0	.500	331	379
New England	5	11	0	.313	297	391
N.Y. Jets	4	12	0	.250	253	411

Central Division

	W	L	T	Pct.	Pts.	OP
Cleveland	9	6	1	.594	334	254
Houston*	9	7	0	.563	365	412
Pittsburgh*	9	7	0	.563	265	326
Cincinnati	8	8	0	.500	404	285

Western Division

	W	L	T	Pct.	Pts.	OP
Denver	11	5	0	.688	362	226
Kansas City	8	7	1	.531	318	286
L.A. Raiders	8	8	0	.500	315	297
Seattle	7	9	0	.438	241	327
San Diego	6	10	0	.375	266	290

NATIONAL CONFERENCE

Eastern Division

	W	L	T	Pct.	Pts.	OP
N.Y. Giants	12	4	0	.750	348	252
Philadelphia*	11	5	0	.688	342	274
Washington	10	6	0	.625	386	308
Phoenix	5	11	0	.313	258	377
Dallas	1	15	0	.063	204	393

Central Division

	W	L	T	Pct.	Pts.	OP
Minnesota	10	6	0	.625	351	275
Green Bay	10	6	0	.625	362	356
Detroit	7	9	0	.438	312	364
Chicago	6	10	0	.375	358	377
Tampa Bay	5	11	0	.313	320	419

Western Division

	W	L	T	Pct.	Pts.	OP
San Francisco	14	2	0	.875	442	253
L.A. Rams*	11	5	0	.688	426	344
New Orleans	9	7	0	.563	386	301
Atlanta	3	13	0	.188	279	437

**Wild-Card qualifiers for playoffs*

Indianapolis finished ahead of Miami in AFC East because of better conference record (7-5 vs. 6-8). Houston finished ahead of Pittsburgh in AFC Central because of head-to-head sweep (2-0). Minnesota finished ahead of Green Bay in NFC Central because of better division record (6-2 vs. 5-3).

Wild-Card playoff: Pittsburgh 26, HOUSTON 23 (OT)

Divisional playoffs: CLEVELAND 34, Buffalo 30; DENVER 24, Pittsburgh 23

AFC championship: DENVER 37, Cleveland 21

Wild-Card playoff: L.A. Rams 21, PHILADELPHIA 7

Divisional playoffs: L.A. Rams 19, N.Y. GIANTS 13 (OT);
SAN FRANCISCO 41, Minnesota 13

NFC championship: SAN FRANCISCO 30, L.A. Rams 3

Super Bowl XXIV: San Francisco (NFC) 55, Denver (AFC) 10, at Louisiana Superdome, New Orleans, Louisiana.

1988

AMERICAN CONFERENCE

Eastern Division

	W	L	T	Pct.	Pts.	OP
Buffalo	12	4	0	.750	329	237
Indianapolis	9	7	0	.563	354	315
New England	9	7	0	.563	250	284
N.Y. Jets	8	7	1	.531	372	354
Miami	6	10	0	.375	319	380

Central Division

	W	L	T	Pct.	Pts.	OP
Cincinnati	12	4	0	.750	448	329
Cleveland*	10	6	0	.625	304	288
Houston*	10	6	0	.625	424	365
Pittsburgh	5	11	0	.313	336	421

Western Division

	W	L	T	Pct.	Pts.	OP
Seattle	9	7	0	.563	339	329
Denver	8	8	0	.500	327	352
L.A. Raiders	7	9	0	.438	325	369
San Diego	6	10	0	.375	231	332
Kansas City	4	11	1	.281	254	320

NATIONAL CONFERENCE

Eastern Division

	W	L	T	Pct.	Pts.	OP
Philadelphia	10	6	0	.625	379	319
N.Y. Giants	10	6	0	.625	359	304
Washington	7	9	0	.438	345	387
Phoenix	7	9	0	.438	344	398
Dallas	3	13	0	.188	265	381

Central Division

	W	L	T	Pct.	Pts.	OP
Chicago	12	4	0	.750	312	215
Minnesota*	11	5	0	.688	406	233
Tampa Bay	5	11	0	.313	261	350
Detroit	4	12	0	.250	220	313
Green Bay	4	12	0	.250	240	315

Western Division

	W	L	T	Pct.	Pts.	OP
San Francisco	10	6	0	.625	369	294
L.A. Rams*	10	6	0	.625	407	293
New Orleans	10	6	0	.625	312	283
Atlanta	5	11	0	.313	244	315

**Wild-Card qualifiers for playoffs*

Indianapolis finished second in AFC East on basis of better record versus common opponents (7-5) over New England (6-6). Cleveland gained first AFC Wild-Card position based on better division record (4-2) over Houston (3-3). Philadelphia finished first in NFC East on basis of head-to-head sweep over New York Giants. Washington finished third in NFC East on basis of better division record (4-4) over Phoenix (3-5). Detroit finished fourth in NFC Central on basis of head-to-head sweep over Green Bay. San Francisco finished first in NFC West based on better head-to-head record (3-1) over Los Angeles Rams (2-2) and New Orleans (1-3). Los Angeles Rams finished second in NFC West on basis of better division record (4-2) over New Orleans (3-3) and earned Wild-Card position based on better conference record (8-4) over New York Giants (9-5) and New Orleans (6-6).

Wild-Card playoff: Houston 24, CLEVELAND 23

Divisional playoffs: CINCINNATI 21, Seattle 13; BUFFALO 17, Houston 10

AFC championship: CINCINNATI 21, Buffalo 10

Wild-Card playoff: MINNESOTA 28, Los Angeles Rams 17

Divisional playoffs: CHICAGO 20, Philadelphia 12;
SAN FRANCISCO 34, Minnesota 9

NFC championship: San Francisco 28, CHICAGO 3

Super Bowl XXIII: San Francisco (NFC) 20, Cincinnati (AFC) 16, at Joe Robbie Stadium, Miami, Florida.

1987

AMERICAN CONFERENCE

Eastern Division

	W	L	T	Pct.	Pts.	OP
Indianapolis	9	6	0	.600	300	238
New England	8	7	0	.533	320	293
Miami	8	7	0	.533	362	335
Buffalo	7	8	0	.467	270	305
N.Y. Jets	6	9	0	.400	334	360

Central Division

	W	L	T	Pct.	Pts.	OP
Cleveland	10	5	0	.667	390	239
Houston*	9	6	0	.600	345	349
Pittsburgh	8	7	0	.533	285	299
Cincinnati	4	11	0	.267	285	370

Western Division

	W	L	T	Pct.	Pts.	OP
Denver	10	4	1	.700	379	288
Seattle*	9	6	0	.600	371	314
San Diego	8	7	0	.533	253	317
L.A. Raiders	5	10	0	.333	301	289
Kansas City	4	11	0	.267	273	388

NATIONAL CONFERENCE

Eastern Division

	W	L	T	Pct.	Pts.	OP
Washington	11	4	0	.733	379	285
Dallas	7	8	0	.467	340	348
St. Louis	7	8	0	.467	362	368
Philadelphia	7	8	0	.467	337	380
N.Y. Giants	6	9	0	.400	280	312

Central Division

	W	L	T	Pct.	Pts.	OP
Chicago	11	4	0	.733	356	282
Minnesota*	8	7	0	.533	336	335
Green Bay	5	9	1	.367	255	300
Tampa Bay	4	11	0	.267	286	360
Detroit	4	11	0	.267	269	384

Western Division

	W	L	T	Pct.	Pts.	OP
San Francisco	13	2	0	.867	459	253
New Orleans*	12	3	0	.800	422	283
L.A. Rams	6	9	0	.400	317	361
Atlanta	3	12	0	.200	205	436

**Wild-Card qualifiers for playoffs*

Houston gained first AFC Wild-Card position on better conference record (7-4) over Seattle (5-6).

Wild-Card playoff: HOUSTON 23, Seattle 20 (OT)

Divisional playoffs: CLEVELAND 38, Indianapolis 21; DENVER 34, Houston 10

AFC championship: DENVER 38, Cleveland 33

Wild-Card playoff: Minnesota 44, NEW ORLEANS 10

Divisional playoffs: Minnesota 36, SAN FRANCISCO 24; Washington 21, CHICAGO 17

NFC championship: WASHINGTON 17, Minnesota 10

Super Bowl XXII: Washington (NFC) 42, Denver (AFC) 10, at San Diego Jack Murphy Stadium, San Diego, California.

Note: 1987 regular season was reduced from 16 to 15 games for each team due to players' strike.

1986

AMERICAN CONFERENCE

Eastern Division

	W	L	T	Pct.	Pts.	OP
New England	11	5	0	.688	412	307
N.Y. Jets*	10	6	0	.625	364	386
Miami	8	8	0	.500	430	405
Buffalo	4	12	0	.250	287	348
Indianapolis	3	13	0	.188	229	400

Central Division

	W	L	T	Pct.	Pts.	OP
Cleveland	12	4	0	.750	391	310
Cincinnati	10	6	0	.625	409	394
Pittsburgh	6	10	0	.375	307	336
Houston	5	11	0	.313	274	329

Western Division

	W	L	T	Pct.	Pts.	OP
Denver	11	5	0	.688	378	327
Kansas City*	10	6	0	.625	358	326
Seattle	10	6	0	.625	366	293
L.A. Raiders	8	8	0	.500	323	346
San Diego	4	12	0	.250	335	396

NATIONAL CONFERENCE

Eastern Division

	W	L	T	Pct.	Pts.	OP
N.Y. Giants	14	2	0	.875	371	236
Washington*	12	4	0	.750	368	296
Dallas	7	9	0	.438	346	337
Philadelphia	5	10	1	.344	256	312
St. Louis	4	11	1	.281	218	351

Central Division

	W	L	T	Pct.	Pts.	OP
Chicago	14	2	0	.875	352	187
Minnesota	9	7	0	.563	398	273
Detroit	5	11	0	.313	277	326
Green Bay	4	12	0	.250	254	418
Tampa Bay	2	14	0	.125	239	473

Western Division

	W	L	T	Pct.	Pts.	OP
San Francisco	10	5	1	.656	374	247
L.A. Rams*	10	6	0	.625	309	267
Atlanta	7	8	1	.469	280	280
New Orleans	7	9	0	.438	288	287

**Wild-Card qualifiers for playoffs*

New York Jets gained first AFC Wild-Card position on better conference record (8-4) over Kansas City (9-5), Seattle (7-5), and Cincinnati (7-5). Kansas City gained second Wild Card based on better conference record (9-5) over Seattle (7-5) and Cincinnati (7-5).

Wild-Card playoff: NEW YORK JETS 35, Kansas City 15

Divisional playoffs: CLEVELAND 23, New York Jets 20 (OT); DENVER 22, New England 17

AFC championship: Denver 23, CLEVELAND 20 (OT)

Wild-Card playoff: WASHINGTON 19, Los Angeles Rams 7

Divisional playoffs: Washington 27, CHICAGO 13; NEW YORK GIANTS 49, San Francisco 3

NFC championship: NEW YORK GIANTS 17, Washington 0

Super Bowl XXI: New York Giants (NFC) 39, Denver (AFC) 20, at Rose Bowl, Pasadena, California.

1985

AMERICAN CONFERENCE

Eastern Division

	W	L	T	Pct.	Pts.	OP
Miami	12	4	0	.750	428	320
N.Y. Jets*	11	5	0	.688	393	264
New England*	11	5	0	.688	362	290
Indianapolis	5	11	0	.313	320	386
Buffalo	2	14	0	.125	200	381

Central Division

	W	L	T	Pct.	Pts.	OP
Cleveland	8	8	0	.500	287	294
Cincinnati	7	9	0	.438	441	437
Pittsburgh	7	9	0	.438	379	355
Houston	5	11	0	.313	284	412

Western Division

	W	L	T	Pct.	Pts.	OP
L.A. Raiders	12	4	0	.750	354	308
Denver	11	5	0	.688	380	329
Seattle	8	8	0	.500	349	303
San Diego	8	8	0	.500	467	435
Kansas City	6	10	0	.375	317	360

NATIONAL CONFERENCE

Eastern Division

	W	L	T	Pct.	Pts.	OP
Dallas	10	6	0	.625	357	333
N.Y. Giants*	10	6	0	.625	399	283
Washington	10	6	0	.625	297	312
Philadelphia	7	9	0	.438	286	310
St. Louis	5	11	0	.313	278	414

Central Division

	W	L	T	Pct.	Pts.	OP
Chicago	15	1	0	.938	456	198
Green Bay	8	8	0	.500	337	355
Minnesota	7	9	0	.438	346	359
Detroit	7	9	0	.438	307	366
Tampa Bay	2	14	0	.125	294	448

Western Division

	W	L	T	Pct.	Pts.	OP
L.A. Rams	11	5	0	.688	340	277
San Francisco*	10	6	0	.625	411	263
New Orleans	5	11	0	.313	294	401
Atlanta	4	12	0	.250	282	452

**Wild-Card qualifiers for playoffs*

New York Jets gained first AFC Wild-Card position on better conference record (9-3) over New England (8-4) and Denver (8-4). New England gained second AFC Wild-Card position based on better record vs. common opponents (4-2) than Denver (3-3). Dallas won NFC Eastern Division title based on better record (4-0) vs. New York Giants (1-3) and Washington (1-3). New York Giants gained first NFC Wild Card position based on better conference record (8-4) over San Francisco (7-5) and Washington (6-6). San Francisco gained second NFC Wild-Card position based on head-to-head victory over Washington.

Wild-Card playoff: New England 26, NEW YORK JETS 14

Divisional playoffs: MIAMI 24, Cleveland 21; New England 27, LOS ANGELES RAIDERS 20

AFC championship: New England 31, MIAMI 14

Wild-Card playoff: NEW YORK GIANTS 17, San Francisco 3

Divisional playoffs: LOS ANGELES RAMS 20, Dallas 0; CHICAGO 21, New York Giants 0

NFC championship: CHICAGO 24, Los Angeles Rams 0

Super Bowl XX: Chicago (NFC) 46, New England (AFC) 10, at Louisiana Superdome, New Orleans, Louisiana.

1984

AMERICAN CONFERENCE

Eastern Division

	W	L	T	Pct.	Pts.	OP
Miami	14	2	0	.875	513	298
New England	9	7	0	.563	362	352
N.Y. Jets	7	9	0	.438	332	364
Indianapolis	4	12	0	.250	239	414
Buffalo	2	14	0	.125	250	454

Central Division

	W	L	T	Pct.	Pts.	OP
Pittsburgh	9	7	0	.563	387	310
Cincinnati	8	8	0	.500	339	339
Cleveland	5	11	0	.313	250	297
Houston	3	13	0	.188	240	437

Western Division

	W	L	T	Pct.	Pts.	OP
Denver	13	3	0	.813	353	241
Seattle*	12	4	0	.750	418	282
L.A. Raiders*	11	5	0	.688	368	278
Kansas City	8	8	0	.500	314	324
San Diego	7	9	0	.438	394	413

NATIONAL CONFERENCE

Eastern Division

	W	L	T	Pct.	Pts.	OP
Washington	11	5	0	.688	426	310
N.Y. Giants*	9	7	0	.563	299	301
St. Louis	9	7	0	.563	423	345
Dallas	9	7	0	.563	308	308
Philadelphia	6	9	1	.406	278	320

Central Division

	W	L	T	Pct.	Pts.	OP
Chicago	10	6	0	.625	325	248
Green Bay	8	8	0	.500	390	309
Tampa Bay	6	10	0	.375	335	380
Detroit	4	11	1	.281	283	408
Minnesota	3	13	0	.188	276	484

Western Division

	W	L	T	Pct.	Pts.	OP
San Francisco	15	1	0	.938	475	227
L.A. Rams*	10	6	0	.625	346	316
New Orleans	7	9	0	.438	298	361
Atlanta	4	12	0	.250	281	382

**Wild-Card qualifiers for playoffs*

New York Giants clinched Wild-Card berth based on 3-1 record vs. St. Louis's 2-2 and Dallas's 1-3. St. Louis finished ahead of Dallas based on better division record (5-3 to 3-5).

Wild-Card playoff: SEATTLE 13, Los Angeles Raiders 7

Divisional playoffs: MIAMI 31, Seattle 10; Pittsburgh 24, DENVER 17

AFC championship: MIAMI 45, Pittsburgh 28

Wild-Card playoff: New York Giants 16, LOS ANGELES RAMS 13

Divisional playoffs: SAN FRANCISCO 21, New York Giants 10; Chicago 23, WASHINGTON 19

NFC championship: SAN FRANCISCO 23, Chicago 0

Super Bowl XIX: San Francisco (NFC) 38, Miami (AFC) 16, at Stanford Stadium, Stanford, California.

PAST STANDINGS

1983

AMERICAN CONFERENCE

Eastern Division

	W	L	T	Pct.	Pts.	OP
Miami	12	4	0	.750	389	250
New England	8	8	0	.500	274	289
Buffalo	8	8	0	.500	283	351
Baltimore	7	9	0	.438	264	354
N.Y. Jets	7	9	0	.438	313	331

Central Division

	W	L	T	Pct.	Pts.	OP
Pittsburgh	10	6	0	.625	355	303
Cleveland	9	7	0	.563	356	342
Cincinnati	7	9	0	.438	346	302
Houston	2	14	0	.125	288	460

Western Division

	W	L	T	Pct.	Pts.	OP
L.A. Raiders	12	4	0	.750	442	338
Seattle*	9	7	0	.563	403	397
Denver*	9	7	0	.563	302	327
San Diego	6	10	0	.375	358	462
Kansas City	6	10	0	.375	386	367

NATIONAL CONFERENCE

Eastern Division

	W	L	T	Pct.	Pts.	OP
Washington	14	2	0	.875	541	332
Dallas*	12	4	0	.750	479	360
St. Louis	8	7	1	.531	374	428
Philadelphia	5	11	0	.313	233	322
N.Y. Giants	3	12	1	.219	267	347

Central Division

	W	L	T	Pct.	Pts.	OP
Detroit	9	7	0	.563	347	286
Green Bay	8	8	0	.500	429	439
Chicago	8	8	0	.500	311	301
Minnesota	8	8	0	.500	316	348
Tampa Bay	2	14	0	.125	241	380

Western Division

	W	L	T	Pct.	Pts.	OP
San Francisco	10	6	0	.625	432	293
L.A. Rams*	9	7	0	.563	361	344
New Orleans	8	8	0	.500	319	337
Atlanta	7	9	0	.438	370	389

**Wild-Card qualifiers for playoffs*

Seattle and Denver gained Wild-Card berths over Cleveland because of their victories over the Browns.

Wild-Card playoff: SEATTLE 31, Denver 7

Divisional playoffs: Seattle 27, MIAMI 20; LOS ANGELES RAIDERS 38, Pittsburgh 10

AFC championship: LOS ANGELES RAIDERS 30, Seattle 14

Wild-Card playoff: Los Angeles Rams 24, DALLAS 17

Divisional playoffs: SAN FRANCISCO 24, Detroit 23; WASHINGTON 51, L.A. Rams 7

NFC championship: WASHINGTON 24, San Francisco 21

Super Bowl XVIII: Los Angeles Raiders (AFC) 38, Washington (NFC) 9, at Tampa Stadium, Tampa, Florida.

1982

AMERICAN CONFERENCE

	W	L	T	Pct.	Pts.	OP
L.A. Raiders	8	1	0	.889	260	200
Miami	7	2	0	.778	198	131
Cincinnati	7	2	0	.778	232	177
Pittsburgh	6	3	0	.667	204	146
San Diego	6	3	0	.667	288	221
N.Y. Jets	6	3	0	.667	245	166
New England	5	4	0	.556	143	157
Cleveland	4	5	0	.444	140	182
Buffalo	4	5	0	.444	150	154
Seattle	4	5	0	.444	127	147
Kansas City	3	6	0	.333	176	184
Denver	2	7	0	.222	148	226
Houston	1	8	0	.111	136	245
Baltimore	0	8	1	.056	113	236

NATIONAL CONFERENCE

	W	L	T	Pct.	Pts.	OP
Washington	8	1	0	.889	190	128
Dallas	6	3	0	.667	226	145
Green Bay	5	3	1	.611	226	169
Minnesota	5	4	0	.556	187	198
Atlanta	5	4	0	.556	183	199
St. Louis	5	4	0	.556	135	170
Tampa Bay	5	4	0	.556	158	178
Detroit	4	5	0	.444	181	176
New Orleans	4	5	0	.444	129	160
N.Y. Giants	4	5	0	.444	164	160
San Francisco	3	6	0	.333	209	206
Chicago	3	6	0	.333	141	174
Philadelphia	3	6	0	.333	191	195
L.A. Rams	2	7	0	.222	200	250

As the result of a 57-day players' strike, the 1982 NFL regular season schedule was reduced from 16 weeks to 9. At the conclusion of the regular season, the NFL conducted a 16-team postseason Super Bowl Tournament. Eight teams from each conference were seeded 1-8 based on their records during the season.

Miami finished ahead of Cincinnati based on better conference record (6-1 to 6-2). Pittsburgh won common games tie-breaker with San Diego (3-1 to 2-1) after New York Jets were eliminated from three-way tie based on conference record (Pittsburgh and San Diego 5-3 vs. Jets 2-3). Cleveland finished ahead of Buffalo and Seattle based on better conference record (4-3 to 3-3 to 3-5). Minnesota (4-1), Atlanta (4-3), St. Louis (5-4), Tampa Bay (3-3) seeds were determined by best won-lost record in conference games. Detroit finished ahead of New Orleans and the New York Giants based on better conference record (4-4 to 3-5 to 3-5).

First round playoff: MIAMI 28, New England 13
LOS ANGELES RAIDERS 27, Cleveland 10
New York Jets 44, CINCINNATI 17
San Diego 31, PITTSBURGH 28

Second round playoff: New York Jets 17, LOS ANGELES RAIDERS 14
MIAMI 34, San Diego 13

AFC championship: MIAMI 14, New York Jets 0

First round playoff: WASHINGTON 31, Detroit 7
GREEN BAY 41, St. Louis 16
MINNESOTA 30, Atlanta 24
DALLAS 30, Tampa Bay 17

Second round playoff: WASHINGTON 21, Minnesota 7
DALLAS 37, Green Bay 26

NFC championship: WASHINGTON 31, Dallas 17

Super Bowl XVII: Washington (NFC) 27, Miami (AFC) 17, at Rose Bowl, Pasadena, California.

1981

AMERICAN CONFERENCE

Eastern Division

	W	L	T	Pct.	Pts.	OP
Miami	11	4	1	.719	345	275
N.Y. Jets*	10	5	1	.656	355	287
Buffalo*	10	6	0	.625	311	276
Baltimore	2	14	0	.125	259	533
New England	2	14	0	.125	322	370

Central Division

	W	L	T	Pct.	Pts.	OP
Cincinnati	12	4	0	.750	421	304
Pittsburgh	8	8	0	.500	356	297
Houston	7	9	0	.438	281	355
Cleveland	5	11	0	.313	276	375

Western Division

	W	L	T	Pct.	Pts.	OP
San Diego	10	6	0	.625	478	390
Denver	10	6	0	.625	321	289
Kansas City	9	7	0	.563	343	290
Oakland	7	9	0	.438	273	343
Seattle	6	10	0	.375	322	388

NATIONAL CONFERENCE

Eastern Division

	W	L	T	Pct.	Pts.	OP
Dallas	12	4	0	.750	367	277
Philadelphia*	10	6	0	.625	368	221
N.Y. Giants*	9	7	0	.563	295	257
Washington	8	8	0	.500	347	349
St. Louis	7	9	0	.438	315	408

Central Division

	W	L	T	Pct.	Pts.	OP
Tampa Bay	9	7	0	.563	315	268
Detroit	8	8	0	.500	397	322
Green Bay	8	8	0	.500	324	361
Minnesota	7	9	0	.438	325	369
Chicago	6	10	0	.375	253	324

Western Division

	W	L	T	Pct.	Pts.	OP
San Francisco	13	3	0	.813	357	250
Atlanta	7	9	0	.438	426	355
Los Angeles	6	10	0	.375	303	351
New Orleans	4	12	0	.250	207	378

**Wild-Card qualifiers for playoffs*

San Diego won AFC Western title over Denver on the basis of a better division record (6-2 to 5-3). Buffalo won a Wild-Card playoff berth over Denver as the result of a 9-7 victory in head-to-head competition.

Wild-Card playoff: Buffalo 31, NEW YORK JETS 27

Divisional playoffs: San Diego 41, MIAMI 38 (OT); CINCINNATI 28, Buffalo 21

AFC championship: CINCINNATI 27, San Diego 7

Wild-Card playoff: New York Giants 27, PHILADELPHIA 21

Divisional playoffs: DALLAS 38, Tampa Bay 0; SAN FRANCISCO 38, New York Giants 24

NFC championship: SAN FRANCISCO 28, Dallas 27

Super Bowl XVI: San Francisco (NFC) 26, Cincinnati (AFC) 21, at Silverdome, Pontiac, Michigan.

1980

AMERICAN CONFERENCE

Eastern Division

	W	L	T	Pct.	Pts.	OP
Buffalo	11	5	0	.688	320	260
New England	10	6	0	.625	441	325
Miami	8	8	0	.500	266	305
Baltimore	7	9	0	.438	355	387
N.Y. Jets	4	12	0	.250	302	395

Central Division

	W	L	T	Pct.	Pts.	OP
Cleveland	11	5	0	.688	357	310
Houston*	11	5	0	.688	295	251
Pittsburgh	9	7	0	.563	352	313
Cincinnati	6	10	0	.375	244	312

Western Division

	W	L	T	Pct.	Pts.	OP
San Diego	11	5	0	.688	418	327
Oakland*	11	5	0	.688	364	306
Kansas City	8	8	0	.500	319	336
Denver	8	8	0	.500	310	323
Seattle	4	12	0	.250	291	408

NATIONAL CONFERENCE

Eastern Division

	W	L	T	Pct.	Pts.	OP
Philadelphia	12	4	0	.750	384	222
Dallas*	12	4	0	.750	454	311
Washington	6	10	0	.375	261	293
St. Louis	5	11	0	.313	299	350
N.Y. Giants	4	12	0	.250	249	425

Central Division

	W	L	T	Pct.	Pts.	OP
Minnesota	9	7	0	.563	317	308
Detroit	9	7	0	.563	334	272
Chicago	7	9	0	.438	304	264
Tampa Bay	5	10	1	.344	271	341
Green Bay	5	10	1	.344	231	371

Western Division

	W	L	T	Pct.	Pts.	OP
Atlanta	12	4	0	.750	405	272
Los Angeles*	11	5	0	.688	424	289
San Francisco	6	10	0	.375	320	415
New Orleans	1	15	0	.063	291	487

**Wild-Card qualifiers for playoffs*

Philadelphia won division title over Dallas on the basis of best net points in division games (plus 84 net points to plus 50). Minnesota won division title because of a better conference record than Detroit (8-4 to 9-5). Cleveland won division title because of a better conference record than Houston (8-4 to 7-5). San Diego won division title over Oakland on the basis of best net points in division games (plus 60 net points to plus 37).

Wild-Card playoff: OAKLAND 27, Houston 7

Divisional playoffs: SAN DIEGO 20, Buffalo 14; Oakland 14, CLEVELAND 12

AFC championship: Oakland 34, SAN DIEGO 27

Wild-Card playoff: DALLAS 34, Los Angeles 13

Divisional playoffs: PHILADELPHIA 31, Minnesota 16; Dallas 30, ATLANTA 27

NFC championship: PHILADELPHIA 20, Dallas 7

Super Bowl XV: Oakland (AFC) 27, Philadelphia (NFC) 10, at Louisiana Superdome, New Orleans, Louisiana.

1979

AMERICAN CONFERENCE

Eastern Division

	W	L	T	Pct.	Pts.	OP
Miami	10	6	0	.625	341	257
New England	9	7	0	.563	411	326
N.Y. Jets	8	8	0	.500	337	383
Buffalo	7	9	0	.438	268	279
Baltimore	5	11	0	.313	271	351

Central Division

	W	L	T	Pct.	Pts.	OP
Pittsburgh	12	4	0	.750	416	262
Houston*	11	5	0	.688	362	331
Cleveland	9	7	0	.563	359	352
Cincinnati	4	12	0	.250	337	421

Western Division

	W	L	T	Pct.	Pts.	OP
San Diego	12	4	0	.750	411	246
Denver*	10	6	0	.625	289	262
Seattle	9	7	0	.563	378	372
Oakland	9	7	0	.563	365	337
Kansas City	7	9	0	.438	238	262

NATIONAL CONFERENCE

Eastern Division

	W	L	T	Pct.	Pts.	OP
Dallas	11	5	0	.688	371	313
Philadelphia*	11	5	0	.688	339	282
Washington	10	6	0	.625	348	295
N.Y. Giants	6	10	0	.375	237	323
St. Louis	5	11	0	.313	307	358

Central Division

	W	L	T	Pct.	Pts.	OP
Tampa Bay	10	6	0	.625	273	237
Chicago*	10	6	0	.625	306	249
Minnesota	7	9	0	.438	259	337
Green Bay	5	11	0	.313	246	316
Detroit	2	14	0	.125	219	365

Western Division

	W	L	T	Pct.	Pts.	OP
Los Angeles	9	7	0	.563	323	309
New Orleans	8	8	0	.500	370	360
Atlanta	6	10	0	.375	300	388
San Francisco	2	14	0	.125	308	416

**Wild-Card qualifiers for playoffs*

Dallas won division title because of a better conference record than Philadelphia (10-2 to 9-3). Tampa Bay won division title because of a better division record than Chicago (6-2 to 5-3). Chicago won a Wild-Card berth over Washington on the basis of best net points in all games (plus 57 net points to plus 53).

Wild-Card playoff: HOUSTON 13, Denver 7
Divisional playoffs: Houston 17, SAN DIEGO 14; PITTSBURGH 34, Miami 14
AFC championship: PITTSBURGH 27, Houston 13
Wild-Card playoff: PHILADELPHIA 27, Chicago 17
Divisional playoffs: TAMPA BAY 24, Philadelphia 17; Los Angeles 21, DALLAS 19
NFC championship: Los Angeles 9, TAMPA BAY 0
Super Bowl XIV: Pittsburgh (AFC) 31, Los Angeles (NFC) 19, at Rose Bowl, Pasadena, California.

1978

AMERICAN CONFERENCE

Eastern Division

	W	L	T	Pct.	Pts.	OP
New England	11	5	0	.688	358	286
Miami*	11	5	0	.688	372	254
N.Y. Jets	8	8	0	.500	359	364
Buffalo	5	11	0	.313	302	354
Baltimore	5	11	0	.313	239	421

Central Division

	W	L	T	Pct.	Pts.	OP
Pittsburgh	14	2	0	.875	356	195
Houston*	10	6	0	.625	283	298
Cleveland	8	8	0	.500	334	356
Cincinnati	4	12	0	.250	252	284

Western Division

	W	L	T	Pct.	Pts.	OP
Denver	10	6	0	.625	282	198
Oakland	9	7	0	.563	311	283
Seattle	9	7	0	.563	345	358
San Diego	9	7	0	.563	355	309
Kansas City	4	12	0	.250	243	327

NATIONAL CONFERENCE

Eastern Division

	W	L	T	Pct.	Pts.	OP
Dallas	12	4	0	.750	384	208
Philadelphia*	9	7	0	.563	270	250
Washington	8	8	0	.500	273	283
St. Louis	6	10	0	.375	248	296
N.Y. Giants	6	10	0	.375	264	298

Central Division

	W	L	T	Pct.	Pts.	OP
Minnesota	8	7	1	.531	294	306
Green Bay	8	7	1	.531	249	269
Detroit	7	9	0	.438	290	300
Chicago	7	9	0	.438	253	274
Tampa Bay	5	11	0	.313	241	259

Western Division

	W	L	T	Pct.	Pts.	OP
Los Angeles	12	4	0	.750	316	245
Atlanta*	9	7	0	.563	240	290
New Orleans	7	9	0	.438	281	298
San Francisco	2	14	0	.125	219	350

**Wild-Card qualifiers for playoffs*

New England won division title on the basis of a better division record than Miami (6-2 to 5-3). Minnesota won division title because of a better head-to-head record against Green Bay (1-0-1).

Wild-Card playoff: Houston 17, MIAMI 9
Divisional playoffs: Houston 31, NEW ENGLAND 14; PITTSBURGH 33, Denver 10
AFC championship: PITTSBURGH 34, Houston 5
Wild-Card playoff: ATLANTA 14, Philadelphia 13
Divisional playoffs: DALLAS 27, Atlanta 20; LOS ANGELES 34, Minnesota 10
NFC championship: Dallas 28, LOS ANGELES 0
Super Bowl XIII: Pittsburgh (AFC) 35, Dallas (NFC) 31, at Orange Bowl, Miami, Florida.

1977

AMERICAN CONFERENCE

Eastern Division

	W	L	T	Pct.	Pts.	OP
Baltimore	10	4	0	.714	295	221
Miami	10	4	0	.714	313	197
New England	9	5	0	.643	278	217
N.Y. Jets	3	11	0	.214	191	300
Buffalo	3	11	0	.214	160	313

Central Division

	W	L	T	Pct.	Pts.	OP
Pittsburgh	9	5	0	.643	283	243
Houston	8	6	0	.571	299	230
Cincinnati	8	6	0	.571	238	235
Cleveland	6	8	0	.429	269	267

Western Division

	W	L	T	Pct.	Pts.	OP
Denver	12	2	0	.857	274	148
Oakland*	11	3	0	.786	351	230
San Diego	7	7	0	.500	222	205
Seattle	5	9	0	.357	282	373
Kansas City	2	12	0	.143	225	349

NATIONAL CONFERENCE

Eastern Division

	W	L	T	Pct.	Pts.	OP
Dallas	12	2	0	.857	345	212
Washington	9	5	0	.643	196	189
St. Louis	7	7	0	.500	272	287
Philadelphia	5	9	0	.357	220	207
N.Y. Giants	5	9	0	.357	181	265

Central Division

	W	L	T	Pct.	Pts.	OP
Minnesota	9	5	0	.643	231	227
Chicago*	9	5	0	.643	255	253
Detroit	6	8	0	.429	183	252
Green Bay	4	10	0	.286	134	219
Tampa Bay	2	12	0	.143	103	223

Western Division

	W	L	T	Pct.	Pts.	OP
Los Angeles	10	4	0	.714	302	146
Atlanta	7	7	0	.500	179	129
San Francisco	5	9	0	.357	220	260
New Orleans	3	11	0	.214	232	336

**Wild-Card qualifier for playoffs*

Baltimore won division title on the basis of a better conference record than Miami (9-3 to 8-4). Chicago won a Wild-Card berth over Washington on the basis of best net points in conference games (plus 48 net points to plus 4).

Divisional playoffs: DENVER 34, Pittsburgh 21; Oakland 37, BALTIMORE 31 (OT)
AFC championship: DENVER 20, Oakland 17
Divisional playoffs: DALLAS 37, Chicago 7; Minnesota 14, LOS ANGELES 7
NFC championship: DALLAS 23, Minnesota 6
Super Bowl XII: Dallas (NFC) 27, Denver (AFC) 10, at Louisiana Superdome, New Orleans, Louisiana.

1976

AMERICAN CONFERENCE

Eastern Division

	W	L	T	Pct.	Pts.	OP
Baltimore	11	3	0	.786	417	246
New England*	11	3	0	.786	376	236
Miami	6	8	0	.429	263	264
N.Y. Jets	3	11	0	.214	169	383
Buffalo	2	12	0	.143	245	363

Central Division

	W	L	T	Pct.	Pts.	OP
Pittsburgh	10	4	0	.714	342	138
Cincinnati	10	4	0	.714	335	210
Cleveland	9	5	0	.643	267	287
Houston	5	9	0	.357	222	273

Western Division

	W	L	T	Pct.	Pts.	OP
Oakland	13	1	0	.929	350	237
Denver	9	5	0	.643	315	206
San Diego	6	8	0	.429	248	285
Kansas City	5	9	0	.357	290	376
Tampa Bay	0	14	0	.000	125	412

NATIONAL CONFERENCE

Eastern Division

	W	L	T	Pct.	Pts.	OP
Dallas	11	3	0	.786	296	194
Washington*	10	4	0	.714	291	217
St. Louis	10	4	0	.714	309	267
Philadelphia	4	10	0	.286	165	286
N.Y. Giants	3	11	0	.214	170	250

Central Division

	W	L	T	Pct.	Pts.	OP
Minnesota	11	2	1	.821	305	176
Chicago	7	7	0	.500	253	216
Detroit	6	8	0	.429	262	220
Green Bay	5	9	0	.357	218	299

Western Division

	W	L	T	Pct.	Pts.	OP
Los Angeles	10	3	1	.750	351	190
San Francisco	8	6	0	.571	270	190
Atlanta	4	10	0	.286	172	312
New Orleans	4	10	0	.286	253	346
Seattle	2	12	0	.143	229	429

**Wild-Card qualifier for playoffs*

Baltimore won division title on the basis of a better division record than New England (7-1 to 6-2). Pittsburgh won division title because of a two-game sweep over Cincinnati. Washington won Wild-Card berth over St. Louis because of a two-game sweep over Cardinals.

Divisional playoffs: OAKLAND 24, New England 21; Pittsburgh 40, BALTIMORE 14
AFC championship: OAKLAND 24, Pittsburgh 7
Divisional playoffs: MINNESOTA 35, Washington 20; Los Angeles 14, DALLAS 12
NFC championship: MINNESOTA 24, Los Angeles 13
Super Bowl XI: Oakland (AFC) 32, Minnesota (NFC) 14, at Rose Bowl, Pasadena, California.

PAST STANDINGS

1975

AMERICAN CONFERENCE

Eastern Division

	W	L	T	Pct.	Pts.	OP
Baltimore	10	4	0	.714	395	269
Miami	10	4	0	.714	357	222
Buffalo	8	6	0	.571	420	355
New England	3	11	0	.214	258	358
N.Y. Jets	3	11	0	.214	258	433

Central Division

	W	L	T	Pct.	Pts.	OP
Pittsburgh	12	2	0	.857	373	162
Cincinnati*	11	3	0	.786	340	246
Houston	10	4	0	.714	293	226
Cleveland	3	11	0	.214	218	372

Western Division

	W	L	T	Pct.	Pts.	OP
Oakland	11	3	0	.786	375	255
Denver	6	8	0	.429	254	307
Kansas City	5	9	0	.357	282	341
San Diego	2	12	0	.143	189	345

NATIONAL CONFERENCE

Eastern Division

	W	L	T	Pct.	Pts.	OP
St. Louis	11	3	0	.786	356	276
Dallas*	10	4	0	.714	350	268
Washington	8	6	0	.571	325	276
N.Y. Giants	5	9	0	.357	216	306
Philadelphia	4	10	0	.286	225	302

Central Division

	W	L	T	Pct.	Pts.	OP
Minnesota	12	2	0	.857	377	180
Detroit	7	7	0	.500	245	262
Chicago	4	10	0	.286	191	379
Green Bay	4	10	0	.286	226	285

Western Division

	W	L	T	Pct.	Pts.	OP
Los Angeles	12	2	0	.857	312	135
San Francisco	5	9	0	.357	255	286
Atlanta	4	10	0	.286	240	289
New Orleans	2	12	0	.143	165	360

**Wild-Card qualifier for playoffs*

Baltimore won division title on the basis of a two-game sweep over Miami.

Divisional playoffs: PITTSBURGH 28, Baltimore 10; OAKLAND 31, Cincinnati 28

AFC championship: PITTSBURGH 16, Oakland 10

Divisional playoffs: LOS ANGELES 35, St. Louis 23; Dallas 17, MINNESOTA 14

NFC championship: Dallas 37, LOS ANGELES 7

Super Bowl X: Pittsburgh (AFC) 21, Dallas (NFC) 17, at Orange Bowl, Miami, Florida.

1974

AMERICAN CONFERENCE

Eastern Division

	W	L	T	Pct.	Pts.	OP
Miami	11	3	0	.786	327	216
Buffalo*	9	5	0	.643	264	244
New England	7	7	0	.500	348	289
N.Y. Jets	7	7	0	.500	279	300
Baltimore	2	12	0	.143	190	329

Central Division

	W	L	T	Pct.	Pts.	OP
Pittsburgh	10	3	1	.750	305	189
Cincinnati	7	7	0	.500	283	259
Houston	7	7	0	.500	236	282
Cleveland	4	10	0	.286	251	344

Western Division

	W	L	T	Pct.	Pts.	OP
Oakland	12	2	0	.857	355	228
Denver	7	6	1	.536	302	294
Kansas City	5	9	0	.357	233	293
San Diego	5	9	0	.357	212	285

NATIONAL CONFERENCE

Eastern Division

	W	L	T	Pct.	Pts.	OP
St. Louis	10	4	0	.714	285	218
Washington*	10	4	0	.714	320	196
Dallas	8	6	0	.571	297	235
Philadelphia	7	7	0	.500	242	217
N.Y. Giants	2	12	0	.143	195	299

Central Division

	W	L	T	Pct.	Pts.	OP
Minnesota	10	4	0	.714	310	195
Detroit	7	7	0	.500	256	270
Green Bay	6	8	0	.429	210	206
Chicago	4	10	0	.286	152	279

Western Division

	W	L	T	Pct.	Pts.	OP
Los Angeles	10	4	0	.714	263	181
San Francisco	6	8	0	.429	226	236
New Orleans	5	9	0	.357	166	263
Atlanta	3	11	0	.214	111	271

**Wild-Card qualifier for playoffs*

St. Louis won division title because of a two-game sweep over Washington.

Divisional playoffs: OAKLAND 28, Miami 26; PITTSBURGH 32, Buffalo 14

AFC championship: Pittsburgh 24, OAKLAND 13

Divisional playoffs: MINNESOTA 30, St. Louis 14; LOS ANGELES 19, Washington 10

NFC championship: MINNESOTA 14, Los Angeles 10

Super Bowl IX: Pittsburgh (AFC) 16, Minnesota (NFC) 6, at Tulane Stadium, New Orleans, Louisiana.

1973

AMERICAN CONFERENCE

Eastern Division

	W	L	T	Pct.	Pts.	OP
Miami	12	2	0	.857	343	150
Buffalo	9	5	0	.643	259	230
New England	5	9	0	.357	258	300
Baltimore	4	10	0	.286	226	341
N.Y. Jets	4	10	0	.286	240	306

Central Division

	W	L	T	Pct.	Pts.	OP
Cincinnati	10	4	0	.714	286	231
Pittsburgh*	10	4	0	.714	347	210
Cleveland	7	5	2	.571	234	255
Houston	1	13	0	.071	199	447

Western Division

	W	L	T	Pct.	Pts.	OP
Oakland	9	4	1	.679	292	175
Denver	7	5	2	.571	354	296
Kansas City	7	5	2	.571	231	192
San Diego	2	11	1	.179	188	386

NATIONAL CONFERENCE

Eastern Division

	W	L	T	Pct.	Pts.	OP
Dallas	10	4	0	.714	382	203
Washington*	10	4	0	.714	325	198
Philadelphia	5	8	1	.393	310	393
St. Louis	4	9	1	.321	286	365
N.Y. Giants	2	11	1	.179	226	362

Central Division

	W	L	T	Pct.	Pts.	OP
Minnesota	12	2	0	.857	296	168
Detroit	6	7	1	.464	271	247
Green Bay	5	7	2	.429	202	259
Chicago	3	11	0	.214	195	334

Western Division

	W	L	T	Pct.	Pts.	OP
Los Angeles	12	2	0	.857	388	178
Atlanta	9	5	0	.643	318	224
New Orleans	5	9	0	.357	163	312
San Francisco	5	9	0	.357	262	319

**Wild-Card qualifier for playoffs*

Cincinnati won division title on the basis of a better conference record than Pittsburgh (8-3 to 7-4). Dallas won division title on the basis of a better point differential vs. Washington (net 13 points).

Divisional playoffs: OAKLAND 33, Pittsburgh 14; MIAMI 34, Cincinnati 16

AFC championship: MIAMI 27, Oakland 10

Divisional playoffs: MINNESOTA 27, Washington 20; DALLAS 27, Los Angeles 16

NFC championship: Minnesota 27, DALLAS 10

Super Bowl VIII: Miami (AFC) 24, Minnesota (NFC) 7, at Rice Stadium, Houston, Texas.

1972

AMERICAN CONFERENCE

Eastern Division

	W	L	T	Pct.	Pts.	OP
Miami	14	0	0	1.000	385	171
N.Y. Jets	7	7	0	.500	367	324
Baltimore	5	9	0	.357	235	252
Buffalo	4	9	1	.321	257	377
New England	3	11	0	.214	192	446

Central Division

	W	L	T	Pct.	Pts.	OP
Pittsburgh	11	3	0	.786	343	175
Cleveland*	10	4	0	.714	268	249
Cincinnati	8	6	0	.571	299	229
Houston	1	13	0	.071	164	380

Western Division

	W	L	T	Pct.	Pts.	OP
Oakland	10	3	1	.750	365	248
Kansas City	8	6	0	.571	287	254
Denver	5	9	0	.357	325	350
San Diego	4	9	1	.321	264	344

NATIONAL CONFERENCE

Eastern Division

	W	L	T	Pct.	Pts.	OP
Washington	11	3	0	.786	336	218
Dallas*	10	4	0	.714	319	240
N.Y. Giants	8	6	0	.571	331	247
St. Louis	4	9	1	.321	193	303
Philadelphia	2	11	1	.179	145	352

Central Division

	W	L	T	Pct.	Pts.	OP
Green Bay	10	4	0	.714	304	226
Detroit	8	5	1	.607	339	290
Minnesota	7	7	0	.500	301	252
Chicago	4	9	1	.321	225	275

Western Division

	W	L	T	Pct.	Pts.	OP
San Francisco	8	5	1	.607	353	249
Atlanta	7	7	0	.500	269	274
Los Angeles	6	7	1	.464	291	286
New Orleans	2	11	1	.179	215	361

**Wild-Card qualifier for playoffs*

Divisional playoffs: PITTSBURGH 13, Oakland 7; MIAMI 20, Cleveland 14

AFC championship: Miami 21, PITTSBURGH 17

Divisional playoffs: Dallas 30, SAN FRANCISCO 28; WASHINGTON 16, Green Bay 3

NFC championship: WASHINGTON 26, Dallas 3

Super Bowl VII: Miami (AFC) 14, Washington (NFC) 7, at Memorial Coliseum, Los Angeles, California.

1971

AMERICAN CONFERENCE

Eastern Division

	W	L	T	Pct.	Pts.	OP
Miami	10	3	1	.769	315	174
Baltimore*	10	4	0	.714	313	140
New England	6	8	0	.429	238	325
N.Y. Jets	6	8	0	.429	212	299
Buffalo	1	13	0	.071	184	394

Central Division

	W	L	T	Pct.	Pts.	OP
Cleveland	9	5	0	.643	285	273
Pittsburgh	6	8	0	.429	246	292
Houston	4	9	1	.308	251	330
Cincinnati	4	10	0	.286	284	265

Western Division

	W	L	T	Pct.	Pts.	OP
Kansas City	10	3	1	.769	302	208
Oakland	8	4	2	.667	344	278
San Diego	6	8	0	.429	311	341
Denver	4	9	1	.308	203	275

NATIONAL CONFERENCE

Eastern Division

	W	L	T	Pct.	Pts.	OP
Dallas	11	3	0	.786	406	222
Washington*	9	4	1	.692	276	190
Philadelphia	6	7	1	.462	221	302
St. Louis	4	9	1	.308	231	279
N.Y. Giants	4	10	0	.286	228	362

Central Division

	W	L	T	Pct.	Pts.	OP
Minnesota	11	3	0	.786	245	139
Detroit	7	6	1	.538	341	286
Chicago	6	8	0	.429	185	276
Green Bay	4	8	2	.333	274	298

Western Division

	W	L	T	Pct.	Pts.	OP
San Francisco	9	5	0	.643	300	216
Los Angeles	8	5	1	.615	313	260
Atlanta	7	6	1	.538	274	277
New Orleans	4	8	2	.333	266	347

**Wild-Card qualifier for playoffs*

Divisional playoffs: Miami 27, KANSAS CITY 24 (OT); Baltimore 20, CLEVELAND 3

AFC championship: MIAMI 21, Baltimore 0

Divisional playoffs: Dallas 20, MINNESOTA 12; SAN FRANCISCO 24, Washington 20

NFC championship: DALLAS 14, San Francisco 3

Super Bowl VI: Dallas (NFC) 24, Miami (AFC) 3, at Tulane Stadium, New Orleans, Louisiana.

1970

AMERICAN CONFERENCE

Eastern Division

	W	L	T	Pct.	Pts.	OP
Baltimore	11	2	1	.846	321	234
Miami*	10	4	0	.714	297	228
N.Y. Jets	4	10	0	.286	255	286
Buffalo	3	10	1	.231	204	337
Boston Patriots	2	12	0	.143	149	361

Central Division

	W	L	T	Pct.	Pts.	OP
Cincinnati	8	6	0	.571	312	255
Cleveland	7	7	0	.500	286	265
Pittsburgh	5	9	0	.357	210	272
Houston	3	10	1	.231	217	352

Western Division

	W	L	T	Pct.	Pts.	OP
Oakland	8	4	2	.667	300	293
Kansas City	7	5	2	.583	272	244
San Diego	5	6	3	.455	282	278
Denver	5	8	1	.385	253	264

NATIONAL CONFERENCE

Eastern Division

	W	L	T	Pct.	Pts.	OP
Dallas	10	4	0	.714	299	221
N.Y. Giants	9	5	0	.643	301	270
St. Louis	8	5	1	.615	325	228
Washington	6	8	0	.429	297	314
Philadelphia	3	10	1	.231	241	332

Central Division

	W	L	T	Pct.	Pts.	OP
Minnesota	12	2	0	.857	335	143
Detroit*	10	4	0	.714	347	202
Chicago	6	8	0	.429	256	261
Green Bay	6	8	0	.429	196	293

Western Division

	W	L	T	Pct.	Pts.	OP
San Francisco	10	3	1	.769	352	267
Los Angeles	9	4	1	.692	325	202
Atlanta	4	8	2	.333	206	261
New Orleans	2	11	1	.154	172	347

**Wild-Card qualifier for playoffs*

Divisional playoffs: BALTIMORE 17, Cincinnati 0; OAKLAND 21, Miami 14

AFC championship: BALTIMORE 27, Oakland 17

Divisional playoffs: DALLAS 5, Detroit 0; San Francisco 17, MINNESOTA 14

NFC championship: Dallas 17, SAN FRANCISCO 10

Super Bowl V: Baltimore (AFC) 16, Dallas (NFC) 13, at Orange Bowl, Miami, Florida.

1969 NFL

EASTERN CONFERENCE

Capitol Division

	W	L	T	Pct.	Pts.	OP
Dallas	11	2	1	.846	369	223
Washington	7	5	2	.583	307	319
New Orleans	5	9	0	.357	311	393
Philadelphia	4	9	1	.308	279	377

Century Division

	W	L	T	Pct.	Pts.	OP
Cleveland	10	3	1	.769	351	300
N.Y. Giants	6	8	0	.429	264	298
St. Louis	4	9	1	.308	314	389
Pittsburgh	1	13	0	.071	218	404

WESTERN CONFERENCE

Coastal Division

	W	L	T	Pct.	Pts.	OP
Los Angeles	11	3	0	.786	320	243
Baltimore	8	5	1	.615	279	268
Atlanta	6	8	0	.429	276	268
San Francisco	4	8	2	.333	277	319

Central Division

	W	L	T	Pct.	Pts.	OP
Minnesota	12	2	0	.857	379	133
Detroit	9	4	1	.692	259	188
Green Bay	8	6	0	.571	269	221
Chicago	1	13	0	.071	210	339

Conference championships: Cleveland 38, DALLAS 14; MINNESOTA 23, Los Angeles 20

NFL championship: MINNESOTA 27, Cleveland 7

Super Bowl IV: Kansas City (AFL) 23, Minnesota (NFL) 7, at Tulane Stadium, New Orleans, Louisiana

1969 AFL

EASTERN DIVISION

	W	L	T	Pct.	Pts.	OP
N.Y. Jets	10	4	0	.714	353	269
Houston	6	6	2	.500	278	279
Boston Patriots	4	10	0	.286	266	316
Buffalo	4	10	0	.286	230	359
Miami	3	10	1	.231	233	332

WESTERN DIVISION

	W	L	T	Pct.	Pts.	OP
Oakland	12	1	1	.923	377	242
Kansas City	11	3	0	.786	359	177
San Diego	8	6	0	.571	288	276
Denver	5	8	1	.385	297	344
Cincinnati	4	9	1	.308	280	367

Divisional playoffs: Kansas City 13, N.Y. JETS 6; OAKLAND 56, Houston 7

AFL championship: Kansas City 17, OAKLAND 7

1968 NFL

EASTERN CONFERENCE

Capitol Division

	W	L	T	Pct.	Pts.	OP
Dallas	12	2	0	.857	431	186
N.Y. Giants	7	7	0	.500	294	325
Washington	5	9	0	.357	249	358
Philadelphia	2	12	0	.143	202	351

Century Division

	W	L	T	Pct.	Pts.	OP
Cleveland	10	4	0	.714	394	273
St. Louis	9	4	1	.692	325	289
New Orleans	4	9	1	.308	246	327
Pittsburgh	2	11	1	.154	244	397

WESTERN CONFERENCE

Coastal Division

	W	L	T	Pct.	Pts.	OP
Baltimore	13	1	0	.929	402	144
Los Angeles	10	3	1	.769	312	200
San Francisco	7	6	1	.538	303	310
Atlanta	2	12	0	.143	170	389

Central Division

	W	L	T	Pct.	Pts.	OP
Minnesota	8	6	0	.571	282	242
Chicago	7	7	0	.500	250	333
Green Bay	6	7	1	.462	281	227
Detroit	4	8	2	.333	207	241

Conference championships: CLEVELAND 31, Dallas 20; BALTIMORE 24, Minnesota 14

NFL championship: Baltimore 34, CLEVELAND 0

Super Bowl III: N.Y. Jets (AFL) 16, Baltimore (NFL) 7, at Orange Bowl, Miami, Florida.

1968 AFL

EASTERN DIVISION

	W	L	T	Pct.	Pts.	OP
N.Y. Jets	11	3	0	.786	419	280
Houston	7	7	0	.500	303	248
Miami	5	8	1	.385	276	355
Boston Patriots	4	10	0	.286	229	406
Buffalo	1	12	1	.077	199	367

WESTERN DIVISION

	W	L	T	Pct.	Pts.	OP
Oakland	12	2	0	.857	453	233
Kansas City	12	2	0	.857	371	170
San Diego	9	5	0	.643	382	310
Denver	5	9	0	.357	255	404
Cincinnati	3	11	0	.214	215	329

Western Division playoff: OAKLAND 41, Kansas City 6

AFL championship: N.Y. JETS 27, Oakland 23

1967 NFL

EASTERN CONFERENCE

Capitol Division

	W	L	T	Pct.	Pts.	OP
Dallas	9	5	0	.643	342	268
Philadelphia	6	7	1	.462	351	409
Washington	5	6	3	.455	347	353
New Orleans	3	11	0	.214	233	379

Century Division

	W	L	T	Pct.	Pts.	OP
Cleveland	9	5	0	.643	334	297
N.Y. Giants	7	7	0	.500	369	379
St. Louis	6	7	1	.462	333	356
Pittsburgh	4	9	1	.308	281	320

WESTERN CONFERENCE

Coastal Division

	W	L	T	Pct.	Pts.	OP
Los Angeles	11	1	2	.917	398	196
Baltimore	11	1	2	.917	394	198
San Francisco	7	7	0	.500	273	337
Atlanta	1	12	1	.077	175	422

Central Division

	W	L	T	Pct.	Pts.	OP
Green Bay	9	4	1	.692	332	209
Chicago	7	6	1	.538	239	218
Detroit	5	7	2	.417	260	259
Minnesota	3	8	3	.273	233	294

Los Angeles won division title on the basis of advantage in points (58-34) in two games vs. Baltimore.

Conference championships: DALLAS 52, Cleveland 14; GREEN BAY 28, Los Angeles 7

NFL championship: GREEN BAY 21, Dallas 17

Super Bowl II: Green Bay (NFL) 33, Oakland (AFL) 14, at Orange Bowl, Miami, Florida.

1967 AFL

EASTERN DIVISION

	W	L	T	Pct.	Pts.	OP
Houston	9	4	1	.692	258	199
N.Y. Jets	8	5	1	.615	371	329
Buffalo	4	10	0	.286	237	285
Miami	4	10	0	.286	219	407
Boston Patriots	3	10	1	.231	280	389

WESTERN DIVISION

	W	L	T	Pct.	Pts.	OP
Oakland	13	1	0	.929	468	233
Kansas City	9	5	0	.643	408	254
San Diego	8	5	1	.615	360	352
Denver	3	11	0	.214	256	409

AFL championship: OAKLAND 40, Houston 7

PAST STANDINGS

1966 NFL

EASTERN CONFERENCE

	W	L	T	Pct.	Pts.	OP
Dallas	10	3	1	.769	445	239
Cleveland	9	5	0	.643	403	259
Philadelphia	9	5	0	.643	326	340
St. Louis	8	5	1	.615	264	265
Washington	7	7	0	.500	351	355
Pittsburgh	5	8	1	.385	316	347
Atlanta	3	11	0	.214	204	437
N.Y. Giants	1	12	1	.077	263	501

WESTERN CONFERENCE

	W	L	T	Pct.	Pts.	OP
Green Bay	12	2	0	.857	335	163
Baltimore	9	5	0	.643	314	226
Los Angeles	8	6	0	.571	289	212
San Francisco	6	6	2	.500	320	325
Chicago	5	7	2	.417	234	272
Detroit	4	9	1	.308	206	317
Minnesota	4	9	1	.308	292	304

NFL championship: Green Bay 34, DALLAS 27
Super Bowl I: Green Bay (NFL) 35, Kansas City (AFL) 10, at Memorial Coliseum, Los Angeles, California.

1966 AFL

EASTERN DIVISION

	W	L	T	Pct.	Pts.	OP
Buffalo	9	4	1	.692	358	255
Boston Patriots	8	4	2	.677	315	283
N.Y. Jets	6	6	2	.500	322	312
Houston	3	11	0	.214	335	396
Miami	3	11	0	.214	213	362

WESTERN DIVISION

	W	L	T	Pct.	Pts.	OP
Kansas City	11	2	1	.846	448	276
Oakland	8	5	1	.615	315	288
San Diego	7	6	1	.538	335	284
Denver	4	10	0	.286	196	381

AFL championship: Kansas City 31, BUFFALO 7

1965 NFL

EASTERN CONFERENCE

	W	L	T	Pct.	Pts.	OP
Cleveland	11	3	0	.786	363	325
Dallas	7	7	0	.500	325	280
N.Y. Giants	7	7	0	.500	270	338
Washington	6	8	0	.429	257	301
Philadelphia	5	9	0	.357	363	359
St. Louis	5	9	0	.357	296	309
Pittsburgh	2	12	0	.143	202	397

WESTERN CONFERENCE

	W	L	T	Pct.	Pts.	OP
Green Bay	10	3	1	.769	316	224
Baltimore	10	3	1	.769	389	284
Chicago	9	5	0	.643	409	275
San Francisco	7	6	1	.538	421	402
Minnesota	7	7	0	.500	383	403
Detroit	6	7	1	.462	257	295
Los Angeles	4	10	0	.286	269	328

Western Conference playoff: GREEN BAY 13, Baltimore 10 (OT)
NFL championship: GREEN BAY 23, Cleveland 12

1965 AFL

EASTERN DIVISION

	W	L	T	Pct.	Pts.	OP
Buffalo	10	3	1	.769	313	226
N.Y. Jets	5	8	1	.385	285	303
Boston Patriots	4	8	2	.333	244	302
Houston	4	10	0	.286	298	429

WESTERN DIVISION

	W	L	T	Pct.	Pts.	OP
San Diego	9	2	3	.818	340	227
Oakland	8	5	1	.615	298	239
Kansas City	7	5	2	.583	322	285
Denver	4	10	0	.286	303	392

AFL championship: Buffalo 23, SAN DIEGO 0

1964 NFL

EASTERN CONFERENCE

	W	L	T	Pct.	Pts.	OP
Cleveland	10	3	1	.769	415	293
St. Louis	9	3	2	.750	357	331
Philadelphia	6	8	0	.429	312	313
Washington	6	8	0	.429	307	305
Dallas	5	8	1	.385	250	289
Pittsburgh	5	9	0	.357	253	315
N.Y. Giants	2	10	2	.167	241	399

WESTERN CONFERENCE

	W	L	T	Pct.	Pts.	OP
Baltimore	12	2	0	.857	428	225
Green Bay	8	5	1	.615	342	245
Minnesota	8	5	1	.615	355	296
Detroit	7	5	2	.583	280	260
Los Angeles	5	7	2	.417	283	339
Chicago	5	9	0	.357	260	379
San Francisco	4	10	0	.286	236	330

NFL championship: CLEVELAND 27, Baltimore 0

1964 AFL

EASTERN DIVISION

	W	L	T	Pct.	Pts.	OP
Buffalo	12	2	0	.857	400	242
Boston Patriots	10	3	1	.769	365	297
N.Y. Jets	5	8	1	.385	278	315
Houston	4	10	0	.286	310	355

WESTERN DIVISION

	W	L	T	Pct.	Pts.	OP
San Diego	8	5	1	.615	341	300
Kansas City	7	7	0	.500	366	306
Oakland	5	7	2	.417	303	350
Denver	2	11	1	.154	240	438

AFL championship: BUFFALO 20, San Diego 7

1963 NFL

EASTERN CONFERENCE

	W	L	T	Pct.	Pts.	OP
N.Y. Giants	11	3	0	.786	448	280
Cleveland	10	4	0	.714	343	262
St. Louis	9	5	0	.643	341	283
Pittsburgh	7	4	3	.636	321	295
Dallas	4	10	0	.286	305	378
Washington	3	11	0	.214	279	398
Philadelphia	2	10	2	.167	242	381

WESTERN CONFERENCE

	W	L	T	Pct.	Pts.	OP
Chicago	11	1	2	.917	301	144
Green Bay	11	2	1	.846	369	206
Baltimore	8	6	0	.571	316	285
Detroit	5	8	1	.385	326	265
Minnesota	5	8	1	.385	309	390
Los Angeles	5	9	0	.357	210	350
San Francisco	2	12	0	.143	198	391

NFL championship: CHICAGO 14, N.Y. Giants 10

1963 AFL

EASTERN DIVISION

	W	L	T	Pct.	Pts.	OP
Boston Patriots	7	6	1	.538	327	257
Buffalo	7	6	1	.538	304	291
Houston	6	8	0	.429	302	372
N.Y. Jets	5	8	1	.385	249	399

WESTERN DIVISION

	W	L	T	Pct.	Pts.	OP
San Diego	11	3	0	.786	399	255
Oakland	10	4	0	.714	363	282
Kansas City	5	7	2	.417	347	263
Denver	2	11	1	.154	301	473

Eastern Division playoff: Boston 26, BUFFALO 8
AFL championship: SAN DIEGO 51, Boston 10

1962 NFL

EASTERN CONFERENCE

	W	L	T	Pct.	Pts.	OP
N.Y. Giants	12	2	0	.857	398	283
Pittsburgh	9	5	0	.643	312	363
Cleveland	7	6	1	.538	291	257
Washington	5	7	2	.417	305	376
Dallas Cowboys	5	8	1	.385	398	402
St. Louis	4	9	1	.308	287	361
Philadelphia	3	10	1	.231	282	356

WESTERN CONFERENCE

	W	L	T	Pct.	Pts.	OP
Green Bay	13	1	0	.929	415	148
Detroit	11	3	0	.786	315	177
Chicago	9	5	0	.643	321	287
Baltimore	7	7	0	.500	293	288
San Francisco	6	8	0	.429	282	331
Minnesota	2	11	1	.154	254	410
Los Angeles	1	12	1	.077	220	334

NFL championship: Green Bay 16, N.Y. GIANTS 7

1962 AFL

EASTERN DIVISION

	W	L	T	Pct.	Pts.	OP
Houston	11	3	0	.786	387	270
Boston Patriots	9	4	1	.692	346	295
Buffalo	7	6	1	.538	309	272
N.Y. Titans	5	9	0	.357	278	423

WESTERN DIVISION

	W	L	T	Pct.	Pts.	OP
Dallas Texans	11	3	0	.786	389	233
Denver	7	7	0	.500	353	334
San Diego	4	10	0	.286	314	392
Oakland	1	13	0	.071	213	370

AFL championship: Dallas Texans 20, HOUSTON 17 (OT)

1961 NFL

EASTERN CONFERENCE

	W	L	T	Pct.	Pts.	OP
N.Y. Giants	10	3	1	.769	368	220
Philadelphia	10	4	0	.714	361	297
Cleveland	8	5	1	.615	319	270
St. Louis	7	7	0	.500	279	267
Pittsburgh	6	8	0	.429	295	287
Dallas Cowboys	4	9	1	.308	236	380
Washington	1	12	1	.077	174	392

WESTERN CONFERENCE

	W	L	T	Pct.	Pts.	OP
Green Bay	11	3	0	.786	391	223
Detroit	8	5	1	.615	270	258
Baltimore	8	6	0	.571	302	307
Chicago	8	6	0	.571	326	302
San Francisco	7	6	1	.538	346	272
Los Angeles	4	10	0	.286	263	333
Minnesota	3	11	0	.214	285	407

NFL championship: GREEN BAY 37, N.Y. Giants 0

1961 AFL

EASTERN DIVISION

	W	L	T	Pct.	Pts.	OP
Houston	10	3	1	.769	513	242
Boston Patriots	9	4	1	.692	413	313
N.Y. Titans	7	7	0	.500	301	390
Buffalo	6	8	0	.429	294	342

WESTERN DIVISION

	W	L	T	Pct.	Pts.	OP
San Diego	12	2	0	.857	396	219
Dallas Texans	6	8	0	.429	334	343
Denver	3	11	0	.214	251	432
Oakland	2	12	0	.143	237	458

AFL championship: Houston 10, SAN DIEGO 3

1960 NFL

EASTERN CONFERENCE

	W	L	T	Pct.	Pts.	OP
Philadelphia	10	2	0	.833	321	246
Cleveland	8	3	1	.727	362	217
N.Y. Giants	6	4	2	.600	271	261
St. Louis	6	5	1	.545	288	230
Pittsburgh	5	6	1	.455	240	275
Washington	1	9	2	.100	178	309

WESTERN CONFERENCE

	W	L	T	Pct.	Pts.	OP
Green Bay	8	4	0	.667	332	209
Detroit	7	5	0	.583	239	212
San Francisco	7	5	0	.583	208	205
Baltimore	6	6	0	.500	288	234
Chicago	5	6	1	.455	194	299
L.A. Rams	4	7	1	.364	265	297
Dallas Cowboys	0	11	1	.000	177	369

NFL championship: PHILADELPHIA 17, Green Bay 13

1960 AFL

EASTERN CONFERENCE

	W	L	T	Pct.	Pts.	OP
Houston	10	4	0	.714	379	285
N.Y. Titans	7	7	0	.500	382	399
Buffalo	5	8	1	.385	296	303
Boston	5	9	0	.357	286	349

WESTERN CONFERENCE

	W	L	T	Pct.	Pts.	OP
L.A. Chargers	10	4	0	.714	373	336
Dallas Texans	8	6	0	.571	362	253
Oakland	6	8	0	.429	319	388
Denver	4	9	1	.308	309	393

AFL championship: HOUSTON 24, L.A. Chargers 16

1959

EASTERN CONFERENCE

	W	L	T	Pct.	Pts.	OP
N.Y. Giants	10	2	0	.833	284	170
Cleveland	7	5	0	.583	270	214
Philadelphia	7	5	0	.583	268	278
Pittsburgh	6	5	1	.545	257	216
Washington	3	9	0	.250	185	350
Chi. Cardinals	2	10	0	.167	234	324

WESTERN CONFERENCE

	W	L	T	Pct.	Pts.	OP
Baltimore	9	3	0	.750	374	251
Chi. Bears	8	4	0	.667	252	196
Green Bay	7	5	0	.583	248	246
San Francisco	7	5	0	.583	255	237
Detroit	3	8	1	.273	203	275
Los Angeles	2	10	0	.167	242	315

NFL championship: BALTIMORE 31, N.Y. Giants 16

1958

EASTERN CONFERENCE

	W	L	T	Pct.	Pts.	OP
N.Y. Giants	9	3	0	.750	246	183
Cleveland	9	3	0	.750	302	217
Pittsburgh	7	4	1	.636	261	230
Washington	4	7	1	.364	214	268
Chi. Cardinals	2	9	1	.182	261	356
Philadelphia	2	9	1	.182	235	306

WESTERN CONFERENCE

	W	L	T	Pct.	Pts.	OP
Baltimore	9	3	0	.750	381	203
Chi. Bears	8	4	0	.667	298	230
Los Angeles	8	4	0	.667	344	278
San Francisco	6	6	0	.500	257	324
Detroit	4	7	1	.364	261	276
Green Bay	1	10	1	.091	193	382

Eastern Conference playoff: N.Y. GIANTS 10, Cleveland 0
NFL championship: Baltimore 23, N.Y. GIANTS 17 (OT)

1957

EASTERN CONFERENCE

	W	L	T	Pct.	Pts.	OP
Cleveland	9	2	1	.818	269	172
N.Y. Giants	7	5	0	.583	254	211
Pittsburgh	6	6	0	.500	161	178
Washington	5	6	1	.455	251	230
Philadelphia	4	8	0	.333	173	230
Chi. Cardinals	3	9	0	.250	200	299

WESTERN CONFERENCE

	W	L	T	Pct.	Pts.	OP
Detroit	8	4	0	.667	251	231
San Francisco	8	4	0	.667	260	264
Baltimore	7	5	0	.583	303	235
Los Angeles	6	6	0	.500	307	278
Chi. Bears	5	7	0	.417	203	211
Green Bay	3	9	0	.250	218	311

Western Conference playoff: Detroit 31, SAN FRANCISCO 27
NFL championship: DETROIT 59, Cleveland 14

1956

EASTERN CONFERENCE

	W	L	T	Pct.	Pts.	OP
N.Y. Giants	8	3	1	.727	264	197
Chi. Cardinals	7	5	0	.583	240	182
Washington	6	6	0	.500	183	225
Cleveland	5	7	0	.417	167	177
Pittsburgh	5	7	0	.417	217	250
Philadelphia	3	8	1	.273	143	215

WESTERN CONFERENCE

	W	L	T	Pct.	Pts.	OP
Chi. Bears	9	2	1	.818	363	246
Detroit	9	3	0	.750	300	188
San Francisco	5	6	1	.455	233	284
Baltimore	5	7	0	.417	270	322
Green Bay	4	8	0	.333	264	342
Los Angeles	4	8	0	.333	291	307

NFL championship: N.Y. GIANTS 47, Chi. Bears 7

1955

EASTERN CONFERENCE

	W	L	T	Pct.	Pts.	OP
Cleveland	9	2	1	.818	349	218
Washington	8	4	0	.667	246	222
N.Y. Giants	6	5	1	.545	267	223
Chi. Cardinals	4	7	1	.364	224	252
Philadelphia	4	7	1	.364	248	231
Pittsburgh	4	8	0	.333	195	285

WESTERN CONFERENCE

	W	L	T	Pct.	Pts.	OP
Los Angeles	8	3	1	.727	260	231
Chi. Bears	8	4	0	.667	294	251
Green Bay	6	6	0	.500	258	276
Baltimore	5	6	1	.455	214	239
San Francisco	4	8	0	.333	216	298
Detroit	3	9	0	.250	230	275

NFL championship: Cleveland 38, LOS ANGELES 14

1954

EASTERN CONFERENCE

	W	L	T	Pct.	Pts.	OP
Cleveland	9	3	0	.750	336	162
Philadelphia	7	4	1	.636	284	230
N.Y. Giants	7	5	0	.583	293	184
Pittsburgh	5	7	0	.417	219	263
Washington	3	9	0	.250	207	432
Chi. Cardinals	2	10	0	.167	183	347

WESTERN CONFERENCE

	W	L	T	Pct.	Pts.	OP
Detroit	9	2	1	.818	337	189
Chi. Bears	8	4	0	.667	301	279
San Francisco	7	4	1	.636	313	251
Los Angeles	6	5	1	.545	314	285
Green Bay	4	8	0	.333	234	251
Baltimore	3	9	0	.250	131	279

NFL championship: CLEVELAND 56, Detroit 10

1953

EASTERN CONFERENCE

	W	L	T	Pct.	Pts.	OP
Cleveland	11	1	0	.917	348	162
Philadelphia	7	4	1	.636	352	215
Washington	6	5	1	.545	208	215
Pittsburgh	6	6	0	.500	211	263
N.Y. Giants	3	9	0	.250	179	277
Chi. Cardinals	1	10	1	.091	190	337

WESTERN CONFERENCE

	W	L	T	Pct.	Pts.	OP
Detroit	10	2	0	.833	271	205
San Francisco	9	3	0	.750	372	237
Los Angeles	8	3	1	.727	366	236
Chi. Bears	3	8	1	.273	218	262
Baltimore	3	9	0	.250	182	350
Green Bay	2	9	1	.182	200	338

NFL championship: DETROIT 17, Cleveland 16

1952

AMERICAN CONFERENCE

	W	L	T	Pct.	Pts.	OP
Cleveland	8	4	0	.667	310	213
N.Y. Giants	7	5	0	.583	234	231
Philadelphia	7	5	0	.583	252	271
Pittsburgh	5	7	0	.417	300	273
Chi. Cardinals	4	8	0	.333	172	221
Washington	4	8	0	.333	240	287

NATIONAL CONFERENCE

	W	L	T	Pct.	Pts.	OP
Detroit	9	3	0	.750	344	192
Los Angeles	9	3	0	.750	349	234
San Francisco	7	5	0	.583	285	221
Green Bay	6	6	0	.500	295	312
Chi. Bears	5	7	0	.417	245	326
Dallas Texans	1	11	0	.083	182	427

National Conference playoff: DETROIT 31, Los Angeles 21
NFL championship: Detroit 17, CLEVELAND 7

1951

AMERICAN CONFERENCE

	W	L	T	Pct.	Pts.	OP
Cleveland	11	1	0	.917	331	152
N.Y. Giants	9	2	1	.818	254	161
Washington	5	7	0	.417	183	296
Pittsburgh	4	7	1	.364	183	235
Philadelphia	4	8	0	.333	234	264
Chi. Cardinals	3	9	0	.250	210	287

NATIONAL CONFERENCE

	W	L	T	Pct.	Pts.	OP
Los Angeles	8	4	0	.667	392	261
Detroit	7	4	1	.636	336	259
San Francisco	7	4	1	.636	255	205
Chi. Bears	7	5	0	.583	286	282
Green Bay	3	9	0	.250	254	375
N.Y. Yanks	1	9	2	.100	241	382

NFL championship: LOS ANGELES 24, Cleveland 17

1950

AMERICAN CONFERENCE

	W	L	T	Pct.	Pts.	OP
Cleveland	10	2	0	.833	310	144
N.Y. Giants	10	2	0	.833	268	150
Philadelphia	6	6	0	.500	254	141
Pittsburgh	6	6	0	.500	180	195
Chi. Cardinals	5	7	0	.417	233	287
Washington	3	9	0	.250	232	326

NATIONAL CONFERENCE

	W	L	T	Pct.	Pts.	OP
Los Angeles	9	3	0	.750	466	309
Chi. Bears	9	3	0	.750	279	207
N.Y. Yanks	7	5	0	.583	366	367
Detroit	6	6	0	.500	321	285
Green Bay	3	9	0	.250	244	406
San Francisco	3	9	0	.250	213	300
Baltimore	1	11	0	.083	213	462

American Conference playoff: CLEVELAND 8, N.Y. Giants 3
National Conference playoff: LOS ANGELES 24, Chi. Bears 14
NFL championship: CLEVELAND 30, Los Angeles 28

1949

EASTERN DIVISION

	W	L	T	Pct.	Pts.	OP
Philadelphia	11	1	0	.917	364	134
Pittsburgh	6	5	1	.545	224	214
N.Y. Giants	6	6	0	.500	287	298
Washington	4	7	1	.364	268	339
N.Y. Bulldogs	1	10	1	.091	153	365

WESTERN DIVISION

	W	L	T	Pct.	Pts.	OP
Los Angeles	8	2	2	.800	360	239
Chi. Bears	9	3	0	.750	332	218
Chi. Cardinals	6	5	1	.545	360	301
Detroit	4	8	0	.333	237	259
Green Bay	2	10	0	.167	114	329

NFL championship: Philadelphia 14, LOS ANGELES 0

1948

EASTERN DIVISION

	W	L	T	Pct.	Pts.	OP
Philadelphia	9	2	1	.818	376	156
Washington	7	5	0	.583	291	287
N.Y. Giants	4	8	0	.333	297	388
Pittsburgh	4	8	0	.333	200	243
Boston	3	9	0	.250	174	372

WESTERN DIVISION

	W	L	T	Pct.	Pts.	OP
Chi. Cardinals	11	1	0	.917	395	226
Chi. Bears	10	2	0	.833	375	151
Los Angeles	6	5	1	.545	327	269
Green Bay	3	9	0	.250	154	290
Detroit	2	10	0	.167	200	407

NFL championship: PHILADELPHIA 7, Chi. Cardinals 0

1947

EASTERN DIVISION

	W	L	T	Pct.	Pts.	OP
Philadelphia	8	4	0	.667	308	242
Pittsburgh	8	4	0	.667	240	259
Boston	4	7	1	.364	168	256
Washington	4	8	0	.333	295	367
N.Y. Giants	2	8	2	.200	190	309

WESTERN DIVISION

	W	L	T	Pct.	Pts.	OP
Chi. Cardinals	9	3	0	.750	306	231
Chi. Bears	8	4	0	.667	363	241
Green Bay	6	5	1	.545	274	210
Los Angeles	6	6	0	.500	259	214
Detroit	3	9	0	.250	231	305

Eastern Division playoff: Philadelphia 21, PITTSBURGH 0
NFL championship: CHI. CARDINALS 28, Philadelphia 21

1946

EASTERN DIVISION

	W	L	T	Pct.	Pts.	OP
N.Y. Giants	7	3	1	.700	236	162
Philadelphia	6	5	0	.545	231	220
Washington	5	5	1	.500	171	191
Pittsburgh	5	5	1	.500	136	117
Boston	2	8	1	.200	189	273

WESTERN DIVISION

	W	L	T	Pct.	Pts.	OP
Chi. Bears	8	2	1	.800	289	193
Los Angeles	6	4	1	.600	277	257
Green Bay	6	5	0	.545	148	158
Chi. Cardinals	6	5	0	.545	260	198
Detroit	1	10	0	.091	142	310

NFL championship: Chi. Bears 24, N.Y. GIANTS 14

1945

EASTERN DIVISION

	W	L	T	Pct.	Pts.	OP
Washington	8	2	0	.800	209	121
Philadelphia	7	3	0	.700	272	133
N.Y. Giants	3	6	1	.333	179	198
Boston	3	6	1	.333	123	211
Pittsburgh	2	8	0	.200	79	220

WESTERN DIVISION

	W	L	T	Pct.	Pts.	OP
Cleveland	9	1	0	.900	244	136
Detroit	7	3	0	.700	195	194
Green Bay	6	4	0	.600	258	173
Chi. Bears	3	7	0	.300	192	235
Chi. Cardinals	1	9	0	.100	98	228

NFL championship: CLEVELAND 15, Washington 14

PAST STANDINGS

1944

EASTERN DIVISION

	W	L	T	Pct.	Pts.	OP
N.Y. Giants	8	1	1	.889	206	75
Philadelphia	7	1	2	.875	267	131
Washington	6	3	1	.667	169	180
Boston	2	8	0	.200	82	233
Brooklyn	0	10	0	.000	69	166

WESTERN DIVISION

	W	L	T	Pct.	Pts.	OP
Green Bay	8	2	0	.800	238	141
Chi. Bears	6	3	1	.667	258	172
Detroit	6	3	1	.667	216	151
Cleveland	4	6	0	.400	188	224
Card-Pitt	0	10	0	.000	108	328

NFL championship: Green Bay 14, N.Y. GIANTS 7

1943

EASTERN DIVISION

	W	L	T	Pct.	Pts.	OP
Washington	6	3	1	.667	229	137
N.Y. Giants	6	3	1	.667	197	170
Phil-Pitt	5	4	1	.556	225	230
Brooklyn	2	8	0	.200	65	234

WESTERN DIVISION

	W	L	T	Pct.	Pts.	OP
Chi. Bears	8	1	1	.889	303	157
Green Bay	7	2	1	.778	264	172
Detroit	3	6	1	.333	178	218
Chi. Cardinals	0	10	0	.000	95	238

Eastern Division playoff: Washington 28, N.Y. GIANTS 0
NFL championship: CHI. BEARS 41, Washington 21

1942

EASTERN DIVISION

	W	L	T	Pct.	Pts.	OP
Washington	10	1	0	.909	227	102
Pittsburgh	7	4	0	.636	167	119
N.Y. Giants	5	5	1	.500	155	139
Brooklyn	3	8	0	.273	100	168
Philadelphia	2	9	0	.182	134	239

WESTERN DIVISION

	W	L	T	Pct.	Pts.	OP
Chi. Bears	11	0	0	1.000	376	84
Green Bay	8	2	1	.800	300	215
Cleveland	5	6	0	.455	150	207
Chi. Cardinals	3	8	0	.273	98	209
Detroit	0	11	0	.000	38	263

NFL championship: WASHINGTON 14, Chi. Bears 6

1941

EASTERN DIVISION

	W	L	T	Pct.	Pts.	OP
N.Y. Giants	8	3	0	.727	238	114
Brooklyn	7	4	0	.636	158	127
Washington	6	5	0	.545	176	174
Philadelphia	2	8	1	.200	119	218
Pittsburgh	1	9	1	.100	103	276

WESTERN DIVISION

	W	L	T	Pct.	Pts.	OP
Chi. Bears	10	1	0	.909	396	147
Green Bay	10	1	0	.909	258	120
Detroit	4	6	1	.400	121	195
Chi. Cardinals	3	7	1	.300	127	197
Cleveland	2	9	0	.182	116	244

Western Division playoff: CHI. BEARS 33, Green Bay 14
NFL championship: CHI. BEARS 37, N.Y. Giants 9

1940

EASTERN DIVISION

	W	L	T	Pct.	Pts.	OP
Washington	9	2	0	.818	245	142
Brooklyn	8	3	0	.727	186	120
N.Y. Giants	6	4	1	.600	131	133
Pittsburgh	2	7	2	.222	60	178
Philadelphia	1	10	0	.091	111	211

WESTERN DIVISION

	W	L	T	Pct.	Pts.	OP
Chi. Bears	8	3	0	.727	238	152
Green Bay	6	4	1	.600	238	155
Detroit	5	5	1	.500	138	153
Cleveland	4	6	1	.400	171	191
Chi. Cardinals	2	7	2	.222	139	222

NFL championship: Chi. Bears 73, WASHINGTON 0

1939

EASTERN DIVISION

	W	L	T	Pct.	Pts.	OP
N.Y. Giants	9	1	1	.900	168	85
Washington	8	2	1	.800	242	94
Brooklyn	4	6	1	.400	108	219
Philadelphia	1	9	1	.100	105	200
Pittsburgh	1	9	1	.100	114	216

WESTERN DIVISION

	W	L	T	Pct.	Pts.	OP
Green Bay	9	2	0	.818	233	153
Chi. Bears	8	3	0	.727	298	157
Detroit	6	5	0	.545	145	150
Cleveland	5	5	1	.500	195	164
Chi. Cardinals	1	10	0	.091	84	254

NFL championship: GREEN BAY 27, N.Y. Giants 0

1938

EASTERN DIVISION

	W	L	T	Pct.	Pts.	OP
N.Y. Giants	8	2	1	.800	194	79
Washington	6	3	2	.667	148	154
Brooklyn	4	4	3	.500	131	161
Philadelphia	5	6	0	.455	154	164
Pittsburgh	2	9	0	.182	79	169

WESTERN DIVISION

	W	L	T	Pct.	Pts.	OP
Green Bay	8	3	0	.727	223	118
Detroit	7	4	0	.636	119	108
Chi. Bears	6	5	0	.545	194	148
Cleveland	4	7	0	.364	131	215
Chi. Cardinals	2	9	0	.182	111	168

NFL championship: N.Y. GIANTS 23, Green Bay 17

1937

EASTERN DIVISION

	W	L	T	Pct.	Pts.	OP
Washington	8	3	0	.727	195	120
N.Y. Giants	6	3	2	.667	128	109
Pittsburgh	4	7	0	.364	122	145
Brooklyn	3	7	1	.300	82	174
Philadelphia	2	8	1	.200	86	177

WESTERN DIVISION

	W	L	T	Pct.	Pts.	OP
Chi. Bears	9	1	1	.900	201	100
Green Bay	7	4	0	.636	220	122
Detroit	7	4	0	.636	180	105
Chi. Cardinals	5	5	1	.500	135	165
Cleveland	1	10	0	.091	75	207

NFL championship: Washington 28, CHI. BEARS 21

1936

EASTERN DIVISION

	W	L	T	Pct.	Pts.	OP
Boston	7	5	0	.583	149	110
Pittsburgh	6	6	0	.500	98	187
N.Y. Giants	5	6	1	.455	115	163
Brooklyn	3	8	1	.273	92	161
Philadelphia	1	11	0	.083	51	206

WESTERN DIVISION

	W	L	T	Pct.	Pts.	OP
Green Bay	10	1	1	.909	248	118
Chi. Bears	9	3	0	.750	222	94
Detroit	8	4	0	.667	235	102
Chi. Cardinals	3	8	1	.273	74	143

NFL championship: Green Bay 21, Boston 6, at Polo Grounds, N.Y.

1935

EASTERN DIVISION

	W	L	T	Pct.	Pts.	OP
N.Y. Giants	9	3	0	.750	180	96
Brooklyn	5	6	1	.455	90	141
Pittsburgh	4	8	0	.333	100	209
Boston	2	8	1	.200	65	123
Philadelphia	2	9	0	.182	60	179

WESTERN DIVISION

	W	L	T	Pct.	Pts.	OP
Detroit	7	3	2	.700	191	111
Green Bay	8	4	0	.667	181	96
Chi. Bears	6	4	2	.600	192	106
Chi. Cardinals	6	4	2	.600	99	97

NFL championship: DETROIT 26, N.Y. Giants 7
One game between Boston and Philadelphia was canceled.

1934

EASTERN DIVISION

	W	L	T	Pct.	Pts.	OP
N.Y. Giants	8	5	0	.615	147	107
Boston	6	6	0	.500	107	94
Brooklyn	4	7	0	.364	61	153
Philadelphia	4	7	0	.364	127	85
Pittsburgh	2	10	0	.167	51	206

WESTERN DIVISION

	W	L	T	Pct.	Pts.	OP
Chi. Bears	13	0	0	1.000	286	86
Detroit	10	3	0	.769	238	59
Green Bay	7	6	0	.538	156	112
Chi. Cardinals	5	6	0	.455	80	84
St. Louis	1	2	0	.333	27	61
Cincinnati	0	8	0	.000	10	243

NFL championship: N.Y. GIANTS 30, Chi. Bears 13

1933

EASTERN DIVISION

	W	L	T	Pct.	Pts.	OP
N.Y. Giants	11	3	0	.786	244	101
Brooklyn	5	4	1	.556	93	54
Boston	5	5	2	.500	103	97
Philadelphia	3	5	1	.375	77	158
Pittsburgh	3	6	2	.333	67	208

WESTERN DIVISION

	W	L	T	Pct.	Pts.	OP
Chi. Bears	10	2	1	.833	133	82
Portsmouth	6	5	0	.545	128	87
Green Bay	5	7	1	.417	170	107
Cincinnati	3	6	1	.333	38	110
Chi. Cardinals	1	9	1	.100	52	101

NFL championship: CHI. BEARS 23, N.Y. Giants 21

1932

	W	L	T	Pct.
Chicago Bears	7	1	6	.875
Green Bay Packers	10	3	1	.769
Portsmouth Spartans	6	2	4	.750
Boston Braves	4	4	2	.500
New York Giants	4	6	2	.400
Brooklyn Dodgers	3	9	0	.250
Chicago Cardinals	2	6	2	.250
Staten Island Stapletons	2	7	3	.222

Chicago Bears and Portsmouth finished regularly scheduled games tied for first place. Bears won playoff game, which counted in standings, 9-0.

1931

	W	L	T	Pct.
Green Bay Packers	12	2	0	.857
Portsmouth Spartans	11	3	0	.786
Chicago Bears	8	5	0	.615
Chicago Cardinals	5	4	0	.556
New York Giants	7	6	1	.538
Providence Steam Roller	4	4	3	.500
Staten Island Stapletons	4	6	1	.400
Cleveland Indians	2	8	0	.200
Brooklyn Dodgers	2	12	0	.143
Frankford Yellow Jackets	1	6	1	.143

1930

	W	L	T	Pct.
Green Bay Packers	10	3	1	.769
New York Giants	13	4	0	.765
Chicago Bears	9	4	1	.692
Brooklyn Dodgers	7	4	1	.636
Providence Steam Roller	6	4	1	.600
Staten Island Stapletons	5	5	2	.500
Chicago Cardinals	5	6	2	.455
Portsmouth Spartans	5	6	3	.455
Frankford Yellow Jackets	4	13	1	.222
Minneapolis Red Jackets	1	7	1	.125
Newark Tornadoes	1	10	1	.091

1929

	W	L	T	Pct.
Green Bay Packers	12	0	1	1.000
New York Giants	13	1	1	.929
Frankford Yellow Jackets	10	4	5	.714
Chicago Cardinals	6	6	1	.500
Boston Bulldogs	4	4	0	.500
Staten Island Stapletons	3	4	3	.429
Providence Steam Roller	4	6	2	.400
Orange Tornadoes	3	5	4	.375
Chicago Bears	4	9	2	.308
Buffalo Bisons	1	7	1	.125
Minneapolis Red Jackets	1	9	0	.100
Dayton Triangles	0	6	0	.000

1928

	W	L	T	Pct.
Providence Steam Roller	8	1	2	.889
Frankford Yellow Jackets	11	3	2	.786
Detroit Wolverines	7	2	1	.778
Green Bay Packers	6	4	3	.600
Chicago Bears	7	5	1	.583
New York Giants	4	7	2	.364
New York Yankees	4	8	1	.333
Pottsville Maroons	2	8	0	.200
Chicago Cardinals	1	5	0	.167
Dayton Triangles	0	7	0	.000

1927

	W	L	T	Pct.
New York Giants	11	1	1	.917
Green Bay Packers	7	2	1	.778
Chicago Bears	9	3	2	.750
Cleveland Bulldogs	8	4	1	.667
Providence Steam Roller	8	5	1	.615
New York Yankees	7	8	1	.467
Frankford Yellow Jackets	6	9	3	.400
Pottsville Maroons	5	8	0	.385
Chicago Cardinals	3	7	1	.300
Dayton Triangles	1	6	1	.143
Duluth Eskimos	1	8	0	.111
Buffalo Bisons	0	5	0	.000

1926

	W	L	T	Pct.
Frankford Yellow Jackets	14	1	2	.933
Chicago Bears	12	1	3	.923
Pottsville Maroons	10	2	2	.833
Kansas City Cowboys	8	3	0	.727
Green Bay Packers	7	3	3	.700
Los Angeles Buccaneers	6	3	1	.667
New York Giants	8	4	1	.667
Duluth Eskimos	6	5	3	.545
Buffalo Rangers	4	4	2	.500
Chicago Cardinals	5	6	1	.455
Providence Steam Roller	5	7	1	.417
Detroit Panthers	4	6	2	.400
Hartford Blues	3	7	0	.300
Brooklyn Lions	3	8	0	.273
Milwaukee Badgers	2	7	0	.222
Akron Pros	1	4	3	.200
Dayton Triangles	1	4	1	.200
Racine Tornadoes	1	4	0	.200
Columbus Tigers	1	6	0	.143
Canton Bulldogs	1	9	3	.100
Hammond Pros	0	4	0	.000
Louisville Colonels	0	4	0	.000

1925

	W	L	T	Pct.
Chicago Cardinals	11	2	1	.846
Pottsville Maroons	10	2	0	.833
Detroit Panthers	8	2	2	.800
New York Giants	8	4	0	.667
Akron Indians	4	2	2	.667
Frankford Yellow Jackets	13	7	0	.650
Chicago Bears	9	5	3	.643
Rock Island Independents	5	3	3	.625
Green Bay Packers	8	5	0	.615
Providence Steam Roller	6	5	1	.545
Canton Bulldogs	4	4	0	.500
Cleveland Bulldogs	5	8	1	.385
Kansas City Cowboys	2	5	1	.286
Hammond Pros	1	4	0	.200
Buffalo Bisons	1	6	2	.143
Duluth Kelleys	0	3	0	.000
Rochester Jeffersons	0	6	1	.000
Milwaukee Badgers	0	6	0	.000
Dayton Triangles	0	7	1	.000
Columbus Tigers	0	9	0	.000

1924

	W	L	T	Pct.
Cleveland Bulldogs	7	1	1	.875
Chicago Bears	6	1	4	.857
Frankford Yellow Jackets	11	2	1	.846
Duluth Kelleys	5	1	0	.833
Rock Island Independents	5	2	2	.714
Green Bay Packers	7	4	0	.636
Racine Legion	4	3	3	.571
Chicago Cardinals	5	4	1	.556
Buffalo Bisons	6	5	0	.545
Columbus Tigers	4	4	0	.500
Hammond Pros	2	2	1	.500
Milwaukee Badgers	5	8	0	.385
Akron Indians	2	6	0	.250
Dayton Triangles	2	6	0	.250
Kansas City Blues	2	7	0	.222
Kenosha Maroons	0	4	1	.000
Minneapolis Marines	0	6	0	.000
Rochester Jeffersons	0	7	0	.000

1923

	W	L	T	Pct.
Canton Bulldogs	11	0	1	1.000
Chicago Bears	9	2	1	.818
Green Bay Packers	7	2	1	.778
Milwaukee Badgers	7	2	3	.778
Cleveland Indians	3	1	3	.750
Chicago Cardinals	8	4	0	.667
Duluth Kelleys	4	3	0	.571
Buffalo All-Americans	5	4	3	.556
Columbus Tigers	5	4	1	.556
Racine Legion	4	4	2	.500
Toledo Maroons	3	3	2	.500
Rock Island Independents	2	3	3	.400
Minneapolis Marines	2	5	2	.286
St. Louis All-Stars	1	4	2	.200
Hammond Pros	1	5	1	.167
Dayton Triangles	1	6	1	.143
Akron Indians	1	6	0	.143
Oorang Indians	1	10	0	.091
Louisville Brecks	0	3	0	.000
Rochester Jeffersons	0	4	0	.000

1922

	W	L	T	Pct.
Canton Bulldogs	10	0	2	1.000
Chicago Bears	9	3	0	.750
Chicago Cardinals	8	3	0	.727
Toledo Maroons	5	2	2	.714
Rock Island Independents	4	2	1	.667
Racine Legion	6	4	1	.600
Dayton Triangles	4	3	1	.571
Green Bay Packers	4	3	3	.571
Buffalo All-Americans	5	4	1	.556
Akron Pros	3	5	2	.375
Milwaukee Badgers	2	4	3	.333
Oorang Indians	3	6	0	.333
Minneapolis Marines	1	3	0	.250
Louisville Brecks	1	3	0	.250
Evansville Crimson Giants	0	3	0	.000
Rochester Jeffersons	0	4	1	.000
Hammond Pros	0	5	1	.000
Columbus Panhandles	0	8	0	.000

1921

	W	L	T	Pct.
Chicago Staleys	9	1	1	.900
Buffalo All-Americans	9	1	2	.900
Akron Pros	8	3	1	.727
Canton Bulldogs	5	2	3	.714
Rock Island Independents	4	2	1	.667
Evansville Crimson Giants	3	2	0	.600
Green Bay Packers	3	2	1	.600
Dayton Triangles	4	4	1	.500
Chicago Cardinals	3	3	2	.500
Rochester Jeffersons	2	3	0	.400
Cleveland Indians	3	5	0	.375
Washington Senators	1	2	0	.333
Cincinnati Celts	1	3	0	.250
Hammond Pros	1	3	1	.250
Minneapolis Marines	1	3	0	.250
Detroit Heralds	1	5	1	.167
Columbus Panhandles	1	8	0	.111
Tonawanda Kardex	0	1	0	.000
Muncie Flyers	0	2	0	.000
Louisville Brecks	0	2	0	.000
New York Giants	0	2	0	.000

1920*

	W	L	T	Pct.
Akron Pros	8	0	3	1.000
Decatur Staleys	10	1	2	.909
Buffalo All-Americans	9	1	1	.900
Chicago Cardinals	6	2	2	.750
Rock Island Independents	6	2	2	.750
Dayton Triangles	5	2	2	.714
Rochester Jeffersons	6	3	2	.667
Canton Bulldogs	7	4	2	.636
Detroit Heralds	2	3	3	.400
Cleveland Tigers	2	4	2	.333
Chicago Tigers	2	5	1	.286
Hammond Pros	2	5	0	.286
Columbus Panhandles	2	6	2	.250
Muncie Flyers	0	1	0	.000

**No official standing was maintained for the 1920 season, and the championship was awarded to the Akron Pros in a League meeting on April 30, 1921. Clubs played schedules which included games against non-league opponents. Records of clubs against all opponents are listed above in alphabetical order.*

ALL-TIME TEAM VS. TEAM RESULTS

RS=REGULAR SEASON
PS=POSTSEASON

***ARIZONA vs. ATLANTA**
RS: Cardinals lead series, 12-6
1966—Falcons, 16-10 (A)
1968—Cardinals, 17-12 (StL)
1971—Cardinals, 26-9 (A)
1973—Cardinals, 32-10 (A)
1975—Cardinals, 23-20 (StL)
1978—Cardinals, 42-21 (StL)
1980—Falcons, 33-27 (StL) OT
1981—Falcons, 41-20 (A)
1982—Cardinals, 23-20 (A)
1986—Falcons, 33-13 (A)
1987—Cardinals, 34-21 (A)
1989—Cardinals, 34-20 (P)
1990—Cardinals, 24-13 (A)
1991—Cardinals, 16-10 (P)
1992—Falcons, 20-17 (A)
1993—Cardinals, 27-10 (A)
1994—Falcons, 10-6 (Atl)
1995—Cardinals, 40-37 (Ariz) OT
(RS Pts.—Cardinals 431, Falcons 356)
**Franchise known as Phoenix prior to 1994 and in St. Louis prior to 1988*

***ARIZONA vs. BUFFALO**
RS: Series tied, 3-3
1971—Cardinals, 28-23 (B)
1975—Bills, 32-14 (StL)
1981—Cardinals, 24-0 (StL)
1984—Cardinals, 37-7 (StL)
1986—Bills, 17-10 (B)
1990—Bills, 45-14 (B)
(RS Pts.—Cardinals 127, Bills 124)
**Franchise known as Phoenix prior to 1994 and in St. Louis prior to 1988*

ARIZONA vs. CAROLINA
RS: Panthers lead series, 1-0
1995—Panthers, 27-7 (C)
(RS Pts.—Panthers 27, Cardinals 7)

***ARIZONA vs. **CHICAGO**
RS: Bears lead series, 52-25-6
(NP denotes Normal Park;
Wr denotes Wrigley Field;
Co denotes Comiskey Park;
So denotes Soldier Field;
all Chicago)
1920—Cardinals, 7-6 (NP)
Staleys, 10-0 (Wr)
1921—Tie, 0-0 (Wr)
1922—Cardinals, 6-0 (Co)
Cardinals, 9-0 (Co)
1923—Bears, 3-0 (Wr)
1924—Bears, 6-0 (Wr)
Bears, 21-0 (Co)
1925—Cardinals, 9-0 (Co)
Tie, 0-0 (Wr)
1926—Bears, 16-0 (Wr)
Bears, 10-0 (So)
Tie, 0-0 (Wr)
1927—Bears, 9-0 (NP)
Cardinals, 3-0 (Wr)
1928—Bears, 15-0 (NP)
Bears, 34-0 (Wr)
1929—Tie, 0-0 (Wr)
Cardinals, 40-6 (Co)
1930—Bears, 32-6 (Co)
Bears, 6-0 (Wr)
1931—Bears, 26-13 (Wr)
Bears, 18-7 (Wr)
1932—Tie, 0-0 (Wr)
Bears, 34-0 (Wr)
1933—Bears, 12-9 (Wr)
Bears, 22-6 (Wr)
1934—Bears, 20-0 (Wr)
Bears, 17-6 (Wr)
1935—Tie, 7-7 (Wr)
Bears, 13-0 (Wr)
1936—Bears, 7-3 (Wr)
Cardinals, 14-7 (Wr)
1937—Bears, 16-7 (Wr)
Bears, 42-28 (Wr)
1938—Bears, 16-13 (So)
Bears, 34-28 (Wr)
1939—Bears, 44-7 (Wr)
Bears, 48-7 (Co)
1940—Cardinals, 21-7 (Co)
Bears, 31-23 (Wr)
1941—Bears, 53-7 (Wr)
Bears, 34-24 (Co)
1942—Bears, 41-14 (Wr)
Bears, 21-7 (Co)
1943—Bears, 20-0 (Wr)
Bears, 35-24 (Co)
1945—Cardinals, 16-7 (Wr)
Bears, 28-20 (Co)
1946—Bears, 34-17 (Co)
Cardinals, 35-28 (Wr)
1947—Cardinals, 31-7 (Co)
Cardinals, 30-21 (Wr)
1948—Bears, 28-17 (Co)
Cardinals, 24-21 (Wr)
1949—Bears, 17-7 (Co)
Bears, 52-21 (Wr)
1950—Bears, 27-6 (Wr)
Cardinals, 20-10 (Co)
1951—Cardinals, 28-14 (Co)
Cardinals, 24-14 (Wr)
1952—Cardinals, 21-10 (Co)
Bears, 10-7 (Wr)
1953—Cardinals, 24-17 (Wr)
1954—Bears, 29-7 (Co)
1955—Cardinals, 53-14 (Co)
1956—Bears, 10-3 (Wr)
1957—Bears, 14-6 (Co)
1958—Bears, 30-14 (Wr)
1959—Bears, 31-7 (So)
1965—Bears, 34-13 (Wr)
1966—Cardinals, 24-17 (StL)
1967—Bears, 30-3 (Wr)
1969—Cardinals, 20-17 (StL)
1972—Bears, 27-10 (StL)
1975—Cardinals, 34-20 (So)
1977—Cardinals, 16-13 (StL)
1978—Bears, 17-10 (So)
1979—Bears, 42-6 (So)
1982—Cardinals, 10-7 (So)
1984—Cardinals, 38-21 (StL)
1990—Bears, 31-21 (P)
1994—Bears, 19-16 (A) OT
(RS Pts.—Bears 1,567, Cardinals 1,014)
**Franchise known as Phoenix prior to 1994, in St. Louis prior to 1988, and in Chicago prior to 1960*
***Franchise in Decatur prior to 1921 and known as Staleys prior to 1922*

***ARIZONA vs. CINCINNATI**
RS: Bengals lead series, 3-2
1973—Bengals, 42-24 (C)
1979—Bengals, 34-28 (C)
1985—Cardinals, 41-27 (StL)
1988—Bengals, 21-14 (C)
1994—Cardinals, 28-7 (A)
(RS Pts.—Cardinals 135, Bengals 131)
**Franchise known as Phoenix prior to 1994 and in St. Louis prior to 1988*

***ARIZONA vs. CLEVELAND**
RS: Browns lead series, 32-10-3
1950—Browns, 34-24 (Cle)
Browns, 10-7 (Chi)
1951—Browns, 34-17 (Chi)
Browns, 49-28 (Cle)
1952—Browns, 28-13 (Cle)
Browns, 10-0 (Chi)
1953—Browns, 27-7 (Chi)
Browns, 27-16 (Cle)
1954—Browns, 31-7 (Cle)
Browns, 35-3 (Chi)
1955—Browns, 26-20 (Chi)
Browns, 35-24 (Cle)
1956—Cardinals, 9-7 (Chi)
Cardinals, 24-7 (Cle)
1957—Browns, 17-7 (Chi)
Browns, 31-0 (Cle)
1958—Browns, 35-28 (Cle)
Browns, 38-24 (Chi)
1959—Browns, 34-7 (Chi)
Browns, 17-7 (Cle)
1960—Browns, 28-27 (Cle)
Tie, 17-17 (StL)
1961—Browns, 20-17 (Cle)
Browns, 21-10 (StL)
1962—Browns, 34-7 (StL)
Browns, 38-14 (Cle)
1963—Cardinals, 20-14 (Cle)
Browns, 24-10 (StL)
1964—Tie, 33-33 (Cle)
Cardinals, 28-19 (StL)
1965—Cardinals, 49-13 (Cle)
Browns, 27-24 (StL)
1966—Cardinals, 34-28 (Cle)
Browns, 38-10 (StL)
1967—Browns, 20-16 (Cle)
Browns, 20-16 (StL)
1968—Cardinals, 27-21 (Cle)
Cardinals, 27-16 (StL)
1969—Tie, 21-21 (Cle)
Browns, 27-21 (StL)
1974—Cardinals, 29-7 (StL)
1979—Browns, 38-20 (StL)
1985—Cardinals, 27-24 (Cle) OT
1988—Browns, 29-21 (P)
1994—Browns, 32-0 (Cle)
(RS Pts.—Browns 1,141, Cardinals 797)
**Franchise known as Phoenix prior to 1994, in St. Louis prior to 1988, and in Chicago prior to 1960*

***ARIZONA vs. DALLAS**
RS: Cowboys lead series, 44-22-1
1960—Cardinals, 12-10 (StL)
1961—Cardinals, 31-17 (D)
Cardinals, 31-13 (StL)
1962—Cardinals, 28-24 (D)
Cardinals, 52-20 (StL)
1963—Cardinals, 34-7 (D)
Cowboys, 28-24 (StL)
1964—Cardinals, 16-6 (D)
Cowboys, 31-13 (StL)
1965—Cardinals, 20-13 (StL)
Cowboys, 27-13 (D)
1966—Tie, 10-10 (StL)
Cowboys, 31-17 (D)
1967—Cowboys, 46-21 (D)
1968—Cowboys, 27-10 (StL)
1969—Cowboys, 24-3 (D)
1970—Cardinals, 20-7 (StL)
Cardinals, 38-0 (D)
1971—Cowboys, 16-13 (StL)
Cowboys, 31-12 (D)
1972—Cowboys, 33-24 (D)
Cowboys, 27-6 (StL)
1973—Cowboys, 45-10 (D)
Cowboys, 30-3 (StL)
1974—Cardinals, 31-28 (StL)
Cowboys, 17-14 (D)
1975—Cowboys, 37-31 (D) OT
Cardinals, 31-17 (StL)
1976—Cardinals, 21-17 (StL)
Cowboys, 19-14 (D)
1977—Cowboys, 30-24 (StL)
Cardinals, 24-17 (D)
1978—Cowboys, 21-12 (D)
Cowboys, 24-21 (StL) OT
1979—Cowboys, 22-21 (StL)
Cowboys, 22-13 (D)
1980—Cowboys, 27-24 (StL)
Cowboys, 31-21 (D)
1981—Cowboys, 30-17 (D)
Cardinals, 20-17 (StL)
1982—Cowboys, 24-7 (StL)
1983—Cowboys, 34-17 (StL)
Cowboys, 35-17 (D)
1984—Cardinals, 31-20 (D)
Cowboys, 24-17 (StL)
1985—Cardinals, 21-10 (StL)
Cowboys, 35-17 (D)
1986—Cowboys, 31-7 (StL)
Cowboys, 37-6 (D)
1987—Cardinals, 24-13 (StL)
Cowboys, 21-16 (D)
1988—Cowboys, 17-14 (P)
Cardinals, 16-10 (D)
1989—Cardinals, 19-10 (D)
Cardinals, 24-20 (P)
1990—Cardinals, 20-3 (P)
Cowboys, 41-10 (D)
1991—Cowboys, 17-9 (P)
Cowboys, 27-7 (D)
1992—Cowboys, 31-20 (D)
Cowboys, 16-10 (P)
1993—Cowboys, 17-10 (P)
Cowboys, 20-15 (D)
1994—Cowboys, 38-3 (D)
Cowboys, 28-21 (A)
1995—Cowboys, 34-20 (D)
Cowboys, 37-13 (A)
(RS Pts.—Cowboys 1,549, Cardinals 1,211)
**Franchise known as Phoenix prior to 1994 and in St. Louis prior to 1988*

***ARIZONA vs. DENVER**
RS: Broncos lead series, 4-0-1
1973—Tie, 17-17 (StL)
1977—Broncos, 7-0 (D)
1989—Broncos, 37-0 (P)
1991—Broncos, 24-19 (D)
1995—Broncos, 38-6 (D)
(RS Pts.—Broncos 123, Cardinals 42)
**Franchise known as Phoenix prior to 1994 and in St. Louis prior to 1988*

***ARIZONA vs. **DETROIT**
RS: Lions lead series, 27-17-5
1930—Tie, 0-0 (Port)
Cardinals, 23-0 (C)
1931—Cardinals, 20-19 (C)
1932—Tie, 7-7 (Port)
1933—Spartans, 7-6 (Port)
1934—Lions, 6-0 (D)
Lions, 17-13 (C)
1935—Tie, 10-10 (D)
Lions, 7-6 (C)
1936—Lions, 39-0 (D)
Lions, 14-7 (C)
1937—Lions, 16-7 (C)
Lions, 16-7 (D)
1938—Lions, 10-0 (D)
Lions, 7-3 (C)
1939—Lions, 21-3 (D)
Lions, 17-3 (C)
1940—Tie, 0-0 (Buffalo)
Lions, 43-14 (C)
1941—Tie, 14-14 (C)
Lions, 21-3 (D)
1942—Cardinals, 13-0 (C)
Cardinals, 7-0 (D)
1943—Lions, 35-17 (D)
Lions, 7-0 (Buffalo)
1945—Lions, 10-0 (Milwaukee)
Lions, 26-0 (D)
1946—Cardinals, 34-14 (C)
Cardinals, 36-14 (D)
1947—Cardinals, 45-21 (C)
Cardinals, 17-7 (D)
1948—Cardinals, 56-20 (C)
Cardinals, 28-14 (D)
1949—Lions, 24-7 (C)
Cardinals, 42-19 (D)
1959—Lions, 45-21 (D)
1961—Lions, 45-14 (StL)
1967—Cardinals, 38-28 (StL)
1969—Lions, 20-0 (D)
1970—Lions, 16-3 (D)
1973—Lions, 20-16 (StL)
1975—Cardinals, 24-13 (D)
1978—Cardinals, 21-14 (StL)
1980—Lions, 20-7 (D)
Cardinals, 24-23 (StL)
1989—Cardinals, 16-13 (D)
1993—Lions, 26-20 (D)
Lions, 21-14 (Phx)
1995—Cardinals, 20-17 (D)
(RS Pts.—Lions 823, Cardinals 696)
**Franchise known as Phoenix prior to*

1994, in St. Louis prior to 1988,
and in Chicago prior to 1960
***Franchise in Portsmouth prior to 1934*
and known as the Spartans

***ARIZONA vs. GREEN BAY**
RS: Packers lead series, 39-21-4
PS: Packers lead series, 1-0
1921—Tie, 3-3 (C)
1922—Cardinals, 16-3 (C)
1924—Cardinals, 3-0 (C)
1925—Cardinals, 9-6 (C)
1926—Cardinals, 13-7 (GB)
Packers, 3-0 (C)
1927—Packers, 13-0 (GB)
Tie, 6-6 (C)
1928—Packers, 20-0 (GB)
1929—Packers, 9-2 (GB)
Packers, 7-6 (C)
Packers, 12-0 (C)
1930—Packers, 14-0 (GB)
Cardinals, 13-6 (C)
1931—Packers, 26-7 (GB)
Cardinals, 21-13 (C)
1932—Packers, 15-7 (GB)
Packers, 19-9 (C)
1933—Packers, 14-6 (C)
1934—Packers, 15-0 (GB)
Cardinals, 9-0 (Mil)
Cardinals, 6-0 (C)
1935—Cardinals, 7-6 (GB)
Cardinals, 3-0 (Mil)
Cardinals, 9-7 (C)
1936—Packers, 10-7 (GB)
Packers, 24-0 (Mil)
Tie, 0-0 (C)
1937—Cardinals, 14-7 (GB)
Packers, 34-13 (Mil)
1938—Packers, 28-7 (Mil)
Packers, 24-22 (Buffalo)
1939—Packers, 14-10 (GB)
Packers, 27-20 (Mil)
1940—Packers, 31-6 (Mil)
Packers, 28-7 (C)
1941—Packers, 14-13 (Mil)
Packers, 17-9 (GB)
1942—Packers, 17-13 (C)
Packers, 55-24 (GB)
1943—Packers, 28-7 (C)
Packers, 35-14 (Mil)
1945—Packers, 33-14 (GB)
1946—Packers, 19-7 (C)
Cardinals, 24-6 (GB)
1947—Cardinals, 14-10 (GB)
Cardinals, 21-20 (C)
1948—Cardinals, 17-7 (Mil)
Cardinals, 42-7 (C)
1949—Cardinals, 39-17 (Mil)
Cardinals, 41-21 (C)
1955—Packers, 31-14 (GB)
1956—Packers, 24-21 (C)
1962—Packers, 17-0 (Mil)
1963—Packers, 30-7 (StL)
1967—Packers, 31-23 (StL)
1969—Packers, 45-28 (GB)
1971—Tie, 16-16 (StL)
1973—Packers, 25-21 (GB)
1976—Cardinals, 29-0 (StL)
1982—**Packers, 41-16 (GB)
1984—Packers, 24-23 (GB)
1985—Cardinals, 43-28 (StL)
1988—Packers, 26-17 (P)
1990—Packers, 24-21 (P)
(RS Pts.—Packers 1,078, Cardinals 823)
(PS Pts.—Packers 41, Cardinals 16)
**Franchise known as Phoenix prior to*
1994, in St. Louis prior to 1988,
and in Chicago prior to 1960
***NFC First-Round Playoff*

***ARIZONA vs. HOUSTON**
RS: Cardinals lead series, 4-2
1970—Cardinals, 44-0 (StL)
1974—Cardinals, 31-27 (H)
1979—Cardinals, 24-17 (H)
1985—Oilers, 20-10 (StL)
1988—Oilers, 38-20 (H)
1994—Cardinals, 30-12 (H)
(RS Pts.—Cardinals 159, Oilers 114)
**Franchise known as Phoenix prior to*
1994 and in St. Louis prior to 1988

***ARIZONA vs. **INDIANAPOLIS**
RS: Cardinals lead series, 6-5
1961—Colts, 16-0 (B)
1964—Colts, 47-27 (B)
1968—Colts, 27-0 (B)
1972—Cardinals, 10-3 (B)
1976—Cardinals, 24-17 (StL)
1978—Colts, 30-17 (StL)
1980—Cardinals, 17-10 (B)
1981—Cardinals, 35-24 (B)
1984—Cardinals, 34-33 (I)
1990—Cardinals, 20-17 (P)
1992—Colts, 16-13 (I)
(RS Pts.—Colts 240, Cardinals 197)
**Franchise known as Phoenix prior to*
1994 and in St. Louis prior to 1988
***Franchise in Baltimore prior to 1984*

***ARIZONA vs. KANSAS CITY**
RS: Chiefs lead series, 4-1-1
1970—Tie, 6-6 (KC)
1974—Chiefs, 17-13 (StL)
1980—Chiefs, 21-13 (StL)
1983—Chiefs, 38-14 (KC)
1986—Cardinals, 23-14 (StL)
1995—Chiefs, 24-3 (A)
(RS Pts.—Chiefs 120, Cardinals 72)
**Franchise known as Phoenix prior to*
1994 and in St. Louis prior to 1988

***ARIZONA vs. MIAMI**
RS: Dolphins lead series, 6-0
1972—Dolphins, 31-10 (M)
1977—Dolphins, 55-14 (StL)
1978—Dolphins, 24-10 (M)
1981—Dolphins, 20-7 (StL)
1984—Dolphins, 36-28 (StL)
1990—Dolphins, 23-3 (M)
(RS Pts.—Dolphins 189, Cardinals 72)
**Franchise known as Phoenix prior to*
1994 and in St. Louis prior to 1988

***ARIZONA vs. MINNESOTA**
RS: Cardinals lead series, 8-5
PS: Vikings lead series, 1-0
1963—Cardinals, 56-14 (M)
1967—Cardinals, 34-24 (M)
1969—Vikings, 27-10 (StL)
1972—Cardinals, 19-17 (M)
1974—Vikings, 28-24 (StL)
**Vikings, 30-14 (M)
1977—Cardinals, 27-7 (M)
1979—Cardinals, 37-7 (StL)
1981—Cardinals, 30-17 (StL)
1983—Cardinals, 41-31 (StL)
1991—Vikings, 34-7 (M)
Vikings, 28-0 (P)
1994—Cardinals, 17-7 (A)
1995—Vikings, 30-24 (A) OT
(RS Pts.—Cardinals 326, Vikings 271)
(PS Pts.—Vikings 30, Cardinals 14)
**Franchise known as Phoenix prior to*
1994 and in St. Louis prior to 1988
***NFC Divisional Playoff*

***ARIZONA vs. **NEW ENGLAND**
RS: Cardinals lead series, 6-2
1970—Cardinals, 31-0 (StL)
1975—Cardinals, 24-17 (StL)
1978—Patriots, 16-6 (StL)
1981—Cardinals, 27-20 (NE)
1984—Cardinals, 33-10 (NE)
1990—Cardinals, 34-14 (P)
1991—Cardinals, 24-10 (P)
1993—Patriots, 23-21 (P)
(RS Pts.—Cardinals 200, Patriots 110)
**Franchise known as Phoenix prior to*
1994 and in St. Louis prior to 1988
***Franchise in Boston prior to 1971*

***ARIZONA vs. NEW ORLEANS**
RS: Cardinals lead series, 10-9
1967—Cardinals, 31-20 (StL)
1968—Cardinals, 21-20 (NO)
Cardinals, 31-17 (StL)
1969—Saints, 51-42 (StL)
1970—Cardinals, 24-17 (StL)
1974—Saints, 14-0 (NO)
1977—Cardinals, 49-31 (StL)
1980—Cardinals, 40-7 (NO)
1981—Cardinals, 30-3 (StL)
1982—Cardinals, 21-7 (NO)
1983—Saints, 28-17 (NO)
1984—Saints, 34-24 (NO)
1985—Cardinals, 28-16 (StL)
1986—Saints, 16-7 (StL)
1987—Cardinals, 24-19 (StL)
1990—Saints, 28-7 (NO)
1991—Saints, 27-3 (P)
1992—Saints, 30-21 (P)
1993—Saints, 20-17 (P)
(RS Pts.—Cardinals 437, Saints 405)
**Franchise known as Phoenix prior to*
1994 and in St. Louis prior to 1988

***ARIZONA vs. N.Y. GIANTS**
RS: Giants lead series, 68-36-2
1926—Giants, 20-0 (NY)
1927—Giants, 28-7 (NY)
1929—Giants, 24-21 (NY)
1930—Giants, 25-12 (NY)
Giants, 13-7 (C)
1935—Cardinals, 14-13 (NY)
1936—Giants, 14-6 (NY)
1938—Giants, 6-0 (NY)
1939—Giants, 17-7 (NY)
1941—Cardinals, 10-7 (NY)
1942—Giants, 21-7 (NY)
1943—Giants, 24-13 (NY)
1946—Giants, 28-24 (NY)
1947—Giants, 35-31 (NY)
1948—Cardinals, 63-35 (NY)
1949—Giants, 41-38 (C)
1950—Cardinals, 17-3 (C)
Giants, 51-21 (NY)
1951—Giants, 28-17 (NY)
Giants, 10-0 (C)
1952—Cardinals, 24-23 (NY)
Giants, 28-6 (C)
1953—Giants, 21-7 (NY)
Giants, 23-20 (C)
1954—Giants, 41-10 (C)
Giants, 31-17 (NY)
1955—Cardinals, 28-17 (C)
Giants, 10-0 (NY)
1956—Cardinals, 35-27 (C)
Giants, 23-10 (NY)
1957—Giants, 27-14 (NY)
Giants, 28-21 (C)
1958—Giants, 37-7 (Buffalo)
Cardinals, 23-6 (NY)
1959—Giants, 9-3 (NY)
Giants, 30-20 (Minn)
1960—Giants, 35-14 (StL)
Cardinals, 20-13 (NY)
1961—Cardinals, 21-10 (NY)
Giants, 24-9 (StL)
1962—Giants, 31-14 (StL)
Giants, 31-28 (NY)
1963—Giants, 38-21 (StL)
Cardinals, 24-17 (NY)
1964—Giants, 34-17 (NY)
Tie, 10-10 (StL)
1965—Giants, 14-10 (NY)
Giants, 28-15 (StL)
1966—Cardinals, 24-19 (StL)
Cardinals, 20-17 (NY)
1967—Giants, 37-20 (StL)
Giants, 37-14 (NY)
1968—Cardinals, 28-21 (NY)
1969—Cardinals, 42-17 (StL)
Giants, 49-6 (NY)
1970—Giants, 35-17 (NY)
Giants, 34-17 (StL)
1971—Giants, 21-20 (StL)
Cardinals, 24-7 (NY)
1972—Giants, 27-21 (NY)
Giants, 13-7 (StL)
1973—Cardinals, 35-27 (StL)
Giants, 24-13 (New Haven)
1974—Cardinals, 23-21 (New Haven)
Cardinals, 26-14 (StL)
1975—Cardinals, 26-14 (StL)
Cardinals, 20-13 (NY)
1976—Cardinals, 27-21 (StL)
Cardinals, 17-14 (NY)
1977—Cardinals, 28-0 (StL)
Giants, 27-7 (NY)
1978—Cardinals, 20-10 (StL)
Giants, 17-0 (NY)
1979—Cardinals, 27-14 (NY)
Cardinals, 29-20 (StL)
1980—Giants, 41-35 (StL)
Cardinals, 23-7 (NY)
1981—Giants, 34-14 (NY)
Giants, 20-10 (StL)
1982—Cardinals, 24-21 (StL)
1983—Tie, 20-20 (StL) OT
Cardinals, 10-6 (NY)
1984—Giants, 16-10 (NY)
Cardinals, 31-21 (StL)
1985—Giants, 27-17 (NY)
Giants, 34-3 (StL)
1986—Giants, 13-6 (StL)
Giants, 27-7 (NY)
1987—Giants, 30-7 (NY)
Cardinals, 27-24 (StL)
1988—Cardinals, 24-17 (P)
Giants, 44-7 (NY)
1989—Giants, 35-7 (NY)
Giants, 20-13 (P)
1990—Giants, 20-19 (NY)
Giants, 24-21 (P)
1991—Giants, 20-9 (NY)
Giants, 21-14 (P)
1992—Giants, 31-21 (NY)
Cardinals, 19-0 (P)
1993—Giants, 19-17 (NY)
Cardinals, 17-6 (P)
1994—Giants, 20-17 (A)
Cardinals, 10-9 (NY)
1995—Giants, 27-21 (NY) OT
Giants, 10-6 (A)
(RS Pts.—Giants 2,343, Cardinals 1,807)
**Franchise known as Phoenix prior to*
1994, in St. Louis prior to 1988,
and in Chicago prior to 1960

***ARIZONA vs. N.Y. JETS**
RS: Cardinals lead series, 2-1
1971—Cardinals, 17-10 (StL)
1975—Cardinals, 37-6 (NY)
1978—Jets, 23-10 (NY)
(RS Pts.—Cardinals 64, Jets 39)
**Franchise known as Phoenix prior to*
1994 and in St. Louis prior to 1988

***ARIZONA vs. **OAKLAND**
RS: Raiders lead series, 2-1
1973—Raiders, 17-10 (StL)
1983—Cardinals, 34-24 (LA)
1989—Raiders, 16-14 (LA)
(RS Pts.—Cardinals 58, Raiders 57)
**Franchise known as Phoenix prior to*
1994 and in St. Louis prior to 1988
***Franchise in Los Angeles from*
1982-1994

***ARIZONA vs. PHILADELPHIA**
RS: Eagles lead series, 46-45-5
PS: Series tied, 1-1
1935—Cardinals, 12-3 (C)
1936—Cardinals, 13-0 (C)
1937—Tie, 6-6 (P)
1938—Eagles, 7-0 (Erie, Pa.)
1941—Eagles, 21-14 (P)
1945—Eagles, 21-6 (P)
1947—Cardinals, 45-21 (P)
**Cardinals, 28-21 (C)
1948—Cardinals, 21-14 (C)
**Eagles, 7-0 (P)
1949—Eagles, 28-3 (P)

ALL-TIME TEAM VS. TEAM RESULTS

1950—Eagles, 45-7 (C)
Cardinals, 14-10 (P)
1951—Eagles, 17-14 (C)
1952—Eagles, 10-7 (P)
Cardinals, 28-22 (C)
1953—Eagles, 56-17 (C)
Eagles, 38-0 (P)
1954—Eagles, 35-16 (C)
Eagles, 30-14 (P)
1955—Tie, 24-24 (C)
Eagles, 27-3 (P)
1956—Cardinals, 20-6 (P)
Cardinals, 28-17 (C)
1957—Eagles, 38-21 (C)
Cardinals, 31-27 (P)
1958—Tie, 21-21 (C)
Eagles, 49-21 (P)
1959—Eagles, 28-24 (Minn)
Eagles, 27-17 (P)
1960—Eagles, 31-27 (P)
Eagles, 20-6 (StL)
1961—Cardinals, 30-27 (P)
Eagles, 20-7 (StL)
1962—Cardinals, 27-21 (P)
Cardinals, 45-35 (StL)
1963—Cardinals, 28-24 (P)
Cardinals, 38-14 (StL)
1964—Cardinals, 38-13 (P)
Cardinals, 36-34 (StL)
1965—Eagles, 34-27 (P)
Eagles, 28-24 (StL)
1966—Cardinals, 16-13 (StL)
Cardinals, 41-10 (P)
1967—Cardinals, 48-14 (StL)
1968—Cardinals, 45-17 (P)
1969—Eagles, 34-30 (StL)
1970—Cardinals, 35-20 (P)
Cardinals, 23-14 (StL)
1971—Eagles, 37-20 (StL)
Eagles, 19-7 (P)
1972—Tie, 6-6 (P)
Cardinals, 24-23 (StL)
1973—Cardinals, 34-23 (P)
Eagles, 27-24 (StL)
1974—Cardinals, 7-3 (StL)
Cardinals, 13-3 (P)
1975—Cardinals, 31-20 (StL)
Cardinals, 24-23 (P)
1976—Cardinals, 33-14 (StL)
Cardinals, 17-14 (P)
1977—Cardinals, 21-17 (P)
Cardinals, 21-16 (StL)
1978—Cardinals, 16-10 (P)
Eagles, 14-10 (StL)
1979—Eagles, 24-20 (StL)
Eagles, 16-13 (P)
1980—Cardinals, 24-14 (StL)
Eagles, 17-3 (P)
1981—Eagles, 52-10 (StL)
Eagles, 38-0 (P)
1982—Cardinals, 23-20 (P)
1983—Cardinals, 14-11 (P)
Cardinals, 31-7 (StL)
1984—Cardinals, 34-14 (P)
Cardinals, 17-16 (StL)
1985—Eagles, 30-7 (P)
Eagles, 24-14 (StL)
1986—Cardinals, 13-10 (StL)
Tie, 10-10 (P) OT
1987—Eagles, 28-23 (StL)
Cardinals, 31-19 (P)
1988—Eagles, 31-21 (P)
Eagles, 23-17 (Phx)
1989—Eagles, 17-5 (Phx)
Eagles, 31-14 (P)
1990—Cardinals, 23-21 (P)
Eagles, 23-21 (Phx)
1991—Cardinals, 26-10 (P)
Eagles, 34-14 (Phx)
1992—Eagles, 31-14 (Phx)
Eagles, 7-3 (P)
1993—Eagles, 23-17 (P)
Cardinals, 16-3 (Phx)
1994—Eagles, 17-7 (P)
Cardinals, 12-6 (A)
1995—Eagles, 31-19 (A)
Eagles, 21-20 (P)
(RS Pts.—Eagles 2,047, Cardinals 1,890)
(PS Pts.—Eagles 28, Cardinals 28)
**Franchise known as Phoenix prior to 1994, in St. Louis prior to 1988, and in Chicago prior to 1960*
***NFL Championship*

***ARIZONA vs. **PITTSBURGH**
RS: Steelers lead series, 29-22-3
1933—Pirates, 14-13 (C)
1935—Pirates, 17-13 (P)
1936—Cardinals, 14-6 (C)
1937—Cardinals, 13-7 (P)
1939—Cardinals, 10-0 (P)
1940—Tie, 7-7 (P)
1942—Steelers, 19-3 (P)
1945—Steelers, 23-0 (P)
1946—Steelers, 14-7 (P)
1948—Cardinals, 24-7 (P)
1950—Steelers, 28-17 (C)
Steelers, 28-7 (P)
1951—Steelers, 28-14 (C)
1952—Steelers, 34-28 (C)
Steelers, 17-14 (P)
1953—Steelers, 31-28 (P)
Steelers, 21-17 (C)
1954—Cardinals, 17-14 (C)
Steelers, 20-17 (P)
1955—Steelers, 14-7 (P)
Cardinals, 27-13 (C)
1956—Steelers, 14-7 (P)
Cardinals, 38-27 (C)
1957—Steelers, 29-20 (P)
Steelers, 27-2 (C)
1958—Steelers, 27-20 (C)
Steelers, 38-21 (P)
1959—Cardinals, 45-24 (C)
Steelers, 35-20 (P)
1960—Steelers, 27-14 (P)
Cardinals, 38-7 (StL)
1961—Steelers, 30-27 (P)
Cardinals, 20-0 (StL)
1962—Steelers, 26-17 (StL)
Steelers, 19-7 (P)
1963—Steelers, 23-10 (P)
Cardinals, 24-23 (StL)
1964—Cardinals, 34-30 (StL)
Cardinals, 21-20 (P)
1965—Cardinals, 20-7 (P)
Cardinals, 21-17 (StL)
1966—Steelers, 30-9 (P)
Cardinals, 6-3 (StL)
1967—Cardinals, 28-14 (P)
Tie, 14-14 (StL)
1968—Tie, 28-28 (StL)
Cardinals, 20-10 (P)
1969—Cardinals, 27-14 (P)
Cardinals, 47-10 (StL)
1972—Steelers, 25-19 (StL)
1979—Steelers, 24-21 (StL)
1985—Steelers, 23-10 (P)
1988—Cardinals, 31-14 (Phx)
1994—Cardinals, 20-17 (A) OT
(RS Pts.—Steelers 1,038, Cardinals 1,003)
**Franchise known as Phoenix prior to 1994, in St. Louis prior to 1988, and in Chicago prior to 1960*
***Steelers known as Pirates prior to 1941*

***ARIZONA vs. **ST. LOUIS**
RS: Rams lead series, 23-19-2
PS: Rams lead series, 1-0
1937—Cardinals, 6-0 (Clev)
Cardinals, 13-7 (Chi)
1938—Cardinals, 7-6 (Clev)
Cardinals, 31-17 (Chi)
1939—Rams, 24-0 (Chi)
Rams, 14-0 (Clev)
1940—Rams, 26-14 (Clev)
Cardinals, 17-7 (Chi)
1941—Rams, 10-6 (Clev)
Cardinals, 7-0 (Chi)
1942—Cardinals, 7-0 (Buffalo)
Rams, 7-3 (Clev)
1945—Rams, 21-0 (Clev)
Rams, 35-21 (Chi)
1946—Cardinals, 34-10 (Chi)
Rams, 17-14 (LA)
1947—Rams, 27-7 (LA)
Cardinals, 17-10 (Chi)
1948—Cardinals, 27-22 (LA)
Cardinals, 27-24 (Chi)
1949—Tie, 28-28 (Chi)
Cardinals, 31-27 (LA)
1951—Rams, 45-21 (LA)
1953—Tie, 24-24 (Chi)
1954—Rams, 28-17 (LA)
1958—Rams, 20-14 (Chi)
1960—Cardinals, 43-21 (LA)
1965—Rams, 27-3 (StL)
1968—Rams, 24-13 (StL)
1970—Rams, 34-13 (LA)
1972—Cardinals, 24-14 (StL)
1975—***Rams, 35-23 (LA)
1976—Cardinals, 30-28 (LA)
1979—Rams, 21-0 (LA)
1980—Rams, 21-13 (StL)
1984—Rams, 16-13 (StL)
1985—Rams, 46-14 (LA)
1986—Rams, 16-10 (StL)
1987—Rams, 27-24 (StL)
1988—Cardinals, 41-27 (LA)
1989—Rams, 37-14 (LA)
1991—Cardinals, 24-14 (LA)
1992—Cardinals, 20-14 (LA)
1993—Cardinals, 38-10 (P)
1994—Rams, 14-12 (LA)
(RS Pts.—Rams 867, Cardinals 742)
(PS Pts.—Rams 35, Cardinals 23)
**Franchise known as Phoenix prior to 1994, in St. Louis prior to 1988, and in Chicago prior to 1960*
***Franchise in Los Angeles prior to 1995 and in Cleveland prior to 1946*
****NFC Divisional Playoff*

***ARIZONA vs. SAN DIEGO**
RS: Chargers lead series, 6-1
1971—Chargers, 20-17 (SD)
1976—Chargers, 43-24 (SD)
1983—Cardinals, 44-14 (StL)
1987—Chargers, 28-24 (SD)
1989—Chargers, 24-13 (P)
1992—Chargers, 27-21 (P)
1995—Chargers, 28-25 (SD)
(RS Pts.—Chargers 184, Cardinals 168)
**Franchise known as Phoenix prior to 1994, in St. Louis prior to 1988,*

***ARIZONA vs. SAN FRANCISCO**
RS: 49ers lead series, 10-9
1951—Cardinals, 27-21 (SF)
1957—Cardinals, 20-10 (SF)
1962—49ers, 24-17 (StL)
1964—Cardinals, 23-13 (SF)
1968—49ers, 35-17 (SF)
1971—49ers, 26-14 (StL)
1974—Cardinals, 34-9 (SF)
1976—Cardinals, 23-20 (StL) OT
1978—Cardinals, 16-10 (SF)
1979—Cardinals, 13-10 (StL)
1980—49ers, 24-21 (SF) OT
1982—49ers, 31-20 (StL)
1983—49ers, 42-27 (StL)
1986—49ers, 43-17 (SF)
1987—49ers, 34-28 (SF)
1988—Cardinals, 24-23 (P)
1991—49ers, 14-10 (SF)
1992—Cardinals, 24-14 (P)
1993—49ers, 28-14 (SF)
(RS Pts.—49ers 431, Cardinals 389)
**Franchise known as Phoenix prior to 1994, in St. Louis prior to 1988, and in Chicago prior to 1960*

***ARIZONA vs. SEATTLE**
RS: Cardinals lead series, 5-0
1976—Cardinals, 30-24 (S)
1983—Cardinals, 33-28 (StL)
1989—Cardinals, 34-24 (S)
1993—Cardinals, 30-27 (S) OT
1995—Cardinals, 20-14 (A) OT
(RS Pts.—Cardinals 147, Seahawks 117)
**Franchise known as Phoenix prior to 1994 and in St. Louis prior to 1988*

***ARIZONA vs. TAMPA BAY**
RS: Series tied, 6-6
1977—Buccaneers, 17-7 (TB)
1981—Buccaneers, 20-10 (TB)
1983—Cardinals, 34-27 (TB)
1985—Buccaneers, 16-0 (TB)
1986—Cardinals, 30-19 (TB)
Cardinals, 21-17 (StL)
1987—Cardinals, 31-28 (StL)
Cardinals, 31-14 (TB)
1988—Cardinals, 30-24 (TB)
1989—Buccaneers, 14-13 (P)
1992—Buccaneers, 23-7 (TB)
Buccaneers, 7-3 (P)
(RS Pts.—Buccaneers 226, Cardinals 217)
**Franchise known as Phoenix prior to 1994 and in St. Louis prior to 1988*

***ARIZONA vs. **WASHINGTON**
RS: Redskins lead series, 62-39-2
1932—Cardinals, 9-0 (B)
Braves, 8-6 (C)
1933—Redskins, 10-0 (C)
Tie, 0-0 (B)
1934—Redskins, 9-0 (B)
1935—Cardinals, 6-0 (B)
1936—Redskins, 13-10 (B)
1937—Cardinals, 21-14 (W)
1939—Redskins, 28-7 (W)
1940—Redskins, 28-21 (W)
1942—Redskins, 28-0 (W)
1943—Redskins, 13-7 (W)
1945—Redskins, 24-21 (W)
1947—Redskins, 45-21 (W)
1949—Cardinals, 38-7 (C)
1950—Cardinals, 38-28 (W)
1951—Redskins, 7-3 (C)
Redskins, 20-17 (W)
1952—Redskins, 23-7 (C)
Cardinals, 17-6 (W)
1953—Redskins, 24-13 (C)
Redskins, 28-17 (W)
1954—Cardinals, 38-16 (C)
Redskins, 37-20 (W)
1955—Cardinals, 24-10 (W)
Redskins, 31-0 (C)
1956—Cardinals, 31-3 (W)
Redskins, 17-14 (C)
1957—Redskins, 37-14 (C)
Cardinals, 44-14 (W)
1958—Cardinals, 37-10 (C)
Redskins, 45-31 (W)
1959—Cardinals, 49-21 (C)
Redskins, 23-14 (W)
1960—Cardinals, 44-7 (StL)
Cardinals, 26-14 (W)
1961—Cardinals, 24-0 (W)
Cardinals, 38-24 (StL)
1962—Redskins, 24-14 (W)
Tie, 17-17 (StL)
1963—Cardinals, 21-7 (W)
Cardinals, 24-20 (StL)
1964—Cardinals, 23-17 (W)
Cardinals, 38-24 (StL)
1965—Cardinals, 37-16 (W)
Redskins, 24-20 (StL)
1966—Cardinals, 23-7 (StL)
Redskins, 26-20 (W)
1967—Cardinals, 27-21 (W)
1968—Cardinals, 41-14 (StL)
1969—Redskins, 33-17 (W)
1970—Cardinals, 27-17 (StL)
Redskins, 28-27 (W)
1971—Redskins, 24-17 (StL)
Redskins, 20-0 (W)

1972—Redskins, 24-10 (W)
Redskins, 33-3 (StL)
1973—Cardinals, 34-27 (StL)
Redskins, 31-13 (W)
1974—Cardinals, 17-10 (W)
Cardinals, 23-20 (StL)
1975—Redskins, 27-17 (W)
Cardinals, 20-17 (StL) OT
1976—Redskins, 20-10 (W)
Redskins, 16-10 (StL)
1977—Redskins, 24-14 (W)
Redskins, 26-20 (StL)
1978—Redskins, 28-10 (StL)
Cardinals, 27-17 (W)
1979—Redskins, 17-7 (StL)
Redskins, 30-28 (W)
1980—Redskins, 23-0 (W)
Redskins, 31-7 (StL)
1981—Cardinals, 40-30 (StL)
Redskins, 42-21 (W)
1982—Redskins, 12-7 (StL)
Redskins, 28-0 (W)
1983—Redskins, 38-14 (StL)
Redskins, 45-7 (W)
1984—Cardinals, 26-24 (StL)
Redskins, 29-27 (W)
1985—Redskins, 27-10 (W)
Redskins, 27-16 (StL)
1986—Redskins, 28-21 (W)
Redskins, 20-17 (StL)
1987—Redskins, 28-21 (W)
Redskins, 34-17 (StL)
1988—Cardinals, 30-21 (P)
Redskins, 33-17 (W)
1989—Redskins, 30-28 (W)
Redskins, 29-10 (P)
1990—Redskins, 31-0 (W)
Redskins, 38-10 (P)
1991—Redskins, 34-0 (W)
Redskins, 20-14 (P)
1992—Cardinals, 27-24 (P)
Redskins, 41-3 (W)
1993—Cardinals, 17-10 (W)
Cardinals, 36-6 (P)
1994—Cardinals, 19-16 (W) OT
Cardinals, 17-15 (A)
1995—Redskins, 27-7 (W)
Cardinals, 24-20 (A)
(RS Pts.—Redskins 2,239, Cardinals 1,893)
Franchise known as Phoenix prior to 1994, in St. Louis prior to 1988, and in Chicago prior to 1960
***Franchise in Boston prior to 1937 and known as Braves prior to 1933*

ATLANTA vs. ARIZONA
RS: Cardinals lead series, 12-6;
See Arizona vs. Atlanta

ATLANTA vs. BUFFALO
RS: Bills lead series, 4-3
1973—Bills, 17-6 (A)
1977—Bills, 3-0 (B)
1980—Falcons, 30-14 (B)
1983—Falcons, 31-14 (A)
1989—Falcons, 30-28 (A)
1992—Bills, 41-14 (B)
1995—Bills, 23-17 (B)
(RS Pts.—Bills 140, Falcons 128)

ATLANTA vs. CAROLINA
RS: Series tied, 1-1
1995—Falcons, 23-20 (A) OT
Panthers, 21-17 (C)
(RS Pts.—Panthers 41, Falcons 40)

ATLANTA vs. CHICAGO
RS: Series tied, 9-9
1966—Bears, 23-6 (C)
1967—Bears, 23-14 (A)
1968—Falcons, 16-13 (C)
1969—Falcons, 48-31 (A)
1970—Bears, 23-14 (A)
1972—Falcons, 37-21 (C)
1973—Falcons, 46-6 (A)
1974—Falcons, 13-10 (A)
1976—Falcons, 10-0 (C)
1977—Falcons, 16-10 (C)
1978—Bears, 13-7 (C)
1980—Falcons, 28-17 (A)
1983—Falcons, 20-17 (C)
1985—Bears, 36-0 (C)
1986—Bears, 13-10 (A)
1990—Bears, 30-24 (C)
1992—Bears, 41-31 (C)
1993—Bears, 6-0 (C)
(RS Pts.—Falcons 340, Bears 333)

ATLANTA vs. CINCINNATI
RS: Bengals lead series, 6-2
1971—Falcons, 9-6 (C)
1975—Bengals, 21-14 (A)
1978—Bengals, 37-7 (C)
1981—Bengals, 30-28 (A)
1984—Bengals, 35-14 (C)
1987—Bengals, 16-10 (A)
1990—Falcons, 38-17 (A)
1993—Bengals, 21-17 (C)
(RS Pts.—Bengals 183, Falcons 137)

ATLANTA vs. CLEVELAND
RS: Browns lead series, 8-2
1966—Browns, 49-17 (A)
1968—Browns, 30-7 (C)
1971—Falcons, 31-14 (C)
1976—Browns, 20-17 (A)
1978—Browns, 24-16 (A)
1981—Browns, 28-17 (C)
1984—Browns, 23-7 (A)
1987—Browns, 38-3 (C)
1990—Browns, 13-10 (C)
1993—Falcons, 17-14 (A)
(RS Pts.—Browns 253, Falcons 142)

ATLANTA vs. DALLAS
RS: Cowboys lead series, 10-6
PS: Cowboys lead series, 2-0
1966—Cowboys, 47-14 (A)
1967—Cowboys, 37-7 (D)
1969—Cowboys, 24-17 (A)
1970—Cowboys, 13-0 (D)
1974—Cowboys, 24-0 (A)
1976—Falcons, 17-10 (A)
1978—*Cowboys, 27-20 (D)
1980—*Cowboys, 30-27 (A)
1985—Cowboys, 24-10 (D)
1986—Falcons, 37-35 (D)
1987—Falcons, 21-10 (D)
1988—Cowboys, 26-20 (D)
1989—Falcons 27-21 (A)
1990—Falcons, 26-7 (A)
1991—Cowboys, 31-27 (D)
1992—Cowboys, 41-17 (A)
1993—Falcons, 27-14 (A)
1995—Cowboys, 28-13 (A)
(RS Pts.—Cowboys 392, Falcons 280)
(PS Pts.—Cowboys 57, Falcons 47)
**NFC Divisional Playoff*

ATLANTA vs. DENVER
RS: Broncos lead series, 5-3
1970—Broncos, 24-10 (D)
1972—Falcons, 23-20 (A)
1975—Falcons, 35-21 (A)
1979—Broncos, 20-17 (A) OT
1982—Falcons, 34-27 (D)
1985—Broncos, 44-28 (A)
1988—Broncos, 30-14 (D)
1994—Broncos, 32-28 (D)
(RS Pts.—Broncos 218, Falcons 189)

ATLANTA vs. DETROIT
RS: Lions lead series, 18-6
1966—Lions, 28-10 (D)
1967—Lions, 24-3 (D)
1968—Lions, 24-7 (A)
1969—Lions, 27-21 (D)
1971—Lions, 41-38 (D)
1972—Lions, 26-23 (A)
1973—Lions, 31-6 (D)
1975—Lions, 17-14 (A)
1976—Lions, 24-10 (D)
1977—Falcons, 17-6 (A)
1978—Falcons, 14-0 (A)
1979—Lions, 24-23 (D)
1980—Falcons, 43-28 (A)
1983—Falcons, 30-14 (D)
1984—Lions, 27-24 (A) OT
1985—Lions, 28-27 (A)
1986—Falcons, 20-6 (D)
1987—Lions, 30-13 (A)
1988—Lions, 31-17 (D)
1989—Lions, 31-24 (A)
1990—Lions, 21-14 (D)
1993—Lions, 30-13 (D)
1994—Lions, 31-28 (D) OT
1995—Falcons, 34-22 (A)
(RS Pts.—Lions 571, Falcons 473)

ATLANTA vs. GREEN BAY
RS: Packers lead series, 10-9
PS: Packers lead series, 1-0
1966—Packers, 56-3 (Mil)
1967—Packers, 23-0 (Mil)
1968—Packers, 38-7 (A)
1969—Packers, 28-10 (GB)
1970—Packers, 27-24 (GB)
1971—Falcons, 28-21 (A)
1972—Falcons, 10-9 (Mil)
1974—Falcons, 10-3 (A)
1975—Packers, 22-13 (GB)
1976—Packers, 24-20 (A)
1979—Falcons, 25-7 (A)
1981—Falcons, 31-17 (GB)
1982—Packers, 38-7 (A)
1983—Falcons, 47-41 (A) OT
1988—Falcons, 20-0 (A)
1989—Packers, 23-21 (Mil)
1991—Falcons, 35-31 (A)
1992—Falcons, 24-10 (A)
1994—Packers, 21-17 (Mil)
1995—*Packers, 37-20 (GB)
(RS Pts.—Packers 439, Falcons 352)
(PS Pts.—Packers 37, Falcons 20)
**NFC First-Round Playoff*

ATLANTA vs. HOUSTON
RS: Falcons lead series, 5-3
1972—Falcons, 20-10 (A)
1976—Oilers, 20-14 (H)
1978—Falcons, 20-14 (A)
1981—Falcons, 31-27 (H)
1984—Falcons, 42-10 (A)
1987—Oilers, 37-33 (H)
1990—Falcons, 47-27 (A)
1993—Oilers, 33-17 (H)
(RS Pts.—Falcons 224, Oilers 178)

ATLANTA vs. *INDIANAPOLIS
RS: Colts lead series, 10-0
1966—Colts, 19-7 (A)
1967—Colts, 38-31 (B)
Colts, 49-7 (A)
1968—Colts, 28-20 (A)
Colts, 44-0 (B)
1969—Colts, 21-14 (A)
Colts, 13-6 (B)
1974—Colts, 17-7 (A)
1986—Colts, 28-23 (A)
1989—Colts, 13-9 (I)
(RS Pts.—Colts 270, Falcons 124)
**Franchise in Baltimore prior to 1984*

ATLANTA vs. KANSAS CITY
RS: Chiefs lead series, 4-0
1972—Chiefs, 17-14 (A)
1985—Chiefs, 38-10 (KC)
1991—Chiefs, 14-3 (KC)
1994—Chiefs, 30-10 (A)
(RS Pts.—Chiefs 99, Falcons 37)

ATLANTA vs. MIAMI
RS: Dolphins lead series, 6-1
1970—Dolphins, 20-7 (A)
1974—Dolphins, 42-7 (M)
1980—Dolphins, 20-17 (A)
1983—Dolphins, 31-24 (M)
1986—Falcons, 20-14 (M)
1992—Dolphins, 21-17 (M)
1995—Dolphins, 21-20 (M)
(RS Pts.—Dolphins 169, Falcons 112)

ATLANTA vs. MINNESOTA
RS: Vikings lead series, 11-6
PS: Vikings lead series, 1-0
1966—Falcons, 20-13 (M)
1967—Falcons, 21-20 (A)
1968—Vikings, 47-7 (M)
1969—Falcons, 10-3 (A)
1970—Vikings, 37-7 (A)
1971—Vikings, 24-7 (M)
1973—Falcons, 20-14 (A)
1974—Vikings, 23-10 (M)
1975—Vikings, 38-0 (M)
1977—Vikings, 14-7 (A)
1980—Vikings, 24-23 (M)
1981—Falcons, 31-30 (A)
1982—*Vikings, 30-24 (M)
1984—Vikings, 27-20 (M)
1985—Falcons, 14-13 (A)
1987—Vikings, 24-13 (M)
1989—Vikings, 43-17 (M)
1991—Vikings, 20-19 (A)
(RS Pts.—Vikings 414, Falcons 246)
(PS Pts.—Vikings 30, Falcons 24)
**NFC First-Round Playoff*

ATLANTA vs. NEW ENGLAND
RS: Falcons lead series, 5-3
1972—Patriots, 21-20 (NE)
1977—Patriots, 16-10 (A)
1980—Falcons, 37-21 (NE)
1983—Falcons, 24-13 (A)
1986—Patriots, 25-17 (NE)
1989—Falcons, 16-15 (A)
1992—Falcons, 34-0 (A)
1995—Falcons, 30-17 (A)
(RS Pts.—Falcons 188, Patriots 128)

ATLANTA vs. NEW ORLEANS
RS: Falcons lead series, 29-24
PS: Falcons lead series, 1-0
1967—Saints, 27-24 (NO)
1969—Falcons, 45-17 (A)
1970—Falcons, 14-3 (NO)
Falcons, 32-14 (A)
1971—Falcons, 28-6 (A)
Falcons, 24-20 (NO)
1972—Falcons, 21-14 (NO)
Falcons, 36-20 (A)
1973—Falcons, 62-7 (NO)
Falcons, 14-10 (A)
1974—Saints, 14-13 (NO)
Saints, 13-3 (A)
1975—Falcons, 14-7 (A)
Saints, 23-7 (NO)
1976—Saints, 30-0 (NO)
Falcons, 23-20 (A)
1977—Saints, 21-20 (NO)
Falcons, 35-7 (A)
1978—Falcons, 20-17 (NO)
Falcons, 20-17 (A)
1979—Falcons, 40-34 (NO) OT
Saints, 37-6 (A)
1980—Falcons, 41-14 (NO)
Falcons, 31-13 (A)
1981—Falcons, 27-0 (A)
Falcons, 41-10 (NO)
1982—Falcons, 35-0 (A)
Saints, 35-6 (NO)
1983—Saints, 19-17 (A)
Saints, 27-10 (NO)
1984—Falcons, 36-28 (NO)
Saints, 17-13 (A)
1985—Falcons, 31-24 (A)
Falcons, 16-10 (NO)
1986—Falcons, 31-10 (NO)
Saints, 14-9 (A)
1987—Saints, 38-0 (A)
1988—Saints, 29-21 (A)
Saints, 10-9 (NO)
1989—Saints, 20-13 (NO)
Saints, 26-17 (A)
1990—Falcons, 28-27 (A)
Saints, 10-7 (NO)
1991—Saints, 27-6 (A)
Falcons, 23-20 (NO) OT
*Falcons, 27-20 (NO)

1992—Saints, 10-7 (A)
Saints, 22-14 (NO)
1993—Saints, 34-31 (A)
Falcons, 26-15 (NO)
1994—Saints, 33-32 (NO)
Saints, 29-20 (A)
1995—Falcons, 27-24 (NO) OT
Falcons, 19-14 (A)
(RS Pts.—Falcons 1,145, Saints 987)
(PS Pts.—Falcons 27, Saints 20)
NFC First-Round Playoff

ATLANTA vs. N.Y. GIANTS
RS: Series tied, 6-6
1966—Falcons, 27-16 (NY)
1968—Falcons, 24-21 (A)
1971—Giants, 21-17 (A)
1974—Falcons, 14-7 (New Haven)
1977—Falcons, 17-3 (A)
1978—Falcons, 23-20 (A)
1979—Giants, 24-3 (NY)
1981—Giants, 27-24 (A) OT
1982—Falcons, 16-14 (NY)
1983—Giants, 16-13 (A) OT
1984—Giants, 19-7 (A)
1988—Giants, 23-16 (A)
(RS Pts.—Giants 211, Falcons 201)

ATLANTA vs. N.Y. JETS
RS: Falcons lead series, 4-3
1973—Falcons, 28-20 (NY)
1980—Jets, 14-7 (A)
1983—Falcons, 27-21 (NY)
1986—Jets, 28-14 (A)
1989—Jets, 27-7 (NY)
1992—Falcons, 20-17 (A)
1995—Falcons, 13-3 (A)
(RS Pts.—Jets 130, Falcons 116)

ATLANTA vs. *OAKLAND
RS: Raiders lead series, 5-3
1971—Falcons, 24-13 (A)
1975—Raiders, 37-34 (O) OT
1979—Raiders, 50-19 (O)
1982—Raiders, 38-14 (A)
1985—Raiders, 34-24 (A)
1988—Falcons, 12-6 (LA)
1991—Falcons, 21-17 (A)
1994—Raiders, 30-17 (LA)
(RS Pts.—Raiders 225, Falcons 165)
Franchise in Los Angeles from 1982-1994

ATLANTA vs. PHILADELPHIA
RS: Eagles lead series, 8-7-1
PS: Falcons lead series, 1-0
1966—Eagles, 23-10 (P)
1967—Eagles, 38-7 (A)
1969—Falcons, 27-3 (P)
1970—Tie, 13-13 (P)
1973—Falcons, 44-27 (P)
1976—Eagles, 14-13 (A)
1978—*Falcons, 14-13 (A)
1979—Falcons, 14-10 (P)
1980—Falcons, 20-17 (P)
1981—Eagles, 16-13 (P)
1983—Eagles, 28-24 (A)
1984—Falcons, 26-10 (A)
1985—Eagles, 23-17 (P) OT
1986—Eagles, 16-0 (A)
1988—Falcons, 27-24 (P)
1990—Eagles, 24-23 (A)
1994—Falcons, 28-21 (A)
(RS Pts.—Eagles 307, Falcons 306)
(PS Pts.—Falcons 14, Eagles 13)
NFC First-Round Playoff

ATLANTA vs. PITTSBURGH
RS: Steelers lead series, 9-1
1966—Steelers, 57-33 (A)
1968—Steelers, 41-21 (A)
1970—Falcons, 27-16 (A)
1974—Steelers, 24-17 (P)
1978—Steelers, 31-7 (P)
1981—Steelers, 34-20 (A)
1984—Steelers, 35-10 (P)
1987—Steelers, 28-12 (A)
1990—Steelers, 21-9 (P)
1993—Steelers, 45-17 (A)
(RS Pts.—Steelers 332, Falcons 173)

ATLANTA vs. *ST. LOUIS
RS: Rams lead series, 37-19-2
1966—Rams, 19-14 (A)
1967—Rams, 31-3 (A)
Rams, 20-3 (LA)
1968—Rams, 27-14 (LA)
Rams, 17-10 (A)
1969—Rams, 17-7 (LA)
Rams, 38-6 (A)
1970—Tie, 10-10 (LA)
Rams, 17-7 (A)
1971—Tie, 20-20 (LA)
Rams, 24-16 (A)
1972—Falcons, 31-3 (A)
Rams, 20-7 (LA)
1973—Rams, 31-0 (LA)
Falcons, 15-13 (A)
1974—Rams, 21-0 (LA)
Rams, 30-7 (A)
1975—Rams, 22-7 (LA)
Rams, 16-7 (A)
1976—Rams, 30-14 (A)
Rams, 59-0 (LA)
1977—Falcons, 17-6 (A)
Rams, 23-7 (LA)
1978—Rams, 10-0 (LA)
Falcons, 15-7 (A)
1979—Rams, 20-14 (LA)
Rams, 34-13 (A)
1980—Falcons, 13-10 (A)
Rams, 20-17 (LA) OT
1981—Rams, 37-35 (A)
Rams, 21-16 (LA)
1982—Falcons, 34-17 (A)
1983—Rams, 27-21 (LA)
Rams, 36-13 (A)
1984—Falcons, 30-28 (LA)
Rams, 24-10 (A)
1985—Rams, 17-6 (LA)
Falcons, 30-14 (A)
1986—Falcons, 26-14 (A)
Rams, 14-7 (LA)
1987—Falcons, 24-20 (A)
Rams, 33-0 (LA)
1988—Rams, 33-0 (A)
Rams, 22-7 (LA)
1989—Rams, 31-21 (A)
Rams, 26-14 (LA)
1990—Rams, 44-24 (LA)
Falcons, 20-13 (A)
1991—Falcons, 31-14 (A)
Falcons, 31-14 (LA)
1992—Falcons, 30-28 (A)
Rams, 38-27 (LA)
1993—Falcons, 30-24 (A)
Falcons, 13-0 (LA)
1994—Falcons, 31-13 (A)
Falcons, 8-5 (LA)
1995—Rams, 21-19 (StL)
Falcons, 31-6 (A)
(RS Pts.—Rams 1,249, Falcons 883)
Franchise in Los Angeles prior to 1995

ATLANTA vs. SAN DIEGO
RS: Falcons lead series, 4-1
1973—Falcons, 41-0 (SD)
1979—Falcons, 28-26 (SD)
1988—Chargers, 10-7 (A)
1991—Falcons, 13-10 (SD)
1994—Falcons, 10-9 (A)
(RS Pts.—Falcons 99, Chargers 55)

ATLANTA vs. SAN FRANCISCO
RS: 49ers lead series, 35-22-1
1966—49ers, 44-7 (A)
1967—49ers, 38-7 (SF)
49ers, 34-28 (A)
1968—49ers, 28-13 (SF)
49ers, 14-12 (A)
1969—Falcons, 24-12 (A)
Falcons, 21-7 (SF)
1970—Falcons, 21-20 (A)
49ers, 24-20 (SF)
1971—Falcons, 20-17 (A)
49ers, 24-3 (SF)
1972—49ers, 49-14 (A)
49ers, 20-0 (SF)
1973—49ers, 13-9 (A)
Falcons, 17-3 (SF)
1974—49ers, 16-10 (A)
49ers, 27-0 (SF)
1975—Falcons, 17-3 (SF)
Falcons, 31-9 (A)
1976—49ers, 15-0 (SF)
Falcons, 21-16 (A)
1977—Falcons, 7-0 (SF)
49ers, 10-3 (A)
1978—Falcons, 20-17 (SF)
Falcons, 21-10 (A)
1979—49ers, 20-15 (SF)
Falcons, 31-21 (A)
1980—Falcons, 20-17 (SF)
Falcons, 35-10 (A)
1981—Falcons, 34-17 (A)
49ers, 17-14 (SF)
1982—Falcons, 17-7 (SF)
1983—49ers, 24-20 (SF)
Falcons, 28-24 (A)
1984—49ers, 14-5 (SF)
49ers, 35-17 (A)
1985—49ers, 35-16 (SF)
49ers, 38-17 (A)
1986—Tie, 10-10 (A) OT
49ers, 20-0 (SF)
1987—49ers, 25-17 (A)
49ers, 35-7 (SF)
1988—Falcons, 34-17 (SF)
49ers, 13-3 (A)
1989—49ers, 45-3 (SF)
49ers, 23-10 (A)
1990—49ers, 19-13 (SF)
49ers, 45-35 (A)
1991—Falcons, 39-34 (SF)
Falcons, 17-14 (A)
1992—49ers, 56-17 (SF)
49ers, 41-3 (A)
1993—49ers, 37-30 (SF)
Falcons, 27-24 (A)
1994—49ers, 42-3 (A)
49ers, 50-14 (SF)
1995—49ers, 41-10 (SF)
Falcons, 28-27 (A)
(RS Pts.—49ers 1,367, Falcons 935)

ATLANTA vs. SEATTLE
RS: Seahawks lead series, 4-1
1976—Seahawks, 30-13 (S)
1979—Seahawks, 31-28 (A)
1985—Seahawks, 30-26 (S)
1988—Seahawks, 31-20 (A)
1991—Falcons, 26-13 (A)
(RS Pts.—Seahawks 135, Falcons 113)

ATLANTA vs. TAMPA BAY
RS: Falcons lead series, 8-6
1977—Falcons, 17-0 (TB)
1978—Buccaneers, 14-9 (TB)
1979—Falcons, 17-14 (A)
1981—Buccaneers, 24-23 (TB)
1984—Buccaneers, 23-6 (TB)
1986—Falcons, 23-20 (TB) OT
1987—Buccaneers, 48-10 (TB)
1988—Falcons, 17-10 (A)
1990—Buccaneers, 23-17 (TB)
1991—Falcons, 43-7 (A)
1992—Falcons, 35-7 (TB)
1993—Buccaneers, 31-24 (A)
1994—Falcons, 34-13 (A)
1995—Falcons, 24-21 (TB)
(RS Pts.—Falcons 299, Buccaneers 255)

ATLANTA vs. WASHINGTON
RS: Redskins lead series, 13-4-1
PS: Redskins lead series, 1-0
1966—Redskins, 33-20 (W)
1967—Tie, 20-20 (A)
1969—Redskins, 27-20 (W)
1972—Redskins, 24-13 (W)
1975—Redskins, 30-27 (A)
1977—Redskins, 10-6 (W)
1978—Falcons, 20-17 (A)
1979—Redskins, 16-7 (A)
1980—Falcons, 10-6 (A)
1983—Redskins, 37-21 (W)
1984—Redskins, 27-14 (W)
1985—Redskins, 44-10 (A)
1987—Falcons, 21-20 (A)
1989—Redskins, 31-30 (A)
1991—Redskins, 56-17 (W)
*Redskins, 24-7 (W)
1992—Redskins, 24-17 (W)
1993—Redskins, 30-17 (W)
1994—Falcons, 27-20 (W)
(RS Pts.—Redskins 472, Falcons 317)
(PS Pts.—Redskins 24, Falcons 7)
NFC Divisional Playoff

BUFFALO vs. ARIZONA
RS: Series tied, 3-3;
See Arizona vs. Buffalo

BUFFALO vs. ATLANTA
RS: Bills lead series, 4-3;
See Atlanta vs. Buffalo

BUFFALO vs. CAROLINA
RS: Bills lead series, 1-0
1995—Bills, 31-9 (B)
(RS Pts.—Bills 31, Panthers 9)

BUFFALO vs. CHICAGO
RS: Bears lead series, 4-2
1970—Bears, 31-13 (C)
1974—Bills, 16-6 (B)
1979—Bears, 7-0 (B)
1988—Bears, 24-3 (C)
1991—Bills, 35-20 (B)
1994—Bears, 20-13 (C)
(RS Pts.—Bears 108, Bills 80)

BUFFALO vs. CINCINNATI
RS: Bengals lead series, 9-7
PS: Bengals lead series, 2-0
1968—Bengals, 34-23 (C)
1969—Bills, 16-13 (B)
1970—Bengals, 43-14 (B)
1973—Bengals, 16-13 (B)
1975—Bengals, 33-24 (C)
1978—Bills, 5-0 (B)
1979—Bills, 51-24 (B)
1980—Bills, 14-0 (C)
1981—Bengals, 27-24 (C) OT
*Bengals, 28-21 (C)
1983—Bills, 10-6 (C)
1984—Bengals, 52-21 (C)
1985—Bengals, 23-17 (B)
1986—Bengals, 36-33 (C) OT
1988—Bengals, 35-21 (C)
**Bengals, 21-10 (C)
1989—Bills, 24-7 (B)
1991—Bills, 35-16 (B)
(RS Pts.—Bengals 365, Bills 345)
(PS Pts.—Bengals 49, Bills 31)
AFC Divisional Playoff
***AFC Championship*

BUFFALO vs. CLEVELAND
RS: Browns lead series, 7-4
PS: Browns lead series, 1-0
1972—Browns, 27-10 (C)
1974—Bills, 15-10 (C)
1977—Browns, 27-16 (B)
1978—Browns, 41-20 (C)
1981—Bills, 22-13 (B)
1984—Browns, 13-10 (B)
1985—Browns, 17-7 (C)
1986—Browns, 21-17 (B)
1987—Browns, 27-21 (C)
1989—*Browns, 34-30 (C)
1990—Bills, 42-0 (C)
1995—Bills, 22-19 (C)
(RS Pts.—Browns 215, Bills 202)
(PS Pts.—Browns 34, Bills 30)
AFC Divisional Playoff

BUFFALO vs. DALLAS
RS: Cowboys lead series, 3-2
PS: Cowboys lead series, 2-0

1971—Cowboys, 49-37 (B)
1976—Cowboys, 17-10 (D)
1981—Cowboys, 27-14 (D)
1984—Bills, 14-3 (B)
1992—*Cowboys, 52-17 (Pasadena)
1993—Bills, 13-10 (D)
**Cowboys, 30-13 (Atlanta)
(RS Pts.—Cowboys 106, Bills 88)
(PS Pts.—Cowboys 82, Bills 30)
Super Bowl XXVII
***Super Bowl XXVIII*

BUFFALO vs. DENVER
RS: Bills lead series, 17-11-1
PS: Bills lead series, 1-0
1960—Broncos, 27-21 (B)
Tie, 38-38 (D)
1961—Broncos, 22-10 (B)
Bills, 23-10 (D)
1962—Broncos, 23-20 (B)
Bills, 45-38 (D)
1963—Bills, 30-28 (D)
Bills, 27-17 (B)
1964—Bills, 30-13 (B)
Bills, 30-19 (D)
1965—Bills, 30-15 (D)
Bills, 31-13 (B)
1966—Bills, 38-21 (B)
1967—Bills, 17-16 (D)
Broncos, 21-20 (B)
1968—Broncos, 34-32 (D)
1969—Bills, 41-28 (B)
1970—Broncos, 25-10 (B)
1975—Bills, 38-14 (B)
1977—Broncos, 26-6 (D)
1979—Broncos, 19-16 (B)
1981—Bills, 9-7 (B)
1984—Broncos, 37-7 (B)
1987—Bills, 21-14 (B)
1989—Broncos, 28-14 (B)
1990—Bills, 29-28 (B)
1991—*Bills, 10-7 (B)
1992—Bills, 27-17 (B)
1994—Bills, 27-20 (B)
1995—Broncos, 22-7 (D)
(RS Pts.—Bills 694, Broncos 640)
(PS Pts.—Bills 10, Broncos 7)
*AFC Championship

BUFFALO vs. DETROIT
RS: Lions lead series, 3-1-1
1972—Tie, 21-21 (B)
1976—Lions, 27-14 (D)
1979—Bills, 20-17 (D)
1991—Lions, 17-14 (B) OT
1994—Lions, 35-21 (D)
(RS Pts.—Lions 117, Bills 90)

BUFFALO vs. GREEN BAY
RS: Bills lead series, 5-1
1974—Bills, 27-7 (GB)
1979—Bills, 19-12 (B)
1982—Packers, 33-21 (Mil)
1988—Bills, 28-0 (B)
1991—Bills, 34-24 (Mil)
1994—Bills 29-20 (B)
(RS Pts.—Bills 158, Packers 96)

BUFFALO vs. HOUSTON
RS: Oilers lead series, 21-13
PS: Bills lead series, 2-0
1960—Bills, 25-24 (B)
Oilers, 31-23 (H)
1961—Bills, 22-12 (H)
Oilers, 28-16 (B)
1962—Oilers, 28-23 (B)
Oilers, 17-14 (H)
1963—Oilers, 31-20 (B)
Oilers, 28-14 (H)
1964—Bills, 48-17 (H)
Bills, 24-10 (B)
1965—Oilers, 19-17 (B)
Bills, 29-18 (H)
1966—Bills, 27-20 (B)
Bills, 42-20 (H)
1967—Oilers, 20-3 (B)
Oilers, 10-3 (H)
1968—Oilers, 30-7 (B)
Oilers, 35-6 (H)
1969—Oilers, 17-3 (B)
Oilers, 28-14 (H)
1971—Oilers, 20-14 (B)
1974—Oilers, 21-9 (B)
1976—Oilers, 13-3 (B)
1978—Oilers, 17-10 (H)
1983—Bills, 30-13 (B)
1985—Bills, 20-0 (B)
1986—Oilers, 16-7 (H)
1987—Bills, 34-30 (B)
1988—*Bills, 17-10 (B)
1989—Bills, 47-41 (H) OT
1990—Oilers, 27-24 (H)
1992—Oilers, 27-3 (H)
**Bills, 41-38 (B) OT
1993—Bills, 35-7 (B)
1994—Bills, 15-7 (H)
1995—Oilers, 28-17 (B)
(RS Pts.—Oilers 710, Bills 648)
(PS Pts.—Bills 58, Oilers 48)
AFC Divisional Playoff
***AFC First-Round Game*

BUFFALO vs. *INDIANAPOLIS
RS: Bills lead series, 28-22-1
1970—Tie, 17-17 (Balt)
Colts, 20-14 (Buff)
1971—Colts, 43-0 (Buff)
Colts, 24-0 (Balt)
1972—Colts, 17-0 (Buff)
Colts, 35-7 (Balt)
1973—Bills, 31-13 (Buff)
Bills, 24-17 (Balt)
1974—Bills, 27-14 (Balt)
Bills, 6-0 (Buff)
1975—Bills, 38-31 (Balt)
Colts, 42-35 (Buff)
1976—Colts, 31-13 (Buff)
Colts, 58-20 (Balt)
1977—Colts, 17-14 (Balt)
Colts, 31-13 (Buff)
1978—Bills, 24-17 (Buff)
Bills, 21-14 (Balt)
1979—Bills, 31-13 (Balt)
Colts, 14-13 (Buff)
1980—Colts, 17-12 (Buff)
Colts, 28-24 (Balt)
1981—Bills, 35-3 (Balt)
Bills, 23-17 (Buff)
1982—Bills, 20-0 (Buff)
1983—Bills, 28-23 (Buff)
Bills, 30-7 (Balt)
1984—Colts, 31-17 (I)
Bills, 21-15 (Buff)
1985—Colts, 49-17 (I)
Bills, 21-9 (Buff)
1986—Bills, 24-13 (Buff)
Colts, 24-14 (I)
1987—Colts, 47-6 (Buff)
Bills, 27-3 (I)
1988—Bills, 34-23 (Buff)
Colts, 17-14 (I)
1989—Colts, 37-14 (I)
Bills, 30-7 (Buff)
1990—Bills, 26-10 (Buff)
Bills, 31-7 (I)
1991—Bills, 42-6 (Buff)
Bills, 35-7 (I)
1992—Bills, 38-0 (Buff)
Colts, 16-13 (I) OT
1993—Bills, 23-9 (Buff)
Bills, 30-10 (I)
1994—Colts, 27-17 (Buff)
Colts, 10-9 (I)
1995—Bills, 20-14 (Buff)
Bills, 16-10 (I)
(RS Pts.—Bills 1,059, Colts 964)
Franchise in Baltimore prior to 1984

BUFFALO vs. *KANSAS CITY
RS: Bills lead series, 16-13-1
PS: Bills lead series, 2-1
1960—Texans, 45-28 (B)
Texans, 24-7 (D)
1961—Bills, 27-24 (B)
Bills, 30-20 (D)
1962—Texans, 41-21 (D)
Bills, 23-14 (B)
1963—Tie, 27-27 (B)
Bills, 35-26 (KC)
1964—Bills, 34-17 (B)
Bills, 35-22 (KC)
1965—Bills, 23-7 (KC)
Bills, 34-25 (B)
1966—Chiefs, 42-20 (B)
Bills, 29-14 (KC)
**Chiefs, 31-7 (B)
1967—Chiefs, 23-13 (KC)
1968—Chiefs, 18-7 (B)
1969—Chiefs, 29-7 (B)
Chiefs, 22-19 (KC)
1971—Chiefs, 22-9 (KC)
1973—Bills, 23-14 (B)
1976—Bills, 50-17 (B)
1978—Bills, 28-13 (B)
Chiefs, 14-10 (KC)
1982—Bills, 14-9 (B)
1983—Bills, 14-9 (KC)
1986—Chiefs, 20-17 (B)
Bills, 17-14 (KC)
1991—Chiefs, 33-6 (KC)
***Bills, 37-14 (B)
1993—Chiefs, 23-7 (KC)
****Bills, 30-13 (B)
1994—Bills, 44-10 (B)
(RS Pts.—Bills 653, Chiefs 643)
(PS Pts.—Bills 74, Chiefs 58)
Franchise in Dallas prior to 1963 and known as Texans
***AFL Championship*
****AFC Divisional Playoff*
*****AFC Championship*

BUFFALO vs. MIAMI
RS: Dolphins lead series, 38-21-1
PS: Bills lead series, 3-0
1966—Bills, 58-24 (B)
Bills, 29-0 (M)
1967—Bills, 35-13 (B)
Dolphins, 17-14 (M)
1968—Tie, 14-14 (M)
Dolphins, 21-17 (B)
1969—Dolphins, 24-6 (M)
Bills, 28-3 (B)
1970—Dolphins, 33-14 (B)
Dolphins, 45-7 (M)
1971—Dolphins, 29-14 (B)
Dolphins, 34-0 (M)
1972—Dolphins, 24-23 (M)
Dolphins, 30-16 (B)
1973—Dolphins, 27-6 (M)
Dolphins, 17-0 (B)
1974—Dolphins, 24-16 (B)
Dolphins, 35-28 (M)
1975—Dolphins, 35-30 (B)
Dolphins, 31-21 (M)
1976—Dolphins, 30-21 (B)
Dolphins, 45-27 (M)
1977—Dolphins, 13-0 (B)
Dolphins, 31-14 (M)
1978—Dolphins, 31-24 (M)
Dolphins, 25-24 (B)
1979—Dolphins, 9-7 (B)
Dolphins, 17-7 (M)
1980—Bills, 17-7 (B)
Dolphins, 17-14 (M)
1981—Bills, 31-21 (B)
Dolphins, 16-6 (M)
1982—Dolphins, 9-7 (B)
Dolphins, 27-10 (M)
1983—Dolphins, 12-0 (B)
Bills, 38-35 (M) OT
1984—Dolphins, 21-17 (B)
Dolphins, 38-7 (M)
1985—Dolphins, 23-14 (B)
Dolphins, 28-0 (M)
1986—Dolphins, 27-14 (M)
Dolphins, 34-24 (B)
1987—Bills, 34-31 (M) OT
Bills, 27-0 (B)
1988—Bills, 9-6 (B)
Bills, 31-6 (M)
1989—Bills, 27-24 (M)
Bills, 31-17 (B)
1990—Dolphins, 30-7 (M)
Bills, 24-14 (B)
*Bills, 44-34 (B)
1991—Bills, 35-31 (B)
Bills, 41-27 (M)
1992—Dolphins, 37-10 (B)
Bills, 26-20 (M)
**Bills, 29-10 (M)
1993—Dolphins, 22-13 (B)
Bills, 47-34 (M)
1994—Bills, 21-11 (B)
Bills, 42-31 (M)
1995—Dolphins, 23-6 (M)
Bills, 23-20 (B)
***Bills, 37-22 (B)
(RS Pts.—Dolphins 1,380, Bills 1,153)
(PS Pts.—Bills 110, Dolphins 66)
AFC Divisional Playoff
***AFC Championship*
****AFC First-Round Playoff*

BUFFALO vs. MINNESOTA
RS: Vikings lead series, 5-2
1971—Vikings, 19-0 (M)
1975—Vikings, 35-13 (B)
1979—Vikings, 10-3 (M)
1982—Bills, 23-22 (B)
1985—Vikings, 27-20 (B)
1988—Bills, 13-10 (B)
1994—Vikings, 21-17 (B)
(RS Pts.—Vikings 144, Bills 89)

BUFFALO vs. *NEW ENGLAND
RS: Patriots lead series, 36-34-1
PS: Patriots lead series, 1-0
1960—Bills, 13-0 (Bos)
Bills, 38-14 (Buff)
1961—Patriots, 23-21 (Buff)
Patriots, 52-21 (Bos)
1962—Tie, 28-28 (Buff)
Patriots, 21-10 (Bos)
1963—Bills, 28-21 (Buff)
Patriots, 17-7 (Bos)
**Patriots, 26-8 (Buff)
1964—Patriots, 36-28 (Buff)
Bills, 24-14 (Bos)
1965—Bills, 24-7 (Buff)
Bills, 23-7 (Bos)
1966—Patriots, 20-10 (Buff)
Patriots, 14-3 (Bos)
1967—Patriots, 23-0 (Buff)
Bills, 44-16 (Bos)
1968—Patriots, 16-7 (Buff)
Patriots, 23-6 (Bos)
1969—Bills, 23-16 (Buff)
Patriots, 35-21 (Bos)
1970—Bills, 45-10 (Bos)
Patriots, 14-10 (Buff)
1971—Patriots, 38-33 (NE)
Bills, 27-20 (Buff)
1972—Bills, 38-14 (Buff)
Bills, 27-24 (NE)
1973—Bills, 31-13 (NE)
Bills, 37-13 (Buff)
1974—Bills, 30-28 (Buff)
Bills, 29-28 (NE)
1975—Bills, 45-31 (Buff)
Bills, 34-14 (NE)
1976—Patriots, 26-22 (Buff)
Patriots, 20-10 (NE)
1977—Bills, 24-14 (NE)
Patriots, 20-7 (Buff)
1978—Patriots, 14-10 (Buff)
Patriots, 26-24 (NE)
1979—Patriots, 26-6 (Buff)
Bills, 16-13 (NE) OT
1980—Bills, 31-13 (Buff)
Patriots, 24-2 (NE)

ALL-TIME TEAM VS. TEAM RESULTS

1981—Bills, 20-17 (Buff)
Bills, 19-10 (NE)
1982—Patriots, 30-19 (NE)
1983—Patriots, 31-0 (Buff)
Patriots, 21-7 (NE)
1984—Patriots, 21-17 (Buff)
Patriots, 38-10 (NE)
1985—Patriots, 17-14 (Buff)
Patriots, 14-3 (NE)
1986—Patriots, 23-3 (Buff)
Patriots, 22-19 (NE)
1987—Patriots, 14-7 (NE)
Patriots, 13-7 (Buff)
1988—Bills, 16-14 (NE)
Bills, 23-20 (Buff)
1989—Bills, 31-10 (Buff)
Patriots, 33-24 (NE)
1990—Bills, 27-10 (NE)
Bills, 14-0 (Buff)
1991—Bills, 22-17 (Buff)
Patriots, 16-13 (NE)
1992—Bills, 41-7 (NE)
Bills, 16-7 (Buff)
1993—Bills, 38-14 (Buff)
Bills, 13-10 (NE) OT
1994—Bills, 38-35 (NE)
Patriots, 41-17 (Buff)
1995—Patriots, 27-14 (NE)
Patriots, 35-25 (Buff)
(RS Pts.—Bills 1,434, Patriots 1,413)
(PS Pts.—Patriots 26, Bills 8)
Franchise in Boston prior to 1971
***Division Playoff*

BUFFALO vs. NEW ORLEANS
RS: Bills lead series, 3-2
1973—Saints, 13-0 (NO)
1980—Bills, 35-26 (NO)
1983—Bills, 27-21 (B)
1989—Saints, 22-19 (B)
1992—Bills, 20-16 (NO)
(RS Pts.—Bills 101, Saints 98)

BUFFALO vs. N.Y. GIANTS
RS: Bills lead series, 4-2
PS: Giants lead series, 1-0
1970—Giants, 20-6 (NY)
1975—Giants, 17-14 (B)
1978—Bills, 41-17 (B)
1987—Bills, 6-3 (B) OT
1990—Bills, 17-13 (NY)
*Giants, 20-19 (Tampa)
1993—Bills, 17-14 (B)
(RS Pts.—Bills 101, Giants 84)
(PS Pts.—Giants 20, Bills 19)
**Super Bowl XXV*

BUFFALO vs. *N.Y. JETS
RS: Bills lead series, 39-31
PS: Bills lead series, 1-0
1960—Titans, 27-3 (NY)
Titans, 17-13 (B)
1961—Bills, 41-31 (B)
Titans, 21-14 (NY)
1962—Titans, 17-6 (B)
Bills, 20-3 (NY)
1963—Bills, 45-14 (B)
Bills, 19-10 (NY)
1964—Bills, 34-24 (B)
Bills, 20-7 (NY)
1965—Bills, 33-21 (B)
Jets, 14-12 (NY)
1966—Bills, 33-23 (NY)
Bills, 14-3 (B)
1967—Bills, 20-17 (B)
Jets, 20-10 (NY)
1968—Bills, 37-35 (B)
Jets, 25-21 (NY)
1969—Jets, 33-19 (B)
Jets, 16-6 (NY)
1970—Bills, 34-31 (B)
Bills, 10-6 (NY)
1971—Jets, 28-17 (NY)
Jets, 20-7 (B)
1972—Jets, 41-24 (B)
Jets, 41-3 (NY)
1973—Bills, 9-7 (B)
Bills, 34-14 (NY)
1974—Bills, 16-12 (B)
Jets, 20-10 (NY)
1975—Bills, 42-14 (B)
Bills, 24-23 (NY)
1976—Jets, 17-14 (NY)
Jets, 19-14 (B)
1977—Jets, 24-19 (B)
Bills, 14-10 (NY)
1978—Jets, 21-20 (B)
Jets, 45-14 (NY)
1979—Bills, 46-31 (B)
Bills, 14-12 (NY)
1980—Bills, 20-10 (B)
Bills, 31-24 (NY)
1981—Bills, 31-0 (B)
Jets, 33-14 (NY)
**Bills, 31-27 (NY)
1983—Jets, 34-10 (B)
Bills, 24-17 (NY)
1984—Jets, 28-26 (B)
Jets, 21-17 (NY)
1985—Jets, 42-3 (NY)
Jets, 27-7 (B)
1986—Jets, 28-24 (B)
Jets, 14-13 (NY)
1987—Jets, 31-28 (B)
Bills, 17-14 (NY)
1988—Bills, 37-14 (NY)
Bills, 9-6 (B) OT
1989—Bills, 34-3 (B)
Bills, 37-0 (NY)
1990—Bills, 30-7 (NY)
Bills, 30-27 (B)
1991—Bills, 23-20 (NY)
Bills, 24-13 (B)
1992—Bills, 24-20 (NY)
Jets, 24-17 (B)
1993—Bills, 19-10 (NY)
Bills, 16-14 (B)
1994—Jets, 23-3 (B)
Jets, 22-17 (NY)
1995—Bills, 29-10 (B)
Bills, 28-26 (NY)
(RS Pts.—Bills, 1,447, Jets 1,376)
(PS Pts.—Bills 31, Jets 27)
**Jets known as Titans prior to 1963*
***AFC First-Round Playoff*

BUFFALO vs. *OAKLAND
RS: Raiders lead series, 15-14
PS: Bills lead series, 2-0
1960—Bills, 38-9 (B)
Raiders, 20-7 (O)
1961—Raiders, 31-22 (B)
Bills, 26-21 (O)
1962—Bills, 14-6 (B)
Bills, 10-6 (O)
1963—Raiders, 35-17 (O)
Bills, 12-0 (B)
1964—Bills, 23-20 (B)
Raiders, 16-13 (O)
1965—Bills, 17-12 (B)
Bills, 17-14 (O)
1966—Bills, 31-10 (O)
1967—Raiders, 24-20 (B)
Raiders, 28-21 (O)
1968—Raiders, 48-6 (B)
Raiders, 13-10 (O)
1969—Raiders, 50-21 (O)
1972—Raiders, 28-16 (O)
1974—Bills, 21-20 (B)
1977—Raiders, 34-13 (O)
1980—Bills, 24-7 (B)
1983—Raiders, 27-24 (B)
1987—Raiders, 34-21 (LA)
1988—Bills, 37-21 (B)
1990—Bills, 38-24 (B)
**Bills, 51-3 (B)
1991—Bills, 30-27 (LA) OT
1992—Raiders, 20-3 (LA)
1993—Raiders, 25-24 (B)
***Bills, 29-23 (B)
(RS Pts.—Raiders 630, Bills 576)
(PS Pts.—Bills 80, Raiders 26)
**Franchise in Los Angeles from 1982-1994*
***AFC Championship*
****AFC Divisional Playoff*

BUFFALO vs. PHILADELPHIA
RS: Eagles lead series, 4-3
1973—Bills, 27-26 (B)
1981—Eagles, 20-14 (B)
1984—Eagles, 27-17 (B)
1985—Eagles, 21-17 (P)
1987—Eagles, 17-7 (P)
1990—Bills, 30-23 (B)
1993—Bills, 10-7 (P)
(RS Pts.—Eagles 141, Bills 122)

BUFFALO vs. PITTSBURGH
RS: Series tied, 7-7
PS: Steelers lead series, 2-1
1970—Steelers, 23-10 (P)
1972—Steelers, 38-21 (B)
1974—*Steelers, 32-14 (P)
1975—Bills, 30-21 (P)
1978—Steelers, 28-17 (B)
1979—Steelers, 28-0 (P)
1980—Bills, 28-13 (B)
1982—Bills, 13-0 (B)
1985—Steelers, 30-24 (P)
1986—Bills, 16-12 (B)
1988—Bills, 36-28 (B)
1991—Bills, 52-34 (B)
1992—Bills, 28-20 (B)
*Bills, 24-3 (P)
1993—Steelers, 23-0 (P)
1994—Steelers, 23-10 (P)
1995—*Steelers, 40-21 (P)
(RS Pts.—Steelers 321, Bills 285)
(PS Pts.—Steelers 75, Bills 59)
**AFC Divisional Playoff*

BUFFALO vs. *ST. LOUIS
RS: Bills lead series, 4-3
1970—Rams, 19-0 (B)
1974—Rams, 19-14 (LA)
1980—Bills, 10-7 (B) OT
1983—Rams, 41-17 (LA)
1989—Bills, 23-20 (B)
1992—Bills, 40-7 (B)
1995—Bills, 45-27 (StL)
(RS Pts.—Bills 149, Rams 140)
**Franchise in Los Angeles prior to 1995*

BUFFALO vs. *SAN DIEGO
RS: Chargers lead series, 16-7-2
PS: Bills lead series, 2-1
1960—Chargers, 24-10 (B)
Bills, 32-3 (LA)
1961—Chargers, 19-11 (B)
Chargers, 28-10 (SD)
1962—Bills, 35-10 (B)
Bills, 40-20 (SD)
1963—Chargers, 14-10 (SD)
Chargers, 23-13 (B)
1964—Bills, 30-3 (B)
Bills, 27-24 (SD)
**Bills, 20-7 (B)
1965—Chargers, 34-3 (B)
Tie, 20-20 (SD)
**Bills, 23-0 (SD)
1966—Chargers, 27-7 (SD)
Tie, 17-17 (B)
1967—Chargers, 37-17 (B)
1968—Chargers, 21-6 (B)
1969—Chargers, 45-6 (SD)
1971—Chargers, 20-3 (SD)
1973—Chargers, 34-7 (SD)
1976—Chargers, 34-13 (B)
1979—Chargers, 27-19 (SD)
1980—Bills, 26-24 (SD)
***Chargers, 20-14 (SD)
1981—Bills, 28-27 (SD)
1985—Chargers, 14-9 (B)
Chargers, 40-7 (SD)
(RS Pts.—Chargers 589, Bills 406)
(PS Pts.—Bills 57, Chargers 27)
**Franchise in Los Angeles prior to 1961*
***AFL Championship*
****AFC Divisional Playoff*

BUFFALO vs. SAN FRANCISCO
RS: Series tied, 3-3
1972—Bills, 27-20 (B)
1980—Bills, 18-13 (SF)
1983—49ers, 23-10 (B)
1989—49ers, 21-10 (SF)
1992—Bills, 34-31 (SF)
1995—49ers, 27-17 (SF)
(RS Pts.—49ers 135, Bills 116)

BUFFALO vs. SEATTLE
RS: Seahawks lead series, 3-2
1977—Seahawks, 56-17 (S)
1984—Seahawks, 31-28 (S)
1988—Bills, 13-3 (S)
1989—Seahawks, 17-16 (S)
1995—Bills, 27-21 (B)
(RS Pts.—Seahawks 128, Bills 101)

BUFFALO vs. TAMPA BAY
RS: Buccaneers lead series, 4-2
1976—Bills, 14-9 (TB)
1978—Buccaneers, 31-10 (TB)
1982—Buccaneers, 24-23 (TB)
1986—Buccaneers, 34-28 (TB)
1988—Buccaneers, 10-5 (TB)
1991—Bills, 17-10 (TB)
(RS Pts.—Buccaneers 118, Bills 97)

BUFFALO vs. WASHINGTON
RS: Redskins lead series, 4-3
PS: Redskins lead series, 1-0
1972—Bills, 24-17 (W)
1977—Redskins, 10-0 (B)
1981—Bills, 21-14 (B)
1984—Redskins, 41-14 (W)
1987—Redskins, 27-7 (B)
1990—Redskins, 29-14 (W)
1991—*Redskins, 37-24 (Minneapolis)
1993—Bills, 24-10 (B)
(RS Pts.—Redskins 148, Bills 104)
(PS Pts.—Redskins 37, Bills 24)
**Super Bowl XXVI*

CAROLINA vs. ARIZONA
RS: Panthers lead series, 1-0;
See Arizona vs. Carolina

CAROLINA vs. ATLANTA
RS: Series tied, 1-1;
See Atlanta vs. Carolina

CAROLINA vs. BUFFALO
RS: Bills lead series, 1-0;
See Buffalo vs. Carolina

CAROLINA vs. CHICAGO
RS: Bears lead series, 1-0
1995—Bears, 31-27 (Chi)
(RS Pts.—Bears 31, Panthers 27)

CAROLINA vs. INDIANAPOLIS
RS: Panthers lead series, 1-0
1995—Panthers, 13-10 (C)
(RS Pts.—Panthers 13, Colts 10)

CAROLINA vs. NEW ENGLAND
RS: Panthers lead series, 1-0
1995—Panthers, 20-17 (NE) OT
(RS Pts.—Panthers 20, Patriots 17)

CAROLINA vs. NEW ORLEANS
RS: Series tied, 1-1;
1995—Panthers, 20-3 (C)
Saints, 34-26 (NO)
(RS Pts.—Panthers 46, Saints 37)

CAROLINA vs. N.Y. JETS
RS: Panthers lead series, 1-0
1995—Panthers, 26-15 (C)
(RS Pts.—Panthers 26, Jets 15)

CAROLINA vs. ST. LOUIS
RS: Rams lead series, 2-0
1995—Rams, 31-10 (C)
Rams, 28-17 (StL)
(RS Pts.—Rams 59, Panthers 27)

CAROLINA vs. SAN FRANCISCO
RS: Series tied, 1-1
1995—Panthers, 13-7 (SF)
49ers, 31-10 (C)

(RS Pts.—49ers 38, Panthers 23)
CAROLINA vs. TAMPA BAY
RS: Buccaneers lead series, 1-0
1995—Buccaneers, 20-13 (C)
(RS Pts.—Buccaneers 20, Panthers 13)
CAROLINA vs. WASHINGTON
RS: Redskins lead series, 1-0
1995—Redskins, 20-17 (W)
(RS Pts.—Redskins 20, Panthers 17)

CHICAGO vs. ARIZONA
RS: Bears lead series, 52-25-6;
See Arizona vs. Chicago
CHICAGO vs. ATLANTA
RS: Series tied, 9-9;
See Atlanta vs. Chicago
CHICAGO vs. BUFFALO
RS: Bears lead series, 4-2;
See Buffalo vs. Chicago
CHICAGO vs. CAROLINA
RS: Bears lead series, 1-0;
See Carolina vs. Chicago
CHICAGO vs. CINCINNATI
RS: Bengals lead series, 4-2
1972—Bengals, 13-3 (Chi)
1980—Bengals, 17-14 (Chi) OT
1986—Bears, 44-7 (Cin)
1989—Bears, 17-14 (Chi)
1992—Bengals, 31-28 (Chi) OT
1995—Bengals, 16-10 (Cin)
(RS Pts.—Bears 116, Bengals 98)
CHICAGO vs. CLEVELAND
RS: Browns lead series, 8-3
1951—Browns, 42-21 (Cle)
1954—Browns, 39-10 (Chi)
1960—Browns, 42-0 (Cle)
1961—Bears, 17-14 (Chi)
1967—Browns, 24-0 (Cle)
1969—Browns, 28-24 (Chi)
1972—Bears, 17-0 (Cle)
1980—Browns, 27-21 (Cle)
1986—Bears, 41-31 (Chi)
1989—Browns, 27-7 (Cle)
1992—Browns, 27-14 (Cle)
(RS Pts.—Browns 301, Bears 172)
CHICAGO vs. DALLAS
RS: Cowboys lead series, 8-6
PS: Cowboys lead series, 2-0
1960—Bears, 17-7 (C)
1962—Bears, 34-33 (D)
1964—Cowboys, 24-10 (C)
1968—Cowboys, 34-3 (C)
1971—Bears, 23-19 (C)
1973—Cowboys, 20-17 (C)
1976—Cowboys, 31-21 (D)
1977—*Cowboys, 37-7 (D)
1979—Cowboys, 24-20 (D)
1981—Cowboys, 10-9 (D)
1984—Cowboys, 23-14 (C)
1985—Bears, 44-0 (D)
1986—Bears, 24-10 (D)
1988—Bears, 17-7 (C)
1991—**Cowboys, 17-13 (C)
1992—Cowboys, 27-14 (D)
(RS Pts.—Cowboys 269, Bears 267)
(PS Pts.—Cowboys 54, Bears 20)
**NFC Divisional Playoff*
***NFC First-Round Playoff*
CHICAGO vs. DENVER
RS: Series tied, 5-5
1971—Broncos, 6-3 (D)
1973—Bears, 33-14 (D)
1976—Broncos, 28-14 (C)
1978—Broncos, 16-7 (D)
1981—Bears, 35-24 (C)
1983—Bears, 31-14 (C)
1984—Bears, 27-0 (C)
1987—Broncos, 31-29 (D)
1990—Bears, 16-13 (D) OT
1993—Broncos, 13-3 (C)
(RS Pts.—Bears 198, Broncos 159)
CHICAGO vs. *DETROIT
RS: Bears lead series, 75-52-5
1930—Spartans, 7-6 (P)
Bears, 14-6 (C)
1931—Bears, 9-6 (C)
Spartans, 3-0 (P)
1932—Tie, 13-13 (C)
Tie, 7-7 (P)
Bears, 9-0 (C)
1933—Bears, 17-14 (C)
Bears, 17-7 (P)
1934—Bears, 19-16 (D)
Bears, 10-7 (C)
1935—Tie, 20-20 (C)
Lions, 14-2 (D)
1936—Bears, 12-10 (C)
Lions, 13-7 (D)
1937—Bears, 28-20 (C)
Bears, 13-0 (D)
1938—Lions, 13-7 (C)
Lions, 14-7 (D)
1939—Lions, 10-0 (C)
Bears, 23-13 (D)
1940—Bears, 7-0 (C)
Lions, 17-14 (D)
1941—Bears, 49-0 (C)
Bears, 24-7 (D)
1942—Bears, 16-0 (C)
Bears, 42-0 (D)
1943—Bears, 27-21 (D)
Bears, 35-14 (C)
1944—Tie, 21-21 (C)
Lions, 41-21 (D)
1945—Lions, 16-10 (D)
Lions, 35-28 (C)
1946—Bears, 42-6 (C)
Bears, 45-24 (D)
1947—Bears, 33-24 (C)
Bears, 34-14 (D)
1948—Bears, 28-0 (C)
Bears, 42-14 (D)
1949—Bears, 27-24 (C)
Bears, 28-7 (D)
1950—Bears, 35-21 (D)
Bears, 6-3 (C)
1951—Bears, 28-23 (D)
Lions, 41-28 (C)
1952—Bears, 24-23 (C)
Lions, 45-21 (D)
1953—Lions, 20-16 (C)
Lions, 13-7 (D)
1954—Lions, 48-23 (D)
Bears, 28-24 (C)
1955—Bears, 24-14 (D)
Bears, 21-20 (C)
1956—Lions, 42-10 (D)
Bears, 38-21 (C)
1957—Bears, 27-7 (D)
Lions, 21-13 (C)
1958—Bears, 20-7 (D)
Bears, 21-16 (C)
1959—Bears, 24-14 (D)
Bears, 25-14 (C)
1960—Bears, 28-7 (C)
Lions, 36-0 (D)
1961—Bears, 31-17 (D)
Lions, 16-15 (C)
1962—Lions, 11-3 (D)
Bears, 3-0 (C)
1963—Bears, 37-21 (D)
Bears, 24-14 (C)
1964—Lions, 10-0 (C)
Bears, 27-24 (D)
1965—Bears, 38-10 (C)
Bears, 17-10 (D)
1966—Lions, 14-3 (D)
Tie, 10-10 (C)
1967—Bears, 14-3 (C)
Bears, 27-13 (D)
1968—Lions, 42-0 (D)
Lions, 28-10 (C)
1969—Lions, 13-7 (D)
Lions, 20-3 (C)
1970—Lions, 28-14 (D)
Lions, 16-10 (C)
1971—Bears, 28-23 (D)
Lions, 28-3 (C)
1972—Lions, 38-24 (C)
Lions, 14-0 (D)
1973—Lions, 30-7 (C)
Lions, 40-7 (D)
1974—Bears, 17-9 (C)
Lions, 34-17 (D)
1975—Lions, 27-7 (D)
Bears, 25-21 (C)
1976—Bears, 10-3 (C)
Lions, 14-10 (D)
1977—Bears, 30-20 (C)
Bears, 31-14 (D)
1978—Bears, 19-0 (D)
Lions, 21-17 (C)
1979—Bears, 35-7 (C)
Lions, 20-0 (D)
1980—Bears, 24-7 (C)
Bears, 23-17 (D) OT
1981—Lions, 48-17 (D)
Lions, 23-7 (C)
1982—Lions, 17-10 (D)
Bears, 20-17 (C)
1983—Lions, 31-17 (D)
Lions, 38-17 (C)
1984—Bears, 16-14 (C)
Bears, 30-13 (D)
1985—Bears, 24-3 (C)
Bears, 37-17 (D)
1986—Bears, 13-7 (C)
Bears, 16-13 (D)
1987—Bears, 30-10 (C)
1988—Bears, 24-7 (D)
Bears, 13-12 (C)
1989—Bears, 47-27 (D)
Lions, 27-17 (C)
1990—Bears, 23-17 (C) OT
Lions, 38-21 (D)
1991—Bears, 20-10 (C)
Lions, 16-6 (D)
1992—Bears, 27-24 (C)
Lions, 16-3 (D)
1993—Bears, 10-6 (D)
Lions, 20-14 (C)
1994—Lions, 21-16 (D)
Bears, 20-10 (C)
1995—Lions, 24-17 (C)
Lions, 27-7 (D)
(RS Pts.—Bears 2,446, Lions 2,238)
**Franchise in Portsmouth prior to 1934 and known as the Spartans*
***CHICAGO vs. GREEN BAY**
RS: Bears lead series, 81-63-6
PS: Bears lead series, 1-0
1921—Staleys, 20-0 (C)
1923—Bears, 3-0 (GB)
1924—Bears, 3-0 (C)
1925—Packers, 14-10 (GB)
Bears, 21-0 (C)
1926—Tie, 6-6 (GB)
Bears, 19-13 (C)
Tie, 3-3 (C)
1927—Bears, 7-6 (GB)
Bears, 14-6 (C)
1928—Tie, 12-12 (GB)
Packers, 16-6 (C)
Packers, 6-0 (C)
1929—Packers, 23-0 (GB)
Packers, 14-0 (C)
Packers, 25-0 (C)
1930—Packers, 7-0 (GB)
Packers, 13-12 (C)
Bears, 21-0 (C)
1931—Packers, 7-0 (GB)
Packers, 6-2 (C)
Bears, 7-6 (C)
1932—Tie, 0-0 (GB)
Packers, 2-0 (C)
Bears, 9-0 (C)
1933—Bears, 14-7 (GB)
Bears, 10-7 (C)
Bears, 7-6 (C)
1934—Bears, 24-10 (GB)
Bears, 27-14 (C)
1935—Packers, 7-0 (GB)
Packers, 17-14 (C)
1936—Bears, 30-3 (GB)
Packers, 21-10 (C)
1937—Bears, 14-2 (GB)
Packers, 24-14 (C)
1938—Bears, 2-0 (GB)
Packers, 24-17 (C)
1939—Packers, 21-16 (GB)
Bears, 30-27 (C)
1940—Bears, 41-10 (GB)
Bears, 14-7 (C)
1941—Bears, 25-17 (GB)
Packers, 16-14 (C)
**Bears, 33-14 (C)
1942—Bears, 44-28 (GB)
Bears, 38-7 (C)
1943—Tie, 21-21 (GB)
Bears, 21-7 (C)
1944—Packers, 42-28 (GB)
Bears, 21-0 (C)
1945—Packers, 31-21 (GB)
Bears, 28-24 (C)
1946—Bears, 30-7 (GB)
Bears, 10-7 (C)
1947—Packers, 29-20 (GB)
Bears, 20-17 (C)
1948—Bears, 45-7 (GB)
Bears, 7-6 (C)
1949—Bears, 17-0 (GB)
Bears, 24-3 (C)
1950—Packers, 31-21 (GB)
Bears, 28-14 (C)
1951—Bears, 31-20 (GB)
Bears, 24-13 (C)
1952—Bears, 24-14 (GB)
Packers, 41-28 (C)
1953—Bears, 17-13 (GB)
Tie, 21-21 (C)
1954—Bears, 10-3 (GB)
Bears, 28-23 (C)
1955—Packers, 24-3 (GB)
Bears, 52-31 (C)
1956—Bears, 37-21 (GB)
Bears, 38-14 (C)
1957—Packers, 21-17 (GB)
Bears, 21-14 (C)
1958—Bears, 34-20 (GB)
Bears, 24-10 (C)
1959—Packers, 9-6 (GB)
Bears, 28-17 (C)
1960—Bears, 17-14 (GB)
Packers, 41-13 (C)
1961—Packers, 24-0 (GB)
Packers, 31-28 (C)
1962—Packers, 49-0 (GB)
Packers, 38-7 (C)
1963—Bears, 10-3 (GB)
Bears, 26-7 (C)
1964—Packers, 23-12 (GB)
Packers, 17-3 (C)
1965—Packers, 23-14 (GB)
Bears, 31-10 (C)
1966—Packers, 17-0 (C)
Packers, 13-6 (GB)
1967—Packers, 13-10 (GB)
Packers, 17-13 (C)
1968—Bears, 13-10 (GB)
Packers, 28-27 (C)
1969—Packers, 17-0 (GB)
Packers, 21-3 (C)
1970—Packers, 20-19 (GB)
Bears, 35-17 (C)
1971—Packers, 17-14 (C)
Packers, 31-10 (GB)
1972—Packers, 20-17 (GB)
Packers, 23-17 (C)
1973—Bears, 31-17 (GB)
Packers, 21-0 (C)
1974—Bears, 10-9 (C)
Packers, 20-3 (Mil)

1975—Bears, 27-14 (C)
Packers, 28-7 (GB)
1976—Bears, 24-13 (C)
Bears, 16-10 (GB)
1977—Bears, 26-0 (GB)
Bears, 21-10 (C)
1978—Packers, 24-14 (GB)
Bears, 14-0 (C)
1979—Bears, 6-3 (C)
Bears, 15-14 (GB)
1980—Packers, 12-6 (GB) OT
Bears, 61-7 (C)
1981—Packers, 16-9 (C)
Packers, 21-17 (GB)
1983—Packers, 31-28 (GB)
Bears, 23-21 (C)
1984—Bears, 9-7 (GB)
Packers, 20-14 (C)
1985—Bears, 23-7 (C)
Bears, 16-10 (GB)
1986—Bears, 25-12 (GB)
Bears, 12-10 (C)
1987—Bears, 26-24 (GB)
Bears, 23-10 (C)
1988—Bears, 24-6 (GB)
Bears, 16-0 (C)
1989—Packers, 14-13 (GB)
Packers, 40-28 (C)
1990—Bears, 31-13 (GB)
Bears, 27-13 (C)
1991—Bears, 10-0 (GB)
Bears, 27-13 (C)
1992—Bears, 30-10 (GB)
Packers, 17-3 (C)
1993—Packers, 17-3 (GB)
Bears, 30-17 (C)
1994—Packers, 33-6 (C)
Packers, 40-3 (GB)
1995—Packers, 27-24 (C)
Packers, 35-28 (GB)
(RS Pts.—Bears 2,539, Packers 2,265)
(PS Pts.—Bears 33, Packers 14)
Bears known as Staleys prior to 1922
***Division Playoff*

CHICAGO vs. HOUSTON
RS: Oilers lead series, 4-3
1973—Bears, 35-14 (C)
1977—Oilers, 47-0 (H)
1980—Oilers, 10-6 (C)
1986—Bears, 20-7 (H)
1989—Oilers, 33-28 (C)
1992—Oilers, 24-7 (H)
1995—Bears, 35-32 (C)
(RS Pts.—Oilers 167, Bears 131)

CHICAGO vs. *INDIANAPOLIS
RS: Colts lead series, 21-16
1953—Colts, 13-9 (B)
Colts, 16-14 (C)
1954—Bears, 28-9 (C)
Bears, 28-13 (B)
1955—Colts, 23-17 (B)
Bears, 38-10 (C)
1956—Colts, 28-21 (B)
Bears, 58-27 (C)
1957—Colts, 21-10 (B)
Colts, 29-14 (C)
1958—Colts, 51-38 (B)
Colts, 17-0 (C)
1959—Bears, 26-21 (B)
Colts, 21-7 (C)
1960—Colts, 42-7 (B)
Colts, 24-20 (C)
1961—Bears, 24-10 (C)
Bears, 21-20 (B)
1962—Bears, 35-15 (C)
Bears, 57-0 (B)
1963—Bears, 10-3 (C)
Bears, 17-7 (B)
1964—Colts, 52-0 (B)
Colts, 40-24 (C)
1965—Colts, 26-21 (C)
Bears, 13-0 (B)
1966—Bears, 27-17 (C)
Colts, 21-16 (B)
1967—Colts, 24-3 (C)
1968—Colts, 28-7 (B)
1969—Colts, 24-21 (C)
1970—Colts, 21-20 (B)
1975—Colts, 35-7 (C)
1983—Colts, 22-19 (B) OT
1985—Bears, 17-10 (C)
1988—Bears, 17-13 (I)
1991—Bears, 31-17 (I)
(RS Pts.—Colts 770, Bears 742)
Franchise in Baltimore prior to 1984

CHICAGO vs. JACKSONVILLE
RS: Bears lead series, 1-0
1995—Bears, 30-27 (J)
(RS Pts.—Bears 30, Jaguars 27)

CHICAGO vs. KANSAS CITY
RS: Bears lead series, 4-2
1973—Chiefs, 19-7 (KC)
1977—Bears, 28-27 (C)
1981—Bears, 16-13 (KC) OT
1987—Bears, 31-28 (C)
1990—Chiefs, 21-10 (C)
1993—Bears, 19-17 (KC)
(RS Pts.—Chiefs 125, Bears 111)

CHICAGO vs. MIAMI
RS: Dolphins lead series, 5-2
1971—Dolphins, 34-3 (M)
1975—Dolphins, 46-13 (C)
1979—Dolphins, 31-16 (M)
1985—Dolphins, 38-24 (M)
1988—Bears, 34-7 (C)
1991—Dolphins, 16-13 (C) OT
1994—Bears, 17-14 (M)
(RS Pts.—Dolphins 186, Bears 120)

CHICAGO vs. MINNESOTA
RS: Vikings lead series, 36-31-2
PS: Bears lead series, 1-0
1961—Vikings, 37-13 (M)
Bears, 52-35 (C)
1962—Bears, 13-0 (M)
Bears, 31-30 (C)
1963—Bears, 28-7 (M)
Tie, 17-17 (C)
1964—Bears, 34-28 (M)
Vikings, 41-14 (C)
1965—Bears, 45-37 (M)
Vikings, 24-17 (C)
1966—Bears, 13-10 (M)
Bears, 41-28 (C)
1967—Bears, 17-7 (M)
Tie, 10-10 (C)
1968—Bears, 27-17 (M)
Bears, 26-24 (C)
1969—Vikings, 31-0 (C)
Vikings, 31-14 (M)
1970—Vikings, 24-0 (C)
Vikings, 16-13 (M)
1971—Bears, 20-17 (M)
Vikings, 27-10 (C)
1972—Bears, 13-10 (C)
Vikings, 23-10 (M)
1973—Vikings, 22-13 (C)
Vikings, 31-13 (M)
1974—Vikings, 11-7 (M)
Vikings, 17-0 (C)
1975—Vikings, 28-3 (M)
Vikings, 13-9 (C)
1976—Vikings, 20-19 (M)
Bears, 14-13 (C)
1977—Vikings, 22-16 (M) OT
Bears, 10-7 (C)
1978—Vikings, 24-20 (C)
Vikings, 17-14 (M)
1979—Bears, 26-7 (C)
Vikings, 30-27 (M)
1980—Vikings, 34-14 (C)
Vikings, 13-7 (M)
1981—Vikings, 24-21 (M)
Bears, 10-9 (C)
1982—Vikings, 35-7 (M)
1983—Vikings, 23-14 (C)
Bears, 19-13 (M)
1984—Bears, 16-7 (C)
Bears, 34-3 (M)
1985—Bears, 33-24 (M)
Bears, 27-9 (C)
1986—Bears, 23-0 (C)
Vikings, 23-7 (M)
1987—Bears, 27-7 (C)
Bears, 30-24 (M)
1988—Vikings, 31-7 (C)
Vikings, 28-27 (M)
1989—Bears, 38-7 (C)
Vikings, 27-16 (M)
1990—Bears, 19-16 (C)
Vikings, 41-13 (M)
1991—Bears, 10-6 (C)
Bears, 34-17 (M)
1992—Vikings, 21-20 (M)
Vikings, 38-10 (C)
1993—Vikings, 10-7 (M)
Vikings, 19-12 (C)
1994—Vikings, 42-14 (C)
Vikings, 33-27 (M) OT
*Bears, 35-18 (M)
1995—Bears, 31-14 (C)
Bears, 14-6 (M)
(RS Pts.—Vikings 1,397, Bears 1,257)
(PS Pts.—Bears 35, Vikings 18)
**NFC First-Round Playoff*

CHICAGO vs. NEW ENGLAND
RS: Patriots lead series, 4-2
PS: Bears lead series, 1-0
1973—Patriots, 13-10 (C)
1979—Patriots, 27-7 (C)
1982—Bears, 26-13 (C)
1985—Bears, 20-7 (C)
*Bears, 46-10 (New Orleans)
1988—Patriots, 30-7 (NE)
1994—Patriots, 13-3 (C)
(RS Pts.—Patriots 113, Bears 73)
(PS Pts.—Bears 46, Patriots 10)
**Super Bowl XX*

CHICAGO vs. NEW ORLEANS
RS: Bears lead series, 9-6
PS: Bears lead series, 1-0
1968—Bears, 23-17 (NO)
1970—Bears, 24-3 (NO)
1971—Bears, 35-14 (C)
1973—Saints, 21-16 (NO)
1974—Bears, 24-10 (C)
1975—Bears, 42-17 (NO)
1977—Saints, 42-24 (C)
1980—Bears, 22-3 (C)
1982—Saints, 10-0 (C)
1983—Saints, 34-31 (NO) OT
1984—Bears, 20-7 (C)
1987—Saints, 19-17 (C)
1990—*Bears, 16-6 (C)
1991—Bears, 20-17 (NO)
1992—Saints, 28-6 (NO)
1994—Bears, 17-7 (C)
(RS Pts.—Bears 321, Saints 249)
(PS Pts.—Bears 16, Saints 6)
**NFC First-Round Playoff*

CHICAGO vs. N.Y. GIANTS
RS: Bears lead series, 25-16-2
PS: Bears lead series, 5-3
1925—Bears, 19-7 (NY)
Giants, 9-0 (C)
1926—Bears, 7-0 (C)
1927—Giants, 13-7 (NY)
1928—Bears, 13-0 (C)
1929—Giants, 26-14 (C)
Giants, 34-0 (NY)
Giants, 14-9 (C)
1930—Giants, 12-0 (C)
Bears, 12-0 (NY)
1931—Bears, 6-0 (C)
Bears, 12-6 (NY)
Giants, 25-6 (C)
1932—Bears, 28-8 (NY)
Bears, 6-0 (C)
1933—Bears, 14-10 (C)
Giants, 3-0 (NY)
*Bears, 23-21 (C)
1934—Bears, 27-7 (C)
Bears, 10-9 (NY)
*Giants, 30-13 (NY)
1935—Bears, 20-3 (NY)
Giants, 3-0 (C)
1936—Bears, 25-7 (NY)
1937—Tie, 3-3 (NY)
1939—Giants, 16-13 (NY)
1940—Bears, 37-21 (NY)
1941—*Bears, 37-9 (C)
1942—Bears, 26-7 (NY)
1943—Bears, 56-7 (NY)
1946—Giants, 14-0 (NY)
*Bears, 24-14 (NY)
1948—Bears, 35-14 (C)
1949—Giants, 35-28 (NY)
1956—Tie, 17-17 (NY)
*Giants, 47-7 (NY)
1962—Giants, 26-24 (C)
1963—*Bears, 14-10 (C)
1965—Bears, 35-14 (NY)
1967—Bears, 34-7 (C)
1969—Giants, 28-24 (NY)
1970—Bears, 24-16 (NY)
1974—Bears, 16-13 (C)
1977—Bears, 12-9 (NY) OT
1985—**Bears, 21-0 (C)
1987—Bears, 34-19 (C)
1990—**Giants, 31-3 (NY)
1991—Bears, 20-17 (C)
1992—Giants, 27-14 (C)
1993—Giants, 26-20 (C)
1995—Bears, 27-24 (NY)
(RS Pts.—Bears 734, Giants 556)
(PS Pts.—Giants 162, Bears 142)
**NFL Championship*
***NFC Divisional Playoff*

CHICAGO vs. N.Y. JETS
RS: Bears lead series, 4-1
1974—Jets, 23-21 (C)
1979—Bears, 23-13 (C)
1985—Bears, 19-6 (NY)
1991—Bears, 19-13 (C) OT
1994—Bears, 19-7 (NY)
(RS Pts.—Bears 101, Jets 62)

CHICAGO vs. *OAKLAND
RS: Raiders lead series, 5-3
1972—Raiders, 28-21 (O)
1976—Raiders, 28-27 (C)
1978—Raiders, 25-19 (C) OT
1981—Bears, 23-6 (O)
1984—Bears, 17-6 (C)
1987—Bears, 6-3 (LA)
1990—Raiders, 24-10 (LA)
1993—Raiders, 16-14 (C)
(RS Pts.—Bears 137, Raiders 136)
**Franchise in Los Angeles from 1982-1994*

CHICAGO vs. PHILADELPHIA
RS: Bears lead series, 24-4-1
PS: Series tied, 1-1
1933—Tie, 3-3 (P)
1935—Bears, 39-0 (P)
1936—Bears, 17-0 (P)
Bears, 28-7 (P)
1938—Bears, 28-6 (P)
1939—Bears, 27-14 (C)
1941—Bears, 49-14 (P)
1942—Bears, 45-14 (C)
1944—Bears, 28-7 (P)
1946—Bears, 21-14 (C)
1947—Bears, 40-7 (C)
1948—Eagles, 12-7 (P)
1949—Bears, 38-21 (C)
1955—Bears, 17-10 (C)
1961—Eagles, 16-14 (P)
1963—Bears, 16-7 (C)
1968—Bears, 29-16 (P)
1970—Bears, 20-16 (C)
1972—Bears, 21-12 (P)
1975—Bears, 15-13 (C)
1979—*Eagles, 27-17 (P)

1980—Eagles, 17-14 (P)
1983—Bears, 7-6 (P)
Bears, 17-14 (C)
1986—Bears, 13-10 (C) OT
1987—Bears, 35-3 (P)
1988—**Bears, 20-12 (C)
1989—Bears, 27-13 (C)
1993—Bears, 17-6 (P)
1994—Eagles, 30-22 (P)
1995—Bears, 20-14 (C)
(RS Pts.—Bears 674, Eagles 322)
(PS Pts.—Eagles 39, Bears 37)
NFC First-Round Playoff
***NFC Divisional Playoff*

CHICAGO vs. *PITTSBURGH
RS: Bears lead series, 16-5-1
1934—Bears, 28-0 (P)
1935—Bears, 23-7 (P)
1936—Bears, 27-9 (P)
Bears, 26-6 (C)
1937—Bears, 7-0 (P)
1939—Bears, 32-0 (P)
1941—Bears, 34-7 (C)
1945—Bears, 28-7 (C)
1947—Bears, 49-7 (C)
1949—Bears, 30-21 (C)
1958—Steelers, 24-10 (P)
1959—Bears, 27-21 (C)
1963—Tie, 17-17 (P)
1967—Steelers, 41-13 (P)
1969—Bears, 38-7 (C)
1971—Bears, 17-15 (C)
1975—Steelers, 34-3 (P)
1980—Steelers, 38-3 (P)
1986—Bears, 13-10 (C) OT
1989—Bears, 20-0 (P)
1992—Bears, 30-6 (C)
1995—Steelers, 37-34 (C) OT
(RS Pts.—Bears 509, Steelers 314)
Steelers known as Pirates prior to 1941

CHICAGO vs. *ST. LOUIS
RS: Bears lead series, 45-30-3
PS: Series tied, 1-1
1937—Bears, 20-2 (Clev)
Bears, 15-7 (C)
1938—Rams, 14-7 (C)
Rams, 23-21 (Clev)
1939—Bears, 30-21 (Clev)
Bears, 35-21 (C)
1940—Bears, 21-14 (Clev)
Bears, 47-25 (C)
1941—Bears, 48-21 (Clev)
Bears, 31-13 (C)
1942—Bears, 21-7 (Clev)
Bears, 47-0 (C)
1944—Rams, 19-7 (Clev)
Bears, 28-21 (C)
1945—Rams, 17-0 (Clev)
Rams, 41-21 (C)
1946—Tie, 28-28 (C)
Bears, 27-21 (LA)
1947—Bears, 41-21 (LA)
Rams, 17-14 (C)
1948—Bears, 42-21 (C)
Bears, 21-6 (LA)
1949—Rams, 31-16 (C)
Rams, 27-24 (LA)
1950—Bears, 24-20 (LA)
Bears, 24-14 (C)
**Rams, 24-14 (LA)
1951—Rams, 42-17 (C)
1952—Rams, 31-7 (LA)
Rams, 40-24 (C)
1953—Rams, 38-24 (LA)
Bears, 24-21 (C)
1954—Rams, 42-38 (LA)
Bears, 24-13 (C)
1955—Bears, 31-20 (LA)
Bears, 24-3 (C)
1956—Bears, 35-24 (LA)
Bears, 30-21 (C)
1957—Bears, 34-26 (C)
Bears, 16-10 (LA)
1958—Bears, 31-10 (C)
Rams, 41-35 (LA)
1959—Rams, 28-21 (C)
Bears, 26-21 (LA)
1960—Bears, 34-27 (C)
Tie, 24-24 (LA)
1961—Bears, 21-17 (LA)
Bears, 28-24 (C)
1962—Bears, 27-23 (LA)
Bears, 30-14 (C)
1963—Bears, 52-14 (LA)
Bears, 6-0 (C)
1964—Bears, 38-17 (C)
Bears, 34-24 (LA)
1965—Rams, 30-28 (LA)
Bears, 31-6 (C)
1966—Rams, 31-17 (LA)
Bears, 17-10 (C)
1967—Rams, 28-17 (C)
1968—Bears, 17-16 (LA)
1969—Rams, 9-7 (C)
1971—Rams, 17-3 (LA)
1972—Tie, 13-13 (C)
1973—Rams, 26-0 (C)
1975—Rams, 38-10 (LA)
1976—Rams, 20-12 (LA)
1977—Bears, 24-23 (C)
1979—Bears, 27-23 (C)
1981—Rams, 24-7 (C)
1982—Bears, 34-26 (LA)
1983—Rams, 21-14 (LA)
1984—Rams, 29-13 (LA)
1985—***Bears, 24-0 (C)
1986—Rams, 20-17 (C)
1988—Rams, 23-3 (LA)
1989—Bears, 20-10 (C)
1990—Bears, 38-9 (C)
1993—Rams, 20-6 (LA)
1994—Bears, 27-13 (C)
1995—Rams, 34-28 (StL)
(RS Pts.—Bears 1,825, Rams 1,606)
(PS Pts.—Bears 38, Rams 24)
Franchise in Los Angeles prior to 1995 and in Cleveland prior to 1946
***Conference Playoff*
****NFC Championship*

CHICAGO vs. SAN DIEGO
RS: Chargers lead series, 4-2
1970—Chargers, 20-7 (C)
1974—Chargers, 28-21 (SD)
1978—Chargers, 40-7 (SD)
1981—Bears, 20-17 (C) OT
1984—Chargers, 20-7 (SD)
1993—Bears, 16-13 (SD)
(RS Pts.—Chargers 138, Bears 78)

CHICAGO vs. SAN FRANCISCO
RS: Series tied, 25-25-1
PS: 49ers lead series, 3-0
1950—Bears, 32-20 (SF)
Bears, 17-0 (C)
1951—Bears, 13-7 (C)
1952—49ers, 40-16 (C)
Bears, 20-17 (SF)
1953—49ers, 35-28 (C)
49ers, 24-14 (SF)
1954—49ers, 31-24 (C)
Bears, 31-27 (SF)
1955—49ers, 20-19 (C)
Bears, 34-23 (SF)
1956—Bears, 31-7 (C)
Bears, 38-21 (SF)
1957—49ers, 21-17 (C)
49ers, 21-17 (SF)
1958—Bears, 28-6 (C)
Bears, 27-14 (SF)
1959—49ers, 20-17 (SF)
Bears, 14-3 (C)
1960—Bears, 27-10 (C)
49ers, 25-7 (SF)
1961—Bears, 31-0 (C)
49ers, 41-31 (SF)
1962—Bears, 30-14 (SF)
49ers, 34-27 (C)
1963—49ers, 20-14 (SF)
Bears, 27-7 (C)
1964—49ers, 31-21 (SF)
Bears, 23-21 (C)
1965—49ers, 52-24 (SF)
Bears, 61-20 (C)
1966—Tie, 30-30 (C)
49ers, 41-14 (SF)
1967—Bears, 28-14 (SF)
1968—Bears, 27-19 (C)
1969—49ers, 42-21 (SF)
1970—49ers, 37-16 (C)
1971—49ers, 13-0 (SF)
1972—49ers, 34-21 (C)
1974—49ers, 34-0 (C)
1975—49ers, 31-3 (SF)
1976—Bears, 19-12 (SF)
1978—Bears, 16-13 (SF)
1979—Bears, 28-27 (SF)
1981—49ers, 28-17 (SF)
1983—Bears, 13-3 (C)
1984—*49ers, 23-0 (SF)
1985—Bears, 26-10 (SF)
1987—49ers, 41-0 (SF)
1988—Bears, 10-9 (C)
*49ers, 28-3 (C)
1989—49ers, 26-0 (SF)
1991—49ers, 52-14 (SF)
1994—**49ers, 44-15 (SF)
(RS Pts.—49ers 1,148, Bears 1,063)
(PS Pts.—49ers 95, Bears 18)
NFC Championship
***NFC Divisional Playoff*

CHICAGO vs. SEATTLE
RS: Seahawks lead series, 4-2
1976—Bears, 34-7 (S)
1978—Seahawks, 31-29 (C)
1982—Seahawks, 20-14 (S)
1984—Seahawks, 38-9 (S)
1987—Seahawks, 34-21 (C)
1990—Bears, 17-0 (C)
(RS Pts.—Seahawks 130, Bears 124)

CHICAGO vs. TAMPA BAY
RS: Bears lead series, 28-8
1977—Bears, 10-0 (TB)
1978—Buccaneers, 33-19 (TB)
Bears, 14-3 (C)
1979—Buccaneers, 17-13 (C)
Bears, 14-0 (TB)
1980—Bears, 23-0 (C)
Bears, 14-13 (TB)
1981—Bears, 28-17 (C)
Buccaneers, 20-10 (TB)
1982—Buccaneers, 26-23 (TB) OT
1983—Bears, 17-10 (C)
Bears, 27-0 (TB)
1984—Bears, 34-14 (C)
Bears, 44-9 (TB)
1985—Bears, 38-28 (C)
Bears, 27-19 (TB)
1986—Bears, 23-3 (TB)
Bears, 48-14 (C)
1987—Bears, 20-3 (C)
Bears, 27-26 (TB)
1988—Bears, 28-10 (C)
Bears, 27-15 (TB)
1989—Buccaneers, 42-35 (TB)
Buccaneers, 32-31 (C)
1990—Bears, 26-6 (TB)
Bears, 27-14 (C)
1991—Bears, 21-20 (TB)
Bears, 27-0 (C)
1992—Bears, 31-14 (C)
Buccaneers, 20-17 (TB)
1993—Bears, 47-17 (C)
Buccaneers, 13-10 (TB)
1994—Bears, 21-9 (C)
Bears, 20-6 (TB)
1995—Bears, 25-6 (TB)
Bears, 31-10 (C)
(RS Pts.—Bears 897, Buccaneers 489)

CHICAGO vs. *WASHINGTON
RS: Bears lead series, 18-12-1
PS: Redskins lead series, 4-3
1932—Tie, 7-7 (B)
1933—Bears, 7-0 (C)
Redskins, 10-0 (B)
1934—Bears, 21-0 (B)
1935—Bears, 30-14 (B)
1936—Bears, 26-0 (B)
1937—**Redskins, 28-21 (C)
1938—Bears, 31-7 (C)
1940—Redskins, 7-3 (W)
**Bears, 73-0 (W)
1941—Bears, 35-21 (C)
1942—**Redskins, 14-6 (W)
1943—Redskins, 21-7 (W)
**Bears, 41-21 (C)
1945—Redskins, 28-21 (W)
1946—Bears, 24-20 (C)
1947—Bears, 56-20 (W)
1948—Bears, 48-13 (C)
1949—Bears, 31-21 (W)
1951—Bears, 27-0 (W)
1953—Bears, 27-24 (W)
1957—Redskins, 14-3 (C)
1964—Redskins, 27-20 (W)
1968—Redskins, 38-28 (C)
1971—Bears, 16-15 (C)
1974—Redskins, 42-0 (W)
1976—Bears, 33-7 (C)
1978—Bears, 14-10 (W)
1980—Bears, 35-21 (C)
1981—Redskins, 24-7 (C)
1984—***Bears, 23-19 (W)
1985—Bears, 45-10 (C)
1986—***Redskins, 27-13 (C)
1987—***Redskins, 21-17 (C)
1988—Bears, 34-14 (W)
1989—Redskins, 38-14 (W)
1990—Redskins, 10-9 (W)
1991—Redskins, 20-7 (C)
(RS Pts.—Bears 666, Redskins 503)
(PS Pts.—Bears 194, Redskins 130)
Franchise in Boston prior to 1937 and known as Braves prior to 1933
***NFL Championship*
****NFC Divisional Playoff*

CINCINNATI vs. ARIZONA
RS: Bengals lead series, 3-2;
See Arizona vs. Cincinnati

CINCINNATI vs. ATLANTA
RS: Bengals lead series, 6-2;
See Atlanta vs. Cincinnati

CINCINNATI vs. BUFFALO
RS: Bengals lead series, 9-7
PS: Bengals lead series, 2-0;
See Buffalo vs. Cincinnati

CINCINNATI vs. CHICAGO
RS: Bengals lead series, 4-2;
See Chicago vs. Cincinnati

CINCINNATI vs. CLEVELAND
RS: Browns lead series, 27-24
1970—Browns, 30-27 (Cle)
Bengals, 14-10 (Cin)
1971—Browns, 27-24 (Cin)
Browns, 31-27 (Cle)
1972—Browns, 27-6 (Cle)
Browns, 27-24 (Cin)
1973—Browns, 17-10 (Cle)
Bengals, 34-17 (Cin)
1974—Bengals, 33-7 (Cin)
Bengals, 34-24 (Cle)
1975—Bengals, 24-17 (Cin)
Browns, 35-23 (Cle)
1976—Bengals, 45-24 (Cle)
Bengals, 21-6 (Cin)
1977—Browns, 13-3 (Cin)
Bengals, 10-7 (Cle)
1978—Browns, 13-10 (Cle) OT
Bengals, 48-16 (Cin)
1979—Browns, 28-27 (Cle)
Bengals, 16-12 (Cin)
1980—Browns, 31-7 (Cle)
Browns, 27-24 (Cin)

ALL-TIME TEAM VS. TEAM RESULTS

1981—Browns, 20-17 (Cin)
Bengals, 41-21 (Cle)
1982—Bengals, 23-10 (Cin)
1983—Browns, 17-7 (Cle)
Bengals, 28-21 (Cin)
1984—Bengals, 12-9 (Cin)
Bengals, 20-17 (Cle) OT
1985—Bengals, 27-10 (Cin)
Browns, 24-6 (Cle)
1986—Bengals, 30-13 (Cle)
Browns, 34-3 (Cin)
1987—Browns, 34-0 (Cin)
Browns, 38-24 (Cle)
1988—Bengals, 24-17 (Cin)
Browns, 23-16 (Cle)
1989—Bengals, 21-14 (Cin)
Bengals, 21-0 (Cle)
1990—Bengals, 34-13 (Cle)
Bengals, 21-14 (Cin)
1991—Browns, 14-13 (Cle)
Bengals, 23-21 (Cin)
1992—Bengals, 30-10 (Cin)
Browns, 37-21 (Cle)
1993—Browns, 27-14 (Cle)
Browns, 28-17 (Cin)
1994—Browns, 28-20 (Cin)
Browns, 37-13 (Cle)
1995—Browns, 29-26 (Cin) OT
Browns, 26-10 (Cle)
(RS Pts.—Bengals 1,053, Browns 1,052)

CINCINNATI vs. DALLAS
RS: Cowboys lead series, 4-2
1973—Cowboys, 38-10 (D)
1979—Cowboys, 38-13 (D)
1985—Bengals, 50-24 (C)
1988—Bengals, 38-24 (D)
1991—Cowboys, 35-23 (D)
1994—Cowboys, 23-20 (C)
(RS Pts.—Cowboys 182, Bengals 154)

CINCINNATI vs. DENVER
RS: Broncos lead series, 11-6
1968—Bengals, 24-10 (C)
Broncos, 10-7 (D)
1969—Broncos, 30-23 (C)
Broncos, 27-16 (D)
1971—Bengals, 24-10 (D)
1972—Bengals, 21-10 (C)
1973—Broncos, 28-10 (D)
1975—Bengals, 17-16 (D)
1976—Bengals, 17-7 (C)
1977—Broncos, 24-13 (C)
1979—Broncos, 10-0 (D)
1981—Bengals, 38-21 (C)
1983—Broncos, 24-17 (D)
1984—Broncos, 20-17 (D)
1986—Broncos, 34-28 (D)
1991—Broncos, 45-14 (D)
1994—Broncos, 15-13 (D)
(RS Pts.—Broncos 341, Bengals 299)

CINCINNATI vs. DETROIT
RS: Series tied, 3-3
1970—Lions, 38-3 (D)
1974—Lions, 23-19 (C)
1983—Bengals, 17-9 (C)
1986—Bengals, 24-17 (D)
1989—Bengals, 42-7 (C)
1992—Lions, 19-13 (C)
(RS Pts.—Bengals 118, Lions 113)

CINCINNATI vs. GREEN BAY
RS: Series tied, 4-4
1971—Packers, 20-17 (GB)
1976—Bengals, 28-7 (C)
1977—Bengals, 17-7 (Mil)
1980—Packers, 14-9 (GB)
1983—Bengals, 34-14 (C)
1986—Bengals, 34-28 (Mil)
1992—Packers, 24-23 (GB)
1995—Packers, 24-10 (GB)
(RS Pts.—Bengals 172, Packers 138)

CINCINNATI vs. HOUSTON
RS: Oilers lead series, 27-26-1
PS: Bengals lead series, 1-0
1968—Oilers, 27-17 (C)
1969—Tie, 31-31 (H)
1970—Oilers, 20-13 (C)
Bengals, 30-20 (H)
1971—Oilers, 10-6 (H)
Bengals, 28-13 (C)
1972—Bengals, 30-7 (C)
Bengals, 61-17 (H)
1973—Bengals, 24-10 (C)
Bengals, 27-24 (H)
1974—Oilers, 34-21 (C)
Oilers, 20-3 (H)
1975—Bengals, 21-19 (H)
Bengals, 23-19 (C)
1976—Bengals, 27-7 (H)
Bengals, 31-27 (C)
1977—Bengals, 13-10 (C) OT
Oilers, 21-16 (H)
1978—Bengals, 28-13 (C)
Oilers, 17-10 (H)
1979—Oilers, 30-27 (C) OT
Oilers, 42-21 (H)
1980—Oilers, 13-10 (C)
Oilers, 23-3 (H)
1981—Oilers, 17-10 (H)
Bengals, 34-21 (C)
1982—Bengals, 27-6 (C)
Bengals, 35-27 (H)
1983—Bengals, 55-14 (H)
Bengals, 38-10 (C)
1984—Bengals, 13-3 (C)
Bengals, 31-13 (H)
1985—Oilers, 44-27 (H)
Bengals, 45-27 (C)
1986—Bengals, 31-28 (C)
Oilers, 32-28 (H)
1987—Oilers, 31-29 (C)
Oilers, 21-17 (H)
1988—Bengals, 44-21 (C)
Oilers, 41-6 (H)
1989—Oilers, 26-24 (H)
Bengals, 61-7 (C)
1990—Oilers, 48-17 (H)
Bengals, 40-20 (C)
*Bengals, 41-14 (C)
1991—Oilers, 30-7 (C)
Oilers, 35-3 (H)
1992—Oilers, 38-24 (C)
Oilers, 26-10 (H)
1993—Oilers, 28-12 (H)
Oilers, 38-3 (C)
1994—Oilers, 20-13 (H)
Bengals, 34-31 (C)
1995—Oilers, 38-28 (C)
Bengals, 32-25 (H)
(RS Pts.—Bengals 1,299, Oilers 1,240)
(PS Pts.—Bengals 41, Oilers 14)
**AFC First Round Playoff*

CINCINNATI vs.*INDIANAPOLIS
RS: Colts lead series, 9-6
PS: Colts lead series, 1-0
1970—**Colts, 17-0 (B)
1972—Colts, 20-19 (C)
1974—Bengals, 24-14 (B)
1976—Colts, 28-27 (B)
1979—Colts, 38-28 (B)
1980—Bengals, 34-33 (C)
1981—Bengals, 41-19 (B)
1982—Bengals, 20-17 (B)
1983—Colts, 34-31 (C)
1987—Bengals, 23-21 (I)
1989—Colts, 23-12 (C)
1990—Colts, 34-20 (C)
1992—Colts, 21-17 (C)
1993—Colts, 9-6 (C)
1994—Colts, 17-13 (C)
1995—Bengals, 24-21 (I) OT
(RS Pts.—Colts 349, Bengals 339)
(PS Pts.—Colts 17, Bengals 0)
**Franchise in Baltimore prior to 1984*
***AFC Divisional Playoff*

CINCINNATI vs. JACKSONVILLE
RS: Bengals lead series, 2-0
1995—Bengals, 24-17 (C)
Bengals, 17-13 (J)
(RS Pts.—Bengals 41, Jaguars 30)

CINCINNATI vs. KANSAS CITY
RS: Chiefs lead series, 11-9
1968—Chiefs, 13-3 (KC)
Chiefs, 16-9 (C)
1969—Bengals, 24-19 (C)
Chiefs, 42-22 (KC)
1970—Chiefs, 27-19 (C)
1972—Bengals, 23-16 (KC)
1973—Bengals, 14-6 (C)
1974—Bengals, 33-6 (C)
1976—Bengals, 27-24 (KC)
1977—Bengals, 27-7 (KC)
1978—Chiefs, 24-23 (C)
1979—Chiefs, 10-7 (C)
1980—Bengals, 20-6 (KC)
1983—Chiefs, 20-15 (KC)
1984—Chiefs, 27-22 (C)
1986—Chiefs, 24-14 (KC)
1987—Bengals, 30-27 (C) OT
1988—Chiefs, 31-28 (KC)
1989—Bengals, 21-17 (KC)
1993—Chiefs, 17-15 (KC)
(RS Pts.—Bengals 396, Chiefs 379)

CINCINNATI vs. MIAMI
RS: Dolphins lead series, 11-3
PS: Dolphins lead series, 1-0
1968—Dolphins, 24-22 (C)
Bengals, 38-21 (M)
1969—Bengals, 27-21 (C)
1971—Dolphins, 23-13 (C)
1973—*Dolphins, 34-16 (M)
1974—Dolphins, 24-3 (M)
1977—Bengals, 23-17 (C)
1978—Dolphins, 21-0 (M)
1980—Dolphins, 17-16 (M)
1983—Dolphins, 38-14 (M)
1987—Dolphins, 20-14 (C)
1989—Dolphins, 20-13 (C)
1991—Dolphins, 37-13 (M)
1994—Dolphins, 23-7 (C)
1995—Dolphins, 26-23 (C)
(RS Pts.—Dolphins 366, Bengals 242)
(PS Pts.—Dolphins 34, Bengals 16)
**AFC Divisional Playoff*

CINCINNATI vs. MINNESOTA
RS: Series tied, 4-4
1973—Bengals, 27-0 (C)
1977—Vikings, 42-10 (M)
1980—Bengals, 14-0 (C)
1983—Vikings, 20-14 (M)
1986—Bengals, 24-20 (C)
1989—Vikings, 29-21 (M)
1992—Vikings, 42-7 (C)
1995—Bengals, 27-24 (C)
(RS Pts.—Vikings 177, Bengals 144)

CINCINNATI vs. *NEW ENGLAND
RS: Patriots lead series, 9-7
1968—Patriots, 33-14 (B)
1969—Patriots, 25-14 (C)
1970—Bengals, 45-7 (C)
1972—Bengals, 31-7 (NE)
1975—Bengals, 27-10 (C)
1978—Patriots, 10-3 (C)
1979—Patriots, 20-14 (C)
1984—Patriots, 20-14 (NE)
1985—Patriots, 34-23 (NE)
1986—Bengals, 31-7 (NE)
1988—Patriots, 27-21 (NE)
1990—Bengals, 41-7 (C)
1991—Bengals, 29-7 (C)
1992—Bengals, 20-10 (C)
1993—Patriots, 7-2 (NE)
1994—Patriots, 31-28 (C)
(RS Pts.—Bengals 357, Patriots 262)
**Franchise in Boston prior to 1971*

CINCINNATI vs. NEW ORLEANS
RS: Saints lead series, 5-3
1970—Bengals, 26-6 (C)
1975—Bengals, 21-0 (NO)
1978—Saints, 20-18 (C)
1981—Saints, 17-7 (NO)
1984—Bengals, 24-21 (NO)
1987—Saints, 41-24 (C)
1990—Saints, 21-7 (C)
1993—Saints, 20-13 (NO)
(RS Pts.—Saints 146, Bengals 140)

CINCINNATI vs. N.Y. GIANTS
RS: Bengals lead series, 4-1
1972—Bengals, 13-10 (C)
1977—Bengals, 30-13 (C)
1985—Bengals, 35-30 (C)
1991—Bengals, 27-24 (C)
1994—Giants, 27-20 (NY)
(RS Pts.—Bengals 125, Giants 104)

CINCINNATI vs. N.Y. JETS
RS: Jets lead series, 9-6
PS: Jets lead series, 1-0
1968—Jets, 27-14 (NY)
1969—Jets, 21-7 (C)
Jets, 40-7 (NY)
1971—Jets, 35-21 (NY)
1973—Bengals, 20-14 (C)
1976—Bengals, 42-3 (NY)
1981—Bengals, 31-30 (NY)
1982—*Jets, 44-17 (C)
1984—Jets, 43-23 (NY)
1985—Jets, 29-20 (C)
1986—Bengals, 52-21 (C)
1987—Jets, 27-20 (NY)
1988—Bengals, 36-19 (C)
1990—Bengals, 25-20 (C)
1992—Jets, 17-14 (NY)
1993—Jets, 17-12 (NY)
(RS Pts.—Jets 363, Bengals 344)
(PS Pts.—Jets 44, Bengals 17)
**AFC First-Round Playoff*

CINCINNATI vs. *OAKLAND
RS: Raiders lead series, 15-7
PS: Raiders lead series, 2-0
1968—Raiders, 31-10 (O)
Raiders, 34-0 (C)
1969—Bengals, 31-17 (C)
Raiders, 37-17 (O)
1970—Bengals, 31-21 (C)
1971—Raiders, 31-27 (O)
1972—Raiders, 20-14 (C)
1974—Raiders, 30-27 (O)
1975—Bengals, 14-10 (C)
**Raiders, 31-28 (O)
1976—Raiders, 35-20 (O)
1978—Raiders, 34-21 (C)
1980—Raiders, 28-17 (O)
1982—Bengals, 31-17 (C)
1983—Raiders, 20-10 (C)
1985—Raiders, 13-6 (LA)
1988—Bengals, 45-21 (LA)
1989—Raiders, 28-7 (LA)
1990—Raiders, 24-7 (LA)
**Raiders, 20-10 (LA)
1991—Raiders, 38-14 (C)
1992—Bengals, 24-21 (C) OT
1993—Bengals, 16-10 (C)
1995—Raiders, 20-17 (C)
(RS Pts.—Raiders 540, Bengals 406)
(PS Pts.—Raiders 51, Bengals 38)
**Franchise in Los Angeles from 1982-1994*
***AFC Divisional Playoff*

CINCINNATI vs. PHILADELPHIA
RS: Bengals lead series, 6-1
1971—Bengals, 37-14 (C)
1975—Bengals, 31-0 (P)
1979—Bengals, 37-13 (C)
1982—Bengals, 18-14 (P)
1988—Bengals, 28-24 (P)
1991—Eagles, 17-10 (P)
1994—Bengals, 33-30 (C)
(RS Pts.—Bengals 194, Eagles 112)

CINCINNATI vs. PITTSBURGH
RS: Steelers lead series, 29-22
1970—Steelers, 21-10 (P)
Bengals, 34-7 (C)
1971—Steelers, 21-10 (P)
Steelers, 21-13 (C)

1972—Bengals, 15-10 (C)
Steelers, 40-17 (P)
1973—Bengals, 19-7 (C)
Steelers, 20-13 (P)
1974—Bengals, 17-10 (C)
Steelers, 27-3 (P)
1975—Steelers, 30-24 (C)
Steelers, 35-14 (P)
1976—Steelers, 23-6 (P)
Steelers, 7-3 (C)
1977—Steelers, 20-14 (P)
Bengals, 17-10 (C)
1978—Steelers, 28-3 (C)
Steelers, 7-6 (P)
1979—Bengals, 34-10 (C)
Steelers, 37-17 (P)
1980—Bengals, 30-28 (C)
Bengals, 17-16 (P)
1981—Bengals, 34-7 (C)
Bengals, 17-10 (P)
1982—Steelers, 26-20 (P) OT
1983—Steelers, 24-14 (C)
Bengals, 23-10 (P)
1984—Steelers, 38-17 (P)
Bengals, 22-20 (C)
1985—Bengals, 37-24 (P)
Bengals, 26-21 (C)
1986—Bengals, 24-22 (C)
Steelers, 30-9 (P)
1987—Steelers, 23-20 (P)
Steelers, 30-16 (C)
1988—Bengals, 17-12 (P)
Bengals, 42-7 (C)
1989—Bengals, 41-10 (C)
Bengals, 26-16 (P)
1990—Bengals, 27-3 (C)
Bengals, 16-12 (P)
1991—Steelers, 33-27 (C) OT
Steelers, 17-10 (P)
1992—Steelers, 20-0 (P)
Steelers, 21-9 (C)
1993—Steelers, 34-7 (P)
Steelers, 24-16 (C)
1994—Steelers, 14-10 (P)
Steelers, 38-15 (C)
1995—Bengals, 27-9 (P)
Steelers, 49-31 (C)
(RS Pts.—Steelers 1,039, Bengals 936)

CINCINNATI vs. *ST. LOUIS
RS: Bengals lead series, 5-2
1972—Rams, 15-12 (LA)
1976—Bengals, 20-12 (C)
1978—Bengals, 20-19 (LA)
1981—Bengals, 24-10 (C)
1984—Rams, 24-14 (C)
1990—Bengals, 34-31 (LA) OT
1993—Bengals, 15-3 (C)
(RS Pts.—Bengals 139, Rams 114)
Franchise in Los Angeles prior to 1995

CINCINNATI vs. SAN DIEGO
RS: Chargers lead series, 13-8
PS: Bengals lead series, 1-0
1968—Chargers, 29-13 (SD)
Chargers, 31-10 (C)
1969—Bengals, 34-20 (C)
Chargers, 21-14 (SD)
1970—Bengals, 17-14 (SD)
1971—Bengals, 31-0 (C)
1973—Bengals, 20-13 (SD)
1974—Chargers, 20-17 (C)
1975—Bengals, 47-17 (C)
1977—Chargers, 24-3 (SD)
1978—Chargers, 22-13 (SD)
1979—Chargers, 26-24 (C)
1980—Chargers, 31-14 (C)
1981—Bengals, 40-17 (SD)
*Bengals, 27-7 (C)
1982—Chargers, 50-34 (SD)
1985—Chargers, 44-41 (C)
1987—Chargers, 10-9 (C)
1988—Bengals, 27-10 (C)
1990—Bengals, 21-16 (SD)
1992—Chargers, 27-10 (SD)
1994—Chargers, 27-10 (SD)
(RS Pts.—Chargers 469, Bengals 449)
(PS Pts.—Bengals 27, Chargers 7)
**AFC Championship*

CINCINNATI vs. SAN FRANCISCO
RS: 49ers lead series, 6-1
PS: 49ers lead series, 2-0
1974—Bengals, 21-3 (SF)
1978—49ers, 28-12 (SF)
1981—49ers, 21-3 (C)
*49ers, 26-21 (Detroit)
1984—49ers, 23-17 (SF)
1987—49ers, 27-26 (C)
1988—**49ers, 20-16 (Miami)
1990—49ers, 20-17 (C)
1993—49ers, 21-8 (SF)
(RS Pts.—49ers 143, Bengals 104)
(PS Pts.—49ers 46, Bengals 37)
**Super Bowl XVI*
***Super Bowl XXIII*

CINCINNATI vs. SEATTLE
RS: Series tied, 7-7
PS: Bengals lead series, 1-0
1977—Bengals, 42-20 (C)
1981—Bengals, 27-21 (C)
1982—Bengals, 24-10 (C)
1984—Seahawks, 26-6 (C)
1985—Seahawks, 28-24 (C)
1986—Bengals, 34-7 (C)
1987—Bengals, 17-10 (S)
1988—*Bengals, 21-13 (C)
1989—Seahawks, 24-17 (C)
1990—Seahawks, 31-16 (S)
1991—Seahawks, 13-7 (C)
1992—Bengals, 21-3 (S)
1993—Seahawks, 19-10 (C)
1994—Bengals, 20-17 (S) OT
1995—Seahawks, 24-21 (S)
(RS Pts.—Bengals 286, Seahawks 253)
(PS Pts.—Bengals 21, Seahawks 13)
**AFC Divisional Playoff*

CINCINNATI vs. TAMPA BAY
RS: Bengals lead series, 3-2
1976—Bengals, 21-0 (C)
1980—Buccaneers, 17-12 (C)
1983—Bengals, 23-17 (TB)
1989—Bengals, 56-23 (C)
1995—Buccaneers, 19-16 (TB)
(RS Pts.—Bengals 128, Buccaneers 76)

CINCINNATI vs. WASHINGTON
RS: Redskins lead series, 4-2
1970—Redskins, 20-0 (W)
1974—Bengals, 28-17 (C)
1979—Redskins, 28-14 (W)
1985—Redskins, 27-24 (W)
1988—Bengals, 20-17 (C) OT
1991—Redskins, 34-27 (C)
(RS Pts.—Redskins 143, Bengals 113)

CLEVELAND vs. ARIZONA
RS: Browns lead series, 32-10-3;
See Arizona vs. Cleveland

CLEVELAND vs. ATLANTA
RS: Browns lead series, 8-2;
See Atlanta vs. Cleveland

CLEVELAND vs. BUFFALO
RS: Browns lead series, 7-4
PS: Browns lead series, 1-0;
See Buffalo vs. Cleveland

CLEVELAND vs. CHICAGO
RS: Browns lead series, 8-3;
See Chicago vs. Cleveland

CLEVELAND vs. CINCINNATI
RS: Browns lead series, 27-24;
See Cincinnati vs. Cleveland

CLEVELAND vs. DALLAS
RS: Browns lead series, 15-9
PS: Browns lead series, 2-1
1960—Browns, 48-7 (D)
1961—Browns, 25-7 (C)
Browns, 38-17 (D)
1962—Browns, 19-10 (C)
Cowboys, 45-21 (D)
1963—Browns, 41-24 (D)
Browns, 27-17 (C)
1964—Browns, 27-6 (C)
Browns, 20-16 (D)
1965—Browns, 23-17 (C)
Browns, 24-17 (D)
1966—Browns, 30-21 (C)
Cowboys, 26-14 (D)
1967—Cowboys, 21-14 (C)
*Cowboys, 52-14 (D)
1968—Cowboys, 28-7 (C)
*Browns, 31-20 (C)
1969—Browns, 42-10 (C)
*Browns, 38-14 (D)
1970—Cowboys, 6-2 (C)
1974—Cowboys, 41-17 (D)
1979—Browns, 26-7 (C)
1982—Cowboys, 31-14 (D)
1985—Cowboys, 20-7 (D)
1988—Browns, 24-21 (C)
1991—Cowboys, 26-14 (C)
1994—Browns, 19-14 (D)
(RS Pts.—Browns 543, Cowboys 455)
(PS Pts.—Cowboys 86, Browns 83)
**Conference Championship*

CLEVELAND vs. DENVER
RS: Broncos lead series, 13-5
PS: Broncos lead series, 3-0
1970—Browns, 27-13 (D)
1971—Broncos, 27-0 (C)
1972—Browns, 27-20 (D)
1974—Browns, 23-21 (C)
1975—Broncos, 16-15 (D)
1976—Broncos, 44-13 (D)
1978—Broncos, 19-7 (C)
1980—Broncos, 19-16 (C)
1981—Broncos, 23-20 (D) OT
1983—Broncos, 27-6 (D)
1984—Broncos, 24-14 (C)
1986—*Broncos, 23-20 (C) OT
1987—*Broncos, 38-33 (D)
1988—Broncos, 30-7 (D)
1989—Browns, 16-13 (C)
*Broncos, 37-21 (D)
1990—Browns, 30-29 (D)
1991—Broncos, 17-7 (C)
1992—Broncos, 12-0 (C)
1993—Broncos, 29-14 (C)
1994—Broncos, 26-14 (D)
(RS Pts.—Broncos 409, Browns 256)
(PS Pts.—Broncos 98, Browns 74)
**AFC Championship*

CLEVELAND vs. DETROIT
RS: Lions lead series, 12-3
PS: Lions lead series, 3-1
1952—Lions, 17-6 (D)
*Lions, 17-7 (C)
1953—*Lions, 17-16 (D)
1954—Lions, 14-10 (C)
*Browns, 56-10 (C)
1957—Lions, 20-7 (D)
*Lions, 59-14 (D)
1958—Lions, 30-10 (C)
1963—Lions, 38-10 (D)
1964—Browns, 37-21 (C)
1967—Lions, 31-14 (D)
1969—Lions, 28-21 (C)
1970—Lions, 41-24 (C)
1975—Lions, 21-10 (D)
1983—Browns, 31-26 (D)
1986—Browns, 24-21 (C)
1989—Lions, 13-10 (D)
1992—Lions, 24-14 (D)
1995—Lions, 38-20 (D)
(RS Pts.—Lions 383, Browns 248)
(PS Pts.—Lions 103, Browns 93)
**NFL Championship*

CLEVELAND vs. GREEN BAY
RS: Packers lead series, 8-6
PS: Packers lead series, 1-0
1953—Browns, 27-0 (Mil)
1955—Browns, 41-10 (C)
1956—Browns, 24-7 (Mil)
1961—Packers, 49-17 (C)
1964—Packers, 28-21 (Mil)
1965—*Packers, 23-12 (GB)
1966—Packers, 21-20 (C)
1967—Packers, 55-7 (Mil)
1969—Browns, 20-7 (C)
1972—Packers, 26-10 (C)
1980—Browns, 26-21 (C)
1983—Packers, 35-21 (Mil)
1986—Packers, 17-14 (C)
1992—Browns, 17-6 (C)
1995—Packers, 31-20 (C)
(RS Pts.—Packers 313, Browns 285)
(PS Pts.—Packers 23, Browns 12)
**NFL Championship*

CLEVELAND vs. HOUSTON
RS: Browns lead series, 30-21
PS: Oilers lead series, 1-0
1970—Browns, 28-14 (C)
Browns, 21-10 (H)
1971—Browns, 31-0 (C)
Browns, 37-24 (H)
1972—Browns, 23-17 (H)
Browns, 20-0 (C)
1973—Browns, 42-13 (C)
Browns, 23-13 (H)
1974—Browns, 20-7 (C)
Oilers, 28-24 (H)
1975—Oilers, 40-10 (C)
Oilers, 21-10 (H)
1976—Browns, 21-7 (H)
Browns, 13-10 (C)
1977—Browns, 24-23 (H)
Oilers, 19-15 (C)
1978—Oilers, 16-13 (C)
Oilers, 14-10 (H)
1979—Oilers, 31-10 (H)
Browns, 14-7 (C)
1980—Oilers, 16-7 (C)
Browns, 17-14 (H)
1981—Oilers, 9-3 (C)
Oilers, 17-13 (H)
1982—Browns, 20-14 (H)
1983—Browns, 25-19 (C) OT
Oilers, 34-27 (H)
1984—Browns, 27-10 (C)
Browns, 27-20 (H)
1985—Browns, 21-6 (H)
Browns, 28-21 (C)
1986—Browns, 23-20 (H)
Browns, 13-10 (C) OT
1987—Oilers, 15-10 (C)
Browns, 40-7 (H)
1988—Oilers, 24-17 (H)
Browns, 28-23 (C)
*Oilers, 24-23 (C)
1989—Browns, 28-17 (C)
Browns, 24-20 (H)
1990—Oilers, 35-23 (C)
Oilers, 58-14 (H)
1991—Oilers, 28-24 (H)
Oilers, 17-14 (C)
1992—Browns, 24-14 (H)
Oilers, 17-14 (C)
1993—Oilers, 27-20 (C)
Oilers, 19-17 (H)
1994—Browns, 11-8 (H)
Browns, 34-10 (C)
1995—Browns, 14-7 (H)
Oilers, 37-10 (C)
(RS Pts.—Browns 1,026, Oilers 907)
(PS Pts.—Oilers 24, Browns 23)
**AFC First-Round Playoff*

CLEVELAND vs. *INDIANAPOLIS
RS: Browns lead series, 13-7
PS: Series tied, 2-2
1956—Colts, 21-7 (C)
1959—Browns, 38-31 (B)
1962—Colts, 36-14 (C)
1964—**Browns, 27-0 (C)
1968—Browns, 30-20 (B)
**Colts, 34-0 (C)
1971—Browns, 14-13 (B)

***Colts, 20-3 (C)
1973—Browns, 24-14 (C)
1975—Colts, 21-7 (B)
1978—Browns, 45-24 (B)
1979—Browns, 13-10 (C)
1980—Browns, 28-27 (B)
1981—Browns, 42-28 (C)
1983—Browns, 41-23 (C)
1986—Browns, 24-9 (I)
1987—Colts, 9-7 (C)
***Browns, 38-21 (C)
1988—Browns, 23-17 (C)
1989—Colts, 23-17 (I) OT
1991—Browns, 31-0 (I)
1992—Colts, 14-3 (I)
1993—Colts, 23-10 (I)
1994—Browns, 21-14 (I)
(RS Pts.—Browns 439, Colts 377)
(PS Pts.—Colts 75, Browns 68)
Franchise in Baltimore prior to 1984
**NFL Championship*
***AFC Divisional Playoff*

CLEVELAND vs. JACKSONVILLE
RS: Jaguars lead series, 2-0
1995—Jaguars, 23-15 (C)
Jaguars, 24-21 (J)
(RS Pts.—Jaguars 47, Browns 36)

CLEVELAND vs. KANSAS CITY
RS: Browns lead series, 8-7-2
1971—Chiefs, 13-7 (KC)
1972—Chiefs, 31-7 (C)
1973—Tie, 20-20 (KC)
1975—Browns, 40-14 (C)
1976—Chiefs, 39-14 (KC)
1977—Browns, 44-7 (C)
1978—Chiefs, 17-3 (KC)
1979—Browns, 27-24 (KC)
1980—Browns, 20-13 (C)
1984—Chiefs, 10-6 (KC)
1986—Browns, 20-7 (C)
1988—Browns, 6-3 (KC)
1989—Tie, 10-10 (C) OT
1990—Chiefs, 34-0 (KC)
1991—Browns, 20-15 (C)
1994—Chiefs, 20-13 (KC)
1995—Browns, 35-17 (C)
(RS Pts.—Chiefs 294, Browns 292)

CLEVELAND vs. MIAMI
RS: Dolphins lead series, 6-4
PS: Dolphins lead series, 2-0
1970—Browns, 28-0 (M)
1972—*Dolphins, 20-14 (M)
1973—Dolphins, 17-9 (C)
1976—Browns, 17-13 (C)
1979—Browns, 30-24 (C) OT
1985—*Dolphins, 24-21 (M)
1986—Browns, 26-16 (C)
1988—Dolphins, 38-31 (M)
1989—Dolphins, 13-10 (M) OT
1990—Dolphins, 30-13 (C)
1992—Dolphins, 27-23 (C)
1993—Dolphins, 24-14 (C)
(RS Pts.—Dolphins 202, Browns 201)
(PS Pts.—Dolphins 44, Browns 35)
AFC Divisional Playoff

CLEVELAND vs. MINNESOTA
RS: Vikings lead series, 8-3
PS: Vikings lead series, 1-0
1965—Vikings, 27-17 (C)
1967—Browns, 14-10 (C)
1969—Vikings, 51-3 (M)
*Vikings, 27-7 (M)
1973—Vikings, 26-3 (M)
1975—Vikings, 42-10 (C)
1980—Vikings, 28-23 (M)
1983—Vikings, 27-21 (C)
1986—Browns, 23-20 (M)
1989—Browns, 23-17 (C) OT
1992—Vikings, 17-13 (M)
1995—Vikings, 27-11 (M)
(RS Pts.—Vikings 292, Browns 161)
(PS Pts.—Vikings 27, Browns 7)
NFL Championship

CLEVELAND vs. NEW ENGLAND
RS: Browns lead series, 10-4
PS: Browns lead series, 1-0
1971—Browns, 27-7 (C)
1974—Browns, 21-14 (NE)
1977—Browns, 30-27 (C) OT
1980—Patriots, 34-17 (NE)
1982—Browns, 10-7 (C)
1983—Browns, 30-0 (NE)
1984—Patriots, 17-16 (C)
1985—Browns, 24-20 (C)
1987—Browns, 20-10 (NE)
1991—Browns, 20-0 (NE)
1992—Browns, 19-17 (NE)
1993—Patriots, 20-17 (C)
1994—Browns, 13-6 (C)
*Browns, 20-13 (C)
1995—Patriots, 17-14 (NE)
(RS Pts.—Browns 278, Patriots 196)
(PS Pts.—Browns 20, Patriots 13)
AFC First-Round Playoff

CLEVELAND vs. NEW ORLEANS
RS: Browns lead series, 9-3
1967—Browns, 42-7 (NO)
1968—Browns, 24-10 (NO)
Browns, 35-17 (C)
1969—Browns, 27-17 (NO)
1971—Browns, 21-17 (NO)
1975—Browns, 17-16 (C)
1978—Browns, 24-16 (NO)
1981—Browns, 20-17 (C)
1984—Saints, 16-14 (C)
1987—Saints, 28-21 (NO)
1990—Saints, 25-20 (NO)
1993—Browns, 17-13 (C)
(RS Pts.—Browns 282, Saints 199)

CLEVELAND vs. N.Y. GIANTS
RS: Browns lead series, 25-17-2
PS: Series tied, 1-1
1950—Giants, 6-0 (C)
Giants, 17-13 (NY)
*Browns, 8-3 (C)
1951—Browns, 14-13 (C)
Browns, 10-0 (NY)
1952—Giants, 17-9 (C)
Giants, 37-34 (NY)
1953—Browns, 7-0 (NY)
Browns, 62-14 (C)
1954—Browns, 24-14 (C)
Browns, 16-7 (NY)
1955—Browns, 24-14 (C)
Tie, 35-35 (NY)
1956—Giants, 21-9 (C)
Browns, 24-7 (NY)
1957—Browns, 6-3 (C)
Browns, 34-28 (NY)
1958—Giants, 21-17 (C)
Giants, 13-10 (NY)
*Giants, 10-0 (NY)
1959—Giants, 10-6 (C)
Giants, 48-7 (NY)
1960—Giants, 17-13 (C)
Browns, 48-34 (NY)
1961—Giants, 37-21 (C)
Tie, 7-7 (NY)
1962—Browns, 17-7 (C)
Giants, 17-13 (NY)
1963—Browns, 35-24 (NY)
Giants, 33-6 (C)
1964—Browns, 42-20 (C)
Browns, 52-20 (NY)
1965—Browns, 38-14 (NY)
Browns, 34-21 (C)
1966—Browns, 28-7 (NY)
Browns, 49-40 (C)
1967—Giants, 38-34 (NY)
Browns, 24-14 (C)
1968—Browns, 45-10 (C)
1969—Browns, 28-17 (C)
Giants, 27-14 (NY)
1973—Browns, 12-10 (C)
1977—Browns, 21-7 (NY)
1985—Browns, 35-33 (NY)
1991—Giants, 13-10 (NY)
1994—Giants, 16-13 (C)
(RS Pts.—Browns 1,000, Giants 808)
(PS Pts.—Giants 13, Browns 8)
Conference Playoff

CLEVELAND vs. N.Y. JETS
RS: Browns lead series, 9-6
PS: Browns lead series, 1-0
1970—Browns, 31-21 (C)
1972—Browns, 26-10 (NY)
1976—Browns, 38-17 (C)
1978—Browns, 37-34 (C) OT
1979—Browns, 25-22 (NY) OT
1980—Browns, 17-14 (C)
1981—Jets, 14-13 (C)
1983—Browns, 10-7 (C)
1984—Jets, 24-20 (C)
1985—Jets, 37-10 (NY)
1986—*Browns, 23-20 (C) OT
1988—Jets, 23-3 (C)
1989—Browns, 38-24 (C)
1990—Jets, 24-21 (NY)
1991—Jets, 17-14 (C)
1994—Browns, 27-7 (C)
(RS Pts.—Browns 330, Jets 295)
(PS Pts.—Browns 23, Jets 20)
AFC Divisional Playoff

CLEVELAND vs. *OAKLAND
RS: Raiders lead series, 8-4
PS: Raiders lead series, 2-0
1970—Raiders, 23-20 (O)
1971—Raiders, 34-20 (C)
1973—Browns, 7-3 (O)
1974—Raiders, 40-24 (C)
1975—Raiders, 38-17 (O)
1977—Raiders, 26-10 (C)
1979—Raiders, 19-14 (O)
1980—**Raiders, 14-12 (C)
1982—***Raiders, 27-10 (LA)
1985—Raiders, 21-20 (C)
1986—Raiders, 27-14 (LA)
1987—Browns, 24-17 (LA)
1992—Browns, 28-16 (LA)
1993—Browns, 19-16 (LA)
(RS Pts.—Raiders 280, Browns 217)
(PS Pts.—Raiders 41, Browns 22)
Franchise in Los Angeles from 1982-1994
**AFC Divisional Playoff*
***AFC First-Round Playoff*

CLEVELAND vs. PHILADELPHIA
RS: Browns lead series, 31-12-1
1950—Browns, 35-10 (P)
Browns, 13-7 (C)
1951—Browns, 20-17 (C)
Browns, 24-9 (P)
1952—Browns, 49-7 (P)
Eagles, 28-20 (C)
1953—Browns, 37-13 (C)
Eagles, 42-27 (P)
1954—Eagles, 28-10 (P)
Browns, 6-0 (C)
1955—Browns, 21-17 (C)
Eagles, 33-17 (P)
1956—Browns, 16-0 (P)
Browns, 17-14 (C)
1957—Browns, 24-7 (C)
Eagles, 17-7 (P)
1958—Browns, 28-14 (C)
Browns, 21-14 (P)
1959—Browns, 28-7 (C)
Browns, 28-21 (P)
1960—Browns, 41-24 (P)
Eagles, 31-29 (C)
1961—Eagles, 27-20 (P)
Browns, 45-24 (C)
1962—Eagles, 35-7 (P)
Tie, 14-14 (C)
1963—Browns, 37-7 (C)
Browns, 23-17 (P)
1964—Browns, 28-20 (P)
Browns, 38-24 (C)
1965—Browns, 35-17 (P)
Browns, 38-34 (C)
1966—Browns, 27-7 (C)
Eagles, 33-21 (P)
1967—Eagles, 28-24 (P)
1968—Browns, 47-13 (C)
1969—Browns, 27-20 (P)
1972—Browns, 27-17 (P)
1976—Browns, 24-3 (C)
1979—Browns, 24-19 (P)
1982—Eagles, 24-21 (C)
1988—Browns, 19-3 (C)
1991—Eagles, 32-30 (C)
1994—Browns, 26-7 (P)
(RS Pts.—Browns 1,120, Eagles 785)

CLEVELAND vs. PITTSBURGH
RS: Browns lead series, 52-40
PS: Steelers lead series, 1-0
1950—Browns, 30-17 (P)
Browns, 45-7 (C)
1951—Browns, 17-0 (C)
Browns, 28-0 (P)
1952—Browns, 21-20 (P)
Browns, 29-28 (C)
1953—Browns, 34-16 (C)
Browns, 20-16 (P)
1954—Steelers, 55-27 (P)
Browns, 42-7 (C)
1955—Browns, 41-14 (C)
Browns, 30-7 (P)
1956—Browns, 14-10 (P)
Steelers, 24-16 (C)
1957—Browns, 23-12 (P)
Browns, 24-0 (C)
1958—Browns, 45-12 (P)
Browns, 27-10 (C)
1959—Steelers, 17-7 (P)
Steelers, 21-20 (C)
1960—Browns, 28-20 (C)
Steelers, 14-10 (P)
1961—Browns, 30-28 (P)
Steelers, 17-13 (C)
1962—Browns, 41-14 (P)
Browns, 35-14 (C)
1963—Browns, 35-23 (C)
Steelers, 9-7 (P)
1964—Steelers, 23-7 (C)
Browns, 30-17 (P)
1965—Browns, 24-19 (C)
Browns, 42-21 (P)
1966—Browns, 41-10 (C)
Steelers, 16-6 (P)
1967—Browns, 21-10 (C)
Browns, 34-14 (P)
1968—Browns, 31-24 (C)
Browns, 45-24 (P)
1969—Browns, 42-31 (C)
Browns, 24-3 (P)
1970—Browns, 15-7 (C)
Steelers, 28-9 (P)
1971—Browns, 27-17 (C)
Steelers, 26-9 (P)
1972—Browns, 26-24 (C)
Steelers, 30-0 (P)
1973—Steelers, 33-6 (P)
Browns, 21-16 (C)
1974—Steelers, 20-16 (P)
Steelers, 26-16 (C)
1975—Steelers, 42-6 (C)
Steelers, 31-17 (P)
1976—Steelers, 31-14 (P)
Browns, 18-16 (C)
1977—Steelers, 28-14 (C)
Steelers, 35-31 (P)
1978—Steelers, 15-9 (P) OT
Steelers, 34-14 (C)
1979—Steelers, 51-35 (C)
Steelers, 33-30 (P) OT
1980—Browns, 27-26 (C)
Steelers, 16-13 (P)
1981—Steelers, 13-7 (P)
Steelers, 32-10 (C)
1982—Browns, 10-9 (C)
Steelers, 37-21 (P)

1983—Steelers, 44-17 (P)
Browns, 30-17 (C)
1984—Browns, 20-10 (C)
Steelers, 23-20 (P)
1985—Browns, 17-7 (C)
Steelers, 10-9 (P)
1986—Browns, 27-24 (P)
Browns, 37-31 (C) OT
1987—Browns, 34-10 (C)
Browns, 19-13 (P)
1988—Browns, 23-9 (P)
Browns, 27-7 (C)
1989—Browns, 51-0 (P)
Steelers, 17-7 (C)
1990—Browns, 13-3 (C)
Steelers, 35-0 (P)
1991—Browns, 17-14 (C)
Steelers, 17-10 (P)
1992—Browns, 17-9 (C)
Steelers, 23-13 (P)
1993—Browns, 28-23 (C)
Steelers, 16-9 (P)
1994—Steelers, 17-10 (C)
Steelers, 17-7 (P)
*Steelers, 29-9 (P)
1995—Steelers, 20-3 (P)
Steelers, 20-17 (C)
(RS Pts.—Browns 1,989, Steelers 1,756)
(PS Pts.—Steelers 29, Browns 9)
AFC Divisional Playoff

CLEVELAND vs. *ST. LOUIS
RS: Browns lead series, 8-7
PS: Browns lead series, 2-1
1950—**Browns, 30-28 (C)
1951—Browns, 38-23 (LA)
**Rams, 24-17 (LA)
1952—Browns, 37-7 (C)
1955—**Browns, 38-14 (LA)
1957—Browns, 45-31 (C)
1958—Browns, 30-27 (LA)
1963—Browns, 20-6 (C)
1965—Rams, 42-7 (LA)
1968—Rams, 24-6 (C)
1973—Rams, 30-17 (LA)
1977—Rams, 9-0 (C)
1978—Browns, 30-19 (C)
1981—Rams, 27-16 (LA)
1984—Rams, 20-17 (LA)
1987—Browns, 30-17 (C)
1990—Rams, 38-23 (C)
1993—Browns, 42-14 (LA)
(RS Pts.—Browns 358, Rams 334)
(PS Pts.—Browns 85, Rams 66)
**Franchise in Los Angeles prior to 1995*
***NFL Championship*

CLEVELAND vs. SAN DIEGO
RS: Chargers lead series, 9-6-1
1970—Chargers, 27-10 (C)
1972—Browns, 21-17 (SD)
1973—Tie, 16-16 (C)
1974—Chargers, 36-35 (SD)
1976—Browns, 21-17 (C)
1977—Chargers, 37-14 (SD)
1981—Chargers, 44-14 (C)
1982—Chargers, 30-13 (C)
1983—Browns, 30-24 (SD) OT
1985—Browns, 21-7 (SD)
1986—Browns, 47-17 (C)
1987—Chargers, 27-24 (SD) OT
1990—Chargers, 24-14 (C)
1991—Browns, 30-24 (SD) OT
1992—Chargers, 14-13 (C)
1995—Chargers, 31-13 (SD)
(RS Pts.—Chargers 392, Browns 336)

CLEVELAND vs. SAN FRANCISCO
RS: Browns lead series, 9-6
1950—Browns, 34-14 (C)
1951—49ers, 24-10 (SF)
1953—Browns, 23-21 (C)
1955—Browns, 38-3 (SF)
1959—49ers, 21-20 (C)
1962—Browns, 13-10 (SF)
1968—Browns, 33-21 (SF)
1970—49ers, 34-31 (SF)
1974—Browns, 7-0 (C)
1978—Browns, 24-7 (C)
1981—Browns, 15-12 (SF)
1984—49ers, 41-7 (C)
1987—49ers, 38-24 (SF)
1990—49ers, 20-17 (SF)
1993—Browns, 23-13 (C)
(RS Pts.—Browns 319, 49ers 279)

CLEVELAND vs. SEATTLE
RS: Seahawks lead series, 9-4
1977—Seahawks, 20-19 (S)
1978—Seahawks, 47-24 (S)
1979—Seahawks, 29-24 (C)
1980—Browns, 27-3 (S)
1981—Seahawks, 42-21 (S)
1982—Browns, 21-7 (S)
1983—Seahawks, 24-9 (C)
1984—Seahawks, 33-0 (S)
1985—Seahawks, 31-13 (S)
1988—Seahawks, 16-10 (C)
1989—Browns, 17-7 (S)
1993—Seahawks, 22-5 (S)
1994—Browns, 35-9 (C)
(RS Pts.—Seahawks 290, Browns 225)

CLEVELAND vs. TAMPA BAY
RS: Browns lead series, 5-0
1976—Browns, 24-7 (TB)
1980—Browns, 34-27 (TB)
1983—Browns, 20-0 (C)
1989—Browns, 42-31 (TB)
1995—Browns, 22-6 (C)
(RS Pts.—Browns 142, Buccaneers 71)

CLEVELAND vs. WASHINGTON
RS: Browns lead series, 32-9-1
1950—Browns, 20-14 (C)
Browns, 45-21 (W)
1951—Browns, 45-0 (C)
1952—Browns, 19-15 (C)
Browns, 48-24 (W)
1953—Browns, 30-14 (W)
Browns, 27-3 (C)
1954—Browns, 62-3 (C)
Browns, 34-14 (W)
1955—Redskins, 27-17 (C)
Browns, 24-14 (W)
1956—Redskins, 20-9 (W)
Redskins, 20-17 (C)
1957—Browns, 21-17 (C)
Tie, 30-30 (W)
1958—Browns, 20-10 (W)
Browns, 21-14 (C)
1959—Browns, 34-7 (C)
Browns, 31-17 (W)
1960—Browns, 31-10 (W)
Browns, 27-16 (C)
1961—Browns, 31-7 (C)
Browns, 17-6 (W)
1962—Redskins, 17-16 (C)
Redskins, 17-9 (W)
1963—Browns, 37-14 (C)
Browns, 27-20 (W)
1964—Browns, 27-13 (W)
Browns, 34-24 (C)
1965—Browns, 17-7 (W)
Browns, 24-16 (C)
1966—Browns, 38-14 (W)
Browns, 14-3 (C)
1967—Browns, 42-37 (C)
1968—Browns, 24-21 (W)
1969—Browns, 27-23 (C)
1971—Browns, 20-13 (W)
1975—Redskins, 23-7 (C)
1979—Redskins, 13-9 (C)
1985—Redskins, 14-7 (C)
1988—Browns, 17-13 (W)
1991—Redskins, 42-17 (W)
(RS Pts.—Browns 1,073, Redskins 667)

DALLAS vs. ARIZONA
RS: Cowboys lead series, 44-22-1;
See Arizona vs. Dallas

DALLAS vs. ATLANTA
RS: Cowboys lead series, 10-6
PS: Cowboys lead series, 2-0;
See Atlanta vs. Dallas

DALLAS vs. BUFFALO
RS: Cowboys lead series, 3-2
PS: Cowboys lead series, 2-0;
See Buffalo vs. Dallas

DALLAS vs. CHICAGO
RS: Cowboys lead series, 8-6
PS: Cowboys lead series, 2-0;
See Chicago vs. Dallas

DALLAS vs. CINCINNATI
RS: Cowboys lead series, 4-2;
See Cincinnati vs. Dallas

DALLAS vs. CLEVELAND
RS: Browns lead series, 15-9
PS: Browns lead series, 2-1;
See Cleveland vs. Dallas

DALLAS vs. DENVER
RS: Cowboys lead series, 4-2
PS: Cowboys lead series, 1-0
1973—Cowboys, 22-10 (Den)
1977—Cowboys, 14-6 (Dal)
*Cowboys, 27-10 (New Orleans)
1980—Broncos, 41-20 (Den)
1986—Broncos, 29-14 (Den)
1992—Cowboys, 31-27 (Den)
1995—Cowboys, 31-21 (Dal)
(RS Pts.—Broncos 134, Cowboys 132)
(PS Pts.—Cowboys 27, Broncos 10)
**Super Bowl XII*

DALLAS vs. DETROIT
RS: Cowboys lead series, 7-6
PS: Series tied, 1-1
1960—Lions, 23-14 (Det)
1963—Cowboys, 17-14 (Dal)
1968—Cowboys, 59-13 (Dal)
1970—*Cowboys, 5-0 (Dal)
1972—Cowboys, 28-24 (Dal)
1975—Cowboys, 36-10 (Det)
1977—Cowboys, 37-0 (Dal)
1981—Lions, 27-24 (Det)
1985—Lions, 26-21 (Det)
1986—Cowboys, 31-7 (Det)
1987—Lions, 27-17 (Det)
1991—Lions, 34-10 (Det)
*Lions, 38-6 (Det)
1992—Cowboys, 37-3 (Det)
1994—Lions, 20-17 (Dal) OT
(RS Pts.—Cowboys 348, Lions 228)
(PS Pts.—Lions 38, Cowboys 11)
**NFC Divisional Playoff*

DALLAS vs. GREEN BAY
RS: Series tied, 8-8
PS: Cowboys lead series, 4-2
1960—Packers, 41-7 (GB)
1964—Packers, 45-21 (D)
1965—Packers, 13-3 (Mil)
1966—*Packers, 34-27 (D)
1967—*Packers, 21-17 (GB)
1968—Packers, 28-17 (D)
1970—Cowboys, 16-3 (D)
1972—Packers, 16-13 (Mil)
1975—Packers, 19-17 (D)
1978—Cowboys, 42-14 (Mil)
1980—Cowboys, 28-7 (Mil)
1982—**Cowboys, 37-26 (D)
1984—Cowboys, 20-6 (D)
1989—Packers, 31-13 (GB)
Packers, 20-10 (D)
1991—Cowboys, 20-17 (Mil)
1993—Cowboys, 36-14 (D)
***Cowboys, 27-17 (D)
1994—Cowboys, 42-31 (D)
***Cowboys, 35-9 (D)
1995—Cowboys, 34-24 (D)
****Cowboys, 38-27 (D)
(RS Pts.—Cowboys 339, Packers 329)
(PS Pts.—Cowboys 181, Packers 134)
**NFL Championship*
***NFC Second-Round Playoff*
****NFC Divisional Playoff*
*****NFC Championship*

DALLAS vs. HOUSTON
RS: Cowboys lead series, 5-3
1970—Cowboys, 52-10 (D)
1974—Cowboys, 10-0 (H)
1979—Oilers, 30-24 (D)
1982—Cowboys, 37-7 (H)
1985—Cowboys, 17-10 (H)
1988—Oilers, 25-17 (D)
1991—Oilers, 26-23 (H) OT
1994—Cowboys, 20-17 (D)
(RS Pts.—Cowboys 200, Oilers 125)

DALLAS vs. *INDIANAPOLIS
RS: Cowboys lead series, 7-2
PS: Colts lead series, 1-0
1960—Colts, 45-7 (D)
1967—Colts, 23-17 (B)
1969—Cowboys, 27-10 (D)
1970—**Colts, 16-13 (Miami)
1972—Cowboys, 21-0 (B)
1976—Cowboys, 30-27 (D)
1978—Cowboys, 38-0 (D)
1981—Cowboys, 37-13 (B)
1984—Cowboys, 22-3 (D)
1993—Cowboys, 27-3 (I)
(RS Pts.—Cowboys 226, Colts 124)
(PS Pts.—Colts 16, Cowboys 13)
**Franchise in Baltimore prior to 1984*
***Super Bowl V*

DALLAS vs. KANSAS CITY
RS: Cowboys lead series, 4-2
1970—Cowboys, 27-16 (KC)
1975—Chiefs, 34-31 (D)
1983—Cowboys, 41-21 (D)
1989—Chiefs, 36-28 (KC)
1992—Cowboys, 17-10 (D)
1995—Cowboys, 24-12 (D)
(RS Pts.—Cowboys 168, Chiefs 129)

DALLAS vs. MIAMI
RS: Dolphins lead series, 6-1
PS: Cowboys lead series, 1-0
1971—*Cowboys, 24-3 (New Orleans)
1973—Dolphins, 14-7 (D)
1978—Dolphins, 23-16 (M)
1981—Cowboys, 28-27 (D)
1984—Dolphins, 28-21 (M)
1987—Dolphins, 20-14 (D)
1989—Dolphins, 17-14 (D)
1993—Dolphins, 16-14 (D)
(RS Pts.—Dolphins 145, Cowboys 114)
(PS Pts.—Cowboys 24, Dolphins 3)
**Super Bowl VI*

DALLAS vs. MINNESOTA
RS: Cowboys lead series, 9-6
PS: Cowboys lead series, 3-1
1961—Cowboys, 21-7 (D)
Cowboys, 28-0 (M)
1966—Cowboys, 28-17 (D)
1968—Cowboys, 20-7 (M)
1970—Vikings, 54-13 (M)
1971—*Cowboys, 20-12 (M)
1973—**Vikings, 27-10 (D)
1974—Vikings, 23-21 (D)
1975—*Cowboys, 17-14 (M)
1977—Cowboys, 16-10 (M) OT
**Cowboys, 23-6 (D)
1978—Vikings, 21-10 (D)
1979—Cowboys, 36-20 (M)
1982—Vikings, 31-27 (M)
1983—Cowboys, 37-24 (M)
1987—Vikings, 44-38 (D) OT
1988—Vikings, 43-3 (D)
1993—Cowboys, 37-20 (M)
1995—Cowboys, 23-17 (M) OT
(RS Pts.—Cowboys 358, Vikings 338)
(PS Pts.—Cowboys 70, Vikings 59)
**NFC Divisional Playoff*
***NFC Championship*

DALLAS vs. NEW ENGLAND
RS: Cowboys lead series, 6-0
1971—Cowboys, 44-21 (D)
1975—Cowboys, 34-31 (NE)
1978—Cowboys, 17-10 (D)
1981—Cowboys, 35-21 (NE)

ALL-TIME TEAM VS. TEAM RESULTS

1984—Cowboys, 20-17 (D)
1987—Cowboys, 23-17 (NE) OT
(RS Pts.—Cowboys 173, Patriots 117)

DALLAS vs. NEW ORLEANS
RS: Cowboys lead series, 14-3
1967—Cowboys, 14-10 (D)
Cowboys, 27-10 (NO)
1968—Cowboys, 17-3 (NO)
1969—Cowboys, 21-17 (NO)
Cowboys, 33-17 (D)
1971—Saints, 24-14 (NO)
1973—Cowboys, 40-3 (D)
1976—Cowboys, 24-6 (NO)
1978—Cowboys, 27-7 (D)
1982—Cowboys, 21-7 (D)
1983—Cowboys, 21-20 (D)
1984—Cowboys, 30-27 (D) OT
1988—Saints, 20-17 (NO)
1989—Saints, 28-0 (NO)
1990—Cowboys, 17-13 (D)
1991—Cowboys, 23-14 (D)
1994—Cowboys, 24-16 (NO)
(RS Pts.—Cowboys 370, Saints 242)

DALLAS vs. N.Y. GIANTS
RS: Cowboys lead series, 43-22-2
1960—Tie, 31-31 (NY)
1961—Giants, 31-10 (D)
Cowboys, 17-16 (NY)
1962—Giants, 41-10 (D)
Giants, 41-31 (NY)
1963—Giants, 37-21 (NY)
Giants, 34-27 (D)
1964—Tie, 13-13 (D)
Cowboys, 31-21 (NY)
1965—Cowboys, 31-2 (D)
Cowboys, 38-20 (NY)
1966—Cowboys, 52-7 (D)
Cowboys, 17-7 (NY)
1967—Cowboys, 38-24 (D)
1968—Giants, 27-21 (D)
Cowboys, 28-10 (NY)
1969—Cowboys, 25-3 (D)
1970—Cowboys, 28-10 (D)
Giants, 23-20 (NY)
1971—Cowboys, 20-13 (D)
Cowboys, 42-14 (NY)
1972—Cowboys, 23-14 (NY)
Giants, 23-3 (D)
1973—Cowboys, 45-28 (D)
Cowboys, 23-10 (New Haven)
1974—Giants, 14-6 (D)
Cowboys, 21-7 (New Haven)
1975—Cowboys, 13-7 (NY)
Cowboys, 14-3 (D)
1976—Cowboys, 24-14 (NY)
Cowboys, 9-3 (D)
1977—Cowboys, 41-21 (D)
Cowboys, 24-10 (NY)
1978—Cowboys, 34-24 (NY)
Cowboys, 24-3 (D)
1979—Cowboys, 16-14 (NY)
Cowboys, 28-7 (D)
1980—Cowboys, 24-3 (D)
Giants, 38-35 (NY)
1981—Cowboys, 18-10 (D)
Giants, 13-10 (NY) OT
1983—Cowboys, 28-13 (D)
Cowboys, 38-20 (NY)
1984—Giants, 28-7 (NY)
Giants, 19-7 (D)
1985—Cowboys, 30-29 (NY)
Cowboys, 28-21 (D)
1986—Cowboys, 31-28 (D)
Giants, 17-14 (NY)
1987—Cowboys, 16-14 (NY)
Cowboys, 33-24 (D)
1988—Giants, 12-10 (D)
Giants, 29-21 (NY)
1989—Giants, 30-13 (D)
Giants, 15-0 (NY)
1990—Giants, 28-7 (D)
Giants, 31-17 (NY)
1991—Cowboys, 21-16 (D)
Giants, 22-9 (NY)
1992—Cowboys, 34-28 (NY)
Cowboys, 30-3 (D)
1993—Cowboys, 31-9 (D)
Cowboys, 16-13 (NY) OT
1994—Cowboys, 38-10 (D)
Giants, 15-10 (NY)
1995—Cowboys, 35-0 (NY)
Cowboys, 21-20 (D)
(RS Pts.—Cowboys 1,531, Giants 1,185)

DALLAS vs. N.Y. JETS
RS: Cowboys lead series, 5-1
1971—Cowboys, 52-10 (D)
1975—Cowboys, 31-21 (NY)
1978—Cowboys, 30-7 (NY)
1987—Cowboys, 38-24 (NY)
1990—Jets, 24-9 (NY)
1993—Cowboys, 28-7 (NY)
(RS Pts.—Cowboys 188, Jets 93)

DALLAS vs. *OAKLAND
RS: Series tied, 3-3
1974—Raiders, 27-23 (O)
1980—Cowboys, 19-13 (O)
1983—Raiders, 40-38 (D)
1986—Raiders, 17-13 (D)
1992—Cowboys, 28-13 (LA)
1995—Cowboys, 34-21 (O)
(RS Pts.—Cowboys 155, Raiders 131)
**Franchise in Los Angeles from 1982-1994*

DALLAS vs. PHILADELPHIA
RS: Cowboys lead series, 43-27
PS: Cowboys lead series, 2-1
1960—Eagles, 27-25 (D)
1961—Eagles, 43-7 (D)
Eagles, 35-13 (P)
1962—Cowboys, 41-19 (D)
Eagles, 28-14 (P)
1963—Eagles, 24-21 (P)
Cowboys, 27-20 (D)
1964—Eagles, 17-14 (D)
Eagles, 24-14 (P)
1965—Eagles, 35-24 (D)
Cowboys, 21-19 (P)
1966—Cowboys, 56-7 (D)
Eagles, 24-23 (P)
1967—Eagles, 21-14 (P)
Cowboys, 38-17 (D)
1968—Cowboys, 45-13 (P)
Cowboys, 34-14 (D)
1969—Cowboys, 38-7 (P)
Cowboys, 49-14 (D)
1970—Cowboys, 17-7 (P)
Cowboys, 21-17 (D)
1971—Cowboys, 42-7 (P)
Cowboys, 20-7 (D)
1972—Cowboys, 28-6 (D)
Cowboys, 28-7 (P)
1973—Eagles, 30-16 (P)
Cowboys, 31-10 (D)
1974—Eagles, 13-10 (P)
Cowboys, 31-24 (D)
1975—Cowboys, 20-17 (P)
Cowboys, 27-17 (D)
1976—Cowboys, 27-7 (D)
Cowboys, 26-7 (P)
1977—Cowboys, 16-10 (P)
Cowboys, 24-14 (D)
1978—Cowboys, 14-7 (D)
Cowboys, 31-13 (P)
1979—Eagles, 31-21 (D)
Cowboys, 24-17 (P)
1980—Eagles, 17-10 (P)
Cowboys, 35-27 (D)
*Eagles, 20-7 (P)
1981—Cowboys, 17-14 (P)
Cowboys, 21-10 (D)
1982—Eagles, 24-20 (D)
1983—Cowboys, 37-7 (D)
Cowboys, 27-20 (P)
1984—Cowboys, 23-17 (D)
Cowboys, 26-10 (P)
1985—Eagles, 16-14 (P)
Cowboys, 34-17 (D)
1986—Cowboys, 17-14 (P)
Eagles, 23-21 (D)
1987—Cowboys, 41-22 (D)
Eagles, 37-20 (P)
1988—Eagles, 24-23 (P)
Eagles, 23-7 (D)
1989—Eagles, 27-0 (D)
Eagles, 20-10 (P)
1990—Eagles, 21-20 (D)
Eagles, 17-3 (P)
1991—Eagles, 24-0 (D)
Cowboys, 25-13 (P)
1992—Eagles, 31-7 (P)
Cowboys, 20-10 (D)
**Cowboys, 34-10 (D)
1993—Cowboys, 23-10 (P)
Cowboys, 23-17 (D)
1994—Cowboys, 24-13 (D)
Cowboys, 31-19 (P)
1995—Cowboys, 34-12 (D)
Eagles, 20-17 (P)
**Cowboys, 30-11 (D)
(RS Pts.—Cowboys 1,622, Eagles 1,252)
(PS Pts.—Cowboys 71, Eagles 41)
**NFC Championship*
***NFC Divisional Playoff*

DALLAS vs. PITTSBURGH
RS: Cowboys lead series, 13-11
PS: Steelers lead series, 2-1
1960—Steelers, 35-28 (D)
1961—Cowboys, 27-24 (D)
Steelers, 37-7 (P)
1962—Steelers, 30-28 (D)
Cowboys, 42-27 (P)
1963—Steelers, 27-21 (P)
Steelers, 24-19 (D)
1964—Steelers, 23-17 (P)
Cowboys, 17-14 (D)
1965—Steelers, 22-13 (P)
Cowboys, 24-17 (D)
1966—Cowboys, 52-21 (D)
Cowboys, 20-7 (P)
1967—Cowboys, 24-21 (P)
1968—Cowboys, 28-7 (D)
1969—Cowboys, 10-7 (P)
1972—Cowboys, 17-13 (D)
1975—*Steelers, 21-17 (Miami)
1977—Steelers, 28-13 (P)
1978—**Steelers, 35-31 (Miami)
1979—Steelers, 14-3 (P)
1982—Steelers, 36-28 (D)
1985—Cowboys, 27-13 (D)
1988—Steelers, 24-21 (P)
1991—Cowboys, 20-10 (D)
1994—Cowboys, 26-9 (P)
1995—***Cowboys, 27-17 (Tempe)
(RS Pts.—Cowboys 532, Steelers 490)
(PS Pts.—Cowboys 75, Steelers 73)
**Super Bowl X*
***Super Bowl XIII*
****Super Bowl XXX*

DALLAS vs. *ST. LOUIS
RS: Rams lead series, 9-8
PS: Series tied, 4-4
1960—Rams, 38-13 (D)
1962—Cowboys, 27-17 (LA)
1967—Rams, 35-13 (D)
1969—Rams, 24-23 (LA)
1971—Cowboys, 28-21 (D)
1973—Rams, 37-31 (LA)
**Cowboys, 27-16 (D)
1975—Cowboys, 18-7 (D)
***Cowboys, 37-7 (LA)
1976—**Rams, 14-12 (D)
1978—Rams, 27-14 (LA)
***Cowboys, 28-0 (LA)
1979—Cowboys, 30-6 (D)
**Rams, 21-19 (D)
1980—Rams, 38-14 (LA)
****Cowboys, 34-13 (D)
1981—Cowboys, 29-17 (D)
1983—****Rams, 24-17 (D)
1984—Cowboys, 20-13 (LA)
1985—**Rams, 20-0 (LA)
1986—Rams, 29-10 (LA)
1987—Cowboys, 29-21 (LA)
1989—Rams, 35-31 (D)
1990—Cowboys, 24-21 (LA)
1992—Rams, 27-23 (D)
(RS Pts.—Rams 413, Cowboys 377)
(PS Pts.—Cowboys 174, Rams 115)
**Franchise in Los Angeles prior to 1995*
***NFC Divisional Playoff*
****NFC Championship*
*****NFC First-Round Playoff*

DALLAS vs. SAN DIEGO
RS: Cowboys lead series, 5-1
1972—Cowboys, 34-28 (SD)
1980—Cowboys, 42-31 (D)
1983—Chargers, 24-23 (SD)
1986—Cowboys, 24-21 (SD)
1990—Cowboys, 17-14 (D)
1995—Cowboys, 23-9 (SD)
(RS Pts.—Cowboys 163, Chargers 127)

DALLAS vs. SAN FRANCISCO
RS: 49ers lead series, 11-6-1
PS: Cowboys lead series, 5-2
1960—49ers, 26-14 (D)
1963—49ers, 31-24 (SF)
1965—Cowboys, 39-31 (D)
1967—49ers, 24-16 (SF)
1969—Tie, 24-24 (D)
1970—*Cowboys, 17-10 (SF)
1971—*Cowboys, 14-3 (D)
1972—49ers, 31-10 (D)
**Cowboys, 30-28 (SF)
1974—Cowboys, 20-14 (D)
1977—Cowboys, 42-35 (SF)
1979—Cowboys, 21-13 (SF)
1980—Cowboys, 59-14 (D)
1981—49ers, 45-14 (SF)
*49ers, 28-27 (SF)
1983—49ers, 42-17 (SF)
1985—49ers, 31-16 (SF)
1989—49ers, 31-14 (D)
1990—49ers, 24-6 (D)
1992—*Cowboys, 30-20 (SF)
1993—Cowboys, 26-17 (D)
*Cowboys, 38-21 (D)
1994—49ers, 21-14 (SF)
*49ers, 38-28 (SF)
1995—49ers, 38-20 (D)
(RS Pts.—49ers 492, Cowboys 396)
(PS Pts.—Cowboys 184, 49ers 148)
**NFC Championship*
***NFC Divisional Playoff*

DALLAS vs. SEATTLE
RS: Cowboys lead series, 4-1
1976—Cowboys, 28-13 (S)
1980—Cowboys, 51-7 (D)
1983—Cowboys, 35-10 (S)
1986—Seahawks, 31-14 (D)
1992—Cowboys, 27-0 (D)
(RS Pts.—Cowboys 155, Seahawks 61)

DALLAS vs. TAMPA BAY
RS: Cowboys lead series, 6-0
PS: Cowboys lead series, 2-0
1977—Cowboys, 23-7 (D)
1980—Cowboys, 28-17 (D)
1981—*Cowboys, 38-0 (D)
1982—Cowboys, 14-9 (D)
**Cowboys, 30-17 (D)
1983—Cowboys, 27-24 (D) OT
1990—Cowboys, 14-10 (D)
Cowboys, 17-13 (TB)
(RS Pts.—Cowboys 123, Buccaneers 80)
(PS Pts.—Cowboys 68, Buccaneers 17)
**NFC Divisional Playoff*
***NFC First-Round Playoff*

DALLAS vs. WASHINGTON
RS: Cowboys lead series, 39-29-2
PS: Redskins lead series, 2-0
1960—Redskins, 26-14 (W)
1961—Tie, 28-28 (D)
Redskins, 34-24 (W)

1962—Tie, 35-35 (D)
Cowboys, 38-10 (W)
1963—Redskins, 21-17 (W)
Cowboys, 35-20 (D)
1964—Cowboys, 24-18 (D)
Redskins, 28-16 (W)
1965—Cowboys, 27-7 (D)
Redskins, 34-31 (W)
1966—Cowboys, 31-30 (W)
Redskins, 34-31 (D)
1967—Cowboys, 17-14 (W)
Redskins, 27-20 (D)
1968—Cowboys, 44-24 (W)
Cowboys, 29-20 (D)
1969—Cowboys, 41-28 (W)
Cowboys, 20-10 (D)
1970—Cowboys, 45-21 (W)
Cowboys, 34-0 (D)
1971—Redskins, 20-16 (D)
Cowboys, 13-0 (W)
1972—Redskins, 24-20 (W)
Cowboys, 34-24 (D)
*Redskins, 26-3 (W)
1973—Redskins, 14-7 (W)
Cowboys, 27-7 (D)
1974—Redskins, 28-21 (W)
Cowboys, 24-23 (D)
1975—Redskins, 30-24 (W) OT
Cowboys, 31-10 (D)
1976—Cowboys, 20-7 (W)
Redskins, 27-14 (D)
1977—Cowboys, 34-16 (D)
Cowboys, 14-7 (W)
1978—Redskins, 9-5 (W)
Cowboys, 37-10 (D)
1979—Redskins, 34-20 (W)
Cowboys, 35-34 (D)
1980—Cowboys, 17-3 (W)
Cowboys, 14-10 (D)
1981—Cowboys, 26-10 (W)
Cowboys, 24-10 (D)
1982—Cowboys, 24-10 (W)
*Redskins, 31-17 (W)
1983—Cowboys, 31-30 (W)
Redskins, 31-10 (D)
1984—Redskins, 34-14 (W)
Redskins, 30-28 (D)
1985—Cowboys, 44-14 (D)
Cowboys, 13-7 (W)
1986—Cowboys, 30-6 (D)
Redskins, 41-14 (W)
1987—Redskins, 13-7 (D)
Redskins, 24-20 (W)
1988—Redskins, 35-17 (D)
Cowboys, 24-17 (W)
1989—Redskins, 30-7 (D)
Cowboys, 13-3 (W)
1990—Redskins, 19-15 (W)
Cowboys, 27-17 (D)
1991—Redskins, 33-31 (D)
Cowboys, 24-21 (W)
1992—Cowboys, 23-10 (D)
Redskins, 20-17 (W)
1993—Redskins, 35-16 (W)
Cowboys, 38-3 (D)
1994—Cowboys, 34-7 (W)
Cowboys, 31-7 (D)
1995—Redskins, 27-23 (W)
Redskins, 24-17 (D)
(RS Pts.—Cowboys, 1,670, Redskins 1,374)
(PS Pts.—Redskins 57, Cowboys 20)
NFC Championship

DENVER vs. ARIZONA
RS: Broncos lead series, 4-0-1;
See Arizona vs. Denver
DENVER vs. ATLANTA
RS: Broncos lead series, 5-3;
See Atlanta vs. Denver
DENVER vs. BUFFALO
RS: Bills lead series, 17-11-1
PS: Bills lead series, 1-0;
See Buffalo vs. Denver

DENVER vs. CHICAGO
RS: Series tied, 5-5;
See Chicago vs. Denver
DENVER vs. CINCINNATI
RS: Broncos lead series, 11-6;
See Cincinnati vs. Denver
DENVER vs. CLEVELAND
RS: Broncos lead series, 13-5
PS: Broncos lead series, 3-0;
See Cleveland vs. Denver
DENVER vs. DALLAS
RS: Cowboys lead series, 4-2
PS: Cowboys lead series, 1-0;
See Dallas vs. Denver
DENVER vs. DETROIT
RS: Broncos lead series, 4-3
1971—Lions, 24-20 (Den)
1974—Broncos, 31-27 (Det)
1978—Lions, 17-14 (Det)
1981—Broncos, 27-21 (Den)
1984—Broncos, 28-7 (Det)
1987—Broncos, 34-0 (Den)
1990—Lions, 40-27 (Det)
(RS Pts.—Broncos 181, Lions 136)
DENVER vs. GREEN BAY
RS: Broncos lead series, 4-2-1
1971—Packers, 34-13 (Mil)
1975—Broncos, 23-13 (D)
1978—Broncos, 16-3 (D)
1984—Broncos, 17-14 (D)
1987—Tie, 17-17 (Mil) OT
1990—Broncos, 22-13 (D)
1993—Packers, 30-27 (GB)
(RS Pts.—Broncos 135, Packers 124)
DENVER vs. HOUSTON
RS: Oilers lead series, 20-11-1
PS: Broncos lead series, 2-1
1960—Oilers, 45-25 (D)
Oilers, 20-10 (H)
1961—Oilers, 55-14 (D)
Oilers, 45-14 (H)
1962—Broncos, 20-10 (D)
Oilers, 34-17 (H)
1963—Oilers, 20-14 (H)
Oilers, 33-24 (D)
1964—Oilers, 38-17 (D)
Oilers, 34-15 (H)
1965—Broncos, 28-17 (D)
Broncos, 31-21 (H)
1966—Oilers, 45-7 (H)
Broncos, 40-38 (D)
1967—Oilers, 10-6 (H)
Oilers, 20-18 (D)
1968—Oilers, 38-17 (H)
1969—Oilers, 24-21 (H)
Tie, 20-20 (D)
1970—Oilers, 31-21 (H)
1972—Broncos, 30-17 (D)
1973—Broncos, 48-20 (H)
1974—Broncos, 37-14 (D)
1976—Oilers, 17-3 (H)
1977—Broncos, 24-14 (H)
1979—*Oilers, 13-7 (H)
1980—Oilers, 20-16 (D)
1983—Broncos, 26-14 (H)
1985—Broncos, 31-20 (D)
1987—Oilers, 40-10 (D)
**Broncos, 34-10 (D)
1991—Oilers, 42-14 (H)
**Broncos, 26-24 (D)
1992—Broncos, 27-21 (D)
1995—Oilers, 42-33 (H)
(RS Pts.—Oilers 879, Broncos 678)
(PS Pts.—Broncos 67, Oilers 47)
**AFC First-Round Playoff*
***AFC Divisional Playoff*
DENVER vs. *INDIANAPOLIS
RS: Broncos lead series, 9-2
1974—Broncos, 17-6 (B)
1977—Broncos, 27-13 (D)
1978—Colts, 7-6 (B)
1981—Broncos, 28-10 (D)
1983—Broncos, 17-10 (B)
Broncos, 21-19 (D)
1985—Broncos, 15-10 (I)
1988—Colts, 55-23 (I)
1989—Broncos, 14-3 (D)
1990—Broncos, 27-17 (I)
1993—Broncos, 35-13 (D)
(RS Pts.—Broncos 230, Colts 163)
**Franchise in Baltimore prior to 1984*
DENVER vs. JACKSONVILLE
RS: Broncos lead series, 1-0
1995—Broncos, 31-23 (D)
(RS Pts.—Broncos 31, Jaguars 23)
DENVER vs. *KANSAS CITY
RS: Chiefs lead series, 41-30
1960—Texans, 17-14 (D)
Texans, 34-7 (Dal)
1961—Texans, 19-12 (D)
Texans, 49-21 (Dal)
1962—Texans, 24-3 (D)
Texans, 17-10 (Dal)
1963—Chiefs, 59-7 (D)
Chiefs, 52-21 (KC)
1964—Broncos, 33-27 (D)
Chiefs, 49-39 (KC)
1965—Chiefs, 31-23 (D)
Chiefs, 45-35 (KC)
1966—Chiefs, 37-10 (KC)
Chiefs, 56-10 (D)
1967—Chiefs, 52-9 (KC)
Chiefs, 38-24 (D)
1968—Chiefs, 34-2 (KC)
Chiefs, 30-7 (D)
1969—Chiefs, 26-13 (D)
Chiefs, 31-17 (KC)
1970—Broncos, 26-13 (D)
Chiefs, 16-0 (KC)
1971—Chiefs, 16-3 (D)
Chiefs, 28-10 (KC)
1972—Chiefs, 45-24 (D)
Chiefs, 24-21 (KC)
1973—Chiefs, 16-14 (KC)
Broncos, 14-10 (D)
1974—Broncos, 17-14 (KC)
Chiefs, 42-34 (D)
1975—Broncos, 37-33 (D)
Chiefs, 26-13 (KC)
1976—Broncos, 35-26 (KC)
Broncos, 17-16 (D)
1977—Broncos, 23-7 (D)
Broncos, 14-7 (KC)
1978—Broncos, 23-17 (KC) OT
Broncos, 24-3 (D)
1979—Broncos, 24-10 (KC)
Broncos, 20-3 (D)
1980—Chiefs, 23-17 (D)
Chiefs, 31-14 (KC)
1981—Chiefs, 28-14 (KC)
Broncos, 16-13 (D)
1982—Chiefs, 37-16 (D)
1983—Broncos, 27-24 (D)
Chiefs, 48-17 (KC)
1984—Broncos, 21-0 (D)
Chiefs, 16-13 (KC)
1985—Broncos, 30-10 (KC)
Broncos, 14-13 (D)
1986—Broncos, 38-17 (D)
Chiefs, 37-10 (KC)
1987—Broncos, 26-17 (KC)
Broncos, 20-17 (D)
1988—Chiefs, 20-13 (KC)
Broncos, 17-11 (D)
1989—Broncos, 34-20 (D)
Broncos, 16-13 (KC)
1990—Broncos, 24-23 (D)
Chiefs, 31-20 (KC)
1991—Broncos, 19-16 (D)
Broncos, 24-20 (KC)
1992—Broncos, 20-19 (D)
Chiefs, 42-20 (KC)
1993—Chiefs, 15-7 (KC)
Broncos, 27-21 (D)
1994—Chiefs, 31-28 (D)
Broncos, 20-17 (KC) OT
1995—Chiefs, 21-7 (D)
Chiefs, 20-17 (KC)
(RS Pts.—Chiefs 1,770, Broncos 1,316)
**Franchise in Dallas prior to 1963 and known as Texans*
DENVER vs. MIAMI
RS: Dolphins lead series, 5-2-1
1966—Dolphins, 24-7 (M)
Broncos, 17-7 (D)
1967—Dolphins, 35-21 (M)
1968—Broncos, 21-14 (D)
1969—Dolphins, 27-24 (M)
1971—Tie, 10-10 (D)
1975—Dolphins, 14-13 (M)
1985—Dolphins, 30-26 (D)
(RS Pts.—Dolphins 161, Broncos 139)
DENVER vs. MINNESOTA
RS: Vikings lead series, 5-3
1972—Vikings, 23-20 (D)
1978—Vikings, 12-9 (M) OT
1981—Broncos, 19-17 (D)
1984—Broncos, 42-21 (D)
1987—Vikings, 34-27 (M)
1990—Vikings, 27-22 (M)
1991—Broncos, 13-6 (M)
1993—Vikings, 26-23 (D)
(RS Pts.—Broncos 175, Vikings 166)
DENVER vs. *NEW ENGLAND
RS: Broncos lead series, 17-12
PS: Broncos lead series, 1-0
1960—Broncos, 13-10 (B)
Broncos, 31-24 (D)
1961—Patriots, 45-17 (B)
Patriots, 28-24 (D)
1962—Patriots, 41-16 (B)
Patriots, 33-29 (D)
1963—Broncos, 14-10 (D)
Patriots, 40-21 (B)
1964—Patriots, 39-10 (D)
Patriots, 12-7 (B)
1965—Broncos, 27-10 (B)
Patriots, 28-20 (D)
1966—Patriots, 24-10 (D)
Broncos, 17-10 (B)
1967—Broncos, 26-21 (D)
1968—Patriots, 20-17 (D)
Broncos, 35-14 (B)
1969—Broncos, 35-7 (D)
1972—Broncos, 45-21 (D)
1976—Patriots, 38-14 (NE)
1979—Broncos, 45-10 (D)
1980—Patriots, 23-14 (NE)
1984—Broncos, 26-19 (D)
1986—Broncos, 27-20 (D)
**Broncos, 22-17 (D)
1987—Broncos, 31-20 (D)
1988—Broncos, 21-10 (D)
1991—Broncos, 9-6 (NE)
Broncos, 20-3 (D)
1995—Broncos, 37-3 (NE)
(RS Pts.—Broncos 658, Patriots 589)
(PS Pts.—Broncos 22, Patriots 17)
**Franchise in Boston prior to 1971*
***AFC Divisional Playoff*
DENVER vs. NEW ORLEANS
RS: Broncos lead series, 4-2
1970—Broncos, 31-6 (NO)
1974—Broncos, 33-17 (D)
1979—Broncos, 10-3 (D)
1985—Broncos, 34-23 (D)
1988—Saints, 42-0 (NO)
1994—Saints, 30-28 (D)
(RS Pts.—Broncos 136, Saints 121)
DENVER vs. N.Y. GIANTS
RS: Series tied, 3-3
PS: Giants lead series, 1-0
1972—Giants, 29-17 (NY)
1976—Broncos, 14-13 (D)
1980—Broncos, 14-9 (NY)
1986—Giants, 19-16 (NY)
*Giants, 39-20 (Pasadena)
1989—Giants, 14-7 (D)
1992—Broncos, 27-13 (D)

(RS Pts.—Giants 97, Broncos 95)
(PS Pts.—Giants 39, Broncos 20)
Super Bowl XXI

DENVER vs. *N.Y. JETS
RS: Series tied, 12-12-1
1960—Titans, 28-24 (NY)
Titans, 30-27 (D)
1961—Titans, 35-28 (NY)
Broncos, 27-10 (D)
1962—Broncos, 32-10 (NY)
Titans, 46-45 (D)
1963—Tie, 35-35 (NY)
Jets, 14-9 (D)
1964—Jets, 30-6 (NY)
Broncos, 20-16 (D)
1965—Broncos, 16-13 (D)
Jets, 45-10 (NY)
1966—Jets, 16-7 (D)
1967—Jets, 38-24 (D)
Broncos, 33-24 (NY)
1968—Broncos, 21-13 (NY)
1969—Broncos, 21-19 (D)
1973—Broncos, 40-28 (NY)
1976—Broncos, 46-3 (D)
1978—Jets, 31-28 (D)
1980—Broncos, 31-24 (D)
1986—Jets, 22-10 (NY)
1992—Broncos, 27-16 (D)
1993—Broncos, 26-20 (NY)
1994—Jets, 25-22 (NY) OT
(RS Pts.—Broncos 615, Jets 591)
Jets known as Titans prior to 1963

DENVER vs. *OAKLAND
RS: Raiders lead series, 48-21-2
PS: Series tied, 1-1
1960—Broncos, 31-14 (D)
Raiders, 48-10 (O)
1961—Raiders, 33-19 (O)
Broncos, 27-24 (D)
1962—Broncos, 44-7 (D)
Broncos, 23-6 (O)
1963—Raiders, 26-10 (D)
Raiders, 35-31 (O)
1964—Raiders, 40-7 (O)
Tie, 20-20 (D)
1965—Raiders, 28-20 (D)
Raiders, 24-13 (O)
1966—Raiders, 17-3 (D)
Raiders, 28-10 (O)
1967—Raiders, 51-0 (O)
Raiders, 21-17 (D)
1968—Raiders, 43-7 (D)
Raiders, 33-27 (O)
1969—Raiders, 24-14 (D)
Raiders, 41-10 (O)
1970—Raiders, 35-23 (O)
Raiders, 24-19 (D)
1971—Raiders, 27-16 (D)
Raiders, 21-13 (O)
1972—Broncos, 30-23 (O)
Raiders, 37-20 (D)
1973—Tie, 23-23 (D)
Raiders, 21-17 (O)
1974—Raiders, 28-17 (D)
Broncos, 20-17 (O)
1975—Raiders, 42-17 (D)
Raiders, 17-10 (O)
1976—Raiders, 17-10 (D)
Raiders, 19-6 (O)
1977—Broncos, 30-7 (O)
Raiders, 24-14 (D)
**Broncos, 20-17 (D)
1978—Broncos, 14-6 (D)
Broncos, 21-6 (O)
1979—Raiders, 27-3 (O)
Raiders, 14-10 (D)
1980—Raiders, 9-3 (O)
Raiders, 24-21 (D)
1981—Broncos, 9-7 (D)
Broncos, 17-0 (O)
1982—Raiders, 27-10 (LA)
1983—Raiders, 22-7 (D)
Raiders, 22-20 (LA)
1984—Broncos, 16-13 (D)
Broncos, 22-19 (LA) OT
1985—Raiders, 31-28 (LA) OT
Raiders, 17-14 (D) OT
1986—Broncos, 38-36 (D)
Broncos, 21-10 (LA)
1987—Broncos, 30-14 (D)
Broncos, 23-17 (LA)
1988—Raiders, 30-27 (D) OT
Raiders, 21-20 (LA)
1989—Broncos, 31-21 (D)
Raiders, 16-13 (LA) OT
1990—Raiders, 14-9 (LA)
Raiders, 23-20 (D)
1991—Raiders, 16-13 (LA)
Raiders, 17-16 (D)
1992—Broncos, 17-13 (D)
Raiders, 24-0 (LA)
1993—Raiders, 23-20 (D)
Raiders, 33-30 (LA) OT
***Raiders, 42-24 (LA)
1994—Raiders, 48-16 (D)
Raiders, 23-13 (LA)
1995—Broncos, 27-0 (D)
Broncos, 31-28 (O)
(RS Pts.—Raiders 1,616, Broncos 1,258)
(PS Pts.—Raiders 59, Broncos 44)
Franchise in Los Angeles from 1982-1994
**AFC Championship*
***AFC First-Round Playoff*

DENVER vs. PHILADELPHIA
RS: Eagles lead series, 6-2
1971—Eagles, 17-16 (P)
1975—Broncos, 25-10 (D)
1980—Eagles, 27-6 (P)
1983—Eagles, 13-10 (D)
1986—Broncos, 33-7 (P)
1989—Eagles, 28-24 (D)
1992—Eagles, 30-0 (P)
1995—Eagles, 31-13 (P)
(RS Pts.—Eagles 163, Broncos 127)

DENVER vs. PITTSBURGH
RS: Broncos lead series, 10-5-1
PS: Series tied, 2-2
1970—Broncos, 16-13 (D)
1971—Broncos, 22-10 (P)
1973—Broncos, 23-13 (P)
1974—Tie, 35-35 (D) OT
1975—Steelers, 20-9 (P)
1977—Broncos, 21-7 (D)
*Broncos, 34-21 (D)
1978—Steelers, 21-17 (D)
*Steelers, 33-10 (P)
1979—Steelers, 42-7 (P)
1983—Broncos, 14-10 (P)
1984—*Steelers, 24-17 (D)
1985—Broncos, 31-23 (P)
1986—Broncos, 21-10 (P)
1988—Steelers, 39-21 (P)
1989—Broncos, 34-7 (D)
*Broncos, 24-23 (D)
1990—Steelers, 34-17 (D)
1991—Broncos, 20-13 (D)
1993—Broncos, 37-13 (D)
(RS Pts.—Broncos 345, Steelers 310)
(PS Pts.—Steelers 101, Broncos 85)
AFC Divisional Playoff

DENVER vs. *ST. LOUIS
RS: Rams lead series, 4-3
1972—Broncos, 16-10 (LA)
1974—Rams, 17-10 (D)
1979—Rams, 13-9 (D)
1982—Broncos, 27-24 (LA)
1985—Rams, 20-16 (LA)
1988—Broncos, 35-24 (D)
1994—Rams, 27-21 (LA)
(RS Pts.—Rams 135, Broncos 134)
Franchise in Los Angeles prior to 1995

DENVER vs. *SAN DIEGO
RS: Broncos lead series, 37-34-1
1960—Chargers, 23-19 (D)
Chargers, 41-33 (LA)
1961—Chargers, 37-0 (SD)
Chargers, 19-16 (D)
1962—Broncos, 30-21 (D)
Broncos, 23-20 (SD)
1963—Broncos, 50-34 (D)
Chargers, 58-20 (SD)
1964—Chargers, 42-14 (SD)
Chargers, 31-20 (D)
1965—Chargers, 34-31 (SD)
Chargers, 33-21 (D)
1966—Chargers, 24-17 (SD)
Broncos, 20-17 (D)
1967—Chargers, 38-21 (D)
Chargers, 24-20 (SD)
1968—Chargers, 55-24 (SD)
Chargers, 47-23 (D)
1969—Broncos, 13-0 (D)
Chargers, 45-24 (SD)
1970—Chargers, 24-21 (SD)
Tie, 17-17 (D)
1971—Broncos, 20-16 (D)
Chargers, 45-17 (SD)
1972—Chargers, 37-14 (SD)
Broncos, 38-13 (D)
1973—Broncos, 30-19 (D)
Broncos, 42-28 (SD)
1974—Broncos, 27-7 (D)
Chargers, 17-0 (SD)
1975—Broncos, 27-17 (SD)
Broncos, 13-10 (D) OT
1976—Broncos, 26-0 (D)
Broncos, 17-0 (SD)
1977—Broncos, 17-14 (SD)
Broncos, 17-9 (D)
1978—Broncos, 27-14 (D)
Chargers, 23-0 (SD)
1979—Broncos, 7-0 (D)
Chargers, 17-7 (SD)
1980—Chargers, 30-13 (D)
Broncos, 20-13 (SD)
1981—Broncos, 42-24 (D)
Chargers, 34-17 (SD)
1982—Chargers, 23-3 (D)
Chargers, 30-20 (SD)
1983—Broncos, 14-6 (D)
Chargers, 31-7 (SD)
1984—Broncos, 16-13 (SD)
Broncos, 16-13 (D)
1985—Chargers, 30-10 (SD)
Broncos, 30-24 (D) OT
1986—Broncos, 31-14 (SD)
Chargers, 9-3 (D)
1987—Broncos, 31-17 (SD)
Broncos, 24-0 (D)
1988—Broncos, 34-3 (D)
Broncos, 12-0 (SD)
1989—Broncos, 16-10 (D)
Chargers, 19-16 (SD)
1990—Chargers, 19-7 (SD)
Broncos, 20-10 (D)
1991—Broncos, 27-19 (D)
Broncos, 17-14 (SD)
1992—Broncos, 21-13 (D)
Chargers, 24-21 (SD)
1993—Broncos, 34-17 (D)
Chargers, 13-10 (SD)
1994—Chargers, 37-34 (D)
Broncos, 20-15 (SD)
1995—Chargers, 17-6 (SD)
Broncos, 30-27 (D)
(RS Pts.—Chargers 1,538, Broncos 1,445)
Franchise in Los Angeles prior to 1961

DENVER vs. SAN FRANCISCO
RS: Broncos lead series, 4-3
PS: 49ers lead series, 1-0
1970—49ers, 19-14 (SF)
1973—49ers, 36-34 (D)
1979—Broncos, 38-28 (SF)
1982—Broncos, 24-21 (D)
1985—Broncos, 17-16 (D)
1988—Broncos, 16-13 (SF) OT
1989—*49ers, 55-10 (New Orleans)
1994—49ers, 42-19 (SF)
(RS Pts.—49ers 175, Broncos 162)
(PS Pts.—49ers 55, Broncos 10)
Super Bowl XXIV

DENVER vs. SEATTLE
RS: Broncos lead series, 22-15
PS: Seahawks lead series, 1-0
1977—Broncos, 24-13 (S)
1978—Broncos, 28-7 (D)
Broncos, 20-17 (S) OT
1979—Broncos, 37-34 (D)
Seahawks, 28-23 (S)
1980—Broncos, 36-20 (D)
Broncos, 25-17 (S)
1981—Seahawks, 13-10 (S)
Broncos, 23-13 (D)
1982—Seahawks, 17-10 (D)
Seahawks, 13-11 (S)
1983—Seahawks, 27-19 (S)
Broncos, 38-27 (D)
*Seahawks, 31-7 (S)
1984—Seahawks, 27-24 (D)
Broncos, 31-14 (S)
1985—Broncos, 13-10 (D) OT
Broncos, 27-24 (S)
1986—Broncos, 20-13 (D)
Seahawks, 41-16 (S)
1987—Broncos, 40-17 (D)
Seahawks, 28-21 (S)
1988—Seahawks, 21-14 (D)
Seahawks, 42-14 (S)
1989—Broncos, 24-21 (S) OT
Broncos, 41-14 (D)
1990—Broncos, 34-31 (D) OT
Seahawks, 17-12 (S)
1991—Broncos, 16-10 (D)
Seahawks, 13-10 (S)
1992—Seahawks, 16-13 (S) OT
Broncos, 10-6 (D)
1993—Broncos, 28-17 (D)
Broncos, 17-9 (S)
1994—Broncos, 16-9 (S)
Broncos, 17-10 (D)
1995—Seahawks, 27-10 (S)
Seahawks, 31-27 (D)
(RS Pts.—Broncos 799, Seahawks 714)
(PS Pts.—Seahawks 31, Broncos 7)
AFC First-Round Playoff

DENVER vs. TAMPA BAY
RS: Broncos lead series, 2-1
1976—Broncos, 48-13 (D)
1981—Broncos, 24-7 (TB)
1993—Buccaneers, 17-10 (D)
(RS Pts.—Broncos 82, Buccaneers 37)

DENVER vs. WASHINGTON
RS: Broncos lead series, 4-3
PS: Redskins lead series, 1-0
1970—Redskins, 19-3 (D)
1974—Redskins, 30-3 (W)
1980—Broncos, 20-17 (D)
1986—Broncos, 31-30 (D)
1987—*Redskins, 42-10 (San Diego)
1989—Broncos, 14-10 (W)
1992—Redskins, 34-3 (W)
1995—Broncos, 38-31 (D)
(RS Pts.—Redskins 171, Broncos 112)
(PS Pts.—Redskins 42, Broncos 10)
Super Bowl XXII

DETROIT vs. ARIZONA
RS: Lions lead series, 27-17-5;
See Arizona vs. Detroit

DETROIT vs. ATLANTA
RS: Lions lead series, 18-6;
See Atlanta vs. Detroit

DETROIT vs. BUFFALO
RS: Lions lead series, 3-1-1;
See Buffalo vs. Detroit

DETROIT vs. CHICAGO
RS: Bears lead series, 75-52-5;
See Chicago vs. Detroit

DETROIT vs. CINCINNATI
RS: Series tied, 3-3;
See Cincinnati vs. Detroit

DETROIT vs. CLEVELAND
RS: Lions lead series, 12-3
PS: Lions lead series, 3-1;
See Cleveland vs. Detroit
DETROIT vs. DALLAS
RS: Cowboys lead series, 7-6
PS: Series tied, 1-1;
See Dallas vs. Detroit
DETROIT vs. DENVER
RS: Broncos lead series, 4-3;
See Denver vs. Detroit
***DETROIT vs. GREEN BAY**
RS: Packers lead series, 66-58-7
PS: Packers lead series, 2-0
1930—Packers, 47-13 (GB)
Tie, 6-6 (P)
1932—Packers, 15-10 (GB)
Spartans, 19-0 (P)
1933—Packers, 17-0 (GB)
Spartans, 7-0 (P)
1934—Lions, 3-0 (GB)
Packers, 3-0 (D)
1935—Packers, 13-9 (Mil)
Packers, 31-7 (GB)
Lions, 20-10 (D)
1936—Packers, 20-18 (GB)
Packers, 26-17 (D)
1937—Packers, 26-6 (GB)
Packers, 14-13 (D)
1938—Lions, 17-7 (GB)
Packers, 28-7 (D)
1939—Packers, 26-7 (GB)
Packers, 12-7 (D)
1940—Lions, 23-14 (GB)
Packers, 50-7 (D)
1941—Packers, 23-0 (GB)
Packers, 24-7 (D)
1942—Packers, 38-7 (Mil)
Packers, 28-7 (D)
1943—Packers, 35-14 (GB)
Packers, 27-6 (D)
1944—Packers, 27-6 (Mil)
Packers, 14-0 (D)
1945—Packers, 57-21 (Mil)
Lions, 14-3 (D)
1946—Packers, 10-7 (Mil)
Packers, 9-0 (D)
1947—Packers, 34-17 (GB)
Packers, 35-14 (D)
1948—Packers, 33-21 (GB)
Lions, 24-20 (D)
1949—Packers, 16-14 (Mil)
Lions, 21-7 (D)
1950—Lions, 45-7 (GB)
Lions, 24-21 (D)
1951—Lions, 24-17 (GB)
Lions, 52-35 (D)
1952—Lions, 52-17 (GB)
Lions, 48-24 (D)
1953—Lions, 14-7 (GB)
Lions, 34-15 (D)
1954—Lions, 21-17 (GB)
Lions, 28-24 (D)
1955—Packers, 20-17 (GB)
Lions, 24-10 (D)
1956—Lions, 20-16 (GB)
Packers, 24-20 (D)
1957—Lions, 24-14 (GB)
Lions, 18-6 (D)
1958—Tie, 13-13 (GB)
Lions, 24-14 (D)
1959—Packers, 28-10 (GB)
Packers, 24-17 (D)
1960—Packers, 28-9 (GB)
Lions, 23-10 (D)
1961—Lions, 17-13 (Mil)
Packers, 17-9 (D)
1962—Packers, 9-7 (GB)
Lions, 26-14 (D)
1963—Packers, 31-10 (Mil)
Tie, 13-13 (D)
1964—Packers, 14-10 (D)
Packers, 30-7 (GB)
1965—Packers, 31-21 (D)
Lions, 12-7 (GB)
1966—Packers, 23-14 (GB)
Packers, 31-7 (D)
1967—Tie, 17-17 (GB)
Packers, 27-17 (D)
1968—Lions, 23-17 (GB)
Tie, 14-14 (D)
1969—Packers, 28-17 (D)
Lions, 16-10 (GB)
1970—Lions, 40-0 (GB)
Lions, 20-0 (D)
1971—Lions, 31-28 (D)
Tie, 14-14 (Mil)
1972—Packers, 24-23 (D)
Packers, 33-7 (GB)
1973—Tie, 13-13 (GB)
Lions, 34-0 (D)
1974—Packers, 21-19 (Mil)
Lions, 19-17 (D)
1975—Lions, 30-16 (Mil)
Lions, 13-10 (D)
1976—Packers, 24-14 (GB)
Lions, 27-6 (D)
1977—Lions, 10-6 (D)
Packers, 10-9 (GB)
1978—Packers, 13-7 (D)
Packers, 35-14 (Mil)
1979—Packers, 24-16 (Mil)
Packers, 18-13 (D)
1980—Lions, 29-7 (Mil)
Lions, 24-3 (D)
1981—Lions, 31-27 (D)
Packers, 31-17 (GB)
1982—Lions, 30-10 (GB)
Lions, 27-24 (D)
1983—Lions, 38-14 (D)
Lions, 23-20 (Mil) OT
1984—Packers, 41-9 (GB)
Lions, 31-28 (D)
1985—Packers, 43-10 (GB)
Packers, 26-23 (D)
1986—Lions, 21-14 (GB)
Packers, 44-40 (D)
1987—Lions, 19-16 (GB) OT
Packers, 34-33 (D)
1988—Lions, 19-9 (Mil)
Lions, 30-14 (D)
1989—Packers, 23-20 (Mil) OT
Lions, 31-22 (D)
1990—Packers, 24-21 (D)
Lions, 24-17 (GB)
1991—Lions, 23-14 (D)
Lions, 21-17 (GB)
1992—Packers, 27-13 (D)
Packers, 38-10 (Mil)
1993—Packers, 26-17 (MIl)
Lions, 30-20 (D)
**Packers, 28-24 (D)
1994—Packers, 38-30 (Mil)
Lions, 34-31 (D)
**Packers, 16-12 (GB)
1995—Packers, 30-21 (GB)
Lions, 24-16 (D)
(RS Pts.—Packers 2,602, Lions 2,380)
(PS Pts.—Packers 44, Lions 36)
**Franchise in Portsmouth prior to 1934 and known as the Spartans*
***NFC First-Round Playoff*
DETROIT vs. HOUSTON
RS: Oilers lead series, 4-3
1971—Lions, 31-7 (H)
1975—Oilers, 24-8 (H)
1983—Oilers, 27-17 (H)
1986—Lions, 24-13 (D)
1989—Oilers, 35-31 (H)
1992—Oilers, 24-21 (D)
1995—Lions, 24-17 (H)
(RS Pts.—Lions 156, Oilers 147)
DETROIT vs. *INDIANAPOLIS
RS: Series tied, 17-17-2
1953—Lions, 27-17 (B)
Lions, 17-7 (D)
1954—Lions, 35-0 (D)
Lions, 27-3 (B)
1955—Colts, 28-13 (B)
Lions, 24-14 (D)
1956—Lions, 31-14 (B)
Lions, 27-3 (D)
1957—Colts, 34-14 (B)
Lions, 31-27 (D)
1958—Colts, 28-15 (B)
Colts, 40-14 (D)
1959—Colts, 21-9 (B)
Colts, 31-24 (D)
1960—Lions, 30-17 (D)
Lions, 20-15 (B)
1961—Lions, 16-15 (B)
Colts, 17-14 (D)
1962—Lions, 29-20 (B)
Lions, 21-14 (D)
1963—Colts, 25-21 (D)
Colts, 24-21 (B)
1964—Colts, 34-0 (D)
Lions, 31-14 (B)
1965—Colts, 31-7 (B)
Tie, 24-24 (D)
1966—Colts, 45-14 (B)
Lions, 20-14 (D)
1967—Colts, 41-7 (B)
1968—Colts, 27-10 (D)
1969—Tie, 17-17 (B)
1973—Colts, 29-27 (D)
1977—Lions, 13-10 (B)
1980—Colts, 10-9 (D)
1985—Colts, 14-6 (I)
1991—Lions, 33-24 (I)
(RS Pts.—Colts 748, Lions 698)
**Franchise in Baltimore prior to 1984*
DETROIT vs. JACKSONVILLE
RS: Lions lead series, 1-0
1995—Lions, 44-0 (D)
(RS Pts.—Lions 44, Jaguars 0)
DETROIT vs. KANSAS CITY
RS: Chiefs lead series, 4-3
1971—Lions, 32-21 (D)
1975—Chiefs, 24-21 (KC) OT
1980—Chiefs, 20-17 (KC)
1981—Lions, 27-10 (D)
1987—Chiefs, 27-20 (D)
1988—Lions, 7-6 (KC)
1990—Chiefs, 43-24 (KC)
(RS Pts.—Chiefs 151, Lions 148)
DETROIT vs. MIAMI
RS: Dolphins lead series, 3-2
1973—Dolphins, 34-7 (M)
1979—Dolphins, 28-10 (D)
1985—Lions, 31-21 (D)
1991—Lions, 17-13 (D)
1994—Dolphins, 27-20 (M)
(RS Pts.—Dolphins 123, Lions 85)
DETROIT vs. MINNESOTA
RS: Vikings lead series, 42-25-2
1961—Lions, 37-10 (M)
Lions, 13-7 (D)
1962—Lions, 17-6 (M)
Lions, 37-23 (D)
1963—Lions, 28-10 (D)
Vikings, 34-31 (M)
1964—Lions, 24-20 (M)
Tie, 23-23 (D)
1965—Lions, 31-29 (M)
Vikings, 29-7 (D)
1966—Lions, 32-31 (M)
Vikings, 28-16 (D)
1967—Tie, 10-10 (M)
Lions, 14-3 (D)
1968—Vikings, 24-10 (M)
Vikings, 13-6 (D)
1969—Vikings, 24-10 (M)
Vikings, 27-0 (D)
1970—Vikings, 30-17 (D)
Vikings, 24-20 (M)
1971—Vikings, 16-13 (D)
Vikings, 29-10 (M)
1972—Vikings, 34-10 (D)
Vikings, 16-14 (M)
1973—Vikings, 23-9 (D)
Vikings, 28-7 (M)
1974—Vikings, 7-6 (D)
Lions, 20-16 (M)
1975—Vikings, 25-19 (M)
Lions, 17-10 (D)
1976—Vikings, 10-9 (D)
Vikings, 31-23 (M)
1977—Vikings, 14-7 (M)
Vikings, 30-21 (D)
1978—Vikings, 17-7 (M)
Lions, 45-14 (D)
1979—Vikings, 13-10 (D)
Vikings, 14-7 (M)
1980—Lions, 27-7 (D)
Vikings, 34-0 (M)
1981—Vikings, 26-24 (M)
Lions, 45-7 (D)
1982—Vikings, 34-31 (D)
1983—Vikings, 20-17 (M)
Lions, 13-2 (D)
1984—Vikings, 29-28 (D)
Lions, 16-14 (M)
1985—Vikings, 16-13 (M)
Lions, 41-21 (D)
1986—Lions, 13-10 (M)
Vikings, 24-10 (D)
1987—Vikings, 34-19 (M)
Vikings, 17-14 (D)
1988—Vikings, 44-17 (M)
Vikings, 23-0 (D)
1989—Vikings, 24-17 (M)
Vikings, 20-7 (D)
1990—Lions, 34-27 (M)
Vikings, 17-7 (D)
1991—Lions, 24-20 (D)
Lions, 34-14 (M)
1992—Lions, 31-17 (D)
Vikings, 31-14 (M)
1993—Lions, 30-27 (M)
Vikings, 13-0 (D)
1994—Vikings, 10-3 (M)
Lions, 41-19 (D)
1995—Vikings, 20-10 (M)
Lions, 44-38 (D)
(RS Pts.—Vikings 1,414, Lions 1,261)
DETROIT vs. NEW ENGLAND
RS: Series tied, 3-3
1971—Lions, 34-7 (NE)
1976—Lions, 30-10 (D)
1979—Patriots, 24-17 (NE)
1985—Patriots, 23-6 (NE)
1993—Lions, 19-16 (NE) OT
1994—Patriots, 23-17 (D)
(RS Pts.—Lions 123, Patriots 103)
DETROIT vs. NEW ORLEANS
RS: Saints lead series, 7-6-1
1968—Tie, 20-20 (D)
1970—Saints, 19-17 (NO)
1972—Lions, 27-14 (D)
1973—Saints, 20-13 (NO)
1974—Lions, 19-14 (D)
1976—Saints, 17-16 (NO)
1977—Lions, 23-19 (D)
1979—Saints, 17-7 (NO)
1980—Lions, 24-13 (D)
1988—Saints, 22-14 (D)
1989—Lions, 21-14 (D)
1990—Lions, 27-10 (NO)
1992—Saints, 13-7 (D)
1993—Saints, 14-3 (NO)
(RS Pts.—Lions 238, Saints 226)
***DETROIT vs. N.Y. GIANTS**
RS: Lions lead series, 18-15-1
PS: Lions lead series, 1-0
1930—Giants, 19-6 (P)
1931—Spartans, 14-6 (P)
Giants, 14-0 (NY)
1932—Spartans, 7-0 (P)
Spartans, 6-0 (NY)
1933—Spartans, 17-7 (P)
Giants, 13-10 (NY)

1934—Lions, 9-0 (D)
1935—**Lions, 26-7 (D)
1936—Giants, 14-7 (NY)
Lions, 38-0 (D)
1937—Lions, 17-0 (NY)
1939—Lions, 18-14 (D)
1941—Giants, 20-13 (NY)
1943—Tie, 0-0 (D)
1945—Giants, 35-14 (NY)
1947—Lions, 35-7 (D)
1949—Lions, 45-21 (NY)
1953—Lions, 27-16 (NY)
1955—Giants, 24-19 (D)
1958—Giants, 19-17 (D)
1962—Giants, 17-14 (NY)
1964—Lions, 26-3 (D)
1967—Lions, 30-7 (NY)
1969—Lions, 24-0 (D)
1972—Lions, 30-16 (D)
1974—Lions, 20-19 (D)
1976—Giants, 24-10 (NY)
1982—Giants, 13-6 (D)
1983—Lions, 15-9 (D)
1988—Giants, 30-10 (NY)
Giants, 13-10 (D) OT
1989—Giants, 24-14 (NY)
1990—Giants, 20-0 (NY)
1994—Lions, 28-25 (NY) OT
(RS Pts.—Lions 556, Giants 449)
(PS Pts.—Lions 26, Giants 7)
Franchise in Portsmouth prior to 1934 and known as the Spartans
***NFL Championship*

DETROIT vs. N.Y. JETS
RS: Lions lead series, 4-3
1972—Lions, 37-20 (D)
1979—Jets, 31-10 (NY)
1982—Jets, 28-13 (D)
1985—Lions, 31-20 (D)
1988—Jets, 17-10 (D)
1991—Lions, 34-20 (D)
1994—Lions, 18-7 (NY)
(RS Pts.—Lions 153, Jets 143)

DETROIT vs. *OAKLAND
RS: Raiders lead series, 5-2
1970—Lions, 28-14 (D)
1974—Raiders, 35-13 (O)
1978—Raiders, 29-17 (O)
1981—Lions, 16-0 (D)
1984—Raiders, 24-3 (D)
1987—Raiders, 27-7 (LA)
1990—Raiders, 38-31 (D)
(RS Pts.—Raiders 167, Lions 115)
Franchise in Los Angeles from 1982-1994

***DETROIT vs. PHILADELPHIA**
RS: Lions lead series, 12-9-2
PS: Eagles lead series, 1-0
1933—Spartans, 25-0 (P)
1934—Lions, 10-0 (P)
1935—Lions, 35-0 (D)
1936—Lions, 23-0 (P)
1938—Eagles, 21-7 (D)
1940—Lions, 21-0 (P)
1941—Lions, 21-17 (D)
1945—Lions, 28-24 (D)
1948—Eagles, 45-21 (P)
1949—Eagles, 22-14 (D)
1951—Lions, 28-10 (P)
1954—Tie, 13-13 (D)
1957—Lions, 27-16 (P)
1960—Eagles, 28-10 (P)
1961—Eagles, 27-24 (D)
1965—Lions, 35-28 (P)
1968—Eagles, 12-0 (D)
1971—Eagles, 23-20 (D)
1974—Eagles, 28-17 (P)
1977—Lions, 17-13 (D)
1979—Eagles, 44-7 (P)
1984—Tie, 23-23 (D) OT
1986—Lions, 13-11 (P)
1995—**Eagles, 58-37 (P)
(RS Pts.—Lions 439, Eagles 405)
(PS Pts.—Eagles 58, Lions 37)
Franchise in Portsmouth prior to 1934 and known as the Spartans
***NFC First-Round Playoff*

DETROIT vs. *PITTSBURGH
RS: Lions lead series, 13-12-1
1934—Lions, 40-7 (D)
1936—Lions, 28-3 (D)
1937—Lions, 7-3 (D)
1938—Lions, 16-7 (D)
1940—Pirates, 10-7 (D)
1942—Steelers, 35-7 (D)
1946—Lions, 17-7 (D)
1947—Steelers, 17-10 (P)
1948—Lions, 17-14 (D)
1949—Steelers, 14-7 (P)
1950—Lions, 10-7 (D)
1952—Lions, 31-6 (P)
1953—Lions, 38-21 (D)
1955—Lions, 31-28 (P)
1956—Lions, 45-7 (D)
1959—Tie, 10-10 (P)
1962—Lions, 45-7 (D)
1966—Steelers, 17-3 (P)
1967—Steelers, 24-14 (D)
1969—Steelers, 16-13 (P)
1973—Steelers, 24-10 (P)
1983—Lions, 45-3 (D)
1986—Steelers, 27-17 (P)
1989—Steelers, 23-3 (D)
1992—Steelers, 17-14 (P)
1995—Steelers, 23-20 (P)
(RS Pts.—Lions 505, Steelers 377)
Steelers known as Pirates prior to 1941

DETROIT vs. *ST. LOUIS
RS: Rams lead series, 39-35-1
PS: Lions lead series, 1-0
1937—Lions, 28-0 (C)
Lions, 27-7 (D)
1938—Rams, 21-17 (C)
Lions, 6-0 (D)
1939—Lions, 15-7 (D)
Rams, 14-3 (C)
1940—Lions, 6-0 (D)
Rams, 24-0 (C)
1941—Lions, 17-7 (D)
Lions, 14-0 (C)
1942—Rams, 14-0 (D)
Rams, 27-7 (C)
1944—Rams, 20-17 (D)
Lions, 26-14 (C)
1945—Rams, 28-21 (D)
1946—Rams, 35-14 (LA)
Rams, 41-20 (D)
1947—Rams, 27-13 (D)
Rams, 28-17 (LA)
1948—Rams, 44-7 (LA)
Rams, 34-27 (D)
1949—Rams, 27-24 (LA)
Rams, 21-10 (D)
1950—Rams, 30-28 (D)
Rams, 65-24 (LA)
1951—Rams, 27-21 (D)
Lions, 24-22 (LA)
1952—Lions, 17-14 (LA)
Lions, 24-16 (D)
**Lions, 31-21 (D)
1953—Rams, 31-19 (D)
Rams, 37-24 (LA)
1954—Lions, 21-3 (D)
Lions, 27-24 (LA)
1955—Rams, 17-10 (D)
Rams, 24-13 (LA)
1956—Lions, 24-21 (D)
Lions, 16-7 (LA)
1957—Lions, 10-7 (D)
Rams, 35-17 (LA)
1958—Rams, 42-28 (D)
Lions, 41-24 (LA)
1959—Lions, 17-7 (LA)
Lions, 23-17 (D)
1960—Rams, 48-35 (LA)
Lions, 12-10 (D)
1961—Lions, 14-13 (D)
Lions, 28-10 (LA)
1962—Lions, 13-10 (D)
Lions, 12-3 (LA)
1963—Lions, 23-2 (LA)
Rams, 28-21 (D)
1964—Tie, 17-17 (LA)
Lions, 37-17 (D)
1965—Lions, 20-0 (D)
Lions, 31-7 (LA)
1966—Rams, 14-7 (D)
Rams, 23-3 (LA)
1967—Rams, 31-7 (D)
1968—Rams, 10-7 (LA)
1969—Lions, 28-0 (D)
1970—Lions, 28-23 (LA)
1971—Rams, 21-13 (D)
1972—Lions, 34-17 (LA)
1974—Rams, 16-13 (LA)
1975—Rams, 20-0 (D)
1976—Rams, 20-17 (D)
1980—Lions, 41-20 (LA)
1981—Rams, 20-13 (LA)
1982—Lions, 19-14 (LA)
1983—Rams, 21-10 (LA)
1986—Rams, 14-10 (LA)
1987—Rams, 37-16 (D)
1988—Rams, 17-10 (LA)
1991—Lions, 21-10 (D)
1993—Lions, 16-13 (LA)
(RS Pts.—Rams 1,436, Lions 1,340)
(PS Pts.—Lions 31, Rams 21)
Franchise in Los Angeles prior to 1995 and in Cleveland prior to 1946
***Conference Playoff*

DETROIT vs. SAN DIEGO
RS: Lions lead series, 3-2
1972—Lions, 34-20 (D)
1977—Lions, 20-0 (D)
1978—Lions, 31-14 (D)
1981—Chargers, 28-23 (SD)
1984—Chargers, 27-24 (SD)
(RS Pts.—Lions 132, Chargers 89)

DETROIT vs. SAN FRANCISCO
RS: 49ers lead series, 27-26-1
PS: Series tied, 1-1
1950—Lions, 24-7 (D)
49ers, 28-27 (SF)
1951—49ers, 20-10 (D)
49ers, 21-17 (SF)
1952—49ers, 17-3 (SF)
49ers, 28-0 (D)
1953—Lions, 24-21 (D)
Lions, 14-10 (SF)
1954—49ers, 37-31 (SF)
Lions, 48-7 (D)
1955—49ers, 27-24 (D)
49ers, 38-21 (SF)
1956—Lions, 20-17 (D)
Lions, 17-13 (SF)
1957—49ers, 35-31 (SF)
Lions, 31-10 (D)
*Lions, 31-27 (SF)
1958—49ers, 24-21 (SF)
Lions, 35-21 (D)
1959—49ers, 34-13 (D)
49ers, 33-7 (SF)
1960—49ers, 14-10 (D)
Lions, 24-0 (SF)
1961—49ers, 49-0 (D)
Tie, 20-20 (SF)
1962—Lions, 45-24 (D)
Lions, 38-24 (SF)
1963—Lions, 26-3 (D)
Lions, 45-7 (SF)
1964—Lions, 26-17 (SF)
Lions, 24-7 (D)
1965—49ers, 27-21 (D)
49ers, 17-14 (SF)
1966—49ers, 27-24 (SF)
49ers, 41-14 (D)
1967—Lions, 45-3 (SF)
1968—49ers, 14-7 (D)
1969—Lions, 26-14 (SF)
1970—Lions, 28-7 (D)
1971—49ers, 31-27 (SF)
1973—Lions, 30-20 (D)
1974—Lions, 17-13 (D)
1975—Lions, 28-17 (SF)
1977—49ers, 28-7 (SF)
1978—Lions, 33-14 (D)
1980—Lions, 17-13 (D)
1981—Lions, 24-17 (D)
1983—**49ers, 24-23 (SF)
1984—49ers, 30-27 (D)
1985—Lions, 23-21 (D)
1988—49ers, 20-13 (SF)
1991—49ers, 35-3 (SF)
1992—49ers, 24-6 (SF)
1993—49ers, 55-17 (D)
1994—49ers, 27-21 (D)
1995—Lions, 27-24 (D)
(RS Pts.—Lions 1,175, 49ers 1,152)
(PS Pts.—Lions 54, 49ers 51)
Conference Playoff
***NFC Divisional Playoff*

DETROIT vs. SEATTLE
RS: Seahawks lead series, 4-2
1976—Lions, 41-14 (S)
1978—Seahawks, 28-16 (S)
1984—Seahawks, 38-17 (S)
1987—Seahawks, 37-14 (D)
1990—Seahawks, 30-10 (S)
1993—Lions, 30-10 (D)
(RS Pts.—Seahawks 157, Lions 128)

DETROIT vs. TAMPA BAY
RS: Lions lead series, 19-17
1977—Lions, 16-7 (D)
1978—Lions, 15-7 (TB)
Lions, 34-23 (D)
1979—Buccaneers, 31-16 (TB)
Buccaneers, 16-14 (D)
1980—Lions, 24-10 (TB)
Lions, 27-14 (D)
1981—Buccaneers, 28-10 (TB)
Buccaneers, 20-17 (D)
1982—Buccaneers, 23-21 (TB)
1983—Lions, 11-0 (TB)
Lions, 23-20 (D)
1984—Buccaneers, 21-17 (TB)
Lions, 13-7 (D) OT
1985—Lions, 30-9 (D)
Buccaneers, 19-16 (TB) OT
1986—Buccaneers, 24-20 (D)
Lions, 38-17 (TB)
1987—Buccaneers, 31-27 (D)
Lions, 20-10 (TB)
1988—Buccaneers, 23-20 (D)
Buccaneers, 21-10 (TB)
1989—Lions, 17-16 (TB)
Lions, 33-7 (D)
1990—Buccaneers, 38-21 (D)
Buccaneers, 23-20 (TB)
1991—Lions, 31-3 (D)
Buccaneers, 30-21 (TB)
1992—Buccaneers, 27-23 (D)
Lions, 38-7 (TB)
1993—Buccaneers, 27-10 (TB)
Lions, 23-0 (D)
1994—Buccaneers, 24-14 (TB)
Lions, 14-9 (D)
1995—Lions, 27-24 (D)
Lions, 37-10 (TB)
(RS Pts.—Lions 768, Buccaneers 626)

***DETROIT vs. **WASHINGTON**
RS: Redskins lead series, 23-8
PS: Redskins lead series, 2-0
1932—Spartans, 10-0 (P)
1933—Spartans, 13-0 (B)
1934—Lions, 24-0 (D)
1935—Lions, 17-7 (B)
Lions, 14-0 (D)
1938—Redskins, 7-5 (D)
1939—Redskins, 31-7 (W)
1940—Redskins, 20-14 (D)
1942—Redskins, 15-3 (D)

1943—Redskins, 42-20 (W)
1946—Redskins, 17-16 (W)
1947—Lions, 38-21 (D)
1948—Redskins, 46-21 (W)
1951—Lions, 35-17 (D)
1956—Redskins, 18-17 (W)
1965—Lions, 14-10 (D)
1968—Redskins, 14-3 (W)
1970—Redskins, 31-10 (W)
1973—Redskins, 20-0 (D)
1976—Redskins, 20-7 (W)
1978—Redskins, 21-19 (D)
1979—Redskins, 27-24 (D)
1981—Redskins, 33-31 (W)
1982—***Redskins, 31-7 (W)
1983—Redskins, 38-17 (W)
1984—Redskins, 28-14 (W)
1985—Redskins, 24-3 (W)
1987—Redskins, 20-13 (W)
1990—Redskins, 41-38 (D)
1991—Redskins, 45-0 (W)
****Redskins, 41-10 (W)
1992—Redskins, 13-10 (W)
1995—Redskins, 36-30 (W) OT
(RS Pts.—Redskins 662, Lions 487)
(PS Pts.—Redskins 72, Lions 17)
Franchise in Portsmouth prior to 1934 and known as the Spartans.
***Franchise in Boston prior to 1937*
****NFC First-Round Playoff*
*****NFC Championship*

GREEN BAY vs. ARIZONA
RS: Packers lead series, 39-21-4
PS: Packers lead series, 1-0;
See Arizona vs. Green Bay

GREEN BAY vs. ATLANTA
RS: Packers lead series, 10-9
PS: Packers lead series, 1-0;
See Atlanta vs. Green Bay

GREEN BAY vs. BUFFALO
RS: Bills lead series, 5-1;
See Buffalo vs. Green Bay

GREEN BAY vs. CHICAGO
RS: Bears lead series, 81-63-6
PS: Bears lead series, 1-0;
See Chicago vs. Green Bay

GREEN BAY vs. CINCINNATI
RS: Series tied, 4-4;
See Cincinnati vs. Green Bay

GREEN BAY vs. CLEVELAND
RS: Packers lead series, 8-6
PS: Packers lead series, 1-0;
See Cleveland vs. Green Bay

GREEN BAY vs. DALLAS
RS: Series tied, 8-8
PS: Cowboys lead series, 4-2;
See Dallas vs. Green Bay

GREEN BAY vs. DENVER
RS: Broncos lead series, 4-2-1;
See Denver vs. Green Bay

GREEN BAY vs. DETROIT
RS: Packers lead series, 66-58-7
PS: Packers lead series, 2-0;
See Detroit vs. Green Bay

GREEN BAY vs. HOUSTON
RS: Series tied, 3-3
1972—Packers, 23-10 (H)
1977—Oilers, 16-10 (GB)
1980—Oilers, 22-3 (GB)
1983—Packers, 41-38 (H) OT
1986—Oilers, 31-3 (GB)
1992—Packers, 16-14 (H)
(RS Pts.—Oilers 131, Packers 96)

GREEN BAY vs. *INDIANAPOLIS
RS: Series tied, 18-18-1
PS: Packers lead series, 1-0
1953—Packers, 37-14 (GB)
Packers, 35-24 (B)
1954—Packers, 7-6 (B)
Packers, 24-13 (Mil)
1955—Colts, 24-20 (Mil)
Colts, 14-10 (B)
1956—Packers, 38-33 (Mil)
Colts, 28-21 (B)
1957—Colts, 45-17 (Mil)
Packers, 24-21 (B)
1958—Colts, 24-17 (Mil)
Colts, 56-0 (B)
1959—Colts, 38-21 (B)
Colts, 28-24 (Mil)
1960—Packers, 35-21 (GB)
Colts, 38-24 (B)
1961—Packers, 45-7 (GB)
Colts, 45-21 (B)
1962—Packers, 17-6 (B)
Packers, 17-13 (GB)
1963—Packers, 31-20 (GB)
Packers, 34-20 (B)
1964—Colts, 21-20 (GB)
Colts, 24-21 (B)
1965—Packers, 20-17 (Mil)
Packers, 42-27 (B)
**Packers, 13-10 (GB) OT
1966—Packers, 24-3 (Mil)
Packers, 14-10 (B)
1967—Colts, 13-10 (B)
1968—Colts, 16-3 (GB)
1969—Colts, 14-6 (B)
1970—Colts, 13-10 (Mil)
1974—Packers, 20-13 (B)
1982—Tie, 20-20 (B) OT
1985—Colts, 37-10 (I)
1988—Colts, 20-13 (GB)
1991—Packers, 14-10 (Mil)
(RS Pts.—Colts 796, Packers 766)
(PS Pts.—Packers 13, Colts 10)
**Franchise in Baltimore prior to 1984*
***Conference Playoff*

GREEN BAY vs. JACKSONVILLE
RS: Packers lead series, 1-0
1995—Packers, 24-14 (J)
(RS Pts.—Packers 24, Jaguars 14)

GREEN BAY vs. KANSAS CITY
RS: Chiefs lead series, 4-1-1
PS: Packers lead series, 1-0
1966—*Packers, 35-10 (Los Angeles)
1973—Tie, 10-10 (Mil)
1977—Chiefs, 20-10 (KC)
1987—Packers, 23-3 (KC)
1989—Chiefs, 21-3 (GB)
1990—Chiefs, 17-3 (GB)
1993—Chiefs, 23-16 (KC)
(RS Pts.—Chiefs 94, Packers 65)
(PS Pts.—Packers 35, Chiefs 10)
**Super Bowl I*

GREEN BAY vs. MIAMI
RS: Dolphins lead series, 8-0
1971—Dolphins, 27-6 (Mia)
1975—Dolphins, 31-7 (GB)
1979—Dolphins, 27-7 (Mia)
1985—Dolphins, 34-24 (GB)
1988—Dolphins, 24-17 (Mia)
1989—Dolphins, 23-20 (Mia)
1991—Dolphins, 16-13 (Mia)
1994—Dolphins, 24-14 (Mil)
(RS Pts.—Dolphins 206, Packers 108)

GREEN BAY vs. MINNESOTA
RS: Vikings lead series, 35-33-1
1961—Packers, 33-7 (Minn)
Packers, 28-10 (Mil)
1962—Packers, 34-7 (GB)
Packers, 48-21 (Minn)
1963—Packers, 37-28 (Minn)
Packers, 28-7 (GB)
1964—Vikings, 24-23 (GB)
Packers, 42-13 (Minn)
1965—Packers, 38-13 (Minn)
Packers, 24-19 (GB)
1966—Vikings, 20-17 (GB)
Packers, 28-16 (Minn)
1967—Vikings, 10-7 (Mil)
Packers, 30-27 (Minn)
1968—Vikings, 26-13 (Mil)
Vikings, 14-10 (Minn)
1969—Vikings, 19-7 (Minn)
Vikings, 9-7 (Mil)
1970—Packers, 13-10 (Mil)
Vikings, 10-3 (Minn)
1971—Vikings, 24-13 (GB)
Vikings, 3-0 (Minn)
1972—Vikings, 27-13 (GB)
Packers, 23-7 (Minn)
1973—Vikings, 11-3 (Minn)
Vikings, 31-7 (GB)
1974—Vikings, 32-17 (GB)
Packers, 19-7 (Minn)
1975—Vikings, 28-17 (GB)
Vikings, 24-3 (Minn)
1976—Vikings, 17-10 (Mil)
Vikings, 20-9 (Minn)
1977—Vikings, 19-7 (Minn)
Vikings, 13-6 (GB)
1978—Vikings, 21-7 (Minn)
Tie, 10-10 (GB) OT
1979—Vikings, 27-21 (Minn) OT
Packers, 19-7 (Mil)
1980—Packers, 16-3 (GB)
Packers, 25-13 (Minn)
1981—Vikings, 30-13 (Mil)
Packers, 35-23 (Minn)
1982—Packers, 26-7 (Mil)
1983—Vikings, 20-17 (GB) OT
Packers, 29-21 (Minn)
1984—Packers, 45-17 (Mil)
Packers, 38-14 (Minn)
1985—Packers, 20-17 (Mil)
Packers, 27-17 (Minn)
1986—Vikings, 42-7 (Minn)
Vikings, 32-6 (GB)
1987—Packers, 23-16 (Minn)
Packers, 16-10 (Mil)
1988—Packers, 34-14 (Minn)
Packers, 18-6 (GB)
1989—Vikings, 26-14 (Minn)
Packers, 20-19 (Mil)
1990—Packers, 24-10 (Mil)
Vikings, 23-7 (Minn)
1991—Vikings, 35-21 (GB)
Packers, 27-7 (Minn)
1992—Vikings, 23-20 (GB) OT
Vikings, 27-7 (Minn)
1993—Vikings, 15-13 (Minn)
Vikings, 21-17 (Mil)
1994—Packers, 16-10 (GB)
Vikings, 13-10 (M) OT
1995—Packers, 38-21 (GB)
Vikings, 27-24 (M)
(RS Pts.—Packers 1,327, Vikings 1,217)

GREEN BAY vs. NEW ENGLAND
RS: Patriots lead series, 3-2
1973—Patriots, 33-24 (NE)
1979—Packers, 27-14 (GB)
1985—Patriots, 26-20 (NE)
1988—Packers, 45-3 (Mil)
1994—Patriots, 17-16 (NE)
(RS Pts.—Packers 132, Patriots 93)

GREEN BAY vs. NEW ORLEANS
RS: Packers lead series, 13-4
1968—Packers, 29-7 (Mil)
1971—Saints, 29-21 (Mil)
1972—Packers, 30-20 (NO)
1973—Packers, 30-10 (Mil)
1975—Saints, 20-19 (NO)
1976—Packers, 32-27 (Mil)
1977—Packers, 24-20 (NO)
1978—Packers, 28-17 (Mil)
1979—Packers, 28-19 (Mil)
1981—Packers, 35-7 (NO)
1984—Packers, 23-13 (NO)
1985—Packers, 38-14 (Mil)
1986—Saints, 24-10 (NO)
1987—Saints, 33-24 (NO)
1989—Packers, 35-34 (GB)
1993—Packers, 19-17 (NO)
1995—Packers, 34-23 (NO)
(RS Pts.—Packers 459, Saints 334)

GREEN BAY vs. N.Y. GIANTS
RS: Packers lead series, 22-20-2
PS: Packers lead series, 4-1
1928—Giants, 6-0 (GB)
Packers, 7-0 (NY)
1929—Packers, 20-6 (NY)
1930—Packers, 14-7 (GB)
Giants, 13-6 (NY)
1931—Packers, 27-7 (GB)
Packers, 14-10 (NY)
1932—Packers, 13-0 (GB)
Giants, 6-0 (NY)
1933—Giants, 10-7 (Mil)
Giants, 17-6 (NY)
1934—Packers, 20-6 (Mil)
Giants, 17-3 (NY)
1935—Packers, 16-7 (GB)
1936—Packers, 26-14 (NY)
1937—Giants, 10-0 (NY)
1938—Giants, 15-3 (NY)
*Giants, 23-17 (NY)
1939—*Packers, 27-0 (Mil)
1940—Giants, 7-3 (NY)
1942—Tie, 21-21 (NY)
1943—Packers, 35-21 (NY)
1944—Giants, 24-0 (NY)
*Packers, 14-7 (NY)
1945—Packers, 23-14 (NY)
1947—Tie, 24-24 (NY)
1948—Giants, 49-3 (Mil)
1949—Giants, 30-10 (GB)
1952—Packers, 17-3 (NY)
1957—Giants, 31-17 (GB)
1959—Giants, 20-3 (NY)
1961—Packers, 20-17 (Mil)
*Packers, 37-0 (GB)
1962—*Packers, 16-7 (NY)
1967—Packers, 48-21 (NY)
1969—Packers, 20-10 (Mil)
1971—Giants, 42-40 (GB)
1973—Packers, 16-14 (New Haven)
1975—Packers, 40-14 (Mil)
1980—Giants, 27-21 (NY)
1981—Packers, 27-14 (NY)
Packers, 26-24 (Mil)
1982—Packers, 27-19 (NY)
1983—Giants, 27-3 (NY)
1985—Packers, 23-20 (GB)
1986—Giants, 55-24 (NY)
1987—Giants, 20-10 (NY)
1992—Giants, 27-7 (NY)
1995—Packers, 14-6 (GB)
(RS Pts.—Giants 752, Packers 704)
(PS Pts.—Packers 111, Giants 37)
**NFL Championship*

GREEN BAY vs. N.Y. JETS
RS: Jets lead series, 5-2
1973—Packers, 23-7 (Mil)
1979—Jets, 27-22 (GB)
1981—Jets, 28-3 (NY)
1982—Jets, 15-13 (NY)
1985—Jets, 24-3 (Mil)
1991—Jets, 19-16 (NY) OT
1994—Packers, 17-10 (GB)
(RS Pts.—Jets 130, Packers 97)

GREEN BAY vs. *OAKLAND
RS: Raiders lead series, 5-2
PS: Packers lead series, 1-0
1967—**Packers, 33-14 (Miami)
1972—Raiders, 20-14 (GB)
1976—Raiders, 18-14 (O)
1978—Raiders, 28-3 (GB)
1984—Raiders, 28-7 (LA)
1987—Raiders, 20-0 (GB)
1990—Packers, 29-16 (LA)
1993—Packers, 28-0 (GB)
(RS Pts.—Raiders 130, Packers 95)
(PS Pts.—Packers 33, Raiders 14)
**Franchise in Los Angeles from 1982-1994*
***Super Bowl II*

GREEN BAY vs. PHILADELPHIA
RS: Packers lead series, 19-8
PS: Eagles lead series, 1-0
1933—Packers, 35-9 (GB)

Packers, 10-0 (P)
1934—Packers, 19-6 (GB)
1935—Packers, 13-6 (P)
1937—Packers, 37-7 (Mil)
1939—Packers, 23-16 (P)
1940—Packers, 27-20 (GB)
1942—Packers, 7-0 (P)
1946—Packers, 19-7 (P)
1947—Eagles, 28-14 (P)
1951—Packers, 37-24 (GB)
1952—Packers, 12-10 (Mil)
1954—Packers, 37-14 (P)
1958—Packers, 38-35 (GB)
1960—*Eagles, 17-13 (P)
1962—Packers, 49-0 (P)
1968—Packers, 30-13 (GB)
1970—Packers, 30-17 (Mil)
1974—Eagles, 36-14 (P)
1976—Packers, 28-13 (GB)
1978—Eagles, 10-3 (P)
1979—Eagles, 21-10 (GB)
1987—Packers, 16-10 (GB) OT
1990—Eagles, 31-0 (P)
1991—Eagles, 20-3 (GB)
1992—Packers, 27-24 (Mil)
1993—Eagles, 20-17 (GB)
1994—Eagles, 13-7 (P)
(RS Pts.—Packers 562, Eagles 410)
(PS Pts.—Eagles 17, Packers 13)
NFL Championship

GREEN BAY vs. *PITTSBURGH
RS: Packers lead series, 18-11
1933—Packers, 47-0 (GB)
1935—Packers, 27-0 (GB)
Packers, 34-14 (P)
1936—Packers, 42-10 (Mil)
1938—Packers, 20-0 (GB)
1940—Packers, 24-3 (Mil)
1941—Packers, 54-7 (P)
1942—Packers, 24-21 (Mil)
1946—Packers, 17-7 (GB)
1947—Steelers, 18-17 (Mil)
1948—Steelers, 38-7 (P)
1949—Steelers, 30-7 (Mil)
1951—Packers, 35-33 (Mil)
Steelers, 28-7 (P)
1953—Steelers, 31-14 (P)
1954—Steelers, 21-20 (GB)
1957—Packers, 27-10 (P)
1960—Packers, 19-13 (P)
1963—Packers, 33-14 (Mil)
1965—Packers, 41-9 (P)
1967—Steelers, 24-17 (GB)
1969—Packers, 38-34 (P)
1970—Packers, 20-12 (P)
1975—Steelers, 16-13 (Mil)
1980—Steelers, 22-20 (P)
1983—Steelers, 25-21 (GB)
1986—Steelers, 27-3 (P)
1992—Packers, 17-3 (GB)
1995—Packers, 24-19 (GB)
(RS Pts.—Packers 689, Steelers 489)
Steelers known as Pirates prior to 1941

GREEN BAY vs. *ST. LOUIS
RS: Rams lead series, 43-37-2
PS: Packers lead series, 1-0
1937—Packers, 35-10 (C)
Packers, 35-7 (GB)
1938—Packers, 26-17 (GB)
Packers, 28-7 (C)
1939—Rams, 27-24 (GB)
Packers, 7-6 (C)
1940—Packers, 31-14 (GB)
Tie, 13-13 (C)
1941—Packers, 24-7 (Mil)
Packers, 17-14 (C)
1942—Packers, 45-28 (GB)
Packers, 30-12 (C)
1944—Packers, 30-21 (GB)
Packers, 42-7 (C)
1945—Rams, 27-14 (GB)
Rams, 20-7 (C)
1946—Rams, 21-17 (Mil)
Rams, 38-17 (LA)
1947—Packers, 17-14 (Mil)
Packers, 30-10 (LA)
1948—Packers, 16-0 (GB)
Rams, 24-10 (LA)
1949—Rams, 48-7 (GB)
Rams, 35-7 (LA)
1950—Rams, 45-14 (Mil)
Rams, 51-14 (LA)
1951—Rams, 28-0 (Mil)
Rams, 42-14 (LA)
1952—Rams, 30-28 (Mil)
Rams, 45-27 (LA)
1953—Rams, 38-20 (Mil)
Rams, 33-17 (LA)
1954—Packers, 35-17 (Mil)
Rams, 35-27 (LA)
1955—Packers, 30-28 (Mil)
Rams, 31-17 (LA)
1956—Packers, 42-17 (Mil)
Rams, 49-21 (LA)
1957—Rams, 31-27 (Mil)
Rams, 42-17 (LA)
1958—Rams, 20-7 (GB)
Rams, 34-20 (LA)
1959—Rams, 45-6 (Mil)
Packers, 38-20 (LA)
1960—Rams, 33-31 (Mil)
Packers, 35-21 (LA)
1961—Packers, 35-17 (GB)
Packers, 24-17 (LA)
1962—Packers, 41-10 (Mil)
Packers, 20-17 (LA)
1963—Packers, 42-10 (GB)
Packers, 31-14 (LA)
1964—Rams, 27-17 (Mil)
Tie, 24-24 (LA)
1965—Packers, 6-3 (Mil)
Rams, 21-10 (LA)
1966—Packers, 24-13 (GB)
Packers, 27-23 (LA)
1967—Rams, 27-24 (LA)
**Packers, 28-7 (Mil)
1968—Rams, 16-14 (Mil)
1969—Rams, 34-21 (LA)
1970—Rams, 31-21 (GB)
1971—Rams, 30-13 (LA)
1973—Rams, 24-7 (LA)
1974—Packers, 17-6 (Mil)
1975—Rams, 22-5 (LA)
1977—Rams, 24-6 (Mil)
1978—Rams, 31-14 (LA)
1980—Rams, 51-21 (LA)
1981—Rams, 35-23 (LA)
1982—Packers, 35-23 (Mil)
1983—Packers, 27-24 (Mil)
1984—Packers, 31-6 (Mil)
1985—Rams, 34-17 (LA)
1988—Rams, 34-7 (GB)
1989—Rams, 41-38 (LA)
1990—Packers, 36-24 (GB)
1991—Rams, 23-21 (LA)
1992—Packers, 28-13 (GB)
1993—Packers, 36-6 (Mil)
1994—Packers, 24-17 (GB)
1995—Rams, 17-14 (GB)
(RS Pts.—Rams 1,951, Packers 1,817)
(PS Pts.—Packers 28, Rams 7)
Franchise in Los Angeles prior to 1995 and in Cleveland prior to 1946
***Conference Championship*

GREEN BAY vs. SAN DIEGO
RS: Packers lead series, 4-1
1970—Packers, 22-20 (SD)
1974—Packers, 34-0 (GB)
1978—Packers, 24-3 (SD)
1984—Chargers, 34-28 (GB)
1993—Packers, 20-13 (SD)
(RS Pts.—Packers 128, Chargers 70)

GREEN BAY vs. SAN FRANCISCO
RS: 49ers lead series, 25-21-1
PS: Packers lead series, 1-0
1950—Packers, 25-21 (GB)
49ers, 30-14 (SF)
1951—49ers, 31-19 (SF)
1952—49ers, 24-14 (SF)
1953—49ers, 37-7 (Mil)
49ers, 48-14 (SF)
1954—49ers, 23-17 (Mil)
49ers, 35-0 (SF)
1955—Packers, 27-21 (Mil)
Packers, 28-7 (SF)
1956—49ers, 17-16 (GB)
49ers, 38-20 (SF)
1957—49ers, 24-14 (Mil)
49ers, 27-20 (SF)
1958—49ers, 33-12 (Mil)
49ers, 48-21 (SF)
1959—Packers, 21-20 (GB)
Packers, 36-14 (SF)
1960—Packers, 41-14 (Mil)
Packers, 13-0 (SF)
1961—Packers, 30-10 (GB)
49ers, 22-21 (SF)
1962—Packers, 31-13 (Mil)
Packers, 31-21 (SF)
1963—Packers, 28-10 (Mil)
Packers, 21-17 (SF)
1964—Packers, 24-14 (Mil)
49ers, 24-14 (SF)
1965—Packers, 27-10 (GB)
Tie, 24-24 (SF)
1966—49ers, 21-20 (SF)
Packers, 20-7 (Mil)
1967—Packers, 13-0 (GB)
1968—49ers, 27-20 (SF)
1969—Packers, 14-7 (Mil)
1970—49ers, 26-10 (SF)
1972—Packers, 34-24 (Mil)
1973—49ers, 20-6 (SF)
1974—49ers, 7-6 (SF)
1976—49ers, 26-14 (GB)
1977—Packers, 16-14 (Mil)
1980—Packers, 23-16 (Mil)
1981—49ers, 13-3 (Mil)
1986—49ers, 31-17 (Mil)
1987—49ers, 23-12 (GB)
1989—Packers, 21-17 (SF)
1990—49ers, 24-20 (GB)
1995—*Packers, 27-17 (SF)
(RS Pts.—49ers 980, Packers 899)
(PS Pts.—Packers 27, 49ers 17)
NFC Divisional Playoff

GREEN BAY vs. SEATTLE
RS: Series tied, 3-3
1976—Packers, 27-20 (Mil)
1978—Packers, 45-28 (Mil)
1981—Packers, 34-24 (GB)
1984—Seahawks, 30-24 (Mil)
1987—Seahawks, 24-13 (S)
1990—Seahawks, 20-14 (Mil)
(RS Pts.—Packers 157, Seahawks 146)

GREEN BAY vs. TAMPA BAY
RS: Packers lead series, 20-13-1
1977—Packers, 13-0 (TB)
1978—Packers, 9-7 (GB)
Packers, 17-7 (TB)
1979—Buccaneers, 21-10 (GB)
Buccaneers, 21-3 (TB)
1980—Tie, 14-14 (TB) OT
Buccaneers, 20-17 (Mil)
1981—Buccaneers, 21-10 (GB)
Buccaneers, 37-3 (TB)
1983—Packers, 55-14 (GB)
Packers, 12-9 (TB) OT
1984—Buccaneers, 30-27 (TB) OT
Packers, 27-14 (GB)
1985—Packers, 21-0 (GB)
Packers, 20-17 (TB)
1986—Packers, 31-7 (Mil)
Packers, 21-7 (TB)
1987—Buccaneers, 23-17 (Mil)
1988—Buccaneers, 13-10 (GB)
Buccaneers, 27-24 (TB)
1989—Buccaneers, 23-21 (GB)
Packers, 17-16 (TB)
1990—Buccaneers, 26-14 (TB)
Packers, 20-10 (Mil)
1991—Packers, 15-13 (GB)
Packers, 27-0 (TB)
1992—Buccaneers, 31-3 (TB)
Packers, 19-14 (Mil)
1993—Packers, 37-14 (TB)
Packers, 13-10 (GB)
1994—Packers, 30-3 (GB)
Packers, 34-19 (TB)
1995—Packers, 35-13 (GB)
Buccaneers, 13-10 (TB) OT
(RS Pts.—Packers 656, Buccaneers 514)

GREEN BAY vs. *WASHINGTON
RS: Packers lead series, 13-12-1
PS: Series tied, 1-1
1932—Packers, 21-0 (B)
1933—Tie, 7-7 (GB)
Redskins, 20-7 (B)
1934—Packers, 10-0 (B)
1936—Packers, 31-2 (GB)
Packers, 7-3 (B)
**Packers, 21-6 (New York)
1937—Redskins, 14-6 (W)
1939—Packers, 24-14 (Mil)
1941—Packers, 22-17 (W)
1943—Redskins, 33-7 (Mil)
1946—Packers, 20-7 (W)
1947—Packers, 27-10 (Mil)
1948—Redskins, 23-7 (Mil)
1949—Redskins, 30-0 (W)
1950—Packers, 35-21 (Mil)
1952—Packers, 35-20 (Mil)
1958—Redskins, 37-21 (W)
1959—Packers, 21-0 (GB)
1968—Packers, 27-7 (W)
1972—Redskins, 21-16 (W)
***Redskins, 16-3 (W)
1974—Redskins, 17-6 (GB)
1977—Redskins, 10-9 (W)
1979—Redskins, 38-21 (W)
1983—Packers, 48-47 (GB)
1986—Redskins, 16-7 (GB)
1988—Redskins, 20-17 (Mil)
(RS Pts.—Packers 459, Redskins 434)
(PS Pts.—Packers 24, Redskins 22)
Franchise in Boston prior to 1937 and known as Braves prior to 1933
***NFL Championship*
****NFC Divisional Playoff*

HOUSTON vs. ARIZONA
RS: Cardinals lead series, 4-2;
See Arizona vs. Houston

HOUSTON vs. ATLANTA
RS: Falcons lead series, 5-3;
See Atlanta vs. Houston

HOUSTON vs. BUFFALO
RS: Oilers lead series, 21-13
PS: Bills lead series, 2-0;
See Buffalo vs. Houston

HOUSTON vs. CHICAGO
RS: Oilers lead series, 4-3;
See Chicago vs. Houston

HOUSTON vs. CINCINNATI
RS: Oilers lead series, 27-26-1
PS: Bengals lead series, 1-0;
See Cincinnati vs. Houston

HOUSTON vs. CLEVELAND
RS: Browns lead series, 30-21
PS: Oilers lead series, 1-0;
See Cleveland vs. Houston

HOUSTON vs. DALLAS
RS: Cowboys lead series, 5-3;
See Dallas vs. Houston

HOUSTON vs. DENVER
RS: Oilers lead series, 20-11-1
PS: Broncos lead series, 2-1;
See Denver vs. Houston

HOUSTON vs. DETROIT
RS: Oilers lead series, 4-3;
See Detroit vs. Houston

HOUSTON vs. GREEN BAY

RS: Series tied, 3-3;
See Green Bay vs. Houston

HOUSTON vs. *INDIANAPOLIS
RS: Series tied, 7-7
1970—Colts, 24-20 (H)
1973—Oilers, 31-27 (B)
1976—Colts, 38-14 (B)
1979—Oilers, 28-16 (B)
1980—Oilers, 21-16 (H)
1983—Colts, 20-10 (B)
1984—Colts, 35-21 (H)
1985—Colts, 34-16 (I)
1986—Oilers, 31-17 (H)
1987—Colts, 51-27 (I)
1988—Oilers, 17-14 (I) OT
1990—Oilers, 24-10 (H)
1992—Oilers, 20-10 (I)
1994—Colts, 45-21 (I)
(RS Pts.—Colts 357, Oilers 301)
Franchise in Baltimore prior to 1984

HOUSTON vs. JACKSONVILLE
RS: Series tied, 1-1
1995—Oilers, 10-3 (J)
Jaguars, 17-16 (H)
(RS Pts.—Oilers 26, Jaguars 20)

HOUSTON vs. *KANSAS CITY
RS: Chiefs lead series, 23-17
PS: Chiefs lead series, 2-0
1960—Oilers, 20-10 (H)
Texans, 24-0 (D)
1961—Texans, 26-21 (D)
Oilers, 38-7 (H)
1962—Texans, 31-7 (H)
Oilers, 14-6 (D)
**Texans, 20-17 (H) OT
1963—Chiefs, 28-7 (KC)
Oilers, 28-7 (H)
1964—Chiefs, 28-7 (KC)
Chiefs, 28-19 (H)
1965—Chiefs, 52-21 (KC)
Oilers, 38-36 (H)
1966—Chiefs, 48-23 (KC)
1967—Chiefs, 25-20 (H)
Oilers, 24-19 (KC)
1968—Chiefs, 26-21 (H)
Chiefs, 24-10 (KC)
1969—Chiefs, 24-0 (KC)
1970—Chiefs, 24-9 (KC)
1971—Chiefs, 20-16 (H)
1973—Chiefs, 38-14 (KC)
1974—Chiefs, 17-7 (H)
1975—Oilers, 17-13 (KC)
1977—Oilers, 34-20 (H)
1978—Oilers, 20-17 (KC)
1979—Oilers, 20-6 (H)
1980—Chiefs, 21-20 (KC)
1981—Chiefs, 23-10 (KC)
1983—Chiefs, 13-10 (H) OT
1984—Oilers, 17-16 (KC)
1985—Oilers, 23-20 (H)
1986—Chiefs, 27-13 (KC)
1988—Oilers, 7-6 (H)
1989—Chiefs, 34-0 (KC)
1990—Oilers, 27-10 (KC)
1991—Oilers, 17-7 (H)
1992—Oilers, 23-20 (H) OT
1993—Oilers, 30-0 (H)
***Chiefs, 28-20 (H)
1994—Chiefs, 31-9 (KC)
1995—Chiefs, 20-13 (KC)
(RS Pts.—Chiefs 852, Oilers 674)
(PS Pts.—Chiefs 48, Oilers 37)
Franchise in Dallas prior to 1963 and known as Texans
***AFL Championship*
****AFC Divisional Playoff*

HOUSTON vs. MIAMI
RS: Series tied, 11-11
PS: Oilers lead series, 1-0
1966—Dolphins, 20-13 (H)
Dolphins, 29-28 (M)
1967—Oilers, 17-14 (H)
Oilers, 41-10 (M)
1968—Oilers, 24-10 (M)
Dolphins, 24-7 (H)
1969—Oilers, 22-10 (H)
Oilers, 32-7 (M)
1970—Dolphins, 20-10 (H)
1972—Dolphins, 34-13 (M)
1975—Oilers, 20-19 (H)
1977—Dolphins, 27-7 (M)
1978—Oilers, 35-30 (H)
*Oilers, 17-9 (M)
1979—Oilers, 9-6 (M)
1981—Dolphins, 16-10 (H)
1983—Dolphins, 24-17 (H)
1984—Dolphins, 28-10 (M)
1985—Oilers, 26-23 (H)
1986—Dolphins, 28-7 (M)
1989—Oilers, 39-7 (H)
1991—Oilers, 17-13 (M)
1992—Dolphins, 19-16 (M)
(RS Pts.—Oilers 420, Dolphins 418)
(PS Pts.—Oilers 17, Dolphins 9)
**AFC First Round Playoff*

HOUSTON vs. MINNESOTA
RS: Vikings lead series, 4-3
1974—Vikings, 51-10 (M)
1980—Oilers, 20-16 (H)
1983—Vikings, 34-14 (M)
1986—Oilers, 23-10 (H)
1989—Vikings, 38-7 (M)
1992—Oilers, 17-13 (M)
1995—Vikings, 23-17 (M) OT
(RS Pts.—Vikings 185, Oilers 108)

HOUSTON vs. *NEW ENGLAND
RS: Patriots lead series, 17-14-1
PS: Oilers lead series, 1-0
1960—Oilers, 24-10 (B)
Oilers, 37-21 (H)
1961—Tie, 31-31 (B)
Oilers, 27-15 (H)
1962—Patriots, 34-21 (B)
Oilers, 21-17 (H)
1963—Patriots, 45-3 (B)
Patriots, 46-28 (H)
1964—Patriots, 25-24 (B)
Patriots, 34-17 (H)
1965—Oilers, 31-10 (H)
Patriots, 42-14 (B)
1966—Patriots, 27-21 (B)
Patriots, 38-14 (H)
1967—Patriots, 18-7 (B)
Oilers, 27-6 (H)
1968—Oilers, 16-0 (B)
Oilers, 45-17 (H)
1969—Patriots, 24-0 (B)
Oilers, 27-23 (H)
1971—Patriots, 28-20 (NE)
1973—Patriots, 32-0 (H)
1975—Oilers, 7-0 (NE)
1978—Oilers, 26-23 (NE)
**Oilers, 31-14 (NE)
1980—Oilers, 38-34 (H)
1981—Patriots, 38-10 (NE)
1982—Patriots, 29-21 (NE)
1987—Patriots, 21-7 (H)
1988—Oilers, 31-6 (H)
1989—Patriots, 23-13 (NE)
1991—Patriots, 24-20 (NE)
1993—Oilers, 28-14 (NE)
(RS Pts.—Patriots 755, Oilers 656)
(PS Pts.—Oilers 31, Patriots 14)
Franchise in Boston prior to 1971
***AFC Divisional Playoff*

HOUSTON vs. NEW ORLEANS
RS: Saints lead series, 4-3-1
1971—Tie, 13-13 (H)
1976—Oilers, 31-26 (NO)
1978—Oilers, 17-12 (NO)
1981—Saints, 27-24 (H)
1984—Saints, 27-10 (H)
1987—Saints, 24-10 (NO)
1990—Oilers, 23-10 (H)
1993—Saints, 33-21 (NO)
(RS Pts.—Saints 172, Oilers 149)

HOUSTON vs. N.Y. GIANTS
RS: Giants lead series, 5-0
1973—Giants, 34-14 (NY)
1982—Giants, 17-14 (NY)
1985—Giants, 35-14 (H)
1991—Giants, 24-20 (NY)
1994—Giants, 13-10 (H)
(RS Pts.—Giants 123, Oilers 72)

HOUSTON vs. *N.Y. JETS
RS: Oilers lead series, 19-12-1
PS: Oilers lead series, 1-0
1960—Oilers, 27-21 (H)
Oilers, 42-28 (NY)
1961—Oilers, 49-13 (H)
Oilers, 48-21 (NY)
1962—Oilers, 56-17 (H)
Oilers, 44-10 (NY)
1963—Jets, 24-17 (NY)
Oilers, 31-27 (H)
1964—Jets, 24-21 (NY)
Oilers, 33-17 (H)
1965—Oilers, 27-21 (H)
Jets, 41-14 (NY)
1966—Jets, 52-13 (NY)
Oilers, 24-0 (H)
1967—Tie, 28-28 (NY)
1968—Jets, 20-14 (H)
Jets, 26-7 (NY)
1969—Jets, 26-17 (NY)
Jets, 34-26 (H)
1972—Oilers, 26-20 (H)
1974—Oilers, 27-22 (NY)
1977—Oilers, 20-0 (H)
1979—Oilers, 27-24 (H) OT
1980—Jets, 31-28 (NY) OT
1981—Jets, 33-17 (NY)
1984—Oilers, 31-20 (H)
1988—Jets, 45-3 (NY)
1990—Jets, 17-12 (H)
1991—Oilers, 23-20 (NY)
**Oilers, 17-10 (H)
1993—Oilers, 24-0 (H)
1994—Oilers, 24-10 (H)
1995—Oilers, 23-6 (H)
(RS Pts.—Oilers 823, Jets 698)
(PS Pts.—Oilers 17, Jets 10)
Jets known as Titans prior to 1963
***AFC First-Round Playoff*

HOUSTON vs. *OAKLAND
RS: Raiders lead series, 20-13
PS: Raiders lead series, 3-0
1960—Oilers, 37-22 (O)
Raiders, 14-13 (H)
1961—Oilers, 55-0 (H)
Oilers, 47-16 (O)
1962—Oilers, 28-20 (O)
Oilers, 32-17 (H)
1963—Raiders, 24-13 (H)
Raiders, 52-49 (O)
1964—Oilers, 42-28 (H)
Raiders, 20-10 (O)
1965—Raiders, 21-17 (O)
Raiders, 33-21 (H)
1966—Oilers, 31-0 (H)
Raiders, 38-23 (O)
1967—Raiders, 19-7 (H)
**Raiders, 40-7 (O)
1968—Raiders, 24-15 (H)
1969—Raiders, 21-17 (O)
***Raiders, 56-7 (O)
1971—Raiders, 41-21 (O)
1972—Raiders, 34-0 (H)
1973—Raiders, 17-6 (H)
1975—Oilers, 27-26 (O)
1976—Raiders, 14-13 (H)
1977—Raiders, 34-29 (O)
1978—Raiders, 21-17 (O)
1979—Oilers, 31-17 (H)
1980—****Raiders, 27-7 (O)
1981—Oilers, 17-16 (H)
1983—Raiders, 20-6 (LA)
1984—Raiders, 24-14 (H)
1986—Raiders, 28-17 (H)
1988—Oilers, 38-35 (H)
1989—Oilers, 23-7 (H)
1991—Oilers, 47-17 (H)
1994—Raiders, 17-14 (LA)
(RS Pts.—Oilers 777, Raiders 737)
(PS Pts.—Raiders 123, Oilers 21)
Franchise in Los Angeles from 1982-1994
***AFL Championship*
****Inter-Divisional Playoff*
*****AFC First-Round Playoff*

HOUSTON vs. PHILADELPHIA
RS: Eagles lead series, 6-0
1972—Eagles, 18-17 (H)
1979—Eagles, 26-20 (H)
1982—Eagles, 35-14 (P)
1988—Eagles, 32-23 (P)
1991—Eagles, 13-6 (H)
1994—Eagles, 21-6 (P)
(RS Pts.—Eagles 145, Oilers 86)

HOUSTON vs. PITTSBURGH
RS: Steelers lead series, 33-18
PS: Steelers lead series, 3-0
1970—Oilers, 19-7 (P)
Steelers, 7-3 (H)
1971—Steelers, 23-16 (P)
Oilers, 29-3 (H)
1972—Steelers, 24-7 (P)
Steelers, 9-3 (H)
1973—Steelers, 36-7 (H)
Steelers, 33-7 (P)
1974—Steelers, 13-7 (H)
Oilers, 13-10 (P)
1975—Steelers, 24-17 (P)
Steelers, 32-9 (H)
1976—Steelers, 32-16 (P)
Steelers, 21-0 (H)
1977—Oilers, 27-10 (H)
Steelers, 27-10 (P)
1978—Oilers, 24-17 (P)
Steelers, 13-3 (H)
*Steelers, 34-5 (P)
1979—Steelers, 38-7 (P)
Oilers, 20-17 (H)
*Steelers, 27-13 (P)
1980—Steelers, 31-17 (P)
Oilers, 6-0 (H)
1981—Steelers, 26-13 (P)
Oilers, 21-20 (H)
1982—Steelers, 24-10 (H)
1983—Steelers, 40-28 (H)
Steelers, 17-10 (P)
1984—Steelers, 35-7 (P)
Oilers, 23-20 (H) OT
1985—Steelers, 20-0 (P)
Steelers, 30-7 (H)
1986—Steelers, 22-16 (H) OT
Steelers, 21-10 (P)
1987—Oilers, 23-3 (P)
Oilers, 24-16 (H)
1988—Oilers, 34-14 (P)
Steelers, 37-34 (H)
1989—Oilers, 27-0 (H)
Oilers, 23-16 (P)
**Steelers, 26-23 (H)
1990—Steelers, 20-9 (P)
Oilers, 34-14 (H)
1991—Steelers, 26-14 (P)
Oilers, 31-6 (H)
1992—Steelers, 29-24 (H)
Steelers, 21-20 (P)
1993—Oilers, 23-3 (H)
Oilers, 26-17 (P)
1994—Steelers, 30-14 (P)
Steelers, 12-9 (H) OT
1995—Steelers, 34-17 (H)
Steelers, 21-7 (P)
(RS Pts.—Steelers 1,021, Oilers 805)
(PS Pts.—Steelers 87, Oilers 41)
**AFC Championship*
***AFC First-Round Playoff*

HOUSTON vs. *ST. LOUIS
RS: Rams lead series, 5-2

1973—Rams, 31-26 (H)
1978—Rams, 10-6 (H)
1981—Oilers, 27-20 (LA)
1984—Rams, 27-16 (LA)
1987—Oilers, 20-16 (H)
1990—Rams, 17-13 (LA)
1993—Rams, 28-13 (H)
(RS Pts.—Rams 149, Oilers 121)
Franchise in Los Angeles prior to 1995

HOUSTON vs. *SAN DIEGO
RS: Chargers lead series, 18-13-1
PS: Oilers lead series, 3-0
1960—Oilers, 38-28 (H)
Chargers, 24-21 (LA)
**Oilers, 24-16 (H)
1961—Chargers, 34-24 (SD)
Oilers, 33-13 (H)
**Oilers, 10-3 (SD)
1962—Oilers, 42-17 (SD)
Oilers, 33-27 (H)
1963—Chargers, 27-0 (SD)
Chargers 20-14 (H)
1964—Chargers, 27-21 (SD)
Chargers, 20-17 (H)
1965—Chargers, 31-14 (SD)
Chargers, 37-26 (H)
1966—Chargers, 28-22 (H)
1967—Chargers, 13-3 (SD)
Oilers, 24-17 (H)
1968—Chargers, 30-14 (SD)
1969—Chargers, 21-17 (H)
1970—Tie, 31-31 (SD)
1971—Oilers, 49-33 (H)
1972—Chargers, 34-20 (SD)
1974—Oilers, 21-14 (H)
1975—Oilers, 33-17 (H)
1976—Chargers, 30-27 (SD)
1978—Chargers, 45-24 (H)
1979—***Oilers, 17-14 (SD)
1984—Chargers, 31-14 (SD)
1985—Oilers, 37-35 (H)
1986—Chargers, 27-0 (SD)
1987—Oilers, 33-18 (H)
1989—Oilers, 34-27 (SD)
1990—Oilers, 17-7 (SD)
1992—Oilers, 27-0 (H)
1993—Chargers, 18-17 (SD)
(RS Pts.—Chargers 781, Oilers 747)
(PS Pts.—Oilers 51, Chargers 33)
Franchise in Los Angeles prior to 1961
***AFL Championship*
****AFC Divisional Playoff*

HOUSTON vs. SAN FRANCISCO
RS: 49ers lead series, 5-3
1970—49ers, 30-20 (H)
1975—Oilers, 27-13 (SF)
1978—Oilers, 20-19 (H)
1981—49ers, 28-6 (SF)
1984—49ers, 34-21 (H)
1987—49ers, 27-20 (SF)
1990—49ers, 24-21 (H)
1993—Oilers, 10-7 (SF)
(RS Pts.—49ers 182, Oilers 145)

HOUSTON vs. SEATTLE
RS: Seahawks lead series, 5-4
PS: Oilers lead series, 1-0
1977—Oilers, 22-10 (S)
1979—Seahawks, 34-14 (S)
1980—Seahawks, 26-7 (H)
1981—Oilers, 35-17 (H)
1982—Oilers, 23-21 (H)
1987—*Oilers, 23-20 (H) OT
1988—Seahawks, 27-24 (S)
1990—Seahawks, 13-10 (S) OT
1993—Oilers, 24-14 (H)
1994—Seahawks, 16-14 (H)
(RS Pts.—Seahawks 178, Oilers 173)
(PS Pts.—Oilers 23, Seahawks 20)
AFC First-Round Playoff

HOUSTON vs. TAMPA BAY
RS: Oilers lead series, 4-1
1976—Oilers, 20-0 (H)
1980—Oilers, 20-14 (H)
1983—Buccaneers, 33-24 (TB)
1989—Oilers, 20-17 (H)
1995—Oilers, 19-7 (H)
(RS Pts.—Oilers 103, Buccaneers 71)

HOUSTON vs. WASHINGTON
RS: Series tied, 3-3
1971—Redskins, 22-13 (W)
1975—Oilers, 13-10 (H)
1979—Oilers, 29-27 (W)
1985—Redskins, 16-13 (W)
1988—Oilers, 41-17 (H)
1991—Redskins, 16-13 (W) OT
(RS Pts.—Oilers 122, Redskins 108)

INDIANAPOLIS vs. ARIZONA
RS: Cardinals lead series, 6-5;
See Arizona vs. Indianapolis

INDIANAPOLIS vs. ATLANTA
RS: Colts lead series, 10-0;
See Atlanta vs. Indianapolis

INDIANAPOLIS vs. BUFFALO
RS: Bills lead series, 28-22-1;
See Buffalo vs. Indianapolis

INDIANAPOLIS vs. CAROLINA
RS: Panthers lead series, 1-0;
See Carolina vs. Indianapolis

INDIANAPOLIS vs. CHICAGO
RS: Colts lead series, 21-16;
See Chicago vs. Indianapolis

INDIANAPOLIS vs. CINCINNATI
RS: Colts lead series, 9-6
PS: Colts lead series, 1-0;
See Cincinnati vs. Indianapolis

INDIANAPOLIS vs. CLEVELAND
RS: Browns lead series, 13-7
PS: Series tied, 2-2;
See Cleveland vs. Indianapolis

INDIANAPOLIS vs. DALLAS
RS: Cowboys lead series, 7-2
PS: Colts lead series, 1-0;
See Dallas vs. Indianapolis

INDIANAPOLIS vs. DENVER
RS: Broncos lead series, 9-2;
See Denver vs. Indianapolis

INDIANAPOLIS vs. DETROIT
RS: Series tied, 17-17-2;
See Detroit vs. Indianapolis

INDIANAPOLIS vs. GREEN BAY
RS: Series tied, 18-18-1
PS: Packers lead series, 1-0;
See Green Bay vs. Indianapolis

INDIANAPOLIS vs. HOUSTON
RS: Series tied, 7-7;
See Houston vs. Indianapolis

INDIANAPOLIS vs. JACKSONVILLE
RS: Colts lead series, 1-0
1995—Colts, 41-31 (J)
(RS Pts.—Colts 41, Jaguars 31)

***INDIANAPOLIS vs. KANSAS CITY**
RS: Chiefs lead series, 6-4
PS: Colts lead series, 1-0
1970—Chiefs, 44-24 (B)
1972—Chiefs, 24-10 (KC)
1975—Colts, 28-14 (B)
1977—Colts, 17-6 (KC)
1979—Chiefs, 14-0 (KC)
Chiefs, 10-7 (B)
1980—Colts, 31-24 (KC)
Chiefs, 38-28 (B)
1985—Chiefs, 20-7 (KC)
1990—Colts, 23-19 (I)
1995—**Colts, 10-7 (KC)
(RS Pts.—Chiefs 213, Colts 175)
(PS Pts.—Colts 10, Chiefs 7)
Franchise in Baltimore prior to 1984
***AFC Divisional Playoff*

***INDIANAPOLIS vs. MIAMI**
RS: Dolphins lead series, 35-17
PS: Dolphins lead series, 1-0
1970—Colts, 35-0 (B)
Dolphins, 34-17 (M)
1971—Dolphins, 17-14 (M)
Colts, 14-3 (B)
**Dolphins, 21-0 (M)
1972—Dolphins, 23-0 (B)
Dolphins, 16-0 (M)
1973—Dolphins, 44-0 (M)
Colts, 16-3 (B)
1974—Dolphins, 17-7 (M)
Dolphins, 17-16 (B)
1975—Colts, 33-17 (M)
Colts, 10-7 (B) OT
1976—Colts, 28-14 (B)
Colts, 17-16 (M)
1977—Colts, 45-28 (B)
Dolphins, 17-6 (M)
1978—Dolphins, 42-0 (B)
Dolphins, 26-8 (M)
1979—Dolphins, 19-0 (M)
Dolphins, 28-24 (B)
1980—Colts, 30-17 (M)
Dolphins, 24-14 (B)
1981—Dolphins, 31-28 (B)
Dolphins, 27-10 (M)
1982—Dolphins, 24-20 (M)
Dolphins, 34-7 (B)
1983—Dolphins, 21-7 (B)
Dolphins, 37-0 (M)
1984—Dolphins, 44-7 (M)
Dolphins, 35-17 (I)
1985—Dolphins, 30-13 (M)
Dolphins, 34-20 (I)
1986—Dolphins, 30-10 (M)
Dolphins, 17-13 (I)
1987—Dolphins, 23-10 (I)
Colts, 40-21 (M)
1988—Colts, 15-13 (I)
Colts, 31-28 (M)
1989—Dolphins, 19-13 (M)
Colts, 42-13 (I)
1990—Dolphins, 27-7 (I)
Dolphins, 23-17 (M)
1991—Dolphins, 17-6 (M)
Dolphins, 10-6 (I)
1992—Colts, 31-20 (M)
Dolphins, 28-0 (I)
1993—Dolphins, 24-20 (I)
Dolphins, 41-27 (M)
1994—Dolphins, 22-21 (M)
Colts, 10-6 (I)
1995—Colts, 27-24 (M) OT
Colts, 36-28 (I)
(RS Pts.—Dolphins 1,180, Colts 845)
(PS Pts.—Dolphins 21, Colts 0)
Franchise in Baltimore prior to 1984
***AFC Championship*

***INDIANAPOLIS vs. MINNESOTA**
RS: Colts lead series, 11-6-1
PS: Colts lead series, 1-0
1961—Colts, 34-33 (B)
Vikings, 28-20 (M)
1962—Colts, 34-7 (M)
Colts, 42-17 (B)
1963—Colts, 37-34 (M)
Colts, 41-10 (B)
1964—Vikings, 34-24 (M)
Colts, 17-14 (B)
1965—Colts, 35-16 (B)
Colts, 41-21 (M)
1966—Colts, 38-23 (M)
Colts, 20-17 (B)
1967—Tie, 20-20 (M)
1968—Colts, 21-9 (B)
**Colts, 24-14 (B)
1969—Vikings, 52-14 (M)
1971—Vikings, 10-3 (M)
1982—Vikings, 13-10 (M)
1988—Vikings, 12-3 (M)
(RS Pts.—Colts 454, Vikings 370)
(PS Pts.—Colts 24, Vikings 14)
Franchise in Baltimore prior to 1984
***Conference Championship*

***INDIANAPOLIS vs. **NEW ENGLAND**
RS: Patriots lead series, 29-22
1970—Colts, 14-6 (Bos)
Colts, 27-3 (Balt)
1971—Colts, 23-3 (NE)
Patriots, 21-17 (Balt)
1972—Colts, 24-17 (NE)
Colts, 31-0 (Balt)
1973—Patriots, 24-16 (NE)
Colts, 18-13 (Balt)
1974—Patriots, 42-3 (NE)
Patriots, 27-17 (Balt)
1975—Patriots, 21-10 (NE)
Colts, 34-21 (Balt)
1976—Colts, 27-13 (NE)
Patriots, 21-14 (Balt)
1977—Patriots, 17-3 (NE)
Colts, 30-24 (Balt)
1978—Colts, 34-27 (NE)
Patriots, 35-14 (Balt)
1979—Colts, 31-26 (Balt)
Patriots, 50-21 (NE)
1980—Patriots, 37-21 (Balt)
Patriots, 47-21 (NE)
1981—Colts, 29-28 (NE)
Colts, 23-21 (Balt)
1982—Patriots, 24-13 (Balt)
1983—Colts, 29-23 (NE) OT
Colts, 12-7 (Balt)
1984—Patriots, 50-17 (I)
Patriots, 16-10 (NE)
1985—Patriots, 34-15 (NE)
Patriots, 38-31 (I)
1986—Patriots, 33-3 (NE)
Patriots, 30-21 (I)
1987—Colts, 30-16 (I)
Patriots, 24-0 (NE)
1988—Patriots, 21-17 (NE)
Colts, 24-21 (I)
1989—Patriots, 23-20 (I) OT
Patriots, 22-16 (NE)
1990—Patriots, 16-14 (I)
Colts, 13-10 (NE)
1991—Patriots, 16-7 (I)
Patriots, 23-17 (NE) OT
1992—Patriots, 37-34 (I) OT
Colts, 6-0 (NE)
1993—Colts, 9-6 (I)
Patriots, 38-0 (NE)
1994—Patriots, 12-10 (I)
Patriots, 28-13 (NE)
1995—Colts, 24-10 (NE)
Colts, 10-7 (I)
(RS Pts.—Patriots 1,129, Colts 917)
Franchise in Baltimore prior to 1984
***Franchise in Boston prior to 1971*

***INDIANAPOLIS vs. NEW ORLEANS**
RS: Series tied, 3-3
1967—Colts, 30-10 (B)
1969—Colts, 30-10 (NO)
1973—Colts, 14-10 (B)
1986—Saints, 17-14 (I)
1989—Saints, 41-6 (NO)
1995—Saints, 17-14 (NO)
(RS Pts.—Colts 108, Saints 105)
Franchise in Baltimore prior to 1984

***INDIANAPOLIS vs. N.Y. GIANTS**
RS: Series tied, 5-5
PS: Colts lead series, 2-0
1954—Colts, 20-14 (B)
1955—Giants, 17-7 (NY)
1958—Giants, 24-21 (NY)
**Colts, 23-17 (NY) OT
1959—**Colts, 31-16 (B)
1963—Giants, 37-28 (B)
1968—Colts, 26-0 (NY)
1971—Colts, 31-7 (NY)
1975—Colts, 21-0 (NY)
1979—Colts, 31-7 (NY)
1990—Giants, 24-7 (I)
1993—Giants, 20-6 (NY)
(RS Pts.—Colts 198, Giants 150)
(PS Pts.—Colts 54, Giants 33)
Franchise in Baltimore prior to 1984
***NFL Championship*

***INDIANAPOLIS vs. N.Y. JETS**
RS: Colts lead series, 30-21

PS: Jets lead series, 1-0
1968—**Jets 16-7 (Miami)
1970—Colts, 29-22 (NY)
Colts, 35-20 (B)
1971—Colts, 22-0 (B)
Colts, 14-13 (NY)
1972—Jets, 44-34 (B)
Jets, 24-20 (NY)
1973—Jets, 34-10 (B)
Jets, 20-17 (NY)
1974—Colts, 35-20 (NY)
Jets, 45-38 (B)
1975—Colts, 45-28 (NY)
Colts, 52-19 (B)
1976—Colts, 20-0 (NY)
Colts, 33-16 (B)
1977—Colts, 20-12 (NY)
Colts, 33-12 (B)
1978—Jets, 33-10 (B)
Jets, 24-16 (NY)
1979—Colts, 10-8 (B)
Jets, 30-17 (NY)
1980—Colts, 17-14 (NY)
Colts, 35-21 (B)
1981—Jets, 41-14 (B)
Jets, 25-0 (NY)
1982—Jets, 37-0 (NY)
1983—Colts, 17-14 (NY)
Jets, 10-6 (B)
1984—Jets, 23-14 (I)
Colts, 9-5 (NY)
1985—Jets, 25-20 (NY)
Jets, 35-17 (I)
1986—Jets, 26-7 (I)
Jets, 31-16 (NY)
1987—Colts, 6-0 (I)
Colts, 19-14 (NY)
1988—Colts, 38-14 (I)
Jets, 34-16 (NY)
1989—Colts, 17-10 (NY)
Colts, 27-10 (I)
1990—Colts, 17-14 (I)
Colts, 29-21 (NY)
1991—Jets, 17-6 (I)
Colts, 28-27 (NY)
1992—Colts, 6-3 (I) OT
Colts, 10-6 (NY)
1993—Jets, 31-17 (I)
Colts, 9-6 (NY)
1994—Jets, 16-6 (NY)
Colts, 28-25 (I)
1995—Colts, 27-24 (NY) OT
Colts, 17-10 (I)
(RS Pts.—Jets 1,013, Colts 1,005)
(PS Pts.—Jets 16, Colts 7)
Franchise in Baltimore prior to 1984
***Super Bowl III*

***INDIANAPOLIS vs **OAKLAND**
RS: Raiders lead series, 5-2
PS: Series tied, 1-1
1970—***Colts, 27-17 (B)
1971—Colts, 37-14 (O)
1973—Raiders, 34-21 (B)
1975—Raiders, 31-20 (B)
1977—****Raiders, 37-31 (B) OT
1984—Raiders, 21-7 (LA)
1986—Colts, 30-24 (LA)
1991—Raiders, 16-0 (LA)
1995—Raiders, 30-17 (O)
(RS Pts.—Raiders 170, Colts 132)
(PS Pts.—Colts 58, Raiders 54)
Franchise in Baltimore prior to 1984
***Franchise in Los Angeles from 1982-1994*
****AFC Championship*
*****AFC Divisional Playoff*

***INDIANAPOLIS vs. PHILADELPHIA**
RS: Series tied, 6-6
1953—Eagles, 45-14 (P)
1965—Colts, 34-24 (B)
1967—Colts, 38-6 (P)
1969—Colts, 24-20 (B)
1970—Colts, 29-10 (B)
1974—Eagles, 30-10 (P)
1978—Eagles, 17-14 (B)
1981—Eagles, 38-13 (P)
1983—Colts, 22-21 (P)
1984—Eagles, 16-7 (P)
1990—Colts, 24-23 (P)
1993—Eagles, 20-10 (I)
(RS Pts.—Eagles 270, Colts 239)
Franchise in Baltimore prior to 1984

***INDIANAPOLIS vs. PITTSBURGH**
RS: Steelers lead series, 11-4
PS: Steelers lead series, 3-0
1957—Steelers, 19-13 (B)
1968—Colts, 41-7 (P)
1971—Colts, 34-21 (B)
1974—Steelers, 30-0 (B)
1975—**Steelers, 28-10 (P)
1976—**Steelers, 40-14 (B)
1977—Colts, 31-21 (B)
1978—Steelers, 35-13 (P)
1979—Steelers, 17-13 (P)
1980—Steelers, 20-17 (B)
1983—Steelers, 24-13 (B)
1984—Colts, 17-16 (I)
1985—Steelers, 45-3 (P)
1987—Steelers, 21-7 (P)
1991—Steelers, 21-3 (I)
1992—Steelers, 30-14 (P)
1994—Steelers, 31-21 (P)
1995—***Steelers, 20-16 (P)
(RS Pts.—Steelers 358, Colts 240)
(PS Pts.—Steelers 88, Colts 40)
Franchise in Baltimore prior to 1984
***AFC Divisional Playoff*
****AFC Championship*

***INDIANAPOLIS vs. **ST. LOUIS**
RS: Colts lead series, 21-16-2
1953—Rams, 21-13 (B)
Rams, 45-2 (LA)
1954—Rams, 48-0 (B)
Colts, 22-21 (LA)
1955—Tie, 17-17 (B)
Rams, 20-14 (LA)
1956—Colts, 56-21 (B)
Rams, 31-7 (LA)
1957—Colts, 31-14 (B)
Rams, 37-21 (LA)
1958—Colts, 34-7 (B)
Rams, 30-28 (LA)
1959—Colts, 35-21 (B)
Colts, 45-26 (LA)
1960—Colts, 31-17 (B)
Rams, 10-3 (LA)
1961—Colts, 27-24 (B)
Rams, 34-17 (LA)
1962—Colts, 30-27 (B)
Colts, 14-2 (LA)
1963—Rams, 17-16 (LA)
Colts, 19-16 (B)
1964—Colts, 35-20 (B)
Colts, 24-7 (LA)
1965—Colts, 35-20 (B)
Colts, 20-17 (LA)
1966—Colts, 17-3 (LA)
Rams, 23-7 (B)
1967—Tie, 24-24 (B)
Rams, 34-10 (LA)
1968—Colts, 27-10 (B)
Colts, 28-24 (LA)
1969—Rams, 27-20 (B)
Colts, 13-7 (LA)
1971—Colts, 24-17 (B)
1975—Rams, 24-13 (LA)
1986—Rams, 24-7 (I)
1989—Rams, 31-17 (LA)
1995—Colts, 21-18 (I)
(RS Pts.—Rams 836, Colts 824)
Franchise in Baltimore prior to 1984
***Franchise in Los Angeles prior to 1995*

***INDIANAPOLIS vs. SAN DIEGO**
RS: Chargers lead series, 10-5
PS: Colts lead series, 1-0
1970—Colts, 16-14 (SD)
1972—Chargers, 23-20 (B)
1976—Colts, 37-21 (SD)
1981—Chargers, 43-14 (B)
1982—Chargers, 44-26 (SD)
1984—Chargers, 38-10 (I)
1986—Chargers, 17-3 (I)
1987—Chargers, 16-13 (I)
Colts, 20-7 (SD)
1988—Colts, 16-0 (SD)
1989—Colts, 10-6 (I)
1992—Chargers, 34-14 (I)
Chargers, 26-0 (SD)
1993—Chargers, 31-0 (I)
1995—Chargers, 27-24 (I)
**Colts, 35-20 (SD)
(RS Pts.—Chargers 347, Colts 223)
(PS Pts.—Colts 35, Chargers 20)
Franchise in Baltimore prior to 1984
***AFC First-Round Playoff*

***INDIANAPOLIS vs. SAN FRANCISCO**
RS: Colts lead series, 22-16
1953—49ers, 38-21 (B)
49ers, 45-14 (SF)
1954—Colts, 17-13 (B)
49ers, 10-7 (SF)
1955—Colts, 26-14 (B)
49ers, 35-24 (SF)
1956—49ers, 20-17 (B)
49ers, 30-17 (SF)
1957—Colts, 27-21 (B)
49ers, 17-13 (SF)
1958—Colts, 35-27 (B)
49ers, 21-12 (SF)
1959—Colts, 45-14 (B)
Colts, 34-14 (SF)
1960—49ers, 30-22 (B)
49ers, 34-10 (SF)
1961—Colts, 20-17 (B)
Colts, 27-24 (SF)
1962—49ers, 21-13 (B)
Colts, 22-3 (SF)
1963—Colts, 20-14 (SF)
Colts, 20-3 (B)
1964—Colts, 37-7 (B)
Colts, 14-3 (SF)
1965—Colts, 27-24 (B)
Colts, 34-28 (SF)
1966—Colts, 36-14 (B)
Colts, 30-14 (SF)
1967—Colts, 41-7 (B)
Colts, 26-9 (SF)
1968—Colts, 27-10 (B)
Colts, 42-14 (SF)
1969—49ers, 24-21 (B)
49ers, 20-17 (SF)
1972—49ers, 24-21 (SF)
1986—49ers, 35-14 (SF)
1989—49ers, 30-24 (I)
1995—Colts, 18-17 (I)
(RS Pts.—Colts 892, 49ers 745)
Franchise in Baltimore prior to 1984

***INDIANAPOLIS vs. SEATTLE**
RS: Colts lead series, 4-1
1977—Colts, 29-14 (S)
1978—Colts, 17-14 (S)
1991—Seahawks, 31-3 (S)
1994—Colts, 17-15 (I)
Colts, 31-19 (S)
(RS Pts.—Colts 97, Seahawks 93)
Franchise in Baltimore prior to 1984

***INDIANAPOLIS vs. TAMPA BAY**
RS: Colts lead series, 5-3
1976—Colts, 42-17 (B)
1979—Buccaneers, 29-26 (B) OT
1985—Colts, 31-23 (TB)
1987—Colts, 24-6 (I)
1988—Colts, 35-31 (I)
1991—Buccaneers, 17-3 (TB)
1992—Colts, 24-14 (TB)
1994—Buccaneers, 24-10 (TB)
(RS Pts.—Colts 195, Buccaneers 161)
Franchise in Baltimore prior to 1984

***INDIANAPOLIS vs. WASHINGTON**
RS: Colts lead series, 16-8
1953—Colts, 27-17 (B)
1954—Redskins, 24-21 (W)
1955—Redskins, 14-13 (B)
1956—Colts, 19-17 (B)
1957—Colts, 21-17 (W)
1958—Colts, 35-10 (B)
1959—Redskins, 27-24 (W)
1960—Colts, 20-0 (B)
1961—Colts, 27-6 (W)
1962—Colts, 34-21 (B)
1963—Colts, 36-20 (W)
1964—Colts, 45-17 (B)
1965—Colts, 38-7 (W)
1966—Colts, 37-10 (B)
1967—Colts, 17-13 (W)
1969—Colts, 41-17 (B)
1973—Redskins, 22-14 (W)
1977—Colts, 10-3 (B)
1978—Colts, 21-17 (B)
1981—Redskins, 38-14 (W)
1984—Redskins, 35-7 (I)
1990—Colts, 35-28 (I)
1993—Redskins, 30-24 (W)
1994—Redskins, 41-27 (I)
(RS Pts.—Colts 607, Redskins 451)
Franchise in Baltimore prior to 1984

JACKSONVILLE vs. CHICAGO
RS: Bears lead series, 1-0;
See Chicago vs. Jacksonville

JACKSONVILLE vs. CINCINNATI
RS: Bengals lead series, 2-0;
See Cincinnati vs. Jacksonville

JACKSONVILLE vs. CLEVELAND
RS: Jaguars lead series, 2-0;
See Cleveland vs. Jacksonville

JACKSONVILLE vs. DENVER
RS: Broncos lead series, 1-0;
See Denver vs. Jacksonville

JACKSONVILLE vs. DETROIT
RS: Lions lead series, 1-0;
See Detroit vs. Jacksonville

JACKSONVILLE vs. GREEN BAY
RS: Packers lead series, 1-0;
See Green Bay vs. Jacksonville

JACKSONVILLE vs. HOUSTON
RS: Series tied, 1-1;
See Houston vs. Jacksonville

JACKSONVILLE vs. INDIANAPOLIS
RS: Colts lead series, 1-0;
See Indianapolis vs. Jacksonville

JACKSONVILLE vs. N.Y. JETS
RS: Jets lead series, 1-0;
1995—Jets, 27-10 (NY)
(RS Pts.—Jets 27, Jaguars 10)

JACKSONVILLE vs. PITTSBURGH
RS: Series tied, 1-1;
1995—Jaguars, 20-16 (J)
Steelers, 24-7 (P)
(RS Pts.—Steelers 40, Jaguars 27)

JACKSONVILLE vs. SEATTLE
RS: Seahawks lead series, 1-0;
1995—Seahawks, 47-30 (J)
(RS Pts.—Seahawks 47, Jaguars 30)

JACKSONVILLE vs. TAMPA BAY
RS: Buccaneers lead series, 1-0;
1995—Buccaneers, 17-16 (TB)
(RS Pts.—Buccaneers 17, Jaguars 16)

KANSAS CITY vs. ARIZONA
RS: Chiefs lead series, 4-1-1;
See Arizona vs. Kansas City

KANSAS CITY vs. ATLANTA
RS: Chiefs lead series, 4-0;
See Atlanta vs. Kansas City

KANSAS CITY vs. BUFFALO
RS: Bills lead series, 16-13-1
PS: Bills lead series, 2-1;
See Buffalo vs. Kansas City

KANSAS CITY vs. CHICAGO
RS: Bears lead series, 4-2;
See Chicago vs. Kansas City

ALL-TIME TEAM VS. TEAM RESULTS

KANSAS CITY vs. CINCINNATI
RS: Chiefs lead series, 11-9;
See Cincinnati vs. Kansas City
KANSAS CITY vs. CLEVELAND
RS: Browns lead series, 8-7-2;
See Cleveland vs. Kansas City
KANSAS CITY vs. DALLAS
RS: Cowboys lead series, 4-2;
See Dallas vs. Kansas City
KANSAS CITY vs. DENVER
RS: Chiefs lead series, 41-30;
See Denver vs. Kansas City
KANSAS CITY vs. DETROIT
RS: Chiefs lead series, 4-3;
See Detroit vs. Kansas City
KANSAS CITY vs. GREEN BAY
RS: Chiefs lead series, 4-1-1
PS: Packers lead series, 1-0;
See Green Bay vs. Kansas City
KANSAS CITY vs. HOUSTON
RS: Chiefs lead series, 23-17
PS: Chiefs lead series, 2-0;
See Houston vs. Kansas City
KANSAS CITY vs. INDIANAPOLIS
RS: Chiefs lead series, 6-4;
PS: Colts lead series, 1-0;
See Indianapolis vs. Kansas City
KANSAS CITY vs. MIAMI
RS: Chiefs lead series, 10-9
PS: Dolphins lead series, 3-0
1966—Chiefs, 34-16 (KC)
Chiefs, 19-18 (M)
1967—Chiefs, 24-0 (M)
Chiefs, 41-0 (KC)
1968—Chiefs, 48-3 (M)
1969—Chiefs, 17-10 (KC)
1971—*Dolphins, 27-24 (KC) OT
1972—Dolphins, 20-10 (KC)
1974—Dolphins, 9-3 (M)
1976—Chiefs, 20-17 (M) OT
1981—Dolphins, 17-7 (KC)
1983—Dolphins, 14-6 (M)
1985—Dolphins, 31-0 (M)
1987—Dolphins, 42-0 (M)
1989—Chiefs, 26-21 (KC)
Chiefs, 27-24 (M)
1990—**Dolphins, 17-16 (M)
1991—Chiefs, 42-7 (KC)
1993—Dolphins, 30-10 (M)
1994—Dolphins, 45-28 (M)
**Dolphins, 27-17 (M)
1995—Dolphins, 13-6 (M)
(RS Pts.—Chiefs 368, Dolphins 337)
(PS Pts.—Dolphins 71, Chiefs 57)
**AFC Divisional Playoff*
***AFC First-Round Playoff*
KANSAS CITY vs. MINNESOTA
RS: Vikings lead series, 3-2
PS: Chiefs lead series, 1-0
1969—*Chiefs, 23-7 (New Orleans)
1970—Vikings, 27-10 (M)
1974—Vikings, 35-15 (KC)
1981—Chiefs, 10-6 (M)
1990—Chiefs, 24-21 (KC)
1993—Vikings, 30-10 (M)
(RS Pts.—Vikings 119, Chiefs 69)
(PS Pts.—Chiefs 23, Vikings 7)
**Super Bowl IV*
***KANSAS CITY vs. **NEW ENGLAND**
RS: Chiefs lead series, 14-7-3
1960—Patriots, 42-14 (B)
Texans, 34-0 (D)
1961—Patriots, 18-17 (D)
Patriots, 28-21 (B)
1962—Texans, 42-28 (D)
Texans, 27-7 (B)
1963—Tie, 24-24 (B)
Chiefs, 35-3 (KC)
1964—Patriots, 24-7 (B)
Patriots, 31-24 (KC)
1965—Chiefs, 27-17 (KC)
Tie, 10-10 (B)
1966—Chiefs, 43-24 (B)
Tie, 27-27 (KC)
1967—Chiefs, 33-10 (B)
1968—Chiefs, 31-17 (KC)
1969—Chiefs, 31-0 (B)
1970—Chiefs, 23-10 (KC)
1973—Chiefs, 10-7 (NE)
1977—Patriots, 21-17 (NE)
1981—Patriots, 33-17 (NE)
1990—Chiefs, 37-7 (NE)
1992—Chiefs, 27-20 (KC)
1995—Chiefs, 31-26 (KC)
(RS Pts.—Chiefs 609, Patriots 434)
**Franchise located in Dallas prior to 1963 and known as Texans*
***Franchise in Boston prior to 1971*
KANSAS CITY vs. NEW ORLEANS
RS: Series tied, 3-3
1972—Chiefs, 20-17 (NO)
1976—Saints, 27-17 (KC)
1982—Saints, 27-17 (NO)
1985—Chiefs, 47-27 (NO)
1991—Saints, 17-10 (KC)
1994—Chiefs, 30-17 (NO)
(RS Pts.—Chiefs 141, Saints 132)
KANSAS CITY vs. N.Y. GIANTS
RS: Giants lead series, 6-2
1974—Giants, 33-27 (KC)
1978—Giants, 26-10 (NY)
1979—Giants, 21-17 (KC)
1983—Chiefs, 38-17 (KC)
1984—Giants, 28-27 (NY)
1988—Giants, 28-12 (NY)
1992—Giants, 35-21 (NY)
1995—Chiefs, 20-17 (KC) OT
(RS Pts.—Giants 205, Chiefs 172)
***KANSAS CITY vs. **N.Y. JETS**
RS: Chiefs lead series, 14-12-1
PS: Series tied, 1-1
1960—Titans, 37-35 (D)
Titans, 41-35 (NY)
1961—Titans, 28-7 (NY)
Texans, 35-24 (D)
1962—Texans, 20-17 (D)
Texans, 52-31 (NY)
1963—Jets, 17-0 (NY)
Chiefs, 48-0 (KC)
1964—Jets, 27-14 (NY)
Chiefs, 24-7 (KC)
1965—Chiefs, 14-10 (NY)
Jets, 13-10 (KC)
1966—Chiefs, 32-24 (NY)
1967—Chiefs, 42-18 (KC)
Chiefs, 21-7 (NY)
1968—Jets, 20-19 (KC)
1969—Chiefs, 34-16 (NY)
***Chiefs, 13-6 (NY)
1971—Jets, 13-10 (NY)
1974—Chiefs, 24-16 (KC)
1975—Jets, 30-24 (KC)
1982—Chiefs, 37-13 (KC)
1984—Jets, 17-16 (KC)
Jets, 28-7 (NY)
1986—****Jets, 35-15 (NY)
1987—Jets, 16-9 (KC)
1988—Tie, 17-17 (NY)
Chiefs, 38-34 (KC)
1992—Chiefs, 23-7 (NY)
(RS Pts.—Chiefs 647, Jets 528)
(PS Pts.—Jets 41, Chiefs 28)
**Franchise in Dallas prior to 1963 and known as Texans*
***Jets known as Titans prior to 1963*
****Inter-Divisional Playoff*
*****AFC First-Round Playoff*
***KANSAS CITY vs. **OAKLAND**
RS: Raiders lead series, 35-34-2
PS: Chiefs lead series, 2-1
1960—Texans, 34-16 (O)
Raiders, 20-19 (D)
1961—Texans, 42-35 (O)
Texans, 43-11 (D)
1962—Texans, 26-16 (O)
Texans, 35-7 (D)
1963—Raiders, 10-7 (O)
Raiders, 22-7 (KC)
1964—Chiefs, 21-9 (O)
Chiefs, 42-7 (KC)
1965—Raiders, 37-10 (O)
Chiefs, 14-7 (KC)
1966—Chiefs, 32-10 (O)
Raiders, 34-13 (KC)
1967—Raiders, 23-21 (O)
Raiders, 44-22 (KC)
1968—Chiefs, 24-10 (KC)
Raiders, 38-21 (O)
***Raiders, 41-6 (O)
1969—Raiders, 27-24 (KC)
Raiders, 10-6 (O)
****Chiefs, 17-7 (O)
1970—Tie, 17-17 (KC)
Raiders, 20-6 (O)
1971—Tie, 20-20 (O)
Chiefs, 16-14 (KC)
1972—Chiefs, 27-14 (KC)
Raiders, 26-3 (O)
1973—Chiefs, 16-3 (KC)
Raiders, 37-7 (O)
1974—Raiders, 27-7 (O)
Raiders, 7-6 (KC)
1975—Chiefs, 42-10 (KC)
Raiders, 28-20 (O)
1976—Raiders, 24-21 (KC)
Raiders, 21-10 (O)
1977—Raiders, 37-28 (KC)
Raiders, 21-20 (O)
1978—Raiders, 28-6 (O)
Raiders, 20-10 (KC)
1979—Chiefs, 35-7 (KC)
Chiefs, 24-21 (O)
1980—Raiders, 27-14 (KC)
Chiefs, 31-17 (O)
1981—Chiefs, 27-0 (KC)
Chiefs, 28-17 (O)
1982—Raiders, 21-16 (KC)
1983—Raiders, 21-20 (LA)
Raiders, 28-20 (KC)
1984—Raiders, 22-20 (KC)
Raiders, 17-7 (LA)
1985—Chiefs, 36-20 (KC)
Raiders, 19-10 (LA)
1986—Raiders, 24-17 (KC)
Chiefs, 20-17 (LA)
1987—Raiders, 35-17 (LA)
Chiefs, 16-10 (KC)
1988—Raiders, 27-17 (KC)
Raiders, 17-10 (LA)
1989—Chiefs, 24-19 (KC)
Raiders, 20-14 (LA)
1990—Chiefs, 9-7 (KC)
Chiefs, 27-24 (LA)
1991—Chiefs, 24-21 (KC)
Chiefs, 27-21 (LA)
†Chiefs, 10-6 (KC)
1992—Chiefs, 27-7 (KC)
Raiders, 28-7 (LA)
1993—Chiefs, 24-9 (KC)
Chiefs, 31-20 (LA)
1994—Chiefs, 13-3 (KC)
Chiefs, 19-9 (LA)
1995—Chiefs, 23-17 (KC) OT
Chiefs, 29-23 (O)
(RS Pts.—Chiefs 1,428, Raiders 1,362)
(PS Pts.—Raiders 54, Chiefs 33)
**Franchise in Dallas prior to 1963 and known as Texans*
***Franchise in Los Angeles from 1982-1994*
****Division Playoff*
*****AFL Championship*
†AFC First-Round Playoff
KANSAS CITY vs. PHILADELPHIA
RS: Series tied, 1-1
1972—Eagles, 21-20 (KC)
1992—Chiefs, 24-17 (KC)
(RS Pts.—Chiefs 44, Eagles 38)
KANSAS CITY vs. PITTSBURGH
RS: Steelers lead series, 13-5
PS: Chiefs lead series, 1-0
1970—Chiefs, 31-14 (P)
1971—Chiefs, 38-16 (KC)
1972—Steelers, 16-7 (P)
1974—Steelers, 34-24 (KC)
1975—Steelers, 28-3 (P)
1976—Steelers, 45-0 (KC)
1978—Steelers, 27-24 (P)
1979—Steelers, 30-3 (KC)
1980—Steelers, 21-16 (P)
1981—Chiefs, 37-33 (P)
1982—Steelers, 35-14 (P)
1984—Chiefs, 37-27 (P)
1985—Steelers, 36-28 (KC)
1986—Chiefs, 24-19 (P)
1987—Steelers, 17-16 (KC)
1988—Steelers, 16-10 (P)
1989—Steelers, 23-17 (P)
1992—Steelers, 27-3 (KC)
1993—*Chiefs, 27-24 (KC) OT
(RS Pts.—Steelers 464, Chiefs 332)
(PS Pts.—Chiefs 27, Steelers 24)
**AFC First-Round Playoff*
KANSAS CITY vs. *ST. LOUIS
RS: Rams lead series, 4-1
1973—Rams, 23-13 (KC)
1982—Rams, 20-14 (LA)
1985—Rams, 16-0 (KC)
1991—Chiefs, 27-20 (LA)
1994—Rams, 16-0 (KC)
(RS Pts.—Rams 95, Chiefs 54)
**Franchise in Los Angeles prior to 1995*
***KANSAS CITY vs. **SAN DIEGO**
RS: Chiefs lead series, 37-33-1
PS: Chargers lead series, 1-0
1960—Chargers, 21-20 (LA)
Texans, 17-0 (D)
1961—Chargers, 26-10 (D)
Chargers, 24-14 (SD)
1962—Chargers, 32-28 (SD)
Texans, 26-17 (D)
1963—Chargers, 24-10 (SD)
Chargers, 38-17 (KC)
1964—Chargers, 28-14 (KC)
Chiefs, 49-6 (SD)
1965—Tie, 10-10 (SD)
Chiefs, 31-7 (KC)
1966—Chiefs, 24-14 (KC)
Chiefs, 27-17 (SD)
1967—Chargers, 45-31 (SD)
Chargers, 17-16 (KC)
1968—Chiefs, 27-20 (KC)
Chiefs, 40-3 (SD)
1969—Chiefs, 27-9 (SD)
Chiefs, 27-3 (KC)
1970—Chiefs, 26-14 (KC)
Chargers, 31-13 (SD)
1971—Chargers, 21-14 (SD)
Chiefs, 31-10 (KC)
1972—Chiefs, 26-14 (SD)
Chargers, 27-17 (KC)
1973—Chiefs, 19-0 (SD)
Chiefs, 33-6 (KC)
1974—Chiefs, 24-14 (SD)
Chargers, 14-7 (KC)
1975—Chiefs, 12-10 (SD)
Chargers, 28-20 (KC)
1976—Chargers, 30-16 (KC)
Chiefs, 23-20 (SD)
1977—Chargers, 23-7 (KC)
Chiefs, 21-16 (SD)
1978—Chargers, 29-23 (SD) OT
Chiefs, 23-0 (KC)
1979—Chargers, 20-14 (KC)
Chargers, 28-7 (SD)
1980—Chargers, 24-7 (KC)
Chargers, 20-7 (SD)
1981—Chargers, 42-31 (KC)
Chargers, 22-20 (SD)
1982—Chiefs, 19-12 (KC)
1983—Chargers, 17-14 (KC)
Chargers, 41-38 (SD)

1984—Chiefs, 31-13 (KC)
Chiefs, 42-21 (SD)
1985—Chargers, 31-20 (SD)
Chiefs, 38-34 (KC)
1986—Chiefs, 42-41 (KC)
Chiefs, 24-23 (SD)
1987—Chiefs, 20-13 (KC)
Chargers, 42-21 (SD)
1988—Chargers, 24-23 (KC)
Chargers, 24-13 (SD)
1989—Chargers, 21-6 (SD)
Chargers, 20-13 (KC)
1990—Chiefs, 27-10 (KC)
Chiefs, 24-21 (SD)
1991—Chiefs, 14-13 (SD)
Chiefs, 20-17 (KC) OT
1992—Chiefs, 24-10 (SD)
Chiefs, 16-14 (KC)
***Chargers, 17-0 (SD)
1993—Chiefs, 17-14 (SD)
Chiefs, 28-24 (KC)
1994—Chargers, 20-6 (SD)
Chargers, 14-13 (KC)
1995—Chiefs, 29-23 (KC) OT
Chiefs, 22-7 (SD)
(RS Pts.—Chiefs 1,510, Chargers 1,388)
(PS Pts.—Chargers 17, Chiefs 0)
Franchise in Dallas prior to 1963 and known as Texans
***Franchise in Los Angeles prior to 1961*
****AFC First-Round Playoff*

KANSAS CITY vs. SAN FRANCISCO
RS: 49ers lead series, 4-2
1971—Chiefs, 26-17 (SF)
1975—49ers, 20-3 (KC)
1982—49ers, 26-13 (KC)
1985—49ers, 31-3 (SF)
1991—49ers, 28-14 (SF)
1994—Chiefs, 24-17 (KC)
(RS Pts.—49ers 139, Chiefs 83)

KANSAS CITY vs. SEATTLE
RS: Chiefs lead series, 22-13
1977—Seahawks, 34-31 (KC)
1978—Seahawks, 13-10 (KC)
Seahawks, 23-19 (S)
1979—Chiefs, 24-6 (S)
Chiefs, 37-21 (KC)
1980—Seahawks, 17-16 (KC)
Chiefs, 31-30 (S)
1981—Chiefs, 20-14 (S)
Chiefs, 40-13 (KC)
1983—Chiefs, 17-13 (KC)
Seahawks, 51-48 (S) OT
1984—Seahawks, 45-0 (S)
Chiefs, 34-7 (KC)
1985—Chiefs, 28-7 (KC)
Seahawks, 24-6 (S)
1986—Seahawks, 23-17 (S)
Chiefs, 27-7 (KC)
1987—Seahawks, 43-14 (S)
Chiefs, 41-20 (KC)
1988—Seahawks, 31-10 (S)
Chiefs, 27-24 (KC)
1989—Chiefs, 20-16 (S)
Chiefs, 20-10 (KC)
1990—Seahawks, 19-7 (S)
Seahawks, 17-16 (KC)
1991—Chiefs, 20-13 (KC)
Chiefs, 19-6 (S)
1992—Chiefs, 26-7 (KC)
Chiefs, 24-14 (S)
1993—Chiefs, 31-16 (S)
Chiefs, 34-24 (KC)
1994—Chiefs, 38-23 (KC)
Seahawks, 10-9 (S)
1995—Chiefs, 34-10 (S)
Chiefs, 26-3 (KC)
(RS Pts.—Chiefs 821, Seahawks 654)

KANSAS CITY vs. TAMPA BAY
RS: Chiefs lead series, 5-2
1976—Chiefs, 28-19 (TB)
1978—Buccaneers, 30-13 (KC)
1979—Buccaneers, 3-0 (TB)
1981—Chiefs, 19-10 (KC)
1984—Chiefs, 24-20 (KC)
1986—Chiefs, 27-20 (KC)
1993—Chiefs, 27-3 (TB)
1995—Chiefs, 24-3 (KC)
(RS Pts.—Chiefs 138, Buccaneers 105)

KANSAS CITY vs. WASHINGTON
RS: Chiefs lead series, 4-1
1971—Chiefs, 27-20 (KC)
1976—Chiefs, 33-30 (W)
1983—Redskins, 27-12 (W)
1992—Chiefs, 35-16 (KC)
1995—Chiefs, 24-3 (KC)
(RS Pts.—Chiefs 131, Redskins 96)

MIAMI vs. ARIZONA
RS: Dolphins lead series, 6-0;
See Arizona vs. Miami

MIAMI vs. ATLANTA
RS: Dolphins lead series, 6-1;
See Atlanta vs. Miami

MIAMI vs. BUFFALO
RS: Dolphins lead series, 38-21-1
PS: Bills lead series, 3-0;
See Buffalo vs. Miami

MIAMI vs. CHICAGO
RS: Dolphins lead series, 5-2;
See Chicago vs. Miami

MIAMI vs. CINCINNATI
RS: Dolphins lead series, 11-3
PS: Dolphins lead series, 1-0;
See Cincinnati vs. Miami

MIAMI vs. CLEVELAND
RS: Dolphins lead series, 6-4
PS: Dolphins lead series, 2-0;
See Cleveland vs. Miami

MIAMI vs. DALLAS
RS: Dolphins lead series, 6-1
PS: Cowboys lead series, 1-0;
See Dallas vs. Miami

MIAMI vs. DENVER
RS: Dolphins lead series, 5-2-1;
See Denver vs. Miami

MIAMI vs. DETROIT
RS: Dolphins lead series, 3-2;
See Detroit vs. Miami

MIAMI vs. GREEN BAY
RS: Dolphins lead series, 8-0;
See Green Bay vs. Miami

MIAMI vs. HOUSTON
RS: Series tied, 11-11
PS: Oilers lead series, 1-0;
See Houston vs. Miami

MIAMI vs. INDIANAPOLIS
RS: Dolphins lead series, 35-17
PS: Dolphins lead series, 1-0;
See Indianapolis vs. Miami

MIAMI vs. KANSAS CITY
RS: Chiefs lead series, 10-9
PS: Dolphins lead series, 3-0;
See Kansas City vs. Miami

MIAMI vs. MINNESOTA
RS: Dolphins lead series, 4-2
PS: Dolphins lead series, 1-0
1972—Dolphins, 16-14 (Minn)
1973—*Dolphins, 24-7 (Houston)
1976—Vikings, 29-7 (Mia)
1979—Dolphins, 27-12 (Minn)
1982—Dolphins, 22-14 (Mia)
1988—Dolphins, 24-7 (Mia)
1994—Vikings, 38-35 (M)
(RS Pts.—Dolphins 131, Vikings 114)
(PS Pts.—Dolphins 24, Vikings 7)
**Super Bowl VIII*

MIAMI vs. *NEW ENGLAND
RS: Dolphins lead series, 36-22
PS: Series tied, 1-1
1966—Patriots, 20-14 (M)
1967—Patriots, 41-10 (B)
Dolphins, 41-32 (M)
1968—Dolphins, 34-10 (B)
Dolphins, 38-7 (M)
1969—Dolphins, 17-16 (B)
Patriots, 38-23 (Tampa)
1970—Patriots, 27-14 (B)
Dolphins, 37-20 (M)
1971—Dolphins, 41-3 (M)
Patriots, 34-13 (NE)
1972—Dolphins, 52-0 (M)
Dolphins, 37-21 (NE)
1973—Dolphins, 44-23 (M)
Dolphins, 30-14 (NE)
1974—Patriots, 34-24 (NE)
Dolphins, 34-27 (M)
1975—Dolphins, 22-14 (NE)
Dolphins, 20-7 (M)
1976—Patriots, 30-14 (NE)
Dolphins, 10-3 (M)
1977—Dolphins, 17-5 (M)
Patriots, 14-10 (NE)
1978—Patriots, 33-24 (NE)
Dolphins, 23-3 (M)
1979—Patriots, 28-13 (NE)
Dolphins, 39-24 (M)
1980—Patriots, 34-0 (NE)
Dolphins, 16-13 (M) OT
1981—Dolphins, 30-27 (NE) OT
Dolphins, 24-14 (M)
1982—Patriots, 3-0 (NE)
**Dolphins, 28-13 (M)
1983—Dolphins, 34-24 (M)
Patriots, 17-6 (NE)
1984—Dolphins, 28-7 (M)
Dolphins, 44-24 (NE)
1985—Patriots, 17-13 (NE)
Dolphins, 30-27 (M)
***Patriots, 31-14 (M)
1986—Patriots, 34-7 (NE)
Patriots, 34-27 (M)
1987—Patriots, 28-21 (NE)
Patriots, 24-10 (M)
1988—Patriots, 21-10 (NE)
Patriots, 6-3 (M)
1989—Dolphins, 24-10 (NE)
Dolphins, 31-10 (M)
1990—Dolphins, 27-24 (NE)
Dolphins, 17-10 (M)
1991—Dolphins, 20-10 (NE)
Dolphins, 30-20 (M)
1992—Dolphins, 38-17 (M)
Dolphins, 16-13 (NE) OT
1993—Dolphins, 17-13 (M)
Patriots, 33-27 (NE) OT
1994—Dolphins, 39-35 (M)
Dolphins, 23-3 (NE)
1995—Dolphins, 20-3 (NE)
Patriots, 34-17 (M)
(RS Pts.—Dolphins 1,344, Patriots 1,117)
(PS Pts.—Patriots 44, Dolphins 42)
**Franchise in Boston prior to 1971*
***AFC First-Round Playoff*
****AFC Championship*

MIAMI vs. NEW ORLEANS
RS: Dolphins lead series, 4-3
1970—Dolphins, 21-10 (M)
1974—Dolphins, 21-0 (NO)
1980—Dolphins, 21-16 (M)
1983—Saints, 17-7 (NO)
1986—Dolphins, 31-27 (NO)
1992—Saints, 24-13 (NO)
1995—Saints, 33-30 (NO)
(RS Pts.—Dolphins 144, Saints 127)

MIAMI vs. N.Y. GIANTS
RS: Giants lead series, 2-1
1972—Dolphins, 23-13 (NY)
1990—Giants, 20-3 (NY)
1993—Giants, 19-14 (M)
(RS Pts.—Giants 52, Dolphins 40)

MIAMI vs. N.Y. JETS
RS: Dolphins lead series, 30-29-1
PS: Dolphins lead series, 1-0
1966—Jets, 19-14 (M)
Jets, 30-13 (NY)
1967—Jets, 29-7 (NY)
Jets, 33-14 (M)
1968—Jets, 35-17 (NY)
Jets, 31-7 (M)
1969—Jets, 34-31 (NY)
Jets, 27-9 (M)
1970—Dolphins, 20-6 (NY)
Dolphins, 16-10 (M)
1971—Jets, 14-10 (M)
Dolphins, 30-14 (NY)
1972—Dolphins, 27-17 (NY)
Dolphins, 28-24 (M)
1973—Dolphins, 31-3 (M)
Dolphins, 24-14 (NY)
1974—Dolphins, 21-17 (M)
Jets, 17-14 (NY)
1975—Dolphins, 43-0 (NY)
Dolphins, 27-7 (M)
1976—Dolphins, 16-0 (M)
Dolphins, 27-7 (NY)
1977—Dolphins, 21-17 (M)
Dolphins, 14-10 (NY)
1978—Jets, 33-20 (NY)
Jets, 24-13 (M)
1979—Jets, 33-27 (NY)
Jets, 27-24 (M)
1980—Jets, 17-14 (NY)
Jets, 24-17 (M)
1981—Tie, 28-28 (M) OT
Jets, 16-15 (NY)
1982—Dolphins, 45-28 (NY)
Dolphins, 20-19 (M)
*Dolphins, 14-0 (M)
1983—Dolphins, 32-14 (NY)
Dolphins, 34-14 (M)
1984—Dolphins, 31-17 (NY)
Dolphins, 28-17 (M)
1985—Jets, 23-7 (NY)
Dolphins, 21-17 (M)
1986—Jets, 51-45 (NY) OT
Dolphins, 45-3 (M)
1987—Jets, 37-31 (NY) OT
Dolphins, 37-28 (M)
1988—Jets, 44-30 (M)
Jets, 38-34 (NY)
1989—Jets, 40-33 (M)
Dolphins, 31-23 (NY)
1990—Dolphins, 20-16 (M)
Dolphins, 17-3 (NY)
1991—Jets, 41-23 (NY)
Jets, 23-20 (M) OT
1992—Jets, 26-14 (NY)
Dolphins, 19-17 (M)
1993—Jets, 24-14 (M)
Jets, 27-10 (NY)
1994—Dolphins, 28-14 (M)
Dolphins, 28-24 (NY)
1995—Dolphins, 52-14 (M)
Jets, 17-16 (NY)
(RS Pts.—Dolphins 1,404, Jets 1,276)
(PS Pts.—Dolphins 14, Jets 0)
**AFC Championship*

MIAMI vs. *OAKLAND
RS: Raiders lead series, 14-5-1
PS: Raiders lead series, 2-1
1966—Raiders, 23-14 (M)
Raiders, 21-10 (O)
1967—Raiders, 31-17 (O)
1968—Raiders, 47-21 (M)
1969—Raiders, 20-17 (O)
Tie, 20-20 (M)
1970—Dolphins, 20-13 (M)
**Raiders, 21-14 (O)
1973—Raiders, 12-7 (O)
***Dolphins, 27-10 (M)
1974—**Raiders, 28-26 (O)
1975—Raiders, 31-21 (M)
1978—Dolphins, 23-6 (M)
1979—Raiders, 13-3 (O)
1980—Raiders, 16-10 (O)
1981—Raiders, 33-17 (M)
1983—Raiders, 27-14 (LA)
1984—Raiders, 45-34 (M)
1986—Raiders, 30-28 (M)
1988—Dolphins, 24-14 (LA)
1990—Raiders, 13-10 (M)

1992—Dolphins, 20-7 (M)
1994—Dolphins, 20-17 (M) OT
(RS Pts.—Raiders 439, Dolphins 350)
(PS Pts.—Dolphins 67, Raiders 59)
Franchise in Los Angeles from 1982-1994
***AFC Divisional Playoff*
****AFC Championship*

MIAMI vs. PHILADELPHIA
RS: Dolphins lead series, 6-2
1970—Eagles, 24-17 (P)
1975—Dolphins, 24-16 (M)
1978—Eagles, 17-3 (P)
1981—Dolphins, 13-10 (M)
1984—Dolphins, 24-23 (M)
1987—Dolphins, 28-10 (P)
1990—Dolphins, 23-20 (M) OT
1993—Dolphins, 19-14 (P)
(RS Pts.—Dolphins 151, Eagles 134)

MIAMI vs. PITTSBURGH
RS: Dolphins lead series, 8-6
PS: Dolphins lead series, 2-1
1971—Dolphins, 24-21 (M)
1972—*Dolphins, 21-17 (P)
1973—Dolphins, 30-26 (M)
1976—Steelers, 14-3 (P)
1979—**Steelers, 34-14 (P)
1980—Steelers, 23-10 (P)
1981—Dolphins, 30-10 (M)
1984—Dolphins, 31-7 (P)
*Dolphins, 45-28 (M)
1985—Dolphins, 24-20 (M)
1987—Dolphins, 35-24 (M)
1988—Steelers, 40-24 (P)
1989—Steelers, 34-14 (M)
1990—Dolphins, 28-6 (P)
1993—Steelers, 21-20 (M)
1994—Steelers, 16-13 (P) OT
1995—Dolphins, 23-10 (M)
(RS Pts.—Dolphins 309, Steelers 272)
(PS Pts.—Dolphins 80, Steelers 79)
**AFC Championship*
***AFC Divisional Playoff*

MIAMI vs. *ST. LOUIS
RS: Dolphins lead series, 6-1
1971—Dolphins, 20-14 (LA)
1976—Rams, 31-28 (M)
1980—Dolphins, 35-14 (LA)
1983—Dolphins, 30-14 (M)
1986—Dolphins, 37-31 (LA) OT
1992—Dolphins, 26-10 (M)
1995—Dolphins, 41-22 (StL)
(RS Pts.—Dolphins 217, Rams 136)
**Franchise in Los Angeles prior to 1995*

MIAMI vs. SAN DIEGO
RS: Chargers lead series, 10-6
PS: Series tied, 2-2
1966—Chargers, 44-10 (SD)
1967—Chargers, 24-0 (SD)
Dolphins, 41-24 (M)
1968—Chargers, 34-28 (SD)
1969—Chargers, 21-14 (M)
1972—Dolphins, 24-10 (M)
1974—Dolphins, 28-21 (SD)
1977—Chargers, 14-13 (M)
1978—Dolphins, 28-21 (SD)
1980—Chargers, 27-24 (M) OT
1981—*Chargers, 41-38 (M) OT
1982—**Dolphins, 34-13 (M)
1984—Chargers, 34-28 (SD) OT
1986—Chargers, 50-28 (SD)
1988—Dolphins, 31-28 (M)
1991—Chargers, 38-30 (SD)
1992—*Dolphins, 31-0 (M)
1993—Chargers, 45-20 (SD)
1994—*Chargers, 22-21 (SD)
1995—Chargers, 24-14 (SD)
(RS Pts.—Chargers 449, Dolphins 371)
(PS Pts.—Dolphins 124, Chargers 76)
**AFC Divisional Playoff*
***AFC Second-Round Playoff*

MIAMI vs. SAN FRANCISCO
RS: Dolphins lead series, 4-3
PS: 49ers lead series, 1-0
1973—Dolphins, 21-13 (M)
1977—Dolphins, 19-15 (SF)
1980—Dolphins, 17-13 (M)
1983—Dolphins, 20-17 (SF)
1984—*49ers, 38-16 (Stanford)
1986—49ers, 31-16 (M)
1992—49ers, 27-3 (SF)
1995—49ers, 44-20 (M)
(RS Pts.—49ers 160, Dolphins 116)
(PS Pts.—49ers 38, Dolphins 16)
**Super Bowl XIX*

MIAMI vs. SEATTLE
RS: Dolphins lead series, 4-1
PS: Series tied, 1-1
1977—Dolphins, 31-13 (M)
1979—Dolphins, 19-10 (M)
1983—*Seahawks, 27-20 (M)
1984—*Dolphins, 31-10 (M)
1987—Seahawks, 24-20 (S)
1990—Dolphins, 24-17 (M)
1992—Dolphins, 19-17 (S)
(RS Pts.—Dolphins 113, Seahawks 81)
(PS Pts.—Dolphins 51, Seahawks 37)
**AFC Divisional Playoff*

MIAMI vs. TAMPA BAY
RS: Dolphins lead series, 4-1
1976—Dolphins, 23-20 (TB)
1982—Buccaneers, 23-17 (TB)
1985—Dolphins, 41-38 (M)
1988—Dolphins, 17-14 (TB)
1991—Dolphins, 33-14 (M)
(RS Pts.—Dolphins 131, Buccaneers 109)

MIAMI vs. WASHINGTON
RS: Dolphins lead series, 5-2
PS: Series tied, 1-1
1972—*Dolphins, 14-7 (Oakland)
1974—Redskins, 20-17 (W)
1978—Dolphins, 16-0 (W)
1981—Dolphins, 13-10 (M)
1982—**Redskins, 27-17 (Pasadena)
1984—Dolphins, 35-17 (W)
1987—Dolphins, 23-21 (M)
1990—Redskins, 42-20 (W)
1993—Dolphins, 17-10 (M)
(RS Pts.—Dolphins 141, Redskins 120)
(PS Pts.—Redskins 34, Dolphins 31)
**Super Bowl VII*
***Super Bowl XVII*

MINNESOTA vs. ARIZONA
RS: Cardinals lead series, 8-5
PS: Vikings lead series, 1-0;
See Arizona vs. Minnesota

MINNESOTA vs. ATLANTA
RS: Vikings lead series, 11-6
PS: Vikings lead series, 1-0;
See Atlanta vs. Minnesota

MINNESOTA vs. BUFFALO
RS: Vikings lead series, 5-2;
See Buffalo vs. Minnesota

MINNESOTA vs. CHICAGO
RS: Vikings lead series, 36-31-2
PS: Bears lead series, 1-0;
See Chicago vs. Minnesota

MINNESOTA vs. CINCINNATI
RS: Series tied, 4-4;
See Cincinnati vs. Minnesota

MINNESOTA vs. CLEVELAND
RS: Vikings lead series, 8-3
PS: Vikings lead series, 1-0;
See Cleveland vs. Minnesota

MINNESOTA vs. DALLAS
RS: Cowboys lead series, 9-6
PS: Cowboys lead series, 3-1;
See Dallas vs. Minnesota

MINNESOTA vs. DENVER
RS: Vikings lead series, 5-3;
See Denver vs. Minnesota

MINNESOTA vs. DETROIT
RS: Vikings lead series, 42-25-2;
See Detroit vs. Minnesota

MINNESOTA vs. GREEN BAY
RS: Vikings lead series, 35-33-1;
See Green Bay vs. Minnesota

MINNESOTA vs. HOUSTON
RS: Vikings lead series, 4-3;
See Houston vs. Minnesota

MINNESOTA vs. INDIANAPOLIS
RS: Colts lead series, 11-6-1
PS: Colts lead series, 1-0;
See Indianapolis vs. Minnesota

MINNESOTA vs. KANSAS CITY
RS: Vikings lead series, 3-2
PS: Chiefs lead series, 1-0;
See Kansas City vs. Minnesota

MINNESOTA vs. MIAMI
RS: Dolphins lead series, 4-2
PS: Dolphins lead series, 1-0;
See Miami vs. Minnesota

MINNESOTA vs. *NEW ENGLAND
RS: Patriots lead series, 4-2
1970—Vikings, 35-14 (B)
1974—Patriots, 17-14 (M)
1979—Patriots, 27-23 (NE)
1988—Vikings, 36-6 (M)
1991—Patriots, 26-23 (NE) OT
1994—Patriots, 26-20 (NE) OT
(RS Pts.—Vikings 151, Patriots 116)
**Franchise in Boston prior to 1971*

MINNESOTA vs. NEW ORLEANS
RS: Vikings lead series, 13-6
PS: Vikings lead series, 1-0
1968—Saints, 20-17 (NO)
1970—Vikings, 26-0 (M)
1971—Vikings, 23-10 (NO)
1972—Vikings, 37-6 (M)
1974—Vikings, 29-9 (M)
1975—Vikings, 20-7 (NO)
1976—Vikings, 40-9 (NO)
1978—Saints, 31-24 (NO)
1980—Vikings, 23-20 (NO)
1981—Vikings, 20-10 (M)
1983—Saints, 17-16 (NO)
1985—Saints, 30-23 (M)
1986—Vikings, 33-17 (M)
1987—*Vikings, 44-10 (NO)
1988—Vikings, 45-3 (M)
1990—Vikings, 32-3 (M)
1991—Saints, 26-0 (NO)
1993—Saints, 17-14 (M)
1994—Vikings, 21-20 (M)
1995—Vikings, 43-24 (M)
(RS Pts.—Vikings 486, Saints 279)
(PS Pts.—Vikings 44, Saints 10)
**NFC First-Round Playoff*

MINNESOTA vs. N.Y. GIANTS
RS: Vikings lead series, 7-4
PS: Giants lead series, 1-0
1964—Vikings, 30-21 (NY)
1965—Vikings, 40-14 (M)
1967—Vikings, 27-24 (M)
1969—Giants, 24-23 (NY)
1971—Vikings, 17-10 (NY)
1973—Vikings, 31-7 (New Haven)
1976—Vikings, 24-7 (M)
1986—Giants, 22-20 (M)
1989—Giants, 24-14 (NY)
1990—Giants, 23-15 (NY)
1993—*Giants, 17-10 (NY)
1994—Vikings, 27-10 (NY)
(RS Pts.—Vikings 268, Giants 186)
(PS Pts.—Giants 17, Vikings 10)
**NFC First-Round Playoff*

MINNESOTA vs. N.Y. JETS
RS: Jets lead series, 4-1
1970—Jets, 20-10 (NY)
1975—Vikings, 29-21 (M)
1979—Jets, 14-7 (NY)
1982—Jets, 42-14 (M)
1994—Jets, 31-21 (M)
(RS Pts.—Jets 128, Vikings 81)

MINNESOTA vs. *OAKLAND
RS: Raiders lead series, 6-2
PS: Raiders lead series, 1-0
1973—Vikings, 24-16 (M)
1976—**Raiders, 32-14 (Pasadena)
1977—Raiders, 35-13 (O)
1978—Raiders, 27-20 (O)
1981—Raiders, 36-10 (M)
1984—Raiders, 23-20 (LA)
1987—Vikings, 31-20 (M)
1990—Raiders, 28-24 (M)
1993—Raiders, 24-7 (LA)
(RS Pts.—Raiders 209, Vikings 149)
(PS Pts.—Raiders 32, Vikings 14)
**Franchise in Los Angeles from 1982-1994*
***Super Bowl XI*

MINNESOTA vs. PHILADELPHIA
RS: Vikings lead series, 10-6
PS: Eagles lead series, 1-0
1962—Vikings, 31-21 (M)
1963—Vikings, 34-13 (P)
1968—Vikings, 24-17 (P)
1971—Vikings, 13-0 (P)
1973—Vikings, 28-21 (M)
1976—Vikings, 31-12 (P)
1978—Vikings, 28-27 (M)
1980—Eagles, 42-7 (M)
*Eagles, 31-16 (P)
1981—Vikings, 35-23 (M)
1984—Eagles, 19-17 (P)
1985—Vikings, 28-23 (P)
Eagles, 37-35 (M)
1988—Vikings, 23-21 (M)
1989—Eagles, 10-9 (P)
1990—Eagles, 32-24 (P)
1992—Eagles, 28-17 (P)
(RS Pts.—Vikings 384, Eagles 346)
(PS Pts.—Eagles 31, Vikings 16)
**NFC Divisional Playoff*

MINNESOTA vs. PITTSBURGH
RS: Vikings lead series, 8-4
PS: Steelers lead series, 1-0
1962—Steelers, 39-31 (P)
1964—Vikings, 30-10 (M)
1967—Vikings, 41-27 (P)
1969—Vikings, 52-14 (M)
1972—Steelers, 23-10 (P)
1974—*Steelers, 16-6 (New Orleans)
1976—Vikings, 17-6 (M)
1980—Steelers, 23-17 (M)
1983—Vikings, 17-14 (P)
1986—Vikings, 31-7 (M)
1989—Steelers, 27-14 (P)
1992—Vikings, 6-3 (P)
1995—Vikings, 44-24 (P)
(RS Pts.—Vikings 310, Steelers 217)
(PS Pts.—Steelers 16, Vikings 6)
**Super Bowl IX*

MINNESOTA vs. *ST. LOUIS
RS: Vikings lead series, 15-11-2
PS: Vikings lead series, 5-1
1961—Rams, 31-17 (LA)
Vikings, 42-21 (M)
1962—Vikings, 38-14 (LA)
Tie, 24-24 (M)
1963—Rams, 27-24 (LA)
Vikings, 21-13 (M)
1964—Rams, 22-13 (LA)
Vikings, 34-13 (M)
1965—Vikings, 38-35 (LA)
Vikings, 24-13 (M)
1966—Vikings, 35-7 (M)
Rams, 21-6 (LA)
1967—Rams, 39-3 (LA)
1968—Rams, 31-3 (M)
1969—Vikings, 20-13 (LA)
**Vikings, 23-20 (M)
1970—Vikings, 13-3 (M)
1972—Vikings, 45-41 (LA)
1973—Vikings, 10-9 (M)
1974—Rams, 20-17 (LA)
***Vikings, 14-10 (M)
1976—Tie, 10-10 (M) OT
***Vikings, 24-13 (M)
1977—Rams, 35-3 (LA)
****Vikings, 14-7 (LA)

1978—Rams, 34-17 (M)
****Rams, 34-10 (LA)
1979—Rams, 27-21 (LA) OT
1985—Rams, 13-10 (LA)
1987—Vikings, 21-16 (LA)
1988—*****Vikings, 28-17 (M)
1989—Vikings, 23-21 (M) OT
1991—Vikings, 20-14 (M)
1992—Vikings, 31-17 (LA)
(RS Pts.—Rams 584, Vikings 583)
(PS Pts.—Vikings 113, Rams 101)
Franchise in Los Angeles prior to 1995
**Conference Championship*
***NFC Championship*
****NFC Divisional Playoff*
*****NFC First-Round Playoff*

MINNESOTA vs. SAN DIEGO
RS: Chargers lead series, 4-3
1971—Chargers, 30-14 (SD)
1975—Vikings, 28-13 (M)
1978—Chargers, 13-7 (M)
1981—Vikings, 33-31 (SD)
1984—Chargers, 42-13 (M)
1985—Vikings, 21-17 (M)
1993—Chargers, 30-17 (M)
(RS Pts.—Chargers 176, Vikings 133)

MINNESOTA vs. SAN FRANCISCO
RS: Series tied, 16-16-1
PS: 49ers lead series, 3-1
1961—49ers, 38-24 (M)
49ers, 38-28 (SF)
1962—49ers, 21-7 (SF)
49ers, 35-12 (M)
1963—Vikings, 24-20 (SF)
Vikings, 45-14 (M)
1964—Vikings, 27-22 (SF)
Vikings, 24-7 (M)
1965—Vikings, 42-41 (SF)
49ers, 45-24 (M)
1966—Tie, 20-20 (SF)
Vikings, 28-3 (SF)
1967—49ers, 27-21 (M)
1968—Vikings, 30-20 (SF)
1969—Vikings, 10-7 (M)
1970—*49ers, 17-14 (M)
1971—49ers, 13-9 (M)
1972—49ers, 20-17 (SF)
1973—Vikings, 17-13 (SF)
1975—Vikings, 27-17 (M)
1976—49ers, 20-16 (SF)
1977—Vikings, 28-27 (M)
1979—Vikings, 28-22 (M)
1983—49ers, 48-17 (M)
1984—49ers, 51-7 (SF)
1985—Vikings, 28-21 (M)
1986—Vikings, 27-24 (SF) OT
1987—*Vikings, 36-24 (SF)
1988—49ers, 24-21 (SF)
*49ers, 34-9 (SF)
1989—*49ers, 41-13 (SF)
1990—49ers, 20-17 (M)
1991—Vikings, 17-14 (M)
1992—49ers, 20-17 (M)
1993—49ers, 38-19 (SF)
1994—Vikings, 21-14 (M)
1995—49ers, 37-30 (SF)
(RS Pts.—49ers 801, Vikings 729)
(PS Pts.—49ers 116, Vikings 72)
NFC Divisional Playoff

MINNESOTA vs. SEATTLE
RS: Seahawks lead series, 3-2
1976—Vikings, 27-21 (M)
1978—Seahawks, 29-28 (S)
1984—Seahawks, 20-12 (M)
1987—Seahawks, 28-17 (S)
1990—Vikings, 24-21 (S)
(RS Pts.—Seahawks 119, Vikings 108)

MINNESOTA vs. TAMPA BAY
RS: Vikings lead series, 25-11
1977—Vikings, 9-3 (TB)
1978—Buccaneers, 16-10 (M)
Vikings, 24-7 (TB)
1979—Buccaneers, 12-10 (M)
Vikings, 23-22 (TB)
1980—Vikings, 38-30 (M)
Vikings, 21-10 (TB)
1981—Buccaneers, 21-13 (TB)
Vikings, 25-10 (M)
1982—Vikings, 17-10 (M)
1983—Vikings, 19-16 (TB) OT
Buccaneers, 17-12 (M)
1984—Buccaneers, 35-31 (TB)
Vikings, 27-24 (M)
1985—Vikings, 31-16 (TB)
Vikings, 26-7 (M)
1986—Vikings, 23-10 (TB)
Vikings, 45-13 (M)
1987—Buccaneers, 20-10 (TB)
Vikings, 23-17 (M)
1988—Vikings, 14-13 (M)
Vikings, 49-20 (TB)
1989—Vikings, 17-3 (M)
Vikings, 24-10 (TB)
1990—Buccaneers, 23-20 (M) OT
Buccaneers, 26-13 (TB)
1991—Vikings, 28-13 (M)
Vikings, 26-24 (TB)
1992—Vikings, 26-20 (M)
Vikings, 35-7 (TB)
1993—Vikings, 15-0 (M)
Buccaneers, 23-10 (TB)
1994—Vikings, 36-13 (TB)
Buccaneers, 20-17 (M) OT
1995—Buccaneers, 20-17 (TB) OT
Vikings, 31-17 (M)
(RS Pts.—Vikings 815, Buccaneers 568)

MINNESOTA vs. WASHINGTON
RS: Redskins lead series, 6-4
PS: Redskins lead series, 3-2
1968—Vikings, 27-14 (M)
1970—Vikings, 19-10 (W)
1972—Redskins, 24-21 (M)
1973—*Vikings, 27-20 (M)
1975—Redskins, 31-30 (W)
1976—*Vikings, 35-20 (M)
1980—Vikings, 39-14 (W)
1982—**Redskins, 21-7 (W)
1984—Redskins, 31-17 (M)
1986—Redskins, 44-38 (W) OT
1987—Redskins, 27-24 (M) OT
***Redskins, 17-10 (W)
1992—Redskins, 15-13 (M)
****Redskins, 24-7 (M)
1993—Vikings, 14-9 (W)
(RS Pts.—Vikings 242, Redskins 219)
(PS Pts.—Redskins 102, Vikings 86)
NFC Divisional Playoff
**NFC Second-Round Playoff*
***NFC Championship*
****NFC First-Round Playoff*

NEW ENGLAND vs. ARIZONA
RS: Cardinals lead series, 6-2;
See Arizona vs. New England

NEW ENGLAND vs. ATLANTA
RS: Falcons lead series, 5-3;
See Atlanta vs. New England

NEW ENGLAND vs. BUFFALO
RS: Patriots lead series, 36-34-1
PS: Patriots lead series, 1-0;
See Buffalo vs. New England

NEW ENGLAND vs. CAROLINA
RS: Panthers lead series, 1-0;
See Carolina vs. New England

NEW ENGLAND vs. CHICAGO
RS: Patriots lead series, 4-2
PS: Bears lead series, 1-0;
See Chicago vs. New England

NEW ENGLAND vs. CINCINNATI
RS: Patriots lead series, 9-7;
See Cincinnati vs. New England

NEW ENGLAND vs. CLEVELAND
RS: Browns lead series, 10-4
PS: Browns lead series, 1-0;
See Cleveland vs. New England

NEW ENGLAND vs. DALLAS
RS: Cowboys lead series, 6-0;
See Dallas vs. New England

NEW ENGLAND vs. DENVER
RS: Broncos lead series, 17-12
PS: Broncos lead series, 1-0;
See Denver vs. New England

NEW ENGLAND vs. DETROIT
RS: Series tied, 3-3;
See Detroit vs. New England

NEW ENGLAND vs. GREEN BAY
RS: Patriots lead series, 3-2;
See Green Bay vs. New England

NEW ENGLAND vs. HOUSTON
RS: Patriots lead series, 17-14-1
PS: Oilers lead series, 1-0;
See Houston vs. New England

NEW ENGLAND vs. INDIANAPOLIS
RS: Patriots lead series, 29-22;
See Indianapolis vs. New England

NEW ENGLAND vs. KANSAS CITY
RS: Chiefs lead series, 14-7-3;
See Kansas City vs. New England

NEW ENGLAND vs. MIAMI
RS: Dolphins lead series, 36-22
PS: Series tied, 1-1;
See Miami vs. New England

NEW ENGLAND vs. MINNESOTA
RS: Patriots lead series, 4-2;
See Minnesota vs. New England

NEW ENGLAND vs. NEW ORLEANS
RS: Patriots lead series, 5-3
1972—Patriots, 17-10 (NO)
1976—Patriots, 27-6 (NE)
1980—Patriots, 38-27 (NO)
1983—Patriots, 7-0 (NE)
1986—Patriots, 21-20 (NO)
1989—Saints, 28-24 (NE)
1992—Saints, 31-14 (NE)
1995—Saints, 31-17 (NE)
(RS Pts.—Patriots 165, Saints 153)

***NEW ENGLAND vs. N.Y. GIANTS**
RS: Giants lead series, 3-1
1970—Giants, 16-0 (B)
1974—Patriots, 28-20 (New Haven)
1987—Giants, 17-10 (NY)
1990—Giants, 13-10 (NE)
(RS Pts.—Giants 66, Patriots 48)
Franchise in Boston prior to 1971

***NEW ENGLAND vs. **N.Y. JETS**
RS: Jets lead series, 39-31-1
PS: Patriots lead series, 1-0
1960—Patriots, 28-24 (NY)
Patriots, 38-21 (B)
1961—Titans, 21-20 (B)
Titans, 37-30 (NY)
1962—Patriots, 43-14 (NY)
Patriots, 24-17 (B)
1963—Patriots, 38-14 (B)
Jets, 31-24 (NY)
1964—Patriots, 26-10 (B)
Jets, 35-14 (NY)
1965—Jets, 30-20 (B)
Patriots, 27-23 (NY)
1966—Tie, 24-24 (B)
Jets, 38-28 (NY)
1967—Jets, 30-23 (NY)
Jets, 29-24 (B)
1968—Jets, 47-31 (Birmingham)
Jets, 48-14 (NY)
1969—Jets, 23-14 (B)
Jets, 23-17 (NY)
1970—Jets, 31-21 (B)
Jets, 17-3 (NY)
1971—Patriots, 20-0 (NE)
Jets, 13-6 (NY)
1972—Jets, 41-13 (NE)
Jets, 34-10 (NY)
1973—Jets, 9-7 (NE)
Jets, 33-13 (NY)
1974—Patriots, 24-0 (NY)
Jets, 21-16 (NE)
1975—Jets, 36-7 (NY)
Jets, 30-28 (NE)
1976—Patriots, 41-7 (NE)
Patriots, 38-24 (NY)
1977—Jets, 30-27 (NY)
Patriots, 24-13 (NE)
1978—Patriots, 55-21 (NE)
Patriots, 19-17 (NY)
1979—Patriots, 56-3 (NE)
Jets, 27-26 (NY)
1980—Patriots, 21-11 (NY)
Patriots, 34-21 (NE)
1981—Jets, 28-24 (NY)
Jets, 17-6 (NE)
1982—Jets, 31-7 (NE)
1983—Patriots, 23-13 (NE)
Jets, 26-3 (NY)
1984—Patriots, 28-21 (NY)
Patriots, 30-20 (NE)
1985—Patriots, 20-13 (NE)
Jets, 16-13 (NY) OT
***Patriots, 26-14 (NY)
1986—Patriots, 20-6 (NY)
Jets, 31-24 (NE)
1987—Jets, 43-24 (NY)
Patriots, 42-20 (NE)
1988—Patriots, 28-3 (NE)
Patriots, 14-13 (NY)
1989—Patriots, 27-24 (NY)
Jets, 27-26 (NE)
1990—Jets, 37-13 (NE)
Jets, 42-7 (NY)
1991—Jets, 28-21 (NE)
Patriots, 6-3 (NY)
1992—Jets, 30-21 (NY)
Patriots, 24-3 (NE)
1993—Jets, 45-7 (NY)
Jets, 6-0 (NE)
1994—Jets, 24-17 (NY)
Patriots, 24-13 (NE)
1995—Patriots, 20-7 (NY)
Patriots, 31-28 (NE)
(RS Pts.—Jets 1,596, Patriots 1,566)
(PS Pts.—Patriots 26, Jets 14)
Franchise in Boston prior to 1971
**Jets known as Titans prior to 1963*
***AFC First-Round Playoff*

NEW ENGLAND vs. *OAKLAND
RS: Raiders lead series, 13-12-1
PS: Series tied, 1-1
1960—Raiders, 27-14 (O)
Patriots, 34-28 (B)
1961—Patriots, 20-17 (B)
Patriots, 35-21 (O)
1962—Patriots, 26-16 (B)
Raiders, 20-0 (O)
1963—Patriots, 20-14 (O)
Patriots, 20-14 (B)
1964—Patriots, 17-14 (O)
Tie, 43-43 (B)
1965—Raiders, 24-10 (B)
Raiders, 30-21 (O)
1966—Patriots, 24-21 (B)
1967—Raiders, 35-7 (O)
Raiders, 48-14 (B)
1968—Raiders, 41-10 (O)
1969—Raiders, 38-23 (B)
1971—Patriots, 20-6 (NE)
1974—Raiders, 41-26 (O)
1976—Patriots, 48-17 (NE)
***Raiders, 24-21 (O)
1978—Patriots, 21-14 (O)
1981—Raiders, 27-17 (O)
1985—Raiders, 35-20 (NE)
***Patriots, 27-20 (LA)
1987—Patriots, 26-23 (NE)
1989—Raiders, 24-21 (LA)
1994—Raiders, 21-17 (NE)
(RS Pts.—Raiders 659, Patriots 554)
(PS Pts.—Patriots 48, Raiders 44)
Franchise in Los Angeles from 1982-1994
**Franchise in Boston prior to 1971*
***AFC Divisional Playoff*

NEW ENGLAND vs. PHILADELPHIA

RS: Eagles lead series, 5-2
1973—Eagles, 24-23 (P)
1977—Patriots, 14-6 (NE)
1978—Patriots, 24-14 (NE)
1981—Eagles, 13-3 (P)
1984—Eagles, 27-17 (P)
1987—Eagles, 34-31 (NE) OT
1990—Eagles, 48-20 (P)
(RS Pts.—Eagles 166, Patriots 132)

NEW ENGLAND vs. PITTSBURGH
RS: Steelers lead series, 10-3
1972—Steelers, 33-3 (P)
1974—Steelers, 21-17 (NE)
1976—Patriots, 30-27 (P)
1979—Steelers, 16-13 (NE) OT
1981—Steelers, 27-21 (P) OT
1982—Steelers, 37-14 (P)
1983—Patriots, 28-23 (P)
1986—Patriots, 34-0 (P)
1989—Steelers, 28-10 (P)
1990—Steelers, 24-3 (P)
1991—Steelers, 20-6 (P)
1993—Steelers, 17-14 (P)
1995—Steelers, 41-27 (P)
(RS Pts.—Steelers 314, Patriots 220)

NEW ENGLAND vs. *ST. LOUIS
RS: Series tied, 3-3
1974—Patriots, 20-14 (NE)
1980—Rams, 17-14 (NE)
1983—Patriots, 21-7 (LA)
1986—Patriots, 30-28 (LA)
1989—Rams, 24-20 (NE)
1992—Rams, 14-0 (LA)
(RS Pts.—Patriots 105, Rams 104)
Franchise in Los Angeles prior to 1995

***NEW ENGLAND vs. **SAN DIEGO**
RS: Patriots lead series, 14-11-2
PS: Chargers lead series, 1-0
1960—Patriots, 35-0 (LA)
Chargers, 45-16 (B)
1961—Chargers, 38-27 (B)
Patriots, 41-0 (SD)
1962—Patriots, 24-20 (B)
Patriots, 20-14 (SD)
1963—Chargers, 17-13 (SD)
Chargers, 7-6 (B)
***Chargers, 51-10 (SD)
1964—Patriots, 33-28 (SD)
Chargers, 26-17 (B)
1965—Tie, 10-10 (B)
Patriots, 22-6 (SD)
1966—Chargers, 24-0 (SD)
Patriots, 35-17 (B)
1967—Chargers, 28-14 (SD)
Tie, 31-31 (SD)
1968—Chargers, 27-17 (B)
1969—Chargers, 13-10 (B)
Chargers, 28-18 (SD)
1970—Chargers, 16-14 (B)
1973—Patriots, 30-14 (NE)
1975—Patriots, 33-19 (SD)
1977—Patriots, 24-20 (SD)
1978—Patriots, 28-23 (NE)
1979—Patriots, 27-21 (NE)
1983—Patriots, 37-21 (NE)
1994—Patriots, 23-17 (NE)
(RS Pts.—Patriots 605, Chargers 530)
(PS Pts.—Chargers 51, Patriots 10)
Franchise in Boston prior to 1971
***Franchise in Los Angeles prior to 1961*
****AFL Championship*

NEW ENGLAND vs. SAN FRANCISCO
RS: 49ers lead series, 7-1
1971—49ers, 27-10 (SF)
1975—Patriots, 24-16 (NE)
1980—49ers, 21-17 (SF)
1983—49ers, 33-13 (NE)
1986—49ers, 29-24 (NE)
1989—49ers, 37-20 (SF)
1992—49ers, 24-12 (NE)
1995—49ers, 28-3 (SF)
(RS Pts.—49ers 215, Patriots 123)

NEW ENGLAND vs. SEATTLE
RS: Seahawks lead series, 7-6
1977—Patriots, 31-0 (NE)
1980—Patriots, 37-31 (S)
1982—Patriots, 16-0 (S)
1983—Seahawks, 24-6 (S)
1984—Patriots, 38-23 (NE)
1985—Patriots, 20-13 (S)
1986—Seahawks, 38-31 (NE)
1988—Patriots, 13-7 (NE)
1989—Seahawks, 24-3 (NE)
1990—Seahawks, 33-20 (NE)
1992—Seahawks, 10-6 (NE)
1993—Seahawks, 17-14 (NE)
Seahawks, 10-9 (S)
(RS Pts.—Patriots 244, Seahawks 230)

NEW ENGLAND vs. TAMPA BAY
RS: Patriots lead series, 3-0
1976—Patriots, 31-14 (TB)
1985—Patriots, 32-14 (TB)
1988—Patriots, 10-7 (NE) OT
(RS Pts.—Patriots 73, Buccaneers 35)

NEW ENGLAND vs. WASHINGTON
RS: Redskins lead series, 4-1
1972—Patriots, 24-23 (NE)
1978—Redskins, 16-14 (NE)
1981—Redskins, 24-22 (W)
1984—Redskins, 26-10 (NE)
1990—Redskins, 25-10 (NE)
(RS Pts.—Redskins 114, Patriots 80)

NEW ORLEANS vs. ARIZONA
RS: Cardinals lead series, 10-9;
See Arizona vs. New Orleans

NEW ORLEANS vs. ATLANTA
RS: Falcons lead series, 29-24
PS: Falcons lead series, 1-0;
See Atlanta vs. New Orleans

NEW ORLEANS vs. BUFFALO
RS: Bills lead series, 3-2;
See Buffalo vs. New Orleans

NEW ORLEANS vs. CAROLINA
RS: Series tied, 1-1
See Carolina vs. New Orleans

NEW ORLEANS vs. CHICAGO
RS: Bears lead series, 9-6
PS: Bears lead series, 1-0;
See Chicago vs. New Orleans

NEW ORLEANS vs. CINCINNATI
RS: Saints lead series, 5-3;
See Cincinnati vs. New Orleans

NEW ORLEANS vs. CLEVELAND
RS: Browns lead series, 9-3;
See Cleveland vs. New Orleans

NEW ORLEANS vs. DALLAS
RS: Cowboys lead series, 14-3;
See Dallas vs. New Orleans

NEW ORLEANS vs. DENVER
RS: Broncos lead series, 4-2;
See Denver vs. New Orleans

NEW ORLEANS vs. DETROIT
RS: Saints lead series, 7-6-1;
See Detroit vs. New Orleans

NEW ORLEANS vs. GREEN BAY
RS: Packers lead series, 13-4;
See Green Bay vs. New Orleans

NEW ORLEANS vs. HOUSTON
RS: Saints lead series, 4-3-1;
See Houston vs. New Orleans

NEW ORLEANS vs. INDIANAPOLIS
RS: Series tied, 3-3;
See Indianapolis vs. New Orleans

NEW ORLEANS vs. KANSAS CITY
RS: Series tied, 3-3;
See Kansas City vs. New Orleans

NEW ORLEANS vs. MIAMI
RS: Dolphins lead series, 4-3;
See Miami vs. New Orleans

NEW ORLEANS vs. MINNESOTA
RS: Vikings lead series, 13-6
PS: Vikings lead series, 1-0;
See Minnesota vs. New Orleans

NEW ORLEANS vs. NEW ENGLAND
RS: Patriots lead series, 5-3;
See New England vs. New Orleans

NEW ORLEANS vs. N.Y. GIANTS
RS: Giants lead series, 10-7
1967—Giants, 27-21 (NY)
1968—Giants, 38-21 (NY)
1969—Saints, 25-24 (NY)
1970—Saints, 14-10 (NO)
1972—Giants, 45-21 (NY)
1975—Giants, 28-14 (NY)
1978—Saints, 28-17 (NO)
1979—Saints, 24-14 (NO)
1981—Giants, 20-7 (NY)
1984—Saints, 10-3 (NY)
1985—Giants, 21-13 (NO)
1986—Giants, 20-17 (NY)
1987—Saints, 23-14 (NO)
1988—Giants, 13-12 (NO)
1993—Giants, 24-14 (NO)
1994—Saints, 27-22 (NO)
1995—Giants, 45-29 (NY)
(RS Pts.—Giants 385, Saints 320)

NEW ORLEANS vs. N.Y. JETS
RS: Series tied, 4-4
1972—Jets, 18-17 (NY)
1977—Jets, 16-13 (NO)
1980—Saints, 21-20 (NY)
1983—Jets, 31-28 (NO)
1986—Jets, 28-23 (NY)
1989—Saints, 29-14 (NO)
1992—Saints, 20-0 (NY)
1995—Saints, 12-0 (NY)
(RS Pts.—Saints 163, Jets 127)

NEW ORLEANS vs. *OAKLAND
RS: Raiders lead series, 4-2-1
1971—Tie, 21-21 (NO)
1975—Raiders, 48-10 (O)
1979—Raiders, 42-35 (NO)
1985—Raiders, 23-13 (LA)
1988—Saints, 20-6 (NO)
1991—Saints, 27-0 (NO)
1994—Raiders, 24-19 (LA)
(RS Pts.—Raiders 164, Saints 145)
Franchise in Los Angeles from 1982-1994

NEW ORLEANS vs. PHILADELPHIA
RS: Eagles lead series, 12-8
PS: Eagles lead series, 1-0
1967—Saints, 31-24 (NO)
Eagles, 48-21 (P)
1968—Eagles, 29-17 (P)
1969—Eagles, 13-10 (P)
Saints, 26-17 (NO)
1972—Saints, 21-3 (NO)
1974—Saints, 14-10 (NO)
1977—Eagles, 28-7 (P)
1978—Eagles, 24-17 (NO)
1979—Eagles, 26-14 (NO)
1980—Eagles, 34-21 (NO)
1981—Eagles, 31-14 (NO)
1983—Saints, 20-17 (P) OT
1985—Saints, 23-21 (NO)
1987—Eagles, 27-17 (P)
1989—Saints, 30-20 (NO)
1991—Saints, 13-6 (P)
1992—Eagles, 15-13 (P)
*Eagles, 36-20 (NO)
1993—Eagles, 37-26 (P)
1995—Eagles, 15-10 (NO)
(RS Pts.—Eagles 445, Saints 365)
(PS Pts.—Eagles 36, Saints 20)
NFC First-Round Playoff

NEW ORLEANS vs. PITTSBURGH
RS: Steelers lead series, 6-5
1967—Steelers, 14-10 (NO)
1968—Saints, 16-12 (P)
Saints, 24-14 (NO)
1969—Saints, 27-24 (NO)
1974—Steelers, 28-7 (NO)
1978—Steelers, 20-14 (P)
1981—Steelers, 20-6 (NO)
1984—Saints, 27-24 (NO)
1987—Saints, 20-16 (P)
1990—Steelers, 9-6 (NO)
1993—Steelers, 37-14 (P)
(RS Pts.—Steelers 218, Saints 171)

NEW ORLEANS vs. *ST. LOUIS
RS: Rams lead series, 28-24
1967—Rams, 27-13 (NO)
1969—Rams, 36-17 (LA)
1970—Rams, 30-17 (NO)
Rams, 34-16 (LA)
1971—Saints, 24-20 (NO)
Rams, 45-28 (LA)
1972—Rams, 34-14 (LA)
Saints, 19-16 (NO)
1973—Rams, 29-7 (LA)
Rams, 24-13 (NO)
1974—Rams, 24-0 (LA)
Saints, 20-7 (NO)
1975—Rams, 38-14 (LA)
Rams, 14-7 (NO)
1976—Rams, 16-10 (NO)
Rams, 33-14 (LA)
1977—Rams, 14-7 (LA)
Saints, 27-26 (NO)
1978—Rams, 26-20 (NO)
Saints, 10-3 (LA)
1979—Rams, 35-17 (NO)
Saints, 29-14 (LA)
1980—Rams, 45-31 (LA)
Rams, 27-7 (NO)
1981—Saints, 23-17 (NO)
Saints, 21-13 (LA)
1983—Rams, 30-27 (LA)
Rams, 26-24 (NO)
1984—Rams, 28-10 (NO)
Rams, 34-21 (LA)
1985—Rams, 28-10 (LA)
Saints, 29-3 (NO)
1986—Saints, 6-0 (NO)
Rams, 26-13 (LA)
1987—Saints, 37-10 (NO)
Saints, 31-14 (LA)
1988—Rams, 12-10 (NO)
Saints, 14-10 (LA)
1989—Saints, 40-21 (LA)
Rams, 20-17 (NO) OT
1990—Saints, 24-20 (LA)
Saints, 20-17 (NO)
1991—Saints, 24-7 (NO)
Saints, 24-17 (LA)
1992—Saints, 13-10 (NO)
Saints, 37-14 (LA)
1993—Saints, 37-6 (LA)
Rams, 23-20 (NO)
1994—Saints, 37-34 (NO)
Saints, 31-15 (LA)
1995—Rams, 17-13 (StL)
Saints, 19-10 (NO)
(RS Pts.—Rams 1,099, Saints 1,013)
Franchise in Los Angeles prior to 1995

NEW ORLEANS vs. SAN DIEGO
RS: Chargers lead series, 5-1
1973—Chargers, 17-14 (SD)
1977—Chargers, 14-0 (NO)
1979—Chargers, 35-0 (NO)
1988—Saints, 23-17 (SD)
1991—Chargers, 24-21 (SD)
1994—Chargers, 36-22 (NO)
(RS Pts.—Chargers 143, Saints 80)

NEW ORLEANS vs. SAN FRANCISCO
RS: 49ers lead series, 36-15-2
1967—49ers, 27-13 (SF)
1969—Saints, 43-38 (NO)
1970—Tie, 20-20 (SF)
49ers, 38-27 (NO)
1971—49ers, 38-20 (NO)
Saints, 26-20 (SF)
1972—49ers, 37-2 (NO)
Tie, 20-20 (SF)
1973—49ers, 40-0 (SF)
Saints, 16-10 (NO)
1974—49ers, 17-13 (NO)
49ers, 35-21 (SF)
1975—49ers, 35-21 (SF)
49ers, 16-6 (NO)

1976—49ers, 33-3 (SF)
49ers, 27-7 (NO)
1977—49ers, 10-7 (NO) OT
49ers, 20-17 (SF)
1978—Saints, 14-7 (SF)
Saints, 24-13 (NO)
1979—Saints, 30-21 (SF)
Saints, 31-20 (NO)
1980—49ers, 26-23 (NO)
49ers, 38-35 (SF) OT
1981—49ers, 21-14 (SF)
49ers, 21-17 (NO)
1982—Saints, 23-20 (SF)
1983—49ers, 32-13 (NO)
49ers, 27-0 (SF)
1984—49ers, 30-20 (SF)
49ers, 35-3 (NO)
1985—Saints, 20-17 (SF)
49ers, 31-19 (NO)
1986—49ers, 26-17 (SF)
Saints, 23-10 (NO)
1987—49ers, 24-22 (NO)
Saints, 26-24 (SF)
1988—49ers, 34-33 (NO)
49ers, 30-17 (SF)
1989—49ers, 24-20 (NO)
49ers, 31-13 (SF)
1990—49ers, 13-12 (NO)
Saints, 13-10 (SF)
1991—Saints, 10-3 (NO)
49ers, 38-24 (SF)
1992—49ers, 16-10 (NO)
49ers, 21-20 (SF)
1993—Saints, 16-13 (NO)
49ers, 42-7 (SF)
1994—49ers, 24-13 (SF)
49ers, 35-14 (NO)
1995—49ers, 24-22 (NO)
Saints, 11-7 (SF)
(RS Pts.—49ers 1,289, Saints 911)

NEW ORLEANS vs. SEATTLE
RS: Saints lead series, 3-2
1976—Saints, 51-27 (S)
1979—Seahawks, 38-24 (S)
1985—Seahawks, 27-3 (NO)
1988—Saints, 20-19 (S)
1991—Saints, 27-24 (NO)
(RS Pts.—Seahawks 135, Saints 125)

NEW ORLEANS vs. TAMPA BAY
RS: Saints lead series, 12-4
1977—Buccaneers, 33-14 (NO)
1978—Saints, 17-10 (TB)
1979—Saints, 42-14 (TB)
1981—Buccaneers, 31-14 (NO)
1982—Buccaneers, 13-10 (NO)
1983—Saints, 24-21 (TB)
1984—Saints, 17-13 (NO)
1985—Saints, 20-13 (NO)
1986—Saints, 38-7 (NO)
1987—Saints, 44-34 (NO)
1988—Saints, 13-9 (NO)
1989—Buccaneers, 20-10 (TB)
1990—Saints, 35-7 (NO)
1991—Saints, 23-7 (NO)
1992—Saints, 23-21 (NO)
1994—Saints, 9-7 (TB)
(RS Pts.—Saints 353, Buccaneers 260)

NEW ORLEANS vs. WASHINGTON
RS: Redskins lead series, 12-5
1967—Redskins, 30-10 (NO)
Saints, 30-14 (W)
1968—Saints, 37-17 (NO)
1969—Redskins, 26-20 (NO)
Redskins, 17-14 (W)
1971—Redskins, 24-14 (W)
1973—Saints, 19-3 (NO)
1975—Redskins, 41-3 (W)
1979—Saints, 14-10 (W)
1980—Redskins, 22-14 (W)
1982—Redskins, 27-10 (NO)
1986—Redskins, 14-6 (NO)
1988—Redskins, 27-24 (W)
1989—Redskins, 16-14 (NO)
1990—Redskins, 31-17 (W)
1992—Saints, 20-3 (NO)
1994—Redskins, 38-24 (NO)
(RS Pts.—Redskins 360, Saints 290)

N.Y. GIANTS vs. ARIZONA
RS: Giants lead series, 68-36-2;
See Arizona vs. N.Y. Giants

N.Y. GIANTS vs. ATLANTA
RS: Series tied, 6-6;
See Atlanta vs. N.Y. Giants

N.Y. GIANTS vs. BUFFALO
RS: Bills lead series, 4-2
PS: Giants lead series, 1-0;
See Buffalo vs. N.Y. Giants

N.Y. GIANTS vs. CHICAGO
RS: Bears lead series, 25-16-2
PS: Bears lead series, 5-3;
See Chicago vs. N.Y. Giants

N.Y. GIANTS vs. CINCINNATI
RS: Bengals lead series, 4-1;
See Cincinnati vs. N.Y. Giants

N.Y. GIANTS vs. CLEVELAND
RS: Browns lead series, 25-17-2
PS: Series tied, 1-1;
See Cleveland vs. N.Y. Giants

N.Y. GIANTS vs. DALLAS
RS: Cowboys lead series, 43-22-2;
See Dallas vs. N.Y. Giants

N.Y. GIANTS vs. DENVER
RS: Series tied, 3-3
PS: Giants lead series, 1-0;
See Denver vs. N.Y. Giants

N.Y. GIANTS vs. DETROIT
RS: Lions lead series, 18-15-1
PS: Lions lead series, 1-0;
See Detroit vs. N.Y. Giants

N.Y. GIANTS vs. GREEN BAY
RS: Packers lead series, 22-20-2
PS: Packers lead series, 4-1;
See Green Bay vs. N.Y. Giants

N.Y. GIANTS vs. HOUSTON
RS: Giants lead series, 5-0;
See Houston vs. N.Y. Giants

N.Y. GIANTS vs. INDIANAPOLIS
RS: Series tied, 5-5
PS: Colts lead series, 2-0;
See Indianapolis vs. N.Y. Giants

N.Y. GIANTS vs. KANSAS CITY
RS: Giants lead series, 6-2;
See Kansas City vs. N.Y. Giants

N.Y. GIANTS vs. MIAMI
RS: Giants lead series, 2-1;
See Miami vs. N.Y. Giants

N.Y. GIANTS vs. MINNESOTA
RS: Vikings lead series, 7-4
PS: Giants lead series, 1-0;
See Minnesota vs. N.Y. Giants

N.Y. GIANTS vs. NEW ENGLAND
RS: Giants lead series, 3-1;
See New England vs. N.Y. Giants

N.Y. GIANTS vs. NEW ORLEANS
RS: Giants lead series, 10-7;
See New Orleans vs. N.Y. Giants

N.Y. GIANTS vs. N.Y. JETS
RS: Jets lead series, 4-3
1970—Giants, 22-10 (NYJ)
1974—Jets, 26-20 (New Haven) OT
1981—Jets, 26-7 (NYG)
1984—Giants, 20-10 (NYJ)
1987—Giants, 20-7 (NYG)
1988—Jets, 27-21 (NYJ)
1993—Jets, 10-6 (NYG)
(RS Pts.—Giants 116, Jets 116)

N.Y. GIANTS vs. *OAKLAND
RS: Raiders lead series, 5-2
1973—Raiders, 42-0 (O)
1980—Raiders, 33-17 (NY)
1983—Raiders, 27-12 (LA)
1986—Giants, 14-9 (LA)
1989—Giants, 34-17 (NY)
1992—Raiders, 13-10 (LA)
1995—Raiders, 17-13 (NY)
(RS Pts.—Raiders 158, Giants 100)
**Franchise in Los Angeles from 1982-1994*

N.Y. GIANTS vs. PHILADELPHIA
RS: Giants lead series, 64-56-2
PS: Giants lead series, 1-0
1933—Giants, 56-0 (NY)
Giants, 20-14 (P)
1934—Giants, 17-0 (NY)
Eagles, 6-0 (P)
1935—Giants, 10-0 (NY)
Giants, 21-14 (P)
1936—Eagles, 10-7 (P)
Giants, 21-17 (NY)
1937—Giants, 16-7 (P)
Giants, 21-0 (NY)
1938—Eagles, 14-10 (P)
Giants, 17-7 (NY)
1939—Giants, 13-3 (P)
Giants, 27-10 (NY)
1940—Giants, 20-14 (P)
Giants, 17-7 (NY)
1941—Giants, 24-0 (P)
Giants, 16-0 (NY)
1942—Giants, 35-17 (NY)
Giants, 14-0 (P)
1944—Eagles, 24-17 (NY)
Tie, 21-21 (P)
1945—Eagles, 38-17 (P)
Giants, 28-21 (NY)
1946—Eagles, 24-14 (P)
Giants, 45-17 (NY)
1947—Eagles, 23-0 (P)
Eagles, 41-24 (NY)
1948—Eagles, 45-0 (P)
Eagles, 35-14 (NY)
1949—Eagles, 24-3 (NY)
Eagles, 17-3 (P)
1950—Giants, 7-3 (NY)
Giants, 9-7 (P)
1951—Giants, 26-24 (NY)
Giants, 23-7 (P)
1952—Giants, 31-7 (P)
Eagles, 14-10 (NY)
1953—Eagles, 30-7 (P)
Giants, 37-28 (NY)
1954—Giants, 27-14 (NY)
Eagles, 29-14 (P)
1955—Eagles, 27-17 (P)
Giants, 31-7 (NY)
1956—Giants, 20-3 (NY)
Giants, 21-7 (P)
1957—Giants, 24-20 (P)
Giants, 13-0 (NY)
1958—Eagles, 27-24 (P)
Giants, 24-10 (NY)
1959—Eagles, 49-21 (P)
Giants, 24-7 (NY)
1960—Eagles, 17-10 (NY)
Eagles, 31-23 (P)
1961—Giants, 38-21 (NY)
Giants, 28-24 (P)
1962—Giants, 29-13 (P)
Giants, 19-14 (NY)
1963—Giants, 37-14 (P)
Giants, 42-14 (NY)
1964—Eagles, 38-7 (P)
Eagles, 23-17 (NY)
1965—Giants, 16-14 (P)
Giants, 35-27 (NY)
1966—Eagles, 35-17 (P)
Eagles, 31-3 (NY)
1967—Giants, 44-7 (NY)
1968—Giants, 34-25 (P)
Giants, 7-6 (NY)
1969—Eagles, 23-20 (NY)
1970—Giants, 30-23 (NY)
Eagles, 23-20 (P)
1971—Eagles, 23-7 (P)
Eagles, 41-28 (NY)
1972—Giants, 27-12 (P)
Giants, 62-10 (NY)
1973—Tie, 23-23 (NY)
Eagles, 20-16 (P)
1974—Eagles, 35-7 (P)
Eagles, 20-7 (New Haven)
1975—Giants, 23-14 (P)
Eagles, 13-10 (NY)
1976—Eagles, 20-7 (P)
Eagles, 10-0 (NY)
1977—Eagles, 28-10 (NY)
Eagles, 17-14 (P)
1978—Eagles, 19-17 (NY)
Eagles, 20-3 (P)
1979—Eagles, 23-17 (P)
Eagles, 17-13 (NY)
1980—Eagles, 35-3 (P)
Eagles, 31-16 (NY)
1981—Eagles, 24-10 (NY)
Giants, 20-10 (P)
*Giants, 27-21 (P)
1982—Giants, 23-7 (NY)
Giants, 26-24 (P)
1983—Eagles, 17-13 (NY)
Giants, 23-0 (P)
1984—Giants, 28-27 (NY)
Eagles, 24-10 (P)
1985—Giants, 21-0 (NY)
Giants, 16-10 (P) OT
1986—Giants, 35-3 (NY)
Giants, 17-14 (P)
1987—Giants, 20-17 (P)
Giants, 23-20 (NY) OT
1988—Eagles, 24-13 (P)
Eagles, 23-17 (NY) OT
1989—Eagles, 21-19 (P)
Eagles, 24-17 (NY)
1990—Giants, 27-20 (NY)
Eagles, 31-13 (P)
1991—Eagles, 30-7 (P)
Eagles, 19-14 (NY)
1992—Eagles, 47-34 (NY)
Eagles, 20-10 (P)
1993—Giants, 21-10 (NY)
Giants, 7-3 (P)
1994—Giants, 28-23 (NY)
Giants, 16-13 (P)
1995—Eagles, 17-14 (NY)
Eagles, 28-19 (P)
(RS Pts.—Giants 2,325, Eagles 2,194)
(PS Pts.—Giants 27, Eagles 21)
**NFC First-Round Playoff*

N.Y. GIANTS vs. *PITTSBURGH
RS: Giants lead series, 42-27-3
1933—Giants, 23-2 (P)
Giants, 27-3 (NY)
1934—Giants, 14-12 (P)
Giants, 17-7 (NY)
1935—Giants, 42-7 (P)
Giants, 13-0 (NY)
1936—Pirates, 10-7 (P)
1937—Giants, 10-7 (P)
Giants, 17-0 (NY)
1938—Giants, 27-14 (P)
Pirates, 13-10 (NY)
1939—Giants, 14-7 (P)
Giants, 23-7 (NY)
1940—Tie, 10-10 (P)
Giants, 12-0 (NY)
1941—Giants, 37-10 (P)
Giants, 28-7 (NY)
1942—Steelers, 13-10 (P)
Steelers, 17-9 (NY)
1945—Giants, 34-6 (P)
Steelers, 21-7 (NY)
1946—Giants, 17-14 (P)
Giants, 7-0 (NY)
1947—Steelers, 38-21 (NY)
Steelers, 24-7 (P)
1948—Giants, 34-27 (NY)
Steelers, 38-28 (P)
1949—Steelers, 28-7 (P)
Steelers, 21-17 (NY)
1950—Giants, 18-7 (P)
Steelers, 17-6 (NY)
1951—Tie, 13-13 (P)

ALL-TIME TEAM VS. TEAM RESULTS

Giants, 14-0 (NY)
1952—Steelers, 63-7 (P)
1953—Steelers, 24-14 (P)
Steelers, 14-10 (NY)
1954—Giants, 30-6 (P)
Giants, 24-3 (NY)
1955—Steelers, 30-23 (P)
Steelers, 19-17 (NY)
1956—Giants, 38-10 (NY)
Giants, 17-14 (P)
1957—Giants, 35-0 (NY)
Steelers, 21-10 (P)
1958—Giants, 17-6 (NY)
Steelers, 31-10 (P)
1959—Giants, 21-16 (P)
Steelers, 14-9 (NY)
1960—Giants, 19-17 (P)
Giants, 27-24 (NY)
1961—Giants, 17-14 (P)
Giants, 42-21 (NY)
1962—Giants, 31-27 (P)
Steelers, 20-17 (NY)
1963—Steelers, 31-0 (P)
Giants, 33-17 (NY)
1964—Steelers, 27-24 (P)
Steelers, 44-17 (NY)
1965—Giants, 23-13 (P)
Giants, 35-10 (NY)
1966—Tie, 34-34 (P)
Steelers, 47-28 (NY)
1967—Giants, 27-24 (P)
Giants, 28-20 (NY)
1968—Giants, 34-20 (P)
1969—Giants, 10-7 (NY)
Giants, 21-17 (P)
1971—Steelers, 17-13 (P)
1976—Steelers, 27-0 (NY)
1985—Giants, 28-10 (NY)
1991—Giants, 23-20 (P)
1994—Steelers, 10-6 (NY)
(RS Pts.—Giants 1,399, Steelers 1,189)
Steelers known as Pirates prior to 1941

N.Y. GIANTS vs. *ST. LOUIS
RS: Rams lead series, 21-9
PS: Series tied, 1-1
1938—Giants, 28-0 (NY)
1940—Rams, 13-0 (NY)
1941—Giants, 49-14 (NY)
1945—Rams, 21-17 (NY)
1946—Rams, 31-21 (NY)
1947—Rams, 34-10 (LA)
1948—Rams, 52-37 (NY)
1953—Rams, 21-7 (LA)
1954—Rams, 17-16 (NY)
1959—Giants, 23-21 (LA)
1961—Giants, 24-14 (NY)
1966—Rams, 55-14 (LA)
1968—Rams, 24-21 (LA)
1970—Rams, 31-3 (NY)
1973—Rams, 40-6 (LA)
1976—Rams, 24-10 (LA)
1978—Rams, 20-17 (NY)
1979—Giants, 20-14 (LA)
1980—Rams, 28-7 (NY)
1981—Giants, 10-7 (NY)
1983—Rams, 16-6 (NY)
1984—Rams, 33-12 (LA)
**Giants, 16-13 (LA)
1985—Giants, 24-19 (NY)
1988—Rams, 45-31 (NY)
1989—Rams, 31-10 (LA)
***Rams, 19-13 (NY) OT
1990—Giants, 31-7 (LA)
1991—Rams, 19-13 (NY)
1992—Rams, 38-17 (LA)
1993—Giants, 20-10 (NY)
1994—Rams, 17-10 (LA)
(RS Pts.—Rams 716, Giants 514)
(PS Pts.—Rams 32, Giants 29)
**Franchise in Los Angeles prior to 1995 and in Cleveland prior to 1946*
***NFC First-Round Playoff*
****NFC Divisional Playoff*

N.Y. GIANTS vs. SAN DIEGO
RS: Giants lead series, 4-3
1971—Giants, 35-17 (NY)
1975—Giants, 35-24 (NY)
1980—Chargers, 44-7 (SD)
1983—Chargers, 41-34 (NY)
1986—Giants, 20-7 (NY)
1989—Giants, 20-13 (SD)
1995—Chargers, 27-17 (NY)
(RS Pts.—Chargers 173, Giants 168)

N.Y. GIANTS vs. SAN FRANCISCO
RS: Series tied, 11-11
PS: Series tied, 3-3
1952—Giants, 23-14 (NY)
1956—Giants, 38-21 (SF)
1957—49ers, 27-17 (NY)
1960—Giants, 21-19 (SF)
1963—Giants, 48-14 (NY)
1968—49ers, 26-10 (NY)
1972—Giants, 23-17 (SF)
1975—Giants, 26-23 (SF)
1977—Giants, 20-17 (NY)
1978—Giants, 27-10 (NY)
1979—Giants, 32-16 (NY)
1980—49ers, 12-0 (SF)
1981—49ers, 17-10 (SF)
*49ers, 38-24 (SF)
1984—49ers, 31-10 (NY)
*49ers, 21-10 (SF)
1985—**Giants, 17-3 (NY)
1986—Giants, 21-17 (SF)
*Giants, 49-3 (NY)
1987—49ers, 41-21 (NY)
1988—49ers, 20-17 (NY)
1989—49ers, 34-24 (SF)
1990—49ers, 7-3 (SF)
***Giants, 15-13 (SF)
1991—Giants, 16-14 (NY)
1992—49ers, 31-14 (NY)
1993—*49ers, 44-3 (SF)
1995—49ers, 20-6 (SF)
(RS Pts.—49ers 451, Giants 427)
(PS Pts.—49ers 119, Giants 118)
**NFC Divisional Playoff*
***NFC First-Round Playoff*
****NFC Championship*

N.Y. GIANTS vs. SEATTLE
RS: Giants lead series, 5-3
1976—Giants, 28-16 (NY)
1980—Giants, 27-21 (S)
1981—Giants, 32-0 (S)
1983—Seahawks, 17-12 (NY)
1986—Seahawks, 17-12 (S)
1989—Giants, 15-3 (NY)
1992—Giants, 23-10 (NY)
1995—Seahawks, 30-28 (S)
(RS Pts.—Giants 177, Seahawks 114)

N.Y. GIANTS vs. TAMPA BAY
RS: Giants lead series, 8-3
1977—Giants, 10-0 (TB)
1978—Giants, 19-13 (TB)
Giants, 17-14 (NY)
1979—Giants, 17-14 (NY)
Buccaneers, 31-3 (TB)
1980—Buccaneers, 30-13 (TB)
1984—Giants, 17-14 (NY)
Buccaneers, 20-17 (TB)
1985—Giants, 22-20 (NY)
1991—Giants, 21-14 (TB)
1993—Giants, 23-7 (NY)
(RS Pts.—Giants 179, Buccaneers 177)

N.Y. GIANTS vs. *WASHINGTON
RS: Giants lead series, 73-50-3
PS: Series tied, 1-1
1932—Braves, 14-6 (B)
Tie, 0-0 (NY)
1933—Redskins, 21-20 (B)
Giants, 7-0 (NY)
1934—Giants, 16-13 (B)
Giants, 3-0 (NY)
1935—Giants, 20-12 (B)
Giants, 17-6 (NY)
1936—Giants, 7-0 (B)
Redskins, 14-0 (NY)
1937—Redskins, 13-3 (W)
Redskins, 49-14 (NY)
1938—Giants, 10-7 (W)
Giants, 36-0 (NY)
1939—Tie, 0-0 (W)
Giants, 9-7 (NY)
1940—Redskins, 21-7 (W)
Giants, 21-7 (NY)
1941—Giants, 17-10 (W)
Giants, 20-13 (NY)
1942—Giants, 14-7 (W)
Redskins, 14-7 (NY)
1943—Giants, 14-10 (NY)
Giants, 31-7 (W)
**Redskins, 28-0 (NY)
1944—Giants, 16-13 (NY)
Giants, 31-0 (W)
1945—Redskins, 24-14 (NY)
Redskins, 17-0 (W)
1946—Redskins, 24-14 (W)
Giants, 31-0 (NY)
1947—Redskins, 28-20 (W)
Giants, 35-10 (NY)
1948—Redskins, 41-10 (W)
Redskins, 28-21 (NY)
1949—Giants, 45-35 (W)
Giants, 23-7 (NY)
1950—Giants, 21-17 (W)
Giants, 24-21 (NY)
1951—Giants, 35-14 (W)
Giants, 28-14 (NY)
1952—Giants, 14-10 (W)
Redskins, 27-17 (NY)
1953—Redskins, 13-9 (W)
Redskins, 24-21 (NY)
1954—Giants, 51-21 (W)
Giants, 24-7 (NY)
1955—Giants, 35-7 (NY)
Giants, 27-20 (W)
1956—Redskins, 33-7 (W)
Giants, 28-14 (NY)
1957—Giants, 24-20 (W)
Redskins, 31-14 (NY)
1958—Giants, 21-14 (W)
Giants, 30-0 (NY)
1959—Giants, 45-14 (NY)
Giants, 24-10 (W)
1960—Tie, 24-24 (NY)
Giants, 17-3 (W)
1961—Giants, 24-21 (W)
Giants, 53-0 (NY)
1962—Giants, 49-34 (NY)
Giants, 42-24 (W)
1963—Giants, 24-14 (W)
Giants, 44-14 (NY)
1964—Giants, 13-10 (NY)
Redskins, 36-21 (W)
1965—Redskins, 23-7 (NY)
Giants, 27-10 (W)
1966—Giants, 13-10 (NY)
Redskins, 72-41 (W)
1967—Redskins, 38-34 (W)
1968—Giants, 48-21 (NY)
Giants, 13-10 (W)
1969—Redskins, 20-14 (W)
1970—Giants, 35-33 (NY)
Giants, 27-24 (W)
1971—Redskins, 30-3 (NY)
Redskins, 23-7 (W)
1972—Redskins, 23-16 (NY)
Redskins, 27-13 (W)
1973—Redskins, 21-3 (New Haven)
Redskins, 27-24 (W)
1974—Redskins, 13-10 (New Haven)
Redskins, 24-3 (W)
1975—Redskins, 49-13 (W)
Redskins, 21-13 (NY)
1976—Redskins, 19-17 (W)
Giants, 12-9 (NY)
1977—Giants, 20-17 (NY)
Giants, 17-6 (W)
1978—Giants, 17-6 (NY)
Redskins, 16-13 (W) OT
1979—Redskins, 27-0 (W)
Giants, 14-6 (NY)
1980—Redskins, 23-21 (NY)
Redskins, 16-13 (W)
1981—Giants, 17-7 (W)
Redskins, 30-27 (NY) OT
1982—Redskins, 27-17 (NY)
Redskins, 15-14 (W)
1983—Redskins, 33-17 (NY)
Redskins, 31-22 (W)
1984—Redskins, 30-14 (W)
Giants, 37-13 (NY)
1985—Giants, 17-3 (NY)
Redskins, 23-21 (W)
1986—Giants, 27-20 (NY)
Giants, 24-14 (W)
***Giants, 17-0 (NY)
1987—Redskins, 38-12 (NY)
Redskins, 23-19 (W)
1988—Giants, 27-20 (NY)
Giants, 24-23 (W)
1989—Giants, 27-24 (W)
Giants, 20-17 (NY)
1990—Giants, 24-20 (W)
Giants, 21-10 (NY)
1991—Redskins, 17-13 (NY)
Redskins, 34-17 (W)
1992—Giants, 24-7 (W)
Redskins, 28-10 (NY)
1993—Giants, 41-7 (W)
Giants, 20-6 (NY)
1994—Giants, 31-23 (NY)
Giants, 21-19 (W)
1995—Giants, 24-15 (W)
Giants, 20-13 (NY)
(RS Pts.—Giants 2,526, Redskins 2,237)
(PS Pts.—Redskins 28, Giants 17)
**Franchise in Boston prior to 1937 and known as Braves prior to 1933*
***Division Playoff*
****NFC Championship*

N.Y. JETS vs. ARIZONA
RS: Cardinals lead series, 2-1;
See Arizona vs. N.Y. Jets

N.Y. JETS vs. ATLANTA
RS: Falcons lead series, 4-3;
See Atlanta vs. N.Y. Jets

N.Y. JETS vs. BUFFALO
RS: Bills lead series, 39-31
PS: Bills lead series, 1-0;
See Buffalo vs. N.Y. Jets

N.Y. JETS vs. CAROLINA
RS: Panthers lead series, 1-0;
See Carolina vs. N.Y. Jets

N.Y. JETS vs. CHICAGO
RS: Bears lead series, 4-1;
See Chicago vs. N.Y. Jets

N.Y. JETS vs. CINCINNATI
RS: Jets lead series, 9-6
PS: Jets lead series, 1-0;
See Cincinnati vs. N.Y. Jets

N.Y. JETS vs. CLEVELAND
RS: Browns lead series, 9-6
PS: Browns lead series, 1-0;
See Cleveland vs. N.Y. Jets

N.Y. JETS vs. DALLAS
RS: Cowboys lead series, 5-1;
See Dallas vs. N.Y. Jets

N.Y. JETS vs. DENVER
RS: Series tied, 12-12-1;
See Denver vs. N.Y. Jets

N.Y. JETS vs. DETROIT
RS: Lions lead series, 4-3;
See Detroit vs. N.Y. Jets

N.Y. JETS vs. GREEN BAY
RS: Jets lead series, 5-2;
See Green Bay vs. N.Y. Jets

N.Y. JETS vs. HOUSTON
RS: Oilers lead series, 19-12-1
PS: Oilers lead series, 1-0;
See Houston vs. N.Y. Jets

N.Y. JETS vs. INDIANAPOLIS
RS: Colts lead series, 30-21
PS: Jets lead series, 1-0;
See Indianapolis vs. N.Y. Jets
N.Y. JETS vs. JACKSONVILLE
RS: Jets lead series, 1-0;
See Jacksonville vs. N.Y. Jets
N.Y. JETS vs. KANSAS CITY
RS: Chiefs lead series, 14-12-1
PS: Series tied, 1-1;
See Kansas City vs. N.Y. Jets
N.Y. JETS vs. MIAMI
RS: Dolphins lead series, 30-29-1
PS: Dolphins lead series, 1-0;
See Miami vs. N.Y. Jets
N.Y. JETS vs. MINNESOTA
RS: Jets lead series, 4-1;
See Minnesota vs. N.Y. Jets
N.Y. JETS vs. NEW ENGLAND
RS: Jets lead series, 39-31-1
PS: Patriots lead series, 1-0;
See New England vs. N.Y. Jets
N.Y. JETS vs. NEW ORLEANS
RS: Series tied, 4-4;
See New Orleans vs. N.Y. Jets
N.Y. JETS vs. N.Y. GIANTS
RS: Jets lead series, 4-3;
See N.Y. Giants vs. N.Y. Jets
***N.Y. JETS vs. **OAKLAND**
RS: Raiders lead series, 15-9-2
PS: Jets lead series, 2-0
1960—Raiders, 28-27 (NY)
Titans, 31-28 (O)
1961—Titans, 14-6 (O)
Titans, 23-12 (NY)
1962—Titans, 28-17 (O)
Titans, 31-21 (NY)
1963—Jets, 10-7 (NY)
Raiders, 49-26 (O)
1964—Jets, 35-13 (NY)
Raiders, 35-26 (O)
1965—Tie, 24-24 (NY)
Raiders, 24-14 (O)
1966—Raiders, 24-21 (NY)
Tie, 28-28 (O)
1967—Jets, 27-14 (NY)
Raiders, 38-29 (O)
1968—Raiders, 43-32 (O)
***Jets, 27-23 (NY)
1969—Raiders, 27-14 (NY)
1970—Raiders, 14-13 (NY)
1972—Raiders, 24-16 (O)
1977—Raiders, 28-27 (NY)
1979—Jets, 28-19 (NY)
1982—****Jets, 17-14 (LA)
1985—Raiders, 31-0 (LA)
1989—Raiders, 14-7 (NY)
1993—Raiders, 24-20 (LA)
1995—Raiders, 47-10 (NY)
(RS Pts.—Raiders 639, Jets 561)
(PS Pts.—Jets 44, Raiders 37)
**Jets known as Titans prior to 1963*
***Franchise in Los Angeles from 1982-1994*
****AFL Championship*
*****AFC Second-Round Playoff*
N.Y. JETS vs. PHILADELPHIA
RS: Eagles lead series, 5-0
1973—Eagles, 24-23 (P)
1977—Eagles, 27-0 (P)
1978—Eagles, 17-9 (P)
1987—Eagles, 38-27 (NY)
1993—Eagles, 35-30 (NY)
(RS Pts.—Eagles 141, Jets 89)
N.Y. JETS vs. PITTSBURGH
RS: Steelers lead series, 12-1
1970—Steelers, 21-17 (P)
1973—Steelers, 26-14 (P)
1975—Steelers, 20-7 (NY)
1977—Steelers, 23-20 (NY)
1978—Steelers, 28-17 (NY)
1981—Steelers, 38-10 (P)
1983—Steelers, 34-7 (NY)
1984—Steelers, 23-17 (NY)
1986—Steelers, 45-24 (NY)
1988—Jets, 24-20 (NY)
1989—Steelers, 13-0 (NY)
1990—Steelers, 24-7 (NY)
1992—Steelers, 27-10 (P)
(RS Pts.—Steelers 342, Jets 174)
N.Y. JETS vs. *ST. LOUIS
RS: Rams lead series, 6-2
1970—Jets, 31-20 (LA)
1974—Rams, 20-13 (NY)
1980—Rams, 38-13 (LA)
1983—Jets, 27-24 (NY) OT
1986—Rams, 17-3 (NY)
1989—Rams, 38-14 (LA)
1992—Rams, 18-10 (LA)
1995—Rams, 23-20 (NY)
(RS Pts.—Rams 198, Jets 131)
**Franchise in Los Angeles prior to 1995*
***N.Y. JETS vs. **SAN DIEGO**
RS: Chargers lead series, 17-9-1
1960—Chargers, 21-7 (NY)
Chargers, 50-43 (LA)
1961—Chargers, 25-10 (NY)
Chargers, 48-13 (SD)
1962—Chargers, 40-14 (SD)
Titans, 23-3 (NY)
1963—Chargers, 24-20 (SD)
Chargers, 53-7 (NY)
1964—Tie, 17-17 (NY)
Chargers, 38-3 (SD)
1965—Chargers, 34-9 (NY)
Chargers, 38-7 (SD)
1966—Jets, 17-16 (NY)
Chargers, 42-27 (SD)
1967—Jets, 42-31 (SD)
1968—Jets, 23-20 (NY)
Jets, 37-15 (SD)
1969—Chargers, 34-27 (SD)
1971—Chargers, 49-21 (SD)
1974—Jets, 27-14 (NY)
1975—Chargers, 24-16 (SD)
1983—Jets, 41-29 (SD)
1989—Jets, 20-17 (SD)
1990—Chargers, 39-3 (NY)
Chargers, 38-17 (SD)
1991—Jets, 24-3 (NY)
1994—Chargers, 21-6 (NY)
(RS Pts.—Chargers 783, Jets 521)
**Jets known as Titans prior to 1963*
***Franchise in Los Angeles prior to 1961*
N.Y. JETS vs. SAN FRANCISCO
RS: 49ers lead series, 6-1
1971—49ers, 24-21 (NY)
1976—49ers, 17-6 (SF)
1980—49ers, 37-27 (NY)
1983—Jets, 27-13 (SF)
1986—49ers, 24-10 (SF)
1989—49ers, 23-10 (NY)
1992—49ers, 31-14 (NY)
(RS Pts.—49ers 169, Jets 115)
N.Y. JETS vs. SEATTLE
RS: Seahawks lead series, 8-4
1977—Seahawks, 17-0 (NY)
1978—Seahawks, 24-17 (NY)
1979—Seahawks, 30-7 (S)
1980—Seahawks, 27-17 (NY)
1981—Seahawks, 19-3 (NY)
Seahawks, 27-23 (S)
1983—Seahawks, 17-10 (NY)
1985—Jets, 17-14 (NY)
1986—Jets, 38-7 (S)
1987—Jets, 30-14 (NY)
1991—Seahawks, 20-13 (S)
1995—Jets, 16-10 (S)
(RS Pts.—Seahawks 226, Jets 191)
N.Y. JETS vs. TAMPA BAY
RS: Jets lead series, 5-1
1976—Jets, 34-0 (NY)
1982—Jets, 32-17 (NY)
1984—Buccaneers, 41-21 (TB)
1985—Jets, 62-28 (NY)
1990—Jets, 16-14 (TB)
1991—Jets, 16-13 (NY)
(RS Pts.—Jets 181, Buccaneers 113)
N.Y. JETS vs. WASHINGTON
RS: Redskins lead series, 4-1
1972—Redskins, 35-17 (NY)
1976—Redskins, 37-16 (NY)
1978—Redskins, 23-3 (W)
1987—Redskins, 17-16 (W)
1993—Jets, 3-0 (W)
(RS Pts.—Redskins 112, Jets 55)

OAKLAND vs. ARIZONA
RS: Raiders lead series, 2-1;
See Arizona vs. Oakland
OAKLAND vs. ATLANTA
RS: Raiders lead series, 5-3;
See Atlanta vs. Oakland
OAKLAND vs. BUFFALO
RS: Raiders lead series, 15-14
PS: Bills lead series, 2-0;
See Buffalo vs. Oakland
OAKLAND vs. CHICAGO
RS: Raiders lead series, 5-3;
See Chicago vs. Oakland
OAKLAND vs. CINCINNATI
RS: Raiders lead series, 15-7
PS: Raiders lead series, 2-0;
See Cincinnati vs. Oakland
OAKLAND vs. CLEVELAND
RS: Raiders lead series, 8-4
PS: Raiders lead series, 2-0;
See Cleveland vs. Oakland
OAKLAND vs. DALLAS
RS: Series tied, 3-3;
See Dallas vs. Oakland
OAKLAND vs. DENVER
RS: Raiders lead series, 48-21-2
PS: Series tied, 1-1;
See Denver vs. Oakland
OAKLAND vs. DETROIT
RS: Raiders lead series, 5-2;
See Detroit vs. Oakland
OAKLAND vs. GREEN BAY
RS: Raiders lead series, 5-2
PS: Packers lead series, 1-0;
See Green Bay vs. Oakland
OAKLAND vs. HOUSTON
RS: Raiders lead series, 20-13
PS: Raiders lead series, 3-0;
See Houston vs. Oakland
OAKLAND vs. INDIANAPOLIS
RS: Raiders lead series, 5-2
PS: Series tied, 1-1;
See Indianapolis vs. Oakland
OAKLAND vs. KANSAS CITY
RS: Raiders lead series, 35-34-2
PS: Chiefs lead series, 2-1;
See Kansas City vs. Oakland
***OAKLAND vs. MIAMI**
RS: Raiders lead series, 14-5-1
PS: Raiders lead series, 2-1
See Miami vs. Oakland
***OAKLAND vs. MINNESOTA**
RS: Raiders lead series, 6-2
PS: Raiders lead series, 1-0
See Minnesota vs. Oakland
***OAKLAND vs. **NEW ENGLAND**
RS: Raiders lead series, 13-12-1
PS: Series tied, 1-1
See New England vs. Oakland
***OAKLAND vs. NEW ORLEANS**
RS: Raiders lead series, 4-2-1
See New Orleans vs. Oakland
***OAKLAND vs. N.Y. GIANTS**
RS: Raiders lead series, 5-2
See N.Y. Giants vs. Oakland
***OAKLAND vs. **N.Y. JETS**
RS: Raiders lead series, 15-9-2
PS: Jets lead series, 2-0
See N.Y. Jets vs. Oakland
***OAKLAND vs. PHILADELPHIA**
RS: Eagles lead series, 4-3
PS: Raiders lead series, 1-0
1971—Raiders, 34-10 (O)
1976—Raiders, 26-7 (P)
1980—Eagles, 10-7 (P)
**Raiders, 27-10 (New Orleans)
1986—Eagles, 33-27 (LA) OT
1989—Eagles, 10-7 (P)
1992—Eagles, 31-10 (P)
1995—Raiders, 48-17 (O)
(RS Pts.—Raiders 159, Eagles 118)
(PS Pts.—Raiders 27, Eagles 10)
**Franchise in Los Angeles from 1982-1994*
***Super Bowl XV*
***OAKLAND vs. PITTSBURGH**
RS: Raiders lead series, 7-5
PS: Series tied, 3-3
1970—Raiders, 31-14 (O)
1972—Steelers, 34-28 (P)
**Steelers, 13-7 (P)
1973—Steelers, 17-9 (O)
**Raiders, 33-14 (O)
1974—Raiders, 17-0 (P)
***Steelers, 24-13 (O)
1975—***Steelers, 16-10 (P)
1976—Raiders, 31-28 (O)
***Raiders, 24-7 (O)
1977—Raiders, 16-7 (P)
1980—Raiders, 45-34 (P)
1981—Raiders, 30-27 (O)
1983—**Raiders, 38-10 (LA)
1984—Steelers, 13-7 (LA)
1990—Raiders, 20-3 (LA)
1994—Steelers, 21-3 (LA)
1995—Steelers, 29-10 (O)
(RS Pts.—Raiders 247, Steelers 227)
(PS Pts.—Raiders 125, Steelers 84)
**Franchise in Los Angeles from 1982-1994*
***AFC Divisional Playoff*
****AFC Championship*
***OAKLAND vs. **ST. LOUIS**
RS: Raiders lead series, 6-2
1972—Raiders, 45-17 (O)
1977—Rams, 20-14 (LA)
1979—Raiders, 24-17 (LA)
1982—Raiders, 37-31 (LA Raiders)
1985—Raiders, 16-6 (LA Rams)
1988—Rams, 22-17 (LA Raiders)
1991—Raiders, 20-17 (LA Raiders)
1994—Raiders, 20-17 (LA Rams)
(RS Pts.—Raiders 193, Rams 147)
**Franchise in Los Angeles from 1982-1994*
***Franchise in Los Angeles prior to 1995*
***OAKLAND vs. **SAN DIEGO**
RS: Raiders lead series, 43-27-2
PS: Raiders lead series, 1-0
1960—Chargers, 52-28 (LA)
Chargers, 41-17 (O)
1961—Chargers, 44-0 (SD)
Chargers, 41-10 (O)
1962—Chargers, 42-33 (O)
Chargers, 31-21 (SD)
1963—Raiders, 34-33 (SD)
Raiders, 41-27 (O)
1964—Chargers, 31-17 (SD)
Raiders, 21-20 (O)
1965—Chargers, 17-6 (O)
Chargers, 24-14 (SD)
1966—Chargers, 29-20 (O)
Raiders, 41-19 (SD)
1967—Raiders, 51-10 (O)
Raiders, 41-21 (SD)
1968—Chargers, 23-14 (O)
Raiders, 34-27 (SD)
1969—Raiders, 24-12 (SD)
Raiders, 21-16 (O)
1970—Tie, 27-27 (SD)
Raiders, 20-17 (O)
1971—Raiders, 34-0 (SD)
Raiders, 34-33 (O)
1972—Tie, 17-17 (O)

Raiders, 21-19 (SD)
1973—Raiders, 27-17 (SD)
Raiders, 31-3 (O)
1974—Raiders, 14-10 (SD)
Raiders, 17-10 (O)
1975—Raiders, 6-0 (SD)
Raiders, 25-0 (O)
1976—Raiders, 27-17 (SD)
Raiders, 24-0 (O)
1977—Raiders, 24-0 (O)
Chargers, 12-7 (SD)
1978—Raiders, 21-20 (SD)
Chargers, 27-23 (O)
1979—Chargers, 30-10 (SD)
Raiders, 45-22 (O)
1980—Chargers, 30-24 (SD) OT
Raiders, 38-24 (O)
***Raiders, 34-27 (SD)
1981—Chargers, 55-21 (O)
Chargers, 23-10 (SD)
1982—Raiders, 28-24 (LA)
Raiders, 41-34 (SD)
1983—Raiders, 42-10 (SD)
Raiders, 30-14 (LA)
1984—Raiders, 33-30 (LA)
Raiders, 44-37 (SD)
1985—Raiders, 34-21 (LA)
Chargers, 40-34 (SD) OT
1986—Raiders, 17-13 (LA)
Raiders, 37-31 (SD) OT
1987—Chargers, 23-17 (LA)
Chargers, 16-14 (SD)
1988—Raiders, 24-13 (LA)
Raiders, 13-3 (SD)
1989—Raiders, 40-14 (LA)
Chargers, 14-12 (SD)
1990—Raiders, 24-9 (SD)
Raiders, 17-12 (LA)
1991—Chargers, 21-13 (LA)
Raiders, 9-7 (SD)
1992—Chargers, 27-3 (SD)
Chargers, 36-14 (LA)
1993—Chargers, 30-23 (LA)
Raiders, 12-7 (SD)
1994—Chargers, 26-24 (LA)
Raiders, 24-17 (SD)
1995—Raiders, 17-7 (O)
Chargers, 12-6 (SD)
(RS Pts.—Raiders 1,681, Chargers 1,521)
(PS Pts.—Raiders 34, Chargers 27)
Franchise in Los Angeles from 1982-1994
***Franchise in Los Angeles prior to 1961*
****AFC Championship*

***OAKLAND vs. SAN FRANCISCO**
RS: Raiders lead series, 5-3
1970—49ers, 38-7 (O)
1974—Raiders, 35-24 (SF)
1979—Raiders, 23-10 (O)
1982—Raiders, 23-17 (SF)
1985—49ers, 34-10 (LA)
1988—Raiders, 9-3 (SF)
1991—Raiders, 12-6 (LA)
1994—49ers, 44-14 (SF)
(RS Pts.—49ers 176, Raiders 133)
**Franchise in Los Angeles from 1982-1994*

***OAKLAND vs. SEATTLE**
RS: Raiders lead series, 20-16
PS: Series tied, 1-1
1977—Raiders, 44-7 (O)
1978—Seahawks, 27-7 (S)
Seahawks, 17-16 (O)
1979—Seahawks, 27-10 (S)
Seahawks, 29-24 (O)
1980—Raiders, 33-14 (O)
Raiders, 19-17 (S)
1981—Raiders, 20-10 (O)
Raiders, 32-31 (S)
1982—Raiders, 28-23 (LA)
1983—Seahawks, 38-36 (S)
Seahawks, 34-21 (LA)
**Raiders, 30-14 (LA)
1984—Raiders, 28-14 (LA)
Seahawks, 17-14 (S)
***Seahawks, 13-7 (S)
1985—Seahawks, 33-3 (S)
Raiders, 13-3 (LA)
1986—Raiders, 14-10 (LA)
Seahawks, 37-0 (S)
1987—Seahawks, 35-13 (LA)
Raiders, 37-14 (S)
1988—Seahawks, 35-27 (S)
Seahawks, 43-37 (LA)
1989—Seahawks, 24-20 (LA)
Seahawks, 23-17 (S)
1990—Raiders, 17-13 (S)
Raiders, 24-17 (LA)
1991—Raiders, 23-20 (S) OT
Raiders, 31-7 (LA)
1992—Raiders, 19-0 (S)
Raiders, 20-3 (LA)
1993—Raiders, 17-13 (S)
Raiders, 27-23 (LA)
1994—Seahawks, 38-9 (LA)
Raiders, 17-16 (S)
1995—Raiders, 34-14 (O)
Seahawks, 44-10 (S)
(RS Pts.—Seahawks 770, Raiders 761)
(PS Pts.—Raiders 37, Seahawks 27)
**Franchise in Los Angeles from 1982-1994*
***AFC Championship*
****AFC First-Round Playoff*

***OAKLAND vs. TAMPA BAY**
RS: Raiders lead series, 3-0
1976—Raiders, 49-16 (O)
1981—Raiders, 18-16 (O)
1993—Raiders, 27-20 (LA)
(RS Pts.—Raiders 94, Buccaneers 52)
**Franchise in Los Angeles from 1982-1994*

***OAKLAND vs. WASHINGTON**
RS: Raiders lead series, 6-2
PS: Raiders lead series, 1-0
1970—Raiders, 34-20 (O)
1975—Raiders, 26-23 (W) OT
1980—Raiders, 24-21 (O)
1983—Redskins, 37-35 (W)
**Raiders, 38-9 (Tampa)
1986—Redskins, 10-6 (W)
1989—Raiders, 37-24 (LA)
1992—Raiders, 21-20 (W)
1995—Raiders, 20-8 (W)
(RS Pts.—Raiders 203, Redskins 163)
(PS Pts.—Raiders 38, Redskins 9)
**Franchise in Los Angeles from 1982-1994*
***Super Bowl XVIII*

PHILADELPHIA vs. ARIZONA
RS: Eagles lead series, 46-45-5
PS: Series tied, 1-1;
See Arizona vs. Philadelphia

PHILADELPHIA vs. ATLANTA
RS: Eagles lead series, 8-7-1
PS: Falcons lead series, 1-0;
See Atlanta vs. Philadelphia

PHILADELPHIA vs. BUFFALO
RS: Eagles lead series, 4-3;
See Buffalo vs. Philadelphia

PHILADELPHIA vs. CHICAGO
RS: Bears lead series, 24-4-1
PS: Series tied, 1-1;
See Chicago vs. Philadelphia

PHILADELPHIA vs. CINCINNATI
RS: Bengals lead series, 6-1;
See Cincinnati vs. Philadelphia

PHILADELPHIA vs. CLEVELAND
RS: Browns lead series, 31-12-1;
See Cleveland vs. Philadelphia

PHILADELPHIA vs. DALLAS
RS: Cowboys lead series, 43-27
PS: Cowboys lead series, 2-1;
See Dallas vs. Philadelphia

PHILADELPHIA vs. DENVER
RS: Eagles lead series, 6-2;
See Denver vs. Philadelphia

PHILADELPHIA vs. DETROIT
RS: Lions lead series, 12-9-2
PS: Eagles lead series, 1-0;
See Detroit vs. Philadelphia

PHILADELPHIA vs. GREEN BAY
RS: Packers lead series, 19-8
PS: Eagles lead series, 1-0;
See Green Bay vs. Philadelphia

PHILADELPHIA vs. HOUSTON
RS: Eagles lead series, 6-0;
See Houston vs. Philadelphia

PHILADELPHIA vs. INDIANAPOLIS
RS: Series tied, 6-6;
See Indianapolis vs. Philadelphia

PHILADELPHIA vs. KANSAS CITY
RS: Series tied, 1-1;
See Kansas City vs. Philadelphia

PHILADELPHIA vs. MIAMI
RS: Dolphins lead series, 6-2;
See Miami vs. Philadelphia

PHILADELPHIA vs. MINNESOTA
RS: Vikings lead series, 10-6
PS: Eagles lead series, 1-0;
See Minnesota vs. Philadelphia

PHILADELPHIA vs. NEW ENGLAND
RS: Eagles lead series, 5-2;
See New England vs. Philadelphia

PHILADELPHIA vs. NEW ORLEANS
RS: Eagles lead series, 12-8
PS; Eagles lead series, 1-0;
See New Orleans vs. Philadelphia

PHILADELPHIA vs. N.Y. GIANTS
RS: Giants lead series, 64-56-2
PS: Giants lead series, 1-0;
See N.Y. Giants vs. Philadelphia

PHILADELPHIA vs. N.Y. JETS
RS: Eagles lead series, 5-0;
See N.Y. Jets vs. Philadelphia

PHILADELPHIA vs. OAKLAND
RS: Eagles lead series, 4-3
PS: Raiders lead series, 1-0;
See Oakland vs. Philadelphia

PHILADELPHIA vs. *PITTSBURGH
RS: Eagles lead series, 43-26-3
PS: Eagles lead series, 1-0
1933—Eagles, 25-6 (Phila)
1934—Eagles, 17-0 (Pitt)
Pirates, 9-7 (Phila)
1935—Pirates, 17-7 (Phila)
Eagles, 17-6 (Pitt)
1936—Pirates, 17-0 (Pitt)
Pirates, 6-0 (Johnstown, Pa.)
1937—Pirates, 27-14 (Pitt)
Pirates, 16-7 (Phila)
1938—Eagles, 27-7 (Buffalo)
Eagles, 14-7 (Charleston, W. Va.)
1939—Eagles, 17-14 (Phila)
Pirates, 24-12 (Pitt)
1940—Pirates, 7-3 (Pitt)
Eagles, 7-0 (Phila)
1941—Eagles, 10-7 (Pitt)
Tie, 7-7 (Phila)
1942—Eagles, 24-14 (Pitt)
Steelers, 14-0 (Phila)
1945—Eagles, 45-3 (Pitt)
Eagles, 30-6 (Phila)
1946—Steelers, 10-7 (Pitt)
Eagles, 10-7 (Phila)
1947—Steelers, 35-24 (Pitt)
Eagles, 21-0 (Phila)
**Eagles, 21-0 (Pitt)
1948—Eagles, 34-7 (Pitt)
Eagles, 17-0 (Phila)
1949—Eagles, 38-7 (Pitt)
Eagles, 34-17 (Phila)
1950—Eagles, 17-10 (Pitt)
Steelers, 9-7 (Phila)
1951—Eagles, 34-13 (Pitt)
Steelers, 17-13 (Phila)
1952—Eagles, 31-25 (Pitt)
Eagles, 26-21 (Phila)
1953—Eagles, 23-17 (Phila)
Eagles, 35-7 (Pitt)
1954—Eagles, 24-22 (Phila)
Steelers, 17-7 (Pitt)
1955—Steelers, 13-7 (Pitt)
Eagles, 24-0 (Phila)
1956—Eagles, 35-21 (Pitt)
Eagles, 14-7 (Phila)
1957—Steelers, 6-0 (Pitt)
Eagles, 7-6 (Phila)
1958—Steelers, 24-3 (Pitt)
Steelers, 31-24 (Phila)
1959—Eagles, 28-24 (Phila)
Steelers, 31-0 (Pitt)
1960—Eagles, 34-7 (Phila)
Steelers, 27-21 (Pitt)
1961—Eagles, 21-16 (Phila)
Eagles, 35-24 (Pitt)
1962—Steelers, 13-7 (Pitt)
Steelers, 26-17 (Phila)
1963—Tie, 21-21 (Phila)
Tie, 20-20 (Pitt)
1964—Eagles, 21-7 (Phila)
Eagles, 34-10 (Pitt)
1965—Steelers, 20-14 (Phila)
Eagles, 47-13 (Pitt)
1966—Eagles, 31-14 (Pitt)
Eagles, 27-23 (Phila)
1967—Eagles, 34-24 (Phila)
1968—Steelers, 6-3 (Pitt)
1969—Eagles, 41-27 (Phila)
1970—Eagles, 30-20 (Phila)
1974—Steelers, 27-0 (Pitt)
1979—Eagles, 17-14 (Phila)
1988—Eagles, 27-26 (Pitt)
1991—Eagles, 23-14 (Phila)
1994—Steelers, 14-3 (Pitt)
(RS Pts.—Eagles 1,362, Steelers 1,021)
(PS Pts.—Eagles 21, Steelers 0)
**Steelers known as Pirates prior to 1941*
***Division Playoff*

PHILADELPHIA vs. *ST. LOUIS
RS: Rams lead series, 15-12-1
PS: Series tied, 1-1
1937—Rams, 21-3 (P)
1939—Rams, 35-13 (Colorado Springs)
1940—Rams, 21-13 (C)
1942—Rams, 24-14 (Akron)
1944—Eagles, 26-13 (P)
1945—Eagles, 28-14 (P)
1946—Eagles, 25-14 (LA)
1947—Eagles, 14-7 (P)
1948—Tie, 28-28 (LA)
1949—Eagles, 38-14 (P)
**Eagles, 14-0 (LA)
1950—Eagles, 56-20 (P)
1955—Rams, 23-21 (P)
1956—Rams, 27-7 (LA)
1957—Rams, 17-13 (LA)
1959—Eagles, 23-20 (P)
1964—Rams, 20-10 (LA)
1967—Rams, 33-17 (LA)
1969—Rams, 23-17 (P)
1972—Rams, 34-3 (P)
1975—Rams, 42-3 (P)
1977—Rams, 20-0 (LA)
1978—Rams, 16-14 (P)
1983—Eagles, 13-9 (P)
1985—Rams, 17-6 (P)
1986—Eagles, 34-20 (P)
1988—Eagles, 30-24 (P)
1989—***Rams, 21-7 (P)
1990—Eagles, 27-21 (LA)
1995—Eagles, 20-9 (P)
(RS Pts.—Rams 586, Eagles 516)
(PS Pts.—Rams 21, Eagles 21)
**Franchise in Los Angeles prior to 1995 and in Cleveland prior to 1946*
***NFL Championship*
****NFC First-Round Playoff*

PHILADELPHIA vs. SAN DIEGO
RS: Chargers lead series, 4-2
1974—Eagles, 13-7 (SD)

1980—Chargers, 22-21 (SD)
1985—Chargers, 20-14 (SD)
1986—Eagles, 23-7 (P)
1989—Chargers, 20-17 (SD)
1995—Chargers, 27-21 (P)
(RS Pts.—Eagles 109, Chargers 103)

PHILADELPHIA vs. SAN FRANCISCO
RS: 49ers lead series, 13-6-1
1951—Eagles, 21-14 (P)
1953—49ers, 31-21 (SF)
1956—Tie, 10-10 (P)
1958—49ers, 30-24 (P)
1959—49ers, 24-14 (SF)
1964—49ers, 28-24 (P)
1966—Eagles, 35-34 (SF)
1967—49ers, 28-27 (P)
1969—49ers, 14-13 (SF)
1971—49ers, 31-3 (P)
1973—49ers, 38-28 (SF)
1975—Eagles, 27-17 (P)
1983—Eagles, 22-17 (SF)
1984—49ers, 21-9 (P)
1985—49ers, 24-13 (SF)
1989—49ers, 38-28 (P)
1991—49ers, 23-7 (P)
1992—49ers, 20-14 (SF)
1993—Eagles, 37-34 (SF) OT
1994—Eagles, 40-8 (SF)
(RS Pts.—49ers 484, Eagles 417)

PHILADELPHIA vs. SEATTLE
RS: Eagles lead series, 4-2
1976—Eagles, 27-10 (P)
1980—Eagles, 27-20 (S)
1986—Seahawks, 24-20 (S)
1989—Eagles, 31-7 (P)
1992—Eagles, 20-17 (S) OT
1995—Seahawks, 26-10 (S)
(RS Pts.—Eagles 135, Seahawks 104)

PHILADELPHIA vs. TAMPA BAY
RS: Eagles lead series, 3-2
PS: Buccaneers lead series, 1-0
1977—Eagles, 13-3 (P)
1979—*Buccaneers, 24-17 (TB)
1981—Eagles, 20-10 (P)
1988—Eagles, 41-14 (TB)
1991—Buccaneers, 14-13 (TB)
1995—Buccaneers, 21-6 (P)
(RS Pts.—Eagles 93, Buccaneers 62)
(PS Pts.—Buccaneers 24, Eagles 17)
NFC Divisional Playoff

PHILADELPHIA vs. *WASHINGTON
RS: Redskins lead series, 66-50-5
PS: Redskins lead series, 1-0
1934—Redskins, 6-0 (B)
Redskins, 14-7 (P)
1935—Eagles, 7-6 (B)
1936—Redskins, 26-3 (P)
Redskins, 17-7 (B)
1937—Eagles, 14-0 (W)
Redskins, 10-7 (P)
1938—Redskins, 26-23 (P)
Redskins, 20-14 (W)
1939—Redskins, 7-0 (P)
Redskins, 7-6 (W)
1940—Redskins, 34-17 (P)
Redskins, 13-6 (W)
1941—Redskins, 21-17 (P)
Redskins, 20-14 (W)
1942—Redskins, 14-10 (P)
Redskins, 30-27 (W)
1944—Tie, 31-31 (P)
Eagles, 37-7 (W)
1945—Redskins, 24-14 (W)
Eagles, 16-0 (P)
1946—Eagles, 28-24 (W)
Redskins, 27-10 (P)
1947—Eagles, 45-42 (P)
Eagles, 38-14 (W)
1948—Eagles, 45-0 (W)
Eagles, 42-21 (P)
1949—Eagles, 49-14 (P)
Eagles, 44-21 (W)
1950—Eagles, 35-3 (P)
Eagles, 33-0 (W)
1951—Redskins, 27-23 (P)
Eagles, 35-21 (W)
1952—Eagles, 38-20 (P)
Redskins, 27-21 (W)
1953—Tie, 21-21 (P)
Redskins, 10-0 (W)
1954—Eagles, 49-21 (W)
Eagles, 41-33 (P)
1955—Redskins, 31-30 (P)
Redskins, 34-21 (W)
1956—Eagles, 13-9 (P)
Redskins, 19-17 (W)
1957—Eagles, 21-12 (P)
Redskins, 42-7 (W)
1958—Redskins, 24-14 (P)
Redskins, 20-0 (W)
1959—Eagles, 30-23 (P)
Eagles, 34-14 (W)
1960—Eagles, 19-13 (P)
Eagles, 38-28 (W)
1961—Eagles, 14-7 (P)
Eagles, 27-24 (W)
1962—Redskins, 27-21 (P)
Eagles, 37-14 (W)
1963—Eagles, 37-24 (W)
Redskins, 13-10 (P)
1964—Redskins, 35-20 (W)
Redskins, 21-10 (P)
1965—Redskins, 23-21 (W)
Eagles, 21-14 (P)
1966—Redskins, 27-13 (P)
Eagles, 37-28 (W)
1967—Eagles, 35-24 (P)
Tie, 35-35 (W)
1968—Redskins, 17-14 (W)
Redskins, 16-10 (P)
1969—Tie, 28-28 (W)
Redskins, 34-29 (P)
1970—Redskins, 33-21 (P)
Redskins, 24-6 (W)
1971—Tie, 7-7 (W)
Redskins, 20-13 (P)
1972—Redskins, 14-0 (W)
Redskins, 23-7 (P)
1973—Redskins, 28-7 (P)
Redskins, 38-20 (W)
1974—Redskins, 27-20 (P)
Redskins, 26-7 (W)
1975—Eagles, 26-10 (P)
Eagles, 26-3 (W)
1976—Redskins, 20-17 (P) OT
Redskins, 24-0 (W)
1977—Redskins, 23-17 (W)
Redskins, 17-14 (P)
1978—Redskins, 35-30 (W)
Eagles, 17-10 (P)
1979—Eagles, 28-17 (P)
Redskins, 17-7 (W)
1980—Eagles, 24-14 (P)
Eagles, 24-0 (W)
1981—Eagles, 36-13 (P)
Redskins, 15-13 (W)
1982—Redskins, 37-34 (P) OT
Redskins, 13-9 (W)
1983—Redskins, 23-13 (P)
Redskins, 28-24 (W)
1984—Redskins, 20-0 (W)
Eagles, 16-10 (P)
1985—Eagles, 19-6 (W)
Redskins, 17-12 (P)
1986—Redskins, 41-14 (W)
Redskins, 21-14 (P)
1987—Redskins, 34-24 (W)
Eagles, 31-27 (P)
1988—Redskins, 17-10 (W)
Redskins, 20-19 (P)
1989—Eagles, 42-37 (W)
Redskins, 10-3 (P)
1990—Redskins, 13-7 (W)
Eagles, 28-14 (P)
**Redskins, 20-6 (P)
1991—Redskins, 23-0 (W)
Eagles, 24-22 (P)
1992—Redskins, 16-12 (W)
Eagles, 17-13 (P)
1993—Eagles, 34-31 (P)
Eagles, 17-14 (W)
1994—Eagles, 21-17 (P)
Eagles, 31-29 (W)
1995—Eagles, 37-34 (P) (OT)
Eagles, 14-7 (W)
(RS Pts.—Eagles 2,450, Redskins 2,411)
(PS Pts.—Redskins 20, Eagles 6)
**Franchise in Boston prior to 1937*
***NFC First-Round Playoff*

PITTSBURGH vs. ARIZONA
RS: Steelers lead series, 29-22-3;
See Arizona vs. Pittsburgh

PITTSBURGH vs. ATLANTA
RS: Steelers lead series, 9-1;
See Atlanta vs. Pittsburgh

PITTSBURGH vs. BUFFALO
RS: Series tied, 7-7
PS: Steelers lead series, 2-1;
See Buffalo vs. Pittsburgh

PITTSBURGH vs. CHICAGO
RS: Bears lead series, 16-5-1;
See Chicago vs. Pittsburgh

PITTSBURGH vs. CINCINNATI
RS: Steelers lead series, 29-22;
See Cincinnati vs. Pittsburgh

PITTSBURGH vs. CLEVELAND
RS: Browns lead series, 52-40
PS: Steelers lead series, 1-0;
See Cleveland vs. Pittsburgh

PITTSBURGH vs. DALLAS
RS: Cowboys lead series, 13-11
PS: Steelers lead series, 2-1;
See Dallas vs. Pittsburgh

PITTSBURGH vs. DENVER
RS: Broncos lead series, 10-5-1
PS: Series tied, 2-2;
See Denver vs. Pittsburgh

PITTSBURGH vs. DETROIT
RS: Lions lead series, 13-12-1;
See Detroit vs. Pittsburgh

PITTSBURGH vs. GREEN BAY
RS: Packers lead series, 18-11;
See Green Bay vs. Pittsburgh

PITTSBURGH vs. HOUSTON
RS: Steelers lead series, 33-18
PS: Steelers lead series, 3-0;
See Houston vs. Pittsburgh

PITTSBURGH vs. INDIANAPOLIS
RS: Steelers lead series, 11-4
PS: Steelers lead series, 3-0;
See Indianapolis vs. Pittsburgh

PITTSBURGH vs. JACKSONVILLE
RS: Series tied, 1-1;
See Jacksonville vs. Pittsburgh

PITTSBURGH vs. KANSAS CITY
RS: Steelers lead series, 13-5
PS: Chiefs lead series, 1-0;
See Kansas City vs. Pittsburgh

PITTSBURGH vs. MIAMI
RS: Dolphins lead series, 8-6
PS: Dolphins lead series, 2-1;
See Miami vs. Pittsburgh

PITTSBURGH vs. MINNESOTA
RS: Vikings lead series, 8-4
PS: Steelers lead series, 1-0;
See Minnesota vs. Pittsburgh

PITTSBURGH vs. NEW ENGLAND
RS: Steelers lead series, 10-3;
See New England vs. Pittsburgh

PITTSBURGH vs. NEW ORLEANS
RS: Steelers lead series, 6-5;
See New Orleans vs. Pittsburgh

PITTSBURGH vs. N.Y. GIANTS
RS: Giants lead series, 42-27-3;
See N.Y. Giants vs. Pittsburgh

PITTSBURGH vs. N.Y. JETS
RS: Steelers lead series, 12-1;
See N.Y. Jets vs. Pittsburgh

PITTSBURGH vs. OAKLAND
RS: Raiders lead series, 7-5
PS: Series tied, 3-3;
See Oakland vs. Pittsburgh

PITTSBURGH vs. PHILADELPHIA
RS: Eagles lead series, 43-26-3
PS: Eagles lead series, 1-0;
See Philadelphia vs. Pittsburgh

***PITTSBURGH vs. **ST. LOUIS**
RS: Rams lead series, 14-4-2
PS: Steelers lead series, 1-0
1938—Rams, 13-7 (New Orleans)
1939—Tie, 14-14 (C)
1941—Rams, 17-14 (Akron)
1947—Rams, 48-7 (P)
1948—Rams, 31-14 (LA)
1949—Tie, 7-7 (P)
1952—Rams, 28-14 (LA)
1955—Rams, 27-26 (LA)
1956—Steelers, 30-13 (P)
1961—Rams, 24-14 (LA)
1964—Rams, 26-14 (P)
1968—Rams, 45-10 (LA)
1971—Rams, 23-14 (P)
1975—Rams, 10-3 (LA)
1978—Rams, 10-7 (LA)
1979—***Steelers, 31-19 (Pasadena)
1981—Steelers, 24-0 (P)
1984—Steelers, 24-14 (P)
1987—Rams, 31-21 (LA)
1990—Steelers, 41-10 (P)
1993—Rams, 27-0 (LA)
(RS Pts.—Rams 418, Steelers 305)
(PS Pts.—Steelers 31, Rams 19)
**Steelers known as Pirates prior to 1941*
***Franchise in Los Angeles prior to 1995 and in Cleveland prior to 1946*
****Super Bowl XIV*

PITTSBURGH vs. SAN DIEGO
RS: Steelers lead series, 15-5
PS: Chargers lead series, 2-0
1971—Steelers, 21-17 (P)
1972—Steelers, 24-2 (SD)
1973—Steelers, 38-21 (P)
1975—Steelers, 37-0 (SD)
1976—Steelers, 23-0 (P)
1977—Steelers, 10-9 (SD)
1979—Chargers, 35-7 (SD)
1980—Chargers, 26-17 (SD)
1982—*Chargers, 31-28 (P)
1983—Steelers, 26-3 (P)
1984—Steelers, 52-24 (P)
1985—Chargers, 54-44 (SD)
1987—Steelers, 20-16 (SD)
1988—Chargers, 20-14 (SD)
1989—Steelers, 20-17 (P)
1990—Steelers, 36-14 (P)
1991—Steelers, 26-20 (P)
1992—Steelers, 23-6 (SD)
1993—Steelers,.16-3 (P)
1994—Chargers, 37-34 (SD)
**Chargers, 17-13 (P)
1995—Steelers, 31-16 (P)
(RS Pts.—Steelers 519, Chargers 340)
(PS Pts.—Chargers 48, Steelers 41)
**AFC First-Round Playoff*
***AFC Championship*

PITTSBURGH vs. SAN FRANCISCO
RS: 49ers lead series, 8-7
1951—49ers, 28-24 (P)
1952—Steelers, 24-7 (SF)
1954—49ers, 31-3 (SF)
1958—49ers, 23-20 (SF)
1961—Steelers, 20-10 (P)
1965—49ers, 27-17 (SF)
1968—49ers, 45-28 (P)
1973—Steelers, 37-14 (SF)
1977—Steelers, 27-0 (P)
1978—Steelers, 24-7 (SF)
1981—49ers, 17-14 (P)
1984—Steelers, 20-17 (SF)
1987—Steelers, 30-17 (P)
1990—49ers, 27-7 (SF)

ALL-TIME TEAM VS. TEAM RESULTS

1993—49ers, 24-13 (P)
(RS Pts.—Steelers 308, 49ers 294)
PITTSBURGH vs. SEATTLE
RS: Seahawks lead series, 6-5
1977—Steelers, 30-20 (P)
1978—Steelers, 21-10 (P)
1981—Seahawks, 24-21 (S)
1982—Seahawks, 16-0 (S)
1983—Steelers, 27-21 (S)
1986—Seahawks, 30-0 (S)
1987—Steelers, 13-9 (P)
1991—Seahawks, 27-7 (P)
1992—Steelers, 20-14 (P)
1993—Seahawks, 16-6 (S)
1994—Seahawks, 30-13 (S)
(RS Pts.—Seahawks 217, Steelers 158)
PITTSBURGH vs. TAMPA BAY
RS: Steelers lead series, 4-0
1976—Steelers, 42-0 (P)
1980—Steelers, 24-21 (TB)
1983—Steelers, 17-12 (P)
1989—Steelers, 31-22 (TB)
(RS Pts.—Steelers 114, Buccaneers 55)
***PITTSBURGH vs. **WASHINGTON**
RS: Redskins lead series, 42-27-3
1933—Redskins, 21-6 (P)
Pirates, 16-14 (B)
1934—Redskins, 7-0 (P)
Redskins, 39-0 (B)
1935—Pirates, 6-0 (P)
Redskins, 13-3 (B)
1936—Pirates, 10-0 (P)
Redskins, 30-0 (B)
1937—Redskins, 34-20 (W)
Pirates, 21-13 (P)
1938—Redskins, 7-0 (P)
Redskins, 15-0 (W)
1939—Redskins, 44-14 (W)
Redskins, 21-14 (P)
1940—Redskins, 40-10 (P)
Redskins, 37-10 (W)
1941—Redskins, 24-20 (P)
Redskins, 23-3 (W)
1942—Redskins, 28-14 (W)
Redskins, 14-0 (P)
1945—Redskins, 14-0 (P)
Redskins, 24-0 (W)
1946—Tie, 14-14 (W)
Steelers, 14-7 (P)
1947—Redskins, 27-26 (W)
Steelers, 21-14 (P)
1948—Redskins, 17-14 (W)
Steelers, 10-7 (P)
1949—Redskins, 27-14 (P)
Redskins, 27-14 (W)
1950—Steelers, 26-7 (W)
Redskins, 24-7 (P)
1951—Redskins, 22-7 (P)
Steelers, 20-10 (W)
1952—Redskins, 28-24 (P)
Steelers, 24-23 (W)
1953—Redskins, 17-9 (P)
Steelers, 14-13 (W)
1954—Steelers, 37-7 (P)
Redskins, 17-14 (W)
1955—Redskins, 23-14 (P)
Redskins, 28-17 (W)
1956—Steelers, 30-13 (P)
Steelers, 23-0 (W)
1957—Steelers, 28-7 (P)
Redskins, 10-3 (W)
1958—Steelers, 24-16 (P)
Tie, 14-14 (W)
1959—Redskins, 23-17 (P)
Steelers, 27-6 (W)
1960—Tie, 27-27 (W)
Steelers, 22-10 (P)
1961—Steelers, 20-0 (P)
Steelers, 30-14 (W)
1962—Steelers, 23-21 (P)
Steelers, 27-24 (W)
1963—Steelers, 38-27 (P)
Steelers, 34-28 (W)
1964—Redskins, 30-0 (P)
Steelers, 14-7 (W)
1965—Redskins, 31-3 (P)
Redskins, 35-14 (W)
1966—Redskins, 33-27 (P)
Redskins, 24-10 (W)
1967—Redskins, 15-10 (P)
1968—Redskins, 16-13 (W)
1969—Redskins, 14-7 (P)
1973—Steelers, 21-16 (P)
1979—Steelers, 38-7 (P)
1985—Redskins, 30-23 (P)
1988—Redskins, 30-29 (W)
1991—Redskins, 41-14 (P)
(RS Pts.—Redskins 1,390, Steelers 1,117)
**Steelers known as Pirates prior to 1941*
***Franchise in Boston prior to 1937*

ST. LOUIS vs. ARIZONA
RS: Rams lead series, 23-19-2
PS: Rams lead series, 1-0;
See Arizona vs. St. Louis
ST. LOUIS vs. ATLANTA
RS: Rams lead series, 37-19-2;
See Atlanta vs. St. Louis
ST. LOUIS vs. BUFFALO
RS: Bills lead series, 4-3;
See Buffalo vs. St. Louis
ST. LOUIS vs. CAROLINA
RS: Rams lead series, 2-0;
See Carolina vs. St. Louis
ST. LOUIS vs. CHICAGO
RS: Bears lead series, 45-30-3
PS: Series tied, 1-1;
See Chicago vs. St. Louis
ST. LOUIS vs. CINCINNATI
RS: Bengals lead series, 5-2;
See Cincinnati vs. St. Louis
ST. LOUIS vs. CLEVELAND
RS: Browns lead series, 8-7
PS: Browns lead series, 2-1;
See Cleveland vs. St. Louis
ST. LOUIS vs. DALLAS
RS: Rams lead series, 9-8
PS: Series tied, 4-4;
See Dallas vs. St. Louis
ST. LOUIS vs. DENVER
RS: Rams lead series, 4-3;
See Denver vs. St. Louis
ST. LOUIS vs. DETROIT
RS: Rams lead series, 39-35-1
PS: Lions lead series, 1-0;
See Detroit vs. St. Louis
ST. LOUIS vs. GREEN BAY
RS: Rams lead series, 43-37-2
PS: Packers lead series, 1-0;
See Green Bay vs. St. Louis
ST. LOUIS vs. HOUSTON
RS: Rams lead series, 5-2;
See Houston vs. St. Louis
ST. LOUIS vs. INDIANAPOLIS
RS: Colts lead series, 21-16-2;
See Indianapolis vs. St. Louis
ST. LOUIS vs. KANSAS CITY
RS: Rams lead series, 4-1;
See Kansas City vs. St. Louis
ST. LOUIS vs. MIAMI
RS: Dolphins lead series, 6-1;
See Miami vs. St. Louis
ST. LOUIS vs. MINNESOTA
RS: Vikings lead series, 15-11-2
PS: Vikings lead series, 5-1;
See Minnesota vs. St. Louis
ST. LOUIS vs. NEW ENGLAND
RS: Series tied, 3-3;
See New England vs. St. Louis
ST. LOUIS vs. NEW ORLEANS
RS: Rams lead series, 28-24;
See New Orleans vs. St. Louis
ST. LOUIS vs. N.Y. GIANTS
RS: Rams lead series, 21-9
PS: Series tied, 1-1;
See N.Y. Giants vs. St. Louis
ST. LOUIS vs. N.Y. JETS
RS: Rams lead series, 6-2;
See N.Y. Jets vs. St. Louis
ST. LOUIS vs. OAKLAND
RS: Raiders lead series, 6-2;
See Oakland vs. St. Louis
ST. LOUIS vs. PHILADELPHIA
RS: Rams lead series, 15-12-1
PS: Series tied, 1-1;
See Philadelphia vs. St. Louis
ST. LOUIS vs. PITTSBURGH
RS: Rams lead series, 14-4-2
PS: Steelers lead series, 1-0;
See Pittsburgh vs. St. Louis
***ST. LOUIS vs. SAN DIEGO**
RS: Series tied, 3-3
1970—Rams, 37-10 (LA)
1975—Rams, 13-10 (SD) OT
1979—Chargers, 40-16 (LA)
1988—Chargers, 38-24 (LA)
1991—Rams, 30-24 (LA)
1994—Chargers, 31-17 (SD)
(RS Pts.—Chargers 153, Rams 137)
**Franchise in Los Angeles prior to 1995*
***ST. LOUIS vs. SAN FRANCISCO**
RS: Rams lead series, 48-42-2
PS: 49ers lead series, 1-0
1950—Rams, 35-14 (SF)
Rams, 28-21 (LA)
1951—49ers, 44-17 (SF)
Rams, 23-16 (LA)
1952—Rams, 35-9 (LA)
Rams, 34-21 (SF)
1953—49ers, 31-30 (SF)
49ers, 31-27 (LA)
1954—Tie, 24-24 (LA)
Rams, 42-34 (SF)
1955—Rams, 23-14 (SF)
Rams, 27-14 (LA)
1956—49ers, 33-30 (SF)
Rams, 30-6 (LA)
1957—49ers, 23-20 (SF)
Rams, 37-24 (LA)
1958—Rams, 33-3 (SF)
Rams, 56-7 (LA)
1959—49ers, 34-0 (SF)
49ers, 24-16 (LA)
1960—49ers, 13-9 (SF)
49ers, 23-7 (LA)
1961—49ers, 35-0 (SF)
Rams, 17-7 (LA)
1962—Rams, 28-14 (SF)
49ers, 24-17 (LA)
1963—Rams, 28-21 (LA)
Rams, 21-17 (SF)
1964—Rams, 42-14 (LA)
49ers, 28-7 (SF)
1965—49ers, 45-21 (LA)
49ers, 30-27 (SF)
1966—Rams, 34-3 (LA)
49ers, 21-13 (SF)
1967—49ers, 27-24 (LA)
Rams, 17-7 (SF)
1968—Rams, 24-10 (LA)
Tie, 20-20 (SF)
1969—Rams, 27-21 (SF)
Rams, 41-30 (LA)
1970—49ers, 20-6 (LA)
Rams, 30-13 (SF)
1971—Rams, 20-13 (SF)
Rams, 17-6 (LA)
1972—Rams, 31-7 (LA)
Rams, 26-16 (SF)
1973—Rams, 40-20 (SF)
Rams, 31-13 (LA)
1974—Rams, 37-14 (LA)
Rams, 15-13 (SF)
1975—Rams, 23-14 (SF)
49ers, 24-23 (LA)
1976—49ers, 16-0 (LA)
Rams, 23-3 (SF)
1977—Rams, 34-14 (LA)
Rams, 23-10 (SF)
1978—Rams, 27-10 (LA)
Rams, 31-28 (SF)
1979—Rams, 27-24 (LA)
Rams, 26-20 (SF)
1980—Rams, 48-26 (LA)
Rams, 31-17 (SF)
1981—49ers, 20-17 (SF)
49ers, 33-31 (LA)
1982—49ers, 30-24 (LA)
Rams, 21-20 (SF)
1983—Rams, 10-7 (SF)
49ers, 45-35 (LA)
1984—49ers, 33-0 (LA)
49ers, 19-16 (SF)
1985—49ers, 28-14 (LA)
Rams, 27-20 (SF)
1986—Rams, 16-13 (LA)
49ers, 24-14 (SF)
1987—49ers, 31-10 (LA)
49ers, 48-0 (SF)
1988—49ers, 24-21 (LA)
Rams, 38-16 (SF)
1989—Rams, 13-12 (SF)
49ers, 30-27 (LA)
**49ers, 30-3 (SF)
1990—Rams, 28-17 (SF)
49ers, 26-10 (LA)
1991—49ers, 27-10 (SF)
49ers, 33-10 (LA)
1992—49ers, 27-24 (SF)
49ers, 27-10 (LA)
1993—49ers, 40-17 (SF)
49ers, 35-10 (LA)
1994—49ers, 34-19 (LA)
49ers, 31-27 (SF)
1995—49ers, 44-10 (StL)
49ers, 41-13 (SF)
(RS Pts.—Rams 2,082, 49ers 2,013)
(PS Pts.—49ers 30, Rams 3)
**Franchise in Los Angeles prior to 1995*
***NFC Championship*
***ST. LOUIS vs. SEATTLE**
RS: Rams lead series, 4-1
1976—Rams, 45-6 (LA)
1979—Rams, 24-0 (S)
1985—Rams, 35-24 (S)
1988—Rams, 31-10 (LA)
1991—Seahawks, 23-9 (S)
(RS Pts.—Rams 144, Seahawks 63)
**Franchise in Los Angeles prior to 1995*
***ST. LOUIS vs. TAMPA BAY**
RS: Rams lead series, 8-3
PS: Rams lead series, 1-0
1977—Rams, 31-0 (LA)
1978—Rams, 26-23 (LA)
1979—Buccaneers, 21-6 (TB)
**Rams, 9-0 (TB)
1980—Buccaneers, 10-9 (TB)
1984—Rams, 34-33 (TB)
1985—Rams, 31-27 (TB)
1986—Rams, 26-20 (LA) OT
1987—Rams, 35-3 (LA)
1990—Rams, 35-14 (TB)
1992—Rams, 31-27 (TB)
1994—Buccaneers, 24-14 (TB)
(RS Pts.—Rams 278, Buccaneers 202)
(PS Pts.—Rams 9, Buccaneers 0)
**Franchise in Los Angeles prior to 1995*
***NFC Championship*
***ST. LOUIS vs. WASHINGTON**
RS: Redskins lead series, 16-5-1
PS: Series tied, 2-2
1937—Redskins, 16-7 (C)
1938—Redskins, 37-13 (W)
1941—Redskins, 17-13 (W)
1942—Redskins, 33-14 (W)
1944—Redskins, 14-10 (W)
1945—**Rams, 15-14 (C)
1948—Rams, 41-13 (W)
1949—Rams, 53-27 (LA)
1951—Redskins, 31-21 (W)
1962—Redskins, 20-14 (W)
1963—Redskins, 37-14 (LA)

1967—Tie, 28-28 (LA)
1969—Rams, 24-13 (W)
1971—Redskins, 38-24 (LA)
1974—Redskins, 23-17 (LA)
***Rams, 19-10 (LA)
1977—Redskins, 17-14 (W)
1981—Redskins, 30-7 (LA)
1983—Redskins, 42-20 (LA)
***Redskins, 51-7 (W)
1986—****Redskins, 19-7 (W)
1987—Rams, 30-26 (W)
1991—Redskins, 27-6 (LA)
1993—Rams, 10-6 (LA)
1994—Redskins, 24-21 (LA)
1995—Redskins, 35-23 (StL)
(RS Pts.—Redskins 554, Rams 424)
(PS Pts.—Redskins 94, Rams 48)
Franchise in Los Angeles prior to 1995 and in Cleveland prior to 1946
***NFL Championship*
****NFC Divisional Playoff*
*****NFC First-Round Playoff*

SAN DIEGO vs. ARIZONA
RS: Chargers lead series, 6-1;
See Arizona vs. San Diego
SAN DIEGO vs. ATLANTA
RS: Falcons lead series, 4-1;
See Atlanta vs. San Diego
SAN DIEGO vs. BUFFALO
RS: Chargers lead series, 16-7-2
PS: Bills lead series, 2-1;
See Buffalo vs. San Diego
SAN DIEGO vs. CHICAGO
RS: Chargers lead series, 4-2;
See Chicago vs. San Diego
SAN DIEGO vs. CINCINNATI
RS: Chargers lead series, 13-8
PS: Bengals lead series, 1-0;
See Cincinnati vs. San Diego
SAN DIEGO vs. CLEVELAND
RS: Chargers lead series, 9-6-1;
See Cleveland vs. San Diego
SAN DIEGO vs. DALLAS
RS: Cowboys lead series, 5-1;
See Dallas vs. San Diego
SAN DIEGO vs. DENVER
RS: Broncos lead series, 37-34-1;
See Denver vs. San Diego
SAN DIEGO vs. DETROIT
RS: Lions lead series, 3-2;
See Detroit vs. San Diego
SAN DIEGO vs. GREEN BAY
RS: Packers lead series, 4-1;
See Green Bay vs. San Diego
SAN DIEGO vs. HOUSTON
RS: Chargers lead series, 18-13-1
PS: Oilers lead series, 3-0;
See Houston vs. San Diego
SAN DIEGO vs. INDIANAPOLIS
RS: Chargers lead series, 10-5
PS: Colts lead series, 1-0;
See Indianapolis vs. San Diego
SAN DIEGO vs. KANSAS CITY
RS: Chiefs lead series, 37-33-1
PS: Chargers lead series, 1-0;
See Kansas City vs. San Diego
SAN DIEGO vs. MIAMI
RS: Chargers lead series, 10-6
PS: Series tied, 2-2;
See Miami vs. San Diego
SAN DIEGO vs. MINNESOTA
RS: Chargers lead series, 4-3;
See Minnesota vs. San Diego
SAN DIEGO vs. NEW ENGLAND
RS: Patriots lead series, 14-11-2
PS: Chargers lead series, 1-0;
See New England vs. San Diego
SAN DIEGO vs. NEW ORLEANS
RS: Chargers lead series, 5-1;
See New Orleans vs. San Diego
SAN DIEGO vs. N.Y. GIANTS
RS: Giants lead series, 4-3;
See N.Y. Giants vs. San Diego
SAN DIEGO vs. N.Y. JETS
RS: Chargers lead series, 17-9-1;
See N.Y. Jets vs. San Diego
SAN DIEGO vs. OAKLAND
RS: Raiders lead series, 43-27-2
PS: Raiders lead series, 1-0;
See Oakland vs. San Diego
SAN DIEGO vs. PHILADELPHIA
RS: Chargers lead series, 4-2;
See Philadelphia vs. San Diego
SAN DIEGO vs. PITTSBURGH
RS: Steelers lead series, 15-5
PS: Chargers lead series, 2-0;
See Pittsburgh vs. San Diego
SAN DIEGO vs. ST. LOUIS
RS: Series tied, 3-3
See St. Louis vs. San Diego
SAN DIEGO vs. SAN FRANCISCO
RS: 49ers lead series, 4-3
PS: 49ers lead series, 1-0;
1972—49ers, 34-3 (SF)
1976—Chargers, 13-7 (SD) OT
1979—Chargers, 31-9 (SD)
1982—Chargers, 41-37 (SF)
1988—49ers, 48-10 (SD)
1991—49ers, 34-14 (SF)
1994—49ers, 38-15 (SD)
*49ers, 49-26 (Miami)
(RS Pts.—49ers 207, Chargers 127)
(PS Pts.—49ers 49, Chargers 26)
**Super Bowl XXIX*
SAN DIEGO vs. SEATTLE
RS: Chargers lead series, 19-15
1977—Chargers, 30-28 (S)
1978—Chargers, 24-20 (S)
Chargers, 37-10 (SD)
1979—Chargers, 33-16 (S)
Chargers, 20-10 (SD)
1980—Chargers, 34-13 (S)
Chargers, 21-14 (SD)
1981—Chargers, 24-10 (SD)
Seahawks, 44-23 (S)
1983—Seahawks, 34-31 (S)
Chargers, 28-21 (SD)
1984—Seahawks, 31-17 (S)
Seahawks, 24-0 (SD)
1985—Seahawks, 49-35 (SD)
Seahawks, 26-21 (S)
1986—Seahawks, 33-7 (S)
Seahawks, 34-24 (SD)
1987—Seahawks, 34-3 (S)
1988—Chargers, 17-6 (SD)
Seahawks, 17-14 (S)
1989—Seahawks, 17-16 (SD)
Seahawks, 10-7 (S)
1990—Chargers, 31-14 (S)
Seahawks, 13-10 (SD) OT
1991—Seahawks, 20-9 (S)
Chargers, 17-14 (SD)
1992—Chargers, 17-6 (SD)
Chargers, 31-14 (S)
1993—Chargers, 18-12 (SD)
Seahawks, 31-14 (S)
1994—Chargers, 24-10 (S)
Chargers, 35-15 (SD)
1995—Chargers, 14-10 (SD)
Chargers, 35-25 (S)
(RS Pts.—Chargers 721, Seahawks 685)
SAN DIEGO vs. TAMPA BAY
RS: Chargers lead series, 6-0
1976—Chargers, 23-0 (TB)
1981—Chargers, 24-23 (TB)
1987—Chargers, 17-13 (TB)
1990—Chargers, 41-10 (SD)
1992—Chargers, 29-14 (SD)
1993—Chargers, 32-17 (TB)
(RS Pts.—Chargers 166, Buccaneers 77)
SAN DIEGO vs. WASHINGTON
RS: Redskins lead series, 5-0
1973—Redskins, 38-0 (W)
1980—Redskins, 40-17 (W)
1983—Redskins, 27-24 (SD)
1986—Redskins, 30-27 (SD)
1989—Redskins, 26-21 (W)
(RS Pts.—Redskins 161, Chargers 89)

SAN FRANCISCO vs. ARIZONA
RS: 49ers lead series, 10-9;
See Arizona vs. San Francisco
SAN FRANCISCO vs. ATLANTA
RS: 49ers lead series, 35-22-1;
See Atlanta vs. San Francisco
SAN FRANCISCO vs. BUFFALO
RS: Series tied, 3-3;
See Buffalo vs. San Francisco
SAN FRANCISCO vs. CAROLINA
RS: Series tied, 1-1;
See Carolina vs. San Francisco
SAN FRANCISCO vs. CHICAGO
RS: Series tied, 25-25-1
PS: 49ers lead series, 3-0;
See Chicago vs. San Francisco
SAN FRANCISCO vs. CINCINNATI
RS: 49ers lead series, 6-1
PS: 49ers lead series, 2-0;
See Cincinnati vs. San Francisco
SAN FRANCISCO vs. CLEVELAND
RS: Browns lead series, 9-6;
See Cleveland vs. San Francisco
SAN FRANCISCO vs. DALLAS
RS: 49ers lead series, 11-6-1
PS: Cowboys lead series, 5-2;
See Dallas vs. San Francisco
SAN FRANCISCO vs. DENVER
RS: Broncos lead series, 4-3
PS: 49ers lead series, 1-0;
See Denver vs. San Francisco
SAN FRANCISCO vs. DETROIT
RS: 49ers lead series, 27-26-1
PS: Series tied, 1-1;
See Detroit vs. San Francisco
SAN FRANCISCO vs. GREEN BAY
RS: 49ers lead series, 25-21-1
PS: Packers lead series, 1-0;
See Green Bay vs. San Francisco
SAN FRANCISCO vs. HOUSTON
RS: 49ers lead series, 5-3;
See Houston vs. San Francisco
SAN FRANCISCO vs. INDIANAPOLIS
RS: Colts lead series, 22-16;
See Indianapolis vs. San Francisco
SAN FRANCISCO vs. KANSAS CITY
RS: 49ers lead series, 4-2;
See Kansas City vs. San Francisco
SAN FRANCISCO vs. MIAMI
RS: Dolphins lead series, 4-3
PS: 49ers lead series, 1-0;
See Miami vs. San Francisco
SAN FRANCISCO vs. MINNESOTA
RS: Series tied, 16-16-1
PS: 49ers lead series, 3-1;
See Minnesota vs. San Francisco
SAN FRANCISCO vs. NEW ENGLAND
RS: 49ers lead series, 7-1;
See New England vs. San Francisco
SAN FRANCISCO vs. NEW ORLEANS
RS: 49ers lead series, 36-15-2;
See New Orleans vs. San Francisco
SAN FRANCISCO vs. N.Y. GIANTS
RS: Series tied, 11-11
PS: Series tied, 3-3;
See N.Y. Giants vs. San Francisco
SAN FRANCISCO vs. N.Y. JETS
RS: 49ers lead series, 6-1;
See N.Y. Jets vs. San Francisco
SAN FRANCISCO vs. OAKLAND
RS: Raiders lead series, 5-3;
See Oakland vs. San Francisco
SAN FRANCISCO vs. PHILADELPHIA
RS: 49ers lead series, 13-6-1;
See Philadelphia vs. San Francisco
SAN FRANCISCO vs. PITTSBURGH
RS: 49ers lead series, 8-7;
See Pittsburgh vs. San Francisco
SAN FRANCISCO vs. ST. LOUIS
RS: Rams lead series, 48-42-2
PS: 49ers lead series, 1-0;
See St. Louis vs. San Francisco
SAN FRANCISCO vs. SAN DIEGO
RS: 49ers lead series, 4-3
PS: 49ers lead series, 1-0;
See San Diego vs. San Francisco
SAN FRANCISCO vs. SEATTLE
RS: 49ers lead series, 4-1
1976—49ers, 37-21 (S)
1979—Seahawks, 35-24 (SF)
1985—49ers, 19-6 (SF)
1988—49ers, 38-7 (S)
1991—49ers, 24-22 (S)
(RS Pts.—49ers 142, Seahawks 91)
SAN FRANCISCO vs. TAMPA BAY
RS: 49ers lead series, 12-1
1977—49ers, 20-10 (SF)
1978—49ers, 6-3 (SF)
1979—49ers, 23-7 (SF)
1980—Buccaneers, 24-23 (SF)
1983—49ers, 35-21 (SF)
1984—49ers, 24-17 (SF)
1986—49ers, 31-7 (TB)
1987—49ers, 24-10 (TB)
1989—49ers, 20-16 (TB)
1990—49ers, 31-7 (SF)
1992—49ers, 21-14 (SF)
1993—49ers, 45-21 (TB)
1994—49ers, 41-16 (SF)
(RS. Pts.—49ers 344, Buccaneers 173)
SAN FRANCISCO vs. WASHINGTON
RS: 49ers lead series, 10-6-1
PS: 49ers lead series, 3-1
1952—49ers, 23-17 (W)
1954—49ers, 41-7 (SF)
1955—Redskins, 7-0 (W)
1961—49ers, 35-3 (SF)
1967—Redskins, 31-28 (W)
1969—Tie, 17-17 (SF)
1970—49ers, 26-17 (SF)
1971—*49ers, 24-20 (SF)
1973—Redskins, 33-9 (W)
1976—Redskins, 24-21 (SF)
1978—Redskins, 38-20 (W)
1981—49ers, 30-17 (W)
1983—**Redskins, 24-21 (W)
1984—49ers, 37-31 (SF)
1985—49ers, 35-8 (W)
1986—Redskins, 14-6 (W)
1988—49ers, 37-21 (SF)
1990—49ers, 26-13 (SF)
*49ers, 28-10 (SF)
1992—*49ers, 20-13 (SF)
1994—49ers, 37-22 (W)
(RS Pts.—49ers 428, Redskins 320)
(PS Pts.—49ers 93, Redskins 67)
**NFC Divisional Playoff*
***NFC Championship*

SEATTLE vs. ARIZONA
RS: Cardinals lead series, 5-0;
See Arizona vs. Seattle
SEATTLE vs. ATLANTA
RS: Seahawks lead series, 4-1;
See Atlanta vs. Seattle
SEATTLE vs. BUFFALO
RS: Seahawks lead series, 3-2;
See Buffalo vs. Seattle
SEATTLE vs. CHICAGO
RS: Seahawks lead series, 4-2;
See Chicago vs. Seattle
SEATTLE vs. CINCINNATI
RS: Series tied, 7-7
PS: Bengals lead series, 1-0;
See Cincinnati vs. Seattle
SEATTLE vs. CLEVELAND
RS: Seahawks lead series, 9-4;
See Cleveland vs. Seattle
SEATTLE vs. DALLAS
RS: Cowboys lead series, 4-1;
See Dallas vs. Seattle
SEATTLE vs. DENVER

ALL-TIME TEAM VS. TEAM RESULTS

RS: Broncos lead series, 22-15
PS: Seahawks lead series, 1-0;
See Denver vs. Seattle
SEATTLE vs. DETROIT
RS: Seahawks lead series, 4-2;
See Detroit vs. Seattle
SEATTLE vs. GREEN BAY
RS: Series tied, 3-3;
See Green Bay vs. Seattle
SEATTLE vs. HOUSTON
RS: Seahawks lead series, 5-4
PS: Oilers lead series, 1-0;
See Houston vs. Seattle
SEATTLE vs. INDIANAPOLIS
RS: Colts lead series, 4-1;
See Indianapolis vs. Seattle
SEATTLE vs. JACKSONVILLE
RS: Seahawks lead series, 1-0;
See Jacksonville vs. Seattle
SEATTLE vs. KANSAS CITY
RS: Chiefs lead series, 22-13;
See Kansas City vs. Seattle
SEATTLE vs. MIAMI
RS: Dolphins lead series, 4-1
PS: Series tied, 1-1;
See Miami vs. Seattle
SEATTLE vs. MINNESOTA
RS: Seahawks lead series, 3-2;
See Minnesota vs. Seattle
SEATTLE vs. NEW ENGLAND
RS: Seahawks lead series, 7-6;
See New England vs. Seattle
SEATTLE vs. NEW ORLEANS
RS: Saints lead series, 3-2;
See New Orleans vs. Seattle
SEATTLE vs. N.Y. GIANTS
RS: Giants lead series, 5-3;
See N.Y. Giants vs. Seattle
SEATTLE vs. N.Y. JETS
RS: Seahawks lead series, 8-4;
See N.Y. Jets vs. Seattle
SEATTLE vs. OAKLAND
RS: Raiders lead series, 20-16
PS: Series tied, 1-1;
See Oakland vs. Seattle
SEATTLE vs. PHILADELPHIA
RS: Eagles lead series, 4-2;
See Philadelphia vs. Seattle
SEATTLE vs. PITTSBURGH
RS: Seahawks lead series, 6-5;
See Pittsburgh vs. Seattle
SEATTLE vs. ST. LOUIS
RS: Rams lead series, 4-1;
See St. Louis vs. Seattle
SEATTLE vs. SAN DIEGO
RS: Chargers lead series, 19-15;
See San Diego vs. Seattle
SEATTLE vs. SAN FRANCISCO
RS: 49ers lead series, 4-1;
See San Francisco vs. Seattle
SEATTLE vs. TAMPA BAY
RS: Seahawks lead series, 3-0
1976—Seahawks, 13-10 (TB)
1977—Seahawks, 30-23 (S)
1994—Seahawks, 22-21 (S)
(RS Pts.—Seahawks 65, Buccaneers 54)
SEATTLE vs. WASHINGTON
RS: Redskins lead series, 5-3
1976—Redskins, 31-7 (W)
1980—Seahawks, 14-0 (W)
1983—Redskins, 27-17 (S)
1986—Redskins, 19-14 (W)
1989—Redskins, 29-0 (S)
1992—Redskins, 16-3 (S)
1994—Seahawks, 28-7 (W)
1995—Seahawks, 27-20 (W)
(RS Pts.—Redskins 149, Seahawks 110)

TAMPA BAY vs. ARIZONA
RS: Series tied, 6-6;
See Arizona vs. Tampa Bay
TAMPA BAY vs. ATLANTA
RS: Falcons lead series, 8-6;
See Atlanta vs. Tampa Bay
TAMPA BAY vs. BUFFALO
RS: Buccaneers lead series, 4-2;
See Buffalo vs. Tampa Bay
TAMPA BAY vs. CAROLINA
RS: Buccaneers lead series, 1-0;
See Carolina vs. Tampa Bay
TAMPA BAY vs. CHICAGO
RS: Bears lead series, 28-8;
See Chicago vs. Tampa Bay
TAMPA BAY vs. CINCINNATI
RS: Bengals lead series, 3-2;
See Cincinnati vs. Tampa Bay
TAMPA BAY vs. CLEVELAND
RS: Browns lead series, 5-0;
See Cleveland vs. Tampa Bay
TAMPA BAY vs. DALLAS
RS: Cowboys lead series, 6-0
PS: Cowboys lead series, 2-0;
See Dallas vs. Tampa Bay
TAMPA BAY vs. DENVER
RS: Broncos lead series, 2-1;
See Denver vs. Tampa Bay
TAMPA BAY vs. DETROIT
RS: Lions lead series, 19-17;
See Detroit vs. Tampa Bay
TAMPA BAY vs. GREEN BAY
RS: Packers lead series, 20-13-1;
See Green Bay vs. Tampa Bay
TAMPA BAY vs. HOUSTON
RS: Oilers lead series, 4-1;
See Houston vs. Tampa Bay
TAMPA BAY vs. INDIANAPOLIS
RS: Colts lead series, 5-3;
See Indianapolis vs. Tampa Bay
TAMPA BAY vs. JACKSONVILLE
RS: Buccaneers lead series, 1-0;
See Jacksonville vs. Tampa Bay
TAMPA BAY vs. KANSAS CITY
RS: Chiefs lead series, 5-2;
See Kansas City vs. Tampa Bay
TAMPA BAY vs. MIAMI
RS: Dolphins lead series, 4-1;
See Miami vs. Tampa Bay
TAMPA BAY vs. MINNESOTA
RS: Vikings lead series, 25-11;
See Minnesota vs. Tampa Bay
TAMPA BAY vs. NEW ENGLAND
RS: Patriots lead series, 3-0;
See New England vs. Tampa Bay
TAMPA BAY vs. NEW ORLEANS
RS: Saints lead series, 12-4;
See New Orleans vs. Tampa Bay
TAMPA BAY vs. N.Y. GIANTS
RS: Giants lead series, 8-3;
See N.Y. Giants vs. Tampa Bay
TAMPA BAY vs. N.Y. JETS
RS: Jets lead series, 5-1;
See N.Y. Jets vs. Tampa Bay
TAMPA BAY vs. OAKLAND
RS: Raiders lead series, 3-0;
See Oakland vs. Tampa Bay
TAMPA BAY vs. PHILADELPHIA
RS: Eagles lead series, 3-2
PS: Buccaneers lead series, 1-0;
See Philadelphia vs. Tampa Bay
TAMPA BAY vs. PITTSBURGH
RS: Steelers lead series, 4-0;
See Pittsburgh vs. Tampa Bay
TAMPA BAY vs. ST. LOUIS
RS: Rams lead series, 8-3
PS: Rams lead series, 1-0;
See St. Louis vs. Tampa Bay
TAMPA BAY vs. SAN DIEGO
RS: Chargers lead series, 6-0;
See San Diego vs. Tampa Bay
TAMPA BAY vs. SAN FRANCISCO
RS: 49ers lead series, 12-1;
See San Francisco vs. Tampa Bay
TAMPA BAY vs. SEATTLE
RS: Seahawks lead series, 3-0;
See Seattle vs. Tampa Bay
TAMPA BAY vs. WASHINGTON
RS: Redskins lead series, 4-3
1977—Redskins, 10-0 (TB)
1982—Redskins, 21-13 (TB)
1989—Redskins, 32-28 (W)
1993—Redskins, 23-17 (TB)
1994—Buccaneers, 26-21 (TB)
Buccaneers, 17-14 (W)
1995—Buccaneers, 14-6 (TB)
(RS Pts.—Redskins 127, Buccaneers 115)

WASHINGTON vs. ARIZONA
RS: Redskins lead series, 62-39-2;
See Arizona vs. Washington
WASHINGTON vs. ATLANTA
RS: Redskins lead series, 13-4-1
PS: Redskins lead series, 1-0;
See Atlanta vs. Washington
WASHINGTON vs. BUFFALO
RS: Redskins lead series, 4-3
PS: Redskins lead series, 1-0;
See Buffalo vs. Washington
WASHINGTON vs. CAROLINA
RS: Panthers lead series, 1-0;
See Carolina vs. Washington
WASHINGTON vs. CHICAGO
RS: Bears lead series, 18-12-1
PS: Redskins lead series, 4-3;
See Chicago vs. Washington
WASHINGTON vs. CINCINNATI
RS: Redskins lead series, 4-2;
See Cincinnati vs. Washington
WASHINGTON vs. CLEVELAND
RS: Browns lead series, 32-9-1;
See Cleveland vs. Washington
WASHINGTON vs. DALLAS
RS: Cowboys lead series, 39-29-2
PS: Redskins lead series, 2-0;
See Dallas vs. Washington
WASHINGTON vs. DENVER
RS: Broncos lead series, 4-3
PS: Redskins lead series, 1-0;
See Denver vs. Washington
WASHINGTON vs. DETROIT
RS: Redskins lead series, 23-8
PS: Redskins lead series, 2-0;
See Detroit vs. Washington
WASHINGTON vs. GREEN BAY
RS: Packers lead series, 13-12-1
PS: Series tied 1-1;
See Green Bay vs. Washington
WASHINGTON vs. HOUSTON
RS: Series tied 3-3;
See Houston vs. Washington
WASHINGTON vs. INDIANAPOLIS
RS: Colts lead series, 16-8;
See Indianapolis vs. Washington
WASHINGTON vs. KANSAS CITY
RS: Chiefs lead series, 4-1;
See Kansas City vs. Washington
WASHINGTON vs. MIAMI
RS: Dolphins lead series, 5-2
PS: Series tied 1-1;
See Miami vs. Washington
WASHINGTON vs. MINNESOTA
RS: Redskins lead series, 6-4
PS: Redskins lead series, 3-2;
See Minnesota vs. Washington
WASHINGTON vs. NEW ENGLAND
RS: Redskins lead series, 4-1;
See New England vs. Washington
WASHINGTON vs. NEW ORLEANS
RS: Redskins lead series, 12-5;
See New Orleans vs. Washington
WASHINGTON vs. N.Y. GIANTS
RS: Giants lead series, 73-50-3
PS: Series tied 1-1;
See N.Y. Giants vs. Washington
WASHINGTON vs. N.Y. JETS
RS: Redskins lead series, 4-1;
See N.Y. Jets vs. Washington
WASHINGTON vs. OAKLAND
RS: Raiders lead series, 6-2
PS: Raiders lead series, 1-0;
See Oakland vs. Washington
WASHINGTON vs. PHILADELPHIA
RS: Redskins lead series, 66-50-5
PS: Redskins lead series, 1-0;
See Philadelphia vs. Washington
WASHINGTON vs. PITTSBURGH
RS: Redskins lead series, 42-27-3;
See Pittsburgh vs. Washington
WASHINGTON vs. ST. LOUIS
RS: Redskins lead series, 16-5-1
PS: Series tied 2-2;
See St. Louis vs. Washington
WASHINGTON vs. SAN DIEGO
RS: Redskins lead series, 5-0;
See San Diego vs. Washington
WASHINGTON vs. SAN FRANCISCO
RS: 49ers lead series, 10-6-1
PS: 49ers lead series, 3-1;
See San Francisco vs. Washington
WASHINGTON vs. SEATTLE
RS: Redskins lead series, 5-3;
See Seattle vs. Washington
WASHINGTON vs. TAMPA BAY
RS: Redskins lead series, 4-3;
See Tampa Bay vs. Washington

RESULTS

Super Bowl	Date	Winner (Share)	Loser (Share)	Score	Site	Attendance
XXX	1-28-96	Dallas ($42,000)	Pittsburgh ($27,000)	27-17	Tempe	76,347
XXIX	1-29-95	San Francisco ($42,000)	San Diego ($26,000)	49-26	Miami	74,107
XXVIII	1-30-94	Dallas ($38,000)	Buffalo ($23,500)	30-13	Atlanta	72,817
XXVII	1-31-93	Dallas ($36,000)	Buffalo ($18,000)	52-17	Pasadena	98,374
XXVI	1-26-92	Washington ($36,000)	Buffalo ($18,000)	37-24	Minneapolis	63,130
XXV	1-27-91	N.Y. Giants ($36,000)	Buffalo ($18,000)	20-19	Tampa	73,813
XXIV	1-28-90	San Francisco ($36,000)	Denver ($18,000)	55-10	New Orleans	72,919
XXIII	1-22-89	San Francisco ($36,000)	Cincinnati ($18,000)	20-16	Miami	75,129
XXII	1-31-88	Washington ($36,000)	Denver ($18,000)	42-10	San Diego	73,302
XXI	1-25-87	N.Y. Giants ($36,000)	Denver ($18,000)	39-20	Pasadena	101,063
XX	1-26-86	Chicago ($36,000)	New England ($18,000)	46-10	New Orleans	73,818
XIX	1-20-85	San Francisco ($36,000)	Miami ($18,000)	38-16	Stanford	84,059
XVIII	1-22-84	L.A. Raiders ($36,000)	Washington ($18,000)	38-9	Tampa	72,920
XVII	1-30-83	Washington ($36,000)	Miami ($18,000)	27-17	Pasadena	103,667
XVI	1-24-82	San Francisco ($18,000)	Cincinnati ($9,000)	26-21	Pontiac	81,270
XV	1-25-81	Oakland ($18,000)	Philadelphia ($9,000)	27-10	New Orleans	76,135
XIV	1-20-80	Pittsburgh ($18,000)	Los Angeles ($9,000)	31-19	Pasadena	103,985
XIII	1-21-79	Pittsburgh ($18,000)	Dallas ($9,000)	35-31	Miami	79,484
XII	1-15-78	Dallas ($18,000)	Denver ($9,000)	27-10	New Orleans	75,583
XI	1-9-77	Oakland ($15,000)	Minnesota ($7,500)	32-14	Pasadena	103,438
X	1-18-76	Pittsburgh ($15,000)	Dallas ($7,500)	21-17	Miami	80,187
IX	1-12-75	Pittsburgh ($15,000)	Minnesota ($7,500)	16-6	New Orleans	80,997
VIII	1-13-74	Miami ($15,000)	Minnesota ($7,500)	24-7	Houston	71,882
VII	1-14-73	Miami ($15,000)	Washington ($7,500)	14-7	Los Angeles	90,182
VI	1-16-72	Dallas ($15,000)	Miami ($7,500)	24-3	New Orleans	81,023
V	1-17-71	Baltimore ($15,000)	Dallas ($7,500)	16-13	Miami	79,204
IV	1-11-70	Kansas City ($15,000)	Minnesota ($7,500)	23-7	New Orleans	80,562
III	1-12-69	N.Y. Jets ($15,000)	Baltimore ($7,500)	16-7	Miami	75,389
II	1-14-68	Green Bay ($15,000)	Oakland ($7,500)	33-14	Miami	75,546
I	1-15-67	Green Bay ($15,000)	Kansas City ($7,500)	35-10	Los Angeles	61,946

SUPER BOWL COMPOSITE STANDINGS

	W	L	Pct.	Pts.	OP
San Francisco 49ers	5	0	1.000	188	89
Green Bay Packers	2	0	1.000	68	24
New York Giants	2	0	1.000	59	39
Chicago Bears	1	0	1.000	46	10
New York Jets	1	0	1.000	16	7
Pittsburgh Steelers	4	1	.800	120	100
Oakland/L.A. Raiders	3	1	.750	111	66
Dallas Cowboys	5	3	.625	221	132
Washington Redskins	3	2	.600	122	103
Baltimore Colts	1	1	.500	23	29
Kansas City Chiefs	1	1	.500	33	42
Miami Dolphins	2	3	.400	74	103
Los Angeles Rams	0	1	.000	19	31
New England Patriots	0	1	.000	10	46
Philadelphia Eagles	0	1	.000	10	27
San Diego Chargers	0	1	.000	26	49
Cincinnati Bengals	0	2	.000	37	46
Buffalo Bills	0	4	.000	73	139
Denver Broncos	0	4	.000	50	163
Minnesota Vikings	0	4	.000	34	95

SUPER BOWL MOST VALUABLE PLAYERS*

Super Bowl I — QB Bart Starr, Green Bay
Super Bowl II — QB Bart Starr, Green Bay
Super Bowl III — QB Joe Namath, N.Y. Jets
Super Bowl IV — QB Len Dawson, Kansas City
Super Bowl V — LB Chuck Howley, Dallas
Super Bowl VI — QB Roger Staubach, Dallas
Super Bowl VII — S Jake Scott, Miami
Super Bowl VIII — RB Larry Csonka, Miami
Super Bowl IX — RB Franco Harris, Pittsburgh
Super Bowl X — WR Lynn Swann, Pittsburgh
Super Bowl XI — WR Fred Biletnikoff, Oakland
Super Bowl XII — DT Randy White and DE Harvey Martin, Dallas
Super Bowl XIII — QB Terry Bradshaw, Pittsburgh
Super Bowl XIV — QB Terry Bradshaw, Pittsburgh
Super Bowl XV — QB Jim Plunkett, Oakland
Super Bowl XVI — QB Joe Montana, San Francisco
Super Bowl XVII — RB John Riggins, Washington
Super Bowl XVIII — RB Marcus Allen, L.A. Raiders
Super Bowl XIX — QB Joe Montana, San Francisco
Super Bowl XX — DE Richard Dent, Chicago
Super Bowl XXI — QB Phil Simms, N.Y. Giants
Super Bowl XXII — QB Doug Williams, Washington
Super Bowl XXIII — WR Jerry Rice, San Francisco
Super Bowl XXIV — QB Joe Montana, San Francisco
Super Bowl XXV — RB Ottis Anderson, N.Y. Giants
Super Bowl XXVI — QB Mark Rypien, Washington
Super Bowl XXVII — QB Troy Aikman, Dallas
Super Bowl XXVIII — RB Emmitt Smith, Dallas
Super Bowl XXIX — QB Steve Young, San Francisco
Super Bowl XXX — CB Larry Brown, Dallas

** Award named Pete Rozelle Trophy since Super Bowl XXV.*

SUPER BOWL XXX

Sun Devil Stadium, Tempe, Arizona
January 28, 1996, Attendance: 76,347

DALLAS 27, PITTSBURGH 17—Cornerback Larry Brown's 2 interceptions led to 14 second-half points and helped lift the Cowboys to their third Super Bowl victory in the last four seasons and their record-tying fifth title overall. Brown's interceptions foiled the comeback efforts of the Steelers, and earned him the Pete Rozelle Trophy as the game's most valuable player. Dallas scored on each of its first three possessions, taking a 13-0 lead on Troy Aikman's 3-yard touchdown pass to Jay Novacek and a pair of field goals by Chris Boniol. Neil O'Donnell's 6-yard touchdown pass to Yancey Thigpen 13 seconds before halftime pulled Pittsburgh within 6 points, and the Steelers had the ball near midfield midway through the third quarter. But O'Donnell's third-down pass was intercepted by Brown at the Cowboys' 38-yard line, and his 44-yard return carried to Pittsburgh's 18. After Aikman's 17-yard completion to Michael Irvin, Emmitt Smith ran 1 yard for the touchdown that put Dallas ahead again by 13 points. The Steelers rallied, though, behind Norm Johnson's 46-yard field goal, a successful surprise onside kick, and Byron (Bam) Morris's 1-yard touchdown run with 6:36 to play in the game. And when they forced a punt and took possession at their own 32-yard line trailing only 20-17 with 4:15 remaining, it appeared they might have a chance to break the NFC's recent domination in the Super Bowl. But on second down, Brown struck again, intercepting O'Donnell's pass at the 39 and returning it 33 yards to the 6. Two plays later, Smith barreled over from 4 yards out for the clinching touchdown with 3:43 to go. Pittsburgh limited the Cowboys' powerful running game to only 56 yards and enjoyed a whopping 201-61 advantage in total yards in the second half, but could not overcome the 3 interceptions (another came on the game's final play) thrown by O'Donnell, the NFL's career leader for fewest interceptions per pass attempt. In all, O'Donnell completed 28 of 49 passes for 239 yards. Morris rushed for a game-high 73 yards on 19 carries. For Dallas, Aikman completed 15 of 23 pass attempts for 209 yards. The Cowboys' victory was the twelfth in a row for NFC teams over AFC teams in the Super Bowl.

Dallas (27)	Offense	Pittsburgh (17)
Kevin Williams	WR	Yancey Thigpen
Mark Tuinei	LT	John Jackson
Nate Newton	LG	Tom Newberry
Derek Kennard	C	Dermontti Dawson
Larry Allen	RG	Brenden Stai
Erik Williams	RT	Leon Searcy
Jay Novacek	TE	Mark Bruener
Michael Irvin	WR	Ernie Mills
Troy Aikman	QB	Neil O'Donnell
Emmitt Smith	RB	Erric Pegram
Daryl Johnston	RB	John L. Williams
	Defense	
Tony Tolbert	LE	Brentson Buckner
Russell Maryland	LT-NT	Joel Steed
Leon Lett	RT-RE	Ray Seals
Charles Haley	RE-LOLB	Kevin Greene
Dixon Edwards	RLB-LILB	Levon Kirkland
Robert Jones	MLB-RILB	Chad Brown
Darrin Smith	RLB-ROLB	Greg Lloyd
Deion Sanders	LCB	Willie Williams
Larry Brown	RCB	Carnell Lake
Darren Woodson	SS	Myron Bell
Brock Marion	FS	Darren Perry

SUBSTITUTIONS

DALLAS—Offense: K—Chris Boniol. P—John Jett. RB—David Lang. WR—Billy Davis, Cory Fleming. TE—Eric Bjornson, Kendell Watkins. G—Dale Hellestrae, Ron Stone. Defense: DE—Hurvin McCormack, Shante Carver. DT—Chad Hennings. LB—Godfrey Myles, Jim Schwantz. CB—Robert Bailey, Alundis Brice. S—Bill Bates, Greg Briggs, Scott Case, Charlie Williams. DNP: QB—Wade Wilson, RB—Sherman Williams. T—George Hegamin.

PITTSBURGH—Offense: K—Norm Johnson. P—Rohn Stark. RB—Tim Lester, Fred McAfee, Byron

(Bam) Morris. WR—Andre Hastings, Corey Holliday, Kordell Stewart. TE—Jonathan Hayes. T—James Parrish. G—Justin Strzelczyk. C—Kendall Gammon. Defense: DE—Kevin Henry. NT—Bill Johnson. LB—Jason Gildon, Donta Jones, Jerry Olsavsky. CB—Deon Figures, Randy Fuller, Chris Oldham, Rod Woodson. S—Lethon Flowers. DNP: QB—Mike Tomczak.

OFFICIALS
Referee—Red Cashion. Umpire—John Keck. Head Linesman—Paul Weidner. Line Judge—Dale Orem. Back Judge—Dick Creed. Field Judge—Don Hakes. Side Judge—Bill Carollo.

SCORING

Dallas (NFC)	10	3	7	7	—	27
Pittsburgh (AFC)	0	7	0	10	—	17

Dall — FG Boniol 42 (2:55)
Dall — Novacek 3 pass from Aikman (Boniol kick) (9:37)
Dall — FG Boniol 35 (8:57)
Pitt — Thigpen 6 pass from O'Donnell (N. Johnson kick) (14:47)
Dall — E. Smith 1 run (Boniol kick) (8:18)
Pitt — FG N. Johnson 46 (3:40)
Pitt — Morris 1 run (N. Johnson kick) (8:24)
Dall — E. Smith 4 run (Boniol kick) (11:17)

TEAM STATISTICS	**Dall.**	**Pitt.**
Total First Downs	15	25
Rushing	5	9
Passing	10	15
Penalty	0	1
Total Net Yardage	254	310
Total Offensive Plays	50	84
Average Gain per Offensive Play	5.1	3.7
Rushes	25	31
Yards Gained Rushing (Net)	56	103
Average Yards per Rush	2.2	3.3
Passes Attempted	23	49
Passes Completed	15	28
Had Intercepted	0	3
Tackled Attempting to Pass	2	4
Yards Lost Attempting to Pass	11	32
Yards Gained Passing (Net)	198	207
Punts	5	4
Average Distance	38.2	44.8
Punt Returns	1	2
Punt Return Yardage	11	18
Kickoff Returns	3	5
Kickoff Return Yardage	37	96
Interception Return Yardage	77	0
Total Return Yardage	125	114
Fumbles	0	2
Own Fumbles Recovered	0	2
Opponent Fumbles Recovered	0	0
Penalties	4	2
Yards Penalized	25	15
Total Points Scored	27	17
Touchdowns	3	2
Rushing	2	1
Passing	1	1
Returns	0	0
Extra Points	3	2
Field Goals	2	1
Field Goals Attempted	2	1
Safeties	0	0
Third-Down Efficiency	2/10	9/19
Fourth-Down Efficiency	1/1	2/4
Time of Possession	26:11	33:49

INDIVIDUAL STATISTICS

Rushing

Dallas	**No.**	**Yds.**	**LG**	**TD**
E. Smith	18	49	23	2
Johnston	2	8	4	0
K. Williams	1	2	2	0
Aikman	4	-3	0	0
Pittsburgh	**No.**	**Yds.**	**LG**	**TD**
Morris	19	73	15	1
Pegram	6	15	4	0
Stewart	4	15	7	0
O'Donnell	1	0	0	0
J. Williams	1	0	0	0

Passing

Dallas	**Att.**	**Comp.**	**Yds.**	**TD**	**Int.**
Aikman	23	15	209	1	0
Pittsburgh	**Att.**	**Comp.**	**Yds.**	**TD**	**Int.**
O'Donnell	49	28	239	1	3

Receiving

Dallas	**No.**	**Yds.**	**LG**	**TD**
Irvin	5	76	20	0
Novacek	5	50	19	1
K. Williams	2	29	22	0
Sanders	1	47	47	0
Johnston	1	4	4	0
E. Smith	1	3	3	0
Pittsburgh	**No.**	**Yds.**	**LG**	**TD**
Hastings	10	98	19	0
Mills	8	78	17	0
Thigpen	3	19	7	1
Morris	3	18	10	0
Holliday	2	19	10	0
J. Williams	2	7	5	0

Interceptions

Dallas	**No.**	**Yds.**	**LG**	**TD**
Brown	2	77	44	0
Marion	1	0	0	0
Pittsburgh	**No.**	**Yds.**	**LG**	**TD**
None	—	—	—	—

Punting

Dallas	**No.**	**Avg.**	**LG**	**Blk.**
Jett	5	38.2	51	0
Pittsburgh	**No.**	**Avg.**	**LG**	**Blk.**
Stark	4	44.8	55	0

Punt Returns

Dallas	**No.**	**FC**	**Yds.**	**LG**	**TD**
Sanders	1	0	11	11	0
Pittsburgh	**No.**	**FC**	**Yds.**	**LG**	**TD**
Hastings	2	0	18	11	0

Kickoff Returns

Dallas	**No.**	**Yds.**	**LG**	**TD**
K. Williams	2	24	18	0
Marion	1	13	13	0
Pittsburgh	**No.**	**Yds.**	**LG**	**TD**
Mills	4	79	22	0
McAfee	1	17	17	0

SUPER BOWL XXIX

Joe Robbie Stadium, Miami, Florida
January 29, 1995, Attendance: 74,107

SAN FRANCISCO 49, SAN DIEGO 26—Steve Young threw a record 6 touchdown passes, and the 49ers became the first team to win five Super Bowls when they routed the Chargers. Young, the game's most valuable player, directed an explosive offense that generated 7 touchdowns, 28 first downs, and 455 total yards. He completed 24 of 36 passes for 325 yards, and broke former 49ers quarterback Joe Montana's previous record of 5 touchdown passes in Super Bowl XXIV. San Francisco wasted little time scoring, taking the lead for good on Young's 44-yard touchdown pass to Jerry Rice only three plays and 1:24 into the game. The next time they had the ball, the 49ers marched 79 yards in four plays, taking a 14-0 lead when Young teamed with running back Ricky Watters on a 51-yard touchdown pass with 10:05 still to play in the opening period. San Diego then put together its most impressive possession of the game, a 13-play, 78-yard drive that consumed more than 7 minutes and was capped by Natrone Means's 1-yard touchdown run, to cut its deficit to 14-7 late in the quarter. But San Francisco countered with a 70-yard drive of its own, and Young's 5-yard touchdown pass to fullback William Floyd made it 21-7. Young's fourth touchdown pass of the half, 8 yards to Watters 4:44 before halftime, increased the advantage to 28-7, and the Chargers could get no closer than 18 points after that. Watters, who ran 9 yards for a touchdown in the third quarter, equaled the Super Bowl record with 3 touchdowns. Rice also scored 3 touchdowns (the second time in his career he'd done that in a Super Bowl) while catching 10 passes for 149 yards. He established career records for receptions, yards, and touchdowns in a Super Bowl. Young, who scrambled 21 yards and 15 yards to set up touchdowns in the first half, was the game's leading rusher with 49 yards on 5 carries. San Diego's Means, who rushed for 1,350 yards during the regular season, was limited to 33 yards on 13 attempts. Chargers quarterback Stan Humphries completed 24 of 49 passes for 275 yards. Rookie Andre Coleman became only the third player in Super Bowl history to return a kickoff for a touchdown, going 98 yards in the third quarter. The 75 points scored by the two teams established another record, breaking the previous mark of 69 set in Dallas's 52-17 victory over Buffalo in XXVII. The 49ers' victory was the eleventh straight for NFC teams over AFC teams in the Super Bowl.

San Diego (AFC)	7	3	8	8	—	26
San Francisco (NFC)	14	14	14	7	—	49

SF — Rice 44 pass from S. Young (Brien kick) (1:24)
SF — Watters 51 pass from S. Young (Brien kick) (4:55)
SD — Means 1 run (Carney kick) (12:16)
SF — Floyd 5 pass from S. Young (Brien kick) (1:58)
SF — Watters 8 pass from S. Young (Brien kick) (10:16)
SD — FG Carney 31 (13:16)
SF — Watters 9 run (Brien kick) (5:25)
SF — Rice 15 pass from S. Young (Brien kick) (11:42)
SD — Coleman 98 kickoff return (Seay pass from Humphries) (11:59)
SF — Rice 7 pass from S. Young (Brien kick) (1:11)
SD — Martin 30 pass from Humphries (Pupunu pass from Humphries) (12:35)

SUPER BOWL XXVIII

Georgia Dome, Atlanta, Georgia
January 30, 1994, Attendance: 72,817

DALLAS 30, BUFFALO 13—Emmitt Smith rushed for 132 yards and 2 second-half touchdowns to power the Cowboys to their second consecutive NFL title. By winning, Dallas joined San Francisco and Pittsburgh as the only franchises with four Super Bowl victories. The Bills, meanwhile, extended a dubious string by losing in the Super Bowl for the fourth consecutive year. To win, the Cowboys had to rally from a 13-6 halftime deficit. Buffalo had forged its lead on Thurman Thomas's 4-yard touchdown run and a pair of field goals by Steve Christie, including a 54-yard kick, the longest in Super Bowl history. But just 55 seconds into the second half, Thomas was stripped of the ball by Dallas defensive tackle Leon Lett. Safety James Washington recovered and weaved his way 46 yards for a touchdown to tie the game at 13-13. After forcing the Bills to punt, the Cowboys began their next possession on their 36-yard line and Smith, the game's most valuable player, took over. He carried 7 times for 61 yards on the ensuing 8-play, 64-yard drive, capping the march with a 15-yard touchdown run to give Dallas the lead for good with 8:42 remaining in the third quarter. Early in the fourth quarter, Washington intercepted Jim Kelly's pass and returned it 12 yards to Buffalo's 34. A penalty moved the ball back to the 39, but Smith carried twice for 10 yards and caught a screen pass for 9, and quarterback Troy Aikman completed a 16-yard pass to Alvin Harper to give the Cowboys a first-and-goal at the 6. Smith took it from there, cracking the end zone on fourth-and-goal from the 1 to put Dallas ahead 27-13 with 9:50 remaining. Eddie Murray's third field goal, from 20 yards with 2:50 left, ended any doubt about the game's outcome. Smith had 30 carries in all, with 19 of his attempts and 92 yards coming after intermission. Washington, normally a reserve who played most of the game because the Cowboys used five defensive backs to combat the Bills' No-Huddle offense, had 11 tackles and forced another fumble by Thomas in the first quarter. Aikman completed 19 of 27 passes for 207 yards. Buffalo's Kelly completed a Super Bowl-record 31 passes in 50 attempts for 260 yards.

Dallas, the first team in NFL history to begin the regular season 0-2 and go on to win the Super Bowl, also became the fifth to win back-to-back titles, following Green Bay, Miami, Pittsburgh (the Steelers did it twice), and San Francisco. Buffalo became the third team, along with Minnesota and Denver, to lose four Super Bowls. The Cowboys' victory was the tenth in succession for the NFC over the AFC.

Dallas (NFC)	6	0	14	10	—	30
Buffalo (AFC)	3	10	0	0	—	13

Dall — FG Murray 41 (2:19)
Buff — FG Christie 54 (4:41)
Dall — FG Murray 24 (11:05)
Buff — Thomas 4 run (Christie kick) (2:34)
Buff — FG Christie 28 (15:00)
Dall — Washington 46 fumble return (Murray kick) (0:55)
Dall — E. Smith 15 run (Murray kick) (6:18)
Dall — E. Smith 1 run (Murray kick) (5:10)
Dall — FG Murray 20 (12:10)

SUPER BOWL XXVII

Rose Bowl, Pasadena, California
January 31, 1993, Attendance: 98,374
DALLAS 52, BUFFALO 17—Troy Aikman threw 4 touchdown passes, Emmitt Smith rushed for 108 yards, and the Cowboys converted 9 turnovers into 35 points while coasting to the victory. Dallas's win was its third in its record sixth Super Bowl appearance; the Bills became the first team to drop three in succession. Buffalo led 7-0 until the first 2 of its record number of turnovers helped the Cowboys take the lead for good late in the opening quarter. First, Dallas safety James Washington intercepted a Jim Kelly pass and returned it 13 yards to the Bills' 47, setting up Aikman's 23-yard touchdown pass to tight end Jay Novacek with 1:36 remaining in the period. On the next play from scrimmage, Kelly was sacked by Charles Haley and fumbled at the Bills' 2-yard line where the Cowboys' Jimmie Jones picked up the loose ball and ran 2 yards for a touchdown. Dallas, which recovered 5 fumbles and intercepted 4 passes, struck just as quickly late in the first half, when Aikman tossed 19- and 18-yard touchdown passes to Michael Irvin 15 seconds apart to give the Cowboys a 28-10 lead at intermission. The second score was set up when Bills running back Thurman Thomas lost a fumble at his 19-yard line. Buffalo scored for the last time when backup quarterback Frank Reich, playing because Kelly was injured while attempting to pass midway through the second quarter, threw a 40-yard touchdown pass to Don Beebe on the final play of the third period to trim the deficit to 31-17. But Dallas put the game out of reach by scoring three times in a span of 2:33 of the fourth quarter. Aikman, the game's most valuable player, completed 22 of 30 passes for 273 yards and was not intercepted. The victory was the ninth in succession for the NFC over the AFC.

Buffalo (AFC)	7	3	7	0	—	17
Dallas (NFC)	14	14	3	21	—	52

Buff — Thomas 2 run (Christie kick) (5:00)
Dall — Novacek 23 pass from Aikman (Elliott kick) (13:24)
Dall — J. Jones 2 fumble recovery return (Elliott kick) (13:39)
Buff — FG Christie 21 (11:36)
Dall — Irvin 19 pass from Aikman (Elliott kick) (13:06)
Dall — Irvin 18 pass from Aikman (Elliott kick) (13:24)
Dall — FG Elliott 20 (6:39)
Buff — Beebe 40 pass from Reich (Christie kick) (15:00)
Dall — Harper 45 pass from Aikman (Elliott kick) (4:56)
Dall — E. Smith 10 run (Elliott kick) (6:48)
Dall — Norton 9 fumble recovery return (Elliott kick) (7:29)

SUPER BOWL XXVI

Metrodome, Minneapolis, Minnesota
January 26, 1992, Attendance: 63,130
WASHINGTON 37, BUFFALO 24—Mark Rypien passed for 292 yards and 2 touchdowns as the Redskins overwhelmed the Bills to win their third Super Bowl in the past 10 years. Rypien, the game's most valuable player, completed 18 of 33 passes, including a 10-yard scoring strike to Earnest Byner and a 30-yard touchdown to Gary Clark. The latter came late in the third quarter after Buffalo had trimmed a 24-0 deficit to 24-10, and effectively put the game out of reach. Washington went on to lead by as much as 37-10 before the Bills made it close wih a pair of touchdowns in the final six minutes. Though the Redskins struggled early, converting their first three drives inside the Bills' 20-yard line into only 3 points, they built a 17-0 halftime lead. And they made it 24-0 just 16 seconds into the second half, after Kurt Gouveia intercepted Buffalo quarterback Jim Kelly's pass on the first play of the third quarter and returned it 23 yards to the Bills' 2. One play later, Gerald Riggs scored his second touchdown of the game to make it 24-0. Kelly, forced to bring Buffalo from behind, completed 28 of a Super Bowl-record 58 passes for 275 yards and 2 touchdowns, but was intercepted 4 times. Bills running back Thurman Thomas, who had an AFC-high 1,407 yards rushing and an NFL-best 2,038 total yards from scrimmage during the regular season, ran for only 13 yards on 10 carries and was limited to 27 yards on 4 receptions. Clark had 7 catches for 114 yards and Art Monk added 7 for 113 for the Redskins, who amassed 417 yards of total offense while limiting the explosive Bills to 283. Washington's Joe Gibbs became only the third head coach to win three Super Bowls.

Washington (NFC)	0	17	14	6	—	37
Buffalo (AFC)	0	0	10	14	—	24

Wash — FG Lohmiller 34 (1:58)
Wash — Byner 10 pass from Rypien (Lohmiller kick) (5:06)
Wash — Riggs 1 run (Lohmiller kick) (7:43)
Wash — Riggs 2 run (Lohmiller kick) (0:16)
Buff — FG Norwood 21 (3:01)
Buff — Thomas 1 run (Norwood kick) (9:02)
Wash — Clark 30 pass from Rypien(Lohmiller kick) (13:36)
Wash — FG Lohmiller 25 (0:06)
Wash — FG Lohmiller 39 (3:24)
Buff — Metzelaars 2 pass from Kelly (Norwood kick) (9:01)
Buff — Beebe 4 pass from Kelly (Norwood kick) (11:05)

SUPER BOWL XXV

Tampa Stadium, Tampa, Florida
January 27, 1991, Attendance: 73,813
NEW YORK GIANTS 20, BUFFALO 19—The NFC champion New York Giants won their second Super Bowl in five years with a 20-19 victory over AFC titlist Buffalo. New York, employing its ball-control offense, had possession for 40 minutes, 33 seconds, a Super Bowl record. The Bills, who scored 95 points in their previous two playoff games leading to Super Bowl XXV, had the ball for less than eight minutes in the second half and just 19:27 for the game. Fourteen of New York's 73 plays came on its initial drive of the third quarter, which covered 75 yards and consumed a Super Bowl-record 9:29 before running back Ottis Anderson ran 1 yard for a touchdown. Giants quarterback Jeff Hostetler kept the long drive going by converting three third-down plays—an 11-yard pass to running back David Meggett on third-and-eight, a 14-yard toss to wide receiver Mark Ingram on third-and-13, and a 9-yard pass to Howard Cross on third-and-four—to give New York a 17-12 lead in the third quarter. Buffalo jumped to a 12-3 lead midway through the second quarter before Hostetler completed a 14-yard scoring strike to wide receiver Stephen Baker to close the score to 12-10 at halftime. Buffalo's Thurman Thomas ran 31 yards for a touchdown on the opening play of the fourth quarter to help Buffalo recapture the lead 19-17. Matt Bahr's 21-yard field goal gave the Giants a 20-19 lead, but Buffalo's Scott Norwood had a chance to win the game with seconds remaining before his 47-yard field-goal attempt sailed wide right. Hostetler completed 20 of 32 passes for 222 yards and 1 touchdown. Anderson rushed 21 times for 102 yards and 1 touchdown to capture the most-valuable-player honors. Thomas totaled 190 scrimmage yards, rushing 15 times for 135 yards and catching 5 passes for 55 yards.

Buffalo (AFC)	3	9	0	7	—	19
N.Y. Giants (NFC)	3	7	7	3	—	20

NYG — FG Bahr 28 (7:46)
Buff — FG Norwood 23 (9:09)
Buff — D. Smith 1 run (Norwood kick) (2:30)
Buff — Safety, B. Smith tackled Hostetler in end zone (6:33)
NYG — Baker 14 pass from Hostetler (Bahr kick) (14:35)
NYG — Anderson 1 run (Bahr kick) (9:29)
Buff — Thomas 31 run (Norwood kick) (0:08)
NYG — FG Bahr 21 (7:40)

SUPER BOWL XXIV

Louisiana Superdome, New Orleans, Louisiana
January 28, 1990, Attendance: 72,919
SAN FRANCISCO 55, DENVER 10—NFC titlist San Francisco won its fourth Super Bowl championship with a 55-10 victory over AFC champion Denver. The 49ers, who also won Super Bowls XVI, XIX, and XXIII, tied the Pittsburgh Steelers for most Super Bowl victories. The Steelers captured Super Bowls IX, X, XIII, and XIV. San Francisco's 55 points broke the previous Super Bowl scoring mark of 46 points by Chicago in Super Bowl XX. San Francisco scored touchdowns on four of its six first-half possessions to hold a 27-3 lead at halftime. Interceptions by Michael Walter and Chet Brooks ended the Broncos' first two possessions of the second half. San Francisco quarterback Joe Montana was named the Super Bowl most valuable player for a record third time. Montana completed 22 of 29 passes for 297 yards and a Super Bowl-record 5 touchdowns. Jerry Rice, Super Bowl XXIII most valuable player, caught 7 passes for 148 yards and three touchdowns. The 49ers' domination included first downs (28 to 12), net yards (461 to 167), and time of possession (39:31 to 20:29).

San Francisco (NFC)	13	14	14	14	—	55
Denver (AFC)	3	0	7	0	—	10

SF — Rice 20 pass from Montana (Cofer kick) (4:54)
Den — FG Treadwell 42 (8:13)
SF — Jones 7 pass from Montana (kick failed) (14:57)
SF — Rathman 1 run (Cofer kick) (7:45)
SF — Rice 38 pass from Montana (Cofer kick) (14:26)
SF — Rice 28 pass from Montana (Cofer kick) (2:12)
SF — Taylor 35 pass from Montana (Cofer kick) (5:16)
Den — Elway 3 run (Treadwell kick) (8:07)
SF — Rathman 3 run (Cofer kick) (0:03)
SF — Craig 1 run (Cofer kick) (1:13)

SUPER BOWL XXIII

Joe Robbie Stadium, Miami, Florida
January 22, 1989, Attendance: 75,129
SAN FRANCISCO 20, CINCINNATI 16—NFC champion San Francisco captured its third Super Bowl of the 1980s by defeating AFC champion Cincinnati 20-16. The 49ers, who also won Super Bowls XVI and XIX, are the first NFC team to win three Super Bowls. Pittsburgh, with four Super Bowl titles (IX, X, XIII, and XIV), and the Oakland/Los Angeles Raiders, with three (XI, XV, and XVIII), lead AFC franchises. Even though San Francisco held an advantage in total net yards (453 to 229), the 49ers found themselves trailing the Bengals late in the game. With the score 13-13, Cincinnati took a 16-13 lead on Jim Breech's 40-yard field goal with 3:20 remaining. It was Breech's third field goal of the day,

following earlier successes from 34 and 43 yards. The 49ers started their winning drive at their 8-yard line. Over the next 11 plays, San Francisco covered 92 yards with the decisive score coming on a 10-yard pass from quarterback Joe Montana to wide receiver John Taylor with 34 seconds remaining. At halftime, the score was 3-3, the first time in Super Bowl history the game was tied at intermission. After the teams traded third-period field goals, the Bengals jumped ahead 13-6 on Stanford Jennings's 93-yard kickoff return for a touchdown with 34 seconds remaining in the quarter. The 49ers didn't waste any time coming back as they covered 85 yards in four plays, concluding with Montana's 14-yard scoring pass to Jerry Rice 57 seconds into the final stanza. Rice was named the game's most valuable player after compiling 11 catches for a Super Bowl-record 215 yards. Montana completed 23 of 36 passes for a Super Bowl-record 357 yards and 2 touchdowns.

Cincinnati (AFC)	0	3	10	3 —	16
San Francisco (NFC)	3	0	3	14 —	20

SF — FG Cofer 41 (11:46)
Cin — FG Breech 34 (13:45)
Cin — FG Breech 43 (9:21)
SF — FG Cofer 32 (14:10)
Cin — Jennings 93 kickoff return (Breech kick) (14:26)
SF — Rice 14 pass from Montana (Cofer kick) (0:57)
Cin — FG Breech 40 (11:40)
SF — Taylor 10 pass from Montana (Cofer kick) (14:26)

SUPER BOWL XXII

San Diego Jack Murphy Stadium, San Diego, California
January 31, 1988, Attendance: 73,302

WASHINGTON 42, DENVER 10—NFC champion Washington won Super Bowl XXII and its second NFL championship of the 1980s with a 42-10 decision over AFC champion Denver. The Redskins, who also won Super Bowl XVII, enjoyed a record-setting second quarter en route to the victory. The Broncos broke in front 10-0 when quarterback John Elway threw a 56-yard touchdown pass to wide receiver Ricky Nattiel on the Broncos' first play from scrimmage. Following a Washington punt, Denver's Rich Karlis kicked a 24-yard field goal to cap a seven-play, 61-yard scoring drive. The Redskins then erupted for 35 points on five straight possessions in the second period and coasted thereafter. The 35 points established an NFL postseason mark for most points in a period, bettering the previous total of 21 by San Francisco in Super Bowl XIX and Chicago in Super Bowl XX. Redskins quarterback Doug Williams led the second-period explosion by throwing a Super Bowl record-tying 4 touchdown passes, including 80- and 50-yard passes to wide receiver Ricky Sanders, a 27-yard toss to wide receiver Gary Clark, and an 8-yard pass to tight end Clint Didier. Washington scored 5 touchdowns in 18 plays with total time of possession of only 5:47. Overall, Williams completed 18 of 29 passes for 340 yards and was named the game's most valuable player. His pass-yardage total eclipsed the Super Bowl record of 331 yards by Joe Montana of San Francisco in Super Bowl XIX. Sanders ended with 193 yards on 8 catches, breaking the previous Super Bowl yardage record of 161 yards by Lynn Swann of Pittsburgh in Game X. Rookie running back Timmy Smith was the game's leading rusher with 22 carries for a Super Bowl-record 204 yards, breaking the previous mark of 191 yards by Marcus Allen of the Raiders in Game XVIII. Smith also scored twice on runs of 58 and 4 yards. Washington's 6 touchdowns and 602 total yards gained also set Super Bowl records. Redskins cornerback Barry Wilburn had 2 of the team's 3 interceptions, and strong safety Alvin Walton had 2 of Washington's 5 sacks.

Washington (NFC)	0	35	0	7 —	42
Denver (AFC)	10	0	0	0 —	10

Den — Nattiel 56 pass from Elway (Karlis kick) (1:57)
Den — FG Karlis 24 (5:51)
Wash — Sanders 80 pass from Williams (Haji-Sheikh kick) (0:53)
Wash — Clark 27 pass from Williams (Haji-Sheikh kick) (4:45)
Wash — Smith 58 run (Haji-Sheikh kick) (8:33)
Wash — Sanders 50 pass from Williams (Haji-Sheikh kick) (11:18)
Wash — Didier 8 pass from Williams (Haji-Sheikh kick) (13:56)
Wash — Smith 4 run (Haji-Sheikh kick) (1:51)

SUPER BOWL XXI

Rose Bowl, Pasadena, California
January 25, 1987, Attendance: 101,063

NEW YORK GIANTS 39, DENVER 20—The NFC champion New York Giants captured their first NFL title since 1956 when they downed the AFC champion Denver Broncos 39-20 in Super Bowl XXI. The victory marked the NFC's fifth NFL title in the past six seasons. The Broncos, behind the passing of quarterback John Elway, who was 13 of 20 for 187 yards in the first half, held a 10-9 lead at intermission, the narrowest halftime margin in Super Bowl history. Denver's Rich Karlis opened the scoring with a Super Bowl record-tying 48-yard field goal. New York drove 78 yards in nine plays on the next series to take a 7-3 lead on quarterback Phil Simms's 6-yard touchdown pass to tight end Zeke Mowatt. The Broncos came right back with a 58-yard scoring drive on six plays capped by Elway's 4-yard touchdown run. The only scoring in the second period was the sack of Elway in the end zone by defensive end George Martin for a New York safety. The Giants produced a key defensive stand early in the second quarter when the Broncos had a first down at the New York 1-yard line, but failed to score on three running plays and Karlis's 23-yard missed field-goal attempt. The Giants took command of the game in the third period en route to a 30-point second half, the most ever scored in one half of Super Bowl play. New York took the lead for good on tight end Mark Bavaro's 13-yard touchdown catch 4:52 into the third period. The nine-play, 63-yard scoring drive included the successful conversion of a fourth-and-1 play on the New York 46-yard line. Denver was limited to only 2 net yards on 10 offensive plays in the third period. Simms set Super Bowl records for most consecutive completions (10) and highest completion percentage (88 percent on 22 completions in 25 attempts). He also passed for 268 yards and 3 touchdowns and was named the game's most valuable player. New York running back Joe Morris was the game's leading rusher with 20 carries for 67 yards. Denver wide receiver Vance Johnson led all receivers with 5 catches for 121 yards. The Giants defeated their three playoff opponents by a cumulative total of 82 points (New York 105, opponents 23), the largest such margin by a Super Bowl winner.

Denver (AFC)	10	0	0	10 —	20
N.Y. Giants (NFC)	7	2	17	13 —	39

Den — FG Karlis 48 (4:09)
NYG — Mowatt 6 pass from Simms (Allegre kick) (9:33)
Den — Elway 4 run (Karlis kick) (12:54)
NYG — Safety, Martin tackled Elway in end zone (12:14)
NYG — Bavaro 13 pass from Simms (Allegre kick) (4:52)
NYG — FG Allegre 21 (11:06)
NYG — Morris 1 run (Allegre kick) (14:36)
NYG — McConkey 6 pass from Simms (Allegre kick) (4:04)
Den — FG Karlis 28 (8:59)
NYG — Anderson 2 run (kick failed) (10:42)
Den — V. Johnson 47 pass from Elway (Karlis kick) (12:54)

SUPER BOWL XX

Louisiana Superdome, New Orleans, Louisiana
January 26, 1986, Attendance: 73,818

CHICAGO 46, NEW ENGLAND 10—The NFC champion Chicago Bears, seeking their first NFL title since 1963, scored a Super Bowl-record 46 points in downing AFC champion New England 46-10 in Super Bowl XX. The previous record for most points in a Super Bowl was 38, shared by San Francisco in XIX and the Los Angeles Raiders in XVIII. The Bears' league-leading defense tied the Super Bowl record for sacks (7) and limited the Patriots to a record-low 7 rushing yards. New England took the quickest lead in Super Bowl history when Tony Franklin kicked a 36-yard field goal with 1:19 elapsed in the first period. The score came about because of Larry McGrew's fumble recovery at the Chicago 19-yard line. However, the Bears rebounded for a 23-3 first-half lead, while building a yardage advantage of 236 total yards to New England's minus 19. Running back Matt Suhey rushed 8 times for 37 yards, including an 11-yard touchdown run, and caught 1 pass for 24 yards in the first half. After the Patriots first drive of the second half ended with a punt to the Bears' 4-yard line, Chicago marched 96 yards in nine plays with quarterback Jim McMahon's 1-yard scoring run capping the drive. McMahon became the first quarterback in Super Bowl history to rush for a pair of touchdowns. The Bears completed their scoring via a 28-yard interception return by reserve cornerback Reggie Phillips, a 1-yard run by defensive tackle/fullback William Perry, and a safety when defensive end Henry Waechter tackled Patriots quarterback Steve Grogan in the end zone. Bears defensive end Richard Dent became the fourth defender to be named the game's most valuable player after contributing 1½ sacks. The Bears' victory margin of 36 points was the largest in Super Bowl history, bettering the previous mark of 29 by the Los Angeles Raiders when they topped Washington 38-9 in Game XVIII. McMahon completed 12 of 20 passes for 256 yards before leaving the game in the fourth period with a wrist injury. The NFL's all-time leading rusher, Bears running back Walter Payton, carried 22 times for 61 yards. Wide receiver Willie Gault caught 4 passes for 129 yards, the fourth-most receiving yards in a Super Bowl. Chicago coach Mike Ditka became the second man (Tom Flores of Raiders was the other) who played in a Super Bowl and coached a team to a victory in the game.

Chicago (NFC)	13	10	21	2 —	46
New England (AFC)	3	0	0	7 —	10

NE — FG Franklin 36 (1:19)
Chi — FG Butler 28 (5:40)
Chi — FG Butler 24 (13:34)
Chi — Suhey 11 run (Butler kick) (14:37)
Chi — McMahon 2 run (Butler kick) (7:36)
Chi — FG Butler 24 (15:00)
Chi — McMahon 1 run (Butler kick) (7:38)
Chi — Phillips 28 interception return (Butler kick) (8:44)
Chi — Perry 1 run (Butler kick) (11:38)
NE — Fryar 8 pass from Grogan (Franklin kick) (1:46)
Chi — Safety, Waechter tackled Grogan in end zone (9:24)

SUPER BOWL XIX

Stanford Stadium, Stanford, California
January 20, 1985, Attendance: 84,059

SAN FRANCISCO 38, MIAMI 16—The San Francisco 49ers captured their second Super Bowl title with a dominating offense and a defense that tamed Miami's explosive passing attack. The Dolphins held a 10-7 lead at the end of the first period, which represented the most points scored by two teams in an opening quarter of a Super Bowl. However, the 49ers used excellent field position in the second period to build a 28-16 halftime lead. Running back Roger Craig set a Super Bowl record by scoring 3 touchdowns on pass receptions of 8 and 16 yards and a run of 2 yards. San Francisco's Joe Montana was voted the game's most valuable player. He joined Green Bay's Bart Starr and Pittsburgh's Terry Bradshaw as the only two-time Super Bowl most valuable players. Montana completed 24 of 35 passes for a Super Bowl-record 331 yards and 3 touchdowns, and rushed 5 times for 59 yards, including a 6-yard touchdown. Craig had 58 yards on 15 carries and caught 7 passes for 77 yards. Wendell Tyler rushed 13 times for 65 yards and had 4 catches for 70 yards. Dwight Clark had 6 receptions for 77 yards, while Russ Francis had 5 for 60. San Francisco's 537 total net yards bettered the previous Super Bowl record of 429 yards by Oakland in Super Bowl XI. The 49ers also held a time of possession advantage over the Dolphins of 37:11 to 22:49.

Miami (AFC)	10	6	0	0 —	16
San Francisco (NFC)	7	21	10	0 —	38

Mia — FG von Schamann 37 (7:36)
SF — Monroe 33 pass from Montana (Wersching kick) (11:48)
Mia — D. Johnson 2 pass from Marino (von Schamann kick) (14:15)
SF — Craig 8 pass from Montana (Wersching kick) (3:26)
SF — Montana 6 run (Wersching kick) (8:02)
SF — Craig 2 run (Wersching kick) (12:55)
Mia — FG von Schamann 31 (14:48)
Mia — FG von Schamann 30 (15:00)
SF — FG Wersching 27 (4:48)
SF — Craig 16 pass from Montana (Wersching kick) (8:42)

SUPER BOWL XVIII

Tampa Stadium, Tampa, Florida
January 22, 1984, Attendance: 72,920

LOS ANGELES RAIDERS 38, WASHINGTON 9—The Los Angeles Raiders dominated the Washington Redskins from the beginning in Super Bowl XVIII and achieved the most lopsided victory in Super Bowl history, surpassing Green Bay's 35-10 win over Kansas City in Super Bowl I. The Raiders took a 7-0 lead 4:52 into the game when Derrick Jensen blocked a Jeff Hayes punt and recovered it in the end zone for a touchdown. With 9:14 remaining in the first half, Raiders quarterback Jim Plunkett threw a 12-yard touchdown pass to wide receiver Cliff Branch to complete a three-play, 65-yard drive. Washington cut the Raiders' lead to 14-3 on a 24-yard field goal by Mark Moseley. With seven seconds left in the first half, Raiders linebacker Jack Squirek intercepted a Joe Theismann pass at the Redskins' 5-yard line and ran it in for a touchdown to give Los Angeles a 21-3 halftime lead. In the third period, running back Marcus Allen, who rushed for a Super Bowl-record 191 yards on 20 carries, increased the Raiders' lead to 35-9 on touchdown runs of 5 and 74 yards, the latter erasing the Super Bowl record of 58 yards set by Baltimore's Tom Matte in Game III. Allen was named the game's most valuable player. The victory over Washington raised Raiders coach Tom Flores' playoff record to 8-1, including a 27-10 win against Philadelphia in Super Bowl XV. The 38 points scored by the Raiders were the highest total by a Super Bowl team. The previous high was 35 points by Green Bay in Game I.

Washington (NFC)	0	3	6	0 —	9
L.A. Raiders (AFC)	7	14	14	3 —	38

Raiders — Jensen recovered blocked punt in end zone (Bahr kick) (4:52)
Raiders — Branch 12 pass from Plunkett (Bahr kick) (5:46)
Wash — FG Moseley 24 (11:55)
Raiders — Squirek 5 interception return (Bahr kick) (14:53)
Wash — Riggins 1 run (kick blocked) (4:08)
Raiders — Allen 5 run (Bahr kick) (7:54)
Raiders — Allen 74 run (Bahr kick) (15:00)
Raiders — FG Bahr 21 (12:36)

SUPER BOWL XVII

Rose Bowl, Pasadena, California
January 30, 1983, Attendance: 103,667

WASHINGTON 27, MIAMI 17—Fullback John Riggins ran for a Super Bowl-record 166 yards on 38 carries to spark Washington to a 27-17 victory over AFC champion Miami. It was Riggins's fourth straight 100-yard rushing game during the playoffs, also a record. The win marked Washington's first NFL title since 1942, and was only the second time in Super Bowl history NFL/NFC teams scored consecutive victories (Green Bay did it in Super Bowls I and II and San Francisco won Super Bowl XVI). The Redskins, under second-year head coach Joe Gibbs, used a balanced offense that accounted for 400 total yards (a Super Bowl-record 276 yards rushing and 124 passing), second in Super Bowl history to 429 yards by Oakland in Super Bowl XI. The Dolphins built a 17-10 halftime lead on a 76-yard touchdown pass from quarterback David Woodley to wide receiver Jimmy Cefalo 6:49 into the first period, a 20-yard field goal by Uwe von Schamann with 6:00 left in the half, and a Super Bowl-record 98-yard kickoff return by Fulton Walker with 1:38 remaining. Washington had tied the score at 10-10 with 1:51 left on a four-yard touchdown pass from Joe Theismann to wide receiver Alvin Garrett. Mark Moseley started the Redskins' scoring with a 31-yard field goal late in the first period, and added a 20-yarder midway through the third period to cut the Dolphins' lead to 17-13. Riggins, who was voted the game's most valuable player, gave Washington its first lead of the game with 10:01 left when he ran 43 yards off left tackle for a touchdown in a fourth-and-1 situation. Wide receiver Charlie Brown caught a six-yard scoring pass from Theismann with 1:55 left to complete the scoring. The Dolphins managed only 176 yards (142 in first half). Theismann completed 15 of 23 passes for 143 yards, with 2 touchdowns and 2 interceptions. For Miami, Woodley was 4 of 14 for 97 yards, with 1 touchdown, and 1 interception. Don Strock was 0 for 3 in relief.

Miami (AFC)	7	10	0	0 —	17
Washington (NFC)	0	10	3	14 —	27

Mia — Cefalo 76 pass from Woodley (von Schamann kick) (6:49)
Wash — FG Moseley 31 (0:21)
Mia — FG von Schamann 20 (9:00)
Wash — Garrett 4 pass from Theismann (Moseley kick) (13:09)
Mia — Walker 98 kickoff return (von Schamann kick) (13:22)
Wash — FG Moseley 20 (6:51)
Wash — Riggins 43 run (Moseley kick) (4:59)
Wash — Brown 6 pass from Theismann (Moseley kick) (13:05)

SUPER BOWL XVI

Pontiac Silverdome, Pontiac, Michigan
January 24, 1982, Attendance: 81,270

SAN FRANCISCO 26, CINCINNATI 21—Ray Wersching's Super Bowl record-tying 4 field goals and Joe Montana's controlled passing helped lift the San Francisco 49ers to their first NFL championship with a 26-21 victory over Cincinnati. The 49ers built a game-record 20-0 halftime lead via Montana's 1-yard touchdown run, which capped an 11-play, 68-yard drive; fullback Earl Cooper's 11-yard scoring pass from Montana, which climaxed a Super Bowl record 92-yard drive on 12 plays; and Wersching's 22- and 26-yard field goals. The Bengals rebounded in the second half, closing the gap to 20-14 on quarterback Ken Anderson's 5-yard run and Dan Ross's 4-yard reception from Anderson, who established Super Bowl passing records for completions (25) and completion percentage (73.5 percent on 25 of 34). Wersching added early fourth-period field goals of 40 and 23 yards to increase the 49ers' lead to 26-14. The Bengals managed to score on an Anderson-to-Ross 3-yard pass with only 16 seconds remaining. Ross set a Super Bowl record with 11 receptions for 104 yards. Montana, the game's most valuable player, completed 14 of 22 passes for 157 yards. Cincinnati compiled 356 yards to San Francisco's 275, which marked the first time in Super Bowl history that the team that gained the most yards from scrimmage lost the game.

San Francisco (NFC)	7	13	0	6 —	26
Cincinnati (AFC)	0	0	7	14 —	21

SF — Montana 1 run (Wersching kick) (9:08)
SF — Cooper 11 pass from Montana (Wersching kick) (8:07)
SF — FG Wersching 22 (14:45)
SF — FG Wersching 26 (14:58)
Cin — Anderson 5 run (Breech kick) (3:35)
Cin — Ross 4 pass from Anderson (Breech kick) (4:54)
SF — FG Wersching 40 (9:35)
SF — FG Wersching 23 (13:03)
Cin — Ross 3 pass from Anderson (Breech kick) (14:44)

SUPER BOWL XV

Louisiana Superdome, New Orleans, Louisiana
January 25, 1981, Attendance: 76,135

OAKLAND 27, PHILADELPHIA 10—Jim Plunkett threw 3 touchdown passes, including an 80-yard strike to Kenny King, as the Raiders became the first wild-card team to win the Super Bowl. Plunkett's touchdown bomb to King—the longest play in Super Bowl history—gave Oakland a decisive 14-0 lead with nine seconds left in the first period. Linebacker Rod Martin had set up Oakland's first touchdown, a 2-yard reception by Cliff Branch, with a 17-yard interception return to the Eagles' 30-yard line. The Eagles never recovered from that early deficit, managing only a Tony Franklin field goal (30 yards) and an 8-yard touchdown pass from Ron Jaworski to Keith Krepfle. Plunkett, who became a starter in the sixth game of the season, completed 13 of 21 for 261 yards and was named the game's most valuable player. Oakland won 9 of 11 games with Plunkett starting, but that was good enough only for second place in the AFC West, although they tied division winner San Diego with an 11-5 record. The Raiders, who had previously won Super Bowl XI over Minnesota, had to win three playoff games to get to the championship game. Oakland defeated Houston 27-7 at home followed by road victories over Cleveland (14-12) and San Diego (34-27). Oakland's Mark van Eeghen was the game's leading rusher with 75 yards on 18 carries. Philadelphia's Wilbert Montgomery led all receivers with 6 receptions for 91 yards. Branch had 5 for 67 and Harold Carmichael of Philadelphia 5 for 83. Martin finished the game with 3 interceptions, a Super Bowl record.

Oakland (AFC)	14	0	10	3 —	27
Philadelphia (NFC)	0	3	0	7 —	10

Oak — Branch 2 pass from Plunkett (Bahr kick) (6:04)
Oak — King 80 pass from Plunkett (Bahr kick) (14:51)
Phil — FG Franklin 30 (4:32)
Oak — Branch 29 pass from Plunkett (Bahr kick) (2:36)
Oak — FG Bahr 46 (10:25)
Phil — Krepfle 8 pass from Jaworski (Franklin kick) (1:01)
Oak — FG Bahr 35 (6:31)

SUPER BOWL XIV

Rose Bowl, Pasadena, California
January 20, 1980, Attendance: 103,985

PITTSBURGH 31, LOS ANGELES 19—Terry Bradshaw completed 14 of 21 passes for 309 yards and set two passing records as the Steelers became the first team to win four Super Bowls. Despite 3 interceptions by the Rams, Bradshaw kept his poise and brought the Steelers from behind twice in the second half. Trailing 13-10 at halftime, Pittsburgh went ahead 17-13 when Bradshaw hit Lynn Swann with a 47-yard touchdown pass after 2:48 of the third quarter. On the Rams' next possession Vince Ferragamo, who completed 15 of 25 passes for 212 yards, responded with a 50-yard pass to Billy Waddy that moved Los Angeles from its 26 to the Steelers' 24. On the following play, Lawrence McCutcheon connected with Ron Smith on a halfback option pass that gave the Rams a 19-17 lead. On Pittsburgh's initial possession of the final period, Bradshaw lofted a 73-yard scoring pass to John Stallworth to put the Steelers in front to stay 24-19. Franco Harris scored on a 1-yard run later in the quarter to seal the verdict. A 45-yard pass from Bradshaw to Stallworth was the key play in the drive to Harris's score. Bradshaw, the game's most valuable player for the second straight year, set career Super Bowl records for most touchdown passes (9) and most passing yards (932). Larry Anderson gave the Steelers excellent field position throughout the game with 5 kickoff returns for a record 162 yards.

Los Angeles (NFC)	7	6	6	0	—	19
Pittsburgh (AFC)	3	7	7	14	—	31

Pitt — FG Bahr 41 (7:29)
LA — Bryant 1 run (Corral kick) (12:16)
Pitt — Harris 1 run (Bahr kick) (2:08)
LA — FG Corral 31 (7:39)
LA — FG Corral 45 (14:46)
Pitt — Swann 47 pass from Bradshaw (Bahr kick) (2:48)
LA — Smith 24 pass from McCutcheon (kick failed) (4:45)
Pitt — Stallworth 73 pass from Bradshaw (Bahr kick) (2:56)
Pitt — Harris 1 run (Bahr kick) (13:11)

SUPER BOWL XIII

Orange Bowl, Miami, Florida
January 21, 1979, Attendance: 79,484

PITTSBURGH 35, DALLAS 31—Terry Bradshaw threw a record 4 touchdown passes to lead the Steelers to victory. The Steelers became the first team to win three Super Bowls, mostly because of Bradshaw's accurate arm. Bradshaw, voted the game's most valuable player, completed 17 of 30 passes for 318 yards, a personal high. Four of those passes went for touchdowns—2 to John Stallworth and the third, with 26 seconds remaining in the second period, to Rocky Bleier for a 21-14 halftime lead. The Cowboys scored twice before intermission on Roger Staubach's 39-yard pass to Tony Hill and a 37-yard fumble return by linebacker Mike Hegman, who stole the ball from Bradshaw. The Steelers broke open the contest with 2 touchdowns in a span of 19 seconds midway through the final period. Franco Harris rambled 22 yards up the middle to give the Steelers a 28-17 lead with 7:10 left. Pittsburgh got the ball right back when Randy White fumbled the kickoff and Dennis Winston recovered for the Steelers. On first down, Bradshaw fired his fourth touchdown pass, an 18-yard pass to Lynn Swann to boost the Steelers' lead to 35-17 with 6:51 to play. The Cowboys refused to let the Steelers run away with the contest. Staubach connected with Billy Joe DuPree on a 7-yard scoring pass with 2:23 left. Then the Cowboys recovered an onside kick and Staubach took them in for another score, passing 4 yards to Butch Johnson with 22 seconds remaining. Bleier recovered another onside kick with 17 seconds left to seal the victory for the Steelers.

Pittsburgh (AFC)	7	14	0	14	—	35
Dallas (NFC)	7	7	3	14	—	31

Pitt — Stallworth 28 pass from Bradshaw (Gerela kick) (5:13)
Dall — Hill 39 pass from Staubach (Septien kick) (15:00)
Dall — Hegman 37 fumble recovery return (Septien kick) (2:52)
Pitt — Stallworth 75 pass from Bradshaw (Gerela kick) (4:35)
Pitt — Bleier 7 pass from Bradshaw (Gerela kick) (14:34)
Dall — FG Septien 27 (12:24)
Pitt — Harris 22 run (Gerela kick) (7:50)
Pitt — Swann 18 pass from Bradshaw (Gerela kick) (8:09)
Dall — DuPree 7 pass from Staubach (Septien kick) (12:37)
Dall — B. Johnson 4 pass from Staubach (Septien kick) (14:38)

SUPER BOWL XII

Louisiana Superdome, New Orleans, Louisiana
January 15, 1978, Attendance: 75,583

DALLAS 27, DENVER 10—The Cowboys evened their Super Bowl record at 2-2 by defeating Denver before a sellout crowd of 75,583, plus 102,010,000 television viewers, the largest audience ever to watch a sporting event. Dallas converted 2 interceptions into 10 points and Efren Herrera added a 35-yard field goal for a 13-0 halftime advantage. In the third period Craig Morton engineered a drive to the Cowboys' 30 and Jim Turner's 47-yard field goal made the score 13-3. After an exchange of punts, Butch Johnson made a spectacular diving catch in the end zone to complete a 45-yard pass from Roger Staubach and put the Cowboys ahead 20-3. Following Rick Upchurch's 67-yard kickoff return, Norris Weese guided the Broncos to a touchdown to cut the Dallas lead to 20-10. Dallas clinched the victory when running back Robert Newhouse threw a 29-yard touchdown pass to Golden Richards with 7:04 remaining in the game. It was the first pass thrown by Newhouse since 1975. Harvey Martin and Randy White, who were named co-most valuable players, led the Cowboys' defense, which recovered 4 fumbles and intercepted 4 passes.

Dallas (NFC)	10	3	7	7	—	27
Denver (AFC)	0	0	10	0	—	10

Dall — Dorsett 3 run (Herrera kick) (10:31)
Dall — FG Herrera 35 (13:29)
Dall — FG Herrera 43 (3:44)
Den — FG Turner 47 (2:28)
Dall — Johnson 45 pass from Staubach (Herrera kick) (8:01)
Den — Lytle 1 run (Turner kick) (9:21)
Dall — Richards 29 pass from Newhouse (Herrera kick) (7:56)

SUPER BOWL XI

Rose Bowl, Pasadena, California
January 9, 1977, Attendance: 103,438

OAKLAND 32, MINNESOTA 14—The Raiders won their first NFL championship before a record Super Bowl crowd plus 81 million television viewers, the largest audience ever to watch a sporting event. The Raiders gained a record-breaking 429 yards, including running back Clarence Davis's 137 rushing yards. Wide receiver Fred Biletnikoff made 4 key receptions, which earned him the game's most valuable player trophy. Oakland scored on three successive possessions in the second quarter to build a 16-0 halftime lead. Errol Mann's 24-yard field goal opened the scoring, then the AFC champions put together drives of 64 and 35 yards, scoring on a 1-yard pass from Ken Stabler to Dave Casper and a 1-yard run by Pete Banaszak. The Raiders increased their lead to 19-0 on a 40-yard field goal in the third quarter, but Minnesota responded with a 12-play, 58-yard drive late in the period, with Fran Tarkenton passing 8 yards to wide receiver Sammy White to cut the deficit to 19-7. Two fourth-quarter interceptions clinched the title for the Raiders. One set up Banaszak's second touchdown run, the other resulted in cornerback Willie Brown's Super Bowl-record 75-yard interception return.

Oakland (AFC)	0	16	3	13	—	32
Minnesota (NFC)	0	0	7	7	—	14

Oak — FG Mann 24 (0:48)
Oak — Casper 1 pass from Stabler (Mann kick) (7:50)
Oak — Banaszak 1 run (kick failed) (11:27)
Oak — FG Mann 40 (9:44)
Minn — S. White 8 pass from Tarkenton (Cox kick) (14:13)
Oak — Banaszak 2 run (Mann kick) (7:21)
Oak — Brown 75 interception return (kick failed) (9:17)
Minn — Voigt 13 pass from Lee (Cox kick) (14:35)

SUPER BOWL X

Orange Bowl, Miami, Florida
January 18, 1976, Attendance: 80,187

PITTSBURGH 21, DALLAS 17—The Steelers won the Super Bowl for the second year in a row on Terry Bradshaw's 64-yard touchdown pass to Lynn Swann and an aggressive defense that snuffed out a late rally by the Cowboys with an end-zone interception on the final play of the game. In the fourth quarter, Pittsburgh ran on fourth down and gave up the ball on the Cowboys' 39 with 1:22 to play. Roger Staubach ran and passed for 2 first downs but his last desperation pass was picked off by Glen Edwards. Dallas's scoring was the result of 2 touchdown passes by Staubach, one to Drew Pearson for 29 yards and the other to Percy Howard for 34 yards. Toni Fritsch had a 36-yard field goal. The Steelers scored on 2 touchdown passes by Bradshaw, 1 to Randy Grossman for 7 yards and the long bomb to Swann. Roy Gerela had 36- and 18-yard field goals. Reggie Harrison blocked a punt through the end zone for a safety. Swann set a Super Bowl record by gaining 161 yards on his 4 receptions.

Dallas (NFC)	7	3	0	7	—	17
Pittsburgh (AFC)	7	0	0	14	—	21

Dall — D. Pearson 29 pass from Staubach (Fritsch kick) (4:36)
Pitt — Grossman 7 pass from Bradshaw (Gerela kick) (9:03)
Dall — FG Fritsch 36 (0:15)
Pitt — Safety, Harrison blocked Hoopes's punt through end zone (3:32)
Pitt — FG Gerela 36 (6:19)
Pitt — FG Gerela 18 (8:23)
Pitt — Swann 64 pass from Bradshaw (kick failed) (11:58)
Dall — P. Howard 34 pass from Staubach (Fritsch kick) (13:12)

SUPER BOWL IX

Tulane Stadium, New Orleans, Louisiana
January 12, 1975, Attendance: 80,997

PITTSBURGH 16, MINNESOTA 6—AFC champion Pittsburgh, in its initial Super Bowl appearance, and NFC champion Minnesota, making a third bid for its first Super Bowl title, struggled through a first half in which the only score was produced by the Steelers' defense when Dwight White downed Vikings' quarterback Fran Tarkenton in the end zone for a safety 7:49 into the second period. The Steelers forced another break and took advantage on the second-half kickoff when Minnesota's Bill Brown fumbled and Marv Kellum recovered for Pittsburgh on the Vikings' 30. After Rocky Bleier failed to gain on first down, Franco Harris carried 3 consecutive times for 24 yards, a loss of 3, and a 9-yard touchdown and a 9-0 lead. Though its offense was completely stymied by Pittsburgh's defense, Minnesota managed to move into a threatening position after 4:27 of the final period when Matt Blair blocked Bobby Walden's punt and Terry Brown recovered the ball in the end zone for a touchdown. Fred Cox's kick failed and the Steelers led 9-6. Pittsburgh wasted no time putting the victory away. The Steelers took the ensuing kickoff and marched 66 yards in 11 plays, climaxed by Terry Bradshaw's 4-yard scoring pass to Larry Brown with 3:31 left. Pittsburgh's defense permitted Minnesota only 119 yards total offense, including a Super Bowl low of 17 rushing yards. The Steelers, meanwhile, gained 333 yards, including Harris's record 158 yards on 34 carries.

Pittsburgh (AFC)	0	2	7	7	—	16
Minnesota (NFC)	0	0	0	6	—	6

Pitt — Safety, White downed Tarkenton in end zone (7:49)
Pitt — Harris 9 run (Gerela kick) (1:35)
Minn — T. Brown recovered blocked punt in end zone (kick failed) (4:27)
Pitt — L. Brown 4 pass from Bradshaw (Gerela kick) (11:29)

SUPER BOWL VIII

Rice Stadium, Houston, Texas
January 13, 1974, Attendance: 71,882

MIAMI 24, MINNESOTA 7—The defending NFL champion Dolphins, representing the AFC for the third straight year, scored the first two times they had possession on marches of 62 and 56 yards while the Miami defense limited the Vikings to only seven plays in the first period. Larry Csonka climaxed the initial 10-play drive with a 5-yard touchdown bolt through right guard after 5:27 had elapsed. Four plays later, Miami began another 10-play scoring drive, which ended with Jim Kiick bursting 1 yard through the middle for another touchdown after 13:38 of the period. Garo Yepremian added a

28-yard field goal midway in the second period for a 17-0 Miami lead. Minnesota then drove from its 20 to a second-and-2 situation on the Miami 7 yard line with 1:18 left in the half. But on two plays, Miami limited Oscar Reed to 1 yard. On fourth-and-1 from the 6, Reed went over right tackle, but Dolphins middle linebacker Nick Buoniconti jarred the ball loose and Jake Scott recovered for Miami to halt the Minnesota threat. The Vikings were unable to muster enough offense in the second half to threaten the Dolphins. Csonka rushed 33 times for a Super Bowl-record 145 yards. Bob Griese of Miami completed 6 of 7 passes for 73 yards.

Minnesota (NFC)	0	0	0	7	—	7
Miami (AFC)	14	3	7	0	—	24

Mia — Csonka 5 run (Yepremian kick) (9:33)
Mia — Kiick 1 run (Yepremian kick) (13:38)
Mia — FG Yepremian 28 (8:58)
Mia — Csonka 2 run (Yepremian kick) (6:16)
Minn — Tarkenton 4 run (Cox kick) (1:35)

SUPER BOWL VII

Memorial Coliseum, Los Angeles, California
January 14, 1973, Attendance: 90,182

MIAMI 14, WASHINGTON 7—The Dolphins played virtually perfect football in the first half as their defense permitted the Redskins to cross midfield only once and their offense turned good field position into 2 touchdowns. On its third possession, Miami opened its first scoring drive from the Dolphins' 37 yard line. An 18-yard pass from Bob Griese to Paul Warfield preceded by three plays Griese's 28-yard touchdown pass to Howard Twilley. After Washington moved from its 17 to the Miami 48 with two minutes remaining in the first half, Dolphins linebacker Nick Buoniconti intercepted a Billy Kilmer pass at the Miami 41 and returned it to the Washington 27. Jim Kiick ran for 3 yards, Larry Csonka for 3, Griese passed to Jim Mandich for 19, and Kiick gained 1 to the 1-yard line. With 18 seconds left until intermission, Kiick scored from the 1. Washington's only touchdown came with 2:07 left in the game and resulted from a misplayed field-goal attempt and fumble by Garo Yepremian, with the Redskins' Mike Bass picking the ball out of the air and running 49 yards for the score. Dolphins safety Jake Scott, who had 2 interceptions, including 1 in the end zone to kill a Redskins' drive, was voted the game's most valuable player.

Miami (AFC)	7	7	0	0	—	14
Washington (NFC)	0	0	0	7	—	7

Mia — Twilley 28 pass from Griese (Yepremian kick) (14:59)
Mia — Kiick 1 run (Yepremian kick) (14:42)
Wash — Bass 49 fumble recovery return (Knight kick) (12:53)

SUPER BOWL VI

Tulane Stadium, New Orleans, Louisiana
January 16, 1972, Attendance: 81,023

DALLAS 24, MIAMI 3—The Cowboys rushed for a record 252 yards and their defense limited the Dolphins to a low of 185 yards while not permitting a touchdown for the first time in Super Bowl history. Dallas converted Chuck Howley's recovery of Larry Csonka's first fumble of the season into a 3-0 advantage and led at halftime 10-3. After Dallas received the second-half kickoff, Duane Thomas led a 71-yard march in eight plays for a 17-3 margin. Howley intercepted Bob Griese's pass at the 50 and returned it to the Miami 9 early in the fourth period, and three plays later Roger Staubach passed 7 yards to Mike Ditka for the final touchdown. Thomas rushed for 95 yards and Walt Garrison gained 74. Staubach, voted the game's most valuable player, completed 12 of 19 passes for 119 yards and 2 touchdowns.

Dallas (NFC)	3	7	7	7	—	24
Miami (AFC)	0	3	0	0	—	3

Dall — FG Clark 9 (13:37)
Dall — Alworth 7 pass from Staubach (Clark kick) (13:45)
Mia — FG Yepremian 31 (14:56)
Dall — D. Thomas 3 run (Clark kick) (5:17)
Dall — Ditka 7 pass from Staubach (Clark kick) (3:18)

SUPER BOWL V

Orange Bowl, Miami, Florida
January 17, 1971, Attendance: 79,204

BALTIMORE 16, DALLAS 13—A 32-yard field goal by rookie kicker Jim O'Brien brought the Baltimore Colts a victory over the Dallas Cowboys in the final five seconds of Super Bowl V. The game between the champions of the AFC and NFC was played on artificial turf for the first time. Dallas led13-6 at the half but interceptions by Rick Volk and Mike Curtis set up a Baltimore touchdown and O'Brien's decisive kick in the fourth period. Earl Morrell relieved an injured Johnny Unitas late in the firsthalf, although Unitas completed the Colts' only scoring pass. It caromed off receiver Eddie Hinton's fingertips, off Dallas defensive back Mel Renfro, and finally settled into the grasp of John Mackey, who went 45 yards to score on a 75-yard play.

Baltimore (AFC)	0	6	0	10	—	16
Dallas (NFC)	3	10	0	0	—	13

Dall — FG Clark 14 (9:28)
Dall — FG Clark 30 (0:08)
Balt — Mackey 75 pass from Unitas (kick blocked) (0:05)
Dall — Thomas 7 pass from Morton (Clark kick) (7:07)
Balt — Nowatzke 2 run (O'Brien kick) (7:25)
Balt — FG O'Brien 32 (14:55)

SUPER BOWL IV

Tulane Stadium, New Orleans, Louisiana
January 11, 1970, Attendance: 80,562

KANSAS CITY 23, MINNESOTA 7—The AFL squared the Super Bowl at two games apiece with the NFL, building a 16-0 halftime lead behind Len Dawson's superb quarterbacking and a powerful defense. Dawson, the fourth consecutive quarterback to be chosen the Super Bowl's top player, called an almost flawless game, completing 12 of 17 passes and hitting Otis Taylor on a 46-yard play for the final Chiefs touchdown. The Kansas City defense limited Minnesota's strong rushing game to 67 yards and had 3 interceptions and 2 fumble recoveries. The crowd of 80,562 set a Super Bowl record, as did the gross receipts of $3,817,872.69.

Minnesota (NFL)	0	0	7	0	—	7
Kansas City (AFL)	3	13	7	0	—	23

KC — FG Stenerud 48 (8:08)
KC — FG Stenerud 32 (1:40)
KC — FG Stenerud 25 (7:08)
KC — Garrett 5 run (Stenerud kick) (9:26)
Minn — Osborn 4 run (Cox kick) (10:28)
KC — Taylor 46 pass from Dawson (Stenerud kick) (13:38)

SUPER BOWL III

Orange Bowl, Miami, Florida
January 12, 1969, Attendance: 75,389

NEW YORK JETS 16, BALTIMORE 7—Jets quarterback Joe Namath "guaranteed" victory on the Thursday before the game, then went out and led the AFL to its first Super Bowl victory over a Baltimore team that had lost only once in 16 games all season. Namath, chosen the outstanding player, completed 17 of 28 passes for 206 yards and directed a steady attack that dominated the NFL champions after the Jets' defense had intercepted Colts quarterback Earl Morrall 3 times in the first half. The Jets had 337 total yards, including 121 rushing yards by Matt Snell. Johnny Unitas, who had missed most of the season with a sore elbow, came off the bench and led Baltimore to its only touchdown late in the fourth quarter after New York led 16-0.

New York Jets (AFL)	0	7	6	3	—	16
Baltimore (NFL)	0	0	0	7	—	7

NYJ — Snell 4 run (Turner kick) (5:57)
NYJ — FG Turner 32 (4:52)
NYJ — FG Turner 30 (11:02)
NYJ — FG Turner 9 (1:34)
Balt — Hill 1 run (Michaels kick) (11:41)

SUPER BOWL II

Orange Bowl, Miami, Florida
January 14, 1968, Attendance: 75,546

GREEN BAY 33, OAKLAND 14—Green Bay, after winning its third consecutive NFL championship, won the Super Bowl title for the second straight year, defeating the AFL champion Raiders in a game that drew the first $3-million gate in football history. Bart Starr again was chosen the game's most valuable player as he completed 13 of 24 passes for 202 yards and 1 touchdown and directed a Packers attack that was in control all the way after building a 16-7 halftime lead. Don Chandler kicked 4 field goals and all-pro cornerback Herb Adderley capped the Green Bay scoring with a 60-yard interception return. The game marked the last for Vince Lombardi as Packers coach, ending nine years at Green Bay in which he won six Western Conference championships, five NFL championships, and two Super Bowls.

Green Bay (NFL)	3	13	10	7	—	33
Oakland (AFL)	0	7	0	7	—	14

GB — FG Chandler 39 (5:07)
GB — FG Chandler 20 (3:08)
GB — Dowler 62 pass from Starr (Chandler kick) (4:10)
Oak — Miller 23 pass from Lamonica (Blanda kick) (8:45)
GB — FG Chandler 43 (14:59)
GB — Anderson 2 run (Chandler kick) (9:06)
GB — FG Chandler 31 (14:58)
GB — Adderley 60 interception return (Chandler kick) (3:57)
Oak — Miller 23 pass from Lamonica (Blanda kick) (5:47)

SUPER BOWL I

Memorial Coliseum, Los Angeles, California
January 15, 1967, Attendance: 61,946

GREEN BAY 35, KANSAS CITY 10—The Green Bay Packers opened the Super Bowl series by defeating the AFL champion Chiefs behind the passing of Bart Starr, the receiving of Max McGee, and a key interception by all-pro safety Willie Wood. Green Bay broke open the game with 3 second-half touchdowns, the first of which was set up by Wood's 50-yard return of an interception to the Chiefs' 5 yard line. McGee, filling in for ailing Boyd Dowler after having caught only 4 passes all season, caught 7 from Starr for 138 yards and 2 touchdowns. Elijah Pitts ran for two other scores. The Chiefs' 10 points came in the second quarter, the only touchdown on a 7-yard pass from Len Dawson to Curtis McClinton. Starr completed 16 of 23 passes for 250 yards and 2 touchdowns and was chosen the most valuable player. The Packers collected $15,000 per man and the Chiefs $7,500—the largest single-game shares in the history of team sports.

Kansas City (AFL)	0	10	0	0	—	10
Green Bay (NFL)	7	7	14	7	—	35

GB — McGee 37 pass from Starr (Chandler kick) (8:56)
KC — McClinton 7 pass from Dawson (Mercer kick) (4:20)
GB — Taylor 14 run (Chandler kick) (10:23)
KC — FG Mercer 31 (14:06)
GB — Pitts 5 run (Chandler kick) (2:27)
GB — McGee 13 pass from Starr (Chandler kick) (14:09)
GB — Pitts 1 run (Chandler kick) (8:25)

AFC CHAMPIONSHIP GAME RESULTS

Includes AFL Championship Games (1960-69)

Season	Date	Winner (Share)	Loser (Share)	Score	Site	Attendance
1995	Jan. 14	Pittsburgh ($27,000)	Indianapolis ($27,000)	20-16	Pittsburgh	61,062
1994	Jan. 15	San Diego ($26,000)	Pittsburgh ($26,000)	17-13	Pittsburgh	61,545
1993	Jan. 23	Buffalo ($23,500)	Kansas City ($23,500)	30-13	Buffalo	76,642
1992	Jan. 17	Buffalo ($18,000)	Miami ($18,000)	29-10	Miami	72,703
1991	Jan. 12	Buffalo ($18,000)	Denver ($18,000)	10-7	Buffalo	80,272
1990	Jan. 20	Buffalo ($18,000)	L.A. Raiders ($18,000)	51-3	Buffalo	80,325
1989	Jan. 14	Denver ($18,000)	Cleveland ($18,000)	37-21	Denver	76,046
1988	Jan. 8	Cincinnati ($18,000)	Buffalo ($18,000)	21-10	Cincinnati	59,747
1987	Jan. 17	Denver ($18,000)	Cleveland ($18,000)	38-33	Denver	76,197
1986	Jan. 11	Denver ($18,000)	Cleveland ($18,000)	23-20*	Cleveland	79,973
1985	Jan. 12	New England ($18,000)	Miami ($18,000)	31-14	Miami	75,662
1984	Jan. 6	Miami ($18,000)	Pittsburgh ($18,000)	45-28	Miami	76,029
1983	Jan. 8	L.A. Raiders ($18,000)	Seattle ($18,000)	30-14	Los Angeles	91,445
1982	Jan. 23	Miami ($18,000)	N.Y. Jets ($18,000)	14-0	Miami	67,396
1981	Jan. 10	Cincinnati ($9,000)	San Diego ($9,000)	27-7	Cincinnati	46,302
1980	Jan. 11	Oakland ($9,000)	San Diego ($9,000)	34-27	San Diego	52,675
1979	Jan. 6	Pittsburgh ($9,000)	Houston ($9,000)	27-13	Pittsburgh	50,475
1978	Jan. 7	Pittsburgh ($9,000)	Houston ($9,000)	34-5	Pittsburgh	50,725
1977	Jan. 1	Denver ($9,000)	Oakland ($9,000)	20-17	Denver	75,044
1976	Dec. 26	Oakland ($8,500)	Pittsburgh ($5,500)	24-7	Oakland	53,821
1975	Jan. 4	Pittsburgh ($8,500)	Oakland ($5,500)	16-10	Pittsburgh	50,609
1974	Dec. 29	Pittsburgh ($8,500)	Oakland ($5,500)	24-13	Oakland	53,800
1973	Dec. 30	Miami ($8,500)	Oakland ($5,500)	27-10	Miami	79,325
1972	Dec. 31	Miami ($8,500)	Pittsburgh ($5,500)	21-17	Pittsburgh	50,845
1971	Jan. 2	Miami ($8,500)	Baltimore ($5,500)	21-0	Miami	76,622
1970	Jan. 3	Baltimore ($8,500)	Oakland ($5,500)	27-17	Baltimore	54,799
1969	Jan. 4	Kansas City ($7,755)	Oakland ($6,252)	17-7	Oakland	53,564
1968	Dec. 29	N.Y. Jets ($7,007)	Oakland ($5,349)	27-23	New York	62,627
1967	Dec. 31	Oakland ($6,321)	Houston ($4,996)	40-7	Oakland	53,330
1966	Jan. 1	Kansas City ($5,309)	Buffalo ($3,799)	31-7	Buffalo	42,080
1965	Dec. 26	Buffalo ($5,189)	San Diego ($3,447)	23-0	San Diego	30,361
1964	Dec. 26	Buffalo ($2,668)	San Diego ($1,738)	20-7	Buffalo	40,242
1963	Jan. 5	San Diego ($2,498)	Boston ($1,596)	51-10	San Diego	30,127
1962	Dec. 23	Dallas ($2,206)	Houston ($1,471)	20-17*	Houston	37,981
1961	Dec. 24	Houston ($1,792)	San Diego ($1,111)	10-3	San Diego	29,556
1960	Jan. 1	Houston ($1,025)	L.A. Chargers ($718)	24-16	Houston	32,183

*Sudden death overtime.

AFC CHAMPIONSHIP GAME COMPOSITE STANDINGS

	W	L	Pct.	Pts.	OP
Cincinnati Bengals	2	0	1.000	48	17
Denver Broncos	4	1	.800	125	101
Buffalo Bills	6	2	.750	180	92
Kansas City Chiefs*	3	1	.750	81	61
Miami Dolphins	5	2	.714	152	115
Pittsburgh Steelers	5	4	.556	186	164
New England Patriots**	1	1	.500	41	65
New York Jets	1	1	.500	27	37
Houston Oilers	2	4	.333	76	140
Indianapolis Colts#	1	2	.333	43	58
Oakland/L.A. Raiders	4	8	.333	228	264
San Diego Chargers***	2	6	.250	128	161
Seattle Seahawks	0	1	.000	14	30
Cleveland Browns	0	3	.000	74	98

*One game played when franchise was in Dallas (Texans). (Won 20-17)

**One game played when franchise was in Boston. (Lost 51-10)

***One game played when franchise was in Los Angeles. (Lost 24-16)

#Two games played when franchise was in Baltimore. (Won 27-17, lost 21-0)

1995 AFC CHAMPIONSHIP GAME

Three Rivers Stadium, Pittsburgh, Pennsylvania
January 14, 1996, Attendance: 61,062

PITTSBURGH 20, INDIANAPOLIS 16—Byron (Bam) Morris ran 1 yard for a touchdown with 1:34 remaining to lift the Steelers to their first AFC championship in 16 years. Despite the late touchdown, however, Pittsburgh didn't secure its Super Bowl berth until Colts quarterback Jim Harbaugh's desperation pass on the game's final play fell incomplete in the end zone. The Steelers, who lost the 1994 AFC title game to San Diego when their final possession ended three yards short of the end zone in the final minute, began their last possession in this game at their own 33-yard line and trailing 16-13 with 3:03 left. Five plays later, quarterback Neil O'Donnell kept the winning drive alive by completing a 9-yard pass to Andre Hastings on fourth-and-3 from the 47. A 37-yard pass to Ernie Mills moved the ball to the Colts' 1, and two plays later Morris bulled his way into the end zone. Indianapolis's final chance began at its 16-yard line with 1:30 to go. Harbaugh passed for 38 yards and scrambled for 17 as the Colts reached Pittsburgh's 29 with five seconds remaining. His final heave into the end zone nearly was caught by Aaron Bailey, but Bailey was not able to cradle the ball as he hit the ground. Harbaugh finished with 21 completions in 33 attempts for 267 yards and 1 touchdown. O'Donnell was 25 of 41 for 205 yards and 1 touchdown for the Steelers. Upstart Indianapolis was bidding to become only the second team (the 1985 Patriots were the first) to win three consecutive road games en route to the Super Bowl.

Indianapolis (16)	Offense	Pittsburgh (20)
Sean Dawkins	WR	Yancey Thigpen
Will Wolford	LT	John Jackson
Randy Dixon	LG	Tom Newberry
Kirk Lowdermilk	C	Dermontti Dawson
Joe Staysniak	RG	Brenden Stai
Jason Mathews	RT	Leon Searcy
Ken Dilger	TE	Mark Bruener
Floyd Turner	WR	Ernie Mills
Jim Harbaugh	QB	Neil O'Donnell
Lamont Warren	RB	Erric Pegram
Zack Crockett	RB-TE	Jonathan Hayes
	Defense	
Bernard Whittington	LE	Brentson Buckner
Tony McCoy	LT-NT	Joel Steed
Tony Siragusa	RT-RE	Ray Seals
Tony Bennett	RE-LOLB	Kevin Greene
Stephen Grant	LLB-LILB	Levon Kirkland
Jeff Herrod	MLB-RILB	Jerry Olsavsky
Quentin Coryatt	RLB-ROLB	Greg Lloyd
Ray Buchanan	LCB	Willie Williams
Ashley Ambrose	RCB	Carnell Lake
David Tate	SS	Myron Bell
Jason Belser	FS	Darren Perry

SUBSTITUTIONS

Indianapolis—Offense: K—Cary Blanchard. P—Chris Gardocki. RB—Clif Groce, Ronald Humphrey. WR—Aaron Bailey, Brian Stablein. TE—Brad Banta, Marcus Pollard. T—Derek West. G—Eric Mahlum, Kipp Vickers. Defense: DE—Freddie Joe Nunn. DT—Ellis Johnson. LB—Trev Alberts, Devon McDonald, Scott Radecic, Trevor Wilmot. CB—Conrad Clarks, Eugene Daniel, Ray McElroy, Damon Watts. S—Derwin Gray. DNP: QB—Craig Erickson.

Pittsburgh—Offense: K—Norm Johnson. P—Rohn Stark. RB—Tim Lester, Fred McAfee, Byron (Bam) Morris, John L. Williams. WR—Andre Hastings, Corey Holliday, Kordell Stewart. TE—Tracy Greene. T—James Parrish, Justin Strzelczyk. C—Kendall Gammon. Defense: DE—Kevin Henry. DT—Bill Johnson. LB—Chad Brown, Jason Gildon, Donta Jones. CB—Deon Figures, Randy Fuller, Chris Oldham. S—Lethon Flowers. DNP: QB—Mike Tomczak

OFFICIALS

Referee—Bernie Kukar. Umpire—Hendi Ancich. Head Linesman—Earnie Frantz. Line Judge—Ron Baynes. Back Judge—Tim Millis. Field Judge—John Robison. Side Judge—Doug Toole.

SCORING

Indianapolis	3	3	3	7	— 16
Pittsburgh	3	7	3	7	— 20

Ind — FG Blanchard 34
Pitt — FG N. Johnson 31
Ind — FG Blanchard 36
Pittt — Stewart 5 pass from O'Donnell (N. Johnson kick)
Ind — FG Blanchard 37
Pitt — FG N. Johnson 36
Ind — Turner 47 pass from Harbaugh (Blanchard kick)
Pitt — Morris 1 run (N. Johnson kick)

TEAM STATISTICS	Ind.	Pitt.
Total First Downs	16	21
Rushing	4	6
Passing	12	12
Penalty	0	3
Total Net Yardage	328	285
Total Offensive Plays	60	66
Average Gain per Offensive Play	5.5	4.3
Rushes	23	24
Yards Gained Rushing (Net)	83	80
Average Yards per Rush	3.6	3.3
Passes Attempted	34	41
Passes Completed	21	25
Had Intercepted	0	1
Tackled Attempting to Pass	3	1
Yards Lost Attempting to Pass	22	0
Yards Gained Passing (Net)	245	205
Punts	4	4
Average Distance	50.0	38.8
Punt Returns	1	3
Punt Return Yardage	5	53
Kickoff Returns	4	4
Kickoff Return Yardage	70	96
Interception Return Yardage	17	0
Total Return Yardage	92	149
Fumbles	1	0
Own Fumbles Recovered	1	0
Opponents Fumbles Recovered	0	0
Penalties	5	4
Yards Penalized	57	25
Total Points Scored	16	20
Touchdowns	1	2
Rushing	0	1
Passing	1	1
Returns	0	0
Extra Points	1	2
Field Goals	3	2
Field Goals Attempted	4	3
Safeties	0	0
Third-Down Efficiency	5/15	6/14
Fourth-Down Efficiency	1/1	1/1
Time of Possession	30:36	29:24

INDIVIDUAL STATISTICS

Rushing

Indianapolis	No.	Yds.	LG	TD
Warren	15	53	10	0
Harbaugh	6	29	9	0
Crockett	1	2	2	0
Humphrey	1	-1	-1	0
Pittsburgh	**No.**	**Yds.**	**LG**	**TD**
Pegram	10	46	9	0
Stewart	4	12	5	0
Morris	7	9	4	1
J. Williams	1	6	6	0
Mills	1	5	5	0
O'Donnell	1	2	2	0

Passing

Indianapolis	Att.	Comp.	Yds.	TD	Int.
Harbaugh	33	21	267	1	0
Warren	1	0	0	0	0
Pittsburgh	**Att.**	**Comp.**	**Yds.**	**TD**	**Int.**
O'Donnell	41	25	205	1	1

Receiving

Indianapolis	No.	Yds.	LG	TD
Dawkins	7	96	30	0
Warren	7	37	7	0
Turner	2	55	47t	1
Crockett	2	22	12	0
Dilger	1	30	30	0
Stablein	1	18	18	0
Bailey	1	9	9	0
Pittsburgh	**No.**	**Yds.**	**LG**	**TD**
Thigpen	6	65	14	0
J. Williams	4	21	7	0
Morris	4	11	6	0
Mills	3	52	37	0
Hastings	3	21	9	0
Stewart	2	18	13	1
Holliday	1	8	8	0
Bruener	1	6	6	0
Pegram	1	3	3	0

Interceptions

Indianapolis	No.	Yds.	LG	TD
Herrod	1	17	17	0
Pittsburgh	**No.**	**Yds.**	**LG**	**TD**
None	—	—	—	—

Punting

Indianapolis	No.	Avg.	LG	Blk.
Gardocki	4	50.0	53	0
Pittsburgh	**No.**	**Avg.**	**LG**	**Blk.**
Stark	4	38.8	50	0

Punt Returns

Indianapolis	No.	FC	Yds.	LG	TD
Buchanan	1	1	5	5	0
Pittsburgh	**No.**	**FC**	**Yds.**	**LG**	**TD**
Hastings	3	0	53	33	0

Kickoff Returns

Indianapolis	No.	Yds.	LG	TD
Bailey	4	70	22	0
Pittsburgh	**No.**	**Yds.**	**LG**	**TD**
Mills	4	96	26	0

NFC CHAMPIONSHIP GAME RESULTS

Includes NFL Championship Games (1933-69)

Season	Date	Winner (Share)	Loser (Share)	Score	Site	Attendance
1995	Jan. 14	Dallas ($27,000)	Green Bay ($27,000)	38-27	Dallas	65,135
1994	Jan. 15	San Francisco ($26,000)	Dallas ($26,000)	38-28	San Francisco	69,125
1993	Jan. 23	Dallas ($23,500)	San Francisco ($23,500)	38-21	Dallas	64,902
1992	Jan. 17	Dallas ($18,000)	San Francisco ($18,000)	30-20	San Francisco	64,920
1991	Jan. 12	Washington ($18,000)	Detroit ($18,000)	41-10	Washington	55,585
1990	Jan. 20	N.Y. Giants ($18,000)	San Francisco ($18,000)	15-13	San Francisco	65,750
1989	Jan. 14	San Francisco ($18,000)	L.A. Rams ($18,000)	30-3	San Francisco	65,634
1988	Jan. 8	San Francisco ($18,000)	Chicago ($18,000)	28-3	Chicago	66,946
1987	Jan. 17	Washington ($18,000)	Minnesota ($18,000)	17-10	Washington	55,212
1986	Jan. 11	New York Giants ($18,000)	Washington ($18,000)	17-0	East Rutherford	76,891
1985	Jan. 12	Chicago ($18,000)	L.A. Rams ($18,000)	24-0	Chicago	66,030
1984	Jan. 6	San Francisco ($18,000)	Chicago ($18,000)	23-0	San Francisco	61,336
1983	Jan. 8	Washington ($18,000)	San Francisco ($18,000)	24-21	Washington	55,363
1982	Jan. 22	Washington ($18,000)	Dallas ($18,000)	31-17	Washington	55,045
1981	Jan. 10	San Francisco ($9,000)	Dallas ($9,000)	28-27	San Francisco	60,525
1980	Jan. 11	Philadelphia ($9,000)	Dallas ($9,000)	20-7	Philadelphia	71,522
1979	Jan. 6	Los Angeles ($9,000)	Tampa Bay ($9,000)	9-0	Tampa Bay	72,033
1978	Jan. 7	Dallas ($9,000)	Los Angeles ($9,000)	28-0	Los Angeles	71,086
1977	Jan. 1	Dallas ($9,000)	Minnesota ($9,000)	23-6	Dallas	64,293
1976	Dec. 26	Minnesota ($8,500)	Los Angeles ($5,500)	24-13	Minnesota	48,379
1975	Jan. 4	Dallas ($8,500)	Los Angeles ($5,500)	37-7	Los Angeles	88,919
1974	Dec. 29	Minnesota ($8,500)	Los Angeles ($5,500)	14-10	Minnesota	48,444
1973	Dec. 30	Minnesota ($8,500)	Dallas ($5,500)	27-10	Dallas	64,422
1972	Dec. 31	Washington ($8,500)	Dallas ($5,500)	26-3	Washington	53,129
1971	Jan. 2	Dallas ($8,500)	San Francisco ($5,500)	14-3	Dallas	63,409
1970	Jan. 3	Dallas ($8,500)	San Francisco ($5,500)	17-10	San Francisco	59,364
1969	Jan. 4	Minnesota ($7,930)	Cleveland ($5,118)	27-7	Minnesota	46,503
1968	Dec. 29	Baltimore ($9,306)	Cleveland ($5,963)	34-0	Cleveland	78,410
1967	Dec. 31	Green Bay ($7,950)	Dallas ($5,299)	21-17	Green Bay	50,861
1966	Jan. 1	Green Bay ($9,813)	Dallas ($6,527)	34-27	Dallas	74,152
1965	Jan. 2	Green Bay ($7,819)	Cleveland ($5,288)	23-12	Green Bay	50,777
1964	Dec. 27	Cleveland ($8,052)	Baltimore ($5,571)	27-0	Cleveland	79,544
1963	Dec. 29	Chicago ($5,899)	New York ($4,218)	14-10	Chicago	45,801
1962	Dec. 30	Green Bay ($5,888)	New York ($4,166)	16-7	New York	64,892
1961	Dec. 31	Green Bay ($5,195)	New York ($3,339)	37-0	Green Bay	39,029
1960	Dec. 26	Philadelphia ($5,116)	Green Bay ($3,105)	17-13	Philadelphia	67,325
1959	Dec. 27	Baltimore ($4,674)	New York ($3,083)	31-16	Baltimore	57,545
1958	Dec. 28	Baltimore ($4,718)	New York ($3,111)	23-17*	New York	64,185
1957	Dec. 29	Detroit ($4,295)	Cleveland ($2,750)	59-14	Detroit	55,263
1956	Dec. 30	New York ($3,779)	Chi. Bears ($2,485)	47-7	New York	56,836
1955	Dec. 26	Cleveland ($3,508)	Los Angeles ($2,316)	38-14	Los Angeles	85,693
1954	Dec. 26	Cleveland ($2,478)	Detroit ($1,585)	56-10	Cleveland	43,827
1953	Dec. 27	Detroit ($2,424)	Cleveland ($1,654)	17-16	Detroit	54,577
1952	Dec. 28	Detroit ($2,274)	Cleveland ($1,712)	17-7	Cleveland	50,934

PLAYOFF GAMES SUMMARIES

Season	Date	Winner (Share)	Loser (Share)	Score	Site	Attendance
1951	Dec. 23	Los Angeles ($2,108)	Cleveland ($1,483)	24-17	Los Angeles	57,522
1950	Dec. 24	Cleveland ($1,113)	Los Angeles ($686)	30-28	Cleveland	29,751
1949	Dec. 18	Philadelphia ($1,094)	Los Angeles ($739)	14-0	Los Angeles	27,980
1948	Dec. 19	Philadelphia ($1,540)	Chi. Cardinals ($874)	7-0	Philadelphia	36,309
1947	Dec. 28	Chi. Cardinals ($1,132)	Philadelphia ($754)	28-21	Chicago	30,759
1946	Dec. 15	Chi. Bears ($1,975)	New York ($1,295)	24-14	New York	58,346
1945	Dec. 16	Cleveland ($1,469)	Washington ($902)	15-14	Cleveland	32,178
1944	Dec. 17	Green Bay ($1,449)	New York ($814)	14-7	New York	46,016
1943	Dec. 26	Chi. Bears ($1,146)	Washington ($765)	41-21	Chicago	34,320
1942	Dec. 13	Washington ($965)	Chi. Bears ($637)	14-6	Washington	36,006
1941	Dec. 21	Chi. Bears ($430)	New York ($288)	37-9	Chicago	13,341
1940	Dec. 8	Chi. Bears ($873)	Washington ($606)	73-0	Washington	36,034
1939	Dec. 10	Green Bay ($703.97)	New York ($455.57)	27-0	Milwaukee	32,279
1938	Dec. 11	New York ($504.45)	Green Bay ($368.81)	23-17	New York	48,120
1937	Dec. 12	Washington ($225.90)	Chi. Bears ($127.78)	28-21	Chicago	15,870
1936	Dec. 13	Green Bay ($250)	Boston ($180)	21-6	New York	29,545
1935	Dec. 15	Detroit ($313.35)	New York ($200.20)	26-7	Detroit	15,000
1934	Dec. 9	New York ($621)	Chi. Bears ($414.02)	30-13	New York	35,059
1933	Dec. 17	Chi. Bears ($210.34)	New York ($140.22)	23-21	Chicago	26,000

**Sudden death overtime.*

NFC CHAMPIONSHIP GAME COMPOSITE STANDINGS

	W	L	Pct.	Pts.	OP
Philadelphia Eagles	4	1	.800	79	48
Baltimore Colts	3	1	.750	88	60
Green Bay Packers	8	3	.727	250	154
Detroit Lions	4	2	.667	139	141
Minnesota Vikings	4	2	.667	108	80
Washington Redskins*	7	5	.583	222	255
Chicago Bears	7	6	.538	286	245
Dallas Cowboys	8	8	.500	361	319
Phoenix Cardinals**	1	1	.500	28	28
San Francisco 49ers	5	6	.454	235	199
Cleveland Browns	4	7	.364	224	253
New York Giants	5	11	.313	240	322
Los Angeles Rams***	3	9	.250	123	270
Tampa Bay Buccaneers	0	1	.000	0	9

**One game played when franchise was in Boston. (Lost 21-6)*
***Both games played when franchise was in Chicago. (Won 28-21, lost 7-0)*
****One game played when franchise was in Cleveland. (Won 15-14)*

1995 NFC CHAMPIONSHIP GAME

Texas Stadium, Irving, Texas
January 14, 1996, Attendance: 65,135

DALLAS 38, GREEN BAY 27—Emmitt Smith rushed for 150 yards and 3 touchdowns to help the Cowboys reach the Super Bowl for the third time in four years and a record eighth time overall. Dallas, playing in the NFC Championship Game for the fourth consecutive year, jumped to a 14-3 lead in the first quarter on a pair of touchdown passes from Troy Aikman to Michael Irvin. But the Packers rallied behind 2 touchdown passes from Brett Favre, and the score was tied 17-17 late in the first half when Smith took control. With 4:05 left in the second quarter and the Cowboys pinned at their own 1-yard line by a punt that rolled out of bounds, Smith got his team out of the shadow of its goal line with a 25-yard run. Six plays later, Aikman's 28-yard completion to Irvin moved Dallas into scoring position, and Smith capped the 11-play, 99-yard drive with a 1 yard touchdown run 24 seconds before halftime. Green Bay rallied again, taking a 27-24 lead on Chris Jacke's 37-yard field goal and Brett Favre's 1-yard touchdown pass to Robert Brooks, only to see Smith rush for 2 more touchdowns to win the game in the fourth quarter. The first was a 5-yard run that capped a 14-play, 90-yard drive, and the latter was a 16-yard run with 9:28 remaining. It was set up by cornerback Larry Brown's interception and 28-yard return. The Cowboys wore down the Packers by controlling the ball for nearly 39 of the game's 60 minutes. Dallas ran more plays (77-55) for more first downs (27-17) and more total yards (419-328), and did not commit a turnover. Aikman completed 21 of 33 passes for 255 yards. Irvin caught 7 passes for 100 yards. Favre, who misfired on his first six attempts and then had his first two completions go for touchdowns, finished with 21 completions in 39 attempts for 307 yards and 3 touchdowns, but was intercepted twice. Brooks caught 6 passes for 105 yards and 2 touchdowns.

Green Bay (27)	Offense	Dallas (38)
Antonio Freeman	WR	Kevin Williams
Ken Ruettgers	LT	Mark Tuinei
Adam Timmerman	LG	Nate Newton
Frank Winters	C	Derek Kennard
Harry Galbreath	RG	Larry Allen
Earl Dotson	RT	Erik Williams
Robert Brooks	WR-TE	Jay Novacek
Mark Ingram	WR	Michael Irvin
Brett Favre	QB	Troy Aikman
Edgar Bennett	RB	Emmitt Smith
Anthony Morgan	WR-RB	Daryl Johnston
	Defense	
Reggie White	LE	Tony Tolbert
Gilbert Brown	LT	Russell Maryland
John Jurkovic	RT	Leon Lett
Sean Jones	RE	Shante Carver
Wayne Simmons	LLB	Darrin Smith
Fred Strickland	MLB	Godfrey Myles
George Koonce	RLB	Darren Woodson
Craig Newsome	LCB	Deion Sanders
Doug Evans	RCB	Larry Brown
LeRoy Butler	SS	Scott Case
George Teague	FS	Brock Marion

SUBSTITUTIONS

Green Bay—Offense: K—Chris Jacke. P—Craig Hentrich. RB—William Henderson, Travis Jervey, Dorsey Levens, Marcus Wilson. WR—Terry Mickens. TE—Mark Chmura, Keith Jackson, Jeff Thomason. T—Gary Brown. C—Mike Arthur. Defense: DE—Matt LaBounty, Gabe Wilkins. DT—Darius Holland, Bob Kuberski. LB—Bernardo Harris, Brian Williams. CB—Keith Crawford, Lenny McGill, Roderick Mullen. S—Mike Prior. DNP: QB—Jim McMahon.

Dallas—Offense: K—Chris Boniol. P—John Jett. RB—David Lang, Sherman Williams. WR—Billy Davis. TE—Eric Bjornson, Kendell Watkins. G—Ron Stone. C—Dale Hellestrae. Defense: DT—Darren Benson, Chad Hennings, Hurvin McCormack. LB—Dixon Edwards, Robert Jones, Jim Schwantz. CB—Robert Bailey, Alundis Brice. S—Bill Bates, Greg Briggs, Charlie Williams. DNP: QB—Wade Wilson. WR—Cory Fleming. T—George Hegamin.

OFFICIALS

Referee—Ed Hochuli. Umpire—Ron Botchan. Head Linesman—Terry Gierke. Line Judge—Tom Barnes. Back Judge—Jim Poole. Field Judge—Ron Spitler. Side Judge—Tom Fincken.

SCORING

Green Bay	10	7	10	0	— 27
Dallas	14	10	0	14	— 38

GB — FG Jacke 46
Dall — Irvin 6 pass from Aikman (Boniol kick)
Dall — Irvin 4 pass from Aikman (Boniol kick)
GB — R. Brooks 73 pass from Favre (Jacke kick)
GB — Jackson 24 pass from Favre (Jacke kick)
Dall — FG Boniol 34
Dall — E. Smith 1 run (Boniol kick)
GB — FG Jacke 37
GB — R. Brooks 1 pass from Favre (Jacke kick)
Dall — E. Smith 5 run (Boniol kick)
Dall — E. Smith 16 run (Boniol kick)

TEAM STATISTICS	G.B.	Dallas
Total First Downs	17	26
Rushing	3	11
Passing	11	13
Penalty	3	2
Total Net Yardage	328	419
Total Offensive Plays	55	77
Average Gain per Offensive Play	6.0	5.4
Rushes	12	43
Yards Gained Rushing (Net)	48	169
Average Yards per Rush	4.0	3.9
Passes Attempted	39	33
Passes Completed	21	21
Had Intercepted	2	0
Tackled Attempting to Pass	4	1
Yards Lost Attempting to Pass	27	5
Yards Gained Passing (Net)	280	250
Punts	3	5
Average Distance	48.0	36.6
Punt Returns	4	1
Punt Return Yardage	54	6
Kickoff Returns	7	4
Kickoff Return Yardage	148	90
Interception Return Yardage	0	27
Total Return Yardage	202	123
Fumbles	0	0
Own Fumbles Recovered	0	0
Opponents Fumbles Recovered	0	0
Penalties	11	6
Yards Penalized	84	65
Total Points Scored	27	38
Touchdowns	3	5
Rushing	0	3
Passing	3	2
Returns	0	0
Extra Points	3	5
Field Goals	2	1
Field Goals Attempted	2	2
Safeties	0	0
Third-Down Efficiency	2/9	9/16
Fourth-Down Efficiency	0/2	0/0
Time of Possession	21:04	38:56

INDIVIDUAL STATISTICS

Rushing

Green Bay	No.	Yds.	LG	TD
Bennett	9	46	18	0
Henderson	1	2	2	0
Levens	1	1	1	0
Favre	1	-1	-1	0

Dallas	No.	Yds.	LG	TD
E. Smith	35	150	25	3
Johnston	2	8	6	0
Aikman	3	6	9	0
S. Williams	1	3	3	0
Sanders	2	2	3	0

Passing

Green Bay	Att.	Comp.	Yds.	TD	Int.
Favre	39	21	307	3	2
Dallas	**Att.**	**Comp.**	**Yds.**	**TD**	**Int.**
Aikman	33	21	255	2	0

Receiving

Green Bay	No.	Yds.	LG	TD
R. Brooks	6	105	73t	2
Jackson	5	99	54	1
Bennett	3	20	8	0
Mickens	2	38	25	0
Levens	2	11	9	0
Chmura	1	16	16	0
Freeman	1	10	10	0
Ingram	1	8	8	0
Dallas	**No.**	**Yds.**	**LG**	**TD**
Irvin	7	100	36	2
Novacek	5	56	25	0
K. Williams	3	32	15	0
Johnston	3	15	8	0
E. Smith	2	17	16	0
Sanders	1	35	35	0

Interceptions

Green Bay	No.	Yds.	LG	TD
None	—	—	—	—
Dallas	**No.**	**Yds.**	**LG**	**TD**
Brown	1	28	28	0
Lett	1	-1	-1	0

Punting

Green Bay	No.	Avg.	LG	Blk.
Hentrich	3	48.0	57	0
Dallas	**No.**	**Avg.**	**LG**	**Blk.**
Jett	4	45.8	54	1

Punt Returns

Green Bay	No.	FC	Yds.	LG	TD
Freeman	4	0	54	39	0
Dallas	**No.**	**FC**	**Yds.**	**LG**	**TD**
Sanders	1	1	6	6	0

Kickoff Returns

Green Bay	No.	Yds.	LG	TD
Freeman	7	148	28	0
Dallas	**No.**	**Yds.**	**LG**	**TD**
K. Williams	4	90	27	0

AFC DIVISIONAL PLAYOFFS RESULTS

Includes Second-Round Playoff Games (1982), AFC Inter-Divisional Games (1969), and special playoff games to break ties for AFL Division Championships (1963, 1968)

Season	Date	Winner (Share)	Loser (Share)	Score	Site	Attendance
1995	Jan. 7	Indianapolis ($13,000)	Kansas City ($13,000)	10-7	Kansas City	77,594
	Jan. 6	Pittsburgh ($13,000)	Buffalo ($13,000)	40-21	Pittsburgh	59,072
1994	Jan. 8	San Diego ($12,000)	Miami ($12,000)	22-21	San Diego	63,381
	Jan. 7	Pittsburgh ($12,000)	Cleveland ($12,000)	29-9	Pittsburgh	58,185
1993	Jan. 16	Kansas City ($12,000)	Houston ($12,000)	28-20	Houston	64,011
	Jan. 15	Buffalo ($12,000)	L.A. Raiders ($12,000)	29-23	Buffalo	61,923
1992	Jan. 10	Miami ($10,000)	San Diego ($10,000)	31-0	Miami	71,224
	Jan. 9	Buffalo ($10,000)	Pittsburgh ($10,000)	24-3	Pittsburgh	60,407
1991	Jan. 5	Buffalo ($10,000)	Kansas City ($10,000)	37-14	Buffalo	80,182
	Jan. 4	Denver ($10,000)	Houston ($10,000)	26-24	Denver	75,301
1990	Jan. 13	L.A. Raiders ($10,000)	Cincinnati ($10,000)	20-10	Los Angeles	92,045
	Jan. 12	Buffalo ($10,000)	Miami ($10,000)	44-34	Buffalo	77,087
1989	Jan. 7	Denver ($10,000)	Pittsburgh ($10,000)	24-23	Denver	75,477
	Jan. 6	Cleveland ($10,000)	Buffalo ($10,000)	34-30	Cleveland	78,921
1988	Jan. 1	Buffalo ($10,000)	Houston ($10,000)	17-10	Buffalo	79,532
	Dec. 31	Cincinnati ($10,000)	Seattle ($10,000)	21-13	Cincinnati	58,560
1987	Jan. 10	Denver ($10,000)	Houston ($10,000)	34-10	Denver	75,440
	Jan. 9	Cleveland ($10,000)	Indianapolis ($10,000)	38-21	Cleveland	79,372
1986	Jan. 4	Denver ($10,000)	New England ($10,000)	22-17	Denver	75,262
	Jan. 3	Cleveland ($10,000)	N.Y. Jets ($10,000)	23-20*	Cleveland	79,720
1985	Jan. 5	New England ($10,000)	L.A. Raiders ($10,000)	27-20	Los Angeles	87,163
	Jan. 4	Miami ($10,000)	Cleveland ($10,000)	24-21	Miami	74,667
1984	Dec. 30	Pittsburgh ($10,000)	Denver ($10,000)	24-17	Denver	74,981
	Dec. 29	Miami ($10,000)	Seattle ($10,000)	31-10	Miami	73,469
1983	Jan. 1	L.A. Raiders ($10,000)	Pittsburgh ($10,000)	38-10	Los Angeles	90,380
	Dec. 31	Seattle ($10,000)	Miami ($10,000)	27-20	Miami	74,136
1982	Jan. 16	Miami ($10,000)	San Diego ($10,000)	34-13	Miami	71,383
	Jan. 15	N.Y. Jets ($10,000)	L.A. Raiders ($10,000)	17-14	Los Angeles	90,038
1981	Jan. 3	Cincinnati ($5,000)	Buffalo ($5,000)	28-21	Cincinnati	55,420
	Jan. 2	San Diego ($5,000)	Miami ($5,000)	41-38*	Miami	73,735
1980	Jan. 4	Oakland ($5,000)	Cleveland ($5,000)	14-12	Cleveland	78,245
	Jan. 3	San Diego ($5,000)	Buffalo ($5,000)	20-14	San Diego	52,253
1979	Dec. 30	Pittsburgh ($5,000)	Miami ($5,000)	34-14	Pittsburgh	50,214
	Dec. 29	Houston ($5,000)	San Diego ($5,000)	17-14	San Diego	51,192
1978	Dec. 31	Houston ($5,000)	New England ($5,000)	31-14	New England	60,735
	Dec. 30	Pittsburgh ($5,000)	Denver ($5,000)	33-10	Pittsburgh	50,230
1977	Dec. 24	Oakland ($5,000)	Baltimore ($5,000)	37-31*	Baltimore	59,925
	Dec. 24	Denver ($5,000)	Pittsburgh ($5,000)	34-21	Denver	75,059
1976	Dec. 19	Pittsburgh ($)	Baltimore ($)	40-14	Baltimore	59,296
	Dec. 18	Oakland ($)	New England ($)	24-21	Oakland	53,050
1975	Dec. 28	Oakland ($)	Cincinnati ($)	31-28	Oakland	53,030
	Dec. 27	Pittsburgh ($)	Baltimore ($)	28-10	Pittsburgh	49,557
1974	Dec. 22	Pittsburgh ($)	Buffalo ($)	32-14	Pittsburgh	49,841
	Dec. 21	Oakland ($)	Miami ($)	28-26	Oakland	53,023
1973	Dec. 23	Miami ($)	Cincinnati ($)	34-16	Miami	78,928
	Dec. 22	Oakland ($)	Pittsburgh ($)	33-14	Oakland	52,646
1972	Dec. 24	Miami ($)	Cleveland ($)	20-14	Miami	78,916
	Dec. 23	Pittsburgh ($)	Oakland ($)	13-7	Pittsburgh	50,327
1971	Dec. 26	Baltimore ($)	Cleveland ($)	20-3	Cleveland	70,734
	Dec. 25	Miami ($)	Kansas City ($)	27-24*	Kansas City	45,822
1970	Dec. 27	Oakland ($)	Miami ($)	21-14	Oakland	52,594
	Dec. 26	Baltimore ($)	Cincinnati ($)	17-0	Baltimore	49,694
1969	Dec. 21	Oakland ($)	Houston ($)	56-7	Oakland	53,539
	Dec. 20	Kansas City ($)	N.Y. Jets ($)	13-6	New York	62,977
1968	Dec. 22	Oakland ($)	Kansas City ($)	41-6	Oakland	53,605
1963	Dec. 28	Boston ($)	Buffalo ($)	26-8	Buffalo	33,044

**Sudden Death Overtime.*

$ Players received 1/14 of annual salary for playoff appearances.

PLAYOFF GAMES SUMMARIES

1995 AFC DIVISIONAL PLAYOFF GAMES

Arrowhead Stadium, Kansas City, Missouri
January 7, 1996, Attendance: 77,594

INDIANAPOLIS 10, KANSAS CITY 7—Cary Blanchard broke a 7-7 tie with a 30-yard field goal late in the third quarter, and the Colts held on to stun the Chiefs. Kansas City, which had compiled the NFL's best record during the regular season by winning 13 of 16 games, had a chance to tie the game in the final minute, but Lin Elliott's 42-yard field-goal try with 37 seconds left was wide left. Elliott also missed a 35-yard attempt in the first half and a 39-yard try early in the fourth quarter. Indianapolis, which won on the road for the second consecutive week, relied on a ground game that produced 147 yards and a stingy defense that forced 4 turnovers and shut out the Chiefs after the first quarter. Kansas City quarterback Steve Bono completed only 11 of 25 passes for 122 yards and was intercepted 3 times before being lifted in favor of backup Rich Gannon late in the fourth quarter. Colts quarterback Jim Harbaugh did not fare any better, completing only 12 of 27 passes for 112 yards, but tied the game with a 5-yard touchdown pass to Floyd Turner midway through the second quarter and scrambled for 48 yards. The Chiefs' Marcus Allen led all rushers with 94 yards on 21 carries.

Indianapolis	0	7	3	0	—	10
Kansas City	7	0	0	0	—	7

KC — Dawson 20 pass from Bono (Elliott kick)
Ind — Turner 5 pass from Harbaugh (Blanchard kick)
Ind — FG Blanchard 30

Three Rivers Stadium, Pittsburgh, Pennsylvania
January 6, 1996, Attendance: 59,072

PITTSBURGH 40, BUFFALO 21—Neil O'Donnell passed for 262 yards and Byron (Bam) Morris ran for 2 game-clinching touchdowns in the fourth quarter as the Steelers advanced to the AFC Championship Game for the second consecutive year. O'Donnell completed 19 of 35 passes, including a 10-yard touchdown to Ernie Mills to give Pittsburgh a 14-0 lead 42 seconds into the second quarter. Norm Johnson added 3 field goals before halftime and another 6:36 into the second half to increase the Steelers' advantage to 26-7. After the Bills pulled within 26-21 on Jim Kelly's 9-yard touchdown pass to running back Thurman Thomas with 11:23 left in the game, Pittsburgh answered with a 9-play, 76-yard drive capped by Morris's 13-yard touchdown run with 6:16 to go. Moments later, linebacker Levon Kirkland's interception and 4-yard return set up Morris's 2-yard touchdown run at the 1:58 mark. Morris finished with 106 yards on 25 carries, helping the Steelers' balanced offense produce 409 total yards. Buffalo, which had amassed a record 341 rushing yards and more than 500 total yards in its victory over the Dolphins a week earlier, managed only 94 rushing yards and 250 total yards in this one. Quarterback Jim Kelly completed only 14 of 29 passes for 135 yards and was intercepted 3 times. Buffalo played without defensive end Bruce Smith, who missed the game because of the flu.

Buffalo	0	7	7	7	—	21
Pittsburgh	7	16	3	14	—	40

Pitt — J.L. Williams 1 run (N. Johnson kick)
Pitt — Mills 10 pass from O'Donnell (N. Johnson kick)
Pitt — FG N. Johnson 45
Pitt — FG N. Johnson 38
Buff — Thomas 1 run (Christie kick)
Pitt — FG N. Johnson 34
Pitt — FG N. Johnson 39
Buff — Cline 2 pass from Van Pelt (Christie kick)
Buff — Thomas 9 pass from Kelly (Christie kick)
Pitt — Morris 13 run (N. Johnson kick)
Pitt — Morris 2 run (N. Johnson kick)

NFC DIVISIONAL PLAYOFFS RESULTS

Includes Second-Round Playoff Games (1982), NFL Conference Championship Games (1967-69), and special playoff games to break ties for NFL Division or Conference Championships (1941, 1943, 1947, 1950, 1952, 1957, 1958, 1965)

Season	Date	Winner (Share)	Loser (Share)	Score	Site	Attendance
1995	Jan. 7	Dallas ($13,000)	Philadelphia ($13,000)	30-11	Dallas	64,371
	Jan. 6	Green Bay ($13,000)	San Francisco ($13,000)	27-17	San Francisco	69,311
1994	Jan. 8	Dallas ($12,000)	Green Bay ($12,000)	35-9	Dallas	64,745
	Jan. 7	San Francisco ($12,000)	Chicago ($12,000)	44-15	San Francisco	64,644
1993	Jan. 16	Dallas ($12,000)	Green Bay ($12,000)	27-17	Dallas	64,790
	Jan. 15	San Francisco ($12,000)	N.Y. Giants ($12,000)	44-3	San Francisco	67,143
1992	Jan. 10	Dallas ($10,000)	Philadelphia ($10,000)	34-10	Dallas	63,721
	Jan. 9	San Francisco ($10,000)	Washington ($10,000)	20-13	San Francisco	64,991
1991	Jan. 5	Detroit ($10,000)	Dallas ($10,000)	38-6	Detroit	78,290
	Jan. 4	Washington ($10,000)	Atlanta ($10,000)	24-7	Washington	55,181
1990	Jan. 13	N.Y. Giants ($10,000)	Chicago ($10,000)	31-3	East Rutherford	77,025
	Jan. 12	San Francisco ($10,000)	Washington ($10,000)	28-10	San Francisco	65,292
1989	Jan. 7	L.A. Rams ($10,000)	N.Y. Giants ($10,000)	19-13*	East Rutherford	76,526
	Jan. 6	San Francisco ($10,000)	Minnesota ($10,000)	41-13	San Francisco	64,918
1988	Jan. 1	San Francisco ($10,000)	Minnesota ($10,000)	34-9	San Francisco	61,848
	Dec. 31	Chicago ($10,000)	Philadelphia ($10,000)	20-12	Chicago	65,534
1987	Jan. 10	Washington ($10,000)	Chicago ($10,000)	21-17	Chicago	65,268
	Jan. 9	Minnesota ($10,000)	San Francisco ($10,000)	36-24	San Francisco	63,008
1986	Jan. 4	N.Y. Giants ($10,000)	San Francisco ($10,000)	49-3	East Rutherford	75,691
	Jan. 3	Washington ($10,000)	Chicago ($10,000)	27-13	Chicago	65,524
1985	Jan. 5	Chicago ($10,000)	N.Y. Giants ($10,000)	21-0	Chicago	65,670
	Jan. 4	L.A. Rams ($10,000)	Dallas ($10,000)	20-0	Anaheim	66,581
1984	Dec. 30	Chicago ($10,000)	Washington ($10,000)	23-19	Washington	55,431
	Dec. 29	San Francisco ($10,000)	N.Y. Giants ($10,000)	21-10	San Francisco	60,303
1983	Jan. 1	Washington ($10,000)	L.A. Rams ($10,000)	51-7	Washington	54,440
	Dec. 31	San Francisco ($10,000)	Detroit ($10,000)	24-23	San Francisco	59,979
1982	Jan. 16	Dallas ($10,000)	Green Bay ($10,000)	37-26	Dallas	63,972
	Jan. 15	Washington ($10,000)	Minnesota ($10,000)	21-7	Washington	54,593
1981	Jan. 3	San Francisco ($5,000)	N.Y. Giants ($5,000)	38-24	San Francisco	58,360
	Jan. 2	Dallas ($5,000)	Tampa Bay ($5,000)	38-0	Dallas	64,848
1980	Jan. 4	Dallas ($5,000)	Atlanta ($5,000)	30-27	Atlanta	59,793
	Jan. 3	Philadelphia ($5,000)	Minnesota ($5,000)	31-16	Philadelphia	70,178
1979	Dec. 30	Los Angeles ($5,000)	Dallas ($5,000)	21-19	Dallas	64,792
	Dec. 29	Tampa Bay ($5,000)	Philadelphia ($5,000)	24-17	Tampa Bay	71,402
1978	Dec. 31	Los Angeles ($5,000)	Minnesota ($5,000)	34-10	Los Angeles	70,436
	Dec. 30	Dallas ($5,000)	Atlanta ($5,000)	27-20	Dallas	63,406
1977	Dec. 26	Dallas ($5,000)	Chicago ($5,000)	37-7	Dallas	63,260
	Dec. 26	Minnesota ($5,000)	Los Angeles ($5,000)	14-7	Los Angeles	70,203
1976	Dec. 19	Los Angeles ($)	Dallas ($)	14-12	Dallas	63,283
	Dec. 18	Minnesota ($)	Washington ($)	35-20	Minnesota	47,466
1975	Dec. 28	Dallas ($)	Minnesota ($)	17-14	Minnesota	48,050
	Dec. 27	Los Angeles ($)	St. Louis ($)	35-23	Los Angeles	73,459
1974	Dec. 22	Los Angeles ($)	Washington ($)	19-10	Los Angeles	77,925
	Dec. 21	Minnesota ($)	St. Louis ($)	30-14	Minnesota	48,150
1973	Dec. 23	Dallas ($)	Los Angeles ($)	27-16	Dallas	63,272
	Dec. 22	Minnesota ($)	Washington ($)	27-20	Minnesota	48,040
1972	Dec. 24	Washington ($)	Green Bay ($)	16-3	Washington	52,321
	Dec. 23	Dallas ($)	San Francisco ($)	30-28	San Francisco	59,746
1971	Dec. 26	San Francisco ($)	Washington ($)	24-20	San Francisco	45,327
	Dec. 25	Dallas ($)	Minnesota ($)	20-12	Minnesota	47,307
1970	Dec. 27	San Francisco ($)	Minnesota ($)	17-14	Minnesota	45,103
	Dec. 26	Dallas ($)	Detroit ($)	5-0	Dallas	69,613

1969	Dec. 28	Cleveland ($)	Dallas ($)	38-14	Dallas	69,321
	Dec. 27	Minnesota ($)	Los Angeles ($)	23-20	Minnesota	47,900
1968	Dec. 22	Baltimore ($)	Minnesota ($)	24-14	Baltimore	60,238
	Dec. 21	Cleveland ($)	Dallas ($)	31-20	Cleveland	81,497
1967	Dec. 24	Dallas ($)	Cleveland ($)	52-14	Dallas	70,786
	Dec. 23	Green Bay ($)	Los Angeles ($)	28-7	Milwaukee	49,861
1965	Dec. 26	Green Bay ($)	Baltimore ($)	13-10*	Green Bay	50,484
1958	Dec. 21	N.Y. Giants (#)	Cleveland (#)	10-0	New York	61,274
1957	Dec. 22	Detroit (#)	San Francisco (#)	31-27	San Francisco	60,118
1952	Dec. 21	Detroit (#)	Los Angeles (#)	31-21	Detroit	47,645
1950	Dec. 17	Los Angeles (#)	Chicago Bears (#)	24-14	Los Angeles	83,501
	Dec. 17	Cleveland (#)	N.Y. Giants (#)	8-3	Cleveland	33,054
1947	Dec. 21	Philadelphia (#)	Pittsburgh (#)	21-0	Pittsburgh	35,729
1943	Dec. 19	Washington (¢)	N.Y. Giants (¢)	28-0	New York	42,800
1941	Dec. 14	Chicago Bears (¢)	Green Bay (¢)	33-14	Chicago	43,425

* *Sudden Death Overtime.*
$ Players received 1/14 of annual salary for playoff appearances.
 # Players received 1/12 of annual salary for playoff appearances.
¢ Players received 1/10 of annual salary for playoff appearances.

1995 NFC DIVISIONAL PLAYOFF GAMES

Texas Stadium, Irving, Texas
January 7, 1996, Attendance: 64,371

DALLAS 30, PHILADELPHIA 11—Emmitt Smith rushed for 99 yards and 1 touchdown to lead the Cowboys to the NFC Championship Game for the fourth consecutive year. Smith's 1-yard touchdown run 3:42 before halftime capped a 79-yard drive and helped break open the game at 17-3. Quarterback Troy Aikman accounted for most of the yards on the march with a 37-yard completion to wide receiver Kevin Williams and a 26-yard toss to fullback Daryl Johnston. A pair of field goals by Chris Boniol extended Dallas's lead to 23-3 in the third quarter, and Aikman made it 30-3 with a 9-yard touchdown pass to Michael Irvin with 5:43 left in the game. Aikman finished with 17 completions in 24 attempts for 253 yards. Williams caught 6 passes for 124 yards. The Eagles mounted little opposition after tying the game at 3-3 on Gary Anderson's 26-yard field goal on the first play of the second quarter. Starting quarterback Rodney Peete had suffered a concussion on the previous play, and backup Randall Cunningham came on to complete only 11 of 26 passes for 161 yards.

Philadelphia	0	3	0	8	—	11
Dallas	3	14	6	7	—	30

Dall — FG Boniol 24
Phil — FG Anderson 26
Dall — Sanders 21 run (Boniol kick)
Dall — E. Smith 1 run (Boniol kick)
Dall — FG Boniol 18
Dall — FG Boniol 51
Dall — Irvin 9 pass from Aikman (Boniol kick)
Phil — Cunningham 4 run (R. Johnson pass from Cunningham)

3Com Park, San Francisco, California
January 6, 1996, Attendance: 69,311

GREEN BAY 27, SAN FRANCISCO 17—The Packers jumped to a 21-0 lead and never were seriously threatened as they dethroned the defending Super Bowl champions. Green Bay dominated the game early, taking the opening kickoff and maintaining possession for 11 plays and 7:11 before Chris Jacke's 44-yard field-goal attempt was blocked by Tim McDonald. But on the 49ers' first play from scrimmage, fullback Adam Walker fumbled because of a hard hit by linebacker Wayne Simmons, after catching a pass from Steve Young. Packers cornerback Craig Newsome picked up the loose ball and returned it 31 yards for a touchdown. After San Francisco failed to make a first down on its ensuing possession, the Packers took only 4 plays to drive 62 yards to Brett Favre's 3-yard touchdown pass to tight end Keith Jackson. Green Bay scored again the next time it had the ball, with Favre's 13-yard touchdown pass to tight end Mark Chmura coming early in the second quarter. By halftime, Favre had completed 15 of 17 passes for 222 yards. He finished the game 21 of 28 for 299 yards, and was not intercepted. Trailing 21-3, the 49ers opened the second half with an 80-yard, 14-play touchdown drive that consumed 7:14, but Jacke kicked a pair of field goals to keep the game out of reach. San Francisco quarterback Steve Young passed for 328 yards and led all rushers with 77 yards, but was forced to attempt a postseason-record 65 passes and completed only 32. He also was intercepted twice, lost a fumble, was sacked 3 times, and consistently harassed by the Packers' pass rush.

Green Bay	14	7	3	3	—	27
San Francisco	0	3	7	7	—	17

GB — Newsome 31 fumble return (Jacke kick)
GB — Jackson 3 pass from Favre (Jacke kick)
GB — Chmura 13 pass from Favre (Jacke kick)
SF — FG Wilkins 21
SF — Young 1 run (Wilkins kick)
GB — FG Jacke 27
GB — FG Jacke 26
SF — Loville 2 run (Wilkins kick)

AFC WILD CARD PLAYOFF GAMES RESULTS

Season	Date	Winner (Share)	Loser (Share)	Score	Site	Attendance
1995	Dec. 31	Indianapolis ($7,500)	San Diego ($7,500)	35-20	San Diego	61,182
	Dec. 30	Buffalo ($13,000)	Miami ($7,500)	37-22	Buffalo	73,103
1994	Jan. 1	Cleveland ($7,500)	New England ($7,500)	20-13	Cleveland	77,452
	Dec. 31	Miami ($12,000)	Kansas City ($7,500)	27-17	Miami	67,487
1993	Jan. 9	L.A. Raiders ($7,500)	Denver ($7,500)	42-24	Los Angeles	65,314
	Jan. 8	Kansas City ($12,000)	Pittsburgh ($7,500)	27-24*	Kansas City	74,515
1992	Jan. 3	Buffalo ($6,000)	Houston ($6,000)	41-38*	Buffalo	75,141
	Jan. 2	San Diego ($10,000)	Kansas City ($6,000)	17-0	San Diego	58,278
1991	Dec. 29	Houston ($10,000)	N.Y. Jets ($6,000)	17-10	Houston	61,485
	Dec. 28	Kansas City ($6,000)	L.A. Raiders ($6,000)	10-6	Kansas City	75,827
1990	Jan. 6	Cincinnati ($10,000)	Houston ($6,000)	41-14	Cincinnati	60,012
	Jan. 5	Miami ($6,000)	Kansas City ($6,000)	17-16	Miami	67,276
1989	Dec. 31	Pittsburgh ($6,000)	Houston ($6,000)	26-23*	Houston	59,406
1988	Dec. 26	Houston ($6,000)	Cleveland ($6,000)	24-23	Cleveland	75,896
1987	Jan. 3	Houston ($6,000)	Seattle ($6,000)	23-20*	Houston	50,519
1986	Dec. 28	N.Y. Jets ($6,000)	Kansas City ($6,000)	35-15	East Rutherford	75,210
1985	Dec. 28	New England ($6,000)	N.Y. Jets ($6,000)	26-14	East Rutherford	75,945
1984	Dec. 22	Seattle ($6,000)	L.A. Raiders ($6,000)	13-7	Seattle	62,049
1983	Dec. 24	Seattle ($6,000)	Denver ($6,000)	31-7	Seattle	64,275
1982	Jan. 9	N.Y. Jets ($6,000)	Cincinnati ($6,000)	44-17	Cincinnati	57,560
	Jan. 9	San Diego ($6,000)	Pittsburgh ($6,000)	31-28	Pittsburgh	53,546
	Jan. 8	L.A. Raiders ($6,000)	Cleveland ($6,000)	27-10	Los Angeles	56,555
	Jan. 8	Miami ($6,000)	New England ($6,000)	28-13	Miami	68,842
1981	Dec. 27	Buffalo ($3,000)	N.Y. Jets ($3,000)	31-27	New York	57,050
1980	Dec. 28	Oakland ($3,000)	Houston ($3,000)	27-7	Oakland	53,333
1979	Dec. 23	Houston ($3,000)	Denver ($3,000)	13-7	Houston	48,776
1978	Dec. 24	Houston ($3,000)	Miami ($3,000)	17-9	Miami	72,445

**Sudden death overtime.*

PLAYOFF GAMES SUMMARIES

1995 AFC WILD CARD PLAYOFF GAMES

San Diego Jack Murphy Stadium, San Diego, California
December 31, 1995, Attendance: 61,182

INDIANAPOLIS 35, SAN DIEGO 20—Unheralded rookie Zack Crockett rushed for a Colts' playoff-record 147 yards as Indianapolis stunned the defending AFC champions. Crockett, who carried only one time for no yards during the regular season, was in the game because starting running back Marshall Faulk reinjured his knee on the first play from scrimmage, and fullback Roosevelt Potts was out for the season with an injured knee. But the third-round draft choice from Florida State averaged 11.3 yards on his 13 carries against a defense that had allowed only 105.7 rushing yards per game during the regular season. The Chargers, who entered the playoffs with a five-game winning streak, took a 3-0 lead on John Carney's 54-yard field goal 5:32 into the first quarter. The lead changed hands five times after that—once on Crockett's 33-yard touchdown run 1:47 before halftime—until Jim Harbaugh's 42-yard touchdown pass to Sean Dawkins in the final minute of the third quarter put the Colts ahead for good at 21-17. San Diego pulled within 21-20 on Carney's 30-yard field goal with 11:53 to play, but Crockett raced 66 yards for a touchdown on the next play from scrimmage to give Indianapolis a 28-20 lead. Harbaugh's 3-yard touchdown run with 6:55 to play provided the final margin of victory. The Chargers had 429 total yards to Indianapolis's 333, but were victimized by 4 interceptions of quarterback Stan Humphries. Jason Belser had 2 of the thefts, including 1 he returned 33 yards to set up Indianapolis's final touchdown. The Colts' victory was their first in a postseason game since 1971.

Indianapolis	0	14	7	14	—	35
San Diego	3	7	7	3	—	20

SD — FG Carney 54
Ind — Dilger 2 pass from Harbaugh (Blanchard kick)
SD — Pupunu 6 pass from Humphries (Carney kick)
Ind — Crockett 33 run (Blanchard kick)
SD — Jefferson 11 pass from Humphries (Carney kick)
Ind — Dawkins 42 pass from Harbaugh (Blanchard kick)
SD — FG Carney 30
Ind — Crockett 66 run (Blanchard kick)
Ind — Harbaugh 3 run (Blanchard kick)

Rich Stadium, Orchard Park, New York
December 30, 1995, Attendance: 73,103

BUFFALO 37, MIAMI 22—Thurman Thomas ran for 158 yards and 1 touchdown as the Bills routed the Dolphins. Buffalo amassed an NFL postseason-record 341 yards on the ground, averaging 6.6 yards per carry. Reserve running back Darick Holmes gained 87 yards, and seldom-used third-stringer Tim Tindale added 68 yards on only 4 carries, one a 44-yard touchdown. The Bills marched 58 yards to Thomas's 1-yard touchdown run the first time they had the ball, and they never looked back, building a 24-0 advantage by the intermission and leading 27-0 before Miami could score. Buffalo finished with 536 total yards, and combined with the Dolphins' 502 to set another postseason record of 1,038 yards total offense in the game. Most of Miami's yardage came long after the issue was decided, however. Quarterback Dan Marino completed 33 of 64 passes for 422 yards and 2 touchdowns, but was intercepted 3 times. Wide receiver O.J. McDuffie caught 11 passes for 154 yards. For the Bills, Steve Tasker caught 5 passes for a career-high 108 yards. Tasker, a special-teams player most of his 11-year career, was thrust into the lineup at wide receiver because of injuries to others this season. He had 3 catches for 45 yards on Buffalo's opening drive.

Miami	0	0	0	22	—	22
Buffalo	10	14	3	10	—	37

Buff — Thomas 1 run (Christie kick)
Buff — FG Christie 48
Buff — Holmes 21 run (Christie kick)
Buff — Tasker 37 pass from Kelly (Christie kick)
Buff — FG Christie 23
Mia — McDuffie 5 pass from Marino (Stoyanovich kick)
Buff — Tindale 44 run (Christie kick)
Mia — Hill 45 pass from Marino (Stoyanovich kick)
Buff — FG Christie 42
Mia — Kirby 1 run (McDuffie pass from Marino)

NFC WILD CARD PLAYOFF GAMES RESULTS

Season	Date	Winner (Share)	Loser (Share)	Score	Site	Attendance
1995	Dec. 31	Green Bay ($13,000)	Atlanta ($7,500)	37-20	Green Bay	60,453
	Dec. 30	Philadelphia ($7,500)	Detroit ($7,500)	58-37	Philadelphia	66,099
1994	Jan. 1	Chicago ($7,500)	Minnesota ($12,000)	35-18	Minneapolis	60,347
	Dec. 31	Green Bay ($7,500)	Detroit ($7,500)	16-12	Green Bay	58,125
1993	Jan. 9	N.Y. Giants ($7,500)	Minnesota ($7,500)	17-10	East Rutherford	75,089
	Jan. 8	Green Bay ($7,500)	Detroit ($12,000)	28-24	Detroit	68,479
1992	Jan. 3	Philadelphia ($6,000)	New Orleans ($6,000)	36-20	New Orleans	68,893
	Jan. 2	Washington ($6,000)	Minnesota ($10,000)	24-7	Minneapolis	57,353
1991	Dec. 29	Dallas ($6,000)	Chicago ($6,000)	17-13	Chicago	62,594
	Dec. 28	Atlanta ($6,000)	New Orleans ($10,000)	27-20	New Orleans	68,794
1990	Jan. 6	Chicago ($10,000)	New Orleans ($6,000)	16-6	Chicago	60,767
	Jan. 5	Washington ($6,000)	Philadelphia ($6,000)	20-6	Philadelphia	65,287
1989	Dec. 31	L.A. Rams ($6,000)	Philadelphia ($6,000)	21-7	Philadelphia	65,479
1988	Dec. 26	Minnesota ($6,000)	L.A. Rams ($6,000)	28-17	Minnesota	61,204
1987	Jan. 3	Minnesota ($6,000)	New Orleans ($6,000)	44-10	New Orleans	68,546
1986	Dec. 28	Washington ($6,000)	L.A. Rams ($6,000)	19-7	Washington	54,567
1985	Dec. 29	N.Y. Giants ($6,000)	San Francisco ($6,000)	17-3	East Rutherford	75,131
1984	Dec. 23	N.Y. Giants ($6,000)	L.A. Rams ($6,000)	16-3	Anaheim	67,037
1983	Dec. 26	L.A. Rams ($6,000)	Dallas ($6,000)	24-17	Dallas	62,118
1982	Jan. 9	Dallas ($6,000)	Tampa Bay ($6,000)	30-17	Dallas	65,042
	Jan. 9	Minnesota ($6,000)	Atlanta ($6,000)	30-24	Minnesota	60,560
	Jan. 8	Green Bay ($6,000)	St. Louis ($6,000)	41-16	Green Bay	54,282
	Jan. 8	Washington ($6,000)	Detroit ($6,000)	31-7	Washington	55,045
1981	Dec. 27	N.Y. Giants ($3,000)	Philadelphia ($3,000)	27-21	Philadelphia	71,611
1980	Dec. 28	Dallas ($3,000)	Los Angeles ($3,000)	34-13	Dallas	63,052
1979	Dec. 23	Philadelphia ($3,000)	Chicago ($3,000)	27-17	Philadelphia	69,397
1978	Dec. 24	Atlanta ($3,000)	Philadelphia ($3,000)	14-13	Atlanta	59,403

1995 NFC WILD CARD PLAYOFF GAMES

Lambeau Field, Green Bay, Wisconsin
December 31, 1995, Attendance: 60,453

GREEN BAY 37, ATLANTA 20—Edgar Bennett rushed for a club playoff-record 108 yards, and Antonio Freeman returned a punt 76 yards for a touchdown in the Packers' victory. Green Bay led just 14-10 in the second quarter before Freeman's punt return and an 85-yard drive just before halftime broke open the game at 27-10. The latter, a 14-play march capped by Brett Favre's 2-yard touchdown pass to tight end Mark Chmura with 49 seconds left in the second quarter, featured 34 rushing yards by Bennett and completions to seven different receivers. The Falcons pulled within 27-17 on Jeff George's 27-yard touchdown pass to J.J. Birden in the first minute of the fourth quarter, but the Packers countered with another lengthy drive to put the game out of reach. The 12-play, 70-yard march took 6:22 and concluded with Favre's 18-yard touchdown pass to running back Dorsey Levens. Favre, who also threw a 14-yard touchdown pass to Robert Brooks in the first quarter, completed 24 of 35 attempts for 199 yards. Bennett, who carried 24 times, broke the Packers' postseason rushing record of 105 yards shared by Pro Football Hall of Fame members Jim Taylor and Paul Hornung. George completed 30 of 54 passes for 366 yards and 2 touchdowns for the Falcons. Eric Metcalf caught 8 passes for 114 yards.

Atlanta	7	3	0	10	—	20
Green Bay	14	13	0	10	—	37

Atl — Metcalf 65 pass from George (Andersen kick)
GB — Bennett 8 run (Jacke kick)
GB — Brooks 14 pass from Favre (Jacke kick)
Atl — FG Andersen 31
GB — Freeman 76 punt return (bad snap)
GB — Chmura 2 pass from Favre (Jacke kick)
Atl — Birden 27 pass from George (Andersen kick)
GB — Levens 18 pass from Favre (Jacke kick)
Atl — FG Andersen 22
GB — FG Jacke 25

Veterans Stadium, Philadelphia, Pennsylvania
December 30, 1995, Attendance: 66,099

PHILADELPHIA 58, DETROIT 37—Rodney Peete passed for 270 yards and 3 touchdowns as the Eagles blasted the Lions. The game was tied 7-7 before Philadelphia put the game away by exploding for 31 points in the second quarter. Gary Anderson began the onslaught with a 21-yard field goal 2:04 into the second quarter, and just 2:13 later Peete teamed with Fred Barnett on a 22-yard touchdown pass for a 17-7 lead. Two plays after that, cornerback Barry Wilburn returned an interception 24 yards for a touchdown, and when Ricky Watters ran 1 yard for a touchdown 4:59 before halftime, the Eagles led 31-7. They ended any remaining suspense when Peete threw a 43-yard desperation pass for a touchdown to Rob Carpenter on the final play of the second quarter. By midway through the third quarter it was 51-7 and Detroit's seven-game winning streak was in tatters. Peete completed 17 of 25 passes in all and was not intercepted. Lions quarterbacks Scott Mitchell and Don Majkowski, meanwhile, combined for 361 yards and 4 touchdowns, but suffered 6 interceptions. The 95 points scored by the two clubs set an NFL postseason record. Philadelphia's second-quarter barrage has been bettered only once in NFL postseason play. Washington scored 35 points in the second quarter of Super Bowl XXII against Denver.

Detroit	7	0	14	16	—	37
Philadelphia	7	31	13	7	—	58

Phil — Garner 15 run (Anderson kick)
Det — Sloan 32 pass from Mitchell (Hanson kick)
Phil — FG Anderson 21
Phil — Barnett 22 pass from Peete (Anderson kick)
Phil — Wilburn 24 interception return (Anderson kick)
Phil — Watters 1 run (Anderson kick)
Phil — Carpenter 43 pass from Peete (Anderson kick)
Phil — Watters 45 pass from Peete (Anderson kick)
Phil — FG Anderson 31
Phil — FG Anderson 39
Det — Moore 68 pass from Majkowski (Hanson kick)
Det — Morton 7 pass from Majkowski (Hanson kick)
Phil — Thomas 30 interception return (Anderson kick)
Det — Sloan 2 pass from Majkowski (Rivers run)
Det — Rivers 1 run (Moore pass from Majkowski)

AFC-NFC PRO BOWL AT A GLANCE RESULTS (1971-1996)

NFC leads series, 15-11

Year	Date	Winner (Share)	Loser (Share)	Score	Site	Attendance
1996	Feb. 4	NFC ($20,000)	AFC ($10,000)	20-13	Honolulu	50,034
1995	Feb. 5	AFC ($20,000)	NFC ($10,000)	41-13	Honolulu	49,121
1994	Feb. 6	NFC ($20,000)	AFC ($10,000)	17-3	Honolulu	50,026
1993	Feb. 7	AFC ($10,000)	NFC ($5,000)	23-20 (OT)	Honolulu	50,007
1992	Feb. 2	NFC ($10,000)	AFC ($5,000)	21-15	Honolulu	50,209
1991	Feb. 3	AFC ($10,000)	NFC ($5,000)	23-21	Honolulu	50,345
1990	Feb. 4	NFC ($10,000)	AFC ($5,000)	27-21	Honolulu	50,445
1989	Jan. 29	NFC ($10,000)	AFC ($5,000)	34-3	Honolulu	50,113
1988	Feb. 7	AFC ($10,000)	NFC ($5,000)	15-6	Honolulu	50,113
1987	Feb. 1	AFC ($10,000)	NFC ($5,000)	10-6	Honolulu	50,101
1986	Feb. 2	NFC ($10,000)	AFC ($5,000)	28-24	Honolulu	50,101
1985	Jan. 27	AFC ($10,000)	NFC ($5,000)	22-14	Honolulu	50,385
1984	Jan. 29	NFC ($10,000)	AFC ($5,000)	45-3	Honolulu	50,445
1983	Feb. 6	NFC ($10,000)	AFC ($5,000)	20-19	Honolulu	49,883
1982	Jan. 31	AFC ($5,000)	NFC ($2,500)	16-13	Honolulu	50,402
1981	Feb. 1	NFC ($5,000)	AFC ($2,500)	21-7	Honolulu	50,360
1980	Jan. 27	NFC ($5,000)	AFC ($2,500)	37-27	Honolulu	49,800
1979	Jan. 29	NFC ($5,000)	AFC ($2,500)	13-7	Los Angeles	46,281
1978	Jan. 23	NFC ($5,000)	AFC ($2,500)	14-13	Tampa	51,337
1977	Jan. 17	AFC ($2,000)	NFC ($1,500)	24-14	Seattle	64,752
1976	Jan. 26	NFC ($2,000)	AFC ($1,500)	23-20	New Orleans	30,546
1975	Jan. 20	NFC ($2,000)	AFC ($1,500)	17-10	Miami	26,484
1974	Jan. 20	AFC ($2,000)	NFC ($1,500)	15-13	Kansas City	66,918
1973	Jan. 21	AFC ($2,000)	NFC ($1,500)	33-28	Dallas	37,091
1972	Jan. 23	AFC ($2,000)	NFC ($1,500)	26-13	Los Angeles	53,647
1971	Jan. 24	NFC ($2,000)	AFC ($1,500)	27-6	Los Angeles	48,222

1996 AFC-NFC PRO BOWL

Aloha Stadium, Honolulu, Hawaii
February 4, 1996, Attendance: 50,034

NFC 20, AFC 13—Jerry Rice had 6 receptions for 82 yards and 1 touchdown to earn player of the game honors in the NFC's victory. The 49ers' wide receiver, who was named to the Pro Bowl for the tenth consecutive year, caught a 1-yard touchdown pass from Packers quarterback Brett Favre 1:41 into the second quarter to cap an 80-yard drive and give the NFC the lead for good at 10-7. The AFC had taken a 7-0 lead 2:26 into the game when Bengals quarterback Jeff Blake connected with Steelers wide receiver Yancey Thigpen on a Pro Bowl-record 93-yard touchdown pass. The NFC increased its advantage to 20-7 at halftime on Redskins linebacker Ken Harvey's 36-yard interception return for a touchdown and Falcons kicker Morten Andersen's 24-yard field goal. The AFC trimmed its deficit to 20-13 when Colts quarterback Jim Harbaugh teamed with Patriots running back Curtis Martin on a 17-yard touchdown pass in the final minute of the third quarter, but its bid to win or tie was rebuffed twice in the final minutes of the fourth quarter. First, 49ers safety Tim McDonald intercepted Harbaugh's pass in the end zone with 1:50 remaining. Then, after the AFC forced a punt and got the ball back near midfield, Harbaugh drove his team to the NFC's 9-yard line in the closing seconds. But he spiked the ball once to stop the clock and threw 3 consecutive incompletions as time ran out. The AFC outgained the NFC 390 total yards to 287, but its quarterbacks suffered 4 interceptions, including 3 off Harbaugh, the NFL's leading passer during the regular season. The NFC raised its edge to 15-11 in Pro Bowl games since the AFL-NFL merger in 1970.

NFC (20)	Offense	AFC (13)
Jerry Rice (San Francisco)	WR	Carl Pickens (Cincinnati)
Lomas Brown (Detroit)	LT	Richmond Webb (Miami)
Nate Newton (Dallas)	LG	Keith Sims (Miami)
Kevin Glover (Detroit)	C	Dermontti Dawson (Pittsburgh)
Randall McDaniel (Minnesota)	RG	Steve Wisniewski (Oakland)
William Roaf (New Orleans)	RT	Bruce Armstrong (New England)
Mark Chmura (Green Bay)	TE	Ben Coates (New England)
Herman Moore (Detroit)	WR	Tim Brown (Oakland)
Brett Favre (Green Bay)	QB	Jeff Blake (Cincinnati)
Emmitt Smith (Dallas)	RB	Marshall Faulk (Indianapolis)
Barry Sanders (Detroit)	RB	Chris Warren (Seattle)
	Defense	
Reggie White (Green Bay)	LE	Bruce Smith (Buffalo)
John Randle (Minnesota)	IL	Chester McGlockton (Oakland)
Eric Swann (Arizona)	IL	Dan Saleaumua (Kansas City)
Charles Haley (Dallas)	RE	Neil Smith (Kansas City)
Ken Harvey (Washington)	LLB	Bryce Paup (Buffalo)
Jessie Tuggle (Atlanta)	MLB	Junior Seau (San Diego)
Lee Woodall (San Francisco)	RLB	Greg Lloyd (Pittsburgh)
Aeneas Williams (Arizona)	LCB	Dale Carter (Kansas City)
Eric Davis (San Francisco)	RCB	Terry McDaniel (Oakland)
Darren Woodson (Dallas)	SS	Carnell Lake (Pittsburgh)
Merton Hanks (San Francisco)	FS	Steve Atwater (Denver)

SUBSTITUTIONS

NFC—Offense: K—Morten Andersen (Atlanta). P—Jeff Feagles (Arizona). QB—Warren Moon (Minnesota), Steve Young (San Francisco). RB—Craig Heyward (Atlanta), Ricky Watters (Philadelphia). WR—Cris Carter (Minnesota), Michael Irvin (Dallas). TE—Brent Jones (San Francisco). ST—Elbert Shelley (Atlanta). KR—Brian Mitchell (Washington). T—Mark Tuinei (Dallas). G—Larry Allen (Dallas). C—Bart Oates (San Francisco). Defense: DE—Chris Doleman (Atlanta), William Fuller (Philadelphia). DT—Dana Stubblefield (San Francisco). LB—Ken Norton (San Francisco), William Thomas (Philadelphia). CB—Eric Allen (New Orleans). S—Tim McDonald (San Francisco). DNP: None.

AFC—Offense: K—Jason Elam (Denver). P—Darren Bennett (San Diego). QB—Steve Bono (Kansas City), Jim Harbaugh (Indianapolis). RB—Kimble Anders (Kansas City), Curtis Martin (New England). WR—Anthony Miller (Denver), Yancey Thigpen (Pittsburgh). TE—Shannon Sharpe (Denver). ST—Steve Tasker (Buffalo). KR—Glyn Milburn (Denver). T—Will Wolford (Indianapolis). G—Will Shields (Kansas City). C—Mark Stepnoski (Houston). Defense: DE—Leslie O'Neal (San Diego). DT—Cortez Kennedy (Seattle). LB—Bryan Cox (Miami), Kevin Greene (Pittsburgh), Derrick Thomas (Kansas City). CB—Darryll Lewis (Houston). S—Blaine Bishop (Houston). DNP: None.

HEAD COACHES

NFC—Mike Holmgren (Green Bay)
AFC—Ted Marchibroda (Indianapolis)

OFFICIALS

Referee—Tom White. Umpire—Al Conway. Head Linesman—Tom Johnson. Line Judge—Mark Steinkerchner. Back Judge—Van Golmont. Field Judge—Kirk Dornan. Side Judge—Don Wedge.

SCORING

NFC	3	17	0	0	—	20
AFC	7	0	6	0	—	13

AFC — Thigpen 93 pass from Blake (Elam kick)
NFC — FG Andersen 36
NFC — Rice 1 pass from Favre (Andersen kick)
NFC — Harvey 36 interception return (Andersen kick)
NFC — FG Andersen 24
AFC — Martin 17 pass from Harbaugh (kick failed)

TEAM STATISTICS	NFC	AFC
Total First Downs	12	21
Rushing	1	9
Passing	10	9
Penalty	1	3
Total Net Yardage	287	390
Total Offensive Plays	60	69
Average Gain per Offensive Play	4.8	5.7
Rushes	22	25
Yards Gained Rushing (Net)	49	127
Average Yards per Rush	2.2	5.1
Passes Attempted	37	40
Passes Completed	19	19
Had Intercepted	0	4
Tackled Attempting to Pass	1	4
Yards Lost Attempting to Pass	7	25
Yards Gained Passing (Net)	238	263
Punts	6	4
Average Distance	46.5	55.5
Punt Returns	1	1

Punt Return Yardage	17	3
Kickoff Returns	3	3
Kickoff Return Yardage	62	52
Interception Return Yardage	79	0
Total Return Yardage	158	55
Fumbles	0	2
Own Fumbles Recovered	0	2
Opponent Fumbles Recovered	0	0
Penalties	9	5
Yards Penalized	80	25
Total Points Scored	20	13
Touchdowns	2	2
Rushing	0	0
Passing	1	2
Returns	1	0
Extra Points	2	1
Field Goals	2	0
Field Goals Attempted	3	0
Safeties	0	0
Third-Down Efficiency	6/15	7/15
Fourth-Down Efficiency	1/1	0/1
Time of Possession	27:14	32:46

INDIVIDUAL STATISTICS

Rushing

NFC	No.	Yds.	LG	TD
Watters	7	26	29	0
Sanders	7	17	9	0
Smith	5	10	7	0
Moon	2	-2	0	0
Mitchell	1	-2	-2	0
AFC	**No.**	**Yds.**	**LG**	**TD**
Warren	7	43	18	0
Anders	8	42	17	0
Milburn	3	15	10	0
Martin	4	14	11	0
Harbaugh	3	13	6	0

Passing

NFC	Att.	Comp.	Yds.	TD	Int.
Favre	14	7	111	1	0
Young	17	8	103	0	0
Moon	6	4	31	0	0
AFC	**Att.**	**Comp.**	**Yds.**	**TD**	**Int.**
Harbaugh	25	12	144	1	3
Blake	13	6	138	1	0
Bono	2	1	6	0	1

Receiving

NFC	No.	Yds.	LG	TD
Rice	6	82	38	1
Irvin	3	60	51	0
Heyward	2	37	28	0
Moore	2	24	12	0
Carter	2	19	16	0
Chmura	1	15	15	0
Watters	1	6	6	0
Mitchell	1	4	4	0
Sanders	1	-2	-2	0
AFC	**No.**	**Yds.**	**LG**	**TD**
Coates	5	66	36	0
Brown	3	27	17	0
Anders	3	8	6	0
Miller	2	41	22	0
Pickens	2	31	17	0
Martin	2	20	17	1
Thigpen	1	93	93t	1
Warren	1	2	2	0

Interceptions

NFC	No.	Yds.	LG	TD
Harvey	1	36	36t	1
Woodson	1	25	25	0
Allen	1	18	18	0
McDonald	1	0	0	0
AFC	**No.**	**Yds.**	**LG**	**TD**
None	—	—	—	—

Punting

NFC	No.	Avg.	LG	Blk.
Feagles	6	46.5	61	0
AFC	**No.**	**Avg.**	**LG**	**Blk.**
Bennett	4	55.5	64	0

Punt Returns

NFC	No.	FC	Yds.	LG	TD
Mitchell	1	0	17	17	0
AFC	**No.**	**FC**	**Yds.**	**LG**	**TD**
Milburn	1	1	3	3	0

Kickoff Returns

NFC	No.	Yds.	LG	TD
Mitchell	2	51	33	0
Sanders	1	11	11	0
AFC	**No.**	**Yds.**	**LG**	**TD**
Milburn	2	36	20	0
Martin	1	16	16	0

1995 AFC-NFC PRO BOWL

Aloha Stadium, Honolulu, Hawaii
February 5, 1995, Attendance: 49,121

AFC 41, NFC 13—Colts rookie Marshall Faulk rushed for a Pro Bowl-record 180 yards to key the AFC's rout of the NFC. Faulk, who earned the Dan McGuire Trophy as the player of the game, averaged nearly 14 yards on his 13 carries and shattered the previous rushing mark of 112 yards set by O.J. Simpson in the 1973 game. Faulk's 49-yard touchdown run from punt formation in the fourth quarter was the longest in Pro Bowl history. The Seahawks' Chris Warren added 127 yards on 14 carries as the AFC amassed records for rushing yards (400) and total yards (552). Steelers tight end Eric Green caught 2 touchdown passes for the victors. The NFC managed only 196 total yards, a large chunk coming when 49ers quarterback Steve Young and Vikings wide receiver Cris Carter teamed on a 51-yard touchdown pass in the first quarter. That gave the NFC a 10-0 advantage, but the AFC rallied in the second quarter and took the lead for good when the Browns' Leroy Hoard scored on a 4-yard touchdown run 2:07 before halftime.

AFC	0	17	3	21	—	41
NFC	10	0	3	0	—	13

NFC — FG Reveiz 28
NFC — Carter 51 pass from Young (Reveiz kick)
AFC — Green 22 pass from Elway (Carney kick)
AFC — FG Carney 22
AFC — Hoard 4 run (Carney kick)
NFC — FG Reveiz 49
AFC — FG Carney 23
AFC — Warren 11 run (Carney kick)
AFC — Green 16 pass from Hostetler (Carney kick)
AFC — Faulk 49 run (Carney kick)

1994 AFC-NFC PRO BOWL

Aloha Stadium, Honolulu, Hawaii
February 6, 1994, Attendance: 50,026

NFC 17, AFC 3—The NFC converted a blocked punt and a fumble recovery into touchdowns just 2:20 apart in the second half of its victory over the AFC. With the score tied 3-3 late in the third quarter, Saints linebacker Renaldo Turnbull deflected a punt by the Oilers' Greg Montgomery, and the NFC took possession at the AFC's 48-yard line. A 32-yard pass from Bobby Hebert to Falcons teammate Andre Rison positioned Rams running back Jerome Bettis for a 4-yard touchdown run with 1:27 left in the third quarter. Moments later, Rams defensive tackle Sean Gilbert recovered a fumble by Oilers quarterback Warren Moon at the AFC's 19. Hebert then teamed with the Vikings' Cris Carter on a 15-yard touchdown pass 53 seconds into the fourth period. The NFC kept the AFC out of the end zone by maintaining possession for more than 38 minutes and forcing 6 turnovers. Rison earned the Dan McGuire Trophy as the player of the game by catching 6 passes for 86 yards. The victory was the fourth in the last six years for the NFC, which leads the series 14-10.

NFC	3	0	7	7	—	17
AFC	0	3	0	0	—	3

NFC — FG Johnson 35
AFC — FG Anderson 25
NFC — Bettis 4 run (Johnson kick)
NFC — Carter 15 pass from Hebert (Johnson kick)

1993 AFC-NFC PRO BOWL

Aloha Stadium, Honolulu, Hawaii
February 7, 1993, Attendance: 50,007

AFC 23, NFC 20—Nick Lowery's 33-yard field goal 4:09 into overtime gave the American Conference all-stars an unlikely 23-20 victory over the National Conference. Despite being overwhelmed by the NFC in first downs (30-9), total yards (471-114), and time of possession (10:19-23:50), the AFC won because it forced 6 turnovers, bocked a pair of field goals (1 of which was returned for a touchdown), and returned an interception for a score. Special-teams star Steve Tasker of the Bills earned the Dan McGuire Trophy as the player of the game for making 4 tackles, forcing a fumble, and blocking a field goal. The block came with eight minutes left in regulation and the game tied at 13-13. The Raiders' Terry McDaniel picked up the loose ball and ran 28 yards for a touchdown and a 20-13 AFC lead. The NFC rallied behind 49ers quarterback Steve Young, whose fourth-down, 23-yard touchdown pass to Giants running back Rodney Hampton tied the game at 20-20 with 10 seconds left in regulation. Young completed 18 of 32 passes for 196 yards but was intercepted 3 times and lost a fumble when sacked in overtime. Raiders defensive end Howie Long fell on that fumble at the NFC 28-yard line, and five plays later, Lowery converted the winning field goal.

AFC	0	10	3	7	3	— 23
NFC	3	10	0	7	0	— 20

NFC — FG Andersen 27
AFC — Seau 31 interception return (Lowery kick)
NFC — FG Andersen 37
NFC — Irvin 9 pass from Aikman (Andersen kick)
AFC — FG Lowery 42
AFC — FG Lowery 29
AFC — McDaniel 28 blocked field goal return (Lowery kick)
NFC — Hampton 23 pass from Young (Andersen kick)
AFC — FG Lowery 33

1992 AFC-NFC PRO BOWL

Aloha Stadium, Honolulu, Hawaii
February 2, 1992, Attendance: 50,209

NFC 21, AFC 15—Atlanta's Chris Miller threw an 11-yard touchdown pass to San Francisco's Jerry Rice with 4:04 remaining in the game to lift the NFC over the AFC. It was the NFC's thirteenth win in the 22-game series. The AFC had taken a 15-14 lead when the Raiders' Jeff Jaeger kicked a 27-yard field goal 1:49 into the fourth quarter. But the NFC, aided by a key roughing-the-passer penalty on a third-down incompletion from the AFC 24-yard line, drove 85 yards to the winning score. The Cowboys' Michael Irvin, playing in his first Pro Bowl, caught 8 passes for 125 yards, including a 13-yard touchdown in the first quarter, and was named the player of the game. Rice had 7 catches for 77 yards. Mark Rypien of Washington, the Super Bowl most valuable player one week earlier, completed 11 of 18 passes for 165 yards and 2 touchdowns for the NFC, including a 35-yard pass to Redskins teammate Gary Clark just 26 seconds before halftime. Miller completed 7 of his 10 attempts for 85 yards.

NFC	7	7	0	7	—	21
AFC	7	5	0	3	—	15

AFC — Clayton 4 pass from Kelly (Jaeger kick)
NFC — Irvin 13 pass from Rypien (Lohmiller kick)
AFC — Safety, Townsend tackled Byner in end zone
AFC — FG Jaeger 48
NFC — Clark 35 pass from Rypien (Lohmiller kick)
AFC — FG Jaeger 27
NFC — Rice 11 pass from Miller (Lohmiller kick)

1991 AFC-NFC PRO BOWL

Aloha Stadium, Honolulu, Hawaii
February 3, 1991, Attendance: 50,345

AFC 23, NFC 21—Buffalo's Jim Kelly and Houston's Ernest Givins combined for a 13-yard scoring pass late in the fourth quarter to rally the AFC over the NFC. Phoenix rookie Johnny Johnson scored on runs of 1 and 9 yards to put the NFC ahead 14-3 in the third quarter. Buffalo's Andre Reed, who led all receivers with 4 catches for 80 yards, caught a 20-yard scoring reception from Kelly early in the fourth quarter to move the AFC to within 1 point. Barry Sanders ran 22 yards for a touchdown to increase the NFC's lead to 21-13. Miami's Jeff Cross blocked a 46-yard field-goal attempt by New Orleans's Morten Andersen with seven seconds remaining to preserve the win. Buffalo's Bruce Smith recorded 3 sacks and also had a blocked field goal. Kelly, who completed 13 of 19 passes for 210 yards and 2 touchdowns, was presented the Dan McGuire Award as player of the game. The AFC's victory narrowed the NFC's Pro Bowl series lead to 12-9.

AFC	3	0	3	17	—	23
NFC	0	7	7	7	—	21

AFC — FG Lowery 26
NFC — J. Johnson 1 run (Andersen kick)
AFC — FG Lowery 43
NFC — J. Johnson 9 run (Andersen kick)
AFC — Reed 20 pass from Kelly (Lowery kick)
NFC — Sanders 22 run (Andersen kick)
AFC — FG Lowery 34
AFC — Givins 13 pass from Kelly (Lowery kick)

1990 AFC-NFC PRO BOWL

Aloha Stadium, Honolulu, Hawaii
February 4, 1990, Attendance: 50,445

NFC 27, AFC 21—The NFC captured its second straight Pro Bowl as the defense accounted for a pair of touchdowns and forced 5 turnovers before the eleventh consecutive sellout crowd at Aloha Stadium. The AFC held a 7-6 halftime edge on a 1-yard scoring run by Christian Okoye of the Chiefs. The NFC then rallied with 21 unanswered points in the third quarter. David Meggett of the Giants began the comeback with an 11-yard touchdown reception from Philadelphia's Randall Cunningham. The Rams' Jerry Gray followed with a 51-yard interception return for a score and the Vikings' Keith Millard added an 8-yard fumble return for a touchdown four minutes later to give the NFC a commanding 27-7 lead. Seattle's Dave Krieg rallied the AFC with a 5-yard touchdown pass to Miami's Ferrell Edmunds. Cleveland's Mike Johnson then returned an interception 22 yards for a score to pull the AFC to within 27-21. Gray, who was credited with 7 tackles, was given the Dan McGuire Award as player of the game. Krieg led all quarterbacks by completing 15 of 23 for 148 yards and 1 touchdown. Buffalo's Thurman Thomas topped all receivers with 5 catches for 47 yards, while Indianapolis's Eric Dickerson led all rushers with 46 yards on 15 carries. The win gave the NFC a 12-8 advantage in Pro Bowl games since 1971.

NFC	3	3	21	0	—	27
AFC	0	7	0	14	—	21

NFC — FG Murray 23
NFC — FG Murray 41
AFC — Okoye 1 run (Treadwell kick)
NFC — Meggett 11 pass from Cunningham (Murray kick)
NFC — Gray 51 interception return (Murray kick)
NFC — Millard 8 fumble recovery return (Murray kick)
AFC — Edmunds 5 pass from Krieg (Treadwell kick)
AFC — M. Johnson 22 interception return (Treadwell kick)

1989 AFC-NFC PRO BOWL

Aloha Stadium, Honolulu, Hawaii
January 29, 1989, Attendance: 50,113

NFC 34, AFC 3—The NFC scored 34 unanswered points to snap a two-game losing streak to the AFC before the tenth straight sellout crowd in Honolulu's Aloha Stadium. Bills kicker Scott Norwood provided the AFC's only points on a 38-yard field goal 6:23 into the game. Touchdown runs by Dallas's Herschel Walker (4 yards) and Atlanta's John Settle (1) brought the NFC a 14-3 halftime lead. Walker added a 7-yard scoring run, the Saints' Morten Andersen kicked field goals of 27 and 51 yards, and Los Angeles Rams' wide receiver Henry Ellard caught an 8-yard scoring pass from Minnesota quarterback Wade Wilson in the second half to complete the scoring. Chicago running back Neal Anderson and Philadelphia quarterback Randall Cunningham, who were both appearing in their first Pro Bowl, also played major roles in the NFC's victory. Anderson rushed 13 times for 85 yards and had 2 receptions for 17. Cunningham, who was voted the game's outstanding player, completed 10 of 14 passes for 63 yards and rushed for 49 yards. The NFC, which had 5 takeaways, outgained the AFC 355 yards to 167 and held a time-of-possession advantage of 35:18 to 24:42. Houston quarterback Warren Moon completed 13 of 20 passes for 134 yards for the AFC. The win gave the NFC an 11-8 advantage in Pro Bowl games.

AFC	3	0	0	0	—	3
NFC	7	7	10	10	—	34

AFC — FG Norwood 38
NFC — Walker 4 run (Andersen kick)
NFC — Settle 1 run (Andersen kick)
NFC — FG Andersen 27
NFC — Walker 7 run (Andersen kick)
NFC — FG Andersen 51
NFC — Ellard 8 pass from Wilson (Andersen kick)

1988 AFC-NFC PRO BOWL

Aloha Stadium, Honolulu, Hawaii
February 7, 1988, Attendance: 50,113

AFC 15, NFC 6—Led by a tenacious pass rush, the AFC defeated the NFC for the second consecutive year before the ninth straight sellout crowd in Honolulu's Aloha Stadium. Buffalo quarterback Jim Kelly scored the game's lone touchdown on a 1-yard run for a 7-6 halftime lead. Colts kicker Dean Biasucci added field goals from 37 and 30 yards to complete the AFC's scoring. Saints kicker Morten Andersen had 25- and 36-yard field goals to account for the NFC's points. AFC defenders held the NFC to 213 yards and recorded 8 sacks. Bills defensive end Bruce Smith, who had 2 sacks among his 5 tackles, was voted the game's outstanding player. Oilers running back Mike Rozier led all rushers with 49 yards on 9 carries. Jets wide receiver Al Toon had 5 receptions for 75 yards. The AFC generated 341 yards total offense and held a time-of-possession advantage of 34:14 to 25:46. By winning, the AFC cut the NFC's lead in the Pro Bowl series to 10-8.

NFC	0	6	0	0	—	6
AFC	0	7	6	2	—	15

NFC — FG Andersen 25
AFC — Kelly 1 run (Biasucci kick)
NFC — FG Andersen 36
AFC — FG Biasucci 37
AFC — FG Biasucci 30
AFC — Safety, Montana forced out of end zone

1987 AFC-NFC PRO BOWL

Aloha Stadium, Honolulu, Hawaii
February 1, 1987, Attendance: 50,101

AFC 10, NFC 6—The AFC defeated the NFC in the lowest-scoring game in AFC-NFC Pro Bowl history. The AFC took a 10-0 halftime lead on Broncos quarterback John Elway's 10-yard touchdown pass to Raiders tight end Todd Christensen and Patriots kicker Tony Franklin's 26-yard field goal. The AFC defense made the lead stand by forcing the NFC to settle for a pair of field goals from 38 and 19 yards by Saints kicker Morten Andersen after the NFC had first downs at the AFC 31-, 7-, 16-, 15-, 6-, and 7-yard lines. Both AFC scores were set up by fumble recoveries by Seahawks linebacker Fredd Young and Dolphins linebacker John Offerdahl, respectively. Eagles defensive end Reggie White, who tied a Pro Bowl record with 4 sacks among his 7 solo tackles, was voted the game's outstanding player. The AFC victory cut the NFC's lead in the Pro Bowl series to 10-7.

AFC	7	3	0	0	—	10
NFC	0	0	3	3	—	6

AFC — Christensen 10 pass from Elway (Franklin kick)
AFC — FG Franklin 26
NFC — FG Andersen 38
NFC — FG Andersen 19

1986 AFC-NFC PRO BOWL

Aloha Stadium, Honolulu, Hawaii
February 2, 1986, Attendance: 50,101

NFC 28, AFC 24—New York Giants quarterback Phil Simms brought the NFC back from a 24-7 halftime deficit to defeat the AFC. Simms, who completed 15 of 27 passes for 212 yards and 3 touchdowns, was named the most valuable player of the game. The AFC had taken its first-half lead behind a 2-yard run by Los Angeles Raiders running back Marcus Allen, who also threw a 51-yard scoring pass to San Diego wide receiver Wes Chandler, an 11-yard touchdown catch by Pittsburgh wide receiver Louis Lipps, and a 34-yard field goal by Steelers kicker Gary Anderson. Minnesota's Joey Browner accounted for the NFC's only score before halftime with a 48-yard interception return. After intermission, the NFC blanked the AFC while scoring 3 touchdowns via a 15-yard catch by Washington wide receiver Art Monk, a 2-yard reception by Dallas tight end Doug Cosbie, and a 15-yard catch by Tampa Bay tight end Jimmie Giles with 2:47 remaining in the game. The victory gave the NFC a 10-6 Pro Bowl record against the AFC.

NFC	0	7	7	14	—	28
AFC	7	17	0	0	—	24

AFC — Allen 2 run (Anderson kick)
NFC — Browner 48 interception return (Andersen kick)
AFC — Chandler 51 pass from Allen (Anderson kick)
AFC — FG Anderson 34
AFC — Lipps 11 pass from O'Brien (Anderson kick)
NFC — Monk 15 pass from Simms (Andersen kick)
NFC — Cosbie 2 pass from Simms (Andersen kick)
NFC — Giles 15 pass from Simms (Andersen kick)

1985 AFC-NFC PRO BOWL

Aloha Stadium, Honolulu, Hawaii
January 27, 1985, Attendance: 50,385

AFC 22, NFC 14—Defensive end Art Still of the Kansas City Chiefs recovered a fumble and returned it 83 yards for a touchdown to clinch the AFC's victory over the NFC. Still's touchdown came in the fourth period with the AFC trailing 14-12 and was one of several outstanding defensive plays in a Pro Bowl dominated by two record-breaking defenses. The teams combined for a Pro Bowl-record 17 sacks, including 4 by New York Jets defensive end Mark Gastineau, who was named the game's outstanding player. The AFC's first score came on a safety when Gastineau tackled running back Eric Dickerson of the Los Angeles Rams in the end zone. The AFC's second score, a 6-yard pass from Miami's Dan Marino to Los Angeles Raiders running back Marcus Allen, was set up by a partial block of a punt by Seahawks linebacker Fredd Young. The NFC leads the series 9-6.

AFC	0	9	0	13	—	22
NFC	0	0	7	7	—	14

AFC — Safety, Gastineau tackled Dickerson in end zone
AFC — Allen 6 pass from Marino (Johnson kick)
NFC — Lofton 13 pass from Montana (Stenerud kick)
NFC — Payton 1 run (Stenerud kick)
AFC — FG Johnson 33
AFC — Still 83 fumble recovery return (Johnson kick)
AFC — FG Johnson 22

1984 AFC-NFC PRO BOWL

Aloha Stadium, Honolulu, Hawaii
January 29, 1984, Attendance: 50,445

NFC 45, AFC 3—The NFC won its sixth Pro Bowl in the last seven seasons by routing the AFC. The NFC was led by the passing of most valuable player Joe Theismann of Washington, who completed 21 of 27 passes for 242 yards and 3 touchdowns. Theismann set Pro Bowl records for completions and touchdown passes. The NFC established Pro Bowl marks for most points scored and fewest points allowed. Running back William Andrews of Atlanta had 6 carries for 43 yards and caught 4 passes for 49 yards, including scoring receptions of 16 and 2 yards. Los Angeles Rams rookie Eric Dickerson gained 46 yards on 11 carries, including a 14-yard touchdown run, and had 45 yards on 5 catches. Rams safety Nolan Cromwell had a 44-yard interception return for a touchdown early in the third period to give the NFC a commanding 24-3 lead. Green Bay wide receiver James Lofton caught an 8-yard touchdown pass, while tight end teammate Paul Coffman had a 6-yard scoring catch.

NFC	3	14	14	14	—	45
AFC	0	3	0	0	—	3

NFC — FG Haji-Sheikh 23
NFC — Andrews 16 pass from Theismann (Haji-Sheikh kick)
NFC — Andrews 2 pass from Montana (Haji-Sheikh kick)
AFC — FG Anderson 43
NFC — Cromwell 44 interception return (Haji-Sheikh kick)
NFC — Lofton 8 pass from Theismann (Haji-Sheikh kick)
NFC — Coffman 6 pass from Theismann (Haji-Sheikh kick)
NFC — Dickerson 14 run (Haji-Sheikh kick)

1983 AFC-NFC PRO BOWL

Aloha Stadium, Honolulu, Hawaii
February 6, 1983, Attendance: 49,883

NFC 20, AFC 19—Dallas's Danny White threw an 11-yard touchdown pass to the Packers' John Jefferson with 35 seconds remaining to rally the NFC over the AFC. White, who completed 14 of 26 passes for 162 yards, kept the winning 65-yard drive alive with a 14-yard completion to Jefferson on a fourth-and-7 play at the AFC 25. The AFC was ahead 12-10 at halftime and increased the lead to 19-10 in the third period, when Marcus Allen scored on a 1-yard run. San Diego's Dan Fouts, who attempted 30 passes, set Pro Bowl records for most completions (17) and yards (274). Pittsburgh's John Stallworth was the AFC's leading receiver with 7 catches for 67 yards. William Andrews topped the NFC with 5 receptions for 48 yards. Fouts and Jefferson were co-winners of the player of the game award.

AFC	9	3	7	0	—	19
NFC	0	10	0	10	—	20

AFC — Walker 34 pass from Fouts (Benirschke kick)
AFC — Safety, Still tackled Theismann in end zone
NFC — Andrews 3 run (Moseley kick)
NFC — FG Moseley 35
AFC — FG Benirschke 29
AFC — Allen 1 run (Benirschke kick)
NFC — FG Moseley 41
NFC — Jefferson 11 pass from D. White (Moseley kick)

1982 AFC-NFC PRO BOWL

Aloha Stadium, Honolulu, Hawaii
January 31, 1982, Attendance: 50,402

AFC 16, NFC 13—Nick Lowery of Kansas City kicked a 23-yard field goal with three seconds remaining to give the AFC a last-second victory over the NFC. Lowery's kick climaxed a 69-yard drive directed by quarterback Dan Fouts. The NFC gained a 13-13 tie with 2:43 to go when Dallas's Tony Dorsett ran 4 yards for a touchdown. In the drive to the winning field goal, Fouts completed 3 passes, including a 23-yard toss to San Diego teammate Kellen Winslow that put the ball on the NFC's 5-yard line. Two plays later, Lowery kicked the field goal. Winslow, who caught 6 passes for 86 yards, was named co-player of the game along with Tampa Bay defensive end Lee Roy Selmon.

NFC	0	6	0	7	—	13
AFC	0	0	13	3	—	16

NFC — Giles 4 pass from Montana (kick blocked)
AFC — Muncie 2 run (kick failed)
AFC — Campbell 1 run (Lowery kick)
NFC — Dorsett 4 run (Septien kick)
AFC — FG Lowery 23

1981 AFC-NFC PRO BOWL

Aloha Stadium, Honolulu, Hawaii
February 1, 1981, Attendance: 50,360

NFC 21, AFC 7—Eddie Murray kicked 4 field goals and Steve Bartkowski fired a 55-yard scoring pass to Alfred Jenkins to lead the NFC to its fourth straight victory over the AFC and a 7-4 edge in the series. Murray was named the game's most valuable player and missed tying Garo Yepremian's Pro Bowl record of 5 field goals when a 37-yard attempt hit the crossbar with 22 seconds remaining. The AFC's only score came on a 9-yard pass from Brian Sipe to Stanley Morgan in the second period. Bartkowski completed 9 of 21 passes for 173 yards, while Sipe connected on 10 of 15 for 142 yards. Ottis Anderson led all rushers with 70 yards on 10 carries. Earl Campbell, the NFL's leading rusher in 1980, was limited to 24 yards on 8 attempts.

AFC	0	7	0	0	—	7
NFC	3	6	0	12	—	21

NFC — FG Murray 31
AFC — Morgan 9 pass from Sipe (J. Smith kick)
NFC — FG Murray 31
NFC — FG Murray 34
NFC — Jenkins 55 pass from Bartkowski (Murray kick)
NFC — FG Murray 36
NFC — Safety, Shell called for holding in end zone

1980 AFC-NFC PRO BOWL

Aloha Stadium, Honolulu, Hawaii
January 27, 1980, Attendance: 49,800

NFC 37, AFC 27—Running back Chuck Muncie of New Orleans ran for 2 touchdowns and threw a 25-yard option pass for another score to give the NFC its third consecutive victory over the AFC. Muncie, who was selected the game's most valuable player, snapped a 3-3 tie on a 1-yard touchdown run at 1:41 of the second quarter, then scored on an 11-yard run in the fourth quarter for the NFC's final touchdown. Two scoring records were set in the game— 37 points by the NFC, eclipsing the 33 by the AFC in 1973, and the 64 points by both teams, surpassing the 61 scored in 1973.

NFC	3	20	7	7	—	37
AFC	3	7	10	7	—	27

NFC — FG Moseley 37
AFC — FG Fritsch 19
NFC — Muncie 1 run (Moseley kick)
AFC — Pruitt 1 pass from Bradshaw (Fritsch kick)
NFC — D. Hill 13 pass from Manning (kick failed)
NFC — T. Hill 25 pass from Muncie (Moseley kick)
NFC — Henry 86 punt return (Moseley kick)
AFC — Campbell 2 run (Fritsch kick)
AFC — FG Fritsch 29
NFC — Muncie 11 run (Moseley kick)
AFC — Campbell 1 run (Fritsch kick)

1979 AFC-NFC PRO BOWL

Memorial Coliseum, Los Angeles, California
January 29, 1979, Attendance: 46,281

NFC 13, AFC 7—Roger Staubach completed 9 of 15 passes for 125 yards, including the winning touchdown on a 19-yard strike to Dallas Cowboys teammate Tony Hill in the third period. The winning drive began at the AFC's 45-yard line after a shanked punt. Staubach hit Ahmad Rashad with passes of 15 and 17 yards to set up Hill's decisive catch. The victory gave the NFC a 5-4 advantage in Pro Bowl games. Rashad, who accounted for 89 yards on 5 receptions, was named the player of the game. The AFC led 7-6 at halftime on Bob Griese's 8-yard scoring toss to Steve Largent late in the second quarter. Largent finished the game with 5 receptions for 75 yards. The NFC scored first as Archie Manning marched his team 70 yards in 11 plays, capped by Wilbert Montgomery's 2-yard touchdown run. The AFC's Earl Campbell was the game's leading rusher with 66 yards on 12 carries.

AFC	0	7	0	0	—	7
NFC	0	6	7	0	—	13

NFC — Montgomery 2 run (kick failed)
AFC — Largent 8 pass from Griese (Yepremian kick)
NFC — T. Hill 19 pass from Staubach (Corral kick)

1978 AFC-NFC PRO BOWL

Tampa Stadium, Tampa, Florida
January 23, 1978, Attendance: 51,337

NFC 14, AFC 13—Walter Payton, the NFL's leading rusher in 1977, sparked a second-half comeback to give the NFC the win and tie the series between the two conferences at four victories each. Payton, who was the game's most valuable player, gained 77 yards on 13 carries and scored the tying touchdown on a 1-yard burst with 7:37 left in the game. Efren Herrera kicked the winning extra point. The AFC dominated the first half of the game, taking a 13-0 lead on field goals of 21 and 39 yards by Toni Linhart and a 10-yard touchdown pass from Ken Stabler to Oakland teammate Cliff Branch. On the NFC's first possession of the second half, Pat Haden put together the first touchdown drive after Eddie Brown returned Ray Guy's punt to the AFC 46-yard line. Haden connected on all 4 of his passes on that drive, finally hitting Terry Metcalf with a 4-yard scoring toss. The NFC continued to rally and, with Jim Hart at quarterback, moved 63 yards in 12 plays for the go-ahead score. During the winning drive, Hart completed 5 of 6 passes for 38 yards and Payton picked up 20 more on the ground.

AFC	3	10	0	0	—	13
NFC	0	0	7	7	—	14

AFC — FG Linhart 21
AFC — Branch 10 pass from Stabler (Linhart kick)
AFC — FG Linhart 39
NFC — Metcalf 4 pass from Haden (Herrera kick)
NFC — Payton 1 run (Herrera kick)

1977 AFC-NFC PRO BOWL

Kingdome, Seattle, Washington
January 17, 1977, Attendance: 64,752

AFC 24, NFC 14—O.J. Simpson's 3-yard touchdown burst at 7:03 of the first quarter gave the AFC a lead it would not surrender, the victory breaking a two-game NFC win streak and giving the American Conference stars a 4-3 series lead. The AFC took a 17-7 lead midway through the second period on the first of 2 Ken Anderson touchdown passes, a 12-yard toss to Charlie Joiner. But the NFC mounted a 73-yard drive capped by Lawrence McCutcheon's 1-yard touchdown plunge to pull within 17-14 at the half. Following a scoreless third quarter, player of the game Mel Blount thwarted a possible NFC score when he intercepted Jim Hart's pass in the end zone. Less than three minutes later, Blount again picked off a Hart pass, returning it 16 yards to the NFC 27. That set up Anderson's 27-yard touchdown strike to the Raiders' Cliff Branch for the final score.

NFC	0	14	0	0	—	14
AFC	10	7	0	7	—	24

AFC — Simpson 3 run (Linhart kick)
AFC — FG Linhart 31
NFC — Thomas 15 run (Bakken kick)
AFC — Joiner 12 pass from Anderson (Linhart kick)
NFC — McCutcheon 1 run (Bakken kick)
AFC — Branch 27 pass from Anderson (Linhart kick)

1976 AFC-NFC PRO BOWL

Superdome, New Orleans, Louisiana
January 26, 1976, Attendance: 30,546

NFC 23, AFC 20—Mike Boryla, a late substitute who did not enter the game until 5:39 remained, lifted the National Football Conference to the victory over the American Football Conference with 2 touchdown passes in the final minutes. It was the second straight NFC win, squaring the series at 3-3. Until Boryla started firing the ball the AFC was in control, leading 13-0 at the half. Boryla entered the game after Billy Johnson had raced 90 yards with a punt to make the score 20-9 in favor of the AFC. He floated a 14-yard touchdown pass to Terry Metcalf and later fired an 8-yard scoring pass to Mel Gray for the winner.

AFC	0	13	0	7	—	20
NFC	0	0	9	14	—	23

AFC — FG Stenerud 20
AFC — FG Stenerud 35

AFC — Burrough 64 pass from Pastorini (Stenerud kick)
NFC — FG Bakken 42
NFC — Foreman 4 pass from Hart (kick blocked)
AFC — Johnson 90 punt return (Stenerud kick)
NFC — Metcalf 14 pass from Boryla (Bakken kick)
NFC — Gray 8 pass from Boryla (Bakken kick)

1975 AFC-NFC PRO BOWL

Orange Bowl, Miami, Florida
January 20, 1975, Attendance: 26,484

NFC 17, AFC 10—Los Angeles quarterback James Harris, who took over the NFC offense after Jim Hart of St. Louis suffered a laceration above his right eye in the second period, threw 2 touchdown passes early in the fourth period to pace the NFC to its second victory in the five-game Pro Bowl series. The NFC win snapped a three-game AFC victory string. Harris, who was named the player of the game, connected with St. Louis's Mel Gray for an 8-yard touchdown 2:03 into the final period. One minute and 24 seconds later, following a fumble recovery by Washington's Ken Houston, Harris tossed another 8-yard scoring pass to Washington's Charley Taylor for the decisive points.

NFC	0	3	0	14	—	17
AFC	0	0	10	0	—	10

NFC — FG Marcol 33
AFC — Warfield 32 pass from Griese (Gerela kick)
AFC — FG Gerela 33
NFC — Gray 8 pass from J. Harris (Marcol kick)
NFC — Taylor 8 pass from J. Harris (Marcol kick)

1974 AFC-NFC PRO BOWL

Arrowhead Stadium, Kansas City, Missouri
January 20, 1974, Attendance: 66,918

AFC 15, NFC 13—Miami's Garo Yepremian's fifth field goal—a 42-yard kick with 21 seconds remaining—gave the AFC its third straight victory since the NFC won the inaugural game following the 1970 season. The field goal by Yepremian, who was voted the game's outstanding player, offset a 21-yard field goal by Atlanta's Nick Mike-Mayer that had given the NFC a 13-12 advantage with 1:41 remaining. The only touchdown in the game was scored by the NFC on a 14-yard pass from Philadelphia's Roman Gabriel to Lawrence McCutcheon of the Los Angeles Rams.

NFC	0	10	0	3	—	13
AFC	3	3	3	6	—	15

AFC — FG Yepremian 16
NFC — FG Mike-Mayer 27
NFC — McCutcheon 14 pass from Gabriel (Mike-Mayer kick)
AFC — FG Yepremian 37
AFC — FG Yepremian 27
AFC — FG Yepremian 41
NFC — FG Mike-Mayer 21
AFC — FG Yepremian 42

1973 AFC-NFC PRO BOWL

Texas Stadium, Irving, Texas
January 21, 1973, Attendance: 37,091

AFC 33, NFC 28—Paced by the rushing and receiving of player of the game O.J. Simpson, the AFC erased a 14-0 first period deficit and built a commanding 33-14 lead midway through the fourth period before the NFC managed 2 touchdowns in the final minute of play. Simpson rushed for 112 yards and caught 3 passes for 58 more to gain unanimous recognition in the balloting for player of the game. John Brockington scored 3 touchdowns for the NFC.

AFC	0	10	10	13	—	33
NFC	14	0	0	14	—	28

NFC — Brockington 1 run (Marcol kick)
NFC — Brockington 3 pass from Kilmer (Marcol kick)
AFC — Simpson 7 run (Gerela kick)
AFC — FG Gerela 18
AFC — FG Gerela 22
AFC — Hubbard 11 run (Gerela kick)
AFC — O. Taylor 5 pass from Lamonica (kick failed)
AFC — Bell 12 interception return (Gerela kick)
NFC — Brockington 1 run (Marcol kick)
NFC — Kwalick 12 pass from Snead (Marcol kick)

1972 AFC-NFC PRO BOWL

Memorial Coliseum, Los Angeles, California
January 23, 1972, Attendance: 53,647

AFC 26, NFC 13—Kansas City's Jan Stenerud kicked 4 field goals to lead the AFC from a 6-0 deficit to victory. The AFC defense picked off 3 passes. Stenerud was selected as the outstanding offensive player and his Kansas City teammate, linebacker Willie Lanier, was the game's outstanding defensive player.

AFC	0	3	13	10	—	26
NFC	0	6	0	7	—	13

NFC — Grim 50 pass from Landry (kick failed)
AFC — FG Stenerud 25
AFC — FG Stenerud 23
AFC — FG Stenerud 48
AFC — Morin 5 pass from Dawson (Stenerud kick)
AFC — FG Stenerud 42
NFC — V. Washington 2 run (Knight kick)
AFC — F. Little 6 run (Stenerud kick)

1971 AFC-NFC PRO BOWL

Memorial Coliseum, Los Angeles, California
January 24, 1971, Attendance: 48,222

NFC 27, AFC 6—Mel Renfro of Dallas broke open the first meeting between the American Football Conference and National Football Conference all-star teams as he returned a pair of punts 82 and 56 yards for touchdowns in the final period to clinch the NFC victory over the AFC. Renfro was voted the game's outstanding back and linebacker Fred Carr of Green Bay the outstanding lineman.

AFC	0	3	3	0	—	6
NFC	0	3	10	14	—	27

AFC — FG Stenerud 37
NFC — FG Cox 13
NFC — Osborn 23 pass from Brodie (Cox kick)
NFC — FG Cox 35
AFC — FG Stenerud 16
NFC — Renfro 82 punt return (Cox kick)
NFC — Renfro 56 punt return (Cox kick)

PRO BOWL ALL-TIME RESULTS

Date	Result	Site (attendance)	Honored players
Jan. 15, 1939	New York Giants 13, Pro All-Stars 10	Wrigley Field, Los Angeles (20,000)	
Jan. 14, 1940	Green Bay 16, NFL All-Stars 7	Gilmore Stadium, Los Angeles (18,000)	
Dec. 29, 1940	Chicago Bears 28, NFL All-Stars 14	Gilmore Stadium, Los Angeles (21,624)	
Jan. 4, 1942	Chicago Bears 35, NFL All-Stars 24	Polo Grounds, New York (17,725)	
Dec. 27, 1942	NFL All-Stars 17, Washington 14	Shibe Park, Philadelphia (18,671)	
Jan. 14, 1951	American Conf. 28, National Conf. 27	Los Angeles Memorial Coliseum (53,676)	Otto Graham, Cleveland, player of the game
Jan. 12, 1952	National Conf. 30, American Conf. 13	Los Angeles Memorial Coliseum (19,400)	Dan Towler, Los Angeles, player of the game
Jan. 10, 1953	National Conf. 27, American Conf. 7	Los Angeles Memorial Coliseum (34,208)	Don Doll, Detroit, player of the game
Jan. 17, 1954	East 20, West 9	Los Angeles Memorial Coliseum (44,214)	Chuck Bednarik, Philadelphia, player of the game
Jan. 16, 1955	West 26, East 19	Los Angeles Memorial Coliseum (43,972)	Billy Wilson, San Francisco, player of the game
Jan. 15, 1956	East 31, West 30	Los Angeles Memorial Coliseum (37,867)	Ollie Matson, Chi. Cardinals, player of the game
Jan. 13, 1957	West 19, East 10	Los Angeles Memorial Coliseum (44,177)	Bert Rechichar, Baltimore, outstanding back Ernie Stautner, Pittsburgh, outstanding lineman
Jan. 12, 1958	West 26, East 7	Los Angeles Memorial Coliseum (66,634)	Hugh McElhenny, San Francisco, outstanding back Gene Brito, Washington, outstanding lineman
Jan. 11, 1959	East 28, West 21	Los Angeles Memorial Coliseum (72,250)	Frank Gifford, N.Y. Giants, outstanding back Doug Atkins, Chi. Bears, outstanding lineman
Jan. 17, 1960	West 38, East 21	Los Angeles Memorial Coliseum (56,876)	Johnny Unitas, Baltimore, outstanding back Gene (Big Daddy) Lipscomb, Baltimore, outstanding lineman
Jan. 15, 1961	West 35, East 31	Los Angeles Memorial Coliseum (62,971)	Johnny Unitas, Baltimore, outstanding back Sam Huff, N.Y. Giants, outstanding lineman
Jan. 7, 1962	AFL West 47, East 27	Balboa Stadium, San Diego (20,973)	Cotton Davidson, Dallas Texans, player of the game
Jan. 14, 1962	NFL West 31, East 30	Los Angeles Memorial Coliseum (57,409)	Jim Brown, Cleveland, outstanding back Henry Jordan, Green Bay, outstanding lineman
Jan. 13, 1963	AFL West 21, East 14	Balboa Stadium, San Diego (27,641)	Curtis McClinton, Dallas Texans, outstanding offensive player Earl Faison, San Diego, outstanding defensive player
Jan. 13, 1963	NFL East 30, West 20	Los Angeles Memorial Coliseum (61,374)	Jim Brown, Cleveland, outstanding back Gene (Big Daddy) Lipscomb, Pittsburgh, outstanding lineman
Jan. 12, 1964	NFL West 31, East 17	Los Angeles Memorial Coliseum (67,242)	Johnny Unitas, Baltimore, player of the game Gino Marchetti, Baltimore, outstanding lineman
Jan. 19, 1964	AFL West 27, East 24	Balboa Stadium, San Diego (20,016)	Keith Lincoln, San Diego, outstanding offensive player Archie Matsos, Oakland, outstanding defensive player
Jan. 10, 1965	NFL West 34, East 14	Los Angeles Memorial Coliseum (60,598)	Fran Tarkenton, Minnesota, outstanding back Terry Barr, Detroit, outstanding lineman
Jan. 16, 1965	AFL West 38, East 14	Jeppesen Stadium, Houston (15,446)	Keith Lincoln, San Diego, outstanding offensive player Willie Brown, Denver, outstanding defensive player
Jan. 15, 1966	AFL All-Stars 30, Buffalo 19	Rice Stadium, Houston (35,572)	Joe Namath, N.Y. Jets, most valuable player, offense Frank Buncom, San Diego, most valuable player, defense
Jan. 15, 1966	NFL East 36, West 7	Los Angeles Memorial Coliseum (60,124)	Jim Brown, Cleveland, outstanding back Dale Meinert, St. Louis, outstanding lineman
Jan. 21, 1967	AFL East 30, West 23	Oakland-Alameda County Coliseum (18,876)	Babe Parilli, Boston, outstanding offensive player Verlon Biggs, N.Y. Jets, outstanding defensive player
Jan. 22, 1967	NFL East 20, West 10	Los Angeles Memorial Coliseum (15,062)	Gale Sayers, Chicago, outstanding back Floyd Peters, Philadelphia, outstanding lineman
Jan. 21, 1968	AFL East 25, West 24	Gator Bowl, Jacksonville, Fla. (40,103)	Joe Namath and Don Maynard, N.Y. Jets, out. off. players Leslie (Speedy) Duncan, San Diego, out. def. player
Jan. 21, 1968	NFL West 38, East 20	Los Angeles Memorial Coliseum (53,289)	Gale Sayers, Chicago, outstanding back Dave Robinson, Green Bay, outstanding lineman
Jan. 19, 1969	AFL West 38, East 25	Gator Bowl, Jacksonville, Fla. (41,058)	Len Dawson, Kansas City, outstanding offensive player George Webster, Houston, outstanding defensive player
Jan. 19, 1969	NFL West 10, East 7	Los Angeles Memorial Coliseum (32,050)	Roman Gabriel, Los Angeles, outstanding back Merlin Olsen, Los Angeles, outstanding lineman
Jan. 17, 1970	AFL West 26, East 3	Astrodome, Houston (30,170)	John Hadl, San Diego, player of the game
Jan. 18, 1970	NFL West 16, East 13	Los Angeles Memorial Coliseum (57,786)	Gale Sayers, Chicago, outstanding back George Andrie, Dallas, outstanding lineman
Jan. 24, 1971	NFC 27, AFC 6	Los Angeles Memorial Coliseum (48,222)	Mel Renfro, Dallas, outstanding back Fred Carr, Green Bay, outstanding lineman
Jan. 23, 1972	AFC 26, NFC 13	Los Angeles Memorial Coliseum (53,647)	Jan Stenerud, Kansas City, outstanding offensive player Willie Lanier, Kansas City, outstanding defensive player
Jan. 21, 1973	AFC 33, NFC 28	Texas Stadium, Irving (37,091)	O.J. Simpson, Buffalo, player of the game
Jan. 20, 1974	AFC 15, NFC 13	Arrowhead Stadium, Kansas City (66,918)	Garo Yepremian, Miami, player of the game
Jan. 20, 1975	NFC 17, AFC 10	Orange Bowl, Miami (26,484)	James Harris, Los Angeles, player of the game
Jan. 26, 1976	NFC 23, AFC 20	Louisiana Superdome, New Orleans (30,546)	Billy Johnson, Houston, player of the game
Jan. 17, 1977	AFC 24, NFC 14	Kingdome, Seattle (64,752)	Mel Blount, Pittsburgh, player of the game
Jan. 23, 1978	NFC 14, AFC 13	Tampa Stadium (51,337)	Walter Payton, Chicago, player of the game
Jan. 29, 1979	NFC 13, AFC 7	Los Angeles Memorial Coliseum (46,281)	Ahmad Rashad, Minnesota, player of the game
Jan. 27, 1980	NFC 37, AFC 27	Aloha Stadium, Honolulu (49,800)	Chuck Muncie, New Orleans, player of the game
Feb. 1, 1981	NFC 21, AFC 7	Aloha Stadium, Honolulu (50,360)	Eddie Murray, Detroit, player of the game
Jan. 31, 1982	AFC 16, NFC 13	Aloha Stadium, Honolulu (50,402)	Kellen Winslow, San Diego, and Lee Roy Selmon, Tampa Bay, players of the game
Feb. 6, 1983	NFC 20, AFC 19	Aloha Stadium, Honolulu (49,883)	Dan Fouts, San Diego, and John Jefferson, Green Bay, players of the game
Jan. 29, 1984	NFC 45, AFC 3	Aloha Stadium, Honolulu (50,445)	Joe Theismann, Washington, player of the game
Jan. 27, 1985	AFC 22, NFC 14	Aloha Stadium, Honolulu (50,385)	Mark Gastineau, N.Y. Jets, player of the game
Feb. 2, 1986	NFC 28, AFC 24	Aloha Stadium, Honolulu (50,101)	Phil Simms, N.Y. Giants, player of the game
Feb. 1, 1987	AFC 10, NFC 6	Aloha Stadium, Honolulu (50,101)	Reggie White, Philadelphia, player of the game
Feb. 7, 1988	AFC 15, NFC 6	Aloha Stadium, Honolulu (50,113)	Bruce Smith, Buffalo, player of the game
Jan. 29, 1989	NFC 34, AFC 3	Aloha Stadium, Honolulu (50,113)	Randall Cunningham, Philadelphia, player of the game
Feb. 4, 1990	NFC 27, AFC 21	Aloha Stadium, Honolulu (50,445)	Jerry Gray, L.A. Rams, player of the game
Feb. 3, 1991	AFC 23, NFC 21	Aloha Stadium, Honolulu (50,345)	Jim Kelly, Buffalo, player of the game
Feb. 2, 1992	NFC 21, AFC 15	Aloha Stadium, Honolulu (50,209)	Michael Irvin, Dallas, player of the game
Feb. 7, 1993	AFC 23, NFC 20 (OT)	Aloha Stadium, Honolulu (50,007)	Steve Tasker, Buffalo, player of the game
Feb. 6, 1994	NFC 17, AFC 3	Aloha Stadium, Honolulu (50,026)	Andre Rison, Atlanta, player of the game
Feb. 5, 1995	AFC 41, NFC 13	Aloha Stadium, Honolulu (49,121)	Marshall Faulk, Indianapolis, player of the game
Feb. 4, 1996	NFC 20, AFC 13	Aloha Stadium, Honolulu (50,034)	Jerry Rice, San Francisco, player of the game

PRESEASON GAMES/PLAYOFF BOWLS

PRO FOOTBALL HALL OF FAME GAME

1962	New York Giants 21, St. Louis Cardinals 21
1963	Pittsburgh Steelers 16, Cleveland Browns 7
1964	Baltimore Colts 48, Pittsburgh Steelers 17
1965	Washington Redskins 20, Detroit Lions 3
1966	No game
1967	Philadelphia Eagles 28, Cleveland Browns 13
1968	Chicago Bears 30, Dallas Cowboys 24
1969	Green Bay Packers 38, Atlanta Falcons 24
1970	New Orleans Saints 14, Minnesota Vikings 13
1971	Los Angeles Rams (NFC) 17, Houston Oilers (AFC) 6
1972	Kansas City Chiefs (AFC) 23, New York Giants (NFC) 17
1973	San Francisco 49ers (NFC) 20, New England Patriots (AFC) 7
1974	St. Louis Cardinals (NFC) 21, Buffalo Bills (AFC) 13
1975	Washington Redskins (NFC) 17, Cincinnati Bengals (AFC) 9
1976	Denver Broncos (AFC) 10, Detroit Lions (NFC) 7
1977	Chicago Bears (NFC) 20, New York Jets (AFC) 6
1978	Philadelphia Eagles (NFC) 17, Miami Dolphins (AFC) 3
1979	Oakland Raiders (AFC) 20, Dallas Cowboys (NFC) 13
1980*	San Diego Chargers (AFC) 0, Green Bay Packers (NFC) 0
1981	Cleveland Browns (AFC) 24, Atlanta Falcons (NFC) 10
1982	Minnesota Vikings (NFC) 30, Baltimore Colts (AFC) 14
1983	Pittsburgh Steelers (AFC) 27, New Orleans Saints (NFC) 14
1984	Seattle Seahawks (AFC) 38, Tampa Bay Buccaneers (NFC) 0
1985	New York Giants (NFC) 21, Houston Oilers (AFC) 20
1986	New England Patriots (AFC) 21, St. Louis Cardinals (NFC) 16
1987	San Francisco 49ers (NFC) 20, Kansas City Chiefs (AFC) 7
1988	Cincinnati Bengals (AFC) 14, Los Angeles Rams (NFC) 7
1989	Washington Redskins (NFC) 31, Buffalo Bills (AFC) 6
1990	Chicago Bears (NFC) 13, Cleveland Browns (AFC) 0
1991	Detroit Lions (NFC) 14, Denver Broncos (AFC) 3
1992	New York Jets (AFC) 41, Philadelphia Eagles (NFC) 14
1993	Los Angeles Raiders (AFC) 19, Green Bay Packers (NFC) 3
1994	Atlanta Falcons (NFC) 21, San Diego Chargers (AFC) 17
1995	Carolina Panthers (NFC) 20, Jacksonville Jaguars (AFC) 14

*Game called with 5:29 remaining due to severe thunder and lightning.

NFL INTERNATIONAL GAMES

Date	Site	Teams
Aug. 12, 1950	Ottawa, Canada	N.Y. Giants 27, Ottawa Roughriders 6
Aug. 11, 1951	Ottawa, Canada	N.Y. Giants 41, Ottawa Roughriders 18
Aug. 5, 1959	Toronto, Canada	Chi. Cardinals 55, Tor. Argonauts 26
Aug. 3, 1960	Toronto, Canada	Pittsburgh 43, Toronto Argonauts 16
Aug. 15, 1960	Toronto, Canada	Chicago 16, N.Y. Giants 7
Aug. 2, 1961	Toronto, Canada	St. Louis 36, Toronto Argonauts 7
Aug. 5, 1961	Montreal, Canada	Chicago 34, Montreal Allouettes 16
Aug. 8, 1961	Hamilton, Canada	Hamilton Tiger-Cats 38, Buffalo 21
Sept. 11, 1969	Montreal, Canada	Pittsburgh 17, N.Y. Giants 13
Aug. 25, 1969	Montreal, Canada	Detroit 22, Boston 9
Aug. 16, 1976	Tokyo, Japan	St. Louis 20, San Diego 10
Aug. 5, 1978	Mexico City, Mexico	New Orleans 14, Philadelphia 7
Aug. 6, 1983	London, England	Minnesota 28, St. Louis 10
*Aug. 3, 1986	London, England	Chicago 17, Dallas 6
*Aug. 9, 1987	London, England	L.A. Rams 28, Denver 27
*July 31, 1988	London, England	Miami 27, San Francisco 21
Aug. 14, 1988	Goteborg, Sweden	Minnesota 28, Chicago 21
Aug. 18, 1988	Montreal, Canada	N.Y. Jets 11, Cleveland 7
*Aug. 5, 1989	Tokyo, Japan	L.A. Rams 16, San Francisco 13 (OT)
*Aug. 6, 1989	London, England	Philadelphia 17, Cleveland 13
*Aug. 4, 1990	Tokyo, Japan	Denver 10, Seattle 7
*Aug. 5, 1990	London, England	New Orleans 17, L.A. Raiders 10
*Aug. 9, 1990	Montreal, Canada	Pittsburgh 30, New England 14
*Aug. 11, 1990	Berlin, Germany	L.A. Rams 19, Kansas City 3
*July 28, 1991	London, England	Buffalo 17, Philadelphia 13
*Aug. 3, 1991	Berlin, Germany	San Francisco 21, Chicago 7
*Aug. 3, 1991	Tokyo, Japan	Miami 19, L.A. Raiders 17
*Aug. 1, 1992	Tokyo, Japan	Houston 34, Dallas 23
*Aug. 15, 1992	Berlin, Germany	Miami 31, Denver 27
*Aug. 16, 1992	London, England	San Francisco 17, Washington 15
*July 31, 1993	Tokyo, Japan	New Orleans 28, Philadelphia 16
*Aug. 1, 1993	Barcelona, Spain	San Francisco 21, Pittsburgh 14
*Aug. 7, 1993	Berlin, Germany	Minnesota 20, Buffalo 6
*Aug. 8, 1993	London, England	Dallas 13, Detroit 13 (OT)
Aug. 14, 1993	Toronto, Canada	Cleveland 12, New England 9
*July 31, 1994	Barcelona, Spain	L.A. Raiders 25, Denver 22
*Aug. 6, 1994	Tokyo, Japan	Minnesota 17, Kansas City 9
*Aug. 13, 1994	Berlin, Germany	N.Y. Giants 28, San Diego 20
*Aug. 15, 1994	Mexico City, Mexico	Houston 6, Dallas 0
*Aug. 5, 1995	Tokyo, Japan	Denver 24, San Francisco 10
*Aug. 12, 1995	Toronto, Canada	Buffalo 9, Dallas 7

*American Bowl Game

CHICAGO ALL-STAR GAME

Pro teams won 31, lost 9, and tied 2. The game was discontinued after 1976.

Year	Date	Winner	Loser	Attendance
1976*	July 23	Pittsburgh 24	All-Stars 0	52,895
1975	Aug. 1	Pittsburgh 21	All-Stars 14	54,103
1974		No game was played		
1973	July 27	Miami 14	All-Stars 3	54,103
1972	July 28	Dallas 20	All-Stars 7	54,162
1971	July 30	Baltimore 24	All-Stars 17	52,289
1970	July 31	Kansas City 24	All-Stars 3	69,940
1969	Aug. 1	N.Y. Jets 26	All-Stars 24	74,208
1968	Aug. 2	Green Bay 34	All-Stars 17	69,917
1967	Aug. 4	Green Bay 27	All-Stars 0	70,934
1966	Aug. 5	Green Bay 38	All-Stars 0	72,000
1965	Aug. 6	Cleveland 24	All-Stars 16	68,000
1964	Aug. 7	Chicago 28	All-Stars 17	65,000
1963	Aug. 2	All-Stars 20	Green Bay 17	65,000
1962	Aug. 3	Green Bay 42	All-Stars 20	65,000
1961	Aug. 4	Philadelphia 28	All-Stars 14	66,000
1960	Aug. 12	Baltimore 32	All-Stars 7	70,000
1959	Aug. 14	Baltimore 29	All-Stars 0	70,000
1958	Aug. 15	All-Stars 35	Detroit 19	70,000
1957	Aug. 9	N.Y. Giants 22	All-Stars 12	75,000
1956	Aug. 10	Cleveland 26	All-Stars 0	75,000
1955	Aug. 12	All-Stars 30	Cleveland 27	75,000
1954	Aug. 13	Detroit 31	All-Stars 6	93,470
1953	Aug. 14	Detroit 24	All-Stars 10	93,818
1952	Aug. 15	Los Angeles 10	All-Stars 7	88,316
1951	Aug. 17	Cleveland 33	All-Stars 0	92,180
1950	Aug. 11	All-Stars 17	Philadelphia 7	88,885
1949	Aug. 12	Philadelphia 38	All-Stars 0	93,780
1948	Aug. 20	Chi. Cardinals 28	All-Stars 0	101,220
1947	Aug. 22	All-Stars 16	Chi. Bears 0	105,840
1946	Aug. 23	All-Stars 16	Los Angeles 0	97,380
1945	Aug. 30	Green Bay 19	All-Stars 7	92,753
1944	Aug. 30	Chi. Bears 24	All-Stars 21	48,769
1943	Aug. 25	All-Stars 27	Washington 7	48,471
1942	Aug. 28	Chi. Bears 21	All-Stars 0	101,100
1941	Aug. 28	Chi. Bears 37	All-Stars 13	98,203
1940	Aug. 29	Green Bay 45	All-Stars 28	84,567
1939	Aug. 30	N.Y. Giants 9	All-Stars 0	81,456
1938	Aug. 31	All-Stars 28	Washington 16	74,250
1937	Sept. 1	All-Stars 6	Green Bay 0	84,560
1936	Sept. 3	All-Stars 7	Detroit 7 (tie)	76,000
1935	Aug. 29	Chi. Bears 5	All-Stars 0	77,450
1934	Aug. 31	Chi. Bears 0	All-Stars 0 (tie)	79,432

*Game shortened due to thunderstorms.

NFL PLAYOFF BOWL

Western Conference won 8, Eastern Conference won 2.
All games played at Miami's Orange Bowl.

1970	Los Angeles Rams 31, Dallas Cowboys 0
1969	Dallas Cowboys 17, Minnesota Vikings 13
1968	Los Angeles Rams 30, Cleveland Browns 6
1967	Baltimore Colts 20, Philadelphia Eagles 14
1966	Baltimore Colts 35, Dallas Cowboys 3
1965	St. Louis Cardinals 24, Green Bay Packers 17
1964	Green Bay Packers 40, Cleveland Browns 23
1963	Detroit Lions 17, Pittsburgh Steelers 10
1962	Detroit Lions 28, Philadelphia Eagles 10
1961	Detroit Lions 17, Cleveland Browns 16

AFC VS. NFC (REGULAR SEASON), 1970-1995

	1970	1971	1972	1973	1974	1975	1976	1977	1978	1979	1980	1981	1982	1983	1984	1985	1986	1987	1988	1989	1990	1991	1992	1993	1994	1995	Totals
Miami	2-1	3-0	3-0	3-0	2-1	3-0	0-2	2-0	3-1	4-0	4-0	3-1	1-1	3-1	4-0	3-1	2-2	3-0	3-1	2-0	2-2	3-1	2-2	3-1	2-2	2-2	67-22
Oakland	1-2	1-1-1	3-0	2-1	3-0	3-0	3-0	1-1	4-0	4-0	2-2	2-2	3-0	2-2	3-1	3-1	1-3	2-2	1-3	2-2	3-1	2-2	2-2	3-1	3-1	3-1	62-31-1
Pittsburgh	0-3	1-2	2-1	3-0	3-0	2-1	1-1	2-0	3-1	3-1	4-0	3-1	1-0	2-2	3-1	1-3	2-2	2-2	1-3	3-1	3-1	0-4	1-3	2-2	2-2	2-2	52-39
Cincinnati	1-2	1-2	2-1	2-1	2-1	3-0	2-0	2-1	2-2	2-2	2-2	2-2	1-0	3-1	2-2	2-2	3-1	1-2	4-0	2-2	1-3	1-3	1-3	2-2	1-3	2-2	49-42
Denver	2-2	1-3	1-3	0-3-1	2-2	2-1	2-0	1-1	2-2	3-1	3-1	3-1	2-1	0-2	3-1	3-1	3-1	2-1-1	3-1	2-2	1-3	2-0	1-3	1-3	1-3	2-2	48-44-2
Cleveland	0-3	2-1	1-2	1-2	1-2	1-3	2-0	1-1	4-0	3-1	3-1	3-1	0-2	2-2	1-3	1-3	2-2	2-2	4-0	3-1	1-3	0-4	2-2	3-1	3-1	1-3	47-46
Kansas City	0-2-1	2-1	2-1	1-1-1	1-2	2-1	1-1	1-1	0-2	0-2	2-0	2-2	0-3	2-2	1-1	2-2	1-1	1-2	0-2	2-0	4-0	2-2	2-2	2-2	3-1	3-1	39-37-2
San Diego	1-2	2-1	0-3	1-2	1-2	0-3	2-0	1-1	2-2	3-1	2-2	2-2	1-0	2-2	4-0	1-1	0-4	2-0	2-2	2-2	1-1	1-3	2-0	2-2	2-2	3-1	42-41
Seattle								1-0	3-1	3-1	1-3	0-2	1-0	1-3	4-0	2-2	3-1	4-0	1-3	0-4	2-2	1-3	0-4	0-2	2-0	3-1	32-32
Buffalo	0-3	0-3	2-0-1	2-1	2-1	1-2	0-2	1-1	1-1	2-2	3-1	1-3	1-2	1-3	1-3	0-2	1-1	1-2	2-2	1-3	3-1	3-1	4-0	4-0	1-3	3-1	41-44-1
Indianapolis	3-0	2-1	0-3	2-1	1-2	2-1	0-2	1-1	2-2	1-1	1-1	0-4	0-1-1	2-0	0-4	3-1	1-3	1-0	2-2	1-3	2-2	0-4	2-0	0-4	0-2	2-2	31-47-1
New England	0-3	0-3	3-0	2-1	3-0	1-2	1-1	2-0	2-2	3-1	1-3	0-4	0-1	2-2	0-4	3-1	3-1	0-3	2-2	0-4	0-4	1-1	0-4	1-1	4-0	0-4	34-52
N.Y. Jets	2-1	0-3	1-2	0-3	2-1	0-3	0-2	1-1	1-3	3-1	1-3	2-0	4-0	3-1	0-2	2-2	2-2	0-4	2-0	1-3	2-0	2-2	0-4	2-2	1-3	0-4	34-52
Houston	0-3	0-2-1	0-3	0-3	0-3	3-0	2-0	2-0	2-2	2-2	4-0	1-3	0-3	1-3	0-4	1-3	2-2	2-2	3-1	3-1	1-3	1-3	3-1	2-2	0-4	1-3	614-590-8
Tampa Bay							0-1																				0-1
Jacksonville																										0-4	0-4
TOTALS	12-27-1	15-23-2	20-19-1	19-19-2	23-17	23-17	16-12	19-9	31-21	36-16	33-19	24-28	15-14-1	26-26	26-26	27-25	26-26	23-22-1	30-22	24-28	26-26	19-33	22-30	27-25	25-27	27-33	614-590-8

NFC VS. AFC (REGULAR SEASON), 1970-1995

	1970	1971	1972	1973	1974	1975	1976	1977	1978	1979	1980	1981	1982	1983	1984	1985	1986	1987	1988	1989	1990	1991	1992	1993	1994	1995	Totals
Dallas	3-0	3-0	3-0	2-1	2-1	2-1	2-0	1-1	3-1	1-3	3-1	4-0	2-1	2-2	2-2	3-1	1-3	2-1	0-4	0-2	1-1	3-1	4-0	2-2	3-1	4-0	58-30
San Francisco	4-0	2-1	2-1	1-2	0-3	1-2	1-1	0-2	1-3	0-4	2-2	3-1	1-3	2-2	3-1	3-1	4-0	3-1	2-2	4-0	4-0	3-1	3-1	2-2	3-1	3-1	57-38
Philadelphia	2-1	1-2	2-1	2-1	2-1	0-3	0-2	1-1	3-1	2-2	3-1	3-1	2-1	1-1	3-1	1-1	2-2	3-1	2-2	3-1	1-3	4-0	3-1	2-2	1-3	1-3	50-39
Washington	2-1	1-2	1-2	2-1	2-1	1-2	1-1	1-1	2-2	2-2	1-3	1-3	1-2	1-3	3-1	3-1	2-2	1-2	2-2	3-1	2-2	1-3	2-2	2-2	2-2	0-4	48-39
St. Louis	2-1	1-2	1-2	3-0	3-1	3-0	1-1	2-0	2-2	2-2	2-2	2-2		4-0	3-1	4-0	3-1	2-1	1-3	2-2	3-1	4-0	2-2	1-3	1-1	1-3	49-44
N.Y. Giants	3-0	1-2	1-2	1-2	1-2	2-1	0-2	0-2	1-1	1-1	1-3	1-1	1-0	0-4	2-0	2-2	3-1	2-1	1-1	4-0	3-1	3-1	2-2	2-2	3-1	0-4	41-39
Minnesota	2-1	2-1	1-2	2-1	2-1	4-0	2-0	1-1	1-3	1-3	1-3	1-3	1-3	4-0	0-4	2-0	1-3	2-1	2-2	2-2	2-2	0-2	3-1	2-2	2-2	3-1	46-44
Chicago	1-2	1-2	1-2	2-2	0-3	0-3	0-2	1-1	0-4	2-2	0-4	4-0	1-1	1-1	2-2	3-1	4-0	2-2	3-1	2-2	2-2	2-2	1-3	2-2	3-1	2-2	42-49
Detroit	3-0	4-0	2-0-1	0-3	1-2	1-2	2-0	2-0	2-2	0-4	0-2	2-2	0-1	1-3	0-4	2-2	1-3	0-4	1-1	1-3	1-3	4-0	2-2	2-0	2-2	3-1	39-46-1
Arizona	2-0-1	2-1	1-2	0-2-1	2-1	2-1	1-1	0-2	0-4	1-3	1-1	3-1		3-1	3-1	2-2	1-1	0-1	1-3	1-3	2-2	1-1	0-2	1-1	3-1	1-3	34-41-2
New Orleans	0-3	0-1-2	0-3	1-2	0-3	0-3	1-2	0-2	1-3	0-4	1-3	2-2	1-0	1-3	3-1	0-4	1-3	4-0	4-0	4-0	2-2	3-1	3-1	2-2	1-3	4-0	39-51-2
Green Bay	2-1	2-1	2-1	1-1-1	2-1	0-3	0-2	0-3	2-2	1-3	1-3	1-1	1-1-1	2-2	0-4	0-4	1-3	1-2-1	1-3	0-2	1-3	1-3	3-1	3-1	1-3	4-0	33-54-3
Atlanta	1-2	3-0	2-2	2-1	0-3	1-2	0-2	0-2	1-3	1-3	2-2	1-3	1-1	3-1	1-3	0-4	1-3	0-4	1-3	2-2	2-2	3-1	2-2	1-3	1-3	2-2	34-59
Tampa Bay								0-1	2-0	2-0	1-3	0-4	2-1	1-3	1-1	0-4	1-1	0-2	1-3	0-4	0-2	1-3	0-2	1-3	1-1	2-2	16-40
Carolina																										3-1	3-1
Seattle							1-0																				1-0
TOTALS	27-12-1	23-15-2	19-20-1	19-19-2	17-23	17-23	12-16	9-19	21-31	16-36	19-33	28-24	14-15-1	26-26	26-26	25-27	26-26	22-23-1	22-30	28-24	26-26	33-19	30-22	25-27	27-25	33-27	590-614-8

INTERCONFERENCE GAMES

1995 INTERCONFERENCE GAMES

(Home Team in capital letters)

NFC 33, AFC 27

AFC Victories

PITTSBURGH 23, Detroit 20
BUFFALO 31, Carolina 9
KANSAS CITY 20, New York Giants 17 (OT)
CLEVELAND 22, Tampa Bay 6
Oakland 20, WASHINGTON 8
San Diego 27, PHILADELPHIA 21
DENVER 38, Washington 31
OAKLAND 48, Philadelphia 17
Kansas City 24, ARIZONA 3
INDIANAPOLIS 21, St. Louis 18
INDIANAPOLIS 18, San Francisco 17
HOUSTON 19, Tampa Bay 7
DENVER 38, Arizona 6
SEATTLE 30, New York Giants 28
Pittsburgh 37, CHICAGO 34 (OT)
KANSAS CITY 24, Washington 3
BUFFALO 23, Atlanta 17
Oakland 17, NEW YORK GIANTS 13
Seattle 27, WASHINGTON 20
MIAMI 21, Atlanta 20
SEATTLE 26, Philadelphia 14
SAN DIEGO 28, Arizona 25
Buffalo 45, ST. LOUIS 27
CINCINNATI 16, Chicago 10
San Diego 27, NEW YORK GIANTS 17
Miami 41, ST. LOUIS 22
CINCINNATI 27, Minnesota 24

NFC Victories

DALLAS 31, Denver 21
SAN FRANCISCO 28, New England 3
Minnesota 44, PITTSBURGH 24
ATLANTA 13, New York Jets 3
Green Bay 24, JACKSONVILLE 14
ATLANTA 30, New England 17
TAMPA BAY 19, Cincinnati 16
DETROIT 38, Cleveland 20
MINNESOTA 23, Houston 17 (OT)
Chicago 30, JACKSONVILLE 27
Dallas 23, SAN DIEGO 9
NEW ORLEANS 33, Miami 30
CAROLINA 26, New York Jets 15
Carolina 20, NEW ENGLAND 17 (OT)
ARIZONA 20, Seattle 14 (OT)
NEW ORLEANS 17, Indianapolis 14
CHICAGO 35, Houston 32
PHILADELPHIA 31, Denver 13
Dallas 34, OAKLAND 21
Green Bay 31, CLEVELAND 20
TAMPA BAY 17, Jacksonville 16
San Francisco 44, MIAMI 20
DALLAS 24, Kansas City 12
GREEN BAY 24, Cincinnati 10
CAROLINA 13, Indianapolis 10
New Orleans 31, NEW ENGLAND 17
St. Louis 23, NEW YORK JETS 20
SAN FRANCISCO 27, Buffalo 17
MINNESOTA 27, Cleveland 11
Detroit 24, HOUSTON 17
DETROIT 44, Jacksonville 0
New Orleans 12, NEW YORK JETS 0
GREEN BAY 24, Pittsburgh 19

REGULAR SEASON INTERCONFERENCE RECORDS, 1970-1995

AMERICAN FOOTBALL CONFERENCE

Eastern Division	W	L	T	Pct.
Miami	67	22	0	.753
Buffalo	41	44	1	.483
Indianapolis	31	47	1	.399
New England	34	52	0	.395
New York Jets	34	52	0	.395
Central Division				
Pittsburgh	52	39	0	.571
Cincinnati	49	42	0	.538
Cleveland	47	46	0	.505
Houston	36	56	1	.392
Jacksonville	0	4	0	.000
Western Division				
Oakland	62	31	1	.665
Denver	48	44	2	.521
Kansas City	39	37	2	.513
Seattle*	33	32	0	.508
San Diego	42	41	0	.506

NATIONAL FOOTBALL CONFERENCE

Eastern Division	W	L	T	Pct.
Dallas	58	30	0	.659
Philadelphia	50	39	0	.562
Washington	48	39	0	.552
New York Giants	41	39	0	.513
Arizona	34	41	2	.455
Central Division				
Minnesota	46	44	0	.511
Chicago	42	49	0	.462
Detroit	39	46	1	.459
Green Bay	33	54	3	.383
Tampa Bay*	16	41	0	.281
Western Division				
Carolina	3	1	0	.750
San Francisco	57	38	0	.600
St. Louis	49	44	0	.527
New Orleans	39	51	2	.435
Atlanta	34	59	0	.366

** Records include one game played between Seattle and Tampa Bay in their inaugural season (1976) when Seattle competed in the NFC and Tampa Bay in the AFC.*

INTERCONFERENCE VICTORIES, 1970-1995

REGULAR SEASON

	AFC	NFC	Tie
1970	12	27	1
1971	15	23	2
1972	20	19	1
1973	19	19	2
1974	23	17	0
1975	23	17	0
1976	16	12	0
1977	19	9	0
1978	31	21	0
1979	36	16	0
1980	33	19	0
1981	24	28	0
1982	15	14	1
1983	26	26	0
1984	26	26	0
1985	27	25	0
1986	26	26	0
1987	23	22	1
1988	30	22	0
1989	24	28	0
1990	26	26	0
1991	19	33	0
1992	22	30	0
1993	27	25	0
1994	25	27	0
1995	27	33	0
Total	614	590	8

PRESEASON

	AFC	NFC	Tie
1970	21	28	1
1971	28	28	3
1972	27	25	4
1973	23	35	2
1974	35	25	0
1975	30	26	1
1976	30	31	0
1977	38	25	0
1978	20	19	0
1979	25	18	0
1980	22	20	1
1981	18	19	0
1982	25	16	0
1983	15	24	0
1984	16	19	0
1985	10	22	1
1986	22	17	0
1987	22	22	0
1988	23	16	1
1989	16	27	0
1990	15	29	0
1991	19	27	0
1992	30	22	0
1993	17	22	0
1994	22	16	0
1995	19	26	0
Total	588	604	14

RECORDS AFTER BYE WEEKS, 1990-95

AFC

Team	Record	Team	Record
Buffalo	6-1	Miami	6-1
Cincinnati	2-5	New England	2-5
Cleveland	2-5	N.Y. Jets	2-5
Denver	6-1	Oakland	3-4
Houston	4-3	Pittsburgh	4-3
Indianapolis	4-3	San Diego	4-3
Jacksonville	0-1	Seattle	1-6
Kansas City	5-2		

RECORDS AFTER BYE WEEKS, 1990-95

NFC

Team	Record	Team	Record
Arizona	4-3	New Orleans	3-4
Atlanta	6-1	N.Y. Giants	2-5
Carolina	0-1	Philadelphia	5-2
Chicago	5-2	St. Louis	3-4
Dallas	5-2	San Francisco	3-4
Detroit	4-3	Tampa Bay	1-6
Green Bay	2-5	Washington	1-6
Minnesota	6-1		

MONDAY NIGHT FOOTBALL, 1970-1995

(Home Team in capitals, games listed in chronological order.)

1995
Dallas 35, NEW YORK GIANTS 0
Green Bay 27, CHICAGO 24
MIAMI 23, Pittsburgh 10
DETROIT 27, San Francisco 24
Buffalo 22, CLEVELAND 19
KANSAS CITY 29, San Diego 23 (OT)
DENVER 27, Oakland 0
NEW ENGLAND 27, Buffalo 14
Chicago 14, MINNESOTA 6
DALLAS 34, Philadelphia 12
PITTSBURGH 20, Cleveland 3
San Francisco 44, MIAMI 20
SAN DIEGO 12, Oakland 6
DETROIT 27, Chicago 7
MIAMI 13, Kansas City 6
SAN FRANCISCO 37, Minnesota 30
Dallas 37, ARIZONA 13

1994
SAN FRANCISCO 44, Los Angeles Raiders 14
PHILADELPHIA 30, Chicago 22
Detroit 20, DALLAS 17 (OT)
BUFFALO 27, Denver 20
PITTSBURGH 30, Houston 14
Minnesota 27, NEW YORK GIANTS 10
Kansas City 31, DENVER 28
PHILADELPHIA 21, Houston 6
Green Bay 33, CHICAGO 6
DALLAS 38, New York Giants 10
PITTSBURGH 23, Buffalo 10
New York Giants 13, HOUSTON 10
San Francisco 35, NEW ORLEANS 14
Los Angeles Raiders 24, SAN DIEGO 17
MIAMI 45, Kansas City 28
Dallas 24, NEW ORLEANS 16
MINNESOTA 21, San Francisco 14

1993
WASHINGTON 35, Dallas 16
CLEVELAND 23, San Francisco 13
KANSAS CITY 15, Denver 7
Pittsburgh 45, ATLANTA 17
MIAMI 17, Washington 10
BUFFALO 35, Houston 7
Los Angeles Raiders 23, DENVER 20
Minnesota 19, CHICAGO 12
BUFFALO 24, Washington 10
KANSAS CITY 23, Green Bay 16
PITTSBURGH 23, Buffalo 0
SAN FRANCISCO 42, New Orleans 7
San Diego 31, INDIANAPOLIS 0
DALLAS 23, Philadelphia 17
Pittsburgh 21, MIAMI 20
New York Giants 24, NEW ORLEANS 14
SAN DIEGO 45, Miami 20
Philadelphia 37, SAN FRANCISCO 34 (OT)

1992
DALLAS 23, Washington 10
Miami 27, CLEVELAND 23
New York Giants 27, CHICAGO 14
KANSAS CITY 27, Los Angeles Raiders 7
PHILADELPHIA 31, Dallas 7
WASHINGTON 34, Denver 3
PITTSBURGH 20, Cincinnati 0
Buffalo 24, NEW YORK JETS 20
Minnesota 38, CHICAGO 10
San Francisco 41, ATLANTA 3
Buffalo 26, MIAMI 20
NEW ORLEANS 20, Washington 3
SEATTLE 16, Denver 13 (OT)
HOUSTON 24, Chicago 7
MIAMI 20, Los Angeles Raiders 7
Dallas 41, ATLANTA 17
SAN FRANCISCO 24, Detroit 6

1991
NEW YORK GIANTS 16, San Francisco 14
Washington 33, DALLAS 31
HOUSTON 17, Kansas City 7
CHICAGO 19, New York Jets 13 (OT)
WASHINGTON 23, Philadelphia 0
KANSAS CITY 33, Buffalo 6
New York Giants 23, PITTSBURGH 20
BUFFALO 35, Cincinnati 16
KANSAS CITY 24, Los Angeles Raiders 21
PHILADELPHIA 30, New York Giants 7
Chicago 34, MINNESOTA 17
Buffalo 41, MIAMI 27
San Francisco 33, LOS ANGELES RAMS 10
Philadelphia 13, HOUSTON 6
MIAMI 37, Cincinnati 13
NEW ORLEANS 27, Los Angeles Raiders 0
SAN FRANCISCO 52, Chicago 14

1990
San Francisco 13, NEW ORLEANS 12
DENVER 24, Kansas City 23
Buffalo 30, NEW YORK JETS 7
SEATTLE 31, Cincinnati 16
Cleveland 30, DENVER 29
PHILADELPHIA 32, Minnesota 24
Cincinnati 34, CLEVELAND 13
PITTSBURGH 41, Los Angeles Rams 10
New York Giants 24, INDIANAPOLIS 7
PHILADELPHIA 28, Washington 14
Los Angeles Raiders 13, MIAMI 10
HOUSTON 27, Buffalo 24
SAN FRANCISCO 7, New York Giants 3
Los Angeles Raiders 38, DETROIT 31
San Francisco 26, LOS ANGELES RAMS 10
NEW ORLEANS 20, Los Angeles Rams 17

1989
New York Giants 27, WASHINGTON 24
Denver 28, BUFFALO 14
CINCINNATI 21, Cleveland 14
CHICAGO 27, Philadelphia 13
Los Angeles Raiders 14, NEW YORK JETS 7
BUFFALO 23, Los Angeles Rams 20
CLEVELAND 27, Chicago 7
NEW YORK GIANTS 24, Minnesota 14
SAN FRANCISCO 31, New Orleans 13
HOUSTON 26, Cincinnati 24
Denver 14, WASHINGTON 10
SAN FRANCISCO 34, New York Giants 24
SEATTLE 17, Buffalo 16
San Francisco 30, LOS ANGELES RAMS 27
NEW ORLEANS 30, Philadelphia 20
MINNESOTA 29, Cincinnati 21

1988
NEW YORK GIANTS 27, Washington 20
Dallas 17, PHOENIX 14
CLEVELAND 23, Indianapolis 17
Los Angeles Raiders 30, DENVER 27 (OT)
NEW ORLEANS 20, Dallas 17
PHILADELPHIA 24, New York Giants 13
Buffalo 37, NEW YORK JETS 14
CHICAGO 10, San Francisco 9
INDIANAPOLIS 55, Denver 23
HOUSTON 24, Cleveland 17
Buffalo 31, MIAMI 6
SAN FRANCISCO 37, Washington 21
SEATTLE 35, Los Angeles Raiders 27
LOS ANGELES RAMS 23, Chicago 3
MIAMI 38, Cleveland 31
MINNESOTA 28, Chicago 27

1987
CHICAGO 34, New York Giants 19
NEW YORK JETS 43, New England 24
San Francisco 41, NEW YORK GIANTS 21
DENVER 30, Los Angeles Raiders 14
Washington 13, DALLAS 7
CLEVELAND 30, Los Angeles Rams 17
MINNESOTA 34, Denver 27
DALLAS 33, New York Giants 24
NEW YORK JETS 30, Seattle 14
DENVER 31, Chicago 29
Los Angeles Rams 30, WASHINGTON 26
Los Angeles Raiders 37, SEATTLE 14
MIAMI 37, New York Jets 28
SAN FRANCISCO 41, Chicago 0
Dallas 29, LOS ANGELES RAMS 21
New England 24, MIAMI 10

1986
DALLAS 31, New York Giants 28
Denver 21, PITTSBURGH 10
Chicago 25, GREEN BAY 12
Dallas 31, ST. LOUIS 7
SEATTLE 33, San Diego 7
CINCINNATI 24, Pittsburgh 22
NEW YORK JETS 22, Denver 10
NEW YORK GIANTS 27, Washington 20
Los Angeles Rams 20, CHICAGO 17
CLEVELAND 26, Miami 16
WASHINGTON 14, San Francisco 6
MIAMI 45, New York Jets 3
New York Giants 21, SAN FRANCISCO 17
SEATTLE 37, Los Angeles Raiders 0
Chicago 16, DETROIT 13
New England 34, MIAMI 27

1985
DALLAS 44, Washington 14
CLEVELAND 17, Pittsburgh 7
Los Angeles Rams 35, SEATTLE 24
Cincinnati 37, PITTSBURGH 24
WASHINGTON 27, St. Louis 10
NEW YORK JETS 23, Miami 7
CHICAGO 23, Green Bay 7
LOS ANGELES RAIDERS 34, San Diego 21
ST. LOUIS 21, Dallas 10
DENVER 17, San Francisco 16
WASHINGTON 23, New York Giants 21
SAN FRANCISCO 19, Seattle 6
MIAMI 38, Chicago 24
Los Angeles Rams 27, SAN FRANCISCO 20
MIAMI 30, New England 27
L.A. Raiders 16, L.A. RAMS 6

1984
Dallas 20, LOS ANGELES RAMS 13
SAN FRANCISCO 37, Washington 31
Miami 21, BUFFALO 17
LOS ANGELES RAIDERS 33, San Diego 30
PITTSBURGH 38, Cincinnati 17
San Francisco 31, NEW YORK GIANTS 10
DENVER 17, Green Bay 14
Los Angeles Rams 24, ATLANTA 10
Seattle 24, SAN DIEGO 0
WASHINGTON 27, Atlanta 14
SEATTLE 17, Los Angeles Raiders 14
NEW ORLEANS 27, Pittsburgh 24
MIAMI 28, New York Jets 17
SAN DIEGO 20, Chicago 7
Los Angeles Raiders 24, DETROIT 3
MIAMI 28, Dallas 21

MONDAY NIGHT FOOTBALL

1983
Dallas 31, WASHINGTON 30
San Diego 17, KANSAS CITY 14
LOS ANGELES RAIDERS 27, Miami 14
NEW YORK GIANTS 27, Green Bay 3
New York Jets 34, BUFFALO 10
Pittsburgh 24, CINCINNATI 14
GREEN BAY 48, Washington 47
ST. LOUIS 20, New York Giants 20 (OT)
Washington 27, SAN DIEGO 24
DETROIT 15, New York Giants 9
Los Angeles Rams 36, ATLANTA 13
New York Jets 31, NEW ORLEANS 28
MIAMI 38, Cincinnati 14
DETROIT 13, Minnesota 2
Green Bay 12, TAMPA BAY 9 (OT)
SAN FRANCISCO 42, Dallas 17

1982
Pittsburgh 36, DALLAS 28
Green Bay 27, NEW YORK GIANTS 19
LOS ANGELES RAIDERS 28, San Diego 24
TAMPA BAY 23, Miami 17
New York Jets 28, DETROIT 13
Dallas 37, HOUSTON 7
SAN DIEGO 50, Cincinnati 34
MIAMI 27, Buffalo 10
MINNESOTA 31, Dallas 27

1981
San Diego 44, CLEVELAND 14
Oakland 36, MINNESOTA 10
Dallas 35, NEW ENGLAND 21
Los Angeles 24, CHICAGO 7
PHILADELPHIA 16, Atlanta 13
BUFFALO 31, Miami 21
DETROIT 48, Chicago 17
PITTSBURGH 26, Houston 13
DENVER 19, Minnesota 17
DALLAS 27, Buffalo 14
SEATTLE 44, San Diego 23
ATLANTA 31, Minnesota 30
MIAMI 13, Philadelphia 10
OAKLAND 30, Pittsburgh 27
LOS ANGELES 21, Atlanta 16
SAN DIEGO 23, Oakland 10

1980
Dallas 17, WASHINGTON 3
Houston 16, CLEVELAND 7
PHILADELPHIA 35, New York Giants 3
NEW ENGLAND 23, Denver 14
CHICAGO 23, Tampa Bay 0
DENVER 20, Washington 17
Oakland 45, PITTSBURGH 34
NEW YORK JETS 17, Miami 14
CLEVELAND 27, Chicago 21
HOUSTON 38, New England 34
Oakland 19, SEATTLE 17
Los Angeles 27, NEW ORLEANS 7
OAKLAND 9, Denver 3
MIAMI 16, New England 13 (OT)
LOS ANGELES 38, Dallas 14
SAN DIEGO 26, Pittsburgh 17

1979
Pittsburgh 16, NEW ENGLAND 13 (OT)
Atlanta 14, PHILADELPHIA 10
WASHINGTON 27, New York Giants 0
CLEVELAND 26, Dallas 7
GREEN BAY 27, New England 14
OAKLAND 13, Miami 3
NEW YORK JETS 14, Minnesota 7
PITTSBURGH 42, Denver 7
Seattle 31, ATLANTA 28
Houston 9, MIAMI 6
Philadelphia 31, DALLAS 21
LOS ANGELES 20, Atlanta 14
SEATTLE 30, New York Jets 7
Oakland 42, NEW ORLEANS 35
HOUSTON 20, Pittsburgh 17
SAN DIEGO 17, Denver 7

1978
DALLAS 38, Baltimore 0
MINNESOTA 12, Denver 9 (OT)
Baltimore 34, NEW ENGLAND 27
Minnesota 24, CHICAGO 20
WASHINGTON 9, Dallas 5
MIAMI 21, Cincinnati 0
DENVER 16, Chicago 7
Houston 24, PITTSBURGH 17
ATLANTA 15, Los Angeles 7
BALTIMORE 21, Washington 17
Oakland 34, CINCINNATI 21
HOUSTON 35, Miami 30
Pittsburgh 24, SAN FRANCISCO 7
SAN DIEGO 40, Chicago 7
Cincinnati 20, LOS ANGELES 19
MIAMI 23, New England 3

1977
PITTSBURGH 27, San Francisco 0
CLEVELAND 30, New England 27 (OT)
Oakland 37, KANSAS CITY 28
CHICAGO 24, Los Angeles 23
PITTSBURGH 20, Cincinnati 14
LOS ANGELES 35, Minnesota 3
ST. LOUIS 28, New York Giants 0
BALTIMORE 10, Washington 3
St. Louis 24, DALLAS 17
WASHINGTON 10, Green Bay 9
OAKLAND 34, Buffalo 13
MIAMI 17, Baltimore 6
Dallas 42, SAN FRANCISCO 35

1976
Miami 30, BUFFALO 21
Oakland 24, KANSAS CITY 21
Washington 20, PHILADELPHIA 17 (OT)
MINNESOTA 17, Pittsburgh 6
San Francisco 16, LOS ANGELES 0
NEW ENGLAND 41, New York Jets 7
WASHINGTON 20, St. Louis 10
BALTIMORE 38, Houston 14
CINCINNATI 20, Los Angeles 12
DALLAS 17, Buffalo 10
Baltimore 17, MIAMI 16
SAN FRANCISCO 20, Minnesota 16
OAKLAND 35, Cincinnati 20

1975
Oakland 31, MIAMI 21
DENVER 23, Green Bay 13
Dallas 36, DETROIT 10
WASHINGTON 27, St. Louis 17
New York Giants 17, BUFFALO 14
Minnesota 13, CHICAGO 9
Los Angeles 42, PHILADELPHIA 3
Kansas City 34, DALLAS 31
CINCINNATI 33, Buffalo 24
Pittsburgh 32, HOUSTON 9
MIAMI 20, New England 7
OAKLAND 17, Denver 10
SAN DIEGO 24, New York Jets 16

1974
BUFFALO 21, Oakland 20
PHILADELPHIA 13, Dallas 10
WASHINGTON 30, Denver 3
MIAMI 21, New York Jets 17
DETROIT 17, San Francisco 13
CHICAGO 10, Green Bay 9
PITTSBURGH 24, Atlanta 17
Los Angeles 15, SAN FRANCISCO 13
Minnesota 28, ST. LOUIS 24
Kansas City 42, DENVER 34
Pittsburgh 28, NEW ORLEANS 7
MIAMI 24, Cincinnati 3
Washington 23, LOS ANGELES 17

1973
GREEN BAY 23, New York Jets 7
DALLAS 40, New Orleans 3
DETROIT 31, Atlanta 6
WASHINGTON 14, Dallas 7
Miami 17, CLEVELAND 9
DENVER 23, Oakland 23
BUFFALO 23, Kansas City 14
PITTSBURGH 21, Washington 16
KANSAS CITY 19, Chicago 7
ATLANTA 20, Minnesota 14
SAN FRANCISCO 20, Green Bay 6
MIAMI 30, Pittsburgh 26
LOS ANGELES 40, New York Giants 6

1972
Washington 24, MINNESOTA 21
Kansas City 20, NEW ORLEANS 17
New York Giants 27, PHILADELPHIA 12
Oakland 34, HOUSTON 0
Green Bay 24, DETROIT 23
CHICAGO 13, Minnesota 10
DALLAS 28, Detroit 24
Baltimore 24, NEW ENGLAND 17
Cleveland 21, SAN DIEGO 17
WASHINGTON 24, Atlanta 13
MIAMI 31, St. Louis 10
Los Angeles 26, SAN FRANCISCO 16
OAKLAND 24, New York Jets 16

1971
Minnesota 16, DETROIT 13
ST. LOUIS 17, New York Jets 10
Oakland 34, CLEVELAND 20
DALLAS 20, New York Giants 13
KANSAS CITY 38, Pittsburgh 16
MINNESOTA 10, Baltimore 3
GREEN BAY 14, Detroit 14
BALTIMORE 24, Los Angeles 17
SAN DIEGO 20, St. Louis 17
ATLANTA 28, Green Bay 21
MIAMI 34, Chicago 3
Kansas City 26, SAN FRANCISCO 17
Washington 38, LOS ANGELES 24

1970
CLEVELAND 31, New York Jets 21
Kansas City 44, BALTIMORE 24
DETROIT 28, Chicago 14
Green Bay 22, SAN DIEGO 20
OAKLAND 34, Washington 20
MINNESOTA 13, Los Angeles 3
PITTSBURGH 21, Cincinnati 10
Baltimore 13, GREEN BAY 10
St. Louis 38, DALLAS 0
PHILADELPHIA 23, New York Giants 20
Miami 20, ATLANTA 7
Cleveland 21, HOUSTON 10
Detroit 28, LOS ANGELES 23

MONDAY NIGHT WON-LOST RECORDS, 1970-1995

AMERICAN FOOTBALL CONFERENCE

	Buff.	Cin.	Clev.	Den.	Hou.	Ind.	Jax.	K.C.	Mia.	N.E.	N.Y.J.	Oak.	Pitt.	S.D.	Sea.
Total	15-16	7-16	13-11	13-19-1	11-11	9-7	0-0	14-8	31-20	5-12	9-16	31-13-1	22-15	13-11	11-5
1995	1-1		0-2	1-0				1-1	2-1	1-0		0-2	1-1	1-1	
1994	1-1			0-2	0-3			1-1	1-0			1-1	2-0	0-1	
1993	2-1		1-0	0-2	0-1	0-1		2-0	1-2			1-0	3-0	2-0	
1992	2-0	0-1	0-1	0-2	1-0			1-0	2-1		0-1	0-2	1-0		1-0
1991	2-1	0-2			1-1			2-1	1-1		0-1	0-2	0-1		
1990	1-1	1-1	1-1	1-1	1-0	0-1		0-1	0-1		0-1	2-0	1-0		1-0
1989	1-2	1-2	1-1	2-0	1-0						0-1	1-0			1-0
1988	2-0		1-2	0-2	1-0	1-1			1-1		0-1	1-1			1-0
1987			1-0	2-1					1-1	1-1	2-1	1-1		0-2	
1986		1-0	1-0	1-1					1-2	1-0	1-1	0-1	0-2	0-1	2-0
1985		1-0	1-0	1-0					2-1	0-1	1-0	2-0	0-2	0-1	0-2
1984	0-1	0-1		1-0					3-0		0-1	2-1	1-1	1-2	2-0
1983	0-1	0-2						0-1	1-1		2-0	1-0	1-0	1-1	
1982	0-1	0-1			0-1				1-1		1-0	1-0	1-0	1-1	
1981	1-1		0-1	1-0	0-1				1-1	0-1		2-1	1-1	2-1	1-0
1980			1-1	1-2	2-0				1-1	1-2	1-0	3-0	0-2	1-0	0-1
1979			1-0	0-2	2-0				0-2	0-2	1-1	2-0	2-1	1-0	2-0
1978		1-2		1-1	2-0	2-1			2-1	0-2		1-0	1-1	1-0	
1977	0-1	0-1	1-0			1-1		0-1	1-0	0-1		2-0	2-0		
1976	0-2	1-1			0-1	2-0		0-1	1-1	1-0	0-1	2-0	0-1		
1975	0-2	1-0		1-1	0-1			1-0	1-1	0-1	0-1	2-0	1-0	1-0	
1974	1-0	0-1		0-2				1-0	2-0		0-1	0-1	2-0		
1973	1-0		0-1	0-0-1				1-1	2-0		0-1	0-0-1	1-1		
1972			1-0		0-1	1-0		1-0	1-0	0-1	0-1	2-0		0-1	
1971			0-1			1-1		2-0	1-0		0-1	1-0	0-1	1-0	
1970		0-1	2-0		0-1	1-1		1-0	1-0		0-1	1-0	1-0	0-1	

NATIONAL FOOTBALL CONFERENCE

	Ariz.	Atl.	Car.	Chi.	Dall.	Det.	G.B.	Minn.	N.O.	N.Y.G.	Phil.	St. L.	S.F.	T.B.	Wash.
Total	5-9-1	5-14	0-0	13-27	27-20	10-9-1	9-11-1	16-15	6-12	14-21-1	14-10	17-20	25-16	1-2	22-21
1995	0-1			1-2	3-0	2-0	1-0	0-2		0-1	0-1		2-1		
1994				0-2	2-1	1-0	1-0	2-0	0-2	1-2	2-0		2-1		
1993		0-1		0-1	1-1		0-1	1-0	0-2	1-0	1-1		1-2		1-2
1992		0-2		0-3	2-1	0-1		1-0	1-0	1-0	1-0		2-0		1-2
1991				2-1	0-1			0-1	1-0	2-1	2-1	0-1	2-1		2-0
1990						0-1		0-1	1-1	1-1	2-0	0-3	3-0		0-1
1989				1-1				1-1	1-1	2-1	0-2	0-2	3-0		0-2
1988	0-1			1-2	1-1			1-0	1-0	1-0	1-1	1-0	1-1		0-2
1987				1-2	2-1			1-0		0-3		1-2	2-0		1-1
1986	0-1			2-1	2-0	0-1	0-1			2-1		1-0	0-2		1-1
1985	1-1			1-1	1-1		0-1			0-1		2-1	1-2		2-1
1984		0-2		0-1	1-1	0-1	0-1		1-0	0-1		1-1	2-0		1-1
1983	0-0-1	0-1			1-1	2-0	2-1	0-1	0-1	1-1-1		1-0	1-0	0-1	1-2
1982					1-2	0-1	1-0	1-0		0-1				1-0	
1981		1-2		0-2	2-0	1-0		0-3			1-1	2-0			
1980				1-1	1-1				0-1	0-1	1-0	2-0		0-1	0-2
1979		1-2			0-2		1-0	0-1	0-1	0-1	1-1	1-0			1-0
1978	2-0	1-0		0-3	1-1			2-0				0-2	0-1		1-1
1977	0-1			1-0	1-1		0-1	0-1		0-1		1-1	0-2		1-1
1976	0-1				1-0			1-1			0-1	0-2	2-0		2-0
1975	0-1			0-1	1-1	0-1	0-1	1-0		1-0	0-1	1-0			1-0
1974		0-1		1-0	0-1	1-0	0-1	1-0	0-1		1-0	1-1	0-2		2-0
1973	0-1	1-1		0-1	1-1	1-0	1-1	0-1	0-1	0-1		1-0	1-0		1-1
1972	1-1	0-1		1-0	1-0	0-2	1-0	0-2	0-1	1-0	0-1	1-0	0-1		2-0
1971	1-0	1-0		0-1	1-0	0-1-1	0-1-1	2-0		0-1		0-2	0-1		1-0
1970		0-1		0-1	0-1	2-0	1-1	1-0		0-1	1-0	0-2			0-1

THURSDAY-SUNDAY NIGHT FOOTBALL

THURSDAY-SUNDAY NIGHT FOOTBALL, 1974-1995

(Home Team in capitals, games listed in chronological order.)

1995
DENVER 22, Buffalo 7 (Sun.)
Philadelphia 31, ARIZONA 19 (Sun.)
Dallas 23, MINNESOTA 17 (OT) (Sun.)
Green Bay 24, JACKSONVILLE 14 (Sun.)
Oakland 47, NEW YORK JETS 10 (Sun.)
Denver 37, NEW ENGLAND 3 (Sun.)
ST. LOUIS 21, Atlanta 19 (Thurs.)
Cincinnati 27, PITTSBURGH 9 (Thurs.)
New York Giants 24, WASHINGTON 15 (Sun.)
Miami 24, SAN DIEGO 14 (Sun.)
PHILADELPHIA 31, Denver 13 (Sun.)
KANSAS CITY 20, Houston 13 (Sun.)
NEW ORLEANS 34, Carolina 26 (Sun.)
New York Giants 10, ARIZONA 6 (Thurs.)
SAN FRANCISCO 27, Buffalo 17 (Sun.)
TAMPA BAY 13, Green Bay 10 (OT) (Sun.)
SEATTLE 44, Oakland 10 (Sun.)
INDIANAPOLIS 10, New England 7 (Sat.)

1994
San Diego 17, DENVER 34 (Sun.)
New York Giants 20, ARIZONA 17 (Sun.)
Kansas City 30, ATLANTA 10 (Sun.)
Chicago 19, NEW YORK JETS 7 (Sun.)
Miami 23, CINCINNATI 7 (Sun.)
PHILADELPHIA 21, Washington 17 (Sun.)
Cleveland 11, HOUSTON 8 (Thurs.)
MINNESOTA 13, Green Bay 10 (OT) (Thurs.)
ARIZONA 20, Pittsburgh 17 (OT) (Sun.)
KANSAS CITY 13, Los Angeles Raiders 3 (Sun.)
DETROIT 14, Tampa Bay 9 (Sun.)
SAN FRANCISCO 31, Los Angeles Rams 27 (Sun.)
New England 12, INDIANAPOLIS 10 (Sun.)
MINNESOTA 33, Chicago 27 (OT) (Thurs.)
Buffalo 42, MIAMI 31 (Sun.)
New Orleans 29, ATLANTA 20 (Sun.)
Los Angeles Raiders 17, SEATTLE 16 (Sun.)
MIAMI 27, Detroit 20 (Sun.)

1993
NEW ORLEANS 33, Houston 21 (Sun.)
Los Angeles Raiders 17, SEATTLE 13 (Sun.)
Dallas 17, PHOENIX 10 (Sun.)
NEW YORK JETS 45, New England 7 (Sun.)
BUFFALO 17, New York Giants 14 (Sun.)
GREEN BAY 30, Denver 27 (Sun.)
ATLANTA 30, Los Angeles Rams 24 (Thurs.)
MIAMI 41, Indianapolis 27 (Sun.)
Detroit 30, MINNESOTA 27 (Sun.)
WASHINGTON 30, Indianapolis 24 (Sun.)
Chicago 16, SAN DIEGO 13 (Sun.)
TAMPA BAY 23, Minnesota 10 (Sun.)
HOUSTON 23, Pittsburgh 3 (Sun.)
SAN FRANCISCO 21, Cincinnati 8 (Sun.)
Green Bay 20, SAN DIEGO 13 (Sun.)
Philadelphia 20, INDIANAPOLIS 10 (Sun.)
MINNESOTA 30, Kansas City 10 (Sun.)
HOUSTON 24, New York Jets 0 (Sun.)

1992
DENVER 17, Los Angeles Raiders 13 (Sun.)
Philadelphia 31, PHOENIX 14 (Sun.)
BUFFALO 38, Indianapolis 0 (Sun.)
San Francisco 16, NEW ORLEANS 10 (Sun.)
NEW YORK JETS 30, New England 21 (Sun.)
NEW ORLEANS 13, Los Angeles Rams 10 (Sun.)
MINNESOTA 31, Detroit 14 (Thurs.)
Pittsburgh 27, KANSAS CITY 3 (Sun.)
New York Giants 24, WASHINGTON 7 (Sun.)
Cincinnati 31, CHICAGO 28 (OT) (Sun.)
DENVER 27, New York Giants 13 (Sun.)
Kansas City 24, SEATTLE 14 (Sun.)
SAN DIEGO 27, Los Angeles Raiders 3 (Sun.)
NEW ORLEANS 22, Atlanta 14 (Thurs.)
Los Angeles Rams 31, TAMPA BAY 27 (Sun.)
Green Bay 16, HOUSTON 14 (Sun.)
MIAMI 19, New York Jets 17 (Sun.)
HOUSTON 27, Buffalo 3 (Sun.)

1991
WASHINGTON 45, Detroit 0 (Sun.)
Houston 30, CINCINNATI 7 (Sun.)
NEW ORLEANS 24, Los Angeles Rams 7 (Sun.)
Dallas 17, PHOENIX 9 (Sun.)
Denver 13, MINNESOTA 6 (Sun.)
Pittsburgh 21, INDIANAPOLIS 3 (Sun.)
Los Angeles Raiders 23, SEATTLE 20 (Sun.)
Chicago 10, GREEN BAY 0 (Thurs.)
Washington 17, NEW YORK GIANTS 13 (Sun.)
DENVER 20, Pittsburgh 13 (Sun.)
MIAMI 30, New England 20 (Sun.)
HOUSTON 28, Cleveland 24 (Sun.)
Atlanta 23, NEW ORLEANS 20 (OT) (Sun.)
Los Angeles Raiders 9, SAN DIEGO 7 (Sun.)
Minnesota 26, TAMPA BAY 24 (Sun.)
Buffalo 35, INDIANAPOLIS 7 (Sun.)
SEATTLE 23, Los Angeles Rams 9 (Sun.)

1990
NEW YORK GIANTS 27, Philadelphia 20 (Sun.)
PITTSBURGH 20, Houston 9 (Sun.)
TAMPA BAY 23, Detroit 20 (Sun.)
Washington 38, PHOENIX 10 (Sun.)
BUFFALO 38, Los Angeles Raiders 24 (Sun.)
CHICAGO 38, Los Angeles Rams 9 (Sun.)
MIAMI 17, New England 10 (Thurs.)
ATLANTA 38, Cincinnati 17 (Sun.)
MINNESOTA 27, Denver 22 (Sun.)
San Francisco 24, DALLAS 6 (Sun.)
CINCINNATI 27, Pittsburgh 3 (Sun.)
Seattle 13, SAN DIEGO 10 (Sun.)
MINNESOTA 23, Green Bay 7 (Sun.)
MIAMI 23, Philadelphia 20 (Sun.)
DETROIT 38, Chicago 21 (Sun.)
INDIANAPOLIS 35, Washington 28 (Sat.)
SEATTLE 17, Denver 12 (Sun.)
HOUSTON 34, Pittsburgh 14 (Sun.)

1989
Dallas 13, WASHINGTON 3 (Sun.)
SAN DIEGO 14, Los Angeles Raiders 12 (Sun.)
INDIANAPOLIS 27, New York Jets 10 (Sun.)
Los Angeles Rams 20, NEW ORLEANS 17 (Sun.)
MINNESOTA 27, Chicago 16 (Sun.)
MIAMI 31, New England 10 (Sun.)
SEATTLE 23, Los Angeles Raiders 17 (Sun.)
Cleveland 24, HOUSTON 20 (Sat.)

1988
HOUSTON 41, Washington 17 (Sun.)
Los Angeles Raiders 13, SAN DIEGO 3 (Sun.)
Minnesota 34, DALLAS 3 (Sun.)
New England 6, MIAMI 3 (Sun.)
New York Giants 13, NEW ORLEANS 12 (Sun.)
Pittsburgh 37, HOUSTON 34 (Sun.)
SEATTLE 42, Denver 14 (Sun.)
Los Angeles Rams 38, SAN FRANCISCO 16 (Sun.)

1987
NEW YORK GIANTS 17, New England 10 (Sun.)
SAN DIEGO 16, Los Angeles Raiders 14 (Sun.)
Miami 20, DALLAS 14 (Sun.)
SAN FRANCISCO 38, Cleveland 24 (Sun.)
Chicago 30, MINNESOTA 24 (Sun.)
SEATTLE 28, Denver 21 (Sun.)
MIAMI 23, Washington 21 (Sun.)
SAN FRANCISCO 48, Los Angeles Rams 0 (Sun.)

1986
New England 20, NEW YORK JETS 6 (Thurs.)
Cincinnati 30, CLEVELAND 13 (Thurs.)
Los Angeles Raiders 37, SAN DIEGO 31 (OT) (Thurs.)
LOS ANGELES RAMS 29, Dallas 10 (Sun.)
SAN FRANCISCO 24, Los Angeles Rams 14 (Fri.)

1985
KANSAS CITY 36, Los Angeles Raiders 20 (Thurs.)
Chicago 33, MINNESOTA 24 (Thurs.)
Dallas 30, NEW YORK GIANTS 29 (Sun.)
SAN DIEGO 54, Pittsburgh 44 (Sun.)
Denver 27, SEATTLE 24 (Fri.)

1984
Pittsburgh 23, NEW YORK JETS 17 (Thurs.)
Denver 24, CLEVELAND 14 (Sun.)
DALLAS 30, New Orleans 27 (Sun.)
Washington 31, MINNESOTA 17 (Thurs.)
SAN FRANCISCO 19, Los Angeles Rams 16 (Fri.)

1983
San Francisco 48, MINNESOTA 17 (Thurs.)
CLEVELAND 17, Cincinnati 7 (Thurs.)
Los Angeles Raiders 40, DALLAS 38 (Sun.)
Los Angeles Raiders 42, SAN DIEGO 10 (Thurs.)
MIAMI 34, New York Jets 14 (Fri.)

1982
BUFFALO 23, Minnesota 22 (Thurs.)
SAN FRANCISCO 30, Los Angeles Rams 24 (Thurs.)
ATLANTA 17, San Francisco 7 (Sun.)

1981
MIAMI 30, Pittsburgh 10 (Thurs.)
Philadelphia 20, BUFFALO 14 (Thurs.)
DALLAS 29, Los Angeles 17 (Sun.)
HOUSTON 17, Cleveland 13 (Thurs.)

1980
TAMPA BAY 10, Los Angeles 9 (Thurs.)
DALLAS 42, San Diego 31 (Sun.)
San Diego 27, MIAMI 24 (OT) (Thurs.)
HOUSTON 6, Pittsburgh 0 (Thurs.)

1979
Los Angeles 13, DENVER 9 (Thurs.)
DALLAS 30, Los Angeles 6 (Sun.)
OAKLAND 45, San Diego 22 (Thurs.)
MIAMI 39, New England 24 (Thurs.)

1978
New England 21, OAKLAND 14 (Sun.)
Minnesota 21, DALLAS 10 (Thurs.)
LOS ANGELES 10, Pittsburgh 7 (Sun.)
Denver 21, OAKLAND 6 (Sun.)

1977
Minnesota 30, DETROIT 21 (Sat.)

1976
Los Angeles 20, DETROIT 17 (Sat.)

1975
LOS ANGELES 10, Pittsburgh 3 (Sat.)

1974
OAKLAND 27, Dallas 23 (Sat.)

HISTORY OF OVERTIME GAMES

PRESEASON

Aug. 28, 1955	Los Angeles 23, New York Giants 17, at Portland, Oregon
Aug. 24, 1962	Denver 27, Dallas Texans 24, at Fort Worth, Texas
Aug. 10, 1974	San Diego 20, New York Jets 14, at San Diego
Aug. 17, 1974	Pittsburgh 33, Philadelphia 30, at Philadelphia
Aug. 17, 1974	Dallas 19, Houston 13, at Dallas
Aug. 17, 1974	Cincinnati 13, Atlanta 7, at Atlanta
Sept. 6, 1974	Buffalo 23, New York Giants 17, at Buffalo
Aug. 9, 1975	Baltimore 23, Denver 20, at Denver
Aug. 30, 1975	New England 20, Green Bay 17, at Milwaukee
Sept. 13, 1975	Minnesota 14, San Diego 14, at San Diego
Aug. 1, 1976	New England 13, New York Giants 7, at New England
Aug. 2, 1976	Kansas City 9, Houston 3, at Kansas City
Aug. 20, 1976	New Orleans 26, Baltimore 20, at Baltimore
Sept. 4, 1976	Dallas 26, Houston 20, at Dallas
Aug. 13, 1977	Seattle 23, Dallas 17, at Seattle
Aug. 28, 1977	New England 13, Pittsburgh 10, at New England
Aug. 28, 1977	New York Giants 24, Buffalo 21, at East Rutherford, N.J.
Aug. 2, 1979	Seattle 12, Minnesota 9, at Minnesota
Aug. 4, 1979	Los Angeles 20, Oakland 14, at Los Angeles
Aug. 24, 1979	Denver 20, New England 17, at Denver
Aug. 23, 1980	Tampa Bay 20, Cincinnati 14, at Tampa Bay
Aug. 5, 1981	San Francisco 27, Seattle 24, at Seattle
Aug. 29, 1981	New Orleans 20, Detroit 17, at New Orleans
Aug. 28, 1982	Miami 17, Kansas City 17, at Kansas City
Sept. 3, 1982	Miami 16, New York Giants 13, at Miami
Aug. 6, 1983	L.A. Raiders 26, San Francisco 23, at Los Angeles
Aug. 6, 1983	Atlanta 13, Washington 10, at Atlanta
Aug. 13, 1983	St. Louis 27, Chicago 24, at St. Louis
Aug. 18, 1983	New York Jets 20, Cincinnati 17, at Cincinnati
Aug. 27, 1983	Chicago 20, Kansas City 17, at Chicago
Aug. 11, 1984	Pittsburgh 20, Philadelphia 17, at Pittsburgh
Aug. 9, 1985	Buffalo 10, Detroit 10, at Pontiac, Mich.
Aug. 10, 1985	Minnesota 16, Miami 13, at Miami
Aug. 17, 1985	Dallas 27, San Diego 24, at San Diego
Aug. 24, 1985	N.Y. Giants 34, N.Y. Jets 31, at East Rutherford, N.J.
Aug. 15, 1986	Washington 27, Pittsburgh 24, at Washington
Aug. 15, 1986	Detroit 30, Seattle 27, at Detroit
Aug. 23, 1986	Los Angeles Rams 20, San Diego 17, at Anaheim
Aug. 30, 1986	Minnesota 23, Indianapolis 20, at Indianapolis
Aug. 23, 1987	Philadelphia 19, New England 13, at New England
Sept. 5, 1987	Cleveland 30, Green Bay 24, at Milwaukee
Sept. 6, 1987	Kansas City 13, St. Louis 10, at Memphis, Tenn.
Aug. 11, 1988	Seattle 16, Detroit 13, at Detroit
Aug. 19, 1988	Miami 16, Denver 13, at Miami
Aug. 19, 1988	Green Bay 21, Kansas City 21, at Milwaukee
Aug. 20, 1988	Houston 20, Los Angeles Rams 17, at Anaheim
Aug. 21, 1988	Minnesota 19, Phoenix 16, at Phoenix
Aug. 5, 1989	Los Angeles Rams 16, San Francisco 13, at Tokyo, Japan
Aug. 26, 1989	Denver 24, Dallas 21, at Denver
Sept. 1, 1989	N.Y. Jets 15, Kansas City 13, at Kansas City
Aug. 24, 1990	Cincinnati 13, New England 10, at New England
Aug. 16, 1991	Cleveland 24, Washington 21, at Washington
Aug. 17, 1991	Cincinnati 27, Minnesota 24, at Cincinnati
Aug. 23, 1991	Dallas 20, Atlanta 17, at Dallas
Aug. 24, 1991	Cincinnati 19, Green Bay 16, at Green Bay
Aug. 22, 1992	Los Angeles Rams 16, Green Bay 13, at Anaheim
Aug. 8, 1993	Dallas 13, Detroit 13, at London, England
Aug. 12, 1995	Washington 16, Houston 13, at Knoxville, Tenn.
Aug. 19, 1995	Indianapolis 20, Green Bay 17, at Green Bay

REGULAR SEASON

Sept. 22, 1974—Pittsburgh 35, Denver 35, at Denver; Steelers win toss. Gilliam's pass intercepted and returned by Rowser to Denver's 42. Turner misses 41-yard field goal. Walden punts and Greer returns to Broncos' 39. Van Heusen punts and Edwards returns to Steelers' 16. Game ends with Steelers on own 26.

Nov. 10, 1974—New York Jets 26, New York Giants 20, at New Haven, Conn.; Giants win toss. Gogolak misses 42-yard field goal. Namath passes to Boozer for five yards and.touchdown at 6:53.

Sept. 28, 1975—Dallas 37, St. Louis 31, at Dallas; Cardinals win toss. Hart's pass intercepted and returned by Jordan to Cardinals' 37. Staubach passes to DuPree for three yards and touchdown at 7:53.

Oct. 12, 1975—Los Angeles 13, San Diego 10, at San Diego; Chargers win toss. Partee punts to Rams' 14. Dempsey kicks 22-yard field goal at 9:27.

Nov. 2, 1975—Washington 30, Dallas 24, at Washington; Cowboys win toss. Staubach's pass intercepted and returned by Houston to Cowboys' 35. Kilmer runs one yard for touchdown at 6:34.

Nov. 16, 1975—St. Louis 20, Washington 17, at St. Louis; Cardinals win toss. Bakken kicks 37-yard field goal at 7:00.

Nov. 23, 1975—Kansas City 24, Detroit 21, at Kansas City; Lions win toss. Chiefs take over on downs at own 38. Stenerud kicks 26-yard field goal at 6:44.

Nov. 23, 1975—Oakland 26, Washington 23, at Washington; Redskins win toss. Bragg punts to Raiders' 42. Blanda kicks 27-yard field goal at 7:13.

Nov. 30, 1975—Denver 13, San Diego 10, at Denver; Broncos win toss. Turner kicks 25-yard field goal at 4:13.

Nov. 30, 1975—Oakland 37, Atlanta 34, at Oakland; Falcons win toss. James punts to Raiders' 16. Guy punts and Herron returns to Falcons' 41. Nick Mike-Mayer misses 45-yard field goal. Guy punts into Falcons' end zone. James punts to Raiders' 39. Blanda kicks 36-yard field goal at 15:00.

Dec. 14, 1975—Baltimore 10, Miami 7, at Baltimore; Dolphins win toss. Seiple punts to Colts' 4. Linhart kicks 31-yard field goal at 12:44.

Sept. 19, 1976—Minnesota 10, Los Angeles 10, at Minnesota; Vikings win toss. Tarkenton's pass intercepted by Monte Jackson and returned to Minnesota 16. Allen blocks Dempsey's 30-yard field goal attempt, ball rolls into end zone for touchback. Clabo punts and Scribner returns to Rams' 20. Rusty Jackson punts to Vikings' 35. Tarkenton's pass intercepted by Kay at Rams' 1, no return. Game ends with Rams on own 3.

***Sept. 27, 1976—Washington 20, Philadelphia 17,** at Philadelphia; Eagles win toss. Jones punts and E. Brown loses one yard on return to Redskins' 40. Bragg punts 51 yards into end zone for touchback. Jones punts and E. Brown returns to Redskins' 42. Bragg punts and Marshall returns to Eagles' 41. Boryla's pass intercepted by Dusek at Redskins' 37, no return. Bragg punts and Bradley returns. Philadelphia holding penalty moves ball back to Eagles' 8. Boryla pass intercepted by E. Brown and returned to Eagles' 22. Moseley kicks 29-yard field goal at 12:49.

Oct. 17, 1976—Kansas City 20, Miami 17, at Miami; Chiefs win toss. Wilson punts into end zone for touchback. Bulaich fumbles into Kansas City end zone, Collier recovers for touchback. Stenerud kicks 34-yard field goal at 14:48.

Oct. 31, 1976—St. Louis 23, San Francisco 20, at St. Louis; Cardinals win toss. Joyce punts and Leonard fumbles on return, Jones recovers at 49ers' 43. Bakken kicks 21-yard field goal at 6:42.

Dec. 5, 1976—San Diego 13, San Francisco 7, at San Diego; Chargers win toss. Morris runs 13 yards for touchdown at 5:12.

Sept. 18, 1977—Dallas 16, Minnesota 10, at Minnesota; Vikings win toss. Dallas starts on Vikings' 47 after a punt early in the overtime period. Staubach scores seven plays later on a four-yard run at 6:14.

***Sept. 26, 1977—Cleveland 30, New England 27,** at Cleveland; Browns win toss. Sipe throws a 22-yard pass to Logan at Patriots' 19. Cockroft kicks 35-yard field goal at 4:45.

Oct. 16, 1977—Minnesota 22, Chicago 16, at Minnesota; Bears win toss. Parsons punts 53 yards to Vikings' 18. Minnesota drives to Bears' 11. On a first-and-10, Vikings fake a field goal and holder Krause hits Voigt with a touchdown pass at 6:45.

Oct. 30, 1977—Cincinnati 13, Houston 10, at Cincinnati; Bengals win toss. Bahr kicks a 22-yard field goal at 5:51.

Nov. 13, 1977—San Francisco 10, New Orleans 7, at New Orleans; Saints win toss. Saints fail to move ball and Blanchard punts to 49ers' 41. Wersching kicks a 33-yard field goal at 6:33.

Dec. 18, 1977—Chicago 12, New York Giants 9, at East Rutherford, N.J.; Giants win toss. The ball changes hands eight times before Thomas kicks a 28-yard field goal at 14:51.

Sept. 10, 1978—Cleveland 13, Cincinnati 10, at Cleveland; Browns win toss. Collins returns kickoff 41 yards to Browns' 47. Cockroft kicks 27-yard field goal at 4:30.

***Sept. 11, 1978—Minnesota 12, Denver 9,** at Minnesota; Vikings win toss. Danmeier kicks 44-yard field goal at 2:56.

Sept. 24, 1978—Pittsburgh 15, Cleveland 9, at Pittsburgh; Steelers win toss. Cunningham scores on a 37-yard "gadget" pass from Bradshaw at 3:43. Steelers start winning drive on their 21.

Sept. 24, 1978—Denver 23, Kansas City 17, at Kansas City; Broncos win toss. Dilts punts to Kansas City. Chiefs advance to Broncos' 40 where Reed fails to make first down on fourth-and-one situation. Broncos march downfield. Preston scores two-yard touchdown at 10:28.

Oct. 1, 1978—Oakland 25, Chicago 19, at Chicago; Bears win toss. Both teams punt on first possession. On Chicago's second offensive series, Colzie intercepts Avellini's pass and returns it to Bears' 3. Three plays later, Whittington runs two yards for a touchdown at 5:19.

Oct. 15, 1978—Dallas 24, St. Louis 21, at St. Louis; Cowboys win toss. Dallas drives from its 23 into field goal range. Septien kicks 27-yard field goal at 3:28.

Oct. 29, 1978—Denver 20, Seattle 17, at Seattle; Broncos win toss. Ball changes hands four times before Turner kicks 18-yard field goal at 12:59.

Nov. 12, 1978—San Diego 29, Kansas City 23, at San Diego; Chiefs win toss. Fouts hits Jefferson for decisive 14-yard touchdown pass on the last play (15:00) of overtime period.

Nov. 12, 1978—Washington 16, New York Giants 13, at Washington; Redskins win toss. Moseley kicks winning 45-yard field goal at 8:32 after missing first down field goal attempt of 35 yards at 4:50.

Nov. 26, 1978—Green Bay 10, Minnesota 10, at Green Bay; Packers win toss. Both teams have possession of the ball four times.

Dec. 9, 1978—Cleveland 37, New York Jets 34, at Cleveland; Browns win toss. Cockroft kicks 22-yard field goal at 3:07.

Sept. 2, 1979—Atlanta 40, New Orleans 34, at New Orleans; Falcons win toss. Bartkowski's pass intercepted by Myers and returned to Falcons' 46. Erxleben punts to Falcons' 4. James punts to Chandler on Saints' 43. Erxleben punts and

Ryckman returns to Falcons' 28. James punts and Chandler returns to Saints' 36. Erxleben retrieves punt snap on Saints' 1 and attempts pass. Mayberry intercepts and returns six yards for touchdown at 8:22.

Sept. 2, 1979—Cleveland 25, New York Jets 22, at New York; Jets win toss. Leahy's 43-yard field goal attempt goes wide right at 4:41. Evans's punt blocked by Dykes is recovered by Newton. Ramsey punts into end zone for touchback. Evans punts and Harper returns to Jets' 24. Robinson's pass intercepted by Davis and returned 33 yards to Jets' 31. Cockroft kicks 27-yard field goal at 14:45.

***Sept. 3, 1979—Pittsburgh 16, New England 13,** at Foxboro; Patriots win toss. Hare punts to Swann at Steelers' 31. Bahr kicks 41-yard field goal at 5:10.

Sept. 9, 1979—Tampa Bay 29, Baltimore 26, at Baltimore; Colts win toss. Landry fumbles, recovered by Kollar at Colts' 14. O'Donoghue kicks 31-yard, first-down field goal at 1:41.

Sept. 16, 1979—Denver 20, Atlanta 17, at Atlanta; Broncos win toss. Broncos march 65 yards to Falcons' 7. Turner kicks 24-yard field goal at 6:15.

Sept. 23, 1979—Houston 30, Cincinnati 27, at Cincinnati; Oilers win toss. Parsley punts and Lusby returns to Bengals' 33. Bahr's 32-yard field goal attempt is wide right at 8:05. Parsley's punt downed on Bengals' 5. McInally punts and Ellender returns to Bengals' 42. Fritsch's third down, 29-yard field goal attempt hits left upright and bounces through at 14:28.

Sept. 23, 1979—Minnesota 27, Green Bay 21, at Minnesota; Vikings win toss. Kramer throws 50-yard touchdown pass to Rashad at 3:18.

Oct. 28, 1979—Houston 27, New York Jets 24, at Houston; Oilers win toss. Oilers march 58 yards to Jets' 18. Fritsch kicks 35-yard field goal at 5:10.

Nov. 18, 1979—Cleveland 30, Miami 24, at Cleveland; Browns win toss. Sipe passes 39 yards to Rucker for touchdown at 1:59.

Nov. 25, 1979—Pittsburgh 33, Cleveland 30, at Pittsburgh; Browns win toss. Sipe's pass intercepted by Blount on Steelers' 4. Bradshaw pass intercepted by Bolton on Browns' 12. Evans punts and Bell returns to Steelers' 17. Bahr kicks 37-yard field goal at 14:51.

Nov. 25, 1979—Buffalo 16, New England 13, at Foxboro; Patriots win toss. Hare's punt downed on Bills' 38. Jackson punts and Morgan returns to Patriots' 20. Grogan's pass intercepted by Haslett and returned to Bills' 42. Ferguson's 51-yard pass to Butler sets up N. Mike-Mayer's 29-yard field goal at 9:15.

Dec. 2, 1979—Los Angeles 27, Minnesota 21, at Los Angeles; Rams win toss. Clark punts and Miller returns to Vikings' 25. Kramer's pass intercepted by Brown and returned to Rams' 40. Cromwell, holding for 22-yard field goal attempt, runs around left end untouched for winning score at 6:53.

Sept. 7, 1980—Green Bay 12, Chicago 6, at Green Bay; Bears win toss. Parsons punts and Nixon returns 16 yards. Five plays later, Marcol returns own blocked field goal attempt 24 yards for touchdown at 6:00.

Sept. 14, 1980—San Diego 30, Oakland 24, at San Diego; Raiders win toss. Pastorini's first-down pass intercepted by Edwards. Millen intercepts Fouts' first-down pass and returns to San Diego 46. Bahr's 50-yard field goal attempt partially blocked by Williams and recovered on Chargers' 32. Eight plays later, Fouts throws 24-yard touchdown pass to Jefferson at 8:09.

Sept. 14, 1980—San Francisco 24, St. Louis 21, at San Francisco; Cardinals win toss. Swider punts and Robinson returns to 49ers' 32. San Francisco drives 52 yards to St. Louis 16, where Wersching kicks 33-yard field goal at 4:12.

Oct. 12, 1980—Green Bay 14, Tampa Bay 14, at Tampa Bay; Packers win toss. Teams trade punts twice. Lee returns second Tampa Bay punt to Green Bay 42. Dickey completes three passes to Buccaneers' 18, where Birney's 36-yard field goal attempt is wide right as time expires.

Nov. 9, 1980—Atlanta 33, St. Louis 27, at St. Louis; Falcons win toss. Strong runs 21 yards for touchdown at 4:20.

#Nov. 20, 1980—San Diego 27, Miami 24, at Miami; Chargers win toss. Partridge punts into end zone, Dolphins take over on their own 20. Woodley's pass for Nathan intercepted by Lowe and returned 28 yards to Dolphins' 12. Benirschke kicks 28-yard field goal at 7:14.

Nov. 23, 1980—New York Jets 31, Houston 28, at New York; Jets win toss. Leahy kicks 38-yard field goal at 3:58.

Nov. 27, 1980—Chicago 23, Detroit 17, at Detroit; Bears win toss. Williams returns kickoff 95 yards for touchdown at 0:21.

Dec. 7, 1980—Buffalo 10, Los Angeles 7, at Buffalo; Rams win toss. Corral punts and Hooks returns to Bills' 34. Ferguson's 30-yard pass to Lewis sets up N. Mike-Mayer's 30-yard field goal at 5:14.

Dec. 7, 1980—San Francisco 38, New Orleans 35, at San Francisco; Saints win toss. Erxleben's punt downed by Hardy on 49ers' 27. Wersching kicks 36-yard field goal at 7:40.

***Dec. 8, 1980—Miami 16, New England 13,** at Miami; Dolphins win toss. Von Schamann kicks 23-yard field goal at 3:20.

Dec. 14, 1980—Cincinnati 17, Chicago 14, at Chicago; Bengals win toss. Breech kicks 28-yard field goal at 4:23.

Dec. 21, 1980—Los Angeles 20, Atlanta 17, at Los Angeles; Rams win toss. Corral's punt downed at Rams' 37. James punts into end zone for touchback. Corral's punt downed on Falcons' 17. Bartkowski fumbles when hit by Harris, recovered by Delaney. Corral kicks 23-yard field goal on first play of possession at 7:00.

Sept. 27, 1981—Cincinnati 27, Buffalo 24, at Cincinnati; Bills win toss. Cater punts into end zone for touchback. Bengals drive to the Bills' 10 where Breech kicks 28-yard field goal at 9:33.

Sept. 27, 1981—Pittsburgh 27, New England 21, at Pittsburgh; Patriots win toss. Hubach punts and Smith returns five yards to midfield. Four plays later Bradshaw throws 24-yard touchdown pass to Swann at 3:19.

Oct. 4, 1981—Miami 28, New York Jets 28, at Miami; Jets win toss. Teams trade punts twice. Leahy's 48-yard field goal attempt is wide right as time expires.

Oct. 25, 1981—New York Giants 27, Atlanta 24, at Atlanta; Giants win toss. Jennings' punt goes out of bounds at New York 47. Bright returns Atlanta punt to Giants' 14. Woerner fair catches punt at own 28. Andrews fumbles on first play, recovered by Van Pelt. Danelo kicks 40-yard field goal four plays later at 9:20.

Oct. 25, 1981—Chicago 20, San Diego 17, at Chicago; Bears win toss. Teams trade punts. Bears' second punt returned by Brooks to Chargers' 33. Fouts pass intercepted by Fencik and returned 32 yards to San Diego 27. Roveto kicks 27-yard field goal seven plays later at 9:30.

Nov. 8, 1981—Chicago 16, Kansas City 13, at Kansas City; Bears win toss. Teams trade punts. Kansas City takes over on downs on its own 38. Fuller's fumble recovered by Harris on Chicago 36. Roveto's 37-yard field goal wide, but Chiefs penalized for leverage. Roveto's 22-yard field goal attempt three plays later is good at 13:07.

Nov. 8, 1981—Denver 23, Cleveland 20, at Denver; Browns win toss. D. Smith recovers Hill's fumble at Denver 48. Morton's 33-yard pass to Upchurch and 6-yard run by Preston set up Steinfort's 30-yard field goal at 4:10.

Nov. 8, 1981—Miami 30, New England 27, at New England; Dolphins win toss. Orosz punts and Morgan returns six yards to New England 26. Grogan's pass intercepted by Brudzinski who returns 19 yards to Patriots' 26. Von Schamann kicks 30-yard field goal on first down at 7:09.

Nov. 15, 1981—Washington 30, New York Giants 27, at New York; Giants win toss. Nelms returns Giants' punt 26 yards to New York 47. Five plays later Moseley kicks 48-yard field goal at 3:44.

Dec. 20, 1981—New York Giants 13, Dallas 10, at New York; Cowboys win toss and kick off. Jennings punts to Dallas 40. Taylor recovers Dorsett's fumble on second down. Danelo's 33-yard field goal attempt hits right upright and bounces back. White's pass for Pearson intercepted by Hunt and returned seven yards to Dallas 24. Four plays later Danelo kicks 35-yard field goal at 6:19.

Sept. 12, 1982—Washington 37, Philadelphia 34, at Philadelphia; Redskins win toss. Theismann completes five passes for 63 yards to set up Moseley's 26-yard field goal at 4:47.

Sept. 19, 1982—Pittsburgh 26, Cincinnati 20, at Pittsburgh; Bengals win toss. Anderson's pass intended for Kreider intercepted by Woodruff and returned 30 yards to Cincinnati 2. Bradshaw completes two-yard touchdown pass to Stallworth on first down at 1:08.

Dec. 19, 1982—Baltimore 20, Green Bay 20, at Baltimore; Packers win toss. K. Anderson intercepts Dickey's first-down pass and returns to Packers' 42. Miller's 44-yard field goal attempt blocked by G. Lewis. Teams trade punts before Stenerud's 47-yard field goal attempt is wide right. Teams trade punts again before time expires in Colts possession.

Jan. 2, 1983—Tampa Bay 26, Chicago 23, at Tampa; Bears win toss. Parsons punts to T. Bell at Buccaneers' 40. Capece kicks 33-yard field goal at 3:14.

Sept. 4, 1983—Baltimore 29, New England 23, at New England; Patriots win toss. Cooks runs 52 yards with fumble recovery three plays into overtime at 0:30.

Sept. 4, 1983—Green Bay 41, Houston 38, at Houston; Packers win toss. Stenerud kicks 42-yard field goal at 5:55.

Sept. 11, 1983—New York Giants 16, Atlanta 13, at Atlanta; Giants win toss. Dennis returns kickoff 54 yards to Atlanta 41. Haji-Sheikh kicks 30-yard field goal at 3:38.

Sept. 18, 1983—New Orleans 34, Chicago 31, at New Orleans; Bears win toss. Parsons punts and Groth returns five yards to New Orleans 34. Stabler pass intercepted by Schmidt at Chicago 47. Parsons punt downed by Gentry at New Orleans 2. Stabler gains 36 yards in four passes; Wilson 38 on six carries. Andersen kicks 41-yard field goal at 10:57.

Sept. 18, 1983—Minnesota 19, Tampa Bay 16, at Tampa; Vikings win toss. Coleman punts and Bell returns eight yards to Tampa Bay 47. Capece's 33-yard field goal attempt sails wide at 7:26. Dils and Young combine for 48-yard gain to Tampa Bay 27. Ricardo kicks 42-yard field goal at 9:27.

Sept. 25, 1983—Baltimore 22, Chicago 19, at Baltimore; Colts win toss. Allegre kicks 33-yard field goal nine plays later at 4:51.

Sept. 25, 1983—Cleveland 30, San Diego 24, at San Diego; Browns win toss. Walker returns kickoff 33 yards to Cleveland 37. Sipe completes 48-yard touchdown pass to Holt four plays later at 1:53.

Sept. 25, 1983—New York Jets 27, Los Angeles Rams 24, at New York; Jets win toss. Ramsey punts to Irvin who returns to 25 but penalty puts Rams on own 13. Holmes 30-yard interception return sets up Leahy's 26-yard field goal at 3:22.

Oct. 9, 1983—Buffalo 38, Miami 35, at Miami; Dolphins win toss. Von Schamann's 52-yard field goal attempt goes wide at 12:36. Cater punts to Clayton who loses 11 to own 13. Von Schamann's 43-yard field goal attempt sails wide at 5:15. Danelo kicks 36-yard field goal nine plays later at 13:58.

Oct. 9, 1983—Dallas 27, Tampa Bay 24, at Dallas; Cowboys win toss. Septien's 51-yard field goal attempt goes wide but Buccaneers penalized for roughing kicker. Septien kicks 42-yard field goal at 4:38.

Oct. 23, 1983—Kansas City 13, Houston 10, at Houston; Chiefs win toss. Lowery kicks 41-yard field goal 13 plays later at 7:41.

Oct. 23, 1983—Minnesota 20, Green Bay 17, at Green Bay; Packers win toss. Scribner's punt downed on Vikings' 42. Ricardo kicks 32-yard field goal eight plays later at 5:05.

***Oct. 24, 1983—New York Giants 20, St. Louis 20,** at St. Louis; Cardinals win toss. Teams trade punts before O'Donoghue's 44-yard field goal attempt is wide left. Jennings' punt returned by Bird to St. Louis 21. Lomax pass intercepted by Haynes who loses six yards to New York 33. Jennings' punt downed on St. Louis 17. O'Donoghue's 19-yard field goal attempt is wide right. Rutledge's pass intercepted by L. Washington who returns 25 yards to New York 25. O'Donoghue's 42-yard field goal attempt is wide right. Rutledge's pass intercepted by W. Smith at St. Louis 33 to end game.

Oct. 30, 1983—Cleveland 25, Houston 19, at Cleveland; Oilers win toss. Teams trade punts. Nielsen's pass intercepted by Whitwell who returns to Houston 20. Green runs 20 yards for touchdown on first down at 6:34.

Nov. 20, 1983—Detroit 23, Green Bay 20, at Milwaukee; Packers win toss. Scribner punts and Jenkins returns 14 yards to Green Bay 45. Murray's 33-yard field goal attempt is wide left at 9:32. Whitehurst's pass intercepted by Watkins and returned to Green Bay 27. Murray kicks 37-yard field goal four plays later at 8:30.

Nov. 27, 1983—Atlanta 47, Green Bay 41, at Atlanta; Packers win toss. K. Johnson returns interception 31 yards for touchdown at 2:13.

Nov. 27, 1983—Seattle 51, Kansas City 48, at Seattle; Seahawks win toss. Dixon's 47-yard kickoff return sets up N. Johnson's 42-yard field goal at 1:36.

Dec. 11, 1983—New Orleans 20, Philadelphia 17, at Philadelphia; Eagles win toss. Runager punts to Groth who fair catches on New Orleans 32. Stabler completes two passes for 36 yards to Goodlow to set up Andersen's 50-yard field goal at 5:30.

***Dec. 12, 1983—Green Bay 12, Tampa Bay 9,** at Tampa; Packers win toss. Stenerud kicks 23-yard field goal 11 plays later at 4:07.

Sept. 9, 1984—Detroit 27, Atlanta 24, at Atlanta; Lions win toss. Murray kicks 48-yard field goal nine plays later at 5:06.

Sept. 30, 1984—Tampa Bay 30, Green Bay 27, at Tampa; Packers win toss. Scribner punts 44 yards to Tampa Bay 2. Epps returns Garcia's punt three yards to Green Bay 27. Scribner's punt downed on Buccaneers' 33. Ariri kicks 46-yard field goal 11 plays later at 10:32.

Oct. 14, 1984—Detroit 13, Tampa Bay 7, at Detroit; Buccaneers win toss. Tampa Bay drives to Lions' 39 before Wilder fumbles. Five plays later Danielson hits Thompson with 37-yard touchdown pass at 4:34.

Oct. 21, 1984—Dallas 30, New Orleans 27, at Dallas; Cowboys win toss. Septien kicks 41-yard field goal eight plays later at 3:42.

Oct. 28, 1984—Denver 22, Los Angeles Raiders 19, at Los Angeles; Raiders win toss. Hawkins fumble recovered by Foley at Denver 7. Teams trade punts. Karlis's 42-yard field goal attempt is wide left. Teams trade punts. Wilson pass intercepted by R. Jackson at Los Angeles 45, returned 23 yards to Los Angeles 22. Karlis kicks 35-yard field goal two plays later at 15:00.

Nov. 4, 1984—Philadelphia 23, Detroit 23, at Detroit; Lions win toss. Lions drive to Eagles' 3 in eight plays. Murray's 21-yard field goal attempt hits right upright and bounces back. Jaworski's pass intercepted by Watkins at Detroit 5. Teams trade punts. Cooper returns Black's punt five yards to Eagles' 14. Time expires four plays later with Eagles on own 21.

Nov. 18, 1984—San Diego 34, Miami 28, at San Diego; Chargers win toss. McGee scores eight plays later on a 25-yard run at 3:17.

Dec. 2, 1984—Cincinnati 20, Cleveland 17, at Cleveland; Browns win toss. Simmons returns Cox's punt 30 yards to Cleveland 35. Breech kicks 35-yard field goal seven plays later at 4:34.

Dec. 2, 1984—Houston 23, Pittsburgh 20, at Houston; Oilers win toss. Cooper kicks 30-yard field goal 16 plays later at 5:53.

Sept. 8, 1985—St. Louis 27, Cleveland 24, at Cleveland; Cardinals win toss. O'Donoghue kicks 35-yard field goal nine plays later at 5:27.

Sept. 29, 1985—New York Giants 16, Philadelphia 10, at Philadelphia; Eagles win toss. Jaworski's pass tipped by Quick and intercepted by Patterson who returns 29 yards for touchdown at 0:55.

Oct. 20, 1985—Denver 13, Seattle 10, at Denver; Seahawks win toss. Teams trade punts twice. Krieg's pass intercepted by Hunter and returned to Seahawks' 15. Karlis kicks 24-yard field goal four plays later at 9:19.

Nov. 10, 1985—Philadelphia 23, Atlanta 17, at Philadelphia; Falcons win toss. Donnelly's 62-yard punt goes out of bounds at Eagles' 1. Jaworski completes 99-yard touchdown pass to Quick two plays later at 1:49.

Nov. 10, 1985—San Diego 40, Los Angeles Raiders 34, at San Diego; Chargers win toss. James scores on 17-yard run seven plays later at 3:44.

Nov. 17, 1985—Denver 30, San Diego 24, at Denver; Chargers win toss. Thomas' 40-yard field goal attempt blocked by Smith and returned 60 yards by Wright for touchdown at 4:45.

Nov. 24, 1985—New York Jets 16, New England 13, at New York; Jets win toss. Teams trade punts twice. Patriots' second punt returned 46 yards by Sohn to Patriots' 15. Leahy kicks 32-yard field goal one play later at 10:05.

Nov. 24, 1985—Tampa Bay 19, Detroit 16, at Tampa; Lions win toss. Teams trade punts. Lions' punt downed on Buccaneers' 38. Igwebuike kicks 24-yard field goal 11 plays later at 12:31.

Nov. 24, 1985—Los Angeles Raiders 31, Denver 28, at Los Angeles; Raiders win toss. Bahr kicks 32-yard field goal six plays later at 2:42.

Dec. 8, 1985—Los Angeles Raiders 17, Denver 14, at Denver; Broncos win toss. Teams trade punts twice. Elway's fumble recovered by Townsend at Broncos' 8. Bahr kicks 26-yard field goal one play later at 4:55.

Sept. 14, 1986—Chicago 13, Philadelphia 10, at Chicago; Eagles win toss. Crawford's fumble of kickoff recovered by Jackson at Eagles' 35. Butler kicks 23-yard field goal 10 plays later at 5:56.

Sept. 14, 1986—Cincinnati 36, Buffalo 33, at Cincinnati; Bills win toss. Zander intercepts Kelly's first-down pass and returns it to Bills' 17. Breech kicks 20-yard field goal two plays later at 0:56.

Sept. 21, 1986—New York Jets 51, Miami 45, at New York; Jets win toss. O'Brien completes 43-yard touchdown pass to Walker five plays later at 2:35.

Sept. 28, 1986—Pittsburgh 22, Houston 16, at Houston; Oilers win toss. Johnson's punt returned 41 yards by Woods to Oilers' 15. Abercrombie scores on three-yard run three plays later at 2:35.

Sept. 28, 1986—Atlanta 23, Tampa Bay 20, at Tampa; Falcons win toss. Teams trade punts. Luckhurst kicks 34-yard field goal 10 plays later at 12:35.

Oct. 5, 1986—Los Angeles Rams 26, Tampa Bay 20, at Anaheim; Rams win toss. Dickerson scores four plays later on 42-yard run at 2:16.

Oct. 12, 1986—Minnesota 27, San Francisco 24, at San Francisco; Vikings win toss. C. Nelson kicks 28-yard field goal nine plays later at 4:27.

Oct. 19, 1986—San Francisco 10, Atlanta 10, at Atlanta; Falcons win toss. Teams trade punts twice. Donnelly punts to 49ers' 27. The following play Wilson recovers Rice's fumble at 49ers' 46 as time expires.

Nov. 2, 1986—Washington 44, Minnesota 38, at Washington; Redskins win toss. Schroeder completes 38-yard touchdown pass to Clark four plays later at 1:46.

Nov. 20, 1986—Los Angeles Raiders 37, San Diego 31, at San Diego; Raiders win toss. Teams trade punts. Allen scores five plays later on 28-yard run at 8:33.

Nov. 23, 1986—Cleveland 37, Pittsburgh 31, at Cleveland; Browns win toss. Teams trade punts. Six plays later Kosar hits Slaughter with 36-yard touchdown pass at 6:37.

Nov. 30, 1986—Chicago 13, Pittsburgh 10, at Chicago; Bears win toss and kick off. Newsome's punt returned by Barnes to Chicago 49. Butler kicks 42-yard field goal five plays later at 3:55.

Nov. 30, 1986—Philadelphia 33, Los Angeles Raiders 27, at Los Angeles; Eagles win toss. Teams trade punts. Long recovers Cunningham's fumble at Philadelphia 42. Waters returns Allen's fumble 81 yards to Los Angeles 4. Cunningham scores on one-yard run two plays later at 6:53.

Nov. 30, 1986—Cleveland 13, Houston 10, at Cleveland; Oilers win toss and kick off. Gossett punts to Houston 39. Luck's pass intercepted by Minnifield at Cleveland 21. Gossett punts to Houston 34. Luck's pass intercepted by Minnifield at Cleveland 43 who returns 20 yards to Houston 37. Moseley kicks 29-yard field goal nine plays later at 14:44.

Dec. 7, 1986—St. Louis 10, Philadelphia 10, at Philadelphia; Cardinals win toss. White blocks Schubert's 40-yard field goal attempt. Teams trade punts. McFadden's 43-yard field goal attempt is wide left. Schubert's 37-yard field goal attempt is wide right. Cavanaugh's pass intercepted by Carter and returned to Eagles' 48 to end game.

Dec. 14, 1986—Miami 37, Los Angeles Rams 31, at Anaheim; Dolphins win toss. Marino completes 20-yard touchdown pass to Duper six plays later at 3:04.

Sept. 20, 1987—Denver 17, Green Bay 17, at Milwaukee; Packers win toss. Del Greco's 47-yard field goal attempt is short. Teams trade punts. Elway intercepted by Noble who returns 10 yards to Green Bay 34. Davis fumbles on next play and Smith recovers. Two plays later, Karlis's 40-yard field goal attempt is wide left. Time expires two plays later with Packers on own 23.

Oct. 11, 1987—Detroit 19, Green Bay 16, at Green Bay; Lions win toss. Prindle's 42-yard field goal attempt is wide left. Packers punt downed on Detroit 17. Prindle kicks 31-yard field goal 16 plays later at 12:26.

Oct. 18, 1987—New York Jets 37, Miami 31, at New York; Jets win toss. Teams trade punts. Ryan intercepted by Hooper at Jets' 47 who returns 11 yards. Mackey intercepted by Haslett at Jets' 37 who returns 9 yards. Jets punt. Mackey intercepted by Radachowsky who returns 45 yards to Miami 24. Ryan completes eight-yard touchdown pass to Hunter five plays later at 14:26.

Oct. 18, 1987—Green Bay 16, Philadelphia 10, at Green Bay; Packers win toss. Hargrove scores on seven-yard run 10 plays later at 5:04.

Oct. 18, 1987—Buffalo 6, New York Giants 3, at Buffalo; Bills win toss. Schlopy's 28-yard field goal attempt is wide left. Teams trade punts. Rutledge intercepted by Clark who returns 23 yards to Buffalo 40. Schlopy kicks 27-yard field goal nine plays later at 14:41.

Oct. 25, 1987—Buffalo 34, Miami 31, at Miami; Bills win toss. Norwood kicks 27-yard field goal seven plays later at 4:12.

Nov. 1, 1987—San Diego 27, Cleveland 24, at San Diego; Browns win toss. Kosar intercepted by Glenn who returns 20 yards to Browns' 25. Abbott kicks 33-yard field goal three plays later at 2:16.

Nov. 15, 1987—Dallas 23, New England 17, at New England; Cowboys win toss. Walker scores on 60-yard run four plays later at 1:50.

Nov. 26, 1987—Minnesota 44, Dallas 38, at Dallas; Vikings win toss. Coleman's punt downed by Hilton at Cowboys' 37. White intercepted by Studwell who returns 12 yards to Vikings' 37. D. Nelson scores on 24-yard run seven plays later at 7:51.

Nov. 29, 1987—Philadelphia 34, New England 31, at New England; Patriots win toss. Ramsey intercepted by Joyner who returns 29 yards to Eagles' 32. Fryar fair catches Teltschik's punt at Patriots' 13. Franklin's 46-yard field goal attempt is short. McFadden's 39-yard field goal attempt is wide left. Tatupu fumbles on next play and Cobb recovers. McFadden kicks 38-yard field goal four plays later at 12:16.

Dec. 6, 1987—New York Giants 23, Philadelphia 20, at New York; Giants win toss and kick off. Teams trade punts twice. Teltschik's punt is returned 16 yards by McConkey to Eagles' 33. Three plays later, Allegre's 50-yard field goal attempt is blocked by Joyner and returned 25 yards by Hoage to Eagles' 30.

McConkey returns Teltschik's punt four yards to Giants' 44. Allegre kicks 28-yard field goal four plays later at 10:42.

Dec. 6, 1987—Cincinnati 30, Kansas City 27, at Cincinnati; Bengals win toss. Teams trade punts. Breech kicks 32-yard field goal 16 plays later at 9:44.

Dec. 26, 1987—Washington 27, Minnesota 24, at Minnesota; Redskins win toss. Haji-Sheikh kicks 26-yard field goal six plays later at 2:09.

Sept. 4, 1988—Houston 17, Indianapolis 14, at Indianapolis; Colts win toss. Dickerson fumble recovered by Lyles who returns six yards to Colts' 42. Zendejas kicks 35-yard field goal six plays later at 3:51.

***Sept. 26, 1988—Los Angeles Raiders 30, Denver 27,** at Denver; Broncos win toss. Teams trade punts twice. Elway intercepted by Lee who returns 20 yards to Broncos' 31. Bahr kicks 35-yard field goal four plays later at 12:35.

Oct. 2, 1988—New York Jets 17, Kansas City 17, at New York; Chiefs win toss. Chiefs punt goes into end zone for touchback. Leahy's 44-yard field goal attempt is wide right. Chiefs punt is returned by Townsell to Jets' 26. Burruss recovers McNeil's fumble at Chiefs' 11. DeBerg intercepted by Humphery at Jets' 49. Three plays later, time expires.

Oct. 9, 1988—Denver 16, San Francisco 13, at San Francisco; Broncos win toss and kick off. Young intercepted by Haynes at Broncos' 32. Denver punt downed at 49ers' 5. Young intercepted by Wilson who returns seven yards to 49ers' 5. Karlis kicks 22-yard field goal two plays later at 8:11.

Oct. 30, 1988—New York Giants 13, Detroit 10, at Detroit; Lions win toss. James's fumble recovered by Taylor at Lions' 22. Three plays later, McFadden kicks 33-yard field goal at 1:13.

Nov. 20, 1988—Buffalo 9, New York Jets 6, at Buffalo; Jets win toss. Vick's fumble recovered by Bennett at Bills' 32. Norwood kicks 30-yard field goal five plays later at 3:47.

Nov. 20, 1988—Philadelphia 23, New York Giants 17, at New York; Eagles win toss. Philadelphia's punt goes into end zone for touchback. Hostetler intercepted by Hoage who returns 11 yards to Giants' 41. Six plays later, Zendejas's 30-yard field-goal attempt is blocked and ball is recovered behind line of scrimmage by Eagles' Simmons, who runs 15 yards for touchdown at 3:09.

Dec. 11, 1988—New England 10, Tampa Bay 7, at New England; Buccaneers win toss and kick off. Staurovsky kicks 27-yard field goal six plays later at 3:08.

Dec. 17, 1988—Cincinnati 20, Washington 17, at Cincinnati; Bengals win toss. Cincinnati's punt returned by Oliphant to Redskins' 16. Grant recovers Williams's fumble at Redskins' 17. Breech kicks 20-yard field goal three plays later at 7:01.

Sept. 24, 1989—Buffalo 47, Houston 41, at Houston; Oilers win toss. Johnson returns Brady's kickoff 17 yards to Oilers' 19. Oilers drive to Buffalo 25, Zendejas's 37-yard field goal blocked, but Bills offsides and Zendejas's second attempt is wide left. Bills' ball and Kelly completes series of passes, including 28-yard game-winner to Andre Reed, at 8:42.

Oct. 8, 1989—Miami 13, Cleveland 10, at Miami; Browns win toss. Metcalf returns Stoyanovich's kickoff 20 yards to Browns' 28. Browns drive ball 46 yards in eight plays; Bahr wide left on 44-yard field goal attempt. Dolphins ball. Browns called for pass interference on Marino pass to Banks at Cleveland 47. Two plays later, Banks's 20-yard reception at Browns' 23 sets up winning 35-yard field goal by Stoyanovich at 6:23.

Oct. 22, 1989—Denver 24, Seattle 21, at Seattle; Seahawks win toss. Treadwell's 56-yard kickoff returned 18 yards by Jefferson to Seahawks' 27. Seahawks drive to Broncos' 22 in 10 plays, but Johnson's 40-yard field goal attempt wide left. Smith intercepts a Krieg pass and returns it 28 yards to Seahawks' 10. Treadwell kicks winning 27-yard field goal at 7:46.

Oct. 29, 1989—New England 23, Indianapolis 20, at Indianapolis; Patriots win toss. Biasucci kickoff returned 13 yards to Patriots' 23 by Martin. Holding penalty brings ball back to Patriots' 13. After six plays, Feagles punt returned 11 yards by Verdin to Colts' 28. Six plays later, Colts punt to Martin at Patriots' 12. Grogan completes three straight passes to Patriots' 44. Five consecutive runs put New England on Colts' 33. Davis kicks a 51-yard winning field goal for Patriots at 9:46.

Oct. 29, 1989—Green Bay 23, Detroit 20, at Milwaukee; Lions win toss. Sanders touchback on Jacke kickoff. On first play, Murphy intercepts Lions' Peete and returns it three yards to Lions' 26. Fullwood gains five yards on three plays to set up Jacke's 38-yard field goal at 2:14.

Nov. 5, 1989—Minnesota 23, Los Angeles Rams 21, at Minneapolis; Rams win toss. Karlis's kick returned 18 yards by Delpino to Rams' 19. Drive stops at Rams' 28. Merriweather blocks Hatcher's punt at 12. Ball rolls out of end zone for safety.

Nov. 19, 1989—Cleveland 10, Kansas City 10, at Cleveland; Browns win toss. Browns punt three times; Chiefs twice; before Kansas City's Lowery misses 47-yard field goal with 17 seconds remaining in overtime. Kosar's pass intercepted as time expired.

Nov. 26, 1989—Los Angeles Rams 20, New Orleans 17, at New Orleans; Saints win toss. Lansford's kickoff returned 27 yards to Saints' 30. After four plays, Barnhardt punts to Rams' 15. Saints penalized 35 yards for interference to Rams' 43. Three plays later, Everett hits Anderson with 14-yard pass to Saints' 40, then 26-yarder to put Rams in field goal position. Lansford kicks 31-yard field goal at 6:38.

Dec. 3, 1989—Los Angeles Raiders 16, Denver 13, at Los Angeles; Broncos win toss. Bell returns Jaeger kickoff 14 yards to Broncos' 18. Broncos' penalized for illegal block to Broncos' 9. Elway completes three passes for two first downs. On third and eight Elway sacked for 10-yard loss. Horan punts, Adams calls for fair catch at Raiders' 29. Dyal's 26-yard reception moves Raiders to Denver 43. Raiders move ball 34 yards in three plays to set up Jaeger's 26-yard field goal at 7:02.

Dec. 10, 1989—Indianapolis 23, Cleveland 17, at Indianapolis; Browns win toss. Teams trade punts. McNeil returns Colts' punt 42 yards to 42. Seven plays later, Bahr misses 35-yard field goal attempt. Three plays later, Stark punts and McNeil returns ball to 50-yard line. Two plays later, Prior intercepts Kosar's pass at Colts' 42 and returns it 58 yards for touchdown at 10:54.

Dec. 17, 1989—Cleveland 23, Minnesota 17, at Cleveland; Browns win toss. Browns punt to Vikings' 18. Six plays later, Vikings punt to Browns' 22. Nine plays later, Bahr lines up to attempt 31-yard field goal. Holder Pagel takes snap and passes 14 yards to Waiters for touchdown at 9:30.

Sept. 23, 1990—Denver 34, Seattle 31, at Denver; Seahawks win toss. Loville returns kickoff 19 yards to Seahawks' 27. Seahawks drive to Broncos' 26, where Johnson misses 44-yard field goal wide right. Broncos take over and Elway completes series of passes to set up Treadwell's 25-yard field goal at 9:14.

Sept. 30, 1990—Tampa Bay 23, Minnesota 20, at Minnesota; Vikings win toss. Vikings drive to Buccaneers' 31; Igwebuike's 48-yard field goal attempt wide left. Buccaneers drive to Vikings' 43 and punt. Gannon's pass is intercepted at Vikings' 26 by Wayne Haddix. Buccaneers drive to Vikings' 19 to set up Christie's 36-yard field goal at 9:11.

Oct. 7, 1990—Cincinnati 34, Los Angeles Rams 31, at Anaheim; Rams win toss. Berry returns kickoff to Rams' 21. After 3 plays, English punts and Green downs ball at Bengals' 25. After 3 plays, Johnson punts and Sutton downs ball at Rams' 29-yard line. After 3 plays, English punts and Price signals fair catch at Bengals' 47. Esiason completes series of passes to 26-yard line to set up Breech's 44-yard field goal at 11:56.

Nov. 4, 1990—Washington 41, Detroit 38, at Detroit; Redskins win toss. Howard downs kickoff on Redskins' 15. After 3 plays, Mojsiejenko punts to Redskins' 45. After 3 plays, Arnold punts to Redskins' 10. Rutledge completes series of passes to set up Lohmiller's 34-yard field goal at 9:10.

Nov. 18, 1990—Chicago 16, Denver 13, at Denver; Broncos win toss. Ezor returns kickoff to Broncos' 12. Both teams have ball twice and have to punt after each possession. Broncos punt after third possession of overtime and Bailey returns 20 yards to Broncos' 34. Harbaugh completes 10-yard pass to Thornton to set up Butler's 44-yard field goal at 13:14.

Nov. 25, 1990—Seattle 13, San Diego 10, at San Diego; Chargers win toss. Lewis returns kickoff to Chargers' 22. After 2 plays, Cox fumbles and ball is recovered by Porter at Chargers' 23. After two plays, Johnson kicks 40-yard field goal at 3:01.

Dec. 2, 1990—Chicago 23, Detroit 17, at Chicago; Lions win toss. Gray returns kickoff to Lions' 35. After 10 plays, Murray misses 35-yard field goal. Bears take possession at Chicago 20. Harbaugh completes 50-yard game-winning pass to Anderson at 10:57.

Dec. 2, 1990—Seattle 13, Houston 10, at Seattle; Seahawks win toss. Warren returns kickoff to Seahawks' 13. After 5 plays, Donnelly punts to Oilers' 23-yard line. Ford's fumble recovered by Wyman. Seahawks take possession at Oilers' 27. After 2 plays, Johnson kicks 42-yard field goal at 4:25.

Dec. 9, 1990—Miami 23, Philadelphia 20, at Miami; Eagles win toss. After 11 plays, Feagles punts to Dolphins' 26. After 6 plays, Roby punts to Eagles' 14 and Harris returns to 25. After 3 plays, Feagles punts to Dolphins' 43. Marino completes series of passes to Eagles' 22. Stoyanovich kicks 39-yard field goal at 12:32.

Dec. 9, 1990—San Francisco 20, Cincinnati 17, at Cincinnati; 49ers win toss. Carter returns kickoff to 49ers' 19. After 10 plays, Cofer kicks 23-yard field goal at 6:12.

Sept. 24, 1991—Chicago 19, New York Jets 13, at Chicago; Jets win toss. Mathis returns kickoff seven yards to New York's 12. Jets drive to New York 26; Bailey returns punt to Chicago 39. Bears drive to Jets' 44-yard line and punt into the end zone. Jets drive to Bears' 11 where Leahy's 28-yard field goal attempt is wide left. Bears drive from 20 to Jets' 1 where Harbaugh runs for touchdown at 14:42.

Oct. 13, 1991—Los Angeles Raiders 23, Seattle 20, at Seattle. Seahawks win toss. Seahawks begin on 20. After 5 plays, Tuten punts and Brown signals fair catch at Raiders' 24. After 3 plays, Gossett punts and Land downs ball at Seattle 9. After 1 play, Lott intercepts at Seahawks' 19 to set up Jaeger's game-winning 37-yard field goal at 6:37.

Oct. 20, 1991—Cleveland 30, San Diego 24, at San Diego; Chargers win toss. After kickoff, Chargers drive to Browns' 45 and punt to Browns' 6 where Hendrickson downs ball. Browns drive to 38 and punt; Taylor fair catches on Chargers' 14. After 3 plays, Brandon intercepts at Chargers' 30 and scores at 5:58.

Oct. 20, 1991—New England 26, Minnesota 23, at New England; Patriots win toss. Martin returns kickoff 18 yards to New England 22. Patriots drive to Minnesota 19. Staurovsky's 36-yard field goal attempt is wide left. Minnesota drives to the 50 where Newsome punts into end zone. On first play, McMillian intercepts at the 40 for Minnesota. After 2 plays, Marion causes Jordan fumble and Pool recovers at New England 20. New England drives to Minnesota 24 where Staurovsky kicks 42-yard field goal as time expires.

Nov. 3, 1991—New York Jets 19, Green Bay 16, at New York; Packers win toss. Thompson returns kickoff 30 yards to Packers' 39. Green Bay drives to New York 24 where Jacke's 42-yard field goal attempt is wide right. Jets drive to 50. Aguiar's punt is fumbled by Sikahema and recovered by New York at Packers' 23. After 2 plays, Leahy kicks 37-yard field goal at 9:40.

Nov. 3, 1991—Washington 16, Houston 13, at Washington; Redskins win toss. Mitchell returns kickoff 9 yards to Washington 14. After 4 plays, Goodburn punts and Givins returns to Houston 31. After 1 play, Moon's pass is intercepted by Green at Oilers' 35. After 3 plays, Lohmiller kicks 41-yard field goal at 4:01.

Nov. 10, 1991—Houston 26, Dallas 23, at Houston; Oilers win toss. Pinkett returns kickoff 20 yards to Houston 24. After 6 plays, Montgomery punts and Martin returns to Dallas 24. Cowboys drive to Oilers' 24 where Smith fumbles and McDowell recovers at Oilers' 15. Houston drives to Dallas 5 where Del Greco kicks 23-yard field goal at 14:31.

Nov. 10, 1991—Pittsburgh 33, Cincinnati 27, at Cincinnati; Pittsburgh wins toss. Woodson downs kickoff for touchback. After 3 plays, Stryzinski punts and Barber returns 7 yards to Cincinnati 38. Bengals drive to Pittsburgh 37 where Woods fumbles and Lloyd returns recovery to Cincinnati 44. After 2 plays, O'Donnell passes to Green for 26-yard touchdown at 6:32.

Nov. 24, 1991—Atlanta 23, New Orleans 20, at New Orleans; Atlanta wins toss. Falcons begin at 20. After 3 plays, Fulhage punts and Fenerty signals fair catch at New Orleans 43. After 3 plays, Barnhardt punts and Thompson downs ball at Atlanta 23. After 3 plays, Fulhage punts and Fenerty fair catches at New Orleans 25. Saints drive to Atlanta 38 where Andersen misses 55-yard field-goal attempt. After 1 play, Rozier fumbles and Martin recovers on 50. Saints drive to Atlanta 38 where Barnhardt punts to Falcons' 2. Atlanta drives to New Orleans 33 where Johnson kicks 50-yard field goal at 13:03.

Nov. 24, 1991—Miami 16, Chicago 13, at Chicago; Miami wins toss. Butler kicks to Miami 20 where Paige returns kickoff 15 yards to 35. Miami drives to Chicago 9 where Stoyanovich kicks 27-yard field goal at 4:11.

Dec. 8, 1991—Buffalo 30, Los Angeles Raiders 27, at Los Angeles; Raiders win toss. Daluiso kicks into end zone for touchback. On third play, Kelso intercepts for Buffalo and returns ball to Bills' 36. Bills drive to Los Angeles 24 where Norwood kicks 42-yard field goal at 2:34.

Dec. 8, 1991—Kansas City 20, San Diego 17, at Kansas City; Chiefs win toss. Carney kicks to Kansas City 10 where Stradford returns 23 yards to 33. After 3 plays, Barker punts to San Diego 4. Chargers drive to 40 where Kidd punts 60 yards into end zone for touchback. Kansas City drives to San Diego 39 where Barker punts 38 yards to 1. After 3 plays, Kidd punts 41 yards to San Diego 42 where Stradford returns 12 yards to 30. Chiefs drive to San Diego 1 where Lowery kicks 18-yard field goal at 11:26.

Dec. 8, 1991—New England 23, Indianapolis 17, at New England; Indianapolis wins toss. Baumann kicks off to Indianapolis 2 where Martin returns 23 yards to 25. After 3 downs, Stark punts to New England 17 where Henderson returns 8 yards to 25. New England drives to 50 where McCarthy punts and Prior signals fair catch at Indianapolis 15. After 3 plays, Stark punts to New England 40 where Henderson returns 7 yards to 47. After 2 plays, Millen passes to Timpson for 45-yard touchdown at 8:55.

Dec. 22, 1991—Detroit 17, Buffalo 14, at Buffalo; Detroit wins toss. Daluiso kicks off to Detroit 20 where Dozier returns 15 yards to Lions 35. Lions drive to Bills' 3 where Murray kicks 21-yard field goal at 4:23.

Dec. 22, 1991—New York Jets 23, Miami 20, at Miami; Jets win toss. Aguiar kicks to Miami's 30 where Logan returns 3 yards to the 33. After 4 downs, Stoyanovich punts to Jets' 15 where Baty returns 8 yards to 23. Jets drive to Miami 12 where Allegre kicks 30-yard field goal at 6:33.

Sept. 6, 1992—Minnesota 23, Green Bay 20, at Green Bay. Vikings win toss. Nelson returns kickoff 14 yards to the Minnesota 23. After 5 plays, Newsome punts 49 yards to Green Bay 21 where Brooks returns 12 yards to the 33. After 2 plays, Glenn intercepts pass at the Vikings' 48. On first play, Allen fumbles and Billups recovers at Green Bay 35. After 3 plays, McJulien punts 33 yards to Vikings' 35. Vikings drive to Minnesota 48; Newsome punts 52 yards for touchback. After 3 plays, McJulien punts and Parker returns 10 yards to Green Bay 48. Vikings drive to Packers' 9 where Reveiz kicks 26-yard field goal at 10:20.

Sept. 13, 1992—Cincinnati 24, Los Angeles Raiders 21, at Cincinnati. Raiders win toss. Land returns kickoff 13 yards but fumbles at Los Angeles's 20; ball recovered by Bengals' Bennett at Raiders' 21. After 1 play, Breech kicks 34-yard field goal at 1:01.

Sept. 20, 1992—Houston 23, Kansas City 20, at Houston. Chiefs win toss. Carter returns kickoff 25 yards to Kansas City 28. On third play of drive, Birden fumbles at Kansas City 34; ball recovered by Houston's D. Smith at Chiefs' 23. After one play, Del Greco kicks 39-yard field goal at 1:55.

Oct. 11, 1992—Indianapolis 6, New York Jets 3, at Indianapolis. Colts win toss. Verdin returns kickoff 33 yards to Colts' 36. Colts drive to Jets' 30 where Biasucci kicks 47-yard field goal at 3:01.

Nov. 8, 1992—Cincinnati 31, Chicago 28, at Chicago. Bears win toss. Lewis returns kickoff 22 yards to Chicago's 29. Bears drive to Chicago's 46 where Gardocki punts; fair catch by Wright at the Cincinnati 17. Bengals drive to Bears' 18 where Breech kicks 36-yard field goal at 8:39.

Nov. 15, 1992—New England 37, Indianapolis 34, at Indianapolis. Colts win toss. Verdin returns kickoff 10 yards to Colts' 20; holding penalty brings ball back to Colts' 10. After two plays, Henderson intercepts pass at Colts' 38 and returns it 9 yards to the 29. In three plays, Patriots drive to 1 where Baumann kicks 18-yard field goal at 3:25.

Nov. 29, 1992—Indianapolis 16, Buffalo 13, at Indianapolis. Colts win toss. Verdin returns kickoff 24 yards to Colts' 22. Colts drive to Buffalo 22 where Biasucci kicks 40-yard field goal at 3:51.

***Nov. 30, 1992—Seattle 16, Denver 13,** at Seattle. Seahawks win toss. Daluiso kicks through end zone for touchback. After three plays, Tuten punts 53 yards to Denver 18 where Marshall returns for no gain. After three plays, Rodriguez punts 29 yards to Seattle 45 where Warren signals fair catch. Seahawks drive to Denver 15 where Kasay's 33-yard field goal attempt misses. Broncos take over at Denver 20. After three plays, Rodriguez punts 43 yards to Seattle 38 where Warren signals for fair catch. After four plays, Tuten punts 39 yards to Denver 4 where Daniels downs punt. After three plays, Rodriguez punts 46 yards to Denver 48 where Warren returns 10 yards to the 38. Seahawks drive to Denver 14 where Kasay kicks 32-yard field goal at 11:10.

Dec. 13, 1992—Philadelphia 20, Seattle 17, at Seattle. Eagles win toss. Sydner returns kick 12 yards to Eagles' 16; illegal block penalty brings ball back to 8. Eagles drive to Philadelphia 45 where Feagles punts for a touchback. After 6 plays, Tuten punts 45 yards to Philadelphia 22 where Sydner returns 7 yards to 29. After 6 plays, Feagles punts 44 yards to Seattle 26 where Warren returns 5 yards to 31. After 5 plays, Tuten punts 32 yards to Philadelphia 20 where Sydner signals for fair catch. Eagles drive to Seattle 27 where Ruzek kicks 44-yard field goal with no time remaining.

Dec. 27, 1992—Miami 16, New England 13, at New England. Patriots win toss. Lockwood returns kickoff 15 yards to Patriots' 21. After three plays, McCarthy punts 39 yards to Miami 33 where Miller returns 2 yards to the 35. Miami drives to New England 18 where Stoyanovich kicks 35-yard field goal at 8:17.

Sept. 12, 1993—Detroit 19, New England 16, at New England. Patriots win toss. Patriots begin at 20. After 3 plays, Saxon punts 42 yards to Detroit 29 where Gray returns 12 yards to the 41. After 3 plays, Arnold punts 41 yards to New England 12 where Brown returns 16 yards to the 28. Patriots drive to Detroit 44 where Saxon punts into the end zone for a touchback. Detroit drives to New England 20 where Hanson kicks 38-yard field goal at 11:04.

Nov. 7, 1993—Buffalo 13, New England 10, at New England. Patriots win toss. T. Brown returns kickoff 27 yards to Patriots 30. Patriots drive to Buffalo 48 where Bills take over on downs. Bills drive to New England 25 where Metzelaars fumbles, and C. Brown recovers. After 3 plays, Saxon punts 46 yards to Buffalo 24 where Copeland returns 11 yards to the 35. Bills drive to New England 14 where Christie kicks 32-yard field goal at 9:22.

Dec. 19, 1993—Phoenix 30, Seattle 27, at Seattle. Cardinals win toss. Bailey returns kickoff 14 yards to Cardinals 20. Cardinals drive to Seattle 23 where Davis kicks 41-yard field goal at 6:45.

Jan. 2, 1994—Dallas 16, New York Giants 13, at New York. Giants win toss. Meggett returns kickoff 19 yards to Giants 19. After 6 plays, Horan punts 45 yards to Cowboys 25 where Widmer downs punt. Cowboys drive to Giants' 23 where Murray kicks 41-yard field goal at 10:44.

Jan. 2, 1994—New England 33, Miami 27, at New England. Dolphins win toss. McDuffie returns kickoff 21 yards to Miami 27. After 3 plays, Hatcher punts 43 yards to New England 29 where Harris returns 6 yards to the 35. After 2 plays, Brown intercepts pass from Bledsoe and returns 3 yards to Miami 49. After 3 plays, Hatcher punts 37 yards to New England 14 where Harris returns 18 yards to the 32. After 2 plays, Bledsoe passes 36 yards to Timpson for touchdown at 4:44.

Jan. 2, 1994—Los Angeles Raiders 33, Denver 30, at Los Angeles. Broncos win toss. Delpino returns kickoff 12 yards to Denver 25. Broncos drive to Los Angeles 22 where Elam's 40-yard field goal attempt is wide left. Raiders drive to Denver 29 where Jaeger kicks 47-yard field goal at 7:10.

***Jan. 3, 1994—Philadelphia 37, San Francisco 34,** at San Francisco. 49ers win toss. Walker returns kickoff, 19 yards to San Francisco 27. 49ers drive to Philadelphia 14 where Cofer misses 32-yard field goal. Eagles start at their 20-yard line, and, after 3 plays, Feagles punts 48 yards to San Francisco 36 where Carter fumbles and 49ers recover. After 7 plays, Wilmsmeyer punts 57 yards to Philadelphia 6 where Sikahema returns 16 yards to the 22. Eagles drive to San Francisco 10 where Ruzek kicks 28-yard field goal with no time remaining.

Sept. 4, 1994—Detroit 31, Atlanta 28, at Detroit. Falcons win toss. Falcons start at their own 16 after holding penalty on kickoff. After 3 plays, Alexander punts 41 yards to Detroit 39 where Clay returns 12 yards to Atlanta 49. Detroit drives to Atlanta 20 where Hanson kicks 37-yard field goal with 9:46 remaining.

Sept. 11, 1994—New York Jets 25, Denver 22, at New York. Jets win toss. Murrell returns kickoff 24 yards to New York 33. Jets drive to Denver 22 where Lowery kicks 39-yard field goal with 11:03 remaining.

***Sept. 19, 1994—Detroit 20, Dallas 17,** at Dallas. Lions win toss. Gray returns kickoff 24 yards to Detroit 32. Lions drive to Dallas 34 where Hanson's 51-yard field-goal attempt is blocked by Lett. Cowboys take possession at Dallas 42. Cowboys drive to Detroit 37 where Kennard fumbles and Swilling recovers. Lions take possession at Detroit 45. After 6 plays, Montgomery punts 31 yards to Dallas 16. Cowboys drive to Dallas 49 where Aikman fumbles and Thomas recovers at Dallas 43. Lions drive to Dallas 26 where Hanson kicks 44-yard field goal with 27 seconds remaining.

Oct. 16, 1994—Arizona 19, Washington 16, at Washington. Redskins win toss. Mitchell returns kickoff 27 yards to Washington 41. Redskins drive to Arizona 34 where Lohmiller's 51-yard field-goal attempt is blocked by Joyner and recovered by Williams who returns it to the Washington 37. After 5 plays, Peterson's 45-yard field-goal attempt is wide right. Redskins take possession at the Washington 36. After 3 plays, Roby punts 36 yards to the Arizona 37 where Robinson returns 3 yards to the 40. After 3 plays, Feagles punts 51 yards for a touchback. After 1 play, Shuler's pass is intercepted by Hoage who returns it to the Washington 12. Peterson kicks 29-yard field goal with 5:00 remaining.

Oct. 16, 1994—Miami 20, Los Angeles Raiders 17, at Miami. Dolphins win toss. McDuffie returns kickoff 19 yards to Miami 23. Dolphins drive to Los Angeles 12 where Stoyanovich kicks 29-yard field goal with 9:14 remaining.

#**Oct. 20, 1994—Minnesota 13, Green Bay 10,** at Minnesota. Vikings win toss. Ismail returns kickoff 22 yards to Minnesota 29. Vikings drive to Green Bay 9 where Fuad Reveiz kicks 27-yard field goal with 10:34 remaining.

Oct. 30, 1994—Detroit 28, New York Giants 25, at New York. Giants win toss. Lewis returns kickoff 16 yards to New York 27. After 3 plays, Horan punts 42 yards to Detroit 24 where Gray calls for fair catch. Detroit drives to New York 6 where Hanson kicks 24-yard field goal with 8:17 remaining.

Oct. 30, 1994—Arizona 20, Pittsburgh 17, at Arizona. Steelers win toss. Johnson returns kickoff 24 yards to Pittsburgh 30 where he fumbles and Arizona's Merritt recovers at Pittsburgh 32. After 3 plays, Davis kicks 51-yard field goal with 13:20 remaining.

Nov. 6, 1994—Cincinnati 20, Seattle 17, at Seattle. Seahawks win toss. Warren returns kickoff 32 yards to Seattle 33. After 3 plays, Tuten punts 37 yards to Cincinnati 28 where Sawyer calls for fair catch. After 3 plays, Johnson punts 64 yards to Seattle 2 where Truitt downs ball. Seahawks drive to Seattle 38 where Tuten punts 50 yards to Cincinnati 12 and Sawyer returns 5 yards to 17. Blake passes to Scott for 76 yards to Seattle 7. Pelfrey kicks 26-yard field goal with 6:46 remaining.

Nov. 6, 1994—Pittsburgh 12, Houston 9, at Houston. Steelers win toss. Stone returns kickoff 15 yards to Pittsburgh 28. After 3 plays, Royals punts 53 yards to Houston 13 where Givins downs ball. After 3 plays, Camarillo punts 57 yards to Pittsburgh 31 where Woodson returns 20 yards to Houston 49. After 3 plays, Royals punts 43 yards to Houston 15 where Coleman returns 3 yards to 18. After 5 plays, Camarillo punts 57 yards to Pittsburgh 12 where Hastings returns 12 yards to 24. Steelers drive to Houston 41 where Royals punts 29 yards to Houston 12, and Coleman calls for fair catch. Brown fumbles on first play and Jones recovers at Houston 22. After 1 play, Anderson kicks 40-yard field goal with 3:36 remaining.

Nov. 13, 1994—New England 26, Minnesota 20, at New England. Patriots win toss. Thompson returns kickoff 27 yards to New England 33. Patriots drive to Minnesota 14 where Bledsoe passes 14 yards to Turner for touchdown with 10:50 remaining.

Nov. 20, 1994—Pittsburgh 16, Miami 13, at Pittsburgh. Steelers win toss. Stone returns kickoff 15 yards to Pittsburgh 16. Steelers drive to Miami 39 where they lose possession on downs. Dolphins drive to Pittsburgh 47 where Arnold punts 35 yards to Pittsburgh 12 and Oliver downs ball. Steelers drive to Miami 21 where Anderson kicks 39-yard field goal with 4:41 remaining.

Nov. 27, 1994—Chicago 19, Arizona 16, at Arizona. Cardinals win toss. Levy returns kickoff 31 yards to Arizona 45. After 5 plays, Feagles punts 38 yards to the end zone for a touchback. Bears drive to Arizona 10 where Butler kicks 27-yard field goal with 6:49 remaining.

Nov. 27, 1994—Tampa Bay 20, Minnesota 17, at Minnesota. Buccaneers win toss. Harris returns kickoff 12 yards to Tampa Bay 38. After 6 plays, Stryzinski punts 40 yards to Minnesota 4 where Guilford muffs punt and Buccaneers' Brady recovers. Husted kicks 22-yard field goal with 12:52 remaining.

#**Dec. 1, 1994—Minnesota 33, Chicago 27,** at Minnesota. Bears win toss. Lewis returns kickoff 23 yards to Chicago 33. Bears drive to Minnesota 22 where Butler's 40-yard field goal attempt is wide left. After 1 play, Moon passes 65 yards to Carter for touchdown with 9:14 remaining.

Dec. 4, 1994—Denver 20, Kansas City 17, at Kansas City. Broncos win toss. Milburn returns kickoff 24 yards to Denver 29. After 3 plays, Millen fumbles and Phillips recovers at Denver 35. After 4 plays, Allen fumbles and Smith recovers at Denver 27. After 6 plays, Rouen punts 45 yards to Kansas City 25 where Hughes calls for fair catch. After 3 plays, Aguiar punts 33 yards to Denver 42 where Chiefs down ball. Broncos drive to Kansas City 17 where Elam kicks 34-yard field goal with 2:48 remaining.

Sept. 3, 1995—Cincinnati 24, Indianapolis 21, at Indianapolis. Bengals win toss. Dunn returns kickoff 15 yards to Bengals' 17. Cincinnati drives to Indianapolis 29 where Pelfrey kicks 47-yard field goal with 12:24 remaining.

Sept. 3, 1995—Atlanta 23, Carolina 20, at Atlanta. Panthers win toss. Baldwin downs kickoff for touchback. Panthers drive to Carolina 42 where Reich fumbles and ball is recovered by Archambeau at Carolina 31. Falcons drive to Panthers' 16 where Andersen kicks 35-yard field goal with 8:43 remaining.

Sept. 10, 1995—Indianapolis 27, New York Jets 24, at New York. Jets win toss. Carter downs kickoff for touchback. Jets punt downed at Colts' 37. Colts drive to Jets' 35 where Cofer kicks 52-yard field goal with 10:33 remaining.

Sept. 10, 1995—Kansas City 20, New York Giants 17, at Kansas City. Chiefs win toss. Vanover returns kickoff 30 yards to Chiefs' 28. Aguiar punts to Giants' 3. Horan punts to Chiefs' 49. Chiefs drive to Giants' 6 where Elliott kicks 23-yard field goal with 7:11 left.

Sept. 17, 1995—Dallas 23, Minnesota 17, at Minnesota. Cowboys win toss. K. Williams returns kickoff 23 yards to Cowboys' 27. E. Smith scores on 31-yard run with 12:34 left.

Sept. 17, 1995—Kansas City 23, Oakland 17, at Kansas City. Chiefs win toss. Vanover returns kickoff 28 yards to Chiefs' 41. M. Allen fumbles, ball recovered by Robbins at Raiders' 38. Hasty intercepts pass at Chiefs' 36 and returns it 64 yards for touchdown with 10:33 left.

Sept. 17, 1995—Atlanta 27, New Orleans 24, at Atlanta. Saints win toss. Hughes returns kickoff 21 yards to Saints' 17. Metcalf returns Wilmsmeyer's punt 18 yards to Saints' 39. Stryzinski punts, fair catch by Hughes at Saints' 14. Wilmsmeyer punt downed at Falcons' 6. Falcons drive to Saints' 3 where Andersen kicks 21-yard field goal with 7:02 left.

Oct. 8, 1995—Indianapolis 27, Miami 24, at Miami. Colts win toss. Warren returns kickoff 25 yards to Colts' 33. Colts drive to Dolphins' 10 where Blanchard kicks 27-yard field goal with 10:02 left.

Oct. 8, 1995—New York Giants 27, Arizona 21, at New York. Cardinals win toss. Terry returns kickoff 20 yards to Cardinals' 23. Hamilton recovers Krieg's fumble at Cardinals' 36. Lynch recovers Brown's fumble at Cardinals' 38. Armstead intercepts pass at Giants' 42 and returns it 58 yards for touchdown with 10:55 left.

Oct. 8, 1995—Minnesota 23, Houston 17, at Minnesota. Vikings win toss. Palmer returns kickoff 10 yards to Vikings' 15. Saxon's punt downed at Oilers' 8. Washington intercepts pass at Vikings' 47 and returns it 25 yards to Oilers' 28. R. Smith scores on 20-yard run with 7:50 left.

Oct. 8, 1995—Philadelphia 37, Washington 34, at Philadelphia. Redskins win toss. Redskins take possession at their 20 after touchback. Turk punt out of bounds at Eagles' 9. Eagles drive to Redskins' 18 where Anderson kicks 35-yard field goal with 4:54 left.

* **Oct. 9, 1995—Kansas City 29, San Diego 23,** at Kansas City. Chargers win toss. Coleman returns kickoff 24 yards to Chargers' 28. Vanover makes fair catch of Bennett's punt at Chiefs' 15. Coleman makes fair catch of Aguiar's punt at Chargers' 43. Vanover returns Bennett's punt 86 yards for a touchdown with 7:33 left.

Oct. 15, 1995—Tampa Bay 20, Minnesota 17, at Tampa Bay. Buccaneers win toss. Edmonds returns kickoff 19 yards to Buccaneers' 22. A. Lee returns Roby's punt to Vikings' 48. Vikings drive to Tampa Bays' 35 where Reveiz's 53-yard field-goal attempt is wide right. Buccaneers take over at own 43 and drive to Vikings' 33 where Husted kicks 51-yard field goal with 8:37 left.

Oct. 22, 1995—Washington 36, Detroit 30, at Washington. Redskins win toss. B. Mitchell returns kickoff 16 yards to Redskins' 27. Turk's punt downed at Lions' 4. D. Green intercepts S. Mitchell's pass and returns it 7 yards for touchdown with 11:19 left.

Oct. 29, 1995—Carolina 20, New England 17, at New England. Panthers win toss. Baldwin returns kickoff 22 yards to Panthers' 25. Meggett makes fair catch of Barnhardt's punt at Patriots' 9. Guliford returns O'Neill's punt 9 yards to Patriots' 32. Panthers drive to Patriots' 12 where Kasay kicks 29-yard field goal with 7:52 left.

Oct. 29, 1995—Cleveland 29, Cincinnati 26, at Cincinnati. Browns win toss. Hunter returns kickoff 31 yards to Browns' 31. Bieniemy returns Tupa's punt 9 yards to Bengals' 37. McCardell makes fair catch of Johnson's punt at Browns' 12. Bieniemy returns Tupa's punt 0 yards to Bengals' 38. Hall intercepts Blake's pass and returns it 5 yards to Bengals' 45. Browns drive to Bengals' 11 where Stover kicks 28-yard field goal with 8:30 left.

Oct. 29, 1995—Arizona 20, Seattle 14, at Arizona. Cardinals win toss. Dowdell returns kickoff 16 yards to Cardinals' 25. Cardinals drive to Seahawks' 10 where G. Davis' 27-yard field goal attempt is blocked. L. Lynch intercepts Friesz's pass at Cardinals' 28 and returns it 72 yards for a touchdown with 3:44 left.

Nov. 5, 1995—Pittsburgh 37, Chicago 34, at Chicago. Bears win toss. Timpson returns kickoff 23 yards to Bears' 33. Hastings returns Sauerbrun's punt 2 yards to Steelers' 31. Steelers drive to Bears' 6 where N. Johnson kicks 24-yard field goal with 6:41 left.

Nov. 12, 1995—Minnesota 30, Arizona 24, at Arizona. Vikings win toss. A. Lee returns kickoff 20 yards to Vikings' 25. Moon throws 50-yard touchdown pass to Ismail with 12:44 left.

Nov. 26, 1995—Arizona 40, Atlanta 37, at Arizona. Falcons win toss. J. Anderson returns kickoff 20 yards to Falcons' 20. Stryzinski fumbles punt snap. Recovered by England at Falcons' 10 where G. Davis kicks 28-yard field goal with 13:17 left.

Dec. 10, 1995—Tampa Bay 13, Green Bay 10, at Tampa Bay. Buccaneers win toss. Edmonds returns kickoff 24 yards to Buccaneers' 23. Tampa Bay drives to Packers' 29 where Husted kicks 47-yard field goal with 11:14 remaining.

**indicates Monday night game*
#indicates Thursday night game

POSTSEASON

Dec. 28, 1958—Baltimore 23, New York Giants 17, at New York in NFL Championship Game. Giants win toss. Maynard returns kickoff to Giants' 20. Chandler punts and Taseff returns one yard to Colts' 20. Colts win at 8:15 on a 1-yard run by Ameche.

Dec. 23, 1962—Dallas Texans 20, Houston Oilers 17, at Houston in AFL Championship Game. Texans win toss and kick off. Jancik returns kickoff to Oilers' 33. Norton punts and Jackson makes fair catch on Texans' 22. Wilson punts and Jancik makes fair catch on Oilers' 45. Robinson intercepts Blanda's pass and returns 13 yards to Oilers' 47. Wilson's punt rolls dead at Oilers' 12. Hull intercepts Blanda's pass and returns 23 yards to midfield. Texans win at 17:54 on a 25-yard field goal by Brooker.

Dec. 26, 1965—Green Bay 13, Baltimore 10, at Green Bay in NFL Divisional Playoff Game. Packers win toss. Moore returns kickoff to Packers' 22. Chandler punts and Haymond returns nine yards to Colts' 41. Gilburg punts and Wood makes fair catch at Packers' 21. Chandler punts and Haymond returns one yard to Colts' 41. Michaels misses 47-yard field goal. Packers win at 13:39 on 25-yard field goal by Chandler.

Dec. 25, 1971—Miami 27, Kansas City 24, at Kansas City in AFC Divisional Playoff Game. Chiefs win toss. Podolak, after a lateral from Buchanan, returns kickoff to Chiefs' 46. Stenerud's 42-yard field goal is blocked. Seiple punts and Podolak makes fair catch at Chiefs' 17. Wilson punts and Scott returns 18 yards to Dolphins' 39. Yepremian misses 62-yard field goal. Scott intercepts Dawson's pass and returns 13 yards to Dolphins' 46. Seiple punts and Podolak loses one yard to Chiefs' 15. Wilson punts and Scott makes fair catch on Dolphins' 30. Dolphins win at 22:40 on a 37-yard field goal by Yepremian.

Dec. 24, 1977—Oakland 37, Baltimore 31, at Baltimore in AFC Divisional Playoff Game. Colts win toss. Raiders start on own 42 following a punt late in the first overtime. Oakland works way into field-goal range on Stabler's 19-yard pass to Branch at Colts' 26. Four plays later, on the second play of the second overtime, Stabler hits Casper with a 10-yard touchdown pass at 15:43.

Jan. 2, 1982—San Diego 41, Miami 38, at Miami in AFC Divisional Playoff Game. Chargers win toss. San Diego drives from its 13 to Miami 8. On second-and-goal, Benirschke misses 27-yard field goal attempt wide left at 9:15. Miami has the ball twice and San Diego twice more before the Dolphins get their third possession. Miami drives from the San Diego 46 to Chargers' 17 and on fourth-and-two, von Schamann's 34-yard field goal attempt is blocked by San Diego's Winslow after 11:27. Fouts then completes four of five passes, including a 39-yarder to Joiner that puts the ball on Dolphins' 10. On first down, Benirschke kicks a 29-yard field goal at 13:52. San Diego's winning drive covered 74 yards in six plays.

Jan. 3, 1987—Cleveland 23, New York Jets 20, at Cleveland in AFC Divisional Playoff Game. Jets win toss. Jets' punt downed at Browns' 26. Moseley's 23-yard field goal attempt is wide right. Teams trade punts. Jets' second punt downed at Browns' 31. First overtime period expires eight plays later with Browns in possession at Jets' 42. Moseley kicks 27-yard field goal four plays into second overtime at 17:02.

Jan. 11, 1987—Denver 23, Cleveland 20, at Cleveland in AFC Championship Game. Browns win toss. Broncos hold Browns on four downs. Browns' punt returned four yards to Denver's 25. Elway completes 22- and 28-yard passes to set up Karlis's 33-yard field goal nine plays into drive at 5:38.

Jan. 3, 1988—Houston 23, Seattle 20, at Houston in AFC Wild Card Game. Seahawks win toss. Rodriguez punts to K. Johnson who returns one yard to Houston 15. Zendejas kicks 32-yard field goal 12 plays later at 8:05.

Dec. 31, 1989—Pittsburgh 26, Houston 23, at Houston in AFC Wild Card Playoff Game. Steelers win toss. Steelers punt to Oilers. Oilers' fumble recovered by Woodson and returned three yards. Four plays and 13 yards later, Anderson kicks a 50-yard field goal at 3:26.

Jan. 7, 1990—Los Angeles Rams 19, New York Giants 13, at New York in NFC Wild Card Game. Rams win toss. Everett completes two passes to move ball to Giants' 48. White called for pass interference; ball spotted on Giants' 25. Everett hits Anderson with a 30-yard touchdown pass at 1:06.

Jan. 3, 1993—Buffalo 41, Houston 38, at Buffalo in AFC Wild Card Game. Houston wins toss. Oilers begin at 20. After 2 plays, Moon's pass is intercepted by Odomes who returns ball 2 yards to Houston 35. After 2 plays, Christie kicks 32-yard field goal at 3:06.

Jan. 8, 1994—Kansas City 27, Pittsburgh 24, at Kansas City in AFC Wild Card Game. Kansas City wins toss. Hughes returns kickoff 20 yards to Kansas City 25. After 3 plays, Barker punts 48 yards to Pittsburgh 18 where Woodson returns 8 yards to the 26. After 6 plays, Royals punts 30 yards to Kansas City 20. Kansas City drives to Pittsburgh 14 where Lowery kicks 32-yard field goal at 11:03.

NFL POSTSEASON OVERTIME GAMES
(BY LENGTH OF GAME)

Dec. 25, 1971	Miami 27, KANSAS CITY 24	82:40
Dec. 23, 1962	Dallas Texans 20, HOUSTON 17	77:54
Jan. 3, 1987	CLEVELAND 23, New York Jets 20	77:02
Dec. 24, 1977	Oakland 37, BALTIMORE 31	75:43
Jan. 2, 1982	San Diego 41, MIAMI 38	73:52
Dec. 26, 1965	GREEN BAY 13, Baltimore 10	73:39
Jan. 8, 1994	KANSAS CITY 27, Pittsburgh 24	71:03
Dec. 28, 1958	Baltimore 23, N.Y. GIANTS 17	68:15
Jan. 3, 1988	HOUSTON 23, Seattle 20	68:05
Jan. 11, 1987	Denver 23, CLEVELAND 20	65:38
Dec. 31, 1989	Pittsburgh 26, HOUSTON 23	63:26
Jan. 3, 1993	BUFFALO 41, Houston 38	63:06
Jan. 7, 1990	Los Angeles Rams 19, N.Y. GIANTS 13	61:06

Home team in CAPS

OVERTIME WON-LOST RECORDS, 1974-1995
(REGULAR SEASON)

AFC	W	L	T	Pct.
Buffalo	9	4	0	.692
Cincinnati	12	6	0	.667
Cleveland	12	8	1	.595
Denver	12	9	2	.565
Houston	6	12	0	.333
Indianapolis	8	6	1	.567
Jacksonville	0	0	0	.000
Kansas City	7	7	2	.500
Miami	8	13	1	.386
New England	7	14	0	.333
New York Jets	9	7	2	.556
Oakland	10	8	0	.556
Pittsburgh	10	4	1	.700
San Diego	7	10	0	.412
Seattle	4	9	0	.308
NFC	**W**	**L**	**T**	**Pct.**
Arizona	8	6	2	.563
Atlanta	7	9	1	.441
Carolina	1	1	0	.500
Chicago	10	11	0	.476
Dallas	8	5	0	.615
Detroit	9	8	1	.528
Green Bay	5	10	4	.368
Minnesota	12	12	2	.500
New Orleans	2	7	0	.222
New York Giants	7	9	1	.441
Philadelphia	7	8	2	.471
St. Louis	6	5	1	.542
San Francisco	4	5	1	.450
Tampa Bay	8	7	1	.531
Washington	10	5	0	.667

OVERTIME GAMES BY YEAR
(REGULAR SEASON)

1995-21	1989-11	1983-19	1977- 6
1994-16	1988- 9	1982- 4	1976- 5
1993-7	1987-13	1981-10	1975- 9
1992-10	1986-16	1980-13	1974- 2
1991-15	1985-10	1979-12	
1990-10	1984- 9	1978-11	

OVERTIME GAME SUMMARY—1974-1995

There have been 238 overtime games in regular-season play since the rule was adopted in 1974 (21 in 1995 season). Breakdown follows:

178 (16) times both teams had at least one possession (75%)
60 (5) times the team which won the toss drove for winning score (42 FG, 18 TD) (25%)
116 (13) times the team which won the toss won the game (49%)
109 (8) times the team which lost the toss won the game (46%)
162 (13) games were decided by a field goal (68%)
62 (8) games were decided by a touchdown (26%)
1 (0) game was decided by a safety (0.4%)
13 (0) games ended tied (5.5%). Last time: Nov. 19, 1989, Cleveland 10, Kansas City 10, at Cleveland

Note: The number in parentheses represents the 1995 season total in each category.

MOST OVERTIME GAMES, SEASON

5 Green Bay Packers, 1983
4 Denver Broncos, 1985
Cleveland Browns, 1989
Minnesota Vikings, 1994
Arizona Cardinals, 1995
Minnesota Vikings, 1995
3 By many teams, last time: Atlanta Falcons, Indianapolis Colts, Kansas City Chiefs, 1995

LONGEST CONSECUTIVE GAME STREAKS WITHOUT OVERTIME (Current)

92 St. Louis Rams (last OT game, 10/7/90 vs. Cincinnati)
40 Buffalo Bills (last OT game, 11/7/93 vs. New England)
32 San Francisco 49ers (last OT game, 1/3/94 vs. Minnesota)
(Record: 110, Phoenix Cardinals, 12/7/86-12/19/93)

SHORTEST OVERTIME GAMES

0:21 Chicago 23, Detroit 17; 11/27/80—only kickoff return for TD
0:30 Baltimore 29, New England 23; 9/4/83
0:55 New York Giants 16, Philadelphia 10; 9/29/85

There have been 13 overtime postseason games dating back to 1958. In 12 cases, both teams had at least one possession. Last time: 1/8/94, Kansas City 27, Pittsburgh 24.

LONGEST OVERTIME GAMES
(ALL POSTSEASON GAMES)

22:40 Miami 27, Kansas City 24; 12/25/71
17:54 Dallas Texans 20, Houston 17; 12/23/62
17:02 Cleveland 23, New York Jets 20; 1/3/87

OVERTIME SCORING SUMMARY

162 were decided by a field goal
25 were decided by a touchdown pass
19 were decided by a touchdown run

OVERTIME GAMES

9 were decided by interceptions (Atlanta 40, New Orleans 34, 9/2/79; Atlanta 47, Green Bay 41, 11/27/83; New York Giants 16, Philadelphia 10, 9/29/85; Indianapolis 23, Cleveland 17, 12/10/89; Cleveland 30, San Diego 24, 10/20/91; Kansas City 23, Oakland 17, 9/17/95; New York Giants 27, Arizona 21, 10/8/95; Washington 36, Detroit 30, 10/22/95; Arizona 20, Seattle 14, 10/29/95)
2 were decided on a fake field goal/touchdown pass (Minnesota 22, Chicago 16, 10/16/77; Cleveland 23, Minnesota 17, 12/17/89)
1 was decided by a kickoff return (Chicago 23, Detroit 17, 11/27/80)
1 was decided by a punt return (Kansas City 29, San Diego 23, 10/9/95)
1 was decided by a fumble recovery (Baltimore 29, New England 23, 9/4/83)
1 was decided on a fake field goal/touchdown run (Los Angeles Rams 27, Minnesota 21, 12/2/79)
1 was decided on a blocked field goal (Denver 30, San Diego 24, 11/17/85)
1 was decided on a blocked field goal/recovery by kicker (Green Bay 12, Chicago 6, 9/7/80)
1 was decided on a blocked field goal/recovery by kicking team (Philadelphia 23, New York Giants 17, 11/20/88)
1 was decided by a safety (Minnesota 23, Los Angeles Rams 21, 11/5/89)
13 ended tied

OVERTIME RECORDS

Longest Touchdown Pass

99 Yards — Ron Jaworski to Mike Quick, Philadelphia 23, Atlanta 17 (11/10/85)
65 Yards — Warren Moon to Cris Carter, Minnesota 33, Chicago 27 (12/1/94)
50 Yards — Tommy Kramer to Ahmad Rashad, Minnesota 27, Green Bay 21 (9/23/79)
50 Yards — Jim Harbaugh to Neal Anderson, Chicago 23, Detroit 17 (12/2/90)
50 Yards — Warren Moon to Qadry Ismail, Minnesota 30, Arizona 24 (11/12/95)

Longest Touchdown Run

60 Yards — Herschel Walker, Dallas 23, New England 17 (11/15/87)
42 Yards — Eric Dickerson, Los Angeles Rams 26, Tampa Bay 20 (10/5/86)
31 Yards — Emmitt Smith, Dallas 23, Minnesota 17 (9/17/95)

Longest Field Goal

52 Yards — Mike Cofer, Indianapolis 27, N.Y. Jets 24 (9/10/95)
51 Yards — Greg Davis, New England 23, Indianapolis 20 (10/29/89)
Greg Davis, Arizona 20, Pittsburgh 17 (10/30/94)
Michael Husted, Tampa Bay 20, Minnesota 17 (10/15/95)
50 Yards — Morten Andersen, New Orleans 20, Philadelphia 17 (12/11/83)
Norm Johnson, Atlanta 23, New Orleans 20 (11/24/91)

Longest Touchdown Plays

99 Yards — (Pass) Ron Jaworski to Mike Quick, Philadelphia 23, Atlanta 17 (11/10/85)
95 Yards — (Kickoff return) Dave Williams, Chicago 23, Detroit 17 (11/27/80)
86 Yards — (Punt return) Tamarick Vanover, Kansas City 29, San Diego 23 (10/9/95)
72 Yards — (Interception return) Lorenzo Lynch, Arizona 20, Seattle 14 (10/29/95)

NFL PAID ATTENDANCE

For detailed 1995 attendance, see page 235.

Year	Regular Season		Average	Postseason	Total
1995	#15,043,562	(240 games)	#62,682	790,906 (12)	#15,834,468
1994	14,030,435	(224 games)	62,636	779,738 (12)	14,810,173
1993	13,966,843	(224 games)	62,352	814,607 (12)	14,781,450
1992	13,828,887	(224 games)	61,736	815,910 (12)	14,644,797
1991	13,841,459	(224 games)	61,792	813,247 (12)	14,654,706
1990	13,959,896	(224 games)	62,321	847,543 (12)	14,807,439
1989	13,625,662	(224 games)	60,829	685,771 (10)	14,311,433
1988	13,539,848	(224 games)	60,446	658,317 (10)	14,198,165
1987	*11,406,166	(210 games)	54,315	656,977 (10)	12,063,143
1986	13,588,551	(224 games)	60,663	734,002 (10)	14,322,553
1985	13,345,047	(224 games)	59,567	710,768 (10)	14,055,815
1984	13,398,112	(224 games)	59,813	665,194 (10)	14,063,306
1983	13,277,222	(224 games)	59,273	675,513 (10)	13,952,735
1982	**7,367,438	(126 games)	58,472	1,033,153 (16)	8,400,591
1981	13,606,990	(224 games)	60,745	637,763 (10)	14,244,753
1980	13,392,230	(224 games)	59,787	624,430 (10)	14,016,660
1979	13,182,039	(224 games)	58,848	630,326 (10)	13,812,365
1978	12,771,800	(224 games)	57,017	624,388 (10)	13,396,188
1977	11,018,632	(196 games)	56,218	534,925 (8)	11,553,557
1976	11,070,543	(196 games)	56,482	492,884 (8)	11,563,427
1975	10,213,193	(182 games)	56,116	475,919 (8)	10,689,112
1974	10,236,322	(182 games)	56,244	438,664 (8)	10,674,986
1973	10,730,933	(182 games)	58,961	525,433 (8)	11,256,366
1972	10,445,827	(182 games)	57,395	483,345 (8)	10,929,172
1971	10,076,035	(182 games)	55,363	483,891 (8)	10,559,926
1970	9,533,333	(182 games)	52,381	458,493 (8)	9,991,826
1969	6,096,127	(112 games) NFL	54,430	162,279 (3)	6,258,406
	2,843,373	(70 games) AFL	40,620	167,088 (3)	3,010,461
1968	5,882,313	(112 games) NFL	52,521	215,902 (3)	6,098,215
	2,635,004	(70 games) AFL	37,643	114,438 (2)	2,749,442
1967	5,938,924	(112 games) NFL	53,026	166,208 (3)	6,105,132
	2,295,697	(63 games) AFL	36,439	53,330 (1)	2,349,027
1966	5,337,044	(105 games) NFL	50,829	74,152 (1)	5,411,196
	2,160,369	(63 games) AFL	34,291	42,080 (1)	2,202,449
1965	4,634,021	(98 games) NFL	47,286	100,304 (2)	4,734,325
	1,782,384	(56 games) AFL	31,828	30,361 (1)	1,812,745
1964	4,563,049	(98 games) NFL	46,562	79,544 (1)	4,642,593
	1,447,875	(56 games) AFL	25,855	40,242 (1)	1,488,117
1963	4,163,643	(98 games) NFL	42,486	45,801 (1)	4,209,444
	1,208,697	(56 games) AFL	21,584	63,171 (2)	1,271,868
1962	4,003,421	(98 games) NFL	40,851	64,892 (1)	4,068,313
	1,147,302	(56 games) AFL	20,487	37,981 (1)	1,185,283
1961	3,986,159	(98 games) NFL	40,675	39,029 (1)	4,025,188
	1,002,657	(56 games) AFL	17,904	29,556 (1)	1,032,213
1960	3,128,296	(78 games) NFL	40,106	67,325 (1)	3,195,621
	926,156	(56 games) AFL	16,538	32,183 (1)	958,339
1959	3,140,000	(72 games)	43,617	57,545 (1)	3,197,545
1958	3,006,124	(72 games)	41,752	123,659 (2)	3,129,783
1957	2,836,318	(72 games)	39,393	119,579 (2)	2,955,897
1956	2,551,263	(72 games)	35,434	56,836 (1)	2,608,099
1955	2,521,836	(72 games)	35,026	85,693 (1)	2,607,529
1954	2,190,571	(72 games)	30,425	43,827 (1)	2,234,398
1953	2,164,585	(72 games)	30,064	54,577 (1)	2,219,162
1952	2,052,126	(72 games)	28,502	97,507 (2)	2,149,633
1951	1,913,019	(72 games)	26,570	57,522 (1)	1,970,541
1950	1,977,753	(78 games)	25,356	136,647 (3)	2,114,400
1949	1,391,735	(60 games)	23,196	27,980 (1)	1,419,715
1948	1,525,243	(60 games)	25,421	36,309 (1)	1,561,552
1947	1,837,437	(60 games)	30,624	66,268 (2)	1,903,705
1946	1,732,135	(55 games)	31,493	58,346 (1)	1,790,481
1945	1,270,401	(50 games)	25,408	32,178 (1)	1,302,579
1944	1,019,649	(50 games)	20,393	46,016 (1)	1,065,665
1943	969,128	(40 games)	24,228	71,315 (2)	1,040,443
1942	887,920	(55 games)	16,144	36,006 (1)	923,926
1941	1,108,615	(55 games)	20,157	55,870 (2)	1,164,485
1940	1,063,025	(55 games)	19,328	36,034 (1)	1,099,059
1939	1,071,200	(55 games)	19,476	32,279 (1)	1,103,479
1938	937,197	(55 games)	17,040	48,120 (1)	985,317
1937	963,039	(55 games)	17,510	15,878 (1)	978,917
1936	816,007	(54 games)	15,111	29,545 (1)	845,552
1935	638,178	(53 games)	12,041	15,000 (1)	653,178
1934	492,684	(60 games)	8,211	35,059 (1)	527,743

 # Record

**Players' 24-day strike reduced 224-game schedule to 210 games.*

***Players' 57-day strike reduced 224-game schedule to 126 games.*

NFL'S 10 BIGGEST ATTENDANCE WEEKENDS
(Paid Count)

Weekend	Games	Attendance
December 9-11, 1995	15	963,521
November 19-20, 1995	15	962,523
September 17-18, 1995	15	958,105
December 16-18, 1995	15	956,675
November 30, December 3-4, 1995	15	940,032
September 3-4, 1995	15	937,747
October 16-17, 1988	14	934,211
December 23-25, 1995	15	933,880
September 10-11, 1995	15	930,401
November 23, 26-27, 1995	15	928,560

NFL'S 10 HIGHEST SCORING WEEKENDS

Point Total	Date	Weekend
761	October 16-17, 1983	7th
739	November 23, 26-27, 1995	13th
736	October 25-26, 1987	7th
734	November 19-20, 1995	12th
732	November 9-10, 1980	10th
725	November 24, 27-28, 1983	13th
714	September 17-18, 1989	2nd
711	November 26, 29-30, 1987	12th
710	November 28, December 1-2, 1985	13th
705	December 16-18, 1995	16th

TOP 10 TELEVISED SPORTS EVENTS OF ALL-TIME
(Based on A.C. Nielsen Figures)

Program	Date	Network	Share	Rating
Super Bowl XVI	1/24/82	CBS	73.0	49.1
Super Bowl XVII	1/30/83	NBC	69.0	48.6
Winter Olympics	2/23/94	CBS	64.0	48.5
Super Bowl XX	1/26/86	NBC	70.0	48.3
Super Bowl XII	1/15/78	CBS	67.0	47.2
Super Bowl XIII	1/21/79	NBC	74.0	47.1
Super Bowl XVIII	1/22/84	CBS	71.0	46.4
Super Bowl XIX	1/20/85	ABC	63.0	46.4
Super Bowl XIV	1/20/80	CBS	67.0	46.3
Super Bowl XXX	1/28/96	NBC	68.0	46.0

TEN MOST WATCHED TV PROGRAMS & ESTIMATED TOTAL NUMBER OF VIEWERS
(Based on A.C. Nielsen Figures)

Program	Date	Network	*Total Viewers
Super Bowl XXX	Jan. 28, 1996	NBC	138,488,000
Super Bowl XXVIII	Jan. 30, 1994	NBC	134,800,000
Super Bowl XXVII	Jan. 31, 1993	NBC	133,400,000
Super Bowl XX	Jan. 26, 1986	NBC	127,000,000
Winter Olympics	Feb. 23, 1994	CBS	126,686,000
Super Bowl XXIX	Jan. 29, 1995	ABC	125,216,000
Super Bowl XXI	Jan. 25, 1987	CBS	122,640,000
M*A*S*H (Special)	Feb. 28, 1983	CBS	121,624,000
Winter Olympics	Feb. 25, 1994	CBS	119,900,000
Super Bowl XXVI	Jan. 26, 1992	CBS	119,680,000

**Watched some portion of the broadcast*

NFL'S 10 BIGGEST TEAM SINGLE-SEASON HOME ATTENDANCE TOTALS
(Paid Count)

Year	Club	Games	Attendance
1980	Detroit Lions	8	634,204
1988	Buffalo Bills	8	631,818
1991	Buffalo Bills	8	631,786
1992	Buffalo Bills	8	630,978
1994	Kansas City Chiefs	8	626,612
1989	Buffalo Bills	8	626,399
1995	Kansas City Chiefs	8	625,936
1989	Cleveland Browns	8	625,240
1993	Buffalo Bills	8	624,349
1988	Cleveland Browns	8	624,154

TOP FIVE PAID ATTENDANCE TOTALS FOR ALL GAMES (Includes Preseason)

Year	Preseason	Regular Season	Postseason	All Games
1995	3,368,289	15,043,562	790,906	19,202,757
1994	3,200,091	14,030,435	779,738	18,010,264
1993	3,170,381	13,966,843	814,607	17,951,831
1992	3,139,557	13,828,887	815,910	17,784,354
1991	3,097,433	13,841,459	813,247	17,752,139

TEN HIGHEST-RATED ABC NFL MONDAY NIGHT FOOTBALL GAMES OF ALL-TIME
(Based on A.C. Nielsen Figures)

Game	Date	Rating	Share
Chicago at Miami	12/2/85	29.6	46.0
N.Y. Giants at San Francisco	12/3/90	26.9	42.0
Dallas at Washington	10/2/78	26.8	43.0
Pittsburgh at San Diego	12/22/80	25.3	40.0
Philadelphia at Miami	11/30/81	25.3	40.0
Pittsburgh at Houston	12/10/79	25.1	40.0
Dallas at Miami	12/17/84	25.1	40.0
Pittsburgh at Dallas	9/13/82	24.9	42.0
Cincinnati at Oakland	12/6/76	24.7	40.0
Dallas at Washington	10/8/73	24.6	40.0
Minnesota at Atlanta	11/19/73	24.6	40.0

NFL'S TEN BIGGEST SINGLE-GAME ATTENDANCE TOTALS

Date	Site	Game	Teams	Attendance
August 15, 1994	Azteca Stadium	American Bowl (Mexico City)	Cowboys vs. Oilers	112,376
August 22, 1947	Soldier Field	College All-Star	Bears vs. All-Stars	105,840
January 20, 1980	Rose Bowl	Super Bowl XIV	Steelers vs. Rams	103,985
January 30, 1983	Rose Bowl	Super Bowl XVII	Redskins vs. Dolphins	103,667
January 9, 1977	Rose Bowl	Super Bowl XI	Raiders vs. Vikings	103,438
November 10, 1957	L.A. Coliseum	Regular Season	49ers at Rams	102,368
January 25, 1987	Rose Bowl	Super Bowl XXI	Giants vs. Broncos	101,643
August 20, 1948	Soldier Field	College All-Star	Cardinals vs. All-Stars	101,220
August 28, 1942	Soldier Field	College All-Star	Bears vs. All-Stars	101,100
November 2, 1958	L.A. Coliseum	Regular Season	Bears at Rams	100,470

NUMBER-ONE DRAFT CHOICES

Season	Date	Team	Player	Position	College
1996	April 20-21	New York Jets	Keyshawn Johnson	WR	Southern California
1995	April 22-23	Cincinnati	Ki-Jana Carter	RB	Penn State
1994	April 24-25	Cincinnati	Dan Wilkinson	DT	Ohio State
1993	April 25-26	New England	Drew Bledsoe	QB	Washington State
1992	April 26-27	Indianapolis	Steve Emtman	DT	Washington
1991	April 21-22	Dallas	Russell Maryland	DT	Miami
1990	April 22-23	Indianapolis	Jeff George	QB	Illinois
1989	April 23-24	Dallas	Troy Aikman	QB	UCLA
1988	April 24-25	Atlanta	Aundray Bruce	LB	Auburn
1987	April 28-29	Tampa Bay	Vinny Testaverde	QB	Miami
1986	April 29-30	Tampa Bay	Bo Jackson	RB	Auburn
1985	April 30-May 1	Buffalo	Bruce Smith	DE	Virginia Tech
1984	May 1-2	New England	Irving Fryar	WR	Nebraska
1983	April 26-27	Baltimore	John Elway	QB	Stanford
1982	April 27-28	New England	Kenneth Sims	DT	Texas
1981	April 28-29	New Orleans	George Rogers	RB	South Carolina
1980	April 29-30	Detroit	Billy Sims	RB	Oklahoma
1979	May 3-4	Buffalo	Tom Cousineau	LB	Ohio State
1978	May 2-3	Houston	Earl Campbell	RB	Texas
1977	May 3-4	Tampa Bay	Ricky Bell	RB	Southern California
1976	April 8-9	Tampa Bay	Lee Roy Selmon	DE	Oklahoma
1975	January 28-29	Atlanta	Steve Bartkowski	QB	California
1974	January 29-30	Dallas	Ed Jones	DE	Tennessee State
1973	January 30-31	Houston	John Matuszak	DE	Tampa
1972	February 1-2	Buffalo	Walt Patulski	DE	Notre Dame
1971	January 28-29	New England	Jim Plunkett	QB	Stanford
1970	January 27-28	Pittsburgh	Terry Bradshaw	QB	Louisiana Tech
1969	January 28-29	Buffalo (AFL)	O.J. Simpson	RB	Southern California
1968	January 30-31	Minnesota	Ron Yary	T	Southern California
1967	March 14	Baltimore	Bubba Smith	DT	Michigan State
1966	November 27, 1965	Atlanta	Tommy Nobis	LB	Texas
	November 28, 1965	Miami (AFL)	Jim Grabowski	RB	Illinois
1965	November 28, 1964	New York Giants	Tucker Frederickson	RB	Auburn
	November 28, 1964	Houston (AFL)	Lawrence Elkins	E	Baylor
1964	December 2, 1963	San Francisco	Dave Parks	E	Texas Tech
	November 30, 1963	Boston (AFL)	Jack Concannon	QB	Boston College
1963	December 3, 1962	Los Angeles	Terry Baker	QB	Oregon State
	December 1, 1962	Kansas City (AFL)	Buck Buchanan	DT	Grambling
1962	December 4, 1961	Washington	Ernie Davis	RB	Syracuse
	December 2, 1961	Oakland (AFL)	Roman Gabriel	QB	North Carolina State
1961	December 27-28, 1960	Minnesota	Tommy Mason	RB	Tulane
	November 23, 1960	Buffalo (AFL)	Ken Rice	G	Auburn
1960	Secret Draft	Los Angeles	Billy Cannon	RB	Louisiana State
	November 22, December 2, 1959	(AFL had no formal first pick)			
1959	December 2, 1958	Green Bay	Randy Duncan	QB	Iowa
1958	December 2, 1957	Chicago Cardinals	King Hill	QB	Rice
1957	November 27, 1956	Green Bay	Paul Hornung	HB	Notre Dame
1956	November 29, 1955	Pittsburgh	Gary Glick	DB	Colorado A&M
1955	January 27-28	Baltimore	George Shaw	QB	Oregon
1954	January 28	Cleveland	Bobby Garrett	QB	Stanford
1953	January 22	San Francisco	Harry Babcock	E	Georgia
1952	January 17	Los Angeles	Bill Wade	QB	Vanderbilt
1951	January 18-19	New York Giants	Kyle Rote	HB	Southern Methodist
1950	January 21-22	Detroit	Leon Hart	E	Notre Dame
1949	December 21, 1948	Philadelphia	Chuck Bednarik	C	Pennsylvania
1948	December 19, 1947	Washington	Harry Gilmer	QB	Alabama
1947	December 16, 1946	Chicago Bears	Bob Fenimore	HB	Oklahoma A&M
1946	January 14	Boston	Frank Dancewicz	QB	Notre Dame
1945	April 6	Chicago Cardinals	Charley Trippi	HB	Georgia
1944	April 19	Boston	Angelo Bertelli	QB	Notre Dame
1943	April 8	Detroit	Frank Sinkwich	HB	Georgia
1942	December 22, 1941	Pittsburgh	Bill Dudley	HB	Virginia
1941	December 10, 1940	Chicago Bears	Tom Harmon	HB	Michigan
1940	December 9, 1939	Chicago Cardinals	George Cafego	HB	Tennessee
1939	December 8, 1938	Chicago Cardinals	Ki Aldrich	C	Texas Christian
1938	December 12, 1937	Cleveland	Corbett Davis	FB	Indiana
1937	December 12, 1936	Philadelphia	Sam Francis	FB	Nebraska
1936	February 8	Philadelphia	Jay Berwanger	HB	Chicago

Note: From 1947 through 1958, the first selection in the draft was a Bonus pick, awarded to the winner of a random draw. That club, in turn, forfeited its last-round draft choice. The winner of the Bonus choice was eliminated from future draws. The system was abolished after 1958, by which time all clubs had received a Bonus choice.

FIRST-ROUND SELECTIONS

FIRST-ROUND SELECTIONS

If club had no first-round selection, first player drafted is listed with round in parentheses.

ARIZONA CARDINALS

Year	Player, College, Position
1936	Jim Lawrence, Texas Christian, B
1937	Ray Buivid, Marquette, B
1938	Jack Robbins, Arkansas, B
1939	Charles (Ki) Aldrich, Texas Christian, C
1940	George Cafego, Tennessee, B
1941	John Kimbrough, Texas A&M, B
1942	Steve Lach, Duke, B
1943	Glenn Dobbs, Tulsa, B
1944	Pat Harder, Wisconsin, B
1945	Charley Trippi, Georgia, B
1946	Dub Jones, Louisiana State, B
1947	DeWitt (Tex) Coulter, Army, T
1948	Jim Spavital, Oklahoma A&M, B
1949	Bill Fischer, Notre Dame, G
1950	Jack Jennings, Ohio State, T (2)
1951	Jerry Groom, Notre Dame, C
1952	Ollie Matson, San Francisco, B
1953	Johnny Olszewski, California, B
1954	Lamar McHan, Arkansas, B
1955	Max Boydston, Oklahoma, E
1956	Joe Childress, Auburn, B
1957	Jerry Tubbs, Oklahoma, C
1958	King Hill, Rice, B
	John David Crow, Texas A&M, B
1959	Bill Stacy, Mississippi State, B
1960	George Izo, Notre Dame, QB
1961	Ken Rice, Auburn, T
1962	Fate Echols, Northwestern, DT
	Irv Goode, Kentucky, C
1963	Jerry Stovall, Louisiana State, S
	Don Brumm, Purdue, DE
1964	Ken Kortas, Louisville, DT
1965	Joe Namath, Alabama, QB
1966	Carl McAdams, Oklahoma, LB
1967	Dave Williams, Washington, WR
1968	MacArthur Lane, Utah State, RB
1969	Roger Wehrli, Missouri, DB
1970	Larry Stegent, Texas A&M, RB
1971	Norm Thompson, Utah, CB
1972	Bobby Moore, Oregon, RB-WR
1973	Dave Butz, Purdue, DT
1974	J.V. Cain, Colorado, TE
1975	Tim Gray, Texas A&M, DB
1976	Mike Dawson, Arizona, DT
1977	Steve Pisarkiewicz, Missouri, QB
1978	Steve Little, Arkansas, K
	Ken Greene, Washington State, DB
1979	Ottis Anderson, Miami, RB
1980	Curtis Greer, Michigan, DE
1981	E.J. Junior, Alabama, LB
1982	Luis Sharpe, UCLA, T
1983	Leonard Smith, McNeese State, DB
1984	Clyde Duncan, Tennessee, WR
1985	Freddie Joe Nunn, Mississippi, LB
1986	Anthony Bell, Michigan State, LB
1987	Kelly Stouffer, Colorado State, QB
1988	Ken Harvey, California, LB
1989	Eric Hill, Louisiana State, LB
	Joe Wolf, Boston College, G
1990	Anthony Thompson, Indiana, RB (2)
1991	Eric Swann, No College, DE
1992	Tony Sacca, Penn State, QB (2)
1993	Garrison Hearst, Georgia, RB
	Ernest Dye, South Carolina, T
1994	Jamir Miller, UCLA, LB
1995	Frank Sanders, Auburn, WR (2)
1996	Simeon Rice, Illinois, DE

ATLANTA FALCONS

Year	Player, College, Position
1966	Tommy Nobis, Texas, LB
	Randy Johnson, Texas A&I, QB
1967	Leo Carroll, San Diego State, DE (2)
1968	Claude Humphrey, Tennessee State, DE
1969	George Kunz, Notre Dame, T
1970	John Small, Citadel, LB
1971	Joe Profit, Northeast Louisiana, RB
1972	Clarence Ellis, Notre Dame, DB
1973	Greg Marx, Notre Dame, DT (2)
1974	Gerald Tinker, Kent State, WR (2)
1975	Steve Bartkowski, California, QB
1976	Bubba Bean, Texas A&M, RB
1977	Warren Bryant, Kentucky, T
	Wilson Faumuina, San Jose State, DT
1978	Mike Kenn, Michigan, T
1979	Don Smith, Miami, DE
1980	Junior Miller, Nebraska, TE
1981	Bobby Butler, Florida State, DB
1982	Gerald Riggs, Arizona State, RB
1983	Mike Pitts, Alabama, DE
1984	Rick Bryan, Oklahoma, DT
1985	Bill Fralic, Pittsburgh, T
1986	Tony Casillas, Oklahoma, NT
	Tim Green, Syracuse, LB
1987	Chris Miller, Oregon, QB
1988	Aundray Bruce, Auburn, LB
1989	Deion Sanders, Florida State, DB
	Shawn Collins, Northern Arizona, WR
1990	Steve Broussard, Washington State, RB
1991	Bruce Pickens, Nebraska, DB
	Mike Pritchard, Colorado, WR
1992	Bob Whitfield, Stanford, T
	Tony Smith, Southern Mississippi, RB
1993	Lincoln Kennedy, Washington, T
1994	Bert Emanuel, Rice, WR (2)
1995	Devin Bush, Florida State, DB
1996	Shannon Brown, Alabama, DT (3)

BALTIMORE RAVENS

Year	Player, College, Position
1996	Jonathan Ogden, UCLA, T
	Ray Lewis, Miami, LB

BUFFALO BILLS

Year	Player, College, Position
1960	Richie Lucas, Penn State, QB
1961	Ken Rice, Auburn, T
1962	Ernie Davis, Syracuse, RB
1963	Dave Behrman, Michigan State, C
1964	Carl Eller, Minnesota, DE
1965	Jim Davidson, Ohio State, T
1966	Mike Dennis, Mississippi, RB
1967	John Pitts, Arizona State, S
1968	Haven Moses, San Diego State, WR
1969	O.J. Simpson, Southern California, RB
1970	Al Cowlings, Southern California, DE
1971	J.D. Hill, Arizona State, WR
1972	Walt Patulski, Notre Dame, DE
1973	Paul Seymour, Michigan, TE
	Joe DeLamielleure, Michigan State, G
1974	Reuben Gant, Oklahoma State, TE
1975	Tom Ruud, Nebraska, LB
1976	Mario Clark, Oregon, DB
1977	Phil Dokes, Oklahoma State, DT
1978	Terry Miller, Oklahoma State, RB
1979	Tom Cousineau, Ohio State, LB
	Jerry Butler, Clemson, WR
1980	Jim Ritcher, North Carolina State, C
1981	Booker Moore, Penn State, RB
1982	Perry Tuttle, Clemson, WR
1983	Tony Hunter, Notre Dame, TE
	Jim Kelly, Miami, QB
1984	Greg Bell, Notre Dame, RB
1985	Bruce Smith, Virginia Tech, DE
	Derrick Burroughs, Memphis State, DB
1986	Ronnie Harmon, Iowa, RB
	Will Wolford, Vanderbilt, T
1987	Shane Conlan, Penn State, LB
1988	Thurman Thomas, Oklahoma State, RB (2)
1989	Don Beebe, Chadron, Neb., WR (3)
1990	James Williams, Fresno State, DB
1991	Henry Jones, Illinois, DB
1992	John Fina, Arizona, T
1993	Thomas Smith, North Carolina, DB
1994	Jeff Burris, Notre Dame, DB
1995	Ruben Brown, Pittsburgh, G
1996	Eric Moulds, Mississippi State, WR

CAROLINA PANTHERS

Year	Player, College, Position
1995	Kerry Collins, Penn State, QB
	Tyrone Poole, Ft. Valley State, DB
	Blake Brockermeyer, Texas, T
1996	Tim Biakabutuka, Michigan, RB

CHICAGO BEARS

Year	Player, College, Position
1936	Joe Stydahar, West Virginia, T
1937	Les McDonald, Nebraska, E
1938	Joe Gray, Oregon State, B
1939	Sid Luckman, Columbia, QB
	Bill Osmanski, Holy Cross, B
1940	Clyde (Bulldog) Turner, Hardin-Simmons, C
1941	Tom Harmon, Michigan, B
	Norm Standlee, Stanford, B
	Don Scott, Ohio State, B
1942	Frankie Albert, Stanford, B
1943	Bob Steber, Missouri, B
1944	Ray Evans, Kansas, B
1945	Don Lund, Michigan, B
1946	Johnny Lujack, Notre Dame, QB
1947	Bob Fenimore, Oklahoma State, B
	Don Kindt, Wisconsin, B
1948	Bobby Layne, Texas, QB
	Max Bumgardner, Texas, E
1949	Dick Harris, Texas, C
1950	Chuck Hunsinger, Florida, B
	Fred Morrison, Ohio State, B
1951	Bob Williams, Notre Dame, B
	Billy Stone, Bradley, B
	Gene Schroeder, Virginia, E
1952	Jim Dooley, Miami, B
1953	Billy Anderson, Compton (Calif.) J.C., B
1954	Stan Wallace, Illinois, B
1955	Ron Drzewiecki, Marquette, B
1956	Menan (Tex) Schriewer, Texas, E
1957	Earl Leggett, Louisiana State, T
1958	Chuck Howley, West Virginia, G
1959	Don Clark, Ohio State, B
1960	Roger Davis, Syracuse, G
1961	Mike Ditka, Pittsburgh, E
1962	Ronnie Bull, Baylor, RB
1963	Dave Behrman, Michigan State, C
1964	Dick Evey, Tennessee, DT
1965	Dick Butkus, Illinois, LB
	Gale Sayers, Kansas, RB
	Steve DeLong, Tennessee, T
1966	George Rice, Louisiana State, DT
1967	Loyd Phillips, Arkansas, DE
1968	Mike Hull, Southern California, RB
1969	Rufus Mayes, Ohio State, T
1970	George Farmer, UCLA, WR (3)
1971	Joe Moore, Missouri, RB
1972	Lionel Antoine, Southern Illinois, T
	Craig Clemons, Iowa, DB
1973	Wally Chambers, Eastern Kentucky, DE
1974	Waymond Bryant, Tennessee State, LB
	Dave Gallagher, Michigan, DT
1975	Walter Payton, Jackson State, RB
1976	Dennis Lick, Wisconsin, T
1977	Ted Albrecht, California, T
1978	Brad Shearer, Texas, DT (3)
1979	Dan Hampton, Arkansas, DT
	Al Harris, Arizona State, DE
1980	Otis Wilson, Louisville, LB
1981	Keith Van Horne, Southern California, T
1982	Jim McMahon, Brigham Young, QB
1983	Jim Covert, Pittsburgh, T
	Willie Gault, Tennessee, WR
1984	Wilber Marshall, Florida, LB
1985	William Perry, Clemson, DT
1986	Neal Anderson, Florida, RB
1987	Jim Harbaugh, Michigan, QB
1988	Brad Muster, Stanford, RB
	Wendell Davis, Louisiana State, WR
1989	Donnell Woolford, Clemson, DB
	Trace Armstrong, Florida, DE
1990	Mark Carrier, Southern California, DB
1991	Stan Thomas, Texas, T
1992	Alonzo Spellman, Ohio State, DE
1993	Curtis Conway, Southern California, WR

1994	John Thierry, Alcorn State, DE
1995	Rashaan Salaam, Colorado, RB
1996	Walt Harris, Mississippi State, DB

CINCINNATI BENGALS

Year	Player, College, Position
1968	Bob Johnson, Tennessee, C
1969	Greg Cook, Cincinnati, QB
1970	Mike Reid, Penn State, DT
1971	Vernon Holland, Tennessee State, T
1972	Sherman White, California, DE
1973	Isaac Curtis, San Diego State, WR
1974	Bill Kollar, Montana State, DT
1975	Glenn Cameron, Florida, LB
1976	Billy Brooks, Oklahoma, WR
	Archie Griffin, Ohio State, RB
1977	Eddie Edwards, Miami, DT
	Wilson Whitley, Houston, DT
	Mike Cobb, Michigan State, TE
1978	Ross Browner, Notre Dame, DT
	Blair Bush, Washington, C
1979	Jack Thompson, Washington State, QB
	Charles Alexander, Louisiana State, RB
1980	Anthony Muñoz, Southern California, T
1981	David Verser, Kansas, WR
1982	Glen Collins, Mississippi State, DE
1983	Dave Rimington, Nebraska, C
1984	Ricky Hunley, Arizona, LB
	Pete Koch, Maryland, DE
	Brian Blados, North Carolina, T
1985	Eddie Brown, Miami, WR
	Emanuel King, Alabama, LB
1986	Joe Kelly, Washington, LB
	Tim McGee, Tennessee, WR
1987	Jason Buck, Brigham Young, DE
1988	Rickey Dixon, Oklahoma, DB
1989	Eric Ball, UCLA, RB (2)
1990	James Francis, Baylor, LB
1991	Alfred Williams, Colorado, LB
1992	David Klingler, Houston, QB
	Darryl Williams, Miami, DB
1993	John Copeland, Alabama, DE
1994	Dan Wilkinson, Ohio State, DT
1995	Ki-Jana Carter, Penn State, RB
1996	Willie Anderson, Auburn, T

CLEVELAND BROWNS

Year	Player, College, Position
1950	Ken Carpenter, Oregon State, B
1951	Ken Konz, Louisiana State, B
1952	Bert Rechichar, Tennessee, DB
	Harry Agganis, Boston U., QB
1953	Doug Atkins, Tennessee, DE
1954	Bobby Garrett, Stanford, QB
	John Bauer, Illinois, G
1955	Kurt Burris, Oklahoma, C
1956	Preston Carpenter, Arkansas, B
1957	Jim Brown, Syracuse, RB
1958	Jim Shofner, Texas Christian, DB
1959	Rich Kreitling, Illinois, DE
1960	Jim Houston, Ohio State, DE
1961	Bobby Crespino, Mississippi, TE
1962	Gary Collins, Maryland, WR
	Leroy Jackson, Western Illinois, RB
1963	Tom Hutchinson, Kentucky, WR
1964	Paul Warfield, Ohio State, WR
1965	James Garcia, Purdue, T (2)
1966	Milt Morin, Massachusetts, TE
1967	Bob Matheson, Duke, LB
1968	Marvin Upshaw, Trinity, Tex., DT-DE
1969	Ron Johnson, Michigan, RB
1970	Mike Phipps, Purdue, QB
	Bob McKay, Texas, T
1971	Clarence Scott, Kansas State, CB
1972	Thom Darden, Michigan, DB
1973	Steve Holden, Arizona State, WR
	Pete Adams, Southern California, T
1974	Billy Corbett, Johnson C. Smith, T (2)
1975	Mack Mitchell, Houston, DE
1976	Mike Pruitt, Purdue, RB
1977	Robert Jackson, Texas A&M, LB
1978	Clay Matthews, Southern California, LB
	Ozzie Newsome, Alabama, TE
1979	Willis Adams, Houston, WR
1980	Charles White, Southern California, RB
1981	Hanford Dixon, Southern Mississippi, DB
1982	Chip Banks, Southern California, LB
1983	Ron Brown, Arizona State, WR (2)
1984	Don Rogers, UCLA, DB
1985	Greg Allen, Florida State, RB (2)
1986	Webster Slaughter, San Diego State, WR (2)
1987	Mike Junkin, Duke, LB
1988	Clifford Charlton, Florida, LB
1989	Eric Metcalf, Texas, RB
1990	Leroy Hoard, Michigan, RB (2)
1991	Eric Turner, UCLA, DB
1992	Tommy Vardell, Stanford, RB
1993	Steve Everitt, Michigan, C
1994	Antonio Langham, Alabama, DB
	Derrick Alexander, Michigan, WR
1995	Craig Powell, Ohio State, LB

DALLAS COWBOYS

Year	Player, College, Position
1960	None
1961	Bob Lilly, Texas Christian, DT
1962	Sonny Gibbs, Texas Christian, QB (2)
1963	Lee Roy Jordan, Alabama, LB
1964	Scott Appleton, Texas, DT
1965	Craig Morton, California, QB
1966	John Niland, Iowa, G
1967	Phil Clark, Northwestern, DB (3)
1968	Dennis Homan, Alabama, WR
1969	Calvin Hill, Yale, RB
1970	Duane Thomas, West Texas State, RB
1971	Tody Smith, Southern California, DE
1972	Bill Thomas, Boston College, RB
1973	Billy Joe DuPree, Michigan State, TE
1974	Ed (Too Tall) Jones, Tennessee State, DE
	Charley Young, North Carolina State, RB
1975	Randy White, Maryland, LB
	Thomas Henderson, Langston, LB
1976	Aaron Kyle, Wyoming, DB
1977	Tony Dorsett, Pittsburgh, RB
1978	Larry Bethea, Michigan State, DE
1979	Robert Shaw, Tennessee, C
1980	Bill Roe, Colorado, LB (3)
1981	Howard Richards, Missouri, T
1982	Rod Hill, Kentucky State, DB
1983	Jim Jeffcoat, Arizona State, DE
1984	Billy Cannon, Jr., Texas A&M, LB
1985	Kevin Brooks, Michigan, DE
1986	Mike Sherrard, UCLA, WR
1987	Danny Noonan, Nebraska, DT
1988	Michael Irvin, Miami, WR
1989	Troy Aikman, UCLA, QB
1990	Emmitt Smith, Florida, RB
1991	Russell Maryland, Miami, DT
	Alvin Harper, Tennessee, WR
	Kelvin Pritchett, Mississippi, DT
1992	Kevin Smith, Texas A&M, DB
	Robert Jones, East Carolina, LB
1993	Kevin Williams, Miami, WR (2)
1994	Shante Carver, Arizona State, DE
1995	Sherman Williams, Alabama, RB (2)
1996	Kavika Pittman, McNeese State, DE (2)

DENVER BRONCOS

Year	Player, College, Position
1960	Roger LeClerc, Trinity, Conn., C
1961	Bob Gaiters, New Mexico State, RB
1962	Merlin Olsen, Utah State, DT
1963	Kermit Alexander, UCLA, CB
1964	Bob Brown, Nebraska, T
1965	Dick Butkus, Illinois, LB (2)
1966	Jerry Shay, Purdue, DT
1967	Floyd Little, Syracuse, RB
1968	Curley Culp, Arizona State, DE (2)
1969	Grady Cavness, Texas-El Paso, DB (2)
1970	Bob Anderson, Colorado, RB
1971	Marv Montgomery, Southern California, T
1972	Riley Odoms, Houston, TE
1973	Otis Armstrong, Purdue, RB
1974	Randy Gradishar, Ohio State, LB
1975	Louis Wright, San Jose State, DB
1976	Tom Glassic, Virginia, G
1977	Steve Schindler, Boston College, G
1978	Don Latimer, Miami, DT
1979	Kelvin Clark, Nebraska, T
1980	Rulon Jones, Utah State, DE (2)
1981	Dennis Smith, Southern California, DB
1982	Gerald Willhite, San Jose State, RB
1983	Chris Hinton, Northwestern, G
1984	Andre Townsend, Mississippi, DE (2)
1985	Steve Sewell, Oklahoma, RB
1986	Jim Juriga, Illinois, T (4)
1987	Ricky Nattiel, Florida, WR
1988	Ted Gregory, Syracuse, NT
1989	Steve Atwater, Arkansas, DB
1990	Alton Montgomery, Houston, DB (2)
1991	Mike Croel, Nebraska, LB
1992	Tommy Maddox, UCLA, QB
1993	Dan Williams, Toledo, DE
1994	Allen Aldridge, Houston, LB (2)
1995	Jamie Brown, Florida A&M, T (4)
1996	John Mobley, Kutztown, LB

DETROIT LIONS

Year	Player, College, Position
1936	Sid Wagner, Michigan State, G
1937	Lloyd Cardwell, Nebraska, B
1938	Alex Wojciechowicz, Fordham, C
1939	John Pingel, Michigan State, B
1940	Doyle Nave, Southern California, B
1941	Jim Thomason, Texas A&M, B
1942	Bob Westfall, Michigan, B
1943	Frank Sinkwich, Georgia, B
1944	Otto Graham, Northwestern, B
1945	Frank Szymanski, Notre Dame, C
1946	Bill Dellastatious, Missouri, B
1947	Glenn Davis, Army, B
1948	Y.A. Tittle, Louisiana State, B
1949	John Rauch, Georgia, B
1950	Leon Hart, Notre Dame, E
	Joe Watson, Rice, C
1951	Dick Stanfel, San Francisco, G (2)
1952	Yale Lary, Texas A&M, B (3)
1953	Harley Sewell, Texas, G
1954	Dick Chapman, Rice, T
1955	Dave Middleton, Auburn, B
1956	Hopalong Cassady, Ohio State, B
1957	Bill Glass, Baylor, G
1958	Alex Karras, Iowa, T
1959	Nick Pietrosante, Notre Dame, B
1960	John Robinson, Louisiana State, S
1961	Danny LaRose, Missouri, T (2)
1962	John Hadl, Kansas, QB
1963	Daryl Sanders, Ohio State, T
1964	Pete Beathard, Southern California, QB
1965	Tom Nowatzke, Indiana, RB
1966	Nick Eddy, Notre Dame, RB (2)
1967	Mel Farr, UCLA, RB
1968	Greg Landry, Massachusetts, QB
	Earl McCullouch, Southern California, WR
1969	Altie Taylor, Utah State, RB (2)
1970	Steve Owens, Oklahoma, RB
1971	Bob Bell, Cincinnati, DT
1972	Herb Orvis, Colorado, DE
1973	Ernie Price, Texas A&I, DE
1974	Ed O'Neil, Penn State, LB
1975	Lynn Boden, South Dakota State, G
1976	James Hunter, Grambling, DB
	Lawrence Gaines, Wyoming, RB
1977	Walt Williams, New Mexico State, DB (2)
1978	Luther Bradley, Notre Dame, DB
1979	Keith Dorney, Penn State, T
1980	Billy Sims, Oklahoma, RB
1981	Mark Nichols, San Jose State, WR
1982	Jimmy Williams, Nebraska, LB
1983	James Jones, Florida, RB
1984	David Lewis, California, TE
1985	Lomas Brown, Florida, T
1986	Chuck Long, Iowa, QB
1987	Reggie Rogers, Washington, DE
1988	Bennie Blades, Miami, DB
1989	Barry Sanders, Oklahoma State, RB
1990	Andre Ware, Houston, QB
1991	Herman Moore, Virginia, WR
1992	Robert Porcher, South Carolina State, DE

FIRST-ROUND SELECTIONS

1993 Ryan McNeil, Miami, DB (2)
1994 Johnnie Morton, Southern California, WR
1995 Luther Elliss, Utah, DT
1996 Reggie Brown, Texas A&M, LB
Jeff Hartings, Penn State, G

GREEN BAY PACKERS

Year	Player, College, Position
1936	Russ Letlow, San Francisco, G
1937	Eddie Jankowski, Wisconsin, B
1938	Cecil Isbell, Purdue, B
1939	Larry Buhler, Minnesota, B
1940	Harold Van Every, Minnesota, B
1941	George Paskvan, Wisconsin, B
1942	Urban Odson, Minnesota, T
1943	Dick Wildung, Minnesota, T
1944	Merv Pregulman, Michigan, G
1945	Walt Schlinkman, Texas Tech, B
1946	Johnny (Strike) Strzykalski, Marquette, B
1947	Ernie Case, UCLA, B
1948	Earl (Jug) Girard, Wisconsin, B
1949	Stan Heath, Nevada, B
1950	Clayton Tonnemaker, Minnesota, C
1951	Bob Gain, Kentucky, T
1952	Babe Parilli, Kentucky, QB
1953	Al Carmichael, Southern California, B
1954	Art Hunter, Notre Dame, T
	Veryl Switzer, Kansas State, B
1955	Tom Bettis, Purdue, G
1956	Jack Losch, Miami, B
1957	Paul Hornung, Notre Dame, B
	Ron Kramer, Michigan, E
1958	Dan Currie, Michigan State, C
1959	Randy Duncan, Iowa, B
1960	Tom Moore, Vanderbilt, RB
1961	Herb Adderley, Michigan State, CB
1962	Earl Gros, Louisiana State, RB
1963	Dave Robinson, Penn State, LB
1964	Lloyd Voss, Nebraska, DT
1965	Donny Anderson, Texas Tech, RB
	Lawrence Elkins, Baylor, E
1966	Jim Grabowski, Illinois, RB
	Gale Gillingham, Minnesota, T
1967	Bob Hyland, Boston College, C
	Don Horn, San Diego State, QB
1968	Fred Carr, Texas-El Paso, LB
	Bill Lueck, Arizona, G
1969	Rich Moore, Villanova, DT
1970	Mike McCoy, Notre Dame, DT
	Rich McGeorge, Elon, TE
1971	John Brockington, Ohio State, RB
1972	Willie Buchanon, San Diego State, DB
	Jerry Tagge, Nebraska, QB
1973	Barry Smith, Florida State, WR
1974	Barty Smith, Richmond, RB
1975	Bill Bain, Southern California, G (2)
1976	Mark Koncar, Colorado, T
1977	Mike Butler, Kansas, DE
	Ezra Johnson, Morris Brown, DE
1978	James Lofton, Stanford, WR
	John Anderson, Michigan, LB
1979	Eddie Lee Ivery, Georgia Tech, RB
1980	Bruce Clark, Penn State, DE
	George Cumby, Oklahoma, LB
1981	Rich Campbell, California, QB
1982	Ron Hallstrom, Iowa, G
1983	Tim Lewis, Pittsburgh, DB
1984	Alphonso Carreker, Florida State, DE
1985	Ken Ruettgers, Southern California, T
1986	Kenneth Davis, Texas Christian, RB (2)
1987	Brent Fullwood, Auburn, RB
1988	Sterling Sharpe, South Carolina, WR
1989	Tony Mandarich, Michigan State, T
1990	Tony Bennett, Mississippi, LB
	Darrell Thompson, Minnesota, RB
1991	Vinnie Clark, Ohio State, DB
1992	Terrell Buckley, Florida State, DB
1993	Wayne Simmons, Clemson, LB
	George Teague, Alabama, DB
1994	Aaron Taylor, Notre Dame, T
1995	Craig Newsome, Arizona State, DB
1996	John Michels, Southern California, T

HOUSTON OILERS

Year	Player, College, Position
1960	Billy Cannon, Louisiana State, RB
1961	Mike Ditka, Pittsburgh, E
1962	Ray Jacobs, Howard Payne, DT
1963	Danny Brabham, Arkansas, LB
1964	Scott Appleton, Texas, DT
1965	Lawrence Elkins, Baylor, WR
1966	Tommy Nobis, Texas, LB
1967	George Webster, Michigan State, LB
	Tom Regner, Notre Dame, G
1968	Mac Haik, Mississippi, WR (2)
1969	Ron Pritchard, Arizona State, LB
1970	Doug Wilkerson, N. Carolina Central, G
1971	Dan Pastorini, Santa Clara, QB
1972	Greg Sampson, Stanford, DE
1973	John Matuszak, Tampa, DE
	George Amundson, Iowa State, RB
1974	Steve Manstedt, Nebraska, LB (4)
1975	Robert Brazile, Jackson State, LB
	Don Hardeman, Texas A&I, RB
1976	Mike Barber, Louisiana Tech, TE (2)
1977	Morris Towns, Missouri, T
1978	Earl Campbell, Texas, RB
1979	Mike Stensrud, Iowa State, DE (2)
1980	Angelo Fields, Michigan State, T (2)
1981	Michael Holston, Morgan State, WR (3)
1982	Mike Munchak, Penn State, G
1983	Bruce Matthews, Southern California, T
1984	Dean Steinkuhler, Nebraska, T
1985	Ray Childress, Texas A&M, DE
	Richard Johnson, Wisconsin, DB
1986	Jim Everett, Purdue, QB
1987	Alonzo Highsmith, Miami, RB
	Haywood Jeffires, North Carolina St., WR
1988	Lorenzo White, Michigan State, RB
1989	David Williams, Florida, T
1990	Lamar Lathon, Houston, LB
1991	Mike Dumas, Indiana, DB (2)
1992	Eddie Robinson, Alabama State, LB (2)
1993	Brad Hopkins, Illinois, T
1994	Henry Ford, Arkansas, DE
1995	Steve McNair, Alcorn State, QB
1996	Eddie George, Ohio State, RB

INDIANAPOLIS COLTS

Year	Player, College, Position
1953	Billy Vessels, Oklahoma, B
1954	Cotton Davidson, Baylor, B
1955	George Shaw, Oregon, B
	Alan Ameche, Wisconsin, FB
1956	Lenny Moore, Penn State, B
1957	Jim Parker, Ohio State, G
1958	Lenny Lyles, Louisville, B
1959	Jackie Burkett, Auburn, C
1960	Ron Mix, Southern California, T
1961	Tom Matte, Ohio State, RB
1962	Wendell Harris, Louisiana State, S
1963	Bob Vogel, Ohio State, T
1964	Marv Woodson, Indiana, CB
1965	Mike Curtis, Duke, LB
1966	Sam Ball, Kentucky, T
1967	Bubba Smith, Michigan State, DT
	Jim Detwiler, Michigan, RB
1968	John Williams, Minnesota, G
1969	Eddie Hinton, Oklahoma, WR
1970	Norman Bulaich, Texas Christian, RB
1971	Don McCauley, North Carolina, RB
	Leonard Dunlap, North Texas State, DB
1972	Tom Drougas, Oregon, T
1973	Bert Jones, Louisiana State, QB
	Joe Ehrmann, Syracuse, DT
1974	John Dutton, Nebraska, DE
	Roger Carr, Louisiana Tech, WR
1975	Ken Huff, North Carolina, G
1976	Ken Novak, Purdue, DT
1977	Randy Burke, Kentucky, WR
1978	Reese McCall, Auburn, TE
1979	Barry Krauss, Alabama, LB
1980	Curtis Dickey, Texas A&M, RB
	Derrick Hatchett, Texas, DB
1981	Randy McMillan, Pittsburgh, RB
	Donnell Thompson, North Carolina, DT
1982	Johnie Cooks, Mississippi State, LB
	Art Schlichter, Ohio State, QB
1983	John Elway, Stanford, QB
1984	Leonard Coleman, Vanderbilt, DB
	Ron Solt, Maryland, G
1985	Duane Bickett, Southern California, LB
1986	Jon Hand, Alabama, DE
1987	Cornelius Bennett, Alabama, LB
1988	Chris Chandler, Washington, QB (3)
1989	Andre Rison, Michigan State, WR
1990	Jeff George, Illinois, QB
1991	Shane Curry, Miami, DE (2)
1992	Steve Emtman, Washington, DT
	Quentin Coryatt, Texas A&M, LB
1993	Sean Dawkins, California, WR
1994	Marshall Faulk, San Diego State, RB
	Trev Alberts, Nebraska, LB
1995	Ellis Johnson, Florida, DT
1996	Marvin Harrison, Syracuse, WR

JACKSONVILLE JAGUARS

Year	Player, College, Position
1995	Tony Boselli, Southern California, T
	James Stewart, Tennessee, RB
1996	Kevin Hardy, Illinois, LB

KANSAS CITY CHIEFS

Year	Player, College, Position
1960	Don Meredith, Southern Methodist, QB
1961	E.J. Holub, Texas Tech, C
1962	Ronnie Bull, Baylor, RB
1963	Buck Buchanan, Grambling, DT
	Ed Budde, Michigan State, G
1964	Pete Beathard, Southern California, QB
1965	Gale Sayers, Kansas, RB
1966	Aaron Brown, Minnesota, DE
1967	Gene Trosch, Miami, DE-DT
1968	Mo Moorman, Texas A&M, G
	George Daney, Texas-El Paso, G
1969	Jim Marsalis, Tennessee State, CB
1970	Sid Smith, Southern California, T
1971	Elmo Wright, Houston, WR
1972	Jeff Kinney, Nebraska, RB
1973	Gary Butler, Rice, TE (2)
1974	Woody Green, Arizona State, RB
1975	Elmore Stephens, Kentucky, TE (2)
1976	Rod Walters, Iowa, G
1977	Gary Green, Baylor, DB
1978	Art Still, Kentucky, DE
1979	Mike Bell, Colorado State, DE
	Steve Fuller, Clemson, QB
1980	Brad Budde, Southern California, G
1981	Willie Scott, South Carolina, TE
1982	Anthony Hancock, Tennessee, WR
1983	Todd Blackledge, Penn State, QB
1984	Bill Maas, Pittsburgh, DT
	John Alt, Iowa, T
1985	Ethan Horton, North Carolina, RB
1986	Brian Jozwiak, West Virginia, T
1987	Paul Palmer, Temple, RB
1988	Neil Smith, Nebraska, DE
1989	Derrick Thomas, Alabama, LB
1990	Percy Snow, Michigan State, LB
1991	Harvey Williams, Louisiana State, RB
1992	Dale Carter, Tennessee, DB
1993	Will Shields, Nebraska, G (3)
1994	Greg Hill, Texas A&M, RB
1995	Trezelle Jenkins, Michigan, T
1996	Jerome Woods, Memphis, DB

MIAMI DOLPHINS

Year	Player, College, Position
1966	Jim Grabowski, Illinois, RB
	Rick Norton, Kentucky, QB
1967	Bob Griese, Purdue, QB
1968	Larry Csonka, Syracuse, RB
	Doug Crusan, Indiana, T
1969	Bill Stanfill, Georgia, DE
1970	Jim Mandich, Michigan, TE (2)
1971	Otto Stowe, Iowa State, WR (2)
1972	Mike Kadish, Notre Dame, DT
1973	Chuck Bradley, Oregon, C (2)
1974	Donald Reese, Jackson State, DE

1975 Darryl Carlton, Tampa, T
1976 Larry Gordon, Arizona State, LB
Kim Bokamper, San Jose State, LB
1977 A.J. Duhe, Louisiana State, DT
1978 Guy Benjamin, Stanford, QB (2)
1979 Jon Giesler, Michigan, T
1980 Don McNeal, Alabama, DB
1981 David Overstreet, Oklahoma, RB
1982 Roy Foster, Southern California, G
1983 Dan Marino, Pittsburgh, QB
1984 Jackie Shipp, Oklahoma, LB
1985 Lorenzo Hampton, Florida, RB
1986 John Offerdahl, Western Michigan, LB (2)
1987 John Bosa, Boston College, DE
1988 Eric Kumerow, Ohio State, DE
1989 Sammie Smith, Florida State, RB
Louis Oliver, Florida, DB
1990 Richmond Webb, Texas A&M, T
1991 Randal Hill, Miami, WR
1992 Troy Vincent, Wisconsin, DB
Marco Coleman, Georgia Tech, LB
1993 O.J. McDuffie, Penn State, WR
1994 Tim Bowens, Mississippi, DT
1995 Billy Milner, Houston, T
1996 Daryl Gardener, Baylor, DT

MINNESOTA VIKINGS

Year Player, College, Position
1961 Tommy Mason, Tulane, RB
1962 Bill Miller, Miami, WR (3)
1963 Jim Dunaway, Mississippi, T
1964 Carl Eller, Minnesota, DE
1965 Jack Snow, Notre Dame, WR
1966 Jerry Shay, Purdue, DT
1967 Clint Jones, Michigan State, RB
Gene Washington, Michigan State, WR
Alan Page, Notre Dame, DT
1968 Ron Yary, Southern California, T
1969 Ed White, California, G (2)
1970 John Ward, Oklahoma State, DT
1971 Leo Hayden, Ohio State, RB
1972 Jeff Siemon, Stanford, LB
1973 Chuck Foreman, Miami, RB
1974 Fred McNeill, UCLA, LB
Steve Riley, Southern California, T
1975 Mark Mullaney, Colorado State, DE
1976 James White, Oklahoma State, DT
1977 Tommy Kramer, Rice, QB
1978 Randy Holloway, Pittsburgh, DE
1979 Ted Brown, North Carolina State, RB
1980 Doug Martin, Washington, DT
1981 Mardye McDole, Mississippi State, WR (2)
1982 Darrin Nelson, Stanford, RB
1983 Joey Browner, Southern California, DB
1984 Keith Millard, Washington State, DE
1985 Chris Doleman, Pittsburgh, LB
1986 Gerald Robinson, Auburn, DE
1987 D.J. Dozier, Penn State, RB
1988 Randall McDaniel, Arizona State, G
1989 David Braxton, Wake Forest, LB (2)
1990 Mike Jones, Texas A&M, TE (3)
1991 Carlos Jenkins, Michigan State, LB (3)
1992 Robert Harris, Southern University, DE (2)
1993 Robert Smith, Ohio State, RB
1994 DeWayne Washington, N. Carolina St., DB
Todd Steussie, California, T
1995 Derrick Alexander, Florida State, DE
Korey Stringer, Ohio State, T
1996 Duane Clemons, California, DE

NEW ENGLAND PATRIOTS

Year Player, College, Position
1960 Ron Burton, Northwestern, RB
1961 Tommy Mason, Tulane, RB
1962 Gary Collins, Maryland, WR
1963 Art Graham, Boston College, WR
1964 Jack Concannon, Boston College, QB
1965 Jerry Rush, Michigan State, DE
1966 Karl Singer, Purdue, T
1967 John Charles, Purdue, S
1968 Dennis Byrd, North Carolina State, DE
1969 Ron Sellers, Florida State, WR
1970 Phil Olsen, Utah State, DE
1971 Jim Plunkett, Stanford, QB
1972 Tom Reynolds, San Diego State, WR (2)
1973 John Hannah, Alabama, G
Sam Cunningham, So. California, RB
Darryl Stingley, Purdue, WR
1974 Steve Corbett, Boston College, G (2)
1975 Russ Francis, Oregon, TE
1976 Mike Haynes, Arizona State, DB
Pete Brock, Colorado, C
Tim Fox, Ohio State, DB
1977 Raymond Clayborn, Texas, DB
Stanley Morgan, Tennessee, WR
1978 Bob Cryder, Alabama, G
1979 Rick Sanford, South Carolina, DB
1980 Roland James, Tennessee, DB
Vagas Ferguson, Notre Dame, RB
1981 Brian Holloway, Stanford, T
1982 Kenneth Sims, Texas, DT
Lester Williams, Miami, DT
1983 Tony Eason, Illinois, QB
1984 Irving Fryar, Nebraska, WR
1985 Trevor Matich, Brigham Young, C
1986 Reggie Dupard, Southern Methodist, RB
1987 Bruce Armstrong, Louisville, T
1988 John Stephens, Northwestern St., La., RB
1989 Hart Lee Dykes, Oklahoma State, WR
1990 Chris Singleton, Arizona, LB
Ray Agnew, North Carolina State, DE
1991 Pat Harlow, Southern California, T
Leonard Russell, Arizona State, RB
1992 Eugene Chung, Virginia Tech, T
1993 Drew Bledsoe, Washington State, QB
1994 Willie McGinest, Southern California, DE
1995 Ty Law, Michigan, DB
1996 Terry Glenn, Ohio State, WR

NEW ORLEANS SAINTS

Year Player, College, Position
1967 Les Kelley, Alabama, RB
1968 Kevin Hardy, Notre Dame, DE
1969 John Shinners, Xavier, G
1970 Ken Burrough, Texas Southern, WR
1971 Archie Manning, Mississippi, QB
1972 Royce Smith, Georgia, G
1973 Derland Moore, Oklahoma, DE (2)
1974 Rick Middleton, Ohio State, LB
1975 Larry Burton, Purdue, WR
Kurt Schumacher, Ohio State, T
1976 Chuck Muncie, California, RB
1977 Joe Campbell, Maryland, DE
1978 Wes Chandler, Florida, WR
1979 Russell Erxleben, Texas, P-K
1980 Stan Brock, Colorado, T
1981 George Rogers, South Carolina, RB
1982 Lindsay Scott, Georgia, WR
1983 Steve Korte, Arkansas, G (2)
1984 James Geathers, Wichita State, DE
1985 Alvin Toles, Tennessee, LB
1986 Jim Dombrowski, Virginia, T
1987 Shawn Knight, Brigham Young, DT
1988 Craig Heyward, Pittsburgh, RB
1989 Wayne Martin, Arkansas, DE
1990 Renaldo Turnbull, West Virginia, DE
1991 Wesley Carroll, Miami, WR (2)
1992 Vaughn Dunbar, Indiana, RB
1993 Willie Roaf, Louisiana Tech, T
Irv Smith, Notre Dame, TE
1994 Joe Johnson, Louisville, DE
1995 Mark Fields, Washington State, LB
1996 Alex Molden, Oregon, DB

NEW YORK GIANTS

Year Player, College, Position
1936 Art Lewis, Ohio U., T
1937 Ed Widseth, Minnesota, T
1938 George Karamatic, Gonzaga, B
1939 Walt Neilson, Arizona, B
1940 Grenville Lansdell, Southern California, B
1941 George Franck, Minnesota, B
1942 Merle Hapes, Mississippi, B
1943 Steve Filipowicz, Fordham, B
1944 Billy Hillenbrand, Indiana, B
1945 Elmer Barbour, Wake Forest, B
1946 George Connor, Notre Dame, T
1947 Vic Schwall, Northwestern, B
1948 Tony Minisi, Pennsylvania, B
1949 Paul Page, Southern Methodist, B
1950 Travis Tidwell, Auburn, B
1951 Kyle Rote, Southern Methodist, B
Jim Spavital, Oklahoma A&M, B
1952 Frank Gifford, Southern California, B
1953 Bobby Marlow, Alabama, B
1954 Ken Buck, Pacific, C (2)
1955 Joe Heap, Notre Dame, B
1956 Henry Moore, Arkansas, B (2)
1957 Sam DeLuca, South Carolina, T (2)
1958 Phil King, Vanderbilt, B
1959 Lee Grosscup, Utah, B
1960 Lou Cordileone, Clemson, G
1961 Bruce Tarbox, Syracuse, G (2)
1962 Jerry Hillebrand, Colorado, LB
1963 Frank Lasky, Florida, T (2)
1964 Joe Don Looney, Oklahoma, RB
1965 Tucker Frederickson, Auburn, RB
1966 Francis Peay, Missouri, T
1967 Louis Thompson, Alabama, DT (4)
1968 Dick Buzin, Penn State, T (2)
1969 Fred Dryer, San Diego State, DE
1970 Jim Files, Oklahoma, LB
1971 Rocky Thompson, West Texas State, WR
1972 Eldridge Small, Texas A&I, DB
Larry Jacobson, Nebraska, DE
1973 Brad Van Pelt, Michigan State, LB (2)
1974 John Hicks, Ohio State, G
1975 Al Simpson, Colorado State, T (2)
1976 Troy Archer, Colorado, DE
1977 Gary Jeter, Southern California, DT
1978 Gordon King, Stanford, T
1979 Phil Simms, Morehead State, QB
1980 Mark Haynes, Colorado, DB
1981 Lawrence Taylor, North Carolina, LB
1982 Butch Woolfolk, Michigan, RB
1983 Terry Kinard, Clemson, DB
1984 Carl Banks, Michigan State, LB
William Roberts, Ohio State, T
1985 George Adams, Kentucky, RB
1986 Eric Dorsey, Notre Dame, DE
1987 Mark Ingram, Michigan State, WR
1988 Eric Moore, Indiana, T
1989 Brian Williams, Minnesota, C-G
1990 Rodney Hampton, Georgia, RB
1991 Jarrod Bunch, Michigan, RB
1992 Derek Brown, Notre Dame, TE
1993 Michael Strahan, Texas Southern, DE (2)
1994 Thomas Lewis, Indiana, WR
1995 Tyrone Wheatley, Michigan, RB
1996 Cedric Jones, Oklahoma, DE

NEW YORK JETS

Year Player, College, Position
1960 George Izo, Notre Dame, QB
1961 Tom Brown, Minnesota, G
1962 Sandy Stephens, Minnesota, QB
1963 Jerry Stovall, Louisiana State, S
1964 Matt Snell, Ohio State, RB
1965 Joe Namath, Alabama, QB
Tom Nowatzke, Indiana, RB
1966 Bill Yearby, Michigan, DT
1967 Paul Seiler, Notre Dame, T
1968 Lee White, Weber State, RB
1969 Dave Foley, Ohio State, T
1970 Steve Tannen, Florida, CB
1971 John Riggins, Kansas, RB
1972 Jerome Barkum, Jackson State, WR
Mike Taylor, Michigan, LB
1973 Burgess Owens, Miami, DB
1974 Carl Barzilauskas, Indiana, DT
1975 Anthony Davis, Southern California, RB (2)
1976 Richard Todd, Alabama, QB
1977 Marvin Powell, Southern California, T
1978 Chris Ward, Ohio State, T
1979 Marty Lyons, Alabama, DE
1980 Johnny (Lam) Jones, Texas, WR
1981 Freeman McNeil, UCLA, RB
1982 Bob Crable, Notre Dame, LB
1983 Ken O'Brien, Cal-Davis, QB

1984 Russell Carter, Southern Methodist, DB
Ron Faurot, Arkansas, DE
1985 Al Toon, Wisconsin, WR
1986 Mike Haight, Iowa, T
1987 Roger Vick, Texas A&M, RB
1988 Dave Cadigan, Southern California, T
1989 Jeff Lageman, Virginia, LB
1990 Blair Thomas, Penn State, RB
1991 Browning Nagle, Louisville, QB (2)
1992 Johnny Mitchell, Nebraska, TE
1993 Marvin Jones, Florida State, LB
1994 Aaron Glenn, Texas A&M, DB
1995 Kyle Brady, Penn State, TE
Hugh Douglas, Central State, Ohio, DE
1996 Keyshawn Johnson, Southern California, WR

OAKLAND RAIDERS

Year	Player, College, Position
1960	Dale Hackbart, Wisconsin, CB
1961	Joe Rutgens, Illinois, DT
1962	Roman Gabriel, North Carolina State, QB
1963	George Wilson, Alabama, RB (6)
1964	Tony Lorick, Arizona State, RB
1965	Harry Schuh, Memphis State, T
1966	Rodger Bird, Kentucky, S
1967	Gene Upshaw, Texas A&I, G
1968	Eldridge Dickey, Tennessee State, QB
1969	Art Thoms, Syracuse, DT
1970	Raymond Chester, Morgan State, TE
1971	Jack Tatum, Ohio State, S
1972	Mike Siani, Villanova, WR
1973	Ray Guy, Southern Mississippi, P
1974	Henry Lawrence, Florida A&M, T
1975	Neal Colzie, Ohio State, DB
1976	Charles Philyaw, Texas Southern, DT (2)
1977	Mike Davis, Colorado, DB (2)
1978	Dave Browning, Washington, DE (2)
1979	Willie Jones, Florida State, DE (2)
1980	Marc Wilson, Brigham Young, QB
1981	Ted Watts, Texas Tech, DB
	Curt Marsh, Washington, T
1982	Marcus Allen, Southern California, RB
1983	Don Mosebar, Southern California, T
1984	Sean Jones, Northeastern, DE (2)
1985	Jessie Hester, Florida State, WR
1986	Bob Buczkowski, Pittsburgh, DE
1987	John Clay, Missouri, T
1988	Tim Brown, Notre Dame, WR
	Terry McDaniel, Tennessee, DB
	Scott Davis, Illinois, DE
1989	Jeff Francis, Tennessee, QB (6)
1990	Anthony Smith, Arizona, DE
1991	Todd Marinovich, Southern California, QB
1992	Chester McGlockton, Clemson, DE
1993	Patrick Bates, Texas A&M, DB
1994	Rob Fredrickson, Michigan State, LB
1995	Napoleon Kaufman, Washington, RB
1996	Rickey Dudley, Ohio State, TE

PHILADELPHIA EAGLES

Year	Player, College, Position
1936	Jay Berwanger, Chicago, B
1937	Sam Francis, Nebraska, B
1938	Jim McDonald, Ohio State, B
1939	Davey O'Brien, Texas Christian, B
1940	George McAfee, Duke, B
1941	Art Jones, Richmond, B (2)
1942	Pete Kmetovic, Stanford, B
1943	Joe Muha, Virginia Military, B
1944	Steve Van Buren, Louisiana State, B
1945	John Yonaker, Notre Dame, E
1946	Leo Riggs, Southern California, B
1947	Neill Armstrong, Oklahoma A&M, E
1948	Clyde (Smackover) Scott, Arkansas, B
1949	Chuck Bednarik, Pennsylvania, C
	Frank Tripucka, Notre Dame, B
1950	Harry (Bud) Grant, Minnesota, E
1951	Ebert Van Buren, Louisiana State, B
	Chet Mutryn, Xavier, B
1952	Johnny Bright, Drake, B
1953	Al Conway, Army, B (2)
1954	Neil Worden, Notre Dame, B
1955	Dick Bielski, Maryland, B
1956	Bob Pellegrini, Maryland, C
1957	Clarence Peaks, Michigan State, B
1958	Walt Kowalczyk, Michigan State, B
1959	J.D. Smith, Rice, T (2)
1960	Ron Burton, Northwestern, RB
1961	Art Baker, Syracuse, RB
1962	Pete Case, Georgia, G (2)
1963	Ed Budde, Michigan State, G
1964	Bob Brown, Nebraska, T
1965	Ray Rissmiller, Georgia, T (2)
1966	Randy Beisler, Indiana, DE
1967	Harry Jones, Arkansas, RB
1968	Tim Rossovich, Southern California, DE
1969	Leroy Keyes, Purdue, RB
1970	Steve Zabel, Oklahoma, TE
1971	Richard Harris, Grambling, DE
1972	John Reaves, Florida, QB
1973	Jerry Sisemore, Texas, T
	Charle Young, Southern California, TE
1974	Mitch Sutton, Kansas, DT (3)
1975	Bill Capraun, Miami, T (7)
1976	Mike Smith, Florida, DE (4)
1977	Skip Sharp, Kansas, DB (5)
1978	Reggie Wilkes, Georgia Tech, LB (3)
1979	Jerry Robinson, UCLA, LB
1980	Roynell Young, Alcorn State, DB
1981	Leonard Mitchell, Houston, DE
1982	Mike Quick, North Carolina State, WR
1983	Michael Haddix, Mississippi State, RB
1984	Kenny Jackson, Penn State, WR
1985	Kevin Allen, Indiana, T
1986	Keith Byars, Ohio State, RB
1987	Jerome Brown, Miami, DT
1988	Keith Jackson, Oklahoma, TE
1989	Jessie Small, Eastern Kentucky, LB (2)
1990	Ben Smith, Georgia, DB
1991	Antone Davis, Tennessee, T
1992	Siran Stacy, Alabama, RB (2)
1993	Lester Holmes, Jackson State, T
	Leonard Renfro, Colorado, DT
1994	Bernard Williams, Georgia, T
1995	Mike Mamula, Boston College, DE
1996	Jermane Mayberry, Texas A&M-Kingsville, T

PITTSBURGH STEELERS

Year	Player, College, Position
1936	Bill Shakespeare, Notre Dame, B
1937	Mike Basrak, Duquesne, C
1938	Byron (Whizzer) White, Colorado, B
1939	Bill Patterson, Baylor, B (3)
1940	Kay Eakin, Arkansas, B
1941	Chet Gladchuk, Boston College, C (2)
1942	Bill Dudley, Virginia, B
1943	Bill Daley, Minnesota, B
1944	Johnny Podesto, St. Mary's, Calif., B
1945	Paul Duhart, Florida, B
1946	Felix (Doc) Blanchard, Army, B
1947	Hub Bechtol, Texas, E
1948	Dan Edwards, Georgia, E
1949	Bobby Gage, Clemson, B
1950	Lynn Chandnois, Michigan State, B
1951	Butch Avinger, Alabama, B
1952	Ed Modzelewski, Maryland, B
1953	Ted Marchibroda, St. Bonaventure, B
1954	Johnny Lattner, Notre Dame, B
1955	Frank Varrichione, Notre Dame, T
1956	Gary Glick, Colorado A&M, B
	Art Davis, Mississippi State, B
1957	Len Dawson, Purdue, B
1958	Larry Krutko, West Virginia, B (2)
1959	Tom Barnett, Purdue, B (8)
1960	Jack Spikes, Texas Christian, RB
1961	Myron Pottios, Notre Dame, LB (2)
1962	Bob Ferguson, Ohio State, RB
1963	Frank Atkinson, Stanford, T (8)
1964	Paul Martha, Pittsburgh, S
1965	Roy Jefferson, Utah, WR (2)
1966	Dick Leftridge, West Virginia, RB
1967	Don Shy, San Diego State, RB (2)
1968	Mike Taylor, Southern California, T
1969	Joe Greene, North Texas State, DT
1970	Terry Bradshaw, Louisiana Tech, QB
1971	Frank Lewis, Grambling, WR
1972	Franco Harris, Penn State, RB
1973	J.T. Thomas, Florida State, DB
1974	Lynn Swann, Southern California, WR
1975	Dave Brown, Michigan, DB
1976	Bennie Cunningham, Clemson, TE
1977	Robin Cole, New Mexico, LB
1978	Ron Johnson, Eastern Michigan, DB
1979	Greg Hawthorne, Baylor, RB
1980	Mark Malone, Arizona State, QB
1981	Keith Gary, Oklahoma, DE
1982	Walter Abercrombie, Baylor, RB
1983	Gabriel Rivera, Texas Tech, DT
1984	Louis Lipps, Southern Mississippi, WR
1985	Darryl Sims, Wisconsin, DE
1986	John Rienstra, Temple, G
1987	Rod Woodson, Purdue, DB
1988	Aaron Jones, Eastern Kentucky, DE
1989	Tim Worley, Georgia, RB
	Tom Ricketts, Pittsburgh, T
1990	Eric Green, Liberty, TE
1991	Huey Richardson, Florida, DE
1992	Leon Searcy, Miami, T
1993	Deon Figures, Colorado, DB
1994	Charles Johnson, Colorado, WR
1995	Mark Bruener, Washington, TE
1996	Jamain Stephens, North Carolina A&T, T

ST. LOUIS RAMS

Year	Player, College, Position
1937	Johnny Drake, Purdue, B
1938	Corbett Davis, Indiana, B
1939	Parker Hall, Mississippi, B
1940	Ollie Cordill, Rice, B
1941	Rudy Mucha, Washington, C
1942	Jack Wilson, Baylor, B
1943	Mike Holovak, Boston College, B
1944	Tony Butkovich, Illinois, B
1945	Elroy (Crazylegs) Hirsch, Wisconsin, B
1946	Emil Sitko, Notre Dame, B
1947	Herman Wedemeyer, St. Mary's, Calif., B
1948	Tom Keane, West Virginia, B (2)
1949	Bobby Thomason, Virginia Military, B
1950	Ralph Pasquariello, Villanova, B
	Stan West, Oklahoma, G
1951	Bud McFadin, Texas, G
1952	Bill Wade, Vanderbilt, QB
	Bob Carey, Michigan State, E
1953	Donn Moomaw, UCLA, C
	Ed Barker, Washington State, E
1954	Ed Beatty, Cincinnati, C
1955	Larry Morris, Georgia Tech, C
1956	Joe Marconi, West Virginia, B
	Charles Horton, Vanderbilt, B
1957	Jon Arnett, Southern California, B
	Del Shofner, Baylor, E
1958	Lou Michaels, Kentucky, T
	Jim Phillips, Auburn, E
1959	Dick Bass, Pacific, B
	Paul Dickson, Baylor, T
1960	Billy Cannon, Louisiana State, RB
1961	Marlin McKeever, So. California, E-LB
1962	Roman Gabriel, North Carolina State, QB
	Merlin Olsen, Utah State, DT
1963	Terry Baker, Oregon State, QB
	Rufus Guthrie, Georgia Tech, G
1964	Bill Munson, Utah State, QB
1965	Clancy Williams, Washington State, CB
1966	Tom Mack, Michigan, G
1967	Willie Ellison, Texas Southern, RB (2)
1968	Gary Beban, UCLA, QB (2)
1969	Larry Smith, Florida, RB
	Jim Seymour, Notre Dame, WR
	Bob Klein, Southern California, TE
1970	Jack Reynolds, Tennessee, LB
1971	Isiah Robertson, Southern, LB
	Jack Youngblood, Florida, DE
1972	Jim Bertelsen, Texas, RB (2)
1973	Cullen Bryant, Colorado, DB (2)
1974	John Cappelletti, Penn State, RB
1975	Mike Fanning, Notre Dame, DT
	Dennis Harrah, Miami, T
	Doug France, Ohio State, T
1976	Kevin McLain, Colorado State, LB

1977 Bob Brudzinski, Ohio State, LB
1978 Elvis Peacock, Oklahoma, RB
1979 George Andrews, Nebraska, LB
Kent Hill, Georgia Tech, T
1980 Johnnie Johnson, Texas, DB
1981 Mel Owens, Michigan, LB
1982 Barry Redden, Richmond, RB
1983 Eric Dickerson, Southern Methodist, RB
1984 Hal Stephens, East Carolina, DE (5)
1985 Jerry Gray, Texas, DB
1986 Mike Schad, Queen's University, Canada, T
1987 Donald Evans, Winston-Salem, DE (2)
1988 Gaston Green, UCLA, RB
Aaron Cox, Arizona State, WR
1989 Bill Hawkins, Miami, DE
Cleveland Gary, Miami, RB
1990 Bern Brostek, Washington, C
1991 Todd Lyght, Notre Dame, DB
1992 Sean Gilbert, Pittsburgh, DE
1993 Jerome Bettis, Notre Dame, RB
1994 Wayne Gandy, Auburn, T
1995 Kevin Carter, Florida, DE
1996 Lawrence Phillips, Nebraska, RB
Eddie Kennison, Louisiana State, WR

SAN DIEGO CHARGERS

Year Player, College, Position
1960 Monty Stickles, Notre Dame, E
1961 Earl Faison, Indiana, DE
1962 Bob Ferguson, Ohio State, RB
1963 Walt Sweeney, Syracuse, G
1964 Ted Davis, Georgia Tech, LB
1965 Steve DeLong, Tennessee, DE
1966 Don Davis, Cal State-Los Angeles, DT
1967 Ron Billingsley, Wyoming, DE
1968 Russ Washington, Missouri, DT
Jimmy Hill, Texas A&I, DB
1969 Marty Domres, Columbia, QB
Bob Babich, Miami, Ohio, LB
1970 Walker Gillette, Richmond, WR
1971 Leon Burns, Long Beach State, RB
1972 Pete Lazetich, Stanford, DE (2)
1973 Johnny Rodgers, Nebraska, WR
1974 Bo Matthews, Colorado, RB
Don Goode, Kansas, LB
1975 Gary Johnson, Grambling, DT
Mike Williams, Louisiana State, DB
1976 Joe Washington, Oklahoma, RB
1977 Bob Rush, Memphis State, C
1978 John Jefferson, Arizona State, WR
1979 Kellen Winslow, Missouri, TE
1980 Ed Luther, San Jose State, QB (4)
1981 James Brooks, Auburn, RB
1982 Hollis Hall, Clemson, DB (7)
1983 Billy Ray Smith, Arkansas, LB
Gary Anderson, Arkansas, WR
Gill Byrd, San Jose State, DB
1984 Mossy Cade, Texas, DB
1985 Jim Lachey, Ohio State, G
1986 Leslie O'Neal, Oklahoma State, DE
James FitzPatrick, Southern California, T
1987 Rod Bernstine, Texas A&M, TE
1988 Anthony Miller, Tennessee, WR
1989 Burt Grossman, Pittsburgh, DE
1990 Junior Seau, Southern California, LB
1991 Stanley Richard, Texas, DB
1992 Chris Mims, Tennessee, DE
1993 Darrien Gordon, Stanford, DB
1994 Isaac Davis, Arkansas, G (2)
1995 Terrance Shaw, Stephen F. Austin, DB (2)
1996 Bryan Still, Virginia Tech, WR (2)

SAN FRANCISCO 49ERS

Year Player, College, Position
1950 Leo Nomellini, Minnesota, T
1951 Y.A. Tittle, Louisiana State, B
1952 Hugh McElhenny, Washington, B
1953 Harry Babcock, Georgia, E
Tom Stolhandske, Texas, E
1954 Bernie Faloney, Maryland, B
1955 Dickie Moegle, Rice, B
1956 Earl Morrall, Michigan State, B
1957 John Brodie, Stanford, B
1958 Jim Pace, Michigan, B
Charlie Krueger, Texas A&M, T
1959 Dave Baker, Oklahoma, B
Dan James, Ohio State, C
1960 Monty Stickles, Notre Dame, E
1961 Jimmy Johnson, UCLA, CB
Bernie Casey, Bowling Green, WR
Bill Kilmer, UCLA, QB
1962 Lance Alworth, Arkansas, WR
1963 Kermit Alexander, UCLA, CB
1964 Dave Parks, Texas Tech, WR
1965 Ken Willard, North Carolina, RB
George Donnelly, Illinois, DB
1966 Stan Hindman, Mississippi, DE
1967 Steve Spurrier, Florida, QB
Cas Banaszek, Northwestern, T
1968 Forrest Blue, Auburn, C
1969 Ted Kwalick, Penn State, TE
Gene Washington, Stanford, WR
1970 Cedrick Hardman, North Texas State, DE
Bruce Taylor, Boston U., DB
1971 Tim Anderson, Ohio State, DB
1972 Terry Beasley, Auburn, WR
1973 Mike Holmes, Texas Southern, DB
1974 Wilbur Jackson, Alabama, RB
Bill Sandifer, UCLA, DT
1975 Jimmy Webb, Mississippi State, DT
1976 Randy Cross, UCLA, C (2)
1977 Elmo Boyd, Eastern Kentucky, WR (3)
1978 Ken MacAfee, Notre Dame, TE
Dan Bunz, Cal State-Long Beach, LB
1979 James Owens, UCLA, WR (2)
1980 Earl Cooper, Rice, RB
Jim Stuckey, Clemson, DT
1981 Ronnie Lott, Southern California, DB
1982 Bubba Paris, Michigan, T (2)
1983 Roger Craig, Nebraska, RB (2)
1984 Todd Shell, Brigham Young, LB
1985 Jerry Rice, Mississippi Valley State, WR
1986 Larry Roberts, Alabama, DE (2)
1987 Harris Barton, North Carolina, T
Terrence Flagler, Clemson, RB
1988 Danny Stubbs, Miami, DE (2)
1989 Keith DeLong, Tennessee, LB
1990 Dexter Carter, Florida State, RB
1991 Ted Washington, Louisville, DT
1992 Dana Hall, Washington, DB
1993 Dana Stubblefield, Kansas, DT
Todd Kelly, Tennessee, DE
1994 Bryant Young, Notre Dame, DT
William Floyd, Florida State, RB
1995 J.J. Stokes, UCLA, WR
1996 Israel Ifeanyi, Southern California, DE (2)

SEATTLE SEAHAWKS

Year Player, College, Position
1976 Steve Niehaus, Notre Dame, DT
1977 Steve August, Tulsa, G
1978 Keith Simpson, Memphis State, DB
1979 Manu Tuiasosopo, UCLA, DT
1980 Jacob Green, Texas A&M, DE
1981 Ken Easley, UCLA, DB
1982 Jeff Bryant, Clemson, DE
1983 Curt Warner, Penn State, RB
1984 Terry Taylor, Southern Illinois, DB
1985 Owen Gill, Iowa, RB (2)
1986 John L. Williams, Florida, RB
1987 Tony Woods, Pittsburgh, LB
1988 Brian Blades, Miami, WR (2)
1989 Andy Heck, Notre Dame, T
1990 Cortez Kennedy, Miami, DT
1991 Dan McGwire, San Diego State, QB
1992 Ray Roberts, Virginia, T
1993 Rick Mirer, Notre Dame, QB
1994 Sam Adams, Texas A&M, DT
1995 Joey Galloway, Ohio State, WR
1996 Pete Kendall, Boston College, T

TAMPA BAY BUCCANEERS

Year Player, College, Position
1976 Lee Roy Selmon, Oklahoma, DT
1977 Ricky Bell, Southern California, RB
1978 Doug Williams, Grambling, QB
1979 Greg Roberts, Oklahoma, G (2)
1980 Ray Snell, Wisconsin, G
1981 Hugh Green, Pittsburgh, LB
1982 Sean Farrell, Penn State, G
1983 Randy Grimes, Baylor, C (2)
1984 Keith Browner, Southern California, LB (2)
1985 Ron Holmes, Washington, DE
1986 Bo Jackson, Auburn, RB
Roderick Jones, Southern Methodist, DB
1987 Vinny Testaverde, Miami, QB
1988 Paul Gruber, Wisconsin, T
1989 Broderick Thomas, Nebraska, LB
1990 Keith McCants, Alabama, LB
1991 Charles McRae, Tennessee, T
1992 Courtney Hawkins, Michigan State, WR (2)
1993 Eric Curry, Alabama, DE
1994 Trent Dilfer, Fresno State, QB
1995 Warren Sapp, Miami, DT
Derrick Brooks, Florida State, LB
1996 Regan Upshaw, California, DE
Marcus Jones, North Carolina, DT

WASHINGTON REDSKINS

Year Player, College, Position
1936 Riley Smith, Alabama, B
1937 Sammy Baugh, Texas Christian, B
1938 Andy Farkas, Detroit, B
1939 I.B. Hale, Texas Christian, T
1940 Ed Boell, New York U., B
1941 Forest Evashevski, Michigan, B
1942 Orban (Spec) Sanders, Texas, B
1943 Jack Jenkins, Missouri, B
1944 Mike Micka, Colgate, B
1945 Jim Hardy, Southern California, B
1946 Casl Rossi, UCLA, B*
1947 Casl Rossi, UCLA, B
1948 Harry Gilmer, Alabama, B
Lowell Tew, Alabama, B
1949 Rob Goode, Texas A&M, B
1950 George Thomas, Oklahoma, B
1951 Leon Heath, Oklahoma, B
1952 Larry Isbell, Baylor, B
1953 Jack Scarbath, Maryland, B
1954 Steve Meilinger, Kentucky, E
1955 Ralph Guglielmi, Notre Dame, B
1956 Ed Vereb, Maryland, B
1957 Don Bosseler, Miami, B
1958 Mike Sommer, George Washington, B (2)
1959 Don Allard, Boston College, B
1960 Richie Lucas, Penn State, QB
1961 Norman Snead, Wake Forest, QB
Joe Rutgens, Illinois, DT
1962 Ernie Davis, Syracuse, RB
1963 Pat Richter, Wisconsin, TE
1964 Charley Taylor, Arizona State, RB-WR
1965 Bob Breitenstein, Tulsa, T (2)
1966 Charlie Gogolak, Princeton, K
1967 Ray McDonald, Idaho, RB
1968 Jim Smith, Oregon, DB
1969 Eugene Epps, Texas-El Paso, DB (2)
1970 Bill Bundige, Colorado, DT (2)
1971 Cotton Speyrer, Texas, WR (2)
1972 Moses Denson, Maryland State, RB (8)
1973 Charles Cantrell, Lamar, G (5)
1974 Jon Keyworth, Colorado, TE (6)
1975 Mike Thomas, Nevada-Las Vegas, RB (6)
1976 Mike Hughes, Baylor, G (5)
1977 Duncan McColl, Stanford, DE (4)
1978 Tony Green, Florida, RB (6)
1979 Don Warren, San Diego State, TE (4)
1980 Art Monk, Syracuse, WR
1981 Mark May, Pittsburgh, T
1982 Vernon Dean, San Diego State, DB (2)
1983 Darrell Green, Texas A&I, DB
1984 Bob Slater, Oklahoma, DT (2)
1985 Tory Nixon, San Diego State, DB (2)
1986 Markus Koch, Boise State, DE (2)
1987 Brian Davis, Nebraska, DB (2)
1988 Chip Lohmiller, Minnesota, K (2)
1989 Tracy Rocker, Auburn, DT (3)
1990 Andre Collins, Penn State, LB (2)
1991 Bobby Wilson, Michigan State, DT
1992 Desmond Howard, Michigan, WR

FIRST-ROUND SELECTIONS

1993 Tom Carter, Notre Dame, DB
1994 Heath Shuler, Tennessee, QB
1995 Michael Westbrook, Colorado, WR
1996 Andre Johnson, Penn State, T

**Choice lost due to ineligibility*

Records

ALL-TIME RECORDS

Compiled by Elias Sports Bureau

The following records reflect all available official information on the National Football League from its formation in 1920 to date. Also included are all applicable records from the American Football League, 1960-69.

Individuals eligible for Rookie records are players who were in their first season of professional football and had not been on the roster of another professional football team, including teams in other leagues, for any regular-season or postseason games in a previous season. Eligible players, therefore, include those who were under contract to a National Football League club for a previous season but were terminated prior to their club's first regular-season game and not re-signed, or who were placed on Reserve/Injured (or another category of the Reserve List) prior to their club's first regular-season game and were not activated during the rest of the regular season or postseason.

INDIVIDUAL RECORDS

SERVICE

Most Seasons

26 George Blanda, Chi. Bears, 1949, 1950-58; Baltimore, 1950; Houston, 1960-66; Oakland, 1967-75
21 Earl Morrall, San Francisco, 1956; Pittsburgh, 1957-58; Detroit, 1958-64; N.Y. Giants, 1965-67; Baltimore, 1968-71; Miami, 1972-76
20 Jim Marshall, Cleveland, 1960; Minnesota, 1961-79
Jackie Slater, L.A. Rams, 1976-94; St. Louis, 1995

Most Seasons, One Club

20 Jackie Slater, L.A. Rams, 1976-94; St. Louis, 1995
19 Jim Marshall, Minnesota, 1961-79
18 Jim Hart, St. Louis, 1966-83
Jeff Van Note, Atlanta, 1969-86
Pat Leahy, N.Y. Jets, 1974-91

Most Games Played, Career

340 George Blanda, Chi. Bears, 1949, 1950-58; Baltimore, 1950; Houston, 1960-66; Oakland, 1967-75
282 Jim Marshall, Cleveland, 1960; Minnesota, 1961-79
263 Jan Stenerud, Kansas City, 1967-79; Green Bay, 1980-83; Minnesota, 1984-85
Clay Matthews, Cleveland, 1978-93; Atlanta, 1994-95

Most Consecutive Games Played, Career

282 Jim Marshall, Cleveland, 1960; Minnesota, 1961-79
240 Mick Tingelhoff, Minnesota, 1962-78
234 Jim Bakken, St. Louis, 1962-78

SCORING

Most Seasons Leading League

5 Don Hutson, Green Bay, 1940-44
Gino Cappelletti, Boston, 1961, 1963-66
3 Earl (Dutch) Clark, Portsmouth, 1932; Detroit, 1935-36
Pat Harder, Chi. Cardinals, 1947-49
Paul Hornung, Green Bay, 1959-61
2 Jack Manders, Chi. Bears, 1934, 1937
Gordy Soltau, San Francisco, 1952-53
Doak Walker, Detroit, 1950, 1955
Gene Mingo, Denver, 1960, 1962
Jim Turner, N.Y. Jets, 1968-69
Fred Cox, Minnesota, 1969-70
Chester Marcol, Green Bay, 1972, 1974
John Smith, New England, 1979-80

Most Consecutive Seasons Leading League

5 Don Hutson, Green Bay, 1940-44
4 Gino Cappelletti, Boston, 1963-66
3 Pat Harder, Chi. Cardinals, 1947-49
Paul Hornung, Green Bay, 1959-61

POINTS

Most Points, Career

2,002 George Blanda, Chi. Bears, 1949, 1950-58; Baltimore, 1950; Houston, 1960-66; Oakland, 1967-75 (9-td, 943-pat, 335-fg)
1,699 Jan Stenerud, Kansas City, 1967-79; Green Bay, 1980-83; Minnesota, 1984-85 (580-pat, 373-fg)
1,634 Nick Lowery, New England, 1978; Kansas City, 1980-93; N.Y. Jets, 1994-95 (536-pat, 366-fg)

Most Points, Season

176 Paul Hornung, Green Bay, 1960 (15-td, 41-pat, 15-fg)
161 Mark Moseley, Washington, 1983 (62-pat, 33-fg)
155 Gino Cappelletti, Boston, 1964 (7-td, 38-pat, 25-fg)

Most Points, No Touchdowns, Season

161 Mark Moseley, Washington, 1983 (62-pat, 33-fg)
149 Chip Lohmiller, Washington, 1991 (56-pat, 31-fg)
145 Jim Turner, N.Y. Jets, 1968 (43-pat, 34-fg)

Most Seasons, 100 or More Points

11 Nick Lowery, Kansas City, 1981, 1983-86, 1988-93
10 Morten Andersen, New Orleans, 1985-89, 1991-94; Atlanta, 1995
8 Gary Anderson, Pittsburgh, 1983-85, 1988, 1991-94

Most Points, Rookie, Season

144 Kevin Butler, Chicago, 1985 (51-pat, 31-fg)
132 Gale Sayers, Chicago, 1965 (22-td)
128 Doak Walker, Detroit, 1950 (11-td, 38-pat, 8-fg)
Chester Marcol, Green Bay, 1972 (29-pat, 33-fg)

Most Points, Game

40 Ernie Nevers, Chi. Cardinals vs. Chi. Bears, Nov. 28, 1929 (6-td, 4-pat)
36 Dub Jones, Cleveland vs. Chi. Bears, Nov. 25, 1951 (6-td)
Gale Sayers, Chicago vs. San Francisco, Dec. 12, 1965 (6-td)
33 Paul Hornung, Green Bay vs. Baltimore, Oct. 8, 1961 (4-td, 6-pat, 1-fg)

Most Consecutive Games Scoring

190 Morten Andersen, New Orleans, 1982-94; Atlanta, 1995 (current)
186 Jim Breech, Oakland, 1979; Cincinnati, 1980-92
155 Ray Wersching, San Francisco, 1977-87

TOUCHDOWNS

Most Seasons Leading League

8 Don Hutson, Green Bay, 1935-38, 1941-44
3 Jim Brown, Cleveland, 1958-59, 1963
Lance Alworth, San Diego, 1964-66
Emmitt Smith, Dallas, 1992, 1994-95
2 By many players

Most Consecutive Seasons Leading League

4 Don Hutson, Green Bay, 1935-38, 1941-44
3 Lance Alworth, San Diego, 1964-66
2 By many players

Most Touchdowns, Career

156 Jerry Rice, San Francisco, 1985-95 (9-r, 146-p, 1-ret)
126 Jim Brown, Cleveland, 1957-65 (106-r, 20-p)
125 Walter Payton, Chicago, 1975-87 (110-r, 15-p)
Marcus Allen, L.A. Raiders, 1982-92; Kansas City, 1993-95 (103-r, 21-p, 1-ret)

Most Touchdowns, Season

25 Emmitt Smith, Dallas, 1995 (25-r)
24 John Riggins, Washington, 1983 (24-r)
23 O.J. Simpson, Buffalo, 1975 (16-r, 7-p)
Jerry Rice, San Francisco, 1987 (1-r, 22-p)

Most Touchdowns, Rookie, Season

22 Gale Sayers, Chicago, 1965 (14-r, 6-p, 2-ret)
20 Eric Dickerson, L.A. Rams, 1983 (18-r, 2-p)
16 Billy Sims, Detroit, 1980 (13-r, 3-p)

Most Touchdowns, Game

6 Ernie Nevers, Chi. Cardinals vs. Chi. Bears, Nov. 28, 1929 (6-r)
Dub Jones, Cleveland vs. Chi. Bears, Nov. 25, 1951 (4-r, 2-p)
Gale Sayers, Chicago vs. San Francisco, Dec. 12, 1965 (4-r, 1-p, 1-ret)
5 Bob Shaw, Chi. Cardinals vs. Baltimore, Oct. 2, 1950 (5-p)
Jim Brown, Cleveland vs. Baltimore, Nov. 1, 1959 (5-r)
Abner Haynes, Dall. Texans vs. Oakland, Nov. 26, 1961 (4-r, 1-p)
Billy Cannon, Houston vs. N.Y. Titans, Dec. 10, 1961 (3-r, 2-p)
Cookie Gilchrist, Buffalo vs. N.Y. Jets, Dec. 8, 1963 (5-r)
Paul Hornung, Green Bay vs. Baltimore, Dec. 12, 1965 (3-r, 2-p)
Kellen Winslow, San Diego vs. Oakland, Nov. 22, 1981 (5-p)
Jerry Rice, San Francisco vs. Atlanta, Oct. 14, 1990 (5-p)
4 By many players. Last time: Rodney Hampton, N.Y. Giants vs. New Orleans, Sept. 24, 1995 (4-r)

Most Consecutive Games Scoring Touchdowns

18 Lenny Moore, Baltimore, 1963-65
14 O.J. Simpson, Buffalo, 1975
13 John Riggins, Washington, 1982-83
George Rogers, Washington, 1985-86
Jerry Rice, San Francisco, 1986-87

POINTS AFTER TOUCHDOWN

Most Seasons Leading League

8 George Blanda, Chi. Bears, 1956; Houston, 1961-62; Oakland, 1967-69, 1972, 1974
4 Bob Waterfield, Cleveland, 1945; Los Angeles, 1946, 1950, 1952
3 Earl (Dutch) Clark, Portsmouth, 1932; Detroit, 1935-36
Jack Manders, Chi. Bears, 1933-35
Don Hutson, Green Bay, 1941-42, 1945

Most (Kicking) Points After Touchdown Attempted, Career

959 George Blanda, Chi. Bears, 1949, 1950-58; Baltimore, 1950; Houston, 1960-66; Oakland, 1967-75
657 Lou Groza, Cleveland, 1950-59, 1961-67
601 Jan Stenerud, Kansas City, 1967-79; Green Bay, 1980-83; Minnesota, 1984-85

Most (Kicking) Points After Touchdown Attempted, Season

70 Uwe von Schamann, Miami, 1984
65 George Blanda, Houston, 1961
63 Mark Moseley, Washington, 1983

Most (Kicking) Points After Touchdown Attempted, Game

10 Charlie Gogolak, Washington vs. N.Y. Giants, Nov. 27, 1966
9 Pat Harder, Chi. Cardinals vs. N.Y. Giants, Oct. 17, 1948; vs. N.Y.

Bulldogs, Nov. 13, 1949
Bob Waterfield, Los Angeles vs. Baltimore, Oct. 22, 1950
Bob Thomas, Chicago vs. Green Bay, Dec. 7, 1980
8 By many players

Most (One-Point) Points After Touchdown, Career
943 George Blanda, Chi. Bears, 1949, 1950-58; Baltimore, 1950; Houston, 1960-66; Oakland, 1967-75
641 Lou Groza, Cleveland, 1950-59, 1961-67
580 Jan Stenerud, Kansas City, 1967-79; Green Bay, 1980-83; Minnesota, 1984-85

Most (One-Point) Points After Touchdown, Season
66 Uwe von Schamann, Miami, 1984
64 George Blanda, Houston, 1961
62 Mark Moseley, Washington, 1983

Most (One-Point) Points After Touchdown, Game
9 Pat Harder, Chi. Cardinals vs. N.Y. Giants, Oct. 17, 1948
Bob Waterfield, Los Angeles vs. Baltimore, Oct. 22, 1950
Charlie Gogolak, Washington vs. N.Y. Giants, Nov. 27, 1966
8 By many players

Most Consecutive (Kicking) Points After Touchdown
234 Tommy Davis, San Francisco, 1959-65
228 Eddie Murray, Detroit, 1988-91; Kansas City, 1992; Tampa Bay, 1992; Dallas, 1993; Philadelphia, 1994; Washington, 1995 (current)
221 Jim Turner, N.Y. Jets, 1967-70; Denver, 1971-74

Highest (Kicking) Points After Touchdown Percentage, Career (200 points after touchdown)
99.43 Tommy Davis, San Francisco, 1959-69 (350-348)
99.08 Nick Lowery, New England, 1978; Kansas City, 1980-93; N.Y. Jets, 1994-95 (541-536)
99.01 Eddie Murray, Detroit, 1980-91; Kansas City, 1992; Tampa Bay, 1992; Dallas, 1993; Philadelphia, 1994; Washington, 1995 (503-498)

Most (Kicking) Points After Touchdown, No Misses, Season
56 Danny Villanueva, Dallas, 1966
Ray Wersching, San Francisco, 1984
Chip Lohmiller, Washington, 1991
54 Mike Clark, Dallas, 1968
George Blanda, Oakland, 1968
53 Pat Harder, Chi. Cardinals, 1948

Most (Kicking) Points After Touchdown, No Misses, Game
9 Pat Harder, Chi. Cardinals vs. N.Y. Giants, Oct. 17, 1948
Bob Waterfield, Los Angeles vs. Baltimore, Oct. 22, 1950
8 By many players

Most Two-Point Conversions, Career
5 Terance Mathis, Atlanta, 1994-95
4 Gino Cappelletti, Boston, 1960-69
3 Richie Lucas, Buffalo, 1960-61
Dave Kocourek, L.A. Chargers, 1960; San Diego, 1961-65; Miami, 1966; Oakland, 1967-68
Daryle Lamonica, Buffalo, 1963-66; Oakland, 1967-69
Bill Mathis, N.Y. Jets, 1960-69
Gene Prebola, Oakland, 1960; Denver, 1961-63
Ronnie Harmon, San Diego, 1994-95
Haywood Jeffires, Houston, 1994-95
Tom Tupa, Cleveland, 1994-95
Rob Moore, N.Y. Jets, 1994; Arizona, 1995
Brett Perriman, Detroit, 1994-95

Most Two-Point Conversions, Season
3 Gino Cappelletti, Boston, 1960
Richie Lucas, Buffalo, 1961
Ronnie Harmon, San Diego, 1994
Haywood Jeffires, Houston, 1994
Tom Tupa, Cleveland, 1994
Terance Mathis, Atlanta, 1995
2 By many players

Most Two-Point Conversions, Game
2 Brett Perriman, Detroit vs. Green Bay, Nov. 6, 1994

FIELD GOALS

Most Seasons Leading League
5 Lou Groza, Cleveland, 1950, 1952-54, 1957
4 Jack Manders, Chi. Bears, 1933-34, 1936-37
Ward Cuff, N.Y. Giants, 1938-39, 1943; Green Bay, 1947
Mark Moseley, Washington, 1976-77, 1979, 1982
3 Bob Waterfield, Los Angeles, 1947, 1949, 1951
Gino Cappelletti, Boston, 1961, 1963-64
Fred Cox, Minnesota, 1965, 1969-70
Jan Stenerud, Kansas City, 1967, 1970, 1975

Most Consecutive Seasons Leading League
3 Lou Groza, Cleveland, 1952-54
2 Jack Manders, Chi. Bears, 1933-34
Armand Niccolai, Pittsburgh, 1935-36
Jack Manders, Chi. Bears, 1936-37
Ward Cuff, N.Y. Giants, 1938-39
Clark Hinkle, Green Bay, 1940-41
Cliff Patton, Philadelphia, 1948-49
Gino Cappelletti, Boston, 1963-64
Jim Turner, N.Y. Jets, 1968-69
Fred Cox, Minnesota, 1969-70
Mark Moseley, Washington, 1976-77
Chip Lohmiller, Washington, 1991-92
Pete Stoyanovich, Miami, 1991-92

Most Field Goals Attempted, Career
637 George Blanda, Chi. Bears, 1949, 1950-58; Baltimore, 1950; Houston, 1960-66; Oakland, 1967-75
558 Jan Stenerud, Kansas City, 1967-79; Green Bay, 1980-83; Minnesota, 1984-85
488 Jim Turner, N.Y. Jets, 1964-70; Denver, 1971-79

Most Field Goals Attempted, Season
49 Bruce Gossett, Los Angeles, 1966
Curt Knight, Washington, 1971
48 Chester Marcol, Green Bay, 1972
47 Jim Turner, N.Y. Jets, 1969
David Ray, Los Angeles, 1973
Mark Moseley, Washington, 1983

Most Field Goals Attempted, Game
9 Jim Bakken, St. Louis vs. Pittsburgh, Sept. 24, 1967
8 Lou Michaels, Pittsburgh vs. St. Louis, Dec. 2, 1962
Garo Yepremian, Detroit vs. Minnesota, Nov. 13, 1966
Jim Turner, N.Y. Jets vs. Buffalo, Nov. 3, 1968
7 By many players

Most Field Goals, Career
373 Jan Stenerud, Kansas City, 1967-79; Green Bay, 1980-83; Minnesota, 1984-85
366 Nick Lowery, New England, 1978; Kansas City, 1980-93; N.Y. Jets, 1994-95
335 George Blanda, Chi. Bears, 1949, 1950-58; Baltimore, 1950; Houston, 1960-66; Oakland, 1967-75

Most Field Goals, Season
35 Ali Haji-Sheikh, N.Y. Giants, 1983
Jeff Jaeger, L.A. Raiders, 1993
34 Jim Turner, N.Y. Jets, 1968
Nick Lowery, Kansas City, 1990
Jason Hanson, Detroit, 1993
John Carney, San Diego, 1994
Fuad Reveiz, Minnesota, 1994
Norm Johnson, Pittsburgh, 1995
33 Chester Marcol, Green Bay, 1972
Mark Moseley, Washington, 1983
Gary Anderson, Pittsburgh, 1985

Most Field Goals, Rookie, Season
35 Ali Haji-Sheikh, N.Y. Giants, 1983
33 Chester Marcol, Green Bay, 1972
31 Kevin Butler, Chicago, 1985

Most Field Goals, Game
7 Jim Bakken, St. Louis vs. Pittsburgh, Sept. 24, 1967
Rich Karlis, Minnesota vs. L.A. Rams, Nov. 5, 1989 (OT)
6 Gino Cappelletti, Boston vs. Denver, Oct. 4, 1964
Garo Yepremian, Detroit vs. Minnesota, Nov. 13, 1966
Jim Turner, N.Y. Jets vs. Buffalo, Nov. 3, 1968
Tom Dempsey, Philadelphia vs. Houston, Nov. 12, 1972
Bobby Howfield, N.Y. Jets vs. New Orleans, Dec. 3, 1972
Jim Bakken, St. Louis vs. Atlanta, Dec. 9, 1973
Joe Danelo, N.Y. Giants vs. Seattle, Oct. 18, 1981
Ray Wersching, San Francisco vs. New Orleans, Oct. 16, 1983
Gary Anderson, Pittsburgh vs. Denver, Oct. 23, 1988
John Carney, San Diego vs. Seattle, Sept. 5, 1993
John Carney, San Diego vs. Houston, Sept. 19, 1993
Doug Pelfrey, Cincinnati vs. Seattle, Nov. 6, 1994 (OT)
Norm Johnson, Atlanta vs. New Orleans, Nov. 13, 1994
5 By many players

Most Field Goals, One Quarter
4 Garo Yepremian, Detroit vs. Minnesota, Nov. 13, 1966 (second quarter)
Curt Knight, Washington vs. N.Y. Giants, Nov. 15, 1970 (second quarter)
Roger Ruzek, Dallas vs. N.Y. Giants, Nov. 2, 1987 (fourth quarter)
3 By many players

Most Consecutive Games Scoring Field Goals
31 Fred Cox, Minnesota, 1968-70
28 Jim Turner, N.Y. Jets, 1970; Denver, 1971-72
Chip Lohmiller, Washington, 1988-90
23 Morten Andersen, New Orleans, 1986-88

Most Consecutive Field Goals
31 Fuad Reveiz, Minnesota, 1994-95
29 John Carney, San Diego, 1992-93
26 Norm Johnson, Atlanta, 1992-93

Longest Field Goal
63 Tom Dempsey, New Orleans vs. Detroit, Nov. 8, 1970

60 Steve Cox, Cleveland vs. Cincinnati, Oct. 21, 1984
Morten Andersen, New Orleans vs. Chicago, Oct. 27, 1991
59 Tony Franklin, Philadelphia vs. Dallas, Nov. 12, 1979
Pete Stoyanovich, Miami vs. N.Y. Jets, Nov. 12, 1989
Steve Christie, Buffalo vs. Miami, Sept. 26, 1993
Morten Andersen, Atlanta vs. San Francisco, Dec. 24, 1995

Highest Field Goal Percentage, Career (100 field goals)
80.60 Matt Stover, Cleveland, 1991-95 (134-108)
80.44 Nick Lowery, New England, 1978; Kansas City, 1980-93; N.Y. Jets, 1994-95 (455-366)
79.58 John Carney, Tampa Bay, 1988-89; L.A. Rams, 1990; San Diego, 1990-95 (191-152)

Highest Field Goal Percentage, Season (Qualifiers)
100.00 Tony Zendejas, L.A. Rams, 1991 (17-17)
96.43 Chris Boniol, Dallas, 1995 (28-27)
96.30 Norm Johnson, Atlanta, 1993 (27-26)

Most Field Goals, No Misses, Game
7 Rich Karlis, Minnesota vs. L.A. Rams, Nov. 5, 1989 (OT)
6 Gino Cappelletti, Boston vs. Denver, Oct. 4, 1964
Joe Danelo, N.Y. Giants vs. Seattle, Oct. 18, 1981
Ray Wersching, San Francisco vs. New Orleans, Oct. 16, 1983
Gary Anderson, Pittsburgh vs. Denver, Oct. 23, 1988
John Carney, San Diego vs. Seattle, Sept. 5, 1993
John Carney, San Diego vs. Houston, Sept. 19, 1993
Doug Pelfrey, Cincinnati vs. Seattle, Nov. 6, 1994 (OT)
Norm Johnson, Atlanta vs. New Orleans, Nov. 13, 1994
5 By many players

Most Field Goals, 50 or More Yards, Career
30 Morten Andersen, New Orleans, 1982-94; Atlanta, 1995
22 Nick Lowery, New England, 1978; Kansas City, 1980-93; N.Y. Jets, 1994-95
21 Eddie Murray, Detroit, 1980-91; Kansas City, 1992; Tampa Bay, 1992; Dallas, 1993; Philadelphia, 1994; Washington, 1995

Most Field Goals, 50 or More Yards, Season
8 Morten Andersen, Atlanta, 1995
6 Dean Biasucci, Indianapolis, 1988
Chris Jacke, Green Bay, 1993
Tony Zendejas, L.A. Rams, 1993
5 Fred Steinfort, Denver, 1980
Norm Johnson, Seattle, 1986
Kevin Butler, Chicago, 1993
Jason Elam, Denver, 1995

Most Field Goals, 50 or More Yards, Game
3 Morten Andersen, Atlanta vs. New Orleans, Dec. 10, 1995
2 By many players. Last time: Morten Andersen, Atlanta vs. San Francisco, Dec. 24, 1995

SAFETIES

Most Safeties, Career
4 Ted Hendricks, Baltimore, 1969-73; Green Bay, 1974; Oakland, 1975-81; L.A. Raiders, 1982-83
Doug English, Detroit, 1975-79, 1981-85
3 Bill McPeak, Pittsburgh, 1949-57
Charlie Krueger, San Francisco, 1959-73
Ernie Stautner, Pittsburgh, 1950-63
Jim Katcavage, N.Y. Giants, 1956-68
Roger Brown, Detroit, 1960-66; Los Angeles, 1967-69
Bruce Maher, Detroit, 1960-67; N.Y. Giants, 1968-69
Ron McDole, St. Louis, 1961; Houston, 1962; Buffalo, 1963-70; Washington, 1971-78
Alan Page, Minnesota, 1967-78; Chicago, 1979-81
Lyle Alzado, Denver, 1971-78; Cleveland, 1979-81; L.A. Raiders, 1982-85
Rulon Jones, Denver, 1980-88
Steve McMichael, New England, 1980; Chicago, 1981-93; Green Bay, 1994
Kevin Greene, L.A. Rams, 1985-92; Pittsburgh, 1993-95
Burt Grossman, San Diego, 1989-93; Philadelphia, 1994
Eric Swann, Phoenix, 1991-93; Arizona, 1994-95
2 By many players

Most Safeties, Season
2 Tom Nash, Green Bay, 1932
Roger Brown, Detroit, 1962
Ron McDole, Buffalo, 1964
Alan Page, Minnesota, 1971
Fred Dryer, Los Angeles, 1973
Benny Barnes, Dallas, 1973
James Young, Houston, 1977
Tom Hannon, Minnesota, 1981
Doug English, Detroit, 1983
Don Blackmon, New England, 1985
Tim Harris, Green Bay, 1988
Brian Jordan, Atlanta, 1991
Burt Grossman, San Diego, 1992
Rod Stephens, Seattle, 1993

Most Safeties, Game
2 Fred Dryer, Los Angeles vs. Green Bay, Oct. 21, 1973

RUSHING

Most Seasons Leading League
8 Jim Brown, Cleveland, 1957-61, 1963-65
4 Steve Van Buren, Philadelphia, 1945, 1947-49
O.J. Simpson, Buffalo, 1972-73, 1975-76
Eric Dickerson, L.A. Rams, 1983-84, 1986; Indianapolis, 1988
Emmitt Smith, Dallas, 1991-93, 1995
3 Earl Campbell, Houston, 1978-80

Most Consecutive Seasons Leading League
5 Jim Brown, Cleveland, 1957-61
3 Steve Van Buren, Philadelphia, 1947-49
Jim Brown, Cleveland, 1963-65
Earl Campbell, Houston, 1978-80
Emmitt Smith, Dallas, 1991-93
2 Bill Paschal, N.Y. Giants, 1943-44
Joe Perry, San Francisco, 1953-54
Jim Nance, Boston, 1966-67
Leroy Kelly, Cleveland, 1967-68
O.J. Simpson, Buffalo, 1972-73; 1975-76
Eric Dickerson, L.A. Rams, 1983-84

ATTEMPTS

Most Seasons Leading League
6 Jim Brown, Cleveland, 1958-59, 1961, 1963-65
4 Steve Van Buren, Philadelphia, 1947-50
Walter Payton, Chicago, 1976-79
3 Cookie Gilchrist, Buffalo, 1963-64; Denver, 1965
Jim Nance, Boston, 1966-67, 1969
O.J. Simpson, Buffalo, 1973-75
Eric Dickerson, L.A. Rams, 1983, 1986; Indianapolis, 1988
Emmitt Smith, Dallas, 1991, 1994-95

Most Consecutive Seasons Leading League
4 Steve Van Buren, Philadelphia, 1947-50
Walter Payton, Chicago, 1976-79
3 Jim Brown, Cleveland, 1963-65
Cookie Gilchrist, Buffalo, 1963-64; Denver, 1965
O.J. Simpson, Buffalo, 1973-75
2 By many players

Most Attempts, Career
3,838 Walter Payton, Chicago, 1975-87
2,996 Eric Dickerson, L.A. Rams, 1983-87; Indianapolis, 1987-91; L.A. Raiders, 1992; Atlanta, 1993
2,949 Franco Harris, Pittsburgh, 1972-83; Seattle, 1984

Most Attempts, Season
407 James Wilder, Tampa Bay, 1984
404 Eric Dickerson, L.A. Rams, 1986
397 Gerald Riggs, Atlanta, 1985

Most Attempts, Rookie, Season
390 Eric Dickerson, L.A. Rams, 1983
378 George Rogers, New Orleans, 1981
368 Curtis Martin, New England, 1995

Most Attempts, Game
45 Jamie Morris, Washington vs. Cincinnati, Dec. 17, 1988 (OT)
43 Butch Woolfolk, N.Y. Giants vs. Philadelphia, Nov. 20, 1983
James Wilder, Tampa Bay vs. Green Bay, Sept. 30, 1984 (OT)
42 James Wilder, Tampa Bay vs. Pittsburgh, Oct. 30, 1983

YARDS GAINED

Most Yards Gained, Career
16,726 Walter Payton, Chicago, 1975-87
13,259 Eric Dickerson, L.A. Rams, 1983-87; Indianapolis, 1987-91; L.A. Raiders, 1992; Atlanta, 1993
12,739 Tony Dorsett, Dallas, 1977-87; Denver, 1988

Most Seasons, 1,000 or More Yards Rushing
10 Walter Payton, Chicago, 1976-81, 1983-86
8 Franco Harris, Pittsburgh, 1972, 1974-79, 1983
Tony Dorsett, Dallas, 1977-81, 1983-85
7 Jim Brown, Cleveland, 1958-61, 1963-65
Eric Dickerson, L.A. Rams, 1983-86; L.A. Rams-Indianapolis, 1987; Indianapolis, 1988-89
Barry Sanders, Detroit, 1989-95
Thurman Thomas, Buffalo, 1989-95

Most Consecutive Seasons, 1,000 or More Yards Rushing
7 Eric Dickerson, L.A. Rams, 1983-86; L.A. Rams-Indianapolis, 1987; Indianapolis, 1988-89
Barry Sanders, Detroit, 1989-95
Thurman Thomas, Buffalo, 1989-95
6 Franco Harris, Pittsburgh, 1974-79

Walter Payton, Chicago, 1976-81
5 Jim Taylor, Green Bay, 1960-64
O.J. Simpson, Buffalo, 1972-76
Tony Dorsett, Dallas, 1977-81
Emmitt Smith, Dallas, 1991-95
Rodney Hampton, N.Y. Giants, 1991-95

Most Yards Gained, Season
2,105 Eric Dickerson, L.A. Rams, 1984
2,003 O.J. Simpson, Buffalo, 1973
1,934 Earl Campbell, Houston, 1980

Most Yards Gained, Rookie, Season
1,808 Eric Dickerson, L.A. Rams, 1983
1,674 George Rogers, New Orleans, 1981
1,605 Ottis Anderson, St. Louis, 1979

Most Yards Gained, Game
275 Walter Payton, Chicago vs. Minnesota, Nov. 20, 1977
273 O.J. Simpson, Buffalo vs. Detroit, Nov. 25, 1976
250 O.J. Simpson, Buffalo vs. New England, Sept. 16, 1973

Most Games, 200 or More Yards Rushing, Career
6 O.J. Simpson, Buffalo, 1969-77; San Francisco, 1978-79
4 Jim Brown, Cleveland, 1957-65
Earl Campbell, Houston, 1978-84; New Orleans, 1984-85
3 Eric Dickerson, L.A. Rams, 1983-87; Indianapolis, 1987-91; L.A. Raiders, 1992; Atlanta, 1993
Greg Bell, Buffalo, 1984-87; L.A. Rams, 1987-89; L.A. Raiders, 1990

Most Games, 200 or More Yards Rushing, Season
4 Earl Campbell, Houston, 1980
3 O.J. Simpson, Buffalo, 1973
2 Jim Brown, Cleveland, 1963
O.J. Simpson, Buffalo, 1976
Walter Payton, Chicago, 1977
Eric Dickerson, L.A. Rams, 1984
Greg Bell, L.A. Rams, 1989

Most Consecutive Games, 200 or More Yards Rushing
2 O.J. Simpson, Buffalo, 1973, 1976
Earl Campbell, Houston, 1980

Most Games, 100 or More Yards Rushing, Career
77 Walter Payton, Chicago, 1975-87
64 Eric Dickerson, L.A. Rams, 1983-87; Indianapolis, 1987-91; L.A. Raiders, 1992; Atlanta, 1993
58 Jim Brown, Cleveland, 1957-65

Most Games, 100 or More Yards Rushing, Season
12 Eric Dickerson, L.A. Rams, 1984
Barry Foster, Pittsburgh, 1992
11 O.J. Simpson, Buffalo, 1973
Earl Campbell, Houston, 1979
Marcus Allen, L.A. Raiders, 1985
Eric Dickerson, L.A. Rams, 1986
Emmitt Smith, Dallas, 1995
10 Walter Payton, Chicago, 1977
Earl Campbell, Houston, 1980
Walter Payton, Chicago, 1985
Barry Sanders, Detroit, 1994

Most Consecutive Games, 100 or More Yards Rushing
11 Marcus Allen, L.A. Raiders, 1985-86
9 Walter Payton, Chicago, 1985
7 O.J. Simpson, Buffalo, 1972-73
Earl Campbell, Houston, 1979

Longest Run From Scrimmage
99 Tony Dorsett, Dallas vs. Minnesota, Jan. 3, 1983 (TD)
97 Andy Uram, Green Bay vs. Chi. Cardinals, Oct. 8, 1939 (TD)
Bob Gage, Pittsburgh vs. Chi. Bears, Dec. 4, 1949 (TD)
96 Jim Spavital, Baltimore vs. Green Bay, Nov. 5, 1950 (TD)
Bob Hoernschemeyer, Detroit vs. N.Y. Yanks, Nov. 23, 1950 (TD)

AVERAGE GAIN

Highest Average Gain, Career (750 attempts)
5.22 Jim Brown, Cleveland, 1957-65 (2,359-12,312)
5.14 Eugene (Mercury) Morris, Miami, 1969-75; San Diego, 1976 (804-4,133)
5.00 Gale Sayers, Chicago, 1965-71 (991-4,956)

Highest Average Gain, Season (Qualifiers)
8.44 Beattie Feathers, Chi. Bears, 1934 (119-1,004)
7.98 Randall Cunningham, Philadelphia 1990 (118-942)
6.87 Bobby Douglass, Chicago, 1972 (141-968)

Highest Average Gain, Game (10 attempts)
17.09 Marion Motley, Cleveland vs. Pittsburgh, Oct. 29, 1950 (11-188)
16.70 Bill Grimes, Green Bay vs. N.Y. Yanks, Oct. 8, 1950 (10-167)
16.57 Bobby Mitchell, Cleveland vs. Washington, Nov. 15, 1959 (14-232)

TOUCHDOWNS

Most Seasons Leading League
5 Jim Brown, Cleveland, 1957-59, 1963, 1965
4 Steve Van Buren, Philadelphia, 1945, 1947-49
3 Abner Haynes, Dall. Texans, 1960-62
Cookie Gilchrist, Buffalo, 1962-64
Paul Lowe, L.A. Chargers, 1960; San Diego, 1961, 1965
Leroy Kelly, Cleveland, 1966-68
Emmitt Smith, Dallas, 1992, 1994-95

Most Consecutive Seasons Leading League
3 Steve Van Buren, Philadelphia, 1947-49
Jim Brown, Cleveland, 1957-59
Abner Haynes, Dall. Texans, 1960-62
Cookie Gilchrist, Buffalo, 1962-64
Leroy Kelly, Cleveland, 1966-68

Most Touchdowns, Career
110 Walter Payton, Chicago, 1975-87
106 Jim Brown, Cleveland, 1957-65
104 John Riggins, N.Y. Jets, 1971-75; Washington, 1976-79, 1981-85

Most Touchdowns, Season
25 Emmitt Smith, Dallas, 1995
24 John Riggins, Washington, 1983
21 Joe Morris, N.Y. Giants, 1985
Emmitt Smith, Dallas, 1994

Most Touchdowns, Rookie, Season
18 Eric Dickerson, L.A. Rams, 1983
15 Ickey Woods, Cincinnati, 1988
14 Gale Sayers, Chicago, 1965
Barry Sanders, Detroit, 1989
Curtis Martin, New England, 1995

Most Touchdowns, Game
6 Ernie Nevers, Chi. Cardinals vs. Chi. Bears, Nov. 28, 1929
5 Jim Brown, Cleveland vs. Baltimore, Nov. 1, 1959
Cookie Gilchrist, Buffalo vs. N.Y. Jets, Dec. 8, 1963
4 By many players

Most Consecutive Games Rushing for Touchdowns
13 John Riggins, Washington, 1982-83
George Rogers, Washington, 1985-86
11 Lenny Moore, Baltimore, 1963-64
Emmitt Smith, Dallas, 1994-95
Emmitt Smith, Dallas, 1995 (current)
10 Greg Bell, L.A. Rams, 1988-89

PASSING

Most Seasons Leading League
6 Sammy Baugh, Washington, 1937, 1940, 1943, 1945, 1947, 1949
4 Len Dawson, Dall. Texans; 1962; Kansas City, 1964, 1966, 1968
Roger Staubach, Dallas, 1971, 1973, 1978-79
Ken Anderson, Cincinnati, 1974-75, 1981-82
Steve Young, San Francisco, 1991-94
3 Arnie Herber, Green Bay, 1932, 1934, 1936
Norm Van Brocklin, Los Angeles, 1950, 1952, 1954
Bart Starr, Green Bay, 1962, 1964, 1966

Most Consecutive Seasons Leading League
4 Steve Young, San Francisco, 1991-94
2 Cecil Isbell, Green Bay, 1941-42
Milt Plum, Cleveland, 1960-61
Ken Anderson, Cincinnati, 1974-75, 1981-82
Roger Staubach, Dallas, 1978-79

PASS RATING

Highest Pass Rating, Career (1,500 attempts)
96.1 Steve Young, Tampa Bay, 1985-86; San Francisco, 1987-95
92.3 Joe Montana, San Francisco, 1979-90, 1992; Kansas City, 1993-94
88.4 Dan Marino, Miami, 1983-95

Highest Pass Rating, Season (Qualifiers)
112.8 Steve Young, San Francisco, 1994
112.4 Joe Montana, San Francisco, 1989
110.4 Milt Plum, Cleveland, 1960

Highest Pass Rating, Rookie, Season (Qualifiers)
96.0 Dan Marino, Miami, 1983
88.2 Greg Cook, Cincinnati, 1969
84.0 Charlie Conerly, N.Y. Giants, 1948

ATTEMPTS

Most Seasons Leading League
4 Sammy Baugh, Washington, 1937, 1943, 1947-48
Johnny Unitas, Baltimore, 1957, 1959-61
George Blanda, Chi. Bears, 1953; Houston, 1963-65
Dan Marino, Miami, 1984, 1986, 1988, 1992
3 Arnie Herber, Green Bay, 1932, 1934, 1936
Sonny Jurgensen, Washington, 1966-67, 1969
2 By many players

Most Consecutive Seasons Leading League
3 Johnny Unitas, Baltimore, 1959-61
George Blanda, Houston, 1963-65

2 By many players

Most Passes Attempted, Career
6,531 Dan Marino, Miami, 1983-95
6,467 Fran Tarkenton, Minnesota, 1961-66, 1972-78; N.Y. Giants, 1967-71
5,926 John Elway, Denver, 1983-95

Most Passes Attempted, Season
691 Drew Bledsoe, New England, 1994
655 Warren Moon, Houston, 1991
636 Drew Bledsoe, New England, 1995

Most Passes Attempted, Rookie, Season
486 Rick Mirer, Seattle, 1993
439 Jim Zorn, Seattle, 1976
433 Kerry Collins, Carolina, 1995

Most Passes Attempted, Game
70 Drew Bledsoe, New England vs. Minnesota, Nov. 13, 1994 (OT)
68 George Blanda, Houston vs. Buffalo, Nov. 1, 1964
66 Chris Miller, Atlanta vs. Detroit, Dec. 24, 1989

COMPLETIONS

Most Seasons Leading League
5 Sammy Baugh, Washington, 1937, 1943, 1945, 1947-48
Dan Marino, Miami, 1984-86, 1988, 1992
4 George Blanda, Chi. Bears, 1953; Houston, 1963-65
Sonny Jurgensen, Philadelphia, 1961; Washington, 1966-67, 1969
3 Arnie Herber, Green Bay, 1932, 1934, 1936
Johnny Unitas, Baltimore, 1959-60, 1963
John Brodie, San Francisco, 1965, 1968, 1970
Fran Tarkenton, Minnesota, 1975-76, 1978
Warren Moon, Houston, 1990-91; Minnesota, 1995

Most Consecutive Seasons Leading League
3 George Blanda, Houston, 1963-65
Dan Marino, Miami, 1984-86
2 By many players

Most Passes Completed, Career
3,913 Dan Marino, Miami, 1983-95
3,686 Fran Tarkenton, Minnesota, 1961-66, 1972-78; N.Y. Giants, 1967-71
3,409 Joe Montana, San Francisco, 1979-90, 1992; Kansas City, 1993-94

Most Passes Completed, Season
404 Warren Moon, Houston, 1991
400 Drew Bledsoe, New England, 1994
385 Dan Marino, Miami, 1994

Most Passes Completed, Rookie, Season
274 Rick Mirer, Seattle, 1993
214 Drew Bledsoe, New England, 1993
Kerry Collins, Carolina, 1995
208 Jim Zorn, Seattle, 1976

Most Passes Completed, Game
45 Drew Bledsoe, New England vs. Minnesota, Nov. 13, 1994 (OT)
42 Richard Todd, N.Y. Jets vs. San Francisco, Sept. 21, 1980
41 Warren Moon, Houston vs. Dallas, Nov. 10, 1991 (OT)

Most Consecutive Passes Completed
22 Joe Montana, San Francisco vs. Cleveland (5), Nov. 29, 1987; vs. Green Bay (17), Dec. 6, 1987
20 Ken Anderson, Cincinnati vs. Houston, Jan. 2, 1983
Hugh Millen, Denver vs. L.A. Raiders (7), Dec. 11, 1994; vs. San Francisco (13), Dec. 17, 1994
18 Steve DeBerg, Denver vs. L.A. Rams (17), Dec. 12, 1982; vs. Kansas City (1), Dec. 19, 1982
Lynn Dickey, Green Bay vs. Houston, Sept. 4, 1983
Joe Montana, San Francisco vs. L.A. Rams (13), Oct. 28, 1984; vs. Cincinnati (5), Nov. 4, 1984
Don Majkowski, Green Bay vs. New Orleans, Sept. 18, 1989
Boomer Esiason, N.Y. Jets vs. Miami (5), Sept. 12, 1993; vs. New England (13), Sept. 26, 1993

COMPLETION PERCENTAGE

Most Seasons Leading League
8 Len Dawson, Dall. Texans, 1962; Kansas City, 1964-69, 1975
7 Sammy Baugh, Washington, 1940, 1942-43, 1945, 1947-49
5 Joe Montana, San Francisco, 1980-81, 1985, 1987, 1989

Most Consecutive Seasons Leading League
6 Len Dawson, Kansas City, 1964-69
3 Sammy Baugh, Washington, 1947-49
Otto Graham, Cleveland, 1953-55
Milt Plum, Cleveland, 1959-61
2 By many players

Highest Completion Percentage, Career (1,500 attempts)
64.15 Steve Young, Tampa Bay, 1985-86; San Francisco, 1987-95 (2,876-1,845)
63.24 Joe Montana, San Francisco, 1979-90, 1992; Kansas City, 1993-94 (5,391-3,409)
62.81 Troy Aikman, Dallas, 1989-95 (2,713-1,704)

Highest Completion Percentage, Season (Qualifiers)
70.55 Ken Anderson, Cincinnati, 1982 (309-218)
70.33 Sammy Baugh, Washington, 1945 (182-128)
70.28 Steve Young, San Francisco, 1994 (461-324)

Highest Completion Percentage, Rookie, Season (Qualifiers)
58.45 Dan Marino, Miami, 1983 (296-173)
57.14 Jim McMahon, Chicago, 1982 (210-120)
56.38 Rick Mirer, Seattle, 1993 (486-274)

Highest Completion Percentage, Game (20 attempts)
91.30 Vinny Testaverde, Cleveland vs. L.A. Rams, Dec. 26, 1993 (23-21)
90.91 Ken Anderson, Cincinnati vs. Pittsburgh, Nov. 10, 1974 (22-20)
90.48 Lynn Dickey, Green Bay vs. New Orleans, Dec. 13, 1981 (21-19)

YARDS GAINED

Most Seasons Leading League
5 Sonny Jurgensen, Philadelphia, 1961-62; Washington, 1966-67, 1969
Dan Marino, Miami, 1984-86, 1988, 1992
4 Sammy Baugh, Washington, 1937, 1940, 1947-48
Johnny Unitas, Baltimore, 1957, 1959-60, 1963
Dan Fouts, San Diego, 1979-82
3 Arnie Herber, Green Bay, 1932, 1934, 1936
Sid Luckman, Chi. Bears, 1943, 1945-46
John Brodie, San Francisco, 1965, 1968, 1970
John Hadl, San Diego, 1965, 1968, 1971
Joe Namath, N.Y. Jets, 1966-67, 1972

Most Consecutive Seasons Leading League
4 Dan Fouts, San Diego, 1979-82
3 Dan Marino, Miami, 1984-86
2 By many players

Most Yards Gained, Career
48,841 Dan Marino, Miami, 1983-95
47,003 Fran Tarkenton, Minnesota, 1961-66, 1972-78; N.Y. Giants, 1967-71
43,040 Dan Fouts, San Diego, 1973-87

Most Seasons, 3,000 or More Yards Passing
11 Dan Marino, Miami, 1984-92, 1994-95
10 John Elway, Denver, 1985-91, 1993-95
8 Joe Montana, San Francisco, 1981, 1983-85, 1987, 1989-90; Kansas City, 1994
Jim Kelly, Buffalo, 1986, 1988-89, 1991-95
Warren Moon, Houston, 1984, 1986, 1989-91, 1993; Minnesota, 1994-95

Most Yards Gained, Season
5,084 Dan Marino, Miami, 1984
4,802 Dan Fouts, San Diego, 1981
4,746 Dan Marino, Miami, 1986

Most Yards Gained, Rookie, Season
2,833 Rick Mirer, Seattle, 1993
2,717 Kerry Collins, Carolina, 1995
2,571 Jim Zorn, Seattle, 1976

Most Yards Gained, Game
554 Norm Van Brocklin, Los Angeles vs. N.Y. Yanks, Sept. 28, 1951
527 Warren Moon, Houston vs. Kansas City, Dec. 16, 1990
521 Dan Marino, Miami vs. N.Y. Jets, Oct. 23, 1988

Most Games, 400 or More Yards Passing, Career
13 Dan Marino, Miami, 1983-95
7 Joe Montana, San Francisco, 1979-90, 1992; Kansas City, 1993-94
6 Dan Fouts, San Diego, 1973-87
Warren Moon, Houston, 1984-93; Minnesota, 1994-95

Most Games, 400 or More Yards Passing, Season
4 Dan Marino, Miami, 1984
3 Dan Marino, Miami, 1986
2 By many players

Most Consecutive Games, 400 or More Yards Passing
2 Dan Fouts, San Diego, 1982
Dan Marino, Miami, 1984
Phil Simms, N.Y. Giants, 1985

Most Games, 300 or More Yards Passing, Career
52 Dan Marino, Miami, 1983-95
51 Dan Fouts, San Diego, 1973-87
48 Warren Moon, Houston, 1984-93; Minnesota, 1994-95

Most Games, 300 or More Yards Passing, Season
9 Dan Marino, Miami, 1984
Warren Moon, Houston, 1990
8 Dan Fouts, San Diego, 1980
7 Dan Fouts, San Diego, 1981
Bill Kenney, Kansas City, 1983
Neil Lomax, St. Louis, 1984
Dan Fouts, San Diego, 1985
Brett Favre, Green Bay, 1995

Most Consecutive Games, 300 or More Yards Passing
5 Joe Montana, San Francisco, 1982
4 Dan Fouts, San Diego, 1979
Dan Fouts, San Diego, 1980-81

Bill Kenney, Kansas City, 1983
Joe Montana, San Francisco, 1985-86
Joe Montana, San Francisco, 1990
Warren Moon, Houston, 1990
Drew Bledsoe, New England, 1993-94
3 By many players

Longest Pass Completion (All TDs except as noted)
99 Frank Filchock (to Farkas), Washington vs. Pittsburgh, Oct. 15, 1939
George Izo (to Mitchell), Washington vs. Cleveland, Sept. 15, 1963
Karl Sweetan (to Studstill), Detroit vs. Baltimore, Oct. 16, 1966
Sonny Jurgensen (to Allen), Washington vs. Chicago, Sept. 15, 1968
Jim Plunkett (to Branch), L.A. Raiders vs. Washington, Oct. 2, 1983
Ron Jaworski (to Quick), Philadelphia vs. Atlanta, Nov. 10, 1985
Stan Humphries (to Martin), San Diego vs. Seattle, Sept. 18, 1994
Brett Favre (to Brooks), Green Bay vs. Chicago, Sept. 11, 1995
98 Doug Russell (to Tinsley), Chi. Cardinals vs. Cleveland, Nov. 27, 1938
Ogden Compton (to Lane), Chi. Cardinals vs. Green Bay, Nov. 13, 1955
Bill Wade (to Farrington), Chicago Bears vs. Detroit, Oct. 8, 1961
Jacky Lee (to Dewveall), Houston vs. San Diego, Nov. 25, 1962
Earl Morrall (to Jones), N.Y. Giants vs. Pittsburgh, Sept. 11, 1966
Jim Hart (to Moore), St. Louis vs. Los Angeles, Dec. 10, 1972 (no TD)
Bobby Hebert (to Haynes), Atlanta vs. New Orleans, Sept. 12, 1993
97 Pat Coffee (to Tinsley), Chi. Cardinals vs. Chi. Bears, Dec. 5, 1937
Bobby Layne (to Box), Detroit vs. Green Bay, Nov. 26, 1953
George Shaw (to Tarr), Denver vs. Boston, Sept. 21, 1962
Bernie Kosar (to Slaughter), Cleveland vs. Chicago, Oct. 23, 1989
Steve Young (to Taylor), San Francisco vs. Atlanta, Nov. 3, 1991

AVERAGE GAIN

Most Seasons Leading League
7 Sid Luckman, Chi. Bears, 1939-43, 1946-47
4 Steve Young, San Francisco, 1991-94
3 Arnie Herber, Green Bay, 1932, 1934, 1936
Norm Van Brocklin, Los Angeles, 1950, 1952, 1954
Len Dawson, Dall. Texans, 1962; Kansas City, 1966, 1968
Bart Starr, Green Bay, 1966-68

Most Consecutive Seasons Leading League
5 Sid Luckman, Chi. Bears, 1939-43
4 Steve Young, San Francisco, 1991-94
3 Bart Starr, Green Bay, 1966-68

Highest Average Gain, Career (1,500 attempts)
8.63 Otto Graham, Cleveland, 1950-55 (1,565-13,499)
8.42 Sid Luckman, Chi. Bears, 1939-50 (1,744-14,686)
8.16 Norm Van Brocklin, Los Angeles, 1949-57; Philadelphia, 1958-60 (2,895-23,611)

Highest Average Gain, Season (Qualifiers)
11.17 Tommy O'Connell, Cleveland, 1957 (110-1,229)
10.86 Sid Luckman, Chi. Bears, 1943 (202-2,194)
10.55 Otto Graham, Cleveland, 1953 (258-2,722)

Highest Average Gain, Rookie, Season (Qualifiers)
9.411 Greg Cook, Cincinnati, 1969 (197-1,854)
9.409 Bob Waterfield, Cleveland, 1945 (171-1,609)
8.36 Zeke Bratkowski, Chi. Bears, 1954 (130-1,087)

Highest Average Gain, Game (20 attempts)
18.58 Sammy Baugh, Washington vs. Boston, Oct. 31, 1948 (24-446)
18.50 Johnny Unitas, Baltimore vs. Atlanta, Nov. 12, 1967 (20-370)
17.71 Joe Namath, N.Y. Jets vs. Baltimore, Sept. 24, 1972 (28-496)

TOUCHDOWNS

Most Seasons Leading League
4 Johnny Unitas, Baltimore, 1957-60
Len Dawson, Dall. Texans, 1962; Kansas City, 1963, 1965-66
3 Arnie Herber, Green Bay, 1932, 1934, 1936
Sid Luckman, Chi. Bears, 1943, 1945-46
Y.A. Tittle, San Francisco, 1955; N.Y. Giants, 1962-63
Dan Marino, Miami, 1984-86
Steve Young, San Francisco, 1992-94
2 By many players

Most Consecutive Seasons Leading League
4 Johnny Unitas, Baltimore, 1957-60
3 Dan Marino, Miami, 1984-86
Steve Young, San Francisco, 1992-94
2 By many players

Most Touchdown Passes, Career
352 Dan Marino, Miami, 1983-95
342 Fran Tarkenton, Minnesota, 1961-66, 1972-78; N.Y. Giants, 1967-71
290 Johnny Unitas, Baltimore, 1956-72: San Diego, 1973

Most Touchdown Passes, Season
48 Dan Marino, Miami, 1984
44 Dan Marino, Miami, 1986
38 Brett Favre, Green Bay, 1995

Most Touchdown Passes, Rookie, Season
22 Charlie Conerly, N.Y. Giants, 1948
20 Dan Marino, Miami, 1983
19 Jim Plunkett, New England, 1971

Most Touchdown Passes, Game
7 Sid Luckman, Chi. Bears vs. N.Y. Giants, Nov. 14, 1943
Adrian Burk, Philadelphia vs. Washington, Oct. 17, 1954
George Blanda, Houston vs. N.Y. Titans, Nov. 19, 1961
Y.A. Tittle, N.Y. Giants vs. Washington, Oct. 28, 1962
Joe Kapp, Minnesota vs. Baltimore, Sept. 28, 1969
6 By many players. Last time: Mark Rypien, Washington vs. Atlanta, Nov. 10, 1991

Most Games, Four or More Touchdown Passes, Career
20 Dan Marino, Miami, 1983-95
17 Johnny Unitas, Baltimore, 1956-72; San Diego, 1973
13 George Blanda, Chi. Bears, 1949, 1950-58; Baltimore, 1950; Houston, 1960-66; Oakland, 1967-75

Most Games, Four or More Touchdown Passes, Season
6 Dan Marino, Miami, 1984
5 Dan Marino, Miami, 1986
4 George Blanda, Houston, 1961
Vince Ferragamo, Los Angeles, 1980

Most Consecutive Games, Four or More Touchdown Passes
4 Dan Marino, Miami, 1984
2 By many players

Most Consecutive Games, Touchdown Passes
47 Johnny Unitas, Baltimore, 1956-60
30 Dan Marino, Miami, 1985-87
28 Dave Krieg, Seattle, 1983-85

HAD INTERCEPTED

Most Consecutive Passes Attempted, None Intercepted
308 Bernie Kosar, Cleveland, 1990-91
294 Bart Starr, Green Bay, 1964-65
279 Jeff George, Indianapolis, 1993; Atlanta, 1994

Most Passes Had Intercepted, Career
277 George Blanda, Chi. Bears, 1949, 1950-58; Baltimore, 1950; Houston, 1960-66; Oakland, 1967-75
268 John Hadl, San Diego, 1962-72; Los Angeles, 1973-74; Green Bay, 1974-75; Houston, 1976-77
266 Fran Tarkenton, Minnesota, 1961-66, 1972-78; N.Y. Giants, 1967-71

Most Passes Had Intercepted, Season
42 George Blanda, Houston, 1962
35 Vinny Testaverde, Tampa Bay, 1988
34 Frank Tripucka, Denver, 1960

Most Passes Had Intercepted, Game
8 Jim Hardy, Chi. Cardinals vs. Philadelphia, Sept. 24, 1950
7 Parker Hall, Cleveland vs. Green Bay, Nov. 8, 1942
Frank Sinkwich, Detroit vs. Green Bay, Oct. 24, 1943
Bob Waterfield, Los Angeles vs. Green Bay, Oct. 17, 1948
Zeke Bratkowski, Chicago vs. Baltimore, Oct. 2, 1960
Tommy Wade, Pittsburgh vs. Philadelphia, Dec. 12, 1965
Ken Stabler, Oakland vs. Denver, Oct. 16, 1977
Steve DeBerg, Tampa Bay vs. San Francisco, Sept. 7, 1986
6 By many players

Most Attempts, No Interceptions, Game
70 Drew Bledsoe, New England vs. Minnesota, Nov. 13, 1994 (OT)
63 Rich Gannon, Minnesota vs. New England, Oct. 20, 1991 (OT)
60 Davey O'Brien, Philadelphia vs. Washington, Dec. 1, 1940

LOWEST PERCENTAGE, PASSES HAD INTERCEPTED

Most Seasons Leading League, Lowest Percentage, Passes Had Intercepted
5 Sammy Baugh, Washington, 1940, 1942, 1944-45, 1947
3 Charlie Conerly, N.Y. Giants, 1950, 1956, 1959
Bart Starr, Green Bay, 1962, 1964, 1966
Roger Staubach, Dallas, 1971, 1977, 1979
Ken Anderson, Cincinnati, 1972, 1981-82
Ken O'Brien, N.Y. Jets, 1985, 1987-88
2 By many players

Lowest Percentage, Passes Had Intercepted, Career (1,500 attempts)
2.08 Neil O'Donnell, Pittsburgh, 1991-95 (1,871-39)
2.58 Joe Montana, San Francisco, 1979-90, 1992; Kansas City, 1993-94 (5,391-139)
2.61 Bernie Kosar, Cleveland, 1985-93; Dallas, 1993; Miami, 1994-95 (3,333-87)

Lowest Percentage, Passes Had Intercepted, Season (Qualifiers)
0.66 Joe Ferguson, Buffalo, 1976 (151-1)
0.90 Steve DeBerg, Kansas City, 1990 (444-4)
1.16 Steve Bartkowski, Atlanta, 1983 (432-5)

Lowest Percentage, Passes Had Intercepted, Rookie, Season (Qualifiers)
2.03 Dan Marino, Miami, 1983 (296-6)
2.10 Gary Wood, N.Y. Giants, 1964 (143-3)
2.82 Bernie Kosar, Cleveland, 1985 (248-7)

ALL-TIME RECORDS

TIMES SACKED

Times Sacked has been compiled since 1963.

Most Times Sacked, Career

483 Fran Tarkenton, Minnesota, 1961-66, 1972-78; N.Y. Giants, 1967-71
478 Dave Krieg, Seattle, 1980-91; Kansas City, 1992-93; Detroit, 1994; Arizona, 1995
477 Phil Simms, N.Y. Giants, 1979-81, 1983-93

Most Times Sacked, Season

72 Randall Cunningham, Philadelphia, 1986
62 Ken O'Brien, N.Y. Jets, 1985
61 Neil Lomax, St. Louis, 1985

Most Times Sacked, Game

12 Bert Jones, Baltimore vs. St. Louis, Oct. 26, 1980
Warren Moon, Houston vs. Dallas, Sept. 29, 1985
11 Charley Johnson, St. Louis vs. N.Y. Giants, Nov. 1, 1964
Bart Starr, Green Bay vs. Detroit, Nov. 7, 1965
Jack Kemp, Buffalo vs. Oakland, Oct. 15, 1967
Bob Berry, Atlanta vs. St. Louis, Nov. 24, 1968
Greg Landry, Detroit vs. Dallas, Oct. 6, 1975
Ron Jaworski, Philadelphia vs. St. Louis, Dec. 18, 1983
Paul McDonald, Cleveland vs. Kansas City, Sept. 30, 1984
Archie Manning, Minnesota vs. Chicago, Oct. 28, 1984
Steve Pelluer, Dallas vs. San Diego, Nov. 16, 1986
Randall Cunningham, Philadelphia vs. L.A. Raiders, Nov. 30, 1986 (OT)
David Norrie, N.Y. Jets vs. Dallas, Oct. 4, 1987
Troy Aikman, Dallas vs. Philadelphia, Sept. 15, 1991
Bernie Kosar, Cleveland vs. Indianapolis, Sept. 6, 1992
10 By many players

PASS RECEIVING

Most Seasons Leading League

8 Don Hutson, Green Bay, 1936-37, 1939, 1941-45
5 Lionel Taylor, Denver, 1960-63, 1965
3 Tom Fears, Los Angeles, 1948-50
Pete Pihos, Philadelphia, 1953-55
Billy Wilson, San Francisco, 1954, 1956-57
Raymond Berry, Baltimore, 1958-60
Lance Alworth, San Diego, 1966, 1968-69
Sterling Sharpe, Green Bay, 1989, 1992-93

Most Consecutive Seasons Leading League

5 Don Hutson, Green Bay, 1941-45
4 Lionel Taylor, Denver, 1960-63
3 Tom Fears, Los Angeles, 1948-50
Pete Pihos, Philadelphia, 1953-55
Raymond Berry, Baltimore, 1958-60

Most Pass Receptions, Career

942 Jerry Rice, San Francisco, 1985-95
940 Art Monk, Washington, 1980-93; N.Y. Jets, 1994; Philadelphia, 1995
819 Steve Largent, Seattle, 1976-89

Most Seasons, 50 or More Pass Receptions

10 Steve Largent, Seattle, 1976, 1978-81, 1983-87
Gary Clark, Washington, 1985-92; Phoenix, 1993; Arizona, 1994
Jerry Rice, San Francisco, 1986-95
9 Art Monk, Washington, 1980-81, 1984-86, 1988-91
James Lofton, Green Bay, 1979-81, 1983-86; Buffalo, 1991-92
Andre Reed, Buffalo, 1986-94
Henry Ellard, L.A. Rams, 1985, 1987-91, 1993; Washington, 1994-95
8 Ernest Givins, Houston, 1986-93
Bill Brooks, Indianapolis, 1986-91; Buffalo, 1993, 1995

Most Pass Receptions, Season

123 Herman Moore, Detroit, 1995
122 Cris Carter, Minnesota, 1994
Cris Carter, Minnesota, 1995
Jerry Rice, San Francisco, 1995
119 Isaac Bruce, St. Louis, 1995

Most Pass Receptions, Rookie, Season

83 Earl Cooper, San Francisco, 1980
81 Keith Jackson, Philadelphia, 1988
75 Terry Kirby, Miami, 1993

Most Pass Receptions, Game

18 Tom Fears, Los Angeles vs. Green Bay, Dec. 3, 1950
17 Clark Gaines, N.Y. Jets vs. San Francisco, Sept. 21, 1980
16 Sonny Randle, St. Louis vs. N.Y. Giants, Nov. 4, 1962
Jerry Rice, San Francisco vs. L.A. Rams, Nov. 20, 1994

Most Consecutive Games, Pass Receptions

183 Art Monk, Washington, 1980-93; N.Y. Jets, 1994; Philadelphia, 1995 (current)
177 Steve Largent, Seattle, 1977-89
159 Jerry Rice, San Francisco, 1985-95 (current)

YARDS GAINED

Most Seasons Leading League

7 Don Hutson, Green Bay, 1936, 1938-39, 1941-44
6 Jerry Rice, San Francisco, 1986, 1989-90, 1993-95
3 Raymond Berry, Baltimore, 1957, 1959-60
Lance Alworth, San Diego, 1965-66, 1968

Most Consecutive Seasons Leading League

4 Don Hutson, Green Bay, 1941-44
3 Jerry Rice, San Francisco, 1993-95
2 By many players

Most Yards Gained, Career

15,123 Jerry Rice, San Francisco, 1985-95
14,004 James Lofton, Green Bay, 1978-86; L.A. Raiders, 1987-88; Buffalo, 1989-92; L.A. Rams, 1993; Philadelphia, 1993
13,089 Steve Largent, Seattle, 1976-89

Most Seasons, 1,000 or More Yards, Pass Receiving

10 Jerry Rice, San Francisco, 1986-95
8 Steve Largent, Seattle, 1978-81, 1983-86
7 Lance Alworth, San Diego, 1963-69

Most Yards Gained, Season

1,848 Jerry Rice, San Francisco, 1995
1,781 Isaac Bruce, St. Louis, 1995
1,746 Charley Hennigan, Houston, 1961

Most Yards Gained, Rookie, Season

1,473 Bill Groman, Houston, 1960
1,231 Bill Howton, Green Bay, 1952
1,131 Bill Brooks, Indianapolis, 1986

Most Yards Gained, Game

336 Willie Anderson, L.A. Rams vs. New Orleans, Nov. 26, 1989 (OT)
309 Stephone Paige, Kansas City vs. San Diego, Dec. 22, 1985
303 Jim Benton, Cleveland vs. Detroit, Nov. 22, 1945

Most Games, 200 or More Yards Pass Receiving, Career

5 Lance Alworth, San Diego, 1962-70; Dallas, 1971-72
4 Don Hutson, Green Bay, 1935-45
Charley Hennigan, Houston, 1960-66
Jerry Rice, San Francisco, 1985-95
3 Don Maynard, N.Y. Giants, 1958; N.Y. Jets, 1960-72; St. Louis, 1973
Wes Chandler, New Orleans, 1978-81; San Diego, 1981-87; San Francisco, 1988

Most Games, 200 or More Yards Pass Receiving, Season

3 Charley Hennigan, Houston, 1961
2 Don Hutson, Green Bay, 1942
Gene Roberts, N.Y. Giants, 1949
Lance Alworth, San Diego, 1963
Don Maynard, N.Y. Jets, 1968

Most Games, 100 or More Yards Pass Receiving, Career

58 Jerry Rice, San Francisco, 1985-95
50 Don Maynard, N.Y. Giants, 1958; N.Y. Jets, 1960-72; St. Louis, 1973
43 James Lofton, Green Bay, 1978-86; L.A. Raiders, 1987-88; Buffalo, 1989-92; L.A. Rams, 1993; Philadelphia, 1993

Most Games, 100 or More Yards Pass Receiving, Season

11 Michael Irvin, Dallas, 1995
10 Charley Hennigan, Houston, 1961
Herman Moore, Detroit, 1995
9 Elroy (Crazylegs) Hirsch, Los Angeles, 1951
Bill Groman, Houston, 1960
Lance Alworth, San Diego, 1965
Don Maynard, N.Y. Jets, 1967
Stanley Morgan, New England, 1986
Mark Carrier, Tampa Bay, 1989
Robert Brooks, Green Bay, 1995
Isaac Bruce, St. Louis, 1995
Jerry Rice, San Francisco, 1995

Most Consecutive Games, 100 or More Yards Pass Receiving

7 Charley Hennigan, Houston, 1961
Bill Groman, Houston, 1961
Michael Irvin, Dallas, 1995
6 Raymond Berry, Baltimore, 1960
Pat Studstill, Detroit, 1966
Isaac Bruce, St. Louis, 1995
5 Elroy (Crazylegs) Hirsch, Los Angeles, 1951
Bob Boyd, Los Angeles, 1954
Terry Barr, Detroit, 1963
Lance Alworth, San Diego, 1966
Don Maynard, N.Y. Jets, 1968-69
Harold Jackson, Philadelphia, 1971-72

Longest Pass Reception (All TDs except as noted)

99 Andy Farkas (from Filchock), Washington vs. Pittsburgh, Oct. 15, 1939
Bobby Mitchell (from Izo), Washington vs. Cleveland, Sept. 15, 1963
Pat Studstill (from Sweetan), Detroit vs. Baltimore, Oct. 16, 1966
Gerry Allen (from Jurgensen), Washington vs. Chicago, Sept. 15, 1968
Cliff Branch (from Plunkett), L.A. Raiders vs. Washington, Oct. 2, 1983
Mike Quick (from Jaworski), Philadelphia vs. Atlanta, Nov. 10, 1985
Tony Martin (from Humphries), San Diego vs. Seattle, Sept. 18, 1994
Robert Brooks (from Favre), Green Bay vs. Chicago, Sept. 11, 1995
98 Gaynell Tinsley (from Russell), Chi. Cardinals vs. Cleveland,

Nov. 17, 1938
Dick (Night Train) Lane (from Compton), Chi. Cardinals vs. Green Bay, Nov. 13, 1955
John Farrington (from Wade), Chicago vs. Detroit, Oct. 8, 1961
Willard Dewveall (from Lee), Houston vs. San Diego, Nov. 25, 1962
Homer Jones (from Morrall), N.Y. Giants vs. Pittsburgh, Sept. 11, 1966
Bobby Moore (from Hart), St. Louis vs. Los Angeles, Dec. 10, 1972 (no TD)
Michael Haynes (from Hebert), Atlanta vs. New Orleans, Sept. 12, 1993

97 Gaynell Tinsley (from Coffee), Chi. Cardinals vs. Chi. Bears, Dec. 5, 1937
Cloyce Box (from Layne), Detroit vs. Green Bay, Nov. 26, 1953
Jerry Tarr (from Shaw), Denver vs. Boston, Sept. 21, 1962
Webster Slaughter (from Kosar), Cleveland vs. Chicago, Oct. 23, 1989
John Taylor (from Young), San Francisco vs. Atlanta, Nov. 3, 1991

AVERAGE GAIN

Highest Average Gain, Career (200 receptions)
22.26 Homer Jones, N.Y. Giants, 1964-69; Cleveland, 1970 (224-4,986)
20.83 Buddy Dial, Pittsburgh, 1959-63; Dallas, 1964-66 (261-5,436)
20.24 Harlon Hill, Chi. Bears, 1954-61; Pittsburgh, 1962; Detroit, 1962 (233-4,717)

Highest Average Gain, Season (24 receptions)
32.58 Don Currivan, Boston, 1947 (24-782)
31.44 Bucky Pope, Los Angeles, 1964 (25-786)
28.60 Bobby Duckworth, San Diego, 1984 (25-715)

Highest Average Gain, Game (3 receptions)
60.67 Bill Groman, Houston vs. Denver, Nov. 20, 1960 (3-182)
Homer Jones, N.Y. Giants vs. Washington, Dec. 12, 1965 (3-182)
60.33 Don Currivan, Boston vs. Washington, Nov. 30, 1947 (3-181)
59.67 Bobby Duckworth, San Diego vs. Chicago, Dec. 3, 1984 (3-179)

TOUCHDOWNS

Most Seasons Leading League
9 Don Hutson, Green Bay, 1935-38, 1940-44
6 Jerry Rice, San Francisco, 1986-87, 1989-91, 1993
3 Lance Alworth, San Diego, 1964-66

Most Consecutive Seasons Leading League
5 Don Hutson, Green Bay, 1940-44
4 Don Hutson, Green Bay, 1935-38
3 Lance Alworth, San Diego, 1964-66
Jerry Rice, San Francisco, 1989-91

Most Touchdowns, Career
146 Jerry Rice, San Francisco, 1985-95
100 Steve Largent, Seattle, 1976-89
99 Don Hutson, Green Bay, 1935-45

Most Touchdowns, Season
22 Jerry Rice, San Francisco, 1987
18 Mark Clayton, Miami, 1984
Sterling Sharpe, Green Bay, 1994
17 Don Hutson, Green Bay, 1942
Elroy (Crazylegs) Hirsch, Los Angeles, 1951
Bill Groman, Houston, 1961
Jerry Rice, San Francisco, 1989
Cris Carter, Minnesota, 1995
Carl Pickens, Cincinnati, 1995

Most Touchdowns, Rookie, Season
13 Bill Howton, Green Bay, 1952
John Jefferson, San Diego, 1979
12 Harlon Hill, Chi. Bears, 1954
Bill Groman, Houston, 1960
Mike Ditka, Chicago, 1961
Bob Hayes, Dallas, 1965
10 Bill Swiacki, N.Y. Giants, 1948
Bucky Pope, Los Angeles, 1964
Sammy White, Minnesota, 1976
Daryl Turner, Seattle, 1984

Most Touchdowns, Game
5 Bob Shaw, Chi. Cardinals vs. Baltimore, Oct. 2, 1950
Kellen Winslow, San Diego vs. Oakland, Nov. 22, 1981
Jerry Rice, San Francisco vs. Atlanta, Oct. 14, 1990
4 By many players. Last time: Mark Ingram, Miami vs. N.Y. Jets, Nov. 27, 1994

Most Consecutive Games, Touchdowns
13 Jerry Rice, San Francisco, 1986-87
11 Elroy (Crazylegs) Hirsch, Los Angeles, 1950-51
Buddy Dial, Pittsburgh, 1959-60
Carl Pickens, Cincinnati, 1994-95

INTERCEPTIONS BY

Most Seasons Leading League
3 Everson Walls, Dallas, 1981-82, 1985
2 Dick (Night Train) Lane, Los Angeles, 1952; Chi. Cardinals, 1954
Jack Christiansen, Detroit, 1953, 1957
Milt Davis, Baltimore, 1957, 1959
Dick Lynch, N.Y. Giants, 1961, 1963
Johnny Robinson, Kansas City, 1966, 1970
Bill Bradley, Philadelphia, 1971-72
Emmitt Thomas, Kansas City, 1969, 1974
Ronnie Lott, San Francisco, 1986; L.A. Raiders, 1991

Most Interceptions By, Career
81 Paul Krause, Washington, 1964-67; Minnesota, 1968-79
79 Emlen Tunnell, N.Y. Giants, 1948-58; Green Bay, 1959-61
68 Dick (Night Train) Lane, Los Angeles, 1952-53; Chi. Cardinals, 1954-59; Detroit, 1960-65

Most Interceptions By, Season
14 Dick (Night Train) Lane, Los Angeles, 1952
13 Dan Sandifer, Washington, 1948
Orban (Spec) Sanders, N.Y. Yanks, 1950
Lester Hayes, Oakland, 1980
12 By nine players

Most Interceptions By, Rookie, Season
14 Dick (Night Train) Lane, Los Angeles, 1952
13 Dan Sandifer, Washington, 1948
12 Woodley Lewis, Los Angeles, 1950
Paul Krause, Washington, 1964

Most Interceptions By, Game
4 Sammy Baugh, Washington vs. Detroit, Nov. 14, 1943
Dan Sandifer, Washington vs. Boston, Oct. 31, 1948
Don Doll, Detroit vs. Chi. Cardinals, Oct. 23, 1949
Bob Nussbaumer, Chi. Cardinals vs. N.Y. Bulldogs, Nov. 13, 1949
Russ Craft, Philadelphia vs. Chi. Cardinals, Sept. 24, 1950
Bobby Dillon, Green Bay vs. Detroit, Nov. 26, 1953
Jack Butler, Pittsburgh vs. Washington, Dec. 13, 1953
Austin (Goose) Gonsoulin, Denver vs. Buffalo, Sept. 18, 1960
Jerry Norton, St. Louis vs. Washington, Nov. 20, 1960; vs. Pittsburgh, Nov. 26, 1961
Dave Baker, San Francisco vs. L.A. Rams, Dec. 4, 1960
Bobby Ply, Dall. Texans vs. San Diego, Dec. 16, 1962
Bobby Hunt, Kansas City vs. Houston, Oct. 4, 1964
Willie Brown, Denver vs. N.Y. Jets, Nov. 15, 1964
Dick Anderson, Miami vs. Pittsburgh, Dec. 3, 1973
Willie Buchanon, Green Bay vs. San Diego, Sept. 24, 1978
Deron Cherry, Kansas City vs. Seattle, Sept. 29, 1985

Most Consecutive Games, Passes Intercepted By
8 Tom Morrow, Oakland, 1962-63
7 Paul Krause, Washington, 1964
Larry Wilson, St. Louis, 1966
Ben Davis, Cleveland, 1968
6 Dick (Night Train) Lane, Chi. Cardinals, 1954-55
Will Sherman, Los Angeles, 1954-55
Jim Shofner, Cleveland, 1960
Paul Krause, Minnesota, 1968
Willie Williams, N.Y. Giants, 1968
Kermit Alexander, San Francisco, 1968-69
Mel Blount, Pittsburgh, 1975
Lemar Parrish, Washington, 1978-79
Eric Harris, Kansas City, 1980
Lester Hayes, Oakland, 1980
Barry Wilburn, Washington, 1987

YARDS GAINED

Most Seasons Leading League
2 Dick (Night Train) Lane, Los Angeles, 1952; Chi. Cardinals, 1954
Herb Adderley, Green Bay, 1965, 1969
Dick Anderson, Miami, 1968, 1970

Most Yards Gained, Career
1,282 Emlen Tunnell, N.Y. Giants, 1948-58; Green Bay, 1959-61
1,207 Dick (Night Train) Lane, Los Angeles, 1952-53; Chi. Cardinals, 1954-59; Detroit, 1960-65
1,185 Paul Krause, Washington, 1964-67; Minnesota, 1968-79

Most Yards Gained, Season
349 Charlie McNeil, San Diego, 1961
303 Deion Sanders, San Francisco, 1994
301 Don Doll, Detroit, 1949

Most Yards Gained, Rookie, Season
301 Don Doll, Detroit, 1949
298 Dick (Night Train) Lane, Los Angeles, 1952
275 Woodley Lewis, Los Angeles, 1950

Most Yards Gained, Game
177 Charlie McNeil, San Diego vs. Houston, Sept. 24, 1961
170 Louis Oliver, Miami vs. Buffalo, Oct. 4, 1992
167 Dick Jauron, Detroit vs. Chicago, Nov. 18, 1973

Longest Return (All TDs)
103 Vencie Glenn, San Diego vs. Denver, Nov. 29, 1987

Louis Oliver, Miami vs. Buffalo, Oct. 4, 1992
102 Bob Smith, Detroit vs. Chi. Bears, Nov. 24, 1949
Erich Barnes, N.Y. Giants vs. Dall. Cowboys, Oct. 15, 1961
Gary Barbaro, Kansas City vs. Seattle, Dec. 11, 1977
Louis Breeden, Cincinnati vs. San Diego, Nov. 8, 1981
Eddie Anderson, L.A. Raiders vs. Miami, Dec. 14, 1992
Donald Frank, San Diego vs. L.A. Raiders, Oct. 31, 1993
101 Richie Petitbon, Chicago vs Los Angeles, Dec. 9, 1962
Henry Carr, N.Y. Giants vs. Los Angeles, Nov. 13, 1966
Tony Greene, Buffalo vs. Kansas City, Oct. 3, 1976
Tom Pridemore, Atlanta vs. San Francisco, Sept. 20, 1981

TOUCHDOWNS

Most Touchdowns, Career
9 Ken Houston, Houston, 1967-72; Washington, 1973-80
7 Herb Adderley, Green Bay, 1961-69; Dallas, 1970-72
Erich Barnes, Chi. Bears, 1958-60; N.Y. Giants, 1961-64; Cleveland, 1965-70
Lem Barney, Detroit, 1967-77
6 Tom Janik, Denver, 1963-64; Buffalo, 1965-68; Boston, 1969-70; New England, 1971
Miller Farr, Denver, 1965; San Diego, 1965-66; Houston, 1967-69; St. Louis, 1970-72; Detroit, 1973
Bobby Bell, Kansas City, 1963-74
Deion Sanders, Atlanta, 1989-93; San Francisco, 1994; Dallas, 1995

Most Touchdowns, Season
4 Ken Houston, Houston, 1971
Jim Kearney, Kansas City, 1972
Eric Allen, Philadelphia, 1993
3 Dick Harris, San Diego, 1961
Dick Lynch, N.Y. Giants, 1963
Herb Adderley, Green Bay, 1965
Lem Barney, Detroit, 1967
Miller Farr, Houston, 1967
Monte Jackson, Los Angeles, 1976
Rod Perry, Los Angeles, 1978
Ronnie Lott, San Francisco, 1981
Lloyd Burruss, Kansas City, 1986
Wayne Haddix, Tampa Bay, 1990
Robert Massey, Phoenix, 1992
Ray Buchanan, Indianapolis, 1994
Deion Sanders, San Francisco, 1994
2 By many players

Most Touchdowns, Rookie, Season
3 Lem Barney, Detroit, 1967
Ronnie Lott, San Francisco, 1981
2 By many players

Most Touchdowns, Game
2 Bill Blackburn, Chi. Cardinals vs. Boston, Oct. 24, 1948
Dan Sandifer, Washington vs. Boston, Oct. 31, 1948
Bob Franklin, Cleveland vs. Chicago, Dec. 11, 1960
Bill Stacy, St. Louis vs. Dall. Cowboys, Nov. 5, 1961
Jerry Norton, St. Louis vs. Pittsburgh, Nov. 26, 1961
Miller Farr, Houston vs. Buffalo, Dec. 7, 1968
Ken Houston, Houston vs. San Diego, Dec. 19, 1971
Jim Kearney, Kansas City vs. Denver, Oct. 1, 1972
Lemar Parrish, Cincinnati vs. Houston, Dec. 17, 1972
Dick Anderson, Miami vs. Pittsburgh, Dec. 3, 1973
Prentice McCray, New England vs. N.Y. Jets, Nov. 21, 1976
Kenny Johnson, Atlanta vs. Green Bay, Nov. 27, 1983 (OT)
Mike Kozlowski, Miami vs. N.Y. Jets, Dec. 16, 1983
Dave Brown, Seattle vs. Kansas City, Nov. 4, 1984
Lloyd Burruss, Kansas City vs. San Diego, Oct. 19, 1986
Henry Jones, Buffalo vs. Indianapolis, Sept. 20, 1992
Robert Massey, Phoenix vs. Washington, Oct. 4, 1992
Eric Allen, Philadelphia vs. New Orleans, Dec. 26, 1993
Ken Norton, San Francisco vs. St. Louis, Oct. 22, 1995

PUNTING

Most Seasons Leading League
4 Sammy Baugh, Washington, 1940-43
Jerrel Wilson, Kansas City, 1965, 1968, 1972-73
3 Yale Lary, Detroit, 1959, 1961, 1963
Jim Fraser, Denver, 1962-64
Ray Guy, Oakland, 1974-75, 1977
Rohn Stark, Baltimore, 1983; Indianapolis, 1985-86
2 By many players

Most Consecutive Seasons Leading League
4 Sammy Baugh, Washington, 1940-43
3 Jim Fraser, Denver, 1962-64
2 By many players

PUNTS

Most Punts, Career
1,154 Dave Jennings, N.Y. Giants, 1974-84; N.Y. Jets, 1985-87
1,083 John James, Atlanta, 1972-81; Detroit, 1982, Houston, 1982-84
1,072 Jerrel Wilson, Kansas City, 1963-77; New England, 1978

Most Punts, Season
114 Bob Parsons, Chicago, 1981
109 John James, Atlanta, 1978
108 John Teltschik, Philadelphia, 1986
Rick Tuten, Seattle, 1992

Most Punts, Rookie, Season
108 John Teltschik, Philadelphia, 1986
99 Lewis Colbert, Kansas City, 1986
96 Mike Connell, San Francisco, 1978
Chris Norman, Denver, 1984

Most Punts, Game
15 John Teltschik, Philadelphia vs. N.Y. Giants, Dec. 6, 1987 (OT)
14 Dick Nesbitt, Chi. Cardinals vs. Chi. Bears, Nov. 30, 1933
Keith Molesworth, Chi. Bears vs. Green Bay, Dec. 10, 1933
Sammy Baugh, Washington vs. Philadelphia, Nov. 5, 1939
Carl Kinscherf, N.Y. Giants vs. Detroit, Nov. 7, 1943
George Taliaferro, N.Y. Yanks vs. Los Angeles, Sept. 28, 1951
12 By many players. Last time: Rick Tuten, Seattle vs. Denver, Nov. 28, 1993

Longest Punt
98 Steve O'Neal, N.Y. Jets vs. Denver, Sept. 21, 1969
94 Joe Lintzenich, Chi. Bears vs. N.Y. Giants, Nov. 16, 1931
93 Shawn McCarthy, New England vs. Buffalo, Nov. 3, 1991

AVERAGE YARDAGE

Highest Average, Punting, Career (250 punts)
45.10 Sammy Baugh, Washington, 1937-52 (338-15,245)
44.68 Tommy Davis, San Francisco, 1959-69 (511-22,833)
44.29 Yale Lary, Detroit, 1952-53, 1956-64 (503-22,279)

Highest Average, Punting, Season (Qualifiers)
51.40 Sammy Baugh, Washington, 1940 (35-1,799)
48.94 Yale Lary, Detroit, 1963 (35-1,713)
48.73 Sammy Baugh, Washington, 1941 (30-1,462)

Highest Average, Punting, Rookie, Season (Qualifiers)
45.92 Frank Sinkwich, Detroit, 1943 (12-551)
45.66 Tommy Davis, San Francisco, 1959 (59-2,694)
45.57 David Lee, Baltimore, 1966 (49-2,233)

Highest Average, Punting, Game (4 punts)
61.75 Bob Cifers, Detroit vs. Chi. Bears, Nov. 24, 1946 (4-247)
61.60 Roy McKay, Green Bay vs. Chi. Cardinals, Oct. 28, 1945 (5-308)
59.50 Darren Bennett, San Diego vs. Pittsburgh, Oct. 1, 1995 (4-238)

PUNTS HAD BLOCKED

Most Consecutive Punts, None Blocked
623 Dave Jennings, N.Y. Giants, 1976-83
619 Ray Guy, Oakland, 1979-81; L.A. Raiders, 1982-86
578 Bobby Walden, Minnesota, 1964-67; Pittsburgh, 1968-72

Most Punts Had Blocked, Career
14 Herman Weaver, Detroit, 1970-76; Seattle, 1977-80
Harry Newsome, Pittsburgh, 1985-89; Minnesota, 1990-93
12 Jerrel Wilson, Kansas City, 1963-77; New England, 1978
Tom Blanchard, N.Y. Giants, 1971-73; New Orleans, 1974-78; Tampa Bay, 1979-81
11 David Lee, Baltimore, 1966-78

Most Punts Had Blocked, Season
6 Harry Newsome, Pittsburgh, 1988
4 Bryan Wagner, Cleveland, 1990
3 By many players

PUNT RETURNS

Most Seasons Leading League
3 Les (Speedy) Duncan, San Diego, 1965-66; Washington, 1971
Rick Upchurch, Denver, 1976, 1978, 1982
2 Dick Christy, N.Y. Titans, 1961-62
Claude Gibson, Oakland, 1963-64
Billy Johnson, Houston, 1975, 1977
Mel Gray, New Orleans, 1987; Detroit, 1991

PUNT RETURNS

Most Punt Returns, Career
292 Vai Sikahema, St. Louis, 1986-87; Phoenix, 1988-90; Green Bay, 1991; Philadelphia, 1992-93
282 Billy Johnson, Houston, 1974-80; Atlanta, 1982-87; Washington, 1988
269 Tim Brown, L.A. Raiders, 1988-94; Oakland, 1995

Most Punt Returns, Season
70 Danny Reece, Tampa Bay, 1979
62 Fulton Walker, Miami-L.A. Raiders, 1985
58 J.T. Smith, Kansas City, 1979

Greg Pruitt, L.A. Raiders, 1983
Leo Lewis, Minnesota, 1988

Most Punt Returns, Rookie, Season
57 Lew Barnes, Chicago, 1986
54 James Jones, Dallas, 1980
53 Louis Lipps, Pittsburgh, 1984

Most Punt Returns, Game
11 Eddie Brown, Washington vs. Tampa Bay, Oct. 9, 1977
10 Theo Bell, Pittsburgh vs. Buffalo, Dec. 16, 1979
Mike Nelms, Washington vs. New Orleans, Dec. 26, 1982
Ronnie Harris, New England vs. Pittsburgh, Dec. 5, 1993
9 Rodger Bird, Oakland vs. Denver, Sept. 10, 1967
Ralph McGill, San Francisco vs. Atlanta, Oct. 29, 1972
Ed Podolak, Kansas City vs. San Diego, Nov. 10, 1974
Anthony Leonard, San Francisco vs. New Orleans, Oct. 17, 1976
Butch Johnson, Dallas vs. Buffalo, Nov. 15, 1976
Larry Marshall, Philadelphia vs. Tampa Bay, Sept. 18, 1977
Nesby Glasgow, Baltimore vs. Kansas City, Sept. 2, 1979
Mike Nelms, Washington vs. St. Louis, Dec. 21, 1980
Leon Bright, N.Y. Giants vs. Philadelphia, Dec. 11, 1982
Pete Shaw, N.Y. Giants vs. Philadelphia, Nov. 20, 1983
Cleotha Montgomery, L.A. Raiders vs. Detroit, Dec. 10, 1984
Phil McConkey, N.Y. Giants vs. Philadelphia, Dec. 6, 1987 (OT)
Andre Hastings, Pittsburgh vs. Cleveland, Nov. 13, 1995

FAIR CATCHES

Most Fair Catches, Career
102 Willie Wood, Green Bay, 1960-71
99 Phil McConkey, N.Y. Giants, 1984-88; Green Bay, 1986; San Diego, 1989
98 Leo Lewis, Minnesota, 1981-90, 1991; Cleveland, 1990

Most Fair Catches, Season
27 Leo Lewis, Minnesota, 1989
25 Mark Konecny, Philadelphia, 1988
Phil McConkey, N.Y. Giants, 1988
Chris Warren, Seattle, 1992
24 Ken Graham, San Diego, 1969
Brian Mitchell, Washington, 1994

Most Fair Catches, Game
7 Lem Barney, Detroit vs. Chicago, Nov. 21, 1976
Bobby Morse, Philadelphia vs. Buffalo, Dec. 27, 1987
6 Jake Scott, Miami vs. Buffalo, Dec. 20, 1970
Greg Pruitt, L.A. Raiders vs. Seattle, Oct. 7, 1984
Phil McConkey, San Diego vs. Kansas City, Dec. 17, 1989
Gerald McNeil, Houston vs. Pittsburgh, Sept. 16, 1990
5 By many players

YARDS GAINED

Most Seasons Leading League
3 Alvin Haymond, Baltimore, 1965-66; Los Angeles, 1969
2 Bill Dudley, Pittsburgh, 1942, 1946
Emlen Tunnell, N.Y. Giants, 1951-52
Dick Christy, N.Y. Titans, 1961-62
Claude Gibson, Oakland, 1963-64
Rodger Bird, Oakland, 1966-67
J.T. Smith, Kansas City, 1979-80
Vai Sikahema, St. Louis, 1986-87
David Meggett, N.Y. Giants, 1989-90

Most Yards Gained, Career
3,317 Billy Johnson, Houston, 1974-80; Atlanta, 1982-87; Washington, 1988
3,169 Vai Sikahema, St. Louis, 1986-87; Phoenix, 1988-90; Green Bay, 1991; Philadelphia, 1992-93
3,008 Rick Upchurch, Denver, 1975-83

Most Yards Gained, Season
692 Fulton Walker, Miami-L.A. Raiders, 1985
666 Greg Pruitt, L.A. Raiders, 1983
656 Louis Lipps, Pittsburgh, 1984

Most Yards Gained, Rookie, Season
656 Louis Lipps, Pittsburgh, 1984
655 Neal Colzie, Oakland, 1975
608 Mike Haynes, New England, 1976

Most Yards Gained, Game
207 LeRoy Irvin, Los Angeles vs. Atlanta, Oct. 11, 1981
205 George Atkinson, Oakland vs. Buffalo, Sept. 15, 1968
184 Tom Watkins, Detroit vs. San Francisco, Oct. 6, 1963

Longest Punt Return (All TDs)
103 Robert Bailey, L.A. Rams vs. New Orleans, Oct. 23, 1994
98 Gil LeFebvre, Cincinnati vs. Brooklyn, Dec. 3, 1933
Charlie West, Minnesota vs. Washington, Nov. 3, 1968
Dennis Morgan, Dallas vs. St. Louis, Oct. 13, 1974
Terance Mathis, N.Y. Jets vs. Dallas, Nov. 4, 1990
97 Greg Pruitt, L.A. Raiders vs. Washington, Oct. 2, 1983

AVERAGE YARDAGE

Highest Average, Career (75 returns)
12.78 George McAfee, Chi. Bears, 1940-41, 1945-50 (112-1,431)
12.75 Jack Christiansen, Detroit, 1951-58 (85-1,084)
12.55 Claude Gibson, San Diego, 1961-62; Oakland, 1963-65 (110-1,381)

Highest Average, Season (Qualifiers)
23.00 Herb Rich, Baltimore, 1950 (12-276)
21.47 Jack Christiansen, Detroit, 1952 (15-322)
21.28 Dick Christy, N.Y. Titans, 1961 (18-383)

Highest Average, Rookie, Season (Qualifiers)
23.00 Herb Rich, Baltimore, 1950 (12-276)
20.88 Jerry Davis, Chi. Cardinals, 1948 (16-334)
20.73 Frank Sinkwich, Detroit, 1943 (11-228)

Highest Average, Game (3 returns)
47.67 Chuck Latourette, St. Louis vs. New Orleans, Sept. 29, 1968 (3-143)
47.33 Johnny Roland, St. Louis vs. Philadelphia, Oct. 2, 1966 (3-142)
45.67 Dick Christy, N.Y. Titans vs. Denver, Sept. 24, 1961 (3-137)

TOUCHDOWNS

Most Touchdowns, Career
8 Jack Christiansen, Detroit, 1951-58
Rick Upchurch, Denver, 1975-83
6 Billy Johnson, Houston, 1974-80; Atlanta, 1982-87; Washington, 1988
David Meggett, N.Y. Giants, 1989-94; New England, 1995
Brian Mitchell, Washington, 1990-95
Eric Metcalf, Cleveland, 1989-94; Atlanta, 1995
5 Emlen Tunnell, N.Y. Giants, 1948-58; Green Bay, 1959-61

Most Touchdowns, Season
4 Jack Christiansen, Detroit, 1951
Rick Upchurch, Denver, 1976
3 Emlen Tunnell, N.Y. Giants, 1951
Billy Johnson, Houston, 1975
LeRoy Irvin, Los Angeles, 1981
2 By many players

Most Touchdowns, Rookie, Season
4 Jack Christiansen, Detroit, 1951
2 By 10 players

Most Touchdowns, Game
2 Jack Christiansen, Detroit vs. Los Angeles, Oct. 14, 1951; vs. Green Bay, Nov. 22, 1951
Dick Christy, N.Y. Titans vs. Denver, Sept. 24, 1961
Rick Upchurch, Denver vs. Cleveland, Sept. 26, 1976
LeRoy Irvin, Los Angeles vs. Atlanta, Oct. 11, 1981
Vai Sikahema, St. Louis vs. Tampa Bay, Dec. 21, 1986
Todd Kinchen, L.A. Rams vs. Atlanta, Dec. 27, 1992
Eric Metcalf, Cleveland vs. Pittsburgh, Oct. 24, 1993

KICKOFF RETURNS

Most Seasons Leading League
3 Abe Woodson, San Francisco, 1959, 1962-63
2 Lynn Chandnois, Pittsburgh, 1951-52
Bobby Jancik, Houston, 1962-63
Travis Williams, Green Bay, 1967; Los Angeles, 1971
Mel Gray, Detroit, 1991, 1994

KICKOFF RETURNS

Most Kickoff Returns, Career
362 Mel Gray, New Orleans, 1986-88; Detroit, 1989-94; Houston, 1995
275 Ron Smith, Chicago, 1965, 1970-72; Atlanta, 1966-67; Los Angeles, 1968-69; San Diego, 1973; Oakland, 1974
243 Bruce Harper, N.Y. Jets, 1977-84

Most Kickoff Returns, Season
66 Tyrone Hughes, New Orleans, 1995
63 Tyrone Hughes, New Orleans, 1994
62 Andre Coleman, San Diego, 1995

Most Kickoff Returns, Rookie, Season
55 Stump Mitchell, St. Louis, 1981
53 Buster Rhymes, Minnesota, 1985
50 Nesby Glasgow, Baltimore, 1979
Dino Hall, Cleveland, 1979
David Dunn, Cincinnati, 1995

Most Kickoff Returns, Game
9 Noland Smith, Kansas City vs. Oakland, Nov. 23, 1967
Dino Hall, Cleveland vs. Pittsburgh, Oct. 7, 1979
Paul Palmer, Kansas City vs. Seattle, Sept. 20, 1987
8 By many players

YARDS GAINED

Most Seasons Leading League
3 Bruce Harper, N.Y. Jets, 1977-79
2 Marshall Goldberg, Chi. Cardinals, 1941-42
Woodley Lewis, Los Angeles, 1953-54

Al Carmichael, Green Bay, 1956-57
Timmy Brown, Philadelphia, 1961, 1963
Bobby Jancik, Houston, 1963, 1966
Ron Smith, Atlanta, 1966-67
Tyrone Hughes, New Orleans, 1994-95

Most Yards Gained, Career
8,833 Mel Gray, New Orleans, 1986-88; Detroit, 1989-94; Houston, 1995
6,922 Ron Smith, Chicago, 1965, 1970-72; Atlanta, 1966-67; Los Angeles, 1968-69; San Diego, 1973; Oakland, 1974
5,538 Abe Woodson, San Francisco, 1958-64; St. Louis, 1965-66

Most Yards Gained, Season
1,617 Tyrone Hughes, New Orleans, 1995
1,556 Tyrone Hughes, New Orleans, 1994
1,478 Brian Mitchell, Washington, 1994

Most Yards Gained, Rookie, Season
1,345 Buster Rhymes, Minnesota, 1985
1,293 Andre Coleman, San Diego, 1994
1,292 Stump Mitchell, St. Louis, 1981

Most Yards Gained, Game
304 Tyrone Hughes, New Orleans vs. L.A. Rams, Oct. 23, 1994
294 Wally Triplett, Detroit vs. Los Angeles, Oct. 29, 1950
251 Jon Vaughn, Kansas City vs. Miami, Dec. 12, 1994

Longest Kickoff Return (All TDs)
106 Al Carmichael, Green Bay vs. Chi. Bears, Oct. 7, 1956
Noland Smith, Kansas City vs. Denver, Dec. 17, 1967
Roy Green, St. Louis vs. Dallas, Oct. 21, 1979
105 Frank Seno, Chi. Cardinals vs. N.Y. Giants, Oct. 20, 1946
Ollie Matson, Chi. Cardinals vs. Washington, Oct. 14, 1956
Abe Woodson, San Francisco vs. Los Angeles, Nov. 8, 1959
Timmy Brown, Philadelphia vs. Cleveland, Sept. 17, 1961
Jon Arnett, Los Angeles vs. Detroit, Oct. 29, 1961
Eugene (Mercury) Morris, Miami vs. Cincinnati, Sept. 14, 1969
Travis Williams, Los Angeles vs. New Orleans, Dec. 5, 1971
104 By many players

AVERAGE YARDAGE

Highest Average, Career (75 returns)
30.56 Gale Sayers, Chicago, 1965-71 (91-2,781)
29.57 Lynn Chandnois, Pittsburgh, 1950-56 (92-2,720)
28.69 Abe Woodson, San Francisco, 1958-64; St. Louis, 1965-66 (193-5,538)

Highest Average, Season (Qualifiers)
41.06 Travis Williams, Green Bay, 1967 (18-739)
37.69 Gale Sayers, Chicago, 1967 (16-603)
35.50 Ollie Matson, Chi. Cardinals, 1958 (14-497)

Highest Average, Rookie, Season (Qualifiers)
41.06 Travis Williams, Green Bay, 1967 (18-739)
33.08 Tom Moore, Green Bay, 1960 (12-397)
32.88 Duriel Harris, Miami, 1976 (17-559)

Highest Average, Game (3 returns)
73.50 Wally Triplett, Detroit vs. Los Angeles, Oct. 29, 1950 (4-294)
67.33 Lenny Lyles, San Francisco vs. Baltimore, Dec. 18, 1960 (3-202)
65.33 Ken Hall, Houston vs. N.Y. Titans, Oct. 23, 1960 (3-196)

TOUCHDOWNS

Most Touchdowns, Career
6 Ollie Matson, Chi. Cardinals, 1952, 1954-58; L.A. Rams, 1959-62; Detroit, 1963; Philadelphia, 1964
Gale Sayers, Chicago, 1965-71
Travis Williams, Green Bay, 1967-70; Los Angeles, 1971
Mel Gray, New Orleans, 1986-88; Detroit, 1989-94; Houston, 1995
5 Bobby Mitchell, Cleveland, 1958-61; Washington, 1962-68
Abe Woodson, San Francisco, 1958-64; St. Louis, 1965-66
Timmy Brown, Green Bay, 1959; Philadelphia, 1960-67; Baltimore, 1968
4 Cecil Turner, Chicago, 1968-73
Ron Brown, L.A. Rams, 1984-89, 1991; L.A. Raiders, 1990
Jon Vaughn, New England, 1991-92; Seattle, 1993-94; Kansas City, 1994
Andre Coleman, San Diego, 1994-95

Most Touchdowns, Season
4 Travis Williams, Green Bay, 1967
Cecil Turner, Chicago, 1970
3 Verda (Vitamin T) Smith, Los Angeles, 1950
Abe Woodson, San Francisco, 1963
Gale Sayers, Chicago, 1967
Raymond Clayborn, New England, 1977
Ron Brown, L.A. Rams, 1985
Mel Gray, Detroit, 1994
2 By many players

Most Touchdowns, Rookie, Season
4 Travis Williams, Green Bay, 1967
3 Raymond Clayborn, New England, 1977
2 By nine players

Most Touchdowns, Game
2 Timmy Brown, Philadelphia vs. Dallas, Nov. 6, 1966
Travis Williams, Green Bay vs. Cleveland, Nov. 12, 1967
Ron Brown, L.A. Rams vs. Green Bay, Nov. 24, 1985
Tyrone Hughes, New Orleans vs. L.A. Rams, Oct. 23, 1994

COMBINED KICK RETURNS

Most Combined Kick Returns, Career
573 Mel Gray, New Orleans, 1986-88; Detroit, 1989-94; Houston, 1995 (p-211, k-362)
527 Vai Sikahema, St. Louis, 1986-87; Phoenix, 1988-90; Green Bay, 1991; Philadelphia, 1992-93 (p-292, k-235)
510 Ron Smith, Chicago, 1965, 1970-72; Atlanta, 1966-67; Los Angeles, 1968-69; San Diego, 1973; Oakland, 1974 (p-235, k-275)

Most Combined Kick Returns, Season
100 Larry Jones, Washington, 1975 (p-53, k-47)
97 Stump Mitchell, St. Louis, 1981 (p-42, k-55)
94 Nesby Glasgow, Baltimore, 1979 (p-44, k-50)
Tyrone Hughes, New Orleans, 1995 (p-28, k-66)
Tamarick Vanover, Kansas City, 1995 (p-51, k-43)

Most Combined Kick Returns, Game
13 Stump Mitchell, St. Louis vs. Atlanta, Oct. 18, 1981 (p-6, k-7)
Ronnie Harris, New England vs. Pittsburgh, Dec. 5, 1993 (p-10, k-3)
12 Mel Renfro, Dallas vs. Green Bay, Nov. 29, 1964 (p-4, k-8)
Larry Jones, Washington vs. Dallas, Dec. 13, 1975 (p-6, k-6)
Eddie Brown, Washington vs. Tampa Bay, Oct. 9, 1977 (p-11, k-1)
Nesby Glasgow, Baltimore vs. Denver, Sept. 2, 1979 (p-9, k-3)
11 By many players

YARDS GAINED

Most Yards Returned, Career
11,220 Mel Gray, New Orleans, 1986-88; Detroit, 1989-94; Houston, 1995 (p-2,387, k-8,833)
8,710 Ron Smith, Chicago, 1965, 1970-72; Atlanta, 1966-67; Los Angeles, 1968-69; San Diego, 1973; Oakland, 1974 (p-1,788, k-6,922)
8,102 Vai Sikahema, St. Louis, 1986-87; Phoenix, 1988-90; Green Bay, 1991; Philadelphia, 1992-93 (p-3,169, k-4,933)

Most Yards Returned, Season
1,930 Brian Mitchell, Washington, 1994 (p-452, k-1,478)
1,879 Tyrone Hughes, New Orleans, 1995 (p-262, k-1,617)
1,737 Stump Mitchell, St. Louis, 1981 (p-445, k-1,292)
Andre Coleman, San Diego, 1995 (p-326, k-1,411)

Most Yards Returned, Game
347 Tyrone Hughes, New Orleans vs. L.A. Rams, Oct. 23, 1994 (p-43, k-304)
294 Wally Triplett, Detroit vs. Los Angeles, Oct. 29, 1950 (k-294)
Woodley Lewis, Los Angeles vs. Detroit, Oct. 18, 1953 (p-120, k-174)
289 Eddie Payton, Detroit vs. Minnesota, Dec. 17, 1977 (p-105, k-184)

TOUCHDOWNS

Most Touchdowns, Career
9 Ollie Matson, Chi. Cardinals, 1952, 1954-58; Los Angeles, 1959-62; Detroit, 1963; Philadelphia, 1964-66 (p-3, k-6)
Mel Gray, New Orleans, 1986-88; Detroit, 1989-94; Houston, 1995 (p-3, k-6)
8 Jack Christiansen, Detroit, 1951-58 (p-8)
Bobby Mitchell, Cleveland, 1958-61; Washington, 1962-68 (p-3, k-5)
Gale Sayers, Chicago, 1965-71 (p-2, k-6)
Rick Upchurch, Denver, 1975-83 (p-8)
Billy Johnson, Houston, 1974-80; Atlanta, 1982-87; Washington, 1988 (p-6, k-2)
Eric Metcalf, Cleveland, 1989-94; Atlanta, 1995 (p-6, k-2)
7 Abe Woodson, San Francisco, 1958-64; St. Louis, 1965-66 (p-2, k-5)
Travis Williams, Green Bay, 1967-70; Los Angeles, 1971 (p-1, k-6)
David Meggett, N.Y. Giants, 1989-94; New England, 1995 (p-6, k-1)

Most Touchdowns, Season
4 Jack Christiansen, Detroit, 1951 (p-4)
Emlen Tunnell, N.Y. Giants, 1951 (p-3, k-1)
Gale Sayers, Chicago, 1967 (p-1, k-3)
Travis Williams, Green Bay, 1967 (k-4)
Cecil Turner, Chicago, 1970 (k-4)
Billy Johnson, Houston, 1975 (p-3, k-1)
Rick Upchurch, Denver, 1976 (p-4)
3 Verda (Vitamin T) Smith, Los Angeles, 1950 (k-3)
Abe Woodson, San Francisco, 1963 (k-3)
Raymond Clayborn, New England, 1977 (k-3)
Billy Johnson, Houston, 1977 (p-2, k-1)
LeRoy Irvin, Los Angeles, 1981 (p-3)
Ron Brown, L.A. Rams, 1985 (k-3)
Tyrone Hughes, New Orleans, 1993 (p-2, k-1)
Mel Gray, Detroit, 1994 (k-3)
Tamarick Vanover, Kansas City, 1995 (p-1, k-2)

2 By many players

Most Touchdowns, Game

2 Jack Christiansen, Detroit vs. Los Angeles, Oct. 14, 1951 (p-2); vs. Green Bay, Nov. 22, 1951 (p-2)
Jim Patton, N.Y. Giants vs. Washington, Oct. 30, 1955 (p-1, k-1)
Bobby Mitchell, Cleveland vs. Philadelphia, Nov. 23, 1958 (p-1, k-1)
Dick Christy, N.Y. Titans vs. Denver, Sept. 24, 1961 (p-2)
Al Frazier, Denver vs. Boston, Dec. 3, 1961 (p-1, k-1)
Timmy Brown, Philadelphia vs. Dallas, Nov. 6, 1966 (k-2)
Travis Williams, Green Bay vs. Cleveland, Nov. 12, 1967 (k-2); vs. Pittsburgh, Nov. 2, 1969 (p-1, k-1)
Gale Sayers, Chicago vs. San Francisco, Dec. 3, 1967 (p-1, k-1)
Rick Upchurch, Denver vs. Cleveland, Sept. 26, 1976 (p-2)
Eddie Payton, Detroit vs. Minnesota, Dec. 17, 1977 (p-1, k-1)
LeRoy Irvin, Los Angeles vs. Atlanta, Oct. 11, 1981 (p-2)
Ron Brown, L.A. Rams vs. Green Bay, Nov. 24, 1985 (k-2)
Vai Sikahema, St. Louis vs. Tampa Bay, Dec. 21, 1986 (p-2)
Eric Metcalf, Cleveland vs. Pittsburgh, Oct. 24, 1993 (p-2)
Tyrone Hughes, New Orleans vs. L.A. Rams, Oct. 23, 1994 (k-2)

FUMBLES

Most Fumbles, Career

144 Dave Krieg, Seattle, 1980-91; Kansas City, 1992-93; Detroit, 1994; Arizona, 1995
138 Warren Moon, Houston, 1984-93; Minnesota, 1994-95
117 Boomer Esiason, Cincinnati, 1984-92; N.Y. Jets, 1993-95

Most Fumbles, Season

18 Dave Krieg, Seattle, 1989
Warren Moon, Houston, 1990
17 Dan Pastorini, Houston, 1973
Warren Moon, Houston, 1984
Randall Cunningham, Philadelphia, 1989
16 Don Meredith, Dallas, 1964
Joe Cribbs, Buffalo, 1980
Steve Fuller, Kansas City, 1980
Paul McDonald, Cleveland, 1984
Phil Simms, N.Y. Giants, 1985
Dave Krieg, Arizona, 1995

Most Fumbles, Game

7 Len Dawson, Kansas City vs. San Diego, Nov. 15, 1964
6 Sam Etcheverry, St. Louis vs. N.Y. Giants, Sept, 17, 1961
Dave Krieg, Seattle vs. Kansas City, Nov. 5, 1989
5 Paul Christman, Chi. Cardinals vs. Green Bay, Nov. 10, 1946
Charlie Conerly, N.Y. Giants vs. San Francisco, Dec. 1, 1957
Jack Kemp, Buffalo vs. Houston, Oct. 29, 1967
Roman Gabriel, Philadelphia vs. Oakland, Nov. 21, 1976
Randall Cunningham, Philadelphia vs. L.A. Raiders, Nov. 30, 1986 (OT)
Willie Totten, Buffalo vs. Indianapolis, Oct. 4, 1987
Dave Walter, Cincinnati vs. Seattle, Oct. 11, 1987
Dave Krieg, Seattle vs. San Diego, Nov. 25, 1990 (OT)
Andre Ware, Detroit vs. Green Bay, Dec. 6, 1992

FUMBLES RECOVERED

Most Fumbles Recovered, Career, Own and Opponents'

51 Warren Moon, Houston, 1984-93, Minnesota, 1994-95 (51 own)
44 Boomer Esiason, Cincinnati, 1984-92; N.Y. Jets, 1993-95 (44 own)
43 Fran Tarkenton, Minnesota, 1961-66, 1972-78; N.Y. Giants, 1967-71 (43 own)
Dave Krieg, Seattle, 1980-91; Kansas City, 1992-93; Detroit, 1994; Arizona, 1995 (43 own)

Most Fumbles Recovered, Season, Own and Opponents'

9 Don Hultz, Minnesota, 1963 (9 opp)
Dave Krieg, Seattle, 1989 (9 own)
8 Paul Christman, Chi. Cardinals, 1945 (8 own)
Joe Schmidt, Detroit, 1955 (8 opp)
Bill Butler, Minnesota, 1963 (8 own)
Kermit Alexander, San Francisco, 1965 (4 own, 4 opp)
Jack Lambert, Pittsburgh, 1976 (1 own, 7 opp)
Danny White, Dallas, 1981 (8 own)
Dan Marino, Miami, 1988 (7 own, 1 opp)
7 By many players

Most Fumbles Recovered, Game, Own and Opponents'

4 Otto Graham, Cleveland vs. N.Y. Giants, Oct. 25, 1953 (4 own)
Sam Etcheverry, St. Louis vs. N.Y. Giants, Sept. 17, 1961 (4 own)
Roman Gabriel, Los Angeles vs. San Francisco, Oct. 12, 1969 (4 own)
Joe Ferguson, Buffalo vs. Miami, Sept. 18, 1977 (4 own)
Randall Cunningham, Philadelphia vs. L.A. Raiders, Nov. 30, 1986 (OT) (4 own)
3 By many players

OWN FUMBLES RECOVERED

Most Own Fumbles Recovered, Career

51 Warren Moon, Houston, 1984-93; Minnesota, 1994-95
44 Boomer Esiason, Cincinnati, 1984-92; N.Y. Jets, 1993-95
43 Fran Tarkenton, Minnesota, 1961-66, 1972-78; N.Y. Giants, 1967-71
Dave Krieg, Seattle, 1980-91; Kansas City, 1992-93; Detroit, 1994; Arizona, 1995

Most Own Fumbles Recovered, Season

9 Dave Krieg, Seattle, 1989
8 Paul Christman, Chi. Cardinals, 1945
Bill Butler, Minnesota, 1963
Danny White, Dallas, 1981
7 By many players

Most Own Fumbles Recovered, Game

4 Otto Graham, Cleveland vs. N.Y. Giants, Oct. 25, 1953
Sam Etcheverry, St. Louis vs. N.Y. Giants, Sept. 17, 1961
Roman Gabriel, Los Angeles vs. San Francisco, Oct. 12, 1969
Joe Ferguson, Buffalo vs. Miami, Sept. 18, 1977
Randall Cunningham, Philadelphia vs. L.A. Raiders, Nov. 30, 1986 (OT)
3 By many players

OPPONENTS' FUMBLES RECOVERED

Most Opponents' Fumbles Recovered, Career

29 Jim Marshall, Cleveland, 1960; Minnesota, 1961-79
28 Rickey Jackson, New Orleans, 1981-93; San Francisco, 1994-95
25 Dick Butkus, Chicago, 1965-73

Most Opponents' Fumbles Recovered, Season

9 Don Hultz, Minnesota, 1963
8 Joe Schmidt, Detroit, 1955
7 Alan Page, Minnesota, 1970
Jack Lambert, Pittsburgh, 1976
Ray Childress, Houston, 1988
Rickey Jackson, New Orleans, 1990

Most Opponents' Fumbles Recovered, Game

3 Corwin Clatt, Chi. Cardinals vs. Detroit, Nov. 6, 1949
Vic Sears, Philadelphia vs. Green Bay, Nov. 2, 1952
Ed Beatty, San Francisco vs. Los Angeles, Oct. 7, 1956
Ron Carroll, Houston vs. Cincinnati, Oct. 27, 1974
Maurice Spencer, New Orleans vs. Atlanta, Oct. 10, 1976
Steve Nelson, New England vs. Philadelphia, Oct. 8, 1978
Charles Jackson, Kansas City vs. Pittsburgh, Sept. 6, 1981
Willie Buchanon, San Diego vs. Denver, Sept. 27, 1981
Joey Browner, Minnesota vs. San Francisco, Sept. 8, 1985
Ray Childress, Houston vs. Washington, Oct. 30, 1988
John Thierry, Chicago vs. Houston, Oct. 22, 1995
2 By many players

YARDS RETURNING FUMBLES

Longest Fumble Run (All TDs)

104 Jack Tatum, Oakland vs. Green Bay, Sept. 24, 1972
100 Chris Martin, Kansas City vs. Miami, Oct. 13, 1991
99 Don Griffin, San Francisco vs. Chicago, Dec. 23, 1991

TOUCHDOWNS

Most Touchdowns, Career (Total)

4 Bill Thompson, Denver, 1969-81
Jessie Tuggle, Atlanta, 1987-95
3 Ralph Heywood, Detroit, 1947-48; Boston, 1948; N.Y. Bulldogs, 1949
Leo Sugar, Chi. Cardinals, 1954-59; St. Louis, 1960; Philadelphia, 1961; Detroit, 1962
Bud McFadin, Los Angeles, 1952-56; Denver, 1960-63; Houston, 1964-65
Doug Cline, Houston, 1960-66; San Diego, 1966
Bob Lilly, Dall. Cowboys, 1961-74
Chris Hanburger, Washington, 1965-78
Lemar Parrish, Cincinnati, 1970-77; Washington, 1978-81; Buffalo, 1982
Paul Krause, Washington, 1964-67; Minnesota, 1968-79
Brad Dusek, Washington, 1974-81
David Logan, Tampa Bay, 1979-86; Green Bay, 1987
Thomas Howard, Kansas City, 1977-83; St. Louis, 1984-85
Greg Townsend, L.A. Raiders, 1983-93; Philadelphia, 1994
Les Miller, San Diego, 1987-90, 1994; New Orleans, 1991-94
Chris Martin, New Orleans, 1983; Minnesota, 1984-88; Kansas City, 1989-92; L.A. Rams, 1993-94
Seth Joyner, Philadelphia, 1986-93; Arizona, 1994-95
Derrick Thomas, Kansas City, 1989-95
Tony Bennett, Green Bay, 1990-93; Indianapolis, 1994-95
2 By many players

Most Touchdowns, Season (Total)

2 Harold McPhail, Boston, 1934
Harry Ebding, Detroit, 1937
John Morelli, Boston, 1944
Frank Maznicki, Boston, 1947
Fred (Dippy) Evans, Chi. Bears, 1948
Ralph Heywood, Boston, 1948
Art Tait, N.Y. Yanks, 1951

John Dwyer, Los Angeles, 1952
Leo Sugar, Chi. Cardinals, 1957
Doug Cline, Houston, 1961
Jim Bradshaw, Pittsburgh, 1964
Royce Berry, Cincinnati, 1970
Ahmad Rashad, Buffalo, 1974
Tim Gray, Kansas City, 1977
Charles Phillips, Oakland, 1978
Kenny Johnson, Atlanta, 1981
George Martin, N.Y. Giants, 1981
Del Rodgers, Green Bay, 1982
Mike Douglass, Green Bay, 1983
Shelton Robinson, Seattle, 1983
Erik McMillan, N.Y. Jets, 1989
Les Miller, San Diego, 1990
Seth Joyner, Philadelphia, 1991
Robert Goff, New Orleans, 1992
Willie Clay, Detroit, 1993
Tyrone Hughes, New Orleans, 1994

Most Touchdowns, Career (Own recovered)
2 Ken Kavanaugh, Chi. Bears, 1940-41, 1945-50
Mike Ditka, Chicago, 1961-66; Philadelphia, 1967-68; Dallas, 1969-72
Gail Cogdill, Detroit, 1960-68; Baltimore, 1968; Atlanta, 1969-70
Ahmad Rashad, St. Louis, 1972-73; Buffalo, 1974; Minnesota, 1976-82
Jim Mitchell, Atlanta, 1969-79
Drew Pearson, Dallas, 1973-83
Del Rodgers, Green Bay, 1982, 1984; San Francisco, 1987-88

Most Touchdowns, Season (Own recovered)
2 Ahmad Rashad, Buffalo, 1974
Del Rodgers, Green Bay, 1982
1 By many players

Most Touchdowns, Career (Opponents' recovered)
4 Jessie Tuggle, Atlanta, 1987-95
3 Leo Sugar, Chi. Cardinals, 1954-59; St. Louis, 1960; Philadelphia, 1961; Detroit, 1962
Doug Cline, Houston, 1960-66; San Diego, 1966
Bud McFadin, Los Angeles, 1952-56; Denver, 1960-63; Houston, 1964-65
Bob Lilly, Dall. Cowboys, 1961-74
Chris Hanburger, Washington, 1965-78
Paul Krause, Washington, 1964-67; Minnesota, 1968-79
Lemar Parrish, Cincinnati, 1970-77; Washington, 1978-81; Buffalo, 1982
Bill Thompson, Denver, 1969-81
Brad Dusek, Washington, 1974-81
David Logan, Tampa Bay, 1979-86; Green Bay, 1987
Thomas Howard, Kansas City, 1977-83; St. Louis, 1984-85
Greg Townsend, L.A. Raiders, 1983-93; Philadelphia, 1994
Les Miller, San Diego, 1987-90, 1994; New Orleans, 1991-94
Chris Martin, New Orleans, 1983; Minnesota, 1984-88; Kansas City, 1989-92; L.A. Rams, 1993-94
Seth Joyner, Philadelphia, 1986-93; Arizona, 1994-95
Derrick Thomas, Kansas City, 1989-95
Tony Bennett, Green Bay, 1990-93; Indianapolis, 1994-95
2 By many players

Most Touchdowns, Season (Opponents' recovered)
2 Harold McPhail, Boston, 1934
Harry Ebding, Detroit, 1937
John Morelli, Boston, 1944
Frank Maznicki, Boston, 1947
Fred (Dippy) Evans, Chi. Bears, 1948
Ralph Heywood, Boston, 1948
Art Tait, N.Y. Yanks, 1951
John Dwyer, Los Angeles, 1952
Leo Sugar, Chi. Cardinals, 1957
Doug Cline, Houston, 1961
Jim Bradshaw, Pittsburgh, 1964
Royce Berry, Cincinnati, 1970
Tim Gray, Kansas City, 1977
Charles Phillips, Oakland, 1978
Kenny Johnson, Atlanta, 1981
George Martin, N.Y. Giants, 1981
Mike Douglass, Green Bay, 1983
Shelton Robinson, Seattle, 1983
Erik McMillan, N.Y. Jets, 1989
Les Miller, San Diego, 1990
Seth Joyner, Philadelphia, 1991
Robert Goff, New Orleans, 1992
Willie Clay, Detroit, 1993
Tyrone Hughes, New Orleans, 1994

Most Touchdowns, Game (Opponents' recovered)
2 Fred (Dippy) Evans, Chi. Bears vs. Washington, Nov. 28, 1948

COMBINED NET YARDS GAINED

Rushing, receiving, interception returns, punt returns, kickoff returns, and fumble returns

Most Seasons Leading League
5 Jim Brown, Cleveland, 1958-61, 1964
3 Cliff Battles, Boston, 1932-33; Washington, 1937
Gale Sayers, Chicago, 1965-67
Eric Dickerson, L.A. Rams, 1983-84, 1986
Thurman Thomas, Buffalo, 1989, 1991-92
2 By many players

Most Consecutive Seasons Leading League
4 Jim Brown, Cleveland, 1958-61
3 Gale Sayers, Chicago, 1965-67
2 Cliff Battles, Boston, 1932-33
Charley Trippi, Chi. Cardinals, 1948-49
Timmy Brown, Philadelphia, 1962-63
Floyd Little, Denver, 1967-68
James Brooks, San Diego, 1981-82
Eric Dickerson, L.A. Rams, 1983-84
Thurman Thomas, Buffalo, 1991-92
Brian Mitchell, Washington, 1994-95

ATTEMPTS

Most Attempts, Career
4,368 Walter Payton, Chicago, 1975-87
3,351 Tony Dorsett, Dallas, 1977-87; Denver, 1988
3,293 Eric Dickerson, L.A. Rams, 1983-87; Indianapolis, 1987-91; L.A. Raiders, 1992; Atlanta, 1993

Most Attempts, Season
496 James Wilder, Tampa Bay, 1984
449 Marcus Allen, L.A. Raiders, 1985
442 Eric Dickerson, L.A. Rams, 1983

Most Attempts, Rookie, Season
442 Eric Dickerson, L.A. Rams, 1983
395 George Rogers, New Orleans, 1981
390 Joe Cribbs, Buffalo, 1980

Most Attempts, Game
48 James Wilder, Tampa Bay vs. Pittsburgh, Oct. 30, 1983
47 James Wilder, Tampa Bay vs. Green Bay, Sept. 30, 1984 (OT)
46 Gerald Riggs, Atlanta vs. L.A. Rams, Nov. 17, 1985

YARDS GAINED

Most Yards Gained, Career
21,803 Walter Payton, Chicago, 1975-87
16,326 Tony Dorsett, Dallas, 1977-87; Denver, 1988
15,957 Marcus Allen, L.A. Raiders, 1982-92; Kansas City, 1993-95

Most Yards Gained, Season
2,535 Lionel James, San Diego, 1985
2,477 Brian Mitchell, Washington, 1994
2,462 Terry Metcalf, St. Louis, 1975

Most Yards Gained, Rookie, Season
2,317 Tim Brown, L.A. Raiders, 1988
2,272 Gale Sayers, Chicago, 1965
2,212 Eric Dickerson, L.A. Rams, 1983

Most Yards Gained, Game
404 Glyn Milburn, Denver vs. Seattle, Dec. 10, 1995
373 Billy Cannon, Houston vs. N.Y. Titans, Dec. 10, 1961
347 Tyrone Hughes, New Orleans vs. L.A. Rams, Oct. 23, 1994

SACKS

Sacks have been compiled since 1982.

Most Seasons Leading League
2 Mark Gastineau, N.Y. Jets, 1983-84
Reggie White, Philadelphia, 1987-88

Most Sacks, Career
157 Reggie White, Philadelphia, 1985-92; Green Bay, 1993-95
132.5 Lawrence Taylor, N.Y. Giants, 1982-93
128 Rickey Jackson, New Orleans, 1981-93; San Francisco, 1994-95

Most Sacks, Season
22 Mark Gastineau, N.Y. Jets, 1984
21 Reggie White, Philadelphia, 1987
Chris Doleman, Minnesota, 1989
20.5 Lawrence Taylor, N.Y. Giants, 1986

Most Sacks, Rookie, Season
12.5 Leslie O'Neal, San Diego, 1986
12 Charles Haley, San Francisco, 1986
11 Vernon Maxwell, Baltimore, 1983

Most Sacks, Game
7 Derrick Thomas, Kansas City vs. Seattle, Nov. 11, 1990
6 Fred Dean, San Francisco vs. New Orleans, Nov. 13, 1983
5.5 William Gay, Detroit vs. Tampa Bay, Sept. 4, 1983

MISCELLANEOUS

Longest Return of Missed Field Goal (All TDs)

101 Al Nelson, Philadelphia vs. Dallas, Sept. 26, 1971
100 Al Nelson, Philadelphia vs. Cleveland, Dec. 11, 1966
Ken Ellis, Green Bay vs. N.Y. Giants, Sept. 19, 1971
99 Jerry Williams, Los Angeles vs. Green Bay, Dec. 16, 1951
Carl Taseff, Baltimore vs. Los Angeles, Dec. 12, 1959
Timmy Brown, Philadelphia vs. St. Louis, Sept. 16, 1962

TEAM RECORDS

CHAMPIONSHIPS

Most Seasons League Champion

11 Green Bay, 1929-31, 1936, 1939, 1944, 1961-62, 1965-67
9 Chi. Bears, 1921, 1932-33, 1940-41, 1943, 1946, 1963, 1985
6 N.Y. Giants, 1927, 1934, 1938, 1956, 1986, 1990

Most Consecutive Seasons League Champion

3 Green Bay, 1929-31
Green Bay, 1965-67
2 Canton, 1922-23
Chi. Bears, 1932-33
Chi. Bears, 1940-41
Philadelphia, 1948-49
Detroit, 1952-53
Cleveland, 1954-55
Baltimore, 1958-59
Houston, 1960-61
Green Bay, 1961-62
Buffalo, 1964-65
Miami, 1972-73
Pittsburgh, 1974-75
Pittsburgh, 1978-79
San Francisco, 1988-89
Dallas, 1992-93

Most Times Finishing First, Regular Season

18 Clev. Browns, 1950-55, 1957, 1964-65, 1967-69, 1971, 1980, 1985-87, 1989
Chi. Bears, 1921, 1932-34, 1937, 1940-43, 1946, 1956, 1963, 1984-88, 1990
N.Y. Giants, 1927, 1933-35, 1938-39, 1941, 1944, 1946, 1956, 1958-59, 1961-63, 1986, 1989-90
17 Dallas, 1966-71, 1973, 1976-79, 1981, 1985, 1992-95
15 Cleveland/L.A. Rams, 1945, 1949-51, 1955, 1967, 1969, 1973-79, 1985
Green Bay, 1929-31, 1936, 1938-39, 1944, 1960-62, 1965-67, 1972, 1995
San Francisco, 1970-72, 1981, 1983-84, 1986-90, 1992,95

Most Consecutive Times Finishing First, Regular Season

7 Los Angeles, 1973-79
6 Cleveland, 1950-55
Dallas, 1966-71
Minnesota, 1973-78
Pittsburgh, 1974-79
5 Oakland, 1972-76
Chicago, 1984-88
San Francisco, 1986-90

GAMES WON

Most Consecutive Games Won

17 Chi. Bears, 1933-34
16 Chi. Bears, 1941-42
Miami, 1971-73
Miami, 1983-84
15 L.A. Chargers/San Diego, 1960-61
San Francisco, 1989-90

Most Consecutive Games Without Defeat

25 Canton, 1921-23 (won 22, tied 3)
24 Chi. Bears, 1941-43 (won 23, tied 1)
23 Green Bay, 1928-30 (won 21, tied 2)

Most Games Won, Season

15 San Francisco, 1984
Chicago, 1985
14 Frankford, 1926
Miami, 1972
Pittsburgh, 1978
Washington, 1983
Miami, 1984
Chicago, 1986
N.Y. Giants, 1986
San Francisco, 1989
San Francisco, 1990
Washington, 1991
San Francisco, 1992
13 By many teams

Most Consecutive Games Won, Season

14 Miami, 1972
13 Chi. Bears, 1934
12 Minnesota, 1969
Chicago, 1985

Most Consecutive Games Won, Start of Season

14 Miami, 1972, entire season
13 Chi. Bears, 1934, entire season
12 Chicago, 1985

Most Consecutive Games Won, End of Season

14 Miami, 1972, entire season
13 Chi. Bears, 1934, entire season
11 Chi. Bears, 1942, entire season
Cleveland, 1951
Houston, 1993

Most Consecutive Games Without Defeat, Season

14 Miami, 1972 (won 14)
13 Chi. Bears, 1926 (won 11, tied 2)
Green Bay, 1929 (won 12, tied 1)
Chi. Bears, 1934 (won 13)
Baltimore, 1967 (won 11, tied 2)
12 Canton, 1922 (won 10, tied 2)
Canton, 1923 (won 11, tied 1)
Minnesota, 1969 (won 12)
Chicago, 1985 (won 12)

Most Consecutive Games Without Defeat, Start of Season

14 Miami, 1972 (won 14), entire season
13 Chi. Bears, 1926 (won 11, tied 2)
Green Bay, 1929 (won 12, tied 1), entire season
Chi. Bears, 1934 (won 13), entire season
Baltimore, 1967 (won 11, tied 2)
12 Canton, 1922 (won 10, tied 2), entire season
Canton, 1923 (won 11, tied 1), entire season
Chicago, 1985 (won 12)

Most Consecutive Games Without Defeat, End of Season

14 Miami, 1972 (won 14), entire season
13 Green Bay, 1929 (won 12, tied 1), entire season
Chi. Bears, 1934 (won 13), entire season
12 Canton, 1922 (won 10, tied 2), entire season
Canton, 1923 (won 11, tied 1), entire season

Most Consecutive Home Games Won

27 Miami, 1971-74
20 Green Bay, 1929-32
18 Oakland, 1968-70
Dallas, 1979-81

Most Consecutive Home Games Without Defeat

30 Green Bay, 1928-33 (won 27, tied 3)
27 Miami, 1971-74 (won 27)
25 Chi. Bears, 1923-25 (won 19, tied 6)

Most Consecutive Road Games Won

18 San Francisco, 1988-90
11 L.A. Chargers/San Diego, 1960-61
San Francisco, 1987-88
10 Chi. Bears, 1941-42
Dallas, 1968-69
New Orleans, 1987-88

Most Consecutive Road Games Without Defeat

18 San Francisco, 1988-90 (won 18)
13 Chi. Bears, 1941-43 (won 12, tied 1)
12 Green Bay, 1928-30 (won 10, tied 2)

Most Shutout Games Won or Tied, Season

10 Pottsville, 1926 (won 9, tied 1)
N.Y. Giants, 1927 (won 9, tied 1)
9 Akron, 1921 (won 8, tied 1)
Canton, 1922 (won 7, tied 2)
Frankford, 1926 (won 9)
Frankford, 1929 (won 6, tied 3)
8 By many teams

Most Consecutive Shutout Games Won or Tied

13 Akron, 1920-21 (won 10, tied 3)
7 Pottsville, 1926 (won 6, tied 1)
Detroit, 1934 (won 7)
6 Buffalo, 1920-21 (won 5, tied 1)
Frankford, 1926 (won 6)
Detroit, 1926 (won 4, tied 2)
N.Y. Giants, 1926-27 (won 5, tied 1)

GAMES LOST

Most Consecutive Games Lost

26 Tampa Bay, 1976-77
19 Chi. Cardinals, 1942-43, 1945
Oakland, 1961-62

18 Houston, 1972-73

Most Consecutive Games Without Victory
26 Tampa Bay, 1976-77 (lost 26)
23 Rochester, 1922-25 (lost 21, tied 2)
Washington, 1960-61 (lost 20, tied 3)
19 Dayton, 1927-29 (lost 18, tied 1)
Chi. Cardinals, 1942-43, 1945 (lost 19)
Oakland, 1961-62 (lost 19)

Most Games Lost, Season
15 New Orleans, 1980
Dallas, 1989
New England, 1990
Indianapolis, 1991
14 By many teams

Most Consecutive Games Lost, Season
14 Tampa Bay, 1976
New Orleans, 1980
Baltimore, 1981
New England, 1990
13 Oakland, 1962
Pittsburgh, 1969
Indianapolis, 1986
12 Tampa Bay, 1977

Most Consecutive Games Lost, Start of Season
14 Tampa Bay, 1976, entire season
New Orleans, 1980
13 Oakland, 1962
Indianapolis, 1986
12 Tampa Bay, 1977

Most Consecutive Games Lost, End of Season
14 Tampa Bay, 1976, entire season
New England, 1990
13 Pittsburgh, 1969
11 Philadelphia, 1936
Detroit, 1942, entire season
Houston, 1972

Most Consecutive Games Without Victory, Season
14 Tampa Bay, 1976 (lost 14), entire season
New Orleans, 1980 (lost 14)
Baltimore, 1981 (lost 14)
New England, 1990 (lost 14)
13 Washington, 1961 (lost 12, tied 1)
Oakland, 1962 (lost 13)
Pittsburgh, 1969 (lost 13)
Indianapolis, 1986 (lost 13)
12 Dall. Cowboys, 1960 (lost 11, tied 1), entire season
Tampa Bay, 1977 (lost 12)

Most Consecutive Games Without Victory, Start of Season
14 Tampa Bay, 1976 (lost 14), entire season
New Orleans, 1980 (lost 14)
13 Washington, 1961 (lost 12, tied 1)
Oakland, 1962 (lost 13)
Indianapolis, 1986 (lost 13)
12 Dall. Cowboys, 1960 (lost 11, tied 1), entire season
Tampa Bay, 1977 (lost 12)

Most Consecutive Games Without Victory, End of Season
14 Tampa Bay, 1976, (lost 14), entire season
New England, 1990 (lost 14)
13 Pittsburgh, 1969 (lost 13)
12 Dall. Cowboys, 1960 (lost 11, tied 1), entire season

Most Consecutive Home Games Lost
14 Dallas, 1988-89
13 Houston, 1972-73
Tampa Bay, 1976-77
11 Oakland, 1961-62
Los Angeles, 1961-63

Most Consecutive Home Games Without Victory
14 Dallas, 1988-89 (lost 14)
13 Houston, 1972-73 (lost 13)
Tampa Bay, 1976-77 (lost 13)
12 Philadelphia, 1936-38 (lost 11, tied 1)

Most Consecutive Road Games Lost
23 Houston, 1981-84
22 Buffalo, 1983-86
19 Tampa Bay, 1983-85
Atlanta, 1988-91

Most Consecutive Road Games Without Victory
23 Houston, 1981-84 (lost 23)
22 Buffalo, 1983-86 (lost 22)
19 Tampa Bay, 1983-85 (lost 19)
Atlanta, 1988-91 (lost 19)

Most Shutout Games Lost or Tied, Season
8 Frankford, 1927 (lost 6, tied 2)
Brooklyn, 1931 (lost 8)
7 Dayton, 1925 (lost 6, tied 1)
Orange, 1929 (lost 4, tied 3)
Frankford, 1931 (lost 6, tied 1)
6 By many teams

Most Consecutive Shutout Games Lost or Tied
8 Rochester, 1922-24 (lost 8)
7 Hammond, 1922-23 (lost 6, tied 1)
6 Providence, 1926-27 (lost 5, tied 1)
Brooklyn, 1942-43 (lost 6)

TIE GAMES

Most Tie Games, Season
6 Chi. Bears, 1932
5 Frankford, 1929
4 Chi. Bears, 1924
Orange, 1929
Portsmouth, 1932

Most Consecutive Tie Games
3 Chi. Bears, 1932
2 By many teams

SCORING

Most Seasons Leading League
10 Chi. Bears, 1932, 1934-35, 1939, 1941-43, 1946-47, 1956
9 San Francisco, 1953, 1965, 1970, 1987, 1989, 1992-95
6 Green Bay, 1931, 1936-38, 1961-62
L.A. Rams, 1950-52, 1957, 1967, 1973

Most Consecutive Seasons Leading League
4 San Francisco, 1992-1995
3 Green Bay, 1936-38
Chi. Bears, 1941-43
Los Angeles, 1950-52
Oakland, 1967-69
2 By many teams

POINTS

Most Points, Season
541 Washington, 1983
513 Houston, 1961
Miami, 1984
505 San Francisco, 1994

Fewest Points, Season (Since 1932)
37 Cincinnati/St. Louis, 1934
38 Cincinnati, 1933
Detroit, 1942
51 Pittsburgh, 1934
Philadelphia, 1936

Most Points, Game
72 Washington vs. N.Y. Giants, Nov. 27, 1966
70 Los Angeles vs. Baltimore, Oct. 22, 1950
65 Chi. Cardinals vs. N.Y. Bulldogs, Nov. 13, 1949
Los Angeles vs. Detroit, Oct. 29, 1950

Most Points, Both Teams, Game
113 Washington (72) vs. N.Y. Giants (41), Nov. 27, 1966
101 Oakland (52) vs. Houston (49), Dec. 22, 1963
99 Seattle (51) vs. Kansas City (48), Nov. 27, 1983 (OT)

Fewest Points, Both Teams, Game
0 In many games. Last time: N.Y. Giants vs. Detroit, Nov. 7, 1943

Most Points, Shutout Victory, Game
64 Philadelphia vs. Cincinnati, Nov. 6, 1934
62 Akron vs. Oorang, Oct. 29, 1922
60 Rock Island vs. Evansville, Oct. 15, 1922
Chi. Cardinals vs. Rochester, Oct. 7, 1923

Fewest Points, Shutout Victory, Game
2 Green Bay vs. Chi. Bears, Oct. 16, 1932
Chi. Bears vs. Green Bay, Sept. 18, 1938

Most Points Overcome to Win Game
28 San Francisco vs. New Orleans, Dec. 7, 1980 (OT) (trailed 7-35, won 38-35)
25 St. Louis vs. Tampa Bay, Nov. 8, 1987 (trailed 3-28, won 31-28)
24 Philadelphia vs. Washington, Oct. 27, 1946 (trailed 0-24, won 28-24)
Detroit vs. Baltimore, Oct. 20, 1957 (trailed 3-27, won 31-27)
Philadelphia vs. Chi. Cardinals, Oct. 25, 1959 (trailed 0-24, won 28-24)
Denver vs. Boston, Oct. 23, 1960 (trailed 0-24, won 31-24)
Miami vs. New England, Dec. 15, 1974 (trailed 0-24, won 34-27)
Minnesota vs. San Francisco, Dec. 4, 1977 (trailed 0-24, won 28-27)
Denver vs. Seattle, Sept. 23, 1979 (trailed 10-34, won 37-34)
Houston vs. Cincinnati, Sept. 23, 1979 (OT) (trailed 0-24, won 30-27)
L.A. Raiders vs. San Diego, Nov. 22, 1982 (trailed 0-24, won 28-24)
L.A. Raiders vs. Denver, Sept. 26, 1988 (OT) (trailed 0-24, won 30-27)
L.A. Rams vs. Tampa Bay, Dec. 6, 1992 (trailed 3-27, won 31-27)

Most Points Overcome to Tie Game
31 Denver vs. Buffalo, Nov. 27, 1960 (trailed 7-38, tied 38-38)
28 Los Angeles vs. Philadelphia, Oct. 3, 1948 (trailed 0-28, tied 28-28)
Most Points, Each Half
1st: 49 Green Bay vs. Tampa Bay, Oct. 2, 1983
48 Buffalo vs. Miami, Sept. 18, 1966
45 Green Bay vs. Cleveland, Nov. 12, 1967
Indianapolis vs. Denver, Oct. 31, 1988
Houston vs. Cleveland, Dec. 9, 1990
2nd: 49 Chi. Bears vs. Philadelphia, Nov. 30, 1941
48 Chi. Cardinals vs. Baltimore, Oct. 2, 1950
N.Y. Giants vs. Baltimore, Nov. 19, 1950
45 Cincinnati vs. Houston, Dec. 17, 1972
Most Points, Both Teams, Each Half
1st: 70 Houston (35) vs. Oakland (35), Dec. 22, 1963
62 N.Y. Jets (41) vs. Tampa Bay (21), Nov. 17, 1985
59 St. Louis (31) vs. Philadelphia (28), Dec. 16, 1962
2nd: 65 Washington (38) vs. N.Y. Giants (27), Nov. 27, 1966
62 L.A. Raiders (31) vs. San Diego (31), Jan. 2, 1983
58 New England (37) vs. Baltimore (21), Nov. 23, 1980
N.Y. Jets (37) vs. New England (21), Sept. 21, 1987
Most Points, One Quarter
41 Green Bay vs. Detroit, Oct. 7, 1945 (second quarter)
Los Angeles vs. Detroit, Oct. 29, 1950 (third quarter)
37 Los Angeles vs. Green Bay, Sept. 21, 1980 (second quarter)
35 Chi. Cardinals vs. Boston, Oct. 24, 1948 (third quarter)
Green Bay vs. Cleveland, Nov. 12, 1967 (first quarter)
Green Bay vs. Tampa Bay, Oct. 2, 1983 (second quarter)
Most Points, Both Teams, One Quarter
49 Oakland (28) vs. Houston (21), Dec. 22, 1963 (second quarter)
48 Green Bay (41) vs. Detroit (7), Oct. 7, 1945 (second quarter)
Los Angeles (41) vs. Detroit (7), Oct. 29, 1950 (third quarter)
47 St. Louis (27) vs. Philadelphia (20), Dec. 13, 1964 (second quarter)
Most Points, Each Quarter
1st: 35 Green Bay vs. Cleveland, Nov. 12, 1967
31 Buffalo vs. Kansas City, Sept. 13, 1964
28 By seven teams
2nd: 41 Green Bay vs. Detroit, Oct. 7, 1945
37 Los Angeles vs. Green Bay, Sept. 21, 1980
35 Green Bay vs. Tampa Bay, Oct. 2, 1983
3rd: 41 Los Angeles vs. Detroit, Oct. 29, 1950
35 Chi. Cardinals vs. Boston, Oct. 24, 1948
28 By 10 teams
4th: 31 Oakland vs. Denver, Dec. 17, 1960
Oakland vs. San Diego, Dec. 8, 1963
Atlanta vs. Green Bay, Sept. 13, 1981
28 By many teams
Most Points, Both Teams, Each Quarter
1st: 42 Green Bay (35) vs. Cleveland (7), Nov. 12, 1967
35 Dall. Texans (21) vs. N.Y. Titans (14), Nov. 11, 1962
Dallas (28) vs. Philadelphia (7), Oct. 19, 1969
Kansas City (21) vs. Seattle (14), Dec. 11, 1977
Detroit (21) vs. L.A. Raiders (14), Dec. 10, 1990
Dallas (21) vs. Atlanta (14), Dec. 22, 1991
34 Los Angeles (21) vs. Baltimore (13), Oct. 22, 1950
Oakland (21) vs. Atlanta (13), Nov. 30, 1975
2nd: 49 Oakland (28) vs. Houston (21), Dec. 22, 1963
48 Green Bay (41) vs. Detroit (7), Oct. 7, 1945
47 St. Louis (27) vs. Philadelphia (20), Dec. 13, 1964
3rd: 48 Los Angeles (41) vs. Detroit (7), Oct. 29, 1950
42 Washington (28) vs. Philadelphia (14), Oct. 1, 1955
41 Green Bay (21) vs. N.Y. Yanks (20), Oct. 8, 1950
4th: 42 Chi. Cardinals (28) vs. Philadelphia (14), Dec. 7, 1947
Green Bay (28) vs. Chi. Bears (14), Nov. 6, 1955
N.Y. Jets (28) vs. Boston (14), Oct. 27, 1968
Pittsburgh (21) vs. Cleveland (21), Oct. 18, 1969
41 Baltimore (27) vs. New England (14), Sept. 18, 1978
New England (27) vs. Baltimore (14), Nov. 23, 1980
40 Chicago (21) vs. Tampa Bay (19), Nov. 19, 1989
Most Consecutive Games Scoring
290 San Francisco, 1977-95 (current)
274 Cleveland, 1950-71
218 Dallas, 1970-85

TOUCHDOWNS

Most Seasons Leading League, Touchdowns
13 Chi. Bears, 1932, 1934-35, 1939, 1941-44, 1946-48, 1956, 1965
7 Dallas, 1966, 1968, 1971, 1973, 1977-78, 1980
San Francisco, 1953, 1970, 1987, 1992-95
6 Oakland, 1967-69, 1972, 1974, 1977
San Diego, 1963, 1965, 1979, 1981-82, 1985
Most Consecutive Seasons Leading League, Touchdowns
4 Chi. Bears, 1941-44
Los Angeles, 1949-52
San Francisco, 1992-95
3 Chi. Bears, 1946-48
Baltimore, 1957-59
Oakland, 1967-69
2 By many teams
Most Touchdowns, Season
70 Miami, 1984
66 Houston, 1961
San Francisco, 1994
64 Los Angeles, 1950
Fewest Touchdowns, Season (Since 1932)
3 Cincinnati, 1933
4 Cincinnati/St. Louis, 1934
5 Detroit, 1942
Most Touchdowns, Game
10 Philadelphia vs. Cincinnati, Nov. 6, 1934
Los Angeles vs. Baltimore, Oct. 22, 1950
Washington vs. N.Y. Giants, Nov. 27, 1966
9 Chi. Cardinals vs. Rochester, Oct. 7, 1923
Chi. Cardinals vs. N.Y. Giants, Oct. 17, 1948
Chi. Cardinals vs. N.Y. Bulldogs, Nov. 13, 1949
Los Angeles vs. Detroit, Oct. 29, 1950
Pittsburgh vs. N.Y. Giants, Nov. 30, 1952
Chicago vs. San Francisco, Dec. 12, 1965
Chicago vs. Green Bay, Dec. 7, 1980
8 By many teams.
Most Touchdowns, Both Teams, Game
16 Washington (10) vs. N.Y. Giants (6), Nov. 27, 1966
14 Chi. Cardinals (9) vs. N.Y. Giants (5), Oct. 17, 1948
Los Angeles (10) vs. Baltimore (4), Oct. 22, 1950
Houston (7) vs. Oakland (7), Dec. 22, 1963
13 New Orleans (7) vs. St. Louis (6), Nov. 2, 1969
Kansas City (7) vs. Seattle (6), Nov. 27, 1983 (OT)
San Diego (8) vs. Pittsburgh (5), Dec. 8, 1985
N.Y. Jets (7) vs. Miami (6), Sept. 21, 1986 (OT)
Most Consecutive Games Scoring Touchdowns
166 Cleveland, 1957-69
97 Oakland, 1966-73
96 Kansas City, 1963-70

POINTS AFTER TOUCHDOWN

Most (One-Point) Points After Touchdown, Season
66 Miami, 1984
65 Houston, 1961
62 Washington, 1983
Fewest (One-Point) Points After Touchdown, Season
2 Chi. Cardinals, 1933
3 Cincinnati, 1933
Pittsburgh, 1934
4 Cincinnati/St. Louis, 1934
Most (One-Point) Points After Touchdown, Game
10 Los Angeles vs. Baltimore, Oct. 22, 1950
9 Chi. Cardinals vs. N.Y. Giants, Oct. 17, 1948
Pittsburgh vs. N.Y. Giants, Nov. 30, 1952
Washington vs. N.Y. Giants, Nov. 27, 1966
8 By many teams
Most (One-Point) Points After Touchdown, Both Teams, Game
14 Chi. Cardinals (9) vs. N.Y. Giants (5), Oct. 17, 1948
Houston (7) vs. Oakland (7), Dec. 22, 1963
Washington (9) vs. N.Y. Giants (5), Nov. 27, 1966
13 Los Angeles (10) vs. Baltimore (3), Oct. 22, 1950
12 In many games
Most Two-Point Conversions, Season
6 Miami, 1994
5 Arizona, 1995
4 Boston, 1960
Buffalo, 1961
N.Y. Jets, 1967
Cleveland, 1994
Houston, 1994
Minnesota, 1994
Seattle, 1994
Atlanta, 1995
New England, 1995
Most Two-Point Conversions, Game
2 Denver vs. Oakland, Oct. 1, 1961
Oakland vs. San Diego, Sept. 30, 1962
Kansas City vs. Houston, Oct. 24, 1965
Houston vs. N.Y. Jets, Dec. 6, 1969
Seattle vs. Kansas City, Oct. 23, 1994
Tampa Bay vs. San Francisco, Oct. 23, 1994
Detroit vs. Green Bay, Nov. 6, 1994

Washington vs. San Francisco, Nov. 6, 1994
Carolina vs. New Orleans, Nov. 26, 1995
Miami vs. Indianapolis, Nov. 26, 1995

Most Two-Point Conversions, Both Teams, Game
3 Seattle (2) vs. Kansas City (1), Oct. 23, 1994
2 In many games

FIELD GOALS

Most Seasons Leading League, Field Goals
11 Green Bay, 1935-36, 1940-43, 1946-47, 1955, 1972, 1974
8 Washington, 1945, 1956, 1971, 1976-77, 1979, 1982, 1992
7 N.Y. Giants, 1933, 1937, 1939, 1941, 1944, 1959, 1983

Most Consecutive Seasons Leading League, Field Goals
4 Green Bay, 1940-43
3 Cleveland, 1952-54
2 By many teams

Most Field Goals Attempted, Season
49 Los Angeles, 1966
Washington, 1971
48 Green Bay, 1972
47 N.Y. Jets, 1969
Los Angeles, 1973
Washington, 1983

Fewest Field Goals Attempted, Season (Since 1938)
0 Chi. Bears, 1944
2 Cleveland, 1939
Card-Pitt, 1944
Boston, 1946
Chi. Bears, 1947
3 Chi. Bears, 1945
Cleveland, 1945

Most Field Goals Attempted, Game
9 St. Louis vs. Pittsburgh, Sept. 24, 1967
8 Pittsburgh vs. St. Louis, Dec. 2, 1962
Detroit vs. Minnesota, Nov. 13, 1966
N.Y. Jets vs. Buffalo, Nov. 3, 1968
7 By many teams

Most Field Goals Attempted, Both Teams, Game
11 St. Louis (6) vs. Pittsburgh (5), Nov. 13, 1966
Washington (6) vs. Chicago (5), Nov. 14, 1971
Green Bay (6) vs. Detroit (5), Sept. 29, 1974
Washington (6) vs. N.Y. Giants (5), Nov. 14, 1976
10 Denver (5) vs. Boston (5), Nov. 11, 1962
Boston (7) vs. San Diego (3), Sept. 20, 1964
Buffalo (7) vs. Houston (3), Dec. 5, 1965
St. Louis (7) vs. Atlanta (3), Dec. 11, 1966
Boston (7) vs. Buffalo (3), Sept. 24, 1967
Detroit (7) vs. Minnesota (3), Sept. 20, 1971
Washington (7) vs. Houston (3), Oct. 10, 1971
Green Bay (5) vs. St. Louis (5), Dec. 5, 1971
Kansas City (7) vs. Buffalo (3), Dec. 19, 1971
Kansas City (5) vs. San Diego (5), Oct. 29, 1972
Minnesota (6) vs. Chicago (4), Sept. 23, 1973
Cleveland (7) vs. Denver (3), Oct. 19, 1975
Cleveland (5) vs. Denver (5), Oct. 5, 1980
9 In many games

Most Field Goals, Season
35 N.Y. Giants, 1983
L.A. Raiders, 1993
34 N.Y. Jets, 1968
Kansas City, 1990
Detroit, 1993
Minnesota, 1994
San Diego, 1994
Pittsburgh, 1995
33 Green Bay, 1972
Washington, 1983
Pittsburgh, 1985
New Orleans, 1987
Miami, 1991
Atlanta, 1995

Fewest Field Goals, Season (Since 1932)
0 Boston, 1932, 1935
Chi. Cardinals, 1932, 1945
Green Bay, 1932, 1944
N.Y. Giants, 1932
Brooklyn, 1944
Card-Pitt, 1944
Chi. Bears, 1944, 1947
Boston, 1946
Baltimore, 1950
Dallas, 1952

Most Field Goals, Game
7 St. Louis vs. Pittsburgh, Sept. 24, 1967
Minnesota vs. L.A. Rams, Nov. 5, 1989 (OT)
6 Boston vs. Denver, Oct. 4, 1964
Detroit vs. Minnesota, Nov. 13, 1966
N.Y. Jets vs. Buffalo, Nov. 3, 1968
Philadelphia vs. Houston, Nov. 12, 1972
N.Y. Jets vs. New Orleans, Dec. 3, 1972
St. Louis vs. Atlanta, Dec. 9, 1973
N.Y. Giants vs. Seattle, Oct. 18, 1981
San Francisco vs. New Orleans, Oct. 16, 1983
Pittsburgh vs. Denver, Oct. 23, 1988
San Diego vs. Seattle, Sept. 5, 1993
San Diego vs. Houston, Sept. 19, 1993
Cincinnati vs. Seattle, Nov. 6, 1994
Atlanta vs. New Orleans, Nov. 13, 1994
5 By many teams

Most Field Goals, Both Teams, Game
8 Cleveland (4) vs. St. Louis (4), Sept. 20, 1964
Chicago (5) vs. Philadelphia (3), Oct. 20, 1968
Washington (5) vs. Chicago (3), Nov. 14, 1971
Kansas City (5) vs. Buffalo (3), Dec. 19, 1971
Detroit (4) vs. Green Bay (4), Sept. 29, 1974
Cleveland (5) vs. Denver (3), Oct. 19, 1975
New England (4) vs. San Diego (4), Nov. 9, 1975
San Francisco (6) vs. New Orleans (2), Oct. 16, 1983
Seattle (5) vs. L.A. Raiders (3), Dec. 18, 1988
Atlanta (6) vs. New Orleans (2), Nov. 13, 1994
7 In many games

Most Consecutive Games Scoring Field Goals
31 Minnesota, 1968-70
28 Washington, 1988-90
22 San Francisco, 1988-89

SAFETIES

Most Safeties, Season
4 Cleveland, 1927
Detroit, 1962
3 By many teams

Most Safeties, Game
3 L.A. Rams vs. N.Y. Giants, Sept. 30, 1984
2 N.Y. Giants vs. Pottsville, Oct. 30, 1927
Chi. Bears vs. Pottsville, Nov. 13, 1927
Detroit vs. Brooklyn, Dec. 1, 1935
N.Y. Giants vs. Pittsburgh, Sept. 17, 1950
N.Y. Giants vs. Washington, Nov. 5, 1961
Chicago vs. Pittsburgh, Nov. 9, 1969
Dallas vs. Philadelphia, Nov. 19, 1972
Los Angeles vs. Green Bay, Oct. 21, 1973
Oakland vs. San Diego, Oct. 26, 1975
Denver vs. Seattle, Jan. 2, 1983
New Orleans vs. Cleveland, Sept. 13, 1987
Buffalo vs. Denver, Nov. 8, 1987

Most Safeties, Both Teams, Game
3 L.A. Rams (3) vs. N.Y. Giants (0), Sept. 30, 1984
2 Chi. Cardinals (1) vs. Frankford (1), Nov. 19, 1927
Chi. Cardinals (1) vs. Cincinnati (1), Nov. 12, 1933
Chi. Bears (1) vs. San Francisco (1), Oct. 19, 1952
Cincinnati (1) vs. Los Angeles (1), Oct. 22, 1972
Chi. Bears (1) vs. San Francisco (1), Sept. 19, 1976
Baltimore (1) vs. Miami (1), Oct. 29, 1978
Atlanta (1) vs. Detroit (1), Oct. 5, 1980
Houston (1) vs. Philadelphia (1), Oct. 2, 1988
Cleveland (1) vs. Seattle (1), Nov. 14, 1993
Arizona (1) vs. Houston (1), Dec. 4, 1994
(Also see previous record)

FIRST DOWNS

Most Seasons Leading League
9 Chi. Bears, 1935, 1939, 1941, 1943, 1945, 1947-49, 1955
7 San Diego, 1965, 1969, 1980-83, 1985
6 L.A. Rams, 1946, 1950-51, 1954, 1957, 1973

Most Consecutive Seasons Leading League
4 San Diego, 1980-83
3 Chi. Bears, 1947-49
2 By many teams

Most First Downs, Season
387 Miami, 1984
380 San Diego, 1985
379 San Diego, 1981

Fewest First Downs, Season
51 Cincinnati, 1933
64 Pittsburgh, 1935

67 Philadelphia, 1937

Most First Downs, Game

39 N.Y. Jets vs. Miami, Nov. 27, 1988
Washington vs. Detroit, Nov. 4, 1990 (OT)
38 Los Angeles vs. N.Y. Giants, Nov. 13, 1966
37 Green Bay vs. Philadelphia, Nov. 11, 1962

Fewest First Downs, Game

0 N.Y. Giants vs. Green Bay, Oct. 1, 1933
Pittsburgh vs. Boston, Oct. 29, 1933
Philadelphia vs. Detroit, Sept. 20, 1935
N.Y. Giants vs. Washington, Sept. 27, 1942
Denver vs. Houston, Sept. 3, 1966

Most First Downs, Both Teams, Game

62 San Diego (32) vs. Seattle (30), Sept. 15, 1985
59 Miami (31) vs. Buffalo (28), Oct. 9, 1983 (OT)
Seattle (33) vs. Kansas City (26), Nov. 27, 1983 (OT)
N.Y. Jets (32) vs. Miami (27), Sept. 21, 1986 (OT)
N.Y. Jets (39) vs. Miami (20), Nov. 27, 1988
58 Los Angeles (30) vs. Chi. Bears (28), Oct. 24, 1954
Denver (34) vs. Kansas City (24), Nov. 18, 1974
Atlanta (35) vs. New Orleans (23), Sept. 2, 1979 (OT)
Pittsburgh (36) vs. Cleveland (22), Nov. 25, 1979 (OT)
San Diego (34) vs. Miami (24), Nov. 18, 1984 (OT)
Cincinnati (32) vs. San Diego (26), Sept. 22, 1985

Fewest First Downs, Both Teams, Game

7 Chi. Cardinals (2) vs. Detroit (5), Sept. 15, 1940
9 Pittsburgh (1) vs. Boston (8), Oct. 27, 1935
Boston (4) vs. Brooklyn (5), Nov. 24, 1935
N.Y. Giants (3) vs. Detroit (6), Nov. 7, 1943
Pittsburgh (4) vs. Chi. Cardinals (5), Nov. 11, 1945
N.Y. Bulldogs (1) vs. Philadelphia (8), Sept. 22, 1949
10 N.Y. Giants (4) vs. Washington (6), Dec. 11, 1960

Most First Downs, Rushing, Season

181 New England, 1978
177 Los Angeles, 1973
176 Chicago, 1985

Fewest First Downs, Rushing, Season

36 Cleveland, 1942
Boston, 1944
39 Brooklyn, 1943
40 Philadelphia, 1940
Detroit, 1945

Most First Downs, Rushing, Game

25 Philadelphia vs. Washington, Dec. 2, 1951
23 St. Louis vs. New Orleans, Oct. 5, 1980
21 Cleveland vs. Philadelphia, Dec. 13, 1959
Green Bay vs. Philadelphia, Nov. 11, 1962
Los Angeles vs. New Orleans, Nov. 25, 1973
Pittsburgh vs. Kansas City, Nov. 7, 1976
New England vs. Denver, Nov. 28, 1976
Oakland vs. Green Bay, Sept. 17, 1978

Fewest First Downs, Rushing, Game

0 By many teams. Last time: New Orleans vs. N.Y. Jets, Dec. 24, 1995

Most First Downs, Rushing, Both Teams, Game

36 Philadelphia (25) vs. Washington (11), Dec. 2, 1951
31 Detroit (18) vs. Washington (13), Sept. 30, 1951
30 Los Angeles (17) vs. Minnesota (13), Nov. 5, 1961
New Orleans (17) vs. Green Bay (13), Sept. 9, 1979
New Orleans (16) vs. San Francisco (14), Nov. 11, 1979
New England (16) vs. Kansas City (14), Oct. 4, 1981

Fewest First Downs, Rushing, Both Teams, Game

2 Houston (0) vs. Denver (2), Dec. 2, 1962
N.Y. Jets, (1) vs. St. Louis (1), Dec. 3, 1995
3 Philadelphia (1) vs. Pittsburgh (2), Oct. 27, 1957
Boston (1) vs. Buffalo (2), Nov. 15, 1964
Los Angeles (0) vs. San Francisco (3), Dec. 6, 1964
Pittsburgh (1) vs. St. Louis (2), Nov. 13, 1966
Seattle (1) vs. New Orleans (2), Sept. 1, 1991
New Orleans (0) vs. N.Y. Jets (3), Dec. 24, 1995
4 In many games

Most First Downs, Passing, Season

259 San Diego, 1985
251 Houston, 1990
250 Miami, 1986

Fewest First Downs, Passing, Season

18 Pittsburgh, 1941
23 Brooklyn, 1942
N.Y. Giants, 1944
24 N.Y. Giants, 1943

Most First Downs, Passing, Game

29 N.Y. Giants vs. Cincinnati, Oct. 13, 1985
27 San Diego vs. Seattle, Sept. 15, 1985
26 Miami vs. Cleveland, Dec. 12, 1988

Fewest First Downs, Passing, Game

0 By many teams. Last time: Houston vs. Kansas City, Oct. 9, 1988

Most First Downs, Passing, Both Teams, Game

43 San Diego (23) vs. Cincinnati (20), Dec. 20, 1982
Miami (24) vs. N.Y. Jets (19), Sept. 21, 1986 (OT)
42 San Francisco (22) vs. San Diego (20), Dec. 11, 1982
41 San Diego (27) vs. Seattle (14), Sept. 15, 1985
Miami (26) vs. Cleveland (15), Dec. 12, 1988

Fewest First Downs, Passing, Both Teams, Game

0 Brooklyn vs. Pittsburgh, Nov. 29, 1942
1 Green Bay (0) vs. Cleveland (1), Sept. 21, 1941
Pittsburgh (0) vs. Brooklyn (1), Oct. 11, 1942
N.Y. Giants (0) vs. Detroit (1), Nov. 7, 1943
Pittsburgh (0) vs. Chi. Cardinals (1), Nov. 11, 1945
N.Y. Bulldogs (0) vs. Philadelphia (1), Sept. 22, 1949
Chicago (0) vs. Buffalo (1), Oct. 7, 1979
2 In many games

Most First Downs, Penalty, Season

43 Denver, 1994
42 Chicago, 1987
41 Denver, 1986

Fewest First Downs, Penalty, Season

2 Brooklyn, 1940
4 Chi. Cardinals, 1940
N.Y. Giants, 1942, 1944
Washington, 1944
Cleveland, 1952
Kansas City, 1969
5 Brooklyn, 1939
Chi. Bears, 1939
Detroit, 1953
Los Angeles, 1953
Houston, 1982

Most First Downs, Penalty, Game

11 Denver vs. Houston, Oct. 6, 1985
9 Chi. Bears vs. Cleveland, Nov. 25, 1951
Baltimore vs. Pittsburgh, Oct. 30, 1977
N.Y. Jets vs. Houston, Sept. 18, 1988
8 Philadelphia vs. Detroit, Dec. 2, 1979
Cincinnati vs. N.Y. Jets, Oct. 6, 1985
Buffalo vs. Houston, Sept. 20, 1987
Houston vs. Atlanta, Sept. 9, 1990
Kansas City vs. L.A. Raiders, Oct. 3, 1993

Most First Downs, Penalty, Both Teams, Game

11 Chi. Bears (9) vs. Cleveland (2), Nov. 25, 1951
Cincinnati (8) vs. N.Y. Jets (3), Oct. 6, 1985
Denver (11) vs. Houston (0), Oct. 6, 1985
Detroit (6) vs. Dallas (5), Nov. 8, 1987
N.Y. Jets (9) vs. Houston (2), Sept. 18, 1988
Kansas City (8) vs. L.A. Raiders (3), Oct. 3, 1993
10 In many games

NET YARDS GAINED RUSHING AND PASSING

Most Seasons Leading League

12 Chi. Bears, 1932, 1934-35, 1939, 1941-44, 1947, 1949, 1955-56
7 San Diego, 1963, 1965, 1980-83, 1985
6 L.A. Rams, 1946, 1950-51, 1954, 1957, 1973
Baltimore, 1958-60, 1964, 1967, 1976
Dall. Cowboys, 1966, 1968-69, 1971, 1974, 1977

Most Consecutive Seasons Leading League

4 Chi. Bears, 1941-44
San Diego, 1980-83
3 Baltimore, 1958-60
Houston, 1960-62
Oakland, 1968-70
2 By many teams

Most Yards Gained, Season

6,936 Miami, 1984
6,744 San Diego, 1981
6,535 San Diego, 1985

Fewest Yards Gained, Season

1,150 Cincinnati, 1933
1,443 Chi. Cardinals, 1934
1,486 Chi. Cardinals, 1933

Most Yards Gained, Game

735 Los Angeles vs. N.Y. Yanks, Sept. 28, 1951
683 Pittsburgh vs. Chi. Cardinals, Dec. 13, 1958
682 Chi. Bears vs. N.Y. Giants, Nov. 14, 1943

Fewest Yards Gained, Game

–7 Seattle vs. Los Angeles, Nov. 4, 1979
–5 Denver vs. Oakland, Sept. 10, 1967
14 Chi. Cardinals vs. Detroit, Sept. 15, 1940

ALL-TIME RECORDS

Most Yards Gained, Both Teams, Game
1,133 Los Angeles (636) vs. N.Y. Yanks (497), Nov. 19, 1950
1,102 San Diego (661) vs. Cincinnati (441), Dec. 20, 1982
1,087 St. Louis (589) vs. Philadelphia (498), Dec. 16, 1962

Fewest Yards Gained, Both Teams, Game
30 Chi. Cardinals (14) vs. Detroit (16), Sept. 15, 1940
136 Chi. Cardinals (50) vs. Green Bay (86), Nov. 18, 1934
154 N.Y. Giants (51) vs. Washington (103), Dec. 11, 1960

Most Consecutive Games, 400 or More Yards Gained
11 San Diego, 1982-83
6 Houston, 1961-62
San Diego, 1981
San Francisco, 1987
5 Chi. Bears, 1947
Philadelphia, 1953
Chi. Bears, 1955
Oakland, 1968
New England, 1981
Cincinnati, 1986
San Francisco, 1994

Most Consecutive Games, 300 or More Yards Gained
29 Los Angeles, 1949-51
26 Miami, 1983-85
25 Miami, 1993-95

RUSHING

Most Seasons Leading League
16 Chi. Bears, 1932, 1934-35, 1939-42, 1951, 1955-56, 1968, 1977, 1983-86
7 Buffalo, 1962, 1964, 1973, 1975, 1982, 1991-92
6 Cleveland, 1958-59, 1963, 1965-67

Most Consecutive Seasons Leading League
4 Chi. Bears, 1939-42
Chi. Bears, 1983-86
3 Detroit, 1936-38
San Francisco, 1952-54
Cleveland, 1965-67
2 By many teams

ATTEMPTS

Most Rushing Attempts, Season
681 Oakland, 1977
674 Chicago, 1984
671 New England, 1978

Fewest Rushing Attempts, Season
211 Philadelphia, 1982
219 San Francisco, 1982
225 Houston, 1982

Most Rushing Attempts, Game
72 Chi. Bears vs. Brooklyn, Oct. 20, 1935
70 Chi. Cardinals vs. Green Bay, Dec. 5, 1948
69 Chi. Cardinals vs. Green Bay, Dec. 6, 1936
Kansas City vs. Cincinnati, Sept. 3, 1978

Fewest Rushing Attempts, Game
6 Chi. Cardinals vs. Boston, Oct. 29, 1933
7 Oakland vs. Buffalo, Oct. 15, 1963
Houston vs. N.Y. Giants, Dec. 8, 1985
Seattle vs. L.A. Raiders, Nov. 17, 1991
Green Bay vs. Miami, Sept. 11, 1994
8 Denver vs. Oakland, Dec. 17, 1960
Buffalo vs. St. Louis, Sept. 9, 1984
Detroit vs. San Francisco, Oct. 20, 1991
Atlanta vs. Detroit, Sept. 5, 1993

Most Rushing Attempts, Both Teams, Game
108 Chi. Cardinals (70) vs. Green Bay (38), Dec. 5, 1948
105 Oakland (62) vs. Atlanta (43), Nov. 30, 1975 (OT)
104 Chi. Bears (64) vs. Pittsburgh (40), Oct. 18, 1936

Fewest Rushing Attempts, Both Teams, Game
34 Atlanta (12) vs. Houston (22), Dec. 5, 1993
Atlanta (15) vs. San Francisco (19), Dec. 24, 1995
35 Seattle (15) vs. New Orleans (20), Sept. 1, 1991
36 Houston (15) vs. N.Y. Jets (21), Oct. 13, 1991

YARDS GAINED

Most Yards Gained Rushing, Season
3,165 New England, 1978
3,088 Buffalo, 1973
2,986 Kansas City, 1978

Fewest Yards Gained Rushing, Season
298 Philadelphia, 1940
467 Detroit, 1946
471 Boston, 1944

Most Yards Gained Rushing, Game
426 Detroit vs. Pittsburgh, Nov. 4, 1934
423 N.Y. Giants vs. Baltimore, Nov. 19, 1950
420 Boston vs. N.Y. Giants, Oct. 8, 1933

Fewest Yards Gained Rushing, Game
–53 Detroit vs. Chi. Cardinals, Oct. 17, 1943
–36 Philadelphia vs. Chi. Bears, Nov. 19, 1939
–33 Phil-Pitt vs. Brooklyn, Oct. 2, 1943

Most Yards Gained Rushing, Both Teams, Game
595 Los Angeles (371) vs. N.Y. Yanks (224), Nov. 18, 1951
574 Chi. Bears (396) vs. Pittsburgh (178), Oct. 10, 1934
558 Boston (420) vs. N.Y. Giants (138), Oct. 8, 1933

Fewest Yards Gained Rushing, Both Teams, Game
–15 Detroit (–53) vs. Chi. Cardinals (38), Oct. 17, 1943
4 Detroit (–10) vs. Chi. Cardinals (14), Sept. 15, 1940
62 L.A. Rams (15) vs. San Francisco (47), Dec. 6, 1964

AVERAGE GAIN

Highest Average Gain, Rushing, Season
5.74 Cleveland, 1963
5.65 San Francisco, 1954
5.56 San Diego, 1963

Lowest Average Gain, Rushing, Season
0.94 Philadelphia, 1940
1.45 Boston, 1944
1.55 Pittsburgh, 1935

TOUCHDOWNS

Most Touchdowns, Rushing, Season
36 Green Bay, 1962
33 Pittsburgh, 1976
30 Chi. Bears, 1941
New England, 1978
Washington, 1983

Fewest Touchdowns, Rushing, Season
1 Brooklyn, 1934
2 Chi. Cardinals, 1933
Cincinnati, 1933
Pittsburgh, 1934
Philadelphia, 1935
Philadelphia, 1936
Philadelphia, 1937
Philadelphia, 1938
Pittsburgh, 1940
Philadelphia, 1972
N.Y. Jets, 1995
3 By many teams

Most Touchdowns, Rushing, Game
7 Los Angeles vs. Atlanta, Dec. 4, 1976
6 By many teams

Most Touchdowns, Rushing, Both Teams, Game
8 Los Angeles (6) vs. N.Y. Yanks (2), Nov. 18, 1951
Chi. Bears (5) vs. Green Bay (3), Nov. 6, 1955
Cleveland (6) vs. Los Angeles (2), Nov. 24, 1957
7 In many games

PASSING

ATTEMPTS

Most Passes Attempted, Season
709 Minnesota, 1981
699 New England, 1994
686 New England, 1995

Fewest Passes Attempted, Season
102 Cincinnati, 1933
106 Boston, 1933
120 Detroit, 1937

Most Passes Attempted, Game
70 New England vs. Minnesota, Nov. 13, 1994
68 Houston vs. Buffalo, Nov 1, 1964
66 Atlanta vs. Detroit, Dec. 24, 1989

Fewest Passes Attempted, Game
0 Green Bay vs. Portsmouth, Oct. 8, 1933
Detroit vs. Cleveland, Sept. 10, 1937
Pittsburgh vs. Brooklyn, Nov. 16, 1941
Pittsburgh vs. Los Angeles, Nov. 13, 1949
Cleveland vs. Philadelphia, Dec. 3, 1950

Most Passes Attempted, Both Teams, Game
112 New England (70) vs. Minnesota (42), Nov. 13, 1994
104 Miami (55) vs. N.Y. Jets (49), Oct. 18, 1987 (OT)
102 San Francisco (57) vs. Atlanta (45), Oct. 6, 1985

Fewest Passes Attempted, Both Teams, Game
4 Chi. Cardinals (1) vs. Detroit (3), Nov. 3, 1935
Detroit (0) vs. Cleveland (4), Sept. 10, 1937

6 Chi. Cardinals (2) vs. Detroit (4), Sept. 15, 1940
8 Brooklyn (2) vs. Philadelphia (6), Oct. 1, 1939

COMPLETIONS

Most Passes Completed, Season
432 San Francisco, 1995
411 Houston, 1991
409 Minnesota, 1994

Fewest Passes Completed, Season
25 Cincinnati, 1933
33 Boston, 1933
34 Chi. Cardinals, 1934
Detroit, 1934

Most Passes Completed, Game
45 New England vs. Minnesota, Nov. 13, 1994 (OT)
42 N.Y. Jets vs. San Francisco, Sept. 21, 1980
41 Houston vs. Dallas, Nov. 10, 1991 (OT)

Fewest Passes Completed, Game
0 By many teams. Last time: Buffalo vs. N.Y. Jets, Sept. 29, 1974

Most Passes Completed, Both Teams, Game
71 New England (45) vs. Minnesota (26), Nov. 13, 1994
68 San Francisco (37) vs. Atlanta (31), Oct. 6, 1985
66 Cincinnati (40) vs. San Diego (26), Dec. 20, 1982

Fewest Passes Completed, Both Teams, Game
1 Chi. Cardinals (0) vs. Philadelphia (1), Nov. 8, 1936
Detroit (0) vs. Cleveland (1), Sept. 10, 1937
Chi. Cardinals (0) vs. Detroit (1), Sept. 15, 1940
Brooklyn (0) vs. Pittsburgh (1), Nov. 29, 1942
2 Chi. Cardinals (0) vs. Detroit (2), Nov. 3, 1935
Buffalo (0) vs. N.Y. Jets (2), Sept. 29, 1974
Chi. Cardinals (0) vs. Green Bay (2), Nov. 18, 1934
3 In seven games

YARDS GAINED

Most Seasons Leading League, Passing Yardage
10 San Diego, 1965, 1968, 1971, 1978-83, 1985
8 Chi. Bears, 1932, 1939, 1941, 1943, 1945, 1949, 1954, 1964
Washington, 1938, 1940, 1944, 1947-48, 1967, 1974, 1989
7 Houston, 1960-61, 1963-64, 1990-92

Most Consecutive Seasons Leading League, Passing Yardage
6 San Diego, 1978-83
4 Green Bay, 1934-37
3 Miami, 1986-88
Houston, 1990-92

Most Yards Gained, Passing, Season
5,018 Miami, 1984
4,870 San Diego, 1985
4,805 Houston, 1990

Fewest Yards Gained, Passing, Season
302 Chi. Cardinals, 1934
357 Cincinnati, 1933
459 Boston, 1934

Most Yards Gained, Passing, Game
554 Los Angeles vs. N.Y. Yanks, Sept. 28, 1951
530 Minnesota vs. Baltimore, Sept. 28, 1969
521 Miami vs. N.Y. Jets, Oct. 23, 1988

Fewest Yards Gained, Passing, Game
–53 Denver vs. Oakland, Sept. 10, 1967
–52 Cincinnati vs. Houston, Oct. 31, 1971
–39 Atlanta vs. San Francisco, Oct. 23, 1976

Most Yards Gained, Passing, Both Teams, Game
884 N.Y. Jets (449) vs. Miami (435), Sept. 21, 1986 (OT)
883 San Diego (486) vs. Cincinnati (397), Dec. 20, 1982
874 Miami (456) vs. New England (418), Sept. 4, 1994

Fewest Yards Gained, Passing, Both Teams, Game
–11 Green Bay (–10) vs. Dallas (–1), Oct. 24, 1965
1 Chi. Cardinals (0) vs. Philadelphia (1), Nov. 8, 1936
7 Brooklyn (0) vs. Pittsburgh (7), Nov. 29, 1942

TIMES SACKED

Most Seasons Leading League, Fewest Times Sacked
10 Miami, 1973, 1982-90
4 San Diego, 1963-64, 1967-68
San Francisco, 1964-65, 1970-71
N.Y. Jets, 1965-66, 1968, 1993
3 Houston, 1961-62, 1978
St. Louis, 1974-76
Washington, 1966-67, 1991

Most Consecutive Seasons Leading League, Fewest Times Sacked
9 Miami, 1982-90
3 St. Louis, 1974-76
2 By many teams

Most Times Sacked, Season
104 Philadelphia, 1986
72 Philadelphia, 1987
70 Atlanta, 1968

Fewest Times Sacked, Season
7 Miami, 1988
8 San Francisco, 1970
St. Louis, 1975
9 N.Y. Jets, 1966
Washington, 1991

Most Times Sacked, Game
12 Pittsburgh vs. Dallas, Nov. 20, 1966
Baltimore vs. St. Louis, Oct. 26, 1980
Detroit vs. Chicago, Dec. 16, 1984
Houston vs. Dallas, Sept. 29, 1985
11 St. Louis vs. N.Y. Giants, Nov. 1, 1964
Los Angeles vs. Baltimore, Nov. 22, 1964
Denver vs. Buffalo, Dec. 13, 1964
Green Bay vs. Detroit, Nov. 7, 1965
Buffalo vs. Oakland, Oct. 15, 1967
Denver vs. Oakland, Nov. 5, 1967
Atlanta vs. St. Louis, Nov. 24, 1968
Detroit vs. Dallas, Oct. 6, 1975
Philadelphia vs. St. Louis, Dec. 18, 1983
Cleveland vs. Kansas City, Sept. 30, 1984
Minnesota vs. Chicago, Oct. 28, 1984
Atlanta vs. Cleveland, Nov. 18, 1984
Dallas vs. San Diego, Nov. 16, 1986
Philadelphia vs. Detroit, Nov. 16, 1986
Philadelphia vs. L.A. Raiders, Nov. 30, 1986 (OT)
L.A. Raiders vs. Seattle, Dec. 8, 1986
N.Y. Jets vs. Dallas, Oct. 4, 1987
Philadelphia vs. Chicago, Oct. 4, 1987
Dallas vs. Philadelphia, Sept. 15, 1991
Cleveland vs. Indianapolis, Sept. 6, 1992
10 By many teams

Most Times Sacked, Both Teams, Game
18 Green Bay (10) vs. San Diego (8), Sept. 24, 1978
17 Buffalo (10) vs. N.Y. Titans (7), Nov. 23, 1961
Pittsburgh (12) vs. Dallas (5), Nov. 20, 1966
Atlanta (9) vs. Philadelphia (8), Dec. 16, 1984
Philadelphia (11) vs. L.A. Raiders (6), Nov. 30, 1986 (OT)
16 Los Angeles (11) vs. Baltimore (5), Nov. 22, 1964
Buffalo (11) vs. Oakland (5), Oct. 15, 1967

COMPLETION PERCENTAGE

Most Seasons Leading League, Completion Percentage
12 San Francisco, 1952, 1957-58, 1965, 1981, 1983, 1987, 1989, 1992-95
11 Washington, 1937, 1939-40, 1942-45, 1947-48, 1969-70
7 Green Bay, 1936, 1941, 1961-62, 1964, 1966, 1968

Most Consecutive Seasons Leading League, Completion Percentage
4 Washington, 1942-45
Kansas City, 1966-69
San Francisco, 1992-95
3 Cleveland, 1953-55
2 By many teams

Highest Completion Percentage, Season
70.65 Cincinnati, 1982 (310-219)
70.25 San Francisco, 1994 (511-359)
70.19 San Francisco, 1989 (483-339)

Lowest Completion Percentage, Season
22.9 Philadelphia, 1936 (170-39)
24.5 Cincinnati, 1933 (102-25)
25.0 Pittsburgh, 1941 (168-42)

TOUCHDOWNS

Most Touchdowns, Passing, Season
49 Miami, 1984
48 Houston, 1961
46 Miami, 1986

Fewest Touchdowns, Passing, Season
0 Cincinnati, 1933
Pittsburgh, 1945
1 Boston, 1932
Boston, 1933
Chi. Cardinals, 1934
Cincinnati/St. Louis, 1934
Detroit, 1942
2 Chi. Cardinals, 1932
Stapleton, 1932
Chi. Cardinals, 1935
Brooklyn, 1936

Pittsburgh, 1942

Most Touchdowns, Passing, Game

7 Chi. Bears vs. N.Y. Giants, Nov. 14, 1943
Philadelphia vs. Washington, Oct. 17, 1954
Houston vs. N.Y. Titans, Nov. 19, 1961
Houston vs. N.Y. Titans, Oct. 14, 1962
N.Y. Giants vs. Washington, Oct. 28, 1962
Minnesota vs. Baltimore, Sept. 28, 1969
San Diego vs. Oakland, Nov. 22, 1981
6 By many teams.

Most Touchdowns, Passing, Both Teams, Game

12 New Orleans (6) vs. St. Louis (6), Nov. 2, 1969
11 N.Y. Giants (7) vs. Washington (4), Oct. 28, 1962
Oakland (6) vs. Houston (5), Dec. 22, 1963
10 San Diego (5) vs. Seattle (5), Sept. 15, 1985
Miami (6) vs. N.Y. Jets (4), Sept. 21, 1986 (OT)

PASSES HAD INTERCEPTED

Most Passes Had Intercepted, Season

48 Houston, 1962
45 Denver, 1961
41 Card-Pitt, 1944

Fewest Passes Had Intercepted, Season

5 Cleveland, 1960
Green Bay, 1966
Kansas City, 1990
N.Y. Giants, 1990
6 Green Bay, 1964
St. Louis, 1982
Dallas, 1993
7 Los Angeles, 1969

Most Passes Had Intercepted, Game

9 Detroit vs. Green Bay, Oct. 24, 1943
Pittsburgh vs. Philadelphia, Dec. 12, 1965
8 Green Bay vs. N.Y. Giants, Nov. 21, 1948
Chi. Cardinals vs. Philadelphia, Sept. 24, 1950
N.Y. Yanks vs. N.Y. Giants, Dec. 16, 1951
Denver vs. Houston, Dec. 2, 1962
Chi. Bears vs. Detroit, Sept. 22, 1968
Baltimore vs. N.Y. Jets, Sept. 23, 1973
7 By many teams. Last time: Green Bay vs. New Orleans, Sept. 14, 1986

Most Passes Had Intercepted, Both Teams, Game

13 Denver (8) vs. Houston (5), Dec. 2, 1962
11 Philadelphia (7) vs. Boston (4), Nov. 3, 1935
Boston (6) vs. Pittsburgh (5), Dec. 1, 1935
Cleveland (7) vs. Green Bay (4), Oct. 30, 1938
Green Bay (7) vs. Detroit (4), Oct. 20, 1940
Detroit (7) vs. Chi. Bears (4), Nov. 22, 1942
Detroit (7) vs. Cleveland (4), Nov. 26, 1944
Chi. Cardinals (8) vs. Philadelphia (3), Sept. 24, 1950
Washington (7) vs. N.Y. Giants (4), Dec. 8, 1963
Pittsburgh (9) vs. Philadelphia (2), Dec 12, 1965
10 In many games

PUNTING

Most Seasons Leading League (Average Distance)

7 Denver, 1962-64, 1966-67, 1982, 1988
6 Washington, 1940-43, 1945, 1958
Kansas City, 1968, 1971-73, 1979, 1984
5 L.A. Rams, 1946, 1949, 1955-56, 1994

Most Consecutive Seasons Leading League (Average Distance)

4 Washington, 1940-43
3 Cleveland, 1950-52
Denver, 1962-64
Kansas City, 1971-73

Most Punts, Season

114 Chicago, 1981
113 Boston, 1934
Brooklyn, 1934
112 Boston, 1935

Fewest Punts, Season

23 San Diego, 1982
31 Cincinnati, 1982
32 Chi. Bears, 1941

Most Punts, Game

17 Chi. Bears vs. Green Bay, Oct. 22, 1933
Cincinnati vs. Pittsburgh, Oct. 22, 1933
16 Cincinnati vs. Portsmouth, Sept. 17, 1933
Chi. Cardinals vs. Chi. Bears, Nov. 30, 1933
Chi. Cardinals vs. Detroit, Sept. 15, 1940
15 N.Y. Giants vs. Chi. Bears, Nov. 17, 1935
Philadelphia vs. N.Y. Giants, Dec. 6, 1987 (OT)

Fewest Punts, Game

0 By many teams. Last time: Minnesota vs. New Orleans, Nov. 19, 1995

Most Punts, Both Teams, Game

31 Chi. Bears (17) vs. Green Bay (14), Oct. 22, 1933
Cincinnati (17), vs. Pittsburgh (14), Oct. 22, 1933
29 Chi. Cardinals (15) vs. Cincinnati (14), Nov. 12, 1933
Chi. Cardinals (16) vs. Chi. Bears (13), Nov. 30, 1933
Chi. Cardinals (16) vs. Detroit (13), Sept. 15, 1940
28 Philadelphia (14) vs. Washington (14), Nov. 5, 1939

Fewest Punts, Both Teams, Game

0 Buffalo vs. San Francisco, Sept. 13, 1992
1 Baltimore (0) vs. Cleveland (1), Nov. 1, 1959
Dall. Cowboys (0) vs. Cleveland (1), Dec. 3, 1961
Chicago (0) vs. Detroit (1), Oct. 1, 1972
San Francisco (0) vs. N.Y. Giants (1), Oct. 15, 1972
Green Bay (0) vs. Buffalo (1), Dec. 5, 1982
Miami (0) vs. Buffalo (1), Oct. 12, 1986
Green Bay (0) vs. Chicago (1), Dec. 17, 1989
2 In many games

AVERAGE YARDAGE

Highest Average Distance, Punting, Season

47.6 Detroit, 1961 (56-2,664)
47.0 Pittsburgh, 1961 (73-3,431)
46.9 Pittsburgh, 1953 (80-3,752)

Lowest Average Distance, Punting, Season

32.7 Card-Pitt, 1944 (60-1,964)
33.8 Cincinnati, 1986 (59-1,996)
33.9 Detroit, 1969 (74-2,510)

PUNT RETURNS

Most Seasons Leading League (Average Return)

9 Detroit, 1943-45, 1951-52, 1962, 1966, 1969, 1991
7 Chi. Cardinals/St. Louis, 1948-49, 1955-56, 1959, 1986-87
5 Cleveland, 1958, 1960, 1964-65, 1967
Green Bay, 1950, 1953-54, 1961, 1972
Dall. Texans/Kansas City, 1960, 1968, 1970, 1979-80
Washington, 1957, 1963, 1976, 1994-95

Most Consecutive Seasons Leading League (Average Return)

3 Detroit, 1943-45
2 By many teams

Most Punt Returns, Season

71 Pittsburgh, 1976
Tampa Bay, 1979
L.A. Raiders, 1985
67 Pittsburgh, 1974
Los Angeles, 1978
L.A. Raiders, 1984
65 San Francisco, 1976

Fewest Punt Returns, Season

12 Baltimore, 1981
San Diego, 1982
14 Los Angeles, 1961
Philadelphia, 1962
Baltimore, 1982
15 Houston, 1960
Washington, 1960
Oakland, 1961
N.Y. Giants, 1969
Philadelphia, 1973
Kansas City, 1982

Most Punt Returns, Game

12 Philadelphia vs. Cleveland, Dec. 3, 1950
11 Chi. Bears vs. Chi. Cardinals, Oct. 8, 1950
Washington vs. Tampa Bay, Oct. 9, 1977
10 Philadelphia vs. N.Y. Giants, Nov. 26, 1950
Philadelphia vs. Tampa Bay, Sept. 18, 1977
Pittsburgh vs. Buffalo, Dec. 16, 1979
Washington vs. New Orleans, Dec. 26, 1982
Philadelphia vs. Seattle, Dec. 13, 1992 (OT)
New England vs. Pittsburgh, Dec. 5, 1993

Most Punt Returns, Both Teams, Game

17 Philadelphia (12) vs. Cleveland (5), Dec. 3, 1950
16 N.Y. Giants (9) vs. Philadelphia (7), Dec. 12, 1954
Washington (11) vs. Tampa Bay (5), Oct. 9, 1977
15 Detroit (8) vs. Cleveland (7), Sept. 27, 1942
Los Angeles (8) vs. Baltimore (7), Nov. 27, 1966
Pittsburgh (8) vs. Houston (7), Dec. 1, 1974
Philadelphia (10) vs. Tampa Bay (5), Sept. 18, 1977
Baltimore (9) vs. Kansas City (6), Sept. 2, 1979
Washington (10) vs. New Orleans (5), Dec. 26, 1982
L.A. Raiders (8) vs. Cleveland (7), Nov. 16, 1986

FAIR CATCHES

Most Fair Catches, Season

34 Baltimore, 1971
32 San Diego, 1969
30 St. Louis, 1967
Minnesota, 1971

Fewest Fair Catches, Season

0 San Diego, 1975
New England, 1976
Tampa Bay, 1976
Pittsburgh, 1977
Dallas, 1982
1 Cleveland, 1974
San Francisco, 1975
Kansas City, 1976
St. Louis, 1976
San Diego, 1976
L.A. Rams, 1982
St. Louis, 1982
Tampa Bay, 1982
2 By many teams

Most Fair Catches, Game

7 Minnesota vs. Dallas, Sept. 25, 1966
Detroit vs. Chicago, Nov. 21, 1976
Philadelphia vs. Buffalo, Dec. 27, 1987
6 By many teams

YARDS GAINED

Most Yards, Punt Returns, Season

785 L.A. Raiders, 1985
781 Chi. Bears, 1948
774 Pittsburgh, 1974

Fewest Yards, Punt Returns, Season

27 St. Louis, 1965
35 N.Y. Giants, 1965
37 New England, 1972

Most Yards, Punt Returns, Game

231 Detroit vs. San Francisco, Oct. 6, 1963
225 Oakland vs. Buffalo, Sept. 15, 1968
219 Los Angeles vs. Atlanta, Oct. 11, 1981

Fewest Yards, Punt Returns, Game

-28 Washington vs. Dallas, Dec. 11, 1966
-23 N.Y. Giants vs. Buffalo, Oct. 20, 1975
Pittsburgh vs. Houston, Sept. 20, 1970
-20 New Orleans vs. Pittsburgh, Oct. 20, 1968

Most Yards, Punt Returns, Both Teams, Game

282 Los Angeles (219) vs. Atlanta (63), Oct. 11, 1981
245 Detroit (231) vs. San Francisco (14), Oct. 6, 1963
244 Oakland (225) vs. Buffalo (19), Sept. 15, 1968

Fewest Yards, Punt Returns, Both Teams, Game

-18 Buffalo (-18) vs. Pittsburgh (0), Oct. 29, 1972
-14 Miami (-14) vs. Boston (0), Nov. 30, 1969
-13 N.Y. Giants (-13) vs. Cleveland (0), Nov. 14, 1965

AVERAGE YARDS RETURNING PUNTS

Highest Average, Punt Returns, Season

20.2 Chi. Bears, 1941 (27-546)
19.1 Chi. Cardinals, 1948 (35-669)
18.2 Chi. Cardinals, 1949 (30-546)

Lowest Average, Punt Returns, Season

1.2 St. Louis, 1965 (23-27)
1.5 N.Y. Giants, 1965 (24-35)
1.7 Washington, 1970 (27-45)

TOUCHDOWNS RETURNING PUNTS

Most Touchdowns, Punt Returns, Season

5 Chi. Cardinals, 1959
4 Chi. Cardinals, 1948
Detroit, 1951
N.Y. Giants, 1951
Denver, 1976
3 Washington, 1941
Detroit, 1952
Pittsburgh, 1952
Houston, 1975
Los Angeles, 1981
Cleveland, 1993

Most Touchdowns, Punt Returns, Game

2 Detroit vs. Los Angeles, Oct. 14, 1951
Detroit vs. Green Bay, Nov. 22, 1951
Chi. Cardinals vs. Pittsburgh, Nov. 1, 1959
Chi. Cardinals vs. N.Y. Giants, Nov. 22, 1959
N.Y. Titans vs. Denver, Sept. 24, 1961
Denver vs. Cleveland, Sept. 26, 1976
Los Angeles vs. Atlanta, Oct. 11, 1981
St. Louis vs. Tampa Bay, Dec. 21, 1986
L.A. Rams vs. Atlanta, Dec. 27, 1992
Cleveland vs. Pittsburgh, Oct. 24, 1993

Most Touchdowns, Punt Returns, Both Teams, Game

2 Philadelphia (1) vs. Washington (1), Nov. 9, 1952
Kansas City (1) vs. Buffalo (1), Sept. 11, 1966
Baltimore (1) vs. New England (1), Nov. 18, 1979
L.A. Raiders (1) vs. Philadelphia (1), Nov. 30, 1986 (OT)
Cincinnati (1) vs. Green Bay (1), Sept. 20, 1992
(Also see previous record)

KICKOFF RETURNS

Most Seasons Leading League (Average Return)

8 Washington, 1942, 1947, 1962-63, 1973-74, 1981, 1995
6 Chicago Bears, 1943, 1948, 1958, 1966, 1972, 1985
5 N.Y. Giants, 1944, 1946, 1949, 1951, 1953

Most Consecutive Seasons Leading League (Average Return)

3 Denver, 1965-67
2 By many teams

Most Kickoff Returns, Season

88 New Orleans, 1980
86 Minnesota, 1984
Cincinnati, 1994
84 Baltimore, 1981

Fewest Kickoff Returns, Season

17 N.Y. Giants, 1944
20 N.Y. Giants, 1941, 1943
Chi. Bears, 1942
23 Washington, 1942

Most Kickoff Returns, Game

12 N.Y. Giants vs. Washington, Nov. 27, 1966
10 By many teams

Most Kickoff Returns, Both Teams, Game

19 N.Y. Giants (12) vs. Washington (7), Nov. 27, 1966
18 Houston (10) vs. Oakland (8), Dec. 22, 1963
17 Washington (9) vs. Green Bay (8), Oct. 17, 1983
San Diego (9) vs. Pittsburgh (8), Dec. 8, 1985
Detroit (9) vs. Green Bay (8), Nov. 27, 1986
L.A. Raiders (9) vs. Seattle (8), Dec. 18, 1988

YARDS GAINED

Most Yards, Kickoff Returns, Season

1,973 New Orleans, 1980
1,840 New Orleans, 1994
1,824 Houston, 1963

Fewest Yards, Kickoff Returns, Season

282 N.Y. Giants, 1940
381 Green Bay, 1940
424 Chicago, 1963

Most Yards, Kickoff Returns, Game

362 Detroit vs. Los Angeles, Oct. 29, 1950
304 Chi. Bears vs. Green Bay, Nov. 9, 1952
New Orleans vs. L.A. Rams, Oct. 23, 1994
295 Denver vs. Boston, Oct. 4, 1964

Most Yards, Kickoff Returns, Both Teams, Game

560 Detroit (362) vs. Los Angeles (198), Oct. 29, 1950
501 New Orleans (304) vs. L.A. Rams (197), Oct. 23, 1994
453 Washington (236) vs. Philadelphia (217), Sept. 28, 1947

AVERAGE YARDAGE

Highest Average, Kickoff Returns, Season

29.4 Chicago, 1972 (52-1,528)
28.9 Pittsburgh, 1952 (39-1,128)
28.2 Washington, 1962 (61-1,720)

Lowest Average, Kickoff Returns, Season

14.7 N.Y. Jets, 1993 (46-675)
15.8 N.Y. Giants, 1993 (32-507)
15.9 Tampa Bay, 1993 (58-922)

TOUCHDOWNS

Most Touchdowns, Kickoff Returns, Season

4 Green Bay, 1967
Chicago, 1970
Detroit, 1994
3 Los Angeles, 1950
Chi. Cardinals, 1954
San Francisco, 1963
Denver, 1966
Chicago, 1967
New England, 1977
L.A. Rams, 1985

2 By many teams

Most Touchdowns, Kickoff Returns, Game

2 Chi. Bears vs. Green Bay, Sept. 22, 1940
Chi. Bears vs. Green Bay, Nov. 9, 1952
Philadelphia vs. Dallas, Nov. 6, 1966
Green Bay vs. Cleveland, Nov. 12, 1967
L.A. Rams vs. Green Bay, Nov. 24, 1985
New Orleans vs. L.A. Rams, Oct. 23, 1994

Most Touchdowns, Kickoff Returns, Both Teams, Game

2 Washington (1) vs. Philadelphia (1), Nov. 1, 1942
Washington (1) vs. Philadelphia (1), Sept. 28, 1947
Los Angeles (1) vs. Detroit (1), Oct. 29, 1950
N.Y. Yanks (1) vs. N.Y. Giants (1), Nov. 4, 1951 (consecutive)
Baltimore (1) vs. Chi. Bears (1), Oct. 4, 1958
Buffalo (1) vs. Boston (1), Nov. 3, 1962
Pittsburgh (1) vs. Dallas (1), Oct. 30, 1966
St. Louis (1) vs. Washington (1), Sept. 23, 1973 (consecutive)
Atlanta (1) vs. San Francisco (1), Dec. 20, 1987 (consecutive)
Houston (1) vs. Pittsburgh (1), Dec. 4, 1988
(Also see previous record)

FUMBLES

Most Fumbles, Season

56 Chi. Bears, 1938
San Francisco, 1978
54 Philadelphia, 1946
51 New England, 1973

Fewest Fumbles, Season

8 Cleveland, 1959
11 Green Bay, 1944
12 Brooklyn, 1934
Detroit, 1943
Cincinnati, 1982
Minnesota, 1982

Most Fumbles, Game

10 Phil-Pitt vs. N.Y. Giants, Oct. 9, 1943
Detroit vs. Minnesota, Nov. 12, 1967
Kansas City vs. Houston, Oct. 12, 1969
San Francisco vs. Detroit, Dec. 17, 1978
9 Philadelphia vs. Green Bay, Oct. 13, 1946
Kansas City vs. San Diego, Nov. 15, 1964
N.Y. Giants vs. Buffalo, Oct. 20, 1975
St. Louis vs. Washington, Oct. 25, 1976
San Diego vs. Green Bay, Sept. 24, 1978
Pittsburgh vs. Cincinnati, Oct. 14, 1979
Cleveland vs. Seattle, Dec. 20, 1981
Cleveland vs. Pittsburgh, Dec. 23, 1990
8 By many teams

Most Fumbles, Both Teams, Game

14 Washington (8) vs. Pittsburgh (6), Nov. 14, 1937
Chi. Bears (7) vs. Cleveland (7), Nov. 24, 1940
St. Louis (8) vs. N.Y. Giants (6), Sept. 17, 1961
Kansas City (10) vs. Houston (4), Oct. 12, 1969
13 Washington (8) vs. Pittsburgh (5), Nov. 14, 1937
Philadelphia (7) vs. Boston (6), Dec. 8, 1946
N.Y. Giants (7) vs. Washington (6), Nov. 5, 1950
Kansas City (9) vs. San Diego (4), Nov. 15, 1964
Buffalo (7) vs. Denver (6), Dec. 13, 1964
N.Y. Jets (7) vs. Houston (6), Sept. 12, 1965
Houston (8) vs. Pittsburgh (5), Dec. 9, 1973
St. Louis (9) vs. Washington (4), Oct. 25, 1976
Cleveland (9) vs. Seattle (4), Dec. 20, 1981
Green Bay (7) vs. Detroit (6), Oct. 6, 1985
12 In many games

FUMBLES LOST

Most Fumbles Lost, Season

36 Chi. Cardinals, 1959
31 Green Bay, 1952
29 Chi. Cardinals, 1946
Pittsburgh, 1950

Fewest Fumbles Lost, Season

3 Philadelphia, 1938
Minnesota, 1980
4 San Francisco, 1960
Kansas City, 1982
5 Chi. Cardinals, 1943
Detroit, 1943
N.Y. Giants, 1943
Cleveland, 1959
Minnesota, 1982
San Diego, 1993

Most Fumbles Lost, Game

8 St. Louis vs. Washington, Oct. 25, 1976
Cleveland vs. Pittsburgh, Dec. 23, 1990
7 Cincinnati vs. Buffalo, Nov. 30, 1969
Pittsburgh vs. Cincinnati, Oct. 14, 1979
Cleveland vs. Seattle, Dec. 20, 1981
6 By many teams

FUMBLES RECOVERED

Most Fumbles Recovered, Season, Own and Opponents'

58 Minnesota, 1963 (27 own, 31 opp)
51 Chi. Bears, 1938 (37 own, 14 opp)
San Francisco, 1978 (24 own, 27 opp)
50 Philadelphia, 1987 (23 own, 27 opp)

Fewest Fumbles Recovered, Season, Own and Opponents'

9 San Francisco, 1982 (5 own, 4 opp)
11 Cincinnati, 1982 (5 own, 6 opp)
12 Washington, 1994 (6 own, 6 opp)

Most Fumbles Recovered, Game, Own and Opponents'

10 Denver vs. Buffalo, Dec. 13, 1964 (5 own, 5 opp)
Pittsburgh vs. Houston, Dec. 9, 1973 (5 own, 5 opp)
Washington vs. St. Louis, Oct. 25, 1976 (2 own, 8 opp)
9 St. Louis vs. N.Y. Giants, Sept. 17, 1961 (6 own, 3 opp)
Houston vs. Cincinnati, Oct. 27, 1974 (4 own, 5 opp)
Kansas City vs. Dallas, Nov. 10, 1975 (4 own, 5 opp)
Green Bay vs. Detroit, Oct. 6, 1985 (5 own, 4 opp)
8 By many teams

Most Own Fumbles Recovered, Season

37 Chi. Bears, 1938
28 Pittsburgh, 1987
27 Philadelphia, 1946
Minnesota, 1963

Fewest Own Fumbles Recovered, Season

2 Washington, 1958
3 Detroit, 1956
Cleveland, 1959
Houston, 1982
4 By many teams

Most Opponents' Fumbles Recovered, Season

31 Minnesota, 1963
29 Cleveland, 1951
28 Green Bay, 1946
Houston, 1977
Seattle, 1983

Fewest Opponents' Fumbles Recovered, Season

3 Los Angeles, 1974
Green Bay, 1995
4 Philadelphia, 1944
San Francisco, 1982
5 Baltimore, 1982

Most Opponents' Fumbles Recovered, Game

8 Washington vs. St. Louis, Oct. 25, 1976
Pittsburgh vs. Cleveland, Dec. 23, 1990
7 Buffalo vs. Cincinnati, Nov. 30, 1969
Cincinnati vs. Pittsburgh, Oct. 14, 1979
Seattle vs. Cleveland, Dec. 20, 1981
6 By many teams

TOUCHDOWNS

Most Touchdowns, Fumbles Recovered, Season, Own and Opponents'

5 Chi. Bears, 1942 (1 own, 4 opp)
Los Angeles, 1952 (1 own, 4 opp)
San Francisco, 1965 (1 own, 4 opp)
Oakland, 1978 (2 own, 3 opp)
4 Chi. Bears, 1948 (1 own, 3 opp)
Boston, 1948 (4 opp)
Denver, 1979 (1 own, 3 opp)
Atlanta, 1981 (1 own, 3 opp)
Denver, 1984 (4 opp)
St. Louis, 1987 (4 opp)
Minnesota, 1989 (4 opp)
Atlanta, 1991 (4 opp)
Philadelphia, 1995 (4 opp)
3 By many teams

Most Touchdowns, Own Fumbles Recovered, Season

2 Chi. Bears, 1953
New England, 1973
Buffalo, 1974
Denver, 1975
Oakland, 1978
Green Bay, 1982
New Orleans, 1983
Cleveland, 1986

Green Bay, 1989

Most Touchdowns, Opponents' Fumbles Recovered, Season

4 Detroit, 1937
Chi. Bears, 1942
Boston, 1948
Los Angeles, 1952
San Francisco, 1965
Denver, 1984
St. Louis, 1987
Minnesota, 1989
Atlanta, 1991
Philadelphia, 1995
3 By many teams

Most Touchdowns, Fumbles Recovered, Game, Own and Opponents'

2 By many teams

Most Touchdowns, Fumbled Recovered, Game, Both Teams, Own and Opponents'

3 Detroit (2) vs. Minnesota (1), Dec. 9, 1962 (2 own, 1 opp)
Green Bay (2) vs. Dallas (1), Nov. 29, 1964 (3 opp)
Oakland (2) vs. Buffalo (1), Dec. 24, 1967 (3 opp)
Oakland (2) vs. Philadelphia (1), Sept. 24, 1995 (3 opp)

Most Touchdowns, Own Fumbles Recovered, Game

1 By many teams

Most Touchdowns, Opponents' Fumbles Recovered, Game

2 Detroit vs. Cleveland, Nov. 7, 1937
Philadelphia vs. N.Y. Giants, Sept. 25, 1938
Chi. Bears vs. Washington, Nov. 28, 1948
N.Y. Giants vs. Pittsburgh, Sept. 17, 1950
Cleveland vs. Dall. Cowboys, Dec. 3, 1961
Cleveland vs. N.Y. Giants, Oct. 25, 1964
Green Bay vs. Dallas, Nov. 29, 1964
San Francisco vs. Detroit, Nov. 14, 1965
Oakland vs. Buffalo, Dec. 24, 1967
N.Y. Giants vs. Green Bay, Sept. 19, 1971
Washington vs. San Diego, Sept. 16, 1973
New Orleans vs. San Francisco, Oct. 19, 1975
Cincinnati vs. Pittsburgh, Oct. 14, 1979
Atlanta vs. Detroit, Oct. 5, 1980
Kansas City vs. Oakland, Oct. 5, 1980
New England vs. Baltimore, Nov. 23, 1980
Denver vs. Green Bay, Oct. 15, 1984
Miami vs. Kansas City, Oct. 11, 1987
St. Louis vs. New Orleans, Oct. 11, 1987
Minnesota vs. Atlanta, Dec. 10, 1989
Philadelphia vs. Phoenix, Nov. 24, 1991
Cincinnati vs. Seattle, Sept. 6, 1992
Oakland vs. Philadelphia, Sept. 24, 1995
Pittsburgh vs. New England, Dec. 16, 1995

Most Touchdowns, Opponents' Fumbled Recovered, Game, Both Teams

3 Green Bay (2) vs. Dallas (1), Nov. 29, 1964
Oakland (2) vs. Buffalo (1), Dec. 24, 1967
Oakland (2) vs. Philadelphia (1), Sept. 24, 1995

TURNOVERS

(Number of times losing the ball on interceptions and fumbles.)

Most Turnovers, Season

63 San Francisco, 1978
58 Chi. Bears, 1947
Pittsburgh, 1950
N.Y. Giants, 1983
57 Green Bay, 1950
Houston, 1962, 1963
Pittsburgh, 1965

Fewest Turnovers, Season

12 Kansas City, 1982
14 N.Y. Giants, 1943
Cleveland, 1959
N.Y. Giants, 1990
16 San Francisco, 1960
Cincinnati, 1982
St. Louis, 1982
Washington, 1982

Most Turnovers, Game

12 Detroit vs. Chi. Bears, Nov. 22, 1942
Chi. Cardinals vs. Philadelphia, Sept. 24, 1950
Pittsburgh vs. Philadelphia, Dec. 12, 1965
11 San Diego vs. Green Bay, Sept. 24, 1978
10 Washington vs. N.Y. Giants, Dec. 4, 1938
Pittsburgh vs. Green Bay, Nov. 23, 1941
Detroit vs. Green Bay, Oct. 24, 1943
Chi. Cardinals vs. Green Bay, Nov. 10, 1946
Chi. Cardinals vs. N.Y. Giants, Nov. 2, 1952
Minnesota vs. Detroit, Dec. 9, 1962
Houston vs. Oakland, Sept. 7, 1963
Washington vs. N.Y. Giants, Dec. 8, 1963
Chicago vs. Detroit, Sept. 22, 1968
St. Louis vs. Washington, Oct. 25, 1976
N.Y. Jets vs. New England, Nov. 21, 1976
San Francisco vs. Dallas, Oct. 12, 1980
Cleveland vs. Seattle, Dec. 20, 1981
Detroit vs. Denver, Oct. 7, 1984

Most Turnovers, Both Teams, Game

17 Detroit (12) vs. Chi. Bears (5), Nov. 22, 1942
Boston (9) vs. Philadelphia (8), Dec. 8, 1946
16 Chi. Cardinals (12) vs. Philadelphia (4), Sept. 24, 1950
Chi. Cardinals (8) vs. Chi. Bears (8), Dec. 7, 1958
Minnesota (10) vs. Detroit (6), Dec. 9, 1962
Houston (9) vs. Kansas City (7), Oct. 12, 1969
15 Philadelphia (8) vs. Chi. Cardinals (7), Oct. 3, 1954
Denver (9) vs. Houston (6), Dec. 2, 1962
Washington (10) vs. N.Y. Giants (5), Dec. 8, 1963
St. Louis (9) vs. Kansas City (6), Oct. 2, 1983

PENALTIES

Most Seasons Leading League, Fewest Penalties

13 Miami, 1968, 1976-84, 1986, 1990-91
9 Pittsburgh, 1946-47, 1950-52, 1954, 1963, 1965, 1968
7 Boston/New England, 1962, 1964-65, 1973, 1987, 1989, 1993

Most Consecutive Seasons Leading League, Fewest Penalties

9 Miami, 1976-84
3 Pittsburgh, 1950-52
2 By many teams

Most Seasons Leading League, Most Penalties

16 Chi. Bears, 1941-44, 1946-49, 1951, 1959-61, 1963, 1965, 1968, 1976
11 Oakland/L.A. Raiders, 1963, 1966, 1968-69, 1975, 1982, 1984, 1991, 1993-95
6 L.A. Rams, 1950, 1952, 1962, 1969, 1978, 1980

Most Consecutive Seasons Leading League, Most Penalties

4 Chi. Bears, 1941-44, 1946-49
3 Chi. Cardinals, 1954-56
Chi. Bears, 1959-61
Houston, 1988-90
L.A./Oakland Raiders, 1993-95

Fewest Penalties, Season

19 Detroit, 1937
21 Boston, 1935
24 Philadelphia, 1936

Most Penalties, Season

156 L.A. Raiders, 1994
149 Houston, 1989
148 L.A. Raiders, 1993

Fewest Penalties, Game

0 By many teams. Last time: Chicago vs. Philadelphia, Dec. 24, 1995

Most Penalties, Game

22 Brooklyn vs. Green Bay, Sept. 17, 1944
Chi. Bears vs. Philadelphia, Nov. 26, 1944
21 Cleveland vs. Chi. Bears, Nov. 25, 1951
20 Tampa Bay vs. Seattle, Oct. 17, 1976

Fewest Penalties, Both Teams, Game

0 Brooklyn vs. Pittsburgh, Oct. 28, 1934
Brooklyn vs. Boston, Sept. 28, 1936
Cleveland vs. Chi. Bears, Oct. 9, 1938
Pittsburgh vs. Philadelphia, Nov. 10, 1940

Most Penalties, Both Teams, Game

37 Cleveland (21) vs. Chi. Bears (16), Nov. 25, 1951
35 Tampa Bay (20) vs. Seattle (15), Oct. 17, 1976
33 Brooklyn (22) vs. Green Bay (11), Sept. 17, 1944

YARDS PENALIZED

Most Seasons Leading League, Fewest Yards Penalized

13 Miami, 1967-68, 1973, 1977-84, 1990-91
8 Boston/Washington, 1935, 1953-54, 1956-58, 1970, 1985
7 Pittsburgh, 1946-47, 1950, 1952, 1962, 1965, 1968
Boston/New England, 1962, 1964-66, 1987, 1989, 1993

Most Consecutive Seasons Leading League, Fewest Yards Penalized

8 Miami, 1977-84
3 Washington, 1956-58
Boston, 1964-66
2 By many teams

Most Seasons Leading League, Most Yards Penalized

15 Chi. Bears, 1935, 1937, 1939-44, 1946-47, 1949, 1951, 1961-62, 1968
10 Oakland/L.A. Raiders, 1963-64, 1968-69, 1975, 1982, 1984, 1991, 1993-94
6 Buffalo, 1962, 1967, 1970, 1972, 1981, 1983
Houston, 1961, 1985-86, 1988-90

Most Consecutive Seasons Leading League, Most Yards Penalized
6 Chi. Bears, 1939-44
3 Cleveland, 1976-78
Houston, 1988-90
2 By many teams

Fewest Yards Penalized, Season
139 Detroit, 1937
146 Philadelphia, 1937
159 Philadelphia, 1936

Most Yards Penalized, Season
1,274 Oakland, 1969
1,239 Baltimore, 1979
1,209 L.A. Raiders, 1984

Fewest Yards Penalized, Game
0 By many teams. Last time: Chicago vs. Philadelphia, Dec. 24, 1995

Most Yards Penalized, Game
209 Cleveland vs. Chi. Bears, Nov. 25, 1951
191 Philadelphia vs. Seattle, Dec. 13, 1992 (OT)
190 Tampa Bay vs. Seattle, Oct. 17, 1976

Fewest Yards Penalized, Both Teams, Game
0 Brooklyn vs. Pittsburgh, Oct. 28, 1934
Brooklyn vs. Boston, Sept. 28, 1936
Cleveland vs. Chi. Bears, Oct. 9, 1938
Pittsburgh vs. Philadelphia, Nov. 10, 1940

Most Yards Penalized, Both Teams, Game
374 Cleveland (209) vs. Chi. Bears (165), Nov. 25, 1951
310 Tampa Bay (190) vs. Seattle (120), Oct. 17, 1976
309 Green Bay (184) vs. Boston (125), Oct. 21, 1945

DEFENSE

SCORING

Most Seasons Leading League, Fewest Points Allowed
11 N.Y. Giants, 1927, 1935, 1938-39, 1941, 1944, 1958-59, 1961, 1990, 1993
9 Chi. Bears, 1932, 1936-37, 1942, 1948, 1963, 1985-86, 1988
7 Cleveland, 1951, 1953-57, 1994

Most Consecutive Seasons Leading League, Fewest Points Allowed
5 Cleveland, 1953-57
3 Buffalo, 1964-66
Minnesota, 1969-71
2 By many teams

Fewest Points Allowed, Season (Since 1932)
44 Chi. Bears, 1932
54 Brooklyn, 1933
59 Detroit, 1934

Most Points Allowed, Season
533 Baltimore, 1981
501 N.Y. Giants, 1966
487 New Orleans, 1980

Fewest Touchdowns Allowed, Season (Since 1932)
6 Chi. Bears, 1932
Brooklyn, 1933
7 Detroit, 1934
8 Green Bay, 1932

Most Touchdowns Allowed, Season
68 Baltimore, 1981
66 N.Y. Giants, 1966
63 Baltimore, 1950

FIRST DOWNS

Fewest First Downs Allowed Season
77 Detroit, 1935
79 Boston, 1935
82 Washington, 1937

Most First Downs Allowed, Season
406 Baltimore, 1981
371 Seattle, 1981
366 Green Bay, 1983

Fewest First Downs Allowed, Rushing, Season
35 Chi. Bears, 1942
40 Green Bay, 1939
41 Brooklyn, 1944

Most First Downs Allowed, Rushing, Season
179 Detroit, 1985
178 New Orleans, 1980
175 Seattle, 1981

Fewest First Downs Allowed, Passing, Season
33 Chi. Bears, 1943
34 Pittsburgh, 1941
Washington, 1943
35 Detroit, 1940
Philadelphia, 1940, 1944

Most First Downs Allowed, Passing, Season
230 Atlanta, 1995
218 San Diego, 1985
216 San Diego, 1981
N.Y. Jets, 1986

Fewest First Downs Allowed, Penalty, Season
1 Boston, 1944
3 Philadelphia, 1940
Pittsburgh, 1945
Washington, 1957
4 Cleveland, 1940
Green Bay, 1943
N.Y. Giants, 1943

Most First Downs Allowed, Penalty, Season
48 Houston, 1985
46 Houston, 1986
43 L.A. Raiders, 1984

NET YARDS ALLOWED RUSHING AND PASSING

Most Seasons Leading League, Fewest Yards Allowed
8 Chi. Bears, 1942-43, 1948, 1958, 1963, 1984-86
6 N.Y. Giants, 1938, 1940-41, 1951, 1956, 1959
Philadelphia, 1944-45, 1949, 1953, 1981, 1991
Minnesota, 1969-70, 1975, 1988-89, 1993
5 Boston/Washington, 1935-37, 1939, 1946

Most Consecutive Seasons Leading League, Fewest Yards Allowed
3 Boston/Washington, 1935-37
Chicago, 1984-86
2 By many teams

Fewest Yards Allowed, Season
1,539 Chi. Cardinals, 1934
1,703 Chi. Bears, 1942
1,789 Brooklyn, 1933

Most Yards Allowed, Season
6,793 Baltimore, 1981
6,403 Green Bay, 1983
6,352 Minnesota, 1984

RUSHING

Most Seasons Leading League, Fewest Yards Allowed
10 Chi. Bears, 1937, 1939, 1942, 1946, 1949, 1963, 1984-85, 1987-88
7 Detroit, 1938, 1950, 1952, 1962, 1970, 1980-81
Philadelphia, 1944-45, 1947-48, 1953, 1990-91
Dallas, 1966-69, 1972, 1978, 1992
5 N.Y. Giants, 1940, 1951, 1956, 1959, 1986

Most Consecutive Seasons Leading League, Fewest Yards Allowed
4 Dallas, 1966-69
2 By many teams

Fewest Yards Allowed, Rushing, Season
519 Chi. Bears, 1942
558 Philadelphia, 1944
762 Pittsburgh, 1982

Most Yards Allowed, Rushing, Season
3,228 Buffalo, 1978
3,106 New Orleans, 1980
3,010 Baltimore, 1978

Fewest Touchdowns Allowed, Rushing, Season
2 Detroit, 1934
Dallas, 1968
Minnesota, 1971
3 By many teams

Most Touchdowns Allowed, Rushing, Season
36 Oakland, 1961
31 N.Y. Giants, 1980
Tampa Bay, 1986
30 Baltimore, 1981

PASSING

Most Seasons Leading League, Fewest Yards Allowed
8 Green Bay, 1947-48, 1962, 1964-68
7 Washington, 1939, 1942, 1945, 1952-53, 1980, 1985
6 Chi. Bears, 1938, 1943-44, 1958, 1960, 1963
Minnesota, 1969-70, 1972, 1975-76, 1989
Pittsburgh, 1941, 1946, 1951, 1955, 1974, 1990
Philadelphia, 1934, 1936, 1940, 1949, 1981, 1991

Most Consecutive Seasons Leading League, Fewest Yards Allowed
5 Green Bay, 1964-68
2 By many teams

Fewest Yards Allowed, Passing, Season
545 Philadelphia, 1934
558 Portsmouth, 1933
585 Chi. Cardinals, 1934

Most Yards Allowed, Passing, Season
4,541 Atlanta, 1995
4,389 N.Y. Jets, 1986
4,311 San Diego, 1981
Fewest Touchdowns Allowed, Passing, Season
1 Portsmouth, 1932
Philadelphia, 1934
2 Brooklyn, 1933
Chi. Bears, 1934
3 Chi. Bears, 1932
Green Bay, 1932
Green Bay, 1934
Chi. Bears, 1936
New York, 1939
New York, 1944
Most Touchdowns Allowed, Passing, Season
40 Denver, 1963
38 St. Louis, 1969
37 Washington, 1961
Baltimore, 1981

SACKS

Most Seasons Leading League
5 Oakland/L.A. Raiders, 1966-68, 1982, 1986
4 Boston/New England, 1961, 1963, 1977, 1979
Dallas, 1966, 1968-69, 1978
Dallas/Kansas City, 1960, 1965, 1969, 1990
3 San Francisco, 1967, 1972, 1976
L.A. Rams, 1968, 1970, 1988
Most Consecutive Seasons Leading League
3 Oakland, 1966-68
2 Dallas, 1968-69
Most Sacks, Season
72 Chicago, 1984
71 Minnesota, 1989
70 Chicago, 1987
Fewest Sacks, Season
11 Baltimore, 1982
12 Buffalo, 1982
13 Baltimore, 1981
Most Sacks, Game
12 Dallas vs. Pittsburgh, Nov. 20, 1966
St. Louis vs. Baltimore, Oct. 26, 1980
Chicago vs. Detroit, Dec. 16, 1984
Dallas vs. Houston, Sept. 29, 1985
11 N.Y. Giants vs. St. Louis, Nov. 1, 1964
Baltimore vs. Los Angeles, Nov. 22, 1964
Buffalo vs. Denver, Dec. 13, 1964
Detroit vs. Green Bay, Nov. 7, 1965
Oakland vs. Buffalo, Oct. 15, 1967
Oakland vs. Denver, Nov. 5, 1967
St. Louis vs. Atlanta, Nov. 24, 1968
Dallas vs. Detroit, Oct. 6, 1975
St. Louis vs. Philadelphia, Dec. 18, 1983
Kansas City vs. Cleveland, Sept. 30, 1984
Chicago vs. Minnesota, Oct. 28, 1984
Cleveland vs. Atlanta, Nov. 18, 1984
Detroit vs. Philadelphia, Nov. 16, 1986
San Diego vs. Dallas, Nov. 16, 1986
L.A. Raiders vs. Philadelphia, Nov. 30, 1986 (OT)
Seattle vs. L.A. Raiders, Dec. 8, 1986
Chicago vs. Philadelphia, Oct. 4, 1987
Dallas vs. N.Y. Jets, Oct. 4, 1987
Indianapolis vs. Cleveland, Sept. 6, 1992
10 By many teams
Most Opponents Yards Lost Attempting to Pass, Season
666 Oakland, 1967
583 Chicago, 1984
573 San Francisco, 1976
Fewest Opponents Yards Lost Attempting to Pass, Season
72 Jacksonville, 1995
75 Green Bay, 1956
77 N.Y. Bulldogs, 1949

INTERCEPTIONS BY

Most Seasons Leading League
9 N.Y. Giants, 1933, 1937-39, 1944, 1948, 1951, 1954, 1961
8 Green Bay, 1940, 1942-43, 1947, 1955, 1957, 1962, 1965
Chi. Bears, 1935-36, 1941-42, 1946, 1963, 1985, 1990
6 Kansas City, 1966-70, 1974
Most Consecutive Seasons Leading League
5 Kansas City, 1966-70
3 N.Y. Giants, 1937-39
2 By many teams
Most Passes Intercepted By, Season
49 San Diego, 1961
42 Green Bay, 1943
41 N.Y. Giants, 1951
Fewest Passes Intercepted By, Season
3 Houston, 1982
5 Baltimore, 1982
6 Houston, 1972
St. Louis, 1982
Most Passes Intercepted By, Game
9 Green Bay vs. Detroit, Oct. 24, 1943
Philadelphia vs. Pittsburgh, Dec. 12, 1965
8 N.Y. Giants vs. Green Bay, Nov. 21, 1948
Philadelphia vs. Chi. Cardinals, Sept. 24, 1950
N.Y. Giants vs. N.Y. Yanks, Dec. 16, 1951
Houston vs. Denver, Dec. 2, 1962
Detroit vs. Chicago, Sept. 22, 1968
N.Y. Jets vs. Baltimore, Sept. 23, 1973
7 By many teams. Last time: New Orleans vs. Green Bay, Sept. 14, 1986
Most Consecutive Games, One or More Interceptions By
46 L.A. Chargers/San Diego, 1960-63
37 Detroit, 1960-63
36 Boston, 1944-47
Most Yards Returning Interceptions, Season
929 San Diego, 1961
712 Los Angeles, 1952
697 Seattle, 1984
Fewest Yards Returning Interceptions, Season
5 Los Angeles, 1959
37 Dallas, 1989
42 Philadelphia, 1982
Most Yards Returning Interceptions, Game
325 Seattle vs. Kansas City, Nov. 4, 1984
314 Los Angeles vs. San Francisco, Oct. 18, 1964
245 Houston vs. N.Y. Jets, Oct. 15, 1967
Most Yards Returning Interceptions, Both Teams, Game
356 Seattle (325) vs. Kansas City (31), Nov. 4, 1984
338 Los Angeles (314) vs. San Francisco (24), Oct. 18, 1964
308 Dallas (182) vs. Los Angeles (126), Nov. 2, 1952
Most Touchdowns, Returning Interceptions, Season
9 San Diego, 1961
7 Seattle, 1984
6 Cleveland, 1960
Green Bay, 1966
Detroit, 1967
Houston, 1967
Most Touchdowns Returning Interceptions, Game
4 Seattle vs. Kansas City, Nov. 4, 1984
3 Baltimore vs. Green Bay, Nov. 5, 1950
Cleveland vs. Chicago, Dec. 11, 1960
Philadelphia vs. Pittsburgh, Dec. 12, 1965
Baltimore vs. Pittsburgh, Sept. 29, 1968
Buffalo vs. N.Y. Jets, Sept. 29, 1968
Houston vs. San Diego, Dec. 19, 1971
Cincinnati vs. Houston, Dec. 17, 1972
Tampa Bay vs. New Orleans, Dec. 11, 1977
2 By many teams
Most Touchdown Returning Interceptions, Both Teams, Game
4 Philadelphia (3) vs. Pittsburgh (1), Dec. 12, 1965
Seattle (4) vs. Kansas City (0), Nov. 4, 1984
3 Los Angeles (2) vs. Detroit (1), Nov. 1, 1953
Cleveland (2) vs. N.Y. Giants (1), Dec. 18, 1960
Pittsburgh (2) vs. Cincinnati (1), Oct. 10, 1983
Kansas City (2) vs. San Diego (1), Oct. 19, 1986
(Also see previous record)

PUNT RETURNS

Fewest Opponents Punt Returns, Season
7 Washington, 1962
San Diego, 1982
10 Buffalo, 1982
11 Boston, 1962
Most Opponents Punt Returns, Season
71 Tampa Bay, 1976, 1977
69 N.Y. Giants, 1953
68 Cleveland, 1974
Fewest Yards Allowed, Punt Returns, Season
22 Green Bay, 1967
34 Washington, 1962
39 Cleveland, 1959
Washington, 1972

Most Yards Allowed, Punt Returns, Season
932 Green Bay, 1949
913 Boston, 1947
906 New Orleans, 1974

Lowest Average Allowed, Punt Returns, Season
1.20 Chi. Cardinals, 1954 (46-55)
1.22 Cleveland, 1959 (32-39)
1.55 Chi. Cardinals, 1953 (44-68)

Highest Average Allowed, Punt Returns, Season
18.6 Green Bay, 1949 (50-932)
18.0 Cleveland, 1977 (31-558)
17.9 Boston, 1960 (20-357)

Most Touchdowns Allowed, Punt Returns, Season
4 New York, 1959
Atlanta, 1992
3 Green Bay, 1949
Chi. Cardinals, 1951
L.A. Rams, 1951, 1994
Washington, 1952
Dallas, 1952
Pittsburgh, 1959, 1993
N.Y. Jets, 1968
Cleveland, 1977
Atlanta, 1986
Tampa Bay, 1986
2 By many teams

KICKOFF RETURNS

Fewest Opponents Kickoff Returns, Season
10 Brooklyn, 1943
13 Denver, 1992
15 Detroit, 1942
Brooklyn, 1944

Most Opponents Kickoff Returns, Season
91 Washington, 1983
89 New England, 1980
San Francisco, 1994
88 San Diego, 1981
Pittsburgh, 1995

Fewest Yards Allowed, Kickoff Returns, Season
225 Brooklyn, 1943
254 Denver, 1992
293 Brooklyn, 1944

Most Yards Allowed, Kickoff Returns, Season
2,045 Kansas City, 1966
1,912 San Francisco, 1994
1,857 San Francisco, 1995

Lowest Average Allowed, Kickoff Returns, Season
14.3 Cleveland, 1980 (71-1,018)
14.9 Indianapolis, 1993 (37-551)
15.0 Seattle, 1982 (24-361)

Highest Average Allowed, Kickoff Returns, Season
29.5 N.Y. Jets, 1972 (47-1,386)
29.4 Los Angeles, 1950 (48-1,411)
29.1 New England, 1971 (49-1,427)

Most Touchdowns Allowed, Kickoff Returns, Season
3 Minnesota, 1963, 1970
Dallas, 1966
Detroit, 1980
Pittsburgh, 1986
2 By many teams

FUMBLES

Fewest Opponents Fumbles, Season
11 Cleveland, 1956
Baltimore, 1982
12 Green Bay, 1995
13 Los Angeles, 1956
Chicago, 1960
Cleveland, 1963
Cleveland, 1965
Detroit, 1967
San Diego, 1969

Most Opponents Fumbles, Season
50 Minnesota, 1963
San Francisco, 1978
48 N.Y. Giants, 1980
N.Y. Jets, 1986
47 N.Y. Giants, 1977
Seattle, 1984

TURNOVERS

(Number of times losing the ball on interceptions and fumbles.)

Fewest Opponents Turnovers, Season
11 Baltimore, 1982
13 San Francisco, 1982
15 St. Louis, 1982

Most Opponents Turnovers, Season
66 San Diego, 1961
63 Seattle, 1984
61 Washington, 1983

Most Opponents Turnovers, Game
12 Chi. Bears vs. Detroit, Nov. 22, 1942
Philadelphia vs. Chi. Cardinals, Sept. 24, 1950
Philadelphia vs. Pittsburgh, Dec. 12, 1965
11 Green Bay vs. San Diego, Sept. 24, 1978
10 By 14 teams

1,000 YARDS RUSHING IN A SEASON

Year	Player, Team	Att.	Yards	Avg.	Long	TD
1995	Emmitt Smith, Dallas[5]	377	1,773	4.7	60	25
	Barry Sanders, Detroit[7]	314	1,500	4.8	75	11
	*Curtis Martin, New England	368	1,487	4.0	49	14
	Chris Warren, Seattle[4]	310	1,346	4.3	52	15
	Terry Allen, Washington[3]	338	1,309	3.9	28	10
	Ricky Watters, Philadelphia[2]	337	1,273	3.8	57	11
	Errict Rhett, Tampa Bay[2]	332	1,207	3.6	21	11
	Rodney Hampton, N.Y. Giants[5]	306	1,182	3.9	32	10
	*Terrell Davis, Denver	237	1,117	4.7	60	7
	Harvey Williams, Oakland	255	1,114	4.4	60	9
	Craig Heyward, Atlanta	236	1,083	4.6	31	6
	Marshall Faulk, Indianapolis[2]	289	1,078	3.7	40	11
	*Rashaan Salaam, Chicago	296	1,074	3.6	42	10
	Garrison Hearst, Arizona	284	1,070	3.8	38	1
	Edgar Bennett, Green Bay	316	1,067	3.4	23	3
	Thurman Thomas, Buffalo[7]	267	1,005	3.8	49	6
1994	Barry Sanders, Detroit[6]	331	1,883	5.7	85	7
	Chris Warren, Seattle[3]	333	1,545	4.6	41	9
	Emmitt Smith, Dallas[4]	368	1,484	4.0	46	21
	Natrone Means, San Diego	343	1,350	3.9	25	12
	*Marshall Faulk, Indianapolis	314	1,282	4.1	52	11
	Thurman Thomas, Buffalo[6]	287	1,093	3.8	29	7
	Rodney Hampton, N.Y. Giants[4]	327	1,075	3.3	27	6
	Terry Allen, Minnesota[2]	255	1,031	4.0	45	8
	Jerome Bettis, L.A. Rams[2]	319	1,025	3.2	19	3
	*Errict Rhett, Tampa Bay	284	1,011	3.6	27	7
1993	Emmitt Smith, Dallas[3]	283	1,486	5.3	62	9
	*Jerome Bettis, L.A. Rams	294	1,429	4.9	71	7
	Thurman Thomas, Buffalo[5]	355	1,315	3.7	27	6
	Erric Pegram, Atlanta	292	1,185	4.1	29	3
	Barry Sanders, Detroit[5]	243	1,115	4.6	42	3
	Leonard Russell, New England	300	1,088	3.6	21	7
	Rodney Hampton, N.Y. Giants[3]	292	1,077	3.7	20	5
	Chris Warren, Seattle[2]	273	1,072	3.9	45	7
	*Reggie Brooks, Washington	223	1,063	4.8	85	3
	*Ron Moore, Phoenix	263	1,018	3.9	20	9
	Gary Brown, Houston	195	1,002	5.1	26	6
1992	Emmitt Smith, Dallas[2]	373	1,713	4.6	68	18
	Barry Foster, Pittsburgh	390	1,690	4.3	69	11
	Thurman Thomas, Buffalo[4]	312	1,487	4.8	44	9
	Barry Sanders, Detroit[4]	312	1,352	4.3	55	9
	Lorenzo White, Houston	265	1,226	4.6	44	7
	Terry Allen, Minnesota	266	1,201	4.5	51	13
	Reggie Cobb, Tampa Bay	310	1,171	3.8	25	9
	Harold Green, Cincinnati	265	1,170	4.4	53	2
	Rodney Hampton, N.Y. Giants[2]	257	1,141	4.4	63	14
	Cleveland Gary, L.A. Rams	279	1,125	4.0	63	7
	Herschel Walker, Philadelphia[2]	267	1,070	4.0	38	8
	Chris Warren, Seattle	223	1,017	4.6	52	3
	*Ricky Watters, San Francisco	206	1,013	4.9	43	9
1991	Emmitt Smith, Dallas	365	1,563	4.3	75	12
	Barry Sanders, Detroit[3]	342	1,548	4.5	69	16
	Thurman Thomas, Buffalo[3]	288	1,407	4.9	33	7
	Rodney Hampton, N.Y. Giants	256	1,059	4.1	44	10
	Earnest Byner, Washington[3]	274	1,048	3.8	32	5
	Gaston Green, Denver	261	1,037	4.0	63	4
	Christian Okoye, Kansas City[2]	225	1,031	4.6	48	9
1990	Barry Sanders, Detroit[2]	255	1,304	5.1	45	13
	Thurman Thomas, Buffalo[2]	271	1,297	4.8	80	11
	Marion Butts, San Diego	265	1,225	4.6	52	8
	Earnest Byner, Washington[2]	297	1,219	4.1	22	6
	Bobby Humphrey, Denver[2]	288	1,202	4.2	37	7
	Neal Anderson, Chicago[3]	260	1,078	4.1	52	10
	Barry Word, Kansas City	204	1,015	5.0	53	4
	James Brooks, Cincinnati[3]	195	1,004	5.1	56	5
1989	Christian Okoye, Kansas City	370	1,480	4.0	59	12
	*Barry Sanders, Detroit	280	1,470	5.3	34	14
	Eric Dickerson, Indianapolis[7]	314	1,311	4.2	21	7
	Neal Anderson, Chicago[2]	274	1,275	4.7	73	11
	Dalton Hilliard, New Orleans	344	1,262	3.7	40	13
	Thurman Thomas, Buffalo	298	1,244	4.2	38	6
	James Brooks, Cincinnati[2]	221	1,239	5.6	65	7
	*Bobby Humphrey, Denver	294	1,151	3.9	40	7
	Greg Bell, L.A. Rams[3]	272	1,137	4.2	47	15
	Roger Craig, San Francisco[3]	271	1,054	3.9	27	6
	Ottis Anderson, N.Y. Giants[6]	325	1,023	3.1	36	14
1988	Eric Dickerson, Indianapolis[6]	388	1,659	4.3	41	14
	Herschel Walker, Dallas	361	1,514	4.2	38	5
	Roger Craig, San Francisco[2]	310	1,502	4.8	46	9
	Greg Bell, L.A. Rams[2]	288	1,212	4.2	44	16
	*John Stephens, New England	297	1,168	3.9	52	4
	Gary Anderson, San Diego	225	1,119	5.0	36	3
	Neal Anderson, Chicago	249	1,106	4.4	80	12
	Joe Morris, N.Y. Giants[3]	307	1,083	3.5	27	5
	*Ickey Woods, Cincinnati	203	1,066	5.3	56	15
	Curt Warner, Seattle[4]	266	1,025	3.9	29	10
	John Settle, Atlanta	232	1,024	4.4	62	7
	Mike Rozier, Houston	251	1,002	4.0	28	10
1987	Charles White, L.A. Rams	324	1,374	4.2	58	11
	Eric Dickerson, L.A. Rams-Indianapolis[5]	283	1,288	4.6	57	6
1986	Eric Dickerson, L.A. Rams[4]	404	1,821	4.5	42	11
	Joe Morris, N.Y. Giants[2]	341	1,516	4.4	54	14
	Curt Warner, Seattle[3]	319	1,481	4.6	60	13
	*Rueben Mayes, New Orleans	286	1,353	4.7	50	8
	Walter Payton, Chicago[10]	321	1,333	4.2	41	8
	Gerald Riggs, Atlanta[3]	343	1,327	3.9	31	9
	George Rogers, Washington[4]	303	1,203	4.0	42	18
	James Brooks, Cincinnati	205	1,087	5.3	56	5
1985	Marcus Allen, L.A. Raiders[3]	390	1,759	4.6	61	11
	Gerald Riggs, Atlanta[2]	397	1,719	4.3	50	10
	Walter Payton, Chicago[9]	324	1,551	4.8	40	9
	Joe Morris, N.Y. Giants	294	1,336	4.5	65	21
	Freeman McNeil, N.Y. Jets[2]	294	1,331	4.5	69	3
	Tony Dorsett, Dallas[8]	305	1,307	4.3	60	7
	James Wilder, Tampa Bay[2]	365	1,300	3.6	28	10
	Eric Dickerson, L.A. Rams[3]	292	1,234	4.2	43	12
	Craig James, New England	263	1,227	4.7	65	5
	Kevin Mack, Cleveland	222	1,104	5.0	61	7
	Curt Warner, Seattle[2]	291	1,094	3.8	38	8
	George Rogers, Washington[3]	231	1,093	4.7	35	7
	Roger Craig, San Francisco	214	1,050	4.9	62	9
	Earnest Jackson, Philadelphia[2]	282	1,028	3.6	59	5
	Stump Mitchell, St. Louis	183	1,006	5.5	64	7
	Earnest Byner, Cleveland	244	1,002	4.1	36	8
1984	Eric Dickerson, L.A. Rams[2]	379	2,105	5.6	66	14
	Walter Payton, Chicago[8]	381	1,684	4.4	72	11
	James Wilder, Tampa Bay	407	1,544	3.8	37	13
	Gerald Riggs, Atlanta	353	1,486	4.2	57	13
	Wendell Tyler, San Francisco[3]	246	1,262	5.1	40	7
	John Riggins, Washington[5]	327	1,239	3.8	24	14
	Tony Dorsett, Dallas[7]	302	1,189	3.9	31	6
	Earnest Jackson, San Diego	296	1,179	4.0	32	8
	Ottis Anderson, St. Louis[5]	289	1,174	4.1	24	6
	Marcus Allen, L.A. Raiders[2]	275	1,168	4.2	52	13
	Sammy Winder, Denver	296	1,153	3.9	24	4
	*Greg Bell, Buffalo	262	1,100	4.2	85	7
	Freeman McNeil, N.Y. Jets	229	1,070	4.7	53	5
1983	*Eric Dickerson, L.A. Rams	390	1,808	4.6	85	18
	William Andrews, Atlanta[4]	331	1,567	4.7	27	7
	*Curt Warner, Seattle	335	1,449	4.3	60	13
	Walter Payton, Chicago[7]	314	1,421	4.5	49	6
	John Riggins, Washington[4]	375	1,347	3.6	44	24
	Tony Dorsett, Dallas[6]	289	1,321	4.6	77	8
	Earl Campbell, Houston[5]	322	1,301	4.0	42	12
	Ottis Anderson, St. Louis[4]	296	1,270	4.3	43	5
	Mike Pruitt, Cleveland[4]	293	1,184	4.0	27	10
	George Rogers, New Orleans[2]	256	1,144	4.5	76	5
	Joe Cribbs, Buffalo[3]	263	1,131	4.3	45	3
	Curtis Dickey, Baltimore	254	1,122	4.4	56	4
	Tony Collins, New England	219	1,049	4.8	50	10
	Billy Sims, Detroit[3]	220	1,040	4.7	41	7
	Marcus Allen, L.A. Raiders	266	1,014	3.8	19	9
	Franco Harris, Pittsburgh[8]	279	1,007	3.6	19	5
1981	*George Rogers, New Orleans	378	1,674	4.4	79	13
	Tony Dorsett, Dallas[5]	342	1,646	4.8	75	4
	Billy Sims, Detroit[2]	296	1,437	4.9	51	13
	Wilbert Montgomery, Philadelphia[3]	286	1,402	4.9	41	8
	Ottis Anderson, St. Louis[3]	328	1,376	4.2	28	9
	Earl Campbell, Houston[4]	361	1,376	3.8	43	10
	William Andrews, Atlanta[3]	289	1,301	4.5	29	10
	Walter Payton, Chicago[6]	339	1,222	3.6	39	6
	Chuck Muncie, San Diego[2]	251	1,144	4.6	73	19
	*Joe Delaney, Kansas City	234	1,121	4.8	82	3
	Mike Pruitt, Cleveland[3]	247	1,103	4.5	21	7
	Joe Cribbs, Buffalo[2]	257	1,097	4.3	35	3
	Pete Johnson, Cincinnati	274	1,077	3.9	39	12
	Wendell Tyler, Los Angeles[2]	260	1,074	4.1	69	12
	Ted Brown, Minnesota	274	1,063	3.9	34	6
1980	Earl Campbell, Houston[3]	373	1,934	5.2	55	13
	Walter Payton, Chicago[5]	317	1,460	4.6	69	6
	Ottis Anderson, St. Louis[2]	301	1,352	4.5	52	9
	William Andrews, Atlanta[2]	265	1,308	4.9	33	4
	*Billy Sims, Detroit	313	1,303	4.2	52	13
	Tony Dorsett, Dallas[4]	278	1,185	4.3	56	11

	*Joe Cribbs, Buffalo	306	1,185	3.9	48	11
	Mike Pruitt, Cleveland[2]	249	1,034	4.2	56	6
1979	Earl Campbell, Houston[2]	368	1,697	4.6	61	19
	Walter Payton, Chicago[4]	369	1,610	4.4	43	14
	*Ottis Anderson, St. Louis	331	1,605	4.8	76	8
	Wilbert Montgomery, Philadelphia[2]	338	1,512	4.5	62	9
	Mike Pruitt, Cleveland	264	1,294	4.9	77	9
	Ricky Bell, Tampa Bay	283	1,263	4.5	49	7
	Chuck Muncie, New Orleans	238	1,198	5.0	69	11
	Franco Harris, Pittsburgh[7]	267	1,186	4.4	71	11
	John Riggins, Washington[3]	260	1,153	4.4	66	9
	Wendell Tyler, Los Angeles	218	1,109	5.1	63	9
	Tony Dorsett, Dallas[3]	250	1,107	4.4	41	6
	*William Andrews, Atlanta	239	1,023	4.3	23	3
1978	*Earl Campbell, Houston	302	1,450	4.8	81	13
	Walter Payton, Chicago[3]	333	1,395	4.2	76	11
	Tony Dorsett, Dallas[2]	290	1,325	4.6	63	7
	Delvin Williams, Miami[2]	272	1,258	4.6	58	8
	Wilbert Montgomery, Philadelphia	259	1,220	4.7	47	9
	Terdell Middleton, Green Bay	284	1,116	3.9	76	11
	Franco Harris, Pittsburgh[6]	310	1,082	3.5	37	8
	Mark van Eeghen, Oakland[3]	270	1,080	4.0	34	9
	*Terry Miller, Buffalo	238	1,060	4.5	60	7
	Tony Reed, Kansas City	206	1,053	5.1	62	5
	John Riggins, Washington[2]	248	1,014	4.1	31	5
1977	Walter Payton, Chicago[2]	339	1,852	5.5	73	14
	Mark van Eeghen, Oakland[2]	324	1,273	3.9	27	7
	Lawrence McCutcheon, Los Angeles[4]	294	1,238	4.2	48	7
	Franco Harris, Pittsburgh[5]	300	1,162	3.9	61	11
	Lydell Mitchell, Baltimore[3]	301	1,159	3.9	64	3
	Chuck Foreman, Minnesota[3]	270	1,112	4.1	51	6
	Greg Pruitt, Cleveland[3]	236	1,086	4.6	78	3
	Sam Cunningham, New England	270	1,015	3.8	31	4
	*Tony Dorsett, Dallas	208	1,007	4.8	84	12
1976	O.J. Simpson, Buffalo[5]	290	1,503	5.2	75	8
	Walter Payton, Chicago	311	1,390	4.5	60	13
	Delvin Williams, San Francisco	248	1,203	4.9	80	7
	Lydell Mitchell, Baltimore[2]	289	1,200	4.2	43	5
	Lawrence McCutcheon, Los Angeles[3]	291	1,168	4.0	40	9
	Chuck Foreman, Minnesota[2]	278	1,155	4.2	46	13
	Franco Harris, Pittsburgh[4]	289	1,128	3.9	30	14
	Mike Thomas, Washington	254	1,101	4.3	28	5
	Rocky Bleier, Pittsburgh	220	1,036	4.7	28	5
	Mark van Eeghen, Oakland	233	1,012	4.3	21	3
	Otis Armstrong, Denver[2]	247	1,008	4.1	31	5
	Greg Pruitt, Cleveland[2]	209	1,000	4.8	64	4
1975	O.J. Simpson, Buffalo[4]	329	1,817	5.5	88	16
	Franco Harris, Pittsburgh[3]	262	1,246	4.8	36	10
	Lydell Mitchell, Baltimore	289	1,193	4.1	70	11
	Jim Otis, St. Louis	269	1,076	4.0	30	5
	Chuck Foreman, Minnesota	280	1,070	3.8	31	13
	Greg Pruitt, Cleveland	217	1,067	4.9	50	8
	John Riggins, N.Y. Jets	238	1,005	4.2	42	8
	Dave Hampton, Atlanta	250	1,002	4.0	22	5
1974	Otis Armstrong, Denver	263	1,407	5.3	43	9
	*Don Woods, San Diego	227	1,162	5.1	56	7
	O.J. Simpson, Buffalo[3]	270	1,125	4.2	41	3
	Lawrence McCutcheon, Los Angeles[2]	236	1,109	4.7	23	3
	Franco Harris, Pittsburgh[2]	208	1,006	4.8	54	5
1973	O.J. Simpson, Buffalo[2]	332	2,003	6.0	80	12
	John Brockington, Green Bay[3]	265	1,144	4.3	53	3
	Calvin Hill, Dallas[2]	273	1,142	4.2	21	6
	Lawrence McCutcheon, Los Angeles	210	1,097	5.2	37	2
	Larry Csonka, Miami[3]	219	1,003	4.6	25	5
1972	O.J. Simpson, Buffalo	292	1,251	4.3	94	6
	Larry Brown, Washington[2]	285	1,216	4.3	38	8
	Ron Johnson, N.Y. Giants[2]	298	1,182	4.0	35	9
	Larry Csonka, Miami[2]	213	1,117	5.2	45	6
	Marv Hubbard, Oakland	219	1,100	5.0	39	4
	*Franco Harris, Pittsburgh	188	1,055	5.6	75	10
	Calvin Hill, Dallas	245	1,036	4.2	26	6
	Mike Garrett, San Diego[2]	272	1,031	3.8	41	6
	John Brockington, Green Bay[2]	274	1,027	3.7	30	8
	Eugene (Mercury) Morris, Miami	190	1,000	5.3	33	12
1971	Floyd Little, Denver	284	1,133	4.0	40	6
	*John Brockington, Green Bay	216	1,105	5.1	52	4
	Larry Csonka, Miami	195	1,051	5.4	28	7
	Steve Owens, Detroit	246	1,035	4.2	23	8
	Willie Ellison, Los Angeles	211	1,000	4.7	80	4
1970	Larry Brown, Washington	237	1,125	4.7	75	5
	Ron Johnson, N.Y. Giants	263	1,027	3.9	68	8
1969	Gale Sayers, Chicago[2]	236	1,032	4.4	28	8
1968	Leroy Kelly, Cleveland[3]	248	1,239	5.0	65	16
	*Paul Robinson, Cincinnati	238	1,023	4.3	87	8
1967	Jim Nance, Boston[2]	269	1,216	4.5	53	7
	Leroy Kelly, Cleveland[2]	235	1,205	5.1	42	11
	Hoyle Granger, Houston	236	1,194	5.1	67	6
	Mike Garrett, Kansas City	236	1,087	4.6	58	9
1966	Jim Nance, Boston	299	1,458	4.9	65	11
	Gale Sayers, Chicago	229	1,231	5.4	58	8
	Leroy Kelly, Cleveland	209	1,141	5.5	70	15
	Dick Bass, Los Angeles[2]	248	1,090	4.4	50	8
1965	Jim Brown, Cleveland[7]	289	1,544	5.3	67	17
	Paul Lowe, San Diego[2]	222	1,121	5.0	59	7
1964	Jim Brown, Cleveland[6]	280	1,446	5.2	71	7
	Jim Taylor, Green Bay[5]	235	1,169	5.0	84	12
	John Henry Johnson, Pittsburgh[2]	235	1,048	4.5	45	7
1963	Jim Brown, Cleveland[5]	291	1,863	6.4	80	12
	Clem Daniels, Oakland	215	1,099	5.1	74	3
	Jim Taylor, Green Bay[4]	248	1,018	4.1	40	9
	Paul Lowe, San Diego	177	1,010	5.7	66	8
1962	Jim Taylor, Green Bay[3]	272	1,474	5.4	51	19
	John Henry Johnson, Pittsburgh	251	1,141	4.5	40	7
	Cookie Gilchrist, Buffalo	214	1,096	5.1	44	13
	Abner Haynes, Dall. Texans	221	1,049	4.7	71	13
	Dick Bass, Los Angeles	196	1,033	5.3	57	6
	Charlie Tolar, Houston	244	1,012	4.1	25	7
1961	Jim Brown, Cleveland[4]	305	1,408	4.6	38	8
	Jim Taylor, Green Bay[2]	243	1,307	5.4	53	15
1960	Jim Brown, Cleveland[3]	215	1,257	5.8	71	9
	Jim Taylor, Green Bay	230	1,101	4.8	32	11
	John David Crow, St. Louis	183	1,071	5.9	57	6
1959	Jim Brown, Cleveland[2]	290	1,329	4.6	70	14
	J.D. Smith, San Francisco	207	1,036	5.0	73	10
1958	Jim Brown, Cleveland	257	1,527	5.9	65	17
1956	Rick Casares, Chi. Bears	234	1,126	4.8	68	12
1954	Joe Perry, San Francisco[2]	173	1,049	6.1	58	8
1953	Joe Perry, San Francisco	192	1,018	5.3	51	10
1949	Steve Van Buren, Philadelphia[2]	263	1,146	4.4	41	11
	Tony Canadeo, Green Bay	208	1,052	5.1	54	4
1947	Steve Van Buren, Philadelphia	217	1,008	4.6	45	13
1934	*Beattie Feathers, Chi. Bears	119	1,004	8.4	82	8

**First season of professional football.*

200 YARDS RUSHING IN A GAME

Date	Player, Team, Opponent	Att.	Yards	TD
Nov. 13, 1994	Barry Sanders, Detroit vs. Tampa Bay	26	237	0
Dec. 12, 1993	*Jerome Bettis, L.A. Rams vs. New Orleans	28	212	1
Oct. 31, 1993	Emmitt Smith, Dallas vs. Philadelphia	30	237	1
Nov. 24, 1991	Barry Sanders, Detroit vs. Minnesota	23	220	4
Dec. 23, 1990	James Brooks, Cincinnati vs. Houston	20	201	1
Oct. 14, 1990	Barry Word, Kansas City vs. Detroit	18	200	2
Sept. 24, 1990	Thurman Thomas, Buffalo vs. N.Y. Jets	18	214	0
Dec. 24, 1989	Greg Bell, L.A. Rams vs. New England	26	210	1
Sept. 24, 1989	Greg Bell, L.A. Rams vs. Green Bay	28	221	2
Sept. 17, 1989	Gerald Riggs, Washington vs. Philadelphia	29	221	1
Dec. 18, 1988	Gary Anderson, San Diego vs. Kansas City	34	217	1
Nov. 30, 1987	*Bo Jackson, L.A. Raiders vs. Seattle	18	221	2
Nov. 15, 1987	Charles White, L.A. Rams vs. St. Louis	34	213	1
Dec. 7, 1986	Rueben Mayes, New Orleans vs. Miami	28	203	2
Oct. 5, 1986	Eric Dickerson, L.A. Rams vs. Tampa Bay (OT)	30	207	2
Dec. 21, 1985	George Rogers, Washington vs. St. Louis	34	206	1
Dec. 21, 1985	Joe Morris, N.Y. Giants vs. Pittsburgh	36	202	3
Dec. 9, 1984	Eric Dickerson, L.A. Rams vs. Houston	27	215	2
Nov. 18, 1984	*Greg Bell, Buffalo vs. Dallas	27	206	1
Nov. 4, 1984	Eric Dickerson, L.A. Rams vs. St. Louis	21	208	0
Sept. 2, 1984	Gerald Riggs, Atlanta vs. New Orleans	35	202	2
Nov. 27, 1983	*Curt Warner, Seattle vs. Kansas City (OT)	32	207	3
Nov. 6, 1983	James Wilder, Tampa Bay vs. Minnesota	31	219	1
Sept. 18, 1983	Tony Collins, New England vs. N.Y. Jets	23	212	3
Sept. 4, 1983	George Rogers, New Orleans vs. St. Louis	24	206	2
Dec. 21, 1980	Earl Campbell, Houston vs. Minnesota	29	203	1
Nov. 16, 1980	Earl Campbell, Houston vs. Chicago	31	206	0
Oct. 26, 1980	Earl Campbell, Houston vs. Cincinnati	27	202	2
Oct. 19, 1980	Earl Campbell, Houston vs. Tampa Bay	33	203	0
Nov. 26, 1978	*Terry Miller, Buffalo vs. N.Y. Giants	21	208	2
Dec. 4, 1977	*Tony Dorsett, Dallas vs. Philadelphia	23	206	2
Nov. 20, 1977	Walter Payton, Chicago vs. Minnesota	40	275	1
Oct. 30, 1977	Walter Payton, Chicago vs. Green Bay	23	205	2
Dec. 5, 1976	O.J. Simpson, Buffalo vs. Miami	24	203	1
Nov. 25, 1976	O.J. Simpson, Buffalo vs. Detroit	29	273	2
Oct. 24, 1976	Chuck Foreman, Minnesota vs. Philadelphia	28	200	2
Dec. 14, 1975	Greg Pruitt, Cleveland vs. Kansas City	26	214	3
Sept. 28, 1975	O.J. Simpson, Buffalo vs. Pittsburgh	28	227	1
Dec. 16, 1973	O.J. Simpson, Buffalo vs. N.Y. Jets	34	200	1
Dec. 9, 1973	O.J. Simpson, Buffalo vs. New England	22	219	1

Sept. 16, 1973	O.J. Simpson, Buffalo vs. New England	29	250	2
Dec. 5, 1971	Willie Ellison, Los Angeles vs. New Orleans	26	247	1
Dec. 20, 1970	John (Frenchy) Fuqua, Pittsburgh vs. Philadelphia	20	218	2
Nov. 3, 1968	Gale Sayers, Chicago vs. Green Bay	24	205	0
Oct. 30, 1966	Jim Nance, Boston vs. Oakland	38	208	2
Oct. 10, 1964	John Henry Johnson, Pittsburgh vs. Cleveland	30	200	3
Dec. 8, 1963	Cookie Gilchrist, Buffalo vs. N.Y. Jets	36	243	5
Nov. 3, 1963	Jim Brown, Cleveland vs. Philadelphia	28	223	1
Oct. 20, 1963	Clem Daniels, Oakland vs. N.Y. Jets	27	200	2
Sept. 22, 1963	Jim Brown, Cleveland vs. Dallas	20	232	2
Dec. 10, 1961	Billy Cannon, Houston vs. N.Y. Titans	25	216	3
Nov. 19, 1961	Jim Brown, Cleveland vs. Philadelphia	34	237	4
Dec. 18, 1960	John David Crow, St. Louis vs. Pittsburgh	24	203	0
Nov. 15, 1959	Bobby Mitchell, Cleveland vs. Washington	14	232	3
Nov. 24, 1957	*Jim Brown, Cleveland vs. Los Angeles	31	237	4
Dec. 16, 1956	*Tom Wilson, Los Angeles vs. Green Bay	23	223	0
Nov. 22, 1953	Dan Towler, Los Angeles vs. Baltimore	14	205	1
Nov. 12, 1950	Gene Roberts, N.Y. Giants vs. Chi. Cardinals	26	218	2
Nov. 27, 1949	Steve Van Buren, Philadelphia vs. Pittsburgh	27	205	0
Oct. 8, 1933	Cliff Battles, Boston vs. N.Y. Giants	16	215	1

**First season of professional football.*

TIMES 200 OR MORE

60 times by 41 players...Simpson 6; Brown, Campbell 4; Bell, Dickerson 3; Payton, Riggs, Rogers, Sanders 2.

4,000 YARDS PASSING IN A SEASON

Year	Player, Team	Att.	Comp.	Pct.	Yards	TD	Int.
1995	Brett Favre, Green Bay	570	359	63.0	4,413	38	13
	Scott Mitchell, Detroit	583	346	59.3	4,338	32	12
	Warren Moon, Minnesota[4]	606	377	62.2	4,228	33	14
	Jeff George, Atlanta	557	336	60.3	4,143	24	11
1994	Drew Bledsoe, New England	691	400	57.9	4,555	25	27
	Dan Marino, Miami[6]	615	385	62.6	4,453	30	17
	Warren Moon, Minnesota[3]	601	371	61.7	4,264	18	19
1993	John Elway, Denver	551	348	63.2	4,030	25	10
	Steve Young, San Francisco	462	314	68.0	4,023	29	16
1992	Dan Marino, Miami[5]	554	330	59.6	4,116	24	16
1991	Warren Moon, Houston[2]	655	404	61.7	4,690	23	21
1990	Warren Moon, Houston	584	362	62.0	4,689	33	13
1989	Don Majkowski, Green Bay	599	353	58.9	4,318	27	20
	Jim Everett, L.A. Rams	518	304	58.7	4,310	29	17
1988	Dan Marino, Miami[4]	606	354	58.4	4,434	28	23
1986	Dan Marino, Miami[3]	623	378	60.7	4,746	44	23
	Jay Schroeder, Washington	541	276	51.0	4,109	22	22
1985	Dan Marino, Miami[2]	567	336	59.3	4,137	30	21
1984	Dan Marino, Miami	564	362	64.2	5,084	48	17
	Neil Lomax, St. Louis	560	345	61.6	4,614	28	16
	Phil Simms, N.Y. Giants	533	286	53.7	4,044	22	18
1983	Lynn Dickey, Green Bay	484	289	59.7	4,458	32	29
	Bill Kenney, Kansas City	603	346	57.4	4,348	24	18
1981	Dan Fouts, San Diego[3]	609	360	59.1	4,802	33	17
1980	Dan Fouts, San Diego[2]	589	348	59.1	4,715	30	24
	Brian Sipe, Cleveland	554	337	60.8	4,132	30	14
1979	Dan Fouts, San Diego	530	332	62.6	4,082	24	24
1967	Joe Namath, N.Y. Jets	491	258	52.5	4,007	26	28

400 YARDS PASSING IN A GAME

Date	Player, Team, Opponent	Att.	Comp.	Yards	TD
Dec. 18, 1995	Steve Young, San Francisco vs. Minnesota	49	30	425	3
Nov. 26, 1995	Dave Krieg, Arizona vs. Atlanta (OT)	43	27	413	4
Nov. 23, 1995	Scott Mitchell, Detroit vs. Minnesota	45	30	410	4
Oct. 1, 1995	Dan Marino, Miami vs. Cincinnati	48	33	450	2
Nov. 20, 1994	Warren Moon, Minnesota vs. N.Y. Jets	50	33	400	2
Nov. 13, 1994	Drew Bledsoe, New England vs. Minnesota (OT)	70	45	426	3
Nov. 6, 1994	Warren Moon, Minnesota vs. New Orleans	57	33	420	3
Sept. 25, 1994	Dan Marino, Miami vs. Minnesota	54	29	431	3
Sept. 4, 1994	Dan Marino, Miami vs. New England (OT)	42	23	473	5
Sept. 4, 1994	Drew Bledsoe, New England vs. Miami (OT)	51	32	421	4
Dec. 19, 1993	Steve Beuerlein, Phoenix vs. Seattle	53	34	431	3
Dec. 5, 1993	Brett Favre, Green Bay vs. Chicago	54	36	402	2
Nov. 28, 1993	Steve Young, San Francisco vs. L.A. Rams	32	26	462	4
Oct. 31, 1993	Jeff Hostetler, L.A. Raiders vs. San Diego	32	20	424	2
Sept. 13, 1992	Steve Young, San Francisco vs. Buffalo	37	26	449	3
Sept. 13, 1992	Jim Kelly, Buffalo vs. San Francisco	33	22	403	3
Nov. 10, 1991	Warren Moon, Houston vs. Dallas (OT)	56	41	432	0
Nov. 10, 1991	Mark Rypien, Washington vs. Atlanta	31	16	442	6
Oct. 13, 1991	Warren Moon, Houston vs. N.Y. Jets	50	35	423	2
Dec. 16, 1990	Warren Moon, Houston vs. Kansas City	45	27	527	3
Nov. 4, 1990	Joe Montana, San Francisco vs. Green Bay	40	25	411	3
Oct. 14, 1990	Joe Montana, San Francisco vs. Atlanta	49	32	476	6
Oct. 7, 1990	Boomer Esiason, Cincinnati vs. L.A. Rams (OT)	45	31	490	3
Dec. 23, 1989	Warren Moon, Houston vs. Cleveland	51	32	414	2
Dec. 11, 1989	Joe Montana, San Francisco vs. L.A. Rams	42	30	458	3
Nov. 26, 1989	Jim Everett, L.A. Rams vs. New Orleans (OT)	51	29	454	1
Nov. 26, 1989	Mark Rypien, Washington vs. Chicago	47	30	401	4
Oct. 2, 1989	Randall Cunningham, Philadelphia vs. Chicago	62	32	401	1
Sept. 24, 1989	Joe Montana, San Francisco vs. Philadelphia	34	25	428	5
Sept. 24, 1989	Dan Marino, Miami vs. N.Y. Jets	55	33	427	3
Sept. 17, 1989	Randall Cunningham, Phil. vs. Washington	46	34	447	5
Dec. 18, 1988	Dave Krieg, Seattle vs. L.A. Raiders	32	19	410	4
Dec. 12, 1988	Dan Marino, Miami vs. Cleveland	50	30	404	4
Oct. 23, 1988	Dan Marino, Miami vs. N.Y. Jets	60	35	521	3
Oct. 16, 1988	Vinny Testaverde, Tampa Bay vs. Indianapolis	42	25	469	2
Sept. 11, 1988	Doug Williams, Washington vs. Pittsburgh	52	30	430	2
Nov. 29, 1987	Tom Ramsey, New England vs. Philadelphia	53	34	402	3
Nov. 22, 1987	Boomer Esiason, Cincinnati vs. Pittsburgh	53	30	409	0
Sept. 20, 1987	Neil Lomax, St. Louis vs. San Diego	61	32	457	3
Dec. 21, 1986	Boomer Esiason, Cincinnati vs. N.Y. Jets	30	23	425	5
Dec. 14, 1986	Dan Marino, Miami vs. L.A. Rams (OT)	46	29	403	5
Nov. 23, 1986	Bernie Kosar, Cleveland vs. Pittsburgh (OT)	46	28	414	2
Nov. 17, 1986	Joe Montana, San Francisco vs. Washington	60	33	441	0
Nov. 16, 1986	Dan Marino, Miami vs. Buffalo	54	39	404	4
Nov. 10, 1986	Bernie Kosar, Cleveland vs. Miami	50	32	401	0
Nov. 2, 1986	Tommy Kramer, Minnesota vs. Washington (OT)	35	20	490	4
Nov. 2, 1986	Ken O'Brien, N.Y. Jets vs. Seattle	32	26	431	4
Oct. 27, 1986	Jay Schroeder, Washington vs. N.Y. Giants	40	22	420	1
Oct. 12, 1986	Steve Grogan, New England vs. N.Y. Jets	42	23	401	3
Sept. 21, 1986	Ken O'Brien, N.Y. Jets vs. Miami (OT)	43	29	479	4
Sept. 21, 1986	Dan Marino, Miami vs. N.Y. Jets (OT)	50	30	448	6
Sept. 21, 1986	Tony Eason, New England vs. Seattle	45	26	414	3
Dec. 20, 1985	John Elway, Denver vs. Seattle	42	24	432	1
Nov. 10, 1985	Dan Fouts, San Diego vs. L.A. Raiders (OT)	41	26	436	4
Oct. 13, 1985	Phil Simms, N.Y. Giants vs. Cincinnati	62	40	513	1
Oct. 13, 1985	Dave Krieg, Seattle vs. Atlanta	51	33	405	4
Oct. 6, 1985	Phil Simms, N.Y. Giants vs. Dallas	36	18	432	3
Oct. 6, 1985	Joe Montana, San Francisco vs. Atlanta	57	37	429	5
Sept. 19, 1985	Tommy Kramer, Minnesota vs. Chicago	55	28	436	3
Sept. 15, 1985	Dan Fouts, San Diego vs. Seattle	43	29	440	4
Dec. 16, 1984	Neil Lomax, St. Louis vs. Washington	46	37	468	2
Dec. 9, 1984	Dan Marino, Miami vs. Indianapolis	41	29	404	4
Dec. 2, 1984	Dan Marino, Miami vs. L.A. Raiders	57	35	470	4
Nov. 25, 1984	Dave Krieg, Seattle vs. Denver	44	30	406	3
Nov. 4, 1984	Dan Marino, Miami vs. N.Y. Jets	42	23	422	2
Oct. 21, 1984	Dan Fouts, San Diego vs. L.A. Raiders	45	24	410	3
Sept. 30, 1984	Dan Marino, Miami vs. St. Louis	36	24	429	3
Sept. 2, 1984	Phil Simms, N.Y. Giants vs. Philadelphia	30	23	409	4
Dec. 11, 1983	Bill Kenney, Kansas City vs. San Diego	41	31	411	4
Nov. 20, 1983	Dave Krieg, Seattle vs. Denver	42	31	418	3
Oct. 9, 1983	Joe Ferguson, Buffalo vs. Miami (OT)	55	38	419	5
Oct. 2, 1983	Joe Theismann, Washington vs. L.A. Raiders	39	23	417	3
Sept. 25, 1983	Richard Todd, N.Y. Jets vs. L.A. Rams (OT)	50	37	446	2
Dec. 26, 1982	Vince Ferragamo, L.A. Rams vs. Chicago	46	30	509	3
Dec. 20, 1982	Dan Fouts, San Diego vs. Cincinnati	40	25	435	1
Dec. 20, 1982	Ken Anderson, Cincinnati vs. San Diego	56	40	416	2
Dec. 11, 1982	Dan Fouts, San Diego vs. San Francisco	48	33	444	5
Nov. 21, 1982	Joe Montana, San Francisco vs. St. Louis	39	26	408	3
Nov. 15, 1981	Steve Bartkowski, Atlanta vs. Pittsburgh	50	33	416	2
Oct. 25, 1981	Brian Sipe, Cleveland vs. Baltimore	41	30	444	4
Oct. 25, 1981	David Woodley, Miami vs. Dallas	37	21	408	3
Oct. 11, 1981	Tommy Kramer, Minnesota vs. San Diego	43	27	444	4
Dec. 14, 1980	Tommy Kramer, Minnesota vs. Cleveland	49	38	456	4
Nov. 16, 1980	Doug Williams, Tampa Bay vs. Minnesota	55	30	486	4
Oct. 19, 1980	Dan Fouts, San Diego vs. N.Y. Giants	41	26	444	3
Oct. 12, 1980	Lynn Dickey, Green Bay vs. Tampa Bay (OT)	51	35	418	1
Sept. 21, 1980	Richard Todd, N.Y. Jets vs. San Francisco	60	42	447	3
Oct. 3, 1976	James Harris, Los Angeles vs. Miami	29	17	436	2
Nov. 17, 1975	Ken Anderson, Cincinnati vs. Buffalo	46	30	447	2
Nov. 18, 1974	Charley Johnson, Denver vs. Kansas City	42	28	445	2
Dec. 11, 1972	Joe Namath, N.Y. Jets vs. Oakland	46	25	403	1
Sept. 24, 1972	Joe Namath, N.Y. Jets vs. Baltimore	28	15	496	6
Dec. 21, 1969	Don Horn, Green Bay vs. St. Louis	31	22	410	5
Sept. 28, 1969	Joe Kapp, Minnesota vs. Baltimore	43	28	449	7
Sept. 9, 1968	Pete Beathard, Houston vs. Kansas City	48	23	413	2
Nov. 26, 1967	Sonny Jurgensen, Washington vs. Cleveland	50	32	418	3
Oct. 1, 1967	Joe Namath, N.Y. Jets vs. Miami	39	23	415	3
Sept. 17, 1967	Johnny Unitas, Baltimore vs. Atlanta	32	22	401	2
Nov. 13, 1966	Don Meredith, Dallas vs. Washington	29	21	406	2
Nov. 28, 1965	Sonny Jurgensen, Washington vs. Dallas	43	26	411	3
Oct. 24, 1965	Fran Tarkenton, Minnesota vs. San Francisco	35	21	407	3
Nov. 1, 1964	Len Dawson, Kansas City vs. Denver	38	23	435	6
Oct. 25, 1964	Cotton Davidson, Oakland vs. Denver	36	23	427	5
Oct. 16, 1964	Babe Parilli, Boston vs. Oakland	47	25	422	4
Dec. 22, 1963	Tom Flores, Oakland vs. Houston	29	17	407	6

OUTSTANDING PERFORMERS

Nov. 17, 1963	Norm Snead, Washington vs. Pittsburgh	40	23	424	2
Nov. 10, 1963	Don Meredith, Dallas vs. San Francisco	48	30	460	3
Oct. 13, 1963	Charley Johnson, St. Louis vs. Pittsburgh	41	20	428	2
Dec. 16, 1962	Sonny Jurgensen, Philadelphia vs. St. Louis	34	15	419	5
Nov. 18, 1962	Bill Wade, Chicago vs. Dall. Cowboys	46	28	466	2
Oct. 28, 1962	Y.A. Tittle, N.Y. Giants vs. Washington	39	27	505	7
Sept. 15, 1962	Frank Tripucka, Denver vs. Buffalo	56	29	447	2
Dec. 17, 1961	Sonny Jurgensen, Philadelphia vs. Detroit	42	27	403	3
Nov. 19, 1961	George Blanda, Houston vs. N.Y. Titans	32	20	418	7
Oct. 29, 1961	George Blanda, Houston vs. Buffalo	32	18	464	4
Oct. 29, 1961	Sonny Jurgensen, Philadelphia vs. Washington	41	27	436	3
Oct. 13, 1961	Jacky Lee, Houston vs. Boston	41	27	457	2
Dec. 13, 1958	Bobby Layne, Pittsburgh vs. Chi. Cardinals	49	23	409	2
Nov. 8, 1953	Bobby Thomason, Philadelphia vs. N.Y. Giants	44	22	437	4
Oct. 4, 1952	Otto Graham, Cleveland vs. Pittsburgh	49	21	401	3
Sept. 28, 1951	Norm Van Brocklin, Los Angeles vs. N.Y. Yanks	41	27	554	5
Dec. 11, 1949	Johnny Lujack, Chi. Bears vs. Chi. Cardinals	39	24	468	6
Oct. 31, 1948	Sammy Baugh, Washington vs. Boston	24	17	446	4
Oct. 31, 1948	Jim Hardy, Los Angeles vs. Chi. Cardinals	53	28	406	3
Nov. 14, 1943	Sid Luckman, Chi. Bears vs. N.Y. Giants	32	21	433	7

TIMES 400 OR MORE

123 times by 64 players...Marino 13; Montana 7; Fouts, Moon 6; Jurgensen, Krieg 5; Kramer 4; Esiason, Namath, Simms, Young 3; Anderson, Blanda, Bledsoe, Cunningham, Johnson, Kosar, Lomax, Meredith, O'Brien, Rypien, Todd, Williams 2.

100 PASS RECEPTIONS IN A SEASON

Year	Player, Team	No.	Yards	Avg.	Long	TD
1995	Herman Moore, Detroit	123	1,686	13.7	69	14
	Jerry Rice, San Francisco[3]	122	1,848	15.1	81	15
	Cris Carter, Minnesota[2]	122	1,371	11.2	60	17
	Isaac Bruce, St. Louis	119	1,781	15.0	72	13
	Michael Irvin, Dallas	111	1,603	14.4	50	10
	Brett Perriman, Detroit	108	1,488	13.8	91	9
	Eric Metcalf, Atlanta	104	1,189	11.4	62	8
	Robert Brooks, Green Bay	102	1,497	14.7	99	13
	Larry Centers, Arizona	101	962	9.5	32	2
1994	Cris Carter, Minnesota	122	1,256	10.3	65	7
	Jerry Rice, San Francisco[2]	112	1,499	13.4	69	13
	Terance Mathis, Atlanta	111	1,342	12.1	81	11
1993	Sterling Sharpe, Green Bay[2]	112	1,274	11.4	54	11
1992	Sterling Sharpe, Green Bay	108	1,461	13.5	76	13
1991	Haywood Jeffires, Houston	100	1,181	11.8	44	7
1990	Jerry Rice, San Francisco	100	1,502	15.0	64	13
1984	Art Monk, Washington	106	1,372	12.9	72	7
1964	Charley Hennigan, Houston	101	1,546	15.3	53	8
1961	Lionel Taylor, Denver	100	1,176	11.8	52	4

1,000 YARDS PASS RECEIVING IN A SEASON

Year	Player, Team	No.	Yards	Avg.	Long	TD
1995	Jerry Rice, San Francisco[10]	122	1,848	15.1	81	15
	Isaac Bruce, St. Louis	119	1,781	15.0	72	13
	Herman Moore, Detroit[2]	123	1,686	13.7	69	14
	Michael Irvin, Dallas[5]	111	1,603	14.4	50	10
	Robert Brooks, Green Bay	102	1,497	14.7	99	13
	Brett Perriman, Detroit	108	1,488	13.8	91	9
	Cris Carter, Minnesota[3]	122	1,371	11.2	60	17
	Tim Brown, Oakland[3]	89	1,342	15.1	80	10
	Yancey Thigpen, Pittsburgh	85	1,307	15.4	43	5
	Jeff Graham, Chicago	82	1,301	15.9	51	4
	Carl Pickens, Cincinnati[2]	99	1,234	12.5	68	17
	Tony Martin, San Diego	90	1,224	13.6	51	6
	Eric Metcalf, Atlanta	104	1,189	11.4	62	8
	Jake Reed, Minnesota[2]	72	1,167	16.2	55	9
	Quinn Early, New Orleans	81	1,087	13.4	70	8
	Anthony Miller, Denver[5]	59	1,079	18.3	62	14
	Bert Emanuel, Atlanta	74	1,039	14.0	52	5
	*Joey Galloway, Seattle	67	1,039	15.5	59	7
	Terance Mathis, Atlanta[2]	78	1,039	13.3	54	9
	Curtis Conway, Chicago	62	1,037	16.7	76	12
	Henry Ellard, Washington[6]	56	1,005	17.9	59	5
	Mark Carrier, Carolina[2]	66	1,002	15.2	66	3
	Brian Blades, Seattle[4]	77	1,001	13.0	49	4
1994	Jerry Rice, San Francisco[9]	112	1,499	13.4	69	13
	Henry Ellard, Washington[5]	74	1,397	18.9	73	6
	Terance Mathis, Atlanta	111	1,342	12.1	81	11
	Tim Brown, L.A. Raiders[2]	89	1,309	14.7	77	9
	Andre Reed, Buffalo[2]	90	1,303	14.5	83	8
	Irving Fryar, Miami[3]	73	1,270	17.4	54	7
	Cris Carter, Minnesota[2]	122	1,256	10.3	65	7
	Michael Irvin, Dallas[4]	79	1,241	15.7	65	6
	Jake Reed, Minnesota	85	1,175	13.8	59	4
	Ben Coates, New England	96	1,174	12.2	62	7
	Herman Moore, Detroit	72	1,173	16.3	51	11
	Fred Barnett, Philadelphia[2]	78	1,127	14.4	54	5
	Carl Pickens, Cincinnati	71	1,127	15.9	70	11
	Sterling Sharpe, Green Bay[4]	94	1,119	11.9	49	18
	Anthony Miller, Denver[4]	60	1,107	18.5	76	5
	Andre Rison, Atlanta[3]	81	1,088	13.4	69	8
	Brian Blades, Seattle[3]	81	1,088	13.4	45	4
	Rob Moore, N.Y. Jets	78	1,010	12.9	41	6
	Shannon Sharpe, Denver	87	1,010	11.6	44	4
1993	Jerry Rice, San Francisco[8]	98	1,503	15.3	80	15
	Michael Irvin, Dallas[3]	88	1,330	15.1	61	7
	Sterling Sharpe, Green Bay[4]	112	1,274	11.4	54	11
	Andre Rison, Atlanta[3]	86	1,242	14.4	53	15
	Tim Brown, L.A. Raiders	80	1,180	14.8	71	7
	Anthony Miller, San Diego[3]	84	1,162	13.8	66	7
	Cris Carter, Minnesota	86	1,071	12.5	58	9
	Reggie Langhorne, Indianapolis	85	1,038	12.2	72	3
	Irving Fryar, Miami[2]	64	1,010	15.8	65	5
1992	Sterling Sharpe, Green Bay[3]	108	1,461	13.5	76	13
	Michael Irvin, Dallas[2]	78	1,396	17.9	87	7
	Jerry Rice, San Francisco[7]	84	1,201	14.3	80	10
	Andre Rison, Atlanta[2]	93	1,119	12.0	71	11
	Fred Barnett, Philadelphia	67	1,083	16.2	71	6
	Anthony Miller, San Diego[2]	72	1,060	14.7	67	7
	Eric Martin, New Orleans[3]	68	1,041	15.3	52	5
1991	Michael Irvin, Dallas	93	1,523	16.4	66	8
	Gary Clark, Washington[5]	70	1,340	19.1	82	10
	Jerry Rice, San Francisco[6]	80	1,206	15.1	73	14
	Haywood Jeffires, Houston[2]	100	1,181	11.8	44	7
	Michael Haynes, Atlanta	50	1,122	22.4	80	11
	Andre Reed, Buffalo[2]	81	1,113	13.7	55	10
	Drew Hill, Houston[5]	90	1,109	12.3	61	4
	Mark Duper, Miami[4]	70	1,085	15.5	43	5
	James Lofton, Buffalo[6]	57	1,072	18.8	77	8
	Mark Clayton, Miami[5]	70	1,053	15.0	43	12
	Henry Ellard, L.A. Rams[4]	64	1,052	16.4	38	3
	Art Monk, Washington[5]	71	1,049	14.8	64	8
	Irving Fryar, New England	68	1,014	14.9	56	3
	John Taylor, San Francisco[2]	64	1,011	15.8	97	9
	Brian Blades, Seattle[2]	70	1,003	14.3	52	2
1990	Jerry Rice, San Francisco[5]	100	1,502	15.0	64	13
	Henry Ellard, L.A. Rams[3]	76	1,294	17.0	50	4
	Andre Rison, Atlanta	82	1,208	14.7	75	10
	Gary Clark, Washington[4]	75	1,112	14.8	53	8
	Sterling Sharpe, Green Bay[2]	67	1,105	16.5	76	6
	Willie Anderson, L.A. Rams[2]	51	1,097	21.5	55	4
	Haywood Jeffires, Houston	74	1,048	14.2	87	8
	Stephone Paige, Kansas City	65	1,021	15.7	86	5
	Drew Hill, Houston[4]	74	1,019	13.8	57	5
	Anthony Carter, Minnesota[3]	70	1,008	14.4	56	8
1989	Jerry Rice, San Francisco[4]	82	1,483	18.1	68	17
	Sterling Sharpe, Green Bay	90	1,423	15.8	79	12
	Mark Carrier, Tampa Bay	86	1,422	16.5	78	9
	Henry Ellard, L.A. Rams[2]	70	1,382	19.7	53	8
	Andre Reed, Buffalo	88	1,312	14.9	78	9
	Anthony Miller, San Diego	75	1,252	16.7	69	10
	Webster Slaughter, Cleveland	65	1,236	19.0	97	6
	Gary Clark, Washington[3]	79	1,229	15.6	80	9
	Tim McGee, Cincinnati	65	1,211	18.6	74	8
	Art Monk, Washington[4]	86	1,186	13.8	60	8
	Willie Anderson, L.A. Rams	44	1,146	26.0	78	5
	Ricky Sanders, Washington[2]	80	1,138	14.2	68	4
	Vance Johnson, Denver	76	1,095	14.4	69	7
	Richard Johnson, Detroit	70	1,091	15.6	75	8
	Eric Martin, New Orleans[2]	68	1,090	16.0	53	8
	John Taylor, San Francisco	60	1,077	18.0	95	10
	Mervyn Fernandez, L.A. Raiders	57	1,069	18.8	75	9
	Anthony Carter, Minnesota[2]	65	1,066	16.4	50	4
	Brian Blades, Seattle	77	1,063	13.8	60	5
	Mark Clayton, Miami[4]	64	1,011	15.8	78	9
1988	Henry Ellard, L.A. Rams	86	1,414	16.4	68	10
	Jerry Rice, San Francisco[3]	64	1,306	20.4	96	9
	Eddie Brown, Cincinnati	53	1,273	24.0	86	9
	Anthony Carter, Minnesota	72	1,225	17.0	67	6
	Ricky Sanders, Washington	73	1,148	15.7	55	12
	Drew Hill, Houston[3]	72	1,141	15.8	57	10
	Mark Clayton, Miami[3]	86	1,129	13.1	45	14
	Roy Green, Phoenix[3]	68	1,097	16.1	52	7
	Eric Martin, New Orleans	85	1,083	12.7	40	7
	Al Toon, N.Y. Jets[2]	93	1,067	11.5	42	5

	Bruce Hill, Tampa Bay	58	1,040	17.9	42	9
	Lionel Manuel, N.Y. Giants	65	1,029	15.8	46	4
1987	J.T. Smith, St. Louis[2]	91	1,117	12.3	38	8
	Jerry Rice, San Francisco[2]	65	1,078	16.6	57	22
	Gary Clark, Washington[2]	56	1,066	19.0	84	7
	Carlos Carson, Kansas City[3]	55	1,044	19.0	81	7
1986	Jerry Rice, San Francisco	86	1,570	18.3	66	15
	Stanley Morgan, New England[3]	84	1,491	17.8	44	10
	Mark Duper, Miami[3]	67	1,313	19.6	85	11
	Gary Clark, Washington	74	1,265	17.1	55	7
	Al Toon, N.Y. Jets	85	1,176	13.8	62	8
	Todd Christensen, L.A. Raiders[3]	95	1,153	12.1	35	8
	Mark Clayton, Miami[2]	60	1,150	19.2	68	10
	*Bill Brooks, Indianapolis	65	1,131	17.4	84	8
	Drew Hill, Houston[2]	65	1,112	17.1	81	5
	Steve Largent, Seattle[8]	70	1,070	15.3	38	9
	Art Monk, Washington[3]	73	1,068	14.6	69	4
	*Ernest Givins, Houston	61	1,062	17.4	60	3
	Cris Collinsworth, Cincinnati[4]	62	1,024	16.5	46	10
	Wesley Walker, N.Y. Jets[2]	49	1,016	20.7	83	12
	J.T. Smith, St. Louis	80	1,014	12.7	45	6
	Mark Bavaro, N.Y. Giants	66	1,001	15.2	41	4
1985	Steve Largent, Seattle[7]	79	1,287	16.3	43	6
	Mike Quick, Philadelphia[3]	73	1,247	17.1	99	11
	Art Monk, Washington[2]	91	1,226	13.5	53	2
	Wes Chandler, San Diego[4]	67	1,199	17.9	75	10
	Drew Hill, Houston	64	1,169	18.3	57	9
	James Lofton, Green Bay[5]	69	1,153	16.7	56	4
	Louis Lipps, Pittsburgh	59	1,134	19.2	51	12
	Cris Collinsworth, Cincinnati[3]	65	1,125	17.3	71	5
	Tony Hill, Dallas[3]	74	1,113	15.0	53	7
	Lionel James, San Diego	86	1,027	11.9	67	6
	Roger Craig, San Francisco	92	1,016	11.0	73	6
1984	Roy Green, St. Louis[2]	78	1,555	19.9	83	12
	John Stallworth, Pittsburgh[3]	80	1,395	17.4	51	11
	Mark Clayton, Miami	73	1,389	19.0	65	18
	Art Monk, Washington	106	1,372	12.9	72	7
	James Lofton, Green Bay[4]	62	1,361	22.0	79	7
	Mark Duper, Miami[2]	71	1,306	18.4	80	8
	Steve Watson, Denver[3]	69	1,170	17.0	73	7
	Steve Largent, Seattle[6]	74	1,164	15.7	65	12
	Tim Smith, Houston[2]	69	1,141	16.5	75	4
	Stacey Bailey, Atlanta	67	1,138	17.0	61	6
	Carlos Carson, Kansas City[2]	57	1,078	18.9	57	4
	Mike Quick, Philadelphia[2]	61	1,052	17.2	90	9
	Todd Christensen, L.A. Raiders[2]	80	1,007	12.6	38	7
	Kevin House, Tampa Bay[2]	76	1,005	13.2	55	5
	Ozzie Newsome, Cleveland[2]	89	1,001	11.2	52	5
1983	Mike Quick, Philadelphia	69	1,409	20.4	83	13
	Carlos Carson, Kansas City	80	1,351	16.9	50	7
	James Lofton, Green Bay[3]	58	1,300	22.4	74	8
	Todd Christensen, L.A. Raiders	92	1,247	13.6	45	12
	Roy Green, St. Louis	78	1,227	15.7	71	14
	Charlie Brown, Washington	78	1,225	15.7	75	8
	Tim Smith, Houston	83	1,176	14.2	47	6
	Kellen Winslow, San Diego[3]	88	1,172	13.3	46	8
	Earnest Gray, N.Y. Giants	78	1,139	14.6	62	5
	Steve Watson, Denver[2]	59	1,133	19.2	78	5
	Cris Collinsworth, Cincinnati[2]	66	1,130	17.1	63	5
	Steve Largent, Seattle[5]	72	1,074	14.9	46	11
	Mark Duper, Miami	51	1,003	19.7	85	10
1982	Wes Chandler, San Diego[3]	49	1,032	21.1	66	9
1981	Alfred Jenkins, Atlanta[2]	70	1,358	19.4	67	13
	James Lofton, Green Bay[2]	71	1,294	18.2	75	8
	Steve Watson, Denver	60	1,244	20.7	95	13
	Frank Lewis, Buffalo[2]	70	1,244	17.8	33	4
	Steve Largent, Seattle[4]	75	1,224	16.3	57	9
	Charlie Joiner, San Diego[4]	70	1,188	17.0	57	7
	Kevin House, Tampa Bay	56	1,176	21.0	84	9
	Wes Chandler, N.O.-San Diego[2]	69	1,142	16.6	51	6
	Dwight Clark, San Francisco	85	1,105	13.0	78	4
	John Stallworth, Pittsburgh[2]	63	1,098	17.4	55	5
	Kellen Winslow, San Diego[2]	88	1,075	12.2	67	10
	Pat Tilley, St. Louis	66	1,040	15.8	75	3
	Stanley Morgan, New England[2]	44	1,029	23.4	76	6
	Harold Carmichael, Philadelphia[3]	61	1,028	16.9	85	6
	Freddie Scott, Detroit	53	1,022	19.3	48	5
	*Cris Collinsworth, Cincinnati	67	1,009	15.1	74	8
	Joe Senser, Minnesota	79	1,004	12.7	53	8
	Ozzie Newsome, Cleveland	69	1,002	14.5	62	6
	Sammy White, Minnesota	66	1,001	15.2	53	3
1980	John Jefferson, San Diego[3]	82	1,340	16.3	58	13
	Kellen Winslow, San Diego	89	1,290	14.5	65	9
	James Lofton, Green Bay	71	1,226	17.3	47	4
	Charlie Joiner, San Diego[3]	71	1,132	15.9	51	4
	Ahmad Rashad, Minnesota[2]	69	1,095	15.9	76	5
	Steve Largent, Seattle[3]	66	1,064	16.1	67	6
	Tony Hill, Dallas[2]	60	1,055	17.6	58	8
	Alfred Jenkins, Atlanta	57	1,026	18.0	57	6
1979	Steve Largent, Seattle[2]	66	1,237	18.7	55	9
	John Stallworth, Pittsburgh	70	1,183	16.9	65	8
	Ahmad Rashad, Minnesota	80	1,156	14.5	52	9
	John Jefferson, San Diego[2]	61	1,090	17.9	65	10
	Frank Lewis, Buffalo	54	1,082	20.0	55	2
	Wes Chandler, New Orleans	65	1,069	16.4	85	6
	Tony Hill, Dallas	60	1,062	17.7	75	10
	Drew Pearson, Dallas[2]	55	1,026	18.7	56	8
	Wallace Francis, Atlanta	74	1,013	13.7	42	8
	Harold Jackson, New England[3]	45	1,013	22.5	59	7
	Charlie Joiner, San Diego[2]	72	1,008	14.0	39	4
	Stanley Morgan, New England	44	1,002	22.8	63	12
1978	Wesley Walker, N.Y. Jets	48	1,169	24.4	77	8
	Steve Largent, Seattle	71	1,168	16.5	57	8
	Harold Carmichael, Philadelphia[2]	55	1,072	19.5	56	8
	*John Jefferson, San Diego	56	1,001	17.9	46	13
1976	Roger Carr, Baltimore	43	1,112	25.9	79	11
	Cliff Branch, Oakland[2]	46	1,111	24.2	88	12
	Charlie Joiner, San Diego	50	1,056	21.1	81	7
1975	Ken Burrough, Houston	53	1,063	20.1	77	8
1974	Cliff Branch, Oakland	60	1,092	18.2	67	13
	Drew Pearson, Dallas	62	1,087	17.5	50	2
1973	Harold Carmichael, Philadelphia	67	1,116	16.7	73	9
1972	Harold Jackson, Philadelphia[2]	62	1,048	16.9	77	4
	John Gilliam, Minnesota	47	1,035	22.0	66	7
1971	Otis Taylor, Kansas City[2]	57	1,110	19.5	82	7
1970	Gene Washington, San Francisco	53	1,100	20.8	79	12
	Marlin Briscoe, Buffalo	57	1,036	18.2	48	8
	Dick Gordon, Chicago	71	1,026	14.5	69	13
	Gary Garrison, San Diego[2]	44	1,006	22.9	67	12
1969	Warren Wells, Oakland[2]	47	1,260	26.8	80	14
	Harold Jackson, Philadelphia	65	1,116	17.2	65	9
	Roy Jefferson, Pittsburgh[2]	67	1,079	16.1	63	9
	Dan Abramowicz, New Orleans	73	1,015	13.9	49	7
	Lance Alworth, San Diego[7]	64	1,003	15.7	76	4
1968	Lance Alworth, San Diego[6]	68	1,312	19.3	80	10
	Don Maynard, N.Y. Jets[5]	57	1,297	22.8	87	10
	George Sauer, N.Y. Jets[3]	66	1,141	17.3	43	3
	Warren Wells, Oakland	53	1,137	21.5	94	11
	Gary Garrison, San Diego	52	1,103	21.2	84	10
	Roy Jefferson, Pittsburgh	58	1,074	18.5	62	11
	Paul Warfield, Cleveland	50	1,067	21.3	65	12
	Homer Jones, N.Y. Giants[3]	45	1,057	23.5	84	7
	Fred Biletnikoff, Oakland	61	1,037	17.0	82	6
	Lance Rentzel, Dallas	54	1,009	18.7	65	6
1967	Don Maynard, N.Y. Jets[4]	71	1,434	20.2	75	10
	Ben Hawkins, Philadelphia	59	1,265	21.4	87	10
	Homer Jones, N.Y. Giants[2]	49	1,209	24.7	70	13
	Jackie Smith, St. Louis	56	1,205	21.5	76	9
	George Sauer, N.Y. Jets[2]	75	1,189	15.9	61	6
	Lance Alworth, San Diego[5]	52	1,010	19.4	71	9
1966	Lance Alworth, San Diego[4]	73	1,383	18.9	78	13
	Otis Taylor, Kansas City	58	1,297	22.4	89	8
	Pat Studstill, Detroit	67	1,266	18.9	99	5
	Bob Hayes, Dallas[2]	64	1,232	19.3	95	13
	Charlie Frazier, Houston	57	1,129	19.8	79	12
	Charley Taylor, Washington	72	1,119	15.5	86	12
	George Sauer, N.Y. Jets	63	1,081	17.2	77	5
	Homer Jones, N.Y. Giants	48	1,044	21.8	98	8
	Art Powell, Oakland[5]	53	1,026	19.4	46	11
1965	Lance Alworth, San Diego[3]	69	1,602	23.2	85	14
	Dave Parks, San Francisco	80	1,344	16.8	53	12
	Don Maynard, N.Y. Jets[3]	68	1,218	17.9	56	14
	Pete Retzlaff, Philadelphia	66	1,190	18.0	78	10
	Lionel Taylor, Denver[4]	85	1,131	13.3	63	6
	Tommy McDonald, Los Angeles[3]	67	1,036	15.5	51	9
	*Bob Hayes, Dallas	46	1,003	21.8	82	12
1964	Charley Hennigan, Houston[3]	101	1,546	15.3	53	8
	Art Powell, Oakland[4]	76	1,361	17.9	77	11
	Lance Alworth, San Diego[2]	61	1,235	20.2	82	13
	Johnny Morris, Chicago	93	1,200	12.9	63	10
	Elbert Dubenion, Buffalo	42	1,139	27.1	72	10
	Terry Barr, Detroit[2]	57	1,030	18.1	58	9
1963	Bobby Mitchell, Washington[2]	69	1,436	20.8	99	7
	Art Powell, Oakland[3]	73	1,304	17.9	85	16
	Buddy Dial, Pittsburgh[2]	60	1,295	21.6	83	9
	Lance Alworth, San Diego	61	1,205	19.8	85	11

	Del Shofner, N.Y. Giants[4]	64	1,181	18.5	70	9
	Lionel Taylor, Denver[3]	78	1,101	14.1	72	10
	Terry Barr, Detroit	66	1,086	16.5	75	13
	Charley Hennigan, Houston[2]	61	1,051	17.2	83	10
	Sonny Randle, St. Louis[2]	51	1,014	19.9	68	12
	Bake Turner, N.Y. Jets	71	1,009	14.2	53	6
1962	Bobby Mitchell, Washington	72	1,384	19.2	81	11
	Sonny Randle, St. Louis	63	1,158	18.4	86	7
	Tommy McDonald, Philadelphia[2]	58	1,146	19.8	60	10
	Del Shofner, N.Y. Giants[3]	53	1,133	21.4	69	12
	Art Powell, N.Y. Titans[2]	64	1,130	17.7	80	8
	Frank Clarke, Dall. Cowboys	47	1,043	22.2	66	14
	Don Maynard, N.Y. Titans[2]	56	1,041	18.6	86	8
1961	Charley Hennigan, Houston	82	1,746	21.3	80	12
	Lionel Taylor, Denver[2]	100	1,176	11.8	52	4
	Bill Groman, Houston[2]	50	1,175	23.5	80	17
	Tommy McDonald, Philadelphia	64	1,144	17.9	66	13
	Del Shofner, N.Y. Giants[2]	68	1,125	16.5	46	11
	Jim Phillips, Los Angeles	78	1,092	14.0	69	5
	*Mike Ditka, Chicago	56	1,076	19.2	76	12
	Dave Kocourek, San Diego	55	1,055	19.2	76	4
	Buddy Dial, Pittsburgh	53	1,047	19.8	88	12
	R.C. Owens, San Francisco	55	1,032	18.8	54	5
1960	*Bill Groman, Houston	72	1,473	20.5	92	12
	Raymond Berry, Baltimore	74	1,298	17.5	70	10
	Don Maynard, N.Y. Titans	72	1,265	17.6	65	6
	Lionel Taylor, Denver	92	1,235	13.4	80	12
	Art Powell, N.Y. Titans	69	1,167	16.9	76	14
1958	Del Shofner, Los Angeles	51	1,097	21.5	92	8
1956	Bill Howton, Green Bay[2]	55	1,188	21.6	66	12
	Harlon Hill, Chi. Bears[2]	47	1,128	24.0	79	11
1954	Bob Boyd, Los Angeles	53	1,212	22.9	80	6
	*Harlon Hill, Chi. Bears	45	1,124	25.0	76	12
1953	Pete Pihos, Philadelphia	63	1,049	16.7	59	10
1952	*Bill Howton, Green Bay	53	1,231	23.2	90	13
1951	Elroy (Crazylegs) Hirsch, Los Angeles	66	1,495	22.7	91	17
1950	Tom Fears, Los Angeles[2]	84	1,116	13.3	53	7
	Cloyce Box, Detroit	50	1,009	20.2	82	11
1949	Bob Mann, Detroit	66	1,014	15.4	64	4
	Tom Fears, Los Angeles	77	1,013	13.2	51	9
1945	Jim Benton, Cleveland	45	1,067	23.7	84	8
1942	Don Hutson, Green Bay	74	1,211	16.4	73	17

First season of professional football.

250 YARDS PASS RECEIVING IN A GAME

Date	Player, Team, Opponent	No.	Yards	TD
Dec. 18, 1995	Jerry Rice, San Francisco vs. Minnesota	14	289	3
Dec. 11, 1989	John Taylor, San Francisco vs. L.A. Rams	11	286	2
Nov. 26, 1989	Willie Anderson, L.A. Rams vs. New Orleans (OT)	15	336	1
Oct. 18, 1987	Steve Largent, Seattle vs. Detroit	15	261	3
Oct. 4, 1987	Anthony Allen, Washington vs. St. Louis	7	255	3
Dec. 22, 1985	Stephone Paige, Kansas City vs. San Diego	8	309	2
Dec. 20, 1982	Wes Chandler, San Diego vs. Cincinnati	10	260	2
Sept. 23, 1979	*Jerry Butler, Buffalo vs. N.Y. Jets	10	255	4
Nov. 4, 1962	Sonny Randle, St. Louis vs. N.Y. Giants	16	256	1
Oct. 28, 1962	Del Shofner, N.Y. Giants vs. Washington	11	269	1
Oct. 13, 1961	Charley Hennigan, Houston vs. Boston	13	272	1
Oct. 21, 1956	Billy Howton, Green Bay vs. Los Angeles	7	257	2
Dec. 3, 1950	Cloyce Box, Detroit vs. Baltimore	12	302	4
Nov. 22, 1945	Jim Benton, Cleveland vs. Detroit	10	303	1

First season of professional football.

2,000 COMBINED NET YARDS GAINED IN A SEASON

Year	Player, Team	Rushing Att.-Yds.	Pass Rec.	Punt Ret.	Kickoff Ret.	Fum. Runs	Total Yds.
1995	Brian Mitchell, Wash.	46-301	38-324	25-315	55-1,408	0-0	164-2,348
	Emmitt Smith, Dallas	377-1,773	62-375	0-0	0-0	0-0	439-2,148
	Glyn Milburn, Denver	49-266	22-191	31-354	47-1,269	0-0	149-2,080
	Ernie Mills, Pittsburgh	5-39	39-679	0-0	54-1,306	0-0	98-2,024
1994	Brian Mitchell, Wash.	78-311	26-236	32-452	58-1,478	0-0	194-2,477
	Barry Sanders, Detroit	331-1,883	44-283	0-0	0-0	0-0	375-2,166
1992	Thurman Thomas, Buffalo	312-1,487	58-626	0-0	0-0	1-0	371-2,113
	Emmitt Smith, Dallas	373-1,713	59-335	0-0	0-0	1-0	433-2,048
	Barry Foster, Pittsburgh	390-1,690	36-344	0-0	0-0	2-(–20)	428-2,014
1991	Thurman Thomas, Buffalo	288-1,407	62-631	0-0	0-0	0-0	350-2,038
1990	Herschel Walker, Minnesota	184-770	35-315	0-0	44-966	4-0	267-2,051
1988	*Tim Brown, L.A. Raiders	14-50	43-725	49-444	41-1,098	7-0	154-2,317
	Roger Craig, San Fran.	310-1,502	76-534	0-0	2-32	2-0	390-2,068
	Eric Dickerson, Indianapolis	388-1,659	36-377	0-0	0-0	1-0	425-2,036
	Herschel Walker, Dallas	361-1,514	53-505	0-0	0-0	3-0	417-2,019
1986	Eric Dickerson, L.A. Rams	404-1,821	26-205	0-0	0-0	2-0	432-2,026
	Gary Anderson, San Diego	127-442	80-871	25-227	24-482	2-0	258-2,022
1985	Lionel James, San Diego	105-516	86-1,027	25-213	36-779	1-0	253-2,535
	Marcus Allen, L.A. Raiders	380-1,759	67-555	0-0	0-0	2-(–6)	449-2,308
	Roger Craig, San Fran.	214-1,050	92-1,016	0-0	0-0	0-0	306-2,066
	Walter Payton, Chicago	324-1,551	49-483	0-0	0-0	1-0	374-2,034
1984	Eric Dickerson, L.A. Rams	379-2,105	21-139	0-0	0-0	4-15	404-2,259
	James Wilder, Tampa Bay	407-1,544	85-685	0-0	0-0	4-0	496-2,229
	Walter Payton, Chicago	381-1,684	45-368	0-0	0-0	1-0	427-2,052
1983	*Eric Dickerson, L.A. Rams	390-1,808	51-404	0-0	0-0	1-0	442-2,212
	William Andrews, Atlanta	331-1,567	59-609	0-0	0-0	2-0	392-2,176
	Walter Payton, Chicago	314-1,421	53-607	0-0	0-0	2-0	369-2,028
1981	*James Brooks, San Diego	109-525	46-329	22-290	40-949	2-0	219-2,093
	William Andrews, Atlanta	289-1,301	81-735	0-0	0-0	0-0	370-2,036
1980	Bruce Harper, N.Y. Jets	45-126	50-634	28-242	49-1,070	3-0	175-2,072
1979	Wilbert Montgomery, Phil.	338-1,512	41-494	0-0	1-6	2-0	382-2,012
1978	Bruce Harper, N.Y. Jets	58-303	13-196	30-378	55-1,280	1-0	157-2,157
1977	Walter Payton, Chicago	339-1,852	27-269	0-0	2-95	5-0	373-2,216
	Terry Metcalf, St. Louis	149-739	34-403	14-108	32-772	1-0	230-2,022
1975	Terry Metcalf, St. Louis	165-816	43-378	23-285	35-960	2-23	268-2,462
	O.J. Simpson, Buffalo	329-1,817	28-426	0-0	0-0	1-0	358-2,243
1974	Mack Herron, New England	231-824	38-474	35-517	28-629	3-0	335-2,444
	Otis Armstrong, Denver	263-1,407	38-405	0-0	16-386	1-0	318-2,198
	Terry Metcalf, St. Louis	152-718	50-377	26-340	20-623	7-0	255-2,058
1973	O.J. Simpson, Buffalo	332-2,003	6-70	0-0	0-0	0-0	338-2,073
1966	Gale Sayers, Chicago	229-1,231	34-447	6-44	23-718	3-0	295-2,440
	Leroy Kelly, Cleveland	209-1,141	32-366	13-104	19-403	0-0	273-2,014
1965	*Gale Sayers, Chicago	166-867	29-507	16-238	21-660	4-0	236-2,272
1963	Timmy Brown, Philadelphia	192-841	36-487	16-152	33-945	2-3	279-2,428
	Jim Brown, Cleveland	291-1,863	24-268	0-0	0-0	0-0	315-2,131
1962	Timmy Brown, Philadelphia	137-545	52-849	6-81	30-831	4-0	229-2,306
	Dick Christy, N.Y. Titans	114-535	62-538	15-250	38-824	2-0	231-2,147
1961	Billy Cannon, Houston	200-948	43-586	9-70	18-439	2-0	272-2,043
1960	*Abner Haynes, Dall. Texans	156-875	55-576	14-215	19-434	4-0	248-2,100

First season of professional football.

300 COMBINED NET YARDS GAINED IN A GAME

Date	Player, Team, Opponent	No.	Yards	TD
Dec. 25, 1995	Kevin Williams, Dallas vs. Arizona	16	307	2
Dec. 10, 1995	Glyn Milburn, Denver vs. Seattle	33	404	0
Oct. 23, 1994	Tyrone Hughes, New Orleans vs. L.A. Rams	11	347	2
Dec. 11, 1989	John Taylor, San Francisco vs. L.A. Rams	14	321	2
Nov. 26, 1989	Willie Anderson, L.A. Rams vs. New Orleans (OT)	15	336	1
Nov. 28, 1988	*Tim Brown, L.A. Raiders vs. Seattle	12	308	1
Dec. 22, 1985	Stephone Paige, Kansas City vs. San Diego	8	309	2
Nov. 10, 1985	Lionel James, San Diego vs. L.A. Raiders (OT)	23	345	0
Sept. 22, 1985	Lionel James, San Diego vs. Cincinnati	20	316	2
Dec. 21, 1975	*Walter Payton, Chicago vs. New Orleans	32	300	1
Nov. 23, 1975	Greg Pruitt, Cleveland vs. Cincinnati	28	304	2
Nov. 1, 1970	Eugene (Mercury) Morris, Miami vs. Baltimore	17	302	0
Oct. 4, 1970	O.J. Simpson, Buffalo vs. N.Y. Jets	26	303	2
Dec. 6, 1969	Jerry LeVias, Houston vs. N.Y. Jets	18	329	1
Nov. 2, 1969	Travis Williams, Green Bay vs. Pittsburgh	11	314	3
Dec. 18, 1966	Gale Sayers, Chicago vs. Minnesota	20	339	2
Dec. 12, 1965	*Gale Sayers, Chicago vs. San Francisco	17	336	6
Nov. 17, 1963	Gary Ballman, Pittsburgh vs. Washington	12	320	2
Dec. 16, 1962	Timmy Brown, Philadelphia vs. St. Louis	19	341	2
Dec. 10, 1961	Billy Cannon, Houston vs. N.Y. Titans	32	373	5
Nov. 19, 1961	Jim Brown, Cleveland vs. Philadelphia	38	313	4
Dec. 3, 1950	Cloyce Box, Detroit vs. Baltimore	13	302	4
Oct. 29, 1950	Wally Triplett, Detroit vs. Los Angeles	11	331	1
Nov. 22, 1945	Jim Benton, Cleveland vs. Detroit	10	303	1

First season of professional football.

TOP 20 SCORERS

Player	Years	TD	FG	PAT	TP
George Blanda	26	9	335	943	2,002
Jan Stenerud	19	0	373	580	1,699
Nick Lowery	17	0	366	536	1,634
Eddie Murray	18	0	325	498	1,473
Pat Leahy	18	0	304	558	1,470
Gary Anderson	14	0	331	448	1,441
Morten Andersen	14	0	333	441	1,440
Jim Turner	16	1	304	521	1,439
Matt Bahr	17	0	300	522	1,422
Mark Moseley	16	0	300	482	1,382
Jim Bakken	17	0	282	534	1,380
Fred Cox	15	0	282	519	1,365
Lou Groza	17	1	234	641	1,349
Norm Johnson	14	0	277	515	1,346

Player	Years				
Jim Breech	14	0	243	517	1,246
Chris Bahr	14	0	241	490	1,213
Gino Cappelletti	11	42	176	350	1,130
Ray Wersching	15	0	222	456	1,122
Kevin Butler	11	0	243	387	1,116
Don Cockroft	13	0	216	432	1,080

Cappelletti's total includes 4 two-point conversions.

TOP 20 TOUCHDOWN SCORERS

Player	Years	Rush	Rec.	Returns	Total TD
Jerry Rice	11	9	146	1	156
Jim Brown	9	106	20	0	126
Marcus Allen	14	103	21	1	125
Walter Payton	13	110	15	0	125
John Riggins	14	104	12	0	116
Lenny Moore	12	63	48	2	113
Don Hutson	11	3	99	3	105
Steve Largent	14	1	100	0	101
Franco Harris	13	91	9	0	100
Emmitt Smith	6	96	4	0	100
Eric Dickerson	11	90	6	0	96
Jim Taylor	10	83	10	0	93
Tony Dorsett	12	77	13	1	91
Bobby Mitchell	11	18	65	8	91
Leroy Kelly	10	74	13	3	90
Charley Taylor	13	11	79	0	90
Don Maynard	15	0	88	0	88
Lance Alworth	11	2	85	0	87
Ottis Anderson	14	81	5	0	86
Paul Warfield	13	1	85	0	86

TOP 20 RUSHERS

Player	Years	Att.	Yards	Avg.	Long	TD
Walter Payton	13	3,838	16,726	4.4	76	110
Eric Dickerson	11	2,996	13,259	4.4	85	90
Tony Dorsett	12	2,936	12,739	4.3	99	77
Jim Brown	9	2,359	12,312	5.2	80	106
Franco Harris	13	2,949	12,120	4.1	75	91
John Riggins	14	2,916	11,352	3.9	66	104
O.J. Simpson	11	2,404	11,236	4.7	94	61
Marcus Allen	14	2,692	10,908	4.1	61	103
Ottis Anderson	14	2,562	10,273	4.0	76	81
Barry Sanders	7	2,077	10,172	4.9	85	73
Thurman Thomas	8	2,285	9,729	4.3	80	54
Earl Campbell	8	2,187	9,407	4.3	81	74
Emmitt Smith	6	2,007	8,956	4.5	75	96
Jim Taylor	10	1,941	8,597	4.4	84	83
Joe Perry	14	1,737	8,378	4.8	78	53
Roger Craig	11	1,991	8,189	4.1	71	56
Gerald Riggs	10	1,989	8,188	4.1	58	69
Herschel Walker	10	1,938	8,122	4.2	91	60
Larry Csonka	11	1,891	8,081	4.3	54	64
Freeman McNeil	12	1,798	8,074	4.5	69	38

TOP 20 COMBINED YARDS GAINED

	Years	Tot.	Rush.	Rec.	Int. Ret.	Punt Ret.	Kickoff Ret.	Fumble Ret.
Walter Payton	13	21,803	16,726	4,538	0	0	539	0
Tony Dorsett	12	16,326	12,739	3,554	0	0	0	33
Marcus Allen	14	15,957	10,908	5,055	0	0	0	–6
Herschel Walker	10	15,881	8,122	4,621	0	0	3,138	0
Jerry Rice	11	15,676	547	15,123	0	0	6	0
Jim Brown	9	15,459	12,312	2,499	0	0	648	0
Eric Dickerson	11	15,411	13,259	2,137	0	0	0	15
James Brooks	12	14,910	7,962	3,621	0	565	2,762	0
Franco Harris	13	14,622	12,120	2,287	0	0	233	–18
O.J. Simpson	11	14,368	11,236	2,142	0	0	990	0
James Lofton	16	14,277	246	14,004	0	0	0	27
Henry Ellard	13	14,104	50	12,163	0	1,527	364	0
Bobby Mitchell	11	14,078	2,735	7,954	0	699	2,690	0
John Riggins	14	13,435	11,352	2,090	0	0	0	–7
Steve Largent	14	13,396	83	13,089	0	68	156	0
Ottis Anderson	14	13,364	10,273	3,062	0	0	0	29
Thurman Thomas	8	13,351	9,729	3,622	0	0	0	0
Drew Hill	14	13,337	19	9,831	0	22	3,460	5
Greg Pruitt	12	13,262	5,672	3,069	0	2,007	2,514	0
Roger Craig	11	13,143	8,189	4,911	0	0	43	0
Art Monk	16	13,063	332	12,721	0	0	10	0

TOP 20 PASSERS

Player	Years	Att.	Comp.	Pct. Comp.	Yards	TD	Pct. TD	Int.	Pct. Int.	Avg. Gain	Rating
Steve Young	11	2,876	1,845	64.2	23,069	160	5.6	79	2.7	8.02	96.1
Joe Montana	15	5,391	3,409	63.2	40,551	273	5.1	139	2.6	7.52	92.3
Dan Marino	13	6,531	3,913	59.9	48,841	352	5.4	200	3.1	7.48	88.4
Brett Favre	5	2,150	1,342	62.4	14,825	108	5.0	66	3.1	6.90	86.8
Jim Kelly	10	4,400	2,652	60.3	32,657	223	5.1	156	3.5	7.42	85.4
Troy Aikman	7	2,713	1,704	62.8	19,607	98	3.6	85	3.1	7.23	83.5
R. Staubach	11	2,958	1,685	57.0	22,700	153	5.2	109	3.7	7.67	83.4
Neil Lomax	8	3,153	1,817	57.6	22,771	136	4.3	90	2.9	7.22	82.7
S. Jurgensen	18	4,262	2,433	57.1	32,224	255	6.0	189	4.4	7.56	82.6
Len Dawson	19	3,741	2,136	57.1	28,711	239	6.4	183	4.9	7.67	82.6
Dave Krieg	16	4,911	2,866	58.4	35,668	247	5.0	187	3.8	7.26	81.9
Ken Anderson	16	4,475	2,654	59.3	32,838	197	4.4	160	3.6	7.34	81.9
Jeff Hostetler	10	1,792	1,036	57.8	12,983	66	3.7	47	2.6	7.24	81.8
Neil O'Donnell	5	1,871	1,069	57.1	12,867	68	3.6	39	2.1	6.88	81.8
Danny White	13	2,950	1,761	59.7	21,959	155	5.3	132	4.5	7.44	81.7
Bernie Kosar	11	3,333	1,970	59.1	23,093	123	3.7	87	2.6	6.93	81.6
Warren Moon	12	5,753	3,380	58.8	42,177	247	4.3	199	3.5	7.33	81.5
B. Esiason	12	4,680	2,661	56.9	34,149	223	4.8	168	3.6	7.30	80.8
Bart Starr	16	3,149	1,808	57.4	24,718	152	4.8	138	4.4	7.85	80.5
Ken O'Brien	10	3,602	2,110	58.6	25,094	128	3.6	98	2.7	6.97	80.4
F. Tarkenton	18	6,467	3,686	57.0	47,003	342	5.3	266	4.1	7.27	80.4

1,500 or more attempts. The passing ratings are based on performance standards established for completion percentage, interception percentage, touchdown percentage, and average gain. Passers are allocated points according to how their marks compare with those standards.

TOP 20 LEADERS IN PASSES COMPLETED

Dan Marino	3,913
Fran Tarkenton	3,686
Joe Montana	3,409
Warren Moon	3,380
John Elway	3,346
Dan Fouts	3,297
Dave Krieg	2,866
Steve DeBerg	2,844
Johnny Unitas	2,830
Boomer Esiason	2,661
Ken Anderson	2,654
Jim Kelly	2,652
Jim Hart	2,593
Phil Simms	2,576
Jim Everett	2,538
John Brodie	2,469
Sonny Jurgensen	2,433
Joe Ferguson	2,369
Roman Gabriel	2,366
John Hadl	2,363

TOP 20 LEADERS IN PASSING YARDS

Dan Marino	48,841
Fran Tarkenton	47,003
Dan Fouts	43,040
Warren Moon	42,177
John Elway	41,706
Joe Montana	40,551
Johnny Unitas	40,239
Dave Krieg	35,668
Jim Hart	34,665
Boomer Esiason	34,149
Steve DeBerg	33,872
John Hadl	33,503
Phil Simms	33,462
Ken Anderson	32,838
Jim Kelly	32,657
Sonny Jurgensen	32,224
Jim Everett	31,583
John Brodie	31,548
Norm Snead	30,797
Joe Ferguson	29,817

OUTSTANDING PERFORMERS

TOP 20 LEADERS IN TOUCHDOWN PASSES

Dan Marino	352
Fran Tarkenton	342
Johnny Unitas	290
Joe Montana	273
Sonny Jurgensen	255
Dan Fouts	254
Dave Krieg	247
Warren Moon	247
John Hadl	244
Len Dawson	239
George Blanda	236
John Elway	225
Boomer Esiason	223
Jim Kelly	223
John Brodie	214
Terry Bradshaw	212
Y.A. Tittle	212
Jim Hart	209
Roman Gabriel	201
Phil Simms	199

TOP 20 PASS RECEIVERS

Player	Years	No.	Yards	Avg.	Long	TD
Jerry Rice	11	942	15,123	16.1	96	146
Art Monk	16	940	12,721	13.5	79	68
Steve Largent	14	819	13,089	16.0	74	100
James Lofton	16	764	14,004	18.3	80	75
Charlie Joiner	18	750	12,146	16.2	87	65
Henry Ellard	13	723	12,163	16.8	81	59
Andre Reed	11	700	9,848	14.1	83	69
Gary Clark	11	699	10,856	15.5	84	65
Ozzie Newsome	13	662	7,980	12.1	74	47
Charley Taylor	13	649	9,110	14.0	88	79
Drew Hill	14	634	9,831	15.5	81	60
Don Maynard	15	633	11,834	18.7	87	88
Raymond Berry	13	631	9,275	14.7	70	68
Sterling Sharpe	7	595	8,134	13.7	79	65
Harold Carmichael	14	590	8,985	15.2	85	79
Fred Biletnikoff	14	589	8,974	15.2	82	76
Mark Clayton	11	582	8,974	15.4	78	84
Harold Jackson	16	579	10,372	17.9	79	76
Cris Carter	9	571	7,204	12.6	80	66
Ernest Givins	10	571	8,215	14.4	83	49

TOP 20 LEADERS IN RECEPTION YARDS

Player	Yards
Jerry Rice	15,123
James Lofton	14,004
Steve Largent	13,089
Art Monk	12,721
Henry Ellard	12,163
Charlie Joiner	12,146
Don Maynard	11,834
Gary Clark	10,856
Stanley Morgan	10,716
Harold Jackson	10,372
Lance Alworth	10,266
Andre Reed	9,848
Drew Hill	9,831
Raymond Berry	9,275
Charley Taylor	9,110
Harold Carmichael	8,985
Fred Biletnikoff	8,974
Mark Clayton	8,974
Wes Chandler	8,966
Roy Green	8,965

TOP 20 INTERCEPTORS

Player	Years	No.	Yards	Avg.	Long	TD
Paul Krause	16	81	1,185	14.6	81	3
Emlen Tunnell	14	79	1,282	16.2	55	4
Dick (Night Train) Lane	14	68	1,207	17.8	80	5
Ken Riley	15	65	596	9.2	66	5
Ronnie Lott	14	63	730	11.6	83	5
Dick LeBeau	13	62	762	12.3	70	3
Dave Brown	15	62	698	11.3	90	5
Emmitt Thomas	13	58	937	16.2	73	5
Bobby Boyd	9	57	994	17.4	74	4
Johnny Robinson	12	57	741	13.0	57	1
Mel Blount	14	57	736	12.9	52	2
Everson Walls	13	57	504	8.8	40	1
Lem Barney	11	56	1,077	19.2	71	7
Pat Fischer	17	56	941	16.8	69	4
Willie Brown	16	54	472	8.7	45	2
Bobby Dillon	8	52	976	18.8	61	5
Jack Butler	9	52	826	15.9	52	4
Larry Wilson	13	52	800	15.4	96	5
Jim Patton	12	52	712	13.7	51	2
Mel Renfro	14	52	626	12.0	90	3

TOP 20 PUNTERS

Player	Years	No.	Yards	Avg.	Long	Blk.
Sammy Baugh	16	338	15,245	45.1	85	9
Tommy Davis	11	511	22,833	44.7	82	2
Yale Lary	11	503	22,279	44.3	74	4
Bob Scarpitto	8	283	12,408	43.8	87	4
Horace Gillom	7	385	16,872	43.8	80	5
Jerry Norton	11	358	15,671	43.8	78	2
Greg Montgomery	7	373	16,311	43.7	77	7
David Lewis	4	285	12,447	43.7	63	0
Sean Landeta	11	729	31,804	43.6	71	4
Rohn Stark	14	1,044	45,530	43.6	72	7
Reggie Roby	13	792	34,418	43.5	77	4
Don Chandler	12	660	28,678	43.5	90	4
Rick Tuten	7	481	20,876	43.4	73	1
Jerrel Wilson	16	1,072	46,139	43.0	72	12
Norm Van Brocklin	12	523	22,413	42.9	72	3
Danny Villanueva	8	488	20,862	42.8	68	2
Rich Camarillo	15	1,027	43,895	42.7	76	6
Tommy Barnhardt	9	549	23,388	42.6	65	2
Bobby Joe Green	14	970	41,317	42.6	75	3
Sam Baker	15	703	29,938	42.6	72	2

250 or more punts.

TOP 20 PUNT RETURNERS

Player	Years	No.	Yards	Avg.	Long	TD
George McAfee	8	112	1,431	12.8	74	2
Jack Christiansen	8	85	1,084	12.8	89	8
Claude Gibson	5	110	1,381	12.6	85	3
Bill Dudley	9	124	1,515	12.2	96	3
Rick Upchurch	9	248	3,008	12.1	92	8
Billy Johnson	14	282	3,317	11.8	87	6
Mack Herron	3	84	982	11.7	66	0
Billy Thompson	13	157	1,814	11.6	60	0
Mel Gray	10	211	2,387	11.3	80	3
Henry Ellard	13	135	1,527	11.3	83	4
Rodger Bird	3	94	1,063	11.3	78	0
Bosh Pritchard	6	95	1,072	11.3	81	2
Brian Mitchell	6	172	1,938	11.3	84	6
Terry Metcalf	6	84	936	11.1	69	1
Bob Hayes	11	104	1,158	11.1	90	3
Floyd Little	9	81	893	11.0	72	2
Louis Lipps	9	112	1,234	11.0	76	3
Bobby Joe Edmonds	5	134	1,471	11.0	75	1
Les (Speedy) Duncan	11	202	2,201	10.9	95	4
Verda (Vitamin) Smith	5	75	814	10.9	85	1

75 or more returns.

TOP 20 KICKOFF RETURNERS

Player	Years	No.	Yards	Avg.	Long	TD
Gale Sayers	7	91	2,781	30.6	103	6
Lynn Chandnois	7	92	2,720	29.6	93	3
Abe Woodson	9	193	5,538	28.7	105	5
Claude (Buddy) Young	6	90	2,514	27.9	104	2
Travis Williams	5	102	2,801	27.5	105	6
Joe Arenas	7	139	3,798	27.3	96	1
Clarence Davis	8	79	2,140	27.1	76	0
Steve Van Buren	8	76	2,030	26.7	98	3
Lenny Lyles	12	81	2,161	26.7	103	3
Eugene (Mercury) Morris	8	111	2,947	26.5	105	3
Bobby Jancik	6	158	4,185	26.5	61	0
Mel Renfro	14	85	2,246	26.4	100	2
Bobby Mitchell	11	102	2,690	26.4	98	5
Ollie Matson	14	143	3,746	26.2	105	6
Alvin Haymond	10	170	4,438	26.1	98	2
Noland Smith	3	82	2,137	26.1	106	1
Al Nelson	9	101	2,625	26.0	78	0
Tim Brown	10	184	4,781	26.0	105	5
Vic Washington	6	129	3,341	25.9	98	1
Dave Hampton	8	113	2,923	25.9	101	3

75 or more returns.

TOP 20 LEADERS IN SACKS

Player	*Years	No.
Reggie White	11	157.0
Lawrence Taylor	12	132.5
Rickey Jackson	14	128.0
Richard Dent	13	126.5
Bruce Smith	11	126.5
Greg Townsend	12	109.5
Kevin Greene	11	108.0
Sean Jones	12	108.0
Leslie O'Neal	9	105.5
Chris Doleman	11	104.5
Andre Tippett	11	100.0
Pat Swilling	10	99.5
Simon Fletcher	11	97.5
Jacob Green	11	97.5
Dexter Manley	10	97.5
Jim Jeffcoat	13	97.0
Charles Haley	10	96.5
Steve McMichael	13	95.0
Clyde Simmons	10	93.0
Derrick Thomas	7	85.0

**Since NFL began compiling sacks in 1982.*

YEARLY STATISTICAL LEADERS

ANNUAL SCORING LEADERS

Year	Player, Team	TD	FG	PAT	TP
1995	Emmitt Smith, Dallas, NFC	25	0	0	150
	Norm Johnson, Pittsburgh, AFC	0	34	39	141
1994	John Carney, San Diego, AFC	0	34	33	135
	Fuad Reveiz, Minnesota, NFC	0	34	30	132
1993	Jeff Jaeger, L.A. Raiders, AFC	0	35	27	132
	Jason Hanson, Detroit, NFC	0	34	28	130
1992	Pete Stoyanovich, Miami, AFC	0	30	34	124
	Morten Andersen, New Orleans, NFC	0	29	33	120
	Chip Lohmiller, Washington, NFC	0	30	30	120
1991	Chip Lohmiller, Washington, NFC	0	31	56	149
	Pete Stoyanovich, Miami, AFC	0	31	28	121
1990	Nick Lowery, Kansas City, AFC	0	34	37	139
	Chip Lohmiller, Washington, NFC	0	30	41	131
1989	Mike Cofer, San Francisco, NFC	0	29	49	136
	*David Treadwell, Denver, AFC	0	27	39	120
1988	Scott Norwood, Buffalo, AFC	0	32	33	129
	Mike Cofer, San Francisco, NFC	0	27	40	121
1987	Jerry Rice, San Francisco, NFC	23	0	0	138
	Jim Breech, Cincinnati, AFC	0	24	25	97
1986	Tony Franklin, New England, AFC	0	32	44	140
	Kevin Butler, Chicago, NFC	0	28	36	120
1985	*Kevin Butler, Chicago, NFC	0	31	51	144
	Gary Anderson, Pittsburgh, AFC	0	33	40	139
1984	Ray Wersching, San Francisco, NFC	0	25	56	131
	Gary Anderson, Pittsburgh, AFC	0	24	45	117
1983	Mark Moseley, Washington, NFC	0	33	62	161
	Gary Anderson, Pittsburgh, AFC	0	27	38	119
1982	*Marcus Allen, L.A. Raiders, AFC	14	0	0	84
	Wendell Tyler, L.A. Rams, NFC	13	0	0	78
1981	Ed Murray, Detroit, NFC	0	25	46	121
	Rafael Septien, Dallas, NFC	0	27	40	121
	Jim Breech, Cincinnati, AFC	0	22	49	115
	Nick Lowery, Kansas City, AFC	0	26	37	115
1980	John Smith, New England, AFC	0	26	51	129
	*Ed Murray, Detroit, NFC	0	27	35	116
1979	John Smith, New England, AFC	0	23	46	115
	Mark Moseley, Washington, NFC	0	25	39	114
1978	*Frank Corral, Los Angeles, NFC	0	29	31	118
	Pat Leahy, N.Y. Jets, AFC	0	22	41	107
1977	Errol Mann, Oakland, AFC	0	20	39	99
	Walter Payton, Chicago, NFC	16	0	0	96
1976	Toni Linhart, Baltimore, AFC	0	20	49	109
	Mark Moseley, Washington, NFC	0	22	31	97
1975	O.J. Simpson, Buffalo, AFC	23	0	0	138
	Chuck Foreman, Minnesota, NFC	22	0	0	132
1974	Chester Marcol, Green Bay, NFC	0	25	19	94
	Roy Gerela, Pittsburgh, AFC	0	20	33	93
1973	David Ray, Los Angeles, NFC	0	30	40	130
	Roy Gerela, Pittsburgh, AFC	0	29	36	123
1972	*Chester Marcol, Green Bay, NFC	0	33	29	128
	Bobby Howfield, N.Y. Jets, AFC	0	27	40	121
1971	Garo Yepremian, Miami, AFC	0	28	33	117
	Curt Knight, Washington, NFC	0	29	27	114
1970	Fred Cox, Minnesota, NFC	0	30	35	125
	Jan Stenerud, Kansas City, AFC	0	30	26	116
1969	Jim Turner, N.Y. Jets, AFL	0	32	33	129
	Fred Cox, Minnesota, NFL	0	26	43	121
1968	Jim Turner, N.Y. Jets, AFL	0	34	43	145
	Leroy Kelly, Cleveland, NFL	20	0	0	120
1967	Jim Bakken, St. Louis, NFL	0	27	36	117
	George Blanda, Oakland, AFL	0	20	56	116
1966	Gino Cappelletti, Boston, AFL	6	16	35	119
	Bruce Gossett, Los Angeles, NFL	0	28	29	113
1965	*Gale Sayers, Chicago, NFL	22	0	0	132
	Gino Cappelletti, Boston, AFL	9	17	27	132
1964	Gino Cappelletti, Boston, AFL	7	25	36	#155
	Lenny Moore, Baltimore, NFL	20	0	0	120
1963	Gino Cappelletti, Boston, AFL	2	22	35	113
	Don Chandler, N.Y. Giants, NFL	0	18	52	106
1962	Gene Mingo, Denver, AFL	4	27	32	137
	Jim Taylor, Green Bay, NFL	19	0	0	114
1961	Gino Cappelletti, Boston, AFL	8	17	48	147
	Paul Hornung, Green Bay, NFL	10	15	41	146
1960	Paul Hornung, Green Bay, NFL	15	15	41	176
	*Gene Mingo, Denver, AFL	6	18	33	123
1959	Paul Hornung, Green Bay	7	7	31	94
1958	Jim Brown, Cleveland	18	0	0	108
1957	Sam Baker, Washington	1	14	29	77
	Lou Groza, Cleveland	0	15	32	77
1956	Bobby Layne, Detroit	5	12	33	99
1955	Doak Walker, Detroit	7	9	27	96
1954	Bobby Walston, Philadelphia	11	4	36	114
1953	Gordy Soltau, San Francisco	6	10	48	114
1952	Gordy Soltau, San Francisco	7	6	34	94
1951	Elroy (Crazylegs) Hirsch, Los Angeles	17	0	0	102
1950	*Doak Walker, Detroit	11	8	38	128
1949	Pat Harder, Chi. Cardinals	8	3	45	102
	Gene Roberts, N.Y. Giants	17	0	0	102
1948	Pat Harder, Chi. Cardinals	6	7	53	110
1947	Pat Harder, Chi. Cardinals	7	7	39	102
1946	Ted Fritsch, Green Bay	10	9	13	100
1945	Steve Van Buren, Philadelphia	18	0	2	110
1944	Don Hutson, Green Bay	9	0	31	85
1943	Don Hutson, Green Bay	12	3	36	117
1942	Don Hutson, Green Bay	17	1	33	138
1941	Don Hutson, Green Bay	12	1	20	95
1940	Don Hutson, Green Bay	7	0	15	57
1939	Andy Farkas, Washington	11	0	2	68
1938	Clarke Hinkle, Green Bay	7	3	7	58
1937	Jack Manders, Chi. Bears	5	8	15	69
1936	Earl (Dutch) Clark, Detroit	7	4	19	73
1935	Earl (Dutch) Clark, Detroit	6	1	16	55
1934	Jack Manders, Chi. Bears	3	10	31	79
1933	Ken Strong, N.Y. Giants	6	5	13	64
	Glenn Presnell, Portsmouth	6	6	10	64
1932	Earl (Dutch) Clark, Portsmouth	6	3	10	55

*First season of professional football.

#Cappelletti's total includes a two-point conversion.

ANNUAL TOUCHDOWN LEADERS

Year	Player, Team	TD	Rush	Pass	Ret.
1995	Emmitt Smith, Dallas, NFC	25	25	0	0
	Carl Pickens, Cincinnati, AFC	17	0	17	0
1994	Emmitt Smith, Dallas, NFC	22	21	1	0
	*Marshall Faulk, Indianapolis, AFC	12	11	1	0
	Natrone Means, San Diego, AFC	12	12	0	0
1993	Jerry Rice, San Francisco, NFC	16	1	15	0
	Marcus Allen, Kansas City, AFC	15	12	3	0
1992	Emmitt Smith, Dallas, NFC	19	18	1	0
	Thurman Thomas, Buffalo, AFC	12	9	3	0
1991	Barry Sanders, Detroit, NFC	17	16	1	0
	Mark Clayton, Miami, AFC	12	0	12	0
	Thurman Thomas, Buffalo, AFC	12	7	5	0
1990	Barry Sanders, Detroit, NFC	16	13	3	0
	Derrick Fenner, Seattle, AFC	15	14	1	0
1989	Dalton Hilliard, New Orleans, NFC	18	13	5	0
	Christian Okoye, Kansas City, AFC	12	12	0	0
	Thurman Thomas, Buffalo, AFC	12	6	6	0
1988	Greg Bell, L.A. Rams, NFC	18	16	2	0
	Eric Dickerson, Indianapolis, AFC	15	14	1	0
	*Ickey Woods, Cincinnati, AFC	15	15	0	0
1987	Jerry Rice, San Francisco, NFC	23	1	22	0
	Johnny Hector, N.Y. Jets, AFC	11	11	0	0
1986	George Rogers, Washington, NFC	18	18	0	0
	Sammy Winder, Denver, AFC	14	9	5	0
1985	Joe Morris, N.Y. Giants, NFC	21	21	0	0
	Louis Lipps, Pittsburgh, AFC	15	1	12	2
1984	Marcus Allen, L.A. Raiders, AFC	18	13	5	0
	Mark Clayton, Miami, AFC	18	0	18	0
	Eric Dickerson, L.A. Rams, NFC	14	14	0	0
	John Riggins, Washington, NFC	14	14	0	0
1983	John Riggins, Washington, NFC	24	24	0	0
	Pete Johnson, Cincinnati, AFC	14	14	0	0
	*Curt Warner, Seattle, AFC	14	13	1	0
1982	*Marcus Allen, L.A. Raiders, AFC	14	11	3	0
	Wendell Tyler, L.A. Rams, NFC	13	9	4	0
1981	Chuck Muncie, San Diego, AFC	19	19	0	0
	Wendell Tyler, Los Angeles, NFC	17	12	5	0
1980	*Billy Sims, Detroit, NFC	16	13	3	0
	Earl Campbell, Houston, AFC	13	13	0	0
	*Curtis Dickey, Baltimore, AFC	13	11	2	0
	John Jefferson, San Diego, AFC	13	0	13	0
1979	Earl Campbell, Houston, AFC	19	19	0	0
	Walter Payton, Chicago, NFC	16	14	2	0
1978	David Sims, Seattle, AFC	15	14	1	0
	Terdell Middleton, Green Bay, NFC	12	11	1	0
1977	Walter Payton, Chicago, NFC	16	14	2	0
	Nat Moore, Miami, AFC	13	1	12	0
1976	Chuck Foreman, Minnesota, NFC	14	13	1	0
	Franco Harris, Pittsburgh, AFC	14	14	0	0
1975	O.J. Simpson, Buffalo, AFC	23	16	7	0
	Chuck Foreman, Minnesota, NFC	22	13	9	0
1974	Chuck Foreman, Minnesota, NFC	15	9	6	0
	Cliff Branch, Oakland, AFC	13	0	13	0

Year	Player, Team				
1973	Larry Brown, Washington, NFC	14	8	6	0
	Floyd Little, Denver, AFC	13	12	1	0
1972	Emerson Boozer, N.Y. Jets, AFC	14	11	3	0
	Ron Johnson, N.Y. Giants, NFC	14	9	5	0
1971	Duane Thomas, Dallas, NFC	13	11	2	0
	Leroy Kelly, Cleveland, AFC	12	10	2	0
1970	Dick Gordon, Chicago, NFC	13	0	13	0
	MacArthur Lane, St. Louis, NFC	13	11	2	0
	Gary Garrison, San Diego, AFC	12	0	12	0
1969	Warren Wells, Oakland, AFL	14	0	14	0
	Tom Matte, Baltimore, NFL	13	11	2	0
	Lance Rentzel, Dallas, NFL	13	0	12	1
1968	Leroy Kelly, Cleveland, NFL	20	16	4	0
	Warren Wells, Oakland, AFL	12	1	11	0
1967	Homer Jones, N.Y. Giants, NFL	14	1	13	0
	Emerson Boozer, N.Y. Jets, AFL	13	10	3	0
1966	Leroy Kelly, Cleveland, NFL	16	15	1	0
	Dan Reeves, Dallas, NFL	16	8	8	0
	Lance Alworth, San Diego, AFL	13	0	13	0
1965	*Gale Sayers, Chicago, NFL	22	14	6	2
	Lance Alworth, San Diego, AFL	14	0	14	0
	Don Maynard, N.Y. Jets, AFL	14	0	14	0
1964	Lenny Moore, Baltimore, NFL	20	16	3	1
	Lance Alworth, San Diego, AFL	15	2	13	0
1963	Art Powell, Oakland, AFL	16	0	16	0
	Jim Brown, Cleveland, NFL	15	12	3	0
1962	Abner Haynes, Dallas, AFL	19	13	6	0
	Jim Taylor, Green Bay, NFL	19	19	0	0
1961	Bill Groman, Houston, AFL	18	1	17	0
	Jim Taylor, Green Bay, NFL	16	15	1	0
1960	Paul Hornung, Green Bay, NFL	15	13	2	0
	Sonny Randle, St. Louis, NFL	15	0	15	0
	Art Powell, N.Y. Titans, AFL	14	0	14	0
1959	Raymond Berry, Baltimore	14	0	14	0
	Jim Brown, Cleveland	14	14	0	0
1958	Jim Brown, Cleveland	18	17	1	0
1957	Lenny Moore, Baltimore	11	3	7	1
1956	Rick Casares, Chi. Bears	14	12	2	0
1955	*Alan Ameche, Baltimore	9	9	0	0
	Harlon Hill, Chi. Bears	9	0	9	0
1954	*Harlon Hill, Chi. Bears	12	0	12	0
1953	Joseph Perry, San Francisco	13	10	3	0
1952	Cloyce Box, Detroit	15	0	15	0
1951	Elroy (Crazylegs) Hirsch, Los Angeles	17	0	17	0
1950	Bob Shaw, Chi. Cardinals	12	0	12	0
1949	Gene Roberts, N.Y. Giants	17	9	8	0
1948	Mal Kutner, Chi. Cardinals	15	1	14	0
1947	Steve Van Buren, Philadelphia	14	13	0	1
1946	Ted Fritsch, Green Bay	10	9	1	0
1945	Steve Van Buren, Philadelphia	18	15	2	1
1944	Don Hutson, Green Bay	9	0	9	0
	Bill Paschal, N.Y. Giants	9	9	0	0
1943	Don Hutson, Green Bay	12	0	11	1
	*Bill Paschal, N.Y. Giants	12	10	2	0
1942	Don Hutson, Green Bay	17	0	17	0
1941	Don Hutson, Green Bay	12	2	10	0
	George McAfee, Chi. Bears	12	6	3	3
1940	John Drake, Cleveland	9	9	0	0
	Richard Todd, Washington	9	4	4	1
1939	Andrew Farkas, Washington	11	5	5	1
1938	Don Hutson, Green Bay	9	0	9	0
1937	Cliff Battles, Washington	7	5	1	1
	Clarke Hinkle, Green Bay	7	5	2	0
	Don Hutson, Green Bay	7	0	7	0
1936	Don Hutson, Green Bay	9	0	8	1
1935	*Don Hutson, Green Bay	7	0	6	1
1934	*Beattie Feathers, Chi. Bears	9	8	1	0
1933	*Charlie (Buckets) Goldenberg, Green Bay	7	4	1	2
	John (Shipwreck) Kelly, Brooklyn	7	2	3	2
	*Elvin (Kink) Richards, N.Y. Giants	7	4	3	0
1932	Earl (Dutch) Clark, Portsmouth	6	3	3	0
	Red Grange, Chi. Bears	6	3	3	0

**First season of professional football.*

ANNUAL LEADERS—MOST FIELD GOALS MADE

Year	Player, Team	Att.	Made	Pct.
1995	Norm Johnson, Pittsburgh, AFC	41	34	82.9
	Morten Andersen, Atlanta, NFC	37	31	83.8
1994	John Carney, San Diego, AFC	38	34	89.5
	Fuad Reveiz, Minnesota, NFC	39	34	87.2
1993	Jeff Jaeger, L.A. Raiders, AFC	44	35	79.5
	Jason Hanson, Detroit, NFC	43	34	79.1
1992	Pete Stoyanovich, Miami, AFC	37	30	81.1
	Chip Lohmiller, Washington, NFC	40	30	75.0
1991	Pete Stoyanovich, Miami, AFC	37	31	83.8
	Chip Lohmiller, Washington, NFC	43	31	72.1
1990	Nick Lowery, Kansas City, AFC	37	34	91.9
	Chip Lohmiller, Washington, NFC	40	30	75.0
1989	Rich Karlis, Minnesota, NFC	39	31	79.5
	*David Treadwell, Denver, AFC	33	27	81.8
1988	Scott Norwood, Buffalo, AFC	37	32	86.5
	Mike Cofer, San Francisco, NFC	38	27	71.1
1987	Morten Andersen, New Orleans, NFC	36	28	77.8
	Dean Biasucci, Indianpolis, AFC	27	24	88.9
	Jim Breech, Cincinnati, AFC	30	24	80.0
1986	Tony Franklin, New England, AFC	41	32	78.0
	Kevin Butler, Chicago, NFC	41	28	68.3
1985	Gary Anderson, Pittsburgh, AFC	42	33	78.6
	Morten Andersen, New Orleans, NFC	35	31	88.6
	*Kevin Butler, Chicago, NFC	37	31	83.8
1984	*Paul McFadden, Philadelphia, NFC	37	30	81.1
	Gary Anderson, Pittsburgh, AFC	32	24	75.0
	Matt Bahr, Cleveland, AFC	32	24	75.0
1983	*Ali-Haji-Sheikh, N.Y. Giants, NFC	42	35	83.3
	*Raul Allegre, Baltimore, AFC	35	30	85.7
1982	Mark Moseley, Washington, NFC	21	20	95.2
	Nick Lowery, Kansas City, AFC	24	19	79.2
1981	Rafael Septien, Dallas, NFC	35	27	77.1
	Nick Lowery, Kansas City, AFC	36	26	72.2
1980	*Ed Murray, Detroit, NFC	42	27	64.3
	John Smith, New England, AFC	34	26	76.5
	Fred Steinfort, Denver, AFC	34	26	76.5
1979	Mark Moseley, Washington, NFC	33	25	75.8
	John Smith, New England, AFC	33	23	69.7
1978	*Frank Corral, Los Angeles, NFC	43	29	67.4
	Pat Leahy, N.Y. Jets, AFC	30	22	73.3
1977	Mark Moseley, Washington, NFC	37	21	56.8
	Errol Mann, Oakland, AFC	28	20	71.4
1976	Mark Moseley, Washington, NFC	34	22	64.7
	Jan Stenerud, Kansas City, AFC	38	21	55.3
1975	Jan Stenerud, Kansas City, AFC	32	22	68.8
	Toni Fritsch, Dallas, NFC	35	22	62.9
1974	Chester Marcol, Green Bay, NFC	39	25	64.1
	Roy Gerela, Pittsburgh, AFC	29	20	69.0
1973	David Ray, Los Angeles, NFC	47	30	63.8
	Roy Gerela, Pittsburgh, AFC	43	29	67.4
1972	*Chester Marcol, Green Bay, NFC	48	33	68.8
	Roy Gerela, Pittsburgh, AFC	41	28	68.3
1971	Curt Knight, Washington, NFC	49	29	59.2
	Garo Yepremian, Miami, AFC	40	28	70.0
1970	Jan Stenerud, Kansas City, AFC	42	30	71.4
	Fred Cox, Minnesota, NFC	46	30	65.2
1969	Jim Turner, N.Y. Jets, AFL	47	32	68.1
	Fred Cox, Minnesota, NFL	37	26	70.3
1968	Jim Turner, N.Y. Jets, AFL	46	34	73.9
	Mac Percival, Chicago, NFL	36	25	69.4
1967	Jim Bakken, St. Louis, NFL	39	27	69.2
	Jan Stenerud, Kansas City, AFL	36	21	58.3
1966	Bruce Gossett, Los Angeles, NFL	49	28	57.1
	Mike Mercer, Oakland-Kansas City, AFL	30	21	70.0
1965	Pete Gogolak, Buffalo, AFL	46	28	60.9
	Fred Cox, Minnesota, NFL	35	23	65.7
1964	Jim Bakken, St. Louis, NFL	38	25	65.8
	Gino Cappelletti, Boston, AFL	39	25	64.1
1963	Jim Martin, Baltimore, NFL	39	24	61.5
	Gino Cappelletti, Boston, AFL	38	22	57.9
1962	Gene Mingo, Denver, AFL	39	27	69.2
	Lou Michaels, Pittsburgh, NFL	42	26	61.9
1961	Steve Myhra, Baltimore, NFL	39	21	53.8
	Gino Cappelletti, Boston, AFL	32	17	53.1
1960	Tommy Davis, San Francisco, NFL	32	19	59.4
	*Gene Mingo, Denver, AFL	28	18	64.3
1959	Pat Summerall, N.Y. Giants	29	20	69.0
1958	Paige Cothren, Los Angeles	25	14	56.0
	*Tom Miner, Pittsburgh	28	14	50.0
1957	Lou Groza, Cleveland	22	15	68.2
1956	Sam Baker, Washington	25	17	68.0
1955	Fred Cone, Green Bay	24	16	66.7
1954	Lou Groza, Cleveland	24	16	66.7
1953	Lou Groza, Cleveland	26	23	88.5
1952	Lou Groza, Cleveland	33	19	57.6
1951	Bob Waterfield, Los Angeles	23	13	56.5
1950	Lou Groza, Cleveland	19	13	68.4
1949	Cliff Patton, Philadelphia	18	9	50.0
	Bob Waterfield, Los Angeles	16	9	56.3
1948	Cliff Patton, Philadelphia	12	8	66.7

1947	Ward Cuff, Green Bay	16	7	43.8
	Pat Harder, Chi. Cardinals	10	7	70.0
	Bob Waterfield, Los Angeles	16	7	43.8
1946	Ted Fritsch, Green Bay	17	9	52.9
1945	Joe Aguirre, Washington	13	7	53.8
1944	Ken Strong, N.Y. Giants	12	6	50.0
1943	Ward Cuff, N.Y. Giants	9	3	33.3
	Don Hutson, Green Bay	5	3	60.0
1942	Bill Daddio, Chi. Cardinals	10	5	50.0
1941	Clarke Hinkle, Green Bay	14	6	42.9
1940	Clarke Hinkle, Green Bay	14	9	64.3
1939	Ward Cuff, N.Y. Giants	16	7	43.8
1938	Ward Cuff, N.Y. Giants	9	5	55.6
	Ralph Kercheval, Brooklyn	13	5	38.5
1937	Jack Manders, Chi. Bears		8	
1936	Jack Manders, Chi. Bears		7	
	Armand Niccolai, Pittsburgh		7	
1935	Armand Niccolai, Pittsburgh		6	
	Bill Smith, Chi. Cardinals		6	
1934	Jack Manders, Chi. Bears		10	
1933	*Jack Manders, Chi. Bears		6	
	Glenn Presnell, Portsmouth		6	
1932	Earl (Dutch) Clark, Portsmouth		3	

First season of professional football.

ANNUAL RUSHING LEADERS

Year	Player, Team	Att.	Yards	Avg.	TD
1995	Emmitt Smith, Dallas, NFC	377	1,773	4.7	25
	*Curtis Martin, New England, AFC	368	1,487	4.0	14
1994	Barry Sanders, Detroit, NFC	331	1,883	5.7	7
	Chris Warren, Seattle, AFC	333	1,545	4.6	9
1993	Emmitt Smith, Dallas, NFC	283	1,486	5.3	9
	Thurman Thomas, Buffalo, AFC	355	1,315	3.7	6
1992	Emmitt Smith, Dallas, NFC	373	1,713	4.6	18
	Barry Foster, Pittsburgh, AFC	390	1,690	4.3	11
1991	Emmitt Smith, Dallas, NFC	365	1,563	4.3	12
	Thurman Thomas, Buffalo, AFC	288	1,407	4.9	7
1990	Barry Sanders, Detroit, NFC	255	1,304	5.1	13
	Thurman Thomas, Buffalo, AFC	271	1,297	4.8	11
1989	Christian Okoye, Kansas City, AFC	370	1,480	4.0	12
	*Barry Sanders, Detroit, NFC	280	1,470	5.3	14
1988	Eric Dickerson, Indianapolis, AFC	388	1,659	4.3	14
	Herschel Walker, Dallas, NFC	361	1,514	4.2	5
1987	Charles White, L.A. Rams, NFC	324	1,374	4.2	11
	Eric Dickerson, Indianapolis, AFC	223	1,011	4.5	5
1986	Eric Dickerson, L.A. Rams, NFC	404	1,821	4.5	11
	Curt Warner, Seattle, AFC	319	1,481	4.6	13
1985	Marcus Allen, L.A. Raiders, AFC	380	1,759	4.6	11
	Gerald Riggs, Atlanta, NFC	397	1,719	4.3	10
1984	Eric Dickerson, L.A. Rams, NFC	379	2,105	5.6	14
	Earnest Jackson, San Diego, AFC	296	1,179	4.0	8
1983	*Eric Dickerson, L.A. Rams, NFC	390	1,808	4.6	18
	*Curt Warner, Seattle, AFC	335	1,449	4.3	13
1982	Freeman McNeil, N.Y. Jets, AFC	151	786	5.2	6
	Tony Dorsett, Dallas, NFC	177	745	4.2	5
1981	*George Rogers, New Orleans, NFC	378	1,674	4.4	13
	Earl Campbell, Houston, AFC	361	1,376	3.8	10
1980	Earl Campbell, Houston, AFC	373	1,934	5.2	13
	Walter Payton, Chicago, NFC	317	1,460	4.6	6
1979	Earl Campbell, Houston, AFC	368	1,697	4.6	19
	Walter Payton, Chicago, NFC	369	1,610	4.4	14
1978	*Earl Campbell, Houston, AFC	302	1,450	4.8	13
	Walter Payton, Chicago, NFC	333	1,395	4.2	11
1977	Walter Payton, Chicago, NFC	339	1,852	5.5	14
	Mark van Eeghen, Oakland, AFC	324	1,273	3.9	7
1976	O.J. Simpson, Buffalo, AFC	290	1,503	5.2	8
	Walter Payton, Chicago, NFC	311	1,390	4.5	13
1975	O.J. Simpson, Buffalo, AFC	329	1,817	5.5	16
	Jim Otis, St. Louis, NFC	269	1,076	4.0	5
1974	Otis Armstrong, Denver, AFC	263	1,407	5.3	9
	Lawrence McCutcheon, Los Angeles, NFC	236	1,109	4.7	3
1973	O.J. Simpson, Buffalo, AFC	332	2,003	6.0	12
	John Brockington, Green Bay, NFC	265	1,144	4.3	3
1972	O.J. Simpson, Buffalo, AFC	292	1,251	4.3	6
	Larry Brown, Washington, NFC	285	1,216	4.3	8
1971	Floyd Little, Denver, AFC	284	1,133	4.0	6
	*John Brockington, Green Bay, NFC	216	1,105	5.1	4
1970	Larry Brown, Washington, NFC	237	1,125	4.7	5
	Floyd Little, Denver, AFC	209	901	4.3	3
1969	Gale Sayers, Chicago, NFL	236	1,032	4.4	8
	Dickie Post, San Diego, AFL	182	873	4.8	6
1968	Leroy Kelly, Cleveland, NFL	248	1,239	5.0	16
	*Paul Robinson, Cincinnati, AFL	238	1,023	4.3	8
1967	Jim Nance, Boston, AFL	269	1,216	4.5	7
	Leroy Kelly, Cleveland, NFL	235	1,205	5.1	11
1966	Jim Nance, Boston, AFL	299	1,458	4.9	11
	Gale Sayers, Chicago, NFL	229	1,231	5.4	8
1965	Jim Brown, Cleveland, NFL	289	1,544	5.3	17
	Paul Lowe, San Diego, AFL	222	1,121	5.0	7
1964	Jim Brown, Cleveland, NFL	280	1,446	5.2	7
	Cookie Gilchrist, Buffalo, AFL	230	981	4.3	6
1963	Jim Brown, Cleveland, NFL	291	1,863	6.4	12
	Clem Daniels, Oakland, AFL	215	1,099	5.1	3
1962	Jim Taylor, Green Bay, NFL	272	1,474	5.4	19
	Cookie Gilchrist, Buffalo, AFL	214	1,096	5.1	13
1961	Jim Brown, Cleveland, NFL	305	1,408	4.6	8
	Billy Cannon, Houston, AFL	200	948	4.7	6
1960	Jim Brown, Cleveland, NFL	215	1,257	5.8	9
	*Abner Haynes, Dall. Texans, AFL	156	875	5.6	9
1959	Jim Brown, Cleveland	290	1,329	4.6	14
1958	Jim Brown, Cleveland	257	1,527	5.9	17
1957	*Jim Brown, Cleveland	202	942	4.7	9
1956	Rick Casares, Chi. Bears	234	1,126	4.8	12
1955	*Alan Ameche, Baltimore	213	961	4.5	9
1954	Joe Perry, San Francisco	173	1,049	6.1	8
1953	Joe Perry, San Francisco	192	1,018	5.3	10
1952	Dan Towler, Los Angeles	156	894	5.7	10
1951	Eddie Price, N.Y. Giants	271	971	3.6	7
1950	Marion Motley, Cleveland	140	810	5.8	3
1949	Steve Van Buren, Philadelphia	263	1,146	4.4	11
1948	Steve Van Buren, Philadelphia	201	945	4.7	10
1947	Steve Van Buren, Philadelphia	217	1,008	4.6	13
1946	Bill Dudley, Pittsburgh	146	604	4.1	3
1945	Steve Van Buren, Philadelphia	143	832	5.8	15
1944	Bill Paschal, N.Y. Giants	196	737	3.8	9
1943	*Bill Paschal, N.Y. Giants	147	572	3.9	10
1942	*Bill Dudley, Pittsburgh	162	696	4.3	5
1941	Clarence (Pug) Manders, Brooklyn	111	486	4.4	5
1940	Byron (Whizzer) White, Detroit	146	514	3.5	5
1939	*Bill Osmanski, Chicago	121	699	5.8	7
1938	*Byron (Whizzer) White, Pittsburgh	152	567	3.7	4
1937	Cliff Battles, Washington	216	874	4.0	5
1936	*Alphonse (Tuffy) Leemans, N.Y. Giants	206	830	4.0	2
1935	Doug Russell, Chi. Cardinals	140	499	3.6	0
1934	*Beattie Feathers, Chi. Bears	119	1,004	8.4	8
1933	Jim Musick, Boston	173	809	4.7	5
1932	*Cliff Battles, Boston	148	576	3.9	3

First season of professional football.

ANNUAL PASSING LEADERS

(Current rating system implemented in 1973)

Year	Player, Team	Att.	Comp.	Yards	TD	Int.	Rating
1995	Jim Harbaugh, Indianapolis, AFC	314	200	2,575	17	5	100.7
	Brett Favre, Green Bay, NFC	570	359	4,413	38	13	99.5
1994	Steve Young, San Francisco, NFC	461	324	3,969	35	10	112.8
	Dan Marino, Miami, AFC	615	385	4,453	30	17	89.2
1993	Steve Young, San Francisco, NFC	462	314	4,023	29	16	101.5
	John Elway, Denver, AFC	551	348	4,030	25	10	92.8
1992	Steve Young, San Francisco, NFC	402	268	3,465	25	7	107.0
	Warren Moon, Houston, AFC	346	224	2,521	18	12	89.3
1991	Steve Young, San Francisco, NFC	279	180	2,517	17	8	101.8
	Jim Kelly, Buffalo, AFC	474	304	3,844	33	17	97.6
1990	Jim Kelly, Buffalo, AFC	346	219	2,829	24	9	101.2
	Phil Simms, N.Y. Giants, NFC	311	184	2,284	15	4	92.7
1989	Joe Montana, San Francisco, NFC	386	271	3,521	26	8	112.4
	Boomer Esiason, Cincinnati, AFC	455	258	3,525	28	11	92.1
1988	Boomer Esiason, Cincinnati, AFC	388	223	3,572	28	14	97.4
	Wade Wilson, Minnesota, NFC	332	204	2,746	15	9	91.5
1987	Joe Montana, San Francisco, NFC	398	266	3,054	31	13	102.1
	Bernie Kosar, Cleveland, AFC	389	241	3,033	22	9	95.4
1986	Tommy Kramer, Minnesota, NFC	372	208	3,000	24	10	92.6
	Dan Marino, Miami, AFC	623	378	4,746	44	23	92.5
1985	Ken O'Brien, N.Y. Jets, AFC	488	297	3,888	25	8	96.2
	Joe Montana, San Francisco, NFC	494	303	3,653	27	13	91.3
1984	Dan Marino, Miami, AFC	564	362	5,084	48	17	108.9
	Joe Montana, San Francisco, NFC	432	279	3,630	28	10	102.9
1983	Steve Bartkowski, Atlanta, NFC	432	274	3,167	22	5	97.6
	*Dan Marino, Miami, AFC	296	173	2,210	20	6	96.0
1982	Ken Anderson, Cincinnati, AFC	309	218	2,495	12	9	95.5
	Joe Theismann, Washington, NFC	252	161	2,033	13	9	91.3
1981	Ken Anderson, Cincinnati, AFC	479	300	3,754	29	10	98.5
	Joe Montana, San Francisco, NFC	488	311	3,565	19	12	88.2
1980	Brian Sipe, Cleveland, AFC	554	337	4,132	30	14	91.4
	Ron Jaworski, Philadelphia, NFC	451	257	3,529	27	12	90.9
1979	Roger Staubach, Dallas, NFC	461	267	3,586	27	11	92.4
	Dan Fouts, San Diego, AFC	530	332	4,082	24	24	82.6

1978	Roger Staubach, Dallas, NFC	413	231	3,190	25	16	84.9
	Terry Bradshaw, Pittsburgh, AFC	368	207	2,915	28	20	84.8
1977	Bob Griese, Miami, AFC	307	180	2,252	22	13	88.0
	Roger Staubach, Dallas, NFC	361	210	2,620	18	9	87.1
1976	Ken Stabler, Oakland, AFC	291	194	2,737	27	17	103.4
	James Harris, Los Angeles, NFC	158	91	1,460	8	6	89.8
1975	Ken Anderson, Cincinnati, AFC	377	228	3,169	21	11	94.1
	Fran Tarkenton, Minnesota, NFC	425	273	2,994	25	13	91.7
1974	Ken Anderson, Cincinnati, AFC	328	213	2,667	18	10	95.9
	Sonny Jurgensen, Washington, NFC	167	107	1,185	11	5	94.6
1973	Roger Staubach, Dallas, NFC	286	179	2,428	23	15	94.6
	Ken Stabler, Oakland, AFC	260	163	1,997	14	10	88.5
1972	Norm Snead, N.Y. Giants, NFC	325	196	2,307	17	12	
	Earl Morrall, Miami, AFC	150	83	1,360	11	7	
1971	Roger Staubach, Dallas, NFC	211	126	1,882	15	4	
	Bob Griese, Miami, AFC	263	145	2,089	19	9	
1970	John Brodie, San Francisco, NFC	378	223	2,941	24	10	
	Daryle Lamonica, Oakland, AFC	356	179	2,516	22	15	
1969	Sonny Jurgensen, Washington, NFL	442	274	3,102	22	15	
	*Greg Cook, Cincinnati, AFL	197	106	1,854	15	11	
1968	Len Dawson, Kansas City, AFL	224	131	2,109	17	9	
	Earl Morrall, Baltimore, NFL	317	182	2,909	26	17	
1967	Sonny Jurgensen, Washington, NFL	508	288	3,747	31	16	
	Daryle Lamonica, Oakland, AFL	425	220	3,228	30	20	
1966	Bart Starr, Green Bay, NFL	251	156	2,257	14	3	
	Len Dawson, Kansas City, AFL	284	159	2,527	26	10	
1965	Rudy Bukich, Chicago, NFL	312	176	2,641	20	9	
	John Hadl, San Diego, AFL	348	174	2,798	20	21	
1964	Len Dawson, Kansas City, AFL	354	199	2,879	30	18	
	Bart Starr, Green Bay, NFL	272	163	2,144	15	4	
1963	Y.A. Tittle, N.Y. Giants, NFL	367	221	3,145	36	14	
	Tobin Rote, San Diego, AFL	286	170	2,510	20	17	
1962	Len Dawson, Dall. Texans, AFL	310	189	2,759	29	17	
	Bart Starr, Green Bay, NFL	285	178	2,438	12	9	
1961	George Blanda, Houston, AFL	362	187	3,330	36	22	
	Milt Plum, Cleveland, NFL	302	177	2,416	18	10	
1960	Milt Plum, Cleveland, NFL	250	151	2,297	21	5	
	Jack Kemp, L.A. Chargers, AFL	406	211	3,018	20	25	
1959	Charlie Conerly, N.Y. Giants	194	113	1,706	14	4	
1958	Eddie LeBaron, Washington	145	79	1,365	11	10	
1957	Tommy O'Connell, Cleveland	110	63	1,229	9	8	
1956	Ed Brown, Chi. Bears	168	96	1,667	11	12	
1955	Otto Graham, Cleveland	185	98	1,721	15	8	
1954	Norm Van Brocklin, Los Angeles	260	139	2,637	13	21	
1953	Otto Graham, Cleveland	258	167	2,722	11	9	
1952	Norm Van Brocklin, Los Angeles	205	113	1,736	14	17	
1951	Bob Waterfield, Los Angeles	176	88	1,566	13	10	
1950	Norm Van Brocklin, Los Angeles	233	127	2,061	18	14	
1949	Sammy Baugh, Washington	255	145	1,903	18	14	
1948	Tommy Thompson, Philadelphia	246	141	1,965	25	11	
1947	Sammy Baugh, Washington	354	210	2,938	25	15	
1946	Bob Waterfield, Los Angeles	251	127	1,747	18	17	
1945	Sammy Baugh, Washington	182	128	1,669	11	4	
	Sid Luckman, Chi. Bears	217	117	1,725	14	10	
1944	Frank Filchock, Washington	147	84	1,139	13	9	
1943	Sammy Baugh, Washington	239	133	1,754	23	19	
1942	Cecil Isbell, Green Bay	268	146	2,021	24	14	
1941	Cecil Isbell, Green Bay	206	117	1,479	15	11	
1940	Sammy Baugh, Washington	177	111	1,367	12	10	
1939	*Parker Hall, Cleveland	208	106	1,227	9	13	
1938	Ed Danowski, N.Y. Giants	129	70	848	7	8	
1937	*Sammy Baugh, Washington	171	81	1,127	8	14	
1936	Arnie Herber, Green Bay	173	77	1,239	11	13	
1935	Ed Danowski, N.Y. Giants	113	57	794	10	9	
1934	Arnie Herber, Green Bay	115	42	799	8	12	
1933	*Harry Newman, N.Y. Giants	136	53	973	11	17	
1932	Arnie Herber, Green Bay	101	37	639	9	9	

First season of professional football.

ANNUAL PASSING TOUCHDOWN LEADERS

Year	Player, Team	TD
1995	Brett Favre, Green Bay, NFC	38
	Jeff Blake, Cincinnati, AFC	28
1994	Steve Young, San Francisco, NFC	35
	Dan Marino, Miami, AFC	30
1993	Steve Young, San Francisco, NFC	29
	John Elway, Denver, AFC	25
1992	Steve Young, San Francisco, NFC	25
	Dan Marino, Miami, AFC	24
1991	Jim Kelly, Buffalo, AFC	33
	Mark Rypien, Washington, NFC	28
1990	Warren Moon, Houston, AFC	33
	Randall Cunningham, Philadelphia, NFC	30
1989	Jim Everett, L.A. Rams, NFC	29
	Boomer Esiason, Cincinnati, AFC	28
1988	Jim Everett, L.A. Rams, NFC	31
	Boomer Esiason, Cincinnati, AFC	28
	Dan Marino, Miami, AFC	28
1987	Joe Montana, San Francisco, NFC	31
	Dan Marino, Miami, AFC	26
1986	Dan Marino, Miami, AFC	44
	Tommy Kramer, Minnesota, NFC	24
1985	Dan Marino, Miami, AFC	30
	Joe Montana, San Francisco, NFC	27
1984	Dan Marino, Miami, AFC	48
	Neil Lomax, St. Louis, NFC	28
	Joe Montana, San Francisco, NFC	28
1983	Lynn Dickey, Green Bay, NFC	32
	Joe Ferguson, Buffalo, AFC	26
	Brian Sipe, Cleveland, AFC	26
1982	Terry Bradshaw, Pittsburgh, AFC	17
	Dan Fouts, San Diego, AFC	17
	Joe Montana, San Francisco, NFC	17
1981	Dan Fouts, San Diego, AFC	33
	Steve Bartkowski, Atlanta, NFC	30
1980	Steve Bartkowski, Atlanta, NFC	31
	Dan Fouts, San Diego, AFC	30
	Brian Sipe, Cleveland, AFC	30
1979	Steve Grogan, New England, AFC	28
	Brian Sipe, Cleveland, AFC	28
	Roger Staubach, Dallas, NFC	27
1978	Terry Bradshaw, Pittsburgh, AFC	28
	Roger Staubach, Dallas, NFC	25
	Fran Tarkenton, Minnesota, NFC	25
1977	Bob Griese, Miami, AFC	22
	Ron Jaworski, Philadelphia, NFC	18
	Roger Staubach, Dallas, NFC	18
1976	Ken Stabler, Oakland, AFC	27
	Jim Hart, St. Louis, NFC	18
1975	Joe Ferguson, Buffalo, AFC	25
	Fran Tarkenton, Minnesota, NFC	25
1974	Ken Stabler, Oakland, AFC	26
	Jim Hart, St. Louis, NFC	20
1973	Roman Gabriel, Philadelphia, NFC	23
	Roger Staubach, Dallas, NFC	23
	Charley Johnson, Denver, AFC	20
1972	Billy Kilmer, Washington, NFC	19
	Joe Namath, N.Y. Jets, AFC	19
1971	John Hadl, San Diego, AFC	21
	John Brodie, San Francisco, NFC	18
1970	John Brodie, San Francisco, NFC	24
	John Hadl, San Diego, AFC	22
	Daryle Lamonica, Oakland, AFC	22
1969	Daryle Lamonica, Oakland, AFL	34
	Roman Gabriel, Los Angeles, NFL	24
1968	John Hadl, San Diego, AFL	27
	Earl Morrall, Baltimore, NFL	26
1967	Sonny Jurgensen, Washington, NFL	31
	Daryle Lamonica, Oakland, AFL	30
1966	Frank Ryan, Cleveland, NFL	29
	Len Dawson, Kansas City, AFL	26
1965	John Brodie, San Francisco, NFL	30
	Len Dawson, Kansas City, AFL	21
1964	Babe Parilli, Boston, AFL	31
	Frank Ryan, Cleveland, NFL	25
1963	Y.A. Tittle, N.Y. Giants, NFL	36
	Len Dawson, Kansas City, AFL	26
1962	Y.A. Tittle, N.Y. Giants, NFL	33
	Len Dawson, Dallas, AFL	29
1961	George Blanda, Houston, AFL	36
	Sonny Jurgensen, Philadelphia, NFL	32
1960	Al Dorow, N.Y. Titans, AFL	26
	Johnny Unitas, Baltimore, NFL	25
1959	Johnny Unitas, Baltimore	32
1958	Johnny Unitas, Baltimore	19
1957	Johnny Unitas, Baltimore	24
1956	Tobin Rote, Green Bay	18
1955	Tobin Rote, Green Bay	17
	Y.A. Tittle, San Francisco	17
1954	Adrian Burk, Philadelphia	23
1953	Robert Thomason, Philadelphia	21
1952	Jim Finks, Pittsburgh	20
	Otto Graham, Cleveland	20
1951	Bobby Layne, Detroit	26
1950	George Ratterman, N.Y. Yanks	22
1949	Johnny Lujack, Chi. Bears	23

Year	Player, Team	
1948	Tommy Thompson, Philadelphia	25
1947	Sammy Baugh, Washington	25
1946	Sid Luckman, Chi. Bears	17
	Bob Waterfield, Los Angeles	17
1945	Sid Luckman, Chi. Bears	14
	*Bob Waterfield, Cleveland	14
1944	Frank Filchock, Washington	13
1943	Sid Luckman, Chi. Bears	28
1942	Cecil Isbell, Green Bay	24
1941	Cecil Isbell, Green Bay	15
1940	Sammy Baugh, Washington	12
1939	Frank Filchock, Washington	11
1938	Bob Monnett, Green Bay	9
1937	Bernie Masterson, Chi. Bears	9
1936	Arnie Herber, Green Bay	11
1935	Ed Danowski, N.Y. Giants	10
1934	Arnie Herber, Green Bay	8
1933	*Harry Newman, N.Y. Giants	11
1932	Arnie Herber, Green Bay	9

**First season of professional football.*

ANNUAL PASS RECEIVING LEADERS

Year	Player, Team	No.	Yards	Avg.	TD
1995	Herman Moore, Detroit, NFC	123	1,686	13.7	14
	Carl Pickens, Cincinnati, AFC	99	1,234	12.5	17
1994	Cris Carter, Minnesota, NFC	122	1,256	10.3	7
	Ben Coates, New England, AFC	96	1,174	12.2	7
1993	Sterling Sharpe, Green Bay, NFC	112	1,274	11.4	11
	Reggie Langhorne, Indianapolis, AFC	85	1,038	12.2	3
1992	Sterling Sharpe, Green Bay, NFC	108	1,461	13.5	13
	Haywood Jeffires, Houston, AFC	90	913	10.1	9
1991	Haywood Jeffires, Houston, AFC	100	1,181	11.8	7
	Michael Irvin, Dallas, NFC	93	1,523	16.4	8
1990	Jerry Rice, San Francisco, NFC	100	1,502	15.0	13
	Haywood Jeffires, Houston, AFC	74	1,048	14.2	8
	Drew Hill, Houston, AFC	74	1,019	13.8	5
1989	Sterling Sharpe, Green Bay, NFC	90	1,423	15.8	12
	Andre Reed, Buffalo, AFC	88	1,312	14.9	9
1988	Al Toon, N.Y. Jets, AFC	93	1,067	11.5	5
	Henry Ellard, L.A. Rams, NFC	86	1,414	16.4	10
1987	J.T. Smith, St. Louis, NFC	91	1,117	12.3	8
	Al Toon, N.Y. Jets, AFC	68	976	14.4	5
1986	Todd Christensen, L.A. Raiders, AFC	95	1,153	12.1	8
	Jerry Rice, San Francisco, NFC	86	1,570	18.3	15
1985	Roger Craig, San Francisco, NFC	92	1,016	11.0	6
	Lionel James, San Diego, AFC	86	1,027	11.9	6
1984	Art Monk, Washington, NFC	106	1,372	12.9	7
	Ozzie Newsome, Cleveland, AFC	89	1,001	11.2	5
1983	Todd Christensen, L.A. Raiders, AFC	92	1,247	13.6	12
	Roy Green, St. Louis, NFC	78	1,227	15.7	14
	Charlie Brown, Washington, NFC	78	1,225	15.7	8
	Earnest Gray, N.Y. Giants, NFC	78	1,139	14.6	5
1982	Dwight Clark, San Francisco, NFC	60	913	15.2	5
	Kellen Winslow, San Diego, AFC	54	721	13.4	6
1981	Kellen Winslow, San Diego, AFC	88	1,075	12.2	10
	Dwight Clark, San Francisco, NFC	85	1,105	13.0	4
1980	Kellen Winslow, San Diego, AFC	89	1,290	14.5	9
	*Earl Cooper, San Francisco, NFC	83	567	6.8	4
1979	Joe Washington, Baltimore, AFC	82	750	9.1	3
	Ahmad Rashad, Minnesota, NFC	80	1,156	14.5	9
1978	Rickey Young, Minnesota, NFC	88	704	8.0	5
	Steve Largent, Seattle, AFC	71	1,168	16.5	8
1977	Lydell Mitchell, Baltimore, AFC	71	620	8.7	4
	Ahmad Rashad, Minnesota, NFC	51	681	13.4	2
1976	MacArthur Lane, Kansas City, AFC	66	686	10.4	1
	Drew Pearson, Dallas, NFC	58	806	13.9	6
1975	Chuck Foreman, Minnesota, NFC	73	691	9.5	9
	Reggie Rucker, Cleveland, AFC	60	770	12.8	3
	Lydell Mitchell, Baltimore, AFC	60	544	9.1	4
1974	Lydell Mitchell, Baltimore, AFC	72	544	7.6	2
	Charles Young, Philadelphia, NFC	63	696	11.0	3
1973	Harold Carmichael, Philadelphia, NFC	67	1,116	16.7	9
	Fred Willis, Houston, AFC	57	371	6.5	1
1972	Harold Jackson, Philadelphia, NFC	62	1,048	16.9	4
	Fred Biletnikoff, Oakland, AFC	58	802	13.8	7
1971	Fred Biletnikoff, Oakland, AFC	61	929	15.2	9
	Bob Tucker, N.Y. Giants, NFC	59	791	13.4	4
1970	Dick Gordon, Chicago, NFC	71	1,026	14.5	13
	Marlin Briscoe, Buffalo, AFC	57	1,036	18.2	8
1969	Dan Abramowicz, New Orleans, NFL	73	1,015	13.9	7
	Lance Alworth, San Diego, AFL	64	1,003	15.7	4
1968	Clifton McNeil, San Francisco, NFL	71	994	14.0	7
	Lance Alworth, San Diego, AFL	68	1,312	19.3	10
1967	George Sauer, N.Y. Jets, AFL	75	1,189	15.9	6
	Charley Taylor, Washington, NFL	70	990	14.1	9
1966	Lance Alworth, San Diego, AFL	73	1,383	18.9	13
	Charley Taylor, Washington, NFL	72	1,119	15.5	12
1965	Lionel Taylor, Denver, AFL	85	1,131	13.3	6
	Dave Parks, San Francisco, NFL	80	1,344	16.8	12
1964	Charley Hennigan, Houston, AFL	101	1,546	15.3	8
	Johnny Morris, Chicago, NFL	93	1,200	12.9	10
1963	Lionel Taylor, Denver, AFL	78	1,101	14.1	10
	Bobby Joe Conrad, St. Louis, NFL	73	967	13.2	10
1962	Lionel Taylor, Denver, AFL	77	908	11.8	4
	Bobby Mitchell, Washington, NFL	72	1,384	19.2	11
1961	Lionel Taylor, Denver, AFL	100	1,176	11.8	4
	Jim (Red) Phillips, Los Angeles, NFL	78	1,092	14.0	5
1960	Lionel Taylor, Denver, AFL	92	1,235	13.4	12
	Raymond Berry, Baltimore, NFL	74	1,298	17.5	10
1959	Raymond Berry, Baltimore	66	959	14.5	14
1958	Raymond Berry, Baltimore	56	794	14.2	9
	Pete Retzlaff, Philadelphia	56	766	13.7	2
1957	Billy Wilson, San Francisco	52	757	14.6	6
1956	Billy Wilson, San Francisco	60	889	14.8	5
1955	Pete Pihos, Philadelphia	62	864	13.9	7
1954	Pete Pihos, Philadelphia	60	872	14.5	10
	Billy Wilson, San Francisco	60	830	13.8	5
1953	Pete Pihos, Philadelphia	63	1,049	16.7	10
1952	Mac Speedie, Cleveland	62	911	14.7	5
1951	Elroy (Crazylegs) Hirsch, Los Angeles	66	1,495	22.7	17
1950	Tom Fears, Los Angeles	84	1,116	13.3	7
1949	Tom Fears, Los Angeles	77	1,013	13.2	9
1948	*Tom Fears, Los Angeles	51	698	13.7	4
1947	Jim Keane, Chi. Bears	64	910	14.2	10
1946	Jim Benton, Los Angeles	63	981	15.6	6
1945	Don Hutson, Green Bay	47	834	17.7	9
1944	Don Hutson, Green Bay	58	866	14.9	9
1943	Don Hutson, Green Bay	47	776	16.5	11
1942	Don Hutson, Green Bay	74	1,211	16.4	17
1941	Don Hutson, Green Bay	58	738	12.7	10
1940	*Don Looney, Philadelphia	58	707	12.2	4
1939	Don Hutson, Green Bay	34	846	24.9	6
1938	Gaynell Tinsley, Chi. Cardinals	41	516	12.6	1
1937	Don Hutson, Green Bay	41	552	13.5	7
1936	Don Hutson, Green Bay	34	536	15.8	8
1935	*Tod Goodwin, N.Y. Giants	26	432	16.6	4
1934	Joe Carter, Philadelphia	16	238	14.9	4
	Morris (Red) Badgro, N.Y. Giants	16	206	12.9	1
1933	John (Shipwreck) Kelly, Brooklyn	22	246	11.2	3
1932	Ray Flaherty, N.Y. Giants	21	350	16.7	3

**First season of professional football.*

ANNUAL PASS RECEIVING LEADERS (YARDS)

Year	Player, Team	No.	Yards	Avg.	TD
1995	Jerry Rice, San Francisco, NFC	122	1,848	15.1	15
	Tim Brown, Oakland, AFC	89	1,342	15.1	10
1994	Jerry Rice, San Francisco, NFC	112	1,499	13.4	13
	Tim Brown, L.A. Raiders, AFC	89	1,309	14.7	9
1993	Jerry Rice, San Francisco, NFC	98	1,503	15.3	15
	Tim Brown, L.A. Raiders, AFC	80	1,180	14.8	7
1992	Sterling Sharpe, Green Bay, NFC	108	1,461	13.5	13
	Anthony Miller, San Diego, AFC	72	1,060	14.7	7
1991	Michael Irvin, Dallas, NFC	93	1,523	16.4	8
	Haywood Jeffires, Houston, AFC	100	1,181	11.8	7
1990	Jerry Rice, San Francisco, NFC	100	1,502	15.0	13
	Haywood Jeffires, Houston, AFC	74	1,048	14.2	8
1989	Jerry Rice, San Francisco, NFC	82	1,483	18.1	17
	Andre Reed, Buffalo, AFC	88	1,312	14.9	9
1988	Henry Ellard, L.A. Rams, NFC	86	1,414	16.4	10
	Eddie Brown, Cincinnati, AFC	53	1,273	24.0	9
1987	J.T. Smith, St. Louis, NFC	91	1,117	12.3	8
	Carlos Carson, Kansas City, AFC	55	1,044	19.0	7
1986	Jerry Rice, San Francisco, NFC	86	1,570	18.3	15
	Stanley Morgan, New England, AFC	84	1,491	17.8	10
1985	Steve Largent, Seattle, AFC	79	1,287	16.3	6
	Mike Quick, Philadelphia, NFC	73	1,247	17.1	11
1984	Roy Green, St. Louis, NFC	78	1,555	19.9	12
	John Stallworth, Pittsburgh, AFC	80	1,395	17.4	11
1983	Mike Quick, Philadelphia, NFC	69	1,409	20.4	13
	Carlos Carson, Kansas City, AFC	80	1,351	16.9	7
1982	Wes Chandler, San Diego, AFC	49	1,032	21.1	9
	Dwight Clark, San Francisco, NFC	60	913	15.2	5
1981	Alfred Jenkins, Atlanta, NFC	70	1,358	19.4	13
	Frank Lewis, Buffalo, AFC	70	1,244	17.8	4
	Steve Watson, Denver, AFC	60	1,244	20.7	13
1980	John Jefferson, San Diego, AFC	82	1,340	16.3	13

	James Lofton, Green Bay, NFC	71	1,226	17.3	4
1979	Steve Largent, Seattle, AFC	66	1,237	18.7	9
	Ahmad Rashad, Minnesota, NFC	80	1,156	14.5	9
1978	Wesley Walker, N.Y. Jets, AFC	48	1,169	24.4	8
	Harold Carmichael, Philadelphia, NFC	55	1,072	19.5	8
1977	Drew Pearson, Dallas, NFC	48	870	18.1	2
	Ken Burrough, Houston, AFC	43	816	19.0	8
1976	Roger Carr, Baltimore, AFC	43	1,112	25.9	11
	*Sammy White, Minnesota, NFC	51	906	17.8	10
1975	Ken Burrough, Houston, AFC	53	1,063	20.1	8
	Mel Gray, St. Louis, NFC	48	926	19.3	11
1974	Cliff Branch, Oakland, AFC	60	1,092	18.2	13
	Drew Pearson, Dallas, NFC	62	1,087	17.5	2
1973	Harold Carmichael, Philadelphia, NFC	67	1,116	16.7	9
	*Isaac Curtis, Cincinnati, AFC	45	843	18.7	9
1972	Harold Jackson, Philadelphia, NFC	62	1,048	16.9	4
	Rich Caster, N.Y. Jets, AFC	39	833	21.4	10
1971	Otis Taylor, Kansas City, AFC	57	1,110	19.5	7
	Gene Washington, San Francisco, NFC	46	884	19.2	4
1970	Gene Washington, San Francisco, NFC	53	1,100	20.8	12
	Marlin Briscoe, Buffalo, AFC	57	1,036	18.2	8
1969	Warren Wells, Oakland, AFL	47	1,260	26.8	14
	Harold Jackson, Philadelphia, NFL	65	1,116	17.2	9
1968	Lance Alworth, San Diego, AFL	68	1,312	19.3	10
	Roy Jefferson, Pittsburgh, NFL	58	1,074	18.5	11
1967	Don Maynard, N.Y. Jets, AFL	71	1,434	20.3	10
	Ben Hawkins, Philadelphia, NFL	59	1,265	21.4	10
1966	Lance Alworth, San Diego, AFL	73	1,383	18.9	13
	Pat Studstill, Detroit, NFL	67	1,266	18.9	5
1965	Lance Alworth, San Diego, AFL	69	1,602	23.2	14
	Dave Parks, San Francisco, NFL	80	1,344	16.8	12
1964	Charley Hennigan, Houston, AFL	101	1,546	15.3	8
	Johnny Morris, Chicago, NFL	93	1,200	12.9	10
1963	Bobby Mitchell, Washington, NFL	69	1,436	20.8	7
	Art Powell, Oakland, AFL	73	1,304	17.8	16
1962	Bobby Mitchel, Washington, NFL	72	1,384	19.2	11
	Art Powell, N.Y. Titans, AFL	64	1,130	17.6	8
1961	Charley Hennigan, Houston, AFL	82	1,746	21.3	12
	Tommy McDonald, Philadelphia, NFL	64	1,144	17.9	13
1960	*Bill Groman, Houston, AFL	72	1,473	20.5	12
	Raymond Berry, Baltimore, NFL	74	1,298	17.5	10
1959	Raymond Berry, Baltimore	66	959	14.5	14
1958	Del Shofner, Los Angeles	51	1,097	21.5	8
1957	Raymond Berry, Baltimore	47	800	17.0	6
1956	Billy Howton, Green Bay	55	1,188	21.6	12
1955	Pete Pihos, Philadelphia	62	864	13.9	7
1954	Bob Boyd, Los Angeles	53	1,212	22.9	6
1953	Pete Pihos, Philadelphia	63	1,049	16.7	10
1952	*Bill Howton, Green Bay	53	1,231	23.2	13
1951	Elroy (Crazylegs) Hirsch, Los Angeles	66	1,495	22.7	17
1950	Tom Fears, Los Angeles	84	1,116	13.3	7
1949	Bob Mann, Detroit	66	1,014	15.4	4
1948	Mal Kutner, Chi. Cardinals	41	943	23.0	14
1947	Mal Kutner, Chi. Cardinals	43	944	21.9	7
1946	Jim Benton, Los Angeles	63	981	15.5	6
1945	Jim Benton, Cleveland	45	1,067	23.7	8
1944	Don Hutson, Green Bay	58	866	14.6	9
1943	Don Hutson, Green Bay	47	776	16.5	11
1942	Don Hutson, Green Bay	74	1,211	16.4	17
1941	Don Hutson, Green Bay	58	738	12.7	10
1940	*Don Looney, Philadelphia	58	707	12.2	4
1939	Don Hutson, Green Bay	34	846	24.9	6
1938	Don Hutson, Green Bay	32	548	17.1	9
1937	*Gaynell Tinsley, Chi. Cardinals	36	675	18.8	5
1936	Don Hutson, Green Bay	34	526	15.5	8
1935	Charley Malone, Boston	22	433	19.7	2
1934	Harry Ebding, Detroit	9	257	28.6	2
1933	*Paul Moss, Pittsburgh	18	383	21.3	2
1932	Johnny Blood (McNally), Green Bay	19	326	17.2	3

**First season of professional football.*

ANNUAL INTERCEPTION LEADERS

Year	Player, Team	No.	Yards	TD
1995	*Orlando Thomas, Minnesota, NFC	9	108	1
	Willie Williams, Pittsburgh, AFC	7	122	1
1994	Eric Turner, Cleveland, AFC	9	199	1
	Aeneas Williams, Arizona, NFC	9	89	0
1993	Eugene Robinson, Seattle, AFC	9	80	0
	Nate Odomes, Buffalo, AFC	9	65	0
	Deion Sanders, Atlanta, NFC	7	91	0
1992	Henry Jones, Buffalo, AFC	8	263	2
	Audray McMillan, Minnesota, NFC	8	157	2
1991	Ronnie Lott, L.A. Raiders, AFC	8	52	0
	Ray Crockett, Detroit, NFC	6	141	1
	Deion Sanders, Atlanta, AFC	6	119	1
	*Aeneas Williams, Phoenix, NFC	6	60	0
	Tim McKyer, Atlanta, NFC	6	24	0
1990	*Mark Carrier, Chicago, NFC	10	39	0
	Richard Johnson, Houston, AFC	8	100	1
1989	Felix Wright, Cleveland, AFC	9	91	1
	Eric Allen, Philadelphia, NFC	8	38	0
1988	Scott Case, Atlanta, NFC	10	47	0
	Erik McMillan, N.Y. Jets, AFC	8	168	2
1987	Barry Wilburn, Washington, NFC	9	135	1
	Mike Prior, Indianapolis, AFC	6	57	0
	Mark Kelso, Buffalo, AFC	6	25	0
	Keith Bostic, Houston, AFC	6	-14	0
1986	Ronnie Lott, San Francisco, NFC	10	134	1
	Deron Cherry, Kansas City, AFC	9	150	0
1985	Everson Walls, Dallas, NFC	9	31	0
	Albert Lewis, Kansas City, AFC	8	59	0
	Eugene Daniel, Indianapolis, AFC	8	53	0
1984	Ken Easley, Seattle, AFC	10	126	2
	*Tom Flynn, Green Bay, NFC	9	106	0
1983	Mark Murphy, Washington, NFC	9	127	0
	Ken Riley, Cincinnati, AFC	8	89	2
	Vann McElroy, L.A. Raiders, AFC	8	68	0
1982	Everson Walls, Dallas, NFC	7	61	0
	Ken Riley, Cincinnati, AFC	5	88	1
	Bobby Jackson, N.Y Jets, AFC	5	84	1
	Dwayne Woodruff, Pittsburgh, AFC	5	53	0
	Donnie Shell, Pittsburgh, AFC	5	27	0
1981	*Everson Walls, Dallas, NFC	11	133	0
	John Harris, Seattle, AFC	10	155	2
1980	Lester Hayes, Oakland, AFC	13	273	1
	Nolan Cromwell, Los Angeles, NFC	8	140	1
1979	Mike Reinfeldt, Houston, AFC	12	205	0
	Lemar Parrish, Washiongton, NFC	9	65	0
1978	Thom Darden, Cleveland, AFC	10	200	0
	Ken Stone, St. Louis, NFC	9	139	0
	Willie Buchanon, Green Bay, NFC	9	93	1
1977	Lyle Blackwood, Baltimore, AFC	10	163	0
	Rolland Lawrence, Atlanta, NFC	7	138	0
1976	Monte Jackson, Los Angeles, NFC	10	173	3
	Ken Riley, Cincinnati, AFC	9	141	1
1975	Mel Blount, Pittsburgh, AFC	11	121	0
	Paul Krause, Minnesota, NFC	10	201	0
1974	Emmitt Thomas, Kansas City, AFC	12	214	2
	Ray Brown, Atlanta, NFC	8	164	1
1973	Dick Anderson, Miami, AFC	8	163	2
	Mike Wagner, Pittsburgh, AFC	8	134	0
	Bobby Bryant, Minnesota, NFC	7	105	1
1972	Bill Bradley, Philadelphia, NFC	9	73	0
	Mike Sensibaugh, Kansas City, AFC	8	65	0
1971	Bill Bradley, Philadelphia, NFC	11	248	0
	Ken Houston, Houston, AFC	9	220	4
1970	Johnny Robinson, Kansas City, AFC	10	155	0
	Dick LeBeau, Detroit, NFC	9	96	0
1969	Mel Renfro, Dallas, NFL	10	118	0
	Emmitt Thomas, Kansas City, AFL	9	146	1
1968	Dave Grayson, Oakland, AFL	10	195	1
	Willie Williams, N.Y. Giants, NFL	10	103	0
1967	Miller Farr, Houston, AFL	10	264	3
	*Lem Barney, Detroit, NFL	10	232	3
	Tom Janik, Buffalo, AFL	10	222	2
	Dave Whitsell, New Orleans, NFL	10	178	2
	Dick Westmoreland, Miami, AFL	10	127	1
1966	Larry Wilson, St. Louis, NFL	10	180	2
	Johnny Robinson, Kansas City, AFL	10	136	1
	Bobby Hunt, Kansas City, AFL	10	113	0
1965	W.K. Hicks, Houston, AFL	9	156	0
	Bobby Boyd, Baltimore, NFL	9	78	1
1964	Dainard Paulson, N.Y. Jets, AFL	12	157	1
	*Paul Krause, Washington, NFL	12	140	1
1963	Fred Glick, Houston, AFL	12	180	1
	Dick Lynch, N.Y. Giants, NFL	9	251	3
	Roosevelt Taylor, Chicago, NFL	9	172	1
1962	Lee Riley, N.Y. Titans, AFL	11	122	0
	Willie Wood, Green Bay, NFL	9	132	0
1961	Billy Atkins, Buffalo, AFL	10	158	0
	Dick Lynch, N.Y. Giants, NFL	9	60	0
1960	*Austin (Goose) Gonsoulin, Denver, AFL	11	98	0
	Dave Baker, San Francisco, NFL	10	96	0
	Jerry Norton, St. Louis, NFL	10	96	0
1959	Dean Derby, Pittsburgh	7	127	0
	Milt Davis, Baltimore	7	119	1

	Don Shinnick, Baltimore	7	70	0
1958	Jim Patton, N.Y. Giants	11	183	0
1957	Milt Davis, Baltimore	10	219	2
	Jack Christiansen, Detroit	10	137	1
	Jack Butler, Pittsburgh	10	85	0
1956	Linden Crow, Chi. Cardinals	11	170	0
1955	Will Sherman, Los Angeles	11	101	0
1954	Dick (Night Train) Lane, Chi. Cardinals	10	181	0
1953	Jack Christiansen, Detroit	12	238	1
1952	*Dick (Night Train) Lane, Los Angeles	14	298	2
1951	Otto Schnellbacher, N.Y. Giants	11	194	2
1950	Orban (Spec) Sanders, N.Y. Yanks	13	199	0
1949	Bob Nussbaumer, Chi. Cardinals	12	157	0
1948	*Dan Sandifer, Washington	13	258	2
1947	Frank Reagan, N.Y. Giants	10	203	0
	Frank Seno, Boston	10	100	0
1946	Bill Dudley, Pittsburgh	10	242	1
1945	Roy Zimmerman, Philadelphia	7	90	0
1944	*Howard Livingston, N.Y. Giants	9	172	1
1943	Sammy Baugh, Washington	11	112	0
1942	Clyde (Bulldog) Turner, Chi. Bears	8	96	1
1941	Marshall Goldberg, Chi. Cardinals	7	54	0
	*Art Jones, Pittsburgh	7	35	0
1940	Clarence (Ace) Parker, Brooklyn	6	146	1
	Kent Ryan, Detroit	6	65	0
	Don Hutson, Green Bay	6	24	0

First season of professional football.

ANNUAL PUNTING LEADERS

Year	Player, Team	No.	Avg.	Long
1995	Rick Tuten, Seattle, AFC	83	45.0	73
	Sean Landeta, St. Louis, NFC	83	44.3	63
1994	Sean Landeta, L.A. Rams, NFC	78	44.8	62
	Jeff Gossett, L.A. Raiders, AFC	77	43.9	65
1993	Greg Montgomery, Houston, AFC	54	45.6	77
	Jim Arnold, Detroit, NFC	72	44.5	68
1992	Greg Montgomery, Houston, AFC	53	46.9	66
	Harry Newsome, Minnesota, NFC	72	45.0	84
1991	Reggie Roby, Miami, AFC	54	45.7	64
	Harry Newsome, Minnesota, AFC	68	45.5	65
1990	Mike Horan, Denver, AFC	58	44.4	67
	Sean Landeta, N.Y. Giants, NFC	75	44.1	67
1989	Rich Camarillo, Phoenix, NFC	76	43.4	58
	Greg Montgomery, Hounton, AFC	56	43.3	63
1988	Harry Newsome, Pittsburgh, AFC	65	45.4	62
	Jim Arnold, Detroit, NFC	97	42.4	69
1987	Rick Donnelly, Atlanta, NFC	61	44.0	62
	Ralf Mojsiejenko, San Diego, AFC	67	42.9	57
1986	Rohn Stark, Indianapolis, AFC	76	45.2	63
	Sean Landeta, N.Y. Giants, NFC	79	44.8	61
1985	Rohn Stark, Indianapolis, AFC	78	45.9	68
	*Rick Donnelly, Atlanta, NFC	59	43.6	68
1984	Jim Arnold, Kansas City, AFC	98	44.9	63
	*Brian Hansen, New Orleans, NFC	69	43.8	66
1983	Rohn Stark, Baltimore, AFC	91	45.3	68
	Frank Garcia, Tampa Bay, NFC	95	42.2	64
1982	Luke Prestridge, Denver, AFC	45	45.0	65
	Carl Birdsong, St. Louis, NFC	54	43.8	65
1981	Pat McInally, Cincinnati, AFC	72	45.4	62
	Tom Skladany, Detroit, NFC	64	43.5	74
1980	Dave Jennings, N.Y. Giants, NFC	94	44.8	63
	Luke Prestridge, Denver, AFC	70	43.9	57
1979	*Bob Grupp, Kansas City, AFC	89	43.6	74
	Dave Jennings, N.Y. Giants, NFC	104	42.7	72
1978	Pat McInally, Cincinnati, AFC	91	43.1	65
	*Tom Skladany, Detroit, NFC	86	42.5	63
1977	Ray Guy, Oakland, AFC	59	43.3	74
	Tom Blanchard, New Orleans, NFC	82	42.4	66
1976	Marv Bateman, Buffalo, AFC	86	42.8	78
	John James, Atlanta, NFC	101	42.1	67
1975	Ray Guy, Oakland, AFC	68	43.8	64
	Herman Weaver, Detroit, NFC	80	42.0	61
1974	Ray Guy, Oakland, AFC	74	42.2	66
	Tom Blanchard, New Orleans, NFC	88	42.1	71
1973	Jerrel Wilson, Kansas City, AFC	80	45.5	68
	*Tom Wittum, San Francisco, NFC	79	43.7	62
1972	Jerrel Wilson, Kansas City, AFC	66	44.8	69
	Dave Chapple, Los Angeles, NFC	53	44.2	70
1971	Dave Lewis, Cincinnati, AFC	72	44.8	56
	Tom McNeill, Philadelphia, NFC	73	42.0	64
1970	Dave Lewis, Cincinnati, AFC	79	46.2	63
	*Julian Fagan, New Orleans, NFC	77	42.5	64
1969	David Lee, Baltimore, NFL	57	45.3	66
	Dennis Partee, San Diego, AFL	71	44.6	62
1968	Jerrel Wilson, Kansas City, AFL	63	45.1	70
	Billy Lothridge, Atlanta, NFL	75	44.3	70
1967	Bob Scarpitto, Denver, AFL	105	44.9	73
	Billy Lothridge, Atlanta, NFL	87	43.7	62
1966	Bob Scarpitto, Denver, AFL	76	45.8	70
	*David Lee, Baltimore, NFL	49	45.6	64
1965	Gary Collins, Cleveland, NFL	65	46.7	71
	Jerrel Wilson, Kansas City, AFL	69	45.4	64
1964	Bobby Walden, Minnesota, NFL	72	46.4	73
	Jim Fraser, Denver, AFL	73	44.2	67
1963	Yale Lary, Detroit, NFL	35	48.9	73
	Jim Fraser, Denver, AFL	81	44.4	66
1962	Tommy Davis, San Francisco, NFL	48	45.6	82
	Jim Fraser, Denver, AFL	55	43.6	75
1961	Yale Lary, Detroit, NFL	52	48.4	71
	Billy Atkins, Buffalo, AFL	85	44.5	70
1960	Jerry Norton, St. Louis, NFL	39	45.6	62
	*Paul Maguire, L.A. Chargers, AFL	43	40.5	61
1959	Yale Lary, Detroit	45	47.1	67
1958	Sam Baker, Washington	48	45.4	64
1957	Don Chandler, N.Y. Giants	60	44.6	61
1956	Norm Van Brocklin, Los Angeles	48	43.1	72
1955	Norm Van Brocklin, Los Angeles	60	44.6	61
1954	Pat Brady, Pittsburgh	66	43.2	72
1953	Pat Brady, Pittsburgh	80	46.9	64
1952	Horace Gillom, Cleveland	61	45.7	73
1951	Horace Gillom, Cleveland	73	45.5	66
1950	*Fred (Curly) Morrison, Chi. Bears	57	43.3	65
1949	*Mike Boyda, N.Y. Bulldogs	56	44.2	61
1948	Joe Muha, Philadelphia	57	47.3	82
1947	Jack Jacobs, Green Bay	57	43.5	74
1946	Roy McKay, Green Bay	64	42.7	64
1945	Roy McKay, Green Bay	44	41.2	73
1944	Frank Sinkwich, Detroit	45	41.0	73
1943	Sammy Baugh, Washington	50	45.9	81
1942	Sammy Baugh, Washington	37	48.2	74
1941	Sammy Baugh, Washington	30	48.7	75
1940	Sammy Baugh, Washington	35	51.4	85
1939	*Parker Hall, Cleveland	58	40.8	80

First season of professional football.

ANNUAL PUNT RETURN LEADERS

Year	Player, Team	No.	Yards	Avg.	Long	TD
1995	David Palmer, Minnesota, NFC	26	342	13.2	74	1
	Andre Coleman, San Diego, AFC	28	326	11.6	88	1
1994	Brian Mitchell, Washington, NFC	32	452	14.1	78	2
	Darrien Gordon, San Diego, AFC	36	475	13.2	90	2
1993	*Tyrone Hughes, New Orleans, NFC	37	503	13.6	83	2
	Eric Metcalf, Cleveland, AFC	36	464	12.9	91	2
1992	Johnny Bailey, Phoenix, NFC	20	263	13.2	65	0
	Rod Woodson, Pittsburgh, AFC	32	364	11.4	80	1
1991	Mel Gray, Detroit, NFC	25	385	15.4	78	1
	Rod Woodson, Pittsburgh, AFC	28	320	11.4	40	0
1990	Clarence Verdin, Indianapolis, AFC	31	396	12.8	36	0
	*Johnny Bailey, Chicago, NFC	36	399	11.1	95	1
1989	Walter Stanley, Detroit, NFC	36	496	13.8	74	0
	Clarence Verdin, Indianapolis, AFC	23	296	12.9	49	1
1988	John Taylor, San Francisco, NFC	44	556	12.6	95	2
	JoJo Townsell, N.Y. Jets, AFC	35	409	11.7	59	1
1987	Mel Gray, New Orleans, NFC	24	352	14.7	80	0
	Bobby Joe Edmonds, Seattle, AFC	20	251	12.6	40	0
1986	*Bobby Joe Edmonds, Seattle, AFC	34	419	12.3	75	1
	*Vai Sikahema, St. Louis, NFC	43	522	12.1	71	2
1985	Irving Fryar, New England, AFC	37	520	14.1	85	2
	Henry Ellard, L.A. Rams, NFC	37	501	13.5	80	1
1984	Mike Martin, Cincinnati, AFC	24	376	15.7	55	0
	Henry Ellard, L.A. Rams, NFC	30	403	13.4	83	2
1983	*Henry Ellard, L.A. Rams, NFC	16	217	13.6	72	1
	Kirk Springs, N.Y. Jets, AFC	23	287	12.5	76	1
1982	Rick Upchurch, Denver, AFC	15	242	16.1	78	2
	Billy Johnson, Atlanta, NFC	24	273	11.4	71	0
1981	LeRoy Irvin, Los Angeles, NFC	46	615	13.4	84	3
	*James Brooks, San Diego, AFC	22	290	13.2	42	0
1980	J.T. Smith, Kansas City, AFC	40	581	14.5	75	2
	*Kenny Johnson, Atlanta, NFC	23	281	12.2	56	0
1979	John Sciarra, Philadelphia, NFC	16	182	11.4	38	0
	*Tony Nathan, Miami, AFC	28	306	10.9	86	1
1978	Rick Upchurch, Denver, AFC	36	493	13.7	75	1
	Jackie Wallace, Los Angeles, NFC	52	618	11.9	58	0
1977	Billy Johnson, Houston, AFC	35	539	15.4	87	2
	Larry Marshall, Philadelphia, NFC	46	489	10.6	48	0
1976	Rick Upchurch, Denver, AFC	39	536	13.7	92	4

Year	Player, Team	No.	Yards	Avg.	Long	TD
	Eddie Brown, Washington, NFC	48	646	13.5	71	1
1975	Billy Johnson, Houston, AFC	40	612	15.3	83	3
	Terry Metcalf, St. Louis, NFC	23	285	12.4	69	1
1974	Lemar Parrish, Cincinnati, AFC	18	338	18.8	90	2
	Dick Jauron, Detroit, NFC	17	286	16.8	58	0
1973	Bruce Taylor, San Francisco, NFC	15	207	13.8	61	0
	Ron Smith, San Diego, AFC	27	352	13.0	84	2
1972	Ken Ellis, Green Bay, NFC	14	215	15.4	80	1
	Chris Farasopoulos, N.Y. Jets, AFC	17	179	10.5	65	1
1971	Les (Speedy) Duncan, Washington, NFC	22	233	10.6	33	0
	Leroy Kelly, Cleveland, AFC	30	292	9.7	74	0
1970	Ed Podolak, Kansas City, AFC	23	311	13.5	60	0
	*Bruce Taylor, San Francisco, NFC	43	516	12.0	76	0
1969	Alvin Haymond, Los Angeles, NFL	33	435	13.2	52	0
	*Bill Thompson, Denver, AFL	25	288	11.5	40	0
1968	Bob Hayes, Dallas, NFL	15	312	20.8	90	2
	Noland Smith, Kansas City, AFL	18	270	15.0	80	1
1967	Floyd Little, Denver, AFL	16	270	16.9	72	1
	Ben Davis, Cleveland, NFL	18	229	12.7	52	1
1966	Les (Speedy) Duncan, San Diego, AFL	18	238	13.2	81	1
	Johnny Roland, St. Louis, NFL	20	221	11.1	86	1
1965	Leroy Kelly, Cleveland, NFL	17	265	15.6	67	2
	Les (Speedy) Duncan, San Diego, AFL	30	464	15.5	66	2
1964	Bobby Jancik, Houston, AFL	12	220	18.3	82	1
	Tommy Watkins, Detroit, NFL	16	238	14.9	68	2
1963	Dick James, Washington, NFL	16	214	13.4	39	0
	Claude (Hoot) Gibson, Oakland, AFL	26	307	11.8	85	2
1962	Dick Christy, N.Y. Titans, AFL	15	250	16.7	73	2
	Pat Studstill, Detroit, NFL	29	457	15.8	44	0
1961	Dick Christy, N.Y. Titans, AFL	18	383	21.3	70	2
	Willie Wood, Green Bay, NFL	14	225	16.1	72	2
1960	*Abner Haynes, Dall. Texans, AFL	14	215	15.4	46	0
	Abe Woodson, San Francisco, NFL	13	174	13.4	48	0
1959	Johnny Morris, Chi. Bears	14	171	12.2	78	1
1958	Jon Arnett, Los Angeles	18	223	12.4	58	0
1957	Bert Zagers, Washington	14	217	15.5	76	2
1956	Ken Konz, Cleveland	13	187	14.4	65	1
1955	Ollie Matson, Chi. Cardinals	13	245	18.8	78	2
1954	*Veryl Switzer, Green Bay	24	306	12.8	93	1
1953	Charley Trippi, Chi. Cardinals	21	239	11.4	38	0
1952	Jack Christiansen, Detroit	15	322	21.5	79	2
1951	Claude (Buddy) Young, N.Y. Yanks	12	231	19.3	79	1
1950	*Herb Rich, Baltimore	12	276	23.0	86	1
1949	Verda (Vitamin T) Smith, Los Angeles	27	427	15.8	85	1
1948	George McAfee, Chi. Bears	30	417	13.9	60	1
1947	*Walt Slater, Pittsburgh	28	435	15.5	33	0
1946	Bill Dudley, Pittsburgh	27	385	14.3	52	0
1945	*Dave Ryan, Detroit	15	220	14.7	56	0
1944	*Steve Van Buren, Philadelphia	15	230	15.3	55	1
1943	Andy Farkas, Washington	15	168	11.2	33	0
1942	Merlyn Condit, Brooklyn	21	210	10.0	23	0
1941	Byron (Whizzer) White, Detroit	19	262	13.8	64	0

**First season of professional football.*

ANNUAL KICKOFF RETURN LEADERS

Year	Player, Team	No.	Yards	Avg.	Long	TD
1995	Ron Carpenter, N.Y. Jets, AFC	20	553	27.7	58	0
	Brian Mitchell, Washington, NFC	55	1,408	25.6	59	0
1994	Mel Gray, Detroit, NFC	45	1,276	28.4	102	3
	Randy Baldwin, Cleveland, AFC	28	753	26.9	85	1
1993	Robert Brooks, Green Bay, NFC	23	611	26.6	95	1
	*Raghib Ismail, L.A. Raiders, AFC	25	605	24.2	66	0
1992	Jon Vaughn, New England, AFC	20	564	28.2	100	1
	Deion Sanders, Atlanta, NFC	40	1,067	26.7	99	2
1991	Mel Gray, Detroit, NFC	36	929	25.8	71	0
	Nate Lewis, San Diego, AFC	23	578	25.1	95	1
1990	Kevin Clark, Denver, AFC	20	505	25.3	75	0
	David Meggett, N.Y. Giants, NFC	21	492	23.4	58	0
1989	Rod Woodson, Pittsburgh, AFC	36	982	27.3	84	1
	Mel Gray, Detroit, NFC	24	640	26.7	57	0
1988	*Tim Brown, L.A. Raiders, AFC	41	1,098	26.8	97	1
	Donnie Elder, Tampa Bay, NFC	34	772	22.7	51	0
1987	Sylvester Stamps, Atlanta, NFC	24	660	27.5	97	1
	Paul Palmer, Kansas City, AFC	38	923	24.3	95	2
1986	Dennis Gentry, Chicago, NFC	20	576	28.8	91	1
	Lupe Sanchez, Pittsburgh, AFC	25	591	23.6	64	0
1985	Ron Brown, L.A. Rams, NFC	28	918	32.8	98	3
	Glen Young, Cleveland, AFC	35	898	25.7	63	0
1984	*Bobby Humphery, N.Y. Jets, AFC	22	675	30.7	97	1
	Barry Redden, L.A. Rams, NFC	23	530	23.0	40	0
1983	Fulton Walker, Miami, AFC	36	962	26.7	78	0
	Darrin Nelson, Minnesota, NFC	18	445	24.7	50	0
1982	*Mike Mosley, Buffalo, AFC	18	487	27.1	66	0
	Alvin Hall, Detroit, NFC	16	426	26.6	96	1
1981	Mike Nelms, Washington, NFC	37	1,099	29.7	84	0
	Carl Roaches, Houston, AFC	28	769	27.5	96	1
1980	Horace Ivory, New England, AFC	36	992	27.6	98	1
	Rich Mauti, New Orleans, NFC	31	798	25.7	52	0
1979	Larry Brunson, Oakland, AFC	17	441	25.9	89	0
	Jimmy Edwards, Minnesota, NFC	44	1,103	25.1	83	0
1978	Steve Odom, Green Bay, NFC	25	677	27.1	95	1
	*Keith Wright, Cleveland, AFC	30	789	26.3	86	0
1977	*Raymond Clayborn, New England, AFC	28	869	31.0	101	3
	*Wilbert Montgomery, Philadelphia, NFC	23	619	26.9	99	1
1976	*Duriel Harris, Miami, AFC	17	559	32.9	69	0
	Cullen Bryant, Los Angeles, NFC	16	459	28.7	90	1
1975	*Walter Payton, Chicago, NFC	14	444	31.7	70	0
	Harold Hart, Oakland, AFC	17	518	30.5	102	1
1974	Terry Metcalf, St. Louis, NFC	20	623	31.2	94	1
	Greg Pruitt, Cleveland, AFC	22	606	27.5	88	1
1973	Carl Garrett, Chicago, NFC	16	486	30.4	67	0
	*Wallace Francis, Buffalo, AFC	23	687	29.9	101	2
1972	Ron Smith, Chicago, NFC	30	924	30.8	94	1
	*Bruce Laird, Baltimore, AFC	29	843	29.1	73	0
1971	Travis Williams, Los Angeles, NFC	25	743	29.7	105	1
	Eugene (Mercury) Morris, Miami, AFC	15	423	28.2	94	1
1970	Jim Duncan, Baltimore, AFC	20	707	35.4	99	1
	Cecil Turner, Chicago, NFC	23	752	32.7	96	4
1969	Bobby Williams, Detroit, NFL	17	563	33.1	96	1
	*Bill Thompson, Denver, AFL	18	513	28.5	63	0
1968	Preston Pearson, Baltimore, NFL	15	527	35.1	102	2
	*George Atkinson, Oakland, AFL	32	802	25.1	60	0
1967	*Travis Williams, Green Bay, NFL	18	739	41.1	104	4
	*Zeke Moore, Houston, AFL	14	405	28.9	92	1
1966	Gale Sayers, Chicago, NFL	23	718	31.2	93	2
	*Goldie Sellers, Denver, AFL	19	541	28.5	100	2
1965	Tommy Watkins, Detroit, NFL	17	584	34.4	94	0
	Abner Haynes, Denver, AFL	34	901	26.5	60	0
1964	*Clarence Childs, N.Y. Giants, NFL	34	987	29.0	100	1
	Bo Roberson, Oakland, AFL	36	975	27.1	59	0
1963	Abe Woodson, San Francisco, NFL	29	935	32.2	103	3
	Bobby Jancik, Houston, AFL	45	1,317	29.3	53	0
1962	Abe Woodson, San Francisco, NFL	37	1,157	31.3	79	0
	*Bobby Jancik, Houston, AFL	24	826	30.3	61	0
1961	Dick Bass, Los Angeles, NFL	23	698	30.3	64	0
	*Dave Grayson, Dall. Texans, AFL	16	453	28.3	73	0
1960	*Tom Moore, Green Bay, NFL	12	397	33.1	84	0
	Ken Hall, Houston, AFL	19	594	31.3	104	1
1959	Abe Woodson, San Francisco	13	382	29.4	105	1
1958	Ollie Matson, Chi. Cardinals	14	497	35.5	101	2
1957	*Jon Arnett, Los Angeles	18	504	28.0	98	1
1956	*Tom Wilson, Los Angeles	15	477	31.8	103	1
1955	Al Carmichael, Green Bay	14	418	29.9	100	1
1954	Billy Reynolds, Cleveland	14	413	29.5	51	0
1953	Joe Arenas, San Francisco	16	551	34.4	82	0
1952	Lynn Chandnois, Pittsburgh	17	599	35.2	93	2
1951	Lynn Chandnois, Pittsburgh	12	390	32.5	55	0
1950	Verda (Vitamin T) Smith, Los Angeles	22	742	33.7	97	3
1949	*Don Doll, Detroit	21	536	25.5	56	0
1948	*Joe Scott, N.Y. Giants	20	569	28.5	99	1
1947	Eddie Saenz, Washington	29	797	27.5	94	2
1946	Abe Karnofsky, Boston	21	599	28.5	97	1
1945	Steve Van Buren, Philadelphia	13	373	28.7	98	1
1944	Bob Thurbon, Card.-Pitt.	12	291	24.3	55	0
1943	Ken Heineman, Brooklyn	16	444	27.8	69	0
1942	Marshall Goldberg, Chi. Cardinals	15	393	26.2	95	1
1941	Marshall Goldberg, Chi. Cardinals	12	290	24.2	41	0

**First season of professional football.*

ANNUAL LEADERS IN SACKS (SINCE 1982)

Year	Player, Team	Sacks
1995	Bryce Paup, Buffalo, AFC	17.5
	William Fuller, Philadelphia, NFC	13
	Wayne Martin, New Orleans, NFC	13
1994	Kevin Greene, Pittsburgh, AFC	14
	Ken Harvey, Washington, NFC	13.5
1993	Neil Smith, Kansas City, AFC	15
	Renaldo Turnbull, New Orleans, NFC	13
	Reggie White, Green Bay, NFC	13
1992	Clyde Simmons, Philadelphia, NFC	19
	Leslie O'Neal, San Diego, AFC	17
1991	Pat Swilling, New Orleans, NFC	17
	William Fuller, Houston, AFC	15
1990	Derrick Thomas, Kansas City, AFC	20
	Charles Haley, San Francisco, NFC	16

YEARLY STATISTICAL LEADERS

Year	Player	
1989	Chris Doleman, Minnesota, NFC	21
	Lee Williams, San Diego, AFC	14
1988	Reggie White, Philadelphia, NFC	18
	G. Townsend, L.A. Raiders, AFC	11.5
1987	Reggie White, Philadelphia, NFC	21
	Andre Tippett, New England, AFC	12.5
1986	Lawrence Taylor, N.Y. Giants, NFC	20.5
	Sean Jones, L.A. Raiders, AFC	15.5
1985	Richard Dent, Chicago, NFC	17
	Andre Tippett, New England, AFC	16.5
1984	Mark Gastineau, N.Y. Jets, AFC	22
	Richard Dent, Chicago, NFC	17.5
1983	Mark Gastineau, N.Y. Jets, AFC	19
	Fred Dean, San Francisco, NFC	17.5
1982	Doug Martin, Minnesota, NFC	11.5
	Jesse Baker, Houston, AFC	7.5

POINTS SCORED

Year	Team	Points
1995	San Francisco, NFC	457
	Pittsburgh, AFC	407
1994	San Francisco, NFC	505
	Miami, AFC	389
1993	San Francisco, NFC	473
	Denver, AFC	373
1992	San Francisco, NFC	431
	Buffalo, AFC	381
1991	Washington, NFC	485
	Buffalo, AFC	458
1990	Buffalo, AFC	428
	Philadelphia, NFC	396
1989	San Francisco, NFC	442
	Buffalo, AFC	409
1988	Cincinnati, AFC	448
	L.A. Rams, NFC	407
1987	San Francisco, NFC	459
	Cleveland, AFC	390
1986	Miami, AFC	430
	Minnesota, NFC	398
1985	San Diego, AFC	467
	Chicago, NFC	456
1984	Miami, AFC	513
	San Francisco, NFC	475
1983	Washington, NFC	541
	L.A. Raiders, AFC	442
1982	San Diego, AFC	288
	Dallas, NFC	226
	Green Bay, NFC	226
1981	San Diego, AFC	478
	Atlanta, NFC	426
1980	Dallas, NFC	454
	New England, AFC	441
1979	Pittsburgh, AFC	416
	Dallas, NFC	371
1978	Dallas, NFC	384
	Miami, AFC	372
1977	Oakland, AFC	351
	Dallas, NFC	345
1976	Baltimore, AFC	417
	Los Angeles, NFC	351
1975	Buffalo, AFC	420
	Minnesota, NFC	377
1974	Oakland, AFC	355
	Washington, NFC	320
1973	Los Angeles, NFC	388
	Denver, AFC	354
1972	Miami, AFC	385
	San Francisco, NFC	353
1971	Dallas, NFC	406
	Oakland, AFC	344
1970	San Francisco, NFC	352
	Baltimore, AFC	321
1969	Minnesota, NFL	379
	Oakland, AFL	377
1968	Oakland, AFL	453
	Dallas, NFL	431
1967	Oakland, AFL	468
	Los Angeles, NFL	398
1966	Kansas City, AFL	448
	Dallas, NFL	445
1965	San Francisco, NFL	421
	San Diego, AFL	340
1964	Baltimore, NFL	428
	Buffalo, AFL	400
1963	N.Y. Giants, NFL	448
	San Diego, AFL	399
1962	Green Bay, NFL	415
	Dall. Texans, AFL	389
1961	Houston, AFL	513
	Green Bay, NFL	391
1960	N.Y. Titans, AFL	382
	Cleveland, NFL	362
1959	Baltimore	374
1958	Baltimore	381
1957	Los Angeles	307
1956	Chi. Bears	363
1955	Cleveland	349
1954	Detroit	337
1953	San Francisco	372
1952	Los Angeles	349
1951	Los Angeles	392
1950	Los Angeles	466
1949	Philadelphia	364
1948	Chi. Cardinals	395
1947	Chi. Bears	363
1946	Chi. Bears	289
1945	Philadelphia	272
1944	Philadelphia	267
1943	Chi. Bears	303
1942	Chi. Bears	376
1941	Chi. Bears	396
1940	Washington	245
1939	Chi. Bears	298
1938	Green Bay	223
1937	Green Bay	220
1936	Green Bay	248
1935	Chi. Bears	192
1934	Chi. Bears	286
1933	N.Y. Giants	244
1932	Chicago Bears	160

TOTAL YARDS GAINED

Year	Team	Yards
1995	Detroit, NFC	6,113
	Denver, AFC	6,040
1994	Miami, AFC	6,078
	San Francisco, NFC	6,060
1993	San Francisco, NFC	6,435
	Miami, AFC	5,812
1992	San Francisco, NFC	6,195
	Buffalo, AFC	5,893
1991	Buffalo, AFC	6,252
	San Francisco, NFC	5,858
1990	Houston, AFC	6,222
	San Francisco, NFC	5,895
1989	San Francisco, NFC	6,268
	Cincinnati, AFC	6,101
1988	Cincinnati, AFC	6,057
	San Francisco, NFC	5,900
1987	San Francisco, NFC	5,987
	Denver, AFC	5,624
1986	Cincinnati, AFC	6,490
	San Francisco, NFC	6,082
1985	San Diego, AFC	6,535
	San Francisco, NFC	5,920
1984	Miami, AFC	6,936
	San Francisco, NFC	6,366
1983	San Diego, AFC	6,197
	Green Bay, NFC	6,172
1982	San Diego, AFC	4,048
	San Francisco, NFC	3,242
1981	San Diego, AFC	6,744
	Detroit, NFC	5,933
1980	San Diego, AFC	6,410
	Los Angeles, NFC	6,006
1979	Pittsburgh, AFC	6,258
	Dallas, NFC	5,968
1978	New England, AFC	5,965
	Dallas, NFC	5,959
1977	Dallas, NFC	4,812
	Oakland, AFC	4,736
1976	Baltimore, AFC	5,236
	St. Louis, NFC	5,136
1975	Buffalo, AFC	5,467
	Dallas, NFC	5,025
1974	Dallas, NFC	4,983
	Oakland, AFC	4,718
1973	Los Angeles, NFC	4,906
	Oakland, AFC	4,773
1972	Miami, AFC	5,036
	N.Y. Giants, NFC	4,483
1971	Dallas, NFC	5,035
	San Diego, AFC	4,738
1970	Oakland, AFC	4,829
	San Francisco, NFC	4,503
1969	Dallas, NFL	5,122
	Oakland, AFL	5,036
1968	Oakland, AFL	5,696
	Dallas, NFL	5,117
1967	N.Y. Jets, AFL	5,152
	Baltimore, NFL	5,008
1966	Dallas, NFL	5,145
	Kansas City, AFL	5,114
1965	San Francisco, NFL	5,270
	San Diego, AFL	5,188
1964	Buffalo, AFL	5,206
	Baltimore, NFL	4,779
1963	San Diego, AFL	5,153
	N.Y. Giants, NFL	5,024
1962	N.Y. Giants, NFL	5,005
	Houston, AFL	4,971
1961	Houston, AFL	6,288
	Philadelphia, NFL	5,112
1960	Houston, AFL	4,936
	Baltimore, NFL	4,245
1959	Baltimore	4,458
1958	Baltimore	4,539
1957	Los Angeles	4,143
1956	Chi. Bears	4,537
1955	Chi. Bears	4,316
1954	Los Angeles	5,187
1953	Philadelphia	4,811
1952	Cleveland	4,352
1951	Los Angeles	5,506
1950	Los Angeles	5,420
1949	Chi. Bears	4,873
1948	Chi. Cardinals	4,705
1947	Chi. Bears	5,053
1946	Los Angeles	3,793
1945	Washington	3,549
1944	Chi. Bears	3,239
1943	Chi. Bears	4,045
1942	Chi. Bears	3,900
1941	Chi. Bears	4,265
1940	Green Bay	3,400
1939	Chi. Bears	3,988
1938	Green Bay	3,037
1937	Green Bay	3,201
1936	Detroit	3,703
1935	Chi. Bears	3,454
1934	Chi. Bears	3,900
1933	N.Y. Giants	2,973
1932	Chi. Bears	2,755

YARDS RUSHING

Year	Team	Yards
1995	Kansas City, AFC	2,222
	Dallas, NFC	2,201
1994	Pittsburgh, AFC	2,180
	Detroit, NFC	2,080
1993	N.Y. Giants, NFC	2,210
	Seattle, AFC	2,015
1992	Buffalo, AFC	2,436
	Philadelphia, NFC	2,388
1991	Buffalo, AFC	2,381
	Minnesota, NFC	2,201
1990	Philadelphia, NFC	2,556
	San Diego, AFC	2,257
1989	Cincinnati, AFC	2,483
	Chicago, NFC	2,287
1988	Cincinnati, AFC	2,710
	San Francisco, NFC	2,523
1987	San Francisco, NFC	2,237
	L.A. Raiders, AFC	2,197
1986	Chicago, NFC	2,700
	Cincinnati, AFC	2,533
1985	Chicago, NFC	2,761
	Indianapolis, AFC	2,439
1984	Chicago, NFC	2,974
	N.Y. Jets, AFC	2,189
1983	Chicago, NFC	2,727
	Baltimore, AFC	2,695
1982	Buffalo, AFC	1,371
	Dallas, NFC	1,313
1981	Detroit, NFC	2,795
	Kansas City, AFC	2,633
1980	Los Angeles, NFC	2,799
	Houston, AFC	2,635
1979	N.Y. Jets, AFC	2,646
	St. Louis, NFC	2,582
1978	New England, AFC	3,165
	Dallas, NFC	2,783
1977	Chicago, NFC	2,811
	Oakland, AFC	2,627
1976	Pittsburgh, AFC	2,971
	Los Angeles, NFC	2,528
1975	Buffalo, AFC	2,974
	Dallas, NFC	2,432
1974	Dallas, NFC	2,454
	Pittsburgh, AFC	2,417
1973	Buffalo, AFC	3,088
	Los Angeles, NFC	2,925
1972	Miami, AFC	2,960
	Chicago, NFC	2,360
1971	Miami, AFC	2,429
	Detroit, NFC	2,376
1970	Dallas, NFC	2,300
	Miami, AFC	2,082
1969	Dallas, NFL	2,276
	Kansas City, AFL	2,220
1968	Chicago, NFL	2,377
	Kansas City, AFL	2,227
1967	Cleveland, NFL	2,139
	Houston, AFL	2,122
1966	Kansas City, AFL	2,274
	Cleveland, NFL	2,166
1965	Cleveland, NFL	2,331
	San Diego, AFL	2,085
1964	Green Bay, NFL	2,276
	Buffalo, AFL	2,040
1963	Cleveland, NFL	2,639
	San Diego, AFL	2,203
1962	Buffalo, AFL	2,480
	Green Bay, NFL	2,460
1961	Green Bay, NFL	2,350
	Dall. Texans, AFL	2,189
1960	St. Louis, NFL	2,356
	Oakland, AFL	2,056
1959	Cleveland	2,149
1958	Cleveland	2,526
1957	Los Angeles	2,142
1956	Chi. Bears	2,468
1955	Chi. Bears	2,388
1954	San Francisco	2,498
1953	San Francisco	2,230
1952	San Francisco	1,905
1951	Chi. Bears	2,408
1950	N.Y. Giants	2,336
1949	Philadelphia	2,607
1948	Chi. Cardinals	2,560
1947	Los Angeles	2,171
1946	Green Bay	1,765
1945	Cleveland	1,714
1944	Philadelphia	1,661
1943	Phil-Pitt	1,730

Year	Team	Yards
1942	Chi. Bears	1,881
1941	Chi. Bears	2,263
1940	Chi. Bears	1,818
1939	Chi. Bears	2,043
1938	Detroit	1,893
1937	Detroit	2,074
1936	Detroit	2,885
1935	Chi. Bears	2,096
1934	Chi. Bears	2,847
1933	Boston	2,260
1932	Chi. Bears	1,770

YARDS PASSING

Leadership in this category has been based on net yards since 1952.

Year	Team	Yards
1995	San Francisco, NFC	4,608
	Miami, AFC	4,210
1994	New England, AFC	4,444
	Minnesota, NFC	4,324
1993	Miami, AFC	4,353
	San Francisco, NFC	4,302
1992	Houston, AFC	4,029
	San Francisco, NFC	3,880
1991	Houston, AFC	4,621
	San Francisco, NFC	3,997
1990	Houston, AFC	4,805
	San Francisco, NFC	4,177
1989	Washington, NFC	4,349
	Miami, AFC	4,216
1988	Miami, AFC	4,516
	Washington, NFC	4,136
1987	Miami, AFC	3,876
	San Francisco, NFC	3,750
1986	Miami, AFC	4,779
	San Francisco, NFC	4,096
1985	San Diego, AFC	4,870
	Dallas, NFC	3,861
1984	Miami, AFC	5,018
	St. Louis, NFC	4,257
1983	San Diego, AFC	4,661
	Green Bay, NFC	4,365
1982	San Diego, AFC	2,927
	San Francisco, NFC	2,502
1981	San Diego, AFC	4,739
	Minnesota, NFC	4,333
1980	San Diego, AFC	4,531
	Minnesota, NFC	3,688
1979	San Diego, AFC	3,915
	San Francisco, NFC	3,641
1978	San Diego, AFC	3,375
	Minnesota, NFC	3,243
1977	Buffalo, AFC	2,530
	St. Louis, NFC	2,499
1976	Baltimore, AFC	2,933
	Minnesota, NFC	2,855
1975	Cincinnati, AFC	3,241
	Washington, NFC	2,917
1974	Washington, NFC	2,978
	Cincinnati, AFC	2,804
1973	Philadelphia, NFC	2,998
	Denver, AFC	2,519
1972	N.Y. Jets, AFC	2,777
	San Francisco, NFC	2,735
1971	San Diego, AFC	3,134
	Dallas, NFC	2,786
1970	San Francisco, NFC	2,923
	Oakland, AFC	2,865
1969	Oakland, AFL	3,271
	San Francisco, NFL	3,158
1968	San Diego, AFL	3,623
	Dallas, NFL	3,026
1967	N.Y. Jets, AFL	3,845
	Washington, NFL	3,730
1966	N.Y. Jets, AFL	3,464
	Dallas, NFL	3,023
1965	San Francisco, NFL	3,487
	San Diego, AFL	3,103
1964	Houston, AFL	3,527
	Chicago, NFL	2,841
1963	Baltimore, NFL	3,296
	Houston, AFL	3,222
1962	Denver, AFL	3,404
	Philadelphia, NFL	3,385
1961	Houston, AFL	4,392
	Philadelphia, NFL	3,605
1960	Houston, AFL	3,203
	Baltimore, NFL	2,956
1959	Baltimore	2,753
1958	Pittsburgh	2,752
1957	Baltimore	2,388
1956	Los Angeles	2,419
1955	Philadelphia	2,472
1954	Chi. Bears	3,104
1953	Philadelphia	3,089
1952	Cleveland	2,566
1951	Los Angeles	3,296
1950	Los Angeles	3,709
1949	Chi. Bears	3,055
1948	Washington	2,861
1947	Washington	3,336
1946	Los Angeles	2,080
1945	Chi. Bears	1,857
1944	Washington	2,021
1943	Chi. Bears	2,310
1942	Green Bay	2,407
1941	Chi. Bears	2,002
1940	Washington	1,887
1939	Chi. Bears	1,965
1938	Washington	1,536
1937	Green Bay	1,398
1936	Green Bay	1,629
1935	Green Bay	1,449
1934	Green Bay	1,165
1933	N.Y. Giants	1,348
1932	Chi. Bears	1,013

FEWEST POINTS ALLOWED

Year	Team	Points
1995	Kansas City, AFC	241
	San Francisco, NFC	258
1994	Cleveland, AFC	204
	Dallas, NFC	248
1993	N.Y. Giants, NFC	205
	Houston, AFC	238
1992	New Orleans, NFC	202
	Pittsburgh, AFC	225
1991	New Orleans, NFC	211
	Denver, AFC	235
1990	N.Y. Giants, NFC	211
	Pittsburgh, AFC	240
1989	Denver, AFC	226
	N.Y. Giants, NFC	252
1988	Chicago, NFC	215
	Buffalo, AFC	237
1987	Indianapolis, AFC	238
	San Francisco, NFC	253
1986	Chicago, NFC	187
	Seattle, AFC	293
1985	Chicago, NFC	198
	N.Y. Jets, AFC	264
1984	San Francisco, NFC	227
	Denver, AFC	241
1983	Miami, AFC	250
	Detroit, NFC	286
1982	Washington, NFC	128
	Miami, AFC	131
1981	Philadelphia, NFC	221
	Miami, AFC	275
1980	Philadelphia, NFC	222
	Houston, AFC	251
1979	Tampa Bay, NFC	237
	San Diego, AFC	246
1978	Pittsburgh, AFC	195
	Dallas, NFC	208
1977	Atlanta, NFC	129
	Denver, AFC	148
1976	Pittsburgh, AFC	138
	Minnesota, NFC	176
1975	Los Angeles, NFC	135
	Pittsburgh, AFC	162
1974	Los Angeles, NFC	181
	Pittsburgh, AFC	189
1973	Miami, AFC	150
	Minnesota, NFC	168
1972	Miami, AFC	171
	Washington, NFC	218
1971	Minnesota, NFC	139
	Baltimore, AFC	140
1970	Minnesota, NFC	143
	Miami, AFC	228
1969	Minnesota, NFL	133
	Kansas City, AFL	177
1968	Baltimore, NFL	144
	Kansas City, AFL	170
1967	Los Angeles, NFL	196
	Houston, AFL	199
1966	Green Bay, NFL	163
	Buffalo, AFL	255
1965	Green Bay, NFL	224
	Buffalo, AFL	226
1964	Baltimore, NFL	225
	Buffalo, AFL	242
1963	Chicago, NFL	144
	San Diego, AFL	255
1962	Green Bay, NFL	148
	Dall. Texans, AFL	233
1961	San Diego, AFL	219
	N.Y. Giants, NFL	220
1960	San Francisco, NFL	205
	Dall. Texans, AFL	253
1959	N.Y. Giants	170
1958	N.Y. Giants	183
1957	Cleveland	172
1956	Cleveland	177
1955	Cleveland	218
1954	Cleveland	162
1953	Cleveland	162
1952	Detroit	192
1951	Cleveland	152
1950	Philadelphia	141
1949	Philadelphia	134
1948	Chi. Bears	151
1947	Green Bay	210
1946	Pittsburgh	117
1945	Washington	121
1944	N.Y. Giants	75
1943	Washington	137
1942	Chi. Bears	84
1941	N.Y. Giants	114
1940	Brooklyn	120
1939	N.Y. Giants	85
1938	N.Y. Giants	79
1937	Chi. Bears	100
1936	Chi. Bears	94
1935	Green Bay	96
	N.Y. Giants	96
1934	Detroit	59
1933	Brooklyn	54
1932	Chi. Bears	44

FEWEST TOTAL YARDS ALLOWED

Year	Team	Yards
1995	San Francisco, NFC	4,398
	Kansas City, AFC	4,549
1994	Dallas, NFC	4,313
	Pittsburgh, AFC	4,326
1993	Minnesota, NFC	4,406
	Pittsburgh, AFC	4,531
1992	Dallas, NFC	3,931
	Houston, AFC	4,211
1991	Philadelphia, NFC	3,549
	Denver, AFC	4,549
1990	Pittsburgh, AFC	4,115
	N.Y. Giants, NFC	4,206
1989	Minnesota, NFC	4,184
	Kansas City, AFC	4,293
1988	Minnesota, NFC	4,091
	Buffalo, AFC	4,578
1987	San Francisco, NFC	4,095
	Cleveland, AFC	4,264
1986	Chicago, NFC	4,130
	L.A. Raiders, AFC	4,804
1985	Chicago, NFC	4,135
	L.A. Raiders, AFC	4,603
1984	Chicago, NFC	3,863
	Cleveland, AFC	4,641
1983	Cincinnati, AFC	4,327
	New Orleans, NFC	4,691
1982	Miami, AFC	2,312
	Tampa Bay, NFC	2,442
1981	Philadelphia, NFC	4,447
	N.Y. Jets, AFC	4,871
1980	Buffalo, AFC	4,101
	Philadelphia, NFC	4,443
1979	Tampa Bay, NFC	3,949
	Pittsburgh, AFC	4,270
1978	Los Angeles, NFC	3,893
	Pittsburgh, AFC	4,168
1977	Dallas, NFC	3,213
	New England, AFC	3,638
1976	Pittsburgh, AFC	3,323
	San Francisco, NFC	3,562
1975	Minnesota, NFC	3,153
	Oakland, AFC	3,629
1974	Pittsburgh, AFC	3,074
	Washington, NFC	3,285
1973	Los Angeles, NFC	2,951
	Oakland, AFC	3,160
1972	Miami, AFC	3,297
	Green Bay, NFC	3,474
1971	Baltimore, AFC	2,852
	Minnesota, NFC	3,406
1970	Minnesota, NFC	2,803
	N.Y. Jets, AFC	3,655
1969	Minnesota, NFL	2,720
	Kansas City, AFL	3,163
1968	Los Angeles, NFL	3,118
	N.Y. Jets, AFL	3,363
1967	Oakland, AFL	3,294
	Green Bay, NFL	3,300
1966	St. Louis, NFL	3,492
	Oakland, AFL	3,910
1965	San Diego, AFL	3,262
	Detroit, NFL	3,557
1964	Green Bay, NFL	3,179
	Buffalo, AFL	3,878
1963	Chicago, NFL	3,176
	Boston, AFL	3,834
1962	Detroit, NFL	3,217
	Dall. Texans, AFL	3,951
1961	San Diego, AFL	3,726
	Baltimore, NFL	3,782
1960	St. Louis, NFL	3,029
	Buffalo, AFL	3,866
1959	N.Y. Giants	2,843
1958	Chi. Bears	3,066
1957	Pittsburgh	2,791
1956	N.Y. Giants	3,081
1955	Cleveland	2,841
1954	Cleveland	2,658
1953	Philadelphia	2,998
1952	Cleveland	3,075
1951	N.Y. Giants	3,250
1950	Cleveland	3,154
1949	Philadelphia	2,831
1948	Chi. Bears	2,931
1947	Green Bay	3,396
1946	Washington	2,451
1945	Philadelphia	2,073
1944	Philadelphia	1,943
1943	Chi. Bears	2,262
1942	Chi. Bears	1,703
1941	N.Y. Giants	2,368
1940	N.Y. Giants	2,219
1939	Washington	2,116
1938	N.Y. Giants	2,029
1937	Washington	2,123
1936	Boston	2,181
1935	Boston	1,996
1934	Chi. Cardinals	1,539
1933	Brooklyn	1,789

FEWEST RUSHING YARDS ALLOWED

Year	Team	Yards
1995	San Francisco, NFC	1,061
	Pittsburgh, AFC	1,321
1994	Minnesota, NFC	1,090
	San Diego, AFC	1,404

1993	Houston, AFC	1,273
	Minnesota, NFC	1,536
1992	Dallas, NFC	1,244
	Buffalo, AFC	1,395
	San Diego, AFC	1,395
1991	Philadelphia, NFC	1,136
	N.Y. Jets, AFC	1,442
1990	Philadelphia, NFC	1,169
	San Diego, AFC	1,515
1989	New Orleans, NFC	1,326
	Denver, AFC	1,580
1988	Chicago, NFC	1,326
	Houston, AFC	1,592
1987	Chicago, NFC	1,413
	Cleveland, AFC	1,433
1986	N.Y. Giants, NFC	1,284
	Denver, AFC	1,651
1985	Chicago, NFC	1,319
	N.Y. Jets, AFC	1,516
1984	Chicago, NFC	1,377
	Pittsburgh, AFC	1,617
1983	Washington, NFC	1,289
	Cincinnati, AFC	1,499
1982	Pittsburgh, AFC	762
	Detroit, NFC	854
1981	Detroit, NFC	1,623
	Kansas City, AFC	1,747
1980	Detroit, NFC	1,599
	Cincinnati, AFC	1,680
1979	Denver, AFC	1,693
	Tampa Bay, NFC	1,873
1978	Dallas, NFC	1,721
	Pittsburgh, AFC	1,774
1977	Denver, AFC	1,531
	Dallas, NFC	1,651
1976	Pittsburgh, AFC	1,457
	Los Angeles, NFC	1,564
1975	Minnesota, NFC	1,532
	Houston, AFC	1,680
1974	Los Angeles, NFC	1,302
	New England, AFC	1,587
1973	Los Angeles, NFC	1,270
	Oakland, AFC	1,470
1972	Dallas, NFC	1,515
	Miami, AFC	1,548
1971	Baltimore, AFC	1,113
	Dallas, NFC	1,144
1970	Detroit, NFC	1,152
	N.Y. Jets, AFC	1,283
1969	Dallas, NFL	1,050
	Kansas City, AFL	1,091
1968	Dallas, NFL	1,195
	N.Y. Jets, AFL	1,195
1967	Dallas, NFL	1,081
	Oakland, AFL	1,129
1966	Buffalo, AFL	1,051
	Dallas, NFL	1,176
1965	San Diego, AFL	1,094
	Los Angeles, NFL	1,409
1964	Buffalo, AFL	913
	Los Angeles, NFL	1,501
1963	Boston, AFL	1,107
	Chicago, NFL	1,442
1962	Detroit, NFL	1,231
	Dall. Texans, AFL	1,250
1961	Boston, AFL	1,041
	Pittsburgh, NFL	1,463
1960	St. Louis, NFL	1,212
	Dall. Texans, AFL	1,338
1959	N.Y. Giants	1,261
1958	Baltimore	1,291
1957	Baltimore	1,174
1956	N.Y. Giants	1,443
1955	Cleveland	1,189
1954	Cleveland	1,050
1953	Philadelphia	1,117
1952	Detroit	1,145
1951	N.Y. Giants	913
1950	Detroit	1,367
1949	Chi. Bears	1,196
1948	Philadelphia	1,209
1947	Philadelphia	1,329
1946	Chi. Bears	1,060
1945	Philadelphia	817
1944	Philadelphia	558
1943	Phil-Pitt	793
1942	Chi. Bears	519
1941	Washington	1,042
1940	N.Y. Giants	977
1939	Chi. Bears	812
1938	Detroit	1,081
1937	Chi. Bears	933
1936	Boston	1,148
1935	Boston	998
1934	Chi. Cardinals	954
1933	Brooklyn	964

FEWEST PASSING YARDS ALLOWED

Leadership in this category has been based on net yards since 1952.

Year	Team	Yards
1995	N.Y. Jets, AFC	2,740
	Philadelphia, NFC	2,816
1994	Dallas, NFC	2,752
	Houston, AFC	2,795
1993	New Orleans, NFC	2,606
	Cincinnati, AFC	2,798
1992	New Orleans, NFC	2,470
	Kansas City, AFC	2,537
1991	Philadelphia, NFC	2,413
	Denver, AFC	2,755
1990	Pittsburgh, AFC	2,500
	Dallas, NFC	2,639
1989	Minnesota, NFC	2,501
	Kansas City, AFC	2,527
1988	Kansas City, AFC	2,434
	Minnesota, NFC	2,489
1987	San Francisco, NFC	2,484
	L.A. Raiders, AFC	2,727
1986	St. Louis, NFC	2,637
	New England, AFC	2,978
1985	Washington, NFC	2,746
	Pittsburgh, AFC	2,783
1984	New Orleans, NFC	2,453
	Cleveland, AFC	2,696
1983	New Orleans, NFC	2,691
	Cincinnati, AFC	2,828
1982	Miami, AFC	1,027
	Tampa Bay, NFC	1,384
1981	Philadelphia, NFC	2,696
	Buffalo, AFC	2,870
1980	Washington, NFC	2,171
	Buffalo, AFC	2,282
1979	Tampa Bay, NFC	2,076
	Buffalo, AFC	2,530
1978	Buffalo, AFC	1,960
	Los Angeles, NFC	2,048
1977	Atlanta, NFC	1,384
	San Diego, AFC	1,725
1976	Minnesota, NFC	1,575
	Cincinnati, AFC	1,758
1975	Minnesota, NFC	1,621
	Cincinnati, AFC	1,729
1974	Pittsburgh, AFC	1,466
	Atlanta, NFC	1,572
1973	Miami, AFC	1,290
	Atlanta, NFC	1,430
1972	Minnesota, NFC	1,699
	Cleveland, AFC	1,736
1971	Atlanta, NFC	1,638
	Baltimore, AFC	1,739
1970	Minnesota, NFC	1,438
	Kansas City, AFC	2,010
1969	Minnesota, NFL	1,631
	Kansas City, AFL	2,072
1968	Houston, AFL	1,671
	Green Bay, NFL	1,796
1967	Green Bay, NFL	1,377
	Buffalo, AFL	1,825
1966	Green Bay, NFL	1,959
	Oakland, AFL	2,118
1965	Green Bay, NFL	1,981
	San Diego, AFL	2,168
1964	Green Bay, NFL	1,647
	San Diego, AFL	2,518
1963	Chicago, NFL	1,734
	Oakland, AFL	2,589
1962	Green Bay, NFL	1,746
	Oakland, AFL	2,306
1961	Baltimore, NFL	1,913
	San Diego, AFL	2,363
1960	Chicago, NFL	1,388
	Buffalo, AFL	2,124
1959	N.Y. Giants	1,582
1958	Chi. Bears	1,769
1957	Cleveland	1,300
1956	Cleveland	1,103
1955	Pittsburgh	1,295
1954	Cleveland	1,608
1953	Washington	1,751
1952	Washington	1,580
1951	Pittsburgh	1,687
1950	Cleveland	1,581
1949	Philadelphia	1,607
1948	Green Bay	1,626
1947	Green Bay	1,790
1946	Pittsburgh	939
1945	Washington	1,121
1944	Chi. Bears	1,052
1943	Chi. Bears	980
1942	Washington	1,093
1941	Pittsburgh	1,168
1940	Philadelphia	1,012
1939	Washington	1,116
1938	Chi. Bears	897
1937	Detroit	804
1936	Philadelphia	853
1935	Chi. Cardinals	793
1934	Philadelphia	545
1933	Portsmouth	558

Compiled by Elias Sports Bureau

1967: Super Bowl I
1968: Super Bowl II
1969: Super Bowl III
1970: Super Bowl IV
1971: Super Bowl V
1972: Super Bowl VI
1973: Super Bowl VII
1974: Super Bowl VIII
1975: Super Bowl IX
1976: Super Bowl X
1977: Super Bowl XI
1978: Super Bowl XII
1979: Super Bowl XIII
1980: Super Bowl XIV
1981: Super Bowl XV
1982: Super Bowl XVI
1983: Super Bowl XVII
1984: Super Bowl XVIII
1985: Super Bowl XIX
1986: Super Bowl XX
1987: Super Bowl XXI
1988: Super Bowl XXII
1989: Super Bowl XXIII
1990: Super Bowl XXIV
1991: Super Bowl XXV
1992: Super Bowl XXVI
1993: Super Bowl XXVII
1994: Super Bowl XXVIII
1995: Super Bowl XXIX
1996: Super Bowl XXX

INDIVIDUAL RECORDS

SERVICE

Most Games

5 Marv Fleming, Green Bay, 1967-68; Miami, 1972-74
Larry Cole, Dallas, 1971-72, 1976, 1978-79
Cliff Harris, Dallas, 1971-72, 1976, 1978-79
Charles Haley, San Francisco, 1989-90; Dallas, 1993-94, 1996
D.D. Lewis, Dallas, 1971-72, 1976, 1978-79
Preston Pearson, Baltimore, 1969; Pittsburgh, 1975; Dallas, 1976, 1978-79
Charlie Waters, Dallas, 1971-72, 1976, 1978-79
Rayfield Wright, Dallas, 1971-72, 1976, 1978-79
4 By many players

Most Games, Winning Team

5 Charles Haley, San Francisco, 1989-90; Dallas, 1993-94, 1996
4 By many players

Most Games, Coach

6 Don Shula, Baltimore, 1969; Miami, 1972-74, 1983, 1985
5 Tom Landry, Dallas, 1971-72, 1976, 1978-79
4 Bud Grant, Minnesota, 1970, 1974-75, 1977
Chuck Noll, Pittsburgh, 1975-76, 1979-80
Joe Gibbs, Washington, 1983-84, 1988, 1992
Marv Levy, Buffalo, 1991-94

Most Games, Winning Team, Coach

4 Chuck Noll, Pittsburgh, 1975-76, 1979-80
3 Bill Walsh, San Francisco, 1982, 1985, 1989
Joe Gibbs, Washington, 1983, 1988, 1992
2 Vince Lombardi, Green Bay, 1967-68
Tom Landry, Dallas, 1972, 1978
Don Shula, Miami, 1973-74
Tom Flores, Oakland, 1981; L.A. Raiders, 1984
Bill Parcells, N.Y. Giants, 1987, 1991
Jimmy Johnson, Dallas, 1993-94
George Seifert, San Francisco, 1990, 1995

Most Games, Losing Team, Coach

4 Bud Grant, Minnesota, 1970, 1974-75, 1977
Don Shula, Baltimore, 1969; Miami, 1972, 1983, 1985
Marv Levy, Buffalo, 1991-94
3 Tom Landry, Dallas, 1971, 1976, 1979
Dan Reeves, Denver, 1987-88, 1990

SCORING

POINTS

Most Points, Career

42 Jerry Rice, San Francisco, 3 games (7-td)
30 Emmitt Smith, Dallas, 3 games (5-td)
24 Franco Harris, Pittsburgh, 4 games (4-td)
Roger Craig, San Francisco, 3 games (4-td)
Thurman Thomas, Buffalo, 4 games (4-td)

Most Points, Game

18 Roger Craig, San Francisco vs. Miami, 1985 (3-td)
Jerry Rice, San Francisco vs. Denver, 1990 (3-td); vs. San Diego, 1995 (3-td)
Ricky Watters, San Francisco vs. San Diego, 1995 (3-td)
15 Don Chandler, Green Bay vs. Oakland, 1968 (3-pat, 4-fg)
14 Ray Wersching, San Francisco vs. Cincinnati, 1982 (2-pat, 4-fg)
Kevin Butler, Chicago vs. New England, 1986 (5-pat, 3-fg)

TOUCHDOWNS

Most Touchdowns, Career

7 Jerry Rice, San Francisco, 3 games (7-p)
5 Emmitt Smith, Dallas, 3 games (5-r)
4 Franco Harris, Pittsburgh, 4 games (4-r)
Roger Craig, San Francisco, 3 games (2-r, 2-p)
Thurman Thomas, Buffalo, 4 games (4-r)

Most Touchdowns, Game

3 Roger Craig, San Francisco vs. Miami, 1985 (1-r, 2-p)
Jerry Rice, San Francisco. vs. Denver, 1990 (3-p); vs. San Diego, 1995 (3-p)
Ricky Watters, San Francisco vs. San Diego, 1995 (1-r, 2-p)
2 Max McGee, Green Bay vs. Kansas City, 1967 (2-p)
Elijah Pitts, Green Bay vs. Kansas City, 1967 (2-r)
Bill Miller, Oakland vs. Green Bay, 1968 (2-p)
Larry Csonka, Miami vs. Minnesota, 1974 (2-r)
Pete Banaszak, Oakland vs. Minnesota, 1977 (2-r)
John Stallworth, Pittsburgh vs. Dallas, 1979 (2-p)
Franco Harris, Pittsburgh vs. Los Angeles, 1980 (2-r)
Cliff Branch, Oakland vs. Philadelphia, 1981 (2-p)
Dan Ross, Cincinnati vs. San Francisco, 1982 (2-p)
Marcus Allen, L.A. Raiders vs. Washington, 1984 (2-r)
Jim McMahon, Chicago vs. New England, 1986 (2-r)
Ricky Sanders, Washington vs. Denver, 1988 (2-p)
Timmy Smith, Washington vs. Denver, 1988 (2-r)
Tom Rathman, San Francisco vs. Denver, 1990 (2-r)
Gerald Riggs, Washington vs. Buffalo, 1992 (2-r)
Michael Irvin, Dallas vs. Buffalo, 1993 (2-p)
Emmitt Smith, Dallas vs. Buffalo, 1994 (2-r)
Emmitt Smith, Dallas vs. Pittsburgh, 1996 (2-r)

POINTS AFTER TOUCHDOWN

Most (One-Point) Points After Touchdown, Career

9 Mike Cofer, San Francisco, 2 games (10 att)
8 Don Chandler, Green Bay, 2 games (8 att)
Roy Gerela, Pittsburgh, 3 games (9 att)
Chris Bahr, Oakland-L.A. Raiders, 2 games (8 att)
7 Ray Wersching, San Francisco, 2 games (7 att)
Lin Elliott, Dallas, 1 game (7 att)
Doug Brien, San Francisco, 1 game (7 att)

Most (One-Point) Points After Touchdown, Game

7 Mike Cofer, San Francisco vs. Denver, 1990 (8 att)
Lin Elliott, Dallas vs. Buffalo, 1993 (7 att)
Doug Brien, San Francisco vs. San Diego, 1995 (7 att)
6 Ali Haji-Sheikh, Washington vs. Denver, 1988 (6 att)
5 Don Chandler, Green Bay vs. Kansas City, 1967 (5 att)
Roy Gerela, Pittsburgh vs. Dallas, 1979 (5 att)
Chris Bahr, L.A. Raiders vs. Washington, 1984 (5 att)
Ray Wersching, San Francisco vs. Miami, 1985 (5 att)
Kevin Butler, Chicago vs. New England, 1986 (5 att)

Most Two-Point Conversions, Game

1 Mark Seay, San Diego vs. San Francisco, 1995
Alfred Pupunu, San Diego vs. San Francisco, 1995

FIELD GOALS

Field Goals Attempted, Career

6 Jim Turner, N.Y. Jets-Denver, 2 games
Roy Gerela, Pittsburgh, 3 games
Rich Karlis, Denver, 2 games
5 Efren Herrera, Dallas, 1 game
Ray Wersching, San Francisco, 2 games

Most Field Goals Attempted, Game

5 Jim Turner, N.Y. Jets vs. Baltimore, 1969
Efren Herrera, Dallas vs. Denver, 1978
4 Don Chandler, Green Bay vs. Oakland, 1968
Roy Gerela, Pittsburgh vs. Dallas, 1976
Ray Wersching, San Francisco vs. Cincinnati, 1982
Rich Karlis, Denver vs. N.Y. Giants, 1987
Mike Cofer, San Francisco vs. Cincinnati, 1989

Most Field Goals, Career

5 Ray Wersching, San Francisco, 2 games (5 att)
4 Don Chandler, Green Bay, 2 games (4 att)
Jim Turner, N.Y. Jets-Denver, 2 games (6 att)
Uwe von Schamann, Miami, 2 games (4 att)
3 Mike Clark, Dallas, 2 games (3 att)
Jan Stenerud, Kansas City, 1 game (3 att)
Chris Bahr, Oakland-L.A. Raiders, 2 games (4 att)
Mark Moseley, Washington, 2 games (4 att)
Kevin Butler, Chicago, 1 game (3 att)
Rich Karlis, Denver, 2 games (6 att)
Jim Breech, Cincinnati, 2 games (3 att)
Matt Bahr, Pittsburgh-N.Y. Giants, 2 games (3 att)
Chip Lohmiller, Washington, 1 game (3 att)
Steve Christie, Buffalo, 2 games (3 att)
Eddie Murray, Dallas, 1 game (3 att)

Most Field Goals, Game

4 Don Chandler, Green Bay vs. Oakland, 1968
Ray Wersching, San Francisco vs. Cincinnati, 1982
3 Jim Turner, N.Y. Jets vs. Baltimore, 1969
Jan Stenerud, Kansas City vs. Minnesota, 1970
Uwe von Schamann, Miami vs. San Francisco, 1985
Kevin Butler, Chicago vs. New England, 1986
Jim Breech, Cincinnati vs. San Francisco, 1989
Chip Lohmiller, Washington vs. Buffalo, 1992
Eddie Murray, Dallas vs. Buffalo, 1994

SUPER BOWL RECORDS

Longest Field Goal
- 54 Steve Christie, Buffalo vs. Dallas, 1994
- 48 Jan Stenerud, Kansas City vs. Minnesota, 1970
- Rich Karlis, Denver vs. N.Y. Giants, 1987
- 47 Jim Turner, Denver vs. Dallas, 1978

SAFETIES
Most Safeties, Game
- 1 Dwight White, Pittsburgh vs. Minnesota, 1975
- Reggie Harrison, Pittsburgh vs. Dallas, 1976
- Henry Waechter, Chicago vs. New England, 1986
- George Martin, N.Y. Giants vs. Denver, 1987
- Bruce Smith, Buffalo vs. N.Y. Giants, 1991

RUSHING
ATTEMPTS
Most Attempts, Career
- 101 Franco Harris, Pittsburgh, 4 games
- 70 Emmitt Smith, Dallas, 3 games
- 64 John Riggins, Washington, 2 games

Most Attempts, Game
- 38 John Riggins, Washington vs. Miami, 1983
- 34 Franco Harris, Pittsburgh vs. Minnesota, 1975
- 33 Larry Csonka, Miami vs. Minnesota, 1974

YARDS GAINED
Most Yards Gained, Career
- 354 Franco Harris, Pittsburgh, 4 games
- 297 Larry Csonka, Miami, 3 games
- 289 Emmitt Smith, Dallas, 3 games

Most Yards Gained, Game
- 204 Timmy Smith, Washington vs. Denver, 1988
- 191 Marcus Allen, L.A. Raiders vs. Washington, 1984
- 166 John Riggins, Washington vs. Miami, 1983

Longest Run From Scrimmage
- 74 Marcus Allen, L.A. Raiders vs. Washington, 1984 (TD)
- 58 Tom Matte, Baltimore vs. N.Y. Jets, 1969
- Timmy Smith, Washington vs. Denver, 1988 (TD)
- 49 Larry Csonka, Miami vs. Washington, 1973

AVERAGE GAIN
Highest Average Gain, Career (20 attempts)
- 9.6 Marcus Allen, L.A. Raiders, 1 game (20-191)
- 9.3 Timmy Smith, Washington, 1 game (22-204)
- 5.3 Walt Garrison, Dallas, 2 games (26-139)

Highest Average Gain, Game (10 attempts)
- 10.5 Tom Matte, Baltimore vs. N.Y. Jets, 1969 (11-116)
- 9.6 Marcus Allen, L.A. Raiders vs. Washington, 1984 (20-191)
- 9.3 Timmy Smith, Washington vs. Denver, 1988 (22-204)

TOUCHDOWNS
Most Touchdowns, Career
- 5 Emmitt Smith, Dallas, 3 games
- 4 Franco Harris, Pittsburgh, 4 games
- Thurman Thomas, Buffalo, 4 games
- 2 Elijah Pitts, Green Bay, 1 game
- Jim Kiick, Miami, 3 games
- Larry Csonka, Miami, 3 games
- Pete Banaszak, Oakland, 2 games
- Marcus Allen, L.A. Raiders, 1 game
- John Riggins, Washington, 2 games
- Jim McMahon, Chicago, 1 game
- Timmy Smith, Washington, 1 game
- Roger Craig, San Francisco, 3 games
- Tom Rathman, San Francisco, 2 games
- John Elway, Denver, 3 games
- Ottis Anderson, N.Y. Giants, 2 games
- Gerald Riggs, Washington, 1 game
- Joe Montana, San Francisco, 4 games

Most Touchdowns, Game
- 2 Elijah Pitts, Green Bay vs. Kansas City, 1967
- Larry Csonka, Miami vs. Minnesota, 1974
- Pete Banaszak, Oakland vs. Minnesota, 1977
- Franco Harris, Pittsburgh vs. Los Angeles, 1980
- Marcus Allen, L.A. Raiders vs. Washington, 1984
- Jim McMahon, Chicago vs. New England, 1986
- Timmy Smith, Washington vs. Denver, 1988
- Tom Rathman, San Francisco vs. Denver, 1990
- Gerald Riggs, Washington vs. Buffalo, 1992
- Emmitt Smith, Dallas vs. Buffalo, 1994
- Emmitt Smith, Dallas vs. Pittsburgh, 1996

PASSING
PASSER RATING
Highest Passer Rating, Career (40 attempts)
- 127.8 Joe Montana, San Francisco, 4 games
- 122.8 Jim Plunkett, Oakland-L.A. Raiders, 2 games
- 112.8 Terry Bradshaw, Pittsburgh, 4 games

ATTEMPTS
Most Passes Attempted, Career
- 145 Jim Kelly, Buffalo, 4 games
- 122 Joe Montana, San Francisco, 4 games
- 101 John Elway, Denver, 3 games

Most Passes Attempted, Game
- 58 Jim Kelly, Buffalo vs. Washington, 1992
- 50 Dan Marino, Miami vs. San Francisco, 1985
- Jim Kelly, Buffalo vs. Dallas, 1994
- 49 Stan Humphries, San Diego vs. San Francisco, 1995
- Neil O'Donnell, Pittsburgh vs. Dallas, 1996

COMPLETIONS
Most Passes Completed, Career
- 83 Joe Montana, San Francisco, 4 games
- 81 Jim Kelly, Buffalo, 4 games
- 61 Roger Staubach, Dallas, 4 games

Most Passes Completed, Game
- 31 Jim Kelly, Buffalo vs. Dallas, 1994
- 29 Dan Marino, Miami vs. San Francisco, 1985
- 28 Jim Kelly, Buffalo vs. Washington, 1992
- Neil O'Donnell, Pittsburgh vs. Dallas, 1996

Most Consecutive Completions, Game
- 13 Joe Montana, San Francisco vs. Denver, 1990
- 10 Phil Simms, N.Y. Giants vs. Denver, 1987
- Troy Aikman, Dallas vs. Pittsburgh, 1996
- 9 Jim Kelly, Buffalo vs. Dallas, 1994
- Neil O'Donnell, Pittsburgh vs. Dallas, 1996

COMPLETION PERCENTAGE
Highest Completion Percentage, Career (40 attempts)
- 70.0 Troy Aikman, Dallas, 3 games, (80-56)
- 68.0 Joe Montana, San Francisco, 4 games (122-83)
- 63.6 Len Dawson, Kansas City, 2 games (44-28)

Highest Completion Percentage, Game (20 attempts)
- 88.0 Phil Simms, N.Y. Giants vs. Denver, 1987 (25-22)
- 75.9 Joe Montana, San Francisco vs. Denver, 1990 (29-22)
- 73.5 Ken Anderson, Cincinnati vs. San Francisco, 1982 (34-25)

YARDS GAINED
Most Yards Gained, Career
- 1,142 Joe Montana, San Francisco, 4 games
- 932 Terry Bradshaw, Pittsburgh, 4 games
- 829 Jim Kelly, Buffalo, 4 games

Most Yards Gained, Game
- 357 Joe Montana, San Francisco vs. Cincinnati, 1989
- 340 Doug Williams, Washington vs. Denver, 1988
- 331 Joe Montana, San Francisco vs. Miami, 1985

Longest Pass Completion
- 80 Jim Plunkett (to King), Oakland vs. Philadelphia, 1981 (TD)
- Doug Williams (to Sanders), Washington vs. Denver, 1988 (TD)
- 76 David Woodley (to Cefalo), Miami vs. Washington, 1983 (TD)
- 75 Johnny Unitas (to Mackey), Baltimore vs. Dallas, 1971 (TD)
- Terry Bradshaw (to Stallworth), Pittsburgh vs. Dallas, 1979 (TD)

AVERAGE GAIN
Highest Average Gain, Career (40 attempts)
- 11.10 Terry Bradshaw, Pittsburgh, 4 games (84-932)
- 9.62 Bart Starr, Green Bay, 2 games (47-452)
- 9.41 Jim Plunkett, Oakland-L.A. Raiders, 2 games (46-433)

Highest Average Gain, Game (20 attempts)
- 14.71 Terry Bradshaw, Pittsburgh vs. Los Angeles, 1980 (21-309)
- 12.80 Jim McMahon, Chicago vs. New England, 1986 (20-256)
- 12.43 Jim Plunkett, Oakland vs. Philadelphia, 1981 (21-261)

TOUCHDOWNS
Most Touchdown Passes, Career
- 11 Joe Montana, San Francisco, 4 games
- 9 Terry Bradshaw, Pittsburgh, 4 games
- 8 Roger Staubach, Dallas, 4 games

Most Touchdown Passes, Game
- 6 Steve Young, San Francisco vs. San Diego, 1995
- 5 Joe Montana, San Francisco vs. Denver, 1990
- 4 Terry Bradshaw, Pittsburgh vs. Dallas, 1979
- Doug Williams, Washington vs. Denver, 1988
- Troy Aikman, Dallas vs. Buffalo, 1993

HAD INTERCEPTED

Lowest Percentage, Passes Had Intercepted, Career (40 attempts)
- 0.00 Jim Plunkett, Oakland-L.A. Raiders, 2 games (46-0)
- Joe Montana, San Francisco, 4 games (122-0)
- 1.25 Troy Aikman, Dallas, 3 games (80-1)
- 2.13 Bart Starr, Green Bay, 2 games (47-1)

Most Attempts, Without Interception, Game
- 36 Joe Montana, San Francisco vs. Cincinnati, 1989
- Steve Young, San Francisco vs. San Diego, 1995
- 35 Joe Montana, San Francisco vs. Miami, 1985
- 32 Jeff Hostetler, N.Y. Giants vs. Buffalo, 1991

Most Passes Had Intercepted, Career
- 7 Craig Morton, Dallas-Denver, 2 games
- Jim Kelly, Buffalo, 4 games
- 6 Fran Tarkenton, Minnesota, 3 games
- John Elway, Denver, 3 games
- 4 Earl Morrall, Baltimore-Miami, 4 games
- Roger Staubach, Dallas, 4 games
- Terry Bradshaw, Pittsburgh, 4 games
- Joe Theismann, Washington, 2 games

Most Passes Had Intercepted, Game
- 4 Craig Morton, Denver vs. Dallas, 1978
- Jim Kelly, Buffalo vs. Washington, 1992
- 3 By nine players

PASS RECEIVING

RECEPTIONS

Most Receptions, Career
- 28 Jerry Rice, San Francisco, 3 games
- 27 Andre Reed, Buffalo, 4 games
- 20 Roger Craig, San Francisco, 3 games
- Thurman Thomas, Buffalo, 4 games

Most Receptions, Game
- 11 Dan Ross, Cincinnati vs. San Francisco, 1982
- Jerry Rice, San Francisco vs. Cincinnati, 1989
- 10 Tony Nathan, Miami vs. San Francisco, 1985
- Jerry Rice, San Francisco vs. San Diego, 1995
- Andre Hastings, Pittsburgh vs. Dallas, 1996
- 9 Ricky Sanders, Washington vs. Denver, 1988

YARDS GAINED

Most Yards Gained, Career
- 512 Jerry Rice, San Francisco, 3 games
- 364 Lynn Swann, Pittsburgh, 4 games
- 323 Andre Reed, Buffalo, 4 games

Most Yards Gained, Game
- 215 Jerry Rice, San Francisco vs. Cincinnati, 1989
- 193 Ricky Sanders, Washington vs. Denver, 1988
- 161 Lynn Swann, Pittsburgh vs. Dallas, 1976

Longest Reception
- 80 Kenny King (from Plunkett), Oakland vs. Philadelphia, 1981 (TD)
- Ricky Sanders (from Williams), Washington vs. Denver, 1988 (TD)
- 76 Jimmy Cefalo (from Woodley), Miami vs. Washington, 1983 (TD)
- 75 John Mackey (from Unitas), Baltimore vs. Dallas, 1971 (TD)
- John Stallworth (from Bradshaw), Pittsburgh vs. Dallas, 1979 (TD)

AVERAGE GAIN

Highest Average Gain, Career (8 receptions)
- 24.4 John Stallworth, Pittsburgh, 4 games (11-268)
- 23.4 Ricky Sanders, Washington, 2 games (10-234)
- 22.8 Lynn Swann, Pittsburgh, 4 games (16-364)

Highest Average Gain, Game (3 receptions)
- 40.33 John Stallworth, Pittsburgh vs. Los Angeles, 1980 (3-121)
- 40.25 Lynn Swann, Pittsburgh vs. Dallas, 1979 (4-161)
- 38.33 John Stallworth, Pittsburgh vs. Dallas, 1979 (3-115)

TOUCHDOWNS

Most Touchdowns, Career
- 7 Jerry Rice, San Francisco, 3 games
- 3 John Stallworth, Pittsburgh, 4 games
- Lynn Swann, Pittsburgh, 4 games
- Cliff Branch, Oakland-L.A. Raiders, 3 games
- 2 Max McGee, Green Bay, 2 games
- Bill Miller, Oakland, 1 game
- Butch Johnson, Dallas, 2 games
- Dan Ross, Cincinnati, 1 game
- Roger Craig, San Francisco, 3 games
- Ricky Sanders, Washington, 2 games
- John Taylor, San Francisco, 3 games
- Gary Clark, Washington, 2 games
- Don Beebe, Buffalo, 3 games
- Michael Irvin, Dallas, 2 games
- Ricky Watters, San Francisco, 1 game
- Jay Novacek, Dallas, 3 games

Most Touchdowns, Game
- 3 Jerry Rice, San Francisco vs. San Diego, 1995; vs. Denver, 1990
- 2 Max McGee, Green Bay vs. Kansas City, 1967
- Bill Miller, Oakland vs. Green Bay, 1968
- John Stallworth, Pittsburgh vs. Dallas, 1979
- Cliff Branch, Oakland vs. Philadelphia, 1981
- Dan Ross, Cincinnati vs. San Francisco, 1982
- Roger Craig, San Francisco vs. Miami, 1985
- Ricky Sanders, Washington vs. Denver, 1988
- Michael Irvin, Dallas vs. Buffalo, 1993
- Ricky Watters, San Francisco vs. San Diego, 1995

INTERCEPTIONS BY

Most Interceptions By, Career
- 3 Chuck Howley, Dallas, 2 games
- Rod Martin, Oakland-L.A. Raiders, 2 games
- Larry Brown, Dallas, 3 games
- 2 Randy Beverly, N.Y. Jets, 1 game
- Jake Scott, Miami, 3 games
- Mike Wagner, Pittsburgh, 3 games
- Mel Blount, Pittsburgh, 4 games
- Eric Wright, San Francisco, 4 games
- Barry Wilburn, Washington, 1 game
- Brad Edwards, Washington, 1 game
- Thomas Everett, Dallas, 2 games
- James Washington, Dallas, 2 games

Most Interceptions By, Game
- 3 Rod Martin, Oakland vs. Philadelphia, 1981
- 2 Randy Beverly, N.Y. Jets vs. Baltimore, 1969
- Chuck Howley, Dallas vs. Baltimore, 1971
- Jake Scott, Miami vs. Washington, 1973
- Barry Wilburn, Washington vs. Denver, 1988
- Brad Edwards, Washington vs. Buffalo, 1992
- Thomas Everett, Dallas vs. Buffalo, 1993
- Larry Brown, Dallas vs. Pittsburgh, 1996

YARDS GAINED

Most Yards Gained, Career
- 77 Larry Brown, Dallas, 3 games
- 75 Willie Brown, Oakland, 2 games
- 63 Chuck Howley, Dallas, 2 games
- Jake Scott, Miami, 3 games

Most Yards Gained, Game
- 77 Larry Brown, Dallas vs. Pittsburgh, 1996
- 75 Willie Brown, Oakland vs. Minnesota, 1977
- 63 Jake Scott, Miami vs. Washington, 1973

Longest Return
- 75 Willie Brown, Oakland vs. Minnesota, 1977 (TD)
- 60 Herb Adderley, Green Bay vs. Oakland, 1968 (TD)
- 55 Jake Scott, Miami vs. Washington, 1973

TOUCHDOWNS

Most Touchdowns, Game
- 1 Herb Adderley, Green Bay vs. Oakland, 1968
- Willie Brown, Oakland vs. Minnesota, 1977
- Jack Squirek, L.A. Raiders vs. Washington, 1984
- Reggie Phillips, Chicago vs. New England, 1986

PUNTING

Most Punts, Career
- 17 Mike Eischeid, Oakland-Minnesota, 3 games
- 15 Larry Seiple, Miami, 3 games
- Mike Horan, Denver, 3 games
- 14 Ron Widby, Dallas, 2 games
- Ray Guy, Oakland-L.A. Raiders, 3 games
- Chris Mohr, Buffalo, 3 games

Most Punts, Game
- 9 Ron Widby, Dallas vs. Baltimore, 1971
- 7 By eight players

Longest Punt
- 63 Lee Johnson, Cincinnati vs. San Francisco, 1989
- 62 Rich Camarillo, New England vs. Chicago, 1986
- 61 Jerrel Wilson, Kansas City vs. Green Bay, 1967

AVERAGE YARDAGE

Highest Average, Punting, Career (10 punts)
- 46.5 Jerrel Wilson, Kansas City, 2 games (11-511)
- 41.9 Ray Guy, Oakland-L.A. Raiders, 3 games (14-587)
- 41.3 Larry Seiple, Miami, 3 games (15-620)

Highest Average, Punting, Game (4 punts)
- 48.8 Bryan Wagner, San Diego vs. San Francisco, 1995 (4-195)
- 48.5 Jerrel Wilson, Kansas City vs. Minnesota, 1970 (4-194)

46.3 Jim Miller, San Francisco vs. Cincinnati, 1982 (4-185)

PUNT RETURNS

Most Punt Returns, Career

6 Willie Wood, Green Bay, 2 games
Jake Scott, Miami, 3 games
Theo Bell, Pittsburgh, 2 games
Mike Nelms, Washington, 1 game
John Taylor, San Francisco, 3 games
5 Dana McLemore, San Francisco, 1 game
4 By eight players

Most Punt Returns, Game

6 Mike Nelms, Washington vs. Miami, 1983
5 Willie Wood, Green Bay vs. Oakland, 1968
Dana McLemore, San Francisco vs. Miami, 1985
4 By six players

Most Fair Catches, Game

3 Ron Gardin, Baltimore vs. Dallas, 1971
Golden Richards, Dallas vs. Pittsburgh, 1976
Greg Pruitt, L.A. Raiders vs. Washington, 1984
Al Edwards, Buffalo vs. N.Y. Giants, 1991
David Meggett, N.Y. Giants vs. Buffalo, 1991

YARDS GAINED

Most Yards Gained, Career

94 John Taylor, San Francisco, 3 games
52 Mike Nelms, Washington, 1 game
51 Dana McLemore, San Francisco, 1 game

Most Yards Gained, Game

56 John Taylor, San Francisco vs. Cincinnati, 1989
52 Mike Nelms, Washington vs. Miami, 1983
51 Dana McLemore, San Francisco vs. Miami, 1985

Longest Return

45 John Taylor, San Francisco vs. Cincinnati, 1989
34 Darrell Green, Washington vs. L.A. Raiders, 1984
31 Willie Wood, Green Bay vs. Oakland, 1968

AVERAGE YARDAGE

Highest Average, Career (4 returns)

15.7 John Taylor, San Francisco, 3 games (6-94)
10.8 Neal Colzie, Oakland, 1 game (4-43)
10.2 Dana McLemore, San Francisco, 1 game (5-51)

Highest Average, Game (3 returns)

18.7 John Taylor, San Francisco vs. Cincinnati, 1989 (3-56)
12.7 John Taylor, San Francisco vs. Denver, 1990 (3-38)
11.7 Kelvin Martin, Dallas vs. Buffalo, 1993 (3-35)

TOUCHDOWNS

Most Touchdowns, Game

None

KICKOFF RETURNS

Most Kickoff Returns, Career

10 Ken Bell, Denver, 3 games
8 Larry Anderson, Pittsburgh, 2 games
Fulton Walker, Miami, 2 games
Andre Coleman, San Diego, 1 game
7 Preston Pearson, Baltimore-Pittsburgh-Dallas, 5 games
Stephen Starring, New England, 1 game

Most Kickoff Returns, Game

8 Andre Coleman, San Diego vs. San Francisco, 1995
7 Stephen Starring, New England vs. Chicago, 1986
6 Darren Carrington, Denver vs. San Francisco, 1990

YARDS GAINED

Most Yards Gained, Career

283 Fulton Walker, Miami, 2 games
244 Andre Coleman, San Diego, 1 game
207 Larry Anderson, Pittsburgh, 2 games

Most Yards Gained, Game

244 Andre Coleman, San Diego vs. San Francisco, 1995
190 Fulton Walker, Miami vs. Washington, 1983
162 Larry Anderson, Pittsburgh vs. Los Angeles, 1980

Longest Return

98 Fulton Walker, Miami vs. Washington, 1983 (TD)
Andre Coleman, San Diego vs. San Francisco, 1995 (TD)
93 Stanford Jennings, Cincinnati vs. San Francisco, 1989 (TD)
67 Rick Upchurch, Denver vs. Dallas, 1978

AVERAGE YARDAGE

Highest Average, Career (4 returns)

35.4 Fulton Walker, Miami, 2 games (8-283)
30.5 Andre Coleman, San Diego, 1 game (8-244)
25.9 Larry Anderson, Pittsburgh, 2 games (8-207)

Highest Average, Game (3 returns)

47.5 Fulton Walker, Miami vs. Washington, 1983 (4-190)
32.4 Larry Anderson, Pittsburgh vs. Los Angeles, 1980 (5-162)
31.3 Rick Upchurch, Denver vs. Dallas, 1978 (3-94)

TOUCHDOWNS

Most Touchdowns, Game

1 Fulton Walker, Miami vs. Washington, 1983
Stanford Jennings, Cincinnati vs. San Francisco, 1989
Andre Coleman, San Diego vs. San Francisco, 1995

FUMBLES

Most Fumbles, Career

5 Roger Staubach, Dallas, 4 games
4 Jim Kelly, Buffalo, 4 games
3 Franco Harris, Pittsburgh, 4 games
Terry Bradshaw, Pittsburgh, 4 games
John Elway, Denver, 3 games
Frank Reich, Buffalo, 4 games
Thurman Thomas, Buffalo, 4 games

Most Fumbles, Game

3 Roger Staubach, Dallas vs. Pittsburgh, 1976
Jim Kelly, Buffalo vs. Washington, 1992
Frank Reich, Buffalo vs. Dallas, 1993
2 Franco Harris, Pittsburgh vs. Minnesota, 1975
Butch Johnson, Dallas vs. Denver, 1978
Terry Bradshaw, Pittsburgh vs. Dallas, 1979
Joe Montana, San Francisco vs. Cincinnati, 1989
John Elway, Denver vs. San Francisco, 1990
Thurman Thomas, Buffalo vs. Dallas, 1994

RECOVERIES

Most Fumbles Recovered, Career

2 Jake Scott, Miami, 3 games (1 own, 1 opp)
Fran Tarkenton, Minnesota, 3 games (2 own)
Franco Harris, Pittsburgh, 4 games (2 own)
Roger Staubach, Dallas, 4 games (2 own)
Bobby Walden, Pittsburgh, 2 games (2 own)
John Fitzgerald, Dallas, 4 games (2 own)
Randy Hughes, Dallas, 3 games (2 opp)
Butch Johnson, Dallas, 2 games (2 own)
Mike Singletary, Chicago, 1 game (2 opp)
John Elway, Denver, 3 games (2 own)
Jimmie Jones, Dallas, 2 games (2 opp)
Kenneth Davis, Buffalo, 4 games (2 own)

Most Fumbles Recovered, Game

2 Jake Scott, Miami vs. Minnesota, 1974 (1 own, 1 opp)
Roger Staubach, Dallas vs. Pittsburgh, 1976 (2 own)
Randy Hughes, Dallas vs. Denver, 1978 (2 opp)
Butch Johnson, Dallas vs. Denver, 1978 (2 own)
Mike Singletary, Chicago vs. New England, 1986 (2 opp)
Jimmie Jones, Dallas vs. Buffalo, 1993 (2 opp)

YARDS GAINED

Most Yards Gained, Game

64 Leon Lett, Dallas vs. Buffalo, 1993 (opp)
49 Mike Bass, Washington vs. Miami, 1973 (opp)
46 James Washington, Dallas vs. Buffalo, 1994 (opp)

Longest Return

64 Leon Lett, Dallas vs. Buffalo, 1993
49 Mike Bass, Washington vs. Miami, 1973 (TD)
46 James Washington, Dallas vs. Buffalo, 1994 (TD)

TOUCHDOWNS

Most Touchdowns, Game

1 Mike Bass, Washington vs. Miami, 1973 (opp 49 yds)
Mike Hegman, Dallas vs. Pittsburgh, 1979 (opp 37 yds)
Jimmie Jones, Dallas vs. Buffalo, 1993 (opp 2 yds)
Ken Norton, Dallas vs. Buffalo, 1993 (opp 9 yds)
James Washington, Dallas vs. Buffalo, 1994 (opp 46 yds)

COMBINED NET YARDS GAINED

(Rushing, receiving, interception returns, punt returns, kickoff returns, and fumble returns)

ATTEMPTS

Most Attempts, Career

108 Franco Harris, Pittsburgh, 4 games
81 Emmitt Smith, Dallas, 3 games
72 Roger Craig, San Francisco, 3 games
Thurman Thomas, Buffalo, 4 games

Most Attempts, Game

39 John Riggins, Washington vs. Miami, 1983

35 Franco Harris, Pittsburgh vs. Minnesota, 1975
34 Matt Snell, N.Y. Jets vs. Baltimore, 1969
Emmitt Smith, Dallas vs. Buffalo, 1994

YARDS GAINED

Most Yards Gained, Career
527 Jerry Rice, San Francisco, 3 games
468 Franco Harris, Pittsburgh, 4 games
410 Roger Craig, San Francisco, 3 games

Most Yards Gained, Game
235 Ricky Sanders, Washington vs. Denver, 1988
220 Jerry Rice, San Francisco vs. Cincinnati, 1989
213 Timmy Smith, Washington vs. Denver, 1988

SACKS

Sacks have been compiled since 1983.

Most Sacks, Career
4.5 Charles Haley, San Francisco-Dallas, 5 games
3 Danny Stubbs, San Francisco, 2 games
Leonard Marshall, N.Y. Giants, 2 games
Jeff Wright, Buffalo, 4 games
2.5 Dexter Manley, Washington, 3 games

Most Sacks, Game
2 Dwaine Board, San Francisco vs. Miami, 1985
Dennis Owens, New England vs. Chicago, 1986
Otis Wilson, Chicago vs. New England, 1986
Leonard Marshall, N.Y. Giants vs. Denver, 1987
Alvin Walton, Washington vs. Denver, 1988
Charles Haley, San Francisco vs. Cincinnati, 1989
Danny Stubbs, San Francisco vs. Denver, 1990
Jeff Wright, Buffalo vs. Dallas, 1994
Raylee Johnson, San Diego vs. San Francisco, 1995
Chad Hennings, Dallas vs. Pittsburgh, 1996

TEAM RECORDS

GAMES, VICTORIES, DEFEATS

Most Games
8 Dallas, 1971-72, 1976, 1978-79, 1993-94, 1996
5 Miami, 1972-74, 1983, 1985
Washington, 1973, 1983-84, 1988, 1992
San Francisco, 1982, 1985, 1989-90, 1995
Pittsburgh, 1975-76, 1979-80, 1996
4 Minnesota, 1970, 1974-75, 1977
Oakland/L.A. Raiders, 1968, 1977, 1981, 1984
Denver, 1978, 1987-88, 1990
Buffalo, 1991-94

Most Consecutive Games
4 Buffalo, 1991-94
3 Miami, 1972-74
2 Green Bay, 1967-68
Dallas, 1971-72; 1978-79; 1993-94
Minnesota, 1974-75
Pittsburgh, 1975-76, 1979-80
Washington, 1983-84
Denver, 1987-88
San Francisco 1989-90

Most Games Won
5 San Francisco, 1982, 1985, 1989-90, 1995
Dallas, 1972, 1978, 1993-94, 1996
4 Pittsburgh, 1975-76, 1979-80
3 Oakland/L.A. Raiders, 1977, 1981, 1984
Washington, 1983, 1988, 1992

Most Consecutive Games Won
2 Green Bay, 1967-68
Miami, 1973-74
Pittsburgh, 1975-76, 1979-80
San Francisco, 1989-90
Dallas, 1993-94

Most Games Lost
4 Minnesota, 1970, 1974-75, 1977
Denver, 1978, 1987-88, 1990
Buffalo, 1991-94
3 Dallas, 1971, 1976, 1979
Miami, 1972, 1983, 1985
2 Washington, 1973, 1984
Cincinnati, 1982, 1989

Most Consecutive Games Lost
4 Buffalo, 1991-94
2 Minnesota, 1974-75
Denver, 1987-88

SCORING

Most Points, Game
55 San Francisco vs. Denver, 1990
52 Dallas vs. Buffalo, 1993
49 San Francisco vs. San Diego, 1995

Fewest Points, Game
3 Miami vs. Dallas, 1972
6 Minnesota vs. Pittsburgh, 1975
7 By four teams

Most Points, Both Teams, Game
75 San Francisco (49) vs. San Diego (26), 1995
69 Dallas (52) vs. Buffalo (17), 1993
66 Pittsburgh (35) vs. Dallas (31), 1979

Fewest Points, Both Teams, Game
21 Washington (7) vs. Miami (14), 1973
22 Minnesota (6) vs. Pittsburgh (16), 1975
23 Baltimore (7) vs. N.Y. Jets (16), 1969

Largest Margin of Victory, Game
45 San Francisco vs. Denver, 1990 (55-10)
36 Chicago vs. New England, 1986 (46-10)
35 Dallas vs. Buffalo, 1993 (52-17)

Most Points, Each Half
1st: 35 Washington vs. Denver, 1988
2nd: 30 N.Y. Giants vs. Denver, 1987

Most Points, Each Quarter
1st: 14 Miami vs. Minnesota, 1974
Oakland vs. Philadelphia, 1981
Dallas vs. Buffalo, 1993
San Francisco vs. San Diego, 1995
2nd: 35 Washington vs. Denver, 1988
3rd: 21 Chicago vs. New England, 1986
4th: 21 Dallas vs. Buffalo, 1993

Most Points, Both Teams, Each Half
1st: 45 Washington (35) vs. Denver (10), 1988
2nd: 44 Buffalo (24) vs. Washington (20), 1992

Fewest Points, Both Teams, Each Half
1st: 2 Minnesota (0) vs. Pittsburgh (2), 1975
2nd: 7 Miami (0) vs. Washington (7), 1973
Denver (0) vs. Washington (7), 1988

Most Points, Both Teams, Each Quarter
1st: 21 Dallas (14) vs. Buffalo (7), 1993
San Francisco (14) vs. San Diego (7), 1995
2nd: 35 Washington (35) vs. Denver (0), 1988
3rd: 24 Washington (14) vs. Buffalo (10), 1992
4th: 28 Dallas (14) vs. Pittsburgh (14), 1979

TOUCHDOWNS

Most Touchdowns, Game
8 San Francisco vs. Denver, 1990
7 Dallas vs. Buffalo, 1993
San Francisco vs. San Diego, 1995
6 Washington vs. Denver, 1988

Fewest Touchdowns, Game
0 Miami vs. Dallas, 1972
1 By 17 teams

Most Touchdowns, Both Teams, Game
10 San Francisco (7) vs. San Diego (3), 1995
9 Pittsburgh (5) vs. Dallas (4), 1979
San Francisco (8) vs. Denver (1), 1990
Dallas (7) vs. Buffalo (2), 1993
7 N.Y. Giants (5) vs. Denver (2), 1987
Washington (6) vs. Denver (1), 1988
Washington (4) vs. Buffalo (3), 1992

Fewest Touchdowns, Both Teams, Game
2 Baltimore (1) vs. N.Y. Jets (1), 1969
3 In six games

POINTS AFTER TOUCHDOWN

Most (One-Point) Points After Touchdown, Game
7 San Francisco vs. Denver, 1990
Dallas vs. Buffalo, 1993
San Francisco vs. San Diego, 1995
6 Washington vs. Denver, 1988
5 Green Bay vs. Kansas City, 1967
Pittsburgh vs. Dallas, 1979
L.A. Raiders vs. Washington, 1984
San Francisco vs. Miami, 1985
Chicago vs. New England, 1986

Most (One-Point) Points After Touchdown, Both Teams, Game
9 Pittsburgh (5) vs. Dallas (4), 1979
Dallas (7) vs. Buffalo (2), 1993
8 San Francisco (7) vs. Denver (1), 1990
San Francisco (7) vs. San Diego (1), 1995

7 Washington (6) vs. Denver (1), 1988
Washington (4) vs. Buffalo (3), 1992

Fewest (One-Point) Points After Touchdown, Both Teams, Game
2 Baltimore (1) vs. N.Y. Jets (1), 1969
Baltimore (1) vs. Dallas (1), 1971
Minnesota (0) vs. Pittsburgh (2), 1975

Most Two-Point Conversions, Game
2 San Diego vs. San Francisco, 1995

Most Two-Point Conversions, Both Teams, Game
2 San Diego (2) vs. San Francisco (0), 1995

FIELD GOALS

Most Field Goals Attempted, Game
5 N.Y. Jets vs. Baltimore, 1969
Dallas vs. Denver, 1978
4 Green Bay vs. Oakland, 1968
Pittsburgh vs. Dallas, 1976
San Francisco vs. Cincinnati, 1982; 1989
Denver vs. N.Y. Giants, 1987

Most Field Goals Attempted, Both Teams, Game
7 N.Y. Jets (5) vs. Baltimore (2), 1969
San Francisco (4) vs. Cincinnati (3), 1989
6 Dallas (5) vs. Denver (1), 1978
5 Green Bay (4) vs. Oakland (1), 1968
Pittsburgh (4) vs. Dallas (1), 1976
Oakland (3) vs. Philadelphia (2), 1981
Denver (4) vs. N.Y. Giants (1), 1987
Dallas (3) vs. Buffalo (2), 1994

Fewest Field Goals Attempted, Both Teams, Game
1 Minnesota (0) vs. Miami (1), 1974
San Francisco (0) vs. Denver (1), 1990
2 Green Bay (0) vs. Kansas City (2), 1967
Miami (1) vs. Washington (1), 1973
Dallas (1) vs. Pittsburgh (1), 1979
Dallas (1) vs. Buffalo (1), 1993
San Diego (1) vs. San Francisco (1), 1995

Most Field Goals, Game
4 Green Bay vs. Oakland, 1968
San Francisco vs. Cincinnati, 1982
3 N.Y. Jets vs. Baltimore, 1969
Kansas City vs. Minnesota, 1970
Miami vs. San Francisco, 1985
Chicago vs. New England, 1986
Cincinnati vs. San Francisco, 1989
Washington vs. Buffalo, 1992
Dallas vs. Buffalo, 1994

Most Field Goals, Both Teams, Game
5 Cincinnati (3) vs. San Francisco (2), 1989
Dallas (3) vs. Buffalo (2), 1994
4 Green Bay (4) vs. Oakland (0), 1968
San Francisco (4) vs. Cincinnati (0), 1982
Miami (3) vs. San Francisco (1), 1985
Chicago (3) vs. New England (1), 1986
Buffalo (2) vs. N.Y. Giants (2), 1991
Washington (3) vs. Buffalo (1), 1992
3 In nine games

Fewest Field Goals, Both Teams, Game
0 Miami vs. Washington, 1973
Pittsburgh vs. Minnesota, 1975
1 Green Bay (0) vs. Kansas City (1), 1967
Minnesota (0) vs. Miami (1), 1974
Pittsburgh (0) vs. Dallas (1), 1979
Washington (0) vs. Denver (1), 1988
San Francisco (0) vs. Denver (1), 1990
San Francisco (0) vs. San Diego (1), 1995

SAFETIES

Most Safeties, Game
1 Pittsburgh vs. Minnesota, 1975; vs. Dallas, 1976
Chicago vs. New England, 1986
N.Y. Giants vs. Denver, 1987
Buffalo vs. N.Y. Giants, 1991

FIRST DOWNS

Most First Downs, Game
31 San Francisco vs. Miami, 1985
28 San Francisco vs. Denver, 1990
San Francisco vs. San Diego, 1995
25 Washington vs. Denver, 1988
Buffalo vs. Washington, 1992
Pittsburgh vs. Dallas, 1996

Fewest First Downs, Game
9 Minnesota vs. Pittsburgh, 1975
Miami vs. Washington, 1983
10 Dallas vs. Baltimore, 1971
Miami vs. Dallas, 1972
11 Denver vs. Dallas, 1978

Most First Downs, Both Teams, Game
50 San Francisco (31) vs. Miami (19), 1985
49 Buffalo (25) vs. Washington (24), 1992
48 San Francisco (28) vs. San Diego (20), 1995

Fewest First Downs, Both Teams, Game
24 Dallas (10) vs. Baltimore (14), 1971
26 Minnesota (9) vs. Pittsburgh (17), 1975
27 Pittsburgh (13) vs. Dallas (14), 1976

RUSHING

Most First Downs, Rushing, Game
16 San Francisco vs. Miami, 1985
15 Dallas vs. Miami, 1972
14 Washington vs. Miami, 1983
San Francisco vs. Denver, 1990

Fewest First Downs, Rushing, Game
1 New England vs. Chicago, 1986
2 Minnesota vs. Kansas City, 1970; vs. Pittsburgh, 1975; vs. Oakland, 1977
Pittsburgh vs. Dallas, 1979
Miami vs. San Francisco, 1985
3 Miami vs. Dallas, 1972
Philadelphia vs. Oakland, 1981

Most First Downs, Rushing, Both Teams, Game
21 Washington (14) vs. Miami (7), 1983
19 Washington (13) vs. Denver (6), 1988
San Francisco (14) vs. Denver (5), 1990
18 Dallas (15) vs. Miami (3), 1972
Miami (13) vs. Minnesota (5), 1974
San Francisco (16) vs. Miami (2), 1985
N.Y. Giants (10) vs. Buffalo (8), 1991

Fewest First Downs, Rushing, Both Teams, Game
8 Baltimore (4) vs. Dallas (4), 1971
Pittsburgh (2) vs. Dallas (6), 1979
9 Philadelphia (3) vs. Oakland (6), 1981
10 Minnesota (2) vs. Kansas City (8), 1970

PASSING

Most First Downs, Passing, Game
18 Buffalo vs. Washington, 1992
17 Miami vs. San Francisco, 1985
San Francisco vs. San Diego, 1995
16 Denver vs. N.Y. Giants, 1987
San Francisco vs. Cincinnati, 1989

Fewest First Downs, Passing, Game
1 Denver vs. Dallas, 1978
2 Miami vs. Washington, 1983
4 Miami vs. Minnesota, 1974

Most First Downs, Passing, Both Teams, Game
32 Miami (17) vs. San Francisco (15), 1985
31 San Francisco (17) vs. San Diego (14), 1995
30 Buffalo (18) vs. Washington (12), 1992

Fewest First Downs, Passing, Both Teams, Game
9 Denver (1) vs. Dallas (8), 1978
10 Minnesota (5) vs. Pittsburgh (5), 1975
11 Dallas (5) vs. Baltimore (6), 1971
Miami (2) vs. Washington (9), 1983

PENALTY

Most First Downs, Penalty, Game
4 Baltimore vs. Dallas, 1971
Miami vs. Minnesota, 1974
Cincinnati vs. San Francisco, 1982
Buffalo vs. Dallas, 1993
3 Kansas City vs. Minnesota, 1970
Minnesota vs. Oakland, 1977
Buffalo vs. Washington, 1992

Most First Downs, Penalty, Both Teams, Game
6 Cincinnati (4) vs. San Francisco (2), 1982
5 Baltimore (4) vs. Dallas (1), 1971
Miami (4) vs. Minnesota (1), 1974
Buffalo (3) vs. Washington (2), 1992
4 Kansas City (3) vs. Minnesota (1), 1970
Buffalo (4) vs. Dallas (0), 1993

Fewest First Downs, Penalty, Both Teams, Game
0 Dallas vs. Miami, 1972
Miami vs. Washington, 1973
Dallas vs. Pittsburgh, 1976
Miami vs. San Francisco, 1985

1 Green Bay (0) vs. Kansas City (1), 1967
Miami (0) vs. Washington (1), 1983
Cincinnati (0) vs. San Francisco (1), 1989
San Francisco (0) vs. Denver (1), 1990
Dallas (0) vs. Buffalo (1), 1994
Dallas (0) vs. Pittsburgh (1), 1996

NET YARDS GAINED RUSHING AND PASSING

Most Yards Gained, Game
602 Washington vs. Denver, 1988
537 San Francisco vs. Miami, 1985
461 San Francisco vs. Denver, 1990

Fewest Yards Gained, Game
119 Minnesota vs. Pittsburgh, 1975
123 New England vs. Chicago, 1986
156 Denver vs. Dallas, 1978

Most Yards Gained, Both Teams, Game
929 Washington (602) vs. Denver (327), 1988
851 San Francisco (537) vs. Miami (314), 1985
809 San Francisco (455) vs. San Diego (354), 1995

Fewest Yards Gained, Both Teams, Game
452 Minnesota (119) vs. Pittsburgh (333), 1975
481 Washington (228) vs. Miami (253), 1973
Denver (156) vs. Dallas (325), 1978
497 Minnesota (238) vs. Miami (259), 1974

RUSHING

ATTEMPTS

Most Attempts, Game
57 Pittsburgh vs. Minnesota, 1975
53 Miami vs. Minnesota, 1974
52 Oakland vs. Minnesota, 1977
Washington vs. Miami, 1983

Fewest Attempts, Game
9 Miami vs. San Francisco, 1985
11 New England vs. Chicago, 1986
17 Denver vs. Washington, 1988; vs. San Francisco, 1990

Most Attempts, Both Teams, Game
81 Washington (52) vs. Miami (29), 1983
78 Pittsburgh (57) vs. Minnesota (21), 1975
Oakland (52) vs. Minnesota (26), 1977
77 Miami (53) vs. Minnesota (24), 1974
Pittsburgh (46) vs. Dallas (31), 1976

Fewest Attempts, Both Teams, Game
49 Miami (9) vs. San Francisco (40), 1985
51 San Diego (19) vs. San Francisco (32), 1995
53 Kansas City (19) vs. Green Bay (34), 1967

YARDS GAINED

Most Yards Gained, Game
280 Washington vs. Denver, 1988
276 Washington vs. Miami, 1983
266 Oakland vs. Minnesota, 1977

Fewest Yards Gained, Game
7 New England vs. Chicago, 1986
17 Minnesota vs. Pittsburgh, 1975
25 Miami vs. San Francisco, 1985

Most Yards Gained, Both Teams, Game
377 Washington (280) vs. Denver (97), 1988
372 Washington (276) vs. Miami (96), 1983
338 N.Y. Giants (172) vs. Buffalo (166), 1991

Fewest Yards Gained, Both Teams, Game
159 Dallas (56) vs. Pittsburgh (103), 1996
168 Buffalo (43) vs. Washington (125), 1992
171 Baltimore (69) vs. Dallas (102), 1971

AVERAGE GAIN

Highest Average Gain, Game
7.00 L.A. Raiders vs. Washington, 1984 (33-231)
Washington vs. Denver, 1988 (40-280)
6.64 Buffalo vs. N.Y. Giants, 1991 (25-166)
6.22 Baltimore vs. N.Y. Jets, 1969 (23-143)

Lowest Average Gain, Game
0.64 New England vs. Chicago, 1986 (11-7)
0.81 Minnesota vs. Pittsburgh, 1975 (21-17)
2.23 Baltimore vs. Dallas, 1971 (31-69)

TOUCHDOWNS

Most Touchdowns, Game
4 Chicago vs. New England, 1986
3 Green Bay vs. Kansas City, 1967
Miami vs. Minnesota, 1974
San Francisco vs. Denver, 1990
2 Oakland vs. Minnesota, 1977
Pittsburgh vs. Los Angeles, 1980
L.A. Raiders vs. Washington, 1984
San Francisco vs. Miami, 1985
N.Y. Giants vs. Denver, 1987
Washington vs. Denver, 1988; vs. Buffalo, 1992
Buffalo vs. N.Y. Giants, 1991
Dallas vs. Pittsburgh, 1996

Fewest Touchdowns, Game
0 By 17 teams

Most Touchdowns, Both Teams, Game
4 Miami (3) vs. Minnesota (1), 1974
Chicago (4) vs. New England (0), 1986
San Francisco (3) vs. Denver (1), 1990
3 Green Bay (3) vs. Kansas City (0), 1967
Pittsburgh (2) vs. Los Angeles (1), 1980
L.A. Raiders (2) vs. Washington (1), 1984
N.Y. Giants (2) vs. Denver (1), 1987
Buffalo (2) vs. N.Y. Giants (1), 1991
Washington (2) vs. Buffalo (1), 1992
Dallas (2) vs. Buffalo (1), 1994
Dallas (2) vs. Pittsburgh (1), 1996

Fewest Touchdowns, Both Teams, Game
0 Pittsburgh vs. Dallas, 1976
Oakland vs. Philadelphia, 1981
Cincinnati vs. San Francisco, 1989
1 In seven games

PASSING

ATTEMPTS

Most Passes Attempted, Game
59 Buffalo vs. Washington, 1992
55 San Diego vs. San Francisco, 1995
50 Miami vs. San Francisco, 1985
Buffalo vs. Dallas, 1994

Fewest Passes Attempted, Game
7 Miami vs. Minnesota, 1974
11 Miami vs. Washington, 1973
14 Pittsburgh vs. Minnesota, 1975

Most Passes Attempted, Both Teams, Game
93 San Diego (55) vs. San Francisco (38), 1995
92 Buffalo (59) vs. Washington (33), 1992
85 Miami (50) vs. San Francisco (35), 1985

Fewest Passes Attempted, Both Teams, Game
35 Miami (7) vs. Minnesota (28), 1974
39 Miami (11) vs. Washington (28), 1973
40 Pittsburgh (14) vs. Minnesota (26), 1975
Miami (17) vs. Washington (23), 1983

COMPLETIONS

Most Passes Completed, Game
31 Buffalo vs. Dallas, 1994
29 Miami vs. San Francisco, 1985
Buffalo vs. Washington, 1992
28 Pittsburgh vs. Dallas, 1996

Fewest Passes Completed, Game
4 Miami vs. Washington, 1983
6 Miami vs. Minnesota, 1974
8 Miami vs. Washington, 1973
Denver vs. Dallas, 1978

Most Passes Completed, Both Teams, Game
53 Miami (29) vs. San Francisco (24), 1985
52 San Diego (27) vs. San Francisco (25), 1995
50 Buffalo (31) vs. Dallas (19), 1994

Fewest Passes Completed, Both Teams, Game
19 Miami (4) vs. Washington (15), 1983
20 Pittsburgh (9) vs. Minnesota (11), 1975
22 Miami (8) vs. Washington (14), 1973

COMPLETION PERCENTAGE

Highest Completion Percentage, Game (20 attempts)
88.0 N.Y. Giants vs. Denver, 1987 (25-22)
75.0 San Francisco vs. Denver, 1990 (32-24)
73.5 Cincinnati vs. San Francisco, 1982 (34-25)

Lowest Completion Percentage, Game (20 attempts)
32.0 Denver vs. Dallas, 1978 (25-8)
37.9 Denver vs. San Francisco, 1990 (29-11)
38.5 Denver vs. Washington, 1988 (39-15)

YARDS GAINED

Most Yards Gained, Game
341 San Francisco vs. Cincinnati, 1989
326 San Francisco vs. Miami, 1985

322 Washington vs. Denver, 1988

Fewest Yards Gained, Game
35 Denver vs. Dallas, 1978
63 Miami vs. Minnesota, 1974
69 Miami vs. Washington, 1973

Most Yards Gained, Both Teams, Game
615 San Francisco (326) vs. Miami (289), 1985
603 San Francisco (316) vs. San Diego (287), 1995
583 Denver (320) vs. N.Y. Giants (263), 1987

Fewest Yards Gained, Both Teams, Game
156 Miami (69) vs. Washington (87), 1973
186 Pittsburgh (84) vs. Minnesota (102), 1975
205 Dallas (100) vs. Miami (105), 1972

TIMES SACKED

Most Times Sacked, Game
7 Dallas vs. Pittsburgh, 1976
New England vs. Chicago, 1986
6 Kansas City vs. Green Bay, 1967
Washington vs. L.A. Raiders, 1984
Denver vs. San Francisco, 1990
5 Dallas vs. Denver, 1978; vs. Pittsburgh, 1979
Cincinnati vs. San Francisco, 1982; 1989
Denver vs. Washington, 1988
Buffalo vs. Washington, 1992

Fewest Times Sacked, Game
0 Baltimore vs. N.Y. Jets, 1969; vs. Dallas, 1971
Minnesota vs. Pittsburgh, 1975
Pittsburgh vs. Los Angeles, 1980
Philadelphia vs. Oakland, 1981
Washington vs. Buffalo, 1992
1 By 11 teams

Most Times Sacked, Both Teams, Game
10 New England (7) vs. Chicago (3), 1986
9 Kansas City (6) vs. Green Bay (3), 1967
Dallas (7) vs. Pittsburgh (2), 1976
Dallas (5) vs. Denver (4), 1978
Dallas (5) vs. Pittsburgh (4), 1979
Cincinnati (5) vs. San Francisco (4), 1989
8 Washington (6) vs. L.A. Raiders (2), 1984

Fewest Times Sacked, Both Teams, Game
1 Philadelphia (0) vs. Oakland (1), 1981
2 Baltimore (0) vs. N.Y. Jets (2), 1969
Baltimore (0) vs. Dallas (2), 1971
Minnesota (0) vs. Pittsburgh (2), 1975
3 In four games

TOUCHDOWNS

Most Touchdowns, Game
6 San Francisco vs. San Diego, 1995
5 San Francisco vs. Denver, 1990
4 Pittsburgh vs. Dallas, 1979
Washington vs. Denver, 1988
Dallas vs. Buffalo, 1993

Fewest Touchdowns, Game
0 By 16 teams

Most Touchdowns, Both Teams, Game
7 Pittsburgh (4) vs. Dallas (3), 1979
San Francisco (6) vs. San Diego (1), 1995
5 Washington (4) vs. Denver (1), 1988
San Francisco (5) vs. Denver (0), 1990
Dallas (4) vs. Buffalo (1), 1993
4 Dallas (2) vs. Pittsburgh (2), 1976
Oakland (3) vs. Philadelphia (1), 1981
San Francisco (3) vs. Miami (1), 1985
N.Y. Giants (3) vs. Denver (1), 1987
Washington (2) vs. Buffalo (2), 1992

Fewest Touchdowns, Both Teams, Game
0 N.Y. Jets vs. Baltimore, 1969
Miami vs. Minnesota, 1974
Buffalo vs. Dallas, 1994
1 In six games

INTERCEPTIONS BY

Most Interceptions By, Game
4 N.Y. Jets vs. Baltimore, 1969
Dallas vs. Denver, 1978
Washington vs. Buffalo, 1992
Dallas vs. Buffalo, 1993
3 By 11 teams

Most Interceptions By, Both Teams, Game
6 Baltimore (3) vs. Dallas (3), 1971
5 Washington (4) vs. Buffalo (1), 1992
4 In seven games

Fewest Interceptions By, Both Teams, Game
0 Buffalo vs. N.Y. Giants, 1991
1 Oakland (0) vs. Green Bay (1), 1968
Miami (0) vs. Dallas (1), 1972
Minnesota (0) vs. Miami (1), 1974
N.Y. Giants (0) vs. Denver (1), 1987
Cincinnati (0) vs. San Francisco (1), 1989

YARDS GAINED

Most Yards Gained, Game
95 Miami vs. Washington, 1973
91 Oakland vs. Minnesota, 1977
89 Pittsburgh vs. Dallas, 1976

Most Yards Gained, Both Teams, Game
95 Miami (95) vs. Washington (0), 1973
91 Oakland (91) vs. Minnesota (0), 1977
89 Pittsburgh (89) vs. Dallas (0), 1976

TOUCHDOWNS

Most Touchdowns, Game
1 Green Bay vs. Oakland, 1968
Oakland vs. Minnesota, 1977
L.A. Raiders vs. Washington, 1984
Chicago vs. New England, 1986

PUNTING

Most Punts, Game
9 Dallas vs. Baltimore, 1971
8 Washington vs. L.A. Raiders, 1984
7 By seven teams

Fewest Punts, Game
2 Pittsburgh vs. Los Angeles, 1980
Denver vs. N.Y. Giants, 1987
3 By 10 teams

Most Punts, Both Teams, Game
15 Washington (8) vs. L.A. Raiders (7), 1984
13 Dallas (9) vs. Baltimore (4), 1971
Pittsburgh (7) vs. Minnesota (6), 1975
12 In three games

Fewest Punts, Both Teams, Game
5 Denver (2) vs. N.Y. Giants (3), 1987
6 Oakland (3) vs. Philadelphia (3), 1981
7 In five games

AVERAGE YARDAGE

Highest Average, Game (4 punts)
48.75 San Diego vs. San Francisco, 1995 (4-195)
48.50 Kansas City vs. Minnesota, 1970 (4-194)
46.25 San Francisco vs. Cincinnati, 1982 (4-185)

Lowest Average, Game (4 punts)
31.20 Washington vs. Miami, 1973 (5-156)
32.38 Washington vs. L.A. Raiders, 1984 (8-259)
32.40 Oakland vs. Minnesota, 1977 (5-162)

PUNT RETURNS

Most Punt Returns, Game
6 Washington vs. Miami, 1983
5 By five teams

Fewest Punt Returns, Game
0 Minnesota vs. Miami, 1974
Buffalo vs. N.Y. Giants, 1991
Washington vs. Buffalo, 1992
1 By 13 teams

Most Punt Returns, Both Teams, Game
9 Pittsburgh (5) vs. Minnesota (4), 1975
8 Green Bay (5) vs. Oakland (3), 1968
Baltimore (5) vs. Dallas (3), 1971
Washington (6) vs. Miami (2), 1983
7 Green Bay (4) vs. Kansas City (3), 1967
Oakland (4) vs. Minnesota (3), 1977
San Francisco (5) vs. Miami (2), 1985

Fewest Punt Returns, Both Teams, Game
2 Dallas (1) vs. Miami (1), 1972
Denver (1) vs. N.Y. Giants (1), 1987
Buffalo (0) vs. N.Y. Giants (2), 1991
Buffalo (1) vs. Dallas (1), 1994
3 Kansas City (1) vs. Minnesota (2), 1970
Minnesota (0) vs. Miami (3), 1974
Washington (1) vs. Denver (2), 1988
Washington (0) vs. Buffalo (3), 1992
Dallas (1) vs. Pittsburgh (2), 1996
4 L.A. Raiders (2) vs. Washington (2), 1984

Chicago (2) vs. New England (2), 1986
Buffalo (1) vs. Dallas (3), 1993

YARDS GAINED

Most Yards Gained, Game
56 San Francisco vs. Cincinnati, 1989
52 Washington vs. Miami, 1983
51 San Francisco vs. Miami, 1985

Fewest Yards Gained, Game
–1 Dallas vs. Miami, 1972
0 By eight teams

Most Yards Gained, Both Teams, Game
74 Washington (52) vs. Miami (22), 1983
66 San Francisco (51) vs. Miami (15), 1985
61 San Francisco (56) vs. Cincinnati (5), 1989

Fewest Yards Gained, Both Teams, Game
9 Washington (0) vs. Bufffalo (9), 1992
10 Buffalo (5) vs. Dallas (5), 1994
13 Miami (4) vs. Washington (9), 1973
San Diego (1) vs. San Francisco (12), 1995

AVERAGE RETURN

Highest Average, Game (3 returns)
18.7 San Francisco vs. Cincinnati, 1989 (3-56)
12.7 San Francisco vs. Denver, 1990 (3-38)
11.7 Dallas vs. Buffalo, 1993 (3-35)

TOUCHDOWNS

Most Touchdowns, Game
None

KICKOFF RETURNS

Most Kickoff Returns, Game
9 Denver vs. San Francisco, 1990
8 San Diego vs. San Francisco, 1995
7 Oakland vs. Green Bay, 1968
Minnesota vs. Oakland, 1977
Cincinnati vs. San Francisco, 1982
Washington vs. L.A. Raiders, 1984
Miami vs. San Francisco, 1985
New England vs. Chicago, 1986

Fewest Kickoff Returns, Game
1 N.Y. Jets vs. Baltimore, 1969
L.A. Raiders vs. Washington, 1984
Washington vs. Buffalo, 1992
2 By seven teams

Most Kickoff Returns, Both Teams, Game
12 Denver (9) vs. San Francisco (3), 1990
San Diego (8) vs. San Francisco (4), 1995
11 Los Angeles (6) vs. Pittsburgh (5), 1980
Miami (7) vs. San Francisco (4), 1985
New England (7) vs. Chicago (4), 1986
10 Oakland (7) vs. Green Bay (3), 1968

Fewest Kickoff Returns, Both Teams, Game
5 N.Y. Jets (1) vs. Baltimore (4), 1969
Miami (2) vs. Washington (3), 1973
Washington (1) vs. Buffalo (4), 1992
6 In three games

YARDS GAINED

Most Yards Gained, Game
244 San Diego vs. San Francisco, 1995
222 Miami vs. Washington, 1983
196 Denver vs. San Francisco, 1990

Fewest Yards Gained, Game
16 Washington vs. Buffalo, 1992
17 L.A. Raiders vs. Washington, 1984
25 N.Y. Jets vs. Baltimore, 1969

Most Yards Gained, Both Teams, Game
290 San Diego (242) vs. San Francisco (48), 1995
279 Miami (222) vs. Washington (57), 1983
245 Denver (196) vs. San Francisco (49), 1990

Fewest Yards Gained, Both Teams, Game
78 Miami (33) vs. Washington (45), 1973
82 Pittsburgh (32) vs. Minnesota (50), 1975
92 San Francisco (40) vs. Cincinnati (52), 1982

AVERAGE GAIN

Highest Average, Game (3 returns)
44.0 Cincinnati vs. San Francisco, 1989 (3-132)
37.0 Miami vs. Washington, 1983 (6-222)
32.4 Pittsburgh vs. Los Angeles, 1980 (5-162)

TOUCHDOWNS

Most Touchdowns, Game
1 Miami vs. Washington, 1983
Cincinnati vs. San Francisco, 1989
San Diego vs. San Francisco, 1995

PENALTIES

Most Penalties, Game
12 Dallas vs. Denver, 1978
10 Dallas vs. Baltimore, 1971
9 Dallas vs. Pittsburgh, 1979

Fewest Penalties, Game
0 Miami vs. Dallas, 1972
Pittsburgh vs. Dallas, 1976
Denver vs. San Francisco, 1990
1 Green Bay vs. Oakland, 1968
Miami vs. Minnesota, 1974; vs. San Francisco, 1985
Buffalo vs. Dallas, 1994
2 By five teams

Most Penalties, Both Teams, Game
20 Dallas (12) vs. Denver (8), 1978
16 Cincinnati (8) vs. San Francisco (8), 1982
14 Dallas (10) vs. Baltimore (4), 1971
Dallas (9) vs. Pittsburgh (5), 1979

Fewest Penalties, Both Teams, Game
2 Pittsburgh (0) vs. Dallas (2), 1976
3 Miami (0) vs. Dallas (3), 1972
Miami (1) vs. San Francisco (2), 1985
4 Denver (0) vs. San Francisco (4), 1990

YARDS PENALIZED

Most Yards Penalized, Game
133 Dallas vs. Baltimore, 1971
122 Pittsburgh vs. Minnesota, 1975
94 Dallas vs. Denver, 1978

Fewest Yards Penalized, Game
0 Miami vs. Dallas, 1972
Pittsburgh vs. Dallas, 1976
Denver vs. San Francisco, 1990
4 Miami vs. Minnesota, 1974
10 Miami vs. San Francisco, 1985
San Francisco vs. Miami, 1985
Buffalo vs. Dallas, 1994

Most Yards Penalized, Both Teams, Game
164 Dallas (133) vs. Baltimore (31), 1971
154 Dallas (94) vs. Denver (60), 1978
140 Pittsburgh (122) vs. Minnesota (18), 1975

Fewest Yards Penalized, Both Teams, Game
15 Miami (0) vs. Dallas (15), 1972
20 Pittsburgh (0) vs. Dallas (20), 1976
Miami (10) vs. San Francisco (10), 1985
38 Denver (0) vs. San Francisco (38), 1990

FUMBLES

Most Fumbles, Game
8 Buffalo vs. Dallas, 1993
6 Dallas vs. Denver, 1978
Buffalo vs. Washington, 1992
5 Baltimore vs. Dallas, 1971

Fewest Fumbles, Game
0 By 12 teams

Most Fumbles, Both Teams, Game
12 Buffalo (8) vs. Dallas (4), 1993
10 Dallas (6) vs. Denver (4), 1978
8 Dallas (4) vs. Pittsburgh (4), 1976

Fewest Fumbles, Both Teams, Game
0 Los Angeles vs. Pittsburgh, 1980
1 Oakland (0) vs. Minnesota (1), 1977
Oakland (0) vs. Philadelphia (1), 1981
Denver (0) vs. Washington (1), 1988
N.Y. Giants (0) vs. Buffalo (1), 1991
2 In five games

Most Fumbles Lost, Game
5 Buffalo vs. Dallas, 1993
4 Baltimore vs. Dallas, 1971
Denver vs. Dallas, 1978
New England vs. Chicago, 1986
2 In many games

Most Fumbles Lost, Both Teams, Game
7 Buffalo (5) vs. Dallas (2), 1993
6 Denver (4) vs. Dallas (2), 1978
New England (4) vs. Chicago (2), 1986
5 Baltimore (4) vs. Dallas (1), 1971

Fewest Fumbles Lost, Both Teams, Game
- 0 Green Bay vs. Kansas City, 1967
  Dallas vs. Pittsburgh, 1976
  Los Angeles vs. Pittsburgh, 1980
  Denver vs. N.Y. Giants, 1987
  Denver vs. Washington, 1988
  Buffalo vs. N.Y. Giants, 1991
  San Diego vs. San Francisco, 1995
  Dallas vs. Pittsburgh, 1996

Most Fumbles Recovered, Game
- 8 Dallas vs. Denver, 1978 (4 own, 4 opp.)
- 6 Dallas vs. Buffalo, 1993 (1 own, 5 opp.)
- 5 Chicago vs. New England, 1986 (1 own, 4 opp.)

TURNOVERS

(Number of times losing the ball on interceptions and fumbles.)

Most Turnovers, Game
- 9 Buffalo vs. Dallas, 1993
- 8 Denver vs. Dallas, 1978
- 7 Baltimore vs. Dallas, 1971

Fewest Turnovers, Game
- 0 Green Bay vs. Oakland, 1968
  Miami vs. Minnesota, 1974
  Pittsburgh vs. Dallas, 1976
  Oakland vs. Minnesota, 1977; vs. Philadelphia, 1981
  N.Y. Giants vs. Denver, 1987; vs. Buffalo, 1991
  San Francisco vs. Denver, 1990; vs. San Diego, 1995
  Buffalo vs. N.Y. Giants, 1991
  Dallas vs. Pittsburgh, 1996
- 1 By many teams

Most Turnovers, Both Teams, Game
- 11 Baltimore (7) vs. Dallas (4), 1971
  Buffalo (9) vs. Dallas (2), 1993
- 10 Denver (8) vs. Dallas (2), 1978
- 8 New England (6) vs. Chicago (2), 1986

Fewest Turnovers, Both Teams, Game
- 0 Buffalo vs. N.Y. Giants, 1991
- 1 N.Y. Giants (0) vs. Denver (1), 1987
- 2 Green Bay (1) vs. Kansas City (1), 1967
  Miami (0) vs. Minnesota (2), 1974
  Cincinnati (1) vs. San Francisco (1), 1989

Compiled by Elias Sports Bureau

Throughout this all-time postseason record section, the following abbreviations are used to indicate various levels of postseason games:

SB Super Bowl (1966 to date)
AFC AFC Championship Game (1970 to date) or AFL Championship Game (1960-69)
NFC NFC Championship Game (1970 to date) or NFL Championship Game (1933-69)
AFC-D AFC Divisional Playoff Game (1970 to date), AFC Second-Round Playoff Game (1982), AFL Inter-Divisional Playoff Game (1969), or special playoff game to break tie for AFL Division Championship (1963, 1968)
NFC-D NFC Divisional Playoff Game (1970 to date), NFC Second-Round Playoff Game (1982), NFL Conference Championship Game (1967-69), or special playoff game to break tie for NFL Division or Conference Championship (1941, 1943, 1947, 1950, 1952, 1957, 1958, 1965)
AFC-FR AFC First-Round Playoff Game (1978 to date)
NFC-FR NFC First-Round Playoff Game (1978 to date)

POSTSEASON GAME COMPOSITE STANDINGS

	W	L	PCT.	PTS.	OP
Green Bay Packers	17	8	.680	577	432
San Francisco 49ers	21	12	.636	860	632
Dallas Cowboys	31	18	.633	1,197	891
Washington Redskins*	21	14	.600	738	625
Pittsburgh Steelers	19	13	.594	728	635
Oakland Raiders**	21	15	.583	855	659
Miami Dolphins	17	14	.548	697	633
Buffalo Bills	14	12	.538	621	582
Indianapolis Colts***	10	9	.526	346	347
Chicago Bears	14	14	.500	579	552
Denver Broncos	9	10	.474	380	502
Philadelphia Eagles	9	10	.474	359	355
Detroit Lions	7	8	.467	342	357
New York Jets	5	6	.455	216	200
Kansas City Chiefs****	8	10	.444	291	370
New York Giants	14	18	.438	529	593
Seattle Seahawks	3	4	.429	128	139
Minnesota Vikings	13	18	.419	553	646
Cincinnati Bengals	5	7	.417	246	257
Houston Oilers	9	13	.409	371	533
St. Louis Rams†	13	20	.394	501	697
San Diego Chargers††	7	11	.389	332	428
Cleveland Browns	11	19	.367	596	692
New England Patriots†††	4	7	.364	208	278
Atlanta Falcons	2	5	.286	139	181
Tampa Bay Buccaneers	1	3	.250	41	94
Arizona Cardinals††††	1	4	.200	81	134
New Orleans Saints	0	4	.000	56	123

One game played when franchise was in Boston (lost 21-6).

***12 games played when franchise was in Los Angeles (won 6, lost 6, 268 points scored, 224 points allowed).*

****15 games played when franchise was in Baltimore (won 8, lost 7, 264 points scored, 262 points allowed).*

*****One game played when franchise was Dallas Texans (won 20-17).*

†One game played when franchise was in Cleveland (won 15-14), 32 games played when franchise was in Los Angeles (won 12, lost 20, 486 points scored, 683 points allowed).

††One game played when franchise was in Los Angeles (lost 24-16).

†††Two games played when franchise was in Boston (won 26-8, lost 51-10).

††††Two games played when franchise was in Chicago (won 28-21, lost 7-0), three games played when franchise was in St. Louis (lost 30-14, lost 35-23, lost 41-16).

INDIVIDUAL RECORDS

SERVICE

Most Games, Career
27 D.D. Lewis, Dallas (SB 5, NFC 9, NFC-D 12, NFC-FR 1)
26 Larry Cole, Dallas (SB 5, NFC 8, NFC-D 12, NFC-FR 1)
25 Charlie Waters, Dallas (SB 5, NFC 9, NFC-D 10, NFC-FR 1)

Most Games, Head Coach
36 Tom Landry, Dallas
Don Shula, Baltimore-Miami
24 Chuck Noll, Pittsburgh
22 Bud Grant, Minnesota

Most Games Won, Head Coach
20 Tom Landry, Dallas
19 Don Shula, Baltimore-Miami
16 Chuck Noll, Pittsburgh
Joe Gibbs, Washington

Most Games Lost, Head Coach
17 Don Shula, Baltimore-Miami
16 Tom Landry, Dallas
12 Bud Grant, Minnesota

SCORING

POINTS

Most Points, Career
115 George Blanda, Chi. Bears-Houston-Oakland, 19 games (49-pat, 22-fg)
108 Thurman Thomas, Buffalo, 18 games (18-td)
Emmitt Smith, Dallas, 13 games (18-td)
103 Matt Bahr, Pittsburgh-Cleveland-N.Y. Giants-New England, 14 games (40-pat, 21-fg)

Most Points, Game
30 Ricky Watters, NFC-D:San Francisco vs. N.Y. Giants, 1993 (5-td)
19 Pat Harder, NFC-D: Detroit vs. Los Angeles, 1952 (2-td, 4-pat, 1-fg)
Paul Hornung, NFC: Green Bay vs. N.Y. Giants, 1961 (1-td, 4-pat, 3-fg)
18 By many players

Most Consecutive Games Scoring
19 George Blanda, Chi. Bears-Houston-Oakland, 1956-75
15 Roy Gerela, Houston-Pittsburgh, 1969-78
14 Toni Fritsch, Dallas-Houston, 1972-80
Rafael Septien, L.A. Rams-Dallas, 1977-83
Matt Bahr, Pittsburgh-Cleveland-N.Y. Giants-New England, 1979-94 (current)

TOUCHDOWNS

Most Touchdowns, Career
18 Thurman Thomas, Buffalo, 18 games (14-r, 4-p)
Emmitt Smith, Dallas, 13 games (16-r, 2-p)
17 Franco Harris, Pittsburgh, 19 games (16-r, 1-p)
Jerry Rice, San Francisco, 19 games (17-p)
13 Marcus Allen, L.A. Raiders-Kansas City, 15 games (11-r, 2-p)

Most Touchdowns, Game
5 Ricky Watters, NFC-D:San Francisco vs. N.Y. Giants, 1993 (5-r)
3 Andy Farkas, NFC-D: Washington vs. N.Y. Giants, 1943 (3-r)
Tom Fears, NFC-D: Los Angeles vs. Chi. Bears, 1950 (3-p)
Otto Graham, NFC: Cleveland vs. Detroit, 1954 (3-r)
Gary Collins, NFC: Cleveland vs. Baltimore, 1964 (3-p)
Craig Baynham, NFC-D: Dallas vs. Cleveland, 1967 (2-r, 1-p)
Fred Biletnikoff, AFC-D: Oakland vs. Kansas City, 1968 (3-p)
Tom Matte, NFC: Baltimore vs. Cleveland, 1968 (3-r)
Larry Schreiber, NFC-D: San Francisco vs. Dallas, 1972 (3-r)
Larry Csonka, AFC: Miami vs. Oakland, 1973 (3-r)
Franco Harris, AFC-D: Pittsburgh vs. Buffalo, 1974 (3-r)
Preston Pearson, NFC: Dallas vs. Los Angeles, 1975 (3-p)
Dave Casper, AFC-D: Oakland vs. Baltimore, 1977 (OT) (3-p)
Alvin Garrett, NFC-FR: Washington vs. Detroit, 1982 (3-p)
John Riggins, NFC-D: Washington vs. L.A. Rams, 1983 (3-r)
Roger Craig, SB: San Francisco vs. Miami, 1984 (1-r, 2-p)
Jerry Rice, NFC-D: San Francisco vs. Minnesota, 1988 (3-p)
Jerry Rice, SB: San Francisco vs. Denver, 1989 (3-p)
Kenneth Davis, AFC: Buffalo vs. L.A. Raiders, 1990 (3-r)
Andre Reed, AFC-FR: Buffalo vs. Houston, 1992 (OT) (3-p)
Sterling Sharpe, NFC-FR: Green Bay vs. Detroit, 1993 (3-p)
Napoleon McCallum, AFC-FR: L.A. Raiders vs. Denver, 1993 (3-r)
Thurman Thomas, AFC: Buffalo vs. Kansas City, 1993 (3-r)
William Floyd, NFC-D: San Francisco vs. Chicago, 1994 (3-r)
Ricky Watters, SB: San Francisco vs. San Diego, 1994 (1-r, 2-p)
Jerry Rice, SB: San Francisco vs. San Diego, 1994 (3-p)
Emmitt Smith, NFC: Dallas vs. Green Bay, 1995 (3-r)

Most Consecutive Games Scoring Touchdowns
8 John Stallworth, Pittsburgh, 1978-83
7 John Riggins, Washington, 1982-84
Marcus Allen, L.A. Raiders, 1982-85
Thurman Thomas, Buffalo, 1992-95 (current)
Emmitt Smith, Dallas, 1993-95 (current)
5 Duane Thomas, Dallas, 1970-71
Franco Harris, Pittsburgh, 1974-75
Franco Harris, Pittsburgh, 1977-79
James Lofton, Green Bay-Buffalo, 1982-90

POINTS AFTER TOUCHDOWN

Most (One-Point) Points After Touchdown, Career
49 George Blanda, Chi. Bears-Houston-Oakland, 19 games (49 att)
42 Mike Cofer, San Francisco, 12 games (46 att)
41 Rafael Septien, L.A. Rams-Dallas, 15 games (41 att)

Most (One-Point) Points After Touchdown, Game
8 Lou Groza, NFC: Cleveland vs. Detroit, 1954 (8 att)
Jim Martin, NFC: Detroit vs. Cleveland, 1957 (8 att)
George Blanda, AFC-D: Oakland vs. Houston, 1969 (8 att)
7 Danny Villanueva, NFC-D: Dallas vs. Cleveland, 1967 (7 att)

Raul Allegre, NFC-D: N.Y. Giants vs. San Francisco, 1986 (7 att)
Mike Cofer, SB: San Francisco vs. Denver, 1989 (8 att)
Lin Elliott, SB: Dallas vs. Buffalo, 1992 (7 att)
Doug Brien, SB: San Francisco vs. San Diego, 1994 (7 att)
Gary Anderson, NFC-FR: Philadelphia vs. Detroit, 1995 (7 att)
6 George Blair, AFC: San Diego vs. Boston, 1963 (6 att)
Mark Moseley, NFC-D: Washington vs. L.A. Rams, 1983 (6 att)
Uwe von Schamann, AFC: Miami vs. Pittsburgh, 1984 (6 att)
Ali Haji-Sheikh, SB: Washington vs. Denver, 1987 (6 att)
Scott Norwood, AFC: Buffalo vs. L.A. Raiders, 1990 (7 att)
Jeff Jaeger, AFC-FR: L.A. Raiders vs. Denver, 1993 (6 att)

Most (Kicking) Points After Touchdown, No Misses, Career
49 George Blanda, Chi. Bears-Houston-Oakland, 19 games
41 Rafael Septien, L.A. Rams-Dallas, 14 games
33 Chris Bahr, Oakland/L.A. Raiders, 11 games

Most Two-Point Conversions, Game
1 John Tracey, AFC-D: Buffalo vs. Boston, 1963
Mark Seay, SB: San Diego vs. San Francisco, 1994
Alfred Pupunu, SB: San Diego vs. San Francisco, 1994
O.J. McDuffie, AFC-FR: Miami vs. Buffalo, 1995
Herman Moore, NFC-FR: Detroit vs. Philadelphia, 1995
Ron Rivers, NFC-FR: Detroit vs. Philadelphia, 1995
Reggie Johnson, NFC-D: Philadelphia vs. Dallas, 1995

FIELD GOALS

Most Field Goals Attempted, Career
39 George Blanda, Chi. Bears-Houston-Oakland, 19 games
31 Mark Moseley, Washington-Cleveland, 11 games
26 Roy Gerela, Houston-Pittsburgh, 15 games

Most Field Goals Attempted, Game
6 George Blanda, AFC: Oakland vs. Houston, 1967
David Ray, NFC-D: Los Angeles vs. Dallas, 1973
Mark Moseley, AFC-D: Cleveland vs. N.Y. Jets, 1986 (OT)
Matt Bahr, NFC: N.Y. Giants vs. San Francisco, 1990
Steve Christie, AFC: Buffalo vs. Miami, 1992
5 By many players

Most Field Goals, Career
22 George Blanda, Chi. Bears-Houston-Oakland, 19 games
21 Matt Bahr, Pittsburgh-Cleveland-N.Y. Giants-New England, 14 games
20 Toni Fritsch, Dallas-Houston, 14 games

Most Field Goals, Game
5 Chuck Nelson, NFC-D: Minnesota vs. San Francisco, 1987
Matt Bahr, NFC: N.Y. Giants vs. San Francisco, 1990
Steve Christie, AFC: Buffalo vs. Miami, 1992
4 Gino Cappelletti, AFC-D: Boston vs. Buffalo, 1963
George Blanda, AFC: Oakland vs. Houston, 1967
Don Chandler, SB: Green Bay vs. Oakland, 1967
Curt Knight, NFC: Washington vs. Dallas, 1972
George Blanda, AFC-D: Oakland vs. Pittsburgh, 1973
Ray Wersching, SB: San Francisco vs. Cincinnati, 1981
Tony Franklin, AFC-FR: New England vs. N.Y. Jets, 1985
Jess Atkinson, NFC-FR: Washington vs. L.A. Rams, 1986
Luis Zendejas, NFC-D: Philadelphia vs. Chicago, 1988
Gary Anderson, AFC-FR: Pittsburgh vs. Houston, 1989 (OT)
Norm Johnson, AFC-D: Pittsburgh vs. Buffalo, 1995
3 By many players

Most Consecutive Games Scoring Field Goals
13 Toni Fritsch, Dallas-Houston, 1972-79
9 Kevin Butler, Chicago, 1985-91
Scott Norwood, Buffalo, 1988-91
8 Mark Moseley, Washington-Cleveland, 1982-86
Rich Karlis, Denver-Minnesota, 1984-89
Steve Christie, Buffalo, 1993-95
Gary Anderson, Pittsburgh-Philadelphia, 1989-95 (current)

Most Consecutive Field Goals
16 Gary Anderson, Pittsburgh-Philadelphia, 1989-95
15 Rafael Septien, Dallas, 1978-82
9 Chuck Nelson, Minnesota, 1987
Steve Christie, Buffalo, 1993-95

Longest Field Goal
58 Pete Stoyanovich, AFC-FR: Miami vs. Kansas City, 1990
54 Ed Murray, NFC-D: Detroit vs. San Francisco, 1983
Steve Christie, SB: Buffalo vs. Dallas, 1993
John Carney, AFC-FR: San Diego vs. Indianapolis, 1995
53 Al Del Greco, AFC-FR: Houston vs. N.Y. Jets, 1991

Highest Field Goal Percentage, Career (10 field goals)
90.9 Chuck Nelson, L.A. Rams-Minnesota, 6 games (11-10)
85.7 Rafael Septien, L.A. Rams-Dallas, 15 games (21-18)
Steve Christie, Buffalo, 9 games (21-18)
84.0 Matt Bahr, Pittsburgh-Cleveland-N.Y. Giants-New England, 14 games (25-21)

SAFETIES

Most Safeties, Game
1 Bill Willis, NFC-D: Cleveland vs. N.Y. Giants, 1950
Carl Eller, NFC-D: Minnesota vs. Los Angeles, 1969
George Andrie, NFC-D: Dallas vs. Detroit, 1970
Alan Page, NFC-D: Minnesota vs. Dallas, 1971
Dwight White, SB: Pittsburgh vs. Minnesota, 1974
Reggie Harrison, SB: Pittsburgh vs. Dallas, 1975
Jim Jensen, NFC-D: Dallas vs. Los Angeles, 1976
Ted Washington, AFC: Houston vs. Pittsburgh, 1978
Randy White, NFC-D: Dallas vs. Los Angeles, 1979
Henry Waechter, SB: Chicago vs. New England, 1985
Rulon Jones, AFC-FR: Denver vs. New England, 1986
George Martin, SB: N.Y. Giants vs. Denver, 1986
D.D. Hoggard, AFC: Cleveland vs. Denver, 1987
Bruce Smith, SB: Buffalo vs. N.Y. Giants, 1990
Reggie White, NFC-FR: Philadelphia vs. New Orleans, 1992
Willie Clay, NFC-FR: Detroit vs. Green Bay, 1994
Carnell Lake, AFC-D: Pittsburgh vs. Cleveland, 1994
Reuben Davis, AFC-D: San Diego vs. Miami, 1994

RUSHING

ATTEMPTS

Most Attempts, Career
400 Franco Harris, Pittsburgh, 19 games
313 Thurman Thomas, Buffalo, 18 games
302 Tony Dorsett, Dallas, 17 games

Most Attempts, Game
38 Ricky Bell, NFC-D: Tampa Bay vs. Philadelphia, 1979
John Riggins, SB: Washington vs. Miami, 1982
37 Lawrence McCutcheon, NFC-D: Los Angeles vs. St. Louis, 1975
John Riggins, NFC-D: Washington vs. Minnesota, 1982
36 John Riggins, NFC: Washington vs. Dallas, 1982
John Riggins, NFC: Washington vs. San Francisco, 1983

YARDS GAINED

Most Yards Gained, Career
1,556 Franco Harris, Pittsburgh, 19 games
1,383 Tony Dorsett, Dallas, 17 games
1,349 Thurman Thomas, Buffalo, 18 games

Most Yards Gained, Game
248 Eric Dickerson, NFC-D: L.A. Rams vs. Dallas, 1985
206 Keith Lincoln, AFC: San Diego vs. Boston, 1963
204 Timmy Smith, SB: Washington vs. Denver, 1987

Most Games, 100 or More Yards Rushing, Career
6 John Riggins, Washington, 9 games
Thurman Thomas, Buffalo, 18 games
Emmitt Smith, Dallas, 13 games
5 Franco Harris, Pittsburgh, 19 games
Marcus Allen, L.A. Raiders-Kansas City, 15 games
4 Larry Csonka, Miami, 12 games
Chuck Foreman, Minnesota, 13 games

Most Consecutive Games, 100 or More Yards Rushing
6 John Riggins, Washington, 1982-83
4 Thurman Thomas, Buffalo, 1990-91
3 Larry Csonka, Miami, 1973-74
Franco Harris, Pittsburgh, 1974-75
Marcus Allen, L.A. Raiders, 1983
Emmitt Smith, Dallas, 1992

Longest Run From Scrimmage
80 Roger Craig, NFC-D: San Francisco vs. Minnesota, 1988 (TD)
74 Marcus Allen, SB: L.A. Raiders vs. Washington, 1983 (TD)
71 Hugh McElhenny, NFC-D: San Francisco vs. Detroit, 1957
James Lofton, NFC-D: Green Bay vs. Dallas, 1982 (TD)

AVERAGE GAIN

Highest Average Gain, Career (75 attempts)
5.68 Roger Staubach, Dallas, 20 games (76-432)
5.14 Marcus Allen, L.A. Raiders-Kansas City, 15 games (255-1,310)
4.89 Eric Dickerson, L.A. Rams-Indianapolis, 7 games (148-724)

Highest Average Gain, Game (10 attempts)
15.90 Elmer Angsman, NFC: Chi. Cardinals vs. Philadelphia, 1947 (10-159)
15.85 Keith Lincoln, AFC: San Diego vs. Boston, 1963 (13-206)
11.31 Zack Crockett, AFC-FR: Indianapolis vs. San Diego, 1995 (13-147)

TOUCHDOWNS

Most Touchdowns, Career
16 Franco Harris, Pittsburgh, 19 games
Emmitt Smith, Dallas, 13 games
14 Thurman Thomas, Buffalo, 18 games
12 John Riggins, Washington, 9 games

Most Touchdowns, Game
5 Ricky Watters, NFC-D: San Francisco vs. N.Y. Giants, 1993

3 Andy Farkas, NFC-D: Washington vs. N.Y. Giants, 1943
Otto Graham, NFC: Cleveland vs. Detroit, 1954
Tom Matte, NFC: Baltimore vs. Cleveland, 1968
Larry Schreiber, NFC-D: San Francisco vs. Dallas, 1972
Larry Csonka, AFC: Miami vs. Oakland, 1973
Franco Harris, AFC-D: Pittsburgh vs. Buffalo, 1974
John Riggins, NFC-D: Washington vs. L.A. Rams, 1983
Kenneth Davis, AFC: Buffalo vs. L.A. Raiders, 1990
Napoleon McCallum, AFC-FR: L.A. Raiders vs. Denver, 1993
Thurman Thomas, AFC: Buffalo vs. Kansas City, 1993
William Floyd, NFC-D: San Francisco vs. Chicago, 1994
Emmitt Smith, NFC: Dallas vs. Green Bay, 1995

Most Consecutive Games Rushing for Touchdowns
7 John Riggins, Washington, 1982-84
Emmitt Smith, Dallas, 1993-95 (current)
6 Thurman Thomas, Buffalo, 1992-95 (current)
5 Franco Harris, Pittsburgh, 1974-75
Franco Harris, Pittsburgh, 1977-79

PASSING

PASSER RATING

Highest Passer Rating, Career (150 attempts)
104.8 Bart Starr, Green Bay, 10 games
104.3 Troy Aikman, Dallas, 12 games
95.6 Joe Montana, San Francisco-Kansas City, 23 games

ATTEMPTS

Most Passes Attempted, Career
734 Joe Montana, San Francisco-Kansas City, 23 games
518 Dan Marino, Miami, 13 games
513 Jim Kelly, Buffalo, 16 games

Most Passes Attempted, Game
65 Steve Young, NFC-D: San Francisco vs. Green Bay, 1995
64 Bernie Kosar, AFC-D: Cleveland vs. N.Y. Jets, 1986 (OT)
Dan Marino, AFC-FR: Miami vs. Buffalo, 1995
58 Jim Kelly, SB: Buffalo vs. Washington, 1991

COMPLETIONS

Most Passes Completed, Career
460 Joe Montana, San Francisco-Kansas City, 23 games
301 Jim Kelly, Buffalo, 16 games
291 Dan Marino, Miami, 13 games

Most Passes Completed, Game
36 Warren Moon, AFC-FR: Houston vs. Buffalo, 1992 (OT)
33 Dan Fouts, AFC-D: San Diego vs. Miami, 1981 (OT)
Bernie Kosar, AFC-D: Cleveland vs. N.Y. Jets, 1986 (OT)
Dan Marino, AFC-FR: Miami vs. Buffalo, 1995
32 Neil Lomax, NFC-FR: St. Louis vs. Green Bay, 1982
Danny White, NFC-FR: Dallas vs. L.A. Rams, 1983
Warren Moon, AFC-D: Houston vs. Kansas City, 1993
Neil O'Donnell, AFC: Pittsburgh vs. San Diego, 1994
Steve Young, NFC-D: San Francisco vs. Green Bay, 1995

COMPLETION PERCENTAGE

Highest Completion Percentage, Career (150 attempts)
68.3 Troy Aikman, Dallas, 12 games (350-239)
66.3 Ken Anderson, Cincinnati, 6 games (166-110)
64.3 Warren Moon, Houston-Minnesota, 10 games (403-259)

Highest Completion Percentage, Game (15 completions)
88.0 Phil Simms, SB: N.Y. Giants vs. Denver, 1986 (25-22)
86.7 Joe Montana, NFC: San Francisco vs. L.A. Rams, 1989 (30-26)
84.2 David Woodley, AFC-FR: Miami vs. New England, 1982 (19-16)

YARDS GAINED

Most Yards Gained, Career
5,772 Joe Montana, San Francisco-Kansas City, 23 games
3,833 Terry Bradshaw, Pittsburgh, 19 games
3,624 Jim Kelly, Buffalo, 16 games

Most Yards Gained, Game
489 Bernie Kosar, AFC-D: Cleveland vs. N.Y. Jets, 1986 (OT)
433 Dan Fouts, AFC-D: San Diego vs. Miami, 1981 (OT)
422 Dan Marino, AFC-FR: Miami vs. Buffalo, 1995

Most Games, 300 or More Yards Passing, Career
6 Joe Montana, San Francisco-Kansas City, 23 games
5 Dan Fouts, San Diego, 7 games
4 Warren Moon, Houston-Minnesota, 10 games
Troy Aikman, Dallas, 12 games
Dan Marino, Miami, 13 games

Most Consecutive Games, 300 or More Yards Passing
4 Dan Fouts, San Diego, 1979-81
3 Jim Kelly, Buffalo, 1989-90
Warren Moon, Houston, 1991-93
2 Daryle Lamonica, Oakland, 1968
Ken Anderson, Cincinnati, 1981-82
Terry Bradshaw, Pittsburgh, 1979-82
Joe Montana, San Francisco, 1983-84
Dan Marino, Miami, 1984
Troy Aikman, Dallas, 1994

Longest Pass Completion
94 Troy Aikman (to Harper), NFC-D: Dallas vs. Green Bay, 1994 (TD)
93 Daryle Lamonica (to Dubenion), AFC-D: Buffalo vs. Boston, 1963 (TD)
88 George Blanda (to Cannon), AFC: Houston vs. L.A. Chargers, 1960 (TD)

AVERAGE GAIN

Highest Average Gain, Career (150 attempts)
8.65 Troy Aikman, Dallas, 12 games (350-3,029)
8.45 Joe Theismann, Washington, 10 games (211-1,782)
8.43 Jim Plunkett, Oakland/L.A.Raiders, 10 games (272-2,293)

Highest Average Gain, Game (20 attempts)
14.71 Terry Bradshaw, SB: Pittsburgh vs. Los Angeles, 1979 (21-309)
13.33 Bob Waterfield, NFC-D: Los Angeles vs. Chi. Bears, 1950 (21-280)
13.16 Dan Marino, AFC: Miami vs. Pittsburgh, 1984 (32-421)

TOUCHDOWNS

Most Touchdown Passes, Career
45 Joe Montana, San Francisco-Kansas City, 23 games
30 Terry Bradshaw, Pittsburgh, 19 games
29 Dan Marino, Miami, 13 games

Most Touchdown Passes, Game
6 Daryle Lamonica, AFC-D: Oakland vs. Houston, 1969
Steve Young, SB: San Francisco vs. San Diego, 1994
5 Sid Luckman, NFC: Chi. Bears vs. Washington, 1943
Daryle Lamonica, AFC-D: Oakland vs. Kansas City, 1968
Joe Montana, SB: San Francisco vs. Denver, 1989
4 Otto Graham, NFC: Cleveland vs. Los Angeles, 1950
Tobin Rote, NFC: Detroit vs. Cleveland, 1957
Bart Starr, NFC: Green Bay vs. Dallas, 1966
Ken Stabler, AFC-D: Oakland vs. Miami, 1974
Roger Staubach, NFC: Dallas vs. Los Angeles, 1975
Terry Bradshaw, SB: Pittsburgh vs. Dallas, 1978
Don Strock, AFC-D: Miami vs. San Diego, 1981 (OT)
Lynn Dickey, NFC-FR: Green Bay vs. St. Louis, 1982
Dan Marino, AFC: Miami vs. Pittsburgh, 1984
Phil Simms, NFC-D: N.Y. Giants vs. San Francisco, 1986
Doug Williams, SB: Washington vs. Denver, 1987
Jim Kelly, AFC-D: Buffalo vs. Cleveland, 1989
Joe Montana, NFC-D: San Francisco vs. Minnesota, 1989
Warren Moon, AFC-FR: Houston vs. Buffalo, 1992 (OT)
Frank Reich, AFC-FR: Buffalo vs. Houston, 1992 (OT)
Troy Aikman, SB: Dallas vs. Buffalo, 1992

Most Consecutive Games, Touchdown Passes
13 Dan Marino, Miami, 1983-95 (current)
10 Ken Stabler, Oakland, 1973-77
Joe Montana, San Francisco-Kansas City, 1988-93
9 John Elway, Denver, 1984-89

HAD INTERCEPTED

Lowest Percentage, Passes Had Intercepted, Career (150 attempts)
1.41 Bart Starr, Green Bay, 10 games (213-3)
2.15 Phil Simms, N.Y. Giants, 10 games (279-6)
2.27 Steve Young, San Francisco, 16 games (308-7)

Most Attempts Without Interception, Game
54 Neil O'Donnell, AFC: Pittsburgh vs. San Diego, 1994
48 Warren Moon, AFC-FR: Houston vs. Pittsburgh, 1989 (OT)
47 Daryle Lamonica, AFC: Oakland vs. N.Y. Jets, 1968

Most Passes Had Intercepted, Career
27 Jim Kelly, Buffalo, 16 games
26 Terry Bradshaw, Pittsburgh, 19 games
21 Joe Montana, San Francisco-Kansas City, 23 games

Most Passes Had Intercepted, Game
6 Frank Filchock, NFC: N.Y. Giants vs. Chi. Bears, 1946
Bobby Layne, NFC: Detroit vs. Cleveland, 1954
Norm Van Brocklin, NFC: Los Angeles vs. Cleveland, 1955
5 Frank Filchock, NFC: Washington vs. Chi. Bears, 1940
George Blanda, AFC: Houston vs. San Diego, 1961
George Blanda, AFC: Houston vs. Dall. Texans, 1962 (OT)
Y.A. Tittle, NFC: N.Y. Giants vs. Chicago, 1963
Mike Phipps, AFC-D: Cleveland vs. Miami, 1972
Dan Pastorini, AFC: Houston vs. Pittsburgh, 1978
Dan Fouts, AFC-D: San Diego vs. Houston, 1979
Tommy Kramer, NFC-D: Minnesota vs. Philadelphia, 1980
Dan Fouts, AFC-D: San Diego vs. Miami, 1982
Richard Todd, AFC: N.Y. Jets vs Miami, 1982
Gary Danielson, NFC-D: Detroit vs. San Francisco, 1983
Jay Schroeder, AFC: L.A. Raiders vs. Buffalo, 1990
4 By many players

POSTSEASON GAME RECORDS

PASS RECEIVING

RECEPTIONS

Most Receptions, Career

111 Jerry Rice, San Francisco, 19 games
77 Andre Reed, Buffalo, 18 games
74 Michael Irvin, Dallas, 13 games

Most Receptions, Game

13 Kellen Winslow, AFC-D: San Diego vs. Miami, 1981 (OT)
Thurman Thomas, AFC-D: Buffalo vs. Cleveland, 1989
Shannon Sharpe, AFC-FR: Denver vs. L.A. Raiders, 1993
12 Raymond Berry, NFC: Baltimore vs. N.Y. Giants, 1958
Michael Irvin, NFC: Dallas vs. San Francisco, 1994
11 Dante Lavelli, NFC: Cleveland vs. Los Angeles, 1950
Dan Ross, SB: Cincinnati vs. San Francisco, 1981
Franco Harris, AFC-FR: Pittsburgh vs. San Diego, 1982
Steve Watson, AFC-D: Denver vs. Pittsburgh, 1984
John L. Williams, AFC-D: Seattle vs. Cincinnati, 1988
Jerry Rice, SB: San Francisco vs. Cincinnati, 1988
Ernest Givins, AFC-FR: Houston vs. Pittsburgh, 1989 (OT)
Amp Lee, NFC-D: Minnesota vs. Chicago, 1994
Jay Novacek, NFC-D: Dallas vs. Green Bay, 1994
O.J. McDuffie, AFC-FR: Miami vs. Buffalo, 1995
Jerry Rice, NFC-C: San Francisco vs. Green Bay, 1995

Most Consecutive Games, Pass Receptions

22 Drew Pearson, Dallas, 1973-83
19 Jerry Rice, San Francisco, 1985-95 (current)
18 Paul Warfield, Cleveland-Miami, 1964-74
Cliff Branch, Oakland/L.A. Raiders, 1974-83

YARDS GAINED

Most Yards Gained, Career

1,656 Jerry Rice, San Francisco, 19 games
1,289 Cliff Branch, Oakland/L.A. Raiders, 22 games
1,167 Fred Biletnikoff, Oakland, 19 games

Most Yards Gained, Game

227 Anthony Carter, NFC-D: Minnesota vs. San Francisco, 1987
215 Jerry Rice, SB: San Francisco vs. Cincinnati, 1988
198 Tom Fears, NFC-D: Los Angeles vs. Chi. Bears, 1950

Most Games, 100 or More Yards Receiving, Career

7 Jerry Rice, San Francisco, 19 games
5 John Stallworth, Pittsburgh, 18 games
Andre Reed, Buffalo, 18 games
Michael Irvin, Dallas, 13 games
4 Fred Biletnikoff, Oakland, 19 games
Dwight Clark, San Francisco, 7 games
Art Monk, Washington, 15 games
Keith Jackson, Philadelphia-Miami-Green Bay, 10 games

Most Consecutive Games, 100 or More Yards Receiving, Career

3 Tom Fears, Los Angeles, 1950-51
Jerry Rice, San Francisco, 1988-89
2 By many players

Longest Reception

94 Alvin Harper (from Aikman), NFC-D: Dallas vs. Green Bay, 1994 (TD)
93 Elbert Dubenion (from Lamonica), AFC-D: Buffalo vs. Boston, 1963 (TD)
88 Billy Cannon (from Blanda), AFC: Houston vs. L.A. Chargers, 1960 (TD)

AVERAGE GAIN

Highest Average Gain, Career (20 receptions)

27.3 Alvin Harper, Dallas, 10 games (24-655)
23.7 Willie Gault, Chicago-L.A. Raiders, 12 games (21-497)
22.8 Harold Jackson, L.A. Rams-New England-Minnesota-Seattle, 14 games (24-548)

Highest Average Gain, Game (3 receptions)

46.3 Harold Jackson, NFC: Los Angeles vs. Minnesota, 1974 (3-139)
42.7 Billy Cannon, AFC: Houston vs. L.A. Chargers, 1960 (3-128)
42.0 Lenny Moore, NFC: Baltimore vs. N.Y. Giants, 1959 (3-126)

TOUCHDOWNS

Most Touchdowns, Career

17 Jerry Rice, San Francisco, 19 games
12 John Stallworth, Pittsburgh, 18 games
10 Fred Biletnikoff, Oakland, 19 games

Most Touchdowns, Game

3 Tom Fears, NFC-D: Los Angeles vs. Chi. Bears, 1950
Gary Collins, NFC: Cleveland vs. Baltimore, 1964
Fred Biletnikoff, AFC-D: Oakland vs. Kansas City, 1968
Preston Pearson, NFC: Dallas vs. Los Angeles, 1975
Dave Casper, AFC-D: Oakland vs. Baltimore, 1977 (OT)
Alvin Garrett, NFC-FR: Washington vs. Detroit, 1982
Jerry Rice, NFC-D: San Francisco vs. Minnesota, 1988
Jerry Rice, SB: San Francisco vs. Denver, 1989
Andre Reed, AFC-FR: Buffalo vs. Houston, 1992 (OT)
Sterling Sharpe, NFC-FR: Green Bay vs. Detroit, 1993
Jerry Rice, SB: San Francisco vs. San Diego, 1994

Most Consecutive Games, Touchdown Passes Caught

8 John Stallworth, Pittsburgh, 1978-83
5 James Lofton, Green Bay-Buffalo, 1982-90
4 Lynn Swann, Pittsburgh, 1978-79
Harold Carmichael, Philadelphia, 1978-80
Fred Solomon, San Francisco, 1983-84
Jerry Rice, San Francisco, 1988-89
John Taylor, San Francisco, 1988-89

INTERCEPTIONS BY

Most Interceptions, Career

9 Charlie Waters, Dallas, 25 games
Bill Simpson, Los Angeles-Buffalo, 11 games
Ronnie Lott, San Francisco-L.A. Raiders, 20 games
8 Lester Hayes, Oakland/L.A. Raiders, 13 games
7 Willie Brown, Oakland, 17 games
Dennis Thurman, Dallas, 14 games

Most Interceptions, Game

4 Vernon Perry, AFC-D: Houston vs. San Diego, 1979
3 Joe Laws, NFC: Green Bay vs. N.Y. Giants, 1944
Charlie Waters, NFC-D: Dallas vs. Chicago, 1977
Rod Martin, SB: Oakland vs. Philadelphia, 1980
Dennis Thurman, NFC-D: Dallas vs. Green Bay, 1982
A.J. Duhe, AFC: Miami vs. N.Y. Jets, 1982
2 By many players

Most Consecutive Games, Interceptions

3 Warren Lahr, Cleveland, 1950-51
Ken Gorgal, Cleveland, 1950-53
Joe Schmidt, Detroit, 1954-57
Emmitt Thomas, Kansas City, 1969
Mel Renfro, Dallas, 1970
Rick Volk, Baltimore, 1970-71
Mike Wagner, Pittsburgh, 1975-76
Randy Hughes, Dallas, 1977-78
Vernon Perry, Houston, 1979-80
Lester Hayes, Oakland, 1980
Gerald Small, Miami, 1982
Lester Hayes, L.A. Raiders, 1982-83
Fred Marion, New England, 1985
John Harris, Seattle-Minnesota, 1984-87
Felix Wright, Cleveland, 1987-88
Kurt Gouveia, Washington, 1991
Eric Davis, San Francisco, 1994
Deion Sanders, San Francisco-Dallas, 1994-95

YARDS GAINED

Most Yards Gained, Career

196 Willie Brown, Oakland, 17 games
187 Ronnie Lott, San Francisco-L.A.-Raiders, 20 games
151 Glen Edwards, Pittsburgh-San Diego, 17 games

Most Yards Gained, Game

101 George Teague, NFC-FR: Green Bay vs. Detroit, 1993
98 Darrol Ray, AFC-FR: N.Y. Jets vs. Cincinnati, 1982
94 LeRoy Irvin, NFC-FR: L.A. Rams vs. Dallas, 1983

Longest Return

101 George Teague, NFC-FR: Green Bay vs. Detroit, 1993 (TD)
98 Darrol Ray, AFC-FR: N.Y. Jets vs. Cincinnati, 1982 (TD)
94 LeRoy Irvin, NFC-FR: L.A. Rams vs. Dallas, 1983

TOUCHDOWNS

Most Touchdowns, Career

3 Willie Brown, Oakland, 17 games
2 Lester Hayes, Oakland/L.A. Raiders, 13 games
Ronnie Lott, San Francisco-L.A. Raiders, 20 games
Darrell Green, Washington, 16 games
Melvin Jenkins, Seattle-Detroit, 5 games

Most Touchdowns, Game

1 By many players.

PUNTING

Most Punts, Career

111 Ray Guy, Oakland/L.A. Raiders, 22 games
84 Danny White, Dallas, 18 games
73 Mike Eischeid, Oakland-Minnesota, 14 games

Most Punts, Game

14 Dave Jennings, AFC-D: N.Y. Jets vs. Cleveland, 1986 (OT)
12 David Lee, AFC-D: Baltimore vs. Oakland, 1977 (OT)
11 Ken Strong, NFC: N.Y. Giants vs. Chi. Bears, 1933
Jim Norton, AFC: Houston vs. Oakland, 1967
Ode Burrell, AFC-D: Houston vs. Oakland, 1969
Dale Hatcher, NFC: L.A. Rams vs. Chicago, 1985

Longest Punt
76 Ed Danowski, NFC: N.Y. Giants vs. Detroit, 1935
Mike Horan, AFC: Denver vs. Buffalo, 1991
72 Charlie Conerly, NFC-D: N.Y. Giants vs. Cleveland, 1950
Yale Lary, NFC: Detroit vs. Cleveland, 1953
71 Ray Guy, AFC: Oakland vs. San Diego, 1980

AVERAGE YARDAGE
Highest Average, Career (25 punts)
44.5 Rich Camarillo, New England, 6 games (35-1,559)
44.4 Lee Johnson, Cleveland-Cincinnati, 7 games (28-1,244)
43.5 John Kidd, Buffalo-San Diego-Miami, 8 games (37-1,610)
Highest Average, Game (4 punts)
56.0 Ray Guy, AFC: Oakland vs. San Diego, 1980 (4-224)
52.5 Sammy Baugh, NFC: Washington vs. Chi. Bears, 1942 (6-315)
51.6 Lee Johnson, AFC-D: Cincinnati vs. L.A. Raiders, 1990 (5-258)

PUNT RETURNS
Most Punt Returns, Career
25 Theo Bell, Pittsburgh-Tampa Bay, 10 games
21 Gerald McNeil, Cleveland-Houston, 8 games
19 Willie Wood, Green Bay, 10 games
Butch Johnson, Dallas-Denver, 18 games
Phil McConkey, N.Y. Giants, 5 games
Most Punt Returns, Game
7 Ron Gardin, AFC-D: Baltimore vs. Cincinnati, 1970
Carl Roaches, AFC-FR: Houston vs. Oakland, 1980
Gerald McNeil, AFC-D: Cleveland vs. N.Y. Jets, 1986 (OT)
Phil McConkey, NFC-D: N.Y. Giants vs. San Francisco, 1986
6 George McAfee, NFC-D: Chi. Bears vs. Los Angeles, 1950
Eddie Brown, NFC-D: Washington vs. Minnesota, 1976
Theo Bell, AFC: Pittsburgh vs. Houston, 1978
Eddie Brown, NFC: Los Angeles vs. Tampa Bay, 1979
John Sciarra, NFC: Philadelphia vs. Dallas, 1980
Kurt Sohn, AFC: N.Y. Jets vs. Miami, 1982
Mike Nelms, SB: Washington vs. Miami, 1982
Anthony Carter, NFC-FR: Minnesota vs. New Orleans, 1987
5 By many players

YARDS GAINED
Most Yards Gained, Career
259 Anthony Carter, Minnesota-Detroit, 9 games
221 Neal Colzie, Oakland-Miami-Tampa Bay, 10 games
211 Gerald McNeil, Cleveland-Houston, 8 games
Most Yards Gained, Game
143 Anthony Carter, NFC-FR: Minnesota vs. New Orleans, 1987
141 Bob Hayes, NFC-D: Dallas vs. Cleveland, 1967
102 Charley Trippi, NFC: Chi. Cardinals vs. Philadelphia, 1947
Longest Return
84 Anthony Carter, NFC-FR: Minnesota vs. New Orleans, 1987 (TD)
81 Hugh Gallarneau, NFC-D: Chi. Bears vs. Green Bay, 1941 (TD)
79 Bosh Pritchard, NFC-D: Philadelphia vs. Pittsburgh, 1947 (TD)

AVERAGE YARDAGE
Highest Average, Career (10 returns)
15.2 Anthony Carter, Minnesota-Detroit, 9 games (17-259)
14.3 Antonio Freeman, Green Bay, 3 games (10-143)
12.9 Brian Mitchell, Washington, 7 games (11-142)
Highest Average Gain, Game (3 returns)
47.0 Bob Hayes, NFC-D: Dallas vs. Cleveland, 1967 (3-141)
29.0 George (Butch) Byrd, AFC: Buffalo vs. San Diego, 1965 (3-87)
25.3 Bosh Pritchard, NFC-D: Philadelphia vs. Pittsburgh, 1947 (4-101)

TOUCHDOWNS
Most Touchdowns
1 Hugh Gallarneau, NFC-D: Chicago Bears vs. Green Bay, 1941
Bosh Pritchard, NFC-D: Philadelphia vs. Pittsburgh, 1947
Charley Trippi, NFC: Chicago Cardinals vs. Philadelphia, 1947
Verda (Vitamin T) Smith, NFC-D: Los Angeles vs. Detroit, 1952
George (Butch) Byrd, AFC: Buffalo vs. San Diego, 1965
Golden Richards, NFC: Dallas vs. Minnesota, 1973
Wes Chandler, AFC-D: San Diego vs. Miami, 1981 (OT)
Shaun Gayle, NFC-D: Chicago vs. N.Y. Giants, 1985
Anthony Carter, NFC-FR: Minnesota vs. New Orleans, 1987
Darrell Green, NFC-D: Washington vs. Chicago, 1987
Antonio Freeman, NFC-FR: Green Bay vs. Atlanta, 1995

KICKOFF RETURNS
Most Kickoff Returns, Career
29 Fulton Walker, Miami-L.A. Raiders, 10 games
22 Eric Metcalf, Cleveland-Atlanta, 5 games
21 Ken Bell, Denver, 9 games
Most Kickoff Returns, Game
8 Marc Logan, AFC-D: Miami vs. Buffalo, 1990
Andre Coleman, SB: San Diego vs. San Francisco, 1994
7 Don Bingham, NFC: Chi. Bears vs. N.Y. Giants, 1956
Reggie Brown, NFC-FR: Atlanta vs. Minnesota, 1982
David Verser, AFC-FR: Cincinnati vs. N.Y. Jets, 1982
Del Rodgers, NFC-D: Green Bay vs. Dallas, 1982
Henry Ellard, NFC-D: L.A. Rams vs. Washington, 1983
Stephen Starring, SB: New England vs. Chicago, 1985
Darick Holmes, AFC-D: Buffalo vs. Pittsburgh, 1995
Antonio Freeman, NFC: Green Bay vs. Dallas, 1995
6 By many players

YARDS GAINED
Most Yards Gained, Career
677 Fulton Walker, Miami-L.A. Raiders, 10 games
499 Eric Metcalf, Cleveland-Atlanta, 5 games
483 Andre Coleman, San Diego, 4 games
Most Yards Gained, Game
244 Andre Coleman, SB: San Diego vs. San Francisco, 1994
190 Fulton Walker, SB: Miami vs. Washington, 1982
170 Les (Speedy) Duncan, NFC-D: Washington vs. San Francisco, 1971
Longest Return
98 Fulton Walker, SB: Miami vs. Washington, 1982 (TD)
Andre Coleman, SB: San Diego vs. San Francisco, 1994 (TD)
97 Vic Washington, NFC-D: San Francisco vs. Dallas, 1972 (TD)
93 Stanford Jennings, SB: Cincinnati vs. San Francisco, 1988 (TD)

AVERAGE YARDAGE
Highest Average, Career (10 returns)
30.1 Carl Garrett, Oakland, 5 games (16-481)
27.9 George Atkinson, Oakland, 16 games (12-335)
25.7 Nate Lewis, San Diego-Chicago, 4 games (11-283)
Highest Average, Game (3 returns)
56.7 Les (Speedy) Duncan, NFC-D: Washington vs. San Francisco, 1971 (3-170)
51.3 Ed Podolak, AFC-D: Kansas City vs. Miami, 1971 (OT) (3-154)
49.0 Les (Speedy) Duncan, AFC: San Diego vs. Buffalo, 1964 (3-147)

TOUCHDOWNS
Most Touchdowns
1 Vic Washington, NFC-D: San Francisco vs. Dallas, 1972
Nat Moore, AFC-D: Miami vs. Oakland, 1974
Marshall Johnson, AFC-D: Baltimore vs. Oakland, 1977 (OT)
Fulton Walker, SB: Miami vs. Washington, 1982
Stanford Jennings, SB: Cincinnati vs. San Francisco, 1988
Eric Metcalf, AFC-D: Cleveland vs. Buffalo, 1989
Andre Coleman, SB: San Diego vs. San Francisco, 1994

FUMBLES
Most Fumbles, Career
16 Warren Moon, Houston-Minnesota, 10 games
13 Tony Dorsett, Dallas, 17 games
10 Franco Harris, Pittsburgh, 19 games
Terry Bradshaw, Pittsburgh, 19 games
Roger Staubach, Dallas, 20 games
Most Fumbles, Game
5 Warren Moon, AFC-D: Houston vs. Kansas City, 1993
4 Brian Sipe, AFC-D: Cleveland vs. Oakland, 1980
3 By many players

RECOVERIES
Most Own Fumbles Recovered, Career
8 Warren Moon, Houston-Minnesota, 10 games
6 John Elway, Denver, 14 games
5 Roger Staubach, Dallas, 20 games
Most Opponents' Fumbles Recovered, Career
4 Cliff Harris, Dallas, 21 games
Harvey Martin, Dallas, 22 games
Ted Hendricks, Baltimore-Oakland/L.A. Raiders, 21 games
Alvin Walton, Washington, 9 games
Monte Coleman, Washington, 21 games
3 Paul Krause, Minnesota, 19 games
Jack Lambert, Pittsburgh, 18 games
Fred Dryer, Los Angeles, 14 games
Charlie Waters, Dallas, 25 games
Jack Ham, Pittsburgh, 16 games
Mike Hegman, Dallas, 16 games
Tom Jackson, Denver, 10 games
Rich Milot, Washington, 13 games
Mike Singletary, Chicago, 12 games
Darryl Grant, Washington, 16 games
Wes Hopkins, Philadelphia, 3 games
Wilber Marshall, Chicago-Washington, 15 games

2 By many players

Most Fumbles Recovered, Game, Own and Opponents'

3 Jack Lambert, AFC: Pittsburgh vs. Oakland, 1975 (3 opp)
Ron Jaworski, NFC-FR: Philadelphia vs. N.Y. Giants, 1981 (3 own)
2 By many players

YARDS GAINED

Longest Return

93 Andy Russell, AFC-D: Pittsburgh vs. Baltimore, 1975 (opp, TD)
64 Leon Lett, SB: Dallas vs. Buffalo, 1992 (opp)
60 Mike Curtis, NFC-D: Baltimore vs. Minnesota, 1968 (opp, TD)
Hugh Green, NFC-FR: Tampa Bay vs. Dallas, 1982 (opp, TD)

TOUCHDOWNS

Most Touchdowns

1 By many players

COMBINED NET YARDS GAINED

Rushing, receiving, interception returns, punt returns, kickoff returns, and fumble returns.

ATTEMPTS

Most Attempts, Career

454 Franco Harris, Pittsburgh, 19 games
387 Thurman Thomas, Buffalo, 18 games
350 Tony Dorsett, Dallas, 17 games

Most Attempts, Game

40 Lawrence McCutcheon, NFC-D: Los Angeles vs. St. Louis, 1975
39 John Riggins, SB: Washington vs. Miami, 1982
Rodney Hampton, NFC-FR: N.Y. Giants vs. Minnesota, 1993
38 Ricky Bell, NFC-D: Tampa Bay vs. Philadelphia, 1979
Rob Carpenter, NFC-FR: N.Y. Giants vs. Philadelphia, 1981

YARDS GAINED

Most Yards Gained, Career

2,060 Franco Harris, Pittsburgh, 19 games
2,004 Thurman Thomas, Buffalo, 18 games
1,832 Marcus Allen, L.A. Raiders-Kansas City, 15 games

Most Yards Gained, Game

350 Ed Podolak, AFC-D: Kansas City vs. Miami, 1971 (OT)
329 Keith Lincoln, AFC: San Diego vs. Boston, 1963
285 Bob Hayes, NFC-D: Dallas vs. Cleveland, 1967

SACKS

Sacks have been compiled since 1982.

Most Sacks, Career

12 Bruce Smith, Buffalo, 17 games
11 Charles Haley, San Francisco-Dallas, 19 games
10.5 Richard Dent, Chicago-San Francisco, 11 games

Most Sacks, Game

3.5 Rich Milot, NFC-D: Washington vs. Chicago, 1984
Richard Dent, NFC-D: Chicago vs. N.Y. Giants, 1985
3 Richard Dent, NFC-D: Chicago vs. Washington, 1984
Garin Veris, AFC-FR: New England vs. N.Y. Jets, 1985
Gary Jeter, NFC-D: L.A. Rams vs. Dallas, 1985
Carl Hairston, AFC-D: Cleveland vs. N.Y. Jets, 1986 (OT)
Charles Mann, NFC-D: Washington vs. Chicago, 1987
Kevin Greene, NFC-FR: L.A. Rams vs. Minnesota, 1988
Greg Townsend, AFC-D: L.A. Raiders vs. Cincinnati, 1990
Wilber Marshall, NFC: Washington vs. Detroit, 1991
Fred Stokes, NFC-FR: Washington vs. Minnesota, 1992
Pierce Holt, NFC-D: San Francisco vs. Washington, 1992
Tony Casillas, NFC: Dallas vs. San Francisco, 1992
Gerald Williams, AFC-FR: Pittsburgh vs. Kansas City, 1993
2.5 Lyle Alzado, AFC-D: L.A. Raiders vs. Pittsburgh, 1983
Jacob Green, AFC-FR: Seattle vs. L.A. Raiders, 1984
Larry Roberts, NFC-D: San Francisco vs. Minnesota, 1988
Leslie O'Neal, AFC-FR: San Diego vs. Kansas City, 1992

TEAM RECORDS

GAMES, VICTORIES, DEFEATS

Most Seasons Participating in Postseason Games

23 N.Y. Giants, 1933-35, 1938-39, 1941, 1943-44, 1946, 1950, 1956, 1958-59,1961-63, 1981, 1984-86, 1989-90, 1993
Cleveland, 1950-55, 1957-58, 1964-65, 1967-69, 1971-72, 1980, 1982, 1985-89, 1994
Dallas, 1966-73, 1975-83, 1985, 1991-95
22 Cleveland/L.A. Rams, 1945, 1949-52, 1955, 1967, 1969, 1973-80, 1983-86, 1988-89
21 Chicago, 1933-34, 1937, 1940-43, 1946, 1950, 1956, 1963, 1977, 1979, 1984-88, 1990-91, 1994

Most Consecutive Seasons Participating in Postseason Games

9 Dallas, 1975-83
8 Dallas, 1966-73
Pittsburgh, 1972-79
Los Angeles, 1973-80
San Francisco, 1983-90
7 Houston, 1987-93

Most Games

49 Dallas, 1966-73, 1975-83, 1985, 1991-95
36 Oakland/L.A. Raiders, 1967-70, 1973-77, 1980, 1982-85, 1990-91, 1993
35 Boston/Washington, 1936-37, 1940, 1942-43, 1945, 1971-74, 1976-77, 1982-84, 1986-87, 1990-92

Most Games Won

31 Dallas, 1967, 1970-73, 1975, 1977-78, 1980-82, 1991-95
21 Washington, 1937, 1942-43, 1972, 1982-83, 1986-87, 1990-92
Oakland/L.A. Raiders, 1967-70, 1973-77, 1980, 1982-83, 1990, 1993
San Francisco, 1970-71, 1981, 1983-84, 1988-90, 1992-94
19 Pittsburgh, 1972, 1974-76, 1978-79, 1984, 1989, 1994-95

Most Consecutive Games Won

9 Green Bay, 1961-62, 1965-67
7 Pittsburgh, 1974-76
San Francisco, 1988-90
Dallas, 1992-94
6 Miami, 1972-73
Pittsburgh, 1978-79
Washington, 1982-83

Most Games Lost

20 L.A. Rams, 1949-50, 1952, 1955, 1967, 1969, 1973-80, 1983-86, 1988-89
19 Cleveland, 1951-53, 1957-58, 1965, 1967-69, 1971-72, 1980, 1982, 1985-89, 1994
18 N.Y. Giants, 1933, 1935, 1939, 1941, 1943-44, 1946, 1950, 1958-59, 1961-63, 1981, 1984-85, 1989, 1993
Minnesota, 1968-71, 1973-78, 1980, 1982, 1987-89, 1992-94
Dallas, 1966-70, 1972-73, 1975-76, 1978-83, 1985, 1991, 1994

Most Consecutive Games Lost

6 N.Y. Giants, 1939, 1941, 1943-44, 1946, 1950
Cleveland, 1969, 1971-72, 1980, 1982, 1985
5 N.Y. Giants, 1958-59, 1961-63
Los Angeles, 1952, 1955, 1967, 1969, 1973
Denver, 1977-79, 1983-84
Baltimore/Indianapolis, 1971, 1975-77, 1987
Philadelphia, 1980-81, 1988-90
Minnesota, 1988-89, 1992-94 (current)
4 Washington, 1972-74, 1976
Miami, 1974, 1978-79, 1981
Chi. Cardinals/St. Louis, 1948, 1974-75, 1982 (current)
Boston/New England, 1963, 1976, 1978, 1982
New Orleans, 1987, 1990-92 (current)
Detroit, 1991, 1993-95 (current)

SCORING

Most Points, Game

73 NFC: Chi. Bears vs. Washington, 1940
59 NFC: Detroit vs. Cleveland, 1957
58 NFC-FR: Philadelphia vs. Detroit, 1995

Most Points, Both Teams, Game

95 NFC-FR: Philadelphia (58) vs. Detroit (37), 1995
79 AFC-D: San Diego (41) vs. Miami (38), 1981 (OT)
AFC-FR: Buffalo (41) vs. Houston (38), 1992 (OT)
78 AFC-D: Buffalo (44) vs. Miami (34), 1990

Fewest Points, Both Teams, Game

5 NFC-D: Detroit (0) vs. Dallas (5), 1970
7 NFC: Chi. Cardinals (0) vs. Philadelphia (7), 1948
9 NFC: Tampa Bay (0) vs. Los Angeles (9), 1979

Largest Margin of Victory, Game

73 NFC: Chi. Bears vs. Washington, 1940 (73-0)
49 AFC-D: Oakland vs. Houston, 1969 (56-7)
48 AFC: Buffalo vs. L.A. Raiders, 1990 (51-3)

Most Points, Shutout Victory, Game

73 NFC: Chi. Bears vs. Washington, 1940
38 NFC-D: Dallas vs. Tampa Bay, 1981
37 NFC: Green Bay vs. N.Y. Giants, 1961

Most Points Overcome to Win Game

32 AFC-FR: Buffalo vs. Houston, 1992 (trailed 3-35, won 41-38) (OT)
20 NFC-D: Detroit vs. San Francisco, 1957 (trailed 7-27, won 31-27)
18 NFC-D: Dallas vs. San Francisco, 1972 (trailed 3-21, won 30-28)
AFC-D: Miami vs. Cleveland, 1985 (trailed 3-21, won 24-21)

Most Points, Each Half

1st: 41 AFC: Buffalo vs. L.A. Raiders, 1990
38 NFC-D: Washington vs. L.A. Rams, 1983
NFC-FR: Philadelphia vs. Detroit, 1995
35 NFC: Cleveland vs. Detroit, 1954
AFC-D: Oakland vs. Houston, 1969

SB: Washington vs. Denver, 1987
2nd: 45 NFC: Chi. Bears vs. Washington, 1940
35 AFC-FR: Buffalo vs. Houston, 1992
30 SB: N.Y. Giants vs. Denver, 1986
AFC: Cleveland vs. Denver, 1987
NFC-FR: Detroit vs. Philadelphia, 1995

Most Points, Each Quarter
1st: 28 AFC-D: Oakland vs. Houston, 1969
24 AFC-D: San Diego vs. Miami, 1981
21 NFC: Chi. Bears vs. Washington, 1940
AFC: San Diego vs. Boston, 1963
AFC-D: Oakland vs. Kansas City, 1968
AFC: Oakland vs. San Diego, 1980
AFC: Buffalo vs. L.A. Raiders, 1990
NFC: San Francisco vs. Dallas, 1994
2nd: 35 SB: Washington vs. Denver, 1987
31 NFC-FR: Philadelphia vs. Detroit, 1995
26 AFC-D: Pittsburgh vs. Buffalo, 1974
3rd: 28 AFC-FR: Buffalo vs. Houston, 1992
26 NFC: Chi. Bears vs. Washington, 1940
21 NFC-D: Dallas vs. Cleveland, 1967
NFC-D: Dallas vs. Tampa Bay, 1981
AFC-D: L.A. Raiders vs. Pittsburgh, 1983
SB: Chicago vs. New England, 1985
NFC-D: N.Y. Giants vs. San Francisco, 1986
AFC: Cleveland vs. Denver, 1987
AFC: Cleveland vs. Denver, 1989
4th: 27 NFC: N.Y. Giants vs. Chi. Bears, 1934
26 NFC-FR: Philadelphia vs. New Orleans, 1992
24 NFC: Baltimore vs. N.Y. Giants, 1959
OT: 6 NFC: Baltimore vs. N.Y. Giants, 1958
AFC-D: Oakland vs. Baltimore, 1977
NFC-D: L.A. Rams vs. N.Y. Giants, 1989

TOUCHDOWNS

Most Touchdowns, Game
11 NFC: Chi. Bears vs. Washington, 1940
8 NFC: Cleveland vs. Detroit, 1954
NFC: Detroit vs. Cleveland, 1957
AFC-D: Oakland vs. Houston, 1969
SB: San Francisco vs. Denver, 1989
7 AFC: San Diego vs. Boston, 1963
NFC-D: Dallas vs. Cleveland, 1967
NFC-D: N.Y. Giants vs. San Francisco, 1986
AFC: Buffalo vs. L.A. Raiders, 1990
SB: Dallas vs. Buffalo, 1992
SB: San Francisco vs. San Diego, 1994
NFC-FR: Philadelphia vs. Detroit, 1995

Most Touchdowns, Both Teams, Game
12 NFC-FR: Philadelphia (7) vs. Detroit (5), 1995
11 NFC: Chi. Bears (11) vs. Washington (0), 1940
10 NFC: Detroit (8) vs. Cleveland (2), 1957
AFC-D: Miami (5) vs. San Diego (5), 1981 (OT)
AFC: Miami (6) vs. Pittsburgh (4), 1984
AFC-FR: Buffalo (5) vs. Houston (5), 1992 (OT)
SB: San Francisco (7) vs. San Diego (3), 1994

Fewest Touchdowns, Both Teams, Game
0 NFC-D: N.Y. Giants vs. Cleveland, 1950
NFC-D: Dallas vs. Detroit, 1970
NFC: Los Angeles vs. Tampa Bay, 1979
1 NFC: Chi. Cardinals (0) vs. Philadelphia (1), 1948
NFC-D: Cleveland (0) vs. N.Y. Giants (1), 1958
AFC: San Diego (0) vs. Houston (1), 1961
AFC-D: N.Y. Jets (0) vs. Kansas City (1), 1969
NFC-D: Green Bay (0) vs. Washington (1), 1972
NFC-FR: New Orleans (0) vs. Chicago (1), 1990
NFC: N.Y. Giants (0) vs. San Francisco (1), 1990
AFC-FR: L.A. Raiders (0) vs. Kansas City (1), 1991
2 In many games

POINTS AFTER TOUCHDOWN

Most (One-Point) Points After Touchdown, Game
8 NFC: Cleveland vs. Detroit, 1954
NFC: Detroit vs. Cleveland, 1957
AFC-D: Oakland vs. Houston, 1969
7 NFC: Chi. Bears vs. Washington, 1940
NFC-D: Dallas vs. Cleveland, 1967
NFC-D: N.Y. Giants vs. San Francisco, 1986
SB: San Francisco vs. Denver, 1989
SB: Dallas vs. Buffalo, 1992
SB: San Francisco vs. San Diego, 1994
NFC-FR: Philadelphia vs. Detroit, 1995
6 AFC: San Diego vs. Boston, 1963
NFC-D: Washington vs. L.A. Rams, 1983
AFC: Miami vs. Pittsburgh, 1984
SB: Washington vs. Denver, 1987
AFC: Buffalo vs. L.A. Raiders, 1990
AFC-FR: L.A. Raiders vs. Denver, 1993

Most (One-Point) Points After Touchdown, Both Teams, Game
10 NFC: Detroit (8) vs. Cleveland (2), 1957
AFC-D: Miami (5) vs. San Diego (5), 1981 (OT)
AFC: Miami (6) vs. Pittsburgh (4), 1984
AFC-FR: Buffalo (5) vs. Houston (5), 1992 (OT)
NFC-FR: Philadelphia (7) vs. Detroit (3), 1995
9 In many games

Fewest (One-Point) Points After Touchdown, Both Teams, Game
0 NFC-D: N.Y. Giants vs. Cleveland, 1950
NFC-D: Dallas vs. Detroit, 1970
NFC: Los Angeles vs. Tampa Bay, 1979

Most Two-Point Conversions, Game
2 SB: San Diego vs. San Francisco, 1994
NFC-FR: Detroit vs. Philadelphia, 1995
1 AFC-D: Buffalo vs. Boston, 1963
AFC-FR: Miami vs. Buffalo, 1995
NFC-D: Philadelphia vs. Dallas, 1995

FIELD GOALS

Most Field Goals, Game
5 NFC-D: Minnesota vs. San Francisco, 1987
NFC: N.Y. Giants vs. San Francisco, 1990
AFC: Buffalo vs. Miami, 1992
4 AFC-D: Boston vs. Buffalo, 1963
AFC: Oakland vs. Houston, 1967
SB: Green Bay vs. Oakland, 1967
NFC: Washington vs. Dallas, 1972
AFC-D: Oakland vs. Pittsburgh, 1973
SB: San Francisco vs. Cincinnati, 1981
AFC-FR: New England vs. N.Y. Jets, 1985
NFC-FR: Washington vs. L.A. Rams, 1986
NFC-D: Philadelphia vs. Chicago, 1988
AFC-FR: Pittsburgh vs. Houston, 1989 (OT)
AFC-D: Pittsburgh vs. Buffalo, 1995
3 By many teams

Most Field Goals, Both Teams, Game
7 AFC-FR: Pittsburgh (4) vs. Houston (3), 1989 (OT)
NFC: N.Y. Giants (5) vs. San Francisco (2), 1990
6 NFC-D: Minnesota (5) vs. San Francisco (1), 1987
NFC-D: Philadelphia (4) vs. Chicago (2), 1988
AFC: Buffalo (5) vs. Miami (1), 1992
5 In many games

Most Field Goals Attempted, Game
6 AFC: Oakland vs. Houston, 1967
NFC-D: Los Angeles vs. Dallas, 1973
AFC-D: Cleveland vs. N.Y. Jets, 1986 (OT)
NFC: N.Y. Giants vs. San Francisco, 1990
5 By many teams

Most Field Goals Attempted, Both Teams, Game
9 NFC-D: Philadelphia (5) vs. Chicago (4), 1988
8 NFC-D: Los Angeles (6) vs. Dallas (2), 1973
NFC-D: Detroit (5) vs. San Francisco (3), 1983
AFC-D: Cleveland (6) vs. N.Y. Jets (2), 1986 (OT)
NFC-D: Minnesota (5) vs. San Francisco (3), 1987
AFC-FR: Houston (4) vs. Pittsburgh (4), 1989 (OT)
NFC-FR: Chicago (4) vs. New Orleans (4), 1990
NFC: N.Y. Giants (6) vs. San Francisco (2), 1990
7 In many games

SAFETIES

Most Safeties, Game
1 By many teams

Most Safeties, Both Teams, Game
1 In many games

FIRST DOWNS

Most First Downs, Game
34 AFC-D: San Diego vs. Miami, 1981 (OT)
33 AFC-D: Cleveland vs. N.Y. Jets, 1986 (OT)
31 SB: San Francisco vs. Miami, 1984

Fewest First Downs, Game
6 NFC: N.Y. Giants vs. Green Bay, 1961
7 NFC: Green Bay vs. Boston, 1936
NFC-D: Pittsburgh vs. Philadelphia, 1947
NFC: Chi. Cardinals vs. Philadelphia, 1948
NFC: Los Angeles vs. Philadelphia, 1949
NFC-D: Cleveland vs. N.Y. Giants, 1958
AFC-D: Cincinnati vs. Baltimore, 1970

NFC-D: Detroit vs. Dallas, 1970
NFC: Tampa Bay vs. Los Angeles, 1979
8 By many teams

Most First Downs, Both Teams, Game
59 AFC-D: San Diego (34) vs. Miami (25), 1981 (OT)
55 AFC-FR: San Diego (29) vs. Pittsburgh (26), 1982
54 AFC-FR: Buffalo (28) vs. Miami (26), 1995

Fewest First Downs, Both Teams, Game
15 NFC: Green Bay (7) vs. Boston (8), 1936
19 NFC: N.Y. Giants (9) vs. Green Bay (10), 1939
NFC: Washington (9) vs. Chi. Bears (10), 1942
20 NFC-D: Cleveland (9) vs. N.Y. Giants (11), 1950

RUSHING

Most First Downs, Rushing, Game
19 NFC-FR: Dallas vs. Los Angeles, 1980
18 AFC-D: Miami vs. Cincinnati, 1973
AFC: Miami vs. Oakland, 1973
AFC-D: Pittsburgh vs. Buffalo, 1974
AFC-FR: Buffalo vs. Miami, 1995
17 AFC-D: Cincinnati vs. Seattle, 1988
AFC: Buffalo vs. Kansas City, 1993

Fewest First Downs, Rushing, Game
0 NFC: Los Angeles vs. Philadelphia, 1949
AFC-D: Buffalo vs. Boston, 1963
AFC: Oakland vs. Pittsburgh, 1974
NFC-FR: New Orleans vs. Minnesota, 1987
NFC: L.A. Rams vs. San Francisco, 1989
NFC-D: Chicago vs. N.Y. Giants, 1990
1 By many teams

Most First Downs, Rushing, Both Teams, Game
26 AFC: Buffalo (14) vs. L.A. Raiders (12), 1990
25 NFC-FR: Dallas (19) vs. Los Angeles (6), 1980
23 NFC: Cleveland (15) vs. Detroit (8), 1952
AFC-D: Miami (18) vs. Cincinnati (5), 1973
AFC-D: Pittsburgh (18) vs. Buffalo (5), 1974
AFC-FR: Buffalo (18) vs. Miami (5), 1995

Fewest First Downs, Rushing, Both Teams, Game
5 AFC-D: Buffalo (0) vs. Boston (5), 1963
6 NFC: Green Bay (2) vs. Boston (4), 1936
NFC-D: Baltimore (2) vs. Minnesota (4), 1968
AFC-D: Houston (1) vs. Oakland (5), 1969
AFC-FR: N.Y. Jets (1) vs. Houston (5), 1991
7 NFC-D: Washington (2) vs. N.Y. Giants (5), 1943
NFC: Baltimore (3) vs. N.Y. Giants (4), 1959
NFC: Washington (3) vs. Dallas (4), 1972
AFC-FR: N.Y. Jets (3) vs. Buffalo (4), 1981
NFC-D: Detroit (3) vs. Dallas (4), 1991
AFC-D: Kansas City (3) vs. Houston (4), 1993
NFC-FR: Detroit (1) vs. Green Bay (6), 1994
NFC-FR: Atlanta (1) vs. Green Bay (6), 1995

PASSING

Most First Downs, Passing, Game
21 AFC-D: Miami vs. San Diego, 1981 (OT)
AFC-D: San Diego vs. Miami, 1981 (OT)
AFC-D: Cleveland vs. N.Y. Jets, 1986 (OT)
NFC-D: Philadelphia vs. Chicago, 1988
20 NFC-FR: Dallas vs. L.A. Rams, 1983
AFC-D: Buffalo vs. Cleveland, 1989
AFC-FR: Miami vs. Buffalo, 1995
NFC-FR: Detroit vs. Philadelphia, 1995
AFC-FR: San Diego vs. Indianapolis, 1995
19 NFC-FR: St. Louis vs. Green Bay, 1982
NFC-FR: Dallas vs. Tampa Bay, 1982
AFC-FR: Pittsburgh vs. San Diego, 1982
AFC-FR: San Diego vs. Pittsburgh, 1982
NFC: Dallas vs. Washington, 1982
NFC-D: Detroit vs. Dallas, 1991
AFC-FR: Kansas City vs. Pittsburgh, 1993 (OT)

Fewest First Downs, Passing, Game
0 NFC: Philadelphia vs. Chi. Cardinals, 1948
1 NFC-D: N.Y. Giants vs. Washington, 1943
NFC: Cleveland vs. Detroit, 1953
SB: Denver vs. Dallas, 1977
2 By many teams

Most First Downs, Passing, Both Teams, Game
42 AFC-D: Miami (21) vs. San Diego (21), 1981 (OT)
38 AFC-FR: Pittsburgh (19) vs. San Diego (19), 1982
34 NFC-FR: Washington (18) vs. San Francisco (16), 1990
AFC-FR: Kansas City (19) vs. Pittsburgh (15), 1993 (OT)

Fewest First Downs, Passing, Both Teams, Game
2 NFC: Philadelphia (0) vs. Chi. Cardinals (2), 1948
4 NFC-D: Cleveland (2) vs. N.Y. Giants (2), 1950
5 NFC: Detroit (2) vs. N.Y. Giants (3), 1935
NFC: Green Bay (2) vs. N.Y. Giants (3), 1939

PENALTY

Most First Downs, Penalty, Game
7 AFC-D: New England vs. Oakland, 1976
6 AFC-D: Cleveland vs. N.Y. Jets, 1986 (OT)
5 AFC-FR: Cleveland vs. L. A. Raiders, 1982

Most First Downs, Penalty, Both Teams, Game
9 AFC-D: New England (7) vs. Oakland (2), 1976
8 NFC-FR: Atlanta (4) vs. Minnesota (4), 1982
7 AFC-D: Baltimore (4) vs. Oakland (3), 1977 (OT)
AFC-FR: Denver (4) vs. L.A. Raiders (3), 1993

NET YARDS GAINED RUSHING AND PASSING

Most Yards Gained, Game
610 AFC: San Diego vs. Boston, 1963
602 SB: Washington vs. Denver, 1987
569 AFC: Miami vs. Pittsburgh, 1984

Fewest Yards Gained, Game
86 NFC-D: Cleveland vs. N.Y. Giants, 1958
99 NFC: Chi. Cardinals vs. Philadelphia, 1948
114 NFC-D: N.Y. Giants vs. Washington, 1943

Most Yards Gained, Both Teams, Game
1,038 AFC-FR: Buffalo (536) vs. Miami (502), 1995
1,036 AFC-D: San Diego (564) vs. Miami (472), 1981 (OT)
1,024 AFC: Miami (569) vs. Pittsburgh (455), 1984

Fewest Yards Gained, Both Teams, Game
331 NFC: Chi. Cardinals (99) vs. Philadelphia (232), 1948
332 NFC-D: N.Y. Giants (150) vs. Cleveland (182), 1950
336 NFC: Boston (116) vs. Green Bay (220), 1936

RUSHING

ATTEMPTS

Most Attempts, Game
65 NFC: Detroit vs. N.Y. Giants, 1935
61 NFC: Philadelphia vs. Los Angeles, 1949
59 AFC: New England vs. Miami, 1985

Fewest Attempts, Game
8 AFC-D: Miami vs. San Diego, 1994
9 SB: Miami vs. San Francisco, 1984
10 NFC: L.A. Rams vs. San Francisco, 1989
NFC-FR: Atlanta vs. Green Bay, 1995

Most Attempts, Both Teams, Game
109 NFC: Detroit (65) vs. N.Y. Giants (44), 1935
97 AFC-D: Baltimore (50) vs. Oakland (47), 1977 (OT)
91 NFC: Philadelphia (57) vs. Chi. Cardinals (34), 1948

Fewest Attempts, Both Teams, Game
32 AFC-D: Houston (14) vs. Kansas City (18), 1993
38 NFC-D: Detroit (16) vs. Dallas (22), 1991
39 NFC-FR: Atlanta (10) vs. Green Bay (29), 1995

YARDS GAINED

Most Yards Gained, Game
382 NFC: Chi. Bears vs. Washington, 1940
341 AFC-FR: Buffalo vs. Miami, 1995
338 NFC-FR: Dallas vs. Los Angeles, 1980

Fewest Yards Gained, Game
–4 NFC-FR: Detroit vs. Green Bay, 1994
7 AFC-D: Buffalo vs. Boston, 1963
SB: New England vs. Chicago, 1985
17 SB: Minnesota vs. Pittsburgh, 1974

Most Yards Gained, Both Teams, Game
430 NFC-FR: Dallas (338) vs. Los Angeles (92), 1980
426 NFC: Cleveland (227) vs. Detroit (199), 1952
411 AFC-FR: Buffalo (341) vs. Miami (70), 1995

Fewest Yards Gained, Both Teams, Game
77 NFC-FR: Detroit (–4) vs. Green Bay (81), 1994
90 AFC-D: Buffalo (7) vs. Boston (83), 1963
106 NFC: Boston (39) vs. Green Bay (67), 1936

AVERAGE GAIN

Highest Average Gain, Game
9.94 AFC: San Diego vs. Boston, 1963 (32-318)
9.29 NFC-D: Green Bay vs. Dallas, 1982 (17-158)
7.35 NFC-FR: Dallas vs. Los Angeles, 1980 (46-338)

Lowest Average Gain, Game
–0.27 NFC-FR: Detroit vs. Green Bay, 1994 (15-(–4))
0.58 AFC-D: Buffalo vs. Boston, 1963 (12-7)
0.64 SB: New England vs. Chicago, 1985 (11-7)

TOUCHDOWNS

Most Touchdowns, Game

7 NFC: Chi. Bears vs. Washington, 1940
6 NFC-D: San Francisco vs. N.Y. Giants, 1993
5 NFC: Cleveland vs. Detroit, 1954
NFC-D: San Francisco vs. Chicago, 1994

Most Touchdowns, Both Teams, Game

7 NFC: Chi. Bears (7) vs. Washington (0), 1940
6 NFC: Cleveland (5) vs. Detroit (1), 1954
NFC-D: San Francisco (6) vs. N.Y. Giants (0), 1993
NFC-D: San Francisco (5) vs. Chicago (1), 1994
5 NFC: Chi. Cardinals (3) vs. Philadelphia (2), 1947
AFC: San Diego (4) vs. Boston (1), 1963
AFC-D: Cincinnati (3) vs. Buffalo (2), 1981

PASSING

ATTEMPTS

Most Attempts, Game

66 AFC-FR: Miami vs. Buffalo, 1995
65 AFC-D: Cleveland vs. N.Y. Jets, 1986 (OT)
NFC-D: San Francisco vs. Green Bay, 1995
61 NFC-FR: Minnesota vs. Chicago, 1994

Fewest Attempts, Game

5 NFC: Detroit vs. N.Y. Giants, 1935
6 AFC: Miami vs. Oakland, 1973
7 SB: Miami vs. Minnesota, 1973

Most Attempts, Both Teams, Game

102 AFC-D: San Diego (54) vs. Miami (48), 1981 (OT)
96 AFC: N.Y. Jets (49) vs. Oakland (47), 1968
95 AFC-D: Cleveland (65) vs. N.Y. Jets (30), 1986 (OT)

Fewest Attempts, Both Teams, Game

18 NFC: Detroit (5) vs. N.Y. Giants (13), 1935
23 NFC: Chi. Cardinals (11) vs. Philadelphia (12), 1948
24 NFC-D: Cleveland (9) vs. N.Y. Giants (15), 1950

COMPLETIONS

Most Completions, Game

36 AFC-FR: Houston vs. Buffalo, 1992 (OT)
34 AFC-D: Cleveland vs. N.Y. Jets, 1986 (OT)
AFC-FR: Miami vs. Buffalo, 1995
33 AFC-D: San Diego vs. Miami, 1981 (OT)
NFC-FR: Minnesota vs. Chicago, 1994

Fewest Completions, Game

2 NFC: Detroit vs. N.Y. Giants, 1935
NFC: Philadelphia vs. Chi. Cardinals, 1948
3 NFC: N.Y. Giants vs. Chi. Bears, 1941
NFC: Green Bay vs. N.Y. Giants, 1944
NFC: Chi. Cardinals vs. Philadelphia, 1947
NFC: Chi. Cardinals vs. Philadelphia, 1948
NFC-D: Cleveland vs. N.Y. Giants, 1950
NFC-D: N.Y. Giants vs. Cleveland, 1950
NFC: Cleveland vs. Detroit, 1953
AFC: Miami vs. Oakland, 1973
4 NFC: N.Y. Giants vs. Detroit, 1935
NFC-D: N.Y. Giants vs. Washington, 1943
NFC-D: Pittsburgh vs. Philadelphia, 1947
NFC-D: Dallas vs. Detroit, 1970
AFC: Miami vs. Baltimore, 1971
SB: Miami vs. Washington, 1982
AFC-FR: Seattle vs. L.A. Raiders, 1984

Most Completions, Both Teams, Game

64 AFC-D: San Diego (33) vs. Miami (31), 1981 (OT)
57 AFC-FR: Houston (36) vs. Buffalo (21), 1992 (OT)
56 NFC-D: Dallas (28) vs. Green Bay (28), 1993

Fewest Completions, Both Teams, Game

5 NFC: Philadelphia (2) vs. Chi. Cardinals (3), 1948
6 NFC: Detroit (2) vs. N.Y. Giants (4), 1935
NFC-D: Cleveland (3) vs. N.Y. Giants (3), 1950
11 NFC: Green Bay (3) vs. N.Y. Giants (8), 1944
NFC-D: Dallas (4) vs. Detroit (7), 1970

COMPLETION PERCENTAGE

Highest Completion Percentage, Game (20 attempts)

88.0 SB: N.Y. Giants vs. Denver, 1986 (25-22)
87.1 NFC: San Francisco vs. L.A. Rams, 1989 (31-27)
80.0 NFC-D: Washington vs. L.A. Rams, 1983 (25-20)

Lowest Completion Percentage, Game (20 attempts)

18.5 NFC: Tampa Bay vs. Los Angeles, 1979 (27-5)
20.0 NFC-D: N.Y. Giants vs. Washington, 1943 (20-4)
25.8 NFC: Chi. Bears vs. Washington, 1937 (31-8)

YARDS GAINED

Most Yards Gained, Game

483 AFC-D: Cleveland vs. N.Y. Jets, 1986 (OT)
435 AFC: Miami vs. Pittsburgh, 1984
432 AFC-FR: Miami vs. Buffalo, 1995

Fewest Yards Gained, Game

3 NFC: Chi. Cardinals vs. Philadelphia, 1948
7 NFC: Philadelphia vs. Chi. Cardinals, 1948
9 NFC-D: N.Y. Giants vs. Cleveland, 1950
NFC: Cleveland vs. Detroit, 1953

Most Yards Gained, Both Teams, Game

809 AFC-D: San Diego (415) vs. Miami (394), 1981 (OT)
747 AFC: Miami (435) vs. Pittsburgh (312), 1984
666 AFC-D: Cleveland (483) vs. N.Y. Jets (183), 1986 (OT)

Fewest Yards Gained, Both Teams, Game

10 NFC: Chi. Cardinals (3) vs. Philadelphia (7), 1948
38 NFC-D: N.Y. Giants (9) vs. Cleveland (29), 1950
102 NFC-D: Dallas (22) vs. Detroit (80), 1970

TIMES SACKED

Most Times Sacked, Game

9 AFC: Kansas City vs. Buffalo, 1966
NFC: Chicago vs. San Francisco, 1984
AFC-D: N.Y. Jets vs. Cleveland, 1986 (OT)
AFC-D: Houston vs. Kansas City, 1993
8 NFC: Green Bay vs. Dallas, 1967
NFC: Minnesota vs. Washington, 1987
7 NFC-D: Dallas vs. Los Angeles, 1973
SB: Dallas vs. Pittsburgh, 1975
AFC-FR: Houston vs. Oakland, 1980
NFC-D: Washington vs. Chicago, 1984
SB: New England vs. Chicago, 1985
AFC-FR: Kansas City vs. San Diego, 1992
AFC-D: Pittsburgh vs. Buffalo, 1992

Most Times Sacked, Both Teams, Game

13 AFC: Kansas City (9) vs. Buffalo (4), 1966
AFC-D: N.Y. Jets (9) vs. Cleveland (4), 1986 (OT)
12 NFC-D: Dallas (7) vs. Los Angeles (5), 1973
NFC-D: Washington (7) vs. Chicago (5), 1984
NFC: Chicago (9) vs. San Francisco (3), 1984
AFC-FR: Kansas City (7) vs. San Diego (5), 1992
11 AFC-D: Houston (9) vs. Kansas City (2), 1993

Fewest Times Sacked, Both Teams, Game

0 AFC-D: Buffalo vs. Pittsburgh, 1974
AFC-FR: Pittsburgh vs. San Diego, 1982
AFC: Miami vs. Pittsburgh, 1984
AFC-D: Buffalo vs. Miami, 1990
AFC-D: Denver vs. Houston, 1991
AFC-FR: Buffalo vs. Miami, 1995
1 In many games

TOUCHDOWNS

Most Touchdowns, Game

6 AFC-D: Oakland vs. Houston, 1969
SB: San Francisco vs. San Diego, 1994
5 NFC: Chi. Bears vs. Washington, 1943
NFC: Detroit vs. Cleveland, 1957
AFC-D: Oakland vs. Kansas City, 1968
SB: San Francisco vs. Denver, 1989
4 By many teams

Most Touchdowns, Both Teams, Game

8 AFC-FR: Buffalo (4) vs. Houston (4), 1992 (OT)
7 NFC: Chi. Bears (5) vs. Washington (2), 1943
AFC-D: Oakland (6) vs. Houston (1), 1969
SB: Pittsburgh (4) vs. Dallas (3), 1978
AFC-D: Miami (4) vs. San Diego (3), 1981 (OT)
AFC: Miami (4) vs. Pittsburgh (3), 1984
AFC-D: Buffalo (4) vs. Cleveland (3), 1989
SB: San Francisco (6) vs. San Diego (1), 1994
NFC-FR: Detroit (4) vs. Philadelphia (3), 1995
6 NFC-FR: Green Bay (4) vs. St. Louis (2), 1982
AFC: Cleveland (3) vs. Denver (3), 1987
AFC-D: Buffalo (3) vs. Miami (3), 1990
AFC-FR: Denver (3) vs. L.A. Raiders (3), 1993

INTERCEPTIONS BY

Most Interceptions By, Game

8 NFC: Chi. Bears vs. Washington, 1940
7 NFC: Cleveland vs. Los Angeles, 1955
6 NFC: Green Bay vs. N.Y. Giants, 1939
NFC: Chi. Bears vs. N.Y. Giants, 1946
NFC: Cleveland vs. Detroit, 1954
AFC: San Diego vs. Houston, 1961

AFC: Buffalo vs. L.A. Raiders, 1990
NFC-FR: Philadelphia vs. Detroit, 1995

Most Interceptions By, Both Teams, Game

10 NFC: Cleveland (7) vs. Los Angeles (3), 1955
AFC: San Diego (6) vs. Houston (4), 1961
9 NFC: Green Bay (6) vs. N.Y. Giants (3), 1939
8 NFC: Chi. Bears (8) vs. Washington (0), 1940
NFC: Chi. Bears (6) vs. N.Y. Giants (2), 1946
NFC: Cleveland (6) vs. Detroit (2), 1954
AFC-FR: Buffalo (4) vs. N.Y. Jets (4), 1981
AFC: Miami (5) vs. N.Y. Jets (3), 1982

YARDS GAINED

Most Yards Gained, Game

138 AFC-FR: N.Y. Jets vs. Cincinnati, 1982
136 AFC: Dall. Texans vs. Houston, 1962 (OT)
130 NFC-D: Los Angeles vs. St. Louis, 1975

Most Yards Gained, Both Teams, Game

156 NFC: Green Bay (123) vs. N.Y. Giants (33), 1939
149 NFC: Cleveland (103) vs. Los Angeles (46), 1955
141 AFC-FR: Buffalo (79) vs. N.Y. Jets (62), 1981

TOUCHDOWNS

Most Touchdowns, Game

3 NFC: Chi. Bears vs. Washington, 1940
2 NFC-D: Los Angeles vs. St. Louis, 1975
NFC-FR: Philadelphia vs. Detroit, 1995
1 In many games

Most Touchdowns, Both Teams, Game

3 NFC: Chi. Bears (3) vs. Washington (0), 1940
2 NFC-D: Los Angeles (2) vs. St. Louis(0), 1975
NFC-D: Dallas (1) vs. Green Bay (1), 1982
NFC-D: Minnesota (1) vs. San Francisco (1), 1987
NFC-FR: Detroit (1) vs. Green Bay (1), 1993
NFC-FR: Philadelphia (2) vs. Detroit (0), 1995
1 In many games

PUNTING

Most Punts, Game

14 AFC-D: N.Y. Jets vs. Cleveland, 1986 (OT)
13 NFC: N.Y. Giants vs. Chi. Bears, 1933
AFC-D: Baltimore vs. Oakland, 1977 (OT)
11 AFC: Houston vs. Oakland, 1967
AFC-D: Houston vs. Oakland, 1969
NFC: L.A. Rams vs. Chicago, 1985

Fewest Punts, Game

0 NFC-FR: St. Louis vs. Green Bay, 1982
AFC-FR: N.Y. Jets vs. Cincinnati, 1982
1 NFC-D: Cleveland vs. Dallas, 1969
AFC: Miami vs. Oakland, 1973
AFC-D: Oakland vs. Cincinnati, 1975
AFC-D: Pittsburgh vs. Baltimore, 1976
AFC: Pittsburgh vs. Houston, 1978
NFC-FR: Green Bay vs. St. Louis, 1982
AFC-FR: Miami vs. New England, 1982
AFC-FR: San Diego vs. Pittsburgh, 1982
AFC-D: Cleveland vs. Indianapolis, 1987
AFC-D: Buffalo vs. Miami, 1990
AFC-FR: L.A. Raiders vs. Kansas City, 1991
NFC-FR: Atlanta vs. New Orleans, 1991
NFC-FR: Chicago vs. Dallas, 1991
AFC-D: Houston vs. Denver, 1991
NFC: San Francisco vs. Dallas, 1992
NFC: Dallas vs. San Francisco, 1994
2 In many games

Most Punts, Both Teams, Game

23 NFC: N.Y. Giants (13) vs. Chi. Bears (10), 1933
22 AFC-D: N.Y. Jets (14) vs. Cleveland (8), 1986 (OT)
21 AFC-D: Baltimore (13) vs. Oakland (8), 1977 (OT)
NFC: L.A. Rams (11) vs. Chicago (10), 1985

Fewest Punts, Both Teams, Game

1 NFC-FR: St. Louis (0) vs. Green Bay (1), 1982
2 AFC-FR: N.Y. Jets (0) vs. Cincinnati (2), 1982
3 AFC: Miami (1) vs. Oakland (2), 1973
AFC-FR: San Diego (1) vs. Pittsburgh (2), 1982
AFC-D: Buffalo (1) vs. Miami (2), 1990
AFC-FR: L.A. Raiders (1) vs. Kansas City (2), 1991
AFC-D: Houston (1) vs. Denver (2), 1991

AVERAGE YARDAGE

Highest Average, Punting, Game (4 punts)

56.0 AFC: Oakland vs. San Diego, 1980
52.5 NFC: Washington vs. Chi. Bears, 1942
51.6 AFC-D: Cincinnati vs. L.A. Raiders, 1990

Lowest Average, Punting, Game (4 punts)

24.9 NFC: Washington vs. Chi. Bears, 1937
25.3 AFC-FR: Pittsburgh vs. Houston, 1989
25.5 NFC: Green Bay vs. N.Y. Giants, 1962

PUNT RETURNS

Most Punt Returns, Game

8 NFC: Green Bay vs. N.Y. Giants, 1944
7 By eight teams

Most Punt Returns, Both Teams, Game

13 AFC-FR: Houston (7) vs. Oakland (6), 1980
11 NFC: Green Bay (8) vs. N.Y. Giants (3), 1944
NFC-D: Green Bay (6) vs. Baltimore (5), 1965
10 In many games

Fewest Punt Returns, Both Teams, Game

0 NFC: Chi. Bears vs. N.Y. Giants, 1941
AFC: Boston vs. San Diego, 1963
NFC-FR: Green Bay vs. St. Louis, 1982
AFC-FR: Houston vs. N.Y. Jets, 1991
AFC-D: Denver vs. Houston, 1991
NFC-D: San Francisco vs. Washington, 1992
1 In many games

YARDS GAINED

Most Yards Gained, Game

155 NFC-D: Dallas vs. Cleveland, 1967
150 NFC: Chi. Cardinals vs. Philadelphia, 1947
143 NFC-FR: Minnesota vs. New Orleans, 1987

Fewest Yards Gained, Game

–10 NFC: Green Bay vs. Cleveland, 1965
–9 NFC: Dallas vs. Green Bay, 1966
AFC-D: Kansas City vs. Oakland, 1968
–5 AFC-D: Miami vs. Oakland, 1970
NFC-D: San Francisco vs. Dallas, 1972
NFC: Dallas vs. Washington, 1972

Most Yards Gained, Both Teams, Game

166 NFC-D: Dallas (155) vs. Cleveland (11), 1967
160 NFC: Chi. Cardinals (150) vs. Philadelphia (10), 1947
146 NFC-D: Philadelphia (112) vs. Pittsburgh (34), 1947

Fewest Yards Gained, Both Teams, Game

–9 NFC: Dallas (–9) vs. Green Bay (0), 1966
–6 AFC-D: Miami (–5) vs. Oakland (–1), 1970
–3 NFC-D: San Francisco (–5) vs. Dallas (2), 1972

TOUCHDOWNS

Most Touchdowns, Game

1 By 11 teams

KICKOFF RETURNS

Most Kickoff Returns, Game

10 NFC-D: L.A. Rams vs. Washington, 1983
NFC-FR: Detroit vs. Philadelphia, 1995
9 NFC: Chi. Bears vs. N.Y. Giants, 1956
AFC: Boston vs. San Diego, 1963
AFC: Houston vs. Oakland, 1967
SB: Denver vs. San Francisco, 1989
AFC-D: Miami vs. Buffalo, 1990
AFC: L.A. Raiders vs. Buffalo, 1990
8 By many teams

Most Kickoff Returns, Both Teams, Game

15 AFC-D: Miami (9) vs. Buffalo (6), 1990
14 NFC-FR: Detroit (10) vs. Philadelphia (4), 1995
13 NFC-D: Green Bay (7) vs. Dallas (6), 1982

Fewest Kickoff Returns, Both Teams, Game

1 NFC: Green Bay (0) vs. Boston (1), 1936
AFC-FR: San Diego (0) vs. Kansas City (1), 1992
2 NFC-D: Los Angeles (0) vs. Chi. Bears (2), 1950
AFC: Houston (0) vs. San Diego (2), 1961
AFC-D: Oakland (1) vs. Pittsburgh (1), 1972
AFC-D: N.Y. Jets (0) vs. L.A. Raiders (2), 1982
AFC: Miami (1) vs. N.Y. Jets (1), 1982
NFC: N.Y. Giants (0) vs. Washington (2), 1986
3 In many games

YARDS GAINED

Most Yards Gained, Game

244 SB: San Diego vs. San Francisco, 1994
225 NFC: Washington vs. Chi. Bears, 1940
222 SB: Miami vs. Washington, 1982

Most Yards Gained, Both Teams, Game

379 AFC-D: Baltimore (193) vs. Oakland (186), 1977 (OT)
321 NFC-D: Dallas (173) vs. Green Bay (148), 1982

318 AFC-D: Miami (183) vs. Oakland (135), 1974

Fewest Yards Gained, Both Teams, Game
5 AFC-FR: San Diego (0) vs. Kansas City (5), 1992
15 NFC: N.Y. Giants (0) vs. Washington (15), 1986
31 NFC-D: Los Angeles (0) vs. Chi. Bears (31), 1950

TOUCHDOWNS

Most Touchdowns, Game
1 NFC-D: San Francisco vs. Dallas, 1972
AFC-D: Miami vs. Oakland, 1974
AFC-D: Baltimore vs. Oakland, 1977 (OT)
SB: Miami vs. Washington, 1982
SB: Cincinnati vs. San Francisco, 1988
AFC-D: Cleveland vs. Buffalo, 1989
SB: San Diego vs. San Francisco, 1994

PENALTIES

Most Penalties, Game
17 AFC-FR: L.A. Raiders vs. Denver, 1993
14 AFC-FR: Oakland vs. Houston, 1980
NFC-D: San Francisco vs. N.Y. Giants, 1981
13 AFC-FR: Houston vs. Cleveland, 1988
AFC-D: Houston vs. Denver, 1991

Fewest Penalties, Game
0 NFC: Philadelphia vs. Green Bay, 1960
NFC-D: Detroit vs. Dallas, 1970
AFC-D: Miami vs. Oakland, 1970
SB: Miami vs. Dallas, 1971
NFC-D: Washington vs. Minnesota, 1973
SB: Pittsburgh vs. Dallas, 1975
NFC: San Francisco vs. Chicago, 1988
SB: Denver vs. San Francisco, 1989
AFC-D: L.A. Raiders vs. Cincinnati, 1990
AFC-D: Miami vs. San Diego, 1992
1 By many teams

Most Penalties, Both Teams, Game
27 AFC-FR: L.A. Raiders (17) vs. Denver (10), 1993
22 AFC-FR: Oakland (14) vs. Houston (8), 1980
NFC-D: San Francisco (14) vs. N.Y. Giants (8), 1981
AFC-FR: Houston (13) vs. Cleveland (9), 1988
21 AFC-D: Oakland (11) vs. New England (10), 1976

Fewest Penalties, Both Teams, Game
1 AFC-D: L.A. Raiders (0) vs. Cincinnati (1), 1990
2 NFC: Washington (1) vs. Chi. Bears (1), 1937
NFC-D: Washington (0) vs. Minnesota (2), 1973
SB: Pittsburgh (0) vs. Dallas (2), 1975
3 AFC: Miami (1) vs. Baltimore (2), 1971
NFC: San Francisco (1) vs. Dallas (2), 1971
SB: Miami (0) vs. Dallas (3), 1971
AFC-D: Pittsburgh (1) vs. Oakland (2), 1972
AFC-D: Miami (1) vs. Cincinnati (2), 1973
SB: Miami (1) vs. San Francisco (2), 1984
NFC: San Francisco (0) vs. Chicago (3), 1988

YARDS PENALIZED

Most Yards Penalized, Game
145 NFC-D: San Francisco vs. N.Y. Giants, 1981
133 SB: Dallas vs. Baltimore, 1970
130 AFC-FR: L.A. Raiders vs. Denver, 1993

Fewest Yards Penalized, Game
0 By 10 teams

Most Yards Penalized, Both Teams, Game
227 AFC-FR: L.A. Raiders (130) vs. Denver (97), 1993
206 NFC-D: San Francisco (145) vs. N.Y. Giants (61), 1981
193 AFC-FR: Houston (118) vs. Cleveland (75), 1988

Fewest Yards Penalized, Both Teams, Game
5 AFC-D: L.A. Raiders (0) vs. Cincinnati (5), 1990
9 NFC-D: Washington (0) vs. Minnesota (9), 1973
15 SB: Miami (0) vs. Dallas (15), 1971

FUMBLES

Most Fumbles, Game
8 SB: Buffalo vs. Dallas, 1992
7 AFC-D: Houston vs. Kansas City, 1993
6 By 11 teams

Most Fumbles, Both Teams, Game
12 AFC: Houston (6) vs. Pittsburgh (6), 1978
SB: Buffalo (8) vs. Dallas (4), 1992
10 NFC: Chi. Bears (5) vs. N.Y. Giants (5), 1934
SB: Dallas (6) vs. Denver (4), 1977
9 NFC-D: San Francisco (6) vs. Detroit (3), 1957
NFC-D: San Francisco (5) vs. Dallas (4), 1972
NFC: Dallas (5) vs. Philadelphia (4), 1980

Most Fumbles Lost, Game
5 SB: Buffalo vs. Dallas, 1992
4 NFC: N.Y. Giants vs. Baltimore, 1958 (OT)
AFC: Kansas City vs. Oakland, 1969
SB: Baltimore vs. Dallas, 1970
AFC: Pittsburgh vs. Oakland, 1975
SB: Denver vs. Dallas, 1977
AFC: Houston vs. Pittsburgh, 1978
AFC: Miami vs. New England, 1985
SB: New England vs. Chicago, 1985
NFC-FR: L.A. Rams vs. Washington, 1986
3 By many teams

Fewest Fumbles, Both Teams, Game
0 NFC: Green Bay vs. Cleveland, 1965
AFC-D: Houston vs. San Diego, 1979
NFC-D: Dallas vs. Los Angeles, 1979
SB: Los Angeles vs. Pittsburgh, 1979
AFC-D: Buffalo vs. Cincinnati, 1981
NFC-D: San Francisco vs. Washington, 1990
NFC: Dallas vs. Green Bay, 1995
1 In many games

RECOVERIES

Most Total Fumbles Recovered, Game
8 SB: Dallas vs. Denver, 1977 (4 own, 4 opp)
7 NFC: Chi. Bears vs. N.Y. Giants, 1934 (5 own, 2 opp)
NFC-D: San Francisco vs. Detroit, 1957 (4 own, 3 opp)
NFC-D: San Francisco vs. Dallas, 1972 (4 own, 3 opp)
AFC: Pittsburgh vs. Houston, 1978 (3 own, 4 opp)
6 AFC: Houston vs. San Diego, 1961 (4 own, 2 opp)
AFC-D: Cleveland vs. Baltimore, 1971 (4 own, 2 opp)
AFC-D: Cleveland vs. Oakland, 1980 (5 own, 1 opp)
NFC: Philadelphia vs. Dallas, 1980 (3 own, 3 opp)
SB: Dallas vs. Buffalo, 1992 (1 own, 5 opp)

Most Own Fumbles Recovered, Game
5 NFC: Chi. Bears vs. N.Y. Giants, 1934
AFC-D: Cleveland vs. Oakland, 1980
4 By many teams

TURNOVERS

Numbers of times losing the ball on interceptions and fumbles.

Most Turnovers, Game
9 NFC: Washington vs. Chi. Bears, 1940
NFC: Detroit vs. Cleveland, 1954
AFC: Houston vs. Pittsburgh, 1978
SB: Buffalo vs. Dallas, 1992
8 NFC: N.Y. Giants vs. Chi. Bears, 1946
NFC: Los Angeles vs. Cleveland, 1955
NFC: Cleveland vs. Detroit, 1957
SB: Denver vs. Dallas, 1977
NFC-D: Minnesota vs. Philadelphia, 1980
7 In many games

Fewest Turnovers, Game
0 By many teams

Most Turnovers, Both Teams, Game
14 AFC: Houston (9) vs. Pittsburgh (5), 1978
13 NFC: Detroit (9) vs. Cleveland (4), 1954
AFC: Houston (7) vs. San Diego (6), 1961
12 AFC: Pittsburgh (7) vs. Oakland (5), 1975

Fewest Turnovers, Both Teams, Game
0 SB: Buffalo vs. N.Y. Giants, 1990
FR: Kansas City vs Pittsburgh, 1993 (OT)
NFC-FR: Detroit vs. Green Bay, 1994
1 AFC-D: Baltimore (0) vs. Cincinnati (1), 1970
AFC-D: Pittsburgh (0) vs. Buffalo (1), 1974
AFC: Oakland (0) vs. Pittsburgh (1), 1976
NFC-D: Minnesota (0) vs. Washington (1), 1982
NFC-D: Chicago (0) vs. N.Y. Giants (1), 1985
SB: N.Y. Giants (0) vs. Denver (1), 1986
NFC: Washington (0) vs. Minnesota (1), 1987
AFC-D: Cincinnati (0) vs. L.A. Raiders (1), 1990
NFC: N.Y. Giants (0) vs. San Francisco (1), 1990
NFC-FR: N.Y. Giants (0) vs. Minnesota (1), 1993
AFC-FR: L.A. Raiders (0) vs. Denver (1), 1993
NFC: Dallas (0) vs. San Francisco (1), 1993
AFC: Indianapolis (0) vs. Pittsburgh (1), 1995
2 In many games

AFC-NFC PRO BOWL RECORDS

Compiled by Elias Sports Bureau

INDIVIDUAL RECORDS

SERVICE

Most Games

10 Lawrence Taylor, N.Y. Giants, 1982-91
Ronnie Lott, San Francisco, 1982-85, 1987-91; L.A. Raiders 1992
Mike Singletary, Chicago, 1984-93
9 *Ken Houston, Houston, 1971-73; Washington, 1974-79
Joe Greene, Pittsburgh, 1971-77, 1979-80
Jack Lambert, Pittsburgh, 1976-84
Walter Payton, Chicago, 1977-81, 1984-87
Harry Carson, N.Y. Giants, 1979-80, 1982-88
Mike Webster, Pittsburgh, 1979-86, 1988
Anthony Muñoz, Cincinnati, 1982-87, 1989-90, 1992
*Reggie White, Philadelphia, 1987-93; Green Bay, 1994, 1996
8 Tom Mack, Los Angeles, 1971-76, 1978-79
*Franco Harris, Pittsburgh, 1973-76, 1978-81
Lemar Parrish, Cincinnati, 1971-72, 1975-77; Washington, 1978, 1980-81
Art Shell, Oakland, 1973-79, 1981
Ted Hendricks, Baltimore, 1972-74; Green Bay, 1975; Oakland, 1981-82; L.A. Raiders, 1983-84
*John Hannah, New England, 1977, 1979-83, 1985-86
*Randy White, Dallas, 1978, 1980-86
James Lofton, Green Bay, 1979, 1981-86; Buffalo 1992
*Mike Munchak, Houston, 1985-86, 1988-93
Howie Long, L.A. Raiders, 1984-88, 1990, 1993-94
Warren Moon, Houston, 1989-94; Minnesota, 1995-96
**Jerry Rice, San Francisco, 1987-88, 1990-94, 1996
**Also selected, but did not play, in one additional game*
***Also selected, but did not play, in two additional games*

SCORING

POINTS

Most Points, Career

45 Morten Andersen, New Orleans, 1986-89, 1991, 1993; Atlanta, 1996 (15-pat, 10-fg)
30 Jan Stenerud, Kansas City, 1971-72, 1976; Green Bay, 1985 (6-pat, 8-fg)
26 Nick Lowery, Kansas City, 1982, 1991, 1993 (5 pat, 7 fg)

Most Points, Game

18 John Brockington, Green Bay, 1973 (3-td)
15 Garo Yepremian, Miami, 1974 (5-fg)
14 Jan Stenerud, Kansas City, 1972 (2-pat, 4-fg)

TOUCHDOWNS

Most Touchdowns, Career

3 John Brockington, Green Bay, 1972-74 (2-r, 1-p)
Earl Campbell, Houston, 1979-82, 1984 (3-r)
Chuck Muncie, New Orleans, 1980; San Diego, 1982-83 (3-r)
William Andrews, Atlanta, 1981-84 (1-r, 2-p)
Marcus Allen, L.A. Raiders, 1983, 1985-86, 1988; Kansas City, 1994 (2-r, 1-p)
2 By 16 players

Most Touchdowns, Game

3 John Brockington, Green Bay, 1973 (2-r, 1-p)
2 Mel Renfro, Dallas, 1971 (2-ret)
Earl Campbell, Houston, 1980 (2-r)
Chuck Muncie, New Orleans, 1980 (2-r)
William Andrews, Atlanta, 1984 (2-p)
Herschel Walker, Dallas, 1989 (2-r)
Johnny Johnson, Phoenix, 1991 (2-r)
Eric Green, Pittsburgh, 1995 (2-p)

POINTS AFTER TOUCHDOWN

Most Points After Touchdown, Career

15 Morten Andersen, New Orleans, 1986-89, 1991, 1993; Atlanta, 1996 (15 att)
6 Chester Marcol, Green Bay, 1973, 1975 (6 att)
Mark Moseley, Washington, 1980, 1983 (7 att)
Ali Haji-Sheikh, N.Y. Giants, 1984 (6 att)
Jan Stenerud, Kansas City, 1971-72, 1976; Green Bay, 1985 (6 att)
5 Nick Lowery, Kansas City, 1982, 1991, 1993 (5 att)
John Carney, San Diego, 1995 (5 att)

Most Points After Touchdown, Game

6 Ali Haji-Sheikh, N.Y. Giants, 1984 (6 att)
5 John Carney, San Diego, 1995 (5 att)
4 Chester Marcol, Green Bay, 1973 (4 att)
Mark Moseley, Washington, 1980 (5 att)
Morten Andersen, New Orleans, 1986 (4 att), 1989 (4 att)

FIELD GOALS

Most Field Goals Attempted, Career

18 Morten Andersen, New Orleans, 1986-89, 1991, 1993; Atlanta, 1996
15 Jan Stenerud, Kansas City, 1971-72, 1976; Green Bay, 1985
10 Nick Lowery, Kansas City, 1982, 1991, 1993

Most Field Goals Attempted, Game

6 Jan Stenerud, Kansas City, 1972
Eddie Murray, Detroit, 1981
Mark Moseley, Washington, 1983
5 Garo Yepremian, Miami, 1974
4 Jan Stenerud, Kansas City, 1976
Nick Lowery, Kansas City, 1991, 1993
Morten Andersen, New Orleans, 1993

Most Field Goals, Career

10 Morten Andersen, New Orleans, 1986-89, 1991, 1993; Atlanta, 1996
8 Jan Stenerud, Kansas City, 1971-72, 1976; Green Bay, 1985
7 Nick Lowery, Kansas City, 1982, 1991, 1993

Most Field Goals, Game

5 Garo Yepremian, Miami, 1974 (5 att)
4 Jan Stenerud, Kansas City, 1972 (6 att)
Eddie Murray, Detroit, 1981 (6 att)
3 Nick Lowery, Kansas City, 1991 (4 att)
Nick Lowery, Kansas City, 1993 (4 att)

Longest Field Goal

51 Morten Andersen, New Orleans, 1989
49 Fuad Reveiz, Minnesota, 1995
48 Jan Stenerud, Kansas City, 1972
Jeff Jaeger, L.A. Raiders, 1992

SAFETIES

Most Safeties, Game

1 Art Still, Kansas City, 1983
Mark Gastineau, N.Y. Jets, 1985
Greg Townsend, L.A. Raiders, 1992

RUSHING

ATTEMPTS

Most Attempts, Career

81 Walter Payton, Chicago, 1977-81, 1984-87
68 O.J. Simpson, Buffalo, 1973-77
63 Eric Dickerson, L.A. Rams, 1984-85, 1987; Indianapolis, 1988-90

Most Attempts, Game

19 O.J. Simpson, Buffalo, 1974
17 Marv Hubbard, Oakland, 1974
16 O.J. Simpson, Buffalo, 1973
Marcus Allen, L.A. Raiders, 1986

YARDS GAINED

Most Yards Gained, Career

368 Walter Payton, Chicago, 1977-81, 1984-87
356 O.J. Simpson, Buffalo, 1973-77
234 Chris Warren, Seattle, 1994-96

Most Yards Gained, Game

180 Marshall Faulk, Indianapolis, 1995
127 Chris Warren, Seattle, 1995
112 O. J. Simpson, Buffalo, 1973

Longest Run From Scrimmage

49 Marshall Faulk, Indianapolis, 1995 (TD)
41 Lawrence McCutcheon, Los Angeles, 1976
Natrone Means, San Diego, 1995
Marshall Faulk, Indianapolis, 1995
39 Chris Warren, Seattle, 1994

AVERAGE GAIN

Highest Average Gain, Career (20 attempts)

9.36 Chris Warren, Seattle, 1994-96, (25-234)
5.81 Marv Hubbard, Oakland, 1972-74 (36-209)
5.71 Wilbert Montgomery, Philadelphia, 1979-80 (21-120)

Highest Average Gain, Game (10 attempts)

13.85 Marshall Faulk, Indianapolis, 1995 (13-180)
9.07 Chris Warren, Seattle, 1995 (14-127)
7.00 O.J. Simpson, Buffalo, 1973 (16-112)
Ottis Anderson, St. Louis, 1981 (10-70)

TOUCHDOWNS

Most Touchdowns, Career

3 Earl Campbell, Houston, 1979-82, 1984
Chuck Muncie, New Orleans, 1980; San Diego, 1982-83
2 John Brockington, Green Bay, 1972-74
O.J. Simpson, Buffalo, 1973-77
Walter Payton, Chicago, 1977-81, 1984-87
Marcus Allen, L.A. Raiders, 1983, 1985-86, 1988; Kansas City, 1994

Herschel Walker, Dallas, 1988-89
Johnny Johnson, Phoenix, 1991

Most Touchdowns, Game
2 John Brockington, Green Bay, 1973
Earl Campbell, Houston, 1980
Chuck Muncie, New Orleans, 1980
Herschel Walker, Dallas, 1989
Johnny Johnson, Phoenix, 1991

PASSING

ATTEMPTS

Most Attempts, Career
120 Dan Fouts, San Diego, 1980-84, 1986
88 Bob Griese, Miami, 1971-72, 1974-75, 1977, 1979
82 Warren Moon, Houston, 1989-94; Minnesota, 1995-96

Most Attempts, Game
32 Bill Kenney, Kansas City, 1984
Steve Young, San Francisco, 1993
30 Dan Fouts, San Diego, 1983
28 Jim Hart, St. Louis, 1976

COMPLETIONS

Most Completions, Career
63 Dan Fouts, San Diego, 1980-84, 1986
44 Bob Griese, Miami, 1971-72, 1974-75, 1977, 1979
41 Warren Moon, Houston, 1989-94; Minnesota, 1995-96

Most Completions, Game
21 Joe Theismann, Washington, 1984
18 Steve Young, San Francisco, 1993
17 Dan Fouts, San Diego, 1983

COMPLETION PERCENTAGE

Highest Completion Percentage, Career (40 attempts)
68.9 Joe Theismann, Washington, 1983-84 (45-31)
64.4 Jim Kelly, Buffalo, 1988, 1991-92 (45-29)
58.9 Ken Anderson, Cincinnati, 1976-77, 1982-83 (56-33)

Highest Completion Percentage, Game (10 attempts)
90.0 Archie Manning, New Orleans, 1980 (10-9)
77.8 Joe Theismann, Washington, 1984 (27-21)
72.2 Jim Everett, L.A. Rams, 1991 (18-13)

YARDS GAINED

Most Yards Gained, Career
890 Dan Fouts, San Diego, 1980-84, 1986
554 Bob Griese, Miami, 1971-72, 1974-75, 1977, 1979
476 Steve Young, San Francisco, 1993-96

Most Yards Gained, Game
274 Dan Fouts, San Diego, 1983
242 Joe Theismann, Washington, 1984
212 Phil Simms, N.Y. Giants, 1986

Longest Completion
93 Jeff Blake, Cincinnati (to Thigpen, Pittsburgh), 1996 (TD)
64 Dan Pastorini, Houston (to Burrough, Houston), 1976 (TD)
59 Randall Cunningham, Philadelphia (to Jackson, Philadelphia [19 yards] lateral to Byner, Washington [40 yards]), 1991

AVERAGE GAIN

Highest Average Gain, Career (40 attempts)
8.02 Jim Kelly, Buffalo, 1988, 1991-92 (45-361)
7.91 Randall Cunningham, Philadelphia, 1989-91 (44-348)
7.64 Joe Theismann, Washington, 1983-84 (45-344)

Highest Average Gain, Game (10 attempts)
15.27 Randall Cunningham, Philadelphia, 1991 (11-168)
11.40 Ken Anderson, Cincinnati, 1977 (10-114)
11.20 Archie Manning, New Orleans, 1980 (10-112)

TOUCHDOWNS

Most Touchdowns, Career
3 Joe Theismann, Washington, 1983-84
Joe Montana, San Francisco, 1982, 1984-85, 1988
Phil Simms, N.Y. Giants, 1986
Jim Kelly, Buffalo, 1988, 1991-92
2 James Harris, Los Angeles, 1975
Mike Boryla, Philadelphia, 1976
Ken Anderson, Cincinnati, 1976-77, 1982-83
Bob Griese, Miami, 1971-72, 1974-75, 1977, 1979
Mark Rypien, Washington, 1990, 1992
John Elway, Denver, 1987-88, 1994-95
Steve Young, San Francisco, 1993-95

Most Touchdowns, Game
3 Joe Theismann, Washington, 1984
Phil Simms, N.Y. Giants, 1986
2 James Harris, Los Angeles, 1975
Mike Boryla, Philadelphia, 1976
Ken Anderson, Cincinnati, 1977
Jim Kelly, Buffalo, 1991
Mark Rypien, Washington, 1992

HAD INTERCEPTED

Most Passes Had Intercepted, Career
8 Dan Fouts, San Diego, 1980-84, 1986
6 Jim Hart, St. Louis, 1975-78
5 Ken Stabler, Oakland, 1974-75, 1978

Most Passes Had Intercepted, Game
5 Jim Hart, St. Louis, 1977
4 Ken Stabler, Oakland, 1974
3 Dan Fouts, San Diego, 1986
Mark Rypien, Washington, 1990
Steve Young, San Francisco, 1993
Jim Harbaugh, Indianapolis, 1996

Most Attempts, Without Interception, Game
27 Joe Theismann, Washington, 1984
Phil Simms, N.Y. Giants, 1986
26 John Brodie, San Francisco, 1971
Danny White, Dallas, 1983
21 Roman Gabriel, Philadelphia, 1974
Dan Marino, Miami, 1985

PERCENTAGE, PASSES HAD INTERCEPTED

Lowest Percentage, Passes Had Intercepted, Career (40 attempts)
0.00 Joe Theismann, Washington, 1983-84 (45-0)
2.13 Dave Krieg, Seattle, 1985, 1989-90 (47-1)
2.22 Jim Kelly, Buffalo, 1988, 1991-92 (45-1)

PASS RECEIVING

RECEPTIONS

Most Receptions, Career
28 Jerry Rice, San Francisco, 1987-88, 1990-94, 1996
18 Walter Payton, Chicago, 1977-81, 1984-87
Michael Irvin, Dallas, 1992-96
17 Steve Largent, Seattle, 1979, 1982, 1985-88

Most Receptions, Game
8 Steve Largent, Seattle, 1986
Michael Irvin, Dallas, 1992
Andre Rison, Atlanta, 1993
7 John Stallworth, Pittsburgh, 1983
Jerry Rice, San Francisco, 1992
6 John Stallworth, Pittsburgh, 1980
Kellen Winslow, San Diego, 1982
Gary Clark, Washington, 1991
Keith Byars, Miami, 1994
Andre Rison, Atlanta, 1994
Jerry Rice, San Francisco, 1996

YARDS GAINED

Most Yards Gained, Career
399 Jerry Rice, San Francisco, 1987-88, 1990-94, 1996
274 Michael Irvin, Dallas, 1992-96
236 Steve Largent, Seattle, 1979, 1982, 1985-88

Most Yards Gained, Game
125 Michael Irvin, Dallas, 1992
114 Wes Chandler, San Diego, 1986
96 Ken Burrough, Houston, 1976

Longest Reception
93 Yancey Thigpen, Pittsburgh (from Blake, Cincinnati), 1996 (TD)
64 Ken Burrough, Houston (from Pastorini, Houston), 1976 (TD)
59 Keith Jackson, Philadelphia (19 yards) lateral to Earnest Byner, Washington (40 yards) (from Cunningham, Philadelphia), 1991

TOUCHDOWNS

Most Touchdowns, Career
2 Mel Gray, St. Louis, 1975-78
Cliff Branch, Oakland, 1975-78
Terry Metcalf, St. Louis, 1975-76, 1978
Tony Hill, Dallas, 1979-80, 1986
William Andrews, Atlanta, 1981-84
James Lofton, Green Bay, 1979, 1981-86; Buffalo 1992
Jimmie Giles, Tampa Bay, 1981-83, 1986
Michael Irvin, Dallas, 1992-95
Cris Carter, Minnesota, 1994-95
Eric Green, Pittsburgh, 1994-95
Jerry Rice, San Francisco, 1987-88, 1990-94, 1996

Most Touchdowns, Game
2 William Andrews, Atlanta, 1984
Eric Green, Pittsburgh, 1995

AFC-NFC PRO BOWL RECORDS

INTERCEPTIONS BY

Most Interceptions By, Career

4 Everson Walls, Dallas, 1982-84, 1986
3 Ken Houston, Houston, 1971-73; Washington, 1974-79
Jack Lambert, Pittsburgh, 1976-84
Ted Hendricks, Baltimore, 1972-74; Green Bay, 1975; Oakland, 1981-82; L.A. Raiders, 1983-84
Mike Haynes, New England, 1978-81, 1983; L.A. Raiders, 1985-87
Deion Sanders, Atlanta, 1992-94; San Francisco, 1995
2 By 10 players

Most Interceptions By, Game

2 Mel Blount, Pittsburgh, 1977
Everson Walls, Dallas, 1982, 1983
LeRoy Irvin, L.A. Rams, 1986
David Fulcher, Cincinnati, 1990

YARDS GAINED

Most Yards Gained, Career

77 Ted Hendricks, Baltimore, 1972-74; Green Bay, 1975; Oakland, 1981-82; L.A. Raiders, 1983-84
73 Rod Woodson, Pittsburgh, 1990-94
51 Jerry Gray, L.A. Rams, 1987-90

Most Yards Gained, Game

73 Rod Woodson, Pittsburgh, 1994
65 Ted Hendricks, Baltimore, 1973
51 Jerry Gray, L.A. Rams, 1990

Longest Gain

73 Rod Woodson, Pittsburgh, 1994 (lateral)
65 Ted Hendricks, Baltimore, 1973
51 Jerry Gray, L.A. Rams, 1990 (TD)

TOUCHDOWNS

Most Touchdowns, Game

1 Bobby Bell, Kansas City, 1973
Nolan Cromwell, L.A. Rams, 1984
Joey Browner, Minnesota, 1986
Jerry Gray, L.A. Rams, 1990
Mike Johnson, Cleveland, 1990
Junior Seau, San Diego, 1993
Ken Harvey, Washington, 1996

PUNTING

Most Punts, Career

33 Ray Guy, Oakland, 1974-79, 1981
23 Rohn Stark, Indianapolis, 1986-87, 1991, 1993
22 Reggie Roby, Miami, 1985, 1990; Washington, 1995

Most Punts, Game

10 Reggie Roby, Miami, 1985
9 Tom Wittum, San Francisco, 1974
Rohn Stark, Indianapolis, 1987
8 Jerrel Wilson, Kansas City, 1971
Tom Skladany, Detroit, 1982
Reggie Roby, Washington, 1995

Longest Punt

64 Tom Wittum, San Francisco, 1974
Darren Bennett, San Diego, 1996
61 Reggie Roby, Miami, 1985
Jeff Feagles, Arizona, 1996
60 Ron Widby, Dallas, 1972
Reggie Roby, Washington, 1995

AVERAGE YARDAGE

Highest Average, Career (10 punts)

46.73 Reggie Roby, Miami, 1985, 1990; Washington, 1995 (22-1,028)
45.25 Jerrel Wilson, Kansas City, 1971-73 (16-724)
44.65 Rohn Stark, Indianapolis, 1986-87, 1991, 1993 (23-1,027)

Highest Average, Game (4 punts)

55.50 Darren Bennett, San Diego, 1996 (4-222)
50.13 Reggie Roby, Washington, 1995 (8-401)
49.57 Jim Arnold, Detroit, 1988 (7-347)

PUNT RETURNS

Most Punt Returns, Career

13 Rick Upchurch, Denver, 1977, 1979-80, 1983
11 Vai Sikahema, St. Louis, 1987-88
10 Mike Nelms, Washington, 1981-83

Most Punt Returns, Game

7 Vai Sikahema, St. Louis, 1987
6 Henry Ellard, L.A. Rams, 1985
Gerald McNeil, Cleveland, 1988
Eric Metcalf, Cleveland, 1995
5 Rick Upchurch, Denver, 1980
Mike Nelms, Washington, 1981
Carl Roaches, Houston, 1982
Johnny Bailey, Phoenix, 1993

Most Fair Catches, Game

2 Jerry Logan, Baltimore, 1971
Dick Anderson, Miami, 1974
Henry Ellard, L.A. Rams, 1985

YARDS GAINED

Most Yards Gained, Career

183 Billy Johnson, Houston, 1976, 1978; Atlanta, 1984
138 Mel Renfro, Dallas, 1971-72, 1974
Rick Upchurch, Denver, 1977, 1979-80, 1983
125 Eric Metcalf, Cleveland, 1994-95

Most Yards Gained, Game

159 Billy Johnson, Houston, 1976
138 Mel Renfro, Dallas, 1971
117 Wally Henry, Philadelphia, 1980

Longest Punt Return

90 Billy Johnson, Houston, 1976 (TD)
86 Wally Henry, Philadelphia, 1980 (TD)
82 Mel Renfro, Dallas, 1971 (TD)

AVERAGE YARDAGE

Highest Average, Career (4 returns)

22.88 Billy Johnson, Houston, 1976, 1978; Atlanta, 1984 (8-183)
21.50 Tony Green, Washington, 1979 (4-86)
14.00 Mel Gray, Detroit, 1991-92, 1995 (5-70)

Highest Average, Game (3 returns)

39.75 Billy Johnson, Houston, 1976 (4-159)
39.00 Wally Henry, Philadelphia, 1980 (3-117)
21.50 Tony Green, Washington, 1979 (4-86)

TOUCHDOWNS

Most Touchdowns, Game

2 Mel Renfro, Dallas, 1971
1 Billy Johnson, Houston, 1976
Wally Henry, Philadelphia, 1980

KICKOFF RETURNS

Most Kickoff Returns, Career

14 Mel Gray, Detroit, 1991-92, 1995
10 Rick Upchurch, Denver, 1977, 1979-80, 1983
Greg Pruitt, Cleveland, 1974-75, 1977-78; L.A. Raiders, 1984
8 Mike Nelms, Washington, 1981-83

Most Kickoff Returns, Game

7 Mel Gray, Detroit, 1995
6 Greg Pruitt, L.A. Raiders, 1984
5 Les (Speedy) Duncan, Washington, 1972
Ron Smith, Chicago, 1973
Herb Mul-Key, Washington, 1974
Mel Gray, Detroit, 1991

YARDS GAINED

Most Yards Gained, Career

309 Greg Pruitt, Cleveland, 1974-75, 1977-78; L.A. Raiders, 1984
294 Mel Gray, Detroit, 1991-92, 1995
222 Rick Upchurch, Denver, 1977, 1979-80, 1983

Most Yards Gained, Game

192 Greg Pruitt, L.A. Raiders, 1984
175 Les (Speedy) Duncan, Washington, 1972
162 Mel Gray, Detroit, 1995

Longest Kickoff Return

62 Greg Pruitt, L.A. Raiders, 1984
61 Eugene (Mercury) Morris, Miami, 1972
55 Ron Smith, Chicago, 1973

AVERAGE YARDAGE

Highest Average, Career (4 returns)

35.00 Les (Speedy) Duncan, Washington, 1972 (5-175)
31.25 Eugene (Mercury) Morris, Miami, 1972 (3-93)
30.90 Greg Pruitt, Cleveland, 1974-75, 1977-78; L.A. Raiders, 1984 (6-192)

Highest Average, Game (3 returns)

35.00 Les (Speedy) Duncan, Washington, 1972 (5-175)
32.00 Greg Pruitt, L.A. Raiders, 1984 (6-192)
31.00 Eugene (Mercury) Morris, Miami, 1972 (3-93)

TOUCHDOWNS

Most Touchdowns, Game

None

FUMBLES

Most Fumbles, Career

6 Dan Fouts, San Diego, 1980-84, 1986

4 Lawrence McCutcheon, Los Angeles, 1974-78
Franco Harris, Pittsburgh, 1973-76, 1978-81
Jay Schroeder, Washington, 1987
Vai Sikahema, St. Louis, 1987-88
3 O.J. Simpson, Buffalo, 1973-77
William Andrews, Atlanta, 1981-84
Joe Montana, San Francisco, 1982, 1984-85, 1988
Walter Payton, Chicago, 1977-81, 1984-87
Neil Lomax, St. Louis, 1985, 1988
Jim Kelly, Buffalo, 1988, 1991-92

Most Fumbles, Game
4 Jay Schroeder, Washington, 1987
3 Dan Fouts, San Diego, 1982
Vai Sikahema, St. Louis, 1987
2 By 11 players

RECOVERIES
Most Fumbles Recovered, Career
3 Harold Jackson, Philadelphia, 1973; Los Angeles, 1974, 1976, 1978 (3-own)
Dan Fouts, San Diego, 1980-84, 1986 (3-own)
Randy White, Dallas, 1978, 1980-86 (3-opp)
2 By many players

Most Fumbles Recovered, Game
2 Dick Anderson, Miami, 1974 (1-own, 1-opp)
Harold Jackson, Los Angeles, 1974 (2-own)
Dan Fouts, San Diego, 1982 (2-own)
Joey Browner, Minnesota, 1990 (2-opp)

YARDAGE
Longest Fumble Return
83 Art Still, Kansas City, 1985 (TD, opp)
51 Phil Villapiano, Oakland, 1974 (opp)
37 Sam Mills, New Orleans, 1988 (opp)

TOUCHDOWNS
Most Touchdowns, Game
1 Art Still, Kansas City, 1985
Keith Millard, Minnesota, 1990

SACKS
Sacks have been compiled since 1983.

Most Sacks, Career
9.5 Reggie White, Philadelphia, 1987-93; Green Bay, 1994
9 Howie Long, L.A. Raiders, 1984-88, 1990, 1993-1994
7 Mark Gastineau, N.Y. Jets, 1983-86

Most Sacks, Game
4 Mark Gastineau, N.Y. Jets, 1985
Reggie White, Philadelphia, 1987
3 Richard Dent, Chicago, 1985
Bruce Smith, Buffalo, 1991
2 By many players

TEAM RECORDS

SCORING
Most Points, Game
45 NFC, 1984

Fewest Points, Game
3 AFC, 1984, 1989, 1994

Most Points, Both Teams, Game
64 NFC (37) vs. AFC (27), 1980

Fewest Points, Both Teams, Game
16 NFC (6) vs. AFC (10), 1987

TOUCHDOWNS
Most Touchdowns, Game
6 NFC, 1984

Fewest Touchdowns, Game
0 AFC, 1971, 1974, 1984, 1989, 1994
NFC, 1987, 1988

Most Touchdowns, Both Teams, Game
8 AFC (4) vs. NFC (4), 1973
NFC (5) vs. AFC (3), 1980

Fewest Touchdowns, Both Teams, Game
1 AFC (0) vs. NFC (1), 1974
NFC (0) vs. AFC (1), 1987
NFC (0) vs. AFC (1), 1988

POINTS AFTER TOUCHDOWN
Most Points After Touchdown, Game
6 NFC, 1984

Most Points After Touchdown, Both Teams, Game
7 NFC (4) vs. AFC (3), 1973
NFC (4) vs. AFC (3), 1980
NFC (4) vs. AFC (3), 1986

FIELD GOALS
Most Field Goals Attempted, Game
6 AFC, 1972
NFC, 1981, 1983

Most Field Goals Attempted, Both Teams, Game
9 NFC (6) vs. AFC (3), 1983

Most Field Goals, Game
5 AFC, 1974

Most Field Goals, Both Teams, Game
7 AFC (5) vs. NFC (2), 1974

NET YARDS GAINED RUSHING AND PASSING
Most Yards Gained, Game
552 AFC, 1995

Fewest Yards Gained, Game
114 AFC, 1993

Most Yards Gained, Both Teams, Game
811 AFC (466) vs. NFC (345), 1983

Fewest Yards Gained, Both Teams, Game
424 AFC (202) vs. NFC (222), 1987

RUSHING
ATTEMPTS
Most Attempts, Game
50 AFC, 1974

Fewest Attempts, Game
14 AFC, 1994

Most Attempts, Both Teams, Game
80 AFC (50) vs. NFC (30), 1974

Fewest Attempts, Both Teams, Game
47 NFC (22) vs. AFC (25), 1996

YARDS GAINED
Most Yards Gained, Game
400 AFC, 1995

Fewest Yards Gained, Game
28 NFC, 1992

Most Yards Gained, Both Teams, Game
441 AFC (400) vs. NFC (41), 1995

Fewest Yards Gained, Both Teams, Game
131 NFC (28) vs. AFC (103), 1992

TOUCHDOWNS
Most Touchdowns, Game
3 NFC, 1989, 1991
AFC, 1995

Most Touchdowns, Both Teams, Game
4 AFC (2) vs. NFC (2), 1973
AFC (2) vs. NFC (2), 1980

PASSING
ATTEMPTS
Most Attempts, Game
55 NFC, 1993

Fewest Attempts, Game
17 NFC, 1972

Most Attempts, Both Teams, Game
94 AFC (50) vs. NFC (44), 1983

Fewest Attempts, Both Teams, Game
42 NFC (17) vs. AFC (25), 1972

COMPLETIONS
Most Completions, Game
32 NFC, 1993

Fewest Completions, Game
7 NFC, 1972, 1982

Most Completions, Both Teams, Game
55 AFC (31) vs. NFC (24), 1983

Fewest Completions, Both Teams, Game
18 NFC (7) vs. AFC (11), 1972

YARDS GAINED
Most Yards Gained, Game
387 AFC, 1983

Fewest Yards Gained, Game
42 NFC, 1982

Most Yards Gained, Both Teams, Game
608 AFC (387) vs. NFC (221), 1983

AFC-NFC PRO BOWL RECORDS

Fewest Yards Gained, Both Teams, Game
215 NFC (89) vs. AFC (126), 1972

TIMES SACKED

Most Times Sacked, Game
9 NFC, 1985

Fewest Times Sacked, Game
0 NFC, 1971

Most Times Sacked, Both Teams, Game
17 NFC (9) vs. AFC (8), 1985

Fewest Times Sacked, Both Teams, Game
3 AFC (1) vs. NFC (2), 1995

TOUCHDOWNS

Most Touchdowns, Game
4 NFC, 1984

Most Touchdowns, Both Teams, Game
5 NFC (3) vs. AFC (2), 1986

INTERCEPTIONS BY

Most Interceptions By, Game
6 AFC, 1977

Most Interceptions By, Both Teams, Game
7 AFC (6) vs. NFC (1), 1977

YARDS GAINED

Most Yards Gained, Game
103 AFC, 1994

Most Yards Gained, Both Teams, Game
116 AFC (103) vs. NFC (13), 1994

TOUCHDOWNS

Most Touchdowns, Game
1 AFC, 1973, 1990, 1993
NFC, 1984, 1986, 1990, 1996

PUNTING

Most Punts, Game
10 AFC, 1985

Fewest Punts, Game
0 NFC, 1989

Most Punts, Both Teams, Game
16 AFC (10) vs. NFC (6), 1985

Fewest Punts, Both Teams, Game
4 NFC (1) vs. AFC (3), 1992

PUNT RETURNS

Most Punt Returns, Game
7 NFC, 1985, 1987
AFC, 1995

Fewest Punt Returns, Game
0 AFC, 1984, 1989

Most Punt Returns, Both Teams, Game
11 NFC (7) vs. AFC (4), 1985

Fewest Punt Returns, Both Teams, Game
2 AFC (1) vs. NFC (1), 1996

YARDS GAINED

Most Yards Gained, Game
177 AFC, 1976

Fewest Yards Gained, Game
–1 NFC, 1991

Most Yards Gained, Both Teams, Game
263 AFC (177) vs. NFC (86), 1976

Fewest Yards Gained, Both Teams, Game
16 AFC (0) vs. NFC (16), 1984

TOUCHDOWNS

Most Touchdowns, Game
2 NFC, 1971

KICKOFF RETURNS

Most Kickoff Returns, Game
8 NFC, 1995

Fewest Kickoff Returns, Game
1 NFC, 1971, 1984, 1994
AFC, 1988, 1991

Most Kickoff Returns, Both Teams, Game
12 NFC (8) vs. AFC (4), 1995

Fewest Kickoff Returns, Both Teams, Game
5 NFC (2) vs. AFC (3), 1979
AFC (1) vs. NFC (4), 1988
NFC (2) vs. AFC (3), 1992
NFC (1) vs. AFC (4), 1994

YARDS GAINED

Most Yards Gained, Game
215 AFC, 1984

Fewest Yards Gained, Game
6 NFC, 1971

Most Yards Gained, Both Teams, Game
293 NFC (200) vs. AFC (93), 1972

Fewest Yards Gained, Both Teams, Game
99 NFC (48) vs. AFC (51), 1987

TOUCHDOWNS

Most Touchdowns, Game
None

FUMBLES

Most Fumbles, Game
10 NFC, 1974

Most Fumbles, Both Teams, Game
15 NFC (10) vs. AFC (5), 1974

RECOVERIES

Most Fumbles Recovered, Game
10 NFC, 1974 (6 own, 4 opp)

Most Fumbles Lost, Game
4 AFC, 1974, 1988
NFC, 1974

YARDS GAINED

Most Yards Gained, Game
87 AFC, 1985

TOUCHDOWNS

Most Touchdowns, Game
1 AFC, 1985
NFC, 1990

TURNOVERS

(Number of times losing the ball on interceptions and fumbles.)

Most Turnovers, Game
8 AFC, 1974

Fewest Turnovers, Game
0 AFC, 1991
NFC, 1991, 1995, 1996

Most Turnovers, Both Teams, Game
12 AFC (8) vs. NFC (4), 1974

Fewest Turnovers, Both Teams, Game
0 AFC vs. NFC, 1991

Rules

OFFICIALS

1996 NFL ROSTER OF OFFICIALS

Jerry Seeman, Director of Officiating
Al Hynes, Supervisor of Officials
Jack Reader, Supervisor of Officials
Ron DeSouza, Supervisor of Officials

No.	Name	Position	College
115	Ancich, Hendi	Umpire	Harbor College
81	Anderson, Dave	Line Judge	Salem College
66	Anderson, Walt	Line Judge	Sam Houston State
34	Austin, Gerald	Referee	Western Carolina
22	Baetz, Paul	Back Judge	Heidelberg
91	Baker, Ken	Field Judge	Eastern Illinois
26	Baltz, Mark	Head Linesman	Ohio University
55	Barnes, Tom	Line Judge	Minnesota
56	Baynes, Ron	Line Judge	Auburn
32	Bergman, Jeff	Line Judge	Robert Morris
40	Bible, Jon	Side Judge	Texas
7	Blum, Ron	Referee	Marin College
90	Borgard, Mike	Side Judge	St. Louis
18	Boston, Byron	Line Judge	Austin
110	Botchan, Ron	Umpire	Occidental
101	Boylston, Bob	Umpire	Alabama
31	Brown, Chad	Umpire	East Texas State
126	Carey, Don	Field Judge	U.C.-Riverside
94	Carey, Mike	Referee	Santa Clara
39	Carlsen, Don	Side Judge	Cal State-Chico
63	Carollo, Bill	Side Judge	Wisconsin
11	Carroll, Duke	Back Judge	Ithaca
43	Cashion, Red	Referee	Texas A&M
41	Cheek, Boris	Back Judge	Morgan State
45	Coleman, George	Back Judge	Bishop College
65	Coleman, Walt	Referee	Arkansas
27	Conway, Al	Umpire	Army
99	Corrente, Tony	Back Judge	Cal State-Fullerton
71	Coukart, Ed	Umpire	Northwestern
61	Creed, Dick	Back Judge	Louisville
75	Daopoulos, Jim	Back Judge	Kentucky
70	Dawson, Scott	Umpire	Virginia Tech
78	Demmas, Art	Umpire	Vanderbilt
113	Dorkowski, Don	Field Judge	Cal State-Los Angeles
6	Dornan, Kirk	Field Judge	Central Washington
74	Duke, James	Umpire	Howard
89	Dunn, Neely	Side Judge	South Carolina State
57	Fiffick, Ed	Umpire	Marquette
47	Fincken, Tom	Side Judge	Kansas State
111	Frantz, Earnie	Head Linesman	No College
50	Gereb, Neil	Umpire	California
72	Gierke, Terry	Head Linesman	Portland State
3	Golmont, Van	Back Judge	Miami
19	Green, Scott	Field Judge	Delaware
23	Grier, Johnny	Referee	University of D.C.
96	Hakes, Don	Field Judge	Bradley
104	Hamer, Dale	Referee	California, Pa.
105	Hantak, Dick	Referee	Southeast Missouri
125	Hayes, Laird	Side Judge	Princeton
54	Hayward, George	Head Linesman	Missouri Western
85	Hochuli, Ed	Referee	Texas-El Paso
114	Johnson, Tom	Head Linesman	Miami, Ohio
97	Jones, Nate	Side Judge	Lewis & Clark
106	Jury, Al	Back Judge	San Bernardino Valley
67	Keck, John	Umpire	Cornell College
86	Kukar, Bernie	Referee	St. John's
120	Lane, Gary	Referee	Missouri
127	Leavy, Bill	Field Judge	San Jose State
76	Liebsack, Ron	Side Judge	Regis
49	Look, Dean	Side Judge	Michigan State
98	Lovett, Bill	Back Judge	Maryland
59	Luckett, Phil	Field Judge	Texas-El Paso
9	Markbreit, Jerry	Referee	Illinois
38	Maurer, Bruce	Line Judge	Ohio State
95	McElwee, Bob	Referee	Navy
35	McGrath, Bob	Head Linesman	Western Kentucky
64	McPeters, Lloyd	Line Judge	Oklahoma State
80	Millis, Timmie	Back Judge	Millsaps
117	Montgomery, Ben	Line Judge	Morehouse
36	Moore, Bob	Back Judge	Dayton
60	Moore, Tommy	Side Judge	Stephen F. Austin
20	Nemmers, Larry	Referee	Upper Iowa
51	Orem, Dale	Line Judge	Louisville
15	Patterson, Rick	Side Judge	Wofford
77	Pereira, Mike	Side Judge	Santa Clara
10	Phares, Ron	Head Linesman	Virginia Tech
79	Pointer, Aaron	Head Linesman	Pacific Lutheran
5	Quirk, Jim	Umpire	Delaware
83	Reels, Richard	Field Judge	No College
53	Reynolds, Bill	Line Judge	West Chester State
44	Rice, Jeff	Umpire	Northwestern
68	Richard, Louis	Back Judge	Southwest Louisiana
121	Rivers, Sanford	Head Linesman	Youngstown State
46	Robison, John	Field Judge	Utah
33	Roe, Howard	Referee	Wichita State
58	Saracino, Jim	Back Judge	Northern Colorado
21	Schleyer, John	Head Linesman	Millersville
122	Schmitz, Bill	Field Judge	Colorado State
109	Semon, Sid	Head Linesman	Southern California
118	Sifferman, Tom	Back Judge	Seattle
73	Skelton, Bobby	Field Judge	Alabama
30	Slaughter, Gary	Head Linesman	East Texas State
29	Slavin, Howard	Side Judge	Southern California
2	Smith, Billy	Field Judge	East Carolina
124	Speight, Leslie	Side Judge	No College
119	Spitler, Ron	Field Judge	Panhandle State
12	Spyksma, Bill	Line Judge	South Dakota
24	Stabile, Tom	Head Linesman	Slippery Rock
88	Steenson, Scott	Back Judge	North Texas
84	Steinkerchner, Mark	Field Judge	Akron
62	Stewart, Charles	Line Judge	Long Beach State
103	Stuart, Rex	Umpire	Appalachian State
4	Toole, Doug	Side Judge	Utah State
42	Triplette, Jeff	Field Judge	Wake Forest
37	Upson, Larry	Line Judge	Prince George C.C.
93	Vaughan, Jack	Field Judge	Mississippi State
52	Veteri, Tony	Head Linesman	Manhattan College
100	Wagner, Bob	Umpire	Penn State
87	Weidner, Paul	Head Linesman	Cincinnati
123	White, Tom	Referee	Temple
8	Williams, Dale	Head Linesman	Cal State-Northridge
82	Winter, Ron	Line Judge	Michigan State
16	Wyant, David	Side Judge	Virginia

NUMERICAL ROSTER

No.	Name	Position
2	Billy Smith	FJ
3	Van Golmont	BJ
4	Doug Toole	SJ
5	Jim Quirk	U
6	Kirk Dornan	FJ
7	Ron Blum	R
8	Dale Williams	HL
9	Jerry Markbreit	R
10	Ron Phares	HL
11	Duke Carroll	BJ
12	Bill Spyksma	LJ
15	Rick Patterson	SJ
16	David Wyant	SJ
18	Byron Boston	LJ
19	Scott Green	FJ
20	Larry Nemmers	R
21	John Schleyer	HL
22	Paul Baetz	BJ
23	Johnny Grier	R
24	Tom Stabile	HL
26	Mark Baltz	HL
27	Al Conway	U
29	Howard Slavin	SJ
30	Gary Slaughter	HL
31	Chad Brown	U
32	Jeff Bergman	LJ
33	Howard Roe	R
34	Gerry Austin	R
35	Bob McGrath	HL
36	Bob Moore	BJ
37	Larry Upson	LJ
38	Bruce Maurer	LJ
39	Don Carlsen	SJ
40	Jon Bible	SJ
41	Boris Cheek	BJ
42	Jeff Triplette	FJ
43	Red Cashion	R
44	Jeff Rice	U
45	George Coleman	BJ
46	John Robison	FJ
47	Tom Fincken	SJ
49	Dean Look	SJ
50	Neil Gereb	U
51	Dale Orem	LJ
52	Tony Veteri	HL
53	Bill Reynolds	LJ
54	George Hayward	HL
55	Tom Barnes	LJ
56	Ron Baynes	LJ
57	Ed Fiffick	U
58	Jim Saracino	BJ
59	Phil Luckett	FJ
60	Tommy Moore	SJ
61	Dick Creed	BJ
62	Charles Stewart	LJ
63	Bill Carollo	SJ
64	Lloyd McPeters	LJ
65	Walt Coleman	R
66	Walt Anderson	LJ
67	John Keck	U
68	Louis Richard	BJ
70	Scott Dawson	U
71	Ed Coukart	U
72	Terry Gierke	HL
73	Bobby Skelton	FJ
74	James Duke	U
75	Jim Daopoulos	BJ
76	Ron Liebsack	SJ
77	Mike Pereira	SJ
78	Art Demmas	U
79	Aaron Pointer	HL
80	Timmie Millis	BJ
81	Dave Anderson	LJ
82	Ron Winter	LJ
83	Richard Reels	FJ
84	Mark Steinkerchner	FJ
85	Ed Hochuli	R
86	Bernie Kukar	R
87	Paul Weidner	HL
88	Scott Steenson	BJ
89	Neely Dunn	SJ
90	Mike Borgard	SJ
91	Ken Baker	FJ
93	Jack Vaughan	FJ
94	Mike Carey	R
95	Bob McElwee	R
96	Don Hakes	FJ
97	Nate Jones	SJ
98	Bill Lovett	BJ
99	Tony Corrente	BJ
100	Bob Wagner	U
101	Bob Boylston	U
103	Rex Stuart	U
104	Dale Hamer	R
105	Dick Hantak	R
106	Al Jury	BJ
109	Sid Semon	HL
110	Ron Botchan	U
111	Earnie Frantz	HL
113	Don Dorkowski	FJ
114	Tom Johnson	HL
115	Hendi Ancich	U
117	Ben Montgomery	LJ
118	Tom Sifferman	BJ
119	Ron Spitler	FJ
120	Gary Lane	R
121	Sanford Rivers	HL
122	Bill Schmitz	FJ
123	Tom White	R
124	Leslie Speight	SJ
125	Laird Hayes	SJ
126	Don Carey	FJ
127	Bill Leavy	FJ

1996 OFFICIALS AT A GLANCE

REFEREES

Gerry Austin, No. **34,** Western Carolina, president, leadership development group, 15th year.
Ron Blum, No. **7,** Marin College, professional golfer, 12th year.
Mike Carey, No. **94,** Santa Clara, owner, skiing accessories, 7th year.
Red Cashion, No. **43,** Texas A&M, chairman, insurance company, 25th year.
Walt Coleman, No. **65,** Arkansas, president, dairy processor, 8th year.
Johnny Grier, No. **23,** University of D.C., planning engineer, 16th year.
Dale Hamer, No. **104,** California (Pa.) University, consultant, 18th year.
Dick Hantak, No. **105,** Southeast Missouri, educator, 19th year.
Ed Hochuli, No. **85,** Texas-El Paso, attorney, 7th year.
Bernie Kukar, No. **86,** St. John's, sales representative, employees benefit plan, 13th year.
Gary Lane, No. **120,** Missouri, vice president, medical supplies, former NFL player, 15th year.
Jerry Markbreit, No. **9,** Illinois, corporate consultant, 21st year.
Bob McElwee, No. **95,** Navy, owner, heavy construction firm, 21st year.
Larry Nemmers, No. **20,** Upper Iowa, motivational speaker, 12th year.
Howard Roe, No. **33,** Wichita State, director, administration and finance, 13th year.
Tom White, No. **123,** Temple, president, athletic sportswear, 8th year.

UMPIRES

Hendi Ancich, No. **115,** Harbor, longshoreman, 15th year.
Ron Botchan, No. **110,** Occidental, college professor, former AFL player, 17th year.
Bob Boylston, No. **101,** Alabama, stockbroker, 19th year.
Chad Brown, No. **31,** East Texas State, director, intramural/sports clubs, 5th year.
Al Conway, No. **27,** Army, director of manufacturing, 28th year.
Ed Coukart, No. **71,** Northwestern, president, commercial bank, 8th year.
Scott Dawson, No. **70,** Virginia Tech, owner, commercial construction company, 2nd year.
Art Demmas, No. **78,** Vanderbilt, Southern coordinator, National Football Foundation and College Hall of Fame, 29th year.
James Duke, No. **74,** Howard, regional manager, department of recreation and parks, 4th year.
Ed Fiffick, No. **57,** Marquette, podiatric physician, 18th year.
Neil Gereb, No. **50,** California, project manager, aircraft company, 16th year.
John Keck, No. **67,** Cornell, petroleum distributor, 25th year.
Jim Quirk, No. **5,** Delaware, senior vice president, securities, 9th year.
Jeff Rice, No. **44,** Northwestern, attorney, 2nd year.
Rex Stuart, No. **103,** Appalachian State, insurance agent, 13th year.
Bob Wagner, No. **100,** Penn State, executive director, cardiovascular institute, 12th year.

HEAD LINESMEN

Mark Baltz, No. **26,** Ohio University, manufacturer's representative, 8th year.
Earnie Frantz, No. **111,** no college, vice president and manager, insurance company, 16th year.
Terry Gierke, No. **72,** Portland State, real estate broker, 16th year.
George Hayward, No. **54,** Missouri Western, vice president and manager, warehouse company, 6th year.
Tom Johnson, No. **114,** Miami, Ohio, retired educator, president/owner, security company, 15th year.
Bob McGrath, No. **35,** Western Kentucky, sales representative, fund raiser, 4th year.
Ron Phares, No. **10,** Virginia Tech, president, construction company, 12th year.
Aaron Pointer, No. **79,** Pacific Lutheran, park department administrator, 10th year.
Sanford Rivers, No. **121,** Youngstown State, assistant vice president, school administration, 8th year.
John Schleyer, No. **21,** Millersville, medical sales, 7th year.
Sid Semon, No. **109,** Southern California, physical educational consultant, 19th year.
Gary Slaughter, No. **30,** East Texas State, assistant plant manager, 1st year.
Tom Stabile, No. **24,** Slippery Rock, secondary educational administrator, 2nd year.
Tony Veteri, No. **52,** Manhattan, director of athletics, 5th year.
Paul Weidner, No. **87,** Cincinnati, marketing manager, 11th year.
Dale Williams, No. **8,** Cal State-Northridge, athletic official, 17th year.

LINE JUDGES

Dave Anderson, No. **81,** Salem, insurance executive, 13th year.
Walt Anderson, No. **66,** Sam Houston State, dentist, orthodontics, 1st year.
Tom Barnes, No. **55,** Minnesota, manufacturing representative, 11th year.
Ron Baynes, No. **56,** Auburn, school administrator, coach, 10th year.
Jeff Bergman, No. **32,** Robert Morris, president and chief executive officer, medical services, 6th year.
Byron Boston, No. **18,** Austin, operations consultant, 2nd year.
Bruce Maurer, No. **38,** Ohio State, administrator and associate director, recreational sports, 10th year.
Lloyd McPeters, No. **64,** Oklahoma State, business insurance sales, 4th year.
Ben Montgomery, No. **117,** Morehouse, school administrator, 15th year.
Dale Orem, No. **51,** Louisville, chairman of the board, bank, 17th year.
Bill Reynolds, No. **53,** West Chester State, educator, 22nd year.
Bill Spyksma, No. **12,** South Dakota, commercial real estate, construction sales, 2nd year.
Mark Steinkerchner, No. **84,** Akron, vice president, 3rd year.
Charles Stewart, No. **62,** Long Beach State, human services administrator, 5th year.
Larry Upson, No. **37,** Prince George City College, senior personnel management specialist, 6th year.
Ron Winter, No. **82,** Michigan State, university professor, 2nd year.

BACK JUDGES

Paul Baetz, No. **22,** Heidelberg, financial consultant, 19th year.
Duke Carroll, No. **11,** Ithaca, president, insurance agency, 2nd year.
Boris Cheek, No. **41,** Morgan State, director, operations and management, 1st year.
George Coleman, No. **45,** Bishop College, executive director, YMCA, 4th year.
Tony Corrente, No. **99,** Cal State-Fullerton, educator, 2nd year.
Richard Creed, No. **61,** Louisville, manager, real estate, 19th year.
Jim Daopoulos, No. **75,** Kentucky, mortgage broker, 8th year.
Van Golmont, No. **3,** Miami, regional manager, marketing development, 6th year.
Al Jury, No. **106,** San Bernardino Valley, state traffic officer, 19th year.
Bill Lovett, No. **98,** Maryland, managing partner, financial sales, 7th year.
Timmie Millis, No. **80,** Millsaps, financial investigative consultant, 8th year.
Bob Moore, No. **36,** Dayton, municipal judge, 13th year.
Louis Richard, No. **68,** Southwestern Louisiana, sales manager, 11th year.
Jim Saracino, No. **58,** Northern Colorado, secondary educator, 2nd year.
Tom Sifferman, No. **118,** Seattle, manufacturer's representative, 11th year.
Scott Steenson, No. **88,** North Texas State, commercial real estate broker, 6th year.

SIDE JUDGES

Jon Bible, No. **40,** Texas, attorney/college educator, 3rd year.
Mike Borgard, No. **90,** St. Louis, president, sales promotions, 7th year.
Don Carlsen, No. **39,** Cal State-Chico, assistant superintendent, county schools, 8th year.
Bill Carollo, No. **63,** Wisconsin, marketing executive, 8th year.
Neely Dunn, No. **89,** South Carolina State, principal, 2nd year.
Tom Fincken, No. **47,** Emporia State, retired educational administrator, 13th year.
Laird Hayes, No. **125,** Princeton, associate professor, physical education/athletics, 2nd year.
Nate Jones, No. **97,** Lewis and Clark, high school principal, 20th year.
Ron Liebsack, No. **76,** Regis, manager, telecommunications, 2nd year.
Dean Look, No. **49,** Michigan State, consultant, medical manufacturing, former AFL player, 24th year.
Tommy Moore, No. **60,** Stephen F. Austin, marketing, manufacturing, representative, 5th year.
Rick Patterson, No. **15,** Wofford, banker, 1st year.
Mike Pereira, No. **77,** Santa Clara, supervisor of officials, owner, sportswear apparel, 1st year.
Howard Slavin, No. **29,** Southern California, attorney, 10th year.
Leslie Speight, No. **124,** No college, high school teacher, 2nd year.
Doug Toole, No. **4,** Utah State, physical therapist, orthopedic and sports medicine, 9th year.
David Wyant, No. **16,** Virginia, director, technology transfer center, 6th year.

FIELD JUDGES

Ken Baker, No. **91,** Eastern Illinois, college educator, 6th year.
Don Carey, No. **126,** California-Riverside, contract manager, 2nd year.
Don Dorkowski, No. **113,** Cal State-Los Angeles, work experience coordinator, 11th year.
Kirk Dornan, No. **6,** Central Washington, managing partner, 3rd year.
Scott Green, No. **19,** Delaware, vice president, government relations, 6th year.
Don Hakes, No. **96,** Bradley, retired educator, 20th year.
Bill Leavy, No. **127,** San Jose State, firefighter, 2nd year.
Phil Luckett, No. **59,** Texas-El Paso, computer program analyst, federal civil services, 6th year.
Richard Reels, No. **83,** Chicago State, director of security, court services, 4th year.
John Robison, No. **46,** Utah, junior high school counselor, 9th year.
Bill Schmitz, No. **122,** Colorado State, general sales manager, 8th year.
Bobby Skelton, No. **73,** Alabama, industrial representative, 12th year.
Billy Smith, No. **2,** East Carolina, federal government, 3rd year.
Ron Spitler, No. **119,** Panhandle State, owner, service center, 15th year.
Jeff Triplette, No. **42,** Wake Forest, general manager, real estate, 1st year.
Jack Vaughan, No. **93,** Mississippi State, marketing consultant, 20th year.

OFFICIAL SIGNALS

1

TOUCHDOWN, FIELD GOAL, or SUCCESSFUL TRY
Both arms extended above head.

2

SAFETY
Palms together above head.

3

FIRST DOWN
Arm pointed toward defensive team's goal.

4

CROWD NOISE, DEAD BALL, or NEUTRAL ZONE ESTABLISHED
One arm above head with an open hand.
With fist closed: **Fourth Down.**

5

BALL ILLEGALLY TOUCHED, KICKED OR BATTED
Fingertips tap both shoulders.

6

TIME OUT
Hands crisscrossed above head.

Same signal followed by placing one hand on top of cap: **Referee's Time Out.**

Same signal followed by arm swung at side: **Touchback.**

7

NO TIME OUT or TIME IN WITH WHISTLE
Full arm circled to simulate moving clock.

8

DELAY OF GAME or EXCESS TIME OUT
Folded arms.

9

FALSE START, ILLEGAL FORMATION, or KICKOFF OR SAFETY KICK OUT OF BOUNDS
Forearms rotated over and over in front of body.

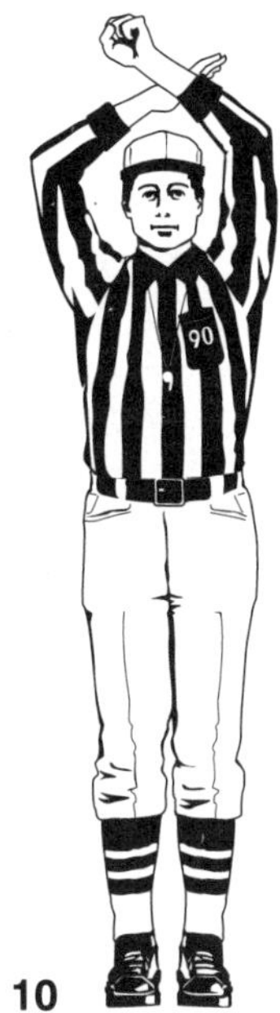

10

PERSONAL FOUL
One wrist striking the other above head.

Same signal followed by swinging leg: **Roughing the Kicker.**

Same signal followed by raised arm swinging forward: **Roughing the Passer.**

Same signal followed by grasping face mask: **Major Face Mask.**

11

HOLDING
Grasping one wrist, the fist clenched, in front of chest.

12

ILLEGAL USE OF HANDS, ARMS, OR BODY
Grasping one wrist, the hand open and facing forward, in front of chest.

13

PENALTY REFUSED, INCOMPLETE PASS, PLAY OVER, or MISSED FIELD GOAL OR EXTRA POINT
Hands shifted in horizontal plane.

14

PASS JUGGLED INBOUNDS AND CAUGHT OUT OF BOUNDS
Hands up and down in front of chest (following incomplete pass signal).

15

ILLEGAL FORWARD PASS
One hand waved behind back followed by loss of down signal (23).

16

INTENTIONAL GROUNDING OF PASS
Parallel arms waved in a diagonal plane across body. Followed by loss of down signal (23).

OFFICIAL SIGNALS

17

INTERFERENCE WITH FORWARD PASS OR FAIR CATCH
Hands open and extended forward from shoulders with hands vertical.

18

INVALID FAIR-CATCH SIGNAL
One hand waved above head.

19

INELIGIBLE RECEIVER OR INELIGIBLE MEMBER OF KICKING TEAM DOWNFIELD
Right hand touching top of cap.

20

ILLEGAL CONTACT
One open hand extended forward.

21

OFFSIDE, ENCROACHMENT, or NEUTRAL ZONE INFRACTION
Hands on hips.

22

ILLEGAL MOTION AT SNAP
Horizontal arc with one hand.

23

LOSS OF DOWN
Both hands held behind head.

24

INTERLOCKING INTERFERENCE, PUSHING, or HELPING RUNNER
Pushing movement of hands to front with arms downward.

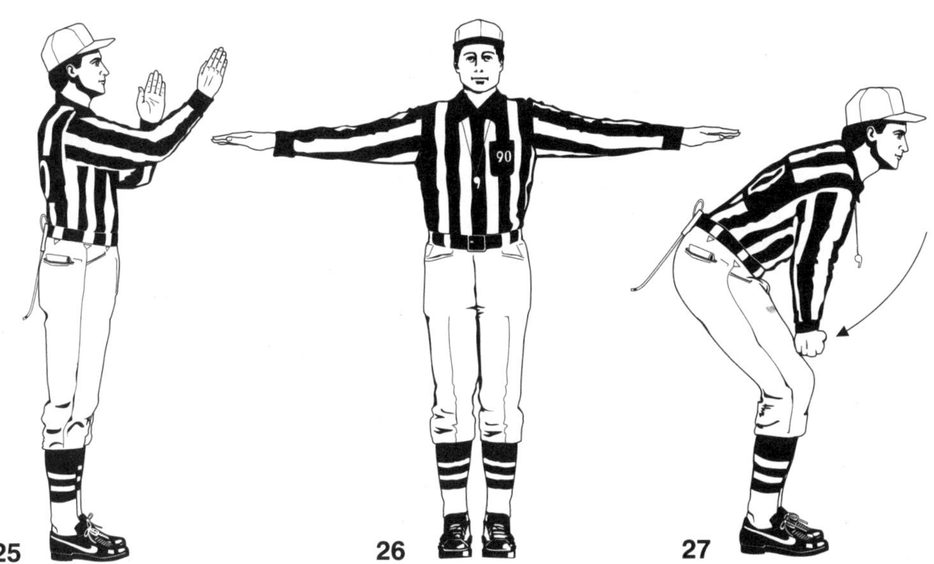

25

TOUCHING A FORWARD PASS OR SCRIMMAGE KICK
Diagonal motion of one hand across another.

26

UNSPORTSMANLIKE CONDUCT
Arms outstretched, palms down.

27

ILLEGAL CUT
Hand striking front of thigh
ILLEGAL BLOCK BELOW THE WAIST
One hand striking front of thigh preceded by personal-foul signal (10).
CHOP BLOCK
Both hands striking side of thighs preceded by personal-foul signal (10).
CLIPPING
One hand striking back of calf preceded by personal-foul signal (10).

28

ILLEGAL CRACKBACK
Strike of an open right hand against the right mid-thigh preceded by personal foul signal (10).

29

PLAYER DISQUALIFIED
Ejection signal.

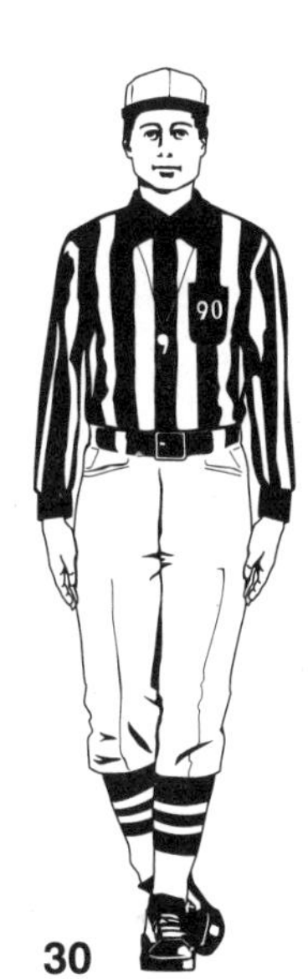

30

TRIPPING
Repeated action of right foot in back of left heel.

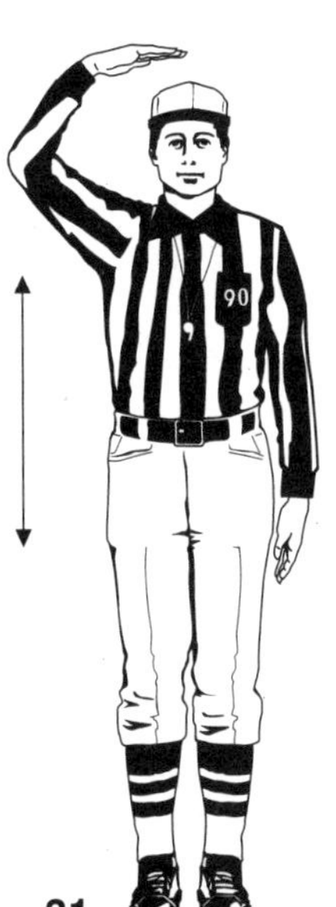

31

UNCATCHABLE FORWARD PASS
Palm of right hand held parallel to ground above head and moved back and forth.

32

ILLEGAL SUBSTITUTION or TOO MANY MEN ON THE FIELD
Both hands on top of head.

OFFICIAL SIGNALS

33

FACE MASK
Grasping face mask with one hand.

34

ILLEGAL SHIFT
Horizontal arcs with two hands.

35

RESET PLAY CLOCK–25 SECONDS
Pump one arm vertically.

36

RESET PLAY CLOCK–40 SECONDS
Pump two arms vertically.

NFL DIGEST OF RULES

This Digest of Rules of the National Football League has been prepared to aid players, fans, and members of the press, radio, and television media in their understanding of the game.

It is not meant to be a substitute for the official rule book. In any case of conflict between these explanations and the official rules, the rules always have precedence.

In order to make it easier to coordinate the information in this digest, the topics discussed generally follow the order of the rule book.

OFFICIALS' JURISDICTIONS, POSITIONS, AND DUTIES

Referee—General oversight and control of game. Gives signals for all fouls and is final authority for rule interpretations. Takes a position in backfield 10 to 12 yards behind line of scrimmage, favors right side (if quarterback is right-handed passer). Determines legality of snap, observes deep back(s) for legal motion. On running play, observes quarterback during and after handoff, remains with him until action has cleared away, then proceeds downfield, checking on runner and contact behind him. When runner is downed, Referee determines forward progress from wing official and, if necessary, adjusts final position of ball.

On pass plays, drops back as quarterback begins to fade back, picks up legality of blocks by near linemen. Changes to complete concentration on quarterback as defenders approach. Primarily responsible to rule on possible roughing action on passer and if ball becomes loose, rules whether ball is free on a fumble or dead on an incomplete pass.

During kicking situations, Referee has primary responsibility to rule on kicker's actions and whether or not any subsequent contact by a defender is legal. The Referee will announce on the microphone when each period is ended.

Umpire—Primary responsibility to rule on players' equipment, as well as their conduct and actions on scrimmage line. Lines up approximately four to five yards downfield, varying position from in front of weakside tackle to strongside guard. Looks for possible false start by offensive linemen. Observes legality of contact by both offensive linemen while blocking and by defensive players while they attempt to ward off blockers. Is prepared to call rule infractions if they occur on offense or defense. Moves forward to line of scrimmage when pass play develops in order to insure that interior linemen do not move illegally downfield. If offensive linemen indicate screen pass is to be attempted, Umpire shifts his attention toward screen side, picks up potential receiver in order to insure that he will legally be permitted to run his pattern and continues to rule on action of blockers. Umpire is to assist in ruling on incomplete or trapped passes when ball is thrown overhead or short.

Head Linesman—Primarily responsible for ruling on offside, encroachment, and actions pertaining to scrimmage line prior to or at snap. Keys on closest setback on his side of the field. On pass plays, Linesman is responsible to clear his receiver approximately seven yards downfield as he moves to a point five yards beyond the line. Linesman's secondary responsibility is to rule on any illegal action taken by defenders on any delay receiver moving downfield. Has full responsibility for ruling on sideline plays on his side, e.g., pass receiver or runner in or out of bounds. Together with Referee, Linesman is responsible for keeping track of number of downs and is in charge of mechanics of his chain crew in connection with its duties.

Linesman must be prepared to assist in determining forward progress by a runner on play directed toward middle or into his side zone. He, in turn, is to signal Referee or Umpire what forward point ball has reached. Linesman is also responsible to rule on legality of action involving any receiver who approaches his side zone. He is to call pass interference when the infraction occurs and is to rule on legality of blockers and defenders on plays involving ball carriers, whether it is entirely a running play, a combination pass and run, or a play involving a kick.

Line Judge—Straddles line of scrimmage on side of field opposite Linesman. Keeps time of game as a backup for clock operator. Along with Linesman is responsible for offside, encroachment, and actions pertaining to scrimmage line prior to or at snap. Line Judge keys on closest setback on his side of field. Line Judge is to observe his receiver until he moves at least seven yards downfield. He then moves toward backfield side, being especially alert to rule on any back in motion and on flight of ball when pass is made (he must rule whether forward or backward). Line Judge has primary responsibility to rule whether or not passer is behind or beyond line of scrimmage when pass is made. He also assists in observing actions by blockers and defenders who are on his side of field. After pass is thrown, Line Judge directs attention toward activities that occur in back of Umpire. During punting situations, Line Judge remains at line of scrimmage to be sure that only the end men move downfield until kick has been made. He also rules whether or not the kick crossed line and then observes action by members of the kicking team who are moving downfield to cover the kick. The Line Judge will advise the Referee when time has expired at the end of each period.

Back Judge—Operates on same side of field as Line Judge, 20 yards deep. Keys on wide receiver on his side. Concentrates on path of end or back, observing legality of his potential block(s) or of actions taken against him. Is prepared to rule from <u>deep</u> position on holding or illegal use of hands by end or back or on defensive infractions committed by player guarding him. Has primary responsibility to make decisions involving sideline on his side of field, e.g., pass receiver or runner in or out of bounds.

Back Judge makes decisions involving catching, recovery, or illegal touching of a loose ball beyond line of scrimmage; rules on plays involving pass receiver, including legality of catch or pass interference; assists in covering actions of runner, including blocks by teammates and that of defenders; calls clipping on punt returns; and, together with Field Judge, rules whether or not field goal attempts are successful.

Side Judge—Operates on same side of field as Linesman, 20 yards deep. Keys on wide receiver on his side. Concentrates on path of end or back, observing legality of his potential block(s) or of actions taken against him. Is prepared to rule from <u>deep</u> position on holding or illegal use of hands by end or back or on defensive infractions committed by player guarding him. Has primary responsibility to make decisions involving sideline on his side of field, e.g., pass receiver or runner in or out of bounds.

Side Judge makes decisions involving catching, recovery, or illegal touching of a loose ball beyond line of scrimmage; rules on plays involving pass receiver, including legality of catch or pass interference; assists in covering actions of runner, including blocks by teammates and that of defenders; and calls clipping on punt returns. On field goals and point after touchdown attempts, he becomes a double umpire.

Field Judge—Takes a position 25 yards downfield. In general, favors the tight end's side of field. Keys on tight end, concentrates on his path and observes legality of tight end's potential block(s) or of actions taken against him. Is prepared to rule from <u>deep</u> position on holding or illegal use of hands by end or back or on defensive infractions committed by player guarding him.

Field Judge times interval between plays on 40/25-second clock plus intermission between two periods of each half; makes decisions involving catching, recovery, or illegal touching of a loose ball beyond line of scrimmage; is responsible to rule on plays involving end line; calls pass interference, fair catch infractions, and clipping on kick returns; and, together with Back Judge, rules whether or not field goals and conversions are successful.

DEFINITIONS

1. **Chucking:** Warding off an opponent who is in front of a defender by contacting him with a quick extension of arm or arms, followed by the return of arm(s) to a flexed position, thereby breaking the original contact.
2. **Clipping:** Throwing the body across the back of an opponent's leg or hitting him from the back below the waist while moving up from behind unless the opponent is a runner or the action is in close line play.
3. **Close Line Play:** The area between the positions normally occupied by the offensive tackles, extending three yards on each side of the line of scrimmage.
4. **Crackback:** Eligible receivers who take or move to a position more than two yards outside the tackle may not block an opponent below the waist if they then move back inside to block.
5. **Dead Ball:** Ball not in play.
6. **Double Foul:** A foul by each team during the same down.
7. **Down:** The period of action that starts when the ball is put in play and ends when it is dead.
8. **Encroachment:** When a player enters the neutral zone and makes <u>contact</u> with an opponent before the ball is snapped.
9. **Fair Catch:** An unhindered catch of a kick by a member of the receiving team who must raise one arm a full length above his head while the kick is in flight.
10. **Foul:** Any violation of a playing rule.
11. **Free Kick:** A kickoff, kick after a safety, or kick after a fair catch. It may be a placekick, dropkick, or punt, except a punt may <u>not</u> be used on a kickoff.
12. **Fumble:** The loss of possession of the ball.
13. **Game Clock:** Scoreboard game clock.
14. **Impetus:** The action of a player that gives momentum to the ball.
15. **Live Ball:** A ball legally free kicked or snapped. It continues in play until the down ends.
16. **Loose Ball:** A live ball not in possession of any player.
17. **Muff:** The touching of a loose ball by a player in an <u>unsuccessful</u> attempt to obtain possession.
18. **Neutral Zone:** The space the length of a ball between the two scrimmage lines. The offensive team and defensive team must remain behind their end of the ball.
    Exception: The offensive player who snaps the ball.
19. **Offside:** A player is offside when any part of his body is beyond his scrimmage or free kick line <u>when the ball is snapped.</u>
20. **Own Goal:** The goal a team is guarding.
21. **Play Clock:** 40/25 second clock.
22. **Pocket Area:** Applies from a point two yards outside of either offensive tackle and includes the tight end if he drops off the line of scrimmage to pass protect. Pocket extends longitudinally behind the line back to offensive team's own end line.
23. **Possession:** When a player controls the ball throughout the act of <u>clearly</u> touching both feet, or any other part of his body other than his hand(s), to the ground inbounds.
24. **Post-Possession Foul:** A foul by the receiving team that occurs after a ball is legally kicked from scrimmage prior to possession changing. The ball must cross the line of scrimmage and the receiving team must retain possession of the kicked ball.
25. **Punt:** A kick made when a player drops the ball and kicks it while it is in flight.
26. **Safety:** The situation in which the ball is dead on or behind a team's own goal if the <u>impetus</u> comes from a player on that team. Two points are scored for the opposing team.
27. **Shift:** The movement of two or more offensive players at the same time before the snap.
28. **Striking:** The act of swinging, clubbing, or propelling the arm or forearm in contacting an opponent.

DIGEST OF RULES

29. **Sudden Death:** The continuation of a tied game into sudden death overtime in which the team scoring first (by safety, field goal, or touchdown) wins.
30. **Touchback:** When a ball is dead on or behind a team's own goal line, provided the impetus came from an opponent and provided it is not a touchdown or a missed field goal.
31. **Touchdown:** When any part of the ball, legally in possession of a player inbounds, is on, above, or over the opponent's goal line, provided it is not a touchback.
32. **Unsportsmanlike Conduct:** Any act contrary to the generally understood principles of sportsmanship.

SUMMARY OF PENALTIES

Automatic First Down

1. Awarded to offensive team on all defensive fouls with these exceptions:
   (a) Offside.
   (b) Encroachment.
   (c) Delay of game.
   (d) Illegal substitution.
   (e) Excessive time out(s).
   (f) Incidental grasp of facemask.
   (g) Neutral zone infraction.
   (h) Running into the kicker.

Loss of Down (No yardage)

1. Second forward pass behind the line.
2. Forward pass strikes ground, goal post, or crossbar.
3. Forward pass goes out of bounds.
4. Forward pass is first touched by eligible receiver who has gone out of bounds and returned.
5. Forward pass touches or is caught by an ineligible receiver on or behind line.
6. Forward pass thrown from behind line of scrimmage after ball once crossed the line.

Five Yards

1. Defensive holding or illegal use of hands (automatic first down).
2. Delay of game.
3. Delay of kickoff.
4. Encroachment.
5. Excessive time out(s).
6. False start.
7. Illegal formation.
8. Illegal shift.
9. Illegal motion.
10. Illegal substitution.
11. First onside kickoff out of bounds between goal lines and not touched.
12. Invalid fair catch signal.
13. More than 11 players on the field at snap for either team.
14. Less than seven men on offensive line at snap.
15. Offside.
16. Failure to pause one second after shift or huddle.
17. Running into kicker.
18. More than one man in motion at snap.
19. Grasping facemask of the ball carrier or quarterback.
20. Player out of bounds at snap.
21. Ineligible member(s) of kicking team going beyond line of scrimmage before ball is kicked.
22. Illegal return.
23. Failure to report change of eligibility.
24. Neutral zone infraction.
25. Loss of team time out(s) or five-yard penalty on the defense for excessive crowd noise.
26. Ineligible player downfield during passing down.

10 Yards

1. Offensive pass interference.
2. Holding, illegal use of hands, arms, or body by offense.
3. Tripping by a member of either team.
4. Helping the runner.
5. Deliberately batting or punching a loose ball.
6. Deliberately kicking a loose ball.

15 Yards

1. Chop block.
2. Clipping below the waist.
3. Fair catch interference.
4. Illegal crackback block by offense.
5. Piling on (automatic first down).
6. Roughing the kicker (automatic first down).
7. Roughing the passer (automatic first down).
8. Twisting, turning, or pulling an opponent by the facemask.
9. Unnecessary roughness.
10. Unsportsmanlike conduct.
11. Delay of game at start of either half.
12. Illegal low block.
13. A tackler using his helmet to butt, spear, or ram an opponent.
14. Any player who uses the top of his helmet unnecessarily.
15. A punter, placekicker, or holder who simulates being roughed by a defensive player.
16. A defender who takes a running start from beyond the line of scrimmage in an attempt to block a field goal or point after touchdown and lands on players at the line of scrimmage.

Five Yards and Loss of Down

1. Forward pass thrown from beyond line of scrimmage.

10 Yards and Loss of Down

1. Intentional grounding of forward pass (safety if passer is in own end zone). If foul occurs more than 10 yards behind line, play results in loss of down at spot of foul.

15 Yards and Loss of Coin Toss Option

1. Team's late arrival on the field prior to scheduled kickoff.
2. Captains not appearing for coin toss.

15 Yards (and disqualification if flagrant)

1. Striking opponent with fist.
2. Kicking or kneeing opponent.
3. Striking opponent on head or neck with forearm, elbow, or hands whether or not the initial contact is made below the neck area.
4. Roughing kicker.
5. Roughing passer.
6. Malicious unnecessary roughness.
7. Unsportsmanlike conduct.
8. Palpably unfair act. (Distance penalty determined by the Referee after consultation with other officials.)

15 Yards and Automatic Disqualification

1. Using a helmet (not worn) as a weapon.

Suspension From Game For One Down

1. Illegal equipment. (Player may return after one down when legally equipped.)

Touchdown Awarded (Palpably Unfair Act)

1. When Referee determines a palpably unfair act deprived a team of a touchdown. (Example: Player comes off bench and tackles runner apparently en route to touchdown.)

FIELD

1. Sidelines and end lines are out of bounds. The goal line is actually in the end zone. A player with the ball in his possession scores when the ball is on, above, or over the goal line.
2. The field is rimmed by a white border, six feet wide, along the sidelines. All of this is out of bounds.
3. The hashmarks (inbound lines) are 70 feet, 9 inches from each sideline.
4. Goal posts must be single-standard type, offset from the end line and painted bright gold. The goal posts must be 18 feet, 6 inches wide and the top face of the crossbar must be 10 feet above the ground. Vertical posts extend at least 30 feet above the crossbar. A ribbon 4 inches by 42 inches long is to be attached to the top of each post. The actual goal is the plane extending indefinitely above the crossbar and between the outer edges of the posts.
5. The field is 360 feet long and 160 feet wide. The end zones are 30 feet deep. The line used in try-for-point plays is two yards out from the goal line.
6. Chain crew members and ball boys must be uniformly identifiable.
7. All clubs must use standardized sideline markers. Pylons must be used for goal line and end line markings.
8. End zone markings and club identification at 50 yard line must be approved by the Commissioner to avoid any confusion as to delineation of goal lines, sidelines, and end lines.

BALL

1. Thirty-six approved footballs will be used in games played outdoors (24 indoors).

COIN TOSS

1. The toss of coin will take place within three minutes of kickoff in center of field. The toss will be called by the visiting captain. The winner may choose one of two privileges and the loser gets the other:
   (a) Receive or kick
   (b) Goal his team will defend
2. Immediately prior to the start of the second half, the captains of both teams must inform the officials of their respective choices. The loser of the original coin toss gets first choice.

TIMING

1. The stadium game clock is official. In case it stops or is operating incorrectly, the Line Judge takes over the official timing on the field.
2. Each period is 15 minutes. The intermission between the periods is two minutes. Halftime is 12 minutes, unless otherwise specified.
3. On charged team time outs, the Field Judge starts watch and blows whistle after 1 minute 50 seconds, unless television does not utilize the time for commercial. In this case the length of the time out is reduced to 40 seconds.
4. The Referee will allow necessary time to attend to an injured player, or repair a legal player's equipment.
5. Each team is allowed three time outs each half.
6. Time between plays will be 40 seconds from the end of a given play until the

snap of the ball for the next play, or a 25-second interval after certain administrative stoppages and game delays.

7. Clock will start running when ball is snapped following all changes of team possession.
8. With the exception of the last two minutes of the first half and the last five minutes of the second half, the game clock will be restarted following a kickoff return, a player going out of bounds on a play from scrimmage, or after declined penalties when appropriate on the referee's signal.
9. Consecutive team time outs can be taken by opposing teams but the length of the second time out will be reduced to 40 seconds.
10. When, in the judgment of the Referee, the level of crowd noise prevents the offense from hearing its signals, he can institute a series of procedures which can result in a loss of team time outs or a five-yard penalty against the defensive team.

SUDDEN DEATH

1. The sudden death system of determining the winner shall prevail when score is tied at the end of the regulation playing time of all NFL games. The team scoring first during overtime play shall be the winner and the game automatically ends upon any score (by safety, field goal, or touchdown) or when a score is awarded by Referee for a palpably unfair act.
2. At the end of regulation time the Referee will immediately toss coin at center of field in accordance with rules pertaining to the usual pregame toss. The captain of the visiting team will call the toss.
3. Following a three-minute intermission after the end of the regulation game, play will be continued in 15-minute periods or until there is a score. There is a two-minute intermission between subsequent periods. The teams change goals at the start of each period. Each team has three time outs per half and all general timing provisions apply as during a regular game. Disqualified players are not allowed to return.
   Exception: In preseason and regular season games there shall be a maximum of 15 minutes of sudden death with two time outs instead of three. General provisions that apply for the fourth quarter will prevail.

TIMING IN FINAL TWO MINUTES OF EACH HALF

1. On kickoff, clock does not start until the ball has been legally touched by player of either team in the field of play. (In all other cases, clock starts with kickoff.)
2. A team cannot buy an excess time out for a penalty. However, a fourth time out is allowed without penalty for an injured player, who must be removed immediately. A fifth time out or more is allowed for an injury and a five-yard penalty is assessed if the clock was running. Additionally, if the clock was running and the score is tied or the team in possession is losing, the ball cannot be put in play for at least 10 seconds on the fourth or more time out. The half or game can end while those 10 seconds are run off on the clock.
3. If the defensive team is behind in the score and commits a foul when it has no time outs left in the final 30 seconds of either half, the offensive team can decline the penalty for the foul and have the time on the clock expire.
4. Fouls that occur in the last five minutes of the fourth quarter as well as the last two minutes of the first half will result in the clock starting on the snap.

TRY

1. After a touchdown, the scoring team is allowed a try during one scrimmage down. The ball may be spotted anywhere between the inbounds lines, two or more yards from the goal line. The successful conversion counts one point by kick; two points for a successful conversion by touchdown; or one point for a safety.
2. The defensive team never can score on a try. As soon as defense gets possession or the kick is blocked or a touchdown is not scored, the try is over.
3. Any distance penalty for fouls committed by the defense that prevent the try from being attempted can be enforced on the succeeding try or succeeding kickoff. Any foul committed on a successful try will result in a distance penalty being assessed on the ensuing kickoff.
4. Only the fumbling player can recover and advance a fumble during a try.

PLAYERS-SUBSTITUTIONS

1. Each team is permitted 11 men on the field at the snap.
2. Unlimited substitution is permitted. However, players may enter the field only when the ball is dead. Players who have been substituted for are not permitted to linger on the field. Such lingering will be interpreted as unsportsmanlike conduct.
3. Players leaving the game must be out of bounds on their own side, clearing the field between the end lines, before a snap or free kick. If player crosses end line leaving field, it is delay of game (five-yard penalty).
4. Substitutes who remain in the game must move onto the field as far as the inside of the field numerals before moving to a wide position.
5. With the exception of the last two minutes of either half, the offensive team, while in the process of substitution or simulated substitution, is prohibited from rushing quickly to the line and snapping the ball with the obvious attempt to cause a defensive foul; i.e., too many men on the field.

KICKOFF

1. The kickoff shall be from the kicking team's 30-yard line at the start of each half and after a field goal and try-for-point. A kickoff is one type of free kick.
2. A one-inch tee may be used (no tee permitted for field goal or try attempt) on a kickoff. The ball is put in play by a placekick or dropkick.
3. If the kickoff clears the opponent's goal posts it is not a field goal.
4. A kickoff is illegal unless it travels 10 yards OR is touched by the receiving team. Once the ball is touched by the receiving team it is a free ball. Receivers may recover and advance. Kicking team may recover but NOT advance UNLESS receiver had possession and lost the ball.
5. When a kickoff goes out of bounds between the goal lines without being touched by the receiving team, the ball belongs to the receivers 30 yards from the spot of the kick or at the out-of-bounds spot unless the ball went out-of-bounds the first time an onside kick was attempted. In this case the kicking team is to be penalized five yards and the ball must be kicked again.
6. When a kickoff goes out of bounds between the goal lines and is touched last by receiving team, it is receiver's ball at out-of-bounds spot.

FREE KICK

1. In addition to a kickoff, the other free kicks are a kick after a safety and a kick after a fair catch. In both cases, a dropkick, placekick, or punt may be used (a punt may not be used on a kickoff).
2. On a free kick after a fair catch, captain of receiving team has the option to put ball in play by punt, dropkick, or placekick without a tee, or by snap. If the placekick or dropkick goes between the uprights a field goal is scored.
3. On a free kick after a safety, the team scored upon puts ball in play by a punt, dropkick, or placekick without tee. No score can be made on a free kick following a safety, even if a series of penalties places team in position. (A field goal can be scored only on a play from scrimmage or a free kick after a fair catch.)

FIELD GOAL

1. All field goals attempted (kicker) and missed from beyond the 20-yard line will result in the defensive team taking possession of the ball at the spot of the kick. On any field goal attempted and missed where the spot of the kick is on or inside the 20-yard line, ball will revert to defensive team at the 20-yard line.

SAFETY

1. The important factor in a safety is impetus. Two points are scored for the opposing team when the ball is dead on or behind a team's own goal line if the impetus came from a player on that team.

Examples of Safety:

(a) Blocked punt goes out of kicking team's end zone. Impetus was provided by punting team. The block only changes direction of ball, not impetus.
(b) Ball carrier retreats from field of play into his own end zone and is downed. Ball carrier provides impetus.
(c) Offensive team commits a foul and spot of enforcement is behind its own goal line.
(d) Player on receiving team muffs punt and, trying to get ball, forces or illegally kicks (creating new impetus) it into end zone where it goes out of the end zone or is recovered by a member of the receiving team in the end zone.

Examples of Non-Safety:

(a) Player intercepts a pass with both feet inbounds in the field of play and his momentum carries him into his own end zone. Ball is put in play at spot of interception.
(b) Player intercepts a pass in his own end zone and is downed in the end zone, even after recovering in the end zone. Impetus came from passing team, not from defense. (Touchback)
(c) Player passes from behind his own goal line. Opponent bats down ball in end zone. (Incomplete pass)

MEASURING

1. The forward point of the ball is used when measuring.

POSITION OF PLAYERS AT SNAP

1. Offensive team must have at least seven players on line.
2. Offensive players, not on line, must be at least one yard back at snap. **(Exception:** player who takes snap.)
3. No interior lineman may move after taking or simulating a three-point stance.
4. No player of either team may invade neutral zone before snap.
5. No player of offensive team may charge or move, after assuming set position, in such manner as to lead defense to believe snap has started.
6. If a player changes his eligibility, the Referee must alert the defensive captain after player has reported to him.
7. All players of offensive team must be stationary at snap, except one back who may be in motion parallel to scrimmage line or backward (not forward).
8. After a shift or huddle all players on offensive team must come to an absolute stop for at least one second with no movement of hands, feet, head, or swaying of body.
9. Quarterbacks can be called for a false start penalty (five yards) if their actions are judged to be an obvious attempt to draw an opponent offside.

USE OF HANDS, ARMS, AND BODY

1. No player on offense may assist a runner except by blocking for him. There

shall be no interlocking interference.

2. A runner may ward off opponents with his hands and arms but no other player on offense may use hands or arms to obstruct an opponent by grasping with hands, pushing, or encircling any part of his body during a block. Hands (open or closed) can be thrust forward to initially contact an opponent on or outside the opponent's frame, but the blocker must work to bring his hands on or inside the frame.
   Note: Pass blocking: Hand(s) thrust forward that slip outside the body of the defender will be legal if blocker worked to bring them back inside. Hand(s) or arm(s) that encircle a defender—i.e., hook an opponent—are to be considered illegal and officials are to call a foul for holding.
   Blocker cannot use his hands or arms to push from behind, hang onto, or encircle an opponent in a manner that restricts his movement as the play develops.
3. Hands cannot be thrust forward above the frame to contact an opponent on the neck, face or head.
   Note: The frame is defined as the part of the opponent's body below the neck that is presented to the blocker.
4. A defensive player may not tackle or hold an opponent other than a runner. Otherwise, he may use his hands, arms, or body only:
   (a) To defend or protect himself against an obstructing opponent.
   Exception: An eligible receiver is considered to be an obstructing opponent ONLY to a point five yards beyond the line of scrimmage unless the player who receives the snap clearly demonstrates no further intention to pass the ball. Within this five-yard zone, a defensive player may make contact with an eligible receiver that may be maintained as long as it is continuous and unbroken up until a point when the receiver is beyond the defender. The defensive player cannot use his hands or arms to push from behind, hang onto, or encircle an eligible receiver in a manner that restricts movement as the play develops. Beyond this five-yard limitation, a defender may use his hands or arms ONLY to defend or protect himself against impending contact caused by a receiver. In such reaction, the defender may not contact a receiver who attempts to take a path to evade him.
   (b) To push or pull opponent out of the way on line of scrimmage.
   (c) In actual attempt to get at or tackle runner.
   (d) To push or pull opponent out of the way in a legal attempt to recover a loose ball.
   (e) During a legal block on an opponent who is not an eligible pass receiver.
   (f) When legally blocking an eligible pass receiver above the waist.
   Exception: Eligible receivers lined up within two yards of the tackle, whether on or immediately behind the line, may be blocked below the waist at or behind the line of scrimmage. NO eligible receiver may be blocked below the waist after he goes beyond the line. (Illegal cut)
   Note: Once the quarterback hands off or pitches the ball to a back, or if the quarterback leaves the pocket area, the restrictions (illegal chuck, illegal cut) on the defensive team relative to the offensive receivers will end, provided the ball is not in the air.
5. A defensive player may not contact an opponent above the shoulders with the palm of his hand except to ward him off on the line. This exception is permitted only if it is not a repeated act against the same opponent during any one contact. In all other cases the palms may be used on head, neck, or face only to ward off or push an opponent in legal attempt to get at the ball.
6. Any offensive player who pretends to possess the ball or to whom a teammate pretends to give the ball may be tackled provided he is crossing his scrimmage line between the ends of a normal tight offensive line.
7. An offensive player who lines up more than two yards outside his own tackle or a player who, at the snap, is in a backfield position and subsequently takes a position more than two yards outside a tackle may not clip an opponent anywhere nor may he contact an opponent below the waist if the blocker is moving toward the ball and if contact is made within an area five yards on either side of the line.
8. A player of either team may block at any time provided it is not pass interference, fair catch interference, or unnecessary roughness.
9. A player may not bat or punch:
   (a) A loose ball (in field of play) toward his opponent's goal line or in any direction in either end zone.
   (b) A ball in player possession.
   Note: If there is any question as to whether a defender is stripping or batting a ball in player possession, the official(s) will rule the action as a legal act (stripping the ball).
   Exception: A forward or backward pass may be batted, tipped, or deflected in any direction at any time by either the offense or the defense.
   Note: A pass in flight that is controlled or caught may only be thrown backward, if it is thrown forward it is considered an illegal bat.
10. No player may deliberately kick any ball except as a punt, dropkick, or placekick.

FORWARD PASS

1. A forward pass may be touched or caught by any eligible receiver. All members of the defensive team are eligible. Eligible receivers on the offensive team are players on either end of line (other than center, guard, or tackle) or players at least one yard behind the line at the snap. A T-formation quarterback is not eligible to receive a forward pass during a play from scrimmage.
   Exception: T-formation quarterback becomes eligible if pass is previously touched by an eligible receiver.
2. An offensive team may make only one forward pass during each play from scrimmage (Loss of down).
3. The passer must be behind his line of scrimmage (Loss of down and five yards, enforced from the spot of pass).
4. Any eligible offensive player may catch a forward pass. If a pass is touched by one offensive player and touched or caught by a second eligible offensive player, pass completion is legal. Further, all offensive players become eligible once a pass is touched by an eligible receiver or any defensive player.
5. The rules concerning a forward pass and ineligible receivers:
   (a) If ball is touched accidentally by an ineligible receiver on or behind his line: loss of down.
   (b) If ineligible receiver is illegally downfield: loss of five yards.
   (c) If touched or caught (intentionally or accidentally) by ineligible receiver beyond the line: loss of 10 yards or loss of down.
6. The player who first controls and continues to maintain control of a pass will be awarded the ball even though his opponent later establishes joint control of the ball.
7. Any forward pass becomes incomplete and ball is dead if:
   (a) Pass hits the ground or goes out of bounds.
   (b) Hits the goal post or the crossbar of either team.
   (c) Is caught by offensive player after touching ineligible receiver.
   (d) An illegal pass is caught by the passer.
8. A forward pass is complete when a receiver clearly possesses the pass and touches the ground with both feet inbounds while in possession of the ball. If a receiver would have landed inbounds with both feet but is carried or pushed out of bounds while maintaining possession of the ball, pass is complete at the out-of-bounds spot.
9. If an eligible receiver goes out of bounds accidentally or is forced out by a defender and returns to first touch and catch a pass, the play is regarded as a pass caught out of bounds. (Loss of down, no yardage.)
10. On a fourth down pass—when the offensive team is inside the opposition's 20-yard line—an incomplete pass results in a loss of down at the line of scrimmage.
11. If a personal foul is committed by the defense prior to the completion of a pass, the penalty is 15 yards from the spot where ball becomes dead.
12. If a personal foul is committed by the offense prior to the completion of a pass, the penalty is 15 yards from the previous line of scrimmage.

INTENTIONAL GROUNDING OF FORWARD PASS

1. Intentional grounding of a forward pass is a foul: loss of down and 10 yards from previous spot if passer is in the field of play or loss of down at the spot of the foul if it occurs more than 10 yards behind the line or safety if passer is in his own end zone when ball is released.
2. Intentional grounding will be called when a passer, facing an imminent loss of yardage due to pressure from the defense, throws a forward pass without a realistic chance of completion.
3. Intentional grounding will not be called when a passer, while out of the pocket and facing an imminent loss of yardage, throws a pass that lands beyond the line of scrimmage, even if no offensive player(s) have a realistic chance to catch the ball (including if the ball lands out of bounds over the sideline or end line).

PROTECTION OF PASSER

1. By interpretation, a pass begins when the passer—with possession of ball—starts to bring his hand forward. If ball strikes ground after this action has begun, play is ruled an incomplete pass. If passer loses control of ball prior to his bringing his hand forward, play is ruled a fumble.
2. No defensive player may run into a passer of a legal forward pass after the ball has left his hand (15 yards). The Referee must determine whether opponent had a reasonable chance to stop his momentum during an attempt to block the pass or tackle the passer while he still had the ball.
3. No defensive player who has an unrestricted path to the quarterback may hit him flagrantly in the area of the knee(s) when approaching in any direction.
4. Officials are to blow the play dead as soon as the quarterback is clearly in the grasp and control of any tackler, and his safety is in jeopardy.

PASS INTERFERENCE

1. There shall be no interference with a forward pass thrown from behind the line. The restriction for the passing team starts with the snap. The restriction on the defensive team starts when the ball leaves the passer's hand. Both restrictions end when the ball is touched by anyone.
2. The penalty for defensive pass interference is an automatic first down at the spot of the foul. If interference is in the end zone, it is first down for the offense on the defense's 1-yard line. If previous spot was inside the defense's 1-yard line, penalty is half the distance to the goal line.
3. The penalty for offensive pass interference is 10 yards from the previous spot.
4. It is pass interference by either team when any player movement beyond the offensive line significantly hinders the progress of an eligible player or such player's opportunity to catch the ball during a legal forward pass. When players are competing for position to make a play on the ball, any contact by

hands, arms, or body shall be considered incidental unless prohibited. Prohibited conduct shall be when a player physically restricts or impedes the opponent in such a manner that is visually evident and materially affects the opponent's opportunity to gain position or retain his position to catch the ball. If a player has gained position, he shall not be considered to have impeded or restricted his opponent in a prohibited manner if all of his actions are a bona fide effort to go to and catch the ball. Provided an eligible player is not interfered with in such a manner, the following exceptions to pass interference will prevail:

(a) If neither player is looking for the ball and there is incidental contact in the act of moving to the ball that does not materially affect the route of an eligible player, there is no interference. If there is any question whether the incidental contact materially affects the route, the ruling shall be no interference.
Note: Inadvertent tripping is not a foul in this situation.

(b) Any eligible player looking for and intent on playing the ball who initiates contact, however severe, while attempting to move to the spot of completion or interception will not be called for interference.

(c) Any eligible player who makes contact, however severe, with one or more eligible players while looking for and making a genuine attempt to catch or bat a reachable ball, will not be called for interference.

(d) It must be remembered that defensive players have as much right to the ball as offensive eligible receivers.

(e) Pass interference by the defense is not to be called when the forward pass is clearly uncatchable.

(f) Note: There is no defensive pass interference behind the line.

BACKWARD PASS

1. Any pass not forward is regarded as a backward pass or lateral. A pass parallel to the line is a backward pass. A runner may pass backward at any time. Any player on either team may catch the pass or recover the ball after it touches the ground.
2. A backward pass that strikes the ground can be recovered and advanced by either team.
3. A backward pass caught in the air can be advanced by either team.
4. A backward pass in flight may not be batted forward by an offensive player.

FUMBLE

1. The distinction between a fumble and a muff should be kept in mind in considering rules about fumbles. A fumble is the loss of possession of the ball. A muff is the touching of a loose ball by a player in an unsuccessful attempt to obtain possession.
2. A fumble may be advanced by any player on either team regardless of whether recovered before or after ball hits the ground.
3. A fumble that goes forward and out of bounds will return to the fumbling team at the spot of the fumble unless the ball goes out of bounds in the opponent's end zone. In this case, it is a touchback.
4. On a play from scrimmage, if an offensive player fumbles anywhere on the field during fourth down, only the fumbling player is permitted to recover and/or advance the ball. If any player fumbles after the two-minute warning in a half, only the fumbling player is permitted to recover and/or advance the ball. If recovered by any other offensive player, the ball is dead at the spot of the fumble unless it is recovered behind the spot of the fumble. In that case, the ball is dead at the spot of recovery. Any defensive player may recover and/or advance any fumble at any time.

KICKS FROM SCRIMMAGE

1. Any kick from scrimmage must be made from behind the line to be legal.
2. Any punt or missed field goal that touches a goal post is dead.
3. During a kick from scrimmage, only the end men, as eligible receivers on the line of scrimmage at the time of the snap, are permitted to go beyond the line before the ball is kicked.
Exception: An eligible receiver who, at the snap, is aligned or in motion behind the line and more than one yard outside the end man on his side of the line, clearly making him the outside receiver, replaces that end man as the player eligible to go downfield after the snap. All other members of the kicking team must remain at the line of scrimmage until the ball has been kicked.
4. Any punt that is blocked and does not cross the line of scrimmage can be recovered and advanced by either team. However, if offensive team recovers it must make the yardage necessary for its first down to retain possession if punt was on fourth down.
5. The kicking team may never advance its own kick even though legal recovery is made beyond the line of scrimmage. Possession only.
6. A member of the receiving team may not run into or rough a kicker who kicks from behind his line unless contact is:
(a) Incidental to and after he had touched ball in flight.
(b) Caused by kicker's own motions.
(c) Occurs during a quick kick, or a kick made after a run, or after kicker recovers a loose ball. Ball is loose when kicker muffs snap or snap hits ground.
(d) Defender is blocked into kicker.
The penalty for running into the kicker is 5 yards. For roughing the kicker: 15 yards, an automatic first down and disqualification if flagrant.
7. If a member of the kicking team attempting to down the ball on or inside opponent's 5-yard line carries the ball into the end zone, it is a touchback.
8. Fouls during a punt are enforced from the previous spot (line of scrimmage).
Exception: Illegal touching, illegal fair catch, invalid fair catch signal, and fouls by the receiving team during loose ball after ball is kicked.
9. While the ball is in the air or rolling on the ground following a punt or field goal attempt and receiving team commits a foul before gaining possession, receiving team will retain possession and will be penalized for its foul.
10. It will be illegal for a defensive player to jump or stand on any player, or be picked up by a teammate or to use a hand or hands on a teammate to gain additional height in an attempt to block a kick (Penalty: 15 yards, unsportsmanlike conduct).
11. A punted ball remains a kicked ball until it is declared dead or in possession of either team.
12. Any member of the punting team may down the ball anywhere in the field of play. However, it is illegal touching (Official's time out and receiver's ball at spot of illegal touching). This foul does not offset any foul by receivers during the down.
13. Defensive team may advance all kicks from scrimmage (including unsuccessful field goal) whether or not ball crosses defensive team's goal line. Rules pertaining to kicks from scrimmage apply until defensive team gains possession.

FAIR CATCH

1. The member of the receiving team must raise one arm a full length above his head and wave it from side to side while kick is in flight. (Failure to give proper sign: receivers' ball five yards behind spot of signal.) **Note:** It is legal for the receiver to shield his eyes from the sun by raising one hand no higher than the helmet.
2. No opponent may interfere with the fair catcher, the ball, or his path to the ball. Penalty: 15 yards from spot of foul and fair catch is awarded.
3. A player who signals for a fair catch is not required to catch the ball. However, if a player signals for a fair catch, he may not block or initiate contact with any player on the kicking team until the ball touches a player. Penalty: snap 15 yards behind spot of foul.
4. If ball hits ground or is touched by member of kicking team in flight, fair catch signal is off and all rules for a kicked ball apply.
5. Any undue advance by a fair catch receiver is delay of game. No specific distance is specified for undue advance as ball is dead at spot of catch. If player comes to a reasonable stop, no penalty. For violation, five yards.
6. If time expires while ball is in play and a fair catch is awarded, receiving team may choose to extend the period with one free kick down. However, placekicker may not use tee.

FOUL ON LAST PLAY OF HALF OR GAME

1. On a foul by defense on last play of half or game, the down is replayed if penalty is accepted.
2. On a foul by the offense on last play of half or game, the down is not replayed and the play in which the foul is committed is nullified.
Exception: Fair catch interference, foul following change of possession, illegal touching. No score by offense counts.
3. On double foul on last play of half or game, down is replayed.

SPOT OF ENFORCEMENT OF FOUL

1. There are four basic spots at which a penalty for a foul is enforced:
(a) Spot of foul: The spot where the foul is committed.
(b) Previous spot: The spot where the ball was put in play.
(c) Spot of snap, pass, fumble, return kick, or free kick: The spot where the act connected with the foul occurred.
(d) Succeeding spot: The spot where the ball next would be put in play if no distance penalty were to be enforced.
Exception: If foul occurs after a touchdown and before the whistle for a try-for-point, succeeding spot is spot of next kickoff.
2. All fouls committed by offensive team behind the line of scrimmage and in the field of play shall be penalized from the previous spot.
3. When spot of enforcement for fouls involving defensive holding or illegal use of hands by the defense is behind the line of scrimmage, any penalty yardage to be assessed on that play shall be measured from the line if the foul occurred beyond the line.

DOUBLE FOUL

1. If there is a double foul during a down in which there is a change of possession, the team last gaining possession may keep the ball unless its foul was committed prior to the change of possession.
2. If double foul occurs after a change of possession, the defensive team retains the ball at the spot of its foul or dead ball spot.
3. If one of the fouls of a double foul involves disqualification, that player must be removed, but no penalty yardage is to be assessed.
4. If the kickers foul during a kick before possession changes and the receivers foul after possession changes, the receivers will retain the ball after enforcement of its foul.

PENALTY ENFORCED ON FOLLOWING KICKOFF

1. When a team scores by touchdown, field goal, extra point, or safety and either team commits a personal foul, unsportsmanlike conduct, or obvious unfair act during the down, the penalty will be assessed on the following kickoff.

DIGEST OF RULES

EMERGENCIES AND UNFAIR ACTS

Emergencies—Policy

The National Football League requires all League personnel, including game officials, Leauge office employees, players, coaches, and other club employees to use best effort to see that each game—preseason, regular season, and postseason—is played to its conclusion. The League recognizes, however, that emergencies may arise that make a game's completion impossible or inadvisable. Such circumstances may include, but are not limited to, severely inclement weather, natural or manmade disaster, power failure, and spectator interference. Games should be suspended, cancelled, postponed, or terminated when circumstances exist such that comencement or continuation of play would pose a threat to the safety of participants or spectators.

Authority of Commissioner's Office

1. Authority to cancel, postpone, or terminate games is vested only in the Commissioner and the League President (other League office representatives and referees may suspend play temporarily; see point No. 3 under this section and point No. 1 under "Authority of Referee" below). The following definitions apply:
   - **Cancel.** To cancel a game is to nullify it either before or after it begins and to make no provision for rescheduling it or for including its score or other performance statistics in League records.
   - **Postpone.** To postpone a game is (a) to defer its starting time to a later date, or (b) to suspend it after play has begun and to make provision to resume at a later date with all scores and other performance statistics up to the point of postponement added to those achieved in the resumed portion of the game.
   - **Terminate.** To terminate a game is to end it short of a full 60 minutes of play, to record it officially as a completed game, and to make no provision to resume it at a later date. The Commissioner or League President may terminate a game in an emergency if, in his opinion, it is reasonable to project that its resumption (a) would not change its ultimate result or (b) would not adversely affect any other interteam competitive issue.
   - **Forfeit.** The Commissioner, (except in cases of disciplinary action; see last section on "Removing Team from Field"), League President, and their representatives, including referees, are not authorized unilaterally to declare forfeits. A forfeit occurs only when a game is not played because of the failure or refusal of *one* team to participate. In that event, the other team, if ready and willing to play, is the winner by a score of 2-0.
2. If an emergency arises that may require cancellation, postponement, or termination (see above), the highest ranking representative from the Commissioner's office working the game in a "control" capacity will consult with the Commissioner, League President, or game-day duty officer designated by the League (by telephone, if that person is not in attendance) concerning such decision. If circumstances warrant, the League representative should also attempt to consult with the weather bureau and with appropriate security personnel of the League, club, stadium, and local authorities. If no representative from the Commissioner's office is working the game in a "control" capacity, the referee will be in charge (see "Authority of Referee" below).
3. In circumstances where safety is of immediate concern, the Commissioner's-office representative may, after consulting with the referee, authorize a temporary suspension in play and, if warranted, removal of the participants from the playing field. The representative should be mindful of the safety of spectators, players, game officials, nonplayer personnel in the bench areas, and other field-level personnel such as photographers and cheerleaders.
4. If possible, the League-office representative should consult with authorized representatives of the two participating clubs before any decision involving cancellation, postponement, or termination is made by the Commissioner or League President.
5. If the Commissioner or League President decides to cancel, postpone, or terminate a game, his representative at the game or the game-day duty officer will then determine the method(s) for announcing such decision, e.g., by public-address anouncement over referee's wireless microphone, by public-address announcement by home club, or by communication to radio, television, and other news media.

Authority of Referee

1. If a referee determines that an emergency warrants immediate removal of participants from the playing field for safety reasons, he may do so on his own authority. If, however, circumstances allow him the time, he must reach the highest ranking full-time League office representative working at the game in a "control" capacity or the game-day duty officer designated by the League (by telephone, if that person is not in attendance) and discuss the actual or potential emergency with such representative or duty officer. That representative or duty officer then will make the final decision on removal of participants from the field or obtain a decision from the Commissioner or League President.
2. If a referee removes participants from the playing field under No. 1 above, he may order them to their respective bench areas or to their locker rooms, whichever is appropriate in the circumstances.
3. After appropriate consultation under No. 1 above, the referee must advise the two participating head coaches of the nature of the emergency and the action contemplated (if the decision has not yet been reached) or of the final decision.
4. The referee must *not*, before a decision is reached, make an announcement on his microphone concerning the possibility of a cancellation, postponement, or termination unless instructed to do so by an appropriate representative of the Commissioner's office.
5. The referee must *not* discuss a forfeit with head coaches or club personnel and must *not* use that term over the referee's microphone (see definition of *forfeit* under No. 1 of "Authority of Commissioner's Office" above).
6. The referee must *not* assess an unsportsmanlike-conduct penalty on the home team for actions of fans that cause or contribute to an emergency.
7. The referee should be mindful of the safety of not only players and officials, but also of the spectators and other nonparticipants.
8. If an emergency involves spectator interference (for example, nonparticipants on the field or thrown objects), the referee immediately should contact the appropriate club or League representative for additional security assistance, including, if applicable, involvement of the League's security representative(s) assigned to the game.
9. The referee may order the resumption of play when he deems conditions safe for all concerned and, if circumstances warrant, after consultation with appropriate representatives of the Commissioner's office.
10. Under no circumstances is the referee authorized to cancel, postpone, terminate, or declare forfeiture of a game unilaterally.

Procedures for Starting and Resuming Games

Subject to the points of authority listed above, League personnel and referees will be guided by the following procedures for starting and resuming games that are affected by emergencies.

1. If, because of an emergency, a regular-season or postseason game is not started at its scheduled time and cannot be played at any later time that same day, the game nevertheless must be played on a subsequent date to be determined by the Commissioner.
2. If an emergency threatens to occur during the playing of a game (for example, an incoming tropical storm), the starting time of the game will not be moved to an earlier time unless there is clearly sufficient time to make an orderly change.
3. All games that are suspended temporarily and resumed on the same day, and all suspended games that are postponed to a later date, will be resumed at the point of suspension. On suspension, the referee will call timeout and make a record of the following: team possessing the ball, direction in which its offense was headed, position of the ball on the field, down, distance, period, time remaining in the period, and any other pertinent information required for an orderly and equitable resumption of play.
4. For regular-season postponements, the Commissioner will make every effort to set the game for no later than two days after its originally scheduled date and at the same site. If unable to schedule at the same site, he will select an appropriate alternative site. If it is impossible to schedule the game within two days after its original date, the Commissioner will attempt to schedule it on the Tuesday of the next calendar week. The Commissioner will keep in mind the potential for competitive inequities if one or both of the involved clubs has already been scheduled for a game close to the Tuesday of that week (for example, a Thursday game).
5. For postseason postponements, the Commissioner will make every effort to set the game as soon as possible after its originally scheduled date and at the same site. If unable to schedule at the same site, he will select an appropriate alternative site.
6. Whenever postponement is attributable to negligence by a club, the negligent club is responsible for all home club costs and expenses, including, subject to approval by the Commissioner, gate receipts and television-contract income. [See Section 19.11 (C) of the NFL Constitution and Bylaws.]
7. Each home club is strictly responsible for having the playing surface of its stadium well maintained and suitable for NFL play.

UNFAIR ACTS

Commissioner's Authority

The Commissioner has sole authority to investigate and to take appropriate disciplinary or corrective measures if any club action, nonparticipant interference, or emergency occurs in an NFL game which he deems so unfair or outside the accepted tactics encountered in professional football that such action has a major effect on the result of a game.

No Club Protests

The authority and measures provided for in this section (UNFAIR ACTS) do not constitute a protest machinery for NFL clubs to dispute the result of a game. The Commissioner will conduct an investigation under this section only to review an act or occurrence that he deems so unfair that the result of the game in question may be inequitable to one of the participating teams. The Commissioner will not apply his authority under this section when a club registers a complaint concerning judgmental errors or routine errors of omission by game officials. Games involving such complaints will continue to stand as completed.

Penalties for Unfair Acts

The Commissioner's powers under this section (UNFAIR ACTS) include the imposition of monetary fines and draft choice forfeitures, suspension of persons involved, and, if appropriate, the reversal of a game's result or the rescheduling of a game, either from the beginning or from the point at which the extraordinary act occurred. In the event of rescheduling a game, the Commissioner will be guided by the procedures specified above ("Procedures for Starting and Resuming Games" under EMERGENCIES). In all cases, the Commissioner will conduct a full investigation, including the opportunity for hearings, use of game videotape, and any other procedures he deems appropriate.

REMOVING TEAM FROM FIELD

No player, coach, or other person affiliated with a club may remove that club's team from the field during the playing of any game, including preseason, except at the direction of the referee. Any club violating this rule will be subject to disciplinary action by the Commissioner, including possible game forfeiture and sole liability for financial losses suffered by the opposing club and any other affected member clubs of the League. [See Section 9.1 (E) of the NFL Constitution and Bylaws.]

NOTES

NOTES

NOTES

NOTES

NOTES